W9-BOK-955
3 3420 00634 506 1

Illumination from the Psalter of St. Elizabeth, *thirteenth century.*
(© Gianni Dagli Orti/CORBIS)

NEW CATHOLIC ENCYCLOPEDIA

NEW CATHOLIC ENCYCLOPEDIA

SECOND EDITION

5
Ead–Fre

Detroit • New York • San Diego • San Francisco • Cleveland • New Haven, Conn. • Waterville, Maine • London • Munich

in association with
THE CATHOLIC UNIVERSITY OF AMERICA • WASHINGTON, D.C.

The New Catholic Encyclopedia, Second Edition

Project Editors
Thomas Carson, Joann Cerrito

Editorial
Erin Bealmear, Jim Craddock, Stephen Cusack, Miranda Ferrara, Kristin Hart, Melissa Hill, Margaret Mazurkiewicz, Carol Schwartz, Christine Tomassini, Michael J. Tyrkus

Permissions
Edna Hedblad, Shalice Shah-Caldwell

Imaging and Multimedia
Randy Bassett, Dean Dauphinais, Robert Duncan, Leitha Etheridge-Sims, Mary K. Grimes, Lezlie Light, Dan Newell, David G. Oblender, Christine O'Bryan, Luke Rademacher, Pamela Reed

Product Design
Michelle DiMercurio

Data Capture
Civie Green

Manufacturing
Rhonda Williams

Indexing
Victoria Agee, Victoria Baker, Lynne Maday, Do Mi Stauber, Amy Suchowski

For more information, contact
The Gale Group, Inc.
27500 Drake Rd.
Farmington Hills, MI 48331-3535
Or you can visit our Internet site at
http://www.gale.com

LIBRARY OF CONGRESS CATALOGING-IN-PUBLICATION DATA

New Catholic encyclopedia.—2nd ed.
p. cm.
Includes bibliographical references and indexes.
ISBN 0-7876-4004-2
1. Catholic Church—Encyclopedias. I. Catholic University of America.
BX841 .N44 2002
282′ .03—dc21
2002000924

ISBN: 0-7876-4004-2 (set)
0-7876-4005-0 (v. 1)
0-7876-4006-9 (v. 2)
0-7876-4007-7 (v. 3)
0-7876-4008-5 (v. 4)
0-7876-4009-3 (v. 5)
0-7876-4010-7 (v. 6)
0-7876-4011-5 (v. 7)
0-7876-4012-3 (v. 8)
0-7876-4013-1 (v. 9)
0-7876-4014-x (v. 10)
0-7876-4015-8 (v. 11)
0-7876-4016-6 (v. 12)
0-7876-4017-4 (v. 13)
0-7876-4018-2 (v. 14)
0-7876-4019-0 (v. 15)

Printed in the United States of America
10 9 8 7 6 5 4 3 2 1

Foreword

This revised edition of the *New Catholic Encyclopedia* represents a third generation in the evolution of the text that traces its lineage back to the *Catholic Encyclopedia* published from 1907 to 1912. In 1967, sixty years after the first volume of the original set appeared, The Catholic University of America and the McGraw-Hill Book Company joined together in organizing a small army of editors and scholars to produce the *New Catholic Encyclopedia*. Although planning for the *NCE* had begun before the Second Vatican Council and most of the 17,000 entries were written before Council ended, Vatican II enhanced the encyclopedia's value and importance. The research and the scholarship that went into the articles witnessed to the continuity and richness of the Catholic Tradition given fresh expression by Council. In order to keep the *NCE* current, supplementary volumes were published in 1972, 1978, 1988, and 1995. Now, at the beginning of the third millennium, The Catholic University of America is proud to join with The Gale Group in presenting a new edition of the *New Catholic Encyclopedia*. It updates and incorporates the many articles from the 1967 edition and its supplements that have stood the test of time and adds hundreds of new entries.

As the president of The Catholic University of America, I cannot but be pleased at the reception the *NCE* has received. It has come to be recognized as an authoritative reference work in the field of religious studies and is praised for its comprehensive coverage of the Church's history and institutions. Although Canon Law no longer requires encyclopedias and reference works of this kind to receive an *imprimatur* before publication, I am confident that this new edition, like the original, reports accurate information about Catholic beliefs and practices. The editorial staff and their consultants were careful to present official Church teachings in a straightforward manner, and in areas where there are legitimate disputes over fact and differences in interpretation of events, they made every effort to insure a fair and balanced presentation of the issues.

The way for this revised edition was prepared by the publication, in 2000, of a Jubilee volume of the *NCE*, heralding the beginning of the new millennium. In my foreword to that volume I quoted Pope John Paul II's encyclical on Faith and Human Reason in which he wrote that history is "the arena where we see what God does for humanity." The *New Catholic Encyclopedia* describes that arena. It reports events, people, and ideas—"the things we know best and can verify most easily, the things of our everyday life, apart from which we cannot understand ourselves" (*Fides et ratio,* 12).

Finally, I want to express appreciation on my own behalf and on the behalf of the readers of these volumes to everyone who helped make this revision a reality. We are all indebted to The Gale Group and the staff of The Catholic University of America Press for their dedication and the alacrity with which they produced it.

Very Reverend David M. O'Connell, C.M., J.C.D.
President
The Catholic University of America

Preface to the Revised Edition

When first published in 1967 the *New Catholic Encyclopedia* was greeted with enthusiasm by librarians, researchers, and general readers interested in Catholicism. In the United States the *NCE* has been recognized as the standard reference work on matters of special interest to Catholics. In an effort to keep the encyclopedia current, supplementary volumes were published in 1972, 1978, 1988, and 1995. However, it became increasingly apparent that further supplements would not be adequate to this task. The publishers subsequently decided to undertake a thorough revision of the *NCE,* beginning with the publication of a Jubilee volume at the start of the new millennium.

Like the biblical scribe who brings from his storeroom of knowledge both the new and the old, this revised edition of the *New Catholic Encyclopedia* incorporates material from the 15-volume original edition and the supplement volumes. Entries that have withstood the test of time have been edited, and some have been amended to include the latest information and research. Hundreds of new entries have been added. For all practical purposes, it is an entirely new edition intended to serve as a comprehensive and authoritative work of reference reporting on the movements and interests that have shaped Christianity in general and Catholicism in particular over two millennia.

SCOPE

The title reflects its outlook and breadth. It is the *New Catholic Encyclopedia,* not merely a new encyclopedia of Catholicism. In addition to providing information on the doctrine, organization, and history of Christianity over the centuries, it includes information about persons, institutions, cultural phenomena, religions, philosophies, and social movements that have affected the Catholic Church from within and without. Accordingly, the *NCE* attends to the history and particular traditions of the Eastern Churches and the Churches of the Protestant Reformation, and other ecclesial communities. Christianity cannot be understood without exploring its roots in ancient Israel and Judaism, nor can the history of the medieval and modern Church be understood apart from its relationship with Islam. Interfaith dialogue requires an appreciation of Buddhism and other world religions, as well as some knowledge of the history of religion in general.

On the assumption that most readers and researchers who use the *NCE* are individuals interested in Catholicism in general and the Church in North America in particular, its editorial content gives priority to the Western Church, while not neglecting the churches in the East; to Roman Catholicism, acknowledging much common history with Protestantism; and to Catholicism in the United States, recognizing that it represents only a small part of the universal Church.

Scripture, Theology, Patrology, Liturgy. The many and varied articles dealing with Sacred Scripture and specific books of the Bible reflect contemporary biblical scholarship and its concerns. The *NCE* highlights official church teachings as expressed by the Church's magisterium. It reports developments in theology, explains issues and introduces ecclesiastical writers from the early Church Fathers to present-day theologians whose works exercise major influence on the development of Christian thought. The *NCE* traces the evolution of the Church's worship with special emphasis on rites and rituals consequent to the liturgical reforms and renewal initiated by the Second Vatican Council.

Church History. From its inception Christianity has been shaped by historical circumstances and itself has become a historical force. The *NCE* presents the Church's history from a number of points of view against the background of general political and cultural history. The revised edition reports in some detail the Church's missionary activity as it grew from a small community in Jerusalem to the worldwide phenomenon it is today. Some entries, such as those dealing with the Middle Ages, the Reformation, and the Enlightenment, focus on major time-periods and movements that cut across geographical boundaries. Other articles describe the history and structure of the Church in specific areas, countries, and regions. There are separate entries for many dioceses and monasteries which by reason of antiquity, size, or influence are of special importance in ecclesiastical history, as there are for religious orders and congregations. The *NCE* rounds out its comprehensive history of the Church with articles on religious movements and biographies of individuals.

Canon and Civil Law. The Church inherited and has safeguarded the precious legacy of ancient Rome, described by Virgil, "to rule people under law, [and] to establish the way of peace." The *NCE* deals with issues of ecclesiastical jurisprudence and outlines the development of legislation governing communal practices and individual obligations, taking care to incorporate and reference the 1983 *Code of Canon Law* throughout and, where appropriate, the *Code of Canons for the Eastern Churches.* It deals with issues of Church-State relations and with civil law as it impacts on the Church and Church's teaching regarding human rights and freedoms.

Philosophy. The Catholic tradition from its earliest years has investigated the relationship between faith and reason. The *NCE* considers at some length the many and varied schools of ancient, medieval, and modern philosophy with emphasis, when appropriate, on their relationship to theological positions. It pays particular attention to the scholastic tradition, particularly Thomism, which is prominent in Catholic intellectual history. Articles on many major and lesser philosophers contribute to a comprehensive survey of philosophy from pre-Christian times to the present.

Biography and Hagiography. The *NCE,* making an exception for the reigning pope, leaves to other reference works biographical information about living persons. This revised edition presents biographical sketches of hundreds of men and women, Christian and non-Christian, saints and sinners, because of their significance for the Church. They include: Old and New Testament figures; the Fathers of the Church and ecclesiastical writers; pagan and Christian emperors; medieval and modern kings; heads of state and other political figures; heretics and champions of orthodoxy; major and minor figures in the Reformation and Counter Reformation; popes, bishops, and priests; founders and members of religious orders and congregations; lay men and lay women; scholars, authors, composers, and artists. The *NCE* includes biographies of most saints whose feasts were once celebrated or are currently celebrated by the universal church. The revised edition relies on Butler's *Lives of the Saints* and similar reference works to give accounts of many saints, but the *NCE* also provides biographical information about recently canonized and beatified individuals who are, for one reason or another, of special interest to the English-speaking world.

Social Sciences. Social sciences came into their own in the twentieth century. Many articles in the *NCE* rely on data drawn from anthropology, economics, psychology and sociology for a better understanding of religious structures and behaviors. Papal encyclicals and pastoral letters of episcopal conferences are the source of principles and norms for Christian attitudes and practice in the field of social action and legislation. The *NCE* draws attention to the Church's organized activities in pursuit of peace and justice, social welfare and human rights. The growth of the role of the laity in the work of the Church also receives thorough coverage.

ARRANGEMENT OF ENTRIES

The articles in the *NCE* are arranged alphabetically by the first substantive word using the word-by-word method of alphabetization; thus "New Zealand" precedes "Newman, John Henry," and "Old Testament Literature" precedes "Oldcastle, Sir John." Monarchs, patriarchs, popes, and others who share a Christian name and are differentiated by a title and numerical designation are alphabetized by their title and then arranged numerically. Thus, entries for Byzantine emperors Leo I through IV precede those for popes of the same name, while "Henry VIII, King of England" precedes "Henry IV, King of France."

Maps, Charts, and Illustrations. The *New Catholic Encyclopedia* contains nearly 3,000 illustrations, including photographs, maps, and tables. Entries focusing on the Church in specific countries contain a map of the country as well as easy-to-read tables giving statistical data and, where helpful, lists of archdioceses and dioceses. Entries on the Church in U.S. states also contain tables listing archdioceses and dioceses where appropriate. The numerous photographs appearing in the *New Catholic Encyclopedia* help to illustrate the history of the Church, its role in modern societies, and the many magnificent works of art it has inspired.

SPECIAL FEATURES

Subject Overview Articles. For the convenience and guidance of the reader, the *New Catholic Encyclopedia* contains several brief articles outlining the scope of major fields: "Theology, Articles on," "Liturgy, Articles on," "Jesus Christ, Articles on," etc.

Cross-References. The cross-reference system in the *NCE* serves to direct the reader to related material in other articles. The appearance of a name or term in small capital letters in text indicates that there is an article of that title elsewhere in the encyclopedia. In some cases, the name of the related article has been inserted at the appropriate point as a *see* reference: (*see* THOMAS AQUINAS, ST.). When a further aspect of the subject is treated under another title, a *see also* reference is placed at the end of the article. In addition to this extensive cross-reference system, the comprehensive index in volume 15 will greatly increase the reader's ability to access the wealth of information contained in the encyclopedia.

Abbreviations List. Following common practice, books and versions of the Bible as well as other standard works by selected authors have been abbreviated throughout the text. A guide to these abbreviations follows this preface.

The Editors

Abbreviations

The system of abbreviations used for the works of Plato, Aristotle, St. Augustine, and St. Thomas Aquinas is as follows: Plato is cited by book and Stephanus number only, e.g., Phaedo 79B; Rep. 480A. Aristotle is cited by book and Bekker number only, e.g., Anal. post. 72b 8–12; Anim. 430a 18. St. Augustine is cited as in the Thesaurus Linguae Latinae, e.g., C. acad. 3.20.45; Conf. 13.38.53, with capitalization of the first word of the title. St. Thomas is cited as in scholarly journals, but using Arabic numerals. In addition, the following abbreviations have been used throughout the encyclopedia for biblical books and versions of the Bible.

Books

Acts	Acts of the Apostles
Am	Amos
Bar	Baruch
1–2 Chr	1 and 2 Chronicles (1 and 2 Paralipomenon in Septuagint and Vulgate)
Col	Colossians
1–2 Cor	1 and 2 Corinthians
Dn	Daniel
Dt	Deuteronomy
Eccl	Ecclesiastes
Eph	Ephesians
Est	Esther
Ex	Exodus
Ez	Ezekiel
Ezr	Ezra (Esdras B in Septuagint; 1 Esdras in Vulgate)
Gal	Galatians
Gn	Genesis
Hb	Habakkuk
Heb	Hebrews
Hg	Haggai
Hos	Hosea
Is	Isaiah
Jas	James
Jb	Job
Jdt	Judith
Jer	Jeremiah
Jgs	Judges
Jl	Joel
Jn	John
1–3 Jn	1, 2, and 3 John
Jon	Jonah
Jos	Joshua
Jude	Jude
1–2 Kgs	1 and 2 Kings (3 and 4 Kings in Septuagint and Vulgate)
Lam	Lamentations
Lk	Luke
Lv	Leviticus
Mal	Malachi (Malachias in Vulgate)
1–2 Mc	1 and 2 Maccabees
Mi	Micah
Mk	Mark
Mt	Matthew
Na	Nahum
Neh	Nehemiah (2 Esdras in Septuagint and Vulgate)
Nm	Numbers
Ob	Obadiah
Phil	Philippians
Phlm	Philemon
Prv	Proverbs
Ps	Psalms
1–2 Pt	1 and 2 Peter
Rom	Romans
Ru	Ruth
Rv	Revelation (Apocalypse in Vulgate)
Sg	Song of Songs
Sir	Sirach (Wisdom of Ben Sira; Ecclesiasticus in Septuagint and Vulgate)
1–2 Sm	1 and 2 Samuel (1 and 2 Kings in Septuagint and Vulgate)
Tb	Tobit
1–2 Thes	1 and 2 Thessalonians
Ti	Titus
1–2 Tm	1 and 2 Timothy
Wis	Wisdom
Zec	Zechariah
Zep	Zephaniah

Versions

Apoc	Apocrypha
ARV	American Standard Revised Version
ARVm	American Standard Revised Version, margin
AT	American Translation
AV	Authorized Version (King James)
CCD	Confraternity of Christian Doctrine
DV	Douay-Challoner Version

ERV	English Revised Version
ERVm	English Revised Version, margin
EV	English Version(s) of the Bible
JB	Jerusalem Bible
LXX	Septuagint
MT	Masoretic Text
NAB	New American Bible
NEB	New English Bible
NIV	New International Version
NJB	New Jerusalem Bible
NRSV	New Revised Standard Version
NT	New Testament
OT	Old Testament
RSV	Revised Standard Version
RV	Revised Version
RVm	Revised Version, margin
Syr	Syriac
Vulg	Vulgate

E

EADMER OF CANTERBURY

Benedictine monk, historian, theologian, biographer of St. Anselm; b. in or near Canterbury, *c.* 1060; d. Canterbury, *c.* 1130. He entered Christ Church, Canterbury, as a child and experienced the transformation in monastic life that took place under the inspiration of Archbishop LANFRANC. When ANSELM became archbishop of Canterbury in 1093, he made Eadmer his chaplain. The two men were never separated until Anselm's death in 1109. During their years together Eadmer acted as a secretary and amanuensis of the archbishop; above all he recorded Anselm's sayings, took notes for a history of his times, the *Historia novorum,* and began to write the *Vita s. Anselmi.* Meanwhile he continued his hagiographical work for the church of Canterbury and began a series of devotional writings in the manner of St. Anselm. In 1120 Eadmer was nominated as bishop of St. Andrews, but he left his see after several months of fruitless argument about the rights of Canterbury over the Scottish church. He spent his last years at Canterbury in the office of precentor, in which he continued to serve his church as a hagiographer and devotional writer. The most important work of these years was his *Tractatus de conceptione sanctae Mariae,* which contains the first theological defense of the doctrine of the IMMACULATE CONCEPTION and foreshadows in a remarkable way some of the later arguments on this theme. Eadmer's main claim to fame is undoubtedly as a historian and biographer of St. Anselm. He was the first notable English historian after BEDE, and as a biographer he showed a talent for vivid and intimate delineation of character seldom surpassed in the Middle Ages.

Bibliography: General works collected in *Patrologia Latina* 158:49–118; 159:301–318, 347–580, 587–606, 709–812. Devotional works, ed. A. WILMART in *Revue des sciences religieuses* 15 (1935) 184–219, 354–379. Editions. *Tractatus de conceptione sanctae Mariae,* ed. H. THURSTON and T. SLATER (Freiburg 1904); *The Life of St. Anselm,* ed. and tr. R. W. SOUTHERN (New York 1962); *History of Recent Events in England,* tr. G. BOSANQUET (London 1964). For a study of his works as a whole and of his relationship with St. Anselm, see R. W. SOUTHERN, *Saint Anselm and His Biographer* (Cambridge, Eng. 1963).

[R. W. SOUTHERN]

EALDRED (ALDRED) OF YORK

A monk of Winchester (d. Sept. 11, 1069), abbot of Tavistock (*c.* 1027), bishop of WORCESTER (1046), and then archbishop of York (1060), Ealdred was a power in both Church and State. He warred against the Welsh and Norse, served on royal embassies to Rome and Germany, and probably crowned Harold II. He administered the dioceses of Hereford and Ramsbury while holding Worcester, but was forced to surrender Worcester before Pope Nicholas granted him the pallium for York. Nonetheless, Ealdred reformed and strengthened his dioceses, especially York, Worcester, Gloucester, Southwell, and Beverley. He submitted to WILLIAM I at Berkhamstead and consecrated him king (Christmas 1066) and Matilda queen (1068), subsequently serving the conqueror loyally, though protesting against any oppression. Sources for his life include the *Anglo-Saxon Chronicle,* Folcard's *Vita* of JOHN OF BEVERLEY, FLORENCE OF WORCESTER, SIMEON OF DURHAM, WILLIAM OF MALMESBURY, and the *Chronica Pontificum of the Church of York* (ed. J. Raine Historians . . . York 2, *Rerum Britannicarum medii aevi scriptores,* London 1858–96).

Bibliography: *The Dictionary of National Biography from the Earliest Times to 1900* (London 1885–1900) 1:249–251. E. A. FREEMAN, *History of the Norman Conquest,* 6 v. (Oxford 1867–79) v.2, 3, 4. F. E. HARMER, ed. and tr., *Anglo-Saxon Writs* (Manchester, Eng. 1952).

[W. A. CHANEY]

EALING ABBEY

Benedictine abbey in Ealing, a suburb of London, England; dedicated to St. Benedict. At the request of Car-

Stone carving statue of female cycladic idol. (©Gianni Dagli Orti/CORBIS)

dinal Herbert VAUGHAN, monks from DOWNSIDE established in Ealing a parish and a small school (1895), which became priory (1916), autonomous (1947), and an abbey (1955). The neo-Gothic church, damaged during World War II, has been restored (1962). Wolstan Pearson was the first prior; Charles Pontifex, the first abbot. In 1963 the community numbered 30 monks; the parish, 7,000 Catholics; and the public school, 700 boys.

Bibliography: *The Tablet* 205 (May, June 1955). *The Benedictine Almanac and Guide 1963* (London 1963).

[J. STÉPHAN]

EARTH-MOTHER, WORSHIP OF THE

Turkish excavations in Asia Minor in the first half of the twentieth century showed that the female idols, which can be connected in part at least with the cult of the Earth-Mother, go back to the fourth millennium B.C. The persistence of her cult in Asia Minor is evident from its various offshoots of the Magna Mater type (*see* MYSTERY RELIGIONS, GRECO-ORIENTAL), for these offshoots all exhibit a common foundation, and in its various manifestations this cult continues to the end of antiquity. The concept of the Earth-Mother was given a more intellectual and spiritual character as soon as she came to be identified with the ancestor-mother of mankind. Ethnological research holds that this fusion took place at an early date. The Celtic worshipers of the *Matres*, or *Matronae*, evidently felt a closer, family relationship with these divinities (*see* CELTIC RELIGION).

The Greeks may have brought with them a disposition to worship the Earth as an inheritance from the common religion of the Indo-Europeans. In India Prithivī, ''the broad'' (earth, as a flat surface), is a divine figure. Among the Persians earth worship is probably retained in the cult of the four elements. The Greeks, who entered Greece from the north in several waves, had certainly become acquainted with an earlier farming culture in the Danube area and had come under the influence of its mentality. In Greece they found themselves in the sphere of a common culture that in the third millennium, despite all local variations, dominated the whole region from Palestine, Cyprus, Crete, and the islands of the Aegean Sea as far west as lower Italy. In the second millennium this culture is called the Minoan-Mycenaean, and the worship of a Mistress of Nature, who can be regarded as an hypostasis of the Asianic goddess of life, was one of its characteristic features. The connection with the earth was strongly emphasized.

For the most part, Homer, the poet of the aristocracy, ignored the earth cult in any form. On the other hand, Hesiod, the peasant poet, stressed the religion of the oppressed class. By emphasizing this predominantly agricultural religion—and by advertence to her significant role in his *Theogony*—he raised the figure of personified Earth to higher recognition. In Hesiod Gaia, it is true, Earth is only the Mother of the Titans (by Uranus), and later—without a father being named—of the Giants. Since Zeus, the son of one of the Titans (Chronus), seizes the rule of the world, she thus appears as one of the great primitive principles. However, her mythology and personification is at first very vague. If the extent of her worship is taken as a norm for divine rank, it must be said in general that Gaia (Ge) as a goddess did not have much significance. The opposing thesis of W. Otto and E. Peterich, his pupil, has been rightly rejected by M. Nilsson (M. P. Nilsson, *Geschichte der griechischen Religion* 1:428). The position of Earth in law as a guarantee of an oath (already in Homer) is higher than in religion. The occasional appeals to her in tragedy are to be regarded as poetic testimony with a philosophical slant [A. Dieterich, *Mutter Erde* (Leipzig 1925); Nilsson, *op. cit.* 432].

The separation of Demeter and of Rhea (the mother of Zeus) from Gaia as more personal figures indicates that Gaia, being conceived as an all too physical and impersonal magnitude, offered insufficient support to religious demands and especially to those of an eschatological nature. The same holds true of Roman Tellus. However, Tellus as a symbol of the vegetative life-force enjoyed a higher esteem in the early Roman farming population than the shadowy and mythless consorts of the gods [F. Altheim, *Terra Mater* (Giessen 1931)].

Bibliography: M. ELIADE, *Patterns in Comparative Religion*, tr. R. SHEED (New York 1958) esp. 239–247. W. DREXLER, ''Gaia,'' *Ausführliches Lexikon der griechischen und röischen Mythologie*, ed. W. H. ROSCHER, (Leipzig 1884–1937) 1.2:1566–86. S. EITREM, ''Gaia,'' *Paulys Realenzyklopädie der klassischen Altertumswissenschaft*, ed. G. WISSOWA et al. (Stuttgart 1910) 7.1:467–479.

[K. PRÜMM]

EAST ASIAN PASTORAL INSTITUTE

Located on the campus of the Jesuit University of Ateneo de Manila in Quezon City, Philippines and sponsored by the Jesuit Conference of East Asia and Oceania (JCEAO), the East Asian Pastoral Institute (EAPI) is an international multicultural center for spiritual renewal, pastoral training and leadership formation for laity, religious, and clergy in the Asia–Pacific region. In addition to organizing sabbatical, theological reflection, and spiritual renewal programs, it focuses on the training and formation of lay leaders and catechists for service in the local churches of Asia–Pacific. It also offers masters and doctorate programs in theology as part of the Manila Theological Consortium.

History. The EAPI was the brainchild of Johannes HOFINGER, S.J., an Austrian Jesuit missionary to China who was expelled by the Communists in 1949. In 1953, he and a small band of fellow Jesuits established the Institute for Missionary Apologetics in army barracks which formerly housed a World War II Japanese concentration camp. In 1961, this institute was renamed the East Asian Pastoral Institute, and its mission was broadened to include training and formation in catechetics and liturgy. On Aug. 15, 1965, the Jesuit General, Pedro Arrupe reorganized EAPI in response to calls by various Asian bishops, missionaries, and religious superiors for the establishment of an international formation and training center in Asia to implement the pastoral vision of Vatican II. Arrupe appointed a Jesuit missionary in Japan, Alfonso Nebreda as its first director with a mandate to oversee the relocation of the institute to new premises on the campus of Ateneo de Manila university, and to initiate new pastoral and leadership training programs. The relocation was completed with the inauguration of the new building complex in 1968.

Publications. In 1962, the fledging institute launched its first publication, a quarterly entitled *Good Tidings*. In 1964 two new journals were inaugurated: *Amen,* which focused on liturgical renewal, and *Teaching All Nations,* which sought to articulate and promote mission catechetics and liturgy. At the end of 1979, *Good Tidings* and *Teaching All Nations* were merged into a new journal, the *East Asian Pastoral Review* (EAPR). EAPI also publishes a newsletter, *The Bridge*.

Bibliography: H. CZARKOWSKI, ''Zur Bedeutung und Situation der Pastoralinstitute in der Dritten Welt,'' *Zeitschrift für Missionswissenschaft und Religionswissenschaft* 59 (1975) 112–126. A. M. DE LA CRUZ, ''Johannes Hofinger Remembered, 1905–1984,'' *Living Light,* 20 (1984) 345–347. F. X. CLARK, ''Johannes Hofinger, S.J., (1905–1984), Life and Bibliography,'' *East Asian Pastoral Review* 21 (1984) 103–120. A. M. NEBREDA, ''Johannes Hofinger: Catalyst and Pioneer,'' *East Asian Pastoral Review,* 21 (1984) 120–127.

[J. Y. TAN]

EAST SYRIAN LITURGY

The liturgical tradition that evolved from the usages of Edessa, the ancient center of the Syriac-speaking Christian Church. It is the liturgical tradition of the ASSYRIAN CHURCH OF THE EAST and the CHALDEAN CATHOLIC CHURCH. In addition, the SYRO-MALABAR CHURCH in India and in diaspora traces its liturgy directly back to the East Syrian rite. The variety of nomenclature for the churches of the East Syrian or Assyrian Church of the East tradition merits a preliminary comment. As a result of a complex ecclesial climate at the time of the Councils of Ephesus (431) and Chalcedon (451), the ancient Oriental church was branded ''Nestorian,'' an inaccurate designation that derived from and persisted because of theological misconceptions and regional prejudice (*see* NESTORIANISM). When some factions of the Church of the East united with Rome in the 15th century, the uniates were designated the Chaldean Church or the Chaldean Catholic Church. The Church of the East now designates itself the Assyrian Church of the East or Church of the East, while the uniate Church prefers the title Chaldean Catholic Church. In November 1994 the Assyrian Church of the East and the Chaldean Catholic Church signed a ''Common Christological Declaration,'' ending centuries of discord and paving the way for fuller unity between the two churches that preserve a common liturgical and spiritual patrimony. Members of the Church of the East and the Chaldean Catholic Church are spread throughout the world, with greatest numbers in Iraq, southern Turkey, Iran, and most recently the United States (especially Illinois, Michigan, and California), France, and Australia. This entry will trace the historical development and particularities of the rite, outline the structure of its Eucharistic liturgy, and give brief comment on the daily office, liturgical cycle, and other liturgical celebrations.

Origins of the East Syrian Liturgical Rite. The strongly biblical East Syrian rite developed in the Persian Empire and is also influenced by the culture of Mesopotamia. Debate surrounds the origins of Christianity in the Mesopotamia and Persia, a region torn by turbulent political battles. The Roman Empire expanded its boundaries to the east, acquiring Syria, which became an imperial province in 27 B.C. Further campaigns extended the boundaries to the Euphrates River, which marked the boundary with the Parthian Empire. There were frequent invasions and regressions through the 2d century. Orshoene, with its capital Edessa, became a client kingdom of Rome *c.* A.D. 166. Rome took over Mesopotamia and made it a province, seized Nisibis, and went south to Babylon and Seleucia. The roads that the Roman armies traveled were also the trade routes that linked Antioch in the west with Iran and India in the east. It is likely that Christianity came early on via these trade routes, and they facilitated the Church of the East's missionary activity that extended to India and even to China along the silk route. In the early 3d century, Ardahshir I of the Persian Sassanian dynasty conquered the Parthians and reigned as king from 226 to 241, when he was succeeded by his son Shapur I (241–272). The Sassanid dynasty would reign for 500 more years. This development led to a certain marginalization of the Church of the East from the Greek- and Latin-speaking Great Church of the Mediterranean basin.

A thorough and critical history of the East Syrian liturgy is still wanting. Scholars have generally traced two lines of influence on the development of the early Syriac tradition in general, which were then extended to the East Syrian liturgy in particular. The first line of thinking posits a substantial influence of Jewish liturgical traditions on early Syrian Christianity. The second traces the origins of the Syriac-speaking churches to Antioch, a strongly hellenized church. Following the common line of thinking, East Syrian liturgy has its roots in the liturgical tradition of Antioch influenced by Jewish liturgical usages.

In the late 20th century this thesis was challenged by scholars. Following William Macomber, the ordinary assumption that the East Syrian liturgy is a branch of the Antiochene liturgy is false. Rather, careful study of the Eucharistic and baptismal liturgies suggests that the East Syrian liturgy is *sui generis.* He proposes that around 400, there were three major liturgical centers: Antioch, Jerusalem, and Edessa. While the Antiochene rite was followed by the Greek-speaking region and the Jerusalem rite in Palestine, the Syriac-speaking Christians to the East followed the rite of Edessa. How uniform this rite was, however, is sheer speculation, since the documentary evidence is scarce. The synod held in Seleucia-Ctesiphon in 410 intended to organize the Church of the East following a period of persecution. It called for the rite used by the bishops of the major center of Seleucia-Ctesiphon (near Babylon) and Maypriqaṭ (to the north at the source of the Tigris) to replace local variants. Macomber judges that the rite in question is that of Edessa, which came to prevail throughout the region, but there is little empirical evidence to support his assumption. The upheaval after the Councils of Ephesus and Chalcedon led to further developments. The rise of monophysitism in Edessa resulted in the move of the followers of Theodore of Mopsuestia, subsequently known as ''Nestorians'' because of Theodore's student, to Nisibis where Edessene usage continued in Persia until the Arab invasions in the 7th century forced restructuring.

Few sources survive for tracing the elements and characteristics of the so-called antique Edessene rite. Extant witnesses allow a few generalizations about this rite. First, the early Syriac-speaking Christian communities of the region had a distinctive euchological pattern. The accounts of missionary Eucharist and baptism in the apocryphal *Acts of Thomas* and *Acts of John* are taken by scholars as witnesses for emerging liturgical practice and coalescing oral tradition in the late 3d century. These accounts suggest a developing form of a strongly epicletic and eschatological euchology. To this day, the euchology is also strongly doxological, focused on giving praise and glory to God.

A distinctive euchological pattern also appears in the oldest extant anaphora, the anaphora of Addai and Mari, the core of which dates to the early 3d century and is still used by the Church of the East today. Unlike Antiochene anaphoras whose subgenres are ordered anamnesis-supper narrative-epiclesis-intercession, Addai and Mari places the epiclesis as the last element, leading into the doxology. It is a fairly undeveloped epiclesis, compared to the more lengthy epicleses of the Acts. The anaphora had a Sanctus, and most likely its original form lacked a supper narrative, a tradition preserved by the Assyrian Church of the East. The anaphora has been judged to be an original Syriac composition and has certain affinities to Jewish prayer forms.

The second observation about the formative period of the East Syrian liturgy concerns the development of the liturgy of the word. As the house-church and missionary celebrations gave way to larger-scale public celebrations, the East Syrian Christians built churches—the oldest of which date from the 4th century—whose apses were filled with an altar, rather than the seats for clergy that are found in the rest of the East and West. In the middle of the nave is a large walled-in platform known as the *bêmâ* that contains a throne used for the gospel book and cross and seats for the bishop and clergy and that was the center for the liturgy of the word. Scholars debate the possible influence of the Jewish synagogue on the Christian *bêmâ.*

With regard to what Scripture was read at the *bêmâ,* Anton Baumstark argues that the earliest Syriac lectionary reflects the continuation of a synagogal system that was coming to be replaced by new Christian material drawn from a variety of sources of different provenance. Before the 7th century, several lectionary systems coexisted. One witness, dubbed the early Syriac lectionary (MS London, British Library, Additional 14528), shows an exuberance for Old Testament lections. In the 7th century, the liturgical reform of Ishôᶜyahb III led to a standardization of the lectionary system and fixed the number of reading to four for the East Syrian Church: two Old Testament (one law, one prophets) and two New Testament (one epistle and one Gospel). The revised lectionary reflects the influence of the Jerusalem system and the confluence of cathedral and monastic systems. In addition to psalmody, the singing of *madrāshê* (narrative songs) *sôgyātâ* (dialogue poems) and perhaps *mêmrê* (metrical homilies) complemented the proclamation of Scripture.

The third important and distinctive aspect of the East Syrian rite is its baptismal liturgy. To this day, the baptismal liturgy is dominated by the imagery and theology of the baptism of Jesus in the Jordan, the imagery of divine adoption, messianic configuration, rebirth, and transformation by the Holy Spirit. The original shape of the East Syrian rite is a prebaptismal anointing followed by water bath and Eucharist. In contrast to the Greek rites, the prebaptismal anointing is strongly pneumatic and messianic rather than exorcisitic or apotropaic. The East Syrian rite eventually adopted a postbaptismal chrismation under influence of the West. The early theologies of Eucharist, baptism, and anointing are given classic poetic expression in the hymns of Ephrem (d. 373). Further significant influence on the developing East Syrian liturgy comes from the School of Nisibis and the work of Narsai (d. 502). In addition to his commentary on the holy mysteries, Narsai's literary legacy includes a number of liturgical compositions.

Structuration (6th–7th Centuries): Reform of Ishô-ᶜyahb III. In the aftermath of the doctrinal controversies and ecclesiastical division in the 5th century, the diversity and variety of local usages gradually give way to more consolidation and structuring in the 6th century. The following account draws on the work of A. Baumstark, P. Youssif, W. Macomber, S. Jammo, and J. Mateos. Patriarch Abâ I (540–552) played an important role in the introduction of new elements to the East Syrian rite. Abâ I traveled widely before becoming patriarch in 540 and introduced liturgical souvenirs in the form of the Byzantine Trisagion and the ''Angel of Peace'' litany. He is also reputed to have composed many *mêmrê, tûrgāmê,* and antiphonal *qānônê* (psalmody and refrains). According to headings of later manuscripts, he also introduced two new anaphoras to the liturgy, honorifically attrributed to Theodore of Mopsuestia and Nestorius, respectively. The 6th century also marked the end of the catechumenate and its associated rituals. Crucial information on the period comes from the commentary of Gabriel Qaṭrayâ (615).

A powerful influence on liturgical development following the Arab conquest and collapse of the Persian Empire comes from Ishôᶜyahb III (580–659) at the upper monastery of Mar Gabriel in Mosul. He is credited with an extensive liturgical standardization and reform that involved the liturgical books and the calendar. Ishôᶜyahb III redacted a liturgical book of continuing importance, the *ḥûdrâ* (''cycle'' or ''course''). The *ḥûdrâ* contains all of the propers texts for the office and Eucharist for the Sundays and feasts of the year, except some more recent feasts. It conformed much of the usage to the liturgy of Mar Gabriel, also known as the Upper Monastery, on the bank of the Tigris River near Mosul. Though late in the manuscript tradition, a number of private prayers of the priest-celebrant, called *kûshāconpê,* also came to infiltrate the liturgy, including the anaphora.

Further textual reform by Ishôᶜyahb III fixed the number of anaphoras at three (Addai and Mari, Theodore, and Nestorius) and assigned when they would be used. He is reputed to have drawn up the *ordo* or *euchologion* called the *ṭaksâ.* As he compiled the rites of baptism, pardon, ordination, and consecration of a church/altar, he may well have revised them. Ishôᶜyahb III is also credited with celebrated liturgical refrains and *madrāshê.* Finally, he established norms for the liturgy of the hours.

Information about subsequent interpolations and ritual changes in the liturgy comes from liturgical commentaries. The 7th-century commentary of Gabriel Bar Lipāh Qaṭrāyâ (sections relevant to the Eucharist are in Jammo in Latin translation) describes a liturgy much the same as the modern. His relative Abraham Bar Lipāh Qaṭrāyâ produced basically the same commentary in question-and-answer form, though he occasionally offers his own interpretations (*Corpus scriptorum Christianorum orientalium* 72, SS 29). The most detailed commentary describes the liturgy of a bishop probably in a city-church because of the elaborate ceremony. The author is not identified and so is known conventionally as the *anonymous commentary* (*Corpus scriptorum Christianorum orientalium* 64 and 72); it took on particular weight in the tradition of liturgical commentary in the East Syrian Church. The *terminus a quo* of this commentary is 780, but its *terminus ad quem* is uncertain. It is generally dated to the 9th or 10th century.

Composition and Codification. The 10th to 13th centuries mark the end of effervescent composition and the filling out of the monastic offices. Patriarch Elias III (d. 1190), also known as Abu Ḥalim, composed a number of prayers collected in the eponymous liturgical book *Abu Ḥalim.* George Wardâ crafted poetic refrains, compiled into the eponymous liturgical book, the *wardâ* (literally, ''the rose'') along with similar composition by other contemporaries. Baumstark dated it from the 13th century. The *gazâ* (treasure) also dates from the 13th century and fills out what is missing in the *ḥûdrâ* for night vigils and later other feasts of the Lord not observed on Sunday and some commemorations of the saints.

After this period of composition and codification of liturgical texts, the East Syrian liturgy underwent further developments as a result of unification with Rome, Latinization, and western missionary influence. Two rival patriarchates fostered two distinct styles of performance. Back-and-forth shifts to unity with Rome affected the liturgical life of the Church of the East. W. Macomber has explored these developments. First, the uniates simplified the ritual of their liturgy, while the original patriarchate lines kept more elaborate ritual actions known as the Alqosh usage. The liturgical texts of the two churches, though, remained the same, apart from some minor variants. Nevertheless, the usage of Alqosh eventually supplanted the simplified liturgy of the first uniate patriarchate. The uniate liturgy underwent further Latinizations when the uniate patriarch was established in Diyarbakir. Patriarch Joseph I's successor also introduced several elements from the Maronite liturgy.

In the following two centuries, the Chaldean Catholic patriarchate of Diyarbakir and the nonuniate patriarchate of Alqosh did attempt liturgical unification, but their rivalry impeded its success. With Abdishoᶜ V (1894–1899) a serious reform began, but the liturgy he submitted drew opposition from Diyarbakir because it set out the usage of Alqosh. Under Emmanuel II Thomas (1900–1947) a compromise was reached that essentially retained the rite of Alqosh. Throughout this period, the Assyrian Church of the East suffered from repeated massacres and forced emigration.

A major development for the standardization of the liturgy came with arrival of missionaries in the 18th through early 20th century. Anglicans, Presbyterians, Lutherans, Baptists, Roman Catholics, and Russian Orthodox took great interest in the Church of the East, building schools, welfare centers, and hospitals as well as trying to reclaim the Nestorians. The Lazarist and Anglican missionaries to the East also imported a few Westernisms in the Alqosh liturgy. It was the efforts of these missionaries, however, that led to the printing and publishing of the East Syrian liturgical texts. For the first time in its history, major manuscripts gave way to printed and bound books patterned after the Western breviary and missal.

By the late 20th century, there were nine editions of the missal that, despite the standardization of the printing press, still vary one from the other. Among the missals, the edition of J. Kelaytâ (*The Liturgy of the Church of the East* [Mosul, 1928]) has been considered the most representative of the manuscript missal traditions. This 'missal' (really a *ṭaksâ*) contains the ordinary of the Eucharistic liturgy and several other rites. The propers are found in the *ḥûdrâ* or its supplement. This edition was reissued in 1959 by Archbishop Darmo. It was published again in 1971 by the Chaldeans who cleared away remaining Latinisms and set Alqosh rubrics as part of liturgical renewal inspired by Vatican II. With regard to the *ḥûdrâ,* the Chaldean (Catholic) version reflects the desire of the editors to avoid expressions that could be construed as Nestorian. The Church of the East *ḥûdrâ* has been edited and published by T. Darmo.

Structure of the Current Eucharistic Liturgy. The celebration of the holy mysteries (*rāzê qadishê*) in the current East Syrian rite opens with an office of praise that includes the Lord's Prayer with a refrain that emphasizes God's holiness, psalmody, presidential prayers, the proper anthem of the rails, procession to the *bêmâ,* incensation, the *lakûmarâ* (To you, O Lord) hymn unique to the East Syrian rite, and veneration of the cross. At the *bêmâ* the trisagion is intoned and a presidential collect invokes God as glorious and immortal.

The liturgy of the word includes two Old Testament readings, a verse of psalmody, an exhortation, the epistle reading, imposition of incense, gospel procession, the praise verse and alleluia, Gospel, an optional homily, and the diaconal litanic prayers known as the *karôzûtâ.*

The liturgy of the Eucharist opens with prostration of the ministers and dismissal of the noncommunicants. The transfer of the gifts and procession to the altar are accompanied by the anthem of the mysteries. When the gifts are deposed, the creed with particular variations is intoned. After preparatory prayers of access, the peace is exchanged and the anphora begins after diaconal proclamation. The anaphora itself is interspersed with private prayers of the priest celebrant. Penitential prayers of the priest celebrant follow the conclusion of the anaphora, followed by an incensation and elevation of the elements. The fraction and consignation follow, with a diaconal proclamation, prayer of absolution, and the Lord's prayer. The call to communion is followed by the versicle "Awesome are you," adoring God. The veil is opened and the elements presented to the people. In the Assyrian Church of the East, the clergy take communion after the people; even the clergy do not take communion themselves but receive communion from another minister. Communion is under both forms while the anthem of the *bêmâ* is sung. The praise, *teshbôḥtâ,* follows. Concluding prayers and the blessing end the liturgy.

Daily Prayer. The office has been studied in detail by J. Mateos and R. Taft. The liturgy of the hours of the East Syrian rite has retained an essentially cathedral, or popular, character, with monastic influence noted in the lesser hours celebrated only during Great Fast. In the 7th century at the Synod of Darin the laity were enjoined to come to morning and evening prayer in the local church rather than a monastery or at home. The office also reflect the historical developments traced in the periods above. Several types of vigils, known as *lelyâ* are celebrated depending on the feast day. Morning prayer, *ṣaprâ,* includes fixed morning psalmody, and on festal days incense, the hymn of light, and the hymn known as the Gloria in the Roman West. Evening prayer, *ramshâ,* has had the ninth hour office attached to it over time, but its core reflects the fixed vesperal psalmody, litanies, and a stational procession. The daily and festal office is integral to unfolding of the liturgical cycle and a primary expression of the the Church of the East's rich theology.

Liturgical Cycle. In conjunction with the arrangement of the liturgical material, Ishô^c^yahb III is also reputed to have fixed the liturgical cycle. The East Syrian liturgical cycle is designated *shabo^c^e,* which means "seven," derived from the common way Mesopotamian and West Asian cultures marked time in 50-day periods of seven weeks plus a day. The seasons are as follows: Annunciation (4 weeks), Epiphany (7 weeks), Fast (7 weeks), Resurrection (7 weeks), Apostles (7 weeks), Summer (7 weeks), Elias (7 weeks), Moses (7 weeks), and Dedication (4 weeks), which has an eschatological color. Due to the variable date of Pasch and Epiphany, however, the seasons are often shortened. The Season of Moses is rarely more than four weeks, and often just one Sunday. Summer is markedly penitential.

Other Liturgical Celebrations. The East Syrian rites' unique characteristics are also apparent in its other liturgical celebrations. Its initiation liturgy is noted above. The marriage liturgy has preserved a number of usages, including common drinking of a mixture of ash from a martyr or saint's shrine and wine, blessing of the bridal robes, crowning before the lections, rich hymnody, and the making of the bed chamber. The *henanâ,* a mixture of oil, water, and dust or ash from a saint or martyr's shrine, is given to the sick; unction of the sick has fallen into disuse. Holy Order focuses on the laying on of hands with epicletic prayer, and there are different burial rites for clergy and laity. Penance, though in disuse, retains a public character; in most cases a Rite of Pardon (*taksâ dhûsayâ*) is celebrated in preparation for communion. The Chaldeans, however, adopted and adapted Latin rites for many of the sacramental celebrations.

Bibliography: An extensive bibliography through 1990 is available in P. YOUSIF, ed. *Classified Bibliography on the East Syrian Liturgy/La bibliographie classifiée de la liturgie syrienne orientale* (Rome 1990). S. BROCK, "The 'Nestorian' Church. A Lamentable Misnomer," *Bulletin of the John Rylands University Library of Manchester* 78 (1996) 23–35. A. BAUMSTARK, *Nichtevangelische syrische Perikopenordnungen der ersten Jahrtausends* (Munster 1921); *Geschichte der syrischen Literatur* (Bonn 1968). T. DARMO, ed. *Ktābâ dqdām wdbātar wdḥûdrâ wdkashkôl wdgazâ wqālā d^c^ ûdrānê ^c^ am ktâbâ dmazmôrê,* 3 v. (Trichur 1960–61). A. GELSTON, *The Eucharistic Prayer of Addai and Mari* (Oxford 1992). S. GRIFFITH, "Spirit in the Bread; Fire in the Wine: The Eucharist as 'Living Medicine' in the Thought of Ephraem the Syrian," *Modern Theology* 15 (1999) 225–246. S. Y. H. JAMMO, *La Structure de la Messe Chaldéene du Début jusqu'à l'Anaphore. Étude historique, OCA* 207 (Rome 1979). W. F. MACOMBER, "A Theory on the Origins of the Syrian, Maronite and Chaldean Rites," *OCP* 39 (1973) 235–242; "A History of the Chaldean Mass," *Worship* 51 (1977) 107–120. J. MATEOS, *Lelya-Ṣapra. Les Offices chaldéens de la nuit et du matin,* 2d ed. *OCA* 156 (Rome 1972). E. RENHART, "Encore une Fois: Le Bēmā des Églises de la Syrie du Nord"; *Parole de l'Orient* 20 (1995) 85–94. G. A. M. ROUWHORST, "Jewish Liturgical Traditions in Early Syriac Christianity," *Vigiliae Christianae* 51 (1997) 77–93. P. YOUSIF, "Appunti sulla preghiera liturgica del rito caldeo e malabarese" (Pontificio Istituto Orientale, Rome 1983, photocopy); "The Divine Liturgy According to the Rite of the Assyro-Chaldean Church," in *The Eucharistic Liturgy in the Christian East,* ed. J. MADEY (Kerala and Paderborn 1982) 175–237; "Le Déroulement de la messe chaldéene," in *Eucharistie: Célébrations, rites, piétés,* BELS 79 (Rome 1995); *L'Eucharistie chez saint Éphrem de Nisibe, OCA* 224 (Rome 1984). G. WINKLER, "Zur frühchristlichen Tauftradition in Syrien und Armenien unter Einbezug der Taufe Jesu." *Ostkirchliche Studien* 27 (1978) 154–172; "Weitere Beobachtungen zur frühen Epiklese (den Doxologie und dem Sanctus). Über die Bedeutung der Apokryphen für die Einforschung der Entwicklung der Riten," *Oriens Christianus* 80 (1996) 177–200. R. TAFT, *The Liturgy of the Hours in East and West: The Origins of the Divine Office and Its Meaning for Today* (Collegeville, Minn. 1986).

[R. E. MCCARRON]

EAST TIMOR, THE CATHOLIC CHURCH IN

Also known as Timor Lorosae, East Timor lies in the Lesser Sunda Islands in the Indonesian archipelago, between 8 and 10 degrees eastern longitude and between 123 and 127 degrees northern latitude, 375 km south of the equator, to the north of AUSTRALIA and west of Papua New Guinea.

The Portuguese arrived in Timor sometime between 1512 and 1522. They officially annexed the area as a Portuguese territory with the appointment of a governor for Timor and Solor in 1702. During this period there were frequent and sometimes violent territorial disputes with the Dutch, who also claimed portions of the islands. From 1702 Portugal administered the area from Goa in India and toward the end of the 19th century from Macau in China. Portugal and the Netherlands established the boundary between their respective territories in 1859. In 1896 Portuguese-controlled East Timor received the status of an autonomous district and in 1909 became a Portuguese overseas province with its own governor and with financial and administrative autonomy.

With the departure of the Dutch from their colonial possessions in Southeast Asia, Dutch Timor became part of Indonesia and was renamed West Timor. East Timor remained under Portuguese control until 1975. After the Portuguese withdrew, Indonesia annexed and administered the territory from 1975 to 1999. The local population voted overwhelmingly for independence from Indonesia in a 1999 referendum. Shortly after, Indonesian-backed militias went on a rampage, killing clergy, religious and innocent civilians, destroying the territory's infrastructure and forcibly displacing the local populace. The United Nations intervened, sending peacekeepers and establishing the United Nations Transitional Administration in East Timor (UNTAET) with the objective of assisting the East Timorese to full nationhood.

The first known missioner in East Timor was the Dominican Antonio Taveira, who came from the neighboring island of Flores and baptized some 5,000 Timorese, probably in Lifao, Oe-cusse, shortly before 1556. He and his confreres sought to convert the local chieftains, whose subjects might then also enter the Church. The converted rulers became vassals of Portugal, obliged to pay tribute and supply soldiers during wartime. With the arrival of 20 new missioners in 1641, pastoral work on the coast became more routine. In the 17th century the mission was controlled by the ''black Portuguese,''or Topass, i.e., the royal mestizo families of da Costa and d'Ornay. Only in 1702 was a permanent mission centre established in Timor, at Lifao, which was transferred to Dili in 1769. A minor seminary was established in *Oe-cusse* in 1734. With the Dutch conquest of Portuguese Malacca in 1641, King John V ordered the Portuguese bishop of Malacca to reside in Timor.

The Timor mission was almost totally neglected during the 18th century. Unrest caused the Portuguese to withdraw in 1729, only returning in 1748. In 1754 there were ten Dominicans on Timor and according to contemporary records, Timor had some 50 churches in 1780. From 1811 to 1824 there remained just a single friar, and for the following three years no resident priest at all. During this time Dominicans from Dili also had responsibility for Christians on the neighbouring islands of Flores and Solor. The Dominicans retained some political and commercial power until early in the 19th century. This arrangement caused friction with the lay officials and led to a virtual identification of ecclesial and colonial authority in the eyes of the Timorese.

The anticlericalism of the liberal politicians in Portugal gravely injured the mission during the 19th century. Portugal decreed the expulsion of religious orders in 1834 and the Dominicans departed. Four years later Dili was transferred to Goa from where diocesan clergy arrived. A report (*c.* 1850) speaks of polygamy being the norm and churches empty and unkempt. The situation improved after 1874 when Timor was transferred to Macau, and 11 secular priests arrived. Three years later the first parishes were established. In 1898 four Jesuits arrived and opened a college and meteorological observatory. By 1900 there were 16 schools for boys and four for girls. In 1910 Portugal again expelled religious and restricted the activities of the secular priests, whose numbers declined from 22 in 1910 to ten in 1924. The Salesians (SDB) opened a technical school in 1927 at Fatumaca, near Bacau. The SDB soon became the largest religious congregation in the territory. In 1930 there were 18,984

Capital: Dili.
Size: East Timor (Timor Lorosae) occupies: (1) an area of 14,609 sq. km. comprising the eastern half of the island of Timor, (2) Oe-cusse, an enclave of 524.8 sq. km. on the northern, Indonesian province of West Timor, and (3) the neighboring islands of Atauro and Jaco, totalling 92.8 sq. km.
Population: The local Maubere population is a mix of Negroid, Melanesian and Malay. There is a small ethnic Chinese community.
Languages: Some 31 languages and dialects are spoken in the east and just five in the west of the territory. By far the most widely spoken is Tetum which East Timor shares with the Belu district of West Timor. Dawan is spoken in the Oe-cussi enclave. Other smaller East Timorese languages include Kemak and Bunak on the border with West Timor. These local languages belong to the Austronesian family of languages.
Religions: About 85% of the indigenous East Timorese are Roman Catholics. Protestant Christians are small but growing. The Chinese community is predominantly Taoist and Buddhist. The Muslim community is comprised almost exclusively of migrants from Indonesia who have not fled with the departing Indonesian soldiers and militias in 1999.
Dioceses: (immediately subject to the Holy See): Dili, Bacau, Seme.

Catholics and 958 catechumens. A minor seminary was opened in 1936 at Saibada which, in 1954, was transferred to Dare, where it is today. The graduates continued their higher studies in Macau or Portugal. In 1940 Dili was separated from Macau and established as a diocese in its own right.

Japanese occupation during the Pacific War (1942-45) was traumatic. A reinforcement of 400 Australian troops arrived in December 1941, and this small Australian force squared off against 21,000 Japanese with the support of the Timorese. In response, the Japanese forces sacked Dili and ravaged the countryside. Some 40,000 Timorese died through bombardment and starvation. Three priests were assassinated by the Japanese, six fled to the mountains with their people while ten escaped to Australia. In 1946 the Portuguese returned to East Timor and reasserted their control.

Until the end of the 1960s the majority of the East Timorese, then numbering about 560,000, still clung to their traditional religion. Most of the 5,300 Chinese traders were Buddhists, with just 490 Catholics among them. There were also only 380 Muslim traders and a mere 100 Protestants in the capital at Dili. Catholics totalled 113,500, or approximately 20 percent of the population. They included most land owners and officials, for whom baptism became the avenue for advancement under the Portuguese. There were 44 clergy of whom 30 were diocesan, nine Salesian (SDB) and five Jesuit (SJ). Just seven were indigenous Timorese. Sisters numbered 37 with just six Timorese; there were 12 Brothers. There were three secondary and 41 primary schools. This stable situation was violently disrupted when Indonesia invaded in December 1975.

A bloodless, left-wing coup by the Portuguese army on April 25, 1974, ended the 48-year dictatorship in Lisbon and led to a rapid process of decolonization for East Timor. Civil fighting broke out in August 1975, instigated by Indonesian intelligence operatives under ''Operation Komodo.'' On Dec. 7, 1975, with the support of the United States, Britain and Australia, Indonesia invaded East Timor and formally annexed the territory in July 1976. The brutality and greed of the occupying force led to strong resistance by the Timorese. Through aerial bombardment and a war-related famine, over a third of the population—perhaps as many as 40 percent—perished in two major assaults in 1976 and 1979. The population decreased from over 700,000 to approximately 540,000. This traumatic genocide went virtually unreported in the outside world. Almost 90 percent of livestock belonging to the indigenous community were wiped out.

Martinho da Costa Lopes, apostolic administrator of Dili from 1978 to 1983, became the voice of the voiceless, but, after condemning atrocities, was removed from office by the Vatican under Indonesian pressure. The Salesian Carlos Filipe Ximenes Belo (b. 1948) was appointed his successor in 1983 and ordained bishop in 1988. Within months of his appointment, Bishop Belo himself began condemning Indonesian military atrocities, becoming the one credible voice courageously speaking the truth from within the territory. He maintained that only by acknowledging the authentic ethnic, cultural and religious identity of the Timorese could their human dignity be restored. For 16 years Bishop Belo walked a tightrope between voicing the aspirations of the people and keeping in contact with the occupying forces. Meanwhile from Australia and New York, Jose Ramos-Horta led the campaign for an independent Timorese state. The surreptitiously filmed massacre of Nov. 12, 1991—when 200 to 300 unarmed mourners of the 18-year-old student, Sebastiao Gomes Rangel were gunned down and bayoneted in cold blood at Santa Cruz Cemetery—shocked the world and led to mounting international pressure on the Indonesian authorities. In defiance of worldwide condemnation, the Special Forces Command (Kopassus) under General Prabowo Subianto, Soeharto's son-in-law, instigated further religious conflict in 1995. On Oct 11, 1996, Bishop Belo and Jose Ramos-Horta received the

Bishop Carlos Filipe Ximenes Belo, giving a homily, Dili, East Timor, photograph by Muchtar Zakaria. (AP/Wide World Photos)

Nobel Prize for Peace in recognition of their courageous efforts.

Throughout this period of turmoil, religious congregations came from Indonesia to complement the longstanding Jesuits and Salesians, including the Divine Word Missionaries (SVD) in 1980, the Franciscans (OFM), and diocesan Sisters from Larantuka (PRR) and Ende (CIY) in Flores. The Church was the one bulwark that defended the dignity and rights of the people. Unsurprisingly, the Church grew rapidly to encompass 36 percent of the population by 1985 and 83 percent of the diocese of Dili and 89 percent of the diocese of Bacau by 1999. Meanwhile Protestants grew to 12 percent, while a majority of the approximately 100,000 migrants from Indonesia were Muslim. A training college for teachers of religious education was opened in Bacau in 1984. In Dili a Pastoral Institute was entrusted to the SVD in 1987. By 1996 there were 30 parishes. In November 1996 East Timor was divided into two dioceses; Dili which remained under Bishop Carlos Ximenes Belo while Bishop Basilio Do Nascimenito was ordained for the new Diocese of Bacau.

The monetary crisis in Southeast Asia in 1997 and the toppling of Soeharto after 32 years of dictatorship the following year broke Indonesia's hold on East Timor. Xanana Gusmao, poet, intellectual, and the Timorese resistance leader, who had been imprisoned in Cipinang Prison, Jakarta, since 1992, was released to house arrest. In May 1999 agreement was reached with Portugal to hold a referendum under United Nations auspices at the end of August. With virtually no preparation and no withdrawal of the occupying forces, a catastrophe was inevitable. Repeated warnings by Bishop Belo went unheeded. Despite months of intimidation and terrorism by Indonesian trained militia gangs and strategic massacres, the most brutal of which was that at Liquica on April 6, 1999, an overwhelming 78 percent of registered voters chose independence. The result was announced on Sept. 5, 1999. That same evening, Indonesian army personnel, together with the militia thugs they had trained, ravaged the country. Virtually every town and village was set on fire, including the harvest in the fields. Eyewitnesses fleeing the violence reported wholesale massacres by marauding militias, including the cold-blooded slaughter on Sept. 6, 1999, of some 100 Timorese who sought shelter in a Catholic church in Suai and the three priests who attempted to shield them, Fr. Hilario Madeira, Fr. Francisco Tavares dos Reis, and Jesuit Fr. Tarcisius Dewanto. Many priests, nuns, religious and seminarians were executed as a reprisal for the Catholic Church's support of East Timorese independence, including the head of Caritas East Timor, Fr Francisco Barreto, killed on September 9, and Jesuit Fr. Karl Albrecht Karim Arbie, head of the Jesuit Refugee Service, killed on September 11. International condemnation of the massacres led to the deployment of a United Nations peace-keeping force. By the time of their arrival, about 60,000 East Timorese had been massacred, 150,000 were hiding in the hills, and 200,000 (about one-third of the population) had fled to Indonesian-controlled West Timor.

Devastated but free, East Timor as a new nation faced a crisis of immense proportions. Two-thirds of youngsters over 15 years of age had never been to school because schools were closed due to the 1975–78 war. A scarcity of trained teachers resulted from the fact that some 86 percent of junior high school teachers and 97 percent in senior high schools had been ethnic Indonesians who fled back to Indonesia after the 1999 referendum. In 1996 the United Nations reported that East Timor had the worst infant mortality rate of the world's 30 least developed countries, some 135 deaths per 1,000 births. At the beginning of the 21st century, this grim picture remained unchanged.

The Catholic Church continued to play an active role in reconstruction and nation building. To accommodate church growth, a third diocese at Seme was erected in 2001. The Diocese of Dili had begun to run the Timor Kmanek radio station. Missionaries returned to assist in the rebuilding of civil society and the Church, as well as preparing the people for independent nationhood.

Bibliography: C. R. BOXER, *Fidalgos in the Far East 1550-1770* (London 1968); *The Portuguese Seaborn Empire 1415-1825* (London 1969). J. DUNN, *East Timor: A People Betrayed* (Australia 1983). A. S. KOHEN, *From the Place of the Dead. The Epic Struggles of Bishop Belo of East Timor* (New York 1999). R. LENNOX, *Fighting Spirit of East Timor. The Life of Martinho da Costa Lopes* (London 2000). J. G. TAYLOR, *Indonesia's Forgotten War: The Hidden History of East Timor* (London 1991); *East Timor: The Price of Freedom* (London 1999).

[J. M. PRIOR]

EASTER AND ITS CYCLE

Easter is the central liturgical season of the Church year, with the Easter season, the 50 days between Easter Sunday and Pentecost, celebrated as one great feast day, the ''great Sunday.'' Since Bede the Venerable (*De ratione temporum* 1:5) the origin of the term for the feast of Christ's Resurrection has been popularly considered to be from the Anglo-Saxon Eastre, a goddess of spring. Another ancient name that has become more common with the renewal of Biblical studies and the liturgy is Pasch, from the Greek transliteration πάσχα of the Aramaic word for the Hebrew *pesach*, passover. In the first three centuries Pasch referred to the annual celebration

Priest saying Easter Mass, covered baskets in the aisle contain the Easter breakfast food, Morave, Slovenia, 1996. (Bojan Brecelj/ CORBIS)

of Christ's Passion and Death; from the end of the 4th century it designated also the EASTER VIGIL; from the 5th century it was reserved more for Easter itself.

History. In Exodus 12.11 and Numbers 28.16 *pesach* is used to describe the passage of Yahweh or His angel on the night of Israel's deliverance out of Egyptian slavery. The Hebrews had been commanded to slaughter a lamb and sprinkle blood on their doorposts; the angel then passed over their homes to destroy only the first-born sons of the Egyptians. Passover referred also to exodus itself and the entrance into the promised land. The term came to be related to the return from Babylonian captivity as the new passover; it also developed an eschatological note referring to the final messianic deliverance. The Old Testament Passover feast joined these themes with those of a primitive spring harvest feast in which the first fruits of grain and flock were offered to the Lord. The primitive liturgical year was composed simply of the regular Sunday celebrations together with the two annual feasts of the Pasch and Pentecost. This simplicity does not reveal so much a poverty of imagination as the vital characteristic of early Christian spirituality: a deep awareness of the risen Christ ever present, ever coming. Every celebration, both the weekly and the annual, was inspired with this awareness. Both this eschatological emphasis and this simple liturgical structure of the year were developments of the apostolic period. Only later evidence shows a growing tendency that has become characteristic, but that is being balanced by regaining a fuller understanding of the Resurrection and ESCHATOLOGY.

The early Christians celebrated Easter as the commemoration par excellence of Christ's Resurrection, but together with the conviction that by initiation into the Church they too had died and risen and ascended with Christ, that by the celebration of each Eucharist they deepened their assimilation to Christ and called for their definitive and full union with Him before the Father. It was natural that they would transform the annual Jewish Passover into their own principal festival.

Date. Not only was the significance of the Jewish feast changed by the Christians, but also the date. The Jewish method of fixing the date, the 14th day of Nisan, did not confine it to any one day; at a very early time Christians began to assign their Pasch to the Sunday following the Jewish feast. By the end of the 2d century this was the universal custom except in Asia Minor, where the Jewish dating was followed by the so-called QUARTODE-

Easter Week procession, Valletta, Malta. (© Bob Krist/CORBIS)

CIMANS. The EASTER CONTROVERSY was settled to some extent by a series of councils and synods in the late 2d and early 3d centuries under Victor I. The Council of Nicaea attempted to enforce uniformity by establishing the rule that the date of Easter fall on the Sunday following the full moon after the vernal equinox. However, because of divergent methods of reckoning, uniformity of observance was not achieved until DIONYSIUS EXIGUUS's work; and even then some provinces, such as Gaul and Britain, went their own way for some years. There is still a divergency of dating between those who follow the Gregorian calendar and those who follow the Julian.

Theme and Characteristics. The paschal mystery, the death and Resurrection of Christ, is the central theme of the Easter cycle—not merely as a historical commemoration, but as a here-and-now manifestation of His glorification in the Christian assembly, and as a fervent prayer for full realization of the Redemption. Like the Jewish Pasch, Easter celebrated deliverance from the slavery of time, sin, and death. Unlike the later Jewish feast, which looked to the coming messianic times, it celebrated the deliverance as already having been achieved in Christ, and as shared by the Church, the Body of Christ. The richness of this theme began to unfold into others at an early date. Easter was considered the ideal time for the initiation of new members into the community of the saved, for their incorporation into the Body of Christ by Baptism, Confirmation, and first Eucharist. The practice led to the development of a preparatory period for Easter itself called LENT. The catechumens were expected to attend instructions, to undergo exorcisms, and to fast. In imitation, and in the wake of the 4th-century monastic-ascetic movement, there grew a sense of the need for personal preparation for all the faithful, who then began to participate in these exercises. Thus we find the themes of baptismal renewal, of fasting, penance, and prayer, of deepening understanding of and more intensive commitment to the mystery of Christ and the Church. The preparatory period came to be associated with Christ's 40-day fast and with the sorrowful events before His Resurrection (*see* HOLY WEEK). On the other side of Easter there developed more joyful themes associated with the appearances of the risen Christ to His disciples, His Ascension, and finally the sending of the Holy Spirit. Easter Week itself, as Lent, originally grew out of the initiatory practice: to celebrate the neophyte's new life in Christ.

Paschaltide. This period was originally designated Pentecost, from the Greek πεντηκοστή (literally 50th). The term originally referred to the 50-day duration of the Easter celebration. The Latin equivalent was *Quinquagesima.* At least from the beginning of the 3d century the Church celebrated these days as one continuous festival of redemption in Christ. All penitential observances were suspended. It was a transformation of the Jewish celebration between their PASSOVER and PENTECOST, during which they joyfully commemorated their possession of the promised land. It was only later that the first 40 days were seen as the time of the risen Christ with His disciples (the Church) before His Ascension, and the last ten days as a preparation for the descent of the Spirit. Originally, Easter itself was the celebration of the whole paschal mystery, death, Resurrection, Ascension, and sending of the Spirit; the 50 days were an extension of the full joy of the Easter Vigil.

Easter Week. After the example of Jewish practice, Easter enjoyed an octave by the 4th century. This octave seems to have been organized principally in view of the newly baptized, who assembled each day for the Eucharist and catechesis. In Rome a development took place between the 6th and 8th centuries. Since Baptism was celebrated during the Easter Vigil, the octave day was the following Saturday, when the neophytes laid aside their white robes. With the disappearance of adult Baptism the week lost its dominant baptismal character and became more the octave of Easter; in the last half of the 7th century the octave day was changed from Saturday to Sunday.

The Easter Sunday Mass came out of the 6th century to supply for the lack created by anticipating the Vigil earlier on Holy Saturday. With the restoration of the Vigil to its nocturnal setting and to its primacy as *the* Easter celebration, this later Sunday Morning Mass commemorating Christ's Resurrection understandably lost some of the importance it had enjoyed. Two themes characterize this week: that of the Resurrection, heard especially in the lessons, and that of Baptism, especially in the antiphons, taken from Psalms speaking of the exodus out of Egypt and entrance into the promised land.

Low Sunday (2nd Sunday of Easter). Even in early sources Low Sunday is ordinarily considered to be the octave of Easter. The day was also distinguished from the previous days by the fact that the neophytes had laid aside their baptismal robes. The real octave day of Easter was rather the 50th day, Pentecost, after the octave of octaves, emphasizing symbolically the fullness of salvation achieved by Christ in His Resurrection and by the Church in Christ.

Bibliography: T. J. TALLEY, *The Origins of the Liturgical Year* (Collegeville, Minn. 1991). A. J. MARTIMORT, ed. *The Church at Prayer IV: The Liturgy and Time* (Collegeville, Minn. 1986). A. NOCENT, *The Liturgical Year, v. 3, The Paschal Triduum, the Easter Season* (Collegeville, Minn. 1977). J. M. PIERCE, ''Holy Week and Easter in the Middle Ages,'' in *Passover and Easter: Origin and History to Modern Times*, eds. P. F. BRADSHAW and L. A. HOFFMAN (Notre Dame, Ind. 1999) 161–85. A. ADAM, *The Liturgical Year: Its History & Its Meaning after the Reform of the Liturgy* (New York 1981).

[E. JOHNSON/T. KROSNICKI/EDS.]

EASTER CONTROVERSY

Controversy surrounded the determination of the date of Easter from the 2d to the 8th century, and is dealt with here as: (1) the QUARTODECIMAN, (2) the Roman-Alexandrian, and (3) the Celtic Easter controversies.

Quartodeciman Controversy. The Asiatic practice in the 2d century of observing Easter on the day of the Jewish Passover conflicted with the Roman custom of celebrating Easter on Sunday, the day of the Resurrection. Occasionally, the Quartodecimans celebrated Easter on the day that other Christians were observing Good Friday. Originally both observances were allowed, but gradually it was felt incongruous that Christians should celebrate Easter on a Jewish feast, and unity in celebrating the principal Christian feast was called for. However, an attempt by Pope VICTOR I (189–198) to impose Roman usage proved unsuccessful in the face of a determined opposition led by Polycrates, Bishop of Ephesus. Although Quartodecimanism waned in the 3d century, it survived in some Asiatic Churches as late as the 5th century.

Roman-Alexandrian Controversy. In the beginning Christians depended on Jewish authorities to calculate the date of the Passover, and thus of Easter; but by the 3d century some Christians started to determine Easter independently. Since the date of the Passover (14th of Nisan) depends on a lunar calendar, there was a perennial problem of reconciling the shorter lunar calendar year with the longer solar year of the Julian calendar by the periodic addition of an intercalary month. It was obviously desirable to construct a cyclic arrangement so that Easter, a fixed day in the lunar calendar, would occur according to a predetermined pattern in the Julian calendar. Unfortunately, because of the complexities involved in the calculations, the number of years in the proposed cycles varied from place to place; thus the fixing of the date of Easter varied, affording the basis for a new series of controversies.

In Rome HIPPOLYTUS devised a 16-year cycle, beginning with the year 222; since its calculations were defective, it was replaced later in the century with an 84-year cycle. In the East ANATOLIUS OF LAODICEA (d. *c.* 282) constructed a calendar with a 19-year cycle, which was adopted at Alexandria. The Council of Arles (314) hoped to achieve uniformity by observing Easter on the same day as the See of Rome, which was charged with announcing the date in advance through circular letters. A similar effort was made in the East at the Council of Nicaea (325). The exact wording of the Nicene decree is uncertain, but it apparently approved the practice of celebrating Easter on the Sunday after both the 14th of Nisan and the vernal equinox, thus implicitly rejecting both Quartodeciman and Jewish calendars (Eusebius, *Vita Constantini* 3.17–20).

However, no one Easter cycle was universally accepted; rather, different cycles continued to prevail. During the 4th century, this frequently resulted in different dates for Easter (Ambrose, *Epist.* 23), though on occasion Alexandria accepted the Roman date and vice versa. After repeated efforts by Pope St. LEO I (440–461) to achieve uniformity between the divergent cycles of Rome (84 years) and Alexandria (19 years), Victorius of Aquitaine constructed a 532-year cycle under the patronage of Leo's successor, Hilary (461–468). During the Laurentian schism, the cycle of Victorius was followed by the antipope Laurentius; this resulted in the reintroduction of the 84-year cycle by the party of Pope SYMMACHUS (498–514).

In the East, the 19-year Anatolian cycle had been computed by Cyril of Alexandria for five cycles (436–531). Some years prior to its expiration, DIONYSIUS EXIGUUS, a monk in Rome, constructed an extension (to 626), which basically followed the 19-year cycle. Dionysius, however, decided to date his calendar, not from the era of Diocletian as Cyril had done, but from the birth of

Christ. Unfortunately, the calculations of Dionysius in dating the "Christian Era" were inaccurate, but the system still remains in use (A.D. for anno Domini). The acceptance of this cycle in Rome ended Rome's long-standing controversy with Alexandria. Yet it was only in the 8th century that the cycle of Dionysius was universally adopted in Western Europe; according to Gregory of Tours (*Hist. Franc.* 5.17; 10.23), the cycle of Victorius, retained by a minority, resulted in divergent celebrations of Easter in Gaul during the 6th century.

Celtic Easter Controversy. An 84-year cycle had been introduced into Ireland at the time of its Christianization in the 5th century; subsequently, the Irish monks and missionaries introduced their Celtic calendar in the regions where they settled, thus coming into conflict with Christians who followed other calendars. In Gaul, the monasteries established by St. COLUMBAN (*c.* 550–615) followed Celtic usages. This aroused considerable opposition from the Gallic bishops who accused Columban of being a Quartodeciman. Nonetheless, he continued to follow the Celtic practice at his monastery of Luxeuil. Sometime after his death, the Gallic calendar was introduced without any recorded opposition.

The Celtic calendar had been introduced also into England. With the arrival of AUGUSTINE OF CANTERBURY and the Roman missionaries sent by Pope Gregory I (590–604), an attempt to introduce the Roman calendar encountered opposition from the Christians following the Celtic custom. The dispute was carried into the royal family of Northumbria, where King Oswy, following Celtic usage, observed Easter, while Queen Eanfled, according to the Roman calendar, observed Palm Sunday. At an assembly convoked at Whitby (664), King Oswy, after hearing the arguments of St. COLMAN on behalf of the Celtic observance and of WILFRID OF YORK on behalf of the Roman usage, decided in favor of the latter in deference to the authority of St. Peter (Bede, *Ecclesiastical History* 3.25–26). Subsequently, Theodore of Tarsus (*c.* 602–690), Archbishop of Canterbury, undertook to extend the Roman calendar throughout England. In Scotland, the Roman usage was introduced by King Naitan in 710; acceptance followed at Iona a few years later (Bede, *Eccl. Hist.* 5.21–22), and by the 9th century it prevailed in Wales. Uniformity of Easter observance was thus attained in the British Isles.

Bibliography: C. C. RICHARDSON, "New Solution to the Quartodeciman Riddle," *Journal of Theological Studies* ns 24 (1973) 74–84. H. F. VON CAMPENHAUSEN, "Ostertermin oder Osterfasten: Zum Verständnis des Irenausbriefs an Viktor (Eusebius' *Ecclesiastical History* 5, 24,12–17)," *Vigiliae Christianae* 28:2 (1974) R. T. BECKWITH, "The Origin of the Festivals Easter and Whitsun," *Studia Liturgica* 13 (1979) 1–20 114–138. S. G. HALL, "The Origins of Easter," *Studia Patristica* 15:1 (1984) 554–567. W. L. PETERSEN, "Eusebius and the Paschal controversy," in *Eusebius, Christianity, and Judaism* (Detroit 1992) 311–325. K. STRAND, "Sunday Easter and Quartodecimanism in the Early Christian Church," *Andrews University Seminary Studies* 28 (1990) 127–136.

[J. FORD/EDS.]

EASTER VIGIL

Holy Saturday has been from earliest times consecrated to Our Lord's Sabbath rest, His burial in the tomb. The early Church in both East and West commemorated this burial by spending the day in rest, prayer, expectation of the Resurrection, and strict fasting. There was no Eucharistic liturgy or communion service of any kind. Today the Church keeps Holy Saturday in austere and quiet mourning because Christ her Bridegroom has been taken away from her and lies in the tomb. The theme of Morning Prayer on this day is the death and burial of Christ, and the descent into the dead.

Spirit

In the early Church the paschal feast was one unitive commemoration of the paschal mystery, representing the entire saving work of Christ, including the Passion, Resurrection, and the sending of the Spirit. In a very real sense the feast remains so, for it celebrates the whole achievement of the Paschal Lamb "who by dying destroyed our death and by rising restored our life" (Memorial Acclamation #2).

In spite of its name the Easter Vigil is not the vigil of Easter in the modern sense of the day before a feast but in the ancient sense of the night celebration of the greatest feast of the year. The Easter Vigil is not the preparation for Easter but the true celebration of Easter itself. St. Augustine calls the paschal vigil "the mother of all vigils" (*Sermo* 219; *Patrologia Latina*, ed. J. P. Migne, 38:1088), by which he means that this is the most important vigil, or night watch, of the whole year. The reason why Pius XII in 1951 "restored" the Vigil to its proper place was to emphasize once again a truth that had become obscured with the passing of time: the Vigil *is* the Easter Feast.

Time of Celebration. The earliest references to Pascha (the ancient name for the unitive commemoration of the Redemption) show that it was essentially a night celebration. The apocryphal *Epistula Apostolorum* emanating from Asia Minor or Egypt bears witness to the nighttime celebration of the feast in the 2d century (J. Quasten, ed., *Monumenta eucharista et liturgica vetustissima* 336–37). Tertullian, writing about 250, calls the Vigil "abnoctantem" (*Ad uxorem* 2.4; *Patrologia Latina*

1:1294); and the *Apostolic Constitutions* (4th century) tells us that the faithful gathered at Vespers of Saturday and continued the Vigil service to the dawn of Easter Sunday (5.19.1; F. X. Funk, ed., *Didascalia et constitutiones apostolorum* 1:288–90).

Many other statements of Jerome, Augustine, and Paulinus of Nola leave no doubt that this was the consecrated practice both in the East and the West in antiquity [*Comm. in evang. sec. Matt.* 4.25.6 (*Patrologia Latina* 21:192); *Sermo* 219 and 228 (*Patrologia Latina* 38:1088, 1101); *Vita s. Ambrosii* 48 (*Patrologia Latina* 14:43)]. The Eastern Churches in fact never abandoned it, but in the West the Vigil was progressively anticipated, beginning in the 12th century when Roman Ordinal 10 (16; *Patrologia Latina* 78:1014) had the service start at noon. Before the end of the same century it was begun at 11 A.M. Holy Saturday (M. Andrieu, *Le Pontifical Romain au moyen-âge* 1:238).

By 1570 the Vigil had been advanced to the early hours of the morning, and the Missal of Pius V made this law. This was the situation that existed in the West until the reforms of Pius XII in 1951. The principal celebration of the greatest feast of the year was held a whole day ahead of time. This had the unhappy effect of deemphasizing the Easter Vigil and simultaneously eliminating any real observance of Holy Saturday as a day of quiet mourning. In restoring the Easter Vigil to its proper time after sundown on Holy Saturday, Pius XII was not merely reviving an ancient practice; he was restoring the feast of Easter to its proper place in the life of the Church. For the nighttime celebration is hardly a matter of sentiment; it is rooted in the very nature of the events it commemorates.

Reasons for Night Celebration. To answer the question why there is so much insistence on celebrating the paschal festival at night is not easy, because there are several reasons for it, and it is hard to say which one has had the greatest influence upon the practice. All of them have their importance and must be taken into account.

The first reason is that Easter is the feast of the triumph of light over the darkness and so the celebration calls for a setting in which this event can be dramatized by using the symbols of light and darkness to good effect (*see* LIGHT, LITURGICAL USE OF). Another is that Easter commemorates in a special way the Resurrection of Our Lord, and the Resurrection took place during the night.

Probably a night celebration was determined for this feast because Easter is the Christian Passover, the fulfillment of the Jewish Passover. The Jewish feast was always celebrated at night; it is natural that the Christian feast, which replaced it, would also be a nighttime feast. The wording of the *Exsultet* gives considerable support to this.

An important part of the Jewish Passover service was the vigil, or night watch, that commemorated the vigil God Himself is represented as keeping through the night of the Exodus (Ex 12.29). God commanded them to observe the anniversary of the deliverance from Egypt as a festival day. By means of this feast celebrated during the night the people of Israel kept alive all that God had done for them—not only the deliverance but what the deliverance had led to—and especially their birth as a holy nation, for it was on that night that Israel began to exist as a nation.

When the Christian Church took over the feast of the Passover, it gave all this a Christian direction. The Church commemorated not just the deliverance from Egypt but a mightier and more far-reaching one—the ''mighty deed'' of God that had drawn them out of darkness into the kingdom of God's beloved Son. This new deliverance, like the old, was associated with the night and the darkness, for the New Exodus, the death of Christ, took place in the darkness, and the Resurrection that completed our Redemption happened during the night.

Hence, just as the Church, the New Israel, came into being with the death and Resurrection of Christ, so, as in the Jewish feast, the Christian Passover was the commemoration of the beginning of the new People of God. This was probably the real reason for having Baptism during this night, for Baptism is the Sacrament of entrance into the People of God and, at the same time, the way that this People continually renews itself.

But the Israelites who kept the vigil each year on this night were not only recalling the Exodus of the past; they were making ready for a greater exodus and a mightier deliverance to be achieved when God would come again to establish them in His kingdom forever. This would be the true paschal festival, the true and final Passover, not a mere commemoration. Christians, too, continued to look forward to a still more glorious deliverance that they believed would occur on this night, a deliverance of which the Redemption is the pledge and the promise: the final and definitive coming of the Lord who will establish them in glory with Him forever. ''This is the night,'' says Lactantius, ''which we celebrate with a night-long vigil because of the coming of our king and God. This night has a twofold significance; in it Christ received life after dying and in the future He will come into possession of the kingdom of the whole world'' (*De divinis instit.* 7:19; *Patrologia Latina* 6:797). For this reason Christians do on this one night of the year what they should be doing spiritually at all times: waiting and hoping for the coming of the Lord.

Liturgical Ceremonies

The altogether special character of this greatest feast of the Church year is apparent in the beautiful liturgical ceremonies of the night. All of them express the Christian's passing over with Christ from the death of sin to the new life under God.

The Blessing of the New Fire. The introductory rites are a preparation for the Vigil rather than a part of it, and ideally they take place outside the Church. Many of these rites are Gallican in origin. The formula for blessing the new fire originated in Germany in the 10th century, but the practice of kindling the new fire is found there as early as the 8th century. The ancient Roman custom was to bring a light out of hiding for illumination Saturday night. The blessing of the new fire is subordinate to the lighting of the paschal candle and the procession.

The Paschal Candle. The entire first part of the Easter Vigil centers about the paschal candle, the symbol of the risen Lord, and one of the most impressive of the Church's sacramentals. It evokes readily the thought of Christ and His victory, the triumph of light over darkness. Yet the origin of this symbol is uncertain. The idea of symbolizing the Resurrection with lighted lamps appears to have come from the East and particularly from Jerusalem. Nevertheless the paschal candle is not derived from that custom, though its subsequent ritual may have been influenced by this symbolism.

The explanation most favored today is that the candle comes from the ancient practice of lighting and blessing a lamp (or lamps) in the early evening to provide light in the darkness. The ceremony, though practical in origin, became in time an elaborate rite called the *Lucernarium,* ''the lighting of the lamps,'' accompanied by psalms, chants, and prayers. Because this service introduced Vespers, Vespers itself was sometimes called *Lucernarium,* as is the case in the Ambrosian Rite. The lighting and blessing of the paschal candle on the greatest night of the year is thus both a survival and a development of a custom once observed every day. That this is probably the true origin of the paschal candle seems to be borne out by the fact that it is still traditionally the deacon who carries the candle into the church and sets it up there; the lighting of the lamps before evening services was the special function of the deacon.

From what can be gathered from references in the writings of the 4th century Fathers [e.g., Jerome, *Epist.* 28 *ad Presidium* 1; Augustine, *Civ.* 15.22 (*Patrologia Latina* 30:188; 41:467)], the custom of having a paschal candle was observed in other Western rites long before it was adopted in the papal liturgy, for there is no definite evidence of its use there before the 12th century (M. Andreiu, *Le Pontifical Romain au moyen-â* 1:240).

One significant change which Pius XII introduced in 1951 was to have the candle lighted and blessed at the beginning of the service and then to have it lead the procession into the church. Prior to 1955 this rite took place in church and the candle was not even lighted until about halfway through the *Exsultet.* All these changes (many of which were really restorations) gave more meaning to the whole rite; the candle recovers the central position and the prominence it deserves because it is the living symbol of the risen Christ.

The celebrant first prepares the candle to be the symbol of Christ by marking it with the sign of the cross and the monogram of Christ and inserting the grains of incense that represent the five wounds. The cross, the Alpha and Omega, and the year are marked with a stylus. This was originally a 9th-century Gallican usage, later adopted for a time at Rome, which was revived in 1955. When the candle thus marked is lighted with the new fire, it becomes the symbol of the risen Lord triumphing over the darkness and bearing in His risen body the five wounds, trophies of His victory.

The full meaning of the paschal candle as the symbol of Christ is apparent when the candle is carried by the deacon into the dark church, dispelling the darkness. This rite is a vivid dramatization of the Resurrection. Pius XII's Ordinal for Holy Week restored to the procession its proper meaning, the triumph of the risen Christ. The deacon heralds the Resurrection with the words *Lumen Christi* (''Light of Christ''); the community acclaims the risen Lord with the glad cry *Deo gratias* (''Thanks be to God''). All present receive the Easter light from the paschal candle. This signifies that we all participate in the glory of the Resurrection; we are thereby made light bearers, children of the light.

Upon reaching the sanctuary the deacon sings the beautiful hymn in honor of the paschal candle, the *EXSULTET IAM ANGELICA TURBA*. This hymn, in the form and style of the ancient hymn of thanksgiving, has for its theme the victory of the King over death, sin, and hell. All the meaning of the paschal feast is concentrated into this paschal hymn. Originally the Exsultet was extemporized, its composition left to the judgment and inspiration of the one who sang it; many such hymns were composed in the early centuries. The modern version, traditionally attributed to St. Ambrose, sums up the redemptive mystery. The Jewish Passover was the prelude to the true Passover, our Lord's passage from death to life. We partake of this passage; His passage becomes ours through the sacred mysteries of Baptism and the Eucharist. Christ is risen from the dead and we are risen with Him to newness of life.

Service of the Word. The oldest part of the Easter Vigil begins with the readings from Scripture. At Rome all these readings (in the ancient Roman ordinal there were six readings) were centered around Baptism. They were intended to be a scriptural commentary on the meaning of the whole rite of Christian initiation. The Collects after each reading show that the ''wonders of old time'' are renewed in the rite of Baptism. From the Middle Ages onward there were 12 readings, but Pius XII's Holy Week Ordinal reverted to the practice of the time of Gregory I.

Baptismal Rite. Upon the conclusion of the Liturgy of the Word and the homily, the blessing of the baptismal water and the conferring of the Sacraments of Initiation follow immediately. In early centuries the water was blessed only at the time the Sacrament was celebrated, as is still the practice in the Eastern rites. When the administration of Baptism was restricted to the Easter Vigil, the blessing of the water was also confined to that time (and to Pentecost). The modern formula for blessing the water, combining elements from the Gelasian and the Hadrian Sacramentaries, represents a fusion of Roman and Gallican elements. Its general theme is that the water, made productive by the Spirit, gives birth to the divine life in the human race. The font is compared to a womb; it is the womb of Holy Church producing a heavenly offspring conceived in holiness and reborn as a new creation. During the consecratory Preface the priest plunges the candle into the water to show that the waters of Baptism derive their power to sanctify from the Passion and Resurrection of Christ. He pours in the chrism to signify the sanctification of the water by the Holy Spirit who is said to dwell in the chrism. Both these symbolic actions originated in the Middle Ages. Pius XII's Holy Week Ordinal gives greater prominence to the blessing of water by having it take place in the sanctuary so that all can see and hear. The Rite of Christian Initiation (RCIA) follows after the blessing of the water.

Whether the Sacraments of Initiation are celebrated or not, the restored Easter Vigil provides something altogether new, the renewal of the baptismal promises. Our consciousness of being a baptized people has been reawakened by the readings and chants, by the blessing of the water, and especially by the celebration of Baptism itself. Now we give expression to this fresh awareness by repeating the promises we once made to renounce Satan and to serve God faithfully. The whole Lenten observance is intended to lead us up to this moment and to prepare us for a genuine and sincere renewal of our baptismal commitment. Like the other rites of this night it is a symbolic yet real resurrection with Christ to a new life of grace. After the renewal of the promises the priest sprinkles the people with the Easter water as a further reminder of their Baptism.

Mass. The true climax of the Easter Vigil is the celebration of the Eucharist, for the Eucharist is the paschal mystery in its essence. No other way of celebrating our redemption, however beautiful or meaningful, can take its place. In fact everything else that is done in the Easter Vigil is only an unfolding of what is daily celebrated in the Eucharistic mystery. Moreover, the Eucharist that crowns the Paschal Vigil is itself the true and original Easter Mass. All texts speak of the Resurrection and of the new life that the Resurrection brings through the Sacrament of Baptism. The antiquity of this Vigil Mass is shown by the fact that several elements of the Proper and the Ordinary are missing from it. The reason is that this formulary antedates the introduction of these chants into the Mass of the Roman rite.

The singing of the traditional triple ALLELUIA after the Epistle is a special feature of the Easter celebration; it is a song of joyful praise to God chanted at a time when we are most conscious of all the wonders God has wrought on our behalf, especially our redemption. The Easter Preface, sung for the first time on this night, extols the true Paschal Lamb whose sacrifice frees us from sin and enables us to pass with Him to eternal life through the Resurrection.

Bibliography: J. GAILLARD, *Holy Week and Easter,* tr. W. BUSCH (Collegeville, Minn. 1954). W. J. O'SHEA, *The Meaning of Holy Week* (Collegeville, Minn. 1958). H. A. SCHMIDT, *Hebdomada Sancta,* 2 v. (Rome 1956–57). A. OLIVAR, ''Vom Ursprung der römischen Taufwasserweihe,'' *Archiv für Liturgiewissenschaft* 6 (1959) 62–78. R. BERGER and H. HOLLERWEGER, *Celebrating the Easter Vigil* (New York 1983). G. BERTONIÈRE, *The Historical Development of the Easter Vigil and Related Services in the Greek Church* (Rome 1972). T. J. TALLEY, *The Origins of the Liturgical Year* (Collegeville 1991). A. J. MARTIMORT, ed., *The Church at Prayer IV: The Liturgy and Time* (Collegeville 1986). A. NOCENT, *The Liturgical Year, v.3. The Paschal Triduum, the Easter Season* (Collegeville 1977). J. M. PIERCE, ''Holy Week and Easter in the Middle Ages,'' in *Passover and Easter: Origin and History to Modern Times,* eds. P. F. BRADSHAW and L. A. HOFFMAN (Notre Dame, Ind. 1999) 161–85. A. ADAM, *The Liturgical Year: Its History & Its Meaning after the Reform of the Liturgy* (New York 1981).

[W. J. O'SHEA/EDS.]

EASTERN CHURCHES

The term Eastern Churches refers to the Churches that developed in the eastern half of the ROMAN EMPIRE along with those communities that were founded in dependence upon them, even though the dependent Churches were found outside of the boundaries of the empire.

DIOCLETIAN in 293 divided the Roman Empire into four prefectures: Gaul, Italy, Illyricum, and the Orient. Upon the death of Theodosius I (395) the empire was divided into two halves that in practice were separate and independent (*see* BYZANTINE EMPIRE). The eastern half of the empire was made up of the Prefectures of Illyricum and the Orient, which were subdivided into smaller administrative units called dioceses. Illyricum contained the Dioceses of Dacia and Macedonia while the Prefecture of the Orient contained the Dioceses of Thrace, Asia, Pontus, the Orient, and Egypt, with the corresponding capitals, Sardica, Sirmium, Heraclea, Ephesus, Caesarea of Cappadocia, Antioch, and Alexandria. These chief centers of civil administration became the leading ecclesiastical centers as well. Illyricum was divided into an eastern and western portion by an arbitrary decision of Theodosius; the boundary line separating the eastern and western halves of the empire ran along the Sava, Drina, and Zeta Rivers down to the city of Budva and to the Adriatic Sea. All lands west of the line belonged ecclesiastically to the Latin or Western Church, while all lands to the east belonged to the respective Eastern Churches.

FORMATION OF THE EASTERN CHURCHES

All Eastern Churches evolved from the Patriarchates of Constantinople, Alexandria, and Antioch, and the two Churches of Persia and Armenia, respectively, which developed outside the Roman Empire. Five characteristic families of liturgical rites developed within these five ecclesiastical jurisdictions: the Alexandrian, Antiochene (or West Syrian), Byzantine, East Syrian, and Armenian.

The Churches of Constantinople, Alexandria, and Antioch. Byzantium had been a suffragan see of the metropolitan of Heraclea in Thrace. After it was transformed into Constantinople, the New Rome, its civil importance made it the ecclesiastical center first in importance after old Rome. Canon 3 of the ecumenical Council of Constantinople (381) attributed to it a primacy of honor after the ancient See of Rome; and canon 28 of the Council of Chalcedon (451) recognized an equivalence between its civil and ecclesiastical powers, granting to the See of Constantinople jurisdiction over all the dioceses of Thrace, Asia, and Pontus (*see* CONSTANTINOPLE, ECUMENICAL PATRIARCHATE OF; CONSTANTINOPLE). Alexandria was the most ancient patriarchate. Geographical and political factors favored Alexandria as the obvious civil and ecclesiastical center for all of Egypt, Libya, and Pentapolis. The Council of Nicaea I (325) recognized the preeminence of Alexandria. (*See* ALEXANDRIA, PATRIARCHATE OF; ALEXANDRIA.) Antioch enjoyed a lesser civil and ecclesiastical significance but exerted its authority over the Diocese of the Orient. Canon 6 of the Council of Nicaea I (325) speaks of the privileges of the See of Antioch, and canon 2 of the Council of Constantinople (381) confirms its position after that of Rome, Constantinople, and Alexandria. (*See* ANTIOCH, PATRIARCHATE OF; ANTIOCH.) Jerusalem became the last of the ancient Eastern patriarchates when it was recognized as a patriarchate by the Council of Chalcedon (451), thus taking from the jurisdiction of Antioch all of Palestine and the peninsula of Sinai (*see* JERUSALEM, PATRIARCHATE OF).

All the daughter Churches that depended upon the three great Eastern Patriarchates of Constantinople, Alexandria, and Antioch embraced the liturgical rite and came under the ecclesiastical jurisdiction of their mother Churches.

Churches of Persia and Armenia. The fourth of the original Churches emerged in Persia. Christianity reached this region by the 2d century, if not the end of the 1st, from Edessa in Syria. The ecclesiastical center of the Persian Church was the great city of Seleucia-Ctesiphon. Because of its location beyond the eastern borders of the Roman Empire, the Church became known as the Assyrian Church of the East. The bishop of this see (*c.* 400) obtained the primacy over all of Persia, taking the title of catholicos instead of patriarch. The Christian religion was always that of the minority, and the hostile relations between the Persians and the Byzantine emperors made contacts with the Churches within the Byzantine Empire both difficult and dangerous. Under the circumstances and especially because of severe persecutions, the Persian bishops declared themselves an autonomous Church. The Persian Church is the source of the East Syrian liturgical rite, which has preserved a significant amount of archaisms because of its relative isolation from the other churches (*see* EAST SYRIAN LITURGY).

According to tradition St. Bartholomew was the Apostle of Armenia. The Armenian Church was established toward the end of the 3d century from the Church of Caesarea of Cappadocia. St. Gregory the Illuminator converted King TIRIDATES III of Armenia along with the mass of the population (290–295). Christianity became the national religion, and in the 5th century the national language was used in the Armenian liturgy (*see* ARMENIAN CHRISTIANITY; ARMENIAN LITURGY).

DEVELOPMENT OF THE EASTERN CHURCHES

The separate development of the Eastern Churches is due primarily to the divisions caused by doctrinal and political disputes. The presentation here is, for the most part, necessarily chronological.

Assyrian Church of the East (Persia). The Assyrian Church of the East exhibited a vigorous missionary expansion that sent missionaries as far as Mongolia and China, as well as in southern India. In this period of expansion from the 6th to the 11th centuries there were 27 metropolitan sees and more than 200 dioceses. Successive waves of persecutions by Muslim conquerors had reduced the size of this Church. Today, the Assyrian

Christians are located principally in Iraq with scattered members in Syria, Iran, and South India (*see* ASSYRIAN CHURCH OF THE EAST).

Syrian Jacobite Church of Antioch. The Syrian Monophysites are called Jacobites after Jacob Baradai (d. 578), who, during the persecutions waged by Justinian I against Monophysitism, secretly consecrated 27 bishops and some 2,000 priests. The Syrian Jacobite patriarch claims the ancient see of the Patriarchate of Antioch as his legitimate see and resides in Damascus.

Armenian Church. The Armenians are divided into several jurisdictions. The main center of honor and authority is the Catholicate of Etchmiadzin in the Republic of Armenia, U.S.S.R. The Catholicate of Cilicia (Sis) has its present center in Antelias, Lebanon, and is on an equal rank, and in communion with Etchmiadzin.

Coptic Church. The modern Copts of Egypt trace their ancestry to the Egyptian Christians who rejected the Ecumenical Council of Chalcedon (*see* COPTIC CHRISTIANITY). After the Council of Chalcedon (451), those who remained faithful to the byzantine emperor and the teachings of the Chalcedon were originally known as Melkites, while those who rejected Chalcedon formed themselves into the Coptic Oriental Orthodox Church. Both the Melkites and the Copts made use of the liturgical rite of the see of Alexandria. But gradually the Melkites adopted the Byzantine ecclesiastical and liturgical usages, while the original Alexandrian liturgical rite evolved into the present-day Coptic liturgical rite, but with traces of the Greek language and Byzantine usages.

Ethiopian Church. Tradition narrates that in the 5th century there arrived in Ethiopia nine monks from Syria. They founded monasteries and translated the New Testament into Ge'ez, a Semitic language then spoken, but now used only for liturgical services. The Ethiopian Church was under the Coptic patriarch of Alexandria until 1948, when it obtained the privilege of appointing a native Ethiopian as *abuna* or head bishop, who in reality rules the Church. In 1959 the Ethiopian Church was declared a patriarchate completely independent of Alexandria, which retained only the honor of precedence.

Orthodox Churches. The Orthodox Church developed over the centuries as a result of a great diversity of factors, chief among them were the differences of theological and spiritual emphasis and political, cultural, and social variations coupled with a fundamentally different ecclesiology, at least in the development and exercise of the organ of jurisdictional authority. The various Orthodox Churches are covered in detail in articles dealing with the countries in which they have a dominant or major place.

Eastern Catholic Churches. After the gradual estrangement between Constantinople and Rome that became permanent from the 11th century onwards, there existed much tension and conflict between the Christian East and West. In 1181 the Maronites were reconciled with Rome, and the Armenians in Syria in 1198, but in general the arrogance of the Latin Crusaders deepened antagonism between the Orthodox and Catholics, owing principally to the plundering by Crusaders of Orthodox churches and shrines, especially those of Constantinople. The capture of Constantinople in 1204 and the establishment of the Latin Empire of Constantinople created a lasting hostility and bitterness. Two large-scale efforts to heal the separation were made, but unsuccessfully, at the Councils of LYONS (1274) and FLORENCE (1439). Decrees of reunion were signed, only to be shortly afterward repudiated by the great majority of the Orthodox clergy and people. When the Turks sacked Constantinople in 1453, the center of Orthodox unity was destroyed. Twenty years later the union signed at Florence had been repudiated by all parties involved; and Western and Eastern Christians settled into two large and distinct bodies with little effort made thereafter at effecting mutual communion.

Zealous missionary activities among the peoples of the Near East and Slav countries by Catholic religious orders, especially Jesuits, Dominicans, Franciscans, and Capuchins, under the aegis of the Congregation for the PROPAGATION OF THE FAITH bore fruit in the rise of the Catholic church that retained their Eastern ecclesial and liturgical rites and customs. When such groups became large enough, Rome set up a hierarchy—even at times a Catholic patriarchate—corresponding to their Eastern counterparts. The Brest-Litovsk Union of 1595 was the first large-scale formation of Eastern Catholics. By this union Ukrainians and White Russians living in what was then part of the kingdom of Poland and Lithuania were reconciled with Rome and formed the nucleus of the Ukrainian Eastern Catholic Church of today.

Assyrian Christians or Chaldeans, began a slow process of reconciliation with Rome beginning in 1552, when Patriarch John Sulaqa (d. 1555) made a profession of the Catholic faith. He was martyred for his action, but a more lasting union was effected in 1681 in the city of Diarbekir. Rome made Bishop Joseph the Catholic patriarch, but the situation became complicated when, in 1778, the other Assyrian patriarch became Catholic, thus providing two Chaldean Catholic patriarchs. From 1834 there has been only one Chaldean Catholic patriarch. In 1663 the Catholic Patriarchate of Syria was established, and in 1729, that of the Melkite Catholics. The Armenian Catholic Patriarchate was set up in Sis, Cilicia, in 1742, while that of the Coptic Catholics was erected in Cairo in 1895. Smaller groups of Eastern Catholic Churches were established among the Romanians, Yugoslavs, Ruthenians, Bulgars, and Greeks. In 1930, through the zeal of Mar IVANIOS, thousands of Indian Syrian Jacobite Christians formed the Syro-Malankara Catholic Church.

Eastern Christians in North America. Eastern Christianity made an entrance into North America when Russian Orthodox missionaries first evangelized Alaska in 1794. But the Eastern Christians first came in large numbers as immigrants from Europe and Asia in the second half of the 19th century. The majority of Eastern Christians in North America are Byzantine Christians.

In the U.S. the Byzantine Catholic Slovaks, Hungarians and Croatians were grouped under the jurisdiction of the Ruthenian Eastern Catholic bishops, while in Canada the Slovaks, Hungarians, Croatians, and White Russians are under the jurisdiction of the Ukrainian Eastern Catholic bishops.

History of Eastern Catholics in the U.S. Eastern Catholic Churches in the U.S. comprises 11 different ethnic groups representing eight different liturgical rites. The majority of the Eastern Catholics in the U.S. are Byzantine Slavic ethnic groups. A mass immigration of Slavs from the old Austro-Hungarian Empire, who called themselves Ruthenians or Pod-Carpathian Ruthenians, and others from Galicia, who preferred to call themselves Ukrainians, began in 1880. The first Byzantine-Slav Catholic priest arrived in the U.S. (1884), Ivan Volansky, founded the first Eastern Catholic parish in Shenandoah, PA, in the same year. Other Eastern Catholic priests left their native lands to take care of their displaced brethren. Numerous priests of the two European Ruthenian Dioceses of Mukachevo and Presov and of the Ukrainian province of Galicia founded parishes, mostly in the coal-mining areas of Pennsylvania. In 1907 there were 152 parishes and 43 missions. To avoid misunderstanding among the majority of Catholics in the U.S., who were of the Latin rite, the Congregation for the Propagation of the Faith specified that only celibate or widowed priests were to be sent to America. However, with the increase in immigration, married priests also were sent.

Ruthenian and Ukrainian Problems and Their Solution. The lack of their own hierarchy in the beginning, with the necessity of submission to the local Latin bishops, caused great discontent among these Slavic Catholics. The Russian Orthodox had moved their episcopal see from San Francisco to New York in 1905, to be nearer to this source of Orthodox recruitment. Father Alexis TOTH, embittered by the treatment that he had received from Latin bishops, became Orthodox and spent the rest of his life forming Orthodox parishes from Catholic Slav groups. This movement toward the Russian Orthodox jurisdiction spread rapidly on the East coast, so that an estimated 200 Catholic Eastern parishes with nearly 225,000 faithful became Russian Orthodox. By the mid-20th century, this number had increased to at least 400,000, forming about 60 percent or more of Slavic Christian population in the U.S.

The Holy See, alarmed at the high rate of defections among these Eastern Catholic immigrants, appointed in 1907, Soter Ortynsky as the first Byzantine Catholic bishop, resident in Philadelphia. Unfortunately he did not have his own proper jurisdiction, being dependent upon the local Latin bishops in whose dioceses his parishes were found. This jurisdiction was given him in 1913, but all his problems were not solved. Many of the people under him were of the Austro-Hungarian Empire, while Bishop Soter was from Galicia.

This problem of nationalism plagued all groups of Eastern Catholics, but especially the Slavs, until in 1924 each group received its own bishop. Constantine Bohachevsky was appointed bishop for the Ukrainians and resided at Philadelphia, while Basil Takach was appointed bishop of Pittsburgh for the Ruthenians, Slovaks, Croatians, and Hungarians. In 1928, at the request of the U.S. hierarchy of Latin bishops, the Holy Office issued a decree that only unmarried men could be ordained to the priesthood. This, along with the problem of church elders holding church property in their own corporate name rather than in the name of the local Latin Ordinary, caused thousands of Ukrainian and Ruthenian Catholics to come under the jurisdiction of an already existing Orthodox hierarchy or to form their own independent national Church. Other sources of defection from the Eastern Catholic Churches were the lack of Eastern Catholic priests, intermarriage with Latin Catholics, and the desire to be considered more ''American'' by forsaking European traditions.

Vatican II resulted in a renaissance and renewed confidence for Eastern Catholic Churches in the U.S. The decree, *Orientalium Ecclesiarum*, facilitated the retrieval of ancient ecclesial and liturgical usages, as well as stemming the pressure to Latinize the churches.

Bibliography: General works. W. F. ADENEY, *The Greek and Eastern Churches* (New York 1908). D. ATTWATER, *The Christian Churches of the East,* 2 v. (rev. ed. Milwaukee 1961–62). F. E. BRIGHTMAN, *Liturgies Eastern and Western,* v.1 (Oxford 1896). L. M. DUCHESNE, *The Churches Separated from Rome,* tr. A. H. MATHEW (London 1907). A. FORTESCUE, *The Lesser Eastern Churches* (London 1913); *The Uniate Eastern Churches,* ed. G. D. SMITH (New York 1923). M. GORDILLO, *Compendium theologiae orientalis* (3d ed. Rome 1950); *Theologia orientalium cum latinorum comparata* [Orientalia Christiana Analecta (Rome 1935–) 158; 1960]. F. HEILER, *Urkirche und Ostkirche* (Munich 1937). R. JANIN, *Les Églises orientales et les rites orientaux* (Paris 1955). M. JUGIE, *Theologia dogmatica Christianorum ab Ecclesia Catholica dissi-*

dentium, 5 v. (Paris 1926–35). I. H. DALMAIS, *Eastern Liturgies,* tr. D. ATTWATER (New York 1960). B. J. KIDD, *The Churches of Eastern Christendom* (London 1927). A. KING, *The Rites of Eastern Christendom,* 2 v. (London 1950). N. LADOMERSZKY, *Theologia orientalis* (Rome 1953). V. LOSSKY, *The Mystical Theology of the Eastern Church* (London 1957). H. MUSSET, *Histoire du christianisme spécialement en Orient,* 3 v. (Harissa 1948–49). F. J. MCGARRIGLE et al., *The Eastern Branches of the Catholic Church* (New York 1938). P. RONDOT, *Les Chrétiens d'Orient* (Paris 1955). N. ZERNOV, *Eastern Christendom* (New York 1961). The Nestorian Church. G. P. BADGER, *The Nestorians and Their Rituals,* 2 v. (London 1852). L. E. BROWNE, *The Eclipse of Christianity in Asia* (Cambridge, England 1933). H. C. LUKE, *Mosul and Its Minorities* (London 1925). A. J. MACLEAN and W. H. BROWNE, *The Catholics of the East and His People* (*Society for Promoting Christian Knowledge*; London 1892). E. TISSERANT, *Eastern Christianity in India,* tr. E. R. HAMBYE (Westminster, Md. 1957); *Dictionnaire de théologie catholique,* ed. A. VACANT, 15 v. (Paris 1903–50; Tables générales 1951–) 11.1:157–323. A. R. VINE, *The Nestorian Churches* (London 1937). W. A. WIGRAM, *An Introduction to the History of the Assyrian Church* (New York 1910). The Monophysite Churches. E. R. HARDY, *Christian Egypt* (New York 1952). J. MASPERO, *Histoire des patriarches d'Alexandrie* (Paris 1923). W. A. WIGRAM, *The Separation of the Monophysites* (London 1923). J. B. COULBEAUX, *Histoire politique et religieuse de l'Abyssinie,* 3 v. (Paris 1929). J. DORESSE, *Ethiopia,* tr. E. COULT (New York 1959). D. L. O'LEARY, *The Ethiopian Church* (*Society for Promoting Christian Knowledge*; London 1936). H. LAMMENS, *La Syrie: Précis historique,* 2 v. (Beirut 1921). *Christianity in Travancore* (Trivandrum 1901). T. E. DOWLING, *The Armenian Church* (*Society for Promoting Christian Knowledge*; London 1910), repr. 1955). M. ORMANIAN, *The Church of Armenia,* ed. T. POLADIAN, tr. G. M. GREGORY (2d ed. London 1955). H. F. TOURNEBIZE, *Histoire politique et religieuse de l'Arménie* (Paris 1910). Statistics on the Eastern Christians. *Oriente Cattolico* (Vatican City 1962). *World Christian Handbook,* ed. H. W. COXHILL and K. GRUBB (London 1962). F. S. MEAD, *Handbook of Denominations in the United States* (2d rev. ed. Nashville 1961). *Parishes and Clergy of the Orthodox and Other Eastern Churches in North America, Together with the Parishes and Clergy of the Polish National Catholic Church* (Buffalo 1962).

[G. A. MALONEY/EDS.]

EASTERN CHURCHES, CONGREGATION FOR THE

The Congregation for the Eastern Churches (*Congregatio pro Ecclesiis Orientalibus*) was established by Pope Paul VI in 1967 pursuant to the apostolic constitution, *Regimini Ecclesiae Universae*. It replaced the Congregation for the Oriental Church (*Congregatio pro Ecclesia Orientali*) that was established as a separate curial office of the Holy See in 1917, although its nucleus lies in the 16th century. In 1573 Gregory XIII instituted a Congregation for the Affairs of the Greeks. This office was entrusted not only with handling matters pertaining to Greek Catholics, but also with promoting communion and unity between the Holy See and the other churches of the Christian East.

Achille Cardinal Silvestrini, Prefect of the Congregation for the Eastern Churches. (AP/Wide World Photos)

Clement VIII (1592–1605) changed this office to the Congregation for Matters of the Holy Faith and Catholic Religion. Like its predecessor, it was charged with treating the affairs of the Greeks and other Eastern Christians; at the same time there was added to its competency the promotion of the Catholic faith in pagan lands. Thus it became a kind of forerunner of the Congregation for the Propagation of the Faith, which Gregory XV erected on June 22, 1622. Within this Congregation Urban VIII (1623–44) set up two commissions to administer Oriental affairs: the one treating questions of the Eastern Churches; the other, charged with editing their liturgical books, was expanded by Clement XI in 1719 to the Congregation for Editing the Books of the Oriental Church.

In the course of time it became increasingly evident that the same office could not deal with the approach to problems and methods for both the missions among the pagans and the affairs of the Eastern Churches. Accordingly, Pius IX, in 1862, set up a separate department for handling the affairs of the Eastern Christians within the Congregation for the PROPAGATION OF THE FAITH. It was called the Congregation for the Propagation of the Faith for the Matters of the Oriental Rites (*Congregatio de Propaganda Fide pro negotiis ritus orientalis*). The whole office remained under one cardinal prefect, but it was divided into two sections, each with its own secretary, officials, consultors, archives, and office of protocol.

Erection and Competence. This arrangement, however, did not turn out to be entirely satisfactory: the unfavorable impression was created that this department was a mere appendage of the Congregation for the Propagation of the Faith; the work for the Eastern Churches increased to such an extent that an independent congregation was thought to be necessary. On May 1, 1917, Benedict XV, with the motu proprio *Dei Providentis,* erected the Congregation for the Oriental Church (*Congregatio pro Ecclesia Orientali*), reserving to himself the post of prefect.

The Congregation is responsible for all matters pertaining to the Eastern Churches, relations between the Latin and Eastern Churches, and all issues arising from the implementation of the CODE OF CANONS OF THE EASTERN CHURCHES and the production of liturgical texts. These faculties are exercised without derogating from the traditional jurisdictional rights of Patriarchs and their Holy Synods in such matters.

Jurisdiction. The territories in which the Congregation has complete and exclusive jurisdiction are: Egypt and the Sinai Peninsula, Eritrea and northern Ethiopia, southern Albania, Bulgaria, Cyprus, Greece, Iran, Iraq, Lebanon, Palestine, Syria, Jordan, Turkey, and Afghanistan.

Bibliography: Congregatio pro Ecclesia Orientali, *Oriente cattolico, cenni storici e statistiche* (Vatican City 1962).

[R. ETTELDORF/EDS.]

EASTERN SCHISM

The separation between the Roman Catholic and the Eastern Orthodox Churches (*see* EASTERN CHURCHES) traces its origins to different ecclesiastical, theological, political and cultural developments in the western and eastern halves of the former Roman Empire. These differences provoked occasional schisms before the 11th century, but between the 11th and 13th centuries a definitive rupture between the two occurred.

From earliest times, Christianity experienced a flexible tension between unity and diversity. When serious disagreements in doctrine or discipline arose, local church councils were convened, following the precedent of the apostolic council described in Acts 15. After their legal recognition of Christianity in the 4th century, Roman emperors convoked general councils in order to address various heresies that threatened to disrupt the unity of the Church. Besides defining normative doctrine, these councils also enacted canons concerning discipline and administration. Seven of these councils held between the 4th and 8th centuries were accepted as ecumenical, meaning that they were considered binding on the entire Church. These are today recognized as authoritative by both the Roman Catholic and the Eastern Orthodox Churches, as well as by some Protestants. Significant populations in the Christian East rejected two of these councils, EPHESUS (431) and CHALCEDON (451), resulting in the schism of the so-called Nestorian and Monophysite (Oriental Orthodox) Churches, respectively.

As Christianity established itself throughout the Roman Empire and beyond, the churches and the bishops of Rome, Alexandria, and Antioch were especially esteemed for their leadership. Besides representing the Christian populations of three of the most important cities of the empire, their prestige derived from the apostolic foundation and succession of their sees. The Council of NICAEA I (325) granted similar honor to the See of Jerusalem, in recognition of its apostolic origins, and the Councils of CONSTANTINOPLE I (381) and Chalcedon raised the See of Constantinople to second in honor after Rome. The government of the empire had been transferred from Rome to Constantinople in 330, so it was thought fitting to recognize the importance of the new imperial city. The establishment of the patriarchate of Constantinople laid the foundation for ecclesiastical rivalry between ''old'' Rome and the ''new Rome,'' Constantinople. Rome objected to the rationale behind the elevation of Constantinople because it emphasized the political importance of the leading sees rather than their apostolic associations, and for this reason also disapproved of Constantinople's use of the title ''Ecumenical Patriarch.'' The Roman popes cultivated their identity as the heirs to Saint Peter, and their see as the location of the martyrdoms of both Peter and Paul. The five bishops of Rome, Constantinople, Alexandria, Antioch, and Jerusalem, in that order of precedence, came to be recognized as a ''pentarchy'' of patriarchs, with leadership responsibility for the churches in their territories.

Rome was both the highest ranking see in honor and also the sole patriarchate in the Latin-speaking West. The eventual Eastern Schism entailed the separation of the Latin-speaking churches of the West, under the leadership of Rome, from the Greek-speaking churches of the East, under the leadership of Constantinople. This split was facilitated by the collapse of Roman political authority and the establishment of the Germanic kingdoms in the West, the rise of Islam in the East, and the settlement of the Slavs in the Balkans. These factors resulted in decreased familiarity and contact between East and West, especially as knowledge of Greek in the West and Latin in the East declined. The schism of the Monophysite and

Nestorian Churches, as well as the Islamic conquest of Alexandria, Antioch, and Jerusalem, diminished the wider influence of those sees and increased that of Constantinople.

Being the seat of civil government, Constantinople was particularly vulnerable to imperial pressures. The churches of Rome and Constantinople were temporarily split during the ACACIAN SCHISM (482–519), named for Acacius, patriarch of Constantinople (471–89). In an attempt to win back the Monophysites, Emperor Zeno (474–91) issued the *HENOTICON* (482), a compromise formula on the two natures of Christ. Rome rejected this compromise, instead upholding the definition of the Council of Chalcedon. With the exception of Pope HONORIUS I (625–38) during the Monothelite controversy, the Roman see was distinguished by its adherence to orthodoxy during the period of Trinitarian and Christological controversy. Its prestige as the leading see was further enhanced when the heresy of ICONOCLASM was introduced by Emperor Leo III in 726. Rome rejected the Iconoclast Council of Hieria (754) and supported the Iconophile Council of NICAEA II (787), which became the Seventh Ecumenical Council.

The Iconoclastic controversy drove a wedge between the papacy and the Roman emperors. Emperor LEO III punished the Roman see for its opposition to Iconoclasm by removing Calabria, Sicily, and Illyricum (including Greece) from papal jurisdiction and placing them under the patriarchate of Constantinople. Confronted by the Lombard military threat and unable to rely on help from the East, Pope STEPHEN II (752–57) requested aid from the Frankish ruler, Pepin III. The Franks defeated the Lombards and established the papacy as the temporal ruler of lands in Italy. Papal estrangement from the empire reached its height when Pope LEO III (795–816) declared Charlemagne the emperor of the Romans on Christmas of the year 800, creating a ''Holy Roman Empire'' of the West to rival the Eastern Roman, or Byzantine, Empire.

After the empress Theodora restored icon veneration in 843, communion was reestablished between Rome and Constantinople. The Eastern church remained unsettled, however, as the bishops who had acquiesced to Iconoclasm were deposed, and rival factions quarreled over the application of canonical strictness. Then, in 856, Theodora was overthrown by her brother, Bardas, on behalf of her adolescent son, Emperor MICHAEL III (842–67). Ignatius, patriarch of Constantinople (847–58; 867–77), was loyal to Theodora and resigned his office. As his replacement, the rival ecclesiastical parties selected a compromise candidate—PHOTIUS (858–67; 877–86), a learned layman and civil servant. Unfortunately, one of the three bishops who consecrated Photius, Gregory Asbestas of Syracuse, had been deposed by Ignatius. Gregory appealed to the pope, but a decision had not yet been returned. The Constantinopolitan synod rehabilitated Gregory and appeared to have reconciled the opposing parties. Shortly afterwards, however, the extreme followers of Ignatius rejected Photius.

Pope NICHOLAS I (858–67) became involved in the situation when Photius sent him the customary announcement of his elevation as patriarch. Nicholas understood papal primacy to mean that he had jurisdiction over the entire Church, not just within the Western patriarchate. He believed that he had the right to adjudicate the internal affairs of the Byzantine church, and so in 863 he declared Photius's elevation uncanonical, excommunicated him, and recognized Ignatius as patriarch. Thus began the so-called Photian Schism between Rome and Constantinople.

Complicating matters was rivalry between the two sees over the conversion of Bulgaria. Frankish and Byzantine missionaries there criticized each other's ecclesiastical customs, provoking Nicholas and Photius's involvement in the production of the first polemical literature between Latins and Greeks. Particularly noteworthy was conflict over the use of the *FILIOQUE* in the Nicene-Constantinopolitan Creed, which would remain a major issue dividing East and West. At a synod in 867, the emperor Michael III, Photius, and the other Eastern patriarchs condemned Pope Nicholas and asked the Western emperor, Louis II, to depose him. But rather Photius himself was deposed when the co-emperor, Basil I (867–86), succeeded to the Byzantine throne after having murdered Michael III.

The legates of Nicholas's successor, Adrian II, attended the Council of CONSTANTINOPLE IV (869–70), confirming the condemnation of Photius and the legitimacy of Ignatius. Jurisdiction over Bulgaria, however, was awarded to Constantinople. This council was accepted by the Roman church as the Eighth Ecumenical later in the 11th century. Ignatius and Photius eventually reconciled with each other, and Photius succeeded to the patriarchate upon Ignatius's death. Photius was recognized by Pope John VIII, who sent his legates to the ''Union Synod'' of 879–80. The Council of Constantinople IV's condemnation of Photius was at that time annulled.

The Photian Schism was resolved with the understanding that each church would continue to observe its own traditions. But the conflict revealed that East and West had developed different notions of authority in the Church, and no longer shared the same culture of one universal Church coterminous with one universal empire. Their spheres of influence were now clearly two, and they competed for authority in the borderlands of Byzantine southern Italy, the Balkans, and Eastern Europe. As Nicholas I demonstrated, the popes understood papal primacy in a monarchical sense, linked to Peter's primacy, and meaning that they exercised jurisdictional and teaching authority over all bishops in the universal church, including the eastern patriarchs. They also viewed themselves in a position superior to emperors and all other temporal authorities. In the 11th century, the Gregorian reform in the Western church further strengthened this self-conception of the papacy. In contrast, although the Eastern church recognized it as the leading see and had on occasion appealed to Rome over disciplinary or doctrinal matters, the East understood authority in the Church in a collegial sense. Rome was the ''first among equals'' in the pentarchy of patriarchs. Doctrine was properly defined by the ecumenical councils, which required the participation or consent of all five patriarchs.

The *filioque* had also emerged as a point of controversy during the Photian Schism. This phrase was added to the Nicene-Constantinopolitan Creed in the 6th century by the church in Spain in order to combat Arianism. The creed, as originally formulated by the Council of Constantinople I (381), stated that the Holy Spirit ''proceeds from the Father.'' The addition of the *filioque* changed the text to read ''who proceeds from the Father *and the Son.*'' This reflected the development of Trinitarian theology in the West, which stressed the unity of the three Persons in the Trinity. The East had rather tended to emphasize the personal distinction among the three, understanding the Father as the unique source of the other two Persons. The Franks spread the use of the *filioque* throughout the West. Although Pope Leo III had objected to altering the words of the creed and omitted the *filioque* from the inscription he commissioned for Saint Peter's basilica, no pope ever objected to the doctrine that it taught. The *filioque* was adopted in Rome at the time of Pope Benedict VIII (1014–15), under German influence. The East objected both to the doctrine, which seemed to them to posit two sources within the Godhead, and to the fact that the West had unilaterally changed the wording of the universal creed of the Church, which had been approved by the Second and Fourth Ecumenical Councils (Constantinople I and Chalcedon, respectively).

Following the Photian Schism, Rome and Constantinople were again briefly out of communion from 912–23. Defying the decision of Patriarch Nicholas I to forbid a fourth marriage intended to legitimize his son, Constantine VII, as heir to the throne, Emperor Leo VI (886–912) appealed to Pope Sergius III and to the eastern patriarchs for approval. A Constantinopolitan synod accepted Sergius's grant of dispensation for the emperor, provoking the resignation of Nicholas and a schism within the Byzantine church. Nicholas was reinstated as patriarch after the death of Leo VI in 912, and asked that Pope Anastasius III (911–13) condemn his predecessor's action. After receiving no reply, Nicholas removed the pope's name from the diptychs, indicating that the two sees were not in communion. This schism was repaired in 923, when Pope John X accepted the decision of the council held in Constantinople in 920, which anathematized fourth marriages.

The year 1054 has conventionally been given as the starting date of the (Great) Eastern Schism, because of the conflict at that time between Pope Leo IX (1049–54) and Patriarch Michael Cerularius (1043–58). But the precise date of the final schism has eluded scholars. Because contemporaries did not recognize a definitive time at which schism occurred, it has been argued that there was no formal schism in the 11th century at all, and other, later, dates for the final break are suggested. Most scholars see the events of 1054 as one significant occasion in the gradual formation and solidification of the schism, which culminated during the Crusades. Others consider the negotiations between Byzantium and Rome that followed this episode to indicate that a break had occurred. Regardless, it is clear that relations between Rome and Constantinople were extremely tenuous during the 11th century. In 1009 Pope Sergius IV (1009–12) sent a letter to Constantinople, announcing his elevation to the Roman see. It was rejected by Patriarch Sergius II (999–1019) because it contained the *filioque.* Sergius IV's predecessor, John XVIII (1004–9), was the last pope to be commemorated in the Constantinopolitan diptychs.

The conflict between Pope Leo IX and Patriarch Cerularius began when the Synod of Siponto (1050), reflecting the concerns of the reform papacy, condemned Greek religious practices in southern Italy. In response, the patriarch imposed the Greek rite on Latin churches in Constantinople. Differences over the *filioque,* fasting, celibacy of the clergy, and the Eucharistic use of leavened or unleavened bread (*azymes*) were the focus of polemicists on both sides. This last issue was seen as particularly scandalous, because it was a visible sign of Latin and Greek divergence in the sacrament of Christian unity par excellence, and reflected different theological interpretations of this primary act of Christian worship.

In spite of the religious controversy, Emperor Constantine IX (1042–55) arranged an alliance with the papacy against the Normans in southern Italy. Leo IX sent a delegation to Constantinople, headed by Cardinal Humbert of Silva Candida and including Frederick of Lorraine, the future Pope Stephen IX. Patriarch Cerularius took offense to the pope's letter to him, which belittled the position of the Constantinopolitan see and questioned his legitimacy as patriarch, and so refused to receive it. This provoked Humbert to publish a response to Archbishop Leo of Ochrid's anti-Latin letter and to engage in a disputation with Nicetas Stethatos. The papal delegation's visit served only to worsen tension between the two churches. On July 16, 1054, Humbert issued a bull of excommunication directed against Cerularius and his followers and placed it on the altar of Hagia Sophia. Ironically, among his complaints, Humbert accused the Byzantines of omitting the *filioque* from the creed. The patriarch in turn held a synod that refuted Humbert's charges and excommunicated the legates. It is important to note that the excommunications were limited to the people involved, and were not directed by the one church against the other as such. Humbert had acted on his own authority, and in the meantime Pope Leo IX had died. In recognition of these facts, in 1965 Pope Paul VI (1963–78) and Patriarch Athenagoras (1948–72) revoked the excommunications of 1054 as a first step towards healing the schism between the churches; it was not an act that resolved the schism itself.

Efforts to normalize ecclesiastical relations between Rome and Constantinople began shortly after 1054. These negotiations were between the popes and the Byzantine emperors, rather than with the patriarchs of Constantinople, as they were governed by the diplomatic and military concerns of the papacy and the empire. In 1071 the empire was dealt a double blow: a devastating defeat by the Seljuk Turks at Manzikert in Anatolia, and the seizure by the Normans of its last remaining territories in Italy. The Byzantines sought an alliance with the papacy against both the Turks and the Normans. After Emperor Michael VII (1071–78) was overthrown in a palace coup, Pope Gregory VII aligned himself with the Normans and excommunicated the next two emperors. Pope Urban II (1088–99) reversed the excommunication of Emperor Alexius I Comnenus (1081–1118). Alexius convoked a synod in 1089 that concluded that there was no evidence of a formal schism between the two churches. Patriarch Nicholas III (1084–1111) offered to commemorate the pope in the diptychs, provided that he would agree to either come to Constantinople to discuss their religious differences or send a statement of faith. Urban declined to respond, and so his name was not inscribed in the diptychs. Nevertheless, it appears that while Latins and Greeks were conscious of their differences and continued to debate them, there was no general acknowledgement of schism, particularly at the popular level.

In 1095 Urban called on Western Christians to help the Byzantines recover the Holy Land from the Turks. He had hoped thereby to improve relations between the churches, but the resulting Crusades had, unfortunately, the opposite results. The Latins passed through the empire on their way to the East, and the strain of provisioning the troops provoked Latins and Greeks against each other. Complicating matters, the Normans, sworn enemies of Byzantium, were prominent among the Crusaders. Rather than turning their conquests over to the emperor, as they had promised, the Latins established their own principalities. Latin patriarchs were installed at Jerusalem in 1099 and at Antioch in 1100; rival Greek lines of succession existed in exile. At Jerusalem, the Latin hierarch was recognized as legitimate by both Latins and Greeks, until the Latins were expelled and the Greek line restored following Saladin's conquest of the city in 1187. At Antioch, however, the legitimate Greek line was forced out by the Latins, creating two competing hierarchies and an open schism in that see.

Tension between Latins and Greeks escalated in the years leading up to the Fourth Crusade. In 1182 rioters in Constantinople, resentful of the political and economic privileges granted to the Latins, massacred the city's Latin inhabitants. The Norman king of Sicily, William II, then invaded Byzantium, massacred the Greeks of Thessalonica in 1185, and intended to reach Constantinople before being defeated. The immediate pretext for the diversion of the Fourth Crusade to Constantinople was, among others, the promise of a claimant to the Byzantine throne to unite the churches, if the Latins would help install him as emperor. The result was the crusader conquest of that city and the subsequent creation of the Latin empire of Constantinople (1204). The crusaders' sack of Constantinople was particularly brutal and sacrilegious, and the Greeks in the Latin-occupied territories were forced to accept the humiliating ''church union'' of religious submission to their conquerors, the bitterness of which would linger for years to come. As in the Holy Land, the Latins established their own patriarchate, while the Greek patriarchate joined the Byzantine government in exile at Nicaea. The schism was now complete.

While still in exile, Emperor John III Vatatzes (1222–54) began negotiations for church union as a means of returning Byzantine rule to Constantinople. Although these efforts failed, MICHAEL VIII PALAEOLOGUS (1259–82) succeeded in retaking Constantinople in 1261. Michael pursued union, hoping that the papacy could dissuade the Latin powers from attempting a reconquest. In 1274 the emperor's representatives attended the Council of Lyons II, presided over by Pope Gregory X (1271–76). There they agreed to accept the Latin faith, recognizing the primacy of the pope as understood by Rome, the Latin doctrine on the Procession of the Holy Spirit, and the *filioque* addition to the creed. Michael had requested that the Greeks be allowed to preserve their rites, including the use of leavened bread in the Eucharist, and that the only change in their worship be the commemoration of the pope. The Roman church, however, continually pressed Michael to enforce the union by requiring the recitation of the *filioque* in the liturgy. Faced with the opposition of the great majority of the Byzantine clergy and laity, Michael refused to alter the rites of his church, but did cruelly persecute the anti-unionists. Unfortunately, he lost his alliance with the papacy upon the election of Martin IV (1281–85), a Frenchman. Martin was an ally of Charles of Anjou, who hoped to restore the Latin empire of Constantinople. Michael remained faithful to the union, even after Martin excommunicated him in 1281. Charles of Anjou ceased to be a threat to the empire after the Sicilian Vespers uprising in 1282. Emperor Andronicus II (1282–1328) repudiated the union of Lyons immediately following his father's death.

Ironically, Andronicus II reopened union negotiations in the latter years of his reign, as the empire again sought military aid from the West, this time against the Ottoman Turks. Andronicus III (1328–41) continued these discussions, sending the Italian Greek theologian Barlaam of Calabria to France in 1339, to visit both the king and Pope Benedict XII (1334–42). Barlaam explained that the Greeks had rejected the union of Lyons because only the representatives of the emperor, not those of the four Eastern patriarchs or of the laity were present at the council, and even they were not allowed to negotiate—rather, they were forced to submit to the Roman church. Although Barlaam's mission failed to produce results, he had articulated the requirements necessary for the Orthodox to accept any union agreement: negotiation of differences at an ecumenical council, by representatives of all five patriarchs and with the consent of the laity. Contrary to Western notions of Byzantine ''caesaropapism,'' union could not be enforced through the will of the emperor alone.

The papacy saw no reason for calling yet another council to debate questions that had already been defined by the Roman church. Nor was it interested in facilitating military assistance to the schismatic (or heretical) Greeks, before they submitted to its authority. In spite of this stalemate, discussions continued throughout the 14th century. In 1369 at Rome, Emperor John V Palaeologus (1341–91) personally converted to the Roman faith. No union of the churches or military aid resulted from his conversion.

As the Ottomans advanced into southeastern Europe, the Western powers grew alarmed. In 1396 a crusading army led by Sigismund of Hungary was defeated at the battle of Nicopolis. The French king, Charles VI, sent Emperor Manuel II (1391–1425) some troops for Constantinople's defense in 1399. Europe was divided at that time over the Great Schism of the West, in which the Roman and Avignonese lines of the papacy fought for recognition, while the Conciliar Movement challenged papal authority itself. The West was at last motivated to negotiate with the East over terms for convoking an ecumenical council.

The Byzantines were invited by Sigismund, now the Western emperor, to send ambassadors to the Council of Constance (1414–17). This council repaired the Western schism by electing Martin V (1417–31) as sole pope. Discussions begun with Martin came to fruition when Pope Eugenius IV (1431–47) and Emperor John VIII (1425–48) agreed to convene a union council designed to meet Byzantine requirements for ecumenicity. The Greeks chose to negotiate with Eugenius rather than with his rival, the Council of Basel. Although they had desired to hold the council in Constantinople, the Turkish threat made that impossible. The Byzantine delegation to the Council of Ferrara-Florence (1438–39) included Patriarch Joseph II (1416–39), representatives of the three Eastern patriarchs and from the churches of Bulgaria, Georgia, Moldo-Wallachia, and Russia, and distinguished lay philosophers. The papacy pledged economic support for the Orthodox delegation and some military aid for the defense of Constantinople, with more help from the Western powers to follow upon the successful conclusion of union.

Negotiations at the council dragged on, as the emperor hoped for the arrival of official embassies from the Western princes, whose allegiances were split between Eugenius and Basel. In the end, the Greeks accepted the union decree, which defined the controversial points in favor of the Latin doctrine. It declared that the Latin and Greek teachings on the Procession of the Holy Spirit were the same, interpreting the patristic Greek use of the phrase ''through the Son'' as the equivalent in meaning of the Latin ''and the Son.'' The *filioque* was defended as having been rightfully added to the creed, but no mention was made of the Greeks being required to add it. It was also agreed that the Eucharist could be celebrated with either leavened or unleavened bread, each church retaining its own custom. Because the Greeks had not speculated much themselves concerning the intermediate state of the soul after death and before the final judgment, they were required to accept the doctrine of purgatory. Finally, the decree asserted the primacy of the pope as teacher and ruler of the Church, while assuring the rights and privileges of the other four patriarchs.

Although church union was the official policy of the Byzantine emperors and the patriarchs of Constantinople from 1439 until the conquest of the city by the Ottoman Turks in 1453, the union was rejected by the Eastern patriarchs, Russia, and the majority of Byzantines, as a betrayal of their traditional faith. In their view, the Roman church had not given up anything that had caused the schism in the first place. Some military help for the defense of Constantinople was indeed deployed (most notably the Crusade of Varna in 1444), but failed to be successful. The church of Constantinople officially repudiated the Florentine union in 1484.

The agreement at Florence was, however, used as a basis for other reunions with the Roman Catholic Church, most notably that of Brest-Litovsk in 1596 with the Ruthenians of Eastern Europe. Today, the status of the Eastern Catholics is a problem in the ongoing ecumenical dialogue between the Roman Catholic and the Eastern Orthodox Churches. The issues of papal primacy (and since Vatican I, infallibility), as well as the *filioque,* remain major stumbling blocks in the path of union.

Bibliography: F. DVORNIK, *The Photian Schism* (Cambridge, Eng. 1948, 1970); *Byzance et la Primauté romaine* (Paris 1964) (*Byzantium and the Roman Primacy,* tr. E. A. QUAIN [New York 1966, 1979]). D. J. GEANAKOPLOS, *Emperor Michael Palaeologus and the West 1258–1282* (Hamden, Conn. 1973); "The Council of Florence (1438–39) and the Problem of Union between the Byzantine and Latin Churches," and "An Orthodox View of the Councils of Basel (1431–49) and of Florence (1438–39) as Paradigm for the Study of Modern Ecumenical Councils," in *Constantinople and the West* (Madison, Wis. 1989) 224–254, 255–278. J. GILL, *The Council of Florence* (Cambridge 1959). J. M. HUSSEY, *The Orthodox Church in the Byzantine Empire* (Oxford 1986). J. MEYENDORFF, *Byzantine Theology: Historical Trends and Doctrinal Themes,* 2d ed. (New York 1987). A. NICHOLS, *Rome and the Eastern Churches* (Edinburgh, Scotland 1992). S. RUNCIMAN, *The Eastern Schism* (Oxford 1955). M. H. SMITH III, *And Taking Bread . . . Cerularius and the Azyme Controversy of 1054* (Paris 1978). K. T. WARE, *The Orthodox Church* (London 1983).

[C. SCOURTIS]

EBBA, SS.

Two saints of this name in Anglo-Saxon England.

Ebba the Elder, abbess; d. Aug. 25, 683. She was the daughter of Ethelfrid, King of Northumbria, and was forced to go into exile after her father's defeat by EDWIN in 616. She became a Christian and later was professed a nun at the double monastery at Coldingham by Bishop FINAN OF LINDISFARNE. At Coldingham she was visited by St. CUTHBERT OF LINDISFARNE, and by King Egfrid (d. 684) and Queen ERMENBURGA OF NORTHUMBRIA with whom she interceded on behalf of Bishop WILFRID OF YORK. At the urging of ADAMNAN OF IONA, she undertook to reform her convent, which was falling away from a strict observance of the rule. Her relics were translated from Coldingham to Durham in the 11th century.

Feast: Aug. 25; Nov. 2 (translation).

Ebba the Younger, abbess and martyr; d. Coldingham, Berwick, England, 870. According to MATTHEW PARIS, the sole source, the Danes martyred her with the whole community after she attempted to buy a reprieve by mutiliating her own face.

Feast: Aug. 23 and April 2.

Bibliography: Ebba the Elder. *Acta Sanctorum* Aug. 5:194–199. BEDE, *Opera historica,* ed. C. PLUMMER, 2 v. (Oxford 1896) 1:264–265. *Vita S. Cuthberti* in *Two Lives of Saint Cuthbert,* ed. and tr., B. COLGRAVE (Cambridge, Eng. 1940) 79–80, 189–190, 318. EDDIUS STEPHANUS, *Life of Bishop Wilfrid,* ed. and tr. B. COLGRAVE (New York 1927), 79. H. H. E. CRASTER, "The Red Book of Durham," *English Historical Review* 40 (1925) 504–532. H. FARMER, *Dictionnaire d'histoire et de géographie ecclésiastiques* (Paris 1912–), 14;1268–69. A. M. ZIMMERMANN, *Kalendarium Benedictinum: Die Heiligen und Seligen des Benediktinerorderns und seiner Zweige* (Metten 1933–1938), 2:618–620. **Ebba the Younger.** MATTHEW PARIS, *Chronica majora,* ed. H. R. LUARD, 7 v. (*Rerum Brittanicarum medii aevi scriptores* 57; 1872—83) 1:391–392. A. M.. ZIMMERMANN, *Kalendarium Benedictinum: Die Heiligen und Seligen des Benediktinerorderns und seiner Zweige,* 4 v. (Metten 1933–38) 2:5–7. H. FARMER, *Dictionnaire d'histoire et de géographie ecclésiastiques* (Paris 1912–), 14:1269–70.

[V. I. J. FLINT]

EBBINGHAUS, HERMANN

German psychologist, pioneer in the experimental investigation of memory, b. Barmen, Jan. 24, 1850; d. Halle, Feb. 26, 1909. He took his doctorate at Bonn with a dissertation on the philosophy of the unconscious of E. von HARTMANN in 1873. Later, while studying privately, he chanced upon a copy of the *Elemente der Psychophysik* of G. T. Fechner and at once began to adapt Fechner's method to the measurement of learning and memory. He first used himself as a subject and 2,300 nonsense syllables of his own invention for material; later he verified his results and published them in *Ueber das Gedächtnis* (Leipzig 1885). At this time he was at Berlin where, as assistant professor, he founded a psychological laboratory in 1886. Ebbinghaus is memorable also for the construction of a completion test, the type destined for long use in intelligence testing. In 1890, with Arthur König, he founded the *Zeitschrift für Psychologie und Physiologie der Sinnesorgane* (Leipzig). He wrote two highly successful books, a general text, *Die Grundzüge der Psychologie* (Leipzig 1902), and a shorter work, *Abriss der Pscychologie* (Leipzig 1908). His treatise on memory is considered by some as the original impetus for more research in psychology than any other single study.

Bibliography: E.G. BORING, *A History of Experimental Psychology* (New York 1950). R. I. WATSON, *The Great Psychologists* (Philadelphia 1963).

[M. G. KECKEISSEN]

EBBO (EBO) OF REIMS

Archbishop of Reims, France; b. *c.* 775; d. Hildesheim, Germany, March 20, 851. He was the son of a serf from beyond the Rhine and of Himiltruda, nurse of Louis I the Pious. Ebbo was a fellow student of the prince who, on becoming king of Aquitaine, made Ebbo his librarian. When Louis became emperor, he obtained for his companion the archiepiscopal See of REIMS, and Ebbo fulfilled this charge with distinction, organizing the chapter, constructing buildings, including a new cathedral, and reforming the monasteries. He enjoyed great prestige at court and was royal *missus* in his province, but he failed in his missionary effort as legate of Pope PASCHAL I to Denmark in 822–823. Under politico-religious pretexts he tried to dethrone Louis the Pious in favor of Louis's son LOTHAIR I, and at Compiegne in 833, he was at the head of the group of bishops who proclaimed the dethronement of the emperor and put him under obligation to do public penance and accept imprisonment. On the restoration of Louis in 835, Ebbo fled and, despite his recantation, was deposed unanimously by the synod at THIONVILLE in March of 835 and interned in the Abbey of FULDA. On the death of his father in 840, Lothair restored Ebbo to his see, but he was exiled again after the victory of CHARLES II the Bald over Lothair at Fontenoy-en-Puisaye on June 25, 841. Pope SERGIUS II also refused to recognize him since Ebbo had not been reelected according to proper canonical procedure, and the pope went so far as to reduce him to the lay state for having exercised episcopal functions in violation of the canons. After quarreling with Lothair and being deprived of his revenues for having declined a diplomatic mission to Constantinople, Ebbo took refuge with Louis the German and received from him the See of Hildesheim. He did not, however, renounce his claims to Reims, where HINCMAR had been archbishop since 845, and after a reconciliation with Lothair he arranged for the meeting at Trier of a synod consisting of papal envoys and bishops, especially those loyal to Charles the Bald, that would examine his case. But neither Ebbo nor the papal envoys appeared; he died at Hildesheim without having been rehabilitated. The clergy he had ordained at Reims during his brief restoration from 840 to 841 were the cause of many legal disputes between 845 and 867, for in Gaul, contrary to the Roman opinion, the ordinations performed by a deposed bishop were considered invalid.

Ebbo left only several minor works (*Patrologia Latina* v.105; 116). FLODOARD OF REIMS (*Historia Remensis ecclesiae,* 1.2. 19) cited two inscriptions, and the *Appendix ad historiam Remensis ecclesiae* reproduces a regulation for the ''ministers'' of the Church of Reims dating from Ebbo's tenure. In a letter to Haltigar, Bishop of Cambrai (d. 831), he invited this bishop to compose a penitential ritual to restore the administration of penance, and in an *Apologia* the statement he made at the synod of Thionville is partially reproduced. The FALSE DECRETALS, justifying Ebbo's conduct, are no longer considered to be his work. The municipal library of Épernay has preserved the famous *Evangeliarium* of Ebbo (MS 1722), written with perfect regularity in letters of gold on vellum. It originated in the Abbey of Hautvillers in Champagne, where the monks executed it, apparently between 817 and 834, at the request of the archbishop.

Bibliography: M. BOUQUET, *Recueil des historiens des Gaules et de la France (Rerum gallicarum et francicarum scriptores)* v.6, 7. *Histoire littéraire de la France* v.5. É. LESNE, *La Hiérarchie épiscopale in Gaule et en Germanie* (Lille 1905); *L'Origine des menses . . .* (Lille 1910). F. LOT et al., *Les Destinées de l'empire en Occident de* 395 à 888, 2 v. (Paris 1928; new ed. 1940). A. FLICHE and V. MARTIN, eds., *Histoire de l'église depuis les origines jusqu'à nos jours* (Paris 1935–) v.6. L. HALPHEN, *Charlemagne et l'empire carolingien* (Paris 1947). H. LECLERCQ, *Dictionnaire d'archéologie chrétienne et de liturgie*, ed F. CABROL et al, 4.2: 1697–1703; 14.2:2213–90. P. VIARD, *Catholicisme* 3:1224–1225.

[J. DAOUST]

EBBO OF SENS, ST.

Archbishop of Sens; b. Tonnerre; d. Aug. 27 *c.* 740–50. Having been educated at the monastery of Saint-Pierre-le-Vif (Sens), Ebbo succeeded his father as count of Tonnerre, returning to the monastery later as a monk. In 704 he was elected abbot and subsequently succeeded his uncle Goéric as archbishop of Sens (probably in 709). During an Arab raid (725 or 731) Ebbo directed a fiery counterattack. He became interested in a life of solitude, prayer, and penance, and consequently arranged a retreat for himself in the forest of Othe near Arces, about 17 miles from Sens. On Sundays he returned to Sens to celebrate Mass and to instruct the people. He was buried at Saint-Pierre-le-Vif near his sisters, who were former recluses. His relics, exhumed by Archbishop Seguin in 980, were transferred to the cathedral of Sens during the Revolution and are preserved there still. His cult remains active at Arces, site of his grotto and a spring that reputedly cures those ill with fever. Until 1850 there was a solemn procession in his honor each August 27, his feast day.

Bibliography: Sources. *Acta Sanctorum* Aug. 6:94–100. J. MABILLON, *Acta sanctorum ordinis S. Benedicti* (Venice 1733–1740), 3:601–605. *Gallia Christiana* (Paris 1856–1865), 12:12–13. **Literature.** ABBÉ DE MANGIN, *Histoire ecclésiastique et civile du diocèse et Langres*, 3 v. (Paris 1765) v. 1. L. BRULLÉE, ''Notice sur Saint Ebbon, archevêque de Sens, mort en 750,'' *Bulletin de la Société archéologique de Sens* 8 (1863) 16–25.

[P. COUSIN]

EBENDORFER, THOMAS

Austrian historiographer, theologian, and diplomat; b. Haselbach, Korneuburg prefecture, lower Austria, Aug. 10, 1388; d. Vienna, Jan. 12, 1464. The son of a landed peasant family and subject to military duty, he began his studies at the University of Vienna in 1408, where he received a doctorate in theology (1428). He became a canon in St. Stephen's Cathedral in Vienna (1427). Sent to the COUNCIL OF BASEL as a representative of the University, he recorded his activities there in the *Diarium* [ed. E. Birk, *Monumenta conciliorum generalium saec. XV* (1857) 1:701–783], a sort of official diary. As a councilor of Emperor Frederick III, he went on diplomatic missions, but when the two men began to grow apart, Ebendorfer withdrew more and more to teaching and administration at the University and to writing history. In 1442 Frederick commissioned him to write a *Chronicle of the Emperors* [ed. W. Jaroschka (Vienna 1956) and F. Pribram, *Mitteilungen des Instituts für osterreichische Geschichtsforschung* (1890), sup. 3]. In 1451 Ebendorfer delivered the first draft to the Emperor, but he continued to expand the work until his death. His *Austrian Chronicle* (ed. A. Lhotsky, *Monumena Germaniae Historica Scriptores rerum Germanicarum (new series)*), planned originally as the seventh book of the *Chronicle of the Emperors*, developed into a separate major work of five volumes, of which the last section (continued to 1462) was partly in diary form. Ebendorfer belonged to the old school, and there is no trace of the humanistic spirit in his works. His distinguishing features as a historian are a special realism of detail and the use of other than writen sources to an extent then unknown. He wrote also many philosophical, theological, and occasional works (mostly unedited).

Bibliography: H. SCHMIDINGER, *Dictionnaire d'histoire et de géographie ecclésiastiques* 14:1276–81. A. LHOTSKY, *Thomas Ebendorfer, ein österreichischer Geschichtschreiber, Theologe und Diplomat des 15. Jahrhunderts* (Schriften der Monumenta Germaniae historica 15; Stuttgart 1957); *Quellenkunde zur mittelalterlichen Geschichte Österreichs* (Graz 1963).

[M. M. ZYKAN]

EBERBACH, ABBEY OF

Near Wiesbaden, Germany. It was founded by Abp. Adalbert of Mainz in 1116 for Augustinian canons, and was taken over by Cistercians of CLAIRVAUX in 1135. It is certain that the Romanesque church (after Clairvaux II) was built by Achard. Ribbed vaults mark the second phase of building, from 1170 to the consecration in 1186. A Gothic aisle for chapels was added on the south side under Abbot William (1310–46). Almost all the medieval buildings remain: the laybrothers' refectory and the monks' dormitory (13th century); the chapter room (12th–14th); the infirmary (12th); since 1617 the winery with a winepress dating from *c.* 1200. The monastery flourished in the 12th and 13th centuries, with four daughterhouses (1142–74) and an extensive wine trade. In 1206 the monk Conrad, who became abbot in 1221, completed at Eberbach the *Exordium magnum Cisterciense* (ed. B. Griesser, Rome 1961). The Swedes and Hessians plundered the abbey in the Thirty Years' War, carrying off its rich library. Of the productive scriptorium at Eberbach, 62 MSS (*Codices Laudiani*) are in the Bodleian Library and ten MSS (Arundel) are in the British Museum, some with magnificent illuminations. The abbey, secularized in 1803, has been a prison, an insane asylum, and a sanatorium; today it is a state winery and museum.

Bibliography: H. HAHN, *Die frühe Kirchenbaukunst der Zisterzienser* (Berlin 1957). A. BRÜCK, *Lexikon für Theologie und Kirche,* ed. J. HOFER and K. RAHNER, 10 v. (2d, new ed. Freiburg 1957–65) 3:627. A. SCHNEIDER, "Deutsche und französische Cistercienser-Handschriften in englischen Bibliotheken," *Cistercienser-Chronik* 69 (1962) 43–54.

[A. SCHNEIDER]

EBERHARD OF EINSIEDELN, BL.

Abbot; d. August 14, 958. He was born in Swabia of a ducal family and became provost of the cathedral of Strasbourg while still a young man. After establishing a reputation for competence and piety, he gave up this office in 934 to join his friend BENNO OF METZ in the hermitage of EINSIEDELN. As the community grew, Eberhard gave his personal wealth for the building of a monastery, which was named Our Lady of the Hermits, and he became the first abbot of the new foundation. The abbey church was consecrated in 948 by CONRAD OF CONSTANCE and ULRIC OF AUGSBURG. Generosity and prosperity were characteristic of the community under his direction, especially during the great famine of 942. His tomb became a place of pilgrimage, but the relics were lost during the French Revolution.

Feast: Aug. 14.

Bibliography: O. RINGHOLZ, *Geschichte des fürstlichen Benediktinerstiftes U. L. F. von Einsiedeln* (New York 1904), only v.1 pub. A. BUTLER, *The Lives of the Saints,* ed. H. THURSTON and D. ATTWATER, 4 v. (New York 1956) 3:330. A. M. ZIMMERMANN, *Kalendarium Benedictinum: Die Heiligen und Seligen des Benediktinerorderns und seiner Zweige,* 4 v. (Metten 1933–38) 2:572–574. L. BERRA, A. MERCATI and A. PELZER, *Dizionario ecclesiastico,* 3 v. (Turin 1954–58) 1:923. R. HENGGELER, *Dictionnaire d'histoire et de géographie ecclésiastiques,* ed. A. BAUDRILLART (Paris 1912–) 14:1288–89. R. TSCHUDI, *Lexikon für Theologie und Kirche,* ed. J. HOFER and K. RAHNER, 10 v. (2d, new ed. Freiburg 1957–65) 3:628.

[J. F. FAHEY]

The Abbey of Eberbach.

EBERHARD OF ROHRDORF, BL.

Abbot and statesman; b. *c.* 1160; d. June 10, 1245. Descended from the counts of Rohrdorf, in Baden, Germany, he joined the CISTERCIANS at the Abbey of Salem and became the fifth abbot in 1191. Eberhard proved himself both capable and energetic and yet was noted for his humility. His reign was the most famous in the history of the abbey, coinciding with one of the critical eras of German history, from the death of FREDERICK I BARBAROSSA to the end of the Hohenstaufen regime. Eberhard had an influential position in the royal court and was among the earliest and most loyal supporters of the Hohenstaufen. Again and again he appears as a witness to the diplomas of Henry VI and FREDERICK II. Numerous imperial documents of the period were written in Salem, for its scriptorium then had more copyists than the imperial chancellery. The abbot also enjoyed the special favor of the popes. INNOCENT III commissioned him to investigate and report on the most difficult questions of ecclesiastical politics such as the disputed episcopal election in AUGSBURG in 1202 and the settlement of the succession to the archbishopric of Mainz. In 1207 he negotiated a peace between Philip of Swabia (d. 1208) and Pope Innocent III.

Under Eberhard, Salem's holdings were greatly extended, and in 1201 he placed it under the protection of Archbishop Eberhard II of Salzburg (d. 1246). In the Codex Salemitanus, the abbot had the land and legal titles of the abbey noted most meticulously, and this valuable collection of documents is still one of the outstanding sources for the cultural and economic history of upper Swabia. The vigorous growth of the monastic family made possible the foundation of the Abbey of Wettingen in 1227. His monks also provided religious direction for the convents of nuns founded during the abbot's term of office: Wald (1212), Heppach (1230), Kalchrain (1230), Rottenmünster (1223), Heiligkreuzthal (1238), Feldbach (1234), and Gutenzell (1237). In 1240 Eberhard resigned his office because of his great age. He enjoyed the highest regard among his contemporaries, and he was inscribed in the Cistercian martyrology soon after his death.

Feast: April 14 (Cistercians).

Bibliography: *Acta Sanctorum* April 2:200. M. GLONING, *Graf Eberhard von Rohrdorf* (Augsburg 1904). H. D. SIEBERT, "Gründung und Anfänge der Reichsabtei Salem," *Freiburger Dözesan-Archiv* NS 35 (1934) 31–56. A. M.. ZIMMERMANN, *Kalendarium Benedictinum: Die Heiligen und Seligen des Benediktinerorderns und seiner Zweige* (Metten 1933–1938), 2:296. M. A. DIMIER, *Dictionnaire d'histoire et de géographie ecclésiastiques* (Paris 1912–), 14:1291–93.

[C. SPAHR]

EBERHARD OF TÜNTENHAUSEN, ST.

Shepherd; b. Freising; d. c. 1370. Eberhard is an uncanonized folk saint, buried under an altar to his honor in the church at Tüntenhausen (Bavaria, Germany). According to the testimony at hearings (1729–34) at which his cult was approved as immemorial, it was said that the faithful took earth from Eberhard's grave and used it as a medicine for sick cattle, yet the grave mound never diminished. Iron and wooden votive statues of animals were left at his grave, and reportedly live calves also were sacrificed. The first mention of his cult is in a letter of 1428. He is the patron of shepherds and domestic animals, invoked in cases of cattle sickness and for good weather.

Feast: Sept. 12, 28, and 29.

Bibliography: L. H. ZOLLING, "Die Verehrung des heiligen Eberhard in Tüntenhausen," *Frigisinga* (1925) 427–432. L. HEILMAIER, *Die Verehrung des heiligen Eberhard in Tüntenhausen* (Freising 1926). R. KRISS, *Die Volkskunde der altbayrischen Gnadenstätten* (Munich 1953) 1:23–24. J. STABER, *Volksfrömmigkeit und Wallfahrtswesen des Spätmittelalters im Bistum Freising* (Hohenkirchen 1955) 45–46.

[D. ANDREINI]

EBERLIN, JOHANNES

Evangelical preacher and popular writer; b. Kleinkötz, near Günzburg, *c.* 1470; d. Leutershausen, before Oct. 13, 1533. He studied at Basel in 1490 and Freiburg in 1493 and entered a Franciscan monastery in Heilsbronn. He lived thereafter in Tübingen, Ulm, and Freiburg, where in 1520 he encountered Luther's writings. On returning to Ulm, he was expelled from the order. In 1521 he published his famous work, *Die 15 Bundgenossen* (The Fifteen Confederates), combining in a folkish way socio-political and religious demands for reform, and describing a utopian state called Wolfaria. He spent a year in Wittenberg and then traveled as an evangelist to Basel, Rheinfelden, Rottenburg, and Ulm. He married, was called to Erfurt, and at the end of 1525, to Wertheim by Count Georg II. Dismissed on May 6, 1530, he ended his days in Leutershausen, near Ansbach. His greatest importance was his authorship of several volumes of folkish reform tracts and religious treatises.

Bibliography: J. EBERLIN VON GÜNZBURG, *Ausgewählte (sämtliche) Schriften*, ed. L. ENDERS, 3 v. (Halle 1896–1900). B. RIGGENBACH, *Johann Eberlin von Günzburg und sein Reformprogramm* (Tübingen 1874). M. RADLKOFER, *Johann Eberlin von Günzburg and sein Vetter Hans Jakob Wehe von Leipheim* (Nördlingen 1887). J. WERNER, *Johann Eberlin von Günzburg, der evangelisch-soziale Volksfreund* (Heidelberg 1889). G. BEBERMEYER, *Die Religion in Geschichte und Gegenwart*[3] 2:297.

[L. W. SPITZ]

EBIONITES

A Jewish Christian sect that flourished between the first and the fourth century. Despite patristic mention of an Ebion as founder, the word actually refers to the "poor men" (*ebjonim*) of the Beatitude (Mt 5.3; Lk 4.18; 7.22). This group of ascetics emigrated from Palestine to Transjordan and Syria. Like the Nazarenes and Sadocites of the Qumran tradition, they opposed official Judaism and accepted Jesus Christ as the Messiah foretold by Moses and as the true Prophet (cf. Dt 18.15), but considered His selection as the Christ or Anointed One as due to His eminent virtue achieved under the guidance of the Spirit received in the baptism of John whereby He kept the law perfectly (i.e., was a *saddîq*). The Ebionites violently opposed the theology of St. Paul because they believed that he had undergone a demoniacal hallucination when he claimed to have had a vision of Christ, and that he had opposed the conversion of the Jews to a perfect observance of the Mosaic Law as intended by St. James in Jerusalem. The Pauline soteriology also was repudiated by the Ebionites, who considered the sacrifices of the Old Law as abolished by the waters of baptism. Their concept of Christ as Son of Man made Him the great reformer of the Judaic Law whose teaching (*didascalia*) was a critique of the interpolations in the Mosaic Torah.

Devoted to a life of strictest poverty and community of goods, they practiced vegetarianism and ritual ablutions that culminated in the mystical ceremony of baptism. Information about the Ebionites is often inconsistent. They used a so-called Gospel of the Hebrews apparently based on Matthew. Their opposition to St. Paul centered on his apostolate rather than on his theology. The so-called *Gospel of the Ebionites* and portions of Clementines (*Homilies* and *Recognitions*) are thought by some scholars to have had an Ebionite origin. The Ebionites are mentioned by Justin (*Dialogues* 47, 48), Irenaeus (*Adversus haereses* 1.26.2; 2.21.1), Tertullian (*De praescriptio* 33), Hippolytus (*Philosphumena* 7.34;

9.13–17), and Epiphanius of Salamis (*Panarion* 29, 30). They are described as Symmachians (after Symmachus, the biblical translator) by the Latin Fathers of the fourth century and were then still extant in Rome, Egypt, and Asia Minor.

Bibliography: H. J. SCHOEPS, *Dictionnaire d'histoire et de géographie ecclésiastiques*, ed. A. BAUDRILLART et al. (Paris 1912–) 14:1314–19. J. THOMAS, *Le Mouvement baptiste en Palestine et Syrie* (Gembloux 1935). *Revue d'histoire ecclésiastique* 30 (Louvain 1934) 257–296. E. MOLLAND, ''La Circoncision: Le Baptême et l'autorité du décret apostolique,'' *Studia Theologica* 9 (1955) 1–39. A. SALLES, *Revue biblique*, 64 (Paris 1957) 516–551.

[F. X. MURPHY]

EBNER, MARGARETHA, BL.

Mystic, Dominican virgin; b. *c.* 1291, Donauwörth (near Nuremberg), Bavaria, Germany; d. June 20, 1351, Medingen, Bavaria, Germany. A child of the nobility, Margaretha received a classical education at home. She was solemnly professed (1306) at the Dominican convent at Maria-Medingen near Dillingen. Dangerously ill for many years, Ebner offered penances—abstinence from wine, fruit, and the bath—for those who had died in the war devastating the countryside. She was suddenly cured, but then forced with the other sisters to leave the convent during the campaign of Ludwig the Bavarian. Shortly thereafter the death of her nurse, to whom she was emotionally attached, caused Margaretha to grieve inconsolably. But in 1332 she regained her composure through the efforts of Henry of Nördlingen, who then assumed her spiritual direction. The correspondence between them is the first collection of this kind in German. Under his tutelage, she wrote with her own hand a full account of all her revelations and conversations with the Infant Jesus, including the answers she received from him, even in her sleep. This diary is preserved at Medingen in a manuscript that dates to 1353. From her letters and diary we learn that she remained loyal to the excommunicated Ludwig the Bavarian, whose soul she learned in a vision had been saved. Among her other correspondents were many contemporary spiritual leaders, including Johannes Tauler. She is considered one of the leaders of the Friends of God. Her body now rests in a chapel built in 1755 in the Maria-Medingen Convent church. Pope John Paul II praised Ebner, the first person he beatified (Feb. 24, 1979), for her perseverance.

Feast: June 20 (Dominicans).

Bibliography: M. EBNER, *Major Works*, tr. & ed. L. P. HINDSLEY (New York 1993). M. GRABMANN, *Neuaufgefundene lateinische Werke deutscher Mystiker* (Munich 1922). P. STRAUCH, *Margeretha Ebner und Heinrich von Nördlingen* (Amsterdam 1966). A. WALZ, ''Gottesfreunde und Margarete Ebner,'' in *Historisches Jahrbuch* (1953), 72:253–265. L. ZOEPF, *Die mystikerin Margaretha Ebner* (Berlin 1914).

[K. I. RABENSTEIN]

EBRACH, ABBEY OF

In Upper Franconia, Diocese of Würzburg, founded in 1127 as a daughterhouse of the Cistercian Abbey of MORIMOND. It flourished in the 12th and 13th centuries with daughterhouses of its own. The abbey had extensive estates in Franconia. It was secularized in 1803 and has been a prison since 1851. The first church was consecrated in 1134. The early Gothic construction (1200–85), with a rectangular apse and a magnificent rose window on the west façade, was sumptuously decorated in early classical style by Abbot Rosshirt (1773–91) employing the services of Materno Bossi, and is today a Catholic parish church. The monk Conrad (d. 1399), a noted theological writer, taught in the abbey's colleges in Prague and Vienna. A long, bitter struggle with the bishops of Würzburg over full exemption ended in failure in 1522. Valuable manuscripts from Ebrach are in Munich, Bamberg, Würzburg, and Wolfenbüttel.

Bibliography: W. WIEMER, *Die Baugeschichte und Bauhütte der Ebracher Abteikirche* (Kallmünz, Ger. 1958). M. HARTIG, *Lexikon für Theologie und Kirche*, ed. J. HOFER and K. RAHNER, 10 v. (2d, new ed. Freiburg 1957–65) 3:636. K. LAUTERER, ''Konrad von Ebrach, Lebenslauf und Schrifttum,'' *Analecta Sacri Ordinis Cisterciensis* 17 (1961) 151–214; 18 (1962) 60–120.

[A. SCHNEIDER]

ECCE HOMO

The presentation of Christ to the people to be mocked by them concludes His religious and civil trial, which is the last stage of the Passion before the Crucifixion. Crowned with thorns and with the reed scepter in His bound hands, His pitiable figure is exhibited in lonely contrast to the contemptuous horde that views Him.

The iconography of Ecce Homo is derived from Jn 19.4–7. The subject became important in Christian art only after the late Middle Ages and under the influence of mystical interpretation of the Passion of Christ. Thus, the iconography of Ecce Homo developed at the same time as that of the ''Man of Sorrows'' or ''Christ of Pity.''

The first representation of Ecce Homo proper is found in the Codex Egberti (10th century, Trier). From the 11th to the early 12th century the subject occurs in the narrative cycle of the Passion. In the early 15th century it began to enjoy an increasingly more important role in art. Contemporary theology as well as late medieval mystery plays of the Passion stimulated the development of the subject, and it became very popular, especially in northern countries. The figure of Christ was isolated from subsidiary motifs in the narrative representation and formed an *Andachtsbild.* In the 16th century the subject was spread widely by means of graphic art (Dürer, Altdorfer, etc.). Titian painted the full scene three times during his career (1543, Kunsthistorisches Museum, Vienna; 1547, Prado, Madrid; 1565, Hermitage, Leningrad), and there are further examples from the baroque period by Reni, Rubens, and Rembrandt.

Bibliography: K. KÜNSTLE, *Geschichte der byzantinischen Literatur* (Munich 1890; 2d ed. 1897) 1:437–440. O. SCHMITT, *Reallexikon zur deutschen Kunstgeschichte* 4 (Stuttgart 1958) 674–700. L. RÉAU, *Iconographie der l'art chrétien*, 6 v. (Paris 1955–59) 2.2:459–461.

[S. TSUJI]

ECCE IAM NOCTIS TENUATUR UMBRA

An office hymn that was historically sung at Lauds on the Sundays from Pentecost until the end of September. It is considered the counterpart of *Nocte surgentes vigilemus omnes* for Matins of the same season. It is considered the counterpart of the counterpart of *Nocte surgentes vigilemus omnes* for Matins of the same season. Both hymns consist of three strophes in Sapphic and Adonic. Recent scholars attribute the *Ecce* to ALCUIN rather than to GREGORY THE GREAT, among whose works it is found both in manuscripts and printed editions. Its style and thought, however, coincide with that of Alcuin and the cultivated tastes of literary circles in the ninth-century CAROLINGIAN RENAISSANCE.

Bibliography: *Analecta hymnica* 51:31032, text. J. CONNELLY, ed. and tr., *Hymns of the Roman Liturgy* (Westminster, Md. 1957).

[M. M. BEYENKA]

ECCLESIAM SUAM

Encyclical letter, "On the Ways in Which the Church Must Carry out Its Mission in the Contemporary World," promulgated by Pope Paul VI on the feast of the Transfiguration, Aug. 6, 1964. *Ecclesiam suam* was the pope's first encyclical letter. In it, he envisions the role of the Church vis-à-vis the secular world.

The prologue, "The Paths of the Church," outlines the encyclical in terms of "three thoughts, which continually disturb [the pope's] heart" (no. 8). First, "the Church should deepen its consciousness of itself" (no. 9). Second, on the basis of this self-awareness, "there arises the unselfish and almost impatient need for renewal" (no. 11). Third, the pope is concerned about "the relationships, which the Church of today should establish with the world which surrounds it and in which it lives and labors" (no. 12). Along these lines, the encyclical is divided into three parts.

"Ecce Homo," woodcut by Albrecht Dürer from the "Great Passion," series, ca. 1497–1500.

Part one, "Awareness," indicates that "it is a duty today for the Church to deepen the awareness that she must have of herself, of the treasure of truth of which she is heir and custodian, and of her mission in the world" (18). The key to this self-awareness is "vigilance." "Vigilance," says the pope, "should always be present and operative in the conscience of the faithful servant; it determines his or her everyday behavior, characteristic of the Christian in the world" (no. 21). He justifies the "boldness" (no. 23) of this invitation because "the Church needs to reflect on herself" and "to experience Christ in herself" (no. 25). Thus, "the first benefit to be reaped from a deepened awareness of herself by the Church is a renewed discovery of her vital bond of union with Christ" (no. 35). Ultimately, this sacred bond is the "mystery of the Church" (no. 36). This mystery "is not a mere object of theological knowledge; it is something to be lived, something the faithful soul can have a kind of connatural experience of, even before arriving at a clear notion of it'' (no. 37). In consideration of the profound and sacred mystery of the Church, the pope teaches that, ''if we can awaken in ourselves such a strength-giving feeling for the Church and instill it in the faithful by profound and careful instruction, many of the difficulties which today trouble students of Ecclesiology, as for example, how the Church can be at once both visible and spiritual, at once free and subject to discipline, communitarian and hierarchical, already holy and yet still being sanctified, contemplative and active . . . will be overcome in practice and solved by those who, after being enlightened by sound teaching, experience the living reality of the Church herself'' (no. 38).

In the second section, ''Renewal,'' Pope Paul indicates that the source of his impetus for renewal is ''the desire to see the Church of God become what Christ wants her to be: one, holy, and entirely dedicated to the pursuit of perfection to which she is effectively called.'' Despite this lofty vocation and, ''perfect as she is in the ideal conception of her Divine Founder,'' he affirms that the Church should ''tend towards becoming perfect in the *real expression* of her earthly existence'' (no. 41). He cautions that the Church's call to perfection should not be understood ''in the sense of *change*, but of a *stronger determination* to preserve the characteristic features which Christ has impressed on the Church'' (no. 47). In view of these criteria for renewal, he indicates that ''the Church will rediscover her renewed youthfulness, not so much by changing her exterior laws, as by interiorly assimilating her true spirit of obedience to Christ and, accordingly, by observing those laws which the Church prescribes for herself with the intention of following Christ'' (no. 51). Subsequently, the pope identifies two points that provide matter for reflection for the renewal of ecclesiastical life, namely, the ''spirit of poverty'' (nos. 54–55) and the ''spirit of charity'' (nos. 56–57).

The final section, ''Dialogue,'' presents the claim that ''if the Church acquires an ever-growing awareness of itself . . . tries to model itself on the ideal of Christ, the result is that the Church becomes radically different from the human environment in which it . . . lives or which it approaches'' (no. 58). However, ''this distinction is not a separation'' (no. 63). To the extent that ''the Church has a true realization of what the Lord wishes it to be, . . . there arises a unique sense of fullness and a need for outpouring.'' A consequence of this outpouring is the ''duty . . . of spreading, offering, and announcing it to others.'' ''To this internal drive of charity which tends to become the external gift of charity,'' says the pope, ''we will give the name of dialogue'' (no. 64), into which ''the Church should enter . . . with the world in which it exists and labors'' (no. 65). ''Dialogue,'' he affirms, ''ought to characterize our apostolic approach and method as has been handed down to us'' (no. 67). In fact, he claims that dialogue ''is found in the very plan of God'' (no. 70). Identifying its ecclesial significance, the pope explains, ''dialogue is . . . a method of accomplishing the apostolic mission'' (no. 81). As such, dialogue is both fruitful for the Church and for the partners she engages: ''The dialectic of this exercise of thought and of patience will make us discover elements of truth also in the opinions of others, it will force us to express our teaching with great fairness, and it will reward us for the work of having explained it in accordance with the objections of another or despite his or her slow assimilation of our teaching. The dialogue will make us wise; it will make us teachers'' (no. 83).

In his concluding remarks, the pope notes that ''it is a cause of joy and comfort . . . to see that such a dialogue is already in existence in the Church and in the areas which surround it. The Church is more than ever alive'' (no. 117).

[K. GODFREY]

ECCLESIASTES, BOOK OF

A SAPIENTIAL book of the Old Testament canon. This article discusses the meaning of the name, the origin and unity of the book, and the author's teaching.

The Name. The initial phrase, the words of Qoheleth (Heb. *dibrê qōhelet*), forms the title in the Hebrew text of Ecclesiastes. Throughout the book the word *qōhelet* occurs seven times (1.1, 2, 12; 7.27; 12.8, 9, 10), always with reference to the author of the work, very much as though it were a proper name. The word is related to *qāhāl,* which means ''congregation'' or ''community.'' Already the Septuagint translator was perplexed by the term and contributed to its enigmatic character by the choice of an obscure Greek word ἐκκλησιαστής; this term, rare in Greek literature and designating a member of the citizen's assembly, is sometimes translated as preacher. Not having a more acceptable solution to the problem, St. Jerome simply transliterated the Greek word for the title of the book in the Vulgate. The style, mood, and purpose of the author are hardly such as to warrant the title preacher.

Origin, Linguistic Characteristics, and Literary Unity. For centuries Solomon was regarded as the author of this book because of the statements in 1.1, 12, and the general argument of the first two chapters. This view has been universally abandoned; now it is generally agreed that the book comes from a much later period. It has been assigned by critics to every century from that of Zerubbabel to that of HEROD THE GREAT, but the present trend is to date its composition in early Hellenistic times, *c.* 300 to 275 B.C. The author's apparent ignorance of belief in a RESURRECTION OF THE DEAD excludes a date so late as the times of the Maccabees (2nd century B.C.). An earlier date is excluded because, among other reasons, his subjective, individualistic approach would not have been in character during monarchic times when community and national interests were paramount.

The language of Qoheleth is not the Hebrew of the Prophets. An analysis of the text provides an abundance of forms, words, and constructions that are Aramaic in nature or related to that idiom. For several decades one school of thought has advanced the hypothesis that Qoheleth in its present form is a translation from an Aramaic original (e.g., F. C. Burkitt, F. Zimmermann, C. C. Torrey, and H. L. Ginsberg), whereas the case against the translation theory has been defended by R. Gordis, among others (see bibliography). The linguistic problem may be answered by suggesting that Qoheleth was thoroughly conversant with Aramaic and used it as a vernacular tongue, while employing Hebrew in its contemporary state of transition to the later Mishnaic form for his lectures and the composition of his work.

The author's style, even as his thought, follows no neat pattern. Much is prose, although a prose that at times tends to become metrical under a load of poetic nuances. There are proverbs of the traditional type, some original and some from popular wisdom tradition [*see* WISDOM (IN THE BIBLE)]; statements seemingly contrary to each other are juxtaposed, and the reader is left to think out the answer; or Qoheleth cites a proverb and immediately adds his own evaluation. It is with this last form that he is most at home (4.9–12; 7.1–14; 9.4–6).

The question of the book's literary unity has become almost a historical one. Because of the author's seemingly unorthodox questioning of accepted orthodox religious and moral standards and because of the peculiarities of language and style, scholars at the beginning of the 20th century favored hypotheses of multiple authorship. The characteristics of the work are now seen from a more profound psychological and historical viewpoint and are interpreted as prime indications of the book's literary unity. Apart from a few evident exceptions, e.g., the opening words in 1.1, the epilogue in 12.9–14, and perhaps the words, ''says Qoheleth,'' in 1.2; 7.27; 12.8, unity of authorship is now generally maintained.

Content and Teaching. Although Ecclesiastes does have a specific theme, an orderly, logical development of that theme is not in evidence. Perhaps the reader would be more sympathetic to the author on this score, if he would visualize the author as a sage advanced in years musing on his favorite subject, now and then glancing at notes made during years of teaching. As once his school audience, so now his readers may best regard his statements as pearls of wisdom that need no further literary framework to enhance their value.

If there is a key to the understanding of Ecclesiastes, it is to be found in the third verse of the book: ''What profit has man from all the labor which he toils at under the sun?'' Qoheleth had sought to plumb the depths of the mystery of life from the viewpoint of its ultimate worth. He desperately sought for what is permanent, lasting, stable—and failed to find it. Like Augustine, Qoheleth had a ''restless heart;'' unlike Augustine he was not favored with the revelation that the human heart is destined to quiet its restlessness in the divine embrace. By observation and experience he had come to know, not that there is no profit at all in human objectives, but that the fullness of an enduring and satisfying good is simply not to be had.

The author covers various areas of human interest and effort, namely, wealth, pleasure, wisdom, work, government, family relationships, worship, business, women, loyalty, prudence, knowledge—and ever finds the same answer; none of these yields an ultimate value, none provides a lasting, limitless satisfaction. Even the best of them, wisdom, is undone by death. Therefore all is elemental vanity, nothingness, a chasing after wind.

Nevertheless, Qoheleth remains a sober, humble realist. He knows God has a plan in the universe of things, even though man is unable to piece that plan together. Injustice, death, misery, and folly do not place his religious faith in jeopardy. The disciple who added the final six verses to his master's musings, may well have reflected his teacher's deepest conviction: ''Fear God and keep his commandments, for this is man's all; because God will bring to judgment every work, with all its hidden qualities, whether good or bad'' (12.13–14).

There exists no evidence concerning Qoheleth's direct contribution to the development of the doctrine of retribution in AFTERLIFE or of blessed immortality. Nevertheless, his trenchant, devastating formulation of the inadequacy of the traditional teaching on RETRIBUTION in this life, together with his probing of the heart's undying desire for limitless possession of truth, goodness, and happiness cannot but have contributed to the evolution toward the belief in an afterlife.

Bibliography: *Encyclopedic Dictionary of the Bible*, tr. and adap. by L. HARTMAN (New York 1963) 615–617. V. HAMP, *Lexikon für Theologie und Kirche*, ed. J. HOFER and K. RAHNER (Freiberg 1957–65) 8:704. K. GALING and W. WERBECK, *Die Religion in*

Geschichte und Gegenwart (Tübingen 1957–65) 5:510–514. R. GORDIS, *Koheleth: The Man and His World* (New York 1951); ''The Original Language of Qohelet,'' *Jewish Quarterly Review* 37 (1946–47) 67–84; ''The Translation-Theory of Qohelet Reexamined,'' *ibid.* 40 (1949–50) 103–116; ''Qohelet and Qumran: A Study of Style,'' *Biblica* 41 (1960) 395–410. C. C. TORREY, ''The Question of the Original Language of Qoheleth,'' *Jewish Quarterly Review* 39 (1948–49) 151–160. H. L. GINSBERG, *Studies in Koheleth* (New York 1950); ''The Structure and Content . . . ,'' *Vetus Testamentum* 3 (1955) 138–149. R. PATRUEL, *L'Ecclésiaste* (new ed. *Bible de Jérusalem*; 1958). W. ZIMMERLI, *Die Weisheit des Predigers Salamo* (Berlin 1936). A. MILLER, ''Aufbau und Grundproblem des Predigers,'' *Miscellanea Biblica* 2 (Rome 1934) 104–132. D. BUZY, ''La Notion de bonheur dans l'Ecclésiaste,'' *Revue biblique* 43 (1934) 494–511. P. W. SKEHAN, *The Literary Relationship between the Book of Wisdom and the Protocanonical Wisdom Books of the O.T.* (Washington 1938).

[W. G. HEIDT]

ECCLESIASTICUS

The title commonly applied to the Latin translation (from the Greek version) of the Wisdom of Ben Sira, also known as SIRACH. The word Ecclesiasticus, like ἐκκλησιαστικός of Codex 248, a witness to the Greek II form of the book, is an adjective. But from the 3d century A.D. the Latin word came to be used also as a proper noun—St. Cyprian (d. 258) cites Sirach in this fashion: *Apud Salomonem in Ecclesiastico,* or simply *In Ecclesiastico* [*Corpus scriptorum ecclesiasticorum latinorum* 3 (Vienna 1868) 110, 154, 176, 177, 178, 181]. In the Vulgate tradition this same peculiarity is found; one manuscript begins *ecclesiastici liber incipit,* and the editions have either *incipit liber ecclesiastici* or simply *Ecclesiasticus,* whereas other manuscripts contain the more logical *incipit liber ecclesiasticus.* The best witnesses of the Vulgate, however, read *liber Hiesu filii Sirach,* a title more in keeping with most Greek manuscripts. The word Ecclesiasticus—either as an adjective modifying *liber* (expressed or understood), or worse still as a proper noun—cannot be satisfactorily accounted for. Perhaps because the book was so often read in the liturgy, it came to be considered the Church book par excellence; or because it is the most important of the Deuterocanonical books that were rejected from the Jewish canon, The Wisdom of Ben Sira came to be known as the ''Churchly'' book—one accepted by the Church but not by the Jews.

Bibliography: *Sapientia Salomonis, Liber Hiesu filii Sirach* (Biblia sacra iuxta latinam vulgatam versionem 12; Rome 1964), a critical ed.

[A. A. DI LELLA]

ECCLESIOLOGY

The branch of theology that studies the nature and mission of the Church. After considering the history of ecclesiology, this article will survey the major developments and issues that have attracted the attention of theologians since the Second Vatican Council.

History. Formal treatises on ecclesiology appeared somewhat late in the history of the Church (even though some writers did compose books on the Church; e.g., St. Cyprian wrote *De catholicae ecclesiae unitate*). Even scholastic theologians of the Middle Ages, including St. Thomas Aquinas, did not include a special treatise on the Church in their *Summae*. However, the writers of the New Testament, the Fathers, and scholastics reflected deeply on the mystery of the Church and treated explicitly of its different aspects, especially in relation to Christological and soteriological themes. One can, therefore, speak of the ecclesiology of the New Testament, of St. Paul, St. Augustine, etc., meaning by this the point of view from which they contemplated the Church and the aspects of the mystery emphasized or clarified by their writings. Prescholastic ecclesiology has certain definite characteristics: it expresses itself in symbolic language rather than in abstract formulations; it emphasizes the interior mystical reality mediated and manifested in the visible sacramental life of the Church. The great scholastic theologians in their insistence on speculative theology at times tended to overlook the rich symbolism of the Scriptures and Fathers, yet they carried forward many of the same themes. St. Thomas, for example, following Augustine, developed the theme of the headship of Christ, considering the MYSTICAL BODY as the domain, or sphere of influence, of Christ's sanctifying and salvific action.

When formal consideration was given to the Church in the domain of DOGMATIC THEOLOGY and the first treatises came to be written, this was done in response to definite historical challenges, which were to determine the aspects under which the Church would be considered. Thus John of Paris in *De potestate regia et papali* (1302–03) sought to delineate the relationship between the spiritual and temporal powers in the context of the conflict between Boniface VIII and Philip the Fair. In the Middle Ages various movements and writers, in reaction to the many abuses in the Church, began to call in question the authority and mediation of the visible Church (e.g., the Franciscan Spirituals, the Waldensians, John Wyclif and John Hus, the conciliar movement consequent upon the tragedy of the Western Schism). These movements found their fullest expression in the theology of Martin Luther and the Protestant Reformation, which ended in rejecting the visible mediation of the Church, especially its priesthood and the authority of the hierarchy.

As a consequence, Catholic theologians began to treat explicitly of the exterior visible aspects of the Church [see Juan de Torquemada, OP, in his *Summa de ecclesia* (Cologne 1480)]; and when the formal treatises came to be written by the theologians of the Counter Reformation, they placed a strong focus on its visible hierarchical structure (see Cardinal Robert Bellarmine, who set the pace for the others in his *De controversiis*). In the ensuing centuries, during which the Church was faced with new threats from Jansenism, Gallicanism, the rationalism of the 18th century, etc., this ecclesiology, whose interest was primarily apologetical and which has been unflatteringly described as a ''hierarchology,'' continued to hold sway and was the one incorporated in the theological manuals for use in seminaries. It reached its high-water mark at Vatican Council I with the solemn definition of the primacy of jurisdiction and infallibility of the pope.

During the 19th century, however, a new ecclesiology was slowly being formulated that sought to integrate the ecclesiology of the Church's visible structure into a more complete and vital understanding of the mystery as found in the Scriptures and Fathers. The first great center of this ecclesiological revival was the theological faculty of Tübingen in Germany, whose greatest light was Johann Adam Möhler (1796 to 1838). His ecclesiology was characterized by its insistence on the community and the interior reality of the life of grace (see *Die Einheit in der Kirche*, 1825, and *Symbolik*, 1832). This revival was furthered by the Jesuit theologians in Rome, especially Giovanni Perrone (1794 to 1876), Carlo Passaglia (1812 to 1887), Klemens Schrader (1820 to 1875), and Cardinal J. B. Franzelin (1816 to 1886); by Matthias Scheeben (1835 to 1888) in Germany; and Cardinal John Henry Newman (1801 to 1890) in England.

In preparation for Vatican I, a proposed schema on the Church, written largely by Schrader, began by defining the Church as the Mystical Body of Christ. It met with opposition from many of the fathers, and a revised version relegated the image to a secondary consideration, preferring to define the Church as a visible society. The new trends, however, continued to exercise their influence, and between the two world wars there was a greatly renewed interest in the theology of the Mystical Body (of special importance were the works of Karl Adam, Émile Mersch, Romano Guardini, Charles Journet, and Sebastian Tromp). In 1943 Pius XII's great encyclical on the Mystical Body (*MYSTICI CORPORIS*), while warning against excesses that could lead to a sort of panchristism, incorporated the patristic and scholastic insistence on the interior reality of grace with the theology of the Church as a visible hierarchical society. During the next 20 years modern Catholic ecclesiology, strongly influenced by the ecumenical movement and the scriptural and liturgical revival, continued to make many advances. French Dominican Yves Congar, for example, contributed especially to an understanding of historical development and the role of the Holy Spirit in the Church, with implications for ecumenism, structural reform, the laity, and spirituality. Congar's compatriot, Jesuit Henri de Lubac, expressed a multidimensional vision of the Church as both a social body in the world and a mystery revealed by God. The fruit of this further study and research is expressed concretely in Vatican II's Dogmatic Constitution on the Church, *Lumen gentium*, as well as in its Pastoral Constitution on the Church in the Modern World, *Gaudium et spes*.

See Also: CHURCH, II (THEOLOGY OF); CHURCH, ARTICLES ON.

Bibliography: Y. M. J. CONGAR, H. FRIES, ed., *Handbuch theologischer Grundbegriffe*, 2 v. (Munich 1962–63) 1:801–12. O. SEMMELROTH, *Lexikon für theologie und Kirche* 3:781–87. *Dictionnaire de théologie catholique*, ed. A. VACANT et al., 15 v. (Tables générales 1951–) 1:1110–30. F. M. BRAUN, *Aspects nouveaux du problème de l'église* (Fribourg 1942). C. ARÉVALO, *Some Aspects of the Theology of the Mystical Body of Christ in the Ecclesiology of Giovanni Perrone, Carlo Passaglia and Clemens Schrader* (Rome 1959). S. JAKI, *Les Tendances nouvelles de l'ecclésiologie* (Rome 1957). É. MERSCH, *Le Corps mystique du Christ*, 2 v. (2d ed. Paris 1936); Eng. *The Whole Christ*, tr. J. R. KELLEY (Milwaukee 1938; London 1949). M. NEDONCELLE et al., *L'Ecclésiologie au XIX siècle* (Paris 1960). G. THILS, *Les Notes de l'église dans l'apologétique catholique depuis la réforme* (Gembloux 1937). Y. M. J. CONGAR, ''Considération historique sur la rupture du XVI siècle dans ses rapports avec la réalisation catholique de l'unité'' in *Chrétiens en dialogue* (Paris 1964) 409–36. G. WEIGEL, ''Catholic Ecclesiology in Our Time'' in *Christianity Divided*, ed. D. J. CALLAHAN et al. (New York 1961) 177–94. A. DULLES, ''A Half Century of Ecclesiology,'' *Theological Studies* 50 (1989) 419–42. M. HIMES, *Ongoing Incarnation: Johann Adam Möhler and the Beginnings of Modern Ecclesiology* (New York 1997). R. KRIEG, *Romano Guardini: A Precursor of Vatican II* (Notre Dame 1997).

[J. R. LERCH/D. M. DOYLE]

The Nature of the Church. Vatican II did not legislate any one definition of the Church. *Lumen gentium* (LG) insisted that the Church is a mystery and proposed a variety of Biblical images, treating at length the Church as the People of God and as the Body of Christ. It also described the Church as a sacrament and as a communion. This last has come to new prominence while the image of the Church as the People of God seems to have been deemphasized. The 1985 Synod of Bishops, for example, made only one reference to the Church as the People of God. Two reasons may explain this deemphasis: a reaction to the misuse of the People of God by some to justify a ''people's church'' or ''popular church'' that is distinct from the hierarchical Church; and the fear that the People of God image might suggest a purely sociological view of the Church to the neglect of its deeper spiritual nature.

Theologians have followed the lead of the Council, avoiding the ''perfect society ecclesiology'' of the past and preferring an ecclesiology that blends the Biblical sources with historical tradition and contemporary needs. To achieve this end, they search for appropriate images, metaphors, types, and symbols to express the nature of the Church. Avery Dulles has argued persuasively for the use of models in ecclesiology: institution, mystical communion, sacrament, herald, servant, and community of disciples. Others have applied social theory to the study of the Church. Communio ecclesiology, with rich sacramental and pneumatic elements, has become a major theme. The 1985 Synod maintained that the ecclesiology of communion is the central and fundamental idea of the conciliar documents, and used it to explain distribution of power in the Church, the sacramental foundation for collegiality, and the coexistence of unity and pluraformity.

Church and the World. *Gaudium et spes* (GS) focused on the Church in its relationship to the world, calling for a discernment of the ''signs of the times'' (GS 4). The Council distinguished earthly progress from the increase of the Kingdom (GS 39) but did not precisely define the nature of their interrelationship. It also affirmed the solidarity of the human family, the collaboration with all people of good will, and the inculturation of the Church in different areas. Theologians have reflected on the role of the Church in the development of social justice and world peace. Political and liberation theologies concentrate on the duty of the Church to defend human life and promote human rights.

Liberation theology, with its stress on orthopraxis, conscientization, and the preferential option for the poor, sees the Church as an agent of social transformation. The Church has a fourfold mission: to announce the gospel of liberation, to denounce all actions that impede human rights, to initiate actions for justice, and to support these initiatives. Rome has criticized some elements in liberation theology: ecclesiological relativism; politicization of the gospel; confusion over human liberation and final redemption; and the use of Marxism, class struggle, and violence.

Although the Church may have no direct political or economic mission with respect to temporal matters, its moral and religious service extends to the entire world. The Church must defend human rights whenever they are violated. John Paul II and the Code of Canon Law, however, prohibit clerics and religious from engaging in partisan politics. A thin line often exists between political activity and partisan politics. The Church cannot retreat from pressing social concerns, but is should avoid excessive involvement in practical politics.

Several theologians have developed Karl Rahner's assertion that Vatican II began the era of the world Church—the movement from a Western or European center to an actual world religion. Such a global and multicultural Catholicism encourages the autonomy of regional churches, the adoption of new symbols, languages, and behavioral patterns, and the greater appreciation of non-Christian religions. The challenge of forming new structures and methodologies has deep pastoral implications for the Church.

Local and Universal Church. Vatican II did not fully explain the relationship between the local and the universal Church. Is the local church simply a part of the universal Church or does the universal Church come to be from the communion of local churches? The latter explanation is favored by many ecclesiologists who point to *Lumen gentium* 26, *Sacrosanctum concilium* (SC) 41, and *Christus Dominus* (CD) 11. The local church may refer to the regional church, the ritual or patriarchal church, the diocese, the parish, the family, and the smaller eucharistic communities. Some argue that the term local church also applies to non-eucharistic groupings, such as religious communities and basic ecclesial communities so prevalent in Latin America.

The local church is Church because in it Christ is wholly present. The Church of Christ is incarnate in the local church and has no existence apart from it. The universal Church is not a juridical union of local churches but the communion of local churches united in faith and the Holy Spirit. ''In and from such particular churches there comes into being the one and only Catholic Church'' (LG 23).

The theology of the local church raises the issue of unity and diversity. Local churches are mutually interdependent; they are always related to other local churches and especially to the Church of Rome. Local churches throughout the world recognize one another and foster the wider mission of the universal Church. Each local church is deeply imbedded in the life of its own people, but it must also be accountable to its sister churches.

If the local church is truly Church, then it would seem that the principle of subsidiarity is applicable. This principle affirms that smaller groups should not be absorbed by larger social bodies. It implies a division of competencies and cooperation and seeks to prevent excessive domination and to encourage local churches to act freely and responsibly. The practical implementation of the principle of subsidiarity inevitably brings up the problem of the tension between authority and freedom: the balance between the rights of the local church and the rights of the Church of Rome.

Ministries and Mission. The postconciliar period has seen an explosion in the number and diversity of ecclesial ministries. The Council taught that the ordained priesthood differs in essence and not only in degree from the priesthood of the faithful (LG 10). It described the priesthood largely in pastoral and functional terms rather than in the highly sacral language of the post-Tridentine period. An extensive literature exists on the nature of priestly identity, the programs of priestly formation, and the pastoral strategies needed in view of the critical shortage of priests and the increase in priestless parishes. Many of the theologies of the priesthood focus on charism, service, and community rather than on the power of the office and its ontological grounding.

The Council authorized the restoration of the permanent diaconate in Latin rite churches (LG 29). The deacon is a minister of word and sacrament and ordained to serve the community in charity and justice. The debate continues over these roles: is the primary task of the deacon to assist the priest in liturgical celebrations or to perform works of charity and justice as Acts of the Apostles 6 seems to indicate?

The theology of the laity has remained a controversial topic. According to Vatican II, "the lay apostolate is a participation in the saving mission of the Church itself" (LG 33). The Council taught that the Christian faithful, by their Baptism and Confirmation, share a "common dignity" and possess a "true equality" in regards to the building up of the Body of Christ. They share in the prophetic, priestly, and kingly mission of Christ. The Code of Canon Law enumerates the rights and duties of the laity, but it does not give them any effective power. The increase in lay ministries, the shortage of priests, and the involvement of the laity in ecclesial decision-making at all levels may help shape a more balanced theology of the laity in the future. The role of women, especially in regard to the greater utilization of their special contributions to the Church, is a significant aspect of this question.

Evangelization is an essential function of the Church and a duty of all its members, as Paul VI emphasized in *Evangelii nuntiandi* (1975) and as John Paul II proclaimed in *Redemptoris Missio* (1990). But Vatican II further affirmed the positive elements in non-Christian religions and the possibility of salvation for the unevangelized. This new point of view has seriously called into question the traditional understanding of mission work. The number of missionaries declined dramatically since the Council. A debate, unresolved by Vatican II, continues over the primary purpose of missionary activity. Is it the planting of the Church as a sign among the unevangelized or the broader pastoral activity among both the unevangelized and the de-Christianized? Missiology is in a transitional stage as it attempts to answer this question.

Primacy and Collegiality. Church authority, always an intriguing question for theologians, has attracted much attention in the last ten years. Vatican II substantially repeated the doctrine of primacy defined at Vatican I, but contemporary studies examine anew the Biblical, historical, and theological evidence. Particular attention has been paid to the possible limits of the pope's power in the light of revelation, natural and divine law, dogma, and ecclesiastical law—all these look to the very mandate of his office. The voluntary limitation of papal authority is also widely discussed in ecumenical circles.

Primacy cannot be properly understood apart from collegiality, one of the major contributions of Vatican II. The Council stressed that unity and collaboration that should exist between the papal and episcopal offices and described the corporate responsibility which the College of Bishops under papal leadership has for the entire Church. Collegiality rests on the ancient idea of the Church as *communio.* The Council, however, was vague about the consequences of collegiality and how it affects the future of the papacy. The debate centers on LG 22, which stated that the College of Bishops with its head, the pope, is the subject of supreme power in the Church. Some theologians argue that there are two inadequately distinct subjects of authority in the Church: the pope and the College of Bishops, and the pope can decide to act personally or collegially. They point to the *Nota praevia* to support their view. This view seems to break the essential unity of Church authority and to separate the papacy from the episcopacy. Others, also arguing from Vatican II, hold that there is only one subject of supreme power-the College of Bishops. Thus every primatial action is also collegial, since the pope is a member and head of the college. This theory, which has much to recommend it, stresses the unity of power in the Church and the collaboration of the pope and the bishops.

The Synod of Bishops, established by Paul VI in 1965, is a major organ of collegiality. Through 2000, ten general assemblies and eight regional assemblies have been held. The current debate concerns the theological character of the synod: is it a truly collegial act, or is it simply a service to the Pope in his capacity as universal primate? The Code of Canon Law and the history of the synods suggest the latter. The synod is an expression of the collegial spirit (LG 23), but it is merely a consultative body. The pope may grant a deliberative vote to its members, but he has not yet done so.

Episcopal conferences were given formal status at Vatican II (CD 36–38) and made mandatory by Paul VI in 1966. Current discussion focuses on the theological basis of the conferences and their teaching authority. There is no unanimity among theologians on these points. Yet many theologians argue that the conferences have a genuine theological basis as limited expression of the collegial spirit and that they have legitimate authority to teach. In juridical terms the synods and episcopal conferences may not be examples of collegiality in the strict sense. But the life of the Church overflows juridical categories and these collegial expression have greatly benefited the Church.

Magisterium and Disagreement. Another problem in postconciliar ecclesiology is the relationship between the ecclesiastical magisterium and theologians. The Council said little about the authority of theologians. It did teach that the faithful are to accept with ''a religious submission of will and of mind'' (*religiosum voluntatis et intellectus obsequium*) the teachings of the Pope and the bishops, even when these teachings are not infallible (LG 25). It presumed assent to Church teaching and did not discuss the possibility or conditions of disagreement. The issue became more than academic in light of the negative reaction to *Humanae vitae* (1968), the encyclical of Paul VI on birth control. Tensions further increased when the Congregation for the Doctrine of the Faith with papal approval censured such theologians as J. Pohier. H. Küng, E. Schillebeeckx, C. Curran, L. Boff, and T. Balasuriya.

The present debate concerns largely the extent to which public dissent to some authentic but non-infallible teachings of the magisterium is permissible. How are the rights of theologians to explore the faith compatible with the rights of the Church to teach authoritatively? The Church cannot accept a ''free market of ideas'' without limit, nor should it unreasonably suppress theological creativity. Public dissent by theologians, however, should not weaken the effectiveness of the magisterium to be a credible witness to the Gospel. Disputes between the magisterium and theologians may be better resolved by beginning the process at the local level and only, when unsuccessful, by appealing to Rome. There is also need for clearer and more equitable procedures for resolving doctrinal conflicts.

A related question is the meaning of the *sensus fidelium*—the objective sense or mind of the Church. The *sensus fidelium*, what the faithful believe, is a gift of the Holy Spirit to the Church. It is not constitutive of revelation nor is it self-justifying, but it does play an important role in the development and preservation of doctrine. Current discussions focus on the *sensus fidelium* as one among several theological sources, its relationship to the magisterium, and the need for greater consultation of the faithful as part of the process by which the Church teaches.

Ecumenism. The Catholic Church is committed to working for the reunion of all Christians, but the exuberant spirit following Vatican II has been tempered. Sober minds realize that the road to full unity will be long and arduous. One of the principal ecclesiological tasks is to discern the relationship between the Churches, and even non-Christian religious groups such as Jews, Muslims, Hindus, and Buddhists.

The Council stated that the Church of Christ subsists in the Catholic Church (LG 8). This passage was not precisely explained at the Council and diverse interpretations continue to appear. A moderate view suggests that the term ''subsists'' (which replaced ''is'' in an earlier text) means that the Catholic Church, because of its institutional fullness, has all the essential properties of churchliness. The Church of Christ is present in a special manner in the Catholic Church, but it extends beyond any one denomination. Communities separate from Catholicism also possess such ecclesial elements as Scripture, sacraments, prayer, worship, and the gifts of the Holy Spirit. As a result, these communities manifest the Church of Christ in various degrees but not in the subsistent way present in the Catholic Church. The Church of Christ, therefore, includes other Christian churches in the East and the West, although they are not in full communion with the Church of Rome.

Many of the bilateral consultations, such as the Lutheran-Roman Catholic Dialogue in the United States and the Anglican-Roman Catholic International Commission (ARCIC), have addressed critical ecclesiological issues. They have discussed in detail ecclesial authority, papal primacy, INFALLIBILITY, sacraments, and ministries. The World Conference of the Faith and Order Commission of the World Council of Churches held in Santiago de Compostela in August 1993 was devoted to the topic of ecclesiology. John Paul II's 1995 encyclical *Ut unum sint*, which has been hailed as an ecumenical breakthrough, asks Catholics and other Christians to consider together the forms that the Petrine ministry might take (96). In 1999, Roman Catholics and Lutherans worldwide celebrated a landmark document, ''Joint Declaration on the Doctrine of Justification.''

Although significant progress has been made, much work remains to be done. Christian union remains a gift and a task. ''There can be no ecumenism worthy of the name without a change of heart'' (*Unitatis redintegratio* 7).

The decades following Vatican II have witnessed intense and even acrimonious ecclesiological debate. But in the process some fundamental issues have been clarified and developed. The ferment of ideas, the polarization within the Church, and major cultural shifts will continue to shape the way we understand and live the Christian life.

See Also: INFALLIBILITY.

Bibliography: C. E. CURRAN, *Faithful Dissent* (Kansas City, Missouri 1986). P. C. EMPIE, et al., eds., *Teaching Authority and Infallibility in the Church. Lutherans and Catholics in Dialogue VI* (Minneapolis 1978). L. J. O'DONOVAN, ed., *Cooperation between Theologians and the Ecclesiastical Magisterium. A Report of a Joint Committee of CLSA and CTSA* (Washington 1982). F. A. SULLIVAN, *Magisterium. Teaching Office in the Catholic Church* (New York 1983). J. M. R. TILLARD, "Sensus Fidelium," *One in Christ* 11 (1975) 2–29. R. GAILLARDETZ, *Teaching with Authority: A Theology of the Magisterium of the Church* (Collegeville, Minnesota 1997). Sacred Congregation for the Doctrine of the Faith, "Instruction on the Ecclesial Vocation of the Theologian," *Origins* 20 (July 5, 1990) 117–26. R. E. BROWN, et al., eds., *Peter in the New Testament* (Minneapolis and New York 1973). A. DULLES, "Bishops' Conference Documents: What Doctrinal Authority?," *Origins*, v. 14 (Jan. 24, 1985) 528–34. P. GRANFIELD, *The Papacy in Transition* (New York 1980); *The Limits of the Papacy: Authority and Autonomy in the Church* (New York 1987). J. M. R. TILLARD, *The Bishop of Rome*, tr. J. DE SATGÉ (Wilmington, Delaware 1983). J. RATZINGER with V. MESSORI, *The Ratzinger Report: An Exclusive Interview on the State of the Church*, trs. S. ATTANASIO and G. HARRISON (San Francisco 1985). G. CAPRILE, *I Sinodi dei vescovi*, 6 v. (Rome 1969–). R. GAILLARDETZ, *Witnesses to the Faith: Community, Infallibility, and the Ordinary Magisterium of Bishops* (New York 1992). "Reflections on the Position of African Women," *Pro Mundi Vita: African Dossier* 33 (1985). V. DONOVAN, *Christianity Rediscovered* (Maryknoll, New York 1982). L. DOOHAN, *The Laity: A Bibliography* (Wilmington, Delaware 1987). N. MITCHELL, *Mission and Ministry: History and Theology in the Sacrament of Order* (Wilmington, Delaware 1982). D. POWER, *Gifts That Differ: Lay Ministries Established and Unestablished* (New York 1980). R. L. RASHKE, *The Deacon in Search of Identity* (New York 1975). D. SENIOR and C. STUHLMUELLER, *The Biblical Foundations for Mission* (Maryknoll, New York 1983). D. BOSCH, *Transforming Mission: Paradigm Shifts in Theology of Mission* (Maryknoll, New York 1991). United States Conference of Catholic Bishops, *Lay Ecclesial Ministry: The State of the Question* (Washington 1999). L. BOFF, *Ecclesiogenesis. The Base Communities Reinvent the Church*, tr. R. R. BARR (Maryknoll, New York 1986). M. AZEVEDO, *Basic Ecclesial Communities in Brazil: The Challenge of a New Way of Being Church* (Washington 1987). R. SCHREITER, *Constructing Local Theologies* (Maryknoll, New York 1985). H.-M. LEGRAND, "La réalisation de l'Eglise en un lieu," *Initiation à la pratique de la théologie*, v. 3, B. LAURET and F. REFOULE, eds. (Paris 1983) 143–345. *Proceedings of the Catholic Theological Society of America* 35 (1980) and 36 (1981), articles on the local church. J. KOMONCHAK, "The Church Universal as the Communion of Local Churches," *Concilium* 146 (1981) 30–35. R. SCHREITER, *The New Catholicity: Theology between the Global and the Local* (Maryknoll, New York 1997). M. AZEVEDO, *Inculturation and the Challenges of Modernity* (Rome 1982). L. BOFF, *Church: Charism and Power. Liberation Theology and the Institutional Church*, tr. J. W. DIERCKSMEIER (New York 1985). W. BÜHLMANN, *Weltkirche, Neue Dimensionen. Modell für das Jahr 2001* (Graz 1984). M. KOLBENSCHLAG, ed., *Between God and Caesar: Priests, Sisters and Political Office in the United States* (New York 1985). R. MCBRIEN, *Caesar's Coin: Religion and Politics in American* (New York 1987). *Proceedings of the Catholic Theological Society of America* 39 (1984), articles on the world Church. M. HIMES and K. HIMES, *Fullness of Faith: The Public Significance of Theology* (New York 1992). J. RATZINGER, *Kirche,Ökumene und Politik* (Cinisello Balsama 1987); Eng. *Church, Ecumenism, and Politics*, tr. R. NOWELL (New York 1988). D. SCHINDLER, *Heart of the World, Center of the Church: Communio Ecclesiology, Liberalism, and Liberation* (Grand Rapids 1996). A. DULLES and P. GRANFIELD, *The Church: A Bibliography* (New York 1999). Y. CONGAR, *I Believe in the Holy Spirit*, 3 v., tr. D. SMITH (New York 1983). A. DULLES, *Models of the Church*, (expanded edition; Garden City, New York 1987). *Extraordinary Synod of Bishops* (Rome 1985). *A Message to the People of God and the Final Report* (NCCB 1986). B. MONDIN, *Le nuove ecclesiologie* (Rome 1980). J. M. R. TILLARD, *Eglise d'eglises: L'ecclesiologie de communion* (Paris 1987). J. D. ZIZIOULAS, *Being as Communion: Studies in Personhood and the Church* (Crestwood, New York 1985). D. DOYLE, *Communion Ecclesiology: Vision and Versions* (Maryknoll, New York 2000). Anglican-Roman Catholic International Commission, *The Final Report* (Cincinnati and Washington 1982). Y. CONGAR, *Diversity and Communion*, tr. J. BOWDEN (Mystic, Connecticut 1985). P. C. EMPIE and T. A. MURPHY, *Papal Primacy and the Universal Church. Lutherans and Catholics in Dialogue V* (Minneapolis 1974). H. FRIES and K. RAHNER, *Unity of the Churches: An Actual Possibility*, tr. R. C. L. GRITSCH and E. W. GRITSCH (Philadelphia and New York 1985). F. A. SULLIVAN, "'Subsist in': The Significance of Vatican II's Decision to Say of the Church of Christ Not That It 'Is' but That It 'Subsists In' the Roman Catholic Church," *One in Christ* 22 (1986) 115–23. T. BEST, G. GASSMANN, eds., *On the Way to Fuller Koinonia: Official Report of the Fifth World Conference on Faith and Order* (Geneva 1993). JOHN PAUL II, *Ut unum sint, Origins* 25 (June 8, 1995) 49–72. J. PUGLISI, ed., *Petrine Ministry and the Unity of the Church* (Collegeville 1999). Sacred Congregation for the Doctrine of the Faith, *Dominus Iesus, Origins* 30 (Sept. 14, 2000) 209–24.

[P. GRANFIELD/D. M. DOYLE]

ECCLESTON, SAMUEL

Fifth archbishop of Baltimore, Md.; b. Kent County, Md., June 27, 1801; d. Washington, D.C., April 22, 1851. His English grandfather settled in Maryland, where he became a merchant and then a planter. Samuel's parents were members of the Episcopal Church; but after his father died, his mother married a Catholic. As a consequence, Samuel was sent in 1812 to St. Mary's College, Baltimore, conducted by the Sulpician Fathers. While there he became a Catholic, decided to study for the priesthood, and entered St. Mary's Seminary on July 23, 1819, despite opposition from relatives. As a seminarian, he acted as an instructor at St. Mary's College. After ordination on April 24, 1825, he entered the Society of the Priests of St. Sulpice and was sent to Issy, France, for further training.

In 1827 Eccleston returned to St. Mary's College, where he served two years as professor and vice president, and five years as president. He was then named coadjutor of Baltimore, consecrated on Sept. 14, 1834, and succeeded Abp. James WHITFIELD at his death on Oct. 19, 1834. Eccleston served Baltimore for 17 years, playing a significant part in the growth of the Church in the U.S. He presided over five provincial councils, the third to the seventh, which met in Baltimore every third year from 1837 to 1849. He played as active a part in the council of 1849, when there were 25 bishops present, as he did in 1837 when there were only 9.

During his tenure, Eccleston encouraged the establishment of the first American preparatory seminary, St. Charles College, which opened in 1848. Many new churches were founded and work on the cathedral was almost completed. The Visitation Nuns and the Christian Brothers opened schools for girls and boys, respectively, in Baltimore. The number of priests nearly doubled during his episcopate, in part because of the coming of the Redemptorists for German-speaking Catholics and the Lazarists.

Bibliography: P. K. GUILDAY, *A History of the Councils of Baltimore, 1791–1884* (New York 1932). C. G. HERBERMANN, *The Sulpicians in the United States* (New York 1916). M. J. RIORDAN, *Cathedral Records from the Beginning of Catholicism in Baltimore* (Baltimore 1906). J. G. D. SHEA, *The Hierarchy of the Catholic Church in the United States* (New York 1887).

[E. F. SCHMITZ]

ECHTER VON MESPELBRUNN, JULIUS

Prince-bishop of Würzburg; b. Mespelbrunn, Lower Franconia, March 18, 1545; d. Würzburg, Sept. 13, 1617. He came of a noble, strongly Catholic family. He studied in the Netherlands, Italy, France, and in Cologne. In 1569 he became a member of the cathedral chapter of Würzburg and was dean in December 1573 when he was elected prince-bishop. After a preparation of 18 months, he was ordained priest and consecrated bishop in May 1575. The Jesuits helped him in the reform of his diocese, which was predominantly Protestant, and Würzburg became outstanding in the COUNTER REFORMATION. In 1582 Echter made a university of the Jesuit college in Würzburg, and in 1589 he founded a seminary. Having set in order the administration and economy of his diocese, he began, with new priests, to reclaim the Protestants of the diocese for Catholicism. Using strong political pressure he regained 100,000 in three years. He built about 300 churches, in the ''Julius style,'' and the ''Julius hospital'' (1579) shows his interest in social measures. His enthusiasm for the Catholic League (1614) contributed to its success, especially in Fulda and Bamberg. Personally he was ascetic and pious; politically he believed in absolutism. According to the spirit of his time, he persecuted witches. He had early leanings toward humanism, but the claim that he also had inclinations toward Protestantism is erroneous.

Bibliography: G. VON PÖLNITZ, *Julius Echter von Mespelbrunn* (Munich 1934); *Lexikon für Theologie und Kirche*[2] 3:639–640. W. ENGEL, *Die Religion in Geschichte und Gegenwart*[3] 2:301.

[G. J. DONNELLY]

ECHTERNACH, ABBEY OF

Former imperial Benedictine monastery in the present town of Echternach, Luxembourg; it is a pilgrimage site, known for its famous dancing procession to the tomb of St. Willibrord on the Tuesday following Pentecost. An almshouse for itinerant Scottish monks before 689, it was founded as a BENEDICTINE monastery (698–704) by St. WILLIBRORD on an estate of St. IRMINA and her daughter Plectrude, consort of Pepin II. During the 8th century it was the center for missions to the Frisians, and the ''port of entry'' for Irish-Anglo-Saxon culture (MSS in Paris, Trier, Maihingen) to the Continent. In the Carolingian period it acquired extensive property holdings; its greatest abbot was Beornrad (775–797). About 848 the abbey was converted into a collegiate church ruled by lay abbots. Despite subsequent decline, it had a famous school and SCRIPTORIUM. The last lay Abbot, Count Siegfried of Luxembourg, requested Emperor OTTO I to send CLUNIAC REFORM monks to Echternach; these arrived from Sankt Maximin in Trier (973). Under Abbot Humbert the Echternach school of illumination was at its peak (e.g., the Golden Gospel Books in Nuremberg, Uppsala, and the library of the Escorial, the MSS in Darmstadt, Gotha, and Bremen). Another decline in the 14th and 15th centuries occasioned a new reform by monks from Sankt Maximin in Trier in 1496. Echternach was suppressed in 1797 during the French Revolution. The body of St. Willibrord is buried in the abbey church, which was built between 1017 and 1031, restored between 1862 and 1868, made a minor basilica in 1939, and repaired after World War II. Of the former Carolingian basilica only the crypt has been preserved; the remains of the Merovingian abbey church were discovered 1949. The abbey buildings are an impressive creation of the French baroque (1727–36).

Bibliography: L. H. COTTINEAU, *Répertoire topobibliographique des abbayes et prierés*, 2 v. (Mâcon 1935–39) 1:1025–26. C. WAMPACH, *Geschichte der Grundherrschaft Echternach im Frühmittelalter,* 2 v. (Luxembourg 1930); *Dictionnaire d'histoire et de géographie ecclésiastiques*, ed. A. BAUDRILLART et al. (Paris 1912–) 14:1365–75. P. METZ, *The Golden Gospels of Echternach,* tr. I. SCHRIER and P. GORGE (New York 1957).

[P. VOLK]

ECK, JOHANN

Theologian and principal adversary of Luther; b. Eck in Swabia. Nov. 13, 1486; d. Ingolstadt, Feb. 10, 1543.

He was the son of Michael Maier, a magistrate in Eck. Eckius and Eccius are Latinizations of the place name Johann adopted as a surname after 1505. He was educated at Heidelberg (1498), Tübingen (1499), Cologne (1501), and Freiburg im Breisgau (1502). At Freiburg he first contacted the new humanism. In 1506 he lectured on the *Sentences* of Peter Lombard; in 1510 he received his doctorate in theology, having been ordained by special dispensation in 1508 at the age of 22.

The Duke of Bavaria invited Eck to become professor of theology at Ingolstadt in 1510. At the same time he became canon of the cathedral of Eichstätt. He wrote on science, philosophy, and theology. *Chrysopassus,* his principal theological work, treats predestination, grace, and free will; this served to prepare him for his controversy with Luther. He was a prominent figure by 1517. His *Obelisci,* a reply to Martin LUTHER's 95 theses, although intended only for the private use of the bishop of Eichstätt, drew him into the struggle to which he devoted the rest of his life. In May 1518 Karlstadt, an early Lutheran, published theses against Eck's *Obelisci.* Eck challenged Karlstadt to a disputation, which took place in Leipzig under the auspices of Duke George of Saxony. In the meantime Eck drew Luther into the debate through 12 theses subtly attacking Luther's doctrine, especially his practical denial of the Roman primacy.

The debate lasted from June 27 to July 16, 1618. Eck had forced Luther to expose his heretical views. Duke George was confirmed in the Catholic cause thereby, but Luther was lost to it forever. After the discussions at Leipzig, Eck, acknowledged champion of the Catholic cause, wrote a treatise on the primacy. This he took to Rome. Leo X appointed him nuncio with Girolamo ALEANDRO, to publish in Germany the bull of Luther's excommunication, *Exsurge Domine,* which Eck had partially composed.

Eck wrote many treatises refuting Lutheran teaching on Penance, satisfaction, purgatory, and the Mass (against Bucer). Against Melanchthon's *Loci communes,* he wrote a famous *Enchiridion,* which went through 90 editions. He opposed Ulrich ZWINGLI at Baden (1526), and with Konrad K. WIMPINA and Johannes COCHLAEUS represented the Catholic position at Augsburg (1530). In 1537 he made a German translation of Scripture.

Bibliography: *Prima (-quinta) pars operum J. Eckii contra Ludderum,* 6 v. (Augsburg 1530–35); *Enchiridion locorum cōmuniū adversus Lutheranos* (Landshut, Ger. 1525). H. GRISAR, *Martin Luther: His Life and Work,* ed. F. J. EBLE and A. PREUSS (Westminster, Md. 1950). E. ISERLOH, *Lexikon für Theologie und Kirche,* ed. J. HOFER and K. RAHNER (Freiburg 1957–65) 3:642–644; *Dictionnaire d'histoire et de géographie ecclésiastiques,* ed. A. BAUDRILLART et al. (Paris 1912) 14:1375–79.

[C. M. AHERNE]

ECKART, ANSELM VON

Missionary in Brazil and later in Russian Poland; b. Bingen, Upper Rhine, Germany, Aug. 4, 1721; d. at the College at Polotsk, Russia, June 29, 1809. At the age of 19 he entered the Society of Jesus, and in 1753 he was sent to the province of Papa in Brazil. During the short time he labored in Brazil he acquired an intimate knowledge of its geography and language. At Marañon he was distinguished as a missionary by his insight and courage; however, his work was cut short by the growing enmity of the Portuguese minister, Sebastião POMBAL, to the Society of Jesus. On trumped-up charges, which were subsequently completely refuted, Eckart and his companions were seized and returned to Portugal in chains. For the next 18 years he was imprisoned in the underground dungeons of Almeida and St. Julian in Lisbon. In 1777, after the death of Joseph I of Portugal, Pombal fell from power, and Eckart and the other survivors were released. He returned to his native Bingen, where as the friend and correspondent of G. V. Murrs he made numerous contributions to the latter's publications. These include notes on his geographical observations in Brazil, an account of the persecution of the missionaries there as well as their sufferings in the Lisbon prisons, and a history of the Jesuits in Portugal.

By the time of Eckart's release the Society of Jesus had been dissolved by the papal bull *Dominus ac Redemptor* (1773). In Russia, which acquired a large Catholic population with the partition of Poland in 1772, the suppression had not become effective, as the Empress, CATHERINE II, refused to permit publication of the bull of suppression. In this Polish area there existed a number of Jesuit colleges and foundations, including the colleges of Polotsk, Vitebsk, Orsha, and Dünaberg, which were therefore retained by the society. Eckart applied here for readmission to the Polish Jesuits and was received. There he spent the fruitful remaining years of his long life, serving as master of novices in the College of Dünaberg; subsequently he was sent to the College of Polotsk.

Bibliography: A. VON ECKART, *Les Prisons du Marquis de Pombal,* v. 9 of *Documents inédits concernant la Compagnie de Jésus,* ed. A. CARAYON, 23 v. (Poitiers 1863–86). A. HUONDER, *Deutsche Jesuitenmissionäre des 17 und 18 Jahrhunderte* (St. Louis, Mo. 1899). A. WELD, *Suppression of the Society of Jesus in the Portuguese Dominions* (London 1877). C. SOMMERVOGEL, *Bibliothèque de la Compagnie de Jésus* (Brussels-Paris 1890–1932) 3:330–331. J. A. OTTO, *Lexikon für Theologie und Kirche,* ed. J. HOFER and K. RAHNER (Freiburg 1957–65) 3:645.

[A. M. CHRISTENSEN]

ECKBERT OF SCHÖNAU

Abbot and theologian; b. Rhineland, before 1132; d. Abbey of Schönau, near Trier, Germany, March 28,

1184. He came from a noble family of the Rhineland with important connections in the local Church hierarchy and was a fellow student of RAINALD OF DASSEL at the schools of Paris. He became a canon of the church of SS. Cassius and Florentius at Bonn, but in 1155, after a journey to Rome, he entered the BENEDICTINES at the Abbey of Schönau, in the Diocese of Trier, under Abbot Hildelin (d. 1166). Rainald, then archbishop of COLOGNE, summoned Eckbert to debate the doctrines of the CATHARI in his archdiocese; Eckbert's *Sermones contra Catharos* (PL 195:11–98), dedicated to the archbishop, proved to be a remarkably clear and penetrating refutation of the heresy. His *Stimulus amoris* (*Patrologica Latina* 158: 748–761, 184:953–966) is often attributed to BERNARD OF CLAIRVAUX or ANSELM OF CANTERBURY, while another meditation, *Soliloquim seu meditationes* (*Patrologica Latina* 153:773–779; 195:105–114), has been credited to Anselm. The tone of his spiritual writings prefigured the later devotion to the SACRED HEART. Eckbert was spiritual director of his sister, ELIZABETH OF SCHÖNAU, a member of the feminine section of the double monastery at Schönau, and after her death he wrote her biography and an account of her revelations (PL 195:119–194). Eckbert was elected abbot of Schönau in 1166 on the death of Hildelin, and even in this busy post kept up his intellectual warfare against the Cathari. This scholarly abbot's vita was written by his successor, Emecho of Schönau [*Neues Archiv der Gesellschaft für ältere deutsche Geschichtskunde* 11 (1886) 448–454].

Bibliography: Works. *Patrologia Latina* 195:11–194. F. W. E. ROTH, ed., *Die Visionen der hl. Elisabeth und die Schriften der Abte Ekbert und Emecho von Schönau* (2d ed. Würzburg 1886); ed., *Das Gebetbuch der heiligen Elisabeth von Schönau* (Augsburg 1886). A. BARRÉ, ''Une Prière d'Ekbert de Schönau au saint Coeur de Marie,'' *Ephemerides mariologicae* 2 (1952) 409–423. **Literature.** P. SÉJOURNÉ, ''*L'Aiguillon d'amour* de l'Abbé Egbert,'' *Regnabit* 2 (1922) 327–332. U. BERLIÈRE, *La Dévotion au Sacré-Coeur dans l'ordre de Saint Benoît* (Paris 1923) 8, 15–17. A WILMART, *Auteurs spirituels et textes dévots du moyen âge latin* (Paris 1932) 194–195, 421–422. J. DE GHELLINCK, *L'Essor de la littérature latine au XIIe siècle* (Brussels-Paris 1946) 1:160, 169–170. K. KÖSTER, ''Das visionäre Werk Elisabeths von Schönau,'' *Archiv für mittelrheinische Kirchengeschichte* 4 (1952) 79–119. A. BORST, *Die Katharer* (Stuttgart 1953), *passim.* J. C. DIDIER, *Dictionnaire d'histoire et de géographie ecclésiastiques* 14:1472–75.

[B. J. COMASKEY]

ECKHART, MEISTER

Dominican theologian and mystic; b. in one of two villages called Hochheim in Thuringia, *c.* 1260; d. 1327 or 1328. He was probably not of noble parentage. He entered the Dominican Order at Erfurt. In 1277 he was a student of arts at Paris, and before 1280 began studying theology at Cologne. In the years 1293–94, as bachelor of theology at Paris, he commented on the *Sentences* of Peter Lombard. About 1294 he was prior of the house of his order at Erfurt and vicar of the vicariate of Thuringia. He graduated as master of theology at Paris and lectured there as regent master in 1302 and 1303. The story that the mastership was conferred directly upon him by the pope appears to have been discredited (cf. Koch, *Archivum Fratrum Praedicatorum* 17). From 1303 to 1311 he was provincial of the Dominican province of Saxony, and from 1311 to 1313 he was at Paris for a second regency in theology. He was at Strasbourg as professor of theology from 1313 to 1323, probably at the Dominican studium. It was at this time that he became active as a preacher and spiritual director, and was highly regarded by Dominican and Cistercian nuns, Beguines, and others.

Although Meister Eckhart apparently always enjoyed the confidence of his brethren (if we are to judge from the positions of responsibility he occupied), he ran into serious difficulties about his doctrine with ecclesiastical authorities in 1326. Two lists of suspect propositions, taken chiefly from his sermons, were laid before him by inquisitors appointed by Henry of Virneburg, Archbishop of Cologne. The inquisitors were Master Reiner Friso, Canon of Cologne and doctor of theology, and Peter Sommer (de Aestate) OFM, former prior of the Franciscan house at Cologne. Eckhart defended himself vigorously, protesting fidelity to the Church and challenging the competence of the inquisitors because of his exemption as a mendicant friar. He attempted to clear himself by explaining the incriminating propositions in a ''Justificative Report'' (*Rechtfertigungsschrift*), which is of the greatest value for understanding the import of his thought. In January 1327, Eckhart appealed to the Holy See, submitting in advance to its decision, and he left for Avignon where he hoped to defend himself personally. He died, however, before his case was concluded.

The documents of the trial consisted of two lists of propositions, the ''Justificative Report,'' and a third list of propositions taken from Eckhart's commentary on St. John; a fourth and fifth list were added later. At the end of the trial, the Avignon theologians submitted the so-called ''Avignon Report.'' It listed 28 propositions, scarcely a fourth part of the number included in the earlier lists. The report also mentioned the explanations occasionally supplied by Eckhart. Notice was taken that Eckhart had denied having taught two of the propositions. Taking into consideration his submissive attitude and orthodox intention, Pope John XXII condemned the propositions only according to their obvious meaning. The condemnation was promulgated Mar. 27, 1329, by the constitution *In agro dominico.* The 28 propositions are listed somewhat differently than in the Avignon report and are judged more leniently. The first 15 propositions and the last two are condemned as erroneous and tainted with heresy, but the other 11 are declared capable of a Catholic meaning if properly explained.

Doctrine. The doctrine of Meister Eckhart owes much to St. Thomas Aquinas. He was also under the influence of Neoplatonism (particularly that of Plotinus and Proclus), the doctrinal texts of which he knew through the work of St. Albert the Great and through the translations of Proclus by the Dominican William Moerbeke. Eckhart was also well read in the works of St. Bernard of Clairvaux. In short, he reflected the thought of much of the spiritual teaching of his time in the Germanic part of Europe, where everything was not indisputably orthodox, especially among several Free Spirit sects and other similar groups.

It is difficult to make a satisfactory appraisal of Eckhart's doctrine, since his *Opus tripartitum* was never finished. It would certainly be going too far to see in him only a ''spiritualist'' and to reduce his theological doctrine, which generally conforms to Thomist tradition and originates from a definite intellectualism, to no more than a speculative prologue to his spiritual doctrine. To the first of the *Quaestiones Parisienses,* ''Is being in God identical with knowing?'' his answer is affirmative. It was in this intellectual perspective that he envisioned creation. All creatures have been, from all eternity, supported by the Word of God, and all things look to the return of the soul to God. God alone *is,* for being (*esse,* or to be) is God. The creature has no being or existence by itself. Of itself it is nothing. Still the being or existence is not to be confused with the Divine Being.

This sets the fundamental attitude that the soul must assume for its return to God; its ''laying bare'' takes on a condition transcending the realm of psychological and ethical requirements. It is ontologically imposed on the being that by itself is nothing. If the creature wishes to participate in the being that truly is, he must allow the Father to generate the Word in him. This even goes beyond the evangelical ideas of sin, redemption, and grace. It is put on the level of an essential unity of the soul and Divinity. This theme is developed by means of a dialectic that varied little in the course of Eckhart's career. Moreover, it was the speculative character of the dialectic that did most to put him in opposition to spiritualists such as St. Bernard of Clairvaux and other representatives of the mysticism of ''mystical marriage'' (or *Brautm ystik*).

From these presuppositions, Eckhart reached the conclusion that the most elevated part of the soul, that part that engaged in contact with God, was in essence intellectual. This *Kraft* (*virtus*) is a spark, *Seelenfünklein* or *scintilla animae.* The ''foundation of the soul'' (*Grund der Seele*) is ''something'' (*etwas*) uncreated and uncreatable. It is this in man that is equal to God, and the seat of divine life and of the truly contemplative life where the spirit reigns. It is also in this uncreated *etwas* of the soul that the ''birth'' of the Word takes place and resemblance to God is realized. This birth, which is mainly described in Eckhart's commentary on St. John, comes after liberation from sin and the laying bare of the soul; it creates the ''noble man'' and is consummated in ''identity.'' Henceforth the spiritual man is one with the Deity in its true essence, not the God whose idolatrous image we form for ourselves. True contemplation is thus attained. It is an intellectual kind of contemplation, but it unites vision and love in a single act, and man finds ''all bliss uniquely from God, through God, and in God.'' This teaching has been called speculative, or essential, mysticism.

The most daring subjects—the absolute transcendence and unknowability of God, total detachment in order to find the unity and image of God—were already touched upon in his writings before 1300, and his teaching was not considered alarming at that time. Moreover, certain of his expressions were not uncommon among the mystics of the Middle Ages. Why then was he condemned? Among other causes, political influences are discernible. Eckhart clashed not with John XXII but with the Franciscans, who were still unreconciled to the recent canonization of the Dominican St. Thomas Aquinas (1323), and with the partisans of Louis of Bavaria who was hostile to the pope, to whom, in general, the Dominicans were faithful. Eckhart also suffered from the suspicion directed toward the more or less heterodox mystic groups, such as the Beguines (condemned at the Council of Vienne in 1312). Oechslin indicates other causes that contributed to Eckhart's difficulties. He used German in many works, and it was necessary for him to form a mystical terminology in that language. His enemies unfairly failed to check his German statements made in sermons with his formal teaching in Latin works (*Dictionnaire de spiritualité ascétique et mystique. Doctrine et histoire* 4:93–116). Still, the propositions condemned in the *In agro dominico* (cf. H. Denzinger, *Enchiridion symbolorum* 950–980) are hard to defend from the point of view of orthodoxy, and nearly all of them were found in Eckhart's writings.

Influence. Despite Eckhart's propositions 16–19 (*ibid.* 966–969), which, in effect, deny the value of external works, the 16th century reformers, who probably had not read the works of Eckhart directly but only through his disciples, made no use of them. His works were seldom copied after his condemnation. Still he did have an influence upon German speculative mysticism from the

14th to the 16th centuries. John Tauler, Henry Suso, John Ruysbroeck, and others less well known, in Germany, Switzerland, and the Low Countries showed a predilection for topics found in Eckhart's writings. It was through these that some of Eckhart's doctrinal themes passed on to the reformers.

The theory of certain German historians, notably during the period of National Socialism, that Eckhart was the ''father of German speculation'' must be denied. His thought, according to them, presented strictly ''Germanic,'' or ''Aryan,'' characteristics. However, Eckhart, whose mind was not particularly original, belonged to the cultural world of the medieval Church, more international than ours today, and he always professed an unquestionable devotion to the Church and to the Christian faith.

Bibliography: Editions. The most important complete ed. is *Die deutschen und lateinischen Werke,* ed. Deutsche Forschungsgemeinschaft (Stuttgart 1936-), Latin works, ed. J. KOCH et al., v.1–4 (1936–61), v.5–6 (in progress), German works, ed. J. QUINT, v.1 (1936–58), v.5 (1954–62), v.2–4 (in progress). Some tracts have been edited in another edition, *Opera latina,* ed. G. THÉRY (Institutum S. Sabinae; Leipzig 1934). *Meister Eckhart: Werke,* ed. F. PFEIFFER, v.2 *Die deutschen Mystiker* (4th ed. Göttingen 1924). The propositions condemned in the constitution *In agro dominico* are found in H. DENZINGER, *Enchiridion symbolorum*, ed. A. SCHÖNMETZER 501–529. F. PFEIFFER, *Meister Eckhart* (Leipzig 1857), tr. with some omissions and additions, C. DE B. EVANS, 2 v. (London 1924–31); *Meister Eckhart: An Introduction to the Study of His Works With an Anthology of His Sermons,* ed. and tr. J. M. CLARK (London 1957). *M. Eckhart, Selected Treatises and Sermons . . . from Latin and German,* ed. and tr. J. M. CLARK and J. V. SKINNER (London 1958). *Meister Eckhart: A Modern Translation,* ed. and tr. R. B. BLAKNEY (New York 1941). **Literature.** F. VANDENBROUCKE, *Dictionnaire d'histoire et de géographie ecclésiastiques*, ed. A. BAUDRILLART et. al. 14:1385–1403. R. L. OECHSLIN, *Dictionnaire de spiritualité ascétique et mystique. Doctrine et histoire*, ed. M. VILLER et. al. 4:93–116. A. DANIELS, ed., ''Eine lateinische Rechtfertigungsschrift des Meister Eckhart, mit einem Geleitwort von Clemens Bäumker,'' *Beiträge zur Geschichte der Philosophie und Theologie des Mittelalters* 23.5 (1923). F. PELSTER, ''Ein Gutachten aus dem Eckhart-Prozess in Avignon,'' *ibid.* Suppl. 3.2 (1935) 1099–1124. J. KOCH, ''Kritische Studien zum Leben Meister Eckharts,'' *Archivum Fratrum Praedicatorum* 29 (1959) 5–51; 30 (1960) 5–52. P. KELLEY, ''Poverty and the Rhineland Mystics,'' *Downside Review* 74 (1956) 48–66; ''Meister Eckhart's Doctrine of the Divine Subjectivity,'' *ibid.* 76 (1958) 65–103. K. G. KERTZ, ''Meister Eckhart's Teaching on the Birth of the Divine Word in the Soul,'' *Traditio* 15 (1959) 327–363. E. W. MCDONNELL, *Beguines and Beghards in Medieval Culture* (New Brunswick, NJ 1954). J. M. CLARK, *The Great German Mystics* (Oxford 1949). J. ANCELET-HUSTACHE, *Master Eckhart and the Rhineland Mystics,* tr. H. GRAEF (pa. New York 1958).

[F. VANDENBROUCKE]

ECKHEL, JOSEPH HILARIUS VON

Jesuit historian, numismatist; b. Enzesfeld, Austria, Jan. 13, 1737; d. Vienna, May 16, 1798. Eckhel began his studies in the Society of Jesus in 1751 and was ordained in 1764. He taught grammar in Jesuit schools at Loeben, Steyr, and Vienna until 1766. Meanwhile, Father J. Khell, SJ, introduced him to the study of NUMISMATICS; and when, in 1772, Eckhel had to abandon his teaching career because of illness, he turned to the study of archeology and numismatics. He toured Italy and devoted himself to a careful study of the coin collections in Bologna, Florence, and Rome. After suppression of the Society of Jesus in 1773, he was appointed director of the numismatic section of the Imperial Museum at Vienna; and in 1776, professor of antiquities and auxiliary historical sciences at the University of Vienna. His *Doctrina nummorum veterum* (8 v. Vienna 1792–98) was his great work and is regarded as the beginning of the scientific study of numismatics, making that discipline an important source of history. He produced also *Catalogus musei Caesarei Vindobonensis nummorum veterum* (Vienna 1779) and *Descriptio nummorum Antiochiae* (Vienna 1786).

Bibliography: P. LACROIX, *Revue Belge de numismatique et de sigillographie* 35 (1897) 45–49. L. KOCH, *Jesuiten-Lexikon: Die Gesellschaft Jesu einst und jetzt* 1:466–467. P. P. R. FRANKIE, *Neue deutsche Biographie* 4:302–303.

[F. DE SA]

ECLECTICISM

A term deriving from the Greek ἐκλέγειν, which means to pick out, to single out, or to choose. When eclectic is applied to a philosopher, it designates one who selects various doctrines from different thinkers and weaves them into a loose sort of unity. Whereas the classical schools and systems of philosophy are marked by rigorous adherence to the deductions and conclusions that follow from their fundamental positions, an eclectic philosophy is characterized by its acceptance of principles and attitudes that, in the parent philosophies, are either mutually exclusive or at least antagonistic. An eclectic philosophy is thus an attempt to find a workable combination of previously conflicting attitudes by regarding their principles in a less rigid and more conciliatory manner.

History. In Western thought eclecticism made its appearance as a result of the SKEPTICISM of Carneades (214?–129 B.C.), founder of the New Academy. It influenced such Stoics as Panaetius of Rhodes (2d century B.C.) and Posidonius of Apamea (1st century B.C.), the Platonists Philo of Larissa (d. *c.* 80 B.C.) and Antiochus of Ascalon (1st century B.C.), and Peripatetics such as Andronicus of Rhodes (1st century B.C.) and Aristocles of Messene (2d century A.D.).

Early Thought. Roman philosophy, except that of LUCRETIUS, was mostly eclectic in spirit. SENECA, EPIC-

TETUS, and MARCUS AURELIUS were partly Platonic and partly Stoic in their philosophies, while the School of the Sextians—which flourished for a while at Rome during the beginning of the Christian Era—combined aspects of Pythagoreanism, Cynicism, and Stoicism. Cicero (106–43 B.C.), the most influential of the eclectics of antiquity, had syncretized elements of Carneadean epistemology, Platonic theology, and Stoic ethics.

Because PLOTINUS absorbed so much of Platonism, Aristotelianism, and Stoicism into his own system, usually called NEOPLATONISM, he has been regarded by some as an eclectic; those who know his *Enneads*, however, see there a synthesis that is decidedly different from any of its sources. One might designate several of his disciples as eclectic in that they interpreted his doctrine in such a way as to bring it more in line with Pythagoreanism, as did Iamblichus (4th century A.D.); or with Platonism, as did Proclus (A.D. 410?–485); or with Aristotelianism, as did Simplicius (6th century A.D.). Another disciple, Plutarch of Athens (d. A.D. 431), might be called eclectic in that he desired his fellow Neoplatonists to be more concerned with the agreement between Plato and Aristotle than with their differences.

Historians in the past usually described Giovanni PICO DELLA MIRANDOLA as an eclectic because of his intense interest in, and apparent agreement with, the opinions of all thinkers of all eras. More recent studies, especially by Ernst Cassirer, suggest that Pico could well subscribe to seemingly incompatible doctrines because he viewed all human truths as imperfect images and symbols of the Perfect Truth that is God, as variable approximations to the absolute limit that is the Eternal Divine Truth.

Modern Philosophy. The eclectic attitude manifests itself in the thought of G. W. LEIBNIZ, with its constant attempts to reconcile divergent and conflicting viewpoints. Leibniz hoped to bridge the philosophical differences between the rationalists and the empiricists by his monadology and by his doctrine of preestablished harmony. In the domain of religion he also made efforts to mitigate dissensions among various Protestant sects and between Protestants and Catholics. This spirit of syncretism sometimes led him to neglect distinctions between mind and matter, faith and reason, determination and freedom, and grace and nature. The eclectic attitude is seen in other German thinkers of the 18th-century Enlightenment, for example in C. Thomasius, Moses Mendelssohn (1729–86), and Christian Garve (1742–98); this is especially true of C. WOLFF. Following the rationalist tradition of R. Descartes and B. Spinoza, Wolff agreed that philosophy should employ the mathematical method; at the same time, however, he had the empiricist's regard for factual knowledge, insisting that the facts of experience agree wiith the conclusions of reason. Like Spinoza, he viewed the world as a closely concatenated order of efficient causes, although he was also profoundly influenced by the teleological explanations of Leibniz. In explaining the position of Leibniz, he so modified its basic points that he failed to recognize fundamental inconsistencies.

Eclecticism marked the thought not only of followers of Wolff, such as Martin Knutzen (1713–51) the famous mathematician, Alexander Baumgarten (1714–62) the theorist in aesthetics, and Johann Lambert (1728–77) the psychologist, but also that of Wolff's opponents, such as Andreas Rüdiger (1673–1731) and Christian Crusius (1715–75).

But the best-known of the more modern eclectics is Victor COUSIN, who not only was convinced that the French Revolution made necessary new formulations in political life but also demanded a reconstruction in philosophical thought. This reconstruction, he was determined, should be founded upon the method of complete and total observation of consciousness and all its elements. In this way the new philosophy would avoid the imperfections of J. LOCKE, T. REID, and I. KANT, each of whom, in Cousin's judgment, had made only an imperfect analysis of consciousness. Because he was convinced that his method would discover all truths, some of which had been uncovered previously by past philosophies, Cousin called his philosophy eclecticism. Theodore Jouffroy (1796–1842), Étienne Vacherot (1809–97), Paul Janet (1823–99), and Jules Simon (1814–96), his disciples, carried on his work.

Because of the many changes in his philosophical outlook, often brought about by his readings in past and contemporary philosophers, F. W. J. von SCHELLING is judged by some to have been an eclectic; one can nonetheless maintain that he remained an idealist throughout his long and prolific career as a professor of philosophy.

Recent Thought. Much of EXISTENTIALISM could be called eclectic in that it contains elements of Cartesian subjectivism, Kantian moralism, Nietzschean voluntarism, Husserlian phenomenology, and positivistic nominalism. These are held together in different ways by the various existentialists, most of whom deny any validity to systematic thought.

Critique. The history of philosophy shows that the origins of eclecticism are far from uniform. It has arisen, as in the case of the Romans, after a period of skeptical thought has made some men wary of fixed and consistent positions. It has also made its appearance when the human spirit became weary with continuing conflicts among schools of philosophy and was only too ready for a conciliatory approach. This was the case with some of the minor eclectics during the German Enlightenment. In other philosophers it has been engendered by the conviction that each philosophical system contains some truths that can be discovered or recovered by the sympathetic researcher. Leibniz and Cousin could be cited as examples of this attitude. Then, too, eclecticism can be very congenial to a thinker who is sufficiently shallow and superficial to feel at ease with principles that are mutually contradictory. Schelling has been so regarded by some.

As a philosophy, eclecticism makes no appeal to a truly creative spirit, for it lacks the unity and cohesiveness that such a mind demands. For the historian of philosophy it makes an unsatisfactory term of reference since it says nothing positive about the philosopher whom it is attempting to describe; for this reason there is a growing tendency to avoid its use.

Bibliography: F. BARONE, *Enciclopedia filosofica*, 4 v. (Venice-Rome 1957) 1:1794–96. H. KUHN, *Lexikon für Theologie und Kirche*, ed. J. HOFER and K. RAHNER, 10 v. (2d, new ed. Freiburg 1957–65) 3:787–88. K. GOLDAMMER and G. PATZIG, *Die Religion in Geschichte und Gegenwart*, 7 v. (3d ed. Tübingen 1957–65) 2:408–09. F. UEERWEG, *Grundriss der Geschichte der Philosophie*, ed. K. PRAECHTER et al., 5 v. (11th, 12th ed. Berlin 1923–28) 1:34, 410, 486, 565. R. EISLER, *Wörterbuch der philosophischen Begriffe*, 3 v. (4th ed. Berlin 1927–30) 1:316. P. FOULQUIÉ and R. SAINT-JEAN, *Dictionnaire de la langue philsophique* (Paris 1962) 195–96.

[V. M. MARTIN]

ECOFEMINISM AND ECOFEMINIST THEOLOGY

With the awareness of the many threats to the ecological health of Earth, some feminists have broadened their concern beyond the social, economic and political status of women to a fundamental re-envisioning of the whole of reality, including the human relationship to nonhuman nature. The term for this total re-envisioning is ''ecofeminism,'' first coined by Françoise d'Eaubonne in 1974. Ecofeminism draws attention to the connection between the domination of women and the exploitation of nonhuman nature in patriarchal societies. In ecofeminism feminist consciousness is extended beyond specific societal wrongs that diminish women to the recognition that there is no liberation for women and no solution to the ecological crisis within a society whose fundamental model of relationships is one of domination. Ecofeminists, therefore, engage in a twofold advocacy on behalf of (1) the well-being of women and other persons diminished by patriarchy (due to racism, ethnic prejudice, classism and colonialism) and (2) the health of the planet exploited by persons in power for their own economic advantage.

Related to environmentalist movements, the ''eco'' prefix in ecofeminsm reflects a commitment to ecology as an all-encompassing organic and social reality. Although ''environment'' and ''ecology'' sometimes are used interchangeably, ecofeminists argue that they are not synonymous. The term ''environment'' refers to nature set apart from human beings—an object ''out there'' for us to study, control or restore through science and technology. The term ''ecology'' conveys a meaning that is more holistic: the study of and commitment to the earthly home that humans along with other living beings, matter, energy and all life forces share. Ecofeminism stresses that humans have a natural biological connectedness with all of Earth's life forms.

Concern with language and the ideology and behaviors it supports is an important characteristic of ecofeminism. Ecofeminists point out that depicting ''nature'' as external to humans is of one piece with the use of gender metaphors in Western constructions of nature and culture. Ecofeminists identify the nature versus culture dualism as the root of the diminishment of the dignity of women and the destruction of the Earth. The linguistic connection of nature with female subordination and culture with male domination is seen as a manifestation of patriarchy closely associated with Enlightenment thinking and values. Ecofeminists reject the association of women with nature as a faulty cultural construct. They see it as objectifying and commodifying women and nonhuman nature for the advantage of men, especially the men who occupy the top levels of the social and economic hierarchies.

Critique of language patterns by ecofeminists extends beyond those explicitly gender-related to patriarchal perspectives that are both hierarchical and dualistic. Hierarchical analysis, for example, is common in biology and can be benign. Biologists classify species according to a hierarchy of complexity, not necessarily positing that the more complex species have more importance or value than the others. However, in the pervasive mind-set of patriarchy, hierarchies of complexity have been often weighted in favor of the one species designated as the most complex, and therefore the highest of the life forms, *homo sapiens*. Historically, the elevation of *homo sapiens* has been at the expense of other species and Earth's limited resources. Ecofeminists maintain that this form of hierarchical dualism promotes an excessive anthropocentricism. Patriarchal anthropocentricism underlies human attempts to dominate nonhuman nature for the sake of ''progress'' as it is defined by the political and economic leaders of the First World, the countries that have the highest levels of economic wealth. Ecofeminists contend that until anthropocentricism is replaced by a human kinship solidarity with earth's life forms, the ecological crisis will continue.

Ecofeminist Theology. From its inception ecofeminism intersected with religion and theology. In the First World west the ecofeminist criticism of an objectified ''nature'' prompted the recognition that the Earth, once envisioned as sacred, is no longer viewed as such. The loss of the sacrality of the Earth has contributed to the ecological crisis. To provide a corrective, during the 1970s some ecofeminists began developing earth-centered religious practices. Among these women are those who believed that the gender attributed to the divine is important for the well-being of women and the health of the planet. Some argued that there is nothing redeemable about the transcendent male, sovereign-God of Judaism and Christianity. These ecofeminists looked to Goddess-centered religious practices, reviving past traditions of honoring the sacredness of Earth and of celebrating the immanence of the Goddess in Earth's processes. Some of these ecofeminist expressions of religion combine neo-pagan spirituality with witchcraft. Others draw on archeological discoveries to construct visions of prehistoric Old European religion in which Goddess worship supports human harmony with nature. From these diverse resources ecofeminists have articulated Goddess ''thealogies.''

Among ecofeminists are Christians who are critical of the syncretistic Goddess religions, arguing that the ''thealogians'' of these religions have a limited understanding of how God is depicted in the Bible and in extra-biblical Christian sources. Drawing attention to female imagery in the Bible, they believe that Christianity can be a resource for liberating women and nonhuman nature from the effects of patriarchy. Christian ecofeminists acknowledge that the Bible has been used to legitimate human domination of other creatures. The directive that humans exercise ''dominion . . . over every living thing that moves upon the earth'' (Gn 1.28) has been interpreted in patriarchal ways that both ignore the historical situation of the Jewish people exiled and enslaved in Babylon during the 500s B.C. and confuse dominion in that ancient social setting with the domination of which humans are capable in the modern age. The biblical account of the ''Days of Creation'' affirms the deep kinship of humans with all of earth's creatures.

To the important concern about the sacrality of nature, Christian ecofemists theologians provided a variety of responses. Rosemary Radford Ruether, a Catholic theologian, proposes an ecofeminist retrieval of the sacramentality of creation (*Gaia and God*). Her proposal for an ecofeminist sacramentality affirms the intrinsic worth of every facet of creation, apart from the value that a particular group of persons, including those in power, attaches to it. Earth is sacramental because all creatures have their origins in God, are ''holy things'' revelatory of the divine presence, and cannot exist apart from a God who transcends specific male names and images. The sacrality of nature is affirmed also by Sallie McFague, a Protestant theologian, in her reflections on the metaphorical statement: ''the world is God's body'' (*The Body of God*). In speaking of the world as the body of God, McFague does not propose to equate God with the material ''stuff'' of the cosmos. God ''bodies forth the world'' and exceeds the sum of the world's parts. God both transcends the world and is immanent in it. Nothing exists without God nurturing and sustaining it with the divine gift of life, an agency more readily associated with female reality than with male. In their distinctive, yet related, ecofeminist theologies Ruether and McFague find bases for ethical responses to the ecological crisis. For Ruether it is an ethics of ''compassionate solidarity'' and for McFague a ''community care.'' For both, it is a love commitment to an eco-justice of right relations with all creatures.

For non-Western ecofeminists, especially those in the Third World countries, awareness of the sacredness of nature is less of an issue. Traditional spiritualities of pre-colonial indigenous cultures affirmed that creation is a sacred manifestation of the divine. Among traditional beliefs commonly held was that land was given to the people as a group or tribe for their use by divine favor. Therefore, individual ownership of land was unheard of. Land and all that inhabited it was a treasured gift from God for the good of the whole community. Therefore, the people routinely performed rituals signifying that their use of the land was a privilege. When they harvested their crops, they offered prayers of thanksgiving to God. However, the Christianity presented to indigenous peoples was given an imperialistic cast by Western colonizers who presumed that land privately owned by men was the universal norm. Women were often presumed by the colonizers to have no land rights (and by extension no rights in any sphere of societal life). Through means that were often violent, the colonizers appropriated great tracts of the most valuable land from indigenous peoples to extract minerals and grow cash crops. Land acquisition and exploitation resulted in the destruction of delicate ecosystems, the denigration of women and the reduction of land to a resource to be exploited by a few rather than a gift to be shared by all.

In post-colonial Third World countries a revisionist interpretation of the inculturation of Christianity has awakened prophetic voices among women who challenge First World notions of private land ownership, industrial development, economic progress and the desacralization of the land. Some Third World ecofeminist theologians affirm core beliefs of Christianity, such as belief in God as creator and giver of life, while also affirming traditional beliefs, including earth-centered spiritualities that celebrate the sacredness of the land. Although significant differences can be discerned in these spiritualities, Third World ecofeminists share common ethical emphases: (1) a critique of First World models of development and progress that contribute to their own poverty; (2) commitment to the sustainability of nature that is basic to survival, very important to women because gender roles in these countries often give them the strenuous work of collecting water, food and fuel for their families; (3) emphasis on practical remedies to wasteful consumption of limited resources; (4) resolve to live a lifestyle that embodies a holistic vision of creation and a response of gratitude to the Creator.

Advocates of Christian ecofeminist theology present it as a prophetic call: (1) to attend to and to correct the destructive effects of patriarchy, not only on women but also in all creatures because such domination is not of God; (2) to reverence creatures, female and male, human and nonhuman in all their diversity because they together form a delicate organic web of life that is of God and in God; (3) to commit oneself to eco-justice both locally and globally.

See Also: ECOLOGY; FEMINISM.

Bibliography: C. J. ADAMS, ed. *Ecofeminism and the Sacred* (New York 1993). C. P. CHRIST, *Rebirth of the Goddess: Lending Meaning in Feminist Spirituality* (Reading, Mass. 1997). A. M. CLIFFORD, ''When Being Human Becomes Truly Earthly, an Ecofeminist Proposal for Solidarity,'' 173–189, in *In the Embrace of God: Feminist Approaches to Christian Anthropology*, ed. A. O'HARA GRAFF (Maryknoll, N.Y. 1995). F. D'EAUBONNE, *Le féminisme ou la mort* (1974), E.T. ''Ecofeminism or Death,'' 64–67, in *New French Feminisms: An Anthology*, ed. E. MARKS and I. DE COURTIVRON (Amherst, 1980). M. GIMBUTAS, *The Goddesses and Gods of Old Europe* (Berkley 1982). S. MCFAGUE, *The Body of God: An Ecological Theology* (Minneapolis 1993); *Super, Natural Christians: How We Should Love Nature* (Minneapolis 1997). R. RADFORD RUETHER, *Gaia and God: An Ecofeminist Theology of Earth Healing* (San Francisco 1992); *Women Healing Earth: Third World Women on Ecology, Feminism, and Religion* (Maryknoll, N.Y. 1996).

[A. CLIFFORD]

ÉCOLE BIBLIQUE

The École Pratique d'Études Bibliques (The Practical School of Biblical Studies) was founded on Nov. 15, 1890 by Father Marie-Joseph Lagrange, OP (1855–1938) in the premises of the Dominican Monastery of Saint Stephen in Jerusalem. Its name underlines its distinctive methodology. The combination of text and monument should ensure that the Bible was studied in the physical and cultural context in which it had been written.

The name was modified in 1920 when the Académie des Inscriptions et Belles- Lettres, Paris, decided to honor the achievements of the École Pratique d'Études Bibliques by designating it the École Archéologique Française de Jérusalem. The first part of the original title was condensed with the result that the official title became École Biblique et Archéologique Française de Jérusalem. Alone of the national archaeological schools in Jerusalem it has a developed teaching program, and since 1983 it has been accredited by the Congregation of Catholic Education to confer the Doctorate in Sacred Scripture. A grant from the European Commission (1999–2001) brought its celebrated library up to fully professional standards.

Faculty. With the exception of Lagrange, who had studied oriental languages at the University of Vienna, none of the original staff had any professional qualifications. Very quickly, however, from the Dominican novices forced to study in Jerusalem by the French anticlerical law of July 15, 1889, he selected and trained a faculty envied by all academic institutions. Marius Antonin Jaussen (1871–1962) became a pioneering ethnographer. Louis-Hugues Vincent (1872–1960) developed into the preeminent Palestinian archaeologist of his generation. Antoine Raphael Savignac (1874–1951) made his mark as a semitic epigrapher, particularly for his work during the three dangerous expeditions with Jaussen into northern Arabia (1907, 1909, 1910–12). The acute critical judgment of Felix-Marie Abel (1876–1953) focused his vast erudition into unrivalled mastery of the Greek sources for the history and geography of Palestine. Eduard Paul Dhorme (1881–1966) became a noted Assyriologist, and was the first to decipher Ugaratic. Lagrange himself concentrated first on the Old Testament, and then on the New Testament, producing the most authoritative Catholic commentaries of their day on the four gospels, Romans and Galatians. The research generated by the close interdisciplinary cooperation of these scholars appeared primarily in the periodical *Revue Biblique* (1892—) and in the monograph series *Études Bibliques* (1903—).

In addition to intense productivity, they also trained their successors, all French Dominicans, who began to appear in the 1930s. Bernard Couroyer (1900–92) published extensively in Egyptology, but also taught Coptic and Arabic. Roland de Vaux (1903–71) was noted both for biblical scholarship and field archaeology. Raymond Tournay (1912–99) produced the best translation of the Psalms in any language. Highly significant work in the New Testament was done by Pierre Benoit (1906–87) and Marie-Emile Boismard (1916—). It was these, together with the survivors of the first generation, who gave Lagrange's ideal its ultimate expression with the publication of the one-volume *Bible de Jérusalem* (1956).

Only in the third generation did the faculty of the École Biblique become international. Jerome Murphy-O'Connor (1935—) was the first non-Frenchman to be appointed (1967). Others soon followed, and eventually non-Dominican professors were added to the staff. In 2000 there were professors and administrators from Brazil, France, Ireland, Italy, Mexico, New Zealand, Poland, Portugal, Switzerland, and the USA. The multinational student body averages some 30 men and women from as many as 20 different countries and many different religious traditions.

Activities. The École Biblique concentrates it activities in two sectors, textual and archaeological. In the first the principal focus is on the text of the Old and New Testaments, which are studied according to the historico-critical method. The troubles that this approach created for Lagrange in the Modernist period no longer exist. More modern approaches are not excluded, and are catered for by invitations to visiting professors, but in fact the interest of the permanent faculty lies in the evolution of texts and the reliability of their historical information. The Dead Sea Scrolls are taught by one of the editors, Abbé Emile Puech of the CNRS, who also edits the *Revue de Qumran*. All the relevant ancient languages are taught.

Because of the lack of funds for excavations the École Biblique first concentrated its archeological activities on highly fruitful surface exploration of the entire biblical region and on the study of monumental complexes. The latter included the Church of the Nativity in Bethlehem (1914), the Haram al-Khalil in Hebron (1923), and above all the city of Jerusalem (1912–55). A series of small excavations (Amwas, Abu Ghosh, En el-Mamoudiyeh) prepared the École Biblique to attempt a major site. Between 1946 and 1962 de Vaux spent nine seasons at Tell el-Farah (11 km NE of Nablus), which he identified as Tirza, the first capital of the Northern Kingdom of Israel. His work there was interrupted by the need to excavate at Qumran, En Feshkha and Wadi Murrabaat (1949–58) in order to provide an historical context for the Dead Sea Scrolls, whose authenticity was disputed at the time of their discovery in the late 1940s.

The École Biblique became responsible for the publication of the Scrolls by default. The fledgling Jordan Department of Antiquities had no textual expert, and the political situation excluded Jewish cooperation. The task fell to Dominique Barthélemy (1921—) and Josef Milik (1922—), a Polish secular priest studying at the École. They coopted Abbé Maurice Baillet when he arrived as a student in 1952. It soon became apparent that the three could not cope with the mass of material. De Vaux won the assent of the Jordanian Government to the formation of an international and interconfession team of experts, of which he became the coordinator (1954). At his death in 1971 he was succeeded by Pierre Benoit until 1986.

The war of June 1967 brought the École Biblique under Israeli jurisdiction, but after excavating in Israel (Tell Keisan), the École went back to Jordan with Jean-Baptiste Humbert, OP (1940—) as field director (Khirbet es-Samra 1981–85, 1993–93; the Citadel in Amman 1986–89), and subsequently moved to Gaza (1995–99).

One of the treasures of the École Biblique is the photo library of some 20,000 glass slides, digitalized from photos taken at the end of the 19th and the beginning of the 20th century. In addition to archaeological sites that have been destroyed they portray a world that has completely disappeared. To bring them to the attention of scholars Jean-Michel de Tarragon, OP (1945—) organized a series of exhibitions, accompanied by detailed catalogues, at the Institut du Monde Arab, Paris: ''Itineraires Bibliques'' (1995), ''Périple de la mer Morte 1908–1909'' (1997), ''Photographies d'Arabie: Hedjaz 1907–1917'' (1999), which also went to Riyadh and Jeddah, Saudi Arabia, and ''Al Quds al-Sharif'' (2002), which also went to the Emirates of the Gulf.

Bibliography: P. BENOIT, ''French Archaeologists,'' in *Benchmarks in Time and Culture: Essays in Honor of Joseph A. Callaway*, ed. J. F. DRINKARD et al. (Atlanta 1988) 63–86. O. BETZ and R. RIESNER, *Jesus, Qumran and the Vatican* (New York 1994). F.-M. BRAUN, *L'oeuvre de Père Lagrange. Étude et bibliographie* (Fribourg 1943). M.-J. LAGRANGE, *Personal Reflections and Memoirs* (Mahwah 1985). J. MURPHY-O'CONNOR with a contribution by J. TAYLOR, *The Ecole Biblique and the New Testament: A Century of Scholarship (1890–1990)* (NTOA 13; Fribourg and Göttingen 1990). J.-L. VESCO, ed., *L'Ancien Testament. Cent ans d'exégèse à l'Ecole Biblique* (CRB 28; Paris 1990). B. T. VIVIANO, ''Ecole Biblique et Archéologique Française de Jérusalem,'' *Biblical Archaeologist* 54 (1991) 160–67.

[J. MURPHY-O'CONNOR]

ECOLOGY

The term ''ecology'' designates one of the basic divisions of biology and was first employed by Ernst Haeckel, the German zoologist, in the 19th century. In the mid-20th century ecology emerged as one of the primary scientific and ethical concerns of humanity. The word comes from the Greek root oikos (''house'' or ''dwelling'') and refers to the systemic relationship of abiotic environmental factors with biotic components such as plants, animals, and microbes. Ecology, therefore, is the study of the structure and dynamics of the web of life, i.e., the biological processes that compose and sustain the earth's ecosystem.

In contrast with the Newtonian view that nature is simple in structure, mechanistic in behavior, and static in form, an ecological interpretation stresses that nature is diverse in structure, reciprocal in behavior, and dynamic in form. Basic premises of an ecological interpretation include the following: (1) All forms of life exist in interdependent relationships. Life is sustained by reciprocity and mutuality among organisms. (2) Nature is dynamic rather than static. In its adaptation and growth nature shows a constantly changing face. (3) The stability of nature depends upon diversity. Heterogeneous environments have greater possibilities for change and adaptation than homogeneous environments. (4) Nature is fragile and finite. Through intentional or unintentional intervention the ecological balance can be so disturbed as to be irremediable. Moreover, nature has limits, and its supply of resources is not infinite.

In recent years ecologists have shown in considerable detail that many of the organisms and species on earth are either being irretrievably destroyed or are now in danger of extinction because of damage by human beings to the earth's ecosystems. Numerous ecological perils threaten humans and other living beings today. A litany of these usually includes: the rapid destruction of forests; massive erosion of soil; disappearance of sources of fresh water; desertification; pollution of land, air and water; extinction of species; global warming; and the thinning of the stratospheric ozone layer. Overarching all of these is the burgeoning human population which, along with patterns of excessive consumption, compounds every ecological problem the earth faces today.

Theology of Nature. In response to the ecological crisis one of the major developments in contemporary theology has been the attempt to reformulate a theology of nature. Six key themes can be discerned. (1) The biblical doctrine of creation (Gn 1) stresses the goodness of the whole created order. In the divine perspective nature has an implicit value of its own in that it manifests the goodness of God and joins in universal praise of its Creator. Nature, therefore, cannot be reduced to an exclusively instrumental status in the service of humanity. (2) Humans are an integral part of the web of life and not an exception to it. So close is the kinship of the human species to its natural environment that the two live in an inescapable reciprocity. Ecology traces the bonds between the two. While emphasizing human continuity with the nonhuman natural world theologians and scientists also call attention to the unique capacities of humans to reflect upon and to project the future of the natural world. Humans are to be responsible caretakers of the earth (Gn 2.15). Within the created order only humans have the capacity to transcend time and place and hence to exercise stewardship with respect to the creation before the Creator. (3) Human sin is illustrated in the fact that the terrestrial sector of creation bears the consequences of our irresponsibility. The ecological crisis calls our attention to the biblical assertion that ''the whole creation is in travail'' (Rom 8.23). (4) The INCARNATION affirms the value of an individual's personal being before God by affirming simultaneously the significance of earthly life and its natural environment as the context for God's revelation. The Word that became flesh has identity and continuity with the creative Word which called all things into being (Jn 1:3). The New Testament authors extend the LOGOS doctrine into a cosmic view in which Christ is the consummation of all things (Colossians) and the restoration of the cosmos through sanctification (Hebrews). The incarnate Christ restores to the creation its reality and value. (5) Some theologians, notably those influenced by TEILHARD DE CHARDIN or American PROCESS PHILOSOPHY, emphasize a new formulation of the doctrine of divine immanence. Rather than acting from without, God is seen as the source of constant gracious creativity acting, in a manner consistent with the doctrine of the Holy Spirit, from within the on-going world process. In process thought distinctions are made between God's primordial and his consequent nature. According to process theology the world process is included within the life of God, who at the same time transcends the world. In this sense it can be said that God is the world's ''ultimate environment.'' (6) The God of creation is also the Lord of history. Environmental scientists and theologians are concerned that ecological values be seen in their social as well as natural context. An ecological ethic requires the reordering of economic values. An adequate theology of nature will see the natural and the social worlds as existing inextricably together.

Ecological Theology. Official religious bodies, not unlike other institutions, have paid little attention to ecological issues until recently, but they are now doing so more explicitly than ever before. Moreover, ecology has increasingly come to engage the attention of religious thinkers, including Christian theologians. The objective of ecological theology is to spell out, in this case from within the context of Christian tradition, precisely why people of faith should care about the nonhuman natural world. Ecological theology is especially appropriate at a time when some prominent environmentalists are claiming that religion, and particularly Christianity, is indifferent if not inimical to the well-being of nature. Critics often cite the controversial thesis of historian Lynn White, Jr., that the Bible, by giving humans ''dominion'' over the earth (Gn 1.26), has sanctioned our ''domination'' of the natural world. Or they appeal to philosophers like John Passmore, who argues that Christianity will never contribute substantially to ecological ethics without ceasing thereby to be Christian. Preoccupation with the supernatural and with immortality, they argue, has led believers to focus so intensely on the ''other world'' that they pay little attention to this one.

Many theologians agree that the Christian tradition is somewhat ambiguous in its evaluation of nature, but that it still has the resources for a fresh ecological vision. Since the survival of nature was not a major issue during the emergence of biblical religion we should not expect the latter to come with pre-packaged remedies for our ecological problems. Still, even though concern for treating the earth as our home has not been a prominent feature of Christian spirituality, the central teachings of the faith can now be shown to be powerfully relevant to ecology.

It is not immediately obvious, though, precisely how Christianity can be said to be ecologically significant. Like some other religious traditions, it cherishes a spirituality that at times seems to have made terrestrial reality less important than ecological ethicists would require. Like some other religious traditions it has fostered a spirituality in which humans are in via, on a long journey of homeless detachment. And this ideal of religious homelessness easily lends itself to translation into an environmentally noxious cosmic homelessness. Can the religious call to live homelessly be made compatible with the ecological imperative to treat the natural world as our home?

In the Bible, Abraham, the common ancestor of Judaism, Christianity, and Islam, was summoned to leave his ancestral home in order to pursue God's promise. His willingness to endure homelessness for the sake of the promise remained an ideal of Israel's religion which also understood itself in terms of an Exodus journey. Jesus called his own followers to a life of homeless pilgrimage. The Letter to the Hebrews states that faith in the promise makes us ''strangers and aliens on earth,'' seekers of ''a better homeland, a heavenly one'' (11.13–16) Numerous other Christian writings, hymns, and prayers down through the ages have echoed the same theme: sojourning, the sense of not yet being at home, is central to Christian faith. Thus many Christians, perhaps even the majority of them, find it difficult to see the earth as ''home.'' They sometimes even interpret it as though it were little more than a ''vale of soul-making.''

This spiritual interpretation of terrestrial existence turns the natural world into little more than a way-station on an exclusively human path to salvation. It robs earthly reality of intrinsic value, and although the doctrines of creation and incarnation clearly exalt the goodness of nature, Christian spirituality has been largely indifferent to the long-term thriving of the earth as a good in itself. FRANCIS OF ASSISI, IGNATIUS LOYOLA, HILDEGAARD OF BINGEN, MEISTER ECKHART, THOMAS AQUINAS, and many others have emphasized the value of all created things, but concern for the long-term welfare of nature has not been a very explicit part of Christian preaching and teaching.

Nevertheless, some concerned theologians have begun to explore the ecological relevance of Christian faith. They are convinced that ecological ethics requires at least some kind of religious grounding and that religious homelessness need not be turned into a cosmic homelessness. While at first sight a pure naturalism may seem to be the only possible framework in which we could embrace the earth as our true home, under examination naturalism fails to demonstrate in sufficient depth precisely why our natural environment is inherently, and not just instrumentally, a good to be preserved and cherished. On the other hand, Christian theology, in spite of its historical ambiguity on the issue, can provide such a foundation.

For convenience one may distinguish three ways in which this theological premise is now being developed. These are the *apologetic, sacramental, and eschatological* approaches to ecology. None of the three can claim adequacy by itself, and there is some tension among them. But taken together they constitute at least the beginnings of an effective theological response.

The Apologetic Approach. The apologetic approach to ecological theology claims, either explicitly or implicitly, that Scripture and tradition together provide an adequate religious foundation for ecological ethics. Examples are the World Day of Peace Message by Pope John Paul II entitled ''The Ecological Crisis: A Common Responsibility'' (1990), the American Catholic Bishops' pastoral, ''Renewing the Earth'' (1992), and the World Council of Churches' statements on ''Justice, Peace and the Integrity of Creation.'' In addition, a growing body of theological articles and books on ecology voice a similar apologetic concern.

The distinguishing mark of apologetic ecological theology is its sometimes unstated conviction that Christian tradition does not need to undergo drastic revision in order to constitute a sufficiently solid basis for environmental ethics. Its summons to responsible stewardship is a clear signal of biblical religion's concern for the natural world. So our vocation as responsible stewards of creation should provide enough of a religious incentive for Christians to take up the cause of ecology today. Numerous scriptural and traditional texts, many of them passed over before, also demonstrate the considerable extent to which Christian faith quite directly obliges us to protect the environment that we share with all other species of living beings.

This apologetic type of ecological theology also looks for support to the traditional emphasis on timeless religious virtues. Without the practice of love, humility, justice, detachment, and gratitude no alleviation of the ecological crisis is even conceivable. Since human habits of immoderation and injustice have contributed so obviously to pollution and the drain on nonrenewable resources, nothing less than a return by all of humanity to the pursuit of virtue will ultimately restore the earth to health. For this conversion to take place in an effective way people the world over must embrace their role as faithful stewards of the creation, representing God's goodness and care toward all other forms of life.

This approach may be called ''apologetic'' because it places a somewhat defensive shield over traditional religious teachings, claiming that they do not deserve the complaints they sometimes receive from secular ecologists. Apologists imply that Christianity is in essence immune to criticism since environmental abuse stems only from our disobedience to the dictates of faith and not from any deficiencies inherent in Christianity itself. Consequently, the ecological crisis calls less for the readjustment of Christianity than for a straightforward retrieval of its forgotten teachings about stewardship, justice, and other virtues. If we would only allow the eternal values set forth in Scripture and tradition to shape our environmental policies, we could avert the possible calamity that threatens the earth today. The fault is not with the sources of faith but with our failure to accept their message.

The often strident criticisms of Christianity by some ecologists would seem to justify something like an apologetic response. In spite of the well-known arguments concerning the ''religious origins'' of our current ecological crisis, it is by no means evident that religion is itself the main culprit. The widespread destruction of ecosystems may stem much less from specific religious attitudes than from irreligious habits and policies uncensored by a healthy sense of human limits and gratitude for the gift of creation.

Nevertheless, although apologetics must be one aspect of any Christian ecological theology today, a growing number of critics from within the Christian community now consider it to be quite inadequate. They concede that its focus on Scripture and tradition is helpful in bringing to our attention many ecologically significant texts and teachings (e.g., the Wisdom Literature, the Noachic covenant with ''every living creature,'' or the psalms that glorify nature as God's creation, not to mention many texts from the New Testament or from early and medieval Christian writers). However, questions still linger about the religious sufficiency of the theme of stewardship and about the general obliviousness to the cosmos that characterizes so much traditional and modern theology. To an increasing number of theologians the ecological crisis requires that we go beyond apologetic theology.

The Sacramental Approach. The ecological crisis, some theologians argue, is so novel and momentous that it calls for a much more radical transformation of Christian faith than the apologetic approach proposes. These theologians seriously doubt that Christianity can adequately confront the problems facing the natural world simply by calling on such classic themes as stewardship and the practice of virtue, important though these may be. Even the most impressive display of scriptural and traditional texts about God and nature may not be enough to demonstrate Christianity's essential involvement with ecology. Theology needs to undergo a new and unprecedented internal change in its whole approach to nature. In brief, according to this second approach, the ecological situation requires that theology develop a much more profound ''sense of the cosmos,'' especially after several modern centuries in which it has focused its attention almost exclusively on themes of history, subjectivity, society, and freedom—usually to the exclusion of nature. Theology is now being challenged to bring the universe back to the center of its concern.

Advocates of this cosmological transformation of theology base their position on what they take to be the *sacramentality* of nature, a theme already explicit in Scripture and tradition but often subordinated to the biblical emphasis on salvation history. While Scripture and tradition are still essential sources of ecological theology, nature itself is seen here also as powerfully disclosive of God. A fresh acknowledgment of the sacral quality of the cosmos itself is taken as the main reason for our valuing nonhuman nature. The inherently revelatory character of nature gives it an intrinsic, even ''sacred,'' value that should shelter it from exploitative technological and industrial projects undertaken in the name of development and ''progress.''

Thomas Berry is one of the most prominent advocates of this sacramental approach. In his widely influential writings he argues that Scripture and tradition are by themselves an incomplete foundation for ecological spirituality and theology. Instead, he suggests that we base our ecological perspective on the sense that the universe itself is the primary revelation of God. His theology claims a strong pedigree in the sacramental emphasis of Catholic tradition, both western and eastern. However, advocates of both the apologetic and eschatological theologies are unhappy with the subordinate role he gives to the Bible.

The sacramental theme is also taken up into the ''creation-centered'' theology associated especially with Matthew Fox. This theology goes far beyond apologetics. Claiming that the traditional call to stewardship and virtue is not nearly enough, it argues that the ecological crisis requires a more radical rethinking of what it means to be Christian within the framework of the entire earth-community. Our inherited texts and teachings are not alone capable of leading us through the needed shift in our religious thinking and practice. The rhythms and powers of the universe must also be allowed to guide us. A reattunement to nature requires also that we attend to the voices of native peoples who have always lived close to the earth. All of the traditional teachings of Christianity—if we expect them to be effective in an age of ecological sensitivity—need to be recast in a sacramental, cosmological, relational, non-hierarchical, non-patriarchal, and non-dualistic fashion.

More than anything else, however, the biblical theme of creation must now be brought to the very center of Christian theology. According to creation-centered theology, this most ecologically compelling of all doctrines has been eclipsed by the tradition's unbalanced exaggeration of a ''fallen'' world and the need for human redemption. According to Fox, a one-sided Fall/Redemption theology diverted our religious attention away from the intrinsic, original goodness of nature. As long as nature seemed to be vitiated by our own sinfulness we failed to greet its sacramental effusiveness with an appropriate reverence. Moreover, a predominantly Fall/Redemption interpretation of the Bible led us toward an anthropocentrism that distracted us from concern about the nonhuman natural world.

Creation-centered theology, therefore, requires a less human-centered understanding of the cosmos than we find in the apologetic approach. Its relativization of the human even carries over to the notion of sin. Sin refers not only to our estrangement from God and other humans, but as well to nature's alienation from us and from God. Likewise ''reconciliation'' refers not only to the restoration of interhuman bonds, but more fundamentally to the renewal of the entire earth-community to which we belong much more completely than it belongs to us. In this theology Christ is much more than a personal historical savior. First and foremost he is the heart of the whole cosmos, the Word in whose image all of nature was fashioned, and the goal toward which the entire universe moves in its evolution. A cosmic Christology, with its roots in the New Testament writings of John and Paul, as well as in Irenaeus and Teilhard de Chardin, is the deepest foundation of a specifically Christian sacramental approach to ecology.

Countering the ecologically problematic cosmic homelessness of some of the world's religious traditions, creation-centered theology encourages an enjoyment of the natural world as our true home. Accordingly it moves beyond those spiritualities that fostered a sense of discomfort with our embodied existence. It is especially critical of the dualistic strains in Christian tradition that have sanctioned negative attitudes toward nature, women, and the body.

To those who accuse this new theology of advocating a licentious brand of ''neo-paganism,'' sacramental ecologists remind us that their ecological preoccupation exacts a much more difficult kind of renunciation than did the puritanical dualism that defined so much Christian morality in the past. An ecological spirituality imposes upon humans the very strict spiritual discipline of taking into account the implications of all of their actions for the entire natural world and future generations. And while an ecological asceticism does not seek to detach us from the natural world, it does require that we forsake the ideal of autonomous, isolated selfhood with which we have become so comfortable since the Enlightenment. Sacramental ecology is equally intolerant of the privatization of religion. Taking into account the implications of our being intimately intertwined with the wider earth-community, and not just with human society, this eco-spirituality demands personal sacrifices that we have never made before.

Such an ethic also calls for a wider understanding of justice than we find in most previous Christian moral teaching. Its emphasis on ''eco-justice'' reminds us that we cannot respond appropriately to any social inequities without attending also to the prospering of the earth's eco-systems. Likewise a truly ''pro-life'' ethic goes beyond focusing only on issues of human fertility and takes into account the need to protect the earth's complex life-systems without which there will be a complete and final ''death of birth'' (McDonagh).

Finally, since a sacramental perspective on ecology discovers in nature an inherent value, it radically questions utilitarian or naturalist attitudes toward the physical world. Inasmuch as nature is essentially the sacramental manifestation of an ultimate goodness and generosity, its value transcends that of simple raw material at the service of purely human projects. Thus the nurturing of a sacramental vision is one of the most important contributions Christianity can make to the grounding of ecological ethics.

The Eschatological Approach. Nevertheless, an accentuation of the theme of nature's sacramentality may not yet be the most distinctive endowment Christian faith can make to ecology. While any attempt to construct a Christian ecological theology today must build on the sacramental interpretation of nature, several theologians (notably Jürgen Moltmann) have asked whether biblical religion's most fundamental theme, that of a divine promise for future fulfillment, is itself of any relevance here. In other words, does ESCHATOLOGY have a significant role to play in shaping an ecologically sensitive theology?

To some ecologists a concern for the eschatological future, as it has been traditionally understood in Christian theology, is ecologically problematic. Discourse about the end of the world or about life beyond death seems to distract us from engagement with present ecological emergencies. On the other hand, since the theme of promise is the backbone of biblical faith, it is doubtful that we could have a distinctively Christian ecological theology without making eschatology central to it.

By ''eschatology'' theology today no longer means simply the religious concern for a personal destiny beyond death. Instead eschatology refers primarily to the patient, shared hope in God's promise that underlies the stories about Abraham, Moses, Israel's messianic expectations, Jesus' parables of the Reign of God, and the early Christian community's longing for the coming of Christ. Eschatology is not speculation about another world so much as it is the anticipation of God's always surprising and restorative appearance out of the future. It is not a vision that pulls us off the face of the earth, but one that looks toward the renewal of the earth and all of creation. The main theme of eschatology is not escape to the other world, but a new creation of this world, culminating in ''the kingdom that will have no end.''

Therefore, when viewed eschatologically all of reality, including the natural world, is permeated with promise. Even in all of its ambiguity the entire universe hints at future fulfillment. Authentic faith constantly scans the horizon for signs of the coming of a new future into the world, not for a removal of humans from the earth. Biblical faith looks not only for a God sacramentally revealed in present natural harmony but even more for the future coming of God in the eschatological perfection of creation, which of course includes the resurrection of the dead. This eschatological sense of promise may also help ground a Christian ecological theology.

An eschatological approach to ecology looks upon the natural world itself as essentially a promise of future fulfillment. Thus it is not only the world's sacramental character, but its being permeated by promise that bids us to care for it. If a theology of nature is to have a close connection to biblical religion, then the theme of promise must be made central and not subordinated to other theological criteria. Seen eschatologically, the present cosmos is an installment of the ultimate perfection announced by the good news of God's coming. Consequently, nature is not something from which to separate ourselves in order to find a final fulfillment, but a reality to which we are everlastingly related and whose new creation we constantly await.

Standing on the promissory character of nature an eschatological ecology does not displace but instead gives a distinctively futurist orientation to the sacramental contribution discussed above. Sacramentalism has the felicitous effect of bringing the wider cosmos back to the attention of theology. But in the Bible sacramentality is taken up into eschatology. Biblical hope does not look for a complete and final epiphany of the sacred in any present manifestation of natural beauty. Such a revelation of God awaits the eschatological future which even now relativizes all present cosmic realities, including the natural world in all its splendor. Nature's value then consists not only of its being transparent to God, as the sacramental approach rightly argues, but also of its being a promise of the future unfolding of God's vision for the world. Thus, human violence toward nature is by implication not only a sacrilege against the alleged ''sacredness'' of life. It is also despair, the turning away from a promise.

As the American Catholic Bishops' pastoral ''Renewing the Earth'' notes, the fundamental ecological virtue is hope. A genuinely biblical perspective requires that our ecological theology remain deeply connected to the sense of promise. If the sacramental approach seeks to recosmologize Christianity, then the Bible demands that we always embed our cosmology in eschatology. Present cosmic reality is not the conclusive symbolic revelation of God but an intense straining toward a new creation not yet fully manifest.

In its vision of redemptive fulfillment the Bible in fact explicitly includes the entire cosmos, now groaning in the birth pangs of new creation. Following the spirit of Paul in Romans 8.18–22, one may say that the universe is not a mere point of departure for the homeless religious pilgrimage, but in all of its evolution a participant in the human journey into God. Religious homelessness does not have to turn into a cosmic homelessness. The cosmos is not left behind as the children of Abraham pursue the promise. Rather it accompanies us in all of our striving. Nature shares eternally in our fate, and God's incarnational embrace of the world makes the whole universe a perpetual participant in the salvation for which Christian faith hopes. Our own religious longing for future fulfillment, therefore, is not a violation but a blossoming of the cosmos. This way of looking at things should make a difference in how we treat the earth's fragile ecosystems.

Viewing nature as promise, eschatological ecology also allows the universe to have a future that far transcends our purely human aspirations. The cosmic future includes much more than the goals that we humans might formally sketch. According to eschatological ecology, any realization of our plans for the human future must be accomplished in a manner that does not interfere with the promise for a transhuman future that the present cosmos may be carrying within itself. We are ethically obliged to preserve all the diversity of the earth's life systems, irrespective of their value for us, since to destroy them is not only to diminish our own future but that also of the larger world that includes us. As the Wisdom Literature implies—and especially the Book of Job—we are not ourselves the authors of the divine vision that embraces and moves all of creation.

An eschatological interpretation of nature carries two additional implications for ecological theology. In the first place, when the cosmos is viewed as promise nature can claim our respect and conservation without requiring that we prostrate ourselves before it. Sacramentalism, on the other hand, if not carefully tempered by a sense of the future, tends to sacralize nature, at times almost to the point of divinization. Eschatology allows for deficiencies in nature that a purely sacramental ecology may not easily tolerate. When it is taken as promise rather than solely as the present symbolic mediation of God, nature is allowed to be less than perfect. When we do not require the universe at this moment to be fully revelatory of God we will be less surprised and discouraged when it turns out to be bloody as well as beautiful. A sacramental ecology cannot easily accommodate the dark side of nature, whereas an eschatological posture, looking more toward the future than the present for the completion of creation and the final coming of God, can acknowledge the unfinished status of the world.

In the second place, an assimilation of ecology into eschatology allows for, and even demands, a way of thinking about personal life beyond death that will avoid a sense of our final separation from nature. The traditional interpretation of death and beyond was exceedingly problematic from an ecological point of view. In spite of the teaching about bodily resurrection, it has usually pictured human destiny in terms of an immortal human soul abandoning the body on an otherworldly journey to a realm completely beyond nature. This picture could hardly avoid placing the entire natural world, of which the body is a part, in a negative light.

What then would an ecologically satisfying notion of personal immortality look like? Karl RAHNER proposed that a person's death need not imply a separation from the earth and the universe, but rather the possibility of entering into a deeper relationship with nature. Though Rahner's language was still somewhat dualistic, he speculated that in death the soul takes on a "pancosmic" relationship to the world rather than becoming completely detached from it. If it is as persons that we die, Rahner implied, any "personal" survival of death could be construed as a deepening rather than a severing of our connections with the cosmos. In death the person is set free from a shallow relationship to the cosmos and to God in order to assume a more profound one. Such a view is consistent with Christian teachings about resurrection, continuous creation, and divine incarnation, as well as with the sense that nature is filled with promise.

The dualistic anthropology presupposed by much traditional piety, on the other hand, encouraged us to prepare for death by detaching ourselves as thoroughly as possible here and now from the world and the body. Allegedly this ascesis would make us ready for the final flight of the soul from the earth. A spirituality chastened by ecological concern, however, would prepare us for our personal death by having us always cherish and deepen our relationship to the cosmos. We prepare for death not by reducing the degree of our connectedness to the earth-community, but by heightening it. Spiritual discipline should under no circumstances mean a weakening of our sense of being intricately related to nature. Thus, in an ecological spirituality asceticism is not so much a matter of leaving things out of our lives as it is the habit of embracing the otherness around us, including the wildness of nature.

For Christian faith, of course, the archetype of such inclusiveness is Jesus himself. The Gospels present him as one who constantly sought out deeper relationships, especially with those who were no longer connected to life: the outcasts, the sick, the sinners—and the dead. Jesus' life, whose central motif is that of including the unincluded, can serve also as the model of our ecological concern. Ecological ethics then is the extension to all beings of the divine spirit of inclusiveness made manifest in Jesus. It is not essential that the historical Jesus himself have made any references to an "ecological crisis" in order to function as the model of our own ecological spirituality today. It is his eschatological spirit of inclusiveness, whose shape may vary from age to age, that is all important. Jesus' radically relational life is the sacrament of a responsive God whose preservative care and concern for life is the ultimate paradigm of our own ecological ethics.

Implications for Environmental Ethics. In light of the three versions of ecological theology discussed above, Christian theology is able to respond substantively to the suspicions voiced by some critics that it is indifferent to the ecological crisis. The apologetic, sacramental, and eschatological strains of ecological theology not only vigorously dispute such a suggestion, but together they make a strong case that Christian faith is inseparable from concern for ecological integrity.

From the apologetic approach ecological theology learns the significance of stewardship and the need for ecologically sustaining virtues. In spite of naturalistic suspicion of the notion of stewardship as being too ''managerial,'' it would be irresponsible for humans now to abandon their vocation as caretakers of nature. Moreover, recent exegesis has shown that the Bible in no way sanctions the human exploitation of nature that Lynn White, Jr., declared to be the main historical cause of the environmental crisis. The biblical theology of human dominion and stewardship was never intended to make humans anything other than bearers of the image of a just and compassionate God in our relationship to the rest of creation.

On the basis of the sacramental approach ecological theology can make the case that Christian faith is essentially, and not just accidentally, bound to the preservation of nature. The loss of nature leads directly to a loss of our sense of God. It is useful to ask what our religions would look like if we lived on a lunar landscape (Berry). From the beginnings of religious history on earth the mystery of the sacred has been revealed through such natural phenomena as clean water, fresh air, fertile soil, clear skies, bright light, thunder and rain, living trees, plants and animals, and life's fertility. Nature, viewed in sacramental perspective, is not primarily raw material to serve human purposes but essentially the showing forth of a divine goodness and generosity. As such it commands a care and concern that a utilitarian view cannot provide.

Finally, an eschatological emphasis allows us to revere nature without compelling us to worship it. It treasures nature as a promise open to future perfection, and in this way provides a distinctively biblical direction to ecological concern.

Bibliography: I. G. BARBOUR, ed., *Earth Might Be Fair: Reflections on Ethics, Religion and Ecology* (Englewood Cliffs, N.J., 1972). T. BERRY, *The Dream of the Earth* (San Francisco 1988). C. BIRCH and J. B. COBB, JR., *The Liberation of Life* (Cambridge 1981). C. BIRCH, W. EAKIN, and J. MCDANIEL, eds., *Liberating Life* (New York 1990). H. E. DALY and J. B. COBB, JR., *For the Common Good* (Boston 1989). D. EDWARDS, *Jesus the Wisdom of God: An Ecological Theology* (Maryknoll, N.Y., 1995). F. ELDER, *Crisis in Eden: A Religious Study of Man and Environment* (New York 1970). J. F. HAUGHT, *The Promise of Nature* (New York 1993). D. T. HESSEL, ed., *Theology for Earth Community: A Field Guide* (Maryknoll, N.Y.,1996). B. HILL, *Christian Faith and the Environment: Making Vital Connections* (Maryknoll, N.Y., 1998). S. MCDONAGH, *The Greening of the Church* (New York 1990). J. MOLTMANN, *God in Creation*, trans. M. KOHL (San Francisco 1985). C. F. D. MOULE, *Man and Nature in the New Testament: Some Reflections on Biblical Theology* (Philadelphia 1967). J. NASH, *Loving Nature* (Nashville 1991). M. OELSCHLAEGER, *Caring for Creation: An Ecumenical Approach to the Environmental Crisis* (New Haven 1996). K. RAHNER, *On the Theology of Death* (New York 1961). R. R. RUETHER, ed., *Christianity and Ecology: Seeking the Well-Being of Earth and Humans* (Cambridge 2000). P. SANTMIRE, *The Travail of Nature* (Philadelphia 1985). P. SMITH, *What Are They Saying about Environmental Ethics?* (Mahwah, N.J., 1997). L. WHITE, JR. ''The Historical Roots of our Ecological Crisis,'' *Science* 155:1203–1207.

[J. C. LOGAN/J. F. HAUGHT]

ECONOMY, DIVINE

Divine economy is the divine plan (ἡ οἰκονομία, Eph 3.9; cf. 1 Cor 2.7–8) hidden in the intellect of God from all eternity before the creation of the world and revealed in the divine acts of SALVATION, through His Prophets, through Jesus Christ (Rom 16.26), and through His Holy Spirit (1 Cor 2.10). The principal subject of that divine plan, while embracing both the order of nature and of grace (St. Thomas, ST 1a, 22), is salvation realized in and through the INCARNATION of the Person of the WORD, who, coming ''in the likeness of sinful flesh as a sin offering'' (Rom 8.3; cf. 2 Cor 5.21) in a passible human nature, underwent suffering and death and returned to the Father glorified in that flesh through which He had effected for man universal REDEMPTION (Heb 9.12).

Divine economy likewise embraces the mystery of the execution of the divine plan of salvation. Creatures to whom God communicates a participation in His causality are secondary agents through whom He acts in applying the fruits of His redemptive act. Through these created secondary agents acting in His name and often through His priestly power, that act is prolonged in space and time, especially in the created sacramental signs that He has endowed with power to communicate GRACE to men.

Essentially the concept of divine economy is that of the total mystery of Christ (Eph 1.10), whereby both the world of nature and that of grace are ordered through Him to the Trinity. In accordance with this above concept, one of the two major parts of Oriental theology is economy, or ''the study of the restoration of the communion between God and men by Jesus Christ'' (Congar).

The word economy is used also by the Oriental Christians to signify the theory and practice whereby the canonical power of the Church is applied benignly to particular cases (Congar).

See Also: ANTHROPOLOGY, THEOLOGICAL; ELEVATION OF MAN; JESUS CHRIST (IN THEOLOGY) 3, (SPECIAL QUESTIONS), 12; MAN; SUPERNATURAL.

Bibliography: O. MICHEL, οἰκονομία, G. KITTEL, *Theologisches Wöterbuch zum Neuen Testament* (Stuttgart 1935–) 5:154–155. *Dictionnaire de théologie catholique,* ed. A. VACANT et al., 15 v. (Paris 1903–50; Tables générales 1951–), Tables générales 1:1096. W. TRILLING and O. SEMMELROTH, ''Heil,'' H. FRIES, ed. *Handbuch theologischer Grundbegriffe,* 2 v. (Munich 1962–63) 1:623–633. C. V. HÉRIS, *The Mystery of Christ* (Westminster, Md. 1950). Y. CONGAR, *Catholicisme* 3:1305–07.

[M. R. E. MASTERMAN]

ECSTASY

The Greek word *ekstasis* signifies ''being outside oneself.'' Commonly, ecstasy is understood to involve an intense and pleasurable affective state along with a movement beyond and outside the limits of one's individuality. Its cognitive content may range from a radical ''unknowing'' to a sense of infinitely expanded knowledge. Sometimes ecstasy, as a state of maximum arousal, is contrasted to states of minimum arousal such as yoga samadhi. This distinction is not always made, however, and conditions as diverse as trance, frenzy, spirit possession, orgasm, rapture, or a quiet contemplative state of bliss may be presented as examples of ecstasy.

A given instance of ecstasy may appear spontaneous, but more often than not there has been some form of either immediate or long-term preparation; for example, meditation, fasting, physical exercises, or the ingestion of drugs. In many spiritual traditions there are elaborate ritual processes that enact an ''ascent to the heavens'' or a ''descent to the underworld,'' either of which can have an ecstatic quality and effect. Ecstatic experiences may also emerge in either the precipitating or the resolution phases of major psychological crises.

Given its many forms and the vast range of cultural and religious traditions within which they are located, it is not certain that it is possible to define ecstasy in any theoretically consistent way. Nevertheless, in recent decades much research on ecstatic phenomena has been done from the points of view of the history of religions, cultural anthropology, sociology, psychology, and ritual studies.

According to this research, ecstasy is a ''liminal'' phenomenon and this quality of taking a person beyond normal boundaries has significant sociopolitical implications in addition to the perhaps more obvious psychological and spiritual ones. In many premodern cultures, shamans—individuals gifted and trained in the practice of ecstatic liminality— have a central role of power within culture and governance. Their ecstasy is understood as a sacred way of obtaining divine guidance and approval for societal activities. In other cultures, ecstatics typically arise from among the dispossessed and marginal (often women, minorities, or those considered abnormal). In this case, public display of ecstatic behavior or claims of unique ecstatic insight may be a path to a level of prestige and power otherwise unavailable to such persons. The women mystics of medieval Europe are often cited as examples of this.

Frenzied ecstasy of a wildly dancing figure, a follower of Dionysus, god of wine, incised on the back of a bronze mirror, late 5th century B.C.

Within modern cultures, the liminality of ecstatic experience may lead to its identification with psychopathology. Indeed, some schizophrenics and others with serious mental illness have episodes of blissful or bizarre ''going beyond the self.'' Scientific research on ''altered states of consciousness'' has attempted to establish physiological correlates for ecstasy as well as other benign and pathological states. An emerging psychological perspective is that ecstasy manifests a natural and normal human potential for ultimate psychospiritual integration. This view may be bolstered by research on ''near-death experiences,'' which finds many people describing the movement into the ultimate liminal moment of death as both supremely integrating and ecstatic.

In this, a paradox becomes evident: what humans find most fearful (death) and what they find most desirable (ecstasy) are convergent. The ecstatic crossing-out of normal boundaries has an innately perilous quality. For this reason, most who have gone by this path have rooted themselves deeply in some form of spiritual tradition that provides symbols, rituals, interpretations, and companions for such a passage.

Bibliography: E. ARBMAN, *Ecstasy or Religious Trance: In the Experience of the Ecstatics and from the Psychological Point of View,* 3 v. (Stockholm 1963–1970). J. J. COLLINS and M. FISHBANE, eds. *Death, Ecstasy, and Other Worldly Journeys* (Albany, N.Y. 1995). I. CULIANU, *Expériences de l'Extase: Extase, Ascension, et Récit Visionnaire, de l'Hellénisme au Moyen Âge* (Paris 1984). M. ELIADE, *Shamanism: Archaic Techniques of Ecstasy,* tr. W. R. TRASK (Princeton, N.J. 1974). R. FISCHER, ''A Cartography of the Ecstatic and Meditative States,'' *Science* 174 (November 1971) 897–905. J. GOETZ et al., s.v. ''Extase dans les religions nonchrétiennes,'' and ''Extase: Psychologie et faits occasionels,'' *Dictionnaire de Spiritualité* (Paris 1961) 4:2045–2072, 2171–2190. F. D. GOODMAN, *Ecstasy, Ritual, and Alternate Reality: Religion in a Pluralistic World* (Bloomington, Ind. 1988). N. G. HOLM, ed., *Religious Ecstasy* (Stockholm 1982). I. M. LEWIS, *Ecstatic Religion: An Anthropological Study of Spirit Possession and Shamanism* (New York 1989). F. VAUGHN and R. WALSH, *Paths beyond Ego: The Transpersonal Vision* (Los Angeles 1993).

[M. FROHLICH]

ECSTASY (IN CHRISTIAN MYSTICISM)

A concomitant but temporary mystical phenomenon that normally accompanies the prayer of ecstatic union and disappears when the soul enters upon the transforming union. As an external phenomenon it consists in a gentle and progressive swooning that terminates in the total alienation of the senses. The ecstatic person does not hear or see anything and the face is usually radiant, as if the individual has been transported to a scene of great beauty and joy.

A trance or swoon could conceivably be caused by diabolical influence. More common, presumably, is the state of absorption and rapture induced by natural psychological causes and not necessarily associated with religious experience. These conditions are sometimes called ecstasy by reason of the similarity of the external phenomena. This article, however, is concerned only with truly supernatural ecstasy, which always presupposes the elevation of the soul to intimate union with God and its consequent detachment from the sensible world. It admits of two forms: prophetic ecstasy and mystical ecstasy. Prophetic ecstasy is a CHARISM, or *gratia gratis data,* and is therefore not within the normal or concomitant phenomena of the mystical state. It may be given even to one in the state of mortal sin, for it is given by God as an illumination of the intellect so that the individual may transmit a message to others. The ecstasy occurs only as a means of binding the other faculties lest they disturb or misinterpret the message given by God.

Mystical ecstasy, on the other hand, is a truly concomitant phenomenon of the mystical state, and especially of the higher grades of infused contemplation; it therefore enters into the normal activity of mystical prayer, but only for a time. The essential note of mystical ecstasy is the elevation of the soul to God, the soul's awareness of its union with God, and the resulting alienation of the internal and external senses in the ecstatic trance. The cause of mystical ecstasy is the Holy Spirit, working through His gifts, and especially through the gifts of wisdom and understanding. The ecstasy occurs because of the weakness of the body and its powers to withstand the divine illumination of infused contemplation, but as the body is purified and strengthened, ecstasy no longer occurs.

St. Thomas Aquinas distinguished three degrees of ecstasy: suspension of the external senses alone; suspension of both the external and internal senses; direct contemplation of the divine essence (ST 2a2ae, 175. 3 ad 1). Mystical ecstasy may be gentle and delightful, or it may be violent and painful. The delightful ecstasy is called simple ecstasy; the painful and violent ecstasy is called seizure, flight of the spirit, or rapture (see St. Teresa of Avila, *Interior Castle, Sixth Mansions,* ch. 5; St. John of the Cross, *Dark Night,* 2.1–2).

Bibliography: M. DE GOEDT, et al., s.v. ''Extase dans le mystique chrétienne,'' *Dictionnaire de Spiritualité* (Paris 1961) 4:2072–2171. A. FARGES, *Mystical Phenomena Compared with Their Human and Diabolical Counterfeits,* tr. S. P. JACQUES (London 1926). J. MARÉCHAL, *Studies in the Psychology of the Mystics,* tr. A. THOROLD (London 1927). B. MCGINN, *The Presence of God: A History of Western Christian Mysticism,* 5 v. (New York 1991–). A. POULAIN, *The Graces of Interior Prayer,* tr. L. L. YORKE SMITH (St. Louis 1950). E. SCHOLL, ''Going Beyond Oneself: *Excessus mentis* and *raptus,*'' *Cistercian Studies* 31 (1996) 273–286. TERESA OF AVILA, *The Book of Her Life,* tr. K. KAVANAUGH and O. RODRIGUEZ, 2d ed. (Washington, D.C. 1987), ch. 18–21; *The Interior Castle,* tr. K. KAVANAUGH and O. RODRIGUEZ (Washington, D.C. 1979). E. UNDERHILL, *Mysticism: A Study in the Nature and Development of Man's Spiritual Consciousness* (Cleveland 1955).

[J. AUMANN]

ECSTASY (IN THE BIBLE)

Etymologically and literally the word ecstasy (from the Gr. ἔκστασις) indicates a displacement; in the sense here intended it means a psychic displacement and designates a state in which some normal functions are suspended and in which the consciousness is absorbed in emotional or mystic experience. The noun ἔκστασις is derived from the verb ἐξίστημι, to displace, drive one out of one's senses, lose one's senses. Both the verb and the noun occur in both the Septuagint translation of the OT and in the NT, though sometimes in the attenuated sense of simple amazement over some wonderful deed. However, the state of ecstasy may be present even when these words do not occur. In the OT ecstasy is sometimes indicated when it is said that the Spirit of the Lord came upon someone (Nm 11.25; 24.2; 1 Sm 10.6, 10; 19.20; 2 Kgs 3.15; Ez 3.14; 11.24), when Ezechiel is ''led forth'' by the Spirit (Ez 11.24; 37.1), and, in some cases, when an individual is said to ''behave like a PROPHET'' (*hitnabbē'*, as in Nm 11.25; 1 Sm 10.5–6, 10, 13; 19.20). It would seem that in many of the OT examples the trancelike state is induced, at least partially, through natural means, such as the rhythm of liturgical dancing and singing. Thus, the group of prophets that Saul met coming down from a high place (where worship was offered in those early days) and in whose company he fell into a trance were carrying several kinds of musical instruments (1 Sm 10.5); it is said quite explicitly that Elisae (Elisha) employed a minstrel to bring on a prophetic trance (2 Kgs 3.15). False prophets are accused of using intoxicants to induce ecstasy (Is 28.7; see also Mi 2.11). Religious frenzy is found also among non-Israelites (Nm 24.2; 16; 1 Kgs 18.26–29) and may even have been introduced into Israel through foreign influence. This does not mean, however, that the phenomenon need be considered a purely natural happening when found in the authentic spokesmen of Israel; just as covenant, law, and kingship, although they originated outside of Israel, took on a unique aspect in Israel because they became the vehicle of the revelation of God's will and the accomplishment of His plan, so it was with prophetic ecstasy.

In the NT, Jesus is depicted as experiencing a kind of ecstasy at key moments such as his baptism (Mk 1.9–11) and his transfiguration (Mk 9.2–8). Ecstatic visions or trances befall Zechariah (Lk 1.67–69), Stephen (Acts 7.55), Peter (Acts 10.10; 11.5), and John (Rev 1.10). At Pentecost the gathered disciples are dramatically possessed by the Holy Spirit (Acts 2.2–4). The most important NT ecstatic figure, however, is Paul. Luke clearly presents Paul's conversion and other key events in his life as ecstatic (Acts 9.3–19; 16.9–10; 18.9–10; 22.17–21; 26.12–19). Most importantly, Paul's description in 2 Cor 12.1–4 of a man ''caught up to the third heaven'' where he ''heard things that cannot be told'' almost certainly refers to himself. In the latter text and elsewhere, Paul employs imagery and language strongly reminiscent of the depiction of ''heavenly journeys'' in the Jewish mysticism and apocalypticism of his time. This suggests that he may not have been innocent of training in practices that encouraged ecstasy. In 1 Corinthians, however, Paul exhibits a somewhat ambivalent attitude toward the ecstatic phenomena that were prevalent there, making a point of distinguishing the trance-like condition of the tongues-speakers from the prophets' ability to control their expressions (1 Cor 14). In both OT and NT, then, ecstatic phenomena may or may not be signs of possession by the Spirit of the true God; a key element of discernment is whether or not they function to create holiness, good order, and loving community in the relations of the people of God among themselves and with their neighbors.

Bibliography: T. CALLAN, ''Prophecy and Ecstasy in Greco-Roman Religion and in 1 Corinthians,'' *Novum Testamentum* 27 (1985) 125–140. W. GRUDEM, *The Gift of Prophecy in 1 Corinthians* (Washington, D.C. 1982). P. MICHAELSON, ''Ecstasy and Possession in Ancient Israel: A Review of Some Recent Contributions,'' *Scandinavian Journal of the Old Testament* 2 (1989) 28–54. A. F. SEGAL, ''Paul and Ecstasy,'' *Society of Biblical Literature Seminar Papers* 25 (Atlanta 1986). R. R. WILSON, ''Prophecy and Ecstasy: A Reexamination,'' *Journal of Biblical Literature* 98 (1979) 321–337; *Prophecy and Society in Ancient Israel* (Philadelphia 1980).

[M. R. E. MASTERMAN/M. FROHLICH]

ECUADOR, THE CATHOLIC CHURCH IN

A South American nation that takes its name from its geographical position on the equator, the Republic of Ecuador is bordered on the north by Colombia, on the east and south by Peru and on the west by the Pacific Ocean. Formed of a rim of coastal land, two humps of the Andes, and an area of green jungle of unknown size and unsurveyed resources called the Eastern Zone, Ecuador also includes the Galápagos Islands. The coastal plain to the west rises to a highlands region known as the sierra and then falls to rolling hills overtaken by jungle vegetation. Cotopaxi, a mountain located south of Quito in the Andes, is the tallest active volcano in the world.

Natural resources in Ecuador include petroleum reserves, timber, fish and hydropower, while agricultural production consists of bananas, coffee, cocoa, rice, plantains and sugarcane, as well as the raising of livestock. El Niño's effect on agricultural production coupled with unstable oil prices sent the economy into a tailspin during the late 1990s, but hopes were that rising oil prices would aid the new government in stabilizing Ecuador's financial situation in the next decade.

Colonial Period. Europeans first entered Ecuador with Francisco Pizarro in 1531 when he was travelling along the coast on his way to conquer Peru. While Pizarro moved to plunder Cajamarca, Peru, in 1532, the commander of his rear guard, Sebastián de Benalcázar, moved on the Incan kingdom of Quito. Although Pizarro intended that the lieutenant should also found a city there, Benalcázar left in pursuit of gold and emeralds rumored to be near Popayán. Flemish Franciscans, led by Jodoco RICKE, who had been the chaplains of the Benalcázar column, remained in a small settlement called San Miguel

Capital: Quito.
Size: 104,505 sq. miles.
Population: 12,920,090 in 2000.
Languages: Spanish; Quecha and other Amerindian languages are also spoken.
Religions: 12,274,000 Catholics (95%); 387,600 Protestants (3%); 258,490 practice native religions.

de Quito, located near the present city of Quito. In December of 1534 the city of San Francisco de Asís de Quito was founded with 203 Spanish *vecinos* and two African servants. Guayaquil was begun the following year.

Several groups of religious soon made the new city their home. The Franciscans transferred their residence from San Miguel to San Francisco de Quito early in 1535; the Mercedarians established a friary in Quito friary in April 1537; and the Dominicans who also accompanied Benalcázar to the area established their residence there in June of 1541. The Augustinians began to construct their friary in Quito in the summer of 1573, while the Jesuits arrived in July 1586. As was natural, the first missionaries to enter the new territory selected the best spots in which to work. The Franciscans, drawing on their experience in Mexico, quickly spread out among the sierra tribes and were soon teaching almost two-thirds of the people in that area, including the famous Otavalo natives. The Mercedarians undertook organized work among the tribes of the coast, especially in the provinces of Manabí, Puná and Esmeraldas. The Dominicans, arriving in early 1541, finding Gonzalo Pizarro's expedition to the Land of the Cinnamon in the planning stages, sent one of their number, Fray Gaspar de CARVAJAL, along as one of the chaplains. Carvajal wrote an account of the discovery of the Amazon River, and the Dominicans remained to work among the tribes of the Ecuadorean jungle.

Central to each order's task of evangelizing the native people was the establishment of a school, most of which provided a free elementary-level education. The Franciscans, under Jodoco Ricke and inspired by Pedro de GANTE, founded in Quinto the Colegio de San Andrés in 1551, the first school to teach fine arts in Quito and a dominant influence on artists as far away as Colombia and Bolivia. More importantly, perhaps, the Colegio taught natives how to plow, harvest and care for domesticated livestock. In 1603 the Augustinians established the first faculty of theology in the University of San Fulgencio, while in 1622 the Jesuits of Quito opened the doors of the University of San Gregorio Magno, which specialized in the humanities and noted among its graduates such men as Juan de Velasco y Petroche, Eugenio de Santa Cruz y Espejo, and General Ignacio de Escandón. In the late 17th century the Dominicans opened the University of San Fernando, which would evolve into Santo Tomás, the first university in Quito to teach medicine, mathematics and civil jurisprudence. Among its graduates were José Joaquín Olmedo, Coronel Juan de Salinas and José Mejía Lequerica. In 1754 the Jesuits introduced the first printing press in their residence at Ambato.

Diocesan Organization. On Jan. 8, 1545, Pope Paul III erected the Diocese of Quito and named the chaplain of Francisco Pizarro, D. García Díaz Arias, as the first bishop. Díaz Arias was succeeded by another exemplary bishop, the learned Dominican Pedro de la Peña, consecrated in 1565. Although a zealous priest and a trained canonist, Peña's work was cut out for him. In an effort to organize the diocese, he visited his entire territory and in 1570 convoked the first diocesan synod, during which he outlined the basic laws and responsibilities, while at the same time, taking from the friars some native parishes which were then given to the diocesan clergy. During a second *visita*, Peña went in to the jungles to confirm the work of the synod and also to stabilize the reductions of the natives, thus founding most of the towns of modern Ecuador. He died in 1583.

Another outstanding community leader was Bishop Alonso de la PEÑA MONTENEGRO (d. 1687), who is considered the founder of Quinto's Christian economy. In his *Itinerario para párrocos*, the bishop furnished not only the usual instructions for his priests, but also established norms for the payment of indemnities incurred by employees while at work, a just wage, the shortening of the work for the natives on the haciendas; he even set down rules of basic hygiene. Notable, too, was the development of a guild system under the aegis of the Church that protected the rights and health of the workers. Some of these guilds continued to exist into the late 20th century, although diminished in influence.

After the evangelization of the natives living along the coast and in the sierra was completed, missionaries turned to the natives of the headwaters of the Amazon, a far more risky endeavor. In 1563 the Crown established a royal *audiencia* at Quito, practically coterminous with the bishopric of the same name. As the missions spread, so did the territory of Quito, and modern Ecuador. The Dominicans who had accompanied the expedition of Gonzalo Pizarro remained in the area, while the Mercedarians, Franciscans and Jesuits entered it in the late 16th century. While the Franciscans were moderately successful, especially after the foundation of the Mission College of Popayán, the work of the Jesuits was far more significant. Maynas—an area stretching along the courses of the upper Amazon down to the Solimões and well into eastern Peru along the Ucayali and Huallaga Rivers—became the mission field of such workers as Rafael Ferrer, Francisco de Figueroa and Samuel FRITZ. Unfortunately the Brazilians frequently raided the missions of the Solimões, and in 1767 the Quito Jesuits were expelled by the Crown from the remaining areas. In a subsequent decree, the Crown would entrust these missions to the Franciscan Mission College of Ocopa under the jurisdiction of the archbishop of Lima and the viceroy of Peru. From this move Peru gained almost two-thirds of its present territory and Quito, which had governed the area for almost two centuries, retained only the memory of past dominion.

Revolutionary Period. By the end of the 18th century Quito had become a center of intellectual and political fermentation. Bishop José Pérez Calama (1790–92), friend and mentor of Father HIDALGO of Mexico, helped to reorganize the studies of the Dominican University of Santo Tomás in accord with the new philosophy. Santa Cruz y Espejo was spreading his political ideas of complete emancipation while the friars, restless under the *ALTERNATIVA*, longed for the day when they could enjoy free elections. José Joaquín de Olmedo was formulating the projects that would make him famous at the Cortes of Cádiz. Energized by new ideas, the Catholics in Quito were among the first to call out for independence from Spain. The first freedom manifesto was launched on Aug. 10, 1809, in the Quito Augustinian friary. Declaring the region independent of Spain, the bishop of Quito, José de CUERO Y CAICEDO, was elected vice president of the first patriotic junta, and later president. Priests and friars served as the first legislators and the first draft of a constitution was written by a priest, Miguel Rodríguez, disciple of Santa Cruz y Espejo.

Unfortunately, this very first attempt was to presage the fate in store for the Church before independence was ultimately won. The bishop of neighboring Cuenca (erected in 1769), a fanatical royalist, actively persecuted the patriotic priests of his own diocese and also sheltered the royalist priestly sympathizers of Quito. As the fortunes of the civil war swayed to and fro, Cuero y Caicedo was driven from Quito, and other nationalist leaders soon followed. The powers of Church leaders forced to flee the country were exercised by vicars who were no more able to maintain a neutral position than their bishops had been. Royalist opponents simply appointed a new vicar when they came to power so that at one time Cuenca had three vicars, each representing a different political faction and each persecuting the followers of the others. Ongoing military operations only added to the confusion and ruin. On May 24, 1822, the royalists were defeated on the slopes of Mt. Pichincha by Colombian forces that simply annexed the *audiencia* of Ecuador, forming Gran Colombia from Ecuador, Colombia and Venezuela. In 1830 increasing chaos prompted General Juan José Flores, a Venezuelan mestizo and commander of the Colombian army in Ecuador, to declare Ecuador independent.

Archdioceses	Suffragans
Cuenca	Azogues, Loja, Machala.
Guayaquil	Babahoyo.
Portoviejo	Santo Domingo de los Colorados.
Quito	Ambato, Guaranda, Ibarra, Latacunga, Riobamba, Tulacán.

There are apostolic vicariates at Aguarico, Esmeraldas, Méndez, Napo, Puyo, San Miguel de Sucumbíos, and Zamora as well as an apostolic prefecture at Galápagos. The region also contains a military ordinariate.

Independent Ecuador. Previously subject either to Lima or Bogotá, in 1822 the *audiencia* of Quito entered a state of independence lacking any real sense of national consciousness. Without trained corps of political administrators or fixed boundaries, the new nation relied on the Church as the sole cohesive force. While political leaders were forced, from necessity, to use the Church and its institutions, they also felt constrained to bend it to the will of the state. The instrument of this control was the highly regalistic constitution of 1824. Under this document, all Church appointments originated with the state. The state also dictated what textbooks could be used in the seminaries. No Church decrees, not even the decisions of a bishop's court, could be executed unless they had first been ''revised'' by a state-appointed lawyer.

Perhaps the most insidious means adopted by the state to ruin the Church was the application of the *recurso de fuerza* to churchmen. In colonial Spain, the legal codes provided that anyone who felt his rights infringed upon had recourse to the civil courts, or fuerza. During this recourse whatever was causing the injury, whether a decree or some action of another, had to stop until the court arrived at a decision. Following independence, if a priest did not like an order from his ecclesiastical superior, or if a friar or nun was displeased with an order from his or her superior, recourse to the civil court was not only admitted but required, thereby nullifying Church authority. In Ecuador another wrinkle was added: if some person connected with the Church believed his or her superior to be withholding some merited promotion, recourse to civil courts could also be used to force the superior to divulge the reasons for the lack of such promotion. To compound the problem, the state frequently refused to fill vacant sees. Thus Cuenca went without a bishop from 1827 to 1841; Guayaquil, erected a bishopric in 1838,

went without a bishop for ten years; and even Quito frequently suffered lapses of up to five years between bishops, although relations had been restored with the Holy See in 1836.

Under the new constitution the Church became the slave of the state and enthusiasm among the clergy consequently declined. Yet, despite this, the religious remained the best teachers in Ecuador and their schools were crowded.

Another threat to the Church came from Protestant pastors, especially Anglicans and Presbyterians from Great Britain. The Protestants were given full liberty of operation and when Bishop Arteta of Quito protested, he and his diocesan advisers were each fined 2,000 pesos.

The only effective voice of protest was that of Vicente SOLANO, a Franciscan who began a journalistic campaign in defense of the Church in 1828 and persisted until his death in 1865. While in no way subtle, a careful reading of Solano's works showed that he was in many ways far ahead of his times, especially in his judicious assessment of revolutionary leader Simon Bolívar, the *evils* of militarism and the *patronato,* a tradition allowing the government to choose Church leaders. While Solano defended the Church, Gabriel García Moreno (d. 1875) defended the people of Ecuador from the forces corrupting his country. He opened negotiations with the Holy See that led to the concordat of 1866, welcomed the first papal representative to Ecuador, installed good bishops such as CHECA Y BARBA and YEROVI, erected the dioceses of Ibarra, Bolívar, Loja and Portoviejo, reformed the religious orders, and recruited orders to undertake the education of Ecuador's young people. Moreno was largely responsible for encouraging the Daughters of Charity to staff the nation's hospitals and the Redemptorists to assist in teaching the natives.

Between 1875 and 1895 the Church continued to enjoy the protection of the state on the whole. New orders were invited to enter the country—the Salesians entering Ecuador in 1888—and in 1884 Julio María Matovalle founded the Association of Catholic Youth, a forerunner of Catholic Action. Although peace and harmony prevailed, tendencies toward liberalism were present, such as the presidential decree of 1891 that terminated the Church tithe and substituted a three percent tax on landed property. Alerted by such government actions, in June of 1892 Ecuador's bishops issued their manifesto on liberalism, a document generally regarded as one of the most notable of its kind.

The Modern Church and the State. In 1895, after a series of scandals by the conservative leadership, the Liberals came to power in the person of Eloy Alfaro, a friend of Juan Montalvo. For the next 15 years Alfaro became the dominant personality in the country, as Moreno had been previously, and the religious face of Ecuador was changed. The concordat with the Holy See was broken; foreign religious orders were forbidden to enter the country and, for a time, even individual foreign priests were excluded; education was placed under complete state control; the property tax was abolished without restoring the tithe; the old law of 1824 of the *patronato* was restored; and the consecration of the country to the Sacred Heart was officially revoked. In 1904 religious were forbidden to administer their own property and four years later it was confiscated without compensation. In 1906 complete separation of Church and state was decreed with a guarantee of religious liberty; however the Catholic Church was discriminated against and denied the right of incorporation before the law. In 1902 marriage had become a civil ceremony; in 1910 divorce was permitted by mutual consent. The legalization of divorce, as well as a 1935 decree declaring the Church to be without legal representation or protection, caused a near revolution, and the government was forced to negotiate with Rome for a new understanding.

Catholic University of Ecuador residence hall.

On July 24, 1937 a modus vivendi was signed between the Holy See and Ecuador that settled many of the main difficulties and ushered in a period of harmony. Diplomatic representation was resumed after a lapse of more than 40 years, the Church was permitted legal representation under certain circumstances, religious were paid a small amount in compensation for the property taken from them in 1908, and the Holy See was again allowed to appoint bishops directly after informing the government of their choice. The constitution of March 6, 1945, recognized complete separation of Church and state. It also permitted divorce even though this has since been rendered a little more difficult.

The Modern Church. Increasing poverty resulted in political upheaval throughout much of the mid-20th century, and the loss of a war with Peru in 1941 did little to improve the country's stability. José Maria Velasco Ibarra ruled the country during much of the period 1944–1972, and the constitution of 1945 was suspended by a military junta that took power in July of 1963. Oil was discovered in the region in the 1970s, although the wealth it generated did not trickle down to the poorer classes. A series of failed and often corrupt governments ended in 1988 with the election of Rodrigo Borja Cevallos, who nationalized the oil companies. A coalition government in 1992 attempted to institute free-market policies in the country, but cuts in social policies sparked discontent and resulted in the election of populist president Abdala Bucaram (known as ''El Loco'') in 1996. Despite, or perhaps because of such constant political upheaval, by the end of the 20th century the government had once again established strong ties to the Church, which was considered a stabilizing force.

Into the 21st Century. By 2000 Ecuador contained 1,109 parishes, tended by 975 diocesan and 820 religious priests, while its 300 brothers tended to institutions of learning and 4,800 sisters operated schools, hospitals and dispensaries. Education was the greatest preoccupation of the Church, and the government supported the efforts of Catholic schools, although religion was not taught in state-run schools. In addition to primary and secondary schools, the Church operated Catholic training schools

Interior of Catholic Church, with statues standing on gold leaf altar, Ecuador. (©The Purcell Team/CORBIS)

for teachers with official accreditation as well as the Catholic University of Quito.

During the 1990s Church leaders actively assisted in moderating several political standoffs. German-born Ecuadorian bishop, Emile Stehle, served as a mediator in several hostage situations involving a Marxist guerilla group active near the border with Colombia. In 1999 Church leaders aided in peace talks that resolved a border conflict with Peru that had escalated into war in January of 1995 after Ecuadorian troops invaded a northern section of Peruvian jungle territory disputed for over a century. Present at the signing of the peace accords, a representative of the Vatican expressed Pope John Paul II's appreciation for providing ''an opening to lasting peace.'' Ending the conflict allowed Ecuadorian bishops to return to addressing the humanitarian needs of a social fabric stressed by a long-running economic downturn, and criticism was leveled at President Bucaram for his decision to allocate money to foreign debt repayment rather than social programs. Bucaram was ultimately impeached on allegations of corruption in 1997 and Fabian Alarcon appointed his successor. Social issues such as abortion rights and an increase in crime due to drug trafficking continued to be addressed by Church leaders through the Latin American Bishops' Council (CELAM), although the Church's efforts to aid the government in implementing a welfare program resulted in several nonfatal bombings in 1998. Although the poverty of rural areas of Ecuador during the 1960s had provided Protestant evangelical groups with inroads to spread their faith, the Catholic Church was still the professed faith of the majority of Ecuadorians by 2000.

Bibliography: L. LINKE, *Ecuador* (3d ed. New York 1960). J. TOBAR DONOSO, *La Iglesia ecuatoriana en el siglo XIX* (Quito 1934); *La Iglesia modeladora de la nacionalidad* (Quito 1953). J. M. VARGAS, *Historia de la Iglesia en el Ecuador durante el patronato español* (Quito 1962). I. ALONSO et al., *La Iglesia en Venezuela y Ecuador* (Madrid 1962).

[A. S. TIBESAR/EDS.]

ECUMENICAL DIALOGUES

Following the Second Vatican Council, scores of international and national commissions were established to forward the work of ecumenical dialogue, usually with doctrinal questions as the focus of their concern. For the most part, these dialogues were conducted on a ''bilateral'' basis, i.e., engaging two churches or confessional families at a time. The Roman Catholic Church has been an active participant in such dialogues, serving as one of the partners in over a third of them. During the 1960s and 1970s, officially sponsored dialogues between churches or confessional families of churches became a prominent component of the movement toward Christian unity. During that time their number increased and their published reports multiplied.

Alongside the conciliar movement and other important components of the ecumenical movement, ''bilateral dialogues'' continued into the 2000s and revealed further developments of its internal dynamics. From their inception the ecumenical dialogues were aimed at the resolution of issues dividing the church through convergences reaching toward a consensus based on clearer understanding, the exchange of insights, and the discovery of new perspectives that would enable the churches to reappropriate their common Christian heritage. Implicit in this goal was the related but further purpose of moving beyond the attainment of doctrinal consensus to the translation of these agreements into an actual living communion of the churches by way of concrete expressions of church fellowship. In order for this to occur, it became increasingly clear that the findings of the dialogues had to move through a process of "reception" by the churches who sponsored them, and on to decision at appropriate levels of authority. As a preliminary to reception, the churches had to develop adequate means to review and assess the dialogue findings and to respond to them in an official way.

During the 1980s, the churches in certain cases began this new task of official response. The most striking example was provided by hundreds of official responses to the LIMA TEXT on "Baptism, Eucharist and Ministry," published in 1982 by the Faith and Order Commission of the World Council of Churches as the fruit of decades of multilateral dialogues.

Anglican-Roman Catholic dialogue. Among bilaterals, the first ANGLICAN-ROMAN CATHOLIC INTERNATIONAL COMMISSION (ARCIC) took the lead with the publication in 1981 of a final report on the work that it had begun in 1970. This marked the most advanced stage to be reached by any bilateral in which the Roman Catholics had participated. ARCIC I carried out its work in stages, publishing as it proceeded discrete reports of its findings concerning eucharistic doctrine, ministry, and ordination, and also authority in the church. Several years after each of these reports appeared, ARCIC I provided a further "elucidation" for each in which it responded to the various comments, queries, and criticisms its initial statements had provoked. All of this material, plus new material on primatial authority and infallibility, was brought together as a composite whole and submitted to the Anglican and Roman Catholic Churches in the form of "The Final Report."

Work of this significance drew comments from many Anglican and Roman Catholic quarters as it unfolded. The Congregation for the Doctrine of the Faith in Rome, as one instance, had not hesitated to offer its observations from time to time, and it did so again on the work as a whole once "The Final Report" itself was published. Such comments as were received generally focused on specific items of appreciation or critical reservation. But it was obvious that a weightier, overall assessment would also have to be made by the churches.

Thus on March 17, 1982, Johannes Cardinal Willebrands, president of the Secretariat for Promoting Christian Unity, wrote to all the episcopal conferences of the Roman Catholic Church, seeking their appraisal of the work. In his letter, the cardinal pointed out that "the process of evaluation is not one that can be carried out in a short time; the results of over ten years of dialogue call for serious study by the Church." The secretariat asked the episcopal conferences to examine the report as to whether it was consonant in substance with the faith of the Catholic Church. At the same time, Anglican authorities requested all the provinces of the Anglican Communion to undertake a similar study and to respond to a parallel, counterpart question. It was envisaged that this process of evaluation by the Anglican and Roman Catholic Communions would culminate in 1988, the year in which the Anglican bishops of the world would assemble again for a meeting of the Lambeth Conference. In the four years following this request for evaluation, approximately 20 Roman Catholic episcopal conferences submitted their responses to Rome and a similar number were submitted to the Anglican Consultative Council. The National Conference of Catholic Bishops in the United States published its response in 1984; the General Convention of the Episcopal Church in the United States issued its response in 1985. Other notable responses included those of the episcopal conferences of England and Wales, of France and of Scotland (all in 1985); and the responses of the General Synod of the Church of England and of the Church of Ireland (1986).

While this process of evaluation and response went on, the work of ecumenical dialogue between Anglicans and Roman Catholics also continued. In 1982 Pope John Paul II and the archbishop of Canterbury, His Grace, the Rt. Hon. Robert Runcie, issued a "Common Declaration," thereby establishing the second Anglican-Catholic International Commission (ARCIC II). To it they entrusted the task of continuing the work already begun with a view toward the eventual resolution of the outstanding doctrinal differences which still separated Anglicans and Roman Catholics. The new commission was also charged with the task of studying "all that hinders the mutual recognition of the ministries of our Communions, and to recommend what steps will be necessary when, on the basis of our unity in faith, we are able to proceed toward the restoration of full communion."

In July of 1985 Cardinal Willebrands wrote to the co-chairman of ARCIC II, suggesting significant ways in which progress toward this mutual recognition might be accomplished, notwithstanding the negative judgment Pope Leo XIII had reached concerning the validity of Anglican ordinations in the papal bull of 1896, *APOSTOLICAE CURAE*. The cardinal wrote:

> If at the end of this process of evaluation the Anglican Communion as such is able to state formally that it professes the same faith concerning essential matters where doctrine admits no difference and which the Roman Catholic Church also affirms are to be believed and held concerning the Eucharist and the Ordained Ministry, the Roman Catholic Church would acknowledge the possibility that in the context of such a profession of faith the texts of the (1552 Anglican) Ordinal might no longer retain that *nativa indoles* ("native charac-

> ter'') which was at the basis of Pope Leo's judgment. That is to say that, if both Communions were so clearly one in their faith concerning Eucharist and Ministry, the context of this discussion would indeed be changed. In that case such a profession of faith could open the way to a new consideration of the Ordinal (and of subsequent rites of ordination introduced in Anglican Churches), a consideration that could lead to a new evaluation by the Catholic Church of the sufficiency of these Anglican rites as far as concerns future ordinations. Such a study would be concerned with the rites in themselves, prescinding at this stage from the question of the continuity in the apostolic succession of the ordaining bishop. In our view, such a possibility . . . could do much to assist the climate of the whole discussion . . . [and] would be the strongest possible stimulus to find ways to overcome the difficulties which will hinder a mutual recognition of ministries.

In a contemporaneous exchange of letters between Pope John Paul II, the archbishop of Canterbury, and Cardinal Willebrands (December 1984 to June 1986) concerning the ordination of women, it was also agreed that this topic should continue to remain a matter of discussion in the Anglican–Roman Catholic dialogue, with the most immediate question being how the ordination of women in some parts of the Anglican Communion affects progress toward fuller communion between it and the Roman Catholic Church.

As the agenda for dialogue thus continued to expand, ARCIC II in 1986 completed work on its first report, entitled ''Salvation and the Church,'' and published it in 1987. This report focused on the relation of the doctrine of salvation to faith, to JUSTIFICATION, to good works, and to the doctrine of the Church. ARCIC II also produced ''Church as Communion'' (1988), ''Life in Christ: Morals, Communion and the Church'' (1994), and ''The Gift of Authority,'' (1999). Being at the most advanced stage of all ecumenical relations in which the Roman Catholic Church is engaged, the bilateral relationship with the Anglican Communion clearly displayed the characteristics that could come to mark other bilateral dialogues later in the 1980s and 1990s. First, doctrine remained at the heart of the dialogue, though the emphasis gradually shifted from the overcoming of past doctrinal disputes toward setting forth a common profession of the faith. Second, as the findings of dialogue mounted and achieved a certain ''critical mass,'' they called forth serious evaluation and official response from the churches engaged in them. In 1991, the Holy See published its evaluation of the *Final Report*. By 1994 clarifications of some of the questions raised in this response enabled Cardinal Edward Cassidy, then president of the Pontifical Council for Promoting Christian Unity, to say that ''no further work'' was necessary at this time on the themes of Eucharist and ministry.

Third, the agenda of the dialogue was extended to include consideration of concrete steps that could be taken by the churches to effect new and further degrees of actual ecclesial communion between them. In the final stage, the churches would need to find ways to authorize and ratify such steps, thus actualizing a fuller church unity.

Other bilateral dialogues. A number of other dialogues conducted at the international level appeared as though they might move in a similar direction to that taken by the Anglican-Roman Catholic relations. Several have continued to exhibit a wide-ranging survey quality, with discussions touching on numerous subjects and sometimes uncovering important findings in one area or another. They seemed to be in the process of accumulating particular agreements, which over time could coalesce into a whole requiring the response of the churches. An example of such a particular agreement, in this case concerning the Eucharist, is found in the 1977 report of the dialogue co-sponsored by the Holy See and the World Alliance of Reformed Churches. Entitled ''The Presence of Christ in the Church and the World,'' this report surveyed five major areas: Christ's relationship to the church; the teaching authority of the church; the presence of Christ in the world; the Eucharist; and the ministry. Phase II of this dialogue was initiated in 1984, taking up a similarly broad theme: ''The Church: The People of God, the Body of Christ, the Temple of the Spirit.'' Under this theme the bilateral commission investigated such questions as whether there is a God-given structure to the church and prepared a common affirmation of the sole mediatorship of Christ.

The commission that the Holy See co-sponsored with the World Methodist Council (WMC) also set its work in wide parameters. Its reports were timed to coincide with the quinquennial meeting of the WMC and named for the sites in which these meetings were held. Thus after its initial Denver report (1971) and subsequent Dublin report (1976), it went on to issue the Honolulu report in 1981 and the Nairobi report in 1986. The two earlier reports had a certain omnibus quality, providing an overall view of matters of common interest and concern to Methodists and Catholics. The two that followed were more thematically organized. The theme of the Honolulu report was ''Toward an Agreed Statement on the Holy Spirit.'' It took up such matters as: the work of the Holy Spirit; the Holy Spirit, Christian experience and authority; Christian moral decisions; and Christian marriage. The Nairobi report was entitled ''Towards a Statement on the Church'' and dealt with: the nature of the church;

church and sacraments; the call to unity; ways of being one church; structures of ministry; and the Petrine office. This dialogue has produced ''The Apostolic Tradition'' (1991), ''The Word of Life: A Statement on Revelation and Faith'' (1996), and ''Speaking the Truth in Love'' (2001).

The Disciples of Christ-Roman Catholic Dialogue also carried out its work on a five-year basis, completing a series of annual meetings in 1981 with the issuance of an ''Agreed Account'' of the work done. The sessions, in sequence, were devoted to the following: the nature of the church and elements of its unity; baptism; gift and call in the search for unity; faith and tradition in the life of the church; the dynamics of unity and division; and apostolicity and catholicity in the visible unity of the church. A second five-year series of annual sessions began in 1983 with discussion more tightly focused on the single overall theme, ''The Church as Koinonia in Christ.''

The Pentecostal-Roman Catholic Conversations carried out six series of meeting, issuing a ''Final Report'' at the end of the first five. The first of these reports dealt with subjects such as baptism in the Holy Spirit, Christian initiation and the gifts, public worship and the gifts, prayer, and praise. The second dealt with speaking in tongues, faith and experience, Scripture and Tradition, Tradition and traditions, perspectives on Mary, ministry in the church, ordination, apostolic succession, and recognition of ministries. The third dealt with understandings of *Koinonia*. The fourth provided a text ''Evangelization, Proselytism and Common Witness.''

The Evangelical-Roman Catholic Dialogue on Mission held sessions from 1977 to 1984 and published its report under the overall theme of ''mission.'' The following subjects were addressed: revelation and authority; the nature of mission; the gospel of salvation; response in the Holy Spirit—the church—and the gospel; the gospel and culture; and the possibilities of common witness. This last topic was also the subject of a major report on ''Common Witness'' published in 1981 by the Joint Working Group of the World Council of Churches and the Holy See. This study document explored the common ground that enables Christian witness to be a common witness and also discussed occasions and possibilities for the realization of common witness.

Note also must be taken of two international commissions founded in the 1980s that demonstrate the still expanding circle of bilateral dialogues. The International Theological Colloquium between Baptists and Catholics began a five-year series of annual sessions in 1984 under the general theme ''Our Common Witness to the World.'' It was conducted under the auspices of the Baptist World Alliance and the Holy See. The goal of these sessions was set as a mutual understanding of similarities and differences in Baptist and Roman Catholic doctrinal, ecclesial, pastoral, and mission concerns.

The International Catholic-Orthodox Theological Commission was established by the Holy See and 14 autocephalous Orthodox Churches and began its work in 1980. Its first report, published in 1982, ''The Mystery of the Church and the Eucharist in the Light of the Most Holy Trinity'' was followed by a discussion of the sacraments of Christian initiation, reported in ''Faith, Sacraments and the Unity of the Church'' (1987), and by a discussion of ''The Sacrament of Order (Ordination) in the Sacramental Structure of the Church, with Particular Reference to the Importance of Apostolic Succession for the Sanctification and Unity of the People of God'' (1988). The dialogue produced ''Uniatism: Method of Union of the Past, and the Present Search for Full Communion'' (1993).

Even in a review summary such as this, the several dialogues reveal interesting differences in the themes they select and the way they elaborate them. In many cases, it appears that these differences reflect the historical traditions of thought and teaching brought to the bilaterals by the partner churches along with their particular preoccupations. At the same time, there are certain similarities among the dialogues about which it is possible to generalize. It can be observed that many of these bilaterals were engaged in a survey of the ecumenical terrain and took a broad avenue of approach. Rather than focusing sharply on one or another major neuralgic issue, they explored numerous points at issue, sometimes quite insightfully but not with the intent of providing exhaustive, systematic treatments. Their reports underscored the principles on which agreement could be based and were selective in treating specific details. They are generally succinct in the statement of their findings. Many have not yet drawn their findings together into composite and coherent wholes demanding evaluation and official response by the sponsoring churches. Neither have they, for the most part, advanced specific proposals for action by the churches that would create new degrees of church fellowship. Rather they appear to lay a part of the foundation on which in the future such proposals could rest.

Lutheran-Catholic dialogues. The U.S. Lutheran-Catholic Dialogue, which engendered 11 volumes of scholarly studies along with its reports was something of an exception to these generalizations. So, too, was the International Lutheran-Roman Catholic Joint Commission in its pursuit of a distinctive course. This joint commission was established in 1973 by the Lutheran World Foundation and the Holy See and completed its first period of work in 1984. Unlike ARCIC and the U.S. Lutheran-Catholic Dialogue, it did not in this period broach the topics of primatial authority, teaching authority, infallibility, or justification by faith. These important matters remain on the agenda. It did issue three briefer statements: ''Ways to Community'' (1980–81), ''All Under One Christ'' (1980, marking the 450th anniversary of the Augsburg Confession), and ''Martin Luther: Witness to Jesus Christ'' (1983, marking the 500th anniversary of the birth of the Reformer). In addition to these it produced three book length reports: ''The Eucharist'' (1978) ''The Ministry in the Church'' (1981), and ''The Church and Justification,'' (1993). It took up and advanced ecumenical discussion on these pivotal subjects that engage every bilateral at some point. In another major report it undertook a task that no prior dialogue had ever attempted. In ''Facing Unity: Models, Forms and Phases of Catholic-Lutheran Church Fellowship'' (1985) it sought to set forth in some detail an integral process whereby through mutual acts of recognition and mutual exchange the churches could advance toward the community of professed faith, a common sacramental life, and unified structures of decision-making and pastoral ministry. In significant ways the joint commission grounded its proposals for the future on models of church life drawn from the ancient church. In doing so it hoped its proposals would obviate the pitfalls encountered by some other models and forms of church union, many of which it reviewed. It also hoped its proposals would combine essential values found in congregational and episcopal forms of church order. This dialogue also moved from dialogue to authoritative decision by proposing a *Joint Declaration on the Doctrine of Justification*. This text was not itself a dialogue, but a formal distilation of the results of the dialogues on this theme. It was evaluated by the member churches of the Lutheran World Federation and by the Holy See. In 1998 the two communities agreed on the content of the *Joint Declaration,* and the formal signing took place on October 31, 1999 in Augsburg, Germany. This process demonstrates another level of church decision making bringing the two churches into a deeper level of communion.

In a particular way this last named *Joint Declaration* signaled the fact that as shared ecumenical research began to meet the challenges of past divisions, so shared ecumenical imagination must strive to meet the needs of the Christian future.

See Also: FAITH AND ORDER COMMISSION.

Bibliography: J. F. PUGLISI and S. J. VOICU, *A Bibliography of Interchurch and Interreligious Theological Dialogues* (Rome 1984); *First Supplement* (Rome 1985); *Second Supplement* (Rome 1986). H. MEYER and L. VISCHER, eds., *Growth in Agreement: Reports and Agreed Statements of Ecumenical Conversations on a World Level* (New York/Geneva 1984). W. RUSCH, H. MEYER, and J. GROS, eds., *Growth in Agreement II,* (Geneva 2000). J. GROS and J. BURGESS, eds., *Building Unity* (New York 1989). J. BURGESS, and J. GROS, eds., *Growing Consensus* (New York 1995).

[J. F. HOTCHKIN]

ECUMENICAL DIRECTORY

The full title of the ''Ecumenical Directory'' is Directory for the Application of Principles and Norms on Ecumenism. It was approved by Pope John Paul II on March 25, 1993 and published on June 8 by the Pontifical Council for Promoting Christian Unity as a general executive decree of the universal Catholic Church. It supplants the Directory for the Application of the Decisions of the Second Vatican Council Concerning Ecumenical Matters, issued during the pontificate of Pope Paul VI.

Development of the Ecumenical Directory. When the archbishop of Rouen, J. M. Martin, presented the draft of the Decree on Ecumenism (*Unitatis redintegratio*) to the Second Vatican Council, he promised that it would be followed by a directory explaining in greater detail the application of its decisions. The Secretariat for Promoting Christian Unity, charged with the task of making good on this promise, produced the Directory in stages. In 1967 Pope Paul VI ordered the publication of Part I of the Directory, and in 1970 he approved Part II. The first called for setting up ecumenical commissions in Catholic dioceses and episcopal conferences. It addressed the validity of baptism conferred in other churches and ecclesial communities, the fostering of spiritual ecumenism, and the sharing of spiritual resources (prayer, worship, and sacraments) with other Christians. The second par addressed ''Ecumenism in Higher Education'' and, in a particular way, in theological faculties and colleges.

The publication of the new Code of Canon Law in 1983 prompted a revision and updating of the Directory. Addressing the Roman Curia in 1985, John Paul II said:

> Every particular church, every bishop, ought to have solicitude for unity and ought to promote the ecumenical movement. The new Code of Canon Law recently promulgated recalled this in a clearer than usual fashion, because it is a matter of Christ's will (Canon 755). But the church of Rome and its bishop have to attend to this care in a quite special way. . . . It is therefore useful that in the field of ecumenism we take a look at the path which we have so far covered in the direction of unity and draw from its enlivening spirit. Among the initiatives taken within the Catholic Church I recall first of all the Ecumenical Directory. . . . This directory will need to be progressively updated in coming months, account being taken of the new Code of Canon Law and the

progress of the ecumenical movement which the directory is directly intended to serve.

Once begun, it became evident that a revision of the existing directory would not be enough. A new directory that would encompass a wider scope, be more specific and concrete, and recognize the significant diversity found among the particular churches was called for. The new directory had the same aim as its predecessor, namely, the advancement of Vatican II's ecumenical vision of the Church, but it was a difficult challenge. As John Paul II remarked ''it is impossible to translate perfectly into canonical language the conciliar image of the Church'' though that image must always be referred to as the ''primary pattern'' that canonical language ought to ''express insofar as it can'' (*Sacrae disciplinae leges,* 1983).

Outline of the Directory. The directory is addressed first to the bishops of the Catholic Church and, through them, to all the faithful, and to members of other churches and ecclesial bodies who, ''it is hoped,'' will find it useful. The first of its five parts reaffirms the commitment of the Catholic Church to ecumenism based on the principles of the Second Vatican Council, and explains that a real and certain communion bonds the Catholic Church with other Christian churches and ecclesial communities. It emphasizes the duty of all Christians to work and pray that division be healed and overcome. Part two describes the structures, beginning with the Pontifical Council for Promoting Christianity Unity, diocesan officers, and other personnel within the Catholic Church, that are charged with promoting ecumenism. Part three deals with the aims and methods of inspiring Catholics, especially those engaged in pastoral work, with an ecumenical outlook. It identifies categories of people who are to be formed, as well as theological faculties, catechetical institutes, and other centers that must accept the responsibility for this formation. Part four expands on the communion that exists among Christians on the basis of their common baptism. This section describes various ways that Christians share in prayer, worship, and other spiritual activities. Part four also incorporates new guidelines on mixed marriages. Part five speaks of various forms of ecumenical cooperation, dialogue and common witness, and the principles that should guide ecumenical activities. It singles out Bible study, the adoption of common liturgical texts, ecumenical cooperation in catechesis, collaborative research, and collaboration in social and cultural programs.

Pope John Paul II has cited the Directory for the Application of Principles and Norms on Ecumenism on several occasions. It is clear from his 1995 encyclical *Ut unum sint* that he sees the directory as providing both the inspiration and framework for ecumenism in the Catholic Church.

Bibliography: ''Directory for the Application of the Decisions of the Second Vatican Council concerning Ecumenical Matters, Ad Totam Ecclesiam (14 May 1967) in Vatican Council II,'' *The Conciliar and Postconciliar Documents,* ed. A. FLANNERY, (Northport, N.Y. 1987), 483–501. *Directory for the Application of Principles and Norms on Ecumenism,* 25 March 1993 (Vatican City 1993). Also U.S. Catholic Conference Publishing Services (Washington, D.C. 1993); *Origins* 23:9 (29 July 1993): 129; 131–160; *L'Osservatore Romano* (16 June 1993): i-xvii. For the text of *Ut unum sint,* see *Acta Apostolica Sedis* 87 (1995): 921–982.

[J. F. HOTCHKIN]

ECUMENICAL MOVEMENT

The word ''ecumenical'' is derived from the Greek word *oikumene,* meaning the whole of the inhabited world (Acts 17.6; Mt 24.14; Heb 2.5). In traditional Catholic usage it means a general or universal council of the Church. In the 20th century, ecumenical has come to designate the movement that seeks to overcome the scandal of divisions and achieve reconciliation among all Christians. This article deals primarily with the Catholic perspectives and approaches toward the ecumenical movement, as shown in authoritative statements and approved activities, and with the general principles involved.

Since the beginning of the Church there have been heresies and schisms. The Church's attempts to reunite them pertains to general Church history. During the first half of the 20th century, the main impetus in the ecumenical movement came from Protestant church leaders. While representatives of Orthodox churches frequently participated in ecumenical gatherings, Roman Catholic participation was officially restricted although occasionally permitted. This early 20th-century ecumenical movement has two characteristics unique in Christian history: (1) it includes the majority of Orthodox Churches and Protestant communities; (2) it centers in the WORLD COUNCIL OF CHURCHES (WCC), which is itself a convergence of three organizations, the INTERNATIONAL MISSIONARY COUNCIL, LIFE AND WORK, and FAITH AND ORDER.

At the Edinburgh Missionary Conference (1910), conventionally regarded as the birth of the 20th-century Ecumenical Movement, Anglican and Protestant missionaries became more deeply convinced that divisions among Christians were a powerful obstacle to the spread of Christianity. They recognized hostility, contentions, and even differences among Christians as scandals and realized that many causes of these divisions seemed irrelevant in non-Christian lands. The International Missionary Council was formed not only to spread information about effective missionary methods, but also to lessen the scandal of Christian divisions by avoiding competition in non-Christian countries. In 1925 the Life and Work Conference at Stockholm studied the application of Christian principles to international relations and to social, industrial, and economic life. Almost simultaneously the Faith and Order Conferences began to discuss doctrinal matters, with a view to unity in faith and order. From these three organizations was formed in 1948 the WCC, with headquarters at Geneva, Switzerland.

The beginnings were not free from confusion and ambiquity about assumptions and aims. The missionary movement tended to assume that ''the glorious Gospel of the blessed God'' was independent of all denominational tenets. The Life and Work movement coined the phrase: ''service unites but doctrine divides;'' and hence avoided doctrinal discussions. There was a question of whether those planning the Faith and Order Conference at Lausanne (1925) were tacitly assuming that Christians are unaware of the kind of Church unity wanted by Christ and must discover it by discussions, and whether they envisioned a league or federation of independent churches based on doctrinal compromise.

Ambiguities of this type probably accounted for Pope Benedict XV's courteous refusal of an invitation from the EPISCOPAL CHURCH in the U.S. (May 1919) to participate in a Faith and Order meeting. After the Life and Work Conference at Lausanne (1927), Pope PIUS XI issued the encyclical, *Mortalium animos*, (Jan. 6, 1928) on true religious unity, in which he asserted unequivocally that unity must be based upon acceptance of Christ's entire revelation, that doctrinal compromise is utterly inadmissible, and that the Church of Christ cannot be a federation of independent bodies holding different doctrines. The pope forbade Catholics to give any support to such ideas. He also made clear statements on the unity of the Church. The Orthodox delegation at the Lausanne Conference spoke in the same vein as Pius XI, objecting that some reports were based on compromises between conflicting ideas and meanings. This group asserted firmly that compromise has no place in matters of faith and conscience. Pius XI's encyclical caused disappointment at the time among non-Catholic ecumenists. Since then, however, some prominent ecumenists have admitted that Pius XI aided the movement, and have noted the danger of substituting well-intentioned friendliness for unity in truth.

Development. Since 1927 the movement for union among non-Catholics has developed greatly, with many repudiations of any idea of compromise in faith. Faith and Order Conferences at Edinburgh (1937) and Lund (1952) increased realization of the depth of doctrinal differences and of the tenacity of denominational traditions. Paradoxically, efforts at unity have increased denominational loyalties. World associations have been developed by Anglicans, Baptists, Congregationalists, Disciples of Christ, Lutherans, Methodists, Pentocostalists, and Presbyterians. These world ''confessional'' associations had the immediate effect of increasing denominational consciousness; but in the long run they may enable unions to be formed on a wider scale.

Two successful endeavors from the ecumenical movement are: (1) that of Anglicans, Congregationalists, Methodists, and Presbyterians, which resulted in the Church of South India, (1949); (2) that of the Congregationalists, Reformed, and Lutherans, which resulted in the UNITED CHURCH OF CHRIST in the U.S. Negotiations have occurred frequently elsewhere, but actual mergers have been comparatively rare, especially between episcopal and non-episcopal churches. Part of the difficulty in arranging mergers resides in nondoctrinal factors, such as historical traditions, established institutions, and differing customs and ways; but most of it stems from divergent doctrinal convictions.

The Lund Conference of the WCC (1952) listed doctrinal differences under the following heads: definition and limits of the Church; Church continuity and unity; goal of the reunion movement; number and nature of the sacraments and their relation to Church membership; scripture and tradition; infallibility; and priesthood and sacrifice. After stating the diverse views held on all these topics, the conference concluded that the method of ''comparative ecclesiology,'' which is one of comparing and contrasting different convictions, had been pursued to its limits and offered no prospects of arriving at reconciliation. It decided to select the following four main points and study them for at least ten years: union of Christ and the Church; tradition and traditions; ways of worship (liturgy); and institutionalism (the Church as a sociological entity, with its law and customs).

Catholic Attitude. The situation changed so radically that many of the papal strictures of 1928 were no longer applicable.

Pius XI. Pius XI had great interest in the Orthodox Churches. Between 1922 and 1939 he issued 23 documents concerning them. He reorganized the Pontifical Oriental Institute, entrusted it to the Jesuits, and provided it with a new building and a large library. He also established the Ethiopian, Ruthenian, and Russian colleges in Rome. In Catholic universities and major seminaries he instituted courses in Orthodox theology and spirituality. To the Benedictines the pope commended a special interest in the Orthodox, which they manifested by founding the monastery at Amay, Belgium (transferred to CHEVETOGNE in 1939). Repeatedly, Pius XI urged esteem for Orthodox theology, spirituality, rights, and customs. He renewed Benedict XV's condemnation of attempts at "Latinization." In his address to the Italian University Catholic Federation (Jan. 10, 1927) the Holy Father asserted principles of universal application in his references to the Orthodox when he declared that knowledge and fraternal charity are essential preliminaries to reunion and that ignorance and prejudice were responsible for past failures.

Five unofficial but approved Catholic observers attended the Faith and Order Conference at Edinburgh (1937).

Holy Office Instructions. Shortly after the formation of the World Council of Churches (1948), the Holy Office issued an "Instruction on the Ecumenical Movement" (1949). This document contained several warnings and indicated lines of conduct for Catholics. It did not attempt a systematic treatment of ecumenical problems, but accorded the movement formal recognition, declared it of serious interest to the whole Catholic Church, and encouraged Catholics, especially priests, to pray for its success and participate actively in it. The instruction encouraged pastoral letters to educate the faithful on these questions. It exhorted bishops to keep well informed on the subject, to guard against possible dangers while promoting ecumenism and appointing suitable priests to study it.

The instruction permitted Catholics, with the approval of competent ecclesiastical authorities, to meet non-Catholics as equals and discuss matters of faith and morals, each group explaining its own teachings. These gatherings were permitted to begin or end with the common recitation of the Lord's Prayer or some other prayer approved by the Catholic Church.

For interdiocesan, national, or international conferences, according to the instructions, permission of the Holy See is necessary. Within dioceses, bishops must regulate these activities and permit none but competent priests to engage in theological discussions. In dialogues, Catholics were told to present the Church's doctrines in their entirety, to avoid whittling down the faith or giving any semblance of indifference to truth.

This document marked a stage in the Church's attitude toward the ecumenical movement, which, it said, "should daily assume a more significant place within the Church's universal pastoral care."

Participation in Ecumenical Meetings. One hindrance to Catholic ecumenical activities was removed in 1950 when the Central Committee of the WCC issued at Toronto a very significant declaration, entitled "The Ecclesiological Significance of the World Council of Churches," which stated that membership in the WCC does not imply that member churches regard other member churches as "churches in the true and full sense of the word," although they do "recognize in other churches elements of the true Church." This document made clear that the WCC is a purely consultative body and allayed fears lest it make unacceptable assumptions about the nature of the Church. From the beginning, the basis of the World Council of Churches has been acceptance of Christ as God and Savior.

Catholic observers attended the Faith and Order Conferences at Lund (1952); at Oberlin, Ohio (1957); and at St. Andrews, Scotland (1960). At the General Assembly of the World Council of Churches at New Delhi, India (1961), five official Catholic observers were present. Five were also present at the Faith and Order Conference in Montreal (1963), along with 15 Catholic visitors from the North American continent, and about 30 in the press corps. The presence of these officially approved observers indicated a friendly interest by the Catholic Church in the proceedings of the World Council of Churches and its organs. The invitation extended to them, and the friendliness shown to them, demonstrated that the World Council of Churches did not intend to exclude the Catholic Church from its vision of the ultimate unity of all Christians, but on the contrary wished to include the Catholic Church in its counsels and plans.

Catholic Ecumenical Organizations. Other evidences of Catholic interest in ecumenism include the formation during the first half of the 20th century of institutes and associations to promote the union of all Christians. At first interest centered on the Orthodox, but later widened to include all divisions among Christians. This was true of the Benedictine Priory at Chevetogne; the Dominican center, Istina, near Paris; the institute of Byzantine studies in Holland; and the *Eastern Churches Quarterly*, published by English Benedictines at Ramsgate Abbey.

Germany. In Germany the "High Church" movement among some Lutherans; the Nazi persecution of Lutherans, Reformed, and Catholics alike; and the homogeneity of the German forms of Protestantism facilitated a rapprochement, which was brought to a focus by the UNA SANCTA movement. After World War II a group of Catholic and Lutheran scholars began meeting for theological and historical discussions under the leadership of Abp. Lorenz Jaeger of Paderborn.

France. In France Yves Congar, OP, had weighty influence, especially because of his book, *Divided Christendom*, translated into English (1939). Abp. Paul Couturier, who began with a special interest in the Orthodox, in 1932, propagated what he called "spiritual ecumenism," urging prayer for the sanctification of different Christian groups and "for the unity which Christ wills and by the means He chooses." This prayer proved widely acceptable. The WCC, especially its Faith and Order Commission, showed growing awareness of the intractable nature of sectarian divisions and emphasized more and more that one essential means of attaining unity lay in humble and universal prayer.

English-speaking World. In these lands enthusiasm for ecumenism developed slowly. Memories of civil and social disabilities, the hard struggle to maintain the faith and build educational institutions, Anglican convictions about the continuity of the Church of England and the ensuing controversies, a certain tradition of suspicion of "unrealistic" proposals for "corporate reunion," the outstanding service of many individual converts to the faith, lesser contact with the Orthodox, and the greater fragmentation of Protestantism in these countries all tended to perpetuate a defensive mentality and to retard appreciation of ecumenism. After the instruction of 1949, and especially after the advent of Pope John XXIII, interest quickened. Books, pamphlets, periodicals, conferences, and contacts with other churches multiplied.

In several countries bishops set up committees or institutes to foster and guide the movement. The Catholic Conference for Ecumenical Questions, founded in 1952 by the then Rev. J. G. M. Willebrands, has had an impressive though unobtrusive influence, and has worked with the Faith and Order Commission of the WCC. Several Catholics from English-speaking countries were members of this conference and cooperated effectively with it. The Friars of the Society of the Atonement at Graymoor, N.Y., have fostered the Week of Prayer for Unity annually in January, and have also published the English edition of *Unitas*.

Scholarly Trends. In the background of these direct efforts lay a series of developments. Biblical, patristic, and historical scholarship grew more international and freer of denominational prepossessions. Knowledge of the Orthodox increased through emigration from Russia and the foundation of Orthodox seminaries in Paris, New York, and Boston. Study of Orthodoxy, especially of the Byzantine period, deepened with the establishment of institutes in Rome, Paris, Munich, Berlin, Belgrade, Brussels, Athens, Prague, Boston, and Washington, D.C. (Dumbarton Oaks). Orthodox participation in the World Council of Churches increased understanding of the Orthodox tradition.

Catholic scholars in Germany, Holland, France, and the U.S. began to reassess the history of the REFORMATION and to appreciate more positively the religious values that the "reformers" retained. Protestants wrote about the Catholic Church with a new understanding and appreciation of the Catholic position. The era of controversy, and the war mentality that accompanied it, showed signs of ending.

New theological trends were manifest. Theology became more biblical, historical, liturgical, and even sociological. Interest quickened in the role of the laity in the church. Catechism teaching became more kerygmatic. Appreciation of the Church's mission to all mankind deepened. The Orthodox developed a eucharistic ecclesiology and became more conscious, especially in the U.S., of jurisdictional problems. Anglicans and Protestants were much influenced by the new orthodoxy associated with Karl Barth, and they took more interest in tradition, although a "Neoevangelicalism" remained suspicious and aloof. Catholics tended to stress the element of "mystery" in the church, rather than juridical and institutional elements.

John XXIII. Pope JOHN XXIII (1958–63) decisively promoted Christian unity. He deprecated the polemical tone used by some Catholics and frequently spoke about other Christians with respect and affection. His simplicity, openheartedness, optimism, and charity encouraged a general spirit of confidence and friendship. His encyclicals, *Mater et Magistra* and *Pacem in terris*, included statements indicative of his concern for Christian unity.

VATICAN COUNCIL II was summoned by John XXIII to stimulate the movement toward unity, among other things. The pope established a Secretariat for the Promotion of the Unity of Christians (June 5, 1960). Through the good offices of this secretariat, under the leadership of Cardinal Augustin Bea, John XXIII held audiences with the Anglican Archbishop Fisher of Canterbury; the presiding bishop of the Protestant Episcopal Church, Dr. Arthur Lichtenberger; the Moderator of the Church of Scotland, Dr. A. C. Craig; and dignitaries of other churches.

Vatican Council II. At the sessions of Vatican Council II observers were in attendance who represented the Orthodox Churches, various Protestant groups, the Anglican Communion, and the WCC. Others were guests of the secretariat. These delegated observers had access to all documents distributed to the fathers of the council and were present at all the general sessions. Although lacking the right to speak or vote at these sessions, they communicated to the Secretariat for Unity their observations and criticism, which in some cases were passed on to the relevant conciliar commissions. Their presence in a conspicuous place in St. Peter's was a reminder of the council's ecumenical purpose. Several of these delegated observers praised the confidence and friendliness accorded them.

The council promulgated (Nov. 21, 1964) a special decree on ecumenism, that treated the principles and practice of ecumenism, and the two chief types of division in the seamless robe of Christ. As the decree explained, the unity of Christ's Church consists of unity of faith, of sacramental worship, and of the fraternal harmony of the family of God secured by the succession of bishops since the time of St. Peter and the Apostles. The document noted the continuing existence of differences among Christians concerning doctrine, discipline, and Church structure and termed these present-day divisions an open contradiction of Christ's will. The stress of the decree, however, was on the unifying elements that are found among Christians as individuals and as corporate groups. Special emphasis was placed on the gifts and endowments of the Orthodox Churches, whose power to govern themselves according to their own diciplines was recognized. Referring to the Churches in the West, where more numerous differences exist among the various Christian denominations themselves and between all of them and the Catholic Church, the council listed several points that all held in common, but it also declared that the other Churches do not share the Catholic understanding of the eucharistic mystery.

Catholics, to whom the decree was addressed, were urged to avoid anything in speech or action that would render relations with other Christians difficult. Recommended, too, was a conversion of mentality and outlook as well as of moral conduct, a willingness to appraise honestly the elements in the Church needing reform or renewal, a spirit of mutual forgiveness shared by Catholics and other Christians, and cooperation between the two in causes for the good of humanity. Catholics were further asked to recognize gladly all the endowments and gifts of other Christian denominations. With due approval Catholics may offer prayer in common with them and engage in interfaith dialogue. In the confrontation of convictions during dialogue, Catholics were counseled to distinguish carefully between the DEPOSIT OF FAITH and formulations of faith, to keep in mind that various theological expressions of divine revelation are often complementary rather than conflicting, and to recall that there is a hierarchy of truths within revelation itself. At the same time, the council decried a false irenicism that would dilute or compromise truth.

Paul IV. The successor of John XXIII continued his predecessor's program for religious unity. PAUL VI's meeting in Jerusalem (January 1964) with the Ecumenical Patriarch Athenagoras of Constantinople roused worldwide Catholic enthusiasm. It demonstrated the Holy Father's willingness to break with precedent, to express esteem for the Orthodox, and to move toward reconciliation with them. On Dec. 7, 1965, the pope and the patriarch nullified simultaneously the mutual anathemas pronounced by Pope LEO IX and MICHAEL CERULARIUS, patriarch of Constantinople, in 1054, at the start of the EASTERN SCHISM.

As Vatican Council II drew to a close, Paul IV set a papal precedent by participating in interfaith prayer with the non-Catholic observers at the council. During the service in the Basilica of St. Paul-Outside-the-Walls (Dec. 4, 1965) a Methodist minister, a Greek Orthodox archimandrite, and a Catholic priest gave the readings, and a Lutheran hymn was sung.

Ecumenical Principles. The views of non-Catholics and Catholics on the principle of ecumenism have become clearer in the light of study and experience.

World Council of Churches. Since its foundation in 1948 this organization has become increasingly prominent in the ecclesiastical situation. The members generally agree that division among Christians is contrary to God's will and a grave obstacle to the acceptance of Christianity by non-Christians, that Church unity must be visible as well as invisible, and that the Church's unity and mission to non-Christians are inextricably connected; they believe the Church must be supranational, supraregional, and supraracial; that some prevalent organ of conference and council is required and is supplied to the member churches by the WCC itself. In addition they discern a need for closer association with the other Protestant bodies, such as the Southern Baptist Convention and the Missouri Synod Lutherans, and with the Catholic Church. Members aspire to perfect Christian unity. Leaders of the WCC realized from the beginning that this goal involved the inclusion of all other Christian bodies as members of the WCC, or at least as friendly associates in consultation with it.

The conviction has grown that unity must be based upon truth and that friendliness that hides or minimizes differences is not in the long run helpful. It is appreciated, too, that the Eucharist is central to reunion, to Christian worship, and to prayer and that, consequently, there must be a ministry accepted by everyone. Moreover, it is agreed that unity must be stable, continuous, and inclusive of the whole Christian fellowship of all places and ages, but not uniform or rigid structurally, since this would extinguish the spirit. Unity, admittedly, derives from and is governed by the unity of the Word of God Incarnate. Several theologians within the World Council of Churches claim that the Church continues in a real sense the redeeming work of Christ. Catholics share fully all these convictions.

Catholic. Vatican II's *Decree on Ecumenicism* made it clear that promoting endeavors at reconciliation and unity among all Christians is one of the principal concerns of the Second Vatican Council (*Unitatis Redintegratio*, 1). It should be noted that Vatican II intended, not to inaugurate a separate Catholic ecumenical movement, but to encourage all Catholics ''to take an active and intelligent part'' in the existing movement (*Unitatis Redintegratio*, 4).

Catholic Principles relative to ecumenism may be summed up as follows: through the fulfillment of the promises of Christ by the action of the Holy Spirit the Church has never failed and can never fail to be one in faith, in Sacraments, and in ordered, authoritative guidance through the successor of St. Peter and the successors of the Apostles. The Church, although a mystery believed by faith, is a sign lifted up among the nations, containing in itself evidence of its divine foundation. Its unity admits a large variety of languages, ritual forms, local prerogatives, spiritual currents, legitimate institutions, and preferred activities; it is not static or immobile, but dynamic and developing. The Church needs internal renewal and reform occasionally. Like holiness and catholicity, unity exists in essentials, but is not complete and perfect. As the Church's catholicity becomes fuller and more perfect through reconciliation with other Christian churches, the scandal of divisions among Christians make it more difficult for non-Christians to recognize the one true Church of Christ; and so a reconciliation of all Christians would have considerable influence in the confrontation of the Church with the great non-Christian religions and with unbelievers.

The defects and sins of members of the Church, both past and present, affect ecclesiastical institutions and obscure the presence of the Holy Spirit in the Church. Humility is, therefore, an important element among Catholic principles of ecumenism.

Two principles regarding theological formulations are important in ecumenical dialogue. The first is that all theological formulations must be understood in their historical context; the second is that no theological formulation exhausts the fullness of truth. This does not mean that formulation is false; it does mean, however, that in the total vision of Christian truth, formulations of individual truths assume another aspect than what they do when taken in isolation.

Other Christians who have received valid baptism merit the Church's esteem and solicitude as her children and as belonging to her, although not fully. Not only as individuals, but also as corporate entities, churches, or ecclesiastical communities, other Christians share a common patrimony with Catholics. Among its treasure are faith in Jesus Christ and the grace and gifts of the Holy Spirit, who acts to preserve what is true and holy and inspires efforts toward full unity.

In the West, churches and communities that are not in communion with the Apostolic See differ considerably among themselves in doctrine, doctrinal emphasis, and manner of government. Not all are equally interested in the ecumenical movement, nor do all have the same mutual esteem that the ecumenical spirit brings. Almost all of them maintain belief in baptism and in Scripture as the word of God. Their celebration of ''the Lord's Supper'' is reverent, and their worship often retains elements that were conspicuous in the ancient liturgies. Their charitable works show an enormous generosity. The churches within the World Council of Churches have developed a greater appreciation of the visible nature and continuity of the Church, of tradition, of the eucharistic liturgy, of the need for an ordained ministry accepted by all, and of the need for the Church to be able to speak to the world with a concordant witness.

The ecumenical method, which is one of ''dialogue,'' envisions frank, friendly discussions about doctrines, pastoral and missionary methods, spirituality, and the devotional life. There are large areas in which Christians can stand and act in unison to maintain Christian values in a secular environment amid the growth of unreligious outlook and conduct.

Massive obstacles bar attainment of unity in faith, sacraments, and authority. On the Catholic side there is fear of indifference that can best be exorcised by loyalty to the directions of the Holy See and by episcopal initiative and leadership. Orthodox, Anglicans, and Protestants dread ''domination'' by Rome and the more articulated doctrinal convictions of Catholicism. These suspicions can only be allayed by increased knowledge and experience of mutual church life and by cooperation for the defense and spread of the general cause.

The ecumenical movement is essentially a spiritual one, a call to increased holiness, zeal, and union with Christ, into which all intellectual and administrative activities must be integrated. The basis of the movement is the clear will of Christ that all his followers should be united; its method is primarily prayer, and ''dialogue'' in various forms; and its hope rests upon the omnipotence of God.

Social Thought. A factor of considerable importance in the Churches' search for unity has been the desire for a coherent witness and a common action making relevant the gospel message of justice and peace among men and nations; indeed, it was the original motive and basis for the participation of some of the Orthodox churches in the ecumenical movement after World War I. The forces of what were called the SOCIAL GOSPEL or ''applied'' or ''practical'' Christianity sponsored international conferences. They met at Stockholm, Sweden, in

1925 and at Oxford, England, in 1937, before the concerns they represented were officially assumed as an integral function of the WCC at its founding in 1948. Moreover, the basic interests of the World Alliance for Promoting Friendship through the Churches are expressed through the WCC's permanent Commissions of the Churches on International Affairs.

The hope of common action and of coherent witness encounters obstacle in the nature of the WCC, which describes itself as "a fellowship of churches," undertaking only such programs as the member churches authorize. Moreover, the WCC's pronouncements have only the authority of their intrinsic wisdom, the documents of its assemblies being "received and commended to the churches for their serious consideration and appropriate action." In addition, the different theological traditions represented in the WCC give rise to different conceptions of the nature of man, of law, of the state, of the relation of religion to temporal structures, and, in short, of the bases of social ethics. Thus, the attempt to work out an ecumenical consensus with the aid of dispersed and volunteer collaborators, and the need for conciliating viewpoints from opposing social systems, often make the positions taken by the WCC, the organized instrument of the ecumenical community, imprecise and tentative.

The central concept elaborated by the WCC is that of the responsible society, defined as "one where freedom is the freedom of all who acknowledge responsibility to justice and public order, and where those who hold positions of authority or economic power are responsible for its exercise to God and to the people whose welfare is affected by it." The concept envisions a social arrangement that maintains in dynamic equilibrium freedom and order, liberty and justice, while barring the road to tyranny and anarchy. The responsible society, it was noted at the Evanston Assembly of 1954, is not conceived of as "an alternative social or political system, but a criterion by which we judge all existing social orders, while at the same time providing a standard to guide us in specific choices we have to make."

The WCC has taken firm stands against racial segregation and for religious freedom; it has consistently supported the United Nations as the best mechanism for reducing tensions between nations. Because of the character of its organization and its ethical criteria, however, its pronouncements on the social order have been, perforce, generalized ones. They are not for that reason insignificant. Thus, they have indefatigably asserted the essential dignity of man who is the object of a divine and redeeming love, the source of all demands for human rights and social justice for every person. They have asserted an obligation of service to the world because of God's love for all men. They have proclaimed the spiritual solidarity of all mankind, thus challenging the pretensions of absolute national sovereignty, the myths of inevitable class conflict, and the fears of irreconcilable national rivalries. They have declared that economic processes and international affairs are neither beyond control nor self-regulatory; they are subject to norms determined by their ultimate function which is to serve man in fulfilling his destiny. They have taught the equality of all men in a common destiny and divinely certified value, thus voicing the irreducible claims of a common humanity to its common goods, and the rights of the individual to an equality of opportunity in providing himself and his family with the necessities for a truly human existence.

Dialogue. Dialogue is one of the ecumenical movement's most characteristic and important steps toward reconciliation. Replacing long-standing patterns of interdenominational polemics, dialogue attempts to create an atmosphere in which all Christians may come to a genuine understanding of each others' beliefs and traditions. The mutual understanding gained through dialogue does not always result in agreement, for understanding another's beliefs may reveal their disparity with one's own position. Accordingly, ecumenical dialogue should not be accompanied by a false irenicism, for nothing is to be gained by pretending that basic differences do not exist or that basic differences can be overcome simply by good will. Nonetheless, ecumenical dialogue has resulted in a remarkable degree of consensus, or a recognition that positions that were previously considered incompatible, can be seen as complementary expressions of God's revelation.

Ecumenical dialogue is conducted in a variety of ways, ranging from multilateral discussions at international meetings sponsored by the World Council of Churches to informal "living-room dialogues" among a few members of different churches. Sometimes ecumenical dialogue takes the form of formal negotiations aimed at uniting two or more denominations. At any one time, several official union conversations may be under way among various churches throughout the world, under the aegis of the the CONSULTATION ON CHURCH UNION. A number of such negotiations have proved successful; e.g., the union of the Methodist Church and the Evangelical United Brethern in 1967 to form the UNITED METHODIST CHURCH.

Union conversations need to involve every level and locale of the churches participating. Many union proposals have withered for lack of popular support, while other unions have been only partial, since some local churches refused to unite. Even when a union plan is ratified, there is usually a tendency for "denominationalism" to continue in much the same way as previously; thus, a process of continuing dialogue and growing together in union is necessary. In other words, since union involves all the members of the churches uniting—not merely administrators and theologians—''grass roots ecumenicism'' is a pastoral necessity if union is to be really effective.

Roman Catholic Participation in Dialogue. In accord with Vatican II's recommendation of ''fraternal dialogue on points of doctrine and the more pressing pastoral problems of our time'' (*Decree* 18), Catholics have entered into dialogue with their fellow Christians in many places and at many levels.

Noteworthy on the international level are the bilateral conversations arranged by the Secretariat for Promoting Christian Unity and the appropriate officials of four world confessional families: the Anglican Communion, the Lutheran World Federation, the World Methodist Council, and the World Alliance of Reformed Churches. In general, these commissions have studied the doctrinal issues that originally divided the participating churches and have searched for an acceptable consensus that would overcome the legacy of separation. In addition, Catholic representatives have participated in such international meetings of the Faith and Order Commission and the General Assembly of the World Council of Churches. The Roman Catholic Church is a full member of the Faith and Order Commission, and has observer status at the World Council of Churches. In practice, Catholic organizations and individual Catholics participate in many of its projects and the feasibility of Catholic membership has been explored by both sides.

Similar conversations are taking place at national and regional levels. In the United States, seven bilateral conversations are sponsored by the Bishops' Committee on Ecumenical and Interreligious Affairs and the appropriate officials of the churches involved: the American Baptist Convention, the Christian Church (Disciples of Christ), the Episcopal church, Lutheran churches, the United Methodist church, Reformed and Presbyterian churches, and Orthodox and other Eastern churches. The membership of these groups usually consists of a half-dozen or more theologians and administrators from each side. Frequently, the discussions in these groups parallel or augment the efforts of the corresponding international conversation, but in some instances, the particularitics of the American religious scene give a special orientation to the dialogue.

Catholics also participate in other ecumenical conversations, such as the Consultation on Church Union, and are working on ecumenical projects, such as those sponsored by the NATIONAL COUNCIL OF CHURCHES.

Various types of formal and informal dialogues are in operation on the local level. For example, some Catholic dioceses have joined state councils of churches, while individual parishes have become members of local councils of churches. Some Catholic priests have become members of local ministerial associations, while other priests have developed informal contacts with the clergy of other churches. Catholic laity have worked with their fellow Christians on civic projects and have participated in such interchurch activities as businessmen's prayer breakfasts and churchwomen's organizations.

While these different forms of dialogue all aim at improving relations among Christians, each dialogue is usually concerned with some specific area of interest: theology, education, social action, or worship.

Theological Discussion. The primary, although not exclusive, concern of the bilateral conversations is discussion of theological issues. Although the choice of specific topics depends on the historical and theological traditions of the churches represented, in most ecumenical conversations one or more of the following issues tend to surface: (1) Gospel, scripture, and tradition; (2) creeds and confessions; (3) church and ministry; and (4) the Sacraments, particularly the Eucharist.

Each of these topics can be discussed in a variety of ways. For example, discussions on the Church have sometimes focused on the Church in relation to the secular world or the Church's social responsibility; other conversations have centered on the Church's ministry and have treated such matters as the nature and role of the priesthood and episcopate, the validity of ordination, and APOSTOLIC SUCCESSION; still other dialogues have been concerned with freedom and responsibility in the Church and have explored such questions as teaching authority in the Church, the nature and function of the papal office, and the exercise of infallibility. Similar variety enriches the dialogue on other topics, such as the spirituality of the ministry, formation of moral judgments, and the ministry of women in the Church.

A primary aim in theological dialogue is mutual understanding. Frequently, such understanding results in the recognition that doctrinal issues that were previously considered to be conflicting should really be seen as complementary. Doctrinal complementarity was accepted by Vatican II, insofar as ''the heritage handed down by the apostles was received with differences of form and manner, so that from the earliest times of the Church, it was explained variously in different places, owing to diversities of genius and conditions of life'' (*Decree* 14). Accordingly, ecumenical dialogue has benefited from both a variety of theological methods and a plurality of doctrinal expressions.

Doctrinal discussion has also been aided by the recognition of a ''HIERARCHY OF TRUTHS'': since doctrines ''vary in their relation to Christian faith'' (*Decree* 11), theologians may agree on basic tenets while allowing flexibility in the presentation of related issues. Also, since doctrines have developed in the past, there is no reason to preclude the possibility of further development in the future; accordingly, ecumenical theologians are exploring ways in which doctrines might converge in an acceptable consensus.

While areas of more or less serious disagreement still remain in ecumenical theology, this should not detract from the substantial amount of consensus that has been achieved in a comparatively short time. For example, the American Lutheran Roman Catholic and Episcopal-Catholic conversations have achieved remarkable consensus on such topics as the Nicene Creed, Baptism, the Eucharist and ministry, and even the papacy.

While manifesting the progress achieved in theological discussion, the publication of consensus statements raises two crucial questions: what degree of consensus is necessary for two churches to enter officially into some type of union? And to what extent is the consensus achieved by theologians shared by members of the churches they represent? Presently, few church officials seem to have envisioned any policy or procedures to implement the consensus emerging from the dialogues of their theologians with those of other churches.

Despite the many ecumenical advances made thus far, theological obstacles to ecumenical growth and progress still remain. Issues like the papal primacy and jurisdiction, ordination of women, sexuality, and especially homosexuality, and such Marian doctrines as the Immaculate Conception and the Assumption of the Blessed Virgin, and so-called 'nontheological/moral' factors like the dramatic rise of conservatively-oriented groups inside the various Christian Churches, all constitute points of serious contention and barriers to be overcome.

Liturgical Sharing. The sense of Christian brotherhood created by shared experiences in dialogue, education, and social action usually leads to a desire to worship together. While participation in ecumenical prayer services encounters little or no theological objection, in contrast, there is considerable divergence in policy in regard to sharing in liturgical worship (*communicatio in sacris*), particularly eucharistic sharing.

Some churches allow ''open communion,'' inviting all Christians attending the service to receive the Eucharist. Sometimes, two churches have reciprocal bilateral agreements permitting intercommunion. Other churches ordinarily welcome only their own members to the Eucharist but do make exceptions in particular cases. Finally, some churches have a policy of ''closed communion'' which permits only members of that church to communicate. The practice of local churches or particular individuals, however, does not always follow denominational policy.

Present Catholic policy is basically that of closed communion with some exceptions; furthermore, Catholic policy in regard to eucharistic sharing with the Eastern churches differs from that of the Western churches.

Since a basic doctrinal and sacramental commonality exists between the Eastern (i.e., Orthodox and Oriental Orthodox) and Catholic churches, ''some sharing in liturgical worship . . . given suitable circumstances and the approval of church authority'' is officially encouraged. Accordingly, Catholics are permitted to receive not only the Eucharist but also the Sacraments of penance and the anointing of the sick from Orthodox and Oriental Orthodox clergy, and Catholics are permitted to reciprocate. In reality, however, world-wide agreement on such sacramental sharing remains to be reached, although it occurs on occasion.

In contrast, the lack of recognized doctrinal agreement between the Catholic and Western (e.g., Protestant) churches has resulted in a general prohibition against liturgical sharing, although with some exceptions: (1) non-Catholics who are rightly disposed and believe in the Sacraments in harmony with the Catholic Church are allowed to receive them for adequate reasons. While urgent situations, such as danger of death, persecution, or imprisonment, are generally acknowledged cases for allowing sacramental sharing, these comprise unusual situations and are not meant as general practice.

Bibliography: R. ROUSE and S. C. NEILL, eds., *A History of the Ecumenical Movement 1517–1948* (Philadelphia 1954). B. LEEMING, *The Vatican Council and Christian Unity* (New York 1966). R. M. BROWN and D. H. SCOTT, eds., *Challenge to Reunion* (New York 1964). A. H. ARMSTRONG and E. J. B. FRY, *Rediscovering Eastern Christendom* (London 1963). A. BEA, *The Unity of Christians*, ed. B. LEEMING (New York 1963). Anglican/Roman Catholic Commission on the Theology of Marriage and Its Application to Mixed Marriages, *Final Report* (Washington, D.C. 1976). Anglican-Roman Catholic Commission/U.S., *ARC-DOC*, I-IV (Documents on Anglican-Roman Catholic Relations) (Washington, D.C.). Baptist-Catholic Regional Conference, *The Church Inside and Out* (Washington, D.C. 1974). *Consultation on Church Union—A Catholic Perspective* (Washington, D.C. 1970). P. C. EMPIE and T. AUSTIN MURPHY, *Papal Primacy and the Universal Church. Lutherans and Catholics in Dialogue* 5 (Minneapolis 1974). Lutheran-Roman Catholic Theological Consultation, *Lutherans and Catholics in Dialogue*, 1–5 (Washington, D.C.). Roman Catholic/Presbyterian-Reformed Consultation. *The Unity We Seek* (New York 1977). L. SWIDLER, ed., *The Eucharist in Ecumenical Dialogue* (New York 1976). United Methodist-Roman Catholic Dialogue/U.S.A., *Holiness and Spirituality of the Ordained Ministry* (Washington, D.C.

1976). N. H. VANDERWERF, *The Times Were Very Full: A Perspective on the First 25 Years of the National Council of the Churches of Christ in the United States of America, 1950–1975* (New York 1975). JOHN PAUL II, *Addresses and Homilies on Ecumenism,* eds. J. B. SHEERIN and J. F. HOTCHKIN (Washington, D.C. 1981). A. J. VAN DER BRENT, *Major Studies and Themes in the Ecumenical Movement* (Geneva, Switzerland 1981). J. DESSEAUX, *Twenty Centuries of Ecumenism* (New York 1984). W. G. RUSCH, *Ecumenism A Movement Toward Church Unity* (Philadelphia 1985). J. L. SANDIDGE, *Roman Catholic/Pentecostal Dialogue (1977–1982): A Study in Developing Ecumenism* (New York 1987). P. C. PHAN, *Christianity and the Wider Ecumenism* (New York 1990) T. D. HORGAN, *Walking Together: Roman Catholics and Ecumenism Twenty-five Years after Vatican II* (Grand Rapids, Mich. 1990). K. RAISER, *Ecumenism in Transition: A Paradigm Shift in the Ecumenical Movement?* (Geneva, Switzerland 1991). R. GIRAULT, *One Church, One Faith, One Lord: New Perspectives in Ecumenism* (Maynooth, Ireland 1993). K. HAGEN, ed. *The Quadrilog: Tradition and the Future of Ecumenism: Essays in Honor of George H. Tavard* (Collegeville, Minn. 1994). D. BUTLER, *Dying to be One: English Ecumenism History, Theology and the Future* (London 1996). G. WAINWRIGHT, *Worship with One Accord: Where Liturgy and Ecumenism Embrace* (New York 1997). M. KINNAMON, *The Ecumenical Movement: An Anthology of Key Texts and Voices* (Grand Rapid, Mich. 1997). C. E. BRAATEN, *Mother Church: Ecclesiology and Ecumenism* (Minneapolis 1998). L. CUNNINGHAM, *Ecumenism: Present Realities and Future Prospects* (Notre Dame, Ind. 1998). N. SAGOVSKY, *Ecumenism, Christian Origins, and the Practice of Communion* (Cambridge, U.K. 2000). M. VAN ELDEREN, *Finding a Voice: Communicating the Ecumenical Movement* (Grand Rapids, Mich. 2001). J. GROS, *That All May Be One: Ecumenism* (Chicago 2001).

[M. A. BROWN/E. DUFF/J. T. FORD/C. V. LAFONTAINE/EDS.]

EDDY, MARY BAKER

Founder of the CHRISTIAN SCIENCE church; b. Bow, N.H., July 16, 1821; d. Chestnut Hill, Mass., Dec. 3, 1910. After a childhood marked by poor health, she married George Washington Glover in 1843. His death and the birth of her son, in 1844, aggravated her nervous disorder. She married Dr. Daniel Patterson, an itinerant dentist, in 1853, but she received a divorce in 1873 on the grounds of desertion. She was wed for a third time, in 1877, to Asa Gilbert Eddy, a sewing machine salesman who died in 1882.

Mrs. Eddy dated her discovery of the principles of Christian Science from 1866 when she recovered from a fall in Lynn, Mass. She began to teach classes in spiritual healing, borrowing freely from the writings of Dr. Phineas P. Quimby, a healer and mesmerist. Her *Science and Health with Key to the Scriptures,* the textbook of the Christian Science Church, was published in 1875, and the first Christian Science Church was organized in Boston, Mass., in 1879. In 1880 she established the short-lived Massachusetts Metaphysical College to propagate her theories of healing. The official church publication, the *Christian Science Journal,* was founded in 1883, and a

Mary Baker Eddy.

daily newspaper, the *Christian Science Monitor,* was begun in 1908. At the time of her death, the church had enrolled about 100,000 members. Its doctrines denied the reality of sin, sickness, and death and advanced a pantheistic conception of God.

Bibliography: E. F. DAKIN, *Mrs. Eddy: The Biography of a Virginal Mind* (New York 1930). L. P. POWELL, *Mary Baker Eddy* (Boston 1950). A. JOHNSON, *Dictionary of American Biography* 6:7–15.

[W. J. WHALEN]

EDEN, GARDEN OF

Term used for PARADISE in the story of man's creation and fall as told in Gn 2.8–3.24 (*see* PRIMEVAL AGE IN THE BIBLE). The exact term is really ''a garden in Eden'' (Heb *gan-bᵉ 'ēden:* 2.8). The author of the account, therefore, evidently thought of Eden as a certain region ''in the East'' (*miqeddem*), i.e., in MESOPOTAMIA, where ''the Lord God planted a garden . . . and put the

"The Paradise," a panel painting by Lucas Cranach the Elder, depicting various scenes from Genesis involving Adam and Eve in the Garden of Eden, 1530, in the Kunsthistorisches Museum, Vienna. (©Francis G. Mayer/CORBIS)

man whom he had formed'' (2.8); see also 2.10 (''a river rose in Eden''). The Hebrew word *'ēden* is probably connected with the Akkadian word *edinu*, itself a loanword from the Sumerian *edin* meaning ''steppe.'' The same local significance is attached to the Hebrew term *gan-'ēden* (garden of Eden) in Gn 2.15; 2.23–24; see also Gn 4.16, where Cain is said to have ''dwelt in the land of Nod to the east of Eden (*'ēden*).'' The Israelites, however, would naturally connect the term with the native Hebrew word *'ēden*, meaning ''luxury,'' ''delight.'' Hence, the Septuagint translated *gan-'ēden* in Gn 3.23–24 as ὁ παράδεισος τῆς τρυφῆς (park of luxury; hence the word paradise). Similarly, in Is 51.3; Ez 28.13; 31.8–9, 16, 18, Eden (*'ēden*) becomes synonymous with ''Yahweh's garden'' or ''God's garden,'' and in Ez 36.35; Jl 2.3 *gan-'ēden* (garden of Eden) means simply a luxuriant field.

Of quite a different meaning is the Hebrew word *'ēden* in the term *b^e^nê-'eden* (sons of Eden) in 2 Kgs 19.12; Is 37.12. This term designates the Edenites, the inhabitants of the region that is called Eden (*'eden*) in Ez 27.23 and more fully as Beth-Eden (*bêt-'eden*) in Am 1.5, which is the region known in Akkadian as Bit-Adini, on the Euphrates south of Haran.

Bibliography: *Encyclopedic Dictionary of the Bible*, tr. and adap. by L. HARTMAN (New York 1963) 620. O. SCHILLING, *Lexikon für Theologie und Kirche*, ed. J. HOFER and K. RAHNER, 10 v. (2d, new ed. Freiburg 1957–65) 3:657. E. A. SPEISER, *Genesis* (Anchor Bible I; Garden City, N.Y. 1964) 16–20. H. RENCKENS, *Israel's Concept of the Beginning*, tr. C. NAPIER (New York 1964) 193–213.

[I. HUNT]

EDES, ELLA B.

Journalist; b. Dec. 7, 1832; d. Pescina, near Pinerolo, Italy, Feb. 27, 1916. A member of an old New England family, Miss Edes was baptized a Catholic on Feb. 25, 1852. In about 1866 she took up permanent residence in Rome, where she did secretarial work for Cardinal Alessandro Barnabò, prefect of the Congregation for the Propagation of the Faith. After 1870 she became Roman correspondent for various newspapers, including the *Tablet* (London); the *New York Herald;* the *New York World* (as ''Anne Brewster''?); the *Brooklyn Daily Eagle;* the *New York Freeman's Journal and Catholic Register;* and the *Catholic Review* and *Catholic News* (New York). Her interest was in Roman ecclesiastical events. She remained intensely loyal to the successors of her confessor,

Abp. John HUGHES of New York, and placed her reportorial talents at their disposal. As an agent of Abp. Michael A. CORRIGAN and his "conservative party" in their conflict with the "progressive" American bishops, Miss Edes incurred the displeasure of the latter. Increasingly unwell after 1900, she closed her Rome apartment at "Via della Mercede, 21" in 1908, and retired to northern Italy. Some of her correspondence with ecclesiastics has been preserved in the archives of the archdioceses of Baltimore, New York, and St. Paul, the Diocese of Rochester, and the American Catholic Historical Society of Philadelphia.

Bibliography: H. J. BROWNE, *The Catholic Church and the Knights of Labor* (Catholic University of America, *Studies in American Church History* 38; Washington 1949) and D. F. REILLY, *The School Controversy 1891–1893* (Washington 1943) touch on Miss Edes's role in Church conflicts.

[R. F. MCNAMARA]

EDESSA

Arab *al-Ruha',* modern Urfa, in Turkey, the capital in antiquity of the Osrhoene peoples of northern Mesopotamia. Conquered by the Assyrians (8th century B.C.), it was called Ruhu (Syriac, Urhoi). Under Seleucus I (312–280 B.C.) its name was changed to Edessa and under Antiochus (175-162), to Antioch. In 132 B.C. it was the capital of the Kingdom of Edessa, or Osrhoene, under the Arab dynasty that was replaced by the Seleucids. Destroyed by the Romans under Trajan but rebuilt by Hadrian, it became a Roman military colony as *Colonia Marcia Edessenorum* in 217. Controlled by the Kingdom of Palmyra (*c.* 270), it fell to the Persians in 609 but was recaptured by the Byzantines under HERACLIUS in 628, absorbed by the Arabs after 639, and retaken by Byzantium in 1031.

During the First Crusade, it was captured by Baldwin of Flanders (1098) but reverted to the Seljuk Turks in 1144. In 1182 the Sultan Saladin brought it under Egyptian control. It was destroyed by the Mongols (1391) and rebuilt by the Turks in 1637.

Edessa was evangelized by Christians from Palestine. Eusebius of Caesarea cites a legendary letter from the Chronicle of Addai, supposedly written by Abgar V Ukhama of Edessa to Christ, who sent the Apostle Addai to convert the country (*Hist. Eccl.* 1.13.1–22). The Epitaph of ABERCIUS contains the first certain evidence of Christianity. The *Liber legum regionum* (*c.* 250) narrates the conversion of King Abgar IX (179–216), a vassal of Osrhoene, but this evidence is questionable since Eusebius, who cites the text, omitted the conversion passage. However he quotes ORIGEN as saying that the Apostle Thomas preached to the Parthians in eastern Syria and in the 4th century the body of Thomas was venerated at Edessa (*Hist. Eccl.* 3.1.1). Eusebius likewise mentions the churches of Osrhoene as participating in the EASTER CONTROVERSY (5.23.4) and the Chronicle of Edessa mentions the inundation of a church in 202. The first bishop, Palut, was consecrated by Serapion of Antioch (*c.* 200) and spread Christianity in East Syria and Persia. The PESHITTA and Tatian's *Diatessaron* apparently originated in Edessa, as did much of the Syrian apocryphal literature, such as the *Acts of Thomas* (3d century), the *Psalms of Thomas* (partly a Judeo-Christian composition of the 2d century), and apparently also the *Odes of Solomon* and the *Gospel of the Truth.* The primitive Christian monuments excavated at nearby DURA-EUROPOS in Syria indicate that in this region appeared the first Christian buildings dedicated exclusively to religious service whose decorations were influenced by Judaic, Mithraic, and Greek art.

Edessan Christianity in the 3d century showed marks of stringent asceticism as instanced by the *Acts of Thomas* and the *Tract on Virginity,* as well as the vogue of spiritual marriage. TATIAN was there after 170, and also BARDESANES (D. 222), the Gnostic hymn writer. It was affected by the persecutions of Decius and Diocletian.

The school of Edessa, rendered illustrious by EPHREM THE SYRIAN (d. 373), was transferred to Nisibis in 457, and had considerable influence on the spread of Christianity in the Sassanid lands. Bishop RABBULA of Edessa (412–435) was a strong anti-Nestorian, who requested that PROCLUS of Constantinople write his Letter to the Armenians; however, Ibas of Edessa (435–457) was deposed as a Nestorian sympathizer at the Robber Synod of Ephesus (449), restored at the Council of CHALCEDON, but later condemned with the THREE CHAPTERS. The Nestorians were expelled in 457, and in the 6th century the Monophysites prevailed through the intrigues of James BARADAI (541–578).

With the Arab invasion Edessa lost significance but was the see of both a Nestorian bishop and a Jacobite metropolitan (until 1097) and produced the Jacobite James of Edessa (d. 708) and the Maronite Theophilus (d. 785). During the Crusades it likewise had a Latin metropolitan but in modern times has become a titular see. The Mission of the Capuchins opened in Edessa in 1841 was suppressed during World War I.

Bibliography: J. DANIÉLOU and H. MARROU, *Des Origines à saint Grégoire le Grand,* v. 1 of *Nouvelle histoire de l'Église* (Paris 1963—). J. TIXERONT, *Les Origines de l'église d'Édesse* (Paris 1888). A. VON HARNACK, *Die Mission und Ausbreitung des Christentums* (4th ed. Leipzig 1924), Eng. *The Mission and Expansion of Christianity,* ed. and tr. J. MOFFATT (New York 1908). I. ORTIZ DE URBINA, "Le origini del cristianesimo in Edessa," *Gregori-*

anum 15 (1934) 82–91. H. LECLERCQ, *Dictionnaire d'archéologie chrétienne et de liturgie,* ed. F. CABROL, H. LECLERQ and H. I. MARROU (Paris 1907–53) 4.2:2058–2110. F. NAU, *Dictionnaire de théologie catholique,* ed. A. VACANT (Paris 1903–50) 4.2:2102–03. H. RAHNER, *Lexikon für Theologie und Kirche,* ed. J. HOFER and K. RAHNER (Freiburg 1957–65) 3:658–659.

[G. ORLANDI]

EDESSA, CHRONICLE OF

The *Chronicum Edessenum,* an anonymous chronicle of the late 6th century. It begins with an official record of the flooding of the city in A.D. 201. In this flood, says the record, the *ecclesia christianorum* or Christian church was hit by the waters, thus supplying valuable witness to early Christianity in OSRHOENE. This document is the first dated Syriac writing. The chronicler uses generally trustworthy sources for his brief, almost annalistic recital of the main events, the succession of bishops, and other matters pertaining to the history of Edessa. It is thus a fine historical source and is preserved in only one manuscript (*Vat. syr.* 163, 7th century).

Bibliography: I. GUIDI et al., eds. and trs., *Chronica minora,* 6 v. (Corpus scriptorum Chritianorum 1–6, Scriptores syri ser. 3.4; 1903–05); Eng. tr. B. H. COWPER, *The Journal of Sacred Literature,* 4th ser., 4 (1864) 28–45. J. TIXERONT, *Les Origines de l'église d'Édesse* (Paris 1888). I. ORTIZ DE URBINA, *Gregoriana* 15 (1934) 82–81, origins.

[I. ORTIZ DE URBINA]

EDESSA, SCHOOL OF

The current of theological thought and teaching characteristic of the early Church in Syria and Mesopotamia. With the conversion of the royal house to Christianity (*c.* 202), EDESSA became a center of Oriental Christian culture and theological activity. Mention is made of the disciples of BARDESANES and LUCIAN OF ANTIOCH, who had studied exegesis with Macarius of Edessa (*Die griechischen christlichen Schriftsteller der ersten drei Jahrhunderte* 21.184), and Eusebius of Emesa attended lectures on Scripture there (*Patrologia Graeca* 67:1045).

In 363 the Emperor Jovian ceded Nisibis to the Persians and EPHREM THE SYRIAN transferred his school of theology from Nisibis to Edessa and directed it there for ten years. Among his earlier disciples, supposedly, were the alleged heretics Paulona and Arvad, and Zenobius, parts of whose writings have been preserved. Ephrem was a competent scholar and controversialist whose literary style and poetry were quickly recognized as classics of Syrian culture and proved a stimulus to the production of exegetical and doctrinal works among his followers. On the death of Ephrem (373), Qiyôrê took charge of the school and gave courses in exegesis. In the beginning he followed Ephrem's methods; later, however, he used the commentaries of THEODORE OF MOPSUESTIA. Among his disciples were Barsauma of Nisibis and Ma'na of Rêwardašir. Two others, Kûmî and Proba, translated the works of Theodore into Syrian, and the school adopted the Antiochene theology. This caused considerable difficulty with Bishop RABBULA of Edessa (412–435), who was a partisan of CYRIL OF ALEXANDRIA.

Ibas of Edessa (435–457), an instructor at the school, succeeded Rabbula. His famous *Letter to Maris* in which he criticized the Alexandrian Christology became an issue at the Council of CHALCEDON (451) and was condemned as one of the THREE CHAPTERS under JUSTINIAN I (553). Many of the students who were formed in theology during the 5th century at Edessa became bishops in Persia; they included Simeon of Beit Aršam, Marûn 'Eloyoto, Acacius the Aramean, 'Abšuto of Nineveh, John of Beit Garmay, Paul bar Qaqay of Karka, Abraham the Mede, and Narses the Leper. These men contributed to the eventual acceptance of NESTORIANISM in the Persian Church. The Acts of the Synods of Tyre and Berytus and of the Robber Synod of Ephesus (449), as well as of the Council of Chalcedon, reveal the difficulties experienced by Ibas.

Narses of Edessa became head of the school in 437 but was expelled from Edessa (451) as a Nestorian and founded a new school at Nisibis on the invitation of Bishop Bar Sauma. In 489 Bishop Cyrus II (470–498) closed the school of Edessa at the order of the Emperor Zeno. On the site of the destroyed school a church was erected in honor of Mary, the Mother of God.

Little is known of the organization of the school at Edessa. Details concerning its teaching and students in the *Testament* of St. Ephrem have been challenged as interpolations. Its successor, the school of Nisibis, proved to be a stronghold of Nestorian teaching.

Bibliography: *Testament de s. Ephrem,* ed. R. DUVAL, *Journal Asiatique* 18 (1901) 234–319. R. NELZ, *Die theologischen Schulen der morgenländischen Kirchen* (Bonn 1916). A. BAUMSTARK, *Geschichte der syrischen Literatur* (Bonn 1922) 34, 66, 100–107. E. R. HAYES, *L'École d'Édesse* (Paris 1930). H. RAHNER, *Lexicon für Theologie und Kirche,* (Freiburg, 1957–66) 3:658–659. A. VAN ROEY, *Dictionnaire d'histoire et de géographie ecclésiastiques* (Paris 1912) 14:1430–32.

[F. X. MURPHY]

EDGAR THE PEACEFUL

King of the English; b. 943; d. July 8, 975. The son of King Edmund and St. Alfgifu, he succeded his brother

Eadwig in 959. During Edgar's reign England enjoyed internal stability and was spared foreign invasion. He supported Archbishop DUNSTAN OF CANTERBURY and his associates, OSWALD OF YORK and ETHELWOLD OF WINCHESTER, in the reform of the English Church and the revival of monasticism. He improved the parish organization and enforced the payment of tithes. His coronation in 973 followed, for the first time in England, a definite liturgical order and emphasized the spiritual side of the ceremony. Edgar was buried at GLASTONBURY, where he was treated almost as a saint.

Bibliography: C. PLUMMER, *Two of the Saxon Chronicles Parallel* (Oxford 1892–99) 1:113–121; 2:152–163. A. J. ROBERTSON, *The Laws of the Kings of England from Edmund to Henry I* (Cambridge, Eng. 1925) 16–39. W. HUNT, *The Dictionary of National Biography From the Earliest Times to 1900* (London 1885–1900) 6:365–370. R. STANTON, *A Menology of England and Wales* (New York 1887) 326–328. F. M. STENTON, *Anglo-Saxon England* (2d ed. Oxford 1947) 359–367. J. GODFREY, *The Church in Anglo-Saxon England* (Cambridge, Eng. 1962). E. JOHN, ''The Beginning of the Benedictine Reform in England,'' *Revue Bénédictine* 73 (1963) 73–87.

[B. W. SCHOLZ]

EDGEWORTH DE FIRMONT, HENRY ESSEX

Priest; b. Edgeworthtown, County Longford, Ireland, 1745; d. Mitau (or Yelgava), Latvia, May 22, 1807. He was the son of a Protestant pastor who was converted to Catholicism, and who moved with his family to Toulouse in 1749. After studying there under the Jesuits, Edgeworth made his ecclesiastical studies in Paris, was ordained, and then devoted himself in Paris to the direction of consciences. He became the confessor of Madame Elizabeth, sister of the king. During the FRENCH REVOLUTION, when King LOUIS XVI chose him to assist at his last hours, Edgeworth went to the Temple prison, conversed at length with the condemned monarch, heard his confession, celebrated Mass for him, distributed Holy Communion to him, and remained with him on the scaffold (1793). Since Edgeworth's courage and priestly activity made him hateful to the revolutionaries, he had to hide in Choisy-le-Roi, Fontainebleau, and Bayeux before taking refuge in England (1796). After visiting the Count of Artois in Edinburgh, he became chaplain to Louis XVIII at Blackenbourg and then at Mitau. His devotion to wounded French prisoners during Napoleon's campaign in Poland led to his own death through a disease contracted while caring for them.

Bibliography: H. E. EDGEWORTH DE FIRMONT, *Letters from the Abbé Edgeworth to His Friends,* ed. T. B. ENGLAND (London 1818). C. S. EDGEWORTH, *Memoirs of the Abbé Edgeworth, Containing His Narrative of the Last Hours of Louis XVI* (London 1815). V. M. MONTAGU, *The Abbé Edgeworth and His Friends* (London 1913). J. HERISSAY, *Les Aumôniers de la guillotine* (Paris 1954).

[C. LEDRÉ]

EDIFICATION (IN THE BIBLE)

The technical NT term for ''building up'' the Church, ''edification,'' has its roots in the OT interplay of the concepts of building the Temple and of building the people; it was used by Jesus Himself to speak of the building of the new people of God; and finally, it was emphasized by St. Paul as a theological term for the spiritual formation of the Christian community.

Use in the OT. Used in the literal sense of constructing a building, the word received its religious stamp in the OT when used in the sense of building the Temple, which is a house for the Lord (1 Kgs 6.1). Because ''house'' could stand for dynasty, ''building a house'' could also mean establishing a lasting dynasty. This play on words underlies Nathan's response to David's intention to build God a house—God instead will build a house for David, namely, the Davidic dynasty (2 Sm 7.5, 7, 11). ''Building'' thus becomes associated with the future of God's people; God will rebuild them [Ps 146 (147A).2; Jer 31.4; 31.28; 33.7]. But cooperation with the divine construction depends less upon descendence from David than upon fidelity to Yahweh (1 Kgs 11.38), so that even neighboring pagan tribes, if they confess Yahweh to be the true God, ''shall be built up in the midst of my people'' (Jer 12.16).

In the Gospels. The Synoptic tradition (Mk 12.10; Mt 21.42; Lk 20.17) uses the building theme in the image of the stone that the builders rejected; it becomes the keystone or cornerstone of the whole edifice. Rejected by Jewish leaders, Jesus becomes through His Resurrection the center and head of the new people God now builds. Peter is presented as the foundation of the new people whom Jesus calls His own; a church that He Himself will build upon Peter (Mt 16.18). The destruction and rebuilding of the Temple is an important element in the Passion story (Mk 14.58; 15.29; Mt 26.61; 27.40), clarified by Jn 2.19–22 in the light of the Resurrection: Jesus' body is the new temple of God.

In St. Paul. In St. Paul, the organic union effected by Baptism with the risen Christ, in whom the fullness of the Godhead dwells bodily (Col 2.9), makes Christians members of Christ (1 Cor 3.16–17; 6.15), hence the sanctuary indwelt by the Holy Spirit (1 Cor 6.19). Thus ''body of Christ'' and ''temple'' (or ''sanctuary'') of

God become interchangeable terms for the Church, as is illustrated by the mixing of the two figures when Paul says both that the body is built up and that the temple grows (Eph 2.21; 4.12, 16).

The process of ''building up'' this body-temple, therefore, is a sacred act—a far cry from the sentimental or merely ethical sense that ''edification'' has acquired in modern times. It is primarily a divine act; God Himself is the builder (1 Cor 3.10; Acts 20.32). This does not exclude, but rather demands Christ's causality, for He is the foundation (1 Cor 3.11; Col 2.7) and source of all building power in the Church (Eph 4.10–16). It also demands the causality of official ministers, especially the Apostles (Eph 2.20; 4.11). They have divine authority to build up (2 Cor 10.8; 13.10; Rom 15.20). Others share in this power but only subordinately to the Apostles (1 Cor 3.10), particularly the Prophets (inspired spokesmen within the community, Eph 2.20; 4.11; one Cor 14.3), but also other ministers, such as evangelists, shepherds, and teachers whom Christ has given to the Church for its upbuilding (Eph 4.10–16). The work of construction belongs also to all the faithful, whose church-building power the official ministers organize and direct. The building power may be a charismatic gift (of any kind, one Cor 14.12, 17, especially prophecy, 14.3, and interpretation of tongues, 14.5) or the superior gift of fraternal charity (1 Cor 12.31; 13), which all must possess and which is the building power par excellence (1 Cor 8.1; Eph 4.16). Every Christian thus has the responsibility for building up the Church (1 Thes 5.11; Rom 14.19; 15.2), and this is a genuine work of ministry corresponding to Christ's design (Eph 4.12).

''Building up'' in both OT and NT theology means strengthening more than expansion (Col 2.7: ''be . . . built up on him and strengthened in the faith''). Thus, the role of sound teaching is stressed in ''upbuilding'' contexts in contrast to the divisive and weakening effects of heterodoxy (Eph 4.10–16). Pauline texts also evoke a wider understanding of the concept by relating it to the contact and interaction of members of the body (Eph 4.16): a sharing of consolation (1 Thes 5.11; Rom 1.11–12), of joy (2 Cor 2.3; one Cor 12.26), of sufferings that can win life for fellow members (Col 1.24; two Cor 4.12; two Tm 2.10), and of prayer (Phil 1.19; two Cor 1.11; Phlm 22). ''Edification'' involves fraternal correction, encouragement, and support (1 Thes 5.11, 14); seeking what is pleasing to one's neighbor, what helps him advance in good (Rom 15.2); avoidance of foul language and making one's speech an occasion of grace for the listeners (Eph 4.29); and promoting unity in the community (1 Cor 14.26, 40). In short, the building up of the community is a good to which all else is to be directed (1 Cor 14.26).

The process is itself directed to a higher end. As a house is built for the one who will dwell in it, so Christians are being ''built together to become a dwelling place for God in the Spirit'' (Eph 2.22), another way of saying they are growing ''into a temple holy in the Lord'' (2.21). Edification is thus a religious act: its end is the consummate indwelling of the Divine Persons.

Bibliography: J. PFAMMATTER, *Die Kirche als Bau* (*Analecta Gregoriana* 110; 1960). O. MICHEL, in G. KITTEL, *Theologisches Wörterbuch zum Neuen Testament* (Stuttgart 1935–) 5:122–161. P. BONNARD, *Jésus-Christ édifiant son église* (Neuchâtel 1948). G. W. MACRAE, ''Building the House of the Lord,'' *American Ecclesiastical Review* 140 (1959) 361–376. *Encyclopedic Dictionary of the Bible*, tr. and adap. by L. HARTMAN (New York 1963) 286. Y. CONGAR, *The Mystery of the Temple* (Westminster, Md. 1962). P. S. MINEAR, *Images of the Church in the New Testament* (Philadelphia 1960).

[G. T. MONTAGUE]

EDIGNA, BL.

Virgin; d. Puch, near Fürstenfeldbruck, Bavaria, Feb. 26, 1109. According to legend she was the daughter of a French king and fled to Bavaria rather than abandon her vow of virginity and accept marriage as her father directed. She reputedly lived there in a hollow linden tree from which, after her death, holy oil flowed, but when merchants tried to sell the oil, the flow stopped. She is still honored at Puch, where she is buried, as patroness against theft.

Feast: Feb. 26.

Bibliography: *Acta Sanctorum* Feb. 3:674–675. R. BAUERREISS, *Kirchengeschichte Bayerns,* 5 v. (St. Ottilien 1949–55) 3:46–47. M. J. HUFNAGEL, *Lexikon für Theologie und Kirche*[2] 3:660.

[J. C. MOORE]

EDMUND OF ABINGDON, ST.

Archbishop of Canterbury (1234–40) and theologian; b. Abingdon (Berks.), *c.* 1170 of obscure parents; d. Soisy (Seineet-Marne), France, Nov. 16, 1240. He attended the schools of Oxford and Paris, incepted at Paris and taught arts at Oxford *c.* 1194 to 1200, and returned to Paris for theology, which he taught at Oxford *c.* 1214 to 1222. He was appointed treasurer of Salisbury cathedral in 1222, was elected archbishop in 1233, and consecrated April 2, 1234. Elected at a time of national crisis, he averted civil war by his firm leadership, reconciling the party of Richard the Marshal to King HENRY III and forcing the king to reconstruct his council. His episcopate was stormy and litigious. The hagiographical tradition that indicates his withdrawal into voluntary exile, though primitive, lacks historical basis. He was on his way to the papal Curia when he died. He was buried at PONTIGNY abbey, which became the center of his cultus. The only works of his that have been identified are two sermons, his *Moralitates in Psalmos* and the famous *Speculum ecclesiae;* the last is an ascetical treatise designed, in its original form, for religious and inflated with didactic matter of a more elementary kind. It shows a heavy debt to the school of Saint-Victor (*see* VICTORINE SPIRITUALITY), has exerted in turn much influence on later English spiritual writers, and is a real landmark in the history of medieval religious sentiment. He was canonized Dec. 16, 1246.

Feast: Nov. 16 (England, Cistercians).

Bibliography: EDMUND OF ABINGDON, *Libellus qui dicitur Speculum ecclesiae* in M. DE LA BIGNE, *Bibliotheca veterum patrum et auctorum ecclesiasticorum,* 8 v. (3d ed. Paris 1609–10) v. 5. *Saint Edmund's "Merure de seinte église,"* ed. H. W. ROBBINS (Lewisburg, Pa. 1924). *Bibliotheca hagiographica latina antiquae ct mediae aetatis* (Brussels 1898–1901), 1:2404–17. E. MARTÈNE and U. DURAND, *Thesaurus novus anecdotorum* (Paris 1717) 3:1775–1927. M. PARIS, *The life of St. Edmund*, tr. and ed. C. H. LAWRENCE (Oxford 1996). R. ROLLE, *Yorkshire Writers,* ed. C. HORSTMAN, 2 v. (London 1895–96) 1:219–261. C. H. LAWRENCE, *St. Edmund of Abingdon: A Study in Hagiography and History* (Oxford 1960), complete bibliog. and discussion; *Month* NS 29 (1963) 213–229.

[C. H. LAWRENCE]

EDMUND THE MARTYR, KING OF EAST ANGLIA, ST.

Reigned 855 to 870; b. *c.* 841; d. November 20, 870. According to ABBO OF FLEURY, his first biographer (*c.* 987), Edmund was a virtuous king, who was defeated by the Danes. He delivered himself into captivity to save his people. He refused to forswear his faith and was shot with arrows and beheaded at or near Hoxne in Suffolk. Within 40 years he was considered a saint and martyr. In the reign of Athelstan his body was translated to the later BURY-ST.-EDMUNDS. St. Edmund was one of the most widely venerated native saints in Anglo-Saxon England. More than 60 churches were dedicated to him. He is usually represented with crown and arrows and considered a patron against the plague.

The English Benedictines and the Dioceses of Birmingham, Northampton, and Westminster observe his feast on November 20.

Bibliography: Sources. AELFRIC, *Lives of three English saints,* ed. G. I. NEEDHAM (London 1966). *Memorials of St. Edmund's Abbey,* ed. T. ARNOLD (*Rerum Brittanicarum medii aevi scriptores*) 96.1:3–50, 93–103. T. D. HARDY, *Descriptive Catalogue of Materials Relating to the History of Great Britain and Ireland* (*Rerum Brittanicarum medii aevi scriptores*) 26.1.2:526–538. *Bibliotheca hagiographica latina antiquae ct mediae aetatis* (Brussels 1898–1901), 1:2392–2403. JOCELIN DE BRAKELOND, *Chronicle of the Abbey of Bury St Edmunds,* tr. of *Chronica,* tr. D. GREENWAY and J. SAYERS (Oxford 1998). H. KJELLEMAN, *La Vie Seint Edmund le Rei* (Göteborg 1935). M. E. PORTER and J. H. BALTZELL, "The Old French Lives of Saint Edmund King of East Anglia," *Romanic Review* 45 (1954) 81–88. A. BELL, "Notes on Two Anglo-Norman Saints' Lives," *Philological Quarterly* 35 (1956) 48–59. Literature. *La Passiun de Seint Edmund*, ed. J GRANT (London 1978). E. BORDIER, *Des reliques de saint Edmond, roi et martyr* (Paris 1971). R. STANTON, *A Menology of England and Wales* (London 1887) 185–186, 559–561. F. HERVEY, ed., *The History of King Edmund the Martyr* (London 1929). W. BONSER, *An Anglo-Saxon and Celtic Bibliography, 450–1087,* 2 v. (Berkeley 1957) v.1, nos. 1174, 3627, 4326–35, 4411. B. HOUGHTON, *Saint Edmund: King and Martyr* (Levenham 1970). L. RÉAU, *Iconographie de l'art chrétien* (Paris 1955–1959) 3.1:410–411.

[B. W. SCHOLZ]

EDOMITES

A Semitic people who, during OT times, inhabited the highlands east of the ARABA, south of the Dead Sea. Their territory was bounded on the north by the Zared (Zered) Valley, beyond which dwelt the MOABITES. The name Edom (Heb. *'ĕdōm*) is derived from the Semitic root meaning red and was given to the land because of the reddish color of the sandstone of that district. Israelite folklore gave the name first to the eponymous ancestor of the Edomites (whom they identified with ESAU) but, by a popular etymology, derived it from the red stew for which he sold his birthright to the Patriarch JACOB (Gn 25.29–34). The Genesis stories concerning the relations between the twin brothers Jacob and Edom-Esau (25.19–34; 27.1–28.9; 32.4–33.20) reflect the Israelite consciousness of close kinship with the Semitic Edomites as well as the rivalry that existed between these peoples throughout much of their history. The passing of the birthright and blessing from the first-born twin to his junior was seen as an indication of divine election (see Mal 1.2–5) but also reflects the barren nature of the Edomite territory as compared to Israel's and the ascendancy of Israel during much of their history (see Gn 27.24–40).

Little is known with certainty of the origins of the Edomite kingdom. Archeological investigations, especially those of N. Glueck, have shown that nomadic invasions (*c.* 1900 B.C.) destroyed the civilization that had flourished earlier in this region. The invaders may have continued to live there as nomads and may have been the Horrites whom Dt 2.12 says the Edomites drove out when they settled there. At any rate, there was again a settled population there before the close of the 13th century B.C. This archeological finding accords with the Biblical tradition that the Israelites en route to the invasion of Palestine were forced, by the determined opposition of the inhabitants, to detour around Edom (Nm 20.14–21; Dt 2.1–7). A list of eight Edomite kings who ruled before the Israelite monarchy was established is given in Gn 36.31–39 and one Chr 1.43–54, and Gn 36.1–19 lists the clans and subclans of Edom.

The Israelites, under DAVID, conquered the Edomites and annexed their territory (2 Sm 8.13–14). This was a great step forward for the Israelite economy, since the conquest gave them access to trade with Arabia, both overland and through the port at Asiongaber (Eziongeber) on the Gulf of Aqaba; it also gave them access to the rich mineral deposits along the Araba. Solomon exploited these advantages by mining ore and erecting an extensive copper refinery (not mentioned in the Bible) and by building THARSIS (i.e., seagoing) vessels for the Red Sea trade (1 Kgs 9.26–28).

The Edomites, to whom this subjection was hateful, tried on several occasions to rebel against Israel, but as long as Israel remained a united kingdom they were unsuccessful (see 1 Kgs 11.14–22). After the division of the kingdom it would seem that Juda continued to exercise control as far south as the Gulf of Aqaba and may have continued to hold parts of Edom. King Josaphat (*c.* 849 B.C.) ruled Edom and continued to use Asiongaber (1 Kgs 22.48–49); he was able both to pass through Edomite territory when aiding Joram, King of Israel, in his attempt to subdue Moab and to count Edom's king as an ally in this venture (2 Kgs 3.1–27). Under Joram, King of Juda (*c.* 849-*c.* 842 B.C.), Edom successfully revolted (2 Kgs 8.20–22), but was reconquered by Amasia (*c.* 800-*c.* 783 B.C.); Amasia's son Azaria (*c.* 783-*c.* 742 B.C.) reopened Elath—either near Asiongaber or identical with it—and the Red Sea trade (2 Kgs 14.7, 22). During the 8th century B.C. the Edomites, like all their neighbors, came under the power of the ever-expanding empire of the Assyrians; they are listed (see J. B. Pritchard, *Ancient Near Eastern Texts Relating to the Old Testament* [2d rev. ed Princeton 1955] 182) as paying tribute to Tiglath-Pileser III (745-728 B.C.). When the Assyrian Empire had been defeated by the Babylonians, the Edomites became subject to the latter. Later, when the people of Judah had been conquered and exiled by the Babylonians, the Edomites saw an opportunity to take for themselves at least a portion of the defenseless land and they occupied part of the Negeb, thus extending their territory to the west of the Araba. For their hostile attitude toward the Israelites, the Edomites were strongly denounced by the Prophets (Is 34.5–7; 63.1–6; Ez 25.12–14; Book of ABDIA).

In NT times the Edomites, now a mixed people known as Idumeans were ruled by the Herod family. From this dynastic family came HEROD THE GREAT, to whom is attributed the slaughter of the Holy INNOCENTS; his son HEROD ANTIPAS, while tetrarch of Galilee, mocked Christ during His Passion and sent Him back to Pilate to be condemned to death.

''Martyrdom of St. Edmund,'' manuscript illumination from a ''Life of St. Edmund,'' c. 1125–1150.

Bibliography: *Encyclopedic Dictionary of the Bible*, tr. and adap. by L. HARTMAN (New York 1963) 620–624. L. GROLLENBERG, *Lexikon für Theologie und Kirche*, ed. J. HOFER and K. RAHNER, 10 v. (2d new ed. Freiburg1957–65) 3:663–664. M. NOTH, *Die Religion in Geschichte und Gegenwart* (3d ed. Tübingen 1957–65) 2:308–309. F. M. ABEL, *Géographie de la Palestine*, 2 v. (Paris 1933–38) 1: 280–285. A. LEGENDRE, *Dictionnaire de la Bible*, ed. F. VIGOUROUX (Paris 1895–1912) 3.1:830–837. A. MUSIL, *Arabia Petraea,* 3 v. in 4 (Vienna 1907–08), v. 2 *Edom.* V. MAAG, ''Jakob-Esau-Edom,'' *Theologische Zeitschrift* 13 (1957) 418–429. N. GLUECK, ''The Civilization of the Edomites,'' *Biblical Archaeologist* 10 (1947) 77–84. W. F. ALBRIGHT, ''The Horites in Palestine,'' *From the Pyramids to Paul,* ed. L. G. LEARY (New York 1935) 9–26.

[W. M. DUFFY]

EDUCATION (PHILOSOPHY OF)

A term popularized by John Dewey (1859–1952) to signify a study of the fundamental principles of the theory of education, as distinguished from the ''science of education,'' i.e., the empirical study of the educational process, and from the ''art of education,'' i.e., the techniques or methods of educational practice. For Dewey, the philosophy of education dealt principally with the values or goals of education.

The history of educational thought indicates that fundamental questions of a philosophical type have been raised concerning (1) the nature of man as he is capable of being educated, (2) the goal or the character of the truly educated man, (3) the trained abilities that man acquires in achieving this goal, and (4) the agents by which man is educated. In this context the term ''education'' should not be limited to merely academic training, but rather taken in its widest sense of the development of all facets of human personality—physical, moral, and intellectual—in their individual and social aspects. On the other hand, the term ''philosophy of education'' is most properly restricted to a study of education in the light of reason, leaving to a theology of education the profounder questions that can be explored only in terms of a divine revelation concerning the nature and destiny of man.

1. HISTORICAL DEVELOPMENT

Every human culture has provided some form of education by which it has transmitted a cultural heritage to its young and by which it has striven to prepare them as members of society. In primitive cultures and in the ancient civilizations of Mesopotamia, Egypt, etc., this task was conceived primarily as the inculcation of a traditional wisdom and way of life sanctioned by experience and by some divine approval, in contrast with the foolishness of youth or of the wickedness of adulthood. In the great ancient civilizations this came to be embodied in sacred books, which after long development crystallized an accepted way of wisdom. Education then became a process of inculcating these sacred books and expounding their application to the varying circumstances of life. This form of education is not dead but remains at the base of world education. For Christians, the Sacred Scriptures embody the wisdom of a long human past elevated by a prophetic vision of man's ultimate destiny, and they believe that this vision will eventually be the source of cultural unity for the whole world, not destroying other ancient cultures, but integrating them.

With the rise of Greek civilization, however, a more specific conception of a civic or secular education appeared, paralleled, it seems, by something similar in the Confucianist tradition of China. This new view saw education as the preparation of a class of free men who, in societies based on slavery, were prepared to be citizens capable of debating questions of the common good. In such an education the predominant discipline was the art of persuasion, called rhetoric, but this needed to be supported by a broad culture, which made a man conversant with human nature and public affairs. This kind of education was first fostered in Greece by the Sophists and, with the sponsorship of the Stoics, passed to the Roman Empire, where it flourished until the Dark Ages. Renewed in the Carolingian and the12th-century renaissance, it came to dominate the whole educational tradition of Europe from the full Renaissance of the 15th century until the 19th century in the form of the so-called classical or humanistic education (*see* CAROLINGIAN RENAISSANCE).

During the 19th and 20th centuries a markedly different type of education came to occupy a position alongside this old literary education, and then rapidly began to supplant it, namely, scientific education with its emphasis on mathematics and experimental techniques and directed not toward citizenship but toward technology, bringing with it an extension of education to the whole population, in order to integrate it into the industrial scheme. The coexistence of these two different types of education has produced the ''Two Cultures'' made famous by the English writer C. P. Snow. It should not be thought, however, that this second type of education is completely new. It also has a continuous tradition going back through the Renaissance and Middle Ages to Aristotle, Plato and the early Greek physicists.

Pre-Christian Theories. Almost every philosopher in the West has reflected on these practical educational traditions and attempted to criticize and reform them. In each case the philosopher's conception of the nature of man, of human knowledge, human love, and human society, has formed the basis of a theory of human development that can be called his philosophy of education.

Socrates and Plato. The sophistical or rhetorical type of education described above had its first systematic defender in the rhetorician Isocrates (436–388 B.C.). It was vigorously opposed by Socrates (469–339 B.C.), who believed that education can not be founded on traditional wisdom alone, nor can it prepare man for mere success according to accepted social standards, but that it must rest on a profound insight into the nature of reality. The philosopher plays the role of social educator and critic; he is the ''gadfly'' of the republic, who by his searching questions awakens men to responsibility and deep reflection.

Following Socrates' lead, Plato (427–347 B.C.) became the most influential figure in the whole history of the philosophy of education. In his *Gorgias, Protagoras,*

Phaedrus, and *Ion* he vigorously criticized an education based on literary and rhetorical studies, and in the *Republic and Laws* he outlined a system based on the gradual ascent of the mind, by way of mathematical and scientific studies, from traditional and popular opinion to a wisdom based on a vision of eternal principles of truth.

For Plato, man is a spiritual intellect imprisoned in a body, whose education is a revival of an innate knowledge of unchanging reality attained through a critical dialectic, in which one who has attained wisdom guides another who seeks it. Although the goal of this education is the contemplation of the Good, or the One, and is attained perfectly only in a future life, it is directive of this earthly life and results in right social action in the service of the common good.

Education, for Plato, has also a moral aspect, which is inseparably united to its intellectual progress, since the awakening of the soul to truth is accompanied and motivated by a growing love of truth. A man first falls in love with another human being because of physical beauty; then, as he becomes aware of the interior beauty of the other's soul, he comes to love him with a genuine friendship. Led by this friendship he acquires the virtue of temperance as regards sensual pleasure, and then grows to love not only an individual but society. In his love for society he acquires the virtue of fortitude in its defense and of justice in its service. In this way different levels of the soul are brought into harmony and the intellect is set free for its own ascent toward truth. The intellectual curriculum begins with play and with literature and art, in which the student grasps something of truth in images. Here the teacher must exercise a severe censorship lest the impressionable child be injured. From literature (which is a shadow of a shadow) the student passes on to the study of mathematics and astronomy (i.e., the study of a mathematical type of science), in which the mind first awakens to the possibility of genuine and stable truth. From this he goes on to dialectics, or philosophy proper, by which he criticizes all that he knows until with purified mind he awakens to an inner intuition of the Good. Once this ultimate vision is reached, man returns to judge by the light of the first principles all that he has previously learned.

The teacher of highest wisdom, who controls the rest of education, is the philosopher-king, who rules the whole state as a kind of school, arranging its games, its religion, and its laws, not with the purpose of domination but to lead its citizens to a share in his own vision and love. His right to rule is based on his own wisdom, which he has achieved only by the greatest humility and disinterestedness, after the pattern of Socrates. He teaches first by regulation of the environment, then by a mythical propaganda, but ultimately not by indoctrination but by dialectic. Since truth is innate, even in the slave, the teacher can only awaken the student by questioning and by the example of friendship. The teacher has no right to escape the responsibility of public affairs but must be a king or a counselor to kings.

In the 20th century Plato has been criticized as the forerunner of totalitarianism, but to do so is to ignore the fact that totalitarian systems set military and economic power as the goal of society to which men are subjected, while for Plato the goal is contemplation, in which the individual, like Socrates, becomes wholly free of social pressure.

Aristotle. For 20 years Plato's pupil Aristotle accepted this view of education in most of its features, but gave it a different theoretical justification. He denied the theory of innate knowledge on which it rested. For Aristotle all knowledge comes from sense experience since the soul is the form of the body and can know only through the body. Consequently he laid more stress than did Plato on individual differences, going so far as to hold that some men are natural slaves—incapable, at least de facto in Greek society, of a liberal education, although capable of a technical education. Furthermore, most free men who can be liberally educated do not attain to anything more than a small share in contemplation since they are too involved in the duties of the active life. It is only the few who by a rigorous scientific education attain to contemplation; and this, even for them, is not a direct vision of ultimate Truth, but only an indirect knowledge of God as He is reflected in the world.

Moral and intellectual education ought to be proportionate, but a man may be morally good and have little learning, and vice versa. Moral education, according to Aristotle, is much more complex than Plato pictured. Since man has to deal with a diversity of objects and situations, each type of which requires a special virtue, and virtues are acquired only by exercise, man must therefore be subject to diversified training. The ultimate source of MORALITY is to be found not in external laws or in a metaphysical vision, but in prudence, which is an intellectual virtue concerned with discovering the right means to an end in highly varying circumstances. Prudence cannot be taught—it is learned by experience—but it can be assisted by ethical analysis.

Intellectual education is not an ascent toward an ultimate vision; it consists in learning a diversity of arts and sciences, each of which has its own proper method and special purpose. Some people are apt for one discipline, some for another, and it is rare to meet a man who can excel in many. These different disciplines, however, do have a certain order, which the teacher needs to know in order to facilitate learning. Literature and logic come first as necessary tools for further learning. Then comes mathematics, not because it elevates the mind to a higher realm but because it furnishes exercises in exact reasoning concerning simple facts that even the young have experienced. According to Aristotle, next comes the study of natural science, which occupies the central position since all knowledge rests on man's experience of nature and its changes. The ethical or social sciences, which are the proper study of the matured adult citizen, can be only sketched for young students, who lack the experience and objectivity required to deal with such matters. Finally, a learned and experienced man in his 50s is ready for the study of philosophy in the full sense (metaphysics), which attempts to compare and synthesize all kinds of knowledge in order to gain some notion of the ultimate Cause of all things.

The teacher does not arouse innate ideas but seeks to help the student analyze his own experience. He does this by skillful questioning, which helps the student to perceive problems in a given discipline and to apply to them the special principles of that discipline as they are grasped from experience. The art proper to the teacher is logic, which includes literary criticism, rhetoric, and dialectics. The teacher of intellectual disciplines should make no claim to statesmanship. The statesman is a man whose prudence is based on experience of public life. The teacher is a man of wisdom, trained in scientific precision. He is also a man of research, since growth in knowledge can be based only on a more extensive acquaintance with facts. Hence, for Aristotle, moral education is the task of the father of a family and of the statesman, but intellectual education is the work of scholars, who must work together to extend learning. History, he thought, shows progress, but also regress, in knowledge.

Stoics and Early Christian Writers. The Stoics accepted much of this Platonic-Aristotelian scheme, but they insisted that education, far from being a search for truth, means the inculcation of an already achieved dogma, which is the sure guide of life. The goal of life is moral, not contemplative, and is primarily an individual rather than a social accomplishment. The teacher communicates the true doctrine to a pupil, who is thus freed from confusion and disciplined to a set mode of life, which he knows how to defend against all criticism. The early Christian writers, whose ideas were theological rather than philosophical, tended to adopt this same position, as did the Neoplatonic philosophers. The age sought a way of life that was complete and perfect and not subject to further inquiry. This attitude in its neoplatonic form became typical of Byzantine culture and of the Islamic culture derived from it.

In the Latin West, however, more dynamic possibilities eventually opened up. Here Christian writers did not merely juxtapose Greek learning and the study of the Scriptures, but attempted a new synthesis, which resulted in a new conception of education. St. AUGUSTINE (354–430), developing a point of view found already in ORIGEN (182?–251?), which was rooted in Platonic theory, defended the liberal arts and philosophy as a useful preparation for a profound study of the Scriptures (*see* PLATONISM). Boethius (475–525) added to this some elements of the Aristotelian tradition. Eventually, this resulted in the scholastic system of the high Middle Ages, best expressed in the views of St. Thomas Aquinas, which are detailed below (*see* SCHOLASTICISM).

Middle Ages and Renaissance. The educational ideas of the nominalists and the other schools of the 14th century have as yet been little examined by historians. The thinkers of the Renaissance were much concerned with educational theory, since the predominant theme of the period was the idea of human perfectibility. This emphasis was not in itself anti-Christian as is sometimes thought. It was continuous with the medieval view of man as the image of God. The Middle Ages, however, emphasized the notion of God as exemplar, man's fallen condition, and his need for restoration to the divine likeness. The Renaissance, struck with the high degree of human perfection portrayed in pagan literature, and under the leadership of a rising class of educated laymen, wished to emphasize the education of man as a citizen of this world. They found much in Plato and Aristotle to their liking, but drew heavily on Quintillian (35?–95), whose views were those of the old sophistic, rhetorical education. The educational philosophers of the period attempted to paint a picture of the ideal aristocratic gentleman. As a result, to the 20th century their educational theory seems rather narrow and idealistic, as it is found in Giovanni Boccacio (1313–75), Pier Paolo VERGERIO (1349–1420), VITTORINO DA FELTRE (1378–1446), or Bl. John DOMINICI, OP (1356–1419), the last representing a clerical reaction to the general trend. In these writers the accent is on ''the whole man,'' with a tendency to emphasize moral, rather than intellectual cultivation. It is also notable that they were concerned more with education of the very young than with the whole range of education portrayed by Plato and Aristotle. Intellectual culture was thought of as primarily literary and rhetorical, and the study of culture itself was moralistic rather than theological, as, e.g., in ERASMUS (1466–1536) and Juan VIVES (1492–1540). The triumph of this rhetorical approach is to be found in Peter RAMUS (1515–72), but Christian humanism of this general type continued in many writers down to François de la Mothe FÉNELON (1651–1715). Some writers of this tradition, such as John Amos COMENIUS (1592–1670), emphasized child psychology in learning.

Scientific Education. The new intellectual tendency that was ultimately to range scientific education alongside humanism as a powerful competitor appeared clearly with René DESCARTES (1596–1650), although its roots go back to Italian universities and to the Oxford of Thomas Bradwardine (*c.* 1291–1349). It was characterized by its accent on mathematics as the fundamental educational discipline, after which all others were to be modeled. Descartes did not develop an educational theory as such, but his influence was very powerful, with his stress on clarity of thought and on deductive procedure in teaching, and his tendency to regard man's imaginative and emotional life as a hindrance to thought and therefore to be rigorously controlled. Reinforced by Calvinistic views of human sinfulness, Descartes' ideas greatly influenced JANSENISM. In England the Cartesian view was not accepted. Rather, the EMPIRICISM of Francis BACON (1561–1626), with its stress on factual information, practical relevance, and the importance of progress in discovery, came to dominate the intellectual scene, but without greatly influencing education. In the *Essay Concerning Education* of John LOCKE (1632–1704), the humanistic and moralistic tradition is still present, modified only by Locke's emphasis on utility.

Later Developments. The next strikingly new educational approach, and perhaps the most influential for the whole modern period, is that of Jean Jacques ROUSSEAU (1712–78), who reacted sharply against both narrow Cartesian rationalism and British empiricism.

Naturalism. Rousseau put great emphasis on the nature of the child to be educated. Artificial cultivation imposed on the child results not in true education he maintained, but rather in the corruption of the child, just as civilization has been the corruption of mankind. Reviving themes as old as the Greek Cynics, Rousseau insisted that natural man is good (the doctrine of original sin had already been expelled by the rationalists of the preceding century), and should be given a chance to develop his natural potentialities. What is most important in man are the moral qualities, especially the goodness of heart that is spontaneously humanitarian. Intellectual development is of secondary value since the truths by which man lives are naturally sensed by every good man. For Rousseau, as the general good sense of mankind is ultimately the safest guide in moral and social matters, so the best form of government is democracy. In Rousseau's system, little needed to be said about the curriculum. The teacher is above all a good example and a wise friend who permits the student to develop naturally.

Rousseau's philosophy received support from the critical philosophy of I. KANT (1724–1804), who, without accepting Rousseau's permissiveness, nevertheless stressed the moral character of education, which he based on an autonomous sense of duty rather than on an objective norm. At the same time, Kant accepted the remarkable synthesis of mathematicism and empiricism forged by Isaac Newton. Moral life, however, he believed to rest not on science but on a conviction of the existence of God, the immortality of the soul, and the moral law, all of which are not subject to metaphysical proof but are simply demanded by the moral needs of the individual and of society. Education seeks above all to confirm these moral convictions. On the intellectual level the way is open to an education that is highly scientific and technical in character.

Psychological and Idealistic Theories. Johann Herbart (1776–1841) who stressed the view that all new learning must be in the context of what has already been learned by the child from previous experience, devised a practical methodology of teaching based on this principle. Among the practical educators and theorists, Johann Heinrich PESTALOZZI (1746–1827) was the most famous. He attempted to reduce this general point of view to practice in elementary education, laying most stress on letting the child learn from his own experience and interests. It has had a permanent effect through the theories of Maria MONTESSORI (1870–1956) and John Dewey, who both stressed the ''child-centered'' character of education; and it has been greatly reinforced by the rapid advance in child psychology by empirical methods. Although all great modern systems of state education have given lip service to the Rousseauian theory, the pressures of mass education have forced these systems to adhere, in actual practice, to a regimented discipline and curriculum.

The idealistic philosophies of the 19th century and the materialism of Karl Marx (1818–63) also stemmed from Kant and G. W. F. Hegel but took a different road. Idealistic and Marxist thinkers were primarily concerned with the notion of social history as an educative process. The whole human race is undergoing education, they held, and therefore every educational system must be judged relative to the stage in this process that it occupies. This view, which has Christian roots, received some rather fantastic formulations in such thinkers as Friedrich FRÖBEL (1782–1852). It remains of importance today, however, in that most contemporary educational theorists view education in the historical context of progress toward the future.

Nationalism. In such systems the state is usually considered the educator and education is a process of social reform. The child must be saved from an environment that is the product of an outmoded past and developed to play his part in a projected future. Thus, in the Marxist theory, it is stressed that most differences between children are not hereditary but environmental in origin. The goal of education is to produce a citizen of a new communistic society, freed from the oppressive limitations imposed by the class structure of the past. This new man will be, above all, a productive member of his society, fully equipped with the methods of science and advanced technology. The teacher is an instrument of the revolution, who assists this progressive action. (Until recently the family in the Soviet Union has played little part in education.) The teacher should make use of the best methods of modern psychology (i.e., the Pavlovian theory of step-by-step conditioning).

Democratic Education. Like Marx, John Dewey had a Hegelian background. He saw education as a process of social reconstruction. For Dewey, as for Marx, the modern scientific method is the key to control over nature and society. He insists that this method is above all a process of searching, inquiring, and problem solving, a method that does not rest on fixed principles. It is a social process, since this inquiry involves the interplay of many minds engaged in free discussion about common needs. The purpose of education is to develop this type of probing intelligence, which alone will make it possible for man to survive in the evolutionary struggle. This survival will itself be possible only if both society and the school are democratic and if the teacher acts as a guide to help the child to fulfill his potentialities. The child, as a growing organism, product as he is of evolution, naturally seeks this free type of growth. The teacher therefore seeks not to inhibit but to promote growth. The moral aspect of education is found in the development of attitudes and motives reflecting this free intelligence. The child should become open-minded, cooperative, inventive, and self-disciplined. The goal of education is this practical intelligence by which the child is able to enter into an open, progressive society, one that not only seeks concrete goals but, having attained one such goal, seeks others beyond. Vague ideals without practical consequences have no place in education. The curriculum is not something fixed but grows out of the actual practical concerns of the child, who is already beginning to live his life as a citizen of the future.

Dewey's philosophy of education is a synthesis of many themes important in modern thought, particularly in its stress on the value of science, democratic society, and practical control over nature. It has been severely criticized by, among others, Robert Maynard Hutchins (1899–1977), Mortimer Adler (1902–2001), and Jacques Maritain (1882–1973). They see his view as essentially a revival of the old sophistic tradition, with its emphasis on the pragmatic orientation as opposed to the contemplative orientation of the Platonic and Aristotelian traditions. They believe that it constitutes a great narrowing of the cultural heritage of the past, capable of severing the roots of Western civilization. It is also under criticism by the newer existentialist and personalist theories of man, which stress the theme that education must awaken the individual to his responsibility for his own life and to the fundamental importance of relations between persons rather than between persons and things.

Bibliography: H. I. MARROU, *A History of Education in Antiquity,* tr. G. LAMB (New York 1956). W. W. JAEGER, *Paideia: The Ideals of Greek Culture,* tr. G. HIGHET, 3 v. (New York 1939–44; v.1, 2nd ed. 1945). R. ULICH, *History of Educational Thought* (New York 1945). J. S. BRUBACHER, *Modern Philosophies of Education* (3rd ed. New York 1962).

[B. M. ASHLEY]

2. MODERN THEORIES

Humanistic thinking during the Renaissance reflected a decided shift in philosophical emphasis from the metaphysical, eternal, and spiritual to the physical, temporal, and material. In short, the focus of concern became man rather than God. In contrast to the worldly southern humanists, Christian humanists continued to regard individual salvation as supremely important although knowledge was to have direct, practical benefit to the whole of society rather than being an end in itself.

Realism in Education. Desiderius ERASMUS (1466–1536) wrote that the practical application of knowledge to service of the community was an essential end of education, second only to service of God as man's principal duty. Impatient with deductive arguments based on assumptions of preexisting ideas, the Spanish humanist and student of Erasmus, Juan Luis VIVES (1492–1540), stated as the basis of his learning theory that the search for truth began with observations of the external world proceeding through inductive reasoning to its conclusion. Vives was the first to begin with the learner rather than with the subject matter in making proposals concerning the aims and methods of education.

Francis Bacon's (1561–1626) attempt to "make a small globe of the intellectual world" influenced the educational thought of the 17th-century Moravian bishop, John Amos COMENIUS (1592–1671). The latter felt that only through an education designed to bring about self-knowledge, self-control, and self-direction to God could man realize his supernatural destiny. He clung to the doctrine of innate ideas and believed that man's germinal capacities must be developed through years of formal schooling, carefully organized to correspond to stages of natural development. Guided by his concept of *pansophia*—universal wisdom—Comenius developed a detailed methodology by means of which the student might come to acquire a vast array of interrelated factual knowledge.

It remained for John LOCKE (1632–1704), at the time of the English Restoration, to reject the doctrine of innate ideas. On the contrary, Locke argued that man's mind is a *tabula rasa,* a blank slate to be filled in through the effects of sensory experience and later reflection. Holding to the Greek ideal of "a sound mind in a sound body," Locke listed virtue, truth, wisdom, breeding, and learning as the desired endowments of a "gentlemen" and violently criticized the schools of his day for imbalancing this order. To Locke, reason and discipline were all important and the disadvantages of formal schooling seemed to outweigh all the advantages.

Naturalism. In developing his own educational thought, Jean Jacques ROUSSEAU (1712–78), the epitome of romantic naturalism, extended Locke's criticism of formal education. Since Rousseau believed that man was inherently good and absolutely free, the task of education was to return him to his state of unfettered innocence. This in turn was to be achieved by rearing the child as far from the stifling influences of corrupt society as possible. The child must learn truth by himself, supplied by sense impressions and illuminated by his "inner light." Rousseau postulated natural stages of development and argued for recognition of the child's right to a life of his own. Like Rousseau, Johann Bernhard Basedow (1723–90) realized the importance of play in the life of the child and insisted on the fundamental role of the sensory perceptions in the acquisition of knowledge.

Rousseau's work influenced also Heinrich PESTALOZZI (1746–1827) and Friedrich FRÖBEL (1782–1852), even though these later educators rejected Rousseau's isolationist ideas by proclaiming education a socializing process and shared a conception of man as the child of God. The Swiss educator Pestalozzi hoped for the moral regeneration of mankind through love and goodness, advocated education for all, and urged that the school should be homelike and natural. For Fröbel, a German disciple of Pestalozzi, education was a process of self-realization that aids man in unfolding the divine essence within him. The "Father of the Kindergarten," he recognized not only the socializing aspects of play but also the significance of play in developing self-activity. Insisting on the essential unity and interconnectedness of all things internal and external, the highly mystical Fröbel proposed a system of "gifts and occupations" by means of which the child might develop insight into various aspects of his world, and increased power of controlling them.

Scientism. The thought of Pestalozzi was concretized by Johann Friedrich Herbart (1776–1841), who began the development of a "science" of education through the systematic application of psychological principles to actual problems of educational practice. However, Herbart broke completely with all those who adhered to the notion of substantive mind. Rejecting the postulates of faculty psychology, he renounced all theories of innate and a priori truths and stressed instead the importance of the sense perceptions, the effects of experience, and the changes of relationships among ideas. Thus, an important task of education is to structure man's "mind" through the systematic formation of associations among ideas within the "apperceptive mass." Yet with all his stress on intellectual attainments, Herbart considered such training subordinate to the development of morality and virtue as an aim of the educational process. Harmonious social relations, self-discipline, and individual liberty attended by respect for the rights of others were more prized by Herbart than was the mere acquisition of factual knowledge.

During the same century in England, Herbert SPENCER (1820–1903) also discussed "liberty" and "morality" but with a considerable difference in interpretation. Spencer rejected all ultimate ideas and absolute truths and insisted that philosophy must integrate and interpret known scientific facts. He described life as an evolutionary process of endless "adjustment" of internal to external conditions and declared that morally "good" conduct is that which leads to successful adjustment. Spencer considered the function of education to be preparation for "complete living," that is, successful adaptation to one's environment, and he appraised subjects in the curriculum in terms of the contribution each could make toward self-preservation, social and political well-being, and effective use of leisure.

Another ardent evolutionist was the prominent American psychologist and educator, Granville Stanley Hall (1846–1924), who postulated the existence of a "folksoul" and depicted the development of the individual by stages that recapitulate or repeat, on a compressed scale, the entire past experience of the race as a whole. Obsessed with the significance of the peculiar characteristics of childhood, Hall strongly opposed the traditional view of the child as a miniature adult and urged increasing awareness of children's needs. He also warned that the schools must make greater provision for individual differences and interests in order to facilitate the natural evolution of both individuals and social institutions.

Nationalism and Communism. The growing scientific interest in eugenics exemplified by Hall was distorted to a perverted extreme during Adolf Hitler's (1889–1945) National Socialist ("Nazi") regime in 20th-century Germany. Nazi doctrine singled out "Blood and Soil" as the fundamental realities of man's existence in organized society. Specifically, the Nazis sought to ensure the supremacy of the ''Aryan race'' in a world dominated by the German ''folkish state.'' It was believed that not only physical type but also such individual characteristics as intellect, leadership, and even musical ability were racial traits transmitted genetically according to Mendelian principles. Recognizing the difficulty of preserving Nordic racial purity, the state asserted its priority over the rights of the individual, parents, and other social institutions in education as in other matters.

In the Socialist-Communist state, the child has likewise been considered the property of the state, which has responsibility for educating him. However, whereas the German National Socialist ideal was the cultivation of an Aryan elite, the Socialist or Communist holds as his ideal the creation of a classless society. To the Communist the determining influence on the life of society is ''the mode of production of material values,'' so that the program of the schools is to be oriented around the concept of socially useful labor. Russian communism rests on a foundation provided by Karl Marx's (1818–83) dialectical materialism, which postulates that conflict caused by internal contradictions inherent in all natural processes is the fundamental means by which change is wrought in the world. All historical development grows out of conflict arising from competition among different socioeconomic classes in society. Translated into action by Vladimir Lenin (1870–1924), Joseph Stalin (1879–1953), and their successors, Marxist doctrine makes clear that the liberation of the proletariat with simultaneous formation of the ideal Socialist state can take place only through revolution and not through reform. The school, charged with molding citizens of the Socialist state, with disseminating Marxist-Leninist philosophical doctrine, and with providing vast numbers of technically skilled laborers, is inextricably connected with the political machinery of the state.

Progressivism. In 20th-century America, John Dewey (1859–1952) and his followers in the progressive movement in education have argued that democracy and not socialism represents the highest development of society and that individual freedom is to be valued over socialistic collectivism. Giving instrumental emphasis to the pragmatism of Charles PEIRCE (1839–1914) and William JAMES (1852–1910), Dewey rejected traditional metaphysical problems and focused on probability and change rather than on certainty and fixed principles. Although Dewey wholeheartedly accepted the principles of the theory of evolution, he stressed the importance of control and ''reconstruction'' of the environment rather than mere passive adjustment to it. Since at any stage of his existence the individual is growing and truly changing and not merely repeating the predetermined cycle of his species, education is a never ending process rather than a stable product. As ''the continuous reconstruction of experience'' in order to direct future action, education represents the means of continuous growth and not a commodity held passively in storage. In the years following the Depression in the U.S., Dewey and his later interpreters in the progressive movement became the target for increasingly severe criticism from many disparate sources.

Social Reconstruction vs. Tradition. George Counts (1889–1974) and Theodore Brameld (1904–1987) warn that drastic social reform rather than minor social adjustments are called for in the present age of crisis; hence their designation as social reconstructionists. In *Dare the Schools Build a New Social Order?* Counts insists that education must deal with the harsh realities of current social issues. Teachers must seek professional autonomy so that the schools will exert a pervasive influence on national social values and institutions. Stressing the importance of the behavioral sciences in a technological age, Brameld proposes the reformulation of international human goals through the achievement of a ''social consensus'' in which students would participate through a curriculum that focuses on the evaluation of social problems.

In sharp contrast to these critics, educational traditionalists argue that the school should refrain from involvement in immediate social problems and plans for molding the future, and should look instead to the traditions of the past for guidance in carrying on its work most effectively. Despite differences in philosophical orientation, Herman Horne (1874–1946), Isaac Kandel (1881–1965), and Robert Ulich (1890–1977) generally agree on educational goals. The school as a formal institution should concentrate on intellectual development and its course of study should be dictated by the intellectual traditions of all ages. In fact, such classical humanists as Robert Maynard Hutchins (1899–1977) and Mortimer Adler (1902–2001) champion the ''Great Books'' of the past as the logical foundation of the curriculum. Linguistic and mathematical skills are of basic importance, while specialized physical, social, and vocational training are best left to other agencies.

Existentialism and Analytic Philosophy. Radically different from traditional philosophies in their relationship to education, neither existentialism nor analytic philosophy seeks to develop a formal philosophy of education. Not concerned with questions of essence, existentialists such as Martin HEIDEGGER (1889–1976), Jean Paul SARTRE (1905–80), Karl JASPERS (1883–1969), and Gabriel MARCEL (1889–1973) emphasize the nature of human existence as man's fundamental concern. Man possesses absolute freedom to choose among possible courses of action but must also assume absolute responsibility for these choices. Life thus becomes a process of self-realization or, to use a favorite existentialist term, of ''transcendence.'' Since individual involvement in life's situations is at the core of human existence, education must be oriented about the unique individual rather than the group. Hence, the existentialist influence in education makes itself felt as an argument for renewed stress on individual self-realization and responsibility in opposition to all utopian schemes involving collective choice and mass consensus.

Analytic philosophy is a movement seeking to clarify man's utterances through logical or linguistic analysis. One school of analytic philosophers, represented by Bertrand Russell (1872–1970) and his followers, prefers to analyze chains of propositions by means of symbolic logic. A second school, typified by Ludwig WITTGENSTEIN (1889–1951), believes that the clarification of meaning in discourse is the true province of philosophy. Concerned with clarifying problems of logic and of meaning rather than with offering educational prescriptions, both groups attempt to limit themselves to providing methods for the analysis of statements made by educators.

Catholic Philosophy of Education. In close agreement with traditionalist views, Catholic educational commentators, such as Jacques MARITAIN (1882–1973), William Cunningham, CSC (1885–1961), and William McGucken, SJ (1889–1943), emphasize that belief in a personal God is essential to all Catholic thinking on any phase of human activity, including formal education. The general basis of the curriculum remains humanistic and liberal in the traditional sense but with all studies integrated through Christ. In his encyclical letter on Christian education, Pope Pius XI (1857–1939) stressed that the Divine mission of the Church entitles it to precedence over all other agencies with respect to the right to make final decisions concerning educational means and ends. Unlike totalitarian systems of education, however, Catholic philosophy maintains that the family, the state, and the Church all share in the responsibility for the education of youth. Thus, Catholic educational goals require a constant striving for intellectual excellence, social responsibility, and spiritual perfection.

While sharing many insights and methods with other educational systems, Catholic philosophy rejects any position that sacrifices the eternal and supernatural to the temporal and natural. Man is a spiritual as well as a physical being, and only the stable hierarchy of values provided by religion can serve as the integrating principle that unifies these diverse but inseparable elements. Those who follow St. Thomas Aquinas (1225?–74) in believing education to be a lifelong ''process of self-activity, self-direction and self-realization'' respect the child's personal integrity and freedom while providing for necessary adult guidance. The child is the ''principal agent'' in the educational process while the teacher is the ''essential mover'' who brings potentialities to realization by giving extrinsic aid to the natural reason.

The contemplation of truth begins in this life but reaches perfection only in the next. Only when education provides the individual with a vision of the eternal and supernatural as well as an appreciation of the temporal and natural will he understand the purpose of his life on earth and realize his destiny in the life to come. For the Catholic, then, any education that attempts to achieve less than this is incomplete.

Bibliography: T. B. H. BRAMELD, *Philosophies of Education in Cultural Perspective* (New York 1955). J. S. BRUBACHER, *Modern Philosophies of Education* (3rd ed. New York 1962). N. G. MCCLUSKEY, *Catholic Viewpoint on Education* (Garden City, N.Y. 1958; rev. ed. Image Bks. 1962). *National Society for the Study of Education, Forty-first Yearbook, 1942,* pt. 1, *Philosophies of Education; Fifty-Fourth Yearbook, 1955,* pt. 1, *Modern Philosophies and Education.* R. H. G. ULICH, *History of Educational Thought* (New York 1945).

[V. P. LANNIE]

EDUCATION, SCHOLASTIC

A system of education, created by the scholastics of the Middle Ages. The term scholastic, derived from the Latin *schola* (school), designates both the curriculum of studies and the method of teaching employed.

The foundation of scholastic education was the seven LIBERAL ARTS, taught in an elementary way in the grammar school and in greater detail in the arts faculty of the university. In grammar school the principal emphasis was on Latin grammar learned from Priscian and Donatus, verified in the Latin Psalter, and developed in simple composition. In grammar school only the simplest elements of arithmetic were taught; logic and the more difficult parts of the quadrivium were taught in the arts faculty of the university. By the middle of the 13th century the university curriculum was fully formed. Although the arts faculty had lectures on all the major books of Aristotle, the main emphasis was on logic. The reason for this was the prominence given to scholastic disputations in all the faculties, including theology and law; without the tool of logic, such scholastic exercises would have been impossible.

The method of teaching consisted of two distinct features (*see* SCHOLASTIC METHOD). The first feature, the basis, was the lecture (*lectio*), or explanation of an authoritative text. Medieval teachers considered it essential to explain first what great thinkers of the past had contributed to human knowledge. They used Aristotle for logic and philosophy, Cicero for rhetoric, Donatus for grammar, Ptolemy for astronomy, Euclid for geometry, and Boethius for arithmetic and harmonics. The second feature, unique to scholastic education, was the disputation (*disputatio*), or dialectical debate on critical issues arising from or occasioned by the text (*see* DIALECTICS IN THE MIDDLE AGES). The purpose of the formalized *sic et non* debate in all subjects was to secure a deeper rational and critical appreciation of the problem and principles involved. The scholastic disputation followed a strict order of discipline (*ordo disciplinae*) in raising questions for discussion; this order was a re-creation of the original order of discovery (*ordo inventionis*). The conspicuous emphasis on order and logical procedure in scholastic education led to a healthy rationalism in all areas of study, including theology, medicine, law, and philosophy. While the immediate purpose of the scholastic method was KNOWLEDGE and SCIENCE, the masters had the additional obligation to form the morals of their students. For this reason, the vote of the masters on the students was always ''concerning behavior and knowledge'' (*de moribus et scientiis*). Only a small part of scholastic education remains today in Catholic seminaries; authentic scholastic disputations have been replaced, in large measure, by seminars.

See Also: SCHOLASTICISM; SCHOLASTIC PHILOSOPHY; SCHOLASTIC THEOLOGY.

Bibliography: G. A. PARÉ et al., *La Renaissance du XIIe siécle: Les Écoles et l'enseignement (Paris 1933).* H. RASHDALL, *The Universities of Europe in the Middle Ages,* ed. F. M. POWICKE and A. B. EMDEN, 3 v. (new ed. Oxford 1936). F. C. COPLESTON, *History of Philosophy* (Westminster, MD 1946–) v. 2–3. H. O. TAYLOR, *The Mediaeval Mind,* 2 v. (4th ed. London 1938). E. S. DUCKETT, *The Gateway to the Middle Ages,* 3 v. (New York 1938; pa. Ann Arbor 1961).

[E. G. RYAN/J. A. WEISHEIPL]

EDWARD THE CONFESSOR, KING OF ENGLAND, ST.

Reigned 1042 to January 5, 1066, the last Anglo-Saxon king of England and refounder of WESTMINSTER ABBEY; b. Islip, Oxfordshire, 1004. The son of Ethelred II and Queen Emma, he was reared at ELY Abbey until the Danish invasions caused him to be exiled to Normandy. There he stayed until he was elected king of England in 1042. In a difficult situation, surrounded by hostile earls and a divided people, he contrived to keep his position by a mixture of gentleness and cunning. Pious, generous, and unambitious, he lacked the ruthlessness that the political situation required, but he was respected by all for his unworldliness and chastity: it was widely believed that his marriage to Earl Godwin's daughter Edith was never consummated. His patronage of Normans, often criticized, was not extensive, but he did make some promise of the throne to William, Duke of Normandy (WILLIAM I), though on his deathbed, according to Anglo-Saxon sources, he gave it to Godwin's son, Harold, instead. Visions and miracles were attributed to him during his life; after his death his cult was limited to Westminster, political circumstances not favoring its development. His incorrupt body was translated in 1102 by Gundulf, bishop of Rochester, but in 1138 an attempt at obtaining papal canonization failed owing to the civil war. But in 1161 ALEXANDER III canonized him, and from then onward he became one of the most popular of English saints, frequently represented in medieval art. The tradition of his personal appearance, a long, bearded face with fair or white hair, remains constant from the BAYEUX tapestry until the time of Henry VII. His feast was extended to the universal Church by INNOCENT XI; his body rests at Westminster Abbey.

Feast: Oct. 13 (translation) in 1163; formerly Jan. 5.

Bibliography: H. R. LUARD, ed., *The Lives of Edward the Confessor* (*Rerum Brittanicarum medii aevi scriptores* 3; 1858). M. R. JAMES, *La Estoire de Seint Aedward le Rei* (Roxburghe Club 1920). M. BLOCH, ''La Vie de S. Édouard le Confesseur par Osbert de Clare,'' *Analecta Bollandiana* 41 (1923) 5–131. L. E. TANNER, ''Some Representations of St. Edward the Confessor,'' *Journal of the British Archaeological Association* 15 (1952) 1–12. F. BARLOW, ed. and tr., *The Life of King Edward, Who Rests at Westminster* (London 1962, 2d. ed. Oxford 1992); *Edward the Confessor and the Norman conquest* (Bexhill-on-Sea, Sussex 1966); *Edward the Confessor* (London 1970, 1979). AELRED OF RIEVAULX, *Vita S. Edwardi regis et confessoris* tr. as *The life of Saint Edward, king and confessor*, tr. J. BERTRAM (Guildford, Surrey 1990).

[H. FARMER]

EDWARD THE MARTYR, KING OF ENGLAND, ST.

Born *c.* 962; died Corfe, Dorset, March 18, 978. His succession to his father, EDGAR THE PEACEFUL, in 975 was supported by Archbishop DUNSTAN OF CANTERBURY and opposed by a faction that preferred his younger stepbrother, Ethelred, and employed the forces hostile to monasticism. He was murdered when he visited Ethelred. His body was buried at Wareham, and in 980, translated to Shaftesbury, where it was elevated by order of King Ethelred in 1001. The *Vita s. Oswaldi* (*c.* 990–1005) records miracles worked by Edward. In 1008 the king and the witan ordered the observance of his Massday. Edward is listed in the Roman Martyrology; his feast is observed in the Diocese of Plymouth.

Feast: March 18; June 20 (translation).

Bibliography: Sources. T. D. HARDY, *Descriptive Catalogue of Materials Relating to the History of Great Britain and Ireland* (*Rerum Brittanicarum medii aevi scriptores*) 26.1.2:579–581. *Bibliotheca hagiographica latina antiquae et mediae aetatis* (Brussels 1898–1901), 1:2418–20. J. EARLE, *Two of the Saxon Chronicles Parallel,* ed. C. PLUMMER, 2 v. (Oxford 1892–99) 1:121–125; 2:163–169, 181. C. E. WRIGHT, *The Cultivation of Saga in Anglo-Saxon England* (Edinburgh 1939) 146–153, 157–171. Literature. W. HUNT, *The Dictionary of National Biography from the Earliest Times to 1900* (London 1885–1900) 6:423–424. D. J. V. FISHER, ''The Anti-monastic Reaction in the Reign of Edward the Martyr,'' *Cambridge Historical Journal* 10, (1950–52) 254–270. W. BONSER, *An Anglo-Saxon and Celtic Bibliography,* 450–1087, 2 v. (Berkeley 1957) Nos. 1296, 1322, 3589, 4411.

[B. W. SCHOLZ]

St. Edward the Martyr, King of England, (975–978)—after accepting a drink from his stepmother, Elfrida—was stabbed by one of her attendants. (©Bettmann/CORBIS)

EDWARDS, JONATHAN

American Congregationalist theologian and philosopher, whose writings revitalized Calvinist theology and introduced a Christian idealistic philosophy; b. East Windsor, Conn., Oct. 5, 1703; d. Princeton, N.J., March 22, 1758. He was the son of a Congregationalist pastor and experienced early strivings after piety and a precocious interest in natural science. At Yale (A.B.1720, M.A. 1723), where he was greatly influenced by J. LOCKE's *Essay on Human Understanding,* he experienced a religious conversion, disposing him to ''a new sense of things'' and ''a sweet delight in God,'' that was to characterize his later life and writings. In 1727 he was ordained as assistant pastor to his grandfather, Rev. Solomon Stoddard, at Northampton, Mass., and married Sarah Pierrepont. Stoddard had departed from the New England orthodoxy by admitting the unregenerate to the Lord's Supper, seeing it as a means of grace rather than a reward for the faithful, thus carrying the HALF-WAY COVENANT to its logical conclusion. On his grandfather's death in 1729, Edwards succeeded him as pastor, continuing at Northampton until 1750.

A sermon to a ministerial convocation at Boston, stressing that grace is given not primarily for the individual's good, but for God's glory, *God Glorified in the Work of Redemption* (Boston 1731), marked him as a defender of Calvinism and foreshadowed his more mature thought on grace and virtue. A religious revival began (1734) at Northampton, described by Edwards in *A Faithful Narrative of the Surprising Work of God* (Boston 1737). Edwards believed that each individual should have a personal dedication to Christ and not merely assent to a body of doctrine, but he opposed ARMINIANISM and the belief that each man was free to choose his own salvation. For Edwards, the revival was a sign of God's grace rather than a means of obtaining it. He was at first well disposed to the GREAT AWAKENING, which began soon afterward, but drew back from its excesses. He was concerned primarily with the pastoral duty of counseling souls to understand and accept God's grace working on them, never a mere revivalist seeking to make converts. In *The Distinguishing Marks of a Work of the Spirit of God* (Boston 1741) and *Some Thoughts concerning the Present Revival of Religion in New England* (Boston 1742), he attempted to distinguish true piety from false and to defend the revival movement, in its widest sense, as a genuine work of the Holy Spirit. His great work, *A Treatise concerning Religious Affections* (Boston 1746), was a penetrating analysis of the difference between gracious affections and fleeting emotions. He held that a genuine change must take place in the heart and that change must show itself in a lifetime of work and worship.

A strict Calvinist himself, as well as a man of sincere personal piety, Edwards had long labored with the problems raised by his grandfather's innovation. As early as 1734 he preached on the dispositions needed to approach the Holy Table, but by 1748 he had concluded that the sacrament was intended by divine ordinance only for ''*visible* professing Christians,'' excluding those who could not testify to divine regeneration. Edwards, seeking to restore the New England churches to the pure Calvin-

Jonathan Edwards. (The Library of Congress)

ism of a congregation of the saints, evoked a storm of protest and was dismissed from his pastoral charge in 1750. Long interested in missionary work among the Indians—he had written an *Account of the Life of the Late Reverend Mr. David Brainerd,* missionary at Stockbridge, Mass. (Boston 1749)—he accepted (1751) a call as Brainerd's successor. Despite harassment by Northampton enemies, he labored faithfully as pastor and schoolmaster until 1758, finding time also to write his most important works, including *A Careful and Strict Enquiry into the Modern Prevailing Notions of That Freedom of Will, Which Is Supposed to Be Essential to Moral Agency* (Boston 1754), *The Nature of True Virtue,* and other philosophic treatises that were published posthumously. In 1757 Edwards accepted a call to become president of Princeton, but died soon after his arrival in January 1758. Publication of the Yale edition of his *Works,* edited by Perry Miller, was begun in 1957.

Bibliography: *Works,* ed. S. E. DWIGHT, 10 v. (New York 1829–30); *Freedom of the Will,* ed. P. RAMSEY (New Haven 1957); *Religious Affections,* ed. J. E. SMITH (New Haven 1959); *The Nature of True Virtue* (Ann Arbor, Mich. 1960). O. E. WINSLOW, *Jonathan Edwards* (New York 1940). P. MILLER, *Jonathan Edwards* (New York 1949). R. G. TURNBULL, *Jonathan Edwards: The Preacher* (Grand Rapids, Mich. 1958). D. J. ELWOOD, *The Philosophical Theology of Jonathan Edwards* (New York 1960). A. O. ALDRIDGE, *Jonathan Edwards* (New York 1964). P. G. E. MILLER, *Errand into the Wilderness* (New York 1957).

[R. K. MACMASTER]

EDWIN, KING OF NORTHUMBRIA, ST.

B. 585; d. Oct. 12, 633. As king of Deira (616) Edwin first united the Northumbrian kingdoms, and then became overlord of all English peoples south of the Humber except those of Kent. In 625 he married ETHELBURGA, daughter of ETHELBERT OF KENT. After his baptism by his wife's chaplain PAULINUS, Bishop of York, he opened his lands to Christianity (627). But his death in the Battle of Hatfield Chase against the pagan King Penda of Mercia halted missionary activity there. King Edwin was venerated, at least locally, as a martyr.

Feast: Oct. 12; formerly Oct. 4.

Bibliography: Sources. BEDE, *Historia ecclesiastica,* ed. C. PLUMMER (Oxford 1896; reprint 1956) bk. 2, ch. 5, 9–20; bk. 3, ch. 1, 6; *Opera historica,* ed. C. PLUMMER, 2 v. (Oxford 1896) 2:86, 93–117. *Bibliotheca hagiographica latina antiquae ct mediae aetatis* (Brussels 1898–1901), 1:2428. **Literature.** W. HUNT, *The Dictionary of National Biography from the Earliest Times to 1900* (London 1885–1900) 6:550–552. R. STANTON, *A Menology of England and Wales* (London 1887) 487–488, 491. F. M. STENTON, *Anglo-Saxon England* (2d ed. Oxford 1947) 65–66, 79–81. C. J. GODFREY, *The Church in Anglo-Saxon England* (New York 1962).

[B. W. SCHOLZ]

EFFICIENT CAUSALITY

As commonly used, the productive action of the AGENT, or efficient cause, or the relationship of such a cause to its effect. Though philosophers prefer a broader meaning (*see* CAUSALITY), the terms cause and causality are usually taken to mean this sort of thing, and in what follows this usage is adopted. What this general description obscures, however, is that there may be no common or single meaning for what goes under the name of efficient cause or causality. And this may explain why philosophers have argued more over causality than over any comparable topic. The controversy is reflected already in the way such causes are classified, but it becomes yet more pronounced when one attempts to formulate the causal proposition in precise fashion or to specify the origin of man's conviction that nothing happens without a cause.

Classification. One need but review the more commonly used philosophical and theological distinctions to see what diverse meanings are marshaled under the caption of efficient cause. Many of these point up the unique way in which Christian thinkers have come to view God's causal relationship to creatures.

Primary vs. Secondary. This is particularly true of the tendency of Christians to speak of God as the first or primary cause, in comparison to whom all other agents are only secondary causes. What is implied in this way of speaking is that, since God alone is uncaused, only He exercises His causal efficacy in an absolute or independent fashion. All other agents depend on Him not only for their initial existence (as a statue depends on the creative power of the sculptor) but for their remaining in existence (which the art object obviously does not).

Productive vs. Conservative. This leads to the further distinction made by medieval thinkers between causes that are merely productive (e.g., the sculptor) and those that conserve their effect by a kind of continuous creativity. For ARISTOTLE, efficient causes are always productive, whereas the continued existence or conservation of the effect is ascribed to the material, formal, or final causes. In Neoplatonic adaptations of Aristotelian cosmogony, however, all continually creating or conserving causes responsible for the very being or existence of a thing are also classified as efficient causes. ALFARABI, AVICENNA, and AVERROËS, for example, believed God created immediately only the first and most perfect of the pure spirits or intelligences responsible for producing the animated planetary spheres. Each intelligence in turn created the one immediately below it in perfection, as well as the animated planet it moved as an unmoved mover in the manner of a final cause. Thus a hierarchy of pure spirits emanated from the creative mind of God in chainlike fashion through a peculiar type of efficient causality, reminiscent in some respects of the Christian conception of how the divine Son proceeds from the Father by an eternal and necessary form of generation.

Being vs. Becoming. Though Christian thinkers generally, from St. THOMAS AQUINAS to R. DESCARTES, admitted that only God could create in a strict sense, they retained the distinction under the title of cause of being (*causa essendi*) as opposed to the cause of becoming (*causa fiendi*). God is the only instance of the former whereas all other causes, inasmuch as they require some medium or material with which to work, fall into the latter class.

Accidentally vs. Essentially Ordered. Where a chain of such efficient causes is involved, scholastics speak of them as being accidentally ordered to one another in producing their final effect. In a series of procreative causes such as grandfather, father, son, and grandson, for instance, the offspring is not essentially dependent on his ancestors as co-causes in the actual exercise of his own generative powers. On the other hand, causes are essentially ordered to each other if they differ in kind, yet cooperate as a single principle of their common effect. Such would be a causal chain of intelligences as Avicenna described, or male and female in generation, or the mind and object according to some theories of cognition. Here neither cause can exercise its proper causality apart from the co-causality of the other; yet neither owes to this causality what it specifically contributes to the end result.

Essential vs. Coincidental. This distinction should not be confused with another philosophical classification of Aristotle and the scholastics, viz, essential (*per se*) vs. coincidental (*per accidens*) causes. Essential causes produce their effect by deliberate intent or by their very nature. Effects resulting from the chance interplay of natural causes or unintentionally happening to or produced by persons, however, are ascribed to CHANCE and to FORTUNE respectively and are called coincidences or accidents.

Free vs. Natural. This leads to a further subdistinction of essential causes into those that are free (i.e., act with foreknowledge and deliberation) and those that are natural (i.e., once the requisite external conditions are present, act in an automatic or determined fashion by reason of their nature or internal constitution). Nature, as the totality of all such causes, came to be regarded by modern thinkers as acting according to unalterable or deterministic laws, a conviction that went unchallenged until the advent of quantum theory in the 20th century.

Physical vs. Moral. The distinction between physical and moral causes reflects another extension of the notion of efficient causality as regards free agents. A physical cause produces an effect by its own direct action, either immediately or by way of some instrument, e.g., the carpenter who builds a bookshelf or the golfer who putts a ball. A moral cause, however, usually refers to a person who by appeal, threat, or the like, induces a second person to act. Here the agent must be distinguished from the motives he sets forth by way of inducement. The latter come under the category of FINAL CAUSALITY. The expression moral cause is applied also to anyone who is ethically or legally responsible for an action's taking place even though he does not make use of a free agent. Thus the man who turns his dog on a bypasser or the doctor who refuses to give his patient the proper medicine or prescribes some quack remedy instead may each be a moral cause of the damage done.

Proximate vs. Remote. Where a chain or sequence of causes is involved, it is customary to distinguish between the proximate, or immediate, cause of the effect and those more remotely related to it. As Avicenna points out, the true cause should coexist with its effect; yet what commonly goes by the name of cause is not the proximate cause but some more remote event or causal situation preceding it in time.

Univocal vs. Equivocal. Another distinction frequently used by scholastic thinkers is that of univocal and equivocal causes. The latter are unlike their effects, whereas the former produce effects of the same nature as themselves. Parents are univocal causes of their offspring, but God is an equivocal cause of his creatures. Fire applied to combustible material is a univocal cause of the resulting flame, but a painter is an equivocal cause of a portrait.

Immanent vs. Transitive. Immanent causes produce their effects within themselves; transitive causes affect something other than themselves. Any vital activity, for example, is an instance of immanent causality, since it is initiated in and by the organism and tends to perfect it. But the degree of immanence varies accordingly as it applies to the life functions of plants and animals or to such spiritual activities as thinking, feeling, willing, and the like. Divine causality, on the other hand, is described as formally immanent inasmuch as it is identified with the divine nature itself; yet it is virtually transitive inasmuch as its effects are something really distinct and other than God (*see* CAUSALITY, DIVINE).

Total vs. Partial. Another common distinction is that between total and partial cause. Carpenters, plumbers, or plasterers are each a partial cause of the house they construct; man, on the other hand, is said to be the total cause of his own decisions or even of such physical actions as walking, swimming, speaking, and so on.

Principal vs. Instrumental. A peculiar type of partial cause is that known as instrumental. In contrast with the principal cause or agent that produces an effect by virtue of some inherent power or action it initiates, an instrumental cause helps the principal agent do what he could not otherwise do or do so easily. Since the notion of instrument has a measure of vagueness about it, there is also some latitude as to how philosophers and theologians apply it (*see* INSTRUMENTAL CAUSALITY). Some require that the instrument be more or less passive, e.g., the hammer or chisel of the sculptor. Such tools produce their effect only because of the power communicated to them by the principal cause. When power tools are used, or still more, when the surgeon or radiologist merely applies an instrument with a self-contained energy source, the aforementioned interpretation needs some revising. Others extend the notion still further when they speak of all created or secondary causes as being merely instrumental agents with respect to God, and this not because God creates and conserves them, but rather because He cooperates in a special way each time they exercise their causal powers. Scholastics commonly hold this to be the case not only with the natural causes but also with the exercise of free will, though there is no agreement as to how God concurs with man's free decisions (*see* BÁÑEZ AND BAÑEZIANISM; MOLINISM). All agree, however, that unless man is the principal cause of his own actions, he can scarcely be regarded as morally responsible for them. Consequently, many prefer to discuss the divine CONCURRENCE with created causes in terms of the first-named distinction between primary and secondary causality rather than in terms of that between principal and instrumental causality.

Participated vs. Unparticipated. Another way of expressing the fact that creatures exercise their own proper causality, albeit dependently on God, is to say that they share or participate in God's creativity. As the scholastics put it, creatures are called participated causes, whereas God's causality is said to be unparticipated. This medieval usage has its philosophical roots in PLATO and PLOTINUS, for whom the transcendent world of absolute values and ideals (identified by St. AUGUSTINE with the divine mind) is that which most truly exists. Applied specifically to efficient causality, it leads the Christian thinker not only to regard God's causal action as a paradigm case of what cause means but also as that which, despite its uniqueness, is paradoxically most typical. This way of viewing things, however, tends to obscure the fact, stressed by contemporary philosophers of the linguistic school, that this notion of cause and causality is a far cry from what goes by that name in ordinary, nonphilosophical usage. Particularly among the skeptical and the agnostic, it further raises questions as to the propriety of such an extension of the usual meaning of cause and, still more, as to the validity of the traditional causal approach to the existence of God.

Causal Proposition. The force of such contemporary objections concerning the scope of application of causal notions becomes clearer from a consideration of the problems posed by any attempt to express in a general way what all or most instances of efficient causality imply. One such problem is how to put the causal relationship itself in propositional form. Perhaps the most neutral and universally acceptable statement is "Whatever begins to be has an efficient cause." This avoids such trivial and uninformative versions as "Every effect has a cause" or "No effect without a cause," where no factual criterion is given for identifying an effect or instance of efficient causality. On the other hand, it is not limited to a specific sense of cause as is the determinist's manifesto: "If, in the course of time, a state *A* of the universe is once followed by a state *B,* then whenever *A* occurs, *B* will follow it" (P. Frank, 54). How to interpret "efficient cause" still remains to be decided. In Plato's *Phile-*

bus (26E), for example, Socrates asks: ''Does not everything which comes into being of necessity come into being through a cause?'' He goes on to describe the cause or agent as ''leading'' and the effect as ''naturally following.'' If one understands this in a temporal sense, it at best describes a cause of becoming (*fiendi or fieri*) and not a cause of being or existence (*essendi or esse*), although it is the latter that figures in the proofs for the existence of God in Avicenna and Aquinas. It should be obvious that this point must be settled before one can answer satisfactorily another question often raised, viz, whether the causal proposition is a principle or a conclusion.

If PRINCIPLE be taken in its etymological sense of a starting point or first premise that needs no proof because it is either self-evident or its truth is commonly admitted, then the causal proposition may be regarded as a principle (*see* FIRST PRINCIPLES). It was so estimated by Plato, Augustine, and the scholastics, though they rarely called it a principle explicitly; the question of whether its denial is self-contradictory became a philosophical issue only in the 14th century with scholastics such as NICHOLAS OF AUTRECOURT. On the other hand, neoscholastics in the last quarter of the 19th century commonly cited it as a basic principle of metaphysics, and many claimed it to be an analytic truth in the Kantian sense of the term. Most of these, however, worded it in some form equivalent to ''No effect without a cause,'' where it could be shown to be trivially true by virtue of a circular definition of terms. But when ''beginning to be'' or contingency was taken as the hallmark of an effect, the reputed analyticity of the proposition was soon challenged. A few contemporary scholastics influenced by I. KANT speak of it as a synthetic a priori truth, and others as a postulate of reason; the majority, however, justify it as a proposition entailed by other metaphysical doctrines, such as that of the real distinction between essence and existence or that of PARTICIPATION, or by the more general principle of SUFFICIENT REASON. [For a neoscholastic critique of this principle, see Mansuetus a S. Felice, *De discordia systematis rationis sufficientis cum libertate humana . . . dissertationes septem* (Cremona 1775); also A. B. Wolter, *Summula Metaphysicae* (Milwaukee 1958) 53–55.] *See* CAUSALITY, PRINCIPLE OF.

Origin of the Notion of Cause. Still another area where the precise meaning of cause figures in the controversy concerns the origin of the causal notion and the related questions of whether any causes are perceived directly or are immediately experienced or whether all instances of causal efficacy must be inferred. That things begin to be is an incontrovertible fact of experience, but there is no similar unanimity as to why man affirms causality as such. RICHARD OF SAINT-VICTOR, for example, declares that the association of ''caused'' and ''what begins to be'' is not something directly experienced but is the fruit of a rational analysis of logical alternatives. Whatever is or can be, he points out, (1) either exists eternally or not, and (2) either exists of itself or not. Of the four possible ways of combining such disjunctive notions, only the idea of something ''not eternal that exists of itself'' is abhorrent to reason. ''Whatever in time begins to be was once nothing,'' he argues. ''But while it was nothing it had nothing whatsoever nor could it do anything at all. To neither itself nor to another could it give this, that it be. Otherwise it would give what it did not possess and do what it could not accomplish'' (*De Trin.* 1.6). Richard, of course, is speaking of an idea of cause that would apply to God, and one may well grant that *causa esse* is not something experienced.

A. Chollet, who uses a somewhat similar argument to try to prove that the link between ''what begins to be'' and ''cause'' is a logically necessary one, insists that both notions are experienced inasmuch as consciousness reveals the fact of one's own causality. MAINE DE BIRAN had proposed this view previously on purely psychological grounds, arguing that the notion of causal force is not the result of a habit of expectancy, as D. HUME claimed, but is the result of an intuition of self as a primal source of activity. It is only by means of an inference that man transfers to external objects this force felt within himself.

More recently A. E. Michotte conducted an ingenious series of experiments at the University of Louvain, which he contends disprove the theories of both Hume and Maine de Biran. For they seem to show that man is equipped by nature to see what Michotte calls the ''causal effect'' in much the same way as he sees locomotion. Any two perceptual objects (be they physical or phenomenal) that move in a certain way with respect to one another will produce the causal impression. If the stimulus conditions are right, the causal impression arises even when an occurrence is observed but once; if the conditions are not right, no amount of repetition will produce an impression of causality. Like the more familiar phi-phenomenon or stroboscopic movement, this impression can be produced artificially when no actual physical causality obtains. It appears spontaneously under conditions far removed from any normal situation in which the specific effect might conceivably be attributed to learning. Michotte shows the laws governing the perception of such a ''kinematic form'' closely resemble the Gestalt laws for the perception of static forms. His experiments, he admits, are concerned only with the phenomenon referred to as causality, not with the epistemological question of how the illusion of causality is to be distinguished from its reality.

Jean Piaget, on the other hand, believes his independent studies on the evolution of the concept of physical causality in children confirms a modified form of Maine de Biran's thesis. In his view, the origin of the concept of causality does stem from an internal experience, although the child does not recognize it as interior at the outset because the distinction between self and the external world only gradually clarifies itself. Other confirmatory evidence suggests that there is a development in a child's perception of causality, although Michotte argues that this is the result of maturation rather than of learning.

Piaget and Michotte have debated the question publicly without settling their differences, seemingly because they are studying initially different types of efficient causality. From Piaget's description almost anything that answers the question ''Why?'' is regarded as a cause at some stage of a child's intellectual development. Some ''causes'' are subsequent to their ''effects'' in time and take the form of a moral obligation. It is the absolute necessity ascribed to the latter, Piaget suggests, that eventually comes to be associated with the physical causality characteristic of nature. Whether this be so or not, it does seem significant that children pass through an animistic stage during which they invest inanimate objects with the kind of causal behavior they seem to understand best, viz, that of free, morally responsible agents. Michotte's work, on the other hand, leaves little doubt that, at a very early age, man without conscious inference tends to group certain temporally successive events in a causal fashion. It is not clear, however, whether the basis is wholly instinctual or partially conditioned by learning.

All this strongly suggests there are at least two fundamentally distinct empirical sources for causality, one external, the other internal. The first, studied by Michotte, could be called mechanical causality since it concerns phenomenal objects that stand in certain temporal and spatial dynamic relationships to one another. It is this relationship that seems to have been extended and generalized in the form studied by Hume and, as a deterministic postulate antedating Heisenberg's UNCERTAINTY PRINCIPLE, was assumed to hold for the whole of inanimate creation. The other is the notion, studied by Piaget, that underlies the nonmechanical explanations of children involving the attribution of motivation and deliberate intention to inanimate objects. To the extent that these nonmechanical explanations seem to antedate mechanical ones in the gradual evolution of a child's notion of physical causality, it may not be rash to presume that this original notion stems from some primitive awareness of FREE WILL. These original notions may provide the basis for an elaborated and expanded conception of causality, in which each type in its expanded form bears traces of the alternate conception. From such initial data of experience, in fact, all the manifold types of efficient causes listed earlier may be constructed.

Conclusion. Philosophers may disagree on definitions, or challenge particular theories, or become puzzled as to how man knows causes; but few would deny the existence of causes or seriously suggest that all causal terminology be eliminated from ordinary language. L. N. TOLSTOI may well be right in his claim that ''the impulse to seek causes is innate in the soul of man,'' for philosophers down the ages, with Richard of Saint-Victor, seem loathe to admit that something once non-existent can come to be with no originative link with any present or previously existing thing or event. The plethora of causal distinctions is itself indicative of this attitude. Man's very attempt to set up some kind of ''principle of causation'' represents reason's ''demand for *some* deeper sort of inward connection between phenomena than their merely habitual time sequence seems to be'' (W. James, 671).

See Also: GOD, PROOFS FOR THE EXISTENCE OF; MOTION, FIRST CAUSE OF.

Bibliography: M. J. ADLER, ed. *The Great Ideas: A Syntopicon of Great Books of the Western World,* 2 v. 1:155–178. AVICENNA, *Prima philosophia,* tract. 6 in *Logyca, Sufficientia* . . . (Venice 1508) v. 2, fol. 91r-95r. V. F. LENZEN, *Causality in Natural Science* (Springfield, Ill. 1954). C. FABRO, *Participation et causalité selon S. Thomas d'Aquin* (Louvain 1961). L. SWEENEY, *A Metaphysics of Authentic Existentialism* (Englewood Cliffs, N.J. 1965). J. OWENS, ''The Causal Proposition—Principle or Conclusion?'' *The Modern Schooman* 32 (1954–55) 159–171, 257–270, 323–339, excellent bibliog. A. B. WOLTER, presidential address in *American Catholic Philosophical Association. Proceedings of the Annual Meeting* 32 (1958) 1–27. G. SCHULEMAN, *Das Kausalprinzip in der Philosophie des hl. Thomas von Aquin* (*Beiträge zur Geschichte der Philosophie und Theologie des Mittelalters* 13.5; [Münster 1915]). J. GEYSER, *Das Prinzip vom zureichenden Grunde* (Regensburg 1929); *Das Gesetz der Ursache* (Munich 1933). A. CHOLLET, *Dictionnaire de théologie catholique* (Paris 1903–50) 2.2:2014–39. MAINE DE BIRAN, *Oeuvres choisies* (Paris 1942). A. E. MICHOTTE, *The Perception of Causality,* tr. T. R. and E. MILES (London 1963), with critical commentary essays and notes by T. R. MILES. J. PIAGET, *The Child's Conception of Physical Causality* (New York 1952). M. A. BUNGE, *Causality* (Cambridge, Mass. 1959). C. J. DUCASSE, *Nature, Mind and Death* (La Salle, Ill. 1951). V. F. LENZEN, *Causality in Natural Science* (Springfield, Ill. 1954). P. FRANK, *Modern Science and Its Philosophy* (Cambridge, Mass. 1949). L. TOLSTOY, *War and Peace,* Second Epilogue (Great Books 51:675–696). W. JAMES, *The Principles of Psychology* (1890) 2 v. (repr. New York 1962), v.2.

[A. B. WOLTER]

EGAN, MICHAEL

First bishop of Philadelphia, Pa.; b. Limerick, Ireland, 1761; d. Philadelphia, July 22, 1814. When he was 18, he entered the Franciscan Order of the Strict Observance at St. Anthony's College, Louvain, Belgium, and received minor orders and the diaconate at Malines, Belgium. He then went to Immaculate Conception College in Prague, where he was ordained and was awarded the lectorate in theology. A petition of Oct. 23, 1786, indicates that a Pater Michael Egan, one of seven Irish clerics, asked the Belgian government for clothing and funds to make this trip when they were obliged to leave Louvain because the Franciscan College there was closed.

From May 24, 1787, to May 18, 1790, Egan was guardian of St. Isidore's College, Rome. He then became guardian of the following Franciscan friaries in Ireland: Ennis, 1790 and 1794; Roscrea, 1793; and Castelyons, 1796. He immigrated to the U.S., and joined Rev. Louis de Barth at St. Mary's Church, Lancaster, Pa., in January 1802. He then went to Philadelphia, where his brother lived, and on April 12, 1803, the trustees of St. Mary's Church elected him one of their pastors. He was unsuccessful in his efforts to carry out an apostolic rescript, received Sept. 29, 1804, to found a province of the Franciscan Order in the U.S. He became a naturalized citizen of the U.S. in Philadelphia on Sept. 18, 1807.

In 1806 Bp. John CARROLL recommended Egan as ordinary for the new diocese he wished established at Philadelphia. According to Carroll, Egan appeared to be "endowed with all the qualities to discharge with perfection all the functions of the episcopacy, except that he lacks robust health, greater experience and a greater degree of firmness in his disposition. He is a learned, modest, humble priest who maintains the spirit of his Order in his whole conduct." When Pius VII established the Diocese of PHILADELPHIA in 1808, Egan was named its first bishop. Delayed because of the Napoleonic wars in Europe, the papal bulls did not arrive until 1810; Egan was consecrated by Archbishop Carroll in Baltimore, Md., on Oct. 28, 1810.

Egan's administration of Philadelphia was marred from the beginning by the trustee problem at St. Mary's, where Rev. William HAROLD, OP, and his uncle, Rev. James Harold, openly led the trustees against their bishop. Despite poor health, Egan firmly opposed them; schism was averted when the Harolds returned to Ireland in 1813. Egan died in 1814 and was buried in St. Mary's churchyard. His remains were later transferred to the crypt of the Cathedral of SS. Peter and Paul, Philadelphia.

Bibliography: M. I. J. GRIFFIN, *History of Rt. Rev. Michael Egan, First Bishop of Philadelphia* (Philadelphia 1893).

[J. F. CONNELLY]

EGBERT OF IONA, ST.

Abbot bishop; b. 639; d. Easter Sunday, April 24, 729. An Englishman by birth, he repaired to Ireland to study at the monastery of Rath Melsigi in Connacht. When the community was visited by a great plague, he was struck down and vowed that if cured he would willingly exile himself from England and go to Germany as a missionary. In a vision he was told that he had an even harder task to accomplish elsewhere, and he sent WIGBERT and later WILLIBRORD to undertake the mission to Germany and Frisia. He went to Iona (Hy) in Scotland and converted the monks there to the Roman system of determining the Easter date and to the Roman TONSURE.

Feast: April 24.

Bibliography: BEDE, *Ecclesiastical History* 3:27, 4:26; 5:22. T. F. TOUT, *The Dictionary of National Biography from the Earliest Times to 1900* (London 1885–1900) 6:564–565. W. BRIGHT, *A Dictionary of Christian Biography*, ed. W. SMITH and H. WACE, (London 1877–1887) 2:49–50. C. J. GODFREY, *The Church in Anglo-Saxon England* (New York 1962).

[R. T. MEYER]

EGBERT (ECGBERT) OF YORK

Archbishop of York; d. Nov. 19, 766. He was a cousin of Ceolwulf (d. 760) and the brother of Edbert (d. 768), who succeeded Ceolwulf as King of Northumbria. He was educated at Rome and was there ordained a deacon. He became bishop of YORK in 732, and a letter of BEDE in 734 urges him to seek the elevation of his see to an archdiocese, which was granted in 735 by Pope GREGORY III. He fostered the school of York with ETHELBERT, later archbishop, at its head and ALCUIN as a pupil. Egbert corresponded with St. BONIFACE and wrote a *Pontifical* (ed. W. Greenwell, London 1853), possibly a *Penitential* (PL 89:443–454), and a treatise *De iure sacerdotali* (PL 89:379–383). The *Exceptiones* of Canon Law can no longer be attributed to him. He was buried in the cathedral at York. Although he is mentioned in the Benedictine martyrologies, there is no approved cult.

Bibliography: BEDE, *Opera historica,* ed. C. PLUMMER, 2 v. (Oxford 1896) 1:405–423, Bede's letter to Egbert. *English Historical Documents* 1:735–745. A. W. HADDAN and W. STUBBS, eds., *Councils and Ecclesiastical Documents Relating to Great Britain and Ireland,* v. 3 (Oxford 1871) 358–360, 388–390, letters of Boniface; 394–395, letter of Paul I; 403–413, *De iure sacerdotali;* 413–431, *Penitential.* ALCUIN, *De pontificibus et sanctis ecclesiae eboracensis carmen* in *The Historians of the Church of York and Its Archbishops,* ed. J. RAINE (RollsS 71; 1879) 386–387. *Acta Sanctorum* Nov. 3:744–745. H. DAUPHIN, *Dictionnaire d'histoire et de géographie ecclésiastiques* 14:1476–78. A. M. ZIMMERMAN, *Kalendarium Benedictinum* (Metten 1933–38) 3:334. K. WEINZIERL, *Lexikon für Theologie und Kirche* (Freiburg 1957–65) 3:668.

[V. I. J. FLINT]

EGERIA, ITINERARIUM OF

Also known as *Peregrinatio Aetheriae*, or ''Aetheria's Pilgrimage,'' the work is the account of a Christian woman's three-year journey through Egypt, Palestine, Syria and ultimately back across Asia Minor to Constantinople in the fourth century. Originally entitled by its discoverer J. F. Gamurrini as, *Sanctae Silviae Aquitanae Peregrinatio ad loca sancta*, it has come to be more commonly identified as the *Itinerarium Egeriae*, ''Egeriae's Travel Notes.'' Gamurrini discovered the text in 1884 at a religious house in Arezzo, in a manuscript from Monte Cassino that also contained fragments of the hymns of St. Hilary of Poitiers along with Hillary's *Tractatus de mysteriis*. The text of the Itinerarium has numerous lacunae. Both the beginning and the end of the narrative are lacking and at least two leaves from the body of the text as we have it are missing as well. Scholarly conjecture varies as to the date of the journey (late fourth to early fifth century), with the weight of opinion favoring an earlier dating, possibly the years 381–384 A.D. The precise identity of the traveler and her station in life cannot be determined with certitude. Was she a highborn person with ties to the imperial court? Was she a pious but worldly laywoman of the bourgeoisie? Was she a religious woman? Similary, the particular region of the Empire from which she haled (southern Gaul, either Aquitaine or Arles; Galicia in northwestern Spain; or, as has more recently been argued, Normandy) is a matter of conjecture

Literarily, it is in the form of a letter addressed both to a group of women (*dominae sorores*) and to a person in authority, either an ecclesiastic or an imperial official (*vestra affectio*), written in a familiar style that mirrors the vulgar or spoken Latin of the Late Empire. It has proven to be a mine of information for philologists, who have analyzed its Latinity for what it reveals of the morphology, the syntax, the fund of vocabulary, even the phonology of the spoken idiom that was slowly evolving in late antiquity into Proto-Romance, out of which would emerge the medieval and modern family of Romance Languages. It is a critical document as well for liturgists and ecclesiologists, particularly historians of monasticism, for geographers and topographers, for students of travel narrative, even for scholars working in women's studies. Although Egeria tends to efface her authorial self before the data that she records, she does emerge as a writer with a distinct literary personality manifested in a lively style blending the spontaneity of oral speech craft with more learned elements to translate vividly, and at times with some humor and even deep emotion, the multifarious experiences of her journey. Moreover, she is the first Christian woman to have authored a book-length text in Latin, and she testifies to the role played by women, religious in church life, even singling out one by name, the deaconess Marthana, whom she encountered in Jerusalem and subsequently visited at her monastery for women at Seleucia of Isauria in Asia Minor.

The Itinerarium's two parts. The text is divided into two parts. The first, composed of twenty-three chapters, recounts Egeria's travels to various pilgrimage sites in the Judaeo-Christian Near East; the second, slightly longer and divided into twenty-six chapters numbered 24 through 49, gives a detailed account of the liturgy of the Church of Jerusalem. The two parts differ substantially from one another, not only in content, but also in genre, form and style. Generically, the first twenty-three chapters constitute an authentic travel narrative and belong to the sub-genre of the pilgrimage. They are arranged chronologically and present the events of the journey sequentially. Speaking in her own name or in that of her fellow travelers, Egeria recounts four distinct journeys, the first three of which she undertook while based in Jerusalem, with the last being her homeward journey, in the course of which she made an extensive detour to visit Edessa and biblical sites associated with the sojourns of Abraham and Jacob at Harran. Indeed, Egeria's various journeys are exclusively motivated by a desire to see first-hand, and to pray at, sites mentioned in Scripture or hallowed by tradition, and to speak with the ecclesiastical personnel—whether bishop, priest, monks or nuns (*parthenae, virgines*)—associated with these sites. Thus, she travels to Sinai, where the text of the Arezzo manuscript begins, ascends the sacred mountains of Sinai and Horeb, lodges at the monastery, before retracing in reverse the early stages of the Exodus, visiting sites in the Biblical land of Gessen (chs. 1–9). There follow shorter journeys via Jericho to Mount Nebo (chs. 10–12), and by way of the Jordan valley to the reputed site of Job's grave in Idumea, in the course of which she passes through places associated with John the Baptist, Elias and Abraham and Melchisedech (chs. 13–16). Edessa, because of the reputed correspondence between Christ and King Abgar, became the focus of a major pilgrimage, motivating her to interrupt her homeward journey to travel there from Antioch across the Euphrates into Mesopotamia (chs. 17–21). The journey from Antioch to Constantinople (chs. 22–23) is marked by visits to the shrines of Saint Tecla in Seleucia of Isauria and of Saint Euphemia in Chalcedon. The pilgrimage-journey is a never-ending act, however, for, having once reached Constantinople, she informs her correspondents that she is projecting a visit to Ephesus to offer prayer at the tomb of the Apostle John.

The second part of the *Itinerarium*, written largely in the impersonal style of the reporter-witness, represents a summary of what she observed of the religious life of the Christian community of Jerusalem over a three-year period. Her account is ordered according to the unfolding of the daily, Sunday and annual liturgy of that community, with a lengthy excursus (chs. 45–47) on the catechetical instruction given by the bishop to candidates for baptism. Egeria's text (chs. 24–25) is the first to describe the order of a regular daily office, consisting of the *Vigiliae Nocturnae*, divided into two parts; a *Vigilia matutina*, which takes place while it is still night, and a morning office, which begins at daybreak and at which the bishop presides—Sext and Nones; and Vespers (*lucenarium*). In Lent, Tierce is also observed. Except for Vespers, where the laity are numerous, these are essentially monastic offices. On Sundays, there is first a pre-service outside the Anastasis attended by a large crowd of religious and laity, then within the church proper an Office of the Resurrection at which the bishop presides, followed by the morning office and concluding with the celebration of the eucharist in the Martyrium. In her description of these offices, Egeria stresses the aptness of the hymns, prayers and readings and calls attention to the numerous blessings and dismissals.

Unique to the Church of Jerusalem's observance of the liturgical year is the convergence of historical and commemorative space permitting the celebration of feasts to be held on the sites associated with their occurrence, with the result that the ritual is characterized by numerous processions to and from stational churches within and without the city. Egeria begins her description of the liturgical year with an incomplete account of the Epiphany and its Octave (ch. 25), followed by the Feast of the Presentation (ch. 26), before moving on to the ceremonial order of the first seven weeks of Lent culminating in the celebration of Lazarus Saturday (chs. 27–29). The liturgy of Holy Week (*septimana major*) is presented in minute detail: Palm Sunday (chs. 30–31); the commemorative rites associated with the observance of the Monday, Tuesday and Wednesday of Holy Week (chs. 32–34); finally, the elaborate and emotionally-charged celebration of Holy Thursday and Good Friday (chs. 35–37). There follow accounts of the observance of the Easter Vigil (ch. 38), Easter and its Octave (39–40) and the Paschal Season (ch. 41). The Ascension (ch. 42), interestingly, is observed with a Wednesday vigil in Bethlehem followed by a Thursday morning mass in the Church of the Nativity. The daylong observance of Pentecost (ch. 43), which also includes a commemoration of the Ascension, is marked by vast throngs processing to all major stational churches of the city and its environs. This is followed by a summary of liturgical practices in Ordinary Time after Pentecost (ch. 44) and an incomplete account of the Feasts of the Finding of the Cross and the Dedication of the Constantinian basilica (*dies enceniarum*) observed in September, with monks from Egypt, the Thebaid, Syria and Mesopotamia coming up to Jerusalem. What other feasts Egeria may have described we cannot know, since the manuscript breaks off at this point.

By dint of reiteration a detailed liturgico-ecclesiological topography of Jerusalem and environs impresses itself upon the reader. The focus of the Church of Jerusalem's liturgy was the complex of the Anastasis, comprising various churches, chapels and atria to which Egeria repeatedly refers: (1) the Anastasis proper, a church in the round built over the reputed site of Christ's burial and adjoining the bishop's house, which was the chief locus of the daily Office; (2) the atrium of the ante Crucem, the Calvary (ad Crucem) and the area behind (post Crucem), to which the congregation processed daily for the conclusion of vespers and where various ceremonies of numerous feasts, notably the Good Friday liturgy, were observed; (3) the Martyrium (*ecclesia major*), where the Sunday eucharistic liturgy as well as that of most principal feasts were celebrated; and (4) the Quintana Pars, the great doorway opening from the city's major thoroughfare and through which the congregation processed on Pentecost. The Syon, called the mother of all churches and built on the site of the apostles' upper room, was the chief locus of the Pentecost litgurgy and figures prominently as a stational church for great feasts and in the weekly liturgy in Ordinary Time. Outside the city are situated the Eleona on the Mount of Olives, commemorating the place where Christ taught his disciples, with the Imbomon, the traditional site of the Ascension nearby; and Gethsemane, the ''elegant church'' (*ecclesia elegans*). Also mentioned are the chapel on the road to Bethany, where Christ was met by Lazarus's sister and, in Bethany itself, the Lazarion or Church of Lazarus, as well as the grotto of the Nativity in Bethlehem. Not to be forgotten are the numerous churches she mentions in the course of her various journeys, for example, the Opu Melchisech at Sedima (Salem).

Salient points. From Egeria's narrative emerge a number of salient points about the conditions of travel in late antiquity (for example, the use of military escorts in unsure areas; the hospitality afforded travelers in monasteries; the road network and the way stations, *mansiones*, along various itineraries) and about the religious life of eastern Christianity. She stresses, for example, the prevalence and importance of monasticism not only in Jerusalem but wherever she traveled, along with the role of monks and women, religious in the liturgy, without, however, neglecting the participation, especially during great feasts, of the laity. She spells out the rules for fasting at different seasons of the year: Wednesdays and Fridays in Ordinary Time; everyday except Sundays in Lent; none during the Paschal Season. She discusses the daily three-hour catechetical instruction given to catechumens by the bishop throughout Lent as well as during the Easter Octave, when, after baptism, they were initiated into the deeper mysteries (*mysteria Dei secretiora*). Her text is also an important document for the meaning of liturgical and ecclesiological vocabulary, notably for a term like *missa*. Finally, and perhaps most importantly, Egeria embodies in her person the pilgrim-traveler figure, who combines an intrepid spirit of adventure with a reverential quest for the authetification of belief through a vicarious reliving of the mysteries of faith *in situ*.

Bibliography: *Itinera Hierosolymitana saeculi iv–viii,* ed., P. GEYER (*Corpus scriptorum ecclesiasticorum latinorum,* 39, 1898). L. SPITZER, ''The Epic Style of the Pilgrim Aetheria,'' *Comparative Literature,* 3 (1949): 225–58. *Ethérie: Journal de voyage,* ed. and tr., H. PÉTRÉ, (Sources chrétiennes 21, 1948; rev. ed., 1982). *Itinerarium Egeriae,* eds., E. FRANCESCHINI and R. WEBER (Turnhout, Bel. 1958). J. MATEOS, ''La Vigile cathédrale chez Egérie,'' *Orientalia Christiana Periodica,* 27 (1961): 281–312. A. A. R. BASTIAENSEN, *Observations sur le vocabulaire liturgique dans ''l'Itinéraire d'Egérie''* (Nijmegen 1962). P. DEVOS, ''La Date du voyage d'Egérie,'' *Analecta Bollandiana,* 85 (1967): 165–94. *Egeria: Diary of a Pilgrimage*, tr. and annot. G. E. GINGRAS, ACW 38 (Washington, D. C. and Paramus, N. J. 1970). G. E. GINGRAS, ''*Et fit missa ad tertia:* A Textual Problem in the *Itinerarium Egeriae,* XLVI, 4,'' in *Kyriakon. FS Johannes Quasten,* vol. 2, ed., P. GRANFIELD and J. A. JUNGMANN (Munster 1970): 596–603. CHR. MORHMANN, ''Egérie et le monachisme,'' *Corona gratiarum I Misc. Dekkers* (Brugge 1975): 163–80. G. SANDERS, ''Egérie, saint Jérome et la Bible: en marge de l'*Itinerarium Egeriae,* 18,2; 39,5; et 2,2,'' *ibid.,* 181–99. *Egeria's Travels to the Holy Land: Newly Translated with Supporting Documents and Notes by John Wilkinson,* 3d ed. (Warminster, Eng. 1999). P. DEVOS, ''Une Nouvelle Egérie,'' *Analecta Bollandiana* 101 (1983): 43–70. V. VÄÄNÄNEN, *Le Journal-Epitre d'Egérie (''Itinerarium Egériae''). Etude linguistique* (Helsinki 1987). J. SCHWARTZ, ''The Encenia of the Church of the Holy Sepulchre, the Temple of Solomon and the Jews,'' *Theologische Zeitschrift,* 43 (1987): 265–81. C. WEBER, ''Egeria's Norman Homeland,'' *Harvard Studies in Philology,* 92 (1989): 437–56. J. M. SNYDER, *The Woman and the Lyre: Woman Writers in Classical Greece and Rome* (Carbondale and Edwardsville, Ill. 1989): 141–51. *Atti del convegno internazionale sulla Peregrinatio Egeriae. Arezzo 23–25 ottobre 1987* (Arezzo 1990).

[G. E. GINGRAS]

EGIDIO MARIA OF ST. JOSEPH, BL.

Franciscan lay brother; b. near Taranto (Apulia), Italy, Nov. 16, 1729; d. Naples, Feb. 7, 1812. He practiced his father's trade of ropemaking and supported the family after his father's death (1747). Before entering the Alcantarine Franciscans at Taranto (1754) under the impetus of an extraordinary spiritual experience, he led a very devout life and participated zealously in the activities of the Sodality of Our Lady of the Rosary. From 1759 to 1812 Egidio (whose name outside religion was Francesco Pontello) lived at the friary of San Paolo a Chiaia in Naples, where he labored as cook, porter, and alms gatherer (quaestor). His simplicity and serenity won him the affection of the Neapolitan sick and poor, among whom he propagated devotion to Mary and Joseph. He was beatified Feb. 5, 1888.

Feast: Feb. 7.

Bibliography: P. COCO, *Cenni della vita del beato Egidio Maria di S. Giuseppe, taumaturgo di Taranto* (Taranto 1931). M. A. HABIG, *The Franciscan Book of Saints* (Chicago 1959) 89–92. *Acta ordinis minorum* 7 (1888) 18–20.

[C. J. LYNCH]

EGINO, BL.

Benedictine, abbot of SANKT ULRICH at Augsburg, Germany; d. Pisa, July 15, 1120. Because of his opposition to the imperial party, he was banished from his monastery in 1098 and took refuge at SANKT BLASIEN (Switzerland). GEBHARD III, Bishop of Constance, sent him on a confidential mission to Pope PASCHAL II. Following the lifting of the ban against the simoniacal Hermann, bishop of Augsburg, he was able to return to that city in 1106, and three years later he was elected abbot of his monastery. He carried out reforms and was a zealous preacher. However, having broken off relations with Bishop Hermann because of the latter's resumption of his old ways, he was eventually forced, in 1118, to flee from Augsburg. In the early months of 1120 he was received with honor by Pope CALLISTUS II. On his return northward that same year, he died at the Camaldolese monastery of San Michele at Pisa and was buried there.

Feast: July 15.

Bibliography: *Vita,* by his successor UDALSCHALK, *Monumenta Germaniae Historica* (Berlin 1826–) division: Scriptores, 12: 429–448. A. M. ZIMMERMANN, *Kalendarium Benedictinum: Die Heiligen und Seligen des Benediktinerorderns und seiner Zweige* (Metten 1933–38) 2:456, 459, W. FINK, *Dictionnaire d'histoire et de géographie ecclésiastiques*, ed. A. BAUDRILLART, et al. (Paris 1912–) 15:17–18.

[M. R. P. MCGUIRE]

EGMOND (EGMONT), ABBEY OF

Benedictine abbey dedicated to St. ADALBERT THE DEACON, in the Diocese of Haarlem (formerly Utrecht), northern Netherlands. Count Theodoric II of Holland rebuilt *c.* 950 a church dedicated to St. Adalbert (d. 740) and installed there monks from Ghent. In 1130 Egmond accepted the customs of CLUNY, and in 1139 the counts of Holland had the abbey made subject to the Holy See; the privilege of pontificals was obtained in 1251. Intervention by the lords of Egmond in abbey affairs caused serious disorders in the 15th century; attempts at reform from 1451 ended with acceptance of the BURSFELD reform in 1491. The abbey, united to the mensal revenue of the new See of Haarlem (1561) and then neglected, was pillaged in 1567 and 1572 (during the siege of Alkmaar), deserted, and destroyed by Calvinists (1573). Monks of Saint-Paul of Wisques, in refuge at Oosterhout, founded the Priory of Egmond (1935), since 1950 an abbey in the Congregation of SOLESMES. The abbey has published *Egmondiana* (1937–51), called *Benedictijns Tijdschrift voor geestelijk leven en geschiedenis* since 1951.

Bibliography: L. H. COTTINEAU, *Répertoire topobibliographique des abbayes et prieurés,* 2 v. (Mâcon 1935–39) 1:1031–32. R. GAZEAU, *Catholicisme. Hier, aujourd'hui et demain,* ed. G. JACQUEMET (Paris 1947–) 3:1471–72. O. BAUMHAUER, *Lexikon für Theologie und Kirche,* ed. J. HOFER and K. RAHNER, 10 v. (2d, new ed. Freiburg 1957–65) 3:673. A. KOCH, *Dictionnaire d'histoire et de géographie ecclésiastiques,* ed. A. BAUDRILLART et al. (Paris 1912–) 15:23–27. O. L. KAPSNER, *A Benedictine Bibliography: An Author-Subject Union List,* 2 v. (2d ed. Collegeville, Minn. 1962): v. 1, author part; v. 2, subject part, 2:205.

[N. N. HUYGHEBAERT]

EGOISM

Egoism refers primarily to a theory of ethics, although in philosophical usage it sometimes also designates a theory of knowledge. As an epistemological position, egoism is treated under SOLIPSISM. In ethics, egoism maintains that each man should seek his own good and ignore that of others, except when this would be to his disadvantage. It is thus opposed to altruism and to all natural law and theocentric systems. Its more common types are the hedonistic, which teaches that one should live only for one's own pleasure; the will-to-power or superman kind, which makes the achieving of superiority and dominance over others the main goal in life; and perfectionistic egoism, which sees in self-development the only reason for existence. This last form is found especially among literary people and aesthetes.

Main Proponents. In antiquity, the CYRENAICS and the Epicureans were hedonistic egoists. However, they subdued the selfishness that was logically entailed in their doctrines by their emphasis on such virtues as kindliness and friendship.

With the rise of Christianity, egoism died out, to reappear in Renaissance Italy under such forms as the EPICUREANISM of Lorenzo VALLA. It was, however, in the 17th and 18th centuries that the position became especially influential. In England, Thomas HOBBES (1588–1679) espoused materialism and an ethics suitable to it. For him, good is simply the object of men's desires, whereas evil is the object of their hate and aversion. Man's good, given human nature, consists mainly in self-preservation, the increase of personal power, and pleasure. War is thus the natural state of man, for if many desire the same thing, to get it they simply endeavor to destroy or subdue each other. Similar views were defended with biting irony and cynicism by Bernard Mandeville (1670–1733), whose *Fable of the Bees* had as its moral that private vices are public benefits. This egoistic tradition was continued but mellowed by Jeremy BENTHAM (1748–1832), according to whom benevolence is a main source of egoistic satisfaction. In France, Hobbes's contemporary, Pierre GASSENDI (1592–1655), furthered the revival of Epicureanism by proposing it as the most satisfactory foundation for Christian theology. This effort failed, however, since readers either saw its implausibility, or, accepting the fundamental HEDONISM, shrugged off the Christian superstructure. Thus, influenced by Gassendi and the English empiricists, many of the leaders of the French ENLIGHTENMENT advocated a more or less sensual egoism: C. A. Helvétius (1715–71), J. O. de La Mettrie, and P. H. D. HOLBACH.

In the 19th century egoism tended either to be absorbed by altruism or to manifest itself under radically new forms. Thus, Herbert SPENCER (1820–1903) taught that both selfishness and benevolence are normal and necessary to man, and that these will be ultimately reconciled and combined through evolution: man will be altruistic for egoistic reasons, but also self-seeking for altruistic reasons. On the other hand, Friedrich NIETZSCHE (1844–1900) distinguished between slave and master morality. For the slavish masses, the Christian ethics of humility and compassion is suitable. The elite supermen, however, are beyond the usual notions of good and evil; not being subject to any obligations, they creatively determine their own values in expressing their basic will-to-power.

In the 20th century egoism has few philosophers to defend it, but as is often the case it continues to be spread through literary works.

Evaluation. Egoism undeniably incorporates in itself certain basic truths: it is natural for man to love himself; he should moreover do so, since each one is ultimately responsible for himself; pleasure, the development of one's potentialities, and the acquisition of power are normally desirable. Despite this, it remains obvious that egoism has a serious and vitiating error at its core: its view that a man is his own end. Such a position is usually the logical corollary of a materialistic or positivistic rejection of divine Providence. It results also from a misconception of the essential sociality of human nature.

These central faults entail others. Among them is the perversion of the whole moral order. An egoism that is consistent with its principles takes as its virtues a subordination of all others to one's ends, the gratification of one's impulses no matter what the cost to others, a fraudulent appearance of kindness, fairness, and geniality; in short, selfishness that is not obvious enough to cause dislike. Many egoists, finding such a view too inhumane, modify it by introducing into their theories such notions as natural feelings of sympathy or of solidarity with their fellow men. Such additions, however, are made at the expense of coherency. Even the latter forms of egoism have no rational way of justifying one's duties to others; hence its proponents are always liable to revert back to selfish tendencies, or to use their fellowmen to serve their own purposes.

The inadequacy of egoism as a philosophy of life can be seen also in its effects on mental health. Subordinating all things to himself, the egoist is in conflict with the indefeasible demands of society and of his own nature. He can neither love nor fit in, and so becomes frustrated and unhappy.

A valid moral philosophy will be the antithesis of egoism on most points. It will admit the existence of the supreme Creator of the entire universe, all of whose parts He has interrelated and ordered ultimately to Himself. Thus all men have the same ends: to know, love, serve, and possess Him. They have, too, the same nature, needs, and rights. They should then love not only themselves but each other. To do so in a properly rational fashion, they must keep in mind a striking paradox of human nature: man best achieves happiness by forgetting himself in the service of God and his fellow men.

Bibliography: J. LECLERCQ, *Les Grandes lignes de la philosophie morale* (rev. ed. Paris 1954). R. A. TSANOFF, *The Moral Ideals of Our Civilization* (New York 1942). J. NUTTIN, *Psycho-analysis and Personality,* tr. G. LAMB (New York 1953). G. MORRA, *Enciclopedia filosofica* 1:1834–36. R. EISLER, *Wörterbuch der philosophischen Begriffe*, 3 v. (4th ed. Berlin 1927–30) 1:298–301.

[G. J. DALCOURT]

EGREGIE DOCTOR PAULE

Brief office hymn that was traditionally assigned to the feast of St. Paul. In the Roman Breviary of 1632, it was assigned to the feasts of SS. Peter and Paul. It was originally part (stanza 4 and the doxology, stanza 6) of the longer hymn *DECORA LUX AETERNITATIS,* which was in turn a revised version of a Carolingian poem on the Apostles Peter and Paul, *Aurea luce et decore roseo* (*Analecta hymnica* 51:216). In the *Decora* hymn, Paul is addressed as *egregie doctor* (cf. Colossians 3 and 1 Corinthians 12) and is asked to "fashion our lives aright and carry off our hearts with yours to heaven."

Bibliography: J. CONNELLY, *Hymns of the Roman Liturgy* (Westminster, MD, 1957) 168–170. B. STÄBLEIN, *Lexicon für Theologie und Kirche*, ed. J. HOFER and K. RAHNER (Freiburg 1957–65) 3:674. J. SZÖVÉRFFY, *Die Annalen der lateinischen Hymnendichtung* (Berlin 1964–65) 1:122–124.

[J. SZÖVÉRFFY]

EGRES, ABBEY OF

Former Cistercian monastery on the Maros River, near Egres, Hungary, Diocese of Csanád (Latin, *Egresium*). Founded by King Béla III in 1179 and settled by monks from PONTIGNY, it was the second CISTERCIAN abbey to be founded in Hungary. It was richly endowed by the king and soon had daughter foundations: Kerc in Transylvania (1202) and Szentkereszt (*Sancta Crux*) in Slavonia (1214). One of the greatest benefactors of the abbey was King Andrew II of Hungary (1205–35), father of St. ELIZABETH OF HUNGARY: he had the monastery fortified and the church richly appurtenanced. He was buried there (1235) beside his queen and consort Jolanta (1232). The Mongol hordes destroyed the church and monastery in 1241; after they had been rebuilt they were pillaged (1279) by the Cumans, whom King Béla IV had settled in that area. Abbots of Egres were often appointed by 13th-century popes as arbitrators of various quarrels between peasantry, nobility, towns, and monasteries. During the 14th century spiritual and moral decline set in at Egres, especially under Abbot Peter Peyt from Flanders, who was suspected of heresy. By 1357 the monastery had only six monks. Later, Pope Alexander VI handed over a portion of the abbey's holdings to the bishop of Csanád, and then in 1514 King Ladislaus VI made inevitable its total extinction by giving the abbey with all its possessions to the same bishop. Nothing of the abbey now remains.

Bibliography: E. BARTÓK, *Az Egresi cisztercita apátság története* (Budapest 1911). R. BÉKÉFI, *A magyarországi cisztercita rend története* (Budapest 1911) 29–. T. HÜMPFNER, *Les Fils de S. Bernard en Hongrie* (Budapest 1927). K. JUHÁSZ, *Die Stifte der Tschanader Diözese im Mittelalter* (Münster 1927); *A csanádi püspökség története,* 8 v. (Makó 1930–47), *passim.* L. H. COTTINEAU, *Répertoire topobibliographique des abbayes et prieurés*, 2 v. (Mâcon 1935–39) 1:1032. M. A. DIMIER, *Dictionnaire d'histoire et de géographie ecclésiastiques*, ed. A. BAUDRILLART et al. (Paris 1912–) 15:28–30.

[M. CSÁKY]

EGYPT

This article covers the history of Egypt to the present day, including the broadly defined periods of (1) Prehistory, (2) Pharaonic Egypt, (3) Ptolemaic, Roman and Byzantine Egypt, (4) Medieval Egypt and (5) Modern Egypt.

THE LAND

A short account of the geography and natural resources of Egypt is preceded here by an explanation of the various names that have been used to designate this land.

Names. The name Egypt is derived, through the Latin *Aegyptus*, from the Greek Αιγυπτος, an inexact reproduction of the Egyptian term *Hi(t)-Ka-Ptah* [Temple of the soul of (the god) Ptah], which was one of the ancient designations for the capital city Memphis (biblical Noph). In Pharaonic times Egyptians called their country ''The Two Lands'' (from the natural division into Upper and Lower Egypt) and ''The Black Land'' (from the color of the fertile soil of the Nile Valley in contrast to the ''red'' land of the surrounding desert). In the Hebrew Bible Egypt is called *misraim*, of uncertain derivation but related to the Akkadian name *Misir (Musur)* and the Arabic name *Misr* used for Egypt today.

Geography. In the harsh deserts and mountains of northeast Africa, Egypt is the only densely populated area. The Nile River flows north from the mountains of Ethiopia and through the Nubian Desert, where its two tributaries, the Blue and the White Nile, join at Khartoum in modern Sudan. To the west lies the Libyan Desert (*see* LIBYA), with five habitable oases, and to the east, the Eastern Desert and the Sinai Peninsula (*see* SINAI, MOUNT). Prior to the construction of a series of dams at Aswan (ancient Syene) in the 20th century, the Nile's annual summer flood spread from north to south, fed by seasonal rains in Ethiopia. The river deposited fertile silt in the Nile Valley and the Delta and washed harmful salts from the soil, providing the conditions for settled life and bountiful agriculture.

Of the approximately 4,000 miles of the Nile's course, Egypt proper comprises some 600 miles of the lower (northern) part of the river and its widely fanned Delta, where two (in antiquity, seven) branches allow the Nile to flow into the Mediterranean Sea. Egypt's natural southern boundary at Aswan (Syene) is caused by a granite barrier crossing the river bed, creating rapids that make navigation impossible (the first Cataract, of six counted north to south). Egypt falls into two unequal parts, the narrow valley in the south (Upper Egypt) and the wide Delta in the north, which often opposed each other during the country's long history. The meeting point of these two regions is the natural place for a capital, which was Memphis in ancient times and is now Cairo. Important cities in Upper Egypt were Thebes (biblical No-Amon, modern Luxor) and Syene (modern Aswan), where the Elephantine Island marked the southern frontier. Among the cities of the Delta, the eastern site of Tanis (biblical Soan, Zoan) flourished between 1500 and 1000 B.C. due to close contacts with Palestine. In 332 B.C., Alexander the Great founded a new capital at ALEXANDRIA in the northwest Delta, providing Egypt with a coastal harbor.

Capital: Cairo.
Size: 389,900 sq. miles.
Population: 68,359,979 in 2000.
Languages: Arabic; English and French are also spoken.
Religions: 240,000 Catholics (.3%), 3,830,000 Orthodox (5.6%), 60,273,181 Sunni Muslims (89%), 2,649,598 Protestants (3.8%), 1,367,200 practice other faiths or are without religious affiliation.
Ecclesiastical organizations: Egypt is divided between several Catholic sects. The Coptic Catholic Church, the predominant Catholic church, has a patriarchate in Alexandria, with eparchies in Minya, Assuit, Sohag, Thebes-Luxor, and Ismayliah. Greek Melkite Catholics have a patriarchate in Alexandria. Armenian, Maronite, and Syrian Catholics each have an eparchy located in Alexandria, while Chaldean Catholics have an eparchy located in Cairo. Latin Catholics have an apostolic vicariate located at Alexandria.

Natural resources. Agriculture was and is the base of Egypt's economy. The primary ancient crops were emmer wheat and barley, as well as flax for linen. Along the riverbanks were papyrus plants, from which the writing material of ancient times was made (*see* PAPYROLOGY). Today, cotton is the main crop and a valuable export; rice and vegetables are also grown. In ancient times, a series of canals and basins helped floodwaters reach as much arable land as possible. Because the Aswan High Dam holds back the flood and its rich silt, irrigation and chemical fertilizers now support agriculture.

Of the many animals domesticated for agriculture and husbandry, cattle were the most important; sheep played a lesser role than in Palestine. The horse was introduced *c.* 1650 B.C., but its use was restricted in ancient times. Donkeys were a primary resource for transport and travel, as they are today, and camels were used as well from the 5th century B.C. onwards.

The deserts hemming Egypt are rich in minerals, semiprecious stones and building stones such as limestone, sandstone, granite and porphyry. Copper deposits are found in the Eastern Desert and in Sinai, and gold veins in the Eastern and the Nubian Deserts. Wood for ships and buildings was imported from Lebanon to supplement sparse native trees. Bricks of sun-dried mud were the main building material; the Egyptian name for

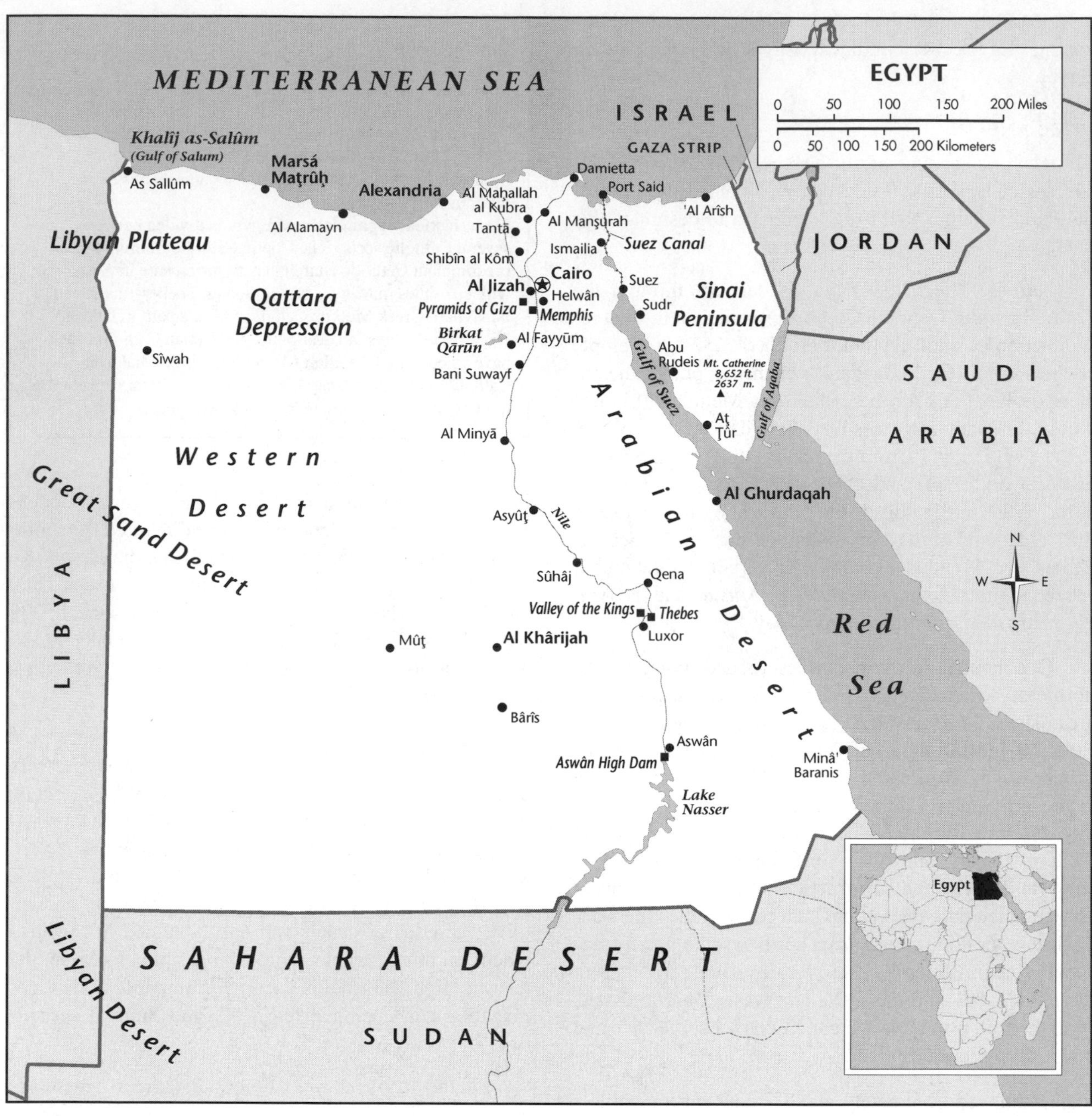

these bricks, *djebet*, passed into Arabic and, via Spain, into Spanish and English as the word adobe.

PREHISTORY

Early humans passed through the Western Desert oases and the Nile Valley as early as the Lower Paleolithic Period, some 500,000 years ago. Over time, the climate changed and turned the swamp-like plains into deserts, and *c.* 10,000 B.C., pastoral settlements began to emerge along the river. Archeologists identify several cultures which flourished as a result of developed agriculture from *c.* 4500 B.C. onwards.

In the north, Merimda, el-Omari and Helwan were centers for a distinctive northern culture. In the Nile Valley at el-Badari, the Badarian culture is known from pit graves where fine pottery vessels and flaked stone tools were buried with the dead. The nearby site of Naqada has yielded important evidence for a culture which spread throughout Upper Egypt from *c.* 4000 to 3200 B.C. During this period, society became increasingly stratified as a small portion of the population consolidated its wealth and power. Grave goods include decorated pottery, terracotta figurines, vessels and weapons worked from hard stones, and tools and combs carved from hippopotamus ivory. Gold and semiprecious stones were used for jewelry. Animal-shaped palettes made of greywacke were used to grind pigments for cosmetics and paint. Decorative motifs like animals, human and divine figures, boats and hunting or battle scenes illustrate the development of religious and social structures. The import of pottery and raw materials like lapis (from Afghanistan) and cedar (from Lebanon) indicate active trade with Palestine and the Near East.

By about 3200 B.C., or a little after, the Naqada culture also saw the creation of the hieroglyphic writing system, perhaps to fill a need for better communication and written records in a more complex society. Such developments paved the way for a Pharaonic Egyptian state.

PHARAONIC EGYPT

After a general introduction, this period is treated under the following subdivisions: Protodynastic and Early Dynastic Period, Old Kingdom, Middle Kingdom, Hyksos Age, New Kingdom, Third Intermediate Period and Cushite Rule, and the Late Period.

General Introduction. Lists of kings (or pharaohs, from the Egyptian *pr-aa*, ''Great House'') were compiled for temple records in antiquity and are a major source for the Pharaonic history of Egypt. In the 3rd century B.C. the Egyptian priest Manetho used older king lists to write a history of Egypt in Greek for the new Ptolemaic rulers, and his work was quoted by other Greek and Latin historians such as Josephus. Manetho is responsible for dividing Egyptian history into 30 dynasties from the initial unification of the country to its conquest by Alexander the Great (332 B.C.), a model followed by modern scholars.

The chronology of Pharaonic Egypt is, for the most part, well established, although some uncertainties persist. A few astronomically fixed points provide a fairly certain framework for the third millennium B.C., and working back from these points the beginning of dynastic history in Egypt is estimated *c.* 3000 B.C.

Protodynastic and Early Dynastic Period (*c.* 3200–2575 B.C.). Modern scholars refer to the period of *c.* 3200 to 3000 B.C. as the Protodynastic Period because during these years, early rulers expanded their power and formed a unified Egyptian state. Some of these rulers are known by name from works of art, such as a ceremonial palette representing king Narmer. Narmer, who came from Upper Egypt, is generally credited with joining the north and south into one nation. On his palette, Narmer is shown defeating enemies associated with the Delta. The king was central to Egyptian religious and political thought because he was responsible for ensuring that *ma'at*, or cosmic order and justice, was maintained in the

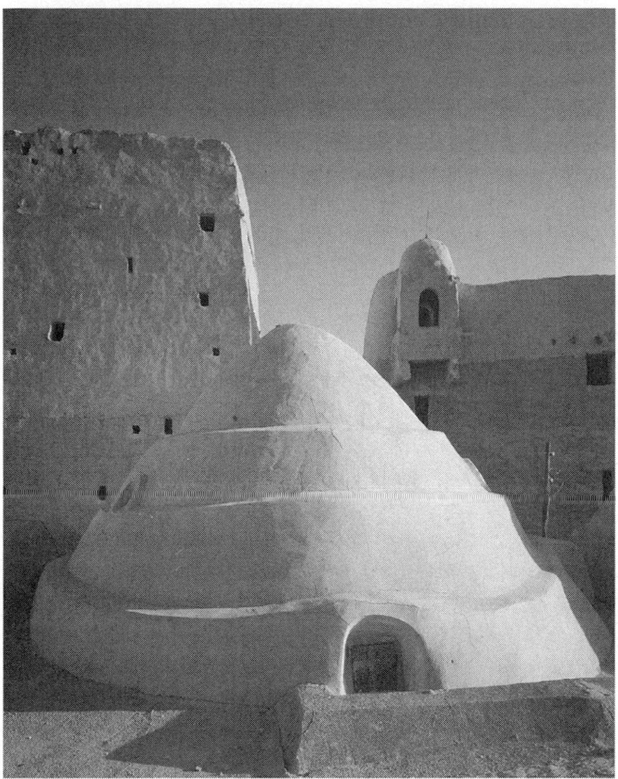

Monastery of St. Anthony, near Za'faranah, Egypt. (©Andrea Jemolo/CORBIS)

universe. As the palette of Narmer shows, even at this early stage in Egyptian history, artists had adopted a canon, or style, of representation which would remain typical of all Egyptian art.

The sequence of numbered dynasties recorded by Manetho begins after the initial unification of Egypt. The first three dynasties (*c.* 3000–2575 B.C.) comprise the Early Dynastic Period, during which the kings strengthened the structure of Egyptian government. In the Third Dynasty (*c.* 2650 B.C.) Egypt reached an important point under the reign of Djoser, who built the first large-scale stone monument for his funerary complex at Saqqara, the cemetery of Memphis (biblical Noph). The center of the complex was a structure of seven graduated layers, the so-called Step Pyramid. Djoser was buried in chambers beneath the pyramid, and buildings around it provided a spiritual 'home' for the dead king where religious rituals ensured his eternal life.

Old Kingdom (*c.* 2575–2140 B.C.). The concentration of Egypt's social, material and artistic skill reached a new height in the Fourth Dynasty (*c.* 2575–2465). Royal funerary monuments were larger and centered around a true pyramid with straight sides. Kings Khufu (Cheops in Greek), Khafra (Chephren) and Menkaure (Mykerinos) built three pyramids at Giza, north of Saqqa-

Head of Pharoah Thutmose III or Queen Hatshepsut, 18th Dynasty

ra. Khufu's is the largest at 481 feet high, and each pyramid with its temples was enclosed by a wall and served by two temples housing statues of the king. Around this complex were the tombs of the king's relatives and nobles. Khafra, a son of Khufu, also built the Sphinx, an enormous figure of the king with a lion's body carved from natural rock. Images like the Sphinx show the dual nature of the king: he was a mortal carrying out a divine office and representing, on earth, the falcon god Horus, who was a king among the gods.

In the Fifth Dynasty (*c.* 2465–2320) kings also explicitly associated themselves with the sun god RA, whose cult was based at Heliopolis (biblical On) in modern Cairo. Kings built smaller pyramid complexes, probably because the larger projects of the Fourth Dynasty had been too expensive and difficult to complete. The number of nobles, or officials, administering the country expanded and many of their tombs are at Saqqara. In the Sixth Dynasty (*c.* 2320–2150), kings began to appoint officials to serve in provinces throughout Egypt, leading to decentralization of the government. Politically, the Sixth Dynasty was very active in Egypt and abroad. Copper and turquoise were mined in Sinai, and close commercial connections existed with BYBLOS (Gebal); trading expeditions penetrated into Africa and sailed the Red Sea. Military campaigns in the western and eastern Delta expanded Egyptian territory. Despite such efforts, though, the devolution of power and the long reign (over 90 years) of King Pepi II hastened a collapse of political order.

The last two dynasties of the Old Kingdom (Dynasties 7 and 8, *c.* 2150–2130) were short-lived and gave way to a group of kings (Dynasties 9 and 10, *c.* 2130–2040) who were based at Heracleopolis in the Faiyum district and controlled only the northern half of Egypt. Scholars refer to this as the First Intermediate Period because Egypt was no longer united. In the south, local officials did not acknowledge the northern kings, instead governing the provinces (called nomes) in their own right. Over time the governors of Thebes (biblical No-amon) in Upper Egypt established Dynasty 11 and competed with the Heracleopolitan kings by gaining dominion over the south as far as the first Cataract.

Middle Kingdom (*c.* 2040–1640). Around 2040 B.C. the rulers of Thebes defeated the Heracleopolitan kings, took control of Lower Egypt and reunited Egypt under King Mentuhotep II of Dynasty 11. This dynasty ended when an official, Amenemhet I (*c.* 1991–1962), claimed the kingship and founded Dynasty 12, which lasted until *c.* 1783 and became the classical age of Pharaonic Egypt. Powerful kings secured the dynastic succession by appointing the heir presumptive as coregent. Egypt annexed Nubia as far south as the second Cataract and built a system of fortresses there. An Egyptian settlement in Sinai worked the mines and included a temple dedicated to the important goddess Hathor. Egypt exercised a strong cultural influence over Palestine and offered political protection to local rulers in the region; ties with Byblos were particularly close. Throughout the Middle Kingdom, Asiatic peoples from Palestine settled in Egypt, especially in the eastern Delta. Close contacts also existed with CRETE, which brought goods and craftsmen to Egypt by boat.

The close of the Middle Kingdom is not well understood. Internal rivalries may have eroded the central government, and Dynasty 13 consisted of a sequence of short reigns. By *c.* 1640, Egypt had disintegrated into several small kingdoms, a time referred to as the Second Intermediate Period.

Hyksos Age. During the Second Intermediate Period (*c.* 1640–1550) the chief rivals in Egypt were a new group of kings at Thebes (Dynasty 17) and a series of kings of Asiatic origin who ruled from the Delta (Dynasties 15 and 16). The Delta kings were known as the Hyksos from the Egyptian term *hekau-khasut* (rulers of foreign lands), signifying their foreign origin. The Hyksos had probably lived in Egypt for some time, however, and they adopted many Egyptian cultural forms alongside their own. Their capital was at Avaris in the northeast Delta, with a palace and fortifications like those also found in Palestine and Syria. It was the Hyksos who introduced horses and chariot-based warfare to Egypt. They made few changes to the administration of Egypt, instead relying on the loyalty of officials in the north and central parts of the country.

New Kingdom (*c.* 1550–1070). Around 1550 B.C., a ruler of the Theban 17th Dynasty, Kamose, led a series of military campaigns against the Hyksos king, Apophis. Under Kamose's brother Ahmose, the Hyksos were defeated and Egypt was reunited at the start of a new dynasty. The 18th Dynasty was a time of unprecedented wealth, and rulers with powerful personalities created an Egyptian empire stretching east to Palestine and south to Nubia, control of which had been lost after the Middle Kingdom.

Hatshepsut and Thutmose III. One important ruler of the 18th Dynasty was Hatshepsut (*c.* 1473–1458), daughter of King Thutmose I and wife of Thutmose II. Hatshepsut was regent for her young stepson, Thutmose III (*c.* 1479–1425), but declared herself king in her own right, one of several women to do so in ancient Egypt. She built a magnificent funerary temple at Deir el-Bahri on the west bank of the Nile at Thebes and sent a large commercial expedition to the land of Punt, in modern Ethiopia.

After Hatshepsut's death (*c.* 1458), the fully grown Thutmose III took sole command of the throne and led an army against Palestine and Syria, where local rulers were rebelling against Egyptian supremacy. For several months Thutmose III besieged MEGIDDO, and on another campaign, he defeated the king of Mitanni in southern Mesopotamia and crossed the Euphrates River, the only pharaoh ever to do so. Egypt did not integrate Syria and Palestine into its government or culture but oversaw these regions through the diplomatic efforts of local officials and garrison towns like Gaza.

Thutmose III also extended Egyptian control further south in Nubia, to the fourth Cataract. Unlike Egypt's Asiatic holdings, Nubia was actively colonized and administered by an Egyptian official, the viceroy of Cush [*see* ETHIOPIANS (CUSHITES)]. Rich gold mines in the Nubian Desert were an important source of wealth for Egypt.

Amenhotep III. A later 18th Dynasty ruler, Amenhotep III (*c.* 1390–1353), ruled the Egyptian empire peacefully. He undertook many building projects, including Luxor Temple and the impressive Hypostyle Hall of Karnak Temple. Two colossal statues of Amenhotep III, called the Colossi of Memnon by the Greeks, mark the site of his destroyed funerary complex near modern Luxor.

Ramses II.

Akhnaton (Amenhotep IV). The son and successor of Amenhotep III ruled from *c.* 1353–1336 and introduced radical political and religious changes. Early in his reign, Amenhotep IV changed his name to Akhnaton, meaning "spirit of the Aton (sun disc)," to reflect his loyalty to the cult of this solar deity. Akhnaton was opposed to the powerful priesthood of the Theban god Amun (or AMON), who was the patron deity of 18th Dynasty kings. Instead, Akhnaton promulgated the Aton religion, which credited the sun disc as the only source of life and positioned the king as sole mediator between this all-powerful god and the people of Egypt. The Aton thus replaced both Amun (Amon) and the ancient sun god Re (Ra).

Although Akhnaton's loyalty to the Aton cult is often attributed to the king's religious conviction, there were political considerations as well: the Aton religion made the king central and unique, rather than a servant of the god, and broke the power of the priests. In the fifth year of his reign, Akhnaton emphasized this new political and religious reality by building a capital city at the previously uninhabited site of Akhet-Aton ("horizon of the Aton"), modern el-Amarna. He also introduced sweeping changes in religious ritual, with ceremonies for the

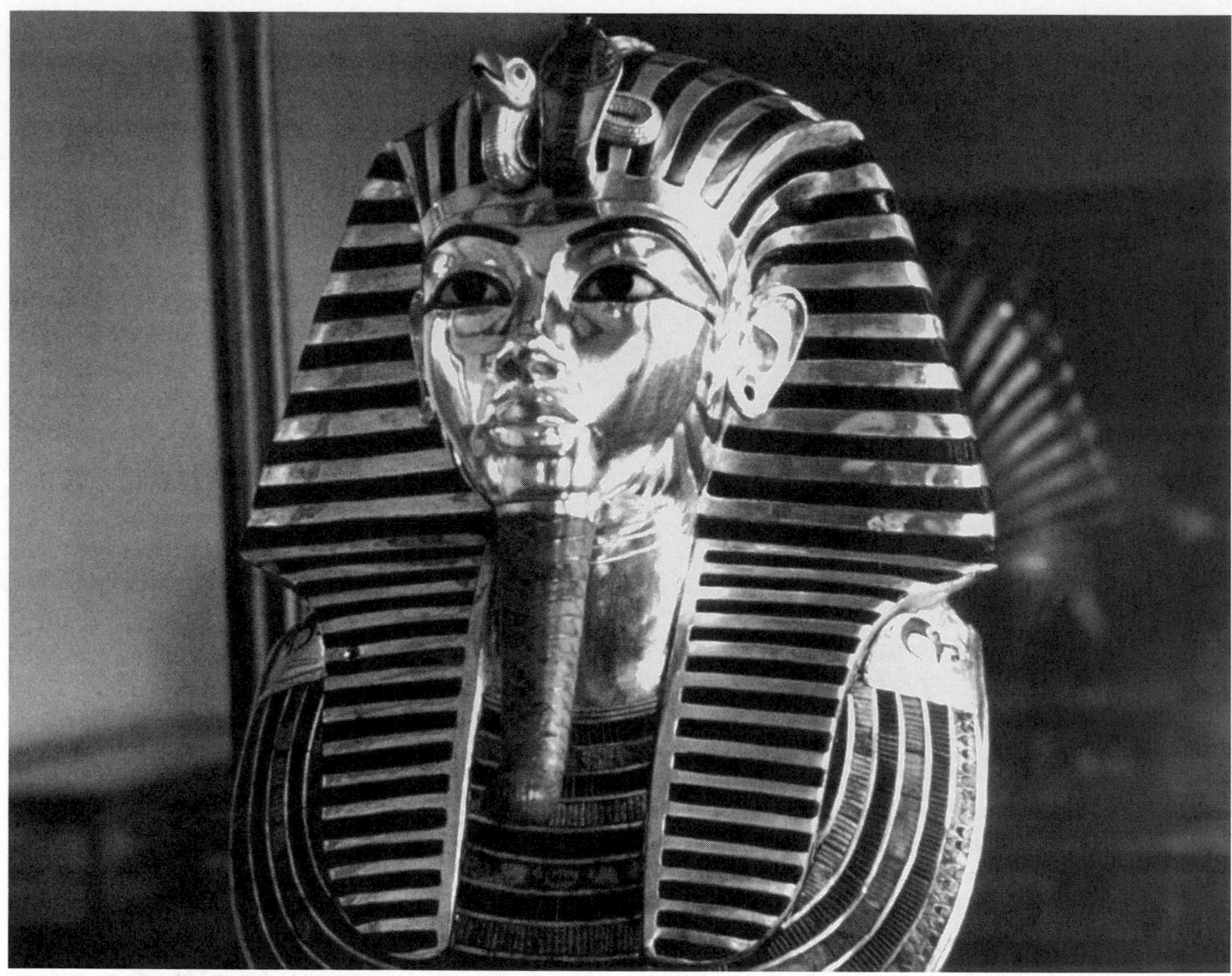

King Tut's burial mask. (Archive Photos)

Aton conducted in the open air, and in art, where stylized physical forms were used to represent Akhnaton, his wife Nefertiti, and their six daughters in the streaming rays of the Aton disc. Officials and private individuals used images of the royal family to make devotions to the Aton.

The novelty of the Aton religion and its opposition to tradition doomed the reforms to failure. Egypt's foreign relations also suffered during Akhnaton's reign, as diplomatic correspondence from some Palestinian rulers (in the so-called Amarna Letters) attests. When Akhnaton died, a new king named Smenkhare, whom some scholars believe was Queen Nefertiti, ruled briefly, followed by a child named Tutankhaton, the son-in-law, and probably also son, of Akhnaton. Representatives of the suppressed Amun priesthood ensured that Tutankhaton renounced the Aton religion and changed his name to Tutankhamun in honor of the Theban god. Tutankhamun (*c.* 1332–1322) died around age 19 and is best known for the 1923 discovery of his tomb, the only royal burial found intact. The so-called ''Amarna Age'' came fully to an end when an army commander named Horemheb (*c.* 1319–1292) claimed the throne and extinguished every trace of the Aton cult, Akhnaton and the city of Akhet-Aton.

Dynasty 19. Horemheb was succeeded by another army commander, Ramses (Ramesses) I, who founded a new line of kings hailing from the northeast Delta. The kings of the 19th Dynasty based themselves there at Tanis (biblical Soan, Zoan), although they continued to build lavish tombs and temples at Thebes. The reestablishment of internal order in Egypt enabled the next king, Seti I (*c.* 1290–1279), to recapture Palestine. Seti I and his son, Ramses II (*c.* 1270–1213), both fought against the Hittite kingdom in Anatolia (in modern Turkey). The Hittite king, Muwatalli, was allied with the city-states of Carchemish, Aleppo and UGARIT. Ramses II fought Muwatalli at the battle of Kadesh, but neither king emerged victorious. They declared a truce, cemented by a diplomatic marriage between Ramses II and a Hittite princess.

For the remainder of Ramses II's long reign Egypt was very prosperous; the king built extensively throughout Egypt and Nubia. Some scholars suggest that Ramses II was the biblical pharaoh confronted by Moses, and builder of the cities of Phithom (Pithom) and Rameses (Pi-Ramesses), but Egyptian sources cannot support this. It is interesting, however, that the only Egyptian reference to Israel occurs in a STELE inscription of Ramses II's successor, Mer-ne-Ptah (*c.* 1213–1204). This stele demonstrates that a people called Israel lived in Palestine at that time, and it was set up to commemorate Mer-ne-Ptah's military victory over Libyans and Sea Peoples (a migratory group from the Near East) in the Delta.

Dynasty 20. The 19th Dynasty was unsettled due to internal problems and foreign attacks like those by the Sea Peoples. In the next dynasty, Ramses III (*c.* 1187–1156) successfully fought off Libyans and more Sea Peoples, among them the PHILISTINES. War depleted Egypt financially, and although several more kings named Ramses (through Ramses XI) complete the 20th Dynasty, central authority waned.

Third Intermediate Period and Cushite Rule. After the end of the 20th Dynasty, the priests of Amun at Thebes styled themselves as kings (Dynasty 21) and governed southern Egypt, *c.* 1075–945. In the north, families originally of Libyan descent founded Dynasty 22 (*c.* 945–715), ruling from the Delta. The first king of the dynasty was Shoshonk (biblical Sesac, Shishak) I, who took a large army into Palestine and sacked Jerusalem, mentioned in 1 Kings 14:25–26 and 2 Chr. 12:2–9. His successors tried to appease Thebes and Upper Egypt but tensions remained, and in the 9th and early 8th centuries B.C., as many as four kings claimed to rule Egypt at once.

While a power vacuum existed in Egypt, Nubia governed itself independently as the kingdom of Cush (or Kush) under a line of rulers based at Napata near the fourth Cataract. One of these rulers, King Piye (*c.* 750–715) swept through Egypt with his army, meeting little resistance, and then withdrew to Napata. Other ethnic Libyan kings reigned briefly as Dynasty 24, but after 715 B.C. the Cushites returned to Egypt under Piye's successor, Shabaqo. Shabaqo established Dynasty 25, made up of Cushite kings who ruled both their native land and all of Egypt.

The Cushites worshipped the Theban god Amon and had strong cultural ties to Egypt due to the long relationship between Egypt and Nubia. The might of the Assyrian Empire was a threat to Cushite rule, however, and the Assyrian kings Sennacherib and Asarhaddon both at-

Coptic icon painted on Monastery of St. Paul, Fafarana, Egypt. (©Bojan Brecelj/CORBIS)

tacked Egypt. Ashurbanipal invaded in 671 B.C., forcing King Taharqo (biblical Tharaca, Tirhakah: 2 Kgs 19:9) to retreat to Napata, where he later died. Taharqo's successor, Tanutamun, re-entered Egypt but was immediately defeated by another Assyrian onslaught, during which Ashurbanipal, with the help of Egyptian vassals, subdued all of Egypt once again.

Late Period. The Assyrians governed the country by appointing Egyptians as vassal rulers. One of these vassals, Psamtek (Psammetichus) I (664–610) of Sais in the Delta, broke free of Assyrian control and established himself as sole ruler of the country, founding Dynasty 26 (664–525). He controlled Thebes by appointing his daughter, Nitocris, there as "divine votaress" of Amon. Psamtek I's success was due in part to the help of Greek (Ionian and Carian) mercenaries in his army, and as Assyria declined, Egypt's contacts with foreign countries grew. Greeks were given a free trading port at Naucratis in the Delta, and Psamtek I led troops to Palestine. Nechao (Necho) II (610–595) continued these policies, campaigning unsuccessfully against the Chaldaeans under NEBUCHADNEZZAR (Nabuchodonosor) and defeating King Josiah of Juda. Subsequently, the Egyptian kings Apries (589–570) and Amasis (570–526) also struggled against the Chaldaeans but were thwarted by

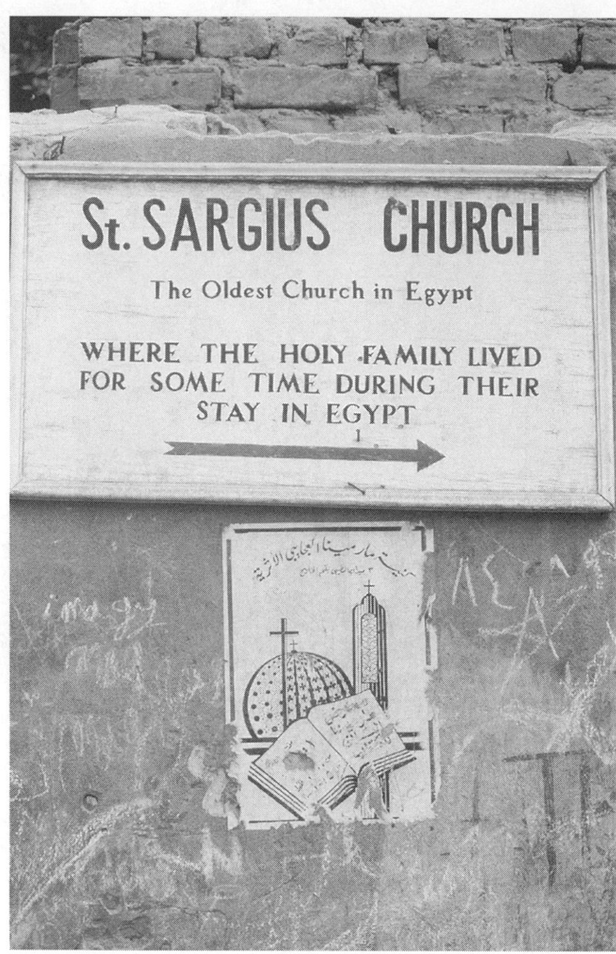

Directional sign pointing way to St. Sargius Coptic Church, Cairo, Egypt. (©Dave Bartruff/CORBIS)

the rise of the Persian Empire under Cyrus the Great in the sixth century B.C.

In 525 B.C., the Persian emperor, Cambyses, pressed west and captured King Psamtek III (526–525) at Pelusium in the eastern Delta. Egypt became part of the Persian Empire, run by an appointed official called the satrap; Manetho termed this period Dynasty 27. The emperor, DARIUS I (522–486), showed some interest in the country, but after his death Egyptian leaders began to wrest power away from Persia. The last three native dynasties (Dynasties 28, 29 and 30), each based in the Delta, attained Egyptian independence and saw a short-lived renaissance of native culture. In 341 B.C., however, Persia reestablished control of Egypt under the emperor Artaxerxes III (358–338), succeeded by Darius III (338–335).

Alexander the Great defeated Darius III at Issus in 333 B.C. and then turned to Egypt, where he was welcomed as liberator. He stayed less than a year, but in that time he was crowned as pharaoh. He founded a harbor on the northwest coast of the Delta, named Alexandria in his honor. In the division of Alexander's empire after his death in 332 B.C., Egypt was given to his general, Ptolemy, son of Lagus, who established himself as Ptolemy I Soter (305–285), king of Egypt and founder of the house of the Ptolemies.

PTOLEMAIC, ROMAN AND BYZANTINE EGYPT

This section surveys Egypt's history as a Hellenistic monarchy and then as part of the Roman and Byzantine empires.

Ptolemaic Period (305–30). The Ptolemaic rulers were Greeks who respected some of Egypt's social and religious traditions while fashioning a Hellenistic monarchy for themselves. Their capital at Alexandria became the greatest intellectual center of its time, with a library of approximately half a million scrolls.

Ptolemy III Euergetes I (246–221) took an interest in Palestine and came into conflict there with the Seleucid Dynasty of Syria. The Syrian wars, combined with feuds among the Ptolemies and native rebellions in the south, weakened Ptolemaic authority. In 170 B.C., Rome intervened on behalf of the Ptolemies against the Seleucid king, ANTIOCHUS IV EPIPHANES (175–164), and as a result Egypt entered more and more into the orbit of the Roman Republic.

The contest between Pompey and Julius Caesar for sole rule over Rome decided Egypt's fate. The last Ptolemaic monarch was Cleopatra VII (51–30), who allied herself first with Caesar and then, after his assassination at Rome in 44 B.C., with Mark Antony in an effort to preserve Egypt's independence. Conflict between Antony and Caesar's heir, Octavian (later Augustus), came to a head at the Battle of Actium off the northwest coast of Greece in 30 B.C. After Antony and Cleopatra's forces were defeated, the pair committed suicide and Octavian claimed Egypt for Rome.

Roman Empire (30 B.C.–A.D. 395). Egypt became a Roman province and was the chief source of grain for the entire empire. Roman rule differed from the Ptolemaic system because the Romans imposed a stricter system of social stratification, privileging a Greek-speaking, city-based elite. Romans did not encourage native Egyptian language, although some Egyptian temples continued to be decorated with representations of Roman "pharaohs" until around A.D. 250. As early as the second century, Christianity began to spread in Egypt, with scholars like Clement and Origen based at Alexandria. Despite Roman attempts to suppress it, Christianity continued to grow, and *c.* 320 St. PACHOMIUS founded the first monastery, in Upper Egypt. MONASTICISM flourished in Egypt as men and women left their homes for these desert settlements.

Byzantine Period. At the partition of the Roman Empire following the death of Emperor Theodosius in 395, Egypt became part of the Eastern Empire and shipped its grain to the capital, Byzantium (Constantinople, modern Istanbul), rather than Rome. Christianity was now the state religion, and under Abbot SHENOUTE OF ATRIPE (Athribis), the Egyptian, or Coptic, Church thrived. Copts continued to adhere to the Monophysite doctrine after this belief in the one divine nature of Christ was condemned at the Fourth Ecumenical Council of CHALCEDON in 451, and Coptic Christianity became separated from mainstream Christianity in the Byzantine Empire.

Under Heraclius (610–641) Byzantine power in the Near East declined, and Arab followers of the new Islamic religion began to filter throughout the region.

MEDIEVAL EGYPT

The following sections cover Egypt from the Arab conquest until 1798: Arab Rule, Fatimid Dynasty, Ayyubid Dynasty, The Mamelukes and Ottoman Egypt.

Arab Rule. In 640, eight years after the death of the prophet MUḤAMMAD, the army of Caliph Umar defeated Byzantine garrisons at Pelusium in the Delta and Fort Babylon (at modern Cairo), bringing Egypt into the Muslim world.

Early Arab rulers maintained much of the Byzantine administrative system and did not force conversions to Islam. The Arabs isolated themselves from the native population and founded a new capital called Fustat (at the site of Fort Babylon), which would grow into Old Cairo. Egypt was ruled by Arab and Turkish governors appointed by the ruling Umayyad caliphs in Damascus, and later the Abbasid caliphs in Baghdad. Gradual Islamization of the country proceeded and most people adopted the Arabic language. In 868, Egypt became the fiefdom of a Turkish general whose stepson, Ahmad Ibn Tulun, went to Egypt and founded the Tulunid Dynasty (868–905), which opposed the Abbasid government and helped Egypt's economy and culture flourish. Ibn Tulun's successors squandered their wealth and power, however, and several years of unrest ensued.

Fatimid Dynasty (969–1171). The Fatimid state, based in North Africa, took control and ruled Egypt as an independent country, setting up its own dynasty at Cairo to rival the Abbasid caliphs in Baghdad. The Fatimids were tolerant of Christians and Jews in their government, except for Caliph el-Hakim (996–1021), who destroyed Christian churches throughout Fatimid territory, including the Church of the Holy Sepulchre in Jerusalem.

The Fatimids followed Shī 'ite Islam (a more esoteric sect which had split off to honor Muḥammad's son-in-law, Caliph Ali), although the majority of Egyptians were, and are, mainstream Sunni Muslims. In the 12th century, struggles within the Fatimid dynasty led to the intervention of Syrian troops, who were Sunni as well. In 1171, the Sunni general, Saladin, wrested control of Egypt and deposed the Fatimids.

Ayyubid Dynasty (1171–1250). Saladin established the Ayyubid dynasty, which restored Egypt to the eastern (Abbasid) caliphate. Under Saladin, Egypt prospered and Cairo became the center of the Arab world. During this period, the CRUSADES touched on Egyptian soil. Damietta in the Delta was captured and occupied for three years (1218–1221) during the Fifth Crusade and again during the Sixth Crusade (1249), when LOUIS IX of France was taken prisoner in Egypt. Saladin was tolerant of Christianity in Egypt and Palestine, and Egypt traded actively with Italian city-states. At the same time, the Ayyubid policy of granting family members control of different parts of the territory encouraged dissent and armed conflict.

The Mamelukes (1250–1517). Ayyubid sultans increasingly purchased Turkish slaves, called Mamelukes, to staff their armies, and in 1250 the Mamelukes took advantage of an Ayyubid feud to elect one of their own men as sultan, backed by Mameluke military strength. The Mameluke Dynasty saw Egypt at the pinnacle of its cultural, economic and political powers. Although the Mamelukes were not ethnically Arab and many did not speak Arabic literature, education and the arts. Mameluke territory in Egypt and Palestine offered a haven to Muslims fleeing Mongol invasions from the Far East, and in part because of this pressure, Christians and Jews were resented and at times persecuted. Conversion to Islam accelerated, and use of the Coptic language declined in favor of Arabic.

Ottoman Egypt (1517–1798). After confrontations between the Mamelukes and the Ottoman Empire over control of Palestine and Syria, the Ottomans defeated the Mamelukes in 1517. Egypt became a province governed from Istanbul (ancient Byzantium, Constantinople) by means of a viceroy, or *pasha*, in Cairo. Mamelukes still constituted a political and financial elite, identified by the title *bey* after their names, and in the late 18th century, Mamelukes tried to reassert power against their Ottoman rulers.

MODERN EGYPT

Egypt's history since the Napleonic invasion of 1798 is treated under these subdivisions: French Occupation, Muhammad Ali and his successors, British Occupation, The Kingdom of Egypt and the Arab Republic of Egypt.

French Occupation (1798–1805). In 1798, NAPOLEON I Bonaparte captured Alexandria with a fleet that included his army as well as a corps of scholars and scientists (savants) interested in Egyptian history and culture. Napoleon claimed to be a friend of the Ottomans who would liberate Egypt from the Mameluke rebels. As the savants set about recording the art, architecture and natural world of Egypt, Napoleon faced the threat of British troops approaching from the Mediterranean and the Ottoman forces from the east. Napoleon slipped by the British and returned to France, leaving his troops behind to hold out against the British until 1801. British forces then withdrew from Egypt in 1803, leaving control of the country to the Ottomans once more.

Although of little military consequence, the French Occupation brought Egypt into close contact with Europe and opened the door for Europeans to study the Egyptian past, most notably through the discovery of the Rosetta Stone—a trilingual Egyptian and Greek inscription which was surrendered to the British—and the publication of the multi-volume *Description de l'Égypte*, which collected the savants' records of ancient and contemporary Egypt.

Muḥammad Ali (1805–1849) and his successors. Amid much debate, Muḥammad Ali was appointed *pasha* and set about establishing himself in a position of almost complete independence from the Ottomans. He restructured the Egyptian administration to break the power of the Mamelukes, effectively making himself chief landowner with an agricultural monopoly. Trade with Europe, especially the British and French, introduced some westernization and opened Egypt to European travelers and archaeologists.

During the reign of Isma'il (1863–1879), a grandson of Muḥammad Ali, the French-designed Suez Canal was opened, making Egypt even more pivotal to Europe and the Ottomans. Isma'il used the title Khedive to distinguish himself from other Ottoman viceroys, and he and his family continued to own most of Egypt's land. Egyptian army leaders and the educated elite, who had been exposed to European administrative ideals, increasingly opposed this autocracy. Under pressure from Britain and France, the Ottomans deposed Isma'il in favor of his son, Tawfiq (1879–1892), which created an opening for further European involvement in Egyptian affairs.

British Occupation (1882–1922). In 1882, British forces occupied Egypt and made it an unofficial, or "veiled," protectorate of the British Empire. Nominally, the Ottoman sultan and the Khedive retained control of Egypt, but Britain installed advisors who oversaw the internal administration, under the direction of the British consul, Lord Cromer.

Khedive Tawfiq was succeeded by his son, Abbas Hilmi II (1892–1914), who at times openly criticized Cromer and General Kitchener, commander of the Egyptian army. In 1898 the army reconquered Sudan and added it to Britain's veiled protection, after which Tawfiq was more conciliatory to the British.

Meanwhile, a growing Egyptian nationalist movement, spearheaded by French-educated lawyer and journalist Mustafa Kamil (1874–1908), turned to the Ottomans for support. The Egyptian upper classes were dissatisfied with the extent and duration of British control, but Cromer did not sympathize with nationalist concerns. By the time Kitchener was appointed consul in 1911, several nationalist factions competed in opposition to the British and to Khedive Abbas Hilmi.

War against the Ottoman Empire was declared in 1914, and Britain made Egypt an official protectorate, deposing the Khedive and appointing his uncle, and later his uncle's brother, as sultan. Kitchener was replaced by a high commissioner, Sir Reginald Wingate, who instituted martial law and abolished the Egyptian assembly.

Two days after the Armistice was signed in November of 1918, an Egyptian delegation (called the *Wafd*) led by nationalist politician Sa'id Zaghlul approached Wingate to plead for Egypt's independence from Britain. When Wingate refused to meet the delegation, revolt broke out and Britain appointed a new commissioner, Lord Allenby, to reassert control. Zaghlul continued to press for independence, and Allenby, hoping to thwart the most radical nationalists, agreed, resulting in a declaration of independence on Feb. 28, 1922.

The Kingdom of Egypt (1922–1952). In March of 1922, the sultan became King Fuad I of Egypt at the head of a constitutional monarchy with a bicameral parliament. However, political struggles continued between the British, the new king and the Wafd, which had become the major nationalist organization with a large popular following.

When World War II broke out in 1939, Egypt was obliged to offer Britain military assistance under the terms of a 1936 treaty, although King Farouk (1936–1952) was hostile to the British; heavy fighting took place in Egypt in 1942–43. Egypt's involvement on behalf of the Arab cause in Palestine (ending in defeat in the first Arab-Israel war of 1948–49) and the formation of the Arab League in 1945 led to further political disagreement with Britain and public demonstrations against the king.

A group of army officers, called the Free Officers, conspired in an armed coup on the night of July 22–23, 1952. Led by Gamal Abdel Nasser, the officers forced King Farouk to abdicate and leave the country.

Arab Republic of Egypt. Nasser and his associates abolished the 1923 constitution. In July of 1953, the Arab

Republic of Egypt was declared (first as the United Arab Republic) and a new constitution was in place by 1956, with Nasser elected as the first president of Egypt.

Nasser (1956–1970). Nasser settled long-standing disputes with Britain over Sudan and the Suez Canal Zone, so that Sudan attained independence and British troops left Suez. Nasser's popular domestic policies were socialist in scope, placing Egyptian industry under state ownership, limiting private landownership and heavily subsidizing commodities like sugar and electricity. He suppressed opposition political organizations, especially the Muslim Brotherhood.

In the postwar political climate, Egypt had an uneasy relationship with the West. In 1956, Nasser provoked a crisis by nationalizing the Suez Canal after the United States and Britain withdrew funding for the Aswan High Dam. With backing from the Soviet Union, the Dam was finally completed in 1968, to provide adequate electricity to Egypt's expanding population.

Antagonism towards the new state of Israel united Egypt and other Arab countries, from whom Israel feared attack. A second Arab-Israeli war in 1956–57 was instigated by the Suez Crisis and ended after American and Soviet intervention convinced Israel to withdraw from territory it had taken in Sinai, bordering the Canal Zone. In June of 1967, the third Arab-Israeli war (called the Six Day War) broke out when Israel launched pre-emptive strikes against Egypt and Jordan. Israeli forces reoccupied the Sinai Peninsula and captured territory in Jordan (the West Bank) and Syria (the Golan Heights).

Sadat (1970–1981). When Nasser died suddenly in September of 1970, vice-president Anwar Sadat succeeded him as president. Sadat inherited an economy struggling with budget deficits, chronic shortages and a military infrastructure nearly destroyed by Israel in the 1967 war.

In October of 1973, a fourth Arab-Israeli war (the October War, or Yom Kippur War) began when Egypt and Syria attacked Israel. To solve the crisis, the United States restored diplomatic relations with Egypt and helped broker a settlement whereby Israel withdrew from Sinai and Egypt fully reopened the Suez Canal to international traffic. Egypt also acknowledged Israel's right to exist. This political victory placed Sadat in a strong position to turn to the West, rather than the Soviet Union, for financial aid. Subsidies and nationalization were curtailed and Western companies began to invest in Egypt, moves which stabilized the economy but were very unpopular. Sadat tried to appease Islamists by giving limited state backing to some religious laws and showing more lenience towards the Muslim Brotherhood.

Sadat also entered into peace negotiations with Israel, and in 1978 he met with the Israeli prime minister, Menachem Begin, and U.S. President James Carter at Camp David near Washington D.C. In March of 1979, Sadat and Begin signed a peace treaty, which brought American support but angered other Arab nations, who immediately excluded Egypt from the Arab League.

Controversial laws adopted in 1980 made it possible for the president to be elected indefinitely, and in September of 1981, members of many opposition groups, including the Muslim Brotherhood, were imprisoned. On Oct. 6, 1981, Sadat was assassinated during a military parade when Islamist army officers opened fire on him.

Mubarak (1981–present). Vice-president Hosni Mubarak survived the attack on Sadat and was immediately elected as the new president. Mubarak restored Egyptian relations with the Arab League in 1989 and has continued to open the Egyptian economy to the West. Mubarak has also used Egypt's pivotal but difficult position with regard to Israel to help further negotiations among moderate Israeli leaders, the Palestinians and other Arab countries, especially during crises like the 1991–92 Persian Gulf War. The activity of Islamist extremists in Egypt remains a serious problem. Coptic Christians in central Egypt have been targeted by radical Islamist militia, and in 1997, members of the outlawed Islamic Jihad group killed more than 60 tourists at Luxor in an attempt to damage the government's vital revenues from travel industry sources. Mubarak was elected to a fourth term as president in 1999.

Bibliography: J. BAINES and J. MALEK, *Cultural Atlas of Ancient Egypt* (2nd ed. New York 2000). *The Oxford History of Ancient Egypt*, ed. I. SHAW (Oxford 2000). *Egypt: The World of the Pharaohs*, ed. R. SCHULZ and M. SEIDEL, tr. P. MANUELIAN (Cologne 1998). B. MIDANT-REYNES, *The Prehistory of Egypt: From the First Egyptians to the First Pharaohs* (Oxford 2000). B. KEMP, *Ancient Egypt: Anatomy of a Civilization* (London and New York 1989). D. REDFORD, *Egypt, Canaan, and Israel in Ancient Times* (Princeton 1992). A. BOWMAN, *Egypt After the Pharaohs* (2nd ed. London 1996). *The Cambridge History of Egypt, volume I: Islamic Egypt, 640–1517 and volume II: Modern Egypt, from 1517 to the End of the Twentieth Century*, ed. M. W. DALY (Cambridge 1998).

[H. GOEDICKE/C. RIGGS]

EGYPT, ANCIENT

This article treats of (1) the religion, (2) the architecture and art, and (3) the language and literature of Pharaonic Egypt.

1. Religion

Herodotus (237) rightfully called the Egyptians the most religious of all men, for religion was one of the most

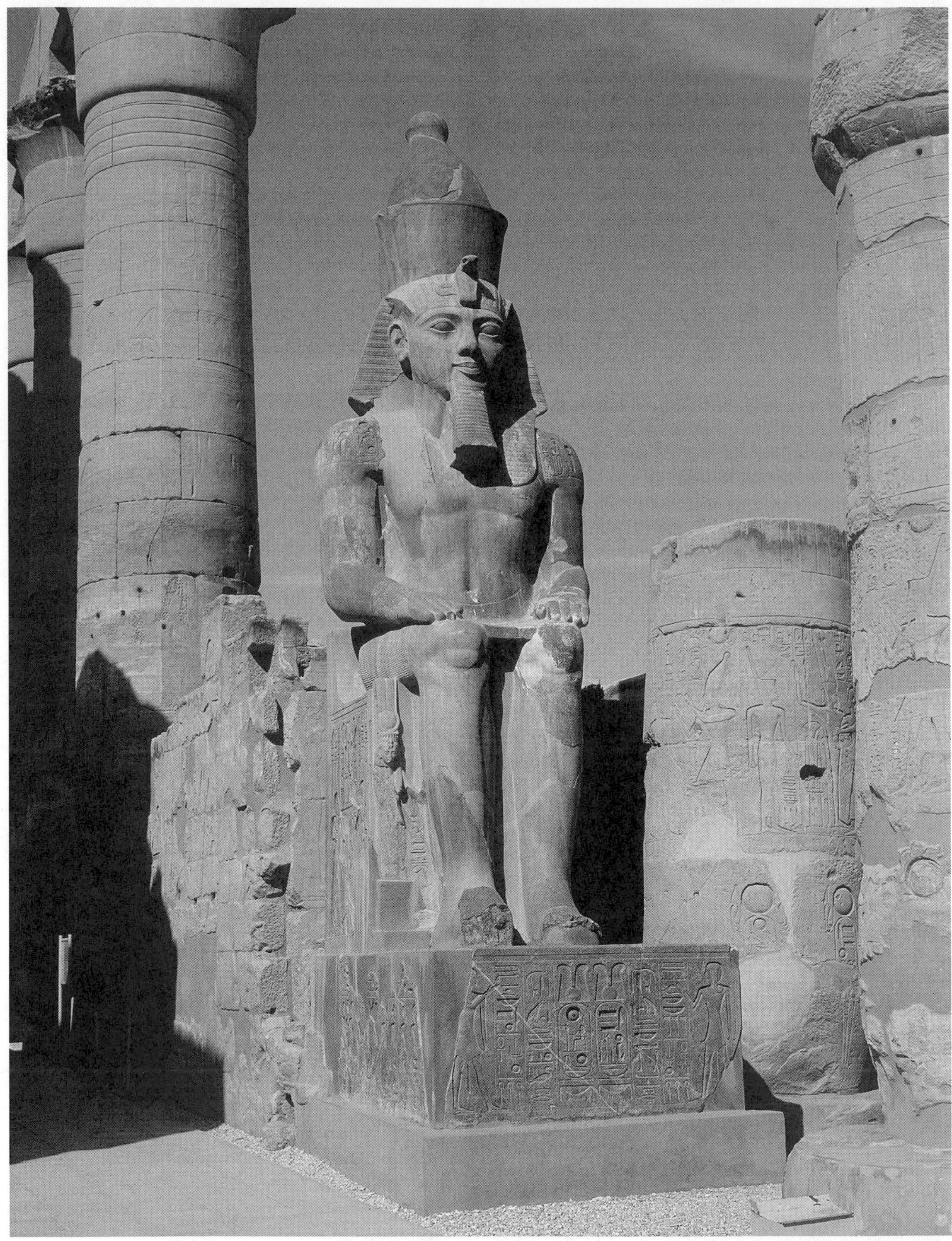

Statue of Ramses II at Luxor Temple, Egypt. (©Papilio/CORBIS)

important elements of ancient Egyptian civilization, playing a major role in the life of the state as well as in the life of the individual. The notion of the divine made its impact felt on the most diverse of human activities. Egypt differs from other ancient Near Eastern nations, for example, in that the majority of the names for its territorial divisions or nomes referred to some symbol for the divine. In addition, many of the cities took their names from the local temple or from some epithet or attribute of the god venerated there, and the great majority of the inhabitants bore names referring to the divine in someway.

On the other hand, the fact that the reconstruction of this civilization is based almost entirely on monuments and documents discovered within sacred enclosures, temples, or necropolises must always be borne in mind. Cities of the living, such as Akhet-Aton (el-'Amârna) and the workers' village at Deir el-Medīnah, have yielded relatively few objects to the excavators. As a consequence, the vestiges of the past tend to place a one-sided emphasis on the religious life of the ancient Egyptians; this leaves a knowledge of their religion nonetheless indispensable for a proper understanding of Egyptian civilization as a whole.

The Gods. The gods of the Egyptian pantheon can be divided into three classes. The most important consists of animals or fetishes, each originally venerated in a single city. Because of the tendency to anthropomorphism, these divinities were represented as men or women with animal heads; for example, the jackal Anubis of Saūti (Lycopolis), modern Asyut; the cat Ubastet of Bubastis in the Delta; the hawk Horus; the ram Harsaphes of Heracleopolis Magna, modern Ehnāsya; the cow Hathor of Aphroditopolis, modern Atfīh; the hawk Haroëris or ''Horus the Great'' of Damanhur; the ram Khnum of Hypselis, modern Shūtb, and of Latopolis, modern Esnah; the hawk-headed warrior god Montu of Hermonthis; the vulture-goddess Uto of Butō, modern Kōm el-Farā'īn; the crocodile Sobek (Greek Souchos) of Faiyūm; the lioness Sekhmet of Rehesu, near Letopolis, later venerated at Memphis; the fabulous animal Seth, of Ombos; the mummified hawk Sokaris, of the Memphite necropolis; and the ibis Toth of Hermopolis in the Delta, modern Baklia, and of Hermopolis Magna, modern el-Ashmūnēn. Several goddesses bear on their heads the animals they originally represented. Thus the goddess Mut, from the Karnak region, wears the skin of a vulture, and Selkis wears a scorpion. Satis, the goddess of the Island of Sehel and of Elephantine, often wears the crown of Upper Egypt combined with antelope horns. This type of representation is especially typical of divinities who originated as fetishes: Isis, from Iseion, modern Behbīt el-Hagar, formerly personified the royal throne; Nefertem, from the Memphis region, a lotus flower; and Nēth from Saïs, modern Sān el-Hagar, an archaic shield with two crossed arrows.

Relief carving depicting funeral mourners bearing gifts for tomb, 18th or 19th Dynasty, Egypt, ca. 1350 B.C.

Cosmic gods comprise the second category, represented as a general rule in human form, as for example, Shu, the personification of air; the moon-god Khonsu; the ithyphallic god of fertility, Min; and the chthonian god of fertility, Osiris, also a king in prehistoric times. These gods, however, were identified also with local divinities of animal origin. Thus, Shu forms with Tefnut, the personification of moisture, a pair of lions, and the goddess of the sky, Nut, is considered a cow-goddess.

To the third category belong gods personifying abstractions in human form: Atum, from Heliopolis, who expresses the concept of universality; AMON, from Karnak, whose name means ''the hidden one''; Ptah of Memphis, god of industrial labor and the arts; and, finally, the goddess Ma'at, personification of cosmic order, manifested in human society in the ethical notions of

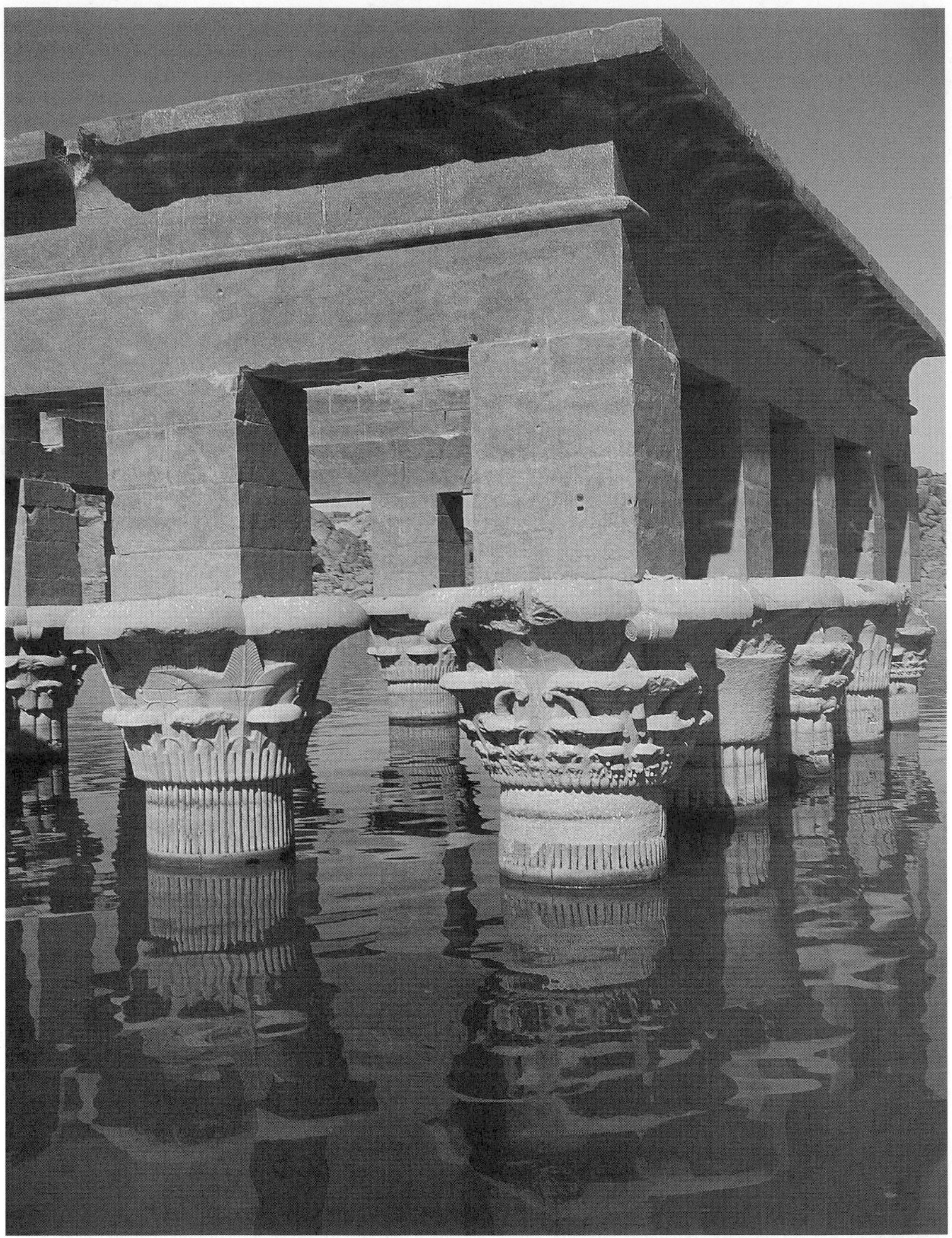

Submerged ruins of Egyptian temple, Philae, Egypt. (©Otto Lang/CORBIS)

truth and justice [see J. B. Pritchard, *The Ancient Near East in Pictures Relating to the Old Testament,* (Princeton 1954) 573].

Theology and the Myths. As a consequence of the political evolution, which brought the cities in closer contact, the problem of the relationships between these local gods, each supreme master in its locale, developed with increasing urgency. The establishment of divine families was a first solution. These families frequently formed a triad, composed of father, mother, and son: thus Ptah, Sekhmet, and Nefertem were brought together at Memphis; and Amon, Mut, and Khonsu, at Thebes. Families consisting of eight or nine divinities appear later. How did the Egyptians reconcile the supremacy of the local god with the existence of the gods of other cities, whose power they never dreamed of contesting? The phenomenon of syncretism, or the identification of the gods, came into play here—the other divinities were considered manifestations or emanations of the local god. There is a text, for example, which in regard to the primordial god Atum, indicates that the other gods are his names, created by him. Similar statements are made concerning other gods, in particular Amon. Syncretism seems to be based on the idea that the divine nature is one and universal. J. Vandier (228–229) concluded from this: ''It is all as though the Egyptians had believed in one god, capable of manifesting himself in different forms. . . . Were the Egyptians in the last analysis monotheists unawares?''

Other writers claim to have discovered more palpable proofs of the existence of monotheism. The ''Monument of Memphite theology'' is of primary concern. H. Junker points out in the god Ur, ''the Great,'' mentioned here, a god of the sky who was venerated as a single god during the prehistoric epoch and was later split up into the numerous divinities of the Memphite pantheon [*Die Götterlehre von Memphis,* in *Abhandlungen der Deutschen (Preussischen, to 1944) Akademie der Wissenschaften zu Berlin (1815–), Phil.-hist.Kl. 23* (1939)].

On the other hand, in the wisdom literature, the divinity is most of the time evoked by the word netter, simply ''God.'' Basing his argument on this fact, and on the ideas expressed in these texts, É. Drioton has defended the hypothesis that the Egyptians, from the beginning of the Old Kingdom, had the idea ''of a God named without determination [and consequently thought of as unique], master of events, provident guardian of men, judge of good and evil actions, and giver of just rewards'' [*La religion égyptienne dans ses grandes signes,* excerpt from *La Revue du Caire,* 1945, in *Pages d'Égyptologie* (Cairo 1957) 79]. In *Le monothéisme de l'ancienne Égypte* [*Cahiers d'histoire égyptienne* (Cairo, Jan. 1949) 168] he formulated his judgment as follows: ''The official Egyptian religion was always polytheism acted upon by the philosophical monotheism of its faithful; for the most enlightened among these, the private religion was most frequently monotheism tainted with polytheism.''

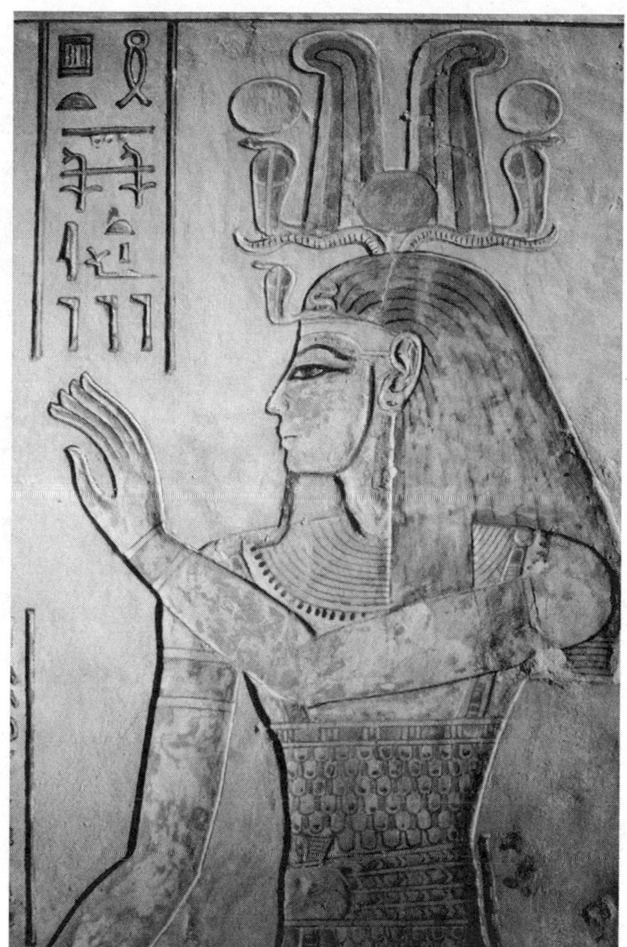

Fresco painting of a god, in Egyptian tomb, Valley of the Kings, Luxor, Egypt. (©Bojan Brecelj/CORBIS)

Theological Systems. Five theological systems can be reconstructed from the texts, each explaining in its own way the origin of the universe, the gods, and men.

According to one cosmogony, not related to any center of worship, the god of the earth, Geb, and the goddess of the sky, Nut, of unspecified origin, created the sun. Each evening, Nut receives him into hiding for the night, and each morning she gives him back to the world.

The system from On-Heliopolis teaches that Atum-Rē came forth from the primordial ocean, Nun, by his own power. He climbed a hill and raised himself up on the *benben* stone at Heliopolis. He then drew out from himself, by masturbating, the first divine couple, Shu and Tefnut (air and moisture). These gods brought into the world Geb and Nut, who gave birth to Osiris, Isis, Seth,

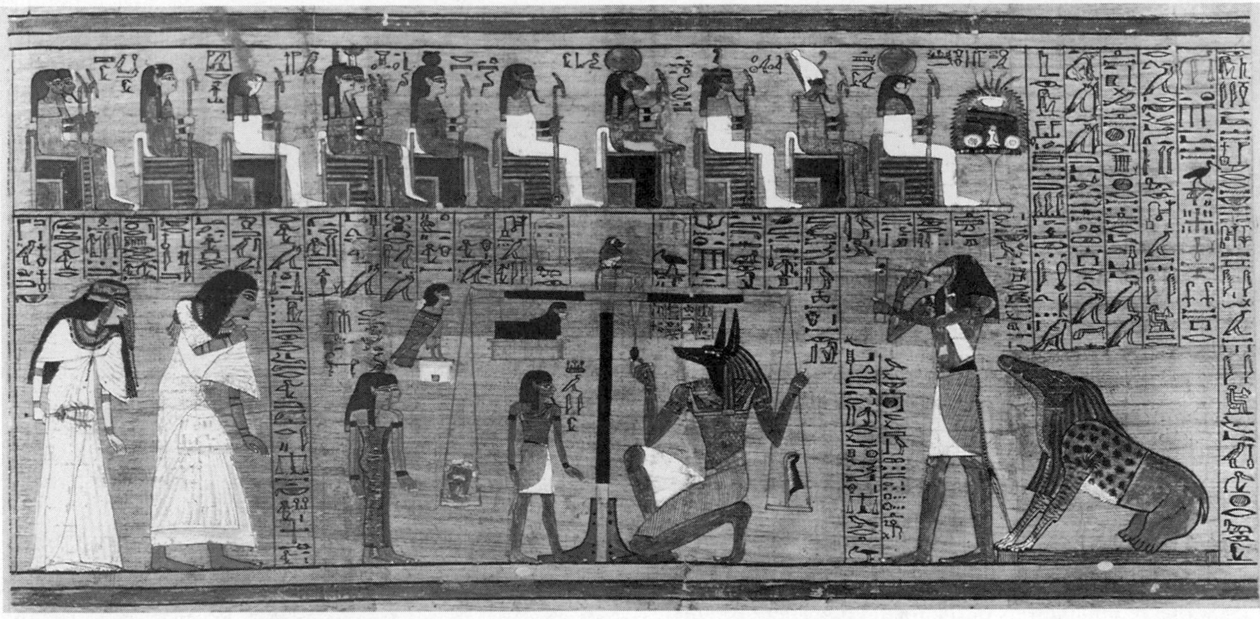

Detail of the "Papyrus of Ani" (Papyrus 10470) from a "Book of the Dead," 18th Dynasty

and Nephthys. The members of this Ennead governed the country, father succeeding son.

The ancient name Shmūn of the city Ashmūnēn (Hermopolis) means "eight," referring to the four divine couples venerated in this place. These divinities, represented in the form of serpents and frogs, set themselves on the primordial mound, which had come forth from Nun at Shmūn, in order to create light, that is, Rē. According to other texts, the Ogdoad created an egg and placed it on the mound. The sun was born from that egg, and in turn created and ordered the world. Among these gods, Amon afterward met with extraordinary fortune when, during the First Intermediate Period, he became the local god of Thebes, and later, the supreme god of Egypt. The system was then transformed as follows. In the beginning there was a serpent-god Kem-atef (he who finished his time) who was assimilated by the great Amon of Karnak. This serpent died and left to his son, the serpent Ir-ta (the creator of the earth), the care of creating the Ogdoad. Ir-ta was assimilated by the ithyphallic Amon of Luxor. Amon, the member of the Ogdoad, is then his son. The eight gods swam from Thebes to Hermopolis, where they created the sun, and came to die later not far from Medīnct Habu. Later, Horus was linked to this cycle as son and heir of the Ogdoad.

The Memphite system is the only one among these Egyptian cosmogonies that does not have to be laboriously reconstructed from the Pyramid Texts and other religious documents, some funerary, some not. It is preserved in the form of doctrine in stele no. 797 of the British Museum, dating from the reign of Shabaka (Twenty-fifth Dynasty). The original text of this "Monument of Memphite theology," however, was composed, according to H. Junker, between the Third and Fifth Dynasties, and was a fusion of the two preceding systems. Ptah finds himself at the head of eight primordial gods, who are only "forms that exist within Ptah." Ur-Atum, the manifestation of Ptah, accomplishes the work of creation with his heart (the seat of intelligence) and his tongue (instrument of the will). The demiurge first creates the other gods of the Ennead, then the *kas* and the *hemsut*, that is, the powers which sustain life, and finally "he caused the cities to rise up and founded the nomes."

Veneration of the sun-god (solar religion) appears alongside the other cults encountered throughout the religious history of Egypt. The name Rē probably originated as the common name for the sun. It was associated with several other gods, in particular with Amon and Atum. Rē-Atum is the sun who disappears during the night; Rē is the star of the day. Khepré (he who is becoming) and Rē-Hor-Akhte (Rē-Horus, dwelling on the horizon) personify the sun that rises in the morning. The Pyramid Texts indicate that the solar religion existed from the most ancient times and that by syncretism with Atum it was integrated into the doctrine of On-Heliopolis. It flourished especially under the Fourth and Fifth Dynasties. During that time several kings bore names formed of compounds based on the name of Rē; and from that time a part of the king's title was *sa-Rē* or "son of Rē"; the kings of the Fifth Dynasty built solar temples near Abū-Gūrab. A story from the Papyrus Westcar (in the

Berlin Museum) tells how the first three kings of that dynasty were born from the union of Rē with the wife of a priest of Rē; the eldest was high priest at Heliopolis before becoming king. Under the Middle Empire, besides Amon-Rē, the names of Khnum-Rē, Min-Rē, and Sobek-Rē appear, attesting to the gradual ascendancy of the solar religion over the other cults. It took on new forms during the New Empire, and even became, under AKHNATON, the only officially tolerated religion.

Myths. The cosmogonical systems, as has just been seen, attributed an uncontested supremacy to the gods. In the myths, on the contrary, they are exposed to all sorts of ambushes and attacks by their adversaries. These legends surround two personages: the sun-god Rē, and Osiris, the god of fertility, lord of the kingdom of the dead. Their vicissitudes are doubtless inspired by the spectacle of nature, in which light and darkness, life and death struggle in unceasing combat.

The ''Destruction of Mankind'' is an important myth from the solar cycle. Rē sent his eye, the goddess Hathor, against the men who had plotted against him. She caused such a massacre that Rē was obliged to have recourse to a trick in order to rescue the survivors. Wounded by such ingratitude, Rē abandoned the government of the world. His daughter, Nut, the divine cow, carried him up to the sky on her back, but while looking at the earth, she was overcome by vertigo. Rē then ordered Shu to hold her up from underneath.

In the Osirian legend, as in certain solar myths, Horus and Seth are the protagonists. Horus, however, is here the son of Osiris and Isis: he is Horus the child. This legend has been transmitted in its most complete form by Plutarch, *De Iside et Osiride.* This version describes the benevolent reign of Osiris, which attracted the jealousy of Seth and his supporters. These succeeded by a trick in enclosing him in a coffin, which they threw into the river. The coffin, borne by the waters to Byblos, in Phoenicia, ran aground near a tree, which grew miraculously around it. Isis, gone in search of her husband, found the coffin, after many adventures, and brought it back to Egypt. But after she arrived at Butō close to her son Horus, Seth discovered the coffin and cut up the cadaver into 40 pieces which he scattered. Isis buried the pieces in the places where she found them. Osiris left the kingdom of the dead for a time to prepare his son for combat. Grown to maturity, Horus defied his uncle Seth and overcame him in a series of conflicts. Certain details of this account show Osiris assuming the character of a vegetation god. At the same time, as among other peoples, this vegetation god is also the god of the dead. The name of the city of Byblos provides a link also between Osiris and Adonis, the Phoenician god of vegetation and water who was him-

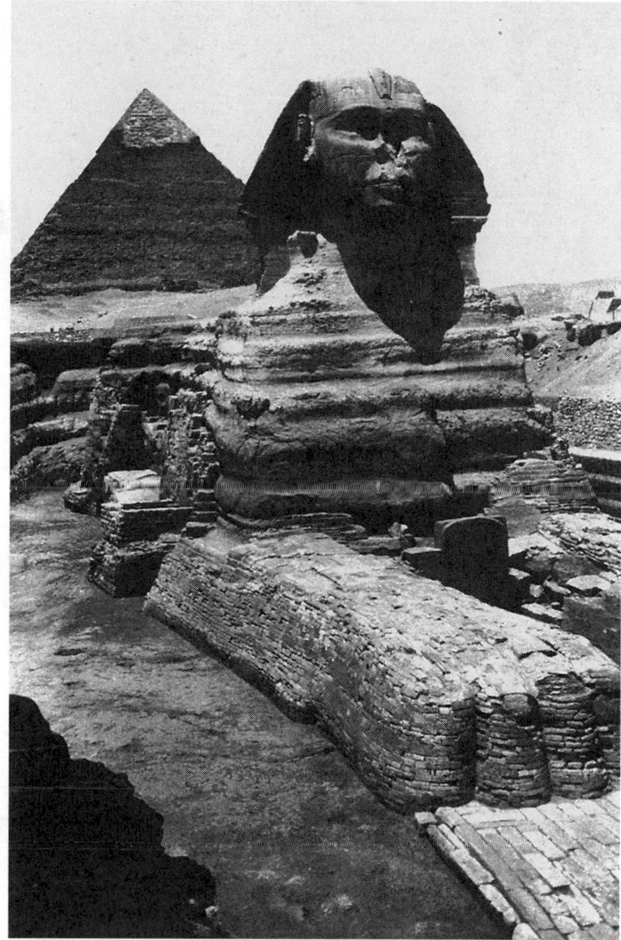

The Sphinx, Cairo, Egypt.

self related to the Canaanite-Mesopotamian god Tammuz.

On the gods and the legends, see H. Kees, *Der Götterglaube im alten Ägypten* (*Mitteil. d. vorderasiat.-äg. Ges.* 45; Leipzig, 1941).

The Cult. Besides the temples and their personnel, the religious calendars of the Egyptian and the routine daily services of worship of their gods are here described.

The Temples. The contrast between the solar religion and the cult of the other gods is reflected clearly in the construction of the sanctuaries. The solar temple of Abū-Gūrab, built by King Ni-User-Rē, of the Fifth Dynasty, is generally thought to be a replica of the sanctuary at Heliopolis. It is basically a large rectangular court, 75 by 100 meters, bounded by a wall, whose entrance is found in the axis of the east façade. In the west end of the court is an obelisk 36 meters high raised above a truncated pyramid 20 meters high. The obelisk is doubtless a reproduction of the *benben* stone at Heliopolis. At its foot was placed the table for offerings. Two passage-

Egyptian pillar monuments, Kalabsha, Egypt. (©Otto Lang/CORBIS)

ways begin at the entrance and follow the enclosure wall, leading in one direction to the substructure of the obelisk, in another to the storehouses set back against the north wall. Both are decorated with reliefs representing the seasons and various scenes from the life of men, as well as animals and plants. Outside the wall is a large ship made of bricks, symbolizing the ship of the sun.

The classic temple, however, was conceived as the palace or house of the god (ḥet-neṯer, per-neṯer). Temples from the New Empire and from the Ptolemaic Epoch are the only ones preserved, but the ruins of a temple built in the southwest of the Faiyūm by Amenhemhet III and IV show that the sanctuaries of the Middle Kingdom were constructed on the same plan. A monumental gateway, flanked by two towers, the so-called pylons, marked the entrance to the temple. Both towers were adorned with notches into which were fitted great poles ornamented with multicolored pennants. An avenue lined with sphinxes, called the ''way of the god,'' often led through the city to the temple. Beyond the pylons opened a great porticoed court. At the end of the court the columned (hypostyle) hall was erected, its ceiling supported by columns whose capitals reproduced the papyrus flower in bloom or bud. Certain ceremonies were performed here attended only by a limited number of privileged persons; the court was the public part of the temple. Behind the hypostyle hall, also called the vestibule, were a variety of rooms containing, among other things, the objects necessary for the ritual and the treasure of the god, as well as constituting chapels of the gods who were his guests (σύνναοι θεοί). The most important section was the holy of holies or the adyton (bu ḏeser or also *set uret*). This chapel forms an independent structure within the temple. It has its own roof and receives no light from the exterior. It contains the naos of granite (*khemu*) in which the statue of the god is placed. On the walls of the vestibule and the other chambers, bas-reliefs depict the ceremonies performed there.

The temple often included a sacred lake in which the priests bathed and purified themselves before celebrating the divine service. Certain ceremonies took place there on feast days. Close by the Ptolemaic temples a small structure was erected, the *mammisi*, to which the mother-goddess was supposed to have withdrawn to await the birth of her son.

The Clergy. In principle, the king, son of the god, was the sole priest, the sole mediator between men and the divinity. Hence, it is always the king who is shown on the walls of temples performing the ceremonies of the daily ritual; in fact, he was replaced in this function by the priests. Their staffs were attached to each temple, more or less numerous depending on the temple's importance. In spite of several different appellations, notably for the high priests, the hierarchical order appears to have been the same for all these groups. A higher clergy, consisting of the ḥem-neṯer, or ''servants of God,'' are generally distinguished from the lower clergy, to which belonged the *wāb*-priests, ''the pure,'' among others. In fact, besides these two orders of priests, the ḥem-neṯer and the *wāb*, there existed several classes of clergymen. By virtue of ordination or rather initiation, expressed by the word *bes*, the priests had the right to enter the adyton and the naos to perform the ceremonies of the cult there. The ritual of Amon indicates that the *wāb* celebrated the divine service, and comparison of the Onomasticon of Amenophis with the circumlocutions employed by the Decrees of Canopus and Memphis lead to the same conclusion.

Among the clergymen, in the first place, were the *kheri-ḥeb* or ''readers,'' ritualists, as their name indicates, who performed secondary tasks in the cult and who were responsible for the proper regulation of the ceremonies. These men were doubtless preparing themselves for the priesthood by familiarizing themselves with all branches of knowledge in a school attached to the temple, the ''House of Life,'' in which the *kheri-ḥeb-ḥeri-tep* or ''chief readers'' and the scribes of the divine book were probably the professors. They also played an important part in the funerary cult, particularly in mummification. The subordinate staff consisted of musicians, chanters, sistrum players, and singers. It is difficult to establish whether the latter were permanently attached to the temple or if they held positions in civil life and came in for a month at a time, three times a year. This was the case with the *kautiu* and the *unutiu.* The former performed all kinds of heavy work, such as cleaning the temple, probably acting as porters and participating as well in the management of the goods. The latter kept watch day and night, probably also crying the hour, thus assuring the punctuality of the ceremonies. It is generally held that these three classes of personnel were made up of pious lay people who benevolently offered their services. But comparison of the passage of the Decree of Memphis N16 with that of Canopus 3 makes it appear possible that, as members of the priestly families they belonged to the ''sacred tribes'' and were considered *wāb,* in the later sense of the term, that is, members of the clergy.

The monthly rotation of duty pertained not only to the subordinate staff, but also to the readers and the *wāb*-priests. For this reason all these members of the clergy were divided into four ''tribes'' or phylae. From the Twenty-first Dynasty up to the close of the Saïte era, the *ḥem-neṯer* or ''prophets'' became so numerous that they were likewise divided into tribes. But during other epochs, there were only four prophets in each great temple. The *ḥem-neṯer* thus may have been simply the heads of the phylae. The Decree of Canopus did, in fact, establish a fifth phyle and place at its head a prophet ''as in the other phylae.'' The prophets were ranked in ascending order from the fourth to the first prophet, who was ordinarily the high priest or chief of the temple.

On the organization of the clergy, see J. Vergote, *Joseph en Égypte* (Louvain 1959) 74–94.

Feasts and Daily Ritual. Several liturgical calendars have been preserved in the temple inscriptions, at Medīnet-Habu, Edfu, and Denderah, for example. Unfortunately these acquaint us, in most instances, only with the names of the numerous feasts listed, rarely indicating anything of the nature of the ceremonies. Processions, however, do seem to have been an especially characteristic feature of these feasts. At Edfu, the statue of the god was carried up to the roof of the temple. At Karnak, Amon left his naos to reside several days in his harem (*opet*) in the South, the temple of Luxor. Descriptions of these feasts may be found in H. W. Fairman, ''Worship and Festivals in an Egyptian Temple,'' *The Bulletin of the John Rylands Library* (Manchester 1903) 37 (1954) 165–203; W. Wolf, *Das schöne Fest von Opet* (Leipzig 1931); H. Gauthier, *Les fêtes du dieu Min* (Cairo 1931).

Two papyri from Berlin (no. 3055, 2014, and 3053), which describe the ritual of the temples of Amon and Mut at Karnak, provide better information concerning the daily worship of the divinity. These are in agreement with the inscriptions and representations in the chapels of Amon and five other gods at Abydos, demonstrating a fair degree of uniformity in the rituals honoring different gods. A. Moret explores this data in *Le rituel du culte journalier en Égypte (Annales du Musée Guimet. Bibl. d'Études* 14; Paris 1902). G. Roeder has slightly altered the order of the ceremonies in his translation of the texts from Abydos: *Kulte, Orakel und Naturverehrung im alten Ägypten* (Zürich-Stuttgart 1960) 72–141. To these documents has since been added a papyrus preserved partially in Cairo and partially in Turin, as well as the Chester Beatty Papyrus IX in the British Museum. H. Nelson studied these texts in relation to the bas-reliefs in the two great temples of Thebes: ''Certain Reliefs at Karnak and Medinet Habu and the Ritual of Amenophis I,'' *Journal of Near Eastern Studies*, 8 (1949) 201–232, 309–345. The rite of Horus at Edfu included similar ceremonies (see Fairman, *supra*). The holy office, celebrated each morning, consisted in the opening of the naos, the adoration and purification of the god with water and incense, and the dressing of the statue, which was then rouged and perfumed. Food and drink were then offered or presented as a sort of meal for the god. Certain texts indicate these offerings may have been made only symbolically, speaking of the offering of Ma'at (in the ritual of Amon) or of the presentation of myrrh (in the ritual of Edfu), for instance. Owing to a ceremony called the ''giving back of the offerings,'' the food was next offered to such other beneficiaries as deceased kings, then carried outside the temple for distribution among the priests, according to their rank. Little is known concerning the makeup of the noonday or evening services.

Piety, Magic, and Morality. Some attention should be directed to the religious life of the people as complementary to the official religion. Unfortunately, the monuments from the early period have yielded little information regarding popular devotion. The wisdom literature is the sole source. This, however, shows, contrary to what has often been said, that the Egyptians of the Old Kingdom had already formed an elevated conception of God and of morality. The New Empire witnessed a change in the relationship that had been formed between the divinities and the faithful. Prayers preserved on the steles depict Amon as the protector of men, the shepherd who watches his flock and who runs to the aid of those who call upon him [e.g., the prayer of Neb-Rē, see J. B. Pritchard, *Ancient Near Eastern Texts Relating to the Old Testament,* (Princeton 1955) 380b]. The great number of ex-votoes, statuettes of the gods, amulets (not all magical), and scarabs with religious devices bears witness to a widespread piety among the people, who addressed themselves by preference to such minor gods as Hapi, the god of the Nile flood; Nepri, god of the wheat; Renenutet, goddess of the harvest; Meskhenet and the seven Hathors, patronesses of women in labor; Taït, goddess of weaving; and Bes and Toëris, protectors of the hearth. The dream books and the ostraca with questions for the oracles demonstrate the wide variety of circumstances that brought the Egyptians into consultation with the deity. Finally, by their personal names they placed themselves under divine protection or proved that they took an active part in the celebration of the religious feasts.

In comparison with prayer, an expression of the dependence of the individual on the divine being, magical incantation treated the god as though subject to certain laws and occult powers. The magician, identifying himself with a god, presumptuously claimed the right to give orders to another god. The Egyptians had no notion of the fundamental contradiction between these two attitudes. Magic, consequently, always played an important part. In their ardent desire to attain their goals, they sometimes alternated sublime prayers with magical injunctions. This practice made itself felt regularly in the rituals and the funerary documents: the Pyramid Texts, the Coffin Texts, and the BOOK OF THE DEAD.

A highly developed moral sense is expressed in the so-called negative confession, in chapter 125 of the Book of the Dead and in the autobiographies represented in the tombs. This witnesses to the innocence of the deceased, before the divine judges, of a wide range of misconduct.

The Life Beyond. Two doctrines concerning life beyond the grave opposed each other, the first being supplanted quite early by the second. According to the Pyramid Texts, the deceased king rose into the sky, taking his place in the solar barque and uniting himself to Rē. The souls of other humans mingled with the stars after death, partaking of their eternal life. The passages toward this heavenly world are located in the East; for that reason this world is called the *Dat* or *Duat,* a word also meaning ''morning.'' The life of those who have been thus ''glorified'' is sometimes depicted as a sojourn in some type of land of plenty, the ''field of reeds'' or the ''field of the offerings.'' According to the second doctrine, the world of the dead is a subterranean world over which Osiris rules. The roads leading there are the roads to the West; this world is called *Imentet* (Coptic *Amente*) or the ''West.'' This conception appears already in a secondary position in the Pyramid Texts, into which it was permitted to penetrate with no little opposition on the part of the supporters of the solar doctrine. It teaches that the dead person must render an account of his good and bad deeds to Osiris. The soul or *ba* of the just, who is *ma'a kheru* or ''justified by his voice,'' lives in the tomb close to the mummified body and the statues, or ''bodies of eternity,'' destined to act in lieu of the body in the event that it begins to decay. His happiness consists in ''coming into the daylight,'' in moving among men and gods and ''doing what the living do.'' In the evening, the soul reenters the subterranean world, which Rē then visits and entertains throughout the night. The Book of the Dead contains the magic formulas giving the power to overcome the obstacles that could prevent the soul from coming and going. According to the position generally taken, the survival of the soul is dependent upon the preservation of the body or its magic counterparts; the soul disappears into nothingness in the event of their destruction. It is, however, difficult to reconcile this opinion with the notion that the survival of the *ma'a kheru* is the reward for a virtuous life. On the other hand, the texts from the "skeptics" do not indicate doubt that the soul is immortal: they simply deny that the Osirian funerals guarantee the *ba* its freedom of movement and they claim that the soul is eternally enclosed in the darkness of the subterranean world. See H. Kees, "Ein Klagelied über das Jenseits," *Zeitschrift für ägyptische Sprache* 62 (1927) 73–79. In the *Dialogue of the Pessimistic Man with his Soul,* the *ba* only threatens to abandon the body if it should perish by fire. There is reason, therefore, to raise the question whether or not the Egyptians did believe in the full immortality of the soul independently of the preservation of the body. There is not, however, any opposition regarding this point between the ancient solar doctrine and the Osirian doctrine. The aim of the Osirian funerals would have been eternal prolongation of life on earth, which, consequently, must have appeared to them as the greatest good. If the body were annihilated, the soul would go toward the field of reeds, where it knew a beatitude that was, in their eyes, happiness only to a certain limited extent.

If, from the beginning, the soul was not subject to death, that would not mean for the Egyptians that the soul is indestructible. Numerous passages in the funerary texts speak of the destruction of the soul, of the "second death," etc. This was the lot reserved for certain ones among those who were found guilty before the tribunal of Osiris, and perhaps for those who were not protected by magic against the enemies from beyond. These texts were assembled by J. Zandee, *Death as an Enemy, according to Egyptian Conceptions* (Leiden 1960). It must be noted that these texts do not indicate that the destruction of the soul is an effect of the disappearance of the body.

If one accepts this interpretation of the Osirian funerals, a new meaning is given to the Egyptian civilization as it appears to us, preserved essentially in its necropolises. Rather than the appanage of a people both morosely and morbidly preoccupied with death, these cities of the dead must be seen as homage and a hymn to life, loved by the Egyptians, it seems, more than by all the rest of mankind. See G. A. Reisner, *The Egyptian Conception of Immortality* (Boston 1912); H. Kees, *Totenglauben und Jenseitsvorstellungen der alten Ägypter* (Leipzig 1926); A. H. Gardiner, *The Attitude of the Ancient Egyptians to Death and the Dead* (Cambridge 1942).

Bibliography: J. H. BREASTED, *Development of Religion and Thought in Ancient Egypt* (New York 1912). A. ERMAN, *Die Religion der Ägypter* (Leipzig 1934), Fr. *La Religion des Égyptiens,* tr. H. WILD (Paris 1937). J. VANDIER, *La Religion égyptienne,* ("Mana" 1.1; Paris 1949). C. DESROCHES-NOBLECOURT, "Les Religions égyptiennes," M. M. GORCE and R. MORTIER, eds., *Histoire générale des religions,* 4 v. (Paris 1944–48) v. 4. H. FRANKFORT, *Ancient Egyptian Religion* (New York 1948). É. DRIOTON, "La Religion égyptienne," M. BRILLANT and R. AIGRAIN, eds., *Histoire des religions,* 5 v. (Paris 1953–56) 3:7–147, 433–437. H. BONNET, *Reallexikon der ágyptischen Religionsgeschichte* (Berlin 1952). S. MORENZ, *Ägyptische Religion* (Stuttgart 1960), Fr. *La Religion égyptienne,* tr. L. JOSPIN (Paris 1962).

[J. VERGOTE]

2. Architecture And Art

Egyptian culture reaches back into the 5th millennium B.C., when neolithic settlements existed in the Faiyûm region at Deir Tasa and Beni Salâma (Merimda). About 3600 B.C. a new, much more advanced culture originated at Gerza and other sites in the north. This chalcolithic period produced some copper pots and some amulets representing gods in the shapes of various animals. Villages turned into towns and districts (the so-called nomes). Two powerful states developed along the banks of the Nile: Upper Egypt in the south, embracing 22 nomes; and Lower Egypt or the Delta land in the north, embracing 20 nomes. Each of these had its totemic symbols of animals or flowers.

Protodynastic Period. During this period (*c.* 2850–*c.* 2615 B.C.) the two Egypts were united in a single kingdom by Menes, also called Narmer, who was, according to the historian Manetho of the 3rd century B.C., the founder of the First Dynasty. This event is documented with great aesthetic, as well as historic, value by one of the earliest objects of Egyptian art: the Palette of Narmer (Cairo Museum) (*see* KINGSHIP IN THE ANCIENT NEAR EAST). Egyptian palettes were plates on which cosmetics were prepared, especially the cosmetic made of powdered malachite mixed with oil, which served as a germicidal eye paint similar to the black ointment that is still put on eyelids in the fly-infested regions of the modern Orient. This 22-inch slate object is decorated on both sides. On one side the king is depicted wearing the tall, white crown of Upper Egypt, as he is about to smite a foe with his lifted mace, while two enemies are fleeing below. The reverse shows Narmer crowned, wearing the red crown of Lower Egypt and surveying two rows of decapitated enemies, whose heads are neatly placed between their feet. Above him the cow heads symbolize the goddess Hathor, protectress of Narmer. Below, the intertwined long necks of two mythical animals form the container in which the ointment was mixed. Even in this early work the convention that was to rule Egyptian art for centuries is already present. The ruler, since he was considered divine, towers high over his vizier and his soldiers. The bodies are represented from the front, whereas the head and legs are seen in profile. This characteristic persists throughout the entire history of Egyptian relief sculpture and painting.

Artistically, the history of Egypt can be divided into three periods corresponding to the Old, the Middle, and the New Kingdoms. The first, called also the Pyramid Age, lasted from *c.* 2850 to *c.* 2140 B.C. Since his life was ruled by religion, the art of the Egyptian naturally reflected his faith.

Old Kingdom. Belief in an afterworld, for which he prepared during his whole lifetime, in a resurrection, and in a last judgment necessitated the preservation of his body. According to his prominence in society the Egyptian built his tomb: in the shape of a truncated pyramid called the mastaba or, as in the case of Djosher, the first king of the Third Dynasty, a series of five mastabas on top of one another, which formed his so-called Step Pyramid at Saqqâra (*see* EGYPT). Out of this structure the true pyramids developed.

Pyramids. The best-known pyramids are those of Khufu (Cheops), Khafra (Chephren), and Menkaure (Mycerinos) at El Gîza. The largest one is the pyramid of Khufu, originally 481 feet high (some of it now covered by sand), on which about 100,000 men labored for 30 years, usually during the period of inundation, when agricultural work was at rest. The core is of yellow limestone, the funeral chamber is lined with granite, and the outer casing, now almost completely stripped off, was once of exquisitely fitted, polished, white limestone that reflected the sun, the sacred emblem of which was a pyramidal shape—a fitting memorial because the kings considered themselves sons of Ra (Re), the sun god. Next to the pyramid a mortuary temple, of which only the foundations are left, was erected. Since tombs were sealed after the body was laid to rest, the temple was used for memorial services. Khafra, who succeeded Khufu, erected a sphinx next to his pyramid as a symbolic guardian of the tomb. The sphinx is a composite figure, lion-bodied with a human head representing the king wearing the linen headdress and the cobra, emblems of royalty. East of the pyramid is Khafra's mortuary temple, to which a causeway once reached from the Nile.

Tombs. Inside the tomb, whether pyramid of king or mastaba of noble, arrangements were made for the comfort and entertainment of the soul of the deceased. The Ka, or life force, was believed to live on in the shape of a bird, the manifestation of the soul after death, called the Ba, and to visit the tomb periodically until the time for last judgment, when the deceased would have to account for his deeds. His heart was balanced against truth before the assembly of gods. If the judgment were favorable, he would become a transfigured spirit and exist in a sphere beyond humanity; if not, he was annihilated by demons. The visiting Ka needed a likeness of the deceased into which it could enter, so portrait statues were placed in each tomb. Those of the kings and nobles were highly stylized and idealized, as, for example, Khafra or the courtier Rahotep and his wife, Nofret. All three statues are in the Cairo Museum. The artist worked from a rectangular block of stone as it came from the quarry, and the result is almost cubistic simplicity. The figures of Rahotep and Nofret were polychromed; the man has a brownish tan all over his body, whereas his lady, who is dressed in a white sheath and wears lavish jewelry, has a light olive complexion. Their eyes are made of crystal, on which the iris is painted, so that they have a startlingly lifelike appearance. The representations of commoners were much more realistic; for example, the limestone figures of the Seated Scribe in the Louvre, whose flabby body witnesses to a sedentary occupation, or the wooden statuette of the portly Ka-aper (Sheikel-Beled, "the mayor"), now in the Cairo Museum.

The walls of the tomb chamber were decorated by polychromed relief sculpture or painting, representing the property or favorite occupations of the deceased. Ti, a court official whose tomb is at Saqqâra, is represented on a hippopotamus hunt, standing up in his reed boat, while his servants attack the animals with spears. Fish swim in the water below, and the papyrus thicket is alive with birds and small beasts above their heads. Another relief from the same tomb represents cattle herded across a river; a herdsman carries a newborn calf, whose head is turned back anxiously toward its lowing mother. It is interesting to observe that, whereas the figure of the deceased Ti is stylized, the herdsmen and especially the animals are quite realistic on these limestone reliefs. A variation in wood is the relief of Hesire in the Cairo Museum, which comes from his brick mastaba at Saqqâra and shows a high degree of technical accomplishment.

Painting at that time was used mostly as an accessory to relief. The painter did not wish to create an illusion; rather he achieved an effect of polychrome harmony. Illustrated papyrus copies of the BOOK OF THE DEAD also are found in the tombs. They served as magical passports that recalled the virtues of the deceased and pleaded for eternal life. They established the formal, archaic style of painting in the Old Kingdom.

Middle Kingdom. During the Middle Kingdom (*c.* 1989–1776 B.C.) the traditional forms of architecture and sculpture were used, and mortuary temples and pyramids were erected; but none of them was as impressive as those at El Gîza. Sesostris I caused an obelisk to be raised in Heliopolis as a homage to the sun. The pyramidion on top, like the pyramids, was an emblem of the sun. Most of the great architectural projects of this time have disappeared because of rebuilding by rulers of the New Kingdom. In the minor arts the Middle Kingdom reached a very high technical excellence, of which the magnificent collection of jewels in the Metropolitan Museum, New York City, bears witness.

New Kingdom. This period (*c.* 1570–*c.* 1150 B.C.), which began after the Hyksos invaders had been driven out of the country, was architecturally the most brilliant period in Egyptian history. The pharaohs built vast temples instead of the huge pyramids to immortalize their names. Plunder of the tombs cautioned the rulers to hide rather than expose their last resting places. These were still magnificently appointed, containing beautiful reliefs, paintings, and all the paraphernalia the Ka might desire; but they were cut deep in the rock and hidden from covetous eyes. The so-called Valley of the Kings and Valley of the Queens near Thebes contain the most grandiose of these rock-cut funeral vaults; but the tombs of nobles at El Ashraf and Deir-el-Medina, though smaller, are artistically just as important and interesting because of their less formal and, at times, impressionistic decoration representing daily life.

Hatshepsut's Temple. The mortuary temple of Queen Hatshepsut at Deir-el-Bahri is one of the most conspicuous monuments of its kind (*see* TEMPLES). She wished to firmly establish her divine origin in order to sustain her unprecedented position as Lady Pharaoh. Colonnaded porticoes built of white limestone, terraces planted with trees and flowers imported from Punt, which had to be watered laboriously, attempted to transform the arid cliff landscape into an earthly paradise of the sun-god Amon-Ra. The noble Senmut, Hatshepsut's chief architect, built sanctuaries to Anubis, the jackal-headed god of the dead, and to the sky-goddess Hathor. The main shrine was dedicated to AMON, and under this the Queen planned her own resting place. However, because of difficulties in cutting the rock, her mortuary chapel was built south of the main sanctuary. She also caused two obelisks to be erected at Karnak, one of which, the largest in all Egypt, is still standing; it is 97 ½ feet high and contains 180 cubic yards of granite.

Thutmose III, the stepson whom Hatshepsut kept from ruling, avenged himself by decapitating all the Queen's likenesses, erasing her name, and letting her beautiful gardens die.

Temples at Karnak and Luxor. On the eastern shore of the Nile the huge temples of Karnak and Luxor bear witness to the building zeal of the rulers during the Empire Period (1570–1211 B.C.). Usually the approach to the temple was from the river, along a processional way lined by guardian spirits, sphinxes, or rams. The pylon gate was formed by two towerlike stone structures with sloping sides decorated by laudatory reliefs and chased vertically to form flag bases for banners. Cedar doors covered by bronze, gold, or electrum led into the colonnaded forecourt, where the public festivals were held. Beyond it was the hypostyle hall, or hall of appearances, the roof of which was supported by rows of columns. Behind the hall was the small inner sanctuary of the god, to which only the priests were admitted. Within the sacred precinct were also the priests' offices, treasury, and storerooms.

Building on the enormous temple of Amon at Karnak went on for centuries. Within the sacred precinct are smaller temples to Khonsu and Ptah, deities of procreative power, and a sacred lake. The great hypostyle hall was started by Seti I and completed by his son, Ramses II. It is 54,000 sq. feet, the largest columnar hall in the world. It has 16 rows of columns, the two central ones of which supported the clerestory. The height of each column is 79 feet; the diameter is 11 ¾ feet; each papyrus capital could accommodate 100 standing men. Like Karnak, the temple of Luxor is dedicated to Amon-Ra. Amenhotep III built the first temple, but Ramses II made many additions, among others six colossal granite figures of himself, two obelisks, and an avenue of sphinxes leading to Karnak, which are presently being excavated. Within the sacred precinct there is a chapel of Alexander the Great, the remains of a Christian shrine, and a mosque; each era has thus paid homage to divinity.

Temples of Ramses II and III. The mortuary temple of Ramses II, the Ramesseum, was built on the opposite side of the Nile, west of Thebes. Even today the grandeur of the ruins, covering 870 by 570 feet, amazes the visitor. Behind the temple are a series of granaries covered by barrel vaults constructed of mudbrick, probably the earliest vaults in the history of architecture. Nearby, at Madînet Habu, Ramses III built his mortuary temple, which is, in concept, similar to that of his predecessor but much better preserved. A series of two courts with statues of the king led to the hypostyle hall, which was followed by smaller halls leading to the sanctuary. A small palace with audience hall and apartments opened to the south of the main court. The thick stone wall surrounding the precinct had fortified gates on western and eastern sides. The gateways contained apartments in the upper stories. The sculptural decoration was enlivened by rich paint, which is especially well preserved in the sheltered places.

At Abu Simbel, between the second and third cataracts of the Nile, Ramses II caused a temple to be hewn out of the rock above the river. Four colossal portraits of the king (64 feet high) decorate the front, and a smaller representation of the sun-god stands above the entrance. By the legs of the sitting colossi eight small figures represent the Pharao's mother, his beloved wife, Nefertari (a Hittite princess), and their children. The door leads into a great hall, 55 by 50 feet, beyond which is a smaller room and a sanctuary with cult statues of Ramses himself, the sun-god Ra-Harakhti, and the chief gods of Thebes and Memphis, Amon and Ptah. Adjacent is the smaller temple of Queen Nefertari, decorated by six colossi (30 feet high), of which four represent Ramses II, and two, the Queen. The interior contains two small halls dedicated to the cow-goddess Hathor, goddess of love, music, and dance. The construction of the Aswân High Dam, which was to transform the Nile to the south into Lake Nasser, threatened these monuments with inundation. At the completion of the dam, the water level would be 120 feet above the heads of the colossi of Ramses II. To save Abu Simbel for posterity, a $36 million project was undertaken whereby the temples and statues were cut into sections and reassembled as much as possible in their ancient form on a plateau 200 feet above the original site. Forty-eight nations of the world responded to the plea of the United Arab Republic to help salvage these important cultural treasures. The U.S. donated $12 million to the cause.

Naturalism. New Kingdom sculpture, while traditional in its frontality and poses, shows a tendency toward naturalism and portrait likeness. Although Hatshepsut is represented on her statue that is now in the Metropolitan Museum as enthroned and wearing the formal headdress and short, pleated linen skirt of a ruler, she is made to appear femininely delicate both in features and in body. Realism was practiced during the reign of Amenhotep IV, who changed his name to AKHNATON, ''useful to Aton.'' He was unique among ancient Egyptian rulers for his monotheism. He rejected the Egyptian pantheon and proclaimed Aton, represented by the sun disk, the sole deity (*see* SUN WORSHIP). The new capital that he built at Tell el 'Amârna he called Akhet-Aton, ''Horizon of Aton.'' Search for truth was his doctrine, and this is mirrored in the numerous portraits of Akhnaton, which show a remarkable lack of flattery; the philosopher-poet king is depicted with a slight paunch typical of a man of sedentary habits. His lovely wife, Nefretiti, and his daughters were the subjects of several works of art. The painted limestone bust of the queen in Berlin is the best known of these, but several unfinished portraits have been found that bear witness to her exquisite beauty. Warm family devotion is depicted on a relief in Cairo, which represents the royal spouses seated, holding their children on their laps, the king kissing one; in the background the sun extends its beneficent rays toward them, and each ray ends in a blessing hand. Tutankhamon, who married one of these princesses, had to renounce Akhnaton's monotheism after a religious upheaval and return to the cult of the old gods of Egypt. The tomb of this young ruler, discovered in 1922, yielded the richest find yet of minor art objects, jewelry, lamps, furniture, chariots, etc.

At Thebes, the reliefs of the tomb of Ramose, who was vizier during the rules of Amenhotep III and his son, Akhnaton, reflect the transition from refined formality, as depicted by the festive gathering in which his brother takes part, to a realistic style, which is illustrated by the later decoration of the burial chamber, representing the funeral procession with priests, offerings, and professional mourners.

Late Period. Relief became progressively flat and turned into deeply incised contour lines with only slight modeling during the late period. Nevertheless, the traditional Egyptian style survived the Greek and Roman conquests and their enormous influence over the art of the provinces. The temple of Isis on the small island of Philae, which is now under water during a great part of the year (because of the Aswan Dam), was started by Ptolemy II in the 3rd century B.C.; but its decoration continued during Roman rule as the cult of Isis became popular with the Romans. It was closed finally by Justinian in A.D. 543. The Horus temple at Edfu (*c.* 200 *B.C.*) is another example of the survival of traditional architecture and sculpture in Ptolemaic times.

Egyptian Paintings. Painting in the New Kingdom was often applied directly, and the relief was omitted. Earth colors and mineral pigments were used with the *al secco* technique. Gum arabic, egg white, glue, wax, or honey served as medium. The figures were sketched in with a red or black outline; there is evidence that a grid was used for proportions. After the application of the color, the contour was outlined again with red and white lines. When the subject matter was mythological or ritual, as it usually was when a royal sepulchre was decorated, the drawing was based on traditional conventions resembling the style of the Book of the Dead. When it was biographical, depicting the favorite events of the life of the deceased, as in the more than 400 private tombs near Thebes, the artist invented his own iconography, and the result was a free, lively style of genre painting. These scenes of banquets, musicians, beautiful ladies, pleasure gardens with pools full of carp and lotus flowers, hunters, fishers, harvesters, and artisans at their toil all present posterity with a valuable document that reflects the high civilization of ancient Egypt.

Bibliography: K. LANGE and M. HIRMER, *Egypt, Architecture, Sculpture, Painting in Three Thousand Years,* tr. R. H. BOOTHROYD (London 1956). A. MEKHITARIAN, *Egyptian Painting,* tr. S. GILBERT (New York 1954). W. S. SMITH, *The Art and Architecture of Ancient Egypt* in *Pelican History of Art,* ed. N. PEVSNER (Baltimore 1958). S. BOSTICCO and H. W. MÜLLER, *Encyclopedia of World Art* (New York 1959) 4:572–710; plates 319–392. J. WILSON, *The Burden of*

Egypt: An Interpretation of Ancient Egyptian Culture (Chicago 1951). S. LLOYD, *The Art of the Ancient Near East* (New York 1961).

[I. E. ELLINGER]

3. Language and Literature

The language of ancient Egypt is related both to the Semitic languages of Southeast Asia and to the Hamitic languages of North Africa (Berber, Somali, Galla). This can be explained either by the fusion of intrusive Semitic elements with the Hamitic African substratum or by the remote common origin of the Semitic and Hamitic language families, which split off at an early date and left Egyptian in between.

Language and Script. Texts of different periods make it possible to detect the stages in the history of the Egyptian written languages from the Archaic Period (*c.* 3000 B.C.) to the Christian era.

History of the Language. Old Egyptian, the language of the Old Kingdom (before 2200 B.C.), was the language of the Pyramid Texts and the earliest biographical inscriptions, which developed probably around the North Egyptian cultural centers of Memphis and Heliopolis.

Middle Egyptian was in general use from the First Intermediate Period to the end of the Eighteenth Dynasty (*c.* 2200–*c.* 1350 B.C.) and survived in the late periods as the language of monumental inscriptions and religious literature. Middle Egyptian probably developed in the Herakleopolitan center and was regarded as the classical form of the Egyptian language.

Late Egyptian, apparently the spoken language of Upper Egypt, was first written in the private letters and administrative documents of the Amarna Period (*c.* 1370–*c.* 1350 B.C.); in the Ramesside Period (13th century B.C.) it replaced Middle Egyptian elsewhere in nonreligious literature. Demotic was the Late Egyptian of the cursive scripts between 750 B.C. and A.D. 320. The popular language in the Late Egyptian Period developed into Coptic.

Types of Script. The Egyptian hieroglyphic script developed from pictographic signs in the Late Predynastic (Gerzean) Period (last quarter of the 4th millennium B.C.), possibly under the influence of Protoliterate Mesopotamian civilization. The earliest known hieroglyphic inscriptions were written at the beginning of the First Dynasty (Kings Narmer and Aha) and already comprised the standard forms of phonetic signs, which changed very little throughout the whole of ancient Egyptian civilization. The hieroglyphic writing included word signs, phonetic symbols, ideographic determinatives, and a complete decimal numerical system.

From the Old Kingdom to the Roman Empire highly decorative hieroglyphic texts were carved or painted on walls and steles as well as on wooden coffins and papyri of religious significance.

The hieratic script developed early from the cursive hieroglyphic signs and, beginning with the Archaic Period, was used on pottery, wood, and papyrus, undergoing considerable stylistic changes in subsequent periods of Egyptian history.

The demotic script developed in the Saitic Period (663–525 B.C.) and later. It gradually replaced the hieratic script in administration, legal records, letters, and folk stories, and remained in general use to the end of the Roman Empire.

Old-Egyptian Literature. The most dynamic age in the formation of ancient Egyptian civilization began in the Late Predynastic (Gerzean) Period and continued until it reached its summit and achieved stabilization in the Pyramid Age, probably before 2500 B.C. There is no doubt that a complex Egyptian literature existed in the Third Dynasty (*c.* 2615–*c.* 2565), especially in the time of King Djoser and his chief architect, Imhotep, who was credited with the authorship of medical texts, books of wisdom, and magic formulas [J. B. Pritchard, *Ancient Near Eastern Texts Relating to the Old Testament,*[2] (Princeton 1954) 419–420].

Later texts, particularly those of a religious, scientific, magical, and didactic character, were intentionally archaized and claimed great antiquity in order to gain esteem, while really ancient texts were carefully preserved, transcribed, and imitated. The authenticity of their early sources can be verified on the basis of linguistic and circumstantial evidence. At least two such texts, the *Memphite Theology* [J. B. Pritchard, *Ancient Near Eastern Texts Relating to the Old Testament,*[2] (Princeton 1955) 4–6], transcribed in the 6th century B.C. by the order of Shabaka (hence known as the Shabaka Stone), and the *Edwin Smith Surgical Papyrus,* both following originals of the Third to the Fifth Dynasties, are listed among the highest achievements of ancient Egyptian civilization, showing the speculative mind and scientific approach so alien to the Egyptian literature of later periods. The Old Kingdom *Teaching of Ptah-hotep* [J. B. Pritchard, *Ancient Near Eastern Texts Relating to the Old Testament,*[2] (Princeton 1955) 412–414], the vizier of King Izezi of the Fifth Dynasty, known from several manuscripts of the Middle Kingdom and later, became the model for Egyptian wisdom literature.

The largest body of the Old Kingdom literature is found in the Pyramid Texts [J. B. Pritchard, *Ancient Near Eastern Texts Relating to the Old Testament,*[2] (Princeton

1955) 326–328], which include magic spells, incantations, and the earliest examples of hymns, with frequent references to cosmic myths but very little narrative. The other largest domain of the Old Kingdom literature is the tomb inscriptions, including the narrative biographical texts of Uni, Heri-Khuf, Sabni, and others, which could have served as prototypes for the best Middle Kingdom stories.

No Old Egyptian tales are known, with the possible exception of the *Story of Cheops* [or Khufu] *and the Magicians.* Circumstantial evidence makes it probable that the stories were first composed in the Fifth or early Sixth Dynasty, but the only manuscript, the Westcar Papyrus, dates from the Hyksos times, and its language is characteristic of the late Middle Kingdom. The text includes several magic adventures told or demonstrated to King Cheops, and it concludes with the alleged prophetic story of the miraculous birth of the first three rulers of the Fifth Dynasty.

Middle Egyptian Literature. The fall of the Old Kingdom authority, the deep crisis of the ancient political and moral order, and the social chaos of the civil war were reflected in the literature of the time of transition, and particularly in the *Admonitions of Ipu-wer* and the *Prophecy of Nefer-rohu* (or Neferti); see J. B. Pritchard, *Ancient Near Eastern Texts Relating to the Old Testament,*[2] (Princeton 1955) 441–446 and Posenor, *Littérature et politique.* The imaginative descriptions of disturbance and total disaster were sometimes concluded with a prophecy of the new ruler or ''the shepherd,'' who would restore order and justice to Egypt. But all the above-mentioned texts are known only from much later manuscripts, and the circumstantial evidence suggests that the original texts were composed not earlier than the Twelfth Dynasty as a kind of political propaganda for the new rulers of the appeased country. In any case, they reflect the awakening of social and national consciousness and a tendency to establish new order in the country. Special emphasis was laid upon rightness or justice, personified as the goddess Ma'at.

Wisdom Literature. An important part in the Egyptian renaissance was played by wisdom literature. The ideas of just rule were expressed in the *Instructions for Meri-ka-re* [J. B. Pritchard, *Ancient Near Eastern Texts Relating to the Old Testament,*[2] (Princeton 1955) 414–418], the Herakleopolitan king of the Tenth Dynasty, and much shorter *Instructions of Amen-em-het I* (*ibid.* 418–419), the first king of the Twelfth Dynasty, assassinated in a palace revolt; and in the *Satire de metièrs* or *Teaching of Kheti* (or Akhtoy), son of Duaf, known from numerous corrupt late copies, describing the dignity of the scribe's profession in comparison with other kinds of work. The same ideas were expressed in the Middle Kingdom Egyptian tales.

The *Philosophical Dispute of the Misanthrope* with his soul is a strange psychological drama of a split personality discussing with his soul (Ba) the problem of death. It includes a sharp criticism of the existing social order, resembling *Admonitions of Nefer-rohu and Ipu-wer.* The *Story of the Eloquent Peasant* [J. B. Pritchard, *Ancient Near Eastern Texts Relating to the Old Testament,*[2] (Princeton 1955) 407–410] was used only as a framework for nine speeches on justice addressed by a complaining peasant to the royal officials.

Travel Stories. Two Middle Kingdom travel stories, of *Si-nuhe* [J. B. Pritchard, *Ancient Near Eastern Texts Relating to the Old Testament,*[2] 18–22] and the *Ship-wrecked Sailor,* deal with the patriotic nostalgia that the Egyptians felt when in foreign lands. Si-nuhe was an Egyptian refugee who attained a high position in the Kingdom of Retenu (Syria or Palestine) but finally returned home to die in his own country. The *Story of Si-nuhe* was considered a classic piece of Egyptian literature, and the large number of preserved manuscripts indicates its great popularity. The language and composition are clear, free from verbosity and unnecessary ornamentation, but effective and picturesque, giving good glimpses into the daily life of the time in Egypt and in the land of Retenu. Everything could have actually happened just as described in the story. The *Ship-wrecked Sailor* is a fantastic story of a sailor's adventures and homesickness on the strange enchanted island of a snake king.

Poetry. Egyptian poetic compositions have apparent strophic arrangement, rhythmic devices, emphasized by periodic repetitions and parallel statements, word play, and alliteration. Some of the Old Kingdom spells of the Pyramid Texts were certainly poems, and the biographical text of Uni (from the early Sixth Dynasty) contains a triumphal hymn, written on the occasion of Uni's happy return from a Nubian expedition, in which every strophe is introduced by a brief clause: ''This army returned in safety. . . .''

The great religious hymns to the sun-god RA (Re), the hymn to the crocodile-god Sobek, the ritual *Hymn to the Crowns,* the *Hymn to Osiris,* the god of vegetation, the *Hymn to the Nile* [J. B. Pritchard, *Ancient Near Eastern Texts Relating to the Old Testament,*[2] (Princeton 1955) 372–373]—these and other hymns, some of which may have originated in the Old Kingdom Pyramid Texts, certainly existed in the Middle Kingdom, although they are known mainly from later manuscripts. The hymns of victory are included in the historical royal records. The best known of such hymns, dedicated to Sesostris III

(1878–1843), had a rigid strophic form and repetitions, possibly intended for a choir. Four elegiac hymns are included in the philosophical *Dispute over Suicide* [J. B. Pritchard, *Ancient Near Eastern Texts Relating to the Old Testament,*[2] (Princeton 1955) 405–407]. Their structure is similar, although they were hardly composed for choral singing.

Religious drama in ancient Egypt, reenacting mythological scenes on special occasions, is attested by some texts with dialogues and presumed stage devices. The Middle Kingdom papyrus from the Ramesseum contains the *Coronation Play,* based on the myth of Horus and Set. A brief account of a similar dramatic performance held on the occaison of seasonal festivals at Abydos is recorded on the stele of Ikhernofret, an official of Sesostris III.

New Kingdom and Late Egyptian Literature. New Kingdom literature did not break with the ancient heritage. The ancient wisdom literature (of Ptah-hotep, Amenemhet I, and Kheti, son of Duaf), the Middle Kingdom poetry, such as religious hymns and the *Harper's Song* [J. B. Pritchard, *Ancient Near Eastern Texts Relating to the Old Testament,*[2] (Princeton 1955) 467], and the best stories (e.g., *Si-nuhe*) were copied and imitated, serving as literary models in the scribal schools. Middle Egyptian remained the language of monumental inscriptions and sacred literature, which used the traditional phraseology.

Historical records of the Empire include vivid narrations of achievements and adventures and poems glorifying the victories [J. B. Pritchard, *Ancient Near Eastern Texts Relating to the Old Testament,*[2] (Princeton 1955) 234–263]. The hymn from the poetic stele of Thutmose III was rewritten with some minor alteration for several later pharaos.

Religious hymnal literature reached the highest level in the solar *Hymn to Amon-Ra* of Suty and Hor [J. B. Pritchard, *Ancient Near Eastern Texts Relating to the Old Testament,*[2] 365–366], composed under Amenhotep III; and in the famous *Hymn to Aton* of the Amarna Period (*ibid.* 369–371), ascribed to King AKHNATON himself and best preserved in the abandoned tomb of It-nṯr Ay (or Eye).

A new literary form, particularly popular in the time of the empire, is represented by charming love songs with clear poetic devices: strophic arrangement, similes, metaphors, play on words, often with humor and satire.

New Kingdom narrative literature must include the historical records of war expeditions and other activities inscribed on the walls of the temples and commemorative steles, especially the records of the Syrian expeditions of Thutmose I and III [J. B. Pritchard, *Ancient Near Eastern Texts Relating to the Old Testament,*[2] (Princeton 1955) 234–241], the *Sportive Stele* of Amenhotep II (*ibid.* 244–245), the *Battle of Kadesh* of Ramses II (*ibid.* 255–256), once known as the *Epic of Pentawer.*

Among the Late Egyptian stories there is the *Story of the Two Brothers* [J. B. Pritchard, *Ancient Near Eastern Texts Relating to the Old Testament,*[2] (Princeton 1955) 23–25], which begins as a folk tale of peasant life and develops in a continuous narrative of magic, adventures, and reincarnations. The *Story of the Foredoomed Prince* (Papyrus Harris 500, see J. B. Pritchard, *Ancient Near Eastern Texts Relating to the Old Testament,*[2] 22b) resembles the European tales of the *Glass Mound* and *Sleeping Beauty.* There are at least two historical folk tales: the *Story of Sekenenre and Apopis* and the *Capture of Joppe.* The long *Story of Wen-Amon* [J. B. Pritchard, *Ancient Near Eastern Texts Relating to the Old Testament,*[2] (Princeton 1955) 25–29] might have been a true account of the travel adventures of an Egyptian official sent from Thebes to Lebanon to bring wood for the sacred bark of Amon. There are also an allegorical *Story of the Blinding of Truth* and several long mythological stories, such as the *Deliverance of Mankind from Destruction* (*ibid.*) inscribed on the shrine of Tutankhamun and on the walls of the royal tombs (Seti I, Ramses II and III), the *Tale of Horus and Seth* (*ibid.* 14–17), with their long quarrel before the divine tribunal, and *How Isis Gained Magic Power over Ra, the King of Gods.* (The last two are preserved on Twentieth-Dynasty papyri in the Chester Beatty collection.)

The Late Egyptian wisdom literature, such as the *Instruction of Ani* [J. B. Pritchard, *Ancient Near Eastern Texts Relating to the Old Testament,*[2] (Princeton 1955) 420–421] and the *Wisdom of Amen-em-ope* (*ibid.* 421–424), reflect the new attitudes of the period, which J. H. Breasted called the ''Age of Personal Piety,'' emphasizing humility, meekness, and total dependence on divine mercy. The Late Egyptian miscellanies include a large number of school texts, copying, quoting, or imitating earlier instructions, together with model letters, didactic or satirical, advocating learning, obedience, and modesty.

The New Kingdom texts of prayers of this period, which include confession of guilt, reconciliation, supplication, and thanksgiving, have been the subject of a fascinating study by B. Gunn, ''Religion of the Poor'' [*The Journal of Egyptian Archaeology,* 3 (1916) 81–94].

Demotic Literature. The Egyptian literature of the latest periods on demotic manuscripts preserves the memory of the glorious past in the cycles of historical novels: the *Story of Setne* (or Khaemwase), the son of

Ramses II, continued in the *Story of Si-Osiris,* his son, two stories from the *Cycle of Petubastis,* and fragments of *Amasis Tales* and of the *Story of Patese.*

The late demotic Papyrus of Leiden contains the long mythological or allegorical *Story of the Solar Eye* or the *Flight of Hathor-Tefnut to Nubia,* which includes several philosophical discourses and animal fables interwoven in the plot of the story. At least one fable of the Leiden Papyrus, *The Mouse and the Lion,* is known from Greek sources ascribed to Aesop. No animal fables have been found in Egyptian literature outside of the Leiden Papyrus, but their existence and popularity in the New Kingdom is evident from drawings representing animals in human attitudes.

Demotic texts of the Ptolemaic and Roman period include a later version of the *BOOK OF THE DEAD* and some fragments copied from lost ancient sources, such as the *Lamentations of Isis and Nephtys* and even the *Wisdom of Hor-dedef* from the Fourth Dynasty [J. B. Pritchard, *Ancient Near Eastern Texts Relating to the Old Testament,*[2] (Princeton 1955) 419–420) and the demotic adaptation of the Memphite Theology, showing the deeply rooted traditions of the ancient Egyptian civilization.

Bibliography: Language. A. H. GARDINER, *Egyptian Grammar* (London 1957). E. EDEL, *Altägyptische Grammatik,* 2 v. (Analecta orientalia 34, 39; Rome 1955–64). A. ERMAN, *Neuägyptische Grammatik* (Leipzig 1933). F. LEXA, *Grammaire démotique* (Prague 1947–51). A. ERMAN and H. GRAPOW, eds., *Wörterbuch der aegyptischen Sprache,* 12 v. (Leipzig 1926–55). H. KEES, ed., *Ägyptologie* (Handbuch der Orientalistik 1.1; Leiden 1959). **Literature.** A. ERMAN, *The Literature of the Ancient Egyptians,* tr. A. M. BLACKMAN (London 1927). G. LEFEBVRE, ed. and tr., *Romans et contes égyptiens de l'époque pharaonique* (Paris 1949). S. SCHOTT, ed. and tr., *Altägyptische Liebeslieder mit Märchen und Liebesgeschichten* (Zurich 1950). E. BRUNNERTRAUT, ed. and tr., *Altägyptische Märchen* (Düsseldorf-Cologne 1963). J. A. WILSON, in J. B. PRITCHARD, *Ancient Near Eastern Texts Relating to the Old Testament,*[2], passim. G. POSENER, ''Recherches littéraires,'' *Revue d'Égyptologie* 6 (1951) 27–48; 7 (1950) 71–84; 8 (1951) 171–189; 9 (1952) 109–120; *Littérature et politique dans l'Égypte de la XIIe dynastie* (Paris 1956).

[B. MARCZUK]

EGYPT, EARLY CHURCH IN

There is no direct evidence for the presence of Christian communities in Egypt before the 2d century A.D. At Alexandria, the greatest port of the eastern Mediterranean, there was a considerable Jewish colony that flourished in the commingling of Oriental, Egyptian, and Greek cultures. This Hellenistic influence produced the Septuagint, and an apologetic literature intended to make Jewish revelation comprehensible to Greek rationalism; there was a considerable body of literature written or translated into Greek. This last class was later held suspect by the Jewish tradition because it had prepared the way for the universality of the New Testament.

The letter of Emperor Claudius (A.D. 41) regarding the influx of Jews from Syria is no longer considered evidence that Christians were dwelling in Egypt at that date; but Egyptians are mentioned among those who heard the Apostles ''speak with foreign tongues'' at Pentecost (Acts 2.10). A later passage of the Acts (18.24–25) is concerned with Apollos, a Jew of Alexandria, ''who had been instructed [in his country] in the Way of the Lord.'' If the words ''in his country'' found in some manuscripts of Acts are authentic, they bear witness to the antiquity of Christian propaganda in Egypt. The tradition that the Church of Alexandria was founded by St. Mark would be conclusive if it had been mentioned by CLEMENT OF ALEXANDRIA or ORIGEN, but the earliest report is that of Eusebius in the 4th century (*Ecclesiastical History* 2.16). It is impossible that Clement and Origen could have ignored the foundation of St. Mark. At the moment that the Church of Egypt entered history toward the end of the 2d century, it appeared solidly organized, drawing its members especially from the Hellenic milieu.

The peril of the Christians, regarded with hostility by the Jews, considered a Jewish sect by the Greeks, and banned by the Roman government, was great. Toward the end of the 2d century, the Gnostic writers Valentinus and Basilides spread their doctrines at Alexandria. GNOSTICISM was not primarily a Christian aberration, but these two writers were Christian heretics. During the late 2d century, a catechetical school was established at Alexandria that seems to give evidence of a considerable Christian community. Once secure at Alexandria, Christianity spread up the Nile Valley. There is no evidence found in papyri dealing with administration or economic life, but numerous literary papyri bear witness to the presence of Christian communities even in Upper Egypt (*Harvard Theological Review* 37 [1944] 201).

Early Persecution of Christians. During the early part of the 3d century, Emperor Septimius Severus took action against the Christians. According to Eusebius (*Ecclesiastical History* 6.2), Christian athletes, that is, the confessors who had the constancy to face torture and death, were brought from the THEBAID and all parts of Egypt to Alexandria for trial and execution. In the course of the 3d century, the gospel spread further into the country places, and Bp. DIONYSIUS OF ALEXANDRIA devoted himself to converting the Egyptians or ''Copts''. The word ''Copt'' is a corruption of the Greek Αἴγυπτιος (Egyptian), which passed first through the Arabic *qoubt.* The country people were called Egyptian to distinguish them from the city dwellers in Alexandria.

More precise information on the spread of Christianity in the countryside may be gathered from documents of the persecution of the emperor DECIUS (249–251), even though the *libelli* (*see* LIBELLATICI) or certificates of sacrifice were required of the whole population, not only of Christians. Almost all certificates have come from Fayyûm. It seems that at this period Coptic translations of the Sacred Scriptures existed, at least of the books used in the liturgical ceremonies (Psalter, Gospel Book); but the problems raised by these books relative to their origin and spread have not been resolved.

The recorded history of the Church in Egypt begins with Bp. Demetrius of Alexandria (189–231). (*See* DEMETRIUS, SS.) It is probable that until his time the only bishop in Egypt was at Alexandria and that he governed the Christians through their local priests and deacons (*Ecclesiastical History* 7.24). According to Eutyches (*Annales; Patrologia Graeca* 111:982), Demetrius was the first to consecrate bishops outside his own capital. That the Egyptian episcopate was the result of a division of the jurisdiction that had formerly belonged entirely to Alexandria explains the absolute authority its bishop enjoyed among his colleagues. His position was confirmed by the sixth canon of the Council of Nicaea (325): ''The old customs in use in Egypt, in Libya, and in the Pentapolis shall continue to exist; that is, the Bishop of Alexandria shall have jurisdiction over all these provinces, for theirs is a similar relation to the Bishop of Rome'' (*Histoire des conciles d'après les documents originaux,* 1:389). The power and authority of the bishop, later the patriarch, of Alexandria was exercised and recognized repeatedly until the Arab conquest. After the Council of CHALCEDON (451), the Monophysites disputed the see, and there were often two or more claimants: one, nominated by the emperor, called ''melkite'' or the king's man, was presumably faithful to the terms of Chalcedon; the other, a Monophysite, was chosen by the Egyptians themselves on the basis of his fidelity to the teachings of Cyril and Dioscorus.

Egyptian Monasticism. In the 3d century, Egypt saw the rise of MONASTICISM. This institution was first associated with the Thebaid, to which many Christians had retired during the persecution of Decius. According to St. JEROME, the first ascetic to settle permanently in the desert was Paul of Thebes (d. *c.* 341). The *Vita Pauli* by Jerome is a romantic story of monasticism, but the *Vita Antonii* written by St. ATHANASIUS (*c.* 357) is essentially trustworthy. Under Anthony common life began to take the place of the purely eremitical life. With Pachomius, monasticism in its cenobitical form became a permanent institution. From the Thebaid, monasticism spread to Lower Egypt; Ammon of Alexandria (d. *c.* 356) trained many disciples in the Nitrian mountains; Macarius (d. *c.* 390) did the same in the desert of Scete. These monasteries were visited by famous pilgrims, particularly in the late 4th and early part of the 5th century, such as Jerome, Rufinus, the two Melanias, Aetheria, John Cassian, Palladius, and Evagrius. The movement continued to attract famous and obscure recruits until the Arab invasions in the 7th century.

Athanasius. The early years of the 4th century had witnessed the persecution of bishops under Maximin Daia, the schism of Meletius, bishop of Lycopolis (*see* MELETIAN SCHISM) and leader of a policy of rigorism toward repentant LAPSI, and the rise of the heresy of ARIUS. The dominant personality of the period was Athanasius of Alexandria, who took part in the Council of Nicaea, called to condemn Arianism. In the persecution leveled against him by the semi-Arian emperors, Athanasius had the support of the monks, approval expressed by Anthony's visit in 339 or 354. The monks continued to support succeeding patriarchs of Alexandria, regarding them as the highest depositaries of religious authority.

Monophysite Troubles. During the late 4th and the 5th century the patriarchs played a crucial part in the ecclesiastical politics of the age. THEOPHILUS OF ALEXANDRIA had JOHN CHRYSOSTOM deposed at the Synod of the OAK (403); Cyril acted as Pope Celestine's delegate at the Council of EPHESUS (431) and excommunicated NESTORIUS, while DIOSCORUS attempted to rehabilitate EUTYCHES at the Robber Council of Ephesus in 449. The patriarchate was the center of the struggle over the Monophysite controversy all during the 6th and 7th centuries. While Emperor JUSTIN I (518–527) did not attempt to dislodge the Monophysite leaders, JUSTINIAN I (527–565) frequently changed the patriarchs and resorted to strong measures or repression. The monasteries outside Alexandria became a refuge for exiled Monophysites, and those in the Nile Valley were taken over by the Aphthartodocetists, followers of JULIAN OF HALICARNASSUS.

In 543 the exiled Monophysite patriarch Theodosius performed an episcopal consecration of great historical importance. The Arab vassal Prince Harith had asked for a bishop for his Christian tribes. At the request of THEODORA (1), Theodosius sent him the monk Theodore as bishop of the wandering Arab peoples and consecrated James BARADAI as bishop of Edessa. The latter exercised a roving commission among the Monophysites of the Mediterranean world, turning a discouraged party into a determined sect. The division of the Egyptians into Orthodox and Monophysite, and the disagreements of the Monophysites among themselves made the Persian conquest (617) inevitable. Under HERACLIUS I (610–641), the Persians were forced to evacuate Egypt (628), but the imperial victory was short lived. On Sept. 29, 642, 10 years after the death of Muhammad, the Arab conquerors replaced the Roman armies in Egypt.

Bibliography: J. DANIÉLOU and H. I. MARROU, *The First Six Hundred Years,* tr. V. CRONIN, v. 1 of *The Christian Centuries* (New York 1964–) 1:127–368. J. LEBRETON and J. ZEILLER, *The History of the Primitive Church,* tr. E. C. MESSENGER, 4 bks. in 2 (New York 1949) 1:365–500; 2:766–1205. J. R. PALANQUE et al., *The Church in the Christian Roman Empire,* tr. E. C. MESSENGER, 2 v. in 1 (New York 1953) 73–337. H. I. BELL, *Cults and Creeds in Graeco-Roman Egypt* (Liverpool 1953) 50–105; *Egypt* (Oxford 1948) 85–134. G. BARDY, *Catholicisme. Hier, aujourd'hui et demain,* ed. G. JACQUEMET (Paris 1947–) 3:1489–97; ibid. 1:310–314, s.v. Alexandrie. E. R. HARDY, *Christian Egypt: Church and People* (New York 1952). H. LECLERCQ, *Dictionnaire d'archéologie chrétienne et de liturgie,* ed. F. CABROL, H. LECLERCQ, and H. I. MARROU, 15 v. (Paris 1907–53) 4.2:2401–2571. A. C. MCGIFFERT, ed. and tr., *The Church History of Eusebius* (*A Select Library of the Nicene and Post-Nicene Fathers,* ed. P. SCHAFF, 14 v. [New York 1886–1900]; 2d series, ed. P. SCHAFF and H. WACE [1890–1900] ser. 2, v.1; 1890) 116–331. J. QUASTEN, *Patrology,* 4 v. (Westminster, Md. 1950–86) 1:254–277; 2:1–120; 3:6–189. R. RÉMONDON, *Dictionnaire de spiritualité ascétique et mystique. Doctrine et histoire,* ed. M. VILLER et al. (Paris 1932) 4:532–548. E. STEIN, *Histoire du Bas-Empire,* tr. J. R. PALANQUE, 2 v. in 3 (Paris 1949–59) v. 2. J. MASPERO, *Histoire des patriarches d'Alexandrie* (Paris 1923). L. DUCHESNE, *L'Église au VI*[e] *siècle* (Paris 1925). H. I. BELL, *Harvard Theological Review* 37 (1944) 185–208. C. J. VON HEFELE, *Histoire des conciles d'après les documents originaux,* tr. and continued by H. LECLERCQ, 10 v. in 19 (Paris 1907–38) 1:193–194, 211–212, 335–363; v. 3.

[M. C. HILFERTY]

EHRHARD, ALBERT

Church historian, patrologist, Byzantinist; b. Herbitzheim, Alsace, March 14, 1862; d. Bonn, Germany, Sept. 23, 1940. After his ordination in 1885, he studied at the University of Würzburg, where he became a friend of Hermann SCHELL, receiving his doctor's degree in theology in 1888. After further studies in Munich and Rome, he was appointed professor of Church history at the Grand Seminaire in Strasbourg (1889). In 1892 he was made professor of Church history at the University of Würzburg. He taught at Vienna (1898), Freiburg im Breisgau (1902), the University of Strasbourg (1903), and the University of Bonn (1920–27). Ehrhard's special interest was the editing of the sources of theology, hagiography, and homiletic literature of the Greek Church: *Forschungen zur Hagiographie der griechischen Kirche* (1897); *Die altchristliche Literatur und ihre Erforschung seit 1880* (1894); ''Geschichte der byzantinischen Theologie,'' in K. Krumbacher, *Geschichte der byzantinischen Literatur* (2d ed. 1897) 37–218. The continuation of his main work, *Ueberlieferung und Bestand der hagiographischen und homiletischen Literatur der griechischen Kirche* (3 v. 1936–52), was made possible by the discovery of his MS after World War II [see J. M. Hoeck, ''Der Nachlass Albert Ehrhards und seine Bedeutung für die Byzantinistik,'' *Byzantion* 21 (1951) 171–178].

Ehrhard's critical presentation of the history of the Church contributed to the creation of a new concept of ecclesiastical history. The advance toward precision took form in his teaching and in such publications as *Stellung und Aufgabe der Kirchengeschichte in der Gegenwart* (1898), *Des Mittelalter und seine kirchliche Entwicklung* (1908), *Die Kirche der Märtyrer* (1932), *Urkirche und Frühkatholizismus* (1935), *Die griechische und die lateinische Kirche* (1937).

He was also a theologian. A concern with the task of the Church in modern society issued in *Der Katholizismus und das 20. Jahrhundert* (1901; 12th ed. 1902), in which he aimed to relate the tradition of Catholic belief to modern outlooks in philosophical, historical, and social sciences. Opposition to it appeared in conservative circles, where he was accused of MODERNISM, a charge that he answered in his *Liberaler Katholizismus?* (1902) and *Katholisches Christentum und Kultur* (1907). Since he did not hesitate to criticize the papal encyclical *Pascendi,* he was deprived of the title of domestic prelate, although it was later restored.

Bibliography: H. LEINEN, ''Ehrhards Abschiedsvorlesung,'' *Academia* 40 (1927) 13. B. ALTANER, *Historisches Jahrbuch der Görres-Gesellschaft* 61 (1941) 459–464. A. DEMPF, *Albert Ehrhard: Der Mann und sein Werk* (Colmar 1944), with bibliog. J. QUASTEN, *Deutsche Literaturzeitung* 76 (1955) 490–493.

[J. QUASTEN]

EHRLE, FRANZ

Cardinal and medievalist; b. Isny (Württemberg), Oct. 17, 1845; d. Rome, March 31, 1934. After entering the Society of Jesus in 1861, he studied in Germany and in England, where he was ordained in 1876. He was assigned to the editorial staff of *Stimmen aus Maria Laach* until he went to Rome in 1880 to pursue intensive studies in medieval thought. There he collaborated with H. DENIFLE in publishing *Archiv für Literatur und Kirchengeschichte des Mittelalters* (7 v. Freiburg im Breisgau 1885–1900). While prefect of the Vatican Library (1895–1914), he published many important texts and studies on medieval thought, libraries, and Roman topography. During World War I, he was in Munich as editor of *Stimmen der Zeit,* but in 1919 he returned to Rome as lecturer in paleography at the Biblical Institute and (1920) the Gregorianum. In 1922 he was created cardinal and in 1929 was given the position of librarian and archivist of the Roman Church, which he retained until his death. He was widely acclaimed for his vast erudition, and he received honorary doctorates from the Universities of Oxford, Cambridge, Münster, Munich, Cologne, Tübingen, and Louvain.

See Also: SCHOLASTICISM.

Bibliography: ''Miscellanea Francesco Ehrle,'' *Studi e Testi* 42 (1924) 37–41. F. PELSTER, *La civiltà cattolica* 85.2 (1934) 449–461; 85.3 (1934) 17–27. M. GRABMANN, ''Heinrich Denifle O. P. und Kardinal Franz Ehrle S. J.,'' *Philosophisches Jahrbuch der Görres-Gesellschaft* 56 (1946) 9–26; *Stimmen der Zeit* 127 (1934) 217–225.V. CATTANEO, *Enciclopedia Filosofica* 1:1838–39. F. STEGMÜLLER, *Lexikon für Theologie und Kirche*, ed. J. HOFER and K. RAHNER (Freiburg 1957–65) 3:719.

[A. M. WALZ]

EINHARD

The biographer and royal counselor of CHARLEMAGNE; b. *c.* 770; d. Seligenstadt, March 14, 840. Einhard, educated first at Fulda, was eventually sent to Charlemagne's palace school at Aachen, where he continued his education under ALCUIN. His talent and industry won the favor of Charlemagne, who entrusted him with supervision of the royal building program and with important diplomatic missions. After Louis the Pious became emperor in 814, Einhard remained as a trusted court official, serving especially as adviser to Louis's son LOTHAIR. In 830 Einhard retired from the court and devoted himself to founding a monastery at Seligenstadt.

In addition to his active career, Einhard wrote extensively. His chief work was his *Life of Charlemagne,* the best biography written in the early Middle Ages. Modeling his work after Suetonius and injecting into it his intimate personal knowledge of Charlemagne, Einhard produced a biography that lauded the great emperor in a dignified, sober fashion. His *Translatio SS. Marcellini et Petri,* describing the events surrounding the bringing of relics from Rome to Seligenstadt, provides remarkable insight into the religious sentiments of the Carolingian age. A considerable number of his letters also survive and are useful in reconstructing the history of the age of Louis the Pious. All of Einhard's writings reflect the cultural effect of the CAROLINGIAN RENAISSANCE.

Bibliography: Sources. EINHARD, *Vita Karoli Magni,* ed. O. HOLDER-EGGER, *Monumenta Germaniae Historica*: *Scriptores rerum Germanicarum* 24, tr. S. E. TURNER (Ann Arbor 1960); *Translatio et miracula Ss. Marcellini et Petri,* ed. G. WAITZ, *Monumenta Germaniae Historica*: *Scriptores* 15:238–264, Eng. *The History of the Translation of the Blessed Martyrs of Christ,* tr. B. WENDELL (Cambridge, Mass. 1926). *Epistolae,* ed. K. HAMPE, *Monumenta Germaniae Historica*, *Epistolae* (Berlin 1826–) 5:105–149. Literature. L. HALPHEN, *Études critiques sur l'histoire de Charlemagne* (Paris 1921). M. BUCHNER, *Einhards Künstler- und Gelehrtenleben* (Bonn 1922). A. J. KLEINCLAUSZ, Éginhard (Paris 1942). W. WATTENBACH, *Deutschlands Geschichtesquellen im Mittelalter. Vorzeit und Karolinger*, ed. W. LEVISON and H. LÖWE, 2:266–280. E. S. DUCKETT, *Carolingian Portraits: A Study in the Ninth Century* (Ann Arbor 1962).

[R. E. SULLIVAN]

EINSIEDELN, ABBEY OF

Benedictine abbey *nullius* dedicated to Our Lady of the Hermits near Schwyz, Diocese of Chur, central Switzerland. St. MEINRAD came from REICHENAU *c.* 835 to live as a hermit in the forest there and was slain by robbers (861). Eberhart (934–958) was the first abbot of a community under the Benedictine Rule. The Dukes of Swabia and the Ottos favored the abbey; Otto I granted it immunity and made the abbot a prince of the Empire. Under Gregory (964–996) there was a famous school with St. WOLFGANG OF REGENSBURG. The abbey was destroyed by fire five times (1029–1577); and after a long struggle it lost half its territory to Schwyz (1350), which in 1424 replaced the Hapsburgs as *advocati* of Einsiedeln. The bishops of Constance contested exemptions of the abbey because of its famous pilgrimage until a compromise was reached (1452–1782). Restriction of novices to the nobility limited the monks to fewer than five after 1350, divine services and the care of pilgrims being entrusted to secular chaplains. Zwingli became a parish priest in Einsiedeln (1516–18). Abbot Ludwig Blarer (1526–44) introduced reform from SANKT GALLEN, Joachim Eichorn (1544–69) restored the cloister, and Augustine Hofmann (1600–29) helped found the Swiss Benedictine congregation. Printing was introduced (1664), and Abbot Augustine Reding (1670–92) was a noted theologian. French troops plundered the abbey and destroyed the chapel (1798), but the monks returned (1801). Abbot Heinrich Schmid (1846–74) founded ST. MEINRAD, New Subiaco, and Richardton in the U.S. In 1948 the Priory of Los Toldos was founded in Argentina. Pius X made Einsiedeln an abbey *nullius* (1907). The abbot ranks with bishops of the Swiss Bishops Conference.

The baroque convent was built (1704–18) after plans by Caspar Moosbrugger; the church (1719–26) was consecrated in 1735 and restored in 1840, 1911, and 1943. The abbey cares for 12 parishes, a theological school for monks, and colleges at Einsiedeln (320 pupils), Ascona in Ticino (200 pupils), and Pfäffikon (180 agricultural students); the four Benedictine nuns' monasteries under Einsiedeln include Fahr. Einsiedeln settled the Abbeys of PETERSHAUSEN (983), MURI (1027), Schaffhausen (1050), and HIRSAU (1065). According to 14th-century

Benedictine Monastery of Einsiedeln, Switzerland. (©Paul Almasy/CORBIS)

legend, the chapel of St. Meinrad, around which the church was built, was consecrated in 948 by Christ Himself. PILGRIMAGES to Einsiedeln have been popular from the 13th century; the Black Madonna dates from *c.* 1400.

Bibliography: R. HENGGELER, *Professbuch der fürstlichen Benediktinerabtei Unserer Lieben Frau zu Einsiedeln* (Monasticon-Benedictinum Helvetiae 3; Einsiedeln 1934); *Dictionnaire historique et biographique de la Suisse,* v.2 (Neuchâtel 1924) 762–765, illus.; *Einsiedeln: Our Lady of Hermits* (4th ed. Munich 1962), illus. guide. O. RINGHOLZ, *Geschichte der fürstlichen Benediktinerstiftes U. L. F. von Einsiedeln,* v.1 (to 1526) (New York 1904), no more pub. L. BIRCHLER, *Kunstdenkmäler der Schweiz,* v.1 (Basel 1927) 17–238, with illus. R. TSCHUDI, *Das Kloster Einsiedeln unter den Aebten Ludwig II. Blarer und Joachim Eichhorn 1526–69* (Diss. Fribourg 1946); *Our Lady of Einsiedeln in Switzerland* (Shrines of the World; Saint Paul, Minn. 1958); *Lexikon für Theologie und Kirche*, ed. J. HOFER and K. RAHNER, 10 v. (2d, new ed. Freiburg 1957–65) 3:766–767. L. H. COTTINEAU, *Répertoire topobibliographique des abbayes et prieurés*, 2 v. (Mâcon 1935–39) 1:1034–39. O. L. KAPSNER, *A Benedictine Bibliography: An Author-Subject Union List*, 2 v. (2d ed. Collegeville, Minn. 1962) 2:205–209. *Annuario Pontificio* (1965) 729.

[A. MAISSEN]

EINSTEIN, ALBERT

Outstanding physicist of the 20th century, author of more than 300 scientific papers and books, and a humanist who fought against man's brutality to man; b. Ulm, Bavaria, March 14, 1879; d. Princeton, N.J., April 18, 1955.

Life and Works. His parents were only nominally of the Jewish faith, and Albert was educated first at a Catholic elementary school in Munich, then at the Luitpold Gymnasium of that city. After an unsuccessful attempt to enter an institution of higher learning without a gymnasium diploma, he obtained one by study at the Swiss town of Aarau and entered the Swiss Federal Polytechnic School at Zurich. On completion of his work there, Einstein was unable to obtain a position either as an assistant to a professor or as a secondary teacher. Having been appointed as engineer in the patent office in Bern, Switzerland, he simultaneously undertook the research that brought him rapid fame. At about the same time he acquired Swiss citizenship and married a fellow student; they had two sons. He also immediately began to publish one or two papers each year on theoretical physics in the *Annalen der Physik.* In 1905 he published three of particular note: ''Über einen die Erzeugung und Verwandlung des Lichtes betreffenden heuristischen Gesichtspunkt'' (On a Heuristic Point of View concerning the Generation and Transmission of Light, *Annalen der Physik,* ser. 4, 17:132–148), in which he described his photon theory of light; ''Über die von der molekularkinetischen Theorie der Wärme geforderte Bewegung von in ruhenden Flussigkeiten suspendierten Teilchen'' (On the Movement of Small Particles Suspended in a Stationary Liquid Demanded by the Molecular Kinetic Theory of Heat, *ibid.* 549–560), on Brownian motion; and ''Elektrodynamik bewegter Körper'' (Electrodynamics of Moving Bodies, *ibid.* 891–921), containing the bases of his theory of relativity. These remarkable publications led to a lectureship at Bern and a series of professorships at the Universities of Zurich (1909) and Prague (1910) and at the Polytechnic School at Zurich (1912). While at Prague, Einstein published many additional papers, including his ''Über den Einfluss der Schwerkraft auf die Ausbreitung des Lichtes'' (Concerning the Influence of Gravitation on the Propagation of Light, *ibid.* 35:898–908). In 1913 he went to Berlin as a member of the Royal Prussian Academy of Science, a professor at the University of Berlin without teaching or administrative obligations, and a member of the Kaiser Wilhelm Research Institute.

During World War I, Einstein acquired a reputation as an anti-militarist. He also remarried, having separated from his first wife, by mutual consent. It was also during the early wartime years that he developed the theory of general relativity, published in his ''Die Grundlage der allgemeinen Relativitätstheorie'' (The Foundation of the Generalized Theory of Relativity, *ibid.* 49:769–822). He predicted that light from stars passing near to the sun would be deflected by a certain amount, a prediction that was confirmed by observations made during an eclipse of the sun in 1919. There was considerable opposition to the relativity theory, however, and when Einstein was awarded the Nobel Prize in 1922, the citation spoke only of his work in photoelectricity and ''in the field of theoretical physics.''

As a public figure, Einstein devoted steadily more and more time to using his prestige to fight for those

Albert Einstein.

ideals in which he believed. Both his relativity theory and his pacificism found many enemies, and when the Nazi terror began in 1932, he was a prime target. He was visiting in the U.S. at the time and did not return to Germany. After a brief stay in Belgium he returned to the U.S. and spent the remainder of his life at the Institute for Advanced Study, Princeton.

Religion and Philosophy. Einstein's views on religion have been the subject of some controversy. He seems to have had a concept of God not unlike that of B. SPINOZA, viz, a cosmic force that produces a harmony of order in the universe but is unconcerned with the affairs of men. Einstein's belief in the rationality of the universe was expressed forcefully in his *Cosmic Religion* (New York 1931). In his address to the first Conference on Science, Philosophy, and Religion, held in New York (1940), he reiterated this theme in a much-quoted phrase, ''science without religion is lame, religion without science is blind'' (see Schilpp, 285). His ''religiosity'' has, for obvious reasons, come under attack by churchmen.

As a philosopher, Einstein has exerted considerable indirect influence, mainly through his theories of relativity. Not himself an advocate of RELATIVISM, he has sometimes been interpreted as giving powerful stimulus to this doctrine. His epistemology seems to have been basically realist, although logical positivists such as P. Frank, V. Lenzen, and H. Reichenbach have seen in it a confirmation of POSITIVISM, and P. W. Bridgman has used it to develop his own system of OPERATIONALISM. Einstein thought that belief in an external world independent of the perceiving subject must be the basis of all natural science, but he was never clear as to how man can know that external world. He held that the concept is ''a free creation of the human mind,'' and yet seemed convinced that man's mathematical insights could somehow mirror the structure of reality. Of less importance as a philosopher than as a stimulator of philosophical thought, Einstein was nonetheless one of the most original thinkers of the 20th century.

Bibliography: P. A. SCHILPP, ed., *Albert Einstein, Philosopher-Scientist,* 2 v. (Evanston, Ill. 1949; New York 1959), complete list of writings to 1950. R. NEIDORF, ''Is Einstein a Positivist?'' *Philosophy of Science* 30 (1963) 173–188.

[D. H. D. ROLLER/W. A. WALLACE]

EISENGREIN, MARTIN AND WILHELM

Uncle and nephew. Martin, theologian and preacher; b. Stuttgart, Dec. 28, 1535; d. Ingolstadt, May 4, 1578. His father, burgomaster of Stuttgart, favored reform ideas and Martin was raised a Protestant. At the University of Vienna where he was a student and later professor of natural philosophy, he abandoned Lutheranism for Catholicism about 1558. In 1560 he was ordained and two years later returned to Ingolstadt as pastor of the university church. Martin, the friend and collaborator of Peter Canisius and Friedrich Staphylus, was repeatedly honored by Pius V, and played a major role in the Catholic Restoration in Bavaria. Duke Albert V sent him on several important missions. From 1563 to 1564 he participated in the deliberations on communion under both species and clerical celibacy held in Vienna. Though Martin held a succession of academic and administrative posts at the University of Ingolstadt, it was in the ministry, especially as a preacher, that he made his reputation. His sermons, discourses on the most debated issues of the day, were published and circulated throughout Germany. He was preacher at the court of Maximilian II from 1568 to 1569.

Wilhelm, church historian; b. Speyer, 1534; d. Rome, 1584. He was a nephew of Martin and is best known for his refutation of Flacius' *Centuries of Magdeburg.* The first two volumes of a projected 16-volume work appeared in 1566 (Ingolstadt) and 1568 (Munich). A later work has the same theme, *Harmonia ecclesiae historica adversus centurias Magdeburg* (Speyer 1576).

Bibliography: L. PFLEGER, ''Wilhelm Eisengrein, ein Gegner des Flacius Illyrikus,'' *Historisches Jahrbuch des Görres–Gesellschaft* 25 (1904) 774–792. V. CONZEMIUS, *Dictionnaire d'histoire et de géographie ecclésiastiques,* ed. A. BAUDRILLAT et al. (Paris 1912–), 15:102–105.

[B. L. MARTHALER]

EKKEHARD OF SANKT GALLEN

The name of three monks of the Abbey of SANKT GALLEN, Switzerland.

Ekkehard I, teacher and poet, of a noble family; b. Thurgau, *c.* 910; d. Sankt Gallen, Jan. 14, 973. When dean of the monastery he was selected as abbot, but he renounced the dignity. He made a pilgrimage to Rome, establishing friendly relations with Pope JOHN XIII. He composed seven sequences and three hymns or religious poems. Doubt has been cast on his authorship of *Waltharius,* a Latin epic based on German folk saga, which has traditionally been attributed to him.

Ekkehard II (*Palatinus,* the Courtier); date of birth unknown; d. Mainz, April 23, 990. He was the nephew and pupil of Ekkehard I. He taught in the monastic school of Sankt Gallen and, later, was Latin tutor to the Duchess Hadwig of Swabia, widow of Burchard II. His influential position with the duchess enabled him to render great services to his monastery. He was also prominent at the court of Emperor OTTO I and became provost of the cathedral of Mainz. He was the author of several sequences, including one in honor of St. Desiderius.

Ekkehard IV, teacher, chronicler; b. Alsace, *c.* 980; d. Oct. 21, *c.* 1060. He studied under NOTKER LABEO at Sankt Gallen and on Labeo's death became the director of the cathedral school at Mainz. He remained there until 1031 and gained favor with the Emperor CONRAD II. He then returned to his monastery, resumed teaching, and continued the ancient chronicle of Sankt Gallen, the *Casus s. Galli,* which had been begun by Ratpert and taken as far as Abbot Salamon (883). Ekkehard brought it down to Notker (972). This famous work is an important source for contemporary events and culture, as well as for the history of Sankt Gallen, but is somewhat tendentious and is full of inaccuracies. Ekkehard's other important literary work is the *Liber benedictionum,* a collection of metrical inscriptions for the walls of the Mainz cathedral, blessings in verse and poems. Of no great literary merit, it nevertheless attests to much learning in monastic studies. Ekkehard also excelled in ecclesiastical music.

Bibliography: M. MANITIUS, *Geschichte der lateinischen Literatur des Mittelalters* 1:609–614. W. STAMMLER and K. LANGOSCH, eds., *Die deutsche Literatur des Mittelalters: Verfasserlexikon* 1:527–541; 5:183–185. F. BRUNHÖLZL and H. F. HAEFELE, *Lexikon für Theologie und Kirche* [2] 3:780–781.

[F. COURTNEY]

EL (GOD)

A singular noun, El (*'ēl*) is the oldest known name for the deity; it was used in varying forms by almost all Semitic peoples as a proper name for God. The Canaanites are known to have worshiped a god whose name was linked with various local sanctuaries (e.g., El-Bethel). The Patriarchs, who also worshiped El, recognized in Him the one true God identified with ELOHIM and YAHWEH who revealed Himself in different ways (Gn 28.10–22; 33.20; 49.25) and who was the author and guarantor of the promises made to them. The significance of the term, which is the same as the Akkadian *ilu*, has been sought in a Semitic root *'yl*, meaning ''to be powerful.''

El is a point of contact between Israel and polytheism. In the Phoenician pantheon described in the texts of UGARIT, El appears as the supreme god; he is the father of the gods and lord of heaven, the chief and utterly transcendent one, of moral and benign character. In the Old Testament, El is less frequently associated with particular cultic sites than is BAAL; his association is mainly with persons. Time and space are not obstacles for Him (in Gn 31.13, He appears to Jacob at great distance from His first appearance). He is different from men and superior to them, and His presence arouses in them feelings of both reverence and awe (Gn 28.17; Nm 23.19; Hos 11.9; Ez 28.2). El is a general component of many names (Gn 4.18; 5.12 etc.).

El is used less than the names Yahweh and Elohim to refer to the God of Israel, but in later Psalms [46(47).3; 49(50).14] and in Job (48 times), El is used as a poetic archaizing element. The plural form *'ēlīm* is used of angels and of pagan gods [Ps 28(29).1; 88(89).7; Ex 15.11]. In English versions El is usually construed to mean ''God.''

Bibliography: W. EICHRODT, *Theology of the Old Testament*, tr. J. A. BAKER (London 1961–). *Encyclopedic Dictionary of the Bible*, tr. and adap. by L. HARTMAN (New York 1963) 633–635.

[R. T. A. MURPHY]

ELBEL, BENJAMIN

Franciscan moral theologian; b. Friedburg, Bavaria, 1690?; d. Soeflingen, near Elm, June 4, 1756. Very little is known of his early life and education. He joined the Order of Friars Minor Recollect and eventually rose to the office of minister provincial of the Strassburg province, serving one term from 1735 to 1738. Elbel taught theology in various seminaries and houses of study of his order, and is best known as a moral theologian. He published his *Theologiae moralis decalogalis et sacramentalis per modum conferentiarum casibus practicis illustrata* (Venice 1731), as well as an account of the history of the Franciscan Order, *Ortus et progressus ordinis minorum S. Francisci ultra quinque saecula* (Monaco 1732). Elbel was a skillful casuist, a probabilist whose works and teaching were sound in doctrine; no controversy attends his name.

Bibliography: H. HURTER, *Nomenclator literarius theologiae catholicae*[3] 4:1635.

[A. J. CLARK]

ELDAD HA-DANI

Traveler and explorer of the second half of the 9th century, who claimed to be a citizen of an independent Jewish state in East Africa, inhabited by the tribes of Dan, Aser (Asher), Gad, and Nephthali (Naphtali). When he visited Babylonia and Kairwan *c.* A.D. 880 and Spain in 883, he told about finding the ''ten lost tribes'' of Israel in his travels and later recorded these tales in writing. Among them were the Bene Moshe (Sons of Moses), depicted as a Utopian society surrounded by the River Sambatyon, which all week fiercely rolled sand and stones but rested on the Sabbath, when it was enclosed in a barrier of fire for half a mile on both sides. Eldad brought from his country a book of Halakot (*see* HALAKAH) widely differing from Talmudic laws and completely in Hebrew, the sole language used by all the tribes. The 14 chapters on the laws of slaughtering and postslaughter inspection were, Eldad asserted, ''learned from the mouth of Joshua ben Nun, Moses, and God.'' The inhabitants of Kairwan were disturbed by the differences between these and Talmudic laws, and they questioned Gaon Zemah ben Hayyim of Sura, but they received his reassurance. Eldad is quoted by Hasdai Ibn Shaprut, RASHI, Abraham ben David, and Abraham ben Maimon. Of the commentators, only Abraham ben Meïr IBN EZRA and Meir of Rothenburg expressed doubts about the validity of his narrative. Several prominent historians expressed their suspicions that he was a Karaite missionary; others refuted this contention by pointing out that certain Halakot he cites regarding examination of slaughtered animals were not accepted by Karaites. Historical research has not yet determined his origin and his personality; it is likely that his story was a historical novel, with a blending of truth and imagination.

Linked with the influence of Eldad's narrative was the apocryphal letter of PRESTER JOHN of the 12th century. Although Eldad had claimed that independent Jewish states existed, the Christian writer told of a priest who ruled over the great kingdom of Ethiopia, to which were subject some Jewish tribes, including the Bene Moshe who lived on the other side of the River Sambatyon.

Bibliography: I. BROYDE, *The Jewish Encyclopedia*, ed. J. SINGER (New York 1901–06) 5:90–92. *Universal Jewish Encyclopedia* (New York 1939–44) 4:46. B. SULER, *Encyclopedia Judaica: Das Judentum in Geschichte und Gegenwart* (Berlin 1928–34) 6:393–399. M. SCHLÖSSINGER, ed., *The Ritual of Eldad Hadani* (New York 1908). A. EPSTEIN, *Eldad Hadani* (Pressburg 1891), in Heb. A. SHOHAT, *Entsiklopedyah Ivrit* 3 (1951) 423–426, in Heb.

[E. SUBAR]

ELDER, GEORGE

Priest, educator; b. Hardin's Creek, Ky., Aug. 11, 1794; d. Bardstown, Ky., Sept. 28, 1838. He was one of eight children of James and Ann (Richards) Elder. His mother was a convert, his father was noted for his wide knowledge of the Bible, and a sister became a nun. George was taught by his father until, at the age of 16, he was sent to Mt. St. Mary's, Emmitsburg, Md. In 1816 he entered St. Mary's Seminary, Baltimore, Md., where he formed a lifetime friendship with William BYRNE. On Sept. 18, 1819, the two friends were ordained at the first ordination ceremony in the Bardstown Cathedral and the first of Bp. John David. Both were founders and first presidents of Kentucky colleges—Byrne of St. Mary's and Elder of St. Joseph's. Elder carried out the ambition of Bp. Benedict J. Flaget to found a school for the boys of Bardstown. It was begun in the basement of St. Joseph Seminary next to the cathedral; a year later (1820) a new wing was added to the building, which by 1823 had become ''the largest and best appointed school structure in the west.'' Many distinguished men from the lower South were educated there. In 1827 Elder was sent to St. Pius parish, Scott County, to settle unrest there; three years later he returned to the presidency of St. Joseph's College. A fire on Jan. 25, 1838, destroyed the college building; Elder's exertions in fighting the fire aggravated a heart condition, causing his death eight months later.

As editor of the Louisville *Catholic Advocate* (founded 1836), he wrote the controversial series titled ''Letters to Brother Jonathan'' and numerous articles on education.

Bibliography: B. J. WEBB, *The Centenary of Catholicity in Kentucky* (Louisville 1884). M. J. SPALDING, *Sketches of the Early Catholic Missions of Kentucky, 1787–1827* (Louisville 1844). J. H. SCHAUINGER, *Cathedrals in the Wilderness* (Milwaukee 1952).

[J. H. SCHAUINGER]

ELDER, WILLIAM HENRY

Archbishop; b. Baltimore, Md., March 22, 1819; d. Cincinnati, Ohio, Oct. 31, 1904. His parents, Basil Spalding and Elizabeth M. (Snowden) Elder, had 13 children; William was the second youngest living. He attended a private school in Baltimore and at 12 entered Mt. St. Mary's College, Emmitsburg, Md., graduating in 1837. He then entered the seminary department of the college, received the diaconate in 1842, and was sent to the Urban College in Rome, where he was ordained on March 29, 1846. Upon his return to the U.S., he was appointed professor of dogmatic theology at Emmitsburg. There he taught theology, Church history, and Scripture, and acted as rector of the seminary until Jan. 9, 1857, when he was named bishop of Natchez, Miss.

Ordinary of Natchez. Elder was consecrated on May 3, 1857, at Baltimore by Abp. Francis P. KENRICK and installed at Natchez, May 31. There he found only 13 priests, two of whom were infirm; 11 churches, one of which was the unfinished cathedral; nine young men preparing for the priesthood; and about 10,000 Catholics in the white population of more than 300,000, and 930 Catholics in the African American population of 309,000. The bishop was the only native American clergyman in the diocese. He organized a total abstinence society and took the pledge himself in order to encourage others. During the Civil War the Northern forces entered Natchez in October 1863. When ordered by the commander of the occupying forces, Brig. Gen. Y. M. Tuttle, to insert a special prayer in the Mass for the President of the U.S. and for the success of the Northern arms, Elder refused and on April 7, 1864, wrote a masterful statement of his position to President Lincoln. Although Tuttle was removed and ultimately replaced by Brig. Gen. M. Brayman, the changes were unrelated to Elder's letter to the president. On July 22, 1864, Brayman ordered the bishop to Vidalia where he was confined for 17 days and wrote a second statement of his position to Secretary of War Edwin M. Stanton, which again elicited no official action.

Elder attended the three Plenary Councils of Baltimore, serving on committees and confirming his own belief in the conciliar method of ecclesiastical administration. In 1868 he went to Europe to assist at the centennial celebration of SS. Peter and Paul; he attended some sessions of Vatican Council I, but did not stay for its conclusion. In 1878, Elder rendered heroic service during the yellow-fever plague, which took the lives of six of his priests and hundreds of the faithful. During this ordeal, he received word that he had been appointed coadjutor to Abp. Joseph ALEMANY of San Francisco, Calif. Because of the critical conditions in Natchez, Elder's appeal for a postponement was approved. However, on Jan. 30, 1880, he was appointed coadjutor with right of succession to Abp. John B. PURCELL of Cincinnati, and he succeeded to that see on July 4, 1883.

Career in Cincinnati. When Elder arrived in CINCINNATI on April 18, 1880, Purcell was already in his last illness, the archdiocese was deeply involved in a bankruptcy action in the courts, and the clergy and faithful were in a state of great uncertainty. As early as 1837, the failure of small savings associations had led to the development of a diocesan project under Rev. Edward Purcell, who accepted the deposits of the faithful and paid six per cent interest. During the 1870s Purcell made large loans to several commercial ventures and when the panic of 1877 brought about the failure of these, the archbishop was thrown into bankruptcy. Legal action was initiated to gain control of all ecclesiastical property, alleging that the debts were diocesan and not those of an individual. The case, tried between April 4, 1882, and June 24, 1882, was not ended until May 11, 1905, almost a year after Archbishop Elder's death.

Elder did not allow this serious financial problem to interfere with his ordinary ecclesiastical activities; in fact he was accused several times of disinterestedness in the church's financial obligations. On March 5, 1882, he presided over the fourth provincial council of Cincinnati, whose decrees were approved by Leo XIII on June 22, 1886. In 1886 and 1898, respectively, Archbishop Elder held the second and third diocesan synods of Cincinnati. He convened the fifth provincial council of Cincinnati on May 19, 1889. In 1887 Mt. St. Mary Seminary, which had been closed for eight years, was reopened, and in 1890, a preparatory seminary dedicated to St. Gregory was established. During his 24-year tenure in Cincinnati, 32 new parishes and missions were founded, with a proportionate growth in the works and institutions of religious. By his wise rule, he restrained the German nationalists in and around Cincinnati. Throughout his life Elder was a prodigious letter writer; his correspondents ranged from cardinals in Rome to poor parishioners of St. Peter's Cathedral in Cincinnati.

Bibliography: *Letters of Archbishop William Henry Elder;* archives of Mt. St. Mary Seminary, Norwood, Ohio; archives of Notre Dame University, South Bend, Ind., diocesan archives at Jackson, Miss.; diocesan archives at Baltimore, Md.; archives of Mt. St. Mary Seminary and College and St. Joseph College, Emmitsburg, Md. R. O. GEROW, *Cradle Days of St. Mary's at Natchez* (Natchez, Miss. 1941). M. M. MELINE and E. F. MCSWEENEY, *The Story of the Mountain,* 2 v. (Emmitsburg, Md. 1911).

[C. R. STEINBICKER]

ELDRAD, ST.

Abbot of Novalese in Piedmont; b. near Aix, Provence; d. March 13, 840–845. Eldrad (Heldrade, Hildradus) was born of an aristocratic family. After a long pilgrimage through Spain and Italy he came to the flourishing Benedictine monastery of Saints. Peter and Andrew at Novalese, near Susa, province of Turin, a cultural center endowed with an excellent library. Elected abbot (*c.* 826), he ruled the monastery till his death. During his career, the abbey became a favored hospice, providing lodging for pilgrims crossing over the Alps into Italy. Two incidents of his tenure as abbot have been recorded: the gift of the monastery of Appagni by LOTHAIR I in 825, and Eldrad's successful negotiations with Count Boso of Turin in 827. His cult was approved in 1702, in 1821, and again in 1903 [*Acta Sanctae Sedis* (Rome 1865–1908) 36 (1904) 424].

Feast: March 13.

Bibliography: *Acta Sanctorum* March 2 326–333. *Bibliotheca hagiographica latina antiquae ct mediae aetatis* (Brussels 1898–1901) 1:2442–46. A. DUMAS, *Dictionnaire d'histoire et de géographie ecclésiastiques* (Paris 1912–) 15:129. DE LABRIOLLE, *Catholicisme* 5:573–574

[J. E. LYNCH]

ELECTION, DIVINE

The general purpose of God in entering into the course of history was to bring about the reparation of man's primal revolt and to reestablish God's kingdom in this world; this He has done through a chosen people and certain chosen individuals. Their story makes up SALVATION HISTORY, which is initiated, directed, and brought to completion by God. The Biblical concept of divine choice or election (Heb. *bāḥar;* Gr. ἐκλογή, ἐκλεκτός) is examined first in the OT, then in the NT.

In the Old Testament. Israel's awareness of being chosen by God goes back to its origins. At Sinai Moses was told by God that the people had been brought there by God Himself and that, ''if you keep my covenant, you shall be my special possession, dearer to me than all other people . . . , a kingdom of priests, a holy nation'' (Ex 19.5–6). The same awareness is shown in Dt 26.18: ''Today the Lord is making this agreement with you, you are to be a people peculiarly his own . . .'' (see also Jos 24.3–13). Election, COVENANT, and promise are three fundamental elements of Israel's faith.

The classic statement regarding Israel's election, however, is the late one found in Dt 7.7–10: ''It was not because you are the largest of all nations that the Lord set his heart upon you and chose you, for you are really the smallest of nations. It was because the Lord loved you and because of his fidelity to the oath he had sworn to your fathers . . . the faithful God who keeps his merciful covenant down to the thousandth generation towards those who love him . . . , but repays with destruction the person who hates him.'' This election was no mystery to the Israelites, any more than focused or selective love is in general. The mystery would be why God loves man at all.

Election is a free act of God, and the OT writers, with their usual honesty and insight, never attribute it to any merit of Israel. J. L. McKenzie rightly says that the divine election confers worthiness rather than presupposes it. Just as the potter freely chooses his clay and forms it into an ''object of whatever sort he pleases'' (Jer 18.4), so the Lord can do with regard to the house of Israel (see also Is 29.16; 45.9–13). The freedom of God's choice is often shown by His choosing the lowly ones of the world, or the younger brother: ''the elder shall serve the younger'' (Gn 25.23). Election is also described as irrevocable and everlasting, ''to the thousandth generation,'' though Israel's response is not compelled and can falter. On Israel's part it unfortunately led to self-righteousness and even to self-sufficiency. The Prophet Amos had to remind them sternly that election meant responsibility, not privilege (3.1–2), and because they had failed their responsibility, they would feel the divine judgment.

The choice of Israel does not mean the rejection of other nations. In the incomparable Servant of the Lord oracles of Deutero-Isaiah, Israel is said to have been chosen by Yahweh for the sake of all the nations (Is 42.1–9; 49.1–6), and a further note is added that its punishment and suffering is even vicarious (52.13–53.12): ''It was our infirmities he bore, our sufferings that he endured.''

Besides the divine election of the people of Israel, many individuals were called and chosen by God. Abraham was blessed and set apart. The Judges, Saul, David, Isaiah, Jeremia, and Ezechiel were all called and chosen by the Lord, not for personal privilege, but to serve God and His people, just as the Israelites were God's instrument for the sake of all nations.

The response God wishes from the people He chooses is faith and fidelity along with service. ''Abraham believed the Lord who credited the act to him as justice'' (Gn 15.6; Rom 4.3). In many places God speaks of Abraham, Moses, Josue, and others as ''my servant'' (e.g., Gn 26.24); and service is seen to be the end for which the Servant of the Lord of Deutero-Isaiah is chosen.

In the New Testament. The chosen people in the NT are the Church of Christ. St. Peter addresses his first epistle to ''the sojourners of the Dispersion . . . chosen unto the sanctification of the Spirit . . .'' (1 Pt 1.1). They are the elect for whom the Lord will shorten the last days (Mt 24.22), and the ''remnant left, selected out of grace'' (λεῖμμα κατ' ἐκλογὴν χάριτος) of Rom 11.5. The Christian community is given names similar to those of OT Israel:''a chosen race, a royal priesthood, a holy nation, a purchased people'' (1 Pt 2.9; cf. Ex 19.5–6). St. James asks, ''Has not God chosen the poor of this world to be rich in faith?'' (Jas 2.5), and St. Paul exhorts: ''Put on therefore as God's chosen ones, holy and beloved, a heart of mercy, kindness, humility, meekness, patience'' (Col 3.12). The statement of our Lord at the end of the parable of the Marriage Feast, ''For many are called, but few are chosen'' (Mt 22.14), must be interpreted as referring to the Church in this world. The kingdom of heaven, which the parable illustrates, is a kingdom in two stages, here and hereafter. The ''chosen'' are those who belong to it in this world, the ''many'' are all the members of the human race. All are invited in the parable: those who respond to the divine call are chosen. Yet the NT use of the word chosen (ἐκλεκτός) always seems to carry with it the notion of favor and choice on the part of God.

All the Apostles are chosen (Mk 3.13), but individual election can be withdrawn, for Judas, like Saul (1 Sm 13.13–14), is finally rejected (Acts 1.25). Peter (Acts 15.7) and Paul (Acts 9.15) are especially chosen. But it is Christ whose election above all others is announced from the cloud at his BAPTISM (Mk 1.9–11) and TRANSFIGURATION (Mk 9.1–7). According to NT thought, Christ and His Church fulfill the role of the Suffering Servant.

Bibliography: *Encyclopedic Dictionary of the Bible*, tr. and adap. by L. HARTMAN (New York 1963) 642–645. R. SCHNACKENBURG, *Lexikon für Theologie und Kirche*, ed. J. HOFER and K. RAHNER, 10 v. (2d new ed. Freiburg1957–65) 3:1061–63. E. L. DIETRICH and J. SCHNEIDER, *Die Religion in Geschichte und Gegenwart* 2:610–614. H. H. ROWLEY, *The Biblical Doctrine of Election* (London 1950). K. GALLING, *Die Erwählungstradition Israels* (Giessen 1928). J. L. MCKENZIE, *The Two-Edged Sword* (Milwaukee 1956) 130–131. J. BRIGHT, *A History of Israel* (Philadelphia 1959). F. PRAT, *Theology of St. Paul,* 2 v. (London 1926–27) 1:436–437. A. JONES, ''God's Choice: Its Nature and Consequences,'' *Scripture* 13 (1961) 35–43. J. BONSIRVEN, *The Theology of the New Testament,* tr. S. F. L. TYE (Westminster, Md. 1963). E. SUTCLIFFE, ''Many Are Called But Few Are Chosen,'' *Irish Theological Quarterly* 28 (1961) 126–131. W. STAERK, ''Zum alttestamentlichen Erwählungsglauben,'' *Zeitschrift für die alttestamentliche Wissenschaft* 55 (1937) 1–36.

[E. LOVELEY]

ELEMENT

An element may be identified in any subject matter that is capable of ANALYSIS AND SYNTHESIS and in any science or art in which such processes are studied. Compounds are known to be such when they can be resolved into simpler parts. The least parts into which anything can be divided, i.e., the ultimate units or parts out of which other things are formed by combination, are called elements. However, elements are only relatively indivisible, that is, in a certain way or context, or from a certain point of view. Thus, the letters of the alphabet and their sounds are elements of speech and writing, although in other respects they are divisible and are not elements.

Element in Philosophy. An element is a kind of material cause from which something is composed in a primary way, as bread is made of flour and water, and a meal of bread and wine (*see* MATTER; MATTER AND FORM). Furthermore, an element is somehow in the compound in a positive way and remains in the compound. It is not like illness, which does not remain in the body after health has been recovered, but rather like nourishing food that does remain after eating. Moreover, an element has a specific character of its own, and one which is simple, that is, not further divisible into other species in the same line of division. Again, just as principles are related to consequences and causes to effects, so elements are related to compounds.

Various Usages. In arithmetic, the unit is the element of which numbers are composed. In geometry, lines determined by points are elements, and also surfaces and solids determined by lines. According to ancient and medieval science, the whole world was thought to be composed of four kinds of elementary bodies—viz, earth, water, air, and fire—all transformable one into another, and further entering into the formation of mixtures and compounds. Moreover it was thought that the animal body in TEMPERAMENT and health depends upon the mixture and proportion of four vital elements or humors, viz, blood, phlegm, yellow bile, and black bile.

In modern biology, cells and tissues are the elements of complex organisms, while simple organisms are resolved into nucleus or nuclear materials and cytoplasm with its organic and inorganic parts. In modern physical science the elements are the chemically simple bodies, about 100 in number of kinds, that are classified with natural sequence in the periodic table (see below).

According to another meaning of the word, the elements of a science or art are its primary conceptions and demonstrations. These are the demonstrations that are made, not by long chains of reasoning, but by simple arguments consisting of three terms and employing only one medium of DEMONSTRATION. In this sense one speaks of the elements of ethics or metaphysics, or of any science or art.

Presence in Compounds. A philosophical problem of importance is concerned with the manner in which elements exist in a compound. Some compounds seem to be mere mixtures of elements that retain their own characteristics and their own identity, as sea water is a mixture of water and various salts. On the other hand, a compound such as water or salt has its own characteristics, and seems to be a natural unit of a kind specifically different from its elements, which do not retain their own characteristics unmodified. In compounds such as these, the elements do not seem to retain their own existence, but have become parts of a new unit and exist in virtue of the new unit (*virtualiter*), somewhat as food becomes part of one organism through digestion and assimilation. If the elements retained their own identity, the compound would not be one in kind, but many.

See Also: ATOMISM; PRINCIPLE; CAUSALITY.

Bibliography: M. J. ADLER, *The Great Ideas: A Syntopicon of Great Books of the Western World* (Chicago 1952) 1:400–412. A. VAN MELSEN, *From Atomos to Atom*, tr. H. J. KOREN (New York 1960). V. MIANO, *Enciclopedia filosofica* (Venice-Rome 1957) 1:1847–50.

[W. H. KANE]

ELEMENTS OF EXISTENCE

Elements of existence are called *khandha* in Pāli and *skandha* in Sanskrit. According to the teachings of the Buddha, all beings are composite, made of parts that are subject to change in time, and therefore impermanent, lacking eternal individuality or soul, and subject to pain. The cause of pain lies in desire, particularly in desire of permanence. The desire of rebirth (*bhāva*) gnaws the believer in the permanence of life and soul (*sessatavādin*), as the desire of annihilation (*vibhāva*) consumes the nihilist (*ucchedavādin*) convinced that death ends all. Desire is extinguished primarily by the right knowledge of the Truths concerning pain in human existence, impermanence, and inexistence of soul. The doctrine of impermanence is basic in Buddhist philosophy, in which becoming takes the place of being. The refutation of the existence of soul is the main theme of the *Kathāvatthu*, an extensive collection of controversial topics attributed to Tissa, the son of Moggāli, and comprised in the *Abhidhammapiṭaka.* To the metaphysical self, Buddhism opposes the transient and metabolic psychic self. Psychophysical life starts with the union of five elements (Pāli, *Pañcakhandha*), one corporeal and the others incorporeal: (1) form or body (*rūpa*); (2) sensation (*vedanā*) arising from the exercise of the six senses—sight, hearing, smell, taste, touch, and mind—upon sense objects; (3) perception (Pāli, *saññā*; Sanskrit *sañjñā*) resulting in the cognition of and reflection upon sensation; (4) disposition (Pāli, *sankhārā*; Sanskrit, *saṁskāra*), including propensity, leaning, proclivity, drive, and passion; (5) consciousness, or conscious thought (Pāli, *viññāna*; Sanskrit *vijñāna*), arising from the interplay of the other psychic components. The individual as a unit of the empirical world consists of an ever-changing combination of the five elements, which consequently keeps him in a state of constant flux. The process whereby life continues in a sequence of dependent origination is sustained by the CHAIN OF CAUSATION.

Bibliography: R. S. COPLESTON, *Buddhism Primitive and Present in Magadha and Ceylon* (2d ed. New York 1908). C. N. E. ELIOT, *Hinduism and Buddhism,* 3 v. (London 1921) v.1; *Japanese Buddhism* (repr. New York 1959). K. J. SAUNDERS, *Epochs in Buddhist History* (Chicago 1924). W. T. DE BARY et al., comps., *Sources of Indian Tradition* (Records of Civilization 56; New York 1958).

[A. S. ROSSO]

ELEUTHERIUS, POPE, ST.

Pontificate: 171 or 177 to 185 or 193. His dates are uncertain. According to Hegesippus, Eleutherius was a deacon under ANICETUS. Eusebius (*Chron.*) places his accession in the seventeenth year of Marcus Aurelius (177) and his death under Pertinax (192), but in his *Ecclesiastical History* (4.22; 5.1, 3–6, 22) he dates Eleutherius' death in the tenth year of Commodus (189). Most authorities agree on a fifteen-year reign. His pontificate was in general a peaceful one. The *Liber pontificalis* says that he was a Greek, the son of Habundius from Nicopolis, and that he maintained that Easter should be celebrated on Sunday. It also attributes to Eleutherius the regulation that no food be rejected as naturally unclean by a Christian, but such a rule was more suitable to fifth-century Rome in view of Manichaean food taboos.

Merely legendary is the strange report in the *Liber* that a King Lucius of Britain asked Eleutherius for missionaries, although it was elaborated by Bede and later medieval chroniclers. However, Rome's growing importance is attested by visits of POLYCARP, JUSTIN MARTYR, and HEGESIPPUS. Its most important visitor at this time was the famous theologian St. Irenaeus, who came to Rome in 177–178 with letters from the Gallic martyrs and the Christians of Lyons asking Eleutherius to judge and mediate the question of MONTANISM.

Tertullian, a convert to Montanism, says that the Roman bishop originally sent out conciliatory letters admitting the authenticity of Montanists' prophetic claims and only later rejected the movement. The pope thus decided in favor of spiritual governance by an institutionalized hierarchy rather than by the charismatic promptings of individual prophets.

Irenaeus's list of Roman bishops, a major source for early Roman Church history, ends with Eleutherius. The statement of the *Liber* that Eleutherius was buried in the Vatican near Peter is not supported by modern excavations under St. Peter's.

Feast: May 26.

Bibliography: *Liber pontificalis,* ed. L. DUCHESNE (Paris 1886–92, 1958) 1:cii–civ, 58–61, 136. A. CLERVAL, *Dictionnaire de théologie catholique.* ed. A. VACANT et al., (Paris 1903–50) 4.2:2319–20. *Acta Sanctorum,* May 3:363–364; May 6:360–362. E. CASPAR, *Geschichte de Papsttums von den Aufängen bis zur Höhe der Weltherrschaft* (Tübingen 1930–33) 1:8, 13, 48, 52. J. HALLER, *Das Papsttum* (Stuttgart 1959–53) v.1. F. X. SEPPELT, *Geschichte der Päpste von den Anfängen bis zur Mitte des 20. Jh.* (Leipzig 1931–41, Munich 1954–59) v.1. E. FERGUSON, ed., *Encyclopedia of Early Christianity* (New York 1997), 1:368. J. N. D KELLY, *Oxford Dictionary of Popes* (New York 1986), 11–12. G. SCHWAGER, *Lexikon für Theologie und Kirche* (Freiburg 1995).

[E. G. WELTIN]

ELEUTHERIUS OF TOURNAI, ST.

Bishop; b. Tournai, 456?; d. 531? According to the *Vita s. Medardi* (2.6) written *c.* 600, Eleutherius, of Gallo-Roman origin, after a youth passed in royal surroundings, became count of Tournai, and then its bishop; only his accession to the episcopate (497–500) seems incontestable. As bishop of Tournai, probably its first, he is credited with the establishment there of an organic Christian community. Since the *vitae* of Eleutherius (the earliest was written toward the end of the ninth century) can be accepted only with the greatest reserve—if at all—the facts of his life are almost impossible to establish. Moreover, both the diocesan synod believed to have been summoned by him (520), and the writings attributed to him (*Patrologia Latina,* ed. J. P. Migne, 217 v. 65:69–82) are spurious.

Feast: Feb. 20.

Bibliography: *Vita s. Medardi, Monumenta Germaniae Auctores antiquissimi* (Berlin 1825–) 4.2:68. *Acta Sanctorum* Feb. 3:190–210. *Historia Tornacensis, Monumenta Germaniae Scriptores* (Berlin 1825–) 14:328–329, 356–357. *Bibliotheca hagiographica latina antiquae ct mediae aetatis* (Brussels 1898–1901) 1:2455–70. H. LECLERCQ, *Dictionnaire d'archéologie chrétienneet de liturgie,* ed. F. CABROL, H. LECLERCQ and H. I. MARROU (Paris 1907–1953) 15.2:2540–43. A. BUTLER, *The Lives of the Saints,* ed. H. THURSTON and D. ATTWATER (New York 1956) 1:381. A. D'HAENENS, *Dictionnaire d'histoire et de géographie ecclésiastiques* (Paris 1912–)15:150–153.

[G. M. COOK]

ELEVATION OF MAN

In the abstract, the elevation of man means God's gratuitous assigning to man of a sole supernatural destiny (the BEATIFIC VISION) together with the means necessary and suitable for the attainment of this end. In the concrete, it means the Father's plan for incorporating man, creature and sinner, into Christ the Savior. In epitome, it means the new Adam, Christ, head and members. From all eternity the Father has predestined us ''to become conformed to the image of his Son, that he should be the firstborn among many brethren'' (Rom 8.29).

Elevation in the First Adam

The Book of Genesis (2.4b–3.24) describes man's origin according to the Yahwistic tradition; the description is primitive, anthropomorphic (Yahweh is a potter working in clay) and contrasts with the later, stylized record of the priestly code preserved for us in Gn 1.1–2.4a (where God has merely to issue a command and things spring into being). Our concern is solely with man's elevation in our first parents. In picturesque and allegorical language, their elevation is depicted as a state of privilege destroyed by sin. Thus Adam is made outside the garden, in the desert, and then transported into Eden, where he lives on terms of familiarity and friendship with Yahweh (what later theology will call the state of grace), enjoying easy access to the tree of life. With Eve he goes about in unblushing nakedness. Sin enters and all is changed. Deprived of their privileges, Adam and Eve are driven out of the garden, back into the desert.

Reflecting on this inspired account, the Church has come to recognize in our first parents what it names the state of ORIGINAL JUSTICE, comprising gifts both SUPERNATURAL (deification) and PRETERNATURAL (immunity from CONCUPISCENCE and from bodily death). Taking their stand on Gn 3.16–19, Fathers of the Church (e.g., Augustine, Chrysostom) and theologians have commonly attributed to Adam a state of felicity exempt from bodily aches and woes, and enriched with the possession not only of the supernatural knowledge of FAITH but also of divinely infused natural knowledge proportioned to his privileged state, necessary for his self-guidance and for his position as founder of the human race (*see* KNOWLEDGE, INFUSED).

However, in crediting Adam with exceptional talents and virtuosities, sobriety is always to be commended. Modern thinkers incline to regard as otiose the elaborate ''might-have-been'' speculations of, say, F. Suárez (*De op. sex dierum* 5; Vivès ed., 3:380–447). The sacred writer was probably not at all trying to report on a particular geographical locality of idyllic amenities where our first parents spent some months of happiness; it may well be that he intended to make no statement either about an actual place or about a considerable sojourn in it. Perhaps his interest was centered exclusively in asserting a state or condition, so that his formal teaching might be condensed as follows: our first parents were invested with high privileges forfeited through their disobedience.

Moreover, an excessive lingering over Adam's situation before the Fall could betray a harmful misplacement of accent. An enlightened Christian does not cultivate a nostalgia for paradise, a sighing for a lost age of gold. He is not a pessimist lamenting Adam's sin as the irreparable primeval catastrophe that casts its melancholy shadow over the whole of subsequent history. Rather he will regard this first phase in man's elevation as radically orientated to the second; he will remember that Adam is no more than the type of Christ to come (τύπος τοῦ μέλλοντος: Rom 5.14).

Restoration in Christ

St. Leo the Great (d. 461) wrote: ''What fell in the first Adam, is raised up in the second'' (*Serm.* 12.1; *Patrologia Latina*, ed. J. P. Migne, 54:168). St. Paul three times compared Christ with Adam: 1 Cor 15.21–22; 44–49; Rom 5.12–21. The elevation of man lost by ORIGINAL SIN is restored by Christ. He, then, is the reconciler, the redeemer, and the renewer. The cumulative force of this trio of typical Pauline expressions means a return to a previously existing state of friendship, freedom, familiarity, or peace [see F. Zorell, *Lexikon Graecum NT* (Paris 1931) under ἀποκαταλλάσσω, καταλλάσσω, καταλλαγή, ἀπολύτρωσις, ἀνακαινόω, ἀνακαίνωσις, ἀνανεόω]. Hence there is some factor common to both elevations, essential to each. What is this common element? It is undoubtedly the state of GRACE or deification, comprising the twofold basic gift of indwelling Spirit (*see* INDWELLING, DIVINE) and created, habitual grace; then the infused theological and moral VIRTUES, together with the seven gifts of the Holy Ghost. Thus arises a divinized man, a sharer in the divine nature, an adoptive son of the heavenly Father, holy, capable of meriting, heir to the beatific vision. Such a precious complex of gifts, whether in the first or second elevation, can issue only from divine love—for the grace-life is nothing but the self-communication of the Triune God out of personal love. But there is a difference. If Adam's grace-life was, like ours, given in love (ἐν ἀγάπῃ: Eph 1.4), it was not given in *the beloved* (ἐν τῷ ἠγαπημένῳ: Eph 1.6), in Christ. If Adam had *gratia Dei,* he did not have *gratia Christi.* The measure of the difference between the first and second elevation is Christ. Restoration, then, means full incorporation into Christ through the Sacraments of Christian initiation (Baptism, Confirmation, and Eucharist) so that man, though stricken with the double unworthiness of creature and sinner, is nevertheless made a full member of the MYSTICAL BODY OF CHRIST. He enters into the Church with its divinely guaranteed teaching and governance of men, with its liturgy (above all, the Mass and the Sacraments). He treats as his own the Scriptures, the Mother of God, and the saints. The specific difference marking man's elevation in Christ can be summed up in the sacramental character—if this is correctly understood: in Adam man was elevated above all by grace; in Christ he is elevated by grace together with the distinct entity of the sacramental character [see *Heythrop Journal* 2 (1961) 318–33].

Relationship between Two Elevations

A triple task confronts us here: first, to explain a negative proposition; second, to explain a positive proposition; third, to assess some difficulties.

Not God's Master Plan. The elevation in Adam was not God's master plan.

First Reason. For this negative assertion, the first reason is based on the sovereignty of God. To identify man's elevation in Adam with God's master plan in the sense that Adam's sin wrecked it, as it were forcing God to concoct some fresh, second-best scheme, is to derogate from God's supremacy. It implies that the will of a creature can be the last and complete explanation of events, whereas in fact it can never wield more than a proximate, partial, and always an essentially subordinate control. Such is the unequivocal teaching of St. Paul. Commenting on God's predilection for Jacob over Esau, he affirms: ''for before the children had yet been born, or had done aught of good or evil, in order that the selective purpose of God might stand, depending not on deeds, but on him who calls, it was said to her [Rebecca], 'The elder shall serve the younger' . . . So then there is question not of him who wills nor of him who runs [τρέχοντος], but of God showing mercy'' (Rom 9.11–16).

Second Reason. That revelation proclaims Christ as the center of all (Col 3.11), the goal of God's eternal decrees, is the second reason for this negative assertion. Though second in the course of time, Christ takes precedence over Adam and all others, being the first-born both of every creature in general and of the dead in particular; all things were made through Him, directed toward Him (εἰς αὐτόν: Col 1.16), and established in Him, head of the Church, redeemer (Col 1.15–20), recapitulator (Eph 1.10).

Third Reason. One is forbidden, thirdly, to identify God's master plan with the elevation in Adam because this latter, while assuredly revealing God's love, does not equally manifest His mercy. Yet revelation lays stress on the manifestation of mercy as God's aim in creating. (A reflection of this appears, e.g., in the Collect, tenth Sunday after Pentecost: ''God, you make known your limitless might above all by sparing and showing pity . . . .'') If God wants to reveal His inmost being through mercy, He has to choose an order into which sin enters. Adam's sin, then, is woven into the pattern of God's plan. Together with the sins that follow, it forms the raw material, so to speak, on which God's mercy works. At the Easter Vigil, the Church pronounces Adam's guilt fortunate—it won for us such and so great a Redeemer: ''O felix culpa quae talem ac tantum meruit habere redemptorem.'' St. Irenaeus (d. *c.* 202) asserted boldly that since the Son of God preexisted from all eternity precisely as Savior, He needed sinners to save, otherwise His role of Savior would be futile: ''Cum enim praeexisteret salvans, oportebat et quod salvaretur fieri, uti non vacuum sit salvans'' (*Adversus haereses* 3.22.3; *Patrologia Graeca*, ed. J. P. Migne, 7:958). The implication, of course, is that the Father, because He predestined His Son precisely as Savior, deliberately chose a scheme in which there would be sinners. Such a notion may jolt any who forget that it is in fact only an echo of St. Paul: ''For God has shut up all in disobedience, that he may have mercy upon all'' (Rom 11.32; cf. Gal 3.22; Rom 3.9–19; 5.20). Further, St. Paul himself has a parallel in the suggestion of many passages from the Gospels: ''For the Son of Man came to seek and to save what was lost'' (Lk 19.10); ''For I have come to call sinners, not the just'' (Mt 9.13). Such words are commonly interpreted as expressions of Our Lord's kind and pitiful heart. They have, in fact, a deeper significance: they bear witness to God's eternal choice of the glorification of mercy as His goal in creating, to His selection of a fallen world as providing scope for His mercy. Christ's characteristic consorting with sinners, so scandalous to the Pharisees, was a visible symbol of His Father's eternal selection of such a world where sin, freely committed by men, abounds in order that redemptive grace might superabound (cf. Rom 5.12–21). The return of the prodigal son is celebrated to the chagrin of the elder, irreproachable brother (Lk 15.25–32)—a predilection that the liturgy (Saturday after second Sunday of Lent) tellingly parallels with the preference shown to Jacob over Esau (Gn 27.6–40). Adam's sin, like Rebecca's trickery, can provoke only divine reprobation—yet both throw open the doors to the Almighty's selective purpose, that mystery of SALVATION kept hidden from the beginning of time in the all-creating mind of God (cf. Eph 3.9).

Thus the elevation in Adam, far from being God's master plan, is not even on a footing of equality and coordination with the later phase. It can claim only a priority of time; its very *raison d'être* and intelligibility depend on the restoration in Christ that it, as a subsidiary and preparatory episode, ushers in.

Superiority of Restoration in Christ. The restoration in Christ enjoys positive superiority over the original elevation in Adam.

St. Paul and the Fathers. This is the emphatic teaching of Rom 5.12–21, where the work of Adam and of

Christ are sharply contrasted. According to Paul, Christ did not merely undo the harm spread by Adam's sin; He goes far beyond readjusting the balance; He endows us with much more than was forfeited in Adam [see Rom 5.15: ". . . much more has the grace of God . . . abounded unto the many (πολλῷ μᾶλλον . . . ἐπερίσσευσεν)"; 20: "grace has abounded yet more (ὑπερεπερίσσευσεν)"]. St. John Chrysostom (d. 407) thus urges Paul's thought: "Christ did not only profit us in the measure in which Adam harmed us, but much more and better (ἀλλὰ καὶ πολλῷ πλεῖον καὶ μεῖζον)" (*In ep. ad Rom. hom.* 10.2; *Patrologia Graeca* 60:476). And again: ". . .Paul did not say grace abounded but superabounded . . . it is as though one did not simply rid a man of his fever but made him handsome, robust and honored; or as though one did not merely feed a hungry man but made him master of much money and constituted him a high-ranking administrator" (*ibid.* 10.3; *Patrologia Graeca* 60:478–79). St. Paul's affirmation of the superiority of our elevation in Christ is caught up and repeated again and again by the writers both of antiquity and of more recent centuries. To mention a few: St. Ambrose [*De instit. virg.* 17.104; *De Jac. et vita beata* 1.6.21; *Ennarr. in ps. 39,* 20 ("Felix ruina, quae reparatur in melius.")], St. Cyril of Alexandria [see H. du Maunoir, *Dogme et spiritualité chez s. Cyrille d'Aléxandrie* (Paris 1944) 175–78, 293–97], St. Leo the Great, and St. Bernard. St. Francis de Sales may be taken as the spokesman of this massive tradition: "Our loss has been to our profit, since in fact mankind has received from its Savior more grace through the Redemption than it would ever have received through the innocence of Adam, had he persevered in this" [*Traité de l'amour de Dieu* (Annecy 1894) 2.5].

Liturgy. Likewise bearing witness to the primacy of the restoration in Christ is the liturgy. At the Offertory of the Mass, mingling water with wine, the priest recites an ancient prayer whose drift is not invariably correctly seized. A comparison is drawn between the wonderful dignity of the first creation and the still more wonderful restoration: *mirabilius reformasti.* It is beyond cavil that in the language of the early Church the dignity of man's creation meant Adam's being equipped with his supernatural and preternatural gifts. In the decrees of the early councils, in patristic literature, in the classical texts of the liturgy man is considered not philosophically or as a rational animal, but historically, i.e., as endowed with God's love in Adam, or as under his curse through original sin. At the Easter Vigil, the prayer concluding the first prophecy expresses exactly the same idea as this Offertory prayer.

Assessment of Difficulties. A number of theological problems arise when one has such an understanding of man's restoration as is outlined above.

God, Author of Sin? If, in order to display mercy, God chooses a world in which sin destroys the elevation in Adam, is not God the author of sin? The answer is negative. God does not cause sin, but He does permit it as consequent upon the free play of man's will. Always and everywhere God seeks the positive good that is Christ and the imitation of Christ; He permits sin only in that perspective. Never could God, without gainsaying His very being, choose sin for its own sake. Man, on the contrary, can will moral evil—the sole thing he can create because it is pure destruction. It might be added that God's foreknowledge of sin does not undermine man's freedom, which God always respects. What violates freedom is an inward constraint on the will. The fact that an event, foreknown by God, inevitably must happen implies a necessity extrinsic, not intrinsic, to the will.

Evils Consequent on Sin. But did not Adam's sin unleash the pack of trials, sorrows, and evils that still affect men? How, then, can the restoration in Christ be anything more than a poor substitute, at best enabling us to save something from all that was lost? Again, even if God, in pardoning the sinner, shows greater liberality and love, is not the very need of mercy sheer loss? Surely it is better not to need, than to need, mercy? Lastly, is not the forgiven sinner, disfigured with the scar of his sin, less resplendent than Adam arrayed in original justice?

To such questions it may be replied that God's pardon is creative. It is not simply a declaration that all is forgiven and forgotten, leaving the sinner inwardly the same. Like the command at the beginning of time that caused the world to exist, God's decree of remission effects an inward change, a regeneration, a miraculous transformation, as St. Paul plainly assures us: "If then any man is in Christ, there is a new creation; the old things have disappeared; something new is there" (2 Cor 5.17). "For his workmanship we are, created in Christ Jesus. . ." (Eph 2.10). Perhaps one should rethink the seemingly paradoxical words of Our Lord: ". . . there will be joy in heaven over one sinner who repents, more than over 99 just who have no need of repentance" (Lk 15.7). In cold reality, how can there be more joy (whether in heaven or on earth) after sin than before it? Is this text to be dismissed as divine hyperbole and rhetoric? Possibly the solution lies in the creativeness of divine forgiveness. Because the miraculous transformation wrought by the Father's mercy in Christ positively transcends in value an innocence never lost, therefore the joy over the conversion of even a solitary sinner eclipses the joy over innocence persevered in. To be quite concrete: a converted sinner (like Paul, Augustine) who, with the utmost generosity, is incorporated into Christ outshines the angels who never sinned; for he is in *Christ Jesus;* they are not. For lovers of God, all things (therefore even sin, as SS. Augustine and Thomas Aquinas expressly maintain in their writings) work together for good (Rom 8.28).

Loss of Preternatural Gifts. Even after the Redemption, concupiscence and death, with their attendant drawbacks, tragedies, and even horrors, reign in the world: surely Adam, equipped with integrity and immortality was much better off.

One way of replying to such a statement is to emphasize that the man incorporated into Christ has incomparably more precious gifts—e.g., the Sacraments. No preternatural gift can do what every Sacrament does—to wit, give, *ex opere operato*, not only a new bond with the Mystical Body but also grace. Penance and the Eucharist in particular, when fittingly and frequently received, aid a man continuously to approach more and more that self-mastery given by integrity; simultaneously, of course, they advance his holiness, his capacity for meriting, and the apostolic worth of his life. Finally, they are his warrant for the eventual resurrection of his flesh.

Furthermore, the trials, sufferings, sorrows, humiliations, weariness, and temptations associated with concupiscence and death take on for the man reborn in Christ a new sense and value. First, they can be used as honorable amends for his own shortcomings and sins; second, properly handled, they can very effectively promote his own holiness; third (and this is the capital consideration here), they have a crusading quality. It was through suffering and death that Christ redeemed the world. He seeks the cooperation of Christians in this supreme work. He invites them to make up in their own flesh what is wanting in His sufferings for the sake of His Body, the Church (Col 1.24). Thus Christ invests the hardships of life with a dynamic and apostolic purpose. Under Him, inspired by His example, in solidarity with Him, Christians are to be cooperators in the salvation of their fellowmen. The means above all to be used, those of Christ Himself, are to the hand of every mortal man—self-denial, suffering, and even death. Christians must accept these not in a spirit of grim stoicism and fatalistic resignation; rather they must welcome them with apostolic joy (''I rejoice now in the sufferings. . .'' Col 1.24; cf. Acts 5.41). They may even go so far as St. Paul—boasting of their frailty, need, and weakness, so that the strength of Christ can rest upon them and be thrown into relief: ''For when I am weak, then I am strong'' (2 Cor 12.10); ''I know whom I have believed'' (2 Tim 1.12); ''I can do all things in him who strengthens me'' (Phil 4.13). They will draw consolation from the thought that Christ has pronounced blessed those who suffer for love of Him (Mt 5.1–12).

Sin and Mercy. If the manifestation of divine mercy is so great a good, then the more of it the better. Hence, ought not a man sin with abandon so as to afford God wider scope for mercy? St. Paul has anticipated this objection; he asks (Rom 6.1) whether it follows that we ought to go on sinning, to give still more occasion for grace. And he answers: ''By no means! For how shall we who are dead to sin still live in it?'' (Rom 6.2; note also the following verses.) Our faith, which prompts us to regard Adam's sin as fortunate for us, likewise teaches us that sin is the chief evil, that the end does not justify the means (cf. Rom 3.8) and that the whole posterity of Adam needs Redemption. In harmony with our faith, St. Thérèse of Lisieux asserted that in preserving her from mortal sin God showed greater love and mercy than in liberating Magdalen from many mortal sins. In an absolutely peerless way, God displayed love and mercy toward His Blessed Mother: all others are at best liberated from sinfulness; she alone was preserved from it in whatever form, being redeemed most eminently. As a daughter of Adam, born into the human race through the normal processes of generation, she ought to have had sin. In fact, by a singular privilege of redemptive grace, she was kept utterly innocent. But while the innocence neither of Adam before the Fall nor of the loyal angels came from the Redemption in Christ, hers did. More closely united to Christ than any other creature, full of grace and therefore (redemptive grace is dynamic and apostolic) the special consort of the Redeemer in the salvation of others, paragon of the redeemed, Mary gives perfect expression to the surpassing excellence of the restoration in Christ.

See Also: FRIENDSHIP WITH GOD; GRACE, ARTICLES ON; GRACE AND NATURE; HOLY SPIRIT, GIFTS OF; INCORPORATION IN CHRIST; JESUS CHRIST (IN THEOLOGY) 3 (SPECIAL QUESTIONS), 12. PRIMACY; JUSTIFICATION; MAN 3; OBEDIENTIAL POTENCY; REBIRTH (IN THE BIBLE); RECAPITULATION IN CHRIST; REDEMPTION; BEATIFIC VISION; DESTINY, SUPERNATURAL.

Bibliography: J. SCHILDENBERGER, *Lexikon für Theologie und Kirche*, ed. J. HOFER and K. RAHNER, 10 v. (2d, new ed. Freiburg 1957–65) 1:127–30. J. CHAINE, *Catholicisme. Hier, aujourd'hui et demain,* ed. G. JACQUEMET (Paris 1947–) 1:127–29. L. VAGANAY, *ibid.* 1:129. THOMAS AQUINAS, *Summa theologiae* 1a, 94–102; 1a2ae, 85.2. C. BOYER, *Tractatus de Deo creante et elevante* (5th ed. Rome 1957). P. GALTIER, *Les Deux Adam* (Paris 1947). F. PRAT, *The Theology of St. Paul,* tr. J. L. STODDARD, 2 v. (Westminster, Md. 1958) v.2. J. F. SAGÜÉS, *Sacrae theologiae summa*, ed. FATHERS OF THE SOCIETY OF JESUS, PROFESSORS OF THE THEOLOGICAL FACILITIES IN SPAIN, v.2 (3d ed. 1958) 2.2:675–812. M. FLICK, ''Il dogma del peccato originale nella teologia contemporanea,'' in *Problemi e orientamenti di teologia dommatica* v.2 (Milan 1957) 89–122. R. CARPENTER, ''Mirabilius reformasti,'' *Nouvelle revue théologique* 61 (1934) 338–49. A. VITTI, ''Christus-Adam,'' *Biblica* 7 (1926) 121–45, 270–85, 384–401.

[J. P. KENNY]

ELFLEDA, ST.

Abbess of Whitby; b. 653; d. Feb. 8, 714. A daughter of Oswy, king of Northumbria, and of St. Eanfled, and the sister of three kings and two queens, Elfleda (or Aelbfled in Bede, Ethelfleda, Edilfleda, Elgiva, Æflaed) was a woman of great sanctity and influence. In fulfillment of a vow following his defeat of King Penda of Mercia, Oswy consecrated his year-old daughter Elfleda to a life of virginity at the abbey of (St.) HILDA, then at Hartlepool. Two years later Hilda purchased land at WHITBY, where she erected her famous double MONASTERY. Elfleda was reared and educated at Whitby; at the death of Hilda (680), she and her mother ruled the monastery.

Elfleda was a friend of the great Northumbrian saints CUTHBERT OF LINDISFARNE, WILFRID OF YORK, and JOHN OF BEVERLEY. John sought her counsel several times, on one occasion spending several days at Whitby. Wilfrid became a ward of King Oswy when he was 13, and it was Queen Eanfled who sent him to study at LINDISFARNE and then to Rome. Because of her great admiration for Cuthbert, Elfleda opposed Wilfrid and his Roman rites. However, when her father declared for the Roman rites and Cuthbert accepted the judgment of the Council of Whitby (664), the difference between Cuthbert and Wilfrid was settled, and throughout the latter part of Wilfrid's stormy life Elfleda became his advocate. It was largely because of her testimony after the death of her brother, King Aldfrith, who repented his treatment of Wilfrid, that as late as 703 he was able to retain his archbishopric of York. Elfleda kept in close touch with Cuthbert throughout her life, even after he retired to FARNE. In 684, at the request of her brother, King Ecgfrith, she met Cuthbert on Coquet Island to try to persuade him to accept the bishopric at Hexham. Elfleda was buried at Whitby, as were her father, mother, and grandfather, St. EDWIN OF NORTHUMBRIA.

Feast: Feb. 8.

There are two other saints of this name: (1) an Anglo-Saxon princess (d. *c.* 936) who became hermit under the obedience of Glastonbury Abbey and was venerated by St. DUNSTAN (feast: Oct. 23); and (2) an abbess at Ramsey Abbey (d. *c.* 1000; feast: Oct. 29).

Bibliography: BEDE, *Ecclesiatical history* 3.24; 4.26. *Acta Sanctorum* Feb. 2:177–186. B. COLGRAVE, ed. and tr., *Two Lives of Saint Cuthbert* (Cambridge, Eng. 1940). A. BUTLER, *The Lives of the Saints,* ed. H. THURSTON and D. ATTWATER (New York 1956) 1:278–279.

[M. E. COLLINS]

Sir Edward Elgar. (The Library of Congress)

ELGAR, EDWARD, SIR

Distinguished Catholic composer; b. Broadheath, near Worcester, England, June 2, 1857; d. Worcester, Feb. 23, 1934. He received most of his musical training from his father, organist at St. George's Catholic Church in Worcester, but was self-taught in composition. After producing several cantatas and orchestral pieces, he emerged as a major musical figure with the ''Enigma'' variations (1899) and *The Dream of Gerontius* (1900), an oratorio setting of Cardinal J. H. NEWMAN's poem. Like *Gerontius,* his Biblical oratorios *The Apostles* (1903) and *The Kingdom* (1906) are affirmations of a deep religious faith in an age of skepticism. They contain many striking passages characterized by excellent vocal and instrumental scoring, richly imaginative (if traditional) harmonies, and magnificent texts, and they are especially effective in depicting states of contemplative tranquility. Like his other extended works, they are criticized mainly for excessive length. His liturgical music consists of a few early motets written for the Worcester church, where he succeeded his father as organist in 1885. Besides the ''Enigma'' variations, his best-known orchestral works are the distinctively English ''Pomp and Circumstance'' marches and the Violin Concerto. He was knighted in 1904, received the Order of Merit in 1911, and was awarded honorary degrees by several English and American universities.

Bibliography: D. MCVEAGH, *Edward Elgar: His Life and Music* (London 1955). P. M. YOUNG, *Elgar, O.M.: A Study of a Musician* (London 1955). D. E. TOVEY et al., *Music and Letters* (London 1920–) 16.1 (Jan. 1935) 1–39, a memorial issue. N. SLONIMSKY, ed., *Baker's Biographical Dictionary of Musicians* (5th ed. New York 1958) 430–432. H. C. COLES, *Grove's Dictionary of Music and Musicians,* ed. E. BLOM, 9 v. (5th ed. London 1954) 2:909–928. B. ADAMS, ''The 'Dark Saying' of the Enigma: Homoeroticism and the Elgarian Paradox,'' *19th-Century Music,* 23 (2000) 218–235. S. LINDLEY, ''This Is the Best of Me . . . ,'' *Organ,* 79 (2000) 136–138. C. E. MCGUIRE, ''Elgar, Judas, and the Theology of Betrayal,'' *19th-Century Music,* 23 (2000) 236–272. B. NEWBOULD, '''Never Done Before': Elgar's Other Enigma,'' *Music and Letters,* 77 (1996) 228–241. A. PAYNE, ''Being Elgar,'' *Tempo,* 204 (1998) 2–3; *Elgar's Third Symphony: The Story of the Reconstruction* (London 1998). A. P. SIMCO, ''Interpreting Elgar's *Enigma Variations,*'' *Percussive Notes: The Journal of the Percussive Arts Society,* 37/1 (1999) 46–48. P. M. YOUNG, *Elgar, Newman, and 'The Dream of Gerontius': In the Tradition of English Catholicism* (Aldershot, Eng. 1995).

[R. M. LONGYEAR]

ELGUERO, FRANCISCO

Mexican lawyer and literary figure; b. Morelia, Michoacán, Mexico, March 14, 1856; d. there, Dec. 17, 1932. He was noted in his legal profession for his devotion to law and justice. Elguero was well read in contemporary thought, especially in philosophy, literary criticism, and the sacred sciences. As a writer on both legal and general topics, he was a staunch defender of the Catholic faith. Above all he was an apologist, as a lecturer, journalist, and author. Elguero linked the defense of Catholicism with the defense of Spanish civilization and held that the purity of the Castilian language was of primary importance because it was the means of transmitting that civilization. He based his opposition to the anti-Catholic laws and institutions of the persecution on a thorough knowledge of Mexican history and published accounts of the arbitrary acts of the various liberal governments Mexico had had. When the revolution of Carranza was successful, Elguero lived in exile in Cuba, where he wrote a series of apologetic articles for *El Diario de la Marina.* On his return to Mexico City, he founded the review *América española,* which stressed Spain's greatness and the Spanish character of Mexican civilization in law, theology, philosophy, and literature. He was a delegate and one of the leaders of the Catholic group in the Madero legislature. A prolific writer, he cultivated all genres—essay, novel, poetry, and oratory. Among his books were *La inmaculada* (Mexico City 1905), *Senilias poéticas* (Havana 1920), *Comentarios a pensamientos religiosos de Luis Veillot* (Mexico City 1924), and *Museo intelectual* (2 v. Mexico City 1930). He also left many unpublished writings. Elguero was a corresponding member of the Academia Mexicana.

[J. GUISA Y AZEVEDO]

ELIADE, MIRCEA

Historian of religion, man of letters; b. Bucharest, March 9, 1907; d. Chicago, April 22,1986. Upon completing the M.A. at the University of Bucharest in 1928 on Italian philosophy, Eliade went to India and studied Sanskrit and Indian thought with the prominent historian of Indian philosophy Surendranath Dasgupta. In 1931 he spent several months in a hermitage in the foothills of the Himalayan mountains. He was awarded the Ph.D. by the University of Bucharest in 1933, where he began his teaching career. He served as cultural attaché for Romania in London and Lisbon during World War II. Following the war he took up residence in Paris and lectured at the Sorbonne and other European universities. In 1957 the University of Chicago appointed him to a faculty position. He founded the journal *History of Religion* and was awarded the Sewell L. Avery Distinguished Service Professorship the following year. His appointment marked the beginning of the so-called Chicago school of the history of religions.

Among the leading historians of religions in the 20th century, he specialized in the study of yoga, shamanism and the myths and rituals of primal societies. Eliade's primary interest was symbolism and its expression through the interplay of myth and ritual. The main sources for his writings are the religious texts of India and the social sciences, especially anthropology, with its rich collection of myths and rituals of preliterate societies. His early research work formed the basis for a series of monographs published in the 1950s and 1960s: *Yoga, Immortality and Freedom* (Fr. 1954, Eng. 1958), based on his doctoral dissertation and revised over two decades, may well be the primary source of his major religious insights; *Patterns in Comparative Religion* (Fr. 1949, Eng. 1958) is his most comprehensive statement on the nature of religious symbol; *Shamanism: Archaic Techniques of Ecstasy* (Fr. 1951, Eng. 1964) reflects his lifelong interest in mysticism and the occult.

The fundamental polarity between the sacred and the profane provided a framework for Eliade's thought. For Eliade religious symbol is studied as a hierophany, i.e., as a manifestation of the sacred. In his scheme of things, a hierophany reveals something other than itself; it is an historical manifestation that may be cosmic, biological, physical or psychological; it is relational insofar as it relates one both to something other than the hierophany and to something other than oneself. Hierophanies are identified by their relational function, which brings the experiencer to a new order of reality, truth, and being—an experience which is not conditioned by ordinary time, space, and existence. Hierophanies make sacred the universe; rituals make sacred or consecrate life (birth, puberty, marriage, death); and myths make sacred the experience of time and space. Eliade maintained that *homo religiosus* seeks that which is beyond ordinary experience and meaning: sacred life and existence, sacred time and space, a sacred universe. Myths transmit from the beginning, *ab origine*, the archetypes or exemplary models which are paradigmatic in religious experience. Ritual imitation and ritual repetition of these archetypes recreate and reactualize a sacred world.

A series of articles on the primal cults and myths of Australia was his major concern in the 1960s. Other important works included *The Quest: History and Meaning in Religion* (1969); *Two Tales of the Occult* (1970); *Zalmoxis, The Vanishing God: Comparative Studies in the Religions and Folklore of Dacia and Eastern Europe* (1972); *Australian Religion: An Introduction* (1973); *Occultism, Witchcraft, and Cultural Fashion: Essays in Comparative Religion* (1976); *No Souvenirs: Journal* (1959–1969); *The Forbidden Forest* (1978); *Journey East, Journey West: 1907–1937* (1981); and *Symbolism, the Sacred, and the Arts* (1985). In the final decade of his life he wrote the three volume *A History of Religious Ideas* (1978, 1981, 1985), an attempt to place his phenomenological work into an historical context, and served as editor in chief of the *Encyclopedia of Religion* (1985), to which he contributed several entries. As a man of letters he wrote numerous essays, novels, short stories, several volumes of autobiography, and edited compilations of classical texts.

Eliade affirmed the history of religions as an autonomous discipline and envisioned its task as that of integration, synthesis, and creativity. He spoke of a creative hermeneutic, not merely as an academic discipline, but as a spiritual discipline in which cultural development is a distinct goal. Recognized as an early phenomenologist or structuralist, methodologically speaking, Eliade was criticized for ahistorical tendencies.

Bibliography: D. ALLEN and D. DOEING, *Mircea Eliade: An Annotated Bibliography 1919–1978* (New York and London 1980).

[W. CENKNER]

ELIAS, PATRIARCH OF JERUSALEM, ST.

Theological controversialist; b. 430; d. 518. Elias, an Arab by birth, was an anchorite in Egypt who fled to Palestine before the Monophysite persecution of TIMOTHY AELURUS, the Patriarch of Alexandria, and was received by Euthymius in his Laura of Sahel. He was appointed patriarch of Jerusalem in 494. He suffered much for his adherence to the Council of CHALCEDON. Refusing to communicate with the Monophysite patriarchs of Antioch and Alexandria, he entered into communion with the Constantinopolitan patriarchs Euphemius (490–496) and Macedonius (496–511) but not with Rome as the ACACIAN schism was still in effect. Elias submitted a profession of faith to Emperor ANASTASIUS I (*c.* 509), and when the emperor interpreted it as an anathema against those who professed the two natures in Christ, Elias protested against this false interpretation and sent another profession based on Chalcedon. At the Synod of Sidon in 511 he was summoned to condemn the doctrine of Chalcedon; but Elias won the majority of the bishops to his side and sent a delegation under (St.) Sabas of Constantinople to defend his position in Jerusalem. Upon the deposition of (St.) Flavian, patriarch of Antioch, for his part in the Synod of Sidon, Sabas successfully defended Elias. When SEVERUS OF ANTIOCH (511–518), the Monophysite usurper, condemned the *Tome* of Pope LEO I and summoned a synod at Tyre to favor his position, Elias broke communion with him and refused to attend the synod. Emperor Anastasius I sent a force under Olympius, governor of Palestine, who ordered Elias to either sign a Monophysite formula or be exiled. When he refused to sign, Elias was exiled to Aila in 516.

Feast: July 20 (Roman Martyrology with St. Flavian); Feb. 18 (Syriac Church).

Bibliography: V. GRUMEL, *Bibliotheca Sanctorum* (Rome 1961) 4:1054–57. *Patrologia Graeca,* ed. J. P. MIGNE (Paris 1857–66) 147:163–174. *Acta Sanctorum* July 2:28–32. J. J. DELANEY and J. E. TOBIN, *Dictionary of Catholic Biography* (New York 1961) 370. E. HONIGMANN, *Évêques et évêches monophysites* (*Corpus scriptorum Christianorum orientalium* 127; 1951). R. JANIN, *Dictionnaire d'histoire et de géographie ecclésiastiques* (Paris 1912–) 15:189–190.

[F. DE SA]

ELIAS BAR SHINĀYĀ

Nestorian metropolitan and one of the most important writers of his age; b. Nisibis (modern Nusaybin in southeastern Turkey, just across the border from Kameshli in Syria), Feb. 11, 975; d. there, shortly after 1049. In his youth he became a monk in the monastery of Michael at Mosul and later in that of Shem'ôn near the Tigris. He was ordained in 994, named bishop of Beit-Nûhadra in 1002, and chosen metropolitan of Nisibis in 1088. His writings belong not only to Syriac literature but also to Arabic Christian literature, since he wrote in both languages. In Syriac he composed certain treatises on canon and civil law, a Syriac grammar, which, in its day, enjoyed great popularity, and various hymns and metrical homilies. In Arabic he wrote the *Book on the Proof of the Truth of the Faith,* a dogmatic treatise written from the viewpoint of Nestorian doctrine, and the *Book on the Removal of Suffering,* teaching the way to acquire interior peace, as well as certain other dissertations. Probably his best-known work, however, is his great *Chronography,* a genuine history of the Church from A.D. 25 to 1018, written both in Arabic and in Syriac; it is valuable especially because it mentions the sources, now mostly lost, from which its author drew his historical material. Another important work of his is the *Book of the Translator,* an Arabic-Syriac dictionary, which is still useful to modern lexicographers. From Elias bar Shināyā are also several pastoral letters, some written in Syriac and some in Arabic, to the clergy and people of Baghdad.

Bibliography: E. BAR SHINAYA, *Des Metropoliten Elias von Nisibis Buch vom Beweis der Wahrheit des Glaubens,* tr. L. HORST (Colmar 1886). R. DUVAL, *La Littérature syriaque* (Anciennes littératures chrétiennes 2; 3d ed. Paris 1907) 395. A. BAUMSTARK, *Geschichte der syrischen literatur* (Bonn 1922) 287–288. E. DELLY, *La Théologie d'Elie bar-Sénaya* (Rome 1957). P. KRÜGER, *Lexikon für Theologie und Kirche* (Freiburg 1957–65) 3:811. F. NAU, *Dictionnaire de théologie catholique* 4.2:2330–31.

[J. M. SOLA-SOLE]

ELIAS EKDIKOS

Twelfth-century Greek theologian frequently confused with Elias, the Metropolitan of Crete, author of scholia on the Homilies of Gregory Nazianzus and John Climacus, and with Elias of Charan. He is probably identical with the hymn writer Elias the monk. Elias Ekdikos is noted for a florilegium, or ascetic collection, called the *Didactic Anthologion,* written under the influence of the great theologian Simon the Younger (11th and 12th centuries). Elias presents a fully developed Byzantine doctrine of the striving of man toward the attainment of perfection. Employing as a metaphor the exodus of the Hebrews from Egypt, he postulates three steps leading toward this achievement: the exodus of the Hebrew people from Egypt as the cleansing of the body; the crossing of the Red Sea as the cleansing of the soul; and the crossing of the desert as the final purification of the spirit, through which man finds perfection in the promised land. Elias wrote also spiritual poetry of which one canon has been published.

Bibliography: *Patrologia Graeca* 90:1401–61; 127:1127–76. K. BAUS, *Lexikon für Theologie und Kirche* [2] 3:812. H. G. BECK, *Kirche und theologische Literatur im byzantinischen Reich,* 588. V. GRUMEL, *Catholicisme* 4:16. M. DISDIER, *Échos d'Orient* 31 (1932) 17–43, 144–164.

[G. LUZNYCKY]

ELIAS OF CORTONA

Franciscan minister general (1221–27 and 1232–39); b. probably at Bivigliano, near Assisi, date unknown; d. Cortona, April 22, 1253. Elias was a notary at Bologna and was among the early companions of Francis; he was received into the Order at Cortona in 1211.

After the first missionary chapter of the brothers in 1217, Elias was chosen to serve as provincial minister for the new venture in the Holy Land. Later, during his own 1219–1220 visit to the East, Francis met Elias and brought him back to Italy. In 1221, after the death of his first vicar, Francis appointed Elias. Elias presided at the famous Chapter of Mats in 1221 and from there he sent a band of brothers under the leadership of Caesar of Spyer on the Order's mission to Germany. From this same chapter he sent Anthony of Padua to Bologna to teach theology. After Francis's death, the Pentecost Chapter of 1227 elected John Parenti, Minister from Spain, to succeed Elias. Pope Gregory IX then enlisted Elias's organizational and architectural skills to oversee the construction of a new basilica in Assisi to honor and celebrate the memory of Francis.

At the 1232 chapter in Rieti, Elias was again elected minister general, succeeding his earlier successor, John Parenti. During this second tenure in office, Elias promoted theological studies in multiple centers throughout Europe, particularly Paris and Oxford, and he furthered missionary expansion into northern and eastern Europe, Asia and Africa. During these years, as the number of brothers increased toward 40,000 and became a powerful force, he completed the building of the basilica. Giving new impulse to developments in Italian art and architecture, he was respected throughout Europe. He won the confidence of Clare of Assisi who, in 1235, wrote to her sister Agnes concerning Elias: ''Follow the counsel of our venerable father, our Brother Elias, the Minister General, that you may walk more securely in the way of the commands of the Lord. Prize it beyond the advice of the others and cherish it as dearer to you than any gift.''

Around 1237, complaints about Elias's leadership began to surface. Because he did not make personal visits throughout the provinces, but sent other brothers as visitators (visitators who were not priests), irritation increased. His refusal to call general chapters every three years as required by the Rule and his demand for funds to finish the basilica increased the opposition. At the general chapter in Rome of 1239, called by Gregory IX, the increasing clerical majority rejected Elias's strong centralized governance and won the day. Elias was deposed. The first priest to hold the office of general minister, Albert of Pisa, succeeded him. Elias returned to Assisi to find himself also deprived of his role as Custos of the Basilica of St. Francis and of the Sacred Convent. He then fled to Pisa to the imperial camp of Emperor Frederick II who was in a struggle with the pope for control of northern parts of Italy. Elias thereby fell under the general excommunication issued by Gregory IX on all those who approached the emperor. This caused great scandal and many brothers considered him an apostate from the Order. Elias died reconciled in the Franciscan friary in Cortona where his remains rest today.

Bibliography: R. B. BROOKE, *Early Franciscan Government: Elias to Bonaventure* (Cambridge, Eng. 1959). P. DALLARI, *Frate Elia, architetto della Basilica d'Assisi e di Cortona* (Milan 1970). T. ECCLESTON, "The Coming of the Friars Minor to England" trans. P. Hermann, in *XIIIth Century Chronicles* (Chicago 1961), 79–191. A. FORTINI, *Francis of Assisi,* tr. H. MOAK (New York 1981). JORDAN OF GIANO, "The Chronicle of Brother Jordan of Giano" tr. P. HERMANN, in *XIIIth Century Chronicles* (Chicago 1961), 17–77. SALIMBENE, *The Chronicle of Salimbene de Adam,* ed. J. L. BAIRD, G. BAGLIVI, and J. KANE (Binghamton, N.Y. 1986).

[J. A. HELLMANN]

ELIAS OF REGGIO, ST.

Known also as Spelaiotes (cave-dweller); b. Reggio di Calabria, Italy, *c.* 865; d. Melicuccà in Calabria, Sept. 11 *c.* 960. At the age of 19 he became a monk, living briefly as a hermit near Rome, then with a companion, Arsenios, at Armo, south of Reggio. Both then spent eight years in a hermitage near Patras. Elias returned to enter the monastery of Saline in Calabria (*see* ELIAS OF THESSALONIKA), but soon settled as a hermit in a cave near Melicuccà, where a group of disciples gathered about him.

Feast: Sept. 11.

Bibliography: *Acta Sanctorum* Sept. 3:848–887. G. MINASI, *Lo Speleota, ovvero S. Elia di Reggio di Calabria, monaco basiliano nel IX. e X. secolo* (Naples 1893). S. BORSARI, *Il monachesimo bizantino nella Sicilia e nell'Italia Meridionale prenormanne* (Naples 1963).

[G. T. DENNIS]

ELIAS OF THESSALONIKA, ST.

Sicilian monk and pilgrim; b. Enna, Sicily, 823; d. Thessalonika, Aug. 17, 903. Elias, baptized John, fled with his family before the Saracen invasion of Sicily (831), but he was taken prisoner (838) and sold into slavery in Africa. On being redeemed, he undertook a pilgrimage to the East and in Jerusalem changed his name to Elias in honor of the Patriarch ELIAS OF JERUSALEM. He visited Alexandria, Antioch, and parts of Persia. On his return to Palermo, he found his mother still living. He established the monastery of Salianae or Aulianae on the west coast of Calabria. Later he set out on another pilgrimage, and visited Sparta and Epirus; later he journeyed to Rome, where he was received by Pope STEPHEN VI. Called to the Byzantine court, he died en route at Thessalonika. His body was returned to the monastery of Salianae, where his cult began almost immediately. His vita is one of the earliest pieces of 10th-century Sicilian hagiography. He is to be distinguished from Elias Spelaiotes (d. 960), a contemporary monk and hermit from Reggio, Calabria, also the subject of a vita (*Acta Sanctorum* Sept. 3:843–888).

Feast: Aug. 17.

Bibliography: *Acta Sanctorum* Aug. 3:479–509. *Bibliotheca hagiographica Graeca,* ed. F. HALKIN, (Brussels 1957) 580. G. MARSOT, *Catholicisme* 4:16. A. BASILE, *Archivio storico della Calabria* 14 (1945) 19–36.

[F. CHIOVARO]

ELIGIUS OF NOYON, ST.

Bishop of Noyon; b. Chaptelat near Limoges, France, *c.* 588; d. Noyon, 660. Apprenticed as a goldsmith, Eligius (or Éloi) entered the service of Kings Chlotar II (d. 629) and Dagobert I (d. 639) as an official of the royal treasury at Paris; his name appears on the third-of-a-sou piece for the period. In 636–637 he was employed on an embassy to Brittany; then in 641 he became bishop of Noyon. He founded the monastery of SOLIGNAC, another house in Noyon where St. Godeberta (d. *c.* 700) was the first abbess, and also an abbey in Paris. He was buried in the cathedral at Noyon. His great friend, St. OUEN OF ROUEN, wrote the first account of his life, parts of which are perhaps incorporated in the existing vita. His cult existed in the eighth century, and he was adopted as the patron saint of metal workers, finding great popularity in the 13th century. His work as a goldsmith is greatly praised by his biographer and seems to have been widely available, but little of it can be identified with certainty today.

Feast: Dec. 1.

Bibliography: *Acta Sanctorum* Jan. 1:154–155; Oct. 13:740–741. *Vita, Monumenta Germaniae Scriptores rerum Merovingicarum* (Berlin 1825–) 4:634–742. Sermons, *ibid.,* 751–761. P. MOREL, *Étude critique de la vie de S. Éloi* (unpublished dissertation Paris 1930) 129–133. J. DUQUESNE, *Saint Eloi* (Paris

Print depicting Elijah carried to heaven in a fiery chariot as Elisha watches, 17th century, Jordan. (©Historical Picture Archive/ CORBIS)

1985). A. BUTLER, *The Lives of the Saints*, ed. H. THURSTON and D. ATTWATER (New York 1956) 4:455–458. É. BROUETTE, *Dictionnaire d'histoire et de géographie ecclésiastiques* (Paris 1912–) 15:260–263.

[V. I. J. FLINT]

ELIJAH

A Prophet from Thisbe (Tishbe) in Galaad, the great champion of the religion of Yahweh during the reign of King Ahab (*c.* 869—*c.* 850) of Israel and his wife Jezebel and that of their son (Ahaziah *c.* 850—*c.* 849). The whole career of Elijah is summed up in his Hebrew name *'ēlîyāh* (*û*), ''my God is Yahweh.'' The actual historical career of Elijah is difficult to reconstruct, because his story (1 Kgs 17.1–19.21; 21.1–29; 2 Kgs 1.2–2.12), which probably came from a once independent cycle of stories about the prophets that the editor of Kings excerpted and incorporated into his book, is overlaid with much legendary material, and since it is apparently drawn from various strands of tradition, it is not always consistent with itself or with other data that can be derived from Biblical and other ancient sources.

Well-known are the stories of the long drought that the prophet brought on the land (to show that Yahweh was superior to Baal, the Canaanite god of fertility); his being fed miraculously by ravens in Wadi Cherith of Transjordan and by the widow in Zarephthah of Phoenicia, whose son he raised from the dead; his triumph over the prophets of Baal on Mt. CARMEL; and his flight to Mt. HOREB, where he witnessed the THEOPHANY in which Yahweh was not in the hurricane or the earthquake but in the ''still small voice'' (to show that Yahweh achieves his purposes quietly and patiently).

The spectacular account of his departure (2 Kgs 2.11) from this world did much to encourage later speculation concerning his role in salvation history. After his return was predicted by Malachi (Mal 3.1, 23–24; see also Sir 48.1–12) as a herald of the DAY OF THE LORD, understood as the precursor of the Messiah, he became a very prominent figure in later Jewish writings. No less than three ''apocalypses'' are known to have been attributed to him. Like Enoch (Gn 5.21–24), who, unlike the other antediluvian Patriarchs, is not said to have died but to have been ''taken by God,'' Elijah was widely believed not to have died but to be ''waiting'' somewhere until God should send him to discharge his role in connection with the establishment of the messianic kingdom. Actually, the NT clearly regards the prediction of Malachi to have been fulfilled in the person of St. JOHN THE BAPTIST (Mt 11.10, 14; 17.10–13; Mk 1.2; 9.10–12; Lk 1.16–17, 76; 7.27), but speculation concerning Elijah continued to flourish, even to the present day, at times taking on a very far-fetched character.

In Christian iconography the figure of Elijah appears frequently both in the Byzantine East and the Latin West. His common attributes are a raven (referring to the birds that fed him during the famine), a flaming sword (alluding to the fire he brought down from heaven on the Mt. Carmel sacrifice), and a fiery chariot (in which he ascended into heaven). The various events of his life, particularly his miracles and his marvelous departure from the earth, have often been portrayed.

Bibliography: V. HAMP et al., *Lexikon für Theologie und Kirche,* ed. J. HOFER and K. RAHNER, 10 v. (2d, new ed. Frieburg 1957–65) 3:806–810. G. FOHRER, *Die Religion in Geischichte und Gegenwart,* 7 v. (3d ed. Tübingen 1957–65) 2:424–427. *Encyclopedic Dictionary of the Bible,* tr. and adap. by L. HARTMAN, (New York 1963), from A. VAN DEN BORN, *Bijbels Woordenboek,* 646–647. L. RÉAU, *Iconographie de l'art chrétien,* 6 v. (Paris 1955–59) 2.1:347–359.

[B. MCGRATH]

ELIJAH (SECOND COMING OF)

''Lo, I will send you Elijah, the prophet, before the day of the Lord comes, the great and terrible day . . .'' (Mal 3.23). This prediction, coupled with the Prophet's dramatic departure from the earth (2 Kgs 2.11), generated a conviction among the Jews that Elijah would return to prepare the day of Yahweh. The Gospels offer evidence of just such a belief in Palestine at the time of Christ. The Jewish levites and priests came to JOHN THE BAPTIST asking if he were Elijah (Jn 1.21); others thought that Jesus Himself might be the Prophet (Mt 16.14; Lk 9.8). And although John denied that he was the Prophet, Christ Himself said of the Baptist: ''And if you are willing to receive it, he is Elijah who was to come'' (Mt 11.14; cf. 17.10–13).

These texts of the Old and New Testaments pose an exegetical problem. According to Christ, John was the long–awaited Elijah; yet the Baptist was obviously not the Prophet himself, for the Scriptures have left a detailed account of his birth and parentage. One is compelled, therefore, to ask the question: is the prophecy of Malachi completely fulfilled in John, or is one to look for Elijah himself to reappear in eschatological times? Quite different answers have been given by patristic writers and by contemporary exegetes.

Perhaps the clearest statement of the patristic view can be found in Augustine. ''As there are two comings of the Judge,'' he writes, ''there will be two heralds. The [Judge] sent before Him the first herald [John] calling him Elijah, because Elijah would be in the Second Coming what John was in the first'' (*In evang. Ioh.* 4.5). In Augustine's interpretation, therefore, John was properly called Elijah because he was a symbol, or type, or the eschatological figure who would precede the Second Coming of Christ (*see* PAROUSIA).

Augustine's view was strongly endorsed by Cardinal Bellarmine and persists in theological manuals. C. Pesch, for instance, identifies the two ''witnesses'' of Rv 11.3 as Elijah and Enoch [*Praelectiones dogmaticae,* v.9 (5th ed. Freiburg 1923) 352].

Modern exegetes, however, have moved away from this older opinion, convinced that it lacks any solid basis in the Scriptures. The prophecy of Malachi, they believe, is not to be understood literally, but rather of one who has the power of Elijah. That the Baptist fulfilled this prophecy was first vaguely indicated by the angel's words to Zechariah ''. . . and he himself shall go before him in the spirit and power of Elijah . . .'' (Lk 1.17). The angel's veiled hint becomes luminously clear in the words of Christ who declared that John was indeed Elijah. Modern exegesis sees no compelling reason to look for any further fulfillment of the prophecy.

Bibliography: *Dictionnaire de théologie catholique,* ed. A. VACANT et al., 15 v. (Paris 1903–50; Tables générales 1951–), Tables générales 1:1154. V. HAMP et al., *Lexikon für Theologie und Kirche,* ed. J. HOFER and K. RAHNER 10 v. (2d, new ed. Freiburg 1957–65) 3:806–810. E. MANGENOT, *Dictionnaire de la Bible,* ed. F. VIGOUROUX, 5 v. (Paris 1895–1912) 2.2:1670–76. G. JACQUEMET, *Catholicisme* 4:10–11. L. CERFAUX and J. CAMBIER, *L'Apocalypse de Saint Jean, lue aux chrétiens* (Paris 1955).

[G. J. DYER]

ELIOT, THOMAS STEARNS

Anglo-American poet and critic; b. St. Louis, Mo., Sept. 26, 1888, d. London, Jan. 4, 1965. He was the seventh and last child of Henry Ware Eliot and Charlotte St-

Thomas Stearns Eliot, London, England, 1956. (AP/Wide World Photos)

earns Eliot, and the grandson of William Greenleaf Eliot, Unitarian minister and founder of Washington University, St. Louis. At Harvard, then under the presidency of his distant relative C. W. Eliot, he encountered DANTE, the metaphysical poets and the French symbolists and commenced writing experimental verse that borrowed its voice from Jules Laforgue and its habits of imagery from late Elizabethan drama. After receiving his bachelor's (1909) and master's (1910) degrees, he spent a year in Paris, where he wrote much of ''The Love Song of J. Alfred Prufrock,'' and then returned to Harvard for graduate study in philosophy (1911–14), envisaging an academic career. Further work in Germany was cut short by World War I, and in 1914 he enrolled at Merton College, Oxford, where he read Aristotle's *Posterior Analytics* and commenced his doctoral thesis on Francis Herbert BRADLEY's theory of knowledge. His marriage to Vivien Haigh-Wood in 1915 marked the termination of his academic career. He submitted the thesis to Harvard in 1916 but never took the degree. Eliot worked in the foreign exchange department at Lloyd's Bank and reviewed numerous books for small sums. These labors, added to the work of equipping himself to be a poet in the contemporary world and the strain of coping with his wife's continual emotional derangements, brought on by 1921 a comprehensive breakdown; during his recuperation at Margate and Lausanne he wrote the first major 20th-century poem in English, *The Waste Land.*

In September 1914 Eliot had met Ezra Pound in London. Pound secured publication of ''Prufrock'' in *Poetry* (Chicago) and during several years' close association accelerated Eliot's assimilation of models and his development of a sharp, unrhetorical, virtuosic verse technique. By 1919 Eliot had blocked out, and in large part occupied, the intellectual territory from which he meant to operate. He had arrived at a workable view of literary tradition: the past that has been deliberately assimilated, the past to the future understanding of which present work in turn, if rightly done, will make an irreversible difference. He had clarified his grasp of the tradition accessible to him, which drew vitality from the Elizabethans and the metaphysicals and from 19th-century France. But he found in Milton a ''Chinese Wall''; in the Romantics, insufficient knowledge; and in the Victorians, diffuse rumination. He had perfected, in a series of poems in quatrains, an aesthetic of sinewy statement, playing against the closed form a rich syntactic variety. And he had defined the dramatic function of rhetoric: a symptom of the speaker's absorption with the figure he is cutting, and so the precise index of a mind's self-consciousness.

Key Poetry. All this knowledge is articulated in *The Waste Land,* in which the poet's awareness of his own plight echoes the weary self-consciousness of the postwar ''mind of Europe,'' stored with resonant fragments and preoccupied with imaginative and spiritual drought. A tough arid eloquence pervades its mosaic of allusions. Shakespeare and St. Augustine, Buddha and Andrew Marvell, the Journey to Emmaus and the Grail-Knight's pilgrimage to a deserted chapel where to inquire after the meaning of symbols is perhaps to resurrect them, all enter a plenum in which the 20th-century imagination has ever since been learning to know its own identity. This poem (1922) and the essays in *The Sacred Wood* (1920) affirmed but did not for some years implement Eliot's authority as the presiding intelligence in literary London and ultimately in the English-speaking West.

''The Hollow Men'' (1925), a dry, dead spiritual void amid which articulation is miraculously sustained, terminated what Eliot expected to be his final collection of verse. He was editing the *Criterion* (1922–39) and working in the publishing firm founded by Geoffrey Faber. In 1927, however, he commenced a new life, naturalized as a British subject; confirmed in the Church of England, of which he was to become his time's most eminent lay communicant; and initiating with ''Journey of the Magi'' (1927) a sequence of religious poems that culminated in *Ash-Wednesday* (1930) and bore autumnal fruit in the major work of his maturity, *Four Quartets* (1935–42).

The church attracted him initially by its embodiment of his idea of tradition, by its transcendental authority in a shifting time, and by its power to define as a meaningful ideal the asceticism that for the poet of *The Waste Land* had been only an appalled refusal of chaotic sensuality. His Magi, in the blank years when the Word on earth has not yet undertaken his ministry, have been accorded not peace but a permanent alienation from the world's satisfactions. His most conspicuously Christian poem, *Ash-Wednesday,* begins by not hoping to turn again (as though going back, not on, would be a good thing if one were permitted to hope for it) and closes in "the dream-crossed twilight between birth and dying," praying to learn "to care and not to care."

Murder in the Cathedral (1935) may be read as a commentary on *Ash-Wednesday.* In this play about the murder of St. Thomas BECKET, the archbishop must learn to care and not to care; for if he merely chooses not to care, and abandons himself to his destroyers, he will be a suicide rather than a martyr. Probably no drama has ever explored so subtle a moral point; but even in the extraordinary scene in which Thomas is tempted by foreknowledge of his own beatification, Eliot's hand is sure—and a Christian drama emerges from what a merely clever writer would have turned into an intellectual puzzle; and a merely theatrical writer, into a thriller.

Out of passages not used in this play grew "Burnt Norton" (1935); out of "Burnt Norton," under the stress of the war years, grew *Four Quartets,* Eliot's comprehensive meditation on the meaning of his own life and that of his ancestors, the contemporary world and the past it fulfils and half disowns, the Christian revelation and the secular pleasures it incorporates, judges, and transcends. The *décor,* like that of Gray's *Elegy,* comes from the 18th-century tradition of the local meditative poem; the structure of each Quartet is drawn from that of "The Waste Land"; the images extend those of Eliot's earlier poems; the whole is quiet, steeped in tradition, and utterly modern, suggesting, as the title implies, a wordless conversation like that among stringed instruments. Only George Herbert's *The Temple* (1633) supplies partial analogies for the quality of feeling in this purest and most characteristic of Eliot's works, and only Rilke's Duino Elegies offers a parallel modern concern for the feel of living in time under eternal sanctions.

Popular Theater. In 1947 Mrs. Eliot died; they had long been legally separated. In 1948 Eliot received the Order of Merit and the Nobel prize for literature. In 1950, with *The Cocktail Party,* a play about contrasting modes of salvation, he reached a large popular audience for the first time. Two more plays for the popular theater followed, *The Confidential Clerk* (1954) and *The Elder Statesman* (1959). In 1957 T. S. Eliot's marriage to Valerie Fletcher inaugurated what were conspicuously the happiest years of his life. He wrote little, traveled much, continued on a reduced schedule his work as a partner of Faber and Faber, and enjoyed, with some irony, the esteem in which he was held as England's most eminent man of letters. His last publication was the long-suppressed 48-year-old doctoral thesis on Bradley's philosophy, which dated from the end of his academic career and the beginning of his life as a poet and man of letters. His ashes were interred in the Somerset village of East Coker, celebrated in *Four Quartets,* where Eliots or Elyots lived for some two centuries before the poet's ancestor Andrew Eliot emigrated in 1667 to found the American branch of the family. "East Coker" begins, "In my beginning is my end," and closes, "In my end is my beginning."

Bibliography: T. S. ELIOT, *Collected Poems, 1909–1962* (New York 1963); *Selected Essays, 1917–1932* (2d ed. New York 1950); *Murder in the Cathedral* (New York 1935); *The Family Reunion* (New York 1939); *The Cocktail Party* (New York 1950); *The Confidential Clerk* (New York 1954); *The Elder Statesman* (New York 1959); *The Use of Poetry and the Use of Criticism* (Cambridge, Mass. 1933); *The Idea of a Christian Society* (New York 1940). D. C. GALLUP, *T. S. Eliot: A Bibliography* (New York 1953). H. KENNER, *The Invisible Poet* (New York 1959); ed., *T. S. Eliot: A Collection of Critical Essays* (Englewood Cliffs, N.J. 1962). N. FRYE, *T. S. Eliot* (New York 1963). G. C. SMITH, *T. S. Eliot's Poetry and Plays* (Chicago 1956). B. RAJAN, ed., *T. S. Eliot: A Study of His Writings by Several Hands* (New York 1948). L. UNGER, *T. S. Eliot: A Selected Critique* (New York 1948). G. WILLIAMSON, *Reader's Guide to T. S. Eliot: A Poem-by-Poem Analysis* (New York 1953). H. HOWARTH, *Notes on Some Figures behind T. S. Eliot* (Boston 1964), contains much biog. material. R. S. KENNEDY, *Working out Salvation with Diligence: The Plays of T. S. Eliot* (Wichita, Kans., 1964). KENNETH ASHER, *T. S. Eliot and Ideology* (Cambridge, U.K., and New York, 1995). ANTHONY JULIUS, *T. S. Eliot, Anti-Semitism, and Literary Form* (Cambridge, U.K., and New York, 1995). CAROLINE PHILLIPS, *The Religious Quest in the Poetry of T. S. Eliot* (Lewiston, N.Y., 1995). NARSINGH SRIVASTAVA, *The Poetry of T. S. Eliot: A Study in Religious Sensibility* (New Delhi, 1991).

[H. KENNER]

ELIPANDUS OF TOLEDO

Chief proponent of the 8th-century heresy of ADOPTIONISM in Spain; b. July 25, 717; d. after 800 (807?). He was appointed archbishop of Toledo *c.* 783. In condemning Migetius for SABELLIANISM (Seville, *c.* 782), Elipandus himself became the author of the Spanish form of adoptionism, claiming that there are two distinct persons in Christ. Felix of Urgel, a contemporary and a subject of Charlemagne, introduced adoptionism into the southern part of Charles's kingdom. He is sometimes considered the author of adoptionism; but ALCUIN blames Elipandus (*Patrologia Latina* 101:231–300). BEATUS OF

LIÉBANA and Etherius, Bishop of Osma [*Symbolum fidei Elipandianae* (785); (*Patrologia Latina* 96:916–920], opposed Elipandus, and Pope ADRIAN I condemned him. CHARLEMAGNE convoked a council at Frankfurt (794), to which the Pope sent legates, and adoptionism was formally condemned. The submission of Elipandus is uncertain, since all documents that assert it derive from a single doubtful source. The error of Elipandus is variously ascribed to Moslem or Nestorian influence or to that of the MOZARABIC RITE. Vernet states, however, that adoptionists had rejected Moslem Christological errors. Some Nestorian influence—real, but hard to trace—and the emphasis of the Mozarabic liturgy seem to be the principal sources of his erroneous theories.

Bibliography: H. FLÓREZ et al, *España sagrada* 5:561–564. C. J. VON HEFELE, *Histoires et conciles d'après les documents originaux*, trans and continued by H. LECLERCQ, 3:985–992. F. VERNET, *Dictionnaire de théologie catholique* 4.2:2330–40. J. F. RIVERA, ''La controversia adopionista del siglo VIII y la ortodoxia de la liturgia Mozárabe,'' *Ephemerides Liturgicae* 47 (1933) 506–536; *Elipando de Toledo* (Toledo 1940). É AMANN, ''L'Adoptionisme espagnol du VIIIe siècle,'' *Revue des sciences religieuses* 16 (1936) 281–317. A. BIGELMAIR, *Lexikon für Theologie und Kirche*, ed. J. HOFER and K. RAHNER (Freiburg 1957–65) 3:815.

[C. M. AHERNE]

ELISHA

Prophet and successor of ELIJAH, Elisha (Heb. 'Ĕlîšā', God saves), from Abel-Mehula (south of Beth-San) was active in the second half of the 9th century B.C. The account of his career is given in 1 Kgs 19.16, 19–21; 2 Kgs 2.1–8.15; 9.1–3; 13.14–21. Much of his story, which once circulated in separate form before it was reworded and incorporated by the editor of Kings into his book, is overlaid with legend. Some of his miracles [*see* MIRACLES (IN THE BIBLE)], for example, have more than a touch of the bizarre about them. Immediately after the ''ascension'' of Elijah, for instance, the story is told how Elisha ''sweetened'' the waters of Jericho (2 Kgs 2.15–22); even today the copious spring at ancient Jericho is pointed out to travelers and pilgrims as the Fountain of Elisha. Following this is the incident of the boys who mocked the Prophet and, at his prayer, were torn apart by bears (2.23–24). The story of his relations with the rich woman of Sunam and his raising of her young son from the dead (2 Kgs 4.1–37) is remarkably similar to the story of Elijah and the widow of Sarephta (1 Kgs 17.9–24). The most significant event in Elisha's career was his designation of Jehu as King of Israel. Even after his death he was credited with working miracles (2 Kgs 13.20–22); but his fame and influence were much less enduring than those of Elijah, who, for example, is mentioned about 30 times in the NT, whereas Elisha is mentioned only once (Lk 4.27), in connection with his curing the leprosy of Naaman the Syrian (2 Kgs 5.1–19).

Bibliography: V. HAMP, *Lexikon für Theologie und Kirche*, ed. J. HOFER and K. RAHNER, 10 v. (2d, new ed. Freiburg 1957–65) 3:821–822. G. FOHRER, *Die Religion in Geschichte und Gegenwart*, 7 v. (3d ed. Tübingen 1957–65) 2:429–431. *Encyclopedic Dictionary of the Bible*, tr. and adap. by L. HARTMAN (New York 1963), from A. VAN DEN BORN, *Bijbels Woordenboek* 650.

[B. MCGRATH]

ELIZABETH, ST.

Wife of Zechariah and mother of JOHN THE BAPTIST. The NT spelling of the name ('Ελισάβετ) represents a late, possibly Aramaic form of the name of the wife of Aaron (Heb. '*ĕlîseba*'; Ex 6.23). Elizabeth was a descendant of her OT namesake, for she was ''of the daughters of Aaron'' (Lk 1.5), i.e., descended from Aaron's line. She is designated as a relative (συγγενίς; Lk 1.36) of Mary, the Mother of Jesus, but it is not possible to ascertain the exact nature of their relationship; according to the legend of the apocryphal *History of Hanna,* Elizabeth's mother, Sophia, was a sister of Mary's mother, Anna. Already advanced in age and sterile (cf. Gn 18.11 for the parallel case of Abraham and Sarah), she and her husband were promised a son by the Angel Gabriel, who appeared to Zachary in the Temple.

The statement that Elizabeth and her husband were ''virtuous before God, walking blamelessly in all the commandments and ordinances of the Lord'' (Lk 1.6) indicates that her sterility was not a result of God's disfavor; she takes her place alongside the holy women of the OT, such as Sarah and Anna, whose barrenness was the prelude to a mighty act of God. Nevertheless, by this phrase, St. Luke intends to contrast her to Mary, who is ''full of grace'' (1.28), and whose Son would be the promised Savior, while the son of Elizabeth was to be His precursor. Like Jeremiah (Jer 1.5), the promised child was to be ''filled with the Holy Spirit from his mother's womb'' (Lk 1.15). This son of her old age would be called a ''prophet of the Most High'' (1.76).

At Mary's visit Elizabeth was six months pregnant. Her greeting to Mary, ''And how have I deserved that the Mother of my Lord should come to me?'' (1.43) indicates her belief that Mary is to be Mother of the Messiah. At Mary's greeting the infant in Elizabeth's womb leapt with joy (1.15). Three months later she gave birth to the son promised to Zachary. At the time of the child's circumcision she insisted that he be called John (''Yahweh is gracious'').

According to legend Elizabeth escaped with her infant son at the time of the massacre of the innocents, and she and her child hid in a cavern, which had opened up to receive them. While there, they were miraculously fed and cared for by angels (Protoevangelium of James, 22).

The principal scene in which Elizabeth is represented in sacred art is the Visitation. There are no representations in the catacombs of the Visitation. She is shown greeting the Blessed Virgin Mary in a carving on a 5th-century sarcophagus at Ravenna and in frescoes from the 6th century in the Church of Sergius at Gaza.

Feast: Nov. 5 (Roman Church); Sept. 8 (Eastern Church).

See Also: VISITATION OF MARY.

Bibliography: P. GAECHTER, *Maria im Erdenleben* (Innsbruck 1953) 98–100. L. RÉAU, *Iconographie de l'art chrétion*, 6 v. (Paris 1955–59) 3.1:415–417.

[M. E. MCIVER]

ELIZABETH I, QUEEN OF ENGLAND

Reigned Nov. 17, 1558, to March 24, 1603; monarch of England's golden age and architect of its final break with the papacy; b. Greenwich, Sept. 7, 1533; d. Richmond. She was the daughter of HENRY VIII and Anne Boleyn. In order to make Anne his wife and in the hope of securing a male heir, Henry repudiated Queen CATHERINE OF ARAGON, rejected papal authority, and became supreme head of the Church in England (1534). The birth of a daughter was a disappointment, and he tired of Anne, who was accused of adultery and executed. Nevertheless Elizabeth had a happy childhood and was educated in the New Learning by such brilliant English humanists as Roger Ascham. Under the rule of her half-sister Mary (1553–58), she was in considerable peril, but it could not be proved that she was implicated in Sir Thomas Wyatt's abortive attempt to overthrow the queen. She conformed to the Catholic religion, but it was fairly clear that she was not a Catholic at heart. The long reign of Elizabeth I was one of the most remarkable in English history, and the queen was a legend in her own lifetime. During these 45 years both English Protestantism and English nationalism achieved success, and England experienced new maritime supremacy, a strengthened economy, and a brilliant literary vitality.

When she became queen (1558) she was illegitimate by both English law and the canons of the Church. If she had wished, she could probably have come to terms with the papacy, but her personal inclinations and, still more, her assessment of the political situation were against it. Elizabeth had no desire to be dependent on either Spain or the papacy, and she decided to throw in her lot with

''Elisha and Gehazi,'' c. 1860s. (©Historical Picture Archives/ CORBIS)

the Protestant cause. The Acts of Supremacy and Uniformity in 1559 declared her Supreme Governor of the Church of England, required the use in all churches of the Book of Common Prayer, and imposed penalties on those who did not attend the parish church on Sundays and holy days. The form of religion that gradually took shape during her reign was uniquely English. It rejected the Church of Rome but retained a great deal of Catholic tradition, although not as much as the queen herself would have liked. Elizabeth was not very interested in theology and not particularly concerned about what men believed in their hearts, but she was determined that they should accept the royal authority in religion and conform outwardly. Though not personally cruel or vindictive, she, like most 16th-century rulers, Catholic and Protestant, was not prepared to tolerate two religions within the state.

In 1570 Pope Pius V excommunicated Elizabeth I and absolved her subjects from their allegiance to her. From Elizabeth further legislation against Catholics followed, but the most ferocious parts of the penal code in the 1580s and 1590s were the product of two other factors—the great success of the missionary priests who began to come into England from 1574 onward and the growing possibility of foreign invasion. The seminary priests and the laity were, with few exceptions, loyal to

"Holy Family with St. Elizabeth and the Infant St. John the Baptist," by Francesco Primaticcio. (©Alexander Burkatowski/CORBIS)

the queen; but Cardinal William ALLEN, the Jesuit Robert PERSONS, and others were working for her overthrow. Persecution increased, and almost 200 priests and laymen were put to death. Many more were imprisoned and fined. (*See* ENGLAND, SCOTLAND, AND WALES, MARTYRS OF.) Elizabeth was generally successful in imposing her religious settlement and by the end of her long reign the Church of England enjoyed national prestige. A large Catholic and a strong Puritan minority survived, nonetheless, and the queen left to her successor, James I, a number of unresolved issues.

Bibliography: The best guide to the vast literature on Elizabeth is C. READ, ed., *Bibliography of British History: Tudor Period, 1485–1603* (2d ed. New York 1959); *Mr. Secretary Walsingham and the Policy of Queen Elizabeth,* 3 v. (Cambridge, MA 1925); *Mr. Secretary Cecil and Queen Elizabeth* (New York 1955). M. CAMPBELL, *The English Yeoman under Elizabeth and the Early Stuarts* (New Haven 1942). E. M. W. TILLYARD, *The Elizabethan World Picture* (New York 1944). M. CREIGHTON, *Queen Elizabeth* (London 1899). J. E. NEALE, *Queen Elizabeth I* (New York 1934; repr. 1959); *Elizabeth I and Her Parliaments,* 2 v. (New York 1959). J. B. BLACK, *The Reign of Elizabeth, 1558–1603* (2d ed. Oxford 1959). E. P. CHEYNEY, *History of England from the Defeat of the Spanish Armada to the Death of Elizabeth,* 2 v. (New York 1914–26). A. L. ROWSE, *The Elizabethan Age,* 2 v. (London 1950–55). J. HURSTFIELD, *Elizabeth I and the Unity of England* (New York 1961). J. B. CODE, *Queen Elizabeth and the English Catholic Historians* (Louvain 1935). M. SCHMIDT, *Die Religion in Geschichte und Gegenwart,* 7 v. (3d ed. Tübingen 1957–65) 2:432. P. HUGHES, *The Reformation in England,* 3 v. in 1 (5th, rev. ed. New York 1963). S. DORAN, *Monarchy and Matrimony* (New York 1996). S. FREY, *Elizabeth I* (New York 1996). C. LEVIN, *The Heart and Stomach of a King* (Philadelphia 1994). W. MACAFFREY, *Elizabeth I* (New York 1993). A. SOMMERSET, *Elizabeth I* (London 1991).

[P. MCGRATH]

Elizabeth I, Queen of England. (© Archive Photos, Inc.)

ELIZABETH OF HUNGARY (THURINGIA), ST.

Hungarian princess, Franciscan penitent, patroness of secular and regular Franciscans; b. 1207; d. Nov. 16/17, 1231. Elizabeth was the daughter of King Andrew II of Hungary and Queen Gertrude. Her sister Mary would marry Asen II, the king of Bulgaria. Her brother Béla would eventually become the king of Hungary. Her maternal aunt was Queen Hedwig of Poland and her first cousin on her father's side was Agnes of Bohemia with whom St. Clare of Assisi corresponded and who is known in these extant letters as Agnes of Prague. Among her other maternal relatives were Mathilda, the abbess of Kitzingen-on-Main, and Eckbert, the bishop of Bamberg. In 1211, at the age of four, she was betrothed to Ludwig IV of Thuringia, son of Duke Hermann and Duchess Sophie of Bavaria. At that time she was brought to the castle in Thuringia, the Wartburg, near Eisenach. There she was raised with her intended husband and his siblings. In 1221, Elizabeth and Ludwig were married. She was fourteen and he twenty. They had three children: a boy, Hermann (1222), and two girls, Sophia (1224) and Gertrude (1227). Ludwig died in 1227 as he was embarking for the Holy Land. Elizabeth died four years later. Pope Gregory IX canonized her in Perugia on May 27, 1235.

Elizabeth's initial contact with Franciscan spirituality dates from 1221 when the friars successfully settled in Germany. Contact with them and a Brother Rodeger, her personal spiritual director for a time, helped develop her sensitivities and dedication in providing food for the poor and hungry and her care for the sick. She built two hospitals, one near Wartburg castle and the other in the town of Marburg. These works of mercy were hallmark activities of the early sisters and brothers of the Order of Penance. Desiring a life of voluntary poverty and humility and anxious for personal involvement in these works of mercy, she was clothed in the grey habit of the Franciscan penitents on Good Friday of 1228. Sometime before her husband's death, Conrad of Marburg took over the role of her spiritual guide. Some few letters from Conrad as well as excerpts from the process of canonization form the nucleus of the earliest records of Elizabeth's life.

Feast: Nov. 17.

St. Elizabeth of Hungary.

Bibliography: J. ANCELET-HUSTACHE, *Gold Tried by Fire: Saint Elizabeth of Hungary,* tr. P. J. OLIGNY and V. O'DONNELL (Chicago 1963). B. CAZELLES, *The Lady as Saint: A Collection of French Hagiographic Romances of the Thirteenth Century* (Philadelphia 1991) 52–171. R. MANSELLI, ''Royal Holiness in the Daily Life of Elizabeth of Hungary: The Testimony of Her Servants,'' tr. E. HAGMANN. *Greyfriars Review* 11 (1997) 311–330. G. SCHINELLI, ''Elizabeth of Hungary: Medieval Princess or Sharper Image?'' *The Cord* 50 (2000), 281–288.

[G. SCHINELLI]

ELIZABETH OF PORTUGAL, ST.

Queen, Franciscan tertiary; b. 1270 or 1271; d. Estremoz, July 4, 1336. Elizabeth (Isabella), daughter of Pedro III and Constance of Aragon, and grandniece of ELIZABETH OF HUNGARY, married King Dinis of Portugal in 1282. She bore his infidelity with loving patience, raised his illegitimate children as her own, and frequently intervened between him and their rebelling son, Alfonso. She devoted herself to the welfare of her subjects, especially the poor, and on several occasions averted war between the kings of Aragon and Castile. When widowed in 1325, she took the habit of the Franciscan Third Order and lived close to the POOR CLARES in Coimbra. She died in Estremoz on her way to make peace between her son and her nephew, Alfonso XI of Castile. Urban VIII canonized her in 1625. Her iconography shows her in regal garb with a dove or olive branch.

Feast: July 4 (formerly July 8).

Bibliography: *Acta Sanctorum* July 2:169–213. A. DE VASCONCELOS, *Evolução do culto de Dona Isabel de Aragão,* 2 v. (Coimbra 1894), reprinted as *Dona Isabel de Arag o: a Rainha Santa,* 2 v. (Coimbra 1993). J. CRESPO, *Santa Isabel na doença e na morte* (Coimbra 1942). P. CANTERO CUADRADO, *Santa Isabel, reina de Portugual* (Zaragoza 1971). A. MUÑOZ FERNÁNDEZ, *Mujer y experiencia religiosa en el marco de la Santidad medieval* (Madrid 1988). D. GIESREGEN, *The Search for St. Elizabeth* (Park Falls, Wis. 1992). F. B. LEITE, *O Rei D. Dinis e a Rainha Santa Isabel* (Coimbra 1993). V. J. MCNABB, *St. Elizabeth of Portugal* (New York 1937). J. BRANQUINHO DE CARRALHO, *As festas da canonização da Rainha Santa Isabel promoridas* (Coimbra 1953). A. BUTLER, *The Lives of the Saints,* ed. H. THURSTON and D. ATTWATER (New York 1956) 3:37–38.

[M. F. LAUGHLIN]

ELIZABETH OF SCHONAU, ST.

Benedictine nun and mystic; b. in the Rhineland, perhaps near Bonn, Germany, 1129; d. Schönau, Hesse, June 18, 1164. She entered the double Benedictine monastery in Schönau at 12, was professed in 1147, and appointed mistress (superior) of the nun's convent in 1157. In 1152, after a serious illness, she had begun to experience extraordinary visions and ecstacies, of which her brother Egbert (*see* ECKBERT OF SCHÖNAU) commanded her to write detailed accounts. He published three books of her *Visiones* with a preface of his own and a chronological list of the visions and most important spiritual experiences. Her second work, the *Liber viarum Dei,* was written in imitation of the *Scivias* of St. HILDEGARD. Both works reveal the controlling hand of Egbert, especially in matters of theology, Church discipline, and politics. Siding with FREDERICK I BARBAROSSA, Elizabeth [Egbert] supported the antipope Victor IV against ALEXANDER III, violently denounced heretics and abuses in the Church, and addressed stern warnings and prophecies of doom to clergy and laity. Her bizarre elaboration of the already fantastic St. URSULA legend (*Visiones,* 2.3), also probably the result of Egbert's influence, was enormously popular in the Middle Ages, as were all her visionary writings, although they were never sanctioned by the Church. Contemporary authorities testify to her sincerity, purity, and genuine zeal. Apparently through a confusion of the two monasteries in Schönau, Cistercian and Benedictine, her name was inscribed as a Cistercian in the Roman MARTYROLOGY in 1584, under GREGORY XIII.

Feast: June 18.

Bibliography: ELISABETH OF SCHÖNAU, *Die Visionen der hl. Elisabeth von Schönau . . . ,* ed. F. W. E. ROTH (Brünn 1884); *Das*

Gebetbuch der hl. Elisabeth von Schönau, ed. F. W. E. ROTH (Augsburg 1886); *Elisabeth of Schönau: The Complete Works,* tr. A. L. CLARK (Mahwah, N.J. 2000). ECKBERT, *Sanctae Elisabeth vita, Patrologia Latina,* ed. J. P. MIGNE, 217 v. (Paris 1878–90) 195: 119–194. *Acta Sanctorum* June 4:499–532; Oct. 9:167–171. A. BUTLER, *The Lives of the Saints,* ed. H. THURSTON and D. ATTWATER (New York 1956) 2:578–580. E. SPIESS, *Ein Zeuge mittelalterlicher Mystik in der Schweiz* (Basel 1935). W. OEHL, *Deutsche Mystikerbriefe* (Munich 1931). W. LEVISON, *Das Werden der Ursula-Legende* (Köln 1928).

[M. F. LAUGHLIN]

ELIZABETH OF THE TRINITY, BL.

Carmelite mystic; (name in the world, Elisabeth Catez) b. July 18, 1880, Camp d'Avor, Bourges, France; d. Nov. 9, 1906, Dijon, France.

Elizabeth Catez is to be distinguished from two other Carmelites of the same name: Elizabeth of the Trinity of the Carmel of Tours (de Quatrebarbes, 1506 to 1660), and Elizabeth of the Trinity of Nantes (E. Duterte de la Coudre, 1881 to 1919). When Elizabeth was seven, her father, a military officer, died; but Elizabeth and her sister Marguerite received an excellent Christian education from their mother, who was much devoted to the writings of St. TERESA OF AVILA. Her mother also encouraged the development of her musical talent by sending her to the Dijon Conservatory. At the age of 14, Elizabeth made a vow of virginity. She entered the Carmel at Dijon Aug. 2, 1901; received the Carmelite habit from Bishop Le Nordez of Dijon on Dec. 8, 1901; and was professed Jan. 11, 1903. On Nov. 21, 1904, she composed her celebrated prayer, ''Oh My God, Trinity Whom I Adore'' (see M. Amabel du Coeur de Jésus; bibliography). About Easter 1905 she discovered in St. Paul her vocation, which was the praising of the glory of the Trinity. She twice received the grace of transforming union, first on the Feast of the Ascension (1906), and again a little later.

At 19, reading the *Way of Perfection* of Teresa of Avila, Elizabeth's attention was drawn to a formula that is the key to the understanding of her interior life and her spiritual doctrine: ''in the heaven of my soul.'' Her personal existence came to be spent entirely in the presence of God, where she wanted nothing to distract her or prevent her life from becoming a continuous prayer. She desired to retire within herself and live in the little cell God had built in her heart, in that little corner of herself where she could see him and have the feeling of his presence.

Two steps mark the rapid spiritual ascension of Elizabeth. In the first she appears in great purity of soul, reaching out to the enjoyment of the presence within her of the Three Divine Persons: ''I have found my heaven upon earth, for heaven is God, and God is in my soul'' (letter to Mme. de Sourdon, June 1902). In the second and more sublime stage she appears passing beyond herself in order to give herself more to the praise of the glory of the Trinity, just as Jesus had no thought but for the glory of the Father: ''Since my soul is a heaven wherein I dwell while awaiting the heavenly Jerusalem, this heaven, too, must sing of the glory of the Eternal, nothing but the glory of the Eternal'' (*Last Retreat,* seventh day). The holy soul devoted to the divine indwelling thus became an apostle of the praise of the glory of the Trinity. The indwelling of the Trinity in the soul was the center of her doctrine as it was of her life. At the root of her teaching, as a condition fundamental to all spiritual life, is inner silence, i.e., a withdrawal from all that is created and a stilling even of the soul in the presence of God. All within should be quieted that the soul may hear the Word and be instructed by him. In this silence the contemplative soul finds the fullness of God. The essential acts of this intimacy with the Guest within consist in a continual exercise of faith and love. Love proves itself by these acts and leads to an absolute fidelity to the will of God even in the slightest matters. The supreme model of this divine life is the Word, perfect praise of the glory of the Father, who wishes to prolong in each of us the mystery of his adoration and redemptive immolation. ''O my Christ . . . crucified for love, I beseech You to identify my soul with all the movements of Your soul, to immerse me, to possess me wholly and to substitute Yourself for me, so that my life is nothing but a ray beaming out from Your life'' (Prayer to the Trinity). Elizabeth saw in the Virgin of the Incarnation all the concentration upon God within her that was her own ideal of holiness. It seemed to her that the attitude of the Virgin during the months between the Annunciation and the Nativity is a model for all interior souls. The issue of this spiritual life is the unceasing praise of the blessed in heaven that is described in the last chapters of Revelations, which became Elizabeth's favorite reading.

This spiritual doctrine concerning what is, in effect, the ultimate unfolding and development of the Christian's baptismal vocation was gathered together in two retreats composed at the end of her life: *How to find Heaven upon Earth* and the *Last Retreat on the Praise of Glory,* which she left as a spiritual last testament.

At the age of 22 she displayed the first signs of Addison's disease, which led to her death at 26. Her last words: ''I go to the light, to love, to life.'' She was beatified on Nov. 25, 1984 by Pope John Paul II.

Feast: Nov. 8 (Carmelites).

Bibliography: Works by St. Elizabeth: The Archives of the Dijon Carmel contain nearly all her original writings. *Souvenirs*

(Dijon 1909); Eng., *The "Praise of Glory:" Reminiscences . . .* (London 1913; repr. Westminster, Md. 1962); *Spiritual Writings,* ed. M. M. PHILIPON, tr. MOTHER ST. AUGUSTINE OF THE SACRED HEART (New York 1962). Complete Works of Elizabeth of the Trinity, *Major Spiritual Writings*, v. 1, tr. A. KANE (repr. Washington, DC 1996); *Letters From Carmel*, v. 2, tr. A. E. NASH (San Diego 1984); *Light Love Life: A Look at a Face and a Heart*, ed. C. DE MEESTER, tr. A. KANE (Washington 1987). Literature. *Acta Apostolicae Sedis* 79 (1987): 1268–73. *L'Osservatore Romano,* English edition, no. 50 (1984). 12, 2. AMABEL DU CŒUR DE JÉSUS, *The Doctrine of the Divine Indwelling: A Commentary on the Prayer of Sister Elizabeth of the Trinity* (Westminster, Md. 1950); *À la lumiére, à l'amour, à la vie* (Paris 1933). H. U. VON BALTHASAR, *Elizabeth of Dijon, An Interpretation of Her Spiritual Mission,* tr. A. V. LITTLEDALE (New York 1956); *Two Sisters in the Spirit: Thérèse of Lisieux & Elizabeth of the Trinity*, tr. D. MARTIN (Fort Collins, Col.: Ignatius, 1997). L. BOUYER, *Women Mystics: Hadewijch of Antwerp, Teresa of Avila, Thérèse of Lisieux, Elizabeth of the Trinity, Edith Stein*, tr. A. E. NASH (Fort Collins, Col. 1993), 155–72. L. BORRIELLO, *The Spiritual Doctrine of Blessed Elizabeth of the Trinity: Apostolic Contemplative*, tr. J. AUMANN (Staten Island, N.Y. 1986). P. M. FÉVOTTE, *Aimer la Bible avec Elisabeth de la Trinité* (Paris 1991); *Virginité, chemin d'amour: à l'école d'Elizabeth de la Trinité* (Paris 1993). J. MOORCROFT, *He Is My Heaven* (Washington, D.C. 2001). M. M. PHILIPON, *The Spiritual Doctrine of Sister Elizabeth of the Trinity* (Westminster, Md. 1947). J. RÉMY, *Ce que croyait Elisabeth de la Trinité* (Paris 1984). E. VANDEUR, *Trinity Whom I Adore: Prayer of Sister Elizabeth of the Trinity* (New York 1953); *Pledge of Glory; Meditations on the Eucharist and the Trinity* (Westminster, Md. 1958).

[M. M. PHILIPON]

ELIZALDE, MIGUEL DE

Jesuit theologian; b. Echalar, Navarre, 1616; d. San Sebastián, Nov. 18, 1678. He entered the Society of Jesus in 1635, and later taught theology and philosophy at Valladolid, Salamanca, and Rome, and for a time was rector of the Jesuit college at Naples. In his *Forma verae religionis quaerendae et inveniendae* (Naples 1662) he ranked himself among the few 17th-century theologians who favored a more rationalistic apologetic, claiming that strict proof of the fact of revelation was possible. This idea was coldly received at the time but took better root in the 19th century and won wide acceptance. But Elizalde is better known for his attack upon PROBABILISM. Without the approval of his religious superiors and in defiance of the criticism and advice of the revisers of the society, he published his *De recta doctrina morum, quatuor libris distincta, quibus accessit: De natura opinionis* under the anagrammatic pseudonym of Antonio Celladei (Lyons 1670). A second and enlarged edition was published posthumously (Fribourg 1684). Elizalde's own moral system is described as PROBABILIORISM, but it could perhaps be better classified as TUTIORISM. On certain points he verged toward Baianist and Jansenist doctrine.

Bibliography: C. SOMMERVOGEL et al., *Bibliothèque de la Compagnie de Jésus* (Brussels-Paris 1890–32) 3:281–383. I. VON DÖLLINGER and F. H. REUSCH, *Geschichte der Moralstreitigkeiten in der römischkatholischen Kirche seit dem sechzehnten Jahrhundert,* 2 v. (Munich 1889) 1:51–56, 141–144, 157, 203, 206; 2:23–45, 47–48.

[P. K. MEAGHER]

ELLARD, GERALD

Liturgist; b. Commonwealth, Wis., Oct. 8, 1894; d. Boston, Mass., April 1, 1963. Gerald was the second of four children born to Hugh Ellard and Margaret Fitzgerald, all four of whom became religious; he followed his older brother, Augustine, into the Society of Jesus, July 27, 1912. In 1925 while studying theology at St. Louis University he met Martin Hellriegel and Virgil MICHEL, and the resulting friendship influenced his determination to do graduate studies in liturgy. He was ordained on June 16, 1926, and began his doctoral studies in the history of liturgy at the University of Munich in 1928. His doctoral dissertation, *Ordination Anointings in the Western Church before 1000 A.D.* (Cambridge, Mass. 1933), was acclaimed as the first scholarly work by a citizen of the United States in the field of liturgy. Research for this work resulted in the publication of another book, *Master Alcuin, Liturgist* (Chicago 1956). While professor of liturgy and Church history at St. Mary's College, St. Marys, Kans. (1932–63), he continued to write and lecture. His most influential work was a textbook for college students, *Christian Life and Worship* (Milwaukee 1933). Other important works were *Men at Work and Worship* (New York 1940), *Mass of the Future* (Milwaukee 1948), which was revised and published as *Mass in Transition* (Milwaukee 1956). He also contributed numerous articles to *Orate Fratres,* later known as *Worship,* of which he was one of the original associate editors.

A charter member of the Liturgical Conference, he served on the board of directors until 1956, and delivered papers at many Liturgical Weeks. He continued to serve the liturgical renewal until his death, which came only a few days after he had given a paper before those gathered at Harvard School of Divinity for a Roman Catholic-Protestant colloquium.

Bibliography: E. A. DIEDERICH, *Yearbook of Literary Studies* (Chapel Hill, NC) 4 (1963) 3–21.

[E. A. DIEDERICH]

ELLIOTT, WALTER

Missionary, author; b. Detroit, Mich., Jan. 6, 1842; d. Washington, D.C., April 18, 1928. He was the ninth child of Robert J. and Frances (O'Shea) Elliott. After attending St. Anne's School, Detroit, and the University of Notre Dame, South Bend, Ind., he began to study law in Cincinnati, Ohio. At the outbreak of the Civil War, he enlisted in the 5th Ohio Infantry, and he fought at Port Republic, Chancellorsville, and Gettysburg. After the war, he resumed his study of law in Detroit where, after admission to the bar, he opened a law office. When Father Isaac HECKER lectured there in May 1868, Elliott was in the audience. Three months later he joined the PAULISTS; he was ordained on May 25, 1872, and began his missionary career, which continued with few interruptions for more than 25 years. An effective preacher, he also became a leader in the temperance crusade and was actively identified with the Catholic Total Abstinence Union.

In 1886 he temporarily left mission work to become Hecker's companion during his declining years. At Abp. John J. KEANE's suggestion, Elliott recorded his conversations with Hecker, using them for a biography of Hecker, which first appeared serially in 1890–91 in the *Catholic World* (v. 51–53). In 1891 it was published in book form as *The Life of Father Hecker.* A French translation and adaptation appeared in 1897 and figured largely in the AMERICANISM controversy.

In 1893 Elliott inaugurated, on a national scale, missions to non-Catholics, organizing for that purpose diocesan mission bands in the dioceses of New York; Cleveland, Ohio; Pittsburgh, Pa.; Hartford, Conn.; and Providence, R.I. To aid the missionaries financially and to disseminate Catholic literature, he and Alexander P. Doyle, CSP, founded the Catholic Missionary Union and the *Missionary* magazine. Elliott also raised funds for the establishment of the Apostolic Mission House, a training center for mission work on the campus of The Catholic University of America, Washington, D.C., and became its first rector in 1902. Except for the years from 1909 to 1912 when he served as general consultor of the Paulist community in New York City, he spent the remainder of his life at the Mission House as rector, professor, and staff writer for the *Missionary.* His published works include *Missions to Non-Catholics* (New York 1893), *The Life of Christ* (New York 1902), *Jesus Crucified* (New York 1906), *Parish Sermons* (New York 1913), *The Spiritual Life* (New York 1914), *Manual of Missions* (Washington 1922), *A Retreat for Priests* (Washington 1924), *A Retreat for Nuns* (Washington 1925), *Mission Sermons* (Washington 1926), and a translation from the German of *The Sermons of John Tauler* (Washington 1910).

Bibliography: Apart from a short sketch of 17 pages in J. MCSORLEY, *Father Hecker and His Friends* (2d ed. St. Louis 1953), there is no published life of Father Elliott. His papers and correspondence are in the Paulist Fathers Archives, New York City.

[V. HOLDEN]

Gerald Ellard.

ELLIS, JOHN TRACY

Priest, pre-eminent historian of the American Catholic community, teacher, writer; b. Seneca, Ill., July 30, 1905; d. Washington, D.C., Oct. 16, 1992. The eldest of two sons of Elmer L. Ellis and Ida Cecilia (née Murphy), Ellis' father owned the local hardware store and was Methodist, his mother was a housewife and Catholic; his brother Norbert (1913–53) continued the family business.

Ellis' early training was local: at St. Patrick's Elementary School (1911–19); Seneca High School (1919–21), and at St. Viator Academy (1921–23) in Bourbonnais, Ill. In 1927 he graduated *magna cum laude* from St. Viator College with a B.A. in English literature. Recipient of a Knights of Columbus Fellowship, he attended The Catholic University of America (1927–30) where he studied under Peter GUILDAY, majoring in medieval history. His master's thesis ''Anti-Papal Legislation in Medieval England 1066–1377'' (1928) was expanded into his doctoral dissertation and published as his first book (1930). In the spring term of 1942, Ellis audited courses in American history at Harvard University as part of his preparations to teach American Catholic history.

His first teaching post was at his *alma mater* St. Viator College (1930–32) where as a layman he taught history. The next two years (1932–34) found him at the College of St. Teresa in Winona, Minn. He returned to Washington, D.C., to study for the priesthood and during this period began his long and fruitful career teaching at The Catholic University of America (1935–64). From 1964 to 1976 he was Professor of Church History at the University of San Francisco. He returned to the Catholic University as Professorial Lecturer in church history (1976–89). He taught summer school at Catholic institutions of learning throughout the United States, and held numerous lectureships: e.g., University of Chicago as Walgreen lecturer (1955), North American College in Rome (1967, 1974–76), Brown University (1967), University of Notre Dame (1970), Graduate Theological Union, Berkeley (1970–71), Gregorian University (1974–75), St. Thomas University—Angelicum (1976), and The Catholic University of America as the first Catholic Daughters of the Americas' visiting professor (1976).

Writings and Influence. A prolific writer, Ellis has published over 150 books, articles, and pamphlets, and over 250 minor works such as book reviews, forewords to books, encyclopedia articles, obituary notices, letters to editors, and reports as secretary of the American Catholic Historical Association. In addition, the archives of The Catholic University of America contain over 100 of his unpublished sermons, commencement addresses, and interviews. A dozen or so books constitute his principal writings. The first three reflect his movement from medieval [*Anti-Papal Legislation in Medieval England [1066–1377]* (1930)], to modern European [*Cardinal Consalvi and Anglo-Papal Relations, [1814–1824]* (1942)], to American church history [*The Formative Years of The Catholic University of America* (1946)]. These were followed by his major work in two volumes based on over three years of extensive archival research *The Life of James Cardinal Gibbons Archbishop of Baltimore, 1834–1921* (1952), which was reissued in a condensed version in 1963 and reprinted in 1987. His survey of the history of the Catholic Church in America that originated in the Walgreen Lectures, *American Catholicism* (1956), was revised in 1969 and has remained for many years one of the principal textbooks in its field. Ellis' admiration for John Lancaster Spalding, bishop of his native diocese, that had earlier led him to write a book on the founding of The Catholic University of America in which this bishop played a significant role, later resulted in a study of this bishop's educational views: *John Lancaster Spalding: First Bishop of Peoria, American Educator* (1961). A collection of about 20 essays on historical and educational themes was published as *Perspectives in American Catholicism* (1963). A projected multivolume history of the Catholic Church in America never progressed beyond *Catholics in Colonial America* (1965). His life-long interest in priestly formation resulted in two major studies: *Essays in Seminary Education* (1967) and a lengthy article in his edited volume *The Catholic Priest in the United States: Historical Investigations* (1971). As important aids to scholars he published *A Select Bibliography of the History of the Catholic Church in the United States* (1947) which was revised as *A Guide to American Catholic History* (1959), and once again revised with Robert Trisco and republished in 1982. Ellis' other major study tool was his *Documents of American Catholic History* (1956), revised in 1962, expanded to two volumes in 1967, and to three in 1987.

Ellis' approach to the writing of church history followed no set method or school of interpretation. His predilection, however, was for biography, for organizing his accounts of the past around the life of a prominent churchman. Although never the subject of one of his own biographies, John Henry Cardinal Newman was a major source of inspiration to him over the years and he strove to imitate the power and beauty of his prose and his total dedication to truth. Ellis' *Commitment to Truth* (1966) set forth eloquently his own ideals of honesty and integrity. His insistence on including in his accounts the historically relevant faults and mistakes of churchmen won Ellis both admirers and critics.

Ellis' influence on the field of American church history was also exercised through his teaching. For over 30 years he guided the work of doctoral students at The Catholic University of America. At least a dozen of these have gone on to publish important books in the field of American Catholic history.

By his numerous sermons, public addresses, essays, interviews, and letters to the editor, Ellis gained stature as one of the principal spokesmen of the Catholic community in America. The most important of these addresses was his ''American Catholics and the Intellectual Life'' (1955) which had a wide circulation and stirred at times a heated debate over the extent and reasons why the American Catholic community has produced so few intellectuals.

Priestly Career. Simultaneous with this academic career was Ellis' life as a priest. In 1934 he joined the Diocese of Winona and began his studies for the priesthood at the Sulpician Seminary (now Theological College) in Washington, D.C. On June 5, 1938, Bishop Francis M. Kelly ordained him a priest at the College of St. Teresa in Winona. On returning to Washington he took up residence (1938–41) in the home of Msgr. Fulton J. SHEEN whom he had served previously as personal secretary. In 1947 he became the first priest incardinated into the newly-formed Archdiocese of Washington. On December 5, 1955, he was named a domestic prelate of Pope Pius XII. Over the years he has assisted nearby parishes or the cathedral on weekends and gained a reputation as an eloquent preacher. Although invited by Robert E. Tracy, Bishop of Baton Rouge, to serve as *peritus* at the Second Vatican Council, he declined. Ellis served the National Conference of Catholic Bishops as chairman of the Sub-committee on History of the Committee on Priestly Life and Ministry (1967–71) and as a member of the Sub-committee on History for the Observance of the Bicentennial (1973–76). In 1988 he was named honorary protonotary apostolic by John Paul II. James Cardinal Hickey presided at his funeral Mass in the National Shrine on Oct. 20, 1992, and Msgr. Thomas Duffy preached the sermon ''A Priestly Ministry to the Truth.'' Ellis was buried in Seneca, Illinois. His rare combination of frankness, courtesy, and deep dedication to the Church helped to make him a personal friend and advisor to many prelates.

Bibliography: For a comprehensive bibliography of Ellis' works (1923–85) see M. A. MILLER, *Studies in Catholic History in Honor of John Tracy Ellis*, eds. N. H. MINNICH, et al. (Wilmington, Del. 1985) 674–738. Life and career. J. T. ELLIS, *Faith and Learning: A Church Historian's Story* (Lanham, Md. 1988); ''Reflections of an Ex-Editor,'' *Catholic Historical Review* 50 (1965) 459–474; ''Fragments from My Autobiography, 1905–1942,'' *Review of Politics* 36 (1974) 565–591; ''The Catholic University of America, 1927–1979: A Personal Memoir,'' *Social Thought* 5 (1979) 35–62; *Catholic Bishops: A Memoir* (Wilmington, Del. 1984). E. C. BIANCHI, ''A Church Historian's Personal Story: An Interview with Monsignor John Tracy Ellis,'' *Records of the American Catholic Historical Society of Philadelphia* 92 (1981) 1–42. G. E. SHERRY, interviews with Ellis, *Our Sunday Visitor* 72 (Feb. 5, 1984), 4–5; 76 (May 3, 1987) 8–9. G. G. HIGGINS, ''John Tracy Ellis, RIP: A Well-Ordered Life,'' *Commonweal* 119 (Nov. 6, 1992) 5–7. T. J. SHELLEY, ''In Memoriam: John Tracy Ellis (1905–1992),'' *America* 167 (Nov. 7, 1992), 340; ''The Young John Tracy Ellis and American Catholic Intellectual Life,'' *U.S. Catholic Historian* 13 (1995) 1–18. *Records of the American Catholic Historical Society of Philadelphia* 104 (1993) 1–18. Historical method. J. D. THOMAS, ''A Century of American Catholic History,'' *U. S. Catholic Historian* 6 (1987) 25–49, especially ''Eclectic Church History: John Tracy Ellis,'' 41–48. J. T. ELLIS, *A Commitment to Truth* (Latrobe, Penn. 1966); ''The Ecclesiastical Historian in the Services of Clio,'' *Church History* 38 (1969) 106–120. Current state of American Catholic intellectual life. D. LIPTAK and T. WALCH, '''American Catholics and the Intellectual Life': An Interview with Monsignor John Tracy Ellis,'' *U. S. Catholic Historian* 4 (1985) 188–194. H. W. BOWDEN, *Church History in an Age of Uncertainty: Historiographical Patterns in the United States, 1906–1990* (Carbondale, Ill. 1991).

[N. H. MINNICH]

ELLIS, PHILIP (MICHAEL)

Benedictine monk of St. Gregory's, Douay, and zealous vicar apostolic of the (English) Western District; b. Waddesdon, Bucks., 1652; d. Segni, Italy, Nov. 16, 1726. As the third son of Rev. John Ellis, he was brought up a Protestant but became a Catholic while a boy at Westminster School. He was known at school and throughout life as ''Jolly Phil.'' He smuggled himself across the English Channel, and entered the Benedictine monastery at Douay, where he was professed on Nov. 30, 1670. One of his brothers was the Protestant bishop of Meath, and another, secretary of state to William III. Later Ellis became chaplain to James II, and was consecrated bishop of Aureliopolis *in partibus* on May 6, 1688, in the chapel of St. James's Palace (then a Benedictine monastery). At the fall of the monarchy, he was imprisoned in Newgate Prison. On his release he went to Rome, was befriended by the Dominican Cardinal Philip Thomas HOWARD, and made assistant prelate at the pontifical throne by Innocent XII. He resigned his vicariate and was made bishop of Segni in 1705 by Clement XI. He labored zealously for his new diocese, founded a seminary there, and held a synod in 1710.

Bibliography: J. GILLOW, *A Literary and Biographical History or Bibliographical Dictionary of the English Catholics from 1534 to the Present Time* 2:161–164. B. HEMPHILL (pseud. for B. WHELAN), *The Early Vicars Apostolic of England, 1685–1750* (London 1954) 20–21. G. OLIVER, *Collections Illustrating the History of the Catholic Religion in the Countries of Cornwall, Devon, Dorset, Somerset, Wilts, and Gloucester* (London 1857). A. À WOOD, *Athenae Oxonienses,* 5 v. (London 1817) 3: 710–711. G. A. ELLIS, *The Ellis Correspondence, 1686–88,* 2 v. (London 1829). N. LUTTRELL, *A Brief Historical Relation of State Affairs from September, 1678 to April, 1714,* 6 v. (Oxford 1857). G. PANZANI, *Memoirs,* tr. J. BERINGTON (Birmingham 1793). J. A. WILLIAMS, ''Bishops Giffard and Ellis and the Western Vicariate, 1688–1715,'' *Journal of Ecclesiastical History* 15 (1964) 218–228.

[B. WHELAN]

ELLUL, JACQUES

Theologian, historian, sociologist, b. Bordeaux, France, Jan. 6, 1912; d. May 29, 1994. Growing up on the docks of Bordeaux, Ellul became a Marxist at age 19, and then at age 22 he converted to Christianity without ever quite letting go of Marxist thought. Ellul was dismissed from his teaching post at the University of Strasbourg by the Vichy government and participated in the French resistance during World War II and the National Liberation Movement in 1944. After the war he served as deputy mayor of Bordeaux and after 1958 devoted much of his energy to working with juvenile delinquents in order to help them be ''positively non-adjusted'' to society. In the 70s and 80s Ellul also became actively engaged in the ecological movement in France and in related issues concerning the use of nuclear energy. Ellul not only wrote a Christian ethic for a technological civilization, he lived it, leaving a rich legacy of word and deed. One of the major Protestant theologians of the 20th century, his primary contribution was to help Christians rethink the meaning of the Gospel for a technological civilization.

Professional Career. Ellul is unusual in that professionally he was not only a theologian, but also an historian and sociologist. He served as professor of law and of the sociology and history of institutions at the University of Bordeaux in France from 1946 until his retirement in 1980. Following in the tradition of Kierkegaard and Karl BARTH, Ellul was one of the leading theologians of the Reformed Church in France. Of the more than 40 books he wrote during his lifetime, approximately half of them were sociological and historical works critically analyzing the impact of modern technological civilization on human life. The other half of his work was a theological response to the issues raised by his critical analysis of modern technology.

Ellul insisted on keeping these two sides of his work separate, so that one reading his sociological works would scarcely have a clue that he was also a theologian. In his theological writing Ellul was deeply influenced by Barth without being an orthodox Barthian, and in his sociological work he was deeply influenced by Karl MARX without being an orthodox Marxist. Ellul described his situation as one of being drawn to both the Gospel and to Marx without ever being able to reconcile the two. Out of that creative tension emerged one of the most thorough and significant Christian theological and ethical critiques of technological civilization in the 20th century.

Scholarly Works. On the sociological side his most important works were *The Technological Society* (1954, English translation [ET] 1964), *Propaganda* (1962, ET 1965), *The Political Illusion*, (1965, ET 1967) and *The New Demons* (1973, ET 1975). His argument in *The Technological Society* was later updated in *The Technological System* (1977, ET 1980) and again in *The Technological Bluff* (1988, ET 1990). On the theological side of his work Ellul responded to the issues raised by his sociological studies in key theological works on the contemporary meaning of various books of scripture. His response to *The Technological Society* was *The Meaning of the City* (1975, ET 1970); to *The Political Illusion it was The Politics of God and the Politics of Man* (1966, ET 1972); to *Propaganda* it was *The Judgment of Jonah* (1952, ET 1971); and to *The New Demons* it was *Apocalypse, the Book of Revelation* (1976, ET 1977). In addition to these scriptural commentaries Ellul wrote a series of theological critiques of life in modern technological civilization, including *The Presence of the Kingdom* (1948, ET 1967), *Hope in Time of Abandonment* (1972, ET 1973), and *The Ethics of Freedom* (1975 and 1984, ET 1976).

The key to understanding Ellul's complex life work at the interface between sociology and theology is his book, *The New Demons*. This is Ellul's masterful work on the sociology of religion in modern technological civilization. What distinguishes it is the thesis that in modern technological civilization, the sociology of religion and the sociology of technology have one and the same subject matter. This is so, he argues, because the sacred that was once embodied in the order of nature is now embodied in the technological order. That is, while human beings once believed that nature was that power that governed their destiny and so treated it with religious awe and subservience, now it is technology that elicits such awe and subservience from human beings.

Technology is out of control, Ellul argues, because human beings have engaged in a religious surrender of their freedom to its demands on the conviction (whether conscious or unconscious) that it offers them their best hope of salvation. The contemporary theological task is to do for a civilization dominated by the myths of technology what Christianity once did for ancient civilizations dominated by the myths of nature: to desacralize its sacred order in the name of the Holy. While the sacred sacralizes the technological order of this world, hope in the Holy One, who is Wholly Other than this world, leads to the desacralization, liberation, and humanization of our technological civilization. Ellul's theological view was also distinctive for his vigorous advocacy of universal salvation, namely, the view that in Christ God brought reconciliation and salvation to the whole human race, not just to believers. At the time of his death he left behind him not only a rich legacy of writings but the witness of an extraordinary life.

Bibliography: Jacques Ellul's works in sociology include: *The Technological Society* (New York 1964); *Propaganda* (New York 1965); *The Political Illusion* (New York 1967); *The New Demons* (New York 1975); *The Technological System* (New York 1980); *The Technological Bluff* (Grand Rapids 1990). Those in theology include: *The Presence of the Kingdom* (New York 1967); *The Judgment of Jonah* (Grand Rapids 1971); *The Politics of God and the Politics of Man* (Grand Rapids 1972); *The Meaning of the City* (Grand Rapids 1970); *Hope in Time of Abandonment* (New York 1973); *The Ethics of Freedom* (Grand Rapids 1976); *Apocalypse the Book of Revelation* (New York 1977). The following are works on Ellul: D. B. CLENDENIN, *Theological Method in Jacques Ellul* (Lanham 1987). D. J. FASCHING, *The Thought of Jacques Ellul* (New York and Toronto 1981). D. GILL, *The Word of God in the Ethics of Jacques Ellul* (Metuchen, NJ and London 1984). J. M. HANKS, *Jacques Ellul: A Comprehensive Bibliography* (Greenwich 1984).

[D. J. FASCHING]

ELLWANGEN, ABBEY OF

Former BENEDICTINE monastery and later a collegiate church, at Ellwangen, Württemberg, Germany, in the former Diocese of Augsburg, currently the Diocese of Rottenburg. The abbey's patrons have been Our Savior, Mary, perhaps Peter and Paul; Sulpicius and Servilianus, whose relics were translated there from Rome between 772 and 795; and Vitus, certainly since 1147. It was founded *c.* 750—according to tradition, specifically in 764—for the purpose of supporting the Carolingian Franks against the Bavarians, celebrating the divine services, and clearing the local forest. The legendary *Vita Hariolfi* (841–851) by ERMENRICH OF PASSAU states that the abbey's founders were two brothers, Bp. Hariolf and Bp. Erlolf of Langres; according to other sources, Erlolf and Hariolf were the same person. However, there appears to be some connection between the abbey and Langres, for both have the same coat of arms. In 817 it was made an imperial abbey; in 979 Ellwangen was taken under papal protection; and in 1215 the abbot was made a prince of the empire. The abbey became embroiled in a war with the local town, which Abbot Rudolph burned to the ground in 1255. First the counts of Oettingen, then from 1370 on, the counts of Württemberg served as lay patrons. In the 15th century deteriorating discipline, bad administration, and a fire (1443) prompted the religious to convert the abbey—with papal approval—into an exempt collegiate church (1460) of secular priests with a prince prior, 12 canons (all of the nobility), and 10 vicars. The dean of the chapter was mitered in 1784. During the Reformation, the prior, Cardinal Otto TRUCHSESS VON WALDBURG (1552–73), called in Peter CANISIUS, and thus Ellwangen remained Catholic. In 1611 a Jesuit house was established there; its college with Gymnasium was built (1721–23), and its church (1724–29), now Lutheran, was decorated by Scheffler.

Ellwangen's Marian shrine church on the Schönenberg was constructed under Bl. Philipp JENINGEN's supervision (1682–86); in 1709 it was destroyed by fire and was rebuilt. A seminary was built there in 1747, but was dissolved in 1798; today the site is held by the Redemptorists. In the secularization of 1802–03, all Ellwangen holdings went to the state of Württemberg, and the collegiate church was dissolved. Ellwangen's jurisdiction over the Catholics of Württemberg (1812–17) and its seminary moved to the new diocesan seat at Rottenburg; the theological school founded at Ellwangen in 1812 became part of the University of TÜBINGEN. The old abbey church (consecrated in 1233) was the prototype of Worms cathedral; it now shows the effect of baroque remodeling in the 17th and 18th centuries. Excavations on the site since 1959 have uncovered a pre-Romanesque reliquary.

Bibliography: L. H. COTTINEAU, *Répertoire topobibliographique des abbayes et prieurés,* 2 v. (Mâcon 1935–39) 1:1042–43. P. SCHMITZ, *Histoire de l'ordre de saint Benoît,* 7 v. (Maredsous 1942–56). K. HALLINGER, *Gorze-Kluny,* 2 v. (Studia anselmiana 22–25; 1950–51). W. SCHWARZ, "Studien zur ältesten Geschichte des Benediktinerklosters Ellwangen" in *Zeitschrift für württembergische Landesgeschichte* 11 (1952) 7–38. B. BUSHART, *Die Stiftskirche in Ellwangen* (Munich 1953). H. PFEIFER, *Verfassungs-und Verwaltungsgeschichte der Fürstpropstei Ellwangen* (Stuttgart 1959). E. H. FISCHER, "Zur kirchlichen Verfassung des Ellwanger Stifts" in *Ellwanger Jahrbuch* 17 (1956–57) 63–84. W. FINK, *Dictionnaire d'histoire et de géographie ecclésiastiques*, ed. A. BAUDRILLART et al. (Paris 1912) 15:242–246. V. BURR, ed., *Ellwangen 764–1964,* 2 v. (Ellwangen 1964).

[G. SPAHR]

ELMO, ST.

Legendary martyr, also known as Erasmus, Rasmus, Ermo. He is probably identified with Erasmus who since the 13th or 14th century has been venerated as one of the FOURTEEN HOLY HELPERS. He is reputed to have been the bishop of Formia in the Campagna, and GREGORY THE GREAT stated that his relics were preserved in the cathedral of that town. When Formia was destroyed by the Saracens in 842, Elmo's remains were moved to Gaëta, where he became patron of that city. Nothing else in the fabulous tales told of St. Elmo has any basis in reality; e.g., that he was the bishop of Antioch who underwent many tortures in DIOCLETIAN's persecution and died after being miraculously transported to Italy. As one of the Fourteen Holy Helpers he finally became a patron against cramps, colic, and all intestinal troubles, and even of women in labor. In Mediterranean countries he became the protector of sailors, and among Neapolitan sailors, the electrical discharges seen around mastheads before and after storms were called ST. ELMO'S FIRE.

Feast: June 2.

Bibliography: *Acta Sanctorum* June 1:206–214. O. ENGELS, *Lexikon für Theologie und Kirche*, ed. J. HOFER and K. RAHNER, 10 v. (2d. new ed. Freiburg 1957–65) 3:955. R. FLAHAUT, *S. Érasme* (Paris 1895). A. BUTLER, *The Lives of the Saints*, rev. ed. H. THURSTON and D. ATTWATER, 4 v. (New York 1956) 2:453–454.

[L. L. RUMMEL]

ELOHIM

The divine name (*'Ĕlōhîm*) most frequently used in the Old Testament, a plural form of Eloah, which appears only in poetical books (34 of the 57 times in Job alone). The form Elohim, when used of the God of Israel, is a plural of majesty, signifying the one God who embodies in Himself all the qualities of divinity, and is almost always accompanied by singular verbs and adjectives. Elohim is used also for other gods in general (Ex 18.11; Dt 10.17) and for particular gods, e.g., Chamos, god of the

Moabites (Jgs 11.24); the goddess ASTARTE of the Sidonians (1 Kgs 11.5); BEELZEBUB, god of Accaron (2 Kgs 1.2). It is used also for the ghost of Samuel (1 Sm 28.13), for Moses (Ex 4.16; 7.1), for the King [Ps 44(45).7], for angels [Ps 8.6; 28(29).1; Jb 1.6; Gn 6.1–4; etc.], for princes and judges [Ps 57(58).2; 81(82).6; cf. Jn 10.34], and for David's dynasty and the Messiah (Za 12.8; Is 9.5).

That Elohim was not a particularly Hebrew name for God is indicated by its appearance in Phoenicia long before its use by the Israelites; both the Amarna Letters and the texts found at UGARIT, where it is sometimes construed with a singular verb referring to the supreme god as representative of all the gods of the pantheon, provide instances of its earlier use. The Israelites, however, used Elohim for their one and only God, who excludes all other genuine deities. He is seen as the creator God endowed with all-embracing power, the ruler of absolute will. YAHWEH, the God of Israel, is the only God, and there is no other (Dt 4.35; 6.4; Is 46.9).

Bibliography: W. EICHRODT, *Theology of the Old Testament*, tr. J. A. BAKER (London 1961–). P. VAN IMSCHOOT, *Théologie de l'Ancien Testament*, 2 v. (Tournai 1954–56).

[R. T. A. MURPHY]

ELOHIST

Name (abbreviated E) given to a certain narrative and legal tradition identifiable in the Pentateuch. It was preserved among the tribes more closely associated with the Exodus and events at Mt. Sinai and developed by them in the northern part of Canaan where they settled. It was given its definitive form about the middle of the eighth century B.C. After 721 B.C. it was conflated with the YAHWIST (J) document in the South. E suffered in this conflation so that it now appears mainly as a supplementary narrative. Its character as an originally independent source, especially in Genesis, was once seriously questioned, but is now generally accepted. E's history, as preserved in the canonical Pentateuch, begins with Abraham (traces perhaps in Genesis ch. 15), continues with the rest of the patriarchs and the story of the Exodus, Sinai covenant, and the wandering in the desert. It carefully uses the name ELOHIM for God (whence its name) in the pre-Sinai narratives (e.g., Ex 3.11–14). Its vocabulary, style, and especially its theological outlook are distinctive. The last includes a concern for the covenant and its stipulations, a resulting stricter morality, a tendency to avoid anthropomorphisms, and an emphasis on an idealized desert existence.

[E. H. MALY]

EL PASO, DIOCESE OF

Suffragan of the Metropolitan See of San Antonio, the Diocese of El Paso *(Elpasensis)* comprises the counties of El Paso, Brewster, Culberson, Hudspeth, Jeff Davis, Loving, Presidio, Reeves, Ward, and Winkler, covering 33,817 square miles in West Texas. It was erected on March 3, 1914, and originally also included 30,617 square miles of southern New Mexico that was separated and designated as the Diocese of Los Cruces in 1982. Approximately 77 percent of the total population were of Hispanic origin. Total Catholic population is estimated to be about 76 percent of the total population.

Diocesan Development. Earliest settlements in this diocese date from 1682, with the Spanish land grant to Tigua Native Americans for the Ysleta Mission and to Piro Native Americans for the Socorro Mission. These two Missions were built following the Spanish government retreat to present day Ciudad Juarez, Mexico, from its northern New Mexico capital of Santa Fe at the time of the Pueblo Rebellion in the year 1680. With the coming of the railroads in the 1880's the population grew rapidly, necessitating the construction of many new churches under the supervision of Rev. Carlos Pinto, SJ, and other Italian Jesuits serving the El Paso area.

Guided by Bishops Anthony J. Schuler, SJ (1915–1942), Sidney M. Metzger (1942–1978), Patricio F. Flores (1978–1979), Raymundo J. Peña (1980–1995) and Armando X. Ochoa (appointed 1996), the Diocese of El Paso has sought to meet the challenges arising from its location on the United States–Mexico border.

The persecution of the Church in Mexico in the early 20th century caused the flight of thousands of Mexican Catholics to the United States. The attempt by Bishop Schuler to harbor numerous priests and religious (among whom was Blessed Miguel Augustin Pro, SJ) led to the near-bankruptcy of the diocese in the 1930s. From the 1940s through the 1970s, Bishop Metzger fought successfully for the rights of miners and garment industry workers. Bishop Peña continued Catholic leadership in social issues on the International Border by his concern for the plight of undocumented immigrants, eventually calling for a ''middle ground'' in the 1994 INS blockade against undocumented immigrants working at low-paying jobs in El Paso.

Many challenges continue to surface in this multicultural, bilingual diocese. To meet these needs, the diocese has devised many strategies and programs, among which are the Tepeyac Institute for ministry training, and a professionally staffed Diocesan Refugee and Migrant Services Office. The El Paso Interreligious Sponsoring Organization (EPISO), with predominantly Catholic support, has launched many successful social, health, and educational initiatives. The Diocesan Office of Peace and Justice promotes Catholic Social teaching and conducts ongoing research into social and environmental issues affecting the border area.

Diocesan offices for Youth Ministry, Marriage and Family Life, Prison and Hospital Ministry, Religious Education, Reverence for Life, Catholic Counseling Services, and a bi-lingual diocesan newspaper (*Rio Grande Catholic*) also contribute to the spiritual and moral well-being of the Church in west Texas. A full-time priest vocation director seeks to deal with the ever growing need for bilingual priests.

In 1999 the diocese began hosting a summer program in Hispanic ministry for seminarians from the Archdiocese of Atlanta. In 2000 this program was expanded to include the academic year. In 2001 the diocese entered a ''pact of solidarity'' with the dioceses of Choluteca (Honduras) and Brownsville (Texas) as a response to the devastation in Honduras by the 1998 hurricane Mitch. Also, in 2001 the Diocese of El Paso established the Catholic Foundation of El Paso to meet growing financial requirements.

Bibliography: C. E. CASTAÑEDA, *Our Catholic Heritage in Texas, 1519–1936*, 7 v. (Austin 1936–58).

[G. CARIE]

ELPHINSTONE, WILLIAM

Bishop, chancellor of Scotland, founder of the University of Aberdeen; b. Glasgow, *c.* 1431; d. Edinburgh, Oct. 25, 1514. Elphinstone graduated (M.A.) from the University of Glasgow in 1462, and later distinguished himself in Canon Law and civil law at Paris and Orléans before returning to Glasgow in 1471. Having been elected rector of the University in 1474, he was appointed senior ecclesiastical judge of Scotland in 1478 and bishop of Ross in 1481, and was transferred to Aberdeen in 1483. A trusted friend of James III, he became chancellor of Scotland in 1488 but was deprived of the office on the king's murder later that year. A skillful diplomat, he negotiated several treaties for the Scottish crown with England, France, and Germany. He founded the University of Aberdeen in 1495, effected a number of important legal and liturgical reforms, and was nominated archbishop of Saint Andrews after the disaster of Flodden in 1513. The most informed, alert, and wisest Scot of his age, he died before his promotion could be ratified.

Bibliography: *Hectoris Boetii Murthlacensium et Aberdonensium episcoporum vitae,* ed. J. MOIR (Aberdeen 1894). L. MACFARLANE, ''William Elphinstone,'' *Aberdeen University Review* 36 (1956) 225–241; 37 (1958) 253–271; 39 (1961) 1–18; *Lexikon für Theologie und Kirche* 2 3:829.

[L. MACFARLANE]

EL SALVADOR, THE CATHOLIC CHURCH IN

Capital: San Salvador.
Size: 8,124 sq. miles.
Population: 6,122,515 in 2000.
Languages: Spanish; Nahua is spoken in some regions.
Religions: 5,265,360 Catholics (86%); 857,152 Protestants (14%).
Metropolitan See: San Salvador, with suffragans Chalatenago, Santa Ana, San Miguel, San Vicente, Santiago María, Sonsonate, and Zacateclouca. There is also a military ordinariate located in El Salvador.

The territory of El Salvador is bounded on the north by Honduras, on the east by Honduras and the Gulf of Fonseca, on the south by a 160-mile stretch of North Pacific Ocean coastline, and on the west by Guatemala. The most densely populated republic in Central America, El Salvador is also the smallest, containing several volcanic mountain ranges in addition to a plateau region and the narrow coastal region. It is characterized by a tropical climate, frequent earthquakes, and regular volcanic activity. The nation still reflects its heritage as a Spanish colony through its inhabitants, most of whom are mestizo; only five percent have pure native blood.

About 63 percent of Salvadorans are engaged in agriculture, the major production of which includes coffee, sugar, corn, and cotton. Textiles and the production of electricity also figure prominently in El Salvador's economic base. Boasting the most developed highway system in all Central America in the early 20th century, El Salvador continued to be easily navigable despite its mountainous terrain.

Originally inhabited by Maya and Pipil tribes, El Salvador's Custatlán region was discovered and subsequently conquered by Pedro de Alvarado, a lieutenant under Spanish conquistador Hernan Cortéz, in 1523. In April 1525 Alvarado founded the city of San Salvador in the Valle de la Bermuda, naming Diego de Holguín the first governor. De Holguín gradually expanded his domain, and the area now know as El Salvador became a province of the Captaincy General of Guatemala in 1542. Religious sent from Spain to administer to the region's Spanish populations also instituted missionary activities, although many of the natives in the region ultimately died as a result of European-introduced diseases.

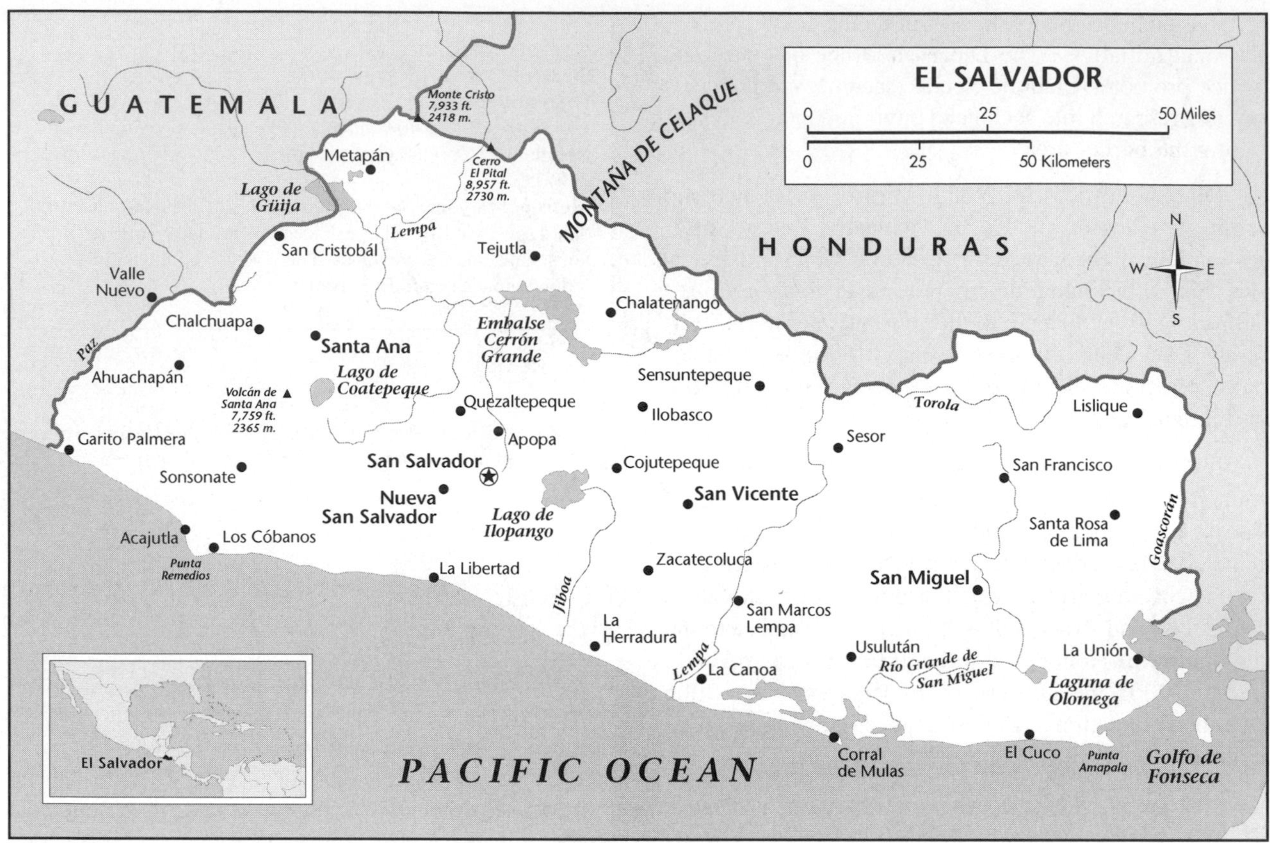

The movement for political independence from Spain first took shape in Custatlán in November of 1811; it failed, as would a second rebellion in 1814. Ultimately, however, the Captaincy General of Guatemala declared its own independence from Spain on Sept. 15, 1821, releasing as it did so each of its provinces. The civilian government of El Salvador opposed the immediate annexation of the newly emancipated Central American states to the Mexican empire of Augustín de Iturbide, and when forced to join, threatened to instead seek incorporation in the United States. The formation of the United Provinces of Central America via a constitution approved on Nov. 22, 1824, resolved the situation, as El Salvador and the other four Central American republics formed a federation of their own. That constitution, on the motion of Salvadorean priest Simeón Canãs, also abolished slavery. Due to internal conflicts, the United Provinces dissolved, leaving El Salvador an independent republic in 1839. Battles between liberal and conservative factions within its civilian government stagnated economic development for the next 70 years.

By the early 20th century El Salvador had developed an elite ruling class, the majority of its citizens exploited and forced to work the coffee plantations. In 1932 peasant unrest resulted in an outbreak of violence, called the Matanza, during which 10,000 lost their lives at the hands of the military. Although a series of military coups wrestled political power and attempted to institute social reforms in the country, their efforts were checked by the financial strength of the nation's landowning families.

In the early 1960s the Church supported efforts by the newly formed Christian Democratic party and the United States to encourage economic development in El Salvador by an infusion of aid to encourage business growth. However, by the early 1970s it became clear to Church leadership that such aid did little to help the poor, but instead contributed to the tradition of exploitation. Rising threats from communist sympathizers spurred on by Cuban dictator Fidel Castro, as well as outbreaks of guerilla-type violence from the Marxist militant group Frente Faravundo Marti de Liberación (FMLN) prompted the United States to back a restrictive, authoritarian regime during the 1980s. During over a decade of civil war 75,000 Salvadorans lost their lives, their tragic deaths documented by the San Salvador Archdiocese human rights office, Tutela Legal, despite government opposition.

As the people of El Salvador struggled against poverty and oppression, they found a leader in Oscar ROMERO, installed as archbishop of San Salvador on Feb.

Church in El Salvador. (©Cory Langley)

23, 1977. Like many Catholic leaders, Romero turned to unionization and education of the peasantry as a way out of El Salvador's economic difficulties, believing it would be by such means that the Church would be a force for liberation. He attempted to end the violence of desperate leftist guerillas as well as powerful right-wing military extremist factions, calling on soldiers to lay down their arms. Unfortunately, such tactics threatened the ruling class, and Church organizations were vilified by the media as reforming priests were expelled from the country or assassinated by paramilitary groups bearing such names as the Wind Warriors Union. Handbills appeared proclaiming ''Be a Patriot. Kill a Priest!'' The violence increased following a bloodless coup by members of the military ostensibly representing Christian Democrat interests on Oct. 15, 1979. During a radio sermon on March 23,1980 Romero reminded soldiers that they were not obligated to obey a law contrary to God's law: ''In the Name of God,'' Romero exhorted, ''stop the repression.'' He was assassinated by a right-wing death squad the next day, as he was offering the sacrifice of the Mass. His funeral procession was met by further violence, as 26 people were killed in gunfire and explosions. On a visit to San Salvador in February 1996, Pope John Paul II would pay homage to the legendary priest and would be presented with a petition requesting Romero's beatification.

Violence against the Church continued into the late 1980s, as priests, nuns, and other religious were systematically killed by right-wing death squads. Fortunately, in 1992 the political situation in El Salvador was defused when guerillas signed a treaty with the pacifist government of President Felix Alfredo Cristiani, ending the era of violence. Aided by such Church leaders as San Salvadoran Archbishop Arturo Rivera Damas, the peace process proved successful, although inclusion of the leftist FMLN resulted in the 1998 introduction of legislation to legalize abortion in the predominately Catholic country. El Salvador continued to operate as a democratic republic under the constitution of Dec. 23, 1983; due to an increase in exports and international financial aid, its economy was in an upturn in 2000.

As El Salvador's government worked to improve the lives of its citizens, it was struck by a series of natural disasters as 1999's Hurricane Mitch was followed two years later by a massive earthquake that left 50,000 families homeless. Church leaders responded in all cases with massive humanitarian aid, and Pope John Paul directed his personal charity, Cor Unum, to send financial aid to the region. During the late 1990s Protestantism began making inroads into this predominately Catholic country. After peace was restored to the region, El Salvador witnessed an increase in missionary activity by the estimated one million Protestant evangelicals entering the country.

Bibliography: F. D. PARKER, *The Central American Republics* (New York 1964).

[L. LAMADRID/EDS.]

ELVIRA, COUNCIL OF

Elvira, the Roman city of Illiberis in southern Spain, near modern Granada, a bishopric in Roman and Visigothic times, was the site of a synod held either in 300–303 (L. Duchesne) or in 309 (H. Gregoire). Attending were 19 bishops and 26 priests representing 37 separate communities, all but five situated in southern Spain, the exceptions being Saragossa, León, Toledo, Calahorra, and Braga. The five provinces of Galicia, Tarragona, Baetica, Lusitania, and Carthagena also were represented. Bishop Felix of Acci (Guadix) presided, and among the delegates was Bishop Hosius of Córdoba. This is the first known council held in Spain, as well as the first council of which the disciplinary canons have been preserved, providing the first real knowledge of the Church in Spain.

The Council was evidently called to deal with disciplinary rather than doctrinal questions. It sought to combat pagan influences in the rapidly increasing Christian body, both by imposing a series of penalties based on exclusion from the Sacraments, and by reinforcing the rights and powers of the hierarchy. The success it achieved is shown by the reproduction of 14 of its 81 canons in the later Councils of ARLES, NICAEA, and SARDICA.

The council has been accused of rigorism; its canons are certainly severe. Most of them deal with penitential discipline. Lesser faults were punished with deprivation of Communion for one, two, three, five, or even ten years. For certain faults no reconciliation was possible even at the hour of death. These faults included idolatry (cc. 1–3), murder by witchcraft (c. 6), repeated fornication or adultery (cc. 7, 47), divorce (c. 8), procuring (c. 12), marriage with pagan priests (c. 17), incest (c. 66), homosexual rape (c. 71), an accusation responsible for the death of the accused (c. 73), and false accusations of the clergy (c. 75).

Definitive exclusion from the Communion in cases of reiterated major sin existed before the council, but it seems to have extended this penalty to cases when the sin was committed for the first time. This severity appears again in the Council of Saragossa (380); it was mitigated by *c.* 400. Until then the Church considered that it did not possess authority to forgive certain sins, and abandoned the sinner to God's mercy.

According to the testimony of the canons, in Spain the catechumenate normally lasted two years (c. 42), but could be extended in doubtful cases (cc. 4, 37). Circus charioteers and actors could not become catechumens without giving up their profession (c. 62). The canons mention Baptism and Confirmation (cc. 38, 77) and the indissolubility of marriage (c. 9). They insist on a holy way of life for the clergy, bishops, priests, deacons, and subdeacons. They are to be carefully selected (cc. 24, 30, 51, 80), are not to immerse themselves in trade (c. 19) or to practice usury (c.20). The purity of their life is stressed (cc. 18, 27). Canon 33 is the oldest legislation enjoining clerical continence in marriage. Canon 53 prohibits one bishop from receiving back into communion a Christian excommunicated by another. Canon 36 prohibits all paintings in churches. This regulation no doubt results from a wish to avoid the appearance of imitating paganism.

Dicing was prohibited since the dice bore images of pagan gods (c. 79). The pagan practice of lighting candles in cemeteries was forbidden (c. 34). Marriage with an ordinary pagan was condemned, but less severely than with Jews or heretics (cc. 15–16). One should not eat with Jews (c. 50), sacrifice with pagans (c. 59), or (ideally) tolerate idols in one's house (c. 41); but a Christian who was killed for public, unprovoked attacks on idols was not thereby a martyr (c. 60). A Christian magistrate was not allowed to take part in church services during his year of office (c. 56). Christians who functioned as pagan priests were more severely disciplined (cc. 2–4, 55).

Bibliography: J. D. MANSI, *Sacrorum Conciliorum nova et amplissima collectio*, 31 v. (Florence-Venice 1757-98) 2:2–406. *Patrologia Latina* 84:301–310. A. C. VEGA, ed., *España Sagrada,* v.56 (Madrid 1957) critical ed.; *ibid.* v.53–54 (Madrid 1961) discussion. J. VIVES et al., *Concilios visigóticos e hispano-romanos* (Madrid 1963) 1–15. C. J. VON HEFELE, *Histoire des conciles d'après les documents originaux*, tr. and continued by H. LECLERCQ, 10 v. in 19 (Paris 1907–38) 1:212–264. G. BARGILLE, *Dictionnaire de théologie catholique* 4.2:2378–97. Z. GARCÍA VILLADA, *Historia eclesiástica de España,* 3 v. in 5 (Madrid 1929–36) 1:301–325. J. GROTZ, *Die Entwicklung des Bussstufenwesens in dervornicänischen Kirche* (Freiburg 1955) 414–427. J. GAUDEMET, *Dictionnaire d'histoire et de géographie ecclésiastiques*, ed. A. BAUDRILLART et al. (Paris 1912–)15:317–347. H. GRÉGOIRE et al., *Les Persécutions dans l'Empire romain* (Brussels 1950).

[J. N. HILLGARTH]

ELWELL, CLARENCE

Educator, bishop; b. Cleveland, Ohio, Feb. 4, 1904, one of six children of George and Josephine Messer Elwell; d. Columbus, Ohio, Feb. 16, 1973. He grew up in Holy Name Parish, Cleveland, where he attended grade and high school.

After attaining his bachelor's degree at John Carroll University, Elwell attended St. Mary Seminary in Cleveland and then went to the University of Innsbruck, Austria, where he was ordained on March 17, 1929.

From 1929 to 1933, Elwell served as assistant pastor at St. Cecilia Parish in Cleveland. He was then appointed assistant superintendent of diocesan school in Cleveland and in 1934 received his master's degree from Western Reserve University. In 1938, he received his doctorate from Harvard. His doctoral dissertation, ''Catholic Religious Education in France 1750–1850,'' was published in book form by Harvard's Graduate School of Education.

In 1938, Elwell was named director of high schools and academies in Cleveland and in 1946 was appointed diocesan school superintendent. He was named a right reverend monsignor in 1949 and a prothonotary apostolic in 1960. At this time, he also received an honorary doctorate from John Carroll University.

Elwell was named auxiliary bishop of Cleveland on Nov. 7, 1962, and was consecrated in St. John Cathedral on December 21. In February 1966 he was named rector of St. John's Cathedral. In November of that year he was named vicar for Catholic education in Cleveland.

Over the years as superintendent of schools, his range of performance was wide indeed as the following would indicate: he returned the schools to the phonics method of teaching reading; he developed a planned acceleration program for the gifted grade school students; he brought more male teachers into the grade schools; he furthered advanced teacher training through the formation of associations for high school teachers; he greatly expanded the diocesan school board, bringing in numerous professionals, including religious and laymen; he developed numerous textbooks and series, which have spread to many dioceses; he established a diocesan radio station to broadcast to the school system's classrooms; he brought about the $22 million high school building program; he expanded the Confraternity of Christian Doctrine program.

On May 29, 1968, Elwell was named the Eighth Ordinary of the Diocese of Columbus. He stated that in Columbus his objective would be to complete already well-established programs. In four years he brought to fruition several religious, educational, charitable, and social programs.

[B. APPLEGATE]

ELY, ANCIENT SEE AND ABBEY OF

In the 8th century Venerable BEDE recorded the main points of the tradition of a Benedictine abbey at Ely (*Hist. Eccl.* 4.19), and the monk of Ely who wrote the 12th-century *Historia Eliensis* amplified Bede's account. Bede noticed the unusual location of Ely in a province of the East Angles surrounded by marshes and the sea, ''in the nature of an island.'' In 649 St. ETHELREDA (Audrey), daughter of Anna, King of the East Angles, received the ''Isle of Ely'' as a marriage gift from her husband Tonbert, chieftain of the South Gyrwe. After his death she married Egfrid of Northumbria, who allowed her to become a nun. Returning to Ely, she built a double monastery (673) on the west bank of the Ouse (16 miles NNE of Cambridge) and ruled over it until her death (679). Her sister Sexburgh succeeded her as abbess.

Marauding Danes destroyed St. Ethelreda's convent *c.* 870. A century later, ETHELWOLD, Bishop of Winchester, persuaded King EDGAR to establish at Ely a Benedictine house for men. Edgar's charter of foundation and liberal endowment created the medieval ''liberty'' of Ely, the territorial base of a quasi-palatine authority enjoyed by subsequent abbots and bishops. This temporal power and responsibility became very significant soon after the Conquest. Ely and the surrounding fenland provided a stronghold for Hereward during his legend-making resistance (1070) to King WILLIAM I. For almost two centuries thereafter Ely was a bordermarch, a citadel that English kings endeavored to protect—not always successfully—against seizure by an opponent. The search for loyal and experienced administrators led to frequent royal interference in abbatial and episcopal elections at Ely.

In October 1109 the Diocese of Ely was separated from that of Lincoln. The Benedictine monks of the conventual cathedral, numbering about 70 at most, formed the bishop's chapter. Bishop Harvey, translated from BANGOR, first ruled the diocese, which included Cambridgeshire as well as the Isle of Ely. Within the ''liberty'' of Ely the bishop performed functions comparable to those of a royal sheriff. A remarkable number of the bishops of Ely (for a list of bishops, see P. Gams, *Series episcoporum ecclesiae catholicae* 188) were appointed to the highest offices in the realm; prior to the 16th-century dissolution, Ely provided eight chancellors and seven royal treasurers.

The cathedral of Ely contains architectural elements representing building styles predominant between 1100 and 1500. The nave and transept are late Norman; the Galilee porch is early English; the lady chapel is in the decorated style and the chantry of Bishop Alcock is an example of perpendicular. The cathedral's most notable feature is a large octagonal tower over the central crossing.

During the bishopric of Thomas Goodrich (1533–54) the monastery at Ely was suppressed (Nov. 18, 1539) and the conventual church transformed into a secular cathedral (1541). Eight prebendaries and the dean thereafter formed the new cathedral chapter. The last Roman Catholic bishop was Thomas Thirlby (1554–59). He was imprisoned by Elizabeth and died in 1570.

Bibliography: THOMAS OF ELY, *Liber Eliensis,* ed. D. J. STEWART (London 1848). *Liber Eliensis,* ed. E. O. BLAKE (Camden Society, ser. 3, v.92; London 1962). J. BENTHAM, *History and Antiquities of the Conventual and Cathedral Church of Ely* (2d ed. Norwich, Eng. 1812). *The Victoria History of the County of Cambridgeshire and the Isle of Ely,* ed. L. F. SALZMAN et al., 4 v. and index (London 1938–60). E. MILLER, *The Abbey and Bishopric of Ely: . . . from the 10th Century to the Early 14th Century* (Cambridge, Eng. 1951). D. J. STEWART, *On the Architectural History of Ely Cathedral* (London 1868). D. KNOWLES and J. K. S. ST. JOSEPH, *Monastic Sites from the Air* (Cambridge, Eng. 1952).

[A. R. HOGUE]

ELZÉAR OF SABRAN, ST.

Count of Ariano (Benevento), Franciscan tertiary(?); b. Ansouis (Provence), France, 1286; d. Paris, Sept. 27, 1323. He married DELPHINA OF SIGNE (1299 or 1300), and in 1316 they each took a vow of chastity. In 1312 Elzéar fought for Naples against Emperor HENRY VII, and he conquered Ariano in 1313. From 1317 on he was counselor to Duke Charles of Calabria, for whom he went in 1323 as ambassador to Paris. He died there and was buried in the Franciscan habit. His remains were brought to Apt the following year. In 1369 he was canonized by his own godchild Urban V, who published the papal bull only in 1371. His remains were transferred to the cathedral of Apt in 1791. Elzéar was a great apostle of Christian charity.

Feast: Sept. 27.

Bibliography: S. BERNARD, *Les époux vierges : Elzéar de Sabran et Delphine de Signe* (Paris 1994). P. A. GIANGROSSO, *Four Franciscan Saints' Lives : German Texts from Codex Sangallensis 589* (Stuttgart 1987).

[L. HARDICK]

EMANATIONISM

A philosophical and theological form of PANTHEISM, according to which all things emanate or flow forth from God as from a primal source or principle. It is opposed to the doctrine of CREATION and of PARTICIPATION, and also to world-formation and evolutionary theories. Whereas the doctrine of creation maintains that the world was formed from nothing (*ex nihilo*), emanationism holds that all things (some immediately, others mediately) proceed from the single substance of God, and this by a type of natural necessity and not by a decree of the divine will. Whereas world-formation theories teach that there is some eternal matter or substrate from which the universe was formed, emanationism maintains that everything is contingent, matter included, and that matter itself emanates from the primal source. In most forms of evolutionism the world principle is regarded as itself undergoing transformation and development and as entering into the constitution of the universe; in emanationism, on the other hand, the primal source or principle remains unchanged as everything else proceeds from it. Again, the process of evolution, at least in its totality, is generally regarded as an ascent, a movement upward toward a greater perfection; emanation, however, is a descent, beginning with the infinitely perfect and yielding emanated beings that are increasingly less pure, less perfect, and less divine. The Infinite is postulated as a starting point, instead of being the goal that the universe continually strives to realize.

History. Vague indications of emanationism are found in ancient mythologies and religions, especially those of India, Egypt, and Persia. Thus in the UPANISHADS things are said to issue from their eternal principle, as the web, from the spider; the plant, from the earth; and the hair, from the skin. Though these and other expressions may be interpreted in the sense of emanationism, however, they are not sufficiently explicit to serve as a basis for the assertion that such systems of philosophy or religion are emanationistic. The teaching of PHILO JUDAEUS on this point is not much clearer. His thought was influenced by two distinct currents: Greek philosophy, especially PLATONISM, and JUDAISM. In his effort to reconcile their teachings, he sometimes falls into inconsistencies and it is difficult to ascertain his true position. According to Philo, God, who is infinitely perfect, cannot act on the world immediately but only through powers or forces (δυνάμεις) that are not identical with Him, but proceed from Him. The primitive divine force is the Logos. Whether the Logos is a substance or only an attribute is not clear in his teaching. From the Logos proceeds the Spirit (πνεῦμα), which is a type of WORLD SOUL. Sometimes God is described as the efficient and active cause of the universe, sometimes also as immanent, as the one and the whole (εἷς καὶ τὸ πᾶν αὐτός ἐστιν).

Neoplatonism. The first clear and systematic expression of emanationism is to be found in the Alexandrian school of NEOPLATONISM. According to PLOTINUS, the most important representative of the school, the first principle of all things is the One. Absolute unity and simplicity is the best expression by which God can be designated. The One is a totally indetermined essence, for any attribute or determination would introduce both limitation and multiplicity. Even intelligence and will cannot belong to this primal reality, for these imply the duality of subject and object, and duality presupposes a higher unity. The One, however, is also described as the First, the Good, the Light, and the Universal Cause. From the One all things proceed; not by creation, which would be an act of the will and therefore incompatible with unity, and not by a spreading of the divine substance, since this would do away with the essential oneness. The One is not all things, but is before all things. Emanation is the process by which all things are derived from the One. The infinite goodness and perfection overflows, as it were; and while remaining within itself and losing nothing of its own perfection, it generates other beings, sending them forth from its own superabundance. Or again, as brightness is produced by the rays of the sun, so everything is a radiation (περίλαμψις) from the Infinite Light. The various emanations form a series, every successive step of which is an image of the preceding one, though inferior to it. The first reality that emanates from the One is the Nous, a pure intelligence, an immanent and changeless thought that effects no activity outside of itself. The Nous is an image of the One and, coming to recognize itself as an image, introduces the first duality, that of subject and object. The Nous includes in itself the intellectual world, or the world of Ideas of PLATO. From the Nous emanates the World Soul, which forms the transition between the world of Ideas and the world of the senses. The World Soul is intelligent, and in this respect similar to the ideal world, but it also tends to realize the Ideas in the material world. It generates particular souls, or rather plastic forces that are the forms of all things. Finally, these souls and their particular forces beget matter, which is of itself indetermined and becomes determined by its union with the forms.

With a few variations in the details, the same essential doctrine of emanation is taught by IAMBLICHUS and PROCLUS. With Plotinus, Iamblichus identifies the One with the Good, but assumes an absolutely first One, which is anterior to the One and is utterly ineffable. From it emanates the One; from the One the intelligible world (Ideas); and from the intelligible world, the intellectual world (thinking beings). According to Proclus, from the One come the unities (ἑνάδες), which alone are related to the world. From the unities emanate the triads of the intelligible essences (being), the intelligible-intellectual essences (life), and the intellectual essences (thought). These again are further differentiated. Matter comes directly from one of the intelligible triads.

Gnosticism. The Gnostics taught that from God, the Father, emanated numberless divine, supramundane Aeons, less and less perfect, which, taken all together, constitute the fullness (πλήρωμα) of divine life (*see* GNOSIS; GNOSTICISM). Wisdom, the last of these, produced an inferior wisdom named Achamoth and also the psychical and material worlds. To denote the mode according to which an inferior is derived from a superior degree, BASILIDES employs the term ἀπόρρια, meaning flowing from, or efflux; and VALENTINUS, the term προβολή, meaning throwing forth or projection.

Christianity. The Fathers of the Church and Christian writers, especially when treating of the divine EXEMPLARISM or of the relations of the three divine Persons in the Trinity, and sometimes when speaking of the origin of the universe, use expressions that remind one of the theory of emanation. Such expressions, however, must be interpreted in light of the doctrine of creation to which they adhered. PSEUDO-DIONYSIUS follows Plotinus and the later Neoplatonists, especially Proclus, and frequently borrows their terminology. Yet he attempts to adapt their views to the teachings of Christianity. For him, God is primarily goodness and love, and other beings are emanations from His goodness, as light is an emanation from the sun.

JOHN SCOTUS ERIGENA took his doctrine from Pseudo-Dionysius and interpreted it in the sense of pantheistic emanationism. For him, there is only one Being, who, by a series of substantial emanations, produces all things. Nature has four divisions, or, more precisely, there are four stages of the one nature: (1) The nature that creates but is not created, i.e., God in His primordial, incomprehensible reality, unknown and unknowable for all beings, even for Himself. God alone truly is, and He is the essence of all things. (2) The nature that is created and also creates, i.e., God considered as containing the ideas, prototypes, or primordial causes of things. This is the ideal world. (3) The nature that is created but does not create, i.e., the world of things existing in space and time. All of these flow, proceed, or emanate from the first principle of being. Creation is a ''procession,'' and creatures and God are but one and the same reality. In creatures God manifests Himself—hence the term *theophania,* by which Erigena describes this process. (4) Nature that neither creates nor is created, i.e., God as the term toward which everything ultimately returns.

Arabian Philosophy. Influenced in many points by Neoplatonism, ARABIAN PHILOSOPHY generally holds much the same form of emanationism, viz, the emanation of the different spheres to which all things celestial and terrestrial belong. According to ALFARABI, from the First Being, conceived as intelligent (and in this Alfarabi departs from Plotinus), the intellect emanates; from the intellect, the world soul; and from the world soul, matter. Avicenna teaches that matter is eternal and uncreated. From the First Cause comes the first intelligence, from which follows a series of processions and emanations of the various celestial spheres down to the earthly sphere on which man dwells. For Averroës, the intellect is not individual but is identical with the universal spirit, which is an emanation from God. A later Arab mystic, IBN 'ARABĪ, illustrates the process of emanation by comparison with a mirror, which receives the features of a man although the man and his features remain united.

Jewish Philosophy. In medieval JEWISH PHILOSOPHY, influences of Neoplatonism are apparent in the teachings of Avicebron and MAIMONIDES. In the CABALA, the doctrine of the Sephiroth, which was developed and systematized early in the 13th century, is essentially a doctrine of emanations. The Sephiroth are the necessary intermediaries between God and the universe, between the intellectual and the material world. They are divided into three groups, the first group of three forming the world of thought; the second group, also of three, the world of soul; and the last group of four, the world of matter.

Catholic Teaching. For Catholics, a discussion of emanationism can only take place in the context of the solutions proposed to the problem of God's nature, especially His simplicity and infinity (*see* GOD; INFINITY OF GOD; SIMPLICITY OF GOD). The doctrine of the Catholic Church is contained in the definition of the dogma of creation by the Fourth Lateran Council (H. Denzinger, *Enchiridion symbolorum*, ed. A. Schönmetzer, 800). VATICAN COUNCIL I also expressly condemns emanationism and anathematizes those who hold ''that finite things, both corporeal and spiritual, or at least spiritual, have emanated from the divine substance'' (*Enchiridion symbolorum* 3024; see also 3002).

See Also: MONISM.

Bibliography: C. A. DUBRAY, *The Catholic Encyclopedia*, ed. C. G. HERBERMANN et al., 16 v. (New York 1907–14) 5:397–99. T. P. ROESER, ''Emanation and Creation,'' *The New Scholasticism* 19 (1945) 85–116. G. FAGGIN, *Enciclopedia filosofica*, 4 v. (Venice-Rome 1957) 1:1861–64. K. JÜSSEN, *Lexikon für Theologie und Kirche*, ed. J. HOFER and K. RAHNER, 10 v. (2d, new ed. Freiburg 1957–65) 3:841–42. H. DÖRRIE, *Die Religion in Geschichte und Gegenwart*, 7 v. (3d ed. Tübingen 1957–65) 2:449–50.

[C. A. DUBRAY/W. A. WALLACE]

EMANCIPATION, CATHOLIC

Term applied to the process, culminating in the Emancipation Act of 1829, whereby Roman Catholics in England, Scotland, and Ireland were relieved of civil disabilities dating back to the 16th century. Although the movement for repeal of anti-Catholic laws was initiated earlier, the term was first employed in the early 19th century by analogy with the British movement for the emancipation of slaves.

Early Relief Acts. Under legislation initiated in the 16th century, commonly known as the penal laws, Roman Catholics in England, Scotland, and Ireland were subjected to severe penalties and disabilities. The measures, varied in character, often were passed to meet the demands of political exigencies and were at times and in different places only partially and sporadically enforced. Nevertheless, they constituted a perpetual threat to Catholics, and the slow and complicated work of repeal did not begin until the reign of George III (1760–1820). Under the Quebec Act of 1774, George III's new subjects in Canada, formerly subjects of Louis XV of France, were accorded nearly all the religious privileges they had previously enjoyed. Catholic bishops might legally exercise their powers, their rights to tithes from their flock being enforceable at law; and the Protestant government was permitted by Rome to exercise a nomination right in the appointment of higher clergy. Little opposition was encountered in the British Parliament during the passage of this measure, save from William Pitt, Earl of Chatham, but the significance of this last is only evident in the establishment of Pitt clubs in the next generation as centers of Protestant resistance to Catholic emancipation. The first real Anglican protest emerged over the proposals to relieve Nonconformist ministers and teachers from subscription to the THIRTY-NINE ARTICLES. In a hostile speech opposing the consequential Parliamentary Relief Bill, Sir Roger Newdigate raised the question whether George III could consent without breaking his coronation oath to maintain the Anglican establishment unimpaired.

Toleration for Catholics, as well as for Nonconformists, really began in the three kingdoms in the atmosphere of revolution in America and in France. During the American War the first concessions were made permitting Catholics to avoid penalties for religious observance, and an act of 1778 (17, 18 George III ch. 49, 60) enabled Catholics to hold long leases and to own landed property. These and all subsequent concessions depended upon subscription to an oath enacted in the Irish Parliament in 1774, testifying to the allegiance of the Catholic subscriber to the Hanoverian line and the Protestant settlement of 1702; denying to the exiled Stuarts any allegiance, and to the Pope any temporal power in the King's dominion; and denying belief in the doctrine that no faith should be kept with heretics, or that it was lawful to kill heretics. The 1778 English act, as well as the Irish, went through the respective Parliaments uneventfully. In Scotland, however, there was a great wave of antipapal feeling stimulated by the Presbyterian clergy, resulting in riots, the burning of the residence in Edinburgh of the Catholic bishop, George Hay, and the burning of Catholic property in Glasgow. The result was an appeal from pro-Catholic authorities to abandon the proposed relief bill. There followed in London the GORDON RIOTS, ten days in June 1780 of burning and looting by an antipopish mob.

Further progress in Catholic relief was necessarily inhibited; Edmund BURKE unsuccessfully appealed to the English Parliament to persevere with the Scottish relief bill. In Ireland, however, the second step taken in 1783 gave Catholic clergy legal protection and extended to the absolute purchase of real property by all Catholics the long lease concessions of 1778. After the outbreak of the French Revolution, England's second move toward international association with Catholicism took place in the flight of the old order from France. Many Catholic exiles took refuge in England. Not merely did the government, Anglican bishops, and landed class give refuge to the *emigré* French clergy, but modest schemes to provide for their support out of public money were set on foot. Privately, in Scotland, pensions were given to the two vicars apostolic and the few parish priests. Small capital building sums also were provided for Hay's seminaries at Alquoheries and Lismore. The third Irish relief bill was passed in 1791, admitting Catholics to the professions. In England the same year saw the passage of a similar measure over which there emerged a division between clergy and laity, as, under the influence of Charles BUTLER (1750–1832), papal pretensions were drastically tailored to Protestant prejudices, and even the Catholic community was for a moment in danger of being statutorily termed ''protesting Catholic Dissenters.'' Ultimately, under episcopal advice, the Irish oath was adopted. Butler responded by founding the Cisalpine Club, arguing that such an organization properly distinguished tolerable Catholic ideas from the ultramontane ones dominated by the Vatican.

In 1793, without a division, Parliament passed the first Scottish relief bill in approximately the same terms as for England and Ireland. In the same year, in the Irish Parliament, an advance was made that was maintained only in that kingdom until the final act of 1829. Catholics were now admitted to the franchise. More professional appointments were open to them, but not membership of Parliament. Proposals in 1795, under the aegis of the Whig Lord Lieutenant, Earl Fitzwilliam (1748–1833), to extend fully the relief measures, were abandoned in consequence of his embarrassing the government over attempting to displace the ruling Dublin clique. Two years later the Irish Parliament, recognizing the termination of Irish ecclesiastical education by the French authorities, approved the establishment of a seminary at home, with a body of trustees nominated in the act. These included the Protestant chief justices, the four Catholic archbishops, and additional bishops, the prelates being nominated personally without reference to their diocesan titles. In consequence, and with government money, there was established the Royal College of St. Patrick of Maynooth.

Act of Union. Regular association, as trustees, with the Catholic archbishops and other bishops gave such statesmen as Lord Castlereagh (1769–1822) considerable insight into the Irish political situation. The rebellion of 1798 was organized by the United Irishmen, a body concerned with political reform, drawing its strength from Dublin Protestants and Belfast Presbyterians, but also including some members of the Catholic Committee, which had played a decisive part in securing mitigation of the laws. After the war with France had commenced, Parliamentary reform had been outlawed, and the United Irishmen had sought support in a revolutionary program linked with Catholic agrarian societies, such as the Defenders, but also with the agnostic French revolutionary government. Few Catholic priests supported the rebellion of 1798; many condemned it, notably bishops, largely because of the association with French revolutionary destruction of organized religion.

Pitt's government, in the light of the French menace under Napoleon, determined to bring about the legislative Union amalgamating the Parliaments. Pitt persuaded the Irish Catholics not to oppose the Act of Union on the understanding that it would be followed by full emancipation. Castlereagh won support for the measure from most of the bishops and also planned a full emancipation scheme involving state payment of clergy and the veto on papal appointments to higher Church positions. The Union passed, and the United Kingdom of Great Britain and Ireland came into being on Jan. 1, 1801. The Protestant Episcopalian Church became the ''United Church of England and Ireland,'' doubly secured in a clause declared to be a fundamental article of the Act of Union. That the Church of Scotland was Presbyterian was tactfully ignored. And nothing was done for the Catholics. The King's susceptibilities regarding his coronation oath emerged nearly 30 years after Newdigate's, and Pitt resigned. When Pitt returned to office in 1804, George III insisted that he promise not to take up Emancipation again. However, the question became of greater significance particularly with the rise in Ireland of the Catholic middle class, until this latter element played the decisive part in forcing on government the solution of 1829.

Veto Question. After Pitt's death, the Whigs again took up Emancipation, sometimes reluctantly, but rarely abandoning it completely. Their ministry ''of all the talents,'' in deference to George III, postponed the issue as long as possible; they then resigned after withdrawing a relief bill. The King again insisted on guarantees of immunity from further ministerial pressure on the Catholic question. About 1808, the desire to dissolve anti-Catholic prejudices led in England to security proposals, such as one that Rome should concede the British government a veto on ecclesiastical appointments. Most of the English prelates agreed, but not so in Ireland, where the ten years since Castlereagh's negotiations had brought about fresh thinking. In particular, lay opinion in the Catholic Committee resented a measure that might result in the diocesan clergy becoming the government's paid agents. In subsequent years the veto proposal commended itself more and more to pro-Catholic Protestant statesmen. Henry Grattan (1746–1820), the leading Irish Whig, sponsored such a measure in 1813, which, however, was not presented on strict party lines, as it gained support from George Canning (1770–1827), the pro-Catholic Tory. Previous to its introduction, the Grattan-Canning bill had been approved by G. B. Quarantotti, Prefect of Propaganda, the Pope being Napoleon's prisoner and not in a position to decide.

Rise of O'Connell. At this stage Daniel O'CONNELL emerged as one of the leading Irish lay exponents of the question on the Catholic Board, as the successor to the Committee was called. He welcomed the bill but deplored the securities. The clergy of the Dublin province had already approved both, expressing themselves, under the influence of James Warren Doyle, Bishop of Kildare and Leighlin (1819–34), in a noncommittal manner. The clergy of the three remaining provinces were hostile in their reactions. O'Connell became the Irish spokesman by insisting that Irish Catholicism, so far as the United Kingdom was concerned, was more orthodox than Rome: ''I confess myself a Catholic, but I deny myself a Papist.'' Many of the Whigs now considered the abandonment of the veto and other securities. After the deaths of George III and Grattan in 1820, optimism prevailed temporarily regarding the possible favor of George IV. William Conyngham Plunket (1764–1854) introduced a further relief bill still maintaining the veto, but it failed to secure more than the approval of the Commons. The general antipathy of the Lords was now clear. George IV also showed himself unwilling to abandon the extreme Protestant position, which under his father had become identified with the maintenance of the prerogative. A bill of 1823 failed. It was now evident that monarchical and aristocratic objections could be maintained indefinitely. The reorganization in Ireland of the Catholic Association, as the Catholic Board had become to evade the law, again made the matter a real political issue. O'Connell's intimidatory tactics and his appeal to the forces of nationalism and democracy aroused fear among the Conservatives. The Whigs again rallied, this time making the mistake of forcing it into a party issue. The result was the revival of antipopery agitation by the ultra-Tories.

Protestant clubs, Pitt clubs, and Brunswick clubs attempted to intimidate the government from the ''open'' system, which, since Lord Liverpool (1770–1828) became Prime Minister in 1812, had permitted ministers to maintain a pro-Catholic attitude while not committing the government. But the absence of ultra-Conservative talent made these conspiracies ineffective. Each successive government after Liverpool's found itself more and more involved. The election of 1826 resulted in an increased number of anti-Catholics being returned to the Commons, indicating how extensive was Protestant antipathy among ordinary British voters. Again it was Ireland that brought about the change. The democratic Catholic Association pushed O'Connell into supporting a political agitation against members unprepared to advocate emancipation. In a few spectacular cases, landlord domination of county constituencies was overthrown. The Whigs and the Tories alike were subjected to strong pressure from their pro-Catholic members, who were virtually under notice from O'Connell that the large Catholic vote would be turned against them and would turn them out if they failed to advocate emancipation.

O'Connell's Election. The fact that O'Connell carefully distinguished the Catholic question from that of Parliamentary reform, to which he did not commit himself until the Tories drove him into the Whig camp, secured the alertness of more Irish members than merely the Whigs. His strength emerged in his successful return at the by-election in Clare when he displaced William Vesey FitzGerald in order to force the government from the ''open'' policy of neutrality through fear of losing Irish support. O'Connell's election in itself was yet a further threat to the ascendancy of Parliament. Whether or not the Duke of Wellington (1769–1852) and Sir Robert Peel (1788–1850), who had in the meantime conceded Nonconformist relief, were correct in thinking that the alternative to granting Catholic emancipation and admitting O'Connell was civil war in Ireland, the fact is that the Union was certainly threatened. The Catholic Association would undoubtedly be able to secure the election of a number of Catholics who might well collectively claim, perhaps at College Green, Dublin, to speak for Ireland and to deny to Westminster any representative character. Thus, to save the Union and to quiet Ireland, emancipation was conceded in the Emancipation Act, which became law on April 13, 1829.

Act of 1829. ''An Act for the relief of his majesty's Roman Catholic subjects'' (10 George IV ch. 7), as it was entitled, abolished the anti-Catholic oaths imposed in former statutes defining the qualifications for membership of the legislature and for public offices (save for a few offices still confined to Protestants, functioning personally for the monarch or in relation to the control of the established church). However, it still remained essential to take an oath of allegiance similar to the Irish oath of 1774, upholding the Protestant succession to the crown, denying the temporal power of the pope within the United Kingdom, and undertaking not to weaken the Protestant establishment. Its immediate positive effects were small. Few Irish and next to no English and Scottish Catholics were returned to Parliament or given high office for more than a generation. Its prestige significance, particularly for Ireland, is almost impossible to exaggerate, and as such it was resented by most of the Anglicans, by contrast with the rest of the Protestants. It was a moral victory in the eyes of Catholic Europe, which gave O'Connell the role of the leading Catholic liberal, particularly as he allied increasingly thereafter with the Whig reformers to compel Protestant vested interests to enforce the act.

In England the resentment of the establishment was evident in the reenactment by the 1829 act of the petty restrictions upon further recruitment to the religious orders, the prohibiting of usage of Church vestments in public or of the robes of public officeholders at Catholic ceremonies, as well as by the banning of the Catholic Association of Ireland and the refusal to admit O'Connell to Parliament until he was again elected. Even the English Catholics reflected the anti-Irish feeling by slighting him, and the Irish hierarchy pointedly ignored him in publicly thanking Wellington for securing the passage of the measure. On a long-term basis the act made possible the building up of the Catholic Church in both countries, though the change was not so apparent in Britain until the great Irish immigration of the mid-century.

Later Relief Acts. In 1844 (7 and 8 Victoria ch. 102) and 1926 (16 and 17 George V ch. 55) most of the remaining obsolescent anti-Catholic laws were repealed. The ineffective Ecclesiastical Titles Act of 1851 (14 and 15 Victoria ch. 60) prohibiting the use of territorial titles by Catholic bishops was repealed in 1871 (34 and 35 Victoria ch. 53). Among the disabilities still retained is the law restraining either the king or the queen of England from being a Roman Catholic. Roman Catholics are barred also from the offices of regent, lord chancellor, and keeper of the great seal, and from a few university places.

Bibliography: W. J. AMHERST, *The History of Catholic Emancipation and the Progress of the Catholic Church in the British Isles . . . from 1771 to 1820,* 2 v. (London 1886). G. F. A. BEST, "The Protestant Constitution and Its Supporters, 1800–1829," *Transactions of the Royal Historical Society,* 5th ser. 8 (London 1958) 105–27. R. D. EDWARDS, *Church and State in Tudor Ireland* (New York 1935); "Minute Book of the Catholic Committee, 1773–1792," in *Archivium Hibernicum* 9 (1942). N. GASH, *Mr. Secretary Peel* (Cambridge, Mass. 1961). É. HALÉVY, *History of the English People in the Nineteenth Century* (London 1924–), v.1–2. U. HENRIQUES, *Religious Toleration in England, 1787–1833* (London 1961). R. B. MCDOWELL, *Public Opinion and Government Policy in Ireland, 1801–1846* (London 1952). G. I. T. MACHIN, *The Catholic Question in English Politics, 1820–1830* (New York 1964). J. A. REYNOLDS, *The Catholic Emancipation Crisis in Ireland, 1823–1829* (New Haven 1954). M. ROBERTS, *The Whig Party, 1807–1812* (New York 1939). H. W. V. TEMPERLEY, "George Canning, the Catholics and the Holy See," in *Dublin Review* 193 (1933). M. WALL, *The Penal Laws, 1691–1760* (Dublin 1961). T. WYSE, *Historical Sketch of the Late Catholic Association of Ireland,* 2 v. (London 1829). D. GWYNN, *The Struggle for Catholic Emancipation, 1750–1829* (London 1928); *A Hundred Years of Catholic Emancipation, 1829–1929* (London 1929). B. N. WARD, *The Dawn of Catholic Emancipation, 1781–1803,* 2 v. (London 1909); *The Eve of Catholic Emancipation, 1808–1839,* 3 v. (London 1911–12); *The Sequel to Catholic Emancipation, 1830–1850,* 2 v. (London 1915).

[R. D. EDWARDS]

EMARD, JOSEPH MÉDARD

Joseph Médard Emard.

Archbishop, educator; b. St. Constant, Canada, April 1, 1853; d. Ottawa, Ontario, Canada, March 28, 1927. He was the son of Médard and Mathilde (Beaudin) Emard.

After pursuing classical studies at the Seminary of St. Thérèse and theology at the Grand Seminary, Montreal, he was ordained at Montreal June 10, 1876, and was appointed curate of Mile End (1876–80). He subsequently spent three years at Rome and received doctorates in theology and Canon Law. Before returning to Canada he toured the Holy Land. From 1880 to 1887 he served as pastor of St. Joseph's parish, Montreal. He lectured in ecclesiastical history at Laval University, Quebec, where he served as vice chancellor (1886–89) and was named chancellor (1889). In 1891 he became a canon of the cathedral and a year later was appointed bishop of Valleyfield when that diocese was established April 5, 1892. He was consecrated by Abp. E. C. Fabre of Montreal on June 9, 1892, and proved to be a talented administrator. He organized diocesan works, wrote several important pastoral letters, and founded a classical college affiliated with Laval University, as well as a kindergarten and a normal school for young women. He also introduced a community of Poor Clares. Emard took an active part in the First Plenary Council of Quebec (1909). While bishop of Valleyfield he served as ordinary for the Canadian armed forces during World War I. He was made assistant to the pontifical throne (1917) and promoted to the archiepiscopal See of Ottawa (June 2, 1922), where he was installed on September 20. He was the author of *Souvenirs d'un voyage en Terre-Sainte* (Montreal 1884), and several short works, instructions, and pastoral letters, which he compiled in his *Oeuvres complètes* (5 v. Montreal 1921–24). His pastoral letter *Congrès Eucharistique de Montreal* was quoted at length by Cardinal Vincenzo Vannutelli during that congress at Montreal in 1910.

[J. T. FLYNN]

EMBER DAYS

By an ancient tradition in the Roman rite, the historical 12 liturgical and penitential days arranged in four triads (*Quattuor tempora,* "the four seasons"). According to this tradition, a Wednesday, Friday, and Saturday in a determined week of each season were constituted Ember Days in the liturgical calendar: winter (the week after the third Sunday of Advent), spring (the week after the first Sunday of Lent), summer (in the week after Pentecost Sunday) and autumn (after the feast of the Holy Cross, September 14). They were observed liturgically in that each Ember Day has its own proper Office and Mass celebrated in violet vestments (red, however, in Pentecost). Though formerly observed as days of fast and total (1917 *Codex iuris canonici* (Rome 1918; repr. Graz 1955) c.1252.2) the Ember Days were not included among the days on which fast or abstinence are required according to the reorganization of penitential discipline contained in Pope Paul VI's apostolic constitution *Poenitemini* of Feb. 17, 1966.

Origin. Though the ultimate origins of the Ember Days are obscure, certain Jewish and pagan influences were operative in their formation. In view of the fact that the roots of the primitive Christian Church were in Judaism, it is not surprising that its religious practice influenced the discipline of the penitential system of the ancient Church. As early as the *Didache*, at the end of the apostolic period, therefore, Wednesday and Friday were observed as fast days, later as stational days, too. The penitential character of Wednesday was very probably inspired by the consideration that it was the day on which the Passion (the arrest of the Lord) commenced, while Friday was the traditional day on which the death of Christ was commemorated by the Church.

According to the *Liber pontificalis* (ed. L. Duchesne, 1:141) Callistus I (d. *c.* 223) created, basically, the Ember Days by constituting Saturday in addition to Wednesday and Friday as a fast day to be observed three times (summer, autumn, winter) in the year "in accordance with the prophecy of grain, wine and oil." We have here an example of Christian practice adapting (paralleling) a much older Roman usage, the so-called pagan feasts of nature, the *feriae messis* (harvest time in June to July), *feriae vindemiales* (vintage time in September), and *feriae sementinae* (seed time in December). But the early Church (e.g., Leo, *Sermo* 90.1; *Patrologia Latina*, ed. J. P. Migne, 54:447) saw also in these fast days a reflection of the ancient Jewish observance of which the book of Zechariah (8.19) speaks: "The fast days of the fourth, the fifth, the seventh and the tenth months shall become occasions of joy and gladness." While the origin of the penitential character of Saturday is somewhat uncertain, it seems probable that it developed through its close association with Friday. Thus Innocent I (d. 417), who extended the Saturday fast to every week of the year, wrote (*Epistola 25 ad Decentium* 4; *Patrologia Latina* 20:555): "Reason shows most clearly that we should fast on Saturday, because it stood between the sadness [of Good Friday] and the joy [of Easter Sunday]." And the *Liber pontificalis* (ed. L. Duchesne, 1.222) reports that Innocent constituted Saturday a fast day "because on Saturday the Lord was placed in the sepulchre and His disciples fasted." In 494 Gelasius I appointed Ember Saturdays as the liturgical days on which ordinations were to take place.

Though Callistus instituted three seasonal fasts, which the Roman Church observed in the fourth (June), the seventh (September) and the tenth (December) months, without however further determining the specific weeks in which these fasts were to be kept, it is not altogether clear when the fourth annual fast was instituted. Primitively the Lenten fast in its totality was regarded as the spring fast. Thus Leo described the practice of the Church that was current in his day: ''The [fasts] are so spread throughout the whole circle of the year that the law of abstinence is operative at all seasons. Thus indeed we observe the spring fast at Lent, the summer fast at Pentecost, the autumn fast in the seventh month, and the winter fast in this month [December] which is the tenth'' (*Sermo* 19.2; *Patrologia Latina* 54:186). Much later, the *Gelasian Sacramentary* (seventh century) gives evidence of a new fast in March, the first month, which was celebrated as a fast distinct from the Lenten observance. By the end of the seventh century this March fast had come to coincide with the fast of the 1st week of Lent [A. Chavasse, ''Les Messes quadragésimales du Sacramentaire Gélasien,'' *Ephemerides liturgicae* 63 (1949) 260–261]. This gradual development was confirmed by Gregory I (d. 604), so that at the end of his pontificate the Church in Rome was observing seasonal (March, June, September, December) fasts of three days (Wednesday, Friday, and Saturday).

The Ember Days, conceived and developed as a product of the Roman Church, were spread throughout northern Europe by missionaries who had been educated in the liturgical traditions of Rome. By the middle of the ninth century the observance of the four groups of Ember Days was widespread in the West. In the time between Gregory I (d. 604) and Gregory VII (d. 1085) the variable factor in the celebration of the Ember Days was the date of their occurrence. Different local churches followed different usages within the broad framework prescribed by Gregory I. The decision of Gregory VII, taken at the Roman Synod of 1078, is believed to represent the first authoritative determination of the specific days of the year on which the Ember Days would be observed by the universal Church in the course of the liturgical cycle (Bernold of Constance, *Micrologus* 24; *Patrologia Latina* 151:995).

Stational Observance. In the ancient church of Rome special churches were assigned for the liturgical observances of these days: the *ecclesia collecta* (where the people gathered) and the *ecclesia stationalis* (whither the people proceeded for the celebration of the liturgy of the day). At the Mass on Ember Wednesday three lessons were read; on Friday, two; and on Saturday, six (plus the Gospel), which may be a vestige of the old title, *Sabbatum in XII lectionibus.* It is possible that at one time 12 lessons were read on Ember Saturday; or it may be that at one time the six lessons were read both in Latin and in Greek. In the early Church Ember Saturday was an all-night (Saturday to Sunday) vigil, which culminated in the ordination rite on Sunday morning so that properly speaking there was no Liturgy celebrated on Saturday itself. Six of the holy orders were conferred, one after each of the first six lessons, the priesthood before the final verse of the Alleluia or the Tract that stands immediately before the Gospel. In terms of Ember Saturday as an ordination day the choice of the traditional stational churches can be explained: St. Mary Major (scrutiny of the candidates on Wednesday), the Twelve Apostles (public approbation of the candidates on Friday), St. Peter's (ordination on Sunday).

Bibliography: A. ADAM, *The Liturgical Year: Its History and Meaning after the Reform of the Liturgy* (Collegeville 1981). A. NOCENT, *The Liturgical Year*, 4 v. (Collegeville 1977). T. J. TALLEY, *The Origins of the Liturgical Year*, rev. ed. (Collegeville 1992). T. J. TALLEY, ''The Origin of the Ember Days: An Inconclusive Postscript,'' *Rituels: mélanges offerts à Pierre-Marie Gy*, ed. P. DE CLERCK and E. PALAZZO (Paris 1990) 465–72. I. H. DALMAIS, P. JOUNEL, and A.G. MARTIMORT, *The Liturgy and Time*, The Church at Prayer v. 4 (Collegeville 1992).

[R. E. MCNALLY/EDS.]

EMBOLISM

Means insertion, interpolation. In the liturgy, although used of other formulas, it usually refers to the prayer appended to the Lord's Prayer. A comparison with other liturgies shows that the Embolism to the Lord's Prayer is very ancient. In Gallican rites, as in the Roman Mass, the Embolism amplified only the last petition of the Our Father. Eastern liturgies (except the Byzantine, which has no Embolism but only a doxology) stress the last two petitions, often by a marked expansion.

In the Roman Rite of the Mass, the Embolism enlarges upon the last petition of the Our Father. The current translation reads: ''Deliver us, Lord from every evil and grant us peace in our day. In your mercy, keep us free from sin and protect us from all anxiety, as we wait in joyful hope for the coming of the Savior, Jesus Christ.''

Bibliography: J. A. JUNGMANN, *The Mass of the Roman Rite*, tr. F. A. BRUNNER, 2 v. (New York 1951–55) 2:284–285, 289.

[F. A. BRUNNER/EDS.]

EMBURY, PHILIP

Founder of the first U.S. Methodist congregation; b. Ballingrane, County Limerick, Ireland, September 1728; d. East Salem, N.Y., August 1773. His parents were German refugees from the Palatinate. He attended the village school and was apprenticed to a carpenter at an early age. Converted at a Methodist meeting in 1752, he became in 1758 an itinerant preacher. In 1760 he and his wife, Margaret Switzer, immigrated to New York City, where Embury taught school and worked as a carpenter. At the request of Mrs. Barbara Heck, he resumed preaching in 1766 and soon formed a congregation. Services were held in his home and in a rigging loft until 1768, when Embury built the first John Street Methodist Church, working on the construction of it himself. In 1770 Embury moved to a farm in Albany (now Washington) County, N.Y.

Bibliography: J. B. WAKELEY, *Lost Chapters Recovered from the Early History of American Methodism* (New York 1858). W. CROOK, *Ireland and the Centenary of American Methodism* (London 1866). S. SEAMAN, *Annals of N.Y. Methodism* (New York 1892).

[R. K. MACMASTER]

EMEBERT OF CAMBRAI, ST.

Identification of Emebert is difficult. Some historians claim that he was bishop of Cambrai-Arras after 627 but before 645 to 652 and that nothing else is known of him (J. Lestoquoy, *Catholicisme* 4:43). Others claim that Emebert was probably the CHORBISHOP of Brabant, son of St. AMALBERGA and the Count of Kontich (Antwerp), and brother of St. GUDULA and St. Renelda (N. Huyghebaert, *Dictionnaire d'histoire et de géographie ecclésiastiques* 15:382–383). Of this Emebert, it is known only that he willed his villa of Merchtem (Brabant) to the church of Our Lady of Cambrai and died after 712 at Ham (Brabant), where he was buried.

Feast: Jan. 15 (Dioceses of Arras, Cambrai, and Lille).

Bibliography: L. DUCHESNE, *Fastes épiscopaux de l'ancienne Gaule* (Paris 1907–1915) 3:108–110. R. PODEVIJN, *De hl. Gudula en hare familie* (Aalst 1927). H. LANCELIN, *Histoire du diocèse de Cambrai* (Valenciennes 1946). M. COENS, ''Le Lieu de naissance de sainte Renelde d'après sa 'Vita,''' *Analecta Bollandiana* 69 (1951) 348–387.

[É. BROUETTE]

EMERIC OF HUNGARY, ST.

Prince (Imre in Hungarian); b. 1007; d. Sept. 2, 1031. He was the son of STEPHEN I, king of HUNGARY, and Gisela. Very little is known about this young prince beyond the fact that he was educated by GERARD OF CSANÁD, made a vow of chastity but was married *c.* 1026 for reasons of state to some foreign princess, and died in a hunting accident. In some sources he appears under the name Henry. Popular in Hungary and Poland, Emeric was canonized in 1083. In the 20th century his cult was revived, particularly in the interwar years when he was honored as the patron saint of Hungarian youth. His legend was written early in the 12th century and his relics are preserved in Székesfehérvár and in Esztergom. Usually he is represented holding a lily.

Feast: Nov. 4.

Bibliography: Sources. *Legenda sancti Emerici ducis,* in *Scriptores rerum Hungaricarum,* ed. I. SZENTPÉTERY, v. 2 (Budapest 1938) 441–460. *Acta Sanctorum* Nov. 2.1:477–491. **Literature.** L. HARSÁNYI, *Az elragadott herceg: Szent Imre herceg életregénye* (Budapest 1990). S. TÓTH, *Magyar és lengyel Imre-legendák* (Acta Universitatis Szegediensis, Acta Historica 11; Szeged 1962). *Szent István Emlékkönyv,* 3 v. (Budapest 1938) 1:412–418, 557–570; 2:570–573. D. VARGHA, *Szent Imre problémák* (Budapest 1931). J. SZALAY, *Catholicisme* 4:44.

[D. SINOR]

EMERSON, RALPH WALDO

Clergyman, essayist, poet, and philosopher; b. Boston, Mass., May 25, 1803; d. Concord, Mass., April 27, 1882. He came of a long line of clergymen; his father had left Calvinism for Unitarianism and was minister at Boston's famous First Church. Emerson entered Harvard College (1817) and upon graduation taught school for a time. He entered Harvard Divinity School (1825), and was appointed pastor of the Second Church (Unitarian) in Boston in 1829. He married in 1829, but his wife died in 1831. He very quickly found himself at odds with Unitarian doctrine and in 1832 resigned his pastorate. The same year he sailed for Europe. After a year of deeply stimulating experiences (he met, among others, COLERIDGE, Wordsworth, and Carlyle, he returned home. He made two more trips abroad, in 1847 and 1872.

In 1836 he published *Nature,* which, like so many of his writings, has a strong manifesto-like quality. It is a challenging declaration of truths toward which many of his contemporaries were groping, and reveals Emerson probing into human reality and the world of nature in order to liberate men from a mechanistic view of the world. Soon there gathered around him a loosely knit group known as Transcendentalists. (*See* TRANSCENDENTALISM, LITERARY.) In 1841 he published *Essays, First Series* and in 1844 *Essays, Second Series.* Then followed *Poems* (1847), *Representative Men* (1850), *English Traits* (1856), *Conduct of Life* (1860), *May Day* (1867), *Society and Solitude* (1870), and *Letters and Social Aims* (1875).

Emerson was to a marked degree universal-minded. Thus he felt drawn to both the Orient and the Occident, as well as to the most advanced movements of thought in his own time. He was always at home in the great literatures, and entered with ease worlds that seemed far removed from his own. It was characteristic of him that he could be carried away by Dante's *Vita Nuova,* which he said "reads like the Book of Genesis." Under great difficulties, this son of the Puritans undertook its translation.

It is significant that Emerson's universality should have blossomed out of a mind so strikingly American. In essays like "The American Scholar" and "Self-Reliance," Emerson speaks for the frontier and not merely for ROMANTICISM; the pioneer spirit was as vital in him as his feeling for his Puritan ancestry and his ties with Coleridge, Wordsworth, and Carlyle. Emerson was moved by this frontier spirit to follow in the footsteps of the Puritan thinker Jonathan EDWARDS. Emerson became passionately attached to the world revealed by the senses, and viewed its perception as integral to spiritual vision itself. Moreover, as with other Americans, the enterprise of carving a new world out of the wilderness left its mark on him, reinforcing to a maximum degree that feeling of the all-embracing unity of life and interconnectedness of things that springs up so spontaneously in man. Again, as were other Americans, he was alert to the dynamism that drives man onward and fills him with a sense of new and strange possibilities that lie ahead.

Man is no alien presence in the world. This is Emerson's resounding message. He therefore applied himself to the business of penetrating to "the aboriginal Self," so that he might lay bare and resuscitate a primal state of consciousness in which one rises to an awareness of higher dimensions within reality as well as of one's own immersion in nature and process.

Given such an outlook, the self-reliance of which Emerson makes so much has little in common with the self-sufficiency of one who remains insensitive to the bond linking him with things and who feels no surge within himself of a world that presses on to new and unforeseeable goals. To Emerson the call to self-reliance was a call to an original confrontation with the universe out of the depths of one's own uniqueness; for, as he saw it, the doorway to life and universality is to be found in selfhood. He was not antisocial. For him it was simply a matter of affirming the truth that society is most healthy when it respects the infinite potentiality of each person, while welcoming diversity and uniqueness.

In his deeper reading of human experience, Emerson could show that personality in its spiritual depths is organically connected with the rocks and the plants and all living creatures, as well as with the divinity that stands behind things. In building his picture of the world, he made use of a doctrine already taught by Jonathan Edwards, which can be traced back to medieval times and beyond, namely that the world is a descending manifestation of spirit. Within such a context Emerson was able to develop his doctrine of the indispensability of organic language, the language of symbolism, to the normal functioning of mind and spirit. In his view, it is through organic language that the world around us evokes answering echoes in the psyche, hinting at realities that escape the grasp of nonpoetic language. Ever close to experience, Emerson believed that symbolic consciousness plays a dominant role in the process by which man seeks to transcend himself toward larger wholeness of life and meaning.

Ralph Waldo Emerson.

See Also: EMANATIONISM; NEOPLATONISM.

Bibliography: *Complete Works,* ed. E. W. EMERSON, 12 v. (Boston 1903–04); *Journals,* ed. E. W. EMERSON and W. E. FORBES, 10 v. (Boston 1909–14); *Letters,* ed. R. L. RUSK, 6 v. (New York 1939). DANTE ALIGHERI, *La Vita Nuova,* tr. R. W. EMERSON, ed. J. C. MATHEWS (Chapel Hill 1960). R. L. RUSK, *The Life of Ralph Waldo Emerson* (New York 1949). F. I. CARPENTER, *Emerson Handbook* (New York 1953). V. C. HOPKINS, *Spires of Form: A Study of Emerson's Aesthetic Theory* (Cambridge, Mass. 1951). S. PAUL, *Emerson's Angle of Vision: Man and Nature in American Experience* (Cambridge, Mass. 1952). S. E. WHICHER, *Freedom and Fate: An Inner Life of Ralph Waldo Emerson* (Philadelphia 1953).

[R. C. POLLOCK]

Jacques André Émery.

ÉMERY, JACQUES ANDRÉ

Sulpician priest outstanding in French ecclesiastical life; b. Gex (Ain), France, Aug. 26, 1732; d. Paris, April 28, 1811. Born into a family notable in the law, he made secondary studies at the Jesuit college in Mâcon, theological studies in Paris, entered the SULPICIANS (1757), and was ordained (1758). The next 34 years were spent training candidates for the priesthood as seminary teacher or superior. This experience enlightened him on contemporary religious and social problems. Disturbed by the inadequacies of current apologetics and spirituality, he published several works, including *L'Esprit de Leibnitz* (1772), and *L'Esprit de Sainte Thérèse* (1775). Elected superior general of the Sulpicians (1782), he succeeded by his wisdom and firmness in reforming the Seminary of Saint-Sulpice in Paris, reserved for younger sons of the nobility destined for the higher clergy.

The FRENCH REVOLUTION, by causing the emigration of almost all the bishops and cutting off relations with Rome, thrust on him a role of highest importance without any official title. His priestly reputation made him the guide and the living conscience of the French clergy deprived of leaders. Very firm in matters of principle, he condemned the CIVIL CONSTITUTION OF THE CLERGY, and the oath to support it. Remaining at his post, he strove to remove the Church from all political compromise with aristocratic and royal counterrevolutionary activities, in order to arrive at a conciliation with the new regime. With this latter aim he authorized taking the oath of Liberty and Equality (1792) by declaring it purely political after studying Gensonné's interpretation of it. After taking it himself, he retracted at peril of his life during the Reign of Terror, when Rome condemned it.

As vicar-general of the Archdiocese of Paris, he kept in communication with its archbishop, M. de Juigné. The interception of one of his letters to the latter led to his arrest (July, 1793) and detention for 15 months in the Conciergerie prison in Paris. During this period he exercised a very active ministry among condemned prisoners. Liberated after Thermidor, Émery worked for religious restoration, recommended what was called "the Parisian method" of reconciling constitutional clergy or priests who had apostatized. He also authorized the clergy to take the various oaths demanded of those exercising religious functions.

During the Consulate and Empire period his line of conduct remained identical. NAPOLEON called him "the little priest," and thereby rendered homage to his action, so priestly and discreet. This man who wanted to be nothing, and who refused several times the episcopate, exercised a profound influence over the clergy. He counseled making the promise of fidelity to the Constitution of the Year VIII (1799), favored the CONCORDAT OF 1801, advised the pre-Revolutionary bishops to resign in accordance with the provisions of this Concordat, and assured nominations of worthy men to the new sees. Most prelates sought his advice, especially FESCH, reformed by him. He reconstituted the Sulpicians, the Seminary of St. Sulpice, and provincial seminaries. When conflict broke out (1806) between Napoleon I and Pius VII, Monsieur Émery, as he was commonly known, courageously defended the pope; opposed the intrusion of MAURY; aided the "black cardinals"; and by his secret correspondence bureau, diffused the letters of Pius VII, brought to him from Savona by the KNIGHTS OF THE FAITH. As a member of the ecclesiastical commissions (1809–11) charged by the emperor to resolve his differences with the pope, Émery refused to sign the decisions of the commissions. Finally, at a famous meeting in the Tuileries (March 17, 1811) attended by leaders in Church and State, Napoleon directed all his questions during a pathetic two-hour dialogue at the septuagenarian, moderate Gallican priest who courageously sustained the cause of Pius VII. So tactful was he that the emperor, far from being irritated, displayed his admiration. Death came the following month.

Bibliography: *Oeuvres complètes de Monsieur Émery,* ed. J. P. MIGNE (Paris 1857). J. LEFLON, *Monsieur Émery,* 2 v. (Paris

1945–46); *Dictionnaire d'histoire et de géographie ecclésiastiques* 15:394–397.

[J. LEFLON]

EMESA (HOMS)

Situated on the Orontes, was the center of the worship of the Syrian sun-god Baal. Roman influence beginning with Pompey and Caesar was firmly established under DOMITIAN. Elagabalus (Heliogabalus), the chief priest of the sun-god who bore that deity's name, was proclaimed imperator in this city by the Syrian troops, assumed the name Marcus Aurelius Antoninus, and ruled from 218 to 222. His debauched reign was ended by a pretorian revolt, and with his demise, efforts to spread the worship of the unconquered sun-god (*Sol Invictus*) in the Roman Empire ceased temporarily. In 272 Aurelian's outnumbered forces gained a significant victory over Zenobia near Emesa. Attributing his success to an apparition of the sun-god who encouraged his troops, Aurelian entered the city, venerated the god, and built a shrine in his honor (*Historia Augusta, Divus Aurelianus* 25).

It is uncertain when Christianity entered this stronghold of pagan worship. The first known bishop of Emesa is Silvanus who suffered martyrdom under DIOCLETIAN (EUSEBIUS, *Ecclesiastical History* 8.13); a later successor, Anatolius, attended the Council of Nicaea. Evidence for the progress of Christianity in Emesa is provided by the so called *Chronicon Paschale* [*Patrologia Graeca*, ed. J. P. Migne (Paris 1857–66) 92:741B], which states that the great church in the city was desecrated under JULIAN THE APOSTATE by the erection of a statue of Dionysus. In Byzantine times Emesa, the home of the renowned hymnographer ROMANUS MELODUS (d. *c.* 560), became famous for the possession of the head of St. John the Baptist.

The see became an autocephalous archbishopric in 452 and, as Homs, has been the administrative center for the patriarchates of the Jacobites and Melchites and for the Roman Catholics. Because of its geographical location commanding the road north from Egypt, Palestine, and Damascus, Emesa experienced the vicissitudes of war from the armies of Arabs, Mongols, Turks, and Crusaders.

Bibliography: *Paulys Realenzyklopädie der klassischen Altertumswissenschaft*, ed. G. WISSOWA et al. (Stuttgart) 5.2 (1905) 2219–22; 10.1 (1917) 948–951. H. LECLERCQ, *Dictionnaire d'archéologie chrétienne et de liturgie* (Paris 1907–53) 4.2:2723–30. R. JANIN, *Dictionnaire d'histoire et de géographie ecclésiastiques*, ed. A. BAUDRILLART et al. (Paris 1912) 15.1:397–399. K. BAUS, *Lexikon für Theologie und Kirche*, ed. J. HOFER and K. RAHNER, 10 v. (2d, new ed. Freiburg 1957–65) 5:470–471. H. G. BECK, *Kirche und theologische Literatur im byzantinischen Reich* (Munich 1959) 195. E. HONIGMANN, *Byzantion* 20 (1950) 64–71. *Annuario Pontificio* (Rome 1964) 183.

[H. DRESSLER]

EMILIANI, JEROME, ST.

Founder of the Order of the Somaschi; b. Venice, Italy, 1486; d. Somascha (Bergamo), Feb. 8, 1537. The son of a patrician family headed by Angelo Emiliani and Eleonora Morosini, he served in the army of the Venetian Republic at Castelnuovo of Quero, where he was taken prisoner. Set free miraculously on Sept. 27, 1511, Jerome left his manacles in thanksgiving at the shrine of the Madonna Grande in Treviso. Joining the Oratory of Divine Love, founded by St. CAJETAN, he took care of the incurables in Venetian hospitals. Later he established institutions for orphans, giving them religious and civil education on a pattern that anticipated the present schools of arts and manual training. Using the question-and-answer method, he taught Christian doctrine to children and peasants, and later he was able to extend his work to Padua, Verona, Como, Milan, and Bergamo. He was joined in these labors by Alessandro Besuzzi and Agostino Barili. In 1534 with numerous other followers he founded the Society of the Servants for the Poor, which was approved in 1540 by PAUL III and promoted to a religious order by St. PIUS V in 1568 as *Clericorum Regularium a Somascha,* with solemn vows, exemption, and the privileges of mendicants.

Jerome also devoted time to prayer and penance in a hermitage that he built in the mountains of Somascha. His spirituality is characterized by love of charity, imitation of Christ in his suffering, and devotion to the Guardian Angels and to the Blessed Virgin, Mother of Orphans. He was beatified by BENEDICT XIV in 1747; canonized July 16, 1767 by CLEMENT XIII; and declared universal patron of orphans and abandoned children by PIUS XI, March 14, 1928.

Feast: Feb. 8 (formerly July 20).

Bibliography: *Vita del clarissimo signor Girolamo Miani gentil huomo venetiano,* tr. as *Life of Jerome Emiliani, most distinguished Venetian nobleman,* tr. Somaschi (Manchester, N.H. 1973). S. ALBANI, *Vita del venerabile e devoto servo di Iddio Ieronimo Miani* (Milan 1600). A. TORTORA, *Vita Hieronymi Aemiliani* (Milan 1620). G. LANDINI, *S. Girolamo Miani* (Rome 1947). *San Girolamo Miani nel V centenario della nascita,* ed. G. SCARABELLO, et al. (Venice 1989). M. HEIMBUCHER, *Die Orden und Kongregationender katholischen Kirche* (Paderborn 1932–1934) 3:275–278.

[P. BIANCHINI]

EMMANUEL

Symbolic name found in Is 7.14; 8.8 (and see 8.10) meaning ''God with us'' (Heb *'immānû-'ēl*). St. Matthew interprets it in a messianic sense and applies it directly to Christ (Mt 1.22). Although exegetes generally agree that Is 7.14 is rightly understood to be a messianic text, they are not wholly in accord in explaining it. Formerly it was widely held that the sign promised to Ahaz, King of Juda, in this passage referred to the VIRGIN BIRTH of Christ and that the sign in question was a miracle in the strict sense of the word. A more critical study of the problem, however, indicates that such an interpretation of the text in the Book of ISAIAH is inaccurate. The sign offered to Achaz was intended to assist him to make a practical decision, i.e., to put his trust in the Lord rather than in Assyria on the occasion of the Syro-Ephraimitic invasion; but the birth of a child 700 years later could hardly be expected to help him. Further, the fact that Christ was miraculously born of a virgin can hardly be used to prove anything to a skeptic, for this is something not open to human observation but is rather an object of faith. Aside from this, the text does not clearly speak of a virgin birth, for the technical Hebrew term for virgin (*b^e^tûlâ*) is not used here, but a more general term (*'almâ*) that means maiden or young woman. Finally, the child is associated with the contemporary scene (7.15–16). Thus, modern interpreters understand the ''sign'' more in accord with the sense that word (Heb *'ôt*) usually has in the Old Testament, i.e., a meaningful, effective indication of God's intervention. Yet, the import of the promise is messianic, for it probably refers to the birth of Hezekiah, son of Ahaz, who would continue the Davidic line, which was the vehicle of God's messianic promises (*see* MESSIANISM; DAVID) at a time when its existence was severely threatened (see Is 7.2–6). The ultimate meaning of the promise, even for Isaiah, would be fulfilled only when the expected messianic deliverance had been realized, and so the oracle continued to look to the future, to the coming of the Son of David par excellence. The Septuagint translators rendered *'almâ* by παρθένος, the technical Greek term for virgin, as an indication that they expected the MESSIAH to have a marvelous birth, and Matthew knew that this did, in fact, come to pass in the birth of Jesus Christ.

Bibliography: *Encyclopedic Dictionary of the Bible*, tr. and adap. by L. HARTMAN (New York 1963) 655–657. H. JUNKER, *Lexikon für Theologie und Kirche*, ed. M. BUCHBERGER, 10 v. (Freiburg 1930–38) 3:847–848. E. JENNI, *Die Religion in Geschichte und Gegenwart*, 7 v. (3d ed. Tübingen 1957–65) 3:677–678. J. COPPENS, ''La Prophétie de la 'Almah, Is 7.14–17,'' *Ephemerides theologicae Lovanienses* 28 (Bruges 1952) 648–678. ''La Prophétie d'Emmanuel,'' *L'Attente du Messie*, ed. L. CERFAUX et al. (Paris 1954) 39–50. F. L. MORIARTY, ''The Emmanuel Prophecies,'' *The Catholic Biblical Quarterly* 19 (Washington 1957) 226–233.

[M. J. CANTLEY]

EMMANUEL, BL.

Bishop; b. Cremona?, *c.* 1225; d. Adwert (Aduard), Holland, Oct. 1, 1298 (feast, Feb. 27). Knowledge about his youth is unreliable, but it is clear that in the 1270s he was professor of Canon Law at the University of Paris. He became archdeacon in Cremona (Italy) and in 1291 or 1292, was bishop there. Having been a staunch defender of the Church against secular encroachment, he was forced to resign in 1295. He spent the last three years of his life at the Cistercian Abbey of Adwert where he was venerated as blessed, although he was never canonized. In 1940 his remains were unearthed and transferred to the Abbey of Notre-Dame de Sion at Diepenveen.

Bibliography: A. ALMA, *Dictionnaire d'histoire et de géographie ecclésiastiques*, ed. A. BAUDRILLART et al. (Paris 1912–) 15:423–424, with bibliography.

[L. J. LEKAI]

EMMERAM, ST.

Marytr, itinerant preacher, possibly bishop, suffered a violent death in Bavaria, perhaps *c.* 660. His original name was Haimhramm. He is the patron of the monastery of SANKT EMMERAM (formerly St. George), where he was buried and was honored as a martyr by 737. No other facts are known about his life. The vita by Bp. Arbeo (Aribo) of Freising (*c.* 772) contains a kernel of fact, but the similarity of most of its details to those in Arbeo's life of CORBINIAN (D. *C.* 725) makes their authenticity improbable. According to Arbeo, Emmeram was bishop of Poitiers (although his name appears on no list) before coming to Bavaria to preach to the Slavs. He was detained at Regensburg by Duke Theodo and eventually murdered by members of the Duke's household on a false accusation to which Emmeram submitted voluntarily. In art, he is shown in episcopal robes, and either pierced by a lance or bound to a ladder and mutilated (as in Arbeo's account of his death).

Feast: Sept. 22.

Bibliography: *Monumenta Germaniae Scriptores rerum Merovingicarum* (Berlin 1825–) 4:452–524. H. C. F. TIMERDING, ed., *Die christliche Frühzeit Deutschlands in den Berichten über die Bekehrer*, 2 v. (Jena 1929) v.1. H. FRANK, *Die Klosterbischöfe des Frankenreiches* (Münster 1932). A. M.. ZIMMERMANN, *Kalendarium Benedictinum: Die Heiligen und Seligen des Benediktinerorderns und seiner Zweige* (Metten 1933–1938) 3:88–91; 4:90. G. JACQUEMET, *Catholicisme* 4:60–61. A. HAUCK, *Kirchengeschichte Deutschlands* (Berlin-Leipzig 1958) 1:352–354. R. BAUERREISS, *Kirchengeschichte Bayerns* (2d ed. St. Ottilien 1958–) 1:53–54.

[M. F. MCCARTHY]

EMMERICH, ANNE CATHERINE

Stigmatic and mystic; b. Flamsche, Westphalia, Sept. 8, 1774; d. Dülmen, Feb. 9, 1824. Her parents were poor, and from childhood her health was not good. At an early age she exhibited phenomena of clairvoyance. In November 1802 she entered the novitiate of the Augustinian nuns at Dülmen; but in 1811 the convent was secularized, and she was received into the house of an emigrant French priest. About a year later she received the stigmata, including a double cross on her breast, and though she tried to hide it, her stigmatization soon became known and aroused not only curiosity but also considerable hostility among unbelievers and rationalists. After years of intermittent investigations by doctors and theologians the civil authorities intervened, and in August 1819 she was forcibly removed to another house and kept under close surveillance for three weeks, but no evidence of fraud came to light.

In the year before this investigation Catherine had been visited by the Romantic poet Clemens Brentano, then recently reconciled to the Church after a period of unbelief, and he was so impressed by her that he decided to remain in Dülmen and to devote himself to writing down the experiences Catherine communicated to him. These activities resulted in two books, *The Dolorous Passion of Our Lord and Saviour Jesus Christ* and the slightly less popular *Life of the Blessed Virgin Mary.* Two facts make the evaluation of these books difficult. First, we do not know how much Brentano communicated or suggested to her in their long conversations. Second, it is impossible to determine exactly what, in Brentano's works, came from her and what from the poet himself. What is certain is that under Brentano's influence her visions became much more elaborate than they had been before. Catherine herself certainly took them very seriously, for she declared that God had commanded her to make them known and that those who had no faith in them would have to render an account for their negligence.

The written reports of the visions themselves contain long descriptions not only of Biblical events but also of apocryphal stories, and they include many historical and topographical details, some of which are correct, others, quite mistaken.

The popular English translation of *The Dolorous Passion* was made from the French translation of the German original and is frequently faulty.

Bibliography: T. WEGENER, *Sister Anne Katherine Emmerich,* tr. F. X. MCGOWAN (New York 1898). H. J. SELLER, *Im Banne des Kreuzes,* ed. I. M. DEITZ (2d ed., Würzburg 1949). W. HÜMPFNER, *Dictionnaire de spiritualité ascétique et mystique* 4.1:622–627, very good for the bibliography of the controversy about her life and works. H. THURSTON, *Surprising Mystics,* ed. J. H. CREHAN (Chicago 1955) 38–99.

[H. GRAEF]

EMMONS, NATHANAEL

Congregationalist minister; b. East Haddam, Conn., April 20, 1745; d. Franklin, Mass., Sept. 23, 1840. He graduated from Yale in 1767, studied theology under Rev. Nathan Strong of Coventry, Conn., and was ordained in 1773 for the Second Church of Wrentham (now Franklin), Mass. He held this charge for 67 years. Emmons trained divinity students in his home and, besides his voluminous published sermons, contributed theological articles to the religious press. An advocate of home and foreign missions, he edited the *Massachusetts Missionary Magazine.* He defended the orthodox Calvinist positions of Jonathan EDWARDS and Samuel Hopkins against the Unitarians and Universalists, and supported Congregational polity against the Presbyterians. In politics he was a Federalist, and characterized Thomas Jefferson as Jeroboam in a famous sermon.

Bibliography: *Complete Works,* 6 v. (Boston 1842), includes an autobiography. E. A. PARK, *Memoir of Nathanael Emmons* (Boston 1861).

[R. K. MACMASTER]

EMOTION (MORAL ASPECT)

Throughout human history, two opposing attitudes toward man's emotional life can be distinguished, the Stoic and the hedonist. The Stoic ideal of the rational man has no place for emotion. The perfect man is "apathetic," indifferent alike to pleasure and pain. For the hedonist, on the contrary, pleasure and pain are the ultimate principles of action. The wise man pursues pleasure as the supreme human value and avoids pain as the ultimate evil. The Christian outlook on emotion is between these two extremes. Christ the perfect man was angry (Mk 3.5) and wept on hearing of the death of Lazarus (Jn 11.33–34).

Use and Misuse of Emotion. Although it is primarily the human will that moves a human being to act, the will is facilitated by the sensitive inclination of the flesh toward what is willed. The role of the emotions is therefore an important and even a necessary one. Without them a man would be relatively inert and slow to move himself to activities needed for change, growth, evolution, or improvement. It is only through the agency of the emotions that a man can tap the reservoirs of his physical powers and energies to enable him to face the crises of life, to defend himself against harm, and to perform with fidelity and thoroughness actions that are necessary to his well-being. But on the other hand, when the emotions get out of control they can lead a man to the gravest disorders and excesses.

Morality. The fact of the baneful consequences of uncontrolled passion no doubt accounts for the suspicion and distrust with which the emotions have been regarded by some, but the necessity of emotions to human life is so manifest that it seems absurd to judge them to be per se evil. In themselves they are morally neutral, neither good nor bad, and they become one or the other only insofar as they influence a man in the direction of good or evil. They are good when, with respect to their quality and intensity, they are appropriate to the objects that arouse them, and they are evil when they are inappropriate, the objects in either case being the objects as they appear in the light of reason judging according to the norms of moral law.

This supposes, however, that the activity of the emotions is in some way subject to the control of man's deliberate will, because nothing that does not proceed, either directly or indirectly, from the deliberate will can rightly be considered to have moral quality. Different instances of emotional activity, however, are differently related to reason and to will, and this may alter considerably the moral character of the emotion itself and of what is done under its influence. Moralists therefore distinguish antecedent and consequent emotion.

Emotion is said to be antecedent if it arises independently of any stimulation or encouragement on the part of the will. It is thus not a voluntary insurgence of the sense appetite, but one that is set off spontaneously on a subvolitional level. It is called antecedent because it arises prior to any act of the will causing or approving it. It anticipates the will act. Since emotion of this kind is not subject to voluntary control, it cannot be accounted voluntary. The man thus impassioned is not responsible for his emotion until it is possible for the will to assume control of it. At the moment when the will deliberately accepts or consents to the emotion, it becomes voluntary and hence ceases to be an antecedent emotion. This also happens when the will, without actually consenting to the emotion, nevertheless neglects to subdue it, in spite of the fact that it could and should do so.

Not all sudden outbursts of emotion can rightly be classified as antecedent. There are cases in which an individual could and should foresee and make suitable provision against events likely to occasion emotional disturbance. If one voluntarily neglects to do this, then the resulting emotion is not antecedent, but is, on the contrary, indirectly voluntary inasmuch as it is a foreseen consequence of the failure to take the measures necessary to forestall it.

It is difficult to determine concretely when one could and should foresee a sudden movement of undesirable emotion and make provision against its occurrence. The majority of medieval theologians inclined to rigorism in this matter and appear to have held that movements of undesirable emotion are always venially sinful, because there is always an element of negligence in the failure to foresee and prevent them, and because the sense appetite shares in some degree in the freedom of the will.

Later theologians took the more benign view that certain sudden movements of emotion are completely beyond the possibility of human control. These they held to be totally devoid of morality. They classified the different movements of sensuality in the following manner: (1) *motus primo-primi,* emotions that are completely beyond the possibility of human control, either because they arise too suddenly or because they are due simply to a bodily condition, and these were held to be amoral in character; (2) *motus secundo-primi,* emotions that are not deliberately willed, but are in some way subject to a man's control and so involve some culpable negligence and are consequently venially sinful; (3) *motus secundi,* disordered emotions that are deliberately willed.

Consequent emotion is voluntary, whether indirectly, as when the will neglects to subdue it, or directly, as happens when the emotion itself is the object of direct desire either for its own sake or as a means to something else. The will can and does on occasion deliberately incite, nourish, encourage, or strengthen emotion, either for the sake of the pleasure to be derived from it, or because it is seen as a means necessary to the accomplishment of something the will wants.

Influence of Emotion upon Responsibility. The moralist is concerned not only with the voluntariness and imputability of an emotional state itself, but also with the bearing emotion may have upon the morality of actions that are performed under its influence. The common position of Catholic moralists on this matter can best be set forth in the following separate conclusions:

(1) Antecedent passion increases the voluntariness of an action proceeding from it, but at the same time diminishes the freedom of that action. It increases the voluntariness of the action because its momentum carries the will with it, so that one performs the action more willingly under its impulse than if such impulse were lacking. But it diminishes the freedom of the action because on the one hand it beclouds the vision of the mind and on the other it weakens the control of the will over the other powers, and this to an extent that may limit materially the possi-

bility of deliberate choice. Since it lessens freedom, it diminishes responsibility also, for one is responsible for what he does to the extent in which he acts freely.

(2) The extent to which antecedent emotion diminishes responsibility will depend upon its violence. If it is of such force or vehemence that it deprives one altogether of the use of reason, then no real freedom remains and the action that occurs cannot be morally blameworthy. In such a case one is, for the time being, in so disturbed a mental state that he is incapable of moral action. Less violent passion, leaving some use of reason, will not totally abolish responsibility, but will diminish it in proportion to the force of the emotional impulse.

(3) Consequent passion, however strong it may be, lessens neither the voluntariness nor the freedom of an action. The reason is that emotion of this kind is itself voluntary, whether directly or indirectly, and in willingly and freely stimulating it or allowing it to exist, one takes upon himself responsibility for the actions to which he can reasonably foresee that it will lead. It might happen, of course, that one's emotion, though voluntary, might reach an unexpected pitch of intensity and thus result in an action more far-reaching than was foreseen. In this case the emotion itself would be partly antecedent and partly consequent. Up to the point to which the person foresees and intends the emotion to reach, it is consequent and voluntary, but the unforeseen excess of emotion would be antecedent and involuntary, and responsibility for actions committed because of it would be accordingly diminished.

Emotion and Virtue. Since the human sensitive appetite has its own act and is, in a sense, rational, because of its intimate association with reason and will, it can be the subject of such virtues as TEMPERANCE and FORTITUDE. The role of such moral virtue is not to destroy or eliminate emotion, but to make the sensitive appetite readily responsive to the dictates of reason. Because of the wounds of original sin, the process of acquiring moral virtue in the sensitive appetite is painful; however, constant effort wears down its resistance, and the continued control of reason leaves its imprint on the appetite. This imprint when fully developed becomes moral virtue. Moral education is an extrinsic help toward this end, but the most important help comes directly from God when He gives grace for the task. Because the whole man, including his sensitivity, has been redeemed, God gives sufficient grace for its control. Indeed, Christian tradition testifies to the infusion at Baptism of the moral virtues of temperance and fortitude.

See Also: CONCUPISCENCE; VIRTUE.

Bibliography: R. E. BRENNAN, *Thomistic Psychology* (New York 1954). J. MARITAIN, *Moral Philosophy* (New York 1964). T. V. MOORE, *The Driving Forces of Human Nature and Their Adjustment* (New York 1948). P. O'BRIEN, *Emotions and Morals* (New York 1950). W. FARRELL, ''Man's Emotional Life,'' *Cross and Crown* 6 (1954) 178–198. R. ALLERS, ''Cognitive Aspect of Emotion,'' *Thomist* 4 (1942) 589–648. P. LUMBRERAS, ''De sensualitatis peccato,'' *Divus Thomas* 32 (1929) 225–240.

[J. CAHILL]

EMPEDOCLES

Empedocles was a Greek philosopher born of an aristocratic family in the Dorian city-state of Akragas on the southern coast of Sicily. The exact dates of his lifetime are a matter of conjecture. It has been argued that he was born *c.* 521 B.C. and died *c.* 461 B.C., but he is usually said to have flourished *c.* 444 B.C. There is little reliable information about his life, but we know that he was banished from his native city. Although Diogenes Laertius reports that he ended his life by leaping into the crater of Mt. Etna, the historian Timaeus tells us that he left Sicily for the Peloponnesus and that the manner of his death is unknown. He was actively engaged in politics, religion, and medicine, and his name was surrounded with an aura of mystic wisdom. He wrote in verse and fairly extensive fragments of two of his poems, one on nature (Περὶ φύσεως), the other on purifications (Καθαρμοί), are extant.

Theory of the Elements. Empedocles's cosmological theory was developed as a response to the Parmenidean insistence on the immutability of being. He agreed with PARMENIDES that whatever exists cannot have come into being nor can it go out of being; yet change is a fact that must be explained. Empedocles's solution rested on a denial of Parmenidean monism. He held that whatever exists is reducible to four basic elements or ''roots'': earth, air, fire, and water. Each minimal unit of these four roots is immutable in its being, and change is the aggregation of these roots into the familiar objects of experience and their subsequent dissolution. In this way Empedocles felt that he could agree with Parmenides that being is immutable and also find room for change in the world of experience.

Furthermore he looked upon the four roots as passive, requiring the imposition of an external force to bring about the combinations and dissolutions of the world of change. Hence he posited the force of love, which is attractive, and the force of hate, which is separative. According to Aristotle (*Meta.* 1075b 1–7), Empedocles assigns to love the dual role of being a material and an efficient cause, since, despite the metaphorical implications of these terms, love and hate were postulated as material forces. Hence Empedoclean cosmology was thoroughly materialistic.

Empedocles envisioned the history of the universe as an eternally recurring cyclic process involving the following four stages: (1) love predominates, and all the elements are thoroughly mixed together; (2) hate progressively expresses itself, and the elements begin to separate out into distinguishable objects; (3) hate predominates, and the four elements are completely separated from each other; and (4) love progressively reasserts itself, and the elements begin to combine into distinguishable objects. This theory of cosmic process enabled him to develop an evolutionary theory of life.

Psychology. He taught the doctrine of the transmigration of souls, a view also found in the Pythagorean school and in the *Dialogues* of Plato. Yet it is not clear how the implication of personal immortality can be made consistent with his doctrine of the cyclic aggregation and separation of the elements. His explanation of perception is, however, a direct consequence of the materialistic commitments of his cosmology. According to Aristotle (*Anim.* 427a 22), Empedocles made no distinction between thought and sense perception. Rather all knowledge is the result of material effluences given off by external objects entering into the pores of the sensory organs. If these effluences are neither too small nor too large in relation to the pores of the sensory organs, then they properly enter into the organs and produce sensation. Empedocles saw that a purely mechanistic theory of knowledge and consciousness is demanded by his materialistic cosmology, and he did not shrink from drawing the consequences.

See Also: GREEK PHILOSOPHY; MATERIALISM; MECHANISM.

Bibliography: For the extant fragments, see H. DIELS, *Die Fragmente der Vorsokratiker: Griechisch und Deutsch*, (10 ed. Berlin 1960–61). English. K. FREEMAN, tr., *Ancilla to the Pre-Socratic Philosophers* (Cambridge, Mass. 1957). EMPEDOCLES, *The Fragments of Empedocles,* tr. W. E. LEONARD (Chicago 1908). Secondary studies. F. C. COPLESTON, *History of Philosophy* (Westminster, Md. 1946) 1:61–65. J. BURNET, *Early Greek Philosophy* (4th ed. London 1930). W. KRANZ, *Empedokles* (Zurich 1949). E. BIGNONE, *Empedocle* (Turin 1916). H. LONG, ''The Unity of Empedocles' Thought,'' *American Journal of Philology* 70 (1949) 142–158.

[R. J. BLACKWELL]

EMPIRICISM

Empiricism, more a philosophical presupposition than a definitive system, insists in general that knowledge begins with the senses and with sense experience. Some empiricists limit all knowledge to sense knowledge and deny the reality of universal ideas, necessary truth, and innate or a priori ideas (*see* SENSISM). This form of empiricism is opposed to RATIONALISM and IDEALISM, which attempt to deduce the nature of reality from the intelligible content of ideas in the mind. A less radical form of empiricism insists that experience be the final test for the validity of any idea or proposition, or holds that any knowledge transcending the data of experience can be only probable. EXPERIENCE itself has different meanings for empiricists. It may refer exclusively to sense data or to man's existential contact with external objects. For Locke, Hume, and Berkeley, it meant the impressions and ideas generated either by external objects or by the mind itself.

This article describes the various forms that empiricism takes in philosophical and scientific thought, surveys the historical development of empiricist attitudes, and concludes with a critical evaluation from the viewpoint of moderate realism.

Types of Empiricism. The principal positions that can be classified as empiricist include strict and relative empiricism, metaphysical empiricism, scientific empiricism, and logical empiricism. These may be characterized in summary fashion as follows:

Strict and Relative Empiricism. A strict or thoroughgoing empiricism refuses to recognize the validity of any knowledge that is not grounded in and verified by sense experience. Denying the validity of METAPHYSICS, it substitutes association and habit for causality, and collections of secondary qualities for substance, tending in general toward SKEPTICISM and AGNOSTICISM. As opposed to this, relative empiricism holds that while sense experience gives rise to ideas, such experience can be intelligently grasped by the intellect to furnish a metaphysical insight into the nature of reality as such.

Metaphysical Empiricism. Relative empiricism can also be termed metaphysical empiricism, although the latter expression has a somewhat different meaning in contemporary philosophy, where it designates a limited metaphysics of finite being growing out of sensible experience. Such a metaphysical empiricism grants the quasi reality of universal ideas or categories, together with the reality of cause and effect, possibility and existence, and substance and accident. At the same time it restricts such categories to the area of finite being and is content with a limited and relative truth about this area. It is strictly opposed to any sort of transcendent metaphysics or to claims for absolute and unchanging truth.

This empiricism purposes to be objective and realistic, and attempts to escape from the skepticism generated by the strict empiricism of Hume and from the subjectivism of KANT. At the same time it refuses to trust the ability of the human mind to rise above the finite and the temporal.

Scientific Empiricism. Scientific empiricists seek to unify the laws of science so as to deduce the laws governing particular sciences from unified principles. Behind this enterprise lies the conviction that only natural science can provide certain knowledge. Scientific empiricism is closely allied to LOGICAL POSITIVISM, linguistic analysis, and contemporary British and American analytical philosophy.

Logical Empiricism. This is the logical counterpart of scientific empiricism. The movement began in the 1920s at the University of Vienna with a group known as the Vienna Circle, composed of men such as M. Schlick, R. Carnap, L. Wittgenstein, P. Frank, and H. Reichenbach. Their aim was to construct a theory of meaning and knowledge that would reconcile the valid elements of rationalism and empiricism through the use of logic and the procedures of natural science. Mathematical or symbolic LOGIC and linguistic analysis were their chief tools. Most logical empiricists adopt Hume's notions of causality and induction, insist on the tautological nature of mathematical and logical truth, and conceive of philosophy as a clarification of everyday language. They usually reject metaphysics as a pseudo-science based on pseudo-problems, having their source in linguistic confusion. One of their principal commitments is to the verifiability principle, which states that only those propositions can be held as true that are capable of actual or possible experiential verification.

Historical Origins. EPICURUS of Athens (341–270 B.C.), from whom EPICUREANISM takes its name, was probably the first radical empiricist. For him, the criteria of truth are sensations, preconceptions, and feelings; and all knowledge is based on sensation. The universe is a void in which atoms move and combine with one another to form material things. These things continually emit minute particles that impinge on the corporeal soul of man and, forming images of themselves there, produce knowledge. His is a crude MATERIALISM, basically reducible to sensism. Zeno of Citium (*c.* 336–264 B.C.), the founder of STOICISM, conceived of the universe as matter penetrated with and guided by an eternal fire. This fire he identifies with nature, the touchstone and key to all knowledge and wisdom.

Medieval Empiricism. The conflict between Platonic and Aristotelian thought was repeated in medieval thought in the persons of St. Augustine (A.D. 354–430) and St. THOMAS AQUINAS (1225–74), respectively. For St. Thomas, as for Aristotle, everything in the intellect is somehow grounded in sense experience; thus, Aquinas finds in the sensible world principles that explain the structure and intelligibility of all being. More empiricist in mentality was WILLIAM OF OCKHAM (1290?–1349), who restricted human certitude to propositions having direct experiential reference. Since only singulars exist, and since all the singulars with which man makes contact are sensible, it is to the sensible world and to the concepts that stand for it that he goes for certitude. All other knowledge, for him, is abstractive and can give no real idea of existence. For example, Ockham sees no way in which either the existence of God or the existence and spirituality of the human soul can be rationally demonstrated. He does admit, however, that one can make an act of faith in the existence of realities transcending sensible experience.

Renaissance Period. The empirical tradition was carried on during the Renaissance chiefly by four thinkers. LEONARDO DA VINCI (1452–1519) conceived of nature as a product of the divine mind. For him, only by an investigation of nature can man return to its source and learn something of divinity. ''Wisdom is the daughter of experience'' was a favorite saying of his, and it is mathematics that enables one to interpret experience and come to an understanding of the rational order operative in nature. Juan Luis VIVES (1492–1540) is often credited with being the father of experimental psychology, since his approach to the human soul was based on introspection and experience. Tomasso CAMPANELLA (1568–1639) was especially interested in harmonizing the new science with both a philosophy based on experience and the teachings of Christianity. He wrote a defense of Galileo in which he stated that if Galileo was to be proved wrong, it must be done by new observations and not by a priori judgments. Galileo GALILEI himself (1564–1639) can be considered an empiricist insofar as he held sense experience to be necessary for ascertaining the existence of objects before mathematical method could be applied to them. Yet experimental verification of mathematical conclusions, while helpful in some cases, was not regarded by him as necessary for those who understood his mathematical method.

British Empiricists. Francis BACON (1561–1626), dissatisfied with rationalism and scholastic philosophy, pleaded for a new system of education based on factual data and conclusions derivable from such data by strictly empirical and scientific methods.

John LOCKE (1632–1704) used a psychological approach, his investigation of experience taking the form of an examination of consciousness. He held that what is known are ideas, and that the whole knowledge process consists in reflecting on the content of these ideas and in discerning their relationships. His empiricism, therefore, is primarily subjective. Locke had to assume a world of things with the power to cause sensible changes in a knowing subject. This world of things he reduced to a minimum of so-called primary qualities, viz, motion, rest, extension, magnitude, and number. Secondary qualities, for him, were the impressions made on the knower, viz, color, taste, sound, odor, resistance. Behind qualities there might be substance; but, since this was never directly sensed, the knowing subject could never account it as more than a collection of secondary sensible qualities. Locke thus thoroughly undermined the foundations of REALISM, and his successors were not slow to remove those foundations entirely.

George BERKELEY (1685–1753) concluded from this that, since man could never know things, but only ideas of things, there were no things at all. God could just as well cause the ideas of things within us as the things themselves.

In his own way, David HUME (1711–76) was no less drastic. Never denying a reality independent of mind, he nonetheless reduced that reality to the barest minimum. Since the human intellect could make no contact with substance, the most that could be asserted was that there were ideas of events, and that these ideas were more or less vivid, more or less closely associated in the human mind. The mind itself was nothing more than a series of ideas, all following each other successively. Since only substance can exercise causality, he argued that causality could mean only a habitually constant association of ideas. This process led him to a hesitant skepticism about the validity of all knowledge.

American Development. In the United States the empirical movement developed chiefly under the influence of Charles Sanders PEIRCE, William JAMES, and John Dewey. Peirce (1839–1914) is generally considered the founder of PRAGMATISM, a form of empiricism in which the emphasis is on activity. According to Peirce, the purpose of thought is to produce belief, and belief has three characteristics: (1) it is something of which man is aware; (2) it appeases the irritation of doubt; and (3) it involves man in establishing habits of action. Thus, beliefs are ordered to action, and different beliefs are distinguished by the diverse actions to which they lead. Hence, sensible effects become the criterion of the content value of any idea. Yet Peirce does attempt to account for abstract and class concepts. The concrete object of experience is for him an exemplification of the possible and as such is able to refer the knower beyond itself; this reference is not sufficient, however, to transcend the order of experience as a whole, and Peirce makes no attempt to do so.

With William James (1842–1930) a more radical form of empiricism appeared, affirming that the only way to settle metaphysical disputes is to refer them to action and practical consequences. James advocated a deemphasis of principles in favor of consequences and facts. He went further than Peirce in stating that its results not only give a proposition meaning, but even make it true. Hence, for him, truth is any activity that enables one to get into practical harmony with his experiential situation. In his preface to *The Meaning of Truth* (New York 1909), James describes his empiricism as consisting of (1) a postulate, (2) a statement of fact, and (3) a generalized conclusion. The postulate states that only those things that can be defined in terms drawn from experience should be debated by philosophers. The statement of fact is that the relations between things are as much part of experience as the things themselves. The conclusion is that the parts of experience are held together by relations that are themselves parts of experience. Thus does James reduce both knowledge and the object of knowledge to the flux of experience.

John Dewey (1859–1952) applied the teachings of Peirce and James to history, sociology, politics, and education. He taught that philosophy must grow out of the philosopher's personal experience in the cultural and historical situation in which he finds himself, this alone being of the real and constituting the real. Yet for Dewey such experience takes place in the naturalistic context of the 19th century, which accepted the Darwinian theory of evolution and regarded mind and man as climactic processes emerging out of the universal dynamism of nature. Experience, in his understanding, cannot be distinguished from nature, and reality is a series of events acting and reacting on one another on a purely physical level. In such a universe, truth is only a precarious balance of interconnecting events that constitute a situation, this situation being constantly modified from within and without. Natural science provides man with the most stable sort of knowledge possible. And faith becomes an act of trust and hope in science, in human intelligence, and in man's quest to unite himself ever more perfectly with the flow of events of which he is a part.

Critical Evaluation. Empiricism is forced to limit KNOWLEDGE to the order of experience and to treat the human INTELLECT simply as a more powerful sense faculty. Yet there is evidence, found in experience, that the intellect transcends the material order. Man does form class concepts, or UNIVERSALS; and, while sense experience may be needed in order to begin, the term of the process, the CONCEPT, is free from the limitations that matter everywhere imposes. A material thing is always individual, and so is a SENSATION. The intellect, however, forms concepts that are predicable of many different individuals in exactly the same way; such concepts abstract from individual differences and particularizations (*see* ABSTRACTION). Since the principle of particularity is matter, to be free from such limitation is to be free from matter (*see* INDIVIDUATION).

The fact of intellectual REFLECTION also indicates that there is more to knowledge than what the senses provide. The intellect is aware of its own act as it places it, but the eye, for example, cannot see itself seeing. Intellectual reflection, too, can identify the principles that structure a sensible thing. There must be more than matter in a material thing; how else can the evident difference between one material thing and another be explained? Material things exist, yet existence and matter are not synonymous; otherwise how can thought that transcends the limitations of matter, but is just as real, be explained?

Empiricism emphasizes a truth without admitting its full implications. The need of experience in the knowing process must be recognized, but it must be recognized too that knowledge cannot be adequately explained merely in terms of the sensible. In fact, the human intellect finds in experience the need to transcend the sensible order and arrive at truths that alone make such experience intelligible.

See Also: KNOWLEDGE; KNOWLEDGE, THEORIES OF; PHENOMENALISM.

Bibliography: F. C. COPLESTON, *Contemporary Philosophy* (Westminster, Md. 1956). J. COLLINS, *A History of Modern European Philosophy* (Milwaukee 1954). G. FAGGIN, *Enciclopedia filosofica* (Venice-Rome 1957) 1:1878–94. É. H. GILSON, *Elements of Christian Philosophy* (New York 1960). S. H. HODGSON, *The Metaphysic of Experience,* 4 v. (New York 1898). G. P. KLUBERTANZ, *The Philosophy of Human Nature* (New York 1953). G. DE SANTILLANA and E. ZILSEL, *The Development of Rationalism and Empiricism* (Chicago 1941). R. EISLER, *Wörterbuch der philosophischen Begriffe* (Berlin 1927–30) 1:334–336.

[H. R. KLOCKER]

EMRYS AP IWAN

Methodist minister, Welsh critic; b. Abergele, March 24, 1851; d. Rhewl, Denbighshire, Jan. 6, 1906. Robert Ambrose Jones (his real name), who was partly of French origin, studied on the Continent, later taught English in Switzerland, and was ordained a Methodist minister in 1883. His vital contribution to Welsh literary studies was the discovery that the definitive period of Welsh classical prose was the renaissance era between the Protestant reform and the Methodist revival that originated with the work of Gruffydd Robert of Milan. This conclusion was the fruit of his search for the finest instrument of clarity and style for the propagation of the Gospel in Welsh. His study of Welsh classical poetry also brought him face to face with the Catholic past of Wales. His esteem for Pascal deepened his interest in Catholicism as he saw its organic and sacramental strength in contrast with divisive tendencies in Nonconformity. But his hatred of clericalism, reinforced by the influence of the French anticlerical pamphleteer Paul Louis Courier, posed a dilemma that he never resolved. However, he objectified it in *Breuddwyd Pabydd Wrth Ei Ewyllys* (posthumous, 1931, A Papist's Wishful Dream), which depicted a future Catholic Wales, reconverted by a native clergy, as the link between Welsh Christian culture and Catholic truth. A proper study of the native language, he thought, would aid in this process. This view involved him in public dispute with Methodist leaders over their policy of opening English churches in predominantly Welsh localities, thereby weakening the currency of the Welsh language. He devoted himself to the education of children through the medium of Welsh, and his uncompromising stand for the purity of Welsh was a Christian defense of the cultural bases of Christianity. He was a prolific writer of homilies, sermons, and essays, a master of a rational and discursive style far removed from the evangelical exhortatory fervor of early Methodism. His works, prophetic in their diagnosis of Welsh cultural developments, continue to exercise great influence in contemporary Wales.

Bibliography: EMRYS AP IWAN, *Detholiad o erthyglau a llythyrau,* ed. D. M. LLOYD, 2 v. (Aberystwyth 1937–40). *Dictionary of Welsh Biography down to 1940* (London 1959) 509–510. J. S. LEWIS, *Ysgrifau dydd Mercher* (Aberystwyth 1945). T. G. JONES, *Cofiant Emrys ap Iwan* (Cardiff 1912).

[C. DANIEL]

EMS, CONGRESS OF

The meeting of the representatives of the three prince-electors of Mainz, Cologne, and Trier, and the prince archbishop of Salzburg at Bad Ems (July 25 to Aug. 25, 1786). Its purpose was to establish a common policy for the German metropolitans against the alleged restrictions of their jurisdiction by the Roman Curia through the accreditation of papal nuncios to various German principalities.

Background. This anti-Roman attitude of the archbishops was as much the result of the enlightened ideas of FEBRONIANISM and GALLICANISM as of the lust for power of the metropolitans that was supported by Emperor JOSEPH II. The immediate occasion for this congress was the erection of a papal nunciature in Munich at the request of the Bavarian Prince-Elector Karl Theodor (Feb. 17, 1785). Its purpose was to limit the jurisdiction of foreign bishops in Bavaria, after the Roman Curia had declined to erect new bishoprics in Bavarian territory. Thereupon the three prince-electors, as well as the archbishop of Salzburg and other bishops, sent a written protest to the pope and to Karl Theodor. The latter, however, assured the churchmen that this new nunciature did not change anything in German Canon Law and, like PIUS VI, he rejected the protest as devoid of application. Then the archbishop of Mainz, Friedrich Karl Joseph von ERTHAL, sent a written complaint to the emperor, requesting him as protector of the German Church to protest to Rome against the sending of a nuncio to Munich. The ruler replied that he recognized the nuncios in Munich and in Cologne only as diplomatic representatives of their secular sovereign, not as the bearers of any ecclesiastical jurisdiction, and he invited the prince-elector of Mainz to let him know his own and his suffragans' objections against the Roman Curia. Encouraged by this answer from the emperor, the German archbishops refused to accept the credentials of the papal nuncios in Cologne and Munich, prohibited any appeal to their tribunals, and declared their jurisdiction in the Reich as ended. When the new nuncios began to exercise their rights anyway, the metropolitans tried to counter this move of the pope by assembling at Ems under the leadership of Erthal.

The Punctation of Ems. The 23 articles of the Ems agreement (Aug. 25, 1786), signed by all delegates, proposed to limit the pope to those rights he had held prior to the time of the False Decretals. Its main resolutions were as follows: The plenary powers of the nuncios in matters of dispensation, inquisitorial proceedings, and acceptance of appeals should in the future pass to the bishops. The episcopal oath prescribed by Gregory IX (1227–41) was declared incompatible with the duties of an imperial prince. Appeals to Rome were to be abolished. Exemptions of religious orders were to be revoked, and their connection with Rome severed. Roman decrees were to require the episcopal *placet.* Roman benefices and Roman legal procedure were to be reformed in favor of the national bishops. Finally, the Vienna concordat agreed to in 1448 by the Holy See and Frederick III would have to be abrogated and replaced by the decrees of the Council of Basel (1431–49) and the Agreement of Aschaffenburg (1447). Early in September of 1786 the articles of the Ems draft agreement were sent to Joseph II, who approved them but suggested a consultation between the metropolitans and their suffragan bishops. (*See* FALSE DECRETALS.)

Opposition to the decrees. Meanwhile, however, a strong party fought the Ems resolutions through fear that a great increase in power of the metropolitans might even cause a schism. The opposition of the bishops was strengthened by the uncompromising attitude of the prince-elector of Bavaria, who in a *Promemoria* directed to the Imperial Diet defended the nuncios and energetically opposed the usurpation of the archbishops. When other secular princes approved this standpoint, there appeared early in 1790 the *Pii Papae VI responsio super nuntiaturis apostolicis* (1789), which refuted the complaints against the papal nunciatures, reprimanded in a paternal way the revolt of the archbishops, and refused to accede to their request for a papal legate to the Imperial Diet, saying that negotiations about this matter were outside the competence of such an envoy. Impressed by this papal declaration, Abp. Clement Wenceslaus of Trier withdrew from the agreement within a month. The metropolitans of Cologne and Salzburg gave up their attempts at ecclesiastical innovations in the wake of the French Revolution. Thus, there remained only the initiator of the congress, Prince-Elector von Erthal of Mainz, who did not want to bow down. But he could not realize his subversive ecclesiastical plans. The victorious French revolutionary armies invaded Germany, annexed a large part of his domains to the French Republic, and drove him and the two other Rhenish metropolitans from their capitals. The Punctation of Ems thus became meaningless.

Bibliography: H. SCHOTTE, "Zur Geschichte des Emser Kongresses," *Historisches Jahrbuch der Görres-Gesellschaft* 35 (1914) 319–348. G. J. JANSEN, *Kurfürst-Erzbischof Max Franz von Köln und die episkopalistischen Bestrebungen seiner Zeit* (Bonn 1933). E. WOLF, *Die Religion in Geschichte und Gegenwart* (3d ed. Tübingen 1957–65) 2:462–463. L. JUST, *Lexikon für Theologie und Kirche,* ed. J. HOFER and K. RAHNER (Freiburg 1957-65) 3:856–57.

[F. MAASS]

EMSER, HIERONYMUS

Humanist and literary adversary of Martin LUTHER; b. Weidenstetten, near Ulm, March 26, 1478; d. Dresden, Nov. 11, 1527. He studied humanities at the University of Tübingen in 1493 and law at the University of Basel in 1497. At this time he became secretary to Cardinal Raimondo Peraudi, who was papal delegate in Germany for the preaching of the jubilee indulgence for a crusade against the Turks. In 1504 he lectured at the University of Erfurt on the comedy of Johann Reuchlin, *Sergius, sive capitis caput,* with Luther as one of his listeners. He was employed in 1509 as secretary to Duke George of Saxony, who sent him to Rome the next year to plead for the canonization of Benno, Bishop of Meissen (d. 1066). On his return Emser wrote the *Vita Bennonis* (1512), claiming that it was based on sources; however, it is unreliable. About 1512 he was ordained and received a benefice at Dresden and at Meissen. Present at the Leipzig disputations of 1519, he became the opponent of Luther, whom he had earlier admired for his courage. To Luther's publicized *Ad aegrocerotem Emserianum M. Lutheri additio* he replied with the harsh *A venatione aegrocerotis assertio.* He was also the adversary of Karlstadt on images, and Zwingli on the Canon of the Mass. Between 1520 and

1527 he wrote eight polemical works. When Luther burned the bull of excommunication at Wittenberg in 1520, he also consigned some of Emser's writings to the flames.

Bibliography: E. L. ENDERS, *Luther und Emser, Ihre Streitschriften aus dem Jahre 1521,* 2 v. (Halle 1890–92). F. LAU, *Die Religion in Geschichte und Gegenwart* (Tübingen 1957–65) 2:462. E. ISERLOH, *Lexikon für Theologie und Kirche*2 3:855–856. A. HUMBERT, *Dictionnaire de théologie catholique* 4.2:2499–2500.

[E. D. MCSHANE]

EMYGDIUS OF ANCONA, ST.

Bishop of Ascoli Piceno, Italy; martyred at Ancona, Aug. 5, 303–4. A legend describing the life, miracles, and death of Emygdius (also Emygdus, Emigdius, Emidius) is extant in several conflicting versions, none earlier than the 11th century. According to the legend, Emygdius was a barbarian from Trier and was converted to Christianity there. At an early age he went to Rome and undertook a vigorous missionary activity under Pope MARCELLUS I. After he provoked popular indignation by his desecration of a statue of Aesculapius, Marcellus consecrated him a bishop and sent him to evangelize the region of Ascoli Piceno. His missionary work was successful. During the persecution of Diocletian, he was beheaded at Ancona with his three companions, SS. Eupolus, Germanus, and Valentinus. His cult spread through Italy, where he is considered an effective protector against earthquakes. Perhaps for this reason he is now venerated in San Francisco and Los Angeles, Calif.

Feast: Aug. 9.

Bibliography: *Acta Sanctorum* Aug. 2:16–36. P. A. APPIANI, *Vita di S. Emidio* (Rome 1702). J. F. MASDEN Y MONTERO, *Difesa critica degli antichi atti del S. Martire Emidio* (Ascoli 1794). A. BUTLER, *The Lives of the Saints,* ed. H. THURSTON and D. ATTWATER (New York 1956–) 3:292–293.

[J. BRÜCKMANN]

EN CLARA VOX REDARGUIT

The office hymn that was historically assigned for Lauds in Advent. Under the title *Vox clara ecce intonat* it originated probably in the fifth century, and is sometimes ascribed to St. Ambrose. The four strophes in iambic dimeter set forth the message of John the Baptist as found in the readings for the first Sunday of Advent (Rom 13.11–14; Lk 21.25–36). After an introductory strophe the call goes out to arouse the slothful soul so that it might see the bright new star, or sun, depending on whether *sidus* refers to the star of Jacob (Num 24.17), or morning star, *stella* (Apoc 22.16), or to the Sun of Justice (Mal 4.2). Since the Lamb of God is sent to pay man's debt (Jn 1.29), man must do penance and ask pardon (Ps 78.9) in the hope of protection (Is 42.8) when Christ comes in glory. In the revised version of this hymn that was found in the Roman Breviary of 1632, only four lines were left unchanged from the original text.

Bibliography: H. A. DANIEL, *Thesaurus hymnologicus,* 5 v. (Halle-Leipzig 1841–56) 1:76, text. J. JULIAN, ed., *A Dictionary of Hymnology* (New York 1957) 2:1228–29. *Analecta hymnica* 51:49. J. CONNELLY, *Hymns of the Roman Liturgy* (Westminster MD 1957) 52–53, Eng. tr.

[M. M. BEYENKA]

EN UT SUPERBA CRIMINUM

An office hymn that was historically prescribed for the Vespers of the feast of the Sacred Heart. It is the work of an anonymous 18th-century author who composed two other ''Ambrosian'' hymns honoring the Sacred Heart, *Auctor beate saeculi* and *COR ARCA LEGEM CONTINENS,* each with five strophes and a doxology. Biblical references (Mt 11.29; Eph 5.2; Heb 6.6) and the teachings of the Fathers provide material for the poet. The hymn declares that through the thrust of the centurion's lance and man's sin, the side of Christ was pierced. Thence was born the Church, Bride of Christ, who sends forth streams of grace in the Sacraments. The faithful Christian will return Christ's love by love and avoid sin, which wounds the Sacred Heart.

Bibliography: J. CONNELLY, *Hymns of the Roman Liturgy* (Westminster, MD 1957) 132–137, text and Eng. tr. M. A. WILLIAMS, *The Sacred Heart in the Life of the Church* (New York 1957). H. LAUSBERG, *Lexicon für Theologie und Kirche*, ed. J. HOFER and K. RAHNER (Freiburg 1957–65) 3:910.

[M. M. BEYENKA]

ENCOMIENDA-DOCTRINA SYSTEM IN SPANISH AMERICA

This system was based on the cooperation of the encomendero and of the doctrinero. The encomendero, usually a conquistador or his descendant, was to supervise the integration of his native wards into the social and economic life of Europe and help the doctrinero (teacher) establish the cultural and religious patterns of Christianity. This cooperative system, as far as we know today, first appeared in Mexico in the 1520s and was based on the often tragic experience of Spain in the three preceding decades in the Antilles. Quite possibly, it was the result solely of this common experience and can not be credited to any individual. However, its prompt establishment in Mexico owes much to the foresight and compassion of Cortés and to the cooperation of Mexico's first priests, the Franciscans.

The Doctrinero. In 16th-century Spanish America the doctrinero was almost always an Augustinian, Dominican, Franciscan, or Mercedarian friar. Royal policy did not favor granting this work to the diocesan clergy. The Jesuits, founded only after the initial conversion of the Americas was well under way, did not share notably in this work. The friar was selected by his provincial, who had to clarify that the individual was adequately trained in theology and in the respective native language. The actual appointment was made by the viceroy or his equivalent in the name of the king. Quite often, the doctrinero was not appointed to a specific doctrina but to a central convent situated near his charges. It was the duty of the superior of this convent to supervise the work of the friars under his care, to appoint each to a definite doctrina, and to visit the doctrinas at least three times each year. He reported to the provincial, who, in turn, had to visit the doctrinas once every three years. The doctrinero had to return to this central convent each Friday for a short theological discussion and for recreation, a humane provision.

The Doctrina. A typical doctrina contained a church, priest's residence, school, hospital, cemetery, and often an *obraje.* No non-native, and this included even the parents of the doctrinero, could remain longer than three days in the doctrina. The cost of the plant was defrayed one-third by the crown, one-third by the encomendero, and one-third by the native tribes. In the hospital the sick were cared for and travelers were given lodging. The quality of the hospitals varied greatly—some were merely miserable huts, while others were richly endowed and staffed with trained surgeons and numerous slaves. Hospital care was free because each native taxpayer gave one tomin a year as part of his head tax. The school was intended to train the sons of the caciques and other prominent families in Christian doctrine, reading and writing Spanish, a little arithmetic, and instrumental and vocal music. The students with their teachers formed the parish choir. The teachers assisted the doctrinero and in his absence even conducted church services, such as funerals, simple Baptisms, and processions. At first, the friars were the teachers. Within a few years, the task was entrusted mostly to trained natives, who were rewarded with the title of Don, exempted from personal services and numerous taxes, and paid in food and clothing. The *obraje* was the village workshop where the natives wove cloth, worked leather or metal, or made pots for sale to pay for a new church or to pay those taxes which were demanded in money so the head of the family would not be forced to labor outside the doctrina to acquire the needed sum. Later these frequently became sweatshops and were often manned by prison labor.

Methods. There was a wide variation in the details of the methods whereby the doctrinero cared for the spiritual instruction and needs of his people. However, on the broad outline there was general agreement. Essentially this agreement was forced by the circumstance that the Indians numbered many millions, the doctrineros, hundreds. To aggravate the problem, the native tribes were scattered over a vast and often inhospitable territory. It was obviously impossible even to think of individual instruction. Group indoctrination was the only feasible solution if the task was to be accomplished with reasonable speed and thoroughness. Even this presented a problem. If each group had to be completely instructed in the faith before Baptism, many decades would certainly pass before the work could be completed and numerous natives would die without the Sacrament. The solution was found in the protracted catechumenate. This system demanded that the native be reduced to living in a town under the control of the encomendero and doctrinero. Then the native could be baptized after instruction in the doctrines which theologians considered essential for salvation, on the supposition that this rudimentary instruction would be perfected in the course of years by enforced attendance at doctrinal classes held at regular intervals, once a week in some places and twice a week in others, and conducted by the doctrinero or his substitute. Therefore, the native was reduced to pueblo life and each pueblo was divided into districts with a native fiscal, or *alguazil,* in charge. On the days when the people of the district were to appear for instruction, the fiscal would knock on their doors to remind them and would then go to the church plaza to check their presence against the official roll. Repeated absences without excuse were punished. No native was forced to be baptized (although at times impatient or stupid doctrineros did use force), but once baptized, he had no choice about attending the classes in doctrine.

In class, great stress was laid on learning by heart a formulary of the main truths that the Spaniards called the *doctrina cristiana.* It consisted of the sign of the cross, the Our Father, the Hail Mary, the Apostles' Creed, the Hail Holy Queen, the 14 articles of faith, the commandments of God, the commandments of the Church, the Sacraments, the spiritual and corporal works of mercy, the theological virtues, the cardinal virtues, the seven capital sins, the enemies of the soul, and the four last things. As an aid to understanding, the doctrinero used charts, pictures, tableaux, mystery plays, reenactments of portions of the Bible, processions, and especially music. Many parts of the formulary as well as translations of some of the hymns of the ancient Church such as the Athanasian

Creed were set to song. The people were encouraged to sing them at home and at work. Many hymns were used for their social dances, a custom in keeping with their pagan rites where the dance was an integral part of their religion. At the same time, the liturgy was conducted with great solemnity. For this purpose, the teachers of the local school were taught to play the part of the canons in the cathedrals and to come to church in the mornings and afternoons. In the morning they chanted a short morning prayer and then a hymn that described some part of the life of Christ. Each day had a different hymn. In the afternoon, they chanted a sort of evensong made up of a few short psalms, an act of contrition, and a petition that God bless them and their village for the night. It was a sort of monastic ritual shared by the people of the whole town.

The doctrinero was supposed to check the knowledge of each native individual at the time of the Easter confession. If it was not satisfactory, the individual could not receive this Sacrament or Communion and ordinarily would be remanded to a special class for intensive instruction. Usually extra priests were sent to help the doctrinero during the Lenten season.

By 1574, the encomienda-doctrina system was found in approximately 9,000 pueblos in Spanish America with about six million inhabitants, according to Juan López de Velasco. These figures are especially valuable because in 1573 the crown forbade the extension of the encomienda beyond the territory in which it was then established. This decree marked the end of the encomienda-doctrina system as a frontier institution. In time, the doctrina was to become simply a parish entrusted to the care of the diocesan clergy under the supervision of the bishop. A new institution would be developed to care for the pagan natives beyond the frontier of Spanish America. It would be called the mission (*see* MISSIONS IN COLONIAL AMERICA).

[A. S. TIBESAR]

ENCUENTROS, NATIONAL PASTORAL

Three national pastoral Encuentros assembled Hispanic Catholics from across the United States in Washington, D.C., in 1972, 1977, and 1985. The meetings were characterized by frank deliberations with broad sociological, anthropological, and ecclesiological implications. After briefly surveying the situation of Hispanic Catholics in the U.S., this entry describes the National Pastoral Encuentros and their outcome.

Latino Identity. Before Vatican II, Latino Church identity was largely regional. Archbishop Robert E. Lucey of San Antonio had helped organize the Bishop's Committee for the Spanish Speaking in 1945, but it was limited to diocesan efforts. Later he guided an interdiocesan outreach to migrant workers, but ethnic concentrations of Puerto Ricans in New York, Cubans in Miami, and Mexicans and Chicanos in the West and Southwest still led the Church to more specific consideration of local challenges and opportunities. Lay involvement was generally restricted to area cofradías and parish organizations. Television and other media, however, made Hispanics of one region more visible to those of other areas. World War II and national civic organizations such as the G. I. Forum strengthened the bonds of national identity. The burgeoning civil rights movement added to the ferment and led to the organization of other national Hispanic publications and conferences.

New theological and ecclesiological dialogue in Catholic South America, reflected at Medellín, also affected U.S. Catholic Hispanics. In 1969 Chicano priests organized Padres Asociados por los Derechos Religiosos, Educativos y Sociales (PADRES) and two years later Chicana Religious formed Las Hermanas. Lay movements such as the Cursillo, Marriage Encounter, and the Christian Family Movement swept the country, creating national networks and training thousands of new leaders. César CHÁVEZ, a cursillista, began to organize farmworkers, and in 1970 Patricio Flores, himself a farmworker, was ordained the first U.S. Hispanic bishop. A coalition of many of these leaders, led by Virgilio Elizondo, founded the Mexican American Cultural Center (MACC) in 1972.

The First National Encuentro. All these events were indirectly essential remote preparation for the first national Encuentro. Its immediate organization began at a 1971 meeting between Robert Stern, director of the Spanish Speaking Apostolate for the Archdiocese of New York, and Edgar Beltrán of the Latin American Episcopal Conference.

The 1972 Encuentro consisted of a few hundred participants, mostly Church leaders, who demanded full participation of Hispanics in all aspects of Church life. As a result, ecclesial authorities began implementing changes. The Division for the Spanish Speaking in the United States Catholic Conference became an independent secretariat with layman Pablo Sedillo as director. Regional offices for Hispanic ministry were initiated or reorganized. More Hispanics were ordained bishops, and dioceses founded agencies for Latino ministry. A permanent committee of Bishops for Hispanic Affairs was also created. These were important steps obtained as a direct result of a national effort of U.S. Hispanic Catholics who worked together toward common objectives.

At the first Encuentro, although there were inevitable tensions between the various ethnic groups later labeled

Hispanic, there was also dialogue. The first Encuentro had a sparse representation of laity, women, youth, or the poor, but it set in motion a national networking and consensus building that continued to grow. Recognition of the importance of the Spanish language and Hispanic culture, and the acknowledgment of Latinos' rightful role and contribution to the entire U.S. Church, accelerated significantly after the First Encuentro.

The Second Encuentro. The process of the second Encuentro addressed many previous tensions. Almost five times as many delegates and observers attended, the fruit of a national consultation of over 100,000 people. Rather than a series of presentations, this Encuentro was a working session of grass roots organizers. Spanish was the official language. The second Encuentro elicited more episcopal participation in its proceedings that were published by the United States Catholic Conference. The conclusions called on both the participants and the entire Church to: (1) continue with the consultative Encuentro process; (2) form Basic Christian Communities; (3) correct injustices within and outside the Church using an option for the poor; (4) promote ecclesial unity based on diversity; and (5) foster lay ministry. Of particular note was the heightened profile of youth.

The Third Encuentro. Unlike the first two, the third Encuentro of 1985 was convoked by a pastoral letter of the National Conference of Catholic Bishops titled The Hispanic Presence: Challenge and Commitment. This was the first NCCB publication dedicated solely to Latino concerns. After an overview of the reality of U.S. Latinos, the bishops summarize the achievements of Hispanic ministry and outline consequent pastoral implications. Further, they make a ''Statement of Commitment'' that pledged to the Church the use of its resources for the temporal and ecclesial needs of the Hispanic community. Finally, they convoke the third Encuentro to help them to ''face our responsibilities well.''

The bishops expressed a desire to draft a National Pastoral Plan for Hispanic Ministry based on the conclusions of this Encuentro. Diocesan and national teams began the process of massive consultation with particular emphasis on previously under represented groups. The great majority of participants had taken part in the exhaustive process of local, diocesan, and regional preparation that reached an estimated 200,000 people through this classic Church event. Efforts paid off in a balanced delegation that included more women and the poor, but young people were still under represented.

Specific themes coalesced into a working document presented to almost 1,200 delegates representing over 130 dioceses. The open and genuine dialogue included some disagreement, for example, several hundred Encuentro delegates staged a protest until the emphasis on the value, equality, and dignity of women was restored to the text of the concluding statement. However, this organized protest itself witnessed to the success that the Encuentro process had achieved in promoting lay leadership in general and women leaders in particular. Ada María Isasi-Díaz, Yolanda Tarango CCVI, Ana María Díaz Stevens, María Luisa Gastón, Rosa Marta Zarate, María Iglesias SC, Ana María Pineda RSM, Olga Villa Parra, Dominga Zapata SH, and countless others witness to the fact that virtually all the extant Hispanic national leadership among women was involved in the Encuentros.

Based on the conclusions of the third Encuentro, the NCCB published the *National Pastoral Plan for Hispanic Ministry* (NPPHM) in 1987. As in the case of the proceedings of the prior Encuentros, the implementation of the NPPHM has been mixed. The process, if not all the documents, however, represents a milestone in the history of the U.S. Church.

Enduring Influence of the Encuentros. Sociologically, the Encuentros fostered greater national networking among Latinos. Numerous diocesan and regional offices attest to this fact, as well as the National Secretariat, and the growing number of national Hispanic Catholic organizations such as the Academy of Catholic Hispanic Theologians of the United States (ACHTUS). Anthropologically these assemblies defended, even celebrated, the right of all Church members to be at once both universally Catholic, and peculiarly distinct in language and culture. No other ethnic group in the country has incarnated this insight as successfully. Ecclesiologically they championed a Church that is communitarian, evangelizing, and missionary. Indeed, some of the Encuentro proceedings predate both of the similarly collaborative U.S. pastoral letters on peace (1983) and the economy (1985).

Only greater historcal perspective will afford a comprehensive evaluation of the Encuentros, but it can already be said that their influence did not end in 1985. The Encuentros gave rise to noted national organizations such as the Instituto de Liturgia Hispana, and they have continued to grow and mature. Many dioceses began their first coordinated efforts at serving and empowering Latinos as a direct result of the *National Pastoral Plan*. The best example of the enduring influence of the Encuentros is the National Catholic Council for Hispanic Ministry. In 1990 some eighteen regional and national Hispanic Catholic associations founded this consortium precisely to continue the collaborative efforts so successfully pioneered at the Encuentros. By 1995 the NCCHM counted forty-nine member organizations. Among their activities was a national Congress held in Los Angeles in 1992, and another in Chicago in 1996. In method and content both the NCCHM and its congresses purposefully follow and consciously continue the three national Encuentros.

The post-Encuentro period has seen a boom in the publication of documents concerning Latinos through the USCC, and other editorials, as well as a plethora of periodicals devoted to Hispanic ministry. Latino representation on theological faculties and in such organizations as the National Conference of Catechetical Leaders, while still small, continues to expand.

Bibliography: J. P. DOLAN and A. F. DECK, *Hispanic Catholic Culture in the U.S.: Issues and Concerns* (Notre Dame 1994). S. GALERON, R. M. ICAZA, and R. URRABAZO, *Prophetic Vision: Pastoral Reflections on the National Pastoral Plan for Hispanic Ministry* (Kansas City 1992). M. SANDOVAL, *On the Move: A History of the Hispanic Church in the United States* (Maryknoll 1990). S. A. PRIVETT, *The U.S. Catholic Church and its Hispanic Members: The Pastoral Vision of Archbishop Robert E. Lucey* (San Antonio 1988). A. M. STEVENS-ARROYO, *Prophets Denied Honor: An Anthology on the Hispanic Church in the United States* (Maryknoll 1980).

[K. G. DAVIS]

ENCYCLICAL

A letter, ''essentially pastoral in character'' (John Paul II, *Ut unum sint* [May 25, 1995], no. 3), written by the pope for the entire Church. Encyclicals have not been used for dogmatic definitions, but rather to give counsel or to shed light on points of doctrine that must be made more precise or that must be taught in view of specific circumstances. For instance, the encyclical *Veritatis splendor* (Aug. 6, 1993), ''limits itself to dealing with certain fundamental questions regarding the Church's moral teaching'' (no. 5).

An encyclical is, first, a papal letter and is therefore distinguished from pastoral letters written by an ordinary for his diocese. Second, it is a letter, and therefore distinguished from other papal documents, such as apostolic constitutions. Since it is a pastoral document, it pertains ordinarily to doctrinal, moral, or disciplinary matters; it is not a legislative text. An encyclical letter is ordinarily addressed either to the bishops or to the entire Church, although at times it is also addressed to those persons who are not members of the Church, but are of ''good will.'' The encyclical letter is also used both in the Orthodox Churches, as is evidenced by the ecumenical patriarch's regular encyclicals for Christmas and Easter, and in the Anglican communion, for instance, at the end of Lambeth Conferences held every 10 years.

History. There have been formal papal letters written for the entire Church from the earliest days of the Christian era. But it seems that the first modern usage of the encyclical as now known was made by Benedict XIV on Dec. 3, 1740, in his encyclical epistle *Ubi primum,* dealing with episcopal duties. It is only in more recent times, from the reign of Pius IX, that encyclicals have become frequent expressions of the pope's ordinary teaching authority.

Authority. The teaching contained in an encyclical has generally not been given as belonging formally to the deposit of revelation, but as Pius XII stated it pertains to Catholic doctrine: ''In writing them, it is true, the Popes do not exercise their teaching authority to the full. But such statements come under the day-to-day teaching of the Church. . . . For the most part the positions advanced and the duties inculcated by these encyclical letters are already bound up, under some other title, with the general body of Catholic teaching'' (see Pius XII, *Humani generis* [Aug. 12, 1950], *AAS* 42 [1950] 568). Because of this, an encyclical is generally considered to be an expression of the pope's ordinary teaching authority; its contents are presumed to belong to the ordinary magisterium unless the opposite is clearly manifested. Because of this, the teaching of an encyclical is capable of being changed on specific points of detail (see Paul VI, *Allocution,* June 23, 1964, *AAS,* 56 [1964] 588).

Pope John Paul II began to use encyclicals to present points of church teaching that are henceforth to be considered ''definitive.'' For instance, in *Evangelium vitae* (March 25, 1995), he used the following formulas: ''Therefore, by the authority which Christ conferred upon Peter and his Successors, and in communion with the Bishops of the Catholic Church, I confirm'' (no. 57). Or, again: ''Therefore, by the authority which Christ conferred upon Peter and his Successors, in communion with the Bishops . . . I declare'' (no. 62). And: ''In harmony with the Magisterium of my Predecessors and in communion with the Bishops of the Catholic Church, I confirm'' (no. 65).

Reception. Although Catholics are to give assent to the moral and doctrinal content of papal encyclicals, three points must be kept in mind. First, encyclicals possess less authority than dogmatic pronouncements made by the extraordinary infallible magisterium (unless otherwise specifically provided). Second, they usually do not contain definitive, or infallible, teaching (unless otherwise clearly stated, as noted above). Finally, the publication of an encyclical does not imply (unless otherwise provided) that the theological issues examined in the encyclical are now closed. An encyclical necessarily expresses a particular theological point of view, but it is usually not a definitive assessment.

Social Encyclicals. Beginning in 1891 with Leo XIII's *Rerum novarum,* the teaching of the Church relating to matters of social justice, human rights, and peace has been expressed in encyclicals. Pius XI issued *Quadragesimo anno* (1931); John XXIII, *Pacem in terris* (1963); Paul VI, *Populorum progressio* (1967). Three major social encyclicals of John Paul II are: *Laborem exercens* (1981), *Sollicitudo rei socialis* (1987), and *Centesimus annus* (1991). These teachings are usually centered on the dignity of the human person and on the gospel message that is a basis and motivation for action (*Centesimus annus,* nos. 53, 57).

Bibliography: R. P. MCBRIEN, ed., *Encyclopedia of Catholicism* (San Francisco 1995), s.v. "Encyclical." F. G. MORRISEY, *Papal and Curial Pronouncements: Their Canonical Significance in Light of the Code of Canon Law* (Ottawa 1995) 11–12.

[F. G. MORRISSEY]

ENCYCLOPEDIAS AND DICTIONARIES, CATHOLIC

An encyclopedia is a comprehensive summary of the significant knowledge of an era. It may either embrace all fields of human interest or be limited to the coverage of a specific subject area. The modern encyclopedia, however, because of the massive volume of facts accumulated in all fields, is less ambitious than its ancient and medieval counterparts.

Ancient Works. To the Greeks, "encyclopaedia" meant "circle of knowledge" or "complete education," a concept exemplified by the extensive works of Aristotle, who attempted to assemble all knowledge available through human observation and thought. With a similar intention, Pliny the Elder claimed to treat in his *Historia naturalis* (A. D. 77) "the subjects included by the Greeks under the name of 'Encyclic Culture.' Naturally, when the Church in the early Middle Ages undertook to preserve and disseminate the knowledge and wisdom of the ancient world, her scholars had at hand ready models for their own compendia.

As early as 551, Cassiodorus, distinguished statesman and secretary to Theodoric, produced the *Institutiones divinarum et humanarum lectionum* after his retirement to his monastery of the Vivarium, later adding notes to his manuscript for the benefit of the "simple and unpolished brothers" of his community.

Medieval Compilations. The standard medieval encyclopedia was the *Etymologiarum libri XX* of Isidore of Seville, completed in 623. The first work to contain a printed map of the known world, the *Etymologies* is a primary source for the modes of thought and factual knowledge of the preceding centuries. Its influence on later encyclopedias can scarcely be overrated. The *De universo* two centuries later of Rabanus Maurus, Abbot of Fulda, was a rearrangement of the *Etymologies* that bowdlerized, as well as plagiarized, it. The greatest achievement of the Middle Ages was undoubtedly the *Speculum maius* of Vincent of Beauvais (1190–1264), written under the patronage of St. Louis of France, who supplied numerous copyists for the many extracts incorporated in it. The first vernacular encyclopedia was the work of Brunetto Latini (d. 1294), a Florentine statesman and friend of Dante who wrote *Li livres dou trésor* during his exile in France.

Other compilers and titles of importance in the medieval period were: Honorius of Autun, *Imago mundi* (1090); Lambert of Saint-Omer, *Liber floridus* (1120); and Alexander Neckham, an Augustinian of St. Albans (1157–1217), who compiled a *De naturis rerum*. The Abbess Herrad of Hohenburg (d. 1195) was the first woman to compile an encyclopedia: her *Hortus deliciarum* was one of the finest illuminated manuscript encyclopedias of which there is record. The *Compendium philosophiae* (c. 1320), with traces of the influence of St. Albert the Great, has been attributed to the Dominican Hugh of Strassburg, author of the well-known *Compendium theologiae*. Pierre Bercheure, a Benedictine friend of Petrarch, compiled a three-part *Reductorium, repertorium, et dictionarium morale utriusque testamenti* (1340), and Gregor Reisch dedicated his *Margarita philosophica* to "ingenuous youth." Giovanni Balbi's *Catholicon* (1460), strongly influenced by the *Etymologies*, was printed, possibly by Gutenberg, "without help of reed, stylus or pen, but by the marvelous concord, proportion, and harmony of punches and types."

Before the late Middle Ages, nearly all these compilations of facts and conjectured facts were written in Latin, and their use was limited to the scholar. Translation into English began in 1480 with William Caxton's *Myrrour of the World*. This was the first illustrated book and one of the first encyclopedias to be printed in England, explaining "how moche the erth hath of heyght, how moche in circuyte, and how thycke in the rnyddle." The term encyclopedia, however, first appeared in English in Sir Thomas Elyot's *The Governour* (1531), which referred to the "circle of doctrine, whiche is in one worde of greke Encyclopaedia."

The *Summas* and the *Mirrours* of the Middle Ages and early Renaissance were followed by the *Treasures* and *Tableaux* of the 16th century. The latter were, in the main, collections of facts showing little or no mastery of the material and giving no evidence of critical research or basic plan.

Influence of Printing. The spread of printing accelerated the encyclopedic movement, yet there was little advance over Vincent's *Speculum*, first printed at Strasbourg (1473–76), then at Basel (1481), Nuremberg (1473–86), Venice (1484, 1494, 1591), and finally by the Benedictines at Douai in 1624. Raffaele Maffei included biographical sketches and an index in his *Commentariorum urbanorum libri XXXVIII* (1506). Francis Bacon was the first to base his work on the philosophy and interrelation of the sciences. Although his *Instauratio magna* (1620–23) was never completed, its comprehensive and well-ordered plan greatly influenced Diderot and D'Alembert in their work on the controversial *Encyclopedie* two centuries later.

Louis Moréri's *Le grand dictionnaire historique* (1674) was deliberately designed as an apologia and defense of the Church. Noteworthy for its new emphasis on geographical and biographical material, it greatly influenced German, Spanish, and English encyclopedias of the period. The *Biblioteca universale sacro-profano* of the Franciscan Vincenzo Maria Coronelli would have been the largest alphabetically arranged encyclopedia in existence, but only seven volumes were completed (1701–06). It is important for its plan and for innovation of the practice of italicizing the titles of books cited in the text.

After Ephraim Chambers' *Cyclopaedia* (1728), ''compiled from the best authors,'' had changed the pattern of encyclopedia publishing from single authorship to collaborative effort, two more Catholic contributions were compiled single-handed. Jacques Paul Migne was responsible for the *Encyclopédie théologique* (1844–66), a series of 168 special *Dictionnaires* covering dogmas, heresies, liturgy, symbolism, and many auxiliary sciences. Gaetano Moroni (1840–79) published his *Dizionario di erudizione*, which, though poorly organized, was rich in notes not found elsewhere. Wetzer and Welte's *Kirchenlexikon* (1847–60; 2d ed. 1882–1903) and *Der Grosse Herder* (1853–57; 5th ed. 1952–56), however, followed the pattern set by Chambers.

Modern Developments. With the 20th century, as knowledge became progressively specialized, practically every country began to produce well-edited encyclopedias for reference in special, as well as in general, fields. The U. S.-edited *Catholic Encyclopedia* (1907–14) was for more than half a century the most significant Catholic reference work in English. The *New Catholic Encyclopedia* (1967) replaced the older work for all practical purposes, but the earlier publication is still useful for historical material in some areas and for specific facts that can be located by means of its excellent index.

In France, Letouzey began (1903) publication of the great French series *Encyclopédie des sciences religieuses*, composed of the following individual works: *Dictionnaire d'archéologie chrétienne et de liturgie* (eds. F. Cabrol and H. LeClereq); *Dictionnaire d'histoire et de géographie ecclésiastiques* (eds. A. Baudrillart et al.); *Dictionnaire de théologie catholique* (eds. A. Vacant, E. Mangenot, and É Amann); *Dictionnaire de la Bible* (ed. F. Vigouroux); and *Dictionnaire du droit canonique* (ed. R. Naz). Since these works have been in progress for over half a century, some of the material is out of date, and some of the bibliographies have been superseded by later publications. The *Dictionnaire de théologie catholique*, however, is being brought up to date by elaborate indices, and the *Dictionnaire de la Bible* is being replaced by the *Supplément* (1928–, ed. L. Pirot), so the series as a whole is still an essential source of information of vast proportions. Beauchesne's *Dictionnaire de spiritualité ascétique et mystique*, ed. M. Viller et al. (1932–), includes many biographies. *Catholicisme hier, aujourd'hui, demain* (1948–), now being issued by Letouzey under the editorship of G. Jacquemet, is the most recent French publication covering these subjects.

The *Lexikon für Theologie und Kirche*, ed. M. Buchberger (1930–38), has been replaced by a new work of the same title, ed. Josef Höfer and Karl Rahner. The Italian *Enciclopedia cattolica*, completed in 1954, covers historical and contemporary matters of concern to the Church. The Netherlands has produced *De katholieke Encyclopaedie* (1950) and the *Encyclopaedie van het Katholicisme* (1955–60); the Jesuits at Sophia University, in collaboration with the German publishing house of Herder, have published the Japanese *Katolikku Daijiten* (1940–53).

The *Staatslexikon* (6th ed. 1959–63) of the Görres-Gesellschaft, the Herder *Lexikon der Pädagogik* (3d ed. 1962), H. Aurenhammer's *Lexikon der christlichen Ikonographie* (1959–), and the *Handbuch Theologischer Grundbegrifle*, ed. Heinrich Fries (1962–63), are typical of the many encyclopedias and dictionaries in special fields published under Catholic auspices.

Since the end of Vatican II in 1965 there have been additions to this list of the encyclopedias and dictionaries. The most extensive of these publications is *Concilium: Theology in the Age of Renewal* which began publication in 1964 and is still in process. With multiple issues per annum there are now more than 220 volumes. It appears in English, French, German, Spanish, Portuguese, and Dutch. Immediately following Vatican II the six volume *Sacramentum Mundi* and the three volume *Sacramentum Verbi*, both published by Herder and Herder, the former edited by Karl Rahner and the latter by Johannes Bauer, were published as encyclopedias, which brought the documents of the Council to bear on theology and biblical theology. One volume abridged versions of these encyclopedias appeared a few years later.

In the United States the short-lived Corpus Publications produced the three volume *Encyclopedic Dictionary of Religion* and the one volume *Corpus Dictionary of Western Churches*. More recently there have been series of one volume encyclopedias on specific topics. Michael O'Carroll, C.S.Sp., has edited a series of five volumes entitled: *Corpus Christi, an Encyclopedia of the Eucharist; Theotokos, a Theological Encyclopedia of the Blessed Virgin Mary; Trinitas, a Theological Encyclopedia of the Holy Trinity; Veni Creator Spiritus, a Theological Encyclopedia of the Holy Spirit*; and *Verbum Caro, an Encyclopedia on Jesus*. In addition Christopher O'Donnell, O. Carm., has edited *Ecclesia, a Theological Encyclopedia of the Church* for this series. These were published by Michael Glazier and The Liturgical Press. The Liturgical Press has also published an extensive series of one volume encyclopedias: *The New Dictionary of Theology; The New Dictionary of Sacramental Worship; The New Dictionary of Catholic Spirituality; The New Dictionary of Catholic Social Thought; Consecrated Phrases: A Latin Theological Dictionary; A Concise Dictionary of Early Christianity*; and *The Liturgical Dictionary of Eastern Christianity*. There is also the *Dictionary of Christian Biography* which is ecumenical in scope.

Mention must also be made of a number of one volume encyclopedias from various publishers. The *Historical Dictionary of Catholicism*, by William J. Collinge (Scarecrow Press, 1997) is no. 12 of the series *Historical Dictionaries of Religions, Philosophies, and Movements*. Michael Glazier and Thomas J. Shelley have published *The Encyclopedia of American Catholic History*, a vast and unique collection of information. There is the specialized *Dictionary of the Liturgy*, edited by J.P. Lang, OFM, published by Our Sunday Visitor. Three one-volume general encyclopedias complete our coverage of American publications. In 1987 Thomas Nelson Publishers gave us *The Catholic Encyclopedia*, edited by Robert C. Broderick. Two years later, Harper-San Francisco produced *The Harper-Collins Encyclopedia of Catholicism*. In 1994 *The Modern Catholic Encyclopedia* was published by The Liturgical Press. These three publications approach Roman Catholicism from differing viewpoints and can be used in conjunction with one another. The multi-volume *New Catholic Encyclopedia* published updated volumes 16 through 19 along with the Jubilee Volume of 2000.

From Italy we have the *Dictionary of Fundamental Theology* (English edition edited by Rene Latourelle). Italy has also given us the multi-volume *Dizionario degli Istituti di Perfezione*, published by Edizioni Paolini beginning in 1973, and the two-volume *Dizionario Patristico e di Antichità Cristiane*, produced by the Institutum Patristicum Augustinianum in 1991. An English translation came out in 1992 as *Encyclopedia of the Early Church*. In the 1990s Germany produced a completely revised edition of the *Lexikon für Theologie und Kirche*. The French continue the work of completing several of the vast encyclopedias mentioned above.

Bibliography: R. BÄUMER, *Lexikon für Theologie und Kirche*, ed. J. HOFER and K. RAHNER (Freiberg 1957–65) 6:998–1001. ''Dictionaires,'' *Catholicisme* 3 (1952) 742–746. R. L. COLLISON, *Encyclopaedias: Their History throughout the Ages* (New York 1964). G. A. ZISCHKA, *Index lexicorum* (Vienna 1959). R. BALLEY, *Guide to Reference Books* (11th ed. Chicago 1996). A. J. WALFORD, *Guide to Reference Material* (London 1961). L. M. MALCLÈS, *Les Sources du travail bibliographique*, 3 v. in 4 (Genève 1950–58). S. P. WALSH, comp., *General Encyclopedias in Print, 1965* (Newark, Del. 1965).

[M. C. CARLEN/R.B. MILLER]

ENCYCLOPEDISTS

Originally the term encyclopedists referred to the contributors to the French *Encyclopédie,* but it has come to be used for all the 18th-century Frenchmen who shared the scientific, political, and religious views popularized in that work.

Origins of the Encyclopedia. The *Encyclopédie, ou Dictionnaire raisonné des sciences, des arts et des métiers, par une société de gens de lettres,* like many revolutionary ideas of its century, had its immediate source in England. In 1728 Ephraim Chambers had published a two-volume work titled *Cyclopedia; or an Universal Dictionary of Arts and Sciences; Containing an Explication of the Terms, and an Account of the Things Signified Thereby, in the Several Arts, both Liberal and Mechanical, and the Several Sciences, Human and Divine . . . the Whole Intended as a Course of Ancient and Modern Learning.* Between 1743 and 1745, John Mills, an Englishman, and Gottfried Sellius, a native of Danzig then residing in Paris, arranged for a French translation of this work, and requested the bookseller André LeBreton to undertake its publication. LeBreton obtained the necessary *privilège royal,* but shortly afterwards eliminated Mills and Sellius from the project, perhaps because their translation was found to be inadequate. In their place he recruited Jean LeRond D'Alembert and Abbé Jean Paul Gua de Malnes. One year later Denis Diderot was added to the staff, and in 1747 he became the general editor. It is generally thought that Diderot was responsible for the decision to enlarge the general scope of the *Encyclopédie;* in his prospectus of 1750 he described it as a compilation ''particularly from the English dictionaries of Chambers, J. Harris [*Lexicon technicum, or an Universal Dictionary of Arts and Sciences,* 1704], and T. Dyche [*A New General English Dictionary*, 1740].''

The first volume of the *Encyclopédie,* published in Paris in 1751, caused great concern among the orthodox, especially the Society of Jesus. Some charged that the JESUITS wished either to destroy the project or to take it into their own hands, pointing out that their *Dictionnaire de Trévoux* was actually a literary competitor, while their *Journal de Trévoux* regularly attacked the *Encyclopédie.* Leading Jansenists also expressed their dismay at the nature of the publication (*see* JANSENISM). However, the work found some favor at court, if only because Mme. de Pompadour cared for neither Jesuits nor Jansenists, and no official action was taken against the *Encyclopédie* until the appearance of the second volume in 1752. At that time the council of LOUIS XV suppressed the two volumes in existence because they contained "maxims tending to destroy the royal authority, to establish a spirit of independence and revolt . . . to build the foundations of error, of moral corruption, of irreligion and of unbelief." Nevertheless, the license to publish further volumes was not revoked, and the work continued with a new volume appearing each year until 1757. During this period the Abbés Tamponnet, Millet, and Cotterel acted as official censors, reviewing all articles, not only those touching theological matters. By 1757 the original list of subscribers had grown from about 2,000 to about 4,000.

In 1759 there was a new suppression of the work, this time by the Parlement of Paris. Later the same year the *privilége* royal was revoked. At this juncture Diderot (D'Alembert had dissociated himself from the project the previous year) proceeded clandestinely with the remaining ten volumes of text, which were published together at Neufchâtel in 1765. These aroused little opposition, however, partly because LeBreton had taken it upon himself, without Diderot's knowledge, to eliminate all passages he thought might offend civil or ecclesiastical authorities. By the time Diderot discovered what had been done it was too late to repair the damage. Marie-Angélique Vandeul, Diderot's daughter, relates that her father ordered LeBreton to print a copy of the ten volumes with the deleted passages restored, but no such copy has ever been found.

Contents and Contributors. The *Encyclopédie,* in its completed form, consists of 17 folio volumes of text and 11 volumes of plates published by LeBreton, four supplementary volumes of text and one of plates published by C. J. Panckoucke in Paris (1776–77), and two volumes of index prepared by Pierre Mouchan and published in Amsterdam (1780). The first volume of the *Encyclopédie* contains D'Alembert's celebrated "Preliminary Discourse," in which he asserted that the purpose of the undertaking was to present the principles and essential details of all the sciences and arts; to provide a ready means of instruction, both for teachers and for those who wished to learn by themselves; and to preserve man's knowledge for posterity. Following Francis BACON, D'Alembert divided all the sciences into three classes, depending on whether they pertained to memory (history), imagination (the *beaux arts*), or reason (philosophy). The entire schema is delineated in a chart in the first volume. There are articles on various phases of biology, chemistry, cooking, gardening, grammar, history, mathematics, medicine, philosophy, physics, and religion, as well as on the trades and manufactures of 18th-century France.

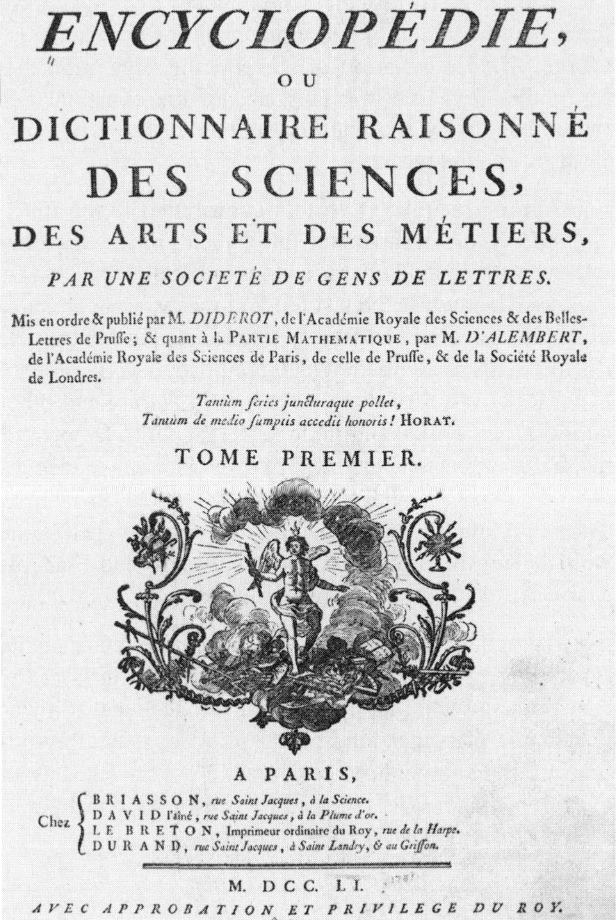
ENCYCLOPÉDIE,

OU

DICTIONNAIRE RAISONNÉ

DES SCIENCES,

DES ARTS ET DES MÉTIERS,

PAR UNE SOCIETÉ DE GENS DE LETTRES.

Mis en ordre & publié par M. *DIDEROT*, de l'Académie Royale des Sciences & des Belles-Lettres de Prusse; & quant à la PARTIE MATHEMATIQUE, par M. *D'ALEMBERT*, de l'Académie Royale des Sciences de Paris, de celle de Prusse, & de la Société Royale de Londres.

Tantùm series juncturaque pollet,
Tantùm de medio sumptis accedit honoris! HORAT.

TOME PREMIER.

A PARIS,

Chez BRIASSON, *rue Saint Jacques, à la Science.*
DAVID l'aîné, *rue Saint Jacques, à la Plume d'or.*
LE BRETON, Imprimeur ordinaire du Roy, *rue de la Harpe.*
DURAND, *rue Saint Jacques, à Saint Landry, & au Griffon.*

M. DCC. LI.

AVEC APPROBATION ET PRIVILEGE DU ROY.

Title page of the first edition of the Encyclopédie, 1751.

In many instances the *Encyclopédie* articles are totally lacking in the objectivity that one expects to find in a 20th-century encyclopedia or dictionary. The authors availed themselves of any and every opportunity to introduce their own political, philosophical, or theological points of view, often in an indirect or satirical manner. While many articles reflect a completely orthodox point of view, others express atheistic or deistic ideas popular among French intellectuals. However, much of what shocked the more conservative segments of society is no longer thought daring, e.g., the advocacy of freedom of the press, the denial of supreme papal power in temporal affairs, the denunciation of slavery, the suggestion that Scripture often uses the language of the common man rather than that of the scientist, and the rejection of INNATISM in knowledge.

Approximately 60 writers contributed to the *Encyclopédie.* Some of the better-known authors are: the Chevalier de Jaucourt, Diderot's chief aid and practically his only assistant while the last ten volumes were in preparation; George Louis Buffon, a naturalist; the Marquis de CONDORCET, mathematician and philosopher; Baron Paul HOLBACH, author of the *Système de la Nature* and other antireligious works; Baron de MONTESQUIEU, famous for his *Esprit des lois* and *Les Lettres Persanes;* Jacques Necker, financier and economist of sorts; Jean-Jacques ROUSSEAU, man of letters and political philosopher; Anne Robert Turgot, economist and statesman; and François Marie Arouet VOLTAIRE, philosopher and *literateur.*

It would be difficult to overestimate the influence the *Encyclopédie* exercised over French intellectuals at the time of its publication; it is generally conceded that it was one of the principal intellectual sources of the Revolution. In the 20th century, of course, it is very dated as an encyclopedia, and its chief value is as a historical document.

Bibliography: *The Encyclopédie of Diderot and D'Alembert: Selected Articles,* ed. J. LOUGH (Cambridge, Eng. 1954). A. M. WILSON, *Diderot: The Testing Years, 1713–1759* (New York 1957). P. GROSCLAUDE, *Un Audacieux Message: L'Encyclopédie* (Paris 1951). F. VENTURI, *Le Origini dell'Enciclopedia* (Florence 1946). J. E. BARKER, *Diderot's Treatment of the Christian Religion in the Encyclopédie* (New York 1941). J. LEGRAS, *Diderot et l'Encyclopédie* (5th ed. Amiens 1928). L. DUCROS, *Les Encyclopédistes* (Paris 1900).

[R. Z. LAUER]

END

A term with many meanings. It frequently has the sense of a terminus or limit, especially of time or place or quantity; so one speaks of the end of an hour, the north end of a city, or the end of a rope. Sometimes end denotes the pure result of a cessation of activity, such as death or the end of a battle. Another meaning, of major importance in philosophy and theology, is end as "the object by virtue of which an event or series of events happens or is said to take place; the final cause" (*Webster's Third New International Dictionary*). End in this sense, as final cause, is that for the sake of which something exists or is done, that for which an AGENT acts or action takes place. A surgical operation has as its end health; a knife is for cutting.

Characteristics. To understand adequately the latter sense of the word end, one must recognize its terminal nature, its causal aspect, its identity with the good, and its relation to means.

End as Terminal. The end as final cause has often been described as that which is first in the order of intention and last in the order of execution or activity. "Last in the order of activity" expresses its terminal quality. Since the end is simply the outcome or goal of what an agent does or seeks, as such it terminates his movement toward that goal; for example, the physician's work is over when the patient returns to health. Even when the goal aimed at is action, as when one plays simply for the action involved in playing, the end, in this case the action itself, completes the agent's striving (St. THOMAS AQUINAS, *C. gent.* 3.2).

End as Causal. Although end is, then, last in the order of activity, it is first in the order of intention; and this primacy in intention has reference to its causal nature (*Summa Theologiae* 1a–2ae, 1.4). When a patient dies in the midst of an operation, death is for him an end in the sense of a terminus; in the same sense, his death terminates the operation. But the patient's death is not the end in the sense of the cause or reason for the operation, since it is not what the surgeon intends.

The intended end, health, is responsible for each step taken by the surgeon in preparing for and carrying out the operation, viz, (1) health is desired; (2) an operation is necessary; (3) thus anesthesia must be administered; and (4) the patient has to be wheeled to surgery. Steps (2), (3), and (4), it should be noted, are chosen only in virtue of the basic aim, health. If health were not intended, they would not be. Moreover, as planned procedures, they exist only as psychic states. In the execution of the acts, the order is inverse: (1) wheeled to surgery, (2) anesthesia, (3) operation, and (4) health. What is first intended (health) is the last thing achieved and what is last intended (wheeled to surgery) is the first thing done. Moreover, what is first intended exercises a determining influence over everything else. The end, then, must be said to be a cause, if it is right to call a cause anything that influences the becoming or existence of a thing (*In 5 meta.* 1.751). Paradoxically, that which is final in the sphere of action is the cause of all the activity leading up to it; hence, the name final cause (*see* FINAL CAUSALITY).

End as Good. The concepts of end and GOOD necessarily involve each other. The end is that which an agent tends to or wills; he intends or wills it because he sees it as good or as suitable to him. In St. Thomas's words, "since the essence of good consists in this that something perfects another as an end, whatever is found to have the character of end also has that of good" (*De ver.* 21.2; see also 1.1).

The essence of good rests in its relation to the power by which one seeks for or desires things, the power called APPETITE. Appetite implies want; want implies incompleteness. Whatever then satisfies appetite (perfects it) is suitable to it, and is therefore desirable. The good is that which completes or perfects appetite.

This concept of good is obviously wider than that of moral good. Man has different levels of appetite, and an object may be good insofar as it is desirable by any one appetite. An object will be morally good only if it fulfills and is suitable to the whole person; it must befit man as man, not simply as he is a sensitive or a living being (*see* MORALITY).

Its desirability is the very reason why the good is a cause. A man can make a desk, read a book, or rob a bank; but, whatever he does, he does it because he thinks it is of value to him, that it will benefit him in some way; in other words, he finds it desirable. The causality of the good is basically a matter of attraction. The good causes by so enticing the agent to itself that he not only intends to get the good but also intends to do whatever is necessary to get it. Aristotle rightly defines the good as ''that at which all things aim'' (*Eth. Nic.* 1094a 3).

End, final cause, and good thus are seen to be identical. One and the same thing is called end because it is the term of an agent's striving, final cause because it influences the agent to act to begin with, and good because it indicates why the agent is so moved.

End as Related to Means. A desire for a good implies both a recognition that the good is attainable (otherwise it is not truly desired but merely wished for) and a resolve to take those measures judged apt for securing it. The measures taken to obtain the end are commonly referred to as the means. In the description of the end as ''that for the sake of which something exists or is done,'' the phrase ''something exists or is done'' designates the means.

A means cannot be understood without referring it to the end in view of which it is chosen. As Aquinas observes, ''the means are good and willed, not in themselves, but as referred to the end. Wherefore the will is directed to them, only in so far as it is directed to the end: so that what it wills in them, is the end'' (*Summa Theologiae* 1a2ae, 8.2). What attracts the agent is not so much the nature of the means as a particular kind of thing as it is its value for achieving the end. In other words, what the agent sees and seeks in the means is basically the goodness of the end itself. Both a biologist and lumberman may value a virgin forest, but for different reasons because their purposes are different.

What influences the agent to desire the end thus influences him to choose the means. The character of the end is then imprinted on the means, so that the means takes on the nature of the end in much the same way that wax takes on the nature of the form impressed on it. Thus, the physical action of walking can be a healthful exercise for a recuperating patient, a punishment for a cadet, or a job for a professional golfer (cf. *Summa Theologiae* 1a2ae,13.1; *De ver.* 22.15).

The means, of course, still retains its own nature as a particular kind of thing, and as such it will have other attributes that may or may not be desirable. A medicine with a high alcoholic content may relieve the cough for which it was taken but also may be otherwise appealing. The initial and basic attraction of the means is its participation in ''the goodness of the end.'' However, one may be additionally inclined or disinclined to it by features that are peculiarly its own. These features may at times prevent the choice of that particular means. But if the means is willed, then willed also are all its known concomitant attributes, desirable or not. They become part of what is intended.

The foregoing analysis of the end may be summed up as follows. A thing is recognized by an agent to be of value to him. It is a good. The attractiveness of the good causes the agent to desire it and to choose the appropriate means to attain it. It is a final cause. When the means have been determined, the order of intention is closed. The agent then begins to execute the means. The appropriate actions are formed until the desired good results. The actions have reached their term, which is called the end.

Kinds of end. While the distinction between ends and means is clear, the reality these terms describe is not so simple. Sometimes a thing may be an end in one respect and a means in another. To deal more precisely with the complexities of the concrete situation, scholastic philosophers make various divisions of end.

Related ends in a given series may be distinguished on the basis of their order of achievement. A proximate end is that for the sake of which something is done directly or immediately. An intermediate end is that in view of which the proximate end is sought and which itself is desired for something else. Both proximate and intermediate ends are also means, each often being referred to as a means-end. The last end in the series is called the ultimate end. A business employee attending night school studies hard to pass a particular course (proximate end). Passing the course will help him earn a degree (intermediate end), which will enable him to get a promotion (ultimate end). An ultimate end is said to be relatively ultimate when the series of which it is the last is subordinate to a higher end or ends. The promotion (relatively ultimate end) may be desired because the salary increase will finance the children's education (a higher end). The absolutely ultimate end—the supreme end—is that to which all of an agent's actions are directed and which is sought for its own sake alone. The supreme end of man is HAPPINESS.

Another division of end is that into objective end (*finis qui*), the good or object itself that is sought, for example, money or knowledge; personal end (*finis cui*), the person for whom the good is desired, for example, health is sought for Peter; formal end (*finis quo*), the act in which the good is possessed or enjoyed, for example, the enjoyment of food is in the eating.

The end of the work (*finis operis*), sometimes called the end of the act, is the normal purpose or function of a thing or action, or the result normally achieved; for example, cutting is the normal function of a knife. The end of the agent (*finis operantis*) is what the agent actually intends when acting, be it identical or not with the end of the work (an agent may use a knife for cutting or as a screwdriver). The end of the work, and also the end of the agent, is called an intrinsic end when it perfects the agent interiorly, for example, knowledge; it is called an extrinsic end when its benefit is felt outside the agent, for example, the doctor's healing felt in the patient. Extrinsic end also may signify the end of the agent when the latter differs from the end of the work.

Natural end is distinguished from supernatural end. Natural end is a good responding to needs within the order of nature and attainable by the natural powers of a being. Supernatural end is one that fulfills a need of supernatural life and is secured only with divine assistance. Natural end has at least two additional meanings: it may signify a good to which a being is inclined by an innate appetite, or it may be used as a synonym for the end of the work (*see* MAN, NATURAL END OF).

Does the end justify the means? The preceding study of end should clarify the issues involved in this question, which, in the history of thought on end, has received considerable attention. Can a morally good intention of itself make an act good?

Scholastic Solution. Attempts to formulate and resolve the question began as early as the twelfth century, when Peter ABELARD took the extreme position that all human acts are in themselves morally neutral and receive whatever morality they have from the agent's intention. PETER LOMBARD partially disagreed, arguing that, although the intention is the principal source of morality, there are intrinsically evil acts that no intention can make good. STEPHEN LANGTON at the start of the thirteenth century assumed the other extreme position, that the morality of an act is determined almost exclusively by its object—that which the act immediately tends to achieve (see ''end of the work,'' above)—and the circumstances in which the act occurs, the intention contributing little or no moral value.

Lombard's solution, given more elaboration and precision especially by St. Thomas Aquinas, prevailed. Discounting certain terminological differences, all the great masters of the thirteenth century maintained that, although the end is the primary moral determinant, both the object (end of the work) and the circumstances of the human act are contributing, and sometimes decisive, moral factors (*Summa Theologiae* 1a2ae, 18–21; *De malo* 2–6).

The end is the chief moral element because it is the very reason for choosing and executing the means-act by which the end is realized. But no end is seen and willed in isolation; it is always willed as viewed through the means, as touched, so to speak, by the character of the means. The means-act is, then, part of what is intended, and its moral nature must be taken into account.

The morality of the means-act is drawn from its object. If what the act immediately tends to achieve conforms to the norm of morality, then the act is good; if contrary to that norm, the act is bad. An objective study of the human act, one made apart from the agent's intention and the circumstances of the individual case, reveals three distinct types of acts: (1) those that are good by nature because they always or normally have a morally good object, for example, acts of charity; (2) those evil by nature because they always or normally have a morally bad object, for example, blasphemy; (3) those morally indifferent by nature, because their object is neutrally related to the norm of morality.

The word ''normally'' in (1) and (2) above is significant, for circumstances alter cases. Just as in the physical order accidents sometimes cause effects other than what nature tends to achieve (e.g., the birth of a malformed child), so in the moral order the circumstances of an individual act may bring about an other than normal moral result. Normally, it is right to return on request something (e.g., a gun) held in trust, but not if the owner has an evil purpose in mind (e.g., to kill his wife). Similarly, the status of normally indifferent acts may be affected by moral CIRCUMSTANCES. In truth, since a means-act is never willed in abstraction but always in particular surroundings, the circumstances are part of the means-act and, consequently, part of the agent's intention.

In sum, if intention is understood to comprehend the whole order of intention, the willed-circumstanced means-for-an-end, then morality is completely in the intention. The intention is good if every part of it is good, and bad if a single feature is bad. However, if intention stands for the agent's purpose in distinction from the means-act chosen to realize it—and only when intention is so understood does the problem of the end justifying the means make sense—then the intention is the primary, but not exclusive, source of morality. It is primary because it is the reason for willing the means-act. A bad end can make a bad means worse, and it can make an indifferent or good means bad. A good end renders a good means better and an indifferent means good. Finally, a good end can never make a bad means good, although it does extenuate the evil. The moral guilt of one who steals to help the poor is certainly not as great as that of one who steals to pamper his sensual appetites.

This solution of the thirteenth-century scholastics to the problem of whether the end justifies the means became and remained the foundation of Catholic moral doctrine. That fact was challenged, however, four centuries later.

Historical Controversy. Defending JANSENISM by means of a strong offensive attack, Blaise PASCAL accused the Jesuits of teaching that the end justifies the means. It is interesting to note that, in the ensuing debate, neither side ever claimed that the end justifies the means; the dispute was solely over whether the Jesuits did in fact teach that it did. When advising confessors on how to assess the extent of a penitent's guilt, certain Jesuit casuists had used the phrase ''direction of intention,'' meaning simply that the penitent's intention must always be examined. Pascal claimed that ''direction of intention'' was actually a methodological principle that enabled the casuists to justify any sin. The charge was categorically denied; but master of irony that he was, Pascal made the charge stick in the public mind. (See G. Goyau, ''La Fin Justifie les Moyens,'' *Dictionnaire apologétique de la foi catholique,* 4 v. [Paris 1911–22] 2:9–17, for a concise but superb history of the controversy.)

The center of the controversy passed quickly from France to Germany, where Pascal's criticisms became the basis of the Protestant polemic against the missionary activity of the Jesuits. The debate heated up measurably from 1850 to 1905, when a considerable prize was offered by two priests (the Jesuit P. Roh in 1852 and Father G. F. Dasbach in 1903) to anyone who could show to a jury of law professors a book authored by a Jesuit that contained the explicit or equivalent formula that the end justifies the means. In 1903 one Paul de Hoensbroech appeared before the Court of Appeals in Cologne to make the only serious attempt to collect the prize. Unable to quote any Jesuit as saying that a good intention justifies a bad means, Hoensbroech contended that certain solutions of some Jesuit casuists proved they held this view. He referred specifically to a dispute among a number of Jesuits over the rightness of counseling a person bent on sinning to do something less evil, for example, to visit a prostitute rather than rape a young virgin. C. HURTADO and M. SA took the negative position because for them the means was bad. G. VAZQUEZ, A. de Escobar y Mendoza, and others argued that what the act of counseling (means) immediately achieved in this instance was simply the lack of a greater evil; it did not cause the evil itself because it did not provoke to sin someone already determined to commit sin. They concluded that the means was morally neutral and therefore the act was good by reason of a good intention. Hoensbroech claimed that the latter solution was based on the principle that the end justifies the means.

The German court ruled against him, and with good cause. As Goyau points out, in the case cited and in all the cases on which the accusations against the Jesuits were founded, the source of the divergent opinions among the casuists themselves and the object of their dialectical subtlety was always the moral nature of the means. Precisely because they firmly held that a good end could not justify a bad means, their entire mental effort was spent on evaluating the morality of the means. However one may disagree with the results of their evaluation, one must admit that the accusations against them were unjust. One may note finally, with Goyau, that since the Reformation, Catholics have been reproached for overemphasizing the objective nature of the moral act, and yet in this controversy they are accused of over-stressing the role of the subjective intention. The real issues are not always what they seem.

See Also: TELEOLOGY; CAUSALITY; HUMAN ACT; MORALITY; VOLUNTARITY.

Bibliography: General. V. J. BOURKE, *Ethics* (New York 1958). M. CRONIN, *The Science of Ethics*, 2 v. (Dublin 1939). É. H. GILSON, *Moral Values and the Moral Life*, tr. L. R. WARD (St. Louis, Mo. 1931; repr. Hamden, Conn. 1961). O. LOTTIN, *Principes de morale*, 2 v. (Louvain 1947). Special. C. DE KONINCK, ''General Standards and Particular Situations in Relation to the Natural Law,'' *Laval Theologique et Philosophique* 6 (1950): 335–338; ''The Nature of Man and His Historical Being,'' *ibid.* 5 (1949): 271–277. C. HOLLENCAMP, *Causa causarum: On the Nature of Good and Final Cause* (Quebec 1949). L. H. KENDZIERSKI, ''Object and Intention in the Moral Act,'' *American Catholic Philosophical Association. Proceedings of the Annual Meeting* 24 (1950): 102–110. O. LOTTIN, *Psychologie et Morale aux XII e et XIIIe siècles,* 3 v. in 4 (Louvain 1942–54) 4:309–517. B. PASCAL, *Provincial Letters*, tr. T. M'CRIE (New York 1941). J. WARREN, ''Nature: A Purposive Agent,'' *The New Scholasticism* 31 (1957): 364–397.

[J. J. WARREN]

END OF THE WORLD

Christian revelation has nothing to say about the end of the world as a purely physical phenomenon that can

"The Dead Risen Out of Their Sepulchres," from "The End of the World and Last Judgment," from "Predis Codex," 1476 manuscript painting by Cristoforo de Predis. (©Archivo Iconografico, S.A./CORBIS)

be forecast or described in scientific terms. To seek such information in the Bible is a waste of time. When references are made to the beginning of the world (Gn 1.1; 2.4; Heb 1.2; 11.3) and the end (1 Thes 4.16; 2 Pt 3.10; Rv 21.1), the sacred writers are dealing with religious truths. Christianity is primarily concerned with the relationship between MAN and GOD, and the material universe is never considered for its own sake, in isolation, but is always to be understood in reference to man's ultimate supernatural DESTINY. Consequently one cannot give a satisfactory account of our belief concerning the end of the world without taking into consideration other truths of revelation and so fitting it into a much wider theological context.

This article deals with (1) the end of the world as the term of salvation history, (*a*) the Messianic Age, present and to come, (*b*) difficulties in describing the future event, (*c*) problems connected with time, (*d*) the importance of the future event; (2) the end of the world and the material creation, (*a*) the part of matter in the redemptive plan, (*b*) the transformation of matter.

End of the World—Term of Salvation History. God is not aloof from the world He has created. He is a Father who intervenes in man's affairs and the supreme intervention was in sending His Son to save mankind.

Messianic Age, Present and to Come. The Messianic Age inaugurated by Christ is the great event of human history, and in a sense the end of the world has already begun. We are in the last days, since the world is in the process of apprehending the Redemption achieved in Christ for which it was created (*see* REDEMPTION). In his first Epistle, St. John says: "It is the last hour" (1.18), and he urges his readers to associate themselves with Christ, the truth and the life, and have no part with the powers of darkness (1.6). The final battle is already joined "so now many antichrists have arisen" (2.18).

This theme is developed in REVELATION, which was written to give encouragement to Christians suffering under the persecution of Domitian. St. John is concerned with spiritual realities, with God as punisher and rewarder. He is not setting out to give a description of the end of the world but rather of the situation with which the Christian will be faced as long as the present age lasts. What he says has a value for any moment in history. No matter how much evil may seem to prevail, God is in control. SATAN has been conquered even though his final overthrow has not yet taken place. This conflict is described in richly symbolic terms. The work of Redemption is still incomplete; only when the heavenly Jerusalem appears in its final glory will the individuals who make up the kingdom attain their full and complete Redemption.

The Gospels express this same truth in their teaching on the kingdom. The term kingdom is to be understood as rule or dominion, so the KINGDOM OF GOD is God's supreme rule or dominion. This was challenged by man at the Fall (*see* ORIGINAL SIN), and the work of Christ is to restore the kingdom. The parables in Matthew 13 indicate something of the complex nature of the kingdom. It will grow like a mustard seed; it will contain good and bad until the final judgment, as a net contains good and bad fish; it involves conflict between good and evil as good seed has to overcome the cockle; it is a leaven working to transform the whole batch; and it is likened to a wedding feast. In other words, the kingdom is not something static; it has a state here on earth and it has a future state of perfection. The perfect reign is still to come, it is not yet realized because the Church is still imperfect, it is not yet without spot and wrinkle. The kingdom in its fullness still lies in the future. So it is that one prays ''Thy kingdom come,'' and because the kingdom is in one sense here and in another yet to come, there is a tension between ''now'' and ''not yet.''

Difficulties in Describing the Future Event. The future and final state involves the last judgment (*see* JUDGMENT, DIVINE), the Second Coming of Christ, the RESURRECTION of the dead; and it implies a transformation that cannot adequately be described in human language. A similar difficulty confronted the PROPHETS of the Old Law when they tried to convey the glories of what was then the future, Messianic Age. They often had recourse to figurative language. This is especially true of the so called apocalyptic literature, such as the books of EZEKIEL and DANIEL. These works deal with God's judgments and they make use of symbolic and stylized phraseology to a much greater extent than normal writing and speaking. As signs of God's judgment there is earthquake (Is 13.13), the sun appearing as sackcloth (Is 50.3), the moon as blood (Jl 3.4), the stars fall from heaven (Is 34.4), the mountains are moved (Jer 4.24), men call upon the mountains to fall upon them (Hos 10.8). These figures found their fulfillment in the various calamities of nature and war that befell Juda and Israel whereby God showed His judgment on the wicked. Such language was used to express times of crisis, and when one finds similar expressions used in Revelation and Our Lord's discourse in Mt 24.5–31, one has to be careful and not interpret them too literally. When one reads in 2 Pt 3.10–13 of the last days described in terms of the elements being dissolved in fire, the convention must be kept in mind. It was not intended to give an exact physical description of the changes that will be wrought in the material universe. The sacred writers are concerned with spiritual values and are anxious to create in the minds of their readers a strong impression that will drive them to practical action in their own lives. They wish to convey certain religious truths in the most effective way. At the end of time God will manifest Himself in a final judgment on mankind.

Problems Connected with Time. The new age that began with the MESSIAH works to its fulfillment in space and time, but the Prophets saw this age as a whole, and the time distinctions were blurred and telescoped so that there is often no clear distinction made between the initial coming of the Messiah and the final consummation. The sacred writers were more concerned with καιρός, the time of opportunity and fulfillment that is in God's hands (cf. Eccl. 3.1–8), than with χρόνος, time as measured in the calendar. Just as one is in danger of accepting certain references to physical happenings too literally, so the Apostles did not always allow for the time distinctions that have to be made if SALVATION HISTORY is to be accomplished in human conditions. They looked for a glorious manifestation of the Messiah all at once, and so in Mt 16.21 Christ made it clear that the triumph of the kingdom would not be established before His own death. At the beginning of Acts it is clear from the questions of the Apostles that they were still expecting the final stage of the kingdom to take place. It was only when they saw the ASCENSION OF JESUS CHRIST that they had final evidence that there would be a Second Coming—a coming that would finally complete the kingdom.

Revelation is silent as to when this event will take place in chronological time. It is only concerned that it *will* take place at the right time, God's time. So one has to be careful not to interpret too literally the signs of the end of the world. That the gospel must be preached to the whole world (Mt 24.14) is obvious when one considers that the Second Coming of Christ is the culmination of the Messianic Age. One cannot hope to deduce a date for this in the future since even St. Paul could speak of the faith of Christians being known to all the world (Rom 1.8). The Jewish tradition that Elia would come again in the days immediately preceding the last days to repeat the scene on Mt. Carmel (1 Kgs 18.36) and manifest the supremacy of Yahweh over false gods finds support in Mal 3.23 and Mt 17.11. But these last days can be interpreted of the Messianic Age itself, and the words of Christ in Mt 17.11–13 indicate that the prophecy is fulfilled, to some extent at least, in JOHN THE BAPTIST. Similarly, the references to a final apostasy (2 Thes 2.3) and the coming of ANTICHRIST can be understood of the continual conflict that assails the followers of Christ.

St. Thomas Aquinas (*Summa theologiae* 3a, suppl., 73) maintains a healthy skepticism as to the interpretation of these signs and does not indulge in some of the fantasies of his contemporaries. Theologians agree as to the suddenness of the end, at least in the sense that it will come about through a divine INTERVENTION and not simply as the result of natural processes. Although it must be admitted that the more one knows of matter, the more he becomes aware of its inner mutability, yet one has to beware of a purely scientific ''proof'' that the world will end some day. Such a view does not take into account the full reality of God's concern in human affairs and can easily lead to a deistic attitude toward creation. Exactly how far God will make use of secondary causes is just as much a problem for the last day as it is for the origins of the human race. It is permissible to hold that God will not dispense entirely from secondary causes any more than He dispensed from them in the origins of life. But it would be rash to read into some of the biblical accounts, 2 Pt, for example, a reference to a vast nuclear explosion.

Importance of the Future Event. The Second Coming of Christ became one of the predominant themes in the early Church, just as in the days before Christ there had been the expectation of the Messiah. This truth was seen to be intimately bound up with the whole of revelation. The certitude that Christ was risen meant that He would certainly come again to judge the world. A belief in the kingdom of God established by Christ meant a belief in the growth of that kingdom and a final manifestation at the last day. The whole prayer life of the Christian was geared to this event in the future. In Gal 6.10 it appears as the spur to charity. There is a close link between the paschal mysteries and the PAROUSIA. What was achieved in Christ at the first Easter will be fully accomplished in men at the last day (Phil 3.20). The liturgical assembly, the breaking of Bread, not only looks to the past, the death and RESURRECTION OF CHRIST, but also to the future coming (1 Cor 11.26). The liturgy transcends time, for Christians are united to the risen Christ now reigning with the Father and the Holy Spirit. It looks to the ''eternal liturgy,'' the worship proffered by the blessed who are outside this world of change and time. So it is that in Revelation, St. John describes the heavenly worship in terms borrowed from the liturgy of his day. One is reminded of the connection between the Eucharist and the last day in the prayer *O sacrum convivium:* ''the memory of His Passion is recalled, the mind is filled with grace, and the pledge of future glory is given to us.'' Some of the early Christians went so far as to expect the Second Coming to take place at night while they were watching at the vigil ceremony for the dawn Eucharist.

The end of the world caused a problem for the Thessalonians. It seemed as if death excluded men from the possibility of sharing in the Parousia. St. Paul (1 Thes 4) answers the difficulty by saying that those who have died in Christ will rise, and then all, the living and the dead, will go together to meet Christ when He returns to earth. He pictures the advent of Christ in terms of a conqueror coming home and all the citizens going to meet him at the city gates. The anxiety of the Thessalonians indicates an appreciation of the Parousia that has been lost. Christ is not only the savior of the individual, but He saves the Church. One's individual SALVATION is to be achieved in the Church and with others. The concern of the Thessalonians that their departed brethren should be present at the last day shows their sense of solidarity and true charity for all.

In this same Epistle one becomes aware of the feeling in those days that the Second Coming could not long be delayed. It should be remembered that the Church of NT times was so near to its origins that the figure of Christ had a great attraction at the purely human level. There were men still alive who had known and loved Him personally, and who could not bear the thought of being separated from Him for long. The beginning of the first Epistle of St. John captures this mood. No wonder that their prayer was ''Come, Lord Jesus.'' They earnestly desired the Second Coming and were perhaps inclined to read their own fallible hopes into the teaching of Christ. But the Second Coming was delayed, Jerusalem was destroyed, and still the Lord had not come. In 2 Pt the assurance that the end will come is given, although one cannot say when. The apparent delay is due not to indecision on God's part, but to the fact that His judgment has to be worked out in time. Time is the measure of human events not of divine ones, and God shows Himself to men in time, as long-suffering and merciful (2 Pt 3.8–10).

As the Church grew and progressed there came a shift of emphasis in relation to the Second Coming. This event was now seen as the term of a long process. There was a realization that the Church had to work in the world, it had to grow according to human laws as well as divine. The significance of the parables of the mustard seed and harvest time was now realized. With the settlement of Constantine there came a growing concern for the transformation and conversion of the world in which the Church found itself. The need was felt to care for material as well as spiritual realities. There was the command to work until the Lord returns. In this way the implications of the INCARNATION were brought out, the idea of God working through human history now, just as He had done in the past. The history of the Church takes on a new significance. Salvation history is ended in so far as there can be no further revelation to supplant that of Christ, but it is still being enacted in so far as the world has yet to be completely sanctified in Christ.

In times of great natural disaster and political upheaval there has been a return to the idea that the end of the world is at hand. This was so in the days of Gregory the Great (d. 604) [see *Hom.* 1.1.5; 1.4.2, PL 76:1080; 1090] and also as the year 1000 approached (reflected in the Cluny liturgy of the dead). But for the most part, the exhortations to watch and the references to the suddenness of the end are now applied to the DEATH of the individual. This different outlook is understandable and good in so far as it brings out the truth that death is the encounter of the individual with the risen Christ, and at death one's eternal lot is determined, judgment is passed on one's life. But there has been a tendency in certain circles since the Renaissance to neglect altogether the consideration of the end of the world and to concentrate exclusively on the fate of the individual Christian. Retreats, missions, spiritual writers often put before the faithful the individual end of each man. Death, judgment, heaven, and hell are seen almost exclusively in reference to the individual (*see* HEAVEN, THEOLOGY OF; HELL, THEOLOGY OF). Perhaps the rather unsatisfactory attempts of fundamentalists to explain the end of the world in terms of physical science contributed to this shift of emphasis (*see* FUNDAMENTALISM). But in recent years there has been a growing appreciation that the sources of revelation are not at all concerned with a description of the physical end of the world. There is a greater awareness of the effects of Christ's saving mission working themselves out in the human situation. The whole of humanity has been incorporated into Christ and has Christ as its goal. This has resulted in the conviction that the teaching of Scripture on the Parousia has certain important social implications and that some sort of synthesis between the theology of the end of the individual and the theology of the end of the world has to be attempted.

End of the World and the Material Creation. One cannot understand the Christian message without a clear grasp of the meaning of the material world and its place in the Redemption. All this has a bearing on the way in which one understands the end of the physical world.

The Part of Matter in the Redemptive Plan. The Redemption was effected through the Incarnation. The fact that God became man and lived a human life, died, and is now in glory with His human body means that there is a theology of MATTER and terrestrial realities (*see* TEMPORAL VALUES, THEOLOGY OF). While holding fast to the primacy of the spirit and being careful to avoid anything that savors of the false MESSIANISM of a purely earthly kingdom or the condemned view of the millennium [H. Denzinger, *Enchiridion symbolorum,* (Freiburg 1963) 3839], nevertheless one must assert that matter has its part to play in the future kingdom. The sacred writers are primarily concerned with spiritual values, but in so far as man has a body he is also part of the material world, and so revelation must have something to say, at least indirectly, about this side of creation. One is assured that man will live on, and man is not a disembodied spirit but body and soul, a totality. The doctrine of the resurrection of the body implies the survival of the material creation in some form or other and it is reasonable to suppose that all matter will have some part in the new world, not only the matter immediately associated with the human body. For the Christian, belief in the end of the world is not belief in the total ANNIHILATION of matter and the survival of purely spiritual realities. Today theologians tend to explain the end in terms of a gradual transformation rather than a discontinuity between this world and the one to come (see G. Thils). The end is a transformation of the world to which one belongs, at least a return to the original harmony of the creation before man sinned. God does not destroy what He has made but He brings it to completion, and the disorders created by man's sin and its consequences will finally be righted in the total victory of Christ. Such a view of the world implies a theology of human history (*see* HISTORY, THEOLOGY OF). God does not save man by withdrawing him from the world, but man is saved in and through history. The story of mankind is the story of a progress toward a final consummation of all things in Christ, the God-man. It is a progress that is only achieved with the help of divine intervention and not by man's unaided efforts. If man had not sinned there would be no such thing as human history as one knows it, and when on the last day all is accomplished, then human history will cease and so eternity will begin. P. TEILHARD DE CHARDIN has some valuable insights into this interpretation of the history of the human race when he speaks of all tending toward the omega point. So it is that a process of continual renewal, an unending series of "ends of the world" such as described by many pagan religions, does not fit in with the biblical idea of time as leading to a definite point in the future that will be the consummation of all [M. Eliade, *Patterns in Comparative Religion,* tr. R. Sheed (New York 1958) 388–409]. From time to time similar theories have been put forward, but they have never found a permanent place in orthodox Christian thought, and on occasion they have been condemned, as for example the Origenist error of a final pardon for the damned [Denz 411]; (*see* APOCATASTASIS).

The account of creation in GENESIS is another indication that the material world was meant to serve man. Man was made lord of creation by God. His dominion is indicated by the naming of the animals in Gn 2.18–20. He brings order into creation. By the Fall, he lost the gift of INTEGRITY and the fact that he is now mortal and subject to disease means that there has been some indirect influence of his sin on nature. Nature has a greater ascendancy over man than it had before the fall of ADAM. Only man fell; creation below man, animate and inanimate, did not sin. But because of his subjection to CONCUPISCENCE, the world and the flesh are instruments of the devil and occasions of sin. It is not so much a question of the rebellion of nature, nature becoming wild, as of man being no longer able to control nature. With the coming of Christ and His conquest of sin at the Resurrection there began the gradual restoration of the lost ascendancy of man over the rest of creation. Through the Incarnation and then through the Resurrection of Christ, matter has been raised and brought into conjunction with the spiritual. The MIRACLES of Christ indicate the transformation foretold in Is 65.17; 66.22. Water is turned into wine, Jesus feeds thousands with a few loaves, He walks on the waters, after His Resurrection He manifests even greater powers over nature. This process is continued by the Church, a human and divine SOCIETY, and by the sacramental system whereby spiritual benefits are conferred by and through matter. At the last day complete integrity will be restored to man when his body rises, and it is hard to see how this cannot but have an effect on the rest of the material universe.

Transformation of Matter. The Resurrection of Christ is the prototype of men's resurrection. It is the promise that the just will one day be fully redeemed in body as well as soul. It is not by putting off the body that man achieves himself but by putting on the risen body. The risen body of Christ is an indication of the future state of man at the end of the world. But one must remember that the Apostles who saw it and testified to it were not themselves risen, and so they could grasp this reality only in an imperfect way. The NT accounts of the Resurrection show one that they did not recognize Him at first; FAITH was required in addition to mere bodily sight (Mt 28.17). It was the same Christ as they had known before His CRUCIFIXION, but He now belonged to a new mode of existence, not indifferent to the material world and its needs, but not constrained by them. To describe such a body baffles the human mind. St. Paul in 1 Cor 15.44 calls it a ''spiritual body,'' that is, a true body but one that fully expresses the spirit.

As Christ is risen and as Mary too is in heaven with her body, the abode of the blessed even now, before the general resurrection, must connote some idea of place (*see* ASSUMPTION OF MARY). But physical space as one experiences it on earth is cramped and limited. For the blessed it is not so limited. Remember, that as Christ and Mary have their bodies, matter even now is already transformed or under the dominion of spirit in some respect. Moreover, the doctrine of the Real Presence in the Eucharist means that transformed matter (Christ's risen body) impinges on the world of man in the sacramental presence.

Despite all this, it would be foolish to try to determine where heaven is located in terms of the universe as one knows it. Since one must hold to the bodily existence of all men after the general resurrection, it is reasonable to suppose that the world will remain in some changed form as the connatural surroundings of risen man, as it is today the connatural surroundings of mortal man.

Quite apart from the teaching on the resurrection of the body there are indications in Scripture that point to a final state of the material universe. In 2 Pt 3 there is reference to a change and transformation of the world rather than annihilation. The end is likened to the new creation after the Flood and the material universe is seen to partake in the final judgment of God on mankind. The Hebrew mentality delighted in associating all of nature with man in his Fall and Redemption and is quite opposed to any Manichaean view of matter as intrinsically evil. Moreover, the traditional teaching that there is real fire in hell, at least in the sense that some material element is used as an instrument of God's justice, could be an indication that matter has some place in the final state of mankind.

Rom 8.19–23 speaks of creation itself groaning and travailing and awaiting deliverance. Many commentators see here some reference to a future renewal of the material creation. Although St. Augustine is one of the few to interpret ''creation'' of mankind alone, nevertheless he does admit (*De civitate Dei*, 22.14, 16) that the material world will assume a new and important role when man's body in a *mirabilis mutatio* will pass out of time into eternity. St. Thomas infers the renewal of the world from the fact that the object of the world is to serve mankind, and when man is transfigured in the resurrection there will be need for the world to be transfigured too (*Summa theologiae* 3a, Suppl., 91.1). With all this in mind one need not hesitate to think of the end of the world in terms of a ''new heaven and new earth'' as found in Rv 21.1.

See Also: ESCHATOLOGY, ARTICLES ON.

Bibliography: E. MANGENOT, *Dictionnaire de théologie catholique*, (Paris 1903–50) 5.2:2504–52. *Dictionnaire de théologie catholique*, Tables générales, (1951–) 1527–30. A. PAUTREL and

D. MOLLAT, *Dictionnaire de la Bible*, suppl. ed. L. PIROT, et. al. 4:1321–94. A. FEUILLET, *ibid.* 6:1331–1419; *Catholicisme* 4:1304–10. G. LANCZKOWSKI et al., *Lexikon für Theologie und Kirche* (Freiburg 1957–65) 3:1083–98. E. PAX and K. RAHNER, *ibid.* 8:120–124. Works of general introduction. R. W. GLEASON, *The World to Come* (New York 1958). J. J. QUINN, *Eschatology* (Foundations of Catholic Theology; Englewood Cliffs, NJ 1965). M. SCHMAUS, *Von den letzten Dingen* (Regensburg 1948); *Katholische Dogmatik,* 5 v. in 8 (5th ed. Munich 1953–59) v.4.2. On salvation history and the end of the world. O. CULLMANN, *Christ and Time,* tr. F. V. FILSON (rev. ed. Philadelphia 1964). J. MARSH in *A Theological Word Book of the Bible,* ed. A. RICHARDSON (New York 1950) 258–267. J. MOUROUX, *The Mystery of Time* (New York 1964). J. DANIÉLOU, *The Lord of History,* tr. N. ABERCROMBIE (Chicago 1958); *Histoire des doctrines chrétiennes avant Nicée* (Paris 1958) v.1, ch. 11. B. RIGAUX, ''La Seconde venue de Jésus,'' *La Venue du Messie: Messianisme et eschatologie* (Récherches Bibliques 6; Bruges 1962) 173–216. R. SCHNACKENBURG, *God's Rule and Kingdom,* tr. J. MURRAY (New York 1963). On the material creation. G. THILS, *Théologie des réalités terrestres,* 2 v. (Louvain 1946–49). K. RAHNER, *Theological Investigations,* v.2, tr. K. H. KRUGER (Baltimore 1964) 203–216; *On the Theology of Death,* tr. C. H. HENKEY (Quaestiones disputatae 2; New York 1961). P. TEILHARD DE CHARDIN, *The Phenomenon of Man,* tr. B. WALL (New York 1959). T. E. CLARKE, ''St. Augustine and Cosmic Redemption,'' *Theological Studies* 19 (1958) 133–164.

[M. E. WILLIAMS]

Shusaku Endo. (AP/Wide World)

ENDO, SHUSAKU

Novelist; b. March 27, 1923, Tokyo, Japan, the son of Tsunehisa Endo, an employee of Yasuda Bank, and Ikuko Endo; d. Sept. 29, 1996. The family moved to Manchuria in 1929 when his father was transferred there. After his parents' marital separation he returned with his mother to the Kobe area of Japan, where they lived with an aunt who was Catholic. His mother became a Catholic, and at her insistence Endo was baptized, receiving the name Paul.

Endo studied French literature at Keio Preparatory School, graduating in 1948. Two years later he went to France and studied modern Catholic literature; he was greatly influenced in methodology by François Mauriac, especially *Thérèse Desqueyroux* and its probing of the depth of human evil, but also Mauriac's break with the Versailles Garden formula of French psychological novels in favor of the realism of Dostoevsky. Existentialism in its myriad forms dominated the philosophical and literary expression of Endo's French world.

His novel *Chinmoku* (*Silence*) appeared in 1966 and established his reputation as a major author. Its story centers on the sixteenth– and seventeenth-century contact of the Jesuit mission with Japan and the subsequent persecution. It was an economic, political, and religious clash of East and West. His *Life of Jesus* was first published in magazine articles designed to introduce Christ to non-Christians; the book enjoyed phenomenal success, yet he felt that it needed continual revision to express his new faith insights.

Endo achieved a reputation as one of Japan's foremost and most prolific writers. His Catholic faith underscored his portrayal of life, the depths of evil together with the aspirations towards divine union. His greatest novel, *Deep River,* traces the religious journey of five Japanese to the Ganges River where God is symbolized with the name ''Onion.'' Otsu, who reflects Endo himself speaks, ''My trust is in the life of the Onion who endured genuine torment for the sake of love . . . as time passes, I feel that trust strengthening within me. I haven't been able to adapt to the thinking and the theology of Europe, but when I suffer all alone I can feel the smiling presence of my Onion, who knows all my trials.'' Endo spent his literary life delving into the unconscious of his characters. There was an East-West contrast throughout, a Buddhist-Christian dialogue, the encounter of world religions, and in it all there was his personal growth in Catholic faith reaching out to all cultures. Endo felt the basic human unity at the unconscious level seeking the ultimate in art, music, language, and culture.

He died Sept. 29, 1996, in the embrace of his Church, receiving the last sacraments from his intimate priest friend Fr. William Johnston, S.J. His influence and the paths he has opened into interreligious dialogue remain a major legacy to be pursued as the Church continues to interact with the great religious traditions of Asia.

Bibliography: The Complete Literary Works of Shusaku Endo in 15 volumes is under way at Shincho Publishing Company. Important works now translated into English include: *Silence* (Kodansha International 1982); *Life of Jesus* (Tokyo 1979); *Deep River* (Tokyo 1994); *Foreign Studies* (Tokyo 1989); *Golden Country* (Tokyo 1970); *The Final Martyrs* (Tokyo 1993); *Scandal* (Tokyo 1988); *The Sea and Poison* (New York 1972); *Volcano* (Tokyo 1979); *When I Whistle* (Tokyo 1974).

[P. O'DONOGHUE]

ENGEL, HANS LUDWIG

Canonist; b. Castle Wagrein, Austria; d. Grillenberg, Austria, April 22,1674. He was a Benedictine of the monastery of Mölk; he studied law at the University of Salzburg, assuming the role of professor of Canon Law, and later, by unanimous consent, that of vice chancellor in 1669. He left Salzburg, returned to Mölk, and died in the parish of Grillenberg. Engel was influential in Germanic circles. His work *Collegium universi juris canonici . . .* published between 1671 and 1674 is admired for its lucidity and profundity. In it he defends the papal supremacy and treats of episcopo-papal relations. Among his more famous works are *Privilegia monasteriorum ex jure communi deducta* (1664), *Tractatus de privilegiis et juribus monasteriorum* (1693), and *Manuale Parochorum* (1661).

Bibliography: G. LEPOINTE, *Dictionnaire de droit canonique* 5:342–343. J. F. VON SCHULTE, *Die Geschichte der Quellen und der Literatur des kanonischen Rechts* 3.1:150–151.

[B. R. PISKULA]

ENGELBERT I OF COLOGNE, ST.

Archbishop; b. *c.* 1185; d. Schwelm, near Gevelsberg, Germany, Nov. 7, 1225. He was a younger son of Engelbert, count of Berg, and because of a medieval abuse whereby even children could receive ecclesiastical benefices, he became provost of St. George and St. Severinus in Cologne and of St. Mary's in Aachen in 1198, and of Cologne Cathedral on April 9, 1203. He was excommunicated and deposed by INNOCENT III in 1206 for supporting Philip of Swabia (d. 1208) against OTTO IV but was restored in 1208, and by way of penance he participated in the crusade against the ALBIGENSES in 1212. His efforts to settle the disputed episcopal succession in Cologne resulted in his own consecration as bishop on Sept. 24, 1217, and he received the PALLIUM on April 24, 1218. In 1220 he was appointed administrator of Germany and guardian of the young Henry, later HENRY VII, the son of FREDERICK II, whom he had supported against Otto IV. As an administrator he struggled indefatigably to establish peace in Germany and in Berg, of which he had become count (1218) upon the death of his brother. As bishop, he was pious and charitable but unpopular because of his zeal for strict monastic discipline and administrative justice. He was murdered by his cousin Frederick of Isenberg, whom he had tried to restrain from injustice toward the nuns of Essen. Though he was never formally canonized, his cult was established on Nov. 7, 1617, when his name was added to the Roman MARTYROLOGY. His relics are in the cathedrals of Cologne and Altenberg. His vita, written in 1226 by CAESARIUS OF HEISTERBACH, still has historical value.

Feast: Nov. 7.

Bibliography: Vita by Caesarius of Heisterbach in *Acta Sanctorum* Nov. 3:644–681, tr. as *Leben, Leiden und Wunder des Heiligen Erzbischofs Engelbert von Köln,* ed. and tr. K. LANGOSCH (Weimar 1955). R. KNIPPING, *Die Regesten der Erzbischöfe von Köln im Mittelalter,* 4 v. (Bonn 1901–15) 3.1:26–88. H. FOERSTER, *Engelbert von Berg der Heilige* (Elberfeld 1925). W. KLEIST, *Der Tod des Erzbischofs Engelbert von Köln* (Diss. Berlin 1918). J. DUBOIS, *Catholicisme* 4:199–200.

[M. F. MCCARTHY]

ENGELBERT OF ADMONT

Abbot and scholar; b. Volkersdorf, Styria, Austria, *c.* 1250; d. Priory of Gallenstein Schloss, in the valley of the Enns, Austria, May 12, 1331. From a consequential family in Styria, he entered the BENEDICTINES *c.* 1267 at the Abbey of ADMONT, a foundation with a proud tradition of scholarship. In 1271 he enrolled in the cathedral school of St. Vitus at Prague, where he studied under Gregory of Hasenberg (d. 1301), but was forced to leave there in 1274, when Ottokar II of Bohemia went to war with the Hapsburg Emperor Rudolph I. Engelbert returned to Admont, where he began a poem in honor of Rudolph's election to the imperial dignity. In 1278 he was at the University of Padua, where he spent the next nine years completing his studies, including four years of theology with the Dominicans. After returning to Austria *c.* 1287, he was elected abbot of the Abbey of SANKT PETER in Salzburg in 1288. Ten years later he was the compromise choice of Archduke Albert of Austria and the archbishop of Salzburg for abbot of Admont. He ruled there for 30 years, fought against the encroachments of the *ministeriales* on the abbey's rights, and, although he rarely left the cloister, was very active intellectually. He resigned his office in 1327 because of his age and retired to Gallenstein Schloss. He was buried in nearby Admont.

His writings cover a wide range of topics, including theology: *De corpore domini* and *De gratiis et virtutibus beatae Mariae virginis;* natural science: translations and commentaries on a number of Aristotle's works; ethics: *De summo bono hominis in hac vita;* politics: *De regimine principum;* history: *De ortu, progressu et fine Romani imperii;* and poetry: *De electione regis Rudolfi.* A number of his works are unpublished. Philosophically and theologically, Engelbert can hardly be labeled an enthusiastic follower of THOMAS AQUINAS; he was rather an eclectic, perhaps even in part a Scotist. Politically, he rejected Ghibelline claims (*see* GUELFS AND GHIBELLINES) and also the GALLICANISM of JOHN (QUIDORT) OF PARIS, against whom he drafted the official Church reply.

Bibliography: Works. *De causis longaevitatis hominum* in *Thesaurus anecdotorum novistimus* (Augsburg 1721–29), ed. B. PEZ, 1.1:439–502; *De gratiis et virtutibus beatae Mariae virginis, ibid.* 1.1:503–762; *Tractatus de libero arbitrio, ibid.* 4.2:119–148. Engelbert's letter listing his works, ed. G. B. FOWLER, in *Recherches de théologie ancienne et médiévale* 29 (1962) 298–306; *Speculum virtutum ad Albertum et Ottonem duces Austriae,* ed. B. PEZ in *Bibliotheca ascetica antiquo-nova,* 12 v. (Regensburg 1723–40) 3:1–498; *Tractatus de providentia Dei, ibid.* 6:49–150; *De passione Domini secundum Matthaeum, ibid.* 7:65–112; *Da statu defunctorum, ibid.* 9:111–192; *De summo bono hominis,* ed. J. C. PEEZ in *Opuscula philosophica* (Regensburg 1725); *Dialogus consupiscentiae et rationis, ibid.; Utrum sapienti competat ducere uxorem, ibid; De ortu, progressu et fine Romani imperii in Maxima bibliotheca Patrum* (Lyons 1668) 25:362–378; *De musica* in M. GERBERT, *Scriptores ecclesiastici de musica sacra potissimum* (Milan 1931) 2:287–369; *Tractatus de officio ancillari Beatae Mariae Virginis,* ed. G. B. FOWLER, *Mitteilungen des Instituts für österreichische Geschichtsforschung* 62 (1954) 379–389. Ed. of E. of A's political writings by G. B. FOWLER, *MGStaatsschriften des späteren Mittelalters* v.1.2. Literature. F. STEGMÜLLER, *Repertorium Commentariorum in Sententias Petri Lombardi* (Würzburg 1947) 2:2240–45. G. B. FOWLER, *Intellectual Interests of Engelbert of Admont* (New York 1947); ''Engelbert of Admont's *Tractatus de officiis et abusionibus eorum,*'' in *Essays in Mediaeval Life and Thought: Festschrift A. P. Evans,* ed. J. H. MUNDY et al. (New York 1955) 109–122; ''Engelbert of Admont and the Universal Idea,'' *Fundamente* 3 (1958); *Dictionnaire de spiritualité ascétique et mystique. Doctrine et histoire*, ed. M. VILLER et al (Paris 1932–) 4.1:745–747; ''MSS of E. of A . . . ,'' *Osiris* 11 (1954) 455–485; ''Additional Notes on MSS of E. of A.,'' *Recherches de théologie ancienne et médiévale* 28 (1961) 269–282; ''A New Dedicatory Preface to the Commentary on Ps. 118 by E. of A.,'' *ibid.* 29 (1962) 306–312.

[B. J. COMASKEY]

ENGELHARDT, ZEPHYRIN

Missionary, historian; b. Bilshausen, Germany, Nov. 13, 1851; d. Santa Barbara, Calif., April 27, 1934. When he was one year old, Charles Anthony, as he was baptized, immigrated with his parents to the U.S. where they settled at Covington, Ky. He joined the Order of Friars Minor at Teutopolis, Ill. (Sept. 22, 1873), and was ordained at St. Louis, Mo. (June 18, 1878). From 1880 to 1900 he was a missionary among the Menominee at Keshina and Superior, Wis., and among the Ottawas at Harbor Springs, Mich. In 1882 he published *Kachkenohamatwon Kesekoch* (Guide to Heaven), a translation from Chippewa to Menominee, and in 1884 his *Kateshim* (Catechism) appeared in the same language. He began in 1896 a monthly journal, *Anishinabe Enamaid* (Praying Indian), written in the Ottawan language. At Harbor Springs, he wrote his first historical works, *The Franciscans in California* (1897) and *The Franciscans in Arizona* (1899).

After 1900 Engelhardt devoted his life to travel and the writing of California mission histories. Stationed principally at Mission Santa Barbara, Calif., he journeyed to Florida, New Mexico, and Mexico. His monumental *Missions and Missionaries of California* was published in four volumes between 1908 and 1915. It was followed by 16 volumes on individual missions and a life of The Holy Man of Santa Clara (1909), Fray Magín Catalá, for whose cause he was vice postulator. He also contributed about 200 historical articles to newspapers and magazines throughout the U.S. Engelhardt's mission histories, which contain abundant translations from original sources, have remained standard works in their field.

Bibliography: Engelhardt Diaries, June 2, 1901–Apr. 21, 1934, Santa Barbara Mission Archives. *Provincial Annals,* ed. M. GEIGER, 6.2 (April 1944), a review of his life and writings. F. B. STECK, *Commonweal* (June 29, 1934) 236–238, an appraisal of the man and his writings.

[M. GEIGER]

ENGELS, FRIEDRICH

Collaborator with Karl Marx in propagandizing socialism; b. Barmen, Prussia, Nov. 28, 1820; d. London, Aug. 5, 1895. He was the oldest of eight children of Friedrich and Elise Engels, whose lineage can be traced in the state of Wuppertal as early as the end of the 16th century. At an early age Engels rebelled against the strict Prussian discipline and somber Lutheran piety in which he had been reared. Upon completion of high school in Elberfeld, he worked for a brief period in his father's textile mill. At the age of 17, at his father's insistence, he took a job as an unsalaried clerk in the export business of Consul Leupold in Bremen. Abundant free time, however, permitted him to develop his own preferences—reading and writing. He learned several languages (he boasted later of being able to converse in 25 tongues) and began contributing to many newspapers and magazines on a variety of subjects ranging from religion and philosophy to politics and military strategy, all self-taught.

Friedrich Engels.

The social consciousness that had its awakening in his firsthand experience with factory conditions in Barmen and later in his father's mill in Manchester, England, came to fruition in his association with Karl Marx, whom he met at Cologne in 1842. Marx was then editor of *Rheinische Zeitung,* a newspaper opposed to the government, which was suppressed by decree in 1843. Together Marx and Engels became political exiles in Switzerland, Paris, Brussels, and finally England.

Although Engels opposed marriage as a bourgeois institution and had no children, he finally married Lizzy Burns on her deathbed in 1878. He had previously lived with her sister Mary, an Irish revolutionary leader, from 1845 until her death in 1863. In 1869 he sold out his share of the Manchester firm and retired at 49; thus, when Marx died in 1883, he was able to devote all his time to editing Marx's *Das Kapital.* However, from 1870 to 1890, through correspondence, pamphlets and articles, and personal contacts, he continued to school leaders of the new and growing European working-class parties in France, Germany, Belgium, Holland, Switzerland, Denmark, Sweden, Norway, Poland, Hungary, Spain, Portugal, Roumania, Bulgaria, Austria, Italy, and finally Russia. Ironically, only England, his adopted homeland, and the U.S. remained outside his sphere of influence, largely because their trade-union and socialist movements believed in parliamentary solutions of economic problems and did not trust his revolutionary determinism.

When Engels died of cancer at his home in London, the proletarian class movement that he and Marx had begun and nurtured lost a dedicated chief of staff, whose talent for stimulating, disseminating, and popularizing highly complicated theories has rarely been equaled.

Engels' proliferation of letters to socialist leaders and articles in newspapers and magazines of almost every industrial center in the world gives a clear picture of his ideas and actions. Although Marx is recognized as the intellectual father of communist thought, Engels was its promulgator and missionary. Dialectical materialism for him filled the void left by his successive abandonment of Lutheranism and Hegelian statism, and he espoused the cause of political and social reform wherever it appeared likely to advance revolutionary communism.

Among his published works are *The Holy Family* (with Marx, 1843), *The Condition of the Working Class in England* (1844), *German Ideology* (with Marx, 1845), *Communist Manifesto* (with Marx, 1848), *Development of Socialism from Utopianism to Science* (with Marx, 1876), and *Marx's Das Kapital* (ed., v.2 1885; v.3 1895).

Bibliography: D. B. GOLDENDACH, *Karl Marx and Friedrich Engels,* tr. J. KUNITZ (New York 1927). G. MAYER, *Friedrich Engels,* tr. G. and H. HIGHET (New York 1936).

[G. W. GRUENBERG]

ENGLAND, JOHN

First bishop of Charleston, S.C., author, orator; b. Cork, Ireland, Sept. 23, 1786; d. Charleston, April 11, 1842. He was the son of Thomas and Honora (Lordan) England. He completed his primary education at Cork and then apprenticed himself to a barrister. After two years, however, he entered (1802) St. Patrick's College, Carlow, where, while still a student, he taught and also preached a Lenten series at the cathedral. By dispensation he was ordained before the prescribed age on Oct. 11, 1808, by Bp. Francis Moylan at St. Mary's Cathedral, Cork. As a priest in Cork he became lecturer at the cathedral; chaplain to the North Presentation Convent, the Magdalen Asylum, and the city prison; inspector of the Catholic poor schools; and teacher of philosophy, and president (1812–17) at St. Mary's College.

During these years he took an active part in the Veto Question, opposing, particularly through the pages of the *Cork Mercantile Chronicle,* of which he was a trustee, any program that would give the British government the right to interfere in the appointment of bishops. He was parish priest at Bandon, 16 miles from Cork, from May 1817 until he resigned in August 1820, when notified that he had been named bishop of Charleston.

Ordinary of Charleston. England was consecrated in St. Finbar's Church, Cork, on Sept. 21, 1820, and arrived in Charleston, Dec. 30, 1820, to take up the administration of a diocese more than 140,000 square miles in area, with about 5,000 Catholics. His first act, after notifying the archbishop of Baltimore of his arrival, was to issue a pastoral letter to the faithful, the first such letter in the history of the American Church. He made a visitation of the Carolinas and Georgia, the three states within his diocese. England was particularly conscious of the need for education and prepared a missal and a catechism to help and instruct his flock. They were printed, not without objections from other U.S. bishops, and distributed.

To combat attacks upon the Church made in the press, he began a newspaper, the *United States Catholic Miscellany,* the first Catholic newspaper in the U.S. It was published weekly, with occasional short lapses, from 1822 until 1861. England wrote the greater part of the material, edited, and even assisted in printing the paper. His writings have been collected from copies of the paper and published on three occasions—one edition running to seven volumes. ''Everything,'' wrote his successor Bp. Ignatius Reynolds, ''which Dr. England published,. . . is worthy of being preserved and read by posterity.'' His statement of the Catholic's duty as a citizen has retained its relevance for more than a century.

His newspaper continued publication with very little support from the rest of the hierarchy. England's ideas were frequently considered radical and at times seemed to be opposed because they were his. Thus, when his diocesan constitution called for an annual convention of the clergy and lay delegates representing the parishes, the program was labeled ''democratic'' by his archbishop, a term that carried a bad connotation in the early 19th century. The constitution was designed to forestall TRUSTEEISM by ensuring an agreeable method of handling temporalities. The only church in Charleston was so entangled by its vestrymen that to make it a cathedral would have been unwise. Accordingly, a procathedral was occupied until an adequate building could be erected.

It was the bishop's hope that the Philosophical and Classical Seminary of Charleston, which began operating in January 1822, would attract vocations to the clergy. St. John the Baptist Seminary, which he opened in 1825, soon provided trained priests for the diocese, four of whom became bishops. In 1829 he organized a diocesan community, the Sisters of Charity of Our Lady of Mercy, to catechize poor children and to care for orphans and the sick. At his invitation, the Ursuline nuns from Blackrock, Cork, opened an academy in 1833. Under England a social welfare program of the Brotherhood of San Marino, the first Catholic society for workingmen in the U.S., undertook the support of a small hospital, staffed by the Sisters of Charity of Our Lady of Mercy, to aid the poor in the fever epidemics. The society and the hospital were short-lived. The bishop's concern for blacks irked the slaveowners who blocked his effort to operate a school for slaves.

National Leadership. In 1833 he was appointed apostolic delegate to Haiti for the purpose of improving the status of the Church there. He was the first U.S. bishop to be chosen by the Holy See for so important a diplomatic mission. It proved, however, to be the one great failure of his career. Nevertheless, Gregory XVI, as a mark of his personal esteem, named England an assistant to the pontifical throne.

His attempt at peacemaking in the Hogan schism in Philadelphia was misinterpreted; his offer of 1822 to accept Rev. William Hogan into the Charleston diocese only served to bring him into disfavor with several U.S. bishops. This experience, and a similar one in connection with the nomination of a successor to Bp. John Connolly of New York, made England press ardently for the calling of a council to achieve a proper understanding among the bishops of the nation. It was almost his insistence alone that finally initiated the Councils of Baltimore.

England visited the chief cities of the Union and traveled to Europe four times, seeking aid in money, vestments, books, and candidates for his convents and seminary. On Jan. 8, 1826, while visiting Washington, D.C., he was invited to address the Congress, the first Catholic clergyman to do so. It was but a month before he received his final papers as a citizen of the U.S.

Pressure of work moved England to request a coadjutor but the choice of William Clancy of St. Patrick's College, Carlow, Ireland, proved unfortunate and Clancy obtained a transfer in 1838, within a year of his arrival. When England died in 1842, the diocese had 14 churches, with three more under construction; 20 priests; and a Catholic population of about 12,000.

Bibliography: P. GUILDAY, *Life and Times of John England,* 2 v. (New York 1927). S. G. MESSMER, ed. *The Works of the Right Reverend John England, First Bishop of Charleston*, 7 v. (Cleveland 1908). P. CLARKE, *A Free Church in a Free Society: The Ecclesiology of John Ireland, Bishop of Charleston, 1820–1842: A Nineteenth Century Bishop in the Southern United States* (Hartsville, SC, 1982)..

[R. C. MADDEN/EDS.]

Bl. John Paine, one of the "Forty Martyrs of England and Wales."

ENGLAND, SCOTLAND, AND WALES, MARTYRS OF

The term, as commonly used, includes all the men and women, priests and laity, belonging to all the older religious orders, the secular clergy, the Society of Jesus, and to every class, trade, or profession, who gave their lives in England and Wales rather than deny their faith. The subjoined chronology includes only those whose cause of beatification or canonization has been formally introduced into the Congregation of Rites, is now pending, or has been concluded: it excludes many who died in prison (e.g., the wife of St. Swithin Wells), others who suffered in reprisal for their part in religious risings (e.g., the PILGRIMAGE OF GRACE, 1536), and about 43 (e.g., Henry GARNET) whose cause has been deferred because of some defect of information. These, known technically as *dilati,* are listed at the end of the chronology. While all could have saved their lives by renouncing their faith, priesthood, or allegiance to the See of Rome, the indictments on which they were found guilty of death varied according to the period and its particular political or religious circumstances: in law all but a few suffered as traitors, whether it was their refusal to take the oath of supremacy or their ordination overseas that made them such.

The protomartyr of the English Reformation was St. John Houghton, prior of the London Charterhouse, executed at Tyburn on May 4, 1535; the last, Bl. William Howard, Viscount Stafford, grandson of St. Philip Howard (d. Oct. 19, 1596), beheaded on Tower Hill, Dec. 29, 1680. Unless otherwise stated in the list, all these martyrs were hanged, drawn, and quartered. This was the death reserved for traitors. The sentence of execution ran: "Ye shall be drawn through the open city to the place of execution, and there be hanged and let down alive, and your privy parts cut off, and your entrails taken out and burnt in your sight; then your head to be cut off and your bodies divided into four parts, to be disposed of at his (her) Majesty's pleasure." In the case of certain martyrs the Sovereign, in the exercise of his prerogative of mercy, commuted the sentence, as with SS. Thomas More and John Fisher, to that of beheading; in others, particularly in the later persecution, the martyrs were permitted to hang until they were dead; but the greater number suffered the full rigors of the sentence. St. Edmund Gennings (d. Dec. 10, 1691), for instance, was heard to invoke St. Gregory, patron of England, while the hangman held the priest's heart in his hand.

Henry VIII. In 1533 HENRY VIII, after failing to secure at Rome a divorce from his lawful wife, CATHERINE OF ARAGON, put her away. In the following year the pope's jurisdiction over England was renounced by Act of Parliament (25 Hen. VIII, *c.* 21). The Act of Succession (*c.* 22), the same year, made it a capital offense to reject or deny the validity of the king's marriage to his mistress, Anne Boleyn, while the Act of Supremacy (1534; 26 Hen. VIII, *c.* 1) made it high treason not to acknowledge the king as "the only Supreme Head on earth of the Church in England." It was under these two Acts that most of the first 50 martyrs in the list suffered death.

Elizabeth I. When Elizabeth I succeeded her half-sister, Mary, on Nov. 17, 1588, a new Act of Supremacy (1 Eliz., *c.* 1) made it treason to maintain the pope's authority in the realm (1 Eliz., *c.* 1) and imposed an oath compelling acknowledgment of the queen as "Supreme Governor as well in all spiritual or ecclesiastical things as temporal"; a new Act of Uniformity (1 Eliz., *c.* 2) restored the Book of Common Prayer (first issued 1549, revised 1552), prohibited the Mass, and made attendance at Protestant service compulsory. In 1569 Dr. William ALLEN (later Cardinal) founded at Douai a seminary for the training of English priests. In November of that year occurred the Northern Rising, which was followed by a wholesale execution of northern Catholics (none of them included in the list below, apart from Bl. Thomas Plumtree, their chaplain). This rising led PIUS V to issue the bull *Regnans in Excelsis* (Feb. 25, 1570) excommunicating the queen, who retaliated by issuing acts

(13 Eliz., *cc.* 1, 2) making it treason to call her a heretic or to introduce papal bulls into the realm.

Under these measures, or on the pretext of alleged complicity in real or feigned plots against the Queen, 38 martyrs suffered between the years 1570 and 1585, including the most famous of them all, St. Edmund Campion and St. Richard Gwyn, the poet, schoolmaster, and protomartyr of Wales.

Without question it was Elizabeth I's intention to supplant the old religion with the new in a bloodless manner. It is significant that there were no martyrs in the first 12 years of her reign, and only five in the years from 1570 to 1577. The entry of new priests into England from the seminaries abroad (the English College in Rome was founded in 1579) induced legislation that increased the number of martyrs. In 1585 a law was passed which the Jesuit historian, Father Pollen, has termed the ''act which made the martyrs.'' This was the famous ''Act against Jesuits, seminary priests and other such like disobedient subjects'' (27 Eliz., *c.* 2), which made it high treason for a native-born subject of the queen, after receiving priestly orders abroad, to return and minister in the realm, unless he gave himself up to the authorities within 48 hours of his landing. Yet Bl. Henry Walpole, executed at York April 7, 1595, suffered for his priesthood, although, as he pleaded, he was captured before the expiration of the statutory time limit. By an extension of this act any lay person who harbored or assisted a priest was liable to the same penalties. All the Acts concerning the persecution are printed, some in full, others in summary, in G. W. Prothero's *Constitutional Documents (1558–1625).*

The following list includes members of the group of 63 martyrs who were beatified equipollently (*per modum cultus*) by Leo XIII on Dec. 29, 1886, and May 13, 1895, as well as those beatified by Pius XI, after a formal process, on Dec. 15, 1929. SS. John Fisher and Thomas More were canonized by the same pope on May 19, 1935. The other saints included in the list are the Forty Martyrs of England and Wales, canonized by Paul VI on June 21, 1970, and the 85 martyrs beatified by John Paul II on Nov. 22, 1987.

After the Low Week meeting of the hierarchy of England and Wales in 1960, in a letter dated April 27, Cardinal Godfrey, as president of the same hierarchy, petitioned John XXIII to reassume the cause of canonization of a selected group of these martyrs. By an understanding with the Holy See only those were included in the list who were (1) already beatified, (2) well-known, and (3) established in the devotion of the faithful. Since that date the cause has been promoted with remarkable results.

In August 2000, a revised liturgical calendar was approved for England and Wales that includes a common feast day (May 4) under the title ''The English Martyrs'' for the 85 martyrs beatified in 1987 and the Forty Martyrs canonized in 1970. This date coincides with a similar feast in the (Anglican) Church of England. Separate feast days are maintained for SS. John Fisher and Thomas More. Individual dioceses and churches may celebrate the memorials of those martyrs of special local interest. The Roman Calendar continues to maintain the feast of the Forty Martyrs of England and Wales on October 25.

The following abbreviations have been used in the appended list: sec. priest for secular priest; sem. priest, seminary priest; b., born; d., died; educ., educated; G.S., Grammar School; Coll., College; ord., ordained; adm., admitted; Engl. miss., English mission; cond., condemned.

Under Henry VIII

1535

St. John Houghton, priest, Carthusian monk, prior of London Charterhouse; b. Essex; educ. Cambridge. d. Tyburn, May 4

St. Robert Lawrence, priest, Carthusian monk, prior of Beauvale, Notts. d. Tyburn, May 4

St. Augustine Webster, priest, Carthusian monk, prior of Axholme, Lincs. d. Tyburn, May 4

St. Richard Reynolds, priest, Bridgettine monk of Syon Abbey, Mddx.; b. Devon; educ. Corpus Christi Coll., Cambridge. d. Tyburn, May 4

Bl. John Haile, secular priest, bachelor of laws; rector of St. Dunstan's, Cranford, vicar of Isleworth, Mddx., canon of Wrigham, Kent. d. Tyburn, May 4

Bl. Humphrey Middlemore, priest, Carthusian monk, vicar of London Charterhouse; b. Edgbaston, Warwicks. d. Tyburn, June 19

Bl. William Exmew, priest, Carthusian monk, procurator of London Charterhouse. d. Tyburn, June 19

Bl. Sebastian Newdigate, priest, Carthusian monk of London Charterhouse; b. Harefield, Mddx.; educ. Cambridge. d. Tyburn, June 19

St. John Fisher, cardinal, bishop of Rochester; b. Beverley, E.R. Yorks.; educ. Cambridge; chancellor of Cambridge University. Beheaded. (Canonized 1935). d. Tower Hill, June 22

St. Thomas More, layman, lord chancellor; b. London; educ. Canterbury Hall, Oxford, and Inns of Court. Beheaded. (Canonized 1935). d. Tower Hill, July 6

1537

Bl. John Rochester, priest, Carthusian monk of London Charterhouse; b. Terling, Essex; educ. Cambridge. Hanged in chains. d. York, May 11

Bl. James Walworth, priest, Carthusian monk of London Charterhouse. Hanged in chains. d. York, May 11

Bl. William Greenwood, Carthusian brother of London Charterhouse. Starved to death. d. Newgate, June 6

Bl. John Davy, deacon, Carthusian monk of London Charterhouse. Starved to death. d. Newgate, June 8

Bl. Robert Salt, Carthusian brother of London Charterhouse. Starved to death. d. Newgate, June 9

Bl. Walter Pierson, Carthusian brother of London Charterhouse. Starved to death. d. Newgate, June 10

Bl. Thomas Green, priest, Carthusian monk of London Charterhouse; fellow of St. John's Coll., Cambridge. Starved to death. d. Newgate, June 10

Bl. Thomas Scryven, Carthusian brother of London Charterhouse. Starved to death. d. Newgate, June 15

Bl. Thomas Redyng, Carthusian brother of London Charterhouse. Starved to death. d. Newgate, June 16

Ven. Antony Brorby (Brookby), priest, Franciscan; educ. Magdalen Coll., Oxford. Strangled in prison. d. Newgate, July 7

Bl. Richard Bere, priest, Carthusian monk of London Charterhouse; b. Glastonbury; educ. Oxford and Inns of Court. Starved to death. d. Newgate, August 9

Bl. Thomas Johnson, priest, Carthusian monk of London Charterhouse. Starved to death. d. Newgate, September 20

Ven. John Travers, sec. priest; educ. Oxford; M.A., D.D.; chancellor of St. Patrick's cathedral, Dublin. Cond. under Act of Supremacy. Executed. d. Dublin, date uncertain

1538

Bl. John Forest, priest, Franciscan, Greenwich Observant Friar; educ. Oxford; confessor to Queen Catherine. Hanged, then burned. d. Smithfield, May 22

Ven. Thomas Cort (Covert), priest, Franciscan, Greenwich Observant Friar. Starved to death. d. Newgate, July 27

Ven. Thomas Belchiam, priest, Franciscan, Greenwich Observant Friar. Starved to death. d. Newgate, August 3

1539

Ven. John Griffith (sometimes misnamed Clark), sec. priest; vicar of Wandsworth, Surrey, and rector of Dolton, Devon. Cond. by Bill of Attainder. d. Southwark, July 8

Ven. John (?) Waire (Maire), priest, Franciscan. Cond. by Bill of Attainder. d. Southwark, July 8

Bl. Adrian Fortescue, Kt. of St. John of Jerusalem, layman; of Punsbourne, Herts., and Stonor Park, Oxford. Cond. by Bill of Attainder. Beheaded. d. Tower Hill, July 9

Ven. Thomas Dingley, Kt. of St. John of Jerusalem, layman; of a Hampshire family. Cond. by Bill of Attainder. Beheaded. d. Tower Hill, July 9

Bl. Richard Whiting, priest, Benedictine, Abbot of Glastonbury; b. Wrington, Somerset; educ. Cambridge. d. Glastonbury, November 15

Bl. John Thorne, priest, Benedictine monk of Glastonbury. d. Glastonbury, November 15

Bl. Roger James, priest, Benedictine monk of Glastonbury. d. Glastonbury, November 15

Bl. Hugh Faringdon (*vere* Cook), priest, Benedictine, Abbot of Reading; b. (prob.) at Faringdon, Berks. d. Reading, November 15

Bl. John Eynon (Onyon), priest, Benedictine monk (of Reading?); priest at St. Giles's, Reading. d. Reading, November 15

Bl. John Rugg, priest, Benedictine monk (of Reading?); prebendary of Chichester. d. Reading, November 15

Bl. John Beche (*vere* Marshall), priest, Benedictine, abbot of Colchester; educ. Oxford. d. Colchester, December 1

St. John Stone, priest, Augustinian monk of Austin Friars, Canterbury. d. Canterbury, not later than December 29

1540

Bl. Thomas Abell, D.D., sec. priest; educ. Oxford; chaplain to Queen Catherine. Cond. by Bill of Attainder. d. Smithfield, July 30

Bl. Edward Powell, D.D., sec. priest; a Welshman; fellow of Oriel Coll., Oxford; headmaster of Eton Coll.; prebendary of Salisbury; vicar of St. Mary Redcliffe, Bristol. Cond. by Bill of Attainder. d. Smithfield, July 30

Bl. Richard Fetherston, D.D., sec. priest; educ. Cambridge; tutor to Princess Mary; archdeacon of Brecknock. Cond. by Bill of Attainder. d. Smithfield, July 30

Bl. William Horne, Carthusian brother of London Charterhouse. Cond. by Bill of Attainder. d. Tyburn, August 4

Ven. Edmund Brindholme, sec. priest; parish priest of the Church of Our Lady, Calais; supporter of Cardinal Pole. Cond. by Bill of Attainder. d. Tyburn, August 4

Ven. Clement Philpot, layman; supporter of Cardinal Pole. Cond. by Bill of Attainder. d. Tyburn, August 4

1541

Bl. Margaret Pole, countess of Salisbury, laywoman; b. Castle Farley, Somerset; of Christchurch and Warblington, Hants.; mother of Cardinal Pole; lady governess of Princess Mary. Cond. by Bill of Attainder. Beheaded. d. Tower of London, May 28

Bl. David Gonson (Gunston or Genson), Kt. of St. John of Jerusalem, layman. Son of Vice-Adm. Gonson. Cond. by Bill of Attainder and under Act of Supremacy. d. Southwark, July 12

1544

Bl. John Larke, sec. priest; rector of St. Ethelburga's, Bishopsgate, then Chelsea. d. Tyburn, March 7

Bl. German Gardiner, layman; educ. Cambridge; secretary to Stephen Gardiner, bishop of Winchester. d. Tyburn, March 7

Bl. John Ireland, sec. priest; chaplain to the Roper Chantry; St. Dunstan's, Canterbury; afterward at Eltham. d. Tyburn, March 7

Ven. Thomas Ashby, layman. Cond. under Act of Supremacy. d. Tyburn, March 19

Under Elizabeth I

1570

Bl. Thomas Plumtree, sec. priest; b. Diocese of Lincoln; educ. Corpus Christi Coll., Oxford; chaplain to the insurgents. d. Durham, January 4

Bl. John Felton, layman; b. Bermondsey; of a Norfolk family. Cond. for publishing the Bull. d. St. Paul's Churchyard, August 8

1571

Bl. John Story, layman, doctor of law; b. Salisbury; educ. Oxford; D.C.L.; president of Broadgates Hall, Oxford; M.P., Hindon, Wilts. Cond. for pretended treason. d. Tyburn, June 1

1572

Bl. Thomas Percy, earl of Northumberland, layman; b. Northumberland. Cond. for the Rising. Beheaded. d. York, August 22

1573

Bl. Thomas Woodhouse, sec. priest and Jesuit. A Marian priest in Lincolnshire; 12 years a prisoner for religion. d. Smithfield, June 19

1577

St. Cuthbert Mayne, sem. priest; b. Yalston, near Barnstaple, Devon; educ. Barnstaple G.S.; St. John's Coll., Oxford; convert minister; Douai; ord. 1575; Engl. miss. at Golden, Cornwall. Cond. under Act of Supremacy and for priesthood. (Protomartyr of the Seminaries.) d. Launceston, November 30

1578

Bl. John Nelson, sem. priest and Jesuit; b. Skelton, near York; educ. Douai; ord. 1575; Engl. miss., London. d. Tyburn, February 3

Bl. Thomas Sherwood, layman, student; b. London; a woolen draper; taken on way to Douai. Cond. under Act of Supremacy (aged 27). d. Tyburn, February 7

1581

Bl. Everard Hanse, sem. priest; b. Northamptonshire; educ. Cambridge; after conversion, Rheims; ord. 1581; taken in London. d. Tyburn, July 31

St. Edmund Campion, priest; b. London; educ. at Bluecoat School; scholar and fellow of St. John's Coll., Oxford; after conversion, Douai; adm. SJ at Rome, 1573; Engl. miss., June 1580–August 1581. Cond. for the fictitious plot in Rome and Flanders. d. Tyburn, December 1

St. Ralph Sherwin, sem. priest; b. Rodsley, Longford, Derbyshire; fellow of Exeter Coll., Oxford; after conversion, Douai and Rome; ord. 1577; Engl. miss., 1580. Cond. for the fictitious plot in Rome and Flanders. (Protomartyr of the English Coll., Rome.) d. Tyburn, December 1

St. Alexander Briant, sem. priest; b. Somersetshire; educ. Hart Hall, Oxford; Douai; Engl. miss., 1578, London; adm. SJ in prison. Cond. for the fictitious plot in Rome and Flanders (aged 25). d. Tyburn, December 1

1582

St. John Paine, sem. priest; b. Diocese of Peterborough; educ. Douai; ord. 1576; Engl. miss., Ingatestone, Essex. Cond. for the fictitious plot in Rome and Flanders. d. Chelmsford, April 2

Bl. Thomas Ford, sem. priest; b. Devon; fellow of Trinity Coll., Oxford; convert; Douai; ord. 1573; Engl. miss., 1576, Oxfordshire and Berks. Cond. for the fictitious plot in Rome and Flanders. d. Tyburn, May 28

Bl. John Shert, sem. priest; b. Shert Hall, near Macclesfield, Cheshire; educ. Brasenose Coll., Oxford; after conversion, Douai and Rome; ord. 1576; Engl. miss., 1579, Cheshire and London. Cond. for the fictitious plot in Rome and Flanders. d. Tyburn, May 28

Bl. Robert Johnson, sem. priest; b. Shropshire; educ. German Coll., Rome and Douai; ord. 1576; Engl. miss., 1580, London. Cond. for the fictitious plot in Rome and Flanders. d. Tyburn, May 28

Bl. William Filby, sem. priest; b. Oxfordshire; educ. Lincoln Coll, Oxford; after conversion, Rheims; ord. 1581; Engl. miss., 1581. Cond. for the fictitious plot in Rome and Flanders. d. Tyburn, May 30

St. Luke Kirby, sem. priest; b. near Richmond, N.R. Yorks. (?); educ. Louvain; after conversion, Douai and Rome; ord. 1577; Engl. miss., 1580. Cond. for the fictitious plot in Rome and Flanders. d. Tyburn, May 30

Bl. Laurence Richardson (*vere* Johnson), sem. priest; b. Great Crosby, Lancs.; educ. Crosby, and Brasenose Coll., Oxford; after conversion, Douai; ord. 1577; Engl. miss., Lancs., etc. Cond. for the fictitious plot in Rome and Flanders. d. Tyburn, May 30

Bl. Thomas Cottam, priest; b. Dilworth or Tarnacre, Lancs.; educ. Brasenose Coll., Oxford; after conversion, Douai; adm. SJ, Rome; Engl. miss., 1580. Cond. for the fictitious plot in Rome and Flanders. d. Tyburn, May 30

Bl. William Lacey, sem. priest; b. Horton, near Settle, W.R. Yorks.; married; on wife's death ord. priest at Rome, 1581; Engl. miss., 1581, Yorks. d. York, August 22

Bl. Richard Kirkman, sem. priest; b. Addingham, near Skipton, W.R. Yorks.; educ. Douai; ord. 1579; Engl. miss., Lincoln and Yorks. d. York, August 22

Bl. James Thompson (alias Hudson), sem. priest; b. York; educ. Rheims; ord. 1581. d. York, November 28

1583

Bl. William Hart, sem. priest; b. Wells, Somerset; educ. Lincoln Coll., Oxford; after conversion, Douai, Rheims, and Rome; ord. 1581; Engl. miss., Yorks. d. York, March 15

Bl. Richard Thirkeld, sem. priest; b. Cunsley (Coniscliffe?), Durham; educ. Queen's Coll., Oxford; Douai and Rheims; ord. 1579; Engl. miss., Yorks., 1579–83. d. York, May 29

Bl. John Slade, layman; b. Milton, Hants.; educ. New Coll., Oxford; schoolmaster. Cond. under Act of Supremacy. d. Winchester, October 30

Bl. John Bodey, layman; b. Wells, Somerset; educ. Winchester, and New Coll., Oxford; after conversion, law student at Douai; schoolmaster. d. Andover, November 2

1584

Bl. William Carter, layman; b. London; printer. Cond. for printing Catholic books. d. Tyburn, January 11

Bl. George Haydock, sem. priest; b. Cottam Hall, near Preston, Lancs.; educ. Rheims and Rome; ord. 1581. d. Tyburn, February 12

Bl. James Fenn, sem. priest; b. Montacute, near Yeovil, Somerset; educ. Corpus Christi Coll., and Gloucester Hall, Oxford; schoolmaster; married; on wife's death went to Rheims; ord. 1580. d. Tyburn, February 12

Bl. Thomas Hemerford, sem. priest; b. Stoke (?), Dorset; educ. St. John's Coll., and Hart Hall, Oxford; Engl. Coll., Rome; ord. 1583. d. Tyburn, February 12

Bl. John Nutter, sem. priest; b. Reedley Hallows, near Burnley, Lancs.; educ. Blackburn, and St. John's Coll., Cambridge; Rheims; ord. 1582. d. Tyburn, February 12

Bl. John Munden, sec. priest; b. Coltley, S. Maperton, Dorset; educ. Winchester and New Coll., Oxford; schoolmaster in Dorset; Rheims; Rome; ord. 1582. d. Tyburn, February 12

Bl. James Bell, sec. priest; b. Warrington, Lancs.; educ. Oxford; a Marian priest, who had conformed, and died for being reconciled (aged 64). d. Lancaster, April 20

Bl. John Finch, layman; a yeoman farmer of Eccleston, Lancs.; convert and harborer of priests. d. Lancaster, April 20

St. Richard Gwyn (alias White); layman; b. Llanidloes, Montgomery; educ. St. John's Coll., Cambridge; schoolmaster in Flints and Denbighshire; convert. (Protomartyr of Wales.) d. Wrexham, October 17

1585

Bl. Thomas Alfield, sem. priest, b. Gloucester; educ. Eton, and King's Coll., Cambridge; after conversion, Douai and Rheims; ord. 1581. Cond. for distributing Allen's book, *Defence of the English Catholics.* Hanged. d. Tyburn, July 6

Ven. Thomas Webley, layman; b. Gloucester; dyer's apprentice; convert. Cond. for distributing Allen's book, *Defence of the English Catholics.* Hanged. d. Tyburn, July 6

Bl. Hugh Taylor, sem. priest; b. Durham; educ. Rheims; ord. 1584. Cond. for priesthood. d. York, November 26

Bl. Marmaduke Bowes, layman; b. Ingram Grange, Ellerbeck, N.R. Yorks. Cond. for harboring a priest. Hanged. d. York, November 27

1586

Bl. Edward Stransham (alias Barber), sem. priest; b. Oxford; educ. St. John's Coll., Oxford; Douai, Rheims; ord. 1580; Engl. miss., 1581, London and Oxford. Cond. for priesthood. d. Tyburn, January 21

Bl. Nicholas Woodfen (alias Devereux, *vere* Wheeler), sem. priest; b. Leominster; educ. Leominster G.S.; Douai, Rheims; ord. 1581; Engl. miss., 1581, London. Cond. for priesthood. d. Tyburn, January 21

St. Margaret Clitherow, laywoman, *nee* Middleton; b. York; convert and receiver of priests. Pressed to death. d. York, March 25

Bl. Richard Sergeant (alias Lea and Long), sem. priest; b. Stone(?), Gloucestershire; educ. Oxford and Rheims; ord. 1583. Cond. for priesthood. d. Tyburn, April 20

Bl. William Thomson (alias Blackburn), sem. priest; b. Blackburn, Lancs.; educ. Rheims; ord. 1584. Cond. for priesthood. d. Tyburn, April 20

Bl. Robert Anderton, sem. priest; b. Isle of Man; educ. Rivington G.S. and Brasenose Coll., Oxford; after conversion, Rheims; ord. 1584. Cond. for priesthood. d. Isle of Wight, April 25

Bl. William Marsden, sem. priest; b. Goosnargh (or Chipping), Lancs.; educ. Rivington G.S., and St. Mary Hall, Oxford; Rheims; ord. 1585. Cond. for priesthood. d. Isle of Wight, April 25

Bl. Francis Ingleby, sem. priest; b. Ripley, W.R. Yorks.; educ. Brasenose Coll., Oxford and Inner Temple; Rheims; ord. 1583; Engl. miss., 1584, Yorks. Cond. for priesthood. d. York, June 3

Bl. Robert Bickerdike, layman; b. Lowhall, near Knaresborough, W.R. Yorks. Cond. for "traitorous" speech. d. York, July 23 (?)

Bl. John Fingley, sem. priest; b. Barnby, near Howden, E.R. Yorks.; educ. Cambridge; Rheims; ord. 1581; Engl. miss., 1581. Cond. for priesthood. d. York, August 8

Bl. John Sandys, sem. priest; b. Lancashire; educ. Rheims; ord. 1584. Cond. for priesthood. d. Gloucester, August 11

Bl. John Lowe, sem. priest; b. London; convert minister; Douai, Rome; ord. 1582; Engl. miss., 1583, London. Cond. for priesthood. d. Tyburn, October 8

Bl. John Adams, sem. priest; b. Martinstown, Dorset; educ. Oxford; convert minister; Rheims; ord. 1580. Cond. for priesthood. d. Tyburn, October 8

Bl. Robert Dibdale, sem. priest; b. Shottery, Warwicks.; educ. Rheims; ord. 1584; Eng. miss., 1584, Denham, Bucks. Cond. for priesthood. d. Tyburn, October 8

Bl. Richard Langley, layman; of Ousethorpe, near Pocklington, E.R. Yorks. Hanged for harboring priests. d. York, December 1

1587

Bl. Thomas Pilcher, sem. priest; b. Battle, Sussex; educ. Balliol Coll., Oxford; after conversion, Rheims; ord. 1583; Engl. miss., 1583, W. Counties. Cond. for priesthood. d. Dorchester, March 21

Bl. Edmund Sykes, sem. priest; b. near Leeds, W.R. Yorks.; educ. Oxford(?); Rheims; ord. 1581; Engl. miss., 1581, Yorks. Cond. for priesthood. d. York, March 23

Bl. Stephen Rowsham (alias Rouse), sem. priest; b. Oxfordshire; educ. Oriel Coll., Oxford; minister at St. Mary's, Oxford; after conversion, Rheims; ord. 1582. Cond. for priesthood. d. Gloucester, April?

Bl. John Hambley, sem. priest; b. St. Mabyn, near Bodmin, Cornwall; convert; Rheims; ord. 1584; Engl. miss., 1585, London and West. Cond. for priesthood. d. Salisbury, April?

Bl. Robert Sutton, sem. priest; b. Burton-on-Trent, Staffs.; educ. Burton, and Christ Church, Oxford; parson of Lutterworth; after conversion, Douai; ord. 1578; Engl. miss., Stafford, nine years. Cond. for priesthood. d. Stafford, July 27

Bl. George Douglas, sem. priest (Franciscan); b. Edinburgh; educ. Paris; ord. *c.* 1560; schoolmaster in Rutland. Cond. under Act of Supremacy. d. York, September 9

Bl. Alexander Crow, sem. priest; b. S. Duffield (or Howden), E.R. Yorks.; shoemaker; student at Rheims; ord. 1583, Engl. miss., Yorks. Cond. for priesthood. d. York, November 30

1588

Bl. Nicholas Garlick, sem. priest; b. Dinting, Derbyshire; educ. Mellor G.S., and Gloucester Hall, Oxford; schoolmaster at Tideswell G.S.; Rheims; ord. 1582; Engl. miss., Midlands. Cond. for priesthood. d. Derby, July 24

Bl. Robert Ludlam, sem. priest; b. Radborne, near Derby; educ. St. John's Coll., Oxford; Rheims; ord. 1581; Engl. miss., 1582, Derbyshire. Cond. for priesthood. d. Derby, July 24

Bl. Richard Simpson (alias Highgate), sem. priest; b. Well, near Ripon, W.R. Yorks.; educ. Gloucester Hall, Oxford; convert minister; Douai; ord. 1577; Engl. miss., ten years. Cond. for priesthood. d. Derby, July 24

Bl. William Dean, sem. priest; b. Linton-in-Craven, W.R. Yorks.; convert minister; Rheims; ord. 1581. Cond. for priesthood. Hanged. d. Mile End Green, August 28

Bl. Henry Webley, layman; b. Gloucester. Hanged for aiding Dean (above). d. Mile End Green, August 28

Bl. William Gunter, sem. priest; b. Raglan, Monmouth; educ. Rheims; ord. 1587. Cond. for priesthood, Hanged. d. Shoreditch, August 28

Bl. Robert Morton, sem. priest; b. Bawtry, W.R. Yorks.; educ. Rheims, Rome; ord. 1587. Cond. for priesthood. Hanged. d. Lincoln's Inn Fields, August 28

Bl. Hugh More, layman; b. Grantham, Lincs.; educ. Broadgates Hall, Oxford and Gray's Inn; convert; Rheims. Hanged for being reconciled. d. Lincoln's Inn Fields, August 28

Bl. Thomas Holford (alias Acton and Bude), sem. priest; b. Aston in parish of Acton, Cheshire; schoolmaster in Herefords.; convert; Rheims; ord. 1583; Engl. miss., London and Cheshire. Cond. for priesthood. Hanged. d. Clerkenwell, August 28

Bl. James Claxton (Clarkson), sem. priest; b. Yorks.; educ. Rheims; ord. 1582. Cond. for priesthood. Hanged. d. Isleworth, August 28

Bl. Thomas Felton, friar minim; b. Bermondsey; son of Bl. John Felton (see above, 1570); educ. Rheims; not yet ord. Hanged for being reconciled. d. Isleworth, August 28

Bl. Richard Leigh (alias Garth or Earth), sem. priest; b. London; educ. Rheims and Rome; ord. 1586. Cond. for priesthood. Hanged. d. Tyburn, August 30

Bl. Edward Shelley, layman; of Warminghurst, Sussex. Hanged for harboring or relieving priests. d. Tyburn, August 30

Bl. Richard Martin, layman; b. Shropshire; educ. Broadgates Hall, Oxford. Hanged for harboring or relieving priests. d. Tyburn, August 30

Bl. Richard Flower (*vere* Lloyd or Floyd), layman; b. Anglesey. Hanged for harboring or relieving priests (aged 22). d. Tyburn, August 30

Bl. John Roche (alias Neale), layman; an Irish waterman. Hanged for harboring or relieving priests. d. Tyburn, August 30

St. Margaret Ward, laywoman; b. Congleton, Cheshire. Cond. for rescuing a priest. Hanged. d. Tyburn, August 30

Bl. William Way (alias Flower, sometimes misnamed Wigges), sem. priest; b. Devon; educ. Rheims; ord. 1586. Cond. for priesthood. d. Kingston-on-Thames, September 23

Bl. Robert Wilcox, sem. priest; b. Chester; educ. Rheims; ord. 1585. Cond. for priesthood. d. Canterbury, October 1

Bl. Edward Campion (*vere* Edwards), sem. priest; b. Ludlow, Shropshire; educ. Jesus Coll., Oxford; after conversion, Rheims; ord. 1587. Cond. for priesthood. d. Canterbury, October 1

Bl. Christopher Buxton, sem. priest; b. Tideswell, Derbyshire; educ. Tideswell G.S.; after conversion Rheims, Rome; ord. 1586. Cond. for priesthood. d. Canterbury, October 1

Bl. Robert Widmerpool, layman; b. Widmerpool, Notts.; educ. Gloucester Hall, Oxford; schoolmaster. Hanged for helping a priest. d. Canterbury, October 1

Bl. Ralph Crockett, sem. priest; b. Barton-on-the-Hill, Cheshire; educ. Christ's Coll., Cambridge, and Gloucester Hall, Oxford; schoolmaster, Norfolk and Suffolk; Rheims; ord. 1586. Cond. for priesthood. d. Chichester, October 1

Bl. Edward James, sem. priest; b. Breaston in parish of Wilne, near Derby; educ. Derby G.S., and St. John's Coll., Oxford; after conversion Rheims, Rome; ord. 1583. Cond. for priesthood. d. Chichester, October 1

Bl. John Robinson, sem. priest; b. Ferrensby, W.R. Yorks.; on wife's death, Rheims; ord. 1585. Cond. for priesthood. d. Ipswich, October 1

Bl. William Hartley, sem. priest; b. Wilne, near Derby; educ. St. John's Coll., Oxford; convert minister; Rheims; ord. 1580. Cond. for priesthood. Hanged. d. Shoreditch, October 5

Bl. Robert Sutton, layman; b. Kegworth, Leicestershire; educ. Oxford(?); schoolmaster in London; convert. Hanged for being reconciled. d. Clerkenwell, October 5

Bl. John Hewett (alias Weldon and Sayell), sem. priest; b. York; educ. Caius Coll., Cambridge; Rheims; ord. 1586. Cond. for priesthood. Hanged. d. Mile End Green, October 5

Bl. Edward Burden, sem. priest; b. Durham; educ. Corpus Christi Coll., Oxford; Rheims; ord. 1584. Cond. for priesthood. d. York, October 31 or November 29

Bl. William Lampley, layman, a Gloucester glover. Cond. for ''persuading to popery.'' d. Gloucester, date unknown

1589

Bl. John Amias (Anne), sem. priest; b. near Wakefield, W.R. Yorks.; clothmonger at Wakefield; married; on wife's death, Rheims; ord. 1581. Cond. for priesthood. d. York, March 15

Bl. Robert Dalby, sem. priest; b. Hemingborough, E.R. Yorks.; convert minister; Rheims; ord. 1588. Cond. for priesthood. d. York, March 15

Bl. George Nichols, sem. priest; b. Oxford; educ. Brasenose Coll., Oxford; master at St. Paul's School; Rheims; ord. 1584; Engl. miss., Oxford. Cond. for priesthood. d. Oxford, July 5

Bl. Richard Yaxley, sem. priest; b. Boston, Lincs.; educ. Rheims; ord. 1586; Engl. miss., Oxford. Cond. for priesthood. d. Oxford, July 5

Bl. Thomas Belson, layman; of Brill, Bucks. Hanged for relieving Nichols and Yaxley (above). d. Oxford, July 5

Bl. Humphrey Pritchard, layman; a Welsh servant. Hanged for relieving Nichols and Yaxley (above). d. Oxford, July 5

Bl. William Spenser, sem. priest; b. Gisburn, W.R. Yorks.; educ. Trinity Coll., Oxford; convert; Rheims; ord. 1583. Cond. for priesthood. d. York, September 24

Bl. Robert Hardesty, layman; a serving-man; b. Yorkshire. Hanged for relieving Spenser (above). d. York, September 24

1590

Bl. Christopher Bales, sem. priest; b. Coniscliffe, Durham; educ. Rome and Rheims; ord. 1587. Cond. for priesthood. d. Fleet Street, March 4

Bl. Nicholas Horner; layman; b. Grantley, W. R. Yorks.; a tailor. Hanged for assisting priests. d. Smithfield, March 4

Bl. Alexander Blake, layman, a London ostler. Hanged for assisting priests. d. Gray's Inn Lane, March 4

Bl. Francis Dickenson (Dicconson), (alias Laurence and Keighley), sem. priest; b. Otley, W.R. Yorks.; convert; educ. Rheims; ord. 1589. Cond. for priesthood. d. Rochester, April 13 or 30

Bl. Miles Gerard (alias William Richardson), sem. priest; b. Ince, near Wigan, Lancs.; schoolmaster; educ. Rheims; ord. 1583. Cond. for priesthood. d. Rochester, April 13 or 30

Bl. Edward Jones, sem. priest; b. Lyndon(?), Diocese of St. Asaph; convert; educ. Rheims; ord. 1588. Cond. for priesthood. d. Fleet Street, May 6

Bl. Antony Middleton, sem. priest; b. Middleton Tyas, N.R. Yorks.; educ. Rheims; ord. 1586. Cond. for priesthood. d. Clerkenwell, May 6

Bl. Edmund Duke, sem. priest; b. Kent; convert; educ. Rheims; Rome; ord. 1589. Cond. for priesthood. d. Durham, May 27

Bl. Richard Hill, sem. priest; a Yorkshireman; educ. Rheims; ord. 1589. Cond. for priesthood. d. Durham, May 27

Bl. John Hogg, sem. priest; b. Cleveland, Yorks.; educ. Rheims; ord. 1589. Cond. for priesthood. d. Durham, May 27

Bl. Richard Holiday, sometimes listed as John Holiday, sem. priest; a Yorkshireman; educ. Rheims; ord. 1589. Cond. for priesthood. d. Durham, May 27

1591

Bl. Robert Thorpe, sem. priest; b. Yorks.; educ. Rheims; ord. 1585. Cond. for priesthood. d. York, May 31

Bl. Thomas Watkinson, yeoman, of Menthrope, E.R. Yorks. Hanged for harboring Thorpe (above). d. York, May 31

Bl. Montford Scott, sem. priest; b. Suffolk; educ. Douai; ord. 1577. Cond. for priesthood. d. Fleet Street, July 1

Bl. George Beesley, sem. priest; b. Goosnargh, Lancs.; educ. Rheims; ord. 1587. Cond. for priesthood. d. Fleet Street, July 1

Bl. Roger Dickenson (Dicconson), sem. priest; b. Lincoln; educ. Rheims; ord. 1583. Cond. for priesthood. d. Winchester, July 7

Bl. Ralph Milner, layman; b. Slackstead, Hants.; husbandman. Hanged for relieving Dickenson (above). d. Winchester, July 7

Bl. Laurence Humphrey, layman; b. Hampshire; convert (aged 20). d. Winchester, date unknown

St. Edmund Gennings (alias Ironmonger), sem. priest; b. Lichfield; convert; educ. Rheims; ord. 1590. Cond. for priesthood. d. Gray's Inn Fields, December 10

St. Swithun Wells, layman; of Brambridge, Hants. Hanged for harboring Gennings (above). d. Gray's Inn Fields, December 10

St. Eustace White, sem. priest; b. Louth, Lincs.; convert; educ. Rheims, Rome; ord. 1588. Cond. for priesthood. d. Tyburn, December 10

St. Polydore Plasden, sem. priest; b. London; educ. Rheims, Rome; ord. 1588. Cond. for priesthood. d. Tyburn, December 10

Bl. Brian Lacey, layman; b. Brockdish, Norfolk. Hanged for relieving priests. d. Tyburn, December 10

Bl. John Mason, layman; b. Kendal, Westmorland. Hanged for relieving priests. d. Tyburn, December 10

Bl. Sidney Hodgson, layman; convert. Hanged for relieving priests. d. Tyburn, December 10

Bl. William Pike, layman; a joiner, of Moors, near Christchurch, Hants. Cond. for being reconciled. Hanged. d. Dorchester, December 22

1592

Bl. William Patenson, sem. priest; b. Durham; educ. Rheims; ord. 1587; Engl. miss., 1589, W. Counties. Cond. for priesthood. d. Tyburn, January 22

Bl. Thomas Pormort (alias Whitgift, White, Pryce, and Meres), sem. priest; b. Little Limber, Lincs.; educ. Cambridge; Rheims, Rome; ord. 1587. Cond. for priesthood. d. St. Paul's Churchyard, February 21

Ven. Richard Williams, sec. priest; a Marian priest who had conformed and been reconciled. d. Tyburn, February 21

Bl. James Bird (Byrd or Beard), layman; b. Winchester; convert; educ. Rheims. Cond. for being reconciled (aged 19). d. Winchester, March 25

Ven. Roger Ashton, layman; b. Croston, Lancs. d. Tyburn, June 23

Bl. Joseph Lambton, sem. priest; b. Malton-in-Rydale, N.R. Yorks.; educ. Rheims, Rome; ord. 1592. Cond. for priesthood. d. Newcastle, July 31

1593

Bl. Edward Waterson, sem. priest; b. London; convert; educ. Rheims; ord. 1592. Cond. for priesthood. d. Newcastle, January 8

Bl. Antony Page, sem. priest; b. Harrow, Mddx; educ. Christ Church, Oxford; Rheims; ord. 1591. Cond. for priesthood. d. York, April 20

Bl. William Davies, sem. priest; b. Croes-yn-Eirias, Caernarvon; educ. St. Edmund Hall, Oxford; Rheims; ord. 1585; miss., N. Wales. Cond. for priesthood. d. Beaumaris, July 27

1594

Bl. John Speed (alias Spence), layman; b. Durham. Hanged for relieving priests. d. Durham, February 4

Bl. William Harrington, sem. priest; b. Mount St. John, Felixkirk, N.R. Yorks.; educ. Rheims; ord. 1592; Engl. miss., London. Cond. for priesthood (aged 27). d. Tyburn, February 18

Bl. John Cornelius (alias O'Mahony and Mohun), sem. priest; b. Bodmin, of Irish parents; fellow of Exeter Coll., Oxford; Rheims, Rome; ord. 1583; Engl. miss., Lanherne, ten years; adm. SJ 1594. Cond. for priesthood. d. Dorchester, July 4

Bl. Thomas Bosgrave, layman, nephew of Sir J. Arundel; b. Cornwall. Hanged for aiding Cornelius (above). d. Dorchester, July 4

Bl. John Carey, layman, Irish serving-man. Hanged for aiding Cornelius (above). d. Dorchester, July 4

Bl. Patrick Salmon, layman, Irish serving-man. Hanged for aiding Cornelius (above). d. Dorchester, July 4

St. John Boste, sem. priest; b. Dufton, Westmorland; educ. Queen's Coll., Oxford; convert minister; Rheims; ord. 1581; Engl. miss., N. Counties, 12 years. Cond. for priesthood. d. Durham, July 24

Bl. John Ingram, sem. priest; b. Stoke Edith, Hereford; convert; educ. New Coll., Oxford; Rheims, Rome; ord. 1589; miss. in Scotland. Cond. for priesthood. d. Gateshead, July 26

Bl. George Swallowell, layman; b. Shadforth, near Durham; educ. Sherburn Hospital; schoolmaster; convert minister. Cond. for being reconciled. d. Darlington, July 26

Bl. Edward Osbaldeston, sem. priest; b. Osbaldeston, near Blackburn, Lancs.; educ. Rheims; ord. 1585; Engl. miss., Yorks. Cond. for priesthood. d. York, November 16

1595

St. Robert Southwell, priest; b. Horsham St. Faith, Norfolk; educ. Douai; Rome; adm. SJ 1578; Engl. miss., London, 1586–92. Cond. for priesthood. d. Tyburn, February 21

Bl. Alexander Rawlins (alias Francis Feriman); sem. priest; b. Oxfordshire; educ. Rheims; ord. 1590; Engl. miss., Yorks. Cond. for priesthood. d. York, April 7

St. Henry Walpole, priest; b. Docking, Norfolk; educ. Norwich G.S., and Peterhouse, Cambridge; Gray's Inn; convert; English Coll., Rome; adm. SJ 1584; ord. Paris, 1588. Cond. for priesthood. d. York, April 7

Bl. William Freeman (alias Mason), sem. priest; b. Menthorpe(?), E.R. Yorks.; educ. Magdalen Coll., Oxford; convert; Rheims; ord. 1587; Engl. miss., Worcester and Warwick. Cond. for priesthood. d. Warwick, August 13

St. Philip Howard, earl of Arundel and Surrey, layman; b. Arundel House, London; prisoner under sentence of death for being reconciled, 1585 till death. d. Tower of London, October 19

1596

Bl. George Errington, layman; b. Hurst, near Morpeth, Northumberland; educ. Oxford. Cond. for "persuading to popery." d. York, November 29

Bl. William Knight, layman; b. S. Duffield(?), E.R. Yorks. Cond. for "persuading to popery." d. York, November 29

Bl. William Gibson, layman; b. near Ripon, W.R. Yorks. Cond. for "persuading to popery." d. York, November 29

1597

Bl. Christopher Robinson, sem. priest; b. Woodside, near Carlisle; educ. Rheims; ord. 1592; Engl. miss., six years in the North. Cond. for priesthood. d. Carlisle, late March or Aug. 19, 1598

Bl. Henry Abbot, layman; of Howden, E.R. Yorks.; convert. Cond. for "persuading to popery." d. York, July 4

Bl. William Andleby (Anlaby), b. Etton, near Beverley, E.R. Yorks.; educ. St. John's Coll., Cambridge; convert; Douai; ord. 1577; Engl. miss., Yorks., 20 years. Cond. for priesthood. d. York, July 4

Bl. Thomas Warcop, layman; of Winston, County Durham. Hanged for harboring. d. York, July 4

Bl. Edward Fulthrop, layman; of Yorkshire. Hanged, drawn, and quartered for being reconciled. d. York, July 4

1598

Bl. John Bretton, layman; b. W. Bretton, near Wakefield, Yorks.; married. Cond. on charge of treasonable language. d. York, April 1

Bl. Peter Snow, sem. priest; b. Ripon, W.R. Yorks.; educ. Rheims; ord. 1591; Engl. miss., Yorks. Cond. for priesthood. d. York, June 15

Bl. Ralph Grimston, yeoman, of Nidd, near Knaresborough, W.R. Yorks. Cond. for harboring. Hanged. d. York, June 15

St. John Jones (alias Buckley), priest, Franciscan; b. Clynog Fawr, Caernarvon; joined Observants at Rome as Father Godfrey Maurice; Engl. miss., London 1592–97. Cond. for priesthood. d. Southwark, July 12

Ven. Richard Horner, sem. priest; b. Bolton Bridge, W.R. Yorks.; educ. Douai; ord. 1595. Cond. for priesthood. d. York, September 4

Ven. John Lion, layman. Cond. for denying Supremacy. d. Oakham, July 16

Ven. James Dowdall, layman; a Waterford merchant; arrested in England. Cond. for denying Supremacy. d. Exeter, August 13

1600

Bl. Christopher Wharton, sem. priest; b. Middleton, near Ilkley, W.R. Yorks.; convert; educ. Trinity Coll., Oxford; Rheims; ord. 1584; Engl. miss., 14 years. Cond. for priesthood. d. York, March 28

St. John Rigby, layman; b. Harrock Hall, near Wigan, Lancs. Cond. for being reconciled. d. Southwark, June 21

Bl. Thomas Sprott (alias Parker), sem. priest; b. Skelsmergh, near Kendal, Westmorland; educ. Douai; ord. 1596. Cond. for priesthood. d. Lincoln, July 1

Bl. Thomas Hunt (alias or *vere* Benstead), sem. priest; b. Norfolk; educ. Valladolid and Seville. Cond. for priesthood. d. Lincoln, July 1

Bl. Robert Nutter (alias Askew and Rowley), sem. priest; b. Reedley Hallows, near Burnley, Lancs.; educ. Blackburn; Rheims; ord. 1581; Engl. miss., 18 years, mostly in prison; adm. OP in prison. Cond. for priesthood. d. Lancaster, July 26

Bl. Edward Thwing, sem. priest; b. Heworth, near York; educ. Rheims; Rome; ord. 1590. Cond. for priesthood. d. Lancaster, July 26

Bl. Thomas Palaser, sem. priest; b. Ellerton-upon-Swale, near Richmond, N.R. Yorks.; educ. Rheims; Valladolid; ord. 1596. Cond. for priesthood. d. Durham, August 9

Bl. John Norton, layman; of Ravensworth, Lamesley, Durham. Hanged for harboring. d. Durham, August 9

Bl. John Talbot, layman; of Thornton-le-Street, N.R. Yorks. Hanged for harboring. d. Durham, August 9

1601

Bl. John Pibush, sem. priest; b. Thirsk, N.R. Yorks.; educ. Rheims; ord. 1587; Engl. miss., 12 years, mostly in prison. Cond. for priesthood. d. Southwark, February 18

Bl. Mark Barkworth (alias Lambert), priest, Benedictine; b. Searby, Lincolnshire; educ. Oxford; after conversion Rome, Valladolid. Cond. for priesthood. d. Tyburn, February 27

Bl. Roger Filcock (alias Arthur), priest; b. Sandwich, Kent; educ. Rheims, Valladolid; adm. SJ in England. Cond. for priesthood. d. Tyburn, February 27

St. Anne Line, laywoman, *nee* Higham; b. Dunmow, Essex; convert. Hanged for harboring. d. Tyburn, February 27

Bl. Thurstan Hunt (alias Greenlow); b. Carlton Hall, Leeds, W.R. Yorks.; educ. Rheims; ord. 1585. Cond. for priesthood. d. Lancaster, April 3

Bl. Robert Middleton, sem. priest; b. York; educ. Douai and Rome; adm. SJ in prison. Cond. for priesthood. d. Lancaster, April 3

Ven. Nicholas Tichborne, layman; b. Hartley Mauditt, Hants. Hanged for rescuing a priest. d. Tyburn, August 24

Ven. Thomas Hackshott (Hawkshaw), layman; a young man from Muresley, Bucks. Hanged for rescuing a priest. d. Tyburn, August 24

1602

Ven. James (or Matthew) *Harrison,* sem. priest; b. Diocese of Lichfield; educ. Rheims; ord. 1583. Cond. for priesthood. d. York, March 22

Ven. Antony Bates (Battie), layman, farmer, of Masham, E.R. Yorks. Hanged for harboring. d. York, March 22

Bl. James Duckett, layman; b. Gilfortrigs, Skelsmergh, Westmorland; convert, bookseller. Cond. for printing Catholic books. Hanged. d. Tyburn, April 19

Ven. Thomas Tichborne, sem. priest; b. Hartley Mauditt, Hants.; educ. Rheims and Rome; ord. 1592; Engl. miss., Hants. Cond. for priesthood. d. Tyburn, April 20

Bl. Robert Watkinson, sem. priest; b. Hemingborough, E.R. Yorks.; educ. Hemingborough and Castleford; Douai; Rome; ord. March 1602. Cond. for priesthood (aged 23). d. Tyburn, April 20

Bl. Francis Page, sem. priest; b. Antwerp; of a Harrow family; educ. Douai; ord. 1600; adm. SJ in prison. Cond. for priesthood. d. Tyburn, April 20

1603

Bl. William Richardson (alias Anderson), sem. priest; b. Wales, near Sheffield, W.R. Yorks.; educ. Valladolid; Seville; ord. 1594. Cond. for priesthood. d. Tyburn, February 17

Under James I

1604

Bl. John Sugar (alias Cox), sem. priest; b. Wombourn, Staffs.; educ. St. Mary Hall, Oxford; convert minister; Douai; ord. 1601; Engl. miss., Midlands. Cond. for priesthood. d. Warwick, July 16

Bl. Robert Grissold, layman; b. Rowington, Warwicks. Cond. for relieving priests. Hanged. d. Warwick, July 16

Ven. Laurence Bailey, layman, a Lancashire miller. Hanged for rescuing a priest. d. Lancaster, August, day unknown

1605

Bl. Thomas Welbourne, layman; b. Hutton Bushel, N.R. Yorks.; schoolmaster. Cond. for "persuading to popery." d. York, August 1

Bl. William Browne, layman; b. Northampton. Cond. for "persuading to popery." d. Ripon, September 5

1606

St. Nicholas Owen, Jesuit brother; b. Oxford; companion to Father Henry Garnet, SJ. Died from torture. d. Tower of London, March 2

Bl. Edward Oldcorne (alias Hunter and Hall), priest; b. York; educ. Rheims; Rome; adm. SJ 1587; Engl. miss., Midlands, 1588–1606. Cond. for alleged complicity in the Gunpowder Plot. d. Worcester, April 7

Bl. Ralph Ashley, Jesuit brother; companion to Oldcorne (above); had been a servant at Rheims and Valladolid. Cond. for alleged complicity in the Gunpowder Plot. d. Worcester, April 7

1607

Bl. Robert Drury, sem. priest; b. Bucks.; educ. Rheims; Valladolid; ord. 1593; Engl. miss., London district. Cond. for priesthood. d. Tyburn, February 26

1608

Bl. Matthew Flathers, sem. priest; b. Weston, near Otley, W.R. Yorks.; educ. Douai; ord. 1606. Cond. for priesthood. d. York, March 21

Bl. George Gervase, priest, Benedictine; b. Bosham, Sussex; educ. Douai; ord. 1603. Cond. for priesthood. d. Tyburn, April 11

St. Thomas Garnet priest; b. Southwark; educ. Horsham; St. Omer; Valladolid; adm. SJ 1604. Cond. for priesthood. (Protomartyr of St. Omer College.) d. Tyburn, June 23

1610

Bl. Roger Cadwallador, sem. priest; b. Stretton, Hereford; educ. Rheims; Valladolid; ord. 1593; Engl. miss., Hereford. Cond. for priesthood. d. Leominster, August 27

Bl. George Napper (Napier), sem. priest; b. Oxford; educ. Corpus Christi Coll., Oxford; Douai; ord. 1596; Engl. miss., Oxford. Cond. for priesthood. d. Oxford, November 9

Bl. Thomas Somers (alias Wilson), sem. priest; b. Skelsmergh, Westmorland; schoolmaster; educ. Douai; ord. 1606; Engl. miss., London district. Cond. for priesthood. d. Tyburn, December 10

St. John Roberts, priest; b. Trawsfynydd, Merioneth; educ. St. John's Coll., Oxford; convert; Valladolid; adm.

OSB, 1599; Engl. miss., London district. Cond. for priesthood. d. Tyburn, December 10

1612

Bl. William Scott, priest; b. Chigwell, Essex; educ. Trinity Hall, Cambridge; convert; adm. OSB in Spain 1604 (Dom Maurus); Engl. miss., London district. Cond. for priesthood. d. Tyburn, May 30

Bl. Richard Newport (alias Smith), sem. priest; b. Ashby St. Legers, Northants.; educ. Rome; ord. 1599; Engl. miss., London district. Cond. for priesthood. d. Tyburn, May 30

St. John Almond, sem. priest; b. Allerton, near Liverpool; educ. Much Woolton; Rheims; Rome; ord. 1598; Engl. miss., 1602–12. Cond. for priesthood. d. Tyburn, December 5

1616

Bl. Thomas Atkinson, sem. priest; b. Leeds; educ. Rheims; ord. 1588; Engl. miss., 1588–1616. Cond. for priesthood. d. York, March 11

Bl. John Thules, sem. priest; b. Whalley, Lancs.; educ. Rheims; Rome; ord. 1592. Cond. for priesthood. d. Lancaster, March 18

Bl. Roger Wrenno, layman, a Chorley weaver. Hanged for relieving priests. d. Lancaster, March 18

Bl. Thomas Maxfield, sem. priest; b. The Mere, Enville, Staffs.; educ. Douai; ord. 1615. Cond. for priesthood. d. Tyburn, July 1

Bl. Thomas Tunstal (alias Helmes and Dyer), priest, Benedictine; b. Whinfell, near Kendal, Westmorland; educ. Douai; ord. 1609. Cond. for priesthood. d. Norwich, July 13

1618

Bl. William Southerne (*Sotheran*), sem. priest; b. Ketton, near Darlington; educ. Valladolid; Seville; Douai; ord. *c.* 1601; Engl. miss. Staffs. Cond. for priesthood. d. Newcastle-upon-Tyne, April 30

Under Charles I

1628

St. Edmund Arrowsmith, priest; b. Haydock, near St. Helen's, Lanes; educ. Douai; ord. 1612; Engl. miss., Lancs., 1613–28; adm. SJ 1623. Cond. for priesthood and "persuading to popery." d. Lancaster, August 28

Bl. Richard Herst (also Hurst or Hayhurst), layman; b. Broughton(?), near Preston, Lancs. Hanged on charge of murder. d. Lancaster, August 29

1641

Bl. William Ward (*vere* Webster), sem. priest; b. Thornby (Thrimby), Westmorland; educ. Douai; ord. 1608; Engl. miss., 33 years (20 in prison). Cond. for priesthood. d. Tyburn, July 26

St. Ambrose (Edward) Barlow, priest; b. Barlow Hall, near Manchester; educ. Douai; Valladolid; professed OSB 1615; Engl. miss., 24 years. Cond. for priesthood. d. Lancaster, September 10

1642

Bl. Richard (Thomas) Reynolds (*vere* Green), sem. priest; b. Warwicks.; educ. Douai; Seville; ord. 1602; Engl. miss., nearly 50 years. Cond. for priesthood (aged about 80). d. Tyburn, January 31

St. Alban (Bartholomew) Roe (Rowe), priest; b. St. Albans; educ. Cambridge(?); after conversion, Douai; professed OSB 1612; Engl. miss., 1615–42. Cond. for priesthood. d. Tyburn, January 31

Ven. John Goodman, sem. priest; b. Bangor; educ. Oxford; convert minister; Douai; ord. in France *c.* 1632. Cond. for priesthood. Died in prison. d. Newgate, April 8

Bl. John Lockwood (alias Lascelles), sem. priest; b. Sowerby, N.R. Yorks.; educ. Rome; ord. 1597; Engl. miss., 1598–1642. Cond. for priesthood (aged 81). d. York, April 13

Bl. Edmund Catherick, sem. priest; of Carlton, near Richmond, N.R. Yorks.; educ. Douai; Engl. miss., 1635–42. Cond. for priesthood. d. York, April 13

Ven. Edward Morgan (alias John Singleton), sem. priest; b. Bettisfield, Flints.; educ. Douai; Rome; Valladolid; ord. 1618; 14 years' prisoner. Cond. for priesthood. d. Tyburn, April 26

Bl. Hugh Green (alias Ferdinand Brooke), sem. priest; b. London; educ. Peterhouse, Cambridge; convert; Douai; ord. 1612; Engl. miss., Dorset. Cond. for priesthood. d. Dorchester, August 19

Bl. Thomas Bullaker, priest; b. Chichester, Sussex; educ. St. Omer; Valladolid; adm. OSF in Spain, 1624 (Father John Baptist). Cond. for priesthood. d. Tyburn, October 12

Bl. Thomas Holland (alias Sanderson and Hammond), priest; b. Sutton, near Prescot, Lancs.; educ. St. Omer; Valladolid; adm. SJ 1624. Cond. for priesthood. d. Tyburn, December 12

1643

Bl. Henry Heath, priest; b. Peterborough; educ. St. Benets, Cambridge; convert minister; Douai; adm. OSF 1622 (Father Paul of St. M. Magdalen). Cond. for priesthood. d. Tyburn, April 17

Bl. Arthur Bell, priest, Franciscan; b. Temple Broughton, Worcester; educ. St. Omer; Valladolid; adm. OSF 1617 (Father Francis); Engl. miss., 1634. Cond. for priesthood. d. Tyburn, December 11

1644

Ven. Robert Price (*Apreece*), layman; of Washingley, Huntingdon. Shot by Puritan soldiers. d. Lincoln, May 7

Bl. John Duckett, sem. priest; b. Underwinder, near Sedbergh, W.R. Yorks.; educ. Douai; ord. 1639; Engl. miss., Durham. Cond. for priesthood. d. Tyburn, September 7

Bl. Ralph Corbie (*vere* Corbington), priest; b. Dublin; educ. St. Omer; Seville; Valladolid; adm. SJ 1631; Engl. miss., Durham. Cond. for priesthood. d. Tyburn, September 7

1645

St. Henry Morse, priest; b. Broome, Suffolk; convert; educ. Inns of Court; Douai; Rome; adm. SJ 1625; Engl. miss., London, etc. Cond. for priesthood. d. Tyburn, February 1

Ven. Brian Cansfield, priest; b. Robert Hall, Tatham, Lancs.; educ. St. Omer; Rome; adm. SJ 1604; Engl. miss., Lincoln and Lancs. Died of ill treatment in prison. d. York, August 3

1646

Bl. Philip Powel (alias Morgan), priest; b. Trallong, Brecknocks; educ. Abergavenny G.S. and Temple; adm. OSB 1614; Engl. miss., 1622, in West. Cond. for priesthood. d. Tyburn, June 30

Bl. Edward Bamber (alias Helmes and Reding), sem. priest; b. Carleton, Blackpool, Lanes; educ. St. Omer; Seville; Engl. miss., Lancs. Cond. for priesthood. d. Lancaster, August 7

Bl. John Woodcock (alias Farington and Thompson), priest; b. Clayton-le-Woods, near Preston, Lancs.; educ. St. Omer; Rome; adm. OSF 1631 (Father Martin). Cond. for priesthood. d. Lancaster, August 7

Bl. Thomas Whitaker (alias Starkie), sem. priest; b. Burnley, Lancs.; educ. St. Omer; Valladolid; ord. 1638; Engl. miss., Lancs. Cond. for priesthood. d. Lancaster, August 7

During The Commonwealth

1651

Bl. Peter Wright, priest; b. Slipton, Northants.; convert; educ. Ghent; Rome; adm. SJ 1629; military chaplain in Civil War. Cond. for priesthood. d. Tyburn, May 19

1654

St. John Southworth, sem. priest; b. Lancs.; connected with Southworths of Samlesbury; educ. Douai; ord. 1619; Engl. miss., Lancs. Cond. for priesthood. d. Tyburn, June 28

Under Charles II

1678

Ven. Edward Mico (alias Harvey), priest; b. Essex; educ. St. Omer; Rome; adm. SJ 1650. Arrested for "the plot." Too ill to be removed from sick-bed, where he died. d. Wild House, London, November 24

Bl. Edward Coleman, layman; b. Suffolk; educ. Peterhouse, Cambridge; convert; secretary to duchess of York. Arrested for "the plot." d. Tyburn, December 3

Ven. Thomas Bedingfeld (alias Mumford, *vere* Downes), priest; b. Norfolk; educ. St. Omer; adm. SJ 1638. Arrested for "the plot." Died in prison. d. Gatehouse, December 21

1679

Bl. William Ireland (*vere* Iremonger), priest; b. Lincs.; educ. St. Omer; adm. SJ, 1655. Arrested for "the plot." d. Tyburn, January 24

Bl. John Grove, layman, servant of Ireland (above). Arrested for "the plot." d. Tyburn, January 24

Ven. Francis Nevill (*vere* Cotton), priest; b. Hants.; adm. SJ 1616; Engl. miss., 1630–79, mostly Midlands. Died in prison for "the plot." d. Stafford, end of February

Bl. Thomas Pickering, Benedictine brother; b. Westmorland(?); professed OSB 1660. Cond. for "the plot." d. Tyburn, May 9

Bl. Thomas Whitbread (alias Harcourt and Harcott), priest; b. Essex; educ. St. Omer; adm. SJ 1635; Engl. miss., 1647–78; Jesuit provincial. Cond. for "the plot." d. Tyburn, June 20

Bl. William Harcourt (alias Waring, *vere* Barrow), priest; b. Weeton-cum-Prees, Kirkham, Lancs.; educ. St. Omer; adm. SJ 1632; Engl. miss., 1645–78, London. Cond. for "the plot." d. Tyburn, June 20

Bl. John Fenwick (*vere* Caldwell), priest; b. Durham; educ. St. Omer; adm. SJ 1656. Cond. for "the plot." d. Tyburn, June 20

Bl. John Gavan, priest; b. London; educ. St. Omer; adm. SJ 1660; Engl. miss., 1671, Staffs. Cond. for "the plot." d. Tyburn, June 20

Bl. Antony Turner, priest; b. Dalby Parva, near Melton Mowbray, Leicester; educ. Cambridge; after conversion, Rome; adm. SJ 1653; Engl. miss., 1661–78, Worcester. Cond. for "the plot." d. Tyburn, June 20

Bl. Richard Langhorne, layman; b. Bedford; educ. Inner Temple; barrister; called to Bar 1654. Cond. for "the plot." d. Tyburn, July 14

St. John (or William) Plessington (Pleasington; alias Scarisbrick), sem. priest; b. Dimples, near Garstang, Lancs.; educ. Scarisbrick School; Valladolid; Engl. miss., Cheshire. Cond. for priesthood. d. Chester, July 19

St. Philip Evans, priest; b. Monmouth; educ. St. Omer; adm. SJ 1665; Welsh miss. Cond. for priesthood. d. Cardiff, July 22

St. John Lloyd, sem. priest; b. Brecknocks; educ. Valladolid; Welsh miss. Cond. for priesthood. d. Cardiff, July 22

Bl. Nicholas Postgate (alias Watson and Whitemore), sem. priest; b. Egton, N.R. Yorks.; educ. Douai; ord. 1628; Engl. miss., Ugthorpe, etc., 50 years. Cond. for priesthood. d. York, August 7

Bl. Charles Meehan, priest; b. in Ireland; Irish Province, OFM; arrested in Wales on way to Ireland. Cond. for priesthood. d. Ruthin, August 12

St. John Wall (alias Francis Webb and Johnson), priest; b. Chingle Hall, Wittingham, Lancs.; educ. Douai; Rome; adm. OSF 1651 (Father Joachim of St. Ann); Engl. miss., Worcester 1656–79. Cond. for priesthood. d. Worcester, August 22

St. John Kemble (alias Holland), sem. priest; b. Pembridge(?), Hereford; educ. Douai; Engl. miss.,1625–79, Hereford. Cond. for priesthood. d. Hereford, August 22

St. David Lewis (alias Charles Baker), priest; b. Abergavenny, Monmouths; educ. Abergavenny G.S.; convert; Rome; adm. SJ 1645; miss., S. Wales, 31 years. Cond. for priesthood. d. Usk, August 27

1680

Ven. Francis Leveson, priest; b. Willenhall, Staffs.; adm. OSF 1664 (Father Ignatius of St. Clare). Arrested for "the plot." Died in prison, Worcester, February 11

Bl. Thomas Thwing (Thweng), sem. priest; b. Heworth, N.R. Yorks.; educ. St. Omer; Douai; ord. 1665; Engl. miss., Yorks., 15 years. Cond. for "the plot." d. York, October 23

Bl. William Howard, Viscount Stafford, layman; grandson of St. Philip HOWARD; b. Strand, London, 1611; married; convert. Cond. for "the plot." Beheaded. d. Tower Hill, December 29

The "Dilati"

Robert Dimock, layman, died in prison, Lincoln, 1580

John Cooper, layman, died in prison, London, 1580

William Tyrwhit, layman, died in prison, London, 1580

William Chaplain, sem. priest, died in prison, place unknown, 1583

Thomas Cotesmore, sem. priest, died in prison, place unknown, 1584

Robert Holmes, sem. priest, died in prison, place unknown, 1584

Roger Wakeman, sem. priest, died in prison, London, 1584

James Lomax, sem. priest, died in prison, place unknown, 1584

Mr. Ailworth, layman, died in prison, London, 1584

Thomas Crowther, sem. priest, died in prison, Southwark, 1585

Edward Pole, sem. priest, died in prison, London, 1585

Laurence Vaux, priest, Can. Reg., died in prison, London, 1585

John Jetter, sem. priest, died in prison, London, 1585

John Harrison, sem. priest, died in prison, place unknown, 1587

Martin Sherson, sem. priest, died in prison, place unknown, 1587

Gabriel Thimelby, layman, died in prison, place unknown, 1587

Thomas Metham, priest, SJ, died in prison, Wisbeach, 1592

James Atkinson, layman, died from torture, London, 1595

Matthew Harrison, sem. priest, executed, York, 1599

Eleanor Hunt, widow, died in prison, York, 1600

Mrs. Swithun Wells, widow, died in prison, London, 1602

Henry Garnet, priest, SJ, executed, London, 1606

John Mawson, layman, executed, Tyburn, 1614

Edward Wilkes, sem. priest, died in prison, York, 1642

Boniface Kemp, priest, OSB, died in prison, Yorkshire, 1642

Ildephonse Hesketh, priest, OSB, died in prison, Yorkshire, 1642

Thomas Vaughan, sem. priest, died in prison, Cardiff, probably 1644

Richard Bradley, priest, SJ, died in prison, Manchester, 1646

John Felton, priest, SJ, died in prison, Lincoln, 1646

Thomas Blount, sem. priest, died in prison, Shrewsbury, probably 1646

Robert Cox, priest, OSB, died in prison, Southwark, 1650

Laurence Hill, layman, executed, Tyburn, 1679

Robert Green, layman, executed, Tyburn, 1679

Thomas Jenison, priest, SJ, died in prison, London, 1679

William Lloyd, sem. priest, died in prison, Brecknock, 1679

Placid Adelham, priest, OSB, died in prison, London, 1680

Richard Birkett, sem., SJ, died in prison, Lancaster, 1680

Richard Lacy, priest, SJ, died in prison, London, 1680

William Atkins, priest, SJ, died in prison, Stafford, 1681

Edward Turner, priest, SJ, died in prison, London, 1681

William Allison, sem. priest, died in prison, York, 1681

Benedict Constable, priest, OSB, died in prison, Durham, 1683

William Bennet, priest, SJ, died in prison, Leicester, 1692

For additional information on martyrs see individual entries.

Bibliography: *The Catholic Martyrs of England and Wales* (London 1985). *L'Osservatore Romano,* English edition, no. 44, (1987): 6–7; no. 48, (1987): 6. R. CHALLONER, *Memoirs of Missionary Priests,* ed. J. H. POLLEN (rev. ed. London 1924; repr. Farnborough 1969). B. CAMM, *Nine Martyr Monks* (London 1931); ed., *Lives of the English Martyrs,* 2 v. (New York 1904–05). P. CARAMAN, *Henry Garnet, 1555–1606, and the Gunpowder Plot* (New York 1965). M. L. CARRAFIELLO, *Robert Parsons and English Catholicism, 1580–1610* (London 1998); *The Catholic Martyrs of England and Wales* (London 1985). P. COLLINSON and J. CRAIG, eds., *The Reformation in English Towns, 1500–1640* (New York 1998). *Acts of the Privy Council* (London 1890–1907). S. DORAN, *Princes, Pastors, and People: The Church and Religion in England, 1529–1689* (London 1991). M. J. DORCY, ''Ven. Robert Nutter,'' *St. Dominic's Family* (Dubuque, Ia. 1964), 341–342. T. P. ELLIS, *The Catholic Martyrs of Wales* (London 1933). Douai, English College, *The First and Second Diaries of the English College Douai,* ed. Fathers of the Congregation of the London Oratory (London 1878). The remaining College Diaries are published by the Catholic Record Society. G. R. ELTON, *Policy and Police: The Enforcement of the Reformation in the Age of Thomas Cromwell* (Cambridge 1972). D. FLYNN, *John Donne and the Ancient Catholic Nobility* (Bloomington, Ind. 1995). H. FOLEY, *Records of the English Province of the Society of Jesus,* 7 v. (London 1877–82). J. FOSTER, *Alumni Oxonienses* (Oxford 1892); *Glover's Visitation of Yorkshire* [London (privately printed), 1875]. J. GIBBONS, *Concertatio Ecclesiae Catholicae in Anglia adversus Calvinpapistas et Puritanos,* ed., M. ROGERS (1588, reprint, Farnborough 1970). GILLOW, *Biblical Dictictionary of English Catholicism,* 5 v. (London and New York 1885–1902). C. HAIGH, *Reformation and Resistance in Tudor Lancashire* (London 1975). F. HEAL & R. O'DAY, eds. *Church and Society in England: Henry VIII to James I,* (London 1977). L. HENDRIKS, *London Charterhouse: Its Monks and Its Martyrs* (London 1889). KNOX, *First and Second Diaries of English College, Douai* (London 1878). D. M. LOADES, *The Oxford Martyrs,* 2 ed. (Bangor, Gwynedd 1992). P. MARSHALL, *The Catholic Priesthood and the English Reformation* (Oxford 1994). T. M. MCCOOG, *The Society of Jesus in Ireland, Scotland, and England: 1541–1588* (New York 1996). J. MORRIS, ed., *The Troubles of Our Catholic Forefathers Related by Themselves,* 3 v. (London 1872–77); *The Catholics of York under Elizabeth* (London 1891). J. H. POLLEN, *Acts of the English Martyrs* (London 1891); *English Martyrs 1584–1683 in Catholic Record Society,* 5 v. (London 1908); *The English Catholics in the Reign of Queen Elizabeth . . . ,* 2nd ed. (New York 1971). M. STANTON, *Menology of England and Wales* (London 1887). J. THADDEUS, *The Franciscans in England 1600– 1859,* 15 v. (London 1898). E. M. THOMPSON, *The Carthusian Order in England* (New York 1930). M. TODD, ed., *Reformation to Revolution: Politics and Religion in Early Modern England* (London 1995). J. N. TYLENDA, *Jesuit Saints & Martyrs* (Chicago 1998), 16–17; 27–32; 65–69; 87–95; 138–40; 155–56; 175–81; 189–92; 198–99; 216–17; 266–70; 288–89; 415–21; 440–42. S. UNDSET, *Stages on the Road,* tr. by A. WALSHAM, *Church Papists: Catholicism, Conformity, and Confessional Polemic in Early Modern England* (Rochester, N.Y. 1993). J. WALSH, *Forty Martyrs of England and Wales* (London 1972). E. I. WATKIN, *Roman Catholicism in England* (New York 1957). WATSON, *Decacordon of Ten Quodlibet Questions* (1602). W. WESTON, *An Autobiography from the Jesuit Underground,* translated by L. E. WHATMORE, *Blessed Carthusian Martyrs* (London 1962). R. WHITING, *Local Responses to the English Reformation* (New York 1998). D. DE YEPES, *Historia Particular de la persecución de Inglaterra* (Madrid 1599).

[P. CARAMAN/EDS.]

ENGLAND, THE CATHOLIC CHURCH IN

One of several kingdoms comprising the United Kingdom of Great Britain and Northern Ireland, England is situated on the largest island in Europe. Bordered on the north by Scotland, on the west by Wales, the Irish

Sea, and the island of Ireland, and on the east by the North Sea, England is separated from France and the European mainland by the English Channel. One of the world' major industrial powers, and with a maritime fleet second to none during the 18th and 19th centuries, England divested itself of its colonial holdings during the early 20th century and has since become a modern nation and a member of the European Union. Although retaining political control of Scotland, Wales, and Northern Ireland, the British parliament granted each of these principalities increasing degrees of political self-determination by the end of the 20th century.

The essay that follows covers the history of Catholicism in England from A.D. 597 to the present. For information specific to Scotland, Wales, or Northern Ireland, please refer to those entries. For information on the Church in England prior to 597, see the entry, BRITAIN, THE EARLY CHURCH IN.

[EDS.]

Capital: London.
Size: 50,333 sq. miles.
Population: 52,563,500 in 2000.
Language: English.
Religions: 4,730,715 Catholics (9%), 25,756,115 Anglicans (49%), 2,102,540 Methodist (4%), 262,000 Sikh (.5%), 270,800 Hindu (.5%), 260,550 Jewish (.5%), 394,230 other (7.5%), 18,786,550 without religious affiliation.

English history before the Reformation can be divided into three epochs, the first of which is a period of conversion or plantation (7th–8th centuries). After almost a century of wars, shifting political boundaries, and Danish invasion, a second period began with Alfred the Great, in which civil and ecclesiastical organization interpenetrated and in which the fortunes of the Church depended greatly upon the king. Finally, during the period from the Conquest onward, the Church in England was drawn into the administrative network of the reformed papacy. From being an outlying part of Christendom in communion with the apostolic see, it became a regional Church (*ecclesia Anglicana*) like all the other churches of Europe, forming part of a unitary system that depended directly upon the papacy for its doctrine, legislation, and discipline.

597 to 880. When GREGORY I became pope all England, save the Cornish coast, was pagan. Christianity had been driven, with the British, into Wales. In Ireland, however, a flourishing Christian population was evangelizing the western isles of Scotland; Wales was also Christian, but the Celtic Church had made no attempt to convert the Anglo-Saxon invaders. Had Gregory not sent AUGUSTINE OF CANTERBURY, Christianity would probably have spread slowly from the north over England; as it was, there was an almost simultaneous entry from north and from south.

While successful at the court of King ETHELBERT OF KENT, the mission of Augustine failed to expand beyond London and south Essex, and a meeting with British ecclesiastics near the Severn failed to achieve a union. After Augustine's death, one of his companions, PAULINUS OF YORK, was sent as bishop to evangelize the north. Having converted the king of the Northumbrians, Paulinus preached and baptized in Lindsey, near York, and as far north as Yeavering in Northumberland. At retirement he left numerous converts, but not an organized church. In East Anglia, the Burgundian Felix of Dunwich and the Irishman FURSEY had more permanent success, and in Wessex BIRINUS founded a church in the upper Thames Valley. Where Paulinus had failed, AIDAN from Iona and his companions succeeded; within 20 years a flourishing Church with Celtic traditions and culture had extended its influence to Mercia in the north Midlands. A clash between the Roman and Celtic traditions was inevitable; while no doctrinal issue was at stake, points of ritual and discipline, including the date of Easter, as well as differences of sentiment, devotions, and ascetic ideals caused disagreement. Union was effected at a debate held at WHITBY in 663, and the victory on disputed points lay with the Roman party, ably represented by WILFRID; but Celtic sanctity, personified by CUTHBERT OF LINDISFARNE, permanently influenced Northumbrian religious sentiment.

Meanwhile England was becoming Christian. The faith was spread and maintained by groups of monks and clergy, living in ''minsters'' and preaching and ministering at crosses and other landmarks before founding churches, which in time became parishes. Monasteries of men and women of the Gallic pattern multiplied, with saintly abbesses such as HILDA OF WHITBY and ETHELREDA OF ELY and hermits such as GUTHLAC OF CROWLAND. A period of loose organization ended with the papal appointment to Canterbury of the elderly Greek monk THEODORE, who, assisted by the African monk HADRIAN, reformed the church, founding new sees and giving it new laws and discipline. Schools began to flourish, and ALDHELM OF MALMESBURY was the first writer. At the same time, the Northumbrian BENEDICT BISCOP took Roman ritual and chant and Benedictine monachism to Jarrow and Wearmouth, where a remarkable flowering of literary and artistic activity was crowned by the writings of BEDE and the calligraphy and illuminations of the LINDISFARNE GOSPELS. The generation following Bede saw a great exodus of missionaries, men and women, from

Metropolitan Sees	Suffragans
Westminster	Brentwood, Northampton, East Anglia, Nottingham
Birmingham	Clifton and Shrewsbury
Liverpool	Hexham and Newcastle, Lancaster, Hallam, Leeds, Middlesbrough, and Salford
Southwark	Plymouth, Portsmouth, Arundel and Brighton.

Northumbrian and Wessex monasteries to Frisia and Germany, with St. BONIFACE of Devon as their chief. The great age of the Anglo-Saxon Church continued in Mercia under Offa and flourished in the north and south till the end of the 8th century, and had its share, through ALCUIN and others, in forming the spirit of the CAROLINGIAN RENAISSANCE.

880 to 1066. The continuity of development was broken from 780 onward by the Danish invasions, which increased in number and strength until the Danes ultimately controlled England north and east of Watling Street. Though Christianity was never exterminated, and the whole of the Danelaw soon became Christian, the country had been shaken and ravaged, and the culture of the past did not return. ALFRED THE GREAT (871–899) inherited a kingdom without schools or monasteries, making the period of recovery slow. A new era of prosperity dawned during the mid-10th century, when the ability and piety of King Athelstan, the patronage of King EDGAR, and the emergence of a trio of saintly and able monk-bishops, DUNSTAN, ETHELWOLD, and OSWALD OF YORK, led to a great rebirth of piety. It issued in and was assisted by a monastic revival on a large scale, leading to the foundation of some 40 houses of men and women, including three cathedrals staffed by monks. A revival of educational, literary, and artistic activity accompanied the monastic movement. This revival owed nothing to Roman or Continental initiative, and though England was traditionally devoted to Rome, the only direct links were the reception of the PALLIUM by each archbishop of Canterbury, the collection of PETER'S PENCE, and frequent pilgrimages to Rome.

In this period civil and ecclesiastical affairs were closely interwoven. Bishops and abbots were members of the royal council or witenagemot, which, presided over by the king, elected bishops, judged important cases, and framed laws on moral and ecclesiastical matters. Bishops would publish their decrees in the shire court, where ecclesiastical as well as civil justice was administered, and were appointed by the king on the advice of the witan.

England was now wholly Christianized, and every village had its church. Yet, as on the Continent, the PROPRIETARY CHURCH was ubiquitous. Parish and field churches as well as domestic chapels were almost all the property of an individual, lay or cleric, or of a monastery, and in the towns they were often owned by a group of burgesses. Everywhere the priest was appointed by the owner. The dioceses, uneven in size and ill-defined, were usually large, preventing bishops from regular contact with their clergy and faithful. While the decadence of the Church remains a debated question, England in the middle decades of the 11th century was certainly an educational and disciplinary (though not an artistic) backwater.

1066 to 1216. The Norman Conquest marked an epoch, not least because it coincided with a great crisis in the history of the Western Church. Its immediate result was to give England, in William the Conqueror and in his archbishop, LANFRANC, two able and energetic men of wide outlook, bent on order and reform. A long-term result was the integration of England into the cultural and religious community of Europe, sharing in and eventually adding to the spiritual and institutional developments of the age. Within 20 years of the Conquest almost all the bishops and abbots were Normans, as were many monks and leading clerks. A great wave of building activity began and cathedrals, abbeys, and parish churches were renewed on a grand scale. After a few decades the new or rejuvenated orders—Austin canons, CISTERCIANS, PREMONSTRATENSIANS, and the native GILBERTINES—were ubiquitous. The number of religious houses, 60 in 1066, had risen to some 600 by 1166. Councils and synods were held, cathedral schools came into existence, the study and observance of Canon Law became common, and canonical episcopal election was recognized as a norm. The Church in England was enriched by men from the Continent, such as the Italians Lanfranc, ANSELM, Faricius of Abingdon (d. 1117), and Vacarius, as well as the French THEOBALD OF CANTERBURY and William of Rievaulx. Those of Norman blood included Gilbert FOLIOT and Thomas BECKET. England returned the obligation with Pope ADRIAN IV (Breakspear), STEPHEN HARDING, JOHN OF SALISBURY, and many others. Lanfranc, above all others, proved himself a great archbishop by establishing metropolitan rights over Wales and attaining similar, although temporary, successes in Ireland and Scotland. Ecclesiastical history, biography, and spiritual writing flourished with EADMER, ORDERICUS VITALIS, WILLIAM OF MALMESBURY, and AELRED of Rievaulx; after an interval, sculpture and illumination flourished also.

The wise rule of WILLIAM I changed to a rough autocracy under WILLIAM II, and Anselm was twice con-

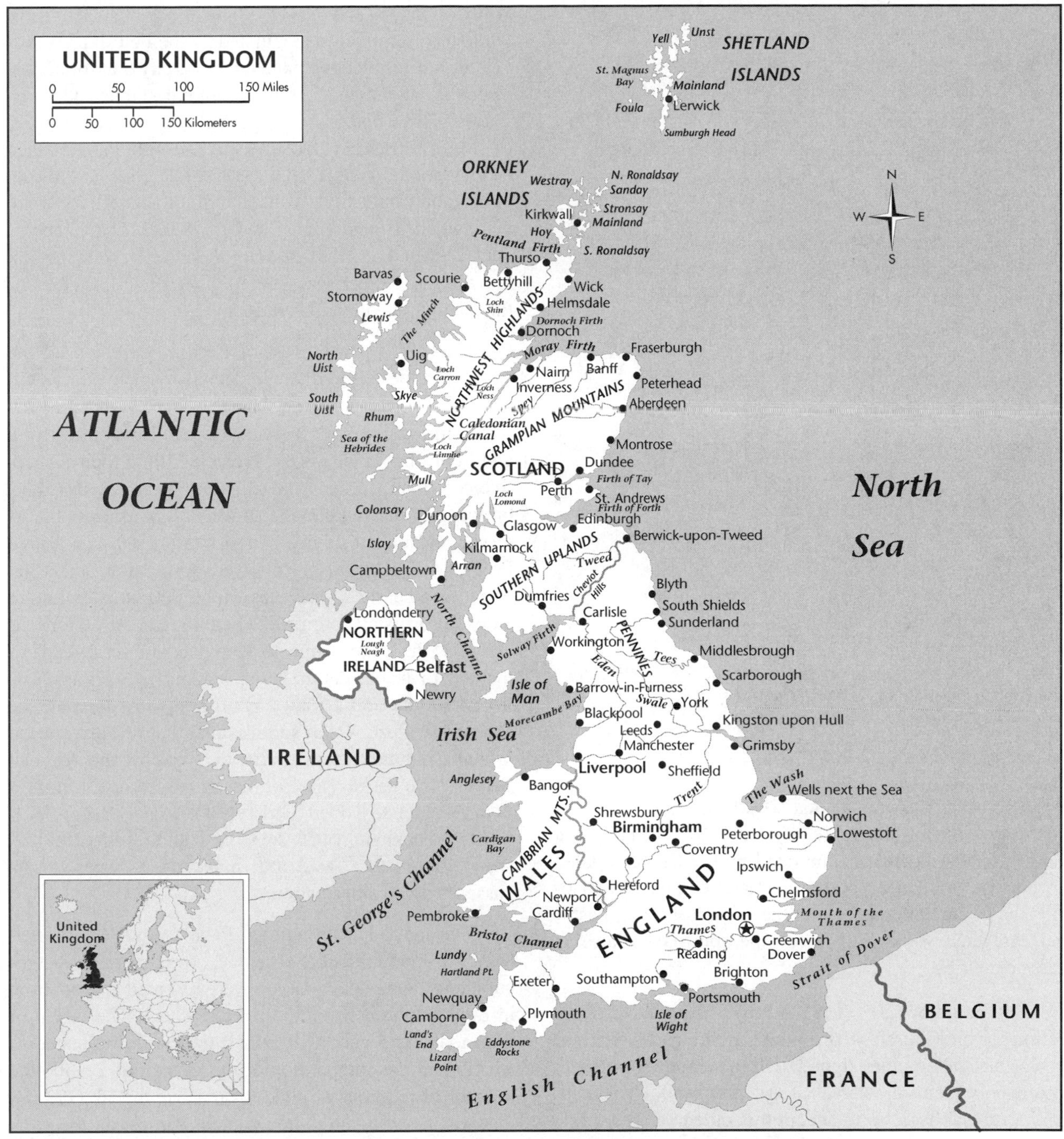

strained to become an exile before a compromise was arranged with Henry I as to the royal appointment of bishops. Tensions existed for the rest of the century between the king endeavoring to retain or reassert the rights exercised by his predecessors and the bishops insisting upon adherence to the new discipline and Canon Law of the GREGORIAN REFORM. Tension flared into conflict when HENRY II, after the eclipse of royal power under King Stephen, attempted to reassert royal control over the Church and over criminal justice in regard to clerks. Archbishop Thomas Becket, after repeated clashes and a long exile in France, was murdered in his cathedral on his return in 1170.

Among the most important social consequences of the Norman Conquest was the feudalization of the Church, which gave bishops and greater abbots liability for feudal dues and military service, while also making them members of the king's council, the body that devel-

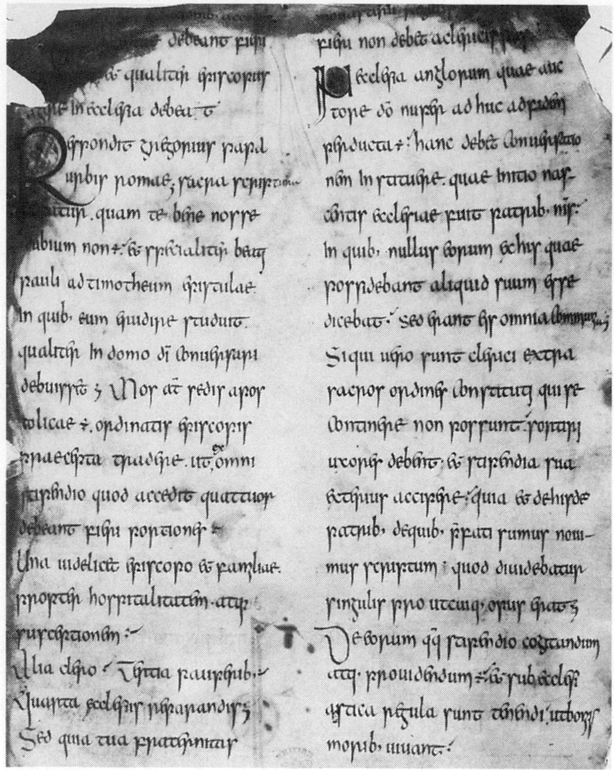

A page from a late 8th-century manuscript of Bede's ''Historia Ecclesiastica Gentis Anglorum.'' The text (from Bk. 2, ch. 1) deals with Augustine's request for a mission to Christianize England.

oped into the Parliament that would become a national institution during the reign of Henry III. Feudalization and the great wealth accumulated by the Church tended to both secularize the prelates concerned and give bishops the double allegiance and the separation from pastoral care that would help cause the spiritual malaise of later centuries.

The reign of JOHN (1199–1216) was a time of tribulation for the Church. A disputed Canterbury election, in which a royal nominee figured, led to an appeal to Rome, the appointment of STEPHEN LANGTON by INNOCENT III, and a refusal by John to accept this outcome. There followed excommunication for the king and an interdict for the country. Even if the miseries of this episode have been exaggerated, it led to the dispersal of some monks, the exile of bishops, and the impoverishment of religious houses at the hands of the king. John's unexpected death brought relaxation, and Pandulf and other papal legates were a harmonizing and reforming influence during the decades that followed.

The Church's Golden Age: 1216–1350. The 13th century was indeed the golden age of the medieval Church in England. Its freedom was guaranteed by the MAGNA CARTA and respected by the pious Henry III, while its discipline was regulated by the Fourth LATERAN COUNCIL. Free election gave it a hierarchy that for almost a century maintained a high level of enlightened administration. Three bishops—Richard of Chichester, EDMUND OF ABINGDON, and THOMAS OF CANTELUPE—attained canonization; ROBERT KILWARDBY, OP; JOHN PECKHAM, OFM; and ROBERT WINCHELSEA, all of Canterbury, were distinguished theologians; and the bench of bishops of which ROBERT GROSSETESTE of Lincoln was the acknowledged leader was perhaps the most illustrious of the English medieval Church.

England, with the rest of Europe, experienced the coming of the friars in the 3d decade of the century. Minors (FRANCISCANS) and Preachers (DOMINICANS) arrived almost simultaneously, settling in London, Oxford, and in all the major towns. Welcomed into their respective communities, they preached and heard confessions, bringing to the middle and lower orders an example of fervor and expert advice. The CARMELITES and Austin Friars (AUGUSTINIANS) followed soon after; by 1300 there were nearly 200 friaries with 5,000 inmates, and in a dozen towns all four orders had houses. At Oxford, as at Paris, the friars came to learn and to serve and remained to teach. As at Paris, leading masters such as ADAM MARSH and ROGER BACON joined their ranks; the fame of Oxford, which soon rivaled that of Paris, rested principally upon them, particularly upon the Minors. Britain gave its full share of masters to Europe: ALEXANDER OF HALES, Robert Grosseteste, Roger Bacon, Kilwardby, Peckham, DUNS SCOTUS, WILLIAM OF OCKHAM, and THOMAS BRADWARDINE make up a series unsurpassed by any other nation.

The age had its difficulties. Papal PROVISION to benefices, the appointment of absentee, foreign, or pluralist incumbents, and papal taxation were resented and opposed in England more strongly than elsewhere. The fervor of the monks and canons declined under the influence of wealth and the competition of the friars, but *c.* 1300 the number of religious of all kinds reached a peak (17,000) that was never again to be attained. Almost all the great abbeys and cathedrals were again reconstructed in part. SALISBURY, built on a virgin site in a single impulse, and WESTMINSTER ABBEY, rebuilt and decorated in the French style, are typical monuments of the purest Gothic.

The rhythm of prosperity slackened in the early 14th century under the influence of economic recession, war, and, in 1348, the Black Death, followed by further visits of pestilence. Clashes between Parliament and Church over papal taxation and provision were sparked by the statutes of PROVISORS (1351) and PRAEMUNIRE (1353), the latter in origin simply a deterrent to clerical appeals to Rome. Earlier still the Statute of MORTMAIN had controlled the engrossing of feudal land by monasteries. In the matter of elections, a compromise was reached by which the canonical body elected a royal nominee, who was then approved and provided by the pope.

1350 to 1485. The 14th century saw the rise of vernacular literature and lay piety. English mystical writers Richard ROLLE (d. 1349), the unknown author of *The Cloud of Unknowing* (*c.* 1375), Walter HILTON (d. 1396), JULIAN OF NORWICH (1342–1416?), and their contemporary, William Langland, to whom *PIERS PLOWMAN* is attributed, all stressed in their different but wholly orthodox ways an individual and uninstitutional spirituality. The same epoch saw a direct attack upon the organized Church, its riches and its claims to special powers and rights. The spokesman of this party was John WYCLIF, a master of Oxford, who, opening with an academic debate on the right of the Church to wealth, went on to attack sacramental and sacerdotal religion and to advocate vernacular preaching and Bible reading. His denial of TRANSUBSTANTIATION and his other heterodox opinions were condemned, though Wyclif himself died unmolested. Externally, the English Church, with its clergy reduced by pestilence, suffered with the rest of Europe the trials of the WESTERN SCHISM which accentuated the insularity already caused by the French war. Among the centralized religious orders the links with European administration were permanently weakened, while many of the ''alien priories'' became denizen, and others were permanently confiscated and their estates transferred to other orders or royal colleges. No new monasteries were founded save a small but fervent group of CARTHUSIAN priories, but colleges of priests and large chantries became popular forms of pious benefaction, as were educational colleges at Oxford and Cambridge. William of WYKEHAM's double foundation at Winchester and New College were notable examples of the trend. In the early 15th century English prelates played a considerable part at the Councils of CONSTANCE and BASEL, but the clergy emerged from the epoch of CONCILIARISM conservative in its attitude toward the papacy. Henry V was characteristic of his country in his severe and orthodox piety, of which SHEEN CHARTERHOUSE and the Bridgettine SYON gave evidence. The century that opened with his reign was perhaps the least distinguished in the history of the English Church. It was as unaffected by the brilliance and paganism of the Italian Renaissance as it was untroubled by the birth pangs of revolution. The DEVOTIO MODERNA of Flanders had no counterpart in England. The administration of the Church was conducted efficiently but mechanically by a group of functionaries in each diocese, who could, when needed, perform all duties for an absentee bishop. Formalism was more ubiquitous than moral laxity or official neglect. The brooding anticlericalism and religious indifference were due to resentment that the higher clergy existed only to judge, to amerce, and to tax. Royal munificence continued to fund great architecture as at Windsor and at King's College, Cambridge, while rich merchants showed their devotion in the churches of Somerset, Gloucestershire, and Suffolk.

Danes invading East Anglia in St. Edmund's reign, illumination in an 11th-century manuscript of ''Life of Saint Edmund,'' written and illuminated probably at the abbey of Bury-St.-Edmunds.

Bibliography: D. WILKINS, *Concilia Magnae Britanniae et Hiberniae,* 4 v. (London 1737, new ed.). A. W. HADDAN and W. STUBBS, eds., *Councils and Ecclesiastical Documents relating to Great Britain and Ireland,* 3 v. in 4 (Oxford 1869–78). F. M. POWICKE and E. B. FRYDE, eds., *Handbook of British Chronology* (2d ed. London 1961). M. DEANESLY, *The Pre-Conquest Church in England* (New York 1961—). *Victoria History of the Counties of England* (London 1900—). BEDE, *Ecclesiastical History,* ed. C. PLUMMER, 2 v. (Oxford 1896). A. H. THOMPSON, ed., *Bede, His Life, Times, and Writings* (Oxford 1935). S. J. CRAWFORD, *Anglo-Saxon Influence on Western Christendom, 600–800* (London 1933). W. LEVISON, *England and the Continent in the 8th Century* (Oxford 1946). MOE. F. BARLOW, *The English Church 1000–1066: A Consti-*

Edward I of England in council with his bishops, illuminated page from a 14th-century manuscript.

tutional History (Hamden, CT 1963). Z. N. BROOKE, *The English Church and the Papacy from the Conquest to the Reign of John* (Cambridge, Eng. 1931). J. R. H. MOORMAN, *Church Life in England in the 13th Century* (Cambridge, Eng. 1945). W. A. PANTIN, *The English Church in the 14th Century* (Cambridge, Eng. 1955). É. PERROY, *L'Angleterre et le grand schisme d'Occident* (Paris 1934). G. R. OWST, *Preaching in Medieval England* (Cambridge, Eng. 1926). A. H. THOMPSON, *The English Clergy and Their Organization in the Later Middle Ages* (Oxford 1947).

[M. D. KNOWLES]

The Early Tudors: 1485 to 1558. The establishment of the Tudor dynasty under its first ruler, Henry VII (1485–1509), introduced a period of strong government and increasing peace and prosperity. This situation was rudely disturbed by the revolt of the king's son, HENRY VIII (1509–47), against the authority of the Catholic Church. During his early years of rule, Henry entrusted the affairs of the Church in England to the hands of Thomas WOLSEY, Lord Chancellor, archbishop of York, and papal legate. The failure of CATHERINE OF ARAGON to present Henry with a male heir and his increasing infatuation with Anne Boleyn led Henry to seek an annulment of his marriage on the grounds that the dispensation that had permitted him to marry his brother's widow had been obtained on false pretenses. Henry's inability to prove his case before a legatine court at Blackfriars, London, presided over by Wolsey and the Roman cardinal, CAMPEGGIO, in 1529, brought on the fall of Wolsey and a successful attempt to subject the Church in England to the king's will.

In 1531, under the threat of PRAEMUNIRE, the bishops recognized the king as ''Supreme Head of the Church in England,'' with the qualifying clause—''insofar as the law of Christ allows''—soon disregarded. In 1532 the clergy virtually abdicated their authority by their submission to the king's demand for a radical revision of Canon Law. On the death of Abp. Warham of Canterbury in this same year, Henry secured the appointment of Thomas CRANMER, already a convinced Protestant, as his successor. Even before Cranmer, at the king's behest, declared the marriage to Catherine null and void, Henry married Anne Boleyn, who in September 1533 gave birth to a daughter, the future Queen ELIZABETH I.

The Statute in Restraint of Appeals of 1532 prevented any appeal to Rome against the judgment of the archbishop's court. Other statutes established the royal supremacy, secured the succession of Elizabeth, and made it treason to deprive the king of any of his titles or dignities. Between the years 1534–45 all who refused to take an oath to accept the supremacy were destroyed, among them Thomas MORE, who had succeeded Wolsey as chancellor; John FISHER, the saintly bishop of Rochester; and a group of Carthusians and Observant friars. In 1535 Henry began to exploit his ecclesiastical authority by a general visitation and valuation of the Church, which soon led to the suppression of the lesser monasteries. The king's agent and vicar-general in the business was Thomas CROMWELL, who had for some time been managing Parliament in Henry's interest.

Henry's treatment of the Church and the fear of worse to come sparked the PILGRIMAGE OF GRACE (1536–37), a rising in the northern counties led by the lawyer, Robert ASKE. The Pilgrimage was at once a protest against the king's marriage, the heretic bishops, the threat to the monasteries, and the repudiation of papal authority. Deceived by royal promises, the rebels dispersed, and Henry took a terrible vengeance. By 1540 every religious house in the country had been suppressed and taken into the king's hands.

Up to this point, apart from rejecting papal authority, Henry had made few innovations in doctrine. Lutheran ideas entered the country with TYNDALE's translation of the New Testament (1526) and COVERDALE's English Bible (1535). The Ten Articles of Religion published in 1536 introduced the Protestant doctrine of justification by faith only, but an official statement of doctrine appearing in 1543, the ''Necessary Erudition of a Christian Man,'' commonly known as the ''King's Book,'' was generally orthodox in tone. Until his death in January 1547, Henry kept strict control over belief in England. The situation was to change dramatically under his son and successor.

The Protestant Edward VI (1547–53) was a child of nine at his succession. Archbishop Cranmer was for the first time free to introduce principles of reform that had long been maturing in his mind. A new ritual, the Order of Communion, appeared in 1548. In January 1549 the Act of Uniformity imposed on the country a new form of worship in the first *BOOK OF COMMON PRAYER*, which preserved the form of the Mass in English, but from which all expressions had been removed that suggested the idea of sacrifice. The attempt to impose this prayer book led to a revolt in the western counties that was ruthlessly suppressed by the government. The first *Book of Common Prayer* was something of a compromise. In 1552 Cranmer produced a more radical edition in which all traces of belief in the sacrifice of the Mass and also of the Real Presence in the Eucharist were absent. An official statement of the new religion, the 42 Articles, appeared in 1553 and was approved by the young king shortly before his death.

The short reign of Edward's sister MARY TUDOR (1553–58) saw a temporary restoration of the Catholic faith and a sharp persecution of the Protestants. One of Mary's first acts was to repeal the religious legislation of the previous reign, but she alienated the sympathy of her people by her marriage to PHILIP II of Spain. Only when the marriage had taken place was Cardinal Reginald POLE, the papal legate, allowed to enter the country and, after receiving the solemn submission of Parliament, to reconcile the nation to the Catholic Church. Mary honorably, but unwisely, attempted to make some restoration to the Church and thereby further antagonized the holders of monastic lands. Finally, in January 1555, the heresy laws were revived, and in the course of the next three years nearly 300 persons, among them Archbishop Cranmer and four other bishops, were burned at the stake as heretics. Many of the leading Protestants had already fled the country and taken refuge in the Protestant cities of Geneva, Frankfurt, Zurich, and Strasbourg, to prepare for the inevitable reaction in England under Mary's successor.

The Reign of Elizabeth: 1558 to 1603. On Nov. 17, 1558, Mary Tudor was succeeded by her half sister, Elizabeth, daughter of Henry VIII and Anne Boleyn. Elizabeth's true religious convictions are a mystery, but from the first she saw clearly that her advantage lay with the party of reform, now reinforced by the returning exiles. A new religious settlement was inevitable, and it was effected in the first Parliament of the reign, which met in January 1559. By the Act of UNIFORMITY, passed in spite

Obverse of the great seal of Edward III of England.

of the protests of the bishops and of the CONVOCATION of the clergy, the second Prayer Book of Edward VI was restored with some slight modifications as the official form of public worship. By the Act of Supremacy, Elizabeth as ''Supreme Governor'' recovered control of the Church.

Bishops who refused to take the oath of supremacy were deprived of their sees and jailed. Those of the clergy who refused to accept the Prayer Book were punished by fines and imprisonment. The laity were commanded under penalty of a fine of 12 pence to attend the Protestant service in their parish churches each Sunday. In 1563 these penalties were increased; a second refusal of the oath was made treason, punishable by death. Royal commissioners toured the country to receive the submission of the clergy. Those who refused to submit were deprived; others went into hiding or exile; but the majority conformed, at least externally, and with this submission the government was for a time satisfied. The general religious situation in the country in the next few years is obscure; many Catholics, particularly in the north,

Anti-Catholic activity during the reign of Edward VI, woodcut from the 1610 edition of Foxe's "Acts and Monuments of the Christian Martyrs."

continued to practice their faith in secret, and there was little overt persecution. After 1568 the situation changed rapidly due to two series of events.

The first was the Northern Rising, an attempt to secure the eventual succession to the English throne of the Catholic MARY STUART, queen of Scots. Led by the Catholic earls of Westmorland and Northumberland, the rising was a disastrous failure and provoked the first executions. In the following year PIUS V was persuaded to support the resistance by issuing the bull, *Regnans in excelsis,* in which he excommunicated Elizabeth as a heretic and supporter of heretics and released her subjects from their allegiance. The effect of the bull was to sharpen the penal laws.

The second event was the arrival in the country in 1574 of the first missionary priests from the English College founded in 1568 at DOUAI by William ALLEN, formerly principal of St. Mary's Hall, Oxford, and a group of English Catholic exiles. The remarkable success of these missionary priests, who from 1580 were supported by a small group of Jesuits led by Edmund CAMPION, alarmed the government. An act of 1581 made it treason to reconcile any of the queen's subjects ''from the religion now by Her Highness' authority established,'' and a further act of 1585 commanded all Jesuits and seminary priests to depart the realm within 40 days under penalty of death.

But nothing could arrest the movement of Catholic revival. Before the end of the reign new seminaries for English students were founded at Rome, Lisbon, Madrid, Seville, and Valladolid. In the course of these years, 189 persons were put to death for the faith in England, among them 111 secular priests and 62 lay men and women. The persecution was further sharpened by the threat of the Spanish Armada in 1588. The toll of the martyrs is the measure of the strength of Catholic resistance to the Protestant government at the end of the century (*see* ENGLAND, SCOTLAND, AND WALES, MARTYRS OF).

The position of English Catholics was weakened in the last years of Elizabeth's reign by serious divisions within the ranks of the clergy. After the death of Thomas Goldwell, the last of the deposed Catholic bishops, in 1585 and of Cardinal Allen in 1594, Catholics were left without a leader. In 1598 the cardinal protector, Tommaso Gaetani, appointed George Blackwell archpriest with full authority over all the clergy in England and with instructions to seek the advice and help of the Jesuit superior in England. A group of the clergy appealed this ruling, asking for the appointment of a bishop. A further appeal in 1601 by a group of 33 priests, later known as the Appellants, was followed by a third appeal, led by Thomas Bluet, this time with the approval of the government

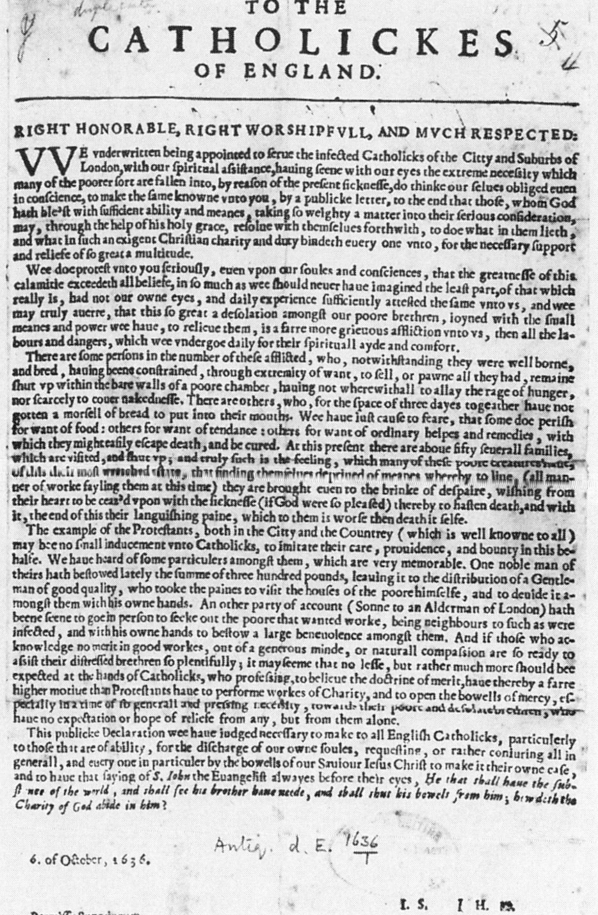

TO THE
CATHOLICKES
OF ENGLAND.

RIGHT HONORABLE, RIGHT WORSHIPFVLL, AND MVCH RESPECTED:

VVE vnderwritten being appointed to serue the infected Catholicks of the Citty and Suburbs of London, with our spiritual assistance, hauing seene with our eyes the extreme necessity which many of the poorer sort are fallen into, by reason of the present sicknesse, do thinke our selues obliged euen in conscience, to make the same knowne vnto you, by a publicke letter, to the end that those, whom God hath ble'st with sufficient ability and meanes, taking so weighty a matter into their serious consideration, may, through the help of his holy grace, resolue with themselues forthwith, to doe what in them lieth, and what in such an exigent Christian charity and duty bindeth euery one vnto, for the necessary support and reliefe of so great a multitude.

Wee doe protest vnto you seriously, euen vpon our soules and consciences, that the greatnesse of this calamitie exceedeth all beliefe, in so much as wee should neuer haue imagined the least part, of that which really is, had not our owne eyes, and daily experience sufficiently attested the same vnto vs, and wee may truly auerre, that this so great a desolation amongst our poore brethren, ioyned with the small meanes and power wee haue, to relieue them, is a farre more grieuous affliction vnto vs, then all the labours and dangers, which wee vndergoe daily for their spirituall ayde and comfort.

There are some persons in the number of these afflicted, who, notwithstanding they were well borne, and bred, hauing beene constrained, through extremity of want, to sell, or pawne all they had, remaine shut vp within the bare walls of a poore chamber, hauing not wherewithall to allay the rage of hunger, nor scarcely to couer nakednesse. There are others, who, for the space of three dayes togeather haue not gotten a morsell of bread to put into their mouths. Wee haue iust cause to feare, that some doe perish for want of food: others for want of tendance: others for want of ordinary helpes and remedies, with which they might easily escape death, and be cured. At this present there are aboue fifty seuerall families, which are visited, and shut vp; and truly such is the feeling, which many of these poore creatures haue, of this their most wretched state, that finding themselues depriued of meanes whereby to liue, (all manner of worke fayling them at this time) they are brought euen to the brinke of despaire, wishing from their heart to be ceaz'd vpon with the sicknesse (if God were so pleased) thereby to hasten death, and with it, the end of this their languishing paine, which to them is worse then death it selfe.

The example of the Protestants, both in the City and the Countrey (which is well knowne to all) may bee no small inducement vnto Catholicks, to imitate their care, prouidence, and bounty in this behalfe. We haue heard of some particulers amongst them, which are very memorable. One noble man of theirs hath bestowed lately the summe of three hundred pounds, leauing it to the distribution of a Gentleman of good quality, who tooke the paines to visit the houses of the poore himselfe, and to deuide it amongst them with his owne hands. An other party of account (Sonne to an Alderman of London) hath beene seene to goe in person to seeke out the poore that wanted worke, being neighbours to such as were infected, and with his owne hands to bestow a large beneuolence amongst them. And if those who acknowledge no merit in good workes, out of a generous minde, or naturall compassion are so ready to assist their distressed brethren so plentifully; it may seeme that no lesse, but rather much more should bee expected at the hands of Catholicks, who professing, to belieue the doctrine of merit, haue thereby a farre higher motiue than Protestants haue to performe workes of Charity, and to open the bowells of mercy, especially in a time of so generall and pressing necessity, towards their poore and desolate brethren, who haue no expectation or hope of reliefe from any, but from them alone.

This publicke Declaration wee haue iudged necessary to make to all English Catholicks, particulerly to those that are of ability, for the discharge of our owne soules, requesting, or rather coniuring all in generall, and euery one in particuler by the bowells of our Sauiour Iesus Christ to make it their owne case, and to haue that saying of *S. Iohn* the Euangelist alwayes before their eyes, *He that shall haue the substance of the world, and shall see his brother haue neede, and shall shut his bowels from him; how doth the Charity of God abide in him?*

6. of October, 1636.

I. S. I. H. M.

Permissu Superiorum.

Henry Morse's appeal ''To the Catholickes of England,'' Oct. 6, 1636.

which sought to profit from the rift between the parties among the clergy. Bluet undertook to secure the recall of the Jesuits from the English mission. Pope Clement VIII, while condemning the association of Bluet and his supporters with the English crown, limited the authority of the archpriest and released him from the obligation of consulting the Jesuits (*see* ARCHPRIEST CONTROVERSY). But the damage was done. Elizabeth ordered all the Jesuits to leave the country and offered a veiled promise of toleration to those of the secular clergy who would, before the last day of January, acknowledge their allegiance to the queen. In spite of the papal prohibition of all dealings with the government, a group of 13 secular priests on the last appointed day made a formal declaration of their allegiance. While professing their undying loyalty to the pope as the successor of St. Peter, they declared their refusal to obey any papal command to take the part of the queen's enemies. With the death of Elizabeth in March 1603 the conflict was temporarily resolved, but the acute division between a party of secular clergy and reli-

Westminster Cathedral, c. 1895, London. (©Hulton/Archive Photos)

gious, notably the Jesuits, was revived later in the century with disastrous consequences.

Under Stuart Kings: 1603 to 1688. Elizabeth was succeeded by JAMES I (1603–25), the son of Mary Queen of Scots. James, a Protestant, began his reign with a promise of toleration that was soon forgotten. As a result of the Gunpowder Plot (1605), the penal laws were revived, and an oath of allegiance that declared the pope's deposing power to be ''impious and heretical,'' was demanded of all Catholics. The question of the legality of the oath was to be a further cause of division in the Catholic body.

Later in James's reign negotiations for the marriage of the king's son, Charles, to a Catholic princess, first the Infanta Maria of Spain, and then Henrietta Maria of France, whom he married, led to a measure of toleration in practice and the hope of further relief. In these years, too, episcopal government was briefly restored to England. In 1623 William Bishop (1544–1624) was consecrated titular bishop of Chalcedon to serve the Catholics in England. He was succeeded by Richard Smith (1566–1655), who soon became involved in a controversy with the regular clergy and in 1631 retired to France and resigned his charge. For the next 50 years English Catholics were left without a bishop.

The early years of Charles I (1625–49) were a time of relative peace. He became deeply attached to his wife, Henrietta Maria, who, by the terms of the marriage treaty, was able to retain a large establishment of priests and chaplains. A movement of conversion developed in the court. Chapels of the Catholic ambassadors in London were well attended, schools and religious houses founded by exiles on the Continent flourished, and the penal laws, by the king's favor, were largely held in abeyance. From 1634 to 1641 a series of Roman agents, ostensibly accredited to the queen, resided in London, and Charles kept up an active correspondence with the court of Rome. There was even talk of reunion, but this possibility was shattered by the outbreak of civil war in 1642, in which the Catholic lords and gentry were royalist almost to a man. After the defeat of the king and his execution in January 1649, the monarchy was abolished and government was assumed first by a Council of State and then by Oliver CROMWELL as lord protector (1653–58). Catholics who had supported the king lost their property, but though the penal laws were revived, only two priests were put to death. Cromwell, in spite of his savage repressions in Ireland, extended a large measure of practical toleration to English Catholics.

The return of the monarchy with CHARLES II (1660–85) brought fresh hopes. Married to a Catholic wife and grateful to the Catholics who had saved his life and helped him to escape to France after the battle of Worcester during the civil war, Charles was prepared to give them support and comfort short of risking his throne. In 1670 he made the secret Treaty of Dover. By the terms of this agreement Charles promised, in return for financial help from Louis XIV of France, to declare himself a Catholic when a suitable opportunity offered. The conversion of his brother James, duke of York, under the influence of the example of his first wife, Anne Hyde (1637–71), herself a convert, alarmed the country, and in 1673 Parliament passed the Test Act, which excluded from office all who refused to take Communion in the Established Church and to deny the doctrine of transubstantiation. A later act of 1678 excluded Catholics from sitting in Parliament. But the great crisis of the reign was the Popish Plot (*see* OATES PLOT) of 1678. Titus Oates, an apostate convert of questionable reputation, revealed an alleged plot of the Jesuits to murder Charles and enthrone the Catholic James. The plot, as Charles well knew, was a fiction, but he made no attempt to protect the accused. Several laymen and priests, including Oliver PLUNKET, archbishop of Armagh, were executed.

On his deathbed, Charles, at the suggestion of his brother, sent for John Huddleston, a Benedictine who had helped save his life after Worcester. The priest heard the dying king's confession, reconciled him to the Church,

The metropolitan cathedral of Christ the King, Liverpool, England, Frederick Gibberd, architect.

and administered the last sacraments. With the accession of his brother JAMES II (1685–88), Protestant England had a Catholic king. It was to prove a disastrous experiment.

James was determined from the outset to secure some measure of toleration, not only for persecuted Catholics, but also for Quakers and Protestant dissenters. Unfortunately, after the first months of his reign, he acted with the greatest imprudence. Catholics were appointed to the Privy Council and given commissions in the army and navy, the king using his dispensing power to protect them from the penalties of the law. At Oxford the master of University College was allowed to continue in office after becoming a Catholic, and at Magdalen College a Catholic president was forced on the unwilling fellows. Tensions flared in 1688 when the Anglican bishops refused to publish the king's "Declaration of Indulgence" granting full civic rights to dissenters. The archbishop of Canterbury and six other bishops were promptly imprisoned in the Tower of London. The birth of James's son at this time aroused fears of a Catholic succession, and the sequel was the REVOLUTION OF 1688 (known as the Glorious Revolution), the flight of the king, and the succession of the Protestant William of Orange (1688–1702), husband of James's daughter Mary.

Not everything gained during James's three-year rule was lost. In 1685 John Leyburn (1620–1702), a former president of Douai College, was made vicar apostolic for England and took up residence in London. Leyburn proved to be an active and able bishop. Three years later, three more vicars apostolic were appointed to the Midland, Western, and London districts. In spite of the vicissitudes of the years immediately following, this form of episcopal government was successfully maintained until the restoration of the hierarchy in 1850.

A Century of Decline: 1688 to 1781. The Protestant Revolution of 1688 was the prelude to the darkest chapter in the history of post-Reformation Catholicism in England. New penal laws prohibited Catholics from bearing arms or possessing a horse above the value of £5, from voting in Parliamentary elections, from practicing as solicitors or barristers, and from inheriting land. A reward of £100 was offered to any informer who secured the conviction of a priest, while an Act of Succession excluded from the throne the many Catholic descendants of Charles II and James II. The effect of this legislation was to exclude the Catholic gentry and middle classes from the professions and from public life. Many, perforce, devoted themselves to the care of their family estates, and with the good will of their Protestant neighbors profited accordingly. Catholics, as a whole, maintained their allegiance to the exiled James II and his sons and successors and played some part in the risings of 1715 and 1745 that attempted the restoration of the Stuart line.

The 18th century saw a sharp decline in Catholic numbers. At the beginning of the period they probably numbered five percent of the population of 6 or 7 million. By 1780 their numbers had decreased to 69,316, served by some 300 priests. The largest concentration was in London, where, in 1742, CHALLONER estimated the Catholic population as 25,000. After London, the greatest numbers were in the north, especially Lancashire. This decline was in large measure due to the extinction or apostasy of many of the old Catholic families who, since the 16th century, had been the chief support of the clergy and who had made possible the continuance of Catholic worship.

The vicars apostolic were imprisoned in 1688 but were soon released. Bishop Philip ELLIS of the Western district then left the country and ended his days as bishop of Segni in Italy. Bishop Bonaventure GIFFORD of the London district was subsequently imprisoned on three separate occasions and lived in constant fear of arrest. Still, with difficulty, the succession was maintained. Although the vicars apostolic of the 18th century were notable for their longevity rather than their accomplishments, there were a few exceptions, among them Richard Challoner, who was in every way distinguished.

Challoner was ordained at Douai (1716) and, after spending some years teaching philosophy and theology, was sent to the London mission in 1730. Here he spent the next 50 years, first as a simple priest, later as coadjutor to Bp. Benjamin PETRE, and from 1758 as vicar apostolic of the London district. His long life was disturbed by two mild outbreaks of persecution: the first in 1745 when Prince Charles Edward, the Stuart Pretender, marched his forces from Scotland as far south as Derby, thus threatening a Catholic restoration; the second in 1767 when John Payne, a Protestant informer, denounced John Baptist Maloney, a priest, who was sentenced to life imprisonment. Challoner was also indicted but the charge failed; the mood of the day no longer favored persecution. Besides his extensive spiritual writings, which did much to mold the piety that would prevail in England for several centuries, Challoner founded two schools for boys, at Standon Lordship in Essex (1749) and at Sedgeley Park, near Wolverhampton (1762). A third school, for girls, was opened at Brook Green.

Relief for persecuted English Catholics came from an unexpected quarter. The revolt of the American colonies obliged the government to seek recruits for the army among Catholic clansmen of the Scottish Highlands and to offer in return a measure of toleration. The crown approached Bishop Challoner as representative of the English Catholics. When Challoner hesitated, the government turned to a committee of laymen, who took over negotiations. It was suggested that in return for the repeal of the penal laws enacted under William III, English Catholics should take an oath of allegiance to the sovereign. Upon Challoner's approval, a petition on these lines was drawn up by Edmund BURKE, and in 1778 a bill for a limited measure of toleration passed both houses of Parliament without difficulty. Passage of this first Relief Act showed the laity what they could do without the bishops, and the lesson was not lost. The act also led to a furious outburst of Protestant bigotry in London when wild rumors of plots against the liberties of Protestant Englishmen circulated in the capital. A Protestant alliance was formed to secure the repeal of the Act. In 1780, under the leadership of Lord George Gordon, an unbalanced nobleman who was also a religious fanatic, a large mob marched on Parliament to present a petition for repeal. A riot followed in which Catholic chapels in the city, including those of the Sardinian and Bavarian embassies, were looted and burned. The rioting spread beyond London. In Bath the house of the vicar apostolic of the Western district, Bishop Walmsley, was destroyed, together with all the archives of the district (*see* GORDON RIOTS). Challoner remained outside London until his death the following January at the age of 90.

Emancipation and Revival: 1781 to 1850. The closing years of the 18th century witnessed a remarkable transformation in the situation of Catholics. The lay committee, largely inspired by its able secretary, Charles BUTLER, and somewhat Gallican in its outlook, continued to seek relief from the penal laws. In 1789 a new bill incorporating an oath rejecting the papal deposing power was drafted. The terms of the oath led to some acute controversies with the vicars apostolic, but in 1791 a new Relief Act authorized the celebration of Mass in registered chapels by priests who had subscribed to the oath.

The outbreak of the French Revolution in 1789 led to the arrival in England of more than 5,500 French clergy; as further evidence of the a new attitude, the English government established a fund for their maintenance. The suppression by France's revolutionary government of English colleges and religious houses on the Continent led to the return of religious orders and seminaries. Students from Douai relocated to Old Hall, Ware, in Hertfordshire, and Ushaw College in County Durham. The Jesuits settled at Stonyhurst in Lancashire, and the Benedictines at Ampleforth and Downside.

An attempt by Prime Minister William Pitt to introduce a bill for Catholic emancipation in 1801 was frustrated by King George III's opposition, but from this year onward, projects for the complete abolition of the penal laws became an almost annual Parliamentary event. Meanwhile Catholics were growing in numbers and influence. By 1811 they numbered some 250,000, a remarkable increase due in part to steady Irish immigration. Between 1791 and 1816 more than 900 chapels were opened. A few Catholics began to attend the universities, and at Cambridge and elsewhere there were a few notable conversions. In 1817 commissions in the army and navy were opened to Catholics. In 1819 John LINGARD published the first three volumes of his *History of England;* this marked the turning of the tide. In 1829, in large measure because of the exertions of Irish Catholic leader Daniel O'CONNELL, an Act of Emancipation was passed restoring to Catholics full rights as citizens, including eligibility for government office and the right to sit in Parliament. Catholic worship and religious activities, however, were prohibited in public. Although religious orders were declared illegal, this clause was never enforced.

An increase in the Catholic population led to an increase in the number of bishops. In 1840 the number of vicariates was raised from four to eight. Even before this date, agitation had begun for the restoration of a diocesan hierarchy and a return to normal episcopal government. In 1835 Nicholas WISEMAN, a former pupil of the newly restored English College in Rome and a brilliant scholar, visited England and delivered a course of sermons for non-Catholics in the chapel of the Sardinian embassy in London. Wiseman soon became the acknowledged leader and spokesman of English Catholics. In 1836 he founded the *Dublin Review* as the organ of English Catholic opinion.

In the following years two devoted Italian missionary priests made a considerable impact on the people of England, Catholic and non-Catholic alike: Luigi Gentili (1801–48), of the Institute of Charity, who was established at Grace-Dieu, and Bl. Dominic BARBERI, a Passionist. Both preached with astonishing success and made many converts, although their introduction of a number of pious Italian practices was less favorably regarded by the older clergy and laity. Augustus Welby PUGIN, a convert, revived the Gothic style of architecture and designed the cathedral church of Southwark.

In 1845 Barberi received into the Church the leader of the OXFORD MOVEMENT, John Henry NEWMAN. Newman and his friends had for some years been engaged in an attempt to find a *via media* between Catholicism and ANGLICANISM. The condemnation of the famous Tract 90 foreshadowed Newman's conversion. He was preceded into the Church by William George WARD, author of *The Ideal of a Christian Church* (1844), a work that held up the Catholic Church as the model of what a church should be. For these opinions Ward was deprived of his degrees by Oxford University. Although a layman, he later taught theology at St. Edmund's, Ware. Newman and Ward were followed into the Church by a large group of Anglican clergy and laity.

In the late 1840s, there came from Ireland, as a result of the potato famine, a tremendous influx of destitute Irish. This immigration swelled enormously the numbers of Catholics in the country; according to the 1851 census England's Catholic population of 679,000 was served by less than 800 priests. The time was ripe for further ecclesiastical reorganization, and in 1850 a diocesan hierarchy was restored. The Holy See created 12 dioceses, with Westminster as the metropolitan see. Wiseman, vicar apostolic of the London district since 1849, became the first cardinal archbishop of Westminster.

Wiseman's pastoral letter from Rome announcing the restoration of the hierarchy was couched in somewhat imprudent terms and roused a flood of protest led by Prime Minister Lord John Russell. Throughout the country effigies of the pope and the cardinal were burned by mobs. In the midst of this no-popery agitation, Wiseman returned to London and issued an ''Appeal to the British People,'' which was published in all the leading newspapers. In it he explained the nature of the new hierarchy's authority and the limitations of his own jurisdiction as archbishop of Westminster; he emphasized the poverty, indeed destitution, of a high percentage of the Catholics of his own diocese. The religious agitation soon subsided, and although Parliament passed an Ecclesiastical Titles Act that imposed a fine of £100 on any person assuming a title to a pretended see in the country, the law was never enforced.

The Modern Church. The new hierarchy met in a synod (1852) at Oscott, where Newman preached his famous sermon on the ''Second Spring,'' but the sanguine hopes of the rapid conversion of England did not materialize. As a result of the Gorham judgment, Archdeacon Henry MANNING and other Anglicans entered the Church (1851), but the stream of conversions was declining. Wiseman, under an increasing strain because of ill health, fell under the influence of Manning, who was ordained a few weeks after reception into the Church and who became in 1865 the second archbishop of Westminster. As archbishop and, from 1875, as cardinal, Manning provided distinguished leadership in primary education and in social work, particularly on the occasion of the great London dock strike (1889). But the hierarchy showed little interest in higher education. Newman's plan to found a Catholic college at Oxford encountered bitter opposition, and Manning's experiment with a Catholic university in Kensington was a failure. Manning showed little understanding of Lord John ACTON or other liberal Catholics, or of Newman. After spending four years in Ireland in connection with the proposed University of Dublin, Newman retired to the Oratory he had established at Birmingham in 1848, and died in 1889.

At VATICAN COUNCIL I (1869–70) Manning was a spokesman for extreme ULTRAMONTANISM. This synod occasioned a mild outbreak of antipapal feeling in England. Bigotry, however, was slowly dying. While religious practice in the country began a long, steady decline, the Catholic body grew in numbers and prospered.

Herbert VAUGHAN, who would succeed Manning at Westminster (1893–1902), founded the first English foreign missionary society, the MILL HILL MISSIONARIES, whose members worked among the African-American population in the United States. Shortly after his appointment to Westminster, Vaughan obtained permission from Rome for Catholics to attend the universities of Oxford and Cambridge, which had abolished all religious tests many years earlier. Vaughan became a cardinal in 1893, and in 1895 he began the construction of Westminster Cathedral. The other outstanding events of his episcopate were the examination of Anglican orders, which were condemned by Leo XIII in *APOSTOLICAE CURAE* (1896), and the cardinal's vigorous defense of denominational schools, which Nonconformists in Parliament wanted to deprive of public financial support.

Vaughan's successor at Westminster was Francis BOURNE, bishop of Southwark from 1897, an excellent diocesan bishop and a builder of schools and churches. In alliance with the Anglicans he defeated an education bill hostile to Catholic schools, which were then increasing rapidly in number. Bourne's long episcopate (1903–35) was disturbed by MODERNISM, which in England was associated with the names of George TYRRELL and Baron Friedrich Von HÜGEL; and later by World War I. During these decades there was a notable increase in Catholics and a reorganization of dioceses. In 1878 the See of Beverley was divided to form the Dioceses of Leeds and Middlesbrough. Portsmouth became a diocese in 1892, and Menevia in 1898. Liverpool and Birmingham were raised to metropolitan status in 1911. In 1916 the Diocese of Newport became the Archdiocese of Cardiff with Menevia as its sole suffragan. Brentwood was created a diocese in 1917, and Lancaster in 1924. The one archdiocese and 12 suffragans of 1850 had thus grown to four metropolitan sees and 14 suffragans.

The number of converts to Catholicism increased steadily. Among the more distinguished during this period were Cyril MARTINDALE, SJ; Ronald KNOX, G. K. CHESTERTON, and Christopher Dawson, while the public champion of the Catholic cause was Hilaire BELLOC. On the initiative of Lord HALIFAX, a group of Anglicans explored the possibilities of reunion in a series of conversations with Catholic theologians at Malines, Belgium, under the presidency of Cardinal Mercier. English Catholics, in general, were not sympathetic, and no tangible results followed from these meetings (*see* MALINES CONVERSATIONS).

Arthur HINSLEY succeeded Bourne at Westminster (1935–43). English to the core and a warmhearted patriot, Hinsley (cardinal from 1937) made a profound impression on the English people, above all by his inspiring broadcast addresses in the early years of World War II. In 1940 he founded the SWORD OF THE SPIRIT, a movement to unite all English Christians in defense of Christian social principles. Early in his episcopate an apostolic delegation was established in London, whose first delegate was Abp. William GODFREY, later archbishop of Westminster (1956–63), succeeding Bernard GRIFFIN. The apostolic delegation performed valuable service in securing information about English prisoners of war. Hinsley's death in 1943 was widely mourned and almost the entire cabinet attended his funeral.

Following World War II there was a steady increase in Catholic ranks, due in part to a considerable influx of Polish and other refugees and to a very large immigration from Ireland. There was also a notable increase in churches and schools. Social legislation considerably improved the material lot of Catholics, most of whom belonged to the working class. Educational reforms and the expansion of the universities resulted in a remarkable increase in the number of Catholic university graduates. They became well represented in academic life and in all the professions.

The work of Vatican Council II aroused a keen awareness of the tragic divisions among Christians and a sincere desire for mutual understanding. Implementation of Vatican II reforms was, however, impeded in England by the resistance of the conservative Church hierarchy, led by Cardinal Godfrey. His successor, Carmel Heenan, was more amenable to the council's message of reconciliation, but, unable to embrace its deeper theological implications, he eventually became disillusioned. At the same time, greater freedom for Catholics in the educational and political realms was undermined by steadily increasing secularism in British society as well as a dramatic exodus of clerics and religious by the late 1980s. The total number of diocesan priests fell from 5,096 in 1966 to 4,457 in 1986 and continued to decline thereafter. Losses were greater in rural areas than in London, where the numbers changed very little. Shortages were felt most acutely in the field of education, as religious were replaced by lay teachers in Catholic schools throughout the country.

Into the Third Millennium. Interestingly, the 1990s sparked a flare-up of age-old questions among British Catholics. The question of whether a Catholic could remain a loyal subject to a divorced monarch—the question that had first surfaced as Henry VIII divorced Catherine of Aragon in the mid-16th century—was raised in 1996 upon the divorce of the heir to the throne, Prince Charles, and Princess Diana. In particular, the role of Queen Elizabeth, leader of the Anglican Church, in backing her son's divorce was called into question. Another issue rooted in Church history was the campaign to repeal the Settlement Act of 1701, which prevents Catholics from gaining the English throne or marrying a British monarch. Several supporters of the repeal within the Anglican Church noted that the role of monarch was political rather than theological, while those opposed noted that eliminating the monarch's position as leader of the Church of England would erode England's traditional claim of being a Christian nation.

Ecumenical efforts between the Anglican Church and the Catholic Church were highlighted in 2000 as leaders from both churches met in Toronto, Canada, in May to ''review and evaluate the accomplishments of 30 years of ecumenical dialogue between the two traditions,'' in the words of Anglican archbishop of Canterbury, George Carey. The meeting occurred six months after Pope John Paul II opened the Holy Door of the Basilica of St. Paul in the presence of Anglican Archbishop Carey and a representative of the World Lutheran Federation. This gesture of peace among the world's Catholic and non-Catholic faiths was a historic moment, a millennial statement intended to bridge the theological gulf created in England five centuries before.

In 2000 England contained 2,495 parish churches, while an additional 1,000 private chapels held Mass at least once per week. There were 3,672 secular and 1,693 religious priests. Of England's approximately 1,950 Catholic schools, 75% educated primary-grade students; in addition, religion remained a required subject in all government-funded schools in both England and Wales. While in 1963 there had been 131,592 Church baptisms, that rate had dropped to 69,712 by 2000, reflecting a continued decline in affiliation with most faiths in England as a whole.

Bibliography: C. READ, ed., *Bibliography of British History: Tudor Period, 1485–1603* (2d ed. New York 1959). G. DAVIS, ed., *Bibliography of British History, Stuart Period, 1603–1714* (Oxford 1928). S. PARGELLIS and D. J. MEDLEY, eds., *Bibliography of British History, 1714–89* (Oxford 1951). D. MATHEW, *Catholicism in England* (2d ed. New York 1950; 3d ed. London 1955). E. I. WATKIN, *Roman Catholicism in England: From the Reformation to 1950* (New York 1957). M. D. R. LEYS, *Catholics in England, 1559–1829: A Social History* (London 1961). H. TOOTELL, *Dodd's Church History of England,* ed. M. A. TIERNEY, 5 v. (London 1839–43). *Biographical Studies 1534–1829* (Bognor Regis, Eng. 1951–56), continued as *Recusant History* (1957—). G. R. ELTON, ed., *The Tudor Constitution* (Cambridge, Eng. 1960). P. HUGHES, *Rome and the Counter-Reformation in England* (London 1942). B. MAGEE, *The English Recusants* (London 1938). P. GUILDAY, *The English Catholic Refugees on the Continent, 1558–1795* (New York 1914). M. J. HAVRAN, *The Catholics in Caroline England* (Stanford, CA 1962). G. ALBION, *Charles I and the Court of Rome* (London 1935). D. MATHEW, *The Age of Charles I* (London 1951). M. V. HAY, *The Jesuits and the Popish Plot* (London 1934). A. C. F. BEALES, *Education under Penalty, 1547–1689* (London 1963). W. R. TRIMBLE, *The Catholic Laity in Elizabethan England 1558–1603* (Cambridge, MA 1964). R. N. HADCOCK, *Map of Monastic Britain* (Chessington, Eng. 1950). B. HEMPHILL (pseud. for B. WHELAN), *The Early Vicars Apostolic of England, 1685–1750* (London 1934). P. HUGHES, *The Catholic Question, 1685–1829* (London 1929). B. N. WARD, *Dawn of the Catholic Revival in England, 1781–1803,* 2 v. (New York 1909); *Eve of Catholic Emancipation,* 3 v. (London 1911–12); *The Sequel to Catholic Emancipation,* 2 v. (New York 1915). G. MACHIN, *The Catholic Question in English Politics, 1820–30* (New York 1964). D. GWYNN, *Lord Shrewsbury, Pugin, and the Catholic Revival* (London 1946). J. ALTHOLZ, *The Liberal Catholic Movement in England: The Rambler and Its Contributors, 1848–1864* (London 1962). G. A. BECK, ed., *The English Catholics 1850–1950* (London 1950). D. MCELRATH, *The Syllabus of Pius IX: Some Reactions in England* (Louvain 1964).

[G. CULKIN/EDS.]

ENGLISH LANGUAGE LITURGICAL CONSULTATION (ELLC)

Established in 1985, the English Language Liturgical Consultation (ELLC) is an international and ecumenical body concerned with English liturgical texts. It is successor to the INTERNATIONAL CONSULTATION ON ENGLISH TEXTS (ICET) which had completed its work in 1975 with a revised edition of *Prayers We Have in Common.* ELLC has a charge going beyond common texts. The new committee was planned to represent, more formally than had ICET, the several existing bodies already established by joint action of the churches in various parts of the English–speaking world.

The first meeting of the ELLC was held in Boston in August 1985, in connection with the biennial congress of Societas Liturgica. The constitutive bodies which agreed to participate were: Australian Consultation on Liturgy (ACOL), CONSULTATION ON COMMON TEXTS (CCT) of North America, INTERNATIONAL COMMISSION ON ENGLISH IN THE LITURGY (ICEL), Joint Liturgical Commission on English in New Zealand, Joint Liturgical Group (JLG) of Great Britain.

The program of ELLC includes reviewing the ICET texts in the light of more than a decade's experience; producing one or more Eucharistic Prayers in common versions; evaluating ecumenical lectionaries, especially those based on the postconciliar Roman lectionary, including the Consultation on Common Texts' *Revised Common Lectionary* that use in North America, and the two–year lectionary of the Joint Liturgical Group; and the future possibility of producing biblical translations appropriate for liturgical proclamation.

In the case of common liturgical texts, extensive consultation with the parent churches was undertaken, with the possibility of adding to the limited corpus of ICET prayers. With regard to any revision of the latter, ELLC agreed that only changes that are certainly necessary should be recommended and that there should be sensitivity to inclusive language in relation to women; the proclamatory quality of texts to be said, heard, and sung; and the pastoral significance of the use of contemporary language. ELLC's revision of ICET's texts was published as *Praying Together: English Language Liturgical Consultation* in 1988.

Bibliography: *Praying Together: English Language Liturgical Consultation* (Nashville 1988). H. R. ALLEN, JR, ''Common texts Revisited,'' *Worship* 60 (1986) 172–175. H. T. ALLEN, JR, ''Common Lectionary : Origins, Assumptions, and Issues,'' *Studia Liturgica* 21 (1991) 14–30.

[F. R. MCMANUS/EDS.]

ENLIGHTENMENT

The Enlightenment was a movement arising from the philosophical systems of the 17th century. It appeared in England in theoretical writings on religion, ethics, and natural law; in France in the books of the *Philosophes;* and in the radical political changes of the American and French Revolutions a century later. Thus it was destined to reach the whole western world and pervade all modern thought, spreading from England and France to North America, and from Portugal and Spain to South America. Though Protestant countries were in general more receptive to the movement, still Catholic Portugal was the first to establish the power of the Enlightenment by means of public law. Her example was followed by the Bourbon states. In the countries of the Orthodox church the influence of the Enlightenment remained limited.

Nature and History. As an intellectual movement, it does not present a harmonious philosophical pattern. According to Kant (''Was ist Aufklärung?'' *Berlinische Monatsschrift,* 1784), the Enlightenment is the emergence of a man from a state of dependence brought about through his own fault. This dependence is the inability to use one's intellect without guidance. The culpability does not lie in lack of intelligence, but in lack of decision and courage to use intelligence without reliance upon someone else. *Sapere aude* (take courage to use your brain) is, therefore, the motto of the Enlightenment.

This characteristic phrase throws light on the position that the Enlightenment assigns to man and to his most valued faculty, the intellect. The advice of the motto presupposes a strong trust in the power of intellect and an optimistic evolutionary faith, and calls for the liberation of man from controls interfering with his independence and his liberty. From these very general ideal premises follow deductions allowing for the most divergent systems and practices, so that a precise evaluation of the Enlightenment is impossible.

Philosophically speaking, the Enlightenment is a specific form of modern individualism and subjectivism. Its precursors are humanism, with its emphasis on what man can do with his own powers, its worship of the ancients, its secularism; and the enlarged view of the world resulting from the opening of new parts of the globe, the extension of commerce, world travel, knowledge of foreign cultures and religions; and the advance of the natural sciences.

The thought processes of the movement revolve around man (anthropocentrism). Observation of nature and man (psychology), analysis of natural law, mathematical thinking, experiment, and comparison: these are the means whereby it seeks to obtain knowledge. It is assumed that knowing must result in acting, since the Enlightenment holds that rational thought and moral act are closely connected. The bond with a positive or moral authority and respect for tradition are rejected. Hence, in spite of its insistence on historical research, the Enlightenment lacks a real instinct for history. The homage it pays to historical antecedents turns out to be mere historicism. The achievements of the past, notably of the Middle Ages, are met with skepticism and criticism.

The Enlightenment was ushered in by the Englishman Bacon of Verulam (*see* BACON, FRANCIS), and the Frenchman René DESCARTES. Bacon, founder of modern experimental philosophy, points the way to the new movement by his statement ''knowledge is power'' (*tantum possumus quantum scimus*), and by his new scientific ideal of an unprejudiced, methodical investigation of nature. Descartes starts his philosophy with methodical doubt, thereby laying the foundation of modern epistemology.

While the movement in England ran in the quiet channels of theoretical discussion, it became stormy in France as a result of political and social conditions. Materialistic and atheistic tendencies, skepticism, destructive criticism of political, social, and ecclesiastical institutions and conditions characterized the French phase of the Enlightenment, from which emerged men like BAYLE, MONTESQUIEU, Diderot, D'Alembert, VOLTAIRE, and ROUSSEAU. The movement finally precipitated the French revolution.

On the other hand, the Enlightenment ran a much quieter course in Germany, where its beginning and its end are marked by the two great thinkers LEIBNIZ and Kant. Leibniz, a man of universal vision, was convinced of the compatibility between the revealed Christian religion and the new insights of natural science. His doctrine of monads is essentially metaphysical, although he makes allowances for rationalism. Christian WOLFF, in trying to shape Leibniz' doctrine into a system, brought about Leibniz' connection with the Enlightenment. In so doing, he created an eclectic, if popular, philosophy, which came to have a wide influence. But the real pioneer of the Enlightenment in Germany was Christian Thomasius, who, following the French formula and especially Samuel von Pufendorf, advocated a doctrine of natural law and political thought independent of ethics and revelation and founded on plain reason. Kant led enlightened rationalism to its high point, but on the other hand pointed out the limits of the faculty of perception (*Kritik der reinen Vernunft,* 1781). He then tried to postulate the existence of God from the view of practical reason, taking as his starting point the fact of moral conscience (*Kritik der praktischen Vernunft,* 1788).

The strong missionary spirit of the Enlightenment spread its influence over a wide area. The secret societies of the Freemasons, the ROSICRUCIANS, and the Illuminati (*see* ILLUMINISM) encouraged a bond among freethinkers. Encyclopedias like Bayle's *Dictionnaire historique et critique* (1695–97) and Diderot and d'Alembert's *Encyclopédie des sciences, des arts et des métiers* (1751–80), periodicals like Christoph Nicolai's *Allgemeine deutsche Bibliothek* (1765–1806) or the *Berlinische Monatsschrift* disseminated, along with aesthetic and popular scientific ideas, the new philosophy in a skillful but also destructive form. Classic German literature, which reached its high point with Lessing, Herder, Schiller, and Goethe, is best seen from this viewpoint.

Philosophy and Religion. The after effects of Ockhamistic thought, together with the impressive progress of natural science, which had made men aware of the regularity of the material course of the universe, urged philosophers to seek a new answer to the question of origin and methods of cognition. Descartes, with his methodical doubt, became not only the originator of philosophical criticism but also, by founding all thought on a consciousness sure of itself (*cogito, ergo sum*) and endowed with so-called innate ideas, made himself the forerunner of all later idealistic-rationalistic systems. Innate ideas are for him the infinite substance, God; and the twofold finite substance is that of thinking man and the extended thing that is thought of. SPINOZA, reuniting this dualism, arrived at pantheism. Thomas HOBBES's sensualistic philosophy is the empiric-naturalistic counterpart to the idealistic system of Descartes. John LOCKE and David HUME derive all cognition from sense experience. Metaphysics is impossible in such a system. The development of such thought ends in the materialism of Claude Helvétius, Paul HOLBACH (*Système de la nature,* 1770) and Julien de La Mettrie (*L'Homme machine,* 1748).

The attitude of these thinkers toward religion is determined partly by tradition and origin, partly by the idealistic or materialistic tendency of each system. When the higher life of man is considered as the effect of bodily organization, when thought and will are said to be sensations resulting from education, the aim of life will be placed in pleasure. Morality, whose source in this purely materialistic view is the physical urge of self-preservation (Holbach, d'Alembert), can be founded only upon considerations of common good and private utility. Real religion has no place (De La Mettrie, Helvétius, Holbach). The idealistic structure of Descartes, on the other hand, appealed as a possible point of development to Jansenists, Oratorians like Malebranche, and some Jesuits. The empiric-inductive method, first demanded by Bacon, required a strict separation of reason and revelation, of knowledge and belief, and led to a natural religion (deism).

HERBERT OF CHERBURY (*De veritate,* 1624) traces all human knowledge to innate common ideas and principles whose criterion of truth is common acceptance. The most important religious-ethical content of innate basic truths is the existence of God, the necessity of divine worship through virtue and piety, expiation of wrongdoing through repentance, and belief in reward and punishment in this life and in the next. Anything that exceeds this is an addition made by positive religions. That is particularly true of dogmas. The more a religion is cleansed of such accretions or the more it approaches a religion whose nature is founded on rationalism, the greater is its value. In such a system religion is not conceived theocentrically as worship of God, but anthropocentrically as moral conduct of the individual, as realization of natural morality, as love of fellow man. Religion thus becomes a stimulus for virtue. But virtue is the happiness of man. All of this is a utilitarian-eudaimonistic way of thinking, leading to the equation: religion=morality.

The concept of a revealed religion and the acceptance of truth on the authority of someone else are repugnant to an Enlightenment based on reason and experience. This explains its attitude toward Christianity. Christ is to be considered as one among many founders of religions. His teaching must be judged by the norm of rational-natural religion and its ethical-humanitarian demands. Consequently, the Bible is a kind of code of ethics, to be studied independently of any alleged divine inspiration and pastoral interpretation. It must be cleansed of anything offensive, notably miracles. This last notion was advocated in particular by the German Protestant Samuel Reimarus in his pamphlet *Apologie oder Schutzschrift für die vernünftigen Verehrer Gottes* (1744–), of which LESSING published seven sections entitled *Wolfenbüttler Fragmente eines Ungenannten* (1744–78). These stirred up great agitation as did the Wertheimer Bible translation of Lorenz Schmidt (1735). The Christian Church is to the adherents of the Enlightenment nothing but one religious association among many others (indifferentism), a society for fostering religion and morality on the basis of the dogma of Christ.

Culture and Education. Man is thus portrayed as a rational, moral being striving for happines and dominated by the urge for knowledge and learning. His knowledge results in actions harmonious with nature and reason; the philosophers call it virtue. And virtue makes for happiness.

This image determines social pedagogy also. Man is good by nature (Rousseau, *Émile,* 1762); nature has implanted in him the germs of a behavior based on social morality. Since he develops freely out of capacities and forces dormant within himself, according to the principle of spontaneity, stress is laid on the subordinate role of pedagogy. Its method has a strong psychological slant, in which the individuality of the pupil is encouraged, and punishment is considered a detriment to his development. Since knowledge and learning occupy a central position in the evolution of an enlightened, progressive man, school attendance is compulsory. The educational standards are further heightened by improving the methods and abilities of teachers. So-called normal schools or teachers' seminars are created after the pattern developed by the Swiss pedagogue, Johann PESTALOZZI.

Not only on the elementary and secondary school levels was the influence of the Enlightenment exerted, but also in universities, where new emphasis was placed upon research, especially in natural sciences. Prototypes in Germany are the Universities of Halle, founded in 1694, and Göttingen, founded in 1737. Parallel with such universities, there also arose special professional institutes, societies, and academies of science. The first university institute was the philological-pedagogical ''seminar'' founded in 1787 at the University of Halle. Scientific academies began with the Royal Society of London (1663), followed by the Prussian Academy of Sciences in Berlin (1700) and the Russian Academy of Sciences in St. Petersburg (1724). The last two had been organized by Leibniz.

The principle of equality among all men as understood by the enlightened philosophers expresses itself in rational morality, humanitarianism, tolerance, and cosmopolitanism. Such attitudes resulted in many praiseworthy developments, such as advances in medicine; the organized care of orphans, the underprivileged, and the handicapped, training for trades within individual capacities; and humanitarian reforms in criminal law and its procedures. The demand grew for abolition of slavery and for the application of ethical principles to colonial peoples. The disabilities that Jews were subjected to were likewise removed. In the U.S. the Jews obtained for the first time complete civil equality in 1776. Finally, cosmopolitanism furthered interest in physical and cultural anthropology, physical and social geography, languages, literature, art, and the civilization of peoples outside the Western cultural cycle.

State and Society. The state ranks highest among social institutions in enlightened thought. It is viewed as the sum of rational individual beings and their rights, and consequently as the totality and actuality of all reason and all law, as the highest and only positive authority. The origin of the state proceeds from the individual, having come about by means of social contract (Rousseau, *Contrat Social,* 1762). Private interest and the desire to keep personal liberty when living together with other men, but without being exposed to their tyranny and quarrelsomeness (loss of freedom, loss of property, war), cause men to band together and to surrender to the state a part of the rights due by nature so that these rights may be protected with better results in favor of the individual. The will of the state is, therefore, the united will of all individuals and is absolute (idea of sovereignty).

The protection of individual rights in the state is best served by the separation of powers into legislative, executive, and judicial. Locke and Rousseau consider popular sovereignty, in opposition to the divine right of kings of a former period, as the supreme norm. A communistic social organization, originating by transference of private property to the state, Rousseau declares indeed compatible with the idea of legality, but psychologically wrong. The possibility of withdrawing rights once transferred to the state is denied, e.g., by Pufendorf and Hobbes, who maintain that power transferred by popular will to the ruler is definite and absolute. From the foregoing it will be seen that the theory of the origin of the state, as proposed by the Enlightenment, admits a development into many different forms of the state: constitutional, absolute, totalitarian.

The purpose of the state is the protection of the individual, his liberty, and his property (administration of justice); the advancement of the individual by encouragement of education through universal compulsory schooling (basis of state monopoly of education); and the improvement of the general standard of living (social welfare). The specific content of individual freedom should consist of freedom of speech, of the press, and of association. These rights include freedom of conscience and freedom of religion, and consequently also the freedom to express collectively a religious belief through a religious community.

State and Church. The Enlightenment, however, has limited its recognition of the corporate liberty of the churches, since it saw therein, especially in the Catholic Church, a danger to the sovereignty of the state. But the various freedoms granted to the individual imply the duty of tolerance, which was now prescribed to the state in its relations with religious corporations. The first popular assembly proclaiming religious parity was that of Catholic Maryland in 1679. As part of a constitution we see parity first in Virginia in 1776; later, in negative wording, in the constitutions of the U.S. (1787–91) and of France (1793), in the Austrian Tolerance Edict (1781), and in the Prussian Common Law (1794). According to the Enlightenment, the state may tolerate only those religious associations that do not contravene the moral norms necessary for maintaining civil society (Locke; cf. wording of many modern constitutions). On this principle England justified its exclusion of atheists and Catholics from tolerance. Catholics were held to disregard the sovereignty of the state because they recognized the alien jurisdiction of the pope and denied the political authority of excommunicated rulers. The former could not bind themselves to an oath of allegiance by calling on God.

As to the actual relation between church and state, philosophers did not disturb the existing Established Church, but rather developed its theory and practice. On the one hand, they wanted to use the influence of religion and church on the moral conduct of men in favor of law and order in the state (Rousseau, Hobbes); on the other, they wanted to establish the sovereignty of the state (absolutism). To this end they developed out of the alleged general rights over the church (*iura maiestatica circa sacra*) a set of special rights, restricting the church. The right of supervision (*ius inspiciendi*) came to include the claim that ecclesiastical jurisdiction districts must not cross state boundaries. The state claimed a right of veto in the appointment of important church functionaries (*ius exclusivae*). Church announcements, in order to take effect, had to have the consent of civil authorities (*placet; ius cavendi*). The effect of ecclesiastical jurisdiction was made illusory by the possibility of appeal to a civil court (*recursus tamquam ab abusu*).

The theory of religion and church as held by the Enlightenment, including the doctrine of absolute state sovereignty, resulted in bitter conflict with the Catholic Church. Hence, it is toward her that the full weight of attack is directed. Obligatory dogmas, the teaching office of the church, supreme papal authority, the character of mystery of the Mass and the Sacraments, monasticism with its vows of obedience, and the contemplative life, were all rejected.

Papacy and Church Organization. Attacks on the papacy were revived by a new conciliar movement manifested in universal and national councils and convocations of clergy, by overemphasis on episcopal power that should stem directly from ordination (*iurisdictio ordinaria episcopi;* the episcopal system), and by the idea of a national church and a national primate. Systems like GALLICANISM, FEBRONIANISM, and JOSEPHINISM represent the relation between the enlightened state and the Church headed by the papacy. In France, during the so-called quarrel about the ''regalia,'' the right of advowson and of disposal of church property, a right conceded to the king in an earlier period, came to be claimed an inherent and inalienable right of the crown. Papal protests were met with a convocation of the French clergy, who signed under duress a fundamental declaration of the Gallican clergy about ecclesiastical power (*Declaratio cleri gallicani de potestate ecclesiastica,* 1682). This declaration affirmed the superiority of general councils and denied the infallibility of the pope in matters of faith. The fact that jurisdictional acts of the pope were to take effect only after consent of the particular national church struck Catholic constitutional law in its vital point, and recognized in principle the notion of a state church.

A theological interpretation of Gallicanism and its application to the territories of the ecclesiastical princes of Germany is given by Febronianism. This system is developed in the book of Febronius, *nom de plume* of the suffragan Bishop of Trier, Nikolaus von Hontheim, *De statu ecclesiae et legitima potestate Romani Pontificis* (1763). Here the pope is thought of as first among equals, as representative of the universal Church or the universal episcopate. In the course of history, the episcopate, deceived by the so-called Pseudo-Isidorian forgery, is said to have transferred to the pope certain rights, express or implied. These rights the episcopate might take back at any time, except the main rights of primacy, which, however, possess no legislative character. On the contrary, in matters of canonical legislation the head of the Church should have the consent of the national churches.

On the basis of this Febronian canon law, the demands of the four German metropolitan bishops were formulated at the Congress of EMS (1786). Accordingly, the archbishops began to introduce arbitrarily the necessary reforms. Their measures reached a climax in the quarrel over the Cologne nunciature.

Similarly, the political church reforms of MARIA THERESA and JOSEPH II in the Hapsburg domains were partly necessary and justified, viz, the secularization of part of numerous monasteries in order to finance new dioceses and parishes and the reorganization of theological studies. But in theory and in practice they were the outcome of enlightened political thought.

Secular and Regular Clergy. The idea of the church as a religious community, part of and subordinate to the state, was bound to result in a lowering of respect for the status of priest and monk. The clergyman became a "servant of religion," whose main task was to be his moral-pedagogic influence on the people. The clergyman as an educator of the masses became an object of interest to the state. Hence, the state claimed the right to prescribe the scholarly training of the clergy and to regulate, to supervise, and even to conduct theological studies according to the needs of the time. In Germany there developed the tendency to require secular and regular clergy to study at the schools of divinity of the state universities. In Austria Joseph II founded general seminaries for this purpose. A study program, in its main outlines still in force today, was set up by Stephan RAUTENSTRAUCH in 1782, commissioned by the Austrian government. It is characterized by emphasis on Biblical and patristic sources and their study in the original languages, introduction of the historical method in the science of theology, and the introduction of history of dogma and of church history in theological instruction, while it minimizes speculative scholastic theology. The interest of the Enlightenment in the teaching and application of knowledge was met by the creation of a new practical subject, namely, pastoral theology.

Generally speaking, contemplation and asceticism were held to have no right to exist, since they did not serve any visible purpose. There was little tolerance for the breviary, for celibacy, or for the fostering of priestly vocations, which was especially harmful to the religious orders. The vow of obedience, by which the regular clergy was bound, was considered incompatible with the task of an educator of the people, and an inadmissible limitation of complete personal liberty. Activities of the regular clergy in pastoral work, education, teaching, and care of the sick were indeed viewed as useful. But the regular clergy who were to form the masses had henceforth to obtain their training at the state universities.

These measures, intensified by the animosity stirred up by literary attacks and the propaganda of the daily press, led many countries to a partial or total secularization of monasteries and orders. In some cases reduction of the number of members was ordered; in other cases the purely contemplative orders were abolished. In 1773 the Bourbon courts successfully forced the Pope, for political reasons, to decree the dissolution of the Jesuit Order. In 1782 Joseph II put through a partial secularization of the monasteries in Austria. A general dissolution of monasteries took place in France from 1789 through the great Revolution and in Germany as a result of a resolution of the Reichstag in 1803 (*Reichsdeputationshauptschluss*).

Divine Service and Pastoral Work. The insistence of the Enlightenment upon the increase of knowledge as the goal of human progress influenced religion in its practical expressions, to the degree that religious instruction became the central point of divine service. The sermon of the Enlightenment was preeminently an appeal to moral conduct. The functions of the priest as mediator to salvation, of the sacrifice of the Mass, and of the Sacraments were thereby often overlooked; everything must edify and stimulate and lead toward practical religiosity and morality. Hence the demand for the use of the vernacular in the liturgy, since people can receive instruction only in a language they all understand. Hence also the demand to rid divine service and the very church building of anything that is nonessential, overdone, strange, or no longer intelligible. That meant a repression of pious folk customs, reduction of the large number of Masses, abolition of Eucharistic exposition during the Mass, and restriction of processions and pilgrimages, of veneration of saints and relics, of indulgences and fraternities. The house of God was invaded by the sober art of classicism (cf. the pastoral letters of the Archbishops of Vienna in 1752, of Salzburg in 1782, and of Augsburg in 1783).

However, not withstanding much bias, the liturgical movement of the Enlightenment somewhat stimulated divine worship for the masses. There arose new rituals and new collections of songs. Furthermore pastoral conferences increased; pastoral periodicals were founded in order to arouse the clergy dedicated to the ministry of souls and to win them over to the new ideas. Thus, while the regular clergy was pushed into the background of Church life, the importance of the official parish ministry increased. Attempts of the episcopate to increase the care of souls and to decrease positions that were not so engaged supported this development. The interest in religious instruction especially benefited the compilation of new catechisms and of methodical catechesis, and its introduction as a required subject in the school curriculum.

Literature. The Enlightenment also affected literary and artistic forms. The literature of the 18th century, for example, was involved in the struggle for supremacy between reason and imagination. Out of this grew a classicism that demanded sobriety as the first canon of literary expression. The emphasis on rational literary style can be found in the effect of Johann Gottsched upon the Leipzig stage; the works of Gotthold Lessing; the *Sturm und Drang* of the middle Rhineland (1770–80), where efforts to restore fantasy never vanquished the strong rational element of the Enlightenment; Voltaire's search for an enlightened Utopia, which led him to teach the need of men's commitment to society, and to reexamine established institutions; and the observations of the master satirist Jonathan Swift on the manner of leading life by reason and without the impulses of emotion.

Evaluation. The positive effects of the Enlightenment lie in the cultivation of a humanitarian and tolerant spirit; an improved administration of law, including a humane criminal law; a pedagogy based on psychology; efforts toward social welfare; stimulation of research, scholarship, and education; and the struggle against ignorance and superstition. As bad effects the following may be counted; the overestimation of intellectual powers (thus Kant), the underestimation of nonintellectual powers (thus Rousseau and Herder), the absolute individualistic idea of liberty as well as statism, the negative attitude toward authority and tradition, religious relativism, and a worldly viewpoint with its ideas of pragmatism and utility. All of which have furthered the secularization of thought and action in all fields, including an exclusively material civilization.

With regard to the Enlightenment the Church has stood partly on the defensive, though partly willing to accept some of its programs. Dangerous consequences have resulted from unrestricted rationalism and liberalism, especially from the rejection of all metaphysics as well as from a conception of the Church based on natural law. On the other hand, it has had its good effects in the advancement of positive theology, especially of theological research; the renewal of the liturgy and of preaching the gospel; concentration on parish work; and the strengthened position of parish priest and bishop. Catholic efforts to fight against superstition and abuses of religious customs, Biblical textual criticism, etc., have often been suspected as unorthodox. To what extent one can speak of healthy progress, or to what extent of hindrance to the Church, must be judged from individual cases.

Bibliography: P. SMITH, *A History of Modern Culture,* 2 v. (New York 1930–34) v.2 *The Enlightenment 1687–1776* (New York 1934). W. E. H. LECKY, *History of the Rise and Influence of the Spirit of Rationalism in Europe,* 2 v. (rev. ed. New York 1925). F. VALJAVEC, *Geschichte der abendländischen Aufklärung* (Vienna 1961). F. UEBERWEG, *Grundriss der Geschichte der Philosophie,* ed. K. PRAECHTER et al., 5 v. (11th, 12th ed. Berlin 1923–28) 3. G. SCHNÜRER, *Katholische Kirche und Kultur im 18. Jahrhundert* (Paderborn 1941). R. N. STROMBERG, *Religious Liberalism in Eighteenth-Century England* (London 1954). R. R. PALMER, *Catholics and Unbelievers in Eighteenth Century France* (Princeton, N.J. 1939). P. HAZARD, *The European Mind: The Critical Years, 1680–1715,* tr. J. L. MAY (New Haven, Conn. 1953); *European Thought in the Eighteenth Century, from Montesquieu to Lessing,* tr. J. L. MAY (New Haven, Conn. 1954). B. GROETHUYSEN, *Die Entstehung der bürgerlichen Welt-und Lebensanschauung in Frankreich,* 2 v. (Halle 1927–30). H. M. WOLFF, *Die Weltanschauung der deutschen Aufklärung in geschichtlicher Entwicklung* (Bern Munich 1949). E. WINTER, *Der Josefinismus und seine Geschichte: Beiträge zur Geistesgeschichte Österreichs 1740–1848* (Brno 1943). F. MAASS, ed., *Der Josephinismus: Quellen zu seiner Geschichte in Österreich 1760–1850,* 5 v. (Fontes rerum Austriacarum II, 71–75; Vienna 1951–61). A. P. WHITAKER, *Latin America and the Enlightenment* (New York 1942). G. JELLINEK, *Die Erklärung der Menschen-und Bürgerrechte: Ein Beitrag zur modernen Verfassungsgeschichte* (4th ed. Munich 1927). D. KNOOP, and G. P. JONES, *The Genesis of Freemasonry* (Manchester, England 1947). A. ANWANDER, *Die allgemeine Religionsgeschichte im katholischen Deutschland während der Aufklärung und Romantik* (Salzburg 1932). W. PHILIPP, *Das Werden der Aufklärung in theologiegeschichtlicher Sicht* (Forschungen zur systematischen Theologie und Religionsphilosophie 3; Göttingen 1957). W. TRAPP, *Vorgeschichte und Ursprung der liturgischen Bewegung* (Regensburg 1940). A. L. MAYER, ''Liturgie, Aufklärung und Klassizismus,'' *Jahrbuch für Liturgiewissenschaft* 9 (1929) 67–127. L. G. CROCKER, ''Recent Interpretations of the French Enlightenment,'' *Journal of World History* 8 (1964) 426–56.

[E. HEGEL]

ENLIGHTENMENT, PHILOSOPHY OF

The ENLIGHTENMENT is a name popularly used to describe the extraordinary scientific, philosophical, religious, and political developments of 18th-century Europe. Like all historical periods, the Enlightenment had no abrupt beginning or end, and the determination of its temporal limits is considerably arbitrary. And like most popular historical nomenclature, the term used to describe this period, while setting in relief a very real aspect of the times, connotes an oversimple and somewhat uncritical view of what actually occurred. The purpose of this article is to outline the philosophical thought that characterized the period; this may be conveniently done in two parts, the first discussing the French and English Enlightenment and the second the German Enlightenment.

French and English Enlightenment

It is undeniable that the scientific developments of 18th-century Europe prompted the wide dissemination of a new spirit, one opposed to a priori solutions and very much given to experimentation. Although the 18th century did not produce any scientific discoveries equaling in importance those of Galileo and Newton, it was a century during which an unusually large number of people began

Carl Linnaeus.

to build on the scientific foundations already provided. The ''scientific method'' began to assume preeminence over all other approaches to important problems, even in moral and religious spheres; and scientific societies, journals, and encyclopedias multiplied their influence as means whereby scientists could exchange information and assist one another in their experimentation. The scientific laboratory became so popular, in fact, that it sometimes assumed the role of a status symbol among the socially elite, particularly in France, and accounts of laboratory experiments became more fashionable in some famous salons than court gossip. Moreover, at this time, in Europe's great universities chairs were founded in such sciences as anatomy, astronomy, botany, and chemistry.

Scientific Progress. Such scientific ferment produced a remarkably large number of concrete results. C. Linnaeus in his *Systema naturae* (Leiden 1735) provided a firm foundation for the complex task of classifying the large number of minerals, plants, and animals that had been discovered and described by him or his assistants, who made voyages to the most distant parts of the earth for this purpose. Also in the field of biology, George Louis Leclerc de Buffon published his *Histoire naturelle, générale et particulière* (44 v. Paris 1749–1804), which argued from the stratification of rocks and the occurrence of fossils at various levels that the planet was of a much greater age than that commonly inferred from Biblical accounts. B. de Maillet (1656–1738) also wrote the very popular *Telliamed* (Amsterdam 1748), in which he proposed the theory that terrestrial forms of life had evolved over long periods of time from aquatic forms. J. B. Lamarck rounded out the century by publishing his *Philosophie zoölogique* (Paris 1809), in which he added to the developing evolutionary theory the notion that evolution was a consequence of adaptation to environment.

Physical Science. In the fields of chemistry and physics, Sir Henry Cavendish (1731–1810) pioneered in experiments with gases, electricity, and heat. He demonstrated the compound nature of water, invented the eudiometer tube, and introduced the use of drying agents in experimentation. Joseph Priestley published a *History of Electricity* (London 1767) and, in the following decade, *Experiments and Observations on Different Kinds of Air* (6 v. London 1774–86). He discovered oxygen, demonstrated the similarity of respiration and combustion, and invented the ''pneumatic trough'' for collecting gases. Priestley was something of a *philosophe* too, writing a *History of the Corruptions of Christianity* (Northumberland, Pa. 1796) and lending his support to the American and French revolutions. A. L. Lavoisier, author of a *Traité élémentaire de chimie* (Paris 1789) and famous for his phlogiston theory of combustion, was also a pioneer in laboratory work and invented, along with P.S. Laplace, a device for measuring linear and cubical expansion due to heat. Laplace is more noted for the ''nebular hypothesis,'' which he proposed in his *Exposition du système du monde* (Paris 1796), and for his pioneering work in probability theory.

The 18th century saw also extraordinary developments in the study of electricity. Benjamin Franklin (1706–90) published his *Experiments and Observations on Electricity* (3 v., London 1754–62). L. Galvani discovered what is now known as the galvanic principle; A. Volta produced the first electrical battery; and at the close of the century A. M. Ampère explained the attraction and repulsion of electrical currents.

Technology. Concurrent with these contributions to physical science, the spirit of the Enlightenment was also producing practical results. Edward Jenner (1749–1823) introduced the practice of vaccination in England; James Watt (1736–1819) developed a steam engine that was such an improvement over the older piston engine of Thomas Newcomen that it could be used to drive all sorts of machinery. And the textile industry was not slow to provide the machines. John Kay had invented the fly-shuttle in 1733; James Hargreaves produced the ''spinning jenny'' in 1764; and Edmund Cartwright developed the power loom in 1785. Finally, Eli Whitney devised his cotton gin in 1793.

Theories of Man. Such successes in science and its applications gave thinkers of the Enlightenment great confidence in human progress. All one needed to make real the Utopias of which others had dreamed was to apply, to the direction of human life, the scientific method that had so successfully dealt with the physical world. It became the fashion to regard man as a very complex machine whose workings, once understood, could be controlled to produce whatever results might be desired. Three of the ENCYCLOPEDISTS were particularly active in providing the new psychological theories: É. B. de CONDILLAC, J. O. de La Mettrie, and P. H. D. HOLBACH. Abbé Condillac, in his *Traité des sensations* (Paris 1754), pushed John Locke's EMPIRICISM to the point of maintaining, against the Englishman's theory of ''ideas of reflection,'' that *all* knowledge is ultimately sensation in one form or another. While Condillac himself was not a materialist in his conception of man, his work was a step in that direction. La Mettrie took the final step in his *L'Homme machine* (Leiden 1748), which was a completely mechanistic analysis of man's psychic activities; thinking, feeling, willing were all proclaimed to be physical functions of a highly complex, completely material mechanism whose motive power was self-love (*see* MATERIALISM).

Holbach, in his *Système de la nature, ou des lois du monde physique et du monde moral* (London 1770), helped popularize La Mettrie's view and emphasized the application of MECHANISM to the realm of morality. Man, Holbach said, is a purely physical being, and ethics is only a matter of considering this physical being from a certain point of view. ''In all he does, a reasonable being ought always set before himself his own happiness and that of his fellows.'' And a consideration of *l'homme machine* from the ethical point of view revealed that ''the source of man's unhappiness is his ignorance of nature.'' Such a conviction made possible a great optimism concerning man's perfectibility. M. J. A. C. CONDORCET gave expression to this optimism in his *Esquisse d'un tableau historique des progrès de l'esprit humain* (Paris 1794), a work that was written, ironically, while Condorcet was in hiding from the Jacobins.

Attitude Toward Religion. Another consequence of the 18th century's confidence in scientific method was an extremely critical attitude toward matters of faith—matters that, by their very nature, could not be subjected to a ''scientific'' critique. Though I. Kant was busy in Germany attempting to provide some rational justification for faith, the general trend of the period was represented by the religious SKEPTICISM of the *philosophes*, particularly Voltaire, J. D'Alembert, and D. Diderot. While these men attacked religion with a vehemence and lack of restraint that induce doubts about their good faith, it must be noted to their credit that much of what they attacked in the religious practices of their day was deserving of criticism, e.g., an excessive love for the miraculous and the bizarre, the Jansenistic view of God as a harsh and exacting master, the bitter rivalries between religious groups, the sentimentalities of some society women who played at being ''spiritual,'' and the failure of powerful and wealthy believers to care for the poor and oppressed. To this extent the *philosophes* can be said to have worked for an ''enlightenment'' in religion and an end to superstition. However, failing to distinguish between genuine religion and its aberrations, they let their enthusiasm for scientific method lead them to characterize all religion based on revelation as superstition. Indeed, when mention is made of the Enlightenment in the 21st century, the characteristic most remembered is the replacement of religious faith by reason—with reason being restricted, in theory if not always in practice, to what was empirically verifiable.

Moses Mendelssohn.

Political Notions. Parallel with the rejection of religious tradition there occurred a similar rejection of political traditions. The general acceptance of hereditary monarchical rule, a privileged class of nobles, and an alliance between the Church and the State gave way, by the end of the century, to the secularized liberty, equality, and fraternity of the French Revolution. The new spirit was epitomized in the 1789 Declaration of the Rights of Man and of the Citizen, which asserted that man had a natural right to liberty, property, security, and resistance to oppression; that sovereignty resided in the nation as a whole rather than in one man; that law was the expression of the general will of the people; and that all citizens were equal before the law. These same principles had guided the American Founding Fathers in severing the ties with monarchical England and in setting up a representative government, principles that had been popularized by Enlightenment writers such as Baron de MONTESQUIEU and J. J. ROUSSEAU. Thomas Jefferson and Benjamin Franklin were deeply imbued with the spirit of the Enlightenment; and Thomas PAINE was active in promoting this spirit, first in America in his *Common Sense* (Philadelphia 1776), afterward in England in his *Rights of Man* (Philadelphia 1791–92), and then in France, where he was elected to the Convention by the Department of Calais. Paine's *The Age of Reason* (London 1794–96) was an expression of the DEISM that became the religion of the Enlightenment.

Bibliography: C. L. BECKER, *The Heavenly City of the Eighteenth-Century Philosophers* (New Haven 1932). R. ROCKWOOD, *Carl Becker's Heavenly City Revisited* (Ithaca, N.Y. 1958). L. I. BREDVOLD, *The Brave New World of the Enlightenment* (Ann Arbor 1961). E. CASSIRER, *The Philosophy of the Enlightenment,* tr. C. A. KOELLN and J. P. PETTEGROVE (Princeton 1951). H. G. NICOLSON, *The Age of Reason* (Garden City, N.Y. 1961). G. HAVENS, *The Age of Ideas: From Reaction to Revolution in 18th-Century France* (New York 1955). P. HAZARD, *European Thought in the Eighteenth Century: From Montesquieu to Lessing,* tr. J. L. MAY (New Haven 1954). C. FRANKEL, *The Faith of Reason: The Idea of Progress in the French Enlightenment* (New York 1948). A. VARTANIAN, *Diderot and Descartes: A Study of Scientific Naturalism in the Enlightenment* (Princeton 1953). R. R. PALMER, *Catholics and Unbelievers in 18th-Century France* (Princeton 1939).

[R. Z. LAUER]

German Enlightenment

The German Enlightenment presents a rather complex intellectual structure in which various currents of thought are discernible ranging all the way from RATIONALISM to PIETISM. This part of the article considers its historical development and concludes with a brief critique.

Historical Development. The history of the German Enlightenment may best be divided into three phases: the early period, that of Wolff and his school, and that of its full development.

Early Period (*1690–1720*). The central figure of this period is Christian Thomasius, with whom the first influence of English EMPIRICISM and PSYCHOLOGISM began to be discernible in German philosophy. In place of the concept of man proposed by traditional metaphysics and moral philosophy, he substituted the notion of man as he actually is, and this particularly in his philosophy of law. Although Thomasius's teacher, Samuel Pufendorff (1632–94) still conceived law as a metaphysical and moral order, for Thomasius law was only a clever balancing of the instinctual and emotional life of man for its purely utilitarian value. Thomasius introduced the separation between law and ethics that was later to prove disastrous.

Wolff and His School (*1720–50*). Christian WOLFF was a typical rationalist—a term used in a pejorative sense by his opponents, particularly the Pietists and orthodox Protestants. Since Martin Luther had placed faith over reason, Pietism treated any religion based on reason as an encroachment upon the freedom and omnipotence of God and of His grace. Understanding and reason thereupon came to be the passwords of Wolff and of his school: through enlightened reason man was to be led to virtue and to happiness. The titles of Wolff's works repeatedly read *Vernünftige Gedanken über. . . .* Actually, however, Wolff's emphasis on reason was not so much the usual rationalist emphasis as it was a return to the type of thought that characterized the school metaphysics of the 17th century and of G. W. LEIBNIZ in particular. Both Leibniz and Wolff were seeking a synthesis of reason and religion, of metaphysics and theology.

Nonetheless, Wolff's Pietistic opponents accused him of being atheistic. In 1723 he was relieved of his position in Halle, where he was professor of philosophy, and he was expelled from the region under threat of being hanged for his teaching. The Hessian University of Marburg received him, however, and there Wolff lived to see his renown reach its climax. In 1740 Frederick II of Prussia brought him back to Halle with full honors. The accusation of atheism was there seen to be completely unjust. Quite the opposite, Wolff had much occupied himself with proofs for the existence of God just as had the proponents of the older metaphysics. The treatment by Wolff, however, was not made in the spirit of the old metaphysics, but rather with a type of purely conceptual analysis that proved too little because it set out to prove too much. More particularly, Wolff understood PROOF (*demonstratio*) in a mathematical sense, overlooking both experience and the inner life of man in the process, and therefore supplying judgments that were analytical and not synthetic.

Wolff's efforts later provoked Kant's criticism of the proofs for the existence of God. When Kant spoke of metaphysics, he usually had in mind the metaphysics of the Leibniz-Wolffian school. For his lectures on metaphysics, in fact, Kant had used a textbook of a student of Wolff, A. G. Baumgarten (1714–62), who is noted also for his work on AESTHETICS. Other students of Wolff include J. C. Gottsched (1700–66), who was similarly occupied with aesthetics; M. Knutzen (1713–51), who taught the young Kant in Königsberg; and G. B. Bilfinger (1693–1750), whose *Philosophische Erleuchtungen* served for a long time as the best textbook of Wolffian metaphysics. In 1737 there were already no less than 107 authors who were writing in a way that identified them as belonging to the Wolffian school. Opponents of Wolff included J. Lange (1670–1744), who was later professor of theology in Halle, as well as A. Rüdiger (1673–1731) and C. A. Crusius (1715–75).

Full Development (c. *1750–80*). In the last phase, the German Enlightenment again fell under the influence of the French and English Enlightenment. Frederick II of Prussia, himself a freethinking litterateur, sent for C. A. Helvetius (1715–71) at Potsdam, made friends with Voltaire, and took Rousseau into his service. Other influences, traceable to John Toland (1670–1722) and Matthew Tindal (1656–1733), encouraged the growth of DEISM. Toland had been in Hanover in 1701 and 1702, while Tindal's work *Christianity as Old as Creation* (London 1730) was translated into German in 1741. In rationalist and Deist circles, the Hamburg Orientalist H. S. Reimarus (1694–1768) criticized the Bible and revelation in his unpublished *Schutzschrift für die vernünftigen Verehrer Gottes.* For him, miracles and revelation are unworthy of God. The thought of Moses Mendelssohn (1729–86) was also Deist.

The greatest figure in this last phase of the German Enlightenment, however, was Mendelssohn's friend G. E. LESSING, the son of a Lutheran pastor in Saxony, a free-lance writer, poet (*Minna von Barnhelm, Emilia Galotti,* and *Nathan der Weise*), secretary of famous personalities, dramatic producer of the Hamburg National Theater, and finally librarian at Wolfenbüttel. His poetry created a new literary taste, while his writings on aesthetics (*Laokoon* and *Hamburger Dramaturgie*) provide a theory of art, especially of drama, that to this day has not become dated. In his *Wolfenbüttler Fragmenten* Lessing published a part of Reimarus's *Schutzschrift* and thereupon provoked a passionate discussion over whether religion should be based on reason or on revelation. Lessing's philosophy saw the divine in the rational ordering of the universe, the moral in reason itself, and the education of the human race in religion and the great religious figures. For him, the religions are not something conclusive, but stages in the vital development of mankind. Everything is undergoing evolution, including religion itself. In particular, there is no final truth for man, but only the constant search for it; this alone gives meaning to the term truth. So as not to shorten this constant search, Lessing taught a repeated existence for man, a palingenesis similar to that of the transmigration of souls. His *Erziehung des Menschengeschlechtes* (Berlin 1780), moreover, contains a philosophy of history and of religion that exerted as much influence on German idealism as it did on liberal Protestant theology of the 19th century.

Alongside the unique and great figure of Lessing stand a long line of popular philosophers of this period, such as the psychologist J. N. Tetens (1736–1807), the moral philosopher J. G. Sulzer (1720–79), the spiritual aphorist G. C. Lichtenberg (1742–99), the Hamburg educator J. B. Basedow, and the still more important Swiss educator J. H. PESTALOZZI. The last-named, however, extends beyond the period of the Enlightenment, and the emotional element in his work takes on more significance than the rational. Those who eventually brought about the overthrow of the Enlightenment were J. G. HAMANN, F. H. JACOBI, and J. G. HERDER.

Critique. The Enlightenment in Germany did much good for education in general and for public instruction in particular. Even catechetical instruction benefited from its lively stimulation, insofar as it replaced rote memory with understanding and encouraged independent thought similar to that of the Socratic method. The cultivation of the humanities and of intellectual tolerance was here served, just as was the battle against biased judgments.

On the other hand, the Enlightenment itself gave rise to new and dangerous prejudices. In this connection one could mention its faith in the omnipotence of reason and of science, its uncritical progressive thinking, and the naïveté of its humanism, which treated man as though he had suffered no blemish from original sin and could work out his own destiny. A similar excess lay in the Enlightenment's Deist conviction that man is able to discern what is possible for God and what is not. Revelation cannot contradict reason, this is true, but man's reason is not the complete and exclusive measure of revelation. The Enlightenment was just as uncomprehending in the face of mystery as it was in the face of history. The enlightened man was faced with the temptation to make himself the measure of all things because he conceived himself as the ideal man. For that reason he regarded parochial education as a second-class effort and thought that a Catholic could not be a complete scholar. One consequence of this attitude is secular education, which is not aware of its peculiar presuppositions and prejudices and to this extent encroaches upon true freedom. ''Enlightened'' thinkers seem unaware that there is no such thing as the ideal man whom they take themselves to be.

See Also: FREETHINKERS; THEISM.

Bibliography: F. C. COPLESTON, *History of Philosophy* (Westminster, Md. 1946–) v.6, Wolff to Kant. H. LEISEGANG, *Lessings Weltanschauung* (Leipzig 1931). H. THIELICKE, *Offenbarung, Vernunft und Existenz: Studien zur Religionsphilosophie Lessings* (Gütersloh 1936; 4th ed. 1959). M. CAMPO, *Cristiano Wolff e il razionalismo precritico,* 2 v. (Milan 1939). M. WUNDT, *Chr. Wolff und die deutsche Aufklärung* (Stuttgart 1941); *Die deutsche Schulphilosophie im Zeitalter der Aufklärung* (Tübingen 1945). H. M. WOLFF, *Die Weltanschauung der deutschen Aufklärung in geschichtlicher Entwicklung* (Bern 1949). R. HAASS, *Die geistige Haltung der katholischen Universitäten Deutschlands im 18. Jahrhundert: Ein Beitrag zur Geschichte der Aufklärung* (Freiburg 1952). W. PHILIPP, *Das Werden der Aufklärung in theologie-geschichtlicher Sicht* (Göttingen 1957).

[J. HIRSCHBERGER]

ENMITY (IN THE BIBLE)

The mutual hostility between persecutor and persecuted, for which the Christian, following Christ's new morality, must substitute a new attitude by which he loves and prays for his enemy (Mt 5.43–48; Lk 6.27–36).

Enmity in the Old Testament. The doctrine of Leviticus demanded that an Israelite respect the rights of his NEIGHBOR and love his fellow Israelites (Leviticus 19.11–18) and even foreigners who lived among them (19.33–34). One was urged to come to the aid of one's enemy when he lost or suffered damage to his livestock (Ex 23.4–5). Besides encouraging a beneficent control over excessive revenge, which was the main purpose of the law of exact retaliation (Ex 21.24; confer, Gn 4.23–24), Hebrew wisdom went further and urged those who had suffered injustice to leave vengeance to God (Prv 20.22), and even to act kindly toward their enemies (Prv 25.21–22). Job, in his ideal innocence, never rejoiced at his enemy's misfortune or, by cursing, wished him dead (Jb 31.29–30). No such command as cited in Matthew 5.43b, "'. . . and shall hate thy enemy,'" can be found in the Old Testament. It is probably a gloss inferred as the opposite of the command to love one's friend (Lv 19.18), and has the tolerative meaning of "and you need not love your enemy."

On the other hand, the disdain in which Israelites held non-Israelites and enemy nations was one of their well-known traits, recorded by Tacitus (*Hist.* 5.5) and exemplified by many Old Testament passages [Dt 7.2; 15.1–3; 23.4–7, 21; 25.17–19; Ps 136(137).7–9]. However, such international enmity is not in question here. Our Lord is contrasting the attitude between a person and his friends to the new attitude of God's sons toward their personal enemies, mainly those who persecute them for religious motives.

In this context of personal enmity Israelites exacted BLOOD VENGEANCE in accordance with their ethical background (Nm 35.19), not even allowing a ransom for the life of a murderer, although such a custom was prevalent in the ancient Near East (Nm 35.31–33). This legitimate vengeance led the Israelites to feel toward unjust aggressors what can be called a justifiable animosity, so vividly depicted in Psalm 108 (109). Since Hebrew law was not only religious but civil, it had to allow for such external manifestations of animus against evil men.

Enmity in the New Testament. In Our Lord's insistence, the new law forbade a Christian to nurture even the best motivated feelings of animosity and demanded instead a benevolence toward enemies, copied after the Father's concern for all men, even the most evil. The enmity to be borne by a member of God's kingdom was especially apt to take the form of religious persecution. The Christian should, indeed, desire that God's enemies desist from opposing God's work in His faithful, but he should desire this without personal hatred for the persecutors. Rather, one should pray for them, a command that should be taken literally and not as a Semitic exaggeration to emphasize a vague moral ideal. Jesus Himself gave His disciples the greatest example of compliance with this command (Lk 23.34), an example later imitated by St. Stephen (Acts 7.60). To love and do good to another who is unfriendly and in opposition to oneself, is, therefore, to imitate in the highest degree the beneficence of God toward His rebellious creatures; it is to reach up and practice God's way of loving, commended to mankind by Christ's destruction of the source of all enmity: ". . . because when as yet we were sinners, Christ died for us" (Rom 5.8–9).

Bibliography: J. A. SANDERS, *The Interpreters' Dictionary of the Bible,* ed. G. A. BUTTRICK, 4 v. (Nashville 1962) 2:101. *Encyclopedic Dictionary of the Bible,* tr. and adap. by L. HARTMAN (New York 1963) 1381.

[J. E. FALLON]

ENNODIUS, MAGNUS FELIX

Ecclesiastical writer and bishop; b. Arles, France, *c.* 473; d. Pavia, Italy, 521. Ennodius, orphaned at an early age, entered the clerical state in Pavia *c.* 494; he then served as secretary to his uncle Laurentius, Bishop of Milan. At a Roman synod in 502 he defended the right of SYMMACHUS to the papal throne; he became bishop of Pavia in 512 or 513. In 515 and again in 517 he headed embassies from Pope HORMISDAS to the Emperor ANASTASIUS I to heal the ACACIAN SCHISM (484), but both missions failed. Known as a zealous pastor he is honored in Pavia as a saint. Ennodius's literary works, written before he became bishop, are often a strange blend of Christian and pagan ideas, so heavily embellished as to be at times unintelligible. His 297 letters are important source material for the early 6th century. His 28 *Dictiones* are model speeches for students, or ''occasional sermons'' to be used by his fellow priests. Among his *Opuscula* are an outstanding life of St. EPIPHANIUS and a sermon in honor of THEODORIC THE GREAT. His 21 poems are grammatically correct but without verve or originality, while some of his 151 epigrams are in questionable taste. His *Eucharisticon de vita sua* is an imitation of the *Confessions* but lacks Augustine's introspection and sincerity. His defense of Symmachus contains the famous sentence: ''God indeed ordained that men should settle the affairs of men; but to pass judgment on the bishop of this see [Rome] He unquestionably reserved to Himself.'' He also urged that the title ''pope'' be restricted to the bishop of Rome.

Feast: July 17.

Bibliography: *Opera Omnia,* ed. G. HARTEL (*Corpus scriptorum ecclesiasticorum latinorum* 6; 1882); *Opera,* ed. F. VOGEL (*Monumenta Germaniae Historica, Auctores antiquissimi* 7; 1885); *The Life of St. Epiphanius,* tr. and ed. G. COOK (Washington 1942). P. C. DE LABRIOLLE, *History and Literature of Christianity,* tr. H. WILSON (New York 1924). M. HADAS, *A History of Latin Literature* (New York 1952). B. ALTANER, *Patrology* (New York 1960) 572–574.

[S. J. MCKENNA]

ENOCH

The son of Cain and the father of Irad, according to the YAHWIST genealogy in Gn 4.17–24. The purpose of this genealogy is to depict the increase of sin and violence in the world from Cain to Lamech (Gn 4.8, 23–24) that came as a result of the Fall (Gn ch. 3). By contrast, the Enoch of the Sethite genealogy of the Pentateuchal PRIESTLY WRITERS in Gn 5.1–32, according to which he is the son of Jared (a variant of Irad) and the father of Mathusale (5.18–24), seems to pertain to the paradisaic era of mankind. The priestly narrative makes no explicit mention of a fall in Adam, but indicates only that by the time of Noah the earth had become corrupt in God's sight and filled with violence (Gn 6.11). Enoch's lifetime belonged to the era when death had not yet touched mankind. ADAM, Seth, and the rest of his ancestors were still alive (5.5–20). During his life on earth, ''Enoch walked with God'' (5.24a). This recalls the Yahwist PARADISE tradition that speaks of Yahweh ''walking in the garden'' (3.8). Enoch, at the end of a perfect life cycle (365 years, by analogy with the solar cycle of 365 days), does not die. All that is said of Enoch is that ''he was seen no more because God took him'' (5.24b). Enoch, belonging to the seventh generation of mankind, seems to mark the apex of the paradisaic era. Thereafter, men will die; corruption will fill the earth.

The Book of Sirach is dependent on Gn 5.21–24 in its praise of Enoch as one who ''walked with the Lord and was taken'' (Sir 44.16; 49.14). Sirach, like Gn 5.21, is extremely reticent with reference to any so-called ascension of Enoch. Whereas Elijah ''went up'' (2 Kgs 2.11), or ''was taken up'' (Sir 48.9), of Enoch the Old Testament says only that God ''took him'' (Gn 5.21; Sir 44.16; 49.14). Sirach also praises Enoch as ''a wonder to succeeding generations by reason of his knowledge,'' i.e., of divine mysteries (Sir 44.16). Here Sirach is perhaps dependent on the various noncanonical traditions that credit Enoch with the reception of special revelations, whether during his lifetime [Enoch (Ethiopic)] or at the time of his so-called ascension to heaven [Enoch (Slavic)]. Traditions concerning Enoch the visionary and revealer of mysteries are preserved in several apocryphal works including the Ethiopic Book of Enoch, written originally in Hebrew or Aramaic about the second century B.C. and preserved only fragmentarily in Greek and Ethiopic translations, and the Slavic Book of Enoch, originally written in Greek by a Jew in the first or second Christian century and probably later revised under Christian influence.

The Epistle of St. JUDE (v. 14) refers to Enoch as a revealer of mysteries and includes a direct citation from Ethiopic Enoch (60.8). The entire passage found in Jude v. 4–15 reveals a dependence on Ethiopic Enoch (Jude v. 4 on 48.10; Jude v. 6 on 12.4; 10.4–6, 11–12; Jude v. 14 on 60.8; Jude v. 14–15 on 1.9). The author of Hebrews praises Enoch's faith and speaks of his transfer or removal (μετάθεσις, not ascension ἀνάλημψις), as a reward of his faith (Heb 11.5). This is a theme that appears frequently in Ethiopic Enoch and also in Jubilees 10.17. The dependence of Heb 11.5 on the apocryphal traditions, however, is not certain. Enoch is also mentioned in the genealogy of Lk 2.23–24 in dependence upon Gn 5.18–24.

Bibliography: H. ODEBERG, G. KITTEL, *Theologisches Wörterbuch zum Neuen Testament* (Stuttgart 1935–) 2:553–557. C. BONNER, *The Last Chapters of Enoch in Greek* (Haverford, Pa. 1937). J. T. MILIK, ''The Dead Sea Scrolls Fragment of the Book of Enoch,'' *Biblica* 32 (1951) 393–400. N. AVIGAD and Y. YADIN, *A Genesis Apocryphon* (Jerusalem 1956). J. DANIÉLOU, *Holy Pagans of the O. T.*, tr. F. FABER (Baltimore 1957) 42–56. D. S. RUSSELL, *The Method and Message of Jewish Apocalyptic* (Philadelphia 1964) 107–118, 327–330. R. H. CHARLES et al., eds., *The Apocrypha and Pseudepigrapha of the O.T. in English,* 2 v. (Oxford 1913) 2:163–164, 425–469. T. W. MANSON, ''The Son of Man in Daniel, Enoch and the Gospels,'' *The Bulletin of the John Rylands Library* 32 (1949–50) 171–193.

[J. PLASTARAS]

ENOCH LITERATURE

The researches of J. T. Milik (see bibliography) on these complicated and fragmentary Aramaic materials have yet to be fully published; and their implications for the Jewish background of Christianity have still to be worked out in detail. One solid inference would seem to be that the absence from the Qumran texts of any trace of the Parables (or, Similitudes) of Enoch (1 Enoch 37–71) is no mere accident. The highly developed portrayal of a messianic ''son of man'' in this part of the composite book needs therefore to be reevaluated as to its date and its relationship to the Gospels.

Insight into the cosmic speculations and apocalyptic hopes in Jewish Palestine before the latest books of the Old Testament were written can be gained from these fragments. In the order of their composition as seen by Milik (except for section 3 below), the several parts of the Enoch collection are as follows: 1. A ''Book of the Heavenly Luminaries'' corresponding to 1 Enoch ch. 72–82. Of four manuscripts (4QEn astr$^{a\text{–}d}$), the oldest is from ±200 B.C., the latest from around the birth of Christ. This material was presented independently in ancient times, and has been greatly reduced before being incorporated into the later book, which also lacks the opening and final portions. It began with a long calendrical treatise, reconciling the solar year with the liturgical year of 364 days adopted into the Book of Jubilees and into Essene worship. This and other lore are presented as taught to Enoch during his earthly life by the angel Uriel. Except for ch. 81 of the later work (still earlier than 100 B.C), this section was composed in the Persian period, fifth–fourth centuries B.C. Its mythical geography is cosmic in scope and shows Babylonian influence. 2. The opening part of 1 Enoch (ch. 1–36) is best described as the ''Book of Watchers,'' i.e., of fallen angels to whom the origin of evil among men is attributed. It includes an older core (ch. 6–19) that contains ''Visions of Enoch.'' Five Qumran manuscripts containing half the text of the 36 chapters prove that the section was already fixed in its content early in the second century B.C. Milik sees it as a third-century B.C. composition, with the ''Visions'' older still. 3. Linked to the ''Book of Watchers'' before 100 B.C. was a ''Book of Giants'' dealing with the legendary antediluvians of Gn 6.1–4. Fragments of this and related texts exist in no less than 15 manuscripts from four different Qumran caves. Taken over by Mani in the third century A.D., it became an accepted part of Manichaean literature, in languages reaching from central Asia to Africa and western Europe. It was still known in the context of the Enoch compilation to Christian writers in Alexandria in the fifth century A.D. The inference lies ready to hand that it was this ''Book of Giants'' with its unsavory Manichaean associations for which the ''Parables of Enoch'' were substituted about the sixth century. Milik dates the ''Parables'' (he prefers ''Discourses'') about A.D. 270, and sees them as written originally in Greek in the style of the Sibylline oracles; they depend on the canonical Gospels. This evaluation will no doubt be controverted. 4. The ''Book of Dreams'' corresponding to 1 Enoch 83–90 comprises two dream visions narrated by Enoch, now thought of as living with his wife in a far-off paradise; he is brought back to earth by angelic guides to instruct his descendants. This section, known from four Qumran manuscripts, is patterned closely on the ''Book of Watchers,'' to which it was composed as a pendant in 164 B.C. (according to Milik). The first dream has to do with the Flood; the second gives a conspectus of world history in highly allegorical terms. From the period of the Exile, 70 successive angelic guardians govern Israel until the end time. A similar scheme (70 generations from Enoch to Christ) underlies the genealogy in Lk 3.23–38. 5. The ''Letter of Enoch'' (1 Enoch 91–105), written in a Hellenistic milieu such as Gaza not later than 100 B.C., is known from two Qumran copies. It transforms the scheme of 70 periods into a cycle of 10 ''weeks of years''; of these, the first seven, a jubilee cycle, comprise world history. The remaining three weeks of years are the eschatological end time. This arrangement combines 70 x 7 elements from a third-century B.C. ''Book of Periods'' with a 10 x 49 pattern from an apocalypse of jubilees transmitted under the name of Ezekiel. Both these sources are known from Qumran; only the former has been partially published. Chapters 106–107 of the Enoch compilation, borrowed from a separate work dealing with the birth of Noah, were already united with the ''Letter'' in a scroll copied late in the first century B.C.

The scroll just mentioned (4QEn^{c}) is that which yields (along with 4QEn Giants^{a}, written by the same scribe) the clearest evidence that the five sections listed above were treated as a two-volume composite work in pre-Christian times: section 1 apart because of its bulk, and sections 2 to 5 combined into a second scroll. Evidence drawn from George Syncellus establishes that this was still the arrangement known in Greek codices to the Christians of Egypt about A.D. 400. The regrouping of the parts into the order 2, ''Parables'' (instead of 3), 4, 1, 5, which produced the *Ethiopic Enoch,* is later, the origin of the last chapter (108) is unexplained.

See Also: QUMRAN COMMUNITY.

Bibliography: J. T. MILIK, ''Problèmes de la Littérature hénochique à la lumière des fragments araméens de Qumrân,'' *Harvard Theological Review* 64 (1971) 333–378, with further references. J. T. MILIK and M. BLACK, *The Books of Enoch, Aramaic Fragments of Qumrân Cave 4* (Oxford in press).

[P. W. SKEHAN]

ENTELECHY

In the usage of Aristotle, entelechy (Gr. 'εντελάεξεια, from 'εν τάελει 'εξειν, to have something in fulfillment; to be complete) is an analogical word. It has two most basic uses: (1) to designate the state of achievement or fulfillment that is like knowledge acquired and possessed (this is its first imposition); and (2) to designate the state of fulfillment, presupposing what is like knowledge possessed, that is like the actual entertaining or considering of knowledge possessed. For example, having acquired, and thus in possession of, knowledge of a geometric proof, one has fulfilled to some extent his natural capacity for learning. But he does not spend the rest of his life thinking through the steps of the proof. Actually thinking through the steps of the proof represents another and distinct sort of fulfillment. Before one has learned the proof, he is capable of learning it. Having learned the proof, he is capable of thinking through its steps. Corresponding to each of these two states of capability is a state of fulfillment, an entelechy. Knowledge possessed is simultaneously, but in different relations, both entelechy and capability. Actually thinking through the steps is impossible without knowledge possessed. This is why what is like knowledge possessed has been called *first* entelechy—first in an ontological sense, that without which something else cannot be or occur. This is also why what is like actually thinking through the steps has been called *second* entelechy. (See Aristotle, *Anim.* 412a 10–12; 417a 21–417b 2.)

Aristotle's purpose in distinguishing these two senses of entelechy was to make clear the sense of the first of his two common definitions of the SOUL: the first entelechy (actuality or ACT is a usual rendering) of a natural body having life potentially in it, i.e., of a natural organized body. The natural organized body of a living thing is related to its soul in the way in which man, taken as a knower, is related to knowledge possessed. The living thing, i.e., the compound of natural organized body and soul, is related to its vital operations (e.g., nourishing, sensing) in the way in which the knowing man, i.e., the compound of human knower and knowledge possessed, is related to actually thinking through the steps. Thus, the natural organized body of a living thing has a twofold entelechy: (1) soul, and (2) vital operations. Soul, being the ontologically prior, i.e., accounting for the ontological status of a living thing as living thing (this is why it is said to be a substantial form), and being that which vital operations presuppose and upon which they depend, is said to be the first entelechy of such a body; a vital operation, a second entelechy.

The suggestion of G. W. LEIBNIZ that his monads may be called entelechies, since they have in themselves a certain perfection consisting in their nonconscious perceptions, represents a usage differing from Aristotle's in that it designates something that is simple and also a substance. Aristotle's designates something simple, indeed; but something related to a substance, and not a substance itself.

Hans Driesch develops a notion of entelechy in the course of a lengthy argument against biological mechanism and for biological vitalism. Entelechy is an elemental agent in nature, over and above physical and chemical agents and configurations thereof, that in the realm of living things accounts for all the order in morphogenesis, and uses the genes as its means to account for inheritance. More generally, it directs life activities and everything material that is used in their performance. It is not a kind of energy, nor is it something quantitative, nor divisible, nor a force; it is not space, but has manifestations in space; it is substance, but only in the sense of what accounts for the ordered wholeness of a living thing; it is a cause, but only in an actual state, as actually accounting for wholeness (since it can also appear in a potential state). Driesch's concept of entelechy is clearly not incompatible with that of Aristotle; but whereas Aristotle's use of entelechy apropos of soul focuses on soul's function as the formal cause constituting a thing a living being, Driesch's can be said to focus on soul's function as efficient or agent cause in relation to the biological development and behavior of the living thing.

See Also: SOUL, HUMAN.

Bibliography: G. GIANNINI, *Enciclopedia filosofica*, 4 v. (Venice-Rome 1957) 1:1919–25. G. W. LEIBNIZ, *The Monadology*, in his *Discourse on Metaphysics, Correspondence with Arnauld, and the Monadology*, tr. G. R. MONTGOMERY (La Salle, Ill. 1962). H. DRIESCH, *The Science and Philosophy of the Organism* (2d ed. London 1929).

[J. BOBIK]

ENUMA ELISH

Babylonian epic of creation. It derives its name from the poem's opening words, *enūma eliš* (when on high). The poem, comprising seven tablets and slightly more than 1,000 lines, narrates the creation and battles of the gods, the creation of man, and the ordering of the cosmos. These themes, however, are subordinate to the poem's primary purpose: to explain how the god MARDUK, patron deity of BABYLON, attained his exalted position in the Babylonian pantheon. Because of its popularity and its annual solemn recital in the liturgy of the 4th day of the New Year's festival, the poem has survived in many copies and can be restored almost in its entirety.

Contents. Enuma Elish begins with a description of the cosmos as it was in the beginning: watery chaos, consisting of three elements—Apsu (the sweet waters), Tiamat (the salt water), and Mummu (probably the mist). From this chaos, with Apsu as father and Tiamat as mother, are born the gods Laḫmu and Laḫamu, who in turn beget gods as their children, have grandchildren, etc. The newly created gods enjoy lively and noisy gatherings, and their hilarity disturbs Apsu and Tiamat, who decide to destroy them. The wise young god Ea, however, learns of their scheme, weaves a spell over Apsu, and kills him, enslaving Mummu at the same time. Ea and his wife then establish their dwelling over the dead Apsu, and there their son Marduk, the hero of the epic, is born.

Meanwhile, some gods incite Tiamat to avenge the death of Apsu. She creates the tremendous army of monsters and places her second husband, Kingu, at its head. Ea, Anu, and Anshar, the three supreme gods, are powerless to overcome Tiamat and her host; and finally an assembly of the gods is called, in which young Marduk is proposed as their champion. Marduk accepts, on the condition that he, instead of the other gods, will henceforth decree all destinies and that his command will be supreme. The gods assent and invest him with the external insignia of kingship.

Marduk then ventures forth against Tiamat, with arrows of lightning, a net held by the four winds, and severe storms as his weapons. Kingu and his army withdraw, and Marduk and Tiamat are pitted in single combat. As she opens her jaws to devour him, he sends in winds to hold them open. Through her open mouth he then shoots an arrow that pierces her heart and kills her. From her dead body he makes the sky and then creates and sets in order the rest of the universe. Kingu is slain, and man is created from his blood by Ea (according to Marduk's plans). The gods are then assigned their various functions by Marduk; and they in return have Babylon and its temple, Esagila, built, where Marduk may reside in majesty. In conclusion, the great gods hold a banquet at which Marduk is seated on a throne, given the tablets of "destinies," and addressed by 50 titles expressing his supreme functions.

Origin. Unlike the GILGAMESH EPIC, Enuma Elish is apparently not derived from earlier Sumerian literary forerunners. It is a distinctly Babylonian creation and was composed in Akkadian sometime during the 2d millennium B.C. In most scholarly circles it is customary to assign the origin of Enuma Elish to approximately the reign of HAMMURABI (Hammurapi), i.e., the 18th century B.C., when the city of Babylon first rose to paramount political importance. The poem is usually viewed as theological underpinning for the rise of an upstart city to become the seat of a mighty empire and for the elevation of its hitherto obscure god to the head of the pantheon in place of the Sumerian god Enlil, who had ruled over the gods previously. Although fragments of the poem have been found in Kish, Uruk, NINEVEH, and Assur (where the Assyrian national god, Ashur, replaces Marduk as hero of the local version), none of these antedate the 1st millennium B.C.; but the faintly archaic language of the poem may be taken as indication of an earlier origin.

Several scholars, however, have presented plausible alternate approaches to the origin of Enuma Elish. W. G. Lambert, for instance, has shown evidence that Marduk was still a relatively minor god in the Babylonian pantheon until about the 13th century B.C. and that he rose to officially sanctioned preeminence only in the late 12th century under Nebuchadnezzar I, on the occasion of a great religious revival in Babylonia. T. Jacobsen, adducing parallels between the Ugaritic epics and Enuma Elish and noting that the sea-storm motif would be much more at home in Syria, has contended that the Babylonian epic—or at least prominent elements of its theomachy—derived from the West Semitic world; he also views Enuma Elish as essentially a cosmogony (with Enlil originally as hero) and only secondarily (after the insertion of Marduk) revised into an apologia for Marduk.

The present state of the epic makes it difficult to adopt, unequivocally, any of these opinions. The original language of the poem is an artificial scribal tongue, thus hard to date precisely. Because of breaks in meter and rhythm at vital points in the verse, traces of extensive later revision may be detected—often to the detriment of the literary qualities of the epic; in this respect it is considerably inferior to the Gilgamesh saga. But it is difficult to date the alleged insertions, and definitive answers to the many problems of origin must await more explicit evidence.

Extra-Babylonian Parallels. Echoes of a primeval divine fight with monsters of the deep can also be found in the OT [e.g., Is 27.1; 51.9–10; Ps 88(89).10–12; Jb 26.12–13] and in Ugaritic literature. (*See* LEVIATHAN). Several other parallels between the Babylonian and OT cosmogony can also be found, e.g., the watery chaos (Akkadian *Tiāmat,* Heb. *t*[e] *hôm*), the existence of light before luminaries, the formation of man as the culminating point of terrestrial creation. [*See* COSMOGONY (IN THE BIBLE)]. But, in general, the dissimilarities between the two accounts are more striking, especially the unequivocal monotheism and sublime grandeur of the Genesis tale as contrasted with the wrangling polytheism (or, at best, henotheism) of the Babylonian tale. The common motifs in creation stories might be explained on the basis of a background of common Semitic folklore or on the basis of known Babylonian literary influence on 2d-millennium Palestine-Syria (or, less plausibly, the reverse). Direct literary borrowing either way seems unlikely from the nature of the sources.

Bibliography: E. A. SPEISER, tr., "The Creation Epic," J. B. PRITCHARD, *Ancient Near Eastern Texts Relating to the Old Testament* (2d rev. ed. Princeton 1955) 60–72. A. HEIDEL, *The Babylonian Genesis* (2d ed. Chicago 1951). W. G. LAMBERT, "The Reign of Nebuchadnezzar I: A Turning Point in the History of Ancient Mesopotamian Religion," *The Seed of Wisdom,* ed. W. S. MCCULLOUGH (Toronto 1964) 3–13. H. FRANKFORT et al., *Before Philosophy* (pa. Baltimore 1959) 182–199.

[J. A. BRINKMAN]

ENVY

Envy is the culpable sadness or displeasure at the spiritual or temporal good of another. In popular usage envy is often not distinguished from jealousy, but jealousy implies a sense of right on the part of the jealous person to the exclusive possession of something. Jealousy, in spite of the pejorative connotation that is usually attached to the term, is not necessarily evil, so long as the right is well founded and the reaction to its violation is expressed in a reasonable manner. The desire of exclusive possession appears at first sight to enter into St. Thomas Aquinas's concept also of envy, for he says that envy makes the good of another an evil to oneself, inasmuch as it lessens one's own excellence (St. Thomas, *Summa Theologiae,* 2a2ae, 36.1). But the point is that the envious person is saddened not precisely because he feels his exclusive right is violated when another possesses the good he envies, but because he feels lessened and humiliated when another is more favored than himself.

Not all displeasure at another's good is sinful: the good may be undeserved, as when an unworthy person is advanced to a position of trust and responsibility; the good may create a nuisance to others, as when the boy next door acquires a bugle; the good may be harmful to the possessor himself, as when sudden affluence comes to a person lacking the virtue to make good use of it.

But if it is supposed that the good is a true good, to be pained or displeased at another's enjoyment of it is sinful. Envy springs from pride, vanity, and ill-regulated self-love. It is sinful because it is opposed to the benevolence essential to charity. Its gravity is dependent on the importance of the good that is envied. The worst envy is that which looks with displeasure upon the spiritual good of another, for such envy has an obviously diabolical character. Envy is a venial sin when it is concerned with trivial goods or when, as is often the case, it is indeliberate or imperfectly voluntary.

From the time of Origen, envy has regularly been numbered among the capital SINS; from it come hatred, calumny, detraction, and many types of malevolent behavior.

Some of the Fathers appear to have regarded envy as an incurable vice [e.g., St. Basil, *Homilia de invidia, Patrologia Graeca,* ed. J. P. Migne, 161 v. (Paris 1857–66) 31:373], or as one curable only by a miracle. However, this must be understood, not of the vice or sin, but of the propensity to envy that is inherent in concupiscence.

The vice of envy is best and most radically remedied by the curbing of the pride, vanity, and self-love from which it comes. Growth in fraternal charity will inevitably weaken the disposition to envy.

Bibliography: L. DESBRUS, *Dictionnaire de théologie catholique,* ed. A. VACANT et al., 15 v. (Paris 1903–50, Tables générales 1951–) 5.1:131–134. É. RANWEZ, *Dictionnaire de spiritualité ascétique et mystique. Doctrine et histoire,* ed. M. VILLER et al. (Paris 1932–) 4.1:774–785.

[W. HERBST]

EOBAN, ST.

Anglo-Saxon missionary and bishop in the Netherlands; d. Dokkum, June 5, 754. Originally a messenger for St. BONIFACE, he later became his amanuensis. He was sent to England by Boniface, and later to Pope Zacharias by King Pepin III. Elevated to the rank of CHORBISHOP, he assisted Boniface in his responsibilities among the Frisians. He is sometimes alluded to as diocesan bishop of Utrecht or Maastricht in 753, although he is not listed in Gams *Series episcoporum.* He accompanied Boniface on the fateful last expedition among the Frisians, and was martyred with him at Dokkum. His relics, originally at Utrecht, were translated first to Fulda and then to Erfurt.

Feast: June 5.

Bibliography: A. M. ZIMMERMANN, *Kalendarium Benedictinum: Die Heiligen und Seligen des Benediktinerorderns und seiner Zweige* (Metten 1933–1938) 2:283–284. W. LEVISON, *England and the Continent in the Eighth Century* (Oxford 1946), *passim.* T. SCHIEFFER, *Winfrid-Bonifatius und die christliche Grundlegung Europas* (Freiburg 1954) 167, 254, 272.

[J. L. DRUSE]

ÉON OF STELLA

Founder of the heretical Eonites (known also as Eons, Eudo, Euno, Evus); b. probably Loudéac, Brittany, 12th century; d. Reims, *c.* 1148. According to WILLIAM OF NEWBURGH, Éon was a simpleton who claimed that in the formula *per eum qui venturus est judicare vivos et mortuos*, the word *eum* designated himself as sovereign judge and Son of God. After recruiting numerous followers, he was cited to appear before EUGENE III at the Synod of Reims (1148). He arrived armed with a forked staff. ''When I raise this staff with its two prongs in the air,'' he explained, ''God governs two-thirds of the world. When I turn it down, I command these two-thirds and God the remainder.'' Éon was condemned to prison and died soon after. He seems to have professed neither MANICHAEISM nor the doctrines of the CATHARI. His opposition to the Church, especially to its wealth, his claim to divine filiation, and his advocacy of communism gained him a tremendous success among the destitute. The arrest and punishment of his followers—for their crimes rather than for their beliefs—in Brittany and Gascony marked the end of the ''Eonite'' heresy.

Bibliography: A. DE LA BORDERIE *Histoire de Bretagne*, 6 v. (Rennes 1905–14) v.3. T. DE CAUZONS, *Histoire de l'Inquisition en France*, 2 v. (Paris 1909–12) v.1. N. R. C. COHN, *The Pursuit of the Millennium* (London 1957). H. TÜCHLE, *Lexikon für Theologie und Kirche* 2 3:1169–70. E. JARRY, *Catholicisme* 4:278–279.

[J. DAOUST]

EPARCHIUS, ST.

Monk and priest (called also Cybard); b. Périgord, France, *c.* 504; d. Angoulême, France, July 1, 581. In spite of parental opposition, he entered a monastery, perhaps Sessac in the Diocese of Saintes, while still young. He served there under Abbot Martin and gained a reputation for virtue and the gift of miracles. Out of humility he left the monastery and went to live in solitude near Angoulême, but his virtues were too well known, and the bishop obliged him to receive ordination to the priesthood. Although a recluse, he accepted disciples who were allowed to do no work or begging but, depending completely on providence, devoted themselves to prayer. GREGORY OF TOURS, the chief source of information, reported a considerable cult of Eparchius in the sixth century and noted that a church was built over his tomb.

Feast: July 1.

Bibliography: *Acta Sanctorum* July 1:97–104. GREGORY OF TOURS, *Historia Francorum,* bk. 6, ch. 8; *De gloria confessorum* ch. (101) 99. A. BUTLER, *The Lives of the Saints,* ed. H. THURSTON and D. ATTWATER (New York 1956) 3: 4. R. AIGRAIN, *Catholicisme* 3:392–394. J. DE LA MARTINIEÈE, *Saint Cybard, étude critique d'hagiographie* (Paris 1908).

[B. CAVANAUGH]

EPHESIANS, EPISTLE TO THE

A New Testament letter traditionally regarded as sent by St. Paul to the Christian community in Ephesus. Two problems, especially perplexing, surround the study of the epistle, viz., its destination and its origin. Despite the title and the address in Eph 1.1, there are solid reasons for questioning its destination as the Ephesian community. The words ''who are at Ephesus'' are lacking in the two major codices, *Vaticanus* and *Sinaiticus,* in important papyri, and in some of the Fathers. Moreover, though purporting to come from Paul, who worked at Ephesus for a fairly long time (Acts 19), it contains no personal references to any of his friends there. Most scholars agree, therefore, that it was not originally written to the Ephesian church. But there is no agreement on the originally intended readers or on how the ''Ephesian'' tradition originated.

Contents and Doctrine. The introductory chapter contains a blessing (1.3–14) and a thanksgiving (1.15–23). In the body of the letter the christology of Colossians is further developed (2.1–3.21). The Church is viewed as a cosmic, universal entity; Christ as the head of the Church is the head of all creation. An important theme of the letter is the reconciliation of Jews and Gentiles (2.11–22), who form one humanity in the body of Christ. The emphasis is on sharing in the resurrection as a present reality rather than as a future hope. Following the exposition is a lengthy section of exhortation (4.1–6.20) that contains traditional materials—a list of vices (5.3–5) and a household code (5.21–6.9).

In content and vocabulary, Ephesians shows literary dependence on Colossians and on other epistles of the Pauline corpus. As in Colossians, the doctrine of Ephesians can be examined under the triple heading of Christ, the Church, and the Christian.

Christ. Colossians had already stated the cosmic dimensions of Christ's supremacy, both in the order of creation and in the order of redemption (Col 1.15–20). This is restated now, although more briefly: all things are to be ''reestablished'' in Christ (Eph 1.10). The term that is used (ἀνακεφαλαιώσασθαι) means ''to sum up'' or ''to bring together under one heading,'' indicating Christ as the source of unity through the one and same salvation. This bringing together in Christ necessarily involves the absolute supremacy of Christ, and the angelic orders are included (1.21). This had been a major point in Colossians, and despite the generally less polemical tone of Ephesians, one can note even here traces of a lack of sympathy with any who would question this doctrine. As in Colossians, πλήρωμα is applied also here to Christ (4.31), but not in the same way. It is always in relationship to the Church and is considered under that heading.

Eph 4.10 states the reason for Christ's achieving the position of being the πλήρωμα: it consists in His descent into the lower regions and His consequent ascension into heaven. By this means He brought His redemptive presence into the whole of the universe.

The Church. The major emphasis of the epistle is on the understanding of the Church. As in Colossians, Christ is explicitly called the head of the Church (Col 1.18; Eph 1.22; 4.15; 5.23) and the Church referred to as the body of Christ (Col 1.18, 24; 3.15; Eph 1.22–23; 4.12, 16; 5.30), the reference in these cases being to the universal Church and not to the particular, local communities. Ephesians further develops the concept. Christ formed His ''body'' by making Jew and Gentile one through the cross (Eph 2.13–16), which destroyed the wall between them (a reference to the wall separating the court of the Gentiles from the court of the Israelites at the Temple of Jerusalem). It is Christ, too, who sees to the ''building up'' of his body, a process that is described in overflowing terms in 4.13–16. The image of head and body has evoked a wealth of other images that bring out the intimate union between Christ and the Church. It is because of this union that the word πλήρωμα and its derivatives can be spoken of the Church, although it is difficult to know precisely what is meant in all of the cases. Christ fills the Church with all things so that she might attain ''to the mature measure of the fullness of Christ'' (4.13). In this way can the Church be called the ''completion of him who fills all with all'' (1.23), although the phrase can also be understood in the more restricted sense in which a ''body'' is the complement of the ''head.'' Both the image and the insistence with which it is applied justify the conclusion that the writer was thinking of a real, organic, though spiritual, union between Christ and the Church and among the various members of the Church.

The intimacy of the union suggested by this image, in turn, evoked the image of a spouse and his bride to describe the relationship between Christ and the Church. The figure is a familiar one from the Old Testament (e.g., Hos 1–3; Ez 16) and is taken up in the New Testament by several writers (e.g., Mk 2.18–20 and parallels; Jn 3.29). Ephesians makes an explicit comparison between Christ's relationship to the Church and a husband's to his wife (5.21–33). Christ's love was such that He delivered Himself up for the Church ''that he might sanctify her, cleansing her in the bath of water by means of the word . . .'' (5.25–26). Thus is the Church presented in ''all her glory, not having spot or wrinkle . . .'' (Eph 5.27). While the writer was concerned in this section primarily with the ordinary husband-wife relationship, the introduction of the Christ-Church analogy has conditioned his whole presentation; the analogy is repeated several times (e.g., 5.24, 25, 29, 32). The climax of the passage, the quotation from Gen 2.24 about the man cleaving to his wife ''and the two shall become one flesh,'' is used to describe the spiritual marriage of Christ and His Church (Eph 5.32). The epistle calls this teaching about the Church a ''great mystery,'' i.e., a part of the whole design of God from the beginning, but hidden until now when it is revealed in Christ.

Ephesians uses still other figures to describe the Church. Eph 2.12–22 proposes a variety of images. In 2.12 the author says that his Gentile readers were at one time ''excluded from the community [πολιτεία] of Israel. . . .'' This is a reference to the theocratic state or commonwealth of the Old Testament that had God as its sovereign and that was to prepare for the coming kingdom of Christ and God (cf. Eph 5.5). Although the Church is not explicitly called a πολιτεία in this passage, such an application can be inferred from the fact that the writer calls the Christians συμπολῖται (fellow citizens) a little later (2.19); the term supposes that a new πολιτεία, the Church with Christ at its head, has been constituted. In the same verse the Christians are said to be ''members of God's household'' (οἰκεῖοι τοῦ θεοῦ), a figure suggestive of a family and based on the adoptive sonship of Christians. The foundation of the household is the apostles and prophets; its chief cornerstone is Jesus Christ (Eph 2.20). The resulting structure is then identified as a ''temple holy in the Lord'' (2.21). This rich combination of images (see 1 Cor 3.10–17) is varied in Eph 4.12, 16, where the ''building up'' is applied to the ''body of Christ.'' These passages take on greater significance in that the images are applied to the universal Church, not to the local church, as is generally the case in Paul's undisputed letters.

The universal character of the Church in Ephesians is most clear from 4.1–16, where the author pointed out three dangers that threaten the unity of the Church (Benoit). These are, first of all, the divisions that can rise up among Christians themselves (4.1–3). They must preserve unity because all Christians together make up ''one body and one Spirit, even as you were called in one hope of your calling'' (4.4). The unity in catholicity is most strikingly stated in the familiar words: ''one Lord, one faith, one baptism; one God and Father of all, who is above all, and throughout all, and in us all'' (4.5–6). The second danger to unity is the variety of gifts within the Church (4.7–11). This variety must be seen as necessary to the perfect building up of Christ's body (4.12) and for the attainment of true unity (4.13). Here there is a strong argument for diversity in unity, even for the necessity of such diversity if true unity is to be attained. The final danger is heretical teaching (4.14) that could interfere seriously with ''growing up in Christ'' (Eph 4.15).

The Christian. The life of the Christian will be greatly influenced by this deeper understanding of the unity of the Church as expressed by the images of the body of Christ, the bride of Christ, the commonwealth and the household of God, the spiritual edifice, and the holy temple. A greater appreciation of the need for love should emerge (4.15–16; 6.23–24); and Christians have the perfect model and stimulus in the love that Christ has shown them (5.2, 25, 29), as well as in the love that the Father manifested in saving them through Christ (2.4–6). This love will be expressed in those virtues that regulate the conduct with one's neighbors (4.2); a further motive is presented in the Christian vocation itself, which is a great thing and calls for correspondingly great actions (4.1). In a fairly long ethical passage the author reminds Christians, first of all, that they are not to imitate the conduct of the Gentiles, since this is not in accord with Christian teaching (4.17–21). Rather, they are to put off the old person entirely, by which is meant anything that is reminiscent of the pagan past, and put on the new person, which means complete correspondence to the life of Christ (4.22–24). This will mean the avoiding of a large number of vices that the epistle lists (4.25–32). The ethical section is continued in chap. 5, which begins with the positive appeal to imitate God as His children and then goes on to show that immorality of any kind is incompatible with their status as ''saints,'' ''children of light,'' and ''filled with the Spirit'' (5.1–20). The writer is aware that it is no easy task to live such a life, but he urges his readers to make use of the extensive armor at their disposal. The passage illustrates the author's genius for making applications of ordinary material objects to the spiritual life (6.10–17).

In three passages in which the epistle deals with domestic morality, it urges the primacy of mutual subjection, something foreign to the pagan society of the time. Beyond the general attitude affecting the relationship of all Christians (5.21), there is a special one affecting that of husband and wife (5.22–33). On the part of the wife it is one of subjection to the husband (5.22). There is no doubt that this subjection would be understood differently in the social order of that day than in the present. That some aspect of this special relationship is essential to the married state seems demanded by the comparison with Christ's relationship to the Church (5.23–24). Once that comparison has been established, the writer uses it again to describe the mutual love between husband and wife as a basic element of the married life (5.25–33).

The second passage concerns children and parents, inculcating obedience on the part of the former and religious disciplining of the children on the part of the latter (6.1–4). The third passage outlines the mutual conduct of Christian masters and slaves. Although the epistle does not declare slavery to be intrinsically evil (such a judgment would have been almost impossible in the social order of that day), it does bring Christian principles into the picture reminding all parties of their responsibility to each other and that they are subject to a Higher Power (6.5–9). Again, these three passages have a parallel in Colossians (Col 3.18–4.1); but in Ephesians the treatment of husbands and wives has been greatly extended.

Time and Place of Writing. The author speaks of himself as a prisoner (3.1; 4.1). Scholars who suppose Pauline authorship, generally place provenance in Rome where Paul would have written it in the early 60s during his imprisonment. The Caesarean or an unrecorded Ephesian imprisonment have been suggested with less convincing arguments (for details, *see* CAPTIVITY EPISTLES). Those who deny Pauline authorship see the epistle as a much later document.

As to its destination, some suggest that it was intended as a circular letter for more than one Christian community (which would account for its strictly epistolary form and lack of personal greetings), or that it was addressed to a community that later became unworthy of it (suggested is Laodicea; cf. Rv 3.14–21; the address would then have been changed to a worthier candidate), or that an unknown author composed it. While none of these opinions can be absolutely excluded, neither can anyone of them be claimed as more probable at the present time.

Despite almost 18 centuries of unanimous, though uncritical acceptance of the Pauline authorship of Ephesians, modern scholars have proposed several serious arguments against it. (1) The vocabulary includes several words that are not used in the seven letters generally recognized as having been written by Paul, as well as an additional number of words that are rarely used by Paul or that are used by Paul with a different meaning. (2) The style is heavy and marked by redundance, unlike the vigorous, hurried style of Paul's letters. (3) The epistle shows a development of thought that is regarded as un-Pauline. (4) The striking surface similarity between Ephesians and Colossians is accompanied by unexplained differences in the meaning of common words and expressions. The last two points have led some scholars to suggest that an unknown author wrote the Epistle to the Ephesians as a summary of Paul's writings or as a conscious development of the doctrine in the Epistle to the Colossians.

Not all scholars find these arguments convincing, but acknowledge the influence of Pauline thought. Among the defenders of scholars who defend Pauline authorship are P. Benoit, L. Cerfaux, Markus Barth, F. F. Bruce, E. H. Maly, and P. T. O'Brien. Scholars who regard the letter as Deutero-Pauline include H. Conzelmann, M. Dibelius, J. Gnilka, E. J. Goodspeed, E. Käsemann, R. Schnackenburg, R. F. Collins, J. A. Fitzmyer, A. T. Lincoln, and M. Y. McDonald. The question of the origin of Ephesians, like that of its destination, remains without a certain solution.

Bibliography: P. J. KOBELSKI, *The Letter to the Ephesians,* in *The New Jerome Biblical Commentary* (Englewood Cliffs, New Jersey 1990). E. J. GOODSPEED, *The Meaning of Ephesians* (New York 1933). K.-M. FISCHER, *Tendenz und Absicht des Epheserbriefes* (Göttingen 1973). A. VAN ROON, *The Authenticity of Ephesians* (Leiden 1974). R. SCHNACKENBURG, *Der Brief an die Epheser* (Neukirchen, 1982). P. BENOIT, ''L'Horizon paulinien de l'épître aux Éphésiens,'' *Revue biblique* 46 (1937) 342–61, 506–25. H. SCHLIER, *Christus und die Kirche im Epheserbrief* (Tübingen 1930). R. F. COLLINS, *Letters That Paul Did Not Write: Letters to the Hebrews and the Pauline Pseudepigrapha* (Wilmington 1988). A. T. LINCOLN, *Ephesians* (Dallas 1990). P. T. O'BRIEN, *The Letter to the Ephesians* (Grand Rapids 1999). M. Y. MACDONALD, *Colossians. Ephesians* (Collegeville 2000). For additional bibliography, *see* CAPTIVITY EPISTLES.

[E. H. MALY/M. P. HORGAN.]

EPHESUS, COUNCIL OF

The Third Ecumenical Council, held at Ephesus in Asia Minor in 431. This article deals with the council's history, its dogma, and its historical and doctrinal significance.

History. Following the difficulties provoked by the preaching of Nestorius against the title THEOTOKOS traditionally applied to the Virgin Mary (*see* NESTORIUS and NESTORIANISM), St. CYRIL OF ALEXANDRIA, acting on a commission given him by Pope CELESTINE I and the Roman synod of Aug. 11, 430, journeyed to Ephesus to preside at the council convoked by the emperor THEODOSIUS II (Nov. 11, 430) at the suggestion of Nestorius. St. Augustine, who had been personally invited, died on August 28 before the opening of the council. Celestine sent legates to preside over the council in his place (*Epist.* 16–19; April 7 and 15, 431), and they were to conduct themselves in accordance with Cyril's wishes.

By June 7, 431, the opening date of the council, many bishops, and particularly the Oriental partisans of Nestorius, had not arrived. Cyril, despite the protests of the bishops and the representative of the emperor, opened the council. The first session (June 22, 431), which was attended by about 150 bishops, approved the doctrine contained in Cyril's letter to Nestorius (*Epist.* 4) but not his 12 anathemas. It condemned the ''blasphemies'' of Nestorius; this action, in Cyril's report, was popularly cheered as a victory of the Lord over the enemies of the faith (*Epist.* 24). On June 26 JOHN OF ANTIOCH and the Oriental bishops arrived and, refusing to join Cyril's assembly, held a council of their own, which excommunicated and deposed Cyril and the bishop of Ephesus, Memnon. Informed of these happenings, Emperor Theodosius in a rescript of June 29 annulled the Cyrillan decisions of June 22.

Upon the arrival of the Roman representatives, the Cyrillan Council met again in their presence; and informed of what had transpired, they expressly approved and confirmed the condemnation of Nestorius, employing the authority of the Apostolic See (July 10–11). On the 16th they excommunicated John of Antioch and his adherents, including THEODORET OF CYR. On July 22 a final session forbade the composition of a formula of faith other than the Nicene Creed and renewed the condemnation of the errors of Nestorius.

In August an imperial rescript requested the bishops to return to their homes and declared that Nestorius, Cyril, and Memnon were deposed and were to be held in arrest. Both parties meanwhile sought the emperor's support. The Oriental bishops presented him with a formula of faith that acknowledged Mary as the Theotokos, but they sought in vain for the condemnation of the anathemas of Cyril. For his part Cyril approached powerful members of the court to whom he sent rich gifts. After a series of theological conferences at Chalcedon, Theodosius dissolved the council in September. Cyril escaped arrest and returned to Alexandria in triumph, while Nestorius was confined to a monastery near Antioch.

In April 433, after lengthy negotiations, Cyril and John of Antioch reached an agreement. John set forth the faith of the Oriental bishops, confessing that the Virgin Mary is the Theotokos, ''because the Word of God has become flesh and is made man.'' In Christ the natures must be distinguished, but they must be united and assigned to one sole person (*prosōpon*). The Oriental bishops anathematized Nestorius and approved his deposition. Cyril joined in the profession of faith with enthusiasm, refrained thereafter from referring to the contested formula of the unique nature, and made no further mention of the anathemas (*Epist.* 38 and 39). Pope SIXTUS III, who had succeeded Celestine (July 31, 432), sent Cyril and John warm congratulations (*Epist.* 5 and 6; Sept. 17, 433).

To the question of which council was in truth the real council of Ephesus—that held by Cyril in such difficult circumstances or that of John and the Oriental bishops—Theodosius and some modern historians have attempted to give an answer by striking a balance between the two. Nevertheless, although Cyril did act in haste and with imprudence, he did not overstep the mandate entrusted to him by Celestine and Theodosius. The Roman emissaries joined him on their arrival; hence, it was Cyril's council and not John's that corresponded with the pope's intention, and that was approved by Sixtus III. Moreover the Church acknowledges the council of Cyril as the one that gave expression of its faith. Thus at the Council of Chalcedon (451) the fathers asserted adherence ''to the ordinances and to all the doctrines of faith of the Holy Synod held long ago at Ephesus under the guidance of Celestine of Rome and Cyril of Alexandria'' (*Acta conciliorum oecumenicorum* 2.1.2:127; and Leo, *Epist.* 93).

Dogma. The council had condemned Nestorius and his ''impious preaching'' in general terms; it did not desire to define or proclaim any other faith than that of Nicaea. But a positive expression of its belief was set forth in Cyril's letter, which was read and approved at the first session. Briefly stated, Cyril maintained that the Being (*physis*) of the Word has not undergone any change in becoming flesh. The Word is united according to the substance (hypostasis) to flesh animated by a rational soul. He is called the Son of Man, although He is so-called neither at one's mere will or one's good pleasure, nor by the assumption of a *prosōpon* (person); the two natures are joined in a true union, and the two constitute one Christ and the one Son. The difference in natures is not suppressed by the union, but the indescribable meeting of divinity and humanity produces one sole Christ. The Word Himself was born of the Virgin and took to Himself the nature of His own proper flesh. It is not the nature of the Word that has suffered; but since His own body has suffered, it can be said that He has suffered and died for us.

There is one sole Christ and Lord, not that the Christian worships a man with the Word, but that he worships a one, only Christ. To reject the union according to the hypostasis is to speak of two sons. Scripture does not say that the Word is united to the *prosōpon* of a man, but that the Word has become flesh. So the Fathers call Mary, the Mother of God, Theotokos. When these formulas are seen in the light of the Apollinarian debate and compared with the Christology of Antioch, they must be acknowledged as having a considerable bearing on what can legitimately pass for a definition by the Council of Ephesus.

Although this letter from Cyril to Nestorius (*Epist.* 17), with the anathemas, was read at the first session of Ephesus, it was not approved by the bishops. The anathemas cannot, then, be considered a solemn definition by the council. Nevertheless, in the entirety of the facts and context, and aside from certain formulas that were still in need of further precision, these anathemas represented the thought of the council. It was thus that the Council of CONSTANTINOPLE II (553) and the whole theological tradition thereafter understood them.

Regarding the maternity of Mary, the council did not give a dogmatic definition in a formal sense. Here again, however, account must be taken of the context and the atmosphere. ''All this debate on the faith,'' says Cyril, ''has only been engaged in because we were convinced that the Blessed Virgin is the Mother of God'' (*Epist.* 39 to John of Antioch in 433). The letter of Cyril that the council adopted as the expression of its faith recalls the traditional use of the word Theotokos and explicitly teaches the divine maternity of Mary in intimate relationship with the mystery of the hypostatic union. Tradition is not wrong in seeing in the decisions of the council the equivalent of a definition.

Significance. Although it had been convoked by Theodosius at the request of Nestorius, the council that was supposed to condemn Cyril resulted in the defeat of Nestorius. To its convocation by the emperor, the pope gave his explicit consent and sent his legates to Ephesus. They were important. The council was in fact an almost exclusively Oriental assembly. Its ecumenical character was constituted by the presence of the Roman delegates, who represented both the Papal See and the Western episcopate whose judgment had been rendered in synod at Rome. Cyril acted more or less as the representative of Pope Celestine. When the delegates of the pope arrived, they intervened with full authority, and Philip the priest relates that all admitted that ''the holy and blessed apostle Peter, prince and leader of apostles, column of the faith, foundation of the Catholic church, had received from Our Lord Jesus Christ, the Savior and Redeemer of mankind, the keys of the kingdom, and the power to bind or forgive sins. It is he who up to now and always lives and gives judgment through his successors.'' These expressions were repeated by Vatican Council I.

The council thus set forth a strong affirmation of the doctrinal authority of the bishop of Rome. It was he who confirmed the conciliar accomplishments. The letters of Sixtus III (*Epist.* 1, 2) to the Oriental bishops and to Cyril have almost the character of an official confirmation: ''*quaecumque sancta synodus, nobis confirmantibus, rejecit*'' (Whatever with our confirmation the holy synod rejected).

In the history of the dogma of the Incarnation, the Council of Ephesus marks a decisive milestone. It acknowledged and sanctified the theology of St. Cyril, the unity of the Incarnate Word, the union of two natures in the unique hypostasis whose difference is not suppressed by the union, the declaration that God the Word was born, suffered, and died in the flesh to which He was united. Certain of these formulas, which did not distinguish sufficiently between nature and hypostasis, were still in need of clarification, and the Orientals would always be tempted to look for APOLLINARIANISM in them, while Eutyches on his part would abuse them by seeing in Christ only one nature after the union. The Council of Chalcedon was to bring a useful counterbalance to the Cyrillan formulas without, however, putting an end to the argument. On the other hand, the divine maternity of Mary was agreed upon by all without discussion, and tradition has not been in error in seeing in the Council of Ephesus the triumph of the Theotokos.

In regard to the Conciliar Acts, Ephesus is the first council of which the original Acta are preserved. These are not the official Acta but individual collections, bringing together the verbal record of the meetings, documents of various kinds, letters, etc. The principal collection preserved was compiled under the direction of Cyril immediately after the council closed and has come down in three Greek collections, the *Vaticana*, the *Segueriana*, and the *Atheniensis*. They were translated into Latin as early as the beginning of the 6th century and were preserved in several collections, e.g., *Turonensis, Palatina, Veronensis, Casinensis* (Monte Cassino). A collection originating in Nestorian circles was translated into Latin by the deacon Rusticus (564–565) and has been preserved under the name Synodicum in the *Casinensis*. Other Latin collections also are known (*Veronensis, Palatina*). The Acts of Ephesus have been published in the older conciliar collections (such as *Sacrorum Conciliorum nova et amplissima collectio* 4–5); but they are now available in the edition of E. Schwartz, *Acta Conciliorum Oecumenicorum*, 5 v. (Berlin 1921–29), v. 1 *Concilium Ephesinum*.

Bibliography: SOCRATES, *Historia ecclesiastica*, 7.29–34; *Patrologia Graeca*, ed. J. P. MIGNE, 161 v. (Paris 1857–66) 67:29–872. EVAGRIUS, *Historia ecclesiastica*, ch. 1.2–7, *Patrologia Graeca*, ed. J. P. MIGNE, 161 v. (Paris 1857–66) 86.2:2419–44. LIBERATUS OF CARTHAGE, *Breviarium causae Nestorianorum et Eutychianorum* (*Acta conciliorum oecumenicorum* 2.5; 1936) 98–141, c. 560, against the religious policy of Justinian. P. T. CAMELOT, *Éphèse et Chalcédoine*, v. 2 of *Histoire des conciles oecuméniques* (Paris 1962). *Le Concile et les conciles* (Chevetogne, Bel. 1960). R. DEVREESSE, "Les Actes du Concile d'Éphèse," *Revue des sciences philosophiques et théologiques* 18 (1929) 223–242, 408–431. P. GALTIER, *Recherches de science religieuse* 21 (1931) 169–199, 269–298. J. LEBON, "Autour de la Définition de la foi au Concile d'Éphèse," *Ephemerides theologicae Lovanienses* 8 (1931) 393–412. G. JOUASSARD, "Marie à travers la patristique," *Maria: Études sur la Sainte Vierge*, ed. H. DU MANIOR, 6 v. (Paris 1949–61) 1:71–216. É. AMANN, "L'Affaire Nestorius vue de Rome," *Revue des sciences religieuses* 23 (1949) 5–37, 207–244; 24 (1950) 28–52, 235–265, a Roman view of Nestorius. A. GRILLMEIER, *Lexikon für Theologie und Kirche*, ed. J. HOFER and K. RAHNER, 10 v. (2d, new ed. Freiburg 1957–65) 3:923–924. PIUS XI, "Lux veritatis" (Encyclical, Dec. 25, 1931) *Acta Apostolicae Sedis* 23 (1931) 493–517. P. L'HUILLIER, *Church of the Ancient Councils: The Disciplinary Work of the First Four Councils* (Crestwood, N.Y. 1995). V. LIMBERIS, "The Council of Ephesus: The Demise of the See of Ephesus and the Rise of the Cult of Theotokos," in *Ephesos: Metropolis of Asia* (Valley Forge, Pa. 1995) 321–340. G. GOULD, "Cyril of Alexandria and the Formula of Reunion," *Downside Review* 106 (1988) 235–252. W. H. C. FREND, *The Rise of the Monophysite Movement* (Cambridge, Eng. 1979), chs. 1 and 4.

[P. T. CAMELOT]

EPHESUS, ROBBER COUNCIL OF

After the condemnation of EUTYCHES by FLAVIAN at the Synod of Constantinople on Nov. 22, 448, THEODOSIUS II, at the suggestion of the eunuch Chrysaphius, Eutyches himself, and DIOSCORUS of Alexandria, decided to call a council to rehabilitate Eutyches, depose Flavian, and "reaffirm the orthodox faith" against the Nestorians, that is, those who, like Theodoret, did not conform to the beliefs of Eutyches. Pope LEO I on invitation sent three legates to the council together with his *Tome to Flavian* (June 13, 449); in the tome he set forth in detail the Catholic doctrine on the mystery of the Incarnation.

The council opened at Ephesus on Aug. 8, 449. In his instructions to Dioscorus, to whom he entrusted the presidency of the council, Theodosius advised him that the assembly was not to add or take away anything from the faith as it had been set forth at the councils of NICAEA and EPHESUS. The bishops who had condemned Eutyches in 448 were present, but were prevented from taking part in the discussions.

Flavian was obviously in the role of the accused; and THEODORET OF CYR had been excluded from the council. In all about 130 bishops, carefully chosen from among the friends of Eutyches and the archimandrite Bar Sauma, an overzealous Cyrillian, accepted the leadership of Dioscorus while the adherents of Flavian were reduced to silence, and the three Roman legates, Julius, bishop of Pozzuoli, the deacon Hilary, and the notary Dulcitius, were handicapped by their lack of a knowledge of Greek.

Immediately at the opening of the council, Julius and Hilary, speaking through an interpreter, asked that the letter from the pope be read. Their request was evaded, and instead the Acts of the Synod of Constantinople at which Eutyches had been condemned were read, frequently interrupted by cries and protests of the bishops, who, at the suggestion of Dioscorus, threatened anathema to anyone who spoke of the two natures of Christ.

In the end, Eutyches was reinstated, and after the Roman representatives twice more in vain demanded that the *Tome* of Leo be read, Dioscorus proposed the deposition of Flavian and of Eusebius of Doryleum. Flavian protested as did the Roman deacon, Hilary, who shouted "*contradicitur*"; a great uproar broke out as the soldiers and the crowd invaded the basilica and disposed of the resistance of the minority by force. When order was restored, the bishops agreed to depose Flavian and Eusebius. Flavian was sent into exile and died en route.

A second session on August 22 dismissed other bishops suspected of Nestorianism—viz, Theodoret of Cyr, Ibas of Edessa, and DOMNUS OF ANTIOCH. The Eutychian party triumphed and the doctrinal agreement between Cyril of Alexandria and John of Antioch reached in 433 was repudiated. On being informed of what had transpired at Ephesus by his deacon Hilary, who had escaped capture and brought an appeal from Flavian, Pope Leo in a local Roman Synod of Sept. 29, 449, denounced the decisions of what he later termed the *latrocinium* or Robber Synod of Ephesus (*Epistles* 95 of July 20, 451).

Bibliography: *Acta conciliorum oecumenicorum* (Berlin 1914–) 2.1.1:68–101; 2.3.1:42–91. P. T. CAMELOT, *Das Konzil von Chalkedon: Geschichte und Gegenwart*, eds. A. GRILLMEIER and H. BACHT, v. 3 (Würzburg 1951–54) 1:213–242. H. BACHT, *ibid.*, 2:197–231.

[P. T. CAMELOT]

EPHPHETA

An Aramaic word spoken by Jesus in the cure of the deaf-mute of Decapolis (Mk 7.31–37). The Greek Gospel text gives ἐφφαθά (7.34), a transliteration of the Aramaic '*etp*[e]*tah* or 'etpattah or of the Hebrew *hippātaḥ* (from the Semitic root *ptḥ*, to open), which Mark translates as διανοίχθητι, ''be thou opened.'' The word is accompanied by sacramental gestures: Jesus touches the man's tongue with spittle and puts His fingers into his ears. The actions of Jesus and His word of command are as a Sacrament, symbolizing the effects to be produced by the divine power using the sacred humanity as an instrument. Hence, it is not surprising to find the Ephpheta ceremony (as it was called from early times) among the rites prescribed by the church in the administration of baptism of infants: with some variations, the ministering priest repeats the actions of Christ and pronounces the solemn Ephpheta.

Bibliography: *Encyclopedic Dictionary of the Bible*, tr. and adap. by L. HARTMAN (New York 1963) 674. I. RABINOWITZ, '''Be opened' = 'Εφφαθά (Mark 7.34): Did Jesus speak Hebrew?'' *Zeitschrift für die neutestamentliche Wissenschaft und die Kunde der äteren Kirche* 53 (1962) 229–238. F. PRAT, *Jesus Christ: His Life, His Teaching, and His Work*, tr. J. J. HEENAN, 2 v. (Milwaukee 1950) 1:399–400. V. TAYLOR, ed., *The Gospel according to St. Mark* (London 1952) 355.

[A. LE HOULLIER]

EPHRAIM

The younger son and younger tribe of Joseph. Situated in the fertile hill-country between Benjamin and the other Joseph tribe, Manasseh, the tribe of Ephraim (Heb. '*epraim,* from root meaning fruitful) was, in the early history of Israel, one of the most numerous and powerful tribes, important for its religious sanctuaries and prime mover in establishing the Northern Kingdom; yet, despite early superiority, Ephraim's leadership of the north was clearly supplanted by Manasseh as early as the 9th century. This article treats in order Ephraim's occupation of the land and its historical role.

Occupation of the land. The Elohist tradition, obviously interested in Ephraim, records how Jacob mistakenly blessed the younger brother in precedence over his older brother Manasseh (Gn 48:5–20). The brothers were the eponymous ancestors of the two Joseph tribes, their double character making up for the tribe of Levi, which received no territory, and thus preserving the classical number 12. The census numbers given for Ephraim and Manasseh in Nm 26:34, 37, as contrasted with those given in Nm 1:33, 35, and the account of Joshua's allotment of territory to Ephraim in a literary context that accords primacy to Manasseh (Jos 16:4; 17:1), reflect Ephraim's later, secondary status, hardly in agreement with its early hegemony (see Phythian-Adams, 231–232). At the Israelite conquest of Canaan, Ephraim gained possession of the strategically located section of north-central hill country bounded by Manasseh on the north, Benjamin and Dan on the south, and extending from the Jordan to the sea (Jos 16:1–9). Strength of numbers led the powerful and warlike Ephraim (Jos 17:14–18) to encroach northward against Manasseh and southeastward to the Canaanite city of Gezer, whose inhabitants they subjected to forced labor and eventually absorbed into the tribe (Jos 16:10; Jgs 1:22–26, 29). The territory is one of the most fruitful in Palestine, as is reflected in its name and in the blessings of Jacob's Oracles (Gn 49:22–26) and Moses' Oracles (Dt 33:13–17).

Historical role. Its access to major zones of movement, superior position in the hill country, and military prowess cast Ephraim in the warrior's role in Israelite history. In the period of occupation Ephraimites fought under Aod against the Moabites (Jgs 3:27), under DEBORAH and Barak against the Canaanite coalition (Jgs 5:14), and under GIDEON against the Madianites (Jgs 7:24). This last episode nearly ended in internal strife because of the insult offered to the martial pride of some Ephraimites (Jgs 8:1–3). A similar incident involving the Judge Jephthah during the Ammonite war erupted into open conflict that resulted in severe Ephraimite losses (Jgs 12:1–6). Ephraim also contributed the Judge Abdon to Israelite history (Jgs 12:13). The presence of the ark at the central shrines of BETHEL and Shiloh further enhanced Ephraimite prestige during this period, as did the renown of Samuel, last of the Judges and reluctant inaugurator of the monarchy (Jos 18:1; Jgs 20:27; 1 Sm 1:1; 4:3). In the political friction after Saul's death (*c.* 1000 B.C.), the Ephraimites remained faithful to his son Is-Baal until his assassination, whereupon they offered their allegiance to David at Hebron (2 Sm 2:9; 5:1; 1 Chr12:30).

The secessionist movement of the northern tribes after Solomon's death (*c.* 922 B.C.) took root in Ephraim, the Prophet Ahijeh instigating Jeroboam I (both Ephraimites) to make the irrevocable break with Judah (1 Kgs 11:26–40). The sheer size and strategic location of Ephraim and Manasseh made them the nucleus of the Northern Kingdom, whose first capital was SHECHEM (1 Kgs 12:25). Despite their alliance, there seems to have been a bitter rivalry between the two (Is 9:20–21), which probably was rooted in the disputes that arose in occupying the land (Jos 17:14–18; see Phythian-Adams, 229–230), and was perhaps reflected in the swift succession of kings and internal instability of the Northern Kingdom. While the subsequent history of the divided monarchy depicts Manasse in the predominant role in the North until its downfall in 721 B.C., early Ephraimite influence was so profound as to make its name synonymous with the Northern Kingdom, Israel, a fact amply attested in prophetic literature (Is 7:2, 5, 8, 17; 9:8; Jer 31:9, 20; Ez 37:16, 19; Hos *passim*).

Bibliography: *Encyclopedic Dictionary of the Bible,* tr. and adap. by L. HARTMAN (New York 1963) 674–675. W. J. PHYTHIAN-ADAMS, ''The Boundary of Ephraim and Manasseh,'' *Palestine Exploration Fund Quarterly* (1929) 228–241. E. ROBERTSON, ''The Period of the Judges: A Mystery Period in the History of Israel,'' *The Bulletin of the John Rylands Library* 30 (1946) 91–114. K. D. SCHUNCK, ''Ophra, Ephron, and Ephraim,'' *Vetus Testamentum* 11 (1961) 188–200.

[R. BARRETT]

EPHREM THE SYRIAN, ST.

Theologian, exegete, and Doctor of the Church; b. NISIBIS, in Mesopotamia, *c.* 306; d. EDESSA, June 373.

Life. Born into a pagan family (though some sources call his parents Christian), Ephrem was baptized at the age of 18 or 28 by the ascetic Bp. (St.) James of Nisibis (303–338), whose influence on his early life was profound. Even more significant was the influence of James' second successor, Vologeses (346–361), with his blending of asceticism and culture; in this period Ephrem was already a famous teacher in the School of Nisibis.

When the Christian Emperor Jovianus was compelled to cede Nisibis to the Persians after the defeat of JULIAN THE APOSTATE (363), Ephrem emigrated with many other Christians to Edessa, where he continued to teach, and became a friend and counselor of Bishop Barses. The exegetical School of Edessa, intermediate in

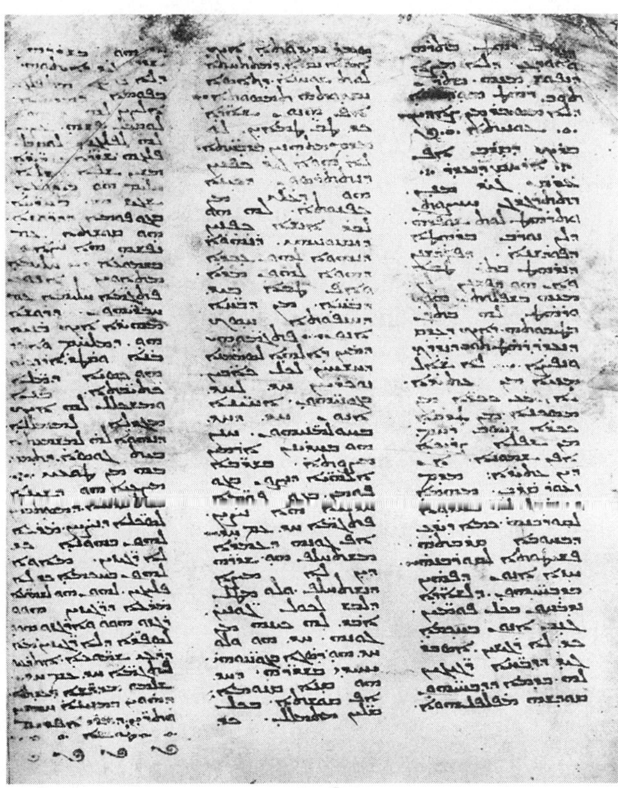

Folio dated 522 of hymns and other writings of St. Ephrem the Syrian (Cod. Vat. Syr. 111, fol. 21v).

method between Antiochene literalism and Alexandrian typology, owes to him its glory and perhaps even its foundation. Ordained a deacon, possibly by James of Nisibis, he apparently never became a priest, and by feigning madness managed to escape episcopal consecration. The Church historian SOZOMEN emphasized Ephrem's reserve in dealing with women and a self–control that made it possible for him to dominate a natural irascibility.

Doctrine. Some historical significance is attached to Ephrem's works against heresies; e.g., the second volume of the Syriac works contains 56 hymns against Marcion, Bardesanes, and Manes, while the third volume has 87 hymns against the ''investigators,'' i.e., skeptics, especially the Arians and Anomeans. More importantly, the hymns and discourses are of interest for the history of dogma. Ephrem's doctrine on man's last end is perfectly orthodox: a particular judgment that fixes the soul's destiny after death; purgatory; and the eternity of hell's punishments. But, like most of the Christian writers down to Pope BENEDICT XII, he saw the souls of the just awaiting the resurrection in a sort of sleep, not enjoying beatitude before the body's resurrection. His forceful, realistic description of the Last Judgment inspired DANTE.

Remarkable as a devotee of the Virgin Mary, Ephrem extoled her cult and believed in her Immaculate

Conception. Other dogmas that find support in him are original sin, free will and its harmony with divine grace, the primacy of Peter, intercession of the saints, and the Real Presence. An antiphon (No. 48) recovered in Armenian reveals the Trinity, especially the Spirit, at work in bringing the glorified humanity of Christ under the Eucharistic species. Our Lord, through the Father's right hand, i.e., the Holy Spirit, is in the Eucharist, and through the Eucharist is in men's hearts, without diminution, in His entirety, adapting Himself to their littleness. For Ephrem, as for many of the Eastern Fathers, the Eucharistic consecration, as well as the Incarnation and Redemption, is the work of the whole Trinity.

Works. Ephrem's literary legacy is still in an early stage of scientific exploration. The edition of J. S. and S. E. Assemani (6 v.: three for the Greek works, three for the Syriac, with Latin translation; Rome 1732–46) is incomplete and inexact, while T. J. Lamy's edition (4 v., Syriac works; Mechlin 1882–1902) omits the works in Assemani. E. Beck undertook a critical edition, with German translation, of the Syriac works in the *Corpus scriptorum Christianorum orientalium* series, which includes the hymns on faith (*Corpus scriptorum Christianorum orientalium* [Paris–Louvain 1903] 154/Syr. 73; 155/Syr. 74), against heresies (169/Syr. 76; 170/Syr. 77), on paradise or against Julian (174/Syr. 78; 175/Syr. 79), on the Nativity and Epiphany (186/Syr. 82; 187/Syr. 83), and on the Church (198/Syr. 84; 199/Syr. 85). C. Tonneau edited the commentaries on Genesis and Exodus (*Corpus scriptorum Christianorum orientalium* [Paris–Louvain 1903] 152–153). The edition of the Greek works by S. G. Mercati produced only one fascicle (Rome 1915). Of the Armenian Ephrem (see below), L. Leloir reedited the commentary on the Diatessaron with a Latin translation (*Corpus scriptorum Christianorum orientalium* [Paris–Louvain 1903] 137 and 145).

Syriac Ephrem. The authentic works in Syriac are the hymns (on faith, against heresies, on virginity, on the Church, on paradise, on the crucifixion), the *Carmina Nisibena* (ed. C. Bickell, Leipzig 1866), some sermons (on faith, on our Lord), and some commentaries (Genesis, Exodus, etc.). Theodoret testifies (*Hist. eccl.* 4.29.3) that Ephrem's hymns ''lent luster to the Christian assemblies,'' and Sozomen reports (*Hist. eccl.* 3.16.7) that the Christians sang them to the music of Harmonius, son of Bardesanes.

Greek Ephrem. Here much is spurious, but certain items are literal translations of Syriac originals that may well stem from Ephrem. Sozomen affirms (*Hist. eccl.* 3.16.2) that ''the Greek translations, which began in his lifetime, lose little if any of their original force.'' The defects of the Greek text—doublets, long and short recensions, interpolations, and omissions—are common to the Syriac. The Greek is ancient, for citations of Greek Ephrem appear in the sixth century. Mme. D. Hemmerdinger–Iliadou distinguishes carefully (1) texts with a Syriac original, (2) texts that offer readings from the Diatessaron, (3) texts that cite apocrypha and agrapha, and (4) items in meter.

Latin Ephrem. Very old, this represents a state of text less reworked than the Greek manuscript tradition.

Armenian Ephrem. To this we are indebted, above all, for the commentaries on the New Testament (the Diatessaron, Acts, Pauline Epistles), but also for poems that are often important for the history of dogma.

For the Georgian, Slavic, Coptic, Arabic, and Syro–Palestinian versions, see J. Kirchmeyer, *Dictionnaire de spiritualité ascétique et mystique. Doctrine et histoire,* ed. M. Viller et al. (Paris 1932–) 4.820–822.

Feast: Jan. 28 (Eastern Church); June 18 (Western Church).

Bibliography: *Textes arméniens relatifs à S. Ephrem*, 2 v., ed. L. TER–PÉTROSSIAN (Louvain 1985). E. BECK et al., *Dictionnaire de spiritualité ascétique et mystique. Doctrine et histoire,* ed. M. VILLER et al. (Paris 1932–) 4.788–822; *Die Theologie des Hl. Ephrem in seinen Hymnen über den Glauben* (*Studia anselmiana* 21; 1949); ''Die Mariologie der echten Schriften Ephrems,'' *Oriens Christianus* 40 (1956) 22–39; *Ephräms Polemik gegen Mani und die Manichäer im Rahmen der zeitgenössischen griechischen Polemik und der des Augustinus* (Louvain 1978); *Ephräms des Syrers Psychologie und Erkenntnislehre* (Louvain 1980); *Ephräms Trinitätslehre im Bild von Sonne/Feuer, Licht und Wärme* (Louvain 1981); *Dōrea und Charis; Die Taufe: zwei Beiträge zur Theologie Ephräms des Syrers* (Louvain 1984). S. P. BROCK, *The Luminous Eye: The Spiritual World Vision of Saint Ephrem* (Rome 1985, rev. ed. Kalamazoo, Mich. 1992). C. M. EDSMAN, *Le Baptême de feu* (Uppsala 1940). P. FÉGHALI, *Les origines du monde et de l'homme dans l'oeuvre de saint Ephrem* (Paris 1997). S. H. GRIFFITH, *Faith Adoring the Mystery: Reading the Bible with St. Ephraem the Syrian* (Milwaukee, Wisc. 1997). M. HOGAN, *The Sermon on the Mount in St. Ephrem's Commentary on the Diatessaron* (Bern 1999). JACOB OF SERUG, *A Metrical Homily on Holy Mar Ephrem*, critical ed. of Syriac text, tr. J. P. AMAR (Turnhout, Belgium 1995). U. POSSEKEL, *Evidence of Greek Philosophical Concepts in the Writings of Ephrem the Syrian* (Louvain 1999). S. SCHIWIETZ, *Das morgenländlische Mönchtum,* v.3 (Mödling bei Wien 1938) 93–179. A. VÖÖBUS, *Literary, Critical, and Historical Studies in Ephrem the Syrian* (Stockholm 1958); *History of Asceticism in the Syrian Orient,* 2 v. (*Corpus scriptorum Christianorum orientalium* 184, 197; 1958–60). P. YOUSIF, *L'Eucharistie chez saint Ephrem de Nisibe* (Rome 1984). A. PALMER, ''The Merchant of Nisibis: Saint Ephrem and His Quest for Union in Numbers,'' *Early Christian Poetry*, J. DEN BOEFT and A. HILHORST eds. (Leiden 1993), 167–233. S. H. GRIFFITH, ''Images of Ephraem: The Syrian Holy Man and His Church,'' *Traditio* 45 (1989–1990): 7–33.

[É. DES PLACES]

EPICLESIS

Liturgy has a dialogical structure, originating in the divine activity within the life of faith. This gift of faith is the source of the Church's expression of praising remembrance of God's deeds in Christ, that grounds the confident petition for God's continuing bestowal of His blessings. The epicletic, or intercessory, aspect reflects the goal of all forms of Christian liturgical activity and is beginning to receive the attention it deserves in the theology of worship.

In ancient pagan and Christian literature, *epiclesis* signifies the invoking of a name (in a liturgical context the name of God) upon a person or thing. The most ancient Christian liturgical epiclesis is that found in all baptismal formulas in which the names of the Three Persons of the Blessed Trinity are invoked over the catechumen. Other forms of epiclesis are found in the rites of Confirmation, Ordination, and the blessing of the baptismal font. This entry discusses the historical and theological dimensions of the epiclesis in the Eucharist.

Term. The principal elements found in the Eucharistic epiclesis as gathered from the various liturgical texts are (1) a simple invocation to God, (2) a petition that God the Father send down the Holy Spirit, (3) a petition that the Holy Spirit transform the bread and wine into the Body and Blood of Christ, (4) a similar petition that the Holy Spirit apply to the faithful the sanctifying fruits of the Eucharist. Often only one or another of these elements is present in the two predominant types of Eucharistic epiclesis: one, a consecratory formula; the other, an application of the sanctifying effects of the Eucharist to the faithful. While the consecratory epiclesis—an invocation to the Holy Spirit to change the elements into the Body of Christ—does not seem to exist in the classical Roman liturgy, it is found in other Latin liturgies, such as the Mozarabic and the Gallican. But in the Eastern liturgies, especially the predominant BYZANTINE rite as typified by the liturgies of St. Basil and St. John Chrysostom, it is fairly universal. The other type of epiclesis, in the sense of an application of the Eucharistic effects, seems to have been the earlier.

Place in the Eucharist. In the Eastern liturgies, the epiclesis follows the Lord's words of institution. In the most widespread Byzantine liturgy of St. John Chrysostom the epiclesis reads: ''And we pray and beseech and entreat You, send down Your Holy Spirit upon us and upon these gifts lying before us. And make this bread the precious Body of Your Christ. Amen. And that which is in the chalice the precious Blood of Your Christ. Amen. Changing them by Your Holy Spirit. Amen, amen, amen.'' The place of the Eastern epiclesis is more logical because it follows the actual historical development of the mysteries as recounted in the same order of events in the Creed. But liturgical development has never been uniform nor always logical, as may be seen in the lack of such a consecratory epiclesis after the words of institution in the Roman rite. There are five highly disputed opinions about whether there is an epiclesis and where it is placed in the classical Roman canon: (1) there is no epiclesis in the Roman Mass, (2) the *Quam oblationem* is the epiclesis coming before the words of institution, (3) the *Supplices te rogamus* is the epiclesis coming after the Consecration through the words of institution, (4) both these are forms of epiclesis, (5) a silent epiclesis occurs in the mere gesture of imposition of hands at the *Hanc igitur*.

Controversy. The early Fathers of the East, in fighting SABELLIANISM and other heretical tendencies of subordinationism, including later attacks against the divinity of the Holy Spirit, stressed the distinction between the Three Persons in the Blessed Trinity. In the Eucharistic Anaphoras of the East, afflicted by heresies against the divinity of the Holy Spirit, there arose an emphasis on the attribution to the Third Person of the power to consecrate and sanctify. Both actions were viewed as fruits of the Eucharist, which had a reference equally well to the faithful as to the gifts offered on the altar. Both in the Eastern liturgies and in the writings of theologians, such as Cyril of Jerusalem (d. 386), Gregory of Nyssa (d. 394), Pseudo-Chrysostom, Theophilus of Alexandria (d. 412), and John Demascene (d. 749), proof can be found of this attribution of consecratory power to the Holy Spirit. But only under the influence of Nicolas Cabasilas (d. 1363) and of Simeon of Thessalonica (d. 1429) did a controversy arise when the Latins attacked the Greeks for holding that the prayer of epiclesis after the words of institution was necessary for consecration. The Latins maintained that the words of institution sufficed. In the reunion council at Florence (1438), John Torquemada (d. 1468), Bessarion (d. 1472), and Isidore (d. 1463), metropolitan of Kiev, tried to reconcile the two opinions. All but Marcus of Ephesus accepted the Latin position that the Sacrament was realized by the Lord's words alone. Marcus pushed Cabasilas's position to the extreme, holding that the words of institution were merely narrative, but the epiclesis was the sole formula of transubstantiation. In the following centuries this became one of the many polemics between the Christian East and West.

In the beginning, the Church was not concerned with the exact point at which transubstantiation took place. The Eucharistic Anaphora was considered as a unity. Later, with the suppression of any consecratory epiclesis in western liturgies and with greater speculation in the West, there was a tendency to define the importance of each prayer of the canon. In the decree of reunion with the Armenians and Jacobites at the Council of Florence (1439–45) there was no question of the epiclesis, but it was stated that the words of institution were the form effecting transubstantiation (H. Denzinger, *Enchiridion symbolorum* 1320, 1352). A similar decree was issued by the Council of Trent (*ibid.* 1654). In 1729 Pope Benedict XIII wrote to the Melkites: ''Not through the invocation of the Holy Spirit but by the words of consecration [i.e., words of institution] is transubstantiation effected.'' The thesis of Prince Maximillian of Saxony, which tried to reconcile the two theories—the words of institution would be the necessary form for the Latin Church; the epiclesis would suffice for the Eastern Church—was condemned by Pius X in 1910 (*ibid.* 3556).

Theological developments since Vatican II. Since the conclusion of the Second Vatican Council, Catholic theologians have attempted to work out the full implications of the dialogue structure, and essentially epicletic nature, of all forms of liturgy: a structure and content that mirror and actualize the covenant relationship between God and the Church, founded on Christ. This entails the rethinking of the christological dimension of worship that is essential for any systematic explanation of the full scope of the theology of Christian liturgical-sacramental activity. There is also the problem of the theological integration of the role of the Holy Spirit into the liturgy so that the complementarity of the activity of Christ and the Holy Spirit is made more understandable. Both the christological and pneumatological aspects are involved in the current discussion on the subject of the theology of liturgy in general, and the epicletic dimension of liturgical-sacramental celebrations in particular.

Traditional Eucharistic prayers. The traditional Eucharistic theologies of the East and West agree that the sanctifying action of the Holy Spirit changes the bread and wine into the Body and Blood of Christ, and that the properly disposed participants of Holy Communion are fully united to Christ through the sanctifying action of the Holy Spirit. All classical Eucharistic Prayers reflect this theology of sanctification by including a twofold invocation: for the sanctification of the bread and wine, and the communicants.

Traditional Eastern Eucharistic Prayers invoke the Father to send the Spirit to change the gifts and the community, while the old Roman Eucharistic Prayer appeals only to ''God.'' This difference between the two traditions no longer remains since the introduction of the epiclesis of the Spirit in the new Eucharistic Prayers of the Roman Missal of Paul VI. However, divergent theological interpretations of the role of the special epiclesis of the Eucharistic Prayer, carried on within the Byzantine Orthodox and Roman Catholic Churches since the Middle Ages, have not been fully resolved at the level of official teaching. Nevertheless, there are hopeful signs that theologians of the two traditions are working toward a consensus over important aspects of this matter. In this regard, developments on the subject of the agent of the divine activity, the role of the presiding minister of the liturgy, and the more recent investigations of the liturgical-theological structure of the Eucharistic Prayer may be singled out for special mention.

Divine Agent of Sanctification. Traditional Western scholastic theology attributes the work of sanctification to the Godhead as such, and ''appropriates'' it to the Holy Spirit, that is, insofar as the name ''Spirit'' evokes the concept of sanctification. In other words, the Holy Spirit is not considered to have a personal mission of sanctification in the Church. There is only the one personal mission of the Word, begun at the Incarnation, and continuing in the Church. From this point of view, the mystery of the transformation of the Eucharistic gifts is attributed to the action of Christ, consecrating the bread and wine, and to the action of the Holy Trinity as such, changing the elements into Christ's Body and Blood. This explanation is still favored in some influential Catholic theological circles.

Traditional Eastern theology, on the other hand, affirms that the Holy Spirit has a personal mission of sanctification in the Church. In virtue of this mission, the Spirit applies the words of Christ to each Eucharist by transforming the elements into Christ's Body and Blood.

The Liturgical Leader. Traditional Eastern and Western theologies agree that through ordination the priest obtains the authority from Christ to act as his representative in the special ministry. Both agree that the priest acts as representative of the Church in the exercise of his ministry. Therefore, both agree that what the priest does in the whole of the Eucharist is done as representative of Christ and the Church.

However, modern Orthodox theology explains that the priest, who presides at the liturgy, always acts directly as the Church's representative in all his official activity. In this way he indirectly represents Christ, the true High Priest of the liturgy of His Church. Consequently, the priest speaks the narrative of institution of the Eucharist as representative of the Church, and thereby as representative of Christ, who relates his words, spoken once for all at the Last Supper, to each Eucharist.

Western theology also holds that the priest always acts as representative of Christ and the Church in all liturgical activity. However, developments in theological reflection on the Eucharist since the 12th century resulted in a new view of how the priest represents the Church and

Christ in this liturgy. According to traditional Western scholastic theology, in the rest of the Eucharistic celebration, before and after the recitation of the words of Christ, the priest directly represents the faith of the Church, and indirectly Christ, the Head. At the recitation of Christ's words, the priest directly represents Christ, and thereby indirectly the Church, insofar as Christ is the Head of the Church. This explanation was favored by Pius XII in his encyclical letter *Mediator Dei* (1947).

From this latter standpoint an epiclesis for the sanctification of the gifts is superfluous after the words of institution. Also the epiclesis before these words cannot be considered an integral sacramental moment of the sanctification of the bread and wine. It represents the desire of the Church, uttered in the name of Christ, for what takes place when the Christ speaks His own words of consecration. Orthodox theology, on the other hand, requires that the epiclesis be considered an integral sacramental moment of the sanctification of the gifts. Both the words of Christ and the epiclesis, taken together, are the sacramental representation of the mystery of the Eucharist. The one expresses the conviction of faith that Christ relates His words of institution to each Eucharist; the other that the Holy Spirit, working with divine and sovereign freedom, applies the words of Christ to the gifts of the Church.

Toward a consensus. There are indications that Orthodox and Roman Catholic theologians are beginning to transcend traditional differences in the theology of the Eucharistic epiclesis.

Orthodox Theology. Leading Orthodox theologians are drawing out more clearly the implications of the active presence of the Risen Lord in the Eucharist. They readily agree that Christ Himself includes the petition of the Church for the coming of the Holy Spirit in His "eternal intercession." Likewise, they make their own the opinion of John Chrysostom, mediated by Nicholas Cabasilas (14th century), that the words of Christ, recorded in the narrative of the Last Supper, are a formula of consecration that retains its power in the present.

Roman Catholic Theology. In modern times Catholic theology has displayed a singular interest in the theology of the Holy Spirit. One of the results has been a growing consensus concerning the personal mission of the Holy Spirit, and the application of this pneumatology to the Eucharist in a way that conforms to the Orthodox approach.

The theology of the role of the minister who presides at the Eucharist has also entered a new stage of development. The notion that the priest is only understandable as embedded in the relation Christ-Church has led many Catholic theologians to discard the sharp distinction between his two representative functions. This means that the priest is best described as the direct representative of the Church, and as indirectly the representative of Christ who is the Head, in all his activities, including that of the Eucharistic Prayer. When the priest recalls the account of institution and intercedes for the coming of the Spirit to apply the words of Christ to this celebration, Christ Himself is understood to relate His words to this liturgy and to include the petition of the Church in His "eternal intercession," since He is the true Host and High Priest of His Eucharist.

Witness of the Eucharistic Prayer. The modern analysis of the literary-theological structure of the classical Eucharistic Prayers has made a notable contribution toward its theology. The commonly accepted results of this investigation can be quickly summarized.

The typical forms of prayer, found in the narrative context in the OT, as well as in traditional Jewish private and public prayer, have anamnetic (praising remembrance) and epicletic (petitionary) sections. The anamnesis of God's mighty acts on behalf of the chosen people grounds their petition for God's continuing support that maintains the covenant relation. Jewish prayer, associated with feasts instituted by God, includes scriptural texts witnessing to the foundation of the feasts. These texts, introduced by way of direct address or allusion, furnish the theological basis of the prayer. The scriptural texts can be found in either the anamnetic or epicletic sections.

This structure of prayer, based on and mirroring the theology of covenant, enables those praying to experience the dynamics of the covenant relationship with God. It was taken over by the Christian Church as the normative structure of her liturgical prayer and, in particular, for the Eucharistic Prayer. Hence the anamnetic and epicletic sections of the Eucharistic Prayer must be considered as units of a single prayer, the confession of the mystery of salvation realized in Christ. Both parts, taken together, express the dynamics of the covenant relation initiated by God and continually actualized in the liturgy of the Church. Classical Eucharistic Prayers, following the pattern of Jewish liturgical prayer, insert the institution of the Eucharist into either the anamnetic or epicletic sections.

The former type, characteristic of the Antiochene tradition, concludes the anamnetic section with the Words of Institution, and an anamnetic-offering prayer that brings out the theological intention of the praising remembrance. This is followed by the epicletic section in which the explicit petition for the sanctification of the gifts can be located before or after the petition ordered to the sanctification of the communicants. The latter type admits of a greater variety. The special epiclesis of sanctification of the gifts can be placed before the Words of Institution and anamnesis-offering prayer, and the one ordered to the sanctification of the communicants afterward, as in the old Roman canon. Sometimes a twofold epiclesis is placed after the institution and anamnesis, as is the case with the Alexandrian anaphora of Mark.

In all Eucharistic Prayers the meaning of the praising remembrance of the saving acts of God in Christ lies primarily in the desire of the Church for fellowship with Christ, the sharing in His saving work, and His glory mediated through the ''food of immortality.'' Hence the presiding minister appears as authorized spokesperson of the community, proclaiming God's deeds in Christ and petitioning that the saving work of Christ be applied in the present. In this activity, he is supported by the ''Amen'' of the liturgical assembly, identifying this prayer as its own.

Centrality of Institution. The institution is the central element in the dynamics of the Eucharistic Prayer. This narrative is the theological center from which the anamnesis-offering prayer draws its inspiration, and the theological center to which the epiclesis for the transformation of the elements is ordered. The epiclesis for the sanctification of the communicants is another center of the Eucharistic Prayer. It enables the community to express at the level of prayer the goal that is attained sacramentally through Holy Communion. The epiclesis for sanctification of the elements can come before or after the institution-anamnesis, but the communion epiclesis only afterward. This shows that the institution is the theological center of the prayer, from which the whole meaning is derived. At the same time, the communion epiclesis always makes clear the goal of the celebration. In Eucharistic Prayers in which the twofold epiclesis is brought together and placed after the institution, the order can be petition for the sanctification of the communicants, followed by petition for the change of the gifts [James (Gr.); Chrysostom (Byz.); Basil (Alex.)]. But even where the petition for the transformation of the gifts is given first consideration, it is always made evident that this is ordered to the benefit of the communicants, not primarily to the change of the gifts as such.

The Eucharistic Prayer expresses the intense desire of the Church to be continually reconciled with God. Following the pattern of the prayer of the OT and Judaism, the Church recalls the narrative of institution, situates it at the climactic summit to confer on her prayer the maximum force. Inspired by the promise that the words of Christ carry, the priest humbly petitions, in the name of the Church, for the transformation of the gifts together with the transformation of the communicants ''for whom'' the change of the gifts is intended. As a person formally deputed for this task, the priest is aptly described as one who represents the Church in the whole of the Eucharistic Prayer. This formulation corresponds best to the liturgical-theological structure of the Eucharistic Prayer and does not deny that Christ Himself is the Host and High Priest of His Church and His Eucharist.

Bibliography: C. VAGAGGINI, *The Canon of the Mass and Liturgical Reform,* tr. ed. P. COUGHLAN (New York 1967). L. VISCHER,''The Epiclesis: Sign of Unity and Renewal,'' *Studia Liturgica* 6 (1969) 30–39. J. H. MCKENNA, ''The Eucharistic Epiclesis in Twentieth Century Theology (1900–1966),'' doc. diss. (Trier 1970). N. CABASILAS, *A Commentary on the Divine Liturgy,* trs. J. M. HUSSEY and P. A. MCNULTY (Crestwood, N.Y. 1977). Y. CONGAR, ''On the Eucharistic Epiclesis,'' *I Believe in the Holy Spirit,* v. 3 (New York 1983). D. COFFEY, ''A Proper Mission of the Holy Spirit,'' *Theological Studies* 47 (1986) 222–250. E. J. KILMARTIN, ''The Active Role of Christ and the Spirit in the Divine Liturgy,'' *Diakonia* 17 (1982) 95–108; ''The Active Role of the Holy Spirit in the Sanctification of the Eucharistic Elements,'' *Theological Studies* 45 (1984) 225–253. H. -J. SCHULTZ, *The Byzantine Liturgy,* tr. M. J. O'CONNELL (New York 1986).

[G. A. MALONEY/E. J. KILMARTIN/EDS.]

EPICTETUS

A younger contemporary of St. Paul, b. Hicropolis of Phyrigia, *c.* A.D. 55; d. *c.* 130. He was taken as a slave boy to Rome by Epaphroditus, a servant of the Emperor Nero, and sent to study under M. Rufus, the Stoic. As a freedman Epictetus opened his own school, but in A.D. 90 he was exiled with all the philosophers of Rome by DOMITIAN. He went to Nicopolis of Epirus near the Ionian Sea; and although Hadrian lifted the ban in 117, Epictetus remained in Asia till his death. Arrian, his devoted pupil, prepared and published his class notes as eight *Discourses.* Four are extant along with a summary, the *Enchiridion,* and some fragments. There is no trace of Christian influence in his thought although he certainly knew of the ''Galileans'' (*Disc.* 4.7). Among the ancients who admired him are M. Aurelius, ORIGEN, St. AUGUSTINE, and St. GREGORY OF NAZIANZUS. His influence on Christian thought has been subtle and profound.

Philosophy begins, for Epictetus, when one realizes the enormous confusion among men about right and happy living. Trained men are unanimous in ideas such as right angles and halftones, to which the ignorant lay no claim. But since everyone is born with some notion of what is good or bad, fine or shameful, right or wrong, each one acts according to his own private impressions as if he knew all. So the philosopher must go in search of what is common to all, the universal basis of judgment, the universal good. He will find it in his own will ultimately, for good and evil are determined by what he can control. Everything else is neutral. The universal good is the truth about human freedom; the essence of good and evil lies in the attitude of the will (*Disc.* 2.92). Men are slaves while ignorant of the true nature of their psychic impressions and their sphere of power; when they choose according to what seems to be, nature resists them and they are frustrated. Men are free when they choose according to the true nature of things; e.g., they cannot resist death, but they can die in peace.

Epictetus's course was divided into three stages similar to the earlier Stoic division into ethics, physics, and logic. The first teaches how to have one's desires in accord with reason, i.e., the right attitude of mind toward external things and events. The second teaches how to conform one's actions to the order of divine providence manifest in creatures. The third stage, for proficients, is a rigorous training in logic to ensure unerring judgment against sophisms and fallacies.

Bibliography: Works. *The Discourses with the Encheiridion and Fragments,* tr. G. LONG (New York 1890); *Complete Extant Writings* in *Stoic and Epicurean Philosophers,* ed. W. J. OATES (New York 1940). Literature. A. JAGU et al., *Dictionnaire de spiritualité ascétique et mystique. Doctrine et histoire* (Paris 1932) 4.1:822–854. M. SPANNEUT, *Reallexikon für Antike und Christentum* (Stuttgart 1950) 5:599–681, bibliog. 678–681. R. D. HICKS, *Stoic and Epicurean* (New York 1910). D. S. SHARP, *Epictetus and the N.T.* (London 1914). B. L. HIJMANS, *Askesis: Notes on E.'s Educational System* (Assen, Neth. 1959). W. A. OLDFATHER, *Contributions toward a Bibliography of Epictetus* (Urbana, Ill. 1952).

[M. J. GIACCHI]

EPICUREANISM

A philosophical school and doctrine founded by EPICURUS. The school resembled a religious community set up for the purpose of diffusing, applying, and perpetuating the writings and way of life of the master. Epicurus encouraged his followers to memorize his basic writings. They were not expected to improve upon or modify his theories deliberately. Hence this exposition of Epicureanism aims basically at reconstructing the philosophy set forth in the original works of Epicurus.

Division of Philosophy. Epicurus divided philosophy into logic, physics, and ethics. Logic, called canonic, is the science of the criterion and principle and is treated in a single book entitled *The Canon.* Physics, dealing with generation, corruption, and nature, is given a variety of presentations according to levels of difficulty; the letters present the subject in an elementary form, while the 37 books *On Nature* constitute a more elaborate treatment. Ethics determines how one should live, what one should do and avoid, and the goal of life (Diogenes 10.30). In his *Letter to Herodotus on Physics* Epicurus sets forth his basic physical doctrines (Diogenes 10.35–84). Another letter (to Menoeceus), also preserved by Diogenes Laertius (10.122–135), presents Epicurus's main teachings on moral matters. As for the canonic, many fragments collected by Usener and others allow one to reconstruct its fundamental principles.

Canonic. The criterion of truth is fourfold: sensations, anticipations, emotions, and images produced in reason. Sensation is the primitive contact of the knower with material reality. It does not involve the intervention of memory or of reason, and is irrefutable and irreducible. Man's thoughts derive from sensations (Diogenes 10:32) through contact, analogy, resemblance, or synthesis; mental discourse also contributes something to the process. In his poem *De rerum natura,* LUCRETIUS—one of the most influential Epicureans—stresses the importance of the senses as a criterion and starting point. In his view, the skeptics, by doubting the validity of sensation, have involved themselves in hopeless contradictions; sensation affords the ultimate means of rectifying errors and therefore merits absolute confidence.

Anticipation involves a number of previous sensations of identical or similar objects, an ''experience'' in terms of which a judgment can be formulated concerning something not as yet perceived or imperfectly perceived, such as the nature of an object, for example, an ox or a horse located at a distance. If such an anticipation is confirmed or at least not contradicted, one's judgment of the object is and was true.

The emotions serve as criteria in matters relating to objects of choice and aversion. Other judgments are verified in terms of images produced in the reason, possibly by the impinging of subtler aspects of objects on the finer rational component of the soul.

Epicurus and his disciples lay great stress on the distinction between judgments based on the criteria of evidence and judgments that do not conform to the criteria. Opinions are corroborated or verified if they state evident facts; they are not corroborated when they run counter to such evidence. However, an opinion may be verified indirectly (that is, not falsified) when it is shown to agree with an evident fact; an example would be the existence of the void, which is linked necessarily with the evident fact of MOTION. To deny the truth of an opinion positing the void, one would have to deny the fact of motion. In this manner Epicurus introduced the possibility of philosophical discourse, that is, the possibility of searching for aspects and structures that are not directly perceptible to the senses or to the mind.

Physics. Physics is studied to secure mental serenity. It is necessary at the outset to determine clearly the primary meanings of words and to refer to the impressions of the senses or to any other criterion (Diogenes 10.38).

The universe is infinite and eternal. It cannot have come from nothing, nor is there anything exterior to it that could change it. It is made up of bodies (revealed by sensation) and of place or void that allows for the possibility of motion. Nothing is conceivable aside from these two constituents. Atomic bodies are immutable substances, while conglomerates of atoms undergo change.

Atomism. Atoms exist in a great variety of shapes, and each shape is possessed by an infinite number of atoms. The atoms move constantly. Their hardness causes them to rebound when they collide because of slight deviations in the direction of their motions. Deviations of atoms were introduced by Epicurus to explain the formation of composite bodies out of atoms separated by the void and moving originally at a uniform speed in the same general downward direction; they explain not only the formation of the universe but also the presence of chance and freedom within it. This may be viewed as an example of a true judgment based on the Epicurean notion of nonfalsification.

Every composite body is a system of atoms moving at the speed of thought, but in constantly changing directions because of collisions with other atoms. Thus the speed of the conglomerate varies as revealed in common experience, without this in any way involving variations in the motions of atoms. The worlds, large and small, arise from concentrations of atoms and dissolve in the same way (Diogenes 10.73). *See* ATOMISM.

Soul. The soul is composed of subtle particles disseminated throughout the body; its existence depends on the body that it animates. The mobility of the living thing results from the smallness and smoothness of its soul atoms. Besides other cruder elements, the soul also comprises, according to Lucretius, a ruling and organizing principle that communicates life to its other parts and, through them, to the body. Any injury that affects this innermost part of the soul brings about the loss of life (*De rerum natura* 3). Once bereft of its protective covering, the soul disintegrates (Diogenes 10.63–64).

Sensitivity arises when the power of the soul becomes fully developed as a result of motion and is communicated to the body. Sensation involves finely textured images emanating from real objects and having the same form as their source. Such images may endure for some time in the atmosphere and traverse long distances at very high speeds (Diogenes 10.46). The fineness of their constituents allows them to pass through obstacles that would stop the cruder atoms. The surfaces of bodies are constantly emitting such images, which retain the order and positions of the atoms in the real object. This is the basic principle underlying the Epicurean theory of sight, hearing, and smell.

Gods. According to Epicurus, there is no need to attribute the regulation of celestial phenomena to divine beings. He firmly rejects the ancient view of the heavenly bodies as endowed with happiness, intelligence, and will. Serenity results not from ascribing the realities of the universe to the influence of divine forces, but from an understanding of its true principles and structure. Only by banishing mythical explanations and the fear of eternal torment or of death can one hope to achieve that imperturbability based on truth that is the goal of philosophy.

However, Epicurus conceives of the gods as awesome images having human forms that are originally perceived in dreams. The gods enjoy happiness and immortality but they are not concerned with the happenings of the physical world. There is no place in Epicureanism for providence or fate, nor is prayer valid save as a recognition of man's subordinate position in nature.

Ethics. Philosophy is the health of the soul (Diogenes 10.122); it opens up a way of life that excludes false opinions on the gods, destiny, and death. Death is nothing to man, and he should not let the fear of it deprive him even of the ephemeral joys of life. "As long as we exist, death is not, and when death is there, we are not" (Diogenes 10.125). The wise man does not fear death; he does not necessarily want the longest life, but he does want the most pleasant.

Epicurus divides desires into natural and empty. Natural desires comprise the necessary and the merely natural. Of necessary desires, some are necessary for happiness, others for bodily well-being, still others for life itself. Since human actions aim at avoiding suffering and fear, such a division of desires allows man to strive only for the things he needs to achieve a happy life.

Pleasure is the beginning and the end of the happy life (Diogenes 10.128–129). It is the principal good of man's nature and therefore determines his objects of choice or aversion. However, some pleasures are rejected (for example, excessive eating) because of the evils they entail; and many pains are judged preferable to certain pleasures because of the heightened pleasure experienced as a result or consequence of the pain. In any case, man must judge in terms of the advantages or disadvantages accompanying the pleasures and pains. Thus Epicurus's ethics may be called a utilitarian HEDONISM. Pleasures must be sought in moderation. Men should be content with little and should not fall into the habit of depending on goods they do not control or over which they may lose their control. Bread and water can be a source of great pleasure to the hungry man (Diogenes 10.131).

The Epicurean conception of pleasure involves moderation and tranquillity. The wise man avoids the orgies of food, drink, and sex. He subordinates his desires and aversions to the vigilance of reason (Diogenes 10.132). Wisdom, in which all other virtues are rooted, makes possible a life of happiness by regulating human actions according to the principles of utilitarian hedonism.

Critique. Epicureanism is remarkable for its firm rejection of superstitions, divination, fate, and some aspects of theological ANTHROPOMORPHISM in an age when most philosophers sought to allow for popular beliefs in their systems. In fact, the Epicureans' hostility to such important elements of folklore and religion may have been largely responsible for the distortions of their doctrines by their contemporaries and for the calumnies to which they were subjected. In this one can but agree with N. De Witt's defense of Epicurus. On the other hand, the quasi-religious approach to Epicurus's teachings and the somewhat crude, dogmatic tone of his pronouncements must have seemed repugnant and even ridiculous to the ancient man of culture. Indeed the Epicurean spokesman in Cicero's philosophical treatises never appears to be taken too seriously. However, A. M. J. Festugière has shown the profoundly human appeal of Epicureanism and the lofty ideals to which Greek MATERIALISM could rise with Epicurus.

See Also: GREEK PHILOSOPHY; STOICISM; KNOWLEDGE, THEORIES OF.

Bibliography: F. C. COPLESTON, *History of Philosophy* (Westminster, Md. 1946) 1:401–412. W. SCHMID, *Reallexikon für Antike und Christentum,* 5:681–819, bibliog. 816–819. DIOGENES LAERTIUS, *Lives of Eminent Philosophers,* bk. 10 on Epicurus (*Loeb Classical Library* 1925) v. 2, Greek text with Eng. tr. R. D. HICKS. A. M. J. FESTUGIÈRE, *Epicurus and His Gods,* tr. C. W. CHILTON (Cambridge, Mass. 1956). N. W. DE WITT, *Epicurus and His Philosophy* (Minneapolis 1954).

[V. CAUCHY]

EPICURUS

Greek philosopher; b. Samos, 341 B.C.; d. Athens, 271 or 270 B.C. His father, Neocles, was an Athenian schoolmaster who had settled in the island of Samos. Epicurus studied there under the Platonist Pamphilus, but at 18 he left the island to go to Athens. Later, when the Athenian settlers were expelled from Samos, Epicurus joined his father in Colophon. His years between 20 and 30 appear to have been formative of his philosophy. He studied for some time under the Democritean Nausiphanes, from whom he is said to have derived his *Canon.* Toward the end of this period, Epicurus underwent an important moral and psychological change; this accounts for the widely divergent opinions of his moral character. His enemies and opponents stress the aggressive and ungrateful bent of his earlier years, while his disciples extol the gentle and considerate master who presided over his philosophical family (see De Witt, ch. 2). At the age of 32 he gathered disciples and founded schools in Mitylene and Lampsacus; five years later he established a school at Athens, where he lived until his death.

Epicurus, 1810 (engraving by George Cooke).

Epicurus wrote about 300 works in which he prides himself on never quoting another author. The list given by Diogenes Laertius enumerates many works on physics, including 37 on Nature, one on the Criterion or the *Canon,* many treatises on ethical matters, and books refuting or expounding other philosophies. The extant works and fragments of Epicurus have been collected and edited by Hermann Usener (*Epicurea,* Leipzig 1887). Diogenes Laertius in his life of Epicurus has preserved for posterity Epicurus's last will, three important letters on physical and ethical subjects, and the principal doctrines—a sort of Epicurean catechism made up of 40 propositions. For an analysis of his teachings and his influence, *see* EPICUREANISM.

Bibliography: F. C. COPLESTON *History of Philosophy* 1:401–412. G. M. POZZO, *Enciclopedia Filosofica* 1:1931–39. N. W. DE WITT, *Epicurus and His Philosophy* (Minneapolis 1954). A. M.

J. FESTUGIÈRE, *Epicurus and His Gods,* tr. C. W. CHILTON (Cambridge, Mass. 1956).

[V. CAUCHY]

EPIGRAPHY, CHRISTIAN

Epigraphy in general is concerned with ancient inscriptions, that is, writings on hard materials, such as stone, metal, clay, bone, and wood. By convention, legends on coins are not included, as they fall within the province of a sister discipline, NUMISMATICS.

Christian Epigraphy and Its Scope. Christian epigraphy, which is primarily concerned with inscriptions written in Greek or Latin, deals with writings on hard materials that can be recognized as being Christian in origin and that fall within the period from the 2d to the 7th century. It includes not only the extant Christian inscriptions themselves, but also copies of inscriptions, now lost, as found in the manuscript tradition, such as the *Itinerarium Einsidlense* and similar documents.

As compared with the some 300,000 profane Greek and Latin inscriptions extant, the Christian Greek and Latin inscriptions comprise a total of some 50,000, the Latin outnumbering the Greek by about five to one. It should be noted both in the case of pagan and Christian inscriptions that the number extant or known through copies represents only a fraction of the total that once existed. The largest number of Christian inscriptions found in any one area come from Rome and its vicinity and total some 20,000. In the 3d century the Greek inscriptions at Rome are as numerous as the Latin, but in the 4th century, the inscriptions are largely Latin, and in the 5th and 6th centuries, Greek disappears from the stones almost completely. The Latin inscriptions from Rome outnumber the Greek by about ten to one. Outside of Rome and Sicily, the number of Christian Greek inscriptions found in the West is very small, but includes the famous PECTORIUS epitaph at Autun. Surprisingly, archeology to date (1965) has brought to light only a relatively limited number of Christian Greek inscriptions on the mainland of Greece, Macedonia, and Thrace, including Constantinople before the 7th century. On the other hand, the finds in Asia Minor, Egypt, Syria, and Palestine have been much more numerous and valuable. The precious inscription of ABERCIUS, for example, comes from Phrygia. Outside of Rome the largest number of Christian Latin inscriptions have been found in Gaul, Africa, the rest of Italy, and Spain. Those from Africa and Gaul are especially important for their rich content. The Christian Latin inscriptions found in Germany are relatively few in number, and the same is generally true for Britain, Switzerland, Illyricum, and the East.

Pagan inscriptions embrace all aspects of public and private life and may be easily classified into a large number of special categories. In contrast, the range of Christian inscriptions is limited. They comprise chiefly funeral inscriptions, pious invocations and acclamations, brief professions of faith, scriptural quotations, and, after the Peace of the Church (313), dedications connected with churches and the cult of saints and martyrs and the graffiti of pious pilgrims. In the period before Constantine, and obviously in times of active persecution, many Christian inscriptions exhibit a guarded or symbolic reference to Christian belief, but by the application of all pertinent criteria these so-called crypto-Christian inscriptions may be identified as Christia without qualification.

On the dogmatic side, Christian inscriptions confirm doctrinal statements and liturgical practices recorded in the literary tradition, but they usually lack the fullness and precision of the patristic writings. On the other hand, they are an invaluable source for the organization of the early Church, for the cult of the martyrs, and, above all, for the daily life and occupations of the rank and file in the Christian communities. T. Mommsen's epigrammatic observation regarding pagan inscriptions applies equally well to the Christian: ''Die Inschriften sind nicht Denkmäler der Literatur sondern des Lebens'' (The inscriptions are not monuments of literature, but of life).

Dating, Letter Forms, Abbreviations, and Linguistic Features. Christian and pagan inscriptions of their very nature have many elements in common that are characteristic of their genre and their age. Funeral inscriptions—and the great majority of Christian inscriptions are in this category—usually do not indicate any form of official date. At Rome, for example, the first dated Latin inscription comes from 217 (E. Diehl, *Inscriptiones Christianae latinae veteres*, 3631b), and the first dated Greek inscription from 235. The number of dated Christian inscriptions in both East and West is very small before 325. When dates are given, the West generally employs consular dating, although one finds also examples of dating according to the Mauretanian Era (A.D. 39) and according to the Era of Spain (38 B.C.) in Africa and Spain respectively. In the East dating by eras was much more frequent, the more common eras in use being: the Seleucid Era (312 B.C.), Era of Antioch (49 B.C.), Era of Bostra (A.D. 105), and Era of Tyre (126 B.C.). In Egypt, Christians introduced an Era of the Martyrs (A.D. 284). The employment of dating by indictions did not become common before the late 5th century A.D. It should be observed that the Christian Era itself was not used before the early Middle Ages. The assignment of dates to undated Christian inscriptions is difficult. However, the converging evidence of letter forms, formulas, and, above all, accompanying archeological evidence, especially

Christian symbols, often make approximate dating reasonably certain. In the case of the catacombs, for example, it has been established that inscriptions found in the topmost galleries are earlier than those found in the lower galleries, which were only dug out later.

Letter Forms. Letter forms in both Christian Greek and Latin inscriptions correspond to the general evolving usage from the 2d to the 7th century. On the whole, the lettering of the earlier Christian inscriptions, especially on the Latin side, is inferior to that in the more or less official pagan inscriptions of the same period (see Grossi Gondi, 8–68, esp. 30–39). An exception must be made later for the elegant Latin capitals created by Furius Dionysius Filocalus for the inscriptions composed by Pope DAMASUS. Funeral inscriptions were normally incised on marble slabs or steles and were often obtained from professional pagan monument makers. This explains in part why a Christian inscription is occasionally found on a slab bearing the conventional pagan dedication *DM* (*Dis manibus*). The Christian *graffiti* of Rome especially are very important. They were made over a long period and furnish direct evidence for the writing habits, religious ideas, and culture of those who scratched them on walls and tombs.

A number of Christian Latin inscriptions found in Rome are written in Greek letters, and some Greek inscriptions were composed by Latin speakers or for Latin speakers. These phenomena are perhaps best explained by the special reverence and prestige attached to Greek as the liturgical language of Rome into the 4th century. It is significant that the extant papal inscriptions—with the exception of that of Cornelius—to the end of the 3d century were written in Greek, although certain other popes listed, as well as Cornelius were not Greek (see Hertling and Kirschbaum, 144).

Abbreviations. Christian inscriptions, especially the Latin, make frequent use—in common with pagan Latin inscriptions—of suspension. Both Greek and Latin Christian inscriptions likewise reveal a frequent employment of what may be called the characteristically Christian form of abbreviation, namely, contraction. Pagan and Christian ligatures occur side by side. Monograms are common also, the most important and the most famous being the Constantinian monogram for Christ (*see* CHI-RHO) which can be dated definitely from the year 323, and which assumes various forms (see Grossi Gondi, 53–68). Of the Christian cryptograms, ΙΧΘΥC is the most widely used (*see* FISH, SYMBOLISM OF). The cryptogram, ΧΜΓ, although not uncommon, has not yet received a generally accepted interpretation (see Testini, 359–60). Psephism occurs in Greek Christian inscriptions, but is rare.

Linguistic Features. Christian Greek inscriptions reflect the contemporary usages of the *koine*—especially the nonliterary *koine*—in phonology, morphology, and syntax. Iotacism—the monophthongization of diphthongs—becomes increasingly common from the 4th century, and local aberrations from the common standard occur in Greek inscriptions found in Asia Minor, Syria, Egypt, and in the post-Constantinian period in Rome. In some instances, mistakes are clearly the result of an imperfect knowledge of Greek on the part of Orientals. The vast majority of Christian Latin inscriptions are written in Vulgar Latin and reflect to a marked degree the spoken Latin of the age in which they were composed. Along with a large number of pagan inscriptions of the same kind they furnish precious information on the evolution of the living Latin into primitive Romance. Sacred inscriptions of a liturgical character, or dedications of churches or other monuments, composed in the second half of the 4th century and in the early 5th, are usually written in the standard Latin prose style of the period. However, Latin funeral inscriptions, especially from the 4th century, and all Latin inscriptions from the second half of the 5th show a steady deterioration in phonology, morphology, and syntax, in some cases becoming almost unintelligible. (See Grossi Gondi, 417–22, but especially the indices in E. Diehl, *Inscriptiones Christianae latinae veteres* 3.) A number of Christian Greek and Latin verse inscriptions are extant, but as a whole—including the epigrams of Pope Damasus—they are more laudable for their pious sentiments than for their poetical quality and metrical accuracy. The most common meters employed are the hexameter, the elegiac couplet, and the iambic trimeter or *senarius*. Some examples are to be classified as accentual rather than metrical verse.

Christian Names, Places of Origin, and Indications of Age. Some definite tendencies or practices can be noted in the inscriptions, but it is impossible to reduce Christian epigraphical nomenclature to a system. In the beginning Christians apparently retained their pagan names. A baptismal name is attested first for Ignatius of Antioch and thereafter the baptismal name becomes common in place of, or often, beside the earlier name. There was a tendency among the Greeks to use a single name. At Rome, however, the traditional usage of three names gave way only gradually to the dominant employment of the single name in the 4th and 5th centuries. Yet it should be noted that converts from the Roman aristocracy, undoubtedly as a mark of humility, adopted a single name as early as the beginning of the 2d century. The types of names found in Christian inscriptions may be classified, in general, under the following heads: (1) profane or mythological, such as Diogenes, Aphrodisia, Asclepiodotus, Apollonius, Galatea, Phoebus, Hermes, such names being fairly common even after 250; (2) Biblical names, such as Susanna, Abel, Martha, Maria, Petrus, Paulus, and Ioannes; these names, however, being relatively rare, and, with few exceptions, late; (3) specifically Christian names, such as Theodorus, Adeodatus, Renatus, Redemptus, Anastasius, Dominica, Fides, Charitas, and, in particular, from Africa, Quodvultdeus, Spesindeo, Habetdeum; (4) names signifying humility or opprobrium, such as Stercorius, Proiectus, Sceleratus; such names commemorated pagan vilification in the age of persecution and were retained as titles of honor, but also of Christian humility; (5) Christian *signa* or nicknames introduced by *qui et* or ὃς καί, and similar formulas, as *Marcellus qui et Exsuperius, Bassa qui et Felix, Anastasia qui et Verula,* Ἀγαθὴ ἡ καὶ Σείρικα, *Muscula quae et Galatea.*

Filiation is normally indicated in Christian Latin inscriptions by the use of *filius* as an appositive preceded or followed by the genitive of the parent's name, as *Novellus Crescentis filius, Primigenia filia Primigenii.* In Christian Greek inscriptions, filiation is indicated by the genitive alone, or by υἱός or θυγάτηρ followed by the genitive. Greek and Latin inscriptions, as their pagan counterparts, often indicate the native region or place of origin of the defunct by a variety of phrases or proper adjectives.

The age lived is indicated commonly by the simple *vixit* or ἔζησε accompanied by the number of years, but Latin inscriptions in particular often include months and days and exhibit specific Christian formulas, as *vixit in saeculo, vixit in pace.* In the fourth and fifth centuries the date of birth is often given according to the consular date. Latin inscriptions, especially, often indicate the age at which Baptism was received or the number of years between Baptism and death. The years lived in marriage are likewise often indicated, and already among the earliest Christian Latin inscriptions. Such information is rarely found in Christian Greek inscriptions.

Family, Civil Status, and Professions. The early Christian inscriptions tend, in general, to ignore distinctions of class and condition, but from the middle of the fourth century data of this kind rapidly became common. They reveal a closely knit Christian family life. Slavery is recognized as a traditional institution but the Christian slave, from the religious point of view, is a person possessing sacred personal rights. Christians are found engaged in a wide range of professions from grammarians and physicians to merchants, bakers, carpenters, dyers, and farmers. They are found also in the higher and lower nobility and as incumbents in all the offices of the imperial administration and in that of the municipalities. (See the lists furnished by Grossi Gondi, 100–19; Leclercq, *Dictionnaire d'archéologie chrétienne et de liturgie*, ed. F. Cabrol, H. Leclerq, and H. I. Marrou, 7.1:750–59; and *Inscriptiones Christianae latinae veteres* 3, *Res Romanae,* 431–58.)

The Church and the Cult of Martyrs and Confessors. With some important exceptions, the pertinent inscriptions—at least the dated ones—belong to the 4th, 5th, and 6th centuries. The Church, the Christian community as a whole, or the Christian communities at the regional or local level, are normally designated by the term ἐκκλησία, *ecclesia,* but often accompanied by a qualifying genitive or by a qualifying adjective. The combination *Ecclesia Catholica* appears first on the stones at Rome in an inscription of Pope Damasus composed in 362. Despite the frequent use of ''Christian'' in the literary tradition from New Testament times, this word occurs rarely in inscriptions outside Asia Minor. A newly baptized or full member of the Christian community is frequently called a νεοφώτιστος, πιστός, *neophytus, fidelis. Puer* and *puella* are sometimes used in the same sense.

The Clergy. The inscriptions furnish evidence for an early distinction between clergy and laity and for clerical ranks. Of the minor orders, that of *lector* is mentioned with the greatest frequency. The major orders are much better represented, and from the pre-Constantinian period come *diaconus* (also called *levita*), *presbyter, episcopus.* The Roman inscriptions include references to the *presbyteri* of the titular churches. For ἐπίσκοπς, *episcopus,* special mention must be made of the early list of the bishops of Rome discovered in the Cemetery of Callistus beginning with ANTEPωC EIII (236) and including one name in Latin letters, CORNELIVS MARTYR EP. Other terms used with some frequency to designate a bishop are *sacerdos, antistes, papa, praesul* (poetic), and *pontifex*—the last, because of its earlier pagan employment, only from the 5th century. Among other words designating ecclesiastical or quasi-ecclesiastical status it will suffice to note *archidiaconus, diaconessa, vidua, fossor;* from monastic life, *monachus, virgo, virgo devota, virgo sacra* or *sacrata.*

Numerous titles or expressions are found that connote devotion or humility: *servus Dei* (used by bishops, lower clergy, and laity), *servus Christi, famulus Dei, ancilla Dei* (often used to indicate a *virgo sacra,* but also applied to unmarried girls and married women), δοῦλος Θεοῦ, δοῦλος Χριστοῦ, δούλη Θεοῦ. *Peccator* is confined largely to ecclesiastical use and is found especially in the *graffiti.*

Cult of the Martyrs and Confessors. The inscriptions reveal an early cult of martyrs and confessors and its steady development. The term confessor is often employed, by Pope Damasus, for example, in the sense of martyr as well as in its stricter meaning. There are no dated examples before the 4th century, as the siglum $\overline{\text{MPT}}$ and the word martyr found in the epitaphs of the popes mentioned above were added later. Yet it seems very probable that a few undated inscriptions referring to martyrs are earlier than Constantine. In any event, from the early 4th century the number of inscriptions honoring martyrs increases rapidly, culminating in the poetic epitaphs of Pope Damasus incised in the beautiful Filocalian letters (see A. Ferrua, *Epigrammata Damasiana*). Martyrs are given the epithets *sanctus, beatus*, or, often in the superlative, *sanctissimus, beatissimus.* Such epithets are frequently given in abbreviated form. However, it should be noted that *sanctus* may be used also in a broader sense to indicate the faithful in general (*sancti*) or an individual pious Christian [see H. Delehaye, *Sanctus* (Brussels 1927)].

Funerary Formulas. The Christian inscriptions, the great majority of which, as already noted, are funerary, exhibit their specific Christian character by their constant expression of an unquestioned belief in a life after death and in the resurrection of the body. Earthly life is a journey, a *peregrinatio,* to the Christian's true homeland (*patria*), heaven. Death is not the end, but the beginning of the true and eternal life with God. Hence the Christian *dies natalis* is not the day of physical birth but the day of death. The passage of the soul or spirit to the other world, to life with God, is indicated by a variety of expressions, for example: *abiit in pace, decessit* (from 234 in Rome), *discessit, evocatus a Domino, excessit, ingressus in pace, migravit de hac luce, recessit, recessit in pace;* in Greek, ἀπεγένετο, ἀπεχώρει πρὸς (τὸν) Κύριον, ἐξῆλθε. It must be emphasized that these expressions are not euphemisms for death but reflect literally the Christian belief mentioned above. Burial is described as a ''storing away'' of the body, or as a rest or sleep, until the resurrection of the dead on the Last Day. This is the meaning conveyed by Latin *depositus est, depositio, conditus in sarcophago, dormit, dormivit in pace, hic iacet, pausat, quiescit, requiescit* (which becomes the basic liturgical word), and by Greek ἀνεπαύσατο, κοίμησις, ἐκοιμήθη, κεῖται.

The Christians, as noted earlier, followed generally the pagan system of dating for years, months, and days. However, there are sporadic and late examples of the use of *dies dominica* for *dies Solis,* of *dies Sabbadi* for *dies Saturni*, and of *feria* for one of the other days of the week.

Inscriptions often praise the virtues or piety of the dead. Expressions like the following are common: *sanctissima femina, benemerenti* (in pagan use also), *devotus obsequiis martyrum, castissima et pudicissima, amator* or *amatrix pauperurm*, μακάριος, θεοπιλέστατος, θεοσεβής.

Christian Dogma and Religious Practices. Because of their brevity, inscriptions do not furnish detailed information on Christian doctrine, yet they contain confirmatory evidence for the major Christian teachings. Thus, they reflect the universal belief in the Trinity, divinity of Christ, Redemption, remission of sins, communion of saints, resurrection of the dead, eternal life. They advocate and contain prayers for the living and the dead. They are particularly valuable for the evidence that they furnish on Baptism, the Eucharist, and Matrimony. They give precious information on the consecration and dedication of churches, on votive offerings, on the veneration of relics, and on the Christian calendar and feasts (especially Easter). Their acclamations, invocations, and prayers in general represent in many respects primitive liturgical formulas. Biblical quotations or adaptations of scriptural passages contribute to our knowledge not only of the early liturgy but also to the textual criticism of the Greek and Latin Bibles. It is hardly necessary to observe that the investigation of Christian inscription must be combined as closely as possible with the study of the accompanying early Christian symbolic art and with that of early Christian literature in all its phases. (For Jewish inscriptions in Greek and Latin, see the works by Frey and Leon cited in the bibliography.)

See Also: ART, EARLY CHRISTIAN; ROSSI, GIOVANNI BATTISTA DE.

Bibliography: Surveys, Manuals, History. W. LARFIELD, *Griechische Epigraphik* (3d ed. Munich 1914). R. BLOCH, *L'Épigraphie latine* (''Que sais-je?'' rev. ed. Paris 1965). R. CAGNAT, *Cours d'épigraphie latine* (4th ed. Paris 1914). H. THYLANDER, *Études sur l'épigraphie latine: Date des inscriptions, noms et dénomination latine, noms et origine des personnes* (Lund 1952). A. FERRUA, ed., *Epigrammata Damasiana* (Vatican City 1942). P. TESTINI, ''Epigrafia,'' in his *Archeologia cristiana* (Rome 1959) 329–543, the most up-to-date comprehensive treatment. L. JALABERT, *Dictionnaire apologétique de la foi catholique*, ed. A. D'ALES et al. (Paris 1912–) 1:1404–53, old but still valuable. L. JALABERT and R. MOUTERDE, ''Inscriptions grecques chrétiennes,'' *Dictionnaire d'archéologie chrétienne et de liturgie*, ed. F. CABROL, H. LECLERCQ, and H. I. MARROU, 15 v. (Paris 1907–53) 7.1:623–94. H. LECLERCQ, ''Inscriptions latines chrétiennes,'' *ibid.* 694–850; ''Inscriptions (Histoire des recueils d'),'' *ibid.* 850–1089. These articles contain a large number of epigraphical texts and are furnished with copious bibliogs. O. MARUCCHI, *Epigrafia cristiana* (Milan 1910), Eng. tr. J. A. WILLIS (Cambridge, Eng. 1912), confined almost entirely to Rome. C. M. KAUFMANN, *Handbuch der altchristlichen Epigraphik* (Freiburg 1917). F. GROSSI GONDI, *Trattato di epigrafia cristiana latina e greca del mondo romano occidentale* (Rome 1920). L. HERTLING and E. KIRSCHBAUM, *The Roman Catacombs and Their Martyrs,* tr. M. J. COSTELLOE (2d ed. London 1960). I. KAJANTO, *Onomastic Studies in the Early Christian Inscriptions of Rome and Carthage* (in Acta Instituti Romani Finlandiae 2.1; Helsinki 1963). A. DEGRASSI, ''Dati demografici in iscrizioni cristiane di Roma,'' *Rendiconti della Classe di Scien-*

ze. . .dell' Accademia dei Lincei 18 (1963) 20–28. Collections, Greek. *Corpus Inscriptionum Graecarum,* ed. A. BOECKH et al., v.4 (Berlin 1959) nos. 8606–9026. In IG the Christian inscriptions are presented *passim.* See esp. v.14. J. S. CREAGHAN and A. E. RAUBITSCHEK, ''Early Christian Epitaphs from Athens,'' *Hesperia* 16 (1947) 1–54. F. HALKIN, ''Inscriptions grecques relatives à l'hagiographie,'' *Analecta Bollandiana* 67 (1949) 87–108; 69 (1951) 67–76; 70 (1952) 116–37, 306–11; 71 (1953) 74–79, 326–58. L. A. JALABERT and R. MOUTERDE, eds., *Inscriptions grecques et latines de la Syrie* (Paris 1929–). No convenient collection of Christian Greek inscriptions corresponding to Diehl (see below) is available. Collections, Latin. E. DIEHL, *Inscriptiones Christianae latinae veters,* 3 v. (Berlin 1925–31), with invaluable index. In *Corpus inscriptionum latinarum* (Berlin 1863–), the Christian Latin inscriptions are omitted from v.6, as they are contained in De Rossi and Silvagni. In the other v. they are presented *passim.* J. B. DE ROSSI, ed., *Inscriptiones christianae Urbis Romae septimo saeculo antiquiores,* 2 v. (Rome 1857–87), new series ed. A. SILVAGNI and A. FERRUA, 3 v. (Rome 1922–57); *Monumenta epigraphica Christiana saec. XII antiquiora quae in Italiae finibus adhuc extant* (Rome 1944). J. VIVES, *Inscripciones cristianas de la España romana y visigoda* (Barcelona 1942). *Sylloge inscriptionum christianorum veterum Musei Vaticani,* ed. H. ZILLACUS et al. (Helsinki 1963). E. DIEHL, *Inscriptiones latinae* (Bonn 1912), plates 32–50. J. B. FREY, *Corus inscriptionum Judaicarum,* ed. J. B. FREY (Rome 1936–). H. J. LEON, *The Jews of Ancient Rome* (Philadelphia 1960). For photographs of Christian inscriptions in addition to those contained in the works listed above, see F. VAN DER MEER and C. MOHRMANN, *Atlas of the Early Christian World,* ed. and tr. M. F. HEDLUND and H. H. ROWLEY (New York 1958), *passim.* For new discoveries and current bibliography, see *Revista di archeologia cristiana* (Rome 1924–) and *L'Année philologique* (Paris 1928–) s.v. ''Épigraphie chrétienne.''

[M. R. P. MCGUIRE]

EPIKEIA

A term derived from the Greek ἐπιείκεια, meaning reasonableness, has undergone a development in moral theology. According to most manuals of theology epikeia is a restrictive interpretation of positive law based on the benign will of the legislator who would not want to bind his subjects in certain circumstances. Recently, theologians have referred to the Thomistic notion of the virtue of epikeia. In a concrete situation the individual invoking a higher law acts against the letter of an imperfect positive law.

St. Thomas Aquinas, following Aristotle, speaks of epikeia as a virtue, which pertains to the virtue of legal justice (*Summa theologiae* 2a2ae, 120.1 ad 2). Human law is imperfect and admits of exceptions because, by its very nature, human law is based on the ordinary course of changing circumstances (*ut in pluribus*). Epikeia safeguards the higher values of the natural law in the face of the imperfections of positive law.

Suárez follows St. Thomas, but under the influence of the medieval jurists, puts special emphasis on the mind of the legislator who would not want to bind his subject in certain circumstances. According to Suárez, epikeia may be used in three cases: (1) when the observance of the law would be sinful by reason of a higher law, epikeia is obligatory; (2) when compliance with the law demands heroism and effort out of proportion to the purpose of the law, epikeia may be used; (3) when particular circumstances unforeseen by the legislator would indicate that it was not his mind or intention to bind the subject, epikeia may be used.

Some modern theologians follow Suárez, but others restrict epikeia solely to the third instance wherein it is purely a question of the mind of the legislator (epikeia in the strict sense). In the first and second instances (epikeia in the wide sense) it is beyond the power of the legislator to bind his subjects. With regard to epikeia in the strict sense, the question of recourse to the legislator is discussed. The general tenor of the teaching is that in cases where there is probability, but no certainty, epikeia may not be used if recourse is possible.

Since 1940, there has been a tendency to revive the notion of epikeia as a virtue connected with legal or social justice. The need for the virtue of epikeia stems from the following conditions: (1) the imperfect nature of human law; (2) the possible tensions between the primary law for the Christian—the internal law of the Spirit—and that law's external expressions; (3) possible conflicts between society seeking the common good and the individual with his inalienable rights and individual good; (4) the imperfection of the human lawgiver. The rapidly changing circumstances of modern society only underscore the need for the virtue of epikeia. Epikeia is not just a way to escape from the obligations of law; it is the response to a higher law (the law of the Spirit or the natural law) against the letter of the positive law. At times, epikeia may demand more than the letter of the positive law.

Epikeia, per se, cannot be used with regard to the natural law, but only with regard to inadequate and imperfect expressions of the natural law. Epikeia can be used with regard to all positive laws, but less often with regard to irritating or invalidating laws. When epikeia is conceived as a virtue, there is no need for recourse to the superior.

See Also: LAWS, CONFLICT OF.

Bibliography: E. HAMEL, ''La Vertu d'Épikie,'' *Sciences ecclésiastiques* 13 (1961) 35–56. L. J. RILEY, *The History, Nature, and Use of Epikeia in Moral Theology* (Washington 1948). R. EGENTER, ''Über die Bedeutung der Epikie im sittlichen Leben,'' *Philosophisches Jahrbuch der Görres-Gesellschaft* 53 (1940) 115–127. J. FUCHS, *Situation und Entscheidung* (Frankfurt 1952) 47–68. A. DI MARINO, ''L'Epikeia Christiana,'' *Divus Thomas* (Piacenza) 55 (1952) 396–424. P. HAYOIT, ''L'Usage de l'epikie,'' *Rev. Dioc. Tournai* 10 (1955) 513–518. J. GIERS, ''Epikie und Sittlichkeit: Gestalt und Gestaltwandel einer Tugend,'' *Der Mensch unter Gottes Anruf und Ordnung: Festgabe für Theodor Muncker,* ed. R. HAUSER and F. SCHOLTZ (Düsseldorf 1958) 51–67. W. SCHÖLLGEN, ''Die Lehrpunkte von der Epikie und vom Kleineren Übel,'' *Anima* 15 (1960) 42–51. B. HÄRING, *The Law of Christ: Moral Theology for Priests and Laity,* tr. E. G. KAISER (Westminster, Md. 1961—) 1:1.74, 247, 269, 281 ff.

[C. E. CURRAN]

EPIKEIA (IN THE BIBLE)

English transliteration of the Greek ἐπιείκεια (that which is of just measure, reasonable, equitable). The Greek word is used in the Septuagint (LXX) only of persons, usually those in authority [Dn 4.24 (LXX: 4.27); Est 3.13; 2 Mc 9.27], and designates the virtue of moderation (prudence) in those who do not rigorously insist upon their rights. Unlike the despot who with want on violence (ὕβρις) presses for his due, the ἐπιεικής ruler manifests toward his subjects a fatherly indulgence and kindness, pardoning offenses and mitigating punishment. As an attribute of God, ἐπιείκεια denotes His mercy (Bar 2.27; Dn 3.42).

In the New Testament, similarly, ἐπιείκεια is attributed to Christ (2 Cor 10.1), to those in authority (Acts 24.4; 1 Pt 2.18; 1 Tm 3.3), and to Christians in general (Phil 4.5; Ti 3.2; Jas 3.17), but it takes on more clearly the nuance of gentleness, meekness, and humility, becoming synonymous with πραΰτης (2 Cor 10.1; Ti 3.2; cf. Wis 2.19). Although the term is not used in Mt 5.39–42 and 1 Cor 6.7, these passages give typical examples of the Christian virtue of ''gladly ceding one's rights.'' Christians must abandon the *lex talionis*; in accordance with the directives of the SERMON on the Mount, they must instead cultivate the generous spirit that does not haggle about one's rights, but has its roots in complete selflessness. Similarly, St. Paul's real concern in writing 1 Cor 6.1–11 was not the administration of justice, but the inculcation of an attitude of living above the law. Christians should renounce their rights rather than give scandal or disturb charitable relations.

The highest example of ἐπιείκεια was given by Christ who, setting aside the glory due His dignity, embraced the condition of a slave and accepted the death of the cross (Phil 2.5–8). Christ, whose mildness (πραΰτης) and gentleness (ἐπιείκεια) Christians must imitate (2 Cor 10.1), is not a weakling, however, but the glorified Lord (Phil 2.9–11) who, instead of jealously guarding His rights, exhibits the mildness that only an omnipotent King can show. His ἐπιείκεια, then, is but the complement of His divine glory and is thoroughly majestic in nature.

Christians, through their heavenly vocation (Phil 3.20), participate in Christ's kingly power and must be guided by His gentleness in their relationship with others. Thus, when St. Paul was accused of being cowardly, he reminded the rebellious Corinthians that he was capable of being stern (2 Cor 10.2), but that he preferred to exercise his authority only in the spirit of the Lord (2 Cor 10.8), i.e., as ἐπιείκεια. The same virtue is required of every Church official (1 Tm 3.3) who, inspired by the gentle wisdom from above (Jas 3.17), must manifest Christ's heavenly glory in his rule. Even more clearly does the majestic aspect of ἐπιείκεια appear in Phil 4.5, where Paul instructs the Philippians to make known their forebearance (τὸ ἐπιεικές) to all since ''the Lord is near.'' The thought of their future glorification must prompt them to maintain their lovable equanimity even in the face of persecution. The Lord will right all wrongs when He returns to establish His universal dominion. Therefore, ἐπιείκεια, which can be rendered as ''kindness, graciousness, the willingness to cede one's rights,'' is an earthly reflection of the heavenly splendor that awaits all who follow Christ's royal example.

Bibliography: H. PREISKER, G. KITTEL *Theologisches Wörterbuch zum Neuen Testament* (Stuttgart 1935–) 2:585–587. C. SPICQ, ''Bénignité, mansuétude, douceur, clémence,'' *Revue biblique* 54 (1947) 321–339. W. BARCLAY, *A N.T. Wordbook* (London 1955) 38–39.

[S. MAKAREWICZ]

EPIPHANIUS, PATRIARCH OF CONSTANTINOPLE

Reigned Feb. 25, 520, to June 5, 535; d. 535. Epiphanius had previously been a *syncellus* in the patriarchal curia and was esteemed for his virtue and knowledge of Scripture, when he was chosen patriarch in 520 in the hope that he would collaborate with the Byzantine Emperors JUSTIN I and JUSTINIAN I to foster better relations with the papacy after the ACACIAN SCHISM (482–519). Soon after his election he sent a profession of faith to Pope HORMISDAS, showing clearly his adherence to the orthodox doctrine of Chalcedon. The next year he wrote to the Pope regarding the deposition of the Patriarch Paul of Antioch. On the occasion of the visit of Pope JOHN I to Constantinople, he had the Pope preside over the celebration of the Easter Liturgy there (April 19, 526). As a result of the colloquy of the orthodox bishops with the Severians held in Constantinople in 532, he requested Pope JOHN II to approve the formula *unus ex trinitate crucifixus* (''One of the Trinity was crucified'') and to condemn those who denied that Mary was truly the Mother of God.

Bibliography: V. GRUMEL, *Les Regestes des actes du patriarcat de Constantinople* 1:217–226. L. BRÉHIER, *Histoire de l'église depuis les origines jusqu'à nos jours* 4:423–442. E. STEIN, *Histoire du Bas-Empire*, ed. J. R. PALANQUE 2:230–231, 378. L. DUCHESNE, *L'Église au VIe siècle* (Paris 1925) 65–70.

[G. T. DENNIS]

EPIPHANIUS OF PAVIA, ST.

Fifth-century Italian bishop; b. *c.* 438–9; d. Pavia, *c.* 496–7. His 30-year episcopate described by his biographer, Bp. Ennodius of Pavia (*c.* 512–521), demonstrates the unlimited charity of the bishops and their influence on civil authority in the difficult years when Roman domination in the West was crumbling. According to the vita, Epiphanius undertook two diplomatic missions: one to reconcile the Roman General Ricimer with the Emperor Anthemius at Rome (467–472); the other for Emperor Nepos with the Visigothic King Euric at Toulouse (474–5).

Epiphanius helped rebuild Pavia after it had been pillaged (476) by the Ostrogothic king of Italy and by the Rugi, and mitigated the sufferings of his people burdened with vexatious laws and intolerable taxes by Odovacar, or led off into captivity. With Bp. Laurentius of Milan he visited the Ostrogothic King THEODORIC (THE GREAT) at Ravenna (493–4) and shortly after, with Bp. Victor of Turin, persuaded the Burgundian King Gundobad at Lyons to release 6,000 Italian captives. His last journey of mercy took him, in midwinter, to Theodoric at Ravenna for the people of the Province of Liguria. When returning to Pavia he fell ill, and he died shortly after he reentered the city. His remains were stolen from Pavia in 962 and placed in the cathedral at Hildesheim.

Feast: Jan. 21.

Bibliography: ENNODIUS OF PAVIA, *Vita and Dictio,* ed. F. VOGEL (*Monumenta Germaniae Auctores antiquissimi* 7; 1885) 84–109; ed. G. HARTEL (*Corpus scriptorum ecclesiasticorum latinorum* 6; 1882) 331–383, 531–539; *The Life of Saint Epiphanius,* tr. G. M. COOK (*Catholic University of America, Studies in Medievel and Renaissance Latin, Language and Literature* 14; 1942); new tr. in *The Fathers of the Church: A New Translation,* ed. R.J. DEFARRARI 15 (1952) 301–351. *Analecta Bollandiana* 17 (1898) 123–127, the Anonymous of Hildesheim. G. H. PERTZ, ed., *Translatio Sancti Epiphanii* (*Monumenta Germaniae Scriptores* (Berlin 1825–) 4; 1841) 248–251. F. SAVIO, *Gli antichi vescovi d'Italia dalle origini al 1300,* 4 v. (1898–1932) 4:350–355. A. RIMOLDI, *Dictionnaire d'histoire et de géographie ecclésiastiques* (Paris 1912–)15:615–617.

[G. M. COOK]

EPIPHANIUS OF SALAMIS, ST.

Church Father; b. near Eleutheropolis, Palestine, *c.* 315; d. at sea, May 402. Epiphanius studied classics in Egypt, and in addition to Syrian, his native language, acquired a knowledge of Coptic and Hebrew; he remained for some time among the monks. On his return to Palestine he founded a monastery near Eleutheropolis that he governed for 30 years and on this basis was ordained. The bishops of CYPRUS selected him for the See of Constantia (Salamis) in 367; he was strongly attached to the doctrine of St. ATHANASIUS (except for the date of Easter) and opposed both the Arians and Origenists with passion but uncritically.

He took part in the MELETIAN SCHISM of Antioch, and broke allegiance with Meletius, whom he accused of refusing to subscribe to the *HOMOOUSIOS* before 363, and of dealing with the Pneumatics. Having tried in vain to win St. BASIL to the cause of Paulinus, he antagonized Vitalis, head of a third Antiochene party. After the Council of CONSTANTINOPLE I (381), over whose beginning Meletius had presided, Epiphanius journeyed to Rome with (St.) JEROME and Paulinus to protest that Council's decisions. Between 387 and 393 he traveled through Palestine with JOHN OF JERUSALEM, and destroyed the painting of a holy image in a church in Jerusalem (*See* PNEUMATOMACHIANS).

Origenism. Epiphanius was aware of Origenistic tendencies among the Palestinian monks (after 374), but in his *Panarion* (ch. 64) he describes ORIGENISM according to the treatise of METHODIUS OF OLYMPUS. He reproaches Origen for teaching SUBORDINATIONISM, the preexistence of souls, and the fall or original sin before the union of the soul with the body. In 393 he attacked Origen in the presence of Bp. JOHN OF JERUSALEM; in the following year, he failed to force John to condemn Origen (Jerome, *Ep.* 51), thus inaugurating a new phase of the Origenistic controversy, and added to his accusations that of the APOCATASTASIS of the devil. He attacked both RUFINUS OF AQUILEIA and Palladius, justly the latter, as he sought to describe contemporary Origenism as a pagan philosophy, or even outright GNOSTICISM.

After the condemnation of Origen in 400, Epiphanius went to Constantinople (402) to agitate against (St.) JOHN CHRYSOSTOM, who had succored the Tall Brothers, expelled from Nitria as Origenists; but when Epiphanius realized that THEOPHILUS OF ALEXANDRIA was involved in the matter, he did not await the Synod of the OAK that deposed Chrysostom, but departed; he died at sea.

Works. Epiphanius, of mediocre Greek culture, was opposed to speculation in theology, and considered philosophy a source of heresy; but his literary style furnishes an interesting example of the contemporary Greek *Koine.*

Ancoratus, 374, deals with the Trinity. It opposes Apollinarianism regarding the Incarnation, and Origenism in reference to the Resurrection and the interpretation of Genesis ch. 1. It closes with a text of the Creed of Nicaea-Constantinople (which a copyist substituted for the original of Nicaea) and a Creed of Epiphanius's own composition (*See* NICENE CREED).

Panarion, a tract against heretics written *c.* 374–76, draws heavily from the *Adv. Haereses* of HIPPOLYTUS and IRENAEUS, as well as original documents. It gives the titles of certain Gnostic works otherwise unknown, and extracts from the *Apostolica* of MARCION or the Montanist Oracles, and includes interesting judgments on his contemporaries.

His *De mensuris et ponderibus* (392) is a manual for the study of the Bible. *De duodecim gemmis* (*c.* 394) is an allegorical interpretation of the 12 jewels on the breastplate of the High Priest. It is preserved in a Georgian translation, and partly in Latin (*Corpus scriptorum ecclesiasticorum latinorum* (Vienna 1866) 35:743–773), with Greek, Coptic, and Ethiopic fragments.

Fragments of three works by Epiphanius against images utilized in the eighth-century controversies over ICONOCLASM have been identified as his: a *Pamphlet against the Images;* a *Letter to Theodosius I;* and the *Testament.* Other of his extant works are letters. One is a *Letter to the Arabs* (Panarion 78.2–25) on the perpetual virginity of Mary; another letter survives in *Ancoratus* (77) and in a Syriac version; and two letters were translated into Latin by Jerome (*Epist.* 51, 91).

In Greek *catenae* there are Epiphanian scholia on the Octateuch; and in Coptic *catenae,* on Mark and Luke. For Arab *catenae,* see G. Graf, *Geschichte der christlichen arabischen Literatur* (Vatican City 1944–1953) 1:356.

Among the works falsely attributed to him are an *Anakephalaiosis,* or summary of the *Panarion;* the *Physiologus* that had great influence on medieval iconography; commentaries on the Old Testament; homilies; and a Life of the Blessed Virgin Mary.

Feast: May 12.

Bibliography: EPIPHANIUS OF SALAMIS, *''Ancoratus'' und ''Panarion,''* ed. K. HOLL, 3 v. (*Die griechischen christlichen Schriftsteller der erstendrei Jahrhunderte* 25, 31, 37; 1915, 1922, 1933); *Texte und Untersuchungenzur Geschichte der altchristlichen Literatur* 36.2 (1910). O. BARDENHEWER, *Geschichte der altkirchlichen Literatur* (Freiburg 1913–1932) 3:293–302. B. E. PERRY, *Paulys Realenzyklopädie der klassischen Altertumswissenschaft,* ed. G. WISSOWA 20.1 (1941) 1074–1129. A. PUECH, *Histoire de la littérature grecque chrétienne,* 3 v. (Paris 1928–30) 3:643–669. B. ALTANER, *Patrology,* tr. H. GRAEF (New York 1960) 365–368. J. QUASTEN, *Patrology* (Westminster, MD 1950) 3:384–396. J. N. D. KELLY, *Early Christian Creeds* (2d ed. London 1960). G. JOUASSARD, *Gregorianum* 42 (1961) 5–36. *Der Physiologus,* tr. and ed. O. SEEL (Zurich 1960). P. NAUTIN, *Dictionnaire d'histoire et de géographie ecclésiastiques* (Paris 1912) 15:617–631. D. FERNÁNDEZ, *De mariologia sancti Epiphanii* (Rome 1968). L. A. ELDRIDGE, *The Gospel Text of Epiphanius of Salamis* (Salt Lake City 1969). G. VALLÉE, *A Study in Anti-Gnostic Polemics* (Waterloo, Ont. 1981). J. F. DECHOW, *Dogma and Mysticism in Early Christianity: Epiphanius of Cyprus and the Legacy of Origen* (Macon, GA 1988). A. POURKIER, *L'hérésiologie chez Epiphane de Salamine* (Paris 1992). M. E. STONE and R. ERVINE, *The Armenian Texts of Epiphanius of Salamis De mensuris et ponderibus* (Sterling, Va. 2000).

[P. CANIVET]

EPIPHANY, THE SOLEMNITY OF

A feast celebrated for most of Christian history on January 6, though—since the reform of the liturgical calendar—marked by most Catholic churches on the Sunday between January 2 and 8, where January 6 is not a holy day of obligation.

Names for the Feast. One of the most ancient annual liturgical feasts, Epiphany has been variously called, in the East, *epiphánia*, *epiphánios*, *theopháneia*, all suggesting divine appearances or manifestations. Other names for the feast—such as *heméra ton photon*, or ''day of lights''—have emphasized the images of sun, stars, and light, long associated with Epiphany and perhaps connected to the period of ''illumination'' in the process of initiation in the early Church. Parallel terms in the Latin West were *dies epiphaniarum*, the ''day of revelations;'' *dies manifestationis*, the ''day of manifestions;'' and simply *apparitio,* ''appearance.'' Also connected to the light imagery was the Latin phrase *dies luminum*, the ''day of lights.''

Before their use in Christian liturgy, the Greek *epiphany* or *theophany* designated a manifestation of a divinity and, later, important events in the life of a ruler, such as a birth, ascension to the throne, or even a visit to a city. The word ''epiphany'' was first used in a Christian sense in the New Testament, referring to both the first and final comings of Christ (see, e.g., Ti 2:11,13). The word was soon after used of the miracles of Christ as manifestations of divine power.

Origins in the Calendar. A feast on January 6 is first mentioned by Clement of Alexandria (around A.D. 215), who said that the Basilidians, a gnostic group, commemorated the baptism of Christ on this day (*Stromata* 4.12; *Die griechischen christlichen Schriftsteller der ersten drei Jahrhunderte* [Leipzig 1897—] 2:284–287). The feast of the Epiphany certainly originated in the East, and it is found in the *Breviarium Syriacum* of 411 *C.E.* (ed. tr. Mariani [Rome 1956] 28). In the West the journals of Ammianus Marcellinus describe a visit in 363 of the Emperor Julian to Gaul ''on the day of the festival in January which the Christians call 'epiphany''' (LCL 2:98–101).

The feast was listed in the Calendar of Carthage, in North Africa (*Dictionnaire d'archéologie chrétienne* 8.2:2286), but not in the Roman Chronograph of 354, where one finds the earliest evidence for Christmas.

In the Egyptian calendar, the winter solstice and a feast of the sun-god were observed on January 6, so it is likely that the Christian date was originally related to draw people away from the pagan celebrations. On the previous night, pagans of Alexandria commemorated the birth of their god Aeon, born of a virgin. Some pagans also believed that the waters of rivers, especially the Nile, acquired miraculous powers and even turned into wine on this night.

Narratives in the East. It is difficult to ascertain if there was originally a single narrative or image for the feast, or if the feast celebrated a variety of epiphanies or manifestations from its origin. By the fourth century the feast embraced the narratives of the birth of Christ, his baptism, the adoration of the Magi, and the miracle at Cana (perhaps linked with the water turned wine in the Egyptian pagan celebration). Epiphanius, fourth-century bishop of Salamis, described the pagan feasts above and accepted January 6 as the date of the birth of Jesus, and he also speaks of the Magi and sign at the wedding in Cana (*Panarion* 51.16).

Two writers of Latin Christianity who traveled in the East give witness to early narratives for the feast. First, the fourth-century travel-diary of Egeria describes the Palestinian celebration of January 6 and its octave. Though a folio is missing, the narrative was likely that of the nativity of Jesus, for the people, monks, and the bishop had gone up from Jerusalem to Bethlehem. There is no mention in Egeria's journal of the baptism or of Cana for this feast (*Journal*, chapter 25). Second, according to John Cassian (*Conferences* 10.2), the Alexandrian ''day of the epiphanies'' commemorated the birth and baptism of Christ.

In ancient Christian Syria the narratives included the birth, the Magi, and the baptism, and the *Apostolic Constitutions* (8.33.7) command that slaves not work ''on the festival of the Epiphany, because on it there came to pass the manifestation of the divinity of Christ . . . at the baptism'' (tr. Grisbrooke, 51).

Narratives in the West. Though some scholars assume that there had been a single narrative at the start to which others were added, it seems more likely that a plurality of objects, all ''manifestations'' of God's presence in Christ, was there from the start. This is supported by the testimony of Bishop Filastrius of Brescia, whose *Diversarum hereseon liber* (c. 383) simultaneously declared that there is only one proper narrative for the feast (the visit of the Magi) and named the feast with the plural *dies epifaniorum*, ''day of the manifestations,'' the plural likely capturing the earlier stratum of more than one narrative even though Filastrius was himself legislating only one for orthodox belief.

Sermons of Augustine indicate that the feast existed in North Africa in his time (*Patrolgia Latina* 38:1026–1039), and eight sermons of Leo the Great (bishop of Rome, 440–461) witness to the feast's observance in Rome in the middle of the fifth century (*Sermons* 31–38; *Patrolgia Latina* 54:234–263). By the time of Augustine and Leo, the date of December 25 for the birth of Christ had been received by most churches, and the narratives of Epiphany had been pared down to the single one of the visit of the Magi, as narrated only in the Gospel of Matthew (2:1–12).

Liturgy. The multiplicity of narratives earlier attached to Epiphany was not manifest in the liturgies of Epiphany in Rome. There the principal narrative was from the earliest sources and still is the visit of the Magi to adore the Christ-child. The narratives of Christ's baptism and of the sign in Cana turning water into wine are secondary.

Early Mass formularies are found in the Würzburg Lectionary (*Dictionnaire d'archéologie chrétienne* 8.2:2286) and in the old Gelasian Sacramentary (ed. Mohlberg 61–68). Although the diary of Egeria testifies to an octave of Epiphany in Palestine, and the Würzburg Lectionary indicates a triduum following January 6, an octave did not enter the Roman liturgy until the eighth century (Gregorian Sacramentary). This octave, together with the vigil, was suppressed in 1956. In the present liturgical calendar of the Roman Catholic church, the Sunday after January 6 is the feast of the Baptism of the Lord, a narrative that had been proclaimed on Epiphany in Egypt in the early Church.

In the Liturgy of the Hours for the feast of Epiphany, the manifestation of Christ's power in the miracle of Cana is commemorated in the Magnificat antiphon on January 6 and in the Gospel of the second Sunday after Epiphany. The espousals of Christ and the Church are mentioned in the same antiphon. This theme enters the Epiphany liturgy because Christ is believed to have sanctified water at his baptism, and it is through the waters of baptism that the church exercises spiritual maternity.

Today the multiplicity is not evident in the texts for the eucharistic liturgy for the celebration of Epiphany. The prayer texts draw only from the Matthean narrative of the Magi. While the prayers maintain the imagery of light and stars, one step removed from the baptismal origins, these are dissociated from their original connection to baptism and the process of illumination. The multiplicity of the feast of manifestation is expressed well, however, in the antiphon for the canticle at morning prayer:

> Today the Bridegroom claims his bride, the Church, since Christ has washed her sins away in Jordan's waters; the Magi hasten with their gifts to the royal wedding; and the wedding guests rejoice, for Christ has changed water into wine, alleluia. This is also so in the antiphon for the canticle at evening prayer:

> Three mysteries mark this holy day: today the star leads the Magi to the infant Christ; today water is changed into wine for the wedding feast; today Christ wills to be baptized by John in the river Jordan to bring us salvation.

Customs. The fourth canon of the Council of Saragossa, Spain, in 380 legislated that ''for 21 continuous days, from December 17 until the day of the feast of Epiphany, which is January 6, no one should be absent from church, or hide at home, withdraw to a dwelling in the country, move to the mountains, or go walking with bare feet. Rather, all should assemble in church.'' (tr. of Mansi, *Sacrorum Conciliorum nova et amplissima collectio* [Paris 1889–1927; repr. Graz 1960] 3:634). These prescriptions both indicate the gravity of the feast and suggest that Christmas itself was not yet observed in Spain in 380, for the three weeks of discipline, during which December 25 would have occurred, would not otherwise have been ''continuous.''

From ancient times the Eastern Church has blessed baptismal water on Epiphany. Antonius of Piacenza (c. 570) testifies that in Palestine the Jordan River itself was blessed (*Itinerarium* 11–12; *Patrologia Latina* 72:903–904), this in commemoration of the baptism of the Lord in the same stream. Antonius testifies that a baptism took place, ships were blessed with the holy water, and ''all descended into the river for blessing, dressed in woven clothes as if for burial.''

As attested by John Cassian, on Epiphany the church of Alexandria announced to other churches the date of the following Easter. Elsewhere the dates of Easter and other movable feasts were announced after the Gospel on the feast of Epiphany. Ambrose testified to a Milanese custom at Epiphany for the enrollment of catechumens. Today, this custom has been revised in some parishes.

Bibliography: A. CHUPUNGCO, ed., *Liturgical Time and Space* (Handbook for Liturgical Studies, v. 5; Collegeville, MN 2000) 135–330. A. ADAM, *The Liturgical Year* (New York 1981) 121–157. T. J. TALLEY, *The Origins of the Liturgical Year* (New York 1986) 79–162. B. BOTTE, *Les origines de la Noël et de L'Épiphanie* (Louvain 1932). M. MERRAS, *The Origins of the Celebration of the Christian Feast of Epiphany: An Ideological, Cultural and Historical Study* (Joensuu, Finland 1995).

[M. F. CONNELL]

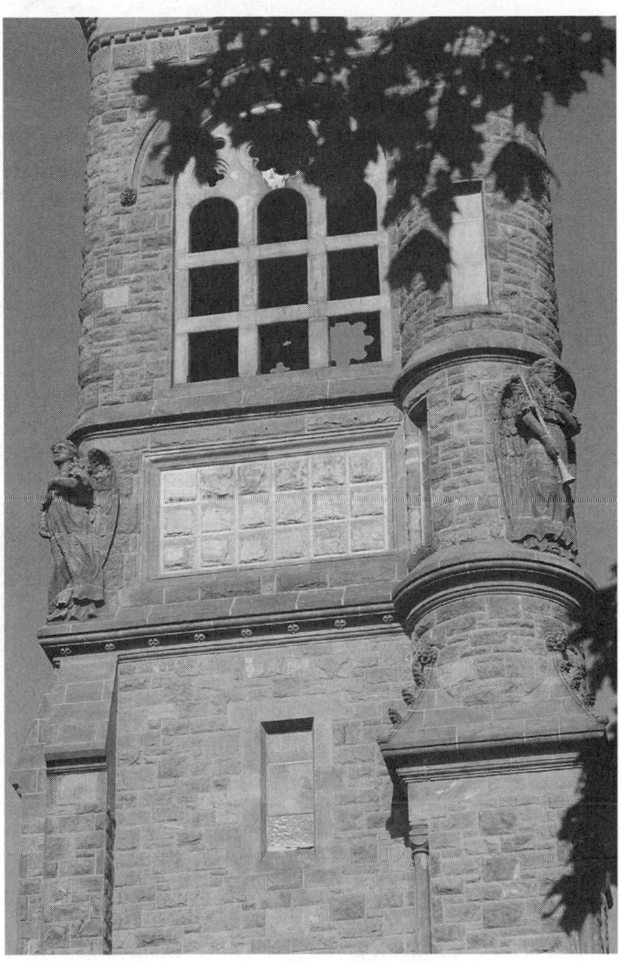

St. Paul's Episcopal Church. (©Lee Snider/CORBIS)

EPISCOPAL CHURCH, U.S.

The Anglican Church in the U.S. since 1789 has been autonomous and independent of the Church of England, but an integral part of the ANGLICAN COMMUNION of churches and joined in kinship of faith, government, and worship to the English mother church (*see* ANGLICANISM).

History. Although the Church of England early made contacts with America through chaplains who accompanied explorers such as Sir Martin Frobisher (1578) and Sir Francis Drake (1579) or unsuccessful colonizers such as Sir Walter Raleigh (1585), the first permanent settlement of the church was begun in 1607 when Rev. Robert Hunt celebrated the Eucharist for the first time in Jamestown. Other foundations followed in Philadelphia (1695), New York City (1697), Boston (1689), Newport, Rhode Island (1702), and Burlington, New Jersey (1705). By the end of the colonial period, the Church of England was represented in all 13 colonies and was officially established in Virginia, Maryland, North and South Caroli-

Cathedral of St. John the Divine, New York. (©CORBIS)

na, and Georgia, although only in the first two was it fully and effectively established. Elsewhere, in the midst of predominantly Nonconformist or non-Anglican communities, the church had to be assisted by the mother church and especially by the SOCIETY FOR THE PROPAGATION OF THE GOSPEL (SPG). To this private organization, founded in 1701 through the efforts of a commissary sent to Maryland by the bishop of London, Thomas Bray, belongs much of the credit for the existence and development of the church during this period.

Early Difficulties. The church in the colonies suffered under three major handicaps. The first was its connection with the state either in England or in America. Where it was established as a state institution in the colonies it suffered from interference by unsympathetic governors or by dominating lay employers, as well as from the inadequacy of funds provided by taxes levied on all members of the colony, whether Anglicans or not. Where it was not established, as in Massachusetts and in Connecticut, the church was a distinct minority suspected by many as the colonial representative of the state Church of England, whose authority and power they had migrated to America to escape.

In this situation the clergy were generally of poor quality. Some had left England to avoid difficulties at home; most lived in conditions of isolation, frontier hardships, and great poverty. A number worked valiantly in the face of grave obstacles, but by and large their standing was inferior and their morale low. To worsen matters, the Anglican mission in the United States was under the direct jurisdiction of the bishop of London throughout English colonial rule. Without a local bishop in the United States during the colonial period, prospective clergymen had to journey to London for their ordination, a prospect that discouraged many candidates.

The American Revolution added a severe crisis of loyalty to the existing troubles. Most of the 250 clergy, together with several thousand of the laity, persisted in their allegiance to the king; and accordingly some were put in prison, some were banished, and some voluntarily departed, going to Canada or back to England. A good percentage of the laity, however, supported the revolution, and two-thirds of those who signed the Declaration of Independence were members of the Episcopal Church. Leaders to the revolutionary cause who were Episcopalians include George Washington, Thomas Jefferson, Patrick Henry, John Jay, Robert Morris, John Marshall, John Randolph, Charles Lee and Harry Lee.

Post-Revolutionary Developments. After the war the church, cut off from Great Britain, disestablished in America, and weakened by losses of clergy and laity, had to develop self-support, a national organization, and especially an American episcopate. The last came about first. Ten of the 14 clergymen in Connecticut voted for Dr. Samuel SEABURY, an American born in Groton, Conn., to go to England for consecration. Put off in England because he could not take an oath of allegiance to the king, Dr. Seabury was consecrated by NONJURING bishops in Aberdeen, Scotland, on Nov. 14, 1784.

Meanwhile, under the leadership of Rev. William White, rector of Christ Church, Philadelphia, a movement arose to constitute a Protestant Episcopal Church for the whole United States. On Sept. 27, 1785, the first general convention met in Philadelphia with delegates from only seven states, but the assembly took important preliminary steps toward the formation of a unifying constitution and the establishment of a hierarchy. Through its efforts Rev. Samuel Provoost and Rev. William White were consecrated in England on Feb. 4, 1787, as bishops for New York and Philadelphia, respectively. Finally, a general convention met in Philadelphia on July 28, 1789, to bring about a united church, but the first session from July 28 to August 8 convened without Bishop Seabury or representatives from New England. The convention then took a number of conciliatory steps, especially the recognition of the validity of Seabury's consecration, thereby succeeding in bringing the bishop and representatives from Massachusetts and New Hampshire to the second session. With united forces the general convention, meeting from September 30 to October 16, adopted a constitution, agreed on and ratified 17 canons, and authorized a BOOK OF COMMON PRAYER. The Episcopal Church of the United States was a reality. To complete the foundation, another bishop, Dr. James Madison, was consecrated in England for Virginia in 1790; and in 1792 all four bishops inaugurated a distinctly American episcopate by uniting in the first consecration in the United States, that of Thomas John Claggett as bishop of Maryland.

For more than 20 years the new church endured many painful trials in its evolution into a sound organism. Many distrusted it as fundamentally an English institution. The loss of the METHODISTS, as well as the demoralizing effects of a long war, weakened its vitality. Formal worship repelled people in an age of emotionalism and freedom in religious expression. Growth was slow and leadership ineffective. However, beginning with the second decade of the 19th century, more effective leadership ushered in a new era of vigorous development. Foremost among the new leaders were the bishops Alexander V. Griswold of the eastern diocese, John H. Hobart of New York, Philander Chase of Ohio, and Richard C. Moore of Virginia. During Griswold's episcopate the parishes in his diocese increased fivefold, and at his death the eastern diocese became the Dioceses of Vermont, Massachusetts, Maine, New Hampshire, and Rhode Island. The four or five active ministers laboring in Virginia when Bishop Moore arrived in Richmond in 1814 increased to nearly 100 during his 27 years of service.

Educational and missionary activities developed, and the early interest in education that had led to the formation (1693) of William and Mary College at Williamsburg, Virginia, blossomed. The General Theological Seminary of New York (1819) and the Theological Seminary of Virginia (1824) were founded. Bishop Chase began Kenyon College in Ohio, and Rev. James L. Breck founded Nashotah Hall, originally an associate mission, but later a theological seminary, in Wisconsin. The Domestic and Foreign Society, organized by the General Convention in 1820, stimulated the work of church extension. Bishop Jackson Kemper, the first officially designated missionary bishop, worked in Indiana, Missouri, Iowa, Wisconsin, and Minnesota. Bishop James H. Otey did missionary work in Tennessee and in the South and Southwest. James L. Breck pushed across the country, establishing foundations along the way, until he reached the Pacific Coast. New dioceses and missionary territories matched the growth of the United States as the church became coextensive with the country, and even went beyond. Missionary zeal led to foundations in Greece, Turkey, Liberia, China, and Japan.

The period of growth was abruptly halted by the Civil War. The Episcopal Church was the only major denomination that did not develop into full-blown schism during the Civil War. Church leaders maintained cordial relations throughout this period. When the split in the Union developed into war, the southern dioceses formed a temporary Protestant Episcopal Church in the Confederate States, holding their first general council in Augusta, Georgia. Nevertheless, both sides still considered themselves one church. Throughout the war both northern and southern sections of the church maintained friendly attitudes. At the 1892 general convention in New York City, the names of the southern bishops were called in, and the 1865 general convention in Philadelphia was attended by some southern delegations. Soon afterward, the unity of the church was quietly restored by the resumption of full relations.

After the Civil War the church continued its progress. In 1866 there were 160,000 Episcopal communicants; in 1900, 720,000. Organized diocesan and missionary work expanded to include the whole of the United States and its dependencies, as well as areas in

Latin America, Africa, and Asia. From 1867 onward the American bishops participated regularly in the meetings of the Anglican Communion known as the LAMBETH CONFERENCES.

With other American churches, the Episcopal Church, particularly since 1900, has championed the cause of a Christian social order. In numerous pronouncements its general conventions have called for social justice, the elimination of poverty and prejudice, opportunity for self-development, and fair shares for all in the gains of progress.

Another and different kind of development came in 1913 when the general convention passed a canon for the recognition of religious communities, significant as the first legislation of its kind since the Reformation (*see* RELIGIOUS ORDERS, ANGLICAN-EPISCOPALIAN) .

Liturgical Reforms. In the 1970s, the Episcopalians engaged in the process of liturgical reform that involved the experimental use of proposed new liturgies, inspired by the liturgical reforms of VATICAN COUNCIL II. In 1976, the general convention approved a measure for the use of the proposed Book of Common Prayer, *ad experimentum.* The proposed prayer book received both accolades and criticisms. Many praised it for its use of contemporary language and its endeavors to incorporate the best of 20th-century historical liturgical scholarship. While a small minority thought that the latter resulted in a prayer book that was more ''Catholic'' than its predecessors, a great majority of its detractors were unhappy with the inclusion of contemporary language in the proposed prayer book, as contrasted with the classic dignity of the Elizabethan idiom. Nevertheless, at the 1979 general convention the new prayer book was passed by an overwhelming majority. This was the first revision of the American Book of Common Prayer which utilized contemporary language (in the Rite B texts), while at the same time retaining the traditional language in the Rite A texts. In conjunction with this revision, a new hymnal was issued in 1982.

Women's Ordination. The controversy over women's ordination became a great concern in the Episcopal Church in the 1970s. Opponents of women's ordination fell into two camps: those who believed that it was theologically impossible for women to be ordained because it ran counter to Scripture and tradition, and those who believed that this was an issue to be decided not by the Episcopal Church on its own, but by the Universal Church at some sort of ecumenical council. Nevertheless, the 1970 general convention authorized the ordination of women deacons. This lead to the ordination of the first woman priest in 1976. The year 1988 witnessed the election of the Rev. Barbara C. Harris as the suffragan bishop of Massachusetts, and she was ordained the first woman bishop in the historic succession in 1989.

Doctrine. The Episcopal Church holds to the Apostles' and Nicene creeds as doctrinal symbols. At its general convention of 1801 it accepted with some modifications the THIRTY-NINE ARTICLES of the Church of England as a general statement of doctrine; but adherence to them as a creed was not demanded. Of the Thirty-Nine Articles, the 21st article is excluded, and the 8th, 35th and 36th articles are accepted in a modified form. The Church expects all of its members to be loyal to the doctrine, discipline, and worship as proposed by the ''one, holy, Catholic, Apostolic Church'' of all ages and as based on the Holy Scriptures. Clergymen must subscribe to the declaration ''I do believe the Holy Scriptures of the Old and New Testaments to be the Word of God, and to contain all things necessary to salvation, and I do solemnly engage to conform to the doctrine, discipline, and worship of the Episcopal Church in the United States of America.'' A wide latitude of interpretation exists, however, in the positions known as HIGH CHURCH, LOW CHURCH, and BROAD CHURCH, differentiated by the relatively high importance or low importance or liberal interpretation given to the episcopate, priesthood, sacraments, and liturgical ceremonies. These positions reflect the ''Catholic'' and ''Evangelical'' elements in the Church: Catholic, as the Anglican Congress of 1954 put it, ''in seeking to do justice to the wholeness of Christian truth, in emphasizing continuity through the Episcopate and in retaining the historic Creeds and Sacraments of undivided Christendom; and Evangelical in its commission to proclaim the Gospel and in its emphasis on personal faith in Jesus Christ as Savior.''

Organization and Structure. The system of ecclesiastical government in the Episcopal Church includes parish or local congregations, dioceses, provinces, and the general convention. Officers of the parish are the rector, who must be a priest; wardens, representing the body of the parish; and members of the vestry, who are the trustees of the parish corporation. The direction of spiritual affairs is exclusively in the hands of the rector. The diocese, consisting of a number of parishes, is governed by a bishop; and the diocesan convention, which is held annually, is presided over by the bishop and is composed of both priests and laity. Each diocese adopts its own constitution for the regulation of its internal affairs, but no canon or regulation may be contrary to the constitution and canons of the general convention. A bishop is elected by the diocese, but the election must be approved by a majority of the standing committees of the dioceses in the United States and by a majority of the bishops having jurisdiction. The bishop may have a coadjutor bishop who has the right of succession as head of the diocese, and may also have suffragan bishops as assistants, but these bishops have limited authority and do not have the right of succession. Missionary bishops are elected by the House of Bishops, subject to confirmation by the House of Deputies if the general convention is in session; if it is not in session, then confirmation must be made by the standing committees of the dioceses.

The supreme governing body is the general convention; it meets every three years and consists of two houses, the House of Bishops and the House of Deputies, each of which sits and deliberates separately. The House of Bishops has as its members all bishops; the House of Deputies is composed of delegates, consisting of not more than four clergy and four laypersons elected from each diocese. In addition, each missionary district within the boundaries of the United States is entitled to one clerical and one lay deputy. Either house may propose new legislation, and all enactments of the convention must be passed by both houses. In this way the laity, ever since the general convention of 1789, has had a responsible share in the legislative action of the Church.

Ecumenical Relations Presenting the Episcopal Church as the best hope for promoting Christian unity in the United States, Rev. William R. Huntington, in *The Church-Idea, An Essay Towards Unity* (1870), offered as a basis for unity what he declared were the Anglican principles: the Scriptures as the word of God, the primitive creeds as the rule of faith, the two Sacraments ordained by Christ, and the episcopate as the keystone of unity. These four points were accepted by the general convention of 1886 meeting in Chicago and became known as the Chicago Quadrilateral. Two years later the third Lambeth Conference offered to the world an almost identical version, which has since been called the LAMBETH QUADRILATERAL.

These early attempts at Christian unity were partially responsible for further attempts in 1910. In that year Charles H. BRENT, then bishop of the Philippine Islands, imbued with a vision obtained at the missionary conference held in Edinburgh, Scotland, made a stirring speech at the U.S. general convention, urging a world meeting on faith and order. The convention appointed a joint commission to attempt such a conference. The first world meeting on faith and order met at Lausanne, Switzerland, in 1927. In 1948 the Faith and Order movement merged with the Life and Work movement to form the WORLD COUNCIL OF CHURCHES, whose avowed purpose is worldwide Christian unity. The Episcopal Church is represented both in the World Council and in the NATIONAL COUNCIL OF THE CHURCHES OF CHRIST in the United States.

In 1960 Rev. Eugene Carson Blake, stated clerk of the United Presbyterian Church, made a formal proposal that his church and the Episcopal Church form ''a plan of church union both catholic and reformed.'' The Episcopal Church accepted the invitation and formed the CONSULTATION ON CHURCH UNION together with the United Presbyterian Church, the United Church of Christ, the Christian Churches (Disciples of Christ), the Methodist Church, and the Evangelical United Brethren Church (which later merged with the Methodist Church to become the United Methodist Church).

Since the 1970s, the Episcopal Church has engaged in formal dialogues with the Roman Catholic, Orthodox, Presbyterian and Lutheran communions. In 1999, the Episcopal Church and the EVANGELICAL LUTHERAN CHURCH IN AMERICA concluded an agreement for full communion partnership.

Bibliography: R. W. ALBRIGHT, *A History of the Protestant Episcopal Church* (New York 1964). E. C. CHORLEY, *Men and Movements in the American Episcopal Church* (New York 1946). G. E. DEMILLE, *The Episcopal Church Since 1900* (New York 1955). J. T. ADDISON, *The Episcopal Church in the United States* (New York 1951). F. V. MILLS, *Bishops by Ballot: An Eighteenth-Century Ecclesiastical Revolution* (New York 1978). R. B. MULLIN, *Episcopal Vision/American Reality: High Church Theology and Social Thought in Evangelical America* (New Haven 1986). D. L. HOLMES, *A Brief History of the Episcopal Church* (Valley Forge, Pa. 1993). C. M. PRELINGER, *Episcopal Women: Gender, Spirituality, and Commitment in an American Mainline Denomination* (New York 1992). P. W. DARLING, *New Wine: The Story of Women Transforming Leadership and Power in the Episcopal Church* (Cambridge, Mass. 1994). N. L. RHODEN, *Revolutionary Anglicanism: The Colonial Church of England Clergy during the American Revolution* (New York 1999). R. W. PRICHARD, *A History of the Episcopal Church,* (rev. ed. Harrisburg, PA 1999). G. S. CADY and C. WEBBER, *Lutherans and Episcopalians Together: A Guide to Understanding* (Cambridge, Mass. 2001).

[R. MATZERATH/C. E. SIMCOX/EDS.]

EPISCOPAL CONFERENCES

Episcopal conferences embody the collegial (conciliar or synodal) exercise of church authority by the bishops of a region or a nation, arising from the recognition in *Lumen gentium,* no. 23, of subsidiarity on one hand and the personal responsibility of archdioceses and dioceses to collaborate on the other. Contemporary determinations about episcopal conferences flow from three historical items: the revision of the Code of Canon Law in 1983; the 1985 Synod of Bishops, held to celebrate the twentieth anniversary of the end of the Second Vatican Council; and *Apostolos suos,* the *motu proprio* of Pope John Paul II on May 21, 1998, that addresses the theological and juridical nature of episcopal conferences.

Conferences of bishops, or national episcopal conferences, originate during the nineteenth century in Europe—for example, Belgium (1830), Germany (1848), Austria (1849), and regional meetings in Italy—but they have deeper roots in the ancient practice of the Church to organize assemblies of bishops at the level of ecclesiastical provinces. In the Eastern Church, these provinces comprise metropolitan and suffragan dioceses; in the Latin Church, the archdioceses and dioceses of a particular geographic region form provinces. The latter have long standing ecclesiastical recognition according to canon 292 of the 1917 Code of Canon Law, while the former received definitive canonical status in 1965 at Vatican Council II with the decree *Christus Dominus,* nos. 37 to 38, and the specifications set forth by Pope Paul VI in his apostolic letter, *Ecclesiae sanctae* of Aug. 5, 1966 (section 1, no. 41).

European assemblies of bishops had their importance recognized as akin to ecclesiastical provinces, but these meetings took place in a historical context of rising European nationalism that often cast liberalism and democracy as oppressors to institutional Catholicism, specifically to the Holy See. In the United States of America, the first national conference of bishops took place in September 1919, although annual meetings of the metropolitan archbishops took place in the final decades of the previous century. In subsequent years, the American episcopate met in annual conference and transacted business first as the National Catholic Welfare Conference and then after Vatican II under two titles: the National Conference of Catholic Bishops and the United States Catholic Conference. In 2000, the episcopate reorganized again as the United States Conference of Catholic Bishops.

1983 Code of Canon Law. Chapter four of book two, ''The People of God,'' of the 1983 Code includes 13 canons (447–59) dealing with the general nature and responsibility of episcopal conferences. The canons are largely derived from the conciliar decree *Christus Dominus* on the pastoral office of bishops in the Church. The canons on national conferences constitute a fourth illustration of the groupings of particular churches, or dioceses, in the organizational structure of the Catholic Church.

The canons embody two aspects of conferences in which they differ from the ancient tradition of particular councils: They are permanent bodies (c. 447), not occasional assemblies, and they have the canonical character of juridic persons in the Church (c. 449, §2). Canons 448 and 450 establish the membership of national conferences, respecting the competence of the Holy See sated in canon 449, §1. Canons 451 to 459 set the composition and operating procedures of the conference. Canon 455 merits particular notice. The canon deals with a great number of practical applications, but it also raises serious theological implications, precisely because it touches the autonomy of individual bishops and the relationship of diocesan bishops with each other and the Holy See. Early recognition of this difficulty appeared in a Nov. 8, 1983 letter of the Cardinal Secretary of State to each national episcopal conference indicating where the conference (a) *may* and (b) *must* issue local norms (see *Communicationes* 15 (1983):135–39.)

1985 Synod of Bishops. With respect to conferences of bishops, the synod members wrestled with two tendencies: one seeing episcopal conferences as a centralizing influence in a nation or region and the other seeing the responsibility and innate power of the bishop of the individual, particular church. A 1988 letter from the Congregation of bishops focused on the theological and the juridic status of national conferences.

On the theological status, the letter repeatedly draws a sharp line between episcopal collegiality (itself the expression of the communion of the local churches) in the full or strict sense and in the partial or limited sense. They are judged collegial only in an analogical and in exact sense. Admitting that the remote foundation of conferences is in the particular (provincial or regional) councils held since the end of the second century, the text sharply distinguishes councils and conferences and dwells upon the pastoral utility of the conferences. The latter are said to lack any proper magisterial office, although their teachings are to be received with a ''religious submission of mind'' in accord with canon 753.

On the juridic status, the Roman letter dealt with the conferences in three sections: (1) restraints on teaching, conceived merely as ''applying pronouncements of the magisterium of the universal Church''; (2) the distinction between the authority of the individual diocesan bishop and the conferences, with the actions of the conferences limited to ''moral authority'' in most instances; and (3) proposals for consensus for nonbinding decisions, with special attention to the danger of a conference's subsidiary organs, commissions, or offices being confused with the conference itself.

Critique of the Roman letter saw many of the concerns as matters of ecclesiastical polity rather than theology and church law. Challenges were made for more precision in terminology and a thorough grounding of both the theological and juridical status of national conferences in conciliar, canonical, papal, historical, and liturgical references. The response of the bishops of the United States was that a new draft should be prepared with the collaboration of representative bishops, canonists, theologians, and historians.

Apostolos suos. The *motu proprio* of May 21, 1998, represents the response to request of the 1988 synod of bishops and subsequent consultations. The document contains four sections. Section one traces major theological-historical moments of the collegial structure or permanent assembly of the apostles as constituted by the Lord Jesus. Section two addresses collegial union among bishops as it touches on the themes of unity, collegiality, and joint pastoral action. Section three sets forth Pope John Paul II's understanding of the conference of bishops as a permanent institution, the issues that currently call for the joint action of the bishops, the manner in which episcopal conferences are to organize territorially, their composition, especially with respect to deliberative or consultative voting power, and finally the authority of the episcopal conference with respect to the authority of the diocesan bishop and the requirements of a *recognitio* of the Apostolic See. Section four sets down complementary norms regarding the conference of bishops.

[A. ESPELAGE]

EPISTEMOLOGY

A term that derives from the Greek ἐπιστήμη and λόγος meaning the science of KNOWLEDGE; in its broadest signification it refers simply to an investigation of knowledge and its problems. A synonymous term is criteriology, from the Greek κρίνω meaning to distinguish or judge, which implies the testing of knowledge to distinguish the true from the false. *See* CRITERION (CRITERIOLOGY). Related to these are the expressions critique of knowledge and GNOSEOLOGY; the former is Kantian in origin and is much used in contemporary philosophy, whereas the latter predominates in European usage. Among scholastics all of these terms are taken to mean the science of true and certain knowledge.

It may be said that epistemology, in its present state of development, is the newest, the most unfinished, and the most unsatisfactory area of philosophical investigation. It is also the most controversial. There is no unanimity about its name, its subject matter, or even the precise problems it attempts to solve. Some important philosophers regard it as a wholly synthetic discipline that owes its existence neither to the demands of reality nor to the exigencies of the human mind, but only to the need for a reaction against false and misleading theories of knowledge. Their point seems to be that an integral REALISM need not be, and even cannot be, critical. Yet the fact remains that there is, and always has been, a critical problem; this is what assures epistemology of its proper place among the philosophical disciplines. The fact that it has become prominent only in modern times and that it was dealt with summarily by ancient and medieval thinkers does not lessen the need to solve the problems associated with its critique of knowledge.

Greek and Medieval Origins. Since men have always asked questions about knowledge and have always been concerned with distinguishing the true from the false, epistemology has a long history. Before the golden age of Greek philosophy, it was natural for men to be less interested in knowledge than in the world of nature. Yet the difficulty of penetrating into nature's secrets gave rise to many different interpretations and conclusions; the very multiplicity of cosmological systems, in fact, prompted the skepticism of the SOPHISTS. Because many mistakes were made, it was easy for the skeptic to find a willing ear for his claim that truth is unattainable. It took the profounder minds of SOCRATES, PLATO, and ARISTOTLE to produce a reaction against this early skepticism, and in their investigations and conclusions are to be found the origins of a genuine scientific epistemology. Particularly with Aristotle was begun the ordered statement of what can now be recognized as the main epistemological tradition, one in accord with the common sense of the ordinary man but going far beyond the latter's primitive indications. The main ideas of this tradition are the recognition of the difference between sensory and intellectual knowledge; a basing of the abstract knowledge of the INTELLECT in a sensory content that depends totally on EXPERIENCE; the denial of INNATISM; the outline of a theory of ABSTRACTION; and, in general, the complex of doctrines that has come to be known as moderate realism, wherein a balanced doctrine of UNIVERSALS makes both PHILOSOPHY and SCIENCE possible. The Aristotelian view allows for a theory of truth and a theory of error, and recognizes that the mind of man is capable of distinguishing between the one and the other.

After Aristotle came a rapid decline toward the MATERIALISM of the Epicureans and the Stoics, with its attendant SKEPTICISM. This attitude persisted roughly to the time of St. AUGUSTINE, with whom there was an accent on the theory of ILLUMINATION and a tendency toward the radical intellectualism of NEOPLATONISM. Augustinian views had a strong influence during the early medieval period. They were counteracted during the high scholastic period, however, as the works of Aristotle were recovered and much of their content incorporated into Western thought. The Aristotelian development reached its zenith in the synthesis of St. THOMAS AQUINAS and the allied realism of DUNS SCOTUS, although it also gave rise to epistemological difficulties associated with the Latin AVERROISM of SIGER OF BRABANT (*see* DOUBLE TRUTH, THEORY OF).

After the golden age of SCHOLASTICISM, Aristotelian realism gave way to NOMINALISM, and this in turn prepared the way for EMPIRICISM and a return to materialism. Attempts were made to revive the older epistemological tradition in the writings of Cardinal Tommaso de Vio CAJETAN, Silvestri FERRARIENSIS, Francisco SUÁREZ, and JOHN OF ST. THOMAS. The results, however, were sporadic and the influence of these men severely limited.

Modern Development. The reversal of the anti-intellectualist trend really began only with René DESCARTES, who initiated a movement to restore the rights of the intellect, and in so doing became the father of modern philosophy. Although a great mathematician, Descartes was a poor epistemologist, if only because he attempted to apply mathematical methodology to all areas of knowledge. His unsound psychology, moreover, left his epistemological doctrines vitiated by assumptions that have plagued the science of knowledge ever since. Descartes denied the true value of SENSATION; he reintroduced the innate ideas of Plato, and is responsible for the representationist conception of knowledge—a conception that has been consistently attributed to scholastics, though they never maintained it. Descartes's intentions were the best; he meant to be a realist and to defend the primacy of reason, but his presuppositions led inevitably to idealism and skepticism, and he succeeded only in fostering an absolute DUALISM of mind and matter that still confuses contemporary thought.

Epistemology degenerated after Descartes until, near the end of the 18th century, I. KANT began a philosophical revolution that proposed to eliminate all unwarranted assumptions and to make a genuine critique of knowledge. Here Kant did not succeed, even though he put at the service of philosophy a penetrating and methodical intelligence, persevering labor, and excellent intention; for he was both profoundly intelligent and ignorant of the long epistemological tradition that had preceded him. Ignoring the fact that man's intellectual knowledge is abstract—a fact that forced Aristotle and St. Thomas to admit an abstractive power in man's intellect—Kant saw no alternative between the innate ideas of Plato and Descartes, which he rejected, and his own theory, which would have intelligence informing the data of sensibility and imposing its own forms upon such data. For him, the mind makes things intelligible and imposes intelligibility upon them; the real in itself is unknowable. Metaphysics, in this view, becomes impossible and knowledge ends in subjectivism and AGNOSTICISM. Anticipating the impasse to which his speculative theory would lead, Kant thereupon developed his critique of practical reason and prepared the way for VOLUNTARISM and PRAGMATISM. Contemporary IDEALISM in epistemology also stems from Kant. At its opposite pole is the line of thought traceable to D. HUME that has accompanied the development of the natural sciences and has manifested itself in various forms such as empiricism, POSITIVISM, SCIENTISM, utilitarianism, and INSTRUMENTALISM.

Epistemological Problems. Textbooks and treatises on epistemology written over the past 50 years frequently contradict one another, offer totally different approaches, and fail to agree even on the basic problems. There are reasons that explain this situation; without doubt a preoccupation with combatting the subjectivism and skepticism that have been the legacy of Descartes, Kant, and Hume has played its part in promoting the general confusion. Defensiveness and negativism have marked most attempts to develop an epistemology within the scholastic tradition. Yet epistemology is not negative; it is a positive investigation of knowledge. Rather than being defensive it must assert the true claims to be made for knowledge in view of reason's nature and role in the life of man.

Although neither Aristotle nor St. Thomas Aquinas wrote treatises that were exclusively epistemological, both consistently made use of a positive and scientifically ordered critique of knowledge in their works. Since this is interwoven with different contents in their writings on many subjects, some effort is required to bring its precise epistemological bearing to light. In what follows an attempt is made to outline the basic epistemological problems implicit in the Aristotelian and Thomistic corpus, relying heavily on an analysis of such problems already provided by L. M. Régis (see bibliog.).

St. Thomas, using Aristotle's method, had pointed out that in a properly scientific investigation of anything only four types of question may be asked. These are: Does the thing exist? What is it? What are its properties? Why does it have these properties? (*In 2 anal. post.* 1.2). The first and second questions have to do with the composition of essence and existence, whereas the third and fourth have to do with the composition of substance and accident. Frequently, the first question does not arise because the existence of the thing may be evident to the senses or to the intelligence. In this case, the answers to the remaining three questions, formulated in series of demonstrations, constitute the science of that particular subject. It is obvious that in many cases the knowledge sought will be extensive and will give rise to a vast number of further questions; it is obvious also that either the imperfections of man's intelligence or the difficulties of the matter under investigation may make it difficult or impossible to proceed to any great length with the inquiry. But the fact remains that these four questions furnish the scientific framework in which any type of research can be pursued.

Applied to epistemology, this basic methodology suggests four questions about knowledge: Is there knowledge? What is knowledge? What are the properties of knowledge? Why does it have these properties? But knowledge is a fact of immediate experience, and thus the first question does not arise. The entire study of epistemology, therefore, may be subsumed under the remaining three questions.

Nature of Knowledge. As to the question, What is knowledge?, knowledge presents itself in man's experience as a complex of activities that occur interiorly and yet put him in contact with the exterior world in which he lives. The investigation of knowledge, as such, belongs properly to psychology, and it is from this science that epistemology accepts its basic principles. Fundamental to an understanding of knowledge is the fact that to know is not a physical, chemical, or mechanical activity, but a vital and immanent activity that is found only in living beings. Irreducibly different from transient activity, it is self-perfecting and terminates in the agent wherein it originates. This means that knowledge is a QUALITY within man, a self-modification whose formal type is specified by its relation to something other than the agent, i.e., the object or thing known.

The subject-object paradox accentuates a mysterious aspect of knowledge that complicates all epistemological problems. The total interiority of knowing stresses the subjective element, to which proper attention must be given—although too much attention here leads to subjectivism and idealism. Simultaneously, knowledge demands that one recognize its exteriority, for knowing makes things other than the knower present to him. The first area of epistemological research, therefore, is the explanation of this subject-object relationship. The elucidation of its interiority and its simultaneous exteriority must be effected and related to the IMMANENCE and self-perfectiveness of cognitive operations (*see* INTENTIONALITY; OBJECTIVITY; CONSCIOUSNESS).

Properties of Knowledge. The second general area of epistemological research is concerned with the answer to the question, What are the properties of knowledge? More precisely, it is concerned with the properties of TRUTH and FALSITY. A kind of truth is associated with apprehensive knowledge on both the sensory and intellectual levels (*see* APPREHENSION, SIMPLE). This truth follows from the necessary relationship between the knowing powers and their respective objects; it is necessary and unavoidable and, in a sense, is built into the cognitive operations, for these may not be false in apprehension. This kind of truth, though naturally guaranteed, is imperfect; indeed, it is as imperfect as the apprehensive knowledge of which it is a property. Apprehensive knowledge, the simple presentation of things, furnishes bits and snatches of reality on both the sensory and intellectual levels. It enables man to grasp isolated aspects of things without unifying these as they are actually found in reality.

The genuine problem of truth is the problem of the unification of this apprehensive knowledge on the intellectual level. The human intelligence has a passion for unity that leads it to integrate the fragmentary bits of knowledge gained through apprehension. This unification is brought about by a JUDGMENT or a series of judgments. When such unification is made in a way that adequates the actual unity found in reality, the mind judging produces a PROPOSITION or statement that is true. When, on the contrary, the proposition is at variance with the mode of being found in reality, the result is falsity. The very possibility of truth is therefore implicit in the difference between the two intellectual functions of apprehension and judgment. Whereas the former simply presents an object to the mind, the latter is a dynamic act wherein the mind not merely reports the things it sees but takes a stand and says something about them. It is in this enunciation that truth or falsity can properly be found. The problems surrounding truth, judgment, enunciation, and the assurance that at least some judgments may be adequated to reality form the second area of epistemological inquiry.

Explanation of Properties. The third general question that faces the epistemologist is: Why must knowledge have either truth or falsity? One may put the question in a different form, e.g., What is infallible knowledge? Seemingly simple, the latter question encompasses a vast series of problems that are extremely complex. The first problem necessarily concerns the very existence of truths that the human intellect must know infallibly, that it cannot miss, that are forced upon it by knowledge it must have and cannot avoid having. If there are such truths, it is important to discover what they are, and then, possessing them, to inquire how they may be used in the further investigation of reality.

St. Thomas was quite certain that FIRST PRINCIPLES exist and can be, in fact, must be known. ''In its origin all knowledge consists in becoming aware of the first indemonstrable principles'' (*De ver.* 10.6). ''Among things apprehended there is to be found a certain order. The notion which we grasp before anything else and which is included in every apprehension is being. And on the notion of being and non-being is based the first indemonstrable principle, namely, that the same thing cannot be affirmed and denied at the same time. On this principle, in turn, are based all other principles'' (*Summa Theologiae* 1a2ae, 94.2). Here begins all CERTITUDE, a property of truth that arises in the first place from necessary judgments. But St. Thomas warns quite clearly that this is not the last word to be said about the subject. The knowledge of these principles is, properly understood, infallible, yet these are ''the beginning and not the end of human enquiry, coming to us from nature and not because of our search for truth'' (*C. gent.* 3.37).

The knowledge of first principles is vague and general; it gives absolutely certain knowledge about the most universal characteristics of all things, yet tells nothing about the more detailed and specific qualities. These must be sought out, and cannot be deduced from the general truths, though the latter always control the more particular truths. The knowledge of first principles does not offer the final answer, but only the starting point from which man's reason, with full knowledge of the controls it has in its possession and assurance of the absolute validity of these principles properly applied, can proceed to the long and often difficult task of searching out more detailed truths. But the first principles of thought are the foundation of all intellectual constructions. There is, moreover, no certitude in the last analysis unless all knowledge be resolved back to first principles whose own certitude is based on immediate evidence.

From further material, supplied by the senses, the intellect perceives other principles that are first within particular orders of knowledge. The precise form these judgments take is analyzed by St. Thomas at the beginning of the *De veritate* (1.1). Such judgments are simply the primary mental assents at which the human mind naturally arrives in its inspection of reality, both in terms of the general modes of being common to everything and the special modes of being proper to the different kinds of things in man's experience. The judgments relating to the general modes of being concern the TRANSCENDENTALS and are the source of all the principles and conclusions of METAPHYSICS. The judgments that relate to the special modes of being concern the categories or various types of reality and are the source of all the principles and conclusions of the special sciences (*see* SCIENCES, CLASSIFICATION OF). The ultimate test of the truth of any judgment, then, is the analytic resolution of that judgment back to first principles, which is the reason that St. Thomas can say: ''There is never falsity in the intellect if the resolution to first principles be rightly carried out'' (*De ver.* 1.12). The human intellect does not learn these principles, nor does it assume them; it arrives at them naturally and necessarily and immediately once it attains a knowledge of the terms that make them up.

The human mind thus attains truth and certitude by grasping first principles and then proceeding from these to conclusions. This does not mean that all knowledge can be deduced from these principles, but only that before anything can be deduced they must be admitted and applied. As regards contingent things, for example, in research in the natural sciences, this means that material things are investigated, weighed, and measured in the light of primary principles—both the first principles of metaphysics and the first principles of the special science involved. The application of these principles to the data of experience produces the conclusions of the particular science.

There is thus a minimum of truth that each man must possess, and from which he can then proceed to knowledge of other truths. In other words, not only can man attain to truth, but to some extent he must attain it; there are certain truths he cannot miss. As St. Thomas says in this regard: ''Although no man can attain to perfect apprehension of truth, yet no one is so completely deprived of it as not to know any at all. The knowledge of truth is easy in this sense, that immediately evident principles by means of which we come to truth are evident for all men'' (*In 2 meta.* 1.275). The epistemological problems that arise in connection with the reasoning process include, e.g., an examination of the process of REASONING itself; an examination of the various types of reasoning, such as ANALYSIS AND SYNTHESIS, INDUCTION and DEDUCTION, and finally the question of the validity of the evidence that conclusions borrow from principles. To many of these problems there are only partial or inadequate solutions, and to some of them there are no solutions at all. The work of the epistemologist is to provide answers to such questions on the basis of a sound logic, psychology, and metaphysics.

See Also: KNOWLEDGE, THEORIES OF; CRITICISM, PHILOSOPHICAL; DOUBT; WONDER; OPINION.

Bibliography: L. M. RÉGIS, *Epistemology,* tr. I. C. BYRNE (New York 1959). R. HOUDE and J. P. MULLALY, eds., *Philosophy of Knowledge* (Philadelphia 1960). J. MARITAIN, *Distinguish to Unite, or The Degrees of Knowledge,* tr. G. B. PHELAN (New York 1959). P. COFFEY, *Epistemology,* 2 v. (New York 1917; repr. Gloucester, MA 1958). G. VAN RIET, *L'Épistémologie thomiste* (Louvain 1946).

[G. C. REILLY]

EPISTLES, NEW TESTAMENT

Twenty-one of the New Testament's 27 books are known as ''epistles.'' The name derives from the Greek and Latin words, *epistolē, epistola*, meaning letter. Tradition ascribes 14 epistles to the Apostle Paul, seven to other authors. Late nineteenth– and early twentieth-century discovery in ancient ruins, rubbish heaps, and tombs included many papyri containing Hellenistic letters. The discovery of these letters enabled biblical scholars to come to a better understanding of the art of letter-writing in the Hellenistic era than had previously been possible.

Pauline Epistles. The oldest of the New Testament epistles is Paul's first letter to the Thessalonians. The earliest Christian communities who expected an imminent Parousia and accepted the Hebrew scriptures as their own scripture experienced no need to produce any literary documentation for their own use. Paul, on the other hand, experienced the need to keep in touch with the communities that he recently evangelized. His letter tells the story of his attempt to stay in contact with the Thessalonians after he had left Macedonia. Unable to return personally to Thessalonica, Paul first sent Timothy as his personal envoy to strengthen and encourage the Thessalonians, then he sent a letter to respond to what was lacking in their faith.

Paul's letter was written in the style of a Hellenistic personal letter. It opens with the name of the sender, the name of the recipient, and a brief greeting—the first things that would be read when the scroll was unrolled and read aloud to the designated recipient(s). Paul omits the customary wish for good health. In its stead he mentions his prayer of thanksgiving for those to whom he was writing as did several other letter-writers of his time. After the body of the letter, containing the specifics of his communication, Paul offers a farewell greeting. Paul did not sign the earliest of his extant letters in his own hand as he would some of the later letters (1 Corinthians; Galatians). Paul's letters frequently address the community as his ''brothers and sisters'' and speak of his desire to be with them. These features of his epistolary style correspond to the norms of Hellenistic letter writing. His contemporaries considered that, in addition to whatever specific message it contained, the major purpose of a letter was to serve as a means being present when absent (*parousia*) and as an expression of the friendship between the letter writer and its recipient (*philophronēsis*). In the largely illiterate Hellenistic world it was customary for a letter-writer to dictate his letters and for a reader, often the one who delivered the letter, to read its contents to its intended audience. The letter was normally ''written'' and ''read'' as an oral composition. The message of a letter (*homilia*), both ancient and contemporary, is always situational. Scholars accordingly speak of the occasional nature of a letter. A letter is always written on a given occasion to a particular recipient and for a specific purpose. These elements of the literary form of a letter must be carefully weighed by those who wish to understand Paul's letters as he wrote them.

Before the first of the canonical gospels had been written, the memory of Paul's creative use of a letter to communicate some aspect of the gospel message had a major influence on the church and was an important piece of church history. The ''apostolic letter'' became a common way to proclaim the gospel. Thus, letters were written by Clement, Polycarp, and Ignatius respectively to the Corinthians, the Philippians, and various churches in Asia Minor.

By the end of the twentieth century biblical scholars generally held that only seven of the 14 New Testament epistles attributed to Paul were actually written by him (Romans, 1–2 Corinthians, Galatians, Philippians, 1 Thessalonians, Philemon). Six of the other epistles attributed to Paul (Ephesians, Colossians, 2 Thessalonians, 1–2 Timothy, Titus), the so-called Pauline pseudepigrapha, have the form of a letter written by Paul but were not written by him. Rather, they were written by disciples of Paul who used Paul's authority to communicate an important message to one or another of his church communities.

The practice of writing in another's name was not altogether unusual in the Hellenistic world. The ancients readily considered as spurious works written in another's name for base motives, for example, for the sake of profit or to discredit an authority. They were not ready to condemn as false works written in another's name when such works were intended to honor the person whose name they bore or when they were intended to use his authority and some of his essential ideas in order to address a situation that he had not personally addressed.

With the acceptance of Ephesians, Colossians, 2 Thessalonians, 1–2 Timothy, and Titus in the Canon, the church expresses a conviction that Paul's authority lies behind these epistles and that they are a legitimate, Spirit-inspired, expression of the Pauline tradition. The cultural and religious situation which allowed anonymous Christian writers to compose the Pauline pseudepigrapha allowed other anonymous authors to write James, 1–2 Peter, 1–2–3 John, Jude, the ''catholic'' or ''general'' epistles of the New Testament. The qualification derives from the fact that these texts were ostensibly intended for various people in the ''dispersion'' (James, 1 Peter), the faithful (2 Peter), or those who had been called (Jude) rather than for specific communities as were Paul's letters. James, 1–2 Peter and Jude have a typical epistolary opening, with mention of the sender, the recipient(s), and a greeting. Otherwise their style and content is quite unlike that of a typical Hellenistic letter. In the case of these letters the form of the apostolic letter was used by anonymous authors to convey authentic early Christian teaching on pertinent topics.

Catholic Epistles. Among the catholic epistles the three Johannine letters form a group apart. The second and third epistle of John are real letters. Their length and their style make them, along with Paul's letter to Philemon, most similar to the letters found among Hellenistic papyri. An anonymous elder wrote 2 John and 3 John, respectively to a church and to Gaius. The First Letter of

John, on the other hand, is totally lacking in epistolary features. This short treatise is included among the Johannine letters because of its similarities with the Fourth Gospel. In this respect it is somewhat similar to the Epistle to the Hebrews which makes no claim to have been a letter nor to have been written by Paul. Only its last three verses bear any real similarity with a letter and these may have later been added to an otherwise self-contained "word of exhortation" (Heb. 13.22).

Other Letters. The New Testament contains eight other epistolary compositions in addition to the traditional 21 epistles. The Book of Revelation contains "letters" to the seven churches of Asia Minor, Ephesus, Smyrna, Pergamum, Thyatira, Sardis, Philadelphia, and Laodicea (2.1–3.22; cf. Rv 1.11). These "letters" are clearly written in the style of the Book of Revelation itself. That they were ostensibly written to churches in the Roman province of Asia where Paul had evangelized and that they are presented as having been written as letters bears testimony to the importance of literary form of Paul's apostolic letter in the early church.

The 29th epistle in the New Testament (Acts 15.23–29) is a communication from an apostolic and presbyteral group in Jerusalem to Gentile Christians in Antioch, Syria, and Cilicia. Luke borrowed the letter from the Antiochene source that he used in the composition of Acts of the Apostles. The letter stipulates the conditions that Gentile Christians must meet if they are to enjoy table fellowship with Jewish Christians. Along among the New Testament letters, this letter to Gentiles opens and closes with the simple "greetings" (*chairein*) and "farewell" (*errōsthe*) of a typical Hellenistic letter.

Bibliography: R. F. COLLINS, *Letters That Paul Did Not Write: The Epistle to the Hebrews and the Pauline Pseudepigrapha* (GNS 28; Wilmington 1988); *The Birth of the New Testament: The Origin and Development of the First Christian Generation* (New York 1993). H. KOSKENNIEMI, *Studien zur idee und Phraseologie des griechischen Briefes bis 400 n. Chr* (AASF B 102/2; Helsinki 1956); J. MURPHY-O'CONNOR, *Paul the Letter-Writer: His World, His Options, His Skills* (GNS 41; Collegeville 1995); J. L. WHITE, *Light from Ancient Letters* (Philadelphia 1986).

[R. F. COLLINS]

EPISTOLAE OBSCURORUM VIRORUM

Humanistic anticlerical satire, the principal literary product of the controversy between Johann REUCHLIN and Johannes PFEFFERKORN and the Cologne theologians, over Pfefferkorn's proposal to destroy all Hebrew books. A bitter pamphlet war followed Pfefferkorn's proposal, and Reuchlin's objections received the support of nearly all humanists (*see* HUMANISM). In 1514 Reuchlin published a collection of commendatory letters, the *Clarorum virorum epistolae*, or *Letters of Famous Men*. The next year there appeared what purported to be a contrary collection of 41 letters written supposedly by Reuchlin's antagonists and addressed to Ortwin GRATIUS, leader of the Cologne theologians. This work, the *Epistolae obscurorum virorum*, or *Letters of Obscure Men*, was really a witty but scurrilous satire, presenting Reuchlin's foes as a self-confessed pack of ignorant obscurantists and unchaste priests. Its deliberately barbarous Latin underlined the charges of ignorance, and the supposed correspondents alternated between complacent descriptions of their own immorality and fatuous discussions of ridiculous "theological" questions. Beyond their indirect pleading of Reuchlin's cause, the letters expressed a mood of dangerous anticlericalism and tended to bring the whole clergy into disrepute. Alongside Gratius and Pfefferkorn, those chiefly attacked were Jacob van Hoogstraten, OP, the inquisitor of Cologne, and Arnold von Tungern, dean of the theological faculty. The *Epistolae* were an immense success among the educated, who did worse than oppose Reuchlin's enemies: they laughed at them. A second edition (1516) had seven additional letters, and in 1517 another 62 were added, and later that year, eight more. The authors remained anonymous. Many suspected ERASMUS, but the *Epistolae* originated in talks between the humanists CROTUS RUBIANUS and Ulrich von HUTTEN, though a number of other persons, including Hermann von dem Bussche and Nikolaus Gerbel, contributed. Crotus wrote most of the first collection; Hutten, most of those added in 1517.

Bibliography: *Epistolae obscurorum virorum*, ed. and tr. F. G. STOKES (London 1909), repr. of English text (New York 1964). H. HOLBORN, *Ulrich von Hutten and the German Reformation*, tr. R. H. BAINTON (New Haven 1937). W. BRECHT, *Die Verfasser der Epistolae obscurorum virorum* (Strasbourg 1904).

[C. G. NAUERT, JR.]

EPITHETS, DIVINE

The names of divinities and the epithets employed to characterize their powers and functions play an essential role in the history of religions. This article is confined to the use of epithets in Greek and Roman religion. The employment of epithets in other religions is treated in the respective articles devoted to them.

Epithets in Greek Religion. They are found frequently in poetry, especially in hymns; however, their occurrence in religious formulas is even more important as these reflect formal and official use. In Greek religion it is necessary to distinguish between epithets that apply to all gods and those that are appropriate for individual divinities. For easier intelligibility, the typical epithets selected are given in transliteration.

General Epithets. As the principle or beginning of all things, god is called *archē* (beginning) *archós, archēgós, archēgétēs*—all with the basic meaning of founder or leader; *prōtos* (first), or *patēr* (father)—defined more precisely by the addition of the adjectives *áphthitos* (imperishable), *pantelēs* (perfect), or *megalōnumos* (illustrious). Gaia and Demeter especially are called *mēter*. The divinity's sanctity is reflected by the epithet *hágios* (holy, replaced later by *hierós* or *hagnós*); his longevity and his immortality, by *présbus* (venerable) and *athánatos* (immortal); his happiness, by *makários* (blessed) and *ólbios* (happy); his power, by *téleios* (all-powerful), and his kindness by *eumenēs, ēpios, híleōs*, and *phílos*. Power and sovereignty are expressed by formulas with *aeí* (always), *mónos* (alone), *pâs* (all), or their compounds. A term like *polutímētos* (very revered) is reserved for divinity.

Epithets Applied to Individual Gods. Some are applied to a group of gods, as *sōtēr* (savior) to Zeus, Apollo, Asclepius, and the Dioscuri; others more particularly to a given god, according to his appearance (an inheritance from ANTHROPOMORPHISM), his attributes, his origin, or his favorite locales. Thus, Apollo is called *akersekómēs* or *chrusokómas* because of his long golden hair, *arguró-toxos* because of his silver bow, *Dēlios* after his birthplace, or *Púthios* after his chief temple at Pytho (Delphi). His sister, Artemis, is called *iochéaira* (archer), *agróteira* (huntress), or *chrusēlakatos* (with golden distaff). Other epithets are rather secondary appellations that are employed alone, as *Lóxias* and *Phoîbos* for Apollo, *Brómios* and *'Iakchos* for Dionysus. Many are unexplained, such as *Diáktoros* and *Erioúnios* for Hermes.

Epithets in Roman Religion. A full index of Latin epithets is given in Carter (see bibliography). Among the general epithets, *sanctus*, which is rare in the literary texts, is very frequent in inscriptions, particularly in votive inscriptions. As regards individual gods, Ceres and Cybele are called *alma*, Apollo, Jupiter, and Mercury, *bonus*; and Liber (Bacchus) is often given the title or epithet *Pater*.

Bibliography: H. J. ROSE, *The Oxford Classical Dictionary*, ed. M. CARY et al. (Oxford 1949) 333–334. C. F. H. BRUCHMANN, ''Epitheta deorum quae apud poetas graecos leguntur,'' *Ausführliches Lexikon der griechischen und römischen Mythologie*, ed. W. H. ROSCHER, Suppl. 1, (Leipzig 1893). J. B. CARTER, ''Epitheta deorum quae apud poetas Latinos leguntur,'' (1902; *ibid.* Suppl. 2), with an excellent index, 107–154. K. KEYSSNER, *Gottesvorstellung im griechischen Hymnus* (Stuttgart 1932). H. DELEHAYE, *Sanctus* (Brussels 1927; reprint 1954).

[É. DES PLACES]

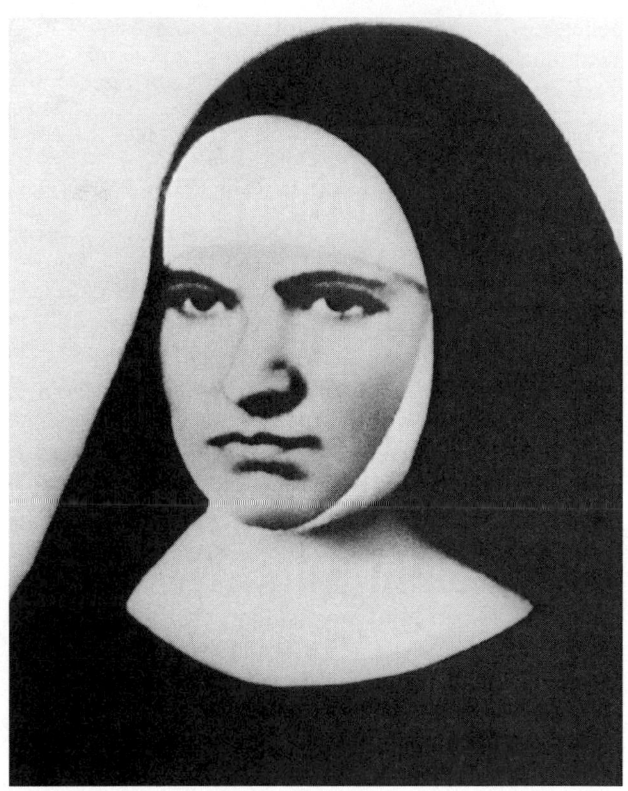

Elisabeth Eppinger.

EPPINGER, ELISABETH

Foundress of the Daughters of the DIVINE REDEEMER; b. Niederbronn, France, Sept. 9, 1814; d. Niederbronn, July 31, 1867. She was the eldest of the 11 children of simple, pious, and poor parents, George and Barbara (Vogt) Eppinger. Her formal education was limited, and she suffered long periods of physical illness as well as severe spiritual trials. In 1846 began a period of visions, revelations, and ecstasies. As the fame of her prophecies and ecstasies spread, she became known as the ''Ecstatic of Niederbronn,'' and her advice was frequently sought. Her energetic and enlightened pastor and confessor, Father Jean Reichard, became convinced that these graces were supernatural; so did Bishop Raess of Strasbourg and the professors at the seminary there. After a remarkable cure of her illness, she was accepted as a postulant in the Sisters of Divine Providence of Ribeauvillé (1846), but before entering the community, heeded her bishop's urging and continued counseling at home. With permission she took the three vows of religion privately (1848). Along with Father Reichard she founded her religious congregation (1849) devoted originally to caring for the sick poor in their homes and aiding other poor persons. As Mother Marie Alphonse, her name in religion, she acted with great competence as superior general until her death, when the congregation had 372 sisters in 74 houses. Her beatification process has been instituted.

Bibliography: L. CRISTIANI, *L'Extatique de Niederbronn* (Paris 1958). A. RICHOMME, *Mère Alphonse-Marie* (Paris 1963). J. LEFLON, *Dictionnaire de spiritualité ascétique et mystique. Doctrine et histoire*, ed. M. VILLER et al. (Paris 1932) 4.1:909–911.

[M. A. VARGA]

EPTADIUS, ST.

B. near Autun, France, *c.* 490; d. Montelon, France, 550. He was a serious boy at 12, a local scholar at 15, and a handsome young bridegroom at 20. Shortly after his marriage, he was struck by a stubborn fever. After a visit by three holy women, his faith and religion revived; he recovered, and then led a life of austerity and penance. Impressed by his virtue, Bp. Flavian (d. 614) of Autun wished to ordain him, but Eptadius fled. King CLOVIS, after making peace with the Burgundian King Gondobad (d. 516), planned to appoint Eptadius bishop of Auxerre. Although elected, Eptadius refused the dignity, compromised enough to accept the priesthood, and withdrew into the monastic community of Cervon, which he had organized. He was noted for his charity and his efforts to ransom captives. It is conjectured that he died at Montelon. Later his relics were taken to the BENEDICTINE monastery at Cervon, which gave rise to the theory that he was a Benedictine himself.

Feast: Aug. 24.

Bibliography: *Acta Sanctorum* Aug. 4:775–781. V. B. HENRY, *Vie de saint Eptade* (Avallon 1863). G. BARDY, *Catholicisme* 4:354–355.

[B. CAVANAUGH]

EQUATORIAL GUINEA, THE CATHOLIC CHURCH IN

Formerly known as either Spanish Guinea or the Province of Fernando Póo, the Republic of Equatorial Guinea includes a portion of the African mainland and five islands located in the Bight of Biafra, in the Gulf of Guinea 20 miles off the coast of CAMEROON. Equatorial Guinea includes the mainland province of Río Muni, bordered on the north by Cameroon, on the east and south by Gabon, and on the west by the Bight of Biafra. Its island territories include Corisco, Great Elobey, Little Elobey, Bioko (formerly Fernando Póo) and Annobón.

With a tropical climate, Equatorial Guinea is frequently visited by strong winds, and flash floods are common. Natural resources include recently discovered oil reserves as well as small gold, manganese and uranium deposits. A volcanic island, Bioko, benefits from more fertile soil than does the Río Muni mainland, and for many years its cocoa, timber and coffee yields served as the region's main exports. In the forested mountainous interior of the island of Bioko live the aboriginal Bubi people. Other ethnic groups include Fang, Duala, Ibibion and Maka, who live on the mainland. Due to a succession of tyrannical and fiscally ineffective leaders, Equatorial Guinea remained one of Africa's poorest nations, its economy dependent on foreign aid from Spain. With the discovery of oil in the late 20th century its economy would stabilize.

Capital: Malabo.
Size: 10,831 sq. miles.
Population: 474,214 in 2000.
Languages: Spanish and French; Fang, Bubi, Ibo, and other tribal languages are spoken in various regions.
Religions: 398,340 Roman Catholics (84%); 4,510 Muslims (1%); 21,340 Protestants (4.5%); 23,710 with traditional beliefs (5%); 26,314 without an organized faith.
Archdiocese: Malabo, on the island of Bioko, with suffragans Bata and Ebebiyin, both on the African mainland.

The island of Bioko was discovered in 1471 and named after Fernando Póo, its Portuguese founder. Portuguese settlements were established in the region during the 16th century and slave trading became common. A Catholic mission established in 1740 failed, and the island was ceded to Spain in 1788. In 1829 Bioko began, with the consent of the Spanish crown, 15 years of British occupation that saw the arrival of English Baptist missionaries. British influences were eliminated in 1844 after control of the region reverted back to Spain. After 1841 the labors of Spanish chaplain Jeronimo de Usera were successful enough to bring other Catholic missionaries to the island. The apostolic prefecture of Annobón, Corisco and Fernando Póo was detached from the vicariate of the Two Guineas in 1855 and entrusted to the Jesuits between 1857 and 1872. Military chaplains were followed by a restored prefecture entrusted to the Claretians in 1882.

From 1857 to 1877 Spanish explorers mapped the nearby regions of the African mainland, and an agreement with the French government in 1900 determined the official boundaries of those regions to be under the control of Spain. With Río Muni now added to its jurisdiction, the region became a vicariate in 1904. The seat of the vicariate, Santa Isabel (now Malabo) on the north coast of Bioko, served as the capital of the region while it remained under Spanish control. Development of the island began in the 1920s, when the mainland became occupied.

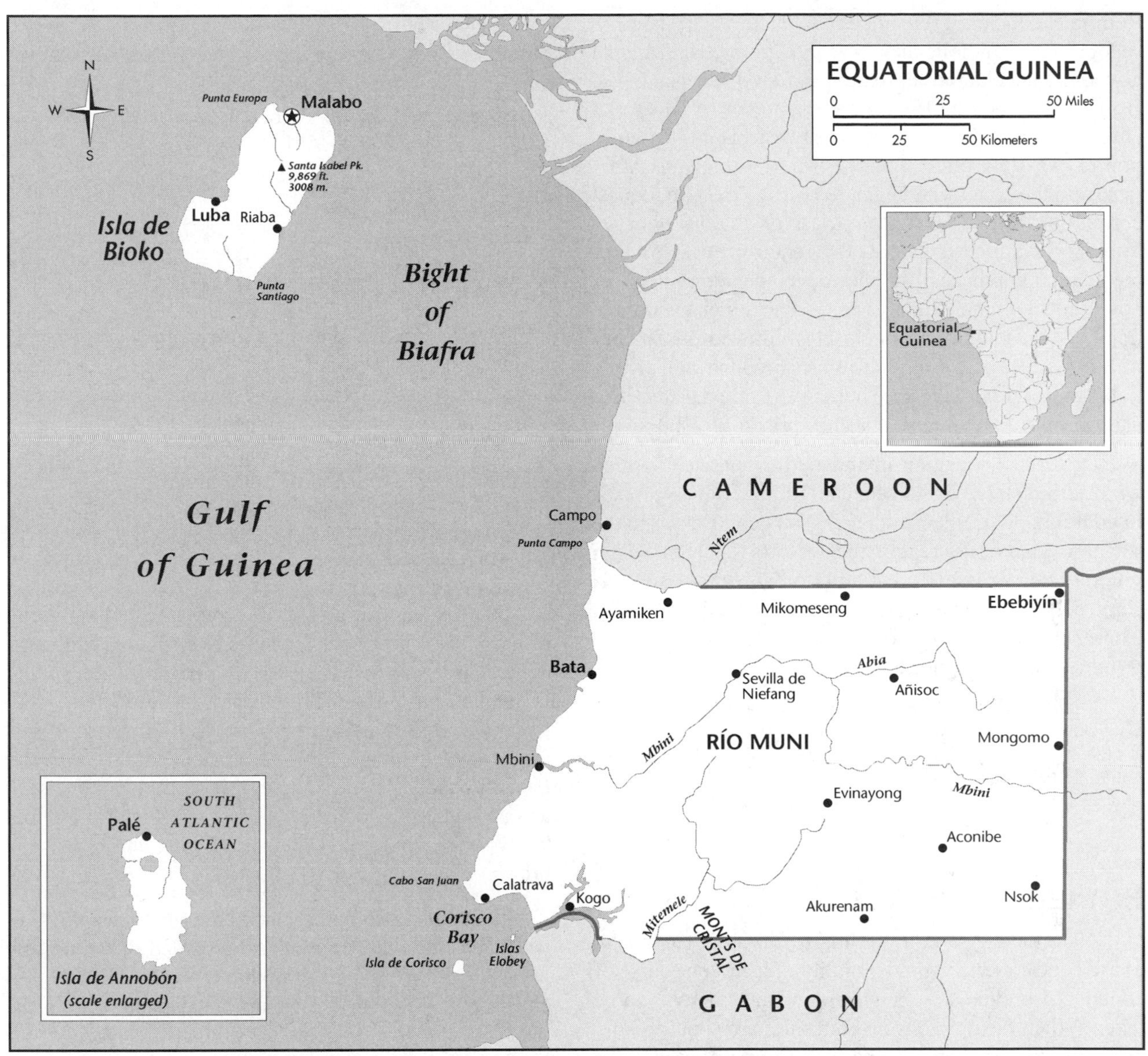

In 1963 Equatorial Guinea was granted the right to limited self-rule, and full independence was granted five years later, on Oct. 12, 1968. Before Río Muni was detached as a separate vicariate in 1965, there were 180,000 Catholics in the vicariate, the highest percentage of Catholics in all of Africa. Unfortunately for those Catholics, as well as for the region's other inhabitants, the first ten years of independence brought death to many under the regime of President Macias Nguema, and the repression of the Catholic Church became one of his main efforts. His nephew, General Teodoro Obiang Nguema Mbasogo, executed Nguema on Aug. 3, 1979 during a military coup that brought about a more peaceful era for the region. Lifting its repression against the Church and encouraged in its sporadic efforts toward democratization by Spain, Equatorial Guinea held its first "free" elections in 1993, where an overwhelming majority elected Teodoro Mbasogo president. Despite this move toward democratization, human rights violations, as well as a questionable election process, remained a concern of the United Nations throughout the 1990s, and the overwhelming election of ruling Democratic Party legislators in the March 1999 election did little to quell suspicions that the democratic process was compromised. In July 1999, 50 bishops from Central Africa met to discuss concerns over the fraud, tribalism and corruption that plagued not only Equatorial Guinea but also several of its African neighbors.

The country's 1995 constitution granted freedom of religion, and Catholicism remained the predominate faith due to its presence in the region over several centuries.

Religious education remained mandatory in all state-run schools and a Catholic mass was incorporated into annual government celebrations of the nation's independence. However, in July of 1998 the government of Equatorial Guinea undertook several repressive measures. In addition to expelling three U.S.-sponsored foreign missionaries from the country, it began requiring priests to request permission before celebrating Mass or holding other assemblies. Church leaders saw this requirement as government retaliation against the open denouncement of government human rights abuses and other manifestations of corruption. It also closely followed the January of 1998 arrest of a Catholic priest in connection with a failed coup attempt the year before; the priest, Father Eduardo Losoha Belope, was still in prison in 2000.

By 2000 the region maintained 53 parishes, which were administered by 43 secular and 52 religious priests. In addition, 36 brothers and 222 sisters contributed to the social welfare of the region, their efforts focused through schools, hospitals and charitable organizations such as Caritas. Despite the escalation of government repression, Church leaders continued to speak out against human rights abuses and other corruption.

Bibliography: A. O. IBÁÑEZ, ''Los misioneros Hijos del Inmaculado Corazón de María en Fernando Po,'' *El Misionero,* 25 (1948) 352–365. *Oriente Cattolico* (Vatican City 1962) 134–135. *Annuario Pontificio* (1964) 748.

[J. A. BELL/EDS.]

EQUIPROBABILISM

The moral system according to which in a doubt of conscience concerning the morality of a certain course of conduct, a middle way between law and liberty is to be taken. When the opinions on both sides are about equally probable, the opinion for liberty may be followed if the doubt concerns the existence of the law (whether there is a law, whether it extends to this case, etc.); but the law must be observed when the doubt concerns the cessation of the law (whether a law that certainly did exist has been fulfilled, whether it has been dispensed with, etc.). For in the former case liberty is in possession, in the latter case the law; and the fundamental principle of this system is ''In a doubt the possessor is to be favored.'' Furthermore, if the opinion for liberty is notably more probable, whether the doubt concerns the existence or the cessation of the law, the opinion for liberty may be followed; if the opinion for law is notably more probable, the law must be observed. The chief defender of this opinion was St. Alphonsus Liguori, the patron of moralists and confessors.

See Also: CONSCIENCE; MORALITY, SYSTEMS OF; REFLEX PRINCIPLES; DOUBT, MORAL.

Bibliography: J. AERTNYS and C. A. DAMEN, *Theologia moralis,* 2 v. (16th ed. Turin 1950) 1:102–119. M. ZALBA, *Theologiae moralis compendium,* 2 v. (Madrid 1958) 1:676. D. M. PRÜMMER, *Manuale theologiae moralis,* ed. E. M. MÜNCH, 3 v. (10th ed. Barcelona 1945–46) 1:347–348. A. LIGUORI, *Theologia moralis,* ed. L. GAUDÉ, 4 v. (Rome 1905–12) 1:54–89.

[F. J. CONNELL]

EQUIVOCATION (LOGIC)

Equivocation, from the Latin *aequa vox* meaning similar sound, is one of the main sources of FALLACY, and may be defined as taking one meaning from a word, whereas another is intended or possible. Thus, it is the acceptance of one definite and particular signification of a term, with or without reflection, although the word in question permits a variety of interpretations. The result is usually a mistake in judgment. Equivocation itself is commonly the result of AMBIGUITY in speech or writing.

The fallacy can arise both from an exact similarity of the word and from a sameness of sound (homonyms). A great number of words in the English language, similar in spelling but different in meaning, lend themselves to this fallacy, such as fire (to burn or to discharge), saw (looked or carpenter's tool), bill (invoice or lip), and rank (station or foul). Even more words are homonyms, such as one and won, soul and sole, fair and fare, nose and knows, steak and stake, might and mite, and bruise and brews.

It should also be remembered that meanings of words change with time or are regarded differently by people in other climates of opinion. A man labeled a liberal in the Victorian era would not pass for one in the 1960s. Words such as democracy, idealism, progress, education, and dictator change in significance with social movements and attitudes. This is why good logic requires that one define terms at the beginning of a debate.

Amphibology is an extension of equivocation in which a whole sentence (instead of one word) takes on a double meaning, usually because of an ambiguity in grammatical construction.

Equivocation has a primary role to play in logic when investigating the possible modes of PREDICATION. There are three modes of predication: the univocal, the analogical, and the equivocal. In the univocal mode, a term is applied to two or more objects in unvarying exactitude of meaning, such as human to Peter and to Pauline, fish to flounder and fluke, or quantity to mountain and mole. In analogical predication, the term is applied to two or more objects not because of an identity of nature, but for some resemblance in characteristics (*see* ANALOGY).

Thus, lamb is applied to Christ because of His resemblance in meekness, gentleness, and purity to a real lamb. In equivocal predication, however, there is neither identity nor resemblance, but only a similarity of word or sound. When the term match is attributed to a wedding and to a lighter, there is no common ground whatsoever in nature or resemblance.

See Also: TERM (LOGIC); PROPOSITION.

Bibliography: J. A. OESTERLE, *Logic: The Art of Defining and Reasoning* (2d ed. Englewood Cliffs, N.J. 1963). S. J. HARTMAN, *Fundamentals of Logic* (St. Louis 1949).

[P. C. PERROTTA]

ERAS, HISTORICAL

By the term era is meant a period dating from a fixed point of time, generally some historical event, and used in reckoning years for chronological purposes. Historical eras are those on which historical chronology is based. A distinction can be made between eras of political or civic origin and those of religious origin.

Eras of Political or Civic Origin. To this class belong eras of empires, eras of cities or provinces, and eras of particular countries or regions.

Eras of Empires. The principal imperial eras are six in number and usually named after rulers or dynasties. The era of Alexander the Great has been made known through inscribed bricks and coins and was distinct from the era of the Seleucids. It began the first of Nisan, 330 B.C., and was connected with Alexander's capture of Persepolis (January 330).

The era of the Seleucids among the Greco-Syrians got its name from Nicator Seleucus, founder of the Dynasty of the SELEUCIDS, who instituted it to commemorate the beginning of his empire (312 B.C.). It was known also by other names: the era of contracts among the Jews, because of its legal character; the era of the Greeks or of Alexander among the Syrian Christians and the Arabs; the era of ''the man with two horns,'' Alexander's epithet among the Arabs; the era of the Chaldeans or the Assyrians; the years of the Syro-Macedonians. The era was first employed in the lunar-solar calendar in use among the Macedonians that began with the first lunar month (ὁ Δῖος, Dios) following the autumnal equinox. The beginning of the era was placed on Dios 1, 312 B.C. When the Greco-Syrians received from Rome the solar calendar with its fixed years of 365 days plus one day every fourth year, they fixed the beginning of the year and consequently that of the era as October 1, and later, *c.* A.D. 460, as September 1, in order to align it with the Byzantine indiction; but this did not affect the Oriental Syrians not subject to Constantinople.

The era of the Seleucids among the Persians began when the Seleucids, having become masters of Persia, imposed their era on it also, yet without changing its calendar, a solar one of 365 days without leap years that continued to proceed as it had before. The beginning of the era was placed on the first of Ferverdin (the first month of the year), which corresponded to Feb. 7, 311 B.C., of the Julian calendar.

The era of the Arsacids, named after Arsacius, the first King of the Parthians, was superimposed on the preceding era of the Persians with the same beginning of the year, the first of Ferverdin. It began on Ferverdin 1, 248 B.C., which corresponded to January 22.

The era of Yezdegird was a continuance of the preceding era and of the same type, having as its point of departure Ferverdin 1 (June 26), A.D. 632. The Jalalaean era ended the era of Yezdegird and was the result of a reform that substituted a fixed solar calendar for the previous one that did not have leap years. The beginning of the year was placed at the vernal equinox, which, being then the 19th of Ferverdin (March 15, 1079, of the Julian calendar), was changed to the first of Ferverdin.

Eras of the Cities or Provinces. Some eras were connected with certain cities. The most important of these were the following.

The era of the Olympiads was named after the city of Olympia, where the Olympic games were held every four years. Each period of four years, at the end of which the games took place, was called an Olympiad. Chronographers, several centuries later (*c.* 300 B.C.), got the idea of using these four-year periods as a measure of chronology. The era of the Olympiads reckoned not directly with individual years, but with the series of four-year periods starting with the institution of the games. The point of departure was the beginning of July 776 B.C. In the concordance tables, the beginning of the year is placed at the beginning of the July that follows January 1 of the corresponding Dionysian year.

The era of the foundation of Rome (*Urbis conditae,* abbreviated U.C.), commonly employed, was determined by Varro (*De gente populi romani,* written *c.* 43 B.C.). It began in 753 B.C. and was reckoned as starting on January 1, even though April 21 was regarded as the actual date of the founding of the city. The Capitoline era was another era based on the traditional founding of Rome. It was established according to the tables of the consuls engraved at the Capitol *c.* 30 B.C. and is one year behind the years of Varro's era. It appears in certain inscriptions and in the works of a few authors.

The Actian era was common to several cities and provinces. It was connected with the victory of Actium, which took place on Sept. 2, 31 B.C.; but in it the beginning of the year varies according to the different calendar (see below).

Egyptian Eras. In Egypt three different eras were in use: the Diocletian, the Alexandrian, and the Oxyrhynchus era (the last variously dated).

The era of Diocletian (also called the era of the martyrs) was common to all of Egypt. Its point of departure was Thoth 1, A.D. 284. In three years out of four, Thoth 1 was August 29; but every fourth year, i.e., in the year after the leap year, it was August 30. (On its origin, *see* CHRONOLOGY, MEDIEVAL.)

The Alexandrian era was an Actian era of which the beginning was fixed on Thoth 1, 30 B.C. Thoth 1 was either August 29 or August 30, as above. The Thoth 1 with which this era began was Aug. 30, 30 B.C. This date also inaugurated the replacement of the Egyptian calendar having 365 days every year with one having 366 days every fourth year.

As for the eras of Oxyrhynchus, as many as eight of these have been noted, of which two are of more importance: A.D. 324, the year Constantius II became emperor, and 355, the year Julian became emperor.

Eras of Syria, Palestine, and Arabia. These include the era of the Seleucids, the Actian era, and the era of the province of Arabia.

The era of the Seleucids was the same as the imperial era mentioned above as common to Syria, Palestine, and Arabia.

The Actian era was common to several cities: Tripoli, Seleucia of Pieria, Laodicea, and Gerasa. Its year began October 1.

The era of the province of Arabia, or the era of Bostra (the capital), commemorated the Emperor Trajan's establishment of Arabia as a province. Its point of departure was March 22, A.D. 106, the vernal equinox falling on that day at that time and thus marking the beginning of the year.

Local Eras. A good number of the local eras commemorated the granting of autonomy to various cities, either by Pompey or Caesar, and for that reason are called Pompeian or Caesarean; their starting dates depend on when these cities received their independence.

Pompeian eras were used in various cities of Syria and Transjordan, especially in the cities of the DECAPOLIS: Abila, Antiochia ad Hippum, Kanatha, Dium, Gerasa, Gadara, Philadelphia, and Pella. The starting date for Gadara was 64 B.C.; for Philadelphia (Ammān), 63 B.C. For the other cities the dates are uncertain, between 64 and 61. Cities outside the Decapolis began their eras about the same time: Antioch and Apamea in 66 B.C.; Demetrias of Phoenicia and Dora in 63; Arethusa in 64 or 63; Epiphania of Cilicia in a year that is uncertain; Gaza on Oct. 28, 61 B.C., following the introduction of a fixed year—an era in use until the 7th century; Tripolis in 64–63; and Scythopolis in 64–63 B.C.

Caesarean eras, with their starting dates, were used in the following cities: Laodicea, Dios (later Oct.) 1, 48 B.C.; Ptolemais, 47; Gabala, Oct. 1, 47 or 46; Antioch (the most important of all), Dios (later Oct.) 1, 49 (Sept. 1, following the adjustment to the Byzantine indiction, *c.* 460); several Syriac writers begin this era Oct. 1, 48 B.C.

Other local eras were used in other cities in Syria and Palestine that had eras of their own: Ascalon, two eras—104 and 57 B.C.; Beirut, 81 B.C. (under Tigrane); Eleutheropolis, A.D. 200; Laodicea, besides the Actian and Caesarean eras already indicated, three other eras—era of freedom under Tigrane, 81–80 B.C.; era of its establishment as a metropolis, A.D. 194; era of the colony, A.D. 197–198 [the last was recently discovered by H. Seyrig, *Syria* 40 (1963) 30–32]; Ptolemais (Accho), besides the Caesarean era indicated, had another era, 174 B.C. (the year of the establishment of the Antiochian colony in the city); Seleucia of Pieria, 109 B.C.; Sidon, 110 or 109 B.C.; Tyre, two eras, 274 and 116 B.C. (independence of the city); the beginning of the year, following the adoption of a fixed year, was October 19.

Eras of Asia Minor. Provinces and cities in Asia Minor that had eras in common were the following.

For Bithynia and Pontus there were the era of the independence of Bithynia, beginning in 297 B.C., and for several cities—Apamea, Myrlea, Bithynium, Nicaea, Nicomedia, Prusa—an era that began in 283 B.C., and came to an end when Bithynia became a Roman province.

In the proconsular province of Asia the era of Sulla, conqueror of the province, began autumn 85 B.C. and was fixed at the equinox, September 24, following the adoption of the solar calendar, later at September 23, the *dies natalis* of Augustus. This era appears in inscriptions from Phrygia, Mysia, Lydia, Pisidia, and Lycia. It continued up to the 6th Christian century.

The era of Galatia, beginning in 25 B.C., was employed in Ancyra, Pessinus, and Tavium.

The era of Pontus Polemoniacus was employed in several cities including Trabezus, Cerasus, Neocaesarea, and Zela. It began October 64 B.C.

Local eras were in use in several of the principal cities: Adana (Antiochia ad Sarum), sometime shortly after

19 B.C.; Amasia, October 3 B.C., annexation to the Roman Empire; Amisus, October 32 B.C., liberation; Anazarbus, 19 B.C.; Gangra, 5 B.C.; Comana, A.D. 34 or 35; Mopsuestia, 68 B.C.; Pompeiopolis, 7 B.C.; and Sinope, which had two eras, 70 and 45 B.C.

Eras of the Balkan Peninsula and the West. Several regions in the Balkans and in western Europe had their own eras.

The era of Upper Moesia began Jan. 1, A.D. 239, when the region was made a Roman province.

The era of Dacia dates from A.D. 246, after the middle of the summer.

Macedonia had two eras—one starting at the time of the Roman conquest, autumn 146 B.C., following the adoption of the solar calendar, the beginning of the year being fixed at October 15; the other an Actian era, beginning Oct. 15, 32 B.C. These two eras are frequently joined in the inscriptions.

The Spanish era began on Jan. 1, 38 B.C. It is found in inscriptions and was current with the chroniclers on the peninsula. It was used in Spain as late as the 14th century and in Portugal until 1422, when it was officially abandoned. It was in use also in the Visigothic provinces of southern Gaul. Its origin has not yet been explained.

The era of Mauretania (Caesarean, Sitifian; for Tingitane Mauretania evidence is lacking) began Jan. 1, A.D. 40, and dates from the annexation of Mauretania by the Roman Empire.

The Carthaginian era is indicated in several inscriptions by the formula *anno N. Kartaginis.* It is now known that the era was connected with the capture of the city by the Vandals in A.D. 439, and not, as was once thought, with its reconquest by the Byzantines. There is no certain evidence for any era connected with this reconquest.

Eras of Religious Character. Certain eras were established with a starting point connected with important events in the histories of various religions. The most important of these are the following.

Era of Abraham. This is used in the Chronicle of Eusebius. It begins with the call of Abraham. The birth of Christ is placed by Eusebius in the year 2015 of this era, 2,014 years after the call of Abraham, two years earlier than in the modern common era, which places it in 2017 of this era; therefore, the era of Abraham begins in 2016 B.C. But this relationship is not constant; it can be shown by cross comparisons that there is a deviation of two years in the calculations of Eusebius from the year 2210 of this era (A.D. 192) to the end of 2343 (A.D. 326), which moves the beginning of his era back from 2016 to 2018 B.C. In St. Jerome's continuation of this era from 2343 to 2395, the deviation is only one year, which brings the beginnings of the era to 2017 B.C.

Christian Eras. Several eras have been established by Christians beginning either on a computed year as the time when the world was created or on a year in the life of Christ.

The Alexandrine, or mundane, era began in the year 5492 B.C., which is considered to have been the year in which the world was created. In this era the year 5501 marks the birth of Christ, which is a starting date also for a Christian era frequently used in conjunction with this world era. The last two digits of any date are the same and always constant in both cases; thus, in this era the year 5965 of creation is the year 465 after the birth of Christ. Since the Alexandrine world era is eight years behind the modern common era, the same is true of its accompanying Christian era. Consequently, the year one in the latter era is A.D. 9 in the Christian. The beginning of its year is the same as that of the world era, i.e., March 25, which marks both the creation of the world and the Incarnation of Christ.

In the Proto-Byzantine era the 1st year was 5509 B.C., and the birth of Christ was placed in the year 5507 (3 B.C.); but this date of the birth of Christ was not used for chronological purposes.

The Byzantine era begins with the creation of the world considered as having taken place in 5507 to 5508 B.C. But Byzantine authors were not uniform in regard to the year of the birth of Christ. At least five different dates can be noted. The principal chronicler (Skilitzes-) Cedrenus placed Christ's birth in 5506 of this era (3–2 B.C.) on December 25 (3 B.C.) and constructed an era of Christ in conjunction with his mundane era, computing it as beginning with the Incarnation on March 25, 5505, of the mundane era, so that the final figure differs by six between the two eras, e.g., the year 5950 of the mundane era is the year 456 of his Christian era.

The common Christian era is known also as the Dionysian era because it was first used by DIONYSIUS EXIGUUS in his paschal table as a substitute for the Diocletian era. The era begins on January 1 of the year of Christ's birth. This year is situated chronologically by its relationship to the Diocletian era in the paschal table mentioned above, in which the year 532 of the Christian era corresponds to the year 248 of the Diocletian era. The Dionysian era spread abroad little by little —first in England, where it was brought by St. Augustine of Canterbury, then in France, and finally in the rest of Europe. It was commonly used by chroniclers in the West from the time of Bede, except in the Iberian Peninsula, where the chroniclers retained the Spanish era for a long time. The beginning of the year differed from place to place: December 25, March 1, Easter, or January 1. By the end of the 16th century January1 was commonly accepted as New Year's Day in this era, following the example of France, where it was made official in 1563.

The era of the Ascension, found among the Greeks and the Syrians, began in A.D. 31.

Jewish World Era. This era began on the first of Tishri 3761 B.C. Its invention appears to go back, at the earliest, to the latter half of the 4th Christian century.

Islamic Era or Era of the Hijra. Year one of this era began on the 1st of Moharem (1st month of the Muslim year), July 16, 622, marking the day arbitrarily set for the commemoration of Muḥammad's HIJIRA, or flight from Mecca to Medina; the flight actually took place 68 days later. The era was instituted by Caliph Omar. It has been in continuous use by Christians living under Muslim rule (in Egypt, Syria, Iraq, and Persia), as well as by the Muslims. Since the Muslim year consists of 12 lunar months totaling 354 or 355 days, special tables must be used for converting a date in the Islamic era into a date in the Christian era. (*See* CALENDARS OF THE ANCIENT NEAR EAST.)

For eras of cyclic origin that, though without historical basis, were nevertheless commonly used in daily life and by the chroniclers, *see* CHRONOLOGY, MEDIEVAL, 1.

Bibliography: F. K. GINZEL, *Handbuch der mathematischen und technischen Chronologie,* 3 v. (Leipzig 1906–14; repr. 1958). A. GIRY, *Manuel de diplomatique* (new ed. Paris 1925). W. KUBITSCHEK, *Paulys Realenzyklopädie der klassischen Altertumswissenschaft*, ed. G. WISSOWA et al. 1.1 (1893) 606–52. H. LECLERCQ, *Dictionnaire d'archéologie chrétienne et de liturgie*, ed. F. CABROL, H. LECLERCQ and H. I. MARROU, 15 v. (Paris 1907–53) 5.1:350–84. H. BRAUNERT, *Lexikon für Theologie und Kirche*, ed. J. HOFER and K. RAHNER, 10 v. (2d, new ed. Freiburg 1957–65) 1:785–86. E. MAHLER, *Chronologische Vergleichungs-Tabellen* (Vienna 1888). L. DE MAS-LATRIE, *Trésor de chronologie* (Paris 1899). P. V. NEUGEBAUER, *Hilfstafeln zur technischen Chronologie* (Kiel 1937). F. RÜHL, *Chronologie des Mittelalters und der Neuzeit* (Berlin 1897). H. SEYRIG, "Antiquités syriennes: Sur les ères de quelques villes de Syrie," *Syria* 27 (1950) 5–50; "Antiquités syriennes: Un Poids de Laodicée," *ibid.* 40 (1963) 31–32. N. DUVAL, "Recherches sur la datation des ères chrétiennes d'Afrique," *Atti del terzo Congresso internazional e di epigrafia greca e latina* (Rome 1959). V. GRUMEL, *La Chronologie* (Paris 1958).

[V. GRUMEL]

ERASMUS, DESIDERIUS

Humanist, classical and patristic scholar, first editor of the Greek New Testament; b. Rotterdam, Holland, Oct. 27, 1466; d. Basel, Switzerland, July 12, 1536. He was an illegitimate child and his father eventually became a priest. Educated first at Gouda, and then from 1475 under the BRETHREN OF THE COMMON LIFE, Erasmus remained at Deventer for eight years; there is no doubt that this tradition shaped his later educational ideals.

Career. In 1483 his parents died; his guardians sent him to a school at s' Hertogenbosch, also maintained by the Brethren. In 1487 he was persuaded, in part by a friend and in part by his guardian, to enter the Augustinian monastery of CANONS REGULAR at Steyn. Although lacking a genuine vocation, he was no doubt partly attracted by the ordered life of the monastery; he found some congenial companions, and he had opportunities for the study of Christian and classical literature. However, even before his ordination (April 25, 1492) he seems to have found the intellectual horizon too confined and was ready to seek a wider opportunity for the development of his intellectual interests. This came in 1494 with an invitation from the bishop of Cambrai to enter his service. Erasmus received a dispensation from residence in his monastery, which he never entered again. Within the year he had persuaded the bishop to allow him to go to Paris to study for a degree in theology.

When Erasmus arrived in Paris in 1495, he took up residence in Montaigu College, where he soon found little to his liking the discipline imposed by the director, Jean Standonck. Equally uncongenial were the lectures on scholastic philosophy and theology at the university. Erasmus tried to escape from this environment by cultivating prominent literary figures, among whom were Italian humanist exiles who were beginning to introduce new standards of taste. At the same time, in order to improve his economic circumstances, he began to take pupils for instruction in Latin. These included some wealthy and highly placed Englishmen, and through one of them he received an invitation to visit England in 1499.

This first visit to England marks a decisive stage in Erasmus's intellectual development. He had an opportunity to meet such men as John COLET, Thomas MORE, and Archbishop WARHAM. Through these friends he came into more direct contact with the heritage of the Italian RENAISSANCE and realized what might be achieved by applying to the great texts of the Christian tradition the same methods of exegesis that the Italian humanists had applied to the classics. To this task Erasmus determined to devote the rest of his life. From his English visit dates his serious application to the study of Greek. A few years later his ambition to provide a more accurate knowledge of the basic texts of the Christian tradition was further confirmed by his discovery in a monastery in the Low Countries of a MS of Lorenzo VALLA's *Annotations on the New Testament.* Erasmus had already been greatly influenced by Valla's ideas on the uses of philology, and he then published the *Annotations* in Paris in 1505 with an enthusiastic introduction.

The English visit was the first of Erasmus's many changes of residence. He returned to France in 1500 and spent some years there and in the Low Countries. A second visit to England in 1505–06 was followed by three years in Italy (1506–09), during which he was associated with the Aldine Academy in Venice and had an opportunity to visit the Rome of JULIUS II. From Rome Erasmus returned to England on the accession of HENRY VIII, in the hope of sharing in the royal patronage. In 1511 he settled in Queen's College, CAMBRIDGE, where he spent two and a half years. Leaving England again in 1514, he went first to Basel and then for brief periods to Louvain and to Holland. In 1521 he returned to Basel, where he remained for the next eight years, his longest residence in one place. The official acceptance of the REFORMATION in Basel in 1529 caused his retreat to Freiburg, where he spent the next six years.

The refusal to identify himself with any of the national cultures in Europe was characteristic of Erasmus. In spite of invitations from France, England, and the Empire he preferred to retain his independence. His increasing literary fame enabled him to lead the life of a man of letters unattached to any institution. The poor scholar who had had to take in pupils for a living became a comparatively wealthy man through the rewards bestowed on him by many patrons.

Works. At the height of his fame, Erasmus occupied a position in the history of European literature rivaled perhaps only by that of VOLTAIRE. In every country, admiring followers accepted his leadership. His letters provide the most comprehensive source for the intellectual history of his age. Of the many works that secured his reputation, the first to bring him public notice was the *Adages.* This collection of classical proverbs with an explanation of their meaning furnished students with a convenient handbook and digest of the subject matter of classical literature, arranged under such headings as misfortune, love, modesty, liberality, war. In 1508 Erasmus brought out at the Aldine Press (*see* MANUTIUS) in Venice a second edition containing three times as many adages as the first and reflecting what he had learned from the refugee Greek scholars at Venice. This remained one of the most popular of Erasmus's works; it went through many editions and its influence can be traced in the vernacular literature of every European country in the 16th century.

In the *Enchiridion militis christiani,* first published in Antwerp (1503), Erasmus expounded his conception of a Christianity infused with the spirit of the Gospels. This little treatise presented life as a struggle between virtue and vice. Here is found the combination of piety and learning, the *docta pietas,* which Erasmus emphasized in so many of his later works. In the analysis of the soul in the *Enchiridion* he follows, on the whole, ORIGEN and the Greek Fathers, who had a profound effect on his thinking. Erasmus later maintained that his chief purpose in writing the book had been to remedy the errors of those who confused ceremonial observances with true piety. The conclusion of the treatise is that there is a regular progression through nature to grace and that the philosophy of Christ depends on the inner action of the spirit rather than on conformity to external rites.

The message of the *Enchiridion* was reiterated in a very different form in the *Praise of Folly,* which has remained the work by which Erasmus is perhaps best known to the general public. It was composed in 1509 while Erasmus was traveling from Italy to England and was dedicated to Thomas More with the pun on his name contained in the title *Encomium moriae.* Erasmus imagined Folly personified delivering a classical oration in her defense. This device gave him an opportunity to satirize many aspects of contemporary society, both ecclesiastical and lay. In the end, however, Folly becomes serious and makes her hearers recognize that what is, in the eyes of the world, the greatest folly, namely Christianity, is in reality the highest wisdom.

The same themes were taken up in many of Erasmus's *Colloquies* of which the first authorized edition was published in 1519. Later the dramatic possibilities of these little dialogues appealed to Erasmus, and he created a whole gallery of characters, through the medium of whose conversation he managed to take up all the great issues of politics and religion of his generation. The style of these compositions was particularly consonant with Erasmus's character. The dialogue form emphasized the rhetorical arts of persuasion that had been so central to the educational curriculum of the Renaissance. Furthermore, this form had the advantage that the views of the author could be concealed beneath those attributed to one of the characters.

The homilies, satires, and colloquies that Erasmus wrote did not interrupt the course of his scholarly work. The number of his editions of classical and patristic works is formidable. Some of these represented no great labor on his part, such was the Basel *Aristotle* of 1531, to which Erasmus contributed only a preface. Others represented years of patient work. What the Aldine Press in Venice had accomplished at the turn of the century for classical literature, FROBEN in Basel aspired to do for patristic literature, and it was upon Erasmus that his establishment chiefly depended. Of the patristic works edited by Erasmus, the most important were the *Jerome* of 1516, the *Augustine* of 1529, the *Chrysostom* of 1530, and the *Origen* of 1536. To the edition of JEROME, with whom he felt a kind of affinity, Erasmus devoted a particular effort, not only emending the text and providing an extensive commentary, but also contributing a preface with an account of the life and works of the translator of the Vulgate.

Erasmus had decided, perhaps as early as his edition of Valla's *Annotations,* to occupy himself with the text of the New Testament. This project grew to be an edition of the Greek text with a new Latin translation and a commentary on which Erasmus was seriously at work from 1512. The *Novum instrumentum,* which appeared in 1516, was the first published version of the Greek text. Erasmus's work is far from the standards of modern scholarship in both method and content. He established his text on a limited number of MSS, rather haphazardly consulted; his knowledge of Greek was insufficient to deal with many philological problems; his footnotes contained frequent irrelevant digressions. The work, nevertheless, was of epoch-making importance. His Greek text was the basis of many of the vernacular versions produced during the sixteenth century.

Erasmus and the Reformation. The *Novum instrumentum* was dedicated to Leo X, whom Erasmus hailed as introducing a new age in which scholarship and the arts would flourish and peace would reign. These hopes, however, were disappointed by the religious revolution in the outbreak of which his own work had played a very large part. His widely read criticism of abuses in the Church, his revolt against formalism, and his appeal for a restoration of an earlier and purer piety awoke an enthusiastic response among his contemporaries and the younger generation. One of his readers was Martin LUTHER, who had sought Erasmus's approval as early as 1516 but felt that ''with him, human things were of greater value than divine'' (''humana praevalent in eo plus quam divina''). In 1519 he begged for Erasmus's support in his struggle with the Curia. Erasmus replied not very cordially, professing ignorance of Luther's writings, but declaring that he had urged moderation in influential quarters.

With the papal condemnation and Luther's treatises of 1520, Erasmus's attitude changed. He feared the consequences of what he now saw to be a revolution, and he deplored Luther's appeal to the general public. As the Lutheran movement took shape and the gap between Rome and Wittenberg widened, Erasmus's position became increasingly uncomfortable. Many of his former friends, such as Dürer and HUTTEN, condemned him for not supporting Luther. Others, such as Aleandro, once his roommate in Venice, accused him of having attacked the basic institutions of the Church and prepared the way for Luther. He was urged by friends on both sides to clarify his position and at first seems to have believed that it was still possible to deal with these great issues in the manner of the *Colloquies.* The *Inquisitio de fide* probably represents his attempt to explore in a dialogue the implications of the religious division. He soon saw, however, that this congenial approach was no longer possible, and he composed his treatise on the freedom of the will, published in 1524, to define his religious position against that of Luther. Luther replied with the *De servo arbitrio,* in which he disdainfully repudiated the theological arguments of Erasmus. This elicited from Erasmus the first and second *Hyperaspistes,* in which he elaborated his original argument. During the same period he had to defend himself from the attacks of his enemies on the other side, especially Alberto Pio, Prince of Carpi, and the Spanish monks.

In spite of these controversies and the bitterness that Erasmus had to face in the last years of his life, he continued his literary and scholarly publications, producing, among other works, in the years at Freiburg the treatise on preaching, *Ecclesiastes,* and the edition of Origen. It was to see these volumes through the press that he returned to Basel in 1535. There he died in the house of Froben, surrounded by his friends. In the absence of a priest, he did not receive the Last Sacraments. He was buried in the cathedral at Basel, which had been converted into a Protestant church.

Significance. Erasmus's significance has been as variously estimated as it was ambiguous in his own lifetime. Rightly regarded as one of those who had prepared the way for the religious revolution, he nevertheless repudiated decisively the work of Luther and ZWINGLI. Although he was offered a cardinal's hat by Paul III, his work was put on the Index by the Council of Trent. To the Enlightenment he appeared a figure in the history of European rationalism. He has often been accused of having been wavering and cowardly in the great crisis of his generation. In fact, however, he maintained with remarkable consistency throughout his life the position defined by his ideals as a Christian humanist. As a Christian, he declared again and again that his whole life had been devoted to the cause of the gospel. He professed always his willingness to submit to the authority of the Church, even though he never committed himself in detail on how that authority was to be defined. Many of the points on which his orthodoxy was questioned were clarified only after his death by the decisions of the Council of TRENT. As a humanist, he believed that even the deepest commitments should be defended, and the cause of truth advanced by persuasion rather than by force. It was the tragedy of his later life that he pleaded for peace and unity in a Christian world that had become so deeply divided that a continuing dialogue was no longer possible.

Bibliography: Works. *Opera omnia,* ed. J. LE CLERC, 10 v. in 11 (Leiden 1703–06); *Opuscula,* ed. W. K. FERGUSON (The Hague 1933); *Ausgewählte Werke,* ed. H. and A. HOLBORN (Munich 1933); *Opus epistolarum,* ed. P. S. ALLEN et al., 12 v. (Oxford 1906–58); *Poems,* ed. C. REEDIJK (Leiden 1956); *Colloquies,* tr. N. BAILEY, ed. E. JOHNSON, 3 v. (London 1900); *Inquisitio de fide,* ed. C. R. THOMPSON (New Haven 1950); *The Education of a Christian Prince,* tr. and ed. L. K. BORN (New York 1936); *Handbook of the Militant Christian,* tr. and ed. J. P. DOLAN (Notre Dame, IN 1962); *The Epistles of E., from his Earliest Letters to his Fifty-first Year, Arranged in Order of Time,* tr. and ed. F. M. NICHOLS, 3 v. (New York 1901–18); *The Free Will* in *Discourse on Free Will,* tr. and ed. E. F. WINTER (New York 1961), treatises by Erasmus and Martin Luther; *The Praise of Folly,* tr. H. H. HUDSON (Princeton 1941); *Colloquies,* tr. C. R. THOMPSON (Chicago 1965). F. F. E. VANDER HAEGHEN et al., 7 v. (Ghent 1897–1908). *Collected Works of Erasmus* (Toronto 1974–). **Studies.** J. HUIZINGA, *Erasmus of Rotterdam* (New York 1952). P. SMITH, *Erasmus: A Study of his Life, Ideals and Place in History* (New York 1923). P. MESTWERDT, *Die Anfänge des E.: Humanismus und ''Devotio moderna,''* ed. H. VON SCHUBERT (Leipzig 1917). A. HYMA, *The Youth of Erasmus* (Ann Arbor 1930). E. F. RICE, ''Erasmus and the Religious Tradition, 1495–1499,'' *Journal of the History of Ideas* 11 (1950) 387–411. Erasmus and the National Traditions. M. BATAILLON, *É. et l'Espagne* (Paris 1937). M. MANN, *É. et les débuts de la réforme française, 1517–1536* (Paris 1934). A. RENAUDET, *É. Et l'Italie* (Geneva 1954); *Préréforme et humanisme à Paris pendant les premières guerres d'Italie, 1494–1517* (2d ed. Paris 1953). L. W. SPITZ, *The Religious Renaissance of the German Humanists* (Cambridge, Mass. 1963). Erasmus and Humanism. R. PFEIFFER, *Humanitas Erasmiana* (Berlin 1931). O. SCHOTTENLOHER, *Erasmus im Ringen um die humanistische Bildungsform* (Münster 1933). M. P. GILMORE, ''Erasmus and the Cause of Christian Humanism: The Last Years, 1529–1536,'' *Humanists and Jurists* (Cambridge, MA 1963) 115–145. S. A. NULLI, *Erasmus e il Rinascimento* (Turin 1955). Religious Thought. L. BOUYER, *Erasmus and his Times,* tr. F. X. MURPHY (Westminster, MD 1959). K. H. OELRICH, *Der späte Erasmus und die Reformation* (Münster 1961). É. V. TELLE, *É. De Rotterdam et le septième Sacrement* (Geneva 1954). H. JEDIN, *History of the Council of Trent,* tr. E. GRAF (St. Louis 1957–60) v.1. D. KNOWLES, *The Religious Orders in England,* 3 v. (Cambridge, England 1948–60) 3:141–156. Special topics. J. HOYOUX, ''Les Moyens d'existence d'É.,'' *Bibliothèque d'Humanisme et Renaissance* NS 5 (1944) 7–59. P. SMITH, *A Key to the Colloquies of Erasmus* (Cambridge, MA 1927). *Bibliotheca Erasmiana,* comp. L. HALKIN, *Erasmus: A Critical Biography,* J. TONKIN, tr. (Oxford 1993). L. JARDINE, *Erasmus, Man of Letters* (Princeton 1993). M. SCREECH, *Erasmus: Ecstacy and the Praise of Folly* (London 1980). J. TRACY, *Erasmus of the Low Countries* (Berkeley 1996); *Erasmus, the Growth of a Mind* (Berkeley 1972).

[M. P. GILMORE]

ERASTIANISM

Erastianism is the doctrine of complete subjection of the Church to the power of the State. This thesis was not specifically held by Thomas Erastus although his name is attached to it.

Career of Erastus. Erastus (Thomas Lüber, Lieber, or Liebler) was born in Baden, Switzerland, on Sept. 7, 1524. Most of his early education was received at Basel, where he was given a patron's aid for his university training. After his recovery from the plague, which had struck Basel, he went first to the University of Bologna and then to the University of Padua where he studied medicine and philosophy. In 1553 he became the court physician to the Prince of Hennenburg, and later to Otto Henry, the Elector of the Palatinate, while he taught medicine at the University of Heidelberg.

Although the subject of his work and teaching was medicine, his chief interest was theology. In the religious controversy that raged at Heidelberg, the Elector Frederick III (1559–76) fostered Calvinism in the Palatinate (*see* REFORMED CHURCHES). At first, Erastus was sympathetic but he opposed the Calvinist party which was led by Caspar Olevianus, when it tried to introduce the Geneva system of church discipline. As a Zwinglian, Erastus was opposed also to the Lutherans on the doctrine of the Eucharist.

Erastus's great work is the *Seventy-Five Theses* (1568) based originally on 100 theses. Seventy-two were against the ideas on excommunication set forth by the English Puritan, George Withers, who was supported by the Calvinists, especially Theodore BEZA. Because of his statements, his opposition to the Presbyterian views, and his alleged Unitarianism Erastus was excommunicated. After a long controversy, he proved the charges false and the excommunication was lifted in 1575. As Lutheranism was restored to the Palatinate by Louis VI in 1579, Erastus resigned from the University of Heidelberg in 1580. He returned to Basel where he taught ethics and medicine until his death, Dec. 31, 1583.

Theories and Doctrines. The central question in the *Theses,* which was written about 1568, was excommunication. The term was used by Erastus not in the Catholic sense of exclusion of a notorious sinner from membership in the Church or communion of the faithful. Erastus wrote against Withers's interpretation of excommunication, which excluded people of bad lives from participation in the Sacrament, on judgment by presbyters or laymen sitting in the name of the whole Church. Erastus insisted that excommunication could not be supported from the Scriptures and that the Sacrament should not be withheld from those who wish to receive it. Erastus argued from the Protestant viewpoint that the Bible is the sole source of faith. The chief argument of his whole system was based on an analogy between the Jewish and Christian dispensations. He noted that the Mosaic Law excluded no one from offering the paschal sacrifice, and that Christ had not excluded Judas from holy communion. Erastus admitted, however, that some exegetes thought that the betrayer left the cenacle before the Holy Eucharist was instituted.

The last three theses state the theory of Church-State relations to which his name is attached, even though the interpretation put upon them was not that of Erastus. He considered the ruler responsible for the external government of the Church, but he limited this responsibility to Christian rulers. Erastus judged that when a ruler is Christian, there is no need for corrective jurisdiction other than that of the State. He thus assigned the ruler the same power he had in the Jewish state. Therefore, according to Erastus, a Christian magistrate might pass judgment on men's conduct, settle disputes, and work with the ministers in admonishing and reproving those who ''live unholy and impure lives,'' but he could not debar anyone who wished to receive the Sacrament. Nowhere did Erastus hold that the interests of religion are subordinate or subservient to those of the State. Nor on the other hand, did he accept the Church as a visible society with its own completely independent government.

Erastus's entire system was never accepted nor promoted by any sect, but his theories on Church-State relations had great influence in Germany and England in the 17th century. The Presbyterians rejected them, but England's Established Church had an Erastian group. The Presbyterians used the term ''Erastian'' as an unfavorable epithet for their opponents in the Westminster Assembly in 1643. The Anglican Richard HOOKER, in his *Of the Laws of Ecclesiastical Polity,* borrowed the Erastian analogy between the Jewish and Christian states to defend the English sovereign's title as head of the Church as well as his appointment of bishops. Hooker required the laity's consent before an ecclesiastical law was binding and believed in a single society that assigned all coercive authority to the civil functionary.

Erastus's real purpose seems to have been to deny to the Church any right to coercive authority apart from the State. He was opposed to any political role for the Church whether that in a theocracy or that of the Church as an independent society within the State. Erastus was not a modern ''Erastian.'' He considered only the case of a state in which a single religion is tolerated as the true one. Moreover, he labored to prevent the Evangelical Church from embracing the Genevan doctrine that the Church is a perfect society in and by itself.

Bibliography: L. C. MCDONALD, *Western Political Theory* (New York 1962). J. Y. EVANS, J. HASTINGS, ed., *Encyclopedia of Religion and Ethics* 13 v. (Edinburgh 1908–27) 5:358–366. R. HOOKER, *Of the Laws of Ecclesiastical Polity,* 2 v. (New York 1925). W. S. CROWLEY, ''Erastianism in England to 1640,'' *Journal of Church and State* 32 (Sum 1990), 549–566. R. E. RODES, ''Last Days of Erastianism: Forms in the American Church State Nexus,'' *Harvard Theological Review* 62 (July 1969), 301–348.

[M. L. FELL]

ERCHEMPERT

Historian, poet, monk of MONTE CASSINO; lived in the second half of the 9th century. The very few biographical details known about Erchempert (namely, those concerning his activities in the years *c.* 880 to 888) derive from his main work, the *Historiola Langobardorum Beneventi degentium,* which traces the history of the southern Italian Lombards, the author's own people, from 774 to 889. The *Historiola* is a primary source for the history of southern Italy in that period. Erchempert himself (*Historiola* c.31) alludes to his poetical work, of which little survives except the dedicatory poem of the *Historiola* [U. Westerbergh, *Beneventan Ninth Century Poetry* (Stockholm 1957) 8–29] and some verses he added to a metrical calendar of Anglo-Saxon origin (*ibid.* 74–90).

Bibliography: P. MEYVAERT, *Dictionnaire d'histoire et de géographie ecclésiastiques* 15:685–687.

[P. MEYVAERT]

ERCONWALD OF LONDON, ST.

Anglo-Saxon bishop of London, monastic founder; b. *c.* 630; d. Barking Abbey, April 30 *c.* 693. Erconwald (Earconwald or Erkenwald) was born in Lindsey of the royal blood of East Anglia. Attracted at an early age to the monastic life, he converted his patrimony into the foundation of two monastic establishments, the abbey at Chertsey under his direction and the abbey at BARKING under the direction of his sister ETHELBURGA. His reputation for sanctity led to his appointment in 675 as bishop of London, where he was consecrated by Abp. THEODORE OF CANTERBURY. As diocesan he enlarged his cathedral church, augmented the revenues of the see, and secured for it papal privileges. He labored to effect the reconciliation of WILFRID OF YORK and Theodore. After 11 years, he retired to Barking. He was buried at SAINT PAUL'S CATHEDRAL, where his shrine was the object of popular pilgrimage during the Middle Ages. In art he is represented in bishop's robes, with no particular distinction.

Feast: May 13 (Dioceses of Westminster, Southwark, and Brentwood); Nov. 14 (translation of 1148); Feb. 1 (translation in 1326).

Bibliography: BEDE, *Ecclesiastical History,* 2 v., tr. J. E. KING based on the version of T. STAPLETON (*Loeb Classical Library*; New York 1930) bk. 4. *Saint Erkenwald,* ed. C. PETERSON (Philadelphia 1977). *The Owl and the Nightingale,* tr. B. STONE (2d ed. London 1988). *The Saint of London: The Life and Miracles of St. Erkenwald,* ed. and tr. E. G. WHATLEY (Binghamton, N.Y. 1989). W. STUBBS, *A Dictionary of Christian Biography*, ed. W. SMITH and H. WACE, (London 1877–1887) 2:177–179.

[J. L. DRUSE]

ERDINGTON, ABBEY OF

Former BENEDICTINE monastery, now a Redemptorist house, in Erdington, a suburb of Birmingham, England, Diocese of Birmingham. Founded in the parish of Father D. H. Haigh in 1876 as a priory of the German Abbey of BEURON, Erdington became an abbey dedicated to Thomas of Canterbury in 1896. In 1899 its first abbot, Dom Anskar Hockelmann (d. 1943), was appointed. There were few English vocations, and the policy of the English government toward citizens of enemy countries living in England resulted in the removal of Abbot Anskar and the appointment of an English abbot, Dom Francis Izard, from 1915 to 1919. Twenty-eight of the monks chose to retire to Germany in 1919, leaving only 11 monks at Erdington. Authorization was obtained from Rome for the sale of the abbey, which was bought by the Redemptorists in 1922; Dom Anskar transferred the Benedictine community to St. Martin of WEINGARTEN in Württemberg.

Bibliography: *Annales O.S.B.,* 28–34 (1920–26) 42–44, 240–242. J. U. SAXTON, ''Die Wiederbelebung der Benediktinerabtei Weingarten,'' *Benediktinische Monatsschrift,* 4 (1922) 316–320; *Bygone Erdington* (Birmingham 1928). H. DAUPHIN, *Dictionnaire d'histoire et de géographie ecclésiastiques,* ed. A. BAUDRILLART et al. (Paris 1912–) 15:688–689.

[V. I. J. FLINT]

ERHARD, ST.

Missionary bishop; b. perhaps Narbonne, France (or Ireland?); d. Regensburg (formerly Ratisbon), Germany, seventh century. The details of this saint's life are unclear, for his vita, which was written in the mid-11th century by a monk, Paul the Jew, perhaps of Fulda of Regensburg, is not completely reliable inasmuch as it borrows freely from the *vitae* of St. ODILIA and St. HIDULF OF MOYENMOUTIER. Erhard may well have been a monk following the rule of COLUMBAN, and it is known that he was certainly a zealous missionary and the founder of seven monasteries. It seems that he was also a regional missionary bishop who died at Regensburg with a great reputation for sanctity; he was buried in the Abbey of Niedermünster. On Oct. 8, 1052, Pope LEO IX, in the presence of Emperor HENRY III, solemnly exhumed the relics

St. Erhard celebrating Mass, miniature from Gospel Book of Abbess Uota, 11th century (Clm 13601, fol. 4r).

of WOLFGANG and Erhard (P. Jaffé, *Regesta pontificum romanorum ab condita ecclesia ad annum post Christum natum 1198,* ed. S. Löwenfeld 1:543), an action that at that time was equivalent to CANONIZATION. While Erhard's cult was overshadowed by that of St. Wolfgang and St. EMMERAM, two famous bishops of Regensburg, his purported crozier and part of his skull are still venerated in Regensburg.

Feast: Jan. 8.

Bibliography: *Monumenta Germaniae Scriptores rerum Merovingicarum* (Berlin 1825–) 6:1–21. *Acta Sanctorum* (Paris 1863–) Jan. 1:533–46. A. SCHÜTTE, *Handbuch der deutschen Heiligen* (Cologne 1941) 113. R. BAUERREISS, *Kirchengeschichte Bayerns,* 5 v. (St. Ottilien 1949–55; 2d ed. Munich 1958–) 1:52–53, 173. KONRAD VON MEGENBERG, *Historia Sancti Erhardi,* ed. R. HANKELN (Ottawa 2000) office for feast. R. VAN DOREN, *Bibliotheca sanctorum* (Rome 1961–) 4:1285–87. A. RAGGI, *ibid.* 1287.

[H. DRESSLER]

ERIC IX JEDVARDSSON, KING OF SWEDEN, ST.

Patron of SWEDEN, reigned from 1150 to *c.* 1160. He was killed, according to legend, in the church of Old-

Reliquary of Saint Eric IX Jedvardsson, who died in 1160, in the Cathedral of Uppsala, Sweden. (©Archivo Iconografico, A.S./ CORBIS)

Uppsala when a Danish prince invaded the country and disputed his right to the throne. This same legend attributes to Eric all the qualities of a good Northern king, i.e., he instituted salutary laws, helped the poor, worked miraculous cures, etc. One of the most famous, although not undisputed, events in the legend, is Eric's ''crusade'' to Finland (*see* HENRY OF UPPSALA). He was honored as the ancestor of a line of Swedish kings. As early as the end of the 12th century, a calendar from the Diocese of Uppsala (Vallentuna) mentioned St. Eric. His *elevatio* took place probably before 1200; he was never formally canonized. Although the surviving legend is of later origin, it seems to be based on records contemporary with the official recognition of his cult. A rhythmical history entitled *Assunt Erici regis sollemnia* (*Analecta Hymnica* 25) and the sequence *Gratulemur dulci prosa* (*Analecta Hymnica* 42) are extant. Numerous paintings, sculptures, and hymns (*Analecta Hymnica* 43) commemorate Eric; his image appears on Swedish coins. His cult was observed not only in Sweden but in Finland, Denmark, Norway, and in the sphere of influence of the BRIGITTINE SISTERS. He is pictured with a sword, palm, and crown. The cathedral of Uppsala, which was once adorned with paintings depicting Eric's life, houses supposedly authentic relics of Eric in a 16th-century shrine.

Feast: May 18.

Bibliography: E. CARLSSON, ''Translacio archiepiscoporum,'' *Uppsala Universitets Årsskrift* (Uppsala 1944) No. 2. A. BUTLER, *The Lives of the Saints,* ed. H. THURSTON and D. ATTWATER (New York 1956–) 2:342–343. B. THORDEMAN, ed., *Erik den Helige: Historia, kult, reliker* (Stockholm 1954), articles by T. SCHMID et al. O. HARTMAN, *Korsfararen; mirakelspel i tre akter* (Stockholm 1962).

[T. SCHMID]

ERITREA, THE CATHOLIC CHURCH IN

Located in northeast Africa, the State of Eritrea is bordered on the north and east by the RED SEA, on the south by ETHIOPIA and DJIBOUTI, and on the west by SUDAN. Including the islands of the Dahlak Archipelago and Zuqar Island, northern coastal plains rising to interior mountains and falling again to rolling plains in the southwest characterize the region. The arid climate of the northern coast cools into the mountains while becoming more arid in the western hills. Subjected to frequent periods of drought and infestations of locusts, agricultural production consists of sorghum, lentils, corn, cotton, tobacco and coffee. Eritrea exports much of it agricultural production, along with textiles, livestock and small manufactured goods, to other nations surrounding the Red Sea.

Annexed to Ethiopia in 1952 as part of a federation, and then made a province, Eritrea began a struggle for independence that lasted three decades. Independence, which was finally achieved on May 24, 1993, was followed by border skirmishes with Ethiopia that escalated into war by 1999. Thousands of refugees lived in camps around the country, prompting such organizations as Caritas to provide much-needed aid. By 2001 peace talks began, accompanied by troop withdrawals from Eritrea's southern border, and the prospect of a lasting peace was viewed as a possibility.

Ecclesiastically, the Ethiopian Orthodox Church has dioceses at Asmara, Barentu and Karen, all of which are suffragans of the Egyptian Archdiocese of Addis Ababa. An Oriental Orthodox Church, it falls under the patriarchy of Constantinople. An apostolic vicariate for the Latin rite is located in the capital city of Asmara.

Part of the ancient Ethopian empire, Eritrea saw the introduction of Christianity in the 4th century. Following a split within the Church at the fourth Ecumenical Council of Chalcedon in 451, Ethiopia joined with the eastern Oriental Orthodox churches. A Coptic rite, the Ethiopian Orthodox Church is monophysite, accepting the doctrine

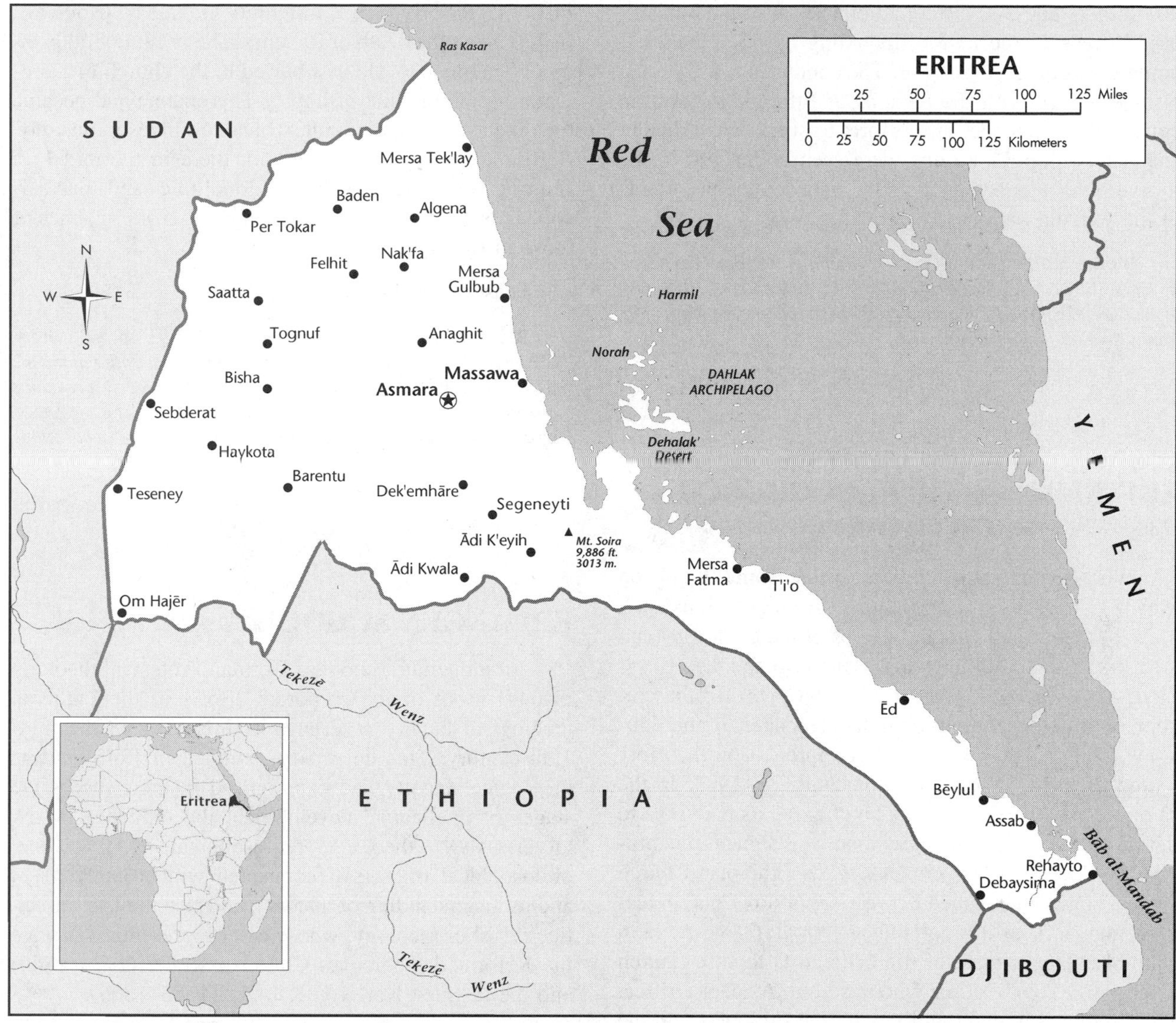

that Christ has, not two, but only a single nature: the divine (*see* MONOPHYTISM). Missionary activity by Ethiopian Orthodox increased in Eritrea during the 19th century; meanwhile Roman Catholicism also made inroads, brought by Italians who colonized the region in 1882. By the 20th century the Latin-rite Church remained a minority faith, numbering only three percent of the population, which otherwise remained divided between Orthodox and Muslim.

In 1935 the region was used as a base for the Italian invasion of Ethiopia, and was incorporated into Italian East Africa the following year. Conquered by the British in 1941, it was federated to Ethiopia in 1952 and was made a northern province of its African neighbor ten years later. Eritrea's incorporation into Ethiopia did much to strengthen the Ethiopian Orthodox Church, which remained the predominate Christian faith even after the nation declared its independence in 1993. In 1995 Orthodox dioceses were established at Barentu and Karen, although difficulties caused in an escalating border war between Eritrea and Ethiopia left them lacking both funding and staff. While the Eritrean government continued to allow the freedom to worship, it prevented religious groups from involvement in politics or other public administration activities. In April 1998, as full-scale war erupted, the troubled Eritrean government postponed announced plans to nationalize the country's private schools and hospitals, most of which were run by the Catholic Church. In April 1999 Pope John Paul II met with bishops of both Ethiopia and Eritrea, urging them to ''support every move toward peace and every effort to restore unity and brotherhood.''

By 2000 the Orthodox Church had 93 parishes under the care of 72 diocesan and 217 religious priests, while

80 brothers and 340 sisters administered to the humanitarian needs of the nation, including the thousands left homeless as the result of war. The country's two Catholic bishops joined with the bishops of Ethiopia to form an episcopal conference, and efforts to work with Muslim and other religious groups were seen as integral in the formation of a peace pact signed between the presidents of the warring nations on Dec. 15, 2000.

Bibliography: E. CERULLI, *Scritti teologici etiopici dei secoli XVI e XVII,* 2 v. (Studi e Testi 198, 204; Vatican City 1958–60). T. KILLION, *Historical Dictionary of Eritrea* (Methchen, NJ 1998). *Annuario Pontificio* (2000).

[P. SHELTON]

ERITREAN ORTHODOX CHURCH (ORIENTAL ORTHODOX)

When Eritrea gained independence from Ethiopia on May 24, 1993 after a long struggle, negotiations took place between the Eritrean bishops of the ETHIOPIAN ORTHODOX CHURCH (ORIENTAL ORTHODOX) and the COPTIC ORTHODOX CHURCH (ORIENTAL ORTHODOX) for the creation of an autocephalous church independent of the Ethiopian Church. This request was approved by the Holy Synod of the Coptic Church on Sept. 28, 1993. In the same month, the Ethiopian Church gave its blessings to the separation. A formal agreement was signed in February 1994 between the primates of the Ethiopian Church and the newly established Eritrean Orthodox Church, recognizing and affirming the AUTOCEPHALY of both churches. The primate of the Eritrean Orthodox Church is the patriarch of Eritrea, who resides in Asmara, Eritrea. This church is in communion with the Ethiopian and the Egyptian Coptic Churches, and accords a primacy of honor to the Coptic Church.

Bibliography: R. ROBERSON, *The Eastern Christian Churches: A Brief Survey*, 6th ed. (Rome 1999).

[EDITORS]

ERKEMBODO, ST.

Benedictine abbot; d. Thérouanne, April 12, 734. He was received into the abbey of Saints. Peter and Paul (SAINT-BERTIN) before 709, and was elected fourth abbot of the monastery in 717. The BENEDICTINE RULE had already replaced the earlier usages of St. COLUMBAN. Erkembodo developed his abbey's liturgical practices and intensified its life of prayer. He increased the property of the monastery by buying neighboring lands, and from Chilperic II and Theodoric IV he obtained confirmation of the privilege of immunity granted by Clovis III. In 720, upon the death of Ravenger, he became fifth bishop of Thérouanne. He was buried in the church of Saint-Omer beside the first bishop of Thérouanne and became the object of a popular cult, which continues to this day. A Romanesque church was built there in the mid-11th century. His present tomb is a monolithic sandstone sarcophagus, with concentric carvings, after the manner of those in Ravenna.

Feast: April 12.

Bibliography: *Acta Sanctorum* April 2:93–95. M. COENS, ''L'Auteur de la *Vita Erkembodonis,*'' *Analecta Bollandiana* 42 (1924) 126–136. L. VAN DER ESSEN, *Étude critique . . . des saints mérovingiens de l'ancienne Belgique* (Louvain 1907). G. COOLEN, ''La Mort de S. E.,'' *Bulletin trimestriel de la société académique des antiquaires de la Morinie* 18 (1957) 641–643.

[G. COOLEN]

ERLANGEN SCHOOL

An influential school of German Protestant theology that grew out of the corporate efforts of the Lutheran theological faculty at Erlangen University in the mid-19th century. This university, founded in 1743, and its theological faculty had experienced in their successive stages of intellectual development the influence of ENLIGHTENMENT theology, philosophical RATIONALISM, philosophical IDEALISM (connected with ROMANTICISM and its understanding of history), and also the late romantic revival of theology, whose chief representatives were the Reformed theologian Christian Krafft (1784–1845) and the scientist Karl von Raumer (1783–1865).

The systematic, theological origin of the Erlangen school was the accomplishment of Gottlieb Adolph von Harless (1806–79), who had been influenced by SCHLEIERMACHER and ''converted'' by Friedrich Tholuck, and who stressed personal ''regeneration.'' This emphasis, the first characteristic mark of the school, received added impetus from Johann Christian von Hofmann (1810–77), who combined the views of PIETISM with a confessional Lutheran outlook and elements of Schleiermacher's thought. Hofmann systematized the regeneration approach and held that all the main parts of classical Lutheran orthodoxy must be constructed in a regressive theological process from the experience of regeneration if the internal testimony of the Holy Spirit has any truth. Theology, he claimed, has met its task if the results of this reconstructive process coincide with the proof from Scripture.

A second characteristic of the school was its systematic interest in biblical interpretation and stress on the promise-fulfillment concept that is the basis of a theology of *Heilsgeschichte* (redemptive history). Hofmann's book, *Weissagung und Erfüllung* (2 v. 184–144), proposed that revelation is God's gradual unfolding of the plan of salvation whereby each step or "fulfillment" is again turned into a promise. Thus, Scripture is to be understood historically, but strictly as a redemptive history with Jesus Christ as its center.

These two characteristics, the emphasis on subjective regeneration and on redemptive history, became the pillars of the impressive system of Franz Hermann von Frank (1827–94), a pupil of Harless and Hofmann. His *System der christlichen Gewissheit* (1870–73) concentrated on the regenerate believer who uncovers the "immanent, transcendent, and transeunt" objects of faith, but his *System der christlichen Wahrheit* (1878–80) proceeded in the opposite direction by unfolding the divine truth (*Wahrheit*) that leads to the individual believer's certainty (*Gewissheit*). Immanent objects of faith, according to Frank, are those the regenerate man finds in himself, such as sin and righteousness; transcendent ones are those causing regeneration, namely the Trinity and the person and work of Christ; and transeunt ones are those that mediate between the immanent and transcendent, such as the Church, Sacraments, and inspiration. This theological system attempted to encompass both Schleiermacher and traditional orthodoxy; it represented the climax of the Erlangen school. Other scholars related to the school, especially Theodosius Harnack (1817–89), Gottfried Thomasius (1802–75), and Theodor von Zahn (1838–1933), did not subscribe fully to Frank's elaborate system.

The school's achievements were effectively attacked by Albrecht RITSCHL and his disciples, but some of its historical and exegetical fruits remained influential. The systematic concept of *Heilsgeschichte* gained new relevance in discussions of typology in Old Testament interpretation.

Bibliography: K. G. STECK, *Evangelisches Kirchenlexicon: Kirchlich-theologisches Handwörterbuch*, ed. H. BRUNOTTE and O. WEBER (Göttingen 1956–61) 1:1123–25. H. GRASS, *Die Religion in Geschichte und Gegenwart* (Tübingen 1957–65) 2:566–568. W. LOHFF, *Lexicon für Theologie und Kirche*, ed. J. HOFER and K. RAHNER (Freiburg 1957–65) 3:981–982.

[D. RITSCHL]

ERLEMBALD, ST.

Lay leader of the Patarines in 11th-century Milan; d. Milan, Italy, Holy Thursday, April 1075. On his return from a pilgrimage to Jerusalem, he decided to become a monk; but with the death of his brother, LANDULF of Cotta, Erlembald resumed his life as a knight, and led the Patarines against the forces of antireform headed by the Milanese Archbishop Guido of Velate.

After the brutal murder of St. ARIALDO, another Patarine leader, in 1066, the movement was to become more militant. Erlembald, now the sole head, sought to avenge his friend's death. Thus, from 1067 on, the word of Arialdo transcended to the sword of Erlembald. By the 1070s, this eagle-eyed, red-bearded soldier of God, who was "like a pope to judge the priests, a king to crumble the peoples," transformed Milan into a battleground.

By 1075 the conflict between Church and State, which had been developing for many decades, was brought into the open by the Milanese situation. Therefore, the Patarines, under Erlembald, served as a catalyst for the INVESTITURE STRUGGLE.

After Erlembald's death in one of the battles, the movement was largely dissipated. Some Patarines went to other cities in Italy, and the rest receded into the twilight for nearly 20 years. Erlembald was canonized by Pope URBAN II, who sought to make a gesture of peace with the remaining die-hards from the Patarine party. He shares the same feast day as his friend, Arialdo.

Feast: June 27.

Bibliography: ANDREW OF STRUMI, "Vita Sancti Arialdi," *Monumenta Germaniae Scriptores* (Berlin 1825–) 30.2. 1047–75. ARNULF, "Gesta archiepiscoporum Mediolanensium," *Monumenta Germaniae Scriptores* (Berlin 1825–) 8.1–31. LANDULF SENIOR, "Historia Mediolanensis," *Monumenta Germaniae Scriptores* (Berlin 1825–) 8.32–100. S. M. BROWN, "Movimenti politico-religiosi a Milano ai tempi della Pataria," *Archivio storico lombardo,* ser. 58, 6 (1931) 227–278. C. CASTIGLIONI, *I santi Arialdo ed Erlembaldo e la Pataria* (Milan 1944). H. E. J. COWDREY, "The Papacy, the Patarenes and the Church of Milan," *Transactions of the Royal Historical Society,* ser. 5, 18 (1968) 25–48. Y. RENOUARD, *Les villes d'Italie de la fin du x*e *siècle au début du xiv*e *siècle,* v. 2 (Paris 1969). E. WERNER, *Pauperes Christi: Studien zu sozial-religiösen bewegungen im zeitalter des reformpapsttums* (Leipzig 1956). J. P. WHITNEY, *Hildebrandine Essays* (Cambridge 1932) 143–157.

[P. M. LEVINE]

ERMELINDE, ST.

Belgian recluse; d. Oct. 29 *c.* 595. She belonged to a rich family in Brabant; her traditional connections with the Carolingian family of Pepin I derive from a unreliable 11th-century vita. According to this legend Ermelinde cut her hair and fled from home to avoid a marriage arranged by her parents. She took up a life of mortification and asceticism in a hermitage, first at Beauvechain and then at Meldaert, near Tirlemont, Belgium. It was later alleged that she founded a monastery at Chaumont near Meldaert. After her death at the age of 48, she was buried at Meldaert, where a chapel was later built in her honor.

Feast: Oct. 29.

Bibliography: *Bibliotheca hagiographica latina antiquae ct mediae aetatis* (Brussels 1898–1901) 1:2605–07. *Acta Sanctorum* Oct. 12:843–872. S. BALAU, *Les Sources de l'histoire de Liège au moyen âge: Étude critique* (Brussels 1903). L. VAN DER ESSEN, *Étude critique . . . des saints mérovingiens de l'ancienne Belgique* (Louvain 1907) 307–309. É. DE MOREAU, *Histoire de l'Église en Belgique* (2d ed. Brussels 1945) 1:196; 2:253, 286; 3:569. J. L. BAUDOT and L. CHAUSSIN, *Vies des saints et des bienheueux selon l'ordre du calendrier avec l'historique des fêtes* (Paris 1935–56) 10:976–977.

[C. P. LOUGHRAN]

ERMENBURGA, ST.

Anglo-Saxon queen and abbess, known also as Domna Ebba or Domneva; d. Thanet, *c.* 695. She was the daughter of Ermenred of the royal line of Kent. In her youth, she was married to Merewald, son of Penda, king of Mercia; by Merewald she had three daughters and one son. Her brothers had been killed in a family struggle in Kent and in compensation, King Egbert of Kent gave her estates on the island of Thanet. After her husband's death she retired there and founded the Abbey of Thanet, being blessed as first abbess by Abp. THEODORE OF CANTERBURY. After a rule of many years she died, and was succeeded as abbess by her daughter, St. MILDRED.

Feast: Nov. 19.

Bibliography: W. STUBBS, *A Dictionary of Christian Biography,* ed. W. SMITH and H. WACE, (London 1877–1887) 2:133. A. M.. ZIMMERMANN, *Kalendarium Benedictinum: Die Heiligen und Seligen des Benediktinerorderns und seiner Zweige* (Metten 1933–1938) 3:329–332.

[J. L. DRUSE]

ERMENRICH OF PASSAU

Benedictine, bishop of Passau; b. *c.* 814; d. Dec. 26, 874. He is perhaps to be identified with the Benedictine monk Ermenrich of ELLWANGEN, who was educated at FULDA under RABANUS MAURUS and Rudolph, at REICHENAU under WALAFRID STRABO, and later at SANKT GALLEN. About 840 Ermenrich composed a life of the Anglo-Saxon monk Sualo (whom he calls Solus), based on oral tradition and historically unimportant. In a dialogue modeled on the *Consolatio* of BOETHIUS, he composed for Gozbald, Bishop of Würzburg (841–855), a legendary account of the founding of the monastery of Ellwangen by Hariolf. Between 850 and 855, he sent to Grimald, Abbot of Sankt Gallen, a letter in which he discussed a wide variety of subjects from grammar and philosophy to mythology and dogma. Though badly organized and overornate in style, the letter shows the breadth of knowledge to be acquired in the monastic schools of the time, contains important historical data, and supplements the chronicles of Sankt Gallen. When sent by Louis the German on a missionary expedition to the court of BORIS I OF BULGARIA (866–867), he worked against the influence of SS. CYRIL and METHODIUS.

Bibliography: E. DÜMMLER in *Forschungen zur deutschen Geschichte,* ed. G. WAITZ, v.13 (Göttingen 1873) 473–485. W. WATTENBACH, *Deutschlands Geschichtsquellen im mittelalter bis zur Mitte des 13 Jh.* (Berlin 1894) 1:282–284. A. HAUCK, *Kirchengeschichte Deutschlands* (Berlin-Leipzig 1958) 2:680–681. V. BURR, ''Ermenrich von Ellwangen,'' *Ellwanger Jahrbuch* 16 (1956) 19–31; *Lexikon für Theologie und Kirche*, ed. J. HOFER and K. RAHNER (Freiburg 1957–65) 3:1031–32. W. SCHWARZ, ''Die Schriften Ermenrichs von Ellwangen,'' *Zeitschrift für Württembergische Landesgeschichte* 12 (1953) 181–189; 15 (1956) 279–281. W. FINK, *Dictionnaire d'histoire et de géographie ecclésiastiques* 15:759–761.

[M. F. MCCARTHY]

ERMIN, ST.

Abbot; b. Herly, Laon, France, late seventh century; d. Lobbes, near Cambrai, Belgium, April 25, 737. He was born of a noble French family and became chaplain and confessor to Madelgar, Bishop of Laon. While in the bishop's service he became a friend of URSMAR, abbot of LOBBES, and entered the BENEDICTINE ORDER at his monastery. When Ursmar resigned in 711 or 712, Ermin succeeded him as abbot bishop of Lobbes. He was buried at Lobbes, and in 1409 his relics were reinterred next to those of St. Ursmar. Together they are the patrons of Lobbes.

Feast: April 18 and 25 (Dioceses of Soissons, Cambrai, Tournai, and Ghent).

Bibliography: *Vita, Monumenta Germaniae Scriptores rerum Merovingicarum* (Berlin 1825–) 6:461–470. J. WARICHEZ, *L'Abbaye de Lobbes* (Tournai 1909). *Analecta Bollandiana* (Brussels 1882–) 50 (1932) 132. W. BÖHNE, *Lexikon für Theologie und Kirche,* ed. J. HOFER and K. RAHNER (Freiburg 1957–1965) 3:1032. A. M.. ZIMMERMANN, *Kalendarium Benedictinum: Die Heiligen und Seligen des Benediktinerorderns und seiner Zweige* (Metten 1933–1938) 2:68–72.

[P. BLECKER]

ERMINFRID, ST.

Frankish monastic founder; seventh century. Born of a noble Frankish family in Franche-Comté, he spent part of his youth at the court of Chlothair II, where his brother Waldalenus became chancellor. In 625 both retired from the court to the area of Cusance for a life of piety. About 627, Erminfrid entered the Celtic monastic life at LUXEUIL. When he inherited the empty nunnery at Islia in Cusance, EUSTACE OF LUXEUIL had him restore the edifice and reestablish monastic life there for men, making it a priory attached to Luxeuil. Erminfrid lived at Cusance, in Franche-Comté (present-day Department of Doubs), to an advanced age and was buried there near his brother.

Feast: Sept. 25.

Bibliography: EGILBERT OF CUSANCE, *Vita, Acta Sanctorum* Sept. 7:106–113. T. W. DAVIDS, *A Dictionary of Christian Biography,* ed. W. SMITH and H. WACE, (London 1877–1887) 2:181. A. M.. ZIMMERMANN, *Kalendarium Benedictinum: Die Heiligen und Seligen des Benediktinerorderns und seiner Zweige* (Metten 1933–1938) 3:101–103. G. BARDY, *Catholicisme* 4:389. J. MARILIER, *Dictionnaire d'histoire et de géographie ecclésiastiques* (Paris 1912) 15:751–752.

[J. L. DRUSE]

ERMINOLD OF PRÜFENING, BL.

Abbot; d. Prüfening, Bavaria, Jan. 6, 1121. Erminold came from the Swabian nobility and, as a youth, entered the BENEDICTINE monastery of HIRSAU under Abbot WILLIAM. He took part in the unsuccessful attempt to reform the Abbey of LORSCH (1106–07) and was appointed (1114) by Bishop OTTO OF BAMBERG to be abbot of the newly founded monastery of Prüfening, near Regensburg. There Erminold implemented a strict reform that led to rebellions by his monks, one of whom finally killed him. In 1283 his relics were disinterred and buried in a catafalque surmounted by a reclining effigy. The sculptor was the ''Erminold Master,'' so called from his connection with this statue, an outstanding example of early German Gothic art.

Feast: Jan. 6.

Bibliography: *Vita Erminoldi, Monumenta Germaniae Historica* (Berlin 1826–) division: Scriptore, 12:480–500. J. SYDOW, *Neue deutsche Biographie* (Berlin 1953–) 4:602. A. M. ZIMMERMANN, *Kalendarium Benedictinum: Die Heiligen und Seligen des Benediktinerorderns und seiner Zweige* (Metten 1933–38) 1:49–51. L. HEIDENHAIN, ''Quellen zum Stil des Ermenoldmeisters,'' *Jahrbuch der Preussischen Kunstsammlungen* 48 (1927) 183–208.

[L KURRAS]

ERNEST OF PARDUBICE (PARDUBITZ)

Archbishop of Prague; b. Hostinné Castle (Czech.), *c.* 1297; d. Roudnice, June 30, 1364. After his education at the Benedictine monastery in Broumov and the bishop's school in Prague, he studied Canon Law at the universities of Bologna and Padua. Following ordination he was named canon, then dean (1338) of the St. Vitus Cathedral Chapter in Prague. He was elected bishop of Prague in 1343, and its first archbishop in 1344. His program of reorganizing and reforming his lax clergy was accomplished through a diocesan synod (1343), enforcing regulations against heretics, and a provincial synod (1349), promulgating statutes concerning ecclesiastical life. He innovated *acta consistorii* to improve administrative procedure in the archdiocese, while at the same time, the DEVOTIO MODERNA was working toward an improvement of moral standards for the laity. He was a trusted friend of Emperor Charles IV, and his frequent emissary to the papal court. The foundation of the new St. Vitus Cathedral (1344) and monasteries at Emmaus (1347) and Kladsko, are credited to Ernest. He was responsible for the foundation of Charles University of Prague (1348), and as its chancellor he secured it privileges and financial support. His desire for retirement obviated the proposal that he be a serious candidate for the papacy in 1362.

Bibliography: E. WINTER, *Tausend Jahre Geisteskampf im Sudetenraum* (Salzburg 1938) 57–98. J. K. VYSKOČIL, *Arnošt z Pardubic* (Prague 1947). S. H. THOMSON, ''Learning at the Court of Charles IV,'' *Speculum* 25 (1950) 1–20.

[L. NEMEC]

ERNEST OF ZWIEFALTEN, ST.

Abbot and martyr; d. Mecca, 1148. His origins are unknown, but for five years he was abbot of ZWIEFALTEN in Swabia. He abdicated in 1146 because of the troublesome factions that were disrupting the life of the monastery. He undertook a pilgrimage to the Holy Land in the retinue of Bishop OTTO OF FREISING, who accompanied the crusade of Conrad III. Legend has it that Ernest was cruelly tortured by the Saracens in MECCA. He is commemorated in Zwiefalten as a martyr, and his cult exists but has never been officially recognized. There are a vita and a *passio* dating from the end of the 12th century [*Acta Sanctorum* (Paris 1863) (1910) Nov. 3:605–617], and he is represented in a large statue and two wall paintings in the abbey church

Feast: Nov. 7.

Bibliography: *Annales maiores Zwifaltenses, Monumenta Germaniae Scriptores* (Berlin 1825) 10:55–56. *Acta Sanctorum* Nov. 3:608–617. A. M.. ZIMMERMANN, *Kalendarium Benedictinum: Die Heiligen und Seligen des Benediktinerorderns und seiner Zweige* (Metten 1933–1938) 3:272–275. H. TÜCHLE, *Kirchengeschichte Schwabens,* 2 v. (Stuttgart 1952–54) 1:245. J. N. HAUNTINGER, *Reise durch Schwaben und Bayern im Jahre 1784,* ed. G. SPAHR

(Weissenhorn 1964). J. E. STADLER and F. J. HEIM, *Vollständiges Heiligenlexikon,* 5 v. (Augsburg 1858–82) 2:87.

[G. SPAHR]

EROTIC LITERATURE

In its widest sense, erotic literature includes all writing that deals to a conspicuous degree with sex and love. Under this norm, there is a vast body of literature that treats these themes from an integral human point of view; that is, sex and love are conceived not merely in terms of their physical aspects, but also as manifestations of the spirit. In this type of literature, the physical is generally quite subordinate to the spiritual aspect. Even when physical details are quite frankly portrayed, they are nevertheless caught up in a total atmosphere that provides aesthetic pleasure, and not sensual titillation. Emotionally immature readers may, of course, read merely to satisfy an unhealthy curiosity, but a sound judgment of the work itself, and of the author's intention as far as it is evident in the work, would conclude that the work is not of its nature seductive or sexually stimulating. Often, as a matter of fact, the very realism of the physical details is a necessary element in bringing alive to the reader the deeper spiritual aspects of the story. Romeo's raptures over Juliet's physical beauty are certainly sensuous, but it would be a most insensitive reader who would think that Romeo did not see much more in Juliet than merely her physical attractions.

Pornography. It can be said that almost all the great literature in the world, and certainly the vast bulk of literature that deals with human relations, is of this erotic type, for the simple reason that love and sex are among the greatest dynamic forces in human life. When these forces get out of hand in literary treatment, they tend to degenerate into writing that is pornographic or obscene. The common quality that runs through all pornographic and obscene writings is emphasis on the physical aspects of sex and love, or on what should be private physical functions, to an extent that makes them the dominant, if not the exclusive, impression on the normal reader. As a result, sex and love become dehumanized and not infrequently disgustingly animalistic. This quality of pornographic writing can often be discerned as the author's deliberate intention (in the so-called ''hard-core'' pornography); but even when the author's intention is not evident, the quality may be manifest by the very nature of the work itself. It is often argued that in works wherein the author's pornographic intent is not evident the literary quality is frequently of such excellence as to make them genuine art and therefore immune from any CENSORSHIP. A sounder view would be that works whose chief, if not exclusive, appeal is to sensuality cannot be works of literary merit.

> Sensual art can very well be great art. Every art is sensual to a certain degree, and it is easy to see that in many arts the sensual is strongly emphasized. But art whose intention is to arouse the senses cannot be great art. On the contrary, the more this is its purpose, the more decidedly it deserts service for the sake of servility or slavery, the further it is from being art at all. Rubens was an artist; the illustrations in an indecent humor magazine are not art, no matter how well they are drawn. Between Boccaccio and Aristophanes and the pornographic novel lies all the difference in the world. [Van der Leeuw, 279.]

PORNOGRAPHY certainly includes all those works that of their nature tend to arouse in the normal reader illicit physical reactions or sexual fancies that of their nature result in such physical reactions (*see* PLEASURE; THOUGHTS, MORALITY OF). Theoretically, and for the sake of precision in argument, it might be better to restrict the definition of pornography to that type of literature that tends to arouse such physical or psychological reactions (*see* H. C. Gardiner, *Norms for the Novel* [rev. ed. Garden City, N.Y. 1960], 62–67). Practically, however, this is not the common understanding of the meaning of the word, nor is it the scope of the meaning almost universally envisioned in law. All civilized countries have laws against obscenity. Some endeavor to draw a distinction between obscenity and pornography. In Germany, for example, the obscene is defined as that which ''offends grossly against the concept of decency, even if it is not pornographic''; in France the obscene is simply that which is *contraire aux bonnes moeurs;* in Belgium, the obscene is variously described as that which is of a nature to *éviller ouá surexciter des passions sensuelles* or that which is of a nature *à produire, à la simple vue, un sentiment de réprobation.* In Japan, the obscene is that which ''stirs up or excites sexual desire, spoils the normal sexual modesty of the ordinary human being, or is contrary to good sexual morals.'' In other countries the obscene is simply that which is ''indecent,'' ''disgusting,'' ''places undue emphasis on sex or crime,'' ''encourages depravity,'' ''offends decency,'' and so on. One German opinion even includes under a definition of obscenity matter that ''extolls wars or racial hatred'' (*see* N. St. John-Stevas, *Obscenity and the Law* [London 1956] appendix 3, 217–359).

Some authors, and generally those whose own works have been accused of being pornographic, have attempted to distinguish between obscenity and pornography. D. H. Lawrence, for example, who claimed that he was a fierce foe of pornography, defended himself against the charge that some of his own works were obscene on the grounds that the use of obscenity is no moral or artistic wrong. It would seem that he and others like him confuse erotic literature, in the sense defined above, with writings that place undue and even revolting emphasis on sex.

Pornography and Censorship. Be that as it may, one fact seems clear: Pornographic-obscene literature, in common understanding, ranges from that which tends to excite to illicit sexual acts or fantasies, through that which tends to debase sex and marriage (this is generally done when woman is portrayed as merely an object of passion, walled off from any love, sympathy, consideration, or esteem), to writings that arouse a justifiable disgust, such as those that dwell on excremental functions. It is evident that a precise definition of pornography does not emerge from these various approaches to it, and this is exactly where, in so many modern societies, the enforcement of laws against obscenity or pornography runs into great difficulty. The search for exactness of legal definition is generally fruitless and frequently not demanded by the nature of the case. St. Thomas Aquinas, for example, has stated this fact succinctly: ''We must not seek the same degree of certainty in all things. Consequently, in contingent matters, it is enough for a thing to be certain, as being true in the great number of instances, though at times and less frequently it may fail'' (*Ethics* 5.2). And the Supreme Court of the U.S. has echoed this principle: ''This Court has consistently held that lack of precision is not itself offensive to the requirements of due process. . . all that is needed is that the language of definitions conveys sufficiently definite warning as to the proscribed conduct when measured by common understanding and practices'' (*Norms for the Novel,* 79). This statement was issued in connection with the 1956 *Roth v. United States* case, wherein this test to determine obscenity was laid down: ''Whether to the average person, applying contemporary community standards, the dominant theme of the material taken as a whole appeals to prurient interest.'' Justice William J. Brennan, Jr., who wrote the decision, continued:

> These words, applied according to the proper standard of judging obscenity . . . give adequate warning of the conduct proscribed and mark. . .boundaries sufficiently distinct for judges and juries fairly to administer the law. . . . That there may be marginal cases in which it is difficult to determine the side of the line on which a particular fact situation falls is no sufficient reason to hold the language too ambiguous to determine a criminal offense. [*Norms for the Novel,* 79.]

Note should be taken of the fact that the presence of the so-called four-letter words does not necessarily make a piece of writing pornographic or obscene. It is true that these words are frequently used in contexts that are obscene; their use betrays vulgarity and crudity, and circumstances under which they are used may make their use sinful (e.g., deliberate use of them to shock or disedify the young and impressionable), but considered merely in themselves, they would not fall under any definition of pornography. Their use is to be reprobated, without doubt, but for the reason that they are vulgar and crude, and even shocking, not because they are *ispo facto* obscene (*see* SPEECH, INDECENT AND VULGAR).

Despite difficulties of definition for purposes of legal control of obscenity, it is clear that the consensus of thought and the universal operation of law in society recognizes that there is such a thing as pornographic and obscene literature. When a work is recognized as definitely such, public authority has the right and the duty to exercise prudent censorship.

See Also: CENSORSHIP OF BOOKS (CANON LAW).

Bibliography: N. ST. JOHN-STEVAS, *Obscenity and the Law* (London 1956). T. J. MURPHY, *Censorship: Government and Obscenity* (Baltimore 1963). M. MEAD, ''Sex and Censorship in Contemporary Society,'' in *New World Writing* (New York 1953). C. R. HEWITT, ed., *Does Pornography Matter?* (London 1961). G. VAN DER LEEUW, *Sacred and Profane Beauty: The Holy in Art,* tr. D. E. GREEN (New York 1963). D. H. LAWRENCE, *Sex, Literature, and Censorship* (New York 1953). H. C. GARDINER, *Norms for the Novel* (rev. ed. Garden City, N.Y. 1960). E. PARTRIDGE, *Shakespeare's Bawdy* (New York 1948).

[H. C. GARDINER]

ERRÁZURIZ Y VALDIVIESO, CRESCENTE

Chilean priest, archbishop, and historian; b. Santiago, CHILE, Nov. 28, 1839; d. there, June 5, 1931. Errázuriz was born into one of Chile's most aristocratic and prominent families of Basque origin, and as a youth was considered by many to lack the temperament to become a distinguished priest. Raised in the mid-19th century when the Church-State controversy was waxing bitter and when his uncle Rafael Valentín Valdivieso y Zañartu was the iron-willed archbishop of Santiago (1845–74), Errázuriz appeared to be too moderate and equable in character, too much the dispassionate scholar, to become the polemicist that clerical leaders at the time, according to the view of many, had to be.

Once ordained, Errázuriz, who suffered frequently from bad health, was content to be a rather inconspicuous and often ignored clergyman. Originally a Dominican, he soon left that order and took up his duties as a secular priest. With enthusiasm he began to study and to write on Chilean Church and colonial history. His historical

Crescente Errázuriz Y Valdivieso.

studies, beginning to appear in the 1870s, refuted the charges of Spanish depravity during the colonial past that had been spread by such liberal, anticlerical Chilean writers as Diego Barros Arana, Miguel Luis Amunátegui, and José Victorino Lastarria. Diligent in his research and objective in his evaluations, Errázuriz found much that was worthy of admiration in Chile's past. Along with history, Errázuriz dedicated himself to journalism, founding in 1874, and becoming the first director of, the newspaper *El Estandarte Católico.* As a journalist charged with defending the Church position on all issues, he disliked having frequently to publish harsh criticisms of old friends.

Church-State Controversy. The relatively obscure clergyman was nominated in 1919 by Pres. Juan Luis Sanfuentes as archbishop of Santiago. The nomination, which was duly approved, had been suggested by the long-time leader of the moderate wing of the Liberal party, Eliodoro Yáñez. Rightly foreseeing that within the next few years the issue of separation of Church and State, which had been under debate for decades, would have to be resolved, Yáñez felt that the times demanded a primate of unusual tolerance, moderation, and wisdom. With the majority of the clergy issuing extreme statements and predicting the moral ruin of Chile if separation occurred, Archbishop Errázuriz himself was for a time swept along by the tide of rising passions. On April 24, 1923, he issued a pastoral admonishing all Catholics to reject *in toto* the attempt to separate Church and State. Such a move, the prelate insisted, would signify an affront to God, a public and solemn declaration on the part of Chileans that God did not exist. Despite this stand, a new constitution providing for Church-State separation was approved in 1925, even though a majority of the registered electorate, for a variety of reasons, boycotted the constitutional plebiscite. Once the new constitution was officially sanctioned, the Chilean hierarchy decided to accept defeat gracefully. The prelates issued a joint pastoral that, reflecting the wishes of the archbishop, expressed the hope for the future safety of the Church and concluded with the confident prediction that the Chilean state would refrain from such acts of persecution as had already been unleashed by separation in other countries.

Fascist Influences. In the late years of his life Errázuriz found grounds for cooperation with dictator Carlos Ibáñez del Campo (1927–31). Avoiding totalitarian expedients, Ibáñez decided against establishing state control over the entire educational structure. In a number of ways he encouraged the expansion of a Church-controlled, private educational system. Errázuriz was highly pleased by this and also came to admire the corporate state ideology that Ibáñez, under the influence of Primo de Rivera and Mussolini, began to advocate. The Errázuriz views on fascism were reflected in the Feb. 16, 1929, edition of the official organ of the Chilean hierarchy, *La Revista Católica.* Not only had Mussolini managed to route the defenders of pseudodemocracy, stated the *Revista;* he had also crushed the doctrines and the parties of international Masonry.

In their concern with the Communist menace, a large majority of the more influential churchmen in Chile had by this time come to accept fascism as a desirable social, political, and economic system, and it was not surprising that the archbishop, in his late 80s, went along with this development, which was by no means without its positive features. Errázuriz cooperated wholeheartedly with the paternalistically administered social reform programs that Catholic Action groups, most of them under the influence of fascist ideology, began to advance in the mid-1920s. Happily death spared Errázuriz the ordeal of witnessing the extremes of violence and racism into which an originally benign Chilean fascism evolved with the rise in that country of a National Socialist or Nazi movement.

However valuable his contributions in preserving calm in the troubled 1920s, Errázuriz's most important role in Chile may, in the final analysis, have been that of historian. By showing a new generation of intellectuals that they could properly feel pride in Chile's colonial past, he helped provide the basis for an integral nationalism and corrected many of the errors of excessively partisan historians. The best insight into the nature of Errázuriz is provided by his autobiographical memoirs, *Algo de lo qué he visto* (posthumous, Santiago de Chile 1934). Among his many historical works appear: *Don García de Mendoza, 1557–61* (1916); *Historia de Chile sin governador: 1554–57* (1912); *Historia de Chile: Pedro de Valdivia* (2 v. 1916); *Orígines de la Iglesia chilena* (1873); and *Seis años de la historia de Chile, 1598–1605* (2 v. 1908).

[F. B. PIKE]

ERRINGTON, GEORGE, BL.

Martyr; b. *c.* 1554 at Hirst (or Herst), Northumberland, England; d. Nov. 29 1596, hanged, drawn, and quartered at York, England. He served as a courier and escort for Catholics traveling between the northeast of England and the Continent, which had to be accomplished furtively. He was imprisoned in the Tower of London from 1585–87 and at York Castle in 1591 and 1593–94, but released. When Errington was again arrested for recusancy and imprisoned at York, a Protestant minister came to him, feigning an interest in Catholicism. Errington was tricked into attempting to persuade the minister to convert. For this reason he was condemned with BB. William KNIGHT and William GIBSON for ''persuading to popery.'' Errington was beatified by Pope John Paul II on Nov. 22, 1987 with George Haydock and Companions.

Feast of the English Martyrs: May 4 (England).

See Also: ENGLAND, SCOTLAND, AND WALES, MARTYRS OF.

Bibliography: R. CHALLONER, *Memoirs of Missionary Priests,* ed. J. H. POLLEN (rev. ed. London 1924). J. H. POLLEN, *Acts of English Martyrs* (London 1891).

[K. I. RABENSTEIN]

ERROR

Truth is commonly defined as the conformity between intellect (knowledge) and reality. As the contrary of truth, error may be defined as a lack of conformity between knowledge and reality. Error is related to FALSITY as the specific to the generic: Falsity may be ontological (falsity in things—possible only in an improper sense); moral (falsity in speech—LYING); or logical (falsity in thought—error). Thus error is logical falsity. As lack of conformity, error is to be distinguished from IGNORANCE, which is defined as lack of knowledge.

Error is positive or negative. Positive error distorts reality. Negative error fails to detect some aspect of reality but does not distort it. If the undetected reality is not connaturally knowable, the error is merely negative. If it is, the error is privative. Thus to judge that white is black is positive error. Not to hear sound waves below a minimum frequency is merely negative error. Not to see a certain color in the spectrum under normal conditions is privative error.

Cognitive powers are naturally ordered to TRUTH. Yet error is possible because KNOWLEDGE is not mere passive reception but an active synthesizing and interpreting of innumerable, diverse data. Among the cognitive acts, JUDGMENT is subject to positive error; under the influence of faulty judgment, conceptualization also is subject to positive error; external sense perception is not subject to positive error. As inherently finite, all cognitive powers are subject to merely negative error; and if a given power is indisposed or poorly applied, to privative error. Error of judgment is error in the strictest sense of the term.

The cause of error is the knower's precipitancy in making unwarranted judgments under the influence of passion, prejudice, haste, inattention, and the like. Avoiding error therefore requires serious effort to attain genuine EVIDENCE and careful vigilance to avoid influences other than evidence when making judgments. As an influence on VOLUNTARITY, error is equivalent in effect to ignorance. Error also has moral relevance in that man's actual sins presuppose an error of judgment equating apparent good with true GOOD.

See Also: INTELLECT; SENSES; CONSCIENCE; ERROR, THEOLOGICAL.

Bibliography: R. P. PHILLIPS, *Modern Thomistic Philosophy,* 2 v. (Westminster, Md. 1948) 2:120–124. F. VAN STEENBERGHEN, *Epistemology,* tr. M. J. FLYNN (2d ed. rev. New York 1949) 172–176. P. COFFEY, *Epistemology*, 2 v. (New York 1917; reprint 1958) 2:366–371. J. GREDT, *Elementa philosophiae Aristotelico-Thomisticae,* ed. E. ZENZEN, 2 v. (13th ed. Freiburg im Br. 1961) 2:681–684. E. VALTON, *Dictionnaire de théologie catholique,* ed. A. VACANT, 15 v. (Paris 1903–50; Tables générales 1951–) 5.1:435–446. L. W. KEELER, ''St. Thomas's Doctrine Regarding Error,'' *The New Scholasticism* 7 (1933) 26–57.

[J. B. NUGENT]

ERROR, THEOLOGICAL

One of the theological censures, i.e., one of the pejorative judgments that indicate a proposition is in some way opposed or harmful to faith or morals. In condemning many propositions of QUESNEL, a censure used by Clement XI was that of ''error'' (H. Denzinger, *Enchiridion symbolorum* 2502). Theologians distinguish various erroneous propositions and speak of them as involving an error in divine faith, in ecclesiastical faith, in Catholic doctrine, or in theology. This last censure, theological error, is generally applied to a proposition that is directly opposed to a strict theological conclusion from a revealed premise. Thus, to maintain that Christ is not capable of laughter would be a theological error.

Rashness is a censure inferior to that of theological error. It is usually applied to a proposition that contravenes a thesis that is not a strict theological conclusion but is well grounded and commonly held by theologians.

See Also: NOTES, THEOLOGICAL.

Bibliography: *Sacrae theologiae summa*, ed. FATHERS OF THE SOCIETY OF JESUS, PROFESSORS OF THE THEOLOGICAL FACULTIES IN SPAIN (Madrid 1962) 1.3:884–913.

[E. J. FORTMAN]

ERTHAL, FRIEDRICH KARL JOSEPH AND FRANZ LUDWIG VON

Friedrich Karl Joseph, prince elector and archbishop of Mainz, primate of Germany and chancellor of the Empire (1774–1802); b. Mainz, Jan. 3, 1719; d. Aschaffenburg, July 25, 1802. He studied at Mainz, Würzburg, and Reims, and became a canon of the cathedral of Mainz (1753) and rector of the university (1754). In 1774 he was elected archbishop of Mainz as well as prince archbishop of Würzburg, but he resigned the latter office in favor of his brother Franz. Karl was most gifted, but worldly, and favorable to the ENLIGHTENMENT. His episcopalist tendencies found expression in the Congress of EMS. As a result of the FRENCH REVOLUTION he lost his territories on the Rhine, and was expelled from Mainz.

Franz Ludwig, prince bishop of Würzburg and Bamberg (1779–95); b. Lohr am Main, Sept. 16, 1730; d. Würzburg, Feb. 14, 1795. After studying theology at Mainz, Würzburg, and Rome, and jurisprudence at Vienna, he was appointed president of the secular administration of the cathedral chapter of Würzburg (1763). In 1779 he was elected unanimously to the double episcopal see of Würzburg and Bamberg. He was loyal to Rome, held strict ecclesiastical views, was solicitous for good training for his clergy, promoted the SPIRITUAL EXERCISES of St. IGNATIUS, and was a zealous preacher and a tireless visitator of both his dioceses. In secular matters he reformed the school system, penal law and administration, and took special care of the poor. To his worldly brother, the prince elector, he proposed the ideal of a ruler in his *Principles of Government,* an ideal that he himself strove to realize completely.

Bibliography: Friedrich Karl Joseph. L. VEZIN, *Die Politik des Mainzer Kurfürsten F. K. von Erthal vom Beginn der Französischen Revolution bis zum Falle von Mainz* (Bonn 1932). Franz Ludwig. F. LEITSCHUH, *L. von Erthal: Fürstbischof von . . . Bamberg, Herzog von Franken* (Bamberg 1894). H. RAAB, *Lexikon für Theologie und Kirche* 2 3:1055–56 bibliog.

[F. MAASS]

ESBJÖRN, LARS PAUL

Pioneer Swedish Lutheran in America; b. Hälsingland, Sweden, Oct. 16, 1808; d. Ostervala, Sweden, July 2, 1870. He was a graduate of Uppsala University and taught school and served as pastor in his homeland for 17 years, during which he was influenced by Pietistic revivalism. Impressed by reports of the spiritual destitution of the Swedes who were then beginning to migrate to America in large numbers, he crossed the Atlantic in 1849 and settled in Illinois. There and in adjacent states he gathered Swedish immigrants into congregations. With other clergymen from Sweden he united these congregations into the Augustana Synod (1860). In the same year, persuaded that the future of Swedish LUTHERANS in America required a native ministry, he helped found Augustana College and Seminary in Chicago (later in Rock Island, Ill.) and was made its president. In his early years in America Esbjörn had fellowship with Methodists because of his own background in Pietistic revivalism, but he resisted proselytizing among Swedish immigrants by Methodists, Baptists, and Episcopalians and in the process became more self-consciously Lutheran in doctrine and practice. Worn out by his labors he returned to Sweden in 1863, where he spent his last seven years as a parish minister.

Bibliography: S. RÖNNEGÅRD, *Prairie Shepherd: Lars Paul Esbjörn,* tr. G. E. ARDEN (Rock Island, Ill. 1952). O. N. OLSON, *The Augustana Lutheran Church in America: Pioneer Period, 1846–1860* (Rock Island, Ill. 1950).

[T. G. TAPPERT]

ESCH, NICHOLAS VAN

Mystical theologian; b. Oosterwijk, Holland, 1507; d. Diest, July 19, 1578. He studied in the College of Pope Adrian VI in Louvain, was ordained priest in 1530, and settled in Cologne. There he tutored and taught philosophy. He had great influence intellectually and spiritually over a group of university students, among them Peter CANISIUS. He was devoted to the Carthusian Order and lived at several different times in the monastery, although his weak health prevented his becoming a member of the order. In 1538 he became pastor at Diest, where he was in charge of the Beguines of St. Catherine. He founded several diocesan seminaries according to the rules of the Council of Trent, and he contributed to the reform of many monasteries and convents by letters, counsel, and visits, on his own initiative or by order of the bishops. His spiritual doctrine, deeply rooted in his own period, was influenced by THOMAS À KEMPIS, Gerard GROOTE, Meister ECKHART, Johannes TAULER, HENRY SUSO, etc. Among his literary works are *Introductio in vitam introversam,* which is the introduction to *Templum animae* (Antwerp 1563) and *Exercitia theologiae mysticae* (Antwerp 1563).

Bibliography: H. HURTER, *Nomenclator literarius theologiae catholicae* 3:133. HERMES in *Wetzer und Welte's Kirchenlexikon,* 12 v. (Freiburg 1882–1903) 4:888–889. D. A. STRACKE in *Ons geestelijk erf* 25 (1951) 59–90. P. GROOTENS, *ibid.* 31 (1957) 51–71. A. AMPE, *ibid.* 32 (1958) 303–330; *Dictionnaire de spiritualité ascétique et mystique* 4:1060–66. A. F. MANNING, *Lexikon für Theologie und Kirche*, ed. J. HOFER and K. RAHNER (Freiburg 1957–65) 3:1109.

[M. M. BARRY]

ESCHATOLOGISM

The explanation of the life and mission of Jesus Christ in terms of His alleged expectation of the full realization of the visible reign of God on earth in the immediate future through His own messianic activity.

In 1892 the German scholar Johannes Weiss published his pioneer work, *Die Predigt Jesu vom Reiche Gottes,* which won for him the distinction of being one of the founders of the "eschatological school." According to J. Weiss, Jesus simply adopted the apocalyptic attitude of His contemporaries. Their eager anticipation of the DAY OF THE LORD was greatly intensified by the preaching of JOHN THE BAPTIST. Gradually Jesus' messianic self-consciousness convinced Him that it would be His own mission that would bring about the coming of the KINGDOM OF GOD in power; this was confirmed by Peter's confession (Mt 16.16). All of the events of Christ's life are viewed by J. Weiss from this perspective.

At the turn of the century another German theologian, Albert Schweitzer, carried this thesis to its logical though extreme conclusion. He maintained that Jesus—firmly convinced that God's judgment on the world was imminent—had no intention of founding a church: such an institution presupposed an extended period of time. Indeed, Jesus did not even look upon Himself as a moral teacher or as the MESSIAH; He saw His earthly task as merely outlining the conditions for entry into the kingdom in the very near future when He would return as the heavenly SON OF MAN. Schweitzer considered the Sermon on the Mount and the other ethical statements of Jesus as provisional, much as a captain's orders to the crew of a sinking ship. The delay of the expected divine intervention forced Him to include His own martyrdom in His plan to precipitate the coming of the kingdom.

Schweitzer expressed these ideas in a book entitled *Von Reimarus zu Wrede: Eine Geschichte der Leben-Jesu-Forschung* (1906). Though actually an attempt to save the "historical" Jesus from the morass of 19th-century rationalism, this work concluded skeptically that the real Jesus cannot be found in the Gospels, but only through personal encounter in the toils and conflicts of His service.

Other scholars, such as M. Werner and R. Otto, were to take up his thesis. Alfred LOISY [*L'Évangile et l'église* (1902), *Autour d'un petit livre* (1903)] used this approach in an attempt to prove a purely natural origin of the NT as a Christian apology for the failure of the expected reign of God to materialize. J. Munck, the Danish scholar, further tried to show that St. Paul shared Jesus' messianic expectation to the extent of concluding that it was his (Paul's) preaching to the Gentiles on which the final consummation of all things depended.

Besides ignoring the many statements of Christ that speak of the presence of the kingdom, this Schweitzerian "unrealized (or consequent) eschatology" nullifies such basic dogmas as the Incarnation, hypostatic union, Redemption, and grace; it denies as well the VISIBILITY OF THE CHURCH. W. D. Davies, a Congregational minister, showed that to connect Jesus with a sectarian apocalyptic movement is "to sever [Him] from the main stream of Judaism." He pointed out, moreover, that the Synoptic Gospels do not support this viewpoint because (1) Jesus' insistence on a strict moral code is too emphatic to pass for an interim ethic; (2) His apocalyptic imagery is borrowed from the OT, not from current apocalypses; and (3) to categorize Christ as a deluded visionary does violence to the Gospel portrayal of Him as "one having authority" (Mt 7.29; cf. 13.54).

Opposed to this futurist interpretation of the life of Jesus is the other extreme sometimes designated as the school of "realized eschatology." Its foremost spokesman in the English-speaking world was C. H. Dodd. Although he did not deny the existence of a future life with God, he saw a perfect fulfillment of the messianic hope in the earthly ministry of Christ. By imitating His obedience, His followers can make the kingdom ''come'' for themselves and attain its fruition. Dodd did not carry this position as far as did the disciples of A. RITSCHL, who equated the kingdom preached by Jesus with the development of man's religious sentiment.

Contrasting with both of these opposing viewpoints is that of the moderate eschatology held by the majority of Christian scholars. Blending realization with unrealization, this position sees Jesus as teaching that the kingdom of God would experience two levels of fulfillment: (1) a genuine but partial fulfillment through His Passion and Resurrection in the conquest of Satan, sin, and death shared sacramentally with His followers; and (2) a future level of perfect fulfillment at the PAROUSIA, when He will reappear in glory to judge mankind and to inaugurate the other-worldly, spiritual phase of the kingdom.

See Also: CHURCH, ARTICLES ON; HOPE OF SALVATION (IN THE BIBLE); MESSIANISM; PEOPLE OF GOD.

Bibliography: F. J. SCHIERSE, *Lexikon für Theologie und Kirche*, ed. M. BUCHBERGER, 10 v. (Freiburg 1930–38) 3:1098–99. J. BONSIRVEN, *The Theology of the New Testament,* tr. S. F. L. TYE (Westminster, Md. 1963) 140–152. W. D. DAVIES, *Christian Origins and Judaism* (Philadelphia 1962) ch. 2, 8. C. H. DODD, *The Parables of the Kingdom* (rev. ed. New York 1961). R. OTTO, *The Kingdom of God and the Son of Man,* tr. F. V. FILSON and B. LEE-WOOLF (rev. ed. London 1943). R. SCHNACKENBURG, *God's Rule and Kingdom,* tr. J. MURRAY (New York 1963). A. SCHWEITZER, *The Mystery of the Kingdom of God,* tr. W. LOWRIE (New York 1950).

[M. K. HOPKINS]

ESCHATOLOGY, ARTICLES ON

The general articles in eschatology are: ESCHATOLOGY (IN THE BIBLE); ESCHATOLOGY (IN THEOLOGY). Classically, eschatology was the science of the four last things: death, judgment, heaven, and hell. Individual articles on these topics include DEATH (IN THE BIBLE); DEATH (THEOLOGY OF); DEATH, PREPARATION FOR; JUDGMENT, DIVINE (IN THE BIBLE); JUDGMENT, DIVINE (IN THEOLOGY); PURGATORY; DEAD, PRAYERS FOR THE; PAROUSIA; END OF THE WORLD; RESURRECTION OF THE DEAD; HEAVEN (IN THE BIBLE); HEAVEN (THEOLOGY OF); BEATIFIC VISION; HELL (IN THE BIBLE); HELL (THEOLOGY OF). Scripture scholarship of the late 19th and 20th centuries focused the question of eschatology on Jesus' preaching of the Kingdom; for the history of this line of thought and its conclusions, see ESCHATOLOGISM; KINGDOM OF GOD. More generally, the meaning of Christian eschatology has been broadened to include the fulfillment of human life and the world not only at death or at the end of history, but as it has been accomplished in Jesus Christ and as it affects the present. This perspective is reflected in such articles as HISTORY, THEOLOGY OF; CREATION; ECOLOGY; THEOLOGY OF HOPE.

[G. F. LANAVE]

ESCHATOLOGY (IN THE BIBLE)

Etymologically, eschatology is the study of the ''last things.'' The difficulty experienced in applying the term in biblical theology stems from the fact that the word ''last'' embodies a more precise concept in modern Western languages than in the categories and thought world of the Bible. ''Last,'' according to Webster's *Third New International Dictionary,* ''designates that which comes at the end of a series; it may imply that no more will follow.'' The variety of viewpoints within the Bible itself can be classified according to the manner in which this ''last in the series'' is envisaged.

General Considerations

Some of the ancient Biblical writers expected a decisive point in history that would end Israel's then-current inconclusive condition and give stable historical existence to the promises that it believed God had given it. Thus, ''last'' for these people meant the complex of events that would mark the end of one historical era and usher in a new one. Some modern scholars refuse to accord the name ''eschatology'' to this outlook. It is, however, the predominant view of the preexilic tradition and already contains within itself the fundamental principle that stands at the basis of all eschatology: that history is incomplete until the moment when God's plan exists fully in its human dimension.

Another Biblical viewpoint looks forward to a Day on which this whole present mode of historical existence will cease in favor of some other ''age'' in which God's rule will be uncontested and supreme. Such an event would necessarily have cosmic repercussions of a much greater extent than those envisaged in the historical eschatology of the first viewpoint, since an end of this age would involve an end of this world as it is now known. This second outlook is called ''cosmic eschatology'' and becomes more prominent in postexilic literature. When the cosmic element is strongly accentuated in a system that tends to stress the dualism between this age and the age to come and to calculate history in terms of periods with the conviction that the ''end'' is imminent, the result is what is known as ''apocalyptic eschatology.'' This type of thinking about the last things characterized late prophetic writing and the intertestamental period. Since all three tendencies shared a common heritage, were composed of much the same elements, and were communicated to the same audience, it is misleading to categorize them too neatly, either chronologically or theologically, into separate compartments. They all witnessed to a unique factor in revealed religion: the conviction that this world of man's experience is destined in and through man for a goal that has been set for it by God and toward which God is directing it.

Biblical Thought Patterns. It has often been noted that modern Western thought categories, e.g., in regard to time and personality, do not coincide with those of the Biblical author [*see* TIME (IN THE BIBLE)]. Though these authors do not present a completely consistent outlook themselves, they do have in common certain characteristics that will be considered briefly before entering upon the main subject.

The most striking feature of this type of thought is the capacity to consider an individual person or thing as the embodiment of a more universal reality and vice versa. Thus, e.g., Israel is both a man and a people (*see* ISRAEL), and the servant of the Lord is both the people Israel and the personal distillation of Israel's vocation (*see* SUFFERING SERVANT, SONGS OF THE). Fundamentally, this ''totality thinking'' is based on an ontological insight into the nature of a concrete universal; and the predication of the total reality, wherever a partial realization of it is discovered, is a form of symbolic analogy. But this procedure is part of an undifferentiated thought process that cannot be expected to conform to the modern more reflective norms of accuracy. In the context of eschatology, there is the interesting example of the term DAY OF THE LORD. This was continually expected to be a definitive event; yet in spite of the fact that many of the aspects of the Day had not been realized, the term was used *post eventum* of the fall of Jerusalem (Lam 1.21; 2.21; Ez 34.12, etc.) while it continued to be predicated as future (Ezekiel ch. 38–39; Jl 2.28–32; etc.).

This same type of thinking can be said to characterize the Israelite views of time. Not only can such words as day, hour, etc., be used with a meaning that is not strictly chronological as is the case in any language, but the very terms in Hebrew for beginning, end, eternity, the end of days, etc., have a relative content that reflects a less objective reference to the world as a norm according to which they are to be judged [*see* WORLD (IN THE BIBLE)]. It might be observed in relation to this view of time that it is not completely foreign to modern philosophical reflections on time that speak of time as ''psychic'' or ''cosmic'' and classify the various depths of time.

Method of Treatment. Modern studies of eschatology usually divide their subject matter into universal or social eschatology and individual eschatology. In the former, they treat of ''the last things'' as they apply to man and his world in general; in the latter, they consider the end of each individual human life in this world. For a more complete treatment of individual eschatology, *see* DEATH (IN THE BIBLE); JUDGMENT, DIVINE (IN THE BIBLE); AFTERLIFE; RESURRECTION OF THE DEAD.

This study traces the historical development of the Biblical concept of eschatology as it acquired greater precision and consistency until it was concentrated in the person and activity of Jesus Christ. For the OT period it follows the standard historical divisions of: preprophetic origins; prophetic teaching in the early, preexilic, and postexilic periods; and the later writings. For the intertestamental period note is made simply of the tendencies and vocabulary that are necessary to understand the NT. For the NT period consideration is given to: the teaching of Jesus; the various accents given to this teaching in the Gospel traditions; Pauline eschatology; and other NT teaching.

In the Old Testament

It seems as though Israel's irrepressible expectation of a future completely ruled by God flows from a consciousness of its own election. This is reflected in Israel's earliest literature.

Preprophetic Origins. The two groups of oracles that are recorded in Genesis ch. 49 (Jacob's Oracles) and Numbers ch. 23–24 (the Oracles of BALAAM) date, in their present form, from the period of the early monarchy and reflect the popular conviction that the promises made to the people by God were then being fulfilled in David and his descendants. The editors who included the poems in the Pentateuch prefaced them by the statement that what is contained therein is to take place ''at the end of days.'' This expression, which is literally ''at the rear of days,'' may reflect a later judgment, that the glories described have yet to be realized. The term is characteristic of later prophetic usage (cf. Is 2.2; Ez 38.16); yet most often it can mean hardly more than ''in times to come'' (cf. Dt 4.30; 31.39). An earlier poem (Judges ch. 5), from the 11th or 12th century B.C., is a victory song celebrating the might of Yahweh and making reference to ''the just deeds of Yahweh'' (Jgs 5.11). Although the term implies some act of judgment on behalf of Israel, such an act could be described as ''just'' only in the context of a covenant relation: a saving act of God is in keeping with the promises made by Him to the people He had chosen (cf. 1 Sm 12.7; Mi 6.5).

The YAHWIST traced the source of this election to God's call of Abraham (Gn 12.1–3) and consistently linked the promise of the land to this mysterious destiny to be a ''blessing'' in his progeny for ''all the tribes of the earth'' (Gn 15.5, 18; 26.3; 28.13). These two factors of land and blessing formed the basis of the Israelites' consciousness of election and provided the foundation for their expectancy of some definitive act of God. In the words of J. Lindblom: ''The historical eschatology originates in the belief in the election of Israel and is unique for the Israelite religion'' [cited by T. Vriezen, *Vetus Testamentum* Supplement 1 (1953) 220, n.1].

Early Prophetic Teaching. Amos, the first prophet whose message has been preserved in writing (*see* AMOS, BOOK OF), built his indictment of the chosen people precisely on the fact of their election (cf. Am 3.2 with Gn 12.1–3). After Amos was convinced that there was no ''turning back'' the doom that threatened not only Israel's enemies but Israel itself (cf. ch. 7–8 with ch. 1–2), he took up the popular expectation of the Day of the Lord and used it to convince his people that they would find themselves among the objects of God's wrath on that Day of Judgment (Am 5.18–20). Perhaps the impact of his discovery led Amos to insist that the decisive event that was to bring about a new historical era would be primarily one of punishment and destruction. Yet even here, the awareness of God's fidelity to his promises forced Amos to hold out a hope that ''it may be'' that a remnant would be rescued (5.4–6, 14–15; and especially 9.11–15, if it is original).

Israel's ingratitude and dullness in the presence of God's loving choice formed the basis for Hosea's conviction of an imminent day of punishment and restoration (*see* HOSEA, BOOK OF). His message to the Northern Kingdom contains a series of threats of unmatched vehemence (Hos 5.14; 10.14–15; 13.7–8; etc.). Yet he sensed the ambiguity of the situation in which a just and angered God cannot act ''reasonably'' because of His love (11.8–9), and thus Hosea's eschatology, like that of Amos, has two aspects. Descriptions of the exact historical consequences of the coming destruction (3.4; 9.4) are found side by side with scathing denunciations of a more general sort (4.4–6; 13.12), and both are balanced against tender promises of restoration (14.2–9) and look to a renewal of the ideal age of the desert wandering and the COVENANT (2.16), as well as to a redundance of this peace into the realm of nature itself (2.23–25). An era is envisaged in which God's spontaneous choice of Israel will be ratified (14.5–9).

Preexilic Prophets. ISAIAH, who saw the fall of the Northern Kingdom, blended in his outlook a realistic, historical actuality with a transcendent sense of divine activity (*see* ISAIAH, BOOK OF). He saw this activity as part of a plan (see especially Is 5.19; 6.9–10; 14.24–27) that necessarily included other nations (since they had to act in regard to Israel), who also would be punished for the same crimes that were bringing about Israel's downfall (2.5–22). This universal outlook was adumbrated by Amos (ch. 2–3), but it became an explicit factor in Isaiah's conviction that, whereas God's judgment on Samaria would be repeated on Jerusalem (Is 28.1–29.6), the whole world stood condemned (14.26–27) and would be restored only through the reinstatement of Jerusalem itself (2.1–4). Isaiah's teaching regarding both aspects of the coming judgment is well typified in the large place he gave to the concept of the Remnant of Israel. This term contained both a threat that some catastrophe was imminent and the assurance that God would be faithful to His promises (1.9). Even granting the antiquity of Gn 49.1–12 and Am 9.11–15, one must still see in Isaiah's connection between the house of David and the light that would shine out of the coming darkness a new note in the prophetic description of God's definitive act in history (Isaiah ch. 7, 9, 11). This conviction was shared by Isaiah's contemporary Micah (Mi 5.1–3) and became part of the prophetic teaching in succeeding generations.

The work of Zephaniah is dependent on the writings of Isaiah and Amos (*see* ZEPHANIAH, BOOK OF); and although there is no new theological contribution in his book, there is in ch. 1 a marked intensity both in the universalism regarding the impending judgment and in Israel's oldest eschatological expectations of a war in which Yahweh would destroy His enemies. In Zephaniah this became the disaster that was about to befall Jerusalem (Zep 1.2–18). Both this intensity and the imagery it evokes became part of later eschatological writing.

JEREMIAH could match the vivid imagery of Zephaniah (*see* JEREMIAH, BOOK OF), and he may indeed have drawn upon the same experience or prophetic tradition in his description of the foe from the north (Jer 4.5–31). He too looked to some definitive event that by then was assumed to include the chastisement of unfaithful Judah. The rise of Babylonian power gave to the generic threats of destruction with which the work abounds a sense of imminence and historical realism. One may, in fact, speak of a sort of ''realized eschatology'' in regard to Jeremiah, who applied all the previous prophetic teaching of a decisive event of divine judgment in history to the actual invasion by NEBUCHADNEZZAR (11.15–17; 15.1–4; 34.8–22; 37.3–10; etc.). It is difficult to establish exactly what Jeremiah thought would happen after the era of judgment, though there is no doubt that he expected that the reprieve promised to those already deported (3.12; 24.5–7) would be extended to the victims of the Babylonian destruction of Jerusalem (32.1–14). Like Isaiah, he built the continuity of the people on an ideal Davidic king (23.1–13, of which at least the core is original); but his own insight consisted in seeing that the reestablishment of Israel would mean the renewal of the covenant in a way that would truly change the hearts of men (31.31–34).

Exilic and Postexilic Prophets. Important developments in Israelite eschatology took place during the Babylonian Exile and in the early postexilic period, as can be seen in the writings of Ezekiel [*see* EZEKIEL, BOOK OF] and the anonymous author of Isaiah ch. 40–55, who is known as Deutero–Isaiah.

Ezekiel. Like Jeremiah, Ezekiel prophesied and witnessed the fall of Jerusalem and saw in it the decisive act of condemnation. Yet one can trace in those writings of Ezekiel that were composed in exile a greater sense of imminence, not only in regard to the traditionally expected judgment on other nations (ch. 25–32), but also in regard to the restoration of Israel that had formed part of the eschatological drama since the teaching of Amos. There is mention of a Davidic ''shepherd'' who would lead the restored people (Ez 34.17–24; 37.24–25) and the insistence that restoration would mean an interior conversion (36.26–27; see also 11.19–20). The accent, however, was placed more on the Temple as the center of the people's life (ch. 40–46), from which there would flow a life-giving stream to all the world (47.1–12). Israel would thus become the ruler of a chastened world (36.1–8, 36–38), and the promise made to the fathers would at last become a reality (47.13–23).

Though the dramatic vision of the resurrection of the dry bones (ch. 37) ought not to be understood in an individual sense, still the problem of individual responsibility was posed by Ezekiel (18.1–32) at about the same time as by Jeremiah (Jer 31.29), and the problem was treated more completely by Ezekiel. There was not yet any direct eschatological application of this individualistic view, though the experience of some men of prayer in Israel had already prepared the way for a different notion of the state of God's friends in the afterlife [Ps 15(16).10; 72(73).25–26]; and the Book of JOB, written in the experience of the exile, challenged the accepted view of RETRIBUTION.

Deutero-Isaiah. This inspired prophet, who wrote at the end of the Exile, seems to have been convinced that the destruction of Jerusalem and the exile constituted the decisive act of judgment foreseen by Jeremiah and Ezekiel. Just as Babylon's growing ascendancy had been the sign of God's impending wrath, so the rise to power of Cyrus and his Persian armies gave historical content to the predictions of a consolation soon to follow.

Deutero-Isaiah was the first to appeal, not only to a plan of God, but also to a notion of time that saw it as having a beginning and an end (Is 41.22–23, 26; 43.13; 46.9; etc.). This plan included the salvation of all the nations and would be brought about by the servant of the Lord, whose mission it was to be a light to the Gentiles and proclaim God's justice to the ends of the earth and whose mysterious suffering and exaltation would bring peace to the many. Jeremiah had seen the land reverting to a state of primeval chaos (Jer 4.23) and had considered that the covenant relation had been severed (31.31–32). Deutero-Isaiah saw the era of restoration as a new creation of both the world and the people (Is 41.17–20; 42.5; 43.1; 45.8; etc.). A restoration of the world was first adumbrated in Hos 2.23 and Is 11.6–9, while the concept of God creating His people by the covenant seems already implied in the use of *qānâ* in Ex 15.16; Dt 32.6. Yet in Deutero-Isaiah there seems to be a concretization of concepts that were previously left undetermined. What, then, is the meaning of this insistence on a cosmic participation in the restoration of the people? It seems that one must apply here the notion of totality thinking mentioned previously, as well as the fact of what can, perhaps, be best termed ''a sliding time scale.'' The cosmic imagery, whether invoked in terms of destruction or renewal, contains within itself the notion that the definitive events in history are effected by a causality that transcends the world of man's control. Yet this thinking clings fast to the ancient conviction that man's inner life has, for good or ill, cosmic repercussions (cf. Gn 3.8–19). It may be granted that Deutero-Isaiah was here writing poetry and using a traditional imagery repeated for its power to evoke an atmosphere rather than propound a dogma; yet it would be false to empty the imagery of all content. Something transcendent is being mediated and certain historical events deserve to be called by its name. Only time can decide whether or not the event that is imminent or even present is in fact the definitive act of God. Not all of what Amos or Hosea or Zephaniah had foretold came to pass; and though the historical nucleus of what Isaiah and Jeremiah expected had in fact transpired, what was described by them as universal (Is 2.2–5) and indeed cosmic (Jer 4.23–26) had not been realized. As men became progressively convinced of the human unattainability of restoration, they looked forward to an event more transcendent than ever.

The sense of actuality that Deutero-Isaiah had initiated primarily in regard to the restoration of Israel was continued and applied more specifically to the expected punishment of the nations. Oracles against the nations had been part of prophetic eschatological preachings since Amos. Yet as the conviction grew that Israel had undergone its judgment and was about to be reinstated, the expectation of a more widespread catastrophe became vivid. Whereas in Isaiah ch. 13 (postexilic) the notion of the holy war and the Day of the Lord is applied to Babylon and in Abdia the same concept is applied to Edom (Abd 15), in both of these writings the aid of cosmic imagery is enlisted, most probably for the reasons mentioned above.

Postexilic Writings. After the Exile, prophecy continued, both in its own right and in the editing and glossing of the older prophetic writings. The disappointment that accompanied the return from Exile forced men to reconsider the full implication of what these older books had taught. Babylon had indeed fallen, and the people had indeed returned to Jerusalem. But there was no miraculous exodus, no universal destruction of the sinful nations who were Israel's enemies, and no worldwide recognition of the might of Yahweh with pilgrimages to a glorious Jerusalem.

Early Postexilic Writers. Haggai and Zechariah [*see* HAGGAI, BOOK OF; ZECHARIAH, BOOK OF] continued to expect the rebuilding of Jerusalem and to look for an anointed ruler (Hg 2.20–23; Zec 6.9–14). Besides, Zechariah introduced a type of symbolism in ch. 1–2 that was later taken up by Daniel and became standard in apocalyptic writing. Joel continued to apply the term ''Day of the Lord'' to judgments against the chosen people (ch. 1–2), while he expected the spiritual renewal spoken of by Jeremiah and Ezekiel and the great judgment of the nations (ch. 3–4). Both of these events were to reveal their transcendent nature by the effects they would have on the cosmos.

Later Postexilic Writers. Trito-Isaiah (the anonymous author of Isaiah ch. 56–66) took these concepts to their limit by ''objectifying'' their cosmic elements and describing a new heaven and a new earth (Isaiah ch.65–66). Deutero-Zechariah (the anonymous author of Zechariah ch. 9–14) developed the mythical elements in Ezekiel ch. 38–39 and applied them to his contemporaries' experience (Za 14.1–21). The collection of oracles known as Malachi [*see* MALACHI, BOOK OF] included more teaching regarding the judgment soon to overtake the nations surrounding Jerusalem, and it inaugurated the notion (Mal 3.23) that the great and terrible Day of the Lord would be preceded by the return of Elijah [*see* ELIJAH (SECOND COMING OF)].

The postexilic author of Isaiah ch. 24–27 (the so-called Apocalypse of Isaiah) elevated ''Babylon'' and ''Moab'' to the status of symbols, much as Ezekiel and Zechariah had done for Jeremiah's ''foe from the north,'' and again the cosmic imagery is in evidence.

Within a long poetic piece that probably derives from the liturgy (Isaiah ch. 26), there occurs what is perhaps the first statement regarding the resurrection of the just in an eschatological context (Is 26.19). As the tension of waiting increased, the problem of the future of those who died without seeing the consolation of Israel finally forced its way into men's consciousness; and the solution, perhaps already stated by the author of Job (Jb 19.25) in the context of personal retribution, was adopted in this larger context.

Writers of the Late OT Period. This solution was repeated in the Book of DANIEL (Dn 12.1–3), with the addition that the incomplete retribution made to both just and unjust in this life, specifically in relation to the expectation of the ''last things,'' would be made good by a resurrection of some of them from the dead. A different solution of this problem in an individual context, not immediately linked with the future of the nation, was adopted by some adherents of the Alexandrian Judaic tradition (such as the author of the Book of WISDOM) that made use of the Greek concept of an imperishable soul to extend the Hebrew notion of *nepeš,* so that the future of a man after death was differentiated according to the deeds he performed on the earth (Wis 3.1–9; 15.3; etc.). The individualizing tendency in the wisdom tradition seems to have applied terms previously restricted to the events of national history to the life of the individual as the Psalms had already done before them [note the ''time of distress,'' the ''day of wrath,'' etc., in Ps 19(20).2; 49(50).15; Jb 15.23; 21.30; Prv 11.4; Wis 3.18; Sir 11.26; etc.]. This outlook provided the basis for a more developed individual eschatology in the intertestamental period.

In the Book of Daniel there is also a certain stable pattern into which traditional elements of prophetic eschatology were fitted in such a way that a new literary genre was created, which developed and became standardized as the normative presentation of this teaching during the two centuries before Christ. Cosmic imagery and a concept of plan were now combined with a greater emphasis on the transcendent nature of the event that would be definitive for all history. Thus, even the vocation of Israel was now concentrated not in a king or a servant, but in a SON OF MAN whose exaltation would have consequences for ''all peoples, nations, and tongues'' (Dn 7.14). The result was an imaginative literature fraught with the conviction, based on careful calculation, that ''the end is near.'' Daniel, one of the earliest APOCALYPTIC writings, already contained the complex imagery and periodic divisions of history. These were not so much the product of a mind taking refuge in fantasy as an effort of faith to adhere to the promises of God and to render them intelligible and actual to an Israel already painfully aware of its true historical dimensions but not less aware of its special vocation within the universalist demands of God's covenant and of the ultimate truth of its confidence in God's justice.

In the Intertestamental Period

Though prophecy had disappeared in the last centuries of pre-Christian Jewish history (1 Mc 4.46), people still awaited the fulfillment of what Deutero-Isaiah had promised. They looked forward to a glorious Jerusalem, the source of salvation for those nations that were left after God's terrible judgment had punished them for their wickedness, especially for their oppression of the Jews. It has been frequently remarked that what Pharisaic zeal effected in relation to the Law, codifying, standardizing, and materializing it, apocalypticism did for prophecy.

The influence of Persian thought has often been assumed for the purpose of explaining a certain dualism that now characterized eschatological thinking. No doubt there was a real and objective content to the distinction between ''this age'' and ''the age to come'' that capitalized on the ''newness'' of the era of restoration as described by the prophets, and this type of objective thinking was apparently injected into the Jewish view of the cosmos by some outside influence. Yet it should be observed that this factor and others that were manifestly dependent for their form on Persian theories (developed angelology, pronounced forensic elements in the judgment, etc.) were well integrated into the Jewish thought system.

Messianic Expectations. The decisive event was now most frequently called ''the end,'' and it was thought of as preceded by a series of woes and calamities (Dn 12.1; Assumption of Moses 10.5; Enoch 80.4–5; Sibylline Oracles 3.806). According to some writings, the final judgment would be presided over by a MESSIAH, and the wars and cosmic convulsions in which he would assert the kingdom of God were called the ''birthpangs'' of the Messiah (cf. Hos 13.13; Is 26.16–19). Sometimes his efforts would be directed specifically against a figure whose traits were derived from the prophetic development of Gog in Ezekiel ch. 38–39 (see also Dn 7.8–14) and perhaps also from Ahriman (Angra Mainyu), the opponent of Ahura Mazda in the Zoroastrian system [*see* AHURA MAZDA (OHRMAZD) AND AHRIMAN], as in the Testament of Issachar 6.1; Enoch 13.1–58; Sibylline Oracles 3.63–65; IQM 1.1–17 (*see* DEAD SEA SCROLLS). The time of this end was calculated on the basis of a reinterpretation of the prophetic writings (cf. Jer 25.11; 29.10 with Dn 9.2, 24–27), which in turn needed to be reinterpreted when the Day failed to appear (cf. Daniel ch. 7 with 4 Esdras 12.11–14; Dn 12.11–13). The restoration of Israel was most often described in terms of a kingdom, though notions about the nature and function of the king differed considerably. In some systems he was easily recognizable as the Davidic ruler described by the prophets, and he now bore the technical designation Messiah, while in still other systems, God Himself was the king without any intermediary. The writings that stressed the other-worldly aspect of the coming new age tended to clothe this figure with heavenly power and give to him a universal dominion. These two figures, the Messiah and the Son of Man, tended to blend into one; and according to some theories, the messianic kingdom on this earth would be succeeded by another that would mark the final entrance of ''the end'' and initiate the age in which God with or without the Messiah would rule forever. Along with this concept of a heavenly man, mention is made of a heavenly Jerusalem, heavenly Sion, etc., which apparently reflected the notion that present earthly realities were only images of their true types, which in the final age would themselves assume human dimensions (Enoch 10.16–19; Psalms of Solomon 17.25; 2 Baruch 4.2–6; 4 Esdras 10.26). This may be but one more aspect of the very realistic, even material expectation of a new heaven and a new earth (Is ch. 66) in which the reign of Satan over the cosmos would be broken and this world would be destroyed.

Retribution in the Hereafter. The awareness of individual eschatology that can already be found in some of the late prophetic and wisdom literatures now received a great deal more attention, though little systematization. The fundamental experiences that, as was shown, forced the problem of individual immortality to consciousness were: the experience of union with God expressed by the Psalmists [e.g., Ps 72(73).25], the experience of the inconclusive nature of retribution in this life (e.g., in Daniel and Job), and the desire that all should share in the realization of the promises (Is 26.19). These, combined with an extra-Biblical anthropology in the late wisdom literature, provided the basis for some integration of the speculations proposed during the period. Again, thinking centered on the concept of judgment, and thus it maintained an intimate link with the events connected with the coming of the kingdom. According to David S. Russell, (357–366), there were four characteristics that marked the change of climate effected during this period. First, the dead were conceived as having individual and conscious existence. Second, they were distinguished on the basis of moral criteria, and the state in which they found themselves as a result of their moral activity in this life was considered by most as irrevocable (Enoch 62.2; 2 Baruch 85.12; Pirke Avoth 4.16; Sifra Leviticus 85; Enoch 71.14–16). Third, in keeping with the changed views regarding the souls of the dead, SHEOL was now regarded as an intermediate state in which men waited for the final judgment. According to most of these writers, the final judgment could not take place until the resurrection, which was usually conceived of as being universal in its proportions but of differing results depending on a man's moral status. According to the systems that envisaged a messianic interregnum, there were sometimes two judgments and even two resurrections, first of some of the just and then of all the dead. Other works, notably the Book of Jubilees (23.31), seem to have dispensed with the notion of resurrection and consequently of a period of waiting. Sheol then became the place of torment for the wicked (Jubilees 7.29; 22.22). The fourth characteristic of these writings followed from the fact of a moral distinction in the hereafter: Sheol was now depicted as having compartments corresponding to the moral and spiritual condition of the souls that went there. The description of these different parts of Sheol drew upon and embellished prophetic imagery and became the source of Christian apocryphal writings and of centuries of subsequent Christian speculation.

In the New Testament

The eschatological concepts of the NT, whether traditional or newly forged, are all dominated by and center on the fact of Christ. The NT asserts unequivocally that the definitive act of judgment, both salvation and condemnation, has been realized in the Passion and Resurrection of Jesus, and yet it looks forward to a Day when this reality will be made fully manifest in each individual and in the whole cosmos. The synthesis of this twofold assertion into some coherent statement that respects the other aspects of revelation is one of the most difficult and, at the same time, most pressing problems of modern Biblical theology.

Confronted with passages that seem alternately to assert and deny the definitive nature of the Christ fact, its present all-sufficiency and its need for future fulfillment, some scholars have been tempted to achieve some sort of consistency by assigning chronological priority to one series and explaining the other series as later additions to the original teaching of Jesus. For the liberals of the 19th century, Jesus was an ethical teacher of unique stature whose subsequent death was given an eschatological interpretation by His disciples. According to Albert Schweitzer and others, Jesus was a ''consistent eschatologist,'' a successor to the apocalyptic theorists, who believed Himself to be the Son of Man and the inaugurator of God's reign on earth. When even His death failed to bring this about, His disciples reinterpreted His message. Charles Dodd, on the other hand, considers that the eschatological imagery is Jesus' own, and He intended by it to assert that its real meaning was being fulfilled in Himself. His followers, who were expecting a more mundane and perhaps a more dramatic manifestation of the Day of the Lord, were led to the conclusion that it would take place in the immediate future; and then, as time wore on, they either continued in their expectations or finally grasped the original meaning of Jesus' message. Rudolf Bultmann, too, maintains that the eschatological imagery originated with Jesus and was continued by His disciples. But Bultmann is convinced that such imagery was the only conceptual equipment available to Jesus at that time through which God's transcendent message could be understood and mediated. Consequently, it is the role of the interpreter today to free this message of its ancient and mythical garb in order to allow it to confront man and elicit from him faith and submission (*see* DEMYTHOLOGIZING). The analyses of Dodd and Bultmann have shed much light on the nature of many passages in the Gospels and have shown how necessary it is to account for the creative activity of the early community and of the Evangelists themselves in any understanding of the message they have passed on. But there is a danger that the desire to achieve a unified view of the Gospel revelation may result in an oversimplification. In order to respect the nature of the Gospel material, one must recognize that in the original teaching of Jesus there is both a realized and a futurist eschatology and that this tension is preserved by the NT authors who developed their own theologies with the aid of concepts traditional in their culture.

Teaching of Jesus. The general tenor of John the Baptist's preaching centered on the theme of restoration and consolation that Deutero-Isaiah had proclaimed on the eve of the return from Babylon and the notion of an impending messianic judgment spoken of in the Book of Malachi (Mk 1.1–8; Mt 3.1–12; Lk 3.1–8; Jn 1.19–34). St. Mark gives the gist of Jesus' early preaching as ''The kingdom of God has come near'' (Mk 1.15; see also Lk 4.18; 7.22; Mt 4.23). This theme was calculated to evoke in the minds of Jesus' hearers the notion of an imminent fulfillment of the prophetic expectations as they were preserved in the thought of His day.

Imminence of the Kingdom. Early in His public life Jesus pointed to His power over demons as proof of the presence of the kingdom (Lk 11.20; Mt 12.28; see also Mk 3.27). He declared those blessed who beheld Him (Mt 13.16; Lk 10.23); He applied the words of Deutero-Isaiah to Himself (Mt 11.2–6; Lk 7.18–23); and He claimed that one greater than Solomon stood before His audience (Mt 12.41–42; Lk 11.31–32). At His entry into Jerusalem, He consciously acted out the fulfillment of Zec 9.9, a passage that was considered messianic by the rabbis; and He appealed to the eschatological universalism of Is 56.7 as well as to Jer 7.11 to establish His right to cleanse the Temple (Mk 11.15 and parallels; see, however, Jn 2.13–17). When Jesus assumed for Himself the prerogative of reinterpreting the Law (e.g., Mt 5.22), He was aware that such a function was expected of the Messiah (Targum Jonathan on Is 12.3; 1QpHab 10.13; CD 1.11; etc.); and when He likened the kingdom of God to His own activity of sowing the word (Mk 4.1–9 and parallels), foreseeing a slow, mysterious growth of that kingdom (Mk 4.30–32), He was undoubtedly claiming to make it present here and now (see also Lk 17.21).

The most predominant feature of Our Lord's preaching, however, seems to have been His stress on the imminent coming of the kingdom of God. Besides being the theme of His early preaching, there are parables from different times of Jesus' life that echo this preoccupation. Among the more outstanding there are: the parable of the Two Men on the Way to Court (Mt 5.25–26; Lk 12.57–59), the Great Feast (Mt 22.1–13; Lk 14.16–24), the Ten Virgins (Mt 25.1–12), and the Vineyard (Mk 12.1–12 and parallels). The parable of the Vineyard was probably propounded during Jesus' last days in Jerusalem. He looked forward to a crucial day in the near future when the ''Bridegroom'' would be taken away from the Disciples (Mk 2.18–20 and parallels). In Mk 9.1 there is recorded a promise of Jesus to His hearers that some of them would see the kingdom of God come in power, and this is most probably an allusion to His forthcoming Passion and Resurrection. Such is undoubtedly the meaning of the symbolic parable that Jesus enacted at the supper the ''night he was betrayed.'' The meal both initiated and foreshadowed the messianic banquet (Lk 22.16), while drawing its meaning from the Passion and Resurrection, which it symbolized. This theme had already sounded in Our Lord's instruction of His disciples. His predictions of imminent suffering for the Son of Man are described in terms of the vocation of the Servant whose sacrifice of Himself as a sin offering (Is 53.10) brings about His own exaltation and the fulfillment of Israel's mission to proclaim God's justice to the ends of the earth (Mk 10.45; see also the ''Passion predictions'' in Mk 8.31; 9.31; 10.32–34; and parallels). At His trial Jesus asserted that men would soon see this exaltation of the Son of Man as Daniel had described Him (Mk 14.62; see also the interpretations in Mt 26.64; Lk 22.69).

Intervening Period. In addition to some other more enigmatic passages that stress the imminence of the kingdom (e.g., Mt 10.23), there is a whole series of passages that reflect Jesus' awareness that there would be a period of time between His death and the final realization of some aspects of the traditional prophetic and apocalyptic teaching. He called about Him a group of disciples, gave them instructions, taught them to pray for the coming of the kingdom (Mt 6.1), and gave them a commission to proclaim His message and suffer for adherence to Him. Jesus endorsed the prevailing view of a general resurrection (Mt 12.41; see also Lk 14.14) and described some of its features (Mk 12.18–27 and parallels). He often spoke of a day of judgment (Mt 10.15; 11.22, 24; etc.) and described the punishments of the wicked in traditional terms (Mt 5.29; Mk 9.45–47; etc.), while also teaching a judgment that follows immediately after death (Lk 16.19–31; see also 12.20). In all of the statements there is a conformity to the common vocabulary of the time; yet there is also a difference. For not only does Jesus assign to Himself the messianic role of judge (Mt 7.22; Lk 6.26; Mt 25.31–46); but more important, as the passages cited imply, a man's future judgment will depend on his present attitude to Jesus. This is stated explicitly in Mk 8.38 (see also parallels and Lk 17.24–26), and it becomes a standard theme in John (Jn 12.48; 5.24; 3.18–21). Moral rectitude is, of course, necessary for entrance into the kingdom (Mt 5.20); yet the newness of Jesus' eschatological preaching lies precisely in His insistence that the future is determined already in the stand one takes now in regard to Him.

It is practically certain that Jesus predicted the fall of Jerusalem (Lk 19.42–44), and it is very probable that the same event forms the frame of reference for the famous ''eschatological discourse'' found in Mark ch. 13 and parallels. The interpretation of this passage is still debated, but it seems to be a good example of the totality thinking and ''sliding time scale'' mentioned previously. The judgment against Jerusalem is described in terms of the Day of the Lord as the Prophets had often done before, and in this same tradition all the imagery reserved for the definitive event of history is applied to this partial realization of it. Thus St. Matthew already transposes the discourse to the ''PAROUSIA and the consummation of the age'' (Mt 24.3).

Theology of the Early Church. In one of the speeches of Peter recorded in Acts, Joel's description of the Day of the Lord (Jl 2.28–32) is applied to the coming of the Holy Spirit (Acts 2.14–36). Peter stated also that Jesus is the source of this gift of the Spirit (Acts 2.33), that He is the future judge of the living and the dead (Acts 10.42; see also 17.31), and that He will be sent from heaven at the time of the restoration of the universe (Acts 3.19–21, a difficult passage).

The tradition first represented in St. Mark's Gospel combines the predictions of the Passion with a description of the vocation of the disciples (Mk 8.34–37; 9.35; 10.39) and continues this assimilation by describing the future suffering of the disciples (13.9–13) in terms reminiscent of the Passion narrative (14.53–65; 15.4–5, 15; etc.). This mystery of the eschatological sufferings of the Son of Man that are continued in the Church is touched on also by St. Paul (2 Cor 4.10; Col 1.24; see also Jn 15.20–21). St. Matthew has a tendency to transpose the sense of imminence in Our Lord's preaching to the expectation of the Parousia (only he among the Evangelists uses the term). Moreover, he employs many words common to the intertestamental apocalyptic tradition (''regeneration,'' Mt 19.28; ''age to come,'' 12.32; see also 13.40, 49). St. Luke capitalizes on some features of Jesus' teaching to insist that the period between the Passion and the consummation of all things is part of God's eschatological plan: it is the era of the Spirit and the Church (cf. Mk 4.17 with Lk 8.13, and cf. Mk 9.1 with Lk 9.27). This same tendency can be seen in the characteristic way Luke records phrases that are in an eschatological context (cf., e.g., Lk 21.20 with Mk 13.14).

St. John actualizes the theme of judgment, as has been seen (see also Jn 16.8–11), and likewise makes the possession of eternal life a present reality (Jn 6.47, 51; 17.20–21; etc.). While he foresees a future ''last day'' of resurrection (6.39–40, 44; 11.24), he also records Jesus as describing Himself as the resurrection and the life (11.25). John alone alludes to the coming sufferings of the disciples as the ''birth pangs'' of the Messiah (16.21), and he applies the term, it seems, both to the definitive hour of the Passion (cf. 19.28–30) and to the future vocation of the disciples. Even the coming of Christ, which John no doubt expected on the last day, is portrayed as an actual reality for the Christian who lives by Christian love (14.3, 19, 21; 16.16–22). Thus, it seems certain that as the actual time of the Parousia was postponed, Christians began to reflect on the full import of Christ's declarations regarding the presence of the kingdom in His own person and activity and to see this reality continued in the Church by the action of the Spirit.

Pauline Eschatology. This same process of penetration can be seen in the writings of St. Paul, who, though he brought to the problem a mind already enriched by the speculations of the rabbis, still required many years to achieve a synthesis.

Individual Eschatology. Paul's strong accent on individual eschatology can be seen in his first answer to the problem of those Christians who die without witnessing the Parousia. Those who die ''through Jesus'' are not only partakers of the ''age to come'' as the rabbis taught; they are now ''with Jesus'' (1 Thes 4.14; see also Phil 1.23). The same preoccupation can be seen in the discussion of the resurrection body in 1 Corinthians ch. 15. The doctrine regarding some kind of identity between the body ''sown'' and that ''reaped'' can also be found in 2 Baruch 49.3; 50.3–4; Sibylline Oracles 4.181; etc.; but the insistence on the unique causality of the risen Lord is at the core of what is peculiar to Christian eschatology. Alongside these early assurances regarding the future of those who ''are asleep,'' i.e., dead, there is a complete scenario of the Day of the Lord that depends on the same tradition as the eschatological discourse in the Synoptics (cf. 1 Thes 5.2 with Mt 24.43) and shares with it the same sense of imminence. In this early period Paul already laid the foundations of his view that the reality of Christ's Resurrection, as imparted now to the believer, conferred on the latter's life an eschatological dimension. It is because ''Jesus died and rose'' that Christians will be brought together with Him (1 Thes 4.14), a togetherness shared also by those who are still ''awake'' (1 Thes 5.9–10). Indeed the power of His Resurrection is at work in those who share the fellowship of His sufferings (Phil 3.10–11), and this power will eventually enable Christ to subject the universe to Himself (Phil 3.20–21).

Future Day of Christ. These three factors of individual union with Christ, cosmic redemption, and actualized eschatology are already being synthesized around the reality of the risen Christ in the letters of the central period of Paul's life. There is still a future day of Christ (1 Cor 1.8; 5.5; 2 Cor 1.14; etc.), which will be a day of judgment (Rom 2.5, 16), a day on which Christ will be revealed (1 Cor 1.7). The events of that day are sketched in 1 Corinthians ch. 15, and in the same letter Paul speaks of the vision that awaits him when the ''now'' of this life gives way to the ''then'' of full maturity (1 Cor 13.12; see also 1 Jn 3.2–3). The power of the risen Christ is stressed again in 2 Cor 3.18 (see also 4.17–18), and there for the first time occurs the apocalyptic hope of a new creation applied to the individual believer (2 Cor 5.17). In the Epistle to the Romans (1.4) the Resurrection, by which Christ was constituted SON OF GOD, is linked to the same Spirit that Christians now possess as a pledge and are thereby already made sons of God. Because Christians possess the Spirit, they are attuned to the groaning of the whole cosmos as it longs to be free of the corruption imposed on it by the folly of man (8.18–24). And it is the presence of the same Spirit deep within Christians that will one day bring their share in the risen life of Christ into a full and definitive human existence, thus transforming the cosmos by conforming them to the image of the Risen One and fulfilling the eternal plan of God.

The same notions are brought to their final synthesis in the Epistles to the Ephesians and the Colossians. The Church is the ''fullness of Christ'' (Eph 1.23; 3.19; 4.13), within which He is now at work subjecting the cosmos and all its demonic forces to Himself (Eph 3.10; 6.12; Col 1.15; 2.8–15; etc.). The beginning and the end of the divine plan, already spoken of by Deutero-Isaiah and sketched in Rom 8.28–30, is now seen to have existed in Christ ''before the creation of the world'' (Eph 1.4; see also 3.9; Col 1.15). The consummation of this plan means the summing up of all things in Christ (Eph 1.10) and the power that achieves this consummation in His Resurrection (Col 1.18; 2.12–13), which is communicated to the believer (Eph 2.6). The PASTORAL EPISTLES, apart from an individualizing tendency in their use of the term Day of Christ (2 Tm 1.12, 18; etc.) and a polemic against some overenthusiastic proponents of ''realized eschatology'' (2 Tm 2.17–18), add nothing to Paul's eschatological teaching. In the Pauline tradition, the Epistle to the Hebrews speaks of the revelation, in these last days, of God in His Son (Heb 1.1), whose death and Resurrection is the definitive act of God on man's behalf (10.12). Christ has not only entered the heavenly realities described by the apocalyptic writers (9.23–24); He has given man access to these same realities (10.19–25). And though this act was performed ''once for all'' (9.26), He is coming again (9.28) on a Day that is drawing near (10.25).

Other New Testament Teaching. In most of the other letters in the NT there seems to be a less dynamic synthesis of the elements that compose the teaching on eschatology. The prevailing terminology is employed, but its full consequences are not investigated. The thought of the glory to come (1 Pt 5.4) or of the punishment reserved for the wicked (2 Pt 2.9–10; Jude 15) is used in a context of moral exhortation. In Jas 5.4 the traditional threat of fire on the ''last days'' is used for the sake of persuading the rich to part with some of their wealth, and in 2 Pt 3.5–13 the same imagery is employed in the unique NT reference to a total destruction of the cosmos by fire.

The Revelation of St. John makes no claim to be counted among the intertestamental writings that are called apocalypses, though it does share much of their imagery in its presentation of the Christian message. The cosmic dimensions of the Christ fact are presented more dramatically in the Revelation than in Paul (Rv 6.12; 16.18–21; 20.11; 21.1), but there is a like insistence on the fact that in Christ God's plan has been definitively realized (Rv 5.9–14; 12.10–12; etc.). Yet Christ is still to come (Rv 1.7; 22.6), and Christians are taught to pray for His coming (Rv 22.17, 20; etc.), even though the LORD'S SUPPER is already a coming of Jesus (3.20). The heavenly Jerusalem, already mentioned by Paul (Gal 4.26), assumes a human dimension (Rv 21.2, 9–27); and enlightened by the Lamb (Rv 8.16), it will be forever the meeting place of God and man. Other images, such as the two stages of the messianic kingdom (e.g., 20.1–15), are not as easy to understand, but they seem to refer to the realized and yet to be realized aspects of Christ's work. (*See* MILLENARIANISM.)

Conclusion. The ''last things'' in Biblical theology are not so much last as ultimate, and their chronological sequence does not correspond to their degree of definitiveness. When the world will have been transformed, then time, as it is now experienced, will cease. There will be such a point in history or rather metahistory, though there are no words that can describe it, and the Scriptures content themselves with clothing it in imagery that insists on its transcendent nature.

The consciousness of being chosen forced Israel to look forward to a Day when God would give them peace and somehow make of them a blessing for the nations. Man's opposition to God's plan was first experienced in the hostility with which the nations resisted Israel's effort at self-realization; they would certainly be punished. Time and failure revealed that the opposition to God was deep within Israel itself, and this brought with it a conviction that God's justice demanded a judgment that would both condemn and save. As one calamity after another befell the chosen people, they became aware of participating in a universal rebellion whose cosmic echoes forced themselves in on man's world; yet they still clung to their vocation and their faith in the promises of God. When even the restoration of Jerusalem failed to end their inconclusive state of existence, men began to look beyond history for a solution. In their overwhelming sense of sin and inadequacy, they mistook God's transcendence for His absence, though they never ceased hoping to see His salvation. Thus, what had begun as a time-bound nationalistic hope now inclined to despair altogether of ever experiencing God's activity within human confines.

The Resurrection of Jesus Christ revealed to man that the transcendence of God's power is at work deep within man's proper dimension. God's judgment has condemned sin in the flesh of His Son, and, in reconciling the world to Himself, He has made good His promise to Abraham. The cosmic dimension of this definitive act can be seen even now in the glory of God on the face of Christ Jesus and can be felt even now in the water and wine and bread that allow man to touch Him. And yet man is saved in hope. The Last Thing is present; yet it does not fully exist. How is it that, though man no longer looks forward to a more decisive divine act, man still groans within himself as he awaits his redemption? Perhaps the best explanation that can be given is that given by Jesus Himself in His description of the tiny mustard seed that must fall into the ground and reveal its promise by dying and transforming all things into itself in the power of its own inner dynamism. What man awaits is not the Christ Himself, but His full manifestation within each man, within the Church, and within the cosmos. ''For you have died, and your life now lies hidden with Christ in God. But when Christ, our life, appears, then you shall appear with him in glory'' (Col 3.3–4).

Bibliography: General. H. GROSS and R. SCHNACKENBURG, *Lexicon für Theologie und Kirche* (Freiburg, 1957–66) 3:1084–93. A. JEPSEN et al., *Die Religion in Geschichte und Gegenwart.* 6 v. (3rd ed. Tübingen 1957–63) 2:655–672. P. AUVRAY, *Catholicisme* 4:410–414. *Encyclopedic Dictionary of the Bible,* tr. and adap. by L. HARTMAN (New York 1963) 677–686. R. PAUTREL and D. MOL-

LAT, "Jugement," *Dictionnaire de la Bible,* suppl. ed. L. PIROT, et al. (Paris 1928) 4:1321–94, with extensive bibliog. up to 1946. Old Testament. W. EICHRODT, *Theology of the O.T.,* tr. J. A. BAKER (Philadelphia 1961). G. VON RAD, *O.T. Theology,* tr. D. STALKER (New York 1962). P. HEINISCH, *Theology of the O.T.,* tr. W. G. HEIDT (Collegeville, Minn. 1950). T. C. VRIEZEN, "Prophecy and Eschatology," *Vetus Testamentum,* Supplement 1 (1953) 199–229. G. A. F. KNIGHT, "Eschatology in the O.T.," *Scottish Journal of Theology* 4 (1951) 355–362. S. O. MOWINCKEL, *He That Cometh,* tr. G. W. ANDERSON (Nashville 1956). L. CERNÝ, *The Day of Yahweh and Some Relevant Problems* (Prague 1948). G. W. BUCHANAN, "Eschatology and the *End of Days,*" *Journal of Near Eastern Studies* 20 (1961) 188–193. R. H. CHARLES, *Eschatology* (New York 1963). J. MOUROUX, *The Mystery of Time,* tr. J. DRURY (New York 1964). J. BARR, *Biblical Words for Time* (Naperville, Ill. 1962). O. CULLMANN, *Christ and Time,* tr. F. V. FILSON (rev. ed. Philadelphia 1964). H. GRESSMAN, *Der Ursprung der israelitisch-jüdischen Eschatologie* (Göttingen 1905); *Der Messias* (Göttingen 1929). G. HÖLSCHER, *Die Ursprünge der jüdischen Eschatologie* (Giessen 1925). L. DÜRR, *Ursprung und Ausbau der israelitisch-jüdischen Heilandserwartung* (Berlin 1925). Intertestamental period. D. S. RUSSELL, *The Method and Message of Jewish Apocalyptic* (Philadelphia 1964), with excellent bibliog. H. H. ROWLEY, *The Relevance of Apocalyptic* (3rd ed. New York 1964). B. VAWTER, "Apocalyptic: Its Relation to Prophecy," *Catholic Biblical Quarterly* 22 (1960) 33–46. T. F. GLASSON, *Greek Influence in Jewish Eschatology* (London 1961). J. BONSIRVEN, *Palestinian Judaism in the Time of Jesus Christ,* tr. W. WOLF (New York 1964). New Testament. J. BONSIRVEN, *The Theology of the N.T.,* tr. S. F. L. TYE (Westminster, Md. 1963). M. MEINERTZ, *Theologie des Neuen Testaments* (Die Heilige Schrift des N.T. 1; Bonn 1950). E. STAUFFER, *N. T. Theology,* tr. J. MARSH (London 1955). R. K. BULTMANN, *Theology of the N.T.,* tr. K. GROBEL, 2 v. (New York 1951–55). A. FEUILLET, *Dictionnaire de la Bible,* suppl. ed. L. PIROT, et al. (Paris 1928) 6:1331–1419, with extensive bibliog. up to 1959. W. G. KÜMMEL, *Promise and Fulfillment,* tr. D. M. BARTON (Naperville, Ill. 1957). C. H. DODD, *The Parables of the Kingdom* (rev. ed. New York 1961); *The Interpretation of the Fourth Gospel* (Cambridge, Eng. 1953; repr. 1960). J. A. T. ROBINSON, *Jesus and His Coming* (Nashville 1958). J. JEREMIAS, *The Parables of Jesus,* tr. S. H. HOOKE (rev. ed. New York 1963). A. WILDER, *Eschatology in the Ethics of Jesus* (rev. ed. New York 1950). H. CONZELMANN, *The Theology of St. Luke,* tr. G. BUSWELL (New York 1960). F. PRAT, *The Theology of St. Paul,* tr. J. L. STODDARD, 2 v. (London 1926–27; repr. Westminster, Md. 1958). R. K. BULTMANN, *Presence of Eternity: History and Eschatology* (New York 1957). R. SCHNACKENBURG, *God's Rule and Kingdom,* tr. J. MURRAY (New York 1963). B. J. LE FROIS, "Eschatological Interpretation of the Apocalypse," *Catholic Biblical Quarterly* 13 (1951) 17–20. R. KOCH, "L'Aspect eschatologique de l'Esprit du Seigneur d'après S. Paul," *Studia Paulina* 1 (1963) 131–141. H. P. OWEN, "Eschatology and Ethics in the N.T.," *Scottish Journal of Theology* 15 (1962) 369–382. W. G. KÜMMEL, "Futuristic and Realized Eschatology in the Earliest Stages of Christianity," *Journal of Religion* 43 (1963) 303–314.

[F. MARTIN]

ESCHATOLOGY (IN THEOLOGY)

The word eschatology is derived from the Greek (ἔσχατος, last) and means the science of the last things. Individual eschatology treats of death, particular judgment, purgatory, heaven, and hell; collective eschatology, of the end of the world, the Second Coming of Christ, the resurrection of the dead, and the general judgment. In the twentieth century the term eschatological began to be used in a wider sense, designating all those aspects of the Christian revelation that transcend this world. In this sense it no longer looks solely to those subjects usually dealt with in the treatise *De novissimis* but includes the Christian's basic attitude to life and his striving to reach fulfillment in the following of the gospel. The first part of this article will survey the ways Christians have historically understood the ultimate realities discussed in eschatology. The second part will present the position of eschatology in recent Catholic theology.

HISTORICAL PERSPECTIVES

One can break down the structure of Christian belief as put forward in the creeds into a present conviction that involves a hope of certain events in the future, justified by reference to past events. The future events are expressed as "From thence He shall come to judge the living and the dead," implying that Christ will come again and man's present moral dispositions will have an important bearing on his ultimate fate, and "I believe in . . . the resurrection of the body and life everlasting," thereby stating that the redeemed will enjoy a never-ending existence in which the body will be present so that man's future condition is not that of a disembodied spirit. The past events that justify this expectation are connected with the life, death, and RESURRECTION OF CHRIST.

Early Church. The close connection between the paschal events and man's final destiny was very much to the fore in early Christianity. There were many treatises on the resurrection. Like St. Paul, Justin, Origen, Hippolytus, Tertullian, and Methodius linked Christ's Resurrection with that of the Christian at the last day. There was special reverence toward the martyrs because they most clearly imitated Christ by laying down their lives, and in the acts of the early martyrs, for instance in the acts of Polycarp, one sees the strong affirmation that those bodies that had been consumed by the flames and dismembered would rise in glory at the last day. The legend of the phoenix arising from the ashes and the peacock as the symbol of immortality are both found among early Church inscriptions. Thus one sees that the Christian belief was something more than the philosophical belief in the immortality of the soul. It was something transcending merely human experience and reason. It was a belief centered on the risen Christ.

The desire and yearning for the accomplishment of God's plan for the world in the definitive victory of Christ meant a recognition of the transience and impermanence of man's present state. It would be an oversimplification to read into this a firm belief and conviction that the END OF THE WORLD was imminent. In the early Church, certainly, a problem was posed by the delay in the Second Coming, but it was soon recognized that the Church had to make use of the period of waiting to convert the world and that in a sense the Christian has already begun to enjoy the future goods in the Resurrection of Christ and his access to God through GRACE. Only the heterodox movements such as MONTANISM looked to a speedy Second Coming that would purge the Church of all its carnal elements.

In those days there was a keen awareness of the social aspect of the future state of mankind, and Origen perhaps more than anyone looked forward to an APOCATASTASIS, the restoration of all things in Christ. He did not fall into the error of CHILIASM as he interpreted Revelation allegorically, but his insistence on the idea of fulfillment led him into supposing that in the end all would find happiness in Christ. Even the devil would be pardoned and hell would be no more. This view was to reappear from time to time in the history of theology. It was taken up by the disciples of Origen, was condemned at the synod of Constantinople in 543 (H. Denzinger, *Enchiridion symbolorum* 411), and was combated by the Fathers. The error is really based on a failure to see that God's glory can be manifested in those who freely reject the divine advances and suffer the consequences. *See* GLORY OF GOD (END OF CREATION). In the West it was St. Augustine who was most conscious of God's action in history, and in books 20 to 22 of *The City of God* one sees this applied to the last things. In his writings against the Pelagians St. Augustine focused attention on the individual's attitude toward death and the last things by his insistence on the gift of final PERSEVERANCE. The importance of the moment of death for the Christian and the need for God's help if man is to enter into eternal life are well brought out in the *De dono perseverantiae.*

Since the time of Nicaea I (325) Christian thinkers had been making use of pagan philosophy to develop the doctrine of man's ultimate end. St. Basil and especially St. Gregory of Nyssa in his *Life of Moses* had helped Christians to recognize that the last things are the conclusion of a long process, not only the progress of mankind through history, but the progress of the individual toward his end, which is God. St. Augustine shows that man cannot but seek his own happiness, that his life is a search for this, and that he can find rest only in God. This individual and collective eschatology have an ultimate harmony.

Middle Ages. Throughout the Middle Ages there continued the same general pattern that was found in the patristic period. Augustine's sense of history is seen in Isidore of Seville, and his influence continued into the 12th century, being particularly marked in Hugh of Saint-Victor. The Manichaean view of matter as evil and consequent denial of the Resurrection were repeated in the heresies of the Catharists and Albigenses.

Monasticism. There has always been a strong witness to the values of life beyond the grave in monasticism. In the 4th century the flight to the desert reminded Christianity that, although it was no longer persecuted, it still had to keep its sights on superterrestrial values. It was a useful corrective of those who like Eusebius of Caesarea tended to identify the Church with the new political order. The prophetic ministry of the Old Testament was continued by the fathers of the desert, who demonstrated that the KINGDOM OF GOD was not yet fully realized. These ideas continued both in the East and in the West. In the East the Hesychastic movement and Gregory Palamas drew men's attention to otherworldly values even to the extent of being thought antihumanist. Their spirituality is founded on two events in the history of man's salvation: one in the past, the INCARNATION; one to come, the resurrection of the last day. This eschatological perspective is essential to their teaching. In Western monastic literature certain eschatological themes are developed. If hell is only alluded to indirectly, it is because this is the place to avoid and is not a subject for contemplation as heaven is. The great wealth of Biblical imagery was used to describe the New Jerusalem. These descriptions of heaven do not convey the idea of a place of disembodied spirits, since the Dionysian tradition had far less influence inside the monasteries than outside them. The mystery of the Transfiguration that patristic tradition had regarded as an anticipation of the Second Coming was a popular subject of devotion, and the feast was introduced into the West by the monks. The Canticle of Canticles was one of the most popular books of the Bible, and the monastic commentators always saw in it the relation between Christ and the individual soul, a tradition that was to continue in the 16th-century mystics. For every Christian the life of grace can be said to be the beginning of union with God, but in a special way the *otium* of the monastic life, the leisure for the things of God, exemption from the cares of the world, was seen as a foretaste of heaven.

Joachim of Fiore. But there was the danger that the monk would idealize the monastic life and deny any value at all to life in the world, and this is what happened with the Abbot Joachim of Fiore. It was not his sense of history nor his harmony between the two Testaments nor his symbolism that were novel but his pessimism concerning any life other than that of the monastery. This led him to overspiritualize the Christian message and look for an immediate Second Coming. The taking of Jerusalem by Saladin in 1187 was a severe blow to Christendom, and, as with previous political happenings of this nature, men's minds were once more recalled to a contemplation of the transitoriness of life. Cyprian, Hilary, Jerome, and Ambrose had spoken of the world growing older, and at the time of Gregory the Great the position of Rome seemed to forebode the end of the world. But these reactions at times of crisis were simply those of the Christian conscience recognizing the precariousness of human existence rather than a definite expectation of the end. In the 12th century there were many allusions to the coming of ANTICHRIST, but often these were nothing more than a literary convention adopted by moralists, reformers, and polemicists dramatizing the situation. Every public misfortune announces the final catastrophe and is another act in the great drama. This is the way the Christian has interpreted St. John's "Antichrist is come already" (cf. 1 Jn 4.3), as an awareness of the power of evil in the world. Any attempt to calculate the date of the end was discouraged, and popular superstition and extreme literalism were always a danger to the true doctrine. Joachim fell into this error of exact calculation and over-ingenious explanation and so was condemned (*see* JOACHIM OF FIORE).

Biblical Commentaries. The traditionally accepted interpretation of the Scriptures included the anagogic sense, which drew the attention of the reader to the significance of the sacred text in reference to Christ's Second Coming. Thus, for the word Jerusalem there would be called to mind the past history of the people of Israel (historic or literal sense); it would recall that the Church is the New Jerusalem (allegoric sense) and that the true city of God is yet to be fully realized (anagogic sense). This anagogy took two forms. For some passages there was the objective doctrinal exposition of the end of the world and the end of the individual, the consideration that man is intended for heaven, that he has yet to enter into his inheritance. But in many cases the anagogic sense was more practical and meant a consideration of the life of prayer and contemplation as a preparation for man's final end.

Scholastics. In his *Book of Sentences,* Peter Lombard considered the main purpose and direction of man's life at the beginning, in the first distinction of the first book. At the end of the work, in book four, distinctions 43 to 50, there is a specific treatment of the themes of resurrection, judgment, heaven, and hell. In the *Summa theologiae,* 1a2ae, 1–5 St. Thomas Aquinas harmonizes the Aristotelian idea of HAPPINESS as the end of man with the Christian teaching that man is created for God. He had reserved a place in the third part for a special treatment of eternal life as the end that one attains through the risen Christ. (Since he never completed the *Summa theologiae,* one has to rely on his commentary on Peter Lombard and on the *Summa contra gentiles* 4.79–97 to ascertain his views on these matters.)

Aquinas's division has the methodological advantage of separating the *finis intentionis* from the *finis executionis.* It gives a unifying principle to the consideration of Christian morality. The danger is that the truths of *De novissimis* may not be sufficiently integrated into Christian life but be considered simply as an appendage. Certain elements of medieval mysticism exaggerated the connection between the two. Thus those movements associated with the names of Meister Eckhart, the Beghards, and the Alumbrados (Illuminati) maintained that in this life one could experience the vision of God. As a reaction against a false mysticism Catholic theology tended to relegate *De novissimis* to an abstract consideration of man's state as it would be in the future.

East and West. The theological disputes in the Middle Ages between East and West concerned the last things only on minor points. There was general agreement on the basic doctrines of man's destiny, but the Council of Florence revealed misunderstanding about the reward or punishment that was given immediately after death, and the nature of the pains of purgatory.

Reformation. It was the doctrine of purgatory that was called into question by the reformers. This was connected as much with the basic Protestant idea of the nature of JUSTIFICATION and an inability to understand temporal punishment as with certain abuses in the practice of Masses for the dead and the use of indulgences.

Since the Reformation. The dispute about the NATURAL ORDER and SUPERNATURAL ORDER has meant discussion as to how far the BEATIFIC VISION can be said to be man's natural end. Against M. Baius the Church has maintained that the destiny to which man has been called completely transcends any exigencies of his nature. In the 17th and 18th centuries the quietist movement neglected the importance of human activity and minimized the role of Christian morality. Counter Reformation theology was characterized by stress on the last things of the individual; there was little about the PAROUSIA. The age was one of individualism, and it is not surprising that personal values were more thought of by theologians. In the *Spiritual Exercises* of St. Ignatius of Loyola, in the writings of St. Grignion de Montfort, in retreats and sermons, the last things are continually referred to; but it is almost exclusively from the point of view of the individual soul. Since the Protestant error had made Catholics insist on the authoritarian and fixed aspect of the Church, it was not surprising that there was little about the Church as still imperfect and on pilgrimage to its final realization at the Parousia.

In the 19th century there came a change. At first it was not seen how there could be any reconciliation between the Church's teaching and contemporary ideas of the progress of mankind. But soon it was appreciated that there is such a thing as a God-directed progress of man. The social encyclicals of Leo XIII and Pius XI testify to the belief that man can attain his fulfillment only in a society that has been transformed and Christianized.

In the 20th century the questions of progress continued to inform reflection upon eschatology. Other trends furthered the integration of eschatology with the whole of theology. Biblical studies came to a better appreciation of the idea of SALVATION HISTORY. Man can reach his fulfillment as an individual only within the framework of society, and society is moving toward the final completion of God's saving plan. Scientific theories of evolution allowed theologians to see a continuity between this world and the next. The notion of a sudden end of the world has been reexamined. Certainly it will be sudden in the sense that it will be due to divine intervention, but it is not necessary to hold to annihilation of the old and creation of something entirely new. The debates about nature and grace produced a better appreciation of the Augustinian concept of the world as being created and destined for a supernatural end.

Biblical studies also uncovered the Semitic idea of man as a totality, which meant less attention was paid to the doctrine of the immortality of the soul and more to the resurrection of the body. Christ came to save the whole man and not just man's soul. The soul is the more important part since it governs and gives form to the rest, but one must not neglect the working out of the Redemption in man's body. Christ's healing of the sick was part of His mission as redeemer. The fall of man meant the loss of the gift of bodily INTEGRITY and immortality of the body. This has been restored to man by Christ, although he does not yet possess it in its totality. As man is body as well as soul, the material creation has a part to play in the redemptive scheme, and one sees this especially in the sacramental system. Much thought has been given in recent years to the Sacraments of the Eucharist, Anointing of the Sick, and Matrimony, all of which have a special reference to the body.

In such a context death is not a liberation from the body so much as a *transitus,* a going over in totality to the new world to which the Christian already belongs in essence by his Baptism. The opposition is not between one place of existence and another so much as between the world as affected by sin and death and the redeemed world of the Spirit. The theology of death began to focus on the call of the Christian to a daily dying as witness to eschatological values. In this the Christian shares in the prophetic mission of Christ, announcing the future event, the Parousia, when Christ will come in glory and the kingdom will be finally and irrevocably established. It is in the religious life that this witness is most clearly seen. The vows of poverty, chastity, and obedience speak to man of another world. The liturgical revival drew attention to the paschal mysteries as the central point of Christianity, which fostered a Christological approach to the last things.

See Also: DEATH (THEOLOGY OF); DESIRE TO SEE GOD, NATURAL; ELEVATION OF MAN; ESCHATOLOGISM; ESCHATOLOGY, ARTICLES ON; HEAVEN (THEOLOGY OF); HELL (THEOLOGY OF); INCARNATIONAL THEOLOGY; INCARNATIONALISM; JUDGMENT, DIVINE (IN THEOLOGY); MAN; PURGATORY; RESURRECTION OF THE DEAD; SANCTION, DIVINE; SUPERNATURAL EXISTENTIAL; TEMPORAL VALUES, THEOLOGY OF.

Bibliography: E. MANGENOT, *Dictionnaire de théologie catholique*, ed. A. VACANT et al. (Paris 1903–50) 5.1:456–457. K. RAHNER, *Lexicon für Theologie und Kirche,* (Freiburg, 1957–66) 3:1094–98. J. A. MACCULLOCH, *Encyclopedia of Religion and Ethics*, ed. J. HASTINGS and J. A. SELBIA (Edinburgh 1908–27) 5:373–391. E. E. KELLETT, *ibid.* 10:757–763. J. GALOT, *Dictionnaire de spiritualité ascétique et mystique. Doctrine et histoire,* ed. M. VILLER et al. (Paris 1932) 4:1020–59. A. WINKLHOFER, *Handbuch theologischer Grundbegriffe*, ed. H. FRIES (Munich 1962–63) 1:327–336. P. AUVRAY, *Catholicisme* 4:410–414. F. L. CROSS, *The Oxford Dictionary of the Christian Church* (London 1957) 462. M. and L. BECQUÉ, *Life after Death,* tr. P. HEPBURNE-SCOTT (New York 1960). R. W. GLEASON, *The World to Come* (New York 1958). M. SCHMAUS, *Katholische Dogmatik,* v.4.2 (5th ed. Munich 1958). On the history of the question. V. DE BROGLIE, *De fine ultimo humanae vitae* (Paris 1948). R. A. KNOX, *Enthusiasm* (New York 1950; repr. 1961). J. LECLERCQ, *The Love of Learning and the Desire for God,* tr. C. MISRAHI (New York 1961). H. DE LUBAC, *Exégèse médiévale,* 2 v. in 4 (Paris 1959–64) 1:621–681; 2:437–558. A. LUNEAU, *L'Histoire du salut chez les pères de l'église* (Paris 1964). On modern problems. B. BESRET, *Incarnation ou eschatologie?* (Paris 1964). L. BOUYER, ''Christianisme et eschatologie,'' *La Vie Intellectuelle* 16 (1948) 6–38; *The Meaning of the Monastic Life,* tr. K. POND (New York 1955). O. CULLMANN, *Immortality of the Soul or Resurrection of the Dead?* (New York 1958). F. X. DURRWELL, *The Resurrection: A Biblical Study,* tr. R. SHEED (New York 1960).

[M. E. WILLIAMS/EDS.]

CONTEMPORARY CATHOLIC THEOLOGY

One of the most significant developments in eschatology in the twentieth century was the rediscovery of the primacy of the advent of the end (the *eschaton*) in Jesus the Christ crucified and risen. It is only in the light of the end of time revealed ''in Christ'' that a truly Christian theology of the last things can be worked out.

In the middle 1960s eschatology was given a new lease on life through the writings of Johann-Baptist Metz and Jürgen Moltmann, who drew attention to the neglect of hope within theology and the need to reintegrate eschatology into the mainstream of Christian theory and praxis. Others, like Karl RAHNER and Wolfhart Pannenberg, emphasized the importance of CHRISTOLOGY for a balanced understanding of eschatology. Since the 1960s there has been a steady stream of literature on eschatology which gathered momentum in the years leading into the celebration of the Jubilee Year 2000 A.D.

To review the contemporary state of eschatology we shall summarize first of all the teaching of the Catholic Church on eschatology from Vatican II onwards. This teaching of the Church will be easily misunderstood if it is not accompanied by some principles of interpretation, and so it will be necessary to outline some hermeneutical guidelines. Mention of interpretation demands that consideration be given to the modern and postmodern contexts in which eschatology exists at present. Since eschatology deals with the destiny of the individual, particular attention must be given to anthropology. The centerpiece of eschatology is Christology, which gives both shape and form to Christian hope. In addressing the relationship between eschatology and Christology some discussion must be given to the current debates about Resurrection. It is impossible to talk about eschatology today without some reference to the contemporary fascination with cosmology. And finally something must be said about the increasing impact of eschatology on the rest of Christian theology.

Church Teaching from Vatican II Onwards. The few eschatological statements that do exist in the Vatican II documents are quite significant and signal a subtle shift in emphasis. The *Dogmatic Constitution on the Church* contains a short chapter devoted to ''The Eschatological Nature of the Pilgrim Church and Her Union with the Heavenly Church'' (Chap. VII). This chapter reminds us that we are living in the end times: ''Already the final age of the world is with us (cf. 1 Cor.10/11) and the renewal of the world is irrevocably underway''(*LG* 48). In the *Pastoral Constitution on the Church and the Modern World* a number of important developments are discernible in articles 38 to 43. Article 38 talks about those who are called ''to give clear witness to the desire for a heavenly home'' whereas others are called ''to dedicate themselves to the earthly service of humanity.'' Of the latter group, it points out they can ''make ready the material of the celestial realm''—thus highlighting the existence of important links between historical existence and eternity. Those who are dedicated to the service of humanity in this life can ''give some kind of foreshadowing of the new age to come'' (39). In the same vein this document points out that ''the expectation of a new earth must not weaken but stimulate our concerns for cultivating this one'' (39). Indeed, the Council describes those who ''knowing that we have no abiding city but seek one which is to come'' as ''mistaken'' (43). Equally significant in this document is the Latin title *Gaudium et spes* which signals the important link between hope and joy: the exercise of Christian hope carries with it an essential element of joy. These shifts opened the way for the development subsequently of political and liberation theologies which in their own different ways gave considerable emphasis to the *praxis* of social justice and its place within the coming Reign of God.

A further emphasis implicit in the eschatology of Vatican II is the way the Council puts Christ at the center, claiming that Christ ''is the goal of human history, the focal point of the longing of history and of civilization, the center of the human race, the joy of every heart and the answer to all its longings'' (a. 43; see also G.S. a.10 and 12; A.G. a. 8). These eschatological references are notable for the way they talk about the *eschaton* rather the *eschata*, for the value they place on the significance of earthly activities for the world to come, and for the focus they give to the possibility of a social eschatology.

In 1979 the Congregation for the Doctrine of the Faith issued an Instruction ''On Certain Questions concerning Eschatology.'' The context of this document was a view being put forward about ''Resurrection in Death'' by the German theologian Ghisbert Greshake initially in 1969 and more extensively in 1977. Greshake's theology of ''Resurrection in Death'' seemed to call into question the need for and the credibility of the classical notion of ''an intermediate state.'' By emphasizing ''Resurrection in Death'' Greshake also appears to eliminate the necessity for a general judgment and the resurrection of humanity at the end of time. In response the Congregation reaffirmed classical eschatology: the general resurrection of the dead at the end of time, the immortality of the soul after death, and the existence of heaven, hell, and purgatory. The immortality of the soul is described in terms of the ''spiritual element (that) survives and subsists after death.'' The same congregation also warns against ''arbitrary imaginative representations'' of the hereafter which can be ''a major cause of difficulties that Christian faith often encounters.'' Instead it must be recognized that ''neither scripture or theology provide sufficient light for a proper picture of life after death.'' This Instruction concludes by emphasizing on the one hand ''a fundamental continuity between our present life in Christ and the future life'' and on the other hand ''a radical difference between the present life and the future.''

The *Catechism of the Catholic Church* set forth its teaching on eschatology by offering a commentary on the last two articles of the Apostles Creed: ''I believe in the Resurrection of the Body and Life everlasting.'' The Catechism outlines what it means by ''Christ's Resurrection and ours'' (992–996). It notes that in death there is a ''separation from the body,'' with the human body decaying and the soul going to meet God (997). The Catechism then goes on to say that God will reunite the body with the soul through the power of Jesus' Resurrection at the end. As to ''how'' the resurrection takes place the Catechism says that this ''exceeds our imagination and understanding'' and ''is accessible only to faith'' (1000). Next the Catechism deals with death, which it says is ''the end of earthly life'' and ''a consequence of sin.'' Death ''shrouded in doubt'' has been transformed through the obedience of Christ unto death.

Under the final article of the Apostles' Creed (viz., life everlasting), the Catechism discusses six areas: particular judgment, heaven, purgatory, hell, last judgment and the hope of the New Heaven and the New Earth. Concerning the New Creation the Catechism ''affirms the profound common destiny of the material world and man'' (1046). The visible universe ''is . . . destined to be transformed'' (1047). The approach of the Catechism in its treatment of eschatology is Trinitarian, Christological, ecclesiological, relational, and communion based. In many respects it could be said that the Catechism expands and elaborates on the content contained in the 1979 CDF *Instruction*.

On a different doctrinal level the International Theological Commission (ITC) published a lengthy document in 1992 entitled ''Some Current Questions in Eschatology.'' The document defends the immortality of the soul after death and the general resurrection of the dead at the end of time. The ITC talks about an ''anthropology of duality'' and an ''eschatology of souls.'' It also refers to the existence of the separated soul as ''half a person,'' as ''not the I,'' and as ''an ontologically incomplete reality'' and uses these descriptions of the separated soul as ways of justifying the need for resurrection at the end of time.

Principles of Interpretation. This teaching of the Church on eschatology will be easily misunderstood unless it is accompanied by some principles of interpretation. The first principle is that eschatology is not some idle speculation about the future, nor is it some kind of report of what goes on in the next world, nor is it a prediction about the end of the world. Instead eschatology is about hope seeking understanding, more specifically about a particular hope-filled interpretation of human experience in the light of the Christ-event. Eschatology seeks to explore, analyze and interpret the potential within human experience insofar as that experience points us towards the future. Eschatology looks at present experience against the background of the salvation offered by Christ to see what it promises for the future.

The key to the interpretation of these experiences is the reality of the life, death and resurrection of Jesus as the Christ summed up in the New Testament and kept alive in the Christian tradition. One way of describing eschatology is to see it as the application of christology to the self, humanity, and creation in a mode of fulfillment. In particular it is the Paschal Christ, the Crucified and Risen One, that gives us an embryonic view of the future of humanity and the world.

A third principle guiding the interpretation of eschatology concerns the question of language. Eschatology statements are symbolic, dialectical and analogical. Symbols point beyond themselves to a dimension of life that is not readily available to human experience. The symbol is not the reality symbolized and yet that reality is only available through the mediating power of symbol. The perspective of dialectic, preferred more by Protestant theologians, highlights the need for negation and usually grounds itself in the cross of Christ. The doctrine of analogy, more favored among Catholic theologians, signals the limitations attaching to all eschatological statements while seeking to assert negatively the truth within its positive statements. Within analogy there is a dynamic movement from affirmation to negation and from negation to further refinement. Of critical importance to analogy is the awareness that we know more by way of negation than by way of affirmation.

A fourth and final principle guiding the understanding of eschatology is the importance of the practical and ethical import of its statements. An authentically Christian eschatology is one that generates a *praxis* of liberation in the present in the name of the coming Reign of God.

The Context of Contemporary Eschatology. One of the most significant contextual shifts within Catholic theology in the twentieth century has been the transition from a classical, fixed understanding of culture to the emergence of a historical consciousness. The culture of historical consciousness recognizes the contingent character of events within history and this clearly has implications for the way we construct a theology of history and providence as underlying suppositions of eschatology. The making of history, which is always self-involving, carries with it a burden of responsibility in the exercise of human agency. History, therefore, is not predetermined but open-ended and therefore subject to the influence of the *praxis* of individual and social liberation. Historical consciousness calls forth a new sense of shared responsibility for the shape of the world in the present and the future. This task for eschatology has been given particular expression in the requests for forgiveness articulated by John Paul II in the Jubilee Year 2000, especially in Jerusalem, and in Athens in 2001.

A second inescapable part of the contemporary context in which eschatology exists today is the new sense of globalization. From an eschatological point of view globalization reminds theology that the destiny of the individual is bound up with the destiny of the whole. Globalization also challenges eschatology to work out an ethic of human justice and ecological sustainability for the well being of the earth in the present.

A third element relating to context concerns the highly ambiguous legacy of the Enlightenment in modernity. The rise of individualism and the cultivation of the shining-self-sufficient-subject of modernity has no need of eschatology. Similarly, modernity's myth of progress, the promise of endless growth, and the politics of social evolution have taken over the role of eschatology in modern theology. Likewise the modern denial of death and the covering over of so much suffering in history has paved the way for the promotion of a purely secular utopia. Lastly, the promises of science in their pursuit of objectivity in the delivery of new freedoms, and the promotion of social reforms have had the effect of sidelining eschatology within contemporary thought.

In recent times these dreams of modernity have been found to be wanting in many respects and in some instances are perceived to be deceptive. This exposure of modernity has given birth to the vague, illusive, and deliberately ill-defined movement known as post-modernity. In contrast to modernity, post-modernity seeks to promote the cultivation of particularity, difference, and otherness. For many the logic of post-modernity seems to be one of radical deconstruction leading to fragmentation, relativism, and ultimately nihilism. One of the most immediate casualties of post-modernity is eschatology insofar as post-modernity dissolves the human subject into an empty site for linguistic exchanges and reduces history to a collection of disconnected fragments. However, it must be noted that there are some affinities between post-modernity and Christian eschatology.

The most obvious affinity is the adoption of the *apophatic*/negative tradition. Both post-modernity and eschatology emphasize what is unknowable, unrepresentable, and unsayable concerning the future. A second affinity between post-modernity and eschatology is the way in which post-modernity deconstructs all affirmations in the name of something other—even though it is impossible to name this other. The nearest post-modernity comes to naming this ''something other'' is to call it the ''possibility of the impossible,'' ''the thought that cannot be thought,'' the future that exists beyond the horizons of the foreseeable. In a somewhat similar fashion some post-modernists are prepared to talk about ''religion without religion'' or ''God without being.'' These positive ''negations'' contain a faint echo with classical eschatology which openly acknowledges that it does not know the future and that it is impossible to express it adequately. There may be some connection between the radical deconstruction of post-modernity and the 'learned ignorance' (*docta ignorantia*) of theology put forward by Aquinas, though it must be pointed out that *docta ignorantia* is a point of arrival in theology and eschatology and not a point of departure.

A third affinity between post-modernity and eschatology is the deep suspicion post-modernity has towards all meta-narratives. Eschatology, of course, cannot succeed without some meta-narrative, especially the narrative of the creation, redemption, and the consummation of all things in Christ. Nonetheless, eschatology shares some suspicion with post-modernity about those narratives that claim to know too much about the end of the world, the nature of the *Parousia*, and the character of eternal life.

Some radical differences between post-modernity and eschatology are the following. Eschatology is constructed in and around the narrative of the unity between the creation, redemption, and the consummation of all things in Christ. Further, eschatology and post-modernity differ significantly on the issue of anthropology. Here eschatology affirms the enduring existence of the self as a conscious, free, and responsible agent both within history and beyond history into eternal life. Lastly, eschatology affirms a unity between the past, the present, and the future within its statements about the meaning of history.

Anthropology. It is most of all in the area of anthropology, namely the question about what it means to be human, that the modern and postmodern contexts of eschatology is most problematic. The exalted and exaggerated self of modernity (going back to Descartes) has given rise to a self-sufficient individualism. This strong individualism has little need of eschatology since as Gabriel MARCEL was fond of pointing out ''hope does not exist at the level of the solitary ego.'' The human self knows that it cannot survive death on its own and that it is only because the self is known and loved by God that it has a future beyond death. It is the experience of loving and being loved that assures a future for the self. However, each of these moves is unavailable to and unnecessary for the shining-self-sufficient-subject of modernity.

At the other end of the spectrum there is the deconstructed self of post-modernity, which is even less available to eschatology. According to post-modernity the human self is something of an empty site around which a great variety of transactions take place, a little like a crossroads that facilitates the movement of traffic. On such a view there can be no coherent anthropology and therefore no viable eschatology. The dissolution of the self carries within itself the dissolution of hope and ultimately the dismantling of eschatology. The sharpness of this deconstruction of the human self highlights the necessity for some form of reconstruction of the human that is able to take account of the positives aspects contained within the modern and postmodern conceptions of the human self, namely the strong sense of human identity within modernity and the equally strong awareness within post-modernity of the presence of so much change in the life of the individual.

The reconstruction of the human required for a viable eschatology needs to take account of the variety of impulses coming from various sources. There is first of all the reaction against the individualism of modernity coming from feminism, ecology, and cosmology. Feminism in its great variety places a strong emphasis on the self as relational. Environmentalists emphasize the ''connected self'' as that which exists in dependence on the rest of nature and creation. Cosmologists talk about the individual as cosmic dust in a state of self-conscious freedom, which is always embodied. These different though complementary perspectives suggest that the whole of life, in particular human life, is organically interconnected, inter-related and inter-dependent. This perspective on human identity prompts the formulation of the following principles in the reconstruction of anthropology: to exist is always to co-exist, to be is always to be in relationship, self discovery comes into being through self surrender to the other.

A second impulse on the nature of the human self comes from the work of Paul RICOEUR as expressed in *One's Self as Another* (Chicago 1992). According to Ricoeur the human self is only available in narrative form and this narrative is more often than not a point of historical arrival rather than a point of departure. What is distinctive for Ricoeur about the human self is the pivotal role that action plays in the constitution of the human self. The self is not available through a process of introspection; rather, the self comes into view through a process of interpersonal action and reaction.

There are at least two different aspects to the self within Ricoeur's philosophy. The historical identity of the human self arises out of a dialectic between the underlying sameness of the self (*idem*) and the ongoing development of selfhood (*ipse*) through a process of mutuality and reciprocity with other selves. Selfhood is never quite as settled or fixed as modernity would suggest; instead, selfhood is far more flexible, as can be seen through the impact of actions associated with a career change, a new relationship, or the death of a spouse. Selfhood is always in process of becoming, open to change and development even though it is the same underlying self that is in motion.

What is significant about these relational and narrative anthropologies is the existence of an active self that is open and unfinished. Given these perspectives on human identity, eschatology emerges not as something additional or extrinsic to anthropology. Instead, eschatology is, as Rahner frequently pointed out, anthropology in a mode of fulfillment or anthropology conjugated in the future. Further, this kind of anthropology, namely a relational anthropology, sees the human subject as one who is in touch with God at the beginning of life and not simply at the end of historical existence. Thirdly, a relational anthropology opens up the way for the development of a social eschatology in both the present and the future.

Christology. The christological focus within eschatology has not always been to the fore in the history of Christian thought. The most obvious example of a break in the link between christology and eschatology is the emphasis often given to the *eschata* at the expense of the advent of the new *eschaton* in Christ. To say that Christ is the hermeneutical principle of eschatological statements (Rahner) means that we must be able to recognize the influence of the Christ-event within eschatological statements. The Christ-event is best summed up in terms of recognizing the theological significance that belongs to the life, death, and resurrection of Jesus as the Christ. This significance can be expressed in a variety of ways. At the Second Vatican Council emphasis was placed on the Paschal Mystery of Christ as the centerpiece of salvation history. Equally, as already noted, Vatican II also described Christ as the goal, ground, and center of human history.

The New Testament points out that God ''has made known to us the mystery of his will, according to his good pleasure that he set forth in Christ, as a plan for the fullness of time, to gather up all things in Him, things in heaven and things on earth'' (Ep. 1.9–10). The letter to the Colossians claims that Christ ''is the image of the invisible God, the first born of all creation . . . in Him all things hold together; He is the beginning, the first born from the dead'' (Col. 1.15). The future, therefore, is christomorphic.

In the early Church there was a sense that an eschatological breakthrough had occurred in the historical life, death, and resurrection of Jesus. The earliest interpretations of the historical life of Jesus are thoroughly eschatological. For example, Paul says that Christ has ''abolished death, brought life and immortality to light'' (2 Tm 1.10). In virtue of the Christ-event we are now living in ''the end of ages'' (1 Cor 10.11) and in the ''latter times'' (1 Tm 4.1) and therefore all are encouraged ''to put away the old man and put on the new man'' (Eph 4.22; Col 3.9). Because Christ is ''the first born among many'' (Rom 8.29; Col 1.18) and ''the first fruits of those who have fallen asleep'' (1 Cor 15.20) Paul can say that since ''all die in Adam, so all will be made alive in Christ'' (1 Cor 15.22).

Further, this experience and understanding of Jesus as the Christ is something that affects not only human existence but also the direction of history as well as material creation itself: ''. . . for creation itself will be set free from its bondage and will obtain the freedom of the glory of the children of God'' (Rom 8.21). The Christ-event, therefore, reconfigures our understanding of God in relation to the future of humanity, of history and of creation.

This sense of eschatological breakthrough is so strong in the early Church that initially Paul believes that the return of Christ (*PAROUSIA*) is imminent and so his early theology emphasizes resurrection and *parousia*. With the passage of time there is a shift from resurrection and *parousia* to death and resurrection, with resurrection taking place after death (2 Cor 5.1–10; Phil 1.21–23; Phil 3.21) to a later theology of being and becoming ''in Christ'' in the present.

Within this theology of Paul there are two key points to be noted. The early Church had a strong awareness and belief that the future has already dawned in Christ and has therefore taken a hold of the present. The future is not something that we are waiting for to take place; instead the future is here already in embryo in the Paschal Mystery of Jesus Christ. Also, in the theology of Paul there is a creative tension between what has ''already'' taken place ''in Christ'' and what is ''not yet'' achieved, between being ''in Christ'' and becoming ''in Christ,'' between the indicative statements such as ''you are in Christ'' and the imperative statements that ''you must put on Christ.'' In Paul there is a dialectic between the already and the not yet, a paradox of dying and rising, a mysticism of being and becoming in Christ. The crucified *and* risen Christ is *one* eschatological reality.

Debates about the Resurrection. The resurrection of Jesus from the dead, so central to eschatology in the early church and in particular in the theology of Paul, needs to be recovered in the twenty-first century. Part of the problem concerning the historicity of resurrection is that the symbol of resurrection has become isolated from other equally important eschatological symbols such as exaltation, glorification, ascension, and Pentecost. The eschatological breakthrough that occurred in the life and death of Jesus can only be grasped in the context of the variety of eschatological symbols employed to capture one and the same post-Calvary experience of Jesus as alive, personally present, gathering, empowering, and missioning the disciples. When resurrection is separated from these other eschatological expressions, then it becomes distorted and literalized.

While it is true to say that the immortality of the soul has captured in the past and continues to capture in the present a most important aspect of eschatology, it must also be recognized that this pre-Christian philosophy needs to be subordinated to the revelation of God's decisive, eschatological action in the life, death, and destiny of Jesus. The resurrection of Jesus is described in explicitly eschatological terms: ''the first fruits of those who have fallen asleep''(1 Cor 15.20), the first born of all creation (Col 1.15), the New Man (Eph 4.22; Col 2.9), and the New Creation (2 Cor 5.17). These images highlight that the Resurrection of Jesus is the beginning of a new process in history, a re-ordering of existence, and the reshaping of creation. The resurrection of Jesus affects all who die, alters the course of history, and reconfigures the destiny of the cosmos. The theological content of these claims of the New Testament cannot be carried adequately by the Platonic doctrine of the immortality of the soul.

The third area of debate about the resurrection concerns the time of resurrection. Between the two positions of resurrection at the end of time (classical view) and resurrection in death (Greshake et al.) there can be found a third position. The perspective of Vatican II, following Paul on the Paschal Mystery and the centrality of communion in Christ, suggests that resurrection is initiated in this life through Baptism and lived out in varying degrees through the paschal process of dying and rising in Christ. This new life ''in Christ'' is deepened in the celebration of the Eucharist and reaches a point of finality in death. In death personal resurrection sets in and is completed, socially and cosmically, with the second coming of Christ, which will effect the final harvesting of humanity, history, and the cosmos into a New Heaven and the New Earth (Rv 21.1–6; Eph 1.9–10). Within this vision there is room for individual resurrection in this life, personal resurrection in death, and the social-cosmic resurrection at the end of time. This position is developed in more detail by Dermot A. Lane in *Keeping Hope Alive: Stirrings in Christian Theology* (New York 1996), 150–162.

Scientific Cosmologies and Christian Eschatologies. It is impossible to discuss Christian eschatology today without giving some consideration to the current fascination with scientific cosmologies. Throughout the twentieth century cosmologists have been attending not only to the beginning but also the ending of the universe. The resulting ''scientific cosmologies'' are increasingly popular and have been taking a hold of the secular imagination. Two very brief sketches will suffice to provide some broad points of comparison with Christian eschatologies.

Freeman Dyson, who works out of an open and expanding universe that will eventually collapse into a cosmic void, emphasizes the importance of adaptability for the future of human life in *Infinite in All Directions* (New York 1988). Dyson suggests that before the onset of cosmic collapse it will be necessary to export life to another planet or galaxy. The nature of life in question would be new forms of human consciousness that could become detached from flesh and blood. These forms of consciousness will be captured through vast systems of organizations and networks made available through computer circuits. For survival it will be necessary for this artificial intelligence to be able to adapt to zero levels of temperature, gravity, and pressure. A second "scientific eschatology" is put forward by Frank Tipler in *The Physics of Immortality* (London 1977). According to Tipler the human mind is a software program within a particular hardware system of the brain. Before the end of time this software program could be transferred to some other hardware system. Tipler claims this transfer of mental software is possible by using the vast quantities of matter and energy that would accumulate just before the collapse of the universe. This transfer would bring into being Omega Point, which would represent the soul as omnipotent, omniscient, and infinite. These summaries do not do justice to the detailed "scientific eschatologies" of these authors. At most they can give a flavor of what is envisaged in terms of creating artificial intelligence and replicating vast banks of information in computer systems about the constitution of human identity which are then presented as expressions of immortality.

A number of observations should be made by way of initial response to these "scientific eschatologies." From an anthropological point of view they seem to be operating out of an understanding of the human as that which is reducible to a gigantic mountain of information-software processes. This perception of the human is explicitly dualistic, presupposing the possibility of disembodied existence in the future, which seems to lack any kind of human subjectivity. In brief the human person is replicated as a vast bank of information, with no sense of the need for healing or wholeness. From a theological perspective it must be noted that these "scientific eschatologies" are secular, making no reference to the creative, redemptive, and consummating God of the Bible; they are "scientific" in that they provide at best speculative information about the future. In contrast theology is not about information but the experience of being grasped and loved by that gracious mystery we call God which refuses to be reduced to propositional data. From an eschatological point of view these "scientific eschatologies" suffer from the absence of human memory as something quite distinct from mechanical memory. Within these predictions there is no memory of the pain, suffering and injustices of former generations that cry out for redemption. There is no memory of the historical Passover of the people of Israel or the Paschal Mystery of Jesus as the Christ, both of which provide sources of hope for the future. Thirdly, there is no memory that the future has already appeared in the death and resurrection of Jesus and that, therefore, the future is already shaping the present. Most of all these secular "scientific eschatologies" are flawed because of the way they disrupt the unity between human memory and imagination. Memory of the past and the future is essential to the credible operations of the imagination. Without memory the human imagination runs the risk of lapsing into fantasy. The capacity of the human imagination to articulate credible alternatives is impaired once it loses contact with tradition and ceases to adhere to the real.

In making this rather negative assessment, it must be acknowledged that these "scientific eschatologies" do provide an opening for an important dialogue between religion and science. The dialogue between Christian eschatology and "scientific eschatologies" has hardly begun, and the distance that exists between the two can be seen in the above points of comparison. It is essential for the credibility of Christian eschatology that this dialogue take place. In particular the dialogue is important to ensure that eschatological claims do not conflict with the established findings of cosmology.

The Growing Influence of Eschatology on the Rest of Theology. In many respects eschatology, understood as hope seeking understanding, is the missing link in a lot of contemporary theology. Metz and Moltmann, Rahner and Pannenberg have sought to bring eschatology to the center of the theological enterprise. This relocation of eschatology is having positive effects on rest of theology.

For instance, eschatology is a powerful reminder of the incompleteness of Christology and that what Christ has set in train continues to be subject to the second coming of Christ. In the area of ecclesiology, eschatology functions as a moderating influence on exaggerated ecclesiological claims, highlighting the fact that the church is always a pilgrim people continually in need of reform and renewal, never to be identified or confused with the coming Reign of God but always seeking to sight and celebrate elements of the Reign of God in the world. In sacramental theology, eschatology is coming more and more to the fore. For example, the eucharist is understood as the sacrament of the *eschaton*: celebrating the past and remembering the future, providing a foretaste of what is to come. In the area of moral theology eschatology provides a grounding for the work of justice, the praxis of liberation, and the care of the earth.

There is an important sense in which the end organizes and unifies the whole of life. Without an end in view, life lapses into empty time (*chronos*). But if there is an end in view, then *chronos* can be transformed into *kairos*, time filled with meaning, a purpose and promise. This, among others, is one of the primary tasks facing eschatology in the twenty-first century.

Bibliography: B. E. DALEY, *The Hope of the Early Church: A Handbook of Patristic Eschatology* (New York 1991). J. P. GALVIN, ed., *Faith and Future: Studies in Eschatology* (New York 1994). J. F. HAUGHT, *The Promise of Nature: Ecology and Cosmic Purpose* (New York 1993). Z. HAYES, *Visions of a Future: A Study of Christian Eschatology* (Wilmington, DE 1989). INTERNATIONAL THEOLOGICAL COMMISSION, ''Some Current Questions in Eschatology,'' *Irish Theological Quarterly* 58 (1992) 209–243. D. A. LANE, ''Anthropology and Eschatology,'' *Irish Theological Quarterly* 61 (1995) 11–28. ''Message of His Holiness John Paul II,'' *Physics, Philosophy and Theology: A Common Quest for Understanding,* eds. R. J. RUSSELL, W. R. STOEGER, and J. V. COYNE (Vatican City 1988). J. NEUNER and J. DUPUIS, eds., *The Christian Faith in Doctrinal Documents of the Catholic Church,* rev. ed. (London 1983). P. C. PHAN, ''Contemporary Contexts and Issues on Eschatology,'' *Theological Studies* 55 (1994) 507–536. J. R. SACHS, ''Current Eschatology: Universal Salvation and the Problem of Hell,'' *Theological Studies* 52 (1991) 227–254. J. RATZINGER, *Eschatology: Death and Eternal Life,* trans. M. WALDSTEIN (Washington, D.C. 1988).

[D. A. LANE]

ESCHMANN, IGNATIUS T.

Dominican philosopher, theologian, and critic; b. Dusseldorf, Nov. 13, 1898; d. Toronto, April 11, 1968. After completing his studies at the Hohenzollern Gymnasium in Dusseldorf in 1916 he was ordered to the trenches as a machine gunner until the end of the First World War, when he was honorably discharged. He joined the Dominican Order and made profession on May 19, 1920. He was sent to Rome to study philosophy and theology at the Angelicum, where he was ordained to the priesthood on July 12, 1925, and where he obtained his doctorate and taught moral philosophy until 1936, gaining the reputation of being a good teacher and a very persuasive preacher. When PIUS XI's encyclical *Mit brennender Sorge* appeared on March 4, 1937, he promulgated its contents as cathedral preacher in Cologne, and found himself at odds with both the police and the German hierarchy. He was ultimately arrested by the civil police and incarcerated in Cologne until the fall of 1938, when he was released and made his way to Canada.

In Ottawa he collaborated with the Canadian Dominicans in preparing the piana edition of the *Summa theologiae* of St. THOMAS AQUINAS, his particular contribution being the sources provided by that edition (1941). Until the end of the war he was under constant surveillance by the Canadian police and suspected by the French Canadian Dominicans as an enemy alien. Invited to join the staff of Laval University, Quebec, he taught for only one year (1939–40), becoming embroiled in a controversy with Cardinal Villeneuve and Charles De Koninck. In 1942 he joined the philosophy department of St. Michael's College and the faculty of the Pontifical Institute of Mediaeval Studies in Toronto. He became a Canadian citizen in Dec. 1945 and devoted the rest of his life to teaching graduate students the riches of St. Thomas and a critical, historical approach to the study of moral philosophy. He pioneered many ideas which have since become part of Catholic scholarship.

Bibliography: L. K. SHOOK, ''Ignatius Eschmann, O.P., 1898–1968,'' *Mediaeval Studies* 30 (1968) v–ix. I. T. ESCHMANN, *The Ethics of Saint Thomas Aquinas: Two Courses,* ed. E. A. SYNAN (Toronto 1997).

[J. A. WEISHEIPL]

ESCOBAR, ANDRÉS DE

Benedictine abbot, bishop, canonist, and theologian; b. Lisbon, 1366 or 1367; d. Florence(?) 1439 or 1440. His writings on the canonical-moral aspects of confessional practice in the Sacrament of PENANCE, on the underlying causes of the EASTERN SCHISM, and on his proposals for the reform of the clerical and lay states of life made him one of the most widely read of Renaissance Churchmen up to the 17th century. This Hispano-Portuguese monk (he was neither a Dominican nor a Franciscan, as some have asserted) earned his master's degree in theology at the University of Vienna. After becoming abbot of Randuf in the Diocese of BRAGA, he began his 40-year career in the papal Curia (*c.* 1397), acting as a papal penitentiary and adviser. He later took part in the councils of CONSTANCE, BASEL, and FLORENCE, and his signature appears on the Decree of Union with the Greeks. In 1408 Pope GREGORY XII made him bishop of Cività (Tempio-Terranova) in Sardinia; in 1422 MARTIN V transferred him to the See of Ajaccio in Corsica. He does not seem to have resided in either see. In May 1428 Martin V transferred him to the titular See of Megara. Besides Randuf, he held the abbeys of San Juan de Pendorada in Oporto and San Rosendo de Celanova in Galicia *in commendam* in order to supplement his meager income.

In his *Gubernaculum conciliorum* (1435) he manifested certain conciliarist views (*see* CONCILIARISM), but Candal asserts that these views must be understood in the light of Escobar's anxiety for the promotion and carrying out of reform in the Church. His authentic attitude appears more sharply defined in his abandonment of the Council of Basel in favor of Pope EUGENE IV and in his defense of papal PRIMACY and INFALLIBILITY in his last treatise, *De Graecis errantibus* (1437). This work, largely derived from St. Thomas Aquinas's *Contra errores Graecorum,* is distinguished for its balanced and sympathetic approach to an understanding of the ritual differences between the Greek and Latin Churches.

Bibliography: The best authority for the facts of Escobar's biography and for a summary view of his writings are his *Tractatus polemico-theologicus de Graecis errantibus,* ed. E. CANDAL (*Concilium florentinum: Documenta et scriptores* 4.1; Rome 1952), and E. CANDAL, ''Andrés de Escobar, Obispo de Megara,'' *Orientalia Christiana periodica* 14 (1948) 80–104.

[R. H. TRAME]

ESCOBAR, MARINA DE, VEN.

Mystic and foundress of the Brigittines in Spain; b. Valladolid, Feb. 8, 1554; d. Valladolid, June 9, 1633. Marina's father, Rodrigo, was a man of deep spirituality, a lawyer at the royal chancellery, and a professor at the university. Her mother, Marguerite, was the daughter of the physician attending Charles V. Marina's adolescence was disturbed somewhat by alterations of fervor, dryness, and scruples. She offered herself totally to God during the Lent of 1587. Three Jesuits were successively her directors: Pedro de Leon; Luis de LA PUENTE, after Pedro's death in 1603; and Miguel de Oreña, who succeeded La Puente. In 1615 Marina conceived the plan of establishing the Brigittines in Spain. With the help of La Puente she drew up an adaptation of the constitutions of St. Brigit, which was approved by Urban VIII, Nov. 28, 1628, and permission was granted for the foundation of the first monastery with Spanish religious from other orders. Although Marina did not live to see the opening of the house in Valladolid in 1637, the Spanish Brigittines nevertheless considered her their foundress.

The last 30 years of Marina's life were spent in small, dark, poorly ventilated quarters, where she was bedridden. She was able to assist at Mass, however, for it was celebrated for her daily in an adjacent room. A small circle of devout women attended to her needs and looked upon her as their spiritual mother. During these years her physical afflictions amounted to a kind of protracted martyrdom, but spiritually she seemed to live two lives—one in which she conversed with those about her, and the other in which she conversed with God, the angels, and the saints. All this is described in what may be called her autobiography, *Vida maravillosa de la Venerable Virgen Doña Marina de Escobar*. This work was put together from notes written at the command of her spiritual directors. The first part, carrying up to the year 1624, was prepared and published by La Puente (Madrid 1655); the second part, by Pinto Ramirez, SJ (Madrid 1673). The two parts were published together in 1766. Besides providing an account of Marina's own extraordinary mystical experience—her participation in the mysteries of the humanity of Christ, including the stigmata, her experience of the divine attributes and of the wonderful ways in which God communicates Himself to the soul, her sufferings of purification—the *Vida* also throws light on many matters of importance in ascetical and mystical theology. The *Vida* was subjected to careful scrutiny by the Jesuits. The first part of it caused the halting of La Puente's process of beatification for 40 years, for the Roman censors thought there was illusion in it and a suggestion of QUIETISM. However, the intervention of the *promotor fidei*, Prospero Lambertini (later Benedict XIV), secured the acceptance of La Puente's text.

Bibliography: C. M. ABAD, *El Venerable Padre Luis de La Puente: Sus libros y su doctrina espiritual* (Comillas 1954) 455–531; *Vida y escritos del V. P. Luis de La Puente* (Comillas 1957) 425–451, 528–550; *Dictionnaire de spiritualité ascétique et mystique. Doctrine et histoire*, ed. M. VILLER et al. (Paris 1932–) 4.1:1083–86.

[J. VERBILLION]

ESCORIAL

Monastery of San Lorenzo, palace, royal mausoleum, college, and monastery, situated 26 miles northwest of Madrid, Spain, on the southern slope of the Guadarrama Mountains near the old village of Escorial. It was founded by Philip II in thanksgiving for the victory of St. Quentin (St. Lawrence's day, Aug. 10, 1557). Begun April 23, 1563 by Juan Bautista de Toledo, a Spanish-born military engineer, it was completed Sept. 13, 1584. The Escorial fulfilled Philip II's promise to provide a mausoleum for the remains of his father Emperor Charles V and provided a residence for the king and a palace for the court; it accommodated community of 100 friars (originally Hieronymites), a seminary, a college, a hospital, a large research library, and a generous basilica.

Architecture of the Escorial. Dissatisfied with the first scheme for the church, Philip II requested plans from a great many architects. Their projects (now lost) were submitted to the Florentine Academy for criticism in 1567. Though parts of some of them may have been incorporated in the building as we see it, visiting Italian military architect Francesco Paciotto submitted the drawings (also lost) according to which the church was built, as we know from José de Sigüenza, official chronicler of the Escorial.

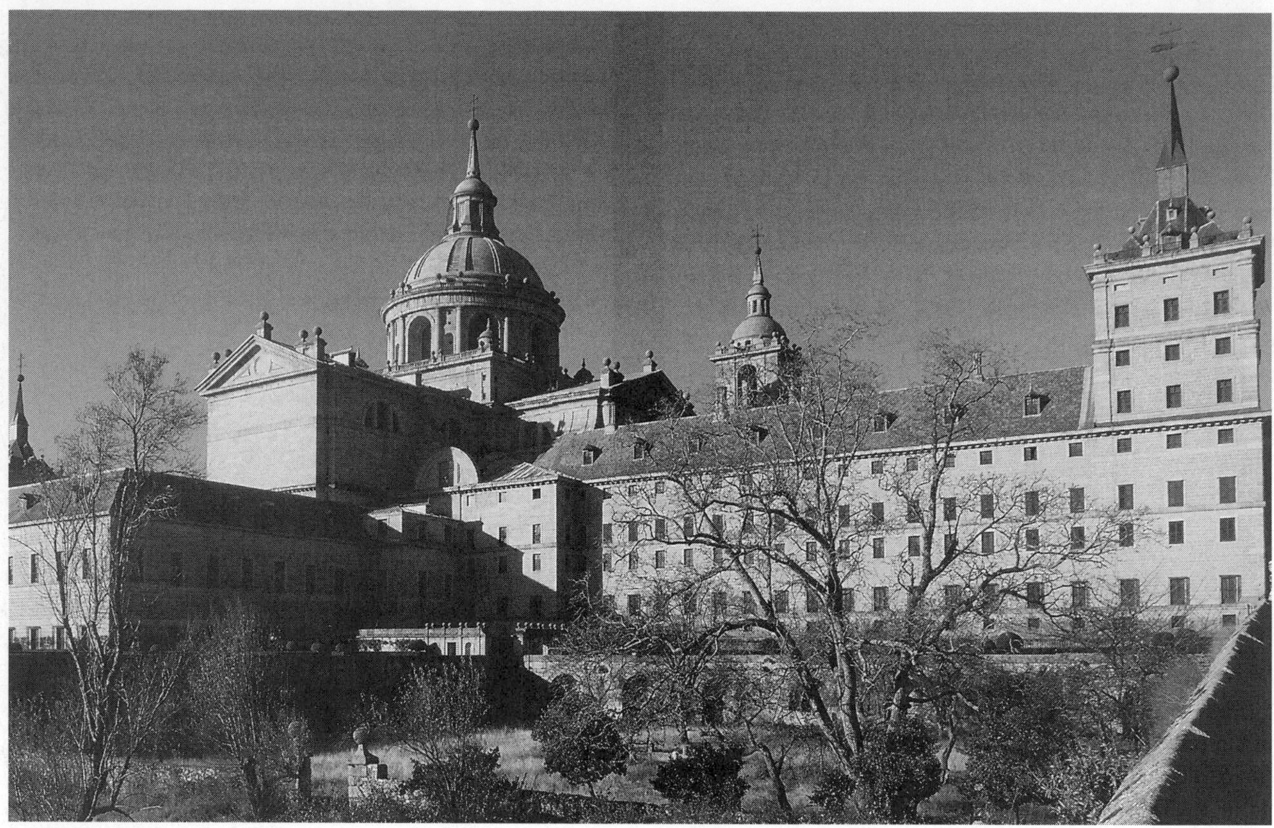

El Escorial Palace and Monastery, San Lorenzo de El Escorial, Spain. (© Nik Wheeler/CORBIS)

Upon the death of de Toledo (May 1567), his assistant Juan de Herrera took charge of the construction. In 1572 Herrera reorganized the entire workshop in order to speed the work, introducing competitive bidding for contracts and requiring stone to be cut to specified dimensions at the quarry rather than on site. Herrera claimed that his methods permitted doing in eight years (1572–84) what by previous methods would have taken 80.

The rectangular building measuring 207 meters by 161 meters consists of three parts: the south portion housed the royal palace and offices; on the north was the monastery with 300 cells and in the middle, the church with 43 altars. The Escorial has remarkable architectural coherence. Built in a coarse granite that permits no refinement of detail, it is contained within clean, simple planes of immense size. The taste and will of Philip II are present everywhere, and he, as much as his architects, is to be credited with the emergence of the severe mode in Spanish architecture (*estilo desornamentado,* or ''bare style''). It contributed a clarity of structure, a love of rectilinear planes, and geometric consonance to subsequent Spanish architecture.

History of the Escorial. The Hieronymites installed by Philip II remained there until their suppression (1854); the monastery was later granted by Isabella II to St. Antonio Maria Claret and a group of secular priests (1859), and by Alfonso XII to the Augustinians (1885), who still hold it. Philip II's ascetic study-bedroom, from which he governed the Spanish Empire and in which he died (1598), is interesting in its simplicity; but Charles III and Charles IV in the 18th century decorated the other rooms and used the building as a hunting lodge. Beneath the church is the pantheon, where most Spanish kings since Charles V are buried with their families in hierarchical order.

The Escorial as a Cultural Center. The Escorial houses some 16,000 oil paintings by Velázquez, Zurbarán, Ribera, Titian, and others; some 540 murals, including that of the battles of Higueruela and St. Quentin (185 feet long); and a world-famous library, which contains about 40,000 books, mostly rare, and 4,742 valuable manuscripts in Arabic, Latin, Greek, Hebrew, and Spanish.

Bibliography: *El Escorial: Eighth Marvel of the World* (Madrid 1967). G. KUBLER, *Building the Escorial* (Princeton 1982). R. MULCAHY, *The Decoration of the Royal Basilica of El Escorial*

(New York 1994). M. CABLE, *El Escorial* (New York 1971). M. LÓPEZ SERRANO, ed., *Trazas de Juan de Herrera* (Madrid 1944). A. PORTABALES-PICHEL, *Maestros mayores, arquitectos y aparejadores de El Escorial* (Madrid 1952). J. QUEVEDO, *Historia del real monasterio de San Lorenzo, llamado comunmente del Escorial* (Madrid 1849). JUAN DE SAN GERÓNIMO, *Memorias sobre la fundación del Escorial y su fábrica* (*Colección de documentos inéditos para la historia de España*, 112 v. (Madrid 1842–95) 7; 1845). JOSÉ DE SIGÜENZA, *Fundación del monasterio de El Escorial* (Madrid 1605; new ed. Madrid 1963). *Historia primitiva y exacta del monasterio del Escorial* (Madrid 1881). *Los Agustinos y el real monasterio de San Lorenzo de El Escorial, 1885–1910* (Madrid 1910). J. ZARCO CUEVAS, *Catálogo de los manuscritos castellanos de la real biblioteca de El Escorial,* 3 v. (Madrid 1924–29).

[G. KUBLER; D. W. LOMAX]

ESCRIVÁ DE BALAGUER Y ALBÁS, JOSEMARÍA, BL.

Founder of the Prelature of the Holy Cross and OPUS DEI; b. Jan. 9, 1902, Barbastro, Spain; d. June 26, 1975, Villa Trevere, Rome, Italy.

One of six children of José Escrivá and Dolores Balaguer, Escrivá studied at the School of Law of the University of Saragossa after high school, subsequently receiving the doctorate in law from the University of Madrid (1939). Once his seminary studies were completed in Saragossa, he was ordained on March 28, 1925. Later he received a doctorate in theology from the Pontifical Lateran University, Rome. His priestly work began in rural parishes and was continued among university students and people from a wide variety of backgrounds in the slums of Saragossa and Madrid.

On Oct. 2, 1928 he founded OPUS DEI, an association whose object is to spread Christian doctrine and virtues in all environments of social and professional life. It provides a spiritual life style for those who want to follow Christ more closely, but who choose to remain in secular society. In 1946, Msgr. Escrivá de Balaguer moved his residence to Rome and traveled throughout Europe to prepare and consolidate the apostolic work of Opus Dei. Between 1970 and 1975, he carried out an extensive work of preaching and catechetical instruction in practically every country of Latin America and in various European nations. In addition to historical, juridical, and theological writings, he is the author of widely read spiritual books, most of which have been translated into several languages, including *The Way* (Chicago 1954), *Holy Rosary* (Chicago 1953), *Conversations with Msgr. Escrivá de Balaguer* (Shannon 1968), *Christ Is Passing By* (Chicago 1974), *Friends of God* (Madrid 1977), and *La Abadesa de las Huelgas* (Madrid 1944). *The Way*, first published in 1934 under the title *Consideraciones espirituales*, by 1999 had sold 4,721,000 copies in 42 languages.

Addressing a crowd of 300,000 faithful gathered on May 17, 1992 in St. Peter's Square for Escrivá's beatification, Pope John Paul II said, "With supernatural intuition, Bl. Josemaría untiringly preached the universal call to holiness and apostolate." Escrivá's body is entombed in the Prelatic Church of Our Lady of Peace at Viale Bruno Buozzi in Rome.

Feast: June 26.

Bibliography: Works by BLESSED JOSEMARÍA ESCRIVÁ: *Children of God: The Life of Spiritual Childhood* (Princeton, N.J. 1998). *Friends of God,* Eng. tr. (Princeton, N.J. 1977). *Furrow* (Princeton, N.J. 1986). *The Forge* (Princeton, N.J. 1987). *The Way of the Cross* (Princeton, N.J. 1981). *The Way,* reprint (Princeton, N.J. 1985). Works about Blessed Josemaría Escrivá: *Así le vieron: testimonios sobre monseñor Escrivá de Balaguer*, ed. R. SERRANO (Madrid 1992). J. H. BENET, *Josemaria Escrivá de Balaguer: un hombre de Dios* (Madrid 1992). P. BERGLAR, *Opus Dei: Life and Work of its Founder* (Princeton, N.J. 1995). S. BERNAL, *Msgr. Josemaría Escrivá de Balaguer* (New York 1977). A. BYRNE, *Sanctifying Ordinary Work* (New York 1975). L. CARANDELL, *Vida y milagros de monseñor Escrivá de Balaguer* (Barcelona 1992). C. CAVALLERI, *Immersed in God: Blessed Josemaria Escriva* (Princeton, N.J. 1996). *Estudios sobre Camino: colección de estudios*, ed. J. MORALES (Madrid 1988). F. GONDRAND, *At God's Pace* (Princeton, N.J. 1982). *Hombre de Dios: testimonios sobre el fundador del Opus Dei* (Madrid 1994). F. OCARIZ BRAÑA, *Canonical Path of Opus Dei* (Princeton, N.J. 1994); *Vivir como hijos de dios: estudios sobre el Beato Josemaría Escrivá* 4th ed. (Pamplona 1999). R. G. PÉREZ, *Trabajando junto al beato Josemaría* (Madrid 1994). *La personalidad del Beato Josemaría Escrivá de Balaguer* (Pamplona 1994). A. DEL PORTILLO, *Immersed in God: Blessed Josemaría Escrivá* (Princeton 1996). J. YNFANTE, *Opus Dei: así en la tierra como en el cielo* (Barcelona 1996).

[M. M. KENNEDY]

ESGLIS, LOUIS PHILIPPE MARIAUCHAU D'

Eighth bishop of Quebec, Canada; b. Quebec, April 24, 1710; d. Saint Pierre, Île d'Orléans, Quebec, June 4, 1788. His father, François Mariauchau d'Esglis, was an army officer who arrived in Canada in 1689. Louis was ordained Sept. 18, 1734, and immediately became the parish priest of Saint Pierre, Île d'Orléans. In 1770 he was approved by the authorities at Rome and London as coadjutor of Quebec and was consecrated by Bp. J. O. Briand July 12, 1772, with the title Bishop of Dorylée. When Briand resigned (1784), d'Esglis, who was the first native-born Canadian bishop, assumed the authority of the see, but remained in his former residence until his death. Too old to administer to the diocese, he had a coadjutor, Jean-François Hubert, appointed as soon as possible.

Bibliography: H. TÊTU, *Les Évêques de Québec* (Quebec 1889). A. H. GOSSELIN, *L'Église du Canada après la conquête,* 2 v. (Quebec 1916–17) v.2.

[H. PROVOST]

Tapestry featuring Opus Dei founder Josemaría Escrivá de Balaguer y Albás. (AP/Wide World Photos)

ESKIL, ST.

Martyr; fl. Sweden, 11th century. He was called Eskillinus by Ailnoth in his *Gesta Suenomagni.* According to a later legend, Eskil was born in England and was stoned to death in the pagan reaction under King Blotsven for having preached the Christian faith under Blotsven's predecessor. The patron of the Diocese of Strängnäs, Sweden, he had a local cultus, in addition to a cultus among the Bridgettines of other countries. The translation of his relics is observed on Oct. 12; a reliquary preserving an arm of the saint is in the State Historical Museum in Stockholm. Bishop Brynolf Algotsson of Skara (d. 1317, beatified 1492) composed a rhymed history and a sequence in Eskil's honor. The town of Eskilstuna (Tuna) bears his name, as does the church in which his remains are buried. Eskil is portrayed in art with the stones of his martyrdom.

Feast: June 12 (Northern Europe).

Bibliography: *Scriptores rerum Suecicarum,* v.2 (Uppsala 1828). *Vitae sanctorum Danorum,* ed. M. C. GERTZ (new ed. Copenhagen 1908–12). *Analecta hymnica* (Leipzig 1886–1922) 42:199–200; 43:130–131. S. LINDQVIST, *Den helige Eskils biskopsdöme* (Stockholm 1915). T. SCHMID, "E., Botvid och David," *Scandia* 4 (1931) 102–114; *Sveriges kristnande* (Stockholm 1934). C. A. MOBERG, *Über die schwedischen Sequenzen,* 2 v. (Uppsala 1927); *Die liturgischen Hymnen in Schweden* (Copenhagen 1947). L. MUSSET, *Les Peuples scandinaves au moyen âge* (Paris 1951).

[T. SCHMID]

ESKIL OF LUND

Archbishop; b. 1100; d. Clairvaux, Sept. 6, 1181. He was the son of high Jutish nobility, and was educated in the cathedral school of Hildesheim (Germany). In 1134, Eskil became bishop of Roskilde (Denmark); in 1138 he succeeded his uncle in the See of LUND; and in 1156 was created primate of Sweden and papal legate for all Scandinavia. He freed his archdiocese from German influence, promoted the GREGORIAN REFORM, converted the pagan Wends, supported ALEXANDER III against FREDERICK I BARBAROSSA, and promoted the settlement of monastic orders, particularly those of the CISTERCIANS and PREMONSTRATENSIANS. For his courageous stand on all these issues, Eskil suffered imprisonment, was forced into exile (1161–67), and, in 1177, retired for the last years of his life to Clairvaux, where he was venerated as a saint.

Bibliography: H. KOCH, *Danmarks kirke i den begyndende Højmiddelalder,* 2 v. (Copenhagen 1936) 1:81–121. W. W. WILLIAMS, *Saint Bernard of Clairvaux* (Westminster, Md. 1952) 88–89. BERNARD OF CLAIRVAUX, *The Letters of St. Bernard of Clairvaux,* tr. B. S. JAMES (Chicago 1953) 493–494. A. OTTO, *Lexikon für Theologie und Kirche* 2 3:1104.

[L. J. LEKAI]

ESPADA Y LANDA, JUAN JOSÉ DÍAZ DE

Reforming Spanish bishop of Havana; b. Arróyave, Alava, Spain, 1756; d. Havana, Aug. 13, 1832. He directed the Diocese of Havana for three decades (1802–32), and was able to ascertain the needs of his diocese with dispatch. To undertake his great work of reform, he requested and obtained the aid of the most outstanding men of merit in the Cuban capital. Because of his fervent apostolic zeal and his great social and intellectual accomplishments, his name was mentioned, *primus inter pares,* with the names of the great prelates of Cuba. Under his pastoral charge, and in large measure under his auspices, Cuban society was able to adapt to the culture and the progress of the period. In his diocese, Bishop Espada contributed a large sum of money and a large plot to establish the first cemetery of Havana. His first pastoral visit (1804–05) produced abundant spiritual fruit, and also permitted him to delineate more exactly the limits of the rural parishes; to allocate, with the greatest possible fairness, the distribution of Church revenue; and to assist impoverished and needy parishes. He was firm in correcting abuses and superstitions, and was a constant protector of charitable institutions and those that favored popular education. He founded schools, reorganized asylums, and directed the Economic Society of Friends of the country, giving it his own vigorous stamp and renewed impetus; he reorganized the seminary; and he encouraged and granted his protection to the famous Father Félix Varela, reformer of philosophical studies, and to Tomás Romay, who introduced and spread vaccination. Espada's outstanding work of reform during two constitutional periods caused him to make bitter and stubborn enemies, who denounced him and reviled him; but most of the people, even those who were in power, honored him. His death occasioned sincere, general manifestations of mourning among all the social classes of a people who loved and respected him.

Bibliography: C. GARCÍA PONS, *El obispo Espada y su influencia en la cultura Cubana* (Havana 1951).

[J. M. PÉREZ CABRERA]

ESPEN, ZEGER BERNHARD VAN

Canonist of wide influence in the Church–State theories of the 18th century; b. Louvain, July 8, 1646; d. Amersfoort, Oct. 2, 1728. After his ecclesiastical studies in Louvain, he was ordained a priest in 1673. In 1675, he received the doctorate in Canon Law and in 1677 he taught that discipline at the Collegium Hadriani VI, University of Louvain, where he was sought out for counsel by many jurists, bishops, and princes. After several influential books and pamphlets that indicated his inclination towards rigorism, he published in 1700 his *Jus ecclesiasticum universum*, an attempt to present in a coherent order all the elements of ecclesiastical discipline. The work strengthened his reputation but also provoked some qualms. In April 1704, it was placed on the list of the Roman Index. Nevertheless, Van Espen continued his work and published a supplement in 1729 (inserted in the 1753 edition). Meanwhile his leanings toward Jansenism and his contacts with prominent members of this movement became evident. Besides, his writings about dispensations, immunities, exemptions and the royal *placet* evinced opinions that provoked violent opposition in many quarters. Moreover, Van Espen had approved, perhaps even caused, the election of the Vicar-General of Utrecht, Cornelius Steenhoven, who had been promoted to archbishop without permission of the Holy See and furthermore by unauthorized electors. When afterward the bishop-elect had himself consecrated by a suspended bishop, assisted by two simple priests, Van Espen, in a letter printed in Holland (*Responsio epistolaris*, 1724), defended this procedure. Thereupon he was suspended and deprived of all claims to his professorship and academic honors.

About the same time, Abp. Thomas Philippe d'Alsace de Boussu submitted to him three questions: (1) whether he adhered sincerely to the confession of faith of Pius IV and was prepared to make it again; (2) whether he was prepared to swear upon the formulary of Alexander VII, in conformity with the Bull *Vineam Domini* (1705); (3) whether he accepted without reservation the constitution *Unigenitus* (1713) and rejected all theses condemned therein. Van Espen responded that he would agree to the first point, but could not to the other two, and appealed to the Governess of the then Austrian Netherlands. But he was sentenced and condemned, and rather than recant, he fled to the northern Netherlands, first to Maastricht, then to Amersfoort, where most Jansenist refugees from France and Belgium had settled. A few months afterward he died.

Bibliography: *Scripta omnia*, 5 v. (Louvain-Paris 1753–68). F. LAURENT, *Van Espen* (Brussels 1860). H. HURTER, *Nomenclator literarius theologiae catholicae* (3d ed. Innsbruck 1903–13) 4: 12181–84. K. WEINZIERL, *Lexikon für Theologie und Kirche*, ed. J. HOFER and K. RAHNER (Freiburg 1957–65) 3:1107. J. LECLERC, *Catholicisme* 4:445. G. LECLERC, Z. B. *Van Espen et l'autorité ecclésiastique* (Zurich 1964). M. NUTTINCK, *La vie et l'oeuvre de Zeger-Bernard Van Espen* (Louvain 1969). G. COOMAN, R. G. W. HUYSMANS, B. WAUTERS, eds., *Zeger-Bernard Van Espen (1646–1728)* (Louvain 2001).

[F. MAASS]

ESPENCE, CLAUDE TOGNIEL DE

Theologian; b. Châlons-sur-Marne, 1511; d. Paris, Oct. 4, 1571. He was rector of the Sorbonne in 1540. Because of his rich qualities he was named in 1544 by Francis I to the theological commission established to prepare agenda for the Council of TRENT, to which he was sent in 1547 as the representative of Henry II. In 1561 he took part in the religious colloquium at Poissy, and because of his spirit of moderation and conciliation was attacked by Protestants and Catholics alike. His most important works were: *De eucharistia eiusque adoratione* (Paris 1573), *Institution du prince chrétien* (Paris 1548), *Traicté contre l'erreur vieil et renouvelé des prédestinés* (Paris 1548).

Bibliography: H. HURTER, *Nomenclator literarius theologiae catholicae* (3d ed. Innsbruck 1903–13) 3:17–19. A. HUMBERT, *Dictionnaire de théologie catholique*, A. VACANT et al. (Paris 1903–50) 5.1:603–605. H. M. FÉRET, *Catholicisme. Hier, aujourd'hui et demain*, ed. G. JACQUEMET (Paris 1947–) 4:445–446. A. BIGELMAIR, *Lexikon für Theologie und Kirche*, ed. J. HOFER and K. RAHNER (2d, new ed. Freiburg 1957–65) 3:1107.

[J. H. MILLER]

ESPINAR, ALONSO DE

Franciscan missionary in the Antilles; place and date of birth unknown; d. at sea, 1513. A friar by this name was vicar of the Franciscan friary of S. Antonio del Jobre in Galicia in 1499, and he may be the same friar who came in 1502 to Santo Domingo with Governor Ovando as the superior of 17 Franciscans. At any rate, Espinar and his friars began the work of evangelization of the New World. In Santo Domingo he began the famous friary of San Francisco, which became the headquarters of the province of the Holy Cross. This was the first province founded by any religious order in the New World, and Espinar seems to have been named the provincial. He helped found the first hospital, La Concepción, in November 1503. He guided the expansion of the friars to Cuba, Puerto Rico, and Jamaica and to the South American continent. He favored the elementary education of the sons of the caciques and other native leaders. By 1512 these students were so numerous that Espinar had shipped from Spain for their use 2,000 primers of reading and writing. In the commotion that resulted in 1511 from the sermon of the Dominican Antonio Montesino, who condemned to hell all Spaniards who held natives, Espinar took a more moderate view and helped to write the laws of Burgos (1512–13) that regulated the labor of the natives. For this he merited the vituperation of Las Casas, although even a prejudiced witness was forced to confess that Espinar was ''a good religious and a venerable person'' and ''that the king had already formed a high opinion of him.'' On a trip to Spain, Espinar requested 40 friars from the king for the work in the New World. The request was readily granted, and the Crown agreed to defray all expenses of the outfitting and of the trip. Espinar was leading eight of these friars to Santo Domingo when he died, as the documents say ''in the middle of the sea'' and was buried there.

Bibliography: A. LÓPEZ, ''Fray Alonso de Espinar, misionero en las Indias,'' *Archivo ibero-americano* 6 (1916) 160–167. A. S. TIBESAR, ''The Franciscan Province of the Holy Cross of Española, 1505–1559,'' *The Americas* 13 (1956–57) 377–397.

[L. G. CANEDO]

ESPINAREDA, PEDRO DE

Pioneer Franciscan missionary in the north of Mexico; b. place and date unknown; d. Zacatecas, Mexico, 1576. Espinareda first appeared in history in the late summer of 1553 traveling from Salamanca in Spain to embark as a Franciscan missionary to the New World. In 1562 he was superior of a small band of Franciscans engaged in settling the nomadic Tepehuan people in the lowlands of Durango and introducing them to the Egyptian plow, which they still use to this day. From his home base at Nombre de Dios he spearheaded the founding of new mission fields farther north. In 1566 he made his historic journey eastward along the northern rim of Spanish conquest to Panuco on the Gulf of Mexico, thereby occasioning further expeditions in that direction and arousing interest in a connecting route between the mines of northwest Mexico and the seaport of Panuco. He was appointed the first commissary of the Inquisition in the newly founded Kingdom of New Vizcaya in 1563, and lived to see his small band of friars grow to become the Custody of Zacatecas, the northern jurisdiction of the Franciscans in Mexico. Tradition tells us that he was the first superior of the custody.

Bibliography: J. L. MECHAM, *Francisco de Ibarra and Nueva Vizcaya* (Durham 1927). J. I. GALLEGOS, *Durango colonial, 1563–1821* (Mexico City 1960).

[I. GALLEGOS]

ESPINOSA, ISIDRO FÉLIX DE

Franciscan missionary and historian; b. Querétaro, Mexico, November 1679; d. there, February 1755. Espinosa entered the Franciscan Order at Querétaro March 18, 1696, and was ordained in February 1703. When sent to the missions in northeast Mexico just below Texas, Espinosa soon became a promoter of reopening the old Franciscan missions. A preliminary exploratory trip (April 1709), of which he wrote his *diario,* helped win a favorable decision, although Espinosa himself was sent back to the college as master of novices. After 1714 Espinosa returned north and with Fray Antonio MARGIL helped to advance the mission frontier to the border of French Louisiana, founding six missions. A French advance in 1718 destroyed these promising centers. In 1721 Espinosa went back to Texas with the Marqués de Aguayo, but his election as guardian of the college forced him to leave and he never returned. He devoted the rest of his life to literary and administrative tasks. In 1726 he was appointed official chronicler of the college of Querétaro and later of all the mission colleges of Mexico. Espinosa's published works are numerous, but the more important are: *El peregrino septentrional atlante. delineado en la exemplarissima vida del Venerable Padre Fray Antonio Margil de Jesús* (Mexico 1737), the basic life of Margil; *Chrónica de la Provincia de Michoacán,* unfinished but printed in 1899; and *Chrónica. . . de todos los colegios de Propaganda Fide de esta Nueva España de misioneros franciscanos* (Mexico 1746). This is the most important work, written in a fluent style carefully documented. A posthumous biography of his brother, the Oratorian Juan Antonio Pérez de Espinosa, was printed in 1942.

Bibliography: I. F. DE ESPINOSA, *Crónica de los Colegios de Propaganda Fide de la Nueva España*, ed., L. GÓMEZ CANEDO (Franciscan Historical Classics 2; new ed. Washington 1964).

[L. G. CANEDO]

ESQUEDA RAMÍREZ, PEDRO, ST.

Martyr, priest; b. Apr. 29, 1887, San Juan de Los Lago, Jalisco, Mexico; d. Nov. 22, 1927, San Miguel el Alto, near Teocaltitlán. Pedro Esqueda, a precocious child, began his formal education at age four. He entered the seminary of Guadalajara (1902), which was seized and closed before he completed his studies. Returning to his home parish, he served as a deacon until his ordination was arranged in 1916 at which time he was named pastor. His passion for catechesis inspired Pedro to found several centers for training catechists. When the persecution of the Church worsened in 1926, Pedro went into hiding, moving from house to house until he was captured in hiding by *federales* on Nov. 18, 1927. They beat the priest, held him incommunicado in the abbey, tortured him for the next few days, and shot him in Teocaltitlán. He was both beatified (Nov. 22, 1992) and canonized (May 21, 2000) with Cristobal MAGALLANES [*see* GUADALAJARA (MEXICO), MARTYRS OF, SS.] by Pope John Paul II.

Feast: May 25 (Mexico).

Bibliography: J. CARDOSO, *Los mártires mexicanos* (Mexico City 1953). J. DÍAZ ESTRELLA, *El movimiento cristero: sociedad y conflicto en los Altos de Jalisco* (México, D.F. 1979).

[K. I. RABENSTEIN]

ESQUIÚ, MAMERTO

Franciscan bishop of Córdoba, patriot, theologian, and orator, whose reputation for sanctity has led to his being considered for beatification; b. San José, Catamarca, Argentina, 1826; d. Córdoba, 1883. He was perhaps the most important Catholic thinker of his country in the 19th century; and his thought, following the tradition of his order, was Neothomistic (*see* NEOSCHOLASTICISM AND NEOTHOMISM). Influenced by Bonaventure, Augustine, and Thomas Aquinas, he tried to stimulate the study of metaphysics. He held that the universe is the revelation of God, whose existence it demonstrates, showing the metaphysical supremacy of Thomas over Aristotle. Dedicating himself to the study of the Scriptures, he explained through them the mysteries of justification and of the laws and grace according to St. JOHN CHRYSOSTOM and the commentaries of St. Thomas on St. Paul; by the Pauline method he resolved the theme of sin and freedom (*libertas a peccato*)—this permitted him to make a thorough criticism of the basis of the liberal thesis that freedom is always the ''servant of love.'' In Christology he was influenced by the Fathers and also by Melchor Cano; in ethics, by St. Alphonsus Liguori. Among the moderns he was well acquainted with Balmes, Donoso Cortés, Bossuet, and the French apologists. On that foundation, he conceived the plan of a theology of history involving the moments of divine conservation and the reparation by the Word, which is historical time; that, in turn, includes the mission of the Apostles (Gospel), the doctrine (Epistles), and the institution of history in Christ. Thus, Christ is the center of society, and the people as such are historically responsible. The influence of *De civitate dei* and of Italian and even German neoscholasticism (Cornoldi) is evident. Man is social, and society is a moral being linked to the infinite; accordingly obedience is a duty, and civil authority is legitimate; but since at bottom the Word sustains everything, the Gospel must be the ultimate law of nations.

Esquiú acquired national fame for his ''Sermon on the Constitution'' (1853), in which he explained the difficulties of submission but also (after a half-century of wars and anarchy) exhorted it. Sovereignty, he said, resides in the people only instrumentally because their origin is from God. In a Catholic people the State must be united to the Church, and he concluded by stating the Marian vocation of America. Esquiú was a mystic whose unitive experiments can be observed in his *Diario;* however, it is not possible to learn whether he reached the transforming union. He was a model bishop and an apostle of confession, who exercised a decisive influence on the organization of Argentina. His unbounded charity and his humility have led the Argentines to consider him a saint. The cause for his beatification was begun Jan. 11, 1952.

Bibliography: M. ESQUIÚ, *Sermones, discursos, cartas pastorales, oraciones fúnebres, etc., correspondencia . . .* , ed. A. ORTIZ 2 v. (Córdoba, Argen. 1883). M. GÁLVEZ, *Vida de fray Mamerto Esquiú* (2d ed. Buenos Aires 1944). A. CATURELLI, *El pensamiento de Mamerto Esquiú* (Córdoba, Arg. 1954).

[A. CATURELLI]

ESSENCE

The word ''essence'' (Lat. *essentia*) is related to the Latin term *ens* (being), which itself implies a relationship to *esse* (to be). Essence is what is, what exists. In this sense, it designates a concrete, singular reality in the act of EXISTENCE. Essence is, moreover, a substantial reality (*see* SUBSTANCE). It is not, properly speaking, that which modifies an existing substance, such as weight, color, and operation, but that which exists in itself, that which sustains itself in existence without the aid of a substratum that receives and supports it. In fact, color, weight, and the like, do not exist: they are accidents; it is through them that substance, or essence, exists as colored, heavy, and so on. (*see* ACCIDENT).

In another sense, essence answers the questions: In what does a particular existing reality consist? What is its DEFINITION? Taken in this meaning, essence expresses the QUIDDITY of a thing, that by which it is immediately intelligible and on which the human mind can focus—because it presents an immobile aspect, the stable FORM of what it really and fully is, viz, a THING.

Since the notion of essence has undergone an evolution in the history of thought and is not uniformly regarded by all philosophers, this article first explains the historical development of the notion, and then treats a problem of interest to scholastic thinkers, viz, the multiplication and individuation of essences. The more difficult historical and doctrinal questions concerning the relationship between essence and existence are treated elsewhere (*see* ESSENCE AND EXISTENCE).

HISTORICAL DEVELOPMENT

The history of the concept of essence may be conveniently divided into periods corresponding to Greek, medieval, modern, and contemporary thought.

Greek thought. For PLATO, essences are the proper object, the only authentic object, of human knowledge.

All else, that is, the world of sensible and moving appearances, is pure illusion: unintelligible in its constant mobility, it really is not; it does not exist. What exists is for Plato the essence of things divested of the various modes they manifest here below; this is realized in an intelligible world separated from the present one, where man may find it by reminiscence. The essence of horse—for example, what exists absolutely as horse, or horse in itself—belongs to the world of archetypal Forms or Ideas, of which the horse sensed here below is only a deceptive partaker, an illusory reflection. Only essence is, with its characteristics of perfection and stability.

Such an idealistic theory found its refutation in the moderate realism of ARISTOTLE, one of Plato's disciples. Aristotle did not admit that what things are and what the mind perceives as unchanged in them exist apart in another world. Rather he extracted essences, definitions, and beings from this separated world and located them in the concrete realities of sensible experience. For Aristotle, essences say what things are; they are not what exists. What exists is concrete essence, that is, essence determined by adventitious secondary elements that make it individual and capable of existence. Horse in itself does not exist, but only particular horses with the essence of horse realized in them.

According to Aristotle, one may speak of essence also as common to all individuals of the same SPECIES. This essence, expressed by the definition, exists formally only in the mind, which abstracts from the individuating notes that clothe an essence in extramental reality (*see* ABSTRACTION). The universal character that essence receives from the mind is itself based on the real presence of the essence in things existing under an individualized mode.

Medieval thought. It is this latter theory that prevailed in Christian philosophy under the name of moderate REALISM, and to which St. THOMAS AQUINAS lent his support. The beings of the world, be they spiritual or material, are none other than realized ideas. Such realization, however, is no longer in the manner described by Plato, but according to a presence immanent within things and through PARTICIPATION in the divine essence, eminent model of all that exists. Essences come into being by way of creation or divine efficiency. The divine essence in its transcendent intelligibility is thus the remote foundation of every created essence.

St. AUGUSTINE was the first to develop the theory of divine ideas as principles and causes of the ideas or essences incarnate in things. The divine ideas are nothing other than the divine essence itself, inasmuch as this is remotely and variously imitable by the beings of nature. This Augustinian conception of ideas is obviously different from that of Plato.

The Thomistic theory of moderate realism did not succeed in rallying all minds. Fourteenth-century philosophers such as WILLIAM OF OCKHAM and NICHOLAS OF AUTRECOURT asserted that the universal essences said to be abstracted from individuals are merely fictions. They refer simply to names, labels that are fixed to individuals of a certain, apparently homogeneous series, but to which no reality corresponds within things. These philosophers have been called nominalists.

Other thinkers, called conceptualists, did not go as far as the nominalists and regarded the common essence as a pure concept, a simple idea in men's minds without any foundation in nature. For them, the mind constructs this idea, starting from a certain sensible similarity, but without anything in existing beings that is really common to them. These two theories of NOMINALISM and CONCEPTUALISM gave rise to the famous problem of UNIVERSALS, which is concerned with the ontological status of the essences of things. The position of St. Thomas is realistic when compared to these theories, while avoiding Plato's exaggerated realism that attributes existence to the universal essence as such.

Modern thought. The fundamental positions adopted with regard to universals are found, with variations, in the philosophical systems of modern thought.

Nominalism underlies all the sensist and empirical systems. For J. S. MILL and D. HUME principally, the real is essentially diverse and is reduced to the purely sensible data of experience. The common essence, which is confused with nature, is no longer perceptible for them. They do not speak of species of things, but only of collections of individuals. Conceptualism takes its roots also and is found with various modalities in the different forms of IDEALISM, ranging from methodical to critical and absolute idealism.

Immanuel KANT was the first, after the success of EMPIRICISM, to admit to the exigencies of universality and determinism in the knowledge of the real. But for him universal essences are not in things, or, at least, man does not reach them in themselves. He grasps only the PHENOMENA; the NOUMENA, which are things in themselves, escape him. Thus the reality of nature comes to him necessarily by sensation, but is known by him only through the a priori forms of sensitivity and the categories of his mind. The essences of beings are reduced to purely subjective constructions that man imposes upon the formless matter of his knowledge. Extramental reality is itself no longer reached; all is contained formally within the knowing subject.

After Kant, the great German idealists, J. G. FICHTE, F. W. J. SCHELLING, and G. W. F. HEGEL, rejecting Kant's ''thing-in-itself'' as a *caput mortuum,* placed all the reality of the world in mind or spirit. For Hegel, especially, essences are completely within man and come from him alone. They express, in their dialectical oppositions and provisional resolutions, the development of the human logos realizing itself progressively to become the Absolute Spirit, God. The Hegelian ''concept'' is certainly not to be confused with an abstract essence; it is a concrete concept in permanent evolution, but it is completely interiorized according to the demands of a radical idealism.

A salutary return to things themselves occurred with E. HUSSERL. Idealism had been given the lie by the brutal realities of World War I. A reassertion of INTENTIONALITY, borrowed by F. BRENTANO from the scholastics, attempted to bring men back into contact with the real external world. The French thinkers Louis LAVELLE and René Le Senne, originators of the ''philosophy of the spirit,'' also attempted to escape from the grip of idealism, and they made way for contemporary EXISTENTIALISM.

Contemporary thought. Karl JASPERS and Martin HEIDEGGER, in Germany, and Jean Paul SARTRE, in France, continued the existentialist movement with its realistic tendency, as did M. MERLEAU-PONTY. These philosophers identified themselves as phenomenologists, and their preoccupation was to go to things themselves as these appear to the mind. They were at the same time fascinated by being, and they professed an ontology wherein being does not come from man; it is really opposed to the grasp of intelligence and is far from being confused with mind. Objective being is seen by them as a sort of milieu that is presented to the mind, but about which nothing can be said except that it is what it is. It excludes from its aggregate all types of distinction, of causality, and of relation: there is being, and that is all. What happens, then, to the essences that seem to divide being into determined portions, into limiting and circumscribing natures? Heidegger's answer is that being, the source of all, precisely as ''historical'' has its effect on the concrete beings of nature. Its effect is not in the manner of the Kantian categories, which are rejected, but no explanation is given as to how the ontological parceling demanded by experience is brought about. While being enjoys an extramental status, essences appear as associated only with the workings of the knowing mind.

The same difficulty of making philosophical contact with concrete reality exists in the ontological phenomenology of Sartre. The distinction of beings, and thus of essences, presents itself to the thinker as an effect of a sort of ''decompression'' of being that the mind carries out by its ability to negate. The mind, which is endowed with freedom, is in fact a being-for-itself that cannot be reduced to the massive being-in-itself of things; it has the power of denying itself, of annihilating, by a type of differentiation that results in the ''ontic'' multiplicity of the beings of nature. This solution does not completely escape from idealism—at least the type of idealism that makes essences a simple determination of man's free activity.

Karl MARX, in complete opposition to the idealist position of Hegel, placed dialectic in matter, which thenceforth became for him the only reality in the world. ''Essences'' evolve in matter according to the process analyzed by Hegel; the knowledge man has of essence is only a reflection, a superstructure. This explanation is incapable of transcending the limitations of dialectical and historical MATERIALISM, with its restrictive view of what is real.

MULTIPLICATION AND INDIVIDUATION

For scholastics, one of the key problems relating to the notion of essence is that of explaining how one essence is shared or multiplied by many individuals. Since essence itself can be applied variously to immaterial entities such as angels, to entities that are composites of matter and spirit such as men, and to purely material entities such as minerals, the different ways in which essence is individualized in each of these categories are here explained, beginning with a consideration of the last category.

Material beings. Such entities appear to man, on the one hand, as obviously individual. On the other hand, they manifest common characteristics in their properties and activities that permit one to classify them scientifically into species, and, in some instances, to formulate certain traits of their underlying nature in definitions. Since essence is both what exists individually and what is common to individuals of the same species, one may, by a kind of abstraction, have a concept of essence that says nothing of the singularity with which it is cloaked within individuals, nor of the universality the mind confers on essence when considering it as present in such individuals. In this manner, essence is neither universal nor singular but is itself an abstraction in which only its constitutive elements are retained.

If one envisages now the multiplicity of individuals having the same specific essence, since the species is given by the form—which is like a number and is not susceptible of more or less without ceasing to be itself—individuality and multiplication can come only from the matter in which the form is received. The material form is not individuated by itself, since, in its contents, it presents only common principles; nor is it individuated by its accidents, either its own or those of the composite, for these are ontologically posterior to the individual essence. Only primary matter can furnish a principle of individuation for form (*see* MATTER AND FORM; INDIVIDUATION).

Matter alone lends itself to potential determinations relative to a QUANTITY about to be realized, which itself is the immediate principle of multiplication and number. Number is, in fact, founded on the numerical unity that accompanies actual and continuous quantity. This quantitative unity must be carefully distinguished from ontological UNITY, which is a transcendental aspect of being (*see* MULTITUDE). Discontinuous quantity receives its proper unity from an essence that is individualized by matter and is made one by its ontological unity. It is by this quantity, primordial accident of substance, that the individual, indivisible in itself, comes to be in the world of space and time.

Spiritual beings. Completely otherwise is the multiplication of created immaterial substances or angels; here quantity plays no role, and yet such substances are perfectly one with an ontological unity. This unity is relative to essence, which fully realizes a creative idea absolutely distinct from all others. It represents a degree of being that stands, in relation to existence, as a really distinct potency that receives and limits existence. Divine existence or *esse divinum*, which in God is supreme act, is thus participated according to the very measure that itself determines the essence. Act and potency are therefore components of all creatures, and at the level of substance itself. Here there is no longer informed matter; real essence plays the role of potency with respect to the act of being. God alone is simple. The immaterial creature is not only composed of an existing reality and its negative limitation; it is really composed of two distinct elements.

Individuation in the angels is thus not effected by a type of matter, as some have held. The ontological idea that such an essence represents, with its full richness, realizes itself in a single individual who is, henceforth, at the same time both species and individual when compared to what takes place in the material world. An angel, for example, Gabriel, is alone in his species, realizing this wholly at the level of singular being that is proper to his essence. Individuation thus proceeds, not from existence, but from essence; the latter adequately corresponds, in its unicity, to a creative idea of God that expresses, without real distinction in Him, the singular mode according to which the divine essence chooses to make itself participable.

The multiplication of spiritual substances has no other source, and their number—better indicated by the term ''multitude''—transcends the entire order of quantity. Multitude is proper to individuated immaterial being: ontologically it expresses nothing more than a group of spiritual beings, which man conceives as analogous to groups of material and numerical entities.

Human beings. Moving finally to individuation within the human species, one finds on a vaster scale what has already been noted concerning purely material species. The human soul, taken essentially and according to its specific definition, is something like the separated substance of the angel; it represents an idea of God that is rich in virtualities. But, in contrast to what takes place in the realm of the immaterial, this idea, to be fully realized—because situated on an ontological level that implies a substantial relation to matter—requires a number of individuals of the same essence, each sharing in the richness of the essence only to the measure determined for it by the particular capacity of the matter it must animate. Thus all human souls are of the same species; their essence is the same specifically. They become incarnate, while retaining their essential spirituality, in the portions of matter that individualize them through their particular relation to quantity. Primary matter and a spiritual soul thus constitute a singular essence, a limiting capacity of *esse* that is one in the order of existence and is numerically one in the quantity of the actually existing composite. The number of men is a number in the proper sense, by reason of the human body that situates individuals in space and time.

What distinguishes spiritual souls such as that of man from infrahuman forms, both living and nonliving, is this: souls individualized by their relation to quantified matter retain their individual character, with their own SUBSISTENCE, at death. They do so because they are made in this way at the moment of their creation and infusion into matter; their number, in this state, more closely approaches the multitude of spiritual substances who have no matter in their constitution.

See Also: ESSENCE AND EXISTENCE; EXISTENCE; ACT; POTENCY; POTENCY AND ACT; IDEA; CONCEPT; NATURE.

Bibliography: A. GAZZANA, *Enciclopedia filosofica,* 4 v. (Venice-Rome 1957) 2:92–103. R. EISLER, *Wörterbuch der philosophischen Begriffe,* 3 v. (4th ed. Berlin 1927–30) 3:538–543. É. H. GILSON, *L'Être et l'essence* (2d ed. Paris 1962). M. D. ROLAND-GOSSELIN, *Le ''De ente et essentia'' de saint Thomas d'Aquin* (Kain, Belg. 1926). R. JOLIVET, *Les Sources de l'idéalisme* (Paris 1936). M. J. ADLER, ''The Hierarchy of Essence,'' *Review of Metaphysics* 6 (1952–53): 3–30.

[M. CORVEZ]

ESSENCE AND EXISTENCE

The relationship between ESSENCE and EXISTENCE poses a problem that was much discussed and controverted in the thirteenth century and continues to be important in the development of scholastic and Thomistic metaphysics. This article surveys the historical origins of the problem, examines in detail the solution proposed by St. Thomas Aquinas, sketches the use made of the doctrine in the Thomistic tradition, and concludes with a briefer account of other solutions.

Historical origins. The remote origins of the controversy over essence and existence are to be found in Greek philosophy, although the problem of the precise relationship between the two concepts was never stated there with the clarity to be found in its later formulations. For PLATO, the problem could not exist, for he conceived essence as the perfect and stable object of the intellect, devoid of the imperfections and changing character of the world of sense. For him, essence alone exists in the strict sense, and this in the world of Ideas; all else that is perceived by the senses is merely an illusion and the occasion for referring back to the world of separated substances or essences.

The rejection by ARISTOTLE of this teaching of his master led him to adumbrate the real distinction between essence and existence, if not to affirm it outright. In his view, essences do not exist in a separated universe but are to be found in the sensible beings of this world, where they have a concrete and singular mode of existence. The essence of horse exists in this individual horse, with the accretion of its particular qualities and of all other accidental determinations that make it to be this singular existent thing. There seems little doubt that, for Aristotle, essence and existence are distinct concepts, since he holds that ''what human nature is and the fact that man exists are not the same thing'' (*Anal. post.* 92b 10–11). Whether his distinction is real or merely rational, however, is disputed (*see* DISTINCTION, KINDS OF). It may be that he affirms only that the singular essence man experiences is in a state of actual existence, and that this serves to differentiate it from the purely possible essence that man's mind may happen to conceive. [For the realistic interpretation, see G. Manser, *Das Wesen des Thomismus* (3d ed. Fribourg 1949) 510.]

Real Distinction. Among the Arab commentators on Aristotle, AVICENNA first brought the problem into focus by teaching explicitly that existence is a kind of ACCIDENT OF ESSENCE, although not in the sense that existence comes to essence as a predicamental accident comes to substance. Rather, Avicenna holds that essence, as ideally conceived, involves an element of necessity, whereas it itself is merely possible when viewed in relation to extramental existence. Existence comes to an essence under the action of the efficient cause, such as is found in the order of nature in GENERATION-CORRUPTION or as is taught in the biblical account of CREATION. Thus, for Avicenna, essence and existence must be really distinct one from the other and not merely distinct in a rational or conceptual way. AVERROËS, it may be noted, disagreed with Avicenna's teaching on this point, reproaching Avicenna for proposing as philosophy what was essentially a theological doctrine of creation.

The first of the scholastics to adopt as his own the position of Avicenna was WILLIAM OF AUVERGNE. Although a severe critic of much of Avicenna's thought, William accepted his teaching on the real distinction and employed it in his *De universo creaturarum* as a proof of the finitude and dependence of creatures (1.3.26; 2.2.8). Gradually the list of adherents grew. To it were added the names of such luminaries of the thirteenth century as St. ALBERT THE GREAT and St. Thomas Aquinas. But the list never became all-inclusive; an appreciable number of thinkers of the thirteenth and subsequent centuries continued to reject this manner of distinguishing between essence and existence.

Opposition to Real Distinction. Foremost among those who opposed the teaching of Avicenna were the heterodox Aristotelians who developed the doctrines of Averroës into the movement that came to be known as Latin AVERROISM. But this was not an isolated group. Certain thirteenth-century theologians of the Augustinian school, among whom were the Dominicans ULRIC OF STRASSBURG, THEODORIC OF FREIBERG, and HARVEY NEDELLEC and the Franciscans PETER JOHN OLIVI and RICHARD OF MIDDLETON, took a firm position against the Avicennian thesis. Like the Latin Averroists, these theologians were motivated by a loyalty to their traditions; they viewed with alarm the tendency to incorporate into the science of theology elements drawn from Islamic and Aristotelian sources. Their opposition, however, although indeed embracing the real distinction, touched it only as part of the larger problem. Not until the advent of Giles of Rome and his controversy with Henry of Ghent did the question of essence and existence become in itself a major issue.

Giles vs. Henry. To GILES OF ROME must go the credit for conferring on the problem a special prominence, for it was he who raised it from its previous ancillary role and treated it on its own merits. Giles saw essence and existence as farther apart than did St. Thomas. For St. Thomas, the two are really distinct; for Giles, they are also separable. Furthermore, Giles insisted, to the annoyance of all who disagreed, that the real distinction is fundamental to philosophy and theology. Without it—and on this point N. del Prado holds that Giles's position is identical to that of St. Thomas—the way was barred against proof of such basic doctrines as creation, the ANALOGY

OF BEING, and the distinction of substance and accidents. Never had so clear and so deliberate a challenge on this issue been hurled, and it did not want for an adversary willing to accept.

In a series of *quodlibets* (1st, 10th, 11th) directly aimed at Giles's position, HENRY OF GHENT countered with his teaching of a rational distinction between essence and existence. And along with his rational distinction, he implicitly rejected, as did all who subscribed to the rational distinction between essence and existence, the major role attributed to the real distinction by Giles. In this teaching he was joined by GODFREY OF FONTAINES, by PETER OF AUVERGNE, and later by John Duns Scotus.

Thomistic doctrine. Although Giles is undoubtedly responsible for bringing the issue to the fore, it is not he, but St. THOMAS AQUINAS, who is recognized as the most important protagonist of the real distinction. Nor is this situation surprising, given the preeminence in theology and philosophy that is rightly accorded Aquinas. In fact, this preeminence not only guaranteed Aquinas a primacy among the defenders of the real distinction, but it constituted a source of embarrassment for those who favored the opposite view. This has not, of course, done away with opposition; in fact it has been the occasion for peculiar maneuvers to which opponents have resorted in an effort to offset St. Thomas's influence.

M. Chossat, for example, sought to erase the problem itself by seriously challenging the traditional understanding of St. Thomas's position, maintaining that Aquinas himself did not teach the real distinction and that the so-called Thomistic position was in fact borrowed from Giles. But with the unearthing of evidence to the contrary through the historical studies of P. MANDONNET and M. GRABMANN this maneuver failed to convince.

Another position, traditionally Suarezian, consists in admitting that the rational distinction is in direct conflict with St. Thomas's teaching and then minimizing the force of the opposition by questioning St. Thomas's competence in dealing with the question. This is the approach of A. d'Ales, who, though accepting the Thomistic view as authentically St. Thomas's, states: "We believe that we must reject the real distinction of essence and existence as the foundation of all metaphysics, but we do not hesitate to affirm that it is the indispensable basis for a thoroughly Thomistic metaphysics." The challenge to Thomistic metaphysics embodied in this statement, namely, that it is a system whose fundamental position is vulnerable, does not find the Thomist submissive. Yet it does corroborate the traditional Thomistic stand by its admission that St. Thomas actually taught the real distinction.

Source of the Doctrine. One looks in vain through the writings of St. Thomas for a treatment of the relationship between essence and existence comparable to that given by Giles. Aquinas does discuss the relationship, but always in contexts that are devoted explicitly to the solutions of other problems. Yet there is abundant evidence of St. Thomas's teaching and his abiding consistency in proposing it. Maturity brought about a shift in St. Thomas's position on some matters, but in the matter of the real distinction the thought of St. Thomas remained unchanged throughout his scholarly career.

More interesting than the number of times that St. Thomas spoke of the real distinction is the question of the source whence he drew his conviction about the distinction. Here two possibilities suggest themselves, one clearly theological, the other philosophical. The first is the text from Exodus 3.14 ("God said to Moses: I am Who am"); the second, the doctrine on potency and act (*see* POTENCY AND ACT). The fact that the greater number of appeals to the real distinction occur in a purely theological context seems to make a good case for the first alternative. That God in a sense defined Himself in the terms "I am Who am" could very well be the source whence St. Thomas drew not only the inspiration to examine the creature in the light of essence and existence but also the assurance of the correctness of his position.

Yet the claim of potency and act is not without merit. Its strongest title to recognition is the constancy with which, and the contextual circumstances in which, St. Thomas the theologian associates potency and act with essence and existence. In the theological works in which he asserts the distinction of essence and existence, he makes frequent mention of the teaching on potency and act. This association of the two is not introduced as a proof of the real distinction. Rather, it is made to emphasize the fact that the essence-existence relation is an instance of the potency-act relation. This is significant, since it reveals that for St. Thomas the two dualities are to be compared with each other as the less known (essence-existence) and the more known (potency-act). Hence the latter could well be a source, if not the principal source, of the surety that distinguishes St. Thomas's commitment to the former.

Formulation of the Teaching. Whenever St. Thomas touches on the relationship between essence and existence—and the number of occasions is impressive—the object of his investigation remains unvaried, namely, the actual existent. His analysis of that object always reaches the same conclusion, although admittedly there are variations in his manner of expressing it. These variations range from (1) explicit identification of the distinction as real (*In Boeth. de hebdom.* 2.32; *De ver.* 27.1 ad 8), to

(2) implicit identification of the reality of the distinction (*Quodl.* 9.4.1.; *In 2 sent.* 16.1.2. ad 5), to (3) the simple statement of a distinction (*In 1 sent.* 8.4.1 sed contra 3; 8.4.2 ad 1; *De ver.* 10.8 ad 12). Such statements are troublesome only if wrenched out of context and understood in an absolute sense. As Aquinas employs them, they are but incidental to the development of some other point of doctrine; upon analysis, the content of each statement is seen to conform to the requirements of the principal question under examination.

St. Thomas's fuller teaching on the real distinction may be summarized as follows. Neither essence nor existence is a THING, nor is either to be identified with the actually existent thing, even though there could be no such thing without benefit of both. In themselves they are principles of being whence the actual existent thing is constituted (*see* PRINCIPLE). Each of these principles is incapable by itself of producing the total result, the actual existent. To effect the actual existent, each principle requires what the other contributes.

Viewed in isolation from existence, essence signifies a mode or manner according to which reality might be fashioned. Or better still—for the essence about which St. Thomas speaks is the essence of the actually existent thing—it stands for all the modes by which reality manifests itself. As a principle of the actual existing thing, it is the element that provides a full explanation of the whatness, or QUIDDITY, of the existent as being, that is, as susceptible of the formal act of being (*esse*). Existence, for its part, makes not the smallest addition to that whatness; moreover, there is no need that it should, since essence provides the complete explanation in its own order. The contribution of existence is in an order entirely different, but complementary, to that wherein essence exercises its influence.

Existence is not simply a factor; it is the primary component of actuality. It is not a FORM but an ACT. In fact, it is act par excellence, the act that perfectly fulfills the notion of act in its most formal sense. For whereas the form as act finalizes in a qualified sense, existence finalizes completely. It is the act that effects the release of essence from a most remote hold on actuality; prior to this release, essence's only claim to actuality is its susceptibility to receive it.

Do the notions of essence and existence represent for St. Thomas reflections of reality itself, or are they notions born solely of the mind's consideration? After the time of St. Thomas, as has been seen, two answers were given to this question. On the one hand, Henry of Ghent maintained that any plurality in this matter was a product of reason alone, that in point of fact there was only a real unity; on the other hand, Giles of Rome insisted not only on a real plurality but also on the separability of the two components. According to Giles, essence and existence are not only distinct independently of the mind's consideration but also capable of existential survival in the event of being severed one from the other. Neither represents St. Thomas's doctrine; Giles departs from it by excess, Henry by defect.

First, St. Thomas saw essence and existence as more than rationally distinct. Second, he never thought of conferring separability on them, either individually or conjunctively. For him, such an attribution would be a complete distortion of the character of essence and existence as principles. He taught merely that the two are really distinct and that their otherness is not the result of reason's consideration alone; reason does not make essence and existence to be two, but discovers that they are two. Despite this otherness, neither can survive the dissolution of their unification. Once their hold on each other is loosened, no trace of either remains in the order of the actual existent.

Supporting Arguments. St. Thomas has recourse to four separate arguments in the comparatively few instances in which he sought to substantiate his position on the real distinction: 1. The argument from the noninclusion of existence within the comprehensive content of essence (*De ente* 4; *De ver.* 10.12; *In 2 sent.*, 1.1.1, 3.1.1). 2. The argument that existence, as the difference distinguishing things that communicate in a generic (or specific) unity, must be really distinct from essence, or quiddity (*In 1 sent.* 8.4.2; *De ver.* 27.1 ad 8). 3. The argument from the identity of essence and existence in God to the distinction of the two in creatures. The real distinction is here emphasized as signifying the basic and universal mode of composition that removes all creatures from the level of perfect simplicity that is proper solely to God (*De ente* 4; *In 1 sent.* 8.5.1–2; *In 2 sent.* 3.1.1; *Quodl.* 9.4.1). 4. The argument involving the notion of PARTICIPATION. Any perfection that is itself common and intrinsically unrestricted but is present in things in a limited fashion must be really distinct from the things in which it is found; this is the case of the perfection of existence (*In 2 sent.* 16.1.1 ad 3, 37.1.2; *De ver.* 21.5; *In Boeth. de hebdom.* 2.31–35).

Although the notions of potency and act are frequently interwoven into the fabric of these arguments, these notions are never of major significance. But wherever potency and act are associated with essence and existence, St. Thomas makes no effort to substantiate the reality of the former composition. This procedure is unintelligible save on the supposition that the reality of the mode of composition of potency and act is better known than that of essence and existence. Indeed, the quasi equation Aquinas makes in the same contexts between essence and existence and potency and act sheds more light on the former than on the latter. To see essence as an instance of potency and existence as a kind of act enables one to understand the unity of the composite of essence and existence and to penetrate to some degree into the notion of existence under the formality of act.

Thomistic tradition. Throughout St. Thomas's writings, the appearance of the doctrine on essence and existence seems always dictated by circumstances other than the doctrine itself. Yet the frequency with which Aquinas made use of this doctrine and the prominence of the contexts in which he employed it are clear expressions both of his conviction and of the high value he placed on it. Nor were these facts lost sight of in his school. Taking their cue from St. Thomas's evaluation of the doctrine, but resetting it in a philosophical context and making explicit what St. Thomas had been content to treat implicitly, Thomists present the doctrine on the real distinction as an indispensable key to a realistic philosophy of being. Within THOMISM, this doctrine is seen as (1) offering a true image of the metaphysical structure of the actual existent, (2) providing a rational basis for the mind's ascent to God, and (3) providing a proof of God's transcendence. [For specific details on the teachings of various individuals, see F. J. Roensch, *Early Thomistic School* (Dubuque, Iowa 1964); G. Manser, *op. cit.*]

Metaphysical Structure of the Actual Existent. The actual existent is a composite of essence and existence. Both are indispensable elements, each making valuable though distinct contributions to the actual existent. A primacy, however, must be granted existence. It is the sole source of the actuality that differentiates the actual existent from merely possible being. Though existence adds nothing to the formal content of essence, essence of itself is incapable of going beyond the range of possibility. Furthermore, it is only by its release from the order of possibility that essence is able to exercise the various functions that belong to it per se. Until actualized by existence, essence is only potentially the subject of the tremendous complex of accidental features that serve to perfect it entitatively and operationally. Existence affords essence the opportunity to function actually as the integrating principle for the sum total of realities that are its accidental modifications. (*See* SUBSISTENCE.)

Rational Basis for Mind's Ascent to God. Because its essence is pure potency with reference to the order of actuality, the actual existent is contingent; hence an efficient cause is needed to explain its presence in the realm of existing things. In the final analysis, this efficient cause must be a Being in whom essence and existence are one and the same (*see* GOD).

Transcendence of God. That the actual existent is composed of essence and existence, while its First Cause demands in itself an identification of these two, does much to demonstrate effectively God's TRANSCENDENCE. The exclusion of entitative composition in God, the cause of being, places Him far beyond the limits of created existent being. This latter participates in actuality, whereas God is essentially actuality. In the created existent, existence is multiplied, whereas the existence of the First Cause is absolutely one and unique. The actual created existent is finite and caused in its existential act, whereas the existence of the First Cause is itself infinite and uncaused. In a word, the difference between the created existent thing and its First Cause in terms of the actuality appropriate to each is the difference between the finite and infinite, the measurable and the immeasurable. Any community discoverable between the two can be only analogical.

Other solutions. The doctrine of St. Thomas on the real distinction found its principal adversary in John Duns Scotus. For Scotus, who thought in perspectives that were somewhat Platonic, essence is existence; thus concrete essence is its own existence. Divine Being is the infinite essence in which all created essences participate; and created essences are real and really existing when God, from the state of simple possibility, puts them into the state of existence. Thus there is no real distinction between existing essence and its act of being (*esse*); existence is only a mode of essence, a degree, an intensity, through which essence has become real. This mode is intrinsic to essence and puts it outside its causes. Existence is no longer the supreme value; it is a modality. Essence overtakes it and leads to a philosophy of essences in which existence plays only an accidental role. Scotus maintained, however, a modal distinction *ex natura rei* between essence and existence. (*See* SCOTISM.)

F. SUÁREZ suppressed even this distinction; for him, *esse* signifies only the placing of essence outside its causes. In Suárez's view, whatever is real is, as such, existent. Man conceives of a distinction between essence and existence because of his own contingency and limitation; in reality, however, the actual essence of a creature is not really distinct from its existence. (*See* SUÁREZIANISM.) Thus, with these two thinkers, SCHOLASTICISM again turned to the direction given it by Henry of Ghent, holding merely for a rational distinction between essence and existence.

Modern Philosophy. As RATIONALISM began to prevail in the modern era, under the influence of R. DESCARTES, substantial forms and essences were gradually rejected. Nothing was left in the visible world but extension and movement; these took the place of essences. Existence, similarly, was the existence of extension and movement—an existence recognized by the scholastics as accidental and thus not adequate to explain the ultimate constituency of being and substance.

For I. KANT and the idealists who followed him, the world of nature interiorized itself more and more. The problem thus became one of knowing how a cosmos created by mind could come to acquire a real or extramental existence. But the philosopher who most transformed the reality of the world and of history into a logos that continually develops itself was G. W. F. HEGEL. For him, an ideal dialectic describes the course of events and enables one to see their ultimate development. The criterion of reality, or of existence, consists in a type of accord with the totality of experience: the true and the existent find their place in the unraveling of facts as synthesized by the mind. The mind proceeds from synthesis to synthesis until it arrives at the ABSOLUTE, Itself the irrefragable guarantee of the real existence of all that is contained within It. Such a system leads to the ultimate form of IDEALISM. Existential reality is there but a backdrop or, even less, a kind of concept that combines with concepts of essence to weave the abstract texture of the real.

Existentialist Reaction. The fact that individual existence has no place in this dialectic prompted the strong reaction of S. A. KIERKEGAARD, who rose to the defense of particular existence—at least of his own existence as a man. The term ''existence,'' for the Danish philosopher as for other existentialists, does not have the same meaning it had for the scholastics. In his view, existence reflects the manner of being proper to man. The prefix ''ex'' no longer signifies the emergence of beings from their causes and from nothingness, but the INTENTIONALITY of CONSCIOUSNESS going toward something different from itself. Still, beneath this ''ex-sistence,'' with its psychological nuance, there is the implication of an ontological aspect that embraces what is or exists fully in extramental reality.

Martin Heidegger, in light of his attempt to situate Being with relation to the human *Dasein*, recognized that he still had not touched the problem of essence and existence as this was posed in the ontological tradition. In fact, Heidegger so separated Being from beings, he so dissociated the ontological from the ontic, that essences appeared to him not as real elements of nature but, after the manner of the idealists, as constructs of the mind. The question of the relation of these essences to real existence thus cannot even be raised in his philosophy. (*See* EXISTENTIALISM)

Nor does J. P. Sartre, scrutinizing the problem in the wake of Heidegger, provide a plausible solution. In his view, existence is pure actuality, the actuality of consciousness going out of itself and refusing to accept the other. By this action, the world exists, as do essences that make up the world, but whose existence is nothing more than the disinterestedness of consciousness. When this table exists, there is the being of table; but the table ''exsists'' only in the sense that it manifests itself to an annihilating consciousness. Things are not exclusively in the mind; they are back to back with being, without thereby having their own being as an ontological reality. It is ultimately consciousness that judges the reality of the type of existence one assigns to things; man has no criterion of truth apart from its ability to be known.

Such, briefly, are the solutions that have been proposed to the problem of the relation between essence and existence. The term ''existence,'' like the term ''essence,'' has been given very different meanings over the centuries. Admittedly, the problem of their relationship is one of the most difficult in philosophy. Yet, since so much depends on it, one might well wish that philosophers had not resigned themselves to so wide a divergence of views.

See Also: BEING; EXISTENTIAL METAPHYSICS; MATTER AND FORM.

Bibliography: N. DEL PRADO, *De veritate fundamentali philosophiae christianae* (Fribourg 1911). M. CHOSSAT, *Dictionnaire de théologie catholique,* 15 v. (Paris 1903–50) 4:1152–1243; ''L'Averroisme de saint Thomas: Notes sur la distinction d'essence et d'existence à la fin du XIIIe siècle,'' *Archives de philosophie* 9.3 (1932) 129–177. A. D'ALES, *Dictionnaire apologétique de la foi catholique,* 4 v. (Paris 1911–22) 4:1667–1713. M. GRABMANN, ''Doctrina S. Thomae de distinctione reali inter essentiam et esse ex documentis ineditis saeculi XIII illustrata,'' in *Acta Hebdomadae Thomisticae Romae* (Rome 1924) 131–190. P. MANDONNET, ''Les Premières disputes sur la distinction réelle, 1276–1287,'' *Revue thomiste* 18 (1910) 741–765. M. D. ROLAND-GOSSELIN, *Le De ente et essentia de saint Thomas d'Aquin* (Kain, Belgium 1926). A. FOREST, *La Structure metaphysique du concret selon S. Thomas d'Aquin* (2d ed. Paris 1956). É. H. GILSON, *Elements of Christian Philosophy* (New York 1960; pa. 1963); *L'Être et l'essence* (2d ed. Paris 1962). É. H. GILSON, *History of Christian Philosophy in the Middle Ages* (New York 1955) 4207–4427. L. SWEENEY, *A Metaphysics of Authentic Existentialism* (Englewood Cliffs, N.J. 1965); ''Existence/Essence in St. Thomas Aquinas's Early Writings,'' *American Catholic Philosophical Association. Proceedings of the Annual Meeting* 37 (1963) 97–131. I. M. BOCHEŃSKI, *Contemporary European Philosophy,* tr. D. NICHOLL and K. ASCHENBRENNER (Berkeley 1956).

[J. C. TAYLOR]

ESSENES

The Essenes, along with the Pharisees and Sadducees, were one of the principal Jewish sects in Christ's time.

Sources. Knowledge of the Essenes is derived principally from the following works: PHILO JUDAEUS, *Quod* *omnis probus liber sit* [*Philonis Opera,* ed. Cohn-Wendland (Berlin 1896) v. 6], par. 75–91; Philo's lost *Apology for the Jews* as preserved in Eusebius, *Praeparatio Evangelica* 8.11.1–18 [K. Mras, *Die greichischen christlichen Schriftsteller der ersten drei Jahrhunderte* (Leipsig 1897–) 43.1:455–457 (1954)]; Flavius Josephus, *Jewish War* (hereafter *B.J.*) 2.8:2–13; *Antiquities* (*Ant.*) 18.1.5; Elder Pliny, *Natural History,* 5.15.73. All these authors seem dependent on earlier common sources, although Josephus (*Life,* 2) claims personal knowledge of the Essenes. The added details on the Essenes in the Slavonic Josephus are of questionable value. The statements that Philo and Josephus make about the Essenes are often inexact generalizations and need to be reexamined in the light of the Essene documents discovered among the DEAD SEA SCROLLS (DSS) of Qumran.

Origins. The name ''Essenes'' comes from Ἐσσηνοί, the Greek form that Josephus uses most frequently and that Pliny Latinizes as *Esseni.* Another form used by Philo and occasionally by Josephus is Ἐσσαῖοι. The derivation of the name is probably from the Aramaic plural (*ḥasên, ḥasayyâ*) of *ḥasyâ,* ''holy, pious,'' the equivalent of the Hebrew *ḥāsîd.*

Pliny located the main Essene settlement above En-Gedi on the west shore of the Dead Sea; this fits well with the ruins discovered at Qumran. Josephus and Philo report that Essenes were scattered about the cities and villages of Palestine. Some manuscripts of Philo mention Syria, separately from Palestine, in connection with Essene settlements, and this may harmonize with the journey to Damascus mentioned in a work connected with the DSS (CDC). Philo (*De vita contemplativa*) also describes the Egyptian THERAPEUTAE, a group like the Essenes.

The Essenes apparently arose as inaugurators of a separate movement in about 150 B.C. Among the supporters of the Machabean revolt of 167 B.C. were the *ḥăsîdîm* (1 Mc 2.42) or ''pious ones.'' (*See* HASIDAEANS.) When the unalloyed motives that sparked the revolt were tarnished by the Machabean usurpation of the high priesthood by Jonathan (152 B.C.), there seems to have been a schism by the more conservative elements among the *ḥăsîdîm.* This schism produced the Essenes who preserved the original name of this group. Josephus's first mention of the Essenes is in relation to the reign of Jonathan (*Ant.* 18.5.9). Both Josephus and Philo estimate their numbers at about 4,000 in the first Christian century. (For subsequent history, *see* QUMRAN COMMUNITY.)

Life. The main group of Essenes lived in community. An ideal of celibacy marked their life, although Josephus (*B.J.* 2.8.13) mentions a group of Essenes who married. There were women at Qumran, but it is not clear whether the marrying Essenes were a separate group or the result of a relaxation of an ideal. Josephus (*B.J.* 2.8.2) says that they adopted children and brought them up as Essenes.

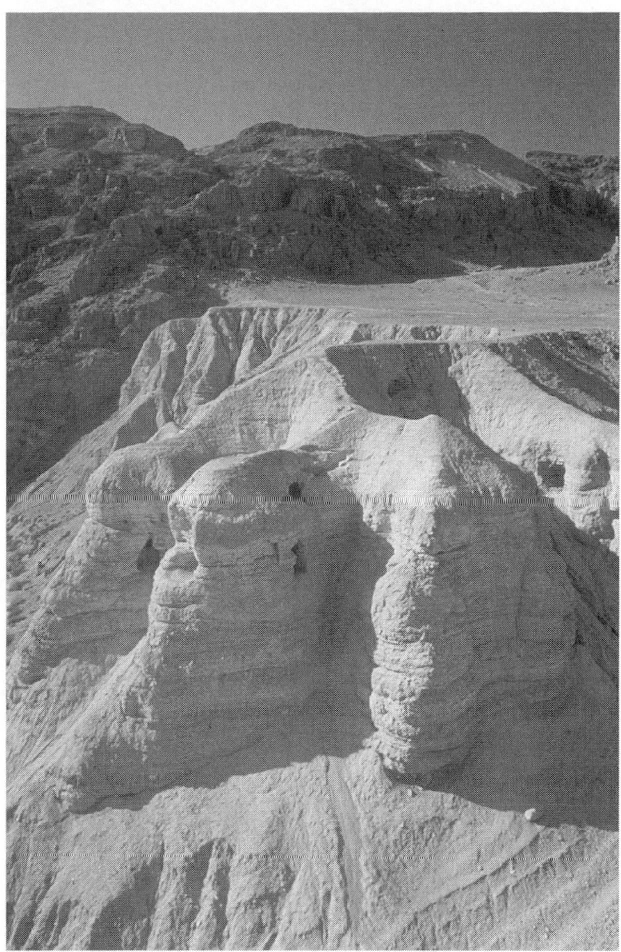

Caves of Essenes, Qumran, Israel. (©Richard T. Nowitz/ CORBIS)

Entrance into the community (*B.J.* 2.8.7) was severely controlled and required a type of novitiate. After a preliminary year of observation, the candidate was admitted to the common meals and to the purifications of the group. Then followed another period of trial (two years according to Josephus, but Qumran indications point to one year) before the candidates were fully accepted. Final entrance was marked by a series of vows covering their duties to God and to fellow Essenes, and their obligations to keep the secrets of the group. They surrendered (all?) their private property to a common treasury.

Prayer and various types of work were compulsory. The common meals were of a religious nature. Josephus (*B.J.* 2.8.5) tells us that the Essenes entered the dining room as if it were a temple, and all waited in silence for the priest to bless the food. Purificatory baths were required before virtually all functions.

Josephus (*B.J.* 2.8.10) mentions four classes of Essenes divided according to seniority. Presiding functionaries (ἐπιμεληταί, ἐπίτροποι, probably equivalent to the Qumran *m*[e]*baqqēr*) were elected by the community. The chief authority among them was the Legislator (*B.J.* 2.8.9); this might be Moses, or perhaps the Qumran Teacher.

Theology. Besides the peculiarities of their way of life, the Essenes had special doctrines that set them apart from other Jews. Here especially, however, we must allow for the inexactitude of our sources. Josephus (*Ant.* 13.5.9) stresses their belief in divine determinism; this may be an exaggeration of the dualistic doctrine found in the DSS. Their cult of the sun (*B.J.* 2.8.5) is still not clear to us, but we know the Qumranites followed a solar calendar and spoke of good and evil in terms of light and darkness.

The Essenes distrusted the regular sacrifices in the Jerusalem Temple (*Ant.* 18.1.5), a distrust flowing from their historic protest against its priesthood. Josephus says they made their own sacrifices, but Philo (*Quod omnis* 75) says that they did not sacrifice animals. Nevertheless, there was a strong priestly element among them. The Essenes maintained the immortality of the soul that had descended from the most pure ethereal substance to be imprisoned in the body (*B.J.* 2.8.11). No real evidence for such a doctrine of preexistence has yet been found in the DSS. Such a doctrine, if true, suggests the possibility of the indirect influence of Greek philosophy on the Essenes (see *Ant.* 15.10.4 for a comparison with the Pythagoreans). In their purifications and angelology, the Essenes present certain parallels with Persian thought, parallels more obvious in the dualism of the DSS. Other common elements were shared by the Essenes and SAMARITANS.

The Essenes had some influence on other branches of Judaism. They seem to have been the channel for preserving and propagating many of the ideas of such apocrypha as *Enoch* and *Jubilees.* Even after their disappearance as a separate group, the Essenes left their traces in Judaeo-Christian sects like the EBIONITES, perhaps in the Mandaeans (*see* MANDAEAN RELIGION), certainly in the Karaites. There have been many unsubstantiated hypotheses about their influence on Christianity. The DSS, however, show grounds for suspecting considerable indirect influence, which does nothing to destroy the originality of Christianity.

Bibliography: S. WAGNER, *Die Essener in der wissenschaftlichen Diskussion* (Berlin 1960), excellent bibliog. A. DUPONT-SOMMER, *The Essene Writings from Qumran* (New York 1962) ch. 1–2. M. BLACK, *The Scrolls and Christian Origins: Studies in the Jewish Background of the New Testament* (London 1961). B. RIGAUX, *Dictionnaire d'histoire et de géographie ecclésiastiques*, ed. A. BAUDRILLART et al. (Paris 1912–) 15:1013–35.

[R. E. BROWN]

ESTE

The famous Italian Este family, of Lombard origin, descended from the Obertenghi. Albert Azzo II (d. 1097) is regarded as the head of the family because he first made Este his residence. His first-born son, made heir of Carinthia by his uncle Guelf III and Duke of Bavaria by Emperor Henry IV, as Guelf IV continued the Guelf family (*see* GUELFS AND GHIBELLINES). In time reduced to the Duchy of Brunswick, in 1714 it emerged as the House of Hanover with George I of England.

Medieval Origins. From Albert's second son, Folco (d. *c.* 1136), descends the Italian line. Folco's son, Obizzo I (d. 1193), inherited FERRARA in 1184 but had to dispute with the Ghibelline Torelli family for the city. Obizzo's nephew, Azzo IV (d. 1212), who sided with Otto IV and then with Innocent III, accompanied Frederick II to Germany in 1212. His first son, Aldobrandino (d. 1215), lost the castle of Este to Padua and was succeeded by the second son, Azzo VII (d. 1264). Their sister, Bl. Beatrice, was a nun. Azzo VII broke with Frederick II and became podesta of Ferrara, establishing the basis of the family's authority. His daughter Beatrice married Andrew II of Hungary. Azzo's son died in prison as a hostage of Frederick II. His grandson, Obizzo II (d. 1293), succeeded; as the ally of Charles of ANJOU, he acquired Modena in 1288 and Reggio in 1289; his daughter Beatrice married Galeazzo VISCONTI. His son, Azzo VIII (d. 1308), had ambitions for Parma and Bologna but lost Modena and Reggio in 1306; he left a disputed succession, and Ferrara came into Angevin hands. In 1317 Rinaldo (d. 1335) regained Ferrara as a fief of the pope. Obizzo III (d. 1352) in 1336 regained Modena, which was conferred on his son Aldobrandino (d. 1361) by Charles IV. Aldobrandino's brother and successor, Albert (d. 1393), founded the University of Ferrara in 1391. Under Albert's son Nicholas III (d. 1441), dissolute and cruel but shrewd, the family became powerful.

Renaissance Greatness. Leonello (d. 1450), Nicholas's son, made Ferrara a major center of culture in the Renaissance. His brother and successor, Borso (d. 1471), Duke of Modena (1452) and of Ferrara (1471), gave his name to one of the world's richest codices, the Bible of Borso in the Biblioteca Estense in Modena. Borso was succeeded by his brother Ercole I (d. 1505), whose children are noteworthy: Beatrice married Ludovico SFORZA; Isabella, known for her culture, married Francesco II GONZAGA, Duke of Mantua; Hippolyte I (d. 1520) was a cardinal; Alfonso I (d. 1534), his successor, Duke of Ferrara, married Lucretia BORGIA, and their son Hippolyte II (d. 1572) was a cardinal. Ercole II (d. 1559), Alfonso's son by his first wife, Anna Sforza, succeeded him. Ercole's son Louis was a cardinal (d. 1586); his daughters Lucretia and Eleanora were praised by Torquato Tasso. With his son Alfonso II (d. 1597), Duke of Ferrara, the legitimate line of Nicholas III became extinct.

The Cesare–Este Line. Clement VIII refused to recognize the illegitimate Cesare (d. 1628), who retained Modena but yielded Ferrara to the Church and French lands to Anne of GUISE. Cesare's son, Alfonso III (d. 1644), married Isabelle of Savoy; he was widowed in 1626, abdicated in 1629, became a Capuchin, and was ordained in 1630. He labored for the apostolate in the Tyrol and in Vienna; his son Louis was cardinal and bishop of Reggio. Another son, Francesco I (d. 1658), fought for both Spain and France in hope of regaining Ferrara. His son, Alfonso IV (d. 1662), a general of Louis XIV, married a niece of Cardinal Mazarin in 1655. Their daughter, Maria Beatrice, married the Duke of York, later JAMES II OF ENGLAND; their son, Francesco II (d. 1694), founded the University of Mantua and the Biblioteca Estense. Since Francesco was without sons, he was succeeded by his uncle Rinaldo (d. 1737), who renounced the cardinalate to marry Charlotte of Brunswick. Rinaldo's son Francesco III (d. 1780) fought for Spain against Austria, but by becoming Austrian administrator general of Lombardy and marrying Beatrice, his niece and heir, to the Archduke Ferdinand, gave up the independence of the duchy. His son Ercole III died in Turin in 1803, an exile from Modena. Ferdinand (d. 1806) and Beatrice (d.1829) inherited the duchy until the Treaty of Vienna gave it to her son Francesco IV (d. 1846). Another son, Ferdinand Charles Joseph (d. 1850), was a famous Austrian general in the Napoleonic wars and governed Galicia (1830–46). Francesco V was dispossessed in 1860 and died in Vienna, Nov. 20, 1875.

The Este Cardinals. The Este family was represented by many cardinals during the period of the high Renaissance. Hippolyte I, a cardinal (b. Ferrara, Nov. 20, 1479; d. Ferrara, Sept. 2, 1520) was, thanks to his aunt, the queen of Matyas Hunyadi of Hungary, archbishop of Esztergom at age seven, cardinal deacon at age 14, archbishop of Milan at age 17, and bishop of Ferrara, Narbonne, Modena, and Capua, as well as a holder of other benefices. He renounced Esztergom for Zagreb in 1497 and yielded Milan to his nephew Hippolyte II in 1520. He conducted successful military operations against Venice in the League of Cambrai (1509) and urged Este to resist Pope Julius II, who wanted it to join the Holy League. When he was summoned to Rome by Julius, he sent in his stead Ariosto, whose patron he was from 1503 to 1517 and who dedicated the *Orlando furioso* to him. Hippolyte was in Hungary from 1517 to 1520. He knew Leonardo da Vinci and was himself a man of great culture.

Beatrice d'Este, 15th-century marble bust by an artist of the school of Milan, now in the Louvre, Paris, France. (Alinari-Art Reference/Art Resource, NY)

Hippolyte II, cardinal (b. Ferrara, Aug. 25, 1509; d. Tivoli, Dec. 2, 1572) was archbishop of Milan at age ten, later bishop of Lyons, Orléans, Autun, Auch, and Morienne, and was made cardinal *in pectore* (thanks to Francis I) in 1538 and publicly proclaimed in 1539. As cardinal protector of France, he represented the French party in Italy and in the sacred college. He was out of favor with Paul IV, but was legate *a latere* for Pius IV to Catherine de Médicis in France (1561–63). He was a great patron of the arts and began the construction of the Villa d'Este at Tivoli. His candidacy for the papacy was defeated in 1550, 1555, and 1561 because reformers who thought him too worldly joined the enemies of France.

Louis, cardinal, (b. Ferrara, Dec. 25, 1538; d. Rome, Dec. 30, 1586) disliked the clerical life, but his family persuaded him to become archbishop of Ferrara and, in 1561, cardinal. In 1558 and in 1581 he sought to leave his orders for marriage, but the pope refused permission. He was protected by the French. From 1565 to 1572 he was the patron of Tasso. Despite his enormous income he was always in debt. He completed the building of the Villa d'Este.

Alexander, cardinal (b. Modena, 1568; d. Rome, 1624) was bishop of Reggio (1621) and a good pastor; he was a learned man, as well as a patron of the arts.

Rinaldo, cardinal (b. Modena, 1618; d. Rome, 1672) left a distinguished military career to become bishop of Reggio and of Montpellier.

Rinaldo, cardinal (b. 1655; d. 1737) was the son of Francesco I. He became cardinal in 1681, but renounced the cardinalate to marry and assure the succession of his family.

The Last Dukes of Ferrara. The power and prestige of the Este family dwindled during the rule of the last Dukes of Ferrara. Alfonso I, Duke of Ferrara (b. Ferrara, July 21, 1476; d. Oct. 1534) was married to Anna Sforza and then Lucretia Borgia; he maintained the duchy by alliances with the pope, France, and the Empire. He traveled in England and Flanders and devoted himself to the arts, commerce, and military science.

Alfonso II, Duke of Ferrara (b. Ferrara, Nov. 22, 1533; d. Ferrara, Oct. 27, 1597) sought in vain to promote the fortunes of Este. From his marriages to the daughters of Cosimo I de Medici in 1560, Emperor Ferdinand I in 1565, and the Duke of Mantua in 1579 he had neither issue nor political advantage. He took part in the civil wars in France; and for his part in the war against the Turks in 1566, Tasso dedicated the *Gerusalemme liberata* to him. He lost supremacy over the small Italian city–states to the Medici. He was disliked despite an anti–Machiavellian program of loyalty and religion, expressed in a *Principe* written by his secretary of state. He died without heirs, and Este escheated to the pope.

Bibliography: L. SIMEONI, *Enciclopedia Italiana di scienzi, littere ed arti,* 36 v. (Rome 1928–39; suppl. 1938–) 14:395–398; 15:857–859. A. MERCATI and A. PELZER, *Dizionario ecclesiastico,* 3 v. (Turin 1954–58) 1:1014–15.

[E. P. COLBERT]

ESTHER, BOOK OF

One of the protocanonical books of the Old Testament, found among the Writings (the third section) in the Jewish Canon, after Lamentations and before Daniel [*see* CANON, BIBLICAL, 2]. It is the last of the five *m^egillôt,* or festive SCROLLS. This article discusses the contents, the text, the origin, and the purpose of the book, and, finally, the canonicity of the Greek additions.

Contents. The dramatic story of Esther recounts the deliverance of the Jewish people from grave danger through the instrumentality of a woman; it is thus similar in theme to the Book of JUDITH. The setting is in Susa, at the palace of the Persian King Xerxes I (486–464 B.C.), given as ''Assuerus'' in the Hebrew text, ''Artaxerxes'' in the Greek. The king, after repudiating Queen Vashti, marries Esther, a young Jewess and the most beautiful girl in the kingdom. Haman, the king's vizier, determines by lot the 13th of Adar (Februrary–March) as the day for slaughtering all of the Jews in the empire. However, Esther and Mordechai, her uncle (or cousin) and foster father, are able to thwart Haman's plans. Haman is hanged on the gallows he had prepared for Mordechai, and Mordechai is promoted to vizier for having uncovered a plot against the king. On the day set for their extermination, the Jews are allowed to defend themselves by slaughtering their enemies. In the provinces the Jews celebrated the victory the following day. But in Susa, Esther requested the king's permission to continue the slaughter on the 14th of Adar and to celebrate on the 15th. Thus, Esther and Mordechai decreed that these events should be commemorated annually by the Feast of PURIM on the 14th and 15th of Adar, at which time the Book of Esther is read.

Text. The Greek Septuagint (LXX) text is much longer than the Hebrew text because of numerous additions. St. Jerome, in translating the Vulgate, followed the Hebrew version, then translated the Greek additions, which he added to the end of the book. According to the Vulgate numbering, which the Douay follows, these Greek additions extend from 10.4 through 16.24. The CCD version, however, gives these sections in the order in which they are found in the LXX but designates them with successive letters of the alphabet, with Arabic numerals for the verses, in order to avoid disturbing the regular chapter and verse enumeration. The major sections are as follows: Mordechai's dream and his discovery of a plot (A.1–17; placed before 1.1); the edict sent out by Haman (B.1–7; placed between 3.13 and 3.14); the prayers of Mordechai and Esther (C.1–30) and Esther's reception by the king (D.1–16; placed after 4.16); the king's edict protecting the Jews (E.1–24; placed between 8.12 and 8.13); and the epilogue (F.1–11; placed at the end of the book).

These different recensions seem to reflect successive stages in the development of the story arising from popular Jewish tradition. The Greek additions (midrashic amplifications; *see* MIDRASH) spiritualize the nonreligious tenor of the more primitive Hebrew text. Even with these additions the largely secular tone of the book and its almost savage nationalism contrasts unfavorably with the far more elevated and religious atmosphere of the Book of Judith.

Origin and Purpose. The story of Esther began to develop from an original nucleus between 300 and 150

Hebrew scroll of the ''Book of Esther,'' showing King Xerxes, Queen Vasthi, Mardochai, Queen Ester, and seven princes of Persia, 17th century.

B.C. in the eastern Jewish DIASPORA and reached its present form *c.* 150–100 B.C. The Greek additions probably date from *c.* 100 B.C. In the past most scholars considered the story based on an event in Jewish history, a threatened pogrom in the Persian Empire from which the Jews escaped. This is the event celebrated annually at Purim. Modern scholars, however, are less willing to see even a minimal basis in history. Many elements of the narrative lack all semblance of verisimilitude, such as the complacence of King Xerxes at the slaughter of tens of thousands of his subjects (9.5–17), to give but one example. The story is possibly a fictional illustration of the firm Jewish belief that those who trust in God will be delivered in all their needs and a concrete illustration of the poetic justice so often prayed for in the Psalms, that the evil doers should perish in the very trap they had set for the innocent (see Est 9.1). Some, however, consider the story a Jewish adaptation of an already existing story of non-Jewish origin. Thus, it could be rooted in an ancient Babylonian myth and festival commemorating the victory of the gods of Babylon over the gods of Elam. Marduk and Ishtar, the chief Babylonian gods, become Mardochai and Esther. Aman and Vashti are derived from Humman and Mashti, the principals of the Elamite pantheon. Others see it stemming from a story in Book 3 of Herodotus. A certain magus (*see* MAGI), Gaumata, upon the death of King Cambyses (530–522 B.C.), usurped the Persian throne by posing as the secretly murdered son of CYRUS, king of Persia. The plot was uncovered by Phaidime, a concubine of the king, and Otanes, her father. Gaumata was executed, and there ensued a wholesale massacre of the Magi. The Persians celebrated this event with a festival, ''The Massacre of the Magi.'' Scholars favoring a non-Jewish origin maintain that the Jews of the Diaspora became familiar with the pagan festival and adopted it. Later the Book of Esther was written to justify and regulate the feast, for which there was no basis in the Torah. At this time the festival became an occasion to fan the flames of Jewish nationalism.

Canonicity of the Greek Additions. Jerome and other Fathers questioned the authenticity of these passages. However, because of the influential position of the LXX, the Greek text with these deuterocanonical additions gradually won acceptance in the Christian Church. The Council of TRENT proclaimed the canonicity of the whole book as contained in the Vulgate.

Bibliography: *Encyclopedic Dictionary of the Bible,* tr. and adap. by L. HARTMAN (New York 1963) 690–693. J. SCHILDENBER-

GER, *Lexikon für Theologie und Kirche,* ed. J. HOFER and K. RAHNER, 10 v. (2d, new ed. Freiburg 1957–65); suppl., *Das Zweite Vatikanische Konzil: Dokumente und kommentare,* ed. H. S. BRECHTER et al., pt. 1 (1966) 3:1115–16. H. BARDTKE and W. WERBECK, *Die Religion in Geschichte und Gegenwart,* 7 v. (3d ed. Tübingen 1957–65) 2:703–708. A. ROBERT, "Historique (Genre)," *Dictionnaire de la Bible,* suppl. ed. L. PIROT, et al. (Paris 1928–) 4:20–23. A. BARUCQ, tr., *Esther* [*Bible de Jérusalem,* 14 (Paris 1952)]. L. SOUBIGOU, *La Sainte Bible,* ed. L. PIROT and A. CLAMER, v.4 (Paris 1952). B. W. ANDERSON, "The Place of the Book of Esther in the Christian Bible," *Journal of Religion,* 30 (Chicago 1950) 32–43. H. RINGGREN, "Esther and Purim," *Svensk exegetisk årsbok* 20 (1955) 5–24.

[E. A. BALLMANN]

ESTIENNE (ÉTIENNE)

A French family of the 16th century renowned as printers and humanists.

Henry Estienne, the founder of the family; b. *c.* 1460; d. Paris, 1520. The family printing press was set up near the Sorbonne University *c.* 1504–05. After Henry's death, since his three sons, Francis, Robert, and Charles, were still quite young, Simon de Colines, a foreman, provisionally took charge of the firm and married their widowed mother in 1521.

Robert, Henry's second son; b. Paris, 1503; d. Geneva, Sept. 7, 1559, collaborated (1522–23) in the printing of a Latin edition of the NT and the Psalms. By 1526 he became head of the family firm. In 1527–28 his first complete Bible in Latin was published, followed by his great *Dictionarium seu linguae latinae thesaurus* in 1531. Francis I appointed him the king's printer in 1539 for Hebrew and Latin works and in 1540 for Greek works. In this official capacity he published many texts of the Latin and Greek classics, as well as those of several early Church writers. Unfortunately, however, Robert became involved in the troubles of the Reformation; his critical and liberal views on religion and the Church ultimately prompted the privy council of Henry II, in 1547, to proscribe the series of Latin Bibles published by his firm. Robert, considering the censorship to be intolerable, became dissatisfied, and in 1548 he visited Geneva, where he conferred with John CALVIN. The following year he became a permanent resident of Geneva and also a member of the Reformed Church. Among his many works published at Geneva were a Greek-Latin NT (1551), in which he introduced the division of the text into verses that is still in use today. He published also a concordance of the whole Bible (1555). In his various editions of the Latin VULGATE (1528–57), Robert Estienne attempted to reestablish critically the authentic text of St. Jerome [*see* BIBLE (TEXTS)]. His contributions to the history of the Vulgate were recognized by H. Quentin in his *Memoir sur l'établissement du texte de la Vulgate* (Rome 1922). During this period Robert published a caustic reply, *Ad censuras theologorum parisiensium responsio* (1552), an answer to the Sorbonne's condemnation of him.

Henry (II) was the eldest son of Robert; b. 1531; d. Lyons, France, January 1598. From 1554 to the time of his death, Henry published a large number of the Greek classics. His greatest work was his Greek dictionary, *Thesaurus graecae linquae*, 5 v. (1572), a masterpiece of lexicography, which reappeared in several editions (Paris 1831–65).

Paul, son of Henry (II); b. 1566; d. 1627, he succeeded his father in charge of the press at Geneva in 1598. He also published a large number of Greek classics. He disappeared from history, however, after his sale of the press in 1627. The Estienne family's activities, both in Geneva and in Paris, ceased after the middle of the 17th century.

Bibliography: F. DRESSLER, *Lexikon für Theologie und Kirche*[2] (Freiburg 1957–65) 3:1116–17. H. R. GUGGISBERG, *Die Religion in Geschichte und Gegenwart*[3] (Tübingen 1957–65) 6:360–361.

[C. H. PICKAR]

ESTIMATIVE POWER

The estimative power (also commonly, estimative sense) is a power of knowledge whose characteristic act is concrete evaluation or estimation. Spoken of as a distinct power of knowledge first by AVICENNA, it was accepted as such by the majority of medieval thinkers. Many later authors, however, have rejected it entirely, or have refused to consider it as distinct from the imagination, e.g., F. SUÁREZ, P. FONSECA, and J. FRÖBES; others consider it of very little importance, e.g., D. MERCIER. In Thomistic philosophy, the estimative power is conceived very much as it was by Avicenna (ST 1a, 78.4). It is the equivalent in animals of the COGITATIVE or DISCURSIVE POWER in man, though man also in some sense has an estimative power, as explained below.

Nature of the Estimative. A certain intelligence or purposiveness is observable in animal activity, and various explanations, such as INSTINCT, are offered for this. Many accept the explanation offered by Aristotle, i.e., that "animals know by nature" (*Phys.* 199a 20–30; *Meta.* 980a 28–981a). Avicenna went further. Having developed an analysis of knowledge in terms of formal objects, he applied this to animal knowledge and activity. He concluded that a distinct power was necessary (*Liber Canonis* 1.1.6.5; *De anima* 1.5, 2.1, 4.1, 4.3).

St. THOMAS AQUINAS followed this analysis closely, but more briefly. Animals, he asserted, have a knowledge of concrete suitability and harmfulness. Such knowledge is not reducible to the external SENSES, which know their objects in directly sensible modes. Consequently, this knowledge cannot be explained by the IMAGINATION either, whose function it is to retain and reproduce what was previously sensed. St. Thomas calls this knowledge ''an unsensed intention'' or ''knowledge-object not able to be grasped by the [external] senses.'' Therefore, a distinct power is required. Nevertheless, an animal does not know the *nature* of good and evil, but only concrete goods and evils which are important to its life and the life of the species (ST 1a, 78.4; *De ver.* 15.1, 25.2; *In 2 de anim.* 13). Another aspect of this knowledge is its unlearned, or ''natural,'' character. Hence, the estimative must be determined by nature to judge certain things as good and others as harmful. St. Thomas sees the evidence for this in the fact that animals of a particular species act in the same way (*De ver.* 24.1, 2; ST 1a2ae, 17.2 ad 3; 13.2 ad 2, 3).

Functions in Animal and Man. Because the kind of knowledge reached by the estimative is evaluative, it is immediately ordered to APPETITE and thus to action (*In 3 sent.* 27.1.2; *De virt. in comm.* 6; ST 1a, 83.1). The ''good'' as known by the animal is concrete and individualized. Consequently, good and evil as thus presented necessarily are followed by acts of appetite: desire, fear, rage, and so on. Hence, the estimative can well be considered to be the guiding, or supreme, power in an animal (*In 3 sent.* 35.1.2.2.1; ST 1a2ae, 31.6).

To a limited extent, we can speak of an estimative power in man (ST 1a, 78.4). For in the earliest years of human life, reason cannot yet guide actions, and sufficient learning has not yet taken place. If the baby responds to concrete good and evil beyond their immediately pleasurable or painful aspects he can do so only to the extent that he also has natural judgments about good and evil.

The area of animal (and human) behavior explained in THOMISM by the estimative power is evidently much the same as that explained by instinct. However, the term instinct for St. Thomas is not a technical term, but a general term for ''innate'' or ''intrinsic'' impulse. The modern doctrine of instinct is a different kind of explanation and has little in common with the estimative power.

See Also: FACULTIES OF THE SOUL; SENSES; COGITATIVE POWER.

Bibliography: G. P. KLUBERTANZ, *The Discursive Power* (St. Louis 1952). M. A. GAFFNEY, *Psychology of the Interior Senses* (St. Louis 1942). R. HAIN, ''De vi aestimativa et de instinctu animalium,'' *Revue de l'Université d'Ottawa* 2.2 (1932) 98–114. D. DE VORGES, ''L'Estimative,'' *Revue néo-scolastique* 11 (1904) 433–454. H. A. WOLFSON, ''The Internal Senses in Latin, Arabic, and Hebrew Philosophic Texts,'' *Harvard Theological Review* 28 (1935) 69–133.

[G. P. KLUBERTANZ]

ESTIUS, GULIELMUS

Exegete, theologian, and hagiographer; b. Gorcum, Holland, 1542; d. Douai, Sept. 20, 1613. After his studies of the classics at Utrecht, he spent 20 years at Louvain, studying sacred sciences and teaching philosophy. He received the S.T.D. in 1580. After his appointment as Professor Primarius at the University of Douai in 1582, he taught Sacred Scripture and served two terms as rector of the seminary. He was chancellor of Douai from 1595 until his death. A profound student, highly esteemed for vast learning, solid judgment, and sincere piety, he was called *Doctor fundatissimus* by Pope Benedict XIV. Among his less famous works are a *History of the Martyrs of Gorcum* (Douai 1603) and an excellent commentary on *Quattuor libri sententiarum Petri Lombardi* (Douai 1615). His greatest work is exegetical, the well-known *In omnes beati Pauli et septem catholicas apostolorum epistolas commentarii* (Douai 1614–16) in which he explained the literal meaning of the NT Epistles with precise judgment, acumen, and erudition. His calm, impartial answers to objections did much to expose the deficiencies of the Protestant Biblical exegesis. His prefaces to each Epistle were particularly valuable for their insight into the exact mind of the authors. Estius's reputation became so great among later scholars that the saying ''Maldonatus on the Gospels, Estius on the Epistles'' became proverbial.

Bibliography: H. HURTER, *Nomenclator literarius theologiae catholicae* 3:484–489. T. LEURIDAN, *Revue des sciences ecclésiastiques* 2 (1895) 120–131, 326–340. L. SALEMBIER, *Dictionnaire de théologie catholique* 5.1:871–878. A. FLEISCHMANN, *Lexikon für Theologie und Kirche* 3:1117.

[J. J. MAHONEY]

ESTONIA, THE CATHOLIC CHURCH IN

A Baltic state, the Republic of Estonia is bound on the north by the Gulf of Finland, on the east by Russia, on the south by LATVIA and the Gulf of Riga, and on the west by the Baltic Sea. With an inland terrain characterized by marshy lowlands, Estonia also includes the two large islands of Hiiumaa (Dägo) and Saaremaa (Ösel) at the mouth of the Gulf of Riga, as well as numerous other

Capital: Tallinn.
Size: 17,410 sq. miles.
Population: 1,431,470 in 2000.
Languages: Estonian, Russian, Ukranian, English, Finnish.
Religions: 4,240 Catholics (.28%), 16,400 Orthodox (1%), 200,900 Lutherans (14%), 3,100 Jews (.2%), 1,206,830 without religious affiliation. Estonia is ministered to by an apostolic administrator.

islands in the Baltic. Natural resources include shale oil, peat, amber and limestone, while agriculturally Estonia's main crops include potatoes, fruits and vegetables, and dairy products.

Estonia was settled by tribal Finno-Ugrian people who formed the bulk of the population by the 11th century. In the Middle Ages it comprised part of Livonia, an area long the center of a power struggle among its more aggressive neighbors. Independent from 1917 to 1941, Estonia was incorporated into the Union of Soviet Socialist Republics (USSR) in 1944 and gained its independence in 1991. The region, which has gone on to develop economic and political ties with Western Europe, possesses a large Russian minority estimated at 30 percent of the population.

Establishment of Christianity. Russian missionaries and traders from Kiev were the first to penetrate Estonia, establishing a post at Tartu about 1030. Sporadic attempts at evangelization were also made by missionaries from Lund, Bremen-Hamburg, Novgorod and Plotsk in the 11th century, but they met with little success. Meinhard of Holstein (d. 1196) was consecrated the first bishop of Livonia in 1186, even before the Germans established a stable political organization in the region. His successor, Berthold of Hanover, died in battle in 1198. Bishop ALBERT I (d. 1229) arrived in 1199 at the head of a German crusade; he began the actual work of settlement and forced conversion of the native population of the area, which he renamed Marienland. The KNIGHTS OF THE SWORD were organized in 1199 at Albert's urging, and the city of Riga was founded as his see in 1201. Theoderich of Treyden, abbot of the Cistercian monastery of Dünamünde, was consecrated missionary bishop of Estonia in early 1211. The Fourth LATERAN COUNCIL (November 1215) made the Livonian church directly subject to Rome, but the bishops, who were also imperial princes, and the Knights divided the newly converted areas between them, largely ignoring the claims of the Holy See. The Danes were also active in the northern part of Estonia and in the islands; in 1219 Waldamar II of Denmark founded the fortified city of Tallinn and, since Bishop Theoderich had been martyred, established his chaplain, Guicelinus, as bishop there. Meanwhile Albert had established his brother, Hermann, in the Estonian bishopric; this see, established at Leal, was moved to Dorpat in 1224. A reaction against the Church came in 1223, but the Knights of the Sword, by cooperating with the bishops, managed to regain their territories and occupy the island of Saarenaa in 1227. Saarenaa was entrusted to the ecclesiastical supervision of Gottfried, another of Albert's kinsmen, and, together with the mainland area of Lääne, became the Diocese of Ösel-Wiek (Latin, *Osiliensis*), the third Estonian diocese, with its seat at Haapsalu. Dorpat and Ösel-Wiek were suffragan to Riga after it became a metropolitan see in 1255, while Revel remained subject to the archbishops of Lund.

The Knights of the Sword, badly decimated by crusading warfare, merged in 1237 with the TEUTONIC KNIGHTS, although the Livonian Knights remained a distinct branch of the order until 1513. Pushing eastward against Novgorod, the order suffered a defeat at the hands of ALEXANDER NEVSKI on the ice of Lake Peipus in 1242. The order remained the dominant political and cultural force in Estonia, although during the 13th century the towns, largely German in population, became increasingly important. Revel, Dorpat, Narva and Fellin (modern Vilyandi) were all members of the Hanseatic League. The vast majority of churchmen, both priests and hierarchy, were Germans, many of them Saxons. In the countryside population, which was becoming rapidly enserfed to the German nobility, indigenous superstitions mixed with Christianity, and the connection between religious faith and serfdom ultimately led a large portion of the population to shun religion altogether. In 1346 Denmark sold its lands in northern Estonia to the Teutonic Knights, prompting the Knights to attempt to annex Livonia to Prussia through the conquest of LITHUANIA. The Knights were defeated in 1410 at the Battle of Tannenberg.

In 1232 the Cistercians founded a monastery at Valkena (German Falkenau), near Dorpat. The Dominicans made foundations at Dorpat, Revel and Narva, while the Franciscans established themselves at Fellin, Dorpat and Wesenberg. By the end of the 16th century there were some 22 monasteries and convents in Estonia.

The Reformation. The bitter conflict between the Teutonic Knights and the Estonian bishops opened the way for the penetration of Lutheran ideas into the country. Lutheran communities were established at Revel, Dorpat and Pernau, where the heresy appealed to the German burgers. Not until the late 1530s did it begin to penetrate the countryside, and even then Protestantism meant little more than the cessation of Catholicism. Preachers and schools, especially for the native population, were lacking. The people followed the lead of their lords, and with the secularization of the order and the bishoprics, they were lost to the faith. The death of Johann von Blankenfield, archbishop of Riga and bishop of Revel and Dorpat, in 1529, marked the end of effective Catholic control in these dioceses.

Worried by the political instability of the area, Ivan (IV) the Terrible of Moscow invaded Estonia in 1558, capturing Narva and Dorpat and carrying the last Catholic bishop of Dorpat, Hermann II Wessal, into captivity. DENMARK and SWEDEN, now Protestant powers, also hoped to achieve territorial gains in Estonia. In 1559 Johann von Münchhausen, bishop of Ösel-Wiek, sold his see to Frederick II of Denmark, who installed his brother, Prince Magnus of Holstein (d. 1583), as the first Protestant prelate. In 1561 the city of Revel, doubting the ability of the order to protect it from Russian advances, submitted to King Eric XIV of Sweden. Their fears were well founded, for in this same year Livonian grand master Gotthard Kettler secularized the order and became duke of Courland, under the protection of King Sigismud Augustus of Poland. In areas under Polish administration, the Jesuit-led COUNTER REFORMATION made remarkable headway, appealing especially to the native population. All this came to an end when, in 1629, Sweden acquired all of mainland Estonia (the islands were added in 1645). Active in the development of the country and the welfare of the native population, Gustavus II of Sweden founded the University of Dorpat in 1634 with a Lutheran theological faculty. In 1721 the Treaty of Nystad confirmed PETER (I) the Great's conquest of the area, and during almost two centuries of Russian rule the Baltic barons, descendants of medieval German conquerors, were once again the dominant economic and political force in Estonia. In the MORAVIAN CHURCH the Estonians first found an opportunity to become pastors to their people. During the period of Russian rule large numbers also entered the Russian ORTHODOX CHURCH. In the last half of the 19th century, the attempts at Russification were met by a rising spirit of nationalism.

The Rise of Communism. The Russian Revolution of 1917 gave Estonia its independence, and in 1918 a truly representative government under Konstantine Päts (d. 1956) came to power. The republic recognized complete freedom of religion, and a Catholic apostolic administration for Estonia was dispatched to Tellinn in 1924. Up until that time there had only been a small number of Polish Catholics in the area, dependent on the Archdiocese of Mogilev. The second administrator, E. Profittlich, SJ, inaugurated a Catholic press with two publications. In 1934 the small Catholic population was organized into six parishes—Tellinn, Tartu, Narva, Valga, Pärnu and Kingisepp—with 12 priests, four of the BYZANTINE rite.

The Russo-German nonaggression pact of 1939 put Estonia, together with Lithuania and Latvia, into the Soviet sphere of influence. In 1940 a people's republic was established to force incorporation into the USSR, although most Western powers refused to recognize this seizure of territory by force.

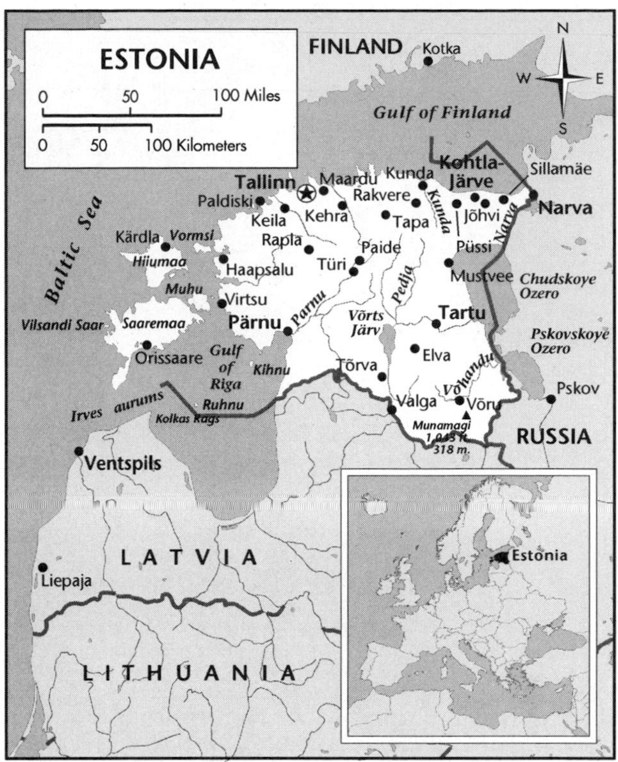

The communist government closed schools and theological institutions throughout Estonia, while at Tartu University religious studies were abolished and thousands of volumes of theological writings were destroyed. The ongoing translation of the New Testament into Estonian was suspended after the appearance of the Gospel of St. Mark. Archbishop Profittich was deported in June 1941, part of Soviet efforts to root out allegedly ''unreliable elements,'' including Catholic, Lutheran and Orthodox clergy. In the Estonian Orthodox Church ties were dissolved with the patriarch of Constantinople and established with the Russian Orthodox Church in Moscow. The Baltic republics, thus plunged into turmoil, welcomed the German invasion of the USSR on June 22, 1941. However, Nazi genocidal policy quickly raised a moral challenge to the Church; by the end of 1941 the Nazis and local collaborators had slaughtered most of Estonia's Jewish population. Throughout World War II, Estonia also suffered heavily in other ways.

Following the Soviet reconquest, the communist hold on the country intensified. The Church, viewed as a fascist agent of Western intelligence services, received much of Soviet dictator Josef Stalin's attention. Mass de-

Saint Nicholas Church, Tallinn, Estonia. (©Ludovic Maisant/CORBIS)

portations between 1945 and 1953 sent thousands to Siberia and other remote regions of the USSR. Prohibitive taxes were levied against the Church, and in 1948 religious instruction in churches was banned. At the same time all Church properties were nationalized, and the buildings ''leased'' to the Church. A new system of supposedly self-governing religious communities responsible to the government was introduced in an attempt to subvert the traditional Catholic parish system and undermine the clergy's leadership of the faithful. The Lutheran, and to a lesser extent, Orthodox Churches also suffered from repression and flight to the West. By the end of World War II only one-third of Estonia's Lutheran pastors and two-thirds of its Orthodox clergy remained in the country.

Coming to power in 1953, Nikita Khrushchev abandoned the terrorism of Stalin. Many deported clergy were allowed to return, and limited official contact with the Holy See was permitted. Unfortunately, this ''thaw'' was short lived, and repressive policies were again in place by the late 1950s, although without the mass terror of the Stalin years. Repression continued, even as the Soviet government sought to normalize relations with the Vatican, and the Holy See sought an ''opening to the east.'' With antireligious propaganda intensifying, in 1957 only one-fourth of ethnic Estonians declared themselves church members; a decade later it was estimated that the country held about 2,500 Catholics in two parishes served by two priests.

Glastnost and the Fall of Communism. During the Gorbachev era (1985–91) the most egregious restrictions on religion were lifted and ultimately eliminated. In February 1990 uprisings against Soviet domination signaled the reinstatement of the 1920 constitution. In September 1991 the USSR recognized Estonia as an independent republic. The resultant fall-off of trade with Russia caused an economic collapse and required rationing. A new constitution was drafted in 1992 that granted religious freedom, although due to the proliferation of evangelical Protestant and fundamentalist groups in the country all churches were required to register with the government. Efforts were also undertaken by the government to return property confiscated under Soviet rule.

In the wake of communism, the Church in Estonia saw its membership drop, a reflection of the decrease in church attendance throughout the country in the late 1990s. Church leaders focused their efforts on reestablishing primary and secondary schools to supplement the government-provided ecumenical religious instruction available in Estonian public schools. In March 1999 an agreement between the Vatican and the Estonian government agreed to give the Church control over appointment of bishops, recognized the legal validity of Catholic marriages, established the right to teach the faith in public schools and allowed foreign priests to enter the country to tend Estonian parishes.

Into the 21st Century. By 2000 Estonia had eight parishes tended by eight secular and five religious priests. In addition, there were approximately 16 brothers and sisters at work in the country. The Estonian Apostolic Orthodox Church, with its patriarchate in Constantinople, and the Russian Orthodox Church, with its patriarchate in Moscow, both claimed followers in Estonia, although the Moscow patriarchate was unable to obtain government registration by 2000. In 1996 tensions between the two churches provoked the Russian Orthodox Church to break ties with Constantinople, and by 2000 the struggle showed signs of dividing along ethnic lines. Pope John Paul II visited Estonia in 1993, during a trip through the newly independent Baltic states.

Bibliography: L. ARBUSON, *Grundriss der Geschichte Liv-Estund Kurlands* (4th ed., Riga 1918); *Die Einführung der Refor-*

mation in Livonia, Estonia und Kurland (Halle 1921). H. KRUUS, *Eesti Kirikulugu*, 3 v. (Tartu 1935–39). A. M. AMMAN, *Kirchenpolitische Wandlungen in Ostbaltikum bis zum Tode Alexander Newskis* (Rome 1936). H. SILD, *Eesti Kirikulugu vanimast ajast olevikumi* (Tartu 1938). E. UUSTALU, *The History of the Estonian People* (London 1952). R. WITTRAM, *Baltische Geschichte; Die Ostseelande Livland, Estland, Kurland, 1180–1918* (Munich 1954). W. KIRCHNER, *The Rise of the Baltic Question* (Newark, DE 1954). J. AUNVER, ''Religious Life and the Church,'' *Aspects of Estonian Culture* (London 1961). R. AUBERT, *Dictionnaire d'histoire et de géographie ecclésiastiques*, ed. A. BAUDRILLART et al. (Paris 1912—) 15:1068–80. F. BENNINGHOVEN, *Der Orden der Schwertbrüder* (Cologne 1964). *The Chronicle of Henry of Livonia*, ed. and tr. J. A. BRUNDAGE (Madison, WI 1961). M. BOURDEAUX, *Land of Crosses* (Chulmleigh, UK 1980). A. LIEVEN, *The Baltic Revolution: Estonia, Latvia, Lithuania, and the Path to Independence* (New Haven, CT 1993). R. J. MISIUNAS and R. TAAGEPERA, *The Baltic States: Years of Dependence 1940–1990* (2d ed. Berkeley, CA 1993). T. RAUN, *Estonia and Estonians* (Stanford, CT 1987). V. S. VARDYS, ''Human Rights Issues in Estonia, Latvia, and Lithuania,'' *Journal of Baltic Studies* 12 (Fall 1981) 275-298. M. HELLMANN, *Lexikon für Theologie und Kirche*[2], eds., J. HOFER and K. RAHNER, 10 v. (2d, new ed. Freiburg 1957–65) 3:1117–19.

[B. J. COMASKEY/EDS.]

ESTOUTEVILLE, GUILLAUME D'

Cardinal, diplomat; b. *c.* 1412; d. Rome, Jan. 22, 1483. He was canon of St.-Maurice of Angers and apostolic notary when EUGENE IV conferred the bishopric of Angers on him (Feb. 20, 1439). The king of France, Charles VII, would not allow such a derogation of the terms of the PRAGMATIC SANCTION of Bourges (1438) and canonically recognized the man elected by the chapter of the cathedral, Jean Michel. Angered by the king's action, Eugene IV made Guillaume a cardinal (1439). PIUS II translated him to the See of Porto (1459), then to Ostia (1461). The Holy See heaped benefices upon him and granted him *in commendam* several bishoprics, especially the Archbishopric of Rouen (1453). NICHOLAS V sent him into France in 1451 as legate *a latere* with the official mandate to work toward the signing of a peace between France and England, but actually he hoped that Guillaume could induce Charles VII to abrogate the Pragmatic Sanction. Charles, however, categorically refused. Guillaume persuaded Charles to open a trial for the reinstatement of JOAN OF ARC and presided personally over the preliminary investigation, May 2 to 3, 1452. He was also able to force the University of PARIS to alter its system of teaching and discipline (*Chartularium universitatis Parisiensis*, ed. H. Denifle and E. Chatelain, 5:713). Thanks to Guillaume's mediation (October 1452), the negotiations between France and Savoy were successful. He managed to effect a *detente* in the persistently stormy relations between the Dauphin of Viennois and Venaissin County. After his return to Rome (January 1453) he went to Rouen (July 18, 1454). In 1455 he was back in Rome. Out of his wealth he gave liberal gifts to many churches.

Bibliography: G. DU F. BEAUCOURT, *Histoire de Charles VII*, v.5 (Paris 1896) 189–219, 353–389. G. BOURGIN, ''Les Cardinaux français et le diaire Caméral de 1439–1486,'' *Mélanges d'archeologie et d'histoire* 24 (1904) 277–316. P. OURLIAC, ''La Pragmatique Sanction et la légation en France du cardinal d'Estouteville (1451–1453),'' *ibid.* 55 (1938) 402–432. N. VALOIS, *Histoire de la Pragmatique Sanction de Bourges sous Charles VII* (Paris 1906) 223–227. W. SCHÜRMEYER, *Das Kardinalkollegium unter Pius II* (Berlin 1914). P. DONCOEUR and Y. LANHERS, eds. and trs., *La Réhabilitation de Jeanne la Pucelle*, 2 v. (Paris 1956–58), v.1 *L'Enquête ordonnée par Charles VII en 1450*, v.2 *L'Enquête du cardinal d'Estouteville en 1452*. G. MOLLAT, *Dictionnaire d'histoire et de géographie ecclésiastiques*, ed. A. BAUDRILLART et al. (Paris 1912–) 15:1080–82.

[G. MOLLAT]

ETERNAL WORD TELEVISION NETWORK (EWTN)

The Eternal Word Television Network (EWTN) transmits religious programming around the clock throughout the world. Its studios are located on the grounds of Our Lady of the Angels Monastery in Birmingham, Alabama. Under Catholic auspices, EWTN uses up-to-date technology to offer services that include television (wired and wireless cable, direct broadcast satellite), short-wave and AM/FM radio, news publishing, and online services (www.etwn.com).

The founder and supervisor of EWTN is Mother Angelica, a Franciscan nun. Born Rita Frances Rizzo on April 20, 1923 in Canton, Ohio, she joined the Poor Clares of Perpetual Adoration (PCPA) in Cleveland on August 15, 1944. From 1946 to 1961 she lived at the Santa Clara Monastery in Canton. With an intense desire to found a new convent, Mother Angelica began exploring possibilities. In 1961 an invitation came from Archbishop Thomas Toolan of the Mobile-Birmingham Diocese to establish a new convent in his diocese. In 1962, the monastery of Our Lady of the Angels was dedicated. During the early years of the Birmingham community, they found a number of ways to raise funds to keep the monastery going. They moved from making fishing lures to roasting peanuts and in 1973 decided to begin a book apostolate based on presentations given by Mother Angelica.

Mother Angelica's involvement in television ministry began in March 1978 when she was interviewed by a Chicago station. Following that interview she began videotaping programs for the Christian Broadcasting Network (CBN). By 1978, Mother Angelica had begun making plans for her own production studio to spread the

Word and called it the Eternal Word Television Studio. Mother Angelica's dream was to reach common persons, teach them the various types of spirituality, provide family programming for children and adults, be a vehicle of expression for various Catholic organizations, and provide inexpensive but high quality programming for dioceses that could not afford to make their own programs. On September 18, 1980, she applied for a license from the Federal Communications Commission to activate the Eternal Word Television Network (EWTN).

When EWTN began transmission on August 15, 1981, the network reached sixty thousand homes; nineteen years later, the program could be seen in more than 59 million homes around the world. In 1983, EWTN launched its flagship series "Mother Angelica Live." Cablecast live three nights each week, this program combined a Bible lesson taught by Mother Angelica with a talk show featuring prominent Catholic theologians, clergy, and lay persons, as well as entertainers and sports figures. Topics discussed ranged from the traditions of the Catholic faith to current church issues.

What began as a beam of faith has evolved into an international network transmitting Christian programs with a Catholic point of view. EWTN, marketed as the global Catholic network, reaches Europe, Africa, and the Pacific Rim. In 1996 EWTN expanded with Spanish television and radio services in the USA market. In 1999 EWTN announced La Red Global Catolica, the twenty-four-hour Spanish cable network, and Radio Catolica Mundial, EWTN Spanish radio network, which are available not only within the United States but in Central and South America. Hispanic programming originates from over a dozen countries and reflects the diversity of the Hispanic community.

A state-of-the-art web site (www.ewtn.com) reflects a diversity of services and select information concerning the Catholic Church. It offers a library of select church documents, recent statements by the pope and church leaders, a gallery of religious art, catalogue for purchasing Catholic publications and religious art, Catholic Headlines News from Catholic World News, Vatican Information Services and Zenit, as well as "Life on the Rock," which is directed toward young people in their search for networking into Catholic youth groups, Catholic colleges, and religious communities. Visitors to the web site can download video and audio programs and clips to their computers.

In 1984, EWTN became the first religious network to receive one of the cable industries' ACE (Award for Cable Excellence) nominations for a series targeted to a specific audience (the family). In the same year, Mother Angelica received the Gabriel Award for Personal Achievement with EWTN from the National Catholic Association of Communicators (Unda-USA).

Bibliography: "The Electronic Church Spreads the Word," *U.S. News & World Report* (April 23, 1984). "Determination," *Cablevision* (Jan. 30,1984). "Satellites that Serve Us," *National Geographic* (Sept. 1983). "A New Cable-TV Network with a Difference," *New York Times* (Aug. 15, 1981). SISTER M. RAPHAEL, *My Life with Mother Angelica* (Our Lady of the Angels Monastery 1982). "The Broadcasting Nun," *New Covenant* (Nov. 1984). D. O'NEIL, *Mother Angelica: Her Life Story* (New York 1986).

[A. A. ZUKOWSKI]

ETERNITY

Although its Greek equivalent, αἰών, first meant fluid of life, then life, then the maximum span of individual life, the eternal usually signifies—from the ancients down to recent times—what endures without beginning or end, or what is inherently timeless, or what is utterly outside the created order of the universe and time.

History. The following survey points out some of the leading views of eternity in ancient, medieval, and modern thought.

Ancient. Major philosophers prior to, or indifferent to, the influence of Christianity ascribed eternity to divine entities that, while above nature, are part and parcel of the universe. For PLATO (*Tim.* 37C), the Forms resident in the domain of being abide unchangeably; they simply are, rather than were or will be. Eternity is the timeless being proper to the Forms. What goes on endlessly is not eternity, but time, a derivative everlasting image of eternity. In ARISTOTLE (*Meta.* 1072b 1–1075a 11), eternity is the perfect all-at-once existence of God, the self-thinking thought. PLOTINUS (*Enn.* 3.1–6) located the Platonic paradigms in the Intellect, the second of the hypostases. In his view, eternity is the unchanging life of Intellect possessing all things all at once in the present; it is the radiation of the manifold of intelligibles concentrated in the Mind.

Capitalizing on the metaphysics latent in Christian revelation, St. AUGUSTINE (*Conf.* 11.1–16) added the dimension of TRANSCENDENCE to eternity. Because God is His own existence, He is immutable and eternal. Hence, eternity is the total presentness of the one incommutable being; indeed, God is His eternity. For Augustine, the Forms of Plato, the Intellect of Plotinus, and the self-thinking thought of Aristotle are supertemporal, but none of them utterly transcends time because none is wholly outside of, and infinitely superior to, a universe produced out of nothing. BOETHIUS (*De cons. phil.* 5.6), also within a Christian framework, formulated a definition that was to become a classic object of medieval commentary: eternity is "the perfect possession of interminable life held wholly all at once.'' Along with Augustine, Boethius regarded total simultaneity as the proper note; eternity is a standing now, in contrast to the flowing now whose never-ceasing course resembles the plenitude of eternity.

Medieval. ALEXANDER OF HALES (*Studia theologica* 1.65) singled out interminability as the distinctive element of eternity. His Franciscan colleague, St. BONAVENTURE (*In 2 sent.* 2.1.1.3), differentiated eternity from time and the *aevum.* Time possesses a before and after with innovation and ''veteration,'' and the *aevum* a before and after without innovation and ''veteration''; but eternity simply lacks a before and after. St. ALBERT THE GREAT (*In 4 phys.* 4.1–4) sharply distinguished the total simultaneity of eternity from that of aeviternity; eternity measures what is utterly invariable. Eternity is the successionless extent—the nonquantitative continuum—of what remains in one mode through all modes. But for St. THOMAS AQUINAS (*Summa theologiae* 1a, 10.1–6), the now rather than a stretch of time serves as the closest natural analogue of eternity: eternity is the uniformity or perfect possession of what is entirely immutable. The section on doctrine below analyzes this definition and its implications. However, according to DUNS SCOTUS (*Quodl.* 6.14 and *Op. oxon.* 1.8.4), life, or actual perfect existence intrinsic to the divine nature, constitutes the subject and foundation of eternity. The other three elements in Boethius's definition, i.e., the interminable, the wholly simultaneous, and perfect possession bespeak extrinsic relations of God. The approach of F. SUÁREZ (*Disp. meta.* 50.1–3) departed further from that of Aquinas. Interminable life, the exclusion of all mutability in existence, is a secondary factor. Eternity is uncreated duration; not the nature of God, but nonorigination from an outside active potency primarily differentiates eternity from created durations.

Modern. The abandonment of a creative God generally entails the loss of a transcendent eternity among certain moderns. Two philosophers committed to this transcendence base their views on moral or religious convictions that are virtually devoid of theoretical content.

B. SPINOZA reached a concept congruent with his quasi-mathematical monism. ''By eternity I understand existence itself insofar as it is conceived to follow necessarily from the definition alone of the eternal thing.'' This formulation is plainly circular; eternal appears in the definition itself. In addition, an outlook relating God and the universe as ground and consequent blurs what is manifestly noneternal with the eternal.

J. LOCKE defined eternity as an infinity of duration, comparable to an infinity of number, achieved when one thinks of a duration ''so much greater as cannot be comprehended.'' But if eternity is merely an unendingly extended time, its potential infinity is irreconcilable with the immaterial infinity of knowledge and power that Locke attributes to God.

I. KANT nullified his acceptance of a transcendent eternity by emptying the idea of God of theoretical import. Unable to know demonstratively that God is, the mind is persuaded by moral faith that God is eternal. In breaking the causal link between time and eternity, Kantian PHENOMENALISM destroyed for many moderns the possibility of regarding eternity as other than a metaphor or a religious symbol.

G. W. F. HEGEL overcame the Kantian divorce of time and eternity by making them diverse attributes of the one Absolute Idea. In itself eternal, the Spirit necessarily expresses itself in nature and history, so that eternity becomes immanent in time. Whereas Spinoza eternalized time, Hegel temporalized eternity. A One necessarily becoming many is really a dynamic manifold, and in a similar fashion an eternity revealing itself in time is really a finite distension.

Reacting against Hegel's absolutism, S. A. KIERKEGAARD put time and eternity at opposite poles. Eternity, the forever present identical with pure being, excludes the becoming and ''either-or'' characteristic of time. Yet existence, one's subjective being, does somehow share in eternity, each moment of decision being filled with eternity. Kierkegaard, somewhat like Kant, posited a theoretically groundless eternity bequeathed by Christian culture to serve the subjective thinker striving for fulfillment. Furthermore, it seems absurd to make each moment big with the plenitude of the eternal.

A. N. WHITEHEAD blended the Platonic Forms with a quasi-Hegelian ingression of the changeless into concretes. Eternal objects, the abstract natures of things, reside in the nontemporal primordial nature of God. Yet in his consequent nature, God is enriched by the creative advance of the universe. Unfortunately, an unconditioned, eternal actuality always potential and subject to time is a self-defeating notion. Eternal objects enmeshed in time are simply constant features of nature abstracted from time.

Doctrine. Four aspects of the realistic account of eternity merit summary exposition: its precise notion, its comparison with noneternal measures, the eternal knowledge of contingents, and the possibility of an *ab aeterno* world.

Notion. As a being of nature, man has his thinking properly attuned to the quiddities of material things. To grasp beings outside nature, his mind must fall back on the negation of natural traits and the modes of causality and excess. In short, man knows not what God is, but what He is not. So with eternity; one knows it not in itself but in virtue of a transcendent negation of the potential in time and the now. TIME is the number of motion according to before and after. The negation of motion, the before and after, and number yields respectively immobility, sameness, and uniformity. Eternity is, then, the uniformity of the utterly immutable. The ascent to eternity can also start from the now, the number of mobile being. The negation of number issues in unity, the negation of mobile being in a being unaffected by mutability; the result is eternity conceived as the unity of an entirely immutable being. The terminus of an approach made from things measured by time coincides with Boethius's definition. Things in time, existing successively, begin and end; what is measured by eternity is successionless. Thus eternity as measure is interminable life existing wholly all at once.

God alone is truly and properly eternal, since He alone is utterly immutable. The word may be said analogously of other beings insofar as they are in some way immutable. However, Plato's Forms and Whitehead's eternal objects are only metaphorically eternal. UNIVERSALS are always and everywhere only in a sheerly negative fashion; for, as known, they are objectified in the human intellect, whose discretely temporal operations exclude eternity. Universals and truths are eternal only as existing in an eternal intellect.

Comparison with Noneternal Measures. The *aevum* is closest to eternity, for it measures angels and human souls, exempt from transmutation. The *aevum* falls short of eternity because joined together with it are successive spiritual actions.

The now recedes even farther from eternity. While subjectively identical, the flowing now is formally other as other. Wedded to the mobile, the now is inexhaustibly potential to a diversity of positions. Eternity, by contrast, measures an immutable infinite act; humanly speaking, it is a *nunc stans,* stationary in that it is perfectly identical without differentiation of phases.

Nevertheless, the now is the moving image of eternity. As indivisible, and therefore most knowable in time, it reflects the perfectly indivisible measure. The now is the point of intersection of eternity and time; it is like the moving point on a circumference whose minimal indivisible act imitates in nature the maximal indivisible act of the transcendent center and measure of all being.

Thus, eternity and the now are analogically one; eternity is to God as the now is to the universal physical cause. The proportional resemblance is founded on the formal causality exercised by eternity with respect to inferior measures. God is so present in other things as the cause of their being that His principal causality does not liquidate, but uses created agents as secondary causes. Similarly, eternity is effective in the now as remote formal cause of its indivisibility, so that the now remains a secondary formal cause unifying cosmic time. Spinoza, Hegel, and Whitehead confuse this causal nexus with an essential unity; Spinoza makes eternity and time one in number, while Hegel and Whitehead make them one in genus or species.

Eternal Knowledge of Contingents. Like the center of a circle directly opposite every designated point on the circumference, eternity is simultaneously present to every instant of time. Each part of time coexists with the whole of eternity, although this part may be past or future in relation to other parts of time. Hence, every event in time is present to eternity; God sees each event actually occurring. Applied to the problem of divine knowledge of future contingents, this means that the copresence to eternity of events past, present, and future assures God an infallible and necessary knowledge of future contingents, including free acts. A contingent event is one actively or passively indeterminate in its causes; its indetermination lies in reference to the future, but once caused, it obviously occurs as this determinate event rather than some other. Socrates need not sit down while lecturing today, but if he is seen sitting down, he is necessarily sitting down. Just as it is evident to any observer that Socrates is now sitting down, so every event in the whole history of the universe is infallibly known by eternal vision, since the whole of time is copresent to the whole of eternity.

Possibility of an Eternal World. An allied problem concerns the eternity, here meaning perpetuity, of the universe. One view, implied by every absolutistic metaphysics, holds that the nature of divine action necessitates an eternal world. An effect must be proportional to its cause, but the conclusion that an eternal cause must produce *ab aeterno* beings is based on the faulty assumption that God generates the universe by natural necessity. God creates according to intellect and will; i.e., He freely determines that the universe will exist after not existing. According to a second opinion, popular with some scholastics, an eternal world is impossible, because to be beginningless is incompatible with being a creature and because an infinite time is untraversable. Indeed creature entails a principle of origin, but not a principle of a duration. Second, since each segment of an eternal time-line would cover a finite distance, it is no more difficult to conceive a time-line without an initial term than one without an end. Thus, an eternal world is neither necessary nor impossible. As God has revealed, the universe was in fact created in time. God so created without necessity and with reason, but the precise reason is hidden in the depths of divine wisdom. (*See* UNIVERSE, ORIGIN OF; CREATION.)

See Also: TIME; NOW.

Bibliography: M. J. ADLER, ed., *The Great Ideas: A Syntopicon of Great Books of the Western World* (Chicago 1952) 1:437–450. R. AMERIO, *Enciclopedia filosofica* (Venice-Rome 1957) 2:166–177. R. EISLER, *Wörterbuch der philosophischen Begriffe* (Berlin 1927–30) 1:420–424. J. GUITTON, *Le Temps et l'éternité chez Plotin et saint Augustin* (3d ed. Paris 1959). J. F. ANDERSON, *The Cause of Being: The Philosophy of Creation in St. Thomas* (St. Louis 1952). B. GERRITY, *Nature, Knowledge, and God* (Milwaukee 1947). H. F. HALLETT, *Aeternitas* (Oxford 1930). R. ONIANS, *The Origins of European Thought* (2d ed. Cambridge, Eng. 1954). I. LECLERC, *Whitehead's Metaphysics* (New York 1958).

[J. M. QUINN]

ETERNITY OF GOD

The eternity of God contains two interrelated aspects. First, God has no beginning and no end. God always was, is, and will be. Second, God is timeless, that is, unlike creatures for whom time marks the changes they experience and undergo, God is immutably the same and so is not subject to the changes marked by time and thus does not experience time. As transcending the created order of change, he is timeless.

Biblical Basis. The Old Testament testifies to the fact that God always was. Abraham called on ''the name of the Lord, the Everlasting God'' (Gn 21:33). The Psalms speak of God being everlasting. Before creation ''from everlasting to everlasting you are God'' (Ps 89/90:2, see Hb 1:12; Is 40:28). God's throne is established from of old for ''you are from everlasting'' (Ps 92/93:2). Unlike creatures and humankind who come to be and perish, ''you, O Lord, are enthroned forever; your name endures to all generations . . . you do endure . . . you are the same, and your years have no end'' (Ps 101/102:12, 24, 26, 27; see Is 63:16). Daniel in his vision sees ''the Ancient of Days'' (Dn 7:13). As creator, God existed prior to all else (see Gn 1, Jb 38, Prv 8). Because God is everlasting and so forever faithful to his promises, he is able to be present to and active within every generation of Israel (see Gn 26:24; 28:13–15; Ex 4:5; 6:3–8; Dt 34:4; Jos 1:3–7; 3:7; 24:2–13). God's mercy, kindness, name, love and salvation are everlasting (Ps 99/100:5, 102/103:17; Is 45:17, 54:8, 56:5; Jer 31:3). God ''inhabits eternity'' (Is 57:15). The New Testament not only testifies to the eternity of the Father but also to the eternity of the Son/Word. It is through the Word or Son that the Father created the universe and so he too is before all else and is thus everlasting (Jn 1:1–3; Heb 1:1–12). The Son possesses eternal life with the Father and it is through the Son that those who believe come to eternal redemption and so share in eternal life (2 Tim 2:10; Heb 5:9, 9:12, 9:15; Mt 25:46; Jn 3:15, 6:54; Rom 6:23, 1 Jn 1:2). This was all in accord with the Father's eternal plan (Eph 3:11). The Holy Spirit is the pledge that guarantees the eternal life of those who believe (Eph 1:13–14, 4:30). God's actions, as narrated within the Old Testament, reveal that he is the everlasting God. This revelation finds its culmination in the New Testament where God is revealed to be an eternal trinity of persons through whose actions humankind is enabled to share in their eternal life. Only if God possesses eternal life in himself is he able to share that life with humankind.

Christian Tradition. While the early Fathers of the Church upheld the eternity of God, it was Augustine who first examined it in any depth, and he did so within his analysis of time. Human beings find it difficult to conceive eternity for their minds are fixed on things that change ''and have a past and future.'' However, ''in the eternal, nothing is transient, but the whole is present. But no time is wholly present . . . Who will lay hold on the human heart to make it still, so that it can see how eternity, in which there is neither future nor past, stands still and dictates future and past times?'' (*Conf.*, XI, 13). For Anselm that which is not subject to space and time is greater than that which is, thus God alone is eternal for he does not come to be or cease to be (*Proslog.*, 13). It is Boethius who provides the classic definition of eternity: ''Eternity is the simultaneously whole and perfect possession of interminable life'' (*The Consolation of Philosophy*, 5). Aquinas argues, following Aristotle's and Augustine's understanding of time, that time is the numbering of before and after within movement. Since God is not in movement in that he does not change from potency to act, he is outside of movement and thus outside of time, and in this ''consists the idea of eternity'' (*Summa Theologiae*, 1, 10, 1). ''The idea of eternity follows immutability, as the idea of time follows movement . . . . Hence, as God is supremely immutable, it supremely belongs to him to be eternal'' (*Summa Theologiae*, 1, 10, 2). For Aquinas, then, because God is being itself (*ipsum esse*) and thus pure act (*actus purus*), he must be eternal in the sense both of having no beginning and no end (interminable life), and of being timeless (no succession). As pure act, God possesses, in accordance with Boethius, the fullness and totality of interminable perfect life simultaneously. The Church attributes eternity to the Godhead as indistinct from the persons (Vatican I, H. Denzinger, *Enchiridion symbolorum*, ed. A. Schönmetzer, 3001). Duration excluding a beginning is exclusively divine (Lateran IV, *Enchiridion symbolorum* 800).

Contemporary Thought. Many of those who deny God's immutability also deny that he is timeless. Some, such as process philosophers and theologians, and, others, like P. Fiddes, N. Pike, R. Swinburne, and K. Ward, argue that God changes through his interaction with the created order and thus there is successive change within him which demands that he experiences time. (*See* IMMUTABILITY OF GOD.) B. Davies argues that while God does not change, there is duration within God. This he believes is more in accord with Aquinas's teaching that God is present to and embraces all time. This understanding would appear to alleviate the problem of how a timeless God can relate to temporal reality. However, in Aquinas's view the reason God is immutable is that he is pure act, and the very notion of pure act abolishes the notion not only of time but also of duration. As pure act everything that God experiences is contained within and experienced as the pure act that he is. While God as pure act endures, there is no duration within pure act for it is the one simultaneous timeless act that God perfectly and total is. One cannot predicate of God not only a past and a future, but also, strictly speaking, "a present", as if God existed in an "eternal now", for this too would imply an everlasting unchanging duration. For God to be eternal, in the sense of being timeless, negates even "the present" within God, for "the present" is a concept founded upon the human experience of time as that which is neither past nor future. For God to be eternal means that God is present to himself and is present to all else in being present to himself, but not in "a present."

While theologians, past and present, have focused their attention on the eternity of God in so far as God is one, yet it must be said that the persons of the Trinity are equally eternal both in that they have no beginning and no end and are timeless. The Father is eternally the Father for he eternally begets the Son and eternally loves the Son in the eternal spiration of the Holy Spirit. The Son is eternally the Son because he is both eternally begotten and in that he eternally loves the Father is the same eternal Spirit. The Holy Spirit is eternally the Holy Spirit because he eternally comes forth from the eternal Father and Son as their love for one another and in that he eternally conforms the Father to be the loving Father of the Son and the loving Son of the Father. The persons of the Trinity then eternally subsist as who they are within their eternal relationships with one another. These subsisting relations which define the persons of the trinity are eternally and fully in act and thus are timeless. The Athanasian Creed (*Quicumque vult*) professes: "The Father is eternal, the Son is eternal, and the Holy Spirit is eternal. Nevertheless, there are not three eternal beings, but one eternal being" (see also Nicaea, *Enchiridion symbolorum* 126; The Council of Rome, *Enchiridion symbolorum* 162; Lateran IV, *Enchiridion symbolorum* 800; Lyon II, *Enchiridion symbolorum* 851–53).

Bibliography: T. AQUINAS, *Summa Theologiae*, I.10.1–6. B. DAVIES, "A Timeless God", *New Blackfriars* 64 (1983) 215–24; *The Thought of Thomas Aquinas* (Oxford 1992). H. GORIS, *Free Creatures of an Eternal God* (Utrecht 1990). W. GUDERSDORF VON JESS, "Divine Eternity in the Doctrine of Augustine," *Augustinian Studies* 6 (1975) 75–96. P. HELM, *Eternal God: A Study of God without Time* (Oxford 1988). C. HUGHES, *On a Complex Theory of a Simple God: An Investigation in Aquinas's Philosophical Theology* (Ithaca, N.Y. 1989). C. PETER, *Participated Eternity in the Vision of God* (Rome 1964). N. PIKE, *God and Timelessness* (London 1970). G. L. PRESTIGE, *God in Patristic Thought* (London 1952). R. SORABJI, *Time, Creation and the Continuum* (Ithaca, N.Y. 1983). E. STUMP and N. KRETZMANN, "Eternity," in *The Concept of God*, ed. T. V. MORRIS (Oxford 1987), 219–52. T. G. WEINANDY, *The Father's Spirit of Sonship: Reconceiving the Trinity* (Edinburgh 1995).

[T. G. WEINANDY]

ETHELBERT, KING OF EAST ANGLIA, ST.

Martyr, d. 794. According to the *Anglo-Saxon Chronicle,* he was killed at the order of Offa II of Mercia, perhaps because he stood for an independent East Anglia. Later hagiographers described him as a pious youth who wished to lead a celibate life, but was persuaded to propose marriage to Elfthryth, Offa's daughter. He was murdered at an interview with the king on the instigation of the queen. His body was later buried in the cathedral of HEREFORD. He became patron saint of Hereford and is honored by extensive services in the *Hereford Breviary* (*Henry Bradshaw Society* 40:167–182; 46:31–36). His feast is now observed in the Dioceses of Cardiff, Wales, and Northampton, England.

Feast: May 20.

Bibliography: T. D. HARDY, *Descriptive Catalogue of Materials Relating to the History of Britain and Ireland,* 3 v. (*Rerum Brittanicarum medii aevi scriptores* (London 1858–1896) 26; London 1862–71) 1.2:494–496. J. EARLE and C. PLUMMER, eds., *Two of the Saxon Chronicles Parallel,* 2 v. (Oxford 1892–99) 1:55, 2:61–62. M. R. JAMES, ed., "Two Lives of St. Ethelbert" *English Historical Review* 32 (1917) 214–244. Landesbibliothek Gotha MS I, No. 81, folios 30–39, see P. GROSJEAN, *Analecta Bollandiana* 58 (1940) 92–93. W. STUBBS, *A Dictionary of Christian Biography,* ed. W. SMITH and H. WACE, (London 1877–1887) 2:215–216. R. STANTON, *A Menology of England and Wales* (New York 1887) 220–221. A. T. BANNISTER, *The Cathedral Church of Hereford* (London 1924).

[B. W. SCHOLZ]

ETHELBERT, KING OF KENT, ST.

Reigned 560 to Feb. 24, 616; b. *c.* 550. The first Christian Anglo-Saxon king and lawgiver of Kent, he was the son of Eormenric, king of Kent, a descendant of

Hengest. The early years of his reign were marked by a struggle with Ceawlin of Wessex for royal supremacy (Bretwaldaship). In pursuit of this objective Ethelbert sought the assistance and prestige of a marriage alliance with the MEROVINGIAN rulers of the Franks and obtained the hand of Bertha, daughter of Charibert, King of the Franks. Since Bertha was a Christian, the marriage arrangements provided for a Frankish bishop as her chaplain, and for the old Roman church of St. Martin in Canterbury as a place for her worship. This Continental connection brought in its wake the mission of AUGUSTINE OF CANTERBURY, sent out by Pope GREGORY I for the conversion of the Angles, Saxons, and Jutes in England. In 597, Augustine was welcomed courteously by Ethelbert, and quarters were assigned him. Later that same year the king accepted Baptism from the hands of the Roman missionary. Ethelbert seems to have been then at the height of his power, having become the acknowledged Bretwalda at the death of Ceawlin.

The king showed himself a paternal benefactor of the Church. He founded churches at Canterbury and Rochester. It was his influence that altered Gregory's plan to make London the primatial see, and the primacy remained at CANTERBURY. He arranged for a second bishopric at ROCHESTER, and endowed the first ST. PAUL'S CATHEDRAL at London. Through his influence the kings of Essex and East Anglia became Christians. In all of this he allowed no forced conversions, and it was probably this same sense of rectitude that lay behind his issuance in 604 of the Kentish laws that bear his name, and which were written in imitation of the old Roman codes. By Bertha he left at least three children, including his successor, the pagan King Eadbald. In religious art he is represented as holding a sword and a church.

Feast: Feb. 25.

Bibliography: BEDE, *Ecclesiastical History,* 2 v., tr. J. E. KING based on the version of T. STAPLETON (*Loeb Classical Library*; New York 1930) bks. 1–2. His dooms are given in F. LIEBERMANN, ed., *Die Gestze der Angelsachsen,* 3 v. (Halle 1898–1916; repr. 1960) 1:3–8. F. M. STENTON, *Anglo-Saxon England* (2d ed. Oxford 1947) 33–112. S. BRECHTER, *Die Quellen zur Angelsachsenmission Gregors des Grossen* (Münster 1941).

[J. L. DRUSE]

"The Baptism of Ethelbert of Kent by St. Augustine," after a fresco painting by William Dyce (1846) in the House of Lords, London, England. (©Baldwin H. Ward and Kathryn C. Ward/ CORBIS)

ETHELBERT OF YORK

Archbishop of York; d. York, England, Nov. 8, *c.* 781. He was related to Archbishop EGBERT, under whom he directed the school of YORK and whom he succeeded in that see. Consecrated in 767, he received the PALLIUM from Pope ADRIAN I in 773. As a teacher of grammar and rhetoric he is referred to with affection by his pupil ALCUIN. Ethelbert traveled to Rome at least once and as archbishop undertook the restoration of the cathedral of York that Alcuin described, seemingly particularly impressed by the 30 altars, many encrusted with precious stones. In his later years Ethelbert consecrated his pupil Eanbald (d. 796) as his successor and retired from active life. He was buried in the cathedral at York, which he had helped to consecrate a short time before his death.

Bibliography: A. W. HADDEN and W. STUBBS, eds., *Councils and Ecclesiastical Documents Relating to Great Britain and Ireland,* 3 v. in 4 (Oxford 1869–78), 3:435–437, letter of Lull to Ethelbert and Ethelbert's reply. ALCUIN, *De pontificibus et sanctis ecclesiae eboracensis carmen in The Historians of the Church of York and Its Archbishops,* ed. J. RAINE, 3 v. (Rolls Series 71; 1879–94) 1:390–397. E. DÜMMLER, ed., *Alcuini sive Albini epistulae, Monumenta Germaniae Historica: Epistolares* 2:112, 114, 116, 121, 143, 148, 200, 232, 233, 271. *Epistulae Bonifacii et Lulli, ibid.* 3:124. H. DAUPHIN, *Dictionnaire d'histoire et de géographie* *ecclésiastiques* (Paris 1912–) 15:1158–59. G. HOCQUARD, *Catholicisme* 1:172.

[V. I. J. FLINT]

ETHELBURGA, SS.

There are three contemporary saints by this name. (1) Ethelburga of Barking; d. *c.* 676. A sister of Bishop ERCONWALD OF LONDON, she was the first abbess of the double monastery at BARKING.

Feast: Oct. 12 (Diocese of Brentwood).

(2) Ethelburga (or Aubierge, Edilburga); d. 695. A sister of St. ETHELREDA, she was abbess of FAREMOUTIERS when she died.

Feast: July 7.

(3) Ethelburga (or Tata) of Lyminge; d. *c.* 644. The daughter of King ETHELBERT and Bertha. In the course of her father's diplomatic and apostolic maneuvers, she married the pagan King EDWIN OF NORTHUMBRIA. Bishop PAULINUS accompanied her to the north as her chaplain and became the first bishop of YORK. Together they labored to spread the knowledge of Christianity throughout Northumbria, their biggest obstacle being the firm paganism of Edwin. Pope BONIFACE V sent her a letter of encouragement. After the birth of a daughter, Edwin renounced his ancestral rites and became a Christian (627), an act that contributed to his death in the Battle of Heathfield in 633. After Ethelburga retired to Kent with her two children, her son was sent on to Gaul, where he died at the court of King Dagobert; her daughter ultimately married Oswy, king of Northumbria. Ethelburga herself founded the Abbey at Lymynge where she died as abbess.

Feast: April 5.

Bibliography: BEDE, *Historia ecclesiastica,* ed. C. PLUMMER (Oxford 1896, repr. 1956) bks. 2, 3, 4. *Acta Sanctorum* Oct. 5:649–652; July 2:481–482. A. BUTLER, *The Lives of the Saints,* ed. H. THURSTON and D. ATTWATER (New York 1956) 4:95–96; 3:34; 2:35. A. M.. ZIMMERMANN, *Kalendarium Benedictinum: Die Heiligen und Seligen des Benediktinerorderns und seiner Zweige* (Metten 1933–1938) 2:20–21. F. L. CROSS, *The Oxford Dictionary of the Christian Church* (London 1957) 465. J. DUBOIS, *Catholicisme* 3:1330.

[J. L. DRUSE]

ETHELHARD (AETHELHEARD) OF CANTERBURY

Archbishop; d. May 12, 805. The creation of the Mercian archbishopric of Lichfield in the 780s at the instigation of King Offa had ended the primacy of CANTERBURY's jurisdiction in southern England. When Ethelhard, Abbot of ''Hlud'' (probably Louth in Lincolnshire), was elevated to Canterbury under Mercian influence following Archbishop Jaenbert's death (Aug. 12, 791), Kentish opposition caused his consecration by Archbishop Hygebert of Lichfield to be postponed until July 21, 793. In 796 a Kentish revolt under the apostate cleric Eadbert Praen forced Ethelhard into exile. Cenwulf, the new king of Mercia, and Ethelhard collaborated in breaking the revolt, and it was their correspondence with Pope LEO III that brought the reassertion of Canterbury's primacy. Journeying to Rome, Ethelhard received papal confirmation of the rights of his see (802), a judgment implemented by Cenwulf and Ethelhard at the Council of Clovesho (803), which abolished the archbishopric of Lichfield and maintained southern English ecclesiastical unity under Canterbury. Episcopal declarations of faith and obedience to the metropolitan apparently began in England during these troubles. Sources for Ethelhard include the *Anglo-Saxon Chronicle,* FLORENCE OF WORCESTER, SIMEON OF DURHAM, and WILLIAM OF MALMESBURY.

Bibliography: A. W. HADDAN and W. STUBBS, *Councils and Ecclesiastical Documents Relating to Great Britain and Ireland,* 3 v. in 4 (Oxford 1869–78) v.3. W. HUNT, *The Dictionary of National Biography from the Earliest Times to 1900* (London 1885–1900) 6:887–889. F. M. STENTON, *Anglo-Saxon England* (2d ed. Oxford 1947).

[W. A. CHANEY]

ETHELNOTH OF CANTERBURY, ST.

Archbishop, called ''the Good''; d. Oct. 29, 1038. Son of ealdorman Aethelmaer, Ethelnoth (or Æthelnoth) was a monk of GLASTONBURY and dean of Christ Church, CANTERBURY, before his consecration to that see by WULFSTAN OF WORCESTER, archbishop of York, (Nov. 13, 1020). BENEDICT VIII received him in Rome ''with much honor'' and gave him the PALLIUM (1022). Archbishop Ethelnoth was chief advisor to King CANUTE OF ENGLAND, who granted him the earliest known writ bestowing judicial and financial authority on an English prelate and presented his gold crown to Ethelnoth's cathedral. The archbishop translated the martyred ALPHEGE OF CANTERBURY's relics from London to Canterbury with great pomp (1023). Ethelnoth's death overwhelmed Bishop Aethelric of Sussex, who did not wish to survive the beloved archbishop and died within a week. Ethelnoth's life is recounted in the *Anglo-Saxon Chronicle* and in the writings of FLORENCE OF WORCESTER, SIMEON OF DURHAM, WILLIAM OF MALMESBURY and GERVASE OF CANTERBURY.

Feast: Oct. 30.

Bibliography: W. HUNT, *The Dictionary of National Biography from the Earliest Times to 1900* (London 1885–1900) 6:889. C. COTTON, *The Saxon Cathedral at Canterbury and the Saxon Saints Buried Therein* (Manchester, Eng. 1929). H. DAUPHIN, *Dictionnaire d'histoire et de géographie ecclésiastiques* (Paris 1912–) 15: 1165–66.

[W. A. CHANEY]

ETHELREDA, QUEEN OF NORTHUMBRIA, ST.

Abbess, most popular of Anglo-Saxon women saints; b. Exning, Suffolk, England, *c.* 630; d. Ely, June 23, 679. Etheldreda (Ediltrudis or Ethelreda) was the daughter of Anna, King of East Anglia. While young she was married to Tonbert, a prince of the Gyrvii who endowed her with the land now called the Isle of Ely. She apparently lived in virginity with him, and after his early death she formally embraced the religious life for five years. Diplomatic considerations brought her out of the convent, and she was married to Egfrid, ultimately king of Northumbria. She seems never to have lived in wedlock with her husband, although there was a spirited argument about her marital duties in which St. WILFRID apparently supported her vocation to virginity. After 12 years Egfrid consented to her return to the convent, and she took the veil at Coldingham from Wilfrid. A year later she returned to ELY where she became abbess. After her death from the plague (which she foretold), her shrine became one of the principal sites of pilgrimage in England. The later form of her name ''Audrey'' gave rise to the word ''tawdry'' because of the cheap souvenirs hawked at her shrine. The church bearing her name in London's Ely Place is the only Catholic church in the metropolis whose structure dates to the Middle Ages. In art, St. Etheldreda is frequently represented as a crowned abbess.

Feast: June 23.

Bibliography: *Acta Sanctorum* June 5 (1863) 417–495. BEDE, *Ecclesiastical History* 4.3. *Liber Eliensis,* ed. E. O. BLAKE (Camden 3d ser., v.92; London 1962). *Liber Eliensis,* ed. E. O. BLAKE (London 1962), attributed variously to THOMAS OF ELY and RICHARD OF ELY. C. W. STUBBS, *Historical Memorials of Ely Cathedral* (New York 1897) 1–94.

[J. L. DRUSE]

ETHELWOLD OF WINCHESTER, ST.

Leader of English monastic revival; b. *c.* 908; d. Aug. 1, 984. He was tonsured and ordained by ALPHEGE ''THE BALD'' OF WINCHESTER, who prophesied Ethelwold's succession to Winchester. Having been a Bene-

St. Ethelreda, Queen of Northumbria, miniature from the ''Benedictional of St. Ethelwold,'' written at Hyde Abbey, c. 965.

dictine of GLASTONBURY, Ethelwold (Æthelwold) was given ABINGDON ABBEY (*c.* 954), which he refounded, introducing Continental, especially Fleury practices (*see* SAINT-BENOÎT-SUR-LOIRE), and creating a model for the monastic revival (*see* DUNSTAN OF CANTERBURY, ST.; OSWALD OF YORK).

In 963 Ethelwold was consecrated bishop of WINCHESTER, where he expelled the worldly clerics and substituted monks at the Old and New Minsters. His harsh methods were perhaps justified by the decayed conditions they met and were supported by King EDGAR THE PEACEFUL, for whom he was tutor and adviser. The ''Father of the Monks,'' Ethelwold restored or founded monasteries at PETERBOROUGH (966), ELY (970), THORNEY (972), and perhaps Chertsey, Milton, CROWLAND, and St. Neot's. Austere but generous and of immense energy, he rebuilt his cathedral, restored ruined minsters, taught and translated, and reformed Church music. He prepared the *Regularis Concordia* (ed. and tr. T. Symons, London 1953) a customary for English religious. A skillful craftsman, he stimulated the Winchester School of manuscript production. The best sources for his life are the *Anglo-Saxon Chronicle* and biographies by Wulfstan of Winchester (*Patrologia Latina* 137:79) and AELFRIC GRAMMATICUS, in the *Chronicon Monasterii de Abingdon* (*Rerum Brittanicarum medii aevi scriptores*), translated by S. H. Gem (1912).

Feast: Aug. 1.

Bibliography: WULFSTAN OF WINCHESTER, *The Life of St. Aethelwold,* ed. M. LAPIDGE and M. WINTERBOTTOM (Oxford 1991). W. HUNT, *The Dictionary of National Biography from the Earliest Times to 1900* (London 1885–1900), 6:901–904. J. A. ROBINSON, *The Times of Saint Dunstan* (Oxford 1923). D. J. V. FISHER, "The Early Biographers of St. E.," *English Historical Review* 67 (1952) 381–391. D. KNOWLES, *The Monastic Order in England 943–1216* (Cambridge, Eng. 1962). M. WINTERBOTTOM, *Three Lives of English Saints* (Toronto 1972). G. B. BRYAN, *Ethelwold and Medieval Music-Drama at Winchester: The Easter Play, its Author, and its Milieu* (Berne 1981). R. DESHMAN, *The Benedictional of Æthelwold* (Princeton, N.J. 1995). M. GRETSCH, *The Intellectual Foundations of the English Benedictine Reform* (Cambridge, U.K. 1999).

[W. A. CHANEY]

ETHICAL FORMALISM

A theory of ETHICS holding that moral value is determined by formal, and not material, considerations. Material and formal are here related by analogy to their physical meanings (*see* MATTER AND FORM). The material aspects of a moral act include what is done and its consequences, while the formal aspects are the law and the attitude and intention of the agent. Usually ethical formalism refers to views of the Kantian type, although intuitionism too is formalistic in a wide sense. A formalistic ethics is called such because it holds that an agent's disposition, taken without reference to any material aspect, determines the morality of his actions, just as form determines the nature of a material subject.

Immanuel KANT is the classic example of a formalist. For him nothing can possibly be conceived as an absolute GOOD, except a good WILL. A will, however, is good only insofar as it does its duty out of sheer dutifulness, and not because of what it achieves or is capable of achieving. Moral goodness is submissiveness to the law that imposes duties. This law is unique, necessary, universal, and inherent in reason itself. It is the CATEGORICAL IMPERATIVE: "Act only on that maxim whereby you can at the same time will that it should become a universal law." It is also purely formal; it does not specify any concrete duties, but merely provides a criterion whereby one can determine what his duties are. And since it does not allow any exceptions, it entails RIGORISM.

By emphasizing the rationality of the moral law, Kant did much to curb the excessive EMPIRICISM and sentimentalism that was current in ethics in his day. He was right also in insisting that morally good acts can proceed only from a free will with a right intention. Again, his categorical imperative expresses a valid insight, that the moral law must be consistent and universal. However, as a norm of morality it is negative and inadequate. With it, Kant may show what cannot be a duty, but when discussing man's obligations in the concrete, he has surreptitiously to introduce considerations of consequences and ends. For it is impossible to divorce, as he tries, the notions of goodness and TELEOLOGY. It is also a serious defect in a moral theory to ignore the nature and circumstances of an act whose morality is to be determined. Again, it is incorrect to identify the good with acting out of mere dutifulness. In a sound ethics the central notions are those of nature, end, and good; duty is a subordinate concept. Many good acts are not duties. The spontaneous, exhilarating love of the good attained in an act may in itself be a better reason for doing it than any duty. Finally, one should point out that only God, by His essence and not merely by His will, is absolutely good and, in addition, also the source of all goodness.

Formalistic views of one type or another have been held also by Jean Jacques ROUSSEAU, Hermann Cohen (1842–1918), Paul Natorp (1854–1924), J. F. HERBART, Josiah ROYCE, and Simone de Beauvoir (b. 1908).

See Also: ETHICS, HISTORY OF; KANTIANISM; NEOKANTIANISM.

Bibliography: J. D. COLLINS, *A History of Modern European Philosophy* (Milwaukee 1954). J. LECLERCQ, *Les Grandes lignes de la philosophie morale* (rev. ed. Paris 1954).

[G. J. DALCOURT]

ETHICS

The philosophical study of voluntary human action, with the purpose of determining what types of activity are good, right, and to be done (or bad, wrong, and not to be done) that man may live well. This article deals with the general features of ethics that are common to most types of classical ethical theory; of the ethics of St. Thomas Aquinas, with variant modern interpretations; and of the main schools of ethics in the Catholic tradition.

General Characteristics. As a philosophical study, ethics is a science, or intellectual habit, that treats information derived from man's natural experience of the problems of human life, from the point of view of natural reasoning. Thus, ethics (etymologically connected with Gr. ἔθος, meaning custom or conduct) is equivalent in meaning to moral philosophy (from Lat. *mos,* meaning custom or behavior). It is also generally regarded as a practical science, in the sense that the objective of the study is not simply to know, but to know which actions should be done and which should be avoided.

The subject matter of ethics is voluntary human conduct: this includes all actions, and also omissions, over which man exercises personal control because he understands and wills these actions (and omissions) in relation to some end he has in view. Such conduct is voluntary, in contrast to not-voluntary activities (digestion of food, accidental falling), which are not under the direction of intellect and will. Included within the scope of ethics, however, are somewhat involuntary activities (e.g., visiting a dentist, doing disagreeable work) that are performed with repugnance, yet involve some degree of personal approval. Perhaps most moral actions are less than perfectly voluntary (*see* VOLUNTARITY). What the ethicist aims at, then, is a reflective, well-considered, and reasonable set of conclusions concerning the kinds of voluntary activities that may be judged GOOD or suitable (or EVIL and unsuitable) for a human agent in the context of man's life as a whole, including his relations to other beings whom his actions influence in some significant way. Most systems of ethics also relate human actions to some overall goal of living: the knowing or loving of the perfect good, the higher welfare of the person or of his society, happiness or pleasure, or some such ideal or real end (*see* GOOD, THE SUPREME).

What distinguishes ethics from other studies of human conduct is the ethicist's interest in what constitutes a good human life, rather than in what makes a person, for example, a successful plumber or painter. The formal objective of ethics implies a distinctive meaning of right and wrong as generally applied to human conduct. Man's actions are studied in other disciplines also, in PSYCHOLOGY, in sociology, even in history, but the primary interest in these areas is not concerned with what man ''ought'' to do but with ''how'' he operates, personally, socially, or in the context of mankind's past. Such studies are non-normative; they do not deal primarily with ''ought'' judgments. Politics treats human action in relation to state welfare; economics relates it to the production and distribution of wealth. In ancient and medieval thought, these two studies were parts of ethics; today, they have become non-normative, and are regarded as outside the scope of ethics. Law and theory of law are closer to ethics; they are normative. However, modern civil and criminal law deal only with activities that have some bearing on public welfare and are capable of regulation by human legislatures and courts.

Thomistic Ethics. By St. THOMAS AQUINAS, ethics is treated in the *Exposition of Aristotle's Nicomachean Ethics.* Some scholars regard this work as an impersonal explanation of Aristotle and not as a personal statement of Aquinas's own views. Others take it as what St. Thomas thought, in philosophy, concerning moral conduct. Aquinas described four kinds of rational order, each requiring a special intellectual habit (*In 1 eth.* 1.2). The habit of the philosophy of nature enables one to think of the order found to exist among all real beings, apart from any effect of man's activity (this habit includes even metaphysics). Next are the habits that enable one to order his own thinking (logic) and the production of useful or beautiful artifacts (art). Finally, there is the habit of ethics: ''The order in voluntary actions belongs to the consideration of moral philosophy.'' Thomas, here, appears to speak personally about ethics, saying something that is not in Aristotle's text. ''And so, to moral philosophy (which we are now treating) it is proper to think about human actions, as they are ordered among themselves and in relation to their ends. Now, I say human operations, those which issue from man's will according to the ordering of reason Just as the subject matter of natural philosophy is motion, or mobile reality, so the subject matter of moral philosophy is human action as ordered to an end, or even man as he is acting voluntarily for the sake of an end'' (*ibid.* 1.3).

From this, it is clear that St. Thomas regards ethics as a practical, even a productive, science: for it brings rational order into the domain of man's own voluntary acts. Yet, there is also a speculative character to Thomistic ethics, particularly in its consideration of the general theory of what constitutes good action. In a famous text (*Summa theologiae* 1a2ae, 94.2) where Thomas explains how we know the most basic judgments of natural moral law, he parallels the work of ethics with that of metaphysics. As the metaphysician starts with the understanding of BEING and bases all his consequent judgments on it, so does the moral scientist start with the meaning of good and move to the initial judgment: ''Good is to be done and sought after; evil [not-good] is to be avoided'' (*ibid.*). This is the starting point of all practical reasoning. Although this statement occurs in a theological work, it explains how a man comes to know what is morally good or evil in a natural way. ''Since the good has the rational character of an end, and evil has the contrary meaning, as a consequence, reason naturally apprehends all things to which man has a natural inclination as goods and, therefore, as things to be sought after in working, and their contraries are apprehended as evils and as things to be avoided'' (*ibid.*). There follows, in the same text, a description of natural inclinations on the level of physical substance, of animal life, and of rational life. This third level is distinctive of man: the good in accord with reason is truly ethical.

More than this start, however, is needed to work out the rules of a good life: they cannot be deduced merely from the notion of good. Experience of the facts of human action, with adequate knowledge of the circumstances in which men operate, form the empirical base from which the ethicist must make practical judgments on the suitability of various kinds of human action. Thomistic ethics is not a deductive rationalism (see Klubertanz, ''The Empiricism . . .'').

Ethics and Moral Theology. Some difference of opinion is found among Thomists on the relation of ethics to MORAL THEOLOGY. Much of the finest moral thought of Aquinas is expressed in his theological writings: the third books of both his *Commentary on the Sentences* and his *Summa contra Gentiles,* the disputed questions *On Evil* and *On the Virtues,* and the *Summa theologiae,* 1a2ae and 2a2ae. All are agreed that moral theology uses data and standards of judgment stemming from supernatural revelation. In the Bible, in the Fathers of the Church, in decisions of popes and councils, in the living tradition of Christianity, are many items of moral wisdom that are accepted on faith by Christians. These have been formed into a rich heritage of moral doctrine by theologians. A purely philosophical ethics cannot use such revealed knowledge. So, the start and the way of thinking of the moral theologian are different from those of the natural ethicist. St. Thomas puts it neatly: ''As sacred doctrine is based on the light of faith, so is philosophy founded on the natural light of reason'' (*In Boeth. de Trin.* 2.3).

Opposing Theories. Yet some Thomists indicate that a purely philosophical ethics would be an inadequate guide for the actual decisions of moral life [Jacques Maritain, *Science and Wisdom* (New York 1940) 174–209]. They suggest that the fall of man and original sin, together with the whole life of grace, are facts of faith that escape the natural ethicist. Consequently, Maritain and others insist that the Christian ethicist should ''philosophize within the faith,'' utilizing certain principles that are known from revelation or from moral theology. A Christian ethics will thus be a more adequate and practical discipline, because it is subalternated to theology.

Other Thomists have criticized Maritain's proposal as destructive of the distinctive character of ethics, or as a fusion of ethics with moral theology [J. M. Ramirez, OP, ''De philosophic morali Christiana,'' *Divus Thomas* 14 (Fribourg 1936) 87–122, 181–204; M. J. Le Guillon, OP, in *Bulletin Thomiste,* 8.1 (1952) 626–629; Klubertanz, ''Ethics and Theology'']. No one denies that it is possible to develop a mixed moral science that would be useful to Christian believers unprepared to study all the details of moral theology. This would be a Christian ethics and not a purely philosophical ethics. It would not be convincing to people without the Catholic faith, and it would not serve as a bridge for ethical discussion with supporters of various types of natural ethics.

Ethical Presuppositions. The ethicist brings to his study certain convictions about the nature of the moral agent (man) and his relations to the rest of reality. Immanuel KANT, in his *Critique of Practical Reason,* claimed that ethics is impossible unless one postulates (or takes for granted) three things: the immortality and freedom of man, and the existence of God [*Kant Selections,* ed. T. M. Greene (New York 1929) 368]. For Kant, the moral agent must be immortal, in order that there be a duration adequate to the fulfilment of moral law; and man must be free, to be able to determine his will according to some law of understanding; finally, ethics must admit a highest good, which implies the existence of God. Kant supposed these three postulates to be so, even though his theoretical philosophy was unable to establish them, for he felt that ethical reasoning needs them. Some modern Catholic writers have adopted this terminology [''The Postulates'' in J. F. Leibell, *Readings in Ethics* (Chicago 1926) 35–152]. There can be no objection to the contention that a valid ethics requires such convictions; however, in Thomism, these truths are not postulated, they are demonstrated in speculative philosophy. Some prior study of the philosophy of man, and possibly of metaphysics, is prerequisite to an understanding of ethics. The foundations of Thomistic ethics rest on the conclusions of the speculative philosophy of Thomas Aquinas.

Morality of Human Action. Thomistic ethics is divided into the consideration of voluntary actions as they are related to the private good of the person (individual ethics) and as they are related to the common good (social ethics). In both divisions, the approach is teleological; that is, ethics treats the HUMAN ACT in terms of the purpose or END (*telos*) to which it is ordered. This is not to say that ''the end justifies the means''; whatever actions, or omissions, may be used to the attainment of an end that is good in itself, these means must also be good (or at least, in the abstract, morally neutral) in themselves, and the real circumstances that surround the action must be morally appropriate. There are, then, three determinants of the moral quality (goodness or evil) of a human action: (1) the end that is intended by the agent must be morally fitting; (2) the kind of action that is performed must be good, in the sense that it is not imprudent, unjust to others, intemperate, cowardly, or uncharitable (this determinant is the formal OBJECT); and (3) all the pertinent circumstances, required for the real context of the activity, must be present and reasonably suited to the nature of a human agent. (*See* MORALITY.)

Human Nature. Each individual moral agent belongs to the human species and has a specific nature in common with his fellow men. One cannot be a human agent unless endowed with certain living capacities to apprehend and desire various aspects of bodily things (SENSE KNOWLEDGE and APPETITE). Every human agent requires an animated body capable of exercising at least some of its animal functions. Thus, men after death are no longer moral agents. Moreover, each moral person must have some use of INTELLECT and WILL, otherwise he is unable to bring about the rational ordering of his activities that entitles him to moral credit for good actions and punishment for evil ones.

While individual differences of mind and body distinguish one human being from another, it is not because of such differences that men are moral beings. Man's specific nature is so designed that certain actions are appropriate, and even peculiar, to his type of being. Briefly, what man does, which no other species does in the same way, is to reason about his experiences so that he may make free decisions to control his mental and bodily actions. His intellection and volition are performed in a distinctively human manner; neither brutes nor angels (man's closest neighbors in the hierarchy of being) understand or will, as man does.

Because of this community of human nature, all humans are subject to one and the same attraction of FINAL CAUSALITY. Irrespective of diversities of individual interest, all have the same specific purpose, or end, determined by their nature. This goal may be described from the viewpoint of man as the fullest possible use of all his capacities, under the direction of reason and will. This is what a Thomist means by HAPPINESS. From the side of that toward which human life is naturally directed, this ultimate goal is some being, great enough to be an inexhaustible object of human knowing and loving. This can only be a perfect being, God. All human actions that bring man nearer to the understanding and love of God are good; actions that remove man from this fulfilment are evil. (*See* MAN, NATURAL END OF.)

Elicited and Imperated Acts. In themselves, human acts are of two general types: elicited and imperated. Elicited actions are voluntary uses of understanding and will: they are begun and completed within the intellect and will of the agent. These are the actions that are most clearly moral. But man is not simply an immaterial being; he is capable of a variety of controlled functions of sensory cognition and appetition, and of many rationally controllable bodily activities. All of these sensory and bodily activities are assumed into moral life when open to rational direction. As such, lower activities are voluntary and are called imperated, or commanded, moral actions.

Both elicited and imperated actions imply moral responsibility in their agent. When reasonable and good, these acts have MERIT, and this entitles their agent to reward; when unreasonable and evil, such acts have demerit, and this calls for punishment. So, all such acts are imputable to their agent; he is responsible for their consequences to himself and to other persons.

Natural Moral Law. Ethical reasoning terminates in judgments that follow the pattern: This kind of action is morally good and should be done; or, this other kind of action is evil and should be omitted. A typical ethical judgment (''Immoderation in eating is to be avoided,'' or ''It is good to help other persons but evil to harm them'') is always somewhat general or universal in form. That is to say, ethical judgments may be regarded as rules for the guidance of any moral agent faced by a problem of a certain type. Such rules are regarded also, in Thomistic ethics, as moral laws. In this sense, LAW means: ''a rational order made by a person who has charge of a community, for the sake of the common good, and promulgated.'' (*Summa theologiae* 1a2ae, 90.4.) ''Promulgated'' here means made available to those subject to such an order.

Right Reason. The primary source of moral laws is God; as First Cause He has fashioned man and his environment so that some kinds of actions are appropriate and others are not. In a secondary sense, since man's intellect enables him to discover reasonable rules of conduct, the human understanding is a proximate source of moral law. The intelligent use of human understanding to work out moral laws is called right reasoning. Since right reason is founded on man's nature and the natures of other things in his environment, and since rational appraisal of the suitability or unsuitability of a given action occurs in the natural course of human life, judgments of right reason also are called natural laws.

Viewed as coming from God, a natural moral law is a participation by the human intellect in God's knowledge of what is right, that is, in eternal law. Seen in terms of human experience, a natural law of morality is simply man's best reasoned judgment of what is generally right or wrong in a given state of affairs. The rules of natural law are, then, ''naturally'' knowable in a double sense: (1) from the point of view of promulgation, they are implanted in the nature of man as a reasoning being; (2) from the point of view of the ''order'' that each moral law embodies, they are expressions of a naturally fitting interrelationship of a given kind of action (or omission) with the nature of man, placed in the real context of his action.

Obligation. Some authors also stress obligation as central to the character of moral law. The emphasis on the will of the lawgiver, in later scholasticism, tended to stress the binding character of law on its subjects. Other Thomistic ethicists think that obligation is not as central as what one might call the reasonable appropriateness of a given type of action. In other words, the ethicist is concerned not merely with what man ''must'' do (the performance of a minimal set of duties) but also with the discovery of what he should do in addition, in order fully to develop his distinctive capacities. Thus considered, the morally good thing transcends a lowest common denominator of what is ethically demanded, and embraces certain types of goodness that are not absolutely required but are nevertheless possible and good for a human agent. Where duty-ethics never requires a man to be a hero or to rise above the ordinary, Thomistic ethics looks to a maximal, or very best, effort on the part of each man as the ideal. Thus, some presentations (Oesterle, Bourke) stress the life of VIRTUE—e.g., perfected habits of intellect, will, and concupiscible and irascible appetites—more than mere conformity to laws. In any case, the judgments of ethics (and of moral theology) must be applied by each person (through moral CONSCIENCE and PRUDENCE) to his own moral problems: this the ethicist cannot do for another person.

Kinds of Ethics. There are various divisions of ethics depending upon the scope of the good that is envisioned. Individual ethics deals with the private good; domestic ethics with the good of a FAMILY; political ethics with the COMMON GOOD of a SOCIETY, state, or nation; and international ethics with the broadest natural common good, that of mankind. A common good embraces not only the sum of private goods of the members of a community, but also the higher goods that can be attained by group activity.

Other Schools. While Thomism is central, various other schools of ethical thinking have enriched Catholic tradition. PLATONISM and STOICISM influenced the early Fathers (e.g., St. Augustine) to subordinate sensory goods to intellectual ones. Peter ABELARD, in the 12th century, stressed internal consent (*intentio*) as most important to the moral act. When Aristotle's *Nicomachean Ethics* became known in the 13th century, Catholic scholars such as St. Albert the Great and Aquinas adopted and modified some of the Aristotelian terminology and analyses of moral action. Franciscan moralists retained much of AUGUSTINIANISM, through the influence of St. BONAVENTURE and JOHN OF LA ROCHELLE. DUNS SCOTUS and WILLIAM OF OCKHAM, in the 14th century, utilized the theme of "right reason," but stressed the Will of God as the source of moral legislation. Francisco SUÁREZ, in the 17th century, emphasized "human nature adequately considered," as the norm of moral judgment. Modern and contemporary ethics has become very diversified.

See Also: ETHICS, HISTORY OF; EXISTENTIAL ETHICS.

Bibliography: J. A. OESTERLE, *Ethics* (Englewood Cliffs, NJ 1957). A. FAGOTHEY, *Right and Reason: Ethics in Theory and Practice* (2d ed. St. Louis 1959). V. J. BOURKE, *Ethics* (New York 1953). THOMAS AQUINAS, *The Pocket Aquinas,* ed. V. J. BOURKE (New York 1960). A. G. SERTILLANGES, *La Philosophie morale de saint Thomas d'Aquin* (rev. ed. Paris 1946). M. WITTMAN, *Die Ethik des hl. Thomas von Aquin* (Munich 1933). J. MARITAIN, *Neuf leçons sur les premières de la philosophie morale* (Paris 1951); *La Philosophie morale* (Paris 1960). J. DE FINANCE, *Ethica generalis* (Rome 1959). J. MESSNER, *Social Ethics: Natural Law in the Modern World,* tr. J. J. DOHERTY (St. Louis 1949). G. P. KLUBERTANZ, "Ethics and Theology," *The Modern Schoolman,* 27 (St. Louis 1949–50) 29–39; "The Empiricism of Thomistic Ethics," *American Catholic Philosophical Association.* Proceedings of the Annual Meeting 31 (Baltimore 1957) 1–24. I. T. ESCHMANN, "St. Thomas's Approach to Moral Philosophy," *ibid.* 25–36. J. LECLERQ, *Les Grandes Lignes de la philosophie morale* (new ed. Paris 1954). T. E. HILL, *Contemporary Ethical Theories* (New York 1950). C. C. BRINTON, *A History of Western Morals* (New York 1959).

[V. J. BOURKE]

ETHICS, HISTORY OF

The science of ETHICS, like other branches of PHILOSOPHY, did not come into being suddenly; rather it has a long and involved history that parallels the development of philosophy itself (*see* PHILOSOPHY, HISTORY OF). This article traces the story of that development through two broad stages: the first deals with ancient and medieval ethical teaching, surveying the origins of ethics among the Greeks and its growth through the patristic and medieval periods; the second is concerned with the evolution of ethical doctrine in modern thought, beginning with the Renaissance and continuing through Kant to the 19th and 20th centuries.

Ancient and Medieval Ethical Teaching

In the 6th century B.C. the Greeks were highly civilized, but had only traditional codes of morality and ideals of behavior which the rising spirit of philosophical criticism did not initially question. This situation changed, however, when growing knowledge of other peoples made known the great differences of custom among them. The resulting contrast helped to initiate ethical inquiry.

Sophists and Socratic Schools. By underlining the relativity of mores, the SOPHISTS generally tended to discredit accepted standards. Yet Sophists like Protagoras wished the contrary, arguing that this very relativity justified each one in following the laws of his own state. They also seem to have implicitly held to a natural law. Other Sophists like Thrasymachus, however, carried their RELATIVISM to radical lengths, even to maintaining that might is right.

SOCRATES (470?–399) rejected such extremes and showed how one could arrive at objective universal knowledge by inductive study. With his ironic dialectic he helped to clarify such basic notions as those of justice and the state. He also held that all men seek happiness and that knowledge is virtue, by which he meant that one who knows what is right will not be voluntarily bad.

Among the lesser disciples of Socrates were the CYNICS and CYRENAICS, each overemphasizing certain aspects of his teaching. Antisthenes (*c.* 445–*c.* 365) held the good life to be one of self-sufficiency and freedom from desires, wants, and conventions—a theme later taken up by the Stoics. Aristippus of Cyrene said pleasure was man's end, a view to be developed by the Epicureans.

Plato and Aristotle. PLATO (428?–347) amplified Socrates's EUDAEMONISM. Man's end is to develop and live in a full and harmonious manner under the guidance of reason. To show how this is done he forged theories of a rational asceticism and of the cardinal virtues. Again, because man is by nature social and capable of achieving perfection and happiness only in society, he discussed in detail the functions of the state, which are to make possible and to promote the good life for the citizens.

ARISTOTLE (384–322) wrote the first systematic treatise of ethics, in which he further developed and modified the Socratic tradition. His method was to compare and contrast the pertinent facts, theories, and opinions, and thereby to sift out the truth. He began by pointing out that the notions of good and end are central in ethics. Accepting the common view that man's end is happiness, he showed that this is to be found only in the activity that is peculiar to man, viz, activity of reason or in accord with reason. He also discussed the conditions of responsibility: knowledge, choice, and lack of compulsion. The theory of the cardinal virtues he replaced with a lengthy consideration of various modes of excellence associated with the operation of the intellect and will: the intellectual and moral virtues. The latter are a mean between excess and defect. Thus, courage is the mean between rashness and cowardice. Justice and friendship he studied in special detail. Disallowing the views that pleasure is *the* good and that all pleasures are bad, he held that as the natural completion of activities, pleasures will be good or bad depending upon the action whence they result. Since the intellect is man's highest faculty, his greatest happiness will be found in a contemplative life provided with a modicum of external goods, health, friends, and pleasure.

Epicureanism and Stoicism. The Platonic and Aristotelian schools were soon eclipsed in popularity by the Epicurean and the Stoic. EPICURUS (342?–270) denied an afterlife and any divine influence on the course of events, and maintained that pleasure is the alpha and omega of blessedness. By pleasure he meant the absence of pain in the body and of trouble in the soul. Debauchery is to be avoided, and blessedness or serenity of soul is to be found especially in sober intellectual pursuits. Of physical goods man should desire only the minimum, and the exercise of virtue is inseparable from a pleasant life. Of the greatest importance, moreover, is true friendship. EPICUREANISM in its original form thus insisted on a high degree of self-discipline, even though this was for egoistic reasons. It flourished for seven centuries and had among its adherents the poets LUCRETIUS and HORACE.

STOICISM was founded by Zeno of Citium (336?–264?) and was systematized by Chrysippus (*c.* 280–206). Man's end is to live virtuously, which is synonymous with living according to nature. Nature is here taken in two senses: rational human nature and the divine law establishing the universal order. Thus man has various duties, such as perfecting himself and propagating the species. Happiness is achieved by practicing the cardinal virtues; which involve each other reciprocally, and consists of apathy, a calm indifference to all emotion and to the vicissitudes of life. This results from understanding and accepting one's role in the cosmic plan. An important aspect of the latter is the universal brotherhood of men. Later Stoics were EPICTETUS and MARCUS AURELIUS. As a school Stoicism died out in the 3d century A.D., but it continued to exert influence throughout the Middle Ages and later, by such doctrines as those of the natural law and the division of virtue.

The Roman moralists CICERO and SENECA had little originality and are of importance mainly as transmitters to the Middle Ages of Greek theories.

Patristic Ethics. In the patristic and medieval periods ethical problems were studied mostly from within the framework of the moral theology that was then developing. Of the purely ethical works the majority are commentaries on Aristotle. Yet Christian moral literature presents decidedly new emphases: on man's relations with God, the dignity and intrinsic worth of individuals, the primacy of love, inner righteousness as contrasted with merely legalistic performance of duty, and the virtues of humility, poverty of spirit, mercy, obedience, and chastity.

More interested in exhortation, the early Christians did not make extensive theoretical studies of morality. St. AMBROSE (340?–397) was their first moralist of note. In his *De officiis ministrorum* he presents a Christianized version of Cicero's *De officiis.* In it the pastoral concern is much more obvious than the scientific. His reduction of all duties to the exercise of the four cardinal virtues became an accepted medieval theme.

Of the Fathers, St. AUGUSTINE (354–430) was the greatest philosopher and moralist. In regard to man's end he accepts the eudaemonism of the Greeks, but insists that happiness can be found only in God. Man attains God not merely through knowledge but especially in a union of love. There is then but one principal virtue, charity, which manifests itself in four ways as the cardinal virtues: as temperance, which is love keeping one's self whole and incorrupt for God; as justice, which is love rightly using all things in the service of God; as fortitude, which is love easily bearing anything for God; as prudence, which is love correctly distinguishing those things that help man reach God from those that would impede him. There is in God the eternal law, which is the divine reason and will requiring man to preserve the natural order of things and forbidding its disturbance. This law, insofar as it is impressed by God in one's heart to illuminate him, is the natural law of which conscience makes him aware. Man, though free, should submit to it. Sin is any transgression of it in deed, word, or desire. Because of the Fall, however, man can achieve moral righteousness only with the help of grace. Freedom of choice is thus different from liberty, which consists in being able to use one's freedom rightly.

Medieval Period. The first major theorist of ethics to appear after Europe recovered from the Dark Ages was Peter ABELARD (1079–1142). In his *Scito Teipsum* (*Know Thyself*) he discusses the nature of morality. He distinguishes sin from the mere inclination to evil, from the pleasure that accompanies acts, from the act itself, from any of its results, and from temptation. To sin is simply to consent to evil. It is intentionally to despise God and His laws. Conversely, a good act is one done with the intention of respecting God's law. Good and evil then depend completely on one's intention. All acts are in themselves morally indifferent. But to avoid the SUBJECTIVISM this might entail, he also holds that an intention is not good if the intended act merely seems good; it must be actually good, that is, in accord with God's law.

Thomism. The century that followed Abelard's death was one of intense research into moral and related psychological questions, culminating with the work of St. THOMAS AQUINAS (1225–74) in the full elaboration of a scientific MORAL THEOLOGY. A major factor in this development was the availability of new translations of Aristotle, especially his works on psychology and ethics. This made necessary the study and evaluation of a number of new concepts and theories concerning the nature of freedom; the psychology of the human act; the relation of the soul to its faculties; the nature and interrelations of synderesis, prudence, and conscience; the nature and properties of the natural law; the intrinsic morality of actions; the indifferences of acts; ignorance as a moral factor; the definition and the classification of the virtues; their interdependence; the nature and types of justice; and the role of reason and of intention in morality. Although the discussion of these problems took place within a theological context, they were primarily philosophical, as were the proposed solutions. Especially important was the work at this time of PHILIP THE CHANCELLOR, the Franciscans, and St. ALBERT THE GREAT.

The greatness of St. Thomas as a moralist lay in his ability to integrate the insights of previous thinkers into a comprehensive, well-articulated, and consistent synthesis. Thus, Thomistic moral theory is fundamentally Aristotelian, but incorporates numerous Stoic and Augustinian elements, the whole of which is unified by Thomas's own manner of conceiving them. Also characteristic are his intellectualist conception of beatitude; his analysis of the voluntary act; his separation of the problems of morality, sin, and merit; his detailed study of the nature and role of the passions; his notion of the moral sense (synderesis) as a habitus of the intellect, rather than a faculty; his theory of virtue; his classic conception of laws, eternal, natural and positive, as ordinances of *reason;* and his reorganization of the whole of moral theology into two parts, one general and the other special, the latter broken down in function of the theological and cardinal virtues.

Scotism and Ockhamism. The end of the Middle Ages was a time of growing SKEPTICISM with regard to the value of philosophy and the capabilities of the intellect. In moral theory this manifested itself in an ever greater emphasis on the divine will in resolving the problem of moral obligation. Thus, John DUNS SCOTUS (1265?–1308), while admitting certain acts to be intrinsically good or evil, held that the obligation itself to do or avoid these acts exists because of the free choice of God's will to impose it. WILLIAM OF OCKHAM (1290?–1349?), on the other hand, denied any ontological connection between the nature of an act and its morality. God in His absolute power and freedom can decree any act to be good or bad, so that the moral law is due to His arbitrary fiat.

Evolution of Ethics in Modern Thought

With the Renaissance, the humanists, in their enthusiasm for the classics, rejected SCHOLASTICISM and revived several of the philosophies of antiquity. Thus, Lorenzo VALLA (*c.* 1407–57) went back to Epicureanism, Justus LIPSIUS (1547–1606) to Stoicism, and Michel de MONTAIGNE (1533–92) to skepticism. The growing dissolution and secularization of standards is, however, best seen in the work of Niccoló MACHIAVELLI (1469–1527), who dissociated public morality from private, and justified, for the prince, policies based on sheer expediency.

Second Scholasticism. But the end of the Renaissance also saw a revival of scholastic philosophy, the moral theories of which were highly original and influential. Bartolomé de MEDINA gave classic formulation to the theory of PROBABILISM. Francisco de VITORIA condemned the slave trade that was again starting to flourish, and developed a doctrine of international law. St. Robert BELLARMINE worked out a theory of Church-State relations. For him, although all authority comes ultimately from God, the popes get theirs directly from Him, whereas civil rulers receive theirs through the mediation of the community. The popes have no direct power over princes, but do have an indirect dominion when spiritual interests clash with temporal. Thus he rejected the theory of the divine right of kings. The most notable of the later scholastics, however, is Francisco SUÁREZ, who worked out a complete and detailed philosophy of law. This period also saw the establishment of special chairs of ethics in the universities, and the development of purely philosophical, logically elaborated, treatises of ethics—the practice up to then having been to treat of moral theory in theology or in the form of commentaries.

Rise of Rationalism. In the 1600s rationalistic views became common on the Continent. Hugo GROTIUS (1583–1645) held that the natural law could be deduced from man's social nature. This theory of a geometrically stable and inferred natural law was widely accepted for over a century. René DESCARTES (1596–1650), ''the father of modern philosophy,'' held that man's goal is rational contentment. To achieve this, one should understand his nature and capabilities, and train his passions so that they are always under the control of the will. Nicolas MALEBRANCHE (1638–1715), a disciple of Descartes and a member of the Oratory, took life to be a constant attempt to avoid the lure of false goods presented to man by the world and the senses; one can succeed only by abandoning the desires of the body, in order to devote one's self to the knowledge and loving fulfillment of the divine order. Baruch SPINOZA (1632–77), attempting to avoid the difficulties of Cartesian dualism, was led to PANTHEISM. For him, beatitude consists in the realization that one is part of the infinite. Man achieves happiness by transcending the opinions that fill most minds to arrive at a true knowledge of the order and unity of the universe. This entails a calm, impersonal acceptance of all that occurs because one understands why it had to. Among the most pernicious of the false opinions men have is acceptance of the authority of institutional religions and monarchs. Gottfried Wilhelm LEIBNIZ (1646–1716) held to psychological DETERMINISM. Man is free from outer determination, but necessarily chooses what seems best. Sin results from a mistaken judgment. Moral perfection, therefore, consists of real understanding of the nature of the universe, and man's main duty is to achieve it.

English and French Theories. The English, meanwhile, were developing their own distinctive approaches to moral problems. Thomas HOBBES (1588–1679) is frankly materialistic and deterministic. Good is whatever a man desires; evil, whatever he hates. In the state of nature before the formation of states, men were more or less equally powerful and, therefore, had equal rights; being fundamentally egoistic, they were in a continual state of war, and this made their lives ''nasty, brutish and short.'' To remedy this situation men agreed to give up their rights to a sovereign who should maintain peace and order. States are thus conventional, not natural, institutions—the source of all law and right. Because it is the most efficient, an absolute monarchy is the best. Bernard Mandeville (1670?–1733) carried on the Hobbesian tradition in maintaining that men were naturally egoistic. He went further, however, to claim that society prospers by pandering to private vices.

After Hobbes most of English ethics consists of refutations of him and the elaboration of alternative solutions to the problems he raised. Among his earlier opponents were the CAMBRIDGE PLATONISTS, Ralph Cudworth and Henry More, who rejected atheistic and mechanistic views in favor of a spiritualist and religious philosophy based on eternal, innate, immutable truths, the contemplation of which unites one with God. Richard Cumberland (1631–1718) denied that the laws of nature were innate, but agreed that they were knowable and unchangeable. Against Hobbes he pointed out that man is by nature social, having benevolent as well as egoistic inclinations. Since individual good is tied in with the common good, man is rationally bound to seek both. John LOCKE (1632–1704) presented moderate views that became widely accepted. On the basis of empirically established notions, he held it possible to deduce ethics and the natural law, which is the ultimate source of obligation. The state of nature was not one of war and license but one of reasonable peace and liberty. In it, all goods at first were for common use, but limited property rights over any portion of it were gained by anyone who would improve it with his labor. States are established by the consent of the people for the protection of their rights; hence the power of rulers should be limited. In the 1700s the English moralists are notable as precursors of altruism and utilitarianism, and for their moral sense theories, their continued opposition to egoistic and voluntaristic conceptions of morality, and their progressive separation of ethics from theology. (*See* BRITISH MORALISTS.)

In France most of the ENCYCLOPEDISTS used Locke's ideas as a foundation for materialistic EGOISM. Yet Jean Jacques ROUSSEAU (1712–78) used a different approach. Man is naturally good but is ineluctably corrupted by society. Despite this, he can feel and maintain his inner integrity by vigorously cleaving to the demands of conscience, the divine instinct that guides even the ignorant.

Kantian Ethics. Immanuel Kant (1724–1804) wanted to show how reason could arrive at necessary and certain truths when it based itself on empirical data. He did this by maintaining that knowledge of this type is gotten through the mind's imposition of its innate forms on such data. This solution, however, made scientific knowledge of nonsensible reality impossible. How then can one have an ethics? Accepting moral obligation as a fact universally admitted, one has only to uncover the principles making it possible. Influenced by Rousseau, Kant held that only a good will is unqualifiedly good. A good will is one that acts solely out of duty, out of respect for the moral law (ETHICAL FORMALISM). Kant distinguishes between hypothetical imperatives, which say what to do if one wishes to attain a given end, and categorical imperatives, which state an unconditional necessity of performing an action. The principle of all morality is the CATEGORICAL IMPERATIVE, which may receive different formulations: ''So act that the maxim of your will can always at the same time be valid as a principle making universal law,'' or ''Act so that you treat humanity, whether in your own person or in that of another, always as an end and never as a means only.'' Moral laws, then, simply state what is rationally necessary. If all men would obey them, one would have a society organized for rational purposes, a kingdom of ends. Acting like members of such a society, men both make and are subject to the laws. Their wills are thus autonomous. This is what gives individual value and dignity. For the moral life to make sense, however, one must postulate that he is free and immortal, and that there is a God. Thus a rational, moral faith can provide man with certitudes that go beyond the limits of science. Kant also reduces all true religion to the community of upright wills.

Idealistic Theories. In the 19th century many of the most influential thinkers developed idealistic and pantheistic systems from a Kantian basis. Ordinarily they rejected Kant's notion of a thing-in-itself behind phenomenon or appearance, and maintained that phenomena have their source in the knowing subject himself, which they then identified in one way or another with the absolute ground of all reality. Their ethics reflect their metaphysics. Johann G. FICHTE (1762–1814) recognized the primacy of the will and of moral action, as did Kant, because through them only does man attain deep insights and perfection. The will freely affirming itself is the primal reality. Since the will is rational and autonomous, morality is its free self-determination to do whatever it sees in any particular situation to be its duty. Georg W. F. HEGEL (1770–1831) held thought to be primal, instead of will. Thus the universe is the dialectical development of the Absolute Idea into self-consciousness, into ''spirit.'' The moral life then is the objectification of the rational exigencies of spirit and, therefore, the gradual self-realization and perfection of individuals and societies. A good man is one who understands that the public good is his own and willingly subordinates himself to it. This does not mean total subjection to the arbitrary demands of a state, but rather that the latter exists to establish and maintain the greatest reasonable, personal freedom of activity. However, the fullest expression of the spirit is achieved, not in the state, but in art, religion, and philosophy. Arthur SCHOPENHAUER (1788–1860), like Fichte, considered the primal reality to be will, but one that is irrational. Its ceaseless craving is the source of unhappiness and makes the majority of men either selfish or malicious. Salvation consists in the denial of will by living a life of compassion, of altruism.

The second half of the century saw the universal dissemination of the Kantian-idealistic tradition (*see* KANTIANISM; NEO-KANTIANISM). It was maintained in Germany by H. Cohen and P. Natorp of the ''Marburg School,'' R. Eucken, and Eduard von HARTMANN; in England, by T. H. Green, F. H. BRADLEY, and B. Bosanquet; in France, by C. B. Renouvier and J. LACHELIER; and in the U.S., by J. ROYCE, G. H. Howison and B. P. Bowne. Its main characteristics are its emphasis on the autonomy and dignity of the person, on social process, and on teleology. It also strongly influenced the development of liberal Protestantism, in which its corrosive effect on dogmas is obvious. This brought leading liberals like F. D. E. SCHLEIERMACHER and A. RITSCHL to emphasize the moral life, which they thought of as the establishment on earth of the Kingdom of God, of a Kingdom of Ends achieved through reason and love. In America these views became widespread under the name of the ''social gospel.''

Naturalist Philosophies. The 19th century also saw the proliferation of naturalistic philosophies of life. The most influential of these was the POSITIVISM of Auguste COMTE (1798–1857), the founder of altruism and of sociology. Some of his more eminent followers, such as J. M. Guyau, Alfred Fouillee, and Émile DURKHEIM, rejected his cult of humanity but continued to develop a sociological approach to ethics. For Durkheim, ethics is a purely inductive study of the rules that society sets up and enforces to maintain itself. In England UTILITARIANISM attracted considerable attention. First developed along the lines of an egoistic HEDONISM by Jeremy BENTHAM (1748–1832) and James MILL (1773–1836), it was transformed by John Stuart MILL (1806–73) into an altruistic hedonism. It received a further critical development in the hands of Henry Sidgwick (1838–1900), who combined it with intuitionism.

The theory of evolution was also made the basis of an ethics. Even before Darwin had put the theory on a solid scientific footing, Herbert SPENCER (1820–1903), the century's most popular English thinker, had made it the central idea of his philosophy. The development of life entails a progressive physical and mental adaptation that will result in the eventual disappearance of evil. Human society is evolving in the direction of complete concord and cooperation, in which egoism and altruism will fuse and mutually support each other. But other evolutionists like T. H. Huxley held such optimism to be unwarranted, because civilization is not the product of evolution but of counterevolution, because ethical progress depends on combating the cosmic process. Friedrich NIETZSCHE (1844–1900) critically overhauled the ideas of Darwin and Schopenhauer: evolution advances by organisms struggling *against* the environment, not by adapting to it; the primal will is not the root of unhappiness and to be negated, but the source of all good. By combining these views he gave EVOLUTION and egoism a radically new interpretation. In evolving, the weaker wills, which are the masses of men, developed the Jewish-Christian ethic, a ''slave-morality,'' because they could not take life as it is. But evolution is producing the ''superman,'' who in his magnanimous strength faces up to the struggles of life, and thereby goes beyond conventional good and evil, transmuting old values into new ones of his own.

Another major naturalistic philosophy of life was socialism. Its earlier utopian forms were due to Claude Henri de SAINT-SIMON, Charles Fourier, and Pierre Proudhon. Rejecting Christianity as one of the main causes of man's debasement, they proclaimed secular schemes for the reorganization of society on the basis of unselfish cooperation and brotherly love, which would do away with all poverty and injustice. Their theories were later overshadowed by the ''scientific'' socialism of Karl MARX (1818–83), the founder of dialectical materialism. Better known as communism, it makes morality completely relative: whatever advances Communist power is good (*see* MATERIALISM, DIALECTICAL AND HISTORICAL).

Neoscholasticism. The latter half of the 19th century also witnessed the rise of neoscholasticism. Its main moralists were L. TAPARELLI D'AZEGLIO and V. CATHREIN. Against the relativism of the idealists and positivists, it maintained the view of a theocentric and immutable natural law. In social ethics it attacked the opposite errors of secularistic socialism and rugged individualism. It was the inspiration of the revolutionary social encyclicals of Pope Leo XIII (*see* SOCIAL THOUGHT, PAPAL).

20th-Century Currents. In the 20th century the main points of view of the 19th found continued support. IDEALISM is represented by B. CROCE, G. GENTILE, H. J. Paton, and E. S. BRIGHTMAN; utilitarianism and intuitionism, by G. E. Moore; evolutionism, by J. Huxley; socialism, by the Communists, Nazis, and Fascists, since the more moderate socialists usually limit themselves to political and economic programs; sociological ethics, by E. Westermarck and A. Kinsey; neoscholasticism, by J. Maritain and J. Leclercq. Besides these, however, there has arisen a multitude of new schools. The more prominent include pragmatism, emotivism, analysis, evolutionism, philosophies of value and spirit, existentialism, and existential ethics.

Pragmatism. At the turn of the century PRAGMATISM was developed and popularized by William JAMES. It was only later, however, due to the efforts of John Dewey, who preferred to call it INSTRUMENTALISM, that it was worked out in detail and gained a widespread following. Dewey rejects any absolute ends, and finds in every concrete situation an end properly to be chosen within it. A good action is one that enables a person to achieve the end he has chosen. But a valid VALUE JUDGMENT is not ordered to the satisfaction of one's immediate or selfish desires. The standard is rather the well-being of both ourselves and the other members of our society.

Emotivism. The 1930s were the heyday of LOGICAL POSITIVISM, as propounded by Moritz Schlick, Rudolf Carnap, Bertrand RUSSELL, and A. J. Ayer. These men are known for their moral theory as emotivists. They maintain that propositions can make sense and be true or false only if they are analytically self-evident, like mathematical statements, or if they are empirically verifiable, like scientific truths. Ethical propositions are neither, and so they are meaningless or ''non-sense.'' They are then only expressions of the emotions of the speaker. The statement ''killing is evil'' merely expresses the speaker's dislike of killing, and his wish that it be avoided. Such assertions, they hold, are basically subjective and cannot be used as universal and objective norms of conduct. Later positivists like C. L. Stevenson have insisted on the emotive character of moral predicates, but have tried to avoid the skepticism entailed in emotivism by emphasizing the importance in life of such noncognitive terms. Since these reflect attitudes that can be discussed and changed, there is a possibility for a valid ethics.

Analysis. In England since World War II the most prominent moral philosophers are of the school loosely referred to as analytical philosophy. They continue the empiricist and positivist tradition, but avoid the crudities of emotivism. They characteristically conceive ethics not as the study of how man should act, but as the study of the language used when talking about how men should act (*see* LINGUISTIC ANALYSIS). Their main representatives are Stephen Toulmin, R. M. Hare and P. H. Nowell-Smith.

Evolutionism. Henri BERGSON was France's most influential philosopher in the 20th century. For him evolution is the result of a living force (*élan vital*) manifesting itself in innumerable forms. In man it has developed two types of morality, the closed and the open. The closed is a common, compulsive morality required by society for its protection and maintained by the habits society inculcates. Open morality results from the visions of prophets and mystics, who see for man a wider ideal than that provided by society, and who would extend his limited social solidarity into a fraternity of all men by transmuting his restricted affections into a universal charity.

Value and Spirit. The philosophy of value is a movement that has attracted a large and variegated following. Taking the notion of value as a central point of reference, it tries to interrelate all things in terms of different kinds and levels of value. It had its inception in the second half of the 19th century with F. BRENTANO and A. Meinong. More recently it was given an idealistic cast by W. Windelband and H. Rickert. It received a highly influential, realistic, and almost Platonic formulation in the hands of Max SCHELER and Nicolai HARTMANN. It was developed spiritualistically by R. LE SENNE and L. LAVELLE, and from a psychologistic and relativistic point of view by C. von EHRENFELS. (*See* VALUE, PHILOSOPHY OF; SPIRIT, MODERN PHILOSOPHIES OF.)

Existentialism. EXISTENTIALISM is likewise a name that covers several different and quite influential views. Although existentialists are much concerned with the individual and his problems, they have produced little in the way of systematic ethics because of their aversion to abstract generalization. This is especially true of M. Heidegger, K. Jaspers, and G. Marcel. On the other hand, however, J. P. Sartre and S. de Beauvoir have outlined their basic positions, which have become known as SITUATIONAL ETHICS. This amounts to a sort of heroic formalism. In general, existentialists insist on the necessity for each man freely to involve himself in his own concrete, uncertain situation, and to make his own decisions.

See Also: MORAL THEOLOGY, HISTORY OF; ILLUMINISM.

Bibliography: F. C. COPLESTON, *History of Philosophy* (Westminster, MD 1946–), see index in each volume. R. A. TSANOFF, *The Moral Ideals of Our Civilization* (New York 1942). O. DITTRICH, *Geschichte der Ethik,* 4 v. (Leipzig 1926–32). F. WAGNER, *Geschichte des Sittlichkeitbegriffes,* 3 v. (Münster in Westfalia 1928–36). J. LECLERCQ, *Les Grandes lignes de la philosophie morale* (rev. ed. Paris 1954). O. LOTTIN, *Psychologie et morale aux XIIe et XIIIe siècles,* 4 v. in 6 (Louvain 1942–54). A. FOREST, et al., *Le Mouvement doctrinal du XIe au XIVe siècle* (Histoire de l'église depuis les origines jusqu'à nos jours 13; Paris 1951). T. E. HILL, *Contemporary Ethical Theories* (New York 1950). J. MACQUARRIE, *Twentieth Century Religious Thought* (New York 1963). A. DIHLE, *Reallexikon für Antike und Christentum,* ed. T. KLAUSER [Stuttgart 1941 (1950–)] 6:646–796.

[G. J. DALCOURT]

ETHIOPIA

Located in northeast Africa, Ethiopia is notable as the only African nation to successfully repel the efforts of European colonialists. It is bordered on the north by Eritrea, on the northeast by Djibouti, on the east by Somalia, on the south by Kenya and on the west by Sudan. Lowlands along Ethiopia's eastern border rise to mountains in the central and southern regions, while the northeast is desert. Natural resources include reserves of gold, platinum and copper, as well as potash and natural gas. Agricultural production, which has been threatened by desertification as well as by overgrazing, deforestation and the diversion of large amounts of money to fund an ongoing border war with Eritrea, accounts for half of Ethiopia's gross domestic product and includes cereals, coffee, oilseed, sugar cane, potatoes and livestock.

Traditionally under the sway of Ethiopian emperors, the region was invaded by Italian forces under Mussolini in 1936. Former Emperor Haile Selassie returned to power in 1941, and the political realm stabilized until an economic downturn in the early 1970s prompted a military junta, the Dergue, to depose Selassie. In 1977 the authoritarian regime of Colonel Mengitsu instituted a centralized Marxist government, which did little to stabilize the economy. Enforcement of the peace was carried out through the Dergue, which caused the murder of numerous political dissidents, including the patriarch of the Ethiopian Orthodox Church, in the late 1970s. Prolonged famine and the outbreak of a guerilla war in the northern province of Eritrea remained unabated, and Mengitsu was forced to resign in 1991. A new government led by the Ethiopian People's Revolutionary Democratic Front was successful in restoring order, until Eritrea voted to secede two years later. The country held its first multiparty elections in 1995 and began a border war with Eritrea three years later that finally showed signs of resolution in the 21st century.

Ecclesiastically, the Ethiopian Catholic Church has an archdiocese in Addis Ababa, with suffragans at Adigrat and at the Eritrean cities of Asmara (1961), Barentu (1995) and Keren (1995). The Latin-rite Church maintains apostolic prefectures at Jimma-Bonga and Gambella, and apostolic vicariates at Asawa, Harar, Meki, Nekemte and Soddo-Hosanna.

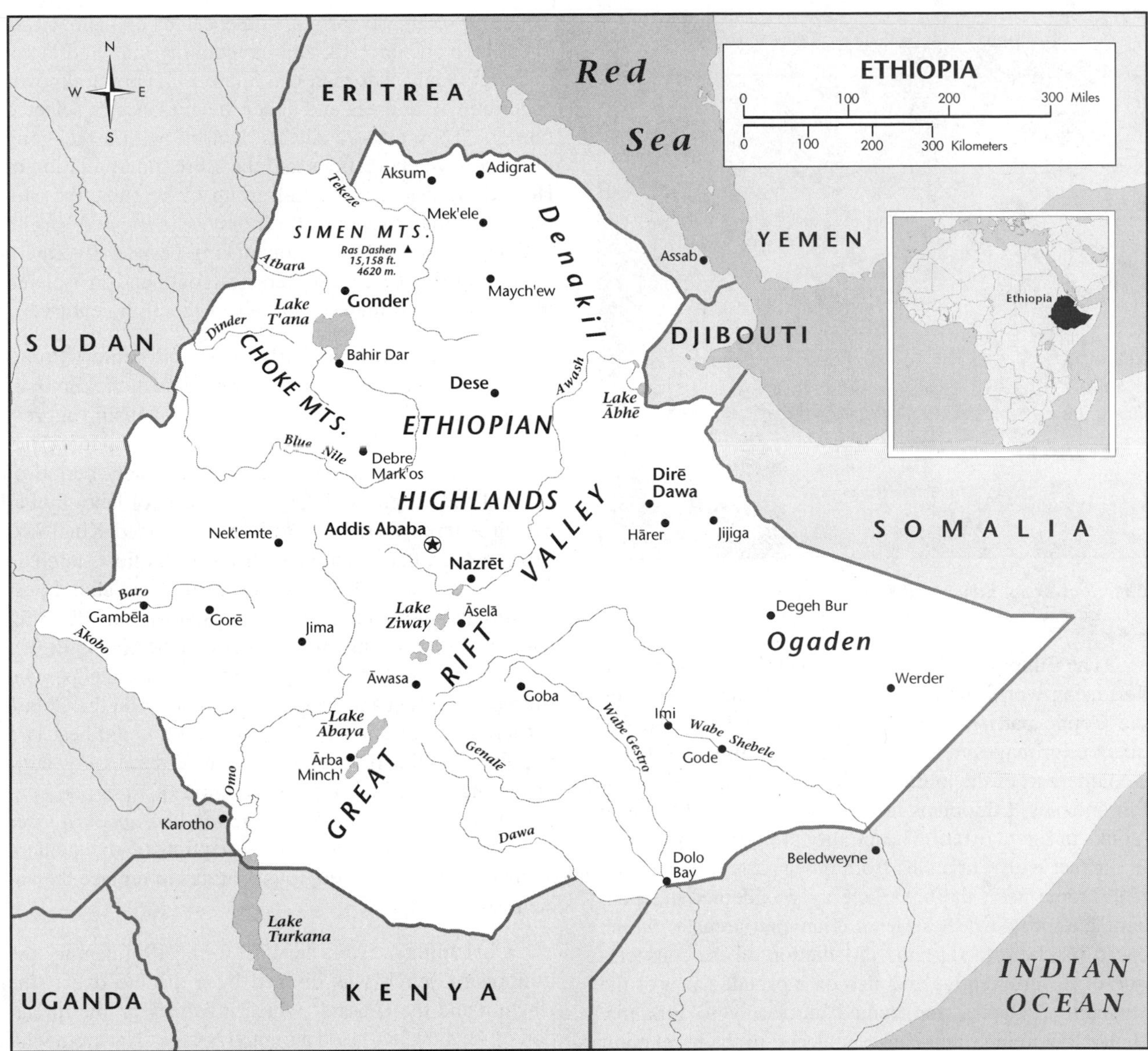

Early History. Christianity was first brought to Ethiopia by Greco-Roman traders from Egypt and Arabia, but large-scale conversion of the inhabitants was the work of St. FRUMENTIUS, consecrated metropolitan of Ethiopia by Athanasius of Alexandria in the early 4th century. Thus from the start Christianity in Ethiopia was connected with the Egyptian Church. Frumentius is credited with converting King 'Ezānā, to whom the Emperor CONSTANTIUS directed a letter, and whose religious progression is recorded on two inscriptions, the one calling him ''Son of the [pagan] God Mahrem,'' and the other styling him a child of the Christian ''Lord of the Heavens.'' The end of the 5th century under King Ella 'Amidā witnessed a revival of the evangelical spirit, but in the 6th century nine missionary ''saints''—Za-Mikâ'êl Aragâwi, Pantalêwon, Isaac Garimâ, Afsê, Gubâ, Alêf, Yem'atâ (or Matâ), Liqânos and Sehmâ—implanted MONOPHYSITISM, which still survives, and established monastic communities.

John of Ephesus records that in the 6th century, King Andog was baptized and asked Justin I or Justinian to send priests and a bishop to Ethiopia. Simultaneously, Cosmas Indicopleustes, visiting the cities of Adulis and Aksum, found a great number of Christians. In 523 King Kalēb (canonized as St. Elesbaan) led an expedition across the Red Sea into Yemen to avenge the massacre of the Christian martyrs of NAJRAN. At this time Ethiopia controlled territory extending over Tigré, Shoa and Amhara. Thereafter, because of a series of revolutions in which records of previous dynasties were destroyed, little else is known until the 13th century.

Church in Axum, Ethiopia. (©Cory Langley)

The Ethiopian Church maintained ties with the Mediterranean world through its hierarchical dependence on the Coptic patriarchate of Alexandria and through frequent pilgrimages to the Holy Land, possibly initiated as a counterpart of the journey to Mecca of Ethiopia's Muslim enemies. Ethiopians in Jerusalem and the Ethiopian monks in Egypt offering hospitality to pilgrims were thus in contact with Christians from other parts of the world. In Ethiopia itself the native clergy was denied independent authority by the Alexandrian patriarchate, which based its claim to supreme jurisdiction on the consecration of St. Frumentius and also on a pseudocanon of the Council of Nicaea that denied autonomy to Ethiopia. Hence the prelates and clerics attached to the royal court used their influence with the king to direct internal politics and were in competition with the regular clergy in the well-landed monasteries, whose authority was concentrated in the provinces.

Church Doctrine Forms. In the 14th century prelates, clerics and regular clergy clashed openly, masking their true interests with theological disputes over such questions as the observance of Christmas and other feasts, fast days and the inheritance by the king of his father's wives. In the second half of the 15th century a settlement was finally reached. The Coptic patriarchate of Egypt was given authority over the whole Ethiopian Church, but the monastic clergy remained under the Ethiopian abbot of the monastery of Dabra Libānos, who was given the title ''ečagē.''

In the 14th and 15th centuries the Ethiopian Church had to contend with two heresies. The Mikaelites taught a doctrine of Gnostic origin, influenced by dualism, citing 1 Tm 6.16 and Jn 1.18, and maintaining that God is not cognizable and that man can approach supreme knowledge only by degrees and under the guidance of selected masters. They elaborated this doctrine with a theogony of successive emanations and the secret interpretation of Holy Scripture. The second group of heretics, the Stephanites, did not venerate the cross or the Blessed Virgin. Although repressed by Ethiopian kings, especially Zare'a Yā'qob (1436–68), these heresies continued in isolated monasteries into the second half of the 16th century.

Western Influence. Early in the 16th century Portugal sent an army to help Ethiopia defeat the Emir of Harar, Ahmed ibn Ibrāhīm, one of many Muslim aggressors over the years. Jesuit missions, sent by St. IGNATIUS OF LOYOLA, soon followed, beginning a new period of cultural and religious history. After years of labor by Patriarch Andrea Oviedo, Pero Páez persuaded King Susneos to conclude a union with the Catholic Church in 1614. After Páez's death, however, the local church, especially the monasteries, raised objections, mainly in regard to the replacing of the ancient ETHIOPIAN (GE'EZ) LITURGY by the Latin liturgy; and King Fāsiladas, who succeeded Susneos in 1632, renewed ties with the Coptic patriarch of Alexandria. The Jesuit mission did bear two important results: first, an increase in Western knowledge of the history, ethnology and religion of Ethiopia, contained in the collection, *Rerum Aethiopicarum Scriptores Occidentales;* and second, the adoption of the modern Amharic language in religious writings to replace the ancient Ge'ez.

Christology. From the 17th to the 19th century the Ethiopian Church was divided by a dispute over ''the Unction and the Union,'' which involved the interpretation of Acts 10.38: ''God anointed Jesus of Nazareth with the Holy Spirit and with power.'' This passage referred to the union of the two natures in Christ and the unction of the Holy Spirit in that union. In 1879 King John IV ended the dispute by making the entire Ethiopian Church accept the Monophysite doctrine of the northern monasteries, which was that of the patriarch of Alexandria. Like the Egyptians, the Ethiopians consider EUTYCHES a heretic, yet remain Monophysite and reject the Catholic doctrine of two natures in Christ. Two schools of thought explain their teaching: the *Walda-qeb* (Sons of Unction) hold that the two natures are radically unified: the divine nature absorbs the human to such an extent that the manhood is merely a phantasm; the Sons of Grace teach that the unification takes place in such a way that the nature of Christ becomes a special nature, and this work is attributed to the Father. The latter school also holds that the unification is completed not through the unction itself but through what is called the adoptive birth of Christ. It recognizes in the Incarnation three kinds of birth: the Word begotten by the Father; Christ begotten of Mary; and finally, the Son of Mary, begotten Son of God, the Father, through adoption, or by His elevation to divinity, and this is accomplished by the Father anointing the Son with the Holy Spirit. Both schools hold that the unification takes place with no blending, no change and no confusion. The contradictions inherent in this dogma are treated as mysteries by Ethiopian theologians.

Except for the problem of the progression of the Holy Ghost (in regard to which the Ethiopians follow the Byzantine teaching) and the humanity of Christ, the Ethiopian Church holds all other articles of faith professed by the Catholic Church.

The Modern Church. In the late 19th century the Ethiopian Church followed the development of the state under the reign of Menelik and renewed contacts with the Western world. In 1878 King John IV had a metropolitan and three bishops—all Egyptians—consecrated for Ethiopia by the Coptic patriarch of Alexandria. In December 1926, on the death of the metropolitan Matthew, the younger clergy demanded an Ethiopian. In June 1929 a compromise was arranged to have an Egyptian, the Abuna Cyril, consecrated as metropolitan, but four Ethiopians consecrated as bishops.

In 1936, while both Ethiopia and Eritrea were under Italian occupation, the Ethiopian clergy ousted Cyril and elected one of its own bishops, the Abuna Abraham, as metropolitan. On Abraham's death in 1939 he was succeeded by the Abuna John. After the British occupied the region in 1941, Cyril returned, and in 1949 an agreement was reached whereby the patriarch of Alexandria would appoint an Ethiopian as metropolitan.

Catholic Missions. After the Jesuit penetration in the 17th century, two Ethiopian Capuchin missionaries were assassinated (1638). The enterprise was abandoned until 1838, when the Vincentian G. Sapeto established a house at Aduwa, and in 1852, 15 native priests were ordained from a seminary established by Giustino de JACOBIS, who had converted more than 5,000 Coptic schismatics at Adawa and Tigré. A persecution under the Negus Theodore resulted in the martyrdom of native priest Abba Ghebré Michael, in 1855.

In 1846 the Capuchins started a mission in the apostolic vicariate of Galla, and the future Cardinal Guglielmo Massaia became the great apostle and opened a seminary at Kaffa. In 1881 Father Taurin Chagne opened a foundation at Harar, and in 1915 Father Marie-Bernard founded an indigenous congregation of sisters.

In 1937 an apostolic delegation was erected at Addis Ababa with nine missions, three vicariates (Addis Ababa, Gimma and Harar) and four prefectures (Dessie, Gondar, Neghelli and Tigré), to which Endeber and Hosanna were added in 1940. The territory north of Addis Ababa was subject to the Congregation for the Oriental Churches, and the rest, to the Congregation of the Propagation of the Faith. On Feb. 12, 1930, Pope Pius XI erected the Ethiopian College, founded in the Vatican in 1919 by Benedict XV, into a Pontifical College confided to the care of the Capuchins under the vicar-general for the Vatican. Addis Ababa was raised to an apostolic internunciature in 1957 and was established as a metropolitan see in 1961. On May 25, 1985 the country gained its first cardinal, Archbishop Paulos Tzadua (b. 1921), who had served as archbishop of Addis Ababa since 1977.

Bronze bishop's crown, 18th century, Azum, Ethiopia. (©Dave Bartruff/CORBIS)

By the late 20th century, with Ethiopia enmeshed in a bloody border war with Eritrea, other problems faced the nation, the result of both wide-scale drought, refugees and the inevitable modernization of its economy. By 2000 a movement was underway by Ethiopian women's groups to legalize abortion, the illegal practice of which

Church of Saint Maryam, 12th–13th Century, Lalibal, Ethiopia. (©Roger Wood/CORBIS)

was touted as a leading cause of death for pregnant women under age 20. Members of both Orthodox and Catholic churches responded that enforcement and counseling should be employed instead. In an effort to counter the effects of an extended famine in the region, in 2001, Pope John Paul II gave $100,000 to Ethiopia through his private charity, Cor Unum.

In 2000 Ethiopia had 192 active parishes, with 142 diocesan and 271 religious priests active among the faithful. In addition, 68 brothers and 719 sisters worked to ensure the health, welfare and spiritual and moral education of all Ethiopians through their humanitarian efforts and the operation of Church schools. Going into the 21st century the Church attempted to foster good relations with Ethiopia's other minority Christian faiths, as well as with the Ethiopian Orthodox Church, as the nation faced the moral and spiritual complexities involved with modernization. By 2001, as efforts between Eritrea and Ethiopia resulted in peace negotiations and the withdrawal of troops, there was hope that both the Church and the government could once again devote full attention to strengthening Ethiopian society and addressing the problems of refugees and of the poor.

Bibliography: *Rerum Aethiopicarum Scriptores Occidentales,* ed. C. BECCARI, 15 v. (Rome 1903–17). E. CERULLI, *Scritti teologici etiopici dei secoli XVI e XVII,* 2 v. (Studi e Testi 198, 204; Vatican City 1958–60); ''Il Mistero della Trinità: Manuale di teologia della Chiesa Etiopica,'' *Orientalia Christiana periodica,* 12 (1946) 47–129.

[F. X. MURPHY/EDS.]

ETHIOPIAN (GE'EZ) CATHOLIC CHURCH

Beginnings. According to Rufinius, a fourth-century Byzantine theologian, Ethiopia's conversion to Christianity began with two Syrian boys, Frumentius and Aedisius, who were aboard a ship in the Red Sea when it was seized off the Ethiopian coast. The boys were taken to Axum where the king, Ella Amida, appointed Aedisius his cupbearer and FRUMENTIUS his secretary. Before his death, Ella Amida gave the two Syrians their freedom. Eventually, Aedisius returned to Tyre, while Frumentius traveled to Alexandria. The young man begged Patriarch ATHANASIUS to send a bishop to provide pastoral care for the growing number of Christians in and around Axum, the capital of Ethiopia. Frumentius was chosen to be that bishop and was duly consecrated bishop of Axum by Athanasius, patriarch of Alexandria. Before returning to Axum at some time around 340, Frumentius had spent approximately five years in Egypt studying liturgy, theology, and the customary practices of the Alexandrian church.

As the first bishop, and recognized as the apostle of Ethiopia, Frumentius, (''Abba Salama Kasasate Berhan,'' ''Peaceable Father, who made Manifest the Light,'' as he is called in Ethiopia) brought with him the celebration of the liturgy that he had been using in Alexandria. The question might be asked: What anaphora did he use? A satisfactory answer to that question may remain unresolved. But working backward from today's liturgy, both Ethiopian Orthodox and Catholic, pride of place is to be given to the very first anaphora of the Ethiopian missal, ''The Anaphora of the Apostles.'' In its present form, that anaphora can be identified as an expanded text of the ancient anaphora in the Apostolic Tradition, commonly attributed to Hippolytus. Of all the churches, only the Ethiopian Church has preserved and used continuously throughout the centuries this ancient anaphora. In the Ethiopian missal the second anaphora is that of ''Our Lord.'' This text is based on a fourth century Syrian document and represents an embellishment of ''The Anaphora of the Apostles.'' With only one exception, today's Ethiopian missal as used by the Ethiopian Orthodox and Catholics is the same. That exception is an inclusion in the Catholic missal of ''The Anaphora of St. Mark,'' but it is not from Alexandria.

Initially, Greek would have been the liturgical language for the simple reason that the liturgy originated in Alexandria, where Greek continued to be the liturgical language until after the Council of Chalcedon. But as Frumentius's apostolic endeavors radiated beyond urban to rural areas, Greek was eventually superceded by Ge'ez, the local language.

Toward the end of the fifth century, the Ethiopian liturgy underwent Syrian and Armenian influences with the arrival of the "Nine Saints" from "Rum," the Byzantine Empire. In all probability the "Nine Saints" were the leaders of a large band of immigrants fleeing persecution in the Byzantine Empire after the Council of CHALCEDON. Whether or not they were anti-Chalcedonian or pro-Chalcedonian is a matter of some conjecture, but in this context their religious affiliation is irrelevant as Eucharistic matters had not been a significant issue at the Council of Chalcedon. These "Saints" are credited with having translated the Gospels and other sacred books into Ge'ez. Confirmation of this Syrian influence lies in the fact that the text of the Gospels translated into Ge'ez was not that used in Alexandria but in Syria.

Centuries of isolation. On 2 Sept. 1441, at the Council of FLORENCE, the head of the Ethiopian delegation from their monastery in Jerusalem told Pope Eugene IV:

> The separation of other Churches was the effect of voluntary rebellion, while the separation of our Church cannot be explained due to rebellion or inconstancy, but due to distance and difficulty of travel in order to reach you. . . . For 800 years, until today, no one before you has addressed a word of greetings to us.

There is not a single document or a single date that indicates Ethiopia's severance from the Apostolic See of Rome and an adoption of, or formal declaration of assent to MONOPHYSITISM. Even today, the Orthodox Church of Ethiopia condemns both Eutyches and Nestorius as heretics. It is, therefore, theologically inaccurate to label the Ethiopian Orthodox Church as being Monophysite. Rather the Church would claim that its christology is based on that of St. CYRIL OF ALEXANDRIA, whose writings predated the Council of Chalcedon.

During those eight hundred years of silence Ethiopia had been isolated from the world outside. Throughout those and subsequent centuries the celebration of the Eucharist in Ethiopia continued, however, in its traditional form. But outside of the country developments had taken place in the celebration of the Eucharist, more so in the Latin Church than in the Oriental Churches. As one of the Oriental Churches, the Church of Ethiopia only gradually became aware of differences in the celebration of the Eucharist as contact was resumed with missionaries from the Latin Church. In the wake of Ahmad ibn Ibrahim's ("Gragn," the left-handed) onslaught into the highlands of Ethiopia that began in 1529 those contacts increased with the arrival of Portuguese military assistance. Within five years of Gragn's final defeat in 1543, the Catholic Church had accepted the celebration of Eucharist according to the Ethiopian liturgical rite. In 1548 Pope Pius III had approved the printing of an Ethiopian missal containing a selection of anaphoras complied by Abba Petros Tesfatsion.

Encounter breeds confrontation. In 1557 Bishop Andre de Oviedo accompanied by five Jesuits and a small party of servants landed at Arkiko. Shortly after arriving at Gondar Bishop Oviedo antagonised the imperial court and was banished to a site between Axum and Adwa, which they called Fremona. They had been forbidden to proselytize among Ethiopians but were permitted to minister to other Portuguese and their offsprings. In that capacity, undoubtedly, they would have used the Latin rite. The last of the Jesuits who had accompanied Bishop Oviedo died at Fremona, aged, 80, in 1597. Only six years later, in 1603, did the next Jesuit, Fr. Pedro Paez, arrive. The following year, on 20th June, and only in response to repeated requests from Emperor Za-Dengel, Fr. Paez celebrated Eucharist in the presence of the emperor according to the Latin rite, read the Gospel in Ge'ez and preached in Amharic.

During his nineteen years in Ethiopia Fr. Paez repeatedly tried to reconcile the different theological terms used by both sides to express their Christology. Perhaps his efforts in this regard bore fruit later as Emperor Fasilidas wrote to the then expelled Patriarch Mendes.

> But this matter (of Christology) is not so important as it is not the reason why the people have withdrawn from us. . . . The cause of dissent is to be found in being deprived of Christ's Blood at Communion. Neither is it for that reason alone that we displeased the people, but also because the Wednesday fast is violated and all the feasts of the year are changed from their established days to other dates. . . .

Fr. Paez does seem, however, to have achieved a degree of mutual understanding during his lifetime with regard to the celebration of Eucharist. In areas that were traditionally Christian, Ethiopian Catholic priests used an Ethiopian Ge'ez missal for the celebration of Eucharist. But only two anaphoras were retained and they had been purified of any anti-Chalcedonian insinuations. The name of Pope Leo, for example, had replaced that of DIOSCORUS. When the Jesuits, however, undertook missionary work beyond the traditional Christian territory, as they did among the Agaw, beginning in 1618, they used the Latin rite, language and vestments.

Three years after the death of Fr. Paez, Patriarch Alfonso Mendes reached Fremona in 1625. From the moment of his arrival Patriarch Mendes vigorously pursued the total Latinization of the Ethiopian Church. To provide pastoral care for the 160,000 Ethiopian Catholics scattered over a vast area, Mendes ordained 20 Ethiopian priests in December 1625. But in the following year, on Feb. 12, he proclaimed that all Ethiopian priests were suspended until such time as he had individually approved each one. He even imposed the use of the Latin rite in monasteries that were traditionally of the Ethiopian liturgical rite. To mollify the mounting hostility to Latinization, Emperor Susenyos, who had become a Catholic in 1622, asked Mendes in 1627 that Ethiopian Catholic priests might be allowed to retain the use of the Ethiopian liturgical rite. His request was refused. Again, in June 1629 and in December of that year, the request was repeated, but on each occasion Mendes refused.

With greater perspicacity than the Patriarch, Emperor Susenyos issued a proclamation in 1631 to the effect that Ethiopians "might follow their ancient customs provided they were not repugnant to the faith." Mendes insisted that the proclamation be rescinded. A ferocious religious battle ensued with the loss of 8000 lives. Even though Susenyos had won the battle he was so depressed that he granted his subjects freedom of religion. Subsequently, Patriarch Mendes and the Jesuits were expelled from Ethiopia.

After his expulsion from Ethiopia, Mendes may have regretted his intransigence, but it was too late. The damage had been done. The deep-seated antagonism between the Ethiopian and the Latin celebration of the Eucharist had taken root; one was indigenous, the other was a foreign imposition. This tragic, sad, historical episode illustrates, however, that, at least in part, there had been at that time a Catholic celebration of the Eucharist according to the Ethiopian liturgical rite.

Renewed initiatives. Over the following 150 years of the approximately twenty papal initiatives to reactivate the mission to Ethiopia, only two are significant to the use of the Ethiopian liturgical rite by the Catholic Church. On May 3, 1640, Fr. James Wemmers, a Flemish Carmelite, was given a papal brief to make the overland journey to Ethiopia. The words of the brief allow for the use of the Ethiopian liturgical rite.

> Wemmers knows well the Ethiopian language and by orders of His Holiness the missionaries have been given instructions not to change the Ethiopian rite, but only to recommend union with the Holy See . . . and (so) with the hope that the priests will be able to appease both the archbishop and the monks as it was they who chased away the Jesuit priests for having changed the rite. . . ."

Wemmers was consecrated Vicar Apostolic of Ethiopia in late 1644 but, unfortunately, died at Naples when about to embark for Egypt.

The second initiative involved an Ethiopian priest, Abba Tobia Ghiorghis Gebreziabhier, who was studying in Rome between 1782 and 1788. On April 21, 1788, the Holy See issued a decree nominating Abba Tobia as the Titular Bishop of Adulis. As a condition to being consecrated bishop the decree specified that the nominee should take an oath to retain the use of the Ethiopian liturgical rite. As if to underline the significance of that oath Abba Tobia was consecrated bishop on June 24, 1788 using the Byzantine liturgical rite. Towards the end of 1789 the bishop arrived in the north of Ethiopia. For the next eight years the bishop led a furtive apostolic life as the Coptic Patriarch of Egypt had sentenced him to death. As he feared dying alone and without the sacraments, Bishop Tobia eventually left Ethiopia in early 1797. In Egypt, on May 7, 1801 he died of the plague. Apart from the robes and episcopal vestments of Bishop Tobia, which are still preserved in the monastery of Debre Damo, there is no trace left in Ethiopia of his years of furtive apostolate.

Abiding initiative. Pope Gregory XVI appointed Justin de Jacobis, C.M., as Prefect Apostolic of Abyssinia on March 10, 1839. Msgr. J. de Jacobis, eventually, arrived at his original residence in Adwa, Tigray, on Oct. 29, 1839. Some seven years later, on May 4, 1846, the original Prefecture was divided by the establishment of the Apostolic Vicariate of the Sudan to the west and the Apostolic Vicariate of the Galla to the south. In the following year, June 19, 1847, the Prefecture of Abyssinia was made the Apostolic Vicariate of Abyssinia, which included Tigray (also Eritrea prior to the colonial occupation), Amhara, Shewa, Wello, Gondar and Gojjam.

While making his journey southwards to his Apostolic Vicariate of the Galla, Msgr. G. Massaia passed through Gual'a, the residence of Msgr. de Jacobis, in late December 1846. Msgr. Massaia, since he had already been consecrated a bishop, performed the ordination of several Ethiopian Catholic priests. Although Msgr. Massaia had been authorized to ordain the priests according to the Latin rite it was understood that they belonged to and would exercise their ministry according to the Ethiopian liturgical rite. For the following Easter Msgr. de Jacobis, together with four of the newly ordained priests, went to Alitiena where they solemnly celebrated Easter according to the Ethiopian liturgical rite. A Papal Bull of July 6, 1847 granted Msgr. De Jacobis permission to carry out "all the sacred functions according to the Abyssinian rite." Pope Pius IX renewed and extended the earlier permission for the use of the Ethiopian liturgical rite in a decree dated April 21, 1850. This decree also stated that: (1) both Msgr. de Jacobis and his missionaries who are of the Latin rite "may carry out the sacred functions in the Abssinian rite," and (2) when they were "celebrating in the Abyssinian rite . . . those who normally use unleavened bread may use leavened bread."

Confirmation of the Vicariate's personnel's use of the Ethiopian liturgical rite and its practices has been provided by Fr. Poussou, C.M., who carried out an official visitation in December 1851. He reported that, in accordance with the practice of the Ethiopian liturgical rite, individual priests did not celebrate a private daily Mass. There was only one Eucharist daily at which the community attended. On Sundays, or major feast days, the bishop usually sang the Eucharist. There was no frequent Communion as members of the community only received on Fridays and Sundays.

Attitude of subsequent vicars apostolic. Monsignor M. Touvier was consecrated in Rome as the fourth Vicar Apostolic of the Vicariate of Abyssinia on April 30, 1870. During an audience with Pope Pius IX on May 4, 1870, the faculties permitting the use of the Ethiopian liturgical rite, as granted to Msgr. Touvier's predecessors, were renewed. In addition, the authorization to celebrate Low Mass, as originally requested by a previous Vicar Apostolic, Msgr. Bel, but never granted, was now conceded.

At that time other Latin practices were introduced such as the use of unleavened bread for the Eucharist and the distribution of Holy Communion under only one species, i.e., bread. This practice, however, was not immediately put into effect. It is on record that for the feast of the Holy Cross on Sept. 27, 1877, Fr. Coulbeaux together with six Ethiopian priests celebrated Eucharist in the Ethiopian liturgical rite at Maibrazio. All the members of the congregation received Holy Communion under both species.

In 1882 Msgr. Massaia wrote a scathing repudiation of the validity of the Ethiopian liturgical rite. Perhaps he had overlooked the repeated renewal by the Holy See of its authorization to use the Ethiopian liturgical rite. Moreover, between 1866 and 1882 there had been at least five authoritative replies addressed to various vicars apostolic clarifying in detail the use and practice of the Ethiopian liturgical rite. Msgr. Touvier was obliged to answer the repudiation of the rite that had been made. He admitted that the thirteen anaphoras of the Eucharist that had been revised and so considered to be "catholic" needed further study.

After Msgr. Touvier's death in August 1888, Msgr. J. Crouzet was consecrated Vicar Apostolic on Oct. 28, 1888. The Holy See asked him to carry out an in-depth review of the Ethiopian liturgical rite. A commission began the work in July 1889. With undue precipitation the Holy See issued a decree on July 10, 1890 that the Latin rite translated into Ge'ez was to replace the Ethiopian liturgical rite. But that did not impede the work of the established commission. Finally, on Nov. 8, 1891 Msgr. Crouzet informed the Holy See that fourteen anaphoras, dated 1890, had been revised, printed and circulated. The Vicar Apostolic explained that he had not given his "imprimatur" to the revised anaphoras, as they could not be considered as definitive. Nevertheless, the priests had been authorized to use the Missal, ad interim, for the celebration of Eucharist. With regard to the administration of the sacraments it is worth noting that only during the time of Msgr. Crouzet was the custom abolished of administering Holy Communion and Confirmation at the rite of Baptism.

The Holy See had not renounced its intention to impose the Latin Mass translated into Ge'ez, as was made clear when Fr. M. da Carbonara, O.F.M. Cap., the new Prefect Apostolic of the Italian colony, was entrusted with that responsibility in February 1895. By as late as 1907, however, when nothing concrete had been forthcoming, the exasperation of the Holy See was expressed in a letter dispatched to the Prefect Apostolic. He replied by stating that for a variety of reasons he was now opposed to the adoption of the Latin liturgy translated into Ge'ez. But perhaps the deathblow to the Holy See's initiative was dealt by Fr. E. Gruson, C.M. who wrote from Alitiena:

> The Latin Mass translated into Ge'ez is not unknown. In the XVIIth century the Jesuits did try to introuce it. And we all know the fate that the Abyssinians's attachment to their traditional rite reserved for it.

When Msgr. C. Carrara succeeded Fr. Da Carbonara in 1912 he wanted to reprint the original missal of 1890. Twenty-two years had passed and eighteen years since the original decision to translate the Latin Mass into Ge'ez, but nothing had come of it. Now for the first time, in a dispatch dated Feb. 25, 1913, the Holy See gave its official approval for the reprinting of the original Mass. Henceforth, the Catholic use of the Ethiopian liturgical rite could no longer be questioned. And in the intervening years it has simply been a matter of editing and reprinting the Catholic Ethiopian missal.

Bibliography: A. ALBERTO, *The Apostolic Vicariate of the Gallas (1846–1938): Three of Its Vicars: Massaja, Cahange, Jarosseau* (Rome 1993). J. BANDRES, "The Ethiopian Anaphora of the Apostles: Historical Considerations," *Proche-Orient Chretien* 36 (1986): 6–13. T. BEINE, *La Politica Cattolica di Seltan Sagad I (1607–1632) e la Missione della Compagnia di Gesu in Etiopia* (Rome 1983). P. CARAMAN, *The Lost Empire: The Story of the Jesuits in Ethiopia, 1555–1634* (Notre Dame 1985). D. CRUMMEY, *Priests and Politicians: Protestant and Catholic Missions in Orthodox Ethiopia, 1830–1868* (Oxford 1971). K. O'MAHONEY, *The Ebullient Phoenix: A History of the Vicariate of Abyssinia*, 3 v. (Asmara, Addis Ababa 1982–1992); "Abune Tobia and His Apostolic Predecessors," *Quaderni di Studi Etiopici* 8–9 (1987–1988): 102–171; *The Spirit and the Bride: A Manual of Church History* (Addis Ababa 1994). A. PAULOS *The Ethiopian Orthodox Tewahido*

Interior of Ethiopian Church, Jerusalem. (©Shai Ginott/CORBIS)

Church: Faith, Order of Worship and Ecumenical Relations (Addis Ababa 1995). A. TAKLA-HAYMANOT, *The Ethiopian Church and Its Christological Doctrine* (Addis Ababa 1982).

[K. O'MAHONEY]

ETHIOPIAN (GE'EZ) LITURGY

The Ethiopic Liturgy is broadly similar to the COPTIC LITURGY, but translated into Ge'ez, ancient Ethiopian. The Ethiopian Divine Liturgy can be divided into two parts: (1) the *Pre-anaphora* including entrance, incensing and preparation of the altar, blessing and offering of the bread and wine, prayers of thanksgiving and petition, trisagion, Epistle, Gospel, dismissal of catechumens, and Creed; and (2) the *Anaphora* including prayer for peace, the Gloria and the Kiss of Peace, the Preface, Sanctus, Consecration, Anamnesis, Epiclesis, fraction, Lord's Prayer, elevation, consignation (a moistening of the Host with the Precious Blood), commingling of the Sacred Species, Communion, prayer of thanksgiving, and the final blessing of the faithful.

Traditionally, there are as many as 17 Anaphoras (Eucharistic Prayers) in the Ethiopian Liturgical Books, although that ''Of the Apostles'' is most commonly used. Church buildings, often with open sides and thatched roof, are generally circular or octagonal in design, although some are rectangular. Church interiors are usually divided into three concentric circles, marked off by high partitions: for the altar, the singers, and the assembly. For liturgical services other than the Divine Liturgy, drum-beating, hand-clapping, and the jangling of sistra set the rhythm of the singing. Fasting is frequent and rigorous. Worthy of note, too, are remnants of an early Jewish influence, e.g., ritual purification for mothers, and distinction between clean and unclean meats.

Bibliography: D. ATTWATER, *The Christian Churches of the East* (rev. ed. Milwaukee 1961) 1:138–146; 2:193–203. S. MERCER, *The Ethiopic Liturgy* (Milwaukee 1915). A. HÄNGGI & I. PAHL, *Prex Eucharistica* (Freiburg 1968).

[E. E. FINN/EDS.]

ETHIOPIANS (CUSHITES)

Inhabitants of ancient Cush (Chus, Heb. kûš), the region between the first and the sixth cataract of the Nile, roughly equivalent to Nubia, i.e., the southern part of modern Egypt and the northern part of modern Sudan.

The Septuagint called the Cushites Αἰθίοπες, which was the Greek term for all swarthy-skinned people south of Egypt; hence the terms *Æthiopes* in the Latin Vulgate and ''Ethiopians'' in the Douay Version of the Bible. But modern ETHIOPIA, which is another name for Abyssinia, is far to the south of ancient Cush.

In several periods during the 3d and 2d millennia B.C., especially when the Egyptians had powerful Pharaohs, as in the 12th and again in the 18th and 19th Dynasties, Cush was made subject to Egypt, so that Egyptian culture exercised considerable influence on Cush. However, from about the 11th century onward Cush was an independent kingdom, with its capital at Meroë on the east bank of the Nile between the 5th and the 6th cataracts. In 716 B.C. its King Pi'ankhi (751–710) invaded Egypt and established there the 25th or Ethiopian Dynasty. His successors, who ruled both at Meroë and at THEBES, Shabako (710–696), Shebteko (696–685), and Taharqo (685–663), called themselves''Kings of Cush and Egypt.'' Although the conquest of Thebes in 671 B.C. put an end to Cushite rule in Egypt, Meroë remained the capital of an independent but ever-weakening kingdom until the 4th century of the Christian Era.

While the kindred terms Cush/Cushites and Ethiopia/Ethiopians occur at least 30 times in the OT, a single reference occurs in the NT (Acts 8.26-40). The terms have a geographic and ethnographic reference. According to the Table of the Nations, Cush was a descendant of Ham (Gn 10.8) and the ancestor of several peoples in southern Arabia (Gn 10.9). According to Gn 2.13, ''all the land of Cush'' was encircled by the Gihon, one of the four legendary rivers of PARADISE. Because of the union of Cush and Egypt in the 8th and 7th centuries B.C., the Prophets often mention Cush in connection with Egypt (Is 20.3–5; 43.3; 45.14; Ez 30.4, 9) or with Phut and Libya (Jer 46.9; Ez 30.5; Na 3.9).

The literary characterization of Ethiopians/Ethiopia in the Bible is variegated. Amos 9:7–8 portrays Ethiopians as a people living at a distance from Israel. While some commentators have assumed that this passage disparages the Ethiopians as an uncivilized nation of slaves, in fact, at the time of Amos' ministry (*c.* 750 B.C.), an Ethiopian dynasty ruled autonomously, and prosperously, in the Upper Nile Valley. Jer 13.23 makes a reference to the swarthy complexion of the Cushites: ''Can the Ethiopian change his skin, or the leopard its spots?''—perhaps a well-known proverb, framed as a rhetorical question. The prophet highlights the immutability of skin color as a hyperbole, to underscore the magnitude of Judah's intransigence.

Ethiopia is renowned in the OT as a land of valiant warriors and military strength (2 Chr 12.2–12; 14.8–13; 16.7–8; Is 20.1–6; Jer 46.2, 8–9; Ez 38.4–5; Na 3.8–10) and is rich in wealth (Is 45.14–15; Dn 11.43; Job 28.17–19). Notwithstanding their reputation, elsewhere, for being a people far-distant from Israel's borders, the OT attests to the historical presence of Ethiopians within Israel/Palestine. They may have arrived there, originally, as war-captives, since Ethiopians frequently served as mercenaries in foreign armies, or possibly as diplomatic envoys (Is 8.1–7). In Israel, they served in the military (1 Sm 18.21–23; 31–32) and even married the indigenous Jews (Jer 36.14; Zep 1.1; Ps 7).

An Ethiopian, Ebed-melech, an official at the royal court in Judah, rescues the prophet Jeremiah from his punishment at the hands of King Zedekiah. The kindness of this outsider to the persecuted prophet dovetails another biblical theme concerning Ethiopians. The Prophets forecast their inclusion among the chosen people, when the Gentile nations gather at Mt. Zion to worship the God of Israel (Is 11.10–11; Jer 39.15–18; Zep 2.10–12; 3.9–10; Ps 68.29–32; 87.1–7).

Acts 8.26–39 recounts the conversion to Christianity of the treasurer of ''Candace, Queen of Ethiopia.'' That Candace is not a personal name, but rather the title of all the queens of the Meroitic kingdom, indicates that the Ethiopian official stands as an emblem or ambassador for his entire nation, a Gentile people, to whom God has gratuitously extended, according to Luke-Acts, the promise of salvation.

Bibliography: M. STACHOW, *''Do You Understand What You Are Reading'' (Acts 8:30): A Historical-Critical Reexamination of the Pericope of Philip and the Ethiopian (Acts 8:26-40)* (Dissertation, The Catholic University of America, Washington D.C. 1998). B. G. TRIGGER, *Ancient Egypt: A Social History* (Cambridge 1983). J. A. FITZMYER, *The Acts of the Apostles, Anchor Bible v. 31* (New York 1998).

[J. B. WHEATON/EDS.]

ETIOLOGY (IN THE BIBLE)

The term may be briefly defined as the assignment of a cause or reason for a custom, a name, etc. This article discusses first the concept of etiology, then the use of etiology in biblical narratives, and finally the question of the historical value of such narratives.

Concept. The word etiology is derived from the Greek αἰτία, which means cause. In the field of literature a narrative is said to be etiological when it attempts to explain the origins of some custom or institution, some monument or natural phenomenon; when it tries to answer the question why or how does it come about that such and such a thing is what it is today. The subject material ranges from the banal (''How did the pig get a curly tail?'') to the basic problems concerning human and cosmic origins. The explanation given is often of a popular, unscientific nature.

In the Bible. Many parts of Scripture abound in etiological narratives, observations, and incidental remarks of all sorts. One simple type of etiology that is found quite often seeks to explain through popular etymology the reason why a particular person or place received such a name: e.g., in Gn 2.23 it is said that ADAM's partner was called woman (Heb. *'iššâ*) because she was taken from man (*'îš*); in 3.20 he named her EVE (*ḥawwâ*) because she was the mother of all the living (*ḥāy*); and Eve called her firstborn Cain (*qayin*) because she had gotten (*qānîtî*) a male child with the help of Yahweh (Gn 4.1); and the city with the half-built tower was called Babel (*see* TOWER OF BABEL) because there Yahweh confused (*bālal*) the builders' language (Gn 11.9). At times more than one explanation is given for the same name: Isaac (*yiṣḥāq*), which means ''he laughs'' or ''may he laugh,'' has given rise to various scenes of laughter in the Genesis narrative. Abraham falls on his face and laughs (*yiṣḥāq*) when God promises him another son, in spite of his age (Gn 17.17); Sara has a similar reaction when she overhears the same promise (Gn 18.9–15); and once Isaac is born, she says that God has given her cause for laughter, and whoever will hear of it will laugh with her (Gn 21.6). There are narratives that explain the origins of sacred places, such as Beer-lahai-roi (Gn 16.7–14) and Bethel (Gn 28.11–22). Others attempt to give an account of various religious practices (CIRCUMCISION, in Gn 17.9–14 and Ex 4.24–26; the SABBATH, in the divine precedent of Gn 2.2–3). The Book of ESTHER intends to show how the feast of PURIM began. An etiological preoccupation is particularly evident in several narratives of the Book of JOSHUA, where the formula, ''and so it has remained to this day,'' or its equivalent, continually recurs (Jos 4.9; 5.9; 6.25; 7.26; 8.28, 29; 9.27; 10.27; etc.). Sometimes a single narrative contains several etiologies: for example, the destruction of Sodom and Gomorrah (Gn 19) succeeds in explaining why the region south of the Dead Sea is so desolate, why there is only one city in that area, why the name of that city is Segor, and how a woman-shaped pillar of salt came into existence. It also explains in a rather disparaging way the origin of the MOABITES and the Ammonites.

The Bible, however, contains etiological material of a much more profound intent. In Gn 2.21–24 the author explains why ''a man leaves his father and mother, and clings to his wife, and the two become one flesh''; by means of the narrative of the rib he suggests that the union of man and woman in marriage is a return to a primitive unity. The story emphasizes that the distinction of the sexes is willed by God [*see* SEX (IN THE BIBLE)] and that marriage is instituted by Him. Chapters 2 and 3 attempt to explain man's present unhappy state, including the fact of DEATH, the hard lot of a farmer trying to eke out a living from a rocky soil, woman's attraction for man in spite of the harsh treatment she received from him in the ancient East [*see* WOMAN (IN THE BIBLE)], and the necessity of wearing clothes (*see* NUDITY), by the story of the fall of man from a far happier state (*see* PRIMEVAL AGE IN THE BIBLE). Similarly, Gn 11.1–9 does not merely explain the origin of the place-name Babel, but seeks to give a reason why humanity, although one in origin, now finds itself dispersed in various localities throughout the world, each people speaking its own language.

Historical Value. The question arises: what is the historical value of such narratives? The profusion and diversity of the material at hand make a general answer impossible. Two points may be made, however. First, the factor of inspiration does not change the character of the literary form utilized; there is no reason to believe that etiology in the Bible has greater historical value than etiology outside the Bible. So the question of historicity is not peculiar to the Scriptures; it must be solved within the broader context of etiology in general. Secondly, each instance of etiology must be examined and judged on its own merits. In the vast majority of cases it will be found (when it is possible to arrive at a definite conclusion—which is not always the case) that the narrative rests simply on the love of word-play so easily observed in the Bible, on the desire to explain a mysterious monument or some feature of the landscape, or on the author's desire to communicate some deeper teaching, rather than on any real historical basis. Yet this is not to be automatically assumed in every case. The universal rejection by M. Noth in *Das Buch Josua* (2d ed. Tübingen 1953) of the historical value of etiological stories has been justly criticized by J. Bright (see bibliog.). The historical value of an etiology in any given case will be open to suspicion and must be confirmed by independent documentary evidence, archeological findings, or other reliable sources, before the genuineness of its tradition can be recognized. There are no universal solutions to this problem; each narrative has to be judged on its own merits.

Bibliography: *Encyclopedic Dictionary of the Bible*, tr. and adap. by L. HARTMAN (New York 1963) 695–697. K. RAHNER, *Lexikon für Theologie und Kirche*, ed. J. HOFER and K. RAHNER (Freiberg 1957–65) 1:1011–12. J. FICHTNER, ''Die etymologische Atiologie in den Namengebungen der geschichtlichen Bücher des A.T.,'' *Vetus Testamentum* 6 (1956) 372–396. J. SCHILDENBERGER, ''Aussageabsicht der inspirierten Geschichtsschreiber des A.T. bei der Komplication von Überlieferungen, sich widersprechenden Doppelberichten und ätiologischen Erzählungen,'' *Sacra Pagina*, ed. J. COPPENS et al., 2 v. (Paris 1959) 1:119–131. J. BRIGHT, *Early Israel in Recent History Writing* (Chicago 1956) 91–100. A. M. DU-

BARLE, *Les Sages d'Israël* (Paris 1946); ''Le Péché originel dans la Genèse,'' *Revue biblique* 64 (1957) 5–34.

[L. F. HARTMAN]

ETRUSCAN RELIGION

Knowledge of Etruscan religion is derived largely from the study of archeological materials. Although there are many extant Etruscan inscriptions, no key to the Etruscan language has yet been found. There are some names of deities on a clay tablet, some apparent curses on lead tablets, an inscribed bronze liver, a rectangular cippus, and a longer text on the wrappings of a mummy. Ancient writers who mention the Etruscans do so in a fragmentary manner and, apparently, are inclined to mix Etruscan with non-Etruscan elements. Roman writers, such as Livy and Cicero, give valuable information, but the works of Claudius Pulcher, Nigidius Figulus, and others who wrote about the Etruscans at length are preserved only in fragments. Some of these writers mention Etruscan books on religious beliefs and practices, but these are likewise lost.

The occurrence in Roman religion of the thunderbolt as a religious manifestation seems to come from the Etruscans. Their chief god, Tinia, and several others, including Juno and Minerva, whom the Romans adopted, were associated with the hurling of thunderbolts that portended events in human life. An Etruscan specialty was hepatoscopy, the interpretation of signs noted in the observation of the livers of animals. The religious expert known as the haruspex was borrowed by the Romans, along with the science of hepatoscopy.

Mural painting on wall of Etruscan tomb in the Tomb of the Jugglers, sixth century B.C., Tarquinia, Rome. (©Charles and Josette Lenars/CORBIS)

Belief in an Afterlife. The Etruscans showed much concern for the dead and for their existence in the afterlife. Throughout the course of Etruscan civilization, the dead are conceived as continuing their lives in the great chamber-tombs that were built and furnished elaborately in imitation of Etruscan dwellings. In the fresco paintings in these tombs, the dead are shown on their journey to the lower world in the company of demons, who are often pictured in horrible forms, however, there is no ground for regarding the lower world of the Etruscans as a place of punishment. The funeral games held for the deceased may have influenced the Roman gladiatorial combats. From the fourth century B.C. on, Greek ideas of the underworld, with Hades and Persephone presiding over it, were known to the Etruscans and, by some, incorporated into their own beliefs. Some of the stone coffins or sarcophagi into which the Etruscans placed the bodies of the deceased have been preserved. The lids of such coffins are frequently adorned with full-length sculptured figures, apparently of the dead persons. In some cases, a couple, apparently man and wife, are similarly sculptured. There is an air of serenity and calm in this Etruscan artwork concerning death that seems to indicate a comforting belief in immortality. However, without any considerable literature to make it intelligible, we do not know whether the Etruscans thought of the next life as a place of happiness and eternal reward or whether, like the classical Greeks, they regarded the next life only as a shadowy and gloomy existence.

Problem of Interpretation. Etruscan religion, because of our limited knowledge, is a complex and difficult subject. Etruscan, Greek, and Italic elements were intermingled, and there are definite traces of an Etruscan connection with the Near East, whence Herodotus and some other ancient writers claim the Etruscans came to settle in Italy. Etruscan hepatoscopy is identical with that of Babylonia, and certain other elements in Etruscan art and religion point to an Eastern origin. Although the deities concerned with their official cults, such as Juno, Minerva, Mars, and others, are known by these names to the Romans, the funerary gods who have to do with the after-life seem to be exclusively Etruscan.

Bibliography: M. PALLOTTINO, *The Etruscans,* tr. J. CAMERON (Baltimore 1955); *Etruscan Painting,* tr. M. E. STANLEY and S. GILBERT (Geneva 1952). C. C. CLEMEN, *Die Religion der Etrusker* (Bonn 1936). R. BLOCH, *Recherches sur les religions de l'Italie antique* (Geneva 1976). G. CAPDEVILLE, ''Les livres sacrés des Étrusques,'' in *Oracles et prophéties dans l'Antiquité* (Paris 1997) 457–508.

[T. A. BRADY/EDS.]

EUBEL, KONRAD

Conventual Franciscan historian; b. Sinning (Bavaria), Jan. 19, 1842; d. Würzburg, Feb. 5, 1923. After being ordained in 1868, he dedicated himself to historical research. In 1887 he was appointed penitentiary at St. Peter's, and during 20 years in Rome continued his historical work. His crowning achievement was his *Hierarchia catholica medii aevi,* a chronological listing of the popes, cardinals, and bishops of all Christianity according to the alphabetical order of the Latin names of the dioceses.

Bibliography: Works. C. EUBEL et al., *Hierarchia Catholica medii (et recentioris) aevi:* v.1, 1198–1431 (2d. ed. Münster 1913); v.2, 1431–1503 (2d. ed. Münster 1914); v.3, 1503–1600 (2d. ed. Münster 1923); v.4, 1592–1667 (Münster 1935); v.5, 1667–1730 (Padua 1952); v.6, 1730–1799 (Padua 1958); *Die avignonesische Obedienz der Mendikanten-Orden* (Paderborn 1900); *Geschichte der kölnischen Minoriten-Ordensprovinz* (Cologne 1906); ed., *Geschichte der oberdeutschen Minoriten-Provinz* (Würzburg 1886); ed., *Bullarium Franciscanum,* v.5–7 (for the years 1303–1431) (Rome 1898–1904); ed., *Bullarii Franciscani epitome* (Quaracchi-Florence 1908). Literature. *Commentarium O.F.M. conventualium* 11 (1923) 22–26. F. DOELLE, ''Die literarische Tätigkeit des P. Konrad Eubel, O.F.M. Conv.,'' *Franziskanische Studien* 5 (Münster-Werl 1918) 307–313. R. RITZLER, ''Die archivalischen Quellen der 'Hierarchia catholica','' *Studi e Testi* 165 (Rome 1952) 51–74.

[J. J. SMITH]

EUCHARIST (BIBLICAL DATA)

This article treats of the origin of the term; then of the Eucharist in its various aspects as found in the Synoptic Gospels and with St. Paul in the First Epistle to the Corinthians; and finally, of the Eucharist as it appears in the Johannine writings.

Origin of the Term. The Jewish form of liturgical blessing (Heb. *berākâ*) that Jesus used at the Last Supper to institute the Eucharist and that has given its name to this sacred rite and its elements had its OT origins in the praise of God that came spontaneously to the lips of one for whom the Lord had performed some great deed; cf., e.g., Gn 24.27: ''Blessed be the Lord''; in Hebrew, *bārûk yhwh;* in the Septuagint (LXX), εὐλογητὸς Κύριος. It could be at the same time a sort of public proclamation of the name of God and an acknowledgement and confession of the power and glory of the Lord (Ex 18.9–11). Such forms lent themselves easily to use in public or private worship; the initial blessing or praise of God came to be followed by a more or less extensive ''remembrance'' (ἀνάμνησις) of God's action in nature and in the history of His people (1 Chr 16.12–14; Neh 9.5–37; Sir 51.1–12). A prayer of petition could often be added (Sir 50.22–24). The LXX often translated these forms of praise and proclamation by εὐλογεῖν (to bless, praise) and ἐξομολογεῖν (to confess, acknowledge, praise); cf. Jesus' use of the latter in Mt 11.25. The verb εὐχαριστεῖν, which in classical and Hellenistic usage meant to give thanks, bestow a favor, also came to be used in this same context; the notion of spontaneous praise preceded that of thanksgiving—a nuance that was later lost on the Hellenistic Christian communities; cf. the miracle of the multiplication of loaves in Mk 8.6–7, where, as at the Last Supper (Mk 14.22–23), εὐλογεῖν and εὐχαριστεῖν appear as synonymous.

This prayer of praise or blessing of God, accompanied by a ''breaking of bread'' and a ''remembrance'' of the manifold benefits of the Lord, preceded the main part of the PASSOVER Meal and other Jewish festive or fraternal meals. A similar blessing followed, spoken over a cup of wine (the ''cup of blessing'' or ''consecrated cup'' of 1 Cor 10.16). In the course of his own *berākâ* (''while blessing''—aorist participle in Mk 14.22 showing simultaneity), Jesus spoke the words of Eucharistic institution that gave new meaning to this ancient rite: ''This is my body; this is my blood.'' (Is this *berākâ* of Jesus to be connected with His high-priestly prayer as given in John ch. 17?) An antecedent Passover HAGGADAH, or didactic exposition of the meaning of the meal, may also have prepared the minds of the disciples for this event. While other early names—the BREAKING OF BREAD, the LORD'S SUPPER—have enjoyed only limited use, this action of blessing, thanksgiving, has given an enduring designation to the sacred rite.

The Sources: Liturgical Traditions of the Institution. The earliest extant account of the Eucharistic celebration in the early Church is found in 1 Cor 11.17–34 (*c.* A.D. 55). On the occasion of abuses that had arisen in the celebration of the Lord's Supper in the Church at Corinth (*see* AGAPE), St. Paul recalled the traditional report that he had received on the true nature of the Eucharist. Paul received this tradition ''from [ἀπό] the Lord'' (1 Cor 11.23), not by some sort of special revelation (whose immediacy would have been better expressed by παρά), but because the Lord Jesus, as institutor of the Eucharist, was the first link in the tradition and because it was by the power and authority of the Lord that the intermediaries, including Paul himself in his role as an Apostle, could be counted on to transmit faithfully the tradition in the Church. To ''receive'' (παραλαμβάνειν) and ''deliver'' (παραδιδόναι) are in fact the equivalents of technical terms for the acceptance and handling on of rabbinical teaching; cf. 1 Cor 15.3–7, where the same terms are clearly used to indicate a historical tradition. This is no denial, however, of the work of Paul himself in fathoming the depths of what he had received.

Plainly, the Pauline account of the institution (11.23–25) is embedded in the framework of a Christian liturgical celebration. The Synoptic accounts (Mk 14.22–24; Mt 26.26–28; Lk 22.19–20), inserted in the course of the Gospel Passion narratives (note the awkward repetition ''and while they were eating'' of Mk 14.18, 22), likewise owe their present form to liturgical use; their laconic structure shows little interest in the details of a Jewish meal that had become superfluous for most Christians. Matthew manifests a close dependence on Mark; Luke's report is inspired by that of Paul, or at least draws on a liturgical source common to both. The mention of the cup ''after the supper'' in Paul (1 Cor 11.25) and Luke (Lk 22.20) seems to reflect the separated sequence of a Jewish meal as described above; liturgical practice has joined cup to bread in Mk 14.22–24 and Mt 26.26–28. Divergence of style and vocabulary precludes a Marcan dependence on Paul. Their fundamental harmony amid difference of detail is a precious sign that they have faithfully transmitted the thought of Jesus in His institution of the Eucharist.

The Passover Meal of the New Covenant. It is not certain that the Eucharistic institution actually took place during a Passover meal in the full sense of the term. In any case, the proximity of the feast has influenced the course of the meal, the accounts that the Synoptics give of it, and its theological significance.

The Jewish Passover meal commemorated the liberation from Egyptian slavery—the first great act of redemption by God for His people (Ex 12.1–28), a redemption that formed the preparatory step for the covenant on Mt. Sinai. At the same time, the meal expressed an eager hope and longing for the definitive coming of the kingdom of God. At the Last Supper, in a clear reference to the actions of Moses in Ex 24.8, Jesus established a new covenant ''in'' (i.e., ''by means of,'' causal) His own blood: ''This is my blood of the covenant'' (Mk 14.24; Mt 26.28); or the more developed form of Paul (1 Cor 11.25) and Luke (22.20): ''This cup is the new covenant in my blood'' (by metonymy, cup stands for blood). The clarifying ''new'' of Paul and Luke recalls the ''new covenant'' of Jer 31.31. This is no distortion; a covenant in the blood of Jesus (''my blood''), replacing the blood of lambs (Ex 12.7) or bulls (Ex 24.5), is of necessity a new covenant. For this theme in the NT see also Rom 11.27; 2 Cor 3.6; Heb 8.6–13; 9.14–15; 9.18–10.39.

The Real Presence and Communion with a Sacrificial Victim. ''Body [flesh] and blood'' is a sacrificial notion: cf. Lv 17.11, 14; Dt 12.23; Ez 39.17–20 (especially important for linking ''flesh and blood'' to a sacrificial meal); Heb 13.11–12. At the Last Supper, the Eucharistic blood in the cup ''is being shed'' (Lk 22.20) or ''will be shed'' (in NT Greek, the present often replaced the future participle; in any case, the thought is clear; it is the same blood of Jesus that will soon be shed on the cross). A mere appeal to the words of institution themselves is insufficient to show the real presence of the body and blood of the Lord. The copula ''is,'' whether expressed or implied (in Aramaic, Jesus would have said simply, ''This my body . . . . This my blood''), is no preclusion of a symbolic meaning; cf. Ez 5.5: ''this is Jerusalem'' (a symbolic action); Mt 13.37–38 (a parable); Jn 15.1, 5 (an allegory).

Among the Semites, however, mere symbols were inadequate for the establishment of a covenant; for this, real victims, not merely signs of them, were required (Gn 15.9–18; Ex 24.5). Added to this is the realistic way in which St. John (see below) and St. Paul speak of the Eucharist. For the latter (1 Cor 10.16–22), it is a ''sharing, partaking'' of the body and blood of the Lord. As ''the table of the Lord, the cup of the Lord,'' the Eucharist is sacrificial food, to be compared to the sacrificial meals of the pagans, which were thought to effect a real contact or communion with the divinity; see Dn 1.8, 13, 15 (LXX) and Mal 1.7, 12 for the OT background of these terms. The Council of Trent saw in Mal 1.11 an anticipation of the perfect sacrifice of the messianic era. Among the Jews, to eat the victim of a sacrifice was to partake of the fruits of the sacrifice (1 Cor 10.18). For the author of the Epistle to the Hebrews (13.10), the Jews have no right to partake of the Christian altar, which is probably to be identified with the (Eucharistic?) body of Christ. In 1 Cor 10.1–6, the manna and the water from the rock (Exodus ch. 16–17; Numbers ch. 20) are ''spiritual,'' both by their supernatural origin and by their existence as prophetic types of the Eucharist. The Eucharist is the food and drink of the Christian in the new Exodus; it is also ''spiritual'' for it contains the risen body of Christ, which, vivified by the Spirit, dispenses spiritual life and strength to those who partake of it.

The Eucharist, like Baptism in the Pauline theology (Rom 6.3–5), is a sharing in the death and Resurrection of the Lord. But a warning is sounded (1 Cor 10.5–6): the reception of the Sacraments does not free one from the demands of the moral law; see the whole context of 1 Corinthians ch. 10–11. In 11.27–34, Paul explains that a judgment on Christians has already commenced by the Eucharistic presence of the Lord; it is an anticipation of His physical presence (PAROUSIA) at the end of time, the reality of which was a chief article of Christian belief—''until he comes'' (11.26).

The Expiatory Sacrifice of the Servant of the Lord. Both the blood shed ''for many'' of Mk 14.24 and the further clarification—''unto the forgiveness of sins''—of Mt 26.28 are allusions to Jesus as the fulfillment of the Isaian ''Servant of the Lord,'' whose vicarious sufferings ''justify'' and ''take away the sins of many,'' i.e., in Semitic idiom, ''an unlimited number, all'' (Is 53.3–6, 11–12; *see* SUFFERING SERVANT, SONGS OF THE). The particularized ''for you'' of Paul (1 Cor 11.24) and Luke (Lk 22.19–20) may well be a liturgical application to Christians present at the Church's Eucharistic celebration; others, however, see in it an original reference to the ''covenant which the Lord has made with you'' of Ex 24.8. On Jesus as the Servant, see also Mt 8.17; 11.4–6; 12.17–21; 20.28; Mk 10.45; Lk 4.17–21; 22.37 (in the context of the Last Supper); Acts 8.32–33; etc.

The substitutive as well as the atoning role of the blood of Jesus is suggested in Mk 14.24, Lk 22.19–20, and 1 Cor 11.24 by the preposition ὑπέρ (for), which can mean not only ''in behalf of,'' ''for the sake of,'' but also ''in place of''; the meanings often merge (cf. Lv 17.11: ''it is the blood, as the seat of life, that makes atonement''; Rom 3.24–25; 5.9). By analogy with the blood, the body of Christ ''is being given for you'' (i.e., in sacrifice: Lk 22.19). In Is 42.6–7; 43.16–21; 49.6, the close union of covenant (communion), Exodus (Passover sacrifice), and Servant (expiation) themes is a preparation for the higher synthesis that Jesus would make in the Eucharist of these distinct yet related ideas. The Servant who is ''a light to the nations'' and who is to bring ''salvation'' to the ''ends of the earth'' is in fact a covenant personified. For cognate ideas, see Is 54.10; 55.3; 56.6; 61.8. Forgiveness of sins is joined to the new covenant in Jer 31.31–34.

The Eucharist as a Permanent Institution in the Church. Although the command to ''do this in remembrance of me'' is probably an elucidation on the part of Paul (1 Cor 11.24–25) and Luke (Lk 22.19) for the benefit of Gentile readers, still the idea of ''remembrance'' (Heb. *zikkārôn*) in the sense of a liturgical reenactment of some past event is deeply rooted in the OT (Ex 12.14, 26–27; 13.3, 8–9; Dt 16.3; Nm 10.10) and must have been present in the thought of Jesus. In this sense, the whole ritual of the Passover meal was a ''remembrance'' of the liberation from Egyptian slavery. It made the past vividly present in word and action: bitter herbs; PASSOVER LAMB; UNLEAVENED BREAD (Dt 16.3; the ἄρτος, literally ''bread in general,'' is therefore no misnomer); and the Passover Haggadah by the head of the family (see Paul's teaching in 1 Cor 5.7–8 on Christ as the Christian Passover). The Last Supper blessing given by Jesus over bread and wine was in turn a proclamation of the new Exodus from the slavery of sin by His own coming death.

After His departure, the disciples were to make liturgically present this same mystery, now not in prophetic action, but in ''remembrance'' of the past. In the words of Paul: ''as often as you shall eat this bread and drink the cup, you proclaim the death of the Lord'' (1 Cor 11.26). This ''proclamation'' has been variously explained: as a recital of a primitive passion narrative in conjunction with the Eucharistic celebration (the verb καταγγέλλειν is used in the NT exclusively for the preaching of the ''good news''); or as a dramatized action, with torn flesh and flowing blood symbolized by broken bread and crimson wine. In reality, it is by the repetition of both the actions and the words of institution contained in Christ's ''remembrance'' that the Eucharist receives its full significance, and that the death is ''proclaimed.'' Christ can no longer die (Heb 9.26–28; 10.12–14), but His sacrificial death is made present (1) by the real presence, under the Eucharistic symbols, of the Christ who once upon a time died, who was raised up, and who is now in glory (the *Christus passus* of St. Thomas Aquinas; see *Summa Theologiae* 3a, 73.3 ad 3), and (2) by the fruits of His death, which Christians receive in partaking of the Eucharist (Mt 26.26–27; 1 Cor 10.16–21; 11.28–29; Jn 6.51c–58); this doctrine was summarized by St. Thomas (ST 3a, 83.1; 22.3 ad 2;73.4 ad 3).

The Eucharist as an Eschatological Meal. Our understanding of the eschatological aspect of the Eucharist is conditioned by the precise meaning of ''kingdom of God'' contained in the various accounts. In Mk 14.25 the Eucharistic meal of which Jesus has just partaken appears as a farewell banquet before His death and as a prefigurement of the messianic banquet in the kingdom of God at the end of time. This figure of the future kingdom under the form of a meal is a frequent one in the Bible [Is 25.6; 55.1–5; 65.13; Ps 22(23).5; Prv 9.1–6; Mt 8.11–12; 22.1–14; 25.10; Lk 14.15–24; Rv 3.20; 19.9]. The ''henceforth'' of Mt 26.29 may hint at the length of time that this interval between the Supper and Parousia had assumed by the time the Gospel was written.

Luke placed the words of Mark before the institution (Lk 22.19b–20 are authentic; their absence from some manuscripts may be due to a confusion over the twofold mention of the ''cup'' in v. 17 and 20) and added to them a notice about a Passover that Jesus will no longer eat until all is ''fulfilled'' in the kingdom of God (22.15–18). Despite the Greek style and Lucan vocabulary, such a combination accords well with the Jewish custom of an initial blessing over the Passover (i.e., meal, not lamb, which need not have been here present) and a first cup of wine. It may thus be either a reworking of a historic pre-Lucan tradition about the actual course of events at the Last Supper, or more probably the playing of a theological variation on themes of Mark (14.25) and Paul (1 Cor 11.24–25) by Luke himself; cf. the artificial position of Lk 22.24–30, found in a different context in the other Synoptics—Mk 10.42–45; Mt 19.28; 20.25–28. In any case, the farewell in Luke is to the Jewish Passover, the fulfillment of which is the Eucharistic meal; the latter is not only an anticipation of the messianic meal at the end of time, as in Mark, but also more immediately of the post-Resurrection meals of the risen Lord in that intermediate phase of the kingdom of God that for Luke is the Church; note his predilection for the mention of such meals (Lk 24.30, 41–43; Acts 1.4).

The eschatological and joyous aspect of the Eucharist appears uppermost in the meager accounts that have been preserved of the liturgical ''breaking of bread'' in the primitive Christian community of Jerusalem (Acts 2.42–47). This is only to be expected. The meals of the risen Lord with His disciples had resumed the series of fraternal repasts that, culminating in the Last Supper, had been broken by His death. After His departure, the disciples, filled with the joy of the Resurrection and the hope of a proximate Parousia, continued to gather and to ''bless God,'' to ''give thanks'' over the bread and wine of the community meal, a meal that would have included a ''remembrance'' of the messianic marvels that they had witnessed, including the events of the Last Supper, Passion and death, which were inseparably bound to the Resurrection (cf. Acts 10.39–41, where the meals with the risen Lord climax the apostolic witness to Jesus' life, death, and Resurrection); the repetition of the words of Eucharistic institution (''do this in remembrance of me'') would render the Lord present once again in their midst.

For St. Paul, the Eucharistic ''breaking of bread'' (Acts 20.7–11—on a Sunday, the day of the Resurrection; 1 Cor 10.16) is likewise situated between the death of the Lord and His Parousia. The phrase, ''you proclaim the death of the Lord until he comes'' (1 Cor 11.26) is an echo of the early Christian hope expressed in the words ''MARANATHA'' (Come, Lord) in 1 Cor 16.22 and ''Come, Lord Jesus!'' in Rv 22.20.

Sacred meals with an aura of eschatological anticipation were in use also among the covenanters of the QUMRAN COMMUNITY (1QS^{a} 2.17–22; perhaps 1QS 6.2–5). They are another poignant testimony to the Jewish longing for that union with God which has in reality been fulfilled in Christ's covenant meal, the Eucharist.

The Eucharist as a Bond of the Church's Unity. The Eucharistic body of Christ has profoundly influenced St. Paul's doctrine on the Church as the body of Christ: ''Because the bread is one, we though many, are one body, all of us who partake of the one bread'' (1 Cor 10.17). The ''one body'' has here the same meaning as ''the body of the Lord'' in the preceding verse, i.e., the real body of the risen Lord. By their contact with the Eucharistic body, Christians come into vital, dynamic union with the person of Christ. That they are identified with the body of Christ is no mere metaphor, borrowed from social or civil life, for the power and life of the Spirit of Christ is present in each of them (1 Cor 6.15; 12.27; Eph 5.30). The communion (κοινωνία sharing, partaking: 1 Cor 10.16) of the individual Christian with the Eucharistic body is thus the cause of their union, communion among themselves (Acts 2.42).

The Eucharist in St. John. The words of Eucharistic institution are lacking in the Last Supper account of the Fourth Gospel (John ch. 13–17). Instead, John's Eucharistic doctrine is concentrated in ch. 6, where, following an account of the multiplication of loaves (v.1–13) and the walking on the sea (v.16–21), Jesus delivers a long discourse of which the principal theme is that of the ''bread of life'' (v.26–72.).

In Part Purely Metaphorical. Despite its literary unity, ch. 6 is not to be regarded as purely and simply a promise of the Eucharist. The themes that Jesus develops from the OT refer, first and foremost, to Himself as the Son who has been sent by the Father into the world (v. 39–40) to give life to it by His person and message (v. 33) and who must metaphorically be eaten by faith. The crowd in 6.14 acclaims Jesus as ''the Prophet,'' namely, the eschatological prophet of Dt 18.15, a theme that played an important role in the early Church's preaching (Acts 3.22–23; 7.37). For the MANNA concept, which is the type of Jesus as the ''bread of life,'' see Ex 16.4, 13–15; Ps 77(78).24; Neh 9.15. According to some Jewish circles, the miracle of the manna was to be repeated at the coming of the Messiah; see the Syriac Apocalypse of Baruch 29.8–30.1 [R. Charles, *The Pseudepigrapha of the OT* (Oxford 1963) 498]. Jesus' words in Jn 6.35, ''He who comes to me shall not hunger, and he who believes in me shall never thirst,'' are an echo of the eschatological ideas found in Is 55.1–2, ''All you who are thirsty, come to the water! You who have no money, come, receive grain and eat,'' and Is 65.13, ''Lo, my servants shall eat, but you shall go hungry; my servants shall drink, but you shall be thirsty.'' The words in Jn 6.45–47, ''And they all shall be taught of God,'' play on a familiar theme of Is 54.13; Jer 31.31–34. Jesus compares Himself to the feast that personified Wisdom prepares for herself in Prv 9.1–6; Sir 24.18–21. The disciple of Christ is likened to the pupil at the feet of Wisdom in the OT.

In Part Purely Literal. The entire discourse, however, cannot be understood in a purely metaphorical sense, although such an interpretation is found among some of the Fathers and later theologians, e.g., Clement of Alexandria and Origen. Cajetan adopted a similar view for the sake of a better defense of the Catholic practice of communion under the species of bread alone: *de spirituali manducatione et potatione . . . est* (''It is a matter of spiritual eating and drinking''; *Commentarium in* ST 3a, 80. 12). The Council of Trent made no decision in the matter. The words in Jn 6.51c–58 (52c–59 in the Vulgate and 1941 Confraternity edition) are in fact far too realistic and contain too many undertones of the words of Eucharistic institution to be merely a metaphor for faith in the person of Christ or for the Redemption brought by him. Ultra-realistic expressions are present: ''I will give'' is a promise for the future, but in John it can also mean ''to give in sacrifice''; ''for [ὑπέρ, on behalf of] the life of the world''; ''bread'' (ἄρτος); ''drink my blood''; ''flesh'' (σάρξ), a more Semitic expression than the σῶμα (body) of the Synoptics and St. Paul; ''he who eats [τρώγειν, literally, gnaw, munch] my flesh.''

Hence, many see in John ch. 6 a uniform transition from reception of Jesus by faith to reception of Him in the Eucharist. Occasioned perhaps by the Passover synagogue readings (6.4, 60) that dealt with the manna in the desert, Jesus would have prepared the minds of the Jews for the Sacrament that he was to institute at the Last Supper.

Double-Meaning Interpretation. The discourse may be envisaged in another fashion. It seems improbable that at such an early date in his ministry Jesus would have demanded, above and beyond a confession of his Messiahship, a belief in the sublime and difficult mystery of the Eucharist. To have done so would be to break the bruised reed and quench the smoking wick (Mt 12.20). One of the characteristics of John's Gospel is that it shows parallels between the Sacraments of the Church and historical events in the life of Jesus. The wine miracle at Cana (Jn 2.1–11), already a sign of the replacement of the Law by the gospel, may point further in John's mind to that greater rite of purification by blood which is the Eucharist; note the proximity of the Passover in 2.13. The miracle of the loaves, a historical event, is described in terms reminiscent of the Last Supper (6.11); this tendency is already to be noted in the Synoptic accounts (Mk 6.41; 8.6; and parallels). The Evangelist, then, would also have seen a deeper sacramental meaning behind a discourse that originally concerned the person of Jesus as Messiah (Jn 6.26–51b, 59–72). To further emphasize the intimate union of faith and Sacrament, the Evangelist or a later editor (cf. ch. 21, which is acknowledged to be a posterior addition) would have inserted 6.51c–58, whose original context lay elsewhere in the Johannine tradition—a version of Jesus' words at the Last Supper, or a Christian homily based on them, whose intention would be to combat a spiritual DOCETISM that would rob the Eucharist of any physical reality.

John's Eucharistic doctrine, like that of the Synoptics and St. Paul, is closely linked to the Passion and death of Jesus and to His second coming (6.54). The efficacy of the Sacraments can in fact come only from the death of Jesus, after he has ''given up his spirit,'' or rather, ''handed over the [Holy] Spirit'' (Jn 19.30). The blood and water flowing from His pierced side is for the Evangelist a type of the Eucharist and Baptism (cf. 1 Jn 5.6, 8 for a similar symbolism). Jesus, the ''true vine'' (Jn 15.1–17), feeds the disciples on His own blood, the ''fruit of the vine'' (Mk 14.25). It is a source for the unity of Christians with Christ and with one another, just as with Paul also the Eucharist makes of Christians ''one body'' (1 Cor 10.17). From the very Incarnation of the Word, in John's thought (Jn 1.14; 1 Jn 4.2), Jesus has been food for those who believe in Him. In the OT itself, the manna had already been a figure for the ''word of life,'' the divine message (Dt 8.3). The Christian ''word of life'' is in turn the Gospel message; Christ is this ''Word of Life'' personified (1 Jn 1.1). Those who believe and listen to this ''Word'' are already nourished by the divine life.

Bibliography: J. BETZ, *Lexikon für Theologie und Kirche,* ed. J. HOFER and K. RAHNER (Freiburg 1957–65) 3:1142–57. J. COPPENS, *Dictionnaire de la Bible* supplement, ed. L. PIROT et al. (Paris 1928–) 2:1146–1215. E. SCHWEIZER, *Die Religion in Geschichte und Gegenwart* (3d ed. Tübingen 1957–65) 1:10–21. G. QUELL and E. STAUFFER, ''ἀγαπάω, ἀγάπη,'' in G. KITTEL, *Theologisches Wörterbuch zum Neuen Testament* (Stuttgart 1935) 1:20–55. G. QUELL and J. BEHM, ''διαθήκη,'' *ibid.* 2:106–137. W. FOERSTER, ''κυριακός,'' *ibid.* 3:1095–96. J. JEREMIAS, ''πάσχα,'' *ibid.* 5:895–903; *The Eucharistic Words of Jesus,* tr. A. EHRHARDT (New York 1955). J. DELORME et al., *The Eucharist in the N.T.,* tr. E. M. STEWART (Baltimore 1964). O. CULLMANN, *Early Christian Worship,* tr. A. S. TODD and J. B. TORRANCE (Chicago 1953). A. J. B. HIGGINS, *The Lord's Supper in the N. T.* (Chicago 1952). F. J. LEENHARDT, *Le Sacrement de la sainte Cène* (Neuchâtel 1948); ''This is My Body,'' *Essays on the Lord's Supper,* tr. J. G. DAVIES (Richmond 1958); ''La Structure du chapitre 6 de l'évangile de Jean,'' *Revue d'histoire et de la philosophie religieuses* 39 (1959) 1–13. J. DUPONT, '''Ceci est mon corps,' 'Ceci est mon sang,''' *Nouvelle revue théologique* 80 (1958) 1025–41. C. VOLLERT, ''The Eucharist: Quests for Insights from Scripture,'' *Theological Studies* 21 (1960) 404–443. B. COOKE, ''Synoptic Presentation of the Eucharist as a Covenant Sacrifice,'' *ibid.* 1–44. A. ARNOLD, *Der Ursprung des christlichen Abendmahls* (2d ed. Freiburg 1939). G. DIX,

The Shape of the Liturgy (2d ed. London 1945; repr. 1960). P. BENOIT, ''Le Récit de la Céne dans Lc. XXII, 15–20,'' *Revue biblique* 48 (1939) 357–393; ''The Holy Eucharist,'' *Scripture* 8 (1956) 97–108; 9 (1957) 1–14. W. GOOSSENS, *Les Origines de l'Eucharistie, Sacrement et sacrifice* (Paris 1931). H. LIETZMANN, *Mass and Lord's Supper*, tr. D. H. G. REEVE (Leiden 1953). G. SLOYAN,'' *Primitive and Pauline* Concepts of the Eucharist,'' *Catholic Biblical Quarterly*23 (1961) 1–13. G. ZIENER, ''Die Brotwunder im Markusevangelium,'' *Biblische Zeitschrift* 4 (1960) 282–285; ''Johannesevangelium und urchristliche Passafeier,'' *Biblische Zeitschrift* 2 (1958) 263–274; ''Weisheitsbuch und Johannesevangelium,'' *Biblica* 38 (1957) 396–418; 39 (1958) 37–60. E. KÄSEMANN, ''The Pauline Doctrine of the Lord's Supper,'' *Essays on N. T. Themes,* tr. W. J. MONTAGUE (pa. Naperville, Ill. 1964) 108–135. C. SPICQ, *L'Épître aux Hébreux*, 2 v. (Études bibliques; Paris 1952–53) 1:316–318; 2:425–426, A. FEUILLET, ''Les Thèmes bibliques majeurs du discours sur le pain de vie (Jn 6),'' *Nouvelle revue théologique* 82 (1960) 803–822, 918–939, 1040–62, repr. in *Études johanniques* (Paris 1962) 47–129. H. SCHÜRMANN, *Eine quellenkritische Untersuchung des lukanischen Abendmahlsberichtes. Lk. 22,7–38,* 3 v. (Münster 1953–57); ''Joh. 6, 51c, ein Schlüssel zur grossen johanneischen Brotrede,'' *Biblische Zeitschrift* 2 (1958) 244–262; ''Abendmahl,'' *Lexikon für Theologie und Kirche,* ed. J. HOFER and K. RAHNER (Freiburg 1957–65) 1:26–31. X. LÉON-DUFOUR, ''Le Mystère du pain de vie (Jean VI),'' *Recherches de science religieuse* 46 (1958) 481–523. B. GERHARDSSON, *Memory and Manuscript,* tr. E. J. SHARPE (Uppsala 1961) 305, 321–322. P. NEUENZEIT, *Das Herrenmahl: Studien zur paulinischen Eucharistieauffassung* (Munich 1960). J. P. AUDET, ''Esquisse historique du genre littéraire de la *bénédiction* juive et de l'*eucharistie* chrétienne,'' *Revue biblique* 65 (1958) 371–399; *La Didachè: Instructions des Apôtres* (Paris 1958). E. J. KILMARTIN, ''Liturgical Influence on John 6,'' *Catholic Biblical Quarterly* 22 (1960) 183–191; ''The Eucharistic Cup in the Primitive Liturgy,'' *ibid.* 24 (1962) 32–43. R. E. BROWN, ''The Johannine Sacramentary Reconsidered,'' *Theological Studies* 23 (1962) 183–206. E. RUCKSTUHL, *Die literarische Einheit des Johannesevangeliums* (Freiburg 1951) 220–271. G. BORNKAMM, ''Die eucharistische Rede im Johannesevangelium,'' *Zeitschrift für die neutestamentliche Wissenschaft und die Kunde der älteren Kirche* 47 (1956) 161–169.

[C. BERNAS]

EUCHARIST, EXPOSITION OF THE

''Exposition of the holy Eucharist, either in the ciborium or in the monstrance, is intended to acknowledge Christ's marvelous presence in the sacrament'' (HCWE 82). In light of the principle found in HCWE 79, however, ''exposition must clearly express the cult of the blessed sacrament in its relationship to the Mass'' (HCWE 82). For that reason, ''Mass is prohibited in the body of the church'' while exposition is taking place (HCWE 83). ''If exposition of the blessed sacrament is extended for an entire day or over several days, it is to be interrupted during the celebration of Mass'' (*ibid.* 83). During the exposition, customary signs of reverence are used (lighted candles, incense) and ''there should be prayers, songs, and readings. . . . To encourage a prayerful spirit, there should be readings from scripture

''The Last Communion of St. Jerome,'' painting by Sandro Botticelli, 15th century. (©Geoffrey Clements/CORBIS)

with a homily or brief exhoration'' (HCWE 85; 93–94). Silence, song, and praying parts of the Liturgy of the Hours are also appropriate (HCWE 95–96). Exposition ordinarily concludes with benediction and reposition of the sacrament in the tabernacle (HCWE 97–100); however, ''exposition which is held exclusively for the giving of benediction is prohibited'' (HCWE 89).

For a more detailed discussion and bibliography in this encyclopedia, *see* EUCHARIST OUTSIDE MASS, WORSHIP OF THE; and EUCHARISTIC DEVOTION.

[N. D. MITCHELL]

EUCHARIST IN CONTEMPORARY CATHOLIC TRADITION

The purpose of this article is not to give a detailed presentation of the history or of the theology of the Eucharist, but to give an overview of directions and trends in Catholic theology in recent years.

Fresh insights and orientations have come from a variety of sources. To begin with, there was the liturgical renewal, starting with the more active participation of congregations and more frequent Communion, and then

"Miraculous Mass," fresco by Simone Martini, part of the freso cycle "Scenes from the Life of St. Martin," in the St. Martin Chapel, Lower Church of San Francesco, Assisi, Italy, 1321. (©Elio Ciol/CORBIS)

moving on to the revision of liturgical books for use in the celebration of the Eucharist. A simultaneous revision took place in many of the Christian Churches of the West. While bringing about considerable liturgical convergence in the manner of celebrating, this went hand-in-hand with an ecumenical dialogue that has gone a long way in resolving historical disputes and unveiling common points of faith and doctrine, even while pointing to the legitimacy of differences, especially over concepts of sacrifice and presence. This meeting of the ways in western communities itself occurs within an openness to the eucharistic traditions of the East.

Dialogue and theological inquiry are, in turn, served by greater historical consciousness, a better knowledge of ancient liturgical rites and prayers, and an appeal to scriptural origins that is affected by historical and literary criticism. Past doctrinal and theological formulations of the mystery of the Eucharist in the Church's tradition are also subjected to historical criticism and can, thus, be reconsidered and assimilated within a larger comprehension, opened up by scriptural, patristic and liturgical research. Catechetically, too, there have been new approaches, especially in putting the mystery of the Eucharist in the context of the mystery of the Church, the Body of Christ and in relating it to the mystery of the Trinity [*see* CHURCH, II (THEOLOGY OF)].

From a historical perspective, it is sometimes said that in the first millennium eucharistic theology was wedded to celebration and in the second became a speculative enterprise that lost touch with celebration. Granting a certain validity to this observation, it is to be noted that even the speculative questions about presence and sacrifice that dominated, first scholastic theology and then post-tridentine, were related to an evolving eucharistic practice that had developed before the theology or the doctrine and which included eucharistic devotions and a new manner of hearing Mass for the faithful. Theology, in other words, took a new turn in the wake of changed liturgical and devotional practice. Not even doctrine or speculative theology, therefore, can be properly understood and interpreted unless seen in the context of ecclesial practice. If contemporary eucharistic theology is often related to a historically critical approach to scriptural reconstruction, to ritual studies, to the study of language, to the study of cultures, or to hermeneutics, this too is because of the need to understand and guide a currently developing practice of eucharistic celebration that shows both convergences and diversities, not only among Churches but within each particular Church.

Taking all of this into account, one could speak of a new orientation in eucharistic theology that can be called doing liturgical theology. This is because the focus is on celebration and on its interpretation within the living and richly diverse tradition of the Church. It is within liturgical theology that history, practice, doctrine, the study of rites and texts, and theological elaboration, come together. One might also speak of this as a hermeneutical approach, since it attends to the Eucharist as an event of God's gift in Christ, a gift that comes to the Church and embodies itself in the Church through an act of "language," that is, through ritual action and spoken word.

With the foregoing in view, a summary of new insights from a variety of fields of eucharistic study will be given under these headings: (1) Eucharist, sacrament of the Body of Christ; (2) Revisiting New Testament origins and background; (3) Eucharistic theology as a liturgical mystagogy, and the study of the Great Eucharistic Prayer; (4) The study of controversies, doctrines and past theologies of the West in historical context; and (5) Orientations in contemporary systematic theologies of the Eucharist.

Eucharist, Sacrament of the Body of Christ

By way of stating a common fundamental principle, one could say that a contemporary liturgical theology looks to the Eucharist as the Sacrament of the Body of Christ, Head and members. This plays a part in historical study and in theological and liturgical revision, which is why it is here considered at the outset. Rather than ask only what Christ does in the eucharistic action, or how his body and blood are present, these questions are put

Manuscript illumination depicting Christ feeding the five thousand with five barley loaves and two fishes, (Jn. 6.9), by Thoros Roslin, American Gospel Book, 1262.

in the larger context of the mystery of the Church as the Body of Christ. This vision is aided by a retrieval of the early Christian vocabulary of *mystérion* and *sacramentum.* Both terms, one Greek and Eastern, the other Latin and Western, derive from the text of the New Testament where they are used in the original language or in translation, to express the divine counsel and action in bringing about the salvation of humankind through the sending of the Son and the Spirit (e.g. Rom 16.25–26; Eph 2.2–3; 3.9). This MYSTERY originates within the Godhead and is ultimately ineffable, but it is manifested in time in visible and symbolic form, beginning with the history of the salvation of Israel and culminating in the incarnation of the Son and the mysteries of his flesh. If the terms are applied in a particular way to the Church's eucharistic celebration in which it keeps memorial of Jesus Christ, this is because in this celebration the mystery is embodied in ritual form at the heart of the Church.

This means that while the Church lives from the life of Christ and the Spirit that come to it through many channels, it expresses its own life and mystery most aptly and most fully in the celebration of the Eucharist. The Eucharist, in turn, is best appreciated when seen as the Sacrament of the Church, Body of Christ. While the eucharistic action includes proclamation, prayers and diverse rituals, its truth was expressed in early Christian centuries through a focus on that which is most central to its purpose, namely on the eating and drinking with thanksgiving at the common table where is received the gift of the Body and Blood of Christ (*see* SACRAMENTAL THEOLOGY).

Contemporary theology points to a number of implications of this vocabulary of mystery and sacrament. Gathering for the Eucharist is an act of the local Church, wherein all members of the community come together. This embodiment of Christ's mystery is essentially do-

Detail of the pope placing the miraculous Host on the Altar from the "Miracle of the Host" by Paolo Uccello. (©Gianni Dagli Orti/CORBIS)

mestic in the character of its ritual rather than sacerdotal. More than a general relation of Eucharist to Church, it is the relation to the local Church that emerges so that a universal communion in Christ is necessarily related to a communion between such eucharistic Churches.

Seen as a gathering and as the mystery of the local Church, the Eucharist is linked to the fellowship of the Church as lived out in practical detail and especially its *diakonia*, that is to its service of the needy in its midst. It also embraces the Church's appeal to a living apostolic tradition, its testimony to the word of God, the testimony of its martyrs, the communion of the living with the dead who have died in the faith of Christ and often fortified by the *VIATICUM* of the sacrament of his Body and Blood. It is related, too, to its travails and its hopes as its members live their earthly pilgrimage in the hope of a divine consummation.

Today, anthropological and ritual studies serve a further appreciation of the symbolism of the bread and wine which expresses the mystery of its communion in Christ. These studies probe the symbolism of meals among peoples, of sharing a common table, and of the bread and wine which are blessed and shared with an invocation of the divinity. Taking a point of departure in ritual, they also enable theology to relate the mystery of the Eucharist, the turns in its celebration and its meaning of life in Christ, to cultural, social and economic realities, and to the place within change of an evocation of past memories and of a people's foundational myths. Placed within this context, the mystery of Christ's embodiment through sacrament and in the body of his Church, is located within the contours of culture and ongoing history.

Revisiting New Testament Origins

In one way or another, the Church in its liturgy, doctrine and theology has regularly taken the Supper Narrative as found in the Synoptics and Saint Paul to be the foundational narrative for eucharistic celebration, especially because of the memorial command. At times this was considered as though one could work chronologically from those texts to trace the development of the Eucharist in the early Church. The first move to a more circumspect approach was occasioned by the influence on the reading of the Scriptures of a historical critical approach. A more hermeneutical approach has now emerged which is more focused on the plot and meaning of the texts and which considers how the memory of the Last Supper is assimilated into the lived memory of diverse Churches, in diverse cultural and historical times.

From Lord's Supper to Last Supper. Scriptural scholars increasingly pointed out that the story as it stands in the New Testament text was much influenced by the practice of the Lord's Supper. This meant the common meals of remembrance at which the faithful came together and in which Christ's death and resurrection were recalled, inclusive of a remembrance of his Last Supper with his disciples on the eve before he was betrayed. These meals were seen, however, to represent a certain diversity from one Church to another and to fit within a larger compass of meal sharing.

Thus consideration of the scriptural roots of the Eucharist took in a larger compass in order to find the right setting in which to place the Supper Narrative. There is what we know of the practice of early communities in keeping memorial of the Lord as they shared the common loaf and the common cup in his name. There are the accounts of the meals of Jesus with others, during his public ministry and after the resurrection, and of the feeding of the crowds, which show that the actions and words of the Last Supper have their setting within Jesus' own continuing relation to sharing a table and to feeding others. Recently, some writers have also drawn attention to the need to relate the narratives of the table action of Jesus on the night before he was betrayed to the account in John's Gospel of the washing of the feet and the love commandment. This Gospel locates these words and action on that same evening of farewell and presents them as another way of expressing the testimony which Jesus, in showing himself in the guise of a servant, left to his disciples.

The Last Supper. In the middle of this attention to other texts, the efforts to reconstruct the events of the Last Supper have not been wanting. The concern to find an accurate historical reconstruction is grounded in a desire to discern the mind and the will of Jesus since discovering this is thought by some to be necessary to the meaning of the Eucharist.

In reconstructing the action, words and significance of the Last Supper, with its memorial command, the usual approach is to relate what was done there to its Jewish setting, of Passover and of table ritual. In general, the meaning of table ritual comes from knowledge of meal practice with its memorial narratives, its blessing prayer, its invocations of memorial commands, and the symbolism of the food and drink that are shared. More particularly, efforts to show that the meal shared by Jesus with his disciples was a Paschal Seder are numerous, just as are the counter efforts. Much of the difficulty of this question lies in a deeper difficulty, that is, the little that is known in a clear way of the seder at the time of Jesus.

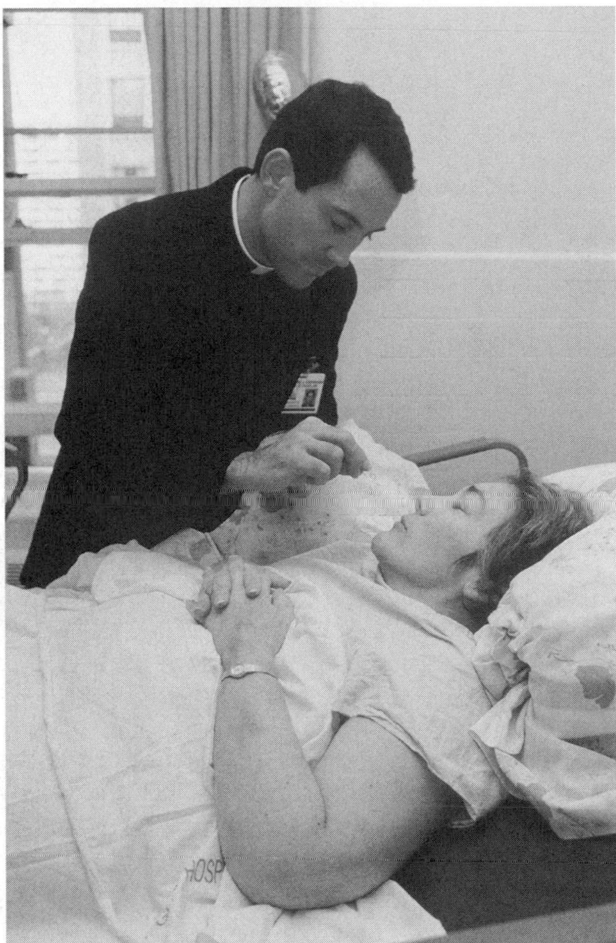

Woman patient receives Communion from priest. (©David H. Wells/CORBIS)

Certainty about such reconstruction, however, is probably impossible. The effort is surmounted by the hermeneutical turn of theology, that is by the realization that the religious significance of the story of the origins of the Church's Eucharist lies in the story itself, not in its historical reconstruction. That is not to say that historical criticism bears no fruit, but this fruit is found in what it shows us of the context for the meaning of the story. Turning to the narrative as narrative, it is clear that the New Testament accounts present the table action as an event which took place at Passover and as a paschal thanksgiving meal which Jesus shares with his disciples in anticipation of his death. They do not allow us to settle the exact order of the meal as Jesus and his followers celebrated it, but they do reveal the reason for the Passover setting. This is meant both to underscore the paschal significance of Jesus' death as evoked in his words and blessing prayer, and to root the Eucharist of the Church in this meal by way of bringing out its memorial and paschal character.

Interior of Buckfast Abbey during Communion services, Devon, England. (©Christopher Cormack/CORBIS)

Memorial command and action. According to one recension of the Supper Narrative, Jesus gave the memorial command at the end of the meal, when he had completed the action with both loaf and cup (Mt 26.26–29). According to another (1 Cor 11.23–26), he gave the command twice, repeating it after each action. There are many examples in Jewish history of feasts kept and meals shared in virtue of a divine command to keep memorial and this provides the background to the memorial command given by Jesus to his disciples. Memorial is done in obedience to God's command, and it is this which gives it its place and power in the life of a community. It is inherent to covenant, a sign of God's fidelity and of the people's fidelity at one and the same time. Finally the actions of table memorial, of which the Paschal Seder is the primary example, combine the gathering of a community that finds identity in the action, narrative, blessing prayer and the ritual action of shared food and drink. Critics rightly point to the departures of Christian Eucharist from Jewish meal services, but this does not derogate from the fact that its true meaning is served by a constant attention to the interaction of the four elements mentioned.

Sacrifice. Attention to Semitic thought-patterns and practices also give us insight into the attachment of sacrificial language both to the death of Jesus and to the celebration kept in his memorial. In giving the bread and cup to his disciples, Jesus is reported to have used abundant sacrificial imagery in speaking of his death, as he had done also at other times. This evokes many strands in the cultic and historical past of Israel. Among the sacrifices recalled are those of the paschal lamb, the sealing of the covenant at Sinai, the levitical peace-offerings and the metaphoric attribution of sacrifice to the suffering of the Servant commemorated in the Servant Songs of the Book of Isaiah. The fact that such language is evoked at a meal also reminds us of the importance of Communion sacrifice and of the presence among the Jewish people at

Jesus' time of those who located true sacrifice in obedience to God's commands, in fellowship and in songs of praise, distancing themselves to some extent in this from the importance given to temple sacrifice. All of this points to the rich and polyvalent significance of the use of sacrificial language which Christians inherited from Jews and which they in turn applied to the death of Jesus, to life lived according to the Gospel, to songs of praise and to their memorial of the death of Jesus at the common table. No narrow definition of sacrifice is possible, but the rich polyvalence of practice and language is pertinent to what is said of Jesus' death and of the memorial supper of Christians.

Eucharistic Mystagogy

It is as difficult to reconstruct the origins and development of the practices of Christian Eucharist as it is to reconstruct the historical facts of the Last Supper. However, we have the written and archeological evidence in hand of Christian celebrations dating over several centuries. We also have evidence in writers such as IRENAEUS OF LYONS, AMBROSE and AUGUSTINE, CYRIL OF JERUSALEM, THEODORE OF MOPSUESTIA and JOHN CHRYSOSTOM that eucharistic theology was developed as a reflection on the words and rites of the liturgical celebration.

Writers today attempt, for their part, either to appropriate this theology or to embark themselves on a reflection that takes its point of departure in rites and texts as these are now known to us from historical research and textual reconstruction. In following this mystagogical line of exposition, authors since early in the 20th century have pointed to the primacy of the sacramental Communion in the body and blood of Christ, noting that the center or focus of the Eucharist is there and not in the words of consecration. In conjunction with this, given the possibilities offered by textual research, liturgical theology includes the analysis of the rich variety of eucharistic prayers from a number of traditions which are now in hand. It is noted that the significance of the prayer comes out only when it is taken as a blessing prayer over food and drink to be shared, and that the meaning of the Communion rite is enriched by knowledge of the eucharistic prayer.

Communion. The *mystérion* or *sacramentum* is located essentially in sacramental Communion, as has been noted above. In other words, the action is of its very nature a communion in the body and blood of Christ, in commemoration of his passion and resurrection and in hope of a part in his now immortal life. The meaning is captured for all time by JUSTIN MARTYR:

> We call this food the Eucharist . . . . Not as common bread or as common drink do we receive these, but just as through the word of God, Jesus Christ, our Saviour, became incarnate and took on flesh and blood for our salvation, so . . . the food over which we give thanks has been given by the prayer of his word, and which nourishes our flesh and blood by assimilation, is both the flesh and blood of that incarnate Jesus (*Apologia* I.66.2: PG 6,428).

Eucharistic Prayer. The text just quoted links the Communion to the ''prayer of his word,'' to the giving of thanks over the food. It is to this that much study and reflection is now given.

The great thanksgiving prayer, also known as the *anaphora*, in its many different forms as known from different Church traditions, provides a rich theology of the Eucharist, as well as of the death and resurrection of Christ, of creation, of salvation history and of the Church. There have been many studies which attempt to reconstruct its early genesis, as well as comparative studies that work within the diversity of texts that have come down to us. The best collection of texts, though by no means complete, remains that of Anton Hänggi and Irmard Pahl, *Prex Eucharistica* as noted below in the bibliography. The most complete analysis of texts is the 1966–68 study of Louis Bouyer, though it has been greatly completed in the intervening years by way of studies of particular texts or traditions.

The genesis of the prayer is still a matter of conjecture, especially in its relation to Jewish blessing prayers. This may be another impossible quest. In the prayers now known to us from early centuries the structure is not always identical or strictly uniform but as a genre the *anaphora* combines praise, thanksgiving and intercession. Though it may not have been there from the very beginning, as traditions were consolidated the Last Supper account, with its memorial command, was placed at the heart of most prayers. Sometimes it is inserted into the prayer's thanksgiving and sometimes, as in the Roman Canon or the Liturgy of Mark, into its intercessions. The reason for the inclusion of the narrative has been clarified through structural studies of the prayer's composition. While Latin theology for a long time held the contrary, it seems that it was introduced into an already constituted prayer. Its purpose is not to give the words of Jesus a power in changing the bread and wine but to highlight the memorial command and the action of Jesus at the Last Supper as that to which eucharistic celebration looks back as foundation. To express this, what is said is that the supper narrative appears in the prayer as an embolism which gives warrant to the eucharistic action by recalling Jesus's memorial command. The sacramental efficacy of the prayer does not, therefore, come from a repetition of Jesus' words but from its inner nature as a memorial prayer.

Textual reconstruction provides only a few texts from the earliest Christian centuries, and it shows them to be very simple in structure, following quite closely the structure of Jewish blessing prayers at meals or in synagogue. Later developments of the prayer habitually included parts that are known as the *anamnesis* and the *epiclesis*, and these are fraught with theological significance. The first is an avowal that in sharing the bread and wine with thanksgiving, the Church is keeping memory of Christ's death, resurrection and ascension, in anticipation of his promised second coming. The second is an invocation that asks for the sending of the Holy Spirit that the prayer and action of the Church may be sacramentally and spiritually efficacious. As insertions into the early simple structure of the blessing prayer, these two sections act as a kind of poetic but theological explicitation of the meaning of Eucharist.

ANAMNESIS and EPICLESIS together relate the mystery commemorated to the time of the community that gathers, but always in eschatological anticipation. The present time, or presence in time, of those gathered is expressed most strongly in its bodily ritual, which refer it to daily time, to historical time and to cosmic time. The prayer allows the time of Christ to enter this time, as it brings it in turn into the time of Christ. Within the ordinary time of a community, the Pasch occurs sacramentally as a kind of irruption, Christ adventing anew to change the very direction of living by pointing it to the anticipation of the fullness of what has been anticipated and promised through the cross and resurrection.

One cannot look only to that section of the prayer called *anamnesis* to see how the mystery of Christ is commemorated. Since it is a later addition to the prayer, it is quite succinct and is usually a brief elenchus of the major moments of Christ's Pasch, such as in the *Anaphora of John Chrysostom* "all the things that were done for us: the cross, the tomb, the resurrection on the third day, the ascension into heaven, the session at the right hand, the second and glorious coming." In the thanksgiving section of the prayers there is a rich variety of metaphors to express the mystery of Christ. For example, the *Anaphora of Basil* recalls the mystery as the mystery of the *kenosis* of the Son, while the *Anaphora of Addai and Mari* posits redemption in the act itself of incarnation for in taking on flesh the Word restored creation, ready though he had to be to endure suffering and death. The prayers of the Alexandrine and Roman liturgies are more explicit in speaking of the sacrifice of Christ, though the sense of this is caught only by evoking the rich variety of Old Testament types, namely the Paschal Lamb, and the sacrifices of Abel, Abraham and Melchizedek. The thanksgiving also provides communities the opportunity to enlarge on what is commemorated by relating the memorial of Christ to the remembrance of creation and God's deeds as recounted in the Old Testament.

The intercessions express the truth of the Communion celebrated, remembering all who in one way or another are gathered into the sacramental commemoration and communion of the mystery of Christ and his Church. The earliest intercession (in the *Didache*) was simply a prayer for the Church that it may be true to its eschatological call. This was expanded to a naming of many persons, or groups of persons, living and dead, all of whom are remembered at the altar because all are one with the Church that makes memorial.

Sacrifice. It is within eucharistic prayers too that a development of sacrificial language is to be found. The Roman Canon is couched primarily in terms of sacrifice, but all texts, east and west, include some sacrificial language. In the first place, the eucharistic prayer is itself a sacrifice of thanksgiving offered by the Church. In the second place, the gifts of bread and wine, the offerings brought for the life of the community and for the poor, are rendered sacrificial by the inclusion of their offering in the prayer. In the third place, through this eucharistic commemoration of the sacrifice of Christ and through the sharing in his body and blood, the Church is taken into the sacrifice of Christ so that in this sacramental action it is shown forth as itself a living sacrifice and a royal priesthood. For these reasons and in these multiple ways, the Eucharist, as such, came to be called a sacrifice. To highlight that the whole action is done as a memorial of Christ's sacrifice and as a participation in it, it was called the sacramental representation of Christ's own sacrifice. As a result it came about in later times that when the Eucharist was called a sacrifice, this was taken to mean that it is the sacrifice of Christ himself, now however sacramentally offered as it was offered once and for all in the flesh upon the Cross. The full significance of such a theology is clear, however, only in the context of the other uses of sacrificial language within the eucharistic prayers of the Church.

As a result of attention to this liturgical history, and as a result of attention to the mystagogical catechesis of the Fathers of the Church, contemporary writers have retrieved the vocabulary of mystery, sacrament, memorial, anamnesis and epiclesis in elaborating theologies that depart from the rigorously definitional vocabulary of scholastic and of manual theologies. This kind of language too has been taken up in ecumenical dialogues as a way of overcoming past controversies within a retrieval of the larger tradition.

Receiving Past Doctrines and Theologies

For a long time, Catholic doctrine and theology were dominated by the concern with presence and sacrifice, while Protestant theology was dominated by a theology of the Word and its proclamation. What these systems meant then, and what they mean now, can be understood only by placing them in their proper historical context, seeing them as integral to the attempt to express eucharistic faith in the midst of controversies and disputes.

Three historical moments in the development of eucharistic thought are here addressed. The first is that of scholastic theology as the systematic resolution of disputes over the truth of Christ's presence in the sacrament that had gone on for some centuries. The second is that of the failed attempt to forge union between East and West at the Council of FLORENCE. The third is that of the 16th-century disputes between Reformers and the Roman Church, with their corresponding formulations of doctrine.

Scholasticism in context. At two different moments of its development, scholastic theology formulated explanations of Christ's eucharistic presence and of the commemoration of Christ's sacrifice that have prevailed in Catholic doctrine and theology until the present. The teaching on Christ's eucharistic presence reached its zenith in the theology and doctrine of transubstantiation of high scholasticism. The teaching on the sacrifice of the Mass owed its final formulation largely to later scholasticism, as is expounded on the practice of the Mass, almost on the eve of the Protestant REFORMATION.

Presence. To understand scholastic thought on Christ's presence in the sacrament, one has to take account of several of its concerns. The first was to meet practical questions such as those that arose from eucharistic devotion and Mass offerings and which had been highlighted by discussions over the manner of Christ's presence. The second was to meet new currents of philosophical thought, especially those marked by the retrieval of the texts of Aristotle. The third was to provide a systematic or scientific presentation as required by the standards of learning at the new universities, and one that would harmonize faith and reason in the presentation of the eucharistic sacrament.

These disputes date back to the ninth-century divergence between the monks RATRAMNUS and PASCHASIUS RADBERTUS and reached some kind of peak in the 11th century-opposition to the ideas of Berengar of Tours. Leaving a presentation of these controversies to others, the issues of scholastic theology may be best understood by seeing what were the questions that were asked when these issues arose.

From the time of Radbertus and Ratramnus, we can list three distinct questions: (a) what do communicants receive under the sign of the bread and wine; (b) how do the faithful participate in the mystery of Christ's passion, in sign and in truth or reality; (c) what is offered in the eucharistic sacrifice. The point that divided Ratramnus and Radbertus had to do with communion in the mystery of Christ's passion and communion in the Church, the body of Christ. The issue on which they divided was that of the relation of the sacrament and of what was received to the historical reality of Jesus. Ratramnus wished to stress that the mystery has to do with the communion between Christ and his members in the Eucharist that followed when his earthly or ''historical'' body had been transformed through the resurrection and now enjoys a glorified state of existence. This body cannot be present on earth as was the body in which he was born, lived and died, but whatever is said about the presence of Christ in the Eucharist has to be related to his communion with the Church as his Body.

Radbertus for his part was also primarily concerned with communion through the Eucharist in the mystery of the passion. In the first place, he said that the passion is present in sign (*in signo*) and in mystery (*in mysterio*) so that all could partake of its fruits and join with Christ in the spiritual offerings through which they imitate it. On the presence of Christ's body, he said that it was present in sign and in reality (*in veritate*). He wished to stress that what is present in the sacrament is indeed the same body in which Christ was born, lived, suffered and died, so that communicants are united with him in the mystery of his passion through communion with this body, in sign and in reality. To stress this reality, he failed to attend to the implications for presence of the glorification and transformation of Christ's body through the resurrection and so to the specific sacramental modality of this presence.

In the debate between BERENGAR and LANFRANC (et alii) there was a twofold practical issue: (a) how do the faithful have communion in the passion of Christ, through the bread and wine, and (b) what reverence is to be shown to the reserved sacrament and how may it be itself the object of cult. This latter question sprang from the emergence, at first within the liturgy and later also outside it, of various devotions surrounding the Sacrament, when it was treated in much the same fashion as the relics of the Cross of Calvary and the relics of saints.

Berengar, citing Augustine, stressed that Christ is present in the Sacrament through sign so that all explanation has to be related to what the sign signifies. However, he posed the question in terms of the disjunction: *aut in signo aut in veritate* (either in sign or in reality), without any third term. He thought that he could use the newly discovered logic of Aristotle to affirm that reality follows appearance, so that what appears is what is present. Hence, in the sacrament of the Eucharist, both the bread and the passion of Christ in which communicants share, are present, the former because of the appearances, the latter because of the sign value, to which Berengar attributed some, unspecified, reality other than subjective.

Whatever Berengar's intentions, he was understood to say that bread and wine are present in reality, and the body and passion of Christ in sign only, even though the sign offers a real communion with Christ in his passion. In response, Lanfranc suggested that some difference can be made between primary substance and secondary substance to explain how bread could appear and serve as sign, not however being present in its primary substance of food, and the body of Christ could be present in its primary substance, but not in its secondary substance of corporeal attributes or appearances.

Apart from these disputes a third element that had to be taken into account by scholastic theology was the inclusion of an article on TRANSUBSTANTIATION in the profession of faith imposed by the Fourth LATERAN COUNCIL (A.D. 1215) on the ALBIGENSIANS (DS 802). What was at issue in the profession was the power of the priest to consecrate bread and wine, changing them into the body and blood of Christ. To define this active agency, the Council used the word *transubstantiate*, which was later taken by scholastic theology to indicate the manner whereby Christ becomes present in the Eucharist and not only the fact of that presence.

In discussing the presence of Christ in the Eucharist, scholastic theologians from PETER LOMBARD onward did not concern themselves much with eucharistic devotions. Their intention was rather to uphold the truth or reality of the gift of Christ's body (and blood if the chalice was still given) in sacramental Communion, as this was expressed in the words "this is my body" and "this is my blood." Their answers to this could of course then be used in relation to his presence when the Sacrament was reserved or used in diverse forms of cult. What needed to be avoided was either a crude physicalism or a reduction of the Sacrament to a sign with referent but no inner reality.

It is important to note that the theories of presence were put in the broader context of the meaning of the Sacrament. By and large, the reason given for the institution of the Sacrament at the Last Supper was twofold: (a) communion with Christ in his passion /transitus /Pasch /sacrifice in faith and loving devotion through the Church's remembrance of the mystery and anticipation of its fulfillment; (b) the communion of the Church as one body in Christ, a communion of faith and charity. In this vein, the fruits of sacramental participation were said to be spiritual nourishment and increase of faith in the passion, communion in love, protection against sin, and the building up of the Church as a community in love.

Explanations of Christ's presence and of the manner in which the bread and wine were changed were couched in ways that showed an appreciation of workings of sign and signification, with due attention given to the reality which appears and is given through the sign. THOMAS AQUINAS was the one who most deeply appropriated the philosophy of Aristotle in explaining the relation between sign, cause and reality, but the concern mentioned is found generally among scholastic writers. What happened, however, was that the larger biblical signification of the paschal background, of the gift of food and drink and of the common table was gradually lost to view. Even though this was still evoked in the *Summa theologiae* of Thomas (III, Q. 73), when he came to the question of meaning and referent he looked solely to the words of Jesus in giving the bread and wine to the apostles (III, Q. 75).

Since these words were taken to point to Christ's body and blood as distinct material realities, what was sought was a philosophical analogy that would allow for the particularity of this unique sacramental presence and the reality of the gift offered to those who approach in faith. In keeping with the use of logic asserted by Berengar, Thomas said that in logic one has to assert a spiritual, not a physical presence, since Christ is physically present in heaven and by all evidence of the senses clearly not physically present in the Eucharist. On the other hand, logic, that is, the meaning of words and sentences in context, is the first and basic indication of what is being offered in this Sacrament, which is truly the body and blood of Christ. The logic of these words points directly to the body and the blood as such, but in virtue of the logic of concomitance, where the body is present, the whole Christ is present, body and blood, soul and divinity. In short, logic indicates a true presence, which is more than presence by sign, but a spiritual presence, which is unlike physical presence. What Aquinas did was to distinguish this from physical presence (*per modum loci*) and from presence purely through recall of the story (*tantum in signo*), neither of which could uphold the truth of the Sacrament. He also refused to accept the theory that affirmed the annihilation of the substance of bread and the substitution under its appearances of the substance of Christ's body, since he found this metaphysically absurd.

The analogy then which he offered in the *Summa theologiae* was that of instant substantial change (exclusion of process by some natural means) and substantial presence. This change is possible because the substance and accident of bread are not totally identifiable and the substantial reality of Christ's body and blood can take on a sacramental and signifying external appearance that is not its own. The negations of this analogy are as important as the affirmations. The analogy has to do with what is present and offered and received in the order of faith, not that of direct physical perception (as though Christ's body and blood in the sacrament could be seen if unveiled) or of reason (as though the object were comprehensible by reason).

DUNS SCOTUS found this explanation philosophically weak and inconsistent with the philosophy of Aristotle to which it appealed. He declared that it is simply impossible to offer an explanation. In line with his thinking of the distinction between God's *potentia absoluta* (what he could do if he so wished) and his *potentia ordinata* (what he did in fact do within his salvific design) he said that God might have brought about the eucharistic change in several ways, some of which would have seemed more reasonable, but that in fact he chose the more mysterious way of transubstantiation. Thus later theology was caught between the positions of Aquinas and Scotus, and it is in its latter form that the doctrine appears to have been known to the 16th-century Reformers.

Eucharistic sacrifice. If the nature of eucharistic sacrifice as an offering emerged as a question distinct from sacramental Communion, this was because of infrequent Communion and of the spreading practice of having priests offer the Mass for specific intentions determined by those who gave stipends to have Masses said. It did not in fact much preoccupy earlier scholastic theologians such as HUGH OF SAINT VICTOR, nor even Thomas Aquinas himself, though he clearly knew of the custom. His theory of sacramental representation in *Summa theologiae* III, q. 83, art. 1, however, could fit the situation, just as it fit the fuller sacramental action in which all took Communion.

In this text, Thomas responded to the question of whether the immolation of Christ is present in the rite of the Mass. He said that the sacrifice of the Cross is made present through representation and through an efficacious communion of its fruits given in reception of the Sacrament. The action in which the sacrifice is represented and the action by which the bread and wine are changed into Christ's body and blood coincide. This is the priest's utterance, speaking in the person of Christ, of the words of Christ over the gifts of bread and wine offered by the faithful. Thus, it is the priest who consummates the sacrifice as it is he, who as instrument of Christ, effects transubstantiation. Through Communion, all present can then benefit from the fruits of the sacrifice represented.

BONAVENTURE seemed more concerned about the offering of sacrifice by priests, both in the *Breviloquium* (VI. 9) and in his writings to members of the Franciscan Order. The latter show that his interest was spurred by the fact that many of them did indeed offer Mass for stipends and with little participation of the faithful. Why should this be important and how does it affect priestly spirituality? In approaching this question, Bonaventure distinguished between sacrifice and sacrament. When Christ becomes present through the signifying words of the priest, his flesh and blood may be offered as a sacrifice of propitiation, and they may be consumed in sacramental reception in a communion of faith, love and devotion.

This sacerdotal explanation of the offering of sacrifice gained great weight and was strongly proposed by Scotus and by Gabriel BIEL. Following Scotus, Biel elaborated on this in discussing the fruits of this offering and their application, since now one had to explain why the priest offered the Mass for specific intentions (*Expositio in Canonem Missae*, lectio 26). As representation of the Sacrifice of the Cross, the Mass is of infinite value but its fruits have to be applied, and this is done through the Mass according to a more restricted measure. In various writers, this was said to have to do with the merits of the Church in its currently living members, the merits of the one who offers the stipend or the merits of the priest. This sort of explanation could even give the impression that the Mass is a distinct offering from that of the Cross, though it is done entirely in dependence on it.

When current theology looks back to scholastic theology, it puts its explanations into historical context. It relates them clearly to the kind of issue that was at stake and to the ways of thinking that were then available. This means that questions about presence and sacrifice may be addressed in new contexts which change the questions and through new ways of thinking, even while respect is shown for what was said at that time. Even in scholastic theology, the question of presence was related to what Christ offered to his disciples and now offers to the Church through the elements of bread and wine, as it was also related to the sign value of offering under the appearances of bread and wine and with the invitation to eat and drink. The question of sacrifice is altered through the retrieval of a patristic perspective, that is, the sacramental representation of Christ's sacrifice is located in the act of giving gift and taking in Communion, not solely in the words spoken by the priest. The issue about the value of the Mass arose from what can only be considered an aberration in eucharistic practice, namely, the celebration of the Eucharist wherein only the priest took Communion.

Catholic and Orthodox Churches: The Council of Florence. The first doctrinal controversy to be taken into account is the formulation of differences between Catholic and Orthodox approaches to the mystery of the Eucharist at the Council of Florence, where attempts at reunion effectively failed (see *Christian Unity: The Council of Florence*, ed. Giuseppe Alberigo. Leuven 1991). As far as sacraments were concerned, the Greeks noted the absence of an *epiclesis* for the Spirit in the Latin eucharistic prayer, as well as the use of leavened bread by the East and of unleavened by the West. The question of purgatory was, likewise, a matter of dispute, and this involved differences over the western practice of offering the Mass for the deceased. In the definition of the synod aimed at union, Greeks and Latins agreed to differ on these practical points, without imposing any uniform procedure.

These points of debate, however, involve the pneumatological and eschatological understanding of the Church and of its sacraments, and are connected with the difference over the inclusion of the *FILIOQUE* in the creed. In confessing the procession of the Spirit from the Father and the Son, Latins took this as the foundation of an ecclesiology which saw a direct relation of the ordained to the Son, both in sacrament and in jurisdiction. At the Mass, the priest was said to speak the words of Christ in Christ's own person (*in persona Christi*), thus effecting consecration and sacrifice. There was no inclusion of the Spirit in the Roman Canon, but if pressed Latin theologians would say that the gift of the Spirit was one of the effects of Mass and sacrament.

In including an invocation for the sending of the Spirit in the Eucharist and in other sacramental prayers, the Eastern Church expressed the belief that Christ operated in the Church, and was united with it, through the action of the Holy Spirit. The Byzantine liturgical commentator, Nicholas CABASILAS, had offered an irenic resolution to the dispute between Greeks and Latins. He attributed the consecration of the bread and wine to the joint action of Word and Holy Spirit, through the words of Christ and the invocation of the Spirit (*A Commentary on the Divine Liturgy*, trans. J. M. Hussey & P. A. McNulty [London 1966] 69–79). The difference however remained. For Latins, the sanctification of gifts and the sanctification of the people are two distinct actions. Greek formulations expressed the view that the people are sanctified with and through the sanctification of their gifts. The invocation of the Spirit, moreover, reflects an ecclesiology which is centered in the Eucharist, where the Spirit is operative, and through which it is formed in the sacrament as the Body of Christ. Communion between Churches could not be attributed, as in the West, to the common submission to the one primatial jurisdiction. It has to come about as a communion between eucharistic communities, so that in some sense each local Church has its own independent, pneumatological and sacramental, center.

The question of eschatology that surfaced in the dispute about making suffrages for the dead is also involved with a sacramental ECCLESIOLOGY. To offer Mass for the dead is to attribute its efficacy for those departed this life to the power of the Church, and to extend ecclesiastical jurisdiction, in some manner, beyond life on this earth. For the East, however, the Communion between the living and the dead has to be seen as sacramental. When the departed are remembered in the Eucharist, it is as members of the communion in the Spirit which binds both the living and the dead, and the sacramental communion of the Body of Christ includes them. If there were disagreements between the Greeks and the Latins over purgatory as a place or state of existence, it had very much to do with this conception of the extension of the authority and power of Church and priesthood.

In recent times, the joint commission for dialogue between the Orthodox and Roman Catholic Churches has issued a statement on "The Mystery of the Church and the Eucharist in the Light of the Mystery of the Holy Trinity" (*The Quest for Unity: Orthodox and Catholics in Dialogue* [Crestwood, N.Y. 1996] 53–64). The document presents the eucharistic celebration as that which makes present the Trinitarian mystery of the Church, or that which draws the Church into the communion between Father, Son and Spirit. It takes due note of the traditional terms of *anamnesis, epiclesis* and *koinonia* to express this active presence of the Trinity in the Eucharist and to show that the Church is nothing other than a visible and earthly participation in their communion. It speaks of how the communion of members in the Church is expressed in the Eucharist. It locates the manifestation of the universal Church in the eucharistic synaxis of the local Church, thus highlighting the importance of the local Church in the mystery of the Eucharist, even while addressing the apostolic communion that needs to exist between local Churches.

Sixteenth Century disputes and teachings. While not wanting to disregard the role of other Churches of the Reformation, attention is given here to the figures of Martin LUTHER and John CALVIN, since it was primarily their teaching that engaged the attention of the Council of Trent.

Martin Luther on the Lord's Supper. In Martin Luther's theology of the Lord's Supper and in his reform of its liturgy one has to keep in mind the fundamental role of doctrine of justification by faith and not by works, and of the importance he gave to preaching and hearing the Word of God. Already in the work, *The Sacrament of the True Body and Blood of Christ and the Brotherhoods* (LW 35, 49–73), he had underlined the link between sign, significance and faith. Fidelity to the sign would require restoration of the chalice to laity. The truth of significance is in the fellowship of communicants and incorporation with Christ and the saints, with serious consequences for the way in which the brotherhoods behave. Faith is no mere assent to doctrine but is found in desire, love and trust, attending to the connection between the gift of Christ's body in the flesh and the spiritual body of which recipients are members.

From early in his career as a reformer, Luther found some eucharistic practices abominable. These were the secret Mass, wherein the words of Christ are not proclaimed to the people, the exclusive use of Latin in the Mass, what he called the Private Mass, or the offering of a Mass at which the faithful do not receive communion. Along with this, there went the denial of the chalice to the laity and the acceptance of stipends.

In his early theological treatise, *Treatise on the New Testament, That Is, the Holy Mass* (LW 35, 94ff), he sketched out his understanding of what he still called the Mass. The Mass as instituted by Christ is a sacrament, not a sacrifice. In the words and signs of Jesus in the Supper Narrative, there is the sign and promise of the forgiveness of sins, to be received in faith, since this alone justifies and not works. This is summed up by Luther in the notion of a testament in which there is testator, heirs, testament, seal or sacrament, bequeathing of blessing of forgiveness of sins, and a command to keep memorial or proclaim the testament.

He sharpened his criticism of Roman practices in *The Babylonian Captivity* (LW 36, 11–57), finding in the Roman Mass as offered by a priest, a typical example of works righteousness. He excoriated the Church for the denial of the chalice to the laity which amounts to a denial of their priesthood and is against the Lord's command. While Luther strongly affirmed the presence of Christ in the sacrament, he found that the doctrine of transubstantiation treats the body and blood of Christ as a thing, destroys the signs of bread and wine and encourages devotions centered on thing, divorced from faith in the promise.

Later in his life, Luther had occasion to take up the cause of real presence against Ulrich ZWINGLI and others, something on which he expanded in the treatise *Against the Fanatics* (LW 36, 335–361), which is a work on the true presence of Christ's body and blood in the Lord's Supper. The terminology he chose to express this presence is that of "in, with and under" the bread and wine. He related it to Christ's Lordship over the Church. To illustrate its manner, meaning and purpose he employs some analogies. He compares it to the presence of an angel in a place, in order to undo any notion of the occupation of a physical location by Christ's body. He also compares it to the mystery of the Incarnation, where the divinity makes itself manifest through the humanity. In this context, he speaks of a communication of properties between the humanity and divinity of Christ through the resurrection, which allows the humanity to share in the divine ubiquity.

John Calvin on the Lord's Supper. For Calvin too, the Roman errors about the Lord's Supper are that the Mass is a sacrifice, the silent recitation of the Mass in which the word of Christ is suppressed, and the teaching on transubstantiation.

As John Calvin explains it in the *Institutes of the Christian Religion*, BK IV.XVII, the doctrine of the Lord's Supper necessarily supposes the doctrine on baptism. In this sacrament, the baptized are made members of God's family, they are promised life, delivered from death and imprinted with the Holy Spirit on their hearts. They are justified by God's free grace and made holy, even though in their works they remain sinners and have nothing of their own on which they can rely. For them, Jesus Christ is the only spiritual nourishment of the soul. This is given in the word of the Gospel and in the visible signs of the bread and the wine added to this word, so that through word and sign the baptized have communion in the body and blood of Jesus Christ. The reason for the institution of the Lord's Supper by Jesus Christ is to seal in the consciences of the baptized the promises of the Gospel, and so to teach reliance in faith on the salvation assured them. In this way, despite their sinfulness they may be led to laud and magnify Christ and strive for the holiness that befits his members.

When he turns to the question as to what is given, Calvin says that it is Jesus Christ, the source and substance of all good, and the fruit and efficacy of his death and passion. The bread is called the body of Christ and the wine his blood, because he is given to those who receive as the substance and foundation of all spiritual benefits. Like Luther, John Calvin rejected the doctrine of transubstantiation as an abomination, but asserted that sacramental Communion is a true communication of Jesus Christ. The bread and wine are visible signs, instruments, representations, of the body and blood which are given, and are signs in no way separable from the reality and substance of what they signify. The body and blood of Jesus Christ, in which he lived on earth, in which he is present in heaven, is made present to the believer by the secret power of the Holy Spirit, who is the bond between Christ and the believer and the bond of the Church which is his Body. Through this gift Jesus Christ operates in the communicant by the Holy Spirit, who is conjoined with the gift and its signs.

The Council of Trent on the Eucharist. When the Council of Trent debated the Eucharist in response to the attacks of the Reformers on Catholic doctrine, it read their own teaching as denials of the truth of the eucharistic sacrament. In the presentation of its own doctrine, it reflected the existing split between offering the Mass and sacramental Communion by dealing with the Sacrifice of the Eucharist and the Sacrament of the Eucharist in two separate decrees. It also failed to resolve the issue of the restoration of the chalice to the laity (and thus of the restoration of the full sacramental sign), but left this as a matter ultimately to be resolved by the pope and the Roman curia. Since the Council was reacting against the Reformers, it also proceeded in large measure by singling out what were considered errors in their writings and by condemning these.

On the subject of Christ's presence, the Council retained and affirmed the standard vocabulary of substantial presence and substantial change, adding that this is aptly called transubstantiation (DS 1636, 1637, 1642). Since the acts of the Council make it clear that the Fathers did not wish to embrace any particular explanation or decide on questions debated between schools of theology, in recent times there is considerable debate as to the exact meaning of this doctrinal teaching, as also about the exact object and meaning of the condemnations pronounced against Reformation teaching.

On a practical level, the Council wished to defend and sustain many of the eucharistic devotions against which the Reformers raged (DS 1643, 1644). However, its explanation of the change that takes place is more closely related to eucharistic celebration than was realized in the manual and catechetical teaching which followed Trent. The exposition of eucharistic faith in the chapters of the decree places the question of Christ's presence in the context of Christ's desire to leave a memorial of his death and spiritual food for his disciples (DS 1638). In interpreting the words of Jesus at the Supper, the offer of his body and blood is related to the blessing (*benedictio*) which he pronounced over the bread and the wine (DS 1632). If this is transposed to the celebration of the Eucharist by the Church, the conciliar teaching shows an awareness of the link between blessing prayer, consecration of the gifts and Communion that was often forgotten in the theology of the post-tridentine era. This is offered as an explanation of the eucharistic gift that is based on words of Jesus at the Last Supper.

In distinguishing between substance and species, preferring this word to accidents, the Council wanted to distinguish between the proper and definitive reality of what results from the priest's blessing or consecration and the way in which the reality presents itself. As made clear in some of the condemnations or anathemas (DS 1651, 1652), for the Council to reduce this to mere spiritual sign or symbolism, or to say that the body of Christ and the bread are present together, would deny both the truth of the sign and the reality offered. While these condemnations do not reflect a careful reading and understanding of Reformation theology, they do interpret the sense of the conciliar decree. Some contemporary theologians think that a clear distinction needs to be made between what is said by the Council and the thought of scholastic theology, despite the similarity in vocabulary. Scholastic theology, especially Thomism, wanted to give an ontological explanation of both presence and change. The explanations of the conciliar decree are intended to be more logical than ontological, that is, assertions that result from the truth value of the words of Jesus. It is to the scriptures that the Council wished ultimately to point for the truth of the mystery, not to medieval theology.

Thus in recent ecumenical dialogue, it has been agreed that the teachings of Luther, Calvin and Trent, despite the acrimony of the time and the mutual condemnations, were three different ways of attempting to safeguard and explain the same fundamental truth. All referred, on the one hand, to the words of Jesus in the New Testament and on the other to the nature of the sacramental sign left to the Church. They all wished to affirm and teach the self-gift of Christ in sacramental Communion, though Trent was also preoccupied about the presence that remains when the celebration ends. Having examined the disputes in historical context to find the reasons for mutual condemnations and for choosing diverse formulas, the partners in the dialogue between Catholics and Lutherans summarizes what could now be said to be the common teaching of the Churches on the presence of Christ: The exalted Lord is present in the Lord's Supper, in the body and blood he gave, with his divinity and his humanity, through the word of promise in the meal gifts of bread and wine, in the power of the Holy Spirit, for reception by the congregation (*Condemnations of the Reformation Era*, 115). Beyond this common teaching, differences of explanation still remain but they are not antithetically opposed to one another as was supposed in the sixteenth century.

When the Council of Trent formulated its doctrine on the Sacrifice of the Mass, it had in mind both the defense of the offering of the Mass by priests for the living and the dead and a statement of teaching that would not fall prey to the Protestant objection that this derogates from the once and for all sufficiency of the sacrifice of the Cross. Hence its main doctrinal proposition is that the sacrifice of the Mass is the memorial and representation of the sacrifice of the Cross, in which priest, victim and offering are the same, and only the sacramental manner of offering different from the bloody offering of Calvary (DS 1739).

It also repeated what was then the standard teaching, that the offering of the Mass by the priest is a sacrifice of propitiation and no mere commemoration (DS 1753), and that this serves as one mode of applying the merits of Christ on the Cross to the living and the dead (DS 1743). This was intended to affirm the value of the offering by the priest, even if no faithful received Communion (DS 1747). The Fathers of the Council, however, chose not to take any position on how this application was effected or on the measure of the value attached to the offering. In short, this is a clear case of wanting to defend a practice without offering much doctrinal explanation of how it operates. As a premise to its treatment of the private Mass, the Council did say that the best manner in which the faithful may receive the fruits of the Eucharist is through sacramental Communion. Nonetheless, its teaching distinguishes between two ways of benefiting from celebration of the memorial of Christ's passion. One is by sacramental Communion, the other by the application of the merits of his passion through the offering made by the priest.

Contemporary readings. In contemporary readings of Trent on sacrifice, Catholic theologians note that its teaching was historically conditioned, both by the liturgical practices of the time and by the defensive attitude it took against the accusations of the Reformers. They see the need to bring sacrifice and sacrament closer together in practice and in theology, recognizing that the ordinary mode of participating in the sacramental mystery is through communion in the body and blood of Christ. The separation of the doctrine of the Eucharist into two decrees has to be overcome. In doing this, it is to be noted that the Council itself took the memorial character of the Eucharist as its starting-point in both decrees and that in both decrees it made some link between eucharistic blessing, offering, sacramental change and communion. In this it was faithful to that fuller eucharistic tradition into which contemporary theology now needs to place the conciliar teaching on the specific points that were its dominant concern.

Ecumenically, it is recognized that liturgical reform has gone a long way in bringing Churches together in their practice and in their eucharistic faith. A liturgical celebration in which proclamation of the word, the prayer of thanksgiving and sacramental Communion by all, have due place provides a new foundation for doctrinal and theological explanation. Doctrinally, to find a common stance, appeal is made to the ideas of memorial, representation and sacramental sacrifice. As it has been put by one agreed statement, ''it has been found possible to state in common our believing conviction about the uniqueness and full sufficiency of Jesus Christ's sacrifice on the cross, as well as the bearing and scope of the *anamnesis* in the eucharistic celebration of the church'' (*The Condemnations of the Reformation Era*, 114). For its part, at the head of its treatment of the sacrament of the Eucharist, *The Catechism of the Catholic Church* chose to place this citation of art. 47 from the *Constitution on the Liturgy* of the Second VATICAN COUNCIL:

> At the Last Supper, on the night he was betrayed, our Saviour instituted the Eucharistic sacrifice of his Body and Blood. This he did in order to perpetuate the sacrifice of the cross throughout the ages until he should come again, and so to entrust to his beloved Spouse, the Church, a memorial of his death and resurrection: a sacrament of love, a sign of unity, a bond of charity, a Paschal banquet in which Christ is consumed, the mind is filled with grace and a pledge of future glory is given to us.

Apart from finding a language on sacrifice that meets with agreement, giving priority to the gift offered by the Father is another way of stating a point of convergence on Christ's presence, one that helps to establish the connection between sacrifice and presence. As stated in the Faith and Order paper no. 111 of the WORLD COUNCIL OF CHURCHES, ''the Eucharist is essentially the sacrament of the gift which God makes to us in Christ through the power of the Holy Spirit''(*Baptism, Eucharist and Ministry*. Geneva: World Council of Churches, 1982, 10).

Past doctrines and theological systems are explained and appropriated into contemporary doctrine and theology in three ways. First, their historical setting is recognized, even as the questions raised are accepted as matters of continued importance. Second, they are read in a new context, one that is in great part constituted by liturgical reforms that bring Churches closer to the early tradition of eucharistic celebration, so that all doctrinal and theological explanation may be related to this. Third, a closer reading of scriptural foundations and patristic teaching offers a new point of departure for critically receiving the formulations and approaches of later eras.

Contemporary Trends in Catholic Theology

Much of Catholic writing on the Eucharist in recent years has to do with revisiting scriptural origins and revisiting the past, as this has been presented here. There has also been a kind of modern liturgical mystagogy, drawing on insights from studies of symbol, ritual, language and culture. There is, however, some move towards a new catechetical and theological synthesis and there have been some important contributions from systematic theologians, of which two will be mentioned here, namely Karl Rahner and Hans Urs von Balthasar, as those who have had the greatest impact on theological thinking about the Eucharist.

As already said, a fundamental principle is that the Eucharist is the Sacrament of the Body of Christ, head and members. What needs to be explained is the communion of Christ with his Church through the celebration of Eucharist in which all take part. The concept of memorial underpins much of the writing about the Eucharist. This seems to be warranted by Scripture, Liturgy and patristics, and it has also proved effective in finding the central point of agreement between Churches of different traditions. With the turn to memorial, the role of the Spirit in the eucharistic liturgy is also emphasized, for it is the gift of the Spirit that makes memorial possible. When it comes to explanation, however, there are diverse ways of understanding what memorial means.

The Second Vatican Council chose to expand on this by attending to the diverse ways in which Christ is present in the liturgy (SC 7), drawing the Church into his mystery, and some theologians have followed this line of thought. Some have followed the orientation of Odo Casel's reading of the patristic and liturgical tradition, by which he speaks of the making present of the Paschal Mystery in the assembly (*Das Mysteriengedächtnis der Messliturgie im Lichte der Tradition* [Münster 1926). Amending this somewhat by reason of a look at Semitic sources and the relation of the Jewish people to the first Pasch, some (e.g. Cesare Giraudo, *Eucaristia per la chiesa*) prefer to speak of the Church's being rendered present to the past event of Christ's *transitus* or passage. There are also those (e.g. Edward Kilmartin, *The Eucharist in the West*) who attribute the continuing efficacy of Christ's Pasch in the Eucharist to the operation of the Holy Spirit, which draws the faithful into the offering of Christ's sacrifice.

The contribution of Karl RAHNER to eucharistic theology remains of importance. In the first place, he noted that all reflection on the Eucharist must derive from the conjunction in one celebration of proclamation of the Word, thanksgiving blessing and eucharistic gift. To this celebration he attributed the notion of event, seeing in it the event of the grace of Christ's Pasch and of God's self-communication in the Church. To explain this event, he used his theory of symbolic causality. Symbolic interaction is the key to human becoming, as it is the key to the presence of one to another. Indeed, the two converge, for one person in becoming present to another, or indeed to a community and a tradition, becomes in the process more fully oneself. By analogy, God can be said to be present to the world through the Word Incarnate and through the symbols by which memorial is kept of his incarnate mysteries. By their own participation in this symbolic interaction, responding to the free and committed offer of the gift of the divine self, the members of the Church become present to God, to each other and to the world. Traditions on eucharistic sacrifice and presence are readily appropriated into this symbolic and dynamic way of looking at the eucharistic memorial.

Building on this, others (see David Power, *The Eucharistic Mystery*) integrate the role of the paschal narrative, or of the supper narrative more fully. These narratives, with the cross and the death of Christ at their center, disrupt the habitual mythical and metaphysical thinking of peoples. They call for a new relation to the possibilities of being and time, a new perspective on the future, and a new way of naming the God who effaces the divine self in the *kenotic* gift of the Son and the operation of the Spirit which enables the Church to keep memorial of this *kenosis*.

Hans Urs von BALTHASAR eschews the language of symbolic causality as an excessive attention to the human and the building of divine analogies on human concepts. Theological language has to find its point of departure in the Cross of Christ and to develop an understanding of the Eucharist that relates to the drama of divine *kenosis*. Eucharistic theology needs to concentrate on the event of spousal encounter between Christ and the Church in the act of the meal, where the sacrament is eaten and God is thanked. This is constitutive of the Church as his Body and constitutive of the Church's relation to the world.

He traces the relation of the Church to Christ as a share in his relation to the Father which is expressed in *eucharistia* and which itself originates within the life of the trinity of persons.

Within their eternal relationship, the Son wishes to be nothing but the icon of the Father. The Son is empty of anything that is peculiar to himself outside his relationship to the Father, of anything that is not reflective of the image of the Father. In his incarnate being and through the Cross, the Son continues to live and to act in this kenotic and iconic relation to the Father. By this he enters into the drama of a sinful world offered redemption by God and it is by such a process that he enters with his humanity into the eternal relation of Father and Son. He left the memorial of this Pasch to the Church so that the Church's eucharistic action could be its participation, as spouse of Christ, in the eternal movement of the Son to the Father as it was lived out in the drama of his presence in the world. It is by this same token, that the Eucharist is the sacrament of Communion, of the communion of the Church in the divine communion of persons. Eucharistic sacrifice is then seen as the Church's entry, by Christ's gift, into the divine drama of *kenosis*, lived out in the world. Transubstantiation, better called substantial conversion, stands for the taking of a form in the present of Christ's engagement with God and with the world, through his spousal communion with his Church. To affirm that Christ is eucharistically present to his Church is to advert to the iconic form in which he offers himself and draws the Church to himself, in his relation to the Father.

Conclusion. The purpose of this entry has been to give an overview of the processes of contemporary Catholic theology in studying and presenting the mystery of the Eucharist. The importance of a renewal of biblical, patristic and liturgical studies was first noted, with some indication of how these have contributed to the celebration and the understanding of the Eucharist. Since Catholic theology depended for several centuries, and up to the present, on scholastic theology and on the teachings of the Council of Trent, it was then shown how these are now being read and integrated into new approaches that are more sensitive to ecumenical dialogue and to contemporary human life. In addition, some information was given about how these approaches affect systematic theology and a brief summary was offered of the contribution of two leading writers of the 20th century.

Bibliography: L. BOUYER, *Eucharist: Theology and Spirituality of the Eucharistic Prayer* (Notre Dame and London 1968). E. DUMOUTET, *Le Christ selon le chair et la vie liturgique au moyen-âge* (Paris 1932). B. A. GERRISH, *Grace and Gratitude: The Eucharistic Theology of John Calvin* (Minneapolis 1993). C. GIRAUDO, *Eucaristia per la chiesa: prospettive teologiche sull'eucaristia a partire della ''lex orandi''* (Rome & Brescia 1986). E. J. KILMARTIN, *The Eucharist in the West: History and Theology* (Collegeville 1998). E. LA VERDIERE, *The Eucharist in the New Testament and the Early Church* (Collegeville 1996). K. LEHMANN, & W. PANNENBERG, eds. *The Condemnations of the Reformation Era: Do They Still Divide?* (Minneapolis 1990). X. LÉON-DUFOUR, *Sharing the Eucharistic Bread: The Witness of the New Testament* (New York/Mahwah 1982). H. R. MCADOO and K. STEVENSON, *The Mystery of the Eucharist in the Anglican Tradition* (Norwich 1995). P. MCPARTLAN, *The Eucharist Makes the Church: Henri de Lubac and John Zizioulas in Dialogue* (Edinburgh 1993). G. MACY, *The Banquet's Wisdom: A Short History of the Theologies of the Lord's Supper* (New York/Mahwah 1992). E. MAZZA, *La Celebrazione eucaristica. Genesi del rito e sviluppo dell'interpretazione* (Milano 1996). H. B. MEYER, *Eucharistie. Gottesdienst der Kirche IV* (Regensburg 1989). N. MITCHELL, *Cult and Controversy: The Worship of the Eucharist outside Mass* (New York 1982). D. N. POWER, *The Eucharistic Mystery: Revitalizing the Tradition* (New York 1992). K. RAHNER, *Theological Investigations* IV (New York 1984). E. SCHILLEBEECKX, *The Eucharist* (New York 1968). A. SCHMEMANN, *The Eucharist: Sacrament of the Kingdom* (Crestwood, New York 1988). H. U. VON BALTHASAR, ''The Mass: A Sacrifice of the Church?'' In *Explorations in Theology*, v. III (San Francisco 1993), 185–243. H. WYBREW, *The Orthodox Liturgy: The Development of the Eucharistic Liturgy in the Byzantine Rite* (New York 1990).

[D. N. POWER]

EUCHARIST OUTSIDE MASS, WORSHIP OF THE

On the feast of Corpus Christi, June 21, 1973, the Congregation of Divine Worship revised the regulations regarding ''Holy Communion and Worship of the Eucharist Outside Mass'' (HCWE). Two decades later (in 1994), certain aspects of the teaching found in HCWE were reiterated in the Catechism of the Catholic Church (CCC). ''Because Christ himself is present in the sacrament of the altar, he is to be honored with the worship of adoration. 'To visit the Blessed Sacrament is . . . a proof of gratitude, an expression of love, and a duty of adoration toward Christ our Lord''' (Paul VI, *Mysterium Fidei* 66)'' (CCC 1418). This article focuses upon the principles and practices described in both these documents.

Hand tooled metal Communion bowl, 10th Century, Museum of Fine Arts, Tbilisi, Russia. (©Dean Conger/Corbis)

Principles. ''Holy Communion and Worship of the Eucharist Outside Mass'' (79, 81) reaffirms the Church's teaching that the liturgical assembly's celebration of Mass is the ''source and culmination of the whole Christian life,'' and that ''prayer before Christ the Lord sacramentally present'' in the reserved Sacrament ''extends the union with Christ which the faithful have reached in Communion.'' Thus the liturgical celebration of Mass is both ''the origin and the goal of the worship which is shown to the Eucharist outside Mass'' (HCWE 2). Thus the altar, not the tabernacle, is the center of Christian worship. But because the Eucharist is reserved, it is fitting and proper that it be adored. The legislation of the Church has always been clear on this point. Participation in the Mass has always been fostered, while exposition of the reserved Eucharist is limited to extraordinary occasions.

The primary and original reason for reservation of the Eucharist is, of course, to provide Communion for the sick and dying (VIATICUM). The secondary reasons are to provide Communion outside Mass and to permit adoration of Christ in the reserved Sacrament. Following the lead of Vatican Council II (*Sacrosanctum Concilium,* 7), HCWE affirms the many presences of Christ in his Church. ''First, he is present in the very assembly of the faithful, gathered together in his name; next he is present in his word, when the Scriptures are read in the Church and explained; then in the person of the minister; finally and above all, in the eucharistic Sacrament'' (HCWE 6). Among these many presences of Christ, the eucharistic presence is distinctive and preeminent: ''In a way that is completely unique, the whole and entire Christ, God and man, is substantially and permanently present in the Sacrament'' (HCWE 6). For this reason, ''it is highly recommended that the place [for the reservation of the Eucharist] be suitable . . . for private adoration and prayer, so that the faithful may easily, fruitfully, and constantly honor the Lord through personal worship'' (HCWE 9). Finally, HCWE notes that because the celebration of Mass is source and summit of the Church's activity, ''Eucharistic devotions should be in harmony with the Sacred Liturgy, take their origin from the Liturgy, and lead people back to the Liturgy'' (HCWE 79).

In light of these principles, HCWE provides liturgical forms for Holy Communion outside Mass (Chapter I), for Communion of the sick and dying (Chapter II), and for worship of the Eucharist outside Mass (Chapter III). Among the latter are exposition and benediction of the Blessed Sacrament, eucharistic processions, and eucharistic congresses.

Exposition and Benediction. ''Exposition of the Holy Eucharist, either in the ciborium or in the monstrance, is intended to acknowledge Christ's marvelous presence in the Sacrament'' (HCWE 82). In light of the principle found in HCWE 79, however, ''exposition must clearly express the cult of the Blessed Sacrament in its relationship to the Mass'' (HCWE 82). For that reason, ''Mass is prohibited in the body of the church'' while exposition is taking place (HCWE 83). ''If exposition of the Blessed Sacrament is extended for an entire day or over several days, it is to be interrupted during the celebration of Mass'' (HCWE 83). During the exposition, customary signs of reverence are used (lighted candles, incense) and ''there should be prayers, songs, and readings . . . To encourage a prayerful spirit, there should be readings from Scripture with a homily or brief exhoration'' (HCWE 85; 93–94). Silence, song, and praying parts of the Liturgy of the Hours are also appropriate (HCWE 95–96).

Exposition ordinarily concludes with benediction and reposition of the Sacrament in the tabernacle (HCWE 97–100); however, ''exposition which is held exclusively for the giving of benediction is prohibited''(HCWE 89). Historically, benediction probably developed from the showing of the Host at the various stations of the Corpus Christi procession. The first known example of Benediction similar to that common today was at Hildesheim in the fifteenth century. It was a response to the growing desire on the part of the faithful to look upon the Host, a desire enhanced by the earlier theological disputes over transubstantiation and the exact moment of consecration. Concurrent with the strengthening of this desire was the gradual introduction of an evening service for the faithful centered around the Salve Regina, which had been composed in the eleventh century. By 1221 it had been joined to Compline in the Dominican monastery in Bologna. As early as 1250, it was part of a popular evening devotion in France. During the next two or three centuries the two devotions, one to the Blessed Mother, the other to the Blessed Sacrament, were combined, whence Benediction is still known in France as Le Salut.

The rite of benediction given in HCWE is simple; it consists of a eucharistic hymn or song, incensation (if the Sacrament is exposed in a monstrance), a brief period of silence, prayer, a blessing of the people with the monstrance (or ciborium) in the form of a cross (the priest or deacon wearing a humeral veil), reposition of the Sacrament, and concluding acclamation (HCWE 97–100).

Processions. It is for the local ordinary to judge whether eucharistic processions are opportune in today's circumstances (HCWE 101). Some processions, such as the annual procession on the feast of Corpus Christi, have ''special importance and meaning for the pastoral life of the parish or city,'' and hence it is ''desirable to continue this procession, in accordance with the law, when today's circumstances permit and when it can truly be a sign of common faith and adoration''(HCWE 102). Such processions ''should be arranged in accordance with local customs'' (HCWE 104). The priest who carries the Sacrament in procession may wear a chasuble (if Mass has just been celebrated) or cope (HCWE 105). Again, ''in accordance with local customs,'' lights and incense accompany the Blessed Sacrament, which is carried under a canopy (HCWE 106). At the end of the procession, benediction is given and the Sacrament is reposed (HCWE 108).

Congresses. Finally, HCWE speaks of ''eucharistic congresses [which] have been introduced into the life of the Church in recent years as a special manifestation of eucharistic worship''(HCWE 109). These large assemblies may be international, national, regional, or local. Their purpose is to deepen understanding of, and devotion to, the Eucharist by gathering ''an individual local church,'' or ''the entire local church,'' or even all the churches ''of a single region or nation or even of the entire world'' for the sake of manifesting ''some aspect of the eucharistic mystery'' and expressing through public worship ''the bond of charity and unity''(HCWE 109). ''Specialists in theological, biblical, liturgical, pastoral, and humane studies'' are to be consulted beforehand concerning the place, theme, and program of the congress (HCWE 110). HCWE also encourages sound catechesis and ''more active participation in the Liturgy'' as appropriate preludes to a congress (HCWE 111). Criteria for celebrating the congress are also provided (HCWE 112). Such gatherings were especially popular in Catholic dioceses during the Jubilee Year 2000.

Historically, the origins of eucharistic congresses can be traced back to the work of Marie Marthe Emilia Tamisier (d. 1910), who first encouraged pilgrimages to places in her native France where eucharistic miracles were commemorated: Avignon, Ars, Douai, Paris, and Paray-le-Monial. The experience of seeing about 60 members of the French Parliament kneel in Margaret Mary Alacoque's chapel at Paray-le-Monial and pledge themselves to resist the secularist policies of the French government, convinced Tamisier of the potential that could be unleashed if Christians were brought together to profess their faith in the Eucharist and in the teachings of Christ. Thus, at the outset there was a socio-political dimension to such gatherings, especially in places where conflict between Church and culture was acute.

A Pontifical Committee for International Eucharistic Congresses was instituted in 1879 by Pope Leo XIII; more than a century later (1986), it was established with new statutes by Pope John Paul II. The first attempts at organizing a eucharistic congress in Europe failed, but one was eventually held at the University of Lille in June of 1881 with 800 people attending from Belgium, England, Spain, France, Holland, and Switzerland. Numerous such meetings followed, and it became customary for the pope ro honor the international eucharistic congress by the presence of a *legate a latere.* After the congress at Lourdes in 1914, meetings were interrupted by World War I. At the congress in Rome, 1922, Pope Pius XI decreed that future meetings be held every two years. From then until World War II regular international congresses were held, including meetings in Africa, South America, Australia, and the Philippines. International congresses were resumed in 1952, and they have continued (at irregular intervals) until the present time.

See Also: EUCHARISTIC CONGRESSES.

Bibliography: N. MITCHELL, *Cult and Controversy: The Worship of the Eucharist Outside Mass* (New York 1982). Pontifical Committee for International Eucharistic Congresses, *I Congressi Eucaristici Internazionali per una Nuova Evangelizzaione* (Città del Vaticano 1991).

[N. D. MITCHELL]

EUCHARISTIC CONGRESSES

These are large assemblies that may be international, national, regional, or local, which seek to deepen understanding of, and devotion to, the eucharist by gathering ''an individual local church,'' or ''the entire local church,'' or even all the churches ''of a single region or nation or even of the entire world'' for the sake of manifesting ''some aspect of the eucharistic mystery'' and expressing through public worship ''the bond of charity and unity'' (HCWE 109).

Historically, the origins of eucharistic congresses can be traced back to the work of Marie Marthe Emilia Tamisier (d. 1910), who first encouraged pilgrimages to places in her native France where Eucharistic miracles were commemorated: Avignon, Ars, Douai, Paris, and Paray-le-Monial. The experience of seeing about 60 members of the French Parliament kneel in Margaret Mary Alacoque's chapel at Paray-le-Monial and pledge themselves to resist the secularist policies of the French government convinced Tamisier of the potential that could be unleashed if Christians were brought together to profess their faith in the Eucharist and in the teachings of Christ. Thus, at the outset there was a sociopolitical dimension to such gatherings, especially in places where conflict between Church and culture was acute.

A Pontifical Committee for International Eucharistic Congresses was instituted in 1879 by Pope Leo XIII. More than a century later (1986), it was established with new statutes by Pope John Paul II. The first attempts at organizing a eucharistic congress in Europe failed, but one was eventually held at the University of Lille in June of 1881 with 800 people attending from Belgium, England, Spain, France, Holland, and Switzerland. Numerous such meetings followed, and it became customary for the pope to honor the international Eucharistic congress by the presence of a legate, *a latere*. After the congress at Lourdes in 1914 meetings were interrupted by World War I. At the congress in Rome, 1922, Pope Pius XI decreed that future meetings be held every two years. From then until World War II regular international congresses were held including meetings in Africa, South America, Australia, and the Philippines. International congresses were resumed in 1952, and have continued (at irregular intervals) until the present time.

A list of international Eucharistic congresses follows: (1) Lille, 1881; (2) Avignon, 1882; (3) Liège, 1883;

Cardinal Rugambua (left) and Cardinal Browne during the 1963 Eucharistic Congress, 'Our Lady' Cathedral, Munich, Germany. (© David Lees/CORBIS)

(4) Fribourg, 1885; (5) Toulouse, 1886; (6) Paris, 1888; (7) Antwerp, 1890; (8) Jerusalem, 1893; (9) Reims, 1894; (10) Paray-le-Monial, 1897; (11) Brussels, 1898; (12) Lourdes, 1899; (13) Angers, 1901; (14) Namur, 1902; (15) Angouleme, 1904; (16) Rome, 1905; (17) Tournai, 1906; (18) Metz, 1907; (19) London, 1908; (20) Cologne, 1909; (21) Montreal, 1910; (22) Madrid, 1911; (23) Vienna, 1912; (24) Malta, 1913; (25) Lourdes, 1914; (26) Rome, 1922; (27) Amsterdam, 1924; (28) Chicago, 1926; (29) Sydney, 1928; (30) Carthage, 1930; (31) Dublin, 1932; (32) Buenos Aires, 1934; (33) Manilla, 1937; (34) Budapest, 1938; (35) Barcelona, 1952; (36) Rio de Janeiro, 1955; (37) Munich, 1960; (38) Bombay, 1964; (39) Bogata, 1968; (40) Melbourne, 1973; (41) Philadelphia, 1976; (42) Lourdes, 1981; (43) Nairobi, 1985; (44) Seoul, 1989; (45) Seville, 1993; (46) Wroclaw, Poland, 1997; (47) Rome, 2000.

Bibliography: N. MITCHELL, *Cult and Controversy: The Worship of the Eucharist outside Mass* (New York 1982). Pontifical Committee for International Eucharistic Congresses, *I Congressi Eucaristici Internazionali per una Nuova Evangelizzaione* (Vatican City 1991).

[N. MITCHELL]

EUCHARISTIC DEVOTION

As Herbert Thurston noted a century ago, a devotional cult of the eucharist outside the liturgy became possible in the Western Church only after the ceremonial reservation of the sacrament developed. While the custom of reserving the sacrament to communicate the sick, the dying, or those absent from the Sunday assembly is itself very ancient (see, e.g., Justin Martyr, First Apology, 65.5), special signs of external adoration (e.g., genuflection, lighted candles) are not. From the first millennium of Church history, there is no reliable evidence for reserving the eucharist so the faithful could ''visit'' it, pray in its presence, or honor it with special marks of devotion. And to this day, the Greek Church knows no devotional cult of the eucharist outside the liturgy.

Visits to the Blessed Sacrament. For more than a millennium there was no uniform manner or place of eucharistic reservation. Sometimes Christians took the sacrament home for communion during the week (*Apostolic Tradition*, 36–38); sometimes clergy reserved it (without ceremony) in the sacristy. Before the 12th century any ritual or private honor to the Eucharist outside Mass was virtually impossible because there were no tabernacles visible in the churches. The Sacrament was kept privately for emergencies, as the Holy Oils are often kept today. But by the beginning of the 13th century devotions toward the reserved eucharist were emerging. The English Ancren Riwle (ca. 1200) tells anchoresses to kneel down each morning and salute the sacrament ''which is over the high altar'' with a prayer that begins, ''Hail, source of our creation!'' Such devotional attention to the eucharist (reserved in church) reflects both a growing consciousness of the important role of Christ's human nature in salvation and a desire by the faithful to see and adore the consecrated Host. Still, there remained considerable variation in the manner of reservation. Vessels of precious metal in the form of a tower or dove (suspended by a cord over the church's principal altar) were common in England and France, while in Germany a ''sacrament house'' was sometimes constructed on the north side of the church.

From the 12th and 13th centuries onward, there is mounting evidence that visits to the Blessed Sacrament were made to honor Christ or to pray for special favors. Thomas Becket told King Henry II that he prayed for him ''before the Majesty of the Body of Christ.'' At the end of the 14th century private devotion at the place of reservation was common among lay Christians, monks, and religious women. Luther and other reformers objected to this adoration. The Council of TRENT in its Decree on the Holy Eucharist, 1551, defended the Feast of Corpus Christi and, in general, the honor and adoration given to the Blessed Sacrament. In the next two centuries there appeared many devotional books advocating visits to the place of reservation, notably St. ALPHONSUS LIGOURI's *Visits to the Blessed Sacrament*, which has gone through more than 2000 editions in 39 languages since 1745.

Nocturnal and Perpetual Adoration. The devotional practice (perpetual or intermittent) of adoring Christ present in the eucharist thus expanded rapidly during medieval and early modern times. Isolated cases of nocturnal adoration had already appeared in the early 13th century. In 1226 the Holy See approved adoration of the Eucharist, veiled on the altar at Avignon, by request of Louis VII to give thanks for his victory over the Albigenses. Certain practices dating back to the 13th and 14th centuries such as watching before the tomb during the last three days of Holy Week, eucharistic processions, and the exposition of the Host may also have entailed nocturnal adoration. By 1393, a branch of Benedictines devoted explicitly to eucharistic adoration had been established. Yet some notable saints hardly mention eucharistic devotion at all. When, for example, in his *Spiritual Exercises*, St. IGNATIUS LOYOLA spoke of God's abiding presence in creation, he said not a word about the reserved Sacrament. During the same historical period, however, Philip II of Spain (1527–98) established a eucharistic ''vigil'' at the Escorial, so that religious, in successive pairs, could pray night and day at the place of reservation.

In time, eucharistic associations emerged whose primary purpose was to promote frequent or perpetual adoration of the reserved Sacrament. In 1810 Giacomo Sinibaldi, Canon of Santa Maria in Via Lata, organized what was to become the Nocturnal Adoration Society, to pay homage to Christ during the night in the various church in which Forty Hours were being held successively. Carmelite Herman Cohen founded a similar society in Paris in 1848. Canonically approved as a pious union in 1851 and raised to the title of archconfraternity in 1858, the Nocturnal Adoration Society promoted the practice of nocturnal adoration through the year and independently of the Forty Hours devotion. In Brussels a movement started in 1848. Under the inspiration of Anna de Meeus became the Archconfraternity of Perpetual Adoration of the Blessed Saccrament and the Work for Need Churches. From this society in 1872 came the Congregation of Perpetual Adorers. At Marseilles in 1859 Peter Julian Eymard established the People's Eucharistic League so that laypeople might share the Eucharistic spirit and work of the religious congregation he had founded. Members promised to make at least one hour of eucharistic adoration each month. The Priests' League for Adoration of the Blessed Sacrament, founded in 1879, was approved at Rome in 1887. In 1950, a society for Perpetual Adoration of the Blessed Sacrament for diocesan priests was canonically erected with headquarters at Rome.

The Forty Hours Devotion. That having been said, the early-modern emphasis on uninterrupted worship of the Blessed Sacrament (''perpetual adoration'')—preferably with the Host solemnly exposed on the altar arose, most probably, in connection with the Forty Hours devotion, a continuous period of public prayer ''before the face of the Lord'' recommended by Pope Clement VII in *Graves et diuturnae* (1592). ''Forty Hours'' seems to have originated in Milan (ca. 1527), where the devotion (involving Masses, eucharistic exposition, processions, litanies and special prayers) rotated through the city's numerous churches, creating a year-round cycle of prayer and supplication. In 1731, Clement XII republished, in Italian, the instructions for Forty Hours ceremonies to be followed as issued two decades earlier by Clement XI. While this ''Clementine Instruction'' was of obligation only in Rome, its use elsewhere was encouraged.

Forty Hours remained popular until the late twentieth century. By decree of June 21, 1973, the Congregation for Divine Worship issued a revised ritual, ''Holy Communion and Worship of the Eucharist Outside Mass

[HCWE].'' HCWE does not specifically mention the Forty Hours Devotion. Instead, it simply recommends with the local Ordinary's consent and when suitable numbers of people will be present, in churches where the Eucharist is regularly reserved solemn exposition of the Blessed Sacrament once a year for an extended, even if not strictly continuous period of time. ''This kind of exposition,'' says HCWE 82, ''must clearly express the cult of the blessed sacrament in its relationship to the Mass. The plan of the exposition should carefully avoid anything which might somehow obscure the principal desire of Christ in instituting the eucharist, namely, to be with us as food, medicine, and comfort.'' When continuous exposition is not possible because of too few worshipers, the Blessed Sacrament may be replaced in the tabernacle during the scheduled periods of adoration, but no more often than twice each day (HCWE, 88). The Host should be consecrated in the Mass which immediately precedes the exposition and after Communion placed in the monstrance upon the altar. Mass ends with the prayer after Communion, and the concluding rites are omitted. The priest then may locate the Blessed Sacrament on an elevated, but not too lofty or distant throne, and incense it (HCWE 93–94). Prayers, scriptural readings, religious silence, homilies or exhortations, congregational singing, and part of the Liturgy of the Hours should be employed during the exposition (HCWE 95–96). This extended exposition is interrupted for Masses celebrated through that period.

Besides exposition, HCWE recommends ''devotional services'' (HCWE 79), processions (HCWE 101–08), and congresses (HCWE 109–12) as suitable forms which help the Christian people to witness their ''faith and devotion toward the sacrament'' and ''to express their worship publicly in the bond of charity and unity'' (HCWE 101, 109). Such devotions are ''strongly encouraged when celebrated according to the regulations of lawful authority,'' and they ''should be in harmony with the sacred liturgy . . . take their bearing from the liturgy, and lead people back to the liturgy'' (HCWE 79).

See Also: EUCHARIST OUTSIDE MASS, WORSHIP OF THE.

Bibliography: E. DUMOUTET, *Le Désir de voir l'hostie* (Paris 1926). N. MITCHELL, *Cult and Controversy: The Worship of the Eucharist Outside Mass* (New York 1982). M. RUBIN, *Corpus Christi: The Eucharist in Late Medieval Culture* (New York 1991).

[N. D. MITCHELL]

EUCHARISTIC ELEVATION

The act of lifting up the eucharistic elements of bread and wine after the consecration in the Roman Rite of the Mass.

The elevation of the bread at this point was introduced into the Mass rite early in the 13th century by Eudes de Sully (d. 1208) or his immediate successor in the Archdiocese of Paris. It was intended to keep the people from adoring the bread before it had been consecrated. During the preceding century many priests held the bread high above the altar while saying the words of consecration. The allegorical tendency of the time saw in this a representation of the lifting up of Christ on the cross, but the simple faithful seeing the eucharistic bread lifted up thought it was already consecrated and proceeded to adore it immediately. To prevent this material idolatry on the part of the people the bishop of Paris forbade priests to elevate the bread until it was consecrated.

At the same time the introduction of the new rite responded to the widespread desire of the people to look at the bread, and it was this desire more than anything else that contributed to the rapid spread of the new rite. Within 50 years, it spread to all the churches of the West and acquired extraordinary importance and popularity.

However, this veneration at times became excessive and often bordered on superstition. People went to any lengths to ensure seeing the elevated host, even calling out to the priest to hold it up higher so that they could see it better. Many exaggerated the efficacy of seeing the elevated host; they even believed that whoever looked at the host in the morning would be protected against misfortune and an unprovided death that day. Many regarded looking at the host as a substitute for receiving the Eucharist; once the Elevation was over they left the church.

The elevation of the chalice became general much later and more gradually, chiefly because the desire of the people to look at the chalice was not as great as their desire to look at the bread. For one thing they could see the bread but not the wine. So we find that the elevation of the chalice was not in common use until the 14th century and was prescribed only with the Missal of Pius V (1570).

The genuflections before and after the elevation were not prescribed until 1570; originally the priest merely made a profound bow at this point. The use of incense at this point in solemn Mass was introduced toward the middle of the 14th century.

The 1969 Roman Rite of the Mass retains the elevation of the bread and the cup at their traditional points during the consecration, followed by a genuflection or profound bow. A second elevation of both the bread and the wine occurs at the doxology of the eucharistic prayer, and a third elevation at the invitation to holy communion.

Bibliography: J. A. JUNGMANN, *The Mass of the Roman Rite,* tr. F. A. BRUNNER (rev. ed. New York 1959) 424–427. j

[W. J. O'SHEA/EDS.]

EUCHARISTIC FAST

Fasting from food and drink before Eucharistic Communion has been a part of Church discipline since the fourth century. Currently the Roman Catholic Church obligates its members to a mitigated form of what at times had been a quite rigorous fast: no food or drink is to be consumed for at least one hour prior to Eucharistic Communion. The discipline, codified in *Codex iuris canonici* Canon 919, does not prohibit drinking water or taking even solid medicine, nor does it bind the sick and aged or those who are occupied in their care. Priests whose pastoral responsibilities require them to celebrate the Eucharist more than once in a day are bound to the fast prior to the first liturgical celebration only.

The 20th century mitigation of the eucharistic fast has occured in several stages. It can best be understood as a response to the liturgical reform set in motion in 1905 with Pope PIUS X's promotion of frequent, even daily, Communion for the laity. At the time of Pius X's decree the communion fast involved abstention from all food and drink, including water, from midnight prior to the reception of Communion. This discipline, in the context of 20th century socio-cultural realities, was judged to be an obstacle to the pastoral implementation of the ideal of regular lay Communion. Pope Pius XII's 1953 apostolic constitution *Christus Dominus* eliminated the prohibition against drinking water; in 1957 he reduced the duration of the fast from food and alcoholic beverages to three hours. After the Second Vatican Council, as part of the renewed effort to promote full and active participation in the eucharistic liturgy, Pope Paul VI decreed in 1964 that the eucharistic fast was further mitigated, binding the Church to abstaining from all food and drink for one hour before Communion; in 1973 he dispensed the sick and their caregivers from even this limited obligation.

History of the Practice. The origins of the discipline are hidden in obscurity. Late fourth century North African councils (Hippo in 393; Carthage in 397) legislated that the Eucharist was to be eaten prior to any other food consumption during a day. St. Augustine, bishop of Hippo, advocates this practice in his letter to Januarius, claiming apostolic origin for it while admitting it was not Jesus' mandate. Some authors have attempted to ground the practice in certain statements of third century Church orders, but recent critical scholarship has cast doubt on the validity of these efforts.

In evaluating the claim for apostolic origin of the practice, liturgical and canonical historians note the witness of I Corinthians and other first century noncanonical writings that in the primitive church the Eucharist was celebrated in the course of a meal. When the Eucharist and meal were separated, the practice of a community agape persisted, although in what relationship to the Church's eucharistic action is unclear. The fourth century legislation specifically notes that on Holy Thursday the sequence of Eucharistic Communion before other eating does not obligate the Church, leading some contemporary commentators to hypothesize an active memory of an earlier practice, if not its persistence. The fact of the fourth century exception is still handed on by St. Thomas Aquinas, in the 13th century, but as a practice long superseded.

In the present state of historical research scholars can only speculate about the ecclesial currents which gave rise to the early discipline. Once in place, the discipline gained in precision and rigor throughout the medieval period. Some medieval legislators ruled that infants at the breast—who according to ancient custom had first received Communion at their Baptisms—were obligated to the fast. Other legislators required a post-communion fast of several hours as well as a pre-communion fast. In some areas, even those lay people who were not communicants were required to keep the communion fast until the priest had communicated on behalf of the Church at the public liturgy of the day.

Reasons for the Eucharistic Fast. The motivation for the communion fast was most commonly discussed in terms of the basic need for respect for the Blessed Sacrament of the Lord's Body and Blood. Aquinas proposed two other motives for the fast: to respond to the Lord's injunction ''Seek first the kingdom of God'' (Mt 6. 33); and to avoid the dangers of vomiting from the intemperance that can accompany eating, for which he cites Paul as authority in I Cor 11.21. When the discipline for the eucharistic fast was introduced into the text of the 1570 Missal of Pius V, the norms enunciated there reflected the tradition as it had been received and interpreted by Aquinas. Aquinas' authority seems also to have stabilized the calculation of the fast from midnight, the start of the Roman day.

Subsequent centuries saw a development of the tradition according to the principles of casuistry operative in moral theology in the post-Tridentine period. Casuists concerned themselves with helping fasters by introducing flexibility into the calculation of midnight (through attention to variables like daylight/standard time and the faster's geographical location in relation to legal time zones). They also debated whether items taken into the mouth but not swallowed (mouthwash, chewing gum, tobacco) or items swallowed accidentally (paper or string) broke the fast and required the ingester to abstain from Communion.

These preoccupations with technical transgression, which shaped much catechesis on the eucharistic fast even in the pre-conciliar period, confirm from another direction the wisdom of the relaxation of the discipline. However, the vestiges of the casuistic attitude have resulted in a discipline lacking firm foundation in Christian religious sensibilities and authentic Christian spirituality. At the onset of the mitigation process in the 1950s, Godfrey Diekmann proposed reaffirmation of the spiritual basis for a eucharistic fast in the paschal character of the mystery of salvation. Self-emptying is a necessary moment prior to receiving the divine fullness. It has also been suggested that the pre-communion fast is a way of ritualizing the spiritual hunger which should characterize all those who gather at the eucharistic table.

Bibliography: INTERNATIONAL COMMISSION ON ENGLISH IN THE LITURGY, *Documents on the Liturgy 1963–79* (Collegeville, Minn. 1982). ST. THOMAS AQUINAS, *Summa Theologiae* 3a 80.8. T. F. ANGLIN, *The Eucharistic Fast: An Historical Synopsis and Commentary* (Washington, D.C. 1941). G. DIEKMANN, "The Fast Ought Not Prevent Communion," *Worship* 27 (1953) 516–23. J. M. FROCHISSE, "A propos des origines de jeñne eucharistique," *Revue d'Histoire Ecclesiastique* 28 (1932) 594–609. J. P. BEAL, J. A. CORIDEN and T. J. GREEN, eds., *New Commentary on the Code of Canon Law* (New York-Mahwah, N.J. 2000).

[M. COLLINS]

EUCHERIUS OF LYONS, ST.

Theologian and bishop of Lyons, 432 to 441; d. Lyons, 449. Eucherius came from a Christian, senatorial family. He received an excellent education, was married to Galla, and had achieved high office in the imperial service when he was chosen (*c.* 432) as bishop of Lyons. His son Salonius became bishop of Geneva before 440; his son (St.) Veranus, who later became bishop of Venice (before 450; d. *c.* 480), accompanied him to the Council of Orange in 441. On agreement with his wife, Eucherius had earlier retired to the monastic life at Lérins and later to a more solitary way of life on the island of Leros.

Eucherius was known for his preaching. Of his writings, two ascetical tracts in letter form have been preserved: *De laude eremi* is addressed to St. HILARY OF ARLES (*C.* 427) and *De contemptu mundi,* to a pagan relative named Valerian. He also dedicated two exegetical works to his sons: for Salonius, an *Instructionum libri duo,* in which he followed JEROME in explaining Greek and Hebrew words; and *Formulae spiritalis intelligentiae,* explaining spiritual exegesis for Veranus. These two works are of importance for the history of the Latin text of the Bible and the VULGATE in France. Eucherius is probably the author of the *Passio Acaunensium martyrum,* the oldest account of the THEBAN LEGION martyrs. The esteem in which Eucherius was held by contemporaries is attested by the dedication of the second part of John CASSIAN's *Collationes* in his honor; as well as by his correspondence with SIDONIUS APOLLINARIS, Hilary of Arles, Rusticus, PAULINUS OF NOLA, and SALVIAN.

Feast: Nov. 16.

Bibliography: *Patrologia Latina,* ed. J. P. MIGNE, 217 v. (Paris 1878–90) 50:686–1214. C. WOTKE, ed., *Corpus scriptorum ecclesiasticorum latinorum* 31.1 (1894), O. BARDENHEWER, *Geschichte der altkirchlichen Literatur* (Freiburg 1913–1932) 4:567–571. B. ALTANER, *Patrology,* tr. H. GRAEF (New York 1960) 541. R. ÉTAIX, *Dictionnaire d'histoire et de géographie ecclésiastiques* (Paris 1912) 15:1315–17. G. BARDY, *Revue biblique* 42 (1933) 14–20. A. MONACI, *Revista di archeologia cristiana* 10 (1933) 19–26, Passio. B. ALTANER, *Miscellanea Isidoriana* (Rome 1936) 11–32. A. E. ANSPACH, *ibid.* 340–343. J. G. HIRTE, *Doctrina scripturistica . . . sancti Eucherii* (Rome 1940). N. K. CHADWICK, *Poetry and Letters in Early Christian Gaul* (London 1955) 151–160. C. CURTI, "La *Passio Acaunensium martyrum,*" *Convivium Dominicum* (Catania 1959) 299–327. S. PRICOCO, *Per una nuova edizione del De contemptu mundi di Eucherio di Lione* (Turin 1967).

[A. NEUWIRTH]

EUCHERIUS OF ORLÉANS, ST.

Bishop; b. late seventh century; d. abbey of Saint-Trond, Belgium, 738. He belonged to an influential MEROVINGIAN family and from his earliest years was destined for the monastic life with the result that he was professed at the BENEDICTINE abbey of JUMIÈGES *c.* 709. Seven years later he was elected, against his will, bishop of Orlèans, where his uncle Suavaric had occupied the episcopal see and where his relatives had powerful support. CHARLES MARTEL, returning from his victory against the Saracens in 732, had him arrested and sent in exile to Cologne because his family was hostile to the party of the mayor of the palace. Eucherius bore his disgrace with great resignation and later obtained permission to retire to the Abbey of SAINT-TROND. He was venerated as a saint from the ninth century.

Feast: Feb. 20.

Bibliography: *Acta Sanctorum* Feb. 3:211–225. *Monumenta Germaniae Scriptores rerum Merovingicarum* (Berlin 1825–) 7.1:41–53. L. DUCHESNE, *Fastes épiscopaux de l'ancienne Gaule* (Paris 1907–1915) 2:462–463. H. LECLERCQ, *Dictionnaire d'archéologie chrétienneet de liturgie,* ed. F. CABROL, H. LECLERCQ and H. I. MARROU (Paris 1907–1953) 12.2:2686. J. L. BAUDOT and L. CHAUSSIN, *Vies des saints et des bienheueux selon l'ordre du calendrier avec l'historique des fêtes* (Paris 1935–1956) 2:428–431. A. DUMAS, *Catholicisme* 4:661. A. M.. ZIMMERMANN, *Kalendarium Benedictinum: Die Heiligen und Seligen des Benediktinerorderns und seiner Zweige* (Metten 1933–1938) 1:234–236.

[É. BROUETTE]

EUDAEMONISM

From the Greek εὐδαιμονία, meaning prosperity or happiness, the ethical theory holding that man's last END, or ultimate GOOD, consists in a state or condition of general well-being or welfare. Throughout the ages this position has been understood in various ways. One may distinguish the ancient version, best represented by Aristotle's treatment in the *Nicomachean Ethics;* the modification made of the Aristotelian position by St. Thomas Aquinas and other medieval schoolmen; and the modern and contemporary positions that make some claim to this identification.

Basically, all eudaemonisms have in common that they are teleological explanations deriving rules and norms for human moral action from some consideration of the end, or destiny, of man. In ordinary usage, the Greek term is often rendered as happiness or its equivalent. Disagreement over the meaning of happiness provides the basis for varieties of eudaemonism. All of the types agree, however, that the notion of a natural end for man guides his ethical theory and behavior and explains the nature of his beatitude. Early forms of eudaemonism stressed the total satisfaction found in the individual life of the morally good person. Medieval theories adapted the ancient interpretations to Christian revelation about man's sanctification and salvation. Modern and contemporary views tend to emphasize the psychological affective aspects of a naturalistic and temporal achievement of a fully human life.

Early Views. The most apt example of the original formulation of eudaemonism is that of Aristotle. Two concepts of ultimate good for man are developed in Aristotle's ethical treatise. The classic idea of personal welfare or happiness as virtuous living can be understood in an ideal sense. ''If happiness is activity in accordance with virtue it is reasonable that it should be in accordance with the highest virtue; and this will be that of the best thing in us. Whether it be reason or something else that is this element which is thought to be our natural ruler and guide and to take thought of things noble and divine, whether it be itself also divine or only the most divine element in us, the activity of this in accordance with its proper virtue will be perfect happiness. That this activity is contemplative we have already said'' (*Eth. Nic. 1177a* 12–18). Here Aristotle founds well-being, or happiness, on well-doing. Thus happiness consists not in merely passive enjoyment but in an action of a kind proper to man, surpassing anything possible to animals. This highest activity appropriate to the nature of man is the best exercise of the supreme power, or faculty, of the human person. Because, for Aristotle, the speculative reason is the noblest power, happiness is an act of knowledge (θεωρία), a constant practice of the intellectual virtues of science, understanding, and wisdom.

Several characteristics mark the activity of contemplation as that best suited to be the ultimate goal of man's striving. Not only is it the full act of the highest power, but it also deals with the most noble reality as object of thought. Contemplative thought is the most continuous occupation possible and offers man the purest and most refined pleasure. It is the most self-sufficient of the virtues, not requiring more than a moderate possession of material goods or necessitating any social relationships for its essential fulfillment. Of all man's actions the most leisurely and unwearied, contemplation is loved for its own sake and not as a means to some further end. A final property of contemplation, which establishes it as the natural beatitude of man, is its likeness to the life of the gods. Its very similarity to the blessed activity of divine beings makes contemplation itself somehow divine.

By reason of this sublimity, however, the life of contemplation is achieved only by those few men who are capable of attaining to philosophical wisdom and who are free from care about the lesser necessaries of life. Therefore, Aristotle proposes a second kind of happiness to be reached by the majority of men: those who live according to the moral virtues are happy men (*ibid.* 1178a 8–1178b 2). The active life is one of harmony and pleasure, which most befits the human estate, that is, the composite nature of man in the midst of his social and political context. Less exalted and less perfect than σοφία is φρόνησις (practical wisdom), but it constitutes the felicity possible to most men.

Medieval Development. Aristotle's eudaemonism was too limited and exclusive to satisfy the Christian view of a common end for all mankind. What was wanting in his theory was supplied by the theologians of the Middle Ages. In the light of divine revelation THOMAS AQUINAS and other schoolmen transformed the Greek position into one of heavenly destiny. Christian eudaemonism placed happiness for man in God as revealed in Scripture and criticized the Greek philosophers for allowing that perfect beatitude could be achieved in this life, for describing it as fully dependent on human effort and achievement, and for their failure to account for the resurrection of the body as part of man's ultimate situation.

Aquinas accommodated all of the positive and some of the negative features of Aristotelian eudaemonism in his treatment of beatitude (ST 1a2ae, 1–5). He agreed that happiness, subjectively considered, could not be merely power, virtue, or state of being; rather it was the activity, or the operation, of the intellect grasping immediately the most intelligible and spiritual object. This reality was identified as the true and living God of revelation, infinite, immutable, and perfectly satisfying all the demands of a good worthy to be happiness objectively considered. No earthly good—neither riches, honors, power, bodily pleasures nor goods of the soul—could so qualify. For Aquinas, the vision of the Divine Essence is supernatural in the sense that it requires the presence of the light of glory (*lumen gloriae*) to assist the natural power of the mind, that it is possible only after physical death, and that it is ultimately gratuitous in the merits of Christ. Joy or delight is the consequence of the possession of God in contemplative knowledge. Both bodily fulfillment in spiritualized integrity and social relationships among the blessed are additions to the essential happiness of the beatific vision.

Modern Trends. With the separation of philosophy from theology accomplished in the modern period, eudaemonistic theory appeared again in naturalistic forms. None of these use the power-activity-object analysis. Instead, they propose an ultimate state or condition that the moral person ought to attain. This may be described as the harmony of the whole life with its human activities and the consequent or concomitant affective states (G. SANTAYANA). Self-realization or self-perfection theories also relate to happiness of the individual. Hedonisms, simple or qualified, identify happiness with pleasure. Some move from the individual to the social perspective, either emphasizing the total evolutionary process (H. SPENCER) or becoming utilitarianisms with happiness as the welfare of the majority (J. BENTHAM, J. S. MILL). Contemporary divisions include psychological value theories and interest and affective state theories. All maintain some teleological element but manifest great diversity in the interpretation of welfare or happiness. (*See* HEDONISM; UTILITARIANISM.)

See Also: MAN, NATURAL END OF; GOOD, THE SUPREME; VALUE, PHILOSOPHY OF.

Bibliography: THOMAS AQUINAS, *Commentary on the Nicomachean Ethics of Aristotle,* tr. C. I. LITZINGER (Chicago 1964), bks. 1, 10; *C.gent.* 3.1–63. J. HIRSCHBERGER, *Lexikon für Theologie und Kirche*, ed. J. HOFER and K. RAHNER, 10 v. (2d, new ed. Freiburg 1957–65) 3:1167–68. K. H. MISKOTTE, *Die Religion in Geschichte und Gegenwart*, 7 v. (3d ed Tübingen 1957–65) 2:723–26. S. PIGNAGNOLI, *Enciclopedia filosofica*, 4 v. (Venice-Rome 1957) 2:204–07. É. H. GILSON, *History of Christian Philosophy in the Middle Ages* (New York 1955). J. M. SCHULHOF, J. HASTINGS, ed., *Encyclopedia of Religion and Ethics*, 13 v. (Edinburgh 1908–27) 5:571–72. T. E. HILL, *Contemporary Ethical Theories* (New York 1950). J. LEONARD, *Le Bonheur chez Aristote* (Brussels 1948). R. SHEEHAN, *The Philosophy of Happiness according to St. Thomas* (Washington 1956). J. MULLANEY, ''The Natural Terrestrial End of Man,'' *The Thomist* 18 (July 1955) 373–95. W. E. MAY, ''The Structure and Argument of the *Nicomachean Ethics,*'' *The New Scholasticism* 36 (1962) 1–28.

[M. G. HUNGERMAN]

EUDES, JOHN, ST.

Missionary in France, founder of seminaries and congregations, spiritual writer and promoter of the devotion to the Sacred Hearts of Jesus and Mary; b. Ri (Orne), France, Nov. 14, 1601; d. Caen, France, Aug. 19, 1680. He came from a devout country family, and was sent to the Jesuit college in Caen in 1615. He took minor orders in 1620 and was received into the congregation by Pierre de BÉRULLE, founder of the Oratory. He was ordained on Dec. 20, 1625, and continued his preparation for a preaching career under Charles de Condren. When an epidemic of the plague broke out in 1627, Eudes volunteered to care for the stricken in his own Diocese of Sées, Normandy. Again in 1631 he heroically shared the lives of the plague victims in the area of Caen.

In 1633 he began his long career as a parish missionary. His unusual gifts as a preacher and confessor made his missions highly successful and earned him a reputation for fervor and eloquence. Though he labored mostly in Normandy, his mission field extended into Brittany, Bourgogne, and the Île-de-France. By 1676 Eudes had preached more than 100 missions, some of them lasting from several weeks to several months.

Eudes also concerned himself with the spiritual improvement of the parish clergy. Beginning in 1641 he gave frequent conferences for priests directed toward the duties of their state in life. He soon realized, however, that the more basic need was the establishment of seminaries for the proper training and spiritual formation of candidates for the priesthood. As superior of the house of the Oratory in Caen, Eudes sought to establish a seminary there and won the approval of the bishop of Bayeux and Cardinal Richelieu. The project had the support of Father de Condren, then superior general, but his successor, Father Bourgoing, opposed the project. After much prayer and counsel, Eudes decided to leave the Oratory, and on March 25, 1643, he founded a society of secular priests (without vows), the Congregation of Jesus and Mary. The new group was dedicated to the formation of a well-trained and virtuous clergy by conducting seminaries for the diocesan priesthood. Through the work of Eudes and his associates seminaries were established at Caen (1644), Coutances (1650), Lisieux (1653), Rouen (1658), Évreux (1667), and Rennes (1670).

Aided by the Visitandines, Eudes founded also a religious society for women. This society, the Congregation of Our Lady of Charity of the Refuge, originated at Caen in 1641 and follows the Rule of St. Augustine. It was intended to provide a refuge for women of ill fame who wished to do penance. The congregation was approved by the bishop of Bayeux (Feb. 8, 1651) and by Pope ALEXANDER VII (bull of Jan. 2, 1666). During Eudes's lifetime three other houses were established in Brittany.

Eudes was a noted spiritual writer. His works include: *La Vie et le royaume de Jésus dans les âmes chrétiennes* (1637), *Le Contrat de l'homme avec Dieu par le saint baptême* (1654), *Le Bon confesseur* (1666), and *Le Mémorial de la vie ecclésiastique* (1681). These practical meditations were built on a simple doctrine, dominated by Jesus as the source of all sanctity and Mary as the model of the Christian life. Drawing inspiration from scriptural texts and from medieval piety, Eudes composed two Offices, one in honor of the Sacred Heart of Mary (1648) and the other in honor of the Sacred Heart of Jesus (1672). He developed the basis for these devotions in his book *Le Coeur admirable de la très sacrée Mère de Dieu,* published posthumously in 1681. His 12th and last book is devoted entirely to the "divine Heart of Jesus." At the time of his beatification in 1909, Eudes was declared by PIUS X to be the "father, doctor, and apostle of the liturgical cultus of the Sacred Hearts." He was canonized by PIUS XI, May 31, 1925.

Feast: Aug. 19.

Bibliography: *Oeuvres complètes,* 12 v. (Paris 1905–09); *Selected Works,* ed. W. E. MYATT and P. J. SKINNER, 6 v. (New York 1946–48); *En tout la volonté de Dieu: saint Jean Eudes à travers ses lettres,* ed. C. GUILLON (Paris 1981); *Le Royaume de Jésus, saint Jean Eudes,* ed. G. OUELLET (Montréal 1988). D. SARGENT, *Their Hearts Be Praised: The Life of St. John Eudes* (New York 1949), bibliog. P. HÉRAMBOURG, *St. John Eudes: A Spiritual Portrait,* tr. R. HAUSER (Westminster, Md. 1960). C. BERTHELOT DU CHESNAY, *Les Missions de Saint Jean Eudes. Contribution à l'histoire des missions en France au XVIIe siècle . . .* (Paris 1967). N. BERMÚDEZ V., *El bautismo en la doctrina de San Juan Eudes* (Madrid 1978). P. MILICENT, *Saint Jean Eudes: un artisan du renouveau chrétien au XVIIe siècle* (Paris 1985).

[C. BERTHELOT DU CHESNAY]

EUDISTS

The Congregation of Jesus and Mary (CJM; Official Catholic Directory #0450), whose members are known as Eudists, is a small society of priests founded in France by St. John EUDES in the 17th century. It is engaged mainly in the training of diocesan clergy and education.

Origin and Development. When the founder initiated the society in 1643, his aim was twofold: to provide seminaries for the formation of clergy according to the decrees of the Council of Trent and to preach parochial missions. The establishment of a seminary in Caen, Normandy, was the immediate reason for the birth of the new society; for Eudes, at that time an ORATORIAN, had not been able to persuade his superiors to start this seminary, then badly needed in that province. Soon other bishops of Normandy and Brittany asked him to establish similar foundations: Coutances (1650), Lisieux (1653), Rouen (1658), Évreux (1667), and Rennes (1670). At the same time Eudes and his confreres carried on their work of preaching parochial missions in towns and villages all over France. After the death of Eudes (1680) and under the rule of his first three successors—Jean Jacques Blouet de Camilly (1680 to 1711), Guy de Fontaines de Neuilly (1711 to 1727), and Pierre Cousin (1727 to 1751)—the society took charge of seven other seminaries in France. After that the number of houses remained practically unchanged under the government of the next four superiors—Jean Prosper Auvray de Saint-André (1751 to 1770), Michel Lefèvre (1770 to 1775), Pierre Le Coq (1775 to 1777), and Pierre Dumont (1777 to 1790).

When the congregation was dissolved in 1790 by the French Revolution, its membership stood at about 100 priests and a few lay brothers. They had charge of the 13 seminaries mentioned above, and in addition, three minor seminaries. The latter were special establishments where seminarians who could not pay for their tuition and support received a combination of classical education and theological instruction. The Eudists also had four colleges of the humanities at Lisieux (1653), Avranches (1693), Domfront (1727), and Valognes (1729); three parishes; and two residence houses, principally for their mission preachers.

One of the main services rendered by the congregation to the Church in France during the 17th century was the strong stand it took against Jansenism; because of this, the clergy in Normandy remained in greater part preserved from the heresy. The traditional devotion of the Eudists to the Holy See caused them to refuse generally to take the schismatic oath imposed upon the French clergy by the Constituent Assembly. Three who were martyred during the massacres of Sept. 2 and 3, 1792, were François Lefranc, famous for his book indicting Masonic plots; Claude Pottier; and François Hébert. Four other Eudists also gave their lives during the persecution.

19th- and 20th-Century Revival. After the Revolution the society was revived in 1826 when Louis Blanchard, former superior of the seminary in Rennes, convened the surviving Eudists and was elected superior general. He died soon afterward (1830); and his successor, Jérôme Louis de la Morinière (1830 to 1849), was able to increase the number of members only to about 40. Upon the request of his friend Bishop Simon BRUTÉ, he sent a few priests to start an establishment in Vincennes, Indiana, but this venture was short-lived. Under Louis Gaudaire (1849 to 1870) the congregation slowly consolidated itself, while remaining centered mainly in Brittany.

New vitality was realized through the leadership of Ange Le Doré, who ruled the society for nearly half a century (1870 to 1916) and whose influence was felt in the general affairs of the Church in France during the struggles with the anticlerical Third Republic. The three seminaries he founded in Mexico were later wiped out by the revolution in that country, but he successfully planted his congregation in Colombia (1883) and in Canada (1890). When he died, the Eudists numbered 270, as against 85 in 1870. Another achievement of Le Doré was the rediscovery of the personality and works of John Eudes, through historical research and the publication of his forgotten spiritual writings. Albert Lucas (1916 to 1930) strove to repair the losses inflicted by World War I; he also revised the constitutions in accord with the 1917 Code of Canon Law.

The congregation remains dedicated chiefly to work in seminaries and education. Like the Oratorians and Sulpicians, the Eudists do not take religious vows and have no special habit distinguishing them from the diocesan clergy.

The generalate is located in Rome; the North American provincialate in Quebec, Canada; and the United States regional headquarters in Seneca, New York.

Bibliography: E. GEORGES, *La Congrégation de Jésus et Marie, dite des Eudistes* (Paris 1933). G. DE LA COTARDIERE, *La Congrégation de Jésus et Marie, Eudistes au Canada, 1890–1940* (Besançon 1946). L. SAMSON, *Les Eudistes en Amérique du Sud, 1883–1926,* 3 v. (Paris 1949–55). C. BERTHELOT DU CHESNAY, *Dictionnaire d'histoire et de géographie ecclésiastiques*, ed. A. BAUDRILLART et al. (Paris 1912–) 15:1331–35.

[G. DE BERTIER DE SAUVIGNY/EDS.]

EUGENDUS OF CONDAT, ST.

Abbot; b. Franche-Compté, *c.* 450; d. Condat, Jan. 1 *c.* 510–17. According to the vita traditionally attributed to a fellow monk and disciple, Eugendus (Oyend) as a child was entrusted to Saints Romanus and Lupicinus, founders of the monastery of Condat (later Saint-Oyend; today, Saint-Claude). There until his death he lived in mortification, study, and prayer, esteemed for his humility and his learning, which included a knowledge of Greek, remarkable for his day. As abbot he rebuilt the monastery, destroyed by fire, and patterned its life on the eastern monasticism of BASIL and John CASSIAN.

Feast: Jan. 1.

Bibliography: *Vita* in J. MABILLON, *Acta sanctorum ordinis. Benedicti* (Venice 1733–40) 1:553–559. *Monumenta Germaniae Scriptores rerum Merovingicarum* (Berlin 1825–) 3:154–166, authenticity questioned by B. KRUSCH; defended by L. DUCHESNE, in *Mélanges d'archéologie et d'histoire* 18 (1898) 5–16. *Analecta Bollandiana* 17 (1898) 367–368. *Vies des páres du Jura,* tr. as *The life of the Jura fathers: The Life and Rule of the Holy Fathers Romanus, Lupicinus, and Eugendus,* tr. T. VIVIAN, K. VIVIAN, and J. B. RUSSELL (Kalamazoo, Mich. 1999). R. POUPARDIN, ''Étude sur les vies des saints fondateurs de Condate et la critique de M. Bruno Krusch,'' *Moyen-âge* 11 (1898) 31–48. A. M.. ZIMMERMANN, *Kalendarium Benedictinum: Die Heiligen und Seligen des Benediktinerorderns und seiner Zweige* (Metten 1933–38) 1:39. J. L. BAUDOT and L. CHAUSSIN, *Vies des saints et des bienheueux selon l'ordre du calendrier avec l'historique des fêtes* (Paris 1935–56) 1:9–11. A. BUTLER, *The Lives of the Saints,* ed. H. THURSTON and D. ATTWATER (New York 1956) 1:5–6.

[G. M. COOK]

EUGENE I, POPE, ST.

Pontificate: Aug. 10, 654 to June 2, 657; d. Rome. His was an aristocratic Roman family; he was a man of conciliatory disposition, outstanding for his sanctity. He accepted election by the Roman clergy after they had resisted pressure by Emperor CONSTANS II for more than a year to replace MARTIN I, who was under arrest. Eugene probably realized Martin would never be restored and feared the possibility of a Monothelite pope. In a letter of July 654 Martin had mentioned three ecclesiastical officials who were his deputies in governing the Church, but in a letter of September 655 he prayed especially ''for the one who is now ruling over the Church,'' a statement interpreted as acquiescence or approval of Eugene's election. The Roman archives begin Eugene's reign in 654, but he cannot be considered incontestably to have been pope until after Martin's death in 655. Eugene sent representatives to negotiate about MONOTHELITISM with Constans, who immediately requested Eugene's recognition of Peter, newly appointed patriarch of Constantinople. Through these representatives Peter forwarded a synodal letter to Eugene, but it was so vague in regard to the two wills in Christ that the clergy and people, assembled to hear it read in St. Mary Major, rejected it and forbade Eugene to begin Mass until he, too, formally renounced it. This so enraged Constans that only a new Arab threat prevented him from arresting Eugene as he had Martin. Eugene was buried at St. Peter's. It was probably Eugene whom WILFRID OF YORK met when he visited Rome, 654.

Feast: June 2.

Bibliography: *Liber pontificalis,* ed. L. DUCHESNE (Paris 1886–1958) 1:341–342. P. JAFFÉ, *Regesta pontificum romanorum ab condita ecclesia ad annum post Christum natum 1198* (Graz 1956) 1:234;2:699, 740. *Patrologia Latina* ed. J. P. MIGNE (Paris 1878–90) 87:129. *Patrologia Graeca,* ed. J. P. MIGNE (Paris 1858–66) 90. *Acta Sanctorum* June 1:214–216. C. J. VON HEFELE, *Histoire des conciles d'après les documents originaux* (Paris 1907–38) 3.1:460. H. K. MANN, *The Lives of the Popes in the Early Middle Ages from 590 to 1304* (London 1902–32) 1.1:406–412. A. CLERVAL, *Dictionnaire de théology catholique,* ed. A. VACANT et al. (Paris 1912) 5.2:1488–89. E. CASPAR, *Geschichte de Papsttums von den Anfängen bis zur Höhe der Weltherrschaft* (Tubingen

1930–33) 2. A. FLICHE and V. MARTIN, eds. *Histoire de l'église depuis les origines jusqu'à nos jours* (Paris 1935) 5. O. BERTOLINI, *Roma di fronte a Bisanzio e ai Longobardi* (Bologna 1941). D. MALLARDO, *Papa sant' Eugenio I* (Naples 1943), and review in *Analecta Bollandiana* 65 (1947) 320. F. X. SEPPELT, *Geschichte der Päpste von den Anfängen bis zur Mitte des 20. Jh.* (Munich 1954–59) 2:67–68. J. HALLER, *Das Papsttum* (Stuttgart 1950–53) 1. P. VIARD, *Catholicisme* 4:673–674. G. SCHWAIGER, *Lexikon für Theologie und Kirche*, ed. J. HOFER and K. RAHNER (Freiburg 1957–65) 3:1171. P. PLANK, *Lexikon des Mittelalters* 6 (München-Zürich 1992–1993). J. M. SANSTERRE, *Dizionario biografico delgi italiani,* 43 (Rome 1993). J. N. D. KELLY, *Oxford Dictionary of Popes* (New York 1986) 75.

[C. M. AHERNE]

EUCENE II, POPE

Pontificate: *c.* Feb.–May 824 to August 827. The *Annales Einhardi* (*Monumenta Germaniae Historica: Scriptores* 1:212) indicate that he was cardinal priest of St. Sabina and enjoyed the support of the local nobility in his contest with another papal candidate; he was upheld also by WALA, counselor of LOUIS THE PIOUS (*Vita Walae* 1:28; *Patrologia Latina* 120:1604). The co-emperor LOTHAIR I met Eugene in Rome and there (November 824) promulgated a *Constitutio Romana* (*Monumenta Germania Historica: Capitularia* 1:322–324) designed to restore order to the papal domains after the troubles under PASCHAL I. Its chief provisions were an oath of fidelity to the emperor on the part of papal subjects, the establishment of a mixed papal-imperial commission to oversee justice, and the guarantee of free papal elections to the Roman citizenry, thus confirming the pact of 817 and eliminating the Roman synodal enactment (769) that such elections be the exclusive business of the clergy. The oath taken by Eugene in ratifying the *constitutio* was henceforth to be taken by his successors before their consecration.

The question of ICONOCLASM arose anew in this pontificate (*Monumenta Germaniae Historica: Concilia* 2:473–551). An embassy of the Byzantine Emperors Michael II (820–829) and THEOPHILUS (829–842) reached Louis the Pious at Rouen (Nov. 17, 824), asking his good offices with the pope in an effort to prohibit the veneration of images. A first Frankish mission had failed to achieve this purpose, but Louis eventually secured papal permission to have his theologians examine the question (Nov. 1, 825). Late that same year, the Western sovereigns dispatched a letter and a new mission to the pope, hinting that he should send a papal commission along with a Frankish legation to Constantinople to affirm the Western position on images. Louis's fear that Eugene would not consent to this (*ibid.* 2:533) was apparently sound; there is evidence neither of papal letters nor of a mission to the East.

Other acts of this pontificate, indicating the return of papal initiative, include a response to BARNARD OF VIENNE (*Patrologia Latina* 105:643–644), an instruction on ordeals (*Patrologia Latina* 129:985–687), a fragment concerning the Abbey of FARFA, and a commendation of St. ANSGAR and companions who commenced their missionary labors in Denmark in the fall of 826. Wide-ranging disciplinary legislation was laid down in 38 canons by the Roman synod of Nov. 14 and 15, 826 (*Monumenta Germaniae Historica: Concilia* 2:552–583).

Bibliography: P. JAFFÉ, *Regesta pontificum romanorum ab condita ecclesia ad annum post Christum natum 1198* (Graz 1956) 1:320–322, 2559, 2564. *Liber Pontificalis,* ed. L. DUCHESNE (Paris 1886–1958) 2:69–70; 3:122. H. K. MANN, *The Lives of the Popes in the Early Middle Ages from 590 to 1304* (London 1902–32) 2.1:156–182. P. BREZZI, *Roma e l'Impero medioevale* (Bologna 1947). J. HALLER, *Das Papsttum* (Stuttgart 1930–33) 2:27–29, 38–39. F. X. SEPPELT, *Geschichte der Päpste von den Anfängen bis zur Mitte des 20. Jh.* (Munich 1954–59) 2:208–214. O. BERTOLINI, in *Studi medioevali in onore di Antonino De Stefano* (Palermo 1956) 43–78. T. NOBLE, ''The Place in Papal History of the Roman Synod of 826,'' *Church History* 45 (1976) 434–54. S. SCHOLTZ, *Lexikon für Theologie und Kirche,* 3d. ed. (Freiburg 1995). J. N. D. KELLY, *Oxford Dictionary of Popes* (New York 1986) 101–102.

[H. G. J. BECK]

EUGENE III, BL. POPE

Pontificate: Feb. 15, 1145, to July 8, 1153; b. Bernardo Pignatelli; d. Tivoli. Bernardo Pignatelli was born near Pisa. He was most likely of humble origin and was probably educated in Pisa. By 1128 he was almost certainly serving as the prior of Saint Zeno. Sometime around 1135 Bernardo met St. BERNARD, joined the CISTERCIAN abbey of CLAIRVAUX, and subsequently became the abbot of Saint Anastasio at Rome. In 1145, on the same day that his predecessor Lucius III died, Bernardo became the first Cistercian pope. He was an unexpected choice, and the precarious political climate at the time of his election made his transition to the Holy Office difficult. The popular commune rejected the pope's temporal powers, and Bernardo's refusal to support the Roman senate forced him to flee to Farfa, where he was consecrated. He then took up residence in VITERBO and remained there until December 1145, when an agreement with Rome permitted him to enter the city. The compromise with the Romans broke down just after Christmas, and in January 1146 he was forced to flee again to Viterbo.

On Dec. 1, 1145, Eugene had proclaimed the Second CRUSADE in a papal bull, *Bulla cruciata.* On March 6, 1146, he renewed the bull and commissioned St. Bernard to preach the crusade. The following year, Eugene himself traveled to France in order to promote the cause, returning to Italy in June 1148. Louis VII of France did take up the cross, and through the influence of St. Bernard, King Conrad III of Germany eventually joined the expedition as well. But the crusade, which became bogged in a futile siege of Damascus, never reached the Holy Land and ended in failure. The circumstances surrounding the Second Crusade, however, did generate some development in medieval political thought; it ultimately led to the classic formulation of the two-swords theory, which can be found in St. Bernard's didactic letters to Eugene.

The pope also rejected a proposal for a new crusade, which was marked by anti-Byzantine bias, and which most probably would never have reached the Holy Land. It was sponsored by Louis VII of France and Roger II of Sicily, an inveterate enemy of Byzantium. Although Roger had been responsible for Eugene's return to Rome in 1149, the pope had no intention of breaking his relationship with Conrad III of Germany, an ally of the Greeks.

Following St. Bernard's advice, Eugene worked to elevate the moral life of both the secular and regular clergy. He held synods at Paris in 1147, Trier in the winter of 1147/48, and Rheims in March 1148. While attending the last, Eugene evaluated the orthodoxy of Gilbert de La Porrée, and under the influence of St. Bernard several of Gilbert's propositions were corrected. Eugene also gave guarded approval of the visions of Hildegard of Bingen, the founder and abbess of the convent at Rupertsberg who was also a noted poet and composer. In 1149 he spotted the talented Nicholas Breakspear (the future Pope Adrian IV) and eventually made him papal legate to Scandinavia. At Cremona, on July 15, 1148, Eugene excommunicated the radical reformer ARNOLD OF BRESCIA, who had become a leader of the Roman Commune and bore some responsibility for Eugene's earlier exile from Rome. The pope also intervened in England and supported Archbishop Theobald of Canterbury in his relations with King Stephen. In addition he deposed William Fitzherbert from the See of York in 1147. Finally, in 1153, Eugene concluded the Treaty of Constance, an accord in which FREDERICK I BARBAROSSA agreed to defend the papacy in return for an imperial coronation. It outlined an arrangement of mutual assistance for pope and emperor but Eugene did not enjoy even the limited benefits of that agreement, since he died in Rome later that same year. Despite his involvement in both diplomatic and ecclesiastical affairs, Eugene managed to continue a life of deep personal devotion and austere simplicity. His cult was authorized by Pius IX in 1872.

Feast: July 8.

Bibliography: *Patrologia Latina,* ed. J. P. MIGNE, 271 v., indexes 4 v. (Paris 1878–90) 180:1013–642. J. D. MANSI, *Sacrorum Conciliorum nova et amplissima collectio,* 31 v. (Florence-Venice 1757–98) v. 21. J. M. WATTERICH, ed., *Pontificum romanorum . . . vitae,* 2 v. (Leipzig 1862) v. 2. P. JAFFÉ, *Regesta pontificum romanorum ab condita ecclesia ad annum post Christum natum 1198,* 882–1198, ed. S. LÖWENFELD, 2 v. (2d ed. Leipzig 1881–88; repr. Graz 1956) 2:20–89. L. DUCHESNE, ed., *Liber pontificalis,* v. 1–2 (Paris 1886–92) v. 2. JOHN OF SALISBURY, *Memoirs of the Papal Court,* ed. and tr. M. CHIBNALL (New York 1956). C. J. VON HEFELE, *Histoire des conciles d'après les documents originaux,* tr. and continued by H. LECLERCQ, 10 v. in 19 (Paris 1907–38) v. 51. H. K. MANN, *The Lives of the Popes in the Early Middle Ages from 590 to 1304,* 18 v. (London 1902–32) v. 9. H. GLEBER, *Papst Eugen III, 1145–1153, unter besonderer Berücksichtigung seiner politischen Tätigkeit* (Jena 1936). A. FLICHE and V. MARTIN, eds., *Histoire de l'église depuis les origines jusqu'à nos jours* (Paris 1935–) v. 9.1. P. BREZZI, *Roma e l'Impero medioevale, 774–1252* (Bologna 1947). F. X. SEPPELT, *Geschichte der Päpste von den Anfängen bis zur Mitte des 20. Jh.* (2d ed. Munich 1956) v. 3. A. JAKOBS, *Eugen III und die Anfänge europäischer Stadtsiegelinebst Anmerkungen zum Bande IV der Germania Pontifica* (Köln 1980). M. HORN, *Studien zur Geschichte Papst Eugens III (1145–1153)* (New York 1992). J. A. WATT, "Spiritual and Temporal Powers," *Cambridge History of Medieval Political Thought,* ed. J. H. BURNS (Cambridge 1988) 367–423.

[J. A. SHEPPARD]

EUGENE IV, POPE

Pontificate: March 3, 1431 to Feb. 23, 1447. b. Gabriel Condulmaro, Venice, *c.* 1383. Condulmaro was a monk who followed the rule of St. AUGUSTINE. Having been brought to the papal court by his uncle GREGORY XII and made cardinal (1408), he went to Constance at his uncle's abdication, July 4, 1415. Under Martin V he governed the March of Ancona and Bologna for a time. As Pope, Eugene confirmed the convocation of the Council of BASEL, but soon prorogued it. The fathers refused to obey, adopted and extended the principle of CONCILIARISM enunciated at the Council of CONSTANCE, and finally forced Eugene to withdraw his dissolution (Dec. 17, 1433). Meantime, continuing his predecessor's negotiations with the Greeks, he agreed to hold a council of union in Constantinople, but yielded to Basel's insistence that it be held in the West. When Basel split on the question of the site (May 7, 1437), Eugene undertook to implement the agreement with the Greeks, hired a fleet, and brought the Emperor, the patriarch, and a retinue of 700 to Ferrara, which he had named as the site (Sept. 18 and Dec. 30, 1437) of the transferred Council of Basel. The council opened on Jan. 8, 1438.

A popular insurrection forced Eugene to abandon Rome. He came to Florence (June 4, 1434), traveled to Bologna (April 22, 1436), and reached Ferrara (Jan. 24, 1438). The Greeks arrived in early March. The council was solemnly inaugurated on April 9, but the doctrinal sessions did not begin until October 8, at the demand of the Greek Emperor, although informal (and inconclusive) discussions on purgatory were held in June and July. In 14 sessions, from October 8 to December 13, there was free debate on the legality of the addition of the FILIOQUE to the Creed, without agreement. In the meantime Eugene, responsible for the upkeep of the Byzantine delegation, was in arrears with his payments and in financial straits. On Jan. 10, 1439, by arrangement with the Greeks, the council moved to FLORENCE, which offered better financial conditions. In March, eight sessions on the doctrine of the Procession of the Holy Spirit produced no agreement, and various other expedients were equally ineffective. On May 27 Eugene spiritedly exhorted the Greeks, thereby giving a new impulse that resulted in agreement on the Procession (June 8) and on PURGATORY, the PRIMACY, and the Eucharist in the following weeks. Union of the two Churches was proclaimed in *Laetentur caeli* on July 6, 1439. Thereafter Armenians, Copts of Egypt, Syrians, and the Chaldeans and Maronites of Cyprus were in turn united with the Holy See. Basel had ''suspended'' Eugene on Jan. 24, 1438, and ''deposed'' him on June 25, 1439. The Pope replied in *Moyses vir Dei* (Sept. 4, 1439), challenging the ecumenicity of the earlier phases of Constance and condemning Basel. At Eugene's death, even though Basel and its antipope FELIX V still continued in schism, most of the Christian West supported him.

Pope Eugene IV receiving a copy of ''Tres Dialoghi'' from the hand of the author, Antonio da Rho.

Eugene always retained the ideals of a religious and as pope lived a simple, regular, and abstemious life. He was charitable to the needy of all classes and readily supported Observant reforms in various religious orders. He was loyal to his ideals in resisting the conciliarism of Basel; to his helpers, even if some of them were less worthy; and to his obligations—supporting René of Anjou at the cost of Aragon's hostility and promoting the crusade against the Turks that ended in defeat at Varna (Nov. 10, 1444). Intelligent without being learned, he was more concerned with rebuilding Rome than with beautifying it. Typically, he desired an unostentatious tomb. He died a poor man. The union with the Greeks achieved by his council was shortlived, but it set the principle for all unions—identity of faith with freedom in matters of rite. It also checked the rabid conciliarism of Basel that threatened to alter the traditional constitution of the Church.

Bibliography: J. GILL, *The Council of Florence* (Cambridge, Eng. 1959), and literature there cited; *Eugenius IV: Pope of Christian Union* (Westminster, Md. 1961). D. BORNSTEIN, ''Giovanni Dominici, the Bianchi, and Venice: Symbolic Action and Interpretive Grids,'' *The Journal of Medieval and Renaissance Studies* 23 (1993) 43–171. A. ESCH, ''Überweisungen an die Apostolische Kammer aus den Diözesen des Reiches unter Einschaltung italienischer und deutscher Kaufleute und Bankiers. Regesten der vatikanischen Archivalien 1431–1475,'' *Quellen und Forchungen aus Italienischen Archiven und Bibliotheken* 78 (1998) 262–387. R. KAY, ''The Concilliar 'Ordo' of Eugenius IV,'' *Councils and Clerical Culture in the Medieval West* 16 (1997). PH. LUISIER, ''La letter du Partiarche Copte Jean XI au Pape Eugèene IV,'' *Orientalia Christiana Periodica* 60 (1994) 87–129. L. SCHMUGGE, ''Salmanticensia Poenitentiariae,'' in *Life, Law, and Letters: Historical Studies in Honour of Antonio García y García* (Rome 1998) 779–93. M. SPREMIC, ''La Serbia gli Stati italiani e la crociata del XV secolo,'' *Clio* 32 (1998) 467–78. J. N. D. KELLY, *Oxford Dictionary of Popes* (New York 1986) 241.

[J. GILL]

EUGENE II (III) OF TOLEDO, ST.

Archbishop; b. Toledo, Spain; d. there, Nov. 13, 657. Born of a royal Visigothic family of Spain, he became a cleric in the cathedral of Toledo and then a monk in the monastery at Saragossa where his uncle (St.) BRAULIO was abbot. There he studied theology and literature and began his career as a writer. When Braulio became bishop (631–656), he appointed Eugene archdeacon of the church of St. Vincent. In 645 King Chindaswinth (641–652) recalled Eugene to Toledo and named him archbishop of that see at the death of Eugene I (646). Eugene's nephew ILDEPHONSUS, who later succeeded him as archbishop, described Eugene as a man of small stature and frail health, but zealous in spiritual and intellectual activity (*De vir. ill.* 14; Patrologia latina 96:204). For 11 years Eugene admirably governed the See of Toledo. He reformed the chant (*see* MOZARABIC RITE), rearranged the feasts of the Spanish liturgy, and played an important role in the Councils of Toledo in 646, 653, 655, and 656; the last two were held under his direction. Eugene was buried in the basilica of St. Leocadia in Toledo. USUARD was the first to include him in his martyrology (875). Eugene's writings included a volume of prose and a treatise *De Trinitate,* both of which are now lost, a collection of short poems on various subjects, two letters, and a revision of Dracontius's *Laudes Dei* and *Satisfactio,* undertaken at the request of Chindaswinth. His poems, which were in the classical tradition, were undistinguished in content but influenced later Christian Latin poets such as Albar of Córdoba.

Feast: Nov. 13.

Bibliography: Works. *Monumenta Germaniae Auctores antiquissimi* (Berlin 1825–) 14:229–291, 300–301. *Patrologia Latina,* ed. J. P. MIGNE, 217 v. (Paris 1878–90) 87:347–418. **Literature.** M. MANITIUS, *Geschichte der lateinischen Literatur des Mittelalters* (Munich 1911–31) 1:194–197. M. MADOZ, "San Eugenio de Toledo," *Historia general de las literaturas hispánicas,* ed. G. DIAZ PLAJA, v.1 (Barcelona 1949) 127–129. F. J. E. RABY, *A History of Christian–Latin Poetry from the Beginnings to the Close of the Middle Ages* (2d ed. Oxford 1953) 127–128. P. B. GAMS, *Die Kirchengeschichte von Spanien,* 3 v. in 5 (Regensburg 1862–79; repr. Graz 1956) 2.2:132–135.

[M. G. MCNEIL]

EUGENIA, ST.

Abbess of Hohenberg (MONT SAINT–ODILE) in Alsace, *c.* 722 to *c.* 735. She succeeded her aunt, St. ODILIA, as abbess. Her father was Duke Adalbert of Alsace, and she seems to have had two sisters, (St.) Attala (*c.* 697–741) and Gunlind, who also became abbesses. Eugenia was revered for her holy life and wise government and was buried in the Chapel of St. John the Baptist close to her aunt, thus sharing in the honor pilgrims paid to the patroness of Alsace. Few of her relics remained after the raids of the Swedes in the Thirty Years' War.

Feast: Sept. 16.

Bibliography: *Acta Sanctorum* Sept. 5:332–335. G. BARDY, *Catholicisme* 4:679.

[F. M. BEACH]

EUGENICUS, MARK, METROPOLITAN OF EPHESUS

Chief Greek opponent of the union achieved in Florence; b. Constantinople, *c.* 1392; d. June 23, 1445. Until he was orphaned at the age of 12, he was educated in his father's school, then by John Chortasmenos and the philosopher Gemistos PLETHON. Mark Eugenicus (baptized Manuel) taught for a time before giving his property to the poor in his 26th year. He then became a monk on the island of Antigone, and took the name of Mark. Forced to return to Constantinople by Turkish troop movements in 1422, he lived in the monastery of the Mangani, where he gained a reputation for learning and sanctity. In view of the Council of FLORENCE he was made metropolitan of Ephesus (*c.* 1436) and procurator of the Patriarchate of Alexandria; he went with the Greeks to Italy, where he first wrote a fervid exhortation to the Pope to eliminate the FILIOQUE, and thus angered the Emperor.

Changed to procurator of Jerusalem and then of Antioch, Mark was chosen as one of six Greek speakers; in all but three sessions at Ferrara and Florence he was the sole Greek speaker. In the discussions on purgatory he became increasingly hostile to Latin doctrine. The addition to the Creed he declared to be the cause of the schism and also illegal because it was forbidden by the Council of Ephesus; he proclaimed that the filioque doctrine was opposed to Scripture, the Councils, and the Fathers. He accused the Latins of falsifying the texts of their own Doctors who taught the filioque.

He was the only Greek prelate consistently to oppose union, did not sign the decree of union, and returned to Constantinople in the Emperor's ship. There he became the center of antiunionism. On the election of the unionist Metrophanes as patriarch, Mark escaped to his episcopal see (May 15, 1440), which he had not yet visited. However, he soon set off for Mt. Athos. After being arrested on imperial orders and confined in a monastery of Lemnos for about two years (during a Turkish siege of the island), he was released probably in mid-1422. Returning to Constantinople, he continued his antiunionist propaganda until at the approach of death, he persuaded George Scholarius (later Patriarch GENNADIUS II) to succeed him in the task. After 14 days of atrocious pain Mark died on June 23, 1445 (or 1444).

Mark was an austere monk and an unflinching champion of orthodoxy as he saw it; he was learned in the Fathers, capable of arguing with the Latins about metaphysics and, strangely, capable also of accusing them of falsifying texts. His prestige assisted his propaganda, which was a skillful blend of serious theological writing and the most blatant *argumenta ad hominem* to suit the people he was addressing, with no little ridicule and invective of opponents. He had a receptive audience in the ill-educated monks and populace of Constantinople. Consequently, he was the most effective single influence that destroyed the union. Soon after his death he was reputed a saint, and his brother wrote a liturgical office for his feast. He was officially canonized by the Orthodox Greek Church in 1734.

Among his writings are 72 Kephalaia (Chapters) explaining his theology. Three discourses on purgatory, 56 syllogisms against the Latins, with a patristic *florilegium,* an address to the Pope, and a confession of faith, mark in part his interventions in the Council of Florence. He wrote a letter to George of Methone against the Latin rite, an encyclical and many tracts against the union, as well as liturgical and homiletic, ascetical, dogmatic, and eulogistic treatises.

Bibliography: *Patrologia Graeca* 160:1080–1200, contains his works. K. MAMONIS, ''Mark Eugenicus, Life and Work,'' *Theologia* 25 (1954) 377–404, 521–575, in Gr. J. GILL, *The Council of Florence* (New York 1959) L. PETIT, ''Documents relatifs au Concile de Florence,'' *Patrologia orientalis* 15.1 (1920) 5–168; 17.2 (1923) 309–522; *Dictionnaire de théologie catholique* 9.2:1968–86. V. LAURENT, *Lexikon für Theologie und Kirche*, ed. J. HOFER and K. RAHNER (Freiburg 1957–65) 7:11–12. V. GRUMEL, *Estudis Franciscans* 36 (1925) 425–448. G. MERCATI, *Opere minori,* 5 v. (Studi e Testi 76–80, 1937–41) 4.101–106. *Kirche und theologische Literatur im byzantinischen Reich* 755–758.

[J. GILL]

EUGENIUS VULGARIUS

Grammarian; place and date of birth and death unknown. He lived in southern Italy and was known for his literary activity during the pontificate of SERGIUS III (904–911). Unlike Sergius, he defended the legality of the election of Pope FORMOSUS (891–896) and the validity of the Holy Orders conferred by him. His arguments as well as his literary form were inspired by AUXILIUS OF NAPLES, although Vulgarius exhibited a greater knowledge of classical and Byzantine culture. Later he abandoned the Formosan cause and composed a submissive letter to SERGIUS III. His writings include *Insimulator et actor* (*Patrologia Latina*, ed. J.P. Migne [Paris 1878–90] 129:1103–12), *De causa formosiana libellus* (Dümmler 117–139), *Letters and Poems* (*Monumenta Germaniae Historica, Poetae* [Berlin 1826–] 4:412–440).

Bibliography: E. DÜMMLER, ed., *Auxilius und Vulgarius* (Leipzig 1866). M. MANITIUS Geschichte der lateinischen Literatur des Mittelalters (Munich 1911–31) 1:433–436. G. BAADER, *Lexikon für Theologie und Kirche* 2 3: 1778–79.

[S. P. LINDEMANS]

EUHEMERUS

Euhemerus of Messene; *c.* 340–260 B.C.; famous for his theory of the natural origin of the gods and religion. His only known work was the *Sacred Record* Ιερὰ ἀναγραφή in at least three books, of which Jacoby identifies 11 fragments, along with 15 more in the remains of Ennius's Latin version. It was an autobiographical romance in which the author claimed to have visited Panchaea, an island in the Indian Ocean. There he found a golden stele with an inscription setting forth the deeds of Uranus, Cronus, and Zeus, just rulers of Panchaea, who had been deified, or had caused themselves to be deified. Euhemerus described also the natural products and social structure of his imaginary kingdom in sober, realistic terms, using the geographical discoveries of Alexander's admirals, details drawn from contemporary knowledge of Persia, Arabia, and Egypt, and utopian theories of government (cf. Hippodamus of Miletus in Aristotle, *Politics* 1267b–1268a). Euhemerus was primarily a rationalistic philosopher of religion, but the realism of his work has sometimes caused him to be regarded as a geographer or historian.

Ennius's translation made Euhemerus known to the Romans, and promoted the development of religious skepticism among them. Christian writers, both Greek and Latin—Clement of Alexandria, Minucius Felix, Lactantius, and Augustine—found him useful in their apologetic against pagan religion and its origins. The term ''Euhemerism'' was coined in the 19th century to signify the rationalistic interpretation of myths and religion.

Bibliography: Fragments in F. JACOBY, *Fragmente der griechischen Historiker* (Berlin 1923) 1: No. 63. F. JACOBY, ''Euemeros (3),'' *Paulys Realenzyklopädie der klassischen Altertumswissenschaft* G. WISSOWA et al. (Stuttgart 1907) 6.1:952–972. J. GEFFCKEN, ''Euhemerism,'' *Encyclopedia of Religion and Ethics*, ed. J. HASTINGS (Edinburgh 1908–27) 5:572–573. J. W. SCHIPPERS, *De ontwikkeling der Euhemeristische godencritiek in de Christelijke Latijnse literatuur* (Groningen 1952).

[H. S. LONG]

EULALIUS, ANTIPOPE

Pontificate: Dec. 27, 418 to April 3, 419. At the death of Pope Zosimus (417–418), a small group of priests and deacons gathered in the Lateran basilica, and on Dec. 27, 418, elected as pope the archdeacon Eulalius who was a Greek like the deceased pope. The next day a sizeable majority of the clergy chose the elderly presbyter Boniface I (418–422). The city prefect supported Eulalius and recommended him to the emperor Honorius (395–423) at Ravenna. When a delegation of Boniface's supporters arrived at court, the emperor thought it best to have both claimants appear at a synod in Ravenna, but the synod proved inconclusive, and Honorius decided upon a second, larger one to be held in Spoleto in June of 419. In the meantime, both claimants were to stay out of Rome. Boniface complied with the imperial order, but Eulalius hoped that if he took up residence in the city while Boniface was absent, he could win popular support. The plan backfired when trouble broke out between the supporters of the two claimants. The prefect expelled Eulalius for vi-

St. Eulogius, Patriarch of Alexandria, manuscript painting in the ''Menologion of Basil II.''

olating the emperor's order, and on April 13, the angry Honorius decreed in favor of Boniface. Eulalius accepted defeat and withdrew from Rome. In 422, as Boniface felt death near, he told the emperor that trouble would arise if Eulalius tried to return to Rome after his death, yet, when the pope died, Eulalius did not return to the city, even though his followers urged him to do so. After the election of Celestine I (422–432), Eulalius accepted a bishopric in Campania, where he died in 423.

Bibliography: H. JEDIN, ed., *History of the Church* (New York 1980), 2:261. J. N. D. KELLY, *Oxford Dictionary of Popes* (New York 1986), 39–40. C. PIETRI, *Roma Christiana* (Rome 1976), 452–455.

[J. F. KELLY]

EULOGIUS, PATRIARCH OF ALEXANDRIA, ST.

Fl. 580 to 607; a theological controversialist; b. Antioch, Syria; d. Alexandria. Eulogius was a monk who became a priest and abbot of the *Deipara*, or Mother of God, monastery at Antioch, and in 580 he became patriarch of Alexandria. He met the future Pope GREGORY I in Constantinople (*c.* 582). Of his correspondence with Pope Gregory between 595 and 600, only Gregory's letters are extant. In one of these, written probably in June 598, the pope gives details of AUGUSTINE OF CANTERBURY's successful mission in England. In 595 the Pope urged Eulogius to oppose the usurpation of the title of universal patriarch by JOHN IV THE FASTER, patriarch of Constantinople (582–595). In *Bibliotheca* PHOTIUS preserved an account of 11 dogmatic orations of Eulogius and of his books against Novatianism (*Patrologia Graeca* 103:532–536) and against the Severian Monophysites (*ibid.* 103:934–955). *See* NOVATIAN AND NOVATIANISM.

In theology Eulogius was a Chalcedonian who followed the doctrine of St. BASIL OF CAESAREA via JOHN THE GRAMMARIAN, whose apology he knew evidently only through long citations in SEVERUS OF ANTIOCH's *Contra Grammaticum.* In contrast with contemporary theological opinion represented by the *De sectis* (*c.* 580), he denied ignorance in Christ, and this doctrine became part of the ordinary magisterium of the Church through Pope Gregory I. The authenticity of his *Homily for Palm Sunday* (*Patrologia Graeca* 103:2408–64) has been challenged, since a similar sermon is attributed to CYRIL OF ALEXANDRIA (*ibid.* 43:427–438) and EPIPHANIUS (*ibid.* 77:1050–72).

Feast: Sept. 13; Feb. 13 (Greek Church).

Bibliography: *Patrologia Graeca,* ed. J. P. MIGNE (Paris 1857–66) 86.2:2937–64. V. N. BENEŠEVIČ, *Revue d'histoire ecclésiastique* 24 (1928) 802. *Acta Sanctorum* Sept. 4:83–94. B. ALTANER, *Patrology,* tr. H. GRAEF (New York 1960) 620. J. J. DELANEY and J. E. TOBIN, eds., *Dictionary of Catholic Biography* (New York 1961) 389. C. MOELLER, *Revue d'histoire ecclésiastique* 46 (1951) 683–688. A. GRILLMEIER and H. BACHT, *Das Konzil von Chalkedon: Geschichte und Gegenwart* (Würzburg 1951–54) 1:691–693. O. BARDENHEWER, *Theologische Quartalschrift* 78 (1896) 353–401.

[F. DE SA]

EUNOMIUS OF CONSTANTINOPLE

Bishop of Cyzicus and chief exponent of Anomoeanism; b. Cappadocia, *c.* 335; d. Dakora, Cappadocia, *c.* 394. Eunomius joined the Arian leader Aëtius in Alexandria as disciple and secretary, and moved with him to Antioch where he was ordained deacon. He became bishop of Cyzicus in 360 (according to Philostorgius) or 366 (according to Socrates), but was soon forced to resign because of his extreme views. After Aëtius died in 366, Eunomius assumed leadership of the radical wing of ARIANISM, organized its communities and defended its doctrine in writing. He was often exiled and changed residence; he died at his family estate at Dakora in Cappadocia. Little remains of his extensive literary production, since the Emperor ARCADIUS ordered it to be burnt in 398. Most of it is known through refutations by Basil of Cappadocia, Gregory of Nyssa, and Apollinaris. Fragments of his Apology have been preserved along with part of a second Apology in answer to Basil's refutation, and a confession of faith addressed to the Emperor Theodosius I in 383. His adversaries accused him of reducing theology to technology: indeed, Eunomius shows himself a subtle dialectician, using Aristotelian methods to defend doctrines of Platonic inspiration, speaking, e.g., of the descending triad of the consubstantial Trinity.

Bibliography: J. QUASTEN, *Patrology* (Westminster MD 1950) 3:306–309, with bibliog. M. SPANNEUT, *Dictionnaire d'histoire et de géographie ecclésiastiques* 15:1399–1405. X. LE BACHELET, *Dictionnaire de théologie catholique* 5.2:1501–14, doctrine.

[V. C. DE CLERCQ]

EUPHEMIA, ST.

Fourth-century martyr under Diocletian; d. Chalcedon, *c.* 303. Her passio, though not historically trustworthy, describes her multiple sufferings; and St. Asterius of Amasea (d. 410) relates that she was ''burnt alive after her teeth were knocked out with a hammer.'' The date of September 16 found in the *Fasti consulares* of Vienne could be that of her martyrdom. In the fourth century a basilica was erected in her honor at Chalcedon and became an important pilgrimage center; both MELANIA THE YOUNGER and the mysterious pilgrim Aetheria visited it. In 451 the Council of CHALCEDON was held in this basilica, and the saint is said to have manifested her miraculous assistance. Shortly before the Persian invasion of the city (617), her relics were taken into Constantinople and placed in the old church of St. Euphemia. Many *encomia* were written in her honor; those by the ninth-century Theodore Bestes and Constantine, bishop of Tion, on the finding of her relics are of some note. Her cult spread rapidly, based as it was on the Council of Chalcedon and the miraculous narrations in her passio. The many authors mentioning her example or her relics include PAULINUS OF NOLA and PETER CHRYSOLOGUS. Many churches were dedicated in her honor: in the East, at Daphne near Antioch, at Oxyrhyncus in Middle Egypt; on the shore of the Adriatic, at Zara, Aquileia, Grado, and Ravenna; in the Mediterranean basin, at Malta and Carthage; and above all in Italy, at Tivoli between 492 and 496, and in Rome, where Pope St. SERGIUS (d. 701) restored the title to the Church of St. Euphemia on the Viminal hill. In the Milanese liturgy she was named in the Canon of the Mass. In the West during the Middle Ages her cult was widespread in Brittany, Alsace, and Austria.

Feast: Sept. 16.

SS. Agatha, Pelagia, and Euphemia, detail of a 6th-century mosaic in S. Apollinare Nuovo, Ravenna.

Bibliography: *Acta Sanctorum* Sept. 5:252–286. A. DELEHAYE, *Les Origines du culte des martyrs* (Brussels 1933). A. S. LEWIS, ed. and tr., *Select Narrations of Holy Women, from the Syro-Antiochene or Sinai Palimpsest,* 2 v. (London 1900). H. LECLERCQ, *Dictionnaire d'archéologie chrétienneet de liturgie*, ed. F. CABROL, H. LECLERCQ, and H. I. MARROU (Paris 1907–53) 5.1:745–746. A. M. SCHNEIDER, A. GRILLMEIER, and H. BACHT, *Das Konzil vom Chalkedon: Geschichte und Gegenwart* (Würzburg 1951–54) 1:291–302.

[L. VEREECKE]

EUPHRASIA, ST.

Virgin and ascetic; b. Constantinople, 380; d. *c.* 410. Euphrasia was the daughter of a senator of Constantinople, Antigonus, who died shortly after her birth, and was related to the Emperor THEODOSIUS I (379–395), who took her and her mother under his protection. Theodosius arranged a betrothal for Euphrasia, at the age of five, to the son of a wealthy senator. Two years later she and her mother withdrew from the court to Egypt, where they settled near a convent of nuns. At age seven Euphrasia, at her own insistence, was given over to the care of the nuns to be trained in the ascetic life; and at 12 she declined her betrothed, who then desired marriage. An heiress, she transferred her fortune to the emperor, probably ARCADIUS (395–408), to be used for charity. She died at the age of 30; St. JOHN DAMASCENE mentions her in his third *Oratio de imaginibus*.

Feast: March 13; July 24 and 25 (Orthodox Church).

Bibliography: G. DE JERPHANION, *Analecta Bollandiana* 55 (1937) 7. *Bibliotheca hagiographica Graeca*, ed. F. HALKIN, (Brussels 1957) 3:631. *Bibliotheca hagiographica latina antiquae ct mediae aetatis* (Brussels 1898–1901) 2718–21.

[E. D. CARTER]

EUSE HOYOS, MARIANO DE JESÚS, BL.

Also known as Fr. Marianito, diocesan priest; b. Oct. 14, 1845, Yarumal (Diocese of Antioquia), northwestern Colombia, and baptized the following day; d. July 12, 1926, Angostura, northeastern Colombia.

The eldest of the seven children of Pedro Euse (of Norman heritage) and Rosalía de Hoyos Echeverri, Mariano was educated at home in order to ensure a Christian formation. Even as a child he took time from his farming duties to teach other children the catechism. When he decided to become a priest (age 16), he was entrusted to the care of his uncle, Fr. Fermín Hoyos. On Feb. 3, 1869, Mariano entered the Medellín seminary. He was ordained (July 14, 1872), assigned as assistant to his uncle at San Pedro (1872–1876), then to Yarumal (1876–78) and Angostura (1878). As assistant to his ailing pastor, Rudesindo Correa, he supervised the completion of the church edifice. Upon Correa's death, Fr. Marianito became pastor and committed himself to caring for the needy during civil war. When his own safety was threatened several times he was forced into hiding. He was known for his poverty, his selfless charity, his simple but effective preaching, and his pastoral zeal, particularly in his ministry to farmers and children. He died after a long illness.

Marianito was buried in the chapel of the Virgin of Carmen, Angostura, which he had constructed. His incorrupt body was translated to the parish church on July 11, 1936. His cause for beatification was introduced Oct. 10, 1980. He was declared venerable (March 3, 1990) and a miracle, the cure of Colombian Fr. Rafael Gildardo Vélez Saldarriaga's prostate cancer, at his intercession approved (March 26, 1999). At his beatification (April 9, 2000) by John Paul II, Marianito became the first Colombian-born blessed.

Feast: July 13.

[K. I. RABENSTEIN]

EUSEBIA OF HAMAY, ST.

Benedictine abbess; d. March 16, 680 or 689. Eusebia, the daughter of St. ADALBALD, was elected abbess of Hamay at the age of 12 (perhaps 23), in accord with the medieval custom of thus gaining for the abbey the patronage of a powerful family. After the murder of Adalbald, Eusebia's mother, St. Rictrude, considering her too young for such responsibility, transferred the entire community of Hamay to Marciennes, whither she had retired with her two younger daughters, and where she was abbess. Eusebia's desire to return to the abandoned monastery induced Rictrude to reestablish the community at Hamay. Eusebia ruled wisely until her death at the age of 40.

Feast: March 16.

Bibliography: *Acta Sanctorum* March 2:445–456. J. MABILLON, *Acta sanctorum ordinis S. Benedicti* (Venice 1733–40) 2:944–951. *Analecta Bollandiana* 20 (1901) 460–463; 62 (1944) 159–164. *Bibliotheca hagiographica latina antiquae et mediae aetatis* (Brussels 1898–1901) 1: 2736–38. G. BARDY, *Catholicisme* 4:710. J. L. BAUDOT and L. CHAUSSIN, *Vies des saints et des bienheueux selon l'ordre du calendrier avec l'historique des fêtes* (Paris 1935–56) 3: 351–352. A. M.. ZIMMERMANN, *Kalendarium Benedictinum: Die Heiligen und Seligen des Benediktinerorderns und seiner Zweige* (Metten 1933–38) 1:333–335.

[M. B. RYAN]

EUSEBIA OF SAINT-CYR, ST.

Abbess and martyr; d. Marseilles, France, 838. She was a BENEDICTINE nun and abbess of Saint-Cyr in Marseilles. According to the legend, which has as its basis her epitaph, she and 39 of her sisters were martyred by the Saracens. She may, however, have lived as early as the sixth or seventh centuries. Her tomb is to be found in the church of SAINT-VICTOR IN MARSEILLES.

Feast: Sept. 20; Oct. 12 (Marseilles).

Bibliography: *Acta Sanctorum* Oct. 4:292–295. A. M.. ZIMMERMANN, *Kalendarium Benedictinum: Die Heiligen und Seligen des Benediktinerorderns und seiner Zweige* (Metten 1933–38) 3:80–82. G. BARDY, *Catholicisme* 4: 710–711. H. LECLERCQ, *Dictionnaire d'archéologie chrétienneet de liturgie,* ed. F. CABROL, H. LECLERCQ and H. I. MARROU (Paris 1907–53) 1.2:1989–91; 10.2:2239–41. S. VERNE, *Sainte Eusébie, abbesse, et ses 40 compagnes martyres à Marseille* (Marseilles 1891).

[P. BLECKER]

EUSEBIUS, POPE, ST.

Pontificate: April 18, 309 to Aug. 17, 309. A violent controversy over the LAPSI, who claimed the right to be received back into ecclesiastical communion without submitting to the customary prolonged penance, was raging when Eusebius succeeded MARCELLUS I. According to the inscriptions of Pope DAMASUS I, the civil authority finally intervened, and Emperor Maxentius exiled both Eusebius and Heraclius, the leader of the opposition, to

Sicily. After Eusebius' death his body was brought back to Rome and buried in the cemetery of Callistus. According to the *Liber pontificalis,* he was a Greek and had been a physician, but little reliable information about him survives.

Feast: Formerly Sept. 26, now Aug. 17.

Bibliography: *Acta Sanctorum,* Sept. 7:245–250. K. BIHLMEYER and H. TÜCHLE, *Kirchengeschichte* (Paderborn 1962) 1:167–168. A. FERRUA, ed., *Epigrammata Damasiana* (Vatican City 1942) 129–136. J. N. D. KELLY *Oxford Dictionary of Popes* (New York 1986), 26. G. SCHWAIGER, *Lexikon für Theologie und Kirche,* 3d. ed. 3 (Freiburg 1995), s.v. ''Eusebius, heilig, Papst.'' B. SODARO, *Santi e beati di Calabria* (Rosarno 1996), 52–56.

[R. K. POETZEL]

EUSEBIUS OF CAESAREA

Bishop of Caesarea in Palestine, apologist, Biblical exegete, and the earliest Church historian; b. *c.* 260; d. *c.* 339. Nothing is known of his family; but it was at Caesarea that he was baptized, as an adult, and entered the ranks of the clergy. In a city where ORIGEN had taught for so many years, Eusebius was heir to a scholarly tradition mediated to him through PAMPHILUS, who had been a pupil of Pierius at Alexandria. Pamphilus had also collected a library, which was a center for scholarly work. So close did Eusebius draw to his older companion in friendship and in the furtherance of literary and textual labors that he adopted the name Eusebius Pamphili, the son or servant of Pamphilus, and it is by this name that he was commonly designated.

Life. The work of the scholars of Caesarea was not disrupted by the persecution of 303 to 313. Eusebius was himself at times away from the city, e.g., at Tyre and in Egypt, where, as at Caesarea itself, he witnessed martyrdoms. The imprisonment (308) and martyrdom (310) of Pamphilus deeply affected him. He commemorated his friend in a *Life,* in three books, no longer extant. He may himself have been imprisoned, but the accusation of apostasy, made long afterward at the Council of Tyre (335), cannot be regarded as more than another of the reckless accusations current at that period; it is most unlikely that an apostate would have been chosen as bishop of Caesarea *c.* 313.

By this time Eusebius was a voluminous writer whose interests covered every field of Christian literary activity. He also had close friendships with other bishops, such as Paulinus of Tyre and Theodotus of Laodicea in Syria. Eusebius preached at the dedication of a church at Tyre *c.* 316.

When the Arian controversy began (*c.* 318), Eusebius had already had occasion to express his opinion on the

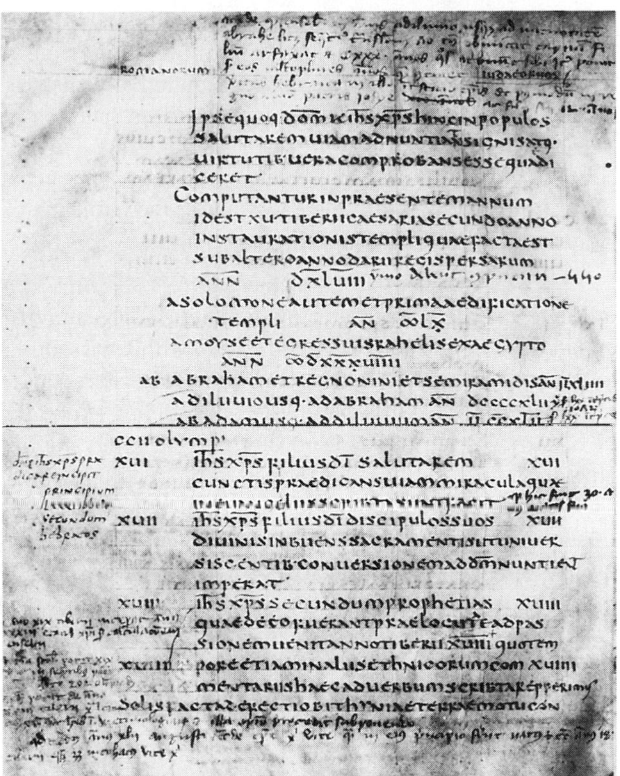

Folio from a 5th- or 6th-century manuscript of Jerome's Latin version of Eusebius's ''Chronicle'' (MS Auct. T. 2. 2.6, fol. 111v).

issues involved, particularly in his *Demonstratio Evangelica.* His support was well worth having; ARIUS (*c.* 320) regarded him as one of his chief supporters. In theology Eusebius was the heir to Origen and later Alexandrian teachers, but in his statement on the relations between Father and Son, it is the SUBORDINATIONISM of Origen that is most prominent. At the Council of Antioch (*c.* 324), Eusebius and two others were provisionally excommunicated for their adherence to Arian views. Their case was referred to a great council called to meet at Ancyra; but Emperor CONSTANTINE I changed the venue of the council to Nicaea. After the council Eusebius explained what had happened in a letter to his own church.

It has commonly been held that Eusebius presented the creed of Caesarea as a basis on which the creed of the council was constructed, but, in view of his personal excommunication, it is more likely that he produced his creed, with a declaration of his lifelong fidelity to it, as evidence of his own right faith. His creed was approved by the emperor, but the Creed of Nicaea, which Eusebius regarded as derived from his own, contains little that is distinctively Caesarean, and the key word *HOMOOUSIOS* and the description of the Son as ''true God'' are not Eusebian.

There is clearly some misunderstanding in Eusebius's letter, or a clumsy endeavor to minimize the consequences of the acceptance of the Council's terms. He appears to have shared the feelings of others that the use of *homoousios* of the Son implied a rending of the divine substance. Eusebius signed both creed and anathemas, more from a desire for peace and under the influence of Constantine than from genuine conviction.

He was soon involved in the quarrels and intrigues of the following years, during which the leading supporters of Nicaea were attacked, and Arius, without assenting to the Nicene decisions, was rehabilitated. Eusebius quarreled with EUSTATHIUS OF ANTIOCH, a leading supporter of Nicaea. Eustathius accused Eusebius of perverting the Nicene faith; and the latter replied with an accusation of SABELLIANISM; the quarrel may also have had its roots in Eustathius's outspoken criticism of Origen. That Eusebius took part in the expulsion of Eustathius about 330 there can be no doubt, but he refused translation to Antioch, a refusal for which he was warmly commended by Constantine.

St. ATHANASIUS and MARCELLUS OF ANCYRA, among others, were also exiled. Athanasius failed to appear at a council called by the emperor in 334 to meet at Caesarea to deal with accusations (nondoctrinal) against him, because of his suspicions of Eusebius; but in 335, under threat of imperial displeasure, he came to the Council of Tyre. Eusebius was one of the judges and was the subject of the taunt about his behavior in the persecution. Athanasius did not wait for condemnation, but appealed to Constantine, who summoned the council to assemble at Constantinople. Eusebius and a few others obeyed after attending the dedication of the church of the Holy Sepulchre at Jerusalem. Athanasius was sent into exile.

Thereafter the celebration of Constantine's *Tricennalia* took place, at which Eusebius delivered a panegyric on the emperor, for whom he had conceived an extreme admiration: he elaborated a new theory of the relations of Church and Empire, made necessary by the changed circumstances of the time. The final controversy of Eusebius's life was with Marcellus of Ancyra, a strong supporter of Nicaea, whose theology was regarded as Sabellian. Marcellus and Eusebius had long been antipathetic to each other: after Marcellus was exiled in 336, Eusebius wrote two works, *Against Marcellus* (2 books) and *On the Theology of the Church* (3 books), in which, while pointing out the errors of Marcellus and defending various friends, he did not himself stand forth as a supporter of Nicaea, though it is clear he had by then moved somewhat nearer to the theology of the council.

Late in his life Eusebius produced his *Theophania,* on the manifestation of God in the work of His Word. The five books are extant in Syriac, and are largely repetitions of passages and topics culled from his other works. After the death of Constantine in 337, Eusebius wrote his *Life of Constantine,* a panegyric on the benefactor of the Church, who had shown singular favor to the author. It is wrong, however, to regard Eusebius as a toady of the Emperor; they probably met only twice, at the Council of Nicea and at the *Tricennalia.* Eusebius was dead by the time of the Council of Antioch in 341. His life, written by Acacius, his pupil and successor at Caesarea, is not extant.

Writings. A noteworthy tendency in his writings is an almost excessive reliance on sources, which sometimes reduces his work to strings of quotations. This may be described as the writing of fully documented apologetic or history, but it can also be considered as a failure to digest what he had read and to consolidate the results of his reading. He himself disclaimed originality. This is not to say that on occasion he did not write well; and in view of prevailing fashions his rhetoric can be excused. In numerous cases he preserved portions of works no longer extant. His works may be grouped under the heads of (1) text, exegesis, and topography of Holy Scripture, (2) apologetic works, and (3) historical works and panegyric.

Exegete. His textual work was undertaken both in collaboration with Pamphilus and by himself. Surviving manuscripts bear witness to this work, carrying inscriptions such as "corrected by the hand of Eusebius Pamphili." It is no wonder that Constantine sent to Eusebius for texts of Scripture for use in the churches of Constantinople.

Eusebius wrote also extensive commentaries, still largely extant, on ISAIAH (after 324) and on the Psalms (*c.* 330–335) and may have written others; his method of exegesis is a blend of allegorism and literalism. He wrote *Gospel Questions and Solutions* (before 312) in which he examined divergencies in the narrative of the Gospels, and a *General Elementary Introduction* in ten books covering the whole course of Christian instruction; four books (7–10) are extant under the title of *Eclogae Propheticae.* Of several works dealing with Biblical topography only the *Onomasticon* survives. This is a geographical dictionary of the Bible, but it has many gaps and shows great inconsistency in the treatment of different entries.

Apologist. Eusebius was primarily an apologist, and this designation of him extends even to his *Ecclesiastical History,* which is a vindication of Christianity against heathens and heretics. Some of his apologetic works were directed to the needs of his own time; such is his *Against Porphyry,* the Neoplatonist detractor of Christianity, in 25 books (before 303). This work is lost, but large portions of it are probably embedded in other writings, as Eusebius constantly reused materials.

In his *Against Hierocles* he refuted the comparison made by Hierocles, a high official and notorious persecutor, between Christ and APOLLONIUS OF TYANA. Pamphilus and Eusebius collaborated in writing a *Defence of Origen,* who had been attacked by METHODIUS OF OLYMPUS and others. Eusebius himself added a sixth book. Only book 1 is extant, in the Latin translation of RUFINUS OF AQUILEIA.

Of wider significance are the *Praeparatio* and *Demonstratio Evangelica* (in 15 and 20 books respectively). The former is a refutation of pagan mythology, oracles, and astrology; an exposition of the Jewish Scripture, with testimonies from heathen writers that support these; and a demonstration of the so-called plagiarisms of the philosophers from the Old Testament and of the contradictions of Greek philosophical teaching. The *Demonstratio* (the first ten books are extant) deals with the fulfillment of prophecy in Christ, His Incarnation and earthly life, and the resumption in Christianity of a pure religion professed by the ancient Patriarchs. *The Theophania* has already been mentioned.

Historian. The *Chronicle* of Eusebius, an epitome of world history down to 303, based partly on the work of JULIUS AFRICANUS, is extant only in Armenian and in Jerome's Latin adaptation (continued to 378). Eusebius prefaced to the actual chronological tables accounts of various nations, in which he made cross-references to events of Jewish history. Chronological works of this kind had long been used by Christians to demonstrate the antiquity of Jewish achievements on which Christianity was based.

This annalistic method was carried over by Eusebius into his *Ecclesiastical History,* in which his narrative is divided by notices of the accessions of Roman emperors and by the episcopal successions of the sees of Rome, Alexandria, Antioch, and Jerusalem. In its final form the *History* consists of ten books and extends to the victory of Constantine over Licinius in 324. But it is clear from indications in certain manuscripts, and from internal evidence of rehandling of material in books 8–10, that earlier editions of the *History* existed. The last three books deal with the years of persecution, followed by peace, from 303 onward, and, with this restriction of subject matter, are very different from the books in which Eusebius dealt with the general history of the Church.

In his preface Eusebius listed the subjects with which he intended to deal, and the last two, the martyrdoms of his own time and the divine succor afforded at the last, look like additions. It is therefore quite likely that the history was first in seven books, down to A.D. 303. Eusebius was well aware that he was a pioneer; while his history is still our chief primary source for its period, it must be noted that Eusebius was limited by the sources available to him. These are practically all Greek sources: he is almost entirely ignorant of the rise and development of the Latin Church. Moreover, it is hardly to be expected that he could handle adequately a subject such as heresy. Mention must be made also of the *Martyrs of Palestine,* which exists in longer and shorter versions: the former is extant only in a Syriac version; the latter is closely attached to book eight of the *Ecclesiastical History.*

Constantinian Panegyric. The *Life of Constantine* must have been written between 337 and 339. It is a panegyric; Eusebius himself regarded it as such and it should not be judged otherwise. But certain doubts have been expressed about this work. It appears to be unknown to other 4th-century authors, and some have thought that it was written much later by someone who embodied genuine documents in it. Others have suspected the genuineness of the documents included by the author; however, one of these has been discovered on papyrus, quite apart from the *Life,* and the tenor of the others is well suited to the Constantinian period. The whole theory of the Christian empire, elaborated in this work (and in Eusebius's oration at the *Tricennalia*), is in keeping with the first days of tolerance and collaboration that were so soon blighted by the reigns of CONSTANTIUS II and JULIAN THE APOSTATE.

Later authors vary in their estimate of Eusebius, as his great services to Christian scholarship were countered by his attachment to the Arians.

Bibliography: Works. *Patrologia Graeca* v.19–24; *Die griechischen christlichen schriftsteller der ersten drei Jahrhunderte* (1902-); Eng. editions of his *Ecclesiastical History,* tr. K. LAKE and J. E. L. OULTON, 2 v. (*Loeb Classical Library*; New York 1926–32:) ed. and tr. H. J. LAWLOR and J. E. L. OULTON, 2 v. (Society for Promoting Christian Knowledge; 1927–28), with introd. and commentary; French ed. and tr. G. BARDY, 4 v. (*Sources Chrétiennes* 31, 41, 55, 73; 1952–60), with introd., nn., and indexes; *Oration at the Tricennalia,* ed. and tr. E. C. RICHARDSON (*A Select Library of the Nicene and Post-Nicene Fathers* 2d ser. 1; 1890) 581–610, rev. tr. with introd. and nn.; *Evangelica Praeparatio,* ed. E. H. GIFFORD, 4 v. in 5 (Oxford 1903), with tr. and nn.; *Evangelica Demonstratio,* tr. W. J. FERRAR, 2 v. (London 1920); *Against Hierocles,* tr. F. C. CONYBEARE in PHILOSTRATUS, *The Life of Apollonius,* 2 v. (*Loeb Classical Library*; New York 1912) 2:484–605; *Life of Constantine,* ed. and tr. E. C. RICHARDSON, *loc. cit.* 411–580. Literature. D. S. WALLACE-HADRILL, *Eusebius of Caesarea* (London 1960), with bibliog. R. LAQUEUR, *Eusebius als Historiker seiner Zeit* (Berlin 1929). H. BERKHOF, *Die Theologie des Eusebius von Caesarea* (Amsterdam 1939). J. N. D. KELLY, *Early Christian Doctrines* (2d ed. New York 1960), theology. J. R. LAURIN, *Orientations maîtresses des Apologistes chrétiens de 270 à 361* (*Analecta Gregoriana* 61; 1954) 94–145, 344–401. N. H. BAYNES, *Byzantine Studies and Other Essays* (New York 1955) 168–172. K. M. SETTON, *Chris-*

tian Attitude towards the Emperor in the 4th Century (New York 1941) 40–56. A. A. T. EHRHARDT, *Politische Metaphysik von Solon bis Augustin,* 2 v. (Tübingen 1959) 2:259–292.

[J. STEVENSON]

EUSEBIUS OF EMESA

Bishop and writer; b. Edessa, *c.* A.D. 300; d. Antioch, before 359. He was educated in Edessa, Scythopolis, Caesarea of Palestine, Alexandria, and Antioch. Eusebius was chosen by the Arians to rule the See of Alexandria in 340; but knowing the popular attachment to the exiled Athanasius, he declined. Shortly afterward he became bishop of EMESA (Homs), capital of Lebanese Phoenicia and ancient center of pagan sun worship. There he was accused of astrology and later, of SABELLIANISM. Resigning his see, he accompanied the Emperor Constantius on an expedition against the Persians *c.* 348, some years before his death.

St. Jerome credits Eusebius with considerable eloquence and mentions his writings against the Jews, pagans, and Novatians, as well as a commentary on Galatians and homilies on the Gospels (*Vir. ill.* 91), but Jerome exaggerates his attachment to ARIANISM (*Chron. an.* 347). Eusebius' writings, the subject of intensive contemporary research (29 discourses in an old Latin version have recently been restored to him), indicate that he was a moderate semi-Arian, dependent on EUSEBIUS OF CAESAREA in his CHRISTOLOGY and Trinitarian theology, more prone to the literal exegesis of Antioch than to Alexandrian allegorism.

Bibliography: J. QUASTEN, *Patrology* 3:348–351. É. M. BUYTAERT, *Eusèbe d'Émèse: Discours conservés en latin,* 2 v. (*Spicilegium sacrum Lovaniense* 26–27; 1953–57); *L'Héritage littéraire d'Eusèbe d'Émèse* (Louvain 1949); ''On the Trinitarian Doctrine of Eusebius of Emesa,'' *Franciscan Studies* 14 (1954) 34–48. D. AMAND DE MENDIETA, ''La Virginité chez Eusèbe d'Émèse et l'ascétisme familial dans la première moitié du IVe siècle,'' *Revue d'histoire ecclésiastique* 50 (1955) 777–820.

[É. DES PLACES]

EUSEBIUS OF NICOMEDIA

Fourth-century bishop, leader of the anti-Nicene reaction; d. *c.* 341. Probably a native of Syria, Eusebius studied with the future heretic ARIUS under LUCIAN OF ANTIOCH; he was first made bishop of Berytus in Phoenicia, then promoted to the metropolitan see of Nicomedia (*c.* 318), where he gained high favor at the court of the Emperor Licinius. He actively supported Arius against ALEXANDER, Patriarch of Alexandria, and was responsible for the rapid spread of the Arian conflict. Eusebius welcomed Arius after Arius's first condemnation, wrote numerous letters to fellow bishops in Arius's defense, and held a synod in Bithynia that nullified Arius's excommunication.

In 324, when CONSTANTINE I defeated Licinius and entered Nicomedia, Eusebius escaped reprisals through the protection of Constantia, wife of Licinius and sister of Constantine. The tone of the Emperor's letter to Bishop Alexander and Arius indicates that his information on the Arian controversy came from Eusebius. At the Council of NICAEA I (325) Eusebius acted as spokesman for the Arian faction; Athanasius constantly referred to it as ''Eusebius and his fellows.'' A document composed by Eusebius was read at the council, causing great indignation among the Fathers. When the Nicene Creed was proposed, he rejected the term *HOMOOUSIOS,* but in the end he signed the creedal statement under pressure from Constantine.

About three months later, according to Philostorgius, Eusebius disavowed his signature and was immediately exiled to Gaul by the Emperor. In 328, having presented a retraction, he was recalled from exile and restored to his see, perhaps by a second assemblage (328) of the Council of Nicaea. He regained his influence at the court and assumed the leadership of a widespread reaction against the Nicene Council and Creed (328–341). Eusebius tried at first to remove the most powerful leaders of the Nicene party. Thus (*c.* 330), EUSTATHIUS OF ANTIOCH was condemned and deposed by a synod held in Antioch. About the same time (or in 336), MARCELLUS OF ANCYRA, under accusation of SABELLIANISM, met with the same fate. But Eusebius's main adversary, ATHANASIUS OF ALEXANDRIA, who had succeeded Alexander in 328, proved difficult to eliminate. Twice he managed to vindicate himself from accusations brought before Constantine; but in 335 the Synod of Tyr, at Eusebius' instigation, condemned Athanasius; he was deposed and sent into exile to Gaul.

Eusebius baptized Constantine at Nicomedia shortly before the Emperor's death in 337. He retained his prominent position under Constantius II and obtained the see of Constantinople, the imperial city from 330. His last known action was to preside over the Dedication Council of ANTIOCH in 341; he died soon afterward. Eusebius left no major writings; three of his letters have been preserved.

Bibliography: ATHANASIUS, *Werke,* ed. H. G. OPITZ, v. 3.1 (Berlin 1934) 15–17, 65–66, letters. A. LICHTENSTEIN, *Eusebius von Nikomedien* (Halle 1903). G. BARDY, *Recherches sur St. Lucien d'Antioche et son école* (Paris 1936) 296–315. G. BAREILLE, *Dictionnaire de théologie catholique* (Paris 1903–50) 5.2:1539–51. J. QUASTEN, *Patrology* 3:190–193. M. SPANNEUT, *Dictionnaire* *d'histoire et de géographie ecclésiastiques* (Paris 1912) 15:1466–71.

[V. C. DE CLERCQ]

EUSEBIUS OF SAMOSATA, ST.

Opponent of ARIANISM; d. 380. Eusebius is mentioned as bishop of Samosata in 361 at the synod of Antioch that elected Meletius as successor to Bishop Eudoxius. When the Arians attempted to seize the acts of the synod, Eusebius met them with heroic and successful refusal (Theodoret of Cyr, *Histoire ecclesiastique* 5.4.8). In 372, with GREGORY OF NAZIANZUS, he aided in the election of BASIL OF CAESAREA and later received several letters from both Basil and Gregory. A sensitive and zealous apostle, he was exiled in Thrace by the Arian-influenced Emperor Valens from 374 to 378; but he was recalled by GRATIAN. A short while later he was killed by a brick thrown by an Arian woman.

Feast: June 21.

Bibliography: *Acta Sanctorum* June 5:204–208. P. BEDJAN, ed., *Acta martyrum,* 7 v. (Paris 1890–97) 6:335–377. A. BUTLER, *The Lives of the Saints,* ed. H. THURSTON and D. ATTWATER (New York 1956) 2:607–608. H. R. REYNOLDS, *A Dictionary of Christian Biography*, ed. W. SMITH and H. WACE, (London 1877–87) 2:369–372. M. SPANNEUT, *Dictionnaire d'histoire et de géographie ecclésiastiques* (Paris 1912–) 15:1473–75. F. L. CROSS, *The Oxford Dictionary of the Christian Church* (London 1957) 475. G. BARDY, *Histoire de l'église depuis les origines jusqu'à nos jours*, ed. A. FLICHE and V. MARTIN (Paris 1935) 3:261–283.

[J. HAMROGUE]

EUSEBIUS OF VERCELLI, ST.

Bishop, monastic founder, and anti-Arian polemicist; b. Sardinia, Italy, early fourth century; d. Vercelli, August 1, 371. He became a member of the Roman clergy under Pope JULIUS. When consecrated first bishop of Vercelli *c.* 344, he established a community life for his clergy, and he is considered a founder of the CANONS REGULAR. He was also instrumental in the establishment of new dioceses near Vercelli, e.g., Turin and Embrun. Eusebius attended the Council of Milan in 355 as legate of Pope LIBERIUS and with Dionysius of Milan upheld the orthodoxy of St. ATHANASIUS against the politically intimidated Western episcopate. He was exiled in the East until the death of CONSTANTIUS II, was liberated under Julian, and in 362 attended the Council of Alexandria with Athanasius and approved its lenient decisions for the reconciliation of compromised bishops. Returned to Italy, he collaborated with HILARY OF POITIERS against the Arians; he died peaceably in his own diocese. Of his correspondence, three letters have been preserved, and the first seven books of a *De Trinitate* previously attributed to Athanasius or Vigilius of Thapsus are now ascribed to him by many patrologists. He also translated *Commentaries on the Psalms* by EUSEBIUS OF CAESAREA (Jerome, *Ep.* 61.2), now lost, and may have authored the pre-Jerome version of the Gospels preserved in the *Codex Vercellensis*.

Feast: Aug. 2 (formerly Dec. 16, anniversary of his consecration).

Bibliography: *De Trinitate* and *Epistulae,* ed. V. BULHART (*Corpus Christianorum. Series latina* 9; 1957) 1–110. *Eusebio di Vercelli e il suo tempo,* ed. E. DAL COVOLO, R. UGLIONE, and G. M. VIAN (Rome 1997). *Patralogiae cursus completus, series latina,* ed. A. HAMMAN (Paris 1957) 1:1741–42, 305–307. B. ALTANER, *Patrology,* tr. H. GRAEF (New York 1960) 429. V. DE CLERCQ, *Dictionnaire d'histoire et de géographie ecclésiastiques* (Paris 1912–) 15:1477–83. *Clavis Patrum latinorum,* ed. E. DEKKERS 105–111.

[V. C. DE CLERCQ]

EUSTACE, MAURICE

Martyr; place and date of birth unknown; d. November 1587. He was the eldest son of John Eustace of Castlemartin and his first wife Elizabeth Pebhard. After being educated at Douai, Maurice entered the Jesuit novitiate at Bruges. His father wrote to his superiors and requested them to send him home, as he was his heir and only son of his first marriage. On returning home, Maurice reminded his father that he could make one of his other children his heir and returned to Bruges against his father's wishes, but was advised by the Jesuits to return home, as his place appeared to be in the world.

His father had him appointed a captain of cavalry. He was denounced as a Jesuit and as a participant in the Baltinglaso rebellion by a younger brother, eager to inherit. His father's will, probated in 1580, named his son William his heir. Maurice denied rebellion, but openly confessed his Catholic faith. Adam Loftus, Lord Chancellor, offered him his daughter in marriage, and a large dowry if he would change his faith. Maurice refused and was executed.

See Also: IRISH CONFESSORS AND MARTYRS.

Bibliography: D. MURPHY, *Our Martyrs* (Dublin 1896). R. BAGWELL, *Ireland under the Tudors,* 3 v. (London 1885–90). Genealogical Office MSS. Dublin: Fisher Wills: Anglo-Irish Pedigrees.

[J. G. BARRY]

EUSTACE OF LUXEUIL, ST.

Abbot; b. Burgundy, *c.* 560; d. Luxeuil, France, April 2, 629. A nephew of Miget, bishop of Langres, he became a monk at the Abbey of LUXEUIL toward the end of the sixth century and was placed in charge of the monastic school there. He followed his abbot, the Irish missionary COLUMBAN, into exile (*c.* 610), but was sent back to take his place as abbot (*c.* 612). Chlotar II later requested him to convince Columban to return to Luxeuil from BOBBIO, but Eustace was unsuccessful. He preached throughout the countryside around the abbey and was a companion of AGIL on a missionary journey to Bavaria. Upon his return (*c.* 617), he found himself forced to oppose the monk Agrestius, who had left the monastery to preach, but now was speaking in open support of the heresy of the THREE CHAPTERS and in opposition to the severity of the abbey's rule. At the Synod of Mâcon the abbot promoted the condemnation of Agrestius and his adherents (626–627). The BENEDICTINE RULE, which Agrestius had advocated, was introduced at Luxeuil only by Eustace's successor, Abbot Waldebert. Eustace was buried at Luxeuil, where his relics remained until *c.* 966, when they were transferred to the Abbey of Vergaville in Lorraine. The body disappeared in 1670, but the site remained a center of pilgrimage until the French Revolution. Eustace's life was written by a contemporary, JONAS OF BOBBIO (*Monumenta Germaniae Historica: Scriptores rerum Merovingicarum*, 4:119–130); he has been mentioned in the martyrologies since the 10th century.

Feast: March 29.

Bibliography: *Acta Sanctorum* (Paris 1863–), March 3:781–787. *Bibliotheca hagiographica latina antiquae et mediae aetatis* (Brussels 1898–1901) 2773–74. C. PERRY, *La Vie de Saint Eustase, 2e abbé de Luxeuil* (Metz 1649). P. A. PIDOUX DE MADUÈRE, *Vie des saints de Franche-Comté,* 4 v. (Lons-le-Saunier 1908–09) 2:178–185. A. M.. ZIMMERMANN, *Kalendarium Benedictinum: Die Heiligen und Seligen des Benediktinerorderns und seiner Zweige* (Metten 1933–38) 1:385–389. J. L. BAUDOT and L. CHAUSSIN, *Vies des saints et des bienheueux selon l'ordre du calendrier avec l'historique des fêtes* (Paris 1935–56) 3:624–626. G. BARDY, *Catholicisme*. 4:714–715. T. DE MOREMBERT, *Dictionnaire d'histoire et de géographie ecclésiastiques* (Paris 1912–) 16:12. *Patrologia Latina,* ed. J. P. MIGNE (Paris 1878–90) 87:1045–56.

[B. J. COMASKEY]

EUSTATHIUS OF ANTIOCH, ST.

Bishop and theologian; b. Side in Pamphylia; d. before 337. Eustathius (or Eustace) was bishop of Beroea in Syria before the Arian conflict, was transferred to the metropolitan See of Antioch (probably 324), and took part in and may even have presided at the Council of Nicaea (325). One of the first and most relentless opponents of Arianism, he was deposed and exiled (*c.* 331) to Trajanopolis in Thrace by Emperor CONSTANTINE; there is no evidence of his return. Some friends, uncompromising Nicaeans, formed a Eustathian faction that survived as a separate group until 482–485. Of his many works 20 titles are known. Extant are one complete exegetical treatise, *On the Witch of Endor against Origen,* and some hundred fragments. His most important work seems to have been *Adversus Arianos,* in at least eight books. Eustathius's Trinitarian theology implies, between God and the Word, a relation of Father to Son. His Christology lays strong stress on the distinction and integrity of the two natures in Christ against the Arians. He was the first to attempt a Logos-Man Christology against the prevalent Logos-Sarx doctrine, and it is in his opposition to the latter theory that he merits a significant place in the history of doctrine. He was not a forerunner of NESTORIUS, for his soteriology and certain nuances of his Christology demand a unicity of person in Christ. In scriptural matters, he cites the Pentateuch and the Gospels in the so-called Lucian recension, denounces the abuses of allegorism, and gives a reasoned and realistic interpretation of the text. In doctrine as well as exegesis, Eustathius would seem to have been an authentic Antiochene.

Feast: July 16.

Bibliography: M. SPANNEUT, ed., *Recherches sur les écrits d'Eustathe d'Antioche* (Lille 1948); *Dictionnaire d'histoire et de géographie ecclésiastiques* (Paris 1912–) 16:13–23. R. V. SELLERS, *Eustathius of Antioch and His Place in the Early History of Christine Doctrine* (Cambridge, Eng. 1928).

[M. SPANNEUT]

EUSTATHIUS OF SEBASTE

Bishop and first promoter of monastic life in eastern Asia Minor; b. *c.* 300; d. 377 or 380. Eustathius, the son of Bishop Eulalius, probably also of Sebaste, Armenia, entered the clergy and studied at Alexandria under ARIUS, whom his father supported at the Council of Nicaea. Probably influenced by Egyptian monasticism, he propagated cenobitism in his native country; but excesses in his ascetical movement, from which Messalianism later derived, brought upon him the censure of his father, and later of various synods. Twenty canons of the Council of Gangra (*c.* 340) are directed against certain practices of the Eustathians, e.g., unbecoming dress, contempt of marriage, and neglect of parental or filial duties. Nevertheless, shortly before 357 Eustathius was promoted to the metropolitan See of Sebaste, and soon afterward he joined efforts with BASIL OF ANCYRA and the Homoiousian party to head off the Anomoeans. He attended all the councils of the time: Ancyra (358), Sirmium (358), Seleucia (359), Constantinople (360), Lampsacus (364), and even Rome (366), where, having signed the Nicene Creed, he was received in communion by Pope LIBERIUS.

After 371 he joined the Pneumatomachian sect and, as a result, engaged in a bitter feud with BASIL THE GREAT, whom he had initiated in the monastic life. At the Council of Cyzicus (376) he signed a creed that affirmed the homoiousios for the Son but denied the full divinity of the Holy Spirit.

See Also: ARIANISM.

Bibliography: F. LOOFS, *Eustathius von Sebaste und die Chronologie der Basilius-Briefe* (Halle 1898). S. SALAVILLE, *Dictionnaire de théologie catholique* 5.2: 1565–74. J. GRIBOMONT, *Dictionnaire de spiritualité ascétique et mystique* 4.2:1708–12; *Dictionnaire d'histoire et de géographie ecclésiastiques* 16:26–33; *Studia Patristica,* v.2 (*Texte und Untersuchungen zur Geschichte der altchristlichen Literatur* 64; 1957) 400–415.

[V. C. DE CLERCQ]

EUSTOCHIA OF PADUA, BL.

Benedictine nun; b. Lucrezia, in Padua, Italy, 1444; d. there, February 13, 1469. She was the daughter of a nun and was born and educated in the convent of San Prosdocimo. After a more observant group replaced the old community there, she sought admission, which was granted reluctantly. Her profession was long delayed because, while she was sometimes obedient, gentle, and charitable, she was often stubborn and ill-tempered, and showed signs of diabolical possession. When suspected of being the cause of the abbess's mysterious illness, she was even in danger of being burned as a witch. Finally a wise and patient confessor intervened, and she took vows and won the respect and even the reverence of the community. Miracles were attributed to her, and her body was found incorrupt when it was transferred several years after her death to a more honorable place. Her cult, confirmed in 1760, is liturgically celebrated at Padua. She is sometimes referred to as Eustochius (or Eustochium), which was her religious name.

Feast: Feb. 13.

Bibliography: G. C. CORDARA, *Vita virtù e miracoli della B. Eustochio vergine padovana* (Venice 1768). A. M. ZIMMERMANN, *Kalendarium Benedictinum: Die Heiligen und Seligen des Benediktinerorderns und seiner Zweige,* 4 v. (Metten 1933–38) 1:207–209. A. BUTLER, *The Lives of the Saints,* ed. H. THURSTON and D. ATTWATER, 4 v. (New York 1956) 1:325–327.

[N. G. WOLF]

EUSTOCHIUM, ST.

Virgin; b. Rome, *c.* 368; d. Bethlehem, Palestine, late 418 or early 419. The third of the four daughters of St. PAULA OF ROME, she consecrated herself to a life of virginity and was trained in the austere life by her widowed mother and St. MARCELLA. Paula and Eustochium Julia were among the noble Roman ladies given spiritual guidance and scriptural instruction by St. JEROME during his stay in Rome (382–385). Upon Jerome's departure, they followed him to the East and, after a trip to Egypt, settled at Bethlehem. In the religious community established there under Jerome's spiritual leadership, Paula supervised three convents for women. Paula died in 404, and Eustochium succeeded to her mother's position. The eulogy on Paula written by Jerome (*Ep.* 108) gives much detail on their life in Bethlehem. Jerome addressed numerous letters to Paula and Eustochium and also dedicated some of his scriptural commentaries to them. Eustochium in her youth was addressee of one of the most famous of Jerome's epistles (*Ep.* 22), a lengthy treatise on virginity. Eustochium and Paula are the ostensible authors of another long letter preserved among Jerome's correspondence (*Ep.* 46), but this letter may actually have been drafted, or rewritten, by Jerome.

Feast: Sept 28.

Bibliography: *Acta Sanctorum* Sept. 7:589–603. JEROME, *Epistulae,* ed. I. HILBERG, 3 v. (*Corpus scriptorum ecclesiasticorum latinorum* 54–56; 1910–18), letters 22, 46, 54, 107, 108, 151, 153, 154; *Letters,* ed. T. C. LAWLER, tr. C. C. MIEROW, v.1 (*Ancient Christian Writers* 33; 1963), *passim.* F. CAVALLERA, *Saint Jérôme,* 2 v. (*Spicilegium sacrum Lovaniense* 1, 2; 1922), *passim.* ST. JEROME, *Epistula di misser sanctu Iheronimu ad Eustochiu,* ed. F. SALMERI (Palermo 1999), letters of Jerome and Eustochium with ample bibliographic references.

[T. C. LAWLER]

EUTHANASIA

The term ''euthanasia,'' from the Greek *eu thanatos* meaning ''well,'' ''good,'' or ''easy'' dying/death, has today become more commonly equated with one form of dying, namely, ''mercy killing,'' considered by the Catholic Church to be *direct* or *active* euthanasia. Official Church teaching describes *direct/active* euthanasia as ''an act or omission which, of itself or by intention, causes death in order to eliminate suffering'' and judges that such an act ''constitutes a murder gravely contrary to the dignity of the human person and to the respect due to the Living God, His Creator.'' (*Catechism of the Catholic Church [CCC],* #2277) The adjectives *direct* and *active* have ethical significance. They are used to distinguish those actions that voluntarily induce death from those *indirect* or *passive* actions of a more palliative nature (e.g., morphine for pain management) that may unintentionally shorten life, or decisions to forego further interventions (omissions) judged to be medically futile in recognition and acceptance of the inevitability and imminence of death. In Catholic moral teaching, indirect and passive euthanasia are considered to be ethical while direct and active euthanasia are unethical.

History. Direct euthanasia has historically deep roots in human society. It was a common practice in ancient Greece, and later in Rome, as evidenced by the suicidal act of Zeno (*c.* 263 B. C.), the founder of the Stoic school of philosophy, who took poison rather than endure an agonizing foot injury. In contrast, physicians in the Hippocratic School of medical ethics opposed euthanasia (and abortion), pledging ''I will neither give a deadly drug to anybody if asked for it, nor will make a suggestion to this effect.'' The later widespread influence of Christianity in Europe reduced the practice of euthanasia, teaching that human life is a gift entrusted to us by God and that direct killing of the innocent violates the commandment ''Thou shalt not kill.'' Nineteenth-century developments in anesthesiology reopened discussions of the ''good death'' with advocacy, for example, of the use of chloroform to end life in cases of hopeless and painful illness.

Pro-euthanasia supporters in the United States began to actively campaign in some states for the legalization of euthanasia. While prominent medical societies opposed euthanasia on the grounds that it was unlawful, ethical arguments were less prominently employed outside the religious communities. The outbreak of World War II and the discovery of the Nazi death camps tended to quiet the voices of advocacy for about a decade.

In the United States legal and ethical discussions about euthanasia and ''the right to die'' became more prominent in the face of the 1975 medical/legal case of Karen Ann Quinlan who went into a coma after allegedly mixing tranquilizers with alcohol, surviving biologically for nine years in a ''persistent vegetative state'' even after New Jersey Supreme Court approval to remove her from a respirator. There developed widespread public concern about ''lives not worth living'' and the possibility of at least voluntary euthanasia if it could be ascertained that the patient would not have wanted to live in this condition. The Vatican's 1980 *Declaration On Euthanasia* affirmed and reiterated the Catholic position that ''nothing and no one can in any way permit the killing of an innocent human being, whether a fetus or an embryo, an infant or an adult, an old person or one suffering from an incurable disease, or a person who is dying.'' The *Declaration* went on to state that ''no one is permitted to ask for this act of killing, either for himself or herself or for another person entrusted to his or her care, nor can he or she consent to it, either explicitly or implicitly. Nor can any authority legitimately recommend or permit such an action. For it is a question of the violation of the divine law, an offence against the dignity of the human person, a crime against life, and an attack on humanity.''

In 1990 retired Michigan pathologist Jack Kevorkian assisted a woman with Alzheimer's disease to end her life, the first of his over 130 reported assisted suicides until his imprisonment in 1999. For some leaders of the euthanasia movement, like England's Derek Humphrey (*Final Exit: The Practicalities of Self- Deliverance and Assisted Suicide for the Dying*), Kevorkian's blatant challenge to existing laws prohibiting euthanasia and assisted suicide and some of his intemperate rhetoric constituted a setback for pro-euthanasia activists. Nonetheless, legislation supporting physician-assisted suicide (PAS) survived a 1997 voter referendum in the State of Oregon.

In April 2001, the Netherlands became the first nation to pass legislation allowing doctors to end the life of patients who are experiencing irremediable and unbearable suffering, who are aware of all other medical options, and who have sought a second professional opinion. The law allows patients to leave a written request for euthanasia, giving doctors discretion to act when patients become too physically or mentally ill to decide for themselves. Several other countries—Switzerland, Colombia, and Belgium—tolerate euthanasia.

Catholic Moral Teaching. Catholic moral teaching on this issue is rooted in the premise that ''human life is the basis of all good, and is the necessary source and condition of every human activity and of all society.'' (*Declaration*) Life is held to be a gift from God, the Creator, who retains ownership of the gift. Human persons are stewards of their gift of life and have an obligation to exercise responsible stewardship. Responsible stewardship includes the limited right of disposal, for example the donation of a non-vital organ or tissue, like skin or one kidney, but not the absolute right of disposal of life itself, as in suicide. The traditional Catholic understanding of responsible stewardship maintains that persons must employ ordinary or proportionate means to preserve life and *may* employ extraordinary or disproportionate means. The latter include all medicines, treatments, and operations that cannot be obtained or used without excessive expense, pain, or other inconvenience, for the patient or for others, or which, if used, would not offer reasonable hope of benefit for the patient.

In this definition the term ''excessive'' is understood as the undue burden associated with pursing the purpose of life, not the burden that the therapy or procedure used to prolong life would entail. The determination of ''disproportionate'' is largely subjective, i.e., what would *this* patient consider to be unduly burdensome? In rejecting or even discontinuing the employment of disproportionate means, ''one does not will to cause death; one's inability to impede it is merely accepted. (*CCC* 2278) To insist upon doing ''everything'' to ward off death when the biological life being sustained will no longer support cognitive function and a potentiality for human and humanizing relationships is a type of vitalism and overly zealous treatment. The Christian belief in personal RESURRECTION and eternal life frees the believer and his or her family and care-givers to allow ''letting go'' of this gift of biological life entrusted to the person by the Creator in order to attain the greater gift of eternal life with God.

The disputed question of omitting or discontinuing the delivery of artificially induced nutrition and hydration has been largely resolved in Catholic teaching within the context of the ''disproportionate means'' principle. The *Ethical and Religious Directives for Catholic Health Care Services* from the United States Conference of Catholic Bishops (June 15, 2001) states: ''There should be a presumption in favor of providing nutrition and hydration to all patients, including patients who require medically assisted nutrition and hydration, as long as this is of sufficient benefit to outweigh the burdens involved to the patient.'' Hydration and nutrition are normally considered part of comfort or palliative care, but in particular cases may become disproportionate medical means and be omitted or discontinued.

In Catholic teaching, all persons are encouraged to provide advance directives for their health care, excluding, of course, requesting being euthanized, in the event they become unable to provide care direction for themselves. Initial Catholic opposition to ''living wills'' and proposed civil legislation to guarantee a patient's right to decline treatment gradually dissipated with the recognition that advances in medical technology, in many instances, could prolong a person's life, at least biologically, to the point where death and dying, not life and living, is prolonged.

In a certain sense, an executed advance directive is a patient's defense against the over technologizing of medical health care. The preferred advance directive is ''durable power of attorney for health care'' that designates or appoints an agent to make health care decisions for the patient and/or gives instructions regarding future health care decisions. This living-agent approach has advantages over the written ''living will'' document that tends to be very specific about treatments or procedures not to be employed, but may not be relevant for the medical situation facing this patient at this time. In durable power of attorney for health care the appointee knows the patient and is better able to make decisions consonant with the values and beliefs of the patient irrespective of specific clinical procedures or treatments.

In the document *EVANGELIUM VITAE* (1995) Pope JOHN PAUL II reiterates the constant teaching of the Catholic Church when he states: ''I confirm that euthanasia is a grave violation of the law of God (emphasis his), since it is deliberate and morally unacceptable killing of a human person. This doctrine is based on the natural law and upon the written word of God, is transmitted by the Church's Tradition and taught by the ordinary and universal Magisterium.'' (*EV* 65) Whether the killing is done by another or is a suicidal act, the rationale for its rejection is that God alone has sovereignty over life and death. The phenomenon of so-called ''assisted suicide,'' especially ''physician assisted suicide,'' has been debated in many countries and has been given legal protection in some, as noted above. However, assisting in the suicide of another places one in the situation of being a formal cooperator in their morally evil act and, therefore, as culpable as the one requesting and carrying out the act. ''Mercy'' and ''compassion'' are offered as the justification for providing a patient a terminal escape from suffering. However, ''even when not motivated by a selfish refusal to be burdened with the life of someone who is suffering, euthanasia must be called a false mercy, and indeed a disturbing 'perversion' of mercy. True 'compassion' leads to sharing another's pain; it does not kill the person whose suffering we cannot bear.'' (*EV* 66) A special perversity is seen in such actions carried out by family members or physicians who, above all, are expected to minister lovingly to a suffering relative or professionally to a patient.

The Church considers the euthanizing of one who has in no way requested it or who has never consented to it to be a form of murder. ''The height of arbitrariness and injustice is reached when certain people, such as physicians or legislators, arrogate to themselves the power to decide who ought to live and who ought to die. . . . Thus, the life of the person who is weak is put into the hands of the one who is strong; in society the sense of justice is lost, and mutual trust, the basis of every authentic interpersonal relationship, is undermined at its root.'' (*EV* 66)

Bibliography: *Declaration on Euthanasia* (Vatican City 1980). *Ethical and Religious Directives for Catholic Health Care Services* (Washington, D.C. 2001). ''Nutrition and Hydration: Moral Considerations'' (Pennsylvania Conference of Catholic Bishops 1992). B. ASHLEY and K. O'ROURKE, *Health Care Ethics: A Theological Analysis,* 4th Edition (Washington, D.C. 1991). P. CATALDO and A. S. MORACZEWSKI, *Catholic Health Care Ethics: A Manual for Ethics Committees* (Boston 2001).

[R. M. FRIDAY]

EUTHYMIUS I, PATRIARCH OF CONSTANTINOPLE

February 907 to May 15, 912; b. Seleucia, Isauria, *c.* 834; d. Constantinople, Aug. 5, 917. Euthymius entered a monastery on Mt. Olympus, Bithynia, as a youth and eventually became abbot of St. Theodora in Constantinople, as well as confessor to Emperor LEO VI the Wise (886–912). He used his influence over the Emperor to protect many of the officials in the party of PHOTIUS from the political reprisals of Stylianus Zautzes, father of Leo's mistress Zoe. He refused to appear at the imperial court, but on being appointed syncellus, he accepted a monastery built for him near the palace. After the death of Leo's first wife, he refused to sanction the Emperor's marriage with Zoe and was banished for two years but was recalled after Zoe's death. When Leo was denied a dispensation for a fourth marriage (*see* BYZANTINE CHURCH, HISTORY OF) by Patriarch NICHOLAS I MYSTICUS, the Emperor appealed to the "four other patriarchs," who granted it. He deposed Nicholas and nominated Euthymius as the new patriarch; but the latter refused the see until he was certain that Nicholas had resigned and that the "four patriarchs" through their representatives had pronounced again in favor of the dispensation. As patriarch he refused to enter the name of the Emperor's fourth wife in the DIPTYCHS and degraded the priest who had blessed their union. After the death of Leo VI, Nicholas was reinstated as patriarch and took revenge on the banished Euthymius. With heroic charity, Euthymius forgave him and the two were reconciled before his death. The life of Euthymius was written by a contemporary, and he was accepted as a saint in the Greek Church in 991. The *Vita* insists on Euthymius's competence as a preacher but only a few of his sermons are certainly authentic: three on the feast of St. Anna (Dec. 9) and one on the Theotokos. He also composed a canon or hymn on the Theotokos and an encomium of Hierotheos. The history ascribed to him of the first seven general councils and the Synod of Photius's rehabilitation (879–880), may have been composed 500 years later by Euthymius II (1410–16).

Bibliography: V. GRUMEL, *Les Regestes des actes du patriarcat de Constantinople* 625–629. P. KARLIN-HAYTER, ed., "Vita S. Euthymii," *Byzantion* 25–37 (1955–57) 1–172; with Eng. tr. *Kirche und theologische Literatur im byzantinischen Reich* 549–550. R. JANIN, *Catholicisme* 4:728–729. M. JUGIE, *Échos d'Orientalia* 16 (1913) 385–395, 481–492; 23 (1924) 286–288; ed. and tr., *Patrologia Orientalis* 16 (1922) 489–514; 19 (1926) 441–445. F. DVORNIK, *The Photian Schism* (Cambridge, Eng. 1948) 111–117. J. DARROUZÈS, *Dictionnaire d'histoire et de géographie ecclésiastiques* 16:58–59. V. GRUMEL, "Observations diverses sur la question photienne," *Diskussionsbeiträge zum 11. Internationalen Byzantinistenkongress, München 1958* (Munich 1961) 48–54.

[M. J. HIGGINS]

St. Euthymius the Great, Monastery at Mount Athos, Greece. (© Chris Hellier/CORBIS)

EUTHYMIUS THE GREAT, ST.

Abbot and Byzantine monastic founder; b. Melitene, Armenia, 377; d. Palestine, Jan. 20, 473. Of a religious family, Euthymius was orphaned early and educated by the bishop of Melitene, Otreus. On his ordination, he was charged with the spiritual care of the ascetics and monasteries of the city, but he fled to Palestine in search of solitude and entered the monastery of Pharan, where he became a friend of St. Theoctistus. Several years later the two monks retired to a hermitage and on being joined by others, Theoctistus (d. 467) founded a laura or cenobitic monastery. The followers of Euthymius later forced him to establish a laura called after him. Its church was consecrated by Bishop Juvenal of Jerusalem in 429. Euthymius organized a way of life in which, after a period of formation, the monk retired to a solitary cell and met with others only for liturgical and spiritual functions. After the death of Euthymius it was reorganized as a cenobium.

By his reputation for sanctity Euthymius converted many nomad Saracens, and had encampment bishoprics (*parembolai*) created to care for them (*Vita* 20–21). His advice was sought by several Oriental bishops who took part in the Councils of EPHESUS (431) and CHALCEDON

(451). Although he appears not to have written any works, his principles of the monastic life and ascetical sayings were recorded by his disciple St. CYRIL OF SCYTHOPOLIS in one of the great early Byzantine hagiographical works, the *Vita s. Euthymii.*

Feast: Jan. 20.

Bibliography: I. HAUSHERR, *Dictionnaire de spiritualité ascétique et mystique. Doctrine et histoire,* ed. M. VILLER (Paris 1932–) 2:2687–90. J. DARROUZÈS, *ibid.* 4:1720–22. R. JANIN, *Dictionnaire d'histoire et de géographie ecclésiastiques* (Paris 1912–) 16:61. E. SCHWARTZ, ed., *Kyrillos von Skythopolis* (Texte und Untersuchungenzur Geschichte der altchristlichen Literatur 49.2; 1939). S. VAILHÉ, ''S. Euthyme le Grand,'' *Revue de l'Orient Chrétien* NS 4 (1909) 256–263. H. CHARLES, *Le Christianisme des Arabes nomades* (Paris 1936) 40–43. H. G. BECK, *Kirche und theologische Literatur im byzantinischen Reich* (Munich 1959) 198, 203. D. CHITTY, *Excavation of the Monastery of St. Euthymius 1929: Quarterly Statement for the Palestine Exploration Fund* (London 1930). A. BARROIS, *Revue Biblique* 39 (1930) 272–275.

[J. BENTIVEGNA]

EUTRAPELIA

From the Greek εὐτραπελία meaning ready wit or liveliness, is a term used by scholastic theologians to signify moderation in the use of recreation. As a virtue *eutrapelia* was introduced into the study of morals by ARISTOTLE (*Eth. Nic.* 4.8), and in modern speech it goes commonly by the name of recreation. Constant work and application cause weariness of mind and body, and the normal cure for this is play. However, this need for relaxation should be in accord with the demands of right reason, which require that recreation involve nothing morally evil, that the participant should not lose self–control altogether, and that the norms of prudence be followed as regards time, circumstances, and social relationship. Defect in the matter of *eutrapelia* would consist in taking too little recreation, which leads to austere moroseness, or in being boorish in one's social relationships. Excess in recreation would occur if one were to become too fascinated by the delight that accompanies play and thus neglect the serious matters of life. St. THOMAS AQUINAS included *eutrapelia* in his scheme of virtues under the potential parts of temperance. Offenses against this virtue ordinarily are not grave, and at most would consist in a hindrance to good social life. Too little play can be worse than too much.

Bibliography: ARISTOTLE, *Nicomachean Ethics* 1128a. THOMAS AQUINAS, ST 2a2ae, 168.2. F. L. B. CUNNINGHAM, ed., *The Christian Life* (Dubuque 1959) 740–741.

[W. HERBST]

EUTYCHES

Constantinopolitan abbot and heretic, considered the father of MONOPHYSITISM; b. *c.* 375; d. 454.

As Archimandrite of an important monastery during the mid-400s in the outskirts of Constantinople, Eutyches enjoyed great influence at the court of Theodosius II through his godson, the eunuch Chrysaphius. In his fidelity to the formula rather than the theology of St. CYRIL OF ALEXANDRIA, and in his anti-Nestorian zeal, he recognized only one nature in Christ. THEODORET OF CYR wrote his *Eranistes* (447) against Eutyches without naming him. He was denounced as a heretic by Eusebius of Doryleum before the *synodos endemousa* on Nov. 8, 448, and at first refused to obey the summons of the Patriarch FLAVIAN. Finally making an appearance on November 22, he obstinately refused to confess that there were two natures in Christ and was condemned and deposed. Pope LEO I confirmed this judgment (*Epist.* 23, 29, 30). Although rehabilitated by the Robber Council of Ephesus in 449, he was exiled after the assumption of emperorship by Marcian and Pulcheria in 451. Nothing further is known of his life.

Pope Leo in his *Tome* to Flavian called Eutyches ''an ignorant, imprudent old man'' for having asserted under questioning at Constantinople that there were two natures before, but only one after the Incarnation. He was thus forced into denying a concrete and individual existence for the human nature of Christ, and into holding that, as the human nature was absorbed by the divinity, Christ's flesh was not consubstantial with ours. St. Leo indicates that Eutyches did not truly understand the theological issue, and, on being challenged, obstinately refused to recede from what he erroneously thought was the opinion of St. Cyril.

Bibliography: M. JUGIE, *Dictionnaire de théologie catholique* 5.2:1582–1609. R. DEVREESSE, ''Les Premières années du monophysisme,'' *Revue des sciences philosophiques et théologiques* 19 (1930) 251–265. R. DRAGUET, ''La Christologie d'Eutychès,'' *Byzantion* 6 (1931) 441–447. P. T. CAMELOT, *Das Konzil von Chalkedon: Geschichte und Gegenwart* 1:229–242. H. BACHT, *ibid.* 2:197–222.

[P. T. CAMELOT]

EUTYCHIAN, POPE, ST.

Pontificate: Jan. 4, 275, to Dec. 7, 283. Beyond the dates of his pontificate, no reliable reports on Eutychian are extant, and no documents ascribed to him are authentic. Despite the fact that no persecution marked his reign, the *Liber pontificalis,* which stated that he was a Tuscan, the son of Marinus, reported that he buried 342 martyrs and ordered that martyrs should be interred in dalmatics. Not a martyr himself, Eutychian was buried in the cemetery of Callistus where his Greek epitaph has been discovered. He is credited, probably erroneously, with establishing the custom whereby first fruits were blessed on the altar.

Bibliography: EUSEBIUS, *Eccesiastical History.* G. SCHWAIGER, *Lexikon für Theologie und Kirche*, ed. J. HOFER and K. RAHNER (Freiberg 1957–65) 3:1214. J. N. D. KELLY, *Oxford Dictionary of Popes* (New York 1986), 23.

[E. G. WELTIN]

EUTYCHIANISM

Eutychianism is a species of MONOPHYSITISM, the Christological heresy that held that in Christ after the hypostatic union, there is only one nature (*physis*). Eutychianism is usually considered to be the strict or authentic type of Monophysitism and is to be distinguished from mitigated forms such as Severian Monophysitism (*see* SEVERUS OF ANTIOCH). Eutychianism thus understood includes, besides the teaching of EUTYCHES himself, doctrines that his opponents commonly attributed to him as well as similar doctrines of later times, whether or not they claim the patronage of Eutyches or have any historical connection with him. Eutychianism so defined embraces all doctrines in which the immutability of the Eternal Word, or the perfect consubstantial integrity of the human nature in Christ, are attacked or denied.

Eutyches was the recognized leader of the mid-5th-century monks at Constantinople. Not a good theologian, but influential in ecclesiastical politics, he engaged in theological controversy to prevent the revival of NESTORIANISM. His own doctrine came under fire when he was accused of heresy by Bp. Eusebius of Doryleum, the man who had been the accuser of NESTORIUS a generation earlier (431).

Eutyches was condemned by FLAVIAN, Patriarch of Constantinople, in the synod of 448. The condemnation was based on Eutyches's refusal to admit that in Christ there are two natures after the union and that Christ's flesh is that "of a man." Eutyches was a friend of CYRIL OF ALEXANDRIA and slavishly devoted to Cyril's terminology, especially the famous phrase: "one nature of the Incarnate Word." The phrase actually had come from the heretic APOLLINARIS OF LAODICEA, but Cyril had been able to interpret and use it correctly. Eutyches was incapable of this.

Eutyches would admit that Christ was of two natures before the union and that Christ's flesh was consubstantial with that of the Blessed Virgin. He held strongly that Christ was true God and true man. He denied any confusion or change of either nature in the union. But he feared that the statement that there were two natures after the union, or that Christ's flesh was the flesh "of a man," involved admitting two persons in Christ, or Nestorianism. Though reinstated by the Robber Council of EPHESUS in 449, he was definitively condemned at the Council of CHALCEDON in 451. He was exiled and thereafter disappears from history.

In the aftermath of opposition to Chalcedon in Egypt and Syria, many doctrines were attributed to Eutyches by his opponents, such as the absorption of Christ's humanity in the divinity, the unreality of Christ's humanity, a heavenly origin of Christ's humanity, the commingling of the humanity and divinity to form a third substance, and transformation of the divinity into the humanity with Christ ceasing to be God. Eutyches did not hold these doctrines, although they did spread among some of the less educated Monophysites. But in refuting them, the orthodox champions often ascribed them to Eutyches himself. The identification of their proponents, except in very few cases, seems to be impossible. Their attribution to Eutyches has no solid foundation. There was more ignorance than malice in his refusal to accept the doctrine of Chalcedon. LEO I characterized him as unlearned, unqualified, and imprudent.

Bibliography: R. V. SELLERS, *The Council of Chalcedon* (London 1953). P. T. CAMELOT, in A. GRILLMEIER and H. BACHT, *Das Konzil von Chalkedon: Geschichte und Gegenwart,* 3 v. (Würzburg 1951–54) 1:229–242; 2:197–222. B. EMMI, *Angelicum* 29 (1952) 1–42. G. BARDY, in A. FLICHE and V. MARTIN, eds., *Histoire de l'égise depuis les origines jusqu'à nos jours* (Paris 1935–) 4:211–222. M. JUGIE, *Dictionnaire de théologie catholique,* ed. A. VACANT et al., 15 v. (Paris 1903–50; Tables générales 1951–) 5.2:1582–1609.

[G. OWENS]

EUTYCHIOS OF ALEXANDRIA

Patriarch of Alexandria, Melchite historian and theologian, whose Arabic name was Sa'īd ibn Batrīq; b. Fosṭāṭ (Cairo), Egypt, Aug. 17, 877; d. Alexandria, May 11, 940. He first dedicated himself to the study of medicine, about which he wrote copiously. On Feb. 7, 933, he was elected patriarch of Alexandria. His literary fame is due mainly to his *Annals* (*Nazm al-Jawhar*). This book, a general history of the world, was begun while he was a layman and was dedicated to his brother, 'Īsā ibn Batrīq, a practicing physician. In it Eutychios follows the pattern of the Byzantine chronologists in writing, without any systematic plan, a religious and profane history from the beginning of the world to his own time, ending with A.D. 938; it was continued down to A.D. 1027 by a relative of his, Yahyā ibn Sa'īd of Antioch. Chief emphasis is given to the history of the Church and of the Muslim Caliphates. The Nestorian and the Monophysite heresies are discussed and refuted at length. The value of *Nazm al-Jawhar* varies with the different sources Eutychios uses for his information. As with other Greek and Syrian writers of that period, he did not hesitate to include many popular legends. However, much factual information relating to contemporary practices cannot be found anywhere else. This alone would make the book invaluable. It soon became very popular, circulated widely, and was used as a source by such different historians as the Copt, al Makīn; the Arab, al Maqrīzī; and the Frenchman, William of Tyre. The author's special views on the heterodoxy of the Copts (Jacobites) and on the early Maronites (whom he identifies as Monothelites) earned for him the severe criticism of their historians.

Eutychios is, most probably, the author of the theological *Book of Demonstration* (*Kitāb al-Burhān*), a work usually attributed in the manuscripts to St. Athanasius the Great. In the first part of this work, the author treats of creation, the destiny of man, the perfections of God, and the Incarnation. In the three other parts, he gathers all the Biblical texts relating to the dogmas described and discussed previously. All four parts were written by one author—a member of the Greek Melchite Church—in Arabic, without traces of any translation, except for Biblical citations, some time before 944. All indications tend to prove Eutychios of Alexandria the sole author of *Kitāb al-Burhān.* Eutychios also wrote *Disputation Between a Christian and a Heretic,* and a book on the creation of the angels.

Bibliography: EUTYCHIOS OF ALEXANDRIA, *Annales,* ed. L. CHEIKHO et al. (*Corpus scriptorum Christianorum orientalium* 50–51, Scriptores arabici, ser. 3, v.6–7; 1906–09), Arabic text only; Latin tr. E. POSOCK (Oxford 1658), repr. *Patrologia Graeca* 111:907–1156; *The Book of Demonstration* (*Kitāb al-Burhān*) *I–II,* ed. P. CACHIA, Eng. tr. W. M. WATT (CSCO 192, 193, 209, 210; Scriptores arabici, v.20–23; 1960–61). G. GRAF, *Geschichte der christlichen arabischen Literatur,* 5 v. (Vatican City 1944–53) 2:32–38. J. M. NEALE, *A History of the Holy Eastern Church,* 2 v. (London 1847) 2:181–183. F. NAU, *Dictionnaire de théologie catholique,* ed. A. VACANT et al. (Paris 1903–50) 5.2: 1609–11.

[L. MALOUF]

EUTYCHIUS, PATRIARCH OF CONSTANTINOPLE

Patriarch from 552 to 565 and 577 to 582; b. Theium, Phrygia, 512; d. Constantinople, April 5, 582. Eutychius made his studies in Constantinople and returned to Amasea, where he was ordained, became a monk and archimandrite or abbot. While stationed as the *apocrisiarius* of the metropolitan of Amasea at Constantinople, he was selected by Justinian I to replace Patriarch Mennas (d. Aug. 24, 552); he entered into relations with Pope Vigilius I, residing in the capital because of the controversy over the Three Chapters, and presided over the Council of Constantinople II (June 553). He was banished by Justinian (565) for his opposition to Aphthartodocetism to which the Emperor had been persuaded in his old age; but was restored as patriarch by Justin II in 577. With the papal *apocrisiarius* at Constantinople, later Pope Gregory I, he engaged in a controversy on the resurrection of the flesh, resulting apparently from a tract on Origenism written by the patriarch that has not been preserved. He likewise wrote against the Monophysite interpretation of the Trisagion. Fragments of a treatise on the Eucharist have been preserved, as have his letter to Pope Vigilius and the decision of the Council of Constantinople prepared under his guidance. He died during Vespers for the octave of Easter, having received a visit from the Emperor Tiberius. His vita was written by his disciple and companion Eustratius; and in 1246 his body was brought to Venice, where it was interred in the church of St. George the Great.

Feast: April 6 (Oriental Church).

Bibliography: *Patrologia Graeca* 86.2:2267–2406. R. JANIN, *Dictionnaire d'histoire et de géographie ecclésiastiques* 16:94–95. *Das Konzil von Chalkidon: Geschichte und Gegenwart. Kirche und theologische Literatur im byzantinischen Reich* 380, 410. K. BAUS, *Lexikon für Theologie und Kirche* 3:1215. *Histoire du Bas-Empire,* ed. J. R. PALANQUE 2:654–681. V. GRUMEL, *Les Regestes des actes du patriarcat de Constantinople* 244–249, 260–263.

[J. BENTIVEGNA]

EVA OF LIÈGE, BL.

Recluse; b. *c.* 1210; d. after 1264. The only source for her life is the *Vita Julianae* (*Acta Sanctorum* April 1:433–475), most of the information for which was contributed by Eva herself. Her influence and affluence indicate that she belonged to a family of high social standing. She was the intimate friend of JULIANA OF LIÈGE and, doubtless encouraged by the latter, she embraced the life of the recluse in a cell attached to the church of St. Martin at Liège. The history of the origin of the Feast of CORPUS CHRISTI demonstrates her constant contact with outstanding theologians of the day. In 1264 she received from Pope URBAN IV, together with the bull *Transiturus,* a personal message and a copy of the Office of the feast composed by THOMAS AQUINAS. Her relics were elevated in the church of St. Martin at Liège in 1622 and her cult was approved by Pope LEO XIII in 1902.

Feast: May 26; March 14 at Liège.

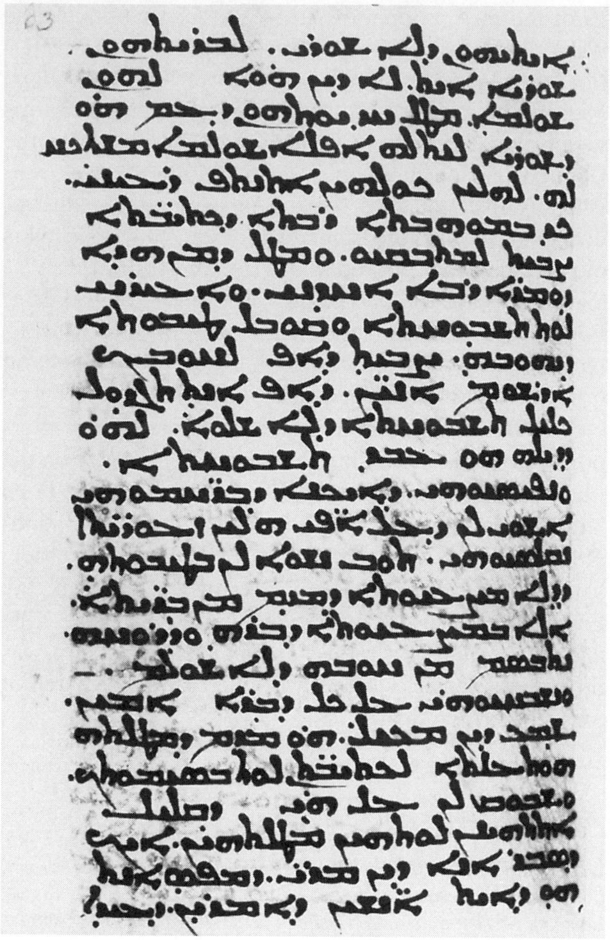

A portion of the second part of Evagrius Ponticus's "Letter to Melania" in a 9th-century Syriac manuscript (Add. MS 17192, fol. 63r).

Bibliography: S. ROISIN, *Dictionnaire d'histoire et de géographie ecclésiastiques,* ed. A. BAUDRILLART (Paris 1912–) 16:114–117. G. MARSOT, *Catholicisme* 4:777–778. ABBÉ JOSEFF, *Vie de sainte Ève, recluse de St. Martin à Liège* (Liège 1903). CLOTILDE DE STE. JULIENNE, *Histoire d'un glorieux passé Julienne de Cornillion, ste. Ève de St-Martin de la Fête-Dieu* (Brussels 1924). A. ERNST, *Zwei Freundinnen Gottes* (Freiburg im Breisgau 1926).

[T. C. CROWLEY]

EVAGRIUS PONTICUS

Fourth-century monk and mystical theologian; b. Ibora in the Hellespont, 345; d. Cellia, Egypt, 399. Although exalted for a time as the equal of the great Church Fathers, he was suspected of heresy after 400, and condemned at the Council of CONSTANTINOPLE II (553); Evagrius's reputation darkened gradually until in 1920 scholars turned renewed attention to him.

Life. Evagrius was selected as a lector by (St.) BASIL, and ordained a deacon by GREGORY OF NAZIANZUS at Constantinople in 379; after assisting at the Council (381), he remained with the Patriarch Nectarius as theologian collaborating in the anti-Eunomian controversy (Palladius, *Hist. laus.* 38). After an interval, he journeyed to Jerusalem (382) and resided in the monastery founded by MELANIA THE ELDER on the Mount of Olives. In 383 he became a monk in Egypt, and he subsequently settled in the Nitrian Valley for two years, and spent 14 years in the Desert of Cellia, supporting himself by copying manuscripts. With Macarius and Ammonius as spiritual fathers, he gradually exercised great influence on the monks through his writings and mystical doctrine.

Works. Besides several treatises preserved in the original Greek, his writings come down in Syriac and Armenian translations or under the name of orthodox teachers such as NILUS OF ANCYRA. Palladius, Socrates (*Hist. Eccl.* 4:23), and Gennadius (*Vir. ill.* 11) mention several collections of his ascetical maxims. One of these, the *Monachikos,* is divided in two sections: the *Praktikos* for uneducated monks (100 ch.) and the *Gnostikos* for cultured ascetics (50 ch.). The *Gnostic Centuries* (*Problemata gnostica*), 600 concise sentences for meditation in six books dealing with ascetic and doctrinal problems—angels, the Trinity, the restoration of all things in God—is extant in two very different versions; one corrected against Origenistic tendencies, the other apparently faithful to the original. The *Antirrhetikos* in eight books described the eight principal vices to be overcome by the monk, and offset them with Scriptural quotations. It is preserved in Syriac and Armenian. The *Mystic Sentences* or *Mirror for Monks and Nuns*, was translated by RUFINUS OF AQUILEIA into Latin (*Patrologia Graeca*, ed. J. P. Migne, 40:1277–86) with an introduction preserved in Evagrius's letters 19 and 20.

Sixty-seven of Evagrius's letters are preserved in Syriac and Armenian. One in Greek (Basil, *Epist.* 8) confutes Arian doctrine on the Trinity, consubstantiality of the Son, and divinity of the Holy Spirit. Of considerable doctrinal importance also is his *Letter to Melania the Elder* (the second part was edited by G. Vitestam, Lund 1964).

The manuscript tradition has preserved a *Hypotyposis* (*Patrologia Graeca* 40:1253–60), *Selecta in Psalmos,* and a *Commentary on Proverbs* culled from the *catenae* of Scripture and other patristic writings and reclaimed for Evagrius by U. v. Balthasar [*Zeitschrift für katholische Theologie* 63 (1939) 86–106; 181–206] and M. Rondeau [*Orientalia Christiana periodica* 26 (1960) 307–40]. Four tracts on monastic perfection—*Ad Eulogium monachum, De malignis cogitationibus, De octo spiritibus malignis,* and *De oratione* (*Patrologia Graeca* 1093–1233)—attributed to St. Nilus have been claimed for Evagrius.

Doctrine. In theology Evagrius follows the *De Principiis* of ORIGEN but in more radical form, constituting the system condemned by the Council of Constantinople II in 553. In the beginning existed a *henade* (oneness) formed by the universe of rational beings created equal, to know God, which is ''essential knowledge.'' Following a fault, these spirits were separated from God, each experiencing a fate in accordance with the degree of the fall. These fallen intellects are called souls and were joined to bodies. By asceticism and contemplation, these intellects can progressively return to God; and there will be a time when all make this return and the original *henade* will be reestablished (APOCATASTASIS). As the body does not belong to the essence of the soul, the resurrection will be only a provisional step. Those ''who see God'' will be incorporeal.

In his earlier works, as in the *Letter to Melania,* the Christology of Evagrius is orthodox following the Cappadocian fathers; but in his later works such as the *Gnostic Centuries,* the *Selecta in Psalmos,* it has been rethought in an Origenistic sense. Christ is only an intellect, similar to those forming the original *henade;* but in contrast to the others he has remained united to the Oneness, and as such is inalterably united to the Word who is God. This intellect has taken a body similar to that of the fallen intellects, to reveal to them ''essential knowledge'' and lead them back to God.

Asceticism and Mysticism. The return to God is accomplished in two steps: the ascetical (*praktikē*) way and the contemplative (gnostikē). The ascetical is the ''spiritual method whose goal is to purify the passionate part of the soul''; it aims at removing obstacles to contemplation, delivering man from his passions, and purifying the intellect of sense reactions; it is directed toward *apatheia* or impassibility. Evagrius analyses the passions and their working with finesse. He popularizes the eight capital vices (reduced later to seven capital sins), viz, gluttony, fornication, avarice, sorrow, anger, discouragement (*acedia*), vainglory, and pride, and distributes these vices according to the tripartite schema of his psychology: the first three deal with the concupiscible appetite, anger with the irascible, and vainglory and pride are attributed to the intellect. Sorrow and discouragement are intermediary vices. Sins and passions are interwoven and follow a rigorous pattern. To overcome them, Evagrius recommends an attack on each in its proper order.

The Contemplative Life is developed in two degrees: natural contemplation (*physikē*), which is subdivided into a contemplation of the body (secondary), and a contemplation of the *logoi* or reasons (primary); and progressive contemplation in which the intellect, by simplifying itself before the undetermined, empties itself of all forms, and comes to see in itself the light of God. ''At the hour of prayer, the contemplative soul resembles the heavens where the light of the Holy Trinity shines'' (*Cent.* suppl. 4). ''The naked intellect [nous] becomes that which sees the Trinity'' (*Cent.* 3.15).

Influence. Evagrius had a profound influence as founder of monastic mysticism, which was spread among the Greeks (St. JOHN CLIMACUS, MAXIMUS CONFESSOR, Dorotheus, and the Hesychasts); among the Latins through John CASSIAN, who adopted his ascetic doctrine; and among the Syrians, the Nestorians and the Monophysites, who consider him their great doctor of mystical theology.

Bibliography: ÉVAGRE LE PONTIQUE, *Traité de l'oraison,* ed. I. HAUSHERR (Paris 1960). J. QUASTEN, *Patrology,* 3 v. (Westminster, Md. 1950–) 3:169–76. S. MARSILI, *G. Cassiano e Evagrio Pontico* (Rome 1936). A. GUILLAUMONT, *Les ''Kephalaia gnostica'' d'Évagre le Pontique* (Paris 1963). A. and C. GUILLAUMONT, *Dictionnaire de spiritualité ascétique et mystique. Doctrine et histoire,* ed. M. VILLER et al. (Paris 1932–) 4.2:1731–44. O. CHADWICK, *John Cassian* (Cambridge, Eng. 1950). F. REFOULÉ, *Orientalia Christiana periodica* 26–27 (1960–61) 221–66; *Revue de l'histoire des religions* 163 (1963) 11–52.

[F. REFOULÉ]

EVAGRIUS SCHOLASTICUS

Sixth-century Byzantine lawyer and historian; b. Epiphania, Coelesyria, 536; d. after August 594. Evagrius wrote an *Ecclesiastical History* that goes from the Council of Ephesus (431) to August 594 and includes secular history also. He is orthodox and reliable (except in chronology), makes use of good sources (listed at the end of book five for books one to four), and was a contemporary and often eyewitness of events in books five and six; his work is important and authoritative. Evagrius was attorney for Gregory, Patriarch of Antioch, drew up his official reports, and accompanied him as professional adviser when he appeared before a synod in Constantinople to clear himself of a charge of incest. He published a collection (now lost) of miscellaneous compositions together with the patriarchal, official reports that earned him an honorary questorship from the Emperor Tiberius II; he was given an honorary prefecture by Emperor Maurice for a panegyric on the occasion of the birth of his first son, Theodosius.

This information is derived from Evagrius's *Ecclesiastical History.* One of his earliest memories was of being taken by his parents as a child of three to Apamea to kiss the relic of the true cross and see it exposed for solemn public veneration. He says that he published his book in his 58th year (594). Two years before, the bubonic plague had come back for the fourth time during his life; he had caught it on its first onslaught 52 years earlier, while still a schoolboy of six, and had lost a daughter and grandchild in the most recent visitation. His wife, and many of his kin, as well as many of his town and country servants, had died of the plague. Pondering the death of his children, he was perplexed as to why the calamities did not happen to pagans with numerous offspring. Although he had not disclosed his doubts to anyone, he received a letter from St. Simeon Stylites the Younger, advising him to abandon such ideas as displeasing to God. Evagrius married a second time, and during the festivities occurred the great earthquake at Antioch of Oct. 29, 589. He says the whole city was taking part in the celebration at public cost; this gives an idea of his prominence in Antioch.

Bibliography: EVAGRIUS SCHOLASTICUS, *The Ecclesiastical History,* ed. J. BIDEZ and J. PARMENTIER (London 1898); Eng. tr. by E. WALFORD, . . . *A History of the Church* (London 1845). B. ALTANER, *Patrology* 277. K. KRUMBACHER *Geschichte der byzantinischen Literatur* 245–247. S. VAILHÉ, *Dictionnaire de théologie catholique* 5.2:1612–13. P. PEETERS, *Analecta Bollandiana* 65 (1947) 35–40. G. MORAVCSIK, *Byzantinoturcica,* 2 v. (2d ed. Berlin 1958), bibliog. M. J. HIGGINS, ''Chosroes II's Votive Offerings at Sergiopolis,'' *Byzantinisches Zeitschrift* 48 (1955) 89–102.

[M. J. HIGGINS]

EVANGELARY (BOOK OF GOSPELS)

Liturgical book containing selected pericopes (Greek *pericope*, for a selection ''cut around'') from the Gospel, arranged in a manner to be read at the Eucharistic Liturgy or Liturgy of the Hours for the feasts and seasons of the liturgical year. Its name comes from the Greek *euaggelion*, meaning Gospel. The evangeliary emerged as a book separate from the Lectionary in the Eastern churches and was designed for the use of the deacon whose task it is to proclaim the Gospel. While some Evangelaries contained the Gospel readings, others contained only tables indicating passages to be read, as well as the Sundays and Holy Days on which they are to be read. Known to the Greeks as an *Evangelistarium*, to the Latins as a *Capitulare*, and elsewhere as a *Synaxarium*, the name Evangelary, though of recent origin, has been universally adopted. The Evangelaries were highly venerated, and therefore text and cover were often richly ornamented.

Following the custom of the Synagogue, the Scriptures of the Old Testament were read at the primitive Christian assemblies. As the Canon of the New Testament was determined, certain extracts from it were included in these readings. Justin relates that when the Christians met together, they read the Memoirs of the Apostles and the writings of the Prophets (Apol., I, lxvii). Tertullian, Cyprian, and other writers bear witness to the same custom; and in the West the order of lector existed as early as the third century. Particular passages were most likely chosen by the presider and it is clear that on certain festivals, the Scripture relating to them would be read. Gradually a more or less definite list would naturally result from this method.

St. John Chrysostom in a homily delivered at Antioch exhorts his hearers to read beforehand the Scripture passages to be read and commented on in the Office of the day (Homilia de Lazaro, iii, c. i). In like manner other Churches would form a table of readings. In the margin of the ms. text it was customary to note the Sunday or festival on which that particular passage would be read, and at the end of the manuscript, the list of such passages, the *Synaxarium* or *Capitulare*, would be added. Transition from this process to the creation of an Evangelary, or collection of all such passages, was easy. Fragments of Evangelaries in Greek date from the fourth, fifth, and sixth centuries, but most of the surviving books date from the ninth century onwards. In like manner, there are Lectionaries in the Latin Churches as early as the fifth century. The *Comes* of the Roman Church dates from before St. Gregory the Great (P.L., XXX, 487–532). From the tenth century onwards Gospel lessons, together with the Epistles and prayers, were united in a new liturgical book, called the Missal.

At the time when the various Gospel passages began to be collected in book form for use in liturgical celebrations, the various families of the Gospel text and its translations were already in existence; and those Evangelaries simply reproduce the particular text favored by the Church which compiled it. Since the Second Vatican Council special provision has been made for a Book of Gospels as distinct from the Sacramentary. The General Instruction of the Roman Missal states that this liturgical book deserves special veneration. Thus it is to be carried in the entrance procession and may be enthroned on the altar. According to traditional liturgical practice the Book of the Gospels is kissed as a sign of veneration and is incensed in the same way as the Most Blessed Sacrament, relics of the holy Cross, images of the Lord exposed for public veneration, gifts for the sacrifice of the Mass, the altar cross, the paschal candle, the priest and the people.

Bibliography: E. DICKMANN, A. HEDWIG, and P. SPRANG, *Das Echternacher Evangelistar Kaiser Heinrichs III.: Staats- und Universitätsbibliothek Bremen Ms. b. 21 /* (Wiesbaden 1995). A. VON EUW, *Liber viventium Fabariensis: Das karolingische Memorialbuch von Pfäfers in seiner liturgie- und kunstgeschichtlichen Bedeutung* (Bern 1989). B. KLÖSSEL-LUCKHARDT, *Das Evangelistar MA 56 des Herzog Anton Ulrich-Museums* (Braunschweig 1992). E. PALAZZO, *A History of Liturgical Books from the Beginning to the Thirteenth Century* (Collegeville 1993). C. VOGEL, *Medieval*

Liturgy: An Introduction to the Sources translated and revised by W. STOREY and N. RASMUSSEN (Washington, DC 1986).

[M. S. DRISCOLL]

EVANGELICAL ALLIANCE

An association formed (1846) at London to unite evangelical Protestants on the basis of their common doctrines; it originated as a reaction to the growth of the OXFORD MOVEMENT within the Church of England and the conversion of John Henry NEWMAN and other leaders to Catholicism. John A. James, pastor of a London Congregationalist church, is credited with having originated the idea of a union of individual Christians on Reformation principles, but Edward Bickersteth, an evangelical Church of England minister long active in the Church Mission Society, became its chief architect. In 1845, after preliminary meetings at Glasgow, Manchester, and London, a Conference on Christian Union was held at Liverpool. The organizational meeting at London in August 1846 was attended by 800 delegates representing 50 separate churches in Europe and America. Friedrich Tholuck of Halle, Adolphe Monod, and the historian J. H. Merle d'AUBIGNÉ were the most influential representatives of Continental Protestantism. The large American delegation included Lyman BEECHER, Samuel H. Cox, and Samuel S. SCHMUCKER, the chief promoter of the Alliance in the U.S. Division over the issue of slavery in America presented one of the meeting's few jarring notes. Agreement on a series of doctrinal propositions was reached, expressing belief in the inspiration, authority, and sufficiency of the Scriptures; private judgment; the unity and Trinity of God; the utter depravity of human nature; the Incarnation, atonement, and mediatorial intercession of Christ; justification by faith alone; the work of the Holy Spirit in conversion; the immortality of the soul; and the divine institution of the Christian ministry, baptism, and the Lord's Supper. Merle d'Aubigné addressed the first conference on the persecution of Lutherans in Russia and later conferences took a leading part in obtaining relief for Protestants in Italy and Spain, for Methodists and Baptists in Sweden, and for Armenian Christians and other victims of intolerance. The Alliance also promoted a week of prayer for Christian unity in January. World conferences were held periodically in Europe and in 1873 at New York.

The composition of the American branch tended to reflect the Presbyterian and Reformed heritage more than other denominational beliefs, and Philip SCHAFF played an important role in its development after the Civil War. He was chiefly responsible for the organization (1867) of the Evangelical Alliance for the U.S., being one of its

St. John the Evangelist on Patmos writing his gospel from "The Book of Hours of the Blessed Virgin Mary." (©Angelo Hornak/ CORBIS)

dominant figures until his death in 1893. Josiah Strong became the executive secretary of the American branch in 1885 and played an important part in focusing its attention on the problems of urban America. National conferences held at Washington in 1887 and at Boston in 1889 dealt with the problems of the unchurched masses, immigration, and social justice. Strong's effort to make the Alliance a vehicle for the SOCIAL GOSPEL proved to be unsuccessful and resulted in his resignation in 1898. The Alliance provided the groundwork for the Federal Council of Churches in the U.S. and was superseded by it in 1908 (*see* NATIONAL COUNCIL OF THE CHURCHES OF CHRIST IN THE U.S.A.).

The World's Evangelical Alliance commemorated its centenary at London in 1946. It continues to be active in Great Britain as a fellowship of evangelical churches dedicated to Christian renewal and ecumenism on a doctrinal basis. Annual reports assess the work of British Evangelicalism, and annual conferences promote evangelical renewal.

Bibliography: Evangelical Alliance, *Report of the Proceedings of the Conference held at Freemasons' Hall* (London 1847). S. S. SCHMUCKER, *True Unity of Christ's Church* (New York 1870); *The Church of the Redeemer* (Philadelphia 1867). D. S. SCHAFF, *The*

Life of Philip Schaff (New York 1897). Evangelical Alliance for U.S.A., *National Perils and Opportunities* (New York 1887); *National Needs and Remedies* (New York 1890). R. ROUSE and S. C. NEILL, eds., *A History of the Ecumenical Movement, 1517–1948* (Philadelphia 1954).

[R. K. MACMASTER/EDS.]

EVANGELICAL AND REFORMED CHURCH

Organized by German Calvinists and Lutherans, it united with the Congregational Christian Church in 1957 to form the UNITED CHURCH OF CHRIST (*see* CALVINISM; LUTHERANISM). As a separate denomination it existed for only 23 years. When formed in 1934 through the union of two churches, the Evangelical Synod of North America and the Reformed Church in the U.S., the combined membership totaled about 620,000.

Immigrants from the Palatinate region of Germany brought their Reformed beliefs with them when they came to the American colonies (*see* REFORMED CHURCHES). Driven from their homeland because of the devastation of the Thirty Years' War and the campaigns of Louis XIV, many of the settlers accepted the hospitality of William PENN. Few ministers accompanied the immigrants; schoolteachers and devout laymen conducted worship services. A teacher, John Philip BOEHM, concluded the first communion service according to the Reformed order on Oct. 15, 1725, at Falkner Swamp, a tiny settlement 40 miles north of Philadelphia. This date is usually taken as the beginning of the Reformed Church in the U.S. Later the Reformed Church of Holland took an interest in these German Reformed colonists and sent Michael SCHLATTER to organize Reformed congregations in 1746 (*see* NETHERLANDS REFORMED CHURCH). He formed a coetus or synod the next year, which remained under Dutch supervision until 1793. When the church achieved its complete independence in that same year it reorganized as the Synod of the German Reformed Church. It expanded into Ohio, Wisconsin, North Carolina, and elsewhere and dropped "German" from its official name in 1869. Philip William OTTERBEIN withdrew from its fellowship to form the UNITED BRETHREN in Christ, and John Winebrenner, to found the General Eldership of the CHURCHES OF CHRIST.

The other denomination in the 1934 merger was established by German immigrants who came to America and settled in the Middle West a century after those who organized the Reformed Church. They sympathized with the union of Lutheran and Reformed traditions that had been ordered by King Frederick of Prussia in 1817. Foreign mission societies in Basel, Switzerland, and Barmen, Germany, sent help and missionaries to these evangelicals in the Mississippi Valley. Rev. Louis Nollau and five others formed a ministerial association in 1840 to which congregations were admitted in 1849. In 1866 this loose federation assumed a synodical character and took the name German Evangelical Synod of the West, later changed to the Evangelical Synod of North America.

The Evangelical Synod and the Reformed Church in the U.S. both drew their memberships from the German-American community, followed the AUGSBURG CONFESSION and Luther's and the HEIDELBERG CATECHISMS, developed a liberal theology, and were governed according to a modified presbyterian polity. In 1929 a plan of union was accepted for the United Brethren in Christ, Reformed Church, and Evangelical Synod but eventually only the latter two bodies merged. This union took place on June 26, 1934, at Cleveland, Ohio.

At the time of the merger the two churches had congregations in 38 states but were especially strong in Pennsylvania and the Middle West. They supported an extensive social welfare program that included ten hospitals, ten children's homes, 18 homes for the aged, and institutions for epileptics. They sponsored three seminaries and eight colleges. In 1934 the Reformed Church reported 345,000 members and the Evangelical Synod 273,000.

The Constitution of the Evangelical and Reformed Church reaffirmed the confessions, catechisms, and creeds of the former churches but added: "Wherever these doctrinal standards differ, ministers, members and congregations, in accordance with the liberty of conscience inherent in the gospel, are allowed to adhere to the interpretation of one of these confessions. However, in each case, the final norm is the word of God."

The church observed the Sacraments of Baptism and the Lord's Supper; the latter was celebrated four times a year and was understood as a memorial service. Several prominent theologians, including Paul TILLICH and Reinhold NIEBUHR, were ordained ministers of the Evangelical and Reformed Church. The local church was governed by elected representatives. An equal number of laymen and clergy attended the annual synod and the general synod, which met every three years. The church was administratively divided into 34 synods. In 1957, it became a part of the UNITED CHURCH OF CHRIST.

[W. J. WHALEN/EDS.]

EVANGELICAL CHURCH

Originally known as the Evangelical Association and the So-Called Albright People. This denomination originated (1800–03) under the leadership of Jacob ALBRIGHT (Albrecht) among German-speaking people in Pennsylvania; it merged in 1946 with the Church of the UNITED BRETHREN to become the Church of the EVANGELICAL UNITED BRETHREN. In April 1968, the Evangelical United Brethren merged with the Methodist Church to become the UNITED METHODIST CHURCH.

When Albright's itinerant preaching career as a Methodist among German-Americans received little encouragement from the Methodist Church, he organized several classes or groups of his followers in 1800. In 1803 a meeting of his supporters ''certified'' Albright as ''a truly evangelical minister,'' but it was only in 1807 that an official conference named Albright's followers as the Newly Formed Methodist Conference. The new organization, however, was technically not a part of the Methodist Church of Francis ASBURY (1745–1816); so the 1809 annual conference changed the name to the So-Called Albright People, a title that became the Evangelical Association in the first general conference of 1816. As the new denomination spread, the English language gradually displaced German in preaching and in religious publications, and vigorous missionary activity was inaugurated. In 1839 a general missionary society was organized, and its efforts extended first to Germany and Switzerland and later to Japan, Russia, Poland-Latvia, and Africa. Between 1891 and 1894 disagreement over polity and administration led two-fifths of the membership to withdraw and form the United Evangelical Church. After nearly three decades of separation, the two groups were reunited in 1922 as the Evangelical Church. The resulting organization entered a new merger in 1946 when it joined a kindred, contemporary denomination, the United Brethren in Christ, to form the Evangelical United Brethren, which in turn merged with the Methodist Church in 1968 to become the United Methodist Church.

The Evangelical Church was Arminian in doctrine and its articles of faith corresponded closely to those of METHODISM (*see* ARMINIANISM). The Evangelicals held firmly to the divinity as well as the humanity of Christ, the sufficiency of Scripture for salvation, and emphasized Christian perfection and sanctification. Two sacraments were professed, Baptism and the Lord's Supper. Baptism was accepted as a sign of the new birth of the Christian; the Lord's Supper was declared to be a representation of man's redemption by the sufferings and death of Christ, while the changing of bread and wine into the body and blood of Christ was denied as unfaithful to Scripture. The organizational structure of the Evangelical Church corresponded generally to that of the Methodist Church. A general conference that met every four years elected bishops who were neither ordained nor consecrated as such, but who presided at the annual conferences and decided all questions of law between general conference sessions. At the time of its merger the Evangelical Church had approximately 250,000 members in 25 states, predominantly in Pennsylvania.

Bibliography: R. W. ALBRIGHT, *A History of the Evangelical Church* (Harrisburg, Pa. 1942). J. BERNESDORFER, *Pietism and Its Influence upon the Evangelical United Brethren Church* (Philadelphia 1951). R. S. WILSON, *Jacob Albright: the Evangelical Pioneer* (Myerstown, Pa. 1940). A. D. GRAEFF et al., *The Pennsylvania Germans,* ed. R. WOOD (Princeton 1942). R. YEAKEL, *History of the Evangelical Association,* 2 v. (Harrisburg, Pa. 1924) v.1, 1750–1850.

[R. MATZERATH/EDS.]

EVANGELICAL CHURCH IN GERMANY (EKD)

In German, *Evangelische Kirche in Deutschland* (EKD), a federation (*Bund*) of Lutheran, Reformed, and United churches comprising the great majority of the Protestant churches in a united Germany. Although it reflects the doctrinal and institutional complexity of German Protestantism in its structure, its foundation in 1948 was a significant ecumenical achievement. At the beginning of the 21st century, the EKD comprises the following 24 Lutheran, Reformed and United ''regional churches'' (*landeskirchen*):

1. Evangelische Landeskirche Anhalts (*Evangelical Church of Anhalt*)
2. Evangelische Landeskirche in Baden (*Evangelical Church of Baden*)
3. Evangelisch-Lutherische Kirche in Bayern (*Evangelical Lutheran Church in Bavaria*)
4. Evangelische Kirche in Berlin-Brandenburg (*Evangelical Church in Berlin-Brandenburg*)
5. Evangelisch-Lutherische Landeskirche in Braunschweig (*Evangelical Lutheran Church in Brunswick*)
6. Bremische Evangelische Kirche (*Evangelical Church of Bremen*)
7. Evangelisch-Lutherische Landeskirche Hannovers (*Evangelical-Lutheran Church of Hanover*)
8. Evangelische Kirche in Hessen und Nassau (*Evangelical Church of Hesse und Nassau*)
9. Evangelische Kirche von Kurhessen-Waldeck (*Evangelical Church of Hesse Electorate-Waldeck*)
10. Lippische Landeskirche (*Church of Lippe*)
11. Evangelisch-Lutherische Landeskirche Mecklenburgs (*Evangelical-Lutheran Church of Mecklenburg*)

12. Nordelbische Evangelisch-Lutherische Kirche (*North Elbian Evangelical Lutheran Church*)

13. Evangelisch-Lutherische Kirche in Oldenburg (*Evangelical-Lutheran Church of Oldenburg*)

14. Evangelische Kirche der Pfalz (*Evangelical Church of the Palatinate*)

15. Pommersche Evangelische Kirche (*Pomeranian Evangelical Church*)

16. Evangelisch-reformierte Kirche (*Evangelical Reformed Church in Bavaria and Northwestern Germany*)

17. Evangelische Kirche im Rheinland (*Evangelical Church of Rhineland*)

18. Evangelische Kirche der Kirchenprovinz Sachsen (*Evangelical Church of the Province of Saxony*)

19. Evangelisch-Lutherische Landeskirche Sachsens (*Evangelical Lutheran Church of Saxony*)

20. Evangelisch-Lutherische Landeskirche Schaumburg-Lippe (*Evangelical-Lutheran Church of Schaumburg-Lippe*)

21. Evangelische Kirche der schlesischen Oberlausitz (*Evangelical Church of Silesian Oberlausitz*)

22. Evangelisch-Lutherische Kirche in Thüringen (*Evangelical Lutheran Church in Thuringia*)

23. Evangelische Kirche von Westfalen (*Evangelical Church of Westphalia*)

24. Evangelische Landeskirche in Württemberg (*Evangelical Church of Württemberg*)

Origin. During the Reformation the Lutheran and Calvinistic churches in the Holy Roman Empire came to be organized as state churches on a territorial basis. What at first had been an emergency solution later became the normal form of church government. Thus various systems of administration by secular authorities (princes, cities) arose. In addition, there was the separation between LUTHERANISM and CALVINISM, which was only partially overcome through the creation of "United" churches (doctrinal or administrative unions of Lutheran and Calvinistic churches) in Prussia and some minor German states in the 19th century. When after the collapse of the monarchy (1918) the Protestant churches reorganized themselves independently, the main problem was to combine a certain degree of national unity with territorial and confessional independence. A rather weak Deutscher Evangelischer Kirchenbund (1922) was superseded by a centralized Deutsche Evangelische Kirche (1933), which, however, was paralyzed by the ensuing struggle against Nazi penetration. It was not until after World War II that a satisfactory solution was found.

Structure. The EKD is based upon the gospel of Jesus Christ as contained in the Scriptures and interpreted by the ancient symbols and whatever confessions of faith are accepted by the member churches, including:

> The Lord's Prayer, The Apostolic creed, The Nicene creed, Luther's 95 Theses, Luther's Small Catechism, The Augsburg Confession of Faith (1530), The Heidelberg Catechism (1563), The Barmen Theological Declaration (1934), The Leuenberg Agreement (1973).

Thus the EKD does not interfere with the confessional affiliation of its members, although the common basis is emphasized.

The EKD is essentially a federation of independent regional churches (*landerskirchen*), which in turn are federations of local churches, without superseding the autonomy, ecclesial heritage, and traditions of its members. Structurally, it comprises the following three administrative levels: the Synod, the Executive Council (*Rat de EKD*) and the Church Conference of member churches. The EKD is also a member of the WORLD COUNCIL OF CHURCHES.

Bibliography: *Amtsblatt der evangelischen Kirche in Deutschland* (1946–). H. BRUNOTTE, *Die Grundordnung der evangelischen Kirche in Deutschland* (Berlin 1954). G. WASSE, *Die Werke und Einrichtungen der evangelischen Kirche* (Göttingen 1954).

[H. SCHÜSSLER/EDS.]

EVANGELICAL LUTHERAN CHURCH IN AMERICA

On Jan. 1, 1988, the Evangelical Lutheran Church in America (ELCA) officially began its life. The constituting of this new Lutheran Church body was the culmination of a long series of efforts to bring diverse Lutheran synods and groups in North America together. The ELCA joined the 2.9 million member Lutheran Church in America (LCA), the 2.3 million member American Lutheran Church (ALC), and the 100,000 member Association of Evangelical Lutheran Churches (AELC). Even though the Lutheran Church-Missouri Synod (LC-MS) is not a part of the ELCA, the new church represents one of the largest bodies in world Lutheranism, with a baptized membership of 5.3 million.

Steps toward Union. Each of the constituting churches had its distinct history. The ALC began its at the constituting convention in Minneapolis in 1960. It was characterized by such distinctive traits as the attempt to integrate the work of theological education; the effort toward Lutheran intersynod cooperation; and the approval of alternate routes to ordained service, with emphasis on members of minorities. The AELC, which had its roots in the LC-MS, began to function in 1977. After a major theological struggle with the Missouri Synod involving the dismissal of personnel from Concordia Seminary in St. Louis, a new church was formed. From the outset the leadership of the AELC considered the denomination as an alternative to the LC-MS and its continuation was to be reviewed every 10 years. The AELC was marked by its commitment to inclusivity and its growth in an understanding of ministry. The LCA, since its inception in 1962, was represented by the incorporation of many ethnic strands. Its desire for inclusivity was highlighted by its social statement on race relations in 1964 and its admission of women to ordination in 1970. The ecumenical thrust of the LCA was dramatically marked by its overture toward union with the ALC and AELC at its convention in Louisville, Kentucky, in 1982.

When the three churches agreed to unite in 1982, they first formed a Commission for a New Lutheran Church. The commission, which consisted of 70 members, planned the merger that was finally approved by church conventions in 1986. At the ELCA constituting convention, held from April 30 to May 3, 1987, in Columbus, Ohio, the Rev. Dr. Herbert W. Chilstrom was elected bishop of the ELCA.

Constitution. The Constitution of the ELCA and that of its synods and regions begins with a Confession of Faith that reaffirms its belief in the Triune God and confesses Jesus Christ as Lord and Savior. The ELCA Statement of Purpose states that the Church is a people created by God in Christ who are empowered, called, and sent. The ELCA Principles of Organization articulate the constitutional commitment to a new church through a mandate to include women, persons of color, and persons whose primary language is other than English in all areas of the life of the church; and a structure that calls for interdependency among congregations, synods, and churchwide organizations as they strive to fulfill their mission to witness to Jesus Christ.

ELCA members form about 11,000 congregations, served by 16,000 clergy. They are divided into 65 synods and 9 regions, and each synod is headed by a bishop. The Conference of Bishops, which consists of the 65 synodical bishops, as well as the bishop and secretary of the ELCA, provides spiritual enrichment and opportunities to discuss issues of importance to the church for those who serve in these roles. The Churchwide Assembly, which is composed of delegates elected by the synods, meets biennially to evaluate ELCA programs, elect officers, and conduct other business of the church.

The work of the main office, located in Chicago, Illinois, is divided among 4 administrative offices, 6 program divisions, 5 supporting commissions, the ELCA Publishing House, the Women of the ELCA, and the Board of Pensions (Address: Evangelical Lutheran Church in America, 8765 West Higgins Road, Chicago, Illinois, 60631).

The ELCA has entered into full communion partnerships with the the Presbyterian Church (USA), the United Church of Christ and the Reformed Church in 1997, the Moravian Church in 1999, and the Episcopal Church in 2000.

Bibliography: H. W. CHILSTROM, *Foundations for the Future: The Evangelical Lutheran Church in America at the Threshold of a New Millennium* (Minneapolis 1988). EVANGELICAL LUTHERAN CHURCH IN AMERICA, *Constitutions, Bylaws, and Continuing Resolutions: Evangelical Lutheran Church in America* (Minneapolis 1988). E. T. BACHMANN, *The Ecumenical Involvement of the LCA Predecessor Bodies: A Brief History 1900–1970* (New York 1983). E. C. NELSON, *Lutheranism in North America 1914–1970* (Minneapolis 1972). W. G. VOLKER, *A Handbook and Directory for Congregational Leaders* (Minneapolis 1988).

[D. J. SWAN/EDS.]

EVANGELICAL UNITED BRETHREN

Two churches founded by German-speaking METHODISTS in the U.S., namely, the Church of the United Brethren in Christ and the Evangelical Church, merged in 1946 to form the Evangelical United Brethren (EUB). In 1968, the EUB merged with the Methodist Church to form the UNITED METHODIST CHURCH. Historically, both the Church of the United Brethren in Christ and the Evangelical Church originated in Pennsylvania in the early 19th century. Their founders preached an Arminian theology to the German immigrants in this area who were mainly Lutherans and Calvinists (*see* ARMINIANISM). Since the Methodist bishops refused to incorporate German-speaking congregations into their church, separate church organizations were established that closely paralleled METHODISM.

Philip William OTTERBEIN (1726–1813), a German Reformed minister, came to America in 1752. Along with a Swiss Mennonite preacher, Martin BOEHM (1725–1812), he conducted revivals in Pennsylvania, Maryland, and Virginia. In 1774 Otterbein became pastor of an independent German congregation in Baltimore, Md. His and Boehm's converts were known as New Reformed German Methodists, or New Mennonites. A conference (1800) drew up plans for the new church, which adopted the name United Brethren in Christ in 1821. A minority seceded in 1889 to form the Church of the UNITED BRETHREN in Christ (Old Constitution).

The Evangelical Church was founded by Jacob ALBRIGHT (1759–1808) who left LUTHERANISM to become a Methodist preacher. He began working among the Germans in Pennsylvania in 1796 and formed an evangelistic association in 1803. This body took more definite form after his death and became known as the Evangelical Association after 1816. Like the United Brethren Church the Evangelical Association underwent a schism. About 40 percent of the members left the main body in 1891, but most of the dissenters returned in 1922. A minority refused to rejoin the parent church and formed the Evangelical Congregational Church. The Evangelical Church served a membership of 250,000 at the time of its merger with the United Brethren in Christ in 1946.

The EUB was essentially Methodistic in doctrine, polity, and liturgy, but it also displayed traces of its Lutheran, Mennonite, and Reformed heritages. For many decades it limited its missionary work to German Americans, but the use of German in worship was curtailed during World War I.

[W. J. WHALEN/EDS.]

EVANGELICALISM

In its widest sense, the term signifies a body of doctrine regarded as the essential message of the Gospel. Although the precise meaning of Evangelicalism has varied with different historical contexts, it is generally applied to the doctrine of salvation by faith in Christ. In the era of the Reformation, those who followed Martin Luther in placing a new stress on this doctrine were commonly designated as Evangelicals. The term was used in this sense to distinguish the churches of the Lutheran tradition from those of the Calvinist tradition, which were commonly known as Reformed. Many Lutheran synods in the United States and Europe use the term ''Evangelical'' as part of their official designation.

The Evangelical Revival in the 18th century, characterized by PIETISM in Germany and METHODISM in England, gave a new sense to the term. Since the 18th century, particularly in English-speaking lands, Evangelicalism has been used to designate the school of Protestantism that maintains that the essence of the Gospel consists in the doctrine of salvation by faith in the atoning death of Christ. In this sense, Evangelicalism has been represented by a tradition within the Anglican communion, as well as by those churches that developed from the 18th-century Evangelical Revival. The Evangelical tradition, in both groups, stressed the authority and inspiration of the Bible and the depravity of fallen nature and its need for a Redeemer, and regarded the sacraments as symbols rather than as means of grace. The Evangelical tradition in worship denied that ordination confers any supernatural power on the minister and stressed the reading of Scripture and the importance of evangelistic preaching.

In England, the Evangelical party found more in common with the Nonconformists than with the High Church wing of the Establishment, and cooperated readily with them in missionary and social-welfare efforts in the 19th century. Similar cooperation among the Protestant churches took place in North America in the same period. From this mutual sharing, the EVANGELICAL ALLIANCE developed as an institution in 1846, and a general sense of a community of Evangelical doctrine shared by many denominations grew up over a longer period. The division between liberals and fundamentalists in the early 20th century, particularly in American Protestantism, brought a somewhat different emphasis to the term. A school of theology, conservative in outlook and closely akin to the fundamentalist view, developed in the United States after 1940 under the general designation of Evangelicalism. Conservative American Protestantism adopted the term, since the forming of the NATIONAL ASSOCIATION OF EVANGELICALS in 1942, as a substitute for fundamentalist or conservative, but with the same meaning.

In England. The Evangelical Revival became influential within the Church of England in 1735. The preaching of John and Charles WESLEY and of George WHITEFIELD stimulated many members of the Established Church to develop a more personal piety and inner religion. The movement was never separatist, and the ordination of Francis ASBURY in 1784 was the first overt step toward separation of the Wesleyan movement from the Church of England. Whitefield found a warm welcome in Scotland, where an Evangelical party developed within the Church of Scotland, and in North America. The GREAT AWAKENING, which swept over the American colonies after 1740, had an impact on all the Protestant churches. The growth of Methodism in England and America and the growth of other closely related churches marked the closing decades of the 18th century. In both countries, the Evangelical movement found reflection in missionary efforts. The English Evangelicals organized the Church Missionary Society and the Religious Tract Society in 1799, as well as the British and Foreign Bible Society in 1804. Through the so-called Clapham Sect, Evangelical churchmen were instrumental in developing reform and social welfare. Henry Ryder, bishop of Gloucester, and Charles Sumner, bishop of Llandaff, brought the Evangelical party to the Bishops' Bench after 1815.

Opposition to the OXFORD MOVEMENT characterized much of the Evangelical activities in the mid-Victorian period. The Parker Society was organized in 1840 to publish the writings of the English Reformers. English Evangelicals stressed home missions and open-air preaching in industrial areas in the latter part of the 19th century; they sponsored the revival meetings of Dwight L. MOODY in 1875. Evangelicalism was somewhat on the defensive in Great Britain in the 20th century, but it experienced a marked revival in 1947 and 1948.

In the United States. Evangelicalism in the United States has been closely linked to efforts at interdenominational cooperation on a basis of shared doctrine. Reflecting the contemporary English development, American Protestants united to form the American Board of Commissioners for Foreign Missions in 1812, the American Bible Society in 1815, and other cooperative ventures. The writings of Samuel S. SCHMUCKER and Philip SCHAFF stressed the common heritage of Evangelical Protestantism, as did the publications of William A. Muhlenberg, who blended Evangelical doctrine and Catholic practice in the Episcopal Church. The development of an American branch of the Evangelical Alliance after the Civil War drew its strength from a shared doctrinal inheritance. After Schaff's death, a new stress on the social Gospel led to the supplanting of the alliance in 1908 by the Federal Council of Churches. To many Evangelicals, the new body was tainted with liberal theology, and they found a more congenial association in the fundamentalist movements.

Several leaders of the fundamentalist crusade were theologians of considerable stature, such as J. Gresham Machen and Benjamin B. WARFIELD, although the movement as a whole was characterized by anti-intellectualism and biblical literalism. These theologians and their successors provided a transition from the older fundamentalism to the new Evangelicalism. Recognizing the blunders of the fundamentalists in their attitude toward science and reason, the modern Evangelicals found spokesmen in Gordon Clark, Bernard Ramm, and Carl F. H. Henry. *The Uneasy Conscience of Modern Fundamentalism,* published by Henry in 1947, had a marked influence in developing a social concern among Evangelicals.

''The Statement of Faith'' adopted by the National Association of Evangelicals in Chicago in 1943 stressed the inspiration and authority of Scripture; the Trinity; the Divinity, Virgin Birth, and Bodily Resurrection of Christ; and his atoning death and message of salvation. The much smaller AMERICAN COUNCIL OF CHRISTIAN CHURCHES, similarly conservative, was formed in 1941. The National Association of Evangelicals sponsored the National Association of Christian Schools (1947) to promote Christian day schools and a National Sunday School Association (1949) to provide uniform lessons. In the field of foreign missions, the Evangelical Foreign Mission Society (1945) centralized the activities of a large number of small mission societies and has been adamant in opposing any concession to local rites or non-Christian customs. The Evangelicals, although recognizing the need for union in Christ, have resisted the ecumenical movement, fearing its tendency to downgrade doctrine for the sake of organizational unity. They claim to have separated from the neo-orthodox and liberal theologians on their understanding of the Bible and from the fundamentalists on questions of social ethics.

Bibliography: L. E. ELLIOTT-BINNS, *The Early Evangelicals* (London 1953). J. D. MURCH, *Cooperation without Compromise: A History of the National Association of Evangelicals* (Grand Rapids, Mich. 1956). M. A. SHIBLEY, *Resurgent Evangelicalism in the United States: Mapping Cultural Change since 1970* (Columbia, S.C. 1996). G. ROSSELL, *The Evangelical Landscape: Essays on the American Evangelical Tradition* (Grand Rapids, Mich. 1996). A. E. MCGRATH, *A Passion for Truth: The Intellectual Coherence of Evangelicalism* (Leicester, Eng. 1996). L. I. SWEET, *The Evangelical Tradition in America* (Macon, Ga. 1997). H. A. HARRIS, *Fundamentalism and Evangelicals* (Oxford/New York 1998). C. SMITH and M. EMERSON, *American Evangelicalism: Embattled and Thriving* (Chicago, Ill. 1998). G. J. DORRIEN, *The Remaking of Evangelical Theology* (Louisville, Ky. 1998). R. STEER, *Church on Fire: The Story of Anglican Evangelicals* (London 1998). R. H. BALMEM, *Blessed Assurance: A History of Evangelicalism in America* (Boston, Mass. 1999). G. CARTER, *Anglican Evangelicals: Protestant Secessions from the Via Media, c. 1800–1850* (Oxford 2000). T. P. RAUSCH, *Catholics and Evangelicals: Do They Share a Common Future?* (New York/Downers Grove, Ill. 2000).

[R. K. MACMASTER/EDS.]

EVANGELII NUNTIANDI

Apostolic exhortation of Pope PAUL VI, ''On Evangelization in the Modern World,'' issued Dec. 8, 1975, following the third ordinary assembly of the Synod of Bishops (Sept. 27 to Oct. 26, 1974). The assembly was charged with clarifying the church's evangelizing identity in a way that did justice both to traditional theology and to the liberationist construction of mission and evangelization. Unable to arrive at a synthetic position and publish a document, it handed the results of its deliberations to Paul VI for his elaboration and study. The exhortation comprises seven chapters.

The exhortation's unifying concern is with the organic nature of evangelization as a fundamental concept and focal image of the mission and ministry of the church. It articulates the answers to three questions: (1) how can ''the hidden energy of the Good News have a powerful effect on the human conscience?''; (2) how and to what extent is ''that evangelical force capable of transforming the people of this century?''; and (3) ''what methods should be followed in order that the power of the Gospel may have its effect?'' (*EN* 4).

In chapter one, the pope roots the church's evangelizing mission in the person and work of Jesus. As evangelization was central to the life of Jesus, so it is to the life of the church. In chapter two, ''What Is Evangelization?'' the concern is to show that ''evangelizing means bringing the Good News into all the strata of humanity and through its influence transforming humanity from within'' (*EN* 16) in a way that permeates cultures ''without being subject to any one of them'' (*EN* 20). In that process, witness is primary but proclamation is necessary to make what is implicit explicit and to make it capable of drawing new members into the Christian community (*EN* 22–23).

Chapter three, ''On the Content of Evangelization,'' confronts both those who overemphasize the inner dimensions of Christian conversion and those who accentuate the public and the political, but downplay the spiritual. This chapter envisages a church vitally inserted in the dramas of the day, armed with an anthropology that is always aware of humanity's tendency to confuse its temporal accomplishments with permanent achievements, while forgetting the need for constant conversion of heart (*EN* 35–37). This emphasis in the exhortation is widely taken as Paul VI's warning that changing social structures that lead to sin and oppression will not suffice as the sole focal image of the Christian mission in the world.

In sections on the ''methods'' (chapter four) ''beneficiaries'' (chapter five) and the ''workers'' (chapter six) of evangelization, Pope Paul advocates the use of all modern means to spread the gospel message among all peoples and all strata of every society, including ''dechristianized'' and non-Christian peoples. In regard to the latter, the pope teaches both that respect is due to followers of other traditions, but also that ''the religion of Jesus . . . objectively places human beings in relation with the plan of God . . . which the other religions do not succeed in doing, even though they have, as it were, their arms stretched out to heaven'' (*EN* 53).

Of special importance in chapter six, where the pope differentiates the proper roles of the various orders of the church in the evangelization of the world, is the stress he places on the role of the laity, whose field of work is ''the vast and complicated world of politics, society and economics, but also the world of culture, of the sciences and the arts, of international life, of the mass media'' (*EN* 70). In chapter seven, the pope emphasizes the action of the Holy Spirit (*EN* 75), displaying his consciousness of the need for a fully Trinitarian theology of religion and evangelization.

[W. BURROWS]

EVANGELIST

A preacher of the gospel or an author of one of the four Gospels. The English word comes, through the Latin *evangelista,* from the Greek noun εὐαγγελιστής, from the verb εὐαγγελίζεσθαι (to announce good news). Evangelist is a title of an activity (not of an office) of early Christian missionaries and proclaimers of the GOSPEL (εὐαγγέλιον, literally ''good news''). Although the words εὐαγγέλιον and εὐαγγελίζεσθαι occur frequently in the New Testament, the word εὐαγγελιστής is found there only three times: (1) Acts 21.8, concerning PHILIP the deacon; (2) in Eph 4.11, where the word appears after ''apostles'' and ''prophets'' and before ''pastors'' and ''teachers'' and where, therefore, it refers to Christian missionaries who have received a special CHARISM; and (3) in 2 Tm 4.5 concerning Timothy (cf. 1 Thes 3.2, where Timothy is called ''a servant of God in the gospel of Christ''). The work of the evangelist consisted more in the proclamation of the glad tidings of Christ's Redemption to those who had not yet heard them than in the instruction and pastoral care of those who had already accepted the faith and been baptized. It was Christ who first announced the glad tidings of salvation (Mt 4.23; 11.5; etc.) and who sent the Apostles for the same purpose (Rom 1.1; 1 Cor 1.17); later the term evangelist was applied to those men whom the Church sent as missionaries to preach the same good news.

The use of the word Evangelist in reference to the authors of the four Holy GOSPELS dates from the third century; it is thus used by St. HIPPOLYTUS OF ROME in speaking of St. Luke (*On Antichrist* 56), and by TERTULLIAN (*Against Praxeas* 21.23) and St. DIONYSIUS OF ALEXANDRIA (Eusebius, *Ecclesiastical History* 7.25.8) in speaking of St. John.

Although originally ''the four living creatures'' of Ez 1.10 and Rv 4.7 had nothing to do with the four Evangelists, the application of these symbolic figures to the four Evangelists began as early as the second century, apparently by St. IRENAEUS (*Her.* 3.11.8). At first there was some inconsistency in the application of the individual symbols; but by the end of the fourth century, thanks especially to the great authority of St. JEROME, the following relationship was fixed: the human-faced figure represented Matthew, because of Matthew's genealogy of the humanity of Christ; the lion-faced figure represented Mark, because of Mark's mention of the voice of the Baptist in the desert; the ox-faced figure represented Luke, because of Luke's mention of the Jewish priest Zachary; and the eagle-faced figure represented John, because of the soaring flight of John's prologue.

In Christian iconography the portrayal of the four Evangelists by these four symbols, usually surrounding the figure of Christ in glory, has been common since the fifth century, both in monumental mosaics in the churches and in miniatures in the Gospel books. However, there has been a concomitant tradition in Christian art of showing the four Evangelists in fully human form.

Bibliography: *Encyclopedic Dictionary of the Bible*, tr. and adap. by L. HARTMAN (New York 1963) 705. G. FRIEDRICH, G. KITTEL *Theologisches Wörterbuch zum Neuen Testament* (Stuttgart 1935–) 2:734–735. J. SCHMID, *Lexikon für Theologie und Kirche*, ed. J. HOFER and K. RAHNER (Freiberg 1957–65) 3:1253–54. Iconography. L. RÉAU, *Iconographie de l'art chrétien* (Paris 1955–59) 3.1:476–480. K. KÜNSTLE, *Ikonographie der christlichen Kunst* (Freiburg 1926–28) 1:609–612. J. H. EMMINGHAUS, *Lexikon für Theologie und Kirche*, ed. J. HOFER and K. RAHNER (Freiberg 1957–65) 3:1254–55.

[M. J. HUNT]

EVANGELISTS, ICONOGRAPHY OF

The Evangelists, as a tetrad, are frequently represented in Christian art, especially in manuscript illumination. They appear in human form or in symbolic guise.

When represented as human figures, the Evangelists are either standing or seated and engaged in composition of the Gospels. Both types were developed from classical figures of philosophers or writers; they were introduced by Christian artists during the 2nd or 3rd century. The seated figure in the posture of meditation is the closest to the classical prototype (Stauronikita cod. 43). Several early Christian sarcophagi contain the first representations of the Evangelists as human figures (sarcophagus of Concordius, Arles). In manuscripts they are usually represented in full–page miniature or as standing portraits, which can sometimes be inserted between text columns. Byzantine artists developed the portrait seen in profile view, while in the West the frontal type was preserved from the classical period. The mosaics in S. Vitale in Ravenna show the Evangelists, each with a codex, in a landscape background. The ivory chair of St. Maximian (Ravenna, 6th century) preserves an excellent example of the early standing portraits; the Evangelists are presented in three–quarter frontal poses, each holding a Gospel Book inscribed with a cross. In the Middle Ages they were represented in typological association with the four great Prophets: Isaiah, Jeremiah, Ezekiel, and Daniel (south transept window, Chartres Cathedral). They were associated in the late medieval period with the four Latin Doctors of the Church: Jerome, Augustine, Ambrose, and Gregory.

The symbolization of the Evangelists by four winged creatures is derived from the vision of Ezekiel and Revelation (4.6–8). To Matthew was assigned the human figure; to Mark, the lion; to Luke, the ox; and to John, the eagle. The Evangelists were assigned their symbols on the basis of the opening passages of each one's Gospel: the man to Matthew, since he narrates the genealogy and birth of Christ; the lion to Mark, because he begins dramatically with the *vox clamantis in deserto* (like the sound of the king of beasts); the calf to Luke, because he describes the sacrifice of Zachary; and the eagle to John, since he commences with the preexistence of the Logos in heaven. The symbolic tetrad stands also for different phases in the life of Christ: the man of Matthew, for the Incarnation; the lion of Mark, for the Resurrection (the medieval lion roared its stillborn cubs to life); the calf of Luke, for the sacrificial death on the cross; and the eagle of John, for the Ascension. These symbols often are represented in apocalyptic scenes like the *Majestas Domini* (mosaics of S. Pudenziana, Rome), as well as Ascensions (Rabbula Codex). A hybrid formation of the Evangelists wearing the heads of their symbols is found chiefly in the

"St. John the Evangelist Writing His Gospel," painting from a 12th-century English Gospel.

''Saint Matthew and Saint John the Evangelist,'' 17th-century painting by Francisco de Ribalta. (©Archivo Iconografico, S.A./ CORBIS)

art of southern France and Spain (Sacramentary of Gellone, 11th century).

Bibliography: F. X. KRAUS, *Real–Encyklopädie der christlichen Alterthümer,* v.1 (Freiburg 1882) 458–463. H. LECLERCQ, *Dictionnaire d'archéologie chrétienne et de liturgie,* ed. F. CABROL, H. LECLERCQ, and H. I. MARROU, 15 v. (Paris 1907–53) 5:845–852. A. M. FRIEND, ''Portraits of the Evangelists in the Greek and Latin Manuscripts,'' *Art Studies* (1927–29). F. VAN DER MEER, *Majestas Domini* (Paris 1938). L. RÉAU, *Iconographie de l'art chrétien,* 6 v. (Paris 1955–59) 3.1:476–480.

[S. TSUJI]

EVANGELIUM VITAE

Pope JOHN PAUL II'S eleventh encyclical letter, ''The Gospel of Life,'' issued on the feast of the ANNUNCIATION, March 25, 1995. In 1991 an extraordinary consistory of the college of cardinals met to discuss ''threats to human life in our day.'' The cardinals asked the pope to affirm the ''value of human life and its inviolability'' with the authority of the Successor of Peter. To this end, the Holy Father wrote a personal letter to each bishop, asking him to cooperate in the development of this encyclical. *Evangelium vitae* appeals to ''each and every person, in the name of God: respect, protect, love and serve life, every human life'' (5).

The encyclical unfolds in four chapters. Chapter one, ''Present-Day Threats to Human Life,'' is an indictment of the growing ''culture of death.'' By applying the story of Cain and Abel to the present-day situation, the pope shows that the fratricidal urge to take the lives of others lies at the heart of abortion and euthanasia, and of other deadly trends, such as the arms race. He shows how the exaggerated and even perverse claims of freedom from constraints in these areas are identical with Cain's self-serving question, ''Am I my brother's keeper?'' Underlying these claims is a mentality that ''carries the concept of subjectivity to an extreme'': the self no longer recognizes the equal rights of other selves, especially those less able to defend themselves. The state, even in democratic countries, risks being subverted by such claims and becoming the tool of the strong, to be used against the weak. The ''sense of God'' is diminishing, along with the sense of human solidarity. The result is a ''practical materialism,'' in which suffering has no value. What is needed is a ''civilization of love and life,'' which cannot exist without self-sacrifice. The Church summons all people to ''choose to be unconditionally pro-life,'' in the name of the Risen Christ, whose ''blood speaks more eloquently than that of Abel.''

Chapter two, ''The Christian Message Concerning Life,'' is a meditation on the proclamation that in Jesus Christ, good is powerful enough to triumph over evil. His death, freely accepted, resulted in new life for himself and for those who believe in him. The biblical teaching on life, from the creation of the world through the Resurrection of Jesus Christ, reveals its triumphant value, without diminishing the central Christian irony that ''life finds its center, its meaning and its fulfillment when it is given up.''

Chapter three, ''God's Holy Law,'' is a reflection on the Fifth Commandment, especially as it regards the death penalty, abortion, and euthanasia. The pope sets out the limits of self-defense for individuals and the state and questions the use of the death penalty: punishment ''ought not go to the extreme of executing the offender except in cases of absolute necessity: in other words, when it would not be possible otherwise to defend society. Today, however, as a result of steady improvements in the organization of the penal system, such cases are very rare, if not practically non-existent.'' If such is the case with regard to the guilty, how much more care should be taken to protect the lives of the innocent? By ''the authority which Christ conferred upon Peter and his Successors, and in communion with the Bishops of the Catholic Church, I confirm that the direct and voluntary killing of an innocent human being is always gravely immoral.'' The acceptance of abortion, in many areas, ''in the popular mind, in behavior and even in law itself,'' is a ''telling sign of an extremely dangerous crisis in the moral sense, which is becoming more and more incapable of distinguishing between good and evil.'' Considering it more necessary than ever to ''to call things by their proper names,'' the pope, using the words of *Gaudium et spes* 51, calls abortion and infanticide ''unspeakable crimes.'' He then reflects in some detail on the innocent victim of abortion, the child, already conceived and genetically distinct and whole. He also considers those involved in the decision to terminate the child's life, including the mother, father, doctor, nurses, and those legislatures that have legalized this ''unspeakable crime'' in many countries. At the other end of life's spectrum lies the question of euthanasia, ''an action or omission which of itself and by intention causes death, with the purpose of eliminating all suffering.'' The pope condemns euthanasia as ''senseless and inhumane,'' although it is often presented as ''logical and humane.'' Another symptom of the culture of death, euthanasia is ''a grave violation of the law of God.'' At the same time, the pope upholds the Church's traditional teaching that one may decide to forego ''aggressive medical treatment'' (extraordinary means) that ''would only secure a precarious and burdensome prolongation of life,'' which he has elsewhere called a ''prolongation of dying.''

Chapter four, ''For a New Culture of Human Life,'' is an outline of the ''culture of life'' based on Matthew 25: ''Whatever you did for one of these least brothers of mine, you did for me.'' It outlines how the People of God can become a ''people of life'': by proclaiming, celebrating, and serving the gospel of life, by making Christian families ''sanctuaries of life,'' and by bringing about a ''transformation of culture.'' Such a transformation calls for a ''general mobilization of consciences and a united ethical effort to activate a great campaign in support of life.'' This gospel of life is for the whole human family; Mary and the Church are revealed as ''mothers,'' that is, bearers of life; and although the forces of evil may menace life, the Resurrection of Jesus Christ means that, ultimately, ''death shall be no more.''

Bibliography: For the text of *Evangelium vitae,* see: *Acta Apostolicae Sedis* 87 (1995): 401–522 (Latin); *Origins* 24, no. 42 (April 6, 1995): 689–727 (English); *The Pope Speaks* 40 (1995): 199–281 (English). For a commentary, see: WM. KEVIN WILDES and ALAN C. MITCHELL, eds., *Choosing Life: A Dialogue on Evangelium Vitae* (Washington, D.C. 1997).

[D. CLARK]

EVANGELIZATION, NEW

The term ''new evangelization'' was first used, it seems, by the Latin American bishops at their general conference at Medellin, Colombia, in 1968. JOHN PAUL II made it a major theme of his pontificate. In an address to the Latin American bishops at Port-au-Prince, Haiti, on March 9, 1983, he called for an evangelization that was ''new in its ardor, its methods, and its expression.'' Evangelization, he insisted, cannot be new in its content, since its theme is always the one gospel given in Jesus Christ. If it arose from ourselves and our situation, he said, it would be a mere human invention, but the ancient and perduring gospel can and must be heralded with new energy and in a language and manner adapted to the people of our day. In his encyclical on missionary activity, REDEMPTORIS MISSIO (1990) he declared: ''I sense that the moment has come to commit all of the Church's energies to a new evangelization and to the mission *ad gentes*. No believer in Christ, no institution of the Church, can avoid this supreme duty: to proclaim Christ to all people'' (RM 3). In the same encyclical and in many other pronouncements, John Paul II linked the new effort of evangelization with the preparation for the Great Jubilee of the year 2000.

The essentials of the program were already identified by PAUL VI, who took the name Paul to signify his intention to model his conduct of the papacy on the ministry of the Apostle of the Gentiles. Wishing to engage the whole Church more decisively in the dissemination of the gospel, he chose as the theme for the Synod of Bishops in 1974 ''the evangelization of the modern world.'' On the basis of materials provided by that synod he issued in 1975 his great apostolic exhortation *Evangelii nuntiandi*. Looking back at the accomplishments of Vatican II, which had ended just ten years earlier, Paul VI declared that the council had sought above all else ''to make the Church of the twentieth century ever better fitted for proclaiming the gospel to the people of the twentieth century'' (EN 2).

The new evangelization has certain features in common with evangelization at any time. By its very nature, evangelization must be Christocentric. Because the traits of Jesus Christ have sometimes been overlaid by secondary and accidental considerations, the new evangelization seeks to start afresh by contemplating the features of Jesus and his central message as set forth in Sacred Scripture. Evangelization clearly proclaims Jesus Christ as its source and goal, and fosters a deep personal relationship to him.

Like all evangelization, again, the new evangelization is governed by the Holy Spirit. Paul VI and John Paul II agree in teaching that the Holy Spirit is the principal agent of evangelization (EN 75; RM 21, 30). ''It was not by chance,'' wrote Paul VI, ''that the great inauguration of evangelization took place on the morning of Pentecost, under the inspiration of the Spirit'' (EN 75). The new evangelization is predicated on the realization that evangelization cannot succeed if it is conducted by purely human efforts. Missionary dynamism, according to John Paul II, is born of the Holy Spirit, who moves the Church to spread its faith.

Besides recalling these constants, the new evangelization has a number of distinctive features, which may be enumerated as follows:

1. Evangelization is broadly conceived so as to include not only the initial announcement of the gospel but the entire process whereby human persons and the world are transformed under its vivifying impact. John Paul II distinguishes three phases. ''First'' or ''primary'' evangelization occurs when the gospel is initially proclaimed to those who do not as yet know Christ. Then, through continuing evangelization, which includes pastoral care, believers are enabled to place their lives ever more fully under the influence of the gospel. In a third phase, the Church undertakes the re-evangelization of those who have fallen away or allowed their faith to grow cold (RM 33). The Church, insofar as it is an institution of men and women here on earth, continually needs to be evangelized (EN 15).

2. Evangelization extends not only to persons but to cultures. It is frequently hindered by an unwholesome split between faith and culture. Paul VI called attention to the need for what he called the ''evangelization of cultures'' (EN 20). John Paul II agreed with Paul VI that cultures themselves need to be regenerated by an encounter with the gospel. At Santo Domingo in 1992 he insisted that the new evangelization must strive to render human cultures harmonious with Christian values and open to the gospel message.

3. Evangelization includes social teaching. In affecting cultures it has an inevitable impact on social structures. Thus no sharp line of demarcation can be made between the spiritual and temporal realms, as though the latter ought to be purely secular and immune to religious or supernatural influence. In evangelizing, the Church cannot remain indifferent to the suffering, inequities, and oppression that afflict so much of the world's population. Paul VI insisted that while the mission of the Church must not be reduced to the dimensions of a purely temporal project, evangelization must concern itself with justice, liberation, development, and peace (EN 31-32). According to John Paul II the Church's mission is primarily to awaken consciences and thereby motivate them to work for a more authentic human development. The Church has no mission to work directly on the economic, technical, or political levels (RM 58).

4. To be effective in our day, evangelization must make use of the mass media of social communication, including the radio, television, and the Internet. These media are not substitutes for the written word or for person-to-person contact, but they serve as needed supplements, gaining audiences who would otherwise not be reached. Paul VI therefore declared that Church would be guilty in God's sight if it failed to use powerful means of communication that are being perfected in our day (EN 45). John Paul II, with a reference to the Apostle Paul's proclamation of the gospel in Ath-

ens, pointed out that the culture of the new media is itself a modern ''Areopagus'' or forum in which the Church's missionary activity must be conducted in order to reach the heart of modern civilization (RM 37).

5. In the new evangelization, special care will be taken to respect the dignity and freedom of the persons being addressed. In earlier times Christian rulers sometimes applied psychological and physical force to induce people to accept the true faith. The new evangelization, by contrast, presupposes acceptance of Vatican II's Declaration on Religious Freedom, which taught that in matters of religion people should be encouraged to make free and responsible judgments without external pressure. Recognizing that the assent of faith must by its very nature be free, the Church avoids offensive proselytization. Both Paul VI and John Paul II have insisted that in evangelizing the Church proposes the truth of the gospel but imposes nothing (EN 80; RM 39). In the last analysis, freedom and truth converge, for, according to the saying of Jesus, ''The truth shall make you free'' (Jn 8:32)—a saying frequently quoted by John Paul II.

6. In the new evangelization, missionary proclamation is combined with dialogue, which respects the point of view of the persons addressed and seeks to meet their real concerns. Dialogue is an aid to proclamation because it enables the evangelizer to discern the dispositions and convictions of the hearers and thus to engage them more effectively. In dialogue both parties are allowed to express themselves with the hope of learning from one another. Dialogue, however, contains an element of proclamation, because it requires each party to express itself frankly and honestly.

Dialogue takes different form according to the audiences being addressed. Paul VI in his encyclical *Ecclesiam suam* (1964) distinguished three circles: humanity as a whole, the monotheistic religions, and non-Catholic Christianity. Since Vatican II official dialogues have been set up with nonbelievers, with non-Christian religions, with the Jews, and with Christian churches and communities. These dialogues are not directly aimed at conversion but at mutual understanding, mutual respect, and convergence. Such dialogues, beneficial though they undoubtedly are, do not take the place of missionary proclamation. In the words of John Paul II, ''Dialogue is not in opposition to the mission *ad gentes*; indeed it has special links with that mission and is one of its expressions'' (RM 55).

Ecumenical dialogue is likewise pertinent to evangelization. It aims to discover, emphasize, and augment the shared beliefs of Christians, with a view to more effective common witness. Paul VI and John Paul II tirelessly reiterated the importance of mutual reconciliation among Christians for the effective proclamation of the gospel to the world (EN 77; RM 50).

7. In the past evangelization has often been seen as the special province of priests and religious professionally dedicated to missionary work. Following in the footsteps of Vatican II, both Paul VI and John Paul II have insisted that it is the whole Church that received the commission to evangelize (EN 15; RM 62, 71). Lay Christians, through incorporation into Christ by baptism, confirmation, and the Eucharist, are called to bear witness to the faith by word and deed. Christian parents are the first evangelizers of their children. The clergy have a special responsibility to organize and oversee the task of evangelization and to stimulate the faithful to rise to their responsibilities. Members of religious orders and congregations dedicated to evangelization are specially called to testify to the radical challenge of the gospel.

The program of the new evangelization introduced by Vatican II and the subsequent popes is one of the most dramatic developments in modern Catholicism. In recent centuries the Catholic Church, polemically arrayed against Protestantism, has insisted more on fine points of doctrine than on the basic Christian message. The faithful, imbued with these defensive attitudes, have found it difficult to rise to the challenge of the new evangelization, which calls for positive proclamation of the basic Christian message. In countries such as the United States terms such as ''evangelization'' appear to have a Protestant ring; they often evoke the image of radio and television preachers whose doctrine and methods are antithetical to Catholic tradition. A further difficulty comes from the preoccupation of some Catholics since Vatican II with projects of inner-church reform. Since their energies are taken up in debates with other Catholics, they tend to lose interest in looking outward beyond the present membership of the Church. Under the influence of modern secularism and agnosticism, some have lost confidence in the saving power of Christ and the gospel.

Notwithstanding these difficulties, the evangelical turn in Catholic official teaching has been welcomed by many Catholics, perhaps especially in eastern Asia, Latin America, and Africa. The bishops of the United States have responded affirmatively in several excellent documents. In 1992 they approved the document ''Go and Make Disciples,'' setting forth a national plan and strategy for evangelization in the United States. Increasing numbers of adults are received into full communion each year, thanks to programs such as ''Renew,'' ''Life in the

Spirit'' seminars, and the Rite of Christian Initiation of Adults.

Bibliography: Paul VI, Apostolic Exhortation ''On Evangelization and the Modern World'' (*Evangelii nuntiandi*) (Washington, D.C. 1975). John Paul II, Encyclical *Mission of the Redeemer (Redemptoris missio)* (Washington, D.C. 1991). R. MARTIN and P. WILLIAMSON, eds., *Pope John Paul II and the New Evangelization* (San Francisco 1995). H. CARRIER, ''Gospel Message and Human Cultures'' (Pittsburgh 1989). A. DULLES, ''John Paul II and the New Evangelization,'' *Studia Missionalia* 48 (1999): 165–80.

[A. DULLES]

EVANGELIZATION OF PEOPLES, CONGREGATION FOR THE

The *Congregatio pro Gentium Evangelizatione*, or Congregation for the Evangelization of the Peoples (CEP) is the successor to the historic Congregation for the Propagation of the Faith. It carries out its predecessor's tasks of coordinating and directing the missionary activity of the Church. This entry covers the history and activities of CEP since 1967. For its history prior to 1967, see under PROPAGATION OF THE FAITH, CONGREGATION FOR THE.

''Propagation of Faith'' Becomes ''Evangelization of Peoples.'' The fifth and sixth chapters of Vatican II's Decree on Missionary Activity (*Ad gentes*, 1965), on the organization of missionary work and cooperation in it, were drafted to overcome the commonly held idea that missionary work was primarily the responsibility of religious orders and societies of apostolic life. That idea had become practically established in the minds of the Catholics over the 500 years since the beginning of the modern missionary movement, and was enshrined in the ''ius commissionis'' approach to foreign missions, whereby mission lands were carved out and assigned to specific religious orders. The centralization of these groups in Rome and their loyalty to the Holy See, moreover, made them ideal centripetal forces to counteract the centrifugal nature of missionary activity as it was conceived in its classic modern period— i.e., as work by professional missionaries that brought the Faith and the Church from Europe to the antipodes of the earth.

Ad gentes brought missionary theology in many respects into harmony with *Lumen gentium* and attempted to establish the principle that mission is the work of the entire church, not just professional missionaries, since ''The Church on earth is by its very nature missionary'' (*Ad gentes* 2). To animate this effort, *Ad gentes* 29 charged the Congregation for the Propagation of the Faith with becoming an ''instrument of administration and an organ of dynamic direction . . . [using] scientific methods and instruments adapted to modern conditions,'' according to norms that were to be laid down by the Pope, aided by ''consultors and experts'' with expertise and experience.

These principles were ratified and implemented by Pope Paul VI in Part III of his *motu proprio Ecclesiae Sanctae* (Aug. 6, 1966), and in his apostolic constitution on the renewal of the Roman Curia, *Regimini ecclesiae universae* (Aug. 15, 1967), articles 81–91. In *Regimini*, the new name of the venerable Congregation is given as the *Congregatio pro Gentium Evangelizatione*. Despite the new name, in both documents, the clear purpose of Pope Paul was to continue its traditional coordinating role, while placing special emphasis on promoting indigenous priestly vocations and helping both missionaries and the whole church appropriate its missionary identity (*Regimini ecclesiae universae* 82). The key words from *Ad gentes* that appear to have characterized the Pope's intentions were to become ''an organ of *dynamic* direction'' of works within its traditional competence, not to take stock of, or begin a radically new kind of evangelization of areas such as Latin America and the traditional European heartlands of Catholicism, which were already in 1967 showing signs of decline from their former levels of activity.

What was new in *Regimini* was the call for three new secretariats founded in the wake of Vatican II to be represented at CEP, and for CEP to have representation in each of them—the Secretariats for Christian unity, for Non-Christians, and for Non-Believers (*Regimini ecclesiae universae* 83). This effectively constitutes the Holy See's recognition that a new era in ecumenical relations had arisen. In it Christian mission had to be carried out with sensitivity to those who in former years were often thought of only as potential ''objects'' of missionary activity, and not as members of venerable faith traditions or followers of sincerely held convictions of non-belief in religions as paths that assisted their members attain transcendent goals. Since 1967, then, CEP has found itself active in the work of the secretariats that have succeeded those mentioned above, namely the Pontifical Councils for Interreligious Dialogue and for Christian Unity, in whose offices is housed the Commission for Religious Relations with the Jews.

CEP Under John Paul II. On June 28, 1988, Pope John Paul II issued the apostolic constitution *Pastor Bonus* (''The Good Shepherd''). Following the promulgation of the New Code of Canon Law on Jan. 2, 1984, *Pastor Bonus* is dedicated to updating the legislation and organization of the Roman Curia. His stated purpose in the long historical-theological introduction (*Pastor Bonus* 1–13) is making the Holy See a ministry of service (*diakonia*) for the entire church, which he refers to as ''a communion'' marked simultaneously with a ''primatial and collegial nature,'' and in which all ''power and authority of the bishops bears the mark of *diakonia* or stewardship'' (*Pastor Bonus* 2). *Pastor Bonus* functions as John Paul's rationale for the authority of the Roman Curia as enjoying ''a truly ecclesial character'' (*Pastor Bonus* 7), exercised ministerially for the benefit of the whole church.

Articles 85 through 92 of *Pastor Bonus* are dedicated to indicating how CEP is to serve. In essence, its tasks remain those that evolved from 1622 to the Second Vatican Council, but they accentuate CEP's role of promoting research in mission theology, spirituality, and pastoral work (*Pastor Bonus* 86). CEP is to care for promoting missionary vocations internationally and in territories it directs and has responsibilities for the education of secular clergy and catechists (*Pastor Bonus* 88). In line with the Pope's overall concern in *Pastor Bonus* to rationalize the work of the Curia, he states that CEP's role in appointing bishops and erecting dioceses in its territories is analogous to that of the Congregation of Bishops (*Pastor Bonus* 90) and is carried out under papal authority and with its approval. Finally CEP is charged with administering its own and funds of others destined to assist the missions.

Of more than passing importance is an issue not raised in the document. Although missiologists by 1988 had come increasingly to speak of mission, including *missio ad gentes*, as transcending *geographical* boundaries, CEP is still charged with directing mission as if it were an activity moving from the so-called ''mature churches'' in Europe and North America for the benefit of the so-called ''young churches'' in Asia, Africa and Latin America. Yet the number of missioners coming from the North was rapidly declining and their average age rising. Between 1968 and 1998, the number of U.S. Catholic missioners, according to the U.S. Catholic Mission Association dropped from 9,655 to 5,883. Between 1992 and 1999, the average age of priests and religious sisters in that group rose from 59.2 to 64.4 and 57.7 to 64.2 respectively. Since figures from Europe are analogous, if CEP's primary role is in directing missionary efforts from the North to the South, its efforts are soon going to be less needed. That is not, however, the entire picture, since there is a rapid growth in the number of *ad gentes* missioners sent into mission *from* Asia, African, and Latin America, lands that hitherto had been thought of as *objects*, and not *subjects* of mission.

Under *Pastor Bonus*, the task of developing structures of ministry that could invigorate evangelization and re-evangelization efforts in areas such as Europe, North America, and Latin America are not within the scope of a geographically and missiologically circumscribed CEP. None of CEP's nor other curial agencies' publications avert to the need to re-examine entrenched attitudes and consider new approaches to mission. Many missiologists argue that sclerotic attitudes hinder the Church from exploring creative ways of bringing in new cohorts of young men and women needed to engage non-Christians and non-practicing Christians effectively in the new areopagi that the Pope and CEP continue to assert should be the objects of mission today.

CEP's Work for Mission. Granted the need to question whether the geographical scope of its activities today correspond to what Pope John Paul II in *Redemptoris Missio* article 37 called the ''new areopagi'' of mission, there is no disputing the fact that CEP has become ever more involved in the work of the world church in the territories it has responsibility for, which include Asia, Oceania, most of Africa, and parts of Latin America and the Caribbean. A great deal of CEP's work is involved with the process of erecting, dividing, and supporting ''mission'' dioceses, as well as in appointing bishops and other key mission leaders, such as seminary rectors. The number of dioceses under CEP's jurisdiction was 1,049 as of October 2000. In a given year, as many as 30 to 40 percent of new Catholic bishops ordained worldwide are carried out under CEP's guidance and nomination for approval by the Holy Father.

Bibliography: B. JACQUELINE, ''Le droit missionnaire après le Concile: observations sur la compétence de la S C pro Gentium Evangelizatione seu de Propaganda Fide,'' *Atti del Congresso internazionale di diritto canonico. La Chiesa dopo il Concilio. Roma, 14–19 gennaio 1970* (Milan 1972) 825–32. A. REUTER, ''Drei nachkonziliäre Instruktionen der S C pro Gentium Evangelizatione,'' *Ius populi dei: Miscellanea in honorem Raymundi Bidagor*, ed. R. BIDAGOR (Rome 1972) 467–518. T. SCALZOTTO, *La sacra congregazione per l'evangelizzazione dei popoli nel decennio del decreto ''Ad gentes.''* (Rome 1975).

[W. R. BURROWS]

EVANS, PHILIP, ST.

Welsh martyr; b. Monmouth, 1645; d. Cardiff, July 22, 1679. Evans was educated at St. Omer and on Sept. 7, 1665, entered the Society of Jesus; after ordination at Liège in 1675 he was sent to work in South Wales. Three years later his zeal made him a marked-man in the fierce outburst of persecution fomented by the fantastic ''plot'' concocted by Titus Oates. In November 1678, John Arnold of Abergavenny, a Calvinist, justice of the peace, and priest hunter, offered, in addition to the customary £50, another £200 for the arrest of Evans. Evans refused to desert his people and was caught on December 2 at the house of Christopher Turberville, at Skier in Glamorgan, where he was then stationed as chaplain.

At Cardiff he refused the oath of allegiance and for three weeks was placed in solitary confinement in an underground cell. For a long time no one would testify to Evans's priesthood until an old woman and her daughter were suborned to swear that they had heard Evans say Mass and preach and had received absolution from him. After six months, on May 3, 1679, Evans was brought to trial. In court the two witnesses repeated their evidence, which was supported by an apostate dwarf, who, at the prompting of Arnold, declared that he had heard Evans say that ''in no short time you will see in England no other religion but the Catholic.'' Evans was found guilty of being a priest and returned to prison, where, being a talented musician, he found consolation in music.

On July 21, when news was brought to him that he was to be executed the next day, he was playing tennis: ''What hurry is there,'' he asked. ''Let me first play out my game.'' On July 22, after bidding farewell to some friends, he was taken to execution with Bl. John Lloyd, with whom he had been tried. The place was Gallows Field (at the northeast end of what is now Richmond Road), Cardiff. Evans, suffering before Lloyd, said to him, ''Adieu, Mr. Lloyd, though for a little time, for we shall shortly meet again.'' Philip Evans was beatified by Pius XI on Dec. 15, 1929, and canonized by Paul VI in 1970.

Feast: July 22.

See Also: ENGLAND, SCOTLAND, AND WALES, MARTYRS OF.

Bibliography: T. P. ELLIS, *Catholic Martyrs of Wales* (London 1933). J. STONOR, *Six Welsh Martyrs* (Postulation pamphlet; London 1961). R. CHALLONER, *Memoirs of Missionary Priests,* ed. J. H. POLLEN (rev. ed. London 1924). A. BUTLER, *The Lives of the Saints*, rev. ed. H. THURSTON and D. ATTWATER (New York 1956) 3:166–167. J. GILLOW, *A Literary and Biographical History or Bibliographical Dictionary of the English Catholics from 1534 to the Present Time.* (London-New York 1885–1902) 2:186–187. H. FOLEY, ed., *Records of the English Province of the Society of Jesus,* 7 v. (London 1877–82) 5.2:882–891.

[G. FITZHERBERT]

EVARISTUS, POPE, ST.

Pontificate: 99 or 96 to 108? According to IRENAEUS (*Adv. Haer.* 3.3), he succeeded CLEMENT I as pope. The LIBERIAN CATALOGUE and other sources list him after Anacletus. A sixth-century recension of the *Liber pontificalis* describes him as a Greek of Antioch, the son of a Jew from Bethlehem. Even if this were not so, his Greek name testifies to the continuing foreign influence in the Roman community. *Liber pontificalis* also ascribes to him the appointment of clergy to the 25 parishes in Rome and the creation of the seven-man college of deacons, a completely unreliable tradition. His episcopacy lasted seven, eight, or nine years according to Eusebius (*Chron. Hist.* 3.34; 4.1; 5.6), nine or 13 years according to different recensions of the *Liber pontificalis*. If Clement died in the third year of TRAJAN'S reign, as Eusebius (3.15) says, Evaristus may have become bishop as late as 101. The tradition that he was martyred is doubtful due to the silence of Irenaeus on the matter. Evaristus is one of the most obscure of popes. Modern excavations indicate that he was not buried near Peter in the Vatican.

Feast: Oct. 26.

Bibliography: EUSEBIUS, *The Ecclesiastical History*, tr. K. LAKE and J. E. L. OULTON, 2 v. [*Loeb Classical Library* (London-New York-Cambridge, Mass.) 1926–32]. L. DUCHESNE, *Liber pontificalis* (Paris 1186–92) 1:XC–XCI. J. P. KIRSCH, *Lexicon für Theologie und Kirche* 2 (Freiburg 1957–65) 3:1260. J. N. D KELLY, *Oxford Dictionary of Popes* (New York 1986) 8.

[E. G. WELTIN]

EVE

The first woman, wife of Adam, and ancestress of all mankind. This article will consider first the biblical data on Eve, and then the place of Eve in dogmatic theology.

In the Bible

The name Eve (Hebrew, *hawwâ*) was given, according to Gn 3.20, by the first man to his wife. It occurs only four other times in the Bible: Gn 4.1, Tb 8.8, 2 Cor 11.3, 1 Tm 2.15. Since Eve is the mother of all the living, by popular etymology, the name is related to the Hebrew word for life, *hayyâ*. The first name given to her by her husband, after God had made her from the man's own body to bring her to him as ''a helper like himself,'' was ''woman [*'iššâ*], for from man [*'îš*] she has been taken'' (Gn 2.23). The profound unity and complementary character of man and woman are, thereby, symbolized by the sacred author.

As mother of all the living, Eve plays a very significant role in the context of Gn 3.20. Man had just been punished by being reduced to his natural state of being mortal. In the author's mind, Eve would seem to be the means by which man may attain at least some sort of continued existence.

The woman's role in the Fall is not that of a temptress, since no such action is described in Gn 3.6b, but, that of the first human transgressor of a covenant law (Gn

2.17). Hence, woman's low condition in Israel society, her pains in childbirth, and her husband's dominion over her (Gn 3.16).

Latin tradition, through a mistranslation of Gn 3.15b, introduced the image of Eve crushing the serpent's head that was later transferred to the Blessed Virgin Mary and became a symbol of her Immaculate Conception (*see* PROTO-EVANGELIUM). Although this meaning is not found in the original text, Eve, nevertheless, as mother of all the living, is an apt figure for the Mother of all those alive in Christ.

Bibliography: E. MAGENOT, *Dictionnaire de théologie catholique* 5.2:1640–55. A. M. DUBARLE, ''Les fondements bibliques du titre marial de nouvelle Eve,'' *Revue du sciences religieuses* 30 (1951) 49–64.

[T. R. HEATH]

In Theology

Among the Fathers of the Church, Justin was the first to add the feminine counterpart to the Christ-Adam parallel. He contrasts MARY, Blessed Virgin, with Eve, seeing in the former obedience and life and in the latter disobedience and death. Clement of Alexandria, Irenaeus, Methodius, Tertullian, and Augustine all commented on Eve, but usually to bring out Mary's greatness. Augustine sees a symbol in the account of Eve's creation from the side of Adam. She is made from man's bone to give her some of man's strength, and in the place of the removed rib the man has flesh to give him some of woman's tenderness (*Gen. ad litt.* 9.18.34, *Patrologia Latina* 34:407). Aquinas writes that the manner of production of the woman from the side of man signifies the social union of man and woman, ''for the woman should neither exercise authority over the man [cf. 1 Tm 2.12] and so she was not made from his head; nor is it right for her to be subject to man's contempt as his slave, and so she was not made from his feet.'' He also sees a Christian sacramental symbol there, ''for from the side of Christ sleeping on the cross the sacraments flowed, namely blood and water, by which the Church was established'' (*Summa theologiae* 1a, 92.3). Scholastics generally follow patristic studies on Eve, seeing her either as a contrasting type of Mary or of the Church.

With the advance of knowledge in scientific fields, especially in those dealing with the origins of man (*see* EVOLUTION), many questions arise. Is Eve only a symbol or a historical personage? Can there be many Eves? Did she share in the gifts given to her husband? While there has never been any formal definition of the Church concerning Eve, the cautions of Pius XII regarding recent teachings on Adam would apply also to her. Whatever is said about Eve must be consistent with Catholic doctrine

''Adam and Eve,'' engraving by William Morris. (©Historical Picture Archive/CORBIS)

on ORIGINAL SIN and the immediate creation of the soul by God [H. Denzinger, *Enchiridion symbolorum*, ed. A. Schönmetzer (32d ed. Freiburg 1963) 3896–97; *see* ADAM (IN THEOLOGY)].

Catholic scholars since M. J. Lagrange have accepted the general theory of the literary form of the creation accounts in Genesis. The woman plays a prominent role both in creation, where her appearance is seen as the finishing touch to all that God has made, and in the paradisal sin, where the beliefs and practices of pagan religions current at the time of the authorship of the account are contrasted. These beliefs deified the female principle and regarded sexual excess in the fertility rites as an act of worship. But in practice, women were treated as socially inferior and the creature of man's pleasure. The CREATION STORY tells us of the dignity of woman, her equality with man, and the divine origin of the differences in sex. The account of the sin warns against woman's idolatrous attempts to share the divine prerogative of procreation by participating in the fertility rites of the pagan gods, since that is abominable to God and punished by Him. The Catholic teaching about the dignity of woman, her vocation as a child of God, equal in nature and grace to man, and the sacredness of the marital relationship is thus seen

Eve plucking the apple from the Tree of the Knowledge of Good and Evil, Burgundian bas relief, c. 1135–40, from the north portal of Autun Cathedral. (Marburg-Art Reference, Art Resource, NY)

grounded in the Genesis story (*see* WOMAN, CATHOLIC TEACHING ON).

See Also: GENESIS, BOOK OF.

Bibliography: *Dictionnaire de théologie catholique.* Tables générales 1:14510–51. H. JUNKER, *Lexikon für Theologie und Kirche*, ed. J. HOFER and K. RAHNER, 10 v. (2d new ed. Freiburg 1957–65) 3:1215–16. THOMAS AQUINAS, *Summa theologiae* 1a, 90–102, and commentary by H. D. GARDEIL in *Somme théologique* I. 90–102: *Les Origines de l'homme,* tr. A. PATFOORT (Paris 1963) 423–451. J. COPPENS, *La Connaissance du bien et du mal et le péché du Paradis* (Louvain 1948). J. DE FRAINE, *The Bible and the Origins of Man* (New York 1962). A. M. DUBARLE, *Le Péché originel dans l'Écriture* (Paris 1958). C. HAURET, *Beginnings: Genesis and Modern Science,* tr. and ed. E. P. EMMANS (2d ed. Dubuque 1964). M. M. LABOURDETTE, *Le Péché originel et les origines de l'homme* (Paris 1953). J. L. MCKENZIE, *Myths and Realities* (Milwaukee 1963) 146–181. R. J. NOGAR, *The Wisdom of Evolution* (Garden City, NY 1963). H. RENCKENS, *Israel's Concept of the Beginning,* tr. C. NAPIER (New York 1964). A. ROBERT and A. TRICOT, *Guide to the Bible*, tr. E. P. ARBEZ and M. P. MCGUIRE, 2 v. (Tournai-New York 1951–55; v. 1, rev. and enl. 1960) 1:174, bibliog. on European and American lit. to 1960. L. F. HARTMAN, ''Sin in Paradise,'' *Catholic Biblical Quarterly* 20 (1958) 26–40, with fine bibliog. C. REILLY, ''Adam and Primitive Man,'' *Irish Theological Quarterly* 26 (1959) 331–345. C. VOLLERT, ''Evolution and the Bible,'' *Symposium on Evolution* (Pittsburgh 1959) 81–119.

[E. H. PETERS]

EVERARD OF YPRES

Writer; b. Ypres, Belgium; d. Clairvaux. Everard studied under GILBERT DE LA PORRÉE at Chartres, Paris, and Poitiers. From 1162 to 1165 he was a cleric in France of Hyacinth, the future CELESTINE III. A teacher at the University of PARIS for most of his life, Everard wrote a compendium (*summula*) of Canon Law sometime after 1180 and addressed a letter to URBAN III (1185–87) to denounce some alleged errors concerning the Trinity and the God-Man. He remained an ardent admirer of his master Gilbert and during the reign of Celestine III (1191–98) wrote his principal work, a Latin *Dialogue between Ratius and Everard,* in which Gilbert's cause is defended by a fictitious Greek, called Ratius, who strongly disagrees with St. Bernard's interpretation of Gilbert's theology. Ratius is also quite critical of certain aspects of monastic life. A letter addressed to Everard by a certain ''Brother B.'' reexamines and questions statements made in the *Dialogue* and in the letter to Urban. Everard spent his last years as a Cistercian at Clairvaux.

Bibliography: N. M. HARING, ''A Latin Dialogue on the Doctrine of Gilbert of Poitiers,'' *Mediaeval Studies* 15 (1953) 243–289: ''The Cistercian Everard of Ypres . . . ,'' *ibid.* 17 (1955) 143–172.

[N. M. HARING]

EVERGISLUS, ST.

Bishop; d. before 594. According to the historically worthless 11th-century vita, Evergislus was the protégé, later archdeacon, of SEVERIN OF COLOGNE. According to the same vita, he stopped to pray one night in a church at Tongres, Belgium, and was set upon by robbers and murdered (*c.* 455). However, Evergislus is rather to be identified with the Bishop Ebregesilus or Eberigisil, whom the more reliable information of GREGORY OF TOURS puts among the emissaries sent by King Childebert II (590) to restore order in a convent of women at Poitiers. Gregory relates also that Evergislus erected a church in honor of St. Mallosus at Birten. The relics of Evergislus are now in the parish church of St. Peter in Cologne. Evergislus is the first bishop of COLOGNE to bear a German name; contrary to the 11th-century report, he seems not to have died a violent death.

Feast: Oct. 24.

Bibliography: *Acta Sanctorum* Oct. 10 650–661. *Bibliotheca hagiographica latina antiquae et mediae aetatis* (Brussels 1898–1901) 1:2365–70. *Analecta Bollandiana* 6 (1887) 193–198 (the incredible 11th century *Vita*). L. DUCHESNE, *Fastes épiscopaux de l'ancienne Gaule* (Paris 1907–15); v.3.

[W. A. JURGENS]

EVERYMAN

An English morality play of the late 15th century, the finest representative of the genre, and the one best known outside the circle of historical scholars (*see* DRAMA, MEDIEVAL, 2). Of undetermined authorship, it is now generally conceded to be a close translation of a Dutch play, *Elckerlijc,* although a number of attempts have been made to prove the priority of the English text. The success of the play with modern audiences is a tribute to the universality of its thematic elements and to the artistry of its dramatic structure. While it is the culmination of a long series of experiments with a nonrepresentational, allegorical drama on the problem of salvation, it transcends the limits of its era to become one of the great plays of all time.

To indicate the indebtedness of the work to a tradition, as well as its artistic superiority to its models, it is necessary to consider, first, its relation to two themes dominant in late medieval art and literature (the DANCE OF DEATH and the *ARS MORIENDI*); secondly, its structure as a theater piece capable of interesting audiences of many types and times.

Everyman accosted by the figure of Death in a woodcut on the opening page of an edition of Everyman, printed by John Scott in St. Paul's Churchyard, London, about 1530.

Relationship to Two Medieval Themes. The Dance of Death, known to Continental literature as the *danse macabre,* has been traced to a French custom of preaching on the theme of death and illustrating the sermon by a solemn processional dance, in which a skeletal figure impersonating Death led one victim after another away toward the tomb, each being garbed as representative of a type, e.g., king, lawyer, shepherd. This graphic exemplification of death as leveler is regarded by some scholars as the origin of the entire morality-play genre, and it is unquestionably a central force in the poetry and painting of late medieval Europe. The somber power of its theme lent itself to meditation on the inevitability of death, but it also invited exploitation of death's horrors, especially in the pictorial representation of physical decay.

A sensationalism of technique in the *danse macabre* brought the theme into disrepute as an excess of flamboyant art, an excess that may account for the development of an *ars moriendi* tradition, an art of dying well, with the emphasis upon spiritual truths and practical preparation for death. This second tradition undoubtedly owed much to late medieval inroads of the epidemics that repeatedly swept away large segments of the population. These catastrophes often meant death unattended by the parish clergyman, who might himself have been among the earliest victims because of his ministrations to the dying. The *ars moriendi* treatise, first associated with the name of the French theologian Jean GERSON and widely imitated throughout Western Europe in the 15th century, was a manual for the dying, intended to assist a person in overcoming the terrors and temptations of the last illness and to console him with thoughts of God's mercy and generosity. It was, therefore, an antidote to the *danse macabre,* whether consciously written for that purpose or not.

Plot and Structure. The first dramatic incident in *Everyman* is an encounter of its hero with Death, who has come suddenly upon the stage to summon him for the final reckoning with God. This event is a restrained but stark confrontation between the soul and the heavenly messenger, and the journey upon which Everyman sets out so reluctantly is an adaptation of the processional Dance of Death. Relentlessly fulfilling his task, Death refuses delay, but concedes that Everyman may have as companion on the journey anyone bold enough to undertake it. There follows a series of encounters with allegorical representations of Everyman's associates and possessions (Fellowship, Kindred, Worldly Goods, etc.), all of whom decline the dubious honor of the invitation. Deserted by all but Good Deeds, Everyman belatedly attempts preparation for death, aided by Knowledge (i.e., self-knowledge) and Confession. In this part of the play, the dramatist has used abstract characters as a means of adapting to the theater the homiletic material of the *ars moriendi* tradition and of structuring into a dramatic conflict the spiritual experiences of the final hours. Accompanied to the edge of the grave by such physical powers as Strength, Five Wits, and Discretion, Everyman enacts a powerful denouement in which he commends his soul into the hands of God.

Structurally, the play is a series of recognitions (in the Aristotelian sense of *anagnorisis*), each followed by a reversal (*peripeteia*). Without postulating that the author had a knowledge of Greek drama, one can nevertheless find in the play these essentials of dramatic design that are universal elements of successful theater. Each recognition is an illumination that Everyman has been evading and each one serves to increase the tension of his conflict with the antagonist, Death, who remains present as an invisible force, although the personified character withdraws after delivering the initial summons.

The recognition of betrayal by one earthly value after another creates a corresponding momentum in the direction of spiritual gain, and thus the falling line of Everyman's physical defeat is counterbalanced by a rising action that culminates in the salvation of his soul. The tension of each crisis is followed by a brief respite as Everyman's self-knowledge assesses the material loss and prepares for the next spiritual gain. The perilous encounters maintain audience suspense until the denouement, the final release of tension. This effects a restoration of tranquility—the catharsis that only great and serious drama achieves.

Implementing the crises and forward movement of the play is a highly complex pattern of speeches ranging from a rapid, stichomythic dialogue through lengthy admonitory expositions by Knowledge and Shrift, reaching greatest dramatic power perhaps in Everyman's own expressions of fear, disillusionment, contrition, and joy. It would be a mistake, however, to exaggerate the naturalism of speech and style, for the morality play is essentially a nonrepresentational art—Knowledge, for example, has no personality and no power of speech in real life. The successful dramatic illusion of reality, however, is created by the literary and mimetic resources of stylized diction and rhythm, carefully modulated according to the rules of an English prosody inherited from the old alliterative poetic tradition. Rhythm, diction, characterization, and incident, then, combine to make this play an art work vastly superior to the Dance of Death, enriched as it is by the spiritual traditions of the *ars moriendi.*

Bibliography: J. Q. ADAMS, ed., *Chief Pre-Shakespearean Dramas* (Boston 1924), text of play. H. CRAIG, *English Religious Drama of the Middle Ages* (Oxford 1955). É. MÂLE, *L'Art religieux de la fin du moyen-âge en France* (5th ed. Paris 1949). G. R. OWST, *Literature and Pulpit in Medieval England* (2d ed. rev. New York 1961). A. P. ROSSITER, *English Drama from Early Times to the Elizabethans* (New York 1950). A. WILLIAMS, *The Drama of Medieval England* (East Lansing 1961).

[E. C. DUNN]

EVESHAM, ABBEY OF

Former Benedictine monastery at Evesham, Worcestershire, England. According to tradition, it was founded by St. Egwin, Bishop of WORCESTER, in 702. From 941 to 969 and from 976 to *c.* 989, during which years it was in lay hands, the abbey church was served by secular priests. BENEDICTINE monks were restored *c.* 989 by the bishop of Worcester. Under Abbot Aelward (1014–44), a relative of King Canute, Evesham began to be independent of the bishops. Abbot Aethelwig (1059–77) regained much land lost under secularization. Aethelwig was an adviser of WILLIAM I (the Conqueror), who entrusted seven Midland counties to him. In 1069 to 1070, during the harrying of the North, Aethelwig made his abbey a relief center for refugees, and in 1073 to 1074 he sent three monks to begin the restoration of monasticism in northern England. He bequeathed money for a new church, which was erected by his successor. In 1095 to 1096 Evesham monks were sent to Denmark to found a priory at Odense. Evesham helped to reform this daughter house in 1174, though contact ceased in the next generation. A cell was founded also at Penwortham, Lancashire, in 1140. In 1189 Roger Norreys, the deposed prior of Canterbury, was transferred to Evesham. The new abbot persecuted the monks and wasted the revenues. An attempted episcopal visitation by the bishop of Worcester, however, united all factions in the abbey. Thomas of Marleberge, the monks' spokesman and a brilliant canonist, won exemption for the abbey during a protracted suit at Rome in 1204 to 1206. This, and the interdict in the following year, prolonged the tyranny of Roger Norreys at Evesham until 1213, when he was deposed by a papal legate. Marleberge himself was abbot of Evesham from 1229 to 1236. He was probably its most learned abbot and coauthor of its chronicle. The abbey's jurisdiction over the churches in the Vale of Evesham was confirmed in 1248. The 14th and 15th centuries were peaceful, though the abbey suffered severely in the Black Death of 1348 to 1349. In 1466 Evesham took over the decayed Abbey of Alcester (Warwickshire), which became a dependency. The abbey was surrendered in 1540. The buildings were demolished and only a detached bell tower remains.

Bibliography: Sources. W. D. MACRAY, ed., *Chronicon abbatiae de Evesham* (*Rerum Britannicarum medii aevi scriptores*, 244 v. 29; 1863). G. R. C. DAVIS, *Medieval Cartularies of Great Britain* (New York 1958) 44. F. WORMALD, ed., *English Kalendars before A.D. 1100* (London 1934–) 1:16.27; *English Benedictine Kalendars after A.D. 1100* (London 1939–) 1:21. H. A. WILSON, ed., *Officium ecclesiasticum abbatum, secundum usum Eveshamensis monasterii* (Henry Bradshaw Society 6; 1893). Literature. *The Victoria History of the County of Worcester,* ed. J. W. WILLIS-BUND et al., 4 v. (Westminster, Eng. 1901–24) v.2. BENEDICTINES OF STANBROOK, *Saint Egwin and his Abbey of Evesham* (London 1904). R. R. DARLINGTON, ''Aethelwig, Abbot of Evesham,'' *English Historical Review* 48 (1933) 1–22, 177–198. L. WEIBULL, ''S:ta Maria i Evesham och s:t Knut i Odense,'' *Scandia* 13 (1940) 196–205. D. KNOWLES, *The Monastic Order in England, 943–1216* (2d ed. Cambridge, Eng. 1962). D. KNOWLES and R. N. HADCOCK, *Medieval Religious Houses: England and Wales* (New York 1953) 58, 65, 63.

[H. P. KING]

EVIL

''Evil'' can be defined as that which opposes, or is the antithesis of, what is good. There is no precise articulation of the nature of evil in the creeds of the Church, nor is there any explicit or definitive Christian doctrine of evil. For biblical writers God's reality was accepted unquestioningly, and evil was accepted as an inevitable aspect of the world. Since evil was (and remains) the source of incredible human suffering and anguish, the biblical response did include appeals to God for understanding, and petitions to God to reduce suffering. The classic example is Job, but there are many other biblical writings that address the issue of understanding God's relationship to evil (cf. Ps 10:1, 22:1, Lam 2:20–22, Jn 9:1–5, Lk 13:1–5, etc.).

In Scripture. While the Scriptures display remarkable consistency and coherence about God and evil, the sacred authors did not produce a systematic theology of evil and suffering, nor did they theorize about God's hidden will in permitting evil and suffering, with a few exceptions (cf. Ps 10:1; Ps 22:1; and Ps 42:9; Lam 2:20–22; Jn 9:1–5, Luke 13:1–5; etc.). Evil is understood predominantly, though by no means exclusively, as divine punishment for sin (cf. Jer 44:22–23; Gal 6:7–8; Mt 7:18–19; Am 3:8; Lam 3:38; Is 45:7; etc.). Other explanations attribute evil andsuffering to divine warnings and tests of faith (2 Cor 8:2; 1 Pt 1:6–7; etc.), to divine discipline (1 Cor 11:32; Dt 7:4–7; Heb 12:5–12; etc.), and as a means of expiation or atonement for sin—as displayed in Israel's sacrificial system of mandatory expiation (Lev 1–7; Jgs 2:18; Jer 8:21; Ps 126:5–6; etc.). The New Testament provides some unique perspectives on evil and its relationship to God; it teaches, for example, that evil has redemptive value, a view inspired especially by the Servant Songs in Isaiah (Is 41:1–4; 49:1–6; 50:4–9; 52:13–53:12), and patterned on Christ's suffering on behalf of all humanity (cf. Mk 10:38–39; Lk 14:27, etc.). Most importantly, perhaps, the New Testament teaches that suffering is not in every instance to be understood as directly attributable to a divine purpose, but that free creatures, both human and angelic, are the source of much, perhaps all, evil. The older view that God causes evils for justifiable reasons was softened, accordingly, by this understanding of human and angelic free will as the source of much suffering. Evil was understood as the result of satanic forces under the leadership of Satan, the personification of evil, yet also an ontological reality: ''the lord of this world'' (cf. Jn 12:31; Jn 14:30; Jn 16:11; Jn 17:31; 2 Cor 4:4; Eph 2:2; 6:12; etc.), ''the adversary'' (1 Pt 5:8), the ''tempter'' (1 Thes 3:5; 2 Cor 11:3), etc., who endlessly goads humanity into sin and brings about trials to discourage us and weaken our resolve for goodness (cf. 1 Thes 2:18; 1 Tm 4:1–7), etc. The human mind was thought to be the battleground for spiritual warfare between God and the demonic (2 Cor 10:3–5; Eph 6:10–12). Christ conducted spiritual warfare in His ministry, exorcizing evil spirits and showing by example that evil is an affront to God and must be resisted. Christian theology holds that Christ defeated Satan by the Cross and Resurrection, freeing us from the bondage to sin and the fear of death (Heb 2:14–15; 1 Cor 15). Christ urged His disciples to continue the fight against evil and He gave them power and authority to do so in His name (cf. Lk 9:1; Lk 10:19; etc.). So focused was Christ's battle against evil powers that St. Paul's letters defined Christ's atoning death as a ransom to Satan (Gal 3:20; 1 Tm 2:6; Col 2:15; Rom 3:25; and cf. Mt 20:28; Heb 2:14; 3:15; 1 Jn 3:8; etc.), a view held by the Church for a millennium until St. Anselm of Canterbury (1033–1109) proposed an alternative view of Christ's death as an atoning satisfaction for humanity's sinful rebellion against God, rather than for a ransom to be paid to Satan (*see* ATONEMENT).

The Source of Evil. Traditionally, Christian theologians have referred to the Adamic Fall (Gn 3) for an understanding of the source of evil, the view that evil emerges from the misuse of human freedom. While this had been foreseen by God, the gift of freedom, nonetheless, was an essential and fundamental gift from God, one that distinguishes humanity from all other creatures and gives man alone the ability to choose good and evil. The misuse of freedom by Adam and Eve (Gn 3) introduced sin and suffering into a world created good (*see* SUFFERING). This "original sin" largely corrupted human nature, though not completely. As St. Augustine explained (*City of God* XIII, 14), the corruption is inherited "seminally" ("in the seed") by Adam and Eve's progeny. Ours is a world, accordingly, in which we are estranged not only from God, but from our spiritual nature, the world itself, and one another. This understanding of the Fall of humanity into corruption and sin became the dominate Christian explanation for evil and suffering. Interestingly, the Old Testament makes no mention of the Adamic Fall after the account in Genesis 3. The account was revived in the intertestamental books of Jubilees and 2 Enoch, and taken into Christianity by St. Paul's image of Christ as the second Adam who had overturned the sin of the first Adam (Rom 5:12–17; 1 Cor 15:21–22; Rom 5:16). The more common Old Testament view is that evil and suffering have their source in the breaking of the covenant established by Yahweh with the patriarchs Abraham and Moses. A further (and much less influential) view of evil's origin is found in the account of the sinful mating of the "sons of God" with "the daughters of men," caused by their "evil imagination" (Gn 6:5), an event that led to God's punishment by the catastrophic flood (Gn 6). The sinful actions noted in Gn 6:5 were elaborated in the Watchers legend in 1 Enoch in the intertestamental period. By the time of Christ, the account of the Fall in Genesis 3 had been coalesced with the "evil imagination" account used in Rabbinic Judaism, and taken up by St. Paul who taught that Adam's Fall was explained by an "evil imagination" that was passed on to his progeny (see Hick, *Evil*, 202–5; see also 2 Esdras 3:21–22: "For the first Adam, burdened with an evil heart, transgressed and was overcome, as were also all who were descended from him"). Augustine developed the theory of *concupiscence* (lust, sexual desire, etc.) as the source of evil within humanity, a theory that was integral to his defense of human freedom and doctrine of original sin (*see* Evans, *Augustine*, 132–67, etc.). St. Thomas later adapted this view, but with a more positive and optimistic emphasis about the condition of the human soul (see *Summa theologiae* I. Qs 81–82; Rahner, "Concupiscentia").

Kinds of Evil. A common division of evil is that into metaphysical, physical, and moral, as explained in the following sections.

Metaphysical Evil. The metaphysical notion of evil comes from LEIBNIZ. This type of evil results, in the opinion of some, from the mere finitude of created beings, i.e., from the absence of a perfection not required for the natural integrity of creatures. According to this conception, evil would affect all created beings universally and without any fault on their part. This view was revived in the twentieth century by several philosophers [cf. M. Heidegger, *Sein und Zeit* (Halle 1927) pp. 175–180; K. Jaspers, *Philosophie* (Berlin 1932) 2: 196–199; J. P. Sartre, *L'Etre et le Néant* (Paris 1943) p. 481], for whom original sin is the universal perception of a nature in anguish, conscious of its limits and native imperfection. Such a metaphysical notion of evil can be contested since finitude in itself is not an evil. It is indeed the negation of a higher perfection (e.g., man is not an angel), but not as a privation (e.g., man is not deprived of the perfections proper to an angel). If there is evil in the notion of metaphysical evil, it may be in the fact that limited and finite creatures inevitably will choose evil over good, and must deal consciously with the inevitability of the ultimate threat of finite existence: death. For the Christian, however, death itself is not an evil, but has been overcome by Christ and eternal life gained. "The last enemy that will be destroyed is death" (1 Cor 15:26).

Physical Evil. Physical evil is that affecting a nature, i.e., a being defined by an essence or by an ensemble of properties. It must not, therefore, be restricted to corporeal evil, for it is much wider in scope, and can be attributed to any nature, corporeal or spiritual, whose integrity it alters. Moral pain or sorrow is a physical evil in that it deprives the soul of its natural equilibrium, just as blindness deprives the body of its natural integrity. The same holds true for all psychological ills affecting spiritual powers, such as psychoses and neuroses.

In this category of physical evil are often included cataclysms—earthquakes, typhoons, epidemics—that afflict greater or lesser areas of the earth. Writers like VOLTAIRE draw arguments against divine providence from these events. Yet evil property so-called does not lie in these cataclysms, which after all flow from natural laws. Evil rather lies in the sufferings, often great and terrible, that accidentally follow in the wake of such phenomena. What is implied here, then, is basically the problem of SUFFERING, with its correlative, that of the PROVIDENCE OF GOD.

Material things can lack the integrity that is proper to their natures. In speaking of non-living things, we sometimes say they are ''altered,'' such as bad wine, i.e., wine that has turned sour or has been diluted. But the evil, properly speaking, is not in such things: howsoever altered or imperfect in their own order, they are what they are by virtue of natural laws. It is man who classifies them as good or bad according as they suit his needs or not. Poison, for instance, is a natural thing, and as such it is good. Evil lies in using poison in a harmful manner, as an instrument of murder. In this case, the evil is in man. Among living beings, natural evil consists in suffering, both physical and moral, that destroys emotional harmony and equilibrium, which constitute the proper perfection of a sensible being as such.

On the matter of suffering, one must distinguish between man and animal. Man is par excellence the subject of suffering; not that he suffers more, quantitatively, than animals, but because he is aware of his suffering. An animal suffers pain without being able to reflect upon it. Awareness of pain serves only to intensify the evil. But this situation provides man with an opportunity to dominate and conquer suffering—an ability that the animal, being identified with suffering and so to speak drowned in it, does not possess. Man can accept suffering as expiation, if he is guilty, or as an act of fortitude, if he is innocent. From this, it should be evident that for man suffering is not an absolute evil, or at least, if it is really *an* evil, it is not *the* evil in itself. Whatever the suffering, it can be either vanquished or diminished by means provided by science, or else overcome by the courage of the one experiencing it, and thus be further ordained to man's moral and spiritual welfare. What would be classifiable as absolute evil, on the other hand, is suffering that could serve no purpose.

The brute animal as subject of suffering does not pose the same problem. Lacking reason, it lacks also a proper finality within itself. The brute is one among many, an instrument in the service of man. Man can use such things for his own advantage, though within the bounds of right reason. Were he unnecessarily to inflict sufferings upon them, he would offend God who requires of man that he make wise use of creation. Man would also degrade himself in seeking perverse satisfaction in the suffering of a sensible creature.

This leads to the problem of DEATH. Death is exclusively the concern of man, for man alone knows that he will die and is capable of anguish as he faces death. Is death an evil? While this problem calls into play all the conceptions of mankind, one may still reduce it to its essential elements. In any event, death cannot be *the* evil. Either man dies completely, or his soul survives the ruin of the bodily organism. If he dies completely, death takes away the problem: evil annihilates itself in its very realization. Moreover, how could death appear as an evil, a privation, for a being destined by nature to die completely? Death appears as evil only to the being that aspires not to die, and perceives this aspiration as fulfilling a need of its nature. This is the case for man, who seems unable to banish the scandal of death. We are here face to face with mystery—a mystery on which Christian faith alone can shed light. For faith teaches us not only that the conditions of man's dying are the result of a fault affecting the destiny of all mankind, but also that the trial that is death is the very door leading the faithful to an eternity of happiness (*De malo* 5.4–5).

Understood biblically, such physical evils are the result of a fallen world, a world corrupted by the prideful evil imagination of humanity (Gn 3). Thus, while historical skeptics like Hume, Voltaire, John Stuart Mill, etc. and contemporary atheists like Michael Martin and William Rowe have argued that the horrors of physical evils are decisive evidence against belief in God, Christians believe that such evils are the price we pay for living in a fallen world. In the writings of St. Augustine and St. Thomas, furthermore, the world is described as an aesthetic whole that is good from God's perspective, while the parts are evils and seen (often) only as such (*see Confessions* VII, 22; *CG* XI, 16–18, 22; etc). Despite the fallen nature of the world, God uses evils for good ends (Rom 8:28), for example, as means for expiation for our sins, or as means by which to achieve good ends not otherwise attainable, etc. Physical evils, moreover, are to be understood as unavoidable byproducts of natural laws that are goods in themselves, being necessary to support human life. As St. Thomas explained: ''Many good things would be taken away if God permitted no evil to exist; for fire would not be generated if air was not corrupted, nor would the life of the lion be preserved unless the ass was killed'' (*Summa theologiae* I. Q48). This, indeed, is a partial explanation for the long-held Christian belief in *o felix culpa* (''O happy fault''), attributed to St. Augustine and others but first used in the 5th century or, perhaps as late as the 7th century (in the *Exsultet* in the

Roman Missal). This belief holds that it is better to have a world in which there is evil than a world without evil, since evil must be seen in the light of Christ's redemptive act. Evil is ''fortunate'' because is has merited such a great and wonderful redeemer (*O felix culpa quae talem ac tantum meruit habere redemptorem*). Physical suffering, then, is not an absolute evil: God remains in sovereign control and ''works together all things for good for those who love God'' (Rom 8:28), as should we (cf. Rom 12:21, etc.). The very nature of physical evils cannot be divorced from the providence of God; we must not attribute these sufferings directly to divine causation, but the good which results is God's work.

Moral Evil. Moral evil, consisting essentially in the disorder of the will, is called fault or sin. This species of evil presents the greatest problem, raising as it does the crucial question: how can its existence be reconciled with the infinitely good providence of God?

In contrast to physical evil, moral evil is that found in a rational and free nature as such. Properly the soul is its immediate subject, or more precisely, the will, with its power of obeying or disobeying the norms of moral conscience and the divine law. Moral evil is therefore a privation of rectitude required by the natural law, a privation affecting a free will, which through its own fault lacks a perfection it ought to have (*De malo* 2.1–2).

Moral evil or the disordered will, however, is itself an ''evil of nature,'' viz, an evil to which a rational and free nature is subject. While this pertains to the general category of physical evil, of which it is a species, its specific nature is such as to justify the distinction between physical and moral evil. Physical evil, as already defined, is always an evil suffered, whether this affects a corporeal or a spiritual nature; such evil is received in a nature whose integrity it violates. Conversely, moral evil results from the voluntary activity of an agent who, in depriving himself of a perfection to which he is obliged by nature, inflicts upon himself a self-mutilation. Moral evil is thus properly constituted by this very activity (*De malo* 1.3).

This point is important in a consideration of evil, for it is precisely in the disordered will that evil assumes its tragic and mysterious character. Though the evil of the world with its attendant sufferings may be a heavy burden on man's reason, the perversity of the will, by which man denies his proper nature and insults God, is an even greater oppression. Thus, it would seem that the essence of evil resides in this perversity, which gives rise also to the evils of the world. In fact, Judeo-Christian revelation considers this moral lapse, inaugurated by Adam and transmitted to all humanity through original sin, as the first cause of all the ills of the world, viz, suffering, interpersonal conflicts, injustice, violence, and wars (cf. St. Augustine, *Vera relig.* 12.23: ''Evil is either sin, or the punishment due to sin'').

Since it is voluntary privation, a refusal to consider here and now the moral rules for right action for the purpose of *a* good that is not *the* good, evil is a consequence of liberty. Such a ''negative positivity,'' such placing of a negation or a refusal, makes the will disordered and defines evil properly so-called (*malum culpae:* moral fault, sin). It is obvious from this that the problem of evil appears primarily as a voluntary perversion; it is the problem of the nature and form of this ''power of nothingness'' that springs from a nature endowed with liberty. Put in this way, the problem of evil is above all a problem for Christians. Pagans, except for those involved in Greco-Oriental religions, were aware only of the physical ills affecting humanity, namely, misery, ignorance, and errancy.

Evil as *Privatio Boni.* The view of evil as ''untruth'' (ARISTOTLE) and as having no reality in itself (PLOTINUS), was developed by St. Augustine in his debates with Manichean dualists who distinguished between spirit and matter, rejecting the flesh (MATTER) as evil and demonic. Augustine defended Christian belief against the Manichean objection that the Christian God, as the creator of all things, must then be the creator of evil as well. AUGUSTINE responded with the *privatio boni* view of evil that he had found in NEOPLATONISM: God, he argued, creates only what is good and, as such, evil has no genuine reality of its own (*ens reale*), but rather, is to be understood as a subjective human concept (*ens rationis*) (*see Enchiridion* XI, etc.; see also St. Thomas, *Summa theologiae* I, Q49; *De Malo* I, 3; etc.), as parasitic on the good and as that that deprives a good creation of its good (*see* Schwarz, *Evil*, ch. 2 and Hick, *Evil*, ch. 3). St. Augustine (cf. *On Nature and Grace; Enchiridion* XI–XIV), and later St. Thomas (*Summa theologiae* I, Q14, 46, etc.), explained this as the corruption of our divinely given ''*telos*,'' the falling away from the good intended for us by God, a view of evil described by St. Augustine variously as *privatio, deprivatio, corruptio, amissio, vitium, defectus, indigentia, and negatia*. What God creates is good and that which deprives the good has no ontological status.

Satan and Evil. Another view of evil gives it a much clearer ontological status, but that has been long neglected by most theologians and rejected by the secular world's fascination with reason and the scientific method during the past three centuries. This view of evil has its basis in the biblical teaching that Satan and his demonic horde of fallen angels (Mt 25:41, 2 Pt 2:4) have been engaged in spiritual warfare against God. It has been argued that after Augustine, the centrality of the spiritual warfare theme was subsumed under the more dominant theme of the all-encompassing providence of God. Rarely has the spiritual warfare theme been exploited by theologians in response to the theodicy issue (*see* Boyd, *God at War*). While God permits satanic evil powers to wreck havoc on the world, the Church has been given ''all power and authority to cast out demons'' (cf. Mt 10:1–8; Mk 16:17; Lk 10:19; Lk 9:1–2) and, indeed, has an obligation to do so. As the ministry of Jesus and his disciples demonstrated, evil is not to be explained away as serving some mysterious divine providence, at least not in every case. Evil, rather, is to be resisted and defeated, except in those instances in which God is enacting just punishment or achieving some greater good through His permission of evil, a permission that allows evil uses of free will in both humanity and satanic forces. Amos 3:6 (''Does evil befall a city unless the Lord has done it?'') warns of God's coming punishment if the people do not repent. By permitting the destruction of the kingdom as a deed of Satan, God accomplished His purpose, since the evil of the people had to be punished (*see* Boyd, *God at War*, 150–52). The point here, however, is that not all evil is to be seen as the means by which God fulfills His purposes. Indeed, the evil misuse of free will by humanity (and satanic powers) causes evils that God does not seek; yet in His incomprehensible goodness, God salvages whatever good can be achieved in these evils (Rom 8:28).

Bibliography: G. BOYD, *God at War* (Downers Grove 1997). G. R. EVANS, *Augustine on Evil* (Cambridge 1982). D. R. GRIFFIN, *God, Power and Evil* (Philadelphia 1976). J. HICK, *Evil and the God of Love,* rev. ed. (New York 1978). G. H. JOYCE, *Principles of Natural Theology* (New York 1972). K. RAHNER, ''Why Does God Allow Us to Suffer,'' *Theological Investigations* XIX (New York 1983); ''Concerning the Relationship between Nature and Grace'' and ''The Theological Concept of Concupiscentia,'' *Theological Investigations* I (Baltimore 1961). H. SCHWARZ, *Evil: A Historical and Theological Perspective*, tr. M. WORTHING (Minneapolis 1995). R. A. SUNGENIS, *Not By Faith Alone: The Biblical Evidence for the Catholic Doctrine of Justification* (Santa Barbara, CA 1997). B. L. WHITNEY, *Theodicy: An Annotated Bibliography on the Problem of Evil, 1960–1991* (Bowling Green State University 1998).

[R. JOLIVET/B. WHITNEY]

EVIL EYE

Belief in the evil eye is a universal phenomenon and is attested to from the remote past. It is found, for example, in ancient Babylonia, Egypt, in the Greco-Roman world, and Talmudic Judaism. The eye is looked upon not only as the window of the soul, but as its visible center from which the rays of sight emanate. Certain human beings (and animals; for example, the serpent) are reputed to be endowed with a glance whose fluid is capable of causing even mortal hurt, deliberately (on the part of sorcerers) or not, to men, especially to young children, to animals (cattle, primarily), and to things (dwellings, harvests, and personal property). The evil eye causes harm through its envy, the venom of which it projects by its glance and thus poisons its object or victim. There are sovereign remedies, which may be permanent (such as representations of the evil eye vanquished by more powerful forces, inscriptions, or amulets of ludicrous or obscene character) or instantaneous (such as an obscene gesture, or spitting). In the early Christian centuries, the evil eye was expanded as the action of the devil, the *Invidus* or Envious One par excellence, and the forms of protection became progressively Christianized (cruciform amulets, Christian abbreviations, inscriptions, invocations to God, to the angels, and to various saints).

Bibliography: F. T. ELWORTHY, *Encyclopedia of Religion and Ethics*, ed. J. HASTINGS (Edinburgh 1908–27) 5:608–615. B. HELLER, ''Böser Blick,'' *Encyclopaedia Judaica: Das Judentum in Geschichte und Gegenwart* (Berlin 1928–34) 4:979–982. D. FREY, *Dämonie des Blickes* (Wiesbaden 1953). B. KÖTTING, ''Böser Blick'' *Reallexikon für Antike und Christentum*, ed. T. KLAUSER (Stuttgart 1941 [1950]–) 2:473–482, with bibliog. S. THOMPSON *Motif-Index of Folk-Literature* (Bloomington, Ind. 1955–58) v.6, s.v. ''Evil Eye.'' S. SELIGMANN, *Die Zauberkraft des Auges und das Berufen* (Hamburg 1922).

[G. M. SANDERS]

EVODIUS OF ANTIOCH, ST.

Bishop of the primitive Church, d. *c.* 64. Eusebius mentions Evodius as the first bishop of Antioch (*Chronology ad ann.* 2058; *Histoire ecclesiastique* 3.22), following the chronicle of JULIUS AFRICANUS (221); while Origen (*Hom. 4 in Lc., Patrologia Graeca,* ed. J. P. Migne 3:938) speaks of him as second bishop of Antioch after St. Peter. He was probably succeeded by IGNATIUS OF ANTIOCH, who speaks of himself as bishop of Syria, indicating that it was the only church in the region at that early date. No ancient document attests to the martyrdom of Evodius; and the attempt to connect him with the Evodias mentioned by St. Paul (Phil 4.2) fails before the fact that this person was almost certainly a woman. The sixth-century chronicler JOHN MALALAS states that Evodius was the first to use the name Christian, and Nicephorus Callistus (*Histoire ecclesiastique* 2.3) mentions Evodius as the author of several writings. But neither of these statements has historical foundation. Evodius is not mentioned in the MARTYROLOGY OF ST. JEROME, or in that of Bede; his name was introduced into the *Martyrologium Romanum parvum* by Ado and thence passed into the later martyrologies.

Feast: May 6 (Latin Church); April 28, June 30, Sept. 7 (Greek Church).

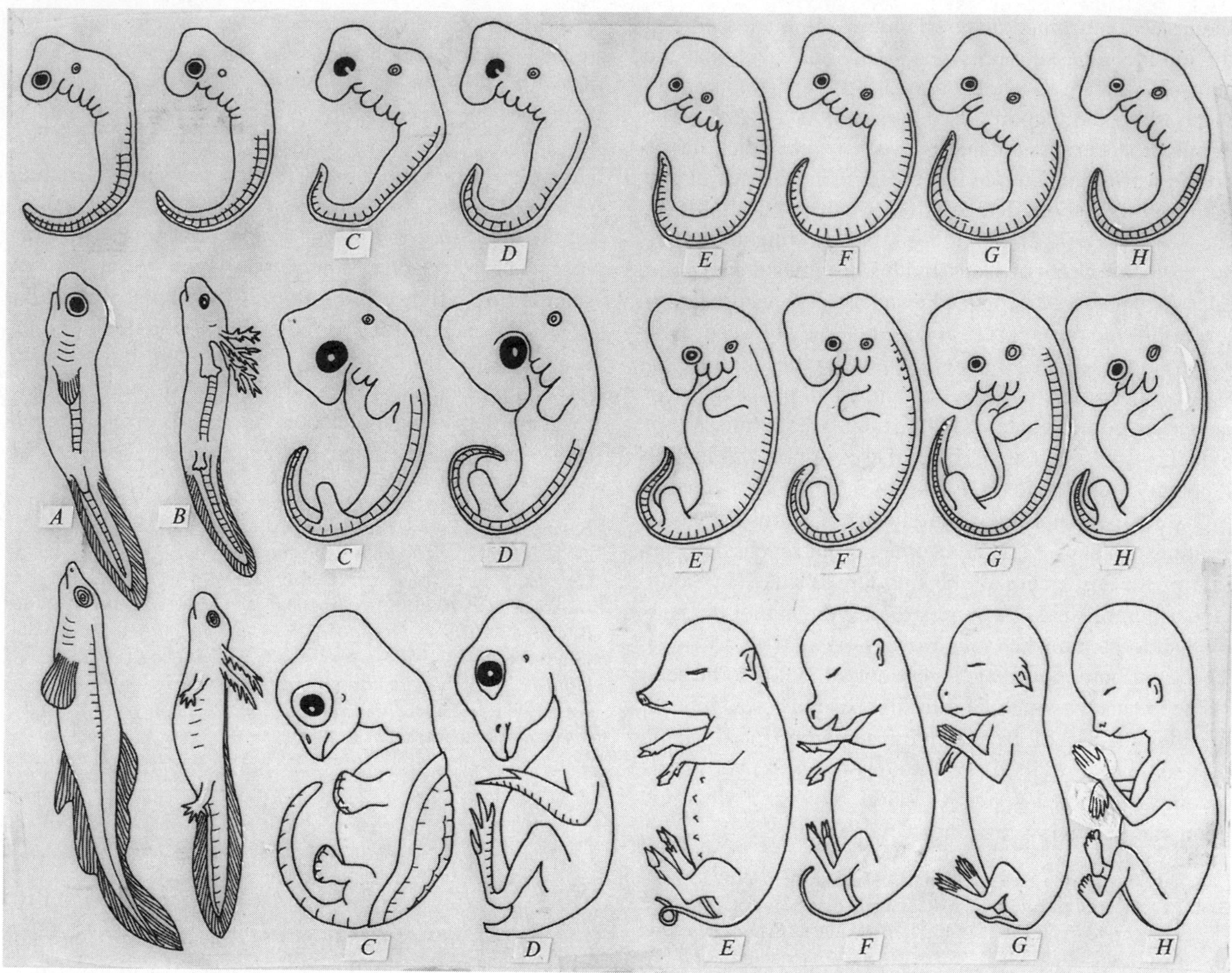

Vertebrate embryos at three comparable stages; development comparison between fish, salamander, tortoise, chick, hog, calf, rabbit, and human. (Catholic University of America)

Bibliography: *Acta Sanctorum* May 2:98. G. SALMON, *A Dictionary of Christian Biography*, ed. W. SMITH and H. WACE, (London 1877–87) 2:428–429. R. AUBERT, *Dictionnaire d'histoire et de géographie ecclésiastiques* (Paris 1912) 16:133. G. BARDY, *Catholicisme* 4:834. A. VON HAUCK, *Geschichte der altchristlichen Litteratur,* 2 v. in 4 (Leipzig 1893–1904) 1.2:781–782; 2.1:116–122.

[J. HAMROGUE]

EVOLUTION

The International Darwin Centennial Convention (Chicago 1959) defined evolution as an irreversible process of developmental change in time, which during its course generates novelty, diversity, and higher levels of organization. It operates in all sectors of the phenomenal universe but has been most fully described in the biological sector. The general statement of evolution explicitly asserts that the natural history of organisms has been and is being accomplished by materials and forces belonging to the organic world, and that no miraculous intrusion is needed to account for the proliferation of new forms.

Philosophical Evaluation

A key issue that contemporary evolutionary theory poses for the philosopher is how best to express both the extent and the limitations of the concept of evolution. Since the publication of Charles DARWIN's *Origin of Species* (1859), a tendency has developed to make of scientific evolution a philosophical principle for evolutionism. But to regard all things as in a state of flux and to make change the sole principle of all knowledge, the sole property of all activity and behavior, and the sole condition of all laws, art, morals, religion, and history is to extend evolution far beyond its documented limits.

Evolution is not a philosophical principle. The value of this theory is great, especially in the biological sciences, but it has important limitations. There is a sense in which all cosmological events have a history, a spatiotemporal context, but of equal importance is the stability of nature and of physical laws. When scientists speak of the evolution of life, of chemical elements, of planets, of the stars and galaxies, the concept of evolution is extended metaphorically. Even in the purely scientific sphere, evolution is not a single-valued term, equally tested in every area of science. For example, in speaking of the evolution of man, one must understand the limited sense in which the term is extended to man's unique psychosocial conditions. Man's spiritual endowments, his intelligence and freedom, necessitate new nonbiological principles of development. Man, in a real sense, fashions his own evolution, his own future niche, his destiny. Though subject to the conditions of time and place, man's work, his art, his language, his morals, his religion, and his history are within man's control and subject to his intelligence and freedom. Evolutionism as a philosophical principle—variously expressed in the ideologies of HISTORICISM, EXISTENTIALISM, and Marxism—cannot derive verification of its assumptions from biological evolution.

Nor is evolution an ultimate explanation of reality. It is not intrinsically bound up with any one metaphysical system. Thus it is not intrinsically materialistic, or mechanistic, or vitalistic; it is not intrinsically atheistic, or pantheistic, or theistic. Yet evolution, like all great scientific theories, needs a philosophical context, and this must be provided by disciplines other than biology and anthropology.

Stability and Change. Although change and its mechanisms have preoccupied evolutionists for many decades, evolutionary change would be meaningless without its corollary, stability. The organic world and its species are amazingly stable. Many representatives of vertebrate families have existed for millions of years unchanged. Although genetic mutation, natural selection, and isolation are natural phenomena, organisms strenuously resist change. And when a variation does come about, the general process is (1) to proliferate, (2) to adapt functionally, (3) to stabilize and find equilibrium, and (4) to become extinct. Extinction of species, so dominant a part of the evolutionary process, is the result of specialization and overstabilization.

The important philosophical insight here is that nature is to be seen in terms of two tendencies, two correlative principles both of being and of knowledge, namely, change and stability. The importance of knowledge of history for the understanding of the cosmos has been clarified by studies of the evolution of organisms. Indeterminism in cosmology and physics, brought to light by relativity and the quantum theory, has meant the death of physical determinism and of the view that the universe is fixed in all of its parts and its development. Nevertheless, science remains founded upon the stability of the cosmos. Hence, science of nature built upon stability alone or change alone must remain fragmentary and illusory. Realism is maintained by applying both correlative principles.

Natural Species. How best to define natural species has always been a problem for both the logician and the naturalist. The theory of evolution has forced the concept of SPECIES to refer to something more fluid and developmental. Traditional philosophies of nature, based upon the teachings of PLATO and ARISTOTLE, tended to define natural species like numbers, claiming that they are immutable, eternal, indivisible, and necessary. The Platonic tradition divided nature into kinds of essences with fixed properties that were, in turn, immutable, eternal, indivisible, and necessary. In his biological works, Aristotle repudiated dialectical classifications that attempted to place all of nature into *sic et non* categories. But until natural history accumulated real evidence for the transformation of organic species, the concept of natural species tended to be identified with that of an immutable, eternal essence.

Although Darwin, and others since, thought that a species was but an arbitrary category for individually distinct organisms, contemporary evolutionists insist that real specific discontinuity exists in nature. Yet, the classical morphological basis of taxonomy is giving way to a more dynamic biological concept of populations. Natural species are not fixed physiological or morphological types, as Linnaeus defined them. They are interbreeding populations isolated reproductively from other interbreeding populations. Where this genetic and ecological definition cannot be applied (e.g., to nonsexual organisms), the old morphological concept is valuable. But the concept of fixed essences has been replaced in biology by a more dynamic concept of relatively stable populations.

This latter concept corresponds favorably with the Aristotelian concept of NATURE, the intrinsic principle of activity and behavior. The term ''ESSENCE'' designates the principle of the being of a thing; the term ''nature'' designates the principle of activity. The physical nature of an organism could be known and its essence remain unknown. Nature is no more fixed than is the relation between the generator and the generated, and, unlike essence, the nature admits of the developmental orientation implied in a true evolution of species. Organisms are not immutable, necessary, eternal, and indivisible. The type of concept that denoted essences of this description is not compatible with evolutionary development, whereas the concept of nature can fully embrace evolutionary theory and a true transformation of natural species.

Higher from Lower. Without reinstituting the debate between Darwin and Lamarck concerning innate tendencies toward perfection, can one say that there is evidence for progress and direction in the known course of evolution? Is there a real sense of evolutionary movement from the lower forms to the higher, from the less perfect to the more perfect? To the biologist, lower and higher or less and more perfect can be judged only in terms of the capacity of the organism to secure its survival. Purpose and finality in evolution are not a priori inferences; but a posteriori, the biologist can observe a direction in evolution in terms of relative survival value. Life has tended to occupy every available niche to ensure the perdurance of the biotic community on this planet. The biologist defines life in terms of an active capacity to transform environmental energies into living energy; in such transformation the organism attains some measure of independence from the environment. Biologically, life is higher and more perfect to the extent that it attains greater independence in any single ecological niche. In this sense, vertebrates are higher than invertebrates, vascular plants than nonvascular plants, reptiles than fishes, birds than reptiles, mammals than birds, and man than other primates.

Furthermore, greater freedom from the control of the environment is achieved by the greater complexity of parts and more integral subordination of parts to the whole organism. This direction to higher complexity and integration is observed also in the fossil record of plants and animals. The general course of evolution has been from the simple forms to the highly complex forms of life. The primary, universal goal of evolution is survival, and although the future of any species cannot be predicted a priori, its history in retrospect can be seen to have followed orderly laws. Those laws have brought forth higher forms from the lower forms in the sense defined. To this extent the natural philosopher may speak of a hierarchy within organic nature.

For the philosopher, the question naturally arises: how can higher organisms arise from lower organisms? The biologist describes the evolutionary process in terms of mutation and selection pressures acting upon an interbreeding population, with isolating mechanisms moving parts of the population further and further from the original through races, varieties, and subspecies all the way to new species. This progress is entirely natural. But the natural philosopher asks for an account of the efficient causes that are sufficient to educe these higher effects. Does this process necessitate the intrusion of nonbiological causes?

The resolution of this problem can be found in the complex interplay of both univocal and equivocal agents acting upon organic matter to produce an effect slightly different from the univocal parent. Mutations are caused by many factors outside the univocal agent, such as cosmic rays and chemical changes caused by atmospheric conditions. Again, many parent-progeny endowments remain latent and are induced only by the requirements of adaptation. No single univocal agent is sufficient to explain the origin of the bird from reptile stock, but a unified complex of univocal and equivocal causes, some acting quite *per accidens* over a long period of gradual change, are sufficient reason for the origin of the new species. This unified convergence of univocal and equivocal causes would be sufficient to explain the natural origin of life by biopoesis, provided that the dynamic order of causes could be accounted for. Although the development of life manifests the presence of some opportunism and randomness, the dynamic order of the whole process must be accounted for.

Chance and Order. In all evolution, CHANCE is an important factor. Environmental forces command adaptation on the part of the organism. The organism itself has very limited power to dominate its ecological niche; moreover, although the environment tends to be stable, it too is subject to chance alterations. Genetic mutations are apparently caused by chance concurrence of environmental events. Does this influence of chance destroy any basic ORDER in the history of organisms? By no means. Evolutionary history cannot be predicted a priori, but neither is it random.

The relation of chance and order in evolution can be compared to the tossing of a coin. In the individual toss, the chance of heads occurring is 50–50, even though one cannot predict the next individual toss. But in 1,000 tosses, one can predict the chances of heads to be about 500 times. Actuarial tables are constructed upon this statistical principle. The same principle applies to evolution. The forces of nature that bring about change and variation are complex and unpredictable in the individual event or phylogeny, but the general process of speciation takes place according to verifiable physical and biological laws. Every biological law restricts evolution. And although the scientist cannot predict the course of evolution from these laws, he can explain the course of evolution that has ever been under the dominance of these laws. The application of the laws of statistics to organic populations has become a very useful tool in analyzing events of the group when cosmic influences upon the individual are too complex to yield orderly treatment. Events, then, that seem to occur quite by chance at the level of the individual are subject to regular laws at the level of the group. Thus, in the general course of evolution, a dynamic order prevails.

Order and God. It is this dynamic order of the organic world—so dependent upon the order of the microcosm on the one hand and upon the order of the megalacosm on the other—that raises for philosophers the question whether or not the ultimate explanation of evolution demands the existence of a transcendent cause as designer. The classical arguments for the existence of God obtain with as much force in a dynamic unfolding order as they do in a universe of static order alone, if not more. Thus, for many thinkers, organic evolution must necessarily be theistic to be complete. This is not to say that God in His intelligent providence and governance of this dynamic order is seen to make a miraculous intrusion upon the natural causes and laws with which He has endowed His creation. In a real sense the laws of nature *are* the operation of His governance. The dynamic order of nature, especially in the unfolding process of evolution, thus makes the inference of a sufficient coordinating and governing cause seem a necessity.

For other thinkers this cause is intrinsic to the cosmos, a conclusion that leads to PANTHEISM. For one who subscribes to ATHEISM, on the other hand, no such cause is needed. Philosophically, neither the pantheistic nor the atheistic position accounts sufficiently for the organization and the governance of the dynamic order of the cosmos, both of which demand the operation of intelligence and will. A being endowed with such faculties would of necessity be spiritual and transcendent to the cosmic order.

Bibliography: R. J. NOGAR, *The Wisdom of Evolution* (New York 1963). P. G. FOTHERGILL, *Evolution and Christians* (New York 1961). J. DE BIVORT DE LA SAUDÉE, ed., *God, Man and the Universe* (New York 1953). F. C. BAWDEN et al., *Symposium on Evolution* (Pittsburgh 1959). E. C. MESSENGER, ed., *Theology and Evolution* (London 1952). C. HAURET, *Beginnings: Genesis and Modern Science,* ed. E. P. EMMANS (Dubuque 1955). B. VAWTER, *A Path through Genesis* (New York 1956). J. LEVIE, *The Bible: Word of God in Words of Men,* tr. S. H. TREMAN (New York 1962). L. R. WARD, *God and World Order* (St. Louis 1961). P. TEILHARD DE CHARDIN, *The Phenomenon of Man,* tr. B. WALL (New York 1959). M. J. ADLER, ed., *The Great Ideas: A Syntopicon of Great Books of the Western World,* 2 v. (Chicago 1952) 1:451–467. A. M. DUBARLE, *The Biblical Doctrine of Original Sin,* tr. E. M. STEWART (New York 1965).

[R. J. NOGAR]

CATHOLIC TEACHING

Man, intelligent, free, graced, and the recipient of revelation, has a relationship beyond other creatures to God, his Creator. Hence, there are theological dimensions to such evolutionary postulates as the historical origin of mankind from lower animal forms, the present state of human nature in a condition of dynamic flux, and future goals of the race to be achieved, perhaps, through man's conscious control of his own evolution.

Pope Pius XII confined the question of man's genesis to "the origin of the human body as coming from preexistent and living matter" (H. Denzinger, *Enchiridion symbolorum,* ed. A. Schönmetzer [32d ed. Freiburg 1963] 3896). The human SOUL, spiritual and immortal, is not explained by purely material antecedents. Man may share biological continuity with lower animals, but there is at least some measure of psychic and moral discontinuity.

To the question "What is the origin of man?" Scripture gives a religious answer. The BOOK OF GENESIS teaches that God is man's Creator and Father and that man is the most excellent of earthly creatures, a creature "made to the image and likeness of God" (Gn 1.3). The Genesis account is a "popular description of the origin of the human race . . . in simple and figurative language adapted to the mentality of a people" in a nontechnological culture (H. Denzinger, *Enchiridion symbolorum* 3898). In his hymn of praise of the Creator, the sacred writer may have taken something (under inspiration) from popular, nonbiblical narrations.

Traditional Idea. For most of Christian history the possibility of evolution in its modern connotation was imagined only as most improbable speculation. The traditional idea that God had created things as they are, fixed in species, did not have a serious rival. Evolution (transformism) came into prominence chiefly through the work of Charles Darwin (*The Origin of Species,* 1859) and Alfred R. Wallace. Early proponents of Darwinism (e.g., T. H. Huxley in England and Ernst Haeckel in Germany) were militant materialists, atheists, or agnostics (Huxley's term). Many churchmen responded to evolution as to an attack upon Christianity, and an unfortunate atmosphere of controversy was the result. In a famous debate, typical of the times, Anglican bishop Samuel Wilberforce confronted Huxley at Oxford in 1860. In Dayton, Tennessee, in 1925 the celebrated "monkey trial" of John T. Scopes saw Clarence Darrow ridicule the fundamentalist ideas of William Jennings Bryan.

Statements of the Fathers and theologians before Darwin are not strictly *ad rem,* since the issue had not even been raised. St. Gregory of Nyssa is sometimes cited as an evolutionist, but he also held that man was privileged above other creatures in being formed by God's own hands. St. John Chrysostom held the view, hardly evolutionary in the modern sense, that Adam's body was lifeless before it received a soul. St. Augustine taught that in the beginning God created *rationes seminales,* the seeds or germs of all things that would eventually develop in time. These seminal causes were postulated to account for the appearance of new things without contradicting the doctrine that God had created all things simultaneously. Augustine also proposed principles applied in 1893 by Pope Leo XIII to cases of apparent conflict between science and the Bible: ''Whatever they [scientists] can really demonstrate to be true of physical nature, let us show to be capable of reconciliation with our Scriptures'' (H. Denzinger, *Enchiridion symbolorum* 3287); and ''the Holy Spirit [in the Scriptures] . . . did not intend to teach men these things in no way profitable unto salvation'' (H. Denzinger, *Enchiridion symbolorum* 3288).

After Darwin. Although churchmen after Darwin regarded evolution as inopportune and dangerous, no official statement of condemnation issued from Rome, and no written work was placed in the INDEX OF FORBIDDEN BOOKS for that reason. The record of the attitudes of theologians, however, shows considerable change since mid-19th century. The provincial council of Cologne (not ecumenical) in 1860 declared that the theory of transformism whereby some lower form spontaneously became a human body was contrary to Scripture and to the faith. Vatican Council I in 1870 was content to repeat the commonsense advice: the same God gives revelation and reason; one truth cannot contradict the other (H. Denzinger, *Enchiridion symbolorum* 3017). In 1909 the Biblical Commission refused to call into question the literal and historical meaning of Genesis in cases ''which touch the fundamental teachings of the Christian religion'' but ruled that one is not bound to seek for scientific exactitude of expression in the first chapter of Genesis and that free discussion of the six days of creation is permitted (June 30, 1909; H. Denzinger, *Enchiridion symbolorum* 3512–19). In 1948 a letter to Cardinal E. Suhard from the secretary of the Biblical Commission noted that the replies of the Biblical Commission in 1909 are ''in no way a hindrance to further truly scientific examination of the problems in accordance with the results acquired in these last 40 years'' (H. Denzinger, *Enchiridion symbolorum* 3862).

In 1950 the encyclical *HUMANI GENERIS* marked the starting point of a new development. Materialism and pantheism were condemned, caution and moderation were counseled in reinterpreting Scripture, but evolution was expressly recognized as a valid hypothesis:

> The teaching authority of the Church does not forbid that, in conformity with the present state of human sciences and sacred theology, research and discussions on the part of men, experienced in both fields take place with regard to the doctrine of evolution. [H. Denzinger, *Enchiridion symbolorum* 3896]

Pope John Paul II, in a discourse to the Pontifical Academy of Sciences (Oct. 22, 1996), reiterated Pius XII's teaching from *Humani generis* on the direct creation of the human soul by God. He cast the whole topic of evolution in the terms of a Christian anthropology, insisting that both theology and the sciences must be judged by what Christian faith knows about human nature: namely, that man is made in the image and likeness of God. The Christian has no objection to evolutionary theories *in se,* but only those that, because of their philosophical principles, do not do justice to who man is. ''The theories of evolution which, because of the philosophies which inspire them, regard the spirit either as emerging from the forces of living matter, or as a simple epiphenomenon of that matter, are incompatible with the truth about man. They are therefore unable to serve as the basis for the dignity of the human person'' (''Discourse,'' 5).

Bibliography: R. COLLIN, *Evolution: Hypotheses and Problems,* tr. S. J. TESTER (New York 1959). D. L. LACK, *Evolutionary Theory and Christian Belief* (London 1957). S. TAX, ed., *Evolution after Darwin,* 3 v. (Chicago 1960).

[O. W. GARRIGAN/EDS.]

EVRARD OF BÉTHUNE

Grammarian, polemicist; b. Béthune, Pas-de-Calais, France. Little is known of his life: several historians have considered him to have been two persons, the first living before 1124, the other dying shortly after 1212. It is certain, however, that his major work, the *Antihaeresis* (ed. J. Gretser, Ingolstadt 1614) could only have been written during the second part of the 12th century or at the beginning of the 13th. This work outlines at length the fundamental beliefs of the CATHARI in order to refute them. In this polemic Evrard successfully criticized the arbitrary scriptural interpretation of the Cathari. Then he discussed the WALDENSES, and finally the Jews, for whom he proposes texts that are difficult to interpret and that he feels might confuse them. His other work, the *Graecismus* [ed. A. J. Wrobel, *Corpus grammaticorum Medii Aevi* (Brussels, 1887) 1], a much-used textbook during the Middle Ages, is a versified Latin grammar based on the interrelationship of Latin and Greek. Evrard aspired to a good style and showed literary knowledge, particularly of early medieval Latin authors; but his writing is mediocre, and his thought not very worthwhile: often he extols faith at the expense of the work at hand. His treatise against the Cathari, however, is extremely helpful for determining their beliefs: J. B. BOSSUET used it in his *Histoire des variations des églises protestantes* to show the differences in doctrine between the Waldenses and the Cathari.

Bibliography: A. WAUTERS in *Biographie nationale de Belgique,* v.6 (1878) 747–751. U. CHEVALIER, *Répertoire des sources* *historiques du moyen-âge* (Paris 1905–07) 1:1261. E. FARAL, *Les Arts poétiques du XIIe et du XIII ^e siècle* (Paris 1924) 38–39. M. MANITIUS, *Geschichte der lateinischen Literatur des Mittelalters* 3:747–751. F. VERNET, *Dictionnaire de théologie catholique* 4.2:1995–98. É. GRIFFE, *Catholicisme* 3:1230. M. GRABMANN, *Lexikon für Theologie und Kirche* (Freiburg 1957–65) 3:627–628.

[É. BROUTTE]

ÉVROUL (EBRULF), ST.

Abbot; b. Bayeux, France, *c.* 617; d. Dec. 29, 706. He had served for some time in the Merovingian royal court. After he and his wife separated, he spent the remaining 22 years of his life as abbot of the Abbey of SAINT-ÉVROULT, which he had founded and which was later named after him. He was also active in missionary work around his monastery, and he founded several other houses in the area. ORDERICUS VITALIS, a monk of Saint-Évroult in the 12th century, mentions Évroul but places him in the sixth century. His relics were lost during the religious wars and the French Revolution, but his cult is still popular in Normandy.

Feast: Dec. 29.

Bibliography: J. MABILLON, *Acta sanctorum ordinis S. Benedicti* (Venice 1733–40) 1:335–342. ORDERICUS VITALIS, *Historia ecclesiastica,* bk. 6, ch. 6–9. *La vie de saint Evroul: poème normand du XIVe siècle,* ed. S. SANDQVIST (Lund 1992). A. M.. ZIMMERMANN, *Kalendarium Benedictinum: Die Heiligen und Seligen des Benediktinerorderns und seiner Zweige* (Metten 1933–38) 3:493–497. L. MUSSET, 1302. T. DE MOREMBERT, *Dictionnaire d'histoire et de géographie ecclésiastiques* (Paris 1912–) 16:220–221.

[P. BLECKER]

ÉVROUL OF SAINT-FUSCIENAU-BOIS, ST.

Abbot; b. Beauvais, France, sixth century; d. near Oroër, France, July 25*c.* 600. His dates are not at all certain, and it has been maintained by some scholars that his activity should be placed a full century later. Reputedly, Évroul (Ebrulf or Evroult) was promoted to sacred orders by the bishop of Beauvais because of his exemplary conduct. Some reports claim that the monks at Saint-Fuscien-au-Bois petitioned that he be appointed their abbot, but other accounts say that royal influence determined the appointment. These uncertainties stem from the fact that this Évroul has at times been confused with ÉVROUL (EBRULF) of Ouche; a vita written centuries after the saint's lifetime contributes little of solid historical evidence. Local tradition reports that Évroul died on his way to Oroër and was buried there, but later (838) his relics were taken to the cathedral in Beauvais. His cult became popular at an early date in the areas in which he had lived and worked.

Feast: July 25; July 27 in Beauvais.

Bibliography: *Acta Sanctorum* July 6:192–198. A. M.. ZIMMERMANN, *Kalendarium Benedictinum: Die Heiligen und Seligen des Benediktinerorderns und seiner Zweige,* 4 v. (Metten 1933–38) 2:505. P. VIARD, *Catholicisme* 4:855; *Bibliotheca sanctorum* (Rome 1961–) 4:892–893. L. H. COTTINEAU, *Répertoire topobibliographique des abbayes et prieurés* (Mâcon 1935–39) 2:2683. *Gallia Christiana,* v.1–13 (Paris 1715–85), v.14–16 (Paris 1856–65) 10: 1302. T. DE MOREMBERT, *Dictionnaire d'histoire et de géographie ecclésiastiques* (Paris 1912) 16:220–221.

[H. DRESSLER]

EWALD, SS.

Two Anglo-Saxon missionaries; d. northwestern Germany, Oct. 3 *c.* 690. According to BEDE (*Histoire ecclesiastique* 5.10) there were two brothers, priests of the English nation bearing the same name, Ewald, who were differentiated by the color of their hair, one called Black Ewald and the other White (Fair) Ewald. Both lived for a time in Ireland and wished to dedicate their lives to the conversion of the Saxons. They arrived in the area somewhat north of the lower regions of the Lippe River and tried to establish contact with the Saxon leaders, but their efforts were thwarted by the local pagans who felled White Ewald with one blow of the sword and tortured Black Ewald before slaying him. According to Bede's account the martyrs' bodies were thrown into the Rhine River but were miraculously recovered by their companions. In the time of Pepin (d. 714) the martyrs' relics were brought to Cologne and placed in the church of St. Clement, now renamed St. Cunibert.

Feast: Oct. 3.

Bibliography: *Acta Sanctorum* Oct. 2:180–207. A. M.. ZIMMERMANN, *Kalendarium Benedictinum: Die Heiligen und Seligen des Benediktinerorderns und seiner Zweige,* 4 v. (Metten 1933–38) 3:127, 129–130. A. SCHÜTTE, *Handbuch der deutschen Heiligen* (Cologne 1941) 120. W. LEVISON, *England and the Continent in the Eighth Century* (Oxford 1946) 58. E. HEGEL, *Kirchliche Vergangenheit in Bistum Essen* (Essen 1960) 13–14, 29. A. FRANZEN, *Dictionnaire d'histoire et de géographie ecclésiastiques* (Paris 1912) 16:221–223.

[H. DRESSLER]

EWING, THOMAS AND CHARLES

Father and son. Thomas was a statesman and lawyer; b. West Liberty, Ohio County, Va., Dec. 28, 1789; d. Lancaster, Ohio, Oct. 26, 1871. Of Scotch-Irish and Presbyterian background, he married Mary Wills Boyle, a Catholic, and was received into the Church (1871) by Abp. J. B. Purcell of Cincinnati, Ohio. As a lawyer Ewing was prominent in important court litigation that tested the validity of charitable trusts, the binding force of national church incorporation, and land titles in the West. He was a friend and adviser of Archbishop Purcell and an opponent of KNOW-NOTHINGISM. Ewing served in the U.S. Senate (1830–36, 1850–51) and was secretary of the treasury (1841); he organized the interior department as its first secretary (1849–50) and was delegate to the Peace Conference of 1861. His son, Thomas, served in the Congress and in the Union Army. His daughter, Ellen, married Gen. William T. Sherman.

Charles was the head of Catholic Indian Missions and a Civil War general; b. Lancaster, Ohio, March 6, 1835; d. Washington, D.C., June 20, 1883. He studied at the Dominican College near Lancaster, Ohio; at Gonzaga College, Washington, D.C.; and at the University of Virginia, Charlottesville. In 1860 he was admitted to the practice of law in St. Louis, Mo., and became a captain in the 13th Infantry Regulars of the Union Army. While fighting in the Arkansas and Mississippi campaigns, he was wounded three times at Vicksburg and was subsequently made a lieutenant colonel. He served as acting inspector general during the Atlanta campaign under Gen. William T. Sherman, his brother-in-law. At the end of this campaign he was cited for gallantry and promoted to brigadier general. After the war he returned to his law practice, and in 1873 he became head of the Bureau of Catholic Indian Missions.

Bibliography: E. E. SHERMAN, *Memorial of Thomas Ewing of Ohio* (New York 1873).

[T. O. HANLEY/J. L. MORRISON]

EX CATHEDRA

Canonized in the language of the Church in the definition of papal infallibility (*Enchiridion symbolorum,* 3074), *ex cathedra* symbolically expresses the supreme authority within the Church of the Roman pontiff. Extended in the form of *ex cathedra Petri,* it symbolizes the Roman pontiff's title to that supreme authority and to the charism of INFALLIBILITY that accompanies it: because he is the successor of Peter, head of the college of Apostles. Where GALLICANISM, abusing the distinction between *sedens* and *sedes,* sought to separate the authority of the Roman pontiff from that of Peter, VATICAN COUNCIL I (*ibid.*) by using the formula *ex cathedra* rejected that separation. Through succession to his chair, or supreme office, in the Church, the authority and infallibility of Peter lives on in the Roman pontiff.

See Also: CHAIR OF PETER; DEFINITION, DOGMATIC; PRIMACY OF THE POPE; TEACHING AUTHORITY OF THE CHURCH (MAGISTERIUM).

Bibliography: A. MICHEL, *Dictionnaire de théologie catholique,* Tables générales 1:916–917. M. J. SCHEEBEN, *Handbuch der katholischen Dogmatik,* v.1 (Freiburg 1948) 231–242.

[E. G. HARDWICK]

EX CORDE ECCLESIAE

Apostolic constitution issued on Aug. 15, 1990 by John Paul II; intended to supplement the apostolic constitution on ecclesiastical faculties and universities, *Sapientia Christiana* (1979), by providing for non-ecclesiastical universities and other Catholic institutions of higher learning a description of their nature and purpose and general norms to govern their activities.

After an introduction (nos. 1–11), the text is divided into two parts. The first, ''Identity and Mission'' (nos. 12–49) briefly describes the nature of a university and locates Catholic identity in the Christian inspiration of individuals and the whole community, ''reflection in the light of the Catholic faith upon the growing treasury of human knowledge, to which it seeks to contribute by its own research,'' ''fidelity to the Christian message as it comes to us through the Church,'' and an institutional commitment to the service both of the People of God and of the whole human family (no. 13). Research undertaken at a Catholic university should be characterized by the search for the integration of knowledge, a dialogue between faith and reason, ethical concern, and a theological perspective (nos. 15–20).

The next sections discuss the university community—teachers, students, and administrators (nos. 21–26)—and the university's place and role in the Church, both universal and local, and the responsibility of bishops to promote and assist in the preservation and strengthening of Catholic identity, with due regard to the autonomy of the sciences, including in theology, and to academic freedom (nos. 27–29).

The mission of the Catholic university is described, first, in terms of its service to Church (no. 31) and to society (nos. 32–37). For the latter the emphasis falls on the university's becoming an ''instrument of cultural progress,'' bringing to bear Christian ''ethical and religious principles,'' promoting social justice, and encouraging interdisciplinary research projects. The Catholic university should also be a place in which pastoral ministry assists an integration of faith and life, demonstrating this by opportunities for community worship and concern for the poor and those suffering injustice (nos. 38–42). The institution should promote the dialogue between the Gospel and culture, with special reference to local cultures and contemporary problems. It should in particular promote a dialogue between Christian thought and the modern sciences. It should encourage and contribute to ecumenical dialogue (nos. 43–47). In all these ways the Catholic university will make an indispensable contribution to the Church's primary task of evangelization (nos. 48, 49).

The second part of the document is devoted to eleven general norms to supplement other ecclesiastical legislation. Article 1 requires that they be applied locally and regionally ''taking into account the statutes of each university or institute and, as far as possible and appropriate, civil law.'' The general norms and local or regional applications to be incorporated into governing documents and university statutes are, as necessary, to be brought into conformity with them. Article 2 legislates for the Catholic identity, which is to be made known in a public document and to be promoted by the influence of Catholic teaching and discipline over all university activities, with due regard taken for the freedom of conscience of each person and for the autonomy and freedom of the various disciplines. Article 3 lists three different ways in which a Catholic university may be established: by the Holy See, an episcopal conference, or a local bishop; by a religious institute or other public juridical person; by other ecclesiastical or lay people. Article 4 entrusts the primary responsibility for maintaining and strengthening Catholic identity to the university itself and its officials. All teachers and administrators are to be informed about this Catholic identity and expected to promote or at least respect it in ways appropriate to the different disciplines. Catholic teachers, particularly in theology, are to be faithful to Catholic doctrine and morals, and others are to respect them; non-Catholic teachers and students are to recognize and respect Catholic identity, and non-Catholic teachers are not to constitute a majority within the institution; education of all students is to include a formation in ethical and religious principles and courses in Catholic doctrine are to be made available.

Article 4 requires that the university remain in communion with the universal Church and with the local Church; bishops are to promote the good of the institution and have a right and duty to supervise the preservation and strengthening of their Catholic identity; the institution is to make periodical reports to the competent church authority on the university and its activities. Article 6 makes provisions for the pastoral ministry at the institution. Article 7 encourages cooperation among Catholic universities and between them and the programs of governments and other national and international organizations on behalf of justice, development, and progress. Articles 8 to 11 provide transitional norms for the application of these norms. The bishops of the United States in November 1999 authorized a set of norms for the application of *Ex corde ecclesiae* and sent these to Rome for approval.

Bibliography: For the text of *Ex corde ecclesiae,* see: *Acta Apostolicae Sedis* 83 (1991): 249–339 (Latin); *Origins* 20, no. 17 (October 4, 1990) (English); *The Pope Speaks* 36 (1991): 21–41 (English).

[J. A. KOMONCHAK]

EX MORE DOCTI MYSTICO

An office hymn which was traditionally prescribed for Matins during Lent until Passion Sunday. It is written in iambic dimeter and has been attributed to GREGORY THE GREAT. The author is preoccupied with the mystical meaning of the number 40 for the days of Lent, as was Gregory, especially in two of his ''Homilies on the Gospels'' (2.24.4 and 2.31.6). The eight strophes and doxology exhort the faithful to observe the fast of Lent. Perhaps the author had in mind the Benedictine Rule (49), where the monk is told during Lent to partake less of speech, food, drink, sleep, and amusement. A prayer for mercy is put on the lips of the assembly, asking that they may please God in this life and hereafter.

Bibliography: *Analecta hymnica* 2:83; 51:55, text. A. S. WALPOLE, ed., *Early Latin Hymns* (Cambridge, Eng. 1922) 321–323. H. LAUSBERG, *Lexicon für Theologie und Kirche*, ed. J. HOFER and K. RAHNER (Freiburg 1957–65) 3:1312.

[M. M. BEYENKA]

EX OMNIBUS AFFLICTIONIBUS

A bull of PIUS V dated Oct. 1, 1567, that condemned the propositions attributed to Michel de Bay, or BAIUS (1513–1589), professor of the university Faculty of Theology at Louvain, Belgium, and to his followers. These propositions had not been numbered at the beginning, with the result that the authors divided them according to circumstances into 76, 79, 80, the division into 76 being the oldest and probably the best. The first 60 were taken, but not always literally, from the writings of Baius. The others must have come from his followers, but no reference is indicated and nowhere is Baius mentioned.

The rejection of these propositions was a rejection of the extreme formulas at which Baius had arrived by holding strictly to the vocabulary and the ideas of the Fathers, especially to those of St. Augustine, and by rejecting in a block all doctrinal development coming from scholastic theology. Thus, he was led to dangerous ambiguities particularly in the notions of natural and SUPERNATURAL. For example, the condemnation of propositions 21 to 24 maintains the free and supernatural character of man's calling to the BEATIFIC VISION, and that of propositions five and six proscribes the idea that before the Fall man could naturally attain to eternal life. Also condemned were various formulas in which Baius seemed to reduce liberty to the simple absence of constraint, and others in which Baius expressed his exaggerated pessimism in regard to the consequences of original sin, maintaining that all the actions of unbelievers are sins and their virtues in reality vices, and also that free will, left to itself, can only sin. On the whole, these propositions treat difficult problems, and their exact interpretation raises complex questions that for a long time were violently debated among theologians. Moreover, the final clause, in which the propositions are qualified in block and in which the meaning changes considerably according to the position of the comma, provoked the famous controversy of the *COMMA PIANUM*. Contrary to common usage, this bull was not printed, but merely transmitted to the Faculty of Theology at Louvain. In 1569 Baius sent to Rome several apologies in which he acknowledged as his own only about 30 of the condemned propositions, which he furthermore claimed to be in accord with the doctrine of the Fathers; and in fact he did not really accept the censure. It was only in 1570 that he somewhat unwillingly signed a disavowal. In view of the cloudy situation, Gregory XIII thought it his duty to renew the condemnation issued by his predecessor. Hence, he reproved the same propositions in the bull, *Provisionis nostrae*, of Jan. 25, 1580, to which Baius submitted the following March 24. Later the bull, *Ex omnibus*, was renewed in the bull, *In eminenti*, of Urban VIII against Jansen in 1642 (date of signing).

See Also: ELEVATION OF MAN; DESTINY, SUPERNATURAL; GRACE, ARTICLES ON; JANSENISM.

Bibliography: H. DENZINGER, *Enchiridion symbolorum*, ed. A. SCHÖENMETZER (32d ed. Freiburg 1963) 1901–80. H. DE LUBAC, *Surnaturel: Études historiques* (Paris 1946); *Augustinisme et théologie moderne* (Paris 1965).

[L. J. COGNET]

EX OPERE OPERANTIS

A technical term literally meaning ''from the work of the doer,'' to be distinguished from EX OPERE OPERATO, which refers to the grace-conferring power inherent in the sacramental rite itself, as an action of Christ. *Ex opere operantis* refers to the role and value of the recipient's or minister's moral condition in causing or receiving sacramental grace.

Peter of Poitiers (d. 1205) first applied to baptism the distinction between the rite that is performed and the one who performs the rite. Graphically, he compares an action in the natural order to the sacramental action: ''When the Jews put Christ to death their deed was evil; but the death of Christ was approved and willed by God'' (*Sententiarum libri quinque* 1, c.16). The application of the principle to the Sacraments was logical, and soon followed. Innocent III (d. 1216) distinguished between sacrilegious action and sacramental celebration: ''Although the action of the one who acts (*opus operans*) is sometimes unclean, yet always the act done (*opus operatum*) is clean'' (*De Sacro Altaris Mysterio* 3.6). In the middle of the 13th century the two formulas were commonly used to point out the difference that exists between Christian Sacraments and Mosaic rites. Actually, the teaching behind the formulas was as old as the doctrine of the objective efficacy of Sacraments, especially of baptism and orders, which Augustine (d. 430) developed against DONATISM, which asserted that Sacraments administered by notoriously unworthy ministers were invalid.

In the 12th century theologians used the distinction to show that Mosaic rites (with the probable exception of circumcision) conferred grace upon the recipient according only to the measure of his faith and fervor, *ex opere operantis;* and that, on the contrary, Christian Sacraments confer grace *ex opere operato* upon the soul capable of receiving it. The Council of Trent (1545–63) defined the term *ex opere operato* in order to deny the Reformers' contention that Sacraments caused grace exactly as did the Mosaic rites, but it did not deny that the faith and fervor of the (adult) recipient condition the measure of grace received.

Ex opere operantis ecclesiae. Theologians commonly teach that the only limit to the measure of grace conferred *ex opere operato* is the degree of faith and fervor in the recipient. This limiting arises, *ex opere operantis,* from the measure of the recipient's cooperation at the time of receiving the rite.

In the 20th century, theologians began a discussion of the recipient's cooperation, specifically his genuine intention to participate together with the minister in the sacramental action, as a necessary element in perfecting a Sacrament as a practical sign of grace. This discussion enlarged the meaning of *ex opere operantis,* and is of particular value in determining precisely the active role of the laity in the offering of Holy Mass.

It should be added that the term is not to be confused another technical phrase, *ex opere operantis Ecclesiae,* that expresses the efficacy of strictly liturgical prayer, an effectiveness that is due to the action of the Church as the Mystical Body of Christ.

Bibliography: P. L. HANLEY, *The Life of the Mystical Body* (Westminster, Md. 1961). C. O'NEIL, "The Role of the Recipient and Sacramental Signification," *Thomist* 21 (1958) 257–301, 508–540.

[P. L. HANLEY]

EX OPERE OPERATO

Scholastic theology employs *ex opere operato* (from the work worked) to distinguish what is accomplished by the minister of a sacrament from the activity of the minister, the *opus operantis* (the work of the one working). This distinction was drawn in order to locate the source of the sanctifying effect in the sacramental rite itself, and not in the holiness of the minister. The Council of Trent used this terminology in its Decree on the Sacraments, Session XIII (1547), canon B: "If anyone says that grace is not conferred *ex opere operato* through the sacraments of the new law . . . let that one be anathema." In the modern ecumenical context, it is worth repeating that Trent's use of *ex opere operato*, while it includes the idea that the efficacy of sacraments does not depend on the holiness of the minister, was primarily intended to oppose those who denied the objective mediation of grace through the sacraments of the Church. This limited use, however, was often overlooked by post-Tridentine Catholic School theology. As a result the theological content of *ex opere operato* was frequently equated with the valid administration of a sacrament.

Christ the Primordial Sacrament. One can begin with the idea that a sacrament, celebrated according to the prescription of the Church, is an objective, infallible offer of the grace signified. All that is needed for a "saving event" to take place is the openness on the part of an apt, and properly disposed, subject, for the reception of the sacramental grace. But this purely juridical interpretation of *ex opere operato* needs to be deepened theologically. Modern Catholic theologians work out the deeper dimension along the lines of THOMAS AQUINAS, who, in his later works, prefers to speak of the efficacy of the sacraments as derived "from the merit, or the passion of Christ," and who never uses *ex opere operato* in his *Summa Theologiae*. This approach is correct because a sacrament can be said to confer grace, or be efficacious, *ex opere operato*, only if it is an act of Christ himself, an authentic sacramental representation of the mystery of Christ's saving work, in and through the community that merits the title church of Christ (E. Schillebeeckx). However, frequently contemporary theologians are content to refer to Christ as the efficient instrumental cause of the sanctifying activity of the Father. This point of view, which stresses the downward movement of the self-communication of the Father through Christ in the Holy Spirit, needs to be broadened.

Christ is not only the primordial sacrament of the divine-human love of humanity and, therefore, the personal cause of the sanctification offered in the Sacraments of the Church. He is also the primordial sacrament of the divine-human love of the Father and, therefore, the reason why the prayer of the Church finds acceptance before the Father. Evidently both of these aspects of the sacramentality of Christ are involved in sacramental celebrations, a theme that is given some consideration in the *Constitution on the Sacred Liturgy*. Moreover, they come into play in an order that corresponds to the sacramental activity of the Church.

Sacramental Incorporation. Sacramental celebrations signify some human and social situations into which the subject of the sacrament is being incorporated (e.g., membership in the Church through Baptism). But, for the eyes of faith, what is denoted is understood to connote a special mode of incorporation into the mystery of the Church: the life of faith in Christ. As social sacrament of salvation, the Church expresses this twofold meaning by reaching out to the subject through the symbolic gesture, and by the accompanying sacramental verbal formulas that explicitly refer to the deeper meaning of the activity. Both gesture and word express the desire of the Church for the sanctification of the subject, and are intended to evoke a corresponding desire in the subject.

As acts of the Church sacraments have an essentially epicletic orientation (*see* EPICLESIS). Some essential verbal formulas of the sacraments are explicit invocations addressed to God (e.g., ordination prayers). But even when the indicative, active form is used (e.g., "I baptize you . . ."), as act of the Church it is only understandable as a petition before God. However, the confidence that the Church manifests is grounded on the conviction of faith that what she does serves as transparency for what Christ is doing in and through the sacramental acts of His Church. Because Christ is the head of the Church, the symbolic action represents Christ reaching out to the subject, and the sacramental word is inserted by Christ himself into His "eternal intercession" before the Father.

When one adds to this consideration the witness of faith of the traditional churches of the East and West that the realization of the sacraments, and the sanctification of the subjects of sacraments, also depend on the work of the Holy Spirit, the full meaning of the term *ex opere operato* is made accessible. It can be stated in this way: sacramental celebrations are efficacious *ex opere operato* because the symbolic actions and intercessory prayer of the Church are the representation and actualization of the twofold aspect of the sacramentality of Christ. The personal source of the correspondence between the activity of the Church and the activity of Christ is the one Holy

Spirit, whom Christ possesses in fullness and shares with His Church. Because the intercession of the Church, made in, with and through Christ the High Priest (sacrament of the divine-human love of the Father), in the power of the Holy Spirit, is always heard by the Father, sacramental celebrations are always the offer of the sanctifying Spirit, made by the Father through the Risen Lord (sacrament of the divine-human love of humanity), in accord with the signification of the sacramental signs instituted by Christ. Consequently, there is a sending of the Spirit by the Father through the Risen Lord to the apt subject, who is open in faith to receive the grace proper to the sacrament.

Bibliography: E. H. SCHILLEBEECKX, *Christ, The Sacrament of the Encounter with God* (New York 1963) 82–89. Constitution on the Sacred Liturgy, *Vatican Council II: The Conciliar and Post Conciliar Documents,* ed. A. FLANNERY (Collegeville 1975) 1–36.

[E. J. KILMARTIN]

EXARCH

Exarch, in Greek, ἔξαρχος, ruler, originally the title given the governor of a province called a diocese under Diocletian's division of the Eastern Prefecture (297). In the organizational development of the Church, patterned in conformity with the political divisions of the Roman Empire, bishops of such dioceses assumed in addition to the title of exarch expanded jurisdiction over those metropolitans within this political unit. In addition to those heads of sees who acquired the patriarchal title at the Council of Nicaea (325), the bishops of Ephesus, Caesarea, and Heraclea, capitals of the respective dioceses of Asia, Cappadocia and Pontus, and Thrace, functioned as exarchs. With the elevation of the See of Constantinople to a patriarchate consequent upon its becoming an imperial residence, conflict arose over the extent of the exarchs' jurisdiction. This was resolved at the Council of Chalcedon (c.9), which reduced their status to that of a metropolitan, permitting their retention of this honorary title and place in the order of precedence next after the five patriarchs. Although mentioned as late as the Council of 680, the office of exarch gradually diminished in importance in the Church's reorganization, being replaced in the West by an apostolic vicar and later primate; in the East it still retained its traditional place. Autocephalous churches, especially those of Cyprus, Ipek, Ochrida, and Trnovo, emphasizing their autonomy, used this title—at times even daring to usurp that of patriarch. In 1870 at the reconstitution of the Bulgarian Orthodox Church, its head, residing in Constantinople, took the title of exarch. Oriental Patriarchs on occasion appoint exarchs with subordinate bishops for semi-independent groups of their jurisdiction throughout the world. The present usage of the term exarch denoting an emissary explains the reason for its being applied even to a minor prelate assigned to a particular mission. Traditionally, Eastern Catholic canonical tradition recognized three kinds of exarchs: (1) those with a territory of their own; (2) apostolic exarchs; and (3) patriarchal or archiepiscopal exarchs who govern a territory not yet constituting a canonically erected diocese.

See Also: EXARCHY.

Bibliography: J. FARIS, *The Eastern Catholic Churches: Constitution and Governance according to the Code of Canons of the Eastern Churches* (Brooklyn 1993). V. POSPISHIL, *Eastern Catholic Church Law* (Brooklyn, NY 1996).

[L. NEMEC]

EXARCHY

The term exarch denotes a delegate and was applied to various higher and lower dignities in the ecclesiastical hierarchy of the Eastern Churches. *Exarchos* was the official title given during the late Roman Empire to the governor of a civil diocese, which was divided into provinces. The ecclesiastical organization was formed parallel to this civil division of the Empire. The bishop was the superior of the *paroikia,* the metropolitan headed the *eparchia,* and the chief bishop of a civil diocese had the position of an exarch.

Besides those sees that later acquired patriarchal title and jurisdiction, namely, Rome, Constantinople, Alexandria, Antioch, and Jerusalem, exarchial jurisdiction was enjoyed by the metropolitans of Ephesus (Diocese of Asia), Caesarea of Cappadocia (Diocese of Pontus), and Heraclea (Diocese of Thrace). However, the bishop of the newly established imperial residence in Constantinople overshadowed them so completely that these exarchs vanished from the scene.

The dignity of supra-metropolitan exarch was revived repeatedly in the Orthodox churches. Orthodox patriarchs appoint exarchs, who have subordinate bishops, for semi-independent groups of their jurisdiction, e.g., the exarchs of the Russian Church in various parts of the world.

The indefinite meaning of the term exarch (delegate) was the reason for its application to other representatives of patriarchs, archbishops, and even bishops; in some places it is a minor honorary title for diocesan priests, conferred upon them by their bishop. The visitors of stauropegial convents, i.e., monasteries that are exempt from the jurisdiction of the local bishop and directly subject to the patriarch, are also called exarchs. They are usually appointed to this office in a permanent manner and supervise all the stauropegial monasteries within the patriarchate.

Historically, Eastern Catholic canonical tradition recognized three kinds of exarch: (1) exarch with a territory of his own, (2) apostolic exarch, and (3) patriarchal (archiepiscopal) exarch.

Independent exarch. The exarch with a territory of his own is equivalent to a territorial abbacy in the Latin canonical tradition and is the superior of an independent monastery (*monasterium sui iuris*). He is in charge of a territory separated from every other diocese, with his own clergy and people. An example is the Exarchial Monastery of the Byzantine Italian Basilian Fathers of St. Mary of Grottaferrata near Rome (Italy), founded by SS. Nilus and Bartholemew in 1004 (*see* GROTTAFERRATA, MONASTERY OF). The exarch-archimandrite is entitled to wear episcopal insignia with the exception of the saccos.

Apostolic exarch. An apostolic exarchy is established outside the patriarchate where the erection of a diocese is not yet feasible. Traditionally, Apostolic exarchs corresponded to the vicars and prefects apostolic of the Latin rite. Due to emigration, groups of Eastern Catholics are now found in all continents, far from their native regions. If their number is sufficiently large, the Holy See might erect ecclesiastical provinces and dioceses, e.g., for the Ukrainians in Canada and the United States. If this is not yet possible, they may be organized in apostolic exarchies.

The apostolic exarchs govern an ecclesiastical territory that is not subject to a Patriarch, Metropolitan or Major Archbishop, when, because of the small number of faithful or for some other grave reason, eparchies (i.e., dioceses) are not established. Such an exarch enjoys the same rights and faculties as residential bishops.

Patriarchal (archiepiscopal) exarch. Such an exarch is appointed in patriarchates and archiepiscopates (i.e., a territory governed by an Oriental archbishop) for a region where an eparchy (diocese) is not yet established. The jurisdiction of this exarch is ordinary but vicarious; i.e., he rules the exarchy in virtue of his office in the name of the patriarch or archbishop major. He is appointed by the patriarch (archbishop) with the advice of the permanent synod of the patriarchate (archiepiscopate) and can be removed only with the consent of the same synod. His rights and duties are equivalent to those of the apostolic exarch, with the difference that he is entirely dependent on his patriarch or archbishop. He has the general jurisdiction of a bishop

Bibliography: J. FARIS, *The Eastern Catholic Churches: Constitution and Governance according to the Code of Canons of the Eastern Churches* (Brooklyn 1993). V. POSPISHIL, *Eastern Catholic Church Law* (Brooklyn, NY 1996).

[V. J. POSPISHIL/EDS.]

EXCLUDED MIDDLE, PRINCIPLE OF THE

The principle of the excluded middle is stated by ARISTOTLE: ''There cannot be an intermediate between contradictions, but of one subject we must either affirm or deny any one predicate'' (*Meta.* 1011b 23–24). His treatment of this PROPOSITION is in Book Γ of the *Metaphysics,* which is devoted largely to the manifestation and defense of the first principles of DEMONSTRATION.

Aristotle's Explanation. The proposition is made clear from the definitions of the true and the false, for it is false to say of what is that it is not, or of what is not that it is; and it is true to say of what is that it is, and of what is not that it is not. If anyone says something is, he either says something true or something false. If he is saying something true, the thing is; if he is saying something false, the thing is not. The same applies if he says something is not. Either the affirmation or the negation is true. The man who holds to an intermediate between contradictions does not grant that one must say of a being that it is or is not, nor of a nonbeing that it is or is not.

Contradictory Opposition. The basis for the principle of the excluded middle is found in the notion of contradictory opposites (*see* OPPOSITION). Things that are opposed as affirmation and negation are such that it is always necessary that one should be true but the other false (*Cat.* 13b 1–3). Since contradiction is a relation between terms opposed as affirmation and negation, it is an opposition between being and nonbeing; thus it makes no difference whether the subject actually exists or not. For example, it always is true or false that Socrates is ill. If Socrates actually exists, he is either ill or not. If he does not actually exist, it is false to say he is ill and true to say he is not ill, for he cannot be ill if he does not exist. Contradictory opposites are therefore quite different from contrary opposites that demand a common subject. The contradictory of ''Socrates is ill'' is not ''Socrates is well,'' but ''Socrates is not ill.'' Contradictory opposition is between being and nonbeing expressed in affirmative and negative statements; it is between being and nonbeing absolutely, and not within a genus. Either of the two opposites may be true or false, but not both true or both false at the same time.

Future Contingents. When two enunciations are in contradictory opposition, is it necessary that one be true and the other false? This question has concerned logicians and philosophers since the time of Aristotle (*Interp.* 18a 28–19b 4). His answer is that propositions about the past or the present must be true or false; likewise, for any universal proposition and its contradictory one must be true and the other false; but for a singular proposition about the future, the case is different. For propositions about the past or the present there is a state of affairs against which the truth or falsity of a proposition can be measured, and this is true regardless of whether the propositions are about necessary or contingent matter. But for singular propositions about the future, there is no state of affairs that can be enunciated truly or falsely. Although singular propositions in necessary or impossible matter do have a determinate truth or falsity, future singular propositions in contingent matter do not.

To illustrate his discussion, Aristotle used the now celebrated example of the sea battle that will or will not take place tomorrow (*ibid.* 18b 24). If it is true now that the sea battle will take place tomorrow and false that it will not take place, a deterministic position is assumed that eliminates CONTINGENCY and makes all events necessary. Aristotle rejects such a position, ''for there is a difference between saying that that which is, when it is, must needs be, and simply saying that all that is must needs be, and similarly in the case of that which is not'' (19a 24–27). Rather, he says that neither contradictory is determinately true or false now. This allows for no intermediate between ''the sea battle will take place'' and ''the sea battle will not take place.'' One or the other of these contradictions will be true and the other false, but neither is so now. The reason lies in the fact that at present the sea battle, however likely it may be, exists only potentially, and there is a possibility that it will never actually come to be.

Other Interpretations. Because of their strict determinism, Stoics held the determinate truth or falsity of every proposition, eliminating the possibility of future contingents. EPICURUS, on the other hand, is reported by Cicero (*De fato* 21) to have denied that every proposition is true or false.

St. THOMAS AQUINAS, in a commentary that exceeds the limits of mere exposition, sheds considerable light on Aristotle's position by analyzing the reasons that account for contingency, namely, the potentiality inherent in matter and the freedom of the human will (*In* 1 *perih.* 13, 14, 15).

Some recent historians of logic have alleged that Aristotle called the principle of the excluded middle into question in that ''he will not allow it to be valid for future contingent events'' (Bocheński, 63) or that he tried to hold the principle of the excluded middle while denying the principle of bivalence (W. C. and M. Kneale, 47–48). The Kneales call the principle that every statement is true or false the principle of bivalence, and formulate the principle of excluded middle, '''Either *P* or not-*P*,' where '*P*' marks a gap into which a declarative sentence may be inserted.'' However, they regard the two principles as equivalent and consider Aristotle's treatment of singular future contingents a mistake. The Kneales' delineation of the mistake is too involved for condensation here; while they regard it as of considerable philosophical interest, they deem it of no logical importance.

Scholz (86–88), following Moritz Schlick, takes the position that ''in every proposition there inheres truth or falsity as a timeless property.'' A statement such as ''Event *E* will occur on such and such a day'' is a timeless statement and is true or false now. But since the truth or falsity of that proposition cannot be calculated on the basis of propositions about present events, we cannot know whether the proposition is true until the point of time has passed. In his view the proposition is true whether we know it or not.

John Stuart Mill (183) denied that an assertion must be either true or false on the ground that there is a third possibility, the unmeaning. He said, for example, ''Abracadabra is a second intention'' is neither true nor false. F. H. BRADLEY (155) countered by pointing out that a proposition without meaning is no proposition, and that if it does mean anything, it is either true or false.

See Also: FIRST PRINCIPLES; CONTRADICTION, PRINCIPLE OF; TRUTH; FALSITY.

Bibliography: G. GIANNINI, *Enciclopedia filosofica,* 4 v. (Venice-Rome 1957) 4:1171–72. J. M. BALDWIN, ed., *Dictionary of Philosophy and Psychology,* 3 v. in 4 (New York 1901–05; repr. Gloucester 1949–57). A. E. BABIN, *The Theory of Opposition in Aristotle* (Notre Dame, Ind. 1940). H. W. B. JOSEPH, *An Introduction to Logic* (2d rev. ed. Oxford 1916). L. S. STEBBING, *A Modern Introduction to Logic* (London 1930). W. C. and M. KNEALE, *The Development of Logic* (Oxford 1962). H. SCHOLZ, *Concise History of Logic,* tr. K. F. LEIDECKER (New York 1961). I. M. BOCHEŃSKI, *A History of Formal Logic,* tr. I. THOMAS (Notre Dame, Ind. 1961). F. H. BRADLEY, *The Principles of Logic,* 2 v. (2d rev. ed. London 1922) v.1. J. S. MILL, *A System of Logic* (New York 1904). N. RESCHER, *Studies in the History of Arabic Logic* (Pittsburgh 1964) ch. 5.

[H. J. DULAC]

EXCOMMUNICATION

The term excommunication (*excommunicatus*—ἀκοινώνητος) first appeared in Church documents in the fourth century. As the term suggests, excommunication involves a varying degree of ''exclusion from the communion of the faithful'' (1917 CIC c.2257.1). From the beginnings of Christianity the central realization and embodiment of ''the communion of the faithful'' has always been the Eucharistic Communion; hence it is from the Eucharist as the center of the common socio-mystical life of the faithful in Christ's Body, the Church, that the excommunicate is primarily excluded. This is the prime factor characterizing excommunication in all the stages of its historical development.

History

New Testament. Faced with the scandal of a gravely sinful brother who resisted all correction and rebuke, the New Testament ἐκκλησία was constrained to isolate such a sinner from its midst (1 Cor 5.2, 13), without necessarily taking away his membership in the community (see 1 Cor 5.11). The Church was, however, no holy remnant ruthlessly ridding itself of sinners (see Mt 13.28–30); rather it remained open to the return of the penitent sinner, so that the segregation of the obdurate sinner had a hopeful outlook (see 2 Thes 3.15; 2 Cor 2.5–11). Even when St. Paul uses a seemingly harsh curse formula, there is still the perspective of hope (see 1 Cor 5.4–5; 1 Tm 1.20).

Mt 18.15–18 is the classical locus in which the Church, after having vainly tried to turn a sinful brother from his ways, is presented as competent to dissociate the sinner from its midst by a judgment that is divinely ratified. If there can be a ''binding'' of the sinner in his sinful alienation from God and from God's people, there always remains the alternative of a ''loosing'' of the same sinner, providing he repents and heeds the voice of the Church (*see* BINDING AND LOOSING).

Patristic and Medieval Period. Two factors distinguish the penitential practice of the ancient Church from that of later ages. First, until about the sixth century the grave sinner was permitted to avail himself of the Church's sacramental penitential procedure only once in his lifetime. Second, the canonico-disciplinary phases of penance, imposed by ecclesiastical authority, were closely inserted into the strictly sacramental elements of penance in a unified procedure. The grave sinner, resolved to make his peace with God in the Church, presented himself to the bishop, who assigned him, by a liturgical excommunication, to a special category of Christians with a separate and juridically inferior status in the Church, i.e., to the class of penitents (*ordo paenitentium*), and imposed on him a varyingly protracted period of public penitential works. At the close of this period of onerous penance, during which the penitent was publicly cut off from the central life of the Church, the bishop lifted the liturgical excommunication, reconciling the penitent to God in the Church, and receiving him once again into communion with the Church, primarily into the Eucharistic life of the Church and then into a sharing in its whole common life. The excommunication of the sinner was thus assumed into the sacramental penitential process, being an integral part of the satisfaction performed in view of an ultimate reconciliation with God in the Church. The ancient Church accordingly wished as little dissociation as possible between what today we would call the internal and the external forums, between sacramental penance and the canonical penalty of excommunication.

The decisive step in the widespread development of a canonical excommunication separated from sacramental penance was the gradual introduction, starting in the sixth and seventh centuries, of a sacramental penitential procedure that was repeatable. Once it became possible for the grave sinner to approach the Sacrament of Penance more than once, then inevitably a more simplified procedure had to be introduced into sacramental penance; and by about the 11th to the 12th centuries the external forms of the administration of Penance had become much the same as we know them today. One result of this development was the gradual, clear emergence, from the 7th century onward, of a canonical disciplinary excommunication, dissociated from its former prominent place within sacramental penance, and as a consequence, applied, not to repentant, but to impenitent sinners. By the high Middle Ages, and for centuries afterward, the interior and exterior forums were, both in theory and in practice, less intimately associated than in patristic times. *See* St. Thomas, *In 4 sent.* 18.2.2 sol. 1.

Conclusion. Once it has become clear that any culpable dissociation from the full visible common life of the Church marks some measure of disruption of the full interior life of grace in the Body of the Lord, there is less likelihood of an excessive separation of delict and sin, and of excommunication and penance. Just as the theology of sacramental penance has regained a firmer ecclesial dimension in that the *res et sacramentum* of the Sacrament is often described as peace with the Church, so too canonical excommunication can be seen in this orientation as a firmer delineation of the sinner's alienation from full communion, and the lifting of the censure can be placed as a preliminary stage to the sacramental absolution conferring on the repentant sinner that peace with the Church which means peace with God.

See Also: ANATHEMA; PENANCE, SACRAMENT OF; SCHISM; SOCIETY (CHURCH AS); VISIBILITY OF THE CHURCH.

Bibliography: B. POSCHMANN, *Penance and the Anointing of the Sick,* tr. and rev. F. COURTNEY (New York 1964). P. ANCIAUX, *The Sacrament of Penance* (New York 1962). W. DOSKOCIL, *Der*

Bann in der Urkirche (Munich 1958). K. RAHNER, *De paenitentia: Tractatus historico-dogmaticus* (3d ed. Innsbruck 1955).

[F. X. LAWLOR]

Canon Law

Breaches of ecclesial faith or order may lead to the declaration or imposition of ecclesiastical penalties. Accordingly, Church members are deprived of certain spiritual or temporal goods of the Church, either temporarily or permanently. Expiatory penalties highlight the ecclesial goods of restoring community order, repairing scandal, and precluding further disciplinary violations. Censures or so-called medicinal penalties are geared much more toward reconciling the offending party with the community.

The most ecclesially significant censure is excommunication, described in the 1917 code as excluding one from the communion of the faithful and entailing various inseparable effects (cc. 2257–2267). The present law does not define this most serious penalty, but simply specifies its inseparable effects, i.e., various prohibitions to one's involvement in the Church's public life (c. 1331). The first part of this canon indicates the effects of any excommunication, and the second describes specific effects of excommunication when there has been a formal intervention by ecclesiastical authority. This may involve either administrative procedure or judicial process before a collegiate court of three judges (c. 1425n1, 2).

An intervention may involve a declaration that an automatic excommunication (*latae sententiae*) has been incurred; or it may entail the infliction of a so-called *ferendae sententiae* excommunication. The intervention of Church authority lends a special solemnity to the legal situation and results in more serious restrictions on the penalized party, e.g., invalidity and not simply illiceity of prohibited acts of ecclesiastical governance.

Some restrictions affecting the excommunicated person are liturgical in character, e.g., prohibition of active ministerial participation in the Eucharist and other acts of public worship and prohibition of celebrating the sacraments or sacramentals or of receiving the sacraments. During the code revision process it had been proposed to exempt penance and anointing from the aforementioned prohibition, but it was finally decided that the excommunicated person needed to have the penalty remitted before receiving any sacraments. Some restrictions flowing from excommunication are governmental in nature, e.g., prohibitions of holding various ecclesiastical offices, exercising various ministries or functions, or positing acts of governance. If an excommunication has been formally inflicted or declared, such a person is also barred from enjoying privileges already acquired, validly acquiring any ecclesiastical dignity, office, or function, and receiving certain ecclesiastical income.

The current law is somewhat circumspect about establishing censures, especially excommunication; such penalties should be reserved for the most serious disciplinary violations (cc. 1318;1349). Not surprisingly the law notably reduces the number of excommunications specified in the 1917 code. Nine ecclesiastical offenses may make a guilty party liable to an excommunication; seven involve *latae sententiae* or automatic penalties; two entail *ferendae sententiae* penalties. The following offenses may lead to a latae sententiae excommunication: apostasy, heresy, schism (c. 1364nl); violation of sacred species (c. 1367); physical attack on the pope (1370); absolution of an accomplice (c. 1378nl); unauthorized episcopal consecration (c. 1382); direct violation of confessional seat by confessor (c. 1388n2); and procuring of an abortion (c. 1398). Finally two offenses may warrant a *ferendae sententiae* excommunication: pretended celebration of Eucharist or conferral of sacramental absolution by one not a priest (c. 1378); and violation of the confessional seal by an interpreter or those other than confessor (c. 1388n2).

Bibliography: T. GREEN, ''Book VI: Sanctions in the Church,'' J. CORIDEN, et al., eds., *The Code of Canon Law: A Text and Commentary* (New York 1985) 906–907; 932.

[T. J. GREEN]

EXEGESIS, BIBLICAL

By Biblical exegesis is meant the exposition of a passage or a book of the Sacred Scriptures. After an introductory section treating of the nature and forms of Biblical exegesis, this article offers an account of its history to show how the Bible was interpreted throughout the centuries.

Since the Bible as a divinely inspired book is a unique work of literature, its exegesis differs in many respects from the interpretation of other ancient documents.

Nature. On the one hand, the Sacred Scriptures are the products of many human authors who lived at various times over at least a millennium and wrote in several different literary genres; on the other hand, all the Scriptures were written under divine inspiration and so have God as their principal author. Therefore, Biblical exegesis employs not only the sciences that are used in the study of other ancient documents that come from a culture differing considerably from the modern, such as philology, history, archeology, and so forth, but also the theological disciplines that enable the exegete to obtain a deeper understanding of God's word and revelation as contained in the Scriptures. A synthesis of the theological exegesis of the Bible forms the basis of BIBLICAL THEOLOGY. Sciences that are auxiliary to Biblical exegesis are the rules of interpretation or Biblical hermeneutics (see section 3, below) and the study of each book as a whole, which is the subject of biblical introductions.

Forms. Even a translation of the Scriptures is, to a certain extent, a form of exegesis; for unless a version is extremely literal, it involves a considerable amount of interpretation in the sense of explanation. The more free or paraphrastic a translation is, the more exegetical it is. Short exegetical notes, usually written on the margin of the page of a Bible, are known as Biblical GLOSSES. In former times an exegetical note, especially if rather long, was known as a SCHOLIUM. A collection of exegetical notes excerpted from the writings of the Church Fathers form so-called Biblical CATENAE.

The fullest form, however, of Biblical exegesis is that of biblical commentaries. The scope of a strictly scientific commentary is to set forth as faithfully as possible the thought of the author by using all available scientific means insofar as they apply, such as textual criticism, literary criticism (to ascertain the specific type of literary genre in which the book is written; *see* FORM CRITICISM, BIBLICAL), philology (*see* BIBLICAL LANGUAGES), geography (*see* PALESTINE), history, and so forth. But since every book of the Bible is not only a human document but also a record of God's revelation, a genuine commentary should set forth also the religious message or KERYGMA of the book. Moralizing conclusions, however, that do not flow directly from the Biblical text belong to HOMILETICS rather than to exegesis. In the Middle Ages such moralizing notes were often called postils or in Latin *postillae,* from the full phrase *post illa verba textus* (after the words of the text).

Bibliography: R. SCHNACKENBURG and K. H. SCHELKE, *Lexicon für Theologie und Kirche* (Freiburg, 1957–66) 3:1273–74. *Encyclopedic Dictionary of the Bible*, tr. and adap. by L. HARTMAN (New York 1963) 1069–71.

[L. F. HARTMAN]

History of Exegesis

In the various periods of history, ever since the Bible was accepted as the inspired word of God, men have endeavored to explain and interpret its meaning through what is known as Biblical exegesis. But every age has had its own characteristic exegesis.

EXEGESIS OF THE OLD TESTAMENT IN THE NEW TESTAMENT

Modern stress on the essential unity of the Bible has drawn attention to the necessity of understanding how and to what extent the OT is used in the NT. The reader of any Bible edited with copious marginal references to OT texts knows how extensively NT writers cite the OT directly or indirectly.

Quotations from the Old Testament. In the NT there are more than 200 direct quotations from the OT, more than half of which, 118, are found in the Pauline Epistles (see L. Venard, *Guide to the Bible* [Tournai–New York 1951–55, rev. and enl. 1960] 1:679). If references of all kinds are counted, the total number is about 350, of which about 300 are cited according to the Septuagint (LXX) version. Matthew's manner of quoting the OT is noteworthy; when he is using Greek sources (i.e., when he depends on Mark) he retains their Greek wording; when working independently, he generally quotes an OT text according to the Hebrew, though on occasion the influence of the LXX can be traced. For example, in Mt 21.16 Psalm 8.3 is cited according to the LXX for apologetic reasons; see A. Wikenhauser, *New Testament Introduction,* tr. J. Cunningham (New York 1958) 195. Except for the author of the Epistle to the Hebrews, who always quotes the LXX exactly, most NT authors show little concern for exactness in their quotations. Their practice of free rendering of OT texts must not be ascribed to memory lapses, but rather to common literary custom or, as in many Pauline texts, to an exegetical purpose; see E. Ellis, *Paul's Use of the OT* (London 1957) 14–15. Some NT writers use interesting combinations in their OT quotations. Paul, for instance, uses three types of combined texts: (1) OT texts strung together to form a single quotation [e.g., Rom 3.10–18 is composed of Ps 13(14).1–3; 5.10; 139(140).4; 9B(10).7; Is 59.7–8; Ps 35(36).2]; (2) chain quotations or *hāraz* (e.g., Rom 9.25–29); (3) looser midrashic commentary (e.g., Romans ch. 9–11; Galatians ch. 3). See Ellis, *op. cit.,* 11, 186 for charts of Pauline combinations.

Interpretations of Old Testament Passages. The NT interpretation of the OT reveals the following characteristics: (1) the allegorical method, so venerated by interpreters of ancient literature and so extensively used by the Alexandrian Jew Philo, is employed only infrequently by NT writers. Paul expressly says that his interpretation of the story of HAGAR and ISHMAEL (Gn 21.9–21) is by way of allegory (Gal 4.21–31). The story of Melchizedek (Gn 14.18–20) receives similar treatment in Heb 7.1–10. Such examples, however, are rare. The allegorical method is not characteristic of NT interpretation of OT texts. (2) Though their interpretations were generally literal in the wide sense of being based on the literal meaning of the OT text, NT writers exercised a great deal of freedom with respect to the original historical sense of the OT text quoted. Nevertheless, these writers were always conscious of the OT as history, and it is not likely that they would ever be unmindful of the historical setting of the OT texts they used; see C. H. Dodd, *The Old Testament in the New* (Philadelphia 1963) 8. (3) Literary allusions to OT words, phraseology, and imagery abound, reflecting the NT writer's familiarity with the OT. (4) OT texts are sometimes cited by way of illustration or analogy, as Dt 21.23 in Gal 3.13. (5) OT texts, especially from the Prophets, are sometimes cited as direct proof of a NT writer's argument. Such is the use of the Servant of the Lord Oracles from Is 42.1–4; 49.1–7; 50.4–11; 52.13–53.12 (*see* SUFFERING SERVANT, SONGS OF THE).

For St. Paul's exegetical method and relation to rabbinical exegesis, see especially: W. D. Davies, *Paul and Rabbinic Judaism* (London 1948, rev. ed. 1955, repr. 1964) and J. Bonsirven, *Exégèse rabbinique et exégèse paulinienne* (Paris 1939). From his study of the NT writers use of the OT, C. H. Dodd [*According to the Scriptures* (London 1952)] concludes that individual passages cited are often only pointers to the OT total context, which is really the basis of the argument.

[L. F. HARTMAN]

JEWISH EXEGESIS

A natural division of the Jewish exegesis of the OT is between that of the Talmudic period (from the beginning of the 1st to the end of the 8th Christian century) and that of the Middle Ages (from *c.* 800 to *c.* 1300).

Talmudic Period. The object of the rabbinical exegesis from the 1st century B.C. to the end of the 8th Christian century was twofold: (1) to determine precisely the true meaning of the text, and (2) to establish the Biblical basis for the HALAKAH or system of jurisprudence composed of traditional legal decisions, commandments of the ancient Fathers, and prescriptions of the Scribes, and to support the HAGGADAH or nonjuridical interpretations and traditions forming an immense literature that was historical, folkloristic, and homiletic in character (see A. Vincent, 42–69; J. Bonsirven, *Dictionnaire de la Bible* suppl. ed. L. Pirot, et al. [Paris] 4:561–569; and A. Robert and A. Tricot, *Guide to the Bible* [Tournai–New York 1951–55] 684–693, especially the translator's notes). To achieve the first object required a literal exegesis, and in fact this became characteristic of Jewish juridical commentaries of the 2nd century of the Christian Era. However, the use of texts as proofs sometimes led to an abuse of the literal sense.

Jewish exegesis is found in a great body of rabbinical literature, which is composed of the following: (1) the MISHNAH and its additions in the TOSEPHTA (explanatory notes on oral traditions not included in the Mishnah); (2) the GEMARAH, written in Aramaic, which commented on, applied, and widely extended the teaching of the Mishnah, as well as incorporating non-Mishnah material; and (3) the midrashim (*see* MIDRASHIC LITERATURE), which were rabbinical commentaries on either the legal texts of the Bible (halakah) or on the historical or moral texts (haggadah). The Mishnah and its commentary, the Gemarah, comprise the TALMUD. See Vincent, 54; and A. Robert and A. Tricot, *Guide to the Bible*, rev. and enl. ed. (Tournai–New York 1960) 1:685–687, footnotes.

The Torah (Mosaic Law) was always considered to be the basis of all prescriptions applied to new circumstances of Jewish life, no matter how far removed from the Law these appeared to be. They were linked to the Law by certain logical rules. Hillel had these seven: (1) from the less to the greater and from the simple to the difficult, (2) from like to like by analogy, (3) according to one passage in the Law, (4) according to two passages in the Law, (5) from the general to the particular and from the particular to the general, (6) explanation of one text by another, and (7) explanation of a text by the context. Rabbi Ishmael ben Elisha (d. *c.* 135) increased these seven to 13; to Rabbi Eliezer ben Yose (d. *c.* 150) 32 are attributed. See Vincent, 46. In spite of its well-known defects, Talmudic exegesis contains much that is of permanent value to Biblical scholarship, as some of the early Fathers, as well as the scholastic and Reformation exegetes, were well aware. Historians of exegesis are not unmindful of the contribution of early rabbinical exegesis to the treasury of Christian interpretation.

Middle Ages. Biblical exegesis in the strict sense, as distinct from the use that the Talmudic rabbis made of the Bible, began among the Jews in the 9th century primarily as a reaction against the Karaites, a Jewish sect that arose toward the end of the 8th century. The Karaites rejected the traditional teachings of the Talmud and demanded a return to the Bible understood in the literal sense. The orthodox rabbis were therefore forced, in defense of traditional Judaism, to study the Hebrew Scriptures and explain their literal sense (*p^e^š-ṭ*) in conformity with orthodox Judaism. A contributing factor was the contact that the rabbis of the time made with Arabic scholars, particularly in Spain, whose grammatical and lexicographical studies in connection with the study of the QUR'ĀN led the Jewish scholars to make similar studies of the Hebrew Bible. An additional reason for the improvement in Jewish exegesis in the Middle Ages was the growing interest among Jews as well as among Muslims and Christians in Aristotelian philosophy, which led to a more rational method in the study of the Sacred Scriptures.

The pioneer of the new Jewish exegesis was the archopponent of the Karaites, Gaon SA'ADIA BEN JOSEPH (822–942). The study of the Scriptures was only one of his many fields of interest, but here, besides his Arabic translation of the Bible, he produced the first Hebrew dictionary and the first Hebrew grammar. In the East, however, where he lived, he had no scholarly successors. His influence was felt, instead, in Spain and later in France. Spanish Jewry of the Middle Ages had several important Hebrew philologists, such as Menachem ben Saruk (*c.* 910–*c.* 970), Dunash ben Labrat (*c.* 920–*c.* 990), Judah ben David Hayyuj (*c.* 940–*c.* 1010), and especially Jonah Marinus (Abū'l Walīd Merwān Ibn-Janah; *c.* 990–*c.* 1050), the greatest Hebrew grammarian of the Middle Ages.

The medieval Jewish exegetes built on the work of these philologists. The most important of the commentators in Spain was Abraham ben Meïr IBN EZRA (*c.* 1092–1167). On the whole, his Biblical commentaries are based on the literal sense, often arrived at by philological or grammatical arguments. A product of the Spanish school, though he spent most of his life in Egypt, was the renowned Jewish scholar MAIMONIDES (Moses ben Maimon; 1135–1204). Although he wrote no commentary, in his works, particularly his *Guide to the Perplexed,* he explained many Biblical passages according to philosophical or even rationalistic principles. The influence of the Jewish exegetes of Spain soon reached France. At Troyes in northern France the renowned Talmudist, RASHI (Rabbi Shelomoh ben Yishaq; 1041–1105), produced popular commentaries on almost all the books of the Hebrew Bible. The commentaries of his grandson, Samuel ben Meïr, known also as Rashbam (*c.* 1085–*c.* 1160), though more diffused, are of greater scientific value. At Narbonne in southern France the Ḳimchi (Ḳimḥi) family, Joseph (*c.* 1105–*c.* 1170) and his sons Moses (d. 1190) and particularly David (*c.* 1160–1235), wrote Biblical commentaries that are still valuable for their philological and grammatical observations. The commentaries of the Spanish Jewish scholar, NAḤMANIDES (Moses ben Naḥman, known also as Ramban; *c.* 1195–*c.* 1270), though containing much valuable material, indulge too often in mystical, cabalistic speculations. After the 13th century medieval Jewish exegesis fell almost completely under the spell of the CABALA, and the works of this period are thus practically worthless from an exegetical viewpoint. But the writings of the earlier Jewish lexicographers, grammarians, and exegetes proved extremely useful to the Christian Hebraists of the later Middle Ages and the Renaissance [*see* HEBREW STUDIES (IN THE CHRISTIAN CHURCH)], and they still merit study by modern Biblical scholars.

[L. F. HARTMAN]

PATRISTIC EXEGESIS

The history of exegesis in the patristic period (extending to the beginning of the 7th century) can best be treated by considering separately the Fathers before Origen, Origen, the school of Alexandria, the school of Antioch, and the Latin Fathers (*see* PATRISTIC STUDIES).

Before Origen. The Apostolic Fathers left no Biblical exegesis in the strict sense. They used the Biblical text either to support their exhortations to lead a fruitful Christian life or, as in the case of Pope St. CLEMENT I in his *First Epistle to the Corinthians* (*c.* A.D. 98), to form a spiritual mosaic of scriptural texts. Generally, the Apostolic Fathers did not attempt to prove their teaching from Biblical texts. A notable exception, however, was the author of the *Epistle of BARNABAS*, who had recourse to an allegorical and typical interpretation of the OT to prove that the Jews failed to understand properly God's will and the Mosaic Law, even its clearest precepts; for example, God's inspired precept regarding abstinence from certain meats really commanded the Jews to flee from the particular vices signified by impure animals (see G. Bardy, *Guide to the Bible*, [Tournai–New York 1951–55; v.1, rev. and enl. 1960] 1:695). The Christians, said the author, were the first to understand the OT properly.

The Apologists of the 2nd century, in addressing unbelievers, could hardly appeal to the OT as proofs of their teaching but had to be content to urge the antiquity of the OT over pagan works. Although it was not characteristic of the Apologists, St. JUSTIN MARTYR (d. *c.* 165) used arguments from the Prophets effectively in both his first *Apology* and his *Dialogue Against Trypho.* Second-century heretics attacked this type of proof by trying to underscore the apparent contradictions between the teaching of the OT and that of Jesus; hence the origin of Marcion's *Antithesis* and Apelles's *Syllogisms.* St. IRENAEUS (*c.* 140–*c.* 202) in his *Adversus Haereses* and TERTULLIAN (*c.* 160–*c.* 230) in his *Contra Marcionem* and in other works defended the OT against the heretics. Heracleon (2nd century), a Gnostic, wrote the oldest commentary on St. John, using principally the allegorical method. Ptolemy, another Gnostic, in a *Letter to Flora,* was probably the first one to attempt to place exegesis on a firm, scientific foundation. (For the light shed on Gnosticism by the discovery of numerous Coptic texts near Nag' Hammâdi in Egypt, *see* CHENOBOSKION, GNOSTIC TEXTS OF.)

Origen. The first Biblical scholar to study critically the LXX was Origen (*c.* 185–*c.* 254), one of the most important figures in the early history of exegesis (*see* ORIGEN AND ORIGENISM). His many exegetical writings appear in scholia (simple notes on difficult or obscure passages; *see* SCHOLIUM), commentaries, and homilies. He wrote scholia on the first four books of the Pentateuch, on Isaiah, Ecclesiastes, the Psalms, Matthew, John, Galatians, and Revelation. He commented on Genesis ch. 1–4, on several Psalms, twice on the Canticle of Canticles, and on Matthew, Luke, John, and the Pauline Epistles except 1 and 2 Corinthians and Timothy. In 1941 at Tura, a few miles south of Cairo, a papyrus containing fragments of the original Greek of Origen's commentary on Romans was discovered. His homilies, about 200 of which have been preserved, were delivered at Caesarea in Palestine.

Unlike his predecessors, Origen set down his ideas on hermeneutics, especially in the fourth book of his *De principiis.* Applying Plato's threefold distinction of body, soul, and spirit to the senses of Scripture, Origen taught that Holy Scripture contained (1) a corporeal or historical sense, which seems to be simply the ordinary proper literal and historical sense that the Biblical text directly conveys; (2) the psychic or moral sense, generally ignored by Origen in practice, which seems to be concerned with moral correction and is often indistinguishable from (3) the spiritual sense, which embraces all other senses that can be derived from the Biblical text. Origen never claimed that all Scripture contained this threefold sense. He believed that it was possible for the sacred author to err, on rare occasions, regarding the corporeal sense, which would then have to be rejected. Again, allegory was not present in every text. Origen thought that the corporeal sense was sufficient for the needs of the simple faithful, but that the perfect sought a deeper meaning hidden beneath the words. At times his allegory is exaggerated, but he made a permanent contribution to textual criticism, typology, and the allegorical method which was to characterize the exegetical school of Alexandria.

School of Alexandria. The foundation of this first Christian theological school (*see* ALEXANDRIA, SCHOOL OF) is commonly attributed to St. PANTAENUS, of whom very little is known. He was born in Sicily and became a convert to Christianity from Stoicism and taught at the exegetical school of Alexandria toward the end of the 2nd century (*c.* 180).

Clement, Dionysius, and Eusebius. Pantaenus was succeeded by his pupil CLEMENT OF ALEXANDRIA (*c.* 150–*c.* 215), a scholar of vast erudition, who was strongly influenced in his exegetical method by the allegorical one of Philo. Clement believed that it was of the very nature of higher truths that they should be communicated only through symbols. He acknowledged three senses of Scripture: the literal, the moral, and the prophetical or allegorical. He believed that all Scripture must be interpreted allegorically. His major works, *Stromata, Paedagogus,* and *Protrepticus* are remarkable for their wealth of Biblical erudition.

St. DIONYSIUS (*c.* 190–265), Bishop of Alexandria from 247 to 265, stated his exegetical principles in a work entitled *On the Promises,* written in response to an attack on the allegorists by a certain Bishop Nepos. St. Dionysius confessed that much in Revelation was beyond his comprehension, but he did not doubt that it contained many profound and hidden senses. It seems that Dionysius wrote commentaries also on Ecclesiastes and Luke.

EUSEBIUS OF CAESAREA (*c.* 260–*c.* 339) as a historian was inclined to the literal sense in his exegesis, but he had received training in the allegorical method from PAMPHILUS (d. 310), a pupil of Origen. In his commentaries on Isaiah, the Psalms, and Luke, Eusebius was generally free from allegorical exaggerations.

Athanasius and Didymus. Of the works of St. ATHANASIUS (*c.* 295–373), who was more a defender of orthodoxy and a shepherd of souls than a professional exegete, we have only fragments, a commentary on the Psalms, and a little work titled *Interpretation of the Psalms,* which reveals his ideas on how to profit best from a prayerful study of the Psalter.

DIDYMUS THE BLIND (*c.* 313–*c.* 398), for many years the head of the school of Alexandria, wrote commentaries on a large number of the books of the OT and the NT, which were highly praised by St. Jerome. The fraction of these commentaries that has been preserved reveals these characteristics: there are two senses of Scripture, the literal and the spiritual; the OT must be interpreted allegorically and, whenever possible, messianically, if it is to be fully understood: his interpretation of the NT is generally according to the literal sense. As a true disciple of Origen, Didymus had learned from experience to control prudently all allegorical applications. G. Bardy (A. Robert and A. Tricot, *Guide to the Bible*, rev. and enl. [Tournai–New York 1960] 1:700) suggests that the commentaries of Didymus on Genesis, Job, and Zechariah have apparently been recovered through the discovery of the papyri at Tura (see above).

Cappadocian Fathers. Among the great Cappadocians who were strongly influenced by Origen and the Alexandrians were St. BASIL (*c.* 329–379), St. GREGORY OF NAZIANZUS (*c.* 330–*c.* 390), and St. GREGORY OF NYSSA (*c.* 335–394), the younger brother of Basil. St. Basil used Scripture primarily for the instruction and edification of the faithful. His homilies *On the Hexameron* as well as those on various Psalms reflect his intention to use the Bible to nourish the spiritual life of his hearers. St. Gregory of Nazianzus used Scripture in much the same fashion. He was above all else a theologian, and he treated the Scriptures primarily as a *locus theologicus* in his conflicts with the Arians and Apollinarists. The finest exegete of all the Cappadocians was the highly gifted St. Gregory of Nyssa. Although he was an allegorist to the core, he nevertheless knew how to use effectively the literal sense when necessary, e.g., in his *De hominis opificio* and *Explicatio Apologetica in Hexaemeron.* His other works include homilies on Ecclesiastes, the Song of Songs, the Lord's Prayer, and the Beatitudes, as well as a homily on the titles of the Psalms, in which he observes that Holy Scripture does not narrate historical facts for their own sakes but in order to teach man how to live virtuously.

Cyril. St. CYRIL OF ALEXANDRIA (d. 444), the great opponent of the Nestorians, was a thoroughgoing allegorist in both his *Adoration and Worship in Spirit and Truth* and *Glaphyra.* The former was written to prove the complete harmony between the OT and the NT, whereas the latter interpreted typically (especially with regard to the person of Christ) passages selected from the Pentateuch. In his commentaries on Isaiah and the Minor Prophets, Cyril leans more toward the historical literal sense, but not always with complete success. His commentary on St. John's Gospel is concerned mainly with doctrinal content and the refutation of heresy.

School of Antioch. The foundation of the Antiochian school (*see* ANTIOCH, SCHOOL OF) at the end of the 3rd century is generally attributed to St. LUCIAN OF ANTIOCH (*c.* 240–317), famous for his role in establishing the Greek *textus receptus.* We know nothing of the exegesis of Lucian. The school's history may be divided into three periods: (1) From Lucian to the coming of Diodore of Tarsus (i.e., from *c.* 280 to 360), (2) from Diodore to Theodore of Mopsuestia (i.e., from 360 to 428), and (3) the period of decline (i.e., from 428 to 500). The exegetical principles of Antioch were directly opposed to those of its rival, Alexandria. Antioch insisted upon expounding the literal and historical meaning of the text. The typical sense (*theoria*) was acknowledged and carefully determined. The allegorical method of Alexandria found little welcome at Antioch.

The following are the more important Antiochians: St. EUSTATHIUS OF ANTIOCH (d. *c.* 335), in his *On the Witch of Endor,* attacked the allegorical method of Origen. DIODORE OF TARSUS (*c.* 330–*c.* 392), the teacher of St. John Chrysostom and Theodore of Mopsuestia and one of the most illustrious of the Antiochians, wrote many exegetical works on the books of the OT and the NT. His exegesis is strictly literal, though he accepts the typical when it is well founded upon the literal and historical sense. The exegesis of St. JOHN CHRYSOSTOM (*c.* 349–407) is found chiefly in this great preacher's homilies. He never formulated any rules of interpretation, but he accepted the literal sense, both proper and improper (i.e., allegorical) and the typical. He was concerned primarily with what he could draw from the sacred text for the good of souls.

THEODORE OF MOPSUESTIA (d. 428) is the best-known Biblical pupil of Diodore. The Council of CONSTANTINOPLE II (553) condemned some of Theodore's opinions on the nature of inspiration and the books to be excluded from the Canon and his restriction of the number of messianic Psalms to four [i.e., Psalm 2; 8; 44 (45); 109 (110)]. Even today it is difficult to evaluate properly his exegetical works. He is well known for his boldness and strict adherence to the literal and historical sense. He explained his exegetical principles in two works now lost: *De allegoria et historia* and *De perfectione operum contra allegoricos.* (But on these works see the translator's note three in A. Robert and A. Tricot, *Guide to the Bible* [Tournai–New York 1960] 1:702.) On the exegetical method of Theodore of Mopsuestia see especially the two works of R. Devreese: ''La Méthode exégètique de Theodore de Mopsueste,'' *Revue biblique* 53 (1946) 207–241, and *Essai sur Theodore de Mopsueste, Studi e Testi* 141 (1948).

THEODORET OF CYR (d. before 466) deserves special mention for his solid interpretation of the Scriptures, which had enduring popularity. He claimed no originality but composed his commentaries only after assiduously studying the best of patristic exegesis. But he was, in fact, far more than a mere copyist and compiler. His many works were often cited in the Biblical CATENAE as authoritative. Faithful to the Antiochian school, he was principally concerned with the literal sense; yet a good deal of solid typology is often expounded in his works. He wrote commentaries on the Psalms, on the Song of Songs, and on all the Prophets, and he considered special questions on the Octateuch and the books of Samuel, Kings, and Chronicles. His exposition of the Pauline Epistles is considered by some to be second only to that made by St. John Chrysostom. Theodoret was the last of the great Antiochians.

Others associated with the School of Antioch were: St. EPHREM THE SYRIAN (*c.* 306–373), who wrote commentaries in Syriac on all the books of the Bible; APOLLINARIS OF LAODICEA (d. *c.* 390); SEVERIAN OF GABALA (d. after 408); and Polychronius of Apamea (d. *c.* 430), the brother of Theodore of Mopsuestia. ADRIANUS (fl. 1st half of the 5th century) composed an *Introduction to Holy Scripture* that set forth the principles of the Antiochians. The insistence of the Antiochians on the historical literal sense proved to be the correct position for sound exegesis according to the mind of the inspired author.

Latin Fathers. The exegetical principles of both Antioch and Alexandria found adherents among commentators of the West. Since no exegetical schools existed there during the patristic period, the following order of authors is simply chronological. TERTULLIAN (d. after 220), who gave the West its theological Latin, wrote no commentaries on Sacred Scripture, but he frequently interpreted

Biblical texts in his writings, generally in the literal sense. St. HIPPOLYTUS OF ROME (d. *c.* 236) wrote many works in Greek that exhibit Alexandrian influence. One would expect allegory in his commentary on the Canticle of Canticles, but it appears also in his work on Daniel. St. VICTORINUS OF PETTAU (d. *c.* 303) commented on many books of the OT and the NT. However, only his work on the Apocalypse has survived. The influence of Origen is reflected also in the works of St. HILARY OF POITIERS (d. 367), whose exegesis is strongly allegorical. A commentary of his on Matthew and another on the Psalms (partly preserved) are extant. A part of his *Tractatus mysteriorum,* a work on OT prophecies, was recovered in 1887. St. AMBROSE (d. 397) composed no commentaries in the strict sense on the books of the Bible. His exegesis, found chiefly in his many homilies on various books of the OT and NT, is allegorical and well balanced, and it reflects the preacher's concern for the formation and salvation of souls.

St. JEROME (d. 419 or 420) is the patron of Biblical studies. His Latin translation of the Bible, his many commentaries on the OT and NT books, especially on the prophetical books, and his knowledge of the principal Biblical languages and of the country and customs of the Holy Land itself have merited for him a special place in the history of Biblical studies. His exegesis, at first strongly allegorical, became more and more literal. We have his commentaries on Ecclesiastes and the Prophets in the OT and on Matthew, Galatians, Ephesians, Titus, and Philippians in the NT. An unknown author referred to as AMBROSIASTER or Pseudo-Ambrose composed an excellent literal commentary on the Pauline Epistles *c.* A.D. 380, probably at Rome. Tyconius the Donatist wrote the first Latin treatise on Biblical HERMENEUTICS, *Liber Regularum, c.* A.D. 370.

St. AUGUSTINE (d. 430) used allegorical and mystical interpretations in his preaching, but he preferred literal exegesis in his theological writings. Though he himself was not well equipped for scientific exegesis, he insisted upon the necessity of learning, and especially of philological training, for the proper study of the written word of God. He interpreted the first few chapters of Genesis four times: *De Genesi contra Manichaeos libri 2* (*c.* 389); *De Genesi ad litteram imperfectus liber* (*c.* 393), more literal than the previous work; the story of creation, allegorically interpreted, in the last three books of his *Confessions* (*c.* 400); and *De Genesi ad litteram libri 12* (*c.* 401), his major work on Genesis. Other important exegetical works of Augustine include: several books of *Quaestiones* and *Locutiones* on the Heptateuch; *Enarrationes in Psalmos,* probably his best exegetical work; *De consensu Evangeliorum,* a study of parallel passages in the Gospels; *Quaestiones* on the Gospels and on certain texts in Romans; and (in treatises or homilies) the Sermon on the Mount, the Gospel of St. John, Galatians, and the beginning of Romans. In his *De doctrina christiana* he set forth his ideas on the nature of exegesis and on the relation of Scripture to theology.

Worthy of mention are also St. PETER CHRYSOLOGUS (d. *c.* 450), who expounded allegorically many NT passages in 176 homilies; Cassiodorus (d. *c.* 580), who interpreted the Psalms and the NT literally; and the long influential St. GREGORY THE GREAT (d. 604), who interpreted allegorically Job (*Moralia*), Ezekiel, and the Gospels and whose primary interest in exegesis was pastoral.

[L. F. HARTMAN]

FROM THE PATRISTIC TO THE MEDIEVAL

Medieval exegesis of Scripture comprehends the Biblical hermeneutic employed by Western theology from about the year 600 to 1500 as well as the Biblical literature, e.g., commentaries, which is the product of this hermeneutic. It poses two questions: How did the medieval theologians interpret Holy Scripture, and in what literary form did they express their exegesis? Because in the course of the Middle Ages the level of culture was so diversified century by century and nation by nation, the extant exegetical literature, of which the larger portion is still unedited, is of very uneven quality. Owing to its rich variety, it is impossible to characterize it accurately in universal terms. Certain traits, however, are clear and salient. It is mystical, in that it held the superiority of the spiritual sense of Scripture over its literal; conservative, in its rigid adherence to the patristic tradition; functional, in its concept of Scripture as the book par excellence for both theological and spiritual formation and for the edification of the Christian faith; and Latin, in that it rested on the text of the *Biblia Vulgata Latina* and the Latin Fathers and used Latin as its literary medium.

Sense of Scripture. Medieval exegesis is firmly rooted in the patristic tradition, which it developed in its own characteristic spirit. Its ultimate inspiration was the school of Alexandria and the hermeneutic of ORIGEN (d. *c.* 254), who, under the influence of the Neoplatonism of PHILO JUDAEUS (d. *c.* 50), taught that a multiplicity of senses (meanings) can be found in the sacred text. ''For just as man,'' he wrote, ''consists of body, soul and spirit, so in the same way does the Scripture, which has been prepared by God to be given for man's salvation'' (*De Principiis* 4.2.4). Thus, according to Origen, the sense of Scripture is threefold: somatic, psychic, and pneumatic. That is, a given text of Scripture may simultaneously yield three different levels of meaning: the literal, the moral, and the spiritual. The transmission of this doctrine to the medieval world was largely indirect, through the

Latin Fathers, since Greek was a virtually unknown language in the Western Church of the early Middle Ages. For example, the teaching of EUCHERIUS OF LYONS (d. 449) in his *Formulae spiritalis intelligentiae* attests to the influence of Origen in the West, when he wrote: ''The body of Sacred Scripture, as it is handed down, is in the letter; its soul is in the moral sense, which is called *tropicus;* its spirit is in the higher understanding, which is called anagogic.'' The concept of the senses of Scripture that John CASSIAN (d. 435) presents in his *Collationes* (8.3) substantially agrees with this teaching. But it is perhaps St. GREGORY THE GREAT (d. 604) who must be regarded as the principal initiator and greatest patron of the medieval doctrine of the four senses. In the second book of his homilies on Ezekiel (*Hom.* 9, n. 8) he explains the functional character of the tetrad of Biblical senses in this way: ''The words of Holy Scripture are square stones, for they can stand on all sides, because on no side are there rough spots. For in every past event that they narrate, in every future event that they foretell, in every moral saying that they speak, and in every spiritual sense they stand, as it were, on a different side, because they have no roughness.'' These two conceptions of the multiple (threefold and fourfold) senses of Scripture dominate medieval exegesis. The fourfold sense was generally preferred to the threefold, to which it was reducible, and the spiritual was invariably preferred to the literal sense. Augustine of Dacia, OP (d. 1282), of the school of St. Thomas, epitomized this medieval hermeneutic in his celebrated distich:

> *Littera gesta docet, quid credis allegoria, Quid agis moralis, quo tendis anagogia.*

This fourfold division of the senses (the literal, the spiritual—including the allegorical, the moral, and the anagogic) of Scripture invaded all areas of medieval life. It was especially appreciated because it harmonized with the Neoplatonic sacramental concept of the universe: the visible (literal) both concealing and revealing a deeper, invisible reality (spiritual). It was also employed as a basic program in library classification (at Salvatorberg), in preaching (Robert de Basevorn), and in education (Hugh of Saint-Victor). It remained classical in Biblical studies until the coming of the Protestant Reformers and the Renaissance humanists, who rejected it with derision in favor of a more direct, historical, literal exegesis. But as late as the end of the 16th century there were still Catholic theologians, e.g., Francisco de TOLEDO (d. 1596), who believed that the doctrine of the fourfold sense of Scripture was to be held *de fide.*

Literal Sense. For the medieval exegete *historia* and *littera* are almost synonymous. Both are to be treated with reverence as the foundation of the higher spiritual sense. Fundamental, therefore, to medieval exegesis is the literal interpretation of Bible history, which included both the past event as well as its inspired narration. For the exegete knew that divine revelation was manifest to mankind in and through historical events and that Scripture was the inspired record of these saving events. His approach to Bible history was religious and theological rather than scientific and critical, though in the high Middle Ages the emphasis began to shift toward the learned element of exegesis. Holy Scripture represented the source book of faith in Christ who was the Lord of history. Literal exegesis was ordered to the discovery in the sacred text of the *res gesta,* divine revelation as a past event. For example, the literal exegesis of the Passion narratives [*see* PASSION OF CHRIST, I (IN THE BIBLE)] concluded to the death of Jesus as a historical event. It avoided its theological significance as pertaining to the spiritual rather than the literal sense of the text. For the medieval exegete history and the historical sense were superficial, exterior, sensible, and though it was a fundamental sense, a deeper, more mystical, theological sense was sought. Once the ultimate meaning or significance of the *res gesta* (the historical event) was grasped, exegesis passed into the spiritual order. To remain on the level of the historical and the literal would be unworthy of the exegete. It would be a betrayal of the primary function of Christian exegesis, the discovery and exposé of the mystery of Christ that must be sought on a higher level than *littera.* Therefore, abandoning the letter (the Jewish exegesis of the Old Law), the Christian exegete turned to the spirit (the Christocentric exegesis of all Scripture). The movement was from the literal to the spiritual sense, from history to allegory; and the validity of this motion was persuaded by the Pauline text: ''The letter kills, but the spirit gives life'' (2 Cor 3.6).

Spiritual Sense. The central task of spiritual exegesis is to uncover the deepest meaning of the *res gesta* that literal exegesis has discovered in the text. Its function is completed in answering three questions: (1) What is the theological (allegorical) meaning of this historical event? (2) What is its moral (tropological) meaning? (3) What is its eschatological (anagogic) meaning? The method is well illustrated by the traditional exegesis of the word Jerusalem: in the literal sense it is the city of the Jews; in the allegorical sense, the Church on earth; in the tropological sense, the virtuous Christian; and in the anagogic sense, the Church in heaven. Discernible in the spiritual sense is an ascending order, from letter to spirit, from the terrestrial to the celestial, from reading to contemplation, from event to reality. Based on history, it rises to faith; through faith Christian virtue is born; by Christian virtue eternal life is attained. These three spiritual senses make up the mystical order. They involve a *conversio,* allegory from the past Christ to the present Christ; tropology, a life reform by the act of Christ; anagogy, a renewal of the present in virtue of the future. Allegory demands a conversion of thought, tropology of morals, anagogy of desires. Allegory builds up the faith, tropology charity, anagogy hope. Allegory yields the sense of dogma, tropology of morality, anagogy of mysticism. Spiritual exegesis, therefore, was essentially ordered to the religious experience.

Despite the apparently systematic character of this hermeneutic, it tended in the course of the Middle Ages to disintegrate. Its understanding of the sacred text was frequently capricious, arbitrary, subjective, and tortured, and in the course of time it tended to drift more and more away from the *sacra pagina* into an uncontrolled mysticism. By the eve of the Reformation it was exhausted, ready to be replaced definitively by a hermeneutic resting on and tied to the literal (historical) sense of the text.

[R. E. MCNALLY]

MONASTIC EXEGESIS

The history of medieval exegesis unfolds in two successive stages of development: the monastic (*c.* 650–1200) and the scholastic (*c.* 1200–1500), which are distinctively different in method, scope, and purpose. In the monastic phase, Biblical studies were ordered to *meditatio* and *contemplatio.* The Bible stood in the center of the monastic liturgy, which was the core of the spiritual life. In the scholastic, *quaestio* and *disputatio* were fundamental to Biblical studies. Up to about 1250 Biblical studies dominated the academic program of monastery and university.

General Characteristics. The monastic approach to Scripture was pious and volitional, whereas the scholastic, learned and intellectual. Representative of the former is the first sermon of St. BERNARD OF CLAIRVAUX (d. 1153), *In Cantica Canticorum* (*Patrologia Latina* 183:785–789), while PETER LOMBARD's (d. 1160) prologue to his Commentary on the Epistles of St. Paul [*Miscellanea Lombardiana* (Novara 1957) 110–12; *Patrologia Latina* 191:1297] illustrates scholastic exegesis. For both monk and schoolman the Bible was the *regina scientiarum,* not only because it contained God's inspiration and revelation, but also because it was the deposit of all true wisdom and piety, the focus of all true education and learning. Its exegesis was an almost infinite task because of its *mira profunditas,* that wondrous profundity, which scarcely any man could ever fathom. But the exegete's progressive uncovering of this profound deposit of truth made possible the progressive development of dogma. Education was ordered to preparing the exegete; and the task of exegesis, the interpretation of Scripture, coincided with the task of theology. Up to the end of the 13th century the terms *theologia* and *Sacra Scriptura* coalesced in meaning. This is illustrated by the way these expressions were used interchangeably. Thus St. THOMAS AQUINAS (d. 1274) wrote: ''Haec est theologia quae sacra scriptura dicitur'' (*In Boeth. de Trin.* 5.4), and St. Bonaventure: ''Sacra scriptura quae theologia dicitur'' (*Breviloquium. Prologus*). Exegesis was accepted only inasmuch as it corresponded to the faith of the Church. Of Scripture, HUGH OF AMIENS (or Rouen; d. 1164) wrote: ''Legit et tenet Ećclesia'' (*Dialogi* 5.12). The Church reads the Holy Scripture, which it holds as its own. It is in terms of this ecclesial point of view that the medieval exegete held the formula: *Sola Scriptura.* All revelation is contained in Scripture, if one listens to it in the sense in which the Church reads it—''in fide Catholica tracta,'' as St. AUGUSTINE (*Gen. ad litt.* 12.37.70) had written.

Irish Monastic Exegesis. One of the most important centers of early medieval exegesis was Ireland, which by the middle of the 7th century had acquired a reputation for learning surpassed only by Visigothic Spain. The high excellence of Ireland is well attested by St. BEDE the Venerable (d. 735), who mentions the number and quality of the young Anglo-Saxons who went there to study the Bible. Representative of the most original Biblical scholarship of early Ireland is the pseudo-Augustinian work (*c.* 650) *De mirabilibus sacrae Scripturae* (*Patrologia Latina* 35:2149–2200), which in its historico-literal approach to the sacred text shows the continuing influence of Antiochene hermeneutics. In fact, from the extant Biblical commentaries of early Ireland it appears that certain of its scholars, with a marked penchant for the learned and the critical, preserved the tradition of Antioch long after it had ceased to be influential elsewhere. In commenting on the sacred text, the Irish stressed the *quaestio,* patristic literature, natural science, and philology. Of the *tres linguae sacrae,* Hebrew, Greek, and Latin, only the last was known; there is no evidence in Irish exegesis of a mastery of Hebrew or Greek. Moreover, despite their scientific pretensions, much of their Biblical literature shows the strong influence of the spiritual element of Alexandria, at times even to the point of fantasy. By establishing Continental centers of learning (e.g., the Abbeys of St. GALL, BOBBIO, Peronne, WÜRZBURG, LUXEUIL) they helped to prepare the subsequent CAROLINGIAN RENAISSANCE of Biblical studies. Outstanding among the early Irish students of the Bible was JOHN SCOTUS ERIGENA (d. *c.* 877), one of the few scholars (besides Sedulius Scotus of Liège and HILDUIN OF SAINT-DENIS) of that day who had a good knowledge of the Greek language.

Benedictine Monastic Exegesis. The Irish monastic movement, which had been initiated by St. COLUMBAN (d. 615), yielded in the course of the 8th century to Benedictinism, under whose aegis a network of monastic schools (e.g., the Abbeys of REICHENAU, FULDA, CORBIE, SAINT-RIQUIER) spread across Europe. True to its tradition, the Benedictine Order concentrated on Biblical studies, even in the face of serious intellectual obstacles. Of necessity, exegesis rested solely on the corrupt text of the *Vulgata latina* of St. Jerome, which, even after the Carolingian revisions (e.g., of ALCUIN, *c.* 800), was still far from perfect. Rare was the scholar who was able to read the Greek text of the NT, and the Septuagint was for all practical purposes an unknown book. By the year 700 Greek had disappeared from the West; and since there had never been in Latin Christendom a strong Hebrew tradition, this important Biblical language played no part in early medieval exegesis. The exegete, therefore, was forced to rely on commentaries such as St. JEROME's *Quaestiones hebraicae in Genesim,* from which various isolated Hebrew and Greek words might be excerpted to support his exegesis. At times, if he was fortunate, he might enjoy the assistance of a Jewish scholar of Hebrew. Early medieval exegesis, therefore, was built neither directly nor immediately on the Biblical languages, nor was it guided by historical, textual, or literary criticism.

Decisive in early medieval exegesis were the Fathers of the Church, authorities par excellence by reason of the official character of their witness to the ancient Christian tradition. But the exegete approached them with a reverence that was disproportionate. Too frequently his reliance on them was servile, unreasoned, narrow, rigorous, and at times simply mechanical even to the point of obscurantism. The intellectual heritage of the Fathers was neither fully transmitted to the medieval world nor fully understood by it. Certain of the works of a few Greek Fathers, such as St. JOHN CHRYSOSTOM, St. GREGORY OF NYSSA, Origen, and EUSEBIUS OF CAESAREA, were disseminated in the Latin translations of St. Jerome, RUFINUS OF AQUILEIA, EUSTATHIUS OF ANTIOCH, DIONYSIUS EXIGUUS, the school (*Vivarium*) of CASSIODORUS. But in general, the writings of the Greek Fathers were not well known. However, a much larger portion of the corpus of the Latin Fathers was transmitted to the early Middle Ages. Here interest centered especially about the works of the golden tetrad: St. AMBROSE, St. Jerome, St. Augustine, and St. Gregory the Great. But many early medieval Bible students were acquainted with these Fathers only partially, through FLORILEGIA, Biblical *CATENAE,* or collections of *sententiae* (e.g., *Liber scintillarum* of Defensor of Ligugé). Their knowledge of the Fathers derived from isolated citations and was in consequence out of context. Thus, until St. ANSELM OF CANTERBURY (d. 1109), no scholar comprehended the theology of St. Augustine as a system of thought. When a Biblical problem was posed, it was solved by citing patristic authorities, generally without identification. Frequently, spurious Bible commentaries were circulated under the names of the Fathers (e.g., Pseudo-Jerome, *Expositio quattuor evangeliorum; Patrologia Latina* 30:531–590) and were used as such. The result at times was naïve and simplistic.

Biblical apocrypha such as *The Book of Henoch, The Assumption of Mary, The Lord's Letter,* and *The Acts of Pilate* also were a factor in early medieval exegesis. Rejected by the Church, they enjoyed no dogmatic authority; their use seems to have been largely confined to supplying those imaginative situations and concrete details of which Scripture is silent.

Exegesis of Carolingian Renaissance. Carolingian Biblical literature can be divided into four general catagories. (1) collections of *quaestiones,* e.g., Wicbod's *Liber quaestionum* (*Patrologia Latina* 96:1105–68); (2) collections of *sententiae,* e.g., SMARAGDUS's *Expositio comitis* (*Patrologia Latina* 102:15–552); (3) Biblical homilies, e.g., REMIGIUS OF AUXERRE's *Homiliae duodecim* (*Patrologia Latina* 131:865–932); and (4) the continuous sustained commentary on the text, e.g., Bede's *In Marci evangelium expositio* (ed., D. Hurst, *Corpus Christianorum. Series latina* 120:431–648). These literary forms, rooted in the patristic tradition, remained despite subsequent development basic to the Middle Ages.

In the early medieval period St. Bede the Venerable stands out as the most competent master of exegesis, Bl. RABANUS MAURUS (d. 856) as the least original but the most prolific. The exegetical work of St. PASCHASIUS RADBERTUS (d. *c.* 860), with his fine sense of the literal, and that of John Scotus Erigena (d. *c.* 877), with his philosophical acumen, is marked by a fresh, advanced approach to the text of Scripture. In these two exegetes the distant future is foreshadowed. The last days of the Carolingians saw the rise of the school of Auxerre under HAIMO (d. *c.* 865), HEIRIC (d. *c.* 876), and his pupil Remigius (d. *c.* 908). The work of the first two shows that ''theological discussion was becoming a normal part of exegesis,'' while Remigius is significant for his contribution to ''the development of Biblical scholarship'' (B. Smalley). In the whole period between 650 and 900 Bible exegesis had made imperceptible but important advances: preservation of the patristic, development of criticism, and discussion of the sacred text in terms of theological problems.

Exegesis of Cathedral Schools. The period from 900 to 1028 forms an interim in the progressive development of Biblical studies. The acute crisis in which civilization had been caught at this time was not conducive to serious study. Furthermore, Cluniac monasticism (*see* CLUNIAC REFORM), so dominant in the religious life of this century, inclined to the liturgical usage of Scripture rather than to its scientific study. In the course of the 10th century the new cathedral schools (e.g., Chartres, Avranches, Paris, Rheims, Tours) tended more and more to take over leadership from the old monastic schools, though the abbey of BEC (Normandy), in the theological tradition of LANFRANC (d. 1089) and St. Anselm (d. 1109), continued supreme. However, in the new cathedral schools, where a vigorous intellectual life was flourishing, academic interest centered, not in Biblical exegesis, but in the arts and sciences. Still, the heavy stress that was placed on secular studies, especially on dialectic, served as a fundamental preparation for the subsequent development of exegesis. By putting at the service of exegesis logic (dialectic), philology (grammar), and criticism (hermeneutic), the school of Chartres under its celebrated master, FULBERT (d. 1028), formulated a program of study that flowered later on in the century.

Exegetical School of Laon. The first half of the 12th century is marked by the rise of two schools of the highest importance in the history of medieval exegesis: the school of ANSELM at Laon (d. *c.* 1117) and the School of St. Victor at Paris. As early as 1100 the school at Laon was a thriving center of learning with a reputation sufficiently high to attract Biblical students from all over Europe. The contribution of this school of exegesis is to be sought principally in Anselm's conception of scientific method: theological and Biblical systematization. The fruition of the program, insofar as it touches theology, came to fullness in the *Liber Sententiarum* of Peter Lombard (d. 1160), a student of Anselm; to perfection in the *Summa Theologiae* of St. Thomas (d. 1274), who had commented on the Sentences of Peter. The Biblical systematization of this school is incarnate in the so-called *Glossa ordinaria,* which is basically the work of Anselm. As it stands today, this glossary (marginal and interlineal) on the whole Bible (individual words, phrases, texts, etc.) represents a compilation that was originally based on *authentica* (the Fathers) but later conflated by *magistralia* (the Doctors). In time (13th–14th centuries) it became one of the most important handbooks for Biblical studies, in fact the backbone of the academic *lectio.*

Exegetical School of Saint-Victor. The school of Saint-Victor (Victorine school) was founded about 1110 by WILLIAM OF CHAMPEAUX (d. 1121), a student of Anselm of Laon. Its most distinguished master, HUGH OF SAINT-VICTOR, lectured there from 1118 until his death in 1141; and by the new program of Biblical studies, which he devised on the basis of St. Augustine's *De doctrina Christiana,* he exerted considerable influence on the development of exegetical method. For Hugh the study of the Bible was to rest on a profound, exact, almost universal education. His *Didascalion,* which presented a full academic propaedeutic to exegesis, put *scientia* at the service of *biblica.* This signified a new understanding of the function of *lectio.* Instead of sharply distinguishing the literal and the spiritual senses and considering the latter as culminating in perfect anagogy (contemplation), Hugh joined history (literal) and allegory (doctrinal) in distinction to morality. In forging this link he emphasized the historical foundation of doctrine; but while insisting on the literal sense as primary and basic to exegesis, he did not exclude the spiritual; for the finality of Bible study is simultaneously realized in knowledge (history and doctrine) and in virtue (morality and contemplation). The task of exegesis is triple: to explain letter, sense, and sentence. On the right understanding of these elements the right exegesis of the text rests. One of the most learned Victorines was ANDREW OF SAINT-VICTOR (d. 1175), whose exegesis (e.g., on the Octateuch) is characterized by its preoccupation with the literal and historical, especially with Hebrew learning. The relatively slender influence of his work, which is the product of an original, objective, critical mind, was out of proportion to its intrinsic value.

Biblical Moral School of Exegesis. The Victorine tradition was continued and developed by ''the Biblical moral school'' of PETER COMESTOR (d. 1179), PETER CANTOR (d. 1197), and STEPHEN LANGTON (d. 1228). For them the spiritual sense is still paramount; but their interest is more in the direction of tropology (moral) than allegory (doctrine), of the practical (homily) more than the speculative (theology). By about 1150 exegesis was in transition from old to new style. St. Bernard stands out as the last great representative of the monastic tradition, while in GILBERT DE LA PORRÉE (d. 1154) and Peter Lombard—both students of Anselm of Laon—the new learning of the university is foreshadowed. Both the traditional method and function of exegesis were being seriously questioned by dialecticians such as PETER OF POITIERS and Adam of the Petit Pont (d. 1181). ROBERT OF MELUN (d. 1164), author of the *Summa sententiarum,* ridiculed the slavish adherence with which the exegetes clung to the *Glossa,* while Peter Comestor criticized the *Liber sententiarum* of Peter Lombard for its excessive dialectic. The Biblical ferment of the mid-12th century would grow into the revolution of the following century, when theology and exegesis would separate as distinct intellectual disciplines.

[R. E. MCNALLY]

SCHOLASTIC EXEGESIS

High Middle Ages. The legacy of the 12th century is the intellectual setting that it created for Bible study. First, under the inspiration of Peter ABELARD (d. 1142) exegesis dared to submit the traditional patristic authorities to a rigorous, critical examination. Second, in posing new *quaestiones* on the basis of textual criticism and probing dialectic, it forced exegesis to reconsider its function, especially in relation to theology. Third, it put at the disposal of exegesis a valuable new learned literature, e.g., the *Historia scholastica* of Peter Comestor, the *Liber sententiarum* of Peter Lombard (both of which Stephen Langton equated in importance), the *Glossa ordinaria* of Anselm, and a series of handbooks for Biblical studies.

From the high Middle Ages on, exegesis was an academic exercise of the *schola,* the *studium generale,* and the university. Students (*auditores*) gathered about the master (*lector*) to hear his exposé of the *sacra pagina.* Their edited transcriptions of the lecture formed the *reportatio,* the source of much modern knowledge of medieval exegesis. The scholastic method of Biblical interpretation was rooted in the old monastic *lectio,* the reading and commenting on Scripture. The *quaestiones* that were posed were answered by citations from the Fathers. Later the *Glossa* provided a standard, traditional interpretation. But in the course of the 12th century the early schoolmen developed a more critical approach to exegesis. The new questions that they posed required a more intensive and learned treatment. In all probability the *disputatio* grew from the tension between *lectio* and *quaestio.* In the second half of the century the *disputatio* extended its scope, becoming more theological, speculative, and dialectical, and tending to drift from the sacred text that it was designed to interpret. Under the influence of Aristotelian dialectics the *quaestiones* became more refined and sophisticated, the *disputationes* more subtle and metaphysical. By the time of Stephen Langton *disput atio* had almost completely broken off from *lectio* to find in the *Liber sententiarum* of Peter Lombard a new center of interest and discussion. By about 1250, at Paris and Oxford, it had definitively separated from *lectio.* While the exegete was left free to concentrate on the text of Scripture, the theologian assumed an independent role and a new theological method: the application of metaphysics to the content of revelation to make it intelligible and systematic. (*See* THEOLOGY, HISTORY OF.)

Throughout the 13th and 14th centuries the Fathers were still cited by the exegete (e.g., St. Thomas's *Catena Aurea*), at times side by side with such authors as Plato, Cicero, Averroës, and others. With the coming of the university system in the early 13th century, exegesis became systematic, especially since Scripture was divided into chapters. Frequently the contents of Scripture were reduced to categories; e.g., *materia, modus, utilitas,* and *intentio* of the author; or according to the causes: *materialis, formalis, finalis,* and *efficiens.* More and more the literal sense was cultivated without neglecting the spiritual. St. ALBERT THE GREAT (d. 1280) insisted on the primacy of the literal sense as the basis of the spiritual, which he conceived as an expository commentary useful for pedagogy. His disciple, St. Thomas Aquinas, faithful in general to traditional exegesis, approached the sacred text from the point of view of its doctrinal content. Perhaps his greatest legacy to exegesis was his *Expositio continua,* a sustained gloss on the Gospels that ranks with the *Glossa ordinaria* of Anselm and the *Glossaria* of Stephen Langton. St. BONAVENTURE (d. 1274) admitted a manifold sense of Scripture but restricted its extension, refusing to see in the sacred text infinite mystical meanings. While accepting the validity of literal and spiritual senses, he insisted that their occurrence and interpretation should be verified in each case.

Late Middle Ages. In the late Middle Ages the *postilla* (*post illa verba* of the text) was developed as a more complete, flowing, detailed, integrated commentary on the text. At the same time, philology was stressed as an indispensable auxiliary to exegesis. Conspicuous here was ROGER BACON (d. 1292), whose *Compendium studii* developed the character of the relation of philology to exegesis as fundamental for scientific progress. His axiom is significant: *Notitia linguarum est prima porta sapientiae.* Philology is not to dominate but to serve exegesis, as dialectic was serving theology. The exegete must interpret Scripture on the basis of the original languages rather than of imperfect Latin translations. In 1311 the Council of VIENNE ordered the cultivation of Hebrew studies for exegesis [*see* HEBREW STUDIES (IN THE CHRISTIAN CHURCH)]; in the course of the 15th century Greek became more common in Biblical studies.

In the history of medieval exegesis no one since St. Jerome (d. 420) knew the Hebrew Old Testament as perfectly as NICHOLAS OF LYRA, OFM (d. 1340), master of Hebrew, Jewish, and Arabic literature. The critical and independent skill with which he explored the sacred text in his commentaries (e.g. *Postillae perpetuae in Vetus et Novum Testamentum*) mark him out as an original scholar. While ready to consult the patristic tradition in his exegesis, he refused to be bound by it. "The writings of the Fathers," he wrote, "are not of such great authority that no one is allowed to think in a contrary sense in those matters which have not been determined by Sacred Scripture itself." But the authentic Catholic spirit that animated his work is beyond question. He knew how to distinguish the scholastic from the ecclesial, the academic from the authoritative, to reject unfounded traditional exegesis, and to repudiate the arbitrary mystical senses in favor of the literal and historical. The influence of his spirit on the Reformers gave rise at a later date to the saying: *Si Lyra non lyrasset, Lutherus non saltasset* (If Lyra had not played on his lyre, Luther would not have danced).

With the coming of the Reformation and humanism, which employed the disciplines of the new learning, criticism, philology, and history, the usefulness of medieval exegesis as a hermeneutical system was virtually terminated. Face to face with this new critical spirit and its scientific technique, medieval exegesis ceased to be relevant and was discarded.

[R. E. MCNALLY]

FROM THE MEDIEVAL TO THE 19TH CENTURY

Renaissance Exegesis. The 14th century produced almost no exegetical works of permanent value. Three outstanding writers of the period were: the Dominicans Meister ECKHART (d. 1327) and NICHOLAS TREVET (d. *c.* 1330) and the Franciscan Nicholas of Lyra (d. 1349). Eckhart wrote two commentaries on Genesis, one literal and the other allegorical, as well as expositions of Exodus, Wisdom, Sirach, and 1 Corinthians and a very long commentary on John. More philosophical and theological than exegetical, these works are heavily indebted to the theology of St. Thomas Aquinas. Nicholas Trevet revealed his good knowledge of Hebrew in his strictly literal commentaries on Genesis, Exodus, Leviticus, Chronicles, and the Psalms.

Nicholas of Lyra's exegesis reflected the beginnings of a new scientific approach to exegesis which, after many vicissitudes in succeeding centuries, would eventually prevail. His best known work, *Postillae perpetuae in Vetus et Novum Testamentum,* exercised wide influence. The *Postillae,* which completed and renewed the *Glossa Ordinaria* of Anselm of Laon, was almost exclusively literal in its interpretations (see Spicq, 336). Lyra refused to accept the interpretations of the Fathers unless, in his judgment, they conformed to the literal sense of the text. During the course of the Middle Ages, Biblical exegesis had made great progress over previous centuries. It had become more and more theological and more than ever before concerned with the literal sense intended by the sacred author. The future would remedy the period's two chief defects: an imperfect knowledge of philology and an inadequate sense of the Bible as the record of God's intervention in history.

The decline in the 15th century of scholastic exegesis and the return to allegory and moralizing is reflected in the works of Jean GERSON (d. 1429) and DENIS THE CARTHUSIAN (d. 1471).

In the 16th century profound changes in Biblical studies took place, caused by the new emphasis on the study of Greek and Hebrew, the improvement in basic scriptural tools, and the exegetical principles of the Reformers, which were partially followed and partially controverted by 16th- and 17th-century Catholic exegetes.

Biblical Philology. Through the efforts of Johann REUCHLIN (d. 1522), the two Johannes Buxtorfs (father d. 1629; son d. 1664), and the Anglican John Lightfoot (d. 1675), Biblical scholars were provided with better Hebrew grammars, dictionaries, Hebrew and Aramaic concordances, and a better knowledge of rabbinical literature. The works of such scholars as Desiderius ERASMUS (d. 1536), Santes PAGNINI (d. 1541), and Robert ESTIENNE (d. 1559) enriched the field of textual criticism. The publication of the first POLYGLOT BIBLES (at Alcalá, 1514–17; Antwerp; 1569–72; Paris, 1628–45; and London, 1653–57) made easier the comparison of different Biblical texts. The principles to be followed in the restoration of the Hebrew text were set forth by the Protestants Jacques Cappel (d.1624) and his brother Louis (d. 1658) in their *Critica Sacra* (1634).

Reformation Exegesis. The translation of the Bible into German by Martin LUTHER (d. 1546) is an admitted literary masterpiece. However, neither his OT commentaries nor those of Huldrych ZWINGLI (d. 1531), Philipp MELANCHTHON (d. 1560), or John CALVIN (d. 1564) made any advance over similar works of their predecessors. The Reformers' polemical aims rendered objective, scientific exegesis difficult. They admitted the inspiration of the Bible but claimed that one's private judgment was sufficient to arrive at its evident sense. Rationalistic exegesis, the logical consequence of this principle, was soon evident in the writings of Hugo GROTIUS (d. 1645) in his *Annotationes in Vetus Testamentum* and in those of Jean LE CLERC (d. 1736) in his *Moysis libri quinque.*

Catholic OT commentaries of the period include: Tommaso de Vio CAJETAN (d. 1534), who commentated on all the OT except the Song of Songs, the deuterocanonical books, and the Prophets, and whose exegetical principles involved him in a celebrated 16th-century controversy [see T. A. Collins, ''Cajetan's Fundamental Biblical Principles,'' *The Catholic Biblical Quarterly* 17 (1955) 363–378]; Johannes MALDONATUS (d. 1583), whose OT exegesis was not equal to that of his famous Gospel commentaries; St. Robert BELLARMINE (d. 1621), who wrote an excellent commentary on the Psalms; Cornelius a LAPIDE (d. 1637), whose voluminous commentaries on all the OT books except Job and the Psalms enshrine what is best in patristic exegesis and provide useful homiletic material; Jacques Bonfrère (d. 1642), who wrote commentaries on the Pentateuch, Joshua, Judges, Ruth, and Chronicles; and, last but not least, Simon de Muis (d. 1644), whose *Commentarius litteralis et historicus in omnes Psalmos et selecta Veteris Testa-*

menti cantica cum versione nova ex Hebraico is surprisingly modern.

For the history of exegesis, however, the most significant 17th-century Catholic Biblical scholar was Richard SIMON (1638–1712), called the founder of Biblical historical criticism. In his *Histoire critique du Vieux Testament* Simon showed his keen awareness of the problems raised by the careful study of the Pentateuch, and he was the first to perceive the organic development of the OT books. His views were bitterly opposed by some as scandalous and a danger to the faith. Despite some serious defects, Simon's work won for its author a permanent place in the history of exegesis.

Eighteenth-Century Exegesis. The 18th century made little positive contribution to the history of exegesis. The works of Augustin CALMET (1672–1757) reached a new peak in Catholic exegesis, but they lacked originality. His literal commentaries on the books of the OT and the NT were solid works of great erudition and exercised great influence especially in France. Textual criticism received contributions from Charles F. Houbigant (d. 1784), Bernard de MONTFAUCON (d. 1741), Pierre SABATIER (d. 1742), Benjamin Kennicott (d. 1783), Robert Holmes (d. 1805), and Giovanni Battista de ROSSI (d. 1831).

[L. F. HARTMAN]

OLD TESTAMENT EXEGESIS IN 19TH AND 20TH CENTURIES

A new era began with Jean ASTRUC's (d. 1766) *Conjectures sur les mémoires originaux dont il parait que Moise s'est servi pour composer le livre de la Genese* (1753). The 19th century would see this literary dissection (of the Pentateuch especially) carried to extremes. Only the principal authors and their proposals can be noted here.

Literary Criticism of Pentateuch. Johann Gottfried Eichhorn (d. 1827) offered the documentary hypothesis, which added other sources to the Yahwistic and Elohistic ones. Alexander GEDDES (d. 1802) proposed the fragment hypothesis in 1792. G. H. A. Ewald (d. 1875) countered with the supplement hypothesis, according to which a fundamental historical document (*Grundschrift*) was supplemented by several other sources. Hermann Hupfeld (d. 1866) further extended the documentary hypothesis in 1853 by distinguishing three basic documents: a basic source called First Elohist, a Yahwistic source, and a Second Elohistic one. In 1854 Eduard Karl August Riehm (d. 1888) proposed Deuteronomy (D) as a fourth source, and in 1869 Theodor Noeldeke (d. 1930) extended the Documentary Hypothesis to the whole Hexateuch. He proposed three sources from the 10th and 9th century B.C. according to the following chronological order: (P) Priestly Code or First Elohist; (E) Second Elohist; (J) Yahwist, and a fourth source (D), dating from just prior to the reform of Josia (621 B.C.). Noeldeke suggested that the Pentateuch attained its final form under Ezra, who successfully promulgated it.

Wellhausen School. The brilliant Julius WELLHAUSEN (d. 1918) championed the ideas of E. G. E. Reuss (d. 1891) and Karl Heinrich Graf (d. 1869) in proposing his own widely accepted hypothesis. The classic Wellhausen thesis of the literary sources of the PENTATEUCH reads as follows: a 9th-century B.C. Yahwistic and an 8th-century B.C. Elohistic source (the latter reflecting the religious traditions of the Northern Kingdom), a fusion of J and E by the Prophets, Deuteronomy, and the Priestly code. S. R. Driver (d. 1914) in England, Léon Gautier (d. 1897) in France, and many leading scholars in Germany promoted the Wellhausen thesis. A pivotal point in the Wellhausen school was the conclusion that the principal codes of Law were composed after, not before, the period of the Prophets, who were the real founders of Israelite monotheism, fraudulently attributed to Moses. The solemn promulgation of the Law was deferred until after the Babylonian Exile. For a fuller history and elaborate bibliography of the history of OT criticism, see J. Coppens, *The Old Testament and the Critics,* tr. E. A. Ryan and E. W. Tribbe (Paterson, N.J. 1942).

In applying their theories to the whole of the Bible members of the Wellhausen school distinguished the literary history of the Israelites into three periods: (1) that of the ancient Prophets, (2) that of the composition of the various codes of the Torah (admitting that some parts of these codes, e.g., the Book of the Covenant, may well have been contemporaneous with the work of the Prophets), and (3) that of the didactic and apocalyptic literature (see Coppens, *op. cit.* 35–36). Wellhausen himself as well as others, notably, Abraham Kuenen (d. 1891) in 1869, Bernhard Duhm (d. 1928) in 1873, and B. Stade in 1905 and 1911, added to the documentary theory a reconstruction of Israel's religious history founded upon the philosophy of G. W. F. HEGEL (d. 1831) as applied to Israel's religion by certain scholars of the school of W. M. L. De Wette (d. 1849), especially J. K. Wilhelm Vatke (d. 1882). According to this school, the history of Israel's religion ought to conform to an evolutionary pattern alleged to be observable in all human history. It was claimed that the religious experience of Israel began with an animism or polydaemonism, evolved into a national henotheism, and finally, under the impetus of the great prophetical movement, as mentioned above, it developed into the ethical monotheism of the exilic and post-exilic periods (see G. E. Wright, ed., *The Bible and the Ancient Near East* [New York 1965] 3–5).

Post-Wellhausen research has considerably altered many positions originally assumed concerning the dates assigned to the four classic sources (J, E, D, P), the unity of these documents and their relative chronology, and the late date assigned by Wellhausen for the origins of all the Deuteronomic or sacerdotal laws. These researches were carried on especially by K. F. R. Budde (1890 and 1902), Immanuel Benzinger (1921), Rudolf Smend (1921), Gustav Holscher (1923), and Otto Eissfeldt (1925), among others. More recently, Gerhard von Rad, R. H. Pfeiffer, P. Romanoff, and Sigmund Mowinckel have sought for other special sources for certain parts of the Torah.

Study of Predocumentary Traditions. At the turn of the century a new phase of critical scholarship began with the work of Hermann GUNKEL (d. 1932) and H. Gressmann (d. 1927), who turned their attention to the study of the individual units of tradition contained within the various documents. It became quickly apparent that the dating of a given document by no means dated the material or traditions contained therein. The modern study of the Patriarchs clearly demonstrates this (see R. de Vaux, *Revue biblique* 53 [1946] 321–348; 55 [1948] 321–347; 56 [1949] 5–36). The new attention being paid to the Biblical traditions in their pre-literary form makes it abundantly clear that, whereas documents containing these traditions may be arranged chronologically, the material they contain cannot be as easily arranged chronologically, and as a consequence they cannot be confidently used to support an evolutionary theory of the development of Israel's religion.

As John Bright has noted (G. E. Wright, ed., *op.cit.* 7–8), all this has led scholars to abandon classical Wellhausenism without abandoning the documentary hypothesis, which stands or falls independently of Wellhausen's views; "and, so far at least, it seems in general to have stood." Opposition to Wellhausen, in whole or in part, came from several outstanding scholars, including E. König (d. 1936) and R. KITTEL (d. 1929). The search for the oral and written sources of the OT books continues.

Catholic Reaction. Catholic scholarship showed little interest in these literary problems until the end of the 19th century. M. J. LAGRANGE (d. 1938) faced the problem squarely in 1898 with his "Les Sources du Pentateuque" [*Revue biblique* 7 (1898) 10–32]. In his last published article, "L'Authenticité mosaïque de la Genèse et la théorie des documents" [*Revue biblique* 47 (1938) 163–183], he acknowledged the existence of documents and proposed that E was used by Moses who sketched the outline for J, which was written by an associate. P was a sort of *Summa* containing only essentials. Many Catholic OT scholars now agree that the documentary hypothesis is valid in principle as at least a partial answer to the problem of the origin of the OT books.

Rationalistic Criticism. In the 19th century another strong current, which came from the 18th century, was rationalistic criticism. Among its principal exponents were: G. E. LESSING (d. 1781), who divorced religion from the Bible; J. S. Semler (d. 1791), who taught that Scripture accommodated itself to contemporary prevailing beliefs; I. KANT (d. 1804), for whom exegesis meant extracting from the Bible ethical truths only; and G. W. F. Hegel, who held that each religion, with its own legends, images, and myths, reflects a stage in a religious evolutionary process; consequently, OT narratives should be interpreted merely as the myths of Israel's religion. The theory of Israel's religious evolution from lesser forms was strengthened by the works of E. B. Tylor (d. 1917) in 1871, H. SPENCER (d. 1903), J. Lippert (d. 1909) in 1881, B. Stade in 1884, and F. Schwally in 1892. Monotheism, the last stage in Israel's religious evolution, was attributed to the work of the Prophets. The panbabylonian school of Hugo Winckler (d. 1913), Friedrich Delitzsch (d. 1922), and others (*see* PANBABYLONIANISM) attributed it to a hidden monotheism in Mesopotamia (see A. Robert and A. Tricot, *Guide to the Bible*, rev. and enl. [Tournai–New York] 1:713–722).

Twentieth-Century Exegesis. At the turn of the 20th century, despite variety concerning details, there was substantial agreement on most OT problems among all leading scholars (see H. H. Rowley, "Trends in OT Study," *The Old Testament and Modern Study* [London 1961] xv–xxxi). After World War I, however, a greater variety of positions on fundamental points emerged. Scholars now recognized a far greater unity in the Bible than before. This led to a renewed interest in the BIBLICAL THEOLOGY of the OT (see R. C. Dentan). During the mid-20th-century there arose new knowledge, new approaches to old problems, new applications of older principles, and new tests of conclusions long since held sacred. A host of new OT scholars won a permanent place in the history of exegesis (W. F. ALBRIGHT, J. Bright, M. Burrows, W. Eichrodt, F. V. Filson, A. Gelin, H. W. Hertzberg, R. A. F. MacKenzie, J. L. McKenzie, S. MOWINCKEL, J. Lindblom, M. Noth, G. von Rad, H. H. Rowley, P. W. SKEHAN, R. de Vaux, and A. Vincent, to name but a few). There was a gradual tendency among 20th-century exegetes to adopt a more conservative opinion on many OT problems.

During this period Catholic Biblical scholarship came of age. Inspired by the directives of the Church, Catholic scholars in both Europe and America won for themselves honored places in Biblical studies. New Catholic Biblical societies were formed, new scientific journals founded, scholarly Biblical faculties erected, and many praiseworthy Catholic OT works continued to appear.

Among the tendencies evident in modern OT studies, the following may be noted: in Pentateuchal criticism new stress was placed on the oral traditions behind the main sources, new sources were discovered, and reconsideration was given to the dates assigned to the old sources; there also existed a widespread tendency to interpret as rituals many historical and prophetical texts as well as many Psalms; there was a strong proposal from the Scandinavian school that the traditio-historical method of investigation were more fruitful than literary criticism in solving various OT problems.

[L. F. HARTMAN]

NEW TESTAMENT EXEGESIS IN 19TH AND 20TH CENTURIES

The exegesis of the principal reformers, M. Luther, J. Calvin, and P. Melanchthon, had ignored the interpretation of the Church and was subjective and mystical in character and far removed from traditional historical enquiry.

Rationalistic Exegesis. The rationalists, in the name of the ''ENLIGHTENMENT,'' sought to emancipate themselves from the ''darkness'' of Christian revelation. Their fundamental principles denied the existence of the supernatural and affirmed that only what is rational is real. In France, England, and Germany charges of fraud and deception were hurled against Christ and His Apostles. H. S. REIMARUS (d. 1768) attributed the beginnings of Christianity to the Apostles, who had idealized the person and teachings of Christ. Heinrich E. G. Paulus (d. 1851) claimed that the Gospels narrated the testimony of witnesses more or less subject to hallucinations. In his *Life of Jesus* (1835) D. F. STRAUSS (d. 1874) held that the Gospel texts, which the rationalists found so difficult, were really mythical in origin. F. C. BAUR (d. 1860) tried to reconstruct the history of the early Church before the appearance of the Gospel myths. Bruno BAUER (d. 1882) maintained that Christ's very existence was a myth. All these writers used Hegelian philosophy as a foundation for their rationalistic exegesis (*see* HEGELIANISM AND NEO-HEGELIANISM).

Reaction to these extreme positions came from J. Ernest RENAN (d. 1892) and especially such liberal Protestants as Bernhard Weiss (d. 1918), Karl Theodor Keim (d. 1878), E. G. E. Reuss (d. 1891), Albert Reville (d. 1906), H. J. HOLTZMANN (d. 1910), and A. von HARNACK (d. 1930). The liberals themselves, however, were opposed by those who wished to free the study of Christ and the Gospels from all philosophies, e.g., Johannes Weiss (d. 1914) and William Wrede (d. 1906). Another strong current at the turn of the 20th century was syncretism, which sought to trace Christian teachings back to various elements in Near Eastern religious speculations, especially those derived from Hellenism. For good summaries of NT trends in the 20th century, see A. Hunter; R. H. Fuller. Only the highlights can be noted here.

Quest for the Historical Jesus. Most influential was the eschatological approach of Albert Schweitzer (d. 1965), in his *Von Reimarus zu Wrede* [1906; *The Quest of the Historical Jesus,* tr. W. Montgomery (New York 1961)], which forced NT scholars to face the problem of eschatology in the Gospels. In his detailed story of the quest for the historical Jesus in the 19th century Schweitzer had revealed the aim of the search: to discover the original teachings of Jesus and through these teachings to test the authenticity of the Church's version of Christianity. The historio-critical method that was used promised objective and scientific results, but unfortunately the method (as it had been used especially by Wrede and Wellhausen) demonstrated quite clearly that the liberals had not reconstructed a very scientific portrait of the historical Jesus after all (see Fuller, 26–27).

Form Criticism. A new and somewhat original approach to the study of the Gospels strongly supported this conclusion. Biblical FORM CRITICISM focused its attention upon the several literary forms or types found in the Gospel narratives. Through an analytical and comparative study of these various literary forms the form critic hopes to be able to retrace the preliterary history of the Gospel traditions. The studies of M. Dibelius, *Die Formgeschichte des Evangeliums* (Tübingen 1919), Eng. tr. by B. L. Woolf, *From Tradition to Gospel* (London and New York 1934); K. L. Schmidt, *Der Rahmen der Geschichte Jesu* (Berlin 1919); R. Bultmann, *Die Geschichte der synoptischen Tradition* (Göttingen 1921), Eng. tr. of 3rd ed., 1957, by John Marsh, *History of the Synoptic Tradition* (New York 1963); and M. Albertz, *Die synoptischen Streitgesprache* (Berlin 1921) showed that the Synoptic Gospels were not written as biographies of Jesus but rather to enshrine the faith of the early Church. The critics claimed that the Gospels could not be used as a source for the reconstruction of the portrait of the historical Jesus because they had been written on a theological rather than an historical basis. These critics claimed further that any quest for the historical Jesus, taking that word historical in its usual modern sense, would prove to be in vain. Dialectical theologians, such as Karl Barth and Martin Kähler, maintained it was unnecessary, since the object of our faith is not the Jesus of history but the Jesus of faith, whose saving action is proclaimed in the KERYGMA. For a balanced judgment and bibliography of form criticism, see A. Wikenhauser, *New Testament Introduction* (New York 1958), Eng. tr. by J. Cunningham, 253–277.

Demythologizing. In 1941 Rudolf Bultmann delivered his now famous lecture, *Neues Testament und Mythologie,* in which he offered an outline of a program to demythologize the NT (*see* DEMYTHOLOGIZING). Much scholarly literature has been published in the course of the debate concerning NT myths (H. W. Bartsch, ed., *Kerygma and Myth* I [London 1960], Eng. tr. by R. H. Fuller, for ''New Testament and Mythology'' [1–44] and bibliography [224–228]). For a dozen years (1941–53) a most heated debate raged over Bultmann's aims and methods.

The New Quest. The debate, while hardly finished, occasioned a return to the quest of the historical Jesus. This began in 1953 when Ernst Käsemann, one of Bultmann's outstanding pupils, delivered a lecture in which he turned his attention to the old problem of the Jesus of history. The story of this new quest, as well as an evaluation of contributions by Käsemann, G. Bornkamm, H. G. Conzelmann, and others has been well told by J. M. Robinson in *A New Quest of the Historical Jesus* (London and Naperville 1959); see also Fuller, 25–53.

Synoptic Studies. Modern studies in the Synoptic Gospels exhibited a significant shift of emphasis in many areas (*see* SYNOPTIC GOSPELS). Formerly little attention was paid to the Evangelists' personal contributions to their Gospels. As Fuller (71) remarked, the Synoptic Evangelists were considered more as simply collectors of oral traditions, as men standing at the end of a pipeline collecting in a bucket what came through, arranging it a little, perhaps, but making little personal contribution to NT theology. By the mid-20th century more attention was paid to the distinctive interpretation each Evangelist applies to the traditions at his disposal and the principles that guide him in the arrangement of these traditions for his own kerygmatic purposes. The problem of distinguishing the main strata or layers of Synoptic material remained only partially solved and continued to invite new and improved solutions. The Synoptic problem intrigued a new generation of NT scholars, as it always did in the past. The scholars in the forefront of modern studies in the Synoptic Gospels were G. Bornkamm, R. Brown, J. M. Robinson, H. G. Conzelmann, and W. Marxsen, among many others. For further details, especially concerning the Lucan writings, see Fuller, 70–100.

Johannine Studies. In Johannine studies, too, a remarkable change took place during the 20th century. No longer were commentators concerned primarily with the questions of authorship, date, and provenance. The earlier critics were intent upon studies of vivisection, partition, and rearrangements of the original order of the Fourth Gospel. Many now agreed with C. H. Dodd that it is ''the duty of an interpreter at least to see what can be done with the document as it has come down to us before attempting to improve upon it.''

Other modern positions on principal Johannine problems may be stated briefly. (1) Regarding authorship, most scholars were content to attribute the Fourth Gospel to an unknown disciple of the Apostle (so, more or less, C. H. Dodd, C. K. Barrett, and R. Bultmann), although R. H. Lightfoot noted that no one has shown it is impossible that the Apostle John was the author. (2) Regarding the date, the general tendency was toward A.D. 100 or even earlier. (3) On the question of John's relation to the Synoptics there was a shift from the older position that claimed John knew and used at least Mark and Luke to the total rejection of any dependence (so Dodd and Bultmann but not Barrett). B. Noack in *Zur Johanneischen Tradition* (Copenhagen 1954) and S. Schulz in *Untersuchungen zur Menschensohn-Christologie im Johannes Evangelium* (Göttingen 1957) made important contributions to the study of pre-Johannine material imbedded in the Johannine discourses (see Fuller, 112–115). (4) Whereas the older view of an Aramaic origin for the Fourth Gospel was received indifferently, few modern scholars rejected entirely M. Black's contention that there are Aramaic logia enshrined in the Fourth Gospel's discourses (see M. Black, *An Aramaic Approach to the Gospels and Acts* [Oxford, 2nd ed. 1954]). (5) Various proposals were offered in the important study of the sources of Johannine theology. The more important sources suggested were: the OT and rabbinic literature (the conservative view), Greek philosophy and Greek religion (the older liberal view), the OT plus Greek influences by way of Hellenistic mysticism (so Dodd, Barrett, and others), and GNOSTICISM (so Bultmann and his school with variations in details) (see Fuller, 118–125).

The discovery of the DEAD SEA SCROLLS opened up new avenues of approach to many Johannine problems. More recent studies arising from the material of the QUM'RAN COMMUNITY seemed to tend, at least in some measure, toward conservative positions in the questions of authorship, date, and provenance.

Pauline Studies. At the beginning of the 20th century the great problem concerning the Pauline Epistles was their authenticity. A century later only the Ephesians and the Pastorals are considered by some to be doubtfully authentic. The old question of the meaning of the term GALATIA is still being debated, though the weight of critical scholarship seems to be on the side of the defenders of the South-Galatian theory, who claim Paul used the term politically (*see* GALATIANS, EPISTLE TO THE). The provenance of the CAPTIVITY EPISTLES, the destination of the

16th chapter of Romans, and the literary unity of 2 Corinthians still exercise NT scholars.

Especially in the mid-20th century new and significant studies were published, including R. Bultmann, *Theology of the New Testament,* tr. K. Grobel (2 v. London 1955–56), which devoted more than 300 pages in v. 1 to an anthropological treatment of Pauline thought; J. Munck, *Paul and the Salvation of Mankind,* tr. F. Clarke (London and Richmond 1959), which stressed the concept of SALVATION HISTORY in Paul's writings [see C. K. Barrett, *From First Adam to Last* (New York 1962) for a similar treatment and R. H. Fuller, 54–68 for an appraisal of both Bultmann and Munck]; and R. Schnackenburg, *New Testament Theology Today,* which was widely consulted for all modern aspects of NT theology.

Catholic Exegesis. In the period following the Council of Trent Catholic exegesis was understandably characterized by a strong apologetic spirit, prompted by the polemical writings of the Protestants. Until about the middle of the 19th century Catholic exegetical works were, for the most part, little more than excellent compilations of Patristic citations fashioned into a strong defense of the chief doctrines of the Church and providing a treasury of homilectic source material. There were, of course, notable exceptions. J. MALDONATUS (d. 1583) composed excellent commentaries on the Gospels, which supplanted all previous Gospel commentaries (see J. M. Bover, ''El P. Juan Maldonado, Theologo y escriturario,'' *Razón y Fe* 34 [1934] 481–504). G. ESTIUS (d. 1613) wrote outstanding expositions of the Pauline and Catholic Epistles, which became classics. The NT commentaries of Cornelius a Lapide (d. 1637) were, like his OT works mentioned above, mosaics of Patristic quotations and references (see R. Galdos, ''De scripturisticis meritis Patris Cornelii a Lapide,'' *Verbum Domini* 17 [1937] 39–44, 88–96).

From the middle of the 19th century Catholic Biblical works of a more learned and scientific nature began to appear. Many now-famous collections had their beginnings after the mid-19th century: *Cursus Sacrae Scripturae, Étude Bibliques, Exegetisches Handbuch zum A.T., Die Hl. Schrift des N.T., Die Hl. Schrift des A.T., Verbum Salutis, Herders Bibel Kommentar: Die Hl. Schrift für das Leben erklart, La Sainte Bible* (Pirot-Clamer), *Regensburger Neues Testament,* and *Die Echter-Bibel.* Also many biblical periodicals under Catholic auspices made their appearance at this time: *Revue Biblique, Biblische Studien, Biblische Zeitschrift, Biblische Zeitfragen, Alttestamentliche Abhandlungen, Biblica, Verbum Domini, The Catholic Biblical Quarterly, Revista Biblica, Estudios Biblicos, Cultura Biblica, Biblische Warte, Lumière et Vie, Bible et Vie Chrétienne,* and *The Bible Today.* Evidence of the vitality of Catholic Biblical studies in the 20th century could be found in Catholic scholars' active participation in both national and international Congresses, whether sponsored by Catholic organizations or others.

Credit for the impetus given to Catholic Biblical studies must be accorded first to the Roman Pontiffs, Leo XIII for his encyclical *PROVIDENTISSIMUS DEUS*, Benedict XV for his encyclical *SPIRITUS PARACLITUS*, and especially Pius XII for his encyclical *DIVINO AFFLANTE SPIRITU*. With full support and encouragement from the Church a new generation of highly equipped NT scholars emerged from such centers of Biblical studies as Rome, Jerusalem, Louvain, Paris, and Washington, D.C. Among the more familiar names of Catholic NT scholars of the latter half of the 20th century are those of B. M. Ahern, P. Benoit, M. E. Boismard, R. Brown, S. Lyonnet, B. Rigaux, K. H. Schelkle, R. Schnackenburg, C. Spicq, D. M. Stanley, B. Vawter, and A. Voegtle, to mention but a few. These and other outstanding scholars faced the more difficult problems of NT exegesis and made significant contributions to such questions as the historicity of the Gospels, the nature of the Evangelical parables, the unfolding and development of Pauline thought, and many thorny questions concerning the interpretation of the Fourth Gospel, as well as such problems as the relation between the Bible and tradition as sources of revelation and the nature of Biblical inspiration.

In discussing the 20th century as a whole, special mention should be made of the rise of Biblical scholarship among American Catholics, who, after slow beginnings, made great progress. The Catholic Biblical Association of America (1936–), especially under its executive secretary L. F. Hartman (1948–), and *The Catholic Biblical Quarterly* (1939–) under a series of capable editors (W. REILLY, M. GRUENTHANER, E. F. Siegman, R. E. Murphy, and B. Vawter) received deserved praise for their efforts in behalf of the study of the Bible in America.

Bibliography: Pontifical Biblical Commission, ''The Interpretation of the Bible in the Church,'' *Origins* 23, no. 29 (Jan. 6, 1994) 497–524. R. M. GRANT, *A Short History of the Interpretation of the Bible* (rev. ed. New York 1963). A. VINCENT, *Judaism,* tr. J. D. SCANLAN (London 1934). W. BACHER, *Die exegetische Terminologie der jüdischen Traditionsliteratur* (Leipzig 1899). W. BACHER, *The Jewish Encyclopedia,* ed. J. SINGER (New York 1901–06) 3:164–174. M. MIELZINER, *Introduction to the Talmud* (New York 1925) 115–187. S. ROSENBLATT, *The Interpretation of the Bible in the Mishnah* (Baltimore 1935). B. SMALLEY, *The Study of the Bible in the Middle Ages* (2nd ed. New York 1952; repr. Notre Dame 1964). C. SPICQ, *Esquisse d'une histoire de l'exégèse latine au moyen âge* (Paris 1944). R. C. DENTAN, *Preface to Old Testament Theology* (rev. ed. New York 1963). H. H. ROWLEY ed., *The Old Testament and Modern Study* (Oxford 1951). R. H. FULLER, *The New Testament in Current Study* (New York 1962). A. M. HUNTER,

Interpreting the New Testament, 1900–1950 (Philadelphia 1951). E. KÄSEMANN, *Essays on New Testament Themes,* tr. W. J. MONTAGUE (London 1964). W. KLASSEN and G. F. SYNDER, eds., *Current Issues in New Testament Interpretation* (New York 1962). R. SCHNACKENBURG, *New Testament Theology Today,* tr. D. ASKEW (New York 1963). A. ALLGEIER, "Exegetische Beiträge zur Geschichte des Griechischen vor dem Humanismus," *Biblica* 24 (1943) 261–288. B. ALTANER, "Zur Kenntnis des Hebräischen im Mittelalter," *Biblische Zeitschrift* 21 (1933) 288–308. B. BISCHOFF, "Wendepunkte in der Geschichte der lateinischen Exegese im Frühmittelalter," *Sacris erudiri* 6 (1954) 189–281. M. D. CHENU, "Les Deux âges de l'allégorisme scriptuaire au moyen âge," *Revue de théologie ancienne et médiévale* 18 (1951) 19–28. H. DE LUBAC, *Exégèse médiévale,* 2 v. in 4 (Paris 1959–64). A. KLEINHANS, "De studio Sacrae Scripturae in ordine Fratrum Minorum saeculo XIII," *Antonianum* 7 (1932) 413–440. M. L. W. LAISTNER, "Antiochene Exegesis in Western Europe during the Middle Ages," *Harvard Theological Review* 40 (1947) 19–31. A. LANDGRAF, "Zur Methode der biblischen Textkritik im 12. Jahrhundert," *Biblica* 10 (1929) 445–474. J. LECLERCQ, *L'Amour des lettres et le désir de Dieu* (Paris 1957). P. MANDONNET, "L'Enseignement de la Bible selon l'usage de Paris," *Revue thomiste* NS 12 (1929) 489–519; "Travaux des Dominicains sur les Saintes Écritures," *Dictionnaire de la Bible*, ed. F. VIGOUROUX 5 v. (Paris 1895–1912) 2.2: 1463–82. R. E. MCNALLY, "Medieval Exegesis," *Theological Studies* 22 (1961) 445–454; *The Bible in the Early Middle Ages* (Woodstock Papers 4; Westminster, Md. 1959). B. SMALLEY, *English Friars and Antiquity in the Early Fourteenth Century* (New York 1960). F. STEGMÜLLER, *Repertorium biblicum medii aevi,* 7 v. (Madrid 1949–61).

[L. F. HARTMAN]

EXEMPLARISM

An epistemological or ontological teaching that makes extensive use of the notion of exemplar in explaining intelligent activity, both human and divine. An exemplar (Lat. *exemplum,* meaning a pattern or model) can be generally described as that in imitation of which something is made (or done) by an agent who himself determines the goal of his activity, i.e., an intelligent agent. According to this description, exemplar refers not only to a pattern or idea according to which a work is made—its usual meaning in philosophy—but also to a model for human action, as when Christ is spoken of as the Divine Exemplar. In any case, an exemplar is something whose likeness an intelligent agent seeks to realize as best he can, either in his action or in his work. Indeed it is a measure in the light of which he works to achieve a determinate effect. As such it exerts its own special type of CAUSALITY (*see* EXEMPLARY CAUSALITY).

The historical importance of this notion lies in the fact that it has figured prominently in theories of ultimate reality proposed by such noted minds as Plato, St. Augustine, and St. Thomas Aquinas, to mention but a few. For the Christian theologian it holds special significance because of its association with the doctrine of the Word, "in Whom all created things take their being" (Col 1.16). This article, however, treats the subject philosophically and is not directly concerned with its theological applications (*see* EXEMPLARITY OF GOD). Its purpose is to trace the main historical development of exemplarism among the philosophers of the West, paying special attention to the doctrine of divine exemplarism found in Augustine and Aquinas. A brief report on the status of that doctrine in modern philosophy is also included, and, where appropriate, some indication given of its possible significance for the individual human person.

Platonic Exemplarism. Among the ancients PLATO is the first to propose a theory of forms or ideas as causes of sensible reality. Rejecting the position of his predecessors that the material universe can be adequately explained in terms of one or more material principles moving about by chance, he proposed instead that the essential distinction and order in things is the result of mind. In the *Timaeus* he holds that the demiurge, being good and wishing to communicate his goodness, fashioned the universe after an ideal pattern (29A). Again, in the *Laws* he maintains that the ruler of the universe has ordered all things with a view to the excellence and preservation of the whole (903B). Thus, according to Plato, the universe has been made and is ruled by an all-powerful and good being who acts in light of a preconceived end.

Subsistent Archetypes. While it would be logical to assume that the universe's plan is in the mind of its ruler and maker, there is good reason to believe that Plato regarded the world's pattern to have its own existence apart from the mind of the demiurge (cf. *Tim.* 28A). This is almost certainly the case with regard to the archetypes of the various classes of sensible reality. In the *Timaeus,* for instance, the statement is made that sensible changing things are "likenesses of real existences modelled after their patterns in a wonderful and inexplicable manner" (50). The "real existences" to which Plato refers are abstracted class concepts that he hypostatized and regarded as co-causes with material elements in the original production of things.

Strictly speaking, then, Plato's demiurge is not a creator, but is conceived as a human maker with the existence of matter (and forms) definitely assumed. Nor, ironically, can it be said that the forms are true exemplars, since they exist apart from the intentional order. In other words, a sensible substance's archetype would have to be that substance's idea existing in the mind of its maker. Still, it is to Plato's credit that he was the first philosopher to recognize that the universe manifests an intelligent plan, thereby revealing the wisdom and goodness of its maker.

Aristotle's Reaction. As generally known, ARISTOTLE, Plato's long-time disciple and friend, found it necessary to repudiate his teacher's doctrine of ideas. According to the Stagirite, the ideas are not needed to explain sensible being and becoming, and furthermore, positing their existence leads to many absurd consequences (cf. *Meta.* 991a 8-b 9). On his part, however, he was unable to pursue the sound suggestion of PARTICIPATION contained in Plato's doctrine. Consequently, for want of a doctrine of CREATION, exemplarism does not figure prominently in his thought, and despite his expressed approval of the view that the universe is ruled by mind, one finds no evidence in Aristotle's writings that he consistently regarded this ruler as governing according to a preconceived plan. Indeed, as more than one Aristotelian scholar has noted, Aristotle's conception of God precludes Him from knowing any being except Himself.

Augustine's Divine Exemplars. With the advent of Christianity, a doctrine of creation enters the mainstream of Western European philosophy, and with it a doctrine of divine exemplarism. St. AUGUSTINE, though sympathetic to much in Plato, as a Christian had to reject the latter's doctrine of ideas, at least in its original form. Thus, according to Augustine, the archetypes of things are not, as Plato had erroneously thought, realities subsisting apart from the divine mind (*Divers. quaest.* 83.46.1–2). Nor are they contained in some intellect distinct from the First Principle, as PLOTINUS had maintained. Consequently, while he admired the Plotinian doctrine of the Nous in view of its close resemblance to the Christian doctrine of the Word, Augustine could not accept the emanation theory underlying it, according to which the universe proceeded by necessity from the One via the Nous and World Soul.

In the Christian view of creation, the universe was made directly by God in light of a plan that He had freely determined upon. Moreover, for Augustine, the ideas of all created things are contained in the Word, the Second Person of the Trinity, who is the same in substance with the Father. As to how one can in any sense acknowledge a plurality of Ideas in the divine intellect without at the same time compromising the divine simplicity, Augustine left no answer. Lacking an existential doctrine of participation, he was unable to root the divine ideas in the divine essence as imitable (Civ. 11.29). Finally, inasmuch as all things are made through Him, there can be nothing that is essentially EVIL—a point worth noting since Augustine, while a Manichean, had held an opposite position.

Exemplarity in Aquinas. While Augustine had relied primarily on his Christian faith to form his views on creation and exemplarism, St. THOMAS AQUINAS, though doubtlessly influenced by revelation, arrived at many of the same truths philosophically. His unique existential approach to reality enabled him to establish quite readily, by reason alone, the existence of an Absolute Being who is at once the ultimate efficient, exemplary, and final cause of all of finite reality. This provided a rational foundation for his Judeo-Christian belief in God as the Self-Existing Being ("I am Who am") and Creator and Lord of the universe.

Doctrine of Creation. In his philosophy of creation, Aquinas sharply opposed both his Greek and Arabian predecessors, all of whom had viewed the universe as necessarily eternal. Although of the opinion that the universe's beginning in time is a truth entirely *de fide,* he also insisted, strictly on metaphysical grounds, that it would always require to be created, and freely (*Summa theologiae* 1a, 46.1). On this last point, St. Thomas took particular issue with the Arabian philosopher, AVICENNA, who taught that the universe proceeded from a plurality of causes by way of a necessary emanation beginning from God, the absolutely simple Being. Aquinas rejected such a theory of the universe's origin for several reasons: (1) It maintained that creatures can create; (2) it reduced God to the finite level by having a creature proceed from Him by natural necessity; and (3), of most concern here, it denied the role of divine wisdom in creation, since, according to this account, the distinction and order found in things proceeds not from the intention of a first agent, but from the accidental convergence of many causes, which is to say from CHANCE (*De pot.* 3.16).

In Aquinas's view, the multitude and distinction of things making up the order of the universe must be traced to the intellect of the first agent, God. For God, who alone is responsible for the original production of things (since only a being in act by its whole substance can produce the whole substance of another being—*ibid.* 3.4) has brought things into existence with a very definite purpose in mind. This purpose could only be to reflect His goodness. And inasmuch as that goodness is more adequately represented by a multitude of beings than it would be by any one creature alone, divine wisdom itself is responsible for the multitude and distinction of created things (*Summa theologiae* 1a, 47.2).

Multitude and Simplicity. In answer to the question posed by Neoplatonists as to how multitude and distinction can arise from an absolutely simple Being, St. Thomas had the following reply. God, in creating, does not act through any natural necessity but through His own intellect and will (*De pot.* 3.16 ad 5). Now in knowing His own essence perfectly, God knows it not only as it is in itself, but also as it can be participated in by creatures according to some degree of likeness. Consequently, in the very act whereby He knows Himself, God also knows the proper type of each and every thing He would and could create. It is in this manner, therefore, that the divine intellect can be said to contain many ideas without detriment, however, to the divine simplicity (*ST* 1a, 15.2).

St. BONAVENTURE, although not employing the notion of participation in his solution to this problem, would appear to be saying basically the same thing as Aquinas when he argues that the divine essence, since it is outside any genus, can be the likeness of each and every creature. (*In 1 sent.* 35.1.2 ad 2). For Aquinas, the divine essence is itself the exemplary cause of all finite reality, insofar as it is understood by God, with the proportion that each creature to be produced has to it (*De ver.* 3.2).

Participation of Existence. As just seen, St. Thomas, like Augustine before him, corrects Plato's theory of ideas by making the divine essence the supreme archetype in light of which each finite being is made and of which it can be said to participate according to some degree of likeness. In a word, the Platonic ideas are rejected in favor of the one Being to whom alone existence is proper. Since such a Being is the fullness of existence, all other beings participate (by way of likeness) in His infinite existence by receiving their existence from Him (*C. gent.* 1.75). Hence, while Aquinas borrowed the notion of participation from Plato, he adapted it to meet the demands of his own existential philosophy, within which context it comes to mean a participation in the perfection of EXISTENCE rather than in some absolute class idea that alone is regarded to be fully real. Since the essence of the finite being is a certain potentiality for existence that receives its actual existence from God, it is originally a possible imitation of the divine essence in the intellect of God (*ibid.* 1.54).

Divine Knowledge. A doctrine of divine exemplarism is therefore employed by St. Thomas to explain the determinate nature that characterizes the existence of each finite being and upon which gradation in being is consequent. Such a doctrine also implies God's providence and eternal law, for existence is conferred upon the creature in a determinate manner so that it can realize in its completed state the measure of the divine goodness for which it has been made. Furthermore, for Aquinas, even matter, although having no actual existence of its own, participates in some way in existence and therefore finds its prototype in God, but as part of the idea of the composite (*De pot.* 3.1 ad 12). Consequently, God's archetypal knowledge includes a knowledge of things, not only according to their specific or class nature, which is consequent upon form, but also according to their very INDIVIDUATION, which is consequent upon matter (*ST* 1a, 14.11; *De ver.* 2.5).

On this particular question Aquinas opposed by anticipation the opinion of WILLIAM OF OCKHAM that seemingly denies to God archetypal knowledge of the various classes of things (for, according to Ockham, only the individual is real), as well as the views of certain ancient Greek philosophers and their followers who denied to God any knowledge of singulars. The importance of St. Thomas's position for the individual human person cannot be overemphasized, since it holds that each individual reality, oneself included, is known and loved by God as a reflection of Himself. As regards evil, since it is a privation of being, it bears no likeness to the divine essence and, consequently, has no exemplary idea in God, even though it is known by God as a certain absence of His goodness in the creature (*De ver.* 3.4).

Ontological Truth. St. Thomas's doctrine of exemplarism also contributes to a better understanding of the TRUTH OF BEING. Since the finite being is said to receive its existence from God, its truth is to be seen in its necessary conformity to the divine intellect. Hence, independent of their conformity to the human intellect, all things are essentially true by virtue of their necessary conformity with their proper mental types in the divine mind (*ibid.* 1.4). As Truth Itself, God is necessarily the ultimate source of the truth or intelligibility of every finite being. Thus is He said to be "the Light of the World," for it is according to an idea of Himself as imitable that all things are made and in Him that all creatures find their truth and ultimate meaning. In theological terms the end of creation is therefore to be seen in the glorification of the God-Man, since "through Him and for Him all things were made" (Col 1.17). In St. Thomas's doctrine of the truth of being there is no room for the RELATIVISM so typical of contemporary thought.

Modern Philosophy. With the emergence of the modern period of Western European philosophy, the doctrine of exemplarism all but totally disappears. True, among the moderns one finds both René DESCARTES and G. W. LEIBNIZ accepting the Christian doctrine of creation, but little provision is made for it in their respective theories of reality. Thus, the proofs they generally advance for God's existence do not proceed from the fact of contingent existence, but from the concept of the perfect being.

Descartes. As regards exemplarism, Descartes maintained, in the voluntarist tradition, that the essences of things and their intrinsic possibility are contingent upon the divine will. Therefore, man's essence, for example, instead of being from all eternity a possible imitation of the divine essence in the divine intellect, is the product of divine decree, for, if God had so willed it, man could have been something other than a rational animal. Such a theory places the divine will beyond the law of contradiction, and in so doing, undermines the possibility of knowing God analogically. In his mechanistic explanation of the physical universe Descartes also dispensed with the need for divine CONCURRENCE and PROVIDENCE.

Leibniz. On the other hand, Leibniz's theory concerning the order of possibles—an order that he regarded as eternal in its own right—went to the opposite extreme of Descartes's position, making the divine will in some way subject to that order. In other words, he also failed to see that the intrinsic possibility of things is rooted in the divine essence as imitable. What is more, his intellectual determinism, according to which one must always choose the greater good, led him to deny of God liberty of specification with respect to His effects. Thus, having willed to create, God must create the best of all possible worlds. Leibniz's error here obviously consisted in not recognizing that the divine goodness is in no way bound to any created order of things, that it can be manifested in some degree in any universe God freely should choose to create.

Other Moderns. B. SPINOZA completely rejected the idea of a free creation, regarding all finite beings as modes of God's infinite substance.

A current of thought quite different from the RATIONALISM of DESCARTES, Spinoza, and Leibniz developed within the British empirical school, whose most notable representatives are T. HOBBES, J. LOCKE, and D. HUME (*see* EMPIRICISM). This school characteristically denied to the intellect any object in reality distinct from that of sense, thereby giving rise to POSITIVISM. Since their theories of knowledge restricted the human mind to the order of sense appearances, thus challenging the very possibility of metaphysics, none of the empiricists can be found supporting a doctrine of ideas.

Nor did this doctrine fare any better with modern IDEALISM, which originates from Immanuel KANT. In the idealistic stream of thought, no sharp distinction is drawn between the world and absolute mind, the result usually being some form of PANTHEISM.

Contemporary Schools. Finally, as regards the status of exemplarism in contemporary philosophy, it need only be noted that a doctrine maintaining the world to be a reflection of God's infinite goodness and beauty can hardly find fertile soil in the current schools of philosophy, all of which question the very possibility of proving God's existence and generally equate reality with the world of change.

See also. EMANATIONISM; NEOPLATONISM.

Bibliography: E. H. GILSON, *The Christian Philosophy of Saint Augustine* (New York 1960). F. C. COPLESTON, *History of Philopsophy* (Westminster, Md. 1946–) 2:71–73, 258–270. J. D. COLLINS, *History of Modern European Philosophy* (Milwaukee 1954). H. PINARD, *Dictionnaire de théologie catholique*, ed. A. VACANT et al., (Paris 1903—50) 3.2:2150–63. G. FAGGIN, *Enciclopedia filosofica* (Venice-Rome 1957) 2:47.

[T. J. KONDOLEON]

EXEMPLARITY OF GOD

The doctrine that God, besides being the efficient and final cause of CREATION, is also its exemplar. An exemplary cause is the model according to which something is made or done. The extramental model, if there be one, responds to an IDEA in the mind of the maker or doer. The exemplary cause is necessarily and intimately united with the final and efficient causes in producing an effect. However, it is properly called an extrinsic formal cause because of its affinity to the intrinsic formal cause, which intrinsically actualizes and specifies the effect. Thus, in educing the form (intrinsic formal cause) out of the clay, the potter (efficient cause) is guided by his idea (exemplary cause) of a vessel which must hold two quarts of water (final cause).

The doctrine of EXEMPLARISM began to be formulated when man first questioned how ''the many'' could come from ''the one,'' or how one exemplar could be multiplied in many individuals. The scholastics solve the difficulty by saying: it is true that no creature can perfectly represent or imitate the divine perfection, which is infinite; but God, who is a voluntary agent, produces many creatures so that what is lacking to one creature's representational capacity is supplied by another's (St. Thomas Aquinas, *Summa theologiae* 1a, 47.1). The degrees of imitation of the divine essence range from the pure potentiality of prime matter to the superior beings which, while they approach God, can never be equal to Him because of His infinity (*Summa contra Gentiles* 2.45, 46). The uncreated ideas are many, and yet do not destroy the divine simplicity because they are identified with the divine essence. They are said to be ''many''—even infinite in number—inasmuch as God knows His essence as imitable by creatures in an infinite number of ways (*Summa theologiae* 1a, 15.1–3; 44.3; *In Dion. de div. nom.* 4.2; 5.3).

The uncreated exemplars can be said to be the total idea that God has of Himself as imitable by creatures. Indeed, the Word is this total idea because He is the perfect expression, always actual, of the infinite number of ways that creatures can imitate God; and, in fact, ''all things were made through him [the Word]'' (Jn 1.3). Hence it is that the Word is *the* exemplar of creation, and that Christ is ''the image of the invisible God, the firstborn of every creature'' (Col 1.15, 16; cf. Prv 8.30; St. Thomas, *In Ioann.* 1.2; *In Col.* 1.4).

See Also: CAUSALITY, DIVINE; EXEMPLARY CAUSALITY; IMAGE OF GOD; LOGOS; SIMILARITY.

Bibliography: A. AMPE, *Dictionnaire de spiritualité ascétique et mystique. Doctrine et histoire*, ed. M. VILLER et al. (Paris 1932—) 4.2:1870–78. L. VAN DER KERKEN, *Lexikon für Theologie und Kirche*, ed. J. HOFER and K. RAHNER (Freiburg 1957–65) 3:1294–95. P. BEILLEVERT, *Catholicisme* 3:276–288. H. VOLK, *Handbuch theologischer Grundbegriffe*, ed. H. FRIES (Munich 1962–63) 2:494–517. T. M. SPARKS, *De divisione causae exemplaris apud S. Thomam* (River Forest, Ill. 1936).

[C. J. CHERESO]

EXEMPLARY CAUSALITY

A special type of CAUSALITY associated with the doctrine of exemplarism and mainly discussed by scholastic philosophers and theologians. It specifies the determination or form of an effect as this is preconceived by an intelligent agent. While scholastics generally agree that the exemplary cause is not itself a fifth type of cause, they part company on the question to which of the traditional four it is more properly reduced. Some conceive it as a type of EFFICIENT CAUSALITY and others classify it under the causality of FORM; a third, and possibly more acceptable, position regards it as an aspect of FINAL CAUSALITY.

A few thinkers, such as DUNS SCOTUS and F. SUÁREZ, regard exemplary causality as within the order of efficient causality, no doubt because of the exemplar's close connection with the will of the intelligent agent. Even St. THOMAS AQUINAS, who considered the exemplar to be a type of formal cause, occasionally refers to it as an operative idea (*De ver.* 2.3 ad 3; *Summa Theologiae* 1a, 15.1 ad 2). This is because the exemplary form or idea exerts its influence upon the effect only through the will (*Summa Theologiae* 1a, 14.8). It thus touches upon the very causality of the efficient cause, whence it is said to be an operative or productive idea.

Strictly speaking, however, since the exemplary cause is of the intentional order, being the idea of some form or determination to be realized in the effect, it is not a type of efficient cause. Rather its function is to direct the agent, measuring his action every step of the way. Because the exemplary cause is the form of the work as preconceived by the intelligent agent, St. Thomas and many of his followers regard it as reducible to the genus of formal cause. However, they then speak of it as being an extrinsic formal cause. While this view is certainly tenable, for the exemplar is a preconceived form, it has the weakness of doing violence to the intrinsic-extrinsic division of causes, according to which division the formal cause is intrinsic to the being of its effect.

Consequently, since the exemplary cause is extrinsic to the effect and exerts its influence as an idea in the intentional order, it is more properly reducible to final cause. Thus, while the final cause considered as a preconceived form of a work exerts an attractive influence upon the will of the agent, it performs at the same time a secondary role of measuring the agent's action; in the latter respect it is an exemplar. Since one might think that the exemplary cause is not always of the intentional order—because the artist often selects for his model something already in existence—it must be noted that the object selected has been assimilated to the intellect of the artist, and that even in this case the artist is working under the influence of an idealized form (cf. *De ver.* 3.2).

Thus, while the exemplary cause does touch upon the areas of efficient and formal causality, precisely as exercising its influence as an idea in the intentional order it can be identified with the final cause.

See Also: EXEMPLARISM; NEOPLATONISM; EMANATIONISM.

Bibliography: C. A. HART, *Thomistic Metaphysics: An Inquiry into the Act of Existing* (Englewood Cliffs, N.J. 1959). G. GIRARDI *Metafisica della causa esemplare in San Tommaso d'Aquino* (Turin 1954). A. FOSSATI, *Enciclopedia Italiana di scienze, littere ed arti*, 36 v. (Rome 1929–39) 2:46–47.

[T. KONDOLEON]

EXEMPLUM

A minor genre of medieval literature; a short moralized narrative used to illustrate the abstract theme of a sermon. Although such a device has probably been used informally by religious teachers in every age of the world, the *exemplum* as a literary type had definite historical associations and a limited period of florescence and decline. It was not characteristic of the PREACHING tradition in Europe until the 12th century, probably because of the strong emphasis on allegorical exegesis in scriptural commentary and homiletic method in the patristic period. The 12th-century renaissance in western Europe, which produced so much historical writing in Latin and such distinguished experiments in vernacular narratives as the *lai* and the romance, provided the impetus and the materials for the rise of the *exemplum*. In the early 13th century the movement of the preaching friars in various countries, committed to religious instruction of lay people through the vernacular sermon, created the great vogue of the *exemplum* for a century and more.

The anecdotes that form the substance of the type could be either religious or secular, and either historically true or fictional. The whole range of human experience was material for this sermon technique, and could be used for the fundamental purpose of providing a moral lesson. Often the exotic legend or the comic fable, by its inherent charm or amusing quality, provided the more disarming vehicle for the applied *moralité*. The personal reminiscenes of the preacher himself, or his reading of a historical literature, gave him the opportunity of creating a reportorial art, and this same skill often enabled him to adapt an anecdote that was centuries old so as to include local details or contemporary reference delightful to the listeners. Surviving *exempla* reveal the fondness for homely realism and a satirical spice that explain much in the comic spirit of late medieval and Renaissance writers such as Chaucer and Boccaccio. Narratives of conjugal life and its tensions humorously presented, antifeminist satire, jests told by the lowly and humble at the expense of the powerful and wealthy—these are the essence of many *exempla*. No better illustration of these qualities can be found than the ''Nonnes Preestes Tale of the Cock and Hen.'' The homely but subtle *exemplum* on pride, told by Chaucer's pilgrim chaplain may well be the masterpiece of the *The Canterbury Tales*.

The 13th century was the era in which manuscript collections of *exempla* were first made and circulated as reference volumes for preachers. Such compilations had various principles of arrangement. Some of them were alphabetized by the virtues and vices commonly discussed in sermons, and contained the relevant anecdotes in serial order. This pattern is found in John of BROMYARD's *Summa predicantium*. Others were organized around a common theme, e.g., the fall of great men, and thus achieved a superior unity, as in Chaucer's ''Monk's Tale,'' in which the repeated catastrophes create a sense of tragic irony. Continental collections are generally regarded as superior to those made in England. Among the best-known are those connected with the names of JACQUES DE VITRY, Étienne de Bourbon, VINCENT OF BEAUVAIS, and CAESARIUS OF HEISTERBACH. One such volume, gathered originally in England is a great work; known as the *GESTA ROMANORUM*, it contained and circulated widely a number of stories later elevated to masterful literary art by Shakespeare.

Bibliography: J. T. WELTER, *L'Exemplum dans la littérature religieuse et didactique du moyen âge* (Paris 1927). J. A. MOSHER, *The Exemplum in the Early Religious and Didactic Literature of England* (New York 1911). G. R. OWST, *Literature and Pulpit in Medieval England* (New York 1961). R. CANTEL and R. RICARD, *Dictionnaire de spiritualité ascétique et mystique. Doctrine et histoire*, ed. M. VILLER et al. (Paris 1932—) 4.2:1892–1902.

[E. C. DUNN]

EXEMPTION, HISTORY OF

Exemption, in general, is a privilege whereby persons, places, or things are removed from the jurisdiction of a superior to whom they would otherwise be subject. Canon Law recognizes exemptions of persons other than institutes of consecrated life (for example, cardinals in *Codex iuris canonici c.* 357 §2), but it is the former which has been of primary interest in the history of the Church. In the Latin Church, the exemption of institutes of consecrated life implies their removal from the governance of the local ordinaries and their subjection to the Supreme Pontiff or other ecclesiastical authority (see *Codex iuris canonici c.* 592). This article traces the development of exemption as a canonical institution. Since this development was largely determined by the evolution of the religious state (*status religiosus*) and by changes in the historical situation of the Church, the five divisions of the article are chronological.

Preparations. The problem of exemption, or more precisely, episcopal exemption, did not arise in an acute form in the earlier centuries of MONASTICISM. It was only with the emergence of predominantly clerical communities after the sixth century, that it became necessary to balance the bishop's right to control the exercise of priestly ministry within his diocese against the rights of an abbot to direct the life and work of his subjects. By the middle of the fifth century, however, certain guiding principles had already emerged: the Council of CHALCEDON (451) decreed that the bishop's permission was needed to erect a monastery and that monks must be subject to the bishop. The Council of ARLES (455) distinguished external affairs and those works of the monastery that were to be subject to the bishop from the monastery's internal affairs, in which the abbot's government was to be free of episcopal interference. During the 6th century this was the basis of most legislation regulating the relationship of monasteries and bishops, although with some local variations (African usage generally favoring greater freedom for the monastery and European usage demanding greater subjection to the bishop). Pope GREGORY THE GREAT (590–604) supported and refined the principle of Arles, especially with regard to monastic freedom from episcopal interference in electing abbots and in administering temporal goods; Gregory's frequent interventions in disputes between bishops and monks gave rise to a firm jurisprudence on many points.

Early Instances of Exemption. The first known instance of episcopal exemption in the proper sense of the term is the one granted by Pope HONORIUS I to the monastery of BOBBIO in 628. The motives for this grant were the personal prestige of its founder, St. COLUMBAN, the traditional monastic organization of the Church in the

British Isles, and the special ethnic and geographical situation at Bobbio; precedents suggesting the juridical possibility of such a grant included the Germanic usage of the *ecclesia propria* (*Eigenkirche,* or PROPRIETARY CHURCH) and the Roman-law institution of *immunitas,* e.g., of military personnel from civilian jurisdiction. Among other early examples of exemption are the two monasteries of Benevento (714 and 741) and those of Fulda (751) and FARFA (775). CLUNY was exempt from its foundation (912) and was later allowed to communicate its exemption to other monasteries joining the CLUNIAC REFORM; this concession by Rome, in support of a particular reform, was later to become a pattern for much wider communication of privileges among religious.

Late Medieval Period. The foundation of the CISTERCIANS (1119) and of the MENDICANT ORDERS a century later, gave rise to new motives for exemption: centrally organized orders working in several dioceses could accomplish their purpose only if they had considerable autonomy. Consequently, in the later medieval period all religious came to enjoy exemption from the authority of the local ordinary. This of course raised difficulties of its own; the wide granting of full exemption seriously weakened the authority of bishops and readily lent itself to abuses. Protests were voiced at the Councils of CONSTANCE (1414–18) and Fifth LATERAN (1512–17), but no legislative changes were found to meet the problem.

Tridentine Period. Strong steps to limit occasions for such abuses were taken at the Council of TRENT (1545–63) and in the papal legislation that followed the council. Some powers over religious (especially over nuns) were given back to bishops; more importantly, the number of persons enjoying exemption was sharply reduced, especially when quasi-religious communities lacking solemn vows were rigorously excluded from any share in the canonical privileges of religious. At the same time (1549) PAUL III, in the constitution *Licet debitum,* granted complete exemption to the JESUITS.

Modern Era. The period following Trent was characterized by the flowering of the great congregations of simple vows. These enjoyed a sort of partial exemption not unlike that which had been favored by GREGORY THE GREAT, i.e., with the internal regime of the community free of the bishop's authority, but with its external works subject to him. A few of the new congregations were actually given the privilege of exemption (e.g., the REDEMPTORISTS and PASSIONISTS), but most managed with a concurrently emerging jurisprudence of their own, whose major steps were the papal constitutions *Quamvis iusto* (BENEDICT XIV, 1749), and *Conditae a Christo* (LEO XIII, 1900). During the 20th century, the differences between exempt and nonexempt religious have been gradually but steadily diminished. The 1917 Code of Canon Law reasserted and strengthened the authority of bishops over all apostolic works in their territories. This authority, reiterated in conciliar and postconciliar documents, found expression in *Codex iuris canonici c.* 678, which subjects members of institutes to the authority of bishops in reference to the care of souls, public exercise of worship and other apostolic works. Further, while the 1983 Code refers to exemption in canon 591, the concept has almost been completed eliminated (see Huels).

Bibliography: A. SCHEUERMANN, *Die Exemtion nach geltendem kirchlichen Recht mit einem Ueberlick über die geschichtliche Entwicklung* (Paderborn 1938). E. FOGLIASSO, ''De extensione iuridici instituti exemptionis religiosorum logice atque historice considerati,'' *Salesianum* 9 (1947) 1–64, 147–206, 318–359; *Dictionnaire de droit canonique,* ed. R. NAZ (Paris 1935–65) 5:637–665. J. D. O'BRIEN, *The Exemption of Religious in Church Law* (Milwaukee 1943). J. HUELS, ''The Demise of Religious Exemption,'' *The Jurist* 54 (1994) 40–55. D. J. KAY, *Exemption: Origins of Exemption and Vatican Council II* (Rome 1990).

[R. W. CROOKER/R. KASLYN]

EXETER, ANCIENT SEE OF

The Ancient See of Exeter was a diocese of southwest England. In 909 Abp. PLEGMUND OF CANTERBURY subdivided the Diocese of Sherborne into three dioceses: Somerset, Cornwall, and Devon (residential city at Crediton). In 1040 Devon and Cornwall were reunited and in 1050 Exeter replaced Crediton as the see city. The Saxon abbey church became the cathedral of Bp. Leofric (1046–70), the first bishop of Exeter. Bishop William Warelwast (1107–37), nephew of William the Conqueror, began building the Norman cathedral that was consecrated in 1133. The present Decorated cathedral, which retained the twin Norman towers over the north and south transepts, was begun *c.* 1275 and finished 90 years later, much of the work being done by Bps. Walter Bronescombe (1258–80), WALTER DE STAPELDON, Peter Quivil (1280–91), and John of Grandisson (1327–69), who added the famous minstrel's gallery in the north clerestory. The clock in the north transept is attributed to Peter Lightfoot, monk of GLASTONBURY. Bishop Peter COURTENAY gave the Peter Bell. Only a few fragments of the original Saxon church remain.

Important manuscripts in the episcopal library include the deed of EDWARD THE CONFESSOR that installed Leofric, the Exeter Book of AS poetry given by Leofric (tr. B. Thorpe, 1842), and the ''Exon Domesday.'' Exeter was apparently the only English cathedral where all dignitaries and canons swore an oath to the bishop. Also, the chapter acknowledged the bishop's rights over a vacant deanery. Exeter was the site of a flourishing theological school. Later bishops included Edmund LACY (1419–55) and the reformer Miles COVERDALE (1551–53). In 1559 Exeter was made an Anglican bishopric.

Bibliography: G. OLIVER, *The History of the City of Exeter,* ed. E. SMIRKE (London 1861). E. A. FREEMAN, *Exeter* (4th ed. New York 1895). R. J. E. BOGGIS, *A History of the Diocese of Exeter* (Exeter 1922). K. EDWARDS, *The English Secular Cathedrals in the Middle Ages* (Manchester, Eng. 1949). V. HOPE and L. J. LLOYD, *Exeter Cathedral: A Short History and Description* (Exeter 1973). N. ORME, *Exeter Cathedral as it Was 1050–1550* (Exeter 1986). M. J. SWANTON and J. ALLAN, *Exeter Cathedral: A Celebration* (Crediton 1991). F. KELLY, *Medieval Art and Architecture at Exeter Cathedral* ([s.l.] 1991).

[N. DENHOLM–YOUNG/EDS.]

Exeter Cathedral, Devon, England. (©Michael Nicholson/ CORBIS)

EXISTENCE

In its root meaning, the word ''existence'' stands for presence or being present, the affirmation, manifestation, or appearance of something in any category, whether this be in nature, where it is known as material existence, or in mind, where it is known as ideal existence.

Notion of existence. Existence thus signifies the fact that something is present in nature or in mind, and this in a precise spatiotemporal way. It therefore preeminently asserts reality in act and points to BEING as the exercise or actualization of reality of any kind. As such, existence is primarily distinguished from and opposed to NONBEING or nothing; only secondarily is it distinguished from the possible (*see* POSSIBILITY). The possible differs from nothing in that nothing cannot be conceptualized and resists passage into being, whereas the possible can be conceptualized by mind and thus pass into being. Yet when the possible does not *de facto* pass into being, it has no existence in reality, that is, no existence in the full, true, and proper sense. Existence thus includes a content and is thereby related to ESSENCE. It is, in fact, the actualization of essence, its *de facto* placement (*existere*) in reality, since essence was possible before being actualized. One may say that essence exists in reality to the extent that it has passed from the sphere of possibility to that of actuality. Since it does not do this by its own power—otherwise possibility would become identical with reality—but through an external principle or cause, such existence implies the agency of some causal principle.

The affirmation of existence can be extended to formal logic and there signifies the attribution of a predicate to a subject. Similarly in the field of mathematics, one speaks of the existence of irrational numbers and of *n*-dimensional space, to the extent that such entities or postulates are logically consistent and imply consequents of use in the mathematical sciences.

Intentional levels of existence. The idea of existence, like that of reality in general, can be located on various intentional levels and distinguished according to its proper content at each level. One can thus speak of experimental existence, which is immediately sensible, and of existence that is imagined or fictive, ideal, logical, artistic, moral, legal and so on, depending on the intentional medium used to represent a particular reality.

Primary Experience of Existence. Existence in its full, proper, and primary sense is that which is affirmed by immediate sensible and mental experience, whether this be direct or indirect and whether it come from experience that is external (objective existence) or from that which is internal (subjective existence). Such existence presents itself to thought in an immediate manifestation. It is in this sense that Aristotle claims it would be ridiculous to try to show the existence of nature (*Phys.* 193a 3) and that St. Thomas Aquinas advances the fact of self-perception against the Averroists (*De unit. intell.* 3). The *de facto* existence of external experience, for example, of the books on the table where I write or of the street I see from the window, is primary and is in a certain sense the foundation for the existence of internal experience (St. Thomas, *In 3 sent.* 23.1.2). But even the existence of internal experience is immediate; it is made evident in reflective awareness of life and activity on the part of the knowing subject. Its focus is the existence of the acts and functions of the subject's perception and of states of his soul, to the extent that these deal with the instinctive and reflective life of the individual (*ibid.* ad 3).

Existence of Soul and Its Faculties. Concomitantly and by implication, the individual comes to an awareness, though indirect and conditioned by his experience, of the proximate principles that produce his knowing acts. These are his powers or faculties, namely, (1) the sense faculties, recognized through sense experience, (2) the intellect, known in the act of understanding, and (3) the will, known in the act of volition (*De malo* 6.1 ad 18). The circle of existential experience, extending all the way to the intellect, is integrated in the unity of the soul's essence (*In 3 sent.* 23.1.2 ad 3). The presence or perception of the existence of these acts and potencies implies the presence of, and thus a profoundly basic insight into, the existence of the soul as a first principle, as well as some knowledge of its nature (*De ver.* 10.8 ad 8 *in contrarium*).

Existence of Privations. Privations are indirectly yet immediately perceived; these include all evils, whether of the physical order (bodily pains, sickness) or of the moral order (the malice of an act, of a bad habit or vice). Although not ''real'' in the strict sense, privations can be said to have existence without a proper essence, inasmuch as they are not ''something,'' but merely indicate the fact of lack or absence in an apt subject. (*See* PRIVATION.)

It should be noted that the various perceptions of existence and the activities that produce them are complementary. In fact, when the structure of the object is disturbed, the subject loses the perception of the existence of the ego itself, and experience runs wild as in a dream world where there is no distinction between appearance and reality.

Mediate Knowledge of Existence. When knowledge of existence does not result from PERCEPTION but from DEMONSTRATION, it is referred to as mediate knowledge of existence. This applies to realities that are not or cannot be immediately present to the knowing subject, either because they are distant (in space) or absent (in time), or because their mode of existence transcends space and time, as for example, spiritual substances and God. Mediate knowledge of the existence of things distant or absent can result from various kinds of demonstration, depending on the type of knowledge proper to such objects, for example, experimentation, physico-mathematical demonstration, and scientific construction. Such demonstration can also convey an immediacy of experience, as seen, for example, in the physical and biological sciences. On the other hand, knowledge of the existence of superior or transcendent beings, for example, God, remains always and solely mediate knowledge, that is, knowledge achieved through demonstration. The starting point is the existence of created things precisely as these reveal themselves as effects of divine omnipotence, and the demonstration itself invokes the principle of CAUSALITY (St. Thomas, *Summa Theologiae* 1a, 2.1–3). Even so-called religious conversion and mystical experience cannot, strictly speaking, provide an immediate perception of the existence of God or of His attributes, but only that of particular effects associated with the spiritual life and its development.

Existence of the Supernatural. The only certain experience of the existence of the supernatural is the experience of the act of faith. In fact, without a special divine revelation no one can be certain of being in grace, but can only have conjectural knowledge of this (*ibid.* 1a2ae, 112.5). But everyone can, and should, have certainty of the existence of faith. Even though supernatural faith depends on a divine influx, it does require an act of man's intellect and will, and he himself can have a direct knowledge of this from both an objective and a subjective standpoint (*ibid.* 1a2ae, 112.5 ad 2; 2a2ae, 2.1 ad 3). The explanation for this lies in the fact that while the intellect is the foundation of man's unity of perception and thus can know both the existence and the nature of all the potencies that are actualized, including acts of the will, the will establishes in man a unity of action (*ibid.* 1a, 82.4 ad 1). For this reason, as S. A. Kierkegaard proved against G. E. LESSING and modern philosophers, the Christian's act of faith constitutes the decisive proof and the surest commitment the human person can have for God.

Formal Existence. In the abstract areas of logic, mathematics, art, morality, and the formal sciences in general, existence is not considered as an extramental and extrasubjective datum and fact. Thus it does not have the same connotation as existence in the strict sense as this is applied to factual reality.

HISTORY OF THE CONCEPT OF EXISTENCE

It is to Aristotle's credit that he distinguished with semantic rigor the problem of existence from that of essence (τὸ ὅτι τὸ διότι). For him, the first is related to the external causes, efficient and final, whereas the second is related to the intrinsic causes, matter and form (*Anal. post.* 78a 22–79a 16; *Meta.* 1041a 15–1041b 33).

Greek thought. In the terminology of ARISTOTLE, existence has two modes of being, potential and actual, since the plant exists in ''some way'' in the seed even before generation, as does the animal in the egg (*Meta.* 1046a 10–36). Yet for Aristotelian thought, which rises above the myth of origins and does not recognize the problem of creation, existence has no meaning in itself. Being means always and only an essence as actualized; spiritual and incorruptible essences are always actual, while material essences pass from potency to act in the eternal cycle of generation and corruption (cf. *Gen. et cor.* 335b 4). On the other hand, since ideas or pure forms do not exist in themselves, temporal existence is the only reality proper to material essences; to speak about the existence of ''separate Ideas'' is ''to use empty words and poetical metaphors'' (*Meta.* 1079b 26). For this reason, and because the world was viewed as eternal and matter as uncreated, Greek thought gave maximum significance to existence as the unique form for real being. In such a context, God Himself exists to the extent that His essence is an act like the property of an essence, or as a pure act of understanding; this distinguishes Him from other substances and forms (*Meta.* 1072b 25; 1074b 33).

For PARMENIDES, as opposed to Aristotle, existence is the process of varied sensations gathered into a unity into the truth of being that is the act of the intellect; likewise for HERACLITUS, the unity and truth of existing things is guaranteed by the logos. Both, therefore, affirm the truth of existence through the agency of the intellect. This truth of being, the pinnacle of Greek thought, was materialized by the Stoics when they identified the λόγος with the πῦρ τεχνικόν or πνεῦμα diffused through nature; thus the development of existence was entailed in the necessary evolution of the destiny (εἱμαρμένη) of the All.

A similar process, but in a direction opposite to that of the Stoics, was the Neoplatonic concept of creation. In the thought of PLOTINUS, there is an emanation of the three primary Hypostases from the overflowing of the One according to the principle that each Thing complete in itself tends to reproduce itself (*Enneads* 5.1.6). According to PROCLUS, this takes the form of a procession that repeats and produces the hierarchy of formal values in the real order of participation (*Elements of Theology,* prop. 25–39). Thus, at the close of Greek philosophy, existence is reabsorbed into essence, real causality into formal derivation, and the πρᾶγμα into the λόγος.

Early Christian conceptions. The passage from the classical to the Christian concept of existence is marked especially by the knowledge of total creation through the free agency of divine will (Gn 1.1). Created existence is thus given an absolute and total dependence on God, and God's role in creation is conceived as a historical intervention, a real relation of temporal reality to the freedom of the divine will. Divine life in this way became transcendent and clearly above involvement in the world. Granting creation, the existence of the world is a contingent fact—as far as God is concerned, because He need not have created it; as far as the world is concerned, because its existence remains always dependent on a continuation of the divine influx (St. Gregory, *Moral.* 16.37; *Patrologia Latina,* 217 v. [Paris 1878–90] 75: 1143).

Thus a new aspect was seen in the concept of existence apart from its dependence on essence: the essence of things is related, according to the EXEMPLARISM of St. AUGUSTINE and of PSEUDO-DIONYSIUS, to the knowledge of God, that is, to the divine intellect insofar as this conceives in itself the forms of the things it creates.

Arabian philosophy. Thus the Christian concept attributed the greatest possible concreteness to existence. On the other hand, ARABIAN PHILOSOPHY, faithful to the Neoplatonic concept of creation as necessary emanation through successive levels, denied God's direct knowledge of, and therefore providence over, the singulars that are the true existents. Yet in the thought of AL-FĀRĀBI and AVICENNA, closer to the theology of the KALĀM, God was conceived as necessary existence and the creature as possible existence. From this followed the basic contingency of existence when cut off completely from essence, so that existence came to be identified with divine causality sustaining the created world (*see* CAUSALITY, DIVINE).

In Arabian philosophy, existence, as an existential affirmation corresponding to the τὸ εἶναι and to the ὅτι of Aristotle, is indicated by the word *annīyya* (the *anitas* of the Latin versions). This can also indicate the concrete existent that is the individual, as well as the subsisting archetypal idea. The Arabs could therefore distinguish essence (*mahīya*), existence as actualization of the essence (*huwīya*), existence as actuality or realized essence (*wugud*), and finally existence as fact and realization of fact (*annīyya*).

Scholasticism. At the beginning of the thirteenth century, the schoolmen followed for the most part the direction of Avicenna and reduced existence to a ''relationship of dependence'' of the creature on God. This formulation appears most clearly in ROBERT GROSSETESTE (*In 2 anal. post.* 1.1). It received almost universal acceptance until recent times, although directly opposed to the Thomistic concept, which is treated fully below. Its chief promoter, HENRY OF GHENT, introduced a new terminology; discussing the structure of the finite, he distinguished a twofold *esse, an esse essentiae,* and an *esse actualis existentiae* (*Quodl.* 1.9). Thus existence, for him, indicated the simple fact of being or, rather, the passage of an essence from possibility to actuality; but since the creature remains ever dependent on divine causality, existence retained also an accidental connotation based on extrinsic participation.

Modern philosophers. This development was jeopardized by modern philosophers, who reduced the ''moment of existence'' to the sphere of PHENOMENA, that is, to immediate sense experience or so-called empirical reality. The significance of methodical doubt from R. DESCARTES to D. HUME, I. KANT, and G. W. F. HEGEL, was that it considered as nonreality the whole realm of immediacy that was suppressed by making a new start with the *cogito.*

In Spinoza's monism, single existents are finite realities, united in the one Substance while themselves remaining multiple and transitory. B. SPINOZA reasserted the scholastic concept of existence under its formal aspect, but without its theological basis, and thus introduced a new rationalist concept of existence. His metaphysical ''indifference,'' assigning existence to the realm of the irrational, was accepted by G. W. LEIBNIZ through the principle of SUFFICIENT REASON, implied both by the creation of this world as the best possible and by the appearance within it of single, real existents. C. WOLFF attempted a further clarification in terms of the realistic principles of the scholastic tradition. Defining existence in the Leibnizian manner as *complementum possibilitatis,* he explains that such completion signifies, in natural theology, dependence on God; in cosmology, the order of contingent things in the material world; and in psychology, the activity of the human mind in conceiving its thoughts.

In his precritical period, Kant found this definition to be too vague, as he did those of A. G. Baumgarten (existence is ''complete inner determination'') and those of C. A. Crusius (who reduced this to spatiotemporal determination), for failing to explain why existence is distinguished from possibility. Kant, therefore, inverted the order: for him, possibility presupposes and bases itself upon existence. Returning then to the Avicennian-scholastic concept that existence cannot be deduced from essence, Kant in the critical writings conceives existence as an a priori category of the mind, a second instance of the modality opposed to nonbeing and situated between possibility-impossibility and necessity-contingency. Thus existence was related to space and time, as in Crusius's exposition, with the difference that the relation was a priori or transcendental (*Critique of Pure Reason* A 80, B 105). Unlike Hume, for whom existence, like substance and causality, is a subjective operation, or ''idea,'' of the imagination derived from experience, Kant relates existence to the operation of the pure intellect as a category.

For existence Kant uses the two terms *Dasein* and *Existenz* almost indifferently; these acquire clearer distinction in the Hegelian dialectic. *Dasein* is the instance of empirical immediacy and multiplicity, and thus of nontruth, of the pure presentation of phenomena as leading to the mediation and to which pure being corresponds as identical to nonbeing; *Existenz,* on the other hand, indicates the instance of what Hegel calls ''second immediacy'' or ''reflected immediacy'' or ''simple essential immediacy,'' which follows upon the mediation of essence and therefore explains the dialectical identity of contraries in action. *Existenz* may be called the instance of externality based on essence (*Wesen*), which is the moment of the underlying interiority, and their synthesis is reality (*Wirklichkeit*). In *Existenz,* the *Sein* of the *Dasein* has been brought back to its foundation (*Grund*), and Hegel can say that essence has ''passed'' into *Existenz.* In more formal terms, *Existenz* is defined as ''the immediate unity of reflection-on-itself and of reflection on something else.''

Contemporary philosophy. In post-Hegelian philosophy, and in particular with S. A. KIERKEGAARD and K. MARX, existence has asserted its primacy through definitions of the truth of being, although in different ways. In Kierkegaard and in Christian EXISTENTIALISM, existence lies in the act of freedom to choose the Absolute and to base oneself on it; in Marxism and in atheistic existentialism, on the other hand, existence is the choice of the finite. In Marxism this choice finds functional expression in the principles of collectivity and of class, while in leftist existentialism it finds expression as a function of the isolated individual.

In this way, existentialism and Marxism represent the distillation of modern philosophy. Putting the source of thought in doubt, they make the will and activity of the subject the foundation for the truth of both knowing and being, and this, as Hegel himself affirmed, following F. H. JACOBI, through a ''leap'' (*Sprung*) that is the dialectic itself. With such a subjective basis for the truth of being, will becomes the essence of the subject himself: modern metaphysics, therefore, as a metaphysics of SUBJECTIVITY, considers the essence of being to lie in the sense of willing. Thus existence passes from simple ''fact,'' ''position,'' ''state,'' or ''mode'' of the real to some principle like the fundamental act of subjectivity.

THOMISTIC NOTION OF ESSE

Greek thought, unable to transcend essence in act or to conceive creation as a total origin of being, limited itself to conceiving existence as a fact. Christian philosophy likewise stopped at the fact of creation and regarded existence as a ''given'' based on the dependence of creatures on divine causality. The scholastic expression of this concept was formulated by thinkers who maintained the real identity of essence and existence, conceding essence and existence the same meaning (and distinction) as the possible and the real. Modern thinkers, making a ''decision'' (will) in favor of radical doubt as the source of thought, progressively freed themselves from essence as ''content'' and foundation, and elevated existence to real and theoretical priority by seeing it as act and related to the structure of being. Thus did the absence of a theoretical basis for existence as act in antithomistic scholasticism influence the rise and development of modern philosophy.

Meaning of esse. St. THOMAS AQUINAS was unique in conceiving being as *id quod est,* that is, the real subsistent that is a synthesis of *essentia* and *esse;* the term *existentia* indicates, for him, the simple ''given'' or fact and has no special theoretical relevance. Aquinas took his point of departure, however, from Avicenna (*In 1 sent.* 8.1.1.4). The synthesis or compounding of *essentia* and *esse* constitutes *ens;* essence is the content and *esse* the activating action, and *ens* is related to and includes both (*In 4 Meta.* 2.558). The concept of *ens commune,* the most common predication for all things, but requiring further determination by generic, specific, and individual notes, differs markedly from the divine *esse,* which is PURE ACT (*De pot.* 7.2 ad 6). The passage from *esse commune* to intensive *esse* is effected through the notion of PARTICIPATION. *Ens* is both concrete and universal in the sense of being the primary participant and the primary participation (*In Boeth. de hebdom.* 2).

In the synthesis that is *ens, esse* is the more formal principle, or *the* ACT par excellence, and this on two distinct levels. In the predicamental sense *esse* is the activation of essence, which itself is related to *esse* as potency (*De pot.* 7.2 ad 9). In the transcendental sense, to the extent that any other act or perfection pre-supposes and is founded on esse, the latter is the actualization of every act and the perfection of all perfections (*Summa Theologiae* 1a, 4.1 ad 3; 1a2ae, 2.5 ad 2). *Esse* is, therefore, the primary act, the simplest, most formal, most intimate, and most immediate (*De anim.* 1 ad 17, 9; *De ver.* 23.4 ad 7; *Summa Theologiae* 1a, 8.1; *C. gent.* 1.23). Consequently, as primary and absolute perfection, in itself including and transcending all perfections, *esse* is the most appropriate of all the names that can be attributed to God, or better—in light of the teaching on ANALOGY—the least inappropriate (*In 1 sent.* 8.1.3; *De pot.* 2.1; *Summa Theologiae* 1a, 13.2). Thus understood, *esse* is the proper effect of God and indicates the radical production of creation that affects not only BECOMING but primary matter itself and pure spiritual substances (*Comp. theol.* 1.68; *C. gent.* 3.66). This can be called the ''intensive notion'' of *esse,* as distinguished from the notion of *existentia* of the formal-predicative kind of Aristotle and the formal-causal (extrinsic) kind of the Augustinian-Avicennian tradition.

Esse and God. Thus, while God is *Esse* as the simplest Pure Act that transcends every finite intellect, a creature is most properly called *ens* in the sense of *id quod habet esse* (*In lib. de caus.* 6). The very nature of the creature, by contrast with God who is the *esse per essentiam,* is to be an *ens per participationem.* This implies both the total dependence of creature on Creator (*Comp. theol.* 1.68) and the composition of essence and esse as two constitutive and really distinct principles, related as potency and act (*De spir. creat.* 1). Both derive from precisely the same metaphysical necessity, and the one presents itself as completing the other. In this unique concept of *esse* the following notions are unified: 1. The Biblical concept of God as ''He Who Is.'' In reserving the name of *esse* for God, St. Thomas follows a constant Hebrew and Christian tradition. The former, beginning with PHILO (*De vita Moysis* 1.14), found technical expression in M. MAIMONIDES (*Dux perplex.* 1.57), while the latter was affirmed among the Latins by St. Augustine and among the Greeks by Pseudo-Dionysius (*De div. nom.* 1, 5) and St. Gregory of Nyssa (*C. Eunomium* 8). 2. The Aristotelian concept of act as perfection and hence affirmation that is prior to and more perfect than potency. Thus, while there can be no potency without an accompanying act, act can well exist without potency (*Meta.* 1049b 10, 1051a 4). This metaphysical principle has its full intelligibility and truth only in the Thomistic concept of the *ipsum esse,* according to which God is called *Esse Subsistens.* The so-called *formae subsistentes,* the intelligences of Aristotelianism and of Neoplatonic EMANATIONISM are subsistent only in the formal sense, that is, as lacking matter, and not in a real way. In Thomism, *esse* is conceptually clarified through the Aristotelian notion of act, just as the speculative exigencies of the Aristotelian notion of act are fully realized only in the Thomistic concept of *esse.* 3. The Platonic concept of participation. The Aristotelian notions of potency and act, like those of matter and form, of SUBSTANCE and ACCIDENT, and of particular and universal, find their basic expression in the difference between the participated and the participating. In *esse* these obtain a theoretical consistency that can be applied to entities whose existence is not subject to change and coming-to-be.

Originality of the Thomistic concept. M. Heidegger makes *esse* the goal and highest end of philosophy, but affirms that the problem is to ''think of being without thought'' [*Der Satz vom Grund* (Pfullingen 1957) 148–156]; St. Thomas, on the other hand, shifting the emphasis from *essentia* to *esse* in his notion of ENS, furnishes a foundation sought in modern thought by radical DOUBT and in IDEALISM by the transcendental.

St. Thomas does not consider *ens,* like other notions that are always determined in themselves, as defined species in a genus, for *ens* transcends genera and species: the principle is already in Aristotle (*Meta.* 998b 22–26), but Aquinas understands it more profoundly. Again, St. Thomas never derives the concept of *ens* from a reflective process of ABSTRACTION, but gives it an absolute priority in the intentional order as the principle through which all other notions and insights are obtained (*De ver.* 1.1). Apprehension of *ens* is the first act of the agent intellect, which becomes the principle of development in the intellectual life (*In 4 Meta.* 6.605). This is followed by that of non-ens (*De pot.* 9.7 ad 15) and by the formulation of the principle of CONTRADICTION, which is the first principle of the intellect (*Summa Theologiae* 1a2ae, 94.2). Thus the notion of *ens* and the principle of contradiction flowing from it appear from the beginning in a transcendental sense and require practically a priori for understanding and furnishing an awareness of reality in terms of object and subject.

The absolute and necessary beginning of thought also finds its intentional expression in *ens.* This concept affirms the unity of perception of the knowing subject in the Thomistic sense of *id quod est* and *id quod habet esse,* and presents itself as the union of empirical experience, revealing being in actuality, and the act of the mind furnishing in a more or less confused way the content of reality as present. This initial evidence of a simultaneous sharing of *ens* between extramental reality and its apprehension by mind as present in act provides a basic reference for the structure of perception in general and for the later determination of the TRUTH of being. The Thomistic notion of *ens,* therefore, expresses not only its original synthesis of essence and *esse,* but attests and guarantees the constitutive sharing of being in man and of man in being, explaining why man seeks himself in being and why being clarifies itself in man. Unlike the transcendental *Ich denke,* which reduces being to the objectivity of the object (see Heidegger, *Der Satz vom Grund,* 154), *ens* links man to reality while setting him apart from himself and from the world, so that he may transcend both the SELF and the world in the search for *Ipsum esse* as the transcendental ABSOLUTE, principle and first cause of all reality and truth.

Knowledge of esse. Some modern authors hold that the Thomistic concept of *esse,* as an act of being in the strict sense, is seized by the mind in the act of JUDGMENT or in the synthesis of subject and predicate (F. Sladeckzek, K. Rahner, M. D. Roland-Gosselin, J. B. Lotz). They do this because they do not distinguish between *existentia* as an empirical datum (*essentia in actu*) and *esse* as a most intimate and profound constitutive principle: The first is accessible to experience and expresses itself in the judgment, whereas the second reveals itself only to the most advanced metaphysical reflection. *Existentia,* therefore, is affirmed either through a judgment of perception that attains the present singulars or through demonstration by means of a principle of causality or of similarity (*per signum*). Essence is known by abstracting the universal from particulars, based on an induction that is a function of the COGITATIVE power influenced by the intellect and above all by the principle of contradiction; thus it expresses itself through DEFINITION and through judgments in the formal order of "nature considered in itself." The activity that unveils *esse* in Thomistic metaphysics has a unique character and could be called a *resolutio* that is proper to metaphysics. When St. Thomas attributes to simple APPREHENSION the knowledge of material essences through abstraction and assigns the *ipsum esse rei* to the second act of the mind (*In Boeth. de Trin.* 5.3), he is speaking of an *esse* that pertains to the ontological, logical, and phenomenological orders, and not strictly of the *esse* that in God is His essence and in creatures is a substantial act distinct from essence and the effect of God Himself.

In Thomistic metaphysics, proceeding as it does from act to act, resolving the less perfect to the more perfect, the *Esse Ipsum* constitutes the final reference for every actuality. Its apprehension is neither intuitive nor abstract but rather a type of "dialectical emergence." Just as the apprehension of *ens* underlies the perception of reality, the apprehension of first principles, and the abstraction of essences, so the apprehension of *esse* as metaphysical act presupposes existential perception as much as intuition and abstraction, and is located at the apex of their convergence. It is obtained, for St. Thomas, by recourse to ARGUMENTATION; this, however, is purely revelatory, bringing to light the originality of *esse* or demonstrating the real distinction between *esse* and essence in creatures and their identity in God. It is a "dialectical" kind of knowledge to the extent that *esse* as such is act and not content; thus the apprehension of *esse* occurs "by emergence," whereby the concept of act is approached as a first principle and foundation, and so reveals the ultimate stage of agreement between intellect and reality.

See Also: EXISTENTIAL METAPHYSICS; ESSENCE AND EXISTENCE; MATTER AND FORM; POTENCY AND ACT.

Bibliography: C. A. HART, *Thomistic Metaphysics* (Englewood Cliffs, N.J. 1959). T. C. O'BRIEN, *Metaphysics and the Existence of God* (Washington 1960). G. P. KLUBERTANZ, *Introduction to the Philosophy of Being* (New York 1955). L. DE RAEYMAEKER, *The Philosophy of Being,* tr. E. H. ZIEGELMEYER (St. Louis 1954). J. F. ANDERSON, *The Bond of Being* (St. Louis, 1949). É. H. GILSON, *L'Être et l'essence* (2d ed. Paris 1962); *Being and Some Philosophers* (2d ed. Toronto 1952). J. MARITAIN, *Existence and the Existent,* tr. L. GALANTIÈRE and G. B. PHELAN (New York 1948). C. FABRO, "La problematica dell 'esse' Tomistico," *Aquinas* 2 (1959) 194–225; *La nozione metafisica di partecipazióne secondo S. Tommaso d'Aquino* (2d ed. Turin 1950); *Participation et causalité selon S. Thomas d'Aquin* (Louvain 1961); *Partecipaziéne e causalité secondo S. Tommaso d'Aquino* (Turin 1960); "Dell'ente di Aristotele all' 'esse' di S. Tommaso," *Aquinas* 1 (1958) 5–39; "Dell'ente, dell'essere e del nulla," *La Philosophie et ses problèmes . . . études . . . offert à R. Jolivet* (Paris 1960); "Per la determinazione dell' ''essere,'' *Tijdschrift voor Philosophie* 23.1 (1961) 97–129; ''The Problem of Being and the Destiny of Man,'' *International Philosophical Quarterly* 1 (1961) 407–436. A. THALHEIMER, *Meaning of the Terms: ''Existence'' and ''Reality''* (Princeton 1920); *Existential Metaphysics* (New York 1960). J. DE FINANCE, *Être et agir dans la philosophie de Saint Thomas* (Paris 1945). J. B. LOTZ, *Das Urteil und das Sein* (Pullach-Munich 1957). J. HEGYI, *Die Bedeutung des Seins* (Pullach-Munich 1959). A. MARC, *L'Idée de l'être chez Saint Thomas et dans la scholastique postérieure* (Paris 1933).

[C. FABRO]

EXISTENTIAL ETHICS

Existential ethics, as distinguished from situational ethics, refers to the contemporary attempt of Catholic theologians, especially in Germany, to work out a concrete, existential, individual ethics that will supplement traditional scholastic ethics, which they regard as limited to an abstract, essential, universal frame of reference. These thinkers, insisting on the uniqueness of the individual moral situation, deny the sufficiency of any straightforward application of universal moral principles to such a situation. According to them, the general moral norms do not cover the existential moment of self-commitment in a concrete situation, and therefore cannot tell the individual what he must do. In other words, the will of God for an existing individual in a concrete situation cannot be adequately expressed in terms of conclusions from the NATURAL LAW. The norms of the natural law can give no more than a ''case'' of the general, and so cannot express the complete moral demands of the individual situation. For there is a positive individual element belonging to the concrete moral act that escapes even the subtlest CASUISTRY.

Individual vs. Situational Ethics. This is not to say that the concrete duty of the individual is not also a case and an application of a universal law or laws. It is indeed this; in fact, it receives a large part of its justification from the general law. But beyond this exemplification of the universal it is the expression of an individual call that demands a comparably individual answer. Or, to put it in another way, whereas the ''cases'' of the universal law can be known and stated in objective universal concepts, the individual, concrete, moral duty has a uniqueness that can be expressed fully only in a kind of nonobjective, peculiarly personal, subjective knowledge. This contrast between objective and subjective existence reflects the existentialist and phenomenological cast of the thinking of the theologians espousing this type of ethics (*see* EXISTENTIALISM; PHENOMENOLOGY).

Existential ethics is similar to situational ethics in this emphasis on the individual and subjective side of moral experience. It is distinguished from situational ethics in that it undertakes its portrayal of the strictly individual duty within the framework of a traditional, universal, essential ethical theory. Existential ethics, then, is best understood as a complement and corrective to traditional Thomistic ethics rather than as a complete, independent system. For this reason, if for no other, it would escape the condemnation of purely situational ethics that was promulgated by the Holy See in 1952 [*Acta Apostolicae Sedis* 44 (1952) 413–19].

Uniqueness of the Situation. Perhaps existential ethics can be best described in terms of the concrete moral challenge each man has to face. This challenge has a double aspect. It can be described according to its content and according to its mode of realization. In both of these aspects the style and approach of phenomenological existentialism exert a strong influence. The content of the moral act is described phenomenologically so that in addition to the objective description of the object and circumstances traditionally discussed, existential ethics adds ''the sense of the concrete situation'' (Heidegger's *Befindlichkeit*). For example, a traditional moralist will give as essential circumstances of stealing that the property belong to someone else and that it be taken against his reasonable will; or of fornication that the two persons be unmarried. The existentialist would say that this describes the objective, ''essential'' situation. To it he adds ''the sense of the concrete situation,'' i.e., the reality out of which the individual's distinct being is formed and which the individual in turn determines. It contains a personal sense of finitude and contingency and a sense of being cast out into the world with no roots or supports of one's own. It is a point of tension with objective and subjective factors. In a sense, it is the point of intersection of the universal laws that apply to a given situation, plus a peculiarly individual law that applies to the person at this specific point of his historical development. From this there comes an individual imperative, tailored to the present state of a soul, an individual arrangement and predetermination for men as individuals standing at particular crossroads of life.

''I-Thou'' Relationship. In addition to this emphasis on the uniqueness of each individual situation, existential ethics lays great stress on the ''I-Thou'' relationship between each person and those who come into his life, and between each person and God. Here, as in every variety of existentialism, we find a sharp distinction drawn between persons and things or objects. Traditionally, we are told, moralists missed the importance of this distinction and tended to treat persons as they did objects. They set up an objective framework of rights and duties that dealt with cold abstractions expressed in universal norms. From this it is difficult to reach down to the warm, living concreteness of moral experience.

The existentialists prefer to have man establish a loving ''I-Thou'' relationship with his neighbor. They claim that man can often know what this personal relationship demands of him without his having to go through any complicated coordination and application of universal moral principles. Love is the key to this intuition of duty. It keeps one from considering the individual as a composite of universals and reveals his unique personal being.

The ''I-Thou'' relationship to God is built around the same loving commitment to another person. No longer is God a remote legislator. Instead, He is the infinite Thou, who calls man personally and immediately. This call is indeed a command, but much more than a universal commandment. God's commanding will is a clear call and is morally binding, even in what have been traditionally considered as matters of counsel. Thus a call to the religious life would seem to bind under pain of sin. This call of God, which can refer to any area of life, religious or secular, is not heard by all men. One has to be well attuned to God's voice to hear His call, and this takes a ''charismatic art'' of discernment of spirits and a special prudence. This discernment and prudence are the outgrowth of a personal immediacy with God that is inspired by faith and love.

In view of this orientation to love rather than law, it is not surprising that the proponents of existential ethics look on morality as a personal challenge to surrender oneself to God that outstrips all objective norms and any purely legal morality. Man must act from his whole heart with a firm grasp of inner truth. He has to be aware of the divine demand on him personally to engage himself totally in the concrete moral challenge. When he does, he will realize that this alone will give him the truly personal life that alone can satisfy him, namely, one in which he comes to grips with absolute, transobjective moral value in direct confrontation with God.

Evaluation and Critique. Historically and ideologically existential ethics can be considered as an attempt to integrate the subjective elements of Protestant theology and the phenomenological insights of existentialism into Catholic moral theology. Taken in this light, it is not an attack on traditional views, but an attack on the exaggerated objectivism of extreme voluntaristic nominalism and its accompanying legalism. Existential ethics emphasizes the personal in a way that augments without contradicting traditional moral theology. It claims to give a less artificial and more realistic moral theory by putting the loving will of God at the center of all morality. Man's personal response to God's personal love for him is not the observance of a commandment but the loving embrace of His will.

The one outstanding figure in the discussion of existential ethics is Karl RAHNER, who exposes this doctrine in his *Gefahren im heutigen Katholizismus* (Einsiedeln 1950) and *Das Dynamische in der Kirche* (Freiburg 1958). Two other moral theologians, Joseph Fuchs and Bernard Häring, lean toward existential ethics, but cannot properly be called proponents of it.

There has been favorable reaction to the proposals of these thinkers among Catholic moral theologians. Many have approved their emphasis on love and have, in their turn, suggested that charity be put at the heart of moral theology. There have been, however, three main objections to the moral theories of existential ethics. First, some theologians—protestations of its proponents to the contrary notwithstanding—think that existential ethics undermines traditional objective morality and falls into a dangerous SUBJECTIVISM. These critics reject the claim that existential ethics is but an extension of traditional Catholic morality, which goes beyond it without denying it. Secondly, and this complaint is more widely voiced, some hold that existential ethics wipes out the distinction between commandment and counsel. For, in some instances at least, it would seem that one is supposed to perceive a command from God to enter the religious life or to marry some particular person, and so understands that he is obliged to enter religion or marry the person in question. Thirdly, some Thomists object that existential ethics is based on a misunderstanding of the role of prudence in the direction of human action, and in reality solves only a pseudo-problem.

It is unlikely that existential ethics will be generally accepted by Catholic theologians until these points are clarified to their general satisfaction.

See Also: PRUDENCE; MORAL THEOLOGY; HUMAN ACT; MORALITY.

Bibliography: F. BÖCKLE, *Lexikon für Theologie und Kirche*, ed. J. HOFER and K. RAHNER, 10 v. (2d, new ed. Freiburg 1957–65) 3:1301–04. J. D. GERKEN, *Toward a Theology of the Layman* (New York 1963) 54–81, 107–52. J. FUCHS, ''Situation Ethics and Theology,'' *Theology Digest* 2 (1954) 25–30. This appeared originally as ''Situationsethik in theologischer Sicht'' in *Scholastik* 27 (1952) 161–83. W. A. WALLACE, ''Existential Ethics: A Thomistic Appraisal,'' *The Thomist* 27 (1963) 493–515.

[J. V. MCGLYNN]

EXISTENTIAL METAPHYSICS

A METAPHYSICS that is existence-oriented, as opposed to one that is essence-oriented. The term is usually applied to the 20th-century emphasis within THOMISM that stresses the existential significance of philosophical (and theological) ideas, i.e., the way in which such ideas indicate or connote forms or aspects of that which either "is" or "can be" (*see* EXISTENCE). Proponents of existential metaphysics have been concerned mainly with ontological doctrines relating to the nature of being and of God, of potency and act, of the transcendentals, of essence, analogy, causality, and substance, as well as with the notions of man, the soul, freedom, nature, time, eternity, morality, the good, love, charity, and grace.

Origins. According to existentialist Thomists, the assertion of the primacy of the act of existing and of the centrality of its significance throughout all areas of knowledge seems novel, not because it is absent from the thought of St. THOMAS AQUINAS, but because that thought was formerly not studied in its original context. As recently as 1929, they point out, MARÉCHAL defined metaphysics in Wolffian fashion as "the science of essences, or of possibles" [*Revue néo-scolastique de philosophie* 31 (1929); reprinted in *Mélanges Joseph Maréchal* (Brussels 1950) 1:106], while three years later R. GARRIGOU-LAGRANGE held that the object of metaphysics is "the intelligible being of sensible things, their essence confusedly known" [*Le réalisme de principe de finalité* (Paris 1932) 30]. These and similar teachings accented ESSENCE as the absolutely certain, self-evident, universal, and necessary ground of the principles of identity, sufficient reason, and causality; they created the impression that SCHOLASTICISM, and Thomism itself, was basically a rationalistic essentialism (*see* RATIONALISM). Such a conception, they stress, missed the capital point, often made by St. Thomas himself, that the act of existing (*esse*) makes anything "to be," and to be all that it "is": "esse est actualitas omnis formae vel naturae" (*st,* 1a, 3.4); "esse est inter omnia perfectissimum . . . perfectio omnium perfectionum" (*De pot.* 7.2 ad 9). Therefore, considered maximally, the act of existing "includes in itself every perfection of being" (*omnem perfectionem essendi*), while transcending them all (*De spir. creat.* 8 ad 3). "Essence," or QUIDDITY, on the other hand, is but "that through which and in which a being [*ens*] has existence [esse]" (*De ente* 1). Thus the term essence in Thomism designates precisely a subject-measure of *esse* [see G. Phelan, "The Being of Creatures," *American Catholic Philosophical Association. Proceedings of the Annual Meeting* 31 (1957), 118–125; W. Carlo, "The Rôle of Essence in Existential Metaphysics," *International Philosophical Quarterly* 2 (1962) 557–590].

Yet the type of Thomistic metaphysical doctrine that may be described as a rationalistic essentialism has never been universally accepted among Thomists. In the early 1930s Jacques Maritain presented Thomism as an "existential" philosophy, always tending toward and terminating in existence [*Sept Leçons sur l'être* (Paris 1934) 28–31]. Somewhat earlier Aimé Forest expounded a "concrete" and "existential" approach to the metaphysics of St. Thomas [*La structure métaphysique du concret selon S. Thomas d'Aquin* (Paris 1931; 2d ed. 1956)], stressing the composition of essence and existence as constituting the primary form of the structure of created being, leading up to God as the universal cause of "being" (*essendi*). At about the same time, André Marc argued that this same composition, or distinction, lies at the very core of the Thomistic notion of being ["L'Idée de l'être chez Saint Thomas et dans la scolastique postérieure," *Archives de philosophie* 10 (1933) 1–144]. A few years later, in the work of Fabro and Geiger, one finds an elaborate interpretation of the Thomistic metaphysics of existential PARTICIPATION, according to which the distinction between essence and *esse* is not a simple application of the Aristotelian doctrine of potency and act, but rather represents an original insight of St. Thomas implying the primacy and centrality of *esse.* For Fabro, in particular, participation means the sharing of *esse;* the creature "is" that which shares *esse* [C. Fabro, *La nozione metafisica di partecipazione secondo S. Tommaso d'Aquino* (Milan 1939); L.-B. Geiger, *La Participation dans la philosophie de S. Thomas d'Aquin* (Paris 1942; 2d ed. 1952)].

For English-speaking audiences, however, it has been principally the work of J. Maritain and É. Gilson that his brought to the fore this notion of an existentially oriented metaphysics (*see* THOMISM, 2, 3). As already noted, Maritain had made this point in the 1930s. In the 1940s he developed it further (e.g., in his *Court Traité de l'existence et de l'existent,* [Paris 1947 Eng. tr. 1948]). Yet the fact remains that the difficulty and the profundity of Maritain's writing have obscured the point for many. In North America, especially, it was left to Gilson to make the matter clear in a series of scholarly works whose influence there, above all, has been unparalleled by that of any other writer. Indeed, the phrase "existential metaphysics of St. Thomas" (as opposed to "essential ontologies," scholastic or other) may be said to be the hallmark of the Gilsonian influence on this continent.

Gilson's Thesis. In the late 1920s and early 1930s Gilson was already insisting that the "philosophy" of St. Thomas could not be divorced from his theology since it in fact existed only within that context; that his integral thought is centered upon Being—which "is" God; and that since philosophy is necessarily about being, it cannot but be, ultimately, about God. For indeed God's self-given name is "He who is" (Ex 3.14), and this means precisely the very act of existing: *ipsum esse,* as St. Thomas explains (*Summa theologiae* 1a, 13.11). Thus Gilson, as early as the Gifford Lectures of 1931–32, was showing that Christianity, in raising man's thoughts to the consideration of the Self-subsisting Act of Being—

ipsum esse, or *ipsum esse per se subsistens,* had revealed to metaphysics the radically existential nature of its object. Accordingly, the problem of being, thanks to revelation, was expressly raised from the Platonic and Aristotelian ''plane of intelligibility'' to the ''plane of existence'' [*L'Esprit de la philosophie mediévale* (Paris 1932) 54–55; Eng. tr. (New York 1940) 51, 80, 82]. As he later remarked, ''to use our own modern terminology let us say that a Christian's philosophy is 'existential' in its own right'' [*God and Philosophy* (New Haven 1941) 4:1]. Detailed application of this general Christian ''existentialism'' to Thomism was made soon thereafter, the author contrasting ''essentialist ontologies,'' which equate being and essence, with ''the existential ontology'' of St. Thomas, which affirms ''the radical primacy of existence over essence [*Le Thomisme* (4th ed. Paris 1942; 5th ed. 1944) part 1, chs. 1, 4].

Such an existentialist metaphysics, however, is not an ''existentialism-without-essence''—a formula that may be said to characterize much contemporary non-Thomistic, and especially atheistic, EXISTENTIALISM, or ''apocryphal existentialism,'' (*''l'existentialisme apocryphe''*) as Maritain calls it [*Court traité* . . . (Paris 1947) 13]. Authentic existentialism is radically different; in fact it is simply the reverse because it affirms that *esse* is in no case without essence, but rather that *esse* is the ''act'' of which ''essence'' is the inseparable measure or mode, save in God, whose essence ''is'' *esse.* In other words, the primacy of the act of existing over essence cannot be understood as a primacy of *esse* over *ens:* to remove *essentia* from *ens* would be to take the ''what'' out of the ''what-is.'' ''There is no real being which is not an actually existing essence and an existent conceivable through the essence which defines it'' [Gilson, ''Existence and Philosophy,'' *American Catholic Philosophical Association. Proceedings of the Annual Meeting* (1946) 9].

Esse, of course, is not *ens,* except in God; but rather is the ''act'' that makes *ens* ''to be,'' and to be totally; whereas *essentia,* in all created things, is the factor within *ens,* or created substance, that makes it to be ''what'' it is. And the ''is'' is prior to the ''what'' as ''act'' is prior to ''potentiality,'' insofar as the latter term is understood to signify a certain receptive capacity relative to the *esse,* or act of existing, that is received (*C. gent.* 2.53; *st* 1a, 77.1).

Christian Philosophy. For Gilson, ''a Christian's philosophy is existential in its own right.'' Such a philosophy, therefore, necessarily, even if implicitly, involves the consideration of being in terms primarily of *esse.* This is so because God Himself, who ''is'' Being, has taught man that His own proper name is *''Esse''* (Ex 3.14). To characterize a philosophy as Christian, Hebrew, Hindu, or Mohammedan is not to define its ''essence,'' but rather to indicate its ''state,'' or its actual condition in the person philosophizing [see Maritain, *De la philosophie Chrétienne* (Paris 1933) 37–39]. For philosophy is a ''work of reason''; indeed, philosophical wisdom, according to St. Thomas, is objectively a perfect work of reason: ''perfectum usum rationis'' (*Summa theologiae* 2a2ae, 45.2). Nevertheless, reason is not any less reason for existing in a Christian, a Hebrew, a Hindu, or a Muslim. Thus it makes sense existentially and historically to designate a philosophy as Christian, Hebrew, Hindu, or Muslim. The concern here is only the first of these, and precisely as formulated in the question: What is the relationship of existential metaphysics to the notion of a philosophy elaborated under the aegis of Christian revelation in general and of the ''I-am-who-am'' in particular?

According to Aquinas, if God is self-subsisting *esse* and if the subject of metaphysics is that whose act is *esse* universally present in everything else (''common being''; *Summa theologiae* 1a, 105.5; *C. gent.* 2.45), then this science in its totality is radically ''existential.'' But that God ''is'' *Esse,* although knowable by natural reason, was known, or known determinately, thanks only to revelation. This is a matter of historical fact. So, in saying that God is ''He who is,'' or *ipsum esse*—only this scholastic exegesis is metaphysically relevant here—revelation, and not reason, was establishing the act of existing (*esse*) ''as the deepest layer of reality as well as the supreme attribute of the divinity'' (GILSON, *God and Philosophy,* 41). Consequently the Christian metaphysician henceforth could not adequately philosophize about being unless his thinking was focused upon the ''act'' (*esse*) that alone makes his object ''to be.'' Indeed, *esse,* as the ''act'' par excellence, is the source of all that deserves the name of ''being.'' At the same time it is in all things the deepest, inmost presence: ''esse est illud quod est magis intimum cuilibet, et quod profundius omnibus inest'' (*Summa theologiae* 1a, 8.1).

These truths about being, and any others that are rationally ascertainable, are not regarded by Aquinas as withdrawn from the domain of philosophy because they happen to have been revealed. For truth about God is twofold, viz, that which can and that which cannot be investigated by reason; and it is fitting that both should be offered to man's belief through a divine revelation (*C. gent.* 1.4, 5). Now, knowledge of God under the aspect of being is accessible to reason because universal ''being'' is the adequate object of the intellect—*intellectus facultas entis; capax universi.* This knowledge of God is, precisely, metaphysics about Him; and it is called natural theology.

Since the ultimate object of philosophy and of theology is the same, viz, God, or the *Ens* that is *Esse,* there is objectively no conflict between them [Gilson, *Elements of Christian Philosophy* (New York 1959)]. In this, however, there is no implication that their subjects are the same. God is not that of which metaphysics formally treats, which is ''common being''; He is its Principal, or extrinsic Cause (*In Boeth. de Trin.* 5.4). Moreover, if metaphysics is ineluctably existential because it concerns that whose ''act'' is ''to be,'' it does not follow that the pure ''To Be,'' which is God, is its starting point. The opposite is true: metaphysics begins its investigation by considering the being of external, sensible things, and ends with God as the absolute Act of Being, who is their Cause.

See Also: CHRISTIAN PHILOSOPHY; FAITH AND REASON; THEOLOGY, NATURAL.

Bibliography: ''The Philosophy of Being,'' *American Catholic Philosophical Association. Proceedings of the Annual Meeting* 21 (1946) 1–207. J. F. ANDERSON, *The Bond of Being* (St. Louis 1949); ''Some Disputed Questions on Our Knowledge of Being,'' *Review of Metaphysics* 11 (1957–58) 550–568. THOMAS AQUINAS, *An Introduction to the Metaphysics of St. Thomas Aquinas,* tr. J. F. ANDERSON (Chicago 1953), selected texts. C. A. HART, *Thomistic Metaphysics* (Englewood Cliffs, N.J. 1959). É. H. GILSON, *L'Être et l'essence* (2d ed. Paris 1962); *Being and Some Philosophers* (2d ed. Toronto 1952); *The Christian Philosophy of St. Thomas Aquinas,* tr. L. K. SHOOK (New York 1956). J. MARITAIN, *Existence and the Existent,* tr. L. GALANTIÈRE and G. B. PHELAN (New York 1948); *A Preface to Metaphysics: Seven Lectures on Being* (New York 1939). E. L. MASCALL, *Existence and Analogy* (New York 1949); *He Who Is* (New York 1948). E. G. SALMON, *The Good in Existential Metaphysics* (Milwaukee 1953).

[J. F. ANDERSON]

EXISTENTIAL PSYCHOLOGY

A comprehensive scientific theory that attempted to integrate the contributions of various behavioral sciences, and should therefore be distinguished from existential philosophy, psychiatry, and psychotherapy. Existential psychology required for its integration basic and comprehensive notions concerning man's nature. It found some of these in its existential attitude toward man, others in its phenomenological approach, and still others in contributions from different schools of psychology and psychiatry. It sought to advance the understanding of human existence by encouraging the dialogue between the behavioral sciences and the phenomenology of man, and by integrating the theories and data of psychology and psychiatry into a science based on knowledge of man's essential nature.

Basic Constructs. The ultimate aim of every science is systematic explanation and orderly understanding. In the 1960s the science of psychology began to move toward the construction of comprehensive theories that could integrate the phenomena and constructs of its various schools. Although such phenomena are interrelated, being themselves expressions of man's nature, the interrelationship can be made explicit only when they are expressed in the same language or—what is analogous—integrated within a common frame of reference. Such a common frame of reference is that provided by a phenomenological description of the original experiences that are differently interpreted by the various schools. The fundamental structures of such experiences, however, require a comprehensive concept for their further integration, and the existential psychologist finds this in the notion of existence.

Existence. The term existence in this context refers to the fact that man's essence is to find himself bodily with others in the world. Man ''ex-sists''—literally, he stands out. Such a notion of existence unites the subjective, physiological, objective, and social aspects of man's behavior. The student of human behavior splits it into many aspects and studies these in isolation, thereby producing a variety of psychologies such as social, behavioral, physiological, introspectional, and psychoanalytical. The reintegration of these aspects presupposes a return to the original experience of behavior in its unity, which is to be found in the notion of existence itself. An integrational construct in existential psychology may be defined as a concept referring to observed phenomena that can be used for the integration of the greatest number and variety of such phenomena, as studied by different schools of psychology and psychiatry.

Subordinated Constructs. While existence (or existential) is one fundamental construct used in this comprehensive theory of psychology, subordinated constructs also are needed to develop a full theory. Examples are: mode of existence, existential world, existential transference, the centered self, ontological security, and insecurity. Such constructs function to connect the phenomena uncovered by various schools of psychology with the fundamental construct of existence.

Relation to Differential Constructs. Existential psychology and its constructs must transcend differential psychologies and their corresponding constructs if it is to integrate these within a common frame of reference. Existential constructs are therefore designed to transcend the predominantly subjective, objective, or situational connotations of differential constructs; they represent instead fundamental human characteristics that are rooted in experience. Rather than being function-oriented, they are person-oriented.

Existential psychology is thus a comprehensive theoretical psychology of human behavior that is conceived as a Gestalt of observable differentiations of an original intentional-behavioral relationship of man to the world. Behavior itself is the observable differentiation of man's intentional relationships. For methodical reasons, one can emphasize in this behavioral relationship three components: (1) the ''intending'' subject-pole, man; (2) the embodiment of this intentionality in measurable behavior; and (3) the ''situated'' object-pole of the resulting intentional behavior.

Differential psychologies concentrate on one or other of the main profiles of man's existence, thereby temporarily abstracting some aspect from the whole of man's behavior. This methodical restriction gives rise to methodically restricted constructs. Such constructs have their own validity and utility, provided they are not proposed as absolute symbols of the whole reality of human behavior.

Dualism and Integration. Scientific psychology was for the most part rooted in IDEALISM or EMPIRICISM, emerging as it did in a cultural atmosphere saturated with Cartesian dualism. Every attempt to found a scientific psychology, therefore, started from either an idealist or an empiricist view of human nature. Idealism led quickly to introspectionism, which considered the contents of CONSCIOUSNESS the legitimate and exclusive object of the new science. Empiricism, on the other hand, gave rise to BEHAVIORISM, which saw quantifiable bodily behavior isolated from consciousness as its exclusive subject matter. To be truly comprehensive, a psychology of existence must use constructs that are neither introspectionist nor behaviorist, but rather transcend the methodical limitations of both. Only in this way can it integrate their findings, without distortion, into a higher unity.

Psychoanalytic Theory. An appraisal of Freudian psychoanalysis from the viewpoint of comprehensive psychology shows that this too was developed within a framework of Cartesian dualism. S. Freud did not assume an original existential unity between man and the world. In Freudian theory, man is biologically fixed by a pattern of innate and instinctive drives, and this prior to his having any dealings with a world that is in principle alien to his being. The world, rather than being constitutive of man's existence, is purely a collection of foreign objects to which his fundamentally fixed biological structure reacts.

Later analytic development is toward a less dualistic view of man and his world, but seems still incapable of transcending the split between man and world on which psychoanalytic theory was originally based. Thus the cultural, interpersonal school of psychoanalytic thought rejects the idea that man's impulsive and emotional behavior emerges from innate instinctive drives within the organismic box. They substitute the perspective of environmental conditions, social pressures, and cultural patterns for the perspective of autonomous instinctual subjectivity; this in itself implies an underestimation of the relatively free subject-pole who interacts with his culture. They elucidate one aspect of human existence and are able to see the whole of human reality in the light of this. The ''situational'' aspect, it is true, is everywhere present in man, even in the innermost reaches of his being, and furnishes a valuable and fruitful insight, even if it is confined to only one aspect of human existence.

Differential Psychologies. Differential psychologies deal with isolated profiles of human behavior. Many of these profiles exhibit features, processes, and laws that have parallels in the activities of animals, plants, and inanimate objects. These similar aspects are abstracted, however, from the whole of man's behavior and objectivized for methodological reasons. The full meaning of such isolated features of behavior can be grasped only when they are reintegrated into the whole. Their sense becomes clear when perceived in the light of the properly human qualities of man as a whole; these characterize all profiles of his behavior and their mutual interdependency. Such comprehensive, all-pervading, specifically human qualities cannot be forced into the mechanical models of differential psychologies concerned with stimulus-response, punishment-reward, tension-reduction, or homeostatic models. Such frames of reference are equally applicable to nonhuman beings. Consequently, mechanistic constructs reflect precisely that in man which is not specifically and exclusively true of human behavior as such. The foundational constructs of existential psychology, on the other hand, point to precisely those unique qualities that set man apart from every other type of being. This puts existential psychology in a privileged position to connect the data and theories of differential psychologies.

Philosophy and Phenomenology. The discipline traditionally concerned with man's fundamental characteristics is philosophy or philosophical anthropology; this studies the being of man in the sense of his nature or his essence. Existential psychology must create similar constructs that represent the specifically human characteristics of behavior. Some constructs, however, are inadequate to this task; when obtained from a merely empirical study of certain groups, for example, they are capable only of integrating the data pertaining to those groups. Constructs obtained from an explicitation of man's very being, on the other hand, are, in principle, broad enough to integrate psychological data from all periods of human history and from all classes of men, even as these are obtained and interpreted by the various differential psychologies.

Theoretical interpretations are incompatible to the extent that they are influenced by incompatible philosophical anthropologies. The criterion that thus determines the selection of existential constructs is the principle of applicability. This principle states that the scientific theorist of human behavior should only borrow philosophical assumptions or constructs that can be used to integrate and explain the findings of differential psychologies. This judgment regarding the adequacy of an assumption or statement is thus a selective one and constitutes a psychological and not a philosophical judgment.

The integration of contributions from differential psychologies presupposes a study of these psychologies to distinguish what is based on real experience from unverified models, hypotheses, and implicit philosophies. The methods used to root such constructs in experience are the methods of natural observation and of phenomenology. Natural observation places one, as it were, in the field of phenomena to be studied, and enables him to describe these phenomena as they first appear. The phenomenological method then leads him to the inner structure of these phenomena, and liberates his perception of this structure from both personal and cultural prejudices that may be present in natural observation and description.

Conclusion. Existential psychology thus studied the intentional-functional behavior of persons who exist with others in a meaningful world. Such behavior also exhibits mechanical features that are abstracted for close observation and study by differential psychologists. Since these features are peripheral and not the unique core of intentional behavior, they are perceived in existential psychology as personal differentiations; as such, they are still permeated by the uniquely human characteristics represented in the fundamental existential constructs.

See Also: PERSONALITY; EXISTENTIALISM; PHENOMENOLOGY.

Bibliography: R. F. CREEGAN, ''A Phenomenological Critique of Psychology,'' *Philosophy and Phenomenological Research* 9 (1948–49) 309–315. V. J. MCGILL, ''The Bearing of Phenomenology on Psychology,'' *ibid.* 7 (1946–47) 357–368. H. P. DAVID and H. VON BRACKEN, eds., *Perspectives in Personality Theory* (New York 1957). A. GURWITSCH, *The Field of Consciousness* (Pittsburgh 1964). A. E. KUENZLI, ed., *The Phenomenological Problem* (New York 1959). R. C. KWANT, *Encounter,* tr. R. C. ADOLPHS (Pittsburgh 1960). W. A. M. LUIJPEN, *Existential Phenomenology* (Pittsburgh 1960). R. MAT et al., eds., *Existence: A New Dimension in Psychiatry and Psychology* (New York 1958). S. STRASSER, *The Philosophy of Behavior* (Pittsburgh 1960); *Phenomenology and the Human Sciences* (Pittsburgh 1963). J. H. VAN DEN BERG, *The Phenomenological Approach to Psychiatry* (Springfield, Ill. 1955). A. L. VAN KAAM, *The Third Force in European Psychology* (Greenville, Del. 1960); ''Assumptions in Psychology,'' *Journal of Individual Psychology* 14 (1958) 22–28; ''The Impact of Existential Phenomenology on the Psychological Literature of Western Europe,'' *Review of Existential Psychology and Psychiatry* 1 (1961) 63–92; ''Existential Psychology as a Comprehensive Theory of Personality,'' *ibid.* 3 (1963) 11–26; ''Humanistic Psychology and Culture,'' *Journal of Humanistic Psychology* 1 (1961) 94–100; *Existential Foundations of Psychology* (Pittsburgh 1966).

[A. L. VAN KAAM]

EXISTENTIAL THEOLOGY

A theological orientation, rather than a systematized body of doctrine, that derives its inspiration from the efforts of Rudolf BULTMANN (1884–1976) to ''DEMYTHOLOGIZE'' the Sacred Scriptures.

The epithet, existential, is based on the outlook postulated by Bultmann for any valid study of the WORD OF GOD in the Bible, especially the New Testament KERYGMA. According to Bultmann, the propositions contained therein can be viewed as theologically significant only insofar as they speak of man's existence. The kerygma thus consists of an organic series of judgments concerning the ''possibilities'' that lie before man. These judgments have the effect of calling to man's attention his properly existential situation. They tell him that he stands before the God who cannot be ''considered,'' i.e., whose being may not be objectivized and thus analyzed, but who is known only in the decision in which He is encountered as another Thou.

This regulative outlook involves peculiar views concerning both the text of the Scriptures and texture of human nature. According to Bultmann and his disciples, the former is a fabric of ''myths'' that must be put to the test of the existential analysis. Here it suffices to understand the mythical character of the Scriptures as expressing a view of the universe radically different from our modern scientific grasp of it. For Bultmann this opposite view included ideas about cosmogonies at variance with one another, as well as differing notions about the eruption into nature of forces foreign to its ordinary processes.

Bultmann's description of human nature as *Dasein* is a frank adoption of the terminology and thought structure of M. Heidegger in this regard (*see* EXISTENTIALISM, 2). To be man is thus to be in such a way that through and in one's own being, being as such is ''put to the test.'' To exist as man, therefore, means to have before oneself the possibility of decision; and when this possibility is realized, man exists authentically. For Bultmann, again, the ''historicity'' of *Dasein* is this very being of man in so far as—distinguished from all other being (*Vorhandensein*)—it can (but need not!) be.

If, then, the Gospels can be ''demythologized'' for modern man, they will be for him—as they are for men of every age—the doorway to faith, i.e., an existential understanding of oneself (*Selbstverständnis*). Thus the existential theologian or exegete sees as his task: (1) to be in vital relation with reality; (2) to examine the sacred text in which this relation is expressed, directly or indirectly; (3) to reexpress this relation so as to make evident the problematic or ''historical'' character of human existence. Whether or not the events represented in the Bible have objective historical validity does not really matter, because their representation has a function altogether different from putting one into contact with something that happened at a given moment in the history of the world. Note that this is not a flat denial on the part of the existential theologian of the historical objectivity of Gospel events. His interest lies elsewhere, and it is dominated by the idea that in the life of Jesus the existential condition of man is laid bare. Faith in Christ consists in the constantly renewed realization that it is possible to accept the grace of God.

To sum up, then, Bultmann attempted to express his understanding of the meaning of the Gospel in terms borrowed from existential (Heideggerian) philosophy. This understanding is based on the idea that, in order validly to speak of God, one must also and of necessity speak of man. The sole content of the Gospel, therefore, is the constant confrontation of man by God in the former's condition of historicity, i.e., the possibility of authentic existence in faith.

The use of the existential analysis to prepare the way for a valid Biblical exegesis also raises the question of the relation between faith and philosophy. Bultmann himself maintained that real confrontation with reality depends on the Biblical word—another distinctively Protestant thesis. The question is then whether or not this is an altogether sound expression of the complete givenness of faith.

Bibliography: H. W. BARTSCH, ed., *Kerygma and Myth,* tr. R. H. FULLER (London 1953). R. MARLÉ, *Bultmann et l'interprétation du Nouveau Testament* (Paris 1956). I. N. WALTY, ''Bulletin du théologie protestante,'' *Revue des sciences philosophiques et théologiques* 42 (1958) 349–370. H. SCHLIER, *Lexikon für Theologie und Kirche*, ed. J. HOFER and K. RAHNER, 10 v. (2d new ed. Freiburg 1957–65) 2:768–769. E. FUCHS, *Die Religion in Geschichte und Gegenwart* 1:1511–1512.

[M. B. SCHEPERS]

EXISTENTIALISM

The philosophy of existentialism, as the name itself implies, indicates a special concern with the problem of EXISTENCE—not with each and every type of existence, but with human existence. Although there may be foreshadowings of existentialism in St. AUGUSTINE, R. DESCARTES, and B. PASCAL, the inspiration of contemporary existentialism is to be found in the writings of the Danish Lutheran S. A. KIERKEGAARD (1813–55). Kierkegaard was convinced that his countrymen had a false notion of what it means to be a Christian. As he saw it, too many of them regarded Christianity as a doctrine to be understood speculatively and to be grasped intellectually. This to him was but the acceptance of the erroneous notion of G. W. F. HEGEL, who had taught that it was the role of speculative philosophy to comprehend all the mysteries of religion, even those of Christianity having to do with the Trinity and the Incarnation.

Kierkegaard for his part insisted that Christianity is not an abstract doctrine to be approached in an impersonal and dispassionate manner as though it were a system of speculative truths. On the contrary, Christianity is a way of life, a mode of living that consists in appropriating and assimilating the message of Christ into one's own existence. If one wanted to call Christianity a doctrine, he should understand that it is a doctrine that proposes to be realized in existence; that the true way of understanding the doctrine of Christianity is to understand its task as one of existing in the doctrine, not of speculating on it.

In his polemic against Hegel and against those Danes who accepted the speculative approach to Christianity, Kierkegaard emphasized a number of ideas, such as existence and the existent, the individual, decision and choice, passion, fear and trembling, dread and despair. These notions have become pivotal for those writers who are usually designated as existential. A partial listing of existentialists whose works have become known to American audiences would include, among the more philosophical, men such as N. BERDĬĀEV (1874–1948), M. BUBER (1878–1965), M. HEIDEGGER (1889–), K. JASPERS (1883–1969), G. MARCEL (1889–1973), J. ORTEGA Y GASSET (1883–1955), J. P. SARTRE (1905–1980), P. TILLICH (1886–1965), and, among the more literary, writers such as E. Albee (1928–), F. Arrabal (1932–), S. Beauvoir (1908–1986), S. Beckett (1906–1989), A. Camus (1913–1960), J. Genet (1910–1986), E. Ionesco (1912–), F. Kafka (1883–1924), H. Pinter (1930–), R. M. Rilke (1875–1926), and M. UNAMUNO Y JUGO (1864–1936).

Although it would be impossible here to give a detailed and adequate exposition of the various teachings of these existentialists, they do adopt certain basic notions that can be indicated in a general way.

Existence and the Individual. First, in all existentialist thought there is an absorbing interest in human existence or human living. This existence is not that of the physical or chemical level or that of the biological realm;

rather the existence in question is what might be designated broadly as ethical or moral existence, for the existentialist is concerned with the problem of what it means really to exist as a man; how does one live a truly human life; what are the characteristics of authentic human endeavor? In Heidegger's expression: other realities are, man alone exists. Questions about the chemical composition of man, the biological functioning of his organs, or the physical constitution of the world in which he lives are of little interest to most existentialists. Their concern is with man and with man's existence, i.e., the existence that marks him off from all the other beings in this universe. Kierkegaard's question: how does one exist as a true Christian, has been broadened into the question: how does one exist as a true human being?

The existence in question here is not that of abstract man, of man in general. Human existence, human living, as the existentialist views it, is always achieved by a man in the here and now, in a concrete situation with a host of particular and accidental circumstances surrounding it. The concern of the existentialist is not with the general and the universal, but with the singular and the individual.

This interest in the individual arises for several reasons. Most existentialists are wary of systems of speculative thought as avenues of approach to problems of human existence. The existentialist regards such systems as abstracting from the particular and unique features in each human situation that make human living the complex and difficult thing it is. This was Kierkegaard's constant complaint against the pure thought of Hegel, and it has been repeated by most existentialists in relation to any abstract view of human existence. The disdain for the universal and the abstract in other existentialists arises from their intense interest in human freedom. Since the very nature of freedom consists in some sort of contingency and indetermination, namely, the power to will something or not to will it, freedom becomes a rather awkward theme in a speculative system such as Hegel's that regards all natures as necessary deductions one from the other. The existentialist sees this determination and necessity as the enemy of all he holds as precious. This is true especially of Sartre and Camus, who make freedom the very essence of man. Then, too, most existentialists see the abstract and the universal as an indignity toward man; for these perspectives degenerate human existence, the human being, the individual person, into an object, a thing, an ''it.'' From such a preoccupation arises the realization of the inhumanity of the view of modern technology wherein man is an impersonal number and a mere member of a group. This protest against the technological attitude is basic to the existentialism of such thinkers as Jaspers and Marcel.

The interest of existentialism in the existing individual not only explains its suspicion of the abstract consideration of human affairs, but also explains why much existentialist writing has taken the form of the novel, the short story, the autobiographical essay, and the play. All these types of literature easily lend themselves to the vivid description and analysis of the human individual groping for an answer to a unique human situation.

Consciousness and Freedom. Because existentialism is concerned with the individual as a conscious self and a responsible agent, as a subject and a ''thou'' rather than as an object and an ''it,'' CONSCIOUSNESS and FREEDOM are central themes in all existentialist thought. Man becomes truly existent only when he lives an intensely conscious life in which he is vividly aware of all the exigencies, decisions, and problems of human living. The existentialist demands that men should become conscious of themselves as reflective beings whose existence must be interpenetrated with thought. He insists that they become fully alive to the richness inherent in each experience; that they live a life that is vibrantly alert to all the anguish, burden, and care of existence.

Too many men, Heidegger complains, are mere followers of the crowd; they are men whose personal judgments are only dull echoes of the anonymous ''they say.'' The man of existence, on the contrary, is the self-thinking man, the man of decision, the free man; for if men should be conscious beings, they should be conscious primarily of their freedom, and of the personal danger into which their freedom plunges them.

One becomes free only by having a personal interest in things, by making decisions, and by consciously following one's choice. Although objective science and the scientific method demand that the knower be disinterested and free from passion, existentialism contends that the individual be personally involved in the situation, that he make his decision with passionate concern. Far from advocating disinterestedness, the existentialist urges that the self become totally engaged in life, that one have a strong and radical commitment to existence, that one consciously, freely, and passionately be involved in one's ultimate concern.

Because the man of existence is fully committed to life and all that it entails, he is aware that his freedom carries with it the heavy burden of responsibility. In Kierkegaard's view, one truly becomes a Christian only when as an adult he assumes full responsibility for all the consequences of his infant Baptism. Sartre sees each individual as the arbiter of all values who must assume therefore the awesome responsibility of being the supreme legislator for his total destiny. Camus regards the real man, the lucid man, as the man who realizes that there are no guilty men, only responsible ones; and, in the existentialism of Heidegger the very existential meaning of the true man is care or concern.

Anguish and Absurdity. Closely intertwined with the notions of freedom, decision, and responsibility are those of abandonment, anguish, dread, fear, and trembling. Because the existentialists have emphasized man in his concreteness and INDIVIDUALITY, there is a tendency among them to describe him as alone, solitary, cut off from his fellowmen. The note of abandonment arises also because for many existentialists there are no objective moral standards to guide man in his choice. Each man is "on his own"; he is abandoned to his own personal decision. If the onerous weight of responsible decision means ANXIETY and anguish of spirit, the existentialist's awareness of the fragile instability of human existence, which can be snuffed out by a myriad of uncontrollable events, adds to that anxiety. There is also in existentialism the insistence on the alienation of modern man, who finds himself estranged from the world of nature by his reflective consciousness and at cross-purposes with his fellowmen by his freedom. Like the stranger of Camus, modern man finds himself a lone outsider for whom the reasons and certainties of a past generation are no longer satisfying or assuring. Existence results in bewilderment, anxiety, and frustration. This searing anguish finds expression in Heidegger's notion of human existence as a movement toward the nothingness of the grave and in Sartre's lament that life is a useless passion.

Another salient theme in existentialism is that of ABSURDITY. In all existentialist literature there is an interest in the nonrational, using that term to signify whatever escapes the comprehension of man. This nonrational element in existence is often called "the absurd." Kierkegaard designates Christ as the absurd; for the fact that God became man out of love for man is something incomprehensible to human reason. The Incarnation cannot be understood by reason; it must be grasped by the leap of faith. Absurdity in Sartre's existentialism signifies the absolute gratuity or contingency of things. Since there is no God to conceive of essences according to the philosophy of Sartre, there is no reason for the things of the physical world, either for their essences or for their existence. They just are; and since they are what they are without reason, they are absurd. In the essays of Camus the notion of absurdity has a somewhat different connotation. Camus admits that there are scientific explanations and descriptions of various parts of the universe, but he denies that there is any all-embracing, comprehensive truth for the whole of reality. There are truths, partial truths, but there is no Truth, no final and decisive reason making the universe a rational whole for man. Marcel makes a distinction between a problem and a mystery: the former is open to human solution, while the latter, as something beyond human comprehension, is a matter for faith. This interest in the absurd is the bond of unity among a number of playwrights such as Genet, Beckett, Ionesco, and Albee, whose plays are portrayals of the absurd in modern existence.

God and Nothingness. Finally, for many of the existentialists the common setting in which human existence seeks its goal is the absence of God. Although Berdi͡aev, Marcel, and Jaspers are theists, the atheistic existentialism of such men as Sartre, Camus, Kafka, Rilke, and the dramatists of the Theater of the Absurd has been more influential. Heidegger's private opinion concerning the existence of God may be open to question, but it is commonly agreed that in his writings he philosophizes as though there were no divinity.

There is little if any attempt made by these existentialists to argue against the traditional proofs for the existence of God; atheism is simply taken for granted. Sartre makes a rather brief attempt to disprove the existence of God, but his procedure clearly indicates that he has misunderstood the traditional notion concerning the divinity. For example, Sartre speaks of God as *Causa Sui;* his explanation of what this definition means indicates that God, in his view, would be a contradictory and self-denying notion. God would be for him an unconscious-conscious being, a full-empty absolute. Camus seems to suggest that the problem of human suffering is the reason for his denial of the existence of a Supreme Being.

Existentialism for these thinkers is a serious attempt to describe an existence from which God has been banished and for which man alone can be the ultimate reason. Man thus becomes the new transcendent for man. He is the unique being through which all being reveals itself; he is the first source of order and meaning in the universe; he is the sole lawgiver in the domain of morality; and he is the creator of all values and ends. Existence is to be what man makes it to be. One can understand the interest of these existentialists in the writings of F. W. NIETZSCHE.

Such ATHEISM could explain the morbid gloom, the heightening anxiety, and the sheer absurdity of life that one often finds in existentialism of this type. Existence has no antecedent explanation nor has it any permanent fulfillment. One strives to be absolutely free, to be consistent with one's fundamental choice; but one should not become serious, to use Sartre's expression, since all human actions are equally doomed to failure.

The absence of God makes death an absolute, an absolute that is regarded by some as an absurd stupidity, by others as a ludicrous monstrosity. In either case, the negation of death, as these writers indicate, should overshadow all the activities of human existence.

Nor is death the only negation. Negativity, negation, and emptiness become recurring themes. Being, as Heidegger envisages it, is filled with nothingness. In Sartre, consciousness is described as a negativity, since consciousness is always consciousness of an object, that is, of something that is not the actually knowing consciousness. Freedom for him is also negation since it is a thrust toward the future goal that is not yet possessed. (*See* NONBEING.)

This note of negation shows itself in another characteristic that is fairly common to existentialists of the atheistic type, viz, an extreme emphasis on the dark side of human existence. Frustration, annoyance, and sorrows are part of all human living, but existentialism seems centered on them. There is very little joy and gladness in existentialist literature, whether one considers the short stories of Kafka, the novels of Sartre, or the plays of Camus. The tragic, the irrational, and the depraved are constantly employed in these works to indicate man's freedom as a crushing responsibility in an existence that is seen more as a condemnation to loneliness than as a call to knowledge, love, and service of others.

Critique. Many critics regard existentialism as an unbalanced view of existence. In their opinion it is a protest that has become too extreme. Arising in Kierkegaard as a warning against the rigid rationalism of Hegel, it has become in many of its adherents a denial of the relevance of any general and abstract truth concerning man, his nature, and his activity. Protesting against the artificiality and hypocrisy of much in bourgeois morality, it has become for some a repudiation of any and every standard of objective morality, including that of Christianity. Morality is said to be completely situational and entirely personal. Aware of the inhumanity that a misguided technology can bring about in modern life by its tendency to regard men as mere numbers, the existentialists have so extolled the inwardness, the subjectivity, and the absolute freedom of the individual that social life becomes philosophically indefensible.

One can well understand why Pope Pius XII on Aug. 12, 1950, in his encyclical *Humani generis* called existentialism ''the new erroneous philosophy.''

See Also: EXISTENTIAL ETHICS; EXISTENTIAL METAPHYSICS; EXISTENTIAL PSYCHOLOGY; EXISTENTIAL THEOLOGY.

Bibliography: E. L. ALLEN, *Existentialism from Within* (London 1953). W. BARRETT, *Irrational Man* (New York 1962). H. J. BLACKHAM, *Six Existentialist Thinkers* (London 1952). J. D. COLLINS, *The Existentialists* (Chicago 1952). M. ESSLIN, *The Theatre of the Absurd* (New York 1961). R. HARPER, *Existentialism: A Theory of Man* (Cambridge, Mass. 1948). F. H. HEINEMANN, *Existentialism and the Modern Predicament* (2d ed. New York 1954). H. KUHN, *Encounter with Nothingness* (Hinsdale, Ill. 1949). V. M. MARTIN, *Existentialism* (Washington 1962). C. MICHALSON, ed., *Christianity and the Existentialists* (New York 1956). K. F. REINHARDT, *The Existentialist Revolt* (Milwaukee 1952). J. A. WAHL, *A Short History of Existentialism,* tr. F. WILLIAMS and S. MARON (New York 1949).

[V. M. MARTIN]

EXMEW, WILLIAM, BL.

Carthusian priest, martyr; d. hanged, drawn, and quartered at Tyburn, London, England, June 19, 1535. William studied Classics at Christ's College, Cambridge, before joining the Carthusians at the London Charterhouse, where he soon became vicar. The year he was named procurator (1534), Henry VIII sought the express acknowledgment from the Carthusians and other prominent subjects of the validity of his marriage to Anne Boleyn and the right of their children to succeed to the throne. Their refusal led to the execution of their prior, St. John HOUGHTON (May 4, 1535). Two days after Houghton's death, Exmew and the vicar Humphrey MIDDLEMORE were denounced to Thomas Cromwell by Thomas Bedyll, a royal commissioner, as being ''obstinately determined to suffer all extremities rather than to alter their opinion'' in regard to papal supremacy in spiritual matters. Both were thrown into Marshalsea prison three weeks later together with their fellow monk Sebastian NEWDIGATE. For 13 days they were manacled in a standing position to a post. Then they were taken to the Tower of London, tried at Westminster (June 11), and condemned to death for high treason for denying Henry's claim to supremacy over the Church of England. Exmew was beatified by Pope Leo XIII on Dec. 9, 1886.

Feast of the English Martyrs: May 4 (England).

See Also: ENGLAND, SCOTLAND, AND WALES, MARTYRS OF.

Bibliography: R. CHALLONER, *Memoirs of Missionary Priests,* ed. J. H. POLLEN (rev. ed. London 1924; repr. Farnborough 1969). L. HENDRIKS, *London Charterhouse: Its Monks and Its Martyrs* (London 1889). J. H. POLLEN, *Acts of English Martyrs* (London 1891).

[K. I. RABENSTEIN]

EXODUS, BOOK OF

The Hebrew title for the second book of the Pentateuch is *w^e'ēlleh š^emôt* (''and these are the names'')—the opening words of the Masoretic Text. The Greek ver-

A scene from Exodus Chapter 32, in which Moses carries the tablets of the Testimony down the mountain to where the Israelites are dancing around the image of a golden calf. (©Historical Picture Archive/CORBIS)

sion took its title from the subject matter of the opening chapters—Ἔξοδος [(the) going out (from Egypt)]. The title of the book in the Vulgate and English Versions—Exodus—is a literal rendering of the Greek title. The contents, origin, and theology of the book will be treated in this article.

Contents. The Book of Exodus may be divided into six sections. The first section (1.1–12.36) tells the story of Israel in Egypt. Here one learns of the oppression of the Israelites, the birth and adoption of MOSES, his flight to Madian and sojourn there, and his call by YAHWEH. Having received instructions regarding his mission and the power to work miracles, Moses returns to Egypt to confront pharaoh with the divine command: ''Let My people go.'' The obduracy of pharaoh and the crescendo of plagues occupy most of the remaining material of this section (*see* PLAGUES OF EGYPT). With the final plague, the death of the first-born of the Egyptians, the Israelites win their freedom, and with the celebration of the Passover ritual (*see* PASSOVER, FEAST OF) they prepare to depart from the land of slavery.

The second section (12.37–18.27) treats the Exodus, itself, and the wandering in the desert. The easy ''Way of the Land of the Philistines'' being excluded, Moses leads his people across the Sea of Reeds on to the rugged terrain of the Sinai Peninsula. Throughout the narrative special emphasis is laid on the divine assistance accorded the Israelites. The victory paean of ch. 15 constitutes a glorious and joyful hymn of praise and simultaneously presents one of the oldest pieces of Hebrew poetry. To the subsequent complaints of the people, Yahweh responds with MANNA, quail, and water from the rock. Through Moses' intercession, He also grants them victory over the Amalekites. The section closes with the institution of the office of Judges [*see* JUDGES (IN THE BIBLE)].

The third and most important section (19.1–24.18) deals with the Covenant. Yahweh summons His chosen leader to Mt. Sinai (*see* THEOPHANY), and through him proposes a unique union with Israel: ". . . you shall be my special possession, dearer to me than all other people, though all the earth is mine'' (19.5). The Decalogue (*see* COMMANDMENTS, TEN) and subsequent Code of Alliance (*see* BOOK OF THE COVENANT) announces the stipulations incumbent upon Israel in view of this union. Having received the Code of Alliance, Moses and the people solemnly ratify this pact with the sprinkling of the sacrificial blood [*see* COVENANT (IN THE BIBLE)].

The fourth section (25.1–31.18) is concerned with instructions for the establishment of worship. Detailed commands concerning the size, construction materials, and adornments of the TENT OF MEETING are listed (*see* ARK OF THE COVENANT). Also in this section are the divine institution of the priesthood, and specific instructions regarding the consecration of priests and their vestments. Further injunctions concern the sacrifices to be offered (*see* SACRIFICE, III).

The rather brief fifth section (32.1–34.35) tells of the chosen people breaking faith with Moses and their erection of the golden calf. The further mediation of Moses averts the destruction of his people and wins a renewal of the covenant with Yahweh. Once again God grants the tablets of the law to his earthly leader.

The sixth and final section (35.1–40.38) describes the fulfillment of the divine instructions. There is extensive repetition of the material contained in the fourth section. The section closes as the cloud (see 24.15.–18) covers the Tent of Meeting and the glory [*see* GLORY (IN THE BIBLE)] of Yahweh fills the dwelling; this is a sign of legitimacy and approval of the newly built sanctuary and represents the proper conclusion of the entire book.

Origin. In antiquity there was little challenge to the Mosaic authorship of Exodus. (The Gnostics in the early ages of the Church objected and maintained that it was an apocryphal Jewish document). Under the influence of renaissance scholarship, however, serious doubts arose. As early as the 16th century, the lawyer Andreas Masius judged that there were non-Mosaic additions to the text. Still greater contributions were made in the 19th century when scholars demonstrated that various sources were employed in the compilation of the text.

Historically, the literary authorship of some parts of the covenant section (19.1–24.18) may perhaps be attributed to Moses. In line with ancient Near Eastern practices, the essentials of this covenant would soon have been put into writing and preserved for periodic renewal on the part of the people (see, e.g., Jos 24.16–28).

Illuminated page of Exodus from a Hebrew Bible, 1299. (©Archivo Iconografico, S.A./CORBIS)

Alongside this written material, an ever-growing body of oral traditions developed. This process continued after the conquest of Canaan. As Hebrew life became more sedentary in Canaan and hence more complex, there was a constant need for new legislative materials. Since these legal developments adhered to the principles instituted by the earlier Mosaic legislation, there was never a problem about attributing these later sections to Moses. With the definitive establishment of the Israelites in Canaan, separate traditions of historical and legal materials began to develop in the north and south of Palestine. There have been numerous efforts to explain these traditions and how they finally found their way into the Pentateuchal text. Most scholars favor the hypothesis according to which the Pentateuch is essentially a compilation of four older written sources, the documents of the YAHWIST, the ELOHIST, the DEUTERONOMIST, and the PRIESTLY WRITERS; on the date and nature of these documents, *see* PENTATEUCH. The sources used in the composition of Exodus are generally divided as follows.

To the Yahwistic source belong: 1.6, 8–12; 2.15–23a; 3.7–8, 16–20; 4.1–16, 19–20a, 22–31; 5.1–23; 6.1; 7.14–18, 23–29; 8.4–11a, 16–28; 9.1–7, 13–21, 23b–34; 10.1–7, 13b–19, 28–29; 11.4–8; 12.21–23, 29–30; 13.21–22; 14.5–7, 10–14, 19–20, 21b, 24–25, 27b, 30–31; 15.22–25, 27; 16.4; 17.1b–2, 7; 19.20; 24.1–2, 9–11; 32.9–14; 33.7–11; 34.1–5, 10–28.

To the Elohistic source belong: 1.15–22; 2.1–14; 3.1–6, 9–15, 21–22; 4.17–18, 20b–21; 7.20b–21a; 9.22–23a, 35; 10.8–13a, 20–27; 11.1–3; 12.31–36, 37b–39; 13.17–19; 15.20–21; 17.3–6, 8–16; 18.1–27; 19.21–25; 20.1–21, 23–26; 21.1–37; 22.1–30; 23.1–32; 24.3–8, 12–15a, 18b; 31.18b; 32.1–8, 15–35; 33.1–6, 12–23; 34.6–9.

To the Priestly source belong: 1.1–5, 7, 13–14; 2.23b–25; 6.2–30; 7.1–13, 19–20a, 21b–22; 8.1–3, 11b–15; 9.8–12; 11.9–10; 12.1–20, 28, 37a, 40–51; 13.1–2, 20; 14.1–4, 8–9, 15–18, 21a, 22–23, 26–27a, 28–29; 16.1–3, 5–36; 17.1a; 19.1–2a; 24.15b–18a; 25.1–40; 26.1–37; 27.1–21; 28.1–43; 29.1–46; 30.1–38; 31.1–18a; 34.29–33; 35.1–35; 36.1–38; 37.1–29; 38.1–31; 39.1–43; 40.1–38.

To later redactors belong: 15.1–19; 19.2b-19; 20.22; 34.34–35. The Deuteronomistic source is not represented in Exodus.

Theology. The Exodus, viewed as a complexus of election, deliverance, and covenant, has long been hailed by biblical scholars as the cardinal dogma of the OT religion. What the Incarnation is to the NT, the Exodus is to the OT; without it the Israelite religion cannot be understood. The basic historical facts of the special election of the Israelites, their rescue from slavery in Egypt, and the singular pact that they sealed with Yahweh are strongly attested; in fact, the whole religious and civil existence of ancient Israel depend on it. The literary form in which the sacred writer conveys these facts may be termed a religious interpretation or explanation of history, and a clear epic tone is noted throughout. Hence, the scenes and imagery should not be interpreted as eyewitness reporting.

The importance of the Exodus complexus cannot be exaggerated. The choice of the Israelites by Yahweh was something unique: ''You alone have I favored more than all the families of the earth'' (Am 3.2). As a consequence of this choice, Israel was the recipient of constant divine benefactions, the first of which was her deliverance from Egypt, a dogma fondly recalled by prophet and psalmist alike: ''It was I who brought you up from the land of Egypt and who led you through the desert for 40 years, to occupy the land of the Amorrites'' (Am 2.10). ''I, the Lord, am your God who led you forth from the land of Egypt; open wide your mouth and I will fill it'' [Ps 80(81).11]. The covenant too was something unique. Other Semitic peoples felt varying degrees of closeness to their deities, a relationship between god and people founded, for example, on imagined ancestry. Not so was the relationship between Yahweh and Israel. Here a strict, formal agreement was entered into. This covenant endowed the Israelites with distinctive prerogatives and made of them God's special possession, a kingdom of priests, and a holy nation (19.5–6).

Of great theological importance, also, is the legal material contained in the book, more specifically, the Decalogue and the Code of the Alliance. Of the Decalogue prescriptions, numbers four to ten provide legislation stemming from the natural law itself and are found already mentioned in earlier Semitic codes. However, the Book of Exodus presents a new approach. In older codes the violation of these precepts was regarded as an offense against a fellow man. In Exodus they also constitute an offense against God. The Decalogue further emphasizes the dogma of monotheism and the duty of honoring the one true God. The liturgical legislation of the book served as the foundation of subsequent Israelite developments in this sphere.

See Also: LAW, MOSAIC.

Bibliography: *La Sainte Bible,* ed. L. PIROT and A. CLAMER, 12 v. (Paris 1935–61). *L'Exode,* M. NOTH, *Exodus,* tr. J. S. BOWDEN (Philadelphia 1962); *Echter Bibel: Altes Testament,* ed. F. NÖTSCHER, 4 v. (Würzburg 1955–59) *Exodus.* J. E. PARK and J. C. RYLAARSDAM, *Exodus,* G. A. BUTTRICK, et al., eds. *The Interpreters' Bible,* (New York 1951–57) 2:188–197. P. W. SKEHAN, ''Exodus in the Samaritan Recension from Qumran,'' *Journal of Biblical Literature* 74 (Boston 1955) 182–187.

[J. E. HUESMAN]

EXOMOLOGESIS

A Greek word for confession, to God or to man, either of God's greatness (Rom 14.11) or of one's sins (Mt 3.6; Didache 14.1). Technically this word designated confession of one's sins as a part of early penitential discipline. It meant (1) the normally private confession to the bishop before receiving a public penance (ST. CYPRIAN, *Enchiridion patristicum* 553); (2) the whole of external exercises of that public penance (TERTULLIAN, *ibid.* 315); or (3) the public general confession prior to the reconciliation granted by the bishop (*Op. cit.* 569).

See Also: CONFESSION, AURICULAR; PENANCE, SACRAMENT OF.

Bibliography: G. W. H. LAMPE, *A Patristic Greek Lexicon* (Oxford 1961—) 1:499–500. E. VACANDARD, *Dictionnaire de* *théologie catholique*, ed. A. VACANT et al., (Paris 1903–50) 3.1:854–861.

[G. GILLEMAN]

EXORCISM

The act of driving out or warding off DEMONS or evil spirits from persons, places, or things that are, or are believed to be, possessed or infested by them or are liable to become victims or instruments of their malice. According to Catholic belief, demons are fallen angels who have rebelled against God. Excluded from friendship with God, they retain, nevertheless, their natural power of acting upon men and the material universe for their own evil purposes. This power is limited by Divine Providence, but it has been given wider scope in consequence of the sin of mankind. Exorcism is nothing more than a prayer to God (sometimes made publicly in the name of the Church, sometimes made privately) to restrain the power of the demons over men and things. This article summarizes the history of and present practice of the church in regard to exorcism, then adds some theological points.

History. The ancient Egyptians and Babylonians as well as other ethnic groups sometimes attributed certain diseases to demoniacal possession, and they believed in the efficacy of magical charms and incantations for banishing the demons. In the Old Testament, the Book of Tobia relates a devil that was said to have killed the seven husbands of Sara (6.14). Subsequently, ''the angel Raphael took the devil, and bound him in the desert of upper Egypt'' (8.3).

Acknowledging the reality of demonic possession, Jesus drove demons out of their victims, not by collusion with Beelzebub, the prince of devils, but by the finger of God (Mt 12.22–30; Mk 3.22–27; Lk 11.14–26). Christ also empowered the Apostles and Disciples to cast out the demons in His name (Mt 10.1; Mk 6.7; Lk 9.1). He committed this same power to believers, generally (Mk 16.17), but the exercise of such power was subject to certain conditions, namely, prayer and fasting (Mt 17.20; Mk 9.28). The Acts of the Apostles records how Paul drove a divining spirit out of a girl who brought her masters much profit by soothsaying (16.16–18; cf. 19.12). No doubt, the other Apostles exercised this power too.

After the apostolic age, the primitive Christians continued to exercise demons. Justin Martyr (100?–165?) speaks of numberless demoniacs throughout the whole world, who were exercised by Christian men in the name of Jesus Christ even though they could not be exorcised by those who used incantations and drugs (2 *Apol.* 6). Tertullian (160?–230?) complains of the ingratitude of

Medieval manuscript illustration of a priest driving out the devil during an exorcism, Chartres, France. (©Christel Gerstenberg/ CORBIS)

the pagans, who called the Christians enemies of the human race, even though the Christians exorcised the pagans without reward or hire (*Apol.* 37). Origen (185?–254?) remarks that the name of Jesus expelled myriad evil spirits from the souls and bodies of men (*Contra Celsum* 1.25). Lactantius (d. beginning of the 4th century) writes that the followers of Christ, in the name of their master and by the sign of His passion, the cross, banished polluted spirits from men (*Instit.* 4.27). Cyril of Jerusalem (315?–386?) notes that the invocation of the name of God scorches and drives out evil spirits like a fierce flame (*Catech.* 20.3). These remarks are typical of the attitude of the early Church, for which an exorcism was an invocation of God against the harassment of devils. Frequently the invocation was accompanied by some symbolic action, such as breathing upon the subject, or laying hands upon him, or signing him with the cross. The invocation might be expressed by calling upon the name of Jesus, or cursing the devil, or commanding him to depart, or reading a passage from Sacred Scripture.

Not only did the early Church exorcise demoniacs, but it also subjected catechumens to exorcism as a preparation for baptism. Catechumens were not considered to be obsessed as demoniacs were; but as a consequence of

"Saint Benedict Exorcises a Demon from a Possessed Man," fresco painting by Il Sodoma, the Abbey of Monteoliveto Maggiore, Siena, Italy. (©Archivo Iconografico, S.A./CORBIS)

original sin (and of personal sin in the case of adults), they were subject more or less to the power of the devil, whose "works" and "pomps" they were called upon to renounce. This exorcism preceding baptism may be explained then in two ways: it was a symbolical anticipation of deliverance from the power of the devil through baptism, and it was a means of restraining the devil from impeding the reception of the Sacramant (cf. St. Thomas, *Summa theologiae* 3a, 71.2). Cyril of Jerusalem describes one manner of exorcism before baptism by which the catechumen was stripped and anointed with exorcised oil from head to foot (*Catech.* 20.3).

Present Practice. Today the Church maintains its traditional attitude toward exorcism. It recognizes the possibility of diabolical possession, and it regulates the manner of dealing with it. The Code of Canon Law allows authorized ministers to perform solemn exorcisms not only over the faithful, but also over non-Catholics and those who are excommunicated (c. 1152). A solemn method of exorcising is given in the Roman Ritual. In most of the Eastern and Western rites, exorcisms continue to serve as a preparation for baptism. Exorcisms also form a part of the blessing of such things as salt, water, and oil; and these, in turn, are used in personal exorcisms and in blessing or consecrating places (e.g., churches) and objects (e.g., altars, sacred vessels, church bells) connected with public worship or intended for private devotion. In exorcising and blessing these objects, the Church prays that those who use them may be protected against the attacks of the devil.

Bibliography: J. FORGET, *Dictionnaire de théologie catholique,* ed. A. VACANT et al. (Paris 1903–50) 5.2:1762–80. A. RODEWYK, *Lexikon für Theologie und Kirche*, ed. J. HOFER and K. RAHNER (Freiburg 1957–65) 3:1314–15. H. LECLERCQ, *Dictionnaire d'archéologie chrétienne et de liturgie*, ed. F. CABROL, H. LECLERCQ, and H. I. MARROU (Paris 1907–53) 5.1:964–978. A. STENZEL, *Die Taufe* (Innsbruck 1958). L. BOUYER, *The Paschal*

Mystery: Meditations on the Last Three Days of Holy Week, tr. M. BENOIT (Chicago 1950).

[E. J. GRATSCH]

Theology. The New Testament's witness to Christ's decisive victory over the powers of evil, a victory proclaimed by the Savior Himself in word and deed (cf. Lk 11.20; Jn 12.31), is the foundation for any theology of exorcism. The authority and ability to cast out devils was entrusted to the Twelve (Mk 3.14–15; cf. Mt 10.1; Lk 9.1), though all ''those who believe'' are also envisioned as sharing this power (Mk 16.17; Lk 10.17–19; cf. Origen, *Contra Celsum* 7.4). Satan's loss of power is, in fact, a continuing sign of man's Redemption (1 Jn 5.18). This conviction is echoed by the Fathers (e.g., Tertullian, *Apol.*; Hilary of Poitiers, *In Ps.* 64.10) and by the schools of the Middle Ages (cf. St. Thomas Aquinas, *Summa theologiae* 2a2ae, 90.2).

In the performance of an exorcism it is always the Church that prays through the instrumentality of the exorcist, so that the efficacy of the rite is analogous to that of the sacramentals. At the same time, it is obvious from the Gospels themselves that the exorcist's faith and integrity play a determining role in the outcome of the exorcism (Mt 17.14–20; Mk 9.13–28; Lk 9.37–43). For this reason the Church exercises the greatest caution in authorizing clerics who have received the power of exorcism through Holy Orders to put it to use. This is not true, of course, of the exorcisms employed during the rite of baptism, but of those uses of the power that an apparently authentic instance of possession has required. Of those cases of possession against which exorcism proves to be ineffective, one can only say that an error of judgement has been made as to the true nature of the phenomenon or that for reasons of His own, God has withheld the rite's efficacy. Recourse to this latter explanation should be infrequent, to say the least, since the question of the Church's ability to carry on the essential work of its founder and master is at issue.

See Also: BAPTISM (LITURGY OF); DIABOLICAL OBSESSION; DIABOLICAL POSSESSION (IN THE BIBLE).

Bibliography: *Satan,* ed. BRUNO DE JÉSUS-MARIA et al. (New York 1952). L. CRISTIANI, *Evidence of Satan in the Modern World,* tr. C. ROLAND (New York 1961).

[L. J. ELMER]

Liturgy. In liturgy and theology an exorcism is the Church's prayer that the power of God's Holy Spirit free a person from sin and evil and from subjection to the devil, the spirit of evil. In popular understanding exorcism generally refers to the driving out of a demon who has possessed a person. The Church, however, is reluctant to admit a supernatural possession in particular cases, since most apparent cases can be explained by pathological conditions. Both modern biblical scholarship and current psychological theory and practice are inclined to admit a supernatural explanation only when a natural explanation has been proved impossible. A practical indication of this reluctance is the 1972 abolition of the office of exorcist with the other minor orders (Paul VI MinQuaedam).

Exorcisms in the form of prayers for protection from evil do remain in the baptismal rituals. The Rite for Infant Baptism (*Ordo Baptismi parvulorum,* May 15, 1969; second *editio typica,* June 24, 1973), for example, contains a prayer of exorcism at the end of the prayer of the faithful and litany, prior to (optional) anointing with the oil of catechumens (which functioned historically as an exorcism). But where the first edition spoke of freedom from the power of darkness (*a potestate tenebrarum*), the second speaks rather of ''original sin'' (*ab originalis culpae labe,* BaptCh 49).

More elaborate exorcisms may be found in the Rite of Christian Initiation of Adults. Exorcism is described as showing the ''true nature of the spiritual life as a battle between flesh and spirit'' (ChrInitAd 101) and the formulas (ibid. 113–118; 373) speak of preservation from sin and evil. The scrutinies, intended to purify and strengthen the candidate (ibid. 154), contain rites of exorcism whereby ''the Church teaches the elect about the mystery of Christ who frees from sin. By exorcism they are freed from the effects of sin and from the influence of the devil, and they are strengthened in their spiritual journey and open their hearts to receive the gifts of the Savior'' (ibid. 156). The ritual's formulas (ibid. 164, 171, 178, 379, 383, 387) reflect this understanding.

Similarly, the blessing of baptismal water in the rituals and the blessing of water at the beginning of the order of Mass in the Sacramentary no longer contain an exorcism of water (or of the salt, use of which is optional).

Scepticism regarding demonic possession and deemphasis of exorcism in no way imply denial of the power of evil customarily spoken of as the devil or Satan.

Bibliography: R. BÉRAUDY, ''Scrutinies and Exorcisms,'' in J. WAGNER, ed., *Adult Baptism and the Catechumenate. Concilium* 22 (1967) 57–61. J. CORTÉS and F. GATTI, *The Case against Possessions and Exorcisms* (New York 1975). L. MITCHELL, *Baptismal Anointing* (London 1966). R. WOODS, *The Occult Revolution* (New York 1971).

[J. DALLEN]

EXPERIENCE

A term rooted in the Greek ἐμπειρία, from which the word empirical is directly derived, and in the Latin *expe-*

rientia, whose verb form *experiri* means to try, to put to the test, to know by experience, and whose past participle furnishes the term expert. Thus, experience is sometimes connotative of a certain wisdom or skill in the practical order. This article explains the philosophical usages of the term, particularly in EPISTEMOLOGY, that are distinctive of Greek, medieval and modern, and contemporary thought.

Greeks. While current practice tends to use the term experience in a sense wide enough to include a solitary chance encounter, with little or no reflection to account for it, this is not exactly the manner in which the Greeks used the term. Their ἐμπειρία is translated as experience. But this translation comes via the Latin *experientia,* and while the Latin tends to retain an implication of being expert, this must be supplied in the English translation. In other words, while the present-day connotation of experience is that of generating knowledge, this was not so for the Greeks. In their view, experience is generated through repetition and is dependent on practical knowledge. Thus, experience for them is more like empirical knowledge. And it is only in this sense that Saint Thomas Aquinas's commentary on Aristotle's *Metaphysics* can be understood: ''In men the next thing above memory is experience, which some animals have only to a small degree. . . . But above experience, which belongs to particular reason, men have as their chief power a universal reason by means of which they live'' (*In 1 meta.* 1). And in like manner, one should understand Aristotle's comparison of experience with art: ''It is from memory that men acquire experience, because the numerous memories of the same thing eventually produce the effect of a single experience. Experience seems very similar to science and art, but actually it is through experience that men acquire science and art'' (*Metaphysics* 981 a 4).

This notion of experience as a certain knowledge of particulars became somewhat modified among the Stoics, a philosophical movement founded by Zeno of Citium (*see* STOICISM). According to Zeno and his followers, experience arises from recollections, which follow from perception. The Stoics maintained that reality consisted only of corporeal objects. Thus, the gods, the soul, and qualities must be interpreted in terms of matter. The Epicureans agreed with the Stoics in this respect; in their development of theories of scientific knowledge, experience became the criterion of judging the truth and falsity of opinion.

Scholastics and Moderns. Through the interpretation of scientific theories in terms of experience, the natural sciences came to be known as *experimental* sciences. For ROGER BACON, experience became the determinant of scientific proof: ''I now wish to unfold the principles of experimental science, since without experience nothing can be sufficiently known. . . . Aristotle's statement, then, that proof is reasoning that causes us to know is to be understood with the proviso that the proof is accompanied by its appropriate experience, and is not to be understood of the bare proof.'' (*Op. mai.* 6.1).

While PHILOSOPHY, since the time of Aristotle, has traditionally been called scientific knowledge, no one in the scholastic tradition made any pretense to identify philosophy with the experimental sciences. However, with the rise in stature of the latter, particularly in England, philosophers such as T. HOBBES, J. LOCKE, D. HUME, and H. SPENCER tended more and more to associate philosophy with the natural sciences. Subsequently, epistemological theories were developed exclusively in the light of the methods of modern science. At least the claims are set forth to develop such theories according to a ''rigorous scientific method.'' Thus, experience becomes a byword in practically all modern theories of knowledge. The classical work of D. J. B. HAWKINS is nothing more than a critique of such usage.

In these theories of knowledge, experience is used in two ways: (l) intrinsically, as a certain conscious awareness, in much the same way as the ancient Stoics used the term; and (2) extrinsically, as pertaining to the things in the world that one encounters.

When experience is considered in the first way, the same naïve problems that beset ancient MATERIALISM reappear in modern interpretation of sense data. Sense data are there not understood as something extrinsic to the knowing subject; rather, they are themselves impressions produced in the senses in the act of PERCEPTION. Hence, the first intimation of CONSCIOUSNESS is not an awareness of something in nature, but the impression that the thing in nature has aroused in man. And the same theory of reconstruction that DEMOCRITUS devised to explain how one can form an IDEA reappears in the writings of B. RUSSELL and of Mao Tse Tung.

Considering experience in the second way, rather than make it something of consciousness alone, John Dewey treats it in much the same way as man's actions are treated in descriptive BEHAVIORISM, viz, strictly in terms of environment. His theory of knowledge regards experience as an extrinsic relation (the referent) to the knowing subject, with no so-called metaphysical structure (e.g., the intellect) to account for the concepts whereby man understands reality. Dewey's unmistakable influence is seen in modern theories of learning, defined in such expressions as ''responses to stimulating situations'' and ''processes of adaptation.''

Contemporaries. Contemporary EXISTENTIALISM tends to give practical philosophy precedence over the speculative. The latter as impugned is static, and thus opposed to the dynamic character of the experience involved in the practical. This development has encouraged the use of phenomenological methods in contemporary scholastic philosophy and theology (*see* PHENOMENOLOGY). There, experience takes on new dimensions as circumscribing the transcendental relation of the ego. Some have been led to reject traditional SCHOLASTICISM because of a resulting erroneous view of the nature of speculative knowledge, as though the human INTELLECT can achieve a contemplation of TRUTH in a completely static state, without a dynamic discursus being necessary to arrive at some type of resolution. As a result of the false dichotomy introduced between dynamism and ''staticism,'' prominence is given to experience in contemporary philosophies that stress the notion of encounter. The metaphysics of Aristotle and Saint Thomas Aquinas, however, rejects such a prominence of dynamism; its aim is to go beyond discovering the truth of being that can be experienced to a discovery of the truth of being that defies sensory perception.

See Also: EMPIRICISM; POSITIVISM; METAPHYSICS, VALIDITY OF; KNOWLEDGE; KNOWLEDGE, THEORIES OF; SENSATION.

Bibliography: M. M. ROSSI, *Enciclopedia filosofica*, 4 v. (Venice-Rome 1957) 2:72–82. R. EISLER, *Wörterbuch der philosophischen Begriff*, 3 v. (4th ed. Berlin 1927–30) 1:357–65, 397–400. D. J. B. HAWKINS, *The Criticism of Experience* (New York 1946). J. L. LENNON, ''The Notion of Experience,'' *The Thomist* 23 (1960) 315–44.

[R. J. MASIELLO]

EXPERIENCE, RELIGIOUS

In its primary signification experience denotes the impression and immutation of a conscious rational subject resulting from actual contact with things, from living through an event or events. The actuality and concreteness of the contact distinguishes experience from what is ideal or imaginary and locates it largely in sensation and feeling, not, however, to the exclusion of intellectual and volitional elements, as long as direct intuitional contact with reality is involved. Every experience would seem to involve at once cognitional and appetitive (both emotional and volitional) elements, with the latter, however, predominating; experience is not mere knowing but more a matter of being affected by the object. As such it is largely subjective, with emphasis upon affectivity. The experience is not limited to the mere passive immutation of the subject but includes as well his vital responses, especially the spontaneous ones. A secondary meaning of the term extends it to signify a state of accumulated experiences, representing achieved habitual attitudes of a cognitional, volitional, or emotive kind. The kinds of experience are numerous and varied. It may be individual or collective; conscious or subconscious; natural or supernatural; and in terms of the area wherein the experience occurs—aesthetic, moral, metaphysical (e.g., the intuition of one's own being), religious, etc.

Religious experience is thus some sort of awareness of and response to the divine, largely achieved in terms of discerning the divine presence or one's total dependence upon divinity. This may be immediate or mediated, but is necessarily subjective either entirely so or with varying degrees of foundation in external reality and history. It is in opposition to abstract rational thought and not infrequently accompanied by such phenomena as revelation, inspiration, voices and visions, conversion, etc.

The Term in History. Religious experience is doubtlessly as old as man himself; yet it is only from the time of the Protestant reformers that it assumes a singular and predominant role in religious life. In the four centuries from Luther to William James there is one common note in all of Western Christianity aside from Catholicism, namely, that religious experience is the ultimate criterion and rule of faith. Every constraint of dogma, authority, and speculative reason is to give way to it.

The Reformers. Martin LUTHER took as his point of departure the doctrine of the Fall as radically corrupting man, despoiling him of even the proper use of his natural powers. Religion is man's experience first of his own sinfulness and then of the bestowal upon him of justification that comes to him from without by an exterior imputation of the merits of Christ. Man, then, is purely passive in his justification, of which, however, he experiences a personal conviction. Faith is no longer a belief in dogmas but a faith in salvation, a sort of confidence or trust. John CALVIN acknowledged this same corruption of man in the *Institutes of the Christian Religion* and explained salvation by recourse to the Holy Spirit, who ''touches'' interiorly the heart of man. The affective satisfaction accompanying these illuminations and inflammations of the Spirit attests to their authenticity against deceptive experiences.

Jansenism. Cornelius JANSEN, M. de Bay (*see* BAIUS AND BAIANISM), and P. Quesnel, loosely grouped together in the movement known as Jansenism, represent a sort of semi-Protestantism within Catholicism. To human nature there is assigned only weakness and corruption; all good originates in the order of grace. But Jansen in the *Augustinus* described grace as an experienced delectation that determines the assent of the will. This was an excessive depreciation of theoretical reason with an extolling of affective life and sentimentality. The soul was represented as capable of an immediate feeling of the rapport between itself and God. The writings of all three of these authors were condemned by the Church (H. Denzinger, *Enchiridion symbolorum*, ed. A. Schönmetzer, 1901–80, 2001–07, 2010–12, 2400–2502). Blaise PASCAL, without being committed to the Jansenist position, did come under its influence and insisted upon salvific knowledge of God as ''felt by the heart, not reason.''

I. Kant and F. D. F. Schleiermacher. The writings of these philosophers introduced a new phase in the Protestant understanding of religious experience. Kant's idealism and agnosticism enhanced religious subjectivity and gave philosophical justification to the Lutheran position on the powerlessness of reason. The norms of religious faith were made to be purely practical and subjective. SCHLEIERMACHER made the very essence of religion to consist in sentiment. According to him, concepts of the speculative reason are no more than superstition. Religious experience is a purely emotive state resulting in an immediate impression of the divine; each experience is at once valid but deficient so that the only authentic form of piety is tolerance. Later writers attempted to regulate this experience by the norms of Scripture (H. Plitt, *Evangelische Glaubenslehre,* 2 v. Gotha 1863–64) or to situate it in the moral crises precipitating conversion (F. R. Franck, *Christian Certainty,* tr. M. J. Evans, Edinburgh 1886).

S. Kierkegaard. Reacting against the pantheism inherent in Hegelian metaphysics, Kierkegaard concerned himself with the personal predicament of man ''existing before God'' (*The Concept of Dread* and *Christian Discourses,* tr. W. Lowrie, London 1944, 1940). In anguish and despair man becomes aware of his lack of self-sufficiency and is thus led to religious experience that consists in an act of commitment to God. This act rests upon an awareness of God that amounts to a personal encounter; historical faith is of no avail here, and the experience cannot be rendered in concepts. Ultimate truth is pure subjectivity, demanding that God ''break in'' upon the soul.

Modernism. A. LOISY and G. TYRRELL were prime spokesmen in a movement that maintained that dogmatic formulas were not valid norms for truth, these being merely the product of a sociological and humanistic experience of the Christian community reflecting upon a revelation it could not grasp. The variance of this from Catholic teaching is noted in the condemnatory decree of the Holy Office *Lamentabili* issued under Pius X (*Enchiridion symbolorum* 3401–66).

Pragmatism. H. BERGSON (*The Two Sources of Morality and Religion,* tr. Andra and Brereton, New York 1954) and W. JAMES (*The Varieties of Religious Experience*) reduced religious faith to the order of subjective utility. Bergson's anti-intellectualism led him to locate religion in experiences arising out of practical activity. Their value is entirely a pragmatic one in a philosophy of pure ''becoming.'' James's contribution consisted in the analysis of the content of such experiences, largely in terms of their psychological manifestations. These occur in the ''subliminal self,'' are largely instances of ''psychological automatism,'' require no belief in a personal God, and are primarily therapeutic in value.

Contemporary Thought. The social crises of the times have provoked even greater concern with subjective religious experience. This is manifest in the purely philosophical writings of many existentialists and phenomenologists, such as E. Husserl, M. Heidegger, and K. Jaspers; it continues to animate the mainstream of orthodox Protestantism as in the crisis-theology of Karl Barth; in Catholicism it has earned the increasing concern of G. Marcel, L. LAVELLE, R. Guardini, K. Rahner, E. Schillebeeckx to mention but a few.

Positive Analysis. Genuine religious experience does hold a place within Catholic theology, never, however, so as to deteriorate into complete subjectivism. Such experience is not, then, a criterion for belief except in a secondary sense, that is, by reference to a historical faith and especially with regard to the Incarnation as a historical event, which is an objective precondition to experience. Three instances will illustrate how such experiences may occur. (1) Human crises—these occur under God's providential guidance effecting those dispositions of soul in which man becomes acutely and intuitively aware of his limitations, his sinfulness, and his need for God. Such experiences can be either preparatory for grace or conducive to further advancement in grace already possessed. They can involve the direct intervention of God (as in the case of Saint Paul struck down on the road to Damascus) but need not do so. (2) Charismatic graces—these are graces that do not as such sanctify the individual but are given rather for the common utility of the Christian community. As visions, private revelations, prophecies, and miracles, they manifest in extraordinary fashion the purposes of God and can occasion a heightened sense of the divine. (3) Faith and the Sacraments—at the very heart of Christianity, common to all in varying degrees of intensity, is a personal awareness of the interrelationships and exchanges with God achieved in an act of belief mediated by the Church and given loving expression in the liturgical acts of shared community worship. This contact depends upon God's saving act toward man realized in the Incarnation, Passion, death, Resurrection, and Ascension of Christ. These events are also utilized by God as instrumental causes in the communication of that grace, which they express symbolically. Religious experience is not this ontological reality introduced into the soul by God with the initial assimilation it achieves; it is rather the personal and quasi-intuitive awareness of what occurs psychologically in man's consciousness. The donation of grace depends (God willing it) upon man's free cooperative response. God's invitational love effects a passive immutation of the soul obscurely open to experience, in which the divine presence is discerned. It then appears possible within the obscurity of faith to know and love in some highly personal and more concrete way the Triune God. The soul thus moves beyond the abstract concepts of faith to a true experience involving interpersonal relationships. This experience is not direct and immediate, not an intuition properly speaking; only the beatific vision is such. Here there is only, at the most, a contuition, a contact in knowledge and love, with God in His very presentiality, but only through the medium of experiencing His created effects within the soul. Saint Thomas characterizes this as quasi-experimental knowledge (In sent. 1.14.2.2 ad 3; *De virt. in comm.* 12 ad 11). In its more sublime instances this becomes infused contemplation elicited by the gift of wisdom (cf. *Summa theologiae* 1a, 43.5 ad 2), which may, but need not be, accompanied by mystical phenomena.

The content of this experience is varied: a sense of sin, of the presence of God, of the victory of Christ, of freedom from the spirit of fear, of fellowship with Christ, of being begotten of God, of sonship, of the indwelling of the Trinity, of entering upon relationships to the Father, in the Spirit, through the Son (Rom 6.4; Gal 2.20; 1 Jn 3.6; Rom 8.15; Col 1.2; Gal 4.6; Rom 5.5).

Faith is not only an intellectual assent to conceptually formulated truth; it is at the same time a loving surrender to a Person. The believing act is an encounter with God, in Christ, and not merely as object but as subject. What is known obscurely is not merely what, but who God is. Such encounter, moreover, cannot be unilateral. The sacramental act, then (above all, in the Eucharist), is first of all a symbolic expression of belief and free acceptance, the vital, conscious response of man to God's initiative in the dialogue of grace. This is undergone in a dark but authentic quasi-intuition of the Person and time-transcending presence of the God-Man.

Bibliography: H. PINARD, *Dictionnaire de théologie catholique*, ed. A. VACANT 5.2:1786–1868. H. M. HUGHES, J. HASTINGS ed., *Encyclopedia of Religion and Ethics*, 13 v. (Edinburgh 1908–27). F. SCHLEIERMACHER, *The Christian Faith,* ed. H. R. MACKINTOSH and J. S. STEWART (Edinburgh 1928; Torchbook 2 v. 1963). W. JAMES, *The Varieties of Religious Experience* (New York 1902; repr. 1963). J. MOUROUX, *The Christian Experience,* tr. G. LAMB (New York 1954). H. PINARD, ''La Théorie de l'expérience religieuse: San évolution de Luther à W. James,'' *Revue d'histoire ecclésiastique* 17 (1921) 63–83, 306–48, 547–74.

[W. J. HILL]

EXPERIENCE THEOLOGY

One of the tendencies in modern Protestantism to affirm that the doctrines of the Christian faith are derived from an analysis of the subjective faith experience. It is clearly discernible in the thought of F. SCHLEIERMACHER and may be traced to his attempt to wed RATIONALISM and philosophical ROMANTICISM. To Schleiermacher's way of thinking, dogma was the rational expression of a certain religious sentiment (this latter being described as the feeling of total dependence on God). He attempted to avoid radically individualistic SUBJECTIVISM, moreover, by observing that authentic religious sentiment includes the experience of Christian fellowship. Christian dogmas, then, will reflect what is common to all such experience. A quasi-tradition is thus established, which, however, Schleiermacher considered to be altogether secondary with reference to the experience.

In the school of Erlangen (K. von Hofmann and F. H. R. Frank) the emphasis is placed more on the genuine experience of rebirth, to which is attributed the objective renewal of faith. Even such thinkers as R. SEEBERG and A. RITSCHL show that they were influenced by these trains of thought, insofar as they make the experience of the awesome power of faith the occasion for the critical interpretation of dogmatic tradition.

The difficulty here, of course, is in discerning precisely how one's own experience is related to what is directly the object of faith. One aspect of this relation is certainly expressed in the term love-knowledge. Communion with God in love is assuredly a principle through which Christian doctrine is better understood; and when such communion is attributed to the Church, we have a factor of dogmatic development. The proponents of experience theology (*Erfahrungstheologie*), however, seem to identify such communion with revelation; and such a position is scarcely tenable.

Bibliography: K. BARTH, *Church Dogmatics,* tr. G. T. THOMSON (New York 1955–) 1.1:6.3. W. LOHFF, *Lexikon für Theologie und Kirche,* ed. J. HOFER and K. RAHNER, 10 v. (2d, new ed. Freibrug 1957–65) 3:981–982. F. E. SCHLEIERMACHER, *The Christian Faith,* ed. H. R. MACKINTOSH and J. S. STEWART (Edinburgh 1928).

[M. B. SCHEPERS]

EXPERIMENTATION, MEDICAL

Principles

Medical experimentation raises a moral question as far as it submits human subjects either to medical treatments not as yet scientifically established or to procedures employed only for the purpose of discovering some truth or of verifying some hypothesis. If the experiment entails any significant risk or hardship for the subject, the matter becomes theologically one of moral rights and duties relative to proper respect for human life and health.

Experimentation admits of two possible objectives: benefit to the individual who submits to experimental measures, or the advance of medical science and consequent benefit to the common good. Accordingly as one or the other purpose is sought exclusively, or at least is paramount in the intention of the participants, two distinct moral problems present themselves.

For the subject's benefit. When the good of the individual patient is the physician's exclusive or predominant concern, the canons of good medicine will dictate the course of a treatment that it is the doctor's duty to provide. Thus, if a sure remedy is available, it should ordinarily be employed in preference to treatment of doubtful efficacy. Or if the only choice of remedy lies among several that are at best doubtful, the most promising should generally be used. The patient is entitled in justice to the surest means reasonably available for achieving the object of his medical contract, viz, the cure or control of his malady.

But it is also true that if a proven remedy would entail exceptional expense, pain, or other hardship, the patient may be justified in choosing instead a treatment whose effectiveness is as yet incompletely established but that circumvents the disadvantage presumably inherent in his using the proven procedure. The patient, in other words, may legitimately run the risk, even though it be considerable, of a less certain remedy, provided there is a proportionately serious reason for so doing. A fortiori, if there is little or no risk involved in accepting a remedy of dubious efficacy, it is undeniably the patient's right to make that choice for any reasonable motive.

But a decision of this kind is the patient's prerogative and not the doctor's. Hence the doctor must prefer the certain to the uncertain remedy, or the more probable to the less probable, unless the patient's rightful choice to the contrary is explicitly expressed either by him or by his legitimate representative, or unless this consent can be reasonably presumed.

For the benefit of others. In order to discern the limitations to be placed on human experimentation undertaken for the benefit of others, one must appreciate two moral truths. The first is simply a denial of that extremist philosophy that we have come to identify as totalitarianism and that would subject the individual completely to the community or state by subordinating all individual rights to the prior claims of the common good. Such a philosophy, in its most blatant form, found expression in the experimental excesses encouraged and practiced under Nazism and later repudiated by the free world in the formulation at Nuremberg of a ten-point statement of limitations to be placed on medical experiments performed on human subjects. Put positively, this principle asserts that, with regard to his life and bodily integrity, each individual possesses a God-given right of immunity from unprovoked attack by any other person. No individual, therefore, can legitimately be considered an expendable member of society to be exploited for the common good. For this reason it follows, in the words of Pius XII, that "the doctor can take no measure or try no course of action without the consent of the patient." Consequently, laudable as may be the desire to contribute to the advancement of medical science, doctors are nonetheless restricted in their human experimentation by this inalienable right of any individual to forbid such use of his organic entity. As the first rule of the Nuremberg Tribunal expresses it, "The voluntary consent of the human subject is absolutely essential."

The second pertinent principle denies what might be called extreme individualism on our part and imposes certain basic limitations on each one's right to dispose of his own life and bodily members. Because of his creaturehood, man must admit himself to be essentially dependent upon his Creator. In context, this dependence means that man is not the absolute master of his body and life. He is not proprietor of himself, but rather a custodian entrusted with the care of "property" that belongs strictly to God. He may, therefore, administer this trust only in compliance with the divine will as manifested to him in various ways.

The first corollary from this principle is the prohibition of the natural law against suicide. To intend directly the termination of one's own life is to usurp a right that belongs exclusively to God. There are circumstances in which we are justified in risking our lives if necessary for the achievement of some momentous good; but in such cases, death, if it should occur, is the unintended byproduct of an act legitimately performed for another reason and is not imputable as a moral evil. Even for the laudable purpose of advancing medical science, no one would be justified in making his own death the intended means to that end.

A second consequence of the same principle relates to bodily damage short of death that for one or another reason one might inflict upon himself or allow another to inflict. We are responsible to God not only for life itself but also for our physical integrity, and only within certain limits may we legitimately mutilate our bodies or suppress their natural functions. According to the principle of totality, for example, one is allowed to sacrifice a bodily member should this be necessary or useful for the good of his own person as a whole. But this principle has no application in a context of investigative procedures undertaken exclusively for the benefit of others. Does any other principle ratify the risking of one's bodily integrity for altruistic motives?

Certainly there are circumstances wherein the principle of charity—i.e., love for fellow man—does legitimatize a certain degree of bodily self-sacrifice on behalf of others. Theologians unanimously agree, for example, that blood transfusions and heterologous skin grafts are morally permissible. On the strength of the same principle, many moralists of highest repute vigorously defend some forms of organic transplantation *inter vivos,* always with certain qualifications that sound medicine would also stipulate. Finally, although one may not intend his own death as a means of saving another's life, it is sometimes permissible deliberately to perform a heroic act that will have two immediate effects, viz, preservation of another's life and the unintended but inevitable loss of one's own. In none of these instances does any bodily benefit accrue to the donor subject. In fact, the contrary is true, especially where the sacrifice of an organ or risk to life is concerned.

Conclusion. It is clear that the immanent teleology of our corporal being does admit of a certain ordination to the benefit of others. In terms of experimental medicine, it would also seem that charity would countenance a limited degree of risk to life or bodily integrity in circumstances that make human experimentation genuinely necessary. But where does one draw the line beyond which one may not licitly go in this regard? No general answer, applicable to all cases indiscriminately, is possible. Each individual case must be judged on its own merits. An attempt must be made to judge whether there is sufficient reason to justify the necessary risk or harm entailed in the particular procedure contemplated. However, the following generic norms can be suggested as morally safe in practice: (1) When bodily damage or risk to life is foreseen as insignificant, there is no valid reason to forbid a willing subject to consent to the procedure in question. (2) No one may legitimately consent to a procedure that entails certain death as a necessary means of achieving the experiment's purpose. (Although it has been suggested by some that a criminal already justly condemned to death might licitly choose this form of execution, such a possibility would represent the sole exception to an otherwise universal rule.)

In the vast intermediate area where hazard to life or health may range from notable to very serious, the maximum limit of permissible risk cannot be sharply defined. But it would seem safe to say that, for a proportionately grave reason, a subject may for the benefit of others authorize and submit to any experimental procedure that will not seriously and permanently impair his functional integrity or cause serious risk of life. Implicit in this concession is the supposition that the procedure has been adequately tested short of human experimentation, that it promises reasonable hope of achieving a good proportionate to the risk, and that all reasonable care is taken to avoid even unintended harm to any who submit to the experiment.

Bibliography: PIUS XII, ''Ce premier Congrès,'' (Address, Sept. 13, 1952) *Acta Apostolicae Sedis* 44 (1952) 779–789; English tr. *Catholic Mind* 51 (May 1953) 305–313; ''Nous sommes heureux,'' (Address, Sept. 30, 1954) *Acta Apostolicae Sedis* 46 (1954) 587–598; English tr. *Catholic Mind* 53 (April 1955) 242–252. G. A. KELLY, *Medico-Moral Problems* (St. Louis, Mo. 1958) 261–269. C. J. MCFADDEN, *Medical Ethics* (5th ed. Philadelphia, Pa. 1961) 249–255. T. J. O'DONNELL, *Morals in Medicine* (2d ed. rev. and enl. Westminster, Md. 1959) 113–120. J. PAQUIN, *Morale et médecine* (3d ed. rev. Montreal 1960) 365–371. J. J. LYNCH, ''Human Experimentation in Medicine: Moral Aspects,'' *Linacre Quarterly* 27 (1960) 62–67.

[J. J. LYNCH]

Recent Developments

Medical and public concern. Medical research and experimentation have provided the physician with considerably improved methods for dealing with human disease and dysfunction. Among these are antimicrobial agents for a variety of infectious diseases; organ transplantation for dealing with total kidney failure and selected heart conditions, as well as other organs such as the liver; better surgical techniques for repair of injuries to tissue and bone; chemotherapy and radiation therapy for cancer control; sophisticated diagnostic techniques such as computerized tomography (CAT); magnetic resonance imaging (MRI), ultrasonography, and numerous other laboratory tests which provide to the physician with more precise information about the condition of his patient; and a host of drugs to deal more effectively with hypertension, anxiety, pain, hormonal deficiencies, allergies, and many other human physical and mental dysfunctions. In addition, the recently completed Human Genome Project promises a bright future for the diagnosis and treatment of diseases at the genetic level.

As the benefits of medical research became more evident in everyday life, increased private and governmental funding has provided the means for still more research. Thus, national support (federal, state, industrial, and private nonprofit) for health research and disease in 1961 was $1.1 billion, while for 1976 it was about $5.1 billion, representing approximately 3.6% of a total health cost of $141.1 billion (National Institutes of Health 1977-Basic Data). The proposed 2002 budget for NIH alone is $23.1 billion (CNN.com).

Parallel with the increase in medical research has been an augmentation in the medical profession's concern about the ethical aspects of human experimentation. One measure of this increased interest is the notable increase in the number of publications in the medical literature which deal with the ethical dimensions of human experimentation. Public and professional interest has also been aroused with the revelation of several apparently flagrant examples of the violation of basic human rights associated with medical research. Such occurrences, it must be stressed, are rare. Recently considerable public interest has developed around the possibility of human cloning (after the announcement in February of 1997 of a cloned sheep, Dolly, with the consequent surfacing of many ethical questions. Similarly, the issue of the use of human stem cells for research and therapy has resulted in intense ethical discussions.

Governmental action. In 1974 Congress passed and the President signed into law, the National Research Act, establishing the National Commission for the Protection of Human Subjects of Biomedical and the Behavioral Research (Title II of Public Law 93–348). The eleven-member commission assumed the task of (1) identifying the basic ethical principles which should undergird research involving human subjects; (2) developing appropriate guidelines; (3) making recommendations for administrative action to the Secretary of the Department of Health, Education, and Welfare (HEW). Over the subsequent years there have been structural changes in the Federal agencies so that the current relevant agency is the Office for Protection from Research Risks located in the Department of Health and Human Services (DHHS). The relevant Federal Regulations may be found in the Code of Federal Regulations, Title 45, Part 46, Protection of Human Subjects.

The early basic regulation governing the protection of human subjects in biomedical and behavioral research were published in the *Federal Register* on May 30, 1974. These regulations required, among other items, that (1) the risks be outweighed by the sum of benefits to the subject and the importance of the knowledge to be gained; (2) the rights and welfare of the subject be adequately protected; (3) legally effective, informed and free consent be obtained; (4) the research be reviewed at timely intervals. Each research site is to set up an Institutional Review Board (IRB) to review every research protocal involving human subjects. Without the IRBs approval that research may not proceed. Other regulations governing research when the subjects are fetuses, pregnant women, or the products of *in vitro* fertilization were issued on Aug. 8, 1975. These were modified and augmented by regulations published on Jan. 11, 1978. Proposed policies governing the use of psychosurgery in practice and research were issued on May 23, 1977, while publication of and invitation of public comment on the report and recommendations of the National Commission regarding research involving children appeared in the *Federal Register* on Jan. 13, 1978. All these regulations have been periodically updated. Part of a refinement and updating process initially included, and continues to include, consultation with the scientific community and interested public groups or individuals. The *Federal Register* remains a reliable information source of changes in Federal Regulations regarding the protection of human subjects in medical research.

Church teaching. Vatican Council II and Popes John XXIII and Paul VI in the area of medical research have primarily applied and reinforced what Pope Pius XII had already said at some length. In his address to the Pontifical Academy of Sciences on April 27, 1968, Pope Paul VI stated: ''The Holy See intends to show that the Catholic Church respects scientific research, recognizes its freedom within its own domain, and looks forward eagerly to its present and future conquests'' (*The Pope Speaks* 13 [1968] 108). In an earlier address to pediatric cardiologists, the pope stated the supreme rule for medical practice and research: ''that man is . . .'the subject, the basis and the end' of life in society . . .'' (May 12, 1967; *The Pope Speaks* 12 [1967] 365). The pope's abiding concern is shown when he addressed the European Association of Hospital Doctors on April 28, 1973 and noted the need to ''reconcile legitimate and necessary research with the personal rights of the patient, who can never be sacrificed as if the matter involved merely a part of humanity ordained to the good of the whole'' (*Pope Speaks* 18 [1973] 69–71). Finally, Pope Paul reiterated his central theme: ''In this field of medical ethics, we would like once more to stress its foundation: unconditional respect for life, from its beginning'' (Paul VI to the doctors of Flanders, April 23, 1977, *Osservatore Rom* May 5, 1977, 9). In his turn, Pope JOHN PAUL II made a number of notable contributions to the field of medical ethics. Among these are the following: *The Splendor of Truth (VERITATIS SPLENDOR)* 1993; *The Gospel of Life (EVANGELIUM VITAE)* 1995; and several documents issued by the Congregation for the Doctrine of the Faith, and aproved by John Paul II, *Declaration on Euthanasia* (1980) and *Instruction on*

Respect for Human Life in Its Origin and on the Dignity of Procreation (*Donum Vitae*) (1987).

From these quotations and other papal statements it is evident that relative to medical research the magisterium asserts three main points: (1) Medical research is necessary and good but must be for the true welfare of human beings. (2) Human life must be respected by the individual and others at all stages of its existence; therefore, research risks are to be limited by the requirements of justice and charity. (3) Human persons are individually of inestimable value and may not under any conditions be used as mere means; consequently, informed and free consent is an absolute condition for human experimentation.

Informed consent. In practice, perhaps the area of greatest difficulty is the process of obtaining truly informed and freely given consent from the potential research subject. Government regulations provide a framework and a mechanism to assure some degree of compliance with the regulations. Nonetheless, ultimately the protection of the subject's basic human rights devolves on those doing the research. The assessment of the risk/benefit ratio depends much on the experimenter's own understanding of the research about to be undertaken. Obtaining appropriate informed consent from the potential research subjects rests in large measure on the researcher's having an attitude of profound respect towards human beings and on his ability to express the expected benefits and reasonably anticipated hazards in a manner that adequately informs and freely elicits the appropriate consent. Special groups such as the poor, the sick, employees, medical and graduate students are considered to be "consent prone" and thus require particular care to assure the absence of coercion. Other groups such as fetuses, the mentally retarded, children, and prisoners are especially vulnerable and thus are generally inappropriate for human experimentation, unless there is serious need and additional safeguards for the good and safety of the individual research subject are rigorously observed and enforced.

Bibliography: B. M ASHLEY and K. D. O'ROURKE, *Health Care Ethics, A Theological Analysis*, 4th ed., T. L. BEAUCHAMP and L. WALTERS, *Contemporary Issues in Bioethics* (Belmont, Calif. 1978). R. L. BOGOMOLNY, *Human Experimentation* (Dallas, Tx. 1976). P. CATALDO and A. S. MORACZEWSKI, *Catholic Health Care Ethics: A Manual for Ethics Committees* (Boston, Mass. 2001). C. FRIED, *Medical Experimentation: Personal Integrity and Social Policy* (New York 1974). B. H. GRAY, *Human Subjects in Medical Experimentation* (New York 1975). N. HERSHEY and R. D. MILLER, *Human Experimentation and the Law* (Germantown, Md. 1976). J KATZ, *Experimentation with Human Beings* (New York 1972). W. E. MAY, *Human Existence, Medicine and Ethics* (Chicago, Ill. 1977). National Academy of Sciences, *Experiments and Research with Humans: Values in Conflict* (Washington, D.C. 1975). T. J. O'DONNEL, *Medicine and Christian Morality* (New York 1976). P. RAMSEY, *The Patient As Person* (New Haven, Conn. and London 1970). S. J. REISER, A. J. DYCK, and W. J. CURRAN, *Ethics in Medicine: Historical Perspectives and Contemporary Concerns* (Cambridge, Mass. 1977). J. J. SHINNERS, *The Morality of Medical Experimentation on Living Human Subjects in the Light of Recent Papal Pronouncements* (Washington, D.C. 1958). M. B. VISSCHER, *Ethical Constraints and Imperatives in Medical Research* (Springfield, Ill. 1975).

[A. S. MORACZEWSKI]

EXPIATION

Expiation is a general concept denoting all acts and means whereby a sacred order to which harm has been done is restored. In any given religious structure the meaning of expiation depends on (1) the nature of the sacred order to which harm has been done—this order can be one that is established by a god, it can be the will of God Himself, or it can also be an impersonally conceived order; (2) the various concepts of the harm or evil that has been done (*see* SIN).

The interdependence of the meanings of expiation, holiness, and sin accounts for the closeness of expiation to other concepts in many contexts. The Latin root word *expiare* means not only to atone for sins but also to placate or appease the wrath of a god. The words expiation, penance, and penalty are often interchangeable. In primitive cultures penal procedure and expiation are often hard to distinguish. The justice of the death penalty for incest in interior Celebes is thought of as self-evident because it confines the evil to the criminals and protects the community. Among the ancient Nordics the same place served as a center for cult and for the execution of justice. Thus sins can be atoned for or punishment inflicted because of the cultic order that protects the common weal. Castigation or self-castigation (in monastic life) to expiate for sin in Christianity, Buddhism, and Jainism is a related phenomenon. In most instances expiation in monastic life, however, is more properly understood as a form of mortification or purification. Purification implies not only the cleansing from evil or sin, but more widely the preparation for the holy, whether in cult and liturgy or in ascetic and monastic life. The confession of sins is probably the most widely attested element of expiation ceremonies. As an integral part of expiation it occurred long before Christianity, e.g., in the Egyptian, Babylonian, Hittite, Israelite, Chinese, and Japanese religions. Outside the Christian sphere of influence, R. Pettazzoni collected evidence of the practice from some 100 primitive tribes scattered over the world. The major emphases in expiation rites and concepts may be presented under four headings.

Concrete Removal of Sins. Expiation rites in primitive religions are often accomplished by such physical means as spitting, vomiting, or drawing of blood. Many ceremonies resemble magic operations, by removing a substance representing the cause of a malady. Among the Kagaba (Colombia, South America) a man who committed a crime is acquitted of his guilt by a process in which pebbles symbolizing the perpetrated evil are removed. Quite common are the burning and ablution of sins. In Brahmanism a priest ritually identifies the guilt of a person with a piece of the wooden, sacrificial post and throws it in the fire, thus physically annihilating the sacrificer's guilt. Ablutions with water, baths, and especially the sprinkling with blood are widely considered effective means of expiation, making people, devotees, and even things free from pollution, impurity, evil, and sin (*see* Ex 12.7). Among the Teutons the sprinkling of blood cleansed the participants in the sacrifice and purified the idols and walls of the temple.

Concreteness in expiation rites is particularly clear in the confession of sins that accompanies or precedes the specific acts. It is particular sins that are declared and are atoned for. Among the Kikuyu (East Africa) the declaration of each sin is followed by expectoration. Bath and confession of sins are both part of the expiatory ceremony among the Bashilange (Congo) and the Thonga (southeast Africa). Although in almost all cases of declaration of sins only the presence of a priest or medicine man is needed, there are, however, exceptions that emphasize the concreteness. Among the Dagari (Upper Guinea) the husband listens to his wife's confession of conjugal infidelities while she is in childbirth. Frequently, expiatory rites with confessions of sins are performed in times of crisis. Sins are feared for their concrete presence and consequences, and their declaration and expiation are to be understood as an equally concrete riddance. The concreteness of these ceremonies is by no means lost in the more advanced cultures and the great religions. Ritual baths and washings occur, for instance, in the religions of Israel, Islam, and Hinduism.

Cultic and Social Forms. The ritualistic writings of Brahmanism describe expiation ceremonies in great detail. The Vedic student who breaks his celibacy wears the skin of an ass and begs for alms while publicly proclaiming his transgression. The function of society in the expiation rite, though not absent elsewhere, is thus strongly accentuated. Religions that are strongly developed on the cultic side often show forms of vicarious expiation. The sins of Israel, e.g., were carried away by the goat for Azazel (Leviticus ch. 16).

In several religions priests play an important mediating role. The most typical example of kings mediating between gods and men and atoning for the transgressions of the people was in Babylon. At the New Year's festival the king did penance on behalf of the people, was divested of his regalia, and was cultically humiliated before being reassured of the god's (Marduk's) favor and reinstated as king. Special penitential prayers and fixed days for expiation rites have a great importance in cults. Brahmanic ritualism developed special rites (*prāyaścitta*) to atone for ritual mistakes. Higher cults in general have special ceremonies and prayers for sins that are unwittingly committed, thus often continuing the concrete concept of sin as a material thing.

Mental Expiation. This form of expiation plays a crucial role in religions and religious institutions that are devoted to meditation and meditation techniques: monasticism, Buddhism, and Indian philosophies such as Sāmkhya and YOGA (*see* INDIAN PHILOSOPHY). In most cases of advanced meditation techniques the purely mental purification is accompanied or preceded by moral purification.

Humiliation before God. Humiliation is the natural concomitant of all religions that are monotheistic or emphasize God's mercy. The act of humiliation is the result of God's mercy and power rather than a means to effect purification. Humble devotion to the god Vishnu has been stressed in India by Rāmānuja and Madhva. (*See* HINDUISM.) The latter and his followers in particular see in *bhakti* the highest bliss. Faith in the most merciful God and the experience of mere creatureliness and sinfulness may make expiation the principal act of man; "Against Thee have we sinned" (Jer 14.7). The act is clearly expressed at the beginning of the Mass in the Confiteor and at the beginning of most Protestant liturgies in the Confession of Sins, followed by the remission of sins or assurance of pardon. Different, yet not unrelated is the basic attitude of Islam (submission).

See Also: EXPIATION (IN THE BIBLE); EXPIATION (IN THEOLOGY).

Bibliography: R. PETTAZZONI, "Confession of Sins: An Attempted General Interpretation," in his *Essays on the History of Religions* (Leiden 1954) 43–54; "Confession of Sins and the Classics," *ibid.* 55–67; *La Confession des péchés,* 2 v. (Paris 1931–32). H. FRANKFORT, *Kingship and the Gods* (Chicago 1948). R. J. THOMPSON, *Penitence and Sacrifice in Early Israel Outside the Levitical Law* (Leiden 1963). H. OLDENBERG, *Die Religion des Veda* (Berlin 1894). F. HEILER, *Das Gebet* (5th ed. Munich 1923). A. MÉDEBIELLE, *Dictionnaire de la Bible,* suppl. ed. L. PIROT, et al. (Paris 1928–) Suppl 3 (1938) 1–262, esp. 3–48, with bibliog. L. H. GRAY et al., J. HASTINGS, ed., *Encyclopedia of Religion and Ethics,* 13 v. (Edinburgh 1908–27) 5:635–671.

[K. W. BOLLE]

EXPIATION (IN THE BIBLE)

A blotting out or removal of sin; hence, the renewal of communion with God. The supreme act of expiation is Christ's death on the cross, the meaning of which is illuminated by a number of Old Testament themes. This article deals first with the idea and practice of expiation in Old Testament times, then with relevant New Testament texts.

In the Old Testament. In Israel a strict correlation is observable between expiation and SIN, and the sense of both is controlled by the COVENANT. Sin is the breaking of the covenantal stipulations, whether moral or ritual; expiation is the wiping out of sin so as to restore the covenantal relationship between the sinner or the sinful people and Yahweh. This stands in pointed contrast to the religions of the world that surrounded Israel during the whole Biblical period—the polytheistic nature-religions of the ancient Near East and the Greek and Hellenistic religions of the Mediterranean. Outside Israel, religion consisted in coming to terms with the gods so as to assure the well-being of the people or of the individual, and the direct purpose of expiatory acts was to allay the gods' often capricious wrath. (*See* SACRIFICE, II). Here as elsewhere, the faith of Israel may be said to account for its own uniqueness inasmuch as it consciously defines itself as a response to the self-revelation of Yahweh, a moral God and Lord of history.

Terminology and Ritual Expiation. In the vocabulary of expiation the Hebrew verb *kippēr* has first importance. Twice in the Old Testament it occurs in a profane sense according to which one placates an angry or ill-disposed man (Gn 32.21; Prv 16.14). As a religious term it has two uses. God expiates sin, i.e., He wipes out, removes, or forgives it; in passive forms of the verb, sin is expiated, i.e., wiped out, removed, forgiven. In liturgical usage *kippēr* means to expiate or to perform expiatory rites. The subject of the verb is Moses, Aaron, or the officiating priest. The object is the sin that is wiped out or the person or place that is cleansed of sin. The object is never God, and the meaning to placate God or His anger is not found.

Despite the relatively late redaction of the Levitical code, expiatory rites are of great antiquity in Israel (see Mi 6.6–7). This is clear from the archaic features in the concept and rite itself of the *ḥaṭṭā't,* or SIN OFFERING, e.g., the idea of the expiatory efficacy of blood that supposed the association of the animal's blood with its life; since the life, which is sacred and a divine gift par excellence, was considered to be in the blood, blood was regarded as peculiarly apt to expiate, i.e., to purify or to win forgiveness. The most important text, Lv 17.11, is part of the Law of HOLINESS, but the concept was certainly much older. [*See* SACRIFICE, III (IN ISRAEL)].

The expiatory ceremonies prescribed in the Book of LEVITICUS are of interest not only in themselves, but also for the light they throw on certain aspects of the New Testament theology of expiation. In the Old Testament ritual, the sin offering is distinguished from other sacrifices by the ritual disposal of the blood (Lv 4.5–7, 16–18, 25, 30, 34; 5.9), of the fat or choice portions (4.8–10, 19, 26, 31, 35), and of the remainder of the victim (4.11–12; etc.). If the sacrifice was offered to expiate the sin of the high priest or of the whole people, the blood was brought into the Holy Place [*see* TENT OF MEETING; TEMPLES (IN THE BIBLE)] and sprinkled before the veil of the HOLY OF HOLIES, smeared on the horns of the altar of incense, and the remainder poured out at the base of the altar of holocausts. The fat was burned on the altar of holocausts, and the ashes were carried outside the camp to a ''clean place'' where the rest of the victim was burned. If the sacrifice was offered for the sin of an individual lay person, the blood was smeared on the horns of the altar of holocausts and the remainder poured out at the base of the altar. The fat was burned on the altar of holocausts, and the remainder was consumed by the priest or priests. There is no evidence that the sacrifice was conceived as a substitute for the sacrifice of the life of the offerer, nor that the shedding of the victim's blood in any way signified a vicarious punishment; and from the disposal of its remains it is clear that the victim was considered holy rather than impure and laden with sin (Lv 6.18–22).

Expiation assumed an ever more dominant role in Israelite religion from the exilic period to the end of the Old Testament period. Nearly half the later legislation on sacrifice was concerned with expiatory offerings: the ancient sin offering (*ḥaṭṭā't*) and guilt offering (*'āšām*) and the HOLOCAUST, which was now given an expiatory significance (Lv 1.4). The same tendency is evident in the importance attached to the Day of ATONEMENT (Lv 16.1–34), distinguished by its expiatory sacrifices, the confession of the people's sins, and the driving of the sin-laden SCAPEGOAT into the desert. However, rites alone do not automatically win forgiveness. Without inner conversion, as the Prophets and later the rabbis frequently insisted, cultic rites are meaningless.

The Servant of the Lord. The peak of the Old Testament theology of expiation is reached in the fourth of the Deutero-Isaian Songs of the SUFFERING SERVANT (Is 52.13–53.12), where the religious tradition stream of ransom and redemption [*see* REDEMPTION (IN THE BIBLE)] converges with that of expiation. The term *'āšām,* which occurs in Is 53.10, had the sense of expiatory offering to God or expiatory sacrifice long before the redaction of the priestly code, as may be seen in 1 Sm 6.3–4, 8, 17. As indicated above, much of the material in the Levitical legislation is very ancient, so much so that, although a distinction of sorts is made between the sin offering (*ḥaṭṭā't*) and guilt offering (*'āšām*), the original distinction (if there was one) had been forgotten by the time of the priestly code's last redaction. Although the LXX changed the meaning of Is 53.10, *'āšām* was nevertheless understood in terms of expiatory sacrifice. In this passage, the suffering and death of the Servant is vicarious, undergone for the sake of others, and so takes on the sense of a ransom for their redemption.

In the Septuagint (LXX) translation of the third century B.C., *kippēr* is rendered mainly by ἐξιλάσκεσθαι; but the meaning of ἐξιλάσκεσθαι in profane Greek, ''to render propitious,'' is lost, and the word is used to express the meanings of *kippēr* discussed above. Other renderings of *kippēr* are ἁγιάζειν (to sanctify), καθαρίζειν (to purify), and ἀφαιρεῖν (to take away). In the three passages in which ἐξιλάσκεσθαι has God for its object (Mal 1.9; Za 7.2; 8.22), the Hebrew verb so rendered is *ḥillâ* (to implore favor), not *kippēr*.

Last Stages of Development. The acute consciousness of sin in late Old Testament Judaism inspired an intense concern with means of expiation. Cultic expiation continued to have first importance, although certain movements on the margin of ''official'' Judaism repudiated the efficacy of the Temple cult (*see* QUMRAN COMMUNITY). Judaism, in the last centuries before Christ, attributed an expiatory value to fasting, alms, prayer, sufferings, and, above all, death, but the efficacy of expiatory sacrifice and of these other means of expiation was understood to depend on the sinner's inner conversion. Death, as the greatest of sufferings, could expiate sin, and the death of the Jewish martyrs had expiatory value for all Israel. It is remarkable, however, that in Judaism this concept remained unrelated to the figure of the Servant of Yahweh until the second Christian century. The idea of a messiah whose suffering and death would have vicarious expiatory value seems to have remained foreign to Jewish thought. The apocrypha attest the expectation that eschatological Israel would be purified of sin, but this is understood to be the result of the messianic judgment; that is, the messiah is pictured not as destroying sin by winning its forgiveness, but as condemning and destroying the sinners themselves.

In the New Testament. The whole mission of Jesus was concerned with the redemption of man from sin [*see* REDEMPTION (IN THE BIBLE)]. His exorcisms, cures, and other miracles were aimed at subverting the dominion of Satan and inaugurating the eschatological kingdom of God. Above all, Jesus conceived His mission as the fulfillment of the role of the Servant whose expiatory death would ransom the world (Mk 10.45; Mt 20.28). This is underscored in the words of institution in the Last Supper accounts, where, beside the theme of the Servant's expiatory self-sacrifice for ''the many,'' i.e., for all (cf. Mk 14.24 with Is 53.12), the death of Jesus is alluded to as the sacrifice that seals the covenant. Conscious reference to the sacrifice of Jesus as PASSOVER LAMB is also probable. As the covenant sacrifice is at the same time an expiatory offering, the *qāhāl,* or eschatological community, born of this covenant is essentially defined by the forgiveness of sins.

The combination of motifs in Is 52.13–53.12 accounts for the diversity of ways in which references to this text find expression in the New Testament. In Mk 10.45 Jesus says He has come to give His life as a ransom (λύτρον) for the world (see 1 Tm 2.6); elsewhere the idea of ransom is replaced by that of expiatory sacrifice (e.g., in Rom 3.25). In either case Jesus freely offers His own life for the forgiveness of the sins of men. This central affirmation was early epitomized in catechetical formulas that drew on the Servant oracles for two motifs: the ''handing over'' of Jesus (Gal 2.20; Rom 4.25; 8.32) and His death ''for our sins'' (1 Cor 15.3) or ''for us'' (Rom 8.32; Eph 5.2). The Servant theme was apparently a significant element in early Christian preaching (Acts 3.13, 26; 8.32–35), and the messianic blessing of the forgiveness of sins (Acts 2.38) no doubt supposes consciousness of the expiatory value of Christ's death, although this theme was not exploited in the early kerygmatic discourses. Christ's definitive expiation of sin is a substantial datum of the theology of St. PAUL, St. John (Jn 1.29; 10.11–15; and *passim*), and the Epistle to the Hebrews (7.27 and *passim*). It is ''in his blood'' that we are justified and saved (Rom 5.9); it is ''the blood of Jesus'' that ''purifies us from all sin'' (1 Jn 1.7; Heb 9.14).

The New Testament writers, in speaking of the expiation of the sins of the world by Christ, understand this to be the work of God Himself in faithfulness to His promises of salvation. The New Testament nowhere depicts Christ as a victim of the Father's anger or displeasure. Christ is never compared to the sin-laden scapegoat, nor is the sacrifice of His life conceived as a punishment reserved for sinners to which He submits in their place. Expiation is seen rather as man's return, in and through Christ, to the Father. It is the forgiveness and reconciliation that only Christ can accomplish and that He does accomplish, out of love and in His blood, for men.

See Also: ROMANS, EPISTLE TO THE.

Bibliography: *Encyclopedic Dictionary of the Bible*, tr. and adap. By L. HARTMAN (New York 1963) 167–175. W. KORNFELD et al., *Lexikon für Theologie und Kirche*, ed. J. HOFER and K. RAHNER (Freiberg 1957–65) 9:1152–56. A. MÉDEBIELLE, *Dictionnaire de la Bible*, suppl. ed. L. PIROT, et al. (Paris 1928–) 3:1–262. K. KOCH et al., *Die Religion in Geschichte und Gegenwart* (Tübingen 1957–65) 6:1368–73. E. SJÖBERG, *Gott und die Sünder im palästinischen Judentum* (Stuttgart 1938). J. JEREMIAS, ''Das Lösegeld für Viele (Mk. 10, 45),'' *Judaica* 3 (1948) 249–264. L. MORALDI, *Espiazione sacrificale e riti espiatori nell'ambiente biblico e* *nell'Antico Testamento* (Rome 1956). S. LYONNET, ''De notione expiationis,'' *Verbum Domini* 37 (1959) 336–352; 38 (1960) 65–75, 241–261; ''Expiation et intercession,'' *Biblica* 40 (1959) 885–901. E. LOHSE, *Märtyrer und Gottesknecht* (2d ed. Göttingen 1963).

[B. F. MEYER]

EXPIATION (IN THEOLOGY)

The concept, expiation, may be considered as it is applied to the work of Christ (in SOTERIOLOGY) or as it is applied to certain works and orientations of Christian SPIRITUALITY.

Soteriology. Christ's redemptive work is many sided. Some of its aspects correspond to those of the SIN it has destroyed. Sin is not only an aversion from God, but also an illicit conversion to a created reality; it gives rise to guilt and penalty. Expiation is an aversion counter to the illicit conversion, and works on the penalty aspect of sin; it is an aversion from a created reality through voluntary suffering and removes the cause of the sinner's alienation from God in order to restore him to holiness and divine favor.

Christ, the Suffering Servant, the new Adam, expiated the penalty of men's sins by His suffering and death, and effected the at-one-ment of man with God. He thereby revealed God's infinite love and mercy, satisfied the divine justice (so exacting because so intimately related to the divine love), and manifested the villainy of sin.

Since there are no consequences of sin in Christ, vicarious expiation does not mean that Christ was punished in man's place; a penalty is a punishment only when paid by the guilty one, and an element of punishment is that it is against the will of the person punished. There is no substitution here of persons but of effects. Christ freely accepted out of love and obedience sufferings that are the penalty exacted for men's sins, but not their punishment.

This doctrine, found in the teaching of the Church [H. Denzinger, *Enchiridion symbolorum*, ed. A. Schönmetzer (Freiburg 1963) 1690, 1691, 1740, 1743, 3438; Pius XI, *Miserentissimus Redemptor, Acta Apostolicae Sedis* 20 (1928) 169–170], is well summed up by Pius XII in *Haurietis aquas:* ''The mystery of the divine Redemption is first and foremost a mystery of love . . . . Since men could in no way expiate their sins, Christ . . . by shedding His precious blood was able to restore and perfect the bond of friendship between God and men . . .'' [*Acta Apostolicae Sedis* 48 (1956) 321–322].

The interpretation of Christ's Person as the Suffering Servant and of His work as a universal expiation valid for all of mankind, since all of mankind is somehow present in Christ, is found both in the Greek and Latin Fathers. The doctrine found in Origen (*Comm. in Rom.* 3.8; *Patrologia Graeca* 14:946–951), Athanasius (*Inc.* 9; *Patrologia Graeca* 25:111), and Eusebius of Caesarea (*Demonstr. evangel.* 10.1; *Patrologia Graeca* 22:724–725) is well expressed by St. Cyril of Alexandria: ''Christ having suffered for us, how could God any longer demand from us the penalty of our sins?'' (*Ador.* 3; *Patrologia Graeca* 68:297). In St. Augustine one finds the whole Latin tradition clearly affirmed: ''By His death, that one most true sacrifice offered on our behalf, He purged, abolished, and extinguished . . . whatever guilt we had'' (*Trin.* 4.13.17; *Patrologia Latina* 42:899).

Although vicarious satisfaction is for Anselm in the *Cur Deus homo*, the essence of Redemption, he does not omit the expiatory aspect. Christ's death was a piacular sacrifice, but not a punishment inflicted by a vindictive God.

For St. Thomas, he who has sinned deserves to be punished, to suffer something contrary to his will (*Summa theologiae* 3a, 86.4). But this penalty, to expiate sin, must be freely accepted. What is most important is not the suffering, but the love with which it is accepted (*Summa theologiae* 3a, 14.1 ad 1). Christ expiated for men because ''the head and members are but one mystical person'' (*Summa theologiae* 3a, 48.2 ad 1).

For the reformers and, more so, for Calvin in whom the doctrine is definitively formulated, Christ's Passion was a punishment substituted for that of guilty mankind. ''. . . Christ . . . took upon Himself and suffered the punishment that by the righteous judgment of God hung over all sinners, and by this expiation the Father has been satisfied'' [*Institutes of the Christian Religion* 2.16; ed. J. T. McNeill, tr. F. L. Battles, 2 v. (Philadelphia 1960) 1:505]. This doctrine, although not generally accepted in contemporary Protestantism, where more emphasis has been given to the divine mystery of love, can still be found in some 19th-century theologians [see R. W. Dale, *The Atonement* (London 1875); J. Denney, *The Christian Doctrine of Reconciliation* (New York 1918)].

Since the Reformation some preachers of the 18th and 19th centuries, such as Bossuet, Bourdaloue, Montsabré, Wiseman, and Faber, have obscured the mystery of Redemption by a too great stress on the penal element [see Philippe de la Trinité, *What is Redemption?* tr. A. Armstrong (New York 1961) 16–37].

Although the great theologians of the 17th and 18th centuries avoided such views, some modern theologians have held that the redemptive value of Christ's death is found primarily in the penal element. C. Pesch [*Das Sühneleiden unseres göttlichen Erlöses* (Freiburg 1916)] was, because of such a doctrine, strongly attacked by J. Rivière, for whom the primal value of Christ's death is to be found in His love. Suffering and love are to one another as matter and form.

Expiation of itself cannot explain the whole of Redemption, but it is an essential element in the salvific work of Christ. It has been absorbed in the satisfaction theory, where it plays the role of an essential material element.

Bibliography: J. RIVIÈRE, *Dictionnaire de théologie catholique,* ed. A. VACANT et al., (Paris 1903–50; Tables générales 1951–) 13.2:1912–2004. L. MORALDI, *Dictionnaire de spiritualité ascétique et mystique. Doctrine et histoire,* ed. M. VILLER et al. (Paris 1932–) 4.2:2026–45. G. JACQUEMET, *Catholicisme* 4:961–963. P. NEUENZEIT, H. FRIES, ed., *Handbuch theologischer Grundbegriffe,* 2 v. (Munich 1962–63) 2:586–596. D. BERTETTO, *Il mistero della colpa secondo S. Tommaso* (Alba 1953). P. EDER, *Sühne* (Basil 1962). P. GRECH, *The Atonement and God: The Main Theories in Modern English Theology* (Rome 1955). P. HARTMANN, *Le Sens plénier de la réparation du péché* (Louvain 1955). T. H. HUGHES, *The Atonement* (London 1949). E. L. KENDALL, *A Living Sacrifice* (London 1960). D. LEWIS, *De necessitate passionis ac mortis Christi ad satisfaciendum pro genere humano, secundum s. Thomam* (Rome 1958). R. T. A. MURPHY, *The Dereliction of Christ on the Cross* (Washington 1940). J. M. O'LEARY, *The Development of the Doctrine of St. Thomas Aquinas on the Passion and Death of our Lord* (Chicago 1952). E. QUARELLO, *Peccato e castigo nella teologia cattolica contemporanea* (Turin 1958). L. RICHARD, *Le Mystère de la Rédemption* (Tournai 1959). H. E. W. TURNER, *The Patristic Doctrine of Redemption* (London 1952). Basilio de San Pablo, ''Irenismo en soteriología,'' in *Semana Española de Teologia,* eleventh, 1951 (Madrid 1952) 455–503. G. GRAYSTONE, ''Modern Theories of the Atonement,'' *The Irish Theological Quarterly* 20 (Dublin 1953) 225–252, 366–388. N. LADOMERSZKY, ''Essai d'étude sur le dogme de la Rédemption dans la théologie contemporaine,'' *Euntes docete* 2 (1949) 321–348. G. OGGIONI, ''Il mistero della redenzione,'' in *Problemi e orientamenti di teologia dommatica,* 2 v. (Milan 1957) 2:237–343. J. RIVIÈRE, ''Un Dossier patristique de l'expiation,'' *Revue des Sciences Religieuses* 2 (1922) 303–315. J. SOLANO, ''Actualidades cristológicosoteriológicas,'' *Estudios eclesiásticos* 24 (1950) 43–69; ''El sentido de la muerte redentora de N.S. Jesu Cristo y algunas corrientes modernos,'' *ibid.* 20 (1964) 399–414.

[L. RICHARD]

In Spiritual theology. The Church, from its beginning, canonized the sentiment that led repentant man to offer God works of expiation, to satisfy for his own sins and the sins of others. The sacrifice of Jesus Christ on the cross was sufficient to satisfy divine justice for all of man's sins. But the followers of Christ are invited to share in their master's work of Redemption by offering to God in Christ's name their good deeds and their penitential works freely assumed, not for themselves only but others also. For it is held that within the Mystical Body the fruit of expiation can be communicated to others, a thought that has inspired many loving and generous souls to voluntary suffering and penitential discipline not for their own sins alone. Through their INCORPORATION IN CHRIST by Baptism, the Christians' own deeds participated in the merits of the Redeemer. Thus every follower of Christ can, by his own actions, extend the forgiving effects of the Savior's suffering and death.

This teaching of the Christian revelation has attracted many people to a life of expiation. Led by a desire to share the work of the Redeemer, they have imposed on themselves a way of mortification, sometimes extreme. Martyrs went to their death gladly with this in view. Virgins dedicated themselves to a life of prayer and fasting in order to bring to needy sinners the justifying effects of Christ's sacrifice. The penances of the early hermits had the same motivation. From these beginnings came monastic life, which organized the practices of those who sought a life of expiation in union with the Savior. Each of the many religious communities in the Church has an expiatory function, in that they offer their members opportunities to practice virtue to win forgiveness of their own and others' sins.

Spiritual writers agree that some expiatory practices are necessary in the life of every Christian. Devotional practices and penitential works, such as attendance at Mass and observance of special times of fast and abstinence, as well as other penitential works, are part of the program of expiation that the Church offers its members. In modern times the popes constantly remind the faithful of their need for expiation by prayer and good deeds, [see, for example, the apostolic constitution *Poenitemini* of Pope Paul VI (Feb. 17, 1966) ch. 1–2]. Expiatory prayers are enriched with indulgences, and the devotions to the Sacred Heart of Jesus, to Our Lady of Lourdes, and of Fatima, which are recommended by the popes, have a strong element of expiation.

See Also: ATONEMENT; REPARATION; SATISFACTION OF CHRIST.

Bibliography: P.POURRAT, *Christian Spirituality,* tr. W. H. MITCHELL et al., 4 v (Westminister, Md. 1953–55) 1:36–48,, 74–129. V. TAYLOR, *Forgiveness and Reconciliation* (2d ed. New York 1946; repr. 1960). PIUS XI, *Miserentissimus Redemptor* (encyclical, May 8, 1928) *Acta Apostolicae Sedis* 20 (Rome 1928) 165–178. PIUS XII, *Fulgens corona* (encyclical, Sept. 8, 1953) *Acta Apostolicae Sedis* 45 (Rome 1953) 577–592. *The Raccolta* (New York 1952) 173–183.

[P. F. MULHERN]

EXSULTET IAM ANGELICA TURBA

The opening words of the *praeconium,* or hymn of praise, sung by the deacon in celebration of Christ's Resurrection after the *Lumen Christi* procession has entered the church for the solemn service of the EASTER VIGIL.

Laus (consecratio, benedictio) cerei, that is, ''praise (consecration, blessing) of the candle,'' is a not infrequent title of this hymn in the oldest MSS, since it is sung in connection with the blessing and offering of the paschal candle, the light of which symbolizes the glory of the risen Christ.

Date, Authorship, Place of Origin, Diffusion. Evidences for this practice date from the late fourth and early fifth centuries. A famous letter in which the author (St. Jerome?) refuses the favor requested by Praesidius, deacon of Piacenza, to help him with the composition of a *laus cerei,* was written in 384. Less than 40 years later, St. Augustine, in his *City of God* (15.22), quoted the first three hexameters of a *laus cerei,* which he had composed years before. Two *Benedictiones cerei* are included among the works of ENNODIUS, Bishop of Pavia (d. 521). From the fact that individual clerics were free to compose their own texts, it may be concluded that at one time variations of this hymn were fairly numerous. Only nine, however, have survived in their entirety: (1) the *Exsultet,* still in use wherever the Roman rite is followed; (2) the formula of the ''Old'' Gelasian Sacramentary (*Incipit: Deus mundi conditor*); (3) the Ambrosian text, still sung in Milan; (4 and 5) the two *Benedictiones* of Ennodius; (6) an interesting text of the Visigothic period preserved in a unique manuscript of the Escorial; (7) the *Vetus Itala* text, called also Beneventan; (8 and 9) the *Benedictio lucernae* and *Benedictio cerei,* comprised in the Visigothic-Hispanic (Mozarabic) Ordinal. To this list may be added a tenth *laus cerei,* of African origin, which, if not complete, seems to lack only an explicit statement of the *celebritas* for which it was composed and the concluding petitions for ecclesiastical and civil authorities, for clergy and people.

Of these texts, the *Exsultet* is considered one of the oldest and by at least one scholar, Dom Pinell of Montserrat, as antedating all the others. On stylistic grounds, notably by reason of the rhythmic clausulae, it is assigned to the fifth century (Di Capua) and by some to the late fourth. This latter date is certainly correct if St. Ambrose (d. 397) was the author. The points of contact in diction and style with his works are numerous enough in the *Exsultet,* the best known and most important being an all but literal quotation from the saint's exposition of Luke (2.41): *Nihil enim nobis nasci profuit* [Ambrose: *Non prodesset nasci] nisi redimi profuisset.* It is not surprising that certain authors are convinced, or at least strongly inclined to believe, that the famous bishop of Milan was the author (Capelle, Pinell). Others, again, find in this *praeconium* stylistic defects that they consider unworthy of Ambrose (Fischer, Huglo). Unless new discoveries of an unexpected sort are made, the debate will probably never be settled. The author, whoever he was, had an intimate knowledge of Ambrose's works, was reared in the same rhetorical tradition and worked in northern Italy or Gaul, this latter possibility being suggested by the occurrence in the Missale Gothicum, a Gallican book written *c.* 700 (but containing older material), of certain passages found in the *Exsultet* to say nothing of stylistic resemblances. In any event, the *Exsultet* was known in Gaul, and it is an interesting fact that what may be called the triumphal course of this remarkable hymn began in Gaul. There it was included by the scribes in copies that they made of liturgical books brought up from Rome—at first, in addition to the Roman text (the second of the ten documents mentioned above), but this latter was finally omitted altogether. ALCUIN, indeed, placed the *Exsultet* at the beginning of his supplement to the Gregorian Sacramentary sent up to Charlemagne by Pope Adrian I, and finally it came into use at Rome itself to the exclusion of the other text.

''Crucifixion,'' miniature painting from a manuscript ''Exsultet Roll'' from the Abbey at Monte Cassino, Italy.

The modern text of the *Exsultet,* i.e., the *praeconium* following the *Lumen Christi procession,* is to be found in any official edition of the Roman Missal published after 1951.

Contents. The *Exsultet* is in two sections, the first being a prologue, which constitutes about one-fifth of the entire composition and has the form of an elaborate invitatory of which the second half is an ''apology'' on the part of the deacon, who requests the aid of his listeners' prayers. This leads into the second section, properly called the *laus cerei,* which is preceded by a dialogue such as is used before the Eucharistic prayer of the Mass. What follows is an elaborate proclamation of this paschal festivity that commemorates the slaying of the true Lamb, a proclamation of this night that destroyed the darkness of sin and restores the faithful to grace and holiness. Adam's sin was ''profitable,'' indeed, and a ''happy fault'' that had so great a Redeemer. (This passage was expunged in certain churches and monasteries for some time during the Middle Ages.) God is asked to accept this burning sacrifice, which Holy Church through its ministers offers by the oblation of a candle, a product of the industry of the bee. (Originally, there followed at this point an elaborate praise of the bee, which was later deleted.) The praise of this night is resumed, the night that despoiled the Egyptians and enriched the Israelites; the night in which things of heaven are joined to things of earth. God is asked that this candle may continue unfailingly to destroy the darkness of this night, that it may mingle with the lights of heaven. In conclusion, there is a brief prayer for the tranquillity of God's servants—the clergy and the devoted people of God—in this paschal celebration.

Pentecost Exsultet. Through many centuries there was sung in the cathedral of Besançon, France, during the vigil of Pentecost, an adaptation of the Easter *Exsultet* to the mystery of Whitsunday—a liturgical curiosity of no little interest. An attempt to introduce this custom at Reims seems to have had short-lived success.

Bibliography: J. BRAUN, ''Osterpräconium u. Osterkerzenweihe,'' *Stimmen aus Maria-Laach* 56 (1899) 273–286. G. MERCATI, *Paralipomena Ambrosiana* (StTest 12; 1904) 24–43. A. FRANZ, *Die kirchlichen Benediktionen im Mittelalter,* 2 v. (Freiburg i. Br. 1909; repr. Graz 1960) 1:519–553. H. M. BANNISTER, ''The *Vetus Itala* Text of the *Exsultet,*'' *Journal of Theological Studies* 11 (1909–10) 43–54. G. MORIN, ''Pour l'authenticité de la lettre de S. Jérôme à Présidius,'' *Bulletin d'ancienne littérature et d'archéologie chrétiennes* 3 (1913) 52–60. F. DI CAPUA, ''Il Ritmo nella prosa liturgica e il *Praeconium Paschale,''* *Didaskaleion* NS 5.2 (1927) 1–23; repr. in *Scritti minori,* 2 v. (Rome 1959) 1:441–459, E. H. KANTOROWICZ, ''A Norman Finale of the *Exultet* and the Rite of Sarum,'' *Harvard Theological Review* 34 (1941) 129–143. B. CAPELLE, ''L' *Exultet* Pascal oeuvre de Saint Ambroise,'' *Miscellania Giovanni Mercati* 1:219–246. B. FISCHER, ''Ambrosius der Verfasser des österlichen *Exultet?*'' *Archiv für Liturgiewissenschaft* 2 (1952) 61–74. C. MOHRMANN, ''Exultent divina mysteria,'' *Ephemerides liturgicae* 66 (1952) 274–281. G. BENOIT-CASTELLI, ''Le *Praeconium paschale,*'' *ibid.* 67 (1953) 309–334. M. HUGLO, ''L'Auteur de l' *Exultet* pascal,'' *Vigilae christianae* 7 (1953) 79–88. A. STRITTMATTER, ''The Pentecost *Exultet* of Reims and Besançon'' in *Studies in Art and Literature for Belle da Costa Greene,* ed. D. MINER (Princeton, N.J. 1954) 384–400. A. GUNY, *Catholicisme* 4:1014–16. H. A. SCHMIDT, *Hebdomada Sancta,* 2 v. (Rome 1956–57) 1:291–292; 2:627–650, 809–826, 976–977. J. M. PINELL, ''La benedicció del ciri pasqual i els seus textos,'' *Liturgica* 2 (1958) 1–119. L. KUNZ and H. LAUSBERG, *Lexikon für Theologie und Kirche,* ed. J. HOFER and K. RAHNER (Freiburg 1957–65) 3: 1318–19. P. VERBRAKEN,'' Une *Laus cerei* africaine,'' *Revue Bénédictine* 70 (1960) 301–312. L. EIZENHÖFER, ''Die Feier der Ostervigil in der Benediktiner Abtei San Silvestro zu Foligno um das Jahr 1100,'' *Archiv für Liturgiewissenschaft* 6 (1960) 349–353. For the study of the Exsultet Rolls (28 and three related rolls are extant): E. BERTAUX, *L'Art dans l'Italie méridionale* (Paris 1904) 213–240. M. AVERY, *The Exultet Rolls of South Italy* (Princeton 1936) v.2, 53 pp. of text, 206 plates, v. 1 unpub. G. B. LADNER, ''The 'Portraits' of Emperors in Southern Italian Exultet Rolls and the Liturgical Commemoration of the Emperor,'' *Speculum* 17 (1942) 181–200. ''Mostra storica nazionale della miniature, palazzo di Venezia (Rome),'' *Catalogo* (Florence 1953) 47–52. J. WETTSTEIN, *Sant' Angelo in Formis et la peinture médiévale en Campanie* (Geneva 1960) 128–151.

[A. STRITTMATTER]

EXSULTET ORBIS GAUDIIS

An office hymn that was traditionally prescribed for Vespers and Lauds on the feasts of Apostles and Evangelists outside Easter time. It is composed of six Ambrosian strophes in iambic dimeter. The author is unknown but the hymn is found as early as the tenth century in a hymnal of Moissac Abbey. It underwent extensive revision in the Roman Breviary of 1632. In contrast to the 1632 revision, the original version, beginning *Exsultet caelum laudibus,* was considered more beautiful. The hymn echoes a number of the scriptural references to the Apostles.

Bibliography: *Analecta hymnica* 51:125–126, for text. J. JULIAN, ed., *A Dictionary of Hymnology* (New York 1957) 1:360–361. M. BRITT, ed., *The Hymns of the Breviary and Missal* (new ed. New York 1948) 354–356. J. CONNELLY, *Hymns of the Roman Liturgy* (Westminster, MD 1957) 140–141, for tr. J. SZÖVÉRFFY, *Die Annalen der lateinischen Hymnendichtung* (Berlin 1964–65) 1:342.

[J. P. MCCORMICK]

EXTENSION

As a primitive term, extension can be defined only ostensively, by pointing to a corporeal substance, the parts of which are distinguished by their positions. But extension is synonymous with neither corporeity nor materiality. To be extended is to be dimensively quantified and this results, formally, in the distinction and ordering of material integral parts. The term is more abstract than corporeity and may refer to both natural (or physical) and mathematical QUANTITY, this latter defining sets of properties and relations that have no immediate physical counterpart. A material principle of SUBSTANCE requires dimensive quantity but is ontologically prior to it.

Though normally referred to continuous quantity, extension may be said of contiguous parts and even of interrupted segments joined by an intermediary. By analogy, the term may refer to nonquantitative measures as in LOGIC, where, opposed to intension, it signifies the magnitude of a nonnumerable multitude or class. In mathematics, extension shares in the analogy of the term SPACE.

Distinctions. Within scholastic philosophy, one finds a distinction between the order of parts of an extended entity relative to a locating boundary on the one hand, and the order of parts relative to the whole of that entity on the other. The former specifies external or local extension; the latter, a mutual externality of parts, specifies internal or situal extension. [*See* PLACE; SITUATION (SITUS).] This distinction emphasizes the factual ordering of dimensive quantity and reflects a controversy. Against the general conviction, some held that extension is primarily a property of occupying space (*see* F. SUÁREZ, *Disp. meta.,* 40.4). The general argument has been that an intrinsic distinguishing order of parts must be prior to any principle of external relation. The theological analysis of the doctrine of the EUCHARIST led to this distinction, since there must be some account given of the natural extension of Christ's Body, which is manifestly not circumscribed in the Sacrament.

Dimensive quantity does not necessarily entail external extension. Physical extension is known sensibly by the perception, usually both visual and tactile, of the external dimensive relations that material substances bear toward their environment, and intellectually it is grasped by the measurability and divisibility that it founds. More detailed physical data raise questions about the type of continuity found in nature and the character of the smallest unit with its relations to complex aggregates.

That extension is an objective attribute of material things is an essential element in a realist philosophy, but apart from a rejection of the dynamistic reduction of extension to forces, positions, and motions of unextended points, there is no agreement upon the ultimate physical matrix of extension (e.g., ether, protomatter, or subnuclear particles), nor upon the character of its dividing boundaries. Such knowledge, depending upon a precise understanding of sensible matter, is never more than dialectical, reflecting the state of research at any given time. Recent physical theory tends to support the notion that the universe is an extended plenum determined generally and in its fundamental units by some formal principles of unity and organization.

Other Views. Unable to conceive of material substances as composed ontologically of principles such as primary matter and substantial form, R. DESCARTES (1596–1650) considered body as such, *res extensa,* a species of substance. He inadequately distinguished substance from its quantitative extension, which he took to be a universal matrix for enfigurement and a requirement for motion. As a result, his philosophy of nature remains ambiguous. Impenetrability or solidity must be attributed by him to some vortex motion in an extended fluidlike plenum; yet this plenum is entirely undifferentiable and, in fact, a mathematical construct.

G. W. LEIBNIZ (1646–1716) was not more concrete, for he understood extension to be an internal representation to each MONAD of the order of coexistence of all monads—the unitary, immaterial, simple substances that constituted his universe. The perception of extension was not, therefore, a sensation, but a God-given harmonious adaptation within each monad.

Influenced, most probably, by this position, I. KANT (1724–1804) thought extension to be an analytical element of the concept body, hence an a priori form or contribution of the mind itself, which orders the content of sense experience, giving the objects and their extensive relations as man knows them. In effect, Kant identified physical and mathematical extension, since both are traced to the internal form of sensuous intuition. The distinction between a sensed objective property and a conception abstracted from the externality of corporeal substance is therefore lost.

Mathematical Extension. The abstraction of the notion of extension can yield either a mathematical or a physical conception; subsequent applications of the notions, especially to realms beyond direct sensation, thereupon become analogical. The mathematical notion, analogical even within that science, is first seen in Euclidean geometry as an abstraction from physical continua, which in three dimensions yield a homogeneous isotropic space. Chronologically, multidimensional spaces were the next analogues, but the concept of extension did not radically change until the arithmetization of geometry.

The essence of this development was the establishment of a correspondence between sets of numbers and geometric elements, so that continuous extension could be represented by continuous algebraic or numeric functions. Successive generalizations of such functions led to interpretations of extension that are far removed from the notion obtained in abstraction. Thus understood, in terms of the analytic properties of algebraic expressions, extension takes on as many meanings as the formal consistency of the multiple systems permits, including systems not having ''smoothness'' or perfect continuity. Finally, the whole of geometry and hence the interpretation of mathematical extension was given a further dialectical interpretation in terms of point sets. Extension then became a set of abstract relations, the link with quantity being the foundation of the opposition between the elements or terms of the relations, otherwise known as situs.

See Also: CONTINUUM; MATHEMATICS, PHILOSOPHY OF.

Bibliography: JOHN OF ST. THOMAS, *Ars Logica,* v.1 of *Cursus philosophicus Thomisticus . . . ,* ed. B. REISER, 3 v. (Turin 1930–37); Eng. tr. *Material Logic: Basic Treatises,* tr. Y. R. SIMON et al. (Chicago 1955). L. A. FOLEY, *Cosmology: Philosophical and Scientific* (Milwaukee 1962). P. BORNE, ''De ente materiale et spirituale sub respectu extensionis et inextensionis,'' *Divus Thomas* 42 (1939) 240–253, 349–369, 461–494.

[C. F. WEIHER]

EXTRAVAGANTES

Extravagantes is a term introduced after the publication of the *Decretum* of GRATIAN to describe all papal texts not found in, but ''circulating outside'' (*extravagantes*), that collection. After Gregory IX had promulgated his authentic series of *extravagantes* in 1234 (*see* GREGORY IX, DECRETALS OF), suppressing all others, the term was used with reference to texts that appeared after his compilation. Similarly, when an authentic collection of post-Gregorian *Extravagantes* was published by Boniface VIII in 1298 in the *LIBER SEXTUS*, to the abrogation of all others, the word *Extravagantes* denoted decretals that came after the Sext. In fact, since the *CLEMENTINAE* that were issued in 1317 were not an exclusive collection like the Decretals and Sext and since no other authentic collection of decretals appeared from 1317 until the Roman edition of the *CORPUS IURIS CANONICI* in 1582, all other papal decretals after 1298 are, properly speaking, *extravagantes* not to the Clementines but to the Sext. However, the *extravagantes* printed in the *Corpus* of 1582 do not cover all papal decrees from the Sext onward, for the *Corpus* simply took over two unofficial collections of post-Sext *extravagantes* that Jean Chappuis, a Parisian lawyer, had published in his edition of the *Corpus* (1500, 1503). These, in fact, did not go beyond 1484 (Sixtus IV).

The first, the *extravagantes* of John XXII, is a collection of 20 decretals of John XXII from 1317 to 1320, which Gesselin de Cassanges put together and glossed in 1325. These *extravagantes,* which were already well known (see, e.g., John Koelner de Vankel, *Summarium Extravagantium Ioannis XXII,* Cologne 1483, 1488, 1493, 1494, 1495), were arranged by Chappuis under 14 titles and 20 chapters taken from the Decretals of Gregory IX.

The second, *Extravagantes communes,* is a collection of 70 decretals from Urban IV (1261–64) to Sixtus IV (1471–84), which Chappuis put together in 1500 from decretals ''commonly circulating'' and to which he added four more in 1503 (one from Benedict XII; three from John XXII, which were also in Gesselin's *extravagantes* but had had an independent existence since 1319, when William of Mont Lauzun composed a commentary on them). Chappuis distributed these *extravagantes* in five books after the manner of the Decretals, but there are no entries in Bk. four on marriage. The bulk of the decretals come from the period 1261 to 1342 (one of Urban IV; one of Martin IV; 11 of Boniface VIII, including *UNAM SANCTAM*; six of Benedict XI; six of Clement V; 33 of John XXII; two of Benedict XII); there are only five from the period 1342 to 1458 (Clement VI, Martin V, Eugene IV, Callistus III), with four from Paul II (1464–71) and six from Sixtus IV (1471–84).

These two sets of *extravagantes* are uneven in quality, on occasion repeating material of the Sext or Clementines. They were never received in the schools, and the Roman edition of 1582 did not authenticate them as collections. The usual citation is by book, title, and chapter for the *Communes* (CorpIurCanExtravagCom 1.8.1) and by title and chapter for those of John XXII (CorpIurCanExtravag Jo XXII 4.1).

Bibliography: E. FOURNIER, *Questions d'histoire du droit canonique* (Paris 1936), pt. 2: ''Les Recueils de décretales 'extravagantes' de 1234 à 1294.'' A. M. STICKLER, *Lexikon für Theologie und Kirche*, ed. J. HOFER and K. RAHNER, 10 v. (2d, new ed. Freiburg 1957–65) 3:67. J. F. VON SCHULTE, *Die Geschichte der Quellen und der Literatur des kanonischen Rechts,* 3 v. in 4 pts. (Stuttgart 1875–80; repr. Graz 1956) 2:59–67. A. M. STICKLER, *Historia iuris canonici latini:* v. 1, *Historia fontium* (Turin 1950) 1:268–272. A. TARDIF, *Histoire des sources du droit canonique* (Paris 1887). A. VAN HOVE, *Commentarium Lovaniense in Codicem iuris canonici 1,* v. 1–5 (Mechlin 1928–); v. 1, Prolegomena (2d ed. 1945) 1:373–375. P. TORQUEBIAU, *Dictionnaire de droit canonique,* ed. R. NAZ, 7 v. (Paris 1935–65) 4:640–643.

[L. E. BOYLE]

EXTRINSICISM

The tendency, especially among philosophers and theologians, to stress the exterior or superficial elements in some complex reality, or to give principal attention to the juridical or moral aspects of a problem rather than to the interior, constitutive, or ontological elements. It is not a definite school of thought on a particular problem, or even a clearly espoused position. Many theological questions have been treated in this way, and the tendency can best be described by seeing its application to three topics: grace, morality, and the Church.

Of all the theological tracts, the one on GRACE has, perhaps, been the most effected by extrinsicism. Pelagianism, an early heresy, involved essentially an extrinsicism. For the Pelagian, grace is not something needed to transform, elevate, and move man to salvation, but rather something that makes salvation easier. There is no necessary connection between grace and salvation for the Pelagian (*see* PELAGIUS AND PELAGIANISM).

In opposition to the Catholic teaching according to which justification involves an interior renewal of man that removes grave sin, the early reformers—such as Luther and Calvin—thought of justification as something entirely extrinsic, not a freeing from sin, but a hiding of sin; not an interior transformation, but an acceptance of the sinner by God (*see* IMPUTATION OF JUSTICE AND MERIT).

St. Thomas Aquinas and his followers considered that by the very presence within man of habitual or sanctifying grace, grave sin is excluded, and man is made an adopted child of God, truly capable of works proportioned to eternal life. The nominalists in general rejected much of this teaching, tending toward a radical extrinsicism. For them grace is only a moral resemblance to God; there is no absolute connection of grace and adoption or grace and sinlessness, and men's works are not—even under grace—truly proportioned to SUPERNATURAL LIFE. They compared grace to money, worthless in itself, but given value by a legal decree of public authority. Scotus held a middle ground, i.e., that grace is connected with men's adoption but does not formally cause it (*see* NOMINALISM).

In the area of moral, or ethical, conduct this extrinsicism can also be found. It is the tendency to give undue importance to the external expression of the law or to the merely exterior observance of the law. It is usually called by some other name, e.g., legalism or Pharisaism. The basic moral code of man is, first of all, interior. This is true both of the NATURAL LAW, which is a participation in the intellectual creature of God's plan for ordering things to their goal (*Summa theologiae* 1a2ae, 91.2), and of the new law, the law revealed by God to lead men to Himself in Christ. This new law is essentially the grace of the Holy Spirit and only secondarily particular precepts or written laws (*Summa theologiae* 1a2ae, 106.1). It would be a mistake, of course, to ignore laws or regulations that govern even exterior conduct, but the underlying directive principle is essentially interior.

Frequently the nature of the Church is expressed inadequately because principal and almost exclusive attention is given to exterior elements: the VISIBILITY OF THE CHURCH, its social structures, laws, external conduct, etc. Part of this may be due to a reaction to early Protestants, who denied these important visible elements and social structures. It is true that these exterior elements do pertain to the Church, but it is, first of all, a community of life with God in Christ. The exterior elements are, as it were, the sacrament of this interior life. *See* CHURCH, II (THEOLOGY OF).

Extrinsicism, then, is a tendency affecting much of philosophical and technological thought. In an extreme case it can involve heresy (e.g., Pelagianism, merely imputed justification). More frequently it involves a less profound analysis of reality, but even here it may cause serious difficulties, both speculative and practical.

[J. HENNESSEY]

EXUPERIUS OF TOULOUSE, ST.

Bishop; date and place of birth uncertain; local tradition places his tomb at Blagnac near Toulouse. As bishop of Toulouse *c.* 405 to 411, Exuperius (or Exsuperius; Spire in French) completed the basilica begun by his predecessor, St. Silvius. It was dedicated to the first bishop of Toulouse, St. Saturninus, whose relics were brought there. St. JEROME dedicated the *Commentarii in Zachariam* to Exuperius, praised his steadfastness during the Vandal invasion (*Epist.* 123), and, in a letter to Rusticus of Marseilles (*Epist.* 125), praised his generosity. Exuperius sought the advice of INNOCENT I on several points of Scripture and discipline. His reply is an important document (P. Jaffé, *Regesta pontificum romanorum ab condita ecclesia ad annum post Christum natum 1198,* ed. S. Löwenfeld and F. Kaltenbrunner n.405). GREGORY OF TOURS (*Historia Francorum* 2:13) took note of his career.

Feast: Sept. 28.

Bibliography: *Acta Sanctorum* Sept. 7:583–589. S. LE NAIN DE TILLEMONT, *Mémoires pour servir à l'histoire ecclésiastique des six premiers siècles* (Paris 1693–1712) 10:617–620, 825–826; 12:268, 285, 322. G. BAREILLE, *Dictionnaire de théologie catholique,* ed. A. VACANT (Paris 1903–50) 5.2:2022–27. A. BUTLER, *The Lives of the Saints,* ed. H. THURSTON and D. ATTWATER (New York 1956) 3:664–665. É.GRIFFE, *La Gaule chrétienne à l'époque romaine,* v.2 (Paris 1957); *Catholicisme* 4:1017.

[G. E. CONWAY]

EYMARD, PIERRE JULIEN, ST.

Religious founder; b. La Mure d'Isére, near Grenoble, France, Feb. 4, 1811; d. there, Aug. 1, 1868. From his early years Eymard had a strong devotion to the Blessed Sacrament. Weak health and paternal opposition were obstacles to his priestly vocation. Illness forced him to leave the novitiate of the Oblates of Mary Immaculate after three months. Subsequent to his father's death

(1831) he entered the major seminary in Grenoble and was ordained in 1834. He served in parish work in the Diocese of Grenoble until 1839 when he joined the MARIST FATHERS. During his 17 years in this congregation he acted as provincial superior and as rector of the College of La Seine-sur-Mer and organized the Third Order of Mary. He sought also to form within the Marists a group dedicated to adoration of line Blessed Sacrament but his superiors did not consider this activity within the proper scope of their apostolate. After gaining permission to leave the Marists, Eymard founded (1856) in Paris the BLESSED SACRAMENT FATHERS and acted as their superior-general for the rest of his life. In 1863 he obtained from the Holy See official approval of the congregation. By 1868 the institute had seven houses in France and two in Belgium, 16 priests, and 34 other members. In 1858 Eymard founded, together with Marguerite Guillot, the Servants of the BLESSED SACRAMENT, a cloistered contemplative congregation for women. Eymard intended perpetual exposition and adoration of the blessed sacrament to be the main purpose of both congregations, but he urged members to engage in any other form of apostolate that would attract souls to the Blessed Sacrament. He founded also the Blessed Sacrament Confraternity, which is still widely popular. His writings consist of the constitutions he composed for his congregations and a posthumously published collection of his sermons and conferences. He was beatified July 22, 1925, and canonized Dec. 9, 1962.

Feast: Aug. 1.

Bibliography: *Eymard Library,* tr. from the French, 9 v. in 10 (New York 1938–48). M. DEMPSEY, *Champion of the Blessed Sacrament: Saint Peter Julian Eymard* (New York 1963). N. B. PELLETIER, *Tomorrow Will Be Too Late: A Life of Saint Peter Julian Eymard* (Cleveland, Ohio 1992).

[J. ROY]

EYRE, THOMAS

First President of Ushaw College; b. Glossop, Derbyshire, 1748; d. Ushaw, May 8, 1810. His education for the priesthood began in 1758, when he and his brothers entered Esquerchin, the preparatory school for the English college at Douai. Following his ordination, Eyre stayed on at Douai as prefect and master of rhetoric and poetry until 1775, when he was assigned to the Stella Mission near Newcastle. Between 1775 and 1794 Eyre combined missionary work with scholarship, editing the works of John Gother and gathering materials for the purpose, unfulfilled, of continuing Dodd's *Church History.* In 1794 Bp. William Gibson, Vicar Apostolic of the Northern District, charged him with the care of the northern students who had been forced to leave Douai during the French Revolution, and were then temporarily installed at Tudhoe under John Lingard (later a great historian). After a few months at Pontop Hall, a new college was founded at Crook Hall, Durham, under Eyre's presidency. In 1803 Gibson obtained the freehold estate of Ushaw, four miles from Durham, and Eyre moved the college there in July 1808. He continued to serve as first president until his death two years later.

Bibliography: *A Literary and Biographical History or Bibliographical Dictionary of the English Catholics from 1534 to the Present Time* 2:199–202. *The Dictionary of National Biography from the Earliest Times to 1900* (London 1885–1900) 6:966–967. R. C. LAING, ed., *Ushaw College Memorial* (Newcastle 1895).

[H. F. GRETSCH]

EYSTON, CHARLES

English antiquarian who wrote about pre-Reformation monastic foundations; b. East Hendred, Berkshire, 1667; d. there, Nov. 5, 1721. Eyston, scion of an ancient Catholic family, succeeded to his father's estate in 1691. He married Winifred Dorothy Fitzherbert in 1692, and of their numerous children, several daughters entered the convent, while one of the sons became a Jesuit. Eyston was devoted to antiquarian researches, and formed a friendship with the famous scholar, Thomas Hearne, who included Eyston's ''A Little Monument to the Once Famous Abbey and Borough of Glastonbury'' in his *History and Antiquities of Glastonbury* (Oxford 1722). This was later reprinted by R. Warner in *History of the Abbey of Glaston and the Town of Glastonbury* (Bath 1826). Hearne's appreciation of Eyston in *Reliquiae Hearnianae* stated: ''He was a Roman Catholick and so charitable to the poor that he is lamented by all who knew anything of him . . . an excellent scholar and so modest that he did not care to have it at any time mentioned.'' Eyston wrote also an unpublished study of ''Old Pious Dissolved Foundations of England . . . ,'' which was in the family library at Hendred for many years.

Bibliography: *A Literary and Biographical History or Bibliographical Dictionary of the English Catholics from 1534 to the Present Time* 2:204–205. T. HEARNE, *Reliquiae Hearnianae* (London 1869). *The Dictionary of National Biography from the Earliest Times to 1900* (London 1885–1900) 6:969–970.

[H. F. GRETSCH]

EYZAGUIRRE, JOSÉ ALEJO

Chilean clerical and political leader; b. Santiago, July 13, 1783; d. there, Aug. 4, 1850. He graduated from the University of San Felipe with a degree in Canon Law and pursued ecclesiastical studies in Lima until his ordination in 1807. When he returned to Chile, he served for three years at the cathedral of Santiago as vicar-general of the bishopric and as canon. Vicar Apostolic MUZI, sent by the Holy See in 1824 to solve various Church problems in Chile, wished to consecrate Eyzaguirre auxiliary bishop of Santiago, but the government, knowing him to be a supporter of the diocesan bishop whom it had just exiled, withheld consent. In 1823 Eyzaguirre was delegate to the constitutional congress, and during the two following years he was president of the congress. He became dean of the ecclesiastical council in 1840. When the Archbishopric of Santiago became vacant in 1843, he was chosen capitular vicar and, in spite of resistance, proposed to the Holy See as archbishop. His refusal to accept government intervention in matters of ecclesiastical authority led him in 1845 to relinquish the government of the archdiocese, which he had administered as archbishop-elect. At the time of his death, he was dean of the cathedral, and also councilor of state, a position he had held since 1844. This priest of great piety and apostolic spirit, who lived a humble and ascetic life, was a bulwark against the abusive meddling of the civil power in ecclesiastical affairs.

Bibliography: L. F. PRIETO DEL RÍO, *Diccionario biográfico del clero secular de Chile* (Santiago de Chile 1922).

[J. EYZAGUIRRE]

EYZAGUIRRE, JOSÉ IGNACIO VÍCTOR DE

Chilean clerical and political leader, founder of the South American College in Rome; b. Santiago, Feb. 25, 1817; d. on board ship in the Mediterranean, Nov. 16, 1875. His family was distinguished in political and religious affairs. He was ordained after becoming a lawyer. At 27 he was chosen a member of the Faculty of Theology of the University of Chile and secretary of its Academy of Sacred Sciences. In 1850 he published *Historia eclesiástica, política y literaria de Chile,* which was awarded a prize by the university and was later translated into French. Between 1847 and 1852 he served as dean of the Faculty of Theology of the University of Chile and vice president of the chamber of deputies.

The violent turn of political events in Chile, which compromised his priestly character, caused him to leave the country and to travel in Europe for four years. These travel experiences, which included a tour of the Holy Land, were described in *El Catolicismo en presencia de sus disidentes* (Paris 1855), translated into various languages and praised by Pius IX, Montalembert, Lacordaire, and García Moreno. The pope wished to make him a titular bishop and to have him join the papal diplomatic service, but Eyzaguirre declined. However, he did offer to assist in the establishment of a seminary in Rome for the education of priests for Latin America. For two years he unselfishly toured all the countries of the vast hemisphere to interest the bishops in the undertaking. In 1858 he was able to inaugurate in Rome the South American College, which has achieved considerable prestige. Pius IX honored Eyzaguirre for his work as founder with the title prothonotary apostolic *ad instar participantium.* In 1859 he published *Los intereses católicos en América,* which contains his travel impressions and reflects the condition of the Church in the New World. The following year, the Holy See utilized his experience and entrusted him with a difficult religious mission in Ecuador, Peru, and Bolivia. At the time of his death he was returning to Rome after having made a pilgrimage to the Holy Land.

Bibliography: C. SILVA COTAPOS, *Monseñor José Ignacio Víctor Eyzaguirre* (Santiago 1919).

[J. EYZAGUIRRE]

EZEKIEL

Third of the Major Prophets of the Old Testament. As an Israelite Prophet, Ezekiel is unique in many ways. He was, as far as is known, the only Prophet to receive his call to prophecy, not in Palestine, but in a foreign land of exile. Unlike any of the canonical Prophets who preceded him, he displays an intense interest in cultic and ritual matters. Other Prophets (Jeremiah, for example) had also been priests, but Ezekiel was the first to prophesy in strictly priestly terms; besides the strong priestly cast of the ch. 40 to 48 complex, his prophetic sermons (e.g., 18.5–23) often read like a priestly *tôrâ*. There is certainly a literary connection between Ezekiel and the Law of HOLINESS (Leviticus ch. 17–26), elaborated in priestly circles during the Babylonian captivity (the direction of the dependence is debated). Nevertheless, Ezekiel was a Prophet before he was a priest. In his employment of the characteristic symbolic action (e.g., Ez 6.11; 21.19; 33.22) he excels all the other Prophets. Strongly tied to the classical prophetic tradition, he also often resembles the older *n*^{e} *bî'îm,* especially in his (probable) influence by ecstatic experience [*see* PROPHETISM (IN THE BIBLE)].

Ministry and Message. It is customary to divide Ezekiel's prophetic ministry into two parts, the point of separation being the destruction of Jerusalem by the Babylonians in 587 B.C. According to Ez 1.2, his call to prophecy took place in Babylonia during the fifth year of King Jehoiachin's captivity, i.e., in 593 B.C. Because the

''The Nativity with the Prophets Isaiah and Ezekiel,'' three part panel from front predella of Maesta altarpiece by Duccio di Buoninsegna. (©Francis G. Mayer/CORBIS)

account in the Book of Ezekiel is composite [*see* EZEKIEL, BOOK OF] and because various of Ezekiel's earlier oracles seem to suppose his presence in Jerusalem, some modern scholars believe that the prophet's initial call took place in Palestine and that only after 587 (and not in 597, the year of Joachin's deportation) did Ezekiel join the Judean exiles in Babylonia. However, this hypothesis is unnecessary if one concedes that Ezekiel could be present in Jerusalem ''in spirit'' (Ez 8.3) and could thus apostrophize its inhabitants from afar. Neither is it necessary to suppose, therefore, that he physically journeyed back and forth between Jerusalem and Babylonia.

Although he was called to be a prophet preeminently to the Israel in exile (Ez 3.4–11), Ezekiel's early prophetic activity much resembles that of Jeremiah. Like Jeremiah he prophesied the inevitability of Jerusalem's destruction for its continued sins, and like Jeremiah he condemned King Zedekiah's suicidal policy of resistance to Babylon. He warned the exiles against their illusory hope of a speedy end of the exile of 597. He, likewise, witnessed against their betrayal of the hopes of Jeremiah, who had seen in them the beginning of the new Israel (Jer ch. 24; 29). Having received generous treatment from their Babylonian conquerors, the displaced Judeans had settled down to adopt their ways as their fathers had the ways of the Canaanites. To the old vices condemned by the preexilic prophets, the exiled ''house of rebellion'' (Ez 2.5–6; 3.9, etc.) added sins of idolatry and religious syncretism.

After the definitive destruction of Jerusalem, Ezekiel's prophecy became one of consolation. Though he entertained no illusions concerning the shortcomings of his fellow exiles, he knew that in them lay the hope of the future and that they must, therefore, be prepared for their destiny. His prophecy of this period includes a utopian constitution of the new Israel, outlining its religion and cult and its economic, political, and moral life. Doubtless one of the most influential aspects of his prophecy was his elaboration of the doctrine of personal retribution (ch. 18; 33). His last dated prophecy (29.17) was of April 26, 571 B.C.

Ezekiel in Christian and Jewish History. Ezekiel's influence on Christianity was pervasive, but indirect rather than direct. He is the prophet least cited or alluded to in the Gospels, probably because in the traditional sense of the word he possessed no messianic teaching (*see* MESSIANISM); as J. Steinmann has said, Ezekiel's ''messiah'' was the new Temple. On the other hand, Ezekiel's work was extensively used by the author of Revelation for its apocalyptic imagery, and through this medium it greatly influenced early Christian art.

Ezekiel is known as the father of JUDAISM. The doctrines of resurrection, personal immortality, and religion of law all have their roots in his prophecy. His often mysterious visions considerably affected the development of apocalyptic and the later mysticism of the CABALA (e.g., the *merkābâ*, the vision of the divine throne in ch. 1; 10). The prophet figures prominently in the art of the famous synagogue of DURA-EUROPOS. On the other hand, however, rabbis of the school of Shammai regarded Ezekiel as an apocryphal book, chiefly because of its conflicts with the Mosaic Law as finally codified in the Pentateuch.

Bibliography: W. ZIMMERLI, *Die Religion in Geschichte und Gegenwart* (Tübingen 1957–65) 2:844–847. *Encyclopedic Dictionary of the Bible*, tr. and adap. by L. HARTMAN (New York 1963) 737–739. For additional bibliography, *see* EZEKIEL, BOOK OF. Iconography. L. RÉAU, *Iconographie de l'art chrétien* (Paris 1955–59) 2.1:373–378. M. D. BECK, *Die Religion in Geschichte und Gegenwart* (Tübingen 1957–65) 2:850–851. A. LEGNER, *Lexikon für Theologie und Kirche*, ed. J. HOFER and K. RAHNER (Freiburg 1957–65) 3:1328.

[B. VAWTER]

EZEKIEL, BOOK OF

Old Testament book containing the message of exilic Prophet EZEKIEL. This article treats of the book's authenticity, structure and contents, literary character, and theology.

Authenticity. From time immemorial the Book of Ezekiel was listed, practically without opposition, in the Jewish canon as one of the Major Prophets; as a matter of course it passed into the canon of the Church. Criticism, too, initially dealt very kindly with the book. Its rigid and straightforward chronology, its logical development from first to last, its distinctive and consistent style, were all taken at face value as proclaiming it throughout the literary work of the exilic Prophet whose life was so thoroughly implicated in the communication of its message.

At the beginning of the 20th century, however, critical opinion began to change. Literary criticism established the redactional character of the book, and on this followed the attempt to determine the quantity of authentic Ezekielian material. Gustav Hölscher (1924) set this material at somewhat less than half the book and assigned its substance to a redactor of the fifth century B.C. The most radical solution was probably that of Charles C. Torrey (1930), for whom the Prophet Ezekiel never existed as a historical personage, and for whom the book was a pseudepigraphon of the Hellenistic age. William A. Irwin (1943) also considered the substance of the book to be Hellenistic; however, he salvaged a Prophet Ezekiel from it by fragmenting the text verse by verse and sometimes word by word, leaving the prophet about one quarter of the work. At least one Catholic author, A. van den Born (1953, 1954), followed the tendency to make the book pseudepigraphical.

Opposing such critics were always others who adhered in varying degrees to the traditional acceptance of the book and its author, and it is this conservative view that has prevailed. Though they may differ on many details, especially concerning the chronology of the Prophet's ministry, most contemporary critics and commentators would probably agree that the substance of Ezekiel goes back to an authentic Prophet of the Exile and portrays with essential accuracy the significance of his prophecy. The redactional character of Ezekiel no longer stands in isolation; this was the rule rather than the exception in the composition of the works of the ''literary'' Prophets, which have reached us through the collections and redactions made by their disciples. By the same token, supplementation and expansion of the prophetic material was the rule rather than the exception in the schools that transmitted it. Thanks to archeology, the exilic experience with which Ezekiel deals is now much better known and understood, and there is less temptation to dismiss or reconstruct the Biblical records. Finally, even though Ezekiel stands out among the preexilic Prophets in his concern for ritual matters, modern-day study of prophetism no longer finds the joining of prophetic and priestly religions the anomaly it was once thought; moreover, this association is typical of the postexilic Prophets, among whom Ezekiel ought perhaps better to be classified.

Structure and Contents. To set the nature of the Book of Ezekiel in clearer light, a detailed analysis of its structure and contents is given here. By its very structure the book falls into three main sections: (1) oracles for Israel before the destruction of Jerusalem: ch. 1–24; (2) oracles against the foreign nations: ch. 25–32; (3) oracles for Israel after the destruction of Jerusalem: ch. 33–48.

Oracles for Israel before the Destruction of Jerusalem: ch. 1–24. Apart from certain redactional insertions from a later period, all the oracles in ch. 1–24 antedate the capture and destruction of Jerusalem by the Babylonians in 587 B.C. In this part of the book the following 20 sections (of unequal length) may be distinguished:

(1) 1.1–3.15 (dated July 31, 593): Ezekiel's vision of the glory of God and his call to prophecy; the account is redactional, and doublets of the same or of similar visions have been combined to form it.

Ezekiel's vision of God, illustration from Ezekiel Chapters 1 and 2. (©Historical Picture Archive/CORBIS)

(2) 3.16a: an introduction that probably went originally with the symbolic actions described in ch. 4–5.

(3) 3.16b–21: an account from a later part of Ezekiel's ministry that has been set at the beginning of the book by the redactor in view of the Prophet's over-all significance for Israel; historically, it belongs with 33.1–20.

(4) 3.22–27: another redactional anticipation; this is the first part of the symbolic dumbness of Ezekiel (when his prophecy consisted in deeds rather than words) before the final fall of Jerusalem; historically it goes with 24.25–27 and 33.21–22.

(5) 4.1–5.15: symbolic actions signifying the coming siege and destruction of Jerusalem.

(6) 6.1–7.27: prophecies in word signifying the same destruction to come; as is true of the preceding, this is a collection of similar prophecies from various occasions.

(7) 8.1–11.21 (dated Sept. 17, 592): Ezekiel's vision of Jerusalem and the Temple; this is a redactional account, composed from multiple visions, which can be separated with some certainty.

(8) 12.1–20: acts symbolic of the Exile from Jerusalem.

(9) 12.21–14.11: a collection of oracles concerning prophecy, true and false, in Judah and Chaldea.

(10) 14.12–23: discourse on personal responsibility.

(11) 15.1–16.52: allegories concerning Jerusalem; to these have been added two passages symbolizing Jerusalem as a vine and as a faithless spouse.

(12) 16.53–63: two prophecies concerning the doom and the future salvation of Israel.

(13) 17.1–19.14: allegories on the kings of Judah; these involve Zedekiah's rebellion against Chaldea (allegory in 17.1–10, explained in 17.11–21), a passage to which a messianic prophecy has been appended

(17.22–24, postexilic, probably not by Ezekiel), and two ''dirges'' over Zedekiah (19.1–9 and 19.10–14); before the dirges a prophetic-priestly discourse or a series of discourses on personal responsibility has been inserted (ch. 18).

(14) 20.1–44 (dated Aug. 14, 591): a discourse or series of discourses on Israel's religious infidelity, concluded with a prophecy of restoration.

(15) 21.1–37: prophecies connected by the catchword ''sword''; these are of mixed character: the sword of Yahweh against Judah (21.1–10; complemented by a symbolic act, 21.11–12), the song of the sword of the Lord (21.13–22), the sword of the Chaldeans against Jerusalem (21.23–28; complemented by an ''antimessianic'' prophecy in 21.29–32), and the sword of the Lord against the Ammonites (21.33–37; topically connected with the preceding, but probably not Ezekiel's).

(16) 22.1–31: a series of prophetic-priestly discourses on the sins of Jerusalem and Israel.

(17) 23.1–49: the allegory of the two sisters, Oholah and Oholibah, representing Samaria and Jerusalem.

(18) 24.1–14 (dated Jan. 15, 588): symbolic action and prophecy announcing the investing of Jerusalem.

(19) 24.15–24: symbolic action prophesying the destruction of the city.

(20) 24.25–27: announcing the end of Ezekiel's dumbness; cf. 3.22–27 above.

Oracles against the Foreign Nations: ch. 25–32. As is usually the case in the postexilic editions of the prophetic works, the prophet's words against foreign nations have been gathered here and used to separate his prophecies against Israel from those that speak of its salvation. Successively they deal with Ammon, Moab, Edom, Philistia, Phoenicia, and Egypt. It is evident that they have been arranged topically rather than chronologically; however, seven of them are dated, including (in 29.17–21, against Egypt) one that bears the latest date of any Ezekielian prophecy (April 26, 571).

Oracles for Israel after the Destruction of Jerusalem: ch. 33–48. In this part of the book the following 12 sections may be distinguished:

(1) 33.1–9: the prophet as watchman; cf. 3.16b–21.

(2) 33.10–20: on individual responsibility.

(3) 33.21–22 (dated Jan. 8, 585): the end of Ezekiel's dumbness; cf. 3.22–27; 24.25–27.

(4) 33.23–29: prophecy against the Judaite survivors.

(5) 33.30–33: against Ezekiel's critics in Babylon.

(6) 34.1–31: the false shepherds of Israel's past and present contrasted with the Lord, the Good Shepherd; the promise of restoration.

(7) 35.1–15: a series of prophecies against Edom, which had cooperated in the Chaldean devastation of Judah.

(8) 36.1–38: prophecies concerning the regeneration of Israel, the land and the people.

(9) 37.1–14: the vision of the dry bones prophesying Israel's resurrection.

(10) 37.15–28: symbolic action portraying the restoration of Israel and Judah.

(11) 38.1–39.29: prophecies against Gog, an apocalyptic and symbolic figure; the eschatological purview probably indicates that these are not Ezekiel's.

(12) 40.1–48.35 (dated April 28, 573): an extended vision of the new Temple-to-be, described in loving detail, together with a utopian view of the new Israel, its laws and institutions; while the nucleus of the material is certainly Ezekiel's, it has doubtless been much expanded and developed by later writers.

Literary Character. As the foregoing analysis indicates, the Book of Ezekiel contains a mixture of many types of prophetical literature, some of them peculiar to this prophet. It abounds in symbolic actions to a greater degree than do the other prophetic books, and the symbolisms tend to be more involved and allegorical and more systematically connected with the prophetic message than was the case with earlier prophets. The allegorical vision, too, is quite typical of Ezekiel; its involved and often bizarre symbolism becomes the model for the subsequent apocalyptic style. A strong priestly influence may be felt in some of the discourses that adopt a legal approach to morality. The same kind of influence is even more apparent in the final chapters with their concern for the Sadocite priesthood, its laws and institutions, and the ritual and practice of the new Temple.

The text of Ezekiel is often very obscure in details and is more than usually overladen with glossings and expansions. Ezekiel's own style is ponderous and baroque, more adapted to prosaic moralizing and discursive description than to the poetry of the prophetic oracle. Most of Ezekiel is, indeed, prose; the attempt to reanalyze it according to the norms of a supposed *Kurzvers* (e.g., by W. Rudolph) has not been entirely convincing, especially as this generally involves considerable rearrangement and deletion in order to support the hypothesis. When Ezekiel does use poetry, it is ordinarily rather rough and poorly sustained; neither his vocabulary nor his choice of images is ''poetic.'' All this is said, however, without prejudice to the genuine prophetic eloquence of the book. Behind the redactional form in which the oracles often appear and despite the overloading of the text, we hear the authentic voice of a passionate and deeply committed man who lived intensely the word that he preached. Not in form, it is true, but in spirit certainly, Ezekiel stands in the great prophetic tradition; it is not ''armchair prophecy.''

Theology. Besides the profound influence that Ezekiel exercised on the development of the spirit and forms of JUDAISM, certain of its theological emphases deserve special note in relation to its place in the record of the history of salvation. Among them are: (1) The concept of the ''glory of the Lord'' (1.1–28; 3.12–15; 8.1–4; 10.1–20; 11.22–23; 43.1–9), represented in a series of visions having as their point of departure the doctrine of the presence of God, signified by the ark of the covenant. This concept, similar to Isaiah's vision of the Lord in the Temple (Is 6.1–13) and allied to other ancient concepts of the divine presence, in Ezekiel strikes a special note of transcendence (the glory of the Lord moves from Jerusalem to Babylonia), while at the same time there is no doubt of its identification with the Temple, which becomes a symbol of the source of all blessings (47.1–12). The combination of these ideas has much influenced later Jewish and Christian theology, including that of the Gospel according to St. JOHN. (2) The personalism involved in the repeated emphasis on individual responsibility was particularly relevant in the emergence of the Judaism of which Ezekiel has been called the father. This doctrine brought to a culmination the prophetic teaching on the remnant of Israel and made possible the Jewish ''church'' that came out of the Exile (*see* ISRAEL). (3) The willingness of Ezekiel to rethink SALVATION HISTORY (*Heilsgeschichte*) in a manner sharply contrasting with that of earlier prophecy (e.g., in ch. 16; 20) indicates both a new attitude to history and an openness to the changes that would be introduced through the development of doctrine leading down to Christianity. As part of this can be included Ezekiel's teaching on the Davidic Messiah, which can in one sense be termed an antimessianism [e.g., Ez 21.23–28 (alluding to Gn 49.10); 46.16–18]. In the concept of Ezekiel there would be a new and spiritual covenant with Israel (Ez 11.19; 36.26) in which, as a matter of course, there would be a Davidic prince (34.23–24; 37.24–25). This prince, however, has been deprived of every trace of the mystique of royalty: he is a lay figure, a servant of the Lord who alone is the Savior of Israel. Ezekiel's doctrine represents a culmination of a prophetic tradition that, as subsequently developed by other Prophets, would be reflected in the antitriumphalist spirit in which Jesus proclaimed the messianic fulfillment.

Bibliography: H. H. ROWLEY, ''The Book of Ezekiel in Modern Study,'' *The Bulletin of the John Rylands Library* 36 (Manchester 1953–54) 146–190, a discussion of the history of criticism of Ezekiel. The most recent critical commentaries are those of G. FOHRER, *Handbuch zum Alten Testament* 13, ed. O. EISSFELDT (Tübingen 1934–) and W. ZIMMERLI, *Ezechiel,* in *Biblischer Kommentar,* ed. M. NOTH (Neukirchen 1955–) v.13. In Eng., G. A. COOKE, *The Book of Ezechiel,* 2 v. (*International Critical Commentary,* ed. S. R. DRIVER et al.; New York 1937), retains its usefulness. Briefer but still serviceable commentaries. H. G. MAY and E. L. ALLEN, G. A. BUTTRICK, et al., eds., *The Interpreters' Bible* (New York 1951–57) 6:40–338. J. MUILENBURG, in *Peake's Commentary on the Bible,* ed. M. BLACK and H. H. ROWLEY (New York 1962) 568–590. E. F. SIEGMAN, *The Book of Ezechiel* (30–31; New York 1961). J. STEINMANN, *Le Prophète Ézéchiel et les débuts de l'exil* (Paris 1953), excellent study of the prophet, his message and meaning, with commentary. H. GESE, *Der Verfassungsentwurf des Ezechiel* (Tübingen 1957), discusses the manifold problems of the final ch. General. W. ZIMMERLI, *Die Religion in Geschichte und Gegenwart,* 7 v. (3d ed. Tübingen 1957–65)2:847–850. J. ZIEGLER, *Lexikon für Theologie und Kirche,* ed. J. HOFER and K. RAHNER (Freiburg 1957–65); suppl., *Das Zweite Vatikanishe Konsil: Dokumente und Kommentare,* ed. H. S. BRECHTER et al. (1966) 3:1327–28. *Encyclopedic Dictionary of the Bible,* tr. and adap. by L. HARTMAN (New York 1963) from A. VAN DEN BORN, *Bijbels Woordenboek,* 739–742.

[B. VAWTER]

EZRA

One of the leading figures in the restoration of the Jewish community in Palestine after the Babylonian Exile. Ezra, whose late-Hebrew or Aramaic name *ezrā* (rendered in Greek as Ἔζ[δ]ρας or Ἐσ[δ]ρα[ς]) means ''help,'' traced his descent from the priestly line of Aaron through Seraiah (Ezr 7.1–5), the high priest who was executed by the Babylonians when they captured Jerusalem in 587 B.C. (2 Kgs 25.18–21).

Priest (Ezr 7.11; 10.10) and ''scribe of the Law of the God of heaven'' (Ezr 7.12, 21), Ezra returned to Jerusalem from Babylon, leading a group composed of over 1,250 Jews from Babylon and Chasphia—laymen, priests, Levites, singers, gatekeepers, and Temple servants (Ezr 7.7; 8.1–20). Disdaining protection from the Persian king Artaxerxes, whose decree authorized Ezra's mission (Ezr 7.1–26), the caravan encamped at the river Ahava, fasted for a time to beg divine protection for the journey, and then proceeded safely to Jerusalem, where the travelers deposited the rich offerings that they had brought for the Temple (Ezr 8.21–36).

According to Ezr 7.7–9, the journey started ''on the first day of the first month'' and ended in Jerusalem ''on the first day of the fifth month'' in the ''seventh year'' of King Artaxerxes. Despite this clear notation, the time of Ezra's arrival and activity in Jerusalem is very much in dispute. If the king mentioned in Ezr 7.7 is Artaxerxes I Longimanus (465–424 B.C.), a ministry in the king's seventh year (458 B.C.) would place Ezra in Palestine before the first mission of NEHEMIAH (definitely dated as 445–433 B.C.). But this seemingly makes a failure of Ezra's mission—contrary to the constant Jewish view of him—since Nehemiah would then have to correct again the abuse of mixed marriages (Nehemiah ch. 13). Several other reasons—e.g., Ezra's reforms seem to have been carried out in an abundant population and a rebuilt city (Ezra ch. 9–10), whereas Nehemiah both rebuilt the city and repopulated it—argue rather for a Nehemiah-Ezra sequence of activity.

To avoid the chronological difficulty, some authors suggest that the king of Ezr 7.7 is Artaxerxes II Mnemon (404–358 B.C.), whose seventh year was 397 B.C. Such a late dating of Ezra's mission, however, makes impossible the coordinated ministries of Ezra and Nehemiah, forcing proponents of this hypothesis to consider Nehemiah's name in Neh 8.9 as a later scribal insertion and to separate in time the material in Nehemiah ch. 10 from what precedes it in ch. 9. Another solution to the problem reads the ''thirty-seventh year'' (428 B.C.) in Ezr 7.7 instead of ''the seventh year,'' the error in number being attributed to faulty textual transmission. This would make Ezra's mission contemporaneous with the second mission of Nehemiah (which began sometime between 433 and 424 B.C.) and would allow time for the rebuilding of the walls and population of Jerusalem.

Part of Ezra's commission from Artaxerxes (Ezr7.11–26) was to regulate religious matters. Accordingly, Ezra, who was shocked to learn how much intermarriage with the peoples of the land had weakened the postexilic principle of Jewish exclusiveness (Ezra ch. 9), called an assembly of the people to tell them that they would have to put away their foreign wives (Ezr 10.1–11; see also Neh 13.23–29). This they did, according to a prearranged system (Ezr 10.12–44).

In another convocation (see Lv 23.24), Ezra read the Law to the people, who celebrated that day as one of joy (Neh 8.1–12). They observed the restored feast of Booths (Neh 8.13–18; cf. Lv 23.33–43). In Neh 9.1–10.40 an account is given of the great covenant with the God of Israel concluded under Ezra's direction. By this covenant the Jews pledged themselves to avoid intermarriage with foreign peoples, to observe the Sabbath and the Sabbatical year, not to exact debts, to pay the Temple tax, and to provide wood, sacrifices, and offerings for the Temple.

Not much else is known about Ezra. He is not mentioned with Nehemiah in the praises of Sir 49.13, but two apocryphal books bear his name. Rabbinic literature hails him as second to Moses in his role of giving the Law. The Talmud even says of him that had not the Law been given through Moses, Ezra would have been worthy to be its vehicle (Sanhedrin 21b), for he restored its legislation when it was forgotten (Sukkah 20a). On the Book of Ezra, *see* CHRONICLER, BIBLICAL.

Bibliography: H. SCHNEIDER, *Lexikon für Theologie und Kirche,* ed. J. HOFER and K. RAHNER, 10 v. (2d, new ed. Freiburg 1957–65) 3:1101–03. *Encyclopedic Dictionary of the Bible,* tr. and adap. by L. HARTMAN (New York 1963), from A. VAN DEN BORN, *Bijbels Woordenboek* 687–688.

[N. J. MCELENEY]

EZRA, BOOK OF

Biblical book that relates the first return of the Jewish exiles from their Babylonian captivity after the edict of Cyrus the Great in 538 B.C.; the rebuilding of the Temple in Jerusalem, a labor completed in 515 B.C.; and the work of the priest-scribe Ezra, who led another group of exiles back to Palestine in the reign of the Persian king Artaxerxes (which Artaxerxes is uncertain). Particular mention is made of Ezra's efforts to preserve the racial purity of the restored Jewish community. (For a more complete treatment of this book, *see* CHRONICLER, BIBLICAL.)

[N. J. MCELENEY]

F

FAÀ DI BRUNO, FRANCESCO, BL.

Mathematician, scientist, inventor, composer, founder of the Sisters of Our Lady of Suffrage, and the Pious Works of Saint Zita, priest; b. March 29, 1825, Alessandria, Piedmont, northern Italy; d. March 27, 1888, Turin, Italy.

Francesco Faà di Bruno, the youngest of the 12 children of Marquis Louis Faà di Bruno, was a remarkable man of great talent and deep faith imbued from his infancy in the ancestral castle at Bruno. Following the death of his mother (1834), Carolina Sappa, Francesco studied at the Collegio San Giorgio di Novi Ligure until his entrance into the Royal Military Academy at Turin (1840). He completed his training, proved his valor in the War of Independence (1848), and rose to the rank of captain–of–staff in the Sardinian Army (1849).

Faà di Bruno was assigned to Paris (1849), but resigned his commission (1853) to study at the Sorbonne under Augustin Louis Cauchy and Urbain Leverrier. There he also became aquainted with Abbé Moigno and Charles Hermite. Upon his return to Turin, he was a professor of mathematics at the university for the rest of his life. In recognition of his achievements as a mathematician, the degree of doctor of science was conferred on him by the Universities of Paris and Turin. In addition to some ascetical writings, the composition of some sacred melodies, and the invention of some scientific apparatuses, Faà di Bruno made numerous and important contributions to mathematics. In 1858, he published a series of seven articles on the religious and pedagogical function of music, as well as a small volume on the topic.

He joined the Saint Vincent de Paul Society (1850) with Cauchy and Adolphe Baudon, and later established a chapter in Turin (1853). Faà di Bruno founded the charitable *Opera Pia Santa Zita* in the San Donato district of Turin (Feb. 2, 1859) to aid house servants and ensure their right to participate in festival liturgies. The society was placed under the patronage of Saint Zita and had Saint John Bosco as its vice president. In addition to this major accomplishment, Faà di Bruno established Saint Joseph's Hospital for the sick and convalescent (1860), a home for aged priests (1862), classes for the vocational education of poor youth (1864), a women's branch of the *Opera* known as the *Congregazione delle Suore Minime di Nostra Signora del Suffragio* (1868), as well as other foundations.

He accomplished all the above as a dedicated layman. On Oct. 22, 1876, at age 51, he was ordained priest. The following month he opened the church he founded (*Chiesa del Suffragio*) to the public (October 30) and celebrated his first Mass as Father Francesco (November 1). Not only was Blessed Francesco a prolific author in both science and music, but his life and works have generated a formidable number of scholarly studies.

Pope John Paul II praised Faà di Bruno on Sept. 25, 1988, for his ability ''to find positive responses to the needs of his time'' (beatification homily).

Bibliography: L. CONDIO, *Francesco Faà di Bruno* (Turin 1932). Facoltà di Teologia dell'Ateneo Romano della Santa Croce, *Il Beato Francesco Faà di Bruno e la donna* (Rome 1991). Istituto Superiore di Scienze Religiose di Torino, *Francesco Faà di Bruno e l'Eucaristia* (Turin 1996). R. LANZAVECCHIA, *Francesco Faà di Bruno* (Alessandria, Italy 1980). V. DEL MAZZA, *Il Coraggio della Carità* (Turin 1988). V. MESSORI, *Un italiano serio: il beato Francesco Faà di Bruno* (Milan 1990); *Ser Cristiano en un mundo hostil*, tr. J. ROUCO and A. MONTERO (Madrid 1997); *Il beato Faà di Bruno—Un cristiano in un mondo ostile* (Milan 1998). P. PALAZZINI, *Francesco Faà di Bruno scienziato e prete* (Rome 1980). Pontificia Università Lateranense, *La Spiritualità di Francesco Faà di Bruno nell'esperienza francese* (Rome 1983). P. RISSO, *Un genio per Cristo: profilo biografico del beato Francesco Faà di Bruno* (Padua 1992). C. TRABUCCO, *Francesco Faà di Bruno, pioniere dell'assistenza sociale* (Rome 1957). Università degli Studi di Torino–Facoltà di Lettere e Filosofia, *Francesco Faà di Bruno e la musica* (Turin 1992). *Acta Apostolicae Sedis* (1988): 1092.

[K. I. RABENSTEIN]

FABER, FREDERICK WILLIAM

Oratorian and popular spiritual writer; b. Calverley, Yorkshire, England, June 28, 1814; d. London, Sept. 26,

Frederick William Faber.

1863. After Harrow, he matriculated at Balliol in 1832, and became a scholar at University College in 1834, and a fellow there in 1837. At his entrance into Oxford he was a Calvinist, but by the end of his 2d year there, he professed Evangelism. By 1837 he had become an Anglican full of hope in the OXFORD MOVEMENT. In 1839 he assisted NEWMAN in translating seven books of St. Optatus for the Library of the Fathers, and on May 26 he received Anglican orders. As pastor of a parish in Elton, he formed the Society of St. Joseph and wrote that he seemed ''to grow more Roman daily.''

In the autumn of 1845, many of his friends, including Newman, were received into the Church, and in November, at Northampton, Bishop Wareing accepted Faber's abjuration of Anglicanism. He founded the Wilfridians in 1846, and was ordained in 1847. When Newman brought the Oratory of St. Philip Neri to Birmingham in 1848, Faber and many of the Wilfridians placed themselves under Newman as novices (*see* ORATORIAN). In 1849 Faber was sent as founder to the oratory on King William Street, London. The two oratories then developed along divergent lines, and Newman and Faber quarreled over Oratorians' hearing nuns' confessions.

The Latin element in Faber's nature was especially revealed in his sermons, which most critics would place in the ''Sweet Flowers of Devotion'' school (the phrase is Cardinal Wiseman's). During a mission in a poor section of Dublin, Faber thus ended an impassioned sermon: ''My dear Irish children, have mercy on your own souls!'' He knelt, the congregation knelt, and a thousand people sobbed.

As a preacher Faber was highly appreciated; Manning compared him with St. Bernard and St. Bernardine of Siena. The skill he demonstrated in adapting spiritual principles to different types of listeners, he also utilized in spiritual direction. He displayed a delicate psychology in shining the light of truth into the darkest recesses of self-love, whether the directed was priest, religious, or lay. He wrote eight volumes in eight years, all composed rapidly with few corrections.

All for Jesus (1853) attained a phenomenal circulation and had ''the goal of making piety bright and happy, especially to laymen.'' While this work gave preliminary techniques for initiating the spiritual life, *Growth in Holiness* (1854) described ''the middle wilderness of long, patient perseverance.'' The third volume in the trilogy, which was to treat of souls within sight of the land of promise, was never written. *The Blessed Sacrament* (1855), *The Creator and the Creature* (1858), *The Foot of the Cross* (1858), *Spiritual Conferences* (1859), *The Precious Blood* (1860), and *Bethlehem* (1860) were all completed and translated rapidly into many European languages. The last book is exceptional in that Faber wrote it to please himself; a study of the Incarnation, it is the most Berullian of his books.

Faber's style is a mixture of erudition, devotional feeling, and poetic fancies. By modern standards, his paragraphs are long and his style florid. His penchant for poetic and archaic words results in a charge of occasional obscurity. The exclamation point is his standby in punctuation. He relies heavily on the emotive and the affective approach. Yet, when allowances are made for external differences, Faber's thought is seen to be relevant to today's spiritual problems, especially in his emphasis on the soul's individuality, man's psychosomatic nature, the indispensability of taking pains with purity of intention, the necessity of spiritual reading (it is a sign of predestination), frequent use of the Sacraments, and friendliness to all men, especially to those not of the faith.

In 1854 the Oratory moved to South Kensington, and there Faber spent the remaining nine years of his life. In July, 1860, the pope conferred on him the degree of doctor of divinity.

Bibliography: F. W. FABER, *A Father Faber Heritage,* ed. M. MERCEDES (Westminister, Md. 1958). R. CHAPMAN, *Father Faber* (Westminster, Md. 1961). J. VERBILLION, ''A New Look at Father Faber,'' *Cross and Crown* 12 (1960) 164–187.

[J. VERBILLION]

FABER, JOHANN AUGUSTANUS

Dominican humanist and theologian; b. Augsburg (not Fribourg, Switzerland), 1475; d. 1530. He made his profession at the Dominican priory at Augsburg, and undertook theological studies in Italy, principally at Venice. In 1507 he was promoted to master of theology in a general chapter at Padua, and in that year returned to Augsburg as prior. In 1511 he was vicar-general of the Dominican Congregation of upper Germany, with the priories of Augsburg, Würzburg, Speyer, Constance, Fribourg, Strassburg, Haguenau, and Zurich under his jurisdiction. From 1512 to 1515 he began the reconstruction of the convent church at Augsburg with funds that accrued from the preaching of a jubilee indulgence conceded by a bull of Leo X. Emperor Maximilian decreed against the bull on March 7, 1515, but reversed his judgment on April 13. In this year Faber disputed with Johann Eck at Bologna on usury and interest, and on his return to Germany was made imperial councilor. Long convinced that thorough classical training was a necessary preparation for a critical study of the Scriptures, the Fathers, and theology, he interested Maximilian in the erection of an Athenaeum at Augsburg, but the Emperor's death on Jan. 12, 1519, brought the project to a standstill. He traveled to the Netherlands with Cardinal Matthäus Lang at the end of 1520 to win the support of the new Emperor Charles V. There he discussed his views with Erasmus. In 1521 he wrote anonymously the *Consilium cuiusdam ex animo cupientis esse consultum et R. pontificis dignitati et christianae religionis tranquillitati,* in which he sympathized with the Lutheran revival of classics. As Luther's theology developed, however, Faber became his firm opponent. This new stand antagonized the humanists and earned him hostility at Augsburg, which he left in 1525, seeking refuge with Cardinal Lang in Salzburg. He returned briefly the next year but again fled.

Bibliography: K. SCHOTTENLOHER, *Bibliographie zur deutschen Geschichte im Zeitalter der Glaubensspaltung* 1:239. J. QUÉTIF and J. ÉCHARD, *Scriptores Ordinis Praedicatorum* (New York 1959) 2.1:80. R. COULON, *Dictionnaire de théologie catholique* (Paris 1903–50) 5.2:2046–50, where the errors in Quétif-Échard are corrected. A. DUVAL, *Catholicisme* 4:1032–33. W. ECKERT, *Lexikon für Theologie und Kirche* (Freiburg 1957–65) 3:1330–31. N. PAULUS, *Die deutschen Dominikaner im Kampfe gegen Luther, 1518–63* (St. Louis, Mo. 1903) 292–313.

[E. D. MCSHANE]

FABER, JOHANNES

Theologian, bishop, opponent of Luther and Zwingli; b. Leutkirch (Swabia),1478; d. Vienna, May 21, 1541. He is sometimes confused with others of the same name. Faber (Heigerlin) studied Canon Law at Tübingen and received a doctorate in theology at Freiburg. Thereafter he was rector at Lindau and Leutkirch, canon at Basel, and vicar-general for Constance (1518). After 1524 he became chaplain and confessor to Archduke Ferdinand and then bishop of Vienna in 1530. At Basel he had been friendly with Erasmus, favored reform of abuses (especially indulgences), and until 1519, sympathized with Zwingli, Oecolampadius, and Melanchthon. From 1522 he opposed Luther with writings such as *Malleus in haeresim Lutheranam* (1524). Representing the bishop of Constance, he debated unsuccessfully against Zwingli at Zurich (1523), and, as an imperial councilor, helped organize a Swiss Catholic party (1526). He attended several imperial diets, including Augsburg (1530), where he examined the AUGSBURG CONFESSION. As bishop of Vienna he preached, worked, and wrote zealously against Protestantism; held regular conferences with his clergy; and provided scholarships for students for the priesthood. He wrote much on doctrinal questions, such as faith and good works, the Mass, and the Eucharist, and also polemics on Hus, Luther, Zwingli, and the Anabaptists.

Bibliography: L. HELBLING *Die Religion in Geschichte und Gegenwart*[3] 2:856. *Allgemeine deutsche Biographie* 14:435–441.

[J. T. GRAHAM]

FABER (FAVRE, LEFÈVRE), PETER, BL.

The first companion of St. IGNATIUS OF LOYOLA; b. Villaret, Savoy, April 13, 1506; d. Rome, Aug. 1, 1546. After early study at Thônes and La Roche he enrolled at St. Barbara's College in the University of Paris in 1525. Here he met and lodged with Francis XAVIER. In 1528 Ignatius of Loyola arrived in Paris and joined Faber and Xavier in firm, deep friendship. On May 30, 1534, Faber was ordained and on Aug. 15, 1534, he said the Mass at which Ignatius and his small band of friends vowed poverty, chastity, and a journey to the Holy Land to work among the Muslims. He then shared the experiences of Ignatius's group in northern Italy and Rome that led to the foundation of the Society of Jesus (*see* JESUITS). When their plans for missionary work among the Muslims were blocked in 1537 by the Turkish war, Faber went with Ignatius to Rome where he was appointed professor of Scripture at the Sapienza.

In 1540 Faber was sent by PAUL III to attend the Diet at Worms and that at Regensburg the following year. At these conferences Faber saw the futility of the hopes of CHARLES V to solve differences between Catholics and Protestants in Germany by discussion and negotiation. He was among the first to respond to the challenge of Lu-

Bl. Peter Faber.

theranism by promoting a genuine reform in the life and discipline of Catholics, both clerical and lay. By preaching and direction, especially by the use of the *Spiritual Exercises* of Ignatius, he brought about many conversions and instilled a new spirit in the Church in the Rhineland, thereby enabling that area to resist the further spread of Protestantism. He founded the first Jesuit residence in Cologne, and received Peter CANISIUS into the Society of Jesus. His labors also took him to Belgium, France, Portugal, and Spain. After being called by Paul III to attend the Council of Trent, he died in Rome.

Because of his profound knowledge and gentle sanctity, Faber was sought out for his counsel, and highly esteemed by Xavier and the early Jesuits. His spiritual diary, the *Memoriale,* is a daily account over a long period of the action of God in his soul. It reveals a deep spiritual refinement, and also the strength and charm of his character that were so important in the success of his work. He was beatified Sept. 5, 1872.

Feast: Aug. 2 (Jesuits).

Bibliography: PETRUS FABER, *Spiritual Writings of Pierre Favre*, ''The Memoriale,'' tr. E. C. MURPHY, ''Selected Letters and Instructions,'' tr. M. E. PALMER (Saint Louis, MO 1996). W. V. BANGERT, *To the Other Towns* (Westminster, Md. 1959), with bibliography. P. FABER, *Mémorial*, tr. M. DE CERTEAU (Collection Christus 4; Paris 1960). C. SOMMERVOGEL, *Bibliotèque de la Compagnie de Jésus* (Brussels-Paris 1890–1932) 4:1657–58; 9:583. *Fabri monumenta: Beati P. F. epistolae, memoriale et processus* (Monumenta historica Societatis Jesu 15; 1914). J. B. KETTENMEYER, ''Aufzeichnungen des Kölner Kartäuserpriors Kalckbrenner über den sel. Peter Faber,'' *Archivum historicum Societatis Jesu* 8 (1939) 86–102. J. N. TYLENDA, *Jesuit Saints & Martyrs* (2d ed. Chicago 1998) 241–45.

[W. V. BANGERT]

FABIAN, POPE, ST.

Pontificate: 236 to Jan. 20, 250. The *Liber pontificalis* describes Fabian as a Roman and credits him with dividing the city into seven ecclesiastical districts with seven deacons and seven subdeacons. The latter were associated with seven notaries to compile the ACTS OF THE MARTYRS. The LIBERIAN CATALOGUE noted his building activities in the Roman cemeteries: *multas fabricas per cimiteria fieri iussit.* These *fabricas* must have included the completion of the bishops' grotto in the cemetery of Calixtus. CYPRIAN OF CARTHAGE describes Fabian as honorable, and praises the integrity of his administration. Fabian approved the condemnation of the African Bishop Privatus of Lambaesis, and apparently did not respond to Origen's letters seeking some measure of reconciliation after his earlier condemnation by Bishop Pontianus.

Getting permission to transfer the bodies of the martyrs PONTIANUS and HIPPOLYTUS from Sardinia and to bury them with honors in Rome, implies that the Roman church had friends in authority, not surprising during the reign of the pro-Christian emperor Philip the Arab (244–249). Ironically, it was Fabian who ordained the future schismatic NOVATIAN. The church historian Eusebius records that when the community sought a successor to ANTERUS, a dove settled on Fabian's head, which the community took to be a sign from God. He died during the persecution of DECIUS, was buried in the cemetery of Callistus, and later translated to the Basilica of St. Sebastian.

Feast: Jan. 20.

Bibliography: EUSEBIUS, *Ecclesiastical History.* 6:29, 34, 36, 39. CYPRIAN, *Correspondance,* ed. and tr. L. BAYARD, (Paris 1925) 1:9, 30. P. GODET, *Dictionnaire de théologie catholique*, ed. A. VACANT et al., (Paris 1903–50) 5:2050–51. E. FERGUSON, *Encyclopedia of Early Christianity* (New York 1997), 1.415. J. N. D. KELLY, *Oxford Dictionary of Popes* (New York 1986), 16–17. G. SCHWAIGER, *Lexikon für Theologie und Kirche,* 3d. ed. 3 (Freiburg 1995), s.v. ''Fabianus, heilig, Papst.''

[E. G. WELTIN]

FABIOLA, ST.

Early Christian benefactress and friend of St. JEROME; d. Rome, 399. She came to the wealthy Roman nobility descended from Julius Maximus and had an extremely passionate nature. Fabiola divorced her first husband because of his vices. To protect herself, she took a second husband, separating herself from Church communion until, as Jerome asserted, the death of her second husband and her public penitence at the church of the Lateran on Easter eve in the presence of the bishop and clergy. She sold her possessions, gave to the poor, and supported monasteries in Italy. In 395 she journeyed to Bethlehem with her relative Oceanus, staying there with SS. PAULA and EUSTOCHIUM.

When the controversy over ORIGENISM divided Jerome and his friends from RUFINUS OF AQUILEIA and Melania, efforts were made to draw Fabiola to the cause of Bp. JOHN OF JERUSALEM, who supported Rufinus (Jerome, *Cont. Ruf.* 3.14); but they proved unsuccessful. Fabiola eagerly attached herself to the teachings of Jerome (*Epist.* 77), who wrote two dissertations for her: one, on the mystical meaning of the dress of the high priest (*Epist.* 64); and another, on the 42 stations (*mansiones*) of the Israelites in the desert (*Epist.* 78). At the rumor of an invasion of the Huns she returned to Rome in 396. A letter from the Roman priest Amandus to Jerome in which he asks Jerome's views on a woman taking a husband while another, although dissolute, husband lives indicates that she may have contemplated a third marriage; but she was discouraged from it by Jerome in his answer to Amandus (*Epist.* 55).

The last three years of her life were spent in charitable activity. She joined PAMMACHIUS in the institution of a hospital at Porto, where she herself cared for the poor and sick. As her restless disposition had found Rome and Italy too small for her charities, she was considering a long journey when she died. The whole of Rome attended the funeral of Fabiola, their great benefactress.

Feast: Dec. 27.

Bibliography: W. H. FREMANTLE, *A Dictionary of Christian Biography,* ed. W. SMITH and H. WACE, (London 1877–87) 2:442–443. H. LECLERCQ, *Dictionnaire d'archéologie chrétienneet de liturgie,* ed. F. CABROL, H. LECLERCQ and H. I. MARROU (Paris 1907–53) 7.2:2274–75. *Patrologia Latina,* ed. J. P. MIGNE (Paris 1878–90) 22:690–698. A. S. D. THIERRY, *Saint Jérôme,* 2 v. (Paris 1867). F. CAVALLERA, *Saint Jérôme,* 2 v. (*Spicilegium sacrum Lovaniense* 1, 2; 1922).

[E. D. CARTER]

FABRI, FILIPPO (FABER)

Theologian, commentator on DUNS SCOTUS; b. Spinata di Brisighella, Italy, 1564; d. Padua, Aug. 27, 1630. He joined the Friars Minor Conventual in 1583. After ordination he studied at the friaries of Ferrara, Padua, and Rome. His fame spread and he became professor of philosophy (1603) and theology (1613) at the University of Padua. Although elected provincial of Bologna (1625–30), he continued to lecture on the teachings of Duns Scotus, becoming renowned for his clear explanations of Scotistic doctrine. Among his writings are: *Philosophia naturalis Duns Scoti* (1601), *Disputationes theologicae* (1620), *Theologicae disputationes de predestinatione* (1623). The *Commen. in XII libros metaphysicorum Aristotelis ad mentem Scoti* and *De primatu Petri, et Pontificis Romani* were published posthumously (Venice 1637). Many of his works are in manuscripts in the Paduan Library. He collaborated in the writing of the Urban Constitutions for the Order of Minor Conventuals.

Bibliography: P. É. D'ALEÇON, *Dictionnaire de théologie catholique,* ed. A. VACANT, 15 v. (Paris 1903–50; Tables générales 1951–) 5.2:2060–61. U. SMEETS, *Lineamenta bibliographiae Scotisticae* (Rome 1942). É. LONGPRÉ, *Catholicisme* 4:1033–34. A. EMMEN, *Lexikon für Theologie und Kirche,* ed. J. HOFER and K. RAHNER, 10 v. (2d, new ed. Freiburg 1957–65) 3:1334. G. FRANCHINI, *Bibliosofia, e memorie letterarie di scrittori francescani conventuali* (Modena 1693). H. HURTER, *Nomenclator literarius theologiae catholicae,* 5 v. in 6 (3d ed. Innsbruck 1903–1913) v.3. J. H. SBARALEA, *Supplementum et castigatio ad scriptores trium ordinum S. Francisci a Waddingo* (Rome 1936) v.2. L. WADDING, *Scriptores Ordinis Minorum* (3d ed. Rome 1906) v.5.

[R. BARTMAN]

FACULTIES OF THE SOUL

The faculties of the soul are often called its potencies. POTENCY, generally speaking, is basically of two sorts, each understood in relation to its corresponding actuality. There is a potency for the actuality that is being, and a potency for the actuality that is making or doing. For example, marble is said to have a potency for being a statue; water in its liquid state has not. Marble has a certain consistency—found also in materials like bronze, wood, and clay—by which it can acquire and maintain the shape of statue. But marble does not make itself into a statue. It is the sculptor who does this. Now, if the sculptor ''does'' this, he ''can do'' it; that is, the sculptor has a potency for making the statue. Thus, just as ''is'' entails ''can be,'' so too ''does'' entails ''can do.'' ''Can be'' is said to be a passive potency; ''can do,'' an active potency, and hence, also a power. The potencies of the soul, like the potency of the sculptor, are active potencies, or powers for doing; they are potencies for the performance of life activities. Because of this they are often called powers of the soul.

How Defined. The powers of the soul are closely related to the soul's definition. The common definition of soul states nothing distinctive of the existent types of soul. To define each type, one must become acquainted with the activities attributed to each; for one comes to know what a thing is by observing what it does. And if it "does," it "can do." One can thus describe the types of soul in terms of their potencies. For example, the vegetative soul is the soul with potencies for nourishing, growing, and reproducing. Yet this has little meaning unless one knows what the activities of nourishing, etc., are. One can get at the nature of these activities by considering the objects on which they bear; for all activities bear on some object. Thus, one can move from object to activity to faculty to type of soul. This does not mean that there are four separate analyses, one each for object, activity, faculty, and type of soul. There is actually only one analysis, that of the object (and of what is implied by it; e.g., an analysis of the sort of natural organized body that this requires); for the activity is defined in terms of the object, the faculty in terms of the activity, and the type of soul in terms of its faculties. To have analyzed the object is to have analyzed the activity and the faculty, hence to have said something about the type of soul and natural organized body.

Vegetative Faculty. The generic object of the vegetative faculty is said to be two different things: (1) food (see Aristotle, *Anim.* 415a 23–416b 30), and (2) the body of which the soul is the first actuality (see St. THOMAS AQUINAS, ST 1a, 78.1). One might wonder about the fact that two different objects are assigned; but the wonder is dispelled if one considers that vegetative activities terminate in this body, but only after having acted upon and affected food. Now, food can be considered in three ways: (1) as nutriment, and so considered it conserves the living body in existence; this is the specific object that defines the activity of nourishing; (2) as augment, and so considered it brings the living body to its quantitative maturity; this is the specific object that defines the activity of growing; and (3) as overflow, and so considered it prepares the living body for producing another like itself; this is the specific object that defines the activity of reproducing.

Although the vegetative faculties use food, they also use the vegetative bodily organs, such as stomach and liver; they also use the natural activities of certain elements and compounds, such as HCl. In spite of such a thorough dependence, there is a degree of transcendence of vegetative activities over the activities of matter in its nonliving states. By its vegetative activities, in which it employs activities that are found also in matter in its nonliving states, a living thing destroys another (food), and by this destruction maintains itself in existence.

Sensitive and Intellectual Faculties. The generic object of the sensitive faculty is whatever is sensible. For sight, it is the visible; for hearing, the audible, etc. The object of the intellectual faculty is whatever is intelligible. This is to say that things in the real world are the objects of sense and intellect; as sensible, they are the objects of senses; as intelligible, the objects of intellect. The sense and the thing as sensible cooperate, as agent and instrument, respectively, in the production within the sense of a form, called the sensible species, by means of which the sense functions, e.g., by means of which sight sees. The intellect and the thing as intelligible (things in the physical world are only potentially intelligible, whereas they are actually sensible) cooperatively produce, as agent and instrument respectively, a form within the intellect, called the intelligible species, by means of which the intellect understands what these things are. This form, unlike the sensible species that is individualized by the bodily matter of the organ of sense, is an absolute form (*see* SPECIES, INTENTIONAL; SOUL, HUMAN, 4).

Although the activities of the sense faculties depend on certain bodily organs (e.g., eye, ear, and nose) and on certain natural activities of elements and compounds (e.g., the photochemical changes in the retina of the eye), these activities nonetheless transcend the activities of matter in its nonliving states. Unlike what happens in the case of changes in the realm of the nonliving and in that of the vegetative, in the case of the change that occurs in a sense when it is actually sensing, a sensible form is produced by, and is present in, a substance that is not the ordinary physical subject of that sensible form. Thus, when the eye sees a tree, there is present in the substance that is the eye a visual form whose ordinary physical subject is the substance that is a tree.

The transcendence of the intellectual faculty is complete, because the form produced by it, and present in it, is an absolute form.

Faculty in General. In addition to questions—What is the faculty of sight, and how does it differ from the faculty of understanding?—raised with a view to making more complete one's account of what soul is, philosophers ask more general questions about the soul's faculties—What is a faculty? And how are the faculties related to the soul? Is the soul constituted out of its faculties as a whole out of parts? Are the faculties substances or accidents?

The faculties of the soul are power parts, as opposed to quantitative parts (*see* SOUL). They are accidents, for the actualities to which they are related, namely, life activities, are accidents, and things related as potency to actuality must be in the same genus. The soul cannot be composed of its faculties as a whole out of parts; for the soul is in the genus of substance, and nothing substantial can be intrinsically constituted of accidents. Although the soul has a plurality of faculties distinct from itself as accidents from something substantial, these are nonetheless united in the soul itself, for in each one living thing there can be but one soul, since the soul is a substantial form. The soul is the one source of all its diverse activities and faculties. Most properly speaking, the living thing, the total living thing, performs life activities; and this it does primarily by means of the soul and its power parts, and secondarily by means of the natural organized body and its bodily parts. The faculties of a living thing are the many accidents of one living substance.

Because of the undesirable connotations of the term faculty, some prefer to use in its stead words like power, potency, capacity, or ability. For in the last two centuries faculty has come, unfortunately and quite in distortion of the Aristotelian-Thomistic notion, to designate tiny independent entities, substancelike, as sources of diverse life activities. More recent PSYCHOLOGY, rightly rejecting the faculties of the faculty psychologists, has at the same time returned to a recognition of the fundamental idea of active potencies or powers. Psychological testing has revealed that human activities are of essentially diverse sorts, and that each sort derives from some tendency or inclination to act in that sort of way. These inclinations appear to be innate, but open to development and differentiation in the individual by means of his experience with the world. It is clear not only that the Aristotelian-Thomistic concept of active potencies is compatible with the concept of innate tendencies or inclinations or capacities, but also that the two concepts are in fact the same, though differently verbalized. Another difference lies in the methodology employed. The Aristotelian-Thomistic concept was arrived at by means at the disposal of the ordinary man, viz, ordinary sense observation and introspection. The contemporary concept, on the other hand, was arrived at by scientific means, through the factor analysis of investigators like C. Spearman (1863–1945), J. McK. Cattell (1860–1944), and L. Thurstone (1887–1955)—an interesting and important scientific confirmation of an age-old philosophical concept.

See Also: INTELLECT; WILL; SENSES; APPETITE.

Bibliography: J. E. ROYCE, *Man and His Nature* (New York 1961), extensive bibliog. F. GAETANI, *Enciclopedia filosofica*, 4 v. (Venice-Rome 1957) 2:250–52. R. ALLERS, ''Functions, Factors and Faculties,'' *The Thomist* 7 (1944) 323–62.

[J. BOBIK]

FACUNDUS OF HERMIANE

Sixth-century African bishop and theologian. Although nothing is known of the origins or early career of Facundus, he belonged to a group of African theologians whose knowledge of the history of the Church and whose theological method, based on the Scriptures and doctrines of the Church Fathers, enabled them to give a clear and logical explanation of the truths of the faith, characteristic of the finest patristic tradition. He likewise stood forth as a champion of the liberty of the Church, asserting its independence of the civil power: ''Since civil affairs are not subject to the church, how can the affairs of the church be subject to the palace?'' (*Pro def. Trium Cap.* 12.4).

Facundus was present in Constantinople when the *acephali,* or semi-Eutychians, as he called the party of THEODORE ASCIDAS, persuaded JUSTINIAN I that by condemning the THREE CHAPTERS he could regain the Monophysites to union with the Catholics; and Facundus maintained that this stratagem was a means of seeking vengeance for the condemnation of ORIGENISM by the Emperor's Edict of 543, brought about by the Roman deacon, later Pope, PELAGIUS I (*ibid.* 1.2; 4.4). Facundus appears to have been present at a synod under Mennas in 546 that discussed the results of the Edict of 544 against the Three Chapters and to have begun writing his 12 books *In Defense of the Three Chapters.* He was one of the 70 bishops who participated in a synod with Pope VIGILIUS I in Constantinople (autumn 547) to discuss the Three Chapters; and in the third session, by his offer to prove that the Council of Chalcedon had accepted the Letter of Ibas of Edessa, caused the Pope to prorogue discussion and ask for the opinions of the bishops in writing. Not yielding to the pressure of the imperial agents, Facundus obtained a seven-day delay in submitting his vote, contrary to the desire of the Emperor.

On later completing his *Defense,* which was addressed and submitted to Justinian, Facundus had to leave the capital. He took part in the general council of Africa (550) that condemned Pope Vigilius until he should rescind the *Judicatum I.* From hiding in exile, he followed the events leading to the Council of CONSTANTINOPLE II (553) and the Pope's submission to the Emperor's pressure (Feb. 23, 554). He directed his *Liber contra Mocianum* against the Pope's turnabout and the intrigue of the government represented by the civil official Mocianus (553 or 558). In 568 he wrote an *Epistola fidei catholicae* summing up his defense of the Three Chapters and attacking Popes Vigilius and Pelagius and the Council of Constantinople II.

The theological argumentation of Facundus's *Defense of the Three Chapters* had been taken into consideration by Justinian in preparing his *Rectae fidei confessio* (July 551), and it was used as the basis for Pope Vigilius's *Constitutum* of May 14, 553, as well as for the *In de-*

fensione Trium Capitulorum of Pelagius. The historical information he supplied for the events leading to the Council of Constantinople and its aftermath is invaluable.

Bibliography: *Patrologia Latina* 67:527–878. G. BARDENHEWER, *Geschichte der altkirchlichen Literatur* 5:320–324. E. CASPAR, *Geschichte de Papsttums von der Anfängen bis zur Höhe der Weltherrschaft* (Tübingen 1930–33) 2:259–261. H. GELZER, *Ausgewählte Kleine Schriften,* ed. H. GELZER, JR. (Leipzig 1907) 73–76. *Histoire du Bas-Empire*, ed. J. R. PALANQUE 2:643–645, 670, 679, 691–692, 824–826, date of *Contra Mocianum.* R. DEVREESSE, *Essai sur Théodore de Mopsueste* (*Studi e Testi* 141; 1948) 210, 221–222. F. TOLLU, *Catholicisme* 4:1053. L. DUCHESNE, *L'Église au VIe siècle* (Paris 1925).

[F. X. MURPHY]

FADICA

Established in 1976, Foundations and Donors Interested in Catholic Activities (FADICA) represents 47 private foundations with shared interests in the church's mission and work. The organization was formed through the leadership of a dozen family foundations convened by the Raskob Foundation of Wilmington Delaware. Three important influences led to FADICA's creation: the Second Vatican Council's vision of the laity with its emphasis on community and service, a trend within American philanthropy favoring collaboration, and growing wealth and influence among American Catholics.

The association, headquartered in Washington, D.C., regularly convenes its members for their continuing education on trends of importance to the church's ministry and internal life. Biannual symposia, research studies, and jointly funded initiatives, enable FADICA's philanthropists to play an active part in Catholic life.

Collective giving on average has exceeded two hundred million dollars. Among FADICA's achievements are its role in launching multi-million dollar programs to address the retirement crisis of American religious; engineering the creation of a U.S. church initiative to aid in the rebuilding of the church in Russia and Central and Eastern Europe; facilitating financial management reforms in the Holy See; persuading the U.S. hierarchy to address the subject of stewardship through a pastoral letter to American Catholics; developing better homiletic curricula in U.S. seminaries; and instituting the first national training course for vocations directors.

On the threshold of a new century, FADICA's shared concerns revolve around questions of how church institutions will maintain their Catholic culture and character as they transition from clergy and religious leadership to lay supervision and governance. There is also the change of attitudes and priorities among the trustees. A new generation of trustees, largely formed in the years after the Second Vatican Council, bring to the foundation an entirely different experience of the church. They have no first-hand memory of the dense Catholic subculture of the twentieth century which gave rise to FADICA. Intentional efforts to reach and mentor a new generation of foundation trustees in Catholic philanthropy are priorities with the FADICA organization.

Bibliography: J. T. ELLIS, *Of Faith and Giving, An Historical Narrative of Catholic Philanthropy* (Washington, D.C. 1981). M. J. OATES, *The Catholic Philanthropic Tradition in America* (Bloomington, Ind. 1995).

[F. J. BUTLER]

FAGNANI, PROSPERO

Italian canonist and theologian, b. S. Angelo, in Vado, Pesaro, Italy, July 2, 1588; d. Rome, Aug. 17, 1678. Of an old and distinguished noble family, he studied at Pavia, where he became doctor of civil and canon law at the age of 20. His brilliance won him the position of professor of law at the Sapienza in Rome, where his teaching enhanced his reputation. When he was 22, he was appointed secretary of the Congregation of the Council by Paul V, thus beginning a long career in which he held the esteem of eight popes and served on 11 congregations. Gregory XV commissioned him to prepare the important bull *Aeterni Patris* (Nov. 15, 1621), which reaffirmed and enlarged the regulations governing the conclave and papal elections. At the age of 44 he became blind but continued his active work with unabated energy. At the order of Alexander VII he undertook his greatest work, *Commentaria absolutissima in quinque libros Decretalium* (8 v. Rome 1661). Written after he had been blind for 28 years, the work reveals tremendous erudition and prodigious memory. The clarity of expression, the moderation and certainty of doctrine, and the exact citations were all the more enhanced by his many practical examples drawn from long experience with the Roman congregations. The index of the *Commentaria* was particularly excellent and has been considered a classic of its type. The work was highly important in the development of Canon Law in the post-Tridentine Church.

Inserted in the *Commentaria* was a treatise, *De opinione probabili,* attacking PROBABILISM, which led St. Alphonsus to call Fagnani the greatest of rigorists.

Bibliography: A. BERTOLA, *Dictionnaire de droit canonique*, ed. R. NAZ (Paris 1935–65) 5:807–809. T. ORTOLAN, *Dictionnaire de théologie catholique* 5.2:2067–69. J. F. VON SCHULTE, *Die Geschichte der Quellen und der Literatur des Kanonischen Rechts*

(Stuttgart 1875–80) 3.1:485. H. HURTER, *Nomenclator literarius theologiae catholicae* 4:253–254.

[J. C. WILLKE]

FAGNANO, JOSÉ

Salesian missionary in Argentina and Chile; b. Rochetta, Italy, March 9, 1844; d. Santiago de Chile, Sept. 18, 1916. As a youth he entered the seminary but soon left to enlist as a soldier in Garibaldi's army, then fighting for Italian unification. Disappointed in the military life, he returned to his classical studies. After becoming a friend of Don Juan BOSCO, founder of the Salesians, he reentered the seminary; he was ordained on Sept. 11, 1868. He received the degree of doctor in fine arts in Turin, and in 1875 went to America with the first Salesian expedition to Argentina. A year later he was director of the first Salesian school in America, established in San Nicolás de los Arroyos, Buenos Aires. Persuaded by Don Bosco, he went to Patagonia in 1880 and started his evangelistic work. He enlisted in General Villega's army, while it was fighting the natives, toward whose pacification and conversion he worked. He was a parish priest in Patagonia in 1860 and in the course of his apostolic work built two schools, the first hospital, and a metereological observatory; he also established a school and a church in Viedma. In 1883 the Holy See named him apostolic delegate to southern Patagonia. He played an important role in the pacification of the natives and built a school and an oratory in Punta Arenas, Tierra del Fuego. He accompanied Ramón Lista's expedition of 1886 and inspected the lake that today bears his name; he carried livestock to Willes Bay and on horseback explored Dawson's Island, supporting in his correspondence the Argentine's right to rule the Falkland Islands. Fagnano died loved and understood by the natives.

Bibliography: R. A. ENTRAIGAS, *Monseñor Fagnano* (Buenos Aires 1945).

[V. O. CUTOLO]

FAITH

As understood in this article, faith means belief in God and acceptance of His revelation as true. The concept of faith will be treated as it is seen in the Bible, in patristic tradition and the teaching of the Church, and in dogmatic theology.

IN THE BIBLE

For the inspired authors of the Sacred Scriptures, faith is indeed an act of the intellect assenting to revealed truth; but since God's revelation in the Bible is often concerned with the future, that is, since the object of divine revelation is frequently God's promises to Israel, biblical faith is often a belief in God's fidelity to His promises and therefore *confidentia* (confidence, trust) as well as *fides* (faith, belief). This can be seen by examining the writings of the older books of the OT, the writings of Judaism, i.e., of the Jews in the last few centuries B.C. and the first Christian century, and finally the writings of the NT.

In the older books of the Old Testament. In these inspired writings, faith plays a very important preparatory role in the SALVATION HISTORY of mankind. At sundry times, God spoke to His chosen people of the OT and demanded of them faith in His word. God thus surpassed the barriers of the natural order and drew aside the veil disclosing the supernatural order of life and truth in Him. Various divinely revealed truths formed a part of Israelite faith and were considered as guiding principles for religious and spiritual conduct. Such truths were, e.g., the existence of one God, the election of Israel as God's chosen people, God's special covenant with Israel, and Israel's ultimate messianic salvation.

Terminology. The most common Hebrew root employed to express Israel's faith in God is *'mn,* of which the basic meaning is firmness, certainty, reliability, and trustworthiness. From this root are derived the adjective *'ēmûn* (faithful: 2 Sm 20.19; trustworthy: Prv 13.17), the nouns *'ĕmûnâ* [steadiness: Ex 17.12; security: Ps 36(37).3; fidelity, faithfulness: 1 Sm 26.23; Hb 2.4, and often predicated of God, as in Dt 32.4; Ps 35(36).6; etc.] and *'ĕmet,* for original *'ement* [trustworthiness: Ex 18.21; Jos 2.12; constancy, fidelity, faithfulness: Gn 24.27, 49; Is 38.18–19; Ps 24(25).10; 39(40).11–12; etc.; truth, reality: Dt 22.20; Jer 9.4; Is 59.14–15], and the adverb *'āmēn* (AMEN or surely, in an assent to something said: Nm 5.22; Dt 27.15–26; Jer. 11.5). As a verb this root is used only in the reflexive (niphal) form *ne'man* (to prove faithful, reliable, true, etc.: Gn 42.20; Dt 7.9; 1 Sm 25.28; etc.) and in the causative (hiphil) form *he'ĕmîn* (to hold as trustworthy, to trust, to believe: Gn 15.6; 45.26; Dt 9.23; etc.).

Since Israel's faith was closely connected with the idea of trust in Yahweh, another verb, when used with God as the object, that implicitly connotes faith is *bāṭaḥ* (to feel secure, to rely, to trust: Dt 28.52; Is 31.1; etc.), with its corresponding noun *beṭaḥ* (security, trust: Is 32.17; Jgs 8.11), which is used mostly as an adverb (securely, confidently: Dt 33.28; Prv 10.9; etc.). A similar verb that may connote the idea of faith is *ḥāsâ* (to seek refuge, to trust: Dt 32.37; Jgs 9.15). Furthermore, since the Israelite's attitude of faith often looked to the future, Hebrew verbs meaning to hope were used (especially in the later OT writings) with a connotation of faith, such as *qāwâ* or *qiwwēh* (e.g., Gn 49.18; Is 40.31; 49.23), *yiḥēl* [e.g., Ps 30(31).25; 32(33).22], *ḥikkēh* (e.g., Is 8.17; 30.18), all of which, with God as the object, signify to wait for Him with confidence, to hope in Him, and therefore, implicitly, to believe in His promises.

Characteristics of Old Testament Faith. The Israelite concept of faith came to denote the peculiar relationship existing between God and Israel, especially the bond of the covenant between them. The faith of Israel was a particular form of life of a people chosen by Him and standing in an active relationship with Him. The Israelite's relationship to God that is designated by the verb *he'ĕmîn* (to believe) often implied an assent of the mind, confidence in the heart, and obedience in the will. Abraham, for instance, who was still childless in his old age, believed without wavering in the Lord's promise that He would give him numerous descendants, and this faith of his was accredited to him as a meritorious deed (Gn 15.6—a passage that is often quoted, to show what true faith is, in Rom 4.3; Gal 3.6; Jas 2.23). Isaiah warned the Israelites that without faith in Yahweh they would not survive (Is 7.9; 28.16). According to Habakkuk, "the just man, because of his faith, shall live" (ab 2.4)—another favorite quotation on faith in the NT (Rom 1.17; Gal 3.11; Heb 10.38). The necessity of faith is seen also in those OT passages that tell of how God's people at times rebelled and refused to believe in Him, so that God had to chastise them for their lack of faith (Nm 14.1–12; Dt 1.26–46; 9.22–24).

Israel's ideal attitude toward God is often described by the term *yir'at yhwh* (Is 11.2–3; Prv 1.7, 29; etc.), traditionally rendered as "the fear of the Lord," although it means rather reverence for Yahweh, the standing in awe of Him, and therefore obeying His word on faith (e.g., Gn 22.12; Dt 6.2; Jos 22.25; etc.), as is clear, e.g., from Ex 14.31: "They feared the Lord and believed in Him." It is a faith that inspires confidence, which forms the theme of many of the Psalms [e.g., Ps 33(34).5–11; 39(40).2–6; 55(56).4–5, 12].

In the OT, to believe in God means to recognize and acknowledge the relationship that God has entered into with Israel. This reciprocal relationship that comes from Israel's encounter with God is of the essence of Israelite faith. God is the originator of the covenant relationship, and the stipulations of the covenant are His commandments (Dt 5.1–4). Faith, then, means the acknowledgment of God's commands and implies obedience on the part of man. Faith, too, expresses the acknowledgment of God's promises and His power to fulfill them [Ex 4.1, 5, 8–9, 30; Ps 105(106).12, 24].

In the OT, therefore, faith in God includes the whole relationship that exists between God and man. It has for its object God's omnipotence, His purpose in choosing His people, His love for them, His constancy and fidelity, and the fulfillment of His promises. Not to believe in God means to become an apostate [Ex 14.31; 19.9; Nm 14.11; Dt 1.32; 32.20; Ps 77(78).22]. Faith thus sums up all the ways by which men express in their lives their relationship to God. According to Isaiah, faith denotes a special form of existence for those who depend on God alone (Is 7.9). The chosen people of God have their particular manner of life and are established through their faith (Is 28.14–16; 30.15). For Israel, faith is the only possible mode of existence; all other attitudes in independence of God or all obligations toward anyone else than God are excluded; God alone, His plan and His will, together with the proper attitude of man, are the only important factors.

In Judaism. In the last few centuries B.C. and in the first Christian century, the ancient OT heritage of faith was taken over, with its leading ideas retained, by both the Palestinian and the Hellenistic Jews. The faith of the Jews was closely related to their past history and thus included the idea of loyalty or fidelity. It was related also to the future in the sense that God would certainly fulfill His promises, which now took on strongly messianic and eschatological overtones. But their faith in God was concerned especially with the present, inasmuch as Israel was called upon to obey God's commandments and remain faithful to His covenant. Faith in God tended, therefore, to determine every aspect of their lives.

The writings of this period show the stress that the Jews put on faith in God. Abraham, Isaac, Jacob, and Moses were signaled out as models and exemplars of faith and obedience (Sir 44.19–23; 1 Mc 5.52; Jdt 8.22–29; Jubilees 6.19; 18.1–19; 21.2; Psalms of Solomon 16.14). Abraham's descendants were distinguished from the godless and impious by reason of their fidelity (Wis 3.9; Sibylline Oracles 5.158, 426; Enoch 46.8; 4 Ezr 7.131). It was stated that to know God is complete justice, and to know His power is the root of immortality (Wis 15.3; see also Enoch 46.8; 4 Ezr 7.131; Apocalypse of Baruch 54.21). In the rabbinical writings, faith was often characterized as obedience to the Law rather than as loyalty to God whose saving acts were experienced in the past or as confidence in Him whom they were called upon to trust in the future. The individual was conscious of the fact that he belonged to God's chosen people and that salvation would be bestowed on the faithful and pious (Syriac Baruch 54.5; 57.22; 2 Ezr 7.24). Other characteristics of faith that were expressed were its simplicity (Wis 1.1), its ultimate victory (2 Ezr 7.34), and its ability to preserve the faithful amid adversity (2 Mc 15.24; 16.22; 17.2).

According to Flavius JOSEPHUS, faith in divine providence meant trust in God (*Ant.* 4.60; *Ap.* 2.170). For

PHILO JUDAEUS, faith was understood within the framework of Hellenistic Judaism; faith meant belief in one God and trust in His providence (*Op. Mund.* 170–172; *Virt.* 216). Philo viewed it as both confidence in God's help and belief in His promises (*Sacr. Ac.* 70; *Vit. Mos.* 1.225; 2.259; *Leg. All.* 3.308; *Mut. Nom.* 166; *Abr.* 275). He understood faith also as a turning away from the world of birth and death and a turning toward God who is eternal, whereby man finds that security which he is seeking. ''To trust God is a true teaching, but to trust our vain reasonings is a lie'' (*Leg. All.* 229). ''He who has sincerely believed in God has learned to disbelieve in all else, all that is created only to perish'' (*Praem. Poen.* 28.30). ''Turning to God is an attitude of the mind'' (*Conf. Ling.* 31) and ''the most perfect of virtues'' (*Rer. Div. Her.* 96; *Virt.* 216; *Abr.* 270). It is no small task to attain this (*Rer. Div. Her.* 93); it is a prize that Abraham acquired (*Migr. Abr.* 44); it is associated with the virtue of piety (*Migr. Abr.* 44); and it is the best sacrifice to be offered to God (*Cher.* 85), who is the best possible truth and the most certain good.

In the New Testament. Here faith is intimately connected with salvation history. To believe in Christ means to accept and have faith in the events of His life, death, Resurrection, and Ascension. It is to believe, not only that these events really took place, but, what is more important, to believe in the significance of these events for man's salvation. These truths were preached by the Apostles and disciples of Christ to men and women of all nations, who were called upon to believe in the Lord Jesus Christ. As a result, in the design of God, a personal relationship came to exist between Christ and His followers. This relationship or attitude of mind is analogous to that which God unfolded in the OT with respect to His chosen people, where faith in God was often expressed in terms of loyalty, trust, and obedience. In the NT, faith means the acceptance and acknowledgment of Christ's existence here and now, as well as the submission of man's mind and will to Him as the cause of Redemption and eternal beatitude.

The LXX had already used the noun πίστις (faith) and the verb πιστεύειν (to believe) to translate the corresponding Hebrew words; the NT continued to use these words in the same way, but here they occur more frequently than they do in the OT. Classical Greek seldom employed these terms in a religious sense, except to indicate a belief in the existence of the gods. In the NT, to believe means to rely on, to trust, or simply to have faith (Mk 13.21; Jn 4.21; Acts 27.25; Rom 4.17). The noun faith can mean loyalty or trust as well as belief (1 Thes 1.8; Phlm 6; Heb 6.1), just as the adjective πιστός (faithful) can mean loyal or trustworthy as well as believing (Mt 25.21, 23; Lk 16.10–11; 1 Tm 3.2; 3 Jn 5; Rv 2.10, 13).

In the Synoptic Gospels and Acts. In the first three Gospels faith often signifies confidence rather than intellectual assent. The faith, for instance, that Christ demanded before performing a miracle was belief in His power and confidence in His goodness (Mk 5.24, 26; 9.23–24). Such is the faith that He rebuked His disciple for lacking (Mt 6.30; 8.26; Mk 4.40; Lk 8.25) the faith that He praised in the centurion of Capharnaum (Mt 8.1). This kind of faith is able to work miracles (Mt 17.20; 21.21; Mk 9.23; Lk 17.6), and the lack of it prevents their performance (Mt 13.58; 17.20; Mk 6.5).

God is the primary object of faith (Mk 11.22–23; Mt 1.22); but faith in Him is intimately related to the mission of His Son in whom God is revealed (Mt 12.28). Thus, faith also in Jesus as the MESSIAH and SON OF GOD is necessary. Belief in Jesus as the Christ and Son of God became the outstanding characteristic of the early Christians, who were called simply ''the believers'' (Acts 2.44; 4.32). Those who hoped to be cured by Jesus acknowledged His power and special relationship to God; they proclaimed Him the Son of God, at least in a broad sense (Mt 8.29; 14.33; Mk 1.24; 3.11; 5.7). Even demoniacs and unclean spirits called Him the Son of God or Messiah (Lk 4.41).

Faith is a free act on the part of man; i.e., it is within man's power to believe and be saved or not to believe and be judged and condemned (Mk 16.15–16). On the first Christian Pentecost, many people believed the gospel and ''accepted the faith'' (Acts 2.41, 44; 6.7). Peter reminded the Jews that they must firmly believe in the divinity of Christ and His mission on God's word, which is more certain than human eyewitness, for God's testimony is greater than that of man (see also 2 Pt 1.16–18).

On occasion, Jesus asked His disciples to acknowledge Him, i.e., to express their belief in His messiahship (Mt 10.32–33; Mk 8.38). Faith in Christ means the remission of sins (Mk 2.5; Lk 7.48–50; Acts 10.43; 26.18); it is a necessary condition for salvation (Acts 4.12; 16.31; 11.17; 15.7–11). Faith in God or in the words of God was sometimes demanded because of His written testimony in the Law and the Prophets (Lk 1.20, 45; Acts 24.14; 26.27; 27.25). Jesus insisted that the testimony of John the Baptist must be accepted and believed as well (Mk 11.31; Mt 21.32). As in the OT, faith in God meant an encounter with God, so also in the NT, to believe in Christ or ''have faith'' in Him means for the Christian to encounter God through Jesus Christ His Son. Even the enemies of Jesus who stood by His cross understood this truth, though they would not accept it (Mt 27.42). Christian converts believed the same (Acts 9.42; 16.31, 34; 18.8), and above all others, St. Paul himself (Acts 22.19).

In the Pauline Epistles. One of the most strongly stressed teachings in the Epistles of St. Paul is the necessity of faith in Christ for salvation—a firm, personal faith that leads a man to receive Baptism and thereby become incorporated into Christ. For Paul, the process of the faith consists in preaching, hearing, accepting, and understanding the gospel, which is the word of God. The faith preached by Paul was proclaimed all over the world (Rom 1.8; 10.17; 1 Cor 2.5; 15.1; 2 Thes 1.3, 5). In the language of Paul, to believe means to become a Christian (1 Cor 1.21; 3.5; 14.22; 15.2–3). While preaching is the contributing cause, faith is really effected by the Spirit of God (1 Cor 2.4–5; 1 Thes 1.4–5). Faith is a free gift of God, and man therefore needs the grace of God if he is to be saved (Eph 2.8). To believe in Christ is to suffer with Him (Phil 1.29); it is the breastplate of the soldier of Christ (1 Thes 5.8) and a shield against all evil (Eph 6.16).

The one true God is the object of faith (1 Thes 1.8–9). Christ as man leads man to the knowledge of God, but Christ as God is the goal of the Christian's life (Rom 10.8–9; Gal 2.16; 1 Cor 3.22–23; 15.24, 28; Phlm 5). The motive for believing God is the testimony of God Himself (Rom 4.3, 23–24; 1 Thes 2.13). There is only one true faith (Eph 4.5), to be defended against false teachers (1 Tm 6.12; 2 Tm 4.7), and one must be ready and willing to die for it (Phil 1.27–30).

Faith in God means the Christian's conviction that God has been and always will be faithful to His promises, which He is all-powerful to fulfill. Therefore, the Christian believes that, since God has loved man and sent His Son into the world to redeem man by His sacrifice on the cross, God will raise the Christian from the dead as He has raised Christ from the dead (Rom 3.25; 4.3–25; 2 Cor 1.9; Gal 3.6; 1 Thes 1.8–9) and that Christ will return at the end of the world to judge the living and the dead (Rom 10.9; 1 Cor 15.1–14; 1 Thes 1.10; 4.14; 5.9–10). Faith is, therefore, first of all an act of man's intellect whereby he freely submits to the authority of God and confesses, at least implicitly, the truth of His divine testimonies (Rom 1.17; Gal 3.11; 1 Thes 2.13).

As an act of the will, faith demands that the Christian make his conduct conform with the teachings of the gospel; in this sense St. Paul often speaks of ''obedience to the gospel'' (Rom 1.5; 10.16; 2 Cor 10.5; 2 Thes 1.8). Christians are called upon to remain firmly grounded in the faith and to persevere in it (Rom 11.20; 1 Cor 15.2; 16.13; 2 Cor 1.23–24; 13.5; Col 1.23; 2.7; 1 Tm 2.15). Their faith must be a living one, of which Paul himself was a model (Gal 2.20; Ti 3.8; 1 Tm 5.8). It must be guarded and protected (Rom 12.3; 11.20–22; 1 Cor 2.14; 2 Cor 6.14–15; 1 Tm 1.19; 6.10). Faith can also be developed and perfected (Rom 10.10; 11.20–22; 2 Cor 10.15; Eph 4.13; Phil 1.25; 2 Thes 1.3).

Faith is closely related to hope and confidence: ''For we in the Spirit wait for the hope of justice in virtue of faith'' (Gal 5.5; see also Rom 4.20; 5.1–2; 1 Thes 1.3; 5.8; 1 Cor 13.13); and as one of the charismatic gifts (1 Cor 12.9; 2 Cor 8.7; *see* CHARISM), faith inspires such confidence as to move mountains and perform miracles (1 Cor 13.2; cf. Mk 11.23). But faith also operates through charity and love (Gal 5.6, 22–23; 6.8–10). Together with hope and charity, faith is one of the triad of virtues that have lasting value on earth and are the means whereby eternal happiness is attained (Rom 10.13–15). However, along with hope, it will give way to the direct vision of God in the future life, where charity alone endures forever (1 Cor 13.13; 2 Cor 5.7).

Since Christ by His death and Resurrection reconciled man with God and effected man's REDEMPTION, faith in Christ and His redemptive work continues to reconcile sinners with God and obtain the forgiveness of their sins (Rom 3.25; 1 Cor 15.17). It is by faith, and not by the works of the Law, that man becomes just and holy in the sight of God (Rom 1.17; 3.28; 4.3; Gal 3.5–6; *See* JUSTIFICATION). Faith, therefore, is the determining element of the Christian life and the characteristic mark of Christian unity (Rom 3.22; Gal 3.7).

In the Epistle to the Hebrews. Faith is defined in Heb 11.1 as ''the substance of things to be hoped for, the evidence of things that are not seen.'' These words are commonly understood in the sense that faith gives the Christian the assurance (ὑπόστασις) that his spiritual hopes will find fulfillment and the conviction (ἔγεγχος) that the divine revelations that surpass knowledge derived from the senses are true. Faith, therefore, is the acceptance of God's word concerning both His promises and the truths He has revealed. The patriarchs and heroes of the OT, by their sufferings and even martyrdom, were exemplars of this faith that rests on God's word (Heb ch. 11). Faith gave them the power and strength to bear adversity patiently. Faith enabled them, as it enables Christians, to grasp the fact that heavenly realities were created by God (Heb 11.3); without faith it is impossible to please God, and he who desires to come to Him must believe that He exists and is the rewarder of the just (11.6).

Faith is also an act of the will, as manifested by the exemplary obedience of those who were renowned for their good deeds and virtuous conduct (11.4–39). ''Fullness of faith'' provides the Christian with assurance of obtaining divine mercy and grace and to believe with unshaken confidence and perfect tranquility that heaven itself will ultimately be possessed (4.16; 10.22–23). Confidence (παρρησία), which has a great reward, must not be lost; it is the source of supernatural life in God (10.35–38). Faith, therefore, inspires and stimulates Christians to orient their whole lives toward Jesus Christ, who is ''the author and finisher of faith'' (12.2).

In the Johannine Writings. Faith is a central theme in the writings of St. John. Although the noun ''faith'' occurs only a few times (1 Jn 5.4; Rv 2.13), the verb ''to believe'' is found frequently. According to St. John, believing is not only an act of the mind, assenting to revealed truths; it is also an act of man's free will. Yet, while man's moral disposition plays a role here, faith is a gift of God (Jn 6.37, 39, 64; 8.47; 1 Jn 4.6; 5.1), for no one can come to the Son unless the Father draws him (Jn 6.44).

In a few instances, according to John, the object of faith is God (Jn 5.24; 12.44; 1 Jn 5.10), but more often it is Christ. To believe in Jesus means to accept Him as the Messiah (1 Jn 5.1); He was sent by the Father (Jn 8.28–29; 11.42; 16.27–30; 17.20–21), and He is the Son of God (3.16, 36; 6.40; 17.27; 20.31). Jesus said to Philip, ''Do you not believe that I am in the Father and the Father in me?'' (14.10–11). For John, Christ is the one mediator between God and man; He is the ''light that has come into the world'' (12.46), ''the life'' whereby everyone lives (11.25–26), and the Savior of the world (4.42; 1 Jn 4.14). Through and by faith the whole man is united to Christ; ''to believe in Christ'' (Jn 3.21; 6.35, 37, 44–45) means to live His life (1 Jn 5.10–12) and to partake of Him as food and drink (Jn 6.35, 50). Faith motivated by charity consists in observing Christ's commandments (1 Jn 2.3–5; 5.3; Jn 8.31, 51; 14.21–23); to believe in Him means to acknowledge and obey Him (Jn 6.69; 10.38; 16.30; 17, 7–8; 1 Jn 4.16). On the other hand, lack of faith in Him is sinful (Jn 16.9; 8.21, 24; 9.41; 15.22–24) and leads to death and eternal damnation (3.18, 36; 5.24, 29). Through faith we become sons of God (1.12; 1 Jn 3.1–2) and heirs of the kingdom of heaven (Jn 3.15–16, 36; 5.24; 6.40, 50; 8.51; 11.25–26). He who believes enjoys a foretaste of everlasting life even here on earth (3.18, 36; 5.24), and Christ, who is the resurrection and the life, will raise up on the last day (5.26; 6.39–40; 11.25).

The faith demanded of a Christian is inspired by the many miracles wrought by Christ in confirmation of His divine origin and mission (2.11; 4.53; 5.36; 9.33; 10.25–38; 11.42; 14.11; 15.24). Faith in Him springs also from His preaching, His predictions, and their fulfillment (2.22; 13.19; 14.29). Moreover, the justification of Christ's claims is attested by God the Father, John the Baptist, and the Scriptures (4.41–42; 5.24; 6.68–69; 17.8, 20; 1 Jn 5.10). Yet Christ Himself says that faith based on His word as preached by His Apostles is better than that inspired by the sight of His miracles (20.29; see also 2.23–24; 4.48). On the part of the believer, good works favor the acceptance of faith (3.21), whereas evil deeds, such as spring from pride and hypocrisy, hinder its reception and operation (3.19–20; 8.44; 5.44; 9.41; 12.42–43).

Finally, in the Revelation to St. John, Christ appears as the faithful witness of God's revelations (Rv 1.5: 19.11); He is the ''Amen'' (3.14; 19.4), i.e., the affirmation that God's words are trustworthy (21.5). Christians who do not ''disown the faith'' (2.13) are united faithfully with Christ, the Lamb of God. If they have ''the patience of the saints,'' keep God's commandments, ''have the faith of Jesus,'' and ''suffer and accept suffering as Christ did'' (2.10–13; 13.10; 14.12), Christ Himself will be their eternal reward (22.20).

Bibliography: P. ANTOINE, *Dictionnaire de la Bible* suppl. ed. L. PIROT (Paris 1928—) 3:276–310. R. SCHNACKENBURG, *Lexikon für Theologie und Kirche,* ed. J. HOFER and K. RAHNER (Freiburg 1957–65) 4:913–917. F. BAUMGÄRTEL and H. BRAUN, *Die Religion in Geschichte und Gegenwart* (Tübingen 1957–65) 2:1588–97. *Encyclopedic Dictionary of the Bible,* tr. and adapt. L. HARTMAN (New York 1963) 744–750. A. GELIN, ''La Foi dans l'A.T.,'' *Lumen Vitae* 22 (1955) 432–442. J. DUPLACY, ''La Foi dans le Judaisme,'' *ibid.* 443–468. P. BENOIT, ''La Foi dans les évangiles synoptiques,'' *ibid.* 469–488. M. BOISMARD, ''La Foi selon Saint Paul,'' *ibid.* 489–514. P. VAN IMSCHOOT, *Théologie de l'Ancien Testament,* 2 v. (Tournai 1954–56) 2:101–103. R. BULTMANN and A. WEISER, *Faith,* tr. D. M. BARTON, in G. KITTEL, *Bible Key Words,* v. 10 (London 1961) 1–33. P. HEINISCH, *Theology of the O.T.*, tr. W. G. HEIDT (Collegeville, Minn. 1955) 43–48. P. MICHALON, ''La Foi, rencontre de Dieu et engagement envers Dieu, selon l'A.T.,'' *Nouvelle revue théologique* 75 (1953) 587–600. J. LEBRETON, *La Vie et l'enseignement de Jésus Christ,* 2 v. (16th ed. Paris 1947) 2:471–490. J. BONSIRVEN, *L'Évangile de saint Paul* (Paris 1948) 177–185, 198–212; *The Theology of the N.T.*, tr. S. F. L. TYE (Westminster, Md. 1963). J. HUBY, ''De la connaissance de foi dans St. Jean,'' *Recherches de science religieuse* 21 (1931) 385–421.

[C. H. PICKAR]

PATRISTIC TRADITION AND TEACHING OF THE CHURCH

Faith in the writings of the Fathers of the Church and in the official magisterium of the Church is treated next, and it is followed by the theological analysis of faith.

Patristic tradition. The Fathers of the Church were more concerned with the content of faith, the gospel of salvation, than with reflective analysis of the act itself. But this very concern with the content of the gospel determined their view of faith: the unwavering assent to the full, correct message of salvation as delivered by the Apostles and their authentic successors (cf. Irenaeus, *Proof of the Apostolic Preaching* 3, ed. S. Weber, Freiburg 1917; Basil, *Moralia* 80.22, *Patrologia Graeca* 31:867–868). However, two parallel ideas contributed to a deepening theology of faith. In one, the apologete, explaining Christianity to an unbelieving world, insists that the gospel is accepted not out of credulity, but out of a reasonable and free commitment. Thus St. Justin (d. 165) devotes lengthy treatises to exposing the reasonableness of such commitment, especially in view of the patent fulfillment of prophecies [*see* PROPHECY (THEOLOGY OF)]. Clement of Alexandria (*c.* 150–215), living in the intellectual capital of the world, head of the first Christian school, advocates philosophy as a useful preparation for faith and proposes Christ as the "Teacher." At the same time, he inaugurates a thesis that becomes a commonplace with the Fathers, especially Augustine. He quotes the Septuagint version of Is 7.9, "unless you believe you will not understand," and notes that since belief precedes understanding even in natural education, it is fitting that knowledge of God should begin with humble acceptance of His revelation [*Stromata* 2.1–6, ed. T. Camelot and C. Mondésert, *Sources Chrétiennes,* ed. H. de Lubac (Paris 1941—) 38]. Thus Christian faith is considered a reasonable, free act of commitment and acknowledgment. A second strain in patristic writing refers to faith as a gift of divine illumination. This stems from the sacramental liturgy, which even in its inception seems to have called Baptism "illumination" (e.g., Eph 5.14; Heb 6.4) and is often found in sermons explaining the baptismal creed (e.g., Cyril of Jerusalem, *Catechesis* 5, *Patrologia Graeca* 33:505–524). Faith is not merely a natural prudential assent to the highly probable but a special gift of God whereby men are enlightened and share in the divine knowledge [cf. Justin, *Dialogue with Trypho* 7, ed. G. Archambault (Paris 1909); Clement of Alexandria, *Stromata* 2.4]. Expressions like "eye of faith" or "light of God penetrating our soul" are common. Faith is not a leap in the dark, but a leap through the dark into light. It is, in fact, a refashioning of human intelligence to the Divine Wisdom and Word, Jesus Christ (Cyril of Alexandria, *Commentary on Isaia* 5.1, *Patrologia Graeca* 70:1188).

Both currents flow into the theology of Augustine. Deceived by the "presumptuous promises of reason" offered by the Manicheans, he learns that humble belief must precede knowledge. Yet, belief is reasonable and appropriate, for it is the intelligent acceptance of the report of a reliable witness, Christ, perfect Wisdom. His treatises in defense of the reasonableness and necessity of belief [e.g., *On Faith in Things Unseen,* ed. F. McDonald (Washington 1950); *On the Utility of Believing,* ed. J. Zycha, *Corpus scriptorum ecclesiasticorum latinorum* 25:1] are complemented by the profound appreciation of the gift of divine illumination and inspiration expressed in the homilies on the writings of St. John [*Tractate on Gospel of St. John* 26.2–7, ed. R. Willems; *Corpus Christianorum* 36; *On the First Epistle of St. John* 3.13, ed. P. Agaësse, Sources Chrétiennes, ed. H. dc Lubac (Paris 1941—) 75]. Faith or belief, made perfect by love, grows into "luminous understanding" of divine truth.

Augustine bequeathed to subsequent theologians a terse definition of faith: "To believe is to think with assent" (*On the Predestination of Saints* 2.5, *Patrologia latina* 44: 962). Medieval theologians utilized this definition within the framework of Aristotelian psychology. These efforts were summed up and perfected by St. Thomas Aquinas, whose theology of faith will be incorporated in a subsequent portion of this essay (*Summa theologiae* 2a2ae, 1–4; *De ver.* 14).

Teaching of the Church. The first official teaching on faith was issued by the Second Council of Orange in 529, and defined against the Semi-Pelagians that faith, although a free act, resulted, even in its beginnings, from the GRACE of God, illumining man's mind (cc. 5–7, H. Denzinger, *Enchiridion symbolorum* 375–377) (*see* SEMIPELAGIANISM). The teaching of Trent is better dealt with elsewhere (*see* JUSTIFICATION). It is sufficient to note that this council makes it clear that the reformers' interpretation of faith *primarily* as trust in God's mercy and forgiveness departs from the traditional emphasis. Rather believers, "awakened and assisted by divine grace, conceive faith from hearing, and they are freely led to God. They believe that the divine revelation and promises are true, especially that the unjustified man is justified by God's grace" (Session VI, ch. 6; H. Denzinger, *Enchiridion symbolorum* 1512).

Vatican I. The most important and complete doctrinal statement on faith was issued by the Vatican Council I. This constitution *De Fide Catholica* was proposed as a remedy for two serious errors that had infected theology during the first half of the 19th century (*see* SEMIRATIONALISM; FIDEISM). The constitution must be read with these errors in mind. It was intended to correct the perspective that they had distorted; it was not an attempt to gather all the elements involved in faith into a perfectly balanced, complete synthesis. The first two chapters of this constitution affirm the existence of God and His self-revelation to men: first in His creation, then in the word that He spoke "in former days by the prophets, and in these days by his Son" (Heb 1.1). The fathers then state that created reason owes to this revelation of Uncreated Truth the complete homage of intellect and will by faith, (*see* REVELATION, THEOLOGY OF). Faith is then defined: "faith, which is 'the beginning of salvation,' the Catholic Church holds to be a supernatural virtue. By it, with the inspiration and help of God's grace, we believe that what He has revealed is true, not because of its intrinsic truth seen by the natural light of reason, but because of the authority of God revealing it, who can neither deceive nor be deceived" (H. Denzinger, *Enchiridion symbolorum* 3008).

Reason and Faith. The intention of the council was to distinguish clearly two orders of knowledge: natural knowledge called *ratio,* and supernatural knowledge called *fides*. This distinction is made first in terms of the source of knowledge or object of the mind: natural reason grasps truth by seeing the intrinsic evidence of things; faith does so in virtue of the authority of God revealing. This is the first definitive statement: faith is an act of real knowledge, but of an order essentially distinct from reason. The phrase ''authority of God revealing'' is expanded only by the words ''who can neither deceive nor be deceived.'' This addition makes explicit the point that ''authority'' does not simply involve the submission of will to power in obedience, but more fully a submission of intellect to an infallible and omniscient witness. Thus the authority of God revealing is in some way a manifestation of His knowledge and veracity.

Second, the council distinguishes the two orders of knowledge by clearly indicating that faith is supernatural, that is, the virtue of faith and its acts are possible for man only by the grace of God. No one, it states forcibly (quoting the Second Council of Orange), ''can consent to the gospel preaching, in the way he must to be saved, without the illumination of the Holy Spirit'' (*ibid.* 3010). Clearly this faith is in the fullest sense a gift of God, not possessed unless given.

This insistence on the essential element of divine grace has three important consequences: (1) The acceptance of the authority of God revealing takes place only by illumination of the intellect by the Holy Spirit. This acceptance is not essentially the work of reason preceding the act of faith, but the work of grace within the very act itself. (2) The faith here spoken of is not only that faith which is informed with charity but ''faith in itself,'' that is, the act of assent that can exist without sanctifying grace. Thus, even if faith is ''dead,'' it is the result of actual grace. (3) The effect of grace is proportioned to the powers informed: intellect is *illumined* and will is *attracted* to the good. It seems then that one can say that grace is so necessary to this act that no miracle alone, not even a resurrection from the dead, can convince and complete belief [*see* MIRACLES (THEOLOGY OF)]. If grace is lacking, the act of faith is not simply less certain or less easy; it is simply impossible. Divine grace does not merely make salutary a natural act of belief; it provides the very intrinsic possibility for faith.

Role of Reason. After such a drastic distinction between faith and reason in terms of object and ability, the fathers of the council might seem to be hard pressed to find any place for reason at all. But they do not hesitate to affirm that this faith, although distinct from reason, is still an intellectual act and that reason has a most important role in the preparation of our minds for faith. They are very realistic in saying this, for God has in fact willed to join to the internal aid of the Holy Spirit certain arguments and signs. These signs—the events of sacred history, miracle, prophecy, the marvelous figure of the living Church—all exist in the natural, visible order. They are open to the scrutiny of man's mind, and study of them will reveal the manifest work of God (*ibid.* 3010).

But even granting that God has provided such external signs of His revelation, what role can they possibly play in an act so utterly under the causality of God's action? The council does not dwell on this problem. It merely states that reason can render revelation credible (*see* FAITH AND REASON).

Summary. The principal elements of this dogmatic statement are (1) faith is an act of knowledge of an essentially different order from natural knowledge; (2) the distinction is one of nature and supernature; faith has as its formal object the authority of God revealing and can be made only with the aid of grace; (3) despite this distinction, faith and reason are in accord and, in fact, cooperate in the human act of response to revelation; (4) since faith is not the inevitable and mathematically unavoidable result of arguments, but due to concurrence and cooperation with grace, faith is a free act; (5) since reasons do not induce supernatural faith as its essential cause, a fortiori no reason is sufficient to induce infidelity; (6) faith is necessary for all men to be saved.

See Also: ANALOGY OF FAITH; APOLOGETICS; CERTITUDE OF FAITH; FAITH AND REASON; GÜNTHER, ANTON; HERMES, GEORG; HERMESIANISM; MYSTERY (IN THEOLOGY); PREAMBLES OF FAITH.

Bibliography: R. AUBERT, *Le Problème de l'acte de foi* (3d ed. Louvain 1958). H. BARS, *The Assent of Faith*, tr. R. HALSTEAD (Baltimore, Md. 1960). G. BRUNHES, *Faith and Its Rational Justification*, tr. W. A. SPENCE (St. Louis, Mo. 1931). G. DE BROGLIE, ''The Preambles of Faith,'' *Theologie und Glaube* 7 (1959) 47–52. H. F. DAVIS, ''The Act of Faith: A Comparative View of Catholic and Protestant Theology,'' *ibid.* 1 (1953) 119–122. J. MOUROUX, *I Believe,* tr. M. TURNER (London 1959). P. A. LIÉGÉ, *Catholicisme* 4: 1370–97. *Dictionnaire de théologie catholique,* ed. A. VACANT et al. (Paris 1903–50), Tables générales (1951) 1537–71. R. SCHNACKENBURG et al., *Lexikon für Theologie und Kirche,* ed. J. HOFER and K. RAHNER (Freiburg 1957–65) 4:913–931. C. H. RATSCHOW, et al., *Die Religion in Geschichte und Gegenwart* (Tübingen 1957–65) 2:1586–1611.

[A. R. JONSEN]

THEOLOGY OF FAITH

The 20th century witnessed a move away from what some theologians regarded as an overly intellectual view of faith, according to which faith tended to be regarded as simply identical to the propositional content of the Church's dogmas. Theologians using the tools of personalist philosophy objected to a primarily intellectual description of faith. The Second Vatican Council, reiterating the doctrine of Vatican I, emphasized that faith is a response of the whole person to God's free revelation (*Dei Verbum* 5). It also suggested that the lack of such a full response was one of the causes of the birth of modern atheism (*Gaudium et spes* 19). After the council, the theologies of liberation made a more direct challenge to the classical account of faith, objecting that it did not take account of the social aspect of faith. For a description of these developments in the late 20th century, see BELIEFS. The present article describes the form and act of faith.

From a semantic analysis of the Greek noun πίστις and the Latin equivalent *fides,* faith in general is to be described as a firm persuasion whereby a person assents to truths that are not seen and cannot be proved but are taken on trust in the reliability of another. This descriptive definition contains two elements: one intellectual, namely, the firm persuasion, and the other affective or fiducial, which is the commitment of oneself to the truthfulness and trustworthiness of a witness. Though the affective element in faith is often stressed more than the cognitive, it is the latter that really takes priority. πειθω, in the passive voice, from which πίστις is derived, primarily means, as does the Latin *credere,* "to be persuaded," which points to an act of the intellect assenting at the command of the will for moral rather than severely intellectual reasons. Furthermore, any act of believing implies the acceptance of something as the truth, and truth is the proper object of the intellect, even though the intellect may assent to it under the influence of the will.

This general notion applies by analogy to believing what men say and believing what God says. In human dealings, one often takes ordinary truths and facts on trust in the reliability of the testimony of another human being. Such faith is a dependable source of much human knowledge as well as a necessary foundation for human relationships, although the noetic value of scientific knowledge strictly so called, is admittedly greater. Divine faith is the fiducial assent to revealed truth given because of the authority of God, who can neither deceive nor be deceived. It is always an infused, supernatural, and essentially mysterious gift, and consequently it cannot be fully comprehended, although it is capable of analogical explanation, and indeed an explanation involving strict analogy and not merely literary metaphor. The psychological elements present in human faith can be applied proportionately to divine faith. Divine faith cannot exist as reserved to the strictly natural order, although it is possible to assent to divine and revealed truth for merely natural and human reasons, but acquired and natural faith of this kind is not formally, but only materially, divine, as would be the faith professed by a rationalist or a formal heretic.

Specific concept of faith. A purely subjective explanation of the nature of faith based on a psychological analysis and phenomenological description of the act of believing is likely to lead, if the method is exclusive, to antidogmatic positions such as are implied by one or another of the following: (1) the purely affective commitment proposed since the time of Martin Luther by many Protestant writers who wished to dissociate themselves from the concept of faith-assent of Catholic theology; (2) a philosophical, rationalist concept of faith based on the criticism of I. Kant; (3) the semirationalist theory of faith proposed by G. HERMES and A. GÜNTHER and condemned by Vatican Council I; (4) the fideist concept of faith proposed by L. E. BAUTAIN, or the traditionalist concept of A. BONNETTY, both of which were also condemned by Vatican Council I; (5) the Modernist and immanentist concepts of faith; (6) the existentialist faith affirmed by S. KIERKEGAARD and Karl Barth.

Catholic tradition recognizes these subjective aspects of the theology of faith and of the act of believing. However, its concept of faith is primarily objective, looking more to who and what is believed.

Formal object of faith. Since faith as such is an assent to truth, divine faith is an assent to First Truth (*Veritas Prima*). This is its proper object. But three phases of truth can be distinguished: ontological truth, or *veritas in essendo,* which is identical with reality; logical truth, or *veritas in cognoscendo,* which is identical with intellectual knowledge; and moral truth, or *veritas in dicendo,* which is the conformity of the external locution to the known truth.

The formal object of Christian faith is God Himself, or First Truth *in essendo,* i.e., taken in the ontological sense. The formal object of any habit of knowledge is the particular aspect of the object that it primarily grasps and is the reason for all that it knows of the object. In the actual economy of salvation in which man is elevated to the supernatural order, the first thing that he knows supernaturally is God Himself, the First Truth *in essendo,* that is, God as He is in Himself, in His essence, His divinity, His innermost life, or briefly, to use the scholastic formula, *Deus sub ratione deitatis.* Although First Truth and the Deity as It is in Itself are abstract theological expressions of a kind that theologians often prefer to concrete ones because of their exactitude, they nevertheless mean God in the concrete, subsisting in three Divine Persons, as these, together with the sum of all divine perfections, have been revealed to man. Consequently God, the First Truth ontologically, is not only the First Truth believed (the *primum credibile*) but also the formal object of faith in all the truths and mysteries that have been revealed. For, as St. Thomas Aquinas pointed out, "nothing comes under faith except in relation to God'' (*Summa theologiae* 2a2ae, 1.1). This is the common and constant doctrine of the Church. The first article of faith, with which in one form or another all the symbols begin and on which all the other articles are based, is: ''I believe in God, One and Triune.''

Formal motive of faith. The formal motive of faith is God Himself speaking, or First Truth *in dicendo,* as this connotes and implies First Truth *in cognoscendo,* or God's own knowing. Like faith itself, the motive of faith is complex and mysterious. Yet in its normal development two preparatory stages can be distinguished, each involving a cumulus of outer motives, before reaching the definite motive for the final assent of the act of believing. The initial dispositive motives, and these are normally indispensable, are to be found in the knowledge of divine revelation, both active and passive, acquired through the consideration of the preambles of faith and the evidences of credibility. This process is known as the *resolutio apologetica* of the motive of faith. In the second stage, also dispositive and normally necessary as preliminary to faith, one learns of the proposition of the revealed truths by the ordinary and solemn magisterium of the Church, which is the infallible rule of faith. This is known as the *resolutio catholica* of the motive. The magisterium, though an integral part of the situation for a Catholic, does not, according to a classical view from which St. Robert Bellarmine and others differ, form an essential component of the motive of faith; it does not decide why one believes, but rather why one's belief is committed to this credal statement rather than that: there is not, then, a specific virtue called ''Catholic faith'' distinct from ''divine faith.''

However, the ultimate and inner motive of faith is the authority of God Himself speaking, who can neither deceive nor be deceived, as was defined dogmatically by Vatican Council I (H. Denzinger, *Enchridion symbolorum* 3008, 3032). This is to be understood as distinct from the objective evidence on which natural, and even religious, knowledge of truth may be based. The dogmatic formula stating the proper and ultimate motive of divine faith agrees with the scholastic formula above, namely, that it is First Truth *in dicendo,* implying First Truth *in cognoscendo.* Thus faith is the firm assent at the command of the will and under the inward motion of God's grace to the saving truths and supernatural mysteries God has revealed, based on the infallible veracity of God's testimony, who cannot deceive (because He is infallibly true) nor be deceived (because He is omniscient). The teachings of the Scriptures are clear and emphatic on this matter. The revelation contained in the Bible carries with it the infallible guarantee of the veracity of the divine communication made to mankind through the patriarchs and Prophets of the Old Law and through Christ and His Apostles in the New. The infallible authority of this revelation is both preceptive, and consequently demands humble obedience, and also magisterial, and therefore demands a firm assent to all its teachings.

Integral object of faith. This includes all that God has revealed. Everything to which the formal motive of faith extends must be embraced by the integral object. The formal reason for believing is the authority of God, and this exists equally with respect to anything and everything that God has in fact revealed. ''By divine and catholic faith, all those things must be believed which are contained in the written word of God and in tradition, and those which are proposed by the Church, either by way of solemn pronouncement or through the exercise of her ordinary and universal teaching power, to be believed as divinely revealed'' (*ibid.* 3011).

[T. URDANOZ/EDS.]

Act of faith and its attributes. The theological treatment of the act of faith goes into the subjective and psychological aspects of faith to which reference was made above. St. Thomas analyzed the psychology of the act of faith with the help of St. Augustine's statement that to believe is to think (*cogitare*) with assent (*Summa theologiae* 2a2ae, 2.1; *In 3 Sent.* 23.2.1; *De ver.* 14.1). St. Thomas's analysis must be seen against the background of opinion on the subject among his immediate predecessors, none of whom had dealt with the problem with a comparable precision.

Peter ABELARD (d. 1142) contented himself with contrasting faith with scientific knowledge: one has knowledge with respect to things he sees, but faith is an intellectual act concerned with things not seen. Other theologians understood Abelard to mean that faith was to be classified with mere opinion. Hugh of Saint-Victor (d. 1142) sought to supply the deficiency and defined faith as a kind of certitude of mind about absent things, stronger than opinion, but weaker than scientific knowledge. For him, the knowledge involved in faith constituted only its material element, the substance of faith consisting in the affective element of the firmness of belief (*Patrologia Latina* 176:35, 531). In this Hugh related faith to the other acts of the mind more broadly, and he made an effort to account for its certitude; but he made the mistake of identifying the act of faith with one of its properties. Alexander of Hales (d. 1245) used the definition of St. Augustine, but he isolated the term ''assent'' and understood the thought (*cogitare*) to apply to the judgment prior to belief. St. Albert the Great also used Augustine's definition, but he did not try to unite the thought and the assent into a single act. The consideration or thought, he held, was not essential to the act of faith itself. It consisted in the search for motives of credibility or in the mind's reflection upon the truth already assented to (St. Albert the Great, *In 3 Sent* 23.3). Like Hugh, Albert saw faith as an affective act because of the lack of evidence for the assent. Faith has knowledge as the material element and the affective act as the formal part.

St. Thomas's Analysis. Faced with this confusion of opinion, Thomas had these things to attempt: the clarification of the relation between faith and the other acts of the mind; a satisfactory explanation of the certitude of faith; a more precise definition of the interrelated roles of intellect and will in the act of faith; and a clear-cut distinction between the intellectual activity preceding the act of faith, that involved in the act itself, and that following upon the act. Substantially he proceeds as follows:

The object of faith is truth. From this it follows that the act of faith belongs to the intellect, and in order to understand its proper nature, one must see it as an intellectual operation. But an act of intellect will either be an act of simple apprehension or an act of composition or division, i.e., an act apprehending the agreement or disagreement between concepts. By simple apprehension, concepts are formed of the natures of things, e.g., man, animal. In this act there is per se neither truth nor falsity, just as there is neither truth nor falsity in simple, incomplex terms. But, as has been shown, the object of faith, per se and formally, is truth; and consequently faith cannot consist in simple apprehension, but must be an act of composition or division, or, in other words, an act of judgment.

Now with respect to a judgment, the intellect may be either determined or undetermined. If undetermined, the indetermination may be negative, in which case there is nescience, and there is neither assent nor thought. Or the indetermination may be positive, as in the case of doubt, in which there is thought without assent and the mind fluctuates between contradictory alternatives.

The intellect determined in its judgment is determined either objectively or subjectively. If it is objectively determined, the determination will be either absolute and total or partial and dependent on some sign or indication of truth. The determination is absolute and total in the case of immediate or intuitive knowledge, in which case there is assent without need of consideration or thought. But the determination is also absolute and total when the knowledge is mediate, as in a conclusion arrived at by demonstration, and in this case there is assent following upon thought. But the determination is partial and incomplete, on the other hand, when the evidence is partial and incomplete. If the evidence is but slight, there is suspicion; if it is weighty but inconclusive, there is opinion, and the mind is inclined to accept one rather than another of contradictory propositions. In these cases, there is at most a limited assent coupled with continued consideration, because the mind is not at rest.

But the intellect may also be determined subjectively, by the choice of the will. Generally in this case the assent is a partial one, accompanied by a recognition of the possibility that one may be wrong. If this possibility is seen as considerable, the limited assent amounts to suspicion. If the possibility is seen as slight, there will be opinion.

So far could St. Thomas go with Aristotle's account of the psychology of judgment. He argued that in the act of divine faith there is a case of the will moving the mind to assent, but to a perfect and complete assent and one that excludes all deliberate fear of being in error. But how account for the perfection of the assent when the intellect is not determined by its proper object? St. Thomas admitted that the intellect cannot be intrinsically satisfied, except when determined by evidence it sees and that in the act of faith it is not so determined. Consequently, the mind's natural inquisitiveness is not set at rest. It remains unsatisfied because it does not see the evidence. Hence, faith essentially allows for reflective consideration, for search, for thought. The believer assents with full certitude, but his intellect is uneasy in the absence of its proper object. Even while it assents, its determination is from without. It is under constraint and continues to look for that which will set it at rest. This search does not result in assent, for the mind already has assented, with an assent caused by the will. The movement of the will is accounted for by the fact that assent appeals to the will as a good. St. Thomas explains the process thus: "Sometimes the intellect cannot be determined to either of the parts of a contradiction, either immediately by understanding the terms (as happens in the case of first principles), or mediately in virtue of the principles (as in the case of conclusions reached by demonstration). It is determined by the will, which chooses to assent to one of the parts because of a consideration sufficient to move it, but not sufficient to move the intellect, namely, that assent seems a good and fitting thing. And such is the disposition of the believer" (*De ver.* 14.1). This is true even of human faith, in which so often it is apparent that a man believes what he wants to believe, i.e., what seems good to him to believe. In the case of divine faith, the good that appeals to the will is the promise of eternal life.

Certitude and Inquietude of Mind. Does the intellect achieve its own good when it is determined thus by the movement of the will? Not immediately in the way most congenial to its nature, for it does not see. But this is more than compensated for by its elevation to an act far beyond the capacity of nature. An object is attained by the intellect through the assent, and in this object and in the certitude of this knowledge the believer's intellect is infinitely elevated above any other human knowledge.

The movement of the will, however, would be unreasonable and imprudent if the intellect were not moved to assent to something true. The will moves reasonably to assent only when a truth not evident is attested by competent witness. There must be evidence of credibility, reasonably satisfying in the circumstances to the mind; otherwise the will, moving the intellect to assent, would be misguided by an imprudent judgment of the mind.

From this one can see the meaning St. Thomas attaches to the thought (*cogitatio*) in his interpretation of Augustine's *credere est cum assensione cogitare.* The thought is a sort of movement of the soul in search of truth it does not fully possess, a straining toward clarity of vision. This is to be carefully distinguished from the thought that precedes the act of faith, i.e., the search and inquiry of the mind into the motives of credibility. The *cogitatio* that belongs to the act of faith itself is the striving for understanding of the things believed and exists simultaneously with the assent.

The utter certitude of faith derives from the fact that the intellect in its assent surrenders itself to God, the First Truth, Subsistent Truth, the source and cause of all created truth. It would be contradictory for the mind to accept God in this light and at the same time to retain fear of error.

Therefore, faith is different from the understanding of first principles or the knowledge derived from demonstration in that, unlike these, its assent is not objectively determined; it is unlike subjectively determined opinion, or human faith, because its assent is not partial or hesitant, but is firm and certain. Hence, the act of faith is an act *sui generis* and, though analogous in some respects to other acts of the mind, is nevertheless reducible to no other act of mind or will.

Involved in this act, on the one hand, is the firmest adherence of the mind and, on the other, searching thought, because the mind's desire is not set at rest. Because there is assent, there ought to be truth for its object, and even truth that is in some sense evident. But because this truth is First Truth, inevident in itself, the mind still strains to see and know. And although it does not see, it nevertheless holds firmly to the truth and has no fear of error. Its perfect determination comes not from an object seen, but from the will. But because the intellectual appetite is not satisfied, the mind in itself is not at rest. In it at the same time are absolute determination and a certain stirring or ferment that comes of its want of satisfaction. There is an assent together with a restlessness of the mind, the assent implying the calm of something settled and fixed, the stirring of mind an inquietude. This antithesis is forced on faith by the character of its object: as true it is deserving of assent; as First Truth, supernatural and inaccessible in itself, it is altogether beyond the grasp of the human mind and hence remains obscure and unseen, and this explains the inquietude.

Supernaturality. Among the ancients, the Pelagians denied the essentially supernatural character of the act of faith and held that no internal grace was necessary either for belief or for progress in faith. The Semi-Pelagians taught that no grace was needed for the beginning of faith or the devout will to believe (*pius credulitatis affectus*), although they did admit that grace was necessary for the complete act. A more modern variant of this error was introduced by G. Hermes and his disciples during the 19th century. They distinguished two kinds of faith: the faith of knowledge and the faith of the heart. The first they understood to be speculative in character, and to coincide more or less with what theologians commonly call *fides informis,* or dead faith, i.e., faith not informed by charity. It was their contention that such faith could be the effect of natural demonstration. But for faith of the heart, which was living, practical faith (*fides formata*), or faith informed by charity, they acknowledged grace to be necessary. Among the Modernists there were those, on the other hand, who tended to deny the need of grace even for faith of the heart, for they looked upon faith as a sense activated by a need for the divine hidden in the subconscious, without the intervention of any judgment of the mind.

According to Catholic teaching, grace is necessary: for the act of faith and its increase (against the Pelagians); for the beginning of faith and the devout will to believe (against the Semi-Pelagians); for *fides informis,* inasmuch as this is supernatural and the gift of God and not the fruit of demonstration (against Hermes). The theological explanation is based on the supernatural character of the mysteries, which are altogether beyond the grasp of natural reason, to which faith assents; reason must be elevated to be capable of grasping them, and this supposes grace. Moreover, the proper effect of faith, which is to initiate supernatural justification and the life of sanctifying grace, is essentially supernatural and demands therefore a supernatural cause.

Reasonableness. Faith is acceptable to reason in the sense that reason perceives the mysteries to which it assents to be worthy of belief. Some have exaggerated the function of reason in faith to the point of identifying faith with knowledge. Such was the mistake of Hermes, Gunther, and J. FROHSCHAMMER during the 19th century. Others have fallen into the opposite error of minimizing the role of reason, to the extent even of claiming that faith is a blind action or movement of the mind. Fideists, traditionalists, Modernists, and others adopted this view in different ways. For fideists, speculative reason can know nothing with certainty. Everything must be held on divine faith, which thus becomes the supreme criterion of truth, even in philosophy. Traditionalists held that reason is impotent so far as the knowledge of religious truth is concerned. Others have maintained that such is the debility of the mind in its apprehension of religious truth that one must look to practical reason and feeling as a basis for faith, thus emphasizing the volitional character of faith at the expense of the intellectual. Some have gone to the length of attributing credibility as well as faith to grace alone, and have conceived rational credibility of a purely natural kind as impossible.

On the other hand, a contrary extreme of opinion is represented in post-Reformation apologetics, which came, particularly in the 19th and early 20th century, to place a great (and some think an undue) emphasis on the function of reason in the steps preparatory to the act of faith [see G. De Broglie, ''La vraie notion thomiste des *praeambula fidei,*'' *Gregorianum* 34 (1953) 341–389]. The motives of credibility tend to become arguments concluding with certainty to the truth of revealed doctrine. One ''proves'' the fact of revelation, and with this established it is difficult to see how the act of faith that follows remains a free or necessarily supernatural act.

All Catholic theologians agree that the truths of faith are worthy and deserving of belief and that this credibility is objectively apparent simply in the natural light of reason, though sometimes it may happen that special grace and the interior assistance of the Holy Spirit may help an individual to come to a sound judgment of credibility on grounds that seem objectively insufficient to justify it. Not only can rational evidence precede the act of faith, but it should. To believe without adequate evidence would be rash. The judgment of credibility is required by man's rational nature, and to believe without it could not be accounted virtuous. There is evidence available to provide grounds for a morally certain judgment of credibility, and in the normal approach to the act of faith there should be as much consideration of that evidence as is necessary to reach such a judgment.

But there is a noteworthy difference among Catholic theologians in their understanding of the nature and object of the judgment of credibility. The earlier theologians, and particularly the Thomists, did not understand the investigation preceding the act of faith as aimed at a certain judgment with regard to the fact of revelation, but at demonstrating the moral fitness and necessity of accepting that fact by faith. It was considered as essentially a prudential judgment, and not one in which the assent of the mind is compelled by the evidence. If this view makes it possible to lay less stress on the demonstrative value of one's thought on the preambles of faith, it does not on that account make the foundation of faith less secure. The certainty and security of faith does not come from the certainty of the reasoning that precedes the act of faith. The act of faith, as St. Thomas saw it, remedies any weakness in one's grasp of the truth of God's existence, and it will also compensate for any insufficiency there may have been in one's perception of the evidences of credibility. ''Faith, considered in itself, sufficiently embraces all things that accompany, follow, or precede it'' (*In 3 Sent.* 24.1.2.2). There is an incomparably clearer perception of credibility that is the effect of faith, than any that could be had by natural argument. ''The faithful see them (the things that are of faith), not as by demonstration, but by the light of faith that makes them see that they ought to believe them'' (*Summa theologiae* 2a2ae, 1.5 ad 1).

Liberty. When Christ preached the gospel, not all believed who saw the miracles and signs. Some of those who heard Paul preach became believers, and some did not (Acts 17.32–34). In fact, faith is invariably represented in the Scriptures as a free, meritorious commitment made to God. That it is essentially a free act was defined by Vatican Council I (H. Denzinger, *Enchiridion symbolorum* 1814). The assent of faith, to be prudent, must be justified by evidence. But the evidence of the motives is not what causes the will to move the intellect to its assent. The act of faith is not in any sense the conclusion to an apodictic syllogism. It is essentially a supernatural thing. The evidence of credibility may indeed be established with moral certainty. But the assent of faith must rest upon a supernatural motive, and to see this motive as supernatural the mind must be enlightened and given a power of perception that it does not have by nature, and the will must be made capable of responding to the attraction of supernatural good. This is effected by grace. But the enlightenment of mind is not such as to compel assent, and grace leaves it within the power of the will to submit itself freely to God's authority.

Certitude. The assent of faith follows upon what is recognized as the divine certification of a truth, and it is, moreover, vivified by a divine grace. From this it follows that the adhesion of the mind to the truth accepted in this way has a firmness greater than can be achieved through the operation of the ordinary laws of thought. There is, consequently, a strength in divine faith, when this is compared with natural opinion, belief, and knowledge, that is altogether unique. Its certitude rests upon a supernatural motive, and as such it is of its nature greater than any natural certitude, even that which is called metaphysical (*see* CERTITUDE). Scientific certitude may indeed have a greater element of indubitability about it; it is possible to doubt a truth of faith, since faith is a free act, while it is impossible to doubt that which is scientifically evident. But as long as one adheres to the proper motive of faith, he has stronger and more trustworthy reason for believing than he has for assenting to the truth of what he sees or has apodictically demonstrated.

Necessity of faith. The act of faith is a contingent fact and does not of its nature require existence. Inquiry here is therefore concerned with hypothetical necessity, or the kind of necessity that arises in consequence of a desire to achieve some end, the end in question being the attainment of salvation. Hypothetical necessity in the strict sense is the necessity of something needed to make the attainment of an end possible, but in a looser sense a thing is sometimes called necessary that merely facilitates the attainment of an end that could, absolutely speaking, be attained without it. In this context, one is concerned with hypothetical necessity in the strict sense, and asks therefore whether the act of faith is strictly necessary to salvation.

In discussing the necessity of anything to salvation, theologians distinguish between a NECESSITY OF MEANS and one of precept. There is a necessity of means when the end cannot be obtained without it. The nexus between means and end may be founded on the very nature of the two, as when sanctifying grace is said to be necessary for salvation; or it may be founded on the fact that God has so ordained it, as when Baptism is said to be necessary for salvation. When there is NECESSITY OF PRECEPT, the means are, by divine prescription, indispensable to the attainment of the end, but provided one is aware of the obligation of employing the means in question and provided also that it is not physically or morally impossible to employ them.

A few theologians, seeing an analogy between the necessity of faith and that of Baptism and pointing to the sufficiency, acknowledged by the Council of Trent, of Baptism of desire when Baptism of water is impossible, have argued that the desire of faith will suffice for salvation. A few others, among whom was Juan de RIPALDA, though he advanced the opinion more for the sake of discussion than for the purpose of defending it as true (*De fide* 17.10.145), have taught that faith in the broad sense (*fides late dicta*) in some circumstances can be sufficient for salvation. By faith in the broad sense they understood natural knowledge of divine and moral truth, acquired from natural sources, but supernaturalized, so to speak, by the help of grace given by God to evoke and to assist the natural processes of reason.

The question is concerned with the necessity of the act of faith. There is no need to inquire about the necessity of the habit, the infused virtue itself, because this must always exist when there is sanctifying grace (H. Denzinger, *Enchiridion symbolorum* 1528, 1561). The act is evidently not necessary to baptized infants who die before reaching the use of reason, for these are saved through no act of their own. The question therefore concerns adults, i.e., those who have reached the use of reason and are morally responsible for their actions.

The Scriptures declare faith as an act to be necessary, and the necessity is clearly one of means. ''My just one lives by faith. . . . Faith is the substance of things to be hoped for, the evidence of things that are not seen. . . . By faith we understand that the world was fashioned by the word of God . . . without faith it is impossible to please God. For he who comes to God must believe that God exists and is the rewarder of those who seek him'' (Heb 10.38–11.6). The faith in question is actual faith: ''By faith we understand.'' That it is a necessity of means appears in the words ''without faith it is impossible to please God'' (cf. also Mk 16.15–16; Gal 2.16). This doctrine has been repeated by the councils. Trent declared faith to be ''the beginning of human salvation, the foundation and root of all justification, without which it is impossible to please God'' (H. Denzinger, *Enchiridion symbolorum* 1532). Vatican I repeated this in the following words: ''And since without faith it is impossible to please God, and to attain to the fellowship of His children, therefore without faith no one has ever attained justification; nor will anyone obtain eternal life, unless he shall have persevered in faith unto the end. And that we may be able to satisfy the obligation of embracing the true faith, and of constantly persevering in it, God has instituted the Church'' (*ibid.* 3012; this passage is also quoted in the *Catechism of the Catholic Church* 161). In these last words at least there is reference to actual faith, but this faith in the context is so closely associated with the faith without which it is impossible to please God—the faith, in other words, that is necessary by a necessity of means—that it is impossible not to identify the two. Furthermore, the necessity of the act of faith for adults not yet justified is declared by the Council of Trent by its inclusion of this act among the steps necessary to justification (H. Denzinger, *Enchiridion symbolorum* 1525, 1532). It is *de fide* that actual faith is necessary, by a necessity of means, to the salvation of adults not yet justified.

It cannot be said that the declarations of the councils refer only to the need of faith, without specifying its object as natural or supernatural, and that therefore the assent with the grace of God to religious truths known through natural reason might satisfy the necessity for those to whom revealed truth has not reached. In 1679 Innocent XI condemned a proposition stating the sufficiency of faith in a broad sense (*ibid.* 2123), and Vatican Council I expressly declared that the faith that is the beginning of man's salvation is a supernatural virtue, whereby inspired and assisted by the grace of God, man believes that the things He has revealed are true because of the authority of Him who reveals them. Therefore the council spoke only of the faith that falls under faith's proper motive, and its object therefore must be revealed truth *qua* revealed.

Similarly, the desire or intention of faith is not sufficient to satisfy the necessity affirmed by the councils. The parallel between the desire of Baptism and the desire of faith will not permit the conclusion that faith in desire can be enough. The desire of Baptism is already an act of supernatural charity, and as such it produces its effect. But the desire of faith is not an act of supernatural charity. Moreover, a person with faith can wish, explicitly or implicitly, to be baptized, and yet be prevented by circumstances from having what he wants. Faith, however, is an internal act, and its desire cannot be frustrated in the same way. If a person seriously wants to believe, he can believe.

Necessity of explicit belief. The necessity of believing something explicitly follows as a corollary from the necessity of the act of faith. In any act of faith, something must be believed explicitly, because one cannot believe anything implicitly without some explicit belief in which the implicit belief is contained. Post-Tridentine theologians not only regard it as *de fide* that there must be some explicit belief, but also that two truths, namely, that God is and that He is the rewarder of those who seek Him (Heb 11.6), must be explicitly believed. It is important that the two truths mentioned be understood in a supernatural sense, that is, as referring to God the author of grace, and to God who holds out a supernatural reward to those who seek him. This is clear from the context in the Epistle to the Hebrews. St. Paul said that one coming to God must believe these truths, and to believe in this immediate context has a precise meaning, for just a few verses before faith is defined as the substance of things hoped for, etc. The things hoped for, the things not seen, are supernatural. They constitute eternal life, which is supernatural beatitude of a kind that no eye has seen, no ear has heard, and no human heart has conceived (1 Cor 2.9).

At all times belief, at least implicit, in the mysteries of the Incarnation and Trinity, is necessary for salvation; and since the Council of Trent, theologians generally add that this is necessary by a necessity of means. "He is that stone, rejected by you, the builders, that has become the chief stone at the corner. Salvation is not found elsewhere; this alone of all the names under heaven has been appointed to men as the one by which we must needs be saved" (Acts 4.11–12; cf. Gal 2.16). Before the coming of Christ, implicit faith in these mysteries sufficed for ordinary men at least, but with the full revelation of grace, explicit faith became necessary. It has been debated among theologians whether explicit belief in the mysteries of the Incarnation, the Trinity, the Redemption is necessary by a necessity of means or of precept. Before the great voyages of discovery in the 15th and 16th centuries, the *orbis terrarum* in the popular consciousness of Europeans was the circle of lands about the Mediterranean. It was possible for men to think that the gospel precept "Going, teach ye all nations" had been more or less adequately fulfilled and that people everywhere had been given a satisfactory opportunity to consider the claims of Christianity. Hence, earlier theologians found no difficulty in reconciling the need of explicit faith with God's mercy and His will respecting the salvation of all men.

But when the geographical discoveries of the 15th and 16th centuries had made Europeans aware of the existence of vast numbers of human beings to whom no word of Christ could possibly have reached through the agency of natural causes, there was a renewed interest in the question of the possibility of salvation for those who had never heard of Christ. There arose, in particular, a controversy concerning the necessity of explicit belief in the mysteries of the Incarnation and the Trinity, and this point has continued to be debated down to the present time. The argument concerns a point of considerable subtlety on which the scriptural evidence is not conclusive, and the whole issue has been more than a little beclouded by ambiguities caused by different senses given by different authors to terms used in the discussion. It is generally admitted by theologians that any view taken on this question is a matter of opinion, and views are advanced by their proponents not as certain, but only as probable, or at most as more probable.

Explicit belief necessary by precept. All theologians agree as to the existence of a divine precept obliging men to believe the truths of the Christian religion. As affirmative, this precept obliges people to learn explicitly and to accept the principal truths of the faith; as negative, it forbids disbelief in any revealed truth. The existence of this precept is evident from the fact of revelation itself. If God communicates truth, it is that men might believe, and to refuse belief is to withhold the honor due to divine wisdom and truth. It is stated explicitly in the Gospel: "Go into the whole world and preach the gospel to every creature. He who believes and is baptized shall be saved, but he who does not believe, shall be condemned" (Mk 16.15–16).

Nevertheless, it is admitted that every man is not obliged to know and believe all revealed truth explicitly.

This would not be possible. It is enough that some revealed truth be believed explicitly, and the rest be accepted implicitly in some general proposition such as "I believe all the truths which God has revealed and which the Holy Catholic Church believes and teaches." To some extent the obligation of explicit belief is a relative one. Those responsible for the instruction of others in the faith—priests, parents, teachers of religion—are obliged ex officio to have a more extensive knowledge of the faith. The well-educated and those who enjoy positions of prominence or leadership in their communities are also expected to have a more thorough instruction in religious truth, partly as a precaution against the dangers to which their faith will be exposed if their religious education does not keep pace with their culture in other matters, and partly because to them is directed more particularly the injunction of St. Peter to be ready at all times with an answer to those who may ask an account of the hope that they cherish (1 Pt 3.15).

The obligation of explicit belief is not altogether relative and variable. There is an absolute minimum to which any normal adult is obligated. In the common opinion of theologians, this minimum includes: (1) Truths necessary to right thinking about Christ and the work of Redemption, or in other words, the truths contained in the Apostles' Creed. That this is obligatory is evident from the constant practice of the Church in requiring an explicit profession of belief in these as a preliminary to Baptism. (2) Truths necessary for right living: the Ten Commandments, the special duties of one's state in life, the laws of the Church that everyone is required to observe. (3) Knowledge of the means of sanctification: the Our Father, the Sacraments that are received by everyone, i.e., Baptism, Reconciliation, the Eucharist, and the other Sacraments when there is occasion to receive them.

The obligation to have explicit knowledge of the above is considered to be grave. There is also an obligation of precept arising from the common custom and practice of the faithful to know the sign of the cross, the Hail Mary, the Our Father, the Creed, and the Commandments by heart, but this is not generally held to bind gravely. Parents and those responsible for the instruction of others are gravely obligated to teach their charges those things necessary for them to know, either by a necessity of means or of precept.

Bibliography: C. MAZZELLA, *De virtutibus infusis* (Rome 1884). C. PESCH, *Praelectiones dogmaticae,* 9 v. (4th ed. Freiburg 1910–22), v. 8. L. BILLOT, *De virtutibus infusis* (Rome 1905). P. LUMBRERAS, *De fide* (Rome 1937). A. LIÉGÉ, "Faith" in *The Virtues and States of Life,* ed. A. M. HENRY (*Theology Library* 4, Chicago, Ill. 1957) 1–59. B. HÄRING, *The Law of Christ: Moral Theology for Priests and Laity,* tr. E. G. KAISER (Westminster, Md. 1961). S. HARENT, *Dictionnaire de théologie catholique,* ed. A. VACANT et al. (Paris 1903–50) 6.1:55–514; 7.2:1726–1930. J. B. BAINVEL, *Dictionnaire apologétique de la foi catholique,* v. 5 (Paris 1911–22) s.v. "Fidéisme," "Foi." J. A. DE ALDAMA, "De virtutibus infusis," *Sacrae theologiae summa,* 4 v. (Madrid 1958–1962) 3:46–219. M. SCHEEBEN, in *Wetzer und Welte's Kirchenlexikon,* 12 v. (2d ed. Freiburg 1882–1901) 5:616–674. R. AUBERT, *Le Problème de l'acte de foi* (3d ed. Louvain 1958). A. STOLZ, *Glaubensgnade und Glaubenslicht nach Thomas von Aquin* (Rome 1933). M. D. CHENU, "La Psychologie de la foi dans la théologie du XIIIe siècle," *Études d'histoire littéraire et doctrinale du XIIIe siècle* 2 (1932) 163–191. B. DUROUX, *La Psychologie de la foi chez s. Thomas d'Aquin* (Tournai 1963). G. DE BROGLIE, *Pour une théorie rationelle de l'acte de foi* (Paris 1955). K. RAHNER, *Schriften zur Theologie,* v. 2 (Einsiedeln 1957) 9–94, 115–141. J. MARITAIN, *La Signification de l'athéisme contemporain* (Paris 1949); *Approaches to God,* tr. P. O'REILLY (New York 1954). J. MOUROUX, *I Believe: The Personal Structure of Faith,* tr. M. TURNER (New York 1959). M. L. GUÉRARD DES LAURIERS, *Dimensions de la foi* (Paris 1952). M. C. D'ARCY, *The Nature of Belief* (New York 1931, new ed. St. Louis 1958); *Belief and Reason* (London 1944). J. H. NEWMAN, *An Essay in Aid of a Grammar of Assent* (New York 1870; pa. 1955). I. FOREST, "The Meaning of Faith," *Thomist* 6 (1943) 230–250. J. C. MURRAY, "The Root of Faith: The Doctrine of M. J. Scheeben," *Theological Studies* 9 (1948) 20–46. J. PIEPER, *Belief and Faith* (New York 1963). H. U. VON BALTHASAR, *Love Alone: The Way of Revelation* (London 1968). JOHN PAUL II, *Fides et ratio* (Vatican City 1998). A. R. DULLES, *Assurance of Things Hoped For: A Theology of Christian Faith* (New York 1994).

[P. K. MEAGHER/EDS.]

FAITH, ACT OF

Faith, the name for the response to revelation, is never faith in the abstract but a human act in a *special* situation, social condition, and historical period. What characterizes faith at the present time is the forms it takes in the context of contemporary atheism, secularism, and religious pluralism, which, as Vatican Council II's Constitution on the Church in the Modern World notes, put belief to a test and refine it (*Gaudium et spes* 19–21). The confrontation is partially due not only to the intrinsic difficulty of faith but also to the neglect or failure of Christians to live up to the Gospel ideal of witnessing to Christ. At the same time present-day problems challenge believers to lead a stronger and purer life of faith. The varieties of contemporary ATHEISM grew out of the 18th-century Enlightenment and the declaration of the "death of God," with human reason and freedom declaimed in God's stead. Man is tempted to believe in his own inevitable progress and perfectibility to the point of an assurance that he can create the world and take destiny into his own hands. To this secular "faith" the universe no longer reflects God; he is increasingly irrelevant to and absent from it. Man has passed from a divinized into a hominized world, into a post-Christian or dechristianized age.

Is real faith, then, possible in a secularized age? The secularism begotten of scientific and technological progress and a sense of human mastery of the world can be beneficial to the Christian faith. It no longer identifies God with the once humanly uncontrollable forces of nature. An earlier and less enlightened faith may have hidden rather than revealed the true face of God. The chief object of the Christian faith remains the same—but through secularization God has been made to recede from the world and to appear more transcendent than ever. The act of faith puts a positive construction upon the rise of secular society and seeks the meaning of the Gospel within it. It looks less to the signs of *space* than to the signs of the *times*, where God proves himself to be the Lord of history. The Christian draws on the heritage of faith to find the answers to the existential questions of the order, meaning, and goal of life.

While there is the shift away from a medieval Christian view, away from a spatial to a temporal view of reality, the act of faith today is no less intellectual than formerly. Even when it does not grapple with questions of the truth and verifiability of how God rules all things ''from above,'' or with a set of propositions for belief, it still has to perceive and acknowledge the mysterious presence of the living God within the events of time. Man is made more responsible to God for the world and society. He is to trust that the unseen is more real than the seen.

In accordance with the New Testament term for faith, πίστεύειη, which can mean ''to rely on, to trust'' as well as ''to believe,'' the element of trust looms larger in the life of faith today. Faith involves risk, insecurity, uncertainty, doubt, a Kierkegaardian ''leap'' into a future that rests with God. It dictates a reliance on the will of the God who knows what is best for human fulfillment. Faith is not only an act of obedience, made once-for-all, but a lifetime commitment to the divine summons. Convinced that the Word of God is trustworthy, the believer faces the unpredictable and incalculable future with courage. He cannot weather the present-day crisis of culture without ''a more personal and explicit adherence to faith,'' which will instill him with ''a more vivid sense of God'' (*Gaudium et spes* 7).

The fact that a child is born into a Christian family, baptized, educated in his environment, does not dispense him from making a free, personal, adult life-decision for or against Christ; he will act upon that decision seriously, superficially, or not at all. The ratification is not so much a matter of a single act or acts as of a basic, life-long orientation to the whole of reality with its values, including God, Christ, his Church.

The total and unconditional surrender to God in the act of faith precludes an exclusively intellectualist view but does not exempt the Catholic from orthodoxy (see Vatican II, *Dei Verbum* 5). It is inaccurate to say that belief stems merely from the will to believe, without consideration of the truths normative for faith. So-called ortho-praxis without orthodoxy will not check the decline or forestall the loss of religious faith. The Catholic ideal is to fuse the two, doctrine and practice: faith ought to be a visible quality of human life, a character development. Genuine faith should affect the whole man and the totality of human living, even if it would be foolish to expect the perfect correlation of belief with life and action.

If faith and secular life are not to be left polarized, then Christians must take the fact of a pluralist world into account. The Christian faith brings home a transcendent way of life rather than a source of theoretical doctrine. A way of life is familial, social, historical, ecclesial. So it is possible for Christians to live together and witness to Christ on the basis of a love-inspired faith. Without disregarding the ecclesial framework of their faith, they must realize they have major interfaith areas where they can live and work for unity of faith. Faith, living and active, leads to the religious experience of love, and love will attract believers spontaneously to the same values, to a sense of what is morally good in interpersonal relationships, to a share in that connatural knowledge which faith and love—the resonance of love in faith's act—make of transcendence, unity, and fidelity.

Bibliography: L. DEWART, *The Future of Belief: Theism in a World Come of Age* (New York 1966). R. PANIKKAR, ''Faith—A Constitutive Dimension of Man,'' *Journal of Ecumenical Studies* 8 (1971) 223–254. K. RAHNER, *Do You believe in God?* (New York 1969). B. SIZEMORE, JR., ''Christian Faith in a Pluralistic World,'' *Journal of Ecumenical Studies* 13 (1976) 405–419. P. SURLIS, ed., *Faith: Its Nature and Meaning* (Dublin 1972). C. WILLIAMS, *Faith in a Secular Age* (New York 1966).

[J. FICHTNER]

FAITH, BEGINNING OF

''Beginning of faith'' is a technical term that had its beginning as a result of the Semi-Pelagian heresy. Although conceding the necessity of God's GRACE for justification, the Semi-Pelagians taught that man could at least desire FAITH and wish to believe without divine help. In other words, these heretics held that ''the beginning of faith'' was natural, not SUPERNATURAL. At issue, of course, was the acquisition of faith in adults, not children.

In opposition to this heresy, the Sccond Council of Orange (529) defined the Church's official position: the increase of faith, the beginning of faith, and even the very desire or wish to believe, is a gift of God (H. Denzinger, *Enchiridion symbolorum,* ed. A. Schönmetzer 375). Thus the council recalled the teaching of St. Paul that faith is a purely gratuitous gift. No one can strictly merit it, i.e., no amount of effort by a human being can force God to give him faith. ''For by grace you have been saved . . . for it is a gift of God'' (Eph 2.8).

The Council of Trent reaffirmed the teaching of Orange and called attention to man's freedom at the beginning of faith. Though always an unmerited gift of God, faith requires man's free and personal assent. The council stated: the Scripture text ''be converted to me . . . and I will turn to you'' (Zec 1.3) shows men that they are free in the act of faith; and when they answer ''Turn to us, O Lord, and we shall be converted to You'' (Lam 5.21), they witness to the fact that the grace of God has first to come to them (*ibid.* 1525).

See Also: SEMI–PELAGIANISM.

Bibliography: É. AMANN, *Dictionnaire de théologie catholique,* ed. A. VACANT et al., 15 v. (Paris 1903–50; Tables générales 1951–) 14.2:1796–1850. S. HARENT, *Dictionnaire de théologie catholique,* ed. A. VACANT et al., 15 v. (Paris 1903–50; Tables générales 1951–) 6.1:55–514. J. AUER, *Lexikon für Theologie und Kirche,* ed. J. HOFER and K. RAHNER, 10 v. (2d, new ed. Freiburg 1957–65) 5:676–677. J. GUILLET, *Themes of the Bible,* tr. A. J. LAMOTHE (South Bend, Ind. 1960). H. LENNERZ, *De gratia Redemptoris* (3d ed. Rome 1949). L. LERCHER, *Institutiones theologiae dogmaticae* 4.1 (5th ed. Barcelona 1951) 253–359. L. CERFAUX, ''La Théologie de la grâce selon saint Paul,'' *La Vie Spirituelle* 83 (1950) 5–19.

[G. N. BUESCHER]

FAITH AND MORALS

The term signifies the object of Catholic FAITH in its entirety. Primarily it includes all the truths revealed by God and proposed by the Church as necessary for men to believe and to act upon if they are to attain eternal salvation, e.g., articles of the Apostles Creed, the commandments of love of God and neighbor. Such truths that are included in the object of Catholic faith are contained in the fonts of Scripture and tradition. Formally revealed truths may be contained in these fonts either explicitly, i.e., according to the manifest meaning of the words, or implicitly, i.e., as known from an analysis or a deeper understanding of the terms themselves.

Secondarily it includes other truths, which are proposed by the Church as necessary to enable men to believe in divine revelation or follow its moral precepts, although these truths have not been divinely revealed, e.g., determination of the canon of Sacred Scripture, canonization of saints, determination of the matter and form of the Sacrament of Holy Orders, some explicitations of the natural law. The Church does not propose these truths as formally revealed but as intimately connected with revealed truths and hence to be accepted on faith.

Historical and Theological Considerations. Many times St. Paul wrote that man is saved by faith rather than by works, i.e., that the supernatural gift of faith unites a man to Christ, and the ''works'' of the religious ceremonies and precepts demanded by the Mosaic Law are useless in effecting this union (Rom ch 3; 9.32; 11.6; Gal 2.16; Eph 2.9). However, the faith in Christ demanded by Paul included avoidance of sin, i.e., GOOD WORKS (Rom ch. 6; 1 Cor ch. 5–8). The Gospels and Epistles demand not only faith but also good works (Mt ch. 5–7; Jn ch. 14–17; Ja ch. 2). St. Clement of Rome (A.D. 95) spoke of sanctification by faith (*1 Clem.* 32, 33) but included good works as the outcome of faith. In the early Christian teaching, faith in Christ was distinguished from ''works,'' i.e., the religious ceremonies of the Mosaic Law. Yet good works, meaning right moral conduct, were always connected with true faith.

After the condemnation in 1520 of Luther's proposition that the Church or pope can determine neither the articles of faith nor the laws of morality or good works (H. Denzinger, *Enchiridion symbolorum,* ed. A. Schönmetzer 1477), the term faith and morals began to appear in Church definitions more regularly. Trent used the term in reference to interpreting Scripture (*ibid.* 1507), while, Vatican I used it in defining the universal jurisdiction of the pope (*ibid.* 3060).

Object of Infallibility. The infallible teaching authority of the Church determines these ''matters of faith and morals'' and proposes them for acceptance by the FAITHFUL of the universal Church, on occasion through the pope speaking as the universal shepherd. This teaching authority preserves, guards, and interprets these truths of the DEPOSIT OF FAITH according to the following categories: (1) The truths revealed directly by God and by Christ, or through His Apostles, and that ordain men to eternal life are preserved, guarded, and transmitted throughout the world, e.g., the Trinity, Christ's birth and Resurrection, the Church as a visible, hierarchical society. Moral matters such as the beatitudes, commands to love God and neighbor, indissolubility of marriage—truths that are principles to guide men's actions toward God—are also defined. These truths are formally and explicitly revealed, that is, they are those that God manifestly intended by the words themselves, considering the nature of human speech and signification of the terms used. (2) Other truths that are formally revealed, but implicitly so, are also transmitted. These truths may be seen from an analysis of the terms of an explicit revelation without bringing in a third term as in a syllogistic form of reasoning. Correlative statements exemplify this: if Jesus Christ, the Word of God, is born of Mary, then Mary is the mother of God; the Council of Ephesus (431) defined this against the heretic Nestorius. Without necessarily declaring exactly how these truths of faith and morals are contained in revelation and without any formally declared logical process, the Church infallibly defines them as part of the deposit of revelation to be accepted on divine faith, and it does this in fulfilling its task of preserving, guarding, and explaining the revealed truths of Scripture and tradition. (3) Truths may be per se revealed, i.e., principally intended by God such as articles of the Creed, or per accidens revealed (Mt 13.1–2; 2 Tm 4.9–16). (4) Faith and morals also includes truths that the Church defines infallibly, though not as part of the revealed deposit, e.g., canon of Sacred Scripture.

Conclusion. Faith and morals primarily includes all divinely revealed truths that God gave to the Church, either directly or through the Apostles, and that are contained in the Scriptures or tradition and that are to be accepted on divine faith as necessary for salvation. Secondarily it includes truths defined by the Church as necessary to preserve and explain the truths formally and directly revealed. The teaching authority of the Church alone determines these truths.

See Also: DOCTRINE; DOGMA; REVELATION, THEOLOGY OF; REVELATION, VIRTUAL; RULE OF FAITH.

Bibliography: E. DUBLANCHY, ''Dépôt de la foi,'' *Dictionnaire de théologie catholique,* ed. A. VACANT, 15 v. (Paris 1903–50; Tables générales 1951–) 4.1: 526–531; ''Dogme,'' *ibid.* 4.2:1576–77; ''Église,'' *ibid.* 2184–85; ''Infaillibilité du Pape,'' *ibid.* 7.2:1699. N. IUNG, ''Révélation,'' *ibid.* 13.2:2616. L. CIAPPI, ''Freedom of the Faith and Papal Infallibility,'' in *Thomist Reader* (Washington 1957) 1–17. C. JOURNET, *The Church of the Word Incarnate,* v.1 tr. A. H. C. DOWNES (New York 1955) 338–342.

[A. E. GREEN]

FAITH AND ORDER COMMISSION

This entry examines the history and accomplishments of the Faith and Order Commission of the WORLD COUNCIL OF CHURCHES (WCC), established in 1927 as the Faith and Order Movement and integrated into the WCC in 1948.

Impetus for the Faith and Order Movement came from the World Missionary Conference in Edinburgh (1910). After the conference, one of its delegates, Bishop Charles H. BRENT of the EPISCOPAL CHURCH, U.S. proposed a conference on matters of faith and order, with a view to working for the unity of all Christians. The General Convention of the Episcopal Church approved his proposal in October 1910. During the next few years, Brent and Robert H. Gardiner, an Episcopal layman, met with the leaders of other churches to lay the foundation for this movement. In 1927 Protestant, Anglican, Old Catholic, and Orthodox delegates met in Lausanne, Switzerland, for the First World Conference on Faith and Order. The Roman Catholic Church was invited but did not participate. The aim of the conference was to ''draw churches out of isolation into conference'' to remove misunderstandings, discuss obstacles to reunion, and issue reports for consideration by the churches. The basis for dialogue was explained as follows: ''We . . . are assembled to consider the things wherein we agree and the things wherein we differ.''

The second World Conference on Faith and Order was held in Edinburgh in 1937 to explore further the possibilities for realizing the unity of Christian churches. Its report distinguished between cooperative action, intercommunion, and organic union, but delegates were unable to agree upon the exact form unity should take. At the Edinburgh conference, concurrently with the Oxford Conference on Life and Work, a proposal for the formation of the WCC was approved. When the WCC was established in 1948, the Faith and Order Movement became a part of this new organization.

The Third World Conference was held in Lund, Sweden, in 1952, followed by the Fourth World Conference in Montreal in 1963. The Montreal conference was a watershed in many respects. For the first time, observers from the Roman Catholic Church and Pentecostal delegates were present, Orthodoxy was widely represented, and Third World representatives were welcomed. The fruitful interaction of the member delegates and external observers at this conference became the basis for the decision made at the commission's 1967 plenary session in Bristol, England, where it revised its rules so that 40 of its 150 members might be invited from churches not currently members of the WCC. This resolution, confirmed at the 1968 meeting of the WCC in Uppsala, Sweden, made it possible for nine Roman Catholic observers to become members of the Faith and Order Commission and to participate at its 1971 meeting in Louvain, Belgium. Additionally, Cardinal Leon-Josef Suenens of Malines-Brussels gave one of the two opening addresses on the theme of this meeting: ''Unity of the Church—Unity of Mankind.''

The theme emerged out of the concerns of earlier conferences. The Bristol meeting posed the question, ''What is the function of the Church in relation to the unifying purpose of God for the world?'' Later the Uppsala assembly noted that the world may hear with skepticism the claim of the Church to be a sign of the coming unity of mankind. Rather, ''to the outsider, the churches often seem remote and irrelevant, busy to the point of tediousness with their own concerns.''

At a 1970 working committee meeting in preparation for Louvain, John Deschner of the United Methodist

Church saw the theme as evidence that Faith and Order was entering into a new stage in its history. It demanded new consideration of the secular import of church unity (its impact on racial, economic, social, generational, and sexist divisions) and of the significance of corporate Christian responses to secular issues.

Upon its introduction at Louvain, the theme was quickly challenged by John Meyendorff of the Orthodox Church in America, chairman of the commission. Highly critical of the more humanistic approach favored at the Uppsala assembly, Meyendorff regarded secular categories of thought as decisive in the ''iconoclastic years'' from the Montreal conference on, during which time ''what F & O represents was largely overshadowed by noisy talk about various social causes.'' Reproving those who reject ''the idea that the Church has a God-given structure [and] think that it must learn from the world how to make the world better,'' he called for a ''Eucharist-centered eschatology'' to regain a place over against false social utopianism.

Rejoinders to this criticism were strongly argued. Thus, José Miguez-Bonino, an Argentinean Methodist, argued that ''the prophetic message [is] that there is no 'Eucharist' outside the conditions of justice and faithfulness . . . which God has covenanted with his People.''

Within the limits of the Louvain meeting it was not possible to reconcile these two perspectives; one more typical of Orthodox spokesmen, the other of Protestants. Neither did it become clear which, if either, perspective held greater favor among the Catholic members present for the first time. Yet the underlying question was urgent and difficult. In response, the commission concluded recommending that further studies be carried out on the main theme and in three other areas: (1) the development of a common expression of the Christian faith (''Giving an Account of the Hope That Is in Us''—1 Pt 3:15), (2) the conceptualization of church unity and models of church union, and (3) the understanding of ministry and sacraments in the local and universal church.

Since then, two general foci of theological research and publication emerged within the commission: working out the details of a visible unity, i.e., the internal ecclesiological life of a united Church; and contextual studies relating the unity of the Church to its role in the mission to the human community. The work on contextual biblical hermeneutics at Louvain contributed to both of these, by amplifying the classical work on doctrine to include contextual as well as biblical and historical methodologies in the pursuit of unity.

Visible Unity. The vision of ''a Conciliar Fellowship of local churches which are themselves truly united,'' articulated at the Nairobi Assembly of the WCC (1975), pictures local unity combined with a worldwide unity focused on a truly ecumenical council recognized as such by Orthodox, Anglican, Protestant, and Roman Catholic Christians. These studies entailed extensive ecumenical research on the early councils, the understanding of ''local church'' among the communions, and the limits of diversity and unity required by the theologies of participating churches in their understanding of the biblical mandate for unity. This vision was the product of studies and consultations of the commission over the previous 50 years.

Three elements are identified as necessary before such unity can be achieved: a common understanding of the APOSTOLIC FAITH as it is to be confessed today; full mutual recognition of one another's baptism, Eucharist, and ordained ministry; and common ways of decision making and teaching authoritatively. At the Accra, Ghana, meeting (1974) work was done on the second of these items and circulated to the churches for their study, feedback, evaluation and revision. This work had been prepared for by detailed work on baptism, Eucharist, and the understanding of ordination throughout the churches and in the biblical and historical sources. The results of this wide theological consultation process produced the statement that was approved for distribution at the Lima meeting of the commission (1982) and the World Council Assembly at Vancouver, British Columbia (1983), called *Baptism, Eucharist and Ministry* and also known as the LIMA TEXT.

In the years following the Stavanger meeting (1985) of the commission, the responses of the churches were published and evaluated in preparation for a World Conference on Faith and Order to take place after the next WCC assembly, in Canberra, Australia (1991). In addition to the wide participation of the churches in the official response process, many popular studies of this document and unofficial reactions from individual scholars and groups have enhanced the material available for digestion and review. During this period extensive research is in progress on the apostolic faith and on the process of reception of the Lima Text in preparation for the third study necessary in the Conciliar Fellowship process, ''Common Ways of Deciding and Acting Together.''

The flowering of the bilateral dialogues between churches and the church union negotiations, such as the CONSULTATION ON CHURCH UNION in the United States, have both contributed to and benefited from the similar themes on which ecumenical research has been carried out in Faith and Order. The rich harvest of bilateral results in the 1970s prepared the ground work for the Lima Text studies of the 1980s. The latter, in turn, has made clear the connection between bilateral, multilateral, and church union dialogues all contributing to the common reconciling purpose and producing a coherent convergence theology for church union. During these same decades the model of visible unity was much debated between the Conciliar Fellowship vision of Nairobi and a Reconciled Diversity vision proposed by the Lutheran World Federation. Subseqent dialogues, including the Lutheran-Roman Catholic *Facing Unity* have pointed the way to reconciling these two visions. Proposals before the churches of the Consultation on Church Union call for giving concrete expression, among these nine U.S. churches, to the Conciliar Fellowship vision realized in concrete stages of covenanting.

As the Third World churches, and voices of women and minority churches in the First World have begun to be heard, along with Orthodox voices from the Second World and the European and American theological efforts, more participatory and contextual styles have been added to the researches of Faith and Order. At the Accra meeting (1974) a study, ''Giving Account of the Hope'' was featured, and brought to fruition at the Bangalore meeting (1978). Likewise, at that meeting a study, ''The Community of Women and Men in the Church,'' was featured, which continued through Lima and Vancouver. This study complemented an ongoing study that was formalized at Lima under the title ''The Unity of the Church and the Renewal of Human Community.'' Major reports on this study were presented at Stavanger and consultations and research continue.

Furthermore, the study process on the Lima Text and the means churches took to make their official responses, as well as the contextual processes used within the apostolic faith study as it moves forward, all relate the work on the internal life of the Church to its mission in the world. Recognizing that the elements of mission and social ministry in the ecumenical movement are contributing in their own way to Christian unity, while the theological research continues, is all part of the one ecumenical vision. The Commission on Faith and Order of the National Council of Churches in the U.S. has assisted the WCC studies for the American churches. Programs have been done on the Lima Text, Apostolic Faith, Conciliar Fellowship, the Community of Women and Men in the Church, and the Unity of the Church and the Renewal of Human Community. In addition, studies on the bilaterals, on spirituality, interreligious dialogue, on such controversial issues as homosexuality, abortion, and the UNIFICATION CHURCH have been undertaken and published.

Bibliography: J. E. SKOGLUND and J. R. NELSON, *Fifty Years of Faith and Order* (New York 1963). L. VISCHER, ed., *A Documentary History of the Faith and Order Movement* (St. Louis 1963). A. DULLES, SJ, ''Faith and Order at Louvain,'' *Theological Studies* 33, 1, 35–67. Meetings of the Faith & Order Commission. 50th Anniversary Celebration, Lausanne, Switzerland (1977); Bangalore, India (Aug. 15–30, 1978); Lima, Peru (Jan. 2–16, 1982); Stavanger, Norway (Aug. 13–26, 1985). Consultations and meetings for ongoing studies have taken place each year, and are reflected in the titles of WCC papers. The following Faith and Order (WCC) Papers are of particular importance: #59 *Faith and Order Louvain 1971* (reports and documents); #60 *Faith and Order Louvain 1971* (minutes of commission and working committee); #69 *What Kind of Unity?* (1974); #72 *Uniting in Hope* (reports and documents) (Accra 1974); #73 *One Baptism, One Eucharist and a Mutually Recognized Ministry: Three Agreed Statements* (1975); #74 *Confessions in Dialogue; Survey of Bilateral Conversations among World Confessional Families, 1959–74,* eds. N. EHRENSTROM and G. GASSMANN (1974); #77 *What Unity Requires* (papers and reports on the unity of the Church) (1976); #81 *Giving Account of the Hope Today,* intro. C. S. SONG (1976); #82 *Lausanne '77: Fifty Years of Faith and Order* (1977); #86 *Giving Account of the Hope Together* (1978); #92 *Sharing in One Hope* (reports and documents) (Bangalore 1978); #93 *Faith and Order, Bangalore 1978* (minutes); #97 *Louisville Consultation on Baptism,* Rev&Exp (Winter 1980); #102 *Episkope and Episcopate in Ecumenical Perspective* (1980); #103 *Spirit of God, Spirit of Christ: Ecumenical Reflections on the Filioque Controversy,* ed. L. VISCHER (1980); #105 *Ordination of Women in Ecumenical Perspective,* ed. C. PARVEY (1980); #111 *Baptism, Eucharist and Ministry* (1982); #112 *Towards Visible Unity: Commission on Faith and Order, Lima, 1982,* v. 1 *Minutes and Addresses;* #113, *ibid.,* v. 2 *Study Papers and Reports;* #114 *Growing Together in Baptism, Eucharist and Ministry. A Study Guide* (1985); #116 *Ecumenical Perspectives on Baptism, Eucharist and Ministry,* ed. M. THURIAN (theological essays) (1985); #117 *Baptism and Eucharist,* eds. M. THURIAN and G. WAINWRIGHT (ecumenical convergence in celebration) (1984); #121 *Minutes of the Standing Commission, Crete, 1984;* #125 *Fourth Forum on Bilateral Conversations Report* (1985); #127 *Called to Be One in Christ,* eds. T. BEST and M. KINNAMON; #129 *Churches Respond to BEM,* v. 1., ed. M. THURIAN (official responses to the *Baptism, Eucharist, and Ministry* text) (1986); #130 *Church, Kingdom, World,* ed. M. THURIAN (The Church as mystery and prophetic sign) (1986); #131 *Faith and Renewal* (Faith and Order Commission meeting held in Stavanger, Norway, Aug. 13–26, 1985); #132 *Churches Respond to BEM,* v. 2 (1986); #135 *ibid.,* v. 3 (1987). *Does Chalcedon Divide or Unite? Towards Convergence in Orthodox Christology,* ed. P. GREGORIOS et al. (1981).

[M. B. HANDSPICKER/J. HOTCHKIN/J. GROS/EDS.]

FAITH, HOPE, AND CHARITY, SS.

A legend states that three sisters, Faith, Hope, and Charity (Latin: Fides, Spes, and Caritas; Greek: Pistis, Elpis, and Agape), at the tender ages of 12, 10, and 9, were boiled in pitch and then beheaded for the faith under the second-century Emperor Hadrian. Their mother, Wisdom (Sapientia or Sophia), was cut down while praying over their bodies. This legendary story was probably inspired by one of two family groups that suffered martyrdom and were buried near Rome: either a family, whose members had the Greek names and were martyred under Hadrian and buried on the Aurelian Way, or a second group with the Latin names, buried in the cemetery of St. Callistus on the Appian Way. The cult of SS. Faith, Hope, and Charity did not exist before the sixth century. The church of St. Sophia in Constantinople was named in honor of the Holy Wisdom of God, Christ the Word, not the Sophia of the legend.

Feast: Aug. 1 (Roman Martyrology).

Bibliography: A. BUTLER, *The Lives of the Saints,* ed. H. THURSTON and D. ATTWATER (New York 1956) 3:238–239.

[E. DAY]

FAITHFUL

As opposed to INFIDEL, faithful is one who believes in God and His revelation in Christ, one who has divine, or Christian, FAITH. Normally this faith is had in the fold of the Catholic Church; but all the baptized who believe in Christ and in good conscience are ''outside the Church'' (separated brethren) also have the faith. [This is the basis of Catholic participation in ecumenism; cf. Vatican II's *Decree on Ecumenism, Unitatis redintegratio* 1; *Acta Apostolicae Sedis* 57 (1964) 90–91.] Nor is it excluded that non-Christians who, without any fault of their own, are ignorant of Christ and His Church should have implicit faith, viz, faith implied in the GRACE they are given when they follow their conscience in doing all that they know God wants of them (cf. H. Denzinger, *Enchiridion symbolorum,* ed. A. Schönmetzer [Freiburg 1963] 2866). They may be anonymous Christians, or infidels in appearance only, without having received any private revelation, but not without the grace of faith transforming their ''natural belief'' in God into divine faith.

In any of these three classes of faithful (Catholics, non-Catholics, and non-Christian believers) faith normally goes together with hope and charity, or the state of grace. The faithful not only believe in Christ; they are also expected to live according to the gospel. Yet faith can exist without the state of grace. It is defined doctrine that when sanctifying grace is lost by grave sin, faith as an infused virtue is not necessarily lost (cf. *Enchiridion symbolorum* 1578); it is lost only by grave sin against faith. Catholic sinners are still faithful and members of the Church, but members that are critically ill. Although theirs is not a living faith, yet it is a gift of God's grace (cf. *Enchiridion symbolorum* 3010, 3035). Theology endeavors to show how it is possible for the infused habit of faith to remain without sanctifying grace and charity; a man can freely assent to God revealing without yet living in accordance with this belief (Virtue is not mere knowledge; it requires, besides, good will and effort), but this ''dead faith'' entails a division of the will, the sinner partly obeying God by believing and partly disobeying God by not doing what He demands. This places his faith in an abnormal and possibly precarious condition.

Because faith is a SUPERNATURAL gift of God that requires one's free cooperation, the faithful who have received the gift of faith must cooperate with that grace. They need not be making acts of faith all the time—this is not possible—but they ought to make such acts whenever required by their Christian duty. Besides, they must take care to have an enlightened faith and to acquire the knowledge of their religion that befits their state in life. Their cooperation with the grace of faith will be wholehearted only when they live in accordance with their belief, i.e., in a state of grace, so that their faith is living, not dead, faith. Nor should they omit to pray for the grace of perseverance, that will help them to make their minds and wills ever more steadfast in the free assent to divine revelation.

See Also: VIRTUE.

Bibliography: S. HARENT, *Dictionnaire de théologie catholique*, ed. A. VACANT et al., (Paris 1903–50) 6.1:357–393, J. TRÜTSCH, *Lexikon für Theologie und Kirche*, ed. J. HOFER and K. RAHNER (Freiberg 1957–65) 4:920–925. G. JACQUEMET, *Catholicisme* 4:1262. J. DUPLACY, *ibid.* 1269–75.

[P. DE LETTER]

FALASHAS

Also known as 'Kayla,' or Beta Israel, a native Jewish sect of ETHIOPIA. Various theories have been proposed about the origin of the Falashas, who are physically and linguistically related to the tribe of the Agaw. According to one tradition, its ancestry traces to Menelik I, son of King Solomon of Israel, and the Queen of Sheba. Some scholars place the date of the sect's origin before the second century B.C., largely because the Ethiopian Jews are unfamiliar with either the Babylonian or Palestinian Talmud. Their Bible is written in an archaic Semitic language known as Ge'ez (the liturgical language of the Ethiopian Coptic Church), and of the Hebrew Scriptures they are most familiar with the Pentateuch. Ethiopian Jews refer to their sect as ''Beta Israel'' (House of Israel) and consider the name ''Falasha,'' which is Amharic for ''exiles'' or ''landless ones,'' a derogatory term.

The religion of the Ethiopian Jews is a modified form of Mosaic Judaism generally unaffected by postbiblical developments. They retain animal sacrifice. They celebrate scriptural and nonscriptural feast days, although the latter are not the same as those celebrated by Jews elsewhere. Their calendar contains the principal Jewish holidays beside several feasts and fast days of their own. One of the sect's nonscriptural feast days, for example, is the Commemoration of Abraham. The Sabbath regulations of Beta Israel are stringent. Members of the sect observe biblical dietary laws, but not the postbiblical rabbinic regulations concerning distinctions between meat and dairy foods. Monogamy is practiced, marriage at a very early age is rare, and marriage outside the religious community is forbidden.

Their religious life, centered in synagogue worship, consists in the recitation of prayers and the reading of the Torah. The chief functionary in each village is the high priest, who is assisted by priests of lower rank. The community appoints their priests, who are not regarded as descended from AARON. There are also monks who live alone or in monasteries, isolated from the other people (Falashas). RABBIS do not exist in the sect.

Until the mid-1980s Ethiopian Jews segregated themselves either in separate villages or in separate quarters in Christian or Islamic towns, in the mountain region of Semen, north of Lake Tana (the source of Blue Nile). They were skilled in agriculture, masonry, pottery, ironworking and weaving. Under the Emperor Haile Selassie I, a few rose to positions of prominence in education and government, but reports of persecution followed the emperor's ouster in 1974. More than 12,000 Ethiopian Jews were airlifted to Israel from late 1984 to early 1985, when the Ethiopian government halted the program. The airlift resumed in 1989, and about 3,500 Falashas immigrated to Israel in 1990. In May 1991, the Israeli government evacuated nearly all of the more than 14,000 Ethiopian Jews remaining in Ethiopia.

Bibliography: S. KAPLAN, *Fils d'Abraham: Les Falashas* (Belgium 1990). S. KAPLAN, "'Falasha' Religion: Ancient Judaism or Evolving Ethiopian Tradition?" *Jewish Quarterly Review* 79 (1988) 49–65. D. KESSLER, *The Falashas: A Short History of the Ethiopian Jews* (London 1996). S. D. MESSING, *The Story of the Falashas: "Black Jews" of Ethiopia* (Yale 1982). T. PARFITT and E. TREVISAN SEMI, eds., *The Beta Israel in Ethiopia and Israel: Studies on Ethiopian Jews* (London 1999). L. RAPOPORT, *Les Falashas d'Ethiopie* (Paris 1983). S. SANDMEL, "Jews, Christians and the Future: What May We Hope For," in D. J. FASCHING, ed., *The Jewish People in Christian Preaching* (Lewiston, NY 1984) 89–104.

[K. HRUBY/T. W. FESUH]

FALCONIERI

Noble family of FLORENCE that included two saints and two able cardinals.

Alexius, St., b. 1200, d. *c.* 1310, was one of seven Florentine nobles who met together for devotions. According to legend, the Virgin appeared to them in 1233 telling them to leave Florence. They returned in 1240 and built a church on the present site of SS. Annunziata. Although their followers increased rapidly in the 13th century, recognition of them as an order was delayed. In 1304, when Pope Benedict XI finally approved the SERVITES, Alexius was the only one of the original seven still living. He was beatified in 1717, the others in 1725; all were canonized in 1888.

Feast: Feb. 12 (Seven Holy Founders of the Servites).

Juliana, St., b. 1270, d. 1341, the niece of St. Alexius, founded the Third Order of the Servites of Mary (*see* MANTELLATE SISTERS) when she was 14 years old. Because of her mother's advanced age, she did not immediately establish a community. Her followers practiced their devotions in their homes. When her mother died in 1302, they began their community life. She was canonized in 1737.

Feast: June 19.

Lelio, cardinal, d. 1648, studied law at the University of Perugia and obtained a degree from the University of Pisa. He became an advocate in Rome, and Popes Paul V, Gregory XV, and URBAN VIII sent him to govern cities and provinces. Urban preferred his counsel in important questions. When he was appointed nuncio to Brussels in 1635, the government considered him pro-French and refused to receive him. In 1643 he was created a cardinal and sent as legate to Bologna. He was an excellent administrator, lessening dissension among the nobles and assisting the poor. He was one of three cardinals who heard the appeal of the delegates from the University of Louvain concerning the *Augustinus* of Cornelius JANSEN.

Alessandro, cardinal, b. 1657, d. 1734, was grandnephew of Lelio. He received his first appointments from Pope INNOCENT XII (1691–1700). In 1702 Pope CLEMENT XI asked him to clear the Roman countryside of persons who made the region unsafe for the inhabitants; in a short time he had restored order. A competent governor of Rome under Clement, he continued in that office during the pontificates of Innocent XIII and Benedict XIII. In 1724 Benedict created him a cardinal and also consecrated his new chapel at the Falconieri villa in Frascati. Both the villa and the palace in Rome are still called by the family name even though they have other owners.

Bibliography: L. PASTOR, *The History of the Popes From the Close of the Middle Ages* (London-St. Louis 1938–61) 29:128, 188; 34:98, 179–180. *Acta Sanctorum* June 4:766–773. L. CÀLLARI, *I palazzi di Roma* (3d ed. Rome 1944). A. M. ROSSI, *ibid.* 11:444–445. A. BUTLER, *The Lives of the Saints*, ed. H. THURSTON and D. ATTWATER (New York 1956) 1:311–313; 2:581–583.

[M. L. SHAY]

FALKNER, TOMÁS

Jesuit missionary; b. Manchester, England, Oct. 17, 1707; d. Plowden Hall, England, Jan. 30, 1784. Falkner studied physical and mathematical sciences with Newton, who was said by a contemporary to have considered him his favorite pupil, and medicine with Richard Mead. As physician for a cargo of slaves, Falkner came to Buenos Aires in 1730 and was converted to Catholicism. He entered the Society of Jesus on May 14, 1732, and was ordained in 1739. Between 1743 and 1751 he worked, with some interruptions, in the Reductions in the pampas and highlands of what is now the province of Buenos Aires. From 1752 to 1756 he was in Santa Fé, and from 1756 to 1767, in Córdoba. During all those years in addition to his priestly labors, he continued to practice medicine, so necessary in those regions where there was a scarcity of medical care. After the expulsion of the Jesuits (1767) he returned to England where he resided until his death. Only two of his writings, both fragmentary and abridged, are extant, but the first is so valuable that it is now considered a classic of its type: *A Description of Patagonia* (London 1774; reprinted by A. Neumann, Chicago 1935), which, according to present-day usage, would now be titled ''A Description of the Province of Buenos Aires.'' The second work is *Of the Patagonians* (Darlington 1788; reedited by G. Furlong, Buenos Aires 1929).

Bibliography: G. FURLONG, *Tomás Falkner y su ''Acerca de los patagones,'' 1788* (Buenos Aires 1954). R. F. DOUBLET, ''An Englishman in Rio de la Plata,'' *Month* 23 (1960) 216–226.

[H. STORNI]

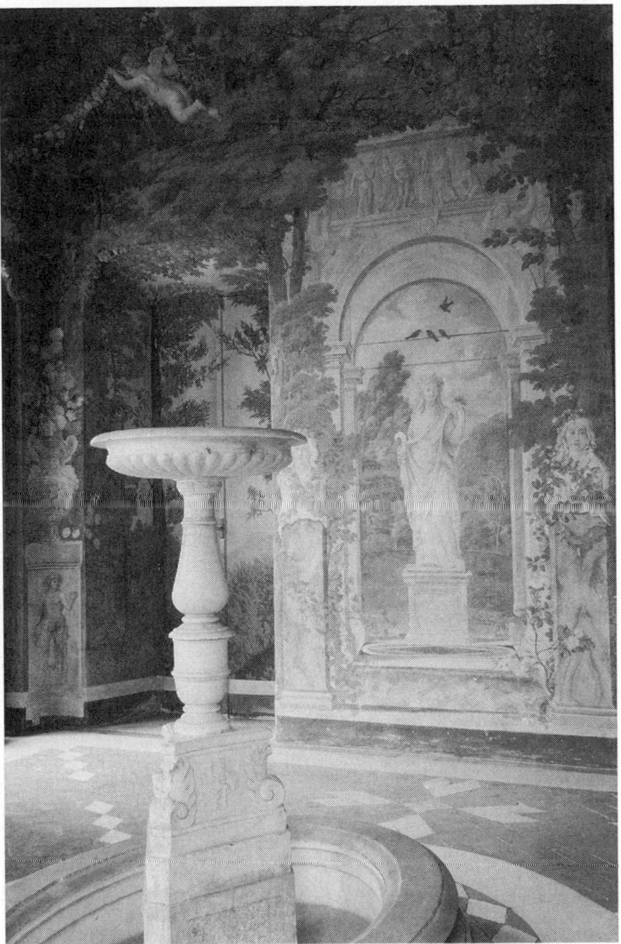

Sala di Primavera at the Villa Faconieri, Frascati, Italy. (©Cuchi White/CORBIS)

FALL RIVER, DIOCESE OF

The Diocese of Fall River (*Riverormensis*) is the suffragan of the metropolitan See of Boston, with jurisdiction over most of southeastern Massachusetts. Fall River, subject to the bishop of the PROVIDENCE, R.I., diocese from 1872 to 1904, was established as a separate see on March 12, 1904.

The Pilgrims were the first settlers in the area, landing at Provincetown on Cape Cod in November 1620. Very few Catholics settled there until the 19th century, when the rise of industry, particularly textiles, created such a demand for labor that hundreds and later thousands of English–Irish immigrants were welcomed. Portuguese, recruited from the Azores for the whaling industry that flourished in Nantucket and New Bedford before the Civil War, later entered the textile industry, and French–Canadians arrived in great numbers at the invitation of mill owners. Between 1820 and 1904, there were 44 parishes established in the area, 18 of them for non–English–language groups. Successive waves of Italians, Poles, Germans, and Lebanese followed, so that of the 13 parishes founded by Fall River's first bishop, nine were national. Catholics soon constituted more than 50 percent of the total population. Under the direction of successive bishops, a well–knit, integrated series of services and institutions provided for every level of need.

William Stang (1854–1907), scholar, theologian, and pulpit orator, was consecrated in Providence, May 1, 1904, as Fall River's first ordinary. During his brief career, he wrote pastoral letters entitled ''The Christian Family'' (1905), ''Christian Marriage'' (1906), and ''Christian Education'' (1907); summoned the first diocesan synod in June 1905; and enforced the *Acerbo nimis* on catechetical instruction, two months after its publication by Pius X. His successor, Daniel F. Feehan, (1855–1934), consecrated Sept. 19, 1907, in Fall River, was particularly concerned with the need for expansion. He established 36 new parishes, 23 of them national, and provided orphanages, day nurseries, camps, and welfare agencies. Catholic Youth Organization (CYO) activities in Fall River stem from his encouragement of them in the late 1920s. In 1930 he was granted an auxiliary, James E. Cassidy (1869–1951), who succeeded as ordinary on July 29, 1934. Cassidy, the workingman's advocate, a stern upholder of temperance and an apostle of charity, founded homes for the aged, CYO centers, and a home for the cancerous poor. In his last years, he presided at the founding of Stonehill College (1948), a four–year coeducational institution conducted by the Holy Cross Fathers.

James L. Connolly (1894–1986), a native of Fall River, was consecrated in 1945, as coadjutor with right of succession; he succeeded to the see on May 17, 1951. It was during his tenure in office that the *Anchor,* a diocesan weekly, was inaugurated in 1957. His successors, Bishop Daniel A. Cronin (1970–1991) and Bishop Sean O'Malley (1992–) witnessed a dramatic increase in the Catholic population, as well as in the number of parishes. The Fall River diocese includes the largest Portuguese community in the United States.

Bibliography: Archives, Diocese of Fall River. F. J. BRADLEY, *Brief History of the Diocese of Fall River* (New York 1931).

[J. L. CONNOLLY/EDS.]

FALLA, MANUEL DE

Foremost 20th-century Andalusian composer; b. Cádiz, Nov. 23, 1876; d. Alta Gracia (Córdoba province), Argentina, Nov. 14, 1946. He studied piano first with his mother, then in 1897 began his training with José Tragó (piano) and Felipe Pedrell (composition)—the leaders of the Spanish national music renewal. His opera *La Vida Breve* won first prize in a national competition in 1905. From 1907 to the outbreak of World War I he lived in Paris, accompanying, teaching piano, and learning from his Impressionist friends, DEBUSSY, Ravel, and Dukas. Once more in Spain, Falla found his stride, turning out a succession of masterful works, such as the ballets *El Amor Brujo* (containing the popular ''Ritual Fire Dance'') and *El Sombrero de Tres Picos* (''The Three-Cornered Hat''); the symphonic ''impressions'' *Noches en los jardines de España* (''Nights in the Gardens of Spain''); a puppet opera based on Cervantes, *El Retablo de Maese Pedro;* a concerto for harpsichord and chamber orchestra; and a suite, *Pedrelliana,* in tribute to his old master. After joining his sister in Argentina in 1939, he concentrated on his miracle-play setting of Jacinto Verdaguer's mystical epic of the birth of America, *L'Atlántida,* unfinished at his death. After services in Córdoba cathedral, his body was interred in the Cádiz cathedral crypt by permission of Pius XII. He was a man of self-effacing austerity and a deep spirituality that issued not so much in church music as in the evocation of the Spanish *mystique* by means of a pure, abstract, lucidly structured style.

Bibliography: M. DE FALLA, *Escritos sobre música y músicos,* ed. F. SOPEÑA (Buenos Aires 1950). J. B. TREND, *Manuel de Falla and the Spanish Music* (New York 1934). J. PAHISSA, *Manuel de Falla* (London 1954). R. ARÍZAGA, *Manuel de Falla* (Buenos Aires 1961). H. WIRTH, *Die Musik in Geschichte und Gegenwart,* ed. F. BLUME (Kassel-Basel 1949–) 3:1747–57. V. SALAS VIU, ''The Mystery of Manuel de Falla's *La Atlántida,*'' *Inter-American Music Bulletin* 33 (Jan. 1963) 1–6. S. DEMARQUEZ, *Manuel de Falla* (Paris 1963). A. BUDWIG, ''The Evolution of Manuel de Falla's *The Three-Cornered Hat,* (1916–20),'' *Journal of Musicological Research* 5 (1984) 191–212. M. CHRISTOFORIDIS, ''El peso de la vanguardia en el proceso creativo del *Concerto* de Manuel de Falla,'' *Revista de Musicología* 20 (1997) 669–682. N. H. LEE, *Manuel de Falla: A Bio-Bibliography* (Westport, Conn. 1998). C. A. HESS, ''Manuel de Falla's *The Three-Cornered Hat* and the Right-Wing Press in Pre-Civil War Spain,'' *Journal of Musicological Research* 15 (1995) 55–84. G. MOSHELL, ''*El Retablo de Maese Pedro* [*Master Peter's Puppet Show*],'' in *International Dictionary of Opera,* ed. C. S. LARUE, 2 v. (Detroit 1993) 1099–1100. Y. NOMMICK, ''Un ejemplo de ambigüedad formal: El *Allegro* del *Concerto* de Manuel de Falla,'' *Revista de Musicología* 21 (1998) 11–35; ''Forma y transformación de las ideas temáticas en las obras instrumentales de Manuel de Falla: Elementos de apreciación,'' *Revista de Musicología* 21 (1998) 573–591. C. URCHEUGUÍA SCHÖLZEL, ''Aspectos compositivos en las *Siete Canciones populares Españolas* de Manuel de Falla (1914/15),'' *Anuario Musical* 51 (1996) 177–201.

[R. STEVENSON]

FALLACY

A fallacy (Lat. *fallacia,* from *fallax,* meaning deceitful, or *fallere,* to deceive) may be defined as a statement or argument that leads one to a false conclusion because of a misconception of the meaning of the words used or a flaw in the reasoning involved. Some terms often used as synonyms of fallacy have different shades of meaning. Thus, a sophism (Gr. σοφός, wise) is a false argument offered with deliberate intent to deceive, a sophist being one who would rather appear to be wise than be wise, i.e., be a trickster (*see* SOPHISTS). A paralogism (Gr. παρά, contrary to, and λόγος, reason) is an unintentional violation of the rules of logic. A PARADOX (Gr. παρά, contrary to, and δόξα, opinion) is a statement that sounds absurd or contradictory, but yet may be true in fact, i.e., ''I die to live.''

Classification. There is no strict agreement among logicians on the classification of fallacies. Some distinguish only two basic types, namely, those ''in diction'' and those ''extra diction.'' Modern writers usually amplify the list with new titles that expand or, in some instances, merely duplicate, the basic concepts. The following outline reflects the more recent methods of classifying fallacies:

I. Fallacies of INDUCTION
  A. Insufficient observation
  B. Unwarranted generalization
  C. False analogy
II. Fallacies of DEDUCTION
  A. Formal
    1. In the proposition
    2. In the syllogism
      a. Illicit premises
      b. Undistributed middle
      c. Extended conclusion
  B. Material
    1. In diction
    2. Extra diction

Regarding inductive fallacies, it is obvious that inadequate observation of particulars cannot lead to a valid generalization. Only after a sufficient number of cases have been carefully checked and rechecked can a safe conclusion be drawn. Again, analogy is good for comparison, but becomes illicit when used to imply identity in nature or characteristics. Children, for example, are as frisky as lambs, but to conclude to an identification of all other characteristics would be unwarranted.

Among deductive fallacies, formal fallacies (paralogisms) arise from violations of the rules of logic regulating the drawing of inferences from propositions and of conclusions from premises in syllogisms. In the case of the PROPOSITION, fallacies may result from improper obversion, conversion, or OPPOSITION, for example, converting "All men are mortal" to "All mortals are men." These are called fallacies of simple inspection. In the case of the SYLLOGISM, formal fallacy may result from violation of any of the rules of syllogistic reasoning. Thus, the syllogism "Man is rational; a woman is not a man; therefore, a woman is not rational," violates the rule that demands only three terms. Some violations—such as having two negative premises, or having two particular premises, or concluding universally from a particular premise or affirmatively from a negative one, or introducing the middle term into the conclusion—are obvious. Others require an expert knowledge of formal logic to detect them.

Fallacies are divided materially into those "in diction" (fallacies of language that arise from an abuse of words) and those "extra diction" (fallacies apart from language that arise from an abuse of reasoning about things). These can be further divided and subdivided in various ways, of which the following are representative.

I. Fallacies in diction.
  A. Equivocation—one word mistaken for another. "He turned the *page.*" (Boy or book?)
  B. Amphibology—double-meaning sentence. "He shot the man with *his* gun." (Whose?)

Manuel de Falla. (©Bettman/CORBIS)

  C. Composition—attributing to the whole what is true only of the part. "*A* is a fine ballplayer; *B* is a fine ballplayer; *C* is a fine ballplayer. . . . *Ergo,* this is a fine team."
  D. Division—attributing to the part what is true only of the whole. "The straw that broke the camel's back."
  E. Metaphor—taking a figure of speech literally or stretching it unduly. "He was as hungry as a horse, so he ate a bucket of oats."
  F. Accent—different stress, tone, or gesture giving a different meaning to a word. "Min*ute* or *min*ute steak?" "Was the priest *in*censed, or in*censed*?"
II. Fallacies extra diction.
  A. Accident—presenting as true in the definite particular what is only generally true. "Americans are a generous people; I am an American; therefore, I am generous."
  B. False absolute—assuming as always true what is true only in its proper field or circumstance. "'Thou shalt not kill.' Therefore, wars are forbidden."
  C. Pretended cause—*post hoc, ergo propter hoc;* a prior event is cited as cause of a subsequent one. "After the U.S. adopted prohibition, the nation prospered."

D. Evading the issue—*ignoratio elenchi.* ''Have you ever been arrested?'' ''Sir, how dare you ask me that?'' This fallacy has many forms, the principal ones of which are:

1. *Argumentum ad hominem*—argument against the person, not the issue.
2. *Argumentum ad populum*—plea based on the arousal of passion and prejudice in a crowd.
3. *Argumentum ad verecundiam* (sense of shame)—embarrassing a speaker by quoting a great name against him. ''Einstein would not agree.''
4. *Argumentum ad misericordiam* (mercy-plea)—''But, Judge, he is of your faith (race).''
5. *Argumentum ad ignorantiam*—taking advantage of one's ignorance. ''It won't hurt, child.''
6. *Argumentum ad baculum* (the big stick)—threatening an opponent, making him concede through fear. ''This, or else!''

E. Begging the question (*petitio principii*)—more than a mere evasion, actually negation or contradiction of the issue. ''A monarchy is the best form of government, because it gives everyone a voice.'' This fallacy is said to have four forms:

1. Flat contradiction—''I do not exist.''
2. *Hysteron-proteron*—a purely empty, negative response taking for granted what needs to be proved. ''Women are incomprehensible—no man can say he understands them.''
3. Tautology—a mere repetition. ''A circle is a line that circles around.''
4. Vicious circle—trying to prove statement *A* by reason of *B,* whose validity depends on *A.* ''A soul is simple because it is nondimensional, and it is nondimensional because it is simple.''

F. The complex question—a ''loaded'' query that cannot be answered by a simple yes or no. ''Have you stopped taking graft?''

Evaluation. These are the most commonly cited fallacies. Their true number, however, is incalculable because some obscurity is to be found in every action and utterance of man, the fallible creature. LOGIC tries to discover the true intent and to detect misconceptions, but only He who is ''the searcher of heart and soul'' (Ps 7.10) can avoid all fallacies.

TRUTH itself is the primary objective of the INTELLECT, just as the good is the goal of the will. Man strives for the truth in many ways—by listening, reading, observing, meditating, and praying. He attains some truths, yet always imperfectly by reason of his first fallacy, the Fall. When he tries to enunciate the truth to others, he encounters the difficulty of choosing the proper, unequivocal word. The hearer, handicapped by his own imperfections, which are sometimes accentuated by prejudice or ill-will, does not always receive the exact meaning intended.

But this fecundity of fallacies, so evident in human affairs, should not make one cynical. In substance, if not in all its details and if not immediately, truth is possible of attainment. Civil courts, historical research, scientific experiments, scriptural exegesis, and philosophical and theological investigation—even such things as panel discussions and public debates—all seek to ferret out the truth. Thus avoidance of fallacy becomes the grand adventure of man's rationality. Truth presents a difficult challenge when compared to the ease of error, but it also offers an exceedingly great reward.

See Also: FALSITY; ANTINOMY; ARGUMENTATION.

Bibliography: S. J. HARTMAN, *Fundamentals of Logic* (St. Louis 1949). R. HOUDE and J. J. FISCHER, *Handbook of Logic* (Dubuque 1954). J. A. OESTERLE, *Logic: The Art of Defining and Reasoning* (2d ed. Englewood Cliffs, N.J. 1963).

[P. C. PERROTTA]

FALLON, MICHAEL FRANCIS

Bishop, educator; b. Kingston, Ontario, Canada, May 17, 1867; d. London, Ontario, Feb. 22, 1931. Fallon was the son of Dominick Fallon, an Irish immigrant. He was educated by the Brothers of Christian Schools and later at Ottawa College where he received his B.A. (1889). He then studied theology at the Gregorian University, Rome, obtaining a doctorate in philosophy and theology. While there, he sought admission to the Oblates of Mary Immaculate; he entered their novitiate in Holland, pronounced his vows June 29, 1894, and was ordained July 29, 1894. On his return to Canada his first assignment was at the University of Ottawa where he was the first to hold the chair of English literature. During this time he served seven years as editor of the *Owl,* a monthly, then one year as editor of the *Union.*

Fallon was renowned for his lectures on Daniel O'Connell, Edmund Burke, and other Irish patriots. He served as vice rector of the University for three years, after which he resigned to become pastor of St. Joseph's, an Irish parish attached to the University (1898–1901). From 1901 to 1904 he was pastor of Holy Angels parish, Buffalo, N.Y. Elected provincial of the American province of Oblates in 1904, he served in that capacity until 1909. He was named bishop of London, Ontario, Dec. 14, 1909, and consecrated there on April 25, 1910, by Abp.

F. P. McEvay of Toronto. During his episcopate, Fallon took an active part in the discussions of public questions; championed the Irish element in the controversy between French and Irish Catholics; and staunchly advocated home rule for Ireland, although he was a strong imperialist on other questions of secular politics. St. Peter's Seminary and Brescia Hall, both affiliated with the University of Western Ontario, were established during his tenure. He edited *Shorter Poems by Catholics* (London 1930).

[J. T. FLYNN]

FALLON, VALÈRE

Economist, moralist, and pioneer of the family movement in Belgium; b. Namur, Belgium, May 24, 1875; d. Louvain, Belgium, Jan. 21, 1955. Fallon entered the Society of Jesus in 1892 and was ordained in 1907. He studied political and social sciences at the Universities of Louvain, Berlin, and Munich from 1909 to 1914 and received a doctorate in political and social sciences in 1913. His thesis, ''La Plus-value et l'impôt,'' received a special award from the Belgian government and the University of Louvain. He taught moral philosophy and economics (1909–43) at the Jesuit college, Louvain, and social economics (1922–49) at the Institut Technique Supérieur Zénobe Gramme, Liège. His *Principes d' économie sociale* ran to seven editions and was translated into Dutch, Spanish, Italian, and English.

Fallon served as chaplain to Belgian forces, from 1914 to 1918 and from 1939 to 1940. With Colonel Lemercier and a few others, he founded (1921) Ligue des Familles Nombreuses and remained its effectual leader until his death. He promoted demographic studies in Belgium and participated in founding the International Population Union in 1928. Among his works are: *Les Allocations familiales en Belgique* (Louvain 1926, translated into Dutch), *La Population belge et son avenir* (Bruxelles 1934), *La Sécurité sociale et les allocations familiales* (Bruxelles 1945), *Les Deux régimes d'allocations familiales* (Bruxelles 1952).

[C. R. MERTENS]

FALSE DECRETALS (PSEUDO-ISIDORIAN FORGERIES)

The False, or Pseudo-Isidorian, Decretals form the principal work among the so-called Pseudo-Isidorian Forgeries, namely, a group of canonical collections that are intimately connected in origin and tendency and that appeared about mid-9th century. The name Pseudo-

Manuscript folio from ''Hispana Gallica Augustodunensis,'' false decretals, 10th century (Cod. Vat, Lat. 1341, fol. 160v).

Isidore (hereinafter Ps.) can be traced back to the 17th century; in the late 19th century B. Simson extended it to the entire group of writings. It is taken from the supposed author of the False Decretals, Isidore Mercator (according to later tradition, Mercatus, Peccator), the name of the collator of generally spurious papal briefs from Clement I until Gregory II. The Middle Ages often took him for St. Isidore of Seville. Among the Ps. Forgeries are numbered: the *Hispana Gallica Augustodunensis* (hereinafter HGA), the *Capitula Angilramni* (hereinafter Cap. Angilr.), the collection of capitularies of BENEDICT THE LEVITE (hereinafter Ben. Lev.), and the Pseudo-Isidorian Decretals (hereinafter Ps. Decretals). But the group of forgeries cannot yet be limited merely to these.

Circumstances and Character of the Forgeries. The four above-named works can be understood in part as representing a reaction to the state of the Church under Louis the Pious (814–840) and his successors: the harmony between Church and State that had existed under Charlemagne had been disturbed by rivalries and attacks by secular leaders on the ecclesiastical establishment and church holdings. Between 818 and 845, several bishops had been deposed or exiled from their sees; reform synods had tried in vain to better the situation (such as Paris, 829; Aachen, 836; Meaux-Paris, 845–846); and there had been all the less reason to hope for any improvement after the definitive fragmentation of the Carolingian Empire in 843.

Tendencies. It would not suffice to consider the Ps. Forgeries simply from the point of view of ecclesiastical politics and jurisprudence: they are more than fabricated legal sources. Attention has been drawn to the plethora of their regulations on the liturgy, doctrine of the Sacraments, the *Vita apostolica* (Möhler), marriage law (Von Scherer), and the hagiographical character of the False Decretals (Davenport); the picture of the Church sketched in the Forgeries has been called ''a vision of a Church in the Golden Age'' (Williams). Judging by the relative amount of time and energy devoted to the various points, the conclusion could be drawn that the principal aim of the Forgeries was to protect the suffragan bishops from the clutches of the metropolitans, provincial synods, and the secular power. The Forgeries complicate immeasurably the procedural rules and the possibility of depositions of bishops who are described panegyrically as *oculi, columnae, throni dei, dii,* etc. To strengthen the position of the bishops, the chorepiscopi, considered as rivals, are relegated to the status of the simple priesthood; and the metropolitans, who are to make decisions only in collaboration with their coprovincials, are jurisdictionally constricted by a newly invented office, that of the *primas,* or *patriarcha.* Accusations against bishops are subtracted from the jurisdiction of the provincial and national synods by being declared *causae maiores,* reserved to the pope, to whom alone belongs likewise the right to ratify the councils. Papal rights are stressed to the extent to which they favor the suffragan bishops.

Unity of the Forgeries. The Ps. Forgeries show evidences, both in tendency and in composition, of a common literary origin, no matter how divergent they may be in their use of sources and in the treatment of specific points. The scope of the sources, the interconnections, and the basic attitude are so uniform that there can be no doubt that the whole group of writings came from the same sort of mind, all the more since the differences between the individual forgeries are partly conditioned by the degree of proficiency of the individual composer and the species of source used in each case. The sequence of the forgeries and the degree of mutual influence have not yet been entirely clarified, but it is probable that the HGA was the earliest product, and that it was used in the Ps. Decretals and the False Capitularies; the Decretals presuppose also the Cap. Angilr. and some at least of the perhaps still unfinished capitularies of Ben. Lev., although Additio IV of the capitularies presupposes the False Decretals.

Individual Forgeries. The HGA, still unedited, is named after the place of origin of the only complete manuscript (Cod. vat. lat. 1341, 10th century; cf. G. Le-Bras, ''Autumn dans l'histoire du droit canonique'' in *Mémoires de la Société Éduenne* 48, autumn 1939). This manuscript is to be treated in the new *Hispana* edition of G. Martinez Diez (cf. *Miscelánea Comillas* 41 [1964]). The same version is contained in a Carolingian addition to Cod. Hamilton 132 (10th century) of the former Prussian State Library (cf. E. A. Lowe, *Codices Latini antiquiores* 8, no. 1047 [1959] 8, 61). It represents a reworking of the *Hispana Gallica,* i.e., the Spanish collection of canons (*Patrologia Latina* v. 84) current in Gaul (of which the only other surviving text is in Cod. Vindobonensis 411). The HGA corrects many meaningless passages in the *Hispana Gallica;* the revision is based in part on genuine sources (*Dionysio-Hadriana,* Irish collection of canons), but there are also typically Ps. additions. The HGA is today generally accepted as a Ps. preliminary work; this contention was initiated by F. Maassen (*Pseudoisidor-Studien I–II, Sitzungsberichte* [Vienna 1884–85] 108–109), after earlier research had taken the HGA to be a *Hispana* with subsequent Ps. interpolations. The period from 845 to 847 is thought to have been the date of composition, 847 being the more probable of the two, although the possibility cannot be excluded of a stratified composition extending beyond even 847.

Capitula Angilramni. The Cap. Angilr. contained 71 (another tradition says 72) brief and relatively moderately falsified laws, almost all dealing with prosecution of clerics, especially bishops (cf. G. May, ''Zu den Anklagebeschränkungen . . . in den capitula Angilramni'' in *Zeitschrift für Kirchengeschichte* 72 [1961]). They have come down in manuscript for the most part together with the A–1 version of the Ps. Decretals and have been edited together with these latter by Hinschius. They claim to have been sent by Pope Adrian I (772–795) to Bp. Angilram of Metz (768–791), hence on occasion the title *Capitula Hadriani* or in Cap. Angilr. 4: *synodus Romana;* in many manuscripts, Pope Adrian is the addressee, but the capitularies have nothing to do with either man. The forger drew heavily upon Roman Law, and used extensively the *Dionysio-Hadriana.* The Cap. Angilr. have been compiled from the sources without any mediation via the Ps. Decretals and at times yield a text that is meaningless for the practice of the Western Church. There are cross-references between the Cap. Angilr. and the capitularies of Ben. Lev., but the priority has not been clarified in all cases. In the Ps. Decretals of Popes Julius and Felix II, the Cap. Angilr. are to a large extent presented as canons of the Council of Nicaea (325).

Capitularies of Benedict the Levite. The Ben. Lev. consists of three books and four additions and claims to be a supplementation of the *Capitularium collectio* of Abbot ANSEGIS of Fontanelle (*Monumenta Germaniae*

Historica: Capitularia 1:394–450), together with which it has often been transmitted and whose numbering of books (1–4, Ansegis; 5–8, Ben. Lev.) it continues (cf. E. Seckel, ''Ben. Lev. decurtatus et excerptus'' in *Festschrift H. Brunner* [Munich-Leipzig 1914]; K. Christ, ''Die Schlossbibliothek von Nikolsburg und die Überlieferung der Kapitularien-Sammlung des Ansegis'' in *Deutsches Archiv* 1 [1937]; W. A. Eckhardt, ''Die von Baluze benutzten Handschriften der Kapitularien-Sammlungen'' in *Mélanges Charles Braibant* [Brussels 1959]). The author claims to have initiated the collection at the order of Abp. Otgar of Mainz (826–847; cf. A. Gerlich, *Rheinische Viertel-jahresblätter* 19 [1954]) and to have found the material mainly in the archives of the Mainz church. The forger clearly wants to insinuate a Mainz origin to the reader: at the beginning of the first book are three genuine fragments from the correspondence of Boniface; and he tries to picture himself to the reader as writing from the right bank of the Rhine (cf. J. Haller, *Nikolaus I. und Pseudoisidor* [Stuttgart 1936] 170). Some authors have given credence to the prologue, and the possibility has been weighed of a Mainz author for the entire forgery as well as for a part of it. But the many cross-references within the forgeries indicate an origin in a single locality and with a single group of persons; and here the West Frankish Kingdom and the opponents of Hincmar of Reims, the partisans of Ebbo of Reims, would be a more reasonable supposition.

The *terminus post quem* that must be accepted is April 21, 847, date of the death of Otgar of Mainz, who is mentioned in the perfect tense in the introductory poem (*Monumenta Germaniae Historica: Poetae* 2:672.2.5–6); the *terminus ante quem* is determined by the date of the capitulary of Quierzy (Feb. 14, 857), which cites false capitularies in its ''capitula domni Karoli et domni Hludowici imperatorum'' (*Monumenta Germaniae Historica: Capitularia* 2:289–291). Although Ben. Lev. calls his product capitularies, he had recourse to a set of sources similar to those used by Ps.; his set of original sources is smaller, but he often goes beyond those of the Ps. Decretals. In the combination of his originals, Ben. Lev. has been diffident; he does not fuse the excerpts as drastically as does Ps. and so is more brittle and less prolix, doing a reasonably good job at imitating the sober style of the Frankish royal chancery.

Pseudo-Isidorian Decretals. The Ps. Decretals include papal briefs and councils from Clement I, who died *c.* 90 (or from Anacletus I, who died *c.* 79 and is here listed as following Clement I) to Gregory II (716–731). The manuscripts, of which almost 100 are known today, have been divided into five classes by Hinschius, the last editor. Class A–1 comprises three parts: (1) after a few introductory fragments, 60 false decretals from Clement to Melchiades (d. 314); (2) councils, beginning with Nicaea I (325) and ending with the Second Council of Seville (619), although Toletanum XIII (683) is latest in point of time; (3) decretals and councils from Sylvester (d. 335) to Gregory II (d. 731)—the second part includes the first part of the *Hispana Gallica,* and the third part includes its second part. Class A–2 contains no portion on the councils and only those decretals from Clement to Damasus (d. 384). Class A/B, wrongly assessed by Hinschius because of the mistake in dating Codex Vat. lat. 630, is close to the genuine *Hispana* and is probably one of the first of the series of forgeries. The later classes, B and C, are derived from A/B. A class C manuscript was the original for J. Merlin's first edition (1524); it is No. 27 of the Bibliothèque de l'Assemblée Nationale and is late 12th century. Ps. avoided any free rendition over large portions of his forgery; rather he put it together in mosaic form out of various, often drastically edited, excerpts (about 10,000). His original sources are: the Bible (in a version diverging from the Vulgate, often not noted by Hinschius); conciliar decisions; decretals; Roman legal sources; common law; capitularies; penitentials; *HIBERNENSIS COLLECTIO;* writings of the Church Fathers, bishops, and private individuals; the Creed of Emperor Justinian I; the *Constitutum Constantini;* the Liber pontificalis; and rules of religious orders. Most of the fragments he took from the HGA or its preliminary forms. Among the general collections, most use is made of the *Quesnelliana* (*Patrologia Latina* 56:359–747) and the *Dionysio-Hadriana,* which was the most widespread collection of canon law in Carolingian days and seems to have been imitated in the invocation and the conclusion of the Ps. Decretals.

Location and Identity of the Forger. The question of the identity and location of the forger centers around the authorship of the False Decretals. The period of composition of the False Decretals has been presumed to lie between 847 and 852, since they included the capitularies of Ben. Lev. finished after April 847 and are cited in writings of Hincmar of Reims, perhaps in 852 and certainly in 857; a material influence of Ps. can be felt in the primacy claim of Thietgaud of Trier, about 852. Of the many, often fantastic, suggestions as to location and identity of the author (e.g., the papal chancery, Pope Joan, someone in Mainz), only the latest will be mentioned. (1) The Diocese of Le Mans in the ecclesiastical province of Tours (first Simson, recently especially Fournier, LeBras, Grand). The forgeries would have provided the bishop of Le Mans with a shield against the attacks of the Breton Duke Nominoe. A main argument is the linguistic similarity of the Ps. Decretals and the contemporary *Gesta Domni Aldrici* and the *Actus pontificum Cenomannis in urbe degentium,* a similarity that Lot (1940–41) chooses to explain in terms of a common schooling. (2) The royal chapel of Charles the Bald, more exactly Hilduin the Younger, Lupus of Ferrières, Wenilo of Sens, and Wulfhad of Bourges. This suggestion, however, offered by Buchner (1937) and approved by Oesterle (1938) has found no partisans. (3) The opponents of Hincmar of Reims and partisans of Ebbo of Reims. Abstracting from the fate of Ebbo, the description of the province fits just as well the ecclesiastical province of Reims, as does the campaign against the chorepiscopi and the solid front of the suffragans against their metropolitans. The question of place and author has stalled on a *Non liquet,* and there is scant hope of giving a conclusive solution simply by suggesting an author or team of authors who were of the same mind as evidenced in the Ps. forgeries. Greater hope of success would attend to a search for the Ps. library, the actual originals used.

Influence and Exposure of the Forgeries. Of all the Ps. Forgeries, the False Decretals gained greatest influence, as can be seen from the manuscript tradition. In the West Frankish Kingdom, Hincmar of Reims was the first to cite them in his writings (852?, 857, 859); in 858, Abbot Lupus of Ferrières inquired in Rome, on the part of several bishops, concerning a Ps. Decretal (*Monumenta Germaniae Historica: Epistolae* 6:114), but a forceful advocate of Ps. Law appeared only in the late 860s in the person of Bp. Hincmar of Laon, nephew and suffragan of Hincmar of Reims (845–882). The battle ended in 871 with the deposition of the bishop of Laon; his defeat was also that of the Ps. party, and the acceptance of the Ps. Decretals made only halting progress in the immediately subsequent decades.

In the kingdom of Lothair II, Thietgaud of Trier (847–863), a bitter opponent of Hincmar of Reims, was the first known to have taken cognizance of them; in the East Frankish Kingdom, the Acts of the Synods of Worms (868), Cologne (887), Metz (893), and Tribur (895) contained Ps. material. Although there was a widespread early tradition of the Ps. Decretals in Italy, signs of cognizance of Ps. appeared only slowly in papal briefs. Perhaps Rothard of Soissons brought Ps. Decretals to Rome in 864; in January 865 Pope Nicholas I presented the decretals of the martyr popes (i.e., the Ps. Decretals) as Roman archive material (P. Jaffé, *Regesta pontificum romanorum*, ed. P. Ewald, v. 2; 2785), without, however, quoting them verbatim. Explicit references to the Ps. Laws are found in the works of his successors Adrian II (867–872), John VIII (872–882), Stephen V (885–891), and John IX (898–900) and in writings connected with the Formosus dispute.

The reform popes made more intensive use of the Ps. Decretals; but it is a mistaken assumption that Leo IX (1049–54) brought the Ps. Forgeries with him from Lorraine, for even his predecessors John XIX (1024–32) and Benedict IX (1032–44) had appealed to Ps. The letters of the early reform popes cited the Ps. Decretals only sparingly, and it was only with Urban II (1088–99) that more intensive use of them began. It is an error to suppose (e.g., Haller) that Gregory VII (1073–86) eagerly sought after Ps. writings. The chief channel of influence was not the papacy but rather the collections of canons.

The broadest stream stemmed from the *Collectio ANSELMO DEDICATA* (*c.* 890); of 1,980 capitula, 507 are Ps. Dissemination proceeded via the Decretum of BURCHARD OF WORMS (1,785 *capitula,* of which 141 are Ps.), and the *Decretum* and the *Panormia* of IVO OF CHARTRES to the *Decretum* of GRATIAN (having 3,500 *capitula,* of which 375 are Ps.). Of the more important collections of canons of the Gregorian reform, the *Diversorum patrum sententiae* have the largest percentage of Ps. (124 out of 315), but Ps. is represented to no inconsiderable extent in the canon law collection of Bp. ANSELM OF LUCCA (264 out of 1150) and the Collection of DEUSDEDIT (143 out of 1173). The Ps. Laws that found their way into all these documents cover many fields: they deal predominantly with questions of trial procedure and accusations, hierarchy and councils. The Ps. Decretals brought no advantages to the suffragan bishops; on the contrary, the reformers included laws that corresponded with their own ideas of the rank and dignity of the papacy and did not always agree with the aspirations of the bishops.

History of Criticism. Already Hincmar of Reims rejected and rebutted some of the Ps. Decretals material (pseudo-Nicene canons); and the spuriousness of certain fragments was wholeheartedly admitted, apart from anonymous writers, by BERNOLD OF CONSTANCE (d. 1100), Peter Comestor (d. *c.* 1179), MARSILIUS OF PADUA (d. 1342 or 1343), Gobelinus Persona (d. 1421), NICHOLAS OF CUSA (d. 1464), and Heinrich Kalteisen (d. 1465). But the discovery of the forgery did not affect their being used. The Magdeburg *centuriatores* under Flacius Illyricus (1559) devoted themselves to proving that the entire body of the pre-Siricius decretals were forgeries; complete success in this endeavor was attained only by the reformed theologian Blondel, who made a meticulous analysis of sources (1628). But the genuinity was still often seriously considered as a possibility, most recently by Dumont (1866–67).

Editions. There is no edition of the HGA. The Ben. Lev. has been edited by G. H. Pertz and F. H. Knust (*Monumenta Germaniae Historica: Leges* 2.2:39–158); a new edition prepared by E. Seckel (d. 1924) for the *Monumenta Germaniae* did not appear, but the question of sources (with the exception of the four additions) has been collated with superlative thoroughness in Seckel's "Studien zu Benedictus Levita I–VIII," *Neues Archiv* 26 (1900); 29 (1904); 31 (1905); 34 (1908); 35 (1909); 39 (1914); 40 (1915); 41 (1917–19) and in his posthumous works published by J. Juncker in *Zeitschrift für Rechtsgeschichte* 23 (1934) and 24 (1935).

The *Decretales Pseudo-Isidorianae et capitula Angilramni* have been edited by Hinschius (Leipzig 1863). This edition is unsatisfactory; its chief shortcoming is that in the council portions it reprints to a large extent the Madrid *Hispana* edition of F. A. Gonzáles. Although Merlin reproduces a later manuscript, his edition is truer to the tradition. And Hinschius's paleographic dating is so faulty that to correct it might involve a shift in the relationship of the classes.

Bibliography: J. MERLIN, ed., *Tomus I quatuor conciliorum generalium,* 2 v. (Paris 1524) v. 1, repr. Cologne 1530 was model for *Patrologia Latina,* ed. J. P. MIGNE, 271 v., indexes 4 v. (Paris 1878–90) v. 130. *Ecclesiastica historia . . . congesta . . . per aliquot studiosos et pios viros in urbe Magdeburgica, centuria II und cent. III* (Basel 1559). D. BLONDEL, *Pseudo-Isidorus et Turrianus vapulantes . . .* (Geneva 1628). J. A. MÖHLER, *Gesammelte Schriften,* ed. J. J. I. DÖLLINGER, 2 v. (Regensburg 1839–40) v. 1. H. WASSERSCHLEBEN, *Beiträge zur Geschichte der Falschen Dekretalen* (Breslau 1844); "Über das Vaterland der Falschen Dekretalen," *Historische Zeitschrift* 64 (1890) 234–250. J. WEIZSÄCKER, "Hincmar und Ps.-Is.," *Zeitschrift für historische Theologie* 28 (1858) 327–430; *Der Kampf gegen den Chorepiskopat des fränkischen Reichs im 9. Jh.* (Tübingen 1859). P. HINSCHIUS, "Der Beiname 'Mercator' in der Vorrede Ps.-Isidors," *Zeitschrift für Kirchenrecht* 6 (1866) 148–152. É. DUMONT, "Les Fausses décrétales," *Revue des questions historiques* 1 (1866) 392–426; 2 (1867) 97–154. A. LAPÔTRE, "Hadrien II et les fausses Décrétales," *ibid.* 27 (1880) 377–431. H. SCHROERS, *Hinkmar, Erzbischof von Reims* (Freiburg 1884). R. VON SCHERER, *Handbuch des Kirchenrechts,* v. 1 (Graz 1885). B. VON SIMSON, *Die Entstehung der pseudoisidorischen Fälschungen in Le Mans* (Leipzig 1886). P. FOURNIER, "Étude sur les Fausses Décrétales," *Revue d'histoire ecclésiastique* 7 (1906) 33–51, 301–316, 543–564, 761–784; 8 (1907) 19–56. H. JÄGER, *Das Kirchenrechtssystem Pseudoisidors* (Doctoral diss. Munich 1908). E. H. DAVENPORT, *The False Decretals* (Oxford 1916). G. HARTMANN, *Der Primat des römischen Bischofs bei Pseudo-Isidor* (Stuttgart 1930). A. DOLD, "Ein altes Konstanzer Handschriftenblatt des 9. Jahrhunderts mit Auszügen aus Pseudoisidor über das Verhalten der Bischöfe in Anklagefällen," *Archiv für katholisches Kirchenrecht* 111 (1931) 17–30. P. FOURNIER and G. LEBRAS, *Histoire des collections canoniques en occident depuis les fausses décrétales jusqu'au Décret de Gratien,* 2 v. (Paris 1931–32) v. 1. C. SILVA-TAROUCA, "Un codice di Pseudo-Isidoro coevo del falso?" *Miscellanea Isidoriana* (Rome 1936) 357–363. J. HALLER, *Nikolaus I. und Pseudoisidor* (Stuttgart 1936). M. BUCHNER, "Pseudoisidor und die Hofkapelle Karls des Kahlen," *Historisches Jahrbuch der Görres-Gesellschaft* 57 (1937) 180–208. G. OESTERLE, "De Pseudo-Isidoro et capella aulica Caroli Calvi," *Jus Pontificium* 18 (1938) 142–150, 219–221. F. LOT, "Textes manceaux et Fausses Décrétales," *Bibliothèque de l'École des Chartes* (Paris 1839–) 101 (1940) 5–48; 102 (1941) 5–34. A. VAN HOVE, *Commentarium Lovaniense in Codicem iuris canonici 1,* v. 1–5 (Mechlin 1928–); v. 1, Prolegomena (2d ed. 1945). A. M. STICKLER, *Historia iuris canonici latini,* v. 1: *Historia fontium* (Turin 1950). R. BUCHNER, *Die Rechtsquellen* (W. WATTENBACH, *Deutschlands Geschichtsquellen im Mittelalter. Vorzeit und Karolinger,* Hefte 1–4, ed. W. LEVISON and H. LÖWE [Weimar 1952– 63] suppl. 1953). S. WILLIAMS, "The Pseudo-Isidorian Problem Today," *Speculum* 29 (1954) 702–707. R. GRAND, "Nouvelles remarques sur l'origine du Pseudo-Isidore, source du *Décret* de Gratien," *Studia Gratiana* 3 (1955) 1–16. H. FUHRMANN, "Die pseudoisidorischen Fälschungen und die Synode von Hohenaltheim," *Zeitschrift für bayerische Landesgeschichte* 20 (1957) 136–151; "Die Fälschungen im Mittelalter," *Historische Zeitschrift* 197 (1963) 529–554. S. WILLIAMS, "The Oldest Text of the *Constitutum Constantini,*" *Traditio* 20 (1964) 448–461. E. SECKEL, J. J. HERZOG, and A. HAUCK, eds., *Realencyklopädie für protestantische Theologie,* 24 v. (3d ed. Leipzig 1896–1913) 16:265–307, the most thorough introd.; "Die erste Zeile Pseudoisidors . . . ," ed. H. FUHRMANN, *Sitzungsberichte der Deutschen (Preussischen* to 1948) *Akademie der Wissenschaften zu Berlin* no. 4 (1959).

[H. FUHRMANN]

FALSITY

Falsity (from Lat. *falsum,* supine of *fallere,* to deceive) is defined by its opposition to TRUTH. Since truth is the conformity or adequation of intellection and being, falsity is their deformity or inadequation. Falsity then is not the same as IGNORANCE, which is the mere absence of KNOWLEDGE conformed to being, as in the newly born child. Nor is it the same as partial or obscure or incomprehensive knowledge, which does not exhaust the knowability of being. In this sense all created knowledge is imperfect or negatively inadequate to being. But falsity is positive inadequation, namely, that between being and knowledge asserting that being is other than it is. Hence falsity is the evil of the intellect, depriving it of the good for which it is made, frustrating its inborn longing for truth. By reason of the duality of terms (intellection and being) in the relation of inadequation that falsity denotes, falsity can be considered either from the point of view of intellection (logical falsity), or from the point of view of being (ontological falsity).

Logical Falsity. Logical falsity, or ERROR, is the deformity of human intellection from being. Since truth is properly and formally in the JUDGMENT, falsity, which is a deprivation of truth, is properly in the judgment only. Logical falsity is therefore a judgment asserting that what is, is not, or that what is not, is. How is it possible for a judgment to be false? St. THOMAS AQUINAS teaches that truth is consciously in the judgment, because the INTELLECT judging knows itself as conformed to being (ST 1a, 16.2). The intellect knows its conformity insofar as in judging it exercises complete reflection on itself (*De ver.* 1.9). Must it not follow then that falsity is properly in the judgment, insofar as the intellect knows itself as deformed from being (see ST 1a, 17.3), and this by reason of its exercised complete reflection? How, then, can the intellect know its falsity without correcting it?

Conformity and Deformity. To state that truth is consciously possessed in the judgment means that the judgment by its very nature presents itself as conformed to being. When, for example, a person says that the paper on which he is writing is white, he knowingly intends to assert that the thing across which his pen moves justifies or verifies what he asserts about it, that it is as he judges it to be. The judgment presents itself as conformed to being, because it involves complete reflection on the intellect's conformity to reality. If the same person inadvertently keeps on his green-tinted sun glasses as he begins to write, he might assert with surprise that the paper on which he is writing is green. In such a case, he knowingly intends to assert that the paper is actually green. He consciously presents his judgment as conformed to being, whereas it is not conformed to, but rather deformed from, being. Thus his erroneous judgment is a conscious deformity from being.

This particular deformity from being is known, but it is known not as deformity (which would equivalently remove the error), but rather as if it were conformity. The core of falsity lies here. The intellect does not avert to its deformity, but confuses this with conformity, and hence takes its partial ignorance for knowledge. In other words it thinks it knows itself to be conformed when actually it does not.

Reflective Awareness. How is this confusion possible if the judgment involves complete reflection and self-knowledge? Firstly, the complete reflection of the human intellect is not the translucent vision of the ANGEL. In knowing, angels are entirely transparent to themselves, because the content of their natural knowledge is entirely from within themselves and so excludes the possibility of error. Man's complete reflection, on the other hand, belongs inseparably to the exercise of his intellection, but it is an exercise whose content is inescapably implicated in a multiplicity of images and sense data that remain necessarily extrinsic to intellection. Hence human intellection must progressively clarify its content by a succession of acts and inferences. The complete reflection objectivizes in general the content of this knowing, and so refers it in general to being and knows itself in general as conformed to being.

But such complete reflection and such general reference to the intellect's conformity to being do not of themselves justify the intellect's particular interpretation of this content (i.e., the objectivizing connection of its elements), on which the truth of the particular judgment depends. Nor do they guarantee the rectitude of the intellect's inferences, nor the logical connection of the various acts by which it concludes to a judgment. The particular interpretation of this content demands reflection on, and sifting of, the sense data (external manifestations of reality) that the content generalizes. It also involves attention to the images (figurative and emotional) evoked by this content, by reason of its similarity to other situations, and a careful weighing of the memory elements involved in the content. The rectitude of its inferences demands that the intellect examine with care each step of its reasoning, and reflect on its connection with, and the validity of, the principles applied.

False Judgment. When the intellect judges falsely, this critical attention to, and discerning reflection on, the data of sense, the association of images, the reliability of memory, the connecting reasoning, and the validity of principles, either is lacking or is insufficient. The intellect judges precipitately without fully reflecting on these sources of its judgment, and so not withholding its assertion until sure it has sufficient EVIDENCE for it. By reason of this insufficient reflection, the intellect asserts as true what only seems to it to be true, and hence it asserts beyond what it knows. It makes such an assertion under the influence of the will. The will, either by reason of its attachment to prejudices, or by its impatience or disinclination to effort, or by not applying its attention, moves the intellect to judge what only seems to be. All falsity lies in this chasm between seeming and being. If something did not seem true, man could not assent to it, since his intellect is a faculty of truth. Yet his intellect can take the seeming true for being true because its judgment is under the influence of the will. From the point of view of the intellect, no error is inevitable.

Ontological Falsity. Ontological falsity is false BEING. Since being is true insofar as it is in conformity to intellection, it is false insofar as it is in deformity to intellection. If being, as being, is true or conformed to intellect, every being is true insofar as it is. How then and in what sense can one speak of false being? Is not false being the same as NONBEING or nothingness? If so, there is no such thing as ontological falsity. Yet one speaks of such things as false prophets, counterfeit coins, sham jewels, artificial silk, synthetic rubber, and false teeth, and these things exist. What is the meaning of their falsity and wherein does it reside?

Being is true as conformed to intellect. If there were no intellect to which being is conformed, being would not be true and so would not be. But if there were no human intellect, being would still be true. Conformity to man's intellect is not essential—it is only accidental to being. If, on the other hand, God's intellect did not exist, being and its truth would cease. Conformity to God's intellect makes being to be. Hence no being can be under any aspect to which God's intellect is not conformed. But a being can be even though man's intellect is deformed from it. As regards God's intellect, therefore, no being is or can be false. Hence no being, as it is in itself, can be false.

The only way, then, that a being can be false is not as it is in itself, but as it is outside itself, i.e., as it appears externally. A thing cannot be false simply, but only under a certain aspect, i.e., under the aspect of its external manifestation. Hence being can be false only in relation to a faculty (intellect) that reaches to what is through appearances, or to an intellect depending on senses, i.e., to a human intellect. Falsity, then, is attributed to a being only as it appears to the human intellect—and that within definite limits. One does not call a tomato a false being because it leads the inexperienced child to mistake it for a rosy apple. A thing is called false only when it would deceive the normal, developed human being, or men in general. The falsity of such things lies in their appearances' being so similar to something else that the average man would not detect the difference. Hence falsity is not in the being of things, but only in their appearances. Moreover, it is in these appearances not formally but only dispositively, in the sense that these appearances tend to provoke men to a false judgment about the reality whose appearances they are. Since the being of what appears is true, and falsity lies only in the appearances of certain beings, ontological falsity is founded in ontological truth.

See Also: TRUTH; ABSURDITY; FALLACY.

Bibliography: L. W. KEELER, *The Problem of Error from Plato to Kant* (*Analecta Gregoriana* 6; 1934). J. H. NICOLAS, ''Le Problème de l'erreur,'' *Revue thomiste* 52 (1952) 328–57, 528–66. M. D. ROLAND-GOSSELIN, ''La Théorie thomiste de l'erreur,'' *Mélanges Thomistes* (*Bibliothèque Thomiste* 3; 1923) 253–74. A. MARC, *Psychologie réflexive* (Brussels 1948) 1:366–75. S. CARMELLA, *Enciclopedia filosofica*, 4 v. (Venice-Rome 1957) 2:30–38, 257–58. E. VALTON, *Dictionnaire de théologie catholique*, ed. A. VACANT et al., 15 v. (Paris 1903–50) 5.1:435–47.

[F. P. O'FARRELL]

FALZON, IGNATIUS, BL.

Catechist; b. July 1, 1813, Valetta, Malta; d., July 1, 1865, Valetta. Ignatius (*Nazju* in Maltese) was born at the time when Malta was in the process of becoming a British colony and naval base. His father was a lawyer and later a judge; his mother was the daughter of a judge. Two of his brothers became priests. Ignatius received degrees in both civil and canon law at the Athenaeum of Malta (1833) and began theological studies, receiving the four minor orders in vogue at the time, but decided against ordination to the priesthood. Ignatius became a member of the Franciscan Third Order.

Ignatius read the signs of the times and studied English. When he realized that the British military personnel stationed in Malta—like the Maltese themselves—lacked a sound formation in the Gospel, he decided to devote his life to catechesis. Ignatius started first by teaching catechism to children and later on to British servicemen. He organized prayer meetings and catechism instruction for the British Catholics and then non–Catholic servicemen as well. Ignatius invited other laymen to help in the catechetical ministry. Some who became priests served as military chaplains in the British army and navy. It is estimated that Ignatius personally prepared at least 650 individuals for reception in the Roman Catholic Church.

Ignatius died on his fifty–second birthday and was buried in the family tomb in the Franciscan church of St. Mary of Jesus in Valetta. Pope John Paul II beatified him when he visited Malta on May 9, 2001. Ignatius' feast is celebrated in Malta on July 1, the day of both his birth and death.

Feast: July 1.

[E. MAGRO]

FAMIAN, ST.

Cistercian priest; b. Cologne, Germany, *c.* 1090; d. Gallese, near Rome, Aug. 8, 1150. As a young man, Famian (Gebhard, Wardo, Quardus) left his wealthy parents for the life of a poor pilgrim. He visited several holy places in Italy and Spain, including Rome and SANTIAGO DE COMPOSTELA. He then lived as a hermit for about 25 years before entering a Cistercian monastery in Osera in northwestern Spain. With his superior's permission, he left for the Holy Land about 1146, returning to Italy in 1150. The first Cistercian to be canonized (1154), he was called ''Famianus'' because of the fame of the miracles reputedly worked at his tomb in Gallese.

Feast: Aug. 8

Bibliography: Sources. *Acta Sanctorum* Aug. 2:389–395. **Literature.** J. L. BAUDOT and L. CHAUSSIN, *Vies des saints et des bienheueux selon l'ordre du calendrier avec l'historique des fêtes* (Paris 1935–56) 8:137. B. BEDINI, *S. Famiano, patrono di Gallese* (Rome 1958). A. M.. ZIMMERMANN, *Kalendarium Benedictinum: Die Heiligen und Seligen des Benediktinerorderns und seiner Zweige* (Metten 1933–38) 2:547–548.

[J. C. MOORE]

FANON

A liturgical garment, in the form of a double humeral cape, oval in shape, the lower part being slightly wider

Fanon worn by Pope Paul VI as he blesses the crowd from the Sedia Gestatoria.

than the upper. It is made of white silk, with red and gold stripes running across it; there is a cross in front and an opening at the top for the head. Historically, it was a secondary papal insignia that was reserved exclusively to the pope, and worn when he was vested in pontificals. The fanon became one of the papal insignia when priests and bishops began to wear the amice under the chasuble. Innocent III called the fanon *orale* (amice) and in his days it seems that it was already a papal vestment, or, more precisely, the papal amice. Later (*c.* 1500), popes began to wear both amice and fanon. During the reign of Pius X, the fanon was separated into two parts, though supposedly forming one vestment. The lower part was put over the alb and the back part of the upper fanon was pulled over the head after the pope received the chasuble; it was then laid on his shoulders and on his breast. Although the separation into two parts simplified the pope's vesting, it also did away with all the remaining traces of the old papal amice.

Bibliography: J. NABUCO, *Ius pontificalium: Introductio in caeremoniale episcoporum* (Tournai 1956) 187–188.

[J. NABUCO/EDS.]

FARA, ST.

Foundress and abbess; b. near Meaux, France, 595; d. 657. Fara (Burgundofara) was the daughter of Count Agneric and sister of SS. Cagnoald of Laon and FARO OF MEAUX. When Fara was a child, St. COLUMBAN—on his way into exile from LUXEUIL—passed her villa and blessed her, whereupon she vowed herself to religious life. Her father later refused to countenance her vow and only after she had persevered through considerable opposition and even persecution did he permit her to found the convent of Evoriacum, later known as FAREMOUTIERS, which he richly endowed. Fara's exemplary life is said to have been responsible for the vocation of her brother Faro.

Feast: April 3; Dec. 7, at Faremoutiers.

Bibliography: J. MABILLON, *Acta sanctorum ordinis S. Benedicti* (Venice 1733–40) 2:420–430. H. M. DELSART, *Sainte Fare* (Paris 1911). J. L. BAUDOT and L. CHAUSSIN, *Vies des saints et des bienheueux selon l'ordre du calendrier avec l'historique des fêtes* (Paris 1935–56) 4:69–72. G. JACQUEMET, *Catholicisme* 4:1094–95.

[B. F. SCHERER]

FAREL, GUILLAUME

Early French Protestant reformer; b. Gap, Dauphiné, 1489; d. Neuchâtel, Switzerland, Sept. 13, 1565. Farel's father was a notary and his background is similar to that of CALVIN, with whom his career as a reformer is later linked. Farel lived and studied in Paris from 1509 to 1521, and there became an ardent disciple of the famous humanist, LEFÈVRE D'ÉTAPLES. With Lefèvre he was a member of the reform circle at Meaux from 1521 to 1523. It was during these years that he adopted Luther's views on grace and justification. To avoid arrest as a heretic Farel left France in 1523 and went to Basel.

His aggressive zeal as a reformer and the complaint of Erasmus caused his expulsion from Basel in 1524. He then preached at Montbéliard where he wrote his most important work, the *Sommaire,* a brief declaration of faith. He went to Strasbourg in 1525, to Berne in late 1526, and on to Aigle, a Bernese dependency that became his center for the next few years. In 1530 he established Protestant reform in Neuchâtel. An initial visit to Geneva in 1532 was unsuccessful, but he returned there in December 1533, with Berne's support, to lay the foundations of Genevan Protestantism. It was Farel who, in July 1536, induced the young Calvin to remain in Geneva and help in the task. Both Farel and Calvin were expelled in 1538. Calvin later returned, but Farel, who had gone back to Neuchâtel, remained there as pastor till the end of his life.

Bibliography: COMITÉ FAREL, ed., *Guillaume Farel, 1489–1565* (Paris 1930), the most exhaustive study. J. DUTILLEUL, *Dictionnaire de théologie catholique*, ed. A. VACANT et al., (Paris 1903–50) 5.2:2081–90. Y. CONGAR, *Catholicisme* 4:1095–96.

[J. C. OLIN]

FAREMOUTIERS, ABBEY OF

Monastery of Benedictine nuns, located in the center of Brie, to the east of Paris, five and a half miles west of Coulommiers, France, in the Diocese of Meaux (patrons, Our Lady; St. Peter). It was founded (*c.* 627) by Agneric, steward of the King of Austrasia and an old friend of St. COLUMBAN, for his daughter FARA, who was made the first abbess under the direction of monks from LUXEUIL. The abbey enjoyed two periods of prosperity. The first, during the early Middle Ages, was marked by many saints: Fara herself, who trained Telchide, Abbess of JOUARRE-EN-BRIE; Fara's successor, Sedride, her half-sister; and ETHELBURGA, as well as the latter's niece, Ercongote. The abbess exercised seigneurial rights over the town formed around the abbey. In 1099 the community, which had grown lax, was reformed by the abbot of MARMOUTIER at the request of the king and IVO OF CHARTRES. During the 12th century the abbey counted 110 nuns. The buildings, destroyed by a fire in 1140, were rebuilt, and the new church was consecrated in 1145. At that time, seven priories were dependent upon Faremoutiers. Toward the end of the 15th century much-needed reform of the abbey by the bishop of Meaux was thwarted by the abbess, on grounds of the abbey's episcopal exemption. Later the reform of FONTEVRAULT was introduced (1518) by Marie Cornu, who arrived from CHELLES with 11 nuns. During the abbey's second period of prosperity, the abbesses, appointed by the king, were remarkable women: Françoise de la Châtre (d. 1643); her niece, Jeanne de Plas (d. 1677), a relative of Fénelon; Madame du Blé d'Uxelles (d. 1685), a friend of Bossuet, who delivered her funeral oration (now lost) and who corresponded with the nuns (150 letters are extant). During the French Revolution the monastery was abolished, the church and convent buildings destroyed. The property, however, was not parceled out. Bishop Gaillard of Meaux recovered possession of this property and on Nov. 5, 1931, restored Faremoutiers, with Benedictine nuns from the priory of Amillis, one of his earlier foundations (September 1924). Today Faremoutiers's community of 40 nuns under a prioress is a minor pontifical cloister. Besides the Divine Office and manual labor, the nuns do catechetical work, visit the poor and sick, and hold closed retreats.

Bibliography: T. DU PLESSIS, *Histoire de l'église de Meaux*, 2 v. (Paris 1731) v.1, *passim.* H. M. DELSART, *Ames saintes du grand siècle* (Maredsous 1931). *Sainte Fare et Faremoutiers: Treize siècles de vie monastique* (Faremoutiers 1957). *Dictionnaire d'histoire et de géographie ecclésiastiques*, ed. A. BAUDRILLART et al. (Paris 1912–), s.v. ''Faremoutiers.''

Umbrian fresco on exterior wall of Santa Maria di Farfa, Farfa Abbey, Lazio, Italy. (©Sandro Vannini/CORBIS)

[P. COUSIN]

FARFA, ABBEY OF

Former Benedictine abbey about 25 miles north of Rome in central Italy. Since 1919 it has been united to ST. PAUL-OUTSIDE-THE-WALLS, which has a group of monks in Farfa to care for the parish and a nearby college. Restoration of the abbey, a national monument since 1929, has brought to light Roman and medieval sections (frescoes of *c.* 700).

Founded on pagan buildings and dedicated to the Blessed Virgin by a bishop of Spoleto, Gregory the Syrian (4th or 6th century) or Lawrence (552–563), Farfa was destroyed by barbarians and restored (690) by St. THOMAS

OF FARFA (of Maurienne). Under Frankish abbots it was fortified; and, endowed by popes, dukes, kings, and emperors, its domain extended from Latium to the Marches. Charlemagne made it an imperial abbey, and its abbots frequented papal and royal courts. After NONANTOLA it was the richest abbey in Italy, with 683 churches and cloisters, 132 castles, two cities, 16 fortified towns, seven ports, and 315 villages. Saracens occupied it (891) and raided Sabina. Abbot Ratfred, who restored the community to the ruined abbey from their refuge in the Marches (940), was poisoned by monks impatient to enjoy the great riches. Hugh (997–1038) introduced the Cluniac reform and made the abbey a spiritual, intellectual, and economic center; his valuable writings generally illustrate a beneficial understanding between Church and State. Berard I completed the basilica, consecrated by Nicholas II (1060). The historian Gregory of Catina revived studies and developed the scriptorium.

Farfa lost importance with the decline of the Empire, with which it had sided in the investiture struggle. Eugene III was consecrated there (1145), Abbot Adinulfus somewhat restored its fortunes and Urban IV made it a *diocesis nullius* (1264); but the abbey's day had passed, and COMMENDATION (1400–1841) only hastened its ruin. Union with the Congregation of MONTE CASSINO (1567) revived it to a degree until it was suppressed by France (1798) and Italy (1862). Bl. Placido RICCARDI was rector of the basilica (1895–1912).

Bibliography: L. H. COTTINEAU, *Répertoire topobibliographique des abbayes et prieurés*, 2 v. (Mâcon 1935–39) 1:1107–09. I. SCHUSTER, *L'imperiale abbazia di Farfa* (Rome 1921). P. MARKTHALER, "Sulle recenti scoperte nell'abbazia imperiale di Farfa," *Revista di archeologia cristiana* 5 (1928) 37–88. G. PENCO, *Storia del monachesimo in Italia* (Rome 1961). J. ROUX, *Catholicisme. Hier, aujourd'hui et demain*, ed. G. JACQUEMET (Paris 1947–) 4:1098–1100. P. VOLK, *Lexikon für Theologie und Kirche*, ed. J. HOFER and K. RAHNER, 10 v. (2d, new ed. Freiburg 1957–65) 4:25–26.

[S. BAIOCCHI]

FARGES, ALBERT

Sulpician philosopher and theologian; b. Beaulieu, department of Corrèze, France, 1848; d. Beaulieu, June 9, 1926. Farges entered the Sulpician seminary in Paris and was ordained in 1872. After teaching in the seminaries of Bruges and Nantes, he filled the position of director of a seminary in Paris for 14 years. In 1896 he became professor of philosophy at the Institut Catholique in Paris and at the Sulpician seminary at Issy. He then became superior of the seminary in Angers.

Two of his works are an outgrowth of lectures in ascetical and mystical theology given at Angers between 1899 and 1905: *Les Phénomènes mystiques, distingués de leurs contrefaçons humaines et diaboliques* (Paris 1920) and *Les Voies ordinaires de la vie spirituelle* (Paris 1925). For both treatises his declared authorities are SS. Teresa and Thomas Aquinas. Farges' greatest contribution was in furthering the revival of Thomistic studies at the end of the 19th century. Under the general title *Études philosophiques pour vulgariser les théories d'Aristote et de S. Thomas et leur accord avec les sciences* (9 v. Paris 1885–1907) he produced a series of individual works devoted to the restoration of Thomism, for which he was highly praised by the French Academy and by Leo XIII. With a fellow Sulpician, Désiré Barbedette, Farges published a compendium of scholastic philosophy in French and Latin that had many editions.

Bibliography: P. POURRAT, *Catholicisme* 4:1100–01.

[M. S. CONLAN]

FARGO, DIOCESE OF

Suffragan of the Metropolitan See of Minneapolis-St. Paul, Minnesota, embracing the eastern part of North Dakota, an area of 35,786 square miles. The Diocese of Fargo *(Fargensis)* was established on Nov. 12, 1889, as the Diocese of Jamestown, but the see city was changed to Fargo, April 6, 1897. When the diocese was established, it embraced all of North Dakota, with about 19,000 Catholics, many of them Native American; 30 priests; 40 churches; one hospital; three parochial schools; and an academy for girls.

The first bishop, John Shanley, was consecrated on Dec. 27, 1889, and governed the new diocese under extreme missionary conditions. His episcopacy was characterized by efforts on behalf of the Native Americans, social reforms, and the movement for temperance. He founded and edited the *Bulletin of the Diocese of Fargo* and contributed an article of historical significance to the Collections of the State Historical Society of North Dakota. When he died on July 16, 1909, there were in the diocese 110 priests, 215 churches, 15 parochial schools, four Native American schools, six academies for girls, five hospitals, and an orphanage.

Prior to the appointment of James O'Reilly as second bishop of Fargo (1910–34), the western part of North Dakota was detached and established in 1910 as the Diocese of Bismarck. O'Reilly, consecrated on May 19, 1910, consolidated the work of his predecessor. Despite the years of drought and depression, which, toward the end of his life, brought many parishes to the brink of bankruptcy, O'Reilly established 34 new parishes and supervised the erection of 56 churches, 54 rectories, 24 schools, and seven hospitals.

On Aug. 10, 1935, Aloisius J. MUENCH was appointed bishop of Fargo and assumed charge of the diocese in the depths of the Depression. He organized the Catholic Church Expansion Fund to refinance mortgaged parishes and to provide credit for future parish development. Muench established the Confraternity of Christian Doctrine and founded *Catholic Action News*, a monthly diocesan newspaper. In 1941 he convened the first diocesan synod and published a Synodal Book of diocesan legislation. He established diocesan scholarships for needy seminarians and the Priests Mutual Aid Fund for sick, disabled, and retired priests. On the national scene he was active in the Catholic Rural Life Movement and the Catholic Central Union (Verein). In 1946 Muench was appointed apostolic visitator to Germany; he was granted the personal title of archbishop in 1950, appointed papal nuncio to Germany in 1951, and created cardinal priest and elevated to the Roman Curia on Dec. 14, 1959. With his appointment to the College of Cardinals, Muench resigned as bishop of Fargo.

During the absence of Muench in Germany, Leo F. Dworschak administered the affairs of the diocese as auxiliary bishop from 1947 to 1959 and succeeded to the see in 1960. During the early years of his episcopacy, ongoing construction of new churches, hospitals, and other Catholic institutions kept pace with the other dioceses in the U.S. Dworschak inaugurated a Diocesan Development Program (DDP) to support diocesan needs and ensure capital expansion. He was present at Vatican II and began the implementation of conciliar reforms in the diocese. Following the council, he established a Diocesan Pastoral Council. In 1969, he oversaw the construction of a high school and college seminary for the Diocese of Fargo that was dedicated in memory of his predecessor. Cardinal Muench Seminary was an ambitious project for a diocese of Fargo's size. In 1969, Dworschak and Bishop Hilary B. Hacker of Bismarck created the North Dakota Catholic Conference, which continues to serve as the liaison of the Catholic community to the political community of the North Dakota.

Upon the retirement of Bishop Dworschak in 1970, his successor, Justin A. Driscoll, was consecrated at Saint Mary's Cathedral, Fargo, on Oct. 28, 1970. Bishop Driscoll's initial responsibilities included the continuing implementation of the various initiatives of the Second Vatican Council. To improve the administration of the diocese, he expanded the number of deaneries from seven to nine. In accord with postconciliar decrees of Pope Paul VI, Driscoll created the first Priest Senate, later known as the Priest Council, in 1972. He instituted the Permanent Diaconate program in 1977 and took an interest in the Catholic press of the diocese, changing the title of the *Catholic Action News* to the *New Earth*. Bishop Driscoll's episcopal ministry came to an unexpected conclusion with his sudden death at an ecumenical conference on Nov. 19, 1984; he was 64.

During Holy Week of 1985, Bishop James S. Sullivan, auxiliary bishop of the Diocese of Lansing, was appointed the sixth bishop of Fargo. One of Sullivan's first duties as bishop was the implementation of the Code of Canon Law of 1983. Following the guidelines of the new Code, Bishop Sullivan commissioned the creation of an all-encompassing diocesan Policy Manual. Sullivan placed great emphasis on priestly vocations. At the peak of his vocational effort, nearly 50 men were studying for the priesthood. He was also responsible for organizing and presiding over the centennial celebrations for the Diocese of Fargo in 1989. Sullivan successfully completed an ambitious capital campaign to provide for the support of retired priests. In the early 1990s, he established the nationally recognized ''Opening Doors, Opening Hearts'' program in which every one of the diocese's 30,000 homes was visited by parish leaders.

Anticipating Sullivan's retirement, the Holy See announced the appointment of Samuel J. Aquila as coadjutor bishop of the Diocese of Fargo on June 17, 2001. Aquila, rector of Saint Vianney Seminary in Denver, Colorado, was consecrated at Saint Mary's Cathedral on August 24 and given charge of the administration of the diocese, thereby allowing Sullivan to assume a more spiritual and pastoral ministry to the people of the diocese. As Aquila began his episcopacy, 25 percent of the total population within the diocesan boundaries were Catholics, organized in 160 parishes administered by 120 priests. Aquila inherited the urgent need to address parish and priestly ministry in light of the rapid demographic shift from rural to urban areas prompted by significant changes in the agricultural economy.

Bibliography: L. PFALLER, *The Catholic Church in Western North Dakota, 1738–1960* (Mandan, ND 1960).

[G. M. WEBER/S. R. W. REISKE]

FARIBAULT PLAN

A compromise school agreement between the local clergy and the public school board in Faribault and Stillwater, Minn., involving the use of tax funds for church-related schools, long a crucial issue in American society. In 1890, to ease the financial burden of Catholics and with the approval of John IRELAND, Archbishop of St. Paul, the pastors of parishes in Faribault and Stillwater leased Catholic schools staffed by sisters to public authorities on an annual basis with renewal optional on the agreement of both parties. Each day the pupils assembled in the parish church for Mass and then proceeded to school to receive secular instruction. Religious instruction was given either before or after the legal public school day. The board of education controlled the secular schooling with the sole proviso that no text be used to which the local ordinary objected (*Civiltá Cattolica,* 1892).

While the Faribault Plan was not the first such experiment in the U.S. (*see* POUGHKEEPSIE PLAN), it stirred up considerable controversy and opposition from both Catholic and Protestant elements and attracted great attention throughout the nation for two reasons: (1) the Faribault and Stillwater communities were within the jurisdiction of the outspoken Archbishop Ireland, sponsor of the project; and (2) it inspired a pamphlet published in 1891 by Rev. Thomas Bouquillon, which aroused strong feelings in the Catholic communities because of its apparent departure from traditional Catholic philosophy (*see* BOUQUILLON CONTROVERSY).

Shortly before the publication of the Bouquillon pamphlet, Ireland had addressed a meeting of the National Education Association (NEA) at St. Paul in the summer of 1890. In his speech, while conceding to the state a right and duty to instruct, Ireland had argued that the exclusion of religion from the classroom would be destructive of religion itself and inimical to the interests of the nation. He then suggested a compromise plan similar to those in effect in England and Prussia or, if this proved to be impossible, an arrangement such as that of Poughkeepsie (NEA Report, 1890). It was the latter suggestion that received the greatest attention and resulted in the experiment being made in Faribault and Stillwater.

The publicity given to the Faribault Plan, however, raised the debate to new vehemence, and the matter was carried to Rome. On April 21, 1892, the Congregation for the Propragation of the Faith issued a decision expressed in words so susceptible to varying interpretations that it provided no solution (*American Ecclesiastical Review,* Suppl. 1892).

Two years later, the division of opinion among Catholics and the strong feelings aroused by the Bouquillon proposition prompted both Catholic and state authorities to terminate the Faribault experiment. Its discontinuance and, later, that of the Poughkeepsie Plan marked the cessation of efforts on the part of Catholic leadership to find a compromise solution to the church-related school financing problem.

While it would be interesting to speculate on what effect an adoption of the compromise at Faribault might have had on the history of American education and of the Church in America, the fact remains that Catholics became committed to the establishment and maintenance of a Catholic school system. Neverthless, although many elements characterizing the American scene at the time of Faribault and Poughkeepsie no longer endure, the controversy surrounding those plans are of import as Catholics debate the adoption of shared-time plans and augmented released-time programs.

Bibliography: J. A. BURNS, *The Growth and Development of the Catholic School System in the United States* (New York 1912). T. J. BOUQUILLON, *Education: To Whom Does It Belong?* (Baltimore 1892). J. H. MOYNIHAN, *The Life of Archhishop John Ireland* (New York 1953).

[O. C. D'AMOUR]

FARINA, GIOVANNI ANTONIO, BL.

Bishop of Vicenza and founder of the Institute of the Sisters Teachers of St. Dorothy, Daughters of the Sacred Heart; b. Gambellara, Vicenza, Italy, Jan.11, 1803; d. Vicenza, March 4, 1888.

Giovanni Antonio was the son of Pietro Farina and Francisca Bellame who entrusted his growth in the faith and education to his uncle, a priest. Farina entered the diocescan seminary at age 15. In 1827 he earned his teaching certificate and was ordained priest. Early in his career he taught in the diocesan seminary for 18 years, ministered in St. Peter's Parish for ten years, and directed the public schools. He founded the first school for the education of girls (1831) and the teaching Sisters of St. Dorothy (1836), who were dedicated to teaching them. The mission of the sisters was later expanded to include the education of the deaf and the blind, and care of the sick elderly. The Rule he wrote for the sisters, approved by Gregory XVI in 1839, remained in effect until 1905.

On January 19, 1851 Fr. Farina was consecrated bishop of Treviso and took as his motto: ''True science consists of the education of the heart, the fear of God.'' During his ten–year episcopacy he made regular pastoral visits, initiated associations in each parish for the care of the needy, propagated the practice of spiritual exercises, and himself participated in the formation of priests and laity. He himself ministered to the physical and spiritual needs of the sick, often taking his priests with him.

On June 18, 1860, he was transferred to the Diocese of Vicenza, where he initiated a renewal of the local Church that included the convocation of the first diocesan synod since 1689. In his efforts to shepherd his flock, he visited villages so remote that they were accessible only by foot or mule. His care for the poor is evidenced by the numerous confraternities he founded. Also notable are his participation in Vatican Council I, his conferral of ordination (1890) on Giuseppe Sarto (the future Pius X), and the patience with which he endured unjust accusations.

The bishop fell gravely ill in 1886 and never fully recovered prior to his death from a stroke. Farina was declared venerable on April 23, 2001. On July 7, 2001, Pope John Paul II approved the miracle necessary for beatification, which occurred on Nov. 4, 2001.

Bibliography: A. I. BASSANI, ed., *Il Vescovo Giovanni Antonio Farina e il suo Istituto nell'Ottocento veneto* (Rome 1988). G. A. CISOTTO, ed., *La visita pastorale di Giovanni Antonio Farina nella Diocesi di Vicenza* (Rome 1977).

[K. I. RABENSTEIN]

FARINGDON, HUGH, BL.

Benedictine priest, abbot of Reading, martyr; *vere* Cook; b. Faringdon (?), Berkshire, England; d. hanged, drawn, and quartered at Reading, Nov. 15, 1539. Hugh, who bore the arms of Cook of Kent, was elected abbot of Reading Abbey in July 1520. He was well-known to Henry VIII as demonstrated by his hosting of the king in January 1521, appointment as a royal chaplain, and receipt of a valuable white leather purse as a New Year's gift from the king in 1532. Faringdon was a member of Parliament (1523–39) when he signed the articles of faith (1536), which virtually acknowledge the royal supremacy. He even sang the Requiem Mass for Queen Jane Seymour (Nov. 4, 1537) and was present for her burial (November 12). Despite these and other signs of a close relationship with the king, he was charged with high treason upon refusing to surrender Reading to the king (1539). Despite his position as a mitred abbot, Chancellor Thomas Cromwell passed Faringdon's death sentence before his trial began. He was executed with BB. John Eynon and John RUGG. He was beatified by Pope Leo XIII on May 13, 1895.

Feast of the English Martyrs: May 4 (England); Dec. 1 (Dioceses of Portsmouth and Westminster; English Benedictines).

See Also: ENGLAND, SCOTLAND, AND WALES, MARTYRS OF.

Bibliography: B. CAMM, ed., *Lives of the English Martyrs,* (New York 1904), I, 338–87. R. CHALLONER, *Memoirs of Missionary Priests,* ed. J. H. POLLEN (rev. ed. London 1924; repr. Farnborough 1969). J. H. POLLEN, *Acts of English Martyrs* (London 1891).

[K. I. RABENSTEIN]

FARLATI, DANIELE

Jesuit church historian; b. San Daniele del Friuli, Italy, Feb. 22, 1690; d. Padua, April 25, 1773. Farlati was admitted into the Society of Jesus at Bologna in 1707. After teaching humanities at the Jesuit college in Padua, he was sent to Rome to complete his theological studies and was ordained there in 1722. He returned to Padua and collaborated with Filippo Riceputi, SJ, on the history of the Church in Illyria. After 20 years of research and with 300 volumes of collected manuscript material, they began their writing. At Riceputi's death in 1742, Farlati was assisted by Giacomo Coleti, SJ. The first volume of the *Illyricum sacrum* was printed at Venice in 1751; while the fifth volume was in press, Farlati died. Coleti completed the work with the eighth volume. In 1910 F. Bulĭc published the *Accessiones et collectiones all' Illyricum sacrum del P. G. Coleti.*

John Cardinal Farley. (©Corbis)

Bibliography: A life of Farlati appears in *Illyricum sacrum* by G. COLETI, v.5 (Venice 1775) vii–xi. C. SOMMERVOGEL et al., *Bibliothéque de la Compagnie de Jésus* (Brussels–Paris 1890–1932) 13:546–547. M. MORSELLETO, A. MERCATI and A. PELZER, *Dizionario ecclesiastico* (Turin 1954–58) 1:1068.

[E. D. MCSHANE]

FARLEY, JOHN MURPHY

Cardinal, fourth archbishop of New York; b. County Armagh, Ireland, Apr. 20, 1842; d. New York, NY, Sept.

17, 1918. John was the fourth and youngest child of Philip and Catherine (Murphy) Farrelly, who died when he was very young. His maternal uncle, Patrick Murphy, had immigrated to New York in 1830 and, prospering in the furniture business, had become interested in educating a nephew for the priesthood. John wrote asking for the opportunity and was trained in the local schools and at St. Macartan's College, Monaghan, the preparatory seminary of the Diocese of Clogher. In 1864 he went to New York and entered Fordham College (University) as a junior. In 1865 he entered St. Joseph's Seminary, Troy, NY, and was sent to the North American College, Rome, in 1866. He was ordained in Rome for the Archdiocese of New York on June 11, 1870, by Cardinal Constantine Patrizi.

On his return to New York he was appointed curate at St. Peter's parish, Staten Island, and remained there until July 1872 when he became secretary to Cardinal John MCCLOSKEY, whom he had met during VATICAN COUNCIL I (1869–70). At this time he changed the spelling of his name from Farrelly to Farley. During the next 30 years, Farley played an important part in the affairs of the archdiocese and moved steadily up the administrative ladder. He was secretary from 1872 until 1884 and vicar general of the archdiocese from 1891 to 1902. In the latter period he was also pastor of St. Gabriel's parish. He became a papal chamberlain in 1884, a domestic prelate in 1892, prothonotary apostolic and titular bishop of Zeugma, successively, in 1895; he was consecrated on Dec. 21, 1895, by Abp. Michael A. CORRIGAN. Finally, on Sept. 25, 1902, he became the fourth archbishop of New York and, on Nov. 27, 1911, cardinal priest with the title church of Santa Maria sopra Minerva.

Two-thirds of Farley's priestly life was spent in close association with McCloskey and Corrigan, whose personalities and careers greatly influenced his own. He admired both, but modeled himself on McCloskey. His dominant traits were caution and the love of peace. The wounds left by the MCGLYNN affair were healed as far as possible.

Farley was the first American ordinary to distribute papal honors widely among those of his clergy who did not hold high administrative posts. He was a pleasing speaker with a wide range of interests, was fluent in French and Italian, and read Spanish. During his administration the number of parochial schools in the archdiocese doubled. He was a friend of The Catholic University of America and a supporter of higher education for women. He was also a patron of the old *Catholic Encyclopedia.* He continued his predecessor's interest in St. Joseph's Seminary, the major seminary of the archdiocese, and carried out his plans for the minor seminary, Cathedral College, which he opened in 1903. He supported the Propagation of the Faith with enthusiasm and welcomed the founders of the Catholic Foreign Mission Society of America (Maryknoll) to New York in 1911. He wrote two books, *The History of St. Patrick's Cathedral* (1908), and *The Life of John Cardinal McCloskey* (1918). He died of pneumonia in 1918 and was buried in St. Patrick's Cathedral.

Bibliography: M. J. LAVELLE, ''John Cardinal Farley, Archbishop of New York,'' *American Ecclesiastical Review* 60 (1919) 113–125. A. J. SHIPMAN, *His Eminence, John, Cardinal Farley* (New York 1912).

[F. D. COHALAN]

FARMER, FERDINAND

Missionary; b. Weissenstein, Württemberg, Germany, Oct. 13, 1720; d. Philadelphia, Pa., Aug. 17, 1786. As Ferdinand Steinmeyer, he abandoned the study of medicine to enter the Society of Jesus at Landsberg in 1743. Ordained about 1750, he was first assigned to China. When the Jesuits in the British colonies in America appealed to the German Jesuit Province for priests to serve the numerous German immigrants in Pennsylvania, Steinmeyer was reassigned to America. He landed in the New World in 1752 and established himself in Lancaster, Pa., as Father Ferdinand Farmer. Using Lancaster as his headquarters, he traveled constantly through eastern Pennsylvania and ministered to all Catholics, serving existing congregations and forming new ones.

In 1758 he transferred his headquarters permanently to old St. Joseph's Church in Philadelphia, continuing his constant missionary journeys, not only in Pennsylvania and Delaware, but also in New Jersey. By the time of the Revolutionary War, he had reached the borders of New York and may have entered New York City. When the British army occupied Philadelphia in 1777, he extended his spiritual ministrations to the Hessian regiments. However, when British headquarters endeavored to raise a regiment of Catholic volunteers and sought to enlist Farmer as their chaplain, he refused.

After the British evacuation in 1778, Farmer extended his missionary expeditions across the Hudson River and gathered the first Catholic congregation in New York City. He had a lifelong interest in natural science, and as an early member of the American Philosophical Society, he corresponded with scholars in Europe. In 1779 he was elected a trustee of the University of Pennsylvania. He is sometimes called the father of the Church in New Jersey and in New York.

Bibliography: J. M. DALEY, ''Pioneer Missionary,'' *Woodstock Letters,* 75 (1946) 103–115, 207–231, 311–321. J. F. QUIRK,

''Father Ferdinand Farmer,'' *Historical Records and Studies of the U. S. Catholic Historical Society of New York* 6.2 (1912) 235–248.

[F. X. CURRAN]

FARNBOROUGH PRIORY

Benedictine priory under PRINKNASH, 37 miles southwest of London, in Hampshire, England; dedicated to St. Michael; it was formerly an abbey in the SOLESMES congregation (1903–47). Empress Eugénie, in residence at Farnborough Hill from 1881, built the neo-Gothic St. Michael Church (1886–87) as a mausoleum for Napoleon III (d. 1873) and their son Prince Louis (slain in the Zulu War 1879). Eugénie was buried there in 1920. French Premonstratensians were replaced as custodians of the shrine by Benedictines of Solesmes (1895). The conventual buildings were completed by 1911. Fernand CABROL, Henri LECLERCQ, Marius FÉROTIN, and André WILMART were among the scholars of Farnborough who produced the *Dictionnaire d'archéologie chrétienne et de liturgie* and other works. After World War I the abbey declined because of the lack of English and French novices. In 1947 the French monks withdrew and were replaced by monks from Prinknash.

Bibliography: R. GAZEAU, *Catholicisme* 4:1103–04. A. SCHMITT, *Lexikon für Theologie und Kirche*, ed. J. HOFER and K. RAHNER, 10 v. (2d, new ed. Freiburg 1957–65) 4:27.

[J. STÉPHAN]

FARNE

Also called Farneland or The Inner Farne, it is the largest of a group of 15 islands near Bamburgh (Northumberland). Its poverty and bleak solitude made it a suitable home of hermit saints. St. AIDAN (d. 651) was its first recorded inhabitant. St. CUTHBERT of Lindisfarne, northern England's most popular saint, lived on Farne (676–684) and died there (687). Parts of the island bear his name as do the island's eider ducks. Farne was deserted during the Danish invasions, but was restored by Edulf of Lindisfarne and occupied by monks of Durham, notably St. Bartholomew of Farne (1151–93). It was made a cell of Durham (1255) and was occupied until the Reformation. It is now a bird and seal sanctuary.

Bibliography: BEDE, *Historia ecclesiastica gentis Anglorum*, ed. C. PLUMMER (1955) 3:16; 4:27–30. GEOFFREY, ''Vita Bartholomaei Farnensis,'' *Symeonis Monachi Opera Omnia*, ed. T. ARNOLD, *Rerum Britannicarum medii aevi scriptores* (New York 1964—) 75.1:295–325. A. WATKIN, ''Farne Island and St. Cuthbert,'' *Downside Review* 70 (1952) 292–307.

[H. FARMER]

Benedictine Monks sing during Blessing of the Silkworm service, Farnborough, Hampshire, England. (©Hulton-Deutsch Collection/CORBIS)

FARNESE

Important Italian family, which, from the late 12th century until 1731 when it became extinct, included Pope Paul III, five cardinals, and the dukes of Parma and Piacenza, notably Alessandro. This family, which became the ducal family of Parma, was neither rich nor important until the early 15th century. Before that the Farnese served Viterbo, Orvieto, and other towns as generals and were always loyal to the papacy. *Pietro II* fought for the GUELFS against Emperor Henry VI, *Pietro III* against Henry VII. *Guido* was bishop of Orvieto from 1302 to 1328.

Ranuccio (d. 1460?) moved to Rome and became senator in 1417 and later general of Pope Eugene IV. The family gained prestige through the fiefs he acquired and through the marriages of his children into the oldest families of Rome. His eldest son, *Pierluigi,* married into the GAETANI family, and his son *Alessandro* was the first cardinal in the family (1493), later becoming Pope PAUL III (1534–49). Paul gave his natural but legitimatized son *Pierluigi* (d. 1547) and his family properties and offices. Pierluigi became duke of Castro and flagbearer of the Church. Two of Pierluigi's sons were created cardinals; *Ottavio,* another son, received Camerino, and his brother

The main portal of the Farnese palace in Rome, designed and built by Antonio da Sangallo the Younger, 1534. Above the balcony is the coat of arms of Pope Paul III. (Alinari-Art Reference/Art Resource, NY)

Orazio was prefect of Rome. Ottavio's marriage with Margaret, the natural daughter of Emperor CHARLES V, was the first international marriage of the Farnese. The family's greatest honor came in 1545 when the pope, after the approval of a consistory, bestowed Parma and Piacenza on Pierluigi with the rank of duke and with right of succession. This marked the end of the old Farnese loyalty to the papacy; Farnese dynastic considerations henceforth came first. From 1545 to 1547, when Duke Pierluigi restricted his nobles, Don Ferrante Gonzaga, Charles V's governor in Milan, encouraged them to rebel. The nobles assassinated Pierluigi, and Don Ferrante occupied Piacenza. Hence Pierluigi's son Ottavio (d. 1586) did not succeed immediately when the duke died in 1547. Instead, the pope, his grandfather, sent Camillo Orsini to govern Parma; Piacenza stayed in the imperialists' hands. In 1550 the new pope JULIUS III restored Parma to Ottavio, but when Ottavio joined with King Henry II of France against the emperor (and the pope), the pope once more deprived him of the duchy. However, French military successes forced Julius to recognize Ottavio as ruler of Parma in 1552. Piacenza was restored to him in 1557; the influence of his wife, Margaret of Parma, and that of her half-brother, King PHILIP II of Spain, was of assistance. Ottavio began the building of the huge Farnese palaces in Piacenza and in Parma. Ottavio's son and successor, *Alessandro* (d. 1592), was the most able member of the ducal family. He had already won a name for himself as a general and governor of the Netherlands for his uncle, Philip II, when he became duke of Parma and Piacenza. He remained in the Spanish Netherlands and never ruled personally in Parma.

His son, Duke *Ranuccio I* (d. 1622), contracted such large debts that his duchy began to decline. *Odoardo* (d. 1646) was ten when his father died, and so his uncle, Cardinal *Odoardo,* served as regent. In time Duke Odoardo proved ambitious. He wished to add Lombardy to his possessions but failed in the attempt. As proud as he was ambitious, he treated the BARBERINI, the nephews of Pope URBAN VIII, with disdain when he visited Rome, and the war for Castro followed. Although he won the war and kept Castro, his debts added a burden to his duchy. *Ranuccio II* (d. 1694) was 16 when he succeeded his father. His uncle, Cardinal *Francesco Maria,* and his mother were regents. In Mazarin's quarrel with Pope INNOCENT X the duke supported France and lost Castro, which became a part of the States of the Church. Duke *Francesco Maria* (d. 1727) succeeded Ranuccio. His brother *Antonio* (d. 1731) was the last duke.

There were five Farnese cardinals (the first date given being that of their cardinalate): *Alessandro* (1534–89), the son of Duke Pierluigi, held several offices; he was vice chancellor in 1535, legate to both Emperor Charles V and King Francis I (1539–41), and to Charles V (1543). He resembled his grandfather, Paul III, in being a great builder. The cardinal completed the Farnese palace, built the Gesù, purchased and completed the Chigi villa, which was renamed the Farnesina, and built the palace at Caprarola. He made the Farnese palace a meeting place in Rome for persons interested in art and literature. *Ranuccio* (1545–65), another son of Duke Pierluigi, was noted for his interest in learning and served as legate in the Marches. *Odoardo* (1591–1626), the son of Duke Alessandro, served as legate in Parma for 20 years and as a member of the first Congregation for the PROPAGATION OF THE FAITH (1622). He built the sacristy of the Gesù. Ludwig von PASTOR described him as one of the outstanding cardinals in 1622 (*see* GREGORY XV). *Francesco Maria* was cardinal from 1645 to 1647. *Girolamo* (1657–68) was nuncio in Switzerland, governor of Rome, and majordomo of Pope ALEXANDER VII before he became a cardinal.

Bibliography: G. MORONI, *Dizionario de erudizione storico-ecclesastica*, 103 v. in 53 (Venice 1840–61) 23:193–215. P. LITTA et al., *Famiglie celebri italiane,* 14 v. (Milan 1819–1923), v.5. L. CALLARI, *I palazzi di Roma* (3d ed. Rome 1944) 212–229. J.

WODKA, *Lexikon für Theologie und Kirche*, ed. J. HOFER and K. RAHNER, 10 v. (2d, new ed. Freiburg 1957–65) 4:27–28.

[M. L. SHAY]

FARO OF MEAUX, ST.

Bishop; d. *c.* 672. He was of Burgundian origin, hence his name Burgundofaro. His sister, St. FARA, founded the double abbey of FAREMOUTIERS. Faro himself had married, but when about 35 years old he determined to embrace the Benedictine life, probably persuaded by his sister. His wife pursued a similar course. Shortly after receiving Holy Orders, he was chosen bishop of Meaux, where he labored many years for the conversion and salvation of souls. The *Vita s. Fari*, written 200 years after his death by Bishop Hildegar of Meaux, is of no great historical value. Likewise, a ballad *Cantilène de Saint Faron*, which has given rise to considerable literature, is without historical foundation. But there are sufficient reliable sources attesting to Faro's existence and work.

Feast: Oct. 28.

Bibliography: *Acta Sanctorum* Oct. 12:593–623. J. MABILLON, *Acta sanctorum ordinis S. Benedicti* (Venice 1733–40) 2:580–598. *Monumenta Germaniae Scriptores rerum Merovingicarum* (Berlin 1825–) 171–203. *Bibliotheca hagiographica latina antiquae ct mediae aetatis* (Brussels 1898–1901) 1:2825–31. J. L. BAUDOT and L. CHAUSSIN, *Vies des saints et des bienheueux selon l'ordre du calendrier avec l'historique des fêtes* (Paris 1935–56) 10:941–945. A. BUTLER, *The Lives of the Saints*, ed. H. THURSTON and D. ATTWATER (New York 1956–) 4:216–217.

[O. L. KAPSNER]

FARRELL, WALTER

Theologian, lecturer, writer; b. Chicago, Ill., July 21, 1902; d. River Forest, Ill., Nov. 23, 1951. Following his education in Chicago at parochial schools and at Quigley Preparatory Seminary, he entered the Dominican Order at Saint Joseph's Priory, Somerset, Ohio, on Sept. 14, 1920. He studied philosophy at St. Rose Priory, Springfield, Ky., and theology at the Dominican House of Studies, Washington, D.C., where he was ordained on June 9, 1927. After obtaining the S.T.Lr. degree in 1928, he pursued graduate studies at the University of Fribourg, Switzerland, from which he received his S.T.D. in 1930. After returning to the U.S., he was professor of dogmatic theology at Somerset until 1933, when he was transferred to the Dominican House of Studies, Washington, D.C. He was appointed regent of studies of the Province of St. Joseph in 1939; the following year he went to Rome and, after a lengthy examination in theology, won the degree of master in sacred theology, the highest honor granted by the Dominican Order. That same year, he was named president of the pontifical faculty of theology at the Dominican House of Studies, Washington, D.C. During World War II, Farrell was a chaplain in the U.S. Navy, serving over a year on the carrier U.S.S. *Yorktown.* Upon leaving the service in 1945, he was assigned to the Dominican House of Studies, River Forest, in the Province of St. Albert the Great. Farrell, an active retreat-master and preacher, was also one of the first lecturers in the Thomist Association, which provided courses in theology for the laity. He helped to launch the *Thomist,* a quarterly speculative review, in April 1939, and contributed frequently to it and to other leading Catholic journals. His best known work was *A Companion to the Summa,* the four volumes of which were published from 1938 to 1942. After his death, his nearly completed life of Christ, together with selections from his earlier writings, was published under the title of *Only Son* (1953).

Bibliography: R. E. BRENNAN, ''Walter Farrell, O.P., Apud Posteros Sacer,'' *The Thomist* (1952) 199–208. R. M. COFFEY, ''The Very Reverend Walter Farrell, O.P., S.T.M.,'' *American Ecclesiastical Review* 126 (1952) 271–278.

[T. C. DONLAN]

FASANI, FRANCESCO ANTONIO, ST.

Baptized Donato Antonio Giovanni Nicolò, known in religion as Francis Antony of Lucera, also called ''Padre Maestro,'' Franciscan priest; b. Aug. 6, 1681, Lucera, Apulia, Italy; d. there Nov. 29, 1742. He was the son of Giuseppe Fasani, a farmer, and Isabella della Monica. After Giuseppe's death (*c.* 1691), Isabella married a man who provided for 'Giovanniello's education. He entered the Conventual Franciscan novitiate at Monte Sant'Angelo Gargano (Foggia) on Aug. 23, 1695, and made his solemn profession one year later. Thereafter he studied literature and philosophy at Venafro (Isernia), Alvito (Frosinone), Montella (Avellino), and Aversa (Caserta), and theology at Agnone (Isernia). Following his ordination at the tomb of St. Francis of Assisi in 1705, he earned a doctorate in theology in Rome (1709), taught theology at the College of St. Bonaventure, then philosophy at St. Francis Convent, Lucera. In addition to his renown as a teacher, Fasani gained a reputation as a lucid preacher, spiritual director, and minister, especially among prisoners and the poor. He served in many offices: guardian at S. Rocco ad Alberona (Foggia, 1709–12) and Lucera (1712–15; 1739–42), and master of novices (Lucera, 1723–29), as well as provincial of Sant'Angelo Province (1720–23). He was known for his simplicity, humility, charity, fidelity to the Franciscan Rule and the spirit of its founder, and devotion to the Immaculate Conception. He composed novenas, including some of the first to the Immaculate Conception, meditations, sermons, Marian hymns, and a pamphlet on the attributes of God. The body of the saint is enshrined under the altar of Lucera's church dedicated to St. Francis. Fasani was beatified in 1951, and canonized by Pope John Paul II on April 13, 1986.

Feast: Nov. 27 (Franciscans).

Bibliography: Works by St Francesco Fasani: *Le 7 Novene Mariane*, ed. F. COSTA (Padua 1986). *Mariale, interpretazione allegorico–spirituale del Cantico dei Cantici*, ed. F. COSTA (Padua 1986). *Il Padre Nostro (Expositio brevis)*, ed. E. GALIGNANO, tr. A. TOLVE and V. PERGOLA (Italian tr. of Fasani's commentary on the Our Father) (Lucera 1996). Literature about St. Francesco Fasani: *Compendium vitae virtum et miraculorum necnon actorum in causa canonizationis beati Francisci A. Fasani, sacerdotis ordinis fratrum minorum conventualium* (Rome 1985). *L'Osservatore Romano,* Eng. ed., no. 16 (1986): 3. A. ANGELINI, *Predestinata!* (Terni, Italy 1968). G. DE ANGELIS, *Prodigio di un sorriso* (Lucera 1991). L. M. BERARDINI, *Il Beato Francesco Antonio Fasani* (Rome 1951). R. COLAPIETRA, *Da Masaniello a Carlo di Borbone, I Convegno Nazionale di Studi su San Francesco A. Fasani* (Lucera 1989). L. DI FONZO, *L'immagine di S. Francesco nei Sermoni e nella vita del Fasani* (Bari 1986); *Santo di Lucera, Profilo cronologico di S. Francesco A. Fasani* (Bari 1986). I. DI GIOVINE, *San Francesco A. Fasani* (Lucera 1989). G. GUASTAMACCHIA, *Il bel San Francesco. La Chiesa del Padre Maestro*, ed. G. PREZIUSO (Lucera 1973). M. MARSICO, *Profilo storico e spirituale di San Francesco A. Fasani* (Rome 1986). B. NONNI, *Francesco Antonio Fasani dei Frati Minori Conventuali* (Lucera 1985). A. ORSITTO, *Il Santo dei poveri* (Lucera 1986). G. STANO, *La stella di Lucera* (Frigento, Italy 1986). T. TOLVE, *Padre Maestro: il cammino dell'amore* (Lucera 1987). G. TRINCUCCI, *Un Santo e la sua città* (Foggia 1988). R. ZAVALLONI, "San Francesco educatore," in *Pedagogia e vita* (Rome 1980). P. ZOLLA, *San Francesco A. Fasani* (Lucera 1986).

[K. I. RABENSTEIN]

FASCE, MARIA TERESA, BL.

Abbess of the Order of Saint Augustine; baptized Marietta; b. Dec. 27, 1881, Torriglia (near Genoa), Italy; d. Jan. 18, 1947, Cascia (near Perugia), Italy. Born into a wealthy family, Teresa served as a catechist in the Augustinian parish of Our Lady of Consolation, Genoa, where she became acquainted with the order's spirituality and captivated by the life of St. RITA OF CASCIA (canonized 1900 when Teresa was 19) Fasce joined the community in June 1906 and professed her vows the following year. She received permission for exclaustration (right to live outside the community) to reflect on her vocation. After ten months with her family, she returned (1911) with a determination to renew the community. Thereafter she professed her solemn vows (1912) and served St. Rita's as novice mistress (1914–17), vicar (1917–20), and abbess (1920–47). She took in orphaned girls whom she called her little bees, which thus gave rise to the name of the orphanage, St. Rita's Hive, which is located next to the church. Fasce worked to relieve suffering in the area. Additionally, she helped to build a new church and nearby an Augustinian seminary, a hospital, and a retreat house. During World War II she courageously and repeatedly opposed the Nazis by denying them access to the convent and those under her protection. Her activity obscures her deeply contemplative vocation, which she encouraged within the community. She wrote the bulletin *Dalle api alle rose* (*From Bees to Roses*) from 1923 in order to spread devotion to St. Rita. Thereafter many pilgrims visited St. Rita's tomb. Mother Maria Teresa died peacefully after suffering for years from a breast tumor, diabetes, and various cardiac and circulatory problems, and was buried in the crypt of St. Rita's Basilica next to her patroness. She was beatified by Pope John Paul II on Oct. 12, 1997.

Feast: Jan. 18.

Bibliography: *Acta Apostolicae Sedis,* no. 20 (1997): 999. *L'Osservatore Romano,* Eng. ed., no. 29 (1995): 5; no. 42 (1997): 1, 2, 11. A. ANGELINI, *Predestinata!* (Terni, Italy 1968).

[K. I. RABENSTEIN]

FAST AND ABSTINENCE

Fasting is here understood as the complete or partial abstention from food, abstinence as the abstention from the eating of meat of certain meat products, when the restraint is undertaken as a religious practice or in accordance with ecclesiastical custom or law. Neither fast nor abstinence is to be confused with the virtue of abstinence, which is a subjective part of temperance that controls the desire and the use of food, although both can be acts of that virtue.

In The Bible. The Biblical concept of fasting embraced both partial and total abstinence from food and drink. The abstention from certain classes of foods that was regulated by dietary law did not fall within the ambit of fasting. The noun used for the term "fast" in the OT was *ṣôm,* a derivative of the verb *ṣûm,* to fast. Such phrases as "not to eat bread" (2 Sm 12.17) and "to mortify oneself" (literally: "to bow down one's soul," Lv 16.29) came into common usage with the Priestly Code and were widely used in post-Biblical Hebrew. Both the Septuagint and the NT employed the verb νηστεύειν to designate fasting as a religious or pious practice. The cognate noun νηστεία was used almost exclusively to denote religious fasting.

Little is known regarding the origin of fasting in Israel. The custom was ancient before it entered legislation.

It appears to have been practiced for a variety of religious motives, especially in times of calamity (in order to give force to prayers for deliverance) and of mourning (1 Sm 7.6; Jl 1.14; Jgs 20.26; 2 Chr 20.3; 1 Kgs 21.9). The Mosaic Law established only one day of fasting, the great Day of ATONEMENT (Lv 16.29–34; Nm 29.7). After the Exile four special days of fasting were added (Zec 8.19).

Christian Practice. Following the examples of Christ (Mt 6.16; Mk 2.20; 9.29) and the Apostles (Acts 13.2; 14.23; 2 Cor 2.27), the earliest Christians practiced both fast and abstinence. In early centuries regular weekly fasts were practiced on Wednesday and Friday (DIDACHE), and abstinence from certain foods, especially flesh meats, was established. The observance of the Friday abstinence in commemoration of the Passion and death of Our Lord was common in both the Eastern and Western Church (Clement of Alexandria, *Stromata*, 6.75; Tertullian, *De jejunio*, 14). Throughout the history of the Church, law and custom regarding fast and abstinence were subject to local variations, both as to the times observed and as to the quantity and quality of food permitted.

In the Western Church. About 400 the Wednesday fast was replaced by that of Saturday, which had come to be regarded also as a day of abstinence, The observance of Lent was of early origin, and the vigil fasts before great feasts, the Ember days, and rogation days eventually came to be observed.

Following the custom of the Jews under the old law, Christians first practiced fasting by abstaining from all food until after sunset or after the recitation of Vespers, when the day's meal would be taken. About the 9th century it began to be customary in some places to take the day's meal after the recitation of None, or about 3 P.M. It had been the custom on days of fasting to say Mass only after the hour of None. This order of the Office was retained, but to make allowance for new customs of fasting the hours of Vespers and None were anticipated, and this led to the celebration of Mass earlier in the day. In the 12th century the custom of breaking one's fast at the hour of None everywhere prevailed, and by the 13th century the practice of taking the meal as early as noon was common.

As the time of the day's meal became earlier and earlier, the exhaustion at the end of the day's labor, unrelieved by the refreshment of food, became more burdensome. In the monasteries, where the days of fasting were much more numerous and where the practice of mid-day meal had also been established, the monks had much earlier distinguished between days of fast prescribed by monastic rule and those observed by the Church. On days of monastic but not Church fast the monks were allowed a slight repast or ''collation'' to be taken during the evening conference (in Latin called *collatio* because the readings were frequently taken from the *Collationes* of Cassian). At first the monastic collation was only a small measure of wine, but later a morsel of bread was added. Monastic practice thus provided the example for general custom. By the 13th century taking something to drink apart from the day's meal was a generally accepted practice, and by the end of the 14th century it was common custom to take a collation of bread, vegetables, or fruit at the end of the day. This collation, however, was never understood to be of sufficient quantity to constitute a normal meal. About the 16th century a very light breakfast was approved. It was understood that at the collation not more than eight ounces of solid food were to be eaten, and at breakfast not more than about two ounces.

Fasting meant not only the observance of the requirements of custom with regard to the quantity of food and the time when it could be eaten, but also abstinence from certain types of food, particularly flesh meat and meat products. Days of fasting were thus days of abstinence although other days might be marked for the observance of abstinence alone. The laws regarding abstinence, like those of fasting, were of unwritten origin and were always subject to variations in custom in time and place. In the early Church abstinence meant refraining from flesh meat and all meat products, including milk, eggs, butter, and cheese. Fish or mollusks, however, were not generally considered to be a form of meat or to fall under the prohibition of abstinence. As early as the 9th century milk, eggs, and milk products began to be exempted either by the force of local custom or by repeated dispensation.

In the Eastern Church. From the earliest times, Wednesday and Friday of each week were observed as days of abstinence in the Greek Church. Other days and seasons were added in the course of time. The major Lent goes back to the 2nd century. In the 4th century it was spoken of as the ''holy forty'' (days), but at some times and in certain places it was a much more extended period. In addition to the great, or major, Lent, three other ''Lents'' have been observed in the Eastern Church: the Lent of the holy Apostles (June 16–28); Mary's Lent (August 1–14); and the Lent preceding Christmas (November 15–December 24). These three minor Lents did not become obligatory before the 8th century; thence to the faithful. Days observed by fasting and abstinence have been numerous in the East; in the Greek Church the total has been as high as 180 in the course of a year.

The practice of abstinence was especially prevalent among the early hermits of the East. St. Anthony and his followers abstained from all food except bread, salt, and water—a practice continued by Pachomius and the Egyptian monks. Monastic fasting and abstinence tended to be extremely rigorous in the East, and this severity had its influence on observance that came to be expected of the faithful. The law of abstinence is referred to as xerophagy, the eating of dry food. In older times on days of abstinence meat and meat products (milk, butter, cheese, eggs), fish, oil, and wine were forbidden. This traditional custom of severe abstinence is still observed by some of the faithful. Rigorous periods of abstinence were often preceded by a week of mitigated abstinence.

In more modern times fast and abstinence in the Eastern Church is often found to be the same both for Churches in union with Rome and for separated Churches.

General Law and U.S. Practice. Until 1917 the general law of the Western Church required the faithful to fast on all the days of Lent except Sunday; on Wednesday, Fridays, and Saturdays of the Ember weeks; and on the vigils of Christmas, Pentecost, Assumption, and All Saints. By custom in many places the Wednesdays and Fridays of Advent were also fast days. By fasting was understood the taking of only one meal a day with abstinence from meat, eggs, and milk products. Moreover, fish was not to be taken along with meat at a meal allowing meat, that is, on the Sundays of Lent, or on normal fast days by those who were otherwise dispensed from meat abstinence. Abstinence without fast was observed on all Fridays and Saturdays throughout the year.

Local dispensations often mitigated these general prohibition. In the U.S. the bishops obtained a number of dispensations. The fathers of the Third Provincial Council of Baltimore in 1837 obtained a dispensation from the custom of fasting on the Wednesdays and Fridays of Advent; and in 1840 the Fourth Provincial Council of Baltimore asked that an indult dispensing from the Saturday abstinence that had been granted for 10 years be made perpetual. Gregory XVI renewed the dispensation for 20 years.

The fathers of the Second Plenary Council of Baltimore in 1866 asked that all dispensations that had been granted to the Province of Baltimore be extended to all other dioceses. However, Pius IX preferred to have the individual bishops seek the indults they needed and give their reasons. Since the Third Plenary Council of Baltimore in 1884 decided that it would be very difficult to pass any uniform legislation on the subject of fast and abstinence, it was left to the individual bishops to determine in provincial councils what seemed best for their territories.

In 1886 Leo XIII granted to all the bishops of the U.S. for 10 years the faculty to dispense each year from the Saturdays abstinence. He also approved a Lenten indult for the U.S. that permitted the taking of meat, eggs, and milk products at all meals on the Sundays of Lent and at the principal meal on Monday, Tuesday, Thursday, and Saturday. Holy Saturday and the Saturdays of Ember weeks were excepted. Fish and meat were never allowed at the same meal, even on Sundays. The use of eggs and milk products at the evening collation and at the principal meal on days when meat was not allowed was permitted. A small piece of bread in the morning could be taken with coffee, tea, chocolate, or any similar beverage. It was permissible to invert the order of the principal meal when this could not be taken at noon. Lard and meat drippings could be used in the preparation of foods. Finally, the faithful who were exempt from the law of fasting could, when the use of meat, eggs, and milk products was permitted, eat such foods more than once a day just as all were permitted to do on the Sundays of Lent when the obligation of fasting did not bind.

In constant use until 1951 was the workingmen's privilege. This was originally granted for 10 years in 1895 and empowered the bishops in the U.S. to permit the use of flesh meat in those circumstances if place and person in which they judged that the common law of abstinence could not be observed without real difficulty. This concession benefited not only the individual workingman but applied also to his family.

In 1917 Benedict XV granted the privilege of transferring abstinence from the Saturdays of Lent to any other day of the week except Ash Wednesday and the Fridays of Lent. In 1941 Pius XII granted to all the bishops of the world the power to dispense entirely from fast and abstinence except on Ash Wednesday and Good Friday. Some restrictions on this faculty were imposed by the Holy See in 1949—namely, that abstinence must be observed on all Fridays of the year; fast and abstinence, on Ash Wednesday, Good Friday, and the vigils of Assumption and Christmas. On days of fast the vigils and abstinence, eggs and milk products could be taken at breakfast and at the collation.

In 1951 a bishops' committee drew up a formula of uniform norms that became the basis for diocesan regulations in the U.S. Regarding abstinence the formula stated: (1) everyone over seven years of age was bound to observe the law of abstinence; (2) complete abstinence was to be observed on Fridays, Ash Wednesday, the vigils of Assumption and Christmas, and Holy Saturday morning. On these days meat and soup or gravy made from meat were not to be taken; (3) partial abstinence was to be observed on Ember Wednesdays and Saturdays, and on the vigils of Pentecost and All Saints. On days of partial abstinence meat and soup or gravy made from meat could be taken only once a day at the principal meal.

In regard to fasting the formula stated: (1) everyone over 21 and under 59 years of age was bound to observe the law of fast; (2) the days of fast were the weekdays of Lent, Ember days, the vigils of Pentecost, Assumption, All Saints, and Christmas; (3) on days of fast only one full meal was allowed. Two other meatless meals, sufficient to maintain strength, were permitted according to each one's needs; but together they should not equal another full meal; (4) meat was permitted at the principal meal on a day of fast except on Fridays, Ash Wednesday, and the vigils of Assumption and Christmas; (5) eating between meals was not permitted; but liquids, including milk and fruit juices, were allowed; (6) when health or ability to work would be seriously affected, the law did not oblige.

In 1956 the bishops of the U.S. slightly modified these norms. Holy Saturdays was excluded as a day of abstinence; the entire day became one only of fast. The vigil of All Saints was no longer listed as a day of fast or of partial abstinence. By decree of the Congregation of the Council in 1957, the law of fast and abstinence that had long been established for the vigil of the Assumption was transferred to the vigil of the Immaculate Conception.

On Dec. 3, 1959, John XXIII granted to all the faithful the faculty of anticipating the obligation of the Christmas Eve fast and abstinence form the 24th to the 23d of December.

Paul VI's Apostolic Constitution and the 1983 Code. Numerous indults obtained for various countries of the world led to widely different ways of observing the law of fast and abstinence until Pope Paul VI reorganized the ecclesiastical discipline. By the apostolic constitution *Poenitemini,* promulgated Feb. 17, 1966, Paul VI sought to renew ''penitential discipline with practices more suited to our times.'' Insisting upon the preeminently interior and religious character of penitence, the pope warns that true penance cannot ever ''prescind from physical asceticism as well.'' The traditional and fundamental means of fulfilling the divine precepts of penance are prayer, fasting, and charity, but the form of penance will vary according to the economic well-being of the locality.

Poenitemini provides the historical, doctrinal, and disciplinary background for canons governing penitential observance in the 1983 Code. The first of the five canons emphasizes the importance for all the faithful to be united by some common observance (c. 1249). Canon 1250 prescribes the penitential days and times observed in the universal church as Fridays throughout the year and the season of Lent. Canon 1251 explains that ''abstinence from eating meat or some other food'' as well as fasting are to be observed without exception on Ash Wednesday and Good Friday. The law of abstinence binds everyone who is 14 and older, and everyone between 18 and 60 must fast (c. 1252). The Code leaves it to the conference of bishops to ''determine more precisely'' particulars regarding the observance of fast and abstinence as well as ''other forms of penance, especially works of charity and exercises of piety'' that might be substituted for abstinence and fast.

In November, 1966 the National Conference of Catholic Bishops issued a statement on regulating penitential discipline in the United States. The obligation to fast and abstain ''from which no Catholic Christian will lightly excuse himself'' binds on Ash Wednesday and Good Friday. ''We preserve for our dioceses the tradition of abstinence from meat on each of the Fridays of Lent, confident that no Catholic Christian will lightly hold himself excused from this penitential practice.'' The bishops strongly recommend participation in daily Mass and a self-imposed program of fasting during Lent.

A few weeks later (Dec. 1, 1966), the bishops' committee on doctrine in answer to two questions responded, that neither the fast-abstinence of Ash Wednesday and Good Friday nor the abstinence of the Fridays of Lent binds gravely as an ecclesiastical law. The divine precept of penitence, however, binds all Catholics in a serious manner. Anyone who claims to be a follower of Christ should approach Him in a spirit of repentance. ''It is obvious that if his disposition is such that he is unwilling to do anything to answer the Lord's call to do penance and follow the pastoral injunctions of his shepherds, he would reveal a mortally serious state of soul, and further specifications would seem to be purely academic.''

Bibliography: T. L. BOUSCAREN and J. I. O'CONNOR, comps., *Canon Law Digest* (Milwaukee 1934–). P. MICHEL et al., *Dictionnaire de théologie catholique,* ed. A. VACANT et al. (Paris 1903–50; Tables générales 1951–) 1.1: 262–277. National Catholic Welfare Conference, *Our Bishops Speak,* ed. R. M. HUBER (Milwaukee 1952). ''Paenitemini,'' *Acta Apostolicae Sedis* 58 (Rome 1966) 177–198; Eng. tr. *Jurist* 26 (1966) 246–258. ''Pastoral Statement of the National Conference of Catholic Bishops on Penitential Observance for the Liturgical Year,'' *Jurist* 27 (1967) 95–100. Congregation of the Council. ''Dubium'' *Acta Apostolicae Sedis* 59 (Rome 1967) 229. A. CARR, ''How Serious the Lenten Fast and Abstinence?'' *Homiletic and Pastoral Review* 67 (New York 1967) 613–615. L. MCREAVY, ''Fasting and Abstinence: How Far Binding?'' *Clergy Review* 52 (London 1967) 642–643. J. O'HARA, ''Christian Fasting,'' Scripture 19 (1967) 3–18, 82–95. M-T. MATHIEU, ''Réflection sur le jeune,'' *Vie Consacrée* 58 (1986) 113–122. J. P. BEAL, J. A. CORIDEN, and T. H. GREEN, eds. *New Commentary on the Code of Canon Law* (New York 2000).

[P. M. J. CLANCY/G. T. KENNEDY/ J. E. LYNCH/EDS.]

FASTRED, BL.

Abbot of Cîteaux; b. Cambron (Belgium); d. Paris, April 21, 1163. A member of the noble Gaviaumer family, he joined the CISTERCIANS at CLAIRVAUX under St. BERNARD. He founded a new monastery in his native Cambron in the diocese of Cambrai in 1148, was elected abbot at Clairvaux in 1157, and in 1161 was promoted to the abbacy of CÎTEAUX. A devoted disciple of St. Bernard, he was a courageous supporter of ALEXANDER III in his fight against FREDERICK I BARBAROSSA. Fastred died in Paris, where Pope Alexander administered the Last Sacraments in the presence of King LOUIS VII, and was buried in Cîteaux. Two of his letters survived and are edited in *Patrologia Latina,* ed. J. P. Migne, 217 v. (Paris 1878–90) 185:704–706; 200:1363–65. Fastred, although never formally canonized, is venerated as blessed among the Cistercians.

Feast: April 21.

Bibliography: J. M. CANIVEZ, *L'Ordre de Cîteaux en Belgique* (Forges lez-Chimay, Belg. 1926) 109–110. S. LENSSEN, *Hagiologium cisterciense,* 2 v. (Tilburg 1948–49; suppl. 1951) 1: 232–234. A. A. KING, *Cîteaux and Her Elder Daughters* (London 1954).

[L. J. LEKAI]

FATE AND FATALISM

According to an ancient concept, all natural events and human actions occur as they do and things are as they are, by the dominance of an absolute principle or cause, more or less conscious, known as fate. While determinism interprets a single fact by linking it necessarily with other single facts, both antecedent and subsequent, fate refers the totality of events to a necessary unique cause. This can even be a free will, therefore an idea of fate is the conclusion of all monistic metaphysics.

Fate, fortune, chance and destiny. Fate is to be distinguished from fortune (τυχή), which ''is not present except in those things which act voluntarily'' (St. Thomas *In 2 phys.* 10); from chance, which may be defined as ''absence of laws,'' [cf., J. Sageret, *Le Hasard et la destinée* (Paris 1927) 142] and which is found only ''in those things which happen from nature''; and finally from destiny, which includes, at least in part, the intervention of even the individual will. In fate, the future is independent of what the individual can will or not will. In the concept of destiny the future is a resultant of that of which human action is also a component. Accordingly, one may say: ''Follow your destiny, fulfill your destiny,'' but not ''Follow your fate.''

The term fate comes from the Latin *fatum,* derived from *fari* (to say). Isidore defines it thus: ''They call fate whatever the gods say, whatever Jupiter says; therefore they say *fatum* is from the verb *fari,* i.e., from a verb meaning to speak'' (*Etymol.* 8.11.90; confer, St. Augustine, *Civ.* 5.9). The Latin *fatum* was employed to translate the Greek terms εἱμαρμένη, αἶσα, and μοῖρα. Cicero defined it as follows: ''I call fate [*fatum*] what the Greeks call εἱμαρμένη, i.e., an orderly series of causes, since cause is connected with cause and each of itself produces an effect. This is an eternal truth coming down from all eternity. . . . Therefore it is understood that fate is that which is called, not through ignorant superstition, but scientifically, 'the eternal cause of things, explaining why more things which have gone before happened, why those which now occur happen, and why those which follow will happen''' (*Divin.* 1.55. 125–126). The Greeks derive εἱμαρμένη either from εἱρμός (series, chain; so Aetius, 1.28.4, ed., H. Diels), or from εἴρομαι (align; confer, Diogenes Laertius 7.149), or from εἴρω (say).

In the history of religious beliefs and of philosophical thought, fatalism has assumed various aspects and meanings. In its early immature and anthropomorphic form, it was mythological fatalism. It became philosophical in its more perfect speculative expression, as in Stoic doctrine. Astrological fatalism may be considered a variant of this form. Finally, one may speak of theological fatalism, as in the case of the various theories involving predestination.

Mythological fatalism. Mythological fatalism, at least as it took shape in Greek thought, is the first form of the doctrine. Above the numerous divinities, whose purposes were often opposed and in conflict, was εἱμαρμένη, a power that dominated even Zeus himself (in Ovid, *Metam.* 9.435, Jupiter says: ''The fates rule me also''). It represented a monistic exigency which was as yet hardly outlined, but which already revealed the need of preserving the cosmic unity which polytheism could not guarantee (confer, Homer, *Iliad* 21.82; 19.186; *Odyssey* 3.226; 11.558). Moreover, this elementary form of fatalism came probably from an early reflection on the ordered and irrevocable movements of the heavenly bodies, a reflection superimposed on simple popular faith. If such was the case, fatalism did not have a religious origin, but was rather the primitive expression of a vague speculative interest, and therefore the most remote antecedent of cosmological mechanism.

Astrological fatalism. The *Quadripartitum* of Claudius Ptolemaeus (2d century A.D.) may be considered the classic text of astrological fatalism, which makes explicit the acceptable astronomical inspirations of mythological fatalism, and thus connects the destiny of the individual with the position of the stars that preside at his birth. Seneca said: ''Our fates lead us, and the hour of birth has de-

"The Fates Gathering in the Stars," painting by Elihu Vedder, ca. 1850–1923. (©Christine's Images/CORBIS)

termined how much time remains for each'' (*De prov.* 5.7). St. Augustine attacked such ideas in ironic vein: ''You will be an adulterer, because you have Venus; you will be a murderer, because you have Mars'' (*In psalm. 140, Patrologia Latina,* 37:1821; confer, *Civ. 5.9*).

Astrological fatalism presumes not only to catch the somatic characteristics and physical vicissitudes of the individual in the net of astral events, but also to predetermine his talent, moral character and feelings. If a sympathetic force (*conspiratio omnium*) connects heaven and earth in a cosmic unity, as astrologers claim their fatalism does, human actions brought under the rigorous law of nature are divested of all moral value. As Gellius says: ''Therefore penalties for the guilty have been wrongfully established by laws, if men do not commit crimes voluntarily, but are led to do so by fate'' (*Noct. Att.* 7.2.5). Astrologers who do not wish to abandon the indisputable doctrine of cosmic *conspiratio,* but who, at the same time, recognize the moral appeals of freedom and responsibility, claim that the power of fate is exercised exclusively on bodies, leaving the will of the ego to function freely (confer, the extracts from BARDESANES, ''Book of the Laws of the Countries,'' or ''Concerning Fate,'' cited by Eusebius, *Praep. Evang.* 6.10). This was a significant question in the consciences of thinkers of the Renaissance, who accepted astrological teachings (*see* PONTANUS, *De rebus coelestibus,* and the attack on astrology made by Pico della Mirandola in his *Disputationes adversus astrologiam*). The same Gnostics who willingly accepted astrological ideas admitted that sages devoted to higher knowledge escape fate (*see* CLEMENT OF ALEXANDRIA, *Exc. Theod.* 78, ed., F. Sagnard, pp. 201–202).

Philosophical fatalism. Philosophical fatalism does not differ substantially from mythological fatalism, of which it may be considered to be the rational and systematic expression, or from astrological fatalism, which is a specific aspect of it and with which it is identified. Among the pre-Socratics, εἱμαρμένη is the necessary bond that connects the parts of the All and guarantees its order and unity. It is the ''cause of things'' (according to Pythagoras, as reported in Diogenes Laertius, 8.27), or it is ''justice, forethought and creator'' (according to Parmenides and Democritus, as cited by Aetius, 1.25.3, ed., H. Diels), or it is ''reason creating from the running of opposite ways of things'' (according to Heraclitus, as quoted by Aetius, 1.7.22). For Anaxagoras, who probably considered εἱμαρμένη an ''empty name'' (cf., Alexander of Aphrodisias, *De fato,* 2), fate shares with other determining causes the government of the world (Aetius, 1.29.7).

After Plato (cf., *Theaet.* 169C; *Tim.* 89C; *Rep.* 619C) and Aristotle (cf., *Eth. Nic.* 7.32 ff.; *Phys.* 2.196a), in whom the concept of fate vanished in the elaboration of a body of thought that was preoccupied with preserving, on the one hand, the freedom and autonomy of the person, and on the other, the teleological ordering of the universe, philosophical fatalism appeared in its most rigorous and systematic form in Stoicism. Works of Zeno, Chrysippus and later of Posidonus and Boethius (fl. 2d century B.C.), were expressly devoted to fate. Zeno defined fate as ''a force which moves matter in a uniform and constant manner,'' whether it be called providence or nature (cf., Theodoret, *Graec. aff. cur.* 6.14). For Chrysippus, it was ''pneumatic power, and the reason of the cosmos . . . according to which what has happened has happened, what happens happens, and what will happen will happen'' (Stobaeus, *Ecl.* 1.5, p. 59, ed., K. Wachsmuth; confer, the definition cited from Cicero *Divin.* above); and also: ''an eternal and unchangeable series of circumstances and a chain rolling and entangling itself through unending and consequential successions from which it is made and with which it is connected'' (Gellius, *Noct. Att.* 7.2.1).

Stoicism, which did not admit any substantial distinction between spirit and matter, explained each and every event by the inexorable rhythm of cyclic time (εἱμαρμένη–κύκλος; see Pseudo-Plutarch, *De fato* 3–4), and it sacrificed all pluralistic and personal demands to its naturalistic monism. Wisdom was found entirely in *amor fati:* ''What then is the duty of the good man? It is to offer himself to fate. It is a great consolation to be swept along with the universe. Whatever it is that has ordered us so to live, so to die, by the same necessity it binds the gods as well. . . . The great creator and ruler of all, it is true, wrote the laws of fate, but he follows them. He obeys forever, he ordered but once'' (Seneca, *De prov.* 5.8). This was the triumph of ''inactive reason'' (*ignava ratio,* ἀργὸς λόγος), which refuses to act and to change the world.

Divination also reveals the future as possible, not for the sake of opening before man the possibility of endless moral activity, but for the sake of rendering him ''as one under compulsion'' (ἀναγκαζόμενος), of binding the chains of his metaphysical subjection more tightly, and of inspiring in him an attitude of apathetic resignation (ἀνάγκη στῆναι). Chrysippus endeavored to distinguish different orders of causes: ''some complete and principal, other auxiliary and proximate'' (cf., Cicero, *Top.* 15.58–59; *id., De fato,* 17.40) through which all that happens, happens ''either through necessity, or through destiny, or through free choice, or through fortune, or through spontaneity'' (Aetius, 1.29.7). But he did not succeed in breaking the iron chain of causes and in preserving the effective freedom of the individual.

Pagan and Christian opposition to fatalism. Fatalism was opposed, especially in its astrological and philosophical forms, by Alexander of Aphrodisias (*De fato*), Plotinus (*Ennead.* 2.3, 3.1), Ammonius (*De fato*) and Proclus [*De providentia et fato et eo quod in nobis,*; see J. C. Orelli, *Alexandri Aphr., Ammonii Hermiae f., Plotini, Bardesanis Syri et G. Gemisti Plethonis de fato* (Turin, 1864)] in defence of the rights of the soul. Plotinus in particular was strong in his opposition. While admitting that the positions of the stars ''announce'' (σημαίνουσι) events, he strove to reconcile cosmic order and the moral autonomy of the individual. In like manner he attacked Epicurean philosophy. The ''swerve'' (*clinamen*), introduced to also make possible the freedom of the will, was considered at best merely an irregular phenomenon that was added to the other elements in the Epicurean system and from which it was impossible to expect a purpose or choice that could really belong to the conscious Ego (*Ennead* 3.1.1). The various treatises on fate by Christian writers (Origen, Minucius Felix, Tertullian, Gregory of Nyssa and John Chrysostom, among others) all exhibited the same hostile attitude. They attacked fatalism to defend not only the rights of man but, above all, the Christian concept of a personal God.

Theological fatalism. Within the ambit of Christian thought, predestination took on the aspect of a theological fatalism in which theistic voluntarism took the place of the impersonal Cosmic Order of the Greeks. The antecedent and positive will of God annulled, not less than the Greek εἱμαρμένη, the freedom of the individual and his moral responsibility. The elect, under the irresistible action of grace, was considered deprived of his freedom: he could do nothing except what was good; the wicked man, on the other hand, deprived of grace, could not help sinning (*non potest non peccare*). Theological fatalism, which had its most common form in Islam, made its first appearances in the Christian world in the Patristic period and the early Middle Ages, but it attained its clearest systematic form in the ideas of Calvin (*Instit.* 3.25.5: non enim pari conditione creantur omnes, sed aliis vita aeterna, aliis damnatio aeterna preordinatur) and, by way of BAIUS, in the Jansenists (cf., P. Quesnel, as cited in the bull *Unigenitus* 32: Jesus Christus se morti tradidit ad liberandum pro semper suo sanguine primogenitos, id est, electos, de manu angeli exterminatoris).

Quietism and occasionalism, can also be brought into close relation with theological fatalism. The first, revived in a Christian setting, the Stoic attitude of inactive resignation (cf., Molinos, *Guía espiritual*); the second introduced into Protestant predestination, motives derived from the mechanism of Descartes (cf., Geulincx, *Ethica:* ''Sum igitur nudus spectator huius machinae. Ita est, ergo ita sit.''). The modern theology of Karl Barth may likewise be considered a true and characteristic form of ''theological occasionalism'' [cf., J. Hamer, *K. Barth* (Paris 1949)]. God's word (*Gottes Wort*) is omnipotent, free and creative, and like the classical fate, it commands man of itself.

Bibliography: R. OTTO, *Paulys Realenzyklopädie der klassischen Altertumswissenschaft,* ed. G. WISSOWA et al., 6.2 (1909) 2047–51. W. GUNDEL, *ibid.,* 7.2 (1912) 2622–45. S. EITREM, *ibid.,* 15.2 (1932) 2449–97. G. FAGGIN, *Enciclopedia filosofica,* 4 v. (Venice-Rome 1957) 2:273–276. H. RINGGREN et al., *Die Religion in Geschichte und Gegenwart*[3], 7 v. (3d ed. Tübingen 1957–65) 3:1404–11. A. DORNER et al., J. HASTINGS, ed., *Encyclopedia of Religion and Ethics,* 13 v. (Edinburgh 1908–27) 5:771–795, comprehensive series of articles. H. VON ARNIM, *Die stoische Lehre von Fatum und Willensfreiheit* (Vienna 1905). W. C. GREENE, *Moira: Fate, Good and Evil in Greek Thought* (Cambridge, Mass. 1944). A. FESTUGIÈRE, *L'Idéal religieux des Grecs et l'Évangile* (Paris 1932). D. AMAND DE MENDIETA, *Fatalisme et liberté dans l'antiquité grecque* (Louvain 1945). V. CIOFFARI, *Fortune and Fate from Democritus to St. Thomas Aquinas* (New York 1949). M. ELIADE, *The Myth of the Eternal Return,* tr., W. R. TRASK (Bollingen Ser. 46; New York 1954). R. GUÉNON, *La Grande Triade* (Paris 1957). G. PFLIGERSDORFFER, ''Fatum und Fortuna,'' *Literaturwissenschaftliches Jahrbuch,* NF 2 (1961) 1–30. M. SPANNEUT, *Le Stoicisme des Pères de l'Église de Clément de Rome à Clément d'Alexandrie* (Paris 1957). *Patrologia Latina,* ed. J. P. MIGNE, 217 V., indexes 4 v. (Paris 1878–90). J. SAGERET, *Le Hasard et la destinée* (Paris 1927) 142. J. HAMER, *K. Barth* (Paris 1949).

[G. FAGGIN]

FATHER (RELIGIOUS TITLE)

The title was in early times given to bishops as teachers possessing authority over the faithful; also, as an early Benedictine rule indicates, to priests as sacramental confessors; finally, to the head of a monastery, the word abbot being derived from abba, father. In modern times it has become the normal mode of address of all priests, whether regular or secular, although previously it had been the exclusive title of mendicant friars. This custom originated in Ireland, whence, as a consequence of Irish immigration, it spread to the English-speaking countries. It was established in England, largely due to Cardinal H. Manning's encouragement, about 1880. This custom is still largely confined to English-speaking countries, in which since 1900 some Anglican clergy also have adopted it. Additional uses today of this title are the continuing ones for a sacramental confessor (compare its liturgical use in the Confiteor) and for religious superiors; it is furthermore used in the form ''council father'' for all bishops and other ecclesiastics who fully participate in an ecumenical council.

Bibliography: *New English Dictionary* (Oxford 1888–1928) 5.2:97, s.v. father, ecclesiastical uses. W. E. ADDIS and T. ARNOLD, *The Catholic Dictionary* (London 1884).

[B. FORSHAW]

FATHERS OF SION

Popular name for the Religious of Our Lady of Sion, a congregation of priests and brothers founded at Paris in 1852 by two brothers, Marie Théodore RATISBONNE and Marie Alphonse RATISBONNE, but not formally organized as a congregation until 1893. The founders sought to promote understanding between Christians and Jews.

The history of the congregation represents the slow but true and progressive evolution of Judeo-Christian relationship in the Church. The earlier activities of the Fathers of Sion included an instruction center for converts in Paris and an orphanage for Jewish children, founded in Jerusalem in 1870. Their work at that time was directed principally toward conversion of religion. But the difficulties arising from such proselytical intent caused the fathers to attempt a new approach in a more ecumenical way by means of studies on Judaism, and collaboration and dialogue with the Jews. Centers of study and dialogue were organized, the best known of which was the *Institute Saint Pierre de Sion* in Jerusalem. In the ensuing years after the Second Vatican Council, the institute, popularly known as the Ratisbonne Institute, became an important ecumenical center for Jewish-Christian relations. In 1985, the congregation transferred the institute to the Holy See, which elevated it to the status of a ''Pontifical Institute'' in 1998.

[M. R. NÔTRE/EDS.]

FATHERS OF THE CHURCH

A technical title applied to certain ecclesiastical writers of Christian antiquity.

Concept. The historical evolution of the term father is not altogether clear. In ancient times the title was given to teachers; the underlying idea is that a teacher is the procreator of a student's spiritual personality (cf. 1 Kgs 20.35; 1 Pt 5.13). The New Testament father is a teacher of spiritual realities, by whose means the soul of man is reborn into the likeness of Christ (1 Cor 4. 14–15). In the first Christian centuries a bishop was emphatically a father in Christ, not primarily because of the parallel between the leader of a community and the head of a family, but because he baptized his flock and was chief teacher of his church. From the late 4th century the term was applied with special pertinence to those bishops of the past who were cited as authoritative witnesses to the Church's tradition. In the 5th-century Christological controversies the ''proof from the fathers'' was for the first time fully exploited, particularly in *FLORILEGIA;* all contending parties, e.g., CYRIL OF ALEXANDRIA (J. D. Mansi, *Sacrorum Conciliorum nova et amplissima collectio,* 31 v. [Florence-Venice 1757–98]) and THEODORET OF CYR (*Monumenta Germaniae* 76:400), appealed to the authority of ''the fathers.''

In a move at once revolutionary and felicitous, AUGUSTINE (*C. Julian.* 1.7.34) included among ''the fathers'' a writer who was not a bishop, JEROME, citing him, by reason of his erudition, as a witness to orthodoxy in the matter of original sin. Recognizing that not all ecclesiastical writers were unexceptionable witnesses, VINCENT OF LÉRINS, the first to develop a theory of patristic proof, applied Augustine's insight more rigidly to ''those approved teachers who, in their respective times and places, abided in the communion and faith of the one catholic Church'' (*Commonit.* 1.3).

A partial list of ''holy fathers,'' including the layman PROSPER OF AQUITAINE, is found in the so-called Gelasian Decree (not a product of Pope Gelasius, but perhaps a faithful reflection of the 6th-century Roman Church), where the accent is on communion: ''those who have not swerved at any point from society with the holy Roman Church, and have not been severed from the faith and preaching that are hers, but by God's grace have shared her fellowship to the last day of their lives'' (4.3).

It is in harmony with this early evolution that the distinctively Catholic conception of the Fathers of the Church has emerged: those ecclesiastical writers of Christian antiquity who are distinguished for orthodoxy of doctrine and holiness of life and have therefore been approved by the Church as witnesses to its faith. In this conception four qualifications are regarded as essential.

Antiquity. The patristic era, as a literary period, opens with the first extant piece of extracanonical literature: in the present state of the evidence, Clement of Rome's *Letter to the Corinthians* (*c.* 96; *see* CLEMENT I, POPE, ST.), unless one persists in assigning an earlier date to the *DIDACHE.* More difficult is the problem of when the age of the Fathers closes. Since the end of the 18th century, Christian antiquity has generally been distinguished from the Middle Ages. Most commonly, Catholic scholars have tended to regard JOHN DAMASCENE (d. *c.* 750) as the last of the Eastern Fathers and ISIDORE OF SEVILLE (d. *c.* 636) as the last of the Western, though some terminate the era as early as the advent of Emperor JUSTINIAN I (527) or the death of Pope GREGORY I (604), or extend it to 850.

The problem is insoluble, for a solution presupposes answers to questions intimately linked with the periodization of history: which factor—the doctrinal or the literary or the cultural or the historical—ought to predominate in delimiting the age of the Fathers? When do the Middle Ages begin? Is the patristic era conterminous with Greco-

Roman culture? How are individual countries and different areas affected in this matter by, for example, Byzantinism, the iconoclast controversy, the Arab conquest, the entrance of Boniface and Columban on the cultural scene?

Orthodoxy. This qualification actually has three facets: excellence of orthodox doctrine. Doctrine in this instance is theological thought externalized in writing: the Fathers are authors. Orthodox doctrine does not imply utter freedom from error, for the Fathers are not simply witnesses to the faith, but in large part are theologians attempting a more or less profound penetration of revelation; rather it demands loyal doctrinal communion with the orthodox Church. The excellence desirable is an elusive quality: it may be originality or profundity or fullness, vigor or clarity or brilliance. It does not necessarily stand comparison with a later age; it does suppose a title to deathlessness on the strength of the author's relative place within the theology of his time.

Holiness. Incontestably, this does not involve formal canonization. Perhaps it does not demand even the spontaneous veneration shown to saints in the early Church. The minimum requisite is ordinary Christian virtue, consistent union with God, revealed concretely in harmony between doctrine and life, between faith and morals. The underlying presupposition is that holiness makes possible, without inescapably guaranteeing, a more exact or a more profound comprehension of divine revelation and Christian tradition.

Ecclesiastical Approval. The Church's approbation may be formal, as when a council or pope or even the martyrology declares an early writer's doctrinal and moral merits; or implicit, as when a council or pope or even the liturgy quotes or cites him approvingly; or virtual, in the presence of a general Christian consensus.

Although this conception of the Fathers is confessedly theological, dogmatic, and to some extent polemic, the scholarly disciplines of patrology and PATRISTIC THEOLOGY have come to cover the same material, from different viewpoints, as the history of ancient Christian literature. Their sphere of interest includes Christian writers whose orthodoxy has been questioned (e.g., Origen) or who abandoned the Church (e.g., Tertullian), pagan authors who attacked the faith (e.g., Celsus and Porphyry), literary genres such as the New Testament apocrypha and the martyr acts. This broader conception of PATRISTIC STUDY stems from a recognition that research into the Fathers will not yield its full theological harvest if it is limited to a compilation of proof texts or seeks only the consensus in doctrine and exegesis that is a privileged sign of authoritative Church teaching; it should reveal significant stages in the development of doctrine, in the Church's understanding and presentation of God's self-communication.

The primitive language of patristic literature was Greek (not classical, but Koine). However, it should be noted that the Greek Fathers and ecclesiastical writers of the 4th and 5th centuries were outstanding representatives of Atticism, so that men such as BASIL and JOHN CHRYSOSTOM were admired by the great Sophist Libanius for their style. In Rome, North Africa, and Gaul the use of Greek was prevalent as late as the 3d century. It was gradually supplanted in the East, outside the Greek area proper, by the national languages, especially Syriac, Coptic, and Armenian, and was displaced in the West by Latin, which apparently had its Christian origins in 2d-century Rome in translations of the Bible—though North Africa's claim to be the cradle of ecclesiastical Latin cannot be rejected out of hand.

Survey of the Literature. Patristic literature may be conveniently divided into three broad periods: its beginnings, to the Rescript of Toleration in 313 or the Council of Nicaea I in 325; its full flowering, to the Council of Chalcedon in 451; and its decline, to the 7th or 8th century.

Antenicene Fathers. Before Nicaea, three sets of writers have been isolated. There is, first, the group styled APOSTOLIC FATHERS because actually or supposedly they had personal contact with the Apostles or were instructed by their disciples. The quantitatively modest legacy of these men—Antioch's impassioned IGNATIUS, Smyrna's more prosaic POLYCARP, Rome's diplomatic Clement, and several others less distinguished—with its pastoral tone, its eschatological emphasis, and its vivid remembrance of Christ, is a genuine reflection and resounding echo of the primitive Christian witness.

Overlapping this intra-Church literature is the apologetical and antiheretical legacy of the 2d century. The Greek APOLOGISTS were born of the Church's reaction to paganism and Judaism. It was Christianity's first literary contact with the outside world, when a remarkable group of cultivated clerics and laymen—notably JUSTIN MARTYR, ATHENAGORAS OF ATHENS, and THEOPHILUS OF ANTIOCH—protested with the pen against imperial sword and mob rumor, presented the New Testament as the fulfillment of the Old, contrasted Christian truth with pagan myth, and pioneered in constructing a bridge between the new revelation and the old philosophy. The antiheretical literature, now in large part lost, was the Church's response to MONTANISM and GNOSTICISM; here the outstanding figure is IRENAEUS, widely regarded as the founder of Christian theology.

Toward A.D. 200 ecclesiastical literature took a new turn: after Irenaeus, the "man of tradition," the dominant characteristic is an impressive effort at comprehensive theological construction, stimulated in part by controversy, but more imperatively by the demands made on Christian intelligence by faith itself. The main centers of theological activity were ALEXANDRIA in the East and CARTHAGE in the West, with Rome playing a secondary but important role. The most striking representatives of this new ferment were CLEMENT OF ALEXANDRIA, pioneer of Christian scholarship; ORIGEN, encyclopedic and insightful; the incisive, passionate, paradoxical TERTULLIAN; CYPRIAN, with his refined ecclesial sense; and to a lesser extent METHODIUS OF OLYMPUS, HIPPOLYTUS OF ROME, and NOVATIAN.

The Golden Age. Licinius's Rescript of Toleration from Nicomedia (more commonly but less accurately termed the Edict of Milan), which officially recognized Christianity's right to exist and conceded to Christians complete freedom of worship, paved the way for the golden age of patristic literature. It is the period of the first four general councils (NICAEA I, CONSTANTINOPLE I, EPHESUS, and CHALCEDON), a constructive, creative period for Christian theology through penetration and elaboration of basic truths with the Trinity and Christology stressed in the East; soteriology and ecclesiology in the West; and a distressing period by reason of the dissensions that rent the Church in ARIANISM, DONATISM, MANICHAEISM, PELAGIANISM, APOLLINARIANISM, NESTORIANISM, and MONOPHYSITISM.

It was also a period of Christian humanism, in that the better authors combined theological competence with broad secular learning and a mastery of literary style. Christian literature flowered on many levels: apologies and dogmatic-polemic treatises, biography and Church history, letters and poetry and sermons, and the Biblical science of the Schools of ALEXANDRIA, ANTIOCH, EDESSA, and NISIBIS.

A select catalogue of first-rate writers is itself an index of this bright hour in the story of literature and theology. In Egypt were the anti-Arian ATHANASIUS and the anti-Nestorian Cyril of Alexandria; the erudite theologian of the Trinity, DIDYMUS THE BLIND; the founder of monastic mysticism, EVAGRIUS PONTICUS; and the ''Platonist in a miter,'' SYNESIUS OF CYRENE. Asia Minor touched new theological heights in the three Cappadocians: the practical BASIL OF CAESAREA, the eloquent GREGORY OF NAZIANZUS, and the speculative GREGORY OF NYSSA. In Antioch and Syria the writers of distinction were EUSEBIUS OF CAESAREA, father of Church history; CYRIL OF JERUSALEM, master of catechetical instruction; EPIPHANIUS OF SALAMIS, insatiable recorder of heresies; and the School of Antioch's most remarkable representatives, DIODORE OF TARSUS, JOHN CHRYSOSTOM, THEODORE OF MOPSUESTIA, and THEODORET OF CYR. In the West the dominant figures were HILARY OF POITIERS, highly effective adversary of Arianism; AMBROSE of Milan, in pulpit and politics one of the most powerful personalities of the 4th century; the learned Biblical scholar and humanist JEROME; LEO I, superb rhetorician and defender of Western civilization; and above all, AUGUSTINE, who ''combined the creative power of Tertullian and the intellectual breadth of Origen with the ecclesiastical sense of Cyprian, the dialectical acumen of Aristotle with the idealistic verve and profound speculation of Plato, the practical sense of the Latin with the intellectual mobility of the Greek'' (Altaner).

Period of Patristic Decline. After Chalcedon a certain decline in constructive theology set in. In part, the cause lay within Christianity itself; for, in the wake of the councils and great Fathers, the central problems of the faith seemed settled, theology appeared to have reached its peak, and so exegesis and speculation grew weak while spirituality and worship came to the fore. In this context, originality and creativity inevitably ebbed; traditionalism, intellectual subservience to the past, was in possession; *catenae* and *florilegia* or collections of texts and citations, multiplied. In part, the explanation is to be sought in the circumstances of the time: the onslaught of barbarians in the West; Caesaropapism in the East; the regrettable rifting of East and West; the culture of Islam laid on Christian ruins. And still the literature is not negligible.

Aristotelian philosophy was put at the service of theological thought, and so the ground was prepared for the flowering of medieval scholasticism. Even the names are not without distinction: BOETHIUS, with his translations of Aristotle; GREGORY THE GREAT, influential interpreter of Scripture and master of sacerdotal spirituality; ISIDORE OF SEVILLE, historian, ascetical writer, and encyclopedist; PSEUDO-DIONYSIUS the Areopagite, profound theologian of the mystical life; MAXIMUS THE CONFESSOR, scholarly adversary of MONOTHELETISM; and JOHN DAMASCENE, synthesizer of Greek patristic wisdom.

This outline, valid enough for the mainstream of patrology, has the disadvantage of disregarding the Oriental area, the literature in languages other than Latin and Greek. Syriac literature, in the Eastern Aramaic dialect of Edessa that became the literary language of Christian writers in northern Syria and western Mesopotamia, found its high point in EPHREM THE SYRIAN, controversialist, dogmatic and ascetical theologian, exegete, and poet; besides the orthodox authors, a number of Nestorian (e.g., NARSES, founder of the School of Nisibis) and Monophysite (e.g., PHILOXENUS OF MABBUGH) theologians are important for the history of theology.

Coptic literature has bequeathed precious Gnostic and Manichaean texts, the genuine and apocryphal Scriptures, the lives of martyrs and monks (e.g., PACHOMIUS and SHENOUTE, the most significant representatives of Egyptian cenobitism), anecdotal accounts such as the APOPHTHEGMATA PATRUM, Church orders, and homiletic and liturgical documents. Georgian literature in its oldest period (4th century to *c.* 700) is strong in translations from the Greek and Armenian, not only the Bible and apocrypha but lives of saints and versions of Fathers (e.g., HIPPOLYTUS); native literature is richest in hagiography.

In Armenian, historians have perhaps the greatest importance (e.g., Agathangelus), though theology is far from negligible (e.g., Eznik of Kolb's *Confutation of the Sects*). The first period of Ethiopic literature (Axumite Empire, 4th to 7th centuries) discloses translations of the Bible, of scriptural apocrypha (e.g., Enoch) and Greek patristic works (e.g., Shepherd of HERMAS), and of monastic rules; whether there was also an indigenous literature is not clear. The oldest extant writings of Arabic Christianity stem from the 8th century, when the language of the Muslim conquerors became the literary and everyday language of the Christians in Palestine, Egypt, and Syria.

Bibliography: Editions and translations. J. P. MIGNE, *Patrologiae cursus completus,* 382 v. (Paris 1844–66). *Corpus scriptorum ecclesiasticorum latinorum* (Vienna 1866–). *Die griechischen christlichen Schriftsteller der ersten Jahrhunderte* (Leipzig 1897–). *Corpus christianorum. Series latina* (Turnhout, Belgium 1953–). *Patrologia orientalis* (Paris 1903–). *Corpus scriptorum christianorum orientalium* (Paris-Louvain 1903–). *Texte und Untersuchungen zur Geschichte der altchristlichen Literatur* (Leipzig 1882–). *Sources chrétiennes* (Paris 1942–). *Ancient Christian Writers* (Westminster, Md. 1946–). *The Fathers of the Church* (Washington 1947–). *A Library of the Fathers of the Holy Catholic Church,* 45 v. (Oxford 1838–88). *The Ante-Nicene Fathers,* 10 v. (American repr. of Edinburgh ed., Buffalo 1884–97). *A Selected Library of Nicene and Post-Nicene Fathers of the Christian Church,* 2 ser., 28 v. (Buffalo-New York 1886–1900; repr. Grand Rapids, Mich. 1952–56). *Bibliothek der Kirchenväter,* 2 ser., 83 v. (Kempten 1911–39). Literature. B. ALTANER, *Patrology,* tr. H. GRAEF from the 5th German ed. (New York 1960). J. QUASTEN, *Patrology,* 3 v. (Westminster, MD 1950–) v.1–3, with French (Paris 1955–) and Spanish (Madrid 1961–) versions that update bibliographies. É. AMANN, *Dictionnaire de théologie catholique,* ed. A. VACANT, 15 v. (Paris 1903–50; Tables générales 1951–) 12:1192–1215. A. STUIBER, *Lexikon für Theologie und Kirche,* ed. J. HOFER and K. RAHNER, 10 v. (2d, new ed. Freiburg 1957–65) 6:272–274. O. BARDENHEWER, *Geschichte der altkirchlichen Literatur,* 5 v. (Freiburg 1913–1932) v.1–5. A. VON HARNACK, *Geschichte der altchristlichen Literatur bis Eusebius,* 2 v. in 4 (Leipzig 1893–1904). H. G. BECK, *Kirche und theologische Literatur im byzantinischen Reich* (Munich 1959). *Die Religion in Geschichte und Gegenwart,* 7 v. (3d ed. Tübingen 1957–65) 1:142–144, Ethiopic; 280–288, Greek and Latin; 529–531, Arabic; 611–612, Armenian; 2:1399–1400, Georgian; 4:8–11, Coptic; 6:581–583, Syriac. J. De Ghellinck, *Patristique et moyenâge: Etudes d'histoire littéraire et doctrinale* v.1 (2d ed. Paris 1949) 3:103–244, 339–484. J. N. D. KELLY, *Early Christian Doctrines* (2d ed. New York 1960). F. UEBERWEG, *Grundriss der Geschichte der Philosophie,* ed. K. PRAECHTER et al., 5 v. (Berlin 1923–28) v.2.

[W. J. BURGHARDT]

Fatima, Portugal. (©Tony Arruza/CORBIS)

FÁTIMA

Parish in the Diocese of Leiria, central Portugal, near the famous cloister Batalha; the name Fátima is Arabic in origin. Since 1917 it has been one of the most famous Marian SHRINES in the world and the destination of numerous pilgrimages. The parish includes the hamlets Aljustrel and Valinhos and the natural depression Cova da Iria (St. IRENE), where the apparition of the Blessed Virgin occurred six times from May 13 to Oct. 13, 1917.

Three shepherd children, Lucia dos Santos (b. 1907) and her cousins Francisco (1908–19) and Jacinta (1910–20), said they saw the figure of a Lady brighter than the sun, standing on a cloud in an evergreen tree. In a conversation that Francisco alone did not hear, though he said he saw the figure, the Lady asked the children to return to the place on the 13th of each month until October, when she would disclose her identity and reveal what she desired. In spite of local incredulity, the children returned as promised, joined by a crowd of spectators that increased from 50 in June, to 1,000 in July, to 18,000 in August, to 30,000 in September, and to 50,000 in October. Only the children saw the Lady, but others reported that they noted movements of the tree and the arrival and departure of the cloud.

Radicals and anticlericals, who were then strong in Portugal, assailed the events. On August 13 the civil prefect of Outrem kidnapped the children and held them for two days, submitting them to interrogation and threats; but the Lady appeared to them on the 19th of the month at nearby Valinhos, promising that in October a great miracle would occur. On that date, in wet and dismal weather, she announced to them that she was Our Lady of the Rosary, and called for amendment in men's lives. Then the sun appeared and seemed to tremble, rotate violently, and finally fall, dancing over the heads of the throng before it returned to normal. Many of the crowd reported having seen this ''Miracle of the Sun'' that was repeated twice more. A journalist who had mocked the events of Fátima in the Lisbon daily *O Seculo* that morning reflected a changed attitude in his report of October 15.

The patriarch of Lisbon had the events watched by Canon Manoel Formigão, who interviewed the children frequently. In 1922 a canonical process of enquiry was opened and lasted seven years. The bishop of Leiria (Oct. 13, 1930) pronounced the 1917 visions at Cova da Iria worthy of credence and authorized the cult of Our Lady of Fátima. Thereafter, Lucia, as a Dorothean lay sister at Túy (Spain), on episcopal command wrote her remembrances in documents dated 1936, 1937, 1941, and 1942, giving further details about the apparitions and the first public information about apparitions of an angel in 1915.

Francisco and Jacinta died of influenza, and in 1948 Lucia entered the Carmelites at Coimbra. The Basilica of Our Lady of Fátima with its lofty tower (1928–53) dominates Cova da Iria. Nearby on the site of the tree is the chapel of the Apparitions, with a statue carved according to Lucia's description. On May 12, 1946, the statue was crowned by the legate of Pope Pius XII, who had been consecrated bishop on May 13, 1917, and who in 1951 chose Fátima for the solemn closing of the Holy Year, attended by more than one million people.

The Third Secret. According to the memoirs written by Sister Lucia in August and December 1941, the first part of the ''secret'' revealed to the three *pastorinhos* of Fatima told of a vision of hell that was interpreted to refer to the two World Wars. The second part of the ''secret'' predicted that Russia would one day return to Christianity, but details of the third part of the secret, recorded by Sister Lucia in January 1944, were not made public until May 12, 2000. The memoir describing the so-called ''third secret'' had been taken to Rome in April 1957 where it was kept in a sealed envelope in the Secret Archives of the Holy Office. Pope John XXIII read the memoir in 1959, Pope Paul VI read it in 1965, and Pope John Paul II read it in July 1981, following the attempt on his life in May of that year. Finally, in May 2000, at Pope John Paul's instructions, a photostat of Sister Lucia's 1944 memoir was made public. It described martyrdom and suffering, including a man ''clothed in white'' who ''falls to the ground apparently dead, under a burst of gunfire.'' At the time Cardinal Angelo Sodano, the Vatican Secretary of State issued a statement to pilgrims who had gathered for the beatification of the two deceased shepherd children that said, after the 1981 assassination attempt by a Turkish gunman in St Peter's Square, ''it appeared evident to his Holiness that it was a motherly hand which guided the bullets past, enabling the Pope to halt at the threshold of death.''

The failed attempt on Pope John Paul's life occurred in 1981 on May 13, the anniversary of the first apparition. After recovering from the gunshot wounds, John Paul had one of the bullets put into the crown of Our Lady's statue. The beatification of Jacinta and Francisco Marto, May 13, 2000 was the occasion for Pope John Paul's third visit to the Fatima shrine.

Bibliography: C. C. MARTINDALE, *The Message of Fatima* (London 1950). J. DE MARCHI, *Era uma Senhora mais brilhante que o sol* (3rd ed. Cova da Iria 1947), Eng. *Fatima, the Facts,* tr. I. M. KINGSBURY (Cork 1950). J. A. PELLETIER, *The Sun Danced at Fatima* (Worcester, Mass. 1951). VISCONDE DE MONTELO (M. N. Formigão), *Os episodios maravilhosos de Fatima* (Lisbon 1921); *As grandes maravilhas de Fatima* (Lisbon 1927). C. RENGERS, *The Youngest Prophet : The Life of Jacinta Marto, Fatima Visionary* (New York 1986). T. TINDAL-ROBERTSON, *Fatima, Russia and Pope John Paul II* (Chulmleigh, England 1992). J. M. ALONSO, ''Histoire ancienne et histoire nouvelle de Fatima,'' in *Vraies et fausses apparitions dans l'église*, ed. B. BILLET (Paris 1973) 55–95.

[H. M. GILLETT/EDS.]

FAUBEL CANO, JUAN BAUTISTA, BL.

Lay martyr, pyrotechnician; b. Jan. 3, 1889, Llíria, Valencia, Spain; d. Aug. 28, 1936, Paterna, Valencia.

Juan Bautista (John Baptist) attended public school, but learned his profession from his parents and completed his formation through private study. He married Patrocinio Beatriz Olba Martínez with whom he had three children: Patrocinio, Josefina, and Juan Bautista. Not only was he considered one of the best pyrotechnicians of the region, but he was known also for his piety, goodness, kindness, and faithfulness in carrying out the work entrusted to him.

From his youth he was an active member of various Catholic groups, including the Third Order of St. Francis, Catholic Action, the Nocturnal Adoration Society, and many others. While he was president of *La Derecha Regional Valenciana* (the Right of the Region of Valencia) he created a section to help the poor.

At the beginning of the Spanish Civil War in 1936, churches, convents, religious objects, and parish records were destroyed. In Liria, the churches left were converted to secular use because the public celebration of the Mass was prohibited. Six priests and 31 lay people of Liria, including Faubel, were assassinated. Although friends advised him to go into hiding at the beginning of the persecution, Faubel declined and continued his daily activities serenely. He was known to say, ''If Our Lord needs my blood, I have no reason to deny Him.''

Aware of the risk he was taking, Juan Bautista, in close collaboration with Fr. Miguel Aliaga Turó, founded la Derecha Regional Valenciana at the beginning of the Republican persecution. La Derecha's purpose was to form youth into authentic Christians by establishing Catholic primary schools. When the sisters of San Miguel Convent were evicted, Faubel provided them refuge in his home. The day they left, Aug. 6, 1936, the militia appeared at his door with pistols to arrest him.

He calmed his wife, took a crucifix in hand, and went with them to an area of Liria called Els Olivarets. There his captors tormented him by discharging their guns into the air and sticking him with needles. For several days he was held in the municipal jail, then transferred to the prison of San Miguel de los Reyes, where he was maltreated but strengthened by covertly receiving the Eucharist on several occasions. He was calm on the evening before his death and arranged for an employee to withdraw his money from his bank account before the authorities took over the account, to provide for his family.

Before dawn on August 28, he was taken with twelve others to a gorge along the highway between Valencia and Ademuz near Paterna, where he was shot with his crucifix in his hand. One of those to be executed, Luis Soler Pérez, managed to escape into the darkness and relate the story of Faubel's martyrdom. Faubel's body was found in the cemetery of Paterna and interred at Liria. He was beatified by Pope John Paul II with José APARICIO SANZ and 232 companions on March 11, 2001.

Feast: Sept. 22.

See Also: SPANISH CIVIL WAR, MARTYRS OF, BB.

Bibliography: V. CÁRCEL ORTÍ, *Martires españoles del siglo XX* (Madrid 1995). W. H. CARROLL, *The Last Crusade* (Front Royal, Va. 1996). J. PÉREZ DE URBEL, *Catholic Martyrs of the Spanish Civil War*, tr. M. F. INGRAMS (Kansas City, Mo. 1993). R. ROYAL, *The Catholic Martyrs of the Twentieth Century* (New York 2000). *L'Osservatore Romano,* Eng. no. 11 (March 14, 2001) 1–4, 12.

[K. I. RABENSTEIN]

FAULHABER, ANDREAS

Martyred for the seal of confession; b. Glatz, Silesia, May 21, 1713; d. Glatz, Dec. 30, 1757. Faulhaber became a priest in 1750. In the fortress town of Glatz, Prussian steps to stamp out Catholic loyalties to the Hapsburgs had led to mutual distrust. A Prussian deserter in the Seven Years' War declared under questioning that Faulhaber had heard his confession and by implication had condoned desertion. This testimony was retracted repeatedly, but it led to the arrest and imprisonment of Faulhaber. While the trial was still pending, Frederick II instructed the commander to execute Faulhaber and not to allow him a confessor. Faulhaber refused to save himself by revealing the deserter's confession. His body, miraculously preserved, was left hanging for 31 months until Austrian troops took it down from the gallows on July 26, 1760, and entombed it in the church in Glatz. In 1930, steps were taken to promote his beatification, but since the ordered expulsion of German clergy from Glatz (now Kłodzko in Southwest Poland), after World War II, efforts seem to be blocked.

Bibliography: L. PASTOR, *The History of the Popes From the Close of the Middle Ages* (London-St. Louis 1938–61) 36:89. E. HENSELER, *P. Faulhaber der Glatzer Kaplan* (Heidelberg 1956). K. ENGELBERT, *Lexikon für Theologie und Kirche*, ed. J. HOFER and K. RAHNER (Freiberg 1957–65) 4:41.

[H. W. L. FREUDENTHAL]

FAULHABER, MICHAEL VON

Cardinal, archbishop of Munich, Germany; b. Klosterheidenfeld, Lower Franconia, Bavaria, March 5, 1869; d. Munich, June 12, 1952. After studying at Schweinfurt and Wurzburg, Faulhaber was ordained in 1892. He was chaplain at Kitzingen for a year before taking his doctorate in theology at the University of Wurzburg, where he remained as a lecturer (1899–1903). He was professor of Old Testament at the University of Strasbourg until 1911, when he was named bishop of Speyer. During World War I he ministered to the Bavarian armies in the field. In 1917 he was transferred to the archdiocese of Munich, and in 1921, made cardinal.

Faulhaber, a monarchist devoted to the Wittelsbach kings of Bavaria, led his people throughout the Nazi era.

His sermons frequently condemned the racism, totalitarianism, and paganism that he described as the basis of the new order. In 1951 the Jewish community formally expressed its appreciation for his attack on anti-Semitism and emphasis on the Jewish background of Christianity during his Advent sermons of 1933. After World War II Faulhaber worked closely with the American occupation forces in the reconstruction of his archdiocese. The highest award of the West German Republic, the Grand Cross of the Order of Merit, was conferred on him by Pres. Theodor Heuss. Faulhaber also published several books.

Bibliography: J. WEISSTHANNER, *Michael Kardinal Faulhaber, 80 Jahre* (2d ed. Munich 1949). M. A. GALLIN, *German Resistance to Hitler* (Washington 1961). M. SCHMAUS, *Staatslexikon*, ed. GÖRRES-GESELLSCHAFT (Freiburg 1957–63) 3:231–233.

[M. A. GALLIN]

FAULT

In popular religious usage, fault is often taken to be synonymous with the various meanings of IMPERFECTION, that is, an act less perfect than it might be, either because it is less good than its alternative, but not against God's law, or against God's law but in a slight matter or is done with little or no deliberation.

In stricter theological usage, fault denotes the objective state of being responsible for a sinful act. The term is then synonymous with culpability or blameworthiness. Theological fault implies at least some realization of wrongdoing and some free choice of the will. In its essence it is a deformity of the agent's will as compared with that of God. It is Catholic teaching that theological fault is removed by perfect contrition or by imperfect contrition with the Sacraments of baptism, penance, or the anointing of the sick. The remission of theological fault does not necessarily imply the remission of all reparation or punishment due to the fault. These and other effects of sin may be removed by good works, especially by reception of the Sacraments and by indulgences. Some Protestant reformers held that fault was never truly removed but only covered over, as it were, by application of the merits of Christ.

As distinct from theological fault, juridical fault is said to be present whenever one performs an act against the law, either knowingly and willingly, or at least in circumstances in which one objectively should have been aware of what he was doing. For a court award for damages to be just, there must be at least some juridical fault. To incur an obligation in justice to pay for damages apart from a court order, there must be theological fault. There can, in certain circumstances, be an obligation in charity to pay for damages of which one is the physical cause even without any fault.

Bibliography: THOMAS AQUINAS, *Summa contra Gentiles* 3.10.

[J. J. FARRAHER]

FAURÉ, GABRIEL URBAIN

Precursor of 20th-century music; b. Pamiers (Ariège), France, May 12, 1845; d. Paris, Nov. 4, 1924. Fauré, sixth child of a nonmusical family, was educated at École Niedermeyer, Paris, an institute dedicated to the betterment of church music. He was both *maître de chapelle* and organist at the Madeleine, as well as professor of composition at the Paris Conservatory, and from 1905, its director. Among his students were Nadia Boulanger, Ravel, and Florent Schmitt. His dramatic compositions are unremarkable, and his work for organ and orchestra is negligible; but his songs, piano works, and chamber music innovated a daring individuality of style whose elements, such as the modality, inventive extensions of harmonic relations, independence in use of dissonance, and preoccupation with rhythm and texture, grew more austere and inventive with his creative maturity. The *Requiem* (1887–88), the climax of some uninspired sacred writings comprising a *Messe Basse* and a few short works, embodied his religious faith and hope for eternal rest. Thus he omitted the Sequence (*Dies Irae*) except for the last line, ''Pie Jesu Domine, dona eis requiem,'' which replaced the *Benedictus.* The work, supported by organ, incorporates his somewhat romanticist early style. It reflects little of the Gregorian tradition, though there is some modal coloring and occasional polyphony. This Mass is a gentle prayer that foretells in its simplicity Fauré's later style and the emotional restraint of the next generation.

Bibliography: *Lettres intimes,* ed. P. FAURÉ-FRÉMIET (Paris 1951). P. FAURÉ-FRÉMIET, *Gabriel Fauré* (new ed. Paris 1957); *Die Musik in Geschichte und Gegenwart,* ed. F. BLUME (Kassel-Basel 1949–) 3:1867–80. C. L. E. KOECHLIN, *Gabriel Fauré, 1845–1924,* tr. L. ORRY (London 1945). N. SUCKLING, *Fauré* (London 1951). M. COOPER, *French Music* (London 1951). C. CABALLERO, ''Fauré and French Musical Aesthetics'' (Ph.D. diss. University of Pennsylvania 1996). R. H. CROUCH, ''The Nocturnes and Barcarolles for Solo Piano of Gabriel Fauré'' (Ph.D. diss. Catholic University 1980). K. JOHANSEN, ''Gabriel Fauré, un art de l'équivoque,'' *Revue de Musicologie,* 85 (1999) 63–96. A. LABUSSIÈRE, ''Gabriel Fauré: 2nd Sonate pour violoncelle et piano op. 117,'' *Analyse Musicale,* 25 (1991) 19–35. M. MACDONALD, ''*Pénélope,*'' in *International Dictionary of Opera,* ed. C. S. LARUE, 2 v. (Detroit 1993) 1002–1003. J.-M. NECTOUX, ''Gabriel (Urbain) Fauré,'' in *The New Grove Dictionary of Music and Musicians,* ed. S. SADIE, v. 6 (New York 1980) 417–428. E. R. PHILLIPS, ''Smoke, Mirrors, and Prisms: Tonal Contradiction in Fauré,'' *Music Analysis,* 12 (1993) 3–24. A. PIOVANO, ''Aspetti della produzione vocale di Gabriel Fauré: il Requiem e le Mélodies,'' *Rassegna Musicale Curci,* 50 (1997) 44–50. D. M.

RANDEL, ed., *The Harvard Biographical Dictionary of Music* (Cambridge, Mass. 1996) 261–262.

[V. RAAD]

FAURE, GIOVANNI BATTISTA

Theologian; b. Rome, Oct. 25, 1702; d. Viterbo, April 5, 1779. Faure entered the Society of Jesus in 1728 and spent most of his life teaching philosophy and theology. It is the opinion of some historians that had he not had a penchant for acrimonious polemic, he would have been regarded as the foremost theologian of his era. A work, *Avviso salutevole* (Naples 1744), in defense of B. Benzi against D. CONCINA, attributed to Faure but never acknowledged as his, was put on the Index in 1744. An acknowledged work, also published anonymously, was his notorious *Commentarium in Bullam Pauli III ''Licet ab initio''* (n.p. 1750), which was also put on the Index in 1757.

Under the pretext of tracing the history of the Inquisition set up by Paul III in 1512, this work bitterly attacks the methods of a number of the inquisitors, most of whom were Dominicans, for their favoritism and arbitrariness in condemning books. It complains also about the censure in 1725 of the faculty of theology at Douai, which was known, the author contends, ''for its devotion to the Holy See.''

Faure's commentary on the *Enchiridion de fide, spe et caritate* of St. Augustine, entitled *Dissertatio dogmatica de praxi quesnelliana,* was stopped in press by order of the Inquisition. Edited and completed by an associate of Faure, this work appeared after his death under the title *In Arnaldi librum de frequenti communione* (Rome 1791). Faure's *Apparatus brevis ad theologiam et jus canonicum* (Rome 1751) underwent many editions. A major work against Jansenism, *Dubitationes theologicae de judicio practico quod super paenitentis . . . dispositione formare sibi potest et debet confessarius* (Lugano 1840), was criticized by some as going too far in permitting the absolution of recidivists (*see* RECIDIVISM). An excellent defense of devotion to the Sacred Heart was offered in Faure's *Bigletti confidenziali critici* (Venice 1772) and *Saggi teologici* (Lugano 1773). His other works include treatises on dogmatic theology, Scripture, Canon Law and Church history.

Faure was imprisoned in the Castel Sant'Angelo near the papal palace in the Vatican after the suppression of the Society of Jesus by Clement XIV in 1773. It was feared his inflammatory writings might foment a rebellion against the papal action. He was liberated by Pius VI in 1775 and spent the rest of his days at Viterbo in peace and quiet.

Gabriel Urbain Fauré.

Bibliography: H. HURTER, *Nomenclator literarius theologiae catholicae* (Innsbruck 1926) 5.1:76–80. J. BRUCKER, *Dictionnaire de théologie catholique*, ed. A. VACANT et al., (Paris 1903–50) 5.2:2100–01. P. BAILLY, *Catholicisme* 4:1117.

[C. R. MEYER]

FAUST, MATHÍAS

Franciscan administrator; b. Oberbimbach, Germany, Dec. 30, 1879; d. New York City, July 27, 1956. Faust's parents, Joseph and Clara (Voelinger) Faust, had him baptized Constantine. He studied at Fulda and Hereveld, Holland, before immigrating to the U.S. in 1896, where he entered the novitiate of the Friars Minor at Paterson, N.J., and was ordained in 1906. Thereafter he served his order, first as novice master, then 12 years as provincial minister, and eight years as assistant provincial. During this time he sent missionaries to China and to the southern part of the U.S., encouraged higher education in the schools of his province, and secured many rare books and manuscripts for his friaries. He was frequently appointed visitator general for other provinces in the U.S., Europe, and Mexico, to which he assigned his own priests to help minister to the people there. He showed a vital interest in the secular Third Order of St. Francis and strongly supported the foundation of St. Anthony

Guild in Paterson, N.J., for the publication of religious works. In 1945 he founded the Academy of American Franciscan History, Washington, D.C., and formed a Commissariate for the Byzantine-Slavonic rite in Connecticut. During World War II, he was delegate general for all Franciscan houses in North and Central America and for four years thereafter was procurator general in Rome. He spent the last four years of his career in New York directing the commissariates of his order in North America.

Bibliography: *Acta Ordinis Fratrum Minorum* 75 (1956) 247–248. A. J. CALLAHAN, *Medieval Francis in Modern America* (New York 1936).

[E. KLAUS]

FAUST LEGEND

The legendary tales that accumulated round the historical figure of George, later Johann, Faust (*c.* 1480–1540) embody one of man's oldest dreams, that of acquiring boundless knowledge and happiness through a spiritual alliance with superhuman forces. This motif appeared in early Christian tradition, e.g., in the story of Simon Magus (Acts ch. 8) and in accounts by Cyprian of Antioch, Theophilius of Adana, Pope Sylvester II, and others that exemplified this kind of temptation. Sorcerers such as Merlin and Klingsor played their sinister roles in medieval courtly literature. The development of the Faust legend, uniquely reflecting the intellectual climate of 16th-century Germany, adds a new dimension to the age-old plot: the total destruction of man's soul brought about by demonic forces.

Religious Climate. The time of the Renaissance and Reformation filled man's mind with the realization of profound changes and revolutions. The theological schism was only one symptom of a general cultural and historical metamorphosis introduced by new scientific discoveries, the humanistic revival of antiquity, and the new spiritual and mystical impulses in religious life. Established systems of values were threatened by new, more dynamic concepts of life that laid the ground for imagining unlimited possibilities of knowledge and power; they also brought about a feeling of unrest and instability. Numerous paintings of this age (e.g., those of Dürer, Grien, and Brueghel) reflect traumatic visions of apocalyptic events and grotesque invasions of demonic forces. The widening horizons in scientific and philosophical knowledge in the thought and discoveries of men such as Nicolaus COPERNICUS, Giordano Bruno, and Johann Kepler grew in their contemporaries' imaginations to titanic notions of human insight into cosmic forces. A significant stimulant for the development of such exalted ideas radiated from the well known but controversial Swiss physician P. A. Paracelsus, whose pansophic system of philosophy attempted to bridge the apparent gap between the natural sciences (which, for him included alchemy and astrology) and Christian theology. He visualized a secret identity of the spiritual and phenomenological world, recognizing two basic forms of human perception: the ''light of grace'' in Christian doctrine and God's second revelation in the ''light of nature'' based on the totality of earthly existence (*Philosophia sagax,* 1537). Such ''advanced'' ideas, reflecting the dynamic, antihierarchical drives of this time, were opposed and passionately condemned as black magic by reactionary and orthodox theologians of both confessions.

Development of the Legend. The remarkable career of Johann Faust, born presumably at Helmstedt, near Heidelberg, coincided with the most crucial years of the reformatory age. He exploited the clandestine fears and superstitions of the people by applying his pretended magical skills to all fields of human knowledge. Since many courts and influential personages employed astrologers, Faust played this role for the lower strata of society by practicing his dubious art in inns and at fairs. He is first mentioned by the Benedictine scholar-abbot Johannes TRITHEMIUS in a letter to the mathematician and Heidelberg court astrologer J. Virdung in 1507. The abbot told his friend that he had met Faust a year before at Gelnhausen and now found this ''vagabond, babbler, and rogue, who deserves to be thrashed,'' at Würzburg, confusing the people by many boastful promises and false divinations. Faust called himself ''the chief of necromancers, astrologer, the second magus, palm-reader, diviner with earth and fire, second in the art of divination with water.'' He appeared shortly afterward in Kreuznach, where he obtained the position of schoolmaster through the influence of Franz von Sickingen, ''a man very fond of mystical lore.'' Discovered to be a sodomite, Faust fled to avoid persecution. Trithemius's characterization of Faust is repeated in a series of subsequent accounts wherein he is reported to cast horoscopes, to make false soothsayings, and fraudulently to practice medicine. But his reputation must have improved toward the end of his life. He was well known, if despised, by leaders of the Reformation, including Luther and Melanchthon. Precisely because he was a resourceful and ambiguous impersonator of many masks, he immensely stimulated the imagination of the people.

Shortly after his death, Faust's image was inflated among the people by being connected with exuberant accounts of all sorts of obscure practices and mysterious dealings with infernal powers that people in that troubled age were able to fancy. The important point for the subsequent development of the legend lies in the fact that these

"Faust in His Study," engraving by Rembrandt, 1652. (©Historical Picture Archive/CORBIS)

mysterious tales were carefully preserved, amended, and used by Protestant theologians. As early as 1548 a Basel minister, Johann Gast, included in his popular *Sermones Convivales* two episodes from Faust's life that expressly illustrate the power of the devil over man. What had not occurred to any of his learned critics during Faust's lifetime now became an unquestionable certainty: Faust had made a compact with the devil and had frivolously bartered away his immortal soul for spiritual power and sensual pleasure. In the fervent explications of preachers Faust obtained the singular honor of being elevated to the ranks of great wizards and magicians of ancient and medieval tradition. He became the embodiment of spiritual pride and of that particular temptation so characteristic of the age: the attributing of greater value to man's own will and intellectual achievement than to the "pure Word of God." It is not accidental that several beginnings of the legend lead to Wittenberg, the spiritual center of the Reformation. Even Luther is said to have felt a threat from Satan and his servant Faust, but "God's word alone overcomes the fiery arrows of the devil and all his temptation." In view of the widespread and fatalistic belief in astrology, the superstitious credulity among the uneducated people, and the increasing uncertainty among learned and responsible persons, it is not surprising that some theologians took seriously the common belief in black magic and used fear and gloomy forebodings to combat spiritual pride, licentiousness, and arrogance. The newly established Protestant church needed the example of the frightful damnation of a human soul to combat what it considered an assembly-line salvation offered by a stagnant institutionalism.

Literary Sources and Treatment. Both the moral implications of the Faust legend and its strange mystical obscurantism account for the immense popularity of the first printed edition of the *Historia von D. Johann Fausten,* by J. Spies (Frankfurt 1587). This collection of episodes was well developed and had circulated widely before its printing; part of it presumably had been recorded and distributed in Latin. Faust's scholarly pursuits are mentioned in the beginning: his "contemplation of the natural elements" and his vain attempt to explore restlessly all the foundations of heaven and earth. The majority of the episodes, however, depicted either low sensual enjoyments or incredible magic feats, recounted in popular balladesque style to serve "all haughty, overcurious and ungodly men as a frightful example, abhorrent illustration, and frank warning." Several new editions followed during the same year, chiefly because the book contained a representative collection of all mystery fables available at that time. A new compilation of Faust stories, greatly expanded by pedantic moral annotations, was edited by G. R. Widemann in 1599. The latest edition appeared in 1674 in Nuremberg, revised by J. H. Pfitzer, and was again published, anonymously, in 1712 by a Christian Believer (*Christlich Meynenden*).

Marlowe's Handling. One of the first English translations of the Faust book was the source of *The Tragical History of the Life and Death of Doctor Faustus* (*c.* 1588) by playwright Christopher Marlowe. His hero is not the boastful rogue and licentious fool of the chapbooks but appears in the more appealing guise of a daring titan rebelling against narrow moral dogmatism. Torn by a furious tension between man and devil, temptation and repentance, revolt and despair, he is overcome by the powers of evil, partly against his will. Marlowe counted on deeper understanding and pity for his hero's grandiose error and thus gave him a more human dimension. Marlowe's dramatization of the Faust legend was brought to the Continent by strolling English players in the early 17th century. But just as the poetically stimulating legend had gradually deteriorated into moralistic chapbooks hawked at fairs, so the tragedy soon changed to a freely improvised comedy and into various puppet plays for the amusement of half-wits and children. The literary critic Johann Gottsched (1700–66) vigorously condemned the harlequinades and fairy tales of Dr. Faustus, which the masses had so long enjoyed. Later the German dramatist G. E. LESSING recognized the truly "national" nature of the Faust plot and tried his own dramatization, of which only a few scenes are preserved. Lessing's treatment favored a rather unorthodox, final salvation of Faust.

Goethe's Version. Only J. von GOETHE, however, succeeded in opening a new dimension in Faust's inner quest for deeper and more meaningful understanding of life. His Faust is tragically driven by an ever unsatisfied yearning for "more than earthly meat and drink." The power of love as well as his continuous search for knowledge gradually develops the potentials of his soul so that Mephistopheles, the chaotic Spirit of Denial, always fails to procure that moment of supreme satisfaction for which Faust would trade his salvation. The devil is "poor" in the face of such a great aspiration for inner fulfillment, and though "man errs as long as he strives," Faust's soul finally ascends into heaven with the help of the "almighty love which forms all things and bears all things." Faust gains in each phase of his existence a new approach toward perfection despite the impossibility of ever achieving such a state in this world.

More recent attempts to revive the Faust legend in poetic form, notably Thomas Mann's novel *Doktor Faustus* (1950), may come closer to the original collection of 16th-century tales in their elevation of a vagrant charlatan to the ranks of powerful rebels of the intellect; Goethe's *Faust,* however, remains the highest expression of the legend, which contained, from the very beginning, the metaphysical question of man's ultimate destiny.

Bibliography: K. ENGEL, *Zusammenstellung der Faust-Schriften vom 16. Jahrhundert bis Mitte 1884* (Oldenburg 1865), 2d ed. of *Bibliotheca Faustiana* (1874). C. KIESEWETTER, *Faust in der Geschichte und Tradition* (Leipzig 1893). H. W. GEISSLER, ed., *Gestaltungen des Faust,* 3 v. (Munich 1927). P. M. PALMER and R. P. MORE, eds. and trs., *The Sources of the Faust Tradition from Simon Magus to Lessing* (New York 1936). E. M. BUTLER, *The Fortunes of Faust* (Cambridge, Eng. 1952).

[K. SCHAUM]

FAUSTUS OF RIEZ

Fifth-century monk, bishop, and theological writer; b. Britain, *c.* 410; d. between 490 and 500. Faustus was a monk at Lérins and became abbot *c.* 433; he took part in the Synod of Arles (455) and was selected as bishop of Riez in Provence *c.* 458. A renowned preacher and opponent of ARIANISM among the Goths, and of Macedonianism, Faustus is considered, with John CASSIAN, a chief proponent of SEMI-PELAGIANISM. He was wrongly accused of favoring a strict predestinationism dependent upon AUGUSTINE OF HIPPO, and, in Synods at Arles (473) and Lyons (474), he successfully opposed the Gallic priest Lucidus, who was condemned for teaching that God withheld grace from those destined for damnation.

Faustus wrote two books *De Spiritu Sancto* against the Macedonians; and two books *De gratia Dei* against Lucidus. Ten of his letters have been preserved, five of them in the correspondence of Bp. Ruricius of Limoges (d. *c.* 508). He is the author of numerous sermons; A. Engelbrecht credits him with 31 (*Corpus scriptorum ecclesiasticorum latinorum* 21), while G. Morin maintains that 75 other sermons attributed to Eusebius of Emesa should be recognized as belonging to Faustus (*Zeitschrift für die neutestamentliche Wissenschaft und die Kunde der älteren Kirche* 1935:92–115).

Faustus interpreted the grace by which the Father draws souls to salvation (Jn 6.44) more as an attraction given through revelation, sermons, and the Scriptures (*De grat.* 1.16); but he combatted Augustine's doctrine of predestination by insisting on God's salvific will for all (*ibid.* 2.4, 10). He saw predestination as based on God's foreknowledge alone (*ibid.* 2.2–3). In the matter of original sin, failing to achieve a notion of total spirituality of the soul, he followed JUSTIN MARTYR, TERTULLIAN, and John CASSIAN and accepted TRADUCIANISM (*Epist.* 3). He was opposed by CLAUDIANUS MAMERTUS (d. 474), whose *De statu animae* reflected Neoplatonist and Augustinian thought on the nature of spiritual reality.

In 477 Faustus was expelled from Gaul by the Arian Visigoth King Euric and lived in exile until 485. He is venerated as a saint in southern France, but his questionable doctrine on grace prevented his cult spreading to the universal Church.

Bibliography: *Patrologia Latina* 58:775–890. A. ENGELBRECHT, ed., *Corpus scriptorum ecclesiasticorum latinorum* 21 (1891). J. HUHN, *Theologische Quartalschrift* 130 (1950) 176–183; 133 (1953) 408–426, de fide. B. ALTANER, *Patrology* 566–567. P. GODET, *Dictionnaire de théologie catholique* 5.2:2101–05. G. WEIGEL, *Faustus of Riez* (Philadelphia 1938). A. G. ELG, *In Faustum Riensen studia* (Upsala 1937); *In epistolam Fausti Riensis tertiam adnotationes* (Lund 1945). H. HAGENDAHL, *La Correspondance de Ruricius* (Göteborg 1952). F. BÖMER, *Der lateinische Neuplatonismus und Neupythagorismus* (Leipzig 1936).

[A. NEUWIRTH]

FAVIER, ALPHONSE

Missionary bishop in China; b. Marsonnay-la-Cote, near Dijon, France, Sept. 22, 1837; d. Beijing, China, April 3, 1905. After joining the VINCENTIANS (1858) Favier went to the Province of Chihli (now Hebei) in northern China (1862), where he remained until 1870 when he was sent to Beijing. In 1897 he became auxiliary bishop of Beijing, and in 1899 vicar apostolic of North Chihli. Favier, who was a good diplomat and linguist, was active in defense of the French protectorate of Chinese Catholic missions. He was largely responsible for the imperial decree (1899) that gave bishops equal rank with mandarins. During the Boxer Rebellion (1900) he inspired 3,500 Christians to withstand a two-month siege in Beijing's Northern Church (Beitang). Afterward he played an important role as mediator between China and the Western powers. Favier's most important writing was *Pékin, Histoire et Déscription* (Lille 1900).

Bibliography: G. GOYAU, *La France missionnaire dans les cinq parties du monde,* v.2 (Paris 1948) 120–124.

[J. KRAHL]

FAY, CYRIL SIGOURNEY WEBSTER

Diplomat; b. Philadelphia, Pa., June 16, 1875; d. New York City, Jan. 10, 1919. Fay was the son of Alfred Forbes and Susan (Hutchinson) Fay. After attending the University of Pennsylvania and the Episcopal Divinity School in Philadelphia, he was ordained in 1903. He became professor of dogmatic and moral theology at Nashotah House, an Episcopal seminary in the Diocese of Fond du Lac, Wis. There Fay joined a group of Anglican clergymen, the ''Companions of the Holy Savior,'' who were led by the Rev. William McGarvey of Philadelphia. In 1907, when the Episcopal convention at Richmond, Va., approved the ''open pulpit'' clause allowing clergy of other denominations to preach in Episcopal churches, McGarvey, Fay, and others in the ''American Oxford Movement'' joined the Catholic Church.

Fay was ordained for the Baltimore Archdiocese by Cardinal James Gibbons, June 21, 1910. He was much in demand as a retreatmaster and preacher; he served as headmaster of the Newman School for Boys, Hackensack, N.J., and in 1917 joined the Red Cross. His work took him to Italy, where he became involved in negotiations to expunge a clause from a secret treaty that excluded the Holy See from participation in the World War I peace conference. Since Fay was a friend of Arthur James Balfour, the British Foreign Minister, and of Sir Eric Drummond and Cecil Dormer, members of the British Commission in Washington, it was decided to undertake further diplomacy in England, rather than approach Pres. Woodrow Wilson. Created a domestic prelate by Benedict XV, Fay returned to the U.S. to prepare for his mission. On the eve of his sailing for London, however, he was stricken with influenza and died.

Bibliography: M. CHANLER, *Autumn in the Valley* (Boston 1936).

[W. K. DUNN]

FAYRFAX, ROBERT

Noted Renaissance composer of liturgical music; b. Deeping Gate, Lincolnshire, England, *c.* 1464; d. probably St. Albans, Oct. 24, 1521. By 1496, if not earlier, he was a gentleman of the chapel royal, and from 1502 was possibly choirmaster at St. Albans, although he retained connections with the chapel royal until his death. He took the degrees Mus.B. (1501) and Mus.D. (1504) at Cambridge and the earliest recorded Mus.D. (1511) at Oxford. He was first singer of the chapel at the Field of Cloth of Gold, June 1520. His works comprise six Masses (of which one is incomplete), two Magnificats, 13 motets, and a few secular songs, lute arrangements, and instrumental pieces. He was highly esteemed by his contemporaries and his music was recopied for a century after his death. His style represents a trend away from the florid manner to a simpler homophonic technique, and is distinguished for great variety in grouping of voices. An edition of his *Collected Works* has been prepared by E. B. Warren for the American Institute of Musicology [(*Corpus mensurablis musicae*, v.17 (Rome 1947–)].

Bibliography: F. L. HARRISON, *Music in Medieval Britain* (New York 1958). ''English Polyphony c. 1470–1540,'' *New Oxford History of Music*, ed. J. A. WESTRUP 11 v. (New York 1957–) 3:303–348. G. REESE, *Music in the Renaissance* (rev. ed. New York 1959) 774–777. A. HUGHES, ''An Introduction to Fayrfax,'' *Musica Disciplina*, 6 (Rome 1952) 83–104. *Grove's Dictionary of Music and Musicians*, ed. E. BLOM, 9 v. (5th ed. London 1954) 3:50–54. D. MATEER and E. NEW, ''*In nomine Jesu*: Robert Fayrfax and the Guild of the Holy Name in St. Paul's Cathedral,'' *Music and Letters* 81 (2000) 507–519. T. MESSENGER, ''Texture and Proportion in the Masses of Robert Fayrfax: Medieval Formal Procedures in the Early Tudor Mass Cycle'' (Ph.D. diss. University of Wales at Bangor, 1979). D. M. RANDEL, ed., *The Harvard Biographical Dictionary of Music* 262 (Cambridge, Massachusetts 1996). N. SANDON, ''Robert Fayrfax'' in *The New Grove Dictionary of Music and Musicians, vol. 6*, ed. S. SADIE (New York 1980) 443–445. N. SLONIMSKY, ed. *Baker's Biographical Dictionary of Musicians, Eighth Edition* (New York 1992) 523.

[S. W. KENNEY]

FEAR

An emotion arising from awareness of something seen as an imminent danger affecting oneself. It has interested philosophers at least from the time of PLATO (*Leges* 644D; 646E) and Aristotle (*Rhetorica* 1382a19–1383b11), and has been the subject of intense study by modern psychologists. Definiteness of an object in fear and the occurrence of this emotion in adequately functioning persons have usually been bases for distinguishing fear from anxiety. Since fears of definite things, however, also appear as signs of mental disturbance (e.g., a phobia for closed places or moving vehicles), presence of an ''attitude of fear'' or a tendency to see danger everywhere better serves to distinguish anxiety from fear.

Moral Aspects. Since responsibility in a moral sense implies the voluntariness of a human act, the question arises as to the influence of fear on the voluntary character of an action. Voluntariness implies some movement on the part of the will, which, in turn, presupposes knowledge, for only a known good moves an appetitive power. A person is morally responsible, then, when he knows what he is doing and retains freedom of action, at least in the sense of having it in his power to do or not to do a given act. Voluntariness implies some movement on the part of the will, which, in turn, presupposes knowledge, for only a known good moves an appetitive power. A person is morally responsible, then, when he knows what he is doing and retains freedom of action, at least in the sense of having it in his power to do or not to do a given act.

In an action done because of fear, there is at least some consent on the part of the will, for we are led to do what we do, not because of the fear itself, but in order to avoid the evil that is feared. Therefore, in an action done out of fear, the voluntary character of the action remains, for it is enough to make an act voluntary that the will contribute something to the action that is done, and this condition is realized in an action done because of fear. It is also clear that fear exerts an influence on the degree of voluntariness of the action, and to the extent that it does, fear diminishes the voluntariness and therefore the responsibility of the action.

To put the matter generally, actions done because of fear remain voluntary and responsible although they become involuntary in a certain respect, and thus lessen responsibility to that extent. What is done out of fear is involuntary in the sense that it is contrary to what would be the will's inclination apart from the circumstances that evoke the fear. A man at gunpoint hands over his wallet to a robber; he would not presumably be willing to dispossess himself in this way except to avoid the evil that threatens him. But the action is, in an absolute sense of the term, voluntary, for the will, in the actual circumstances, prefers to sustain the loss rather than to endure the consequences of resistance. There is thus a mixture of voluntariness and involuntariness in what is done. The action is said to be voluntary simply or absolutely speaking, but involuntary in a certain respect (*secundum quid*). The element of involuntariness shows some goodness in the will, even if the action is an evil one, and to that extent diminishes culpability.

This analysis of fear does not include, however, a situation in which a person is so overcome by an impending evil that fear causes him to lose rational control completely. An action performed by a person in such a condition would not be voluntary at all. Voluntary action is always in some way subject to reason. No degree of fear that falls short of depriving a person of the use of reason renders him incapable of controlling his action. Both civil and ecclesiastical laws expressly recognize the influence of fear where contractual obligations are concerned, and in certain cases declare obligations undertaken under the influence of fear to be either void or voidable.

See Also: APPETITE.

Bibliography: M. B. ARNOLD, *Emotion and Personality,* 2 v. (New York 1960), an extensive and profound analysis of fear and the other emotions. D. B. LINDSLEY, ''Emotion'' in S. S. STEVENS, ed., *Handbook of Experimental Psychology* (New York 1951). M. L. REYMERT, ed., *Feelings and Emotions: The Mooseheart Symposium in Cooperation with the University of Chicago* (New York 1950). R. W. LEEPER, ''A Motivational Theory of Emotion to Replace 'Emotion as Disorganized Response,''' *Psychological Review* 55 (1948) 5–21. A. T. JERSILD, ''Emotional Development'' in L. CARMICHAEL, ed., *Manual of Child Psychology* (2d ed. New York 1954) 833–917. H. SELYE, *The Stress of Life* (New York 1956). THOMAS AQUINAS, *Summa theologiae* 1a2ae, 6.6. H. DAVIS, *Moral and Pastoral Theology,* 4 v. (5th ed. New York 1946). J. A. OESTERLE, *Ethics* (Englewood Cliffs, N.J. 1957) 67–69.

[H. GAVIN/J. A. OESTERLE]

FEAR OF THE LORD

An expression of frequent occurrence indicating the attitude that man should assume toward God.

In the Bible. In the Old Testament the wonderful WORKS OF GOD, ''fearful and terrible deeds'' (Ex 34.10; 2 Sm 7.23), produced a sense of awe and fear in the Israelites who came into contact with Him (Ex 3.6). This was not merely a negative emotion of blind terror, for God's self-revelation is also a disclosure of His salvific purpose. Hence, in Deuteronomy fear of the Lord (Heb. *yir'at yhwh*) is equated with reverence and piety that includes love for God and hatred of sin (Dt 6.1–5)—a synthesis of Old Testament religion. In this sense, the sapiential literature speaks of the fear of the Lord as the ''beginning of wisdom'' [Jb 28.28; Prv 1.7; Ps 110(111).10, Sir 1.16]. In postexilic Judaism to fear God meant in practice to observe the Law (Tb 1.10; Sir 23.27).

In the New Testament the Disciples were filled with awe by the wonderful works of Jesus (Mk 4.39–41; 16.8; Lk 5.26). The early Church lived with a sense of awe (Acts 2.43) not incompatible with joy. Though fear is less emphasized in the New Testament, it remains a necessary quality of the Christian attitude (Acts 9.31; 2 Cor 5.11). Love overcomes worldly fear (1 Jn 4.18), but the Christian must live constantly in reverent fear of God (Rom 11.20; Phil 2.12).

Bibliography: *Encyclopedic Dictionary of the Bible*, tr. and adap. by L. HARTMAN (New York 1963) 766–767. S. TERRIEN, G. A. BUTTRICK, ed., *The Interpreters' Dictionary of the Bible* (Nashville 1962) 2:256–260. É. BOULARAND, *Dictionnaire de spiritualité ascétique et mystique. Doctrine et histoire*, ed. M. VILLER et al. (Paris 1932–) 2.2:2463–75. L. NIEDER, *Lexikon für Theologie und Kirche*, ed. J. HOFER and K. RAHNER (Freiberg 1957–65) 4:1107–08. G. BERTRAM and G. KITTEL, *Theologisches Wörterbuch zum Neuen Testament* (Stuttgart 1935–) 3:124–128. J. FICHTNER and C. MAURER, *Die Religion in Geschichte und Gegenwart* (Tübingen 1957–65) 2:1793–95. H. A. BRONGERS, ''La Crainte du Seigneur,'' *Oudtestamentische Studiën* 5 (1948) 151–173. R. H. PFEIFFER, ''The Fear of God,'' *Israel Exploration Journal* 5 (1955) 41–48. B. OLIVER, *La Crainte de Dieu comme valeur religieuse dans l'A.T.* (Brussels 1960). S. PLATH, Furcht Gottes: Der Begriff Jir'a im A.T. (Stuttgart 1963).

[C. J. PEIFER]

As a Gift of the Holy Spirit. Fear of the Lord strengthens the acts of the virtue of hope. A soul moved by the gift is overwhelmed at the greatness of God and adheres ever more firmly to the divine goodness. A reverence follows that moves the person to fear anything that threatens its union with the Father. This fear is filial, not the servile fear whose concern is punishment; it causes the soul to turn not only from sin, but also from every tendency to refuse God anything. Appreciation of God's goodness increases, and with it grows contempt for self and all created goods. Thus, as the gift adds to hope's certitude, it also perfects humility and temperance. The beatitude corresponding to fear is ''Blessed are the poor in spirit,'' for whoever is moved by fear is blessed in seeking nothing of this world. The fruits of fear are modesty, continence, and chastity, all acts of temperance but as fruits that are perfected by the gift.

Bibliography: B. FROGET, *The Indwelling of the Holy Spirit in the Souls of the Just*, tr. S. A. RAEMERS (Westminister, Md. 1950). A. ROYO, *The Theology of Christian Perfection*, ed. and tr. J. AUMANN (Dubuque 1962) 392–400, 496. THOMAS AQUINAS, *Summa theologiae* 2a2ae, 19.

[P. F. MULHERN]

FEAST OF ASSES

The name sometimes given in medieval France to the FEAST OF FOOLS, celebrated on or about the Feast of the Circumcision (January 1), and sometimes to the Festival of the Flight into Egypt, held within the octave of the Epiphany (January 6). Both feasts, however innocent in origin, were by the 13th century characterized by burlesqued services, in some of which—as at Beauvais, Sens, and Autun—the ass played a part. At Beauvais, two 13th-century MSS, one for the Feast of the Circumcision, the other for the Flight into Egypt, show the normal form of the Mass and the Canonical Office retained, but the text extended by interpolations, or tropes, and the ceremonial including a considerable amount of buffoonery.

The ceremonial for the feast of the Flight into Egypt called for braying by the participants at Mass and, it would appear, the bringing of an ass into church. Both included the Prose of the Ass, *Orientis partibus,* each stanza of which had as refrain some variant of ''Hez, Sire Asne, hez!'' A ''reformed'' version for the feast on January 1, at Sens, although called *asinaria festa* and retaining the Prose of the Ass, omits the coarser elements of revelry and seems to have been entirely serious in its intentions. The ass itself was not necessarily a comic figure; it had served for the flight into Egypt, for Christ's entry into Jerusalem, and was, moreover, associated with the ox in *praesepe* observances.

The relation between the Feast of Asses and plays of the prophets such as that of Balaam and his ass is not altogether clear. Karl Young, while noting that the dramatic *Ordo Prophetarum* came first, denies that the riotous *asinaria festa* was derived from it. It would appear that in the course of time the ass was introduced from the Feast of Fools into the plays of the prophets, and that sometimes, as at Rouen, the *asina* forced upon the pious performance the name *Festum Asinorum.* The Feast of Asses was, of course, included in the ecclesiastical strictures against the Feast of Fools.

See Also: DRAMA, MEDIEVAL.

Bibliography: E. K. CHAMBERS, *The Medieval Stage,* 2 v. (Oxford 1903; reprint 1948) 1:274–335. K. YOUNG, *The Drama of the Medieval Church,* 2 v. (Oxford 1933) 1:104–105, 551; 2:154–170.

[M. N. MALTMAN]

FEAST OF FOOLS

A widely celebrated mock-religious festival of the Middle Ages. It was originally celebrated by the subdeacons of cathedrals, and was held on or about the Feast of the Circumcision (January 1). The name is sometimes applied collectively to the several liturgical revels of the Christmas season, particularly as celebrated by the deacons on the Feast of St. Stephen (December 26), the priests on St. John's Day (December 27), the choirboys on Holy Innocents' (December 28), and by the subdeacons on or about the Circumcision (January 1). Such revels, disputedly claimed to have been a Christian adaptation of the pagan festivities of the Kalends when great license was permitted the lower classes, were widespread in Europe during the Christmas season, and especially at the festivities of the subdeacons, whose feast came to be known specifically as the Feast of Fools. Though observances varied locally, they usually included burlesqued services, censing with unseemly objects, and more or less riotous behavior.

The essence of the feast was inversion of status, the control of the services of the day being given over wholly to the subdeacons. At First Vespers their representative (variously styled Lord, Abbot, Bishop, or Pope of Fools) received the staff of office from the master of ceremonies, assumed his authority, and retained it throughout the feast. Though the feast had its vogue in the French cathedrals, there are records of it in England, notably at Lincoln, Salisbury, and Beverley.

The feast seems to have originated about the 12th century; although official opposition was manifested as early as 1207, it continued in popularity through the 14th century. In 1435 very severe penalties were imposed by the Council of Basle for its observance; it was eventually suppressed, but remnants lingered on well into the 16th century.

See Also: FEAST OF ASSES; BOY BISHOP.

Bibliography: E. K. CHAMBERS, *The Medieval Stage,* 2 v. (Oxford 1903) 1:274–335, 336–389. K. YOUNG, *The Drama of the Medieval Church,* 2 v. (Oxford 1933) 1:104–111. E. WELSFORD, *The Fool: His Social and Literary History* (London 1935) 197–217.

[M. N. MALTMAN]

FEASTS, RELIGIOUS

Feasts or festivals are periodically recurring occasions for the expression of religious joy. Generally they occur annually, but weekly, monthly, and other celebrations are also common.

Pagan Feasts. In remotest antiquity and in primitive societies in general, virtually all feasts are religious in character. They express, on the one hand, a natural desire to rejoice in the blessings of life and nature and to escape briefly the arduous tasks of daily life, and, on the other hand, a striving toward the gods, who have given the gifts of life and nature, and an effort to unite with the world of the divine. The widespread custom of feasting in honor of the dead clearly reflects the role of the feast as a link with another world. Likewise the ritual, symbolism, and mythology of feasts enable the celebrants to participate in the world of mythical origins conceived of as an eternal present. The stories of the creation of the world or the epics of gods and heroes, for example, are ritually recited or reenacted at feasts, which thus serve, not only as bonds of society, but as instruments for handing on religious traditions. Feasts are the external manifestation of religion itself in every culture, and they very often include sacrifice as a prominent part of their ritual.

Feasts may be classified according to their object. Those originating in individual or family life include the celebrations of birth or name-giving, initiation, marriage, and death or burial. Others center about cosmic events: the change of seasons, the appearance of the moon, the sun, and the stars, and especially the new year, which is almost universally observed, though not at a fixed time in all cultures. Closely connected with this category are feasts allied with phases of agricultural life, especially harvest festivals, and those that depend on hunting and fishing seasons and the like. Finally, there are feasts honoring various gods; some of these result from former cosmic or agricultural associations, and others commemorate historical events in the life of a god or prophet or religious founder.

In the developed cultures of antiquity one finds highly complex calendars of feasts that often clearly reveal the connection between agriculture and religious life. This is especially true of Mesopotamia, where numerous monthly and yearly feasts were observed through the centuries. The principal one was the new year festival, in later times the 12-day Babylonian *Akîtu,* with its elaborate ritual of recitation of the creation epic, sacred marriage and fertility drama, public penitence for the past, and divination of the future. The ancient Egyptian feasts were characterized by the cult of the dead and by processions bearing statues of the god being honored, often majestic processions on the Nile River. The festivals of

"Family at the Table for the Passover Meal," manuscript illumination, 15th century. (©Archivo Iconografico, S.A./ CORBIS)

Greece were originally agricultural in character and purely local; in classical times they honored various gods, and eventually some of the Athenian festivals, such as the Dionysiac, spread throughout the country. Especially significant features were the drama and the athletic games. As the traditional Roman religion acquired an increasingly formalized character, its feasts tended to become secular observances, while foreign religions, such as the Syrian, Greek, or Egyptian mysteries, and eventually Christianity, expressed the religious sentiments of the people.

Feasts in Israel. For the principal Hebrew feasts in Old Testament times there are several festival calendars in the Pentateuch and scattered allusions elsewhere in the Bible. The calendars, from the Yahwist, Elohist, Deuteronomic, and Priestly traditions, are found respectively in Ex 34.18–23; Ex 23.14–17; Dt 16.1–17; Lv 23 and the sacrificial legislation based on this in Num 28.9–29.39. Certain important additional Jewish feasts are of later origin.

The weekly and monthly feasts are the SABBATH and the New-Moon Day (*see* NEW-MOON FEAST, HEBREW). Although of uncertain origin, the weekly day of rest was as old as the worship of Yahweh and occupied a very important place in Israelite life because it commemorated the Covenant with Yahweh. The first day of each lunar month was also celebrated with rest from work and special sacrifices. Only the New-Moon Day of the 7th (formerly the 1st) month retained special solemnity in later times, and some of its features were incorporated into the late Jewish New Year's Day, Rosh ha-Shanah, celebrated on the same date but not mentioned in the Old Testaments.

The oldest annual Israelite feasts are the three great pilgrimages (*haggîm*) to the central religious sanctuary—Unleavened Bread, Weeks or Pentecost, and Tabernacles or Booths (*see* PILGRIMAGES, 1). All three are of agricultural origin and were probably adopted from the Canaanites after the Israelite conquest. All three were later historicized, i.e., were associated with events in Israel's history that were then commemorated annually: the deliverance from Egyptian bondage, the giving of the Law, and the wilderness journey, respectively. In the Deuteronomic reform the three pilgrimages were centralized at the Jerusalem Temple and some time later were given definite dates. The Feast of Unleavened Bread, observed for seven days at the beginning of the barley harvest in spring, from the 15th to the 21st of Nisan, was, around the time of the Exile, combined with the Feast of PASSOVER, which took place on the night of the 14th of Nisan. Passover may be even older than Unleavened Bread in Israel's history; it was a nomadic sacrifice that had probably been celebrated privately at home in the time when the earliest festival calendars were drawn up, for they do not mention it. The Feast of Weeks, or of the wheat harvest, was celebrated for one day only, seven weeks after Unleavened Bread. (*See* PENTECOST.) The Feast of Booths, at first the most prominent of the three, was the autumnal harvest festival, originally called the Ingathering. It was observed for seven (later eight) days beginning with the 15th of Tishri. It takes its name from the huts erected in the vineyards and orchards in the harvest season; these were ultimately identified with the tents used as dwelling places in the Exodus sojourn in the desert. *See* BOOTHS (TABERNACLES), FEAST OF.

The solemn Day of Atonement, Yom Kippur, was observed with sacrifices, penance, and fasting five days before Booths and is better classified as a fast day than as a feast. It originated very late in Old Testament times but embodied some ancient rites. *See* ATONEMENT, DAY OF (YOM KIPPUR).

Of the later feasts, two deserve mention because they have survived till the 20th century. The Feast of the Dedication, or Hanukkah, was instituted on the 25th of Kislev, 164 B.C., when Judas Maccabee reconsecrated the altar of the Temple that had been profaned three years before (*see* DEDICATION OF THE TEMPLE, FEAST OF). The story is told in 1 Maccabees 4.36–59 and 2 Maccabees 10.1–8. The origin of the Feast of PURIM, or Lots, celebrated on the 14th and 15th of Adar, is attributed by the Book of Esther to the escape of the Persian Jews from the plot of the wicked Haman. This is not a historical account, however, although the feast, very likely of pagan or at least secular origin in the East, cannot be linked with certainty to specific Persian or Babylonian practice.

Early Christian Feasts. The earliest Christians did not immediately dissociate themselves from the observance of the Jewish feasts. Many references in the New Testament indicate that Jesus and His disciples, as well as the early Palestinian Christian communities, observed the Sabbath and the major annual festivals. This observance had been invested by Christ with a new dimension, however, since He proclaimed His own superiority to the Law and oriented it to the eschatological events. It remained for Saint Paul to proclaim the Christian's independence from the Jewish festival calendar (Colossians 2.16), and with the fall of Jerusalem and the growth of the Church outside Palestine, the Judeo-Christian festival observance ceased except among sectarian groups.

The earliest feast in the Christian calendar was the LORD'S DAY, SUNDAY, which is well attested in the New Testament and the Apostolic Fathers (e.g., Acts of the Apostles 20.7; Revelation 1.10; *Didache* 14; Ignatius, *Magn.* 9.1). It commemorated the Resurrection and was observed with the celebration of the Eucharist; it was not connected in its origins with the Jewish Sabbath. The first annual feast to be observed was Easter, which initially coincided with the Jewish Passover festival but did not retain any of the Jewish meaning except symbolically (*see* EASTER AND ITS CYCLE). The great EASTER CONTROVERSY about the exact date of Easter and the manner of calculating it lasted from the 2d to the 4th century, and in some parts of the world until much later. The Council of Nicaea (325) decided in favor of the Sunday after the vernal equinox, and this date was gradually adopted throughout the Western Church.

The Feast of Pentecost also persisted in the Christian calendar, but again totally dissociated from its Jewish connotations. It commemorated the events of Acts of the Apostles ch. 2; by the 3d century it was a well established observance. The Feast of the ASCENSION OF JESUS CHRIST, 40 days after Easter, is well attested in writings of the 4th century.

The LITURGICAL YEAR IN THE ROMAN RITE, as known today, came into existence only gradually once the Easter and Christmas feasts had been established. There is 3d-century evidence that the Epiphany (January 6) was celebrated in Alexandria as the feast of Christ's baptism (*see* EPIPHANY, FEAST OF). The commemoration of the birthday of the Lord on December 25 spread from Rome throughout the Western Church from the 4th century, and Epiphany remained as the commemoration of the Magi incident recounted in Matthew 2.1–12. (*See* CHRISTMAS AND ITS CYCLE.)

Feasts honoring the saints, including MARIAN FEASTS, came into general use still later. Some of the oldest Marian feasts originated in the Eastern Church and spread to the West in the 6th and 7th centuries. Saints' feasts are rooted in the very early cult of the martyrs and are attested from the 3d and 4th centuries. (*See* SAINTS, DEVOTION TO THE.) Until the end of the Middle Ages the number of Christian feasts grew to considerable proportions; the tendency of modern times has been to reduce the number, both of feasts involving the obligations of Mass and abstinence from work and of other feasts often of only local importance.

Bibliography: J. H. BATESON et al., J. HASTINGS, ed., *Encyclopedia of Religion and Ethics*, 13 v. (Edinburgh 1908–27) 5:835–94. J. K. FOTHERINGHAM et al., *ibid.* 3:61–141, C. M. EDSMAN et al., *Die Religion in Geschichte und Gegenwart*, 7 v. (3d ed. Tübingen 1957–65) 2:906–21. O. SCHROEDER, *Lexikon für Theologie und Kirche*, ed. J. HOFER and K. RAHNER, 10 v. (2d, new ed. Freiburg 1957–65) 4:99–100. H. EISING, and W. LURZ, *ibid.* 95–99. J. H. MILLER, *Fundamentals of the Liturgy* (Notre Dame, Ind. 1960) 345–424. M. ELIADE, *Cosmos and History* (New York 1954). K. KERÉNYT, ''Vom Wesen des Festes,'' *Paideuma* 1 (1938) 59–74. R. DE VAUX, *Ancient Israel, Its Life and Institutions*, tr. J. MCHUGH (New York 1961) 468–517. G. B. GRAY, *Sacrifice in the Old Testament* (Oxford 1925). T. H. GASTER, *Festivals of the Jewish Year* (New York 1953). T. MAERTENS, *C'est fête en l'honneur de Yahvé* (Paris 1961). A. A. MCARTHUR, *The Evolution of the Christian Year* (London 1953). B. STEWART, *The Development of Christian Worship* (New York 1953) 214–51.

[G. W. MACRAE]

FEBRES CORDERO MUÑOZ, MIGUEL FRANCISCO, ST.

Baptized Francisco, also known as Miguel of Ecuador, scholar, author, philologist, poet, member of the Lasallian Institute of the Brothers of Christian Instruction, first Ecuadorian saint; b. Nov. 7, 1854, Cuenca, Ecuador; d. Feb. 9, 1910, Premia del Mar (near Barcelona), Spain. The scion of a politically prominent family of Cuenca headed by Francisco Febres Cordero Montoya and Ana Muñoz, Francisco was among the first students of the Lasallian Brothers at Cuenca (1863). Francisco joined the Lasallian Brothers, in spite of the initial resistance of his family and a physical deformity that made walking difficult. He took the habit at Cuenca, March 24, 1868 at age 13, and took the name Brother Miguel, the first native Ecuadorian in the Institute. Following his formation, he became a beloved teacher of languages (Spanish, French, and English) at the order's schools at Cuenca, then Quito. His pedagogical skills led to his appointment as public examiner and inspector of Quito's schools. His passion, however, was teaching the catechism to boys preparing for the sacraments. Miguel published the first of his many textbooks, a Spanish grammar, when he was 17. His work in the fields of linguistics and literature won him acclaim as a scholar and membership in the National Academies of Ecuador (1892) (which included membership in the Royal Academy of Spain), France (1900), and Venezuela (1906). He also authored a catechism and other pious works, including hymns. At a time boding civil unrest and religious persecution in France, he was assigned first to Paris (March 1907), then to the motherhouse at Lembecq–lez–Hal (near Brussels), Belgium (July 1907) to translate the Institute's documents into Spanish from French. Because the less temperate climate affected his health, he was transferred (1908) to the juniorate at Premia de Mar near Barcelona, where he was noted for his heroic efforts on behalf of his charges and the church during the July 1909 anarchist riots. Shortly thereafter, he contracted pneumonia and died. His body was returned to Quito at the start of the Spanish Civil War. The Ecuadorean government dedicated a monument to his honor in 1955. Miguel of Ecuador, patron of crippled children, was beatified by Pope Paul VI, Oct. 30, 1977, and canonized by Pope John Paul II on Oct. 21, 1984.

Feast: Feb. 9 (Lasallian Brothers).

Bibliography: *Un religieux équatorien, frère Miguel de l'Institut des Frères des écoles chrétiennes, 1854–1910* (Lembecq–lez–Hal, Belgium 1913). G. CEVALLOS GARCÍA, *Salí tras tí, clamando, y eras ido* (Cuenca, Ecuador 1962). R. CRESPO TORAL, *El hermano Miguel de las escuelas cristiana* (Cuenca, Ecuador 1937). R. L. GUIDI, *Un cuore per la scuola: vita di fratel Miguel delle Scuole cristiane* (Vicenza 1977). I. MOSCOSO DÁVILA and M. MALO GONZÁLEZ, *Ramas y floracion de una estirpe gloriosa*, 2 v. (Cuenca, Ecuador 1985–1986). E. MUÑOZ BORRERO, *Antología acerca del Hermano Miguel* (Cuenca, Ecuador 1967); *Un académico en los altares: el beato hermano Miguel de las Escuelas Cristianas* (Quito 1977). M. OLIVÉ, *San Miguel Febres Cordero—ese hermano: 21 de octubre de 1984, fiestas de la canonización* (Caracas, Venezuela 1984). L. PÁEZ FUENTES, *El hermano Miguel, maestro ejemplar* (Quito 1977); *Labor pedagógica, científica y literaria del hermano Miguel* (Quito 1991). L. SALM, *Brother Miguel Febres Cordero, F.S.C.: Teacher, Scholar, Saint* (Romeoville, Ill. 1984). *Acta Apostolicae Sedis* 78 (1986): 5–12. *L'Osservatore Romano*, Eng. ed., no. 45 (1977): 3–9; no. 46 (1984): 6–7.

[K. I. RABENSTEIN]

FEBRONIANISM

A theory of the constitution of the Church and of Church-State relations developed by Johann Nikolaus von HONTHEIM (1701–90), Auxiliary Bishop of Trier, under the pseudonym Justinus Febronius, in *The State of the Church and the Legitimate Authority of the Roman Pontiff, a Book Composed for the Purpose of Uniting in Religion Dissident Christians* (Frankfurt 1763). Professing to be based on accepted teaching, *De statu ecclesiae* (its Latin title) is censorious and bitter in tone, with many quotations from sources condemned as heretical.

Principles. Its thesis is that the PAPACY claims many powers not given by Christ or exercised in the Church of the first eight centuries. The Church is not monarchical. The PRIMACY OF THE POPE is to effect unity, to assure vigilance, and to promulgate laws enacted by a general council. It would be well if each general council would set the date for the next general council to convene. Failing this, a general council may be called by the pope, the emperor, or bishops [*see* BISHOP (IN THE CHURCH)]. As all bishops are equal, the pope has no jurisdiction outside his own see, which need not be Rome. Infallibility resides in the whole Church. Only the consent of the bishops makes papal pronouncements binding. The false decretals of Pseudo-Isidore account for the changed role of the papacy. The Roman Curia is the special object of vituperation. Instruction of the people, national synods, appeal to the royal power, reform in the Church, can bring about conditions necessary for Christian reunion. The effect of Febronianism would be the creation of a national German church, a collegium, or body, subject to the prince, a department of government.

Roots. Febronianism grew out of the ENLIGHTENMENT, GALLICANISM, conciliarism [*see* CONCILIARISM (HISTORY OF)], JANSENISM, regalism, ABSOLUTISM. Hontheim studied at Louvain under the canonist Z. B. van ESPEN, whose *On the Promulgation of Laws,* though it had been placed on the Index, he frequently quotes. He studied too in Leiden, where national and natural law intermingled. He was influenced by J. von Spangenberg, whom he assisted when the Councilor represented Trier at the electoral Diet of Frankfurt in 1742. Spangenberg thought a scholarly work on the *GRAVAMINA* and the German Church necessary. Hontheim's association with G. C. Neller, who came from Würzburg to teach in the seminars of Trier, brought greater familiarity with Gallican literature. Neller's *Principia juris publici ecclesiastici,* placed on the Index in 1750, was a much-used source for Febronius.

The concept of sovereignty that developed during the Enlightenment caused princes to treat papal envoys as diplomats of a foreign power, without status regarding the affairs of the Church in their countries. The rights of papal nuncios in the Rhenish electoral bishoprics and a Roman court's acceptance of a cause not yet judged in the Metz episcopal court of the first instance were under discussion at the time *De statu ecclesiae* appeared.

Response to Book. The book was translated into German, French, Italian, Spanish, and Portuguese. Supplements came out as volumes two to four, 1770 to 1774, and an abridgment by the author in 1777. The first edition was placed on the Index in 1764, and Clement XIII requested German bishops to outlaw it in their dioceses. The response was delayed and fainthearted; the Elector of Trier was among those who complied. After its condemnation, Maria Theresa ordered the suppression of the first Latin and German editions. Through G. van Swieten this was reduced to a simple prohibition, withdrawn in 1769. Even earlier a new canon law based on Febronian principles had developed. JOSEPHINISM antedates, embraces, and extends Febronianism. Congenial to Kaunitz, it was taught in Austrian universities. The dislike of Roman centralism and ultramontane Jesuits increased the popularity of Febronianism in Portugal, Spain, the Austrian Netherlands, Venice, Tuscany, and Naples. The bishop of Coimbra was imprisoned in 1770 for denouncing Febronianism. In 1786 Pius VI's brief *Super soliditate petrae* condemned Febronianism as it appeared in *Was ist der Papst?* (1782) by the Viennese canonist, J. V. Eybel.

Febronius was answered by more than 20 Catholic theologians. Clement XIII sent encouraging briefs to several such defenders. P. BALLERINI, the Dominican T. Mamachi, and the Jesuit F. A. ZACCARIA were among the most prolific. Zaccaria was exiled from Naples for his *Anti-Febronius.*

Klemens Wenzeslaus of Saxony and Poland, grandson of Emperor Joseph I, became bishop of Trier in February 1768. He continued to protect Hontheim as had J. P. von Walendorf, his predecessor, though his auxiliary's identity with Febronius was known to the papal nuncio N. Oddi. In 1775 Klemens Wenzeslaus asked the French clergy's opinion of *De statu ecclesiae.* In their assembly that year, the French clergy repudiated Febronianism; it went far beyond Gallicanism in their opinion.

Protestants also wrote against Febronius. More than the primacy of the pope was at issue between Catholics and ''dissident Christians.'' G. E. LESSING thought the book mere flattery of princes; every argument used against the pope could be used more tellingly against secular rulers.

At the Coblenz Conference of 1769, the elector-bishops of Mainz, Trier, and Cologne, with Hontheim's aid, listed 30 grievances against the Holy See. The importance of Febronianism can be seen in Pius VI's choice of the Christmas consistory of 1778 to announce the long-awaited recantation of Hontheim. Even after this the rumor that the recantation had been forced, denied by Hontheim in the press but supported by his commentary on his recantation, kept the issue alive.

Further Influence. The Congress of EMS, 1786, saw the elector-bishops and the Prince-Bishop of Salzburg draw up the Punctation of Ems along the lines of the Coblenz *Gravamina* to win a greater measure of independence. In the same year the Synod of Pistoia, called by Duke Leopold of Tuscany, brother of Joseph II, drew up resolutions inspired by Bishop Scipione de' RICCI. Based on Febronian-Jansenist principles, they were repudiated by the majority of the Tuscan bishops and condemned in Pius VI's constitution *AUCTOREM FIDEI*, Aug. 28, 1794.

The wars of the French Revolution and Napoleon ended the Rhenish electorates, but the influence of Febronianism continued into the 19th century. After the Congress of Vienna, Metternich hoped for the creation of a German national church, to be constituted at the Frankfurt Bundestag. He used his cousin, Ignaz Heinrich von WESSENBERG, Vicar-General of the Prince-Primate Dalberg for the Diocese of Constance. The effort was revived by Bismarck in the second half of the 19th century. Some even consider that the refusal of a German primate, requested by the 1848 Bishops' Conference at Würzburg, to head a Reich Church was due to Rome's memory of Febronianism and the perfidy of the last primate, Dalberg.

See Also: CHURCH AND STATE.

Bibliography: T. ORTOLAN, *Dictionnaire de théologie catholique*, ed. A. VACANT et al., 15 v. (Paris 1903–50) 5.2:2115–24. L. JUST, *Lexikon für Theologie und Kirche*, ed. J. HOFER and K. RAHNER, 10 v. (2d, new ed. Freiburg 1957–65) 4:4647. H. RAAB, *ibid.* 5:479–80. E. WOLF, *Die Religion in Geschichte und Gegenwart*, 7 v. (3d ed. Tübingen 1957–65) 2:890–91. L. PASTOR, *The History of the Popes From the Close of the Middle Ages*, 40 v. (London-St. Louis 1938–61): v.13–40, from 1st German ed. *Geschichte und Päpste seit dem Ausgang des Mittelalters*, 16 v. in 21 (Freiburg 1885–1933; repr. 1955–) 36:191, 202, 248, 250–78, 287–88; 39:127 56; 40:2–28. H. DENZINGER, *Enchiridion symbolorum*, ed. A. SCHÖNMETZER (32d ed. Freiburg 1963) 2592–97, 2600–2700. E. ALEXANDER, "Church and Society in Germany . . . 1789–1950," tr. T. STOLPER, *Church and Society,* ed. J. N. MOODY (New York 1953). C. J. BLENNERHASSETT, "The Papacy and the Catholic Church," *Cambridge Modern History* (London-New York 1902–12) 10:131–68. R. A. GRAHAM, *Vatican Diplomacy* (Princeton 1959). R. W. GREAVES, "Religion," *New Cambridge Modern History* (2d ed. London-New York 1957–) 7:113–26. L. STURZO, *Church and State,* tr. B. B. CARTER (New York 1939) 325–26, *passim.* R. DUCHON, "De Bossuet à Febronius," *Revue d'histoire ecclésiastique* 65 (1970) 375–422.

[M. O'CALLAGHAN]

FÉCAMP, ABBEY OF

Originally a monastery for nuns, then a Benedictine abbey, on the English Channel, 24 miles northeast of Le Havre, France, Diocese of Rouen (Lat. *Fiscamnum*). In 664 Count WANINGUS founded the abbey for nuns. This monastery was destroyed by the Normans in 841, and the nuns who were not massacred fled to Picardy. Richard II, Duke of Normandy (996–1026), replaced the lax canons whom his father had established in Trinity Church there with Benedictine monks (1001) under WILLIAM OF SAINT-BÉNIGNE OF DIJON. John of Fécamp (1028–78), William's disciple, succeeded him in 1028 and gave a strong impetus to the abbey school (noted for its work in ecclesiastical chant). Generously endowed by Richard II, the abbey was prosperous during the 12th and 13th centuries; an abbey *nullius*, it possessed the three abbeys of BERNAY, ÉVREUX in Normandy, and Blangy in Artois, as well as 30 parish churches and vast material domains in France, England, and Spain. Fécamp, itself, with its reputed relic of the Precious Blood was a pilgrimage center. The 12th-century Romanesque church was burned in 1168, and the present church was erected under Abbots Henry of Sully (1139–87) and Raoul of Argences (1187–1219), the lantern tower over the transept being built under Abbot William of Vaspail (1229–59). The abbey suffered great destruction during the Hundred Years' War. The abbots of the period included Peter Roger (1326–29), who became Pope CLEMENT VI; D'Estouteville (1390–1423), founder of the abbey's celebrated choir of chanters, which survived until 1791; and Gilles de Duremont (1423–44), a creature of the Duke of Bedford and one of the judges who condemned JOAN OF ARC. In the 16th century the Abbot Cardinals Jean Balue and Antoine Bohier, the three cardinals of LORRAINE, and François de Joyeuse continued to attract kings and royalty to Fécamp as before, but the abbey suffered much during the Wars of Religion. The 17th and 18th centuries were again prosperous times for Fécamp; the Maurist reform, desired by the monks as early as 1620, was introduced in 1650 despite the opposition of the grand prior. The church façade was redone in classical style in 1748. In 1768 the abbey numbered 27 MAURISTS; it was suppressed in the French Revolution, and the abbey church became a parish church.

Bibliography: J. VALLERY-RADOT, "La Trinité de Fécamp," *Congrès archéologique de France, 1900–1925* (Paris 1927) 405–458. J. LECLERCQ and J. P. BONNES, *Jean de Fécamp* (Paris 1946). *L'Abbaye bénédictine de Fécamp: Ouvrage scientifique du XIIIème centenaire, 658–1958*, 4 v. (Fécamp 1959–63).

[P. COUSIN]

FEDERATED COLORED CATHOLICS

A militant national organization of black Catholics that sought to eliminate discriminatory practices against African Americans especially in Catholic institutions. The key figure in its foundation was Dr. Thomas W. Turner, a black Catholic educator associated with Hampton Institute, Hampton, Virginia. Early in 1917, he and a small group of black friends organized the Committee against the Extension of Race Prejudice in the Church. To achieve their objectives, these pioneers used written personal appeals to members of the hierarchy to correct discriminatory practices in Catholic churches, societies, schools, and seminaries. In 1919 the committee was enlarged to 25 members, and its name changed to the Committee for the Advancement of Colored Catholics. Since written appeals had borne little fruit, committees were formed to approach key Church leaders personally to plead the cause of black Catholics. The need for expanded membership soon became apparent, and in 1925 the national organization called the Federated Colored Catholics of the United States came into existence. Group membership, by Catholic parishes and parochial organizations, was emphasized in an effort to educate black Catholics regarding their rights and also to increase the effectiveness of the organization as a bargaining influence.

The objectives of the organization were most clearly stated in a resolution adopted at its annual convention in Detroit in 1930. Briefly, these included equal employment opportunities for all regardless of race; elimination of segregation in housing, recreation, and public utilities; Catholic education on all levels for black Catholic children; the breakdown of discriminatory policies in the admission of blacks to all Catholic institutions; admission of black boys and girls to convents and seminaries; the outlawing of discriminatory practices at Catholic church services and social functions; and a plea for the support of all Catholics in obtaining recognition of the dignity of black people as human beings, with constitutional rights to full citizenship.

Until 1930 the leadership in the federation was exclusively black. A membership of more than 100,000 was claimed. Interested whites, clerics, and laymen became increasingly involved, especially in participation at annual conventions. By 1932, when its convention was held in New York, the federation had become much more interracial in membership and leadership; and a new name, the National Catholic Federation for the Promotion of Better Race Relations, was adopted. One year later it was changed to the National Catholic Interracial Federation. By this time the older black leaders, with their emphasis on a direct, militant approach to the solution of racial problems, had lost influence, and new leadership was channeled into the Catholic Interracial Council movement, founded in New York in 1934.

Bibliography: H. M. SMITH, ''Federated Colored Catholics of the U.S.: A Historical Sketch,'' *The Chronicle* 4 (1931) 543–547. H. M. TEABEAU, ''Federated Colored Catholics Make History in New York City Convention,'' *Interracial Review* 5 (1932) 195, 198–200. T. J. HARTE, *Catholic Organizations Promoting Negro-White Race Relations in the United States* (Catholic University of America, Studies in Sociology; Washington 1947) 1–9.

[T. J. HARTE]

FEDERATION OF ASIAN BISHOPS' CONFERENCES

The Federation of Asian Bishops' Conferences (FABC) is a transnational episcopal structure that brings together 14 bishops' conferences from the following regions as full members: Bangladesh, India, Indonesia, Japan, Korea, Laos-Cambodia, Malaysia-Singapore-Brunei, Myanmar (Burma), Pakistan, Philippines, Sri Lanka, Taiwan, Thailand, and Vietnam, as well as ten associate members: Hong Kong, Kazakhstan, Kyrgyzstan, Macau, Mongolia, Nepal, Siberia, Tadjikistan, Turkmenistan, and Uzbekistan. It has ten associate members, drawn from the ecclesiastical jurisdictions of Hong Kong, Kazakhstan, Kyrgyzstan, Macau, Mongolia, Nepal, Siberia, Tadjikistan, Turkmenistan, and Uzbekistan. By virtue of their membership in the Catholic Bishops' Conference of India (CBCI), both the Syro-Malabar and Syro-Malankara Eastern Catholic Churches are also members of, and participate in the leadership and activities of the FABC. West Asia (the Middle East) has its own transnational structure, the Council of Catholic Patriarchs of the Orient (*Conseil des Patriarches Catholiques d'Orient* or CPCO), and does not form part of FABC. The foundation for the FABC was laid at the historic gathering of 180 Asian Catholic Bishops at the Asian Catholic Bishops' Meeting in Manila during the visit of Pope Paul VI to East Asia and Southeast Asia in November of 1970.

Structures and Statements. The supreme body of the federation is the Plenary Assembly, which convenes once in four years with the presidents and official delegates from each member conference. The Plenary Assembly makes major decisions and sets policy. The normal work of FABC is directed through three bodies: the Central Committee, composed of the presidents of the conferences represented, puts into effect the decisions and directives of the Plenary Assembly; the Central Secretariat, located in Hong Kong, coordinates the activities of the Federation and assists the functioning of all its levels; and the Standing Committee, composed of five members elected from various parts of FABC region, executes the directives of the central committee and directs the work of the Central Secretariat. The FABC has no president; rather, there is a "convenor" from the Standing Committee, a general secretary, and an assistant general secretary who coordinates the work from the Hong Kong office.

Every four years the official delegates to the Plenary Assembly take up pastorally relevant questions for study and deliberation. It is customary that two Asian theologians each present a major paper addressing the theme of the assembly. Most of the work is done in sectional workshops for which guideline papers are prepared in advance. Themes of the Plenary Assembly have included the following: "Evangelization in Modern Asia" (Taipei 1974); "Prayer—the Life of the Church in Asia" (Calcutta 1978); "The Church—Community of Faith in Asia" (Bangkok 1982); "The Vocation and Mission of the Laity in the Church and in the World of Asia" (Tokyo 1986); "Journeying Together Toward The Third Millennium" (Bandung 1990);"Christian Discipleship in Asia Today: Service to Life" (Manila 1995); and "A Renewed Church in Asia on a Mission of Love and Service" (Sampran 2000).

Much of the work between the assemblies is done by the various offices of the FABC. In addition to the Office of Theological Concerns (formerly, the Theological Advisory Commission), there are offices for the laity, mission, human development, ecumenical and interreligious affairs, education and student chaplaincy, and social communications. A joint planning meeting that is generally held biennially or more frequently, if needed, encourages fruitful exchange among the offices, and each has taken initiatives to organize a series of workshops for the bishops in its respective field.

Published statements based on the conclusions of these workshops have found echo beyond the FABC and contributed to the Church in other continents. The office for ecumenical and interreligious affairs, for example, conducted a series of institutes called "Bishops' Institute for Religious Affairs" (BIRA). The workshops organized by the office for human development since 1974 are known as the Bishops' Institute for Social Action (BISA). The same office is engaged in a new series of workshops entitled, "Faith Encounter in Social Action" (FEISA), through which bishops are exposed to the faith of peoples of other religious traditions and are led to discover how the Church could collaborate together with them in the transformation of society.

The Office of Theological Concerns responds to the pastoral situation of the region by making up deeper study of certain crucial themes. Composed of theologians nominated by each bishops' conference, the commission has issued many important documents, including theses on interreligious dialogue [FABC Papers 48]; theses on the local church [FABC Papers 60]; Asian perspectives on Church and politics [FABC Papers 63]; Asian Christian perspectives on harmony [FABC Papers 65]; the spirit at work in Asia today [FABC Papers 81]; and methodology for Asian Christian theology [FABC Papers 96]. In April of 1994, the commission brought together some of the distinguished theologians of Asia and representatives from other continents for a colloquium in Pattaya, Thailand, "Being Church in Asia in the Twenty-first Century."

Influence. The FABC has played a significant role among the churches of Asia. It strengthened the bonds of communion among the bishops in the region and contributed to the development of a shared vision about the Church and its mission in Asia. Its influence on the Church throughout the world is witnessed to by the ever-growing interest in the documents it has published. The deliberations of the bishops at the plenary assemblies, shaped by their experience in the various countries and sustained by the work of the offices, have led to the emergence of a certain theological orientation. Major theological contributions of the FABC have been to develop a theology of religions from an Asian perspective; to explore the relationship of Church and reign of God in a multi-religious context; to understand the local Church with particular emphasis on cultural and socio-political aspects; to explore the meaning and significance of dialogue; and to offer new perspectives on mission and evangelization.

Initial impetus for this theological orientation was given by the first plenary assembly (Taipei 1974), which spoke of the need for a threefold dialogue: with the religions of Asia, with the cultures of Asia, and with the poor of Asia. Following developments in the Church and in the region during the 1970s and 1980s, new avenues were explored in the spirit of dialogue. One such initiative was to forge closer understanding and cooperation with the ecumenical organization Christian Conference of Asia (CCA), representing most of the Protestant and Orthodox Churches in Asia. A step in this direction was the conference held in Singapore in July of 1987, where participants from FABC and CCA came together to reflect on "Living and Working Together with Sisters and Brothers of Other Faiths." At a colloquium in Hua Hin, Thailand, in 1993, both organizations agreed to undertake a single and unified structure of collaboration. The 1996 colloquium in Cheung Chau, Hong Kong explored further avenues for collaboration under the theme "Asian Movement for Christian Unity."

Since its inception, the FABC has fostered episcopal collegiality, consultation, and collaboration among the many Catholic bishops' conferences from disparate and diverse regions throughout the vast Asian continent. The FABC has consistently committed itself in service to the daily life experiences of the Asian peoples by recognizing their rich cultural heritage, affirming their intense religiosity, and empowering them in their struggle to attain a better quality of life in the midst of crushing poverty and socio-political marginalization. Nevertheless, much work remains to be done: the relationship between church and state in several countries, especially in countries such as mainland China, Myanmar, Vietnam, Laos, Cambodia, and North Korea; the struggling churches of East Timor, Kazakhstan, Kyrgyzstan, Mongolia, Siberia, Tadjikistan, Turkmenistan, and Uzbekistan; growing ethnic strife and religious conflicts in many parts of Asia; and the pervasive problem of economic exploitation with its disruptive implications in all areas of people's lives. To compound matters, most countries lack funds and resources for training personnel to implement the inspiring vision of the FABC.

Bibliography: The series, FABC Papers, published by the Central Secretariat of the Federation in Hong Kong, offers a wealth of wide-ranging materials that help one to understand the spirit and orientation of FABC. Most of the official documents of the FABC have been collected and published in a convenient two-volume collection: G. B. ROSALES and C. G. ARÉVALO, eds., *For All The Peoples of Asia: Federation of Asian Bishops' Conferences Documents, 1970–1991* (Maryknoll, NY 1992) and F.-J. EILERS, ed., *For All The Peoples of Asia Volume 2: Federation of Asian Bishops' Conferences Documents from 1992 to 1996* (Quezon City 1997). See also: S. BEVANS, ''Inculturation of Theology in Asia (The Federation of Asian Bishops' Conferences, 1970–1995),'' *Studia Missionalia* 45 (1996) 1–23. J. DUPUIS, ''FABC Focus on the Church's Evangelizing Mission in Asia Today,'' *Vidyajyoti* 56 (1992) 449–468. J. KAVUNKAL, ''Local Church in the FABC Statements,'' *Jeevadhara* 27 (1997) 260–271. S. PAINADATH, ''Theological Perspectives of FABC on Interreligious Dialogue,'' *Jeevadhara* 27 (1997) 272–288. P. C. PHAN, ''Human Development and Evangelization (The first to the sixth plenary assembly of the Federation of Asian Bishops' Conferences),'' *Studia Missionalia* 47 (1998) 205–227. J. Y. TAN, ''Theologizing at the Service of Life: The Contextual Theological Methodology of the Federation of Asian Bishops' Conferences (FABC)'' *Gregorianum* 83 no. 3 (2000) 541–575. F. WILFRED, et al., ''What the Spirit Says to the Churches. A Vademecum on the Pastoral and Theological Orientations of the Federation of Asian Bishops' Conferences (FABC),'' *Vidyajyoti* 62 (1998) 124–133.

[F. WILFRED/J. TAN]

FEDERATION OF DIOCESAN LITURGICAL COMMISSIONS

The Federation of Diocesan Liturgical Commissions (FDLC) is a national association encompassing all diocesan liturgical commissions, offices of worship (or comparable diocesan structures) established by the local bishops in the United States. Since September 1980, the national office has been located in Washington, DC.

The bishops' committee on the liturgy and its secretariat gave a strong impetus to the foundation of the FDLC. They hosted a meeting of the heads of diocesan liturgical commissions at the Liturgical Week in Houston in 1966 and Kansas City in 1967. In a similar meeting in Chicago, November 1968, a motion was made that a federation of liturgical commissions be organized. In the Feb. 9, 1969 meeting, the bishops' committee on the liturgy implemented the Chicago motion by directing that two representatives from each of 12 regions be elected from among the chairs and secretaries of all the diocesan commissions in the United States. These elected representatives formed the charter 24.

The charter 24 were convened at the 1969 meeting of the diocesan commissions in Pittsburgh. Temporary officers were elected, and organizing committees were appointed. The first constitutional meeting of the FDLC took place in El Paso, Texas, in conjunction with the 1970 meeting of the Southwest Liturgical Conference. At this time the FDLC was formally established, a constitution was adopted, and permanent officers were elected.

The FDLC views itself as a professional organization seeking to promote the liturgy as the heart of Christian life in the parish and to assist the United States Conference of Catholic Bishops (USCCB), as well as individual bishops in their discharging their responsibilities for fostering liturgical catechesis in their dioceses. Concentrating on the pastoral aspects of liturgical celebration, it places a high priority on gathering, dispensing, and commissioning liturgical materials to aid liturgical renewal and catechetical programs in each diocese. An annual meeting, regional meetings, the *FDLC Newsletters,* and other specially commissioned publications serve as focus points for this effort. To foster closer cooperation between the FDLC and the USCCB, the FDLC Chair and Executive Director attend all plenary meetings of the USCCB.

[J. D. SHAUGHNESSY/J. L. CUNNINGHAM/EDS.]

FEEHAN, PATRICK AUGUSTINE

Archbishop; b. County Tipperary, Ireland, Aug. 29, 1829; d. Chicago, IL, July 12, 1902. He was the son of Patrick and Judith (Cooney) Feehan. Entering Maynooth College, County Kildare, Ireland, in January 1847, he studied philosophy and theology and was appointed to the Dunboyne Establishment, Maynooth, for higher studies. In 1850 his family emigrated to the U.S. When Abp. Peter Kenrick of St. Louis, MO, appealed for candidates for his archdiocese, Feehan volunteered and Kenrick ordained him in St. Louis on Nov. 1, 1852. Feehan's first assignment was to teach moral theology and Sacred Scripture in the Carondelet Seminary, Missouri. In 1854, when Anthony O'Regan was chosen bishop of Chicago, Feehan succeeded him as seminary president. Four years later he was named to the pastorate of St. Michael's Church and then to the Immaculate Conception parish.

During the Civil War, a hospital for the wounded was established in the vicinity, and Feehan's solicitude for the war victims spread his reputation beyond the diocese. Some of the most destructive Civil War battles were fought in Tennessee, and many Catholic churches were ruined. The devastation so overwhelmed Bp. James Whelan of Nashville that he resigned in 1863. Feehan declined the nomination to Nashville in 1864 because he feared the change would prove fatal to his invalid mother who was living near him. However, when she died in July 1865, he accepted the appointment and was consecrated by Archbishop Kenrick in St. Louis on Nov. 1, 1865.

Feehan arrived in Nashville for his installation on November 11 to find that there were only three diocesan priests in Tennessee. During his 15-year administration, he directed the rebuilding of churches and was successful in recruiting clerics from Ireland. He attended Vatican Council I (1869–70). On Sept. 10, 1880, he was appointed the first archbishop of CHICAGO and was installed at Holy Name Cathedral on November 25. During his 22-year episcopate, churches increased from 194 to 298, priests from 205 to 538, and schools from 88 with 25,000 pupils to 166, with a total of 62,723 pupils.

Feehan convened the first archdiocesan synod on Dec. 13, 1887, at which the decrees of the Third Plenary Council of Baltimore were promulgated. In 1892 the *New World,* official Catholic newspaper of the Chicago archdiocese, began publication. Feehan helped to organize the second Catholic Congress held in Chicago from Sept. 4 to 8, 1893, in conjunction with the Columbian Exposition and World's Fair. With the growth of the archdiocese, Feehan saw the need for an auxiliary bishop. Rome first designated Alexander J. McGavick, pastor of St. John's Church, Chicago, to be titular bishop of Narcopolis and auxiliary bishop of Chicago. But soon after his consecration on May 1, 1899, illness incapacitated him, and Peter J. Muldoon, pastor of St. Charles Borromeo Church, Chicago, was made titular bishop of Tamassus and consecrated in Holy Name Cathedral on July 25, 1901. A few of the Irish-born local clergy objected to the selection of a native-born American. Their leader, Jeremiah Crowley, pastor of St. Mary's Church in Oregon, IL, was excommunicated. This friction saddened the last days of the archbishop. When Feehan's death occurred suddenly as the result of an apoplectic stroke, Catholics in the archdiocese numbered 800,000 and, despite the extensive building program, the archdiocese was financially sound.

Bibliography: C. J. KIRKFLEET, *The Life of Patrick Augustine Feehan* (Chicago 1922). J. J. THOMPSON, *The Archdiocese of Chicago* (Des Plaines, IL 1920).

[H. C. KOENIG]

FEENEY, LEONARD

Poet, essayist, founder and superior of a religious congregation of men and women, b. Lynn, Mass., Feb. 15, 1897, and d. Still River, Mass., Jan. 30, 1978. Trained in Jesuit schools, he entered the Society in 1914 and, after completing seminary studies, did graduate work at Oxford. He was ordained at Weston College in 1928.

Feeney quickly attracted attention in the Catholic literary world with his first book of poetry, *In Towns and Little Towns* (1927). This was followed over the next 20 years by a great variety of writings: essays, short stories, sketches, biography, dramatizations, and more poetry. Educated ''in the hard school of wonder,'' as he put it, he was entranced with ''the earthliness of heavenly things and the heavenliness of earthly things.'' With his buoyant, paradoxical style he was called by many the ''American G. K. Chesterton.'' Among Feeney's popular books were: *In Towns and Little Towns* (1927); *Fish on Friday* (1934); *Boundaries* (1936); *Riddle and Reverie* (1936); *Song for a Listener* (1936); *You'd Better Come Quietly* (1939); *Survival Till Seventeen* (1941); *The Leonard Feeney Omnibus* (1943); and *Your Second Childhood* (1945).

Feeney insisted on the primacy of doctrine as the source of theology and devotion. ''And by the way/ Speaking of how to pray,/Dogmas come first, not liturgies.'' Frank Sheed, a long-time friend and one of his publishers, said of his writings, ''For Father Feeney, dogma is not only true; it is breathlessly exciting. That is his special vocation—to make his readers feel the thrill.'' Besides contributing to Catholic periodicals and broadcasting on ''The Catholic Hour,'' Feeney was also literary editor of *America* and president of the Catholic Poetry Society of America. In 1943, at the height of his literary and lecturing career, he was assigned as permanent chaplain to St. Benedict Center, an intellectual and spiritual forum for Harvard and Radcliffe students, founded in 1940 by Catherine Goddard Clarke. His love of dogma made Feeney insist that the doctrine, *extra ecclesiam nulla salus*, must be held and professed without compromise. This stand bred a reaction which led to ecclesiastical censures on him and his followers.

Diogo Antônio Feijó.

On Jan. 17, 1949, with Catherine Goddard Clarke, he founded a religious community of men and women. In 1958, the community moved from Cambridge, Mass., to a farm in Still River, Mass., where they were better able to follow a monastic life of prayer, study, and manual labor according to the Benedictine spirit. In 1972, through the efforts of Bishop Bernard J. Flanagan of Worcester, Cardinal Humberto Medeiros of Boston, and Cardinal John Wright of the Congregation for the Clergy, all ecclesiastical censures against Father Feeney were removed. Subsequently the majority of the members of the community were reconciled with the church.

[S. M. CLARE]

FEIJÓ, DIOGO ANTÔNIO

Priest and regent of Brazil; b. São Paulo, August 1784; d. São Paulo, Nov. 10, 1843. Ordained at São Paulo on Feb. 25, 1809, Feijó was a pious priest and diligent in his duties, always saying Mass and teaching catechism in his three benefices of Campinas, Itú, and São Paulo until 1821, and later, in the intervals in his political and administrative activity. In Itú he taught philosophy, out of which developed a study that was published posthumously by Eugênio Egas. There he also joined with some secular priests who were living a life of study and asceticism, including corporal penances. This association was dissolved under suspicion of Jansenism, although this was never proved.

Studies have been made of the composition of his library, of his two projects for the reform of the clergy, his polemic in favor of a married clergy, and, of his correspondence with the Holy See on the confirmation of a bishop whom he, as regent of the empire, had nominated. The studies demonstrate that, as a result of being chiefly self-taught and influenced by teachers who had been trained in the Luso-Brazilian studies reformed by the enlightened Marquis of Pombal, Feijó held some erroneous beliefs. His pragmatic tendencies as a liberal political reformer furthered such beliefs. He retracted them twice and died with the Last Sacraments.

He was buried in the crypt of the cathedral of São Paulo, where a monument was erected in his honor in 1913. Brazil venerates him as a Cincinnatus in a cassock because, as minister of justice (1831–32), after the tumult over the abdication of Pedro I, he saved Rio de Janeiro and the nation from anarchy without veering from a rule of law; and as regent of the empire (1835–37) he carried on a good administration. He was forced to resign as regent by a revolt in Rio Grande do Sul and by the opposition of the parliament, that, according to the constitution, he might have dissolved. Although already a paralytic, he fought in the unsuccessful liberal revolt of 1842. He served as a deputy to the Cortes of Lisbon in 1821, and to the general assembly from 1826 on; he was a senator at the time of his death.

Bibliography: E. EGAS, *Diogo Antônio Feijó,* 2 v. (São Paulo 1912). O. T. DE SOUSA, *Diogo Antônio Feijó* (Rio de Janeiro 1942). L. CASTANHO DE ALMEIDA, *O sacerdote Diogo Antônio Feijó* (Petropolis n.d.). L. G. NOVELLI, *Feijó, un velho paulista* (Rio de Janeiro 1963).

[L. CASTANHO]

FELBIGER, JOHANN IGNAZ VON

Augustinian canon regular and reformer in the fields of education and religious instruction; b. Gross-Glogau, Nov. 6, 1724; d. Pressburg, May 17, 1788. Felbiger became a Canon Regular of St. Augustine in 1746 and was engaged for a time in the reform of educational methods in the Catholic school system in Silesia and Austria. Becoming an abbot in Sagan, Silesia, in 1758, he undertook the reform of the schools attached to the chapters of collegiate churches in that district and in Prussia. In 1774 he was called by Maria Theresa to Vienna to introduce some needed improvements into the Austrian school system. In 1778, he was named chief director of the Austrian educational system, a position he held until after the death of Maria Theresa. He then was dismissed by Joseph II (1782), who was dissatisfied with Felbiger's adherence to strictly religious principles in education.

Felbiger's chief contributions to education were in the areas of organization and methodization. As an organizer, he is credited with the formation of a new educational system, the establishment of colleges for the training of teachers (a much needed contribution), the substitution of classroom education for the then customary tutorial system, and the establishment of religious instruction as a systematic subject for the schools. As a methodizer, he is noted for his introduction of the Sagan method of teaching, and for substituting the catechizing method for pure memorization. In collaboration with his prior, B. Strauch, he published three graded catechisms under the title *Silesian Catechism* (1766) that enjoyed wide popularity. The most important of his many publications was *Methodenbuch für Lehrer der deutschen Schulen* (1775).

Bibliography: N. A. WEBER, *The Catholic Encyclopedia*, ed. C. G. HERBERMANN et al., (New York 1907–14) 6:27–28. L. BOPP, *Lexikon der Pädagogik*, ed. H. ROMBACH (Freiburg 1962) 1179–80.

[E. LEWIS]

FELICI, PERICLE

Canonist, cardinal, and leading figure at the Second Vatican Council; b. Segni, Italy, Aug. 1, 1911; d. Foggia, Italy, Mar. 22, 1982. Felici studied philosophy and theology in Rome and was ordained to the priesthood on Oct. 28, 1933. His doctoral thesis, *Summa psychanalyseos liniamenta eiusque compendiosa refutatio,* was published in 1937. In 1938 Felici was awarded the doctorate *utroque iure* by the Pontifical University of the Lateran, after defending a brilliant dissertation *De iure poenali interpretando.*

Named rector of the Pontifical Institute of Jurisprudence at St. Apollinaris, for 10 years Felici served as spiritual director for the Pontifical Roman Seminary. In 1943 he began teaching fundamental moral theology at the Lateran University. His treatises on the virtues of justice and religion were greatly admired both for their content and elegant style. Felici was said to be one of the most gifted Latinists in modern times.

In 1947 Pope Pius XII named him an auditor on the Sacred Roman Rota. Pope John XXIII ordained Felici as Titular Archbishop of Samosata (1960), and appointed him to be Secretary General of the Second Vatican Ecumenical Council (1962–65). The post required him not only to prepare extensive preliminary studies, but also to coordinate each meeting and present a synthesis of the council father's oftentimes lengthy discussions. Felici published a collection of his own interventions at Vatican II, *Il lungo cammino del Concilio* (1967).

In 1967, after the Council, Felici presided over the commission for the restoration of the permanent diaconate. In that same year, Pope Paul VI named Felici pro-President of the Pontifical Commission for the revision of the Code of Canon Law. He became its president when raised to the rank of cardinal in June. The cardinal served on various Sacred Commission and Congregations: for the Doctrine of the Faith, for Bishops, for the Sacraments and Divine Worship, for the Causes of Saints, and as head of the Archives of the Vatican. He also served as President of the Court of Appeal at the Vatican, and President of the Commission for the interpretation of the decrees of Vatican Council II. Together with Cardinals VILLOT and Conway he presided over the First Synod of Bishops in 1967.

Between 1967 and 1969 Cardinal Felici published *Freud e il peccato; Concilio vitam alere; Continuità, coerenze, fermezza di dottrina;* and *Il Vaticano II e il celibato sacerdotale.* He likewise contributed articles to various reviews and to the *Dizionario di Teologial Morale Casus Conscientiae* by Palazzini-De Jorio. He was the founder of the review *Communicationes* and contributed frequently to *L'Osservatore Romano.*

On Oct. 21, 1981, Felici presented the integral text of the revised Code of Canon Law to the plenary session of the Cardinals. The following month Pope John Paul II entrusted him with the task of making some final alterations. Unfortunately Cardinal Felici's sudden and unexpected death prevented him from witnessing the Code's promulgation on Jan. 25, 1983.

[J. AUMANN]

FELICISSIMUS AND AGAPITUS, SS.

Deacon martyrs, d. Rome, 258. Nothing is known of their life and death except for that material contained in the poem composed in their honor by Pope DAMASUS I. They were deacons of the Roman Church martyred with Pope SIXTUS II, during the Valerian persecution, and buried in the cemetery of Praetextatus. GREGORY IV gave their bones to the Abbot Gozbald of Niederaltaich for his church at Isarhofen.

Feast: Aug. 7.

Bibliography: *Acta Sanctorum* Aug. 2:124–142. H. LECLERCQ, *Dictionnaire d'archéologie chrétienne et de liturgie,* ed. F. CABROL, H. LECLERCQ and H. I. MARROU (Paris 1907–53) 5:1249–59.

A. FERRUA, ed., *Epigrammata Damasiana* (Vatican City 1942) 152–156.

[R. K. POETZEL]

FELIX, MARCUS ANTONIUS

Roman procurator of Palestine (*c.* A.D. 53–60) who held St. Paul a prisoner at Caesarea. Felix was a freedman of Antonia, Emperor Claudius's mother, and a brother of Pallas, Claudius's favorite. He was first married to Drusilla, the granddaughter of Anthony and Cleopatra, and later to the daughter of Herod AGRIPPA I, also named Drusilla. She had been married for two months to Aziz, King of Emesa (ancient Hamath), before leaving him to marry Felix. Felix was made procurator (governor) of Palestine by Claudius in 52 or 53. His brother's favored position emboldened him to cruelty, lust, greed, and assassination, and saved him from punishment when Nero recalled him to Rome on a charge of maladministration (*c.* A.D. 60).

His misconduct fanned Jewish discontent and eventually led to the Jewish revolt of 66–70. Paul, after his arrest at Jerusalem, was taken to Caesarea in order to be protected against the fanatical Jews in Jerusalem and to stand trial before Felix, who already had ''some accurate knowledge of the Way'' (Acts 23.22–24.23). Some days later Paul terrified Felix and Drusilla by speaking to them on chastity and the judgment to come, but in hope of a bribe, Felix kept him in prison for two years, speaking to him often (23.24–26). When Felix was recalled to Rome, he left Paul in prison for the sake of currying favor with the Jews, although he admitted that he did not find him guilty of any crime. He was succeeded by Porcius FESTUS.

Bibliography: R. VON ROHDEN, *Paulys Realenzyklopädie der klassischen Altertumswissenschaft*, ed. G. WISSOWA et al. 1.2 (1894) 2616–18. F. M. ABEL, *Histoire de la Palestine depuis la Conquête d'Alexandre jusqu'à l'invasion Arabe,* 2 v. (*Études bibliques* 1952) 1:463–468. *Encyclopedic Dictionary of the Bible*, tr. and adap. by L. HARTMAN (New York 1963) 769–770. J. SCHMID, *Lexikon für Theologie und Kirche*, ed. J. HOFER and K. RAHNER (Freiberg 1957–65) 4:70. E. HAENCHEN, *Die Apostelgeschichte* (12th ed. rev. 1959).

[F. J. BUCKLEY]

FELIX I, POPE, ST.

Pontificate: Jan. 5, 269 to Dec. 30, 274. The *Liber pontificalis* states that Felix was a Roman, son of Constantius, but this report is unreliable, as is the assertion that he instituted the celebration of Mass over the sepulchers and memorials of martyrs. This custom had been observed before Felix's time, and he continued the practice.

Early in Felix's reign a letter addressed to his predecessor, Pope DIONYSIUS, arrived in Rome from the synod of Antioch, which had deposed Bishop PAUL OF SAMOSATA for his heretical teachings on the Trinity. Felix probably sent a reply to this report. There is an important sidelight to this event. In 272 Paul appealed his case to the emperor Valerian (270–275) who referred the matter to the bishops in Italy, and particularly Rome. Apparently the matter did not reach Italy, but the emperor's attitude suggests that he was familiar with the Italian churches and was not hostile to them, although he later turned against the Christians. Scholars agree that the epistolary treatise on Christ addressed to Maximus of Alexandria and cited by St. CYRIL OF ALEXANDRIA (*Apol.* 6), the Council of EPHESUS (431), and St. VINCENT OF LÉRINS (*Commonit.* 2.30) is not Felix's letter, but a forgery perpetrated by the followers of APOLLINARIS OF LAODICEA.

The fourth-century Roman calendar of feasts maintained that Felix was buried in the bishops crypt in the catacomb of St. Callixtus. The *Liber pontificalis* erroneously calls him a martyr and claims that he was buried on the Via Aurelia, confusing him with a Roman martyr of the same name.

Feast: May 30.

Bibliography: EUSEBIUS, *Ecclesiastical History* 7.30, 32. E. CASPAR, *Geschichte de Papsttums von den Aufängen bis zur Höhe der Weltherrschaft* (Tübingen 1930–33) 1:43, 84, 468. J. QUASTEN, *Patrology* (Westminster, Md. 1950–) 2:242. E. FERGUSON, *Encyclopedia of Early Christianity* (New York 1997) 1:426. J. N. D. KELLY, *Oxford Dictionary of Popes* (New York 1986) 23. G. SCHWAIGER, *Lexikon für Theologie und Kirche,* 3d. ed. (Freiburg 1995).

[E. G. WELTIN]

FELIX II, ANTIPOPE

Pontificate: 355 to Nov. 22, 366. When the emperor Constantius II (337–361) exiled Pope Liberius (352–366) for opposing his Arianizing policies, the archdeacon Felix led the Roman clergy in proclaiming allegiance to their exiled bishop. The emperor pressured the clergy, who eventually gave way and elected Felix to be pope, probably in the imperial palace at Ravenna. The Romans resisted Felix, and during a visit to Rome in 357, Constantius found the people imploring him to reinstate Liberius. The emperor held on for another year but then decided that he could only maintain peace in the city by allowing Liberius to return—but not as the one pope; only as co-bishop with Felix. The Romans rejected this and drove Felix from the city. He attempted a return, only to be driven away again. He refused to resign and took up residence in the suburbs with a dwindling number of followers. The city prefect made no effort to depose him, preferring instead to keep the two claimants and their followers at a distance so that no trouble would break out. Felix died in 365, a year before Liberius, who avoided trouble by reconciling himself with Felix's clergy, one of whom may have been the future pope Damasus I (366–384).

This antipope had a posthumous influence on papal history, however. The *Liber pontificalis* gives him a favorable entry, and his name is entered in the list of popes, so that the next pope named Felix is styled Felix III or Felix II (III) (483–492), and the third of that name is Felix IV or Felix III (IV) (526–530). No legitimate pope subsequently took that name, although an antipope of the conciliar period styled himself Felix V (1439–1449).

Bibliography: H. JEDIN, ed., *History of the Church* (New York 1980) 2:249–250. J. N. D. KELLY, *Oxford Dictionary of Popes* (New York 1986) 31–32. C. PIETRI, *Roma Christiana* (Rome 1976) 237–268. G. SCHWAIGER, *Lexikon für Theologie und Kirche,* 3d. ed. (Freiburg 1995).

[J. F. KELLY]

FELIX III (II), POPE, ST.

Pontificate: March 13, 483, to Feb. 25, or March 1, 492. Felix, successor to Simplicius and a member of the higher clergy closely allied with the senatorial class, was the son of the titular priest of Fasciola (SS. Nereo e Achilleo). The Praetorian Prefect Basil, acting in the name of King Odoacer, seems to have exerted an influence on his election; and Felix seems to be the first pope who officially announced his election to the emperor (Zeno). Seconded by the archdeacon Gelasius, he adopted a firm stand toward the peril of MONOPHYSITISM in the East. John Talaia, the orthodox Patriarch of Alexandria who fled when Acacius of Constantinople supported Peter Mongus, informed Felix of events in the East. Felix sent to Constantinople legates who demanded the ouster of the Monophysite patriarch. Acacius was summoned to Rome to explain his behavior, but instead of ceding he seems to have perjured himself, and the impression was given that Rome had approved the HENOTIKON. In a Roman council (July 28, 484) Felix excommunicated and deposed Acacius and suspended the legates. The sentence was published in Constantinople through a daring move on the part of the orthodox Akoimetoi monks, and Acacius ordered the pope's name removed from the diptychs.

The ACACIAN SCHISM, thus inaugurated, lasted for 35 years and was the first serious break between East and West. After the death of Acacius (489) and the accession of the Byzantine Emperor ANASTASIUS I (491) efforts were made to resolve the quarrel, but without success. While he did not excommunicate the emperor, who was responsible for imposing the Henotikon, Felix addressed him in a letter that was quite different in tone from the usual court communications and warned him ''to learn divine things from those who are in charge of them, and not to desire to teach them.'' He asserted roundly the superiority of the Church in spiritual matters. This letter was in a sense ''the opening gun fired in the long struggle between papacy and empire.''

Felix also convoked a Lateran council (March 13, 487) that discussed the matter of the reconciliation of laymen, priests, and even bishops who had consented to be rebaptized by the Arians in the face of the fierce persecution of the African church by the VANDALS. Pope Felix was buried in the basilica of St. Paul, in the family crypt, the exact location of which is unknown.

Feast: March 1.

Bibliography: *Patrolgiae cursus completus, series latina,* ed. A. HAMMAN 3:719–722, letters. A. THIEL, ed., *Epistolae romanorum pontificum* (Braunsberg 1868) 1:222–279. *Liber pontificalis,* ed. L. DUCHESNE (Paris 1886–1958) 1:252–254; 3:87. E. CASPAR, *Geschichte de Papsttums von den Anfängen bis zur Höhe der Weltherrschaft* (Tübingen 1930–33) 2:22–44, 749–752. H. LECLERCQ, *Dictionnaire de théologie catholique,* ed. A. VACANT et al. (Paris 1903–50) 13.1:1211. E. SCHWARTZ, *Publizistische Sammlungen zum acacianischen Schisma* (1934). O. BERTOLINI, *Roma di fronte a Bisanzio e ai Longobardi* (Bologna 1941) 31–39. T. G. JALLAND, *The Church and the Papacy* (Society for Promoting Christian Knowledge 1944) 315–321. W. ULLMANN, *The Growth of Papal Government in the Middle Ages* (2d ed. New York 1962). R. U. MONTINI, *Le tombe dei Papi* (Rome 1957) 104. G. SCHWAIGER, *Lexikon für Theologie und Kirche,* 3d. ed. (Freiburg 1995).

[J. CHAPIN]

FELIX IV (III), POPE, ST.

Pontificate: July 12, 526 to Sept. 20 or 22, 530. The harshly treated JOHN I was succeeded as pope by the Roman priest Felix, who was imposed upon the Romans by the Arian Gothic King Theodoric. Shortly after the new pope's consecration, the king died and was succeeded by his grandson Athalaric, whose mother, Queen Amalasuntha, acted as regent during her son's minority. Since the queen was well disposed toward Catholics and Byzantium, the late king's policy of persecution was abandoned, and the Church once again enjoyed good relations with the Arian rulers of Italy. When the Roman clergy complained that the civil authorities had usurped their privileges, a royal edict confirmed the custom requiring that civil or criminal charges brought against the clergy be heard by the pope or by a court appointed by him. He appointed more than fifty priests in fifty months, apparently hoping to populate the Roman clergy with men sympathetic to his views.

Felix IV, detail of the much-restored 6th-century mosaic in the church of SS. Cosmas and Damian in Rome. (Alinari-Art Reference/Art Resource, NY)

Felix sent St. CAESARIUS OF ARLES, at the latter's request, a series of chapters (*capitula*) culled from the Bible and the writings of the Fathers, particularly St. Augustine, defining the teaching of the Church on the subject of grace and free will. These canons, adopted by the Second Council of ORANGE (529) and subsequently approved by Pope BONIFACE II, acquired great dogmatic authority in the Church, and effectively put an end to the controversy over grace, and enshrined Augustine's views.

The adaptation for Christian worship of various buildings of the Roman Forum began under Felix. He received permission from Queen Amalasuntha to convert the Templum Sacrae Urbis and the adjoining small round temple, the so–called ''Heroon Romuli,'' on the Via Sacra into the nave and atrium, respectively, of a church dedicated to the martyrs SS. COSMAS AND DAMIAN, who were associated with healing. Afraid that disorders might break out among factions in the Roman Church after his death, Felix resorted to the unusual procedure of designating his own successor by handing his pallium to the archdeacon Boniface. Word of the pope's choice was then sent to the court at Ravenna, but the Roman senate forbade any discussion of a successor to a living pope. Felix was buried in the portico of St. Peter's. A mosaic portrait in the apse of SS. Cosmas and Damian is the first contemporary papal likeness to have survived, but it has been so much altered by later hands that it does not have much historical value.

Feast: Jan. 30.

Bibliography: *Clavis Patrum latinorum,* ed. E. DEKKERS (2d ed. Streenbrugge 1961) 1686–90. *Patrologia latina,* ed. J. P. MIGNE, 217 v., indexes 4 v. (Paris 1878–90) 65:11–23. *Liber pontificalis,* ed. L. DUCHESNE, v. 1–2 (Paris 1886–92), v. 3 (Paris 1958) 1:279–280; 3:91. H. LECLERCQ, *Dictionnaire d'archéologie chrétienne et de liturgie* (Paris 1907–53) 13.1:1216. G. SCHWAIGER, *Lexikon für Theologie und Kirche* (2d, new ed. Freiburg 1957–65) 4:68–69. R. U. MONTINI, *Le tombe dei papi* (Rome 1957). G. B. LADNER, *Die Papstbildnisse* (Vatican City 1941–). E. FERGUSON, ed., *Encyclopedia of Early Christianity* (New York 1997) 1:426. H. JEDIN, *History of the Church* (New York, 1980) 2:626. J.N.D. KELLY, *Oxford Dictionary of Popes* (New York 1986) 55–56. J. RICHARDS, *Popes and Papacy the Early Middle Ages* (London 1979) 120–125.

[J. CHAPIN]

FELIX V, ANTIPOPE

Pontificate: (sometimes referred to as the pope of Basel) Nov. 5, 1439–April 7, 1449. Duke Amadeus VIII of Savoy was born in Chambéry on Dec. 4, 1383, and died in Geneva on Jan. 7, 1451. After he took over the family's estates in 1391, he expanded them to include the Piedmont and the Ligurian coast. His success brought him more wealth and influence. In 1416 the German king Sigismund (1410–37, emp. 1433) raised Savoy's status to a duchy, and in 1422 the same king granted Amadeus the county of Geneva. Amadeus was an extremely devout layman, and in October 1434, after the deaths of his wife, Maria of Burgundy (1422), and eldest son (1431) he appointed his second son, Ludovico, as regent. He then retired to Ripaille on Lake Geneva. Here, he and five other knights formed the Order of St. Maurice, leading a semi-eremitical life according to a rule written by Amadeus.

Amadeus lived peacefully at Ripaille until a small group of dissenters from the Council of BASEL began negotiating with him to be their pope. The majority of Basel's representatives recognized Pope EUGENE IV (1431–47) and had moved with him to Ferrara/Florence. The group that approached Amadeus had deposed Eugene and now sought a replacement. After much hesitation Amadeus accepted, and was elected on Nov. 5, 1439. He abdicated as Duke of Savoy on Jan. 6, 1440, was ordained priest, and consecrated Felix V (July 24, 1440) by Cardinal d'Allamand of Aries, the only cardinal remaining in Basel. This immediately created a new schism because Eugene had already excommunicated Amadeus on March 23, 1440 at the Council of FLORENCE. Felix's reign was only supported by a scattered group of secondary powers: Savoy, Switzerland, the Dukes of Austria, Tyrol, and Bayern-München, along with the Count of Simmern, various smaller orders (e.g., the Teutonic Knights and the Carthusians), and a few universities with allegiance to the Council of Basel (Cracow, Erfurt, Leipzig, Vienna). The antipope was also not successful in naming cardinals; most of those he nominated turned him down. However, some agreed, including Aeneas Sylvius Piccolomini, later PIUS II (1458–64), who was Felix's secretary for the first two years of his reign. Felix also had monetary problems. He argued with the Council of Basil over his right to claim various revenues and benefices as pope. In November 1442, Felix left Basel for Lausanne and then Geneva, where he could secure an income.

As the situation became more difficult for him and increasingly dangerous for the long-term security of his family's holdings, Felix looked for an amicable way to resign. Finally, through the mediation of Charles VII of France (1422–61), an arrangement was reached with Eugene's successor, NICHOLAS V (1447–55), whereby Felix rescinded all actions and pronouncements he had made as pope. In exchange, Nicholas named Amadeus cardinal bishop of St. Sabina and papal vicar-general (and legate) for Savoy and several surrounding dioceses (Basel, Strasburg, et al.). The last of the antipopes, Felix abdicated on April 7, 1449. He lived in Geneva for another three years. He died there on Jan. 7, 1451, and was buried at Ripaille, where he had founded the Order of St. Maurice.

Bibliography: *Bollario de Felice V*, 8 v. manuscript in the Archivio di Stato in Turin. R. DE MAULDE-LA-CLAVIÈRE, *Concordat ou Transaction passée entre le duc Amédée VIII et le clergé de Savoie, 1433* (Paris 1881). A. ECKSTEIN, *Zur Finanzlage Felix' V. und des Basler Konzils* (Berlin 1912; Aalen 1973). G. MOLLAT, *Dictionnaire d'histoire et de géographie ecclésiastiques* (Paris 1914) 2.1166–74. F. COGNASSO, *Amadeo VIII* (Turin 1930; Milan 1990). F. X. SEPPELT, *Geschichte der Päpste von den Anfängen bis zur Mitte des zwanzigsten Jahrhunderts* (Munich 1956) 4.295–305. F. COGNASSO, *Dizionario biografico degli Italiani* (Rome 1960) 2.749–53. MARIE-JOSÉ, *La Maison de Savoie: Amédée VIII. le duc qui devient pape* (Paris 1962). S. EDMUNDS, "The Missals of Felix V and Early Savoyard Illumination," *Art Bulletin* 46 (1964) 127–41. M. CREIGHTON, *A History of the Papacy from the Great Schism to the Sack of Rome*, v. 1 (London 1897; New York 1969). E. MONGIANO, "Privilegi concessi all' antipapa Felix V," *Rivista de storia del diritto italiano* 52 (1979) 174–87. H. SCHNEIDER, "Die Halbbulle Felix' V: Zur Imitation kurialen Kanzleibrauchs in der Basler Konzilskanzlei," *Annuarium historiae conciliorum* 17 (1985) 457–63. J. N. D. KELLY, *The Oxford Dictionary of Popes* (New York 1986) 243–44. J. HELMRATH, *Das Basler Konzil, 1431–1449: Forschungsstand und Probleme* (Cologne 1987) 153–57. E. MONGIANO, *La cancelleria di un antipapa: il bollario de Felice V* (Torino 1988). B. ANDENMATTEN, et al. *Amédée VIII-Felix V, premier duc de Savoie et pape, 1383–1451: colloque international, Ripaille-Lausanne, 23–26 octobre 1990: études* (Lausanne 1992).

[P. M. SAVAGE]

FELIX OF CANTALICE, ST.

Capuchin lay brother; b. Cantalice (Diocese of Cittaducale), Italy, May 18, 1515; d. Rome, May 18, 1587. Felix was the third of four sons born to devout peasant parents, Santi and Santa Porri. Until his 28th year he labored as a farmhand and shepherd. Felix led a remarkably innocent life, and spent much time in prayer, especially during his long vigils with the flocks. Finally, desirous of imitating the Desert Fathers, he sought admission to the newly formed branch of Friars Minor known as Capuchins.

In the novitiate of the order's Roman province at Anticoli, Felix (who retained his baptismal name) manifested the heroic spirit of charity, prayer, and penance that characterized his entire life despite temptations and a malignant fever that tried his vocation. He pronounced his solemn vows in the friary of Monte San Giovanni, May 18, 1544, and spent three more years in spiritual formation at Tivoli and Viterbo. In 1547 he was sent to the Convent of St. Bonaventure, Rome, where for the next 40 years he served his brethren as questor. This meant that every day Felix had to trudge the streets of Rome, stopping at homes and shops to collect in a sack the food offered by benefactors for St. Bonaventure's large community. The barefoot friar with the huge sack over his shoulder became a celebrity. Children flocked to him, hailed him with his own constant greeting, "Deo gratias." Along the way he converted hardened sinners, consoled sufferers, and fed the poor. The Romans were edified and amused by his accustomed outcry: "Make way for the Capuchins' ass!" One day (St.) Philip NERI deposited his great clerical hat on the brother's cowled head, and obliged him, as a test of humility, to go thus on his rounds. But Felix in return insisted that Philip drink publicly from a huge flagon of wine, to the great glee and merriment of the onlookers.

Felix enjoyed the friendship of other saints and eminent persons. (St.) Charles BORROMEO consulted him, unlettered though he was, on the rule of life to be given his Oblates. Another personal friend was SIXTUS V, who, on the day of Felix's death, urged the process of his beatification. Sixtus declared that he had witnessed 18 miracles wrought by the holy questor, and that he would testify to them personally. Consoled by heavenly visions, Felix died on the feast of his patron, which was also the anniversary of his own birth and religious profession. His body lies in the Capuchin Church of the Immaculate Conception, Rome, on the present Via Veneto. URBAN VIII beatified Felix on Oct. 1, 1625. With his canonization by CLEMENT XI, May 22, 1712, Felix of Cantalice became the first Capuchin saint. He is often depicted according to one of his visions, holding the Infant Jesus, whom the Blessed Virgin has placed in his arms.

Feast: May 18.

Bibliography: B. GITZEN, ''St. Felix of Cantalice,'' *Round Table of Franciscan Research,* 10 (reprint 1949) 99–116. A. KERR, *A Son of St. Francis* (London 1900). *Lexicon Capuccinum* (Rome 1951) 574–575. A. BUTLER, *The Lives of the Saints,* ed. H. THURSTON and D. ATTWATER (New York 1956) 2:344–345. *Acta Sanctorum* May 4:202–292. W. DE PARIS, *Catholicisme* 4:1153–54. *Analecta Ordinis Fratrum Minorum Cappuchinorum* 29 (1913) 283–288.

[T. MACVICAR]

FELIX OF NICOSIA, BL.

Lay brother; b. Nicosia, Sicily, Nov. 5, 1715; d. there, May 31, 1787. His father, Philip Amoroso, a poor shoemaker, and his devout mother, Carmela, had him baptized Giacomo. He followed his father's trade until at 27 he entered the Capuchin Order at Mistretta, Oct. 1, 1743. He received the name Felix after St. Felix of Cantalice, the first Capuchin saint. During the 44 years of his religious life, Felix served his brethren in the duties of a lay brother, especially as a seeker of alms. He was renowned for his charity, especially toward the sick and prisoners, and for his austere penances, constant prayer, and his power of miracles, which earned him the title *thaumaturgus.* For 33 years he lived under a superior who considered it his role to sanctify Felix by subjecting him to relentless severity and fantastic humiliations, all of which he heroically endured. Felix was beatified by Leo XIII, Feb. 12, 1888; three years later his remains were transferred to the Cathedral of Nicosia.

Feast: June 1.

Bibliography: *Lexicon Capuccinum* (Rome 1951) 578.

[T. MACVICAR]

FELIX OF NOLA, ST.

Third-century confessor; b. Nola, near Naples, Italy. Felix, born of a Syrian father, became a priest; he was imprisoned during a persecution, and later released. His reputation for holiness, working miracles, and attracting pilgrims is perpetuated by St. PAULINUS OF NOLA who chose Felix as his patron, erected a basilica in his honor, and wrote many poems (*natalicia*) eulogizing Felix on his feast day. Paulinus consulted St. AUGUSTINE on requests from people desiring to be buried near the tomb of Felix and received Augustine's *De cura gerenda pro mortuis* (*c.* 424) in response. Felix is invoked in finding lost articles, also as the avenger of perjury.

Feast: Jan. 14.

Bibliography: G. LUONGO, *Lo specchio dell'agiografo: S. Felice. . .* (Naples 1992). B. KÖTTING, *Peregrinatio religiosa* (Münster 1950). R. C. GOLDSCHMIDT, ed., *Paulinus' Churches at Nola* (Amsterdam 1940). A. BUTLER, *The Lives of the Saints,* ed. H. THURSTON and D. ATTWATER (New York 1956) 1:80–81.

[A. C. RUSH]

FELIX OF VALOIS, ST.

Cofounder of the Trinitarians; b. 1127; d. 1212. Although with St. JOHN OF MATHA, he is claimed as cofounder of the TRINITARIANS, his very existence is doubtful. The earliest Trinitarians kept no archives, but in the 15th and 16th centuries certain writers of the order compiled fictitious records, which they claimed were based on documents. This earliest ''history'' was further elaborated. According to the account, Felix belonged to the House of Valois. He retired into the forest of Galeresse to live as a hermit and in 1197 he and John of Matha established the Trinitarian Order. He was never officially canonized, though his cult was confirmed in 1666.

Feast: Nov. 20.

Bibliography: J. L. BAUDOT and L. CHAUSSIN, *Vies des saints et des bienheueux selon l'ordre du calendrier avec l'historique des fêtes* (Paris 1935–56) 11:669–671. B. DE GAIFFIER, *Analecta Bollandiana* 73 (1955) 261. A. BUTLER, *The Lives of the Saints,* ed. H. THURSTON and D. ATTWATER (New York 1956) 4:392–393. R. GAZEAU, *Catholicisme* 4:1156–57.

[A. G. BIGGS]

FELTON, JOHN, BL.

Martyr; b. Surrey?, date unknown; d. London, Aug. 8, 1570. He was from an ancient and wealthy Norfolk family, and related by marriage to the Boleyn family. His wife had been lady in waiting to Mary Tudor and was a personal friend of Elizabeth I. The Feltons enjoyed the unusual privilege of keeping a private chaplain under license.

It was John Felton who affixed the declaratory act *Regnans in Excelsis* (by which St. Pius V excommunicated Elizabeth) to the gate of the Bishop of London's palace in May 1570. An immediate search was ordered and a copy of the bull was found in the rooms of a student at Lincoln's Inn. Under torture the young man confessed that he had received the copy from Felton and the latter was arrested. Well aware of what was happening, he made no attempt to escape, to resist, or to deny the charges but, rather, behaved as one looking forward to martyrdom. Despite torture, he admitted nothing other than the publishing of the bull, which, he maintained, was solely his responsibility. He was tried at the Guildhall in August 1570 and executed at St. Paul's Church Yard Aug. 8, 1570. Felton was beatified by Leo XIII in 1886.

Bibliography: S. LEE, *The Dictionary of National Biography from the Earliest Times to 1900,* 63 v. (London 1908) 6:1170–72. R. CHALLONER, *Memoirs of Missionary Priests,* ed. J. H. POLLEN (rev. ed. London 1924). J. H. POLLEN, *Acts of English Martyrs* (London 1891); *English Catholics in the Reign of Queen Elizabeth* (New York 1920).

[B. C. FISHER]

FELTON, THOMAS, BL.

Minim friar, martyr; b. 1567, Bermondsey Abbey, England; hanged at Isleworth, Aug. 28, 1588. Thomas, son of the martyr Bl. John FELTON, left his father's faith for a time to conform to the new religion. Repenting of his sin, he joined the Minims and was tonsured in 1583. He was arrested before being professed, but was tortured horribly and executed for being reconciled to the Church. Thomas was beatified by Pius XI on Dec. 15, 1929.

Feast of the English Martyrs: May 4 (England).

See Also: ENGLAND, SCOTLAND, AND WALES, MARTYRS OF.

Bibliography: R. CHALLONER, *Memoirs of Missionary Priests,* ed. J. H. POLLEN (rev. ed. London 1924; repr. Farnborough 1969). J. H. POLLEN, *Acts of English Martyrs* (London 1891).

[K. I. RABENSTEIN]

FEMINISM

A global movement that draws attention to the many ways in which the full human dignity of women is diminished by patriarchy and its pervasive androcentricism, feminism advocates change on behalf of women's personal and corporate well-being. This general characterization of feminism is overly simplistic unless the history of the development of feminism is taken into account. This history is usually divided into three stages or ''waves'' that rose from changing perceptions of the root causes for women's diminishment and of the best strategies for remedying them. In the nineteenth century, when feminism emerged as a distinct movement, the major goal of feminists was to advocate recognition of women's intrinsic worth and to improve the position of women in the public sphere. This goal was revisited and broadened in the 1960s by feminists who promoted an equal-rights agenda. In both of these eras, the primary spokespersons and beneficiaries were white women. In the last quarter of the twentieth century, however, feminists broadened their goals and became more attuned to the distinctive effects of patriarchy and the complexity of women's experience, shaped by race, ethnicity, and class. During this same period feminists began to recognize that patriarchy not only affects women in destructive ways, it also dehumanizes men and exploits nonhuman nature. Therefore, feminists went beyond an exclusive focus on women's struggles for justice to include ending (a) the oppression of men who suffer under the burden of racism, ethnic prejudice, classism, and colonialism, and (b) the needless destruction by humans of Earth's many life forms.

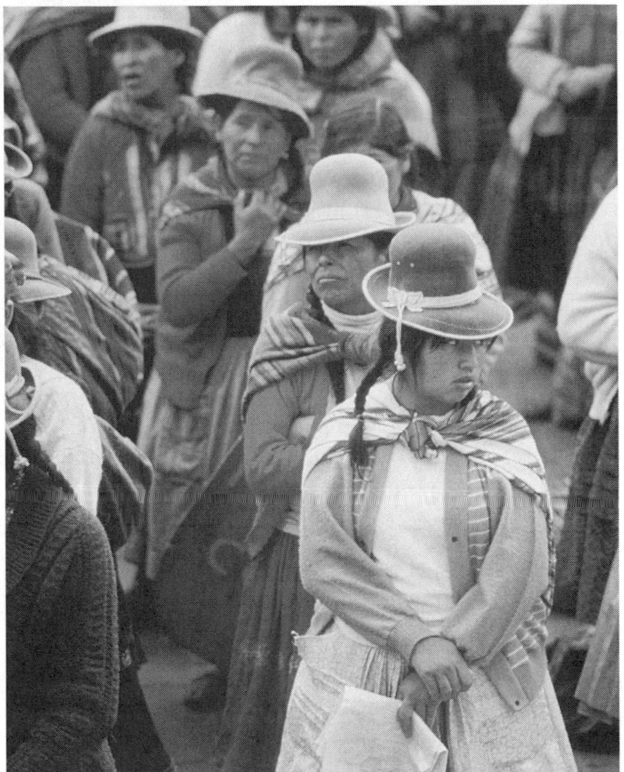

Women's Rights demonstration, Cuzco, Paucartambo, Peru. (©Jeremy Horner/CORBIS)

The First Wave. Late-nineteenth-century movements for women's rights in the United States and Western Europe mark the historical beginnings of feminism. However, long before Hubertine Auclert coined the term in 1882, precursors such as Christine de Pizan (1405) and Mary Wollstonescraft (1792) drew attention to the secondary status of women in society, attributing it not to women's inferior nature, but to their lack of education. In the nineteenth century, educated women in the west began to organize movements to gain an expansion of rights, especially the right of married women to own property and the right of women to vote. Undertaken with religious fervor and commitment to moral reform, the specifics of the first wave of feminism varied from country to country. In many countries, however, the goal of women's suffrage was achieved: in New Zealand (1893), Finland (1906), Britain, Canada and Russia (1917) and the United States (1920). Once this very public goal of liberal democracy was attained, the first wave of feminism waned in the midst of the emergence of pressing world-wide political and economic concerns of the 1930s.

Believing that the secondary status of women would be remedied when women were given the same political rights as men, many women active in nineteenth and early-twentieth-century suffrage movements retained the belief that the proper place for a woman, especially for the married woman with children, was the home. This belief, basic to the ''cult of true womanhood,'' enabled the early promoters of the first wave of feminism to attribute special status to women. It was women who ably cared for children and were the natural guardians of Christian moral values in the home. These same moral values would have a positive effect on the nation when women participated in political decision-making. Some women of this era challenged the ''cult of true womanhood'' point of view, arguing that it failed to take into account the ways in which women are treated as inferiors in their own homes. Among them was Elizabeth Cady Stanton who counted among her many accomplishments *The Woman's Bible* (1895).

The Second Wave. In the 1960s a second wave of feminism began with earnest in the United States in the context of the Civil Rights movement which championed the equality of blacks with whites. The second wave revived and broadened not only women's political struggle for equality of the first wave but also led to the development of feminist studies as a new academic discipline, impacting virtually every area of research, including Christian theology, spirituality, and ethics. During this period there were many forms of grass roots protests of women's oppression with organizations formed to orchestrate them (e.g., the National Organization of Women). Stressing that the oppression of women consists in their lack of political and economic equality with men, the women's liberation movement spread to western Europe and beyond in the 1970s. Women in the academy also became involved in the nascent women's liberation movement with many taking up the task of Simone de Beauvoir, author of *The Second Sex* (1949), to search for a suitable theory to explain women's subordination to men and women's own complicity in their own domination. Kate Millett (*Sexual Politics*, 1969, 1977) and Shulamith Firestone (*The Dialectic of Sex*, 1970, 1979) argued that the economic and political forms of domination given the most attention by women in the movement were relatively superficial when compared to patriarchy and its pervasive effects on all aspects of society.

Feminist theory of the 1970s focused its attention on the distinction between biologically determined sexual traits and culturally defined gender roles. Analysis of gender oppression of women paved the way for feminist scholars to recognize the wide ranging effects of patriarchy: the multifaceted social systems that legitimate and enforce the dominance of white, educated males in a society, giving the men in power responsibility for defining what is masculine and feminine. Although women, particularly well educated Euro-American and European women, at times display patterns of patriarchal domination, especially over children and persons of color, feminist theory attributes the organization of patriarchal societies to men who are its principal beneficiaries.

In second wave secular feminism it is possible to discern at least four major types of responses to patriarchy: liberal feminism, cultural feminism, radical feminism, and socialist feminism.

Liberal feminism has its roots in Enlightenment political theory and is more common in democratic countries. The defining characteristic of liberal feminism is the claim that social inequality in patriarchal societies, especially the lack of equal economic and political rights for women, subverts liberal democracy. True to its nineteenth-century roots, liberal feminism seeks to remove the barriers that deny women full legal, political, economic and civil rights as autonomous adults and to attain equal access for women to all facets of society: political, economic, social, and cultural. Since the 1960s, the liberal feminist struggle for the full equality of women with men has expressed itself in a variety of ways: advocating legislation that insures equity in pay for women; gaining equal access for women to leadership roles that have been traditionally closed to them, such as women holding political offices and being CEOs of major corporations; insuring the right to individual privacy, especially in regard to decisions about a woman's body, including the right of a woman to make choices in matters related to childbearing.

Cultural feminism, sometimes called ''romantic feminism'' or ''reform feminism,'' focuses on the contributions and values traditionally associated with women, like nurturing and compassion, and the contribution women can make to the betterment of all realms of society. Cultural feminism is rooted in two premises that can be traced to the nineteenth-century ''cult of true womanhood'': the presumption of the moral superiority of women, associated with their maternal role, and the need for that moral superiority to make societal life more humane. Cultural feminists envision women as less ambitious and competitive, and more likely to be egalitarian, nurturing, and peacemaking than men. It manifests itself wherever complementarity in masculine and feminine roles rooted in sexual difference is emphasized.

At the opposite end of the spectrum from cultural feminism is radical or separatist feminism which rejects complementarity because it exalts the ideal of woman at the expense of real women and often means that women are expected to carry out male-defined roles. Further, for the radical feminist liberal feminism does not go far enough in its reforms. Liberal feminism accommodates itself to a male-defined liberal state which conceives of rights in terms of individual subjectivity. For the radical feminist, however, ''the personal'' is also always ''the political.'' What makes this type of feminism radical is the belief that male domination of women is the root of all societal problems and the paradigm for all power relationships. Radical feminists actively seek to raise awareness of the pervasiveness of patriarchy in every facet of societal life and to transform that life through extensive reorganization. Radical feminist analysis is particularly critical of male violence toward women tolerated in patriarchal societies. In this analysis attention is focused on overtly violent acts such as rape, pornography, woman battering, war, and ecological destruction and overt violence in support of economic women's dependency and psychological inferiority. To counter these forms of patriarchal violence, some radical feminists advocate creating separatist ''women-centered societies'' which are, as far as possible, exclusively female. Only in such societies can women celebrate their womanhood free from male control. When women absent themselves from patriarchal society, then the power of patriarchy would be overthrown.

The final form of second wave feminism that traces its beginnings to the 1970s is socialist feminism which, in agreement with radical feminism, holds that patriarchy is a pervasive problem affecting all realms of human life. However, socialist feminists regard the movement among some radical feminists to create separate women-centered societies as unrealistic. Influenced by Marxist principles, socialist feminists locate women's oppression within the context of economic class struggle. They emphasize that one cannot ignore the impact of economic class divisions on women's oppression and perceived inferiority. Socialist feminists stress that in capitalist societies those who control the means of production also define the division of labor according to sex, race, and ethnicity. The patriarchy of capitalism manifests itself in the undervaluing of the work of women in child bearing and child rearing, because it is not considered economically productive. Socialist feminists strive to make women's unpaid labor politically and economically relevant. Although socialist feminists embrace Marxist economic analysis, they also fault it for failing to focus sufficiently on the pervasive effects of patriarchy. Socialism does not automatically liberate women. Although in socialist societies women are as free as men to work at any job outside the home and in this regard are man's equal, the vast majority of working women continue to do most of the domestic work in their homes.

The Third Wave. Most of the people who exemplify the characteristics associated with the four types of second-wave feminism are white women of European origin. Although analyzed as distinct types, traits associated with liberal, cultural, radical, and socialist feminisms are often combined by individual feminists. In the late 1970s and early 1980s the concerns of many feminists turned to issues related to female embodiment and the difference that social location makes in the struggles of women. Heretofore white feminists uncritically presumed to speak for all women. However, their universalizing positions failed to take into account the different experiences of women of color and how race, ethnicity and social class affected the conceptions of femininity and masculinity. In the United States the essentialism of European American women was critiqued by African American women. Among them was Audre Lorde, an author and poet, who in 1979 challenged white feminist scholars about their position of privilege and the accompanying neglect of the differences between themselves and black women and other women of color. She questioned how white women proposed to deal with the fact that women who clean their houses and tend their children while they attend conferences on feminist theory were, for the most part, poor women of color.

To distinguish themselves from white women's feminist agenda, African American women chose to name themselves ''womanist,'' a word play on ''womanish'' (meaning a self-assertive African American girl) coined by Alice Walker (*In Search of Our Mother's Garden*, 1983). Other women of color are also naming themselves in ways that draw attention to the difference that their social location makes in their struggle to attain full human dignity. Some women of Latin American origins, for example, have adopted terms such as *Latina* or *mujerista* to name their distinct realities and struggles. Since 1975 a series of United Nations conferences on women have revealed as many differences as similarities among women of the First and Third Worlds, West and East, North and South. Therefore, "difference" has become a major analytical category in feminist thought to account for the stratifications of societies along class, race, ethnic group, and gender lines. Therefore, a logical step in the struggle against patriarchy was to incorporate concern for the men whose race and class locates them with women in the underclass of society. In addition to attention to these people-centered concerns, among third wave feminists are those who seek to end the exploitation of the earth and its living species. Ecofeminism draws attention to the connection between the domination of women and other forms of social domination, and the exploitation of nonhuman nature, arguing that human and nonhuman forms of domination are intimately connected and mutually reinforcing.

In sum, third wave feminism challenges the secondary status of women and of subjugated men on the grounds of their supposed "natural inferiority," while attending to the different culture specific ways in which this supposed inferiority is promoted. It is also reconstructive: (1) in the many ways it supports the full personhood and dignity of women and men by both respecting and bridging difference through solidarity, and (2) in its re-envisioning of the whole of reality in post-patriarchal ways, including human relationship with nonhuman nature.

Christianity and Feminism. In the assessment of some, including Christian religious leaders, feminism is incompatible with the Christian tradition. This judgment is often made in reaction to specific positions held by one or other of the feminist groups, such as the liberal feminists who champion reproductive rights of women and the radical feminists who advocate anti-male separatism. Although not necessarily explicitly religious in nature, the many feminisms that have emerged over the years have often been intertwined not only with religious and moral debates, but also with religious and moral commitments. Many Catholics (women and men) identify themselves as feminists today because they find themselves compelled to live their baptismal vocation by affirming their church's teachings on reverence for life and the inherent dignity of the human person, and to apply the prophetic message of Jesus Christ to all forms of patriarchal injustice, including gender discrimination, racial prejudice, colonial oppression and ecological destruction. A Christian feminist, in company with other feminists, advocates major structural change in all realms of society but does so guided by the Spirit who is the source of authentic wisdom and freeing truth.

See Also: ECOFEMINIST THEOLOGY; LATINA THEOLOGY; WOMANIST THEOLOGY.

Bibliography: S. DE BEAUVOIR, *The Second Sex* (1949; E.T. New York 1974). C. DE PIZAN, *The Book of Ladies* (1405; E.T. New York 1982). G. LERNER, *The Creation of Patriarchy* (New York 1986); *The Creation of Feminist Consciousness* (New York 1993). A. LORDE, *Sister Outsider* (Trumansburg, N.Y. 1984). M. RILEY, *Transforming Feminism* (Kansas City 1989). S. M. SCHNEIDERS, *With Oil in Their Lamps: Faith, Feminism and the Future* (New York 2000). A. WALKER, *In Our Mother's Garden: Womanist Prose* (New York 1983). M. WOLLSTONECRAFT, *A Vindication of the Rights of Women* (1792; London and Rutland, Vt., 1995).

[A. CLIFFORD]

FEMINIST HERMENEUTICS

Broadly speaking, feminist hermeneutics is the theory, art and practice of interpretation in the interest of women. It addresses a broad realm of things, ranging from the Bible and other theological texts to human acts and products, endeavoring to challenge and correct the effects of patriarchy on them. Feminist hermeneutics makes women's many varied experiences the major resource for the hermeneutic process, no matter what expression of human life is the focus. From a theological standpoint, feminist hermeneutics enables women to engage in the critical construction of religious meaning in ways that attend to the complex whole of women's experiences, especially experiences of struggle against dehumanization due to patriarchy. Where texts are concerned, feminist hermeneutics, like most forms of contemporary hermeneutics, holds that the meaning perceived in a text depends on the social setting in which it was produced as well as the social setting in which it is received and handed on. This "double hermeneutic" is evident in the strategies of interpretation employed by feminist theologians. Among the most common strategies used in the construction of religious meaning by feminist scholars are hermeneutics of suspicion, of remembrance and of proclamation.

A *feminist hermeneutics of suspicion* is first and foremost a consciousness-raising activity that requires one to take into account the influence of culturally determined gender roles and attitudes on whatever is being examined. It is concerned with bringing to consciousness the effects of male bias and ideology on understandings of the wider whole of meaning. A feminist hermeneutics of suspicion is concerned not only with critical engagement about what is said about women that may diminish their full human dignity, but also with the silences that presume women's secondary status by ignoring their experiences of the divine.

In the case of Christian feminist theology, the primary application of a feminist hermeneutics of suspicion has been focused on the Bible. The strategy is to interpret a biblical text and its Christian receptions, mindful that both have been largely shaped by male perspectives without attention to those of women. For example, when a biblical text is interpreted one begins by assuming that the text was affected by how the community for whom it was written was structured. Attention to the effects of patriarchal structures on biblical texts does not rule out God's self-communication through the biblical word and its interpretation, but it does explicitly recognize that God speaks to human beings in human fashion. It is reasonable to assume, therefore, that in patriarchal societies androcentricism which neglects women's perspectives affects not only how texts are written but also what is both emphasized and neglected in them. For example, texts like Paul's letters to the Corinthians cannot be understood merely from the dictionary definitions of the ancient Greek words and the mastery of the rules of grammar that he used. Statements such as "women should keep silent in the churches" (1 Cor 14:34) must be understood in relationship to the lives and cultural situation of the author and his audience. In the process the interpreter must also attend to the unique "givenenss" of her (his) hermeneutical situation that is affected by a tradition of reception that may transmit patriarchal presuppositions that are both overt and subtle.

On the positive side, a feminist hermeneutics of suspicion prepares the way for a *feminist hermeneutics of remembrance* that reconstructs historical texts from women's perspectives, restoring women to Christian history and women's religious history to Christianity. In some cases a hermeneutics of remembrance takes the form of the woman who diligently searched for the "sacred coin," which in this case is a "lost" tradition whose liberating potential for women has never been realized. In such cases not only biblical but also extra-biblical ancient texts are used. In other cases a hermeneutics of remembrance reclaims the suffering of women of the past and of all persons subjugated through enslavement, exile, and persecution, and recognizes them to be "dangerous memories" subversive to the *status quo*. Such memories are subversive because even in the midst of crises, women found in their relationship with God and/or Jesus Christ reasons for hope and motivation to be agents for liberation from oppressive sociopolitical establishments and religious institutions. These memories invite corrections to sexist perspectives while preserving the freeing truth of the "Good-news." They also challenge to solidarity with all persons past and present who struggle for human dignity. In short, a hermeneutics of remembrance neither negates the dehumanizing effects of patriarchy on biblical and Christian history nor does it give them the final word. The Bible and many extra-biblical sources, both ancient and modern, provide rich resources for constructing feminist theologies for our time that heal suffering, liberate from struggle and end economic exploitation.

By the end of the 20th century, feminist hermeneutical scholarship of suspicion and remembrance gained acceptance in the academy and in some grassroots Christian groups. Many Christian feminists recognize that the rich insights resulting from the application of a feminist hermeneutics of remembrance can easily be regarded to be mere theory unless a *feminist hermeneutics of proclamation* is used to enact these insights in the Christian community. A performative language, feminist hermeneutics of proclamation gives expression to religious meaning in ways oriented to praxis. Christian feminists recognize that liturgy (conceived here as any form of communal worship) is important to the faith life of Christians. Grounded in the conviction that the interaction and integration of the Bible and worship is the backbone of Christian experience and formation, a hermeneutics of proclamation promotes personal and communal participation, biblical imagination and emancipatory action. Integrating interpretations made possible by the application of feminist hermeneutics of suspicion and remembrance, a feminist hermeneutics of proclamation seeks to give the reconstructed divine Word flesh in liturgical ritual, storytelling, Bible-centered drama, dance, song, preaching and action in ways that are genuinely inclusive of the experiences of women. Whatever the form of the proclamation, the goal is to keep alive the freeing truth of the "Good-news" of the full human dignity of all persons, especially women, and of the intrinsic value of all of creation.

Bibliography: C. CAMP, "Feminist Theological Hermeneutics," in *Searching the Scriptures: A Feminist Introduction*, ed., E. SCHÜSSLER FIORENZA (New York 1993) 154–171. A. M. CLIFFORD, *Introducing Feminist Theology* (Maryknoll, N.Y. 2001). E. SCHÜSSLER FIORENZA, *Bread Not Stone: The Challenge of Feminist Biblical Scholarship* (Boston 1984); *But She Said: Feminist Practices of Biblical Interpretation* (Boston 1992).

[A. CLIFFORD]

FEMINIST THEOLOGY

Feminist theology examines the meaning and implications of Christian faith from the perspective of a commitment to justice for females. An intellectual development with profound spiritual, psychological, and political implications, it shares with Christian theology in general the classic aim of "faith seeking understanding," but is distinguished by two additional features. The first is the assumption that standard theology has been skewed by longstanding sexism in the tradition. According to this analysis, both social arrangements (patriarchy) and ideological biases (androcentrism) have privileged males and failed to do justice to females; thus an intellectually and morally adequate theology requires significant correction of previous work in all theological disciplines. The second distinguishing feature of feminist theology is a methodological commitment to emphasizing women's experience, in all its complexity and diversity, while conducting the tasks of theological reflection. These tasks generally involve three things: *critique* of sexist interpretations and practices; *retrieval* of women's past contributions to ecclesial life and theological reflection; and, *construction* of more just and accurate interpretations and practices.

There are many definitions and types of feminism, and much controversy about the meanings and implications of the various types (*see* FEMINISM). Some definitions emphasize the participation of women as subjects of their own liberative process against the injustice of sexism, while others emphasize that human beings of both sexes are capable of recognizing and opposing this evil. These two types may be designated respectively as ''woman-centered feminism'' and ''inclusive feminism.'' They are different, but each captures true aspects of the movement and has useful practical applications. Feminism is understood here inclusively as a position that involves a solid conviction of the equality of women and men, and a commitment to reform society and to reform the thought systems that legitimate the present social order. Those who espouse feminism, however, differ widely in their analyses of injustice, levels of commitment to liberating action, degrees of explicitness of commitment, and opinions regarding specific problems and their solutions.

This presentation first sketches the main lines of the historical development of feminist theology, and then describes some of its substantive contributions to various fields and topics traditionally explored by theologians. Although the emphasis is on U.S. Roman Catholicism, it is important to recognize that feminist theology has an inherently ecumenical dimension and has engaged the energies of many Catholic and Protestant (and some Orthodox) scholars throughout the world. It has an interfaith dimension as well, sharing concerns with analogous movements among feminist thinkers from Buddhist, Jewish, Muslim, and other traditions. From the beginning, Catholic women in the United States have played a leading role in the development of feminist theology, thanks to the insight and dedication of pioneering laywomen and vowed women religious, and to the intellectual heritage of Catholic women's colleges. These colleges prepared a climate for the practice and reception of feminist theology by establishing a tradition of women's higher learning and leadership unparalleled elsewhere. The exclusion of women from the sacrament of orders has also influenced some women to pursue academic theology, since female leadership has been possible in academic settings, whereas it has been limited in institutional and pastoral settings.

Launching a Movement: 1960–75. Prior to the Second Vatican Council, theology had functioned mainly to educate future priests, who studied Latin texts in classes that were often isolated from wider social and intellectual currents. Some lay persons took courses in neoscholastic philosophy and theology in Catholic colleges and universities, and religious sisters and brothers read some works related to their vocation, but only the clergy had access to doctoral programs that would prepare them for research and teaching at advanced levels in the field. An early exception to this rule was the graduate program inaugurated at St. Mary's College in Indiana by Sister Mary Madeleva Wolff, CSC, in 1944. Only in the 1960s did wider access to theological studies become available to women in the United States. At that time a ''second wave'' of feminism was underway, and papal and conciliar documents were beginning to affirm women's basic equality and political rights in ways that would have astonished those who decades earlier had campaigned for women's suffrage in the face of opposition from the hierarchy.

Several provisions of Vatican II's Pastoral Constitution on the Church in the Modern World (*Gaudium et spes,* or *GS*) were particularly influential in inspiring Catholic women to look critically at their own tradition and undertake theological studies in view of advancing the reforms initiated by the council. The first was the recognition that because of the essential equality of all persons (*homines* in the original Latin, a term that includes females in a manner that ''men'' does not), ''any kind of social or cultural discrimination in basic personal rights on the grounds of sex . . . must be curbed and eradicated as incompatible with God's design'' (#29). Furthermore, the council also affirmed a more dynamic, historically conscious understanding of God's will for humanity than had previously held sway, with all that this implies in terms of openness to the genuinely *new:* ''In each nation and social group there is a growing number of men and women who are conscious that they themselves are the architects and molders of their community's culture. All over the world the sense of autonomy and responsibility increases with effects of the greatest importance for the spiritual and moral maturity of humankind'' (#55). Although *GS* itself retains much of the androcentrism of its time, and hardly anticipates the effects its ideas would have on feminist readers, passages such as the above marked a significant change and opened new vistas for progressive women and men.

Women were not specified in the crucial paragraph (#62), which voices the hope that ''more of the laity will receive adequate theological formation and that some among them will dedicate themselves professionally to these studies and contribute to their advancement.'' The language does not rule out women's participation, and it was soon interpreted inclusively by various Catholic universities and seminaries. Moreover, by affirming intellectual freedom in theology, the final sentence of this paragraph states a principle that contributed both to male support of women's involvement in the discipline and also to the development of feminist positions by theologians: ''But for the proper exercise of this role [of theologian], the faithful, both clerical and lay, should be accorded a lawful freedom of inquiry, of thought, and of expression, tempered by humility and courage in whatever branch of study they have specialized.''

A number of Catholic women had anticipated this conciliar invitation and begun theological studies earlier in the United States or Europe, among whom Mary Daly, Elisabeth Schüssler Fiorenza, and Rosemary Radford Ruether have been particularly influential. Schüssler Fiorenza's *Der vergessene Partner,* a pioneering study of possibilities for women in ministry, was published in 1964. Daly's highly influential *The Church and the Second Sex* appeared in 1968. Drawing on insights of feminist philosopher Simone de Beauvoir, Daly raised critical questions regarding Catholic doctrine and practice and offered some ''modest proposals'' for reform. Within several years Daly moved to a ''postchristian'' religious stance, and in 1973 she leveled a sustained critique of classical theology in *Beyond God the Father.* Meanwhile, many other Catholic women were moving through doctoral studies in various theological disciplines and beginning to publish early examples of feminist theology. These thinkers were influenced by biblical themes and traditional theology as well as by secular feminism and the works of ''critical'' and liberation theologians such as Jürgen Habermas, Gustavo Gutiérrez, and James Cone. By 1975, which had been declared International Women's Year by the United Nations, Ruether and Schüssler Fiorenza had published works that began to enlarge the feminist theological agenda by making connections with concerns about racism, anti-Semitism, colonialism, economic injustice, and ecological well-being; all of which they argued were the effects of patriarchy. The early phase in the U.S. feminist theological movement culminated in two historic events that took place in 1975. First, in late November more than 1,200 persons gathered in Detroit for the first national meeting of the Women's Ordination Conference (WOC), where for the first time a significant number of female theologians joined with male colleagues to probe a question of vital importance to the Church. After this historic meeting WOC sponsored a series of national events, including one to mark its twenty-fifth anniversary in Milwaukee in 2000, and helped to plan an international conference on women's ordination, Women's Ordination Worldwide, held in Dublin, Ireland, in 2001. Second, in December 1975, the Jesuit journal, *Theological Studies,* published a special issue on ''Women: New Dimensions,'' which carried articles by women who would later contribute major works of feminist theology (reprinted in Burghardt 1977).

Gaining Ground: 1975–90. Organizational activities and feminist theological scholarship intensified in the second stage of the movement. North American and European women gained institutional power in colleges, universities, and seminaries, as well as in professional organizations and academic societies. Meanwhile women elsewhere began to claim a voice within the Ecumenical Association of Third World Theologians (EATWOT), which had been founded in 1976. During an EATWOT meeting in Geneva in 1983, attended also by some theologians from Europe and the United States, feminists established a Women's Commission to address the issues of sexism in male liberation theology and racism in the white women's movement. In 1986 the European Society of Women in Theological Research (ESWTR) was established; it meets biennially. Since 1993 ESWTR has published a yearbook of research and reviews; its first issue provided historical information on European feminist theology, including attention to the contributions of such leading scholars as Kari Børresen (Norway), Catharina Halkes (Netherlands), and Mary Grey (Britain).

Increasingly, feminist theologians were contributing full-length books. In 1983 Ruether published the first ''systematic'' work of feminist theology, *Sexism and God-Talk,* which probed topics ranging from method to eschatology, and Schüssler Fiorenza published a feminist theological reconstruction of early Christianity, *In Memory of Her.* Both authors were among a number of feminist theologians who spoke at the first of three national ''women-church'' gatherings organized by Catholic groups that took place first in Chicago (1983), to be followed by assemblies in Cincinnati (1987) and Albuquerque (1993). These gatherings were notable for efforts to provide program information in Spanish as well as English. The first bilingual work of feminist theology appeared in 1988, Ada María Isasi-Díaz and Yolanda Tarango's *Hispanic Women: Prophetic Voice in the Church.*

Meanwhile, feminist theologians were being tenured in colleges and universities and elected to leadership in professional societies. Courses in women's history and feminist theology entered the curriculum, and in 1985 the *Journal of Feminist Studies in Religion* was launched, coedited by Schüssler Fiorenza and Jewish scholar Judith Plaskow. That year Schüssler Fiorenza also coedited, with Mary Collins, the first issue of what became a regular series of the international journal *Concilium* devoted to feminist theology. Subsequent volumes have been coedited by Anne E. Carr, M. Shawn Copeland, and Mary John Mananzan, with articles from these journals collected in *The Power of Naming* (Schüssler Fiorenza 1996). Carr's volume, *Transforming Grace: Christian Tradition and Women's Experience,* probed doctrines of God and Christ as well as questions of theological method, women's ordination, and spirituality. In 1990 the establishment of a women's seminar in constructive theology as a regular part of the annual meeting of the Catholic Theological Society of America marked the solid gains achieved by feminist theologians in North America. Although still overwhelmingly a movement of white women, feminist theology had deepened its recognition of the interstructured nature of oppression, acknowledged the problem of false generalizations about women's experience, and enlarged the critique of patriarchy to include heterosexism as well as sexism, racism, classism, and mistreatment of the environment.

Development and Diversification: Feminist Theologies since 1990. The last decade of the 20th century saw the publication of many influential books and articles in feminist theology, often focused and constructive efforts to advance discussion in particular fields of theological inquiry. In a number of instances white women exhibited a more intense self-critique and greater attention to diversity within the movement, while theology published by women of color voiced concerns of cultural, racial, economic, and gender injustice with a new urgency and power.

Copeland, the first African American woman to give a plenary paper at a national meeting of theologians, set a new agenda in her address to the College Theology Society in 1994. ''Mere rhetoric'' of solidarity is insufficient, she argued; effective solidarity requires a deep-seated conversion, which involves different things for women from different social locations. Although white feminist theologians had acknowledged the links between racism, classism, and sexism for years, they had often written of ''women'' at a level of generality that glossed over significant differences, and had failed to attend to the voices of black, red, yellow, and brown women. By the 1990s some theologians of color had developed particular designations for their writings in order to distinguish them from white feminist theology: womanist (African American), Latina/*mujerista,* and *minjung* (Korean). Other theologians of color retained the designation ''feminist'' and at the same time drew explicitly on their own heritages. The influence of the writings of both groups of women of color on the works of white feminists gives promise of a future when preoccupation with discussions of diversity will give way to sustained and effective collaboration on matters of concern to all (*see* LATINA THEOLOGY; WOMANIST THEOLOGY).

Contributions of Feminist Theologies to Theological Disciplines. By definition feminist theologies seek to overcome injustice, and thus there is an ethical dimension prominent in all of this work. Women theologians with specialized training in other traditional fields of theological studies have made notable contributions to the following areas.

Theological Method. Ruether (1983), Carr (1988), Isasi-Díaz (1988, 1992), and Copeland (1996, 1998) are among those who deal extensively with questions of theological method, and they all regard attention to women's diverse experiences and the employment of sources beyond classical Christian texts as important for progress in the discipline. Isasi-Díaz is distinctive in her efforts to bring the voices of U.S. Latinas from various cultural background directly into theological discussions, employing substantial quotations from these ''grass roots'' Christians in her writings. Concerning the norm for judging the adequacy of theological work, there has been some movement beyond a general insistence that good theology must promote women's human dignity to a more precise claim that good theology leads to the ''flourishing of poor women of color in violent situations'' (Johnson 1993). The overall task of Christian feminist theologies has been aptly described as that of correlating ''the central and liberating themes of biblical and Christian tradition with the experience of women in the contemporary situation'' (Carr 1988).

Biblical Studies, Hermeneutics, and History. Classical Christian texts are of crucial importance to scholars seeking justice for women in the tradition, and considerable work has been done to bring out the liberating potential buried beneath patriarchal records and interpretations of revelation. Whether this involves retrieving lost images and stories, probing possibilities of women's authorship and leadership, criticizing oppressive material, or reading between the lines to discover glimpses of equality in earlier societies, the project of feminist biblical criticism is both technically specialized and wide-ranging in its implications. Likewise, important historical work has been done to correct the record of women's activities, ideas, and influence in the centuries since biblical times, which casts new light on the development of doctrine as well as that of church law and practices. Scholars have made available newly interpreted writings of women from ''patristic'' and medieval times, and have invited reconsideration of the significance of female mystics and monastic movements such as the Beguines, and various other expressions of female creativity and leadership (Schmitt and Kulzer 1996, Kirk 1998, Madigan 1998). They have likewise documented and probed the causes of misogyny and patriarchal efforts to control women—whether by doctrine, law, or violence—and challenged contemporary Christians to overcome these longstanding tendencies to sin. This critical revisionist history carries implications for all areas of Church doctrine and practice, and is particularly powerful when conducted by scholars who attend to the combined effects of racism, colonialism, and sexism. (*See* FEMINIST HERMENEUTICS; WOMEN IN THE BIBLE.)

Doctrine of God. At the heart of theology is the mystery of God, which transcends the human capacity for symbolizing and yet requires symbolic expression. Because the symbol of God functions either to oppress or to liberate, feminist theologians have done extensive work to critique the unjust and idolatrous tendency to think that God is male. Strategies for calling attention to the problem, which is so ingrained that most Christians require some reminder that all speech about God is analogous and incapable of conveying the Mystery, have included referring to the Deity as ''God/ess'' (Ruether 1983), ''G*d,'' (Schüssler Fiorenza 1994), and ''God . . . She'' (Johnson 1993). Strategies for expanding the metaphors beyond the overused ''Father'' have involved personal images (for example, ''Mother,'' ''Lover,'' ''Friend''), the biblical ''Sophia'' (Divine Wisdom), and other terms such as ''Matrix,'' ''Creator,'' ''Liberator,'' and ''Source of All Being,'' as well as such biblical images as ''rock,'' ''fountain,'' ''midwife,'' and ''coin seeker.'' Johnson's comprehensive study, *She Who Is* (1983) considers each person of the Trinity in light of the female-associated term ''Sophia,'' and probes how these ''dense symbols'' convey Her relational, living, and compassionate nature.

Doctrine of Creation and Eschatology. Feminist theologies have stressed the goodness of creation and sought to overcome false dualisms that would value spirit at the expense of matter. They have also placed great emphasis on ecology (*see* ECOFEMINISM AND ECOFEMINIST THEOLOGY). The central theme of Jesus' teaching, the Reign of God, has been understood as a reality affecting the present world, summoning and empowering human efforts to bring about a future of right relationships among all creatures of Earth. Various ways of overcoming patriarchal associations with traditional imagery of ''Kingdom'' have been suggested, including the *mujerista* neologism ''Kin-dom'' (Isasi-Díaz 1996). While characterized by a strong ecological and political emphasis, feminist eschatology also recognizes a transcendent, mysterious dimension to the ultimate future (Ruether 1992). Hope for divine healing of the broken bones of history's victims, especially poor women of color, should impel Christians to the praxis of solidarity in the here-and-now (Copeland 1998).

Theological Anthropology. A faulty understanding of human nature is basic to the racism and sexism that feminist theologies seek to overcome. Although mainstream modern theology has rejected classical notions that males from dominant groups enjoy a higher degree of rationality, and are thus created more closely in the ''image of God'' than females and subordinated males, vestiges of racism and misogyny continue to cause great harm. White feminists initially laid most stress on overcoming stereotypes responsible for sexist attitudes and practices, such as the notions that women are ''property,'' ''temptresses,'' ''irrational,'' of a different and lesser nature thanmen. Instead of blaming Eve for ''original sin,'' they named patriarchy as a primordial sinful system, and argued about how best to articulate an anthropology that did justice to the equality of females and males while also respecting human embodiment and diversity of experience. There has been widespread agreement that notions of ''gender complementarity,'' which tend to idealize females while assigning them ''special'' roles, actually function to limit women to men's ideas of their worth and purpose and fail to respect their essential autonomy and dignity. Contributions by theologians of color have sharpened the critique in recent years, and led to further theorizing on the theological significance of difference and the complexity of women's experience (Graff 1996). ''*La vida cotidiana*'' (''everyday life'') is a newly recognized resource for understanding and praxis (Isasi-Díaz 1996, Aquino 1998), and countering systemic violence against women and children must become the focal purpose of anthropological reflection (Copeland 1998).

Christology. The significance of Christ and the meaning of salvation have been addressed in various ways by feminist scholars. Recognizing that much previous Christology has contributed to injustice to women, and yet disagreeing with Daly's view that male dominance and ''Christolatry'' are essential to the tradition, white theologians have emphasized the prophetic role taken by Jesus in his day (Schüssler Fiorenza 1994) and investigated the ways that gender and redemption have been related in Christian history (Ruether 1998). They have insisted that although the maleness of Jesus is a historical fact, this particularity is transcended in the identity of the Christ and has neither theological nor normative status (Schneiders 1986, Johnson 1992). Christologies by feminists of color have sought to liberate Jesus from the racism and imperialism of dominant theologies and stressed the identification of the historical Jesus with the poor and marginalized (Copeland 1996).

Ecclesiology, Mariology, and Sacraments. While criticizing the oppressive ways in which church structures have functioned, feminist theologians have maintained that Christianity began as a ''discipleship of equals'' (Schüssler Fiorenza 1983); since a ''spirit-filled community'' has long existed in tension with the patriarchal historical institution, the contemporary ''women-church'' movement should seek its ideals without being ultimately separatist (Ruether 1985). Emphasis on an inclusive solidarity that affirms difference within the community as it struggles for justice (Isasi-Díaz 1993) is widely shared in feminist ecclesiologies. Work on embodiment and sacraments has deepened thought on marriage, ministry, Eucharist, and worship, and kept the issue of women's ordination under discussion (Hilkert 1997, Byrne 1998, Ross 1998, Walton 2000). Feminist scholars have also developed new interpretations of Mary (Gebara and Bingemer 1989, Rodriguez 1994, Cunneen 1996) and the saints (Johnson 1998).

Ethics and Moral Theology. The implications of feminist theologies for the way Christians should live have been pondered in many works of feminist ethics, which are now influencing discussions of moral theology more generally (Curran et al. 1996). Among topics of particular concern have been agency (Isasi-Díaz 1993), commitment (Farley 1986), conscience and authority (Patrick 1996), ecology (Ruether 1992, Gebara 1999), economics and work (Andolsen 1989, 1998, Guider 1995), family (Cahill 2000), friendship (Hunt 1991), natural law (Traina 1999), power (Hinze 1995), sexuality and gender (Gudorf 1994, Cahill 1996, Jung 2001), and struggle and violence (Isasi-Díaz 1993, Mananzan 1996). Feminist theologians have brought their commitment to justice for females to many other topics in biomedical and social ethics, ranging from concerns about reproductive issues (Ryan 2001) to matters of war and peace (Cahill 1994).

Spirituality. Because all feminist theologies invite believers to a deep process of conversion, there has been considerable attention to topics in spirituality, which is a concept of wide appeal both within and beyond the churches today. Joann Wolski Conn has dealt with psychological aspects of spiritual growth (1989) and Shawn Madigan (1998) has gathered historically important spiritual writings by women. The lecture series sponsored by St. Mary's College in honor of Sister Madeleva Wolff has resulted in the publication of a new title in women's spirituality annually since 1985; recent overviews from African American, U.S. Latina, and European American perspectives have been contributed by Hayes (1995), Rodriguez (1996), and Schneiders (2000).

That feminist theology as a discipline has come of age is now evident. There is a substantial number of scholarly books by recognized theologians, as well as many introductory texts designed for classroom use. The *Journal of Feminist Studies in Religion* has been published in the United States since 1985, and *Feminist Theology* in Great Britain since 1992. That a dictionary conveying the complexity of feminist theologies (Russell and Clarkson 1996) contains extensive entries under headings that include African, Asian, European, Latin American, North American, Pacific Island, and South Asian, testifies to the global extent of this movement. The challenge now is for theologians from diverse backgrounds to carry forward their critical and constructive work, gain a wider hearing beyond the academic community, and develop an effective solidarity among themselves and among believers more generally, for the sake of building a just and ecologically responsible society.

Bibliography: B. ANDOLSEN, *Daughters of Jefferson, Daughters of Bookblacks: Racism and American Feminism* (Macon, Ga. 1986). M. P. AQUINO, *Our Cry for Life: Feminist Theology from Latin America* (Maryknoll, N.Y. 1993); ''Latin American Feminist Theology,'' *Journal of Feminist Studies in Religion* 14 (1998) 89–107. W. BURGHARDT, ed., *Woman: New Dimensions* (New York 1977). L. BYRNE, *Woman at the Altar* (New York 1998). L. S. CAHILL, *Sex, Gender and Christian Ethics* (Cambridge 1996); *Family: A Christian Social Perspective* (Minneapolis 2000). D. L. CARMODY, *Christian Feminist Theology* (Oxford 1995). A. E. CARR, *Transforming Grace: Christian Tradition and Women's Experience* (San Francisco 1988). A. CLIFFORD, *Introducing Feminist Theology* (Maryknoll, N.Y. 2001). R. COLL, *Christianity and Feminism in Conversation* (Mystic, Conn. 1994). J. W. CONN, *Spirituality and Personal Maturity* (New York 1989). M. S. COPELAND, ''The New Anthropological Subject at the Heart of the Mystical Body of Christ,'' *Catholic Theological Society of America. Proceedings* 53 (1998) 25–47; ''Theologies, Contemporary,'' in *Dictionary of Feminist Theologies,* ed. L. RUSSELL and J. S. CLARKSON (Louisville 1996) 283–287. S. CUNNEEN, *In Search of Mary: The Woman and the Symbol* (New York 1996). M. DALY, *Beyond God the Father* (Boston 1973). V. FABELLA and M. A. ODUYOYE, eds., *With Passion and Compassion: Third World Women Doing Theology* (Maryknoll, N.Y. 1988). V. FABELLA and S. PARK, eds., *We Dare to Dream: Doing Theology as Asian Women* (Maryknoll, N.Y. 1990). V. FABELLA and R. S. SUGIRTHARAJAH, eds., *Dictionary of Third World Theologies* (Maryknoll, N.Y. 2000). A. M. GARDINER, ed., *Women and Catholic Priesthood* (New York 1976). I. GEBARA and M. C. BINGEMER, *Mary: Mother of God, Mother of the Poor* (Maryknoll, N.Y. 1989). A. GRAFF, ed., *In the Embrace of God: Feminist Approaches to Theological Anthropology* (Maryknoll, N.Y. 1995). C. GUDORF, *Body, Sex, and Pleasure: Reconstructing Christian Sexual Ethics* (Cleveland 1994). M. GUIDER, *Daughters of Rahab* (Minneapolis 1995). D. HAYES, *Hagar's Daughters: Womanist Ways of Being in the World* (New York 1995). M. A. HINSDALE and P. KAMINISKI, eds., *Women and Theology* (Maryknoll, N.Y. 1995). C. F. HINZE, *Comprehending Power in Christian Social Ethics* (New York 1995). M. HUNT, *Fierce Tenderness: A Feminist Theology of Friendship* (New York 1991). A. M. ISASI-DÍAZ, *En la Lucha: A His-*

panic Women's Liberation Theology (Minneapolis 1993); *Mujerista Theology: A Theology for the Twenty-First Century* (Maryknoll, N.Y. 1996). A. M. ISASI-DÍAZ and Y. TARANGO, *Hispanic Women: Prophetic Voice in the Church* (San Francisco 1988). U. KING, ed., *Feminist Theology from the Third World* (Maryknoll, N.Y. 1994). P. KIRK, *Sor Juana Inés de la Cruz* (New York 1998). E. JOHNSON, *She Who Is: The Mystery of God in Feminist Theological Discourse* (New York 1992). P. B. JUNG, with J. A. CORAY, eds., *Sexual Diversity and Catholicism* (Collegeville, Minn. 2001). C. LACUGNA, ed., *Freeing Theology: The Essentials of Theology in Feminist Perspective* (San Francisco 1993). S. MADIGAN, ed., *Mystics, Visionaries, and Prophets: A Historical Anthology of Women's Spiritual Writings* (Minneapolis 1998). M. J. MANANZAN et al., eds., *Women Struggling against Violence: A Spirituality for Life* (Maryknoll, N.Y. 1996). A. E. PATRICK, *Liberating Conscience: Feminist Explorations in Catholic Moral Theology* (New York 1996); ''Feminist Ethics in the New Millennium,'' in *Ethical Dilemmas in the New Millennium*, ed. F. EIGO, v. 1 (Villanova, Pa. 2000). S. ROSS, *Extravagant Affections: A Feminist Sacramental Theology* (New York 1998). L. RUSSELL and J. S. CLARKSON, eds., *Dictionary of Feminist Theologies* (Louisville 1996). R. R. RUETHER, *Sexism and God-Talk: Toward a Feminist Theology* (Boston 1983); *Women-Church* (San Francisco 1985); *Gaia and God: An Ecofeminist Theology of Earth Healing* (San Francisco 1992); *Women and Redemption: A Theological History* (Minneapolis 1998). S. SCHNEIDERS, *Women and the Word* (New York 1986); *Beyond Patching: Faith and Feminism in the Catholic Church* (New York 1991); *With Oil in Their Lamps: Faith, Feminism, and the Future* (New York 2000). E. SCHÜSSLER FIORENZA, *In Memory of Her: A Feminist Theological Reconstruction of Christian Origins* (New York 1983); *Discipleship of Equals: A Critical Feminist Ekklesia-Logy of Liberation* (New York 1993); *Jesus: Miriam's Child, Sophia's Prophet* (New York 1994). C. L. H. TRAINA, *Feminist Ethics and Natural Law* (Washington, D.C. 1999). J. WALTON, *Feminist Liturgy: A Matter of Justice* (Collegeville, Minn. 2000).

[A. E. PATRICK]

FENEBERG, JOHANN MICHAEL

Priest and mystic; b. Marktoberdorf (Allgäu), Bavaria, Feb. 9, 1751; d. Vöhringen, Bavaria, Oct. 12, 1812. After studying at Kaufbeuren and the Jesuit Gymnasium at Augsburg, Feneberg was admitted into the Jesuit novitiate at Landsberg a Lech, Bavaria. After the suppression of the Society of Jesus in 1773, he continued his studies toward the priesthood and was ordained in 1775. He taught humanities at the Gymnasium of St. Paul in Regensburg, and at Dillingen, at which time he wrote a plan for studies that caused controversy (*Lehrplan,* Dillingen 1789). In 1793 he, along with some other professors, was removed from teaching on suspicion of Illuminist tendencies. He was given the parish of Seeg (Allgäu), which he administered with great success. His association with the Pietist Martin Boos, who stayed with Feneberg at Seeg for a year, revived suspicions of unorthodox mysticism. Boos tried to convert Feneberg and his assistants, Christof Schmid and Xaver Bayer, to his doctrine of love of God without works. After an ecclesiastical interrogation at Augsburg in August 1797, Feneberg and his assistants were allowed to return to Seeg. In 1805 he exchanged Seeg for the parish of Vöhringen where he translated the New Testament later edited by M. Wittmann (Regensburg 1808).

François de Salignac de la Mothe Fénelon. (©Leonard de Selva/CORBIS)

Bibliography: F. W. BODEMANN, *Leben J.M. Fenebergs* (Bielefeld 1856). J. M. SAILER, *Aus Fenebergs Leben* (Munich 1814). J. A. FISCHER, *Lexikon für Theologie und Kirche*, ed. J. HOFER and K. RAHNER (Freiberg 1957–65) 4:75, bibliog.

[E. D. MCSHANE]

FÉNELON, FRANÇOIS DE SALIGNAC DE LA MOTHE

Educator, theologian, archbishop; b. in the château de Fénelon, near Sarlat in the region of Périgord, Gascony, Aug. 6, 1651; d. Cambrai, Jan. 7, 1715. Fénelon was the thirteenth child of a father whose noble ancestry went back to the tenth century. Because of poor health, he received his early education at home, then at the Jesuit college in Cahors (1663–65); he left his native province in 1666 to study in Paris at the College of Le Plessis. In 1672 or 1673 he entered the Paris Seminary of Saint-Sulpice. Ordained at about 24, he served in the parish of

Saint-Sulpice (1675–78), laying aside his dream of missionary work in Greece. In 1678 Fénelon was appointed superior of the Convent of New Catholics in Paris, a post he occupied (with some interruptions) until 1689. The purpose of the institution was to convert and strengthen in their new faith young girls from Protestant families. Fénelon headed two preaching missions (December 1685 to July 1686, and May to July 1687) in Saintonge and Aunis. These represented efforts to convert the Protestants disturbed by the recent revocation of the Edict of NANTES. Fénelon could not tolerate heterodox religious beliefs, but he preferred gentle persuasion to persecution.

Early Writings. In 1687 Fénelon published his first important work, *Traité de l'Education des filles,* composed at the request of his friends, the Duc and Duchesse de Beauvilliers, for the benefit of their daughters, and partially embodying the results of his pedagogical experiences at the Convent of New Catholics. Although on the whole conservative, the book was a pioneering work. The dignity of women and the necessity of molding young girls for adulthood are the underlying principles. He criticized the harsh methods of his day, preferring a subtly persuasive and engaging technique proportioned to the mentality of the learner. The pupil should not be too conscious of being taught, and reason should as much as possible supplant mere discipline.

By 1687 Fénelon had powerful friends: BOSSUET, the Beauvilliers (the Duc was soon to be made guardian of the Duc de Bourgogne, grandson of the King and second in line to the succession), and the Duc and Duchesse de Chevreuse. He was introduced to Mme. de Maintenon and on Oct. 4, 1688, met Mme. GUYON.

In August 1689, at the suggestion of Mme. de Maintenon and of Beauvilliers, the King chose Fénelon as tutor of his grandson. To this period (1689–99) we owe the *Fables*, the *Dialogues des morts,* and the novel *Télémaque*, most of which was not published until later. Fénelon created these as a series of texts to meet the different stages in the intellectual and moral development of his royal charge: the first book for the child, the second for the adolescent, the third for the boy on the threshold of manhood. The two latter works are courses in the art of ruling well; the central theme is that one must first be a good man in order to be a great king; concrete examples point up lessons in statesmanship and moral idealism. In the novel the examples are adapted from the legends of antiquity, whereas in the dialogues historical figures are the types. Fénelon's method—the inculcation of truth through enjoyment—proved itself in this instance: the spoiled child, subject to tantrums, became a serious, pious boy with admirable self-control. In 1693 Fénelon was elected to the French Academy; in 1695 he was named to the archbishopric of Cambrai and consecrated by Bossuet at Versailles.

The Semiquietism Affair. Ever eager to enrich his spiritual life, Fénelon had been attracted to the teaching of Mme. Guyon. Although not approving the more extreme forms of her thought and charitably discounting her eccentricities and often exaggerated expressions, he thought that she had discovered a method of prayer well suited to bring the individual near to God, and that indeed her doctrine was not too far removed from that of the mystical saints and doctors accepted by the Church. It soon began to be bruited about that the doctrine skirted the line between orthodoxy and heresy, and was close to the QUIETISM recently condemned by Rome. Mme. Guyon's writings were examined by Church authorities (1694–95), but Fénelon could not agree with Bossuet's reaction. The appearance, at the beginning of 1697, of Fénelon's *L'Explication des Maximes des Saints sur la vie intérieure* and, a month later, of Bossuet's interpretation of the doctrine launched the unfortunate polemic between the two.

As a result, Fénelon's favor at court began to decline: Mme. de Maintenon turned against him and the King banished him to Cambrai (1697). He was officially deprived of the title of tutor in January 1699. On March 12 of that fatal year, the papal brief *Cum alias* condemned 23 propositions found in Fénelon's work, as seeming to favor quietism. Fénelon himself had insisted that Rome scrutinize his book, and after months of study the consultors had been equally divided; a majority was secured later. In April the first volume of *Télémaque* appeared in an unauthorized edition, and readers saw in it a veiled criticism of the King and his government. Although Fénelon denied this, the event put the seal on his official disgrace at court, and he spent the remaining years of his life in his diocese.

Despite the loss of royal favor, Fénelon remained greatly influential. At Cambrai he maintained the dignity of his office while he himself lived very simply. He was accessible to all, heard the confessions of the most humble parishoners, and frequently made inspection tours of his large diocese. He corresponded with the Duc de Bourgogne and met him on different occasions. When war swept over his diocese, he succored the enemy wounded as well as the French. Finally, he used the rich revenues of his diocese so well that upon his death he left neither debts nor notable assets. A fever, following a carriage accident in November 1714, brought his noble life to an end two months later.

Social Thought. For an understanding of Fénelon's political thinking, the chief documents are, in addition to his dialogues and novel, the bold *Lettre à Louis XIV* (from internal evidence, written *c.* 1693 or 1694, but very likely never read by the King), *Examen de conscience sur les devoirs de la royauté* (1697 or after), *Discours pour le sacre de l'Electeur de Cologne* (1707), and *Tables de Chaulnes* (1711). The last work was the result of discussions with the Duc de Chevreuse, in which the two men formulated plans for the possible administration of the Duc de Bourgogne, who had just become the heir presumptive. Fénelon knew that a reform of the French monarchy was necessary—to that end he had prepared the young Duke, but his protégé died in 1712. Fénelon detested absolutism, and called for a constitutional monarch restrained by law. He further advocated a number of specific reforms: economic, e.g., the reduction of expenses and a balanced budget; political, e.g., the reestablishment of the Estates General and decentralization; and social, e.g., freedom for the nobility to enter commerce or the magistracy. Industry was to be encouraged, and manufactured goods were to be allowed to compete freely on the world market. Fénelon insisted that the Church be independent of the State, which should protect the Church without being its master. He was not, like Bossuet, a partisan of the Gallican freedom of the Church of France. (*See* GALLICANISM).

It was during the Cambrai period that Fénelon summed up his religious thinking. In the *Traité de l'Existence de Dieu* (Pt. 1, 1712; Pt. 2, 1718 and 1731) he is both an intellectual and a mystic. For him the arguments of the heart were more telling than those of the intellect; he seemed to be erecting a dike against the rationalistic flood that was to come. Fénelon yearned for the vision of God to whom he wished to be united and in whom he would lose himself. Ever a man of apostolic zeal, he strove to improve the faithful, bring back the heretic, and convince the unbeliever. He fought to establish at Cambrai a seminary that would compete with the Jansenist centers at Douai and Louvain (*see* JANSENISM), and, from 1704, wrote much to defend the Augustinian conception of grace against Jansenist misinterpretation. His final polemic in this controversy was the *Instruction pastorale en forme de dialogues contre le système de Jansénius* (1714). Inflexible in controversy, he was charitable in his relations with the Jansenists of his diocese. One of his last writings was the *Lettre sur les occupations de l'Académie française* (1714).

Seminal Influence. Fénelon was not a professional man of letters, but he was a born artist. His style is generally characterized by the qualities of ease, fluidity and grace, harmony, and equilibrium. More important, his ideas were seminal. His educational philosophy foreshadowed that of ROUSSEAU's *Emile.* His desire to break the aesthetic fetters imposed upon writers hastened the literary upheaval then gathering momentum. His thinking on the writing of history anticipated VOLTAIRE. Above all, his criticism of royal absolutism and his ideas on political, economic, and social reforms were to make an impression upon the revolutionary minds that were to follow. Philosophers of the 18th century, unfortunately, interpreted Fénelon to suit themselves. Thus Fénelon's Catholic mysticism was equated with sentimental deism. He would have been surprised at Rousseau's application of his educational theories. Fénelon remains the most likable personality of the closing years of the reign of Louis XIV. It has been asserted that if his constructive reform program had been realized, the French Revolution might have been prevented.

Bibliography: *Oeuvres,* 35 v. (Versailles 1820–30); *Oeuvres complètes,* 10 v. (Paris 1848–52). D. C. CABEEN, ed., *A. Critical Bibliography of French Literature* (Syracuse 1961), contains the most up-to-date annotated bibliography, M. DE LA BEDOYÈRE, *The Archbishop and the Lady: The Story of Fénelon and Madame Guyon* (New York 1956). E. CARCASSONNE, *Fénelon* (Paris 1946), the best biography and general treatment. P. JANET, *Fénelon* (Paris 1892), old, but still good.

[J. W. COSENTINI]

FENG DE, MATTHEW, ST.

Martyr, lay Franciscan; b. 1855, Xiao Bashi, Shuo Xian, Shanxi Province, China; d. July 9, 1900, Taiyüan, Shanxi Province, China. Matthew Feng De (also given as Matthias Fun–Te) was a fervent neophyte. Following his baptism and confirmation, he moved to Taiyüan to aid famine victims (1893). When his failing eyesight made it impossible to support his family, his bishop gave him a job as night watchman for the Taiyüan cathedral. He was among the several dozen trapped inside the cathedral by the Boxers on July 5, 1900, and decapitated four days later. Matthew was beatified by Pope Pius XII (Nov. 24, 1946) and canonized (Oct. 1, 2000) by Pope John Paul II with Augustine Zhao Rong and companions.

Feast: July 4.

Bibliography: L. M. BALCONI, *Le Martiri di Taiyuen* (Milan 1945). *Acta Apostolicae Sedis* 47 (1955) 381–388; *Vita del b. A. Crescitelli* (Milan 1950). M. T. DE BLARER, *Les Bse Marie Hermine de Jésus et ses compagnes, franciscaines missionnaires de Marie, massacrées le 9 juillet 1900 à Tai–Yuan–Fou, Chine* (Paris 1947). *Les Vingt–neuf martyrs de Chine, massacrés en 1900, béatifiés par Sa Sainteté Pie XII, le 24 novembre, 1946* (Rome 1946). L. MINER, *China's Book of Martyrs: A Record of Heroic Martyrdoms and Marvelous Deliverances of Chinese Christians during the Summer of 1900* (Ann Arbor 1994). J. SIMON, *Sous le sabre des Boxers* (Lille 1955). C. TESTORE, *Sangue e palme sul fiume giallo. I beati martiri cinesi nella persecuzione della Boxe Celi Sud–Est, 1900* (Rome 1955). *L'Osservatore Romano,* Eng. Ed. 40 (2000): 1–2, 10.

[K. I. RABENSTEIN]

FENLON, JOHN F.

Sulpician, seminary president; b. Chicago, Ill., June 23, 1873; d. Holland, Mich., July 31, 1943. He was the son of Thomas and Mary (O'Keefe) Fenlon. After early education in a parochial school, he attended St. Ignatius, a Jesuit high school, and at 18 entered St. Mary's Seminary, Baltimore, Md. There he was greatly influenced by Revs. Edward R. Dyer and Alphonse L. Magnien, who guided him through philosophy and theology and, even while he was still a seminarian, sent him for advanced studies in Hebrew to Johns Hopkins University, Baltimore. Ordained in Chicago on June 19, 1896, Fenlon spent two years there as assistant at Holy Name Cathedral and then joined the Sulpicians. He was sent at once to the Minerva (Angelica) University, Rome, where he received a doctorate in theology (1900) and did further study in oriental languages at the Sapienzia under Guidi.

On his return to the U.S. in 1901, Fenlon was assigned to teach dogmatic theology and scripture at St. Joseph's Seminary, Dunwoodie, Yonkers, N.Y. He was appointed to the provincial council of his society (1903) and served as superior of the Sulpician house of studies (1904–11) and as president of Divinity College at the Catholic University of America (1911–24), both in Washington, D.C. While there he acted as secretary at the annual bishops' meeting and helped to establish the National Catholic Welfare Conference. In 1924 he became the president of Theological College at Catholic University and in December 1925 succeeded Dyer as president of St. Mary's Seminary and University and provincial superior of the Sulpicians in the U.S. Under his administration, the new St. Mary's Seminary of Theology was opened in suburban Roland Park, Baltimore, in 1929, and St. Edward's Seminary in Seattle, Wash., was begun in 1932. Fenlon wrote articles for the old *Catholic Encyclopedia,* contributed to many Catholic magazines, and traveled widely in the interest of his society and the institution over which he presided. He was the recipient of honorary degrees from Loyola College, Baltimore (1938), and the University of Montreal, Canada (1943).

Bibliography: P. BOISARD, *Lettre circulaire à l'occasion de la mort de M. Fenlon* (Seminaire Saint Sulpice, Issy, Mar. 18, 1946). *The Voice* (St. Mary's Seminary, Baltimore) 21.1–2 (Oct.-Nov. 1943). J. T. ELLIS, *The Life of James Cardinal Gibbons,* 2 v. (Milwaukee 1952).

[C. M. CUYLER]

FENN, JAMES, BL.

Widower, priest martyr; b. 1540, Montacute, near Yeovil, Somerset, England; d. Feb. 12, 1584. After completing his education at Corpus Christi and Gloucester Hall, Oxford, Fenn was a schoolmaster in Somerset. He married and fathered two children. On the death of his wife, he studied for the priesthood at Rheims, where he was ordained in 1580. He was indicted, Feb. 5, 1584, with Bl. George HAYDOCK, Bl. William DEAN, and six other priests for conspiring against the queen at Rheims. All were adjudged guilty two days later and sentenced to execution. Thereafter he was shackled in "the pit" in the Tower of London. Jesuit Fr. Pollen records an eyewitness account of the execution: "before the cart was driven away, he was stripped of all his apparell saving his shirt only, and presently after the cart was driven away his shirt was pulled of his back, so that he hung stark naked, whereat the people muttered greatly." Fenn's daughter Frances was present at the execution of her father. He was beatified by Pius XI on Dec. 15, 1929.

Feast of the English Martyrs: May 4 (England).

See Also: ENGLAND, SCOTLAND, AND WALES, MARTYRS OF.

Bibliography: R. CHALLONER, *Memoirs of Missionary Priests,* ed. J. H. POLLEN (rev. ed. London 1924; repr. Farnborough 1969). H. FOLEY, *Records of the English Province of the Society of Jesus,* 7 v. (London 1877–82) 74, 103. GILLOW, *Biblical Dictictionary of English Catholicism,* (London and New York 1885–1902) III, 202; cf. III, 265; V, 142, 201. J. H. POLLEN, *Acts of English Martyrs* (London 1891) 252, 253, 304.

[K. I. RABENSTEIN]

FENTON, JOSEPH CLIFFORD

Priest, theologian, editor; b. Springfield, MA, Jan. 16, 1906; d. Chicopee Falls, MA, July 7, 1969. He was the elder son of Michael Francis and Elizabeth (Clifford) Fenton. He received an A.B. from Holy Cross College (1926), an S.T.L. and J.C.B. from the University of Montreal (1930); and an S.T.D. from the Angelicum in Rome (1931). After his ordination as a priest for the diocese of Springfield, MA in 1930, he was a curate at Immaculate Conception Church, Easthampton, MA (1931–33) and St. Joseph's Church, Leicester, MA (1933–34). He taught philosophy at St. Ambrose College, Davenport, IA (1934–35) and theology at St. Bernard's Seminary, Rochester, NY (1936–38). In 1938, Msgr. James Moran Corrigan, the sixth rector of The Catholic University of America, appointed Fenton to the Department of Religious Education. A year later, he transferred to the School of Sacred Theology where he served as dean from 1943 to 1945. He taught fundamental and dogmatic theology at the University until his retirement in 1963 owing to poor health. That same year he was named pastor of St. Patrick's Church in Chicopee Falls, MA. Three years later he died.

Msgr. Fenton—a very large man well over six feet tall—was a familiar figure with his cassock and biretta on the campus of Catholic University for 25 years. His students remember him as an imposing person who lectured dramatically and often intimidated them with unexpected questions. Fenton's colorful expressions and trenchant observations became legendary.

In the 1940s and 1950s Fenton was very active in the American Church. As a charter member of the CATHOLIC THEOLOGICAL SOCIETY OF AMERICA, he became its first secretary (1946–47) and the recipient of the Society's Cardinal Spellman Award for Theology (1958). He published six books: *The Theology of Prayer* (1939), *The Concept of Sacred Theology* (1941), *We Stand with Christ* (1943), *The Calling of a Diocesan Priest* (1944), *The Concept of the Diocesan Priesthood* (1951), and *The Catholic Church and Salvation* (1958).

Serving as editor of *The American Ecclesiastical Review* (1944–63), he wrote over 150 articles on a variety of topics: the nature of theology, biblical scholarship, membership in the Church, the teaching authority of the Church, and the necessity of the Church for salvation. His writing was clear, often polemical, and, at times, intemperate. He wrote with conviction and, on occasion, with humor. A committed traditionalist and passionate defender of magisterial teaching, he vigorously opposed any idea that even suggested liberalism or Modernism. As a controversialist, he is best remembered for his aggressive opposition to John Courtney Murray, S.J., on religious freedom and on the relationship between Church and state.

During his career, Fenton received many ecclesiastical honors from Rome. The Holy See named him a papal chamberlain (1951), a domestic prelate (1954), and a protonotary apostolic (1963). Recipient of the papal medal, *Pro Ecclesia et Pontifice* (1954), he belonged to the Pontifical Roman Theological Academy and served as a counselor to the Sacred Congregation of Seminaries and Universities (1950–67). During the first years of the Second Vatican Council he was a member of the preparatory Theological Commission, the Doctrinal Commission, the Commission on Faith and Morals, and also a *peritus*.

[P. GRANFIELD]

FENWICK, BENEDICT JOSEPH

Educator, second bishop of Boston; b. near Leonardtown, Md., Sept. 3, 1782; d. Boston, Mass., Aug. 11, 1846. Fenwick was the son of Richard and Dorothy (Plowden) Fenwick. He attended Georgetown College (now University), a school newly established by Bp. John Carroll, and in 1806 he was admitted to the Georgetown novitiate of the reestablished Society of Jesus. (*See* JESUITS.) His Jesuit novitiate and studies in theology at St. Mary's Seminary, Baltimore, Md., prepared him for ordination on March 12, 1808. He was assigned to St. Peter's Church, New York City, where, with Anthony Kohlmann, SJ, he was copastor and cofounder of the New York Literary Institution. In 1817 Fenwick was called to Washington, D.C., to serve as president of Georgetown College. There were, however, warring factions in the Church in Charleston, S.C., and Fenwick was sent there in 1818 as peacemaker. He remained after the arrival of Bp. John England, whom he served as vicar-general. His next appointment, in May 1822, was as minister of Georgetown College and procurator general of the Society. From 1822 to 1825 he again served as president of Georgetown.

Having been proposed for the episcopacy several times since 1814, he was named bishop of Boston and consecrated in Baltimore on Nov. 1, 1825. His diocese, which covered all of New England, had three priests, eight churches (some in bad repair), and the cathedral in Boston, with a Catholic population of 9,000. He arranged for a new location for the Ursuline Nuns in Charlestown, Mass., began a small seminary in his own residence, and started a school for boys and girls at the cathedral. The Ursuline convent was destroyed by a Nativist mob in 1834, but Fenwick generally dealt successfully with anti-Catholic forces. He established (1829) a newspaper, the *Jesuit* (later the Boston *Pilot*) to defend Catholic views, and strengthened his diocese by founding (1834) the Catholic Irish colony of Benedicta in Maine.

Fenwick's major contribution to education was the founding in 1843 of the College of Holy Cross, Worcester, Mass., the first Catholic college in New England. Using land and a building given by Rev. James Fitton, Fenwick turned the new college over to the Jesuits. Aided by funds from the Society for the Propagation of the Faith and from the Leopoldine Association of Vienna, he also sent priests throughout New England to build churches and establish parishes. He held the first clerical retreat and the first diocesan synod, both in 1842. During his administration the diocese was transformed from one of the weakest to one of the strongest in the U.S.

Bibliography: R. H. LORD et al., *History of the Archdiocese of Boston . . . 1604 to 1943,* 3 v. (Boston 1945).

[T. F. CASEY]

FENWICK, EDWARD DOMINIC

Missionary, first bishop of Cincinnati, OH; b. St. Mary's County, MD, Aug. 19, 1768; d. Wooster, OH,

Sept. 26, 1832. His father was Ignatius Fenwick, descendant of Cuthbert Fenwick of Maryland; his mother was Sarah Taney, the daughter of Michael and Sarah (Brooke) Taney. Edward received his early education privately on the Fenwick manor and entered Holy Cross College, conducted by English Dominicans at Bornheim, Belgium, where he completed the humanities course in 1788. He entered the Dominican Order and was professed on March 26, 1790. He next studied theology and was ordained probably on Feb. 23, 1793. When he had been teaching at Holy Cross College for a year, the English Dominicans fled to England because of the French Revolution, leaving Fenwick in charge. His American citizenship did not prevent his imprisonment and probably did not influence his later release. On regaining his freedom he joined the English Dominicans at Carshalton, near London, and soon received permission to establish a house of English Dominicans in the U.S. He returned to the U.S. in November 1804.

On the advice of Bp. John Carroll, Fenwick visited Kentucky in early 1805 to investigate the possibilities of a Dominican foundation there. He gave a favorable report and was appointed superior of the incipient Dominican province of St. Joseph in July 1806. Near Springfield, KY, he purchased the John Waller plantation where he began a building program which, on its completion in 1812, included St. Rose's Church and Priory and the College of St. Thomas of Aquin. In 1807, however, he was replaced as superior at his own request; thereafter he devoted himself to missionary work. He traveled throughout Kentucky and in 1808 began his apostolate in Ohio, where he concentrated his efforts after 1816. In 1818, he and Father Nicholas D. Young blessed the first church in Ohio, near Somerset, and from there he served Catholics throughout the state. His missionary wanderings on horseback earned him the titles of "itinerant preacher" and "Apostle of Ohio" and eventually led to his appointment as the first bishop of Cincinnati.

He was consecrated at St. Rose Church, Springfield, KY, on Jan. 13, 1822, by Bp. Benedict Flaget, and, with other Dominican priests, reached Cincinnati in March. In May 1823, feeling the need of clergy and deprived of the Dominicans in Kentucky, Fenwick left for Rome to seek the establishment of a Dominican province in Ohio. Final arrangements concerning the new province were not made until 1828, when the Dominicans of Ohio and Kentucky were united under Fenwick. After his return from Europe in March 1825, Fenwick had sufficient resources to build St. Peter in Chains Cathedral in Cincinnati. In 1829, St. Francis Xavier Seminary was organized and became part of the Athenaeum (a corporation having direction of the seminaries of the archdiocese), which opened in 1831. The same year the first issue of his diocesan paper, the Catholic *Telegraph–Register,* appeared. By this time Fenwick had 24 priests and 22 churches in his diocese. The next year, while returning from his annual visitation through Ohio and Michigan, he died of cholera at Wooster, Ohio. He was buried there, but his remains were later transferred to the Cincinnati cathedral and finally to St. Joseph's Cemetery.

Bibliography: V. F. O'DANIEL, *The Right Rev. Edward Dominic Fenwick, OP* (2d ed. Washington 1921). J. H. LAMOTT, *History of the Archdiocese of Cincinnati, 1821–1921* (New York 1921). M. J. HYNES, *History of the Diocese of Cleveland 1847–1952* (Cleveland 1953).

[J. SAUTER]

FENWICK, JOHN, BL.

Jesuit priest and martyr; *vere* Caldwell; b. Durham, England, 1628; d. hanged, drawn, and quartered at Tyburn (London), June 20, 1679. When John embraced the Catholic faith, his Protestant family disowned him. He made his way to the Jesuit college at St-Omer in about 1654, then entered the Jesuit novitiate at Watten two years later. After completing his theology studies at Liège, he was ordained (1664) then served as procurator of St-Omer. About 1674 he returned to England. While serving in London as procurator, he was arrested (Sept. 28, 1678) with Bl. William IRELAND. He was bound so tightly in irons at Newgate Prison that one of his legs became gangrenous. He was tried at the Old Bailey (Dec. 17, 1678) together with Frs. WHITBREAD and Ireland on the fallacious charge of complicity in the Oates Plot to assassinate the king. The trial was suspended when it appeared the jury would render a verdict in favor of the priests. These Jesuits were joined by others who had been apprehended on the same charge and tried again on June 13, 1679. Upon the instruction of the judge, all were found guilty on perjurous testimony and condemned. After pardoning those who persecuted him, Fenwick said: "I am very willing to and ready to suffer death. I pray God pardon me my sins and save my soul." He was beatified by Pius XI on Dec. 15, 1929.

Feast of the English Martyrs: May 4 (England); Dec. 1 (Jesuits).

See Also: ENGLAND, SCOTLAND, AND WALES, MARTYRS OF.

Bibliography: R. CHALLONER, *Memoirs of Missionary Priests,* ed. J. H. POLLEN (rev. ed. London 1924; repr. Farnborough 1969). J. H. POLLEN, *Acts of English Martyrs* (London 1891). J. N. TYLENDA, *Jesuit Saints & Martyrs* (Chicago 1998) 175–78.

[K. I. RABENSTEIN]

FEODOROV, LEONID

Exarch; b. St. Petersburg, Russia, Nov. 4, 1879; d. Vyatka (or Kirov), Russia, March 7, 1935. Feodorov studied for the priesthood in St. Petersburg at the Orthodox Ecclesiastical Academy, then under the influence of SOLOV'EV, but in 1902 he journeyed to Italy to enter the Catholic Church. On his way, he visited in Lvov Metropolitan Andrĭi SHEPTYTS'KYĬ, under whose guidance he remained all his life. While studying in Rome, he defended the rights of the Ukrainian Rite Catholics in the U.S. In 1911 he was ordained in Constantinople by the Bulgarian Archbishop Mirov, and then entered the Studite monastery of Kamenitza in Bosnia. He took an active part in the conferences in Velegrad concerning reunion. In 1914 he returned to St. Petersburg, but was deported to Tobolsk by the Russian police.

In 1917 he was named exarch of the Russian Catholics of the Russian Rite by Metropolitan Sheptyts'kyĭ. Benedict XV confirmed his nomination and created him prothonotary apostolic (1921). Feodorov then organized the first Russian Catholic communities of this rite. In 1923 he was tried in Moscow with 15 other Catholics for defending the Church's rights and was sentenced to ten years' imprisonment, but he was released in April of 1926. Two months later he was rearrested and sent to the Solovki Islands where he organized a secret liturgical life for the prisoners. He was transferred to Pinega (1929), to Kotlas (1931), and finally to Vyatka (1934).

Unlike the Latin rite clergy in Russia, Feodorov maintained that Russian converts to Catholicism should embrace the Russian rite. He also advocated that this rite be preserved in its purity, unaffected by Latin influence. Before his arrest and while in prison, Feodorov established fraternal contacts with the Orthodox clergy and with Patriarch TIKHON. He used to call his communities of Russian Catholics prototypes of the corporate reunion that would take place some day.

Bibliography: P. A. MAILLEUX, *Exarch Leonid Feodorov, Bridgebuilder between Rome and Moscow* (New York 1964).

[P. A. MAILLEUX]

FERDINAND, BL.

Infante of Portugal; b. Santarém, Portugal, Sept. 29, 1402; d. Fez, Morocco, June 5, 1443. He lived as a monk at the court of his father, John I, and, at 20, became grand master of the Order of AVIZ. He was a model of virtue and chivalry—averse to argumentation, criticism, and swearing—chaste of body and soul. In command of the disastrous Portuguese expedition to capture Tangiers in

Ferdinand II. (©Bettmann/CORBIS)

September 1437, he surrendered himself, his secretary, his confessor, and several pages as hostages to the Moroccans to save his troops. The Portuguese refused to deliver Ceuta as Ferdinand's ransom, and he died after a harsh captivity, which he endured with great patience. In 1451, João Alvarez, his secretary, brought Ferdinand's heart to Lisbon and wrote an account of his captivity (*Acta Sanctorum* June 1:552–581, and Coimbra 1911). The rest of his relics were translated from Morocco to Batalha in 1463. Calderón's *El príncipe constante* dramatizes Ferdinand's career.

Feast: June 5.

Bibliography: A. DE HOLANDA and S. BENING, *A genealogia do Infante Dom Fernando de Portugal* (Porto, Portugal 1984). J. ALVARES, *Obras*, critical edition ed. A. DE ALMEIDA CALADO, 2 v. (Coimbra 1960); *Trautado da vida e feitos do muito vertuoso Sor. ifante D. Fernando*, critical edition ed. A. DE ALMEIDA CALADO, (Coimbra 1960). G. MARSOT, *Catholicisme* 4:1187.

[J. PÉREZ DE URBEL]

FERDINAND II, HOLY ROMAN EMPEROR

Reigned from 1619 to 1637; b. Graz, Styria, July 9, 1578; d. Vienna, Feb. 15, 1637. He was the oldest son of

Archduke Charles of the Inner Austrian line of the Hapsburgs (ruling in Styria, Carinthia, Carniola, etc., since 1576) and Maria, the daughter of Duke Albert V of Bavaria. As a youth he was much influenced by his Bavarian relatives and their policy of aggressive Catholic restoration combined with a weakening of the power (often exerted in the Protestant cause) of the estates. His studies with the Jesuits at Ingolstadt only strengthened his resolve to undo his father's concessions to the Protestants—in the course of a pilgrimage to Rome and to Loreto he took a vow to give up his life and his lands before sacrificing his religious principles. In 1598 he began to carry this program into practice in Styria: Protestants were faced with a choice between conversion and exile; their schools were closed and their churches confiscated for Catholic use. His desire to see such a policy extend to the remaining Hapsburg lands in the area made it difficult for him to find his way through the complexities of the "Brother's Quarrel," when Emperor Rudolf II was faced with a virtual family insurrection against his feeble leadership at a critical time.

When the childless Matthias became emperor (1612), Ferdinand was recognized as his heir (the claims of Philip III of Spain were settled amicably) and was duly elected king of Bohemia (1617) and king of Hungary (1618). It was only a matter of time before his known sympathies and policies led to conflict with the Protestants. The defenestration of Prague (May 23, 1618) was an attack on his program and his representatives in Bohemia; in August 1619 the Bohemians elected Frederick V, elector palatine, as their king in Ferdinand's place. The death of Matthias (1619) helped to make the conflict a general one in the Hapsburg lands: Bohemia, Hungary, Upper Austria, and the Protestants in Lower Austria began to plan for a general confederation of estates and an aristocratic commonwealth favorable to the Protestant cause. Ferdinand's election as emperor (1619) and his agreement with Maximilian I of Bavaria and the Catholic League strengthened his position. On Nov. 8, 1620, the battle of the White Mountain (near Prague) was a triumph for his cause and for the Counter Reformation Catholicism and moderate absolutism he represented. The victory made it possible for him to declare Bohemia a hereditary monarchy, to weaken the power of its estates, and to give vast holdings there to his Catholic supporters.

As the conflict moved into Germany itself, there were signs that Ferdinand would apply to the empire the same policies that had been successful in the Austrian lands and Bohemia. In the first years of the THIRTY YEARS' WAR his armies were victorious over a number of German Protestant princes and their Danish allies; by 1628 his gifted military leader, Count Albrecht von Wallenstein, had reached the shores of the Baltic. In the German courts, Catholic as well as Protestant, there was apprehension now that Ferdinand's victories would establish an absolute monarchy in Germany. His Edict of RESTITUTION (1629) revealed Ferdinand in a most uncompromising mood: the effort to recapture ground lost by the Catholic Church since the Religious Peace of AUGSBURG (1555) could not fail to strengthen the hand of the opposition. At the Diet of Regensburg (1630) it was clear that the high point of his predominance in German affairs had been passed; the princes (Maximilian of Bavaria among them) forced him to dispense with Wallenstein's services.

The entry of Sweden into the war forced him to recall Wallenstein, but he could no longer depend on his loyalty; there was soon plentiful evidence of his treachery, and Ferdinand gave the order to execute him without a formal trial (1634). He was able to conclude the favorable Treaty of Prague (1635) and to ensure that the imperial crown would remain in the possession of his family, when his son Ferdinand was elected king of the Romans (1636) shortly before his death.

Ferdinand, for all his attractive human traits, did not possess the elements of royal greatness. Reluctant to make decisions and much influenced by his advisers, especially his Jesuit confessors, he sought to pursue a policy largely dominated by religious considerations at a time when a more secular approach to politics (*raison d'état*) was making itself felt. Yet with all these limitations, Ferdinand had a large measure of success: he made certain that the great majority of the inhabitants of the Hapsburg dominions would be Catholic in their religious belief and that the future of the Austrian monarchy, thanks to his system of moderate absolutism, would be assured for generations to come.

Bibliography: K. EDER, *Neue Deutsche Biographie* (Berlin 1953–) 5:83–85. H. STURMBERGER, *Kaiser Ferdinand II und das Problem des Absolutismus* (Munich 1957). C. V. WEDGWOOD, *The Thirty Years War* (New Haven 1939). A. DUCH, *Lexikon für Theologie und Kirche*, ed. J. HOFER and K. RAHNER (Freiburg 1957–65) 4:80–81. B. CHUDOBA, *Spain and the Empire, 1519–1643* (Chicago 1952).

[W. B. SLOTTMAN]

FERDINAND III, KING OF CASTILE, ST.

Reigned in Castile from 1217 and León from 1230 to May 30, 1252; b. Valparaiso, June 24, 1198; d. Seville. He definitively united Castile and León and reduced Muslim power in Andalusia to the kingdom of Granada. Ferdinand was born of the second invalid marriage of Alfonso IX of León (1188–1230), that to Berengaria, daughter of Alfonso VIII of Castile (1170–1214). He succeeded to Castile after his mother, inheriting it upon the premature death of her brother Henry I (1214–17), had abdicated. Alfonso IX opposed his son's accession to León. However, by the Concord of Benavente (Dec. 11, 1230) Ferdinand actually succeeded his father. On Nov. 30, 1219, he married Beatrice, daughter of Philip of Swabia.

Ferdinand's measures to quell civil disturbances arising at his accessions interrupted his conquest of Muslim Andalusia. From the expeditions undertaken in 1224 until he received the surrender of Córdoba in 1236 and of Seville on Nov. 23, 1248, his reign constituted a permanent and efficacious crusade. His invasion of Murcia necessitated the Agreement of Almizra with James I of Aragon (1213–76), in which the southern and western boundaries of James's kingdom of Valencia were fixed and Castile was left free to subdue Murcia and ultimately Granada.

Tolerant toward the Jews and Muslims who submitted to his authority, Ferdinand strove to re-Christianize the conquered peoples through the ministry of the new MENDICANT ORDERS. He especially advanced legal studies by his promotion of the University of Salamanca. Having centralized the administration of his two kingdoms, he initiated the production of a uniform code of laws, a project completed by his successor, Alfonso the Wise. He was canonized by CLEMENT X on Feb. 4, 1671.

Feast: May 30.

Bibliography: L. FERNÁNDEZ DE RETANA, *San Fernando III y su época* (Madrid 1941). D. MANSILLA REOYO, *Iglesia castellano-leonesa y Curia romana en los tiempos del rey san Fernando* (Madrid 1945). A. M. BURRIEL, *Memorias para la vida del santo rey Don Fernando III*, ed. M. DE MANUEL RODRÍGUEZ (Barcelona 1974). J. GONZÁLEZ, *Reinado y diplomas de Fernando III,* 3 v. (Córdoba 1980-1986). M. DEL C. FERNÁNDEZ DE CASTRO CABEZA, *The Life of the Very Noble King of Castile and León, Saint Ferdinand III* (Mount Kisco, NY 1987). J. M. DE MENA, *Entre la cruz y la espada: San Fernando* (Sevilla 1990). A. CINTAS DEL BOT, *Iconografía del Rey San Fernando en la pintura de Sevilla* (Sevilla 1991). G. MARTÍNEZ DÍEZ, *Fernando III* (Palencia 1993). F. ANSÓN, *Fernando III, rey de Castilla y León* (Madrid 1998). F. GIL DELGADO, *Andalucía, designio de Fernando III el santo: pregón de San Fernando* (Sevilla 1998). A. DUMAS, *Catholicisme* 4:1186–87.

[R. H. TRAME]

FERMENTUM

The particle of the Eucharistic bread sent by the bishop of Rome to the bishops of other churches as a symbol of unity and intercommunion. According to Eusebius this custom was already known to Irenaeus as a longstanding tradition (*Hist. eccl.* 5.24.16; *Die griechischen christlichen Schriftsteller der ersten drei Jahrhunderte,* 9.1:497). In the 4th century the Council of Laodicea forbade sending the Eucharist abroad. In Rome, however, at the time of Innocent I (402–417), acolytes brought the fermentum to the priests of the titular churches every Sunday. This too was a symbol of the unity between the bishop and his priests. For the same reason, the officiating priest, who represented the pope at the stational Mass, also received the fermentum. When this custom finally fell into disuse, every priest nonetheless continued to drop a particle of consecrated Host into the chalice at the COMMINGLING, but the Host was the one consecrated in the same Mass.

Bibliography: J. A. JUNGMANN, *The Mass of the Roman Rite,* tr. F. A. BRUNNER, 2 v. (New York 1951–55) 2:312–313; ''Fermentum . . . ,'' *Colligere fragmenta: Festschrift Alban Dold,* ed. B. FISCHER and V. FIALA (Beuron 1952) 185–190.

[J. P. DE JONG]

FERNÁNDEZ DE PIEDRAHITA, LUCAS

Bishop and historian; b. Bogotá, Colombia, 1624; d. Panama, 1688. He studied at the Seminary of St. Bartolomé and upon his ordination became curate of the native towns of Fuzagasugá and Paipa. He was named canon of the cathedral. In 1654 when the archbishopric of Santa Fe de Bogotá was vacant, the canons elected him as capitular vicar. He ruled this vast see with great zeal until he turned it over to the new archbishop. Because of the difficulties he had as capitular vicar with the civil authority (especially the incident with the visitor Juan Cornejo), he was accused of malfeasance and sent to Spain to justify his conduct. There everything went very slowly, and Piedrahita took advantage of the time to write *Historia general de las conquistas del Nuevo Reino de Granada.* The first part was published in 1688 in Amberes; the second part was lost. Once the author had died, no one was interested enough to preserve it. The published section (12 volumes divided into chapters) goes up to 1553 and is indispensable to any study of the period. The style is clear and pure. The Spanish court found the conduct of Piedrahita to be proper, and to show its confidence in him, named him bishop of Santa Marta. There he suffered a great deal when the pirates attacked the city. He was later transferred to Panama, where he continued to work with apostolic zeal until his death.

[J. RESTREPO POSADA]

FERNÁNDEZ SOLAR, TERESA DE LOS ANDES, ST.

Baptized Juana Enriquita Josefina de la Corazón Sagrada, known in religion as Teresa of Jesus, Discalced Carmelite mystic, victim soul; b. July 13, 1900, Santiago, Chile; d. April 12, 1920, Los Andes Carmel, Chile. Juana was one of seven children of Miguel Fernández Jaraquemada and Lucía Solar Armstrong. She vowed perpetual virginity at age 15 (1915). Although she was often sick, upon completing her education at the finest schools in Santiago, Juana entered the Carmel of Los Andes and received the name Teresa of Jesus (May 7, 1919) and began her novitiate five months later. At the beginning of March 1920, she predicted her impending death. After she fell gravely ill with typhus on Good Friday, April 2, 1920, arrangements were made for her to make her profession *in articulo mortis* on April 6. She died six days later. She left behind numerous letters and a diary (*Historia de la vida de una de sus hijas,* 1917–20) filled with spiritual wisdom, the fruit of her intense prayer life and mystical gifts. Miracles began to occur at her tomb in Los Andes soon after her death. Teresa, Chile's first saint, was both beatified (April 3, 1987, Santiago) and canonized (March 21, 1993, Rome) by Pope John Paul II. She is a patroness of the sick.

Feast: July 13.

Bibliography: *L'Osservatore Romano,* Eng. ed., no. 18 (1987): 8–9. E. T. GIL DE MURO, *Cada vez que mire el mar* (Burgos 1992). M. D. GRIFFIN, ed., *Testimonies to Blessed Teresa of the Andes* (Washington, D.C. 1991); *God, the Joy of My Life* (Hubertus, Wisc. 1994), includes the saint's spiritual diary. M. ORTEGA RIQUELME, *Teresa de los Andes: testimonio y desafío* (Santiago, Chile 1993). A. M. RISOPATRÓN L., *Teresa de los Andes, Teresa de Chile* (Santiago 1988).

[K. I. RABENSTEIN]

FERNÁNDEZ TRUYOLS, ANDRÉS

Scripture scholar; b. Manacor, Majorca, Dec. 15, 1870; d. Barcelona, Nov. 3, 1961. After his ordination in 1894, Fernández entered the Society of Jesus and continued his studies in Spain and England. He taught Sacred Scripture and Hebrew in St. Beuno's College, North Wales (1905–06), and in Tortosa, Spain, until 1909, when he was summoned to the Pontifical Biblical Institute, then just established in Rome by Pius X. As vice rector (1914–18) and rector (1918–24) of the Roman institute, he laid the groundwork for founding a filial house in Jerusalem where he lived from 1929 to 1947, traveling throughout the Holy Land and conducting Biblical study tours. He pursued his writing career in Rome until 1953, then in Barcelona until his death. His works include 11 books and 120 articles, among which are commentaries on Job, Ezra, and Nehemia, a life of Christ in two editions with translations in English and Italian, and studies on Palestinian topography and geography. He founded the periodicals *Biblica* (1920–) and *Verbum Domini* (1921–), and he was the first (1927) to propound the theory of the *sensus plenior* in Biblical hermeneutics.

Bibliography: A. ARCE, *Vida y escritos del P. Andrés Fernández* (Jerusalem 1944). *Miscelánea Biblica Andrés Fernandez,* v.34 (1960) 133–134 of *Estudios Ecclesiasticos;* F. DE P. SOLÁ, *ibid.* 311–325, contains a list of all his works to 1960.

[P. J. CALDERONE]

FÉROTIN, MARIUS

Benedictine, historian of the liturgy; b. Chateauneuf-du-Rhône, France, Nov. 18, 1855; d. Farnborough, Sept. 15, 1914. Having studied under the monks of Hautecombe, he entered SOLESMES in 1876 and was a monk at SILOS, Spain (1881–92), and FARNBOROUGH, England (1895–1914). An eminent liturgist, he was a specialist in the MOZARABIC RITE and an outstanding historian of Spain. His publications include *Catalogo de los manuscriptos del Padre Sarmiento existentes in Silos [Indice . . . del Padre Sarmiento* (Madrid 1888)]; *Histoire de l'abbaye de Silos* (Paris 1897); *Le Liber Ordinum en usage dans l'église wisigothique et mozarabe* (Paris 1904); *Monumenta ecclesiae liturgica,* v.5; *Le Liber Mozarabicus sacramentorum et les manuscrits mozarabes* (Paris 1912), v.6 of *Mon. eccles. lit.* He collaborated on the *Dictionnaire de la Bible,* on the *Mois bibliographique* (1893–97) v. 1–5; the *Bibliothèque de l'École des Chartes* (1900–02) v. 61–63, a letter of HUGH OF CLUNY to Bernard of Agen; two Visigothic manuscripts in the library of Ferdinand I, in the *Revue des questions historiques* [v. 74 (October 1903)], an important article identifying the real author of the Peregrinatio Aetheriae (Silviae).

Bibliography: F. CABROL, *Journal of Theological Studies* 16 (1914–15) 305–313; *Bulletin de S. Martin et S. Benoît* (Ligugé 1915) 19–24. F. CABROL and H. LECLERCQ, *Dictionnaire d'archéologie chrétienneet de liturgie,* ed. F. CABROL, H. LECLERCQ and H. I. MARROU, 15 v. (Paris 1907–53) 5.1:1382–98.

[J. DAOUST]

FERRAGUD GIRBÉS, JOSÉ RAMÓN, BL.

Lay martyr, farm worker; b. Oct. 10, 1887, Algemesí, Valencia, Spain; d. Sept. 24, 1936, Alzira.

As in other parts of Spain during the civil war of 1936–39, the churches and convents of José Ramón Ferragud's hometown of Algemesí were sacked and burned, and religious objects stolen or destroyed. After July 18 the persecution became more virulent, leading to the execution of many priests and faithful lay people, including Fr. José Pascual Ferrer Botella and the laborers Ferragud and Bl. José Medes Ferrís, and Bl. María Teresa Ferragud Roig, the ancient mother of four religious who were also martyrs: Felicidad, Joaquina, Vicenta, and Agustina.

José Ramón (Joseph Raymond) was baptized two days after his birth in the church of San Jaime, Algemesí, and was confirmed in the same church on May 19, 1889. His parents taught him the faith, while he learned secular subjects in the local public school. On Jan. 21, 1914, he married Josefa Ramona Borrás, who bore him eight children.

With the great simplicity of a saint, José Ramón assisted all in need without hesitation. He cofounded the Union of Catholic Workers (1,800 members in 1936) of which he was secretary in 1931. His faith grew because of his daily period of meditation, participation in the Mass, reception of Holy Communion, recitation of the rosary with his family, and devotion to the Sacred Heart of Jesus and the Blessed Virgin. He belonged to the Nocturnal Adoration Society, Catholic Action, and other groups at San Luis Parish. José Ramón's primary apostolates were the Buena Prensa (Good Press) and as a catechist. Personally he was known for his humility, friendliness, prudence, energy, and valor.

In the days just before the July revolution, José Ramón was aware that religious persecution and probable martyrdom lay ahead. As a union leader he was particularly vulnerable. He was threatened with murder in 1934 because of his defense of sound religious doctrine during the union elections. By February 1936, he believed his fate was sealed. Two months later, Ferragud directly contributed to the failure of a local revolutionary strike directed against the catholic union. Thereafter he learned of the decision to kill him because he would not give up Church rights in favor of workers' rights. Despite the danger surrounding him, he continued his daily activities serenely, trusting that his fate was in the hands of God.

José Ramón was arrested by the militia after midnight on July 28, interrogated at the town hall, then taken to the convent of Fons Salutis, which had been converted into a prison. There he was maltreated physically and psychologically for about a week before being released. When they arrived at his home the second time, the revolutionaries shot the door opened and rushed inside. José Ramón remained incarcerated for 53 days at Fons Salutis during his second stay. At dawn on September 24 about 20 inmates, including Ferragud, were taken by truck to an isolated spot near Alcira called Barraca and executed. The bodies were dumped in Alcira's cemetery, where they were interred. Later Ferragud's remains were transferred to Christ of Calvary crypt in Algemesí.

Three days after his martyrdom, one of his executioners regretted having killed a good worker, and committed to compensating the widow. From that day she was given ten pesetas daily. That same man reported that the martyr exclaimed, ''Long live Christ the King!'', before covering his face with the black shirt he was wearing. José Ramón was beatified by Pope John Paul II with José Aparicio Sanz and 232 companions on March 11, 2001.

Feast: Sept. 22.

See Also: SPANISH CIVIL WAR, MARTYRS OF, BB.

Bibliography: V. CÁRCEL ORTÍ, *Martires españoles del siglo XX* (Madrid 1995). W. H. CARROLL, *The Last Crusade* (Front Royal, Va. 1996). J. PÉREZ DE URBEL, *Catholic Martyrs of the Spanish Civil War*, tr. M. F. INGRAMS (Kansas City, Mo. 1993). R. ROYAL, *The Catholic Martyrs of the Twentieth Century* (New York 2000). ''Hombres de Acción Católica de Valencia,'' *Possumus*, no. 103 (1960), 8. *L'Osservatore Romano,* Eng. no. 11 (March 14, 2001) 1–4, 12.

[K. I. RABENSTEIN]

FERRANDUS OF CARTHAGE

Deacon and ecclesiastical writer; d. Carthage, A. D. 546 or 547. His close association with Fulgentius of Ruspe, of whom he was a pupil, was probably responsible for the unjustified addition of Fulgentius to his own name. In 508 he accompanied Fulgentius into exile in Sardinia, from which a return to Carthage became possible only in 523. Ferrandus is mentioned in laudatory terms as a deacon of Carthage by FACUNDUS OF HERMIANE, VICTOR OF TUNNUNA, and later writers.

He is most probably the author of the excellent *Vita Fulgentii,* which furnishes so much precious information on the man and his age. His *Breviatio canonum* is a systematic and comprehensive exposition of the Canon Law in force in North Africa as based on the decrees of numerous Greek and African councils. Each of the 232 prescriptions is stated and defined, then supported by a number of pertinent canons. The *Breviatio* is an important source for the early history of Canon Law. Of his 12 extant letters, five are short personal notes, but the rest are theological treatises or discussions in epistolary form. Two of these have a special interest. Letter 6 is an answer to the request of the Roman deacons Pelagius and Anatolius for a statement on Justinian's condemnation of the Three Chapters. Ferrandus criticized the emperor's action in strong terms. Letter 7, a reply to Count Reginus, who had asked how a pious soldier should conduct himself in military life, lays down seven rules, *regulae innocentiae,* for his guidance.

Bibliography: *Clavis Patrum latinorum*, ed. E. DEKKERS (Steenbrugge 1961) Nos. 847–848, 1768. H. RAHNER, *Lexikon für Theologie und Kirche*, ed. J. HOFER and K. RAHNER (Freiberg 1957–65) 4:87, with valuable bibliog. A. JÜLICHER, *Paulys Realenzyklopädie der klassischen Altertumswissenschaft*, ed. G. WISSOWA et al. 6.2 (1909) 2219–21. H. R. REYNOLDS, *A Dictionary of Christian Biography*, ed. W. SMITH and H. WACE (London 1877–87) 2:583–584, old but still useful. A. VETULANI, *Dictionnaire de droit canonique*, ed. R. NAZ (Paris 1935–65) 2:1111–13. M. SCHANZ, C. HOSIUS, and G KRÜGER, *Geschichte der römischen Literatur* (Munich 1914–35) 4.2:572–575. O. BARDENHEWER, *Geschichte der altkirchlichen Literatur* (Freiburg 1913–32) 5:316–320. U. MORICCA, *Storia della letteratura latina cristiana,* 3 v. in 5 (Turin 1923–1935) 3.2:1395–1407. G. F. LAPEYRE, *Vie de Saint Fulgence de Ruspe, par Ferrand, diacre de Carthage* (Paris 1929).

[M. R. P. MCGUIRE]

FERRARI, ANDREA CARLO, BL.

Cardinal; archbishop of Milan; founder of the Company of Saint Paul (*Compagnia di San Paolo*); b. Aug. 13, 1850, Lalatta di Protopiano (diocese of Parma), Emilia–Romagna, Italy; d. Feb. 2, 1921, Milan, Lombardy, Italy. Son of Giuseppe Ferrari and Maddalena Langarine, Andrea received both his early education and seminary training at Parma, where he was ordained to the priesthood on Dec. 20, 1873. Thereafter he was appointed vice–rector of Parma's seminary (1873), rector (1876), and cathedral canon (1878). He was named bishop of Guastalla (1890), then transferred to the diocese of Como, Lombardy (1891), where he proved himself a true ''Father of Souls.'' Three years later he was made archbishop of Milan (1894) and created a cardinal. He founded the Company of Saint Paul for pastoral work, many churches, the Catholic University of the Sacred Heart, and charitable institutions. During World War I, Ferrari organized a group to care for soldiers and prisoners, for which he received the Grand Cross of Saints Maurizio and Lazarro (1919). He continued his pastoral work until death, even when bedridden. At his beatification (May 10, 1987) Pope John Paul II likened Ferrari's pastoral heart to that of the Good Shepherd and praised his fervent charity.

Feast: Feb. 1 (Archdiocese of Milan).

Bibliography: G. CARACCIOLO, *La fede e le opere: la figura del cristiano nella pastorale del cardinal Ferrari e nella Compagnia di San Paolo* (Milan 1994). A. MAJO, *A. C. Ferrari: uomo di Dio, uomo di tutti* (Milan 1994); *Il Card. Ferrari, i cattolici e il catechismo nella scuola* (Milan 1995). L. MONTAGNA, *Il cardinale Andrea Carlo Ferrari e l'ora presente* (Milan 1969). G. PONZINI, *Il cardinale A. C. Ferrari a Milano, 1894–1921: fondamenti e linee del suo ministero episcopale* (Milan 1981). G. ROSSI, *Il cardinal Ferrari* (Assisi 1956). C. SNIDER, *L'episcopato del cardinale Andrea C. Ferrari* (Vicenza 1982). *Acta Apostolicae Sedis* (1987): 690. *L'Osservatore Romano,* Eng. ed., no. 21 (1987): 18–19.

[K. I. RABENSTEIN]

FERRARI, BARTOLOMEO, VEN.

Cofounder of the BARNABITES; b. Milan, 1499; d. there, Nov. 25, 1544. He was born of a noble family, but was orphaned as a young child. He studied law at Pavia, and in 1524 he showed much charity and courage in aiding the plague-stricken in Milan. Dedication to works of mercy led him and his friend Antonio Morigia to join the Confraternity of Eternal Wisdom. There with Anthony ZACCARIA they united in the foundation of a congregation of clerks regular to work for moral reform and the defense of the faith against heresy. The strong support of Bartolomeo's brother, Basilio Ferrari, employed in the papal court, helped their project, and the new order was approved by the bull *Vota per quae vos* of Clement VII (Feb. 18, 1533). Ferrari was ordained *c.* 1532 and elected general in 1542. He consolidated the new order, formed new recruits and obtained privileges from Paul III and Emperor Charles V. He was venerated by the people after the declaration of his virtues by Urban VIII in 1634.

Bibliography: I. GOBIO, *Vita del ven. PP. B. Ferrari e G. A. Morigia* (Milan 1858). O. M. PREMOLI, *Storia dei Barnabiti nel cinquencento* (Rome 1913).

[U. M. FASOLA]

FERRARIENSIS (FRANCESCO SILVESTRI)

Theologian; b. Ferrara, *c.* 1474, d. Rennes, France, Sept. 19, 1528. He joined the Dominican order at the age of 14 in the priory of St. Mary of the Angels, Ferrara. He was outstanding in studies. Besides being famous for learning in theology and philosophy, he was also well versed in literature and music. Ferrariensis taught philosophy and theology in various Dominican houses of study and from 1507 to 1508 was master of students at Bologna. He became a master of sacred theology in 1515. He held priorships at Ferrara and Bologna. From 1518 to 1520 Ferrariensis was the vicar-general of the congregation of Lombardy. In 1520 he was appointed regent of the Dominican studium at Bologna. Clement VII appointed him vicar-general of the entire order in 1524, and in June 1525 he was elected master general. As general, he visited the order's provinces in Italy, France, and the Low Countries, zealously seeking to restore primitive fervor and discipline. It is thought that these travels hastened his premature death.

The principal work of Ferrariensis is his monumental commentary on the *Summa contra gentiles* of St. THOMAS AQUINAS. This was written before 1516 and first published at Paris in 1552. Leo XIII, in the preface of the Leonine edition of the *Summa contra gentiles,* describes this commentary as a ''rich and illustrious stream through which the doctrine of Saint Thomas flows.'' Ferrariensis illustrates, defends, and approves the Thomistic doctrine, following the form and substance of Aquinas admirably. Like the *Summa contra gentiles* itself, the commentary is brief in the treatment of each question. Ferrariensis is the great commentator on the *Summa contra gentiles* as Cajetan is on the *Summa Theologiae* of Aquinas. So true is this that in the official Leonine editions of St. Thomas Aquinas, the commentaries of Ferrariensis are annexed to each chapter of the *Summa contra gentiles,* as are Cajetan's to the *Summa Theologiae.*

Among the other works of Ferrariensis are his *Annotations on the eight Books of the Physics of Aristotle and Saint Thomas, and the Commentary on the three Books De Anima of Aristotle and Saint Thomas.* His *Annotations on the Posterior Analytics of Aristotle and Saint Thomas* are also noteworthy. He also wrote an apologetical work *Apologia de convenientia institutorum Romanae ecclesiae cum evangelica libertate,* in which he defended the liberty guiding and guarding the Church against the attacks of Luther. Other writings included works on Blessed Hosanna of Mantua, OP, a Dominican mystic for whom he was the spiritual director; encyclical letters to his order while he was master general; and a collection of prayers.

Ferrariensis arrived on the scholarly scene at the end of the first antischolastic period. He is most important for making the thought of Aquinas available at a critical moment in the European history of thought. HUMANISM was current at the time, and the understanding of St. Thomas helped the Church immeasurably. He was also present for the great arguments with Luther.

In his own right, Ferrariensis was also a remarkable metaphysician. He was an admirer of CAJETAN and emulated him as a philosopher and theologian. Yet he did not hesitate to disagree with Cajetan on important points, such as original justice, the immortality of the soul, fideism, abstraction, analogy, and the principle of individuation, among many things. He wrote a commentary on the *Prima Pars* of the *Summa Theologiae* but destroyed it upon seeing the superior work of Cajetan. Curiously, Cajetan, upon seeing the work of Ferrariensis on the *Summa contra gentiles,* destroyed a commentary he was preparing upon the same work and insisted that the work of Ferrariensis be published.

Bibliography: M. M. GORCE, *Dictionnaire de théologie catholique* (Paris 1903–50) 14.2:2085–87. J. QUÉTIF and J. ÉCHARD, *Scriptores Ordinis Praedicatorum* (New York 1959) 2.1:59–60. C. GIACON, *La seconda scolastica,* 2 v. (Milan 1944–46) 1:37–162.

[E. M. ROGERS]

FERRARIS, LUCIO

Canonist; b. Solero, near Alexandria; d. 1763. He entered the Order of the Friars Minor of the strict observance. He became provincial and then lecturer in theology, synodal examiner, and consultor of the Holy Office. He is renowned for his *Prompa bibliotheca canonica, juridica, moralis, theologica necnon ascetica, polemica, rubristica historica,* prepared at Bologna (1746) in three folio volumes. The principal editions that followed were: Rome 1760–66, 10 v.; 1767, eight v.; Bologna 1763, 1766, nine v.; Venice 1782, with a supplement; Rome 1784–90, nine v. The Benedictines of Monte Cassino put out an edition in 1844, and included the published decrees of the Roman Congregations, which were lacking in the earlier editions. The Congregation of Propaganda with painstaking care published (1885–98) a later edition in nine volumes. The *Bibliotheca* of Ferraris is in alphabetical dictionary form. Schulte, having recognized the value and practical utility of this format, criticized his having spread out under different words, studies referring to the same subject. He also questioned its historical value, but the arrangement in alphabetical order and the citations of jurisprudence made the work useful and easy to consult. Ferraris endeavored to resolve controverted questions with equity, using the principles of probabilism.

Bibliography: J. F. VON SCHULTE, *Die Geschichte der Quellen und der Literatur des kanonischen Rechts* 3.1:531. E. H. VOLLET, *Grande encyclopédie,* ed. A. BERTHELOT, 31 v. (Paris 1886–1902) 17:317. G. LE POINTE, *Dictionnaire de droit canonique* 5:831. A. M. STICKLER, *Historia iuris canonici latini* 320, 349.

[T. D. DOUGHERTY]

FERRATA, DOMENICO

Cardinal, secretary of state of Benedict XV; b. Gradoli (Viterbo), March 4, 1847; d. Rome, Oct. 10, 1914. After receiving in Rome doctorates in Canon Law, theology, and philosophy, he taught Canon Law there at St. Apollinaris (1876) and at the College of Propaganda (1877). He entered the papal diplomatic service at the urging of Pius IX and became auditor in the nunciature in Paris (1879–83). In 1883 he was named director of the Accademia dei nobili ecclesiastici. In the Congregation of Extraordinary Ecclesiastical Affairs, he was undersecretary (1883), and secretary (1889). Leo XIII sent him four times on delicate missions to Switzerland to settle difficulties between dioceses and cantons (1883–88). He was designated titular archbishop of Thessalonica and nuncio to Brussels (1885). When sent as nuncio to Paris (1891), he was the principal architect, as well as executor, of Leo XIII's policy regarding the RALLIEMENT. He became a cardinal in 1896. After returning to Rome (1899), he was named successively prefect of four congregations: Indulgences (1899); Rites (1900); Religious (1902); and Discipline of the Sacraments (1908); and then secretary of the Holy Office (1913). Benedict XV appointed him secretary of state a few weeks before his death. Of his *Mémoires* (3 v., 1920–21) Benedict XV said, ''They should serve as a guide and example for ecclesiastics called to the Church's diplomatic corps.''

Bibliography: U. STUTZ, *Die päpstliche Diplomatie unter Leo XIII nach den Denkwürdigkeiten des Kardinals Domenico Ferrata* (Berlin 1926). G. JACQUEMET, *Catholiscisme* 4:1198–99.

[W. H. PETERS]

FERREOLUS OF UZÈS, ST.

Bishop; b. the first half of the sixth century; d. Jan. 4, 581. GREGORY OF TOURS referred to him as the bishop of Uzès, a man of great sanctity, full of wisdom and intelligence, who wrote several books of letters after the example of SIDONIUS. These letters have not survived. Extant under his name, however, is a monastic rule, which, according to its preface, Ferreolus wrote for a monastery founded by him at Uzès; it shows dependence upon the BENEDICTINE RULE. Fragments of a vita of uncertain date and historical worth ascribe to him remarkable zeal in clerical reform. His activity in converting the Jews of his diocese gave rise to charges of political conspiracy and to a three-year exile, followed by exoneration and restoration to his see.

Feast: Jan. 4.

Bibliography: *Rule, Patrologia Latina,* ed. J. P. MIGNE (Paris 1878–90) 66:959–976. GREGORY OF TOURS, *Historia Francorum,* 6:7, *Monumenta Germaniae Scriptores rerum Merovingicarum* (Berlin 1825–)1.1:276–277; Eng. tr. O. M. DALTON, 2 v. (Oxford 1927). *Bibliotheca hagiographica latina antiquae et mediae aetatis* (Brussels 1898–1901) 1:2901–02. L. DUCHESNE, *Fastes épiscopaux de l'ancienne Gaule* (Paris 1907–15) 1:304. J. CHAPMAN, *St. Benedict and the Sixth Century* (New York 1929). J. L. BAUDOT and L. CHAUSSIN, *Vies des saints et des bienheueux selon l'ordre du calendrier avec l'historique des fêtes* (Paris 1935–56) 1:79.

[G. M. COOK]

FERRER ESTEVE, JOSÉ, BL.

Martyr, priest of the Order of Poor Clerics Regular of the Mother of God of the Pious Schools (Piarists); b. Feb. 17, 1904, in Algemesí, Valencia, Spain; d. Dec. 9, 1936. The novice master in Albarracín for the province of Valencia, José was a joyful, jovial man by nature, and his humor cheered his confreres daily. He also served as organist in Albarracín's cathedral. On July 10 he went to Algeneri for a rest with his parents. He remained there until Dec. 9, when he was arrested. During the night he was taken to a roadside location and shot. He was beatified on Oct. 1, 1995 by Pope John Paul II together with 12 other Piarists (*see* PAMPLONA, DIONISIO AND COMPANIONS, BB.).

Feast: Sept. 22.

Bibliography: ''Decreto Super Martyrio,'' *Acta Apostolicae Sedis* (1995): 651–656. *La Documentation Catholique* 2125 (Nov. 5, 1995): 924.

[L. GENDERNALIK/EDS.]

FERRERI, ZACCARIA

Reform-minded Italian bishop and author; b. Vincenza, *c.* 1479; d. Rome, 1524. His writings indicate a thorough humanistic and theological training. Around 1494 he joined the Benedictines, becoming abbot *c.* 1504, but transferring to the Carthusians in 1508. Dissatisfied with the conditions in the Church, he left the contemplative life and entered politics. Espousing conciliar theory, he became the guiding spirit of a small group of cardinals who, supported by Maximilian I and Louis XII, called a general council (Conciliabulum) to meet at Pisa (1511). As secretary of the sparsely attended council, he published the *Apologia sacri Pisani concilii moderni,* drawing on Jean Gerson's theory of devolution and the decrees *Sacrosancta* and *Frequens.* Pope Julius II deflated the conciliar movement by issuing *Sacrosancta Romanae ecclesiae* (July 1511), convening the Lateran Council (1512), and excommunicating the participants in the Conciliabulum. Ferreri took refuge in France. Upon Leo X's accession (1513), he dedicated a poem to him in which he urged Church reform. He was absolved by Leo and appointed referendary. In 1519 he was named bishop of Guardalfiera, then nuncio to Russia and Poland (1519–21). In Thorn (Torun, 1520) he convened a synod to counter the spread of Lutheranism and published his *Oratorio habita Thuronii* and *Vita Casimiri ex Poloniae* (both Cracow 1521). To Adrian VI he addressed *De reformatione ecclesiae suasoria . . . ad Hadrianum VI* (Venice 1523), impassionately urging Church reform. His *Hymni novi ecclesiastici* (Rome 1525), revisions of hymns, were published as part of a general reform of the Roman Breviary initiated by Leo X. Contemporaries hailed Ferreri's pure Latin style. In humanistic exuberance, he referred to the Holy Trinity as *triforme numen*

Olympi, to the Mother of God as *nympha candidissima,* and to God as *deorum maximus rector.*

Bibliography: B. MORSOLIN, *Zaccaria Ferreri* (Vicenza 1877) J. KLOTZNER, *Kardinal D. Jacobazzi und sein Konzilswerk* (Rome 1948) 227–236. W. MÜLLER, *Lexikon für Theologie und Kirche,* ed. J. HOFER and K. RAHNER (Freiburg 1957–65) 4:91–92.

[F. F. STRAUSS]

FERRETTI, GABRIELE

Cardinal, papal secretary of state; b. Ancona, Italy, Jan. 31, 1795; d. Rome, Sept. 13, 1860. He came from a family of the lower nobility related to the family of Pius IX. After becoming bishop of Rieti (1827), he served as nuncio to Naples (1833–37) and archbishop of Fermo (1837–42) and became a cardinal (1839) and legate to Pesaro (December 1846). His liberal sympathies led Pius IX to name him secretary of state (July 5, to Dec. 31, 1847), succeeding Gizzi. An adherent of NEO-GUELFISM, Ferretti favored the Italian national cause, notably by seeking a tariff union with Piedmont; but he refused to go so far as to declare war on Austria. In the STATES OF THE CHURCH he sought to give some satisfaction to moderate liberal opinion, but contented himself with half-measures. His popularity was very high at the start, but declined rapidly, partly because of his very explosive disposition. After resigning the secretariate of state he was legate to Ravenna for some months before becoming grand penitentiary (1852), and then cardinal bishop of Sabina (1853). His generosity and integrity were widely esteemed.

Bibliography: D. SPADONI, *Dizionario del risorgimento nazionale,* ed. M. ROSI et al., 4 v. (Milan 1930–37) 3:80. A. M. GHISALBERTI, *Enciclopedia Italiana di scienzi, littere ed arti* (Rome 1929–39) 15:63. L. FARINI, *Lo stato romano dal 1815 al 1850,* v.1 (Florence 1854). R. QUAZZA, *Pio IX e Massimo d'Azeglio nelle vicende romane del 1847,* 2 v. (Modena 1954–55).

[R. AUBERT]

FERRIÈRES-EN-GÂTINAIS, ABBEY OF

Former royal Benedictine monastery, in Ferrières, canton Gâtinais, about 40 miles northeast of Orléans, France, in the Diocese of Orléans, ancient Diocese of Sens (patrons, SS. Peter and Paul). About 630 Duke Vandalbert of Étampes installed monks there in a preexisting chapel. But nothing else is known of this monastery before ALCUIN is noted as its abbot during the CAROLINGIAN RENAISSANCE. The abbey is known to have been rebuilt between 814 and 845. The exact affiliation of the original monks is not known, but the BENEDICTINE RULE was introduced there in 817, and Ferrières entered its period of splendor, producing men such as ALDRIC OF SENS, Lupus of Ferrières, and ADO OF VIENNE. After a period of decline it was restored both spiritually and temporally by King Louis VII of France in the 12th century. The calamities of the Hundred Years' War almost ruined the monastic life at the abbey. In 1521, despite the opposition of the monks, the contemporary CLUNIAC REFORM was introduced there, and a certain renewal of religious life resulted. The abbey was sacked by the Calvinists in 1568 to 1569 and had to be restored. It subsequently belonged in some manner to the Reform Congregation of Saint-Vanne (*see* VERDUN-SUR-MEUSE) and the so-called "Congregation of Saint Benedict" before passing to the MAURISTS in the mid-17th century (*see* BENEDICTINES). When the monastery was suppressed in 1790 during the French Revolution, only nine monks were in residence. The abbey church (12th century, partially restored after 1864) is preserved as an ancient monument and used as a parish church. The famed chapel of Notre-Dame-de-Bethléem has been restored and still attracts pilgrims. The claustral buildings were demolished.

Bibliography: *Gallia Christiana,* v.1–13 (Paris 1715–85) 4:370–372. E. MARTÈNE and F. FORTET, *Histoire de la congrégation de Saint-Maur,* ed. G. CHARVIN, 9 v. in 5 (Archives de la France monastique 31–35, 42–43, 46–47; Ligugé 1928–43) 2:286, 3:235. M. AUBERT, *Congrès archéologique de France* 93 (1930) 219–232, with bibliog. R. GAZEAU, *Catholicisme. Hier, aujourd'hui et demain,* ed. G. JACQUEMET (Paris 1947–) 4:1204–05.

[L. GAILLARD]

FERRINI, CONTARDO, BL.

University professor, jurist; b. Milan, April 4, 1859; d. Suna (Novara), Oct. 17, 1902. After receiving a degree in jurisprudence from the University of Pavia (1880), he spent two years at the University of Berlin pursuing graduate studies in ancient classics and ancient law. He was appointed (1887) professor of Roman law at the University of Messina, transferring to the University of Modena (1890) and to the University of Pavia (1894). Ferrini, reared and educated in a devout Catholic family, led a most exemplary life as a layman. He took a vow of celibacy in 1881 and became a Franciscan tertiary. Soon after his death, his reputation of sanctity led to the introduction of his cause before the Congregation of Rites (July 4, 1924). He was beatified April 13, 1947.

As one of the earliest serious Italian students of Byzantine law, he published a critical edition of the Greek *Parafrasi: Institutionum graeca paraphrasis Theophilo antecessori vulgo tributa* (1884–97). His profound knowledge of Oriental languages enabled him to com-

Bl. Contardo Ferrini. (The Catholic University of America)

plete the Latin translation of the *Libro siro-romano.* He collaborated in the edition of books 1–28 of the *Digesta Iustiniani Augusti* (1908). His *Manuale di Pandette* (1900) represents his research on several minor Roman jurists and on aspects of Roman and modern private law. His interest in Roman penal law resulted in the *Esposizione storica e dottrinale del diritto penale romano* (1899). Ferrini reconstructed the personality and doctrines of several Roman jurists in his *Sulle fonti delle istituzioni di Giustiniano.* His legal studies, save for his major works, have been collected in five volumes (Milan 1929–30).

Feast: Oct. 17.

Bibliography: C. PELLEGRINI, *La vita del professor Contardo Ferrini* (2d ed. Turin 1928). B. JARRETT, *Contardo Ferrini* (London 1933). R. DANIELI. A. BUTLER, *The Lives of the Saints,* ed. H. THURSTON and D. ATTWATER, 4 v. (New York 1956) 4: 210–213.

[H. R. MARRARO]

FERTILITY AND VEGETATION CULTS

The descriptive formulation of the subject makes a definition rather superfluous: vegetation and fertility cults are simply the rites concerned with the origin, growth, decay, death, and regeneration of created life. There is no essential difference between vegetation cults and fertility cults; the former are the specific form of the latter in the cultural (and agricultural) environment of planters and peasants.

Universality and Importance. In the history of religions these cults have an enormous importance because of their geographic universality, as well as because of their impact on the totality of religious life within the individual cultures. Although they are eminently typical of the cultures of early planters and later agricultural civilizations, they are not absent from other economic systems. The ceremonies by which hunters try to secure an abundant supply of game belong to a realm of religious experience identical with that of the sowing ceremonies in agriculture. Through their impact on the totality of religious life, for the fecundity of nature (plants, animals) is but an epiphany of the sacred power of life present in everything existing, they constitute a microcosmic participation in the life of the cosmos, ceaselessly regenerating itself.

Since religion is intimately connected with the existential situation of man in the cosmos, the central place of fertility and vegetation cults ought not to cause surprise, for they deal with the mystery of life itself: mortality and regeneration, the solidarity between all levels of existence, the necessity to kill in order to live or preserve life, etc. The cultures and civilizations of agrarian societies are really permeated with this sort of Weltanschauung that has been called ''cosmobiology'': the same divine rhythm that governs the universe governs and determines also human life, thus bringing it into harmony with reality through integrating it into the unity of existence. This rhythm, forcefully present to man in the constant renewal of vegetation, the process of birth and rebirth in nature, the cycle of human fertility, is connected spontaneously with the great cosmic hierophanies, each one of them commanding its own rites.

The Role of the Sky and Sky Gods. There is evidence that in most archaic cultures the sky was the great hierophany of fertility as well as of creation. This is still clear in the mythology of the Indo-Mediterranean religions, where the sky gods are somehow identified with bulls (with the earth as a cow) or with other animals that personify the male power of fecundation, such as the stallion, the ram, or the boar. *Dyaus* was known as *suretah* (good seed), and *Zeus* was the one who sent rain and assured the fertility of the fields. From the hierogamic union of the couple Sky-Earth, *Dhyāvaprthivi*, all life came forth. The earth, of course, is the Great Mother, the foundation of the universe. All things come from and return to the *Tellus Mater*. One of the most striking fertility cults will, therefore, be the ritual reenactment of this hierogamy, which may be consummated in the temple by the king or the priest acting as representatives of the god, and by the queen, the priest's wife, or a maiden who then sometimes remains in the enclosure of the sanctuary to continue her fertility function in sacred prostitution.

It is well known that sky gods, even when they remain as supreme beings in the religious consciousness of believers, have a tendency to become remote gods, *dei otiosi*. They are replaced in cult by more dynamic religious forces that represent or dispense fertility, exuberance of life, and vitality. The most important of such forces is the storm god. He is not ''supreme,'' he does not represent the creation of the cosmos, he may even be second to the Great Goddess, being merely her spouse; but he is the Great Male, the Fecundator, the Bull, characterized by an often orgiastic and bloody cult. The rain is his sowing, and his hierophany is the ceaseless energy of biological renewal. Such are, e.g., *Indra* (the *Sahasramuska,* ''the one with a thousand testicles''), *Teshup* and his Hittite counterpart, *Enlil, Bel,* and others. Similarly, the hierophany of the earth, originally cosmic, became chthonian with the appearance of agriculture. And just as the Sky God was replaced in the cult by the Fecundator-Storm God, so the Earth Mother was replaced by the Great Goddess of vegetation and harvesting (Corn Mother, etc.). Often the Storm God, the Goddess of Fertility, and their son, the God of Vegetation (the famous dying and rising, or vanishing and reappearing god), form a sort of triad in the fertility cults of agricultural societies.

These gods and goddesses of fertility are typically ambivalent, especially the Storm God: their power can be destroying as well as fecundating. *Kālī,* ''the gentle and benevolent one,'' is represented as covered with blood and wearing a necklace of human skulls. This ambivalent character may to some extent explain also the ambivalent character of their cults, in which cruelty and serenity are frequently found together, although other factors—to be noted below—were more decisive. The Earth has the capacity of giving birth unceasingly to whatever is entrusted to her, however lifeless and sterile it may be. This concept has given origin to such rites as the *humi positio* in childbirth, burial in the position of an embryo, burying alive as a sacrifice, etc. There is, in agricultural societies, an obvious solidarity between the fertility of the land and the fertility of woman that commands a striking homology between woman and plowland, as between phallus and plow, and between semen and rain (or seed).

The Role of the Moon, Water, and Stones. Another important hierophany in the realm of vegetation and fertility cults is the moon. Subject to the universal law of becoming, birth, growth, decline, and death, the moon governs the rhythm of life, the cycles of fertility. She is a symbol of immortality, because her death is never final. The moon gives fertility, also, because she governs the fertilizing powers of the seas and the rains. A large number of fertility gods and goddesses have a lunar character. The moon and her animal epiphanies (snake, snail, bear, dog, frog) play an important role in fertility cults. The phallic cult, e.g., is frequently connected with the moon or the snake, or with both.

Water is the great symbol of potentiality, the universal Mother, the source of everything existing, of all life and growth. Immersion rites effect a return to this state of potentiality, a reintegration into preexistence, in order to increase the potential of life that brings about a total regeneration in a new birth.

Stones, such as *cromlechs* and *menhirs,* may have the power to fertilize a sterile woman. Hence the practice of sexual intercourse in front of stones.

The Role of Plants and Trees. Plant hierophanies are very often connected with the idea of a mystical relationship between mankind and vegetation: dead heroes are changed into plants, the human race originates from a vegetable species, there is a hidden herb of immortality, etc. The tree is a most important hierophany of the living cosmos in its endless process of renewal and regeneration. The ritual importance of the cosmic tree, the *axis mundi,* the tree of life, is well known. Vegetation gods are frequently represented as trees. In India and Africa sap-filled trees are theophanies of divine motherhood. They are sought by women who want to become fertile and by the spirits of the dead who want to be reborn. Other rites commanded by this hierophany are: birth at the foot of a tree, placing in or going through the hollow of a tree as a cure for illness, the ''marriage of trees'' in order to procure fertility for a sterile woman, the ceremonial planting or burning of trees, the Maypole ceremonies, etc.

The root crop cultivators developed the central mythic theme of what has been called, since Jensen, the *dema,* a mythical divine or semidivine being, ritually slain, from whose dismembered body the first plants originated. Human, and—sometimes by way of substitution—animal sacrifices, in which the victim may be cut to pieces, reenact this primeval mythical event. Head hunting, cannibalism, and other bloody rites are based in this general ideology.

Ancestors and Fertility Cults. The homology between the seeds and the dead, both buried in the womb of Mother Earth, is basic for the connection of ancestors with vegetation and fertility. Chthonian fertility divinities easily absorb fertility rites, even to the point of turning them into sacrifices to ancestors. The mystery religions are based on this homology and solidarity between the dead and vegetation: redemption through rebirth follows death and disintegration in a larval mode of existence. But all vegetation cults are based on a conscious or unconscious idea that man is regenerated by sharing in the resurrection of vegetal forms of life or, at least, attains a ''created'' immortality, which is not an individual one but rather the endless continuance of his species.

Major Role of Fertility Cults in Agricultural Civilizations. Fertility and vegetation cults found their highest development in the religions of agricultural civilizations. One would be justified in saying that agriculture, farm labor itself, is the fertility cult par excellence. It deals with the holiness of life and actively intervenes in its process, unleashing the holy power of vegetation hidden in the womb of Mother Earth. Sowing, tilling the soil, harvesting, reaping the first or the last sheaf are therefore surrounded with rites. Some of them have a marked propitiatory nature, connected with the anxiety not to exhaust the life of nature by taking its fruits, or with the idea that the sacred forces dwelling in the vegetable world must be reconciled with the destructive human interference by the offering of the first fruits, etc. Some are intended to assist the growth of the plants and hallow the work of the farmer, such as ceremonial nakedness, seminal or phallic symbolism, and similar phenomena.

The application of human sexuality to vegetation is typical: the ritual mating of a couple, reenacting the cosmic hierogamy on plowed land, usually in the spring, in order to stimulate the creative forces of nature. Vice versa, human fertility may also be stimulated by the biocosmic energy present in plant life. The ritual of the hierogamy may be followed by a collective orgy that seems to have a double function: to reenact the creative union of the divine couple but also to reenter the primal, pregerminative state of chaos and dissolution from which new life will originate. Many rites are connected with the reappearance of vegetative life in the spring: the battle between winter and summer, the driving out or killing of winter, the bringing in of spring, surviving in carnival and May celebrations. They all somehow make the primeval act of generation present as the active force of periodical renewal. The basic conviction behind all these cults is that vegetation shares eminently in the creative force of life, ceaselessly manifesting itself in the regeneration of an endless variety of forms.

Bibliography: M. ELIADE, *Patterns in Comparative Religion,* tr. R. SHEED (New York 1958); *Images and Symbols,* tr. P. MAIRET (New York 1961). J. G. FRAZER, *The Golden Bough,* 12 v. (3d ed. London 1911–15). W. LIUNGMAN, *Traditionswanderungen: Euphrat-Rhein,* 2 v. (Helsinki 1937–38). A. E. JENSEN, *Myth and Cult among Primitive Peoples,* tr. M. T. CHOLDIN and W. WEISSLEDER (Chicago 1963). F. M. BERGOUNIOUX and J. GOETZ, *Les Religions des préhistoriques et des Primitifs* (Paris 1958). J. J. MEYER, *Trilogie altindischer Mächte und Feste der Vegetation* (Zurich 1937). A. DIETERICH, *Mutter Erde* (3d ed. Berlin 1925). W. SCHMIDT, *Das Mutterrecht* (Fribourg 1955). C. HENTZE, *Mythes et symboles lunaires* (Antwerp 1932). *La Lune, mythes et rites* (Sources Orientales 5; Paris 1962).

[F. DE GRAEVE]

FERTILITY AND VEGETATION CULTS (IN THE BIBLE)

After Israel's conquest of Canaan one of the greatest dangers to the covenant made with YAHWEH at Mount SINAI was the widespread practice of vegetation and fertility cults by the Canaanites who had not been entirely eliminated by the invading Israelites (Jgs 2.20–23). The Canaanite farmer had been accustomed for ages to attribute a fruitful harvest to the mythical powers of his gods. The sexual activity of the male and female gods, BAAL and Anath (Baalath), were considered by him to be the source of the land's fertility.

The texts discovered at UGARIT from 1929 on give extensive information about this cult (*Ancient Near Eastern Texts Relating to the Old Testament* 129–155). Baal, the god of rain and vegetation, was killed each summer and carried off to the underworld by Mot, the god of death (no rain falls in Palestine from late April to late October). Anath went searching for her brother (and consort), and when she found him, she killed Mot and brought Baal back to life. Because of the reunion of the lovers, the rains returned, mingled with the earth, and stirred up again the powers of fertility. Man was not merely a spectator of this mythical union. By ritually enacting the drama of Baal and Anath through sexual union with a temple prostitute, as it was believed, man aided in bringing the divine pair together again in a fertilizing union, thus assuring a bountiful harvest.

Many of the Israelites in their transition from a nomadic to a sedentary existence were attracted to this cult and turned away from the God of the Sinai covenant to Baal, the lord of the farm lands that they had conquered. The syncretistic adoption of Canaanite fertility superstitions is attested by the numerous mother-goddess figurines uncovered in Israelite archeological sites, although the figurines may not have been used as idols, but merely as amulets assuring successful childbirth. It is attested also by the constant polemic carried on by the Prophets against the worship of Baal, ASTARTE, and Asherah (identified in Israel with Anath).

The struggle against the fertility cults was obviously the source of the characterization of unfaithfulness to Israel's God as adultery and fornication (Hos 2.4–15). In Dt 23.18–19 cultic prostitution is expressly forbidden, undoubtedly as a reaction to the practice of fertility rites in the Temple itself during the reigns of Manasseh and Amon (2 Kgs 23.7). Evidence of the continued popularity of fertility rites, even after the fall of Jerusalem, is found in Jer 44.15–30, where the cult of Ishtar, the queen of heaven (Astarte), is condemned. The main argument against these cults was that Yahweh is the Lord of all in fruitfulness (Gn 27.28; Dt 7.13); He is not part of the process of fertility, has no female consort, but loves Israel as a husband loves his wife (Hos 2.16–3.5; 2.1–3).

Bibliography: C. M. EDSMAN, *Die Religion in Geschichte und Gegenwart*, 7 v. (3d ed. Tübingen 1957–65) 2:1166–68. A. CLOSS, *Lexikon für Theologie und Kirche*, ed. J. HOFER and K. RAHNER, 10 v. (2d new ed. Freiburg 1957–65) 4:410. W. F. ALBRIGHT, *Archaeology and the Religion of Israel* (Baltimore 1946; 4th ed. 1956). J. L. MCKENZIE, *Myths and Realities: Studies in Biblical Theology* (Milwaukee 1963) 85–132. H. G. MAY, "The Fertility Cult in Hosea," *American Journal of Semitic Languages and Literatures* 48 (1931–32) 73–98.

[H. MUELLER]

FESCH, JOSEPH

Cardinal; b. Ajaccio, Corsica, Jan. 3, 1763; d. Rome, May 13, 1839. His father, François, a native of Basel, was a military officer in the service of Geneva. Through his mother, Angela Pietrasanta, he was the half brother of Letizia Ramolino, and uncle of her children NAPOLEON and Joseph BONAPARTE, who were his companions in youth. A priest in 1785, he was archdeacon of Ajaccio at the outbreak of the FRENCH REVOLUTION, and took the oath of obedience to the CIVIL CONSTITUTION OF THE CLERGY (1791). Expelled by his fellow countrymen, he took refuge in France (1793), renounced the ecclesiastical state, and devoted himself for eight years to profitable business enterprises. Napoleon, general of the French army in Italy, helped promote his fortune. When the first consul reestablished Catholicism in France by the CONCORDAT OF 1801, Fesch obtained absolution (April 1802) and reentered the Church. His nephew had him named archbishop of Lyons (July 1802), and then ambassador to the Holy See (1803). Pius VII created him cardinal (1803). He resided in Rome from May 1803 until April 1806. He was the one who induced Pius VII to come to Paris for the imperial consecration and coronation of Napoleon I (Dec. 2, 1804). On the eve of the consecration, he officiated at the marriage of Napoleon and Josephine, but later he pronounced the union null when the emperor decided (1809) to marry Marie Louise of Austria. When he failed to convince the Holy See that it should be part of the Great Empire of the West, he was recalled as ambassador.

He then dwelt at the French court (1806–12) as Grand Almoner and counselor in ecclesiastical affairs. The role of mediator was forced on him during the differences between the emperor and the pope, causing him to be accused in Paris of being complaisant to the Vatican, and at the Vatican, of GALLICANISM. Napoleon confided to Fesch the presidency of the National Council convened in Paris (1811) by the emperor. But, discontent with the weakness of Fesch, and with the resistance of the majority of the bishops, Napoleon brutally dismissed him. Fesch had to return to his diocese, where he had scarcely ever resided, although he had confided it to the care of excellent vicars-general. Thereupon a veritable religious renaissance followed, with six seminaries erected, numerous vocations, and even new congregations. But Napoleon became irritated at the ultramontane and royalist opposition to him among Catholics, and raged against ecclesiastics who were partisans of Pius VII. A persecution seemed imminent when Napoleon's military defeats led to the invasion of French soil. Before the allies reached Lyons, Fesch had fled to seek refuge with the pope himself.

The cardinal had to pass his last 25 years in Rome, leading a pious and retired existence. Pius VII and Leo XII took away his jurisdiction over his diocese, but he persisted in retaining the title archbishop of Lyons. His last will disposed of important legacies to his diocese, where he was generally forgotten by the time of his death.

Bibliography: F. MASSON, *Napoleon et sa famille,* 13 v. (Paris 1897–1919), hostile. A. LATREILLE, *Napoléon et le Saint-Siège: l'ambassade du Cardinal Fesch à Rome* (Paris 1935).

[A. LATREILLE]

FESTA, COSTANZO

Important composer of the first Italian madrigals; b. Rome, *c.* 1490; d. Rome, April 10, 1545. From *c.* 1517 until his death he was a member of the papal chapel choir. The inclusion of four of his works in the French Codex Medici (*c.* 1517–19) and his mention in Rabelais's *Quart Livre* indicate that he was in France as composer to Louis XII (1462–1515) prior to his engagement in Rome. His sacred compositions include most of the Renaissance forms—Masses, motets, hymns, Magnificats, and a four-voice *Te Deum* that is still performed at the Vatican. His style, which had a marked influence on that of PALESTRINA, derives from the Flemish technique, but he introduced homophonic chordal passages and nonimitative counterpoint. His renown as a madrigalist is attested to by the many publications of his works both during and after his lifetime, and he has been called Italy's chief musician in the age of Ariosto and Michelangelo.

Bibliography: *Opera omnia*, ed. A. MAIN, *Corpus Mensurablis musicae*, ed. American Institute of Musicology, v. 25; (Rome 1962–). E. E. LOWINSKY, "The Medici Codex," *Annales Musicologiques* 5 (1957) 61–178. K. JEPPESEN, *Die Musik in Geschichte und Gegenwart*, ed. F. BLUME (Kassel-Basel 1949–) 4:90–102. G. REESE, *Music in the Renaissance* (rev. ed. New York 1959). A. MAIN, "Costanzo Festa" in *The New Grove Dictionary of Music and Musicians, vol. 6*, ed. S. SADIE (New York 1980) 501–504. H. MUSCH, *Costanzo Festa als Madrigalkomponist* (Baden-Baden 1977). D. M. RANDEL, ed., *The Harvard Biographical Dictionary of Music* 265 (Cambridge, Massachusetts 1996). N. SLONIMSKY, ed. *Baker's Biographical Dictionary of Musicians, Eighth Edition* (New York 1992) 534.

[F. J. GUENTNER]

FESTIVIS RESONENT COMPITA VOCIBUS

Office hymn that was formerly prescribed for the Feast of the Precious Blood in the Tridentine liturgical calendar. It is a composition of an unknown author of the 17th century, written in honor of the Precious Blood shed for man's salvation. Its seven strophes employ the asclepiadic meter, with minor asclepiadic in the first three lines of each strophe and glyconic in the fourth.

Bibliography: M. BRITT, ed., *The Hymns of the Breviary and Missal* (new ed. New York 1948) 251–254. J. CONNELLY, *Hymns of the Roman Liturgy* (Westminster MD 1957) 204–205.

[J. P. MCCORMICK]

FESTUS, PORCIUS

Roman procurator of Palestine (*c.* 60–62) who sent St. Paul to Rome for trial at the Emperor's tribunal. He was an honest and capable administrator, but he did not live long enough to lessen the Jewish hostility toward Rome that had grown to dangerous proportions during the preceding decades. During his administration a case of mob violence in Caesarea and a rebellion in the desert was suppressed. The Jews urged Festus to bring Paul, whom his predecessor Marcus Antonius FELIX had left in prison for two years at Caesarea, to Jerusalem for trial before the Sanhedrin (Acts 24.27–25.9); but Paul, knowing that this was merely a ruse for killing him on the way, claimed his right as a Roman citizen to be tried before the Emperor's tribunal in Rome (25.10–12). In order to have a fuller report on the case, Festus had Paul plead his case before Herod AGRIPPA II and Berenice (25.13–26.31). Agrippa's opinion was that "this man might have been set at liberty, if he had not appealed to Caesar" (25.32).

Bibliography: M. LAMBERTZ, *Paulys Realenzyklopädie der klassischen Altertumswissenschaft* 22.1 (1953) 220–227. F. M. ABEL, *Histoire de la Palestine depuis la Conquête d'Alexandre jusqu'à l'invasion Arabe*, 2 v. (*Études bibliques* 1952) 1:468–470. *Encyclopedic Dictionary of the Bible* 770. S. SANDMEL, *The Interpreters' Dictionary of the Bible* 2:265–266. J. SCHMID, *Lexikon für Theologie und Kirche*, ed. J. HOFER and K. RAHNER (Freiburg 1957–65) 4:101.

[F. J. BUCKLEY]

FETHERSTON, RICHARD, BL.

Priest, martyr; d. hanged, drawn, and quartered at Smithfield (London), July 30, 1540. Fr. Fetherston, archdeacon of Brecknock, earned his doctorate in theology at Cambridge. He served as chaplain to Queen Catherine of Aragon and as Latin tutor to Princess Mary, who succeeded her brother Edward to the throne. He spoke in favor of the validity of the marriage of Catherine and Henry VIII during the divorce proceedings and again during a Convocation that began in April 1529. Friction with the king began when he was one of the few members of the Convocation who refused to sign the act declaring the marriage illegal from the beginning. In 1534, upon refusing to take the Oath of Supremacy, he was imprisoned in the Tower of London for six years (Dec. 13, 1534 to July 30, 1540). He was attainted for high treason and executed, together with BB. Thomas ABELL and Edward POWELL, who had also been councillors to Queen Catharine in the divorce proceedings. They were beatified by Pope Leo XIII on Dec. 29, 1886.

Feast of the English Martyrs: May 4 (England); July 30 (Wales).

See Also: ENGLAND, SCOTLAND, AND WALES, MARTYRS OF.

Bibliography: R. CHALLONER, *Memoirs of Missionary Priests*, ed. J. H. POLLEN (rev. ed. London 1924; repr. Farnborough 1969). J. H. POLLEN, *Acts of English Martyrs* (London 1891).

[K. I. RABENSTEIN]

FÉTIS, FRANÇOIS JOSEPH

Composer, critic, and musicographer whose writings exerted a great influence on music in France and Belgium; b. Mons, Belgium, March 25, 1784; d. Brussels, March 26, 1871. Fétis began his music studies with his father, an organist, and continued them at the Paris Conservatory, where he took the Prix de Rome in 1807. He was librarian of the conservatory from 1826 to 1833, and almost single-handedly edited the *Revue Musicale* from 1827 to 1835. When the Brussels Conservatory was founded in 1833, he was appointed director and at the same time chapel master to Leopold I of the Belgians. About 1807 the music of the past had begun to command his attention, probably through the researches of Choron, who had published his first editions of DESPREZ and PALESTRINA in 1805. Fétis himself spent many years preparing a critical edition of GREGORIAN CHANT, which was never brought to completion. His important publications are the eight-volume *Biographie universelle des musiciens et bibliographie générale de la musique* (1835) and five-volume *Histoire générale de la musique depuis les temps les plus anciens* (1869–75). These works, which are still consulted profitably despite their errors and assumptions, bespeak his informed and broad view of music history. Far from regarding the harmonic system of his own time as the only one possible, Fétis recognized the value of non-Western systems and in that respect is one of the great precursors of ethnomusicology. He also foresaw the development of atonality and even of serial (tone-row) technique. Among his own compositions are pianoforte, chamber, and symphonic works; operas and comic operas; and, in the sacred category, a five-voice Mass, several ''easy'' Masses, a Requiem, Te Deum, and Vesper Psalm settings.

Bibliography: R. WANGERMÉE, *François Joseph Fétis* (Brussels 1951); *Die Musik in Geschichte und Gegenwart,* ed. F. BLUME (Kassel-Basel 1949–) 4:129–136. C. R. HALSKI, *Grove's Dictionary of Music and Musicians,* ed. E. BLOM, 9 v. (5th ed. London 1954) 3:75–77. *Histoire de la musique,* ed. ROLAND-MANUEL, 2 v. (Paris 1960–63); v. 9, 16 of *Encyclopédie de la Pléiade* v. 2. M. I. ARLIN, ed. *Esquisse de l'histoire de l'harmonie: An English-Language Translation of the François-Joseph Fétis ''History of Harmony''* (Hillsboro, N.Y. 1994). D. LEWIN, ''Concerning the Inspired Revelation of F.-J. Fétis,'' *Theoria: Historical Aspects of Music Theory,* 2 (1987) 1–12. D. M. RANDEL, ed., *The Harvard Biographical Dictionary of Music* (Cambridge, Mass. 1996) 265. N. SLONIMSKY, ed., *Baker's Biographical Dictionary of Musicians* (8th ed. New York 1992) 534. R. WANGERMÉE, ''François-Joseph Fétis,'' in *The New Grove Dictionary of Music and Musicians* ed. S. SADIE, v. 6 (New York 1980) 511–514.

[S. CORBIN]

FEUDALISM

A much-debated historians' construct, derived etymologically from the term ''fief'' (Latin, *feodum*), used variously to describe legal, political, military, social, and economic features of western European society between the eighth and the fifteenth centuries. Its focus has conventionally been the fief (land as well as the rights and obligations attached to its possession), given conditionally by a lay or clerical lord to a lay or clerical vassal in return for the vassal's oath of homage and fidelity and the ensuing reciprocal obligations on the part of both. The

Peasant paying feudal dues to the clergy of Tournai, 15th Century. (©Bettmann/CORBIS)

military aristocracy (clerical vassals might provide military service or acts of piety that benefited the lord) thus created expressed its identity by rituals of homage and oaths (and by rituals that dissolved the relationship or accomodated loyalty to more than one lord) and by adopting a particular style of life and behavior. It lived from the labor of peasant cultivators whom it reduced from free status to serfdom. The implication of the suffix ''-ism'' is that these institutions were far more coherent and systematic than historians have found them to have been. In casual use the term is sometimes used adjectivally (as feudal) and usually pejoratively to characterize medieval European society as a whole. In a specialized sense derived partly from anthropology it is sometimes used comparatively for the study of features believed to be common to western Europe and other Eurasian civilizations. In a distinctive Marxist sense the term designates a stage of socio-economic history between the slave mode of production of antiquity and the capitalist mode, characterized by the extraction of material resources from an obligated class of inferior agricultural laborers by a class of lords which had appropriated to itself key elements of public authority and lived off tributary labor. The Maxist thesis is now sometimes termed the tributary mode of production.

Different and often conflicting definitions of feudalism appeared very early, in the debates over noble and clerical privilege and royal government in France, as well as their origin and constitutional meaning, between the sixteenth and the late eighteenth centuries. Because different meanings of the term are historically derived, this article will begin with an account of the changing history of the term and its meanings, then isolate the elements that have been thought constitutive of it, outline a typology of definitions, and conclude with a survey of current research.

THE DEBATES OVER FEUDAL LAW AND THE ORIGINS OF FRANCE IN EARLY MODERN EUROPE (1539-1789).

The *Libri Feudorum,* or *Books concerning Fiefs*, was a compilation of twelfth- and thirteenth-century legal texts and opinions from northern Italy concerning property, security of tenure, and heritability. It was often taught and commented on as an appendage to learned Roman Law in European universities after the twelfth century. The fifteenth-century jurist Giacomo Alvarotto (1385–1453) claimed that the *Libri Feudorum* represented universal property law, was a *feudalis scientia,* and that different customs concerning landholding and noble status in different parts of Europe could be reconciled to the principles of that ''feudal science.''

Legal scholars long debated whether this law and the institutions it described and dealt with were originally Roman or an independent post-Roman creation of the Lombards or Franks, and hence Germanic in origin; it therefore became an essential problem for determining the origins of France. The first modern commentary on the work was written by the French jurist Charles Dumoulin in 1539, as part of the debate as to whether French law was independent of Roman law, and therefore autonomous, or indebted to Roman or Lombard law. Dumoulin denied the authority of the *Libri Feudorum,* arguing that it had no standing in France, but he also asserted that the Frankish invention of the fief antedated the *Libri Feudorum* and that the nobility of France was directly descended from ancient Frankish war leaders, while the peasantry was descended from the subjugated Gauls. The problem of the origin of the *fief* and therefore of the French nobility became a question for both historians and jurists. This argument was taken up vigorously by the jurist-publicist François Hotman, who argued for the validity of the living force of customary law as an expression of national identity and the rejection of Roman law. The jurist Jacques Cujas published his edition of the *Libri Feudorum* in 1566 (reissued and revised in 1567 and reprinted in 1773), and Hotman expressed his theory in the *Tripartite Commentary on Fiefs* and the *Francogallia* in 1573.

The views and authority of Dumoulin, Cujas, and Hotman were acknowledged by later French jurists, particularly those specialists known as *feudistes,* in the course of the seventeenth and eighteenth centuries. The *feudistes* specialized in the highly technical law concerning the property and privileges of the nobility and supported the efforts of the nobility to maximize its income by expanding and strictly enforcing ancient claims of privilege. Their work also contributed to the association of the technical legal term *féodalité* with the increasing general hostility to noble and clerical privilege.

At the same time, a number of historians dealt with the origin of the fief from the political perspectives of both nobility and royalty. Particularly influential was the book, *État de la France*, published in 1727 by H. de Boulainvilliers, that claimed for the nobility certain sovereign rights independent of those of the king. According to Boulainvilliers, the nobility was descended from the free and equal Franks who had conquered the enslaved Gauls and elected one of their own, CLOVIS, as king. Boulainvilliers' chief critic, the Abbé Dubos, countered in 1742 with a royalist version of Frankish history according to which the king, not the nobles, originally controlled and distributed lands and rights of justice. Dubos' royalist arguments in turn attracted the criticism of Montesquieu, who, in 1748 in Books XXX and XXXI of *The Spirit of the Laws,* replaced Dubos' strongly royalist interpretation with a mediated history that saw considerable historical cooperation between king and nobles. On the very eve of the French Revolution of 1789, therefore, the questions of the ancient constitution of France and the place of fiefs and the rights of the nobility which held them and the rights pertaining to them were still being vigorously debated.

The debates in sixteenth- and seventeenth-century France were echoed in Scotland and England where Thomas Craig (1538–1608) in his *Jus Feudale* of 1603 and Henry Spelman applied the systematic teaching terminology of French jurists concerning the rules of land tenure, the forfeiture of tenure, and the hereditability of tenure to the property laws of Scotland and England. In England, too, legal arguments of this kind were used in the service of both sides in the debates over the limited-royalist idea of the ancient constitution and the strongly royalist idea of a king-imposed feudal law in the late seventeenth century. From the very outset of discussions of feudal law in France and England in the seventeenth century there was a political dimension to the legal and historical debates.

In a series of decrees issued between Aug. 4 and 11, 1789, the National Constituent Assembly of France claimed that it had ''completely abolished the feudal regime,'' which it considered a particularly dangerous component of the *ancien régime*. The elements of the ''feudal regime'' that it demolished were personal servitude (*mainmorte*), such aristocratic and lordly rights as pertained to restricted areas for hunting, all judicial courts held by aristocrats and their agents, tithes to churches and monasteries as well as perquisites of local priests and financial contributions to Rome, the purchase of public office, unequal payment of taxes because of social or legal status, all guilds, corporations, and universities, and all inequality of birth and access to employment. Other critics even included the survival of numerous regional and local dialects of French and various patois as vestiges of a feudal society. As diverse in origin and character as these elements were, the assembly saw in their combination, nevertheless, a feudal world that had to go. Its most abhorrent features were, according to the Preamble to the Constitution of 1791, ''the institutions that offended against liberty and equal rights.'' According to Alexis de Tocqueville, they ''were commonly referred to under the heading of feudal institutions.'' In early French revolutionary thought it was feudalism that separated the nobles and clergy from the essential French nation—the Third Estate and the king.

The assembly's use of the term ''feudal'' in this context was broad enough to include ecclesiastical property and privilege as well, and it signalled the massive assault on the Roman Catholic church in France (including its Gallican version) that continued under the successive regimes of the revolution and had already appeared among ENLIGHTENMENT thinkers, especially VOLTAIRE. Clerical privilege also became one of the themes in the criticism of reactionary regimes after 1815, especially during the revolutions of 1830 and 1848. Such thought also crossed the Atlantic; from his reading of English and French literature on the subject, for example, the American John Adams wrote his treatise *On the Canon and Feudal Laws.*

HISTORIANS AND FEUDALISM IN THE NINETEENTH AND TWENTIETH CENTURIES.

In the early nineteenth century the adjective feudal (French, *féodal*) was gradually applied by historians to other areas of medieval society, expanding the original seventeenth-century meaning of the French term *féodalité,* originally translated as feudality, but by 1817 converted to feudalism. Already in the late eighteenth century Scots economic theorists—Adam Smith in 1763 and John Millar in the 1790s—had begun to characterize the earlier European economy as based on a system of property and government which conflicted with commerce and a market society, the third of four historical kinds of economy that they recognized: hunting, pastoral, agricultural, and commercial. In his *Wealth of Nations* of 1776, Smith appears to have been the first writer in English to use the phrase ''the feudal system'' as a social and economic category. By 1800 *féodalité*/feudality had come to mean a form of government characterized by the fragmentation of central authority, a socio-economic order, and a general term of contemporary abuse of practices that resembled those of the past. Anti-nobility also became the theme of a number of works by economists in the early nineteenth century, those of Claude-Henri de Saint-Simon (1760-1825) and the historian Augustin Thierry (1795-1856), and their views were broadened by the philosopher G. W. F. HEGEL.

The influence of this approach on Karl MARX produced Marx's savage characterization of feudalism as the seedbed of capitalism, in which the capitalist exploiter of the proletariat replaced the aristocratic exploiter of the peasant and merchant. Beginning with the *German Ideology* of 1845, and continuing with *The Communist Manifesto* of 1848, Marx and Friedrich Engels constructed their sequence of stages in the oppressive modes of production that preceded Socialism, in which feudalism found its Marxist place: Primitive Communist, Asiatic, Slave, Slavonic, Germanic, Feudal, and Capitalist.

But most nineteenth- and early-twentieth-century historians considered feudalism either as a legal, political, or military phenomenon from the perspective of legal or political history, as a socio-economic phenomenon, or as an economic system possessing a particular social structure. The sociologist Max Weber, who posited three forms of legitimate government in human history—the rational, the traditional, and the charismatic—located feudal government in the traditional category, lacking rationality and bureaucracy. It became one of Weber's Ideal Types and is still sometimes used in Weber's sense.

With the growth of academic, professional history in the later nineteenth century, scholars adopted a narrower and less pejorative view of feudalism, one characterized in 1875 by the French scholar Numa Fustel de Coulanges as a conditional possession of land which has been substituted for property in land, the existence of lordships that divided up the land and were ruled by men who had ceased to obey the king, and the dependence of these lordships on each other. The critical elements of the system were the benefice, the request for it and the precarious character of its tenure, patronage, the immunity, and fidelity between man and lord. Both academic historians and legal historians regarded feudalism as a slowly changing set of relations between superiors and inferiors in matters of landholding. Empirical academic historians rejected general theory and ideology, edited and published enormous numbers of texts, chiefly chronicles and private charters conveying land, and they withdrew from the older, broader characterizations of feudalism as a blanket term for the entire middle ages, narrowing to the general period from 800 to 1300 and focusing primarily on western Europe, particularly France. They also greatly expanded the study of the history of the nobility, rulership, and statebuilding. But they remained divided as to whether the phenomena they studied were purely legal and political, on the one hand, or social and economic, on the other.

The legal and political aspect of the problem was reflected in the work of the German constitutional historian, Heinrich Mitteis, and his followers. Mitteis considered the consolidation and ordering of the feudal system the basis for the modern constitutional state. Other historians, like the French scholar Henri Sée, insisted on the primarily economic and social character of feudalism. These two views were most strongly expressed in two works published within five years of each other, Marc Bloch's ambitious and immensely wide-ranging *Feudal Society,* published in two volumes in 1939 and 1940, and François Louis Ganshof's *Feudalism* of 1944. Bloch attempted to combine both the legal/political and social/economic views, including discussions even of the psychology and emotional life of the period, in a vast panorama of European social life between the ninth and the thirteenth centuries. Some of his views were published in an American encyclopedia as early as 1931. Ganshof offered the most concise and abstract institutional-legal account ever written.

Bloch posited two feudal ages, the first extending from the eighth century until around 1050 and the second from 1050 to the early thirteenth century. Bloch hinged the division between the two ages on the devastation caused by the invasions of the ninth and tenth centuries and their impact on the European economy, creating regimes of arbitrary lordship over an oppressed peasantry, the desertion of settlements, the displacement of agricultural populations, and general impoverishment. These in turn led to a privatizing of public authority, the collapse of public justice, the multiplication of knights and castles, the need of powerful men to recruit military servants, and the creative force of what Bloch termed ''the bonds of dependence'' between fighting men and their lords: homage, fief-giving, security of tenure, and the increasing heritability of the fief as an expression of dynastic consciousness. All of these became systematized during the twelfth and thirteenth centuries, giving kings the opportunity to resume a process of statebuilding from the systematized base of the preceding centuries. Bloch included in his idea of feudal society the following elements:

> A subject peasantry; widespread use of the service tenement instead of a salary, which was out of the question; the supremacy of a class of specialized warriors; ties of obedience and protection which bind man to man and, within the warrior class, assume the distinctive form called vassalage; fragmentation of authority leading inevitably to disorder; and, in the midst of all this, the survival of other forms of association, family and State, of which the latter, during the second feudal age, was to acquire renewed strength. (*Feudal Society,* 443–445)

TYPOLOGY OF ELEMENTS ASSOCIATED WITH FEUDALISM.

Since the work of Bloch and Ganshof, the following elements have been used, either alone or in various or total combination, to identify feudalism. Some or all of them are spoken of as expanding between the tenth and the twelfth centuries from a core area between the Loire and Rhine rivers north into the Low Countries, west to England (especially after the Norman Conquest of 1066), south to Norman Sicily, east to Germany and then to the Latin Christian kingdom of Jerusalem during the twelfth century, and southwest into Catalonia.

Chronology and social conditions: The arguments for both the continuity from the CAROLINGIAN period to the twelfth century and for dramatic change around the year 1000 depend upon the analysis of political, economic, and social conditions during the ninth and tenth centuries.

Castellans and warlords. Specialized warriors who assume control over a small or large territory by building private castles and dominating the countryside, assembling a group of warriors around themselves, and depressing the status of the local free peasantry by brute coercion.

Ties of dependence. The establishment of a relationship by an oath-taking and giving ritual between two free men, acknowledging one of them to be superior and the other to be inferior (homage, from Latin, *homagium* [from *homo,* man], French *hommage*) and owing loyalty (fidelity) to the superior, may be understood to indicate the disintegration of a previously stable large-scale society or simply a changing relationship among members of the ruling orders of society.

The provision of military service. As weapons and the expense of acquiring them and training with them increased the need for specialized warriors, lords (from Latin, *dominus*; Old English *hlaford* [the giver of the loaf]; French *seigneur*) who could command and reward specialized warriors could use them to expand their own bases of power and territory.

The fief (from Old High German *fihu,* Latin *feodum,* French *fief,* German *Lehen,* Old English *læn*). Landed property with its attached rights, obligations, and revenues. Although neither fief nor benefice (Latin *beneficium,* French *benefice*) was a necessary part of the establishment of ties of dependence, it was one way of providing the necessary support for fighting men in service to another. The term feudalism itself derives from the fief. Sufficiently large fiefs could be in turn beneficed to vassals of the vassal (from Celtic *qwas,* Latin *vassus,* French *vassal*), a process known as subinfeudation. A vassal might also hold fiefs from more than one lord, leading to the distinction between liege homage and simple hommage, the former taking precedence over the latter.

The joining of fief and vassalage. Reinforces the superior-inferior relationship by the conditional transfer of property from lord to vassal in return for specified services from the vassal, often military.

Aids, Obligations, and Services. Besides military service, vassals were often obligated to pay a relief when the son of a vassal succeeded his father. If the vassal left a minor son or daughter the lord retained the right of wardship, which enabled him to collect the income from the fief and award such children in marriage to a favorite or a wealthy suitor. If the vassal left no heir, the fief was said to have reverted (escheated) to the lord. Other services and obligations included castle-guard, payments to the lord upon the knighting of his eldest son and marriage of his eldest daughter, the responsibility of contributing to the lord's ransom if he were captured, hospitality to the lord and his entourage when they were itinerary, and to offer the lord advice on matters of common interest to lords and vassals.

The segmentation of public authority. The assumption that something resembling a centralized monarchical government existed in the late eighth and ninth centuries and that this government disintegrated, opening the way for the appropriation of formerly public powers by individual, self-interested lords. In the thirteenth century the existence of the elements listed so far enabled rulers to re-establish stronger monarchies using the relationships among lords, between lords and vassals, and between lords and rulers as the basis for a new kind of centralizing state.

Rights of justice. Attached to fiefs, they parallel political decentralization by decentralizing the law, since formerly public rights of justice (the ban, those of the king or his agents, the counts) are now attached to fiefs and administered largely for purposes of personal profit by those who hold them.

Nobility. By linking lords and vassals in relationships based on the military culture of both, the warrior, or knight (Latin, *miles*; French, *chevalier,* German, *Ritter*; Old English, *cniht*) is slowly assimilated to the ranks of the nobility, which include even the highest-ranking dukes and counts, and in some cases the king.

Mentality. The expression of the values and temperament of noble warriors. At the upper levels of this society it is reflected in marriage patterns and dynastic consciousness and the growth of courtly values and a distinctive courtly literature. At the lower levels it characterizes the deliberate distancing on the part of knights from the peasantry. The oppression of disarmed peasants is one sign of the knightly status of the individual.

Seigneurialism. The rule of a local lord over the peasant population from whose compulsory, tributary labor he sustains himself. Lord and peasants together constitute the manorial system, in which the manor court and the power of the lord dominate the agricultural economy. Some historians argue that seigneurialism and manorialism constitute an area of social and economic life distinct from feudalism.

Feudal anarchy or alternate kinds of order? The elements described above have led to very different interpretations of their character. Earlier historians consistently characterized their various combinations as reflections of feudal anarchy, the nearly complete privatization of formerly public, governmental institutions for purely personal benefit. Other historians regard them rather as the imposition of an alternative form of order, one with its own rules and its own forms of stability.

FEUDALISM AFTER BLOCH AND GANSHOF

During the second half of the twentieth century, most historians concentrated more on Bloch's second feudal age as the only age of feudal society, generally discounting Bloch's earlier period as an archaic society with some of whose surviving institutions the lords of the eleventh and twelfth century worked differently. Other historians criticized Bloch's assumptions about the extent of the tenth-century crisis and argued for a much greater degree of continuity between Late Antiquity and the twelfth century, thereby posing the problem as one debated between scholars who argue for a gradual evolution of practices and institutions and those who see a ''feudal revolution'' or ''feudal mutation'' occurring around the turn of the second millennium.

Under the influence of anthropology, a number of scholars have also attempted to consider feudalism as a comparative subject that had European parallels elsewhere in Eurasia, particularly Japan. The new dynamics of the study of Late Antiquity and early medieval Europe made earlier discussions of Roman or Germanic origins of feudal institutions virtually a dead letter and encouraged the new focus on the study of the nobility, lesser military ranks, the peasantry, studies of particular regions, and a reassessment of the tenth- or eleventh-century origins of the new forms of lordship and community.

The influential work of Georges Duby and his students, associates, and successors after 1953 represents the current state of research on the new chronology, based on detailed regional studies, studies of family structures, the study of ecclesiastical grants of land by great monasteries and powerful bishops, not only in northern France and the Rhineland, but in the French Midi, Catalonia, central and southern Italy, and the Low Countries, with England now considered less an exceptional case than it traditionally had been, chiefly because of the strong central rule imposed by WILLIAM I (the Conqueror) and his immediate successors. Most scholars are also more reluctant to assume the existence of all of the elements discussed above as essential to a feudal system. Seigneurialism and manorialism, which focus on the estate or village community and its internal rule, especially tend to be considered independently of those elements that characterize the life of nobles or those rising into the nobility. Instead of feudal anarchy, historians are beginning to find both a cultural and political order in the world of eleventh- and twelfth-century nobles and rulers.

In spite of the complete transformation of both the sources and the methodology of Bloch and Ganshof in the second half of the twentieth century, a number of articulate scholars have continued to urge that the term feudalism be dropped from the historian's vocabulary and mind. Since a famous and widely debated essay published by Elizabeth A. R. Brown in 1974, and especially since the highly critical book by Susan Reynolds, *Fiefs and Vassals,* in 1994, a line has been drawn between historians who accept the idea of a feudal revolution or mutation around the turn of the second millennium and are willing to use the adjective feudal to describe the society that emerged from it, and those who find the abstract term feudalism too imprecise and overloaded with implications of homogeneity and consistency in a period and place that had neither, or else possessed some features that may be properly termed feudal but lacked others. Like most complex scholarly questions, the history ends in a lively and continuing debate.

Bibliography: On the origins of the debate. E. CARCASONNE, *Montesquieu et le problème de la constitution française au XVIII siècle* (Paris 1927). J. G. A. POCOCK, *The Ancient Constitution and the Feudal Law* (Cambridge 1957; repr. New York 1967), esp. chs. 1 and 4. D. KELLEY, *The Foundations of Modern Historical Scholarship* (New York 1970), esp. chs. 6 and 7. J.Q.C. MACKRELL, *The Attack on Feudalism in Eighteenth-Century France* (London-Toronto 1973). P. GOUBERT, *The Ancien Régime: French Society 1600–1750,* tr. S. COX (New York-Evanston 1973). T. CRAIG, *Jus Feudale,* tr. J. A. CLYDE (Edinburgh 1934), with an appended translation of the *Libri Feudorum.* On nineteenth-century development. O. BRUNNER and O. HINTZE in *Lordship and Community in Medieval Europe,* ed. F. L. CHEYETTE (New York 1968). R. BOUTRUCHE, *Seigneurie et féodalité: le premier âge des liens d'homme à homme* (Paris 1968) 1: 11–25. P. OURLIAC, ''La féodalité et son histoire,'' *Revue historique du droit français et étranger* 73 (1995) 1–21. D. HERLIHY, ed., *The History of Feudalism* (New York-London 1970). B. DISTELKAMP, ''Heinrich Mitteis Lehnrecht und Staatsgewalt im Lichte moderner Forschung,'' in *Heinrich Mitteis nach hundert Jahren (1889-1989),* P. LANDAU, H. NEHLSEN, and D. WILLOWEIT, eds. (Munich 1991) 11–22, as well as other essays in the same volume. On the modern divided approach. M. BLOCH, *Feudal Society,* tr. L. A. MANYON (Chicago 1961). F. L. GANSHOF, *Feudalism,* tr. P. GRIERSON (London 1952). G. DUBY, *La société aux XIe et XIIe siècles dans la région mâconnaise* (Paris 1953); *The Three Orders: Feudal Society Examined,* tr. A. GOLDHAMMER (Chicago 1978). J. R. STRAYER, *Feudalism* (Princeton 1965), considers feudalism chiefly in political terms. T. EVERGATES, *Feudal Society in Medieval France: Documents from the County of Champagne* (Philadelphia 1993), the most important collection of documents in English. Recent studies in the tradition of Bloch. J.-P. POLY and E. BOURNAZEL, *The Feudal Transformation, 900–1200,* tr. C. HIGGITT (New York-London 1991). *Past & Present,* 142 (1994), 152 (1996), and 155 (1997), an important series of exchanges among Thomas Bisson, Dominique Barthélemy, Stephen D. White, Timothy Reuter, and Chris Wickham. T. M. BISSON, ''Medieval Lordship,'' *Speculum* 70 (1995). E. BOURNAZEL and J.-P. POLY, eds., *Les féodalités* (Paris 1998). D. BARTHÉLEMY, *La mutation de l'an mil a-t-elle eu lieu?* (Paris 1998). E. MAGNOU-NORTIER, ''The Enemies of the Peace: Reflections on a Vocabulary, 500-1100,'' in *The Peace of God,* T. HEAD and R. LANDES, eds. (Ithaca-London 1992) 58-79. H.-W. GOETZ, ''Serfdom and the Beginnings of a 'Seigneurial System' in the Carolingian Period: A Survey of the Evidence,'' *Early Medieval Europe* 2 (1993) 29–51. P. FOURACRE, *The Age of Charles Martel* (London-New York 2000) 121–154. E. A. R. BROWN, ''The Tyranny of a Construct: Feudalism and Historians of Medieval Europe,'' *American Historical Review* 79 (1974) 1063–1088. S. REYNOLDS, *Fiefs and Vassals* (Oxford 1994); ''Afterthoughts on Fiefs and Vassals,'' *The Haskins Society Journal* 9 (1997, published 2001) 1–15. P. ANDERSON, *Passages from Antiquity to Feudalism* (London 1974). C. WICKHAM, ''The Other Transition: From the Ancient World to Feudalism,'' *Past & Present* 103 (1984) 3–36. R. COULBORN, ed., *Feudalism in History* (Princeton 1956). E. LEACH, S. N. MUKHERJEE, and J. WARD, eds., *Feudalism: Comparative Studies* (Sydney 1985), valuable especially for Ward's detailed typological analysis. H. MUKHIA, *The Feudalism Debate* (Manohar 1999).

[E. PETERS]

FEUERBACH, LUDWIG ANDREAS

German philosopher; b. Landshut, July 28, 1804; d. Rechenberg, near Nürnberg, Sept. 13, 1872; a proponent of atheistic humanism, he prepared the way for Karl Marx's dialectical and historical materialism with his criticisms of Hegelian philosophy.

Feuerbach originally embarked upon a theological course of studies, but abandoned this to study philosophy under HEGEL in Berlin. For a short time he taught at the

University of Erlangen, then withdrew from the faculty after he was discovered and criticized as author of an anonymous work, *Gedanken eines Denkers über Tod und Unsterblichkeit* (1830), which denied the immortality of the soul. He then retired to an estate in the country, where his wife's affluence allowed him to lead a life of private study.

Initially a fervent Hegelian, Feuerbach soon became convinced that Hegel's philosophy is too idealistic and does not pay sufficient attention to man in his physical environment. In an article in the *Hallische Jahrbücher* (1839) that was to determine the further development of left-wing Hegelianism, he attacked Hegel's IDEALISM for spiritualizing nature and taking away its proper reality. According to Hegel, nature has no concrete reality in itself: it is a mere estrangement of the Absolute Spirit. For Feuerbach, the relation between idea and concrete reality is to be reversed; rather than seek the explanation of man in a superhuman, immaterial "Idea," as Hegel did, philosophy should look for the origin of all ideology in man's concrete, material reality.

In his major work, *Das Wesen des Christentums* (1841), Feuerbach applied this principle to the special case of religion. Man in his relation to nature is the first and ultimate reality. But in religion man projects his own nature into an imaginary world above him. To an illusionary Being he ascribes qualities that rightly belong to the human species as a whole; all the attributes predicated of God are therefore derived from man's own nature. The cause of this self-estrangement Feuerbach finds in man's consciousness of his individual limitation. Unable to face limitations that humiliate him personally, man blames the entire human nature for them and attributes the perfections of the species to a Supreme Being. The task of Feuerbach's anthropology is to restore to man all the qualities he has estranged from himself in religion, and to make him aware of the fact that he is his own God.

In an article published in 1842, *Vorläufige Thesen zur Reform der Philosophie,* Feuerbach extended his critique of religion to all speculative philosophy, particularly Hegelianism. Philosophy is in fact a pseudotheology, and Hegel's Idea fulfills the same function as God in religion: it places the essence of man outside man. This article, as well as *Das Wesen des Christentums,* profoundly influenced Marx in his interpretation and use of the Hegelian dialectic. In his later work Feuerbach gradually evolved toward MATERIALISM; more and more he came to see man as a physical being whose thoughts and feelings are determined by his material living conditions. Later, Marx would criticize this materialism in the *Theses on Feuerbach* and distinguish his own, more dialectical position from Feuerbach's.

Historically Feuerbach remains an important figure because he was the first philosopher in the Christian world openly to defend humanistic ATHEISM, and also because his work has influenced the development of Marxism more than that of any other thinker except Hegel. His theory on the origin of religion is simplistic and has been abandoned today. His criticism of Hegel is based on a misunderstanding of Hegel's Idea, which is not solely logical or spiritual, as Feuerbach assumes, but the self-development of reality as well as thought.

See Also: HEGELIANISM AND NEO-HEGELIANISM; MATERIALISM, DIALECTICAL AND HISTORICAL.

Bibliography: L. A. FEUERBACH, *Sämtliche werke,* ed. W. BOLIN and F. JODL, 10 v. (Stuttgart 1959–60); *The Essence of Christianity,* tr. G. ELIOT (New York 1957). W. B. CHAMBERLAIN, *Heaven Wasn't His Destination: The Philosophy of Ludwig Feuerbach* (London 1941).

[L. DUPRÉ]

FEUILLANTS

The Feuillants were founded by Jean de la BARRIÈRE as the reformed branch of the Cistercians in 1577, suppressed in 1791. As regular abbot in 1577, Jean undertook the reform of the Cistercian Monastery of Les Feuillants near Toulouse, and within a decade had transformed it into a flourishing monastery. Sixtus V gave preliminary approval of the reform in 1586 and the movement spread in France and Italy. In 1592 Clement VIII approved the Feuillants (*Fulienses*) as an autonomous order, exempt from Cîteaux, but on his insistence the severe regulations, which exceeded the strictness of Cistercian life, were relaxed somewhat. In 1630, two separate congregations were required, one in France that retained the name Feuillants and one in Italy known as the Reformed Bernardines. Eventually the Feuillants possessed 31 houses and the Bernardines 43. During the 18th century, vocations declined, but the monks remained faithful to their original spirit. The French Revolution suppressed all religious houses in 1791, and the vacant monastery in Paris became the headquarters of a famous revolutionary club. The Bernardines came to an end in 1802. The Feuillantines, a community for women, founded in 1587 by Barrière with the cooperation of Anne and Marguerite de Polastron, were suppressed in 1791.

Feuillant houses were governed by abbots elected for three years. Central control was in a general chapter, held every third year under the presidency of an elected abbot general. Each community consisted of choir monks, lay brothers, and oblates. Their discipline was one of the strictest in monastic history. They retained the Cistercian habit, but went about barefooted and bareheaded; their diet was restricted to bread, water, and vegetables seasoned only with salt; they slept on planks, and having neither chairs nor tables, knelt on the floor to eat. They spent their time in prayer and hard manual labor in strict silence; in time they assumed intellectual work and pastoral duties.

Bibliography: H. HEIMBUCHER, *Die Orden und Kongregationen der katholischen Kirche,* 2 v. (3d ed. Paderborn 1932–34) 1:374–376. B. GRIESSER, *Lexikon für Theologie und Kirche,* ed. J. HOFER and K. RAHNER, 10 v. (2d, new ed. Freiburg 1957–65) 4:113. J. M. CANIVEZ, *Dictionnaire de droit canonique,* ed. R. NAZ, 7 v. (Paris 1935–65) 5:835–836. M. B. BRARD, *Catholicisme* 4:1235–39. M. STANDAERT, *Dictionnaire de spiritualité ascétique et mystique. Doctrine et histoire,* ed. M. VILLER et al. (Paris 1932–) 5:274–287.

[L. J. LEKAI]

FEY, CLARA

Foundress of the Sisters of the POOR CHILD JESUS; b. Aachen, Germany, April 11, 1815; d. Simpelveld, Netherlands, May 8, 1894. In 1837 she and some other zealous women opened a school for poor children in Aachen. To perpetuate and extend the apostolic work, she founded her religious congregation (1844) and until her death served as its superior general, despite frail health and frequent illness. During the KULTURKAMPF she and her community were obliged to flee to the Netherlands. She was noted for her industriousness combined with a deep interior life. The decree introducing her cause for beatification was issued in 1958.

Bibliography: O. PFÜLF, *Mutter Clara Fey und ihre Stiftung* (2d ed. Freiburg 1913). J. SOLZBACHER, ed., *Immer beim Herrn: Wandel in der Gegenwart Gottes nach Mutter Clara Fey* (2d ed. Mödling 1958), tr. M. COLMAN, *Heaven on Earth* (Westminster, Md. 1958).

[J. SOLZBACHER]

FICHTE, JOHANN GOTTLIEB

Founder of absolute transcendental IDEALISM and father of the philosopher Immanuel Hermann Fichte (1796–1879); b. Rammenau in Saxony, May 19, 1762; d. Berlin, Jan. 27, 1814. The elder Fichte received his early education under the patronage of Baron von Miltitz. Agitated and rebellious, he studied theology at Göttingen, Jena, and Leipzig from 1780 to 1784, then devoted nine years to private instruction. Asked to explain Kant's philosophy, he so thoroughly penetrated it that his anonymously published *Versuch einer Kritik aller Offenbarung* (Königsberg 1792) was thought to be Kant's own work. Fichte decided to supply a philosophy of religion for Kant's system. Reducing religion to Kant's "moral law," he held that sensible representations in various religions are an illusion of practical reason. In 1794 he started to teach at the University of Jena, but he was accused of atheism in 1798 and had to cede his position to F. W. J. SCHELLING the following year. Going to Berlin, he began to give courses in philosophy there and at Erlangen (1805). Inciting German nationalism by his *Reden an die deutschen Nation* (1807–08), he eventually became the second rector of the newly established University of Berlin. He died of typhus, which he contracted from his wife.

Teaching. According to Fichte, DOGMATISM abstracts from understanding and proposes the thing in itself as a reality that is the cause of thought, whereas idealism abstracts from the thing and substitutes intelligence in itself for the reality. Thus idealism holds that thoughts are representations accompanied by an awareness of necessity, produced by the intelligence. At the end of a lengthy transcendental deduction, Fichte proposes the Ego, itself transcending objectification, as the condition of all objectifiability and the necessary condition of self-consciousness. The transcendental Ego is attainable only by intellectual intuition, in which it is recognized by its activity within consciousness. Life arises in intellectual intuition, and, without it, there is death.

Fichte's absolute idealism claims a "victory over the opposition between thought and being," as well as between being and action. This victory establishes absolute activism and pure freedom, and morality is absolute and unconditioned. Reason determines its own activity by itself and, from this fact of self-determination, it must recognize that others, too, have freedom. The concept of law, then, is a condition of one's own consciousness. The essential condition for a juridical situation (*Rechtszustand*) is the state, and the law of the state is the principal scope of the philosophy of law. The basis for all life in the state is the "pact of the citizens" (*Staatsbürgervertrag*), which embraces a defense pact (*Schutzvertrag*) and a property pact (*Eigentumsvertrag*). The ultimate complement of this concession is the "closed commercial state," in which work and merit should be divided by the state as such according to a type of socialism. Whoever violates the pact of the state by an infraction of the law will be excluded from the pact of the state.

In accord with DEISM and ILLUMINISM, Fichte makes religion identical with morality and duty. He adopts the formula "faith in the moral order of the world" as the expression of the very essence of religion. Like Kant, he attributes to faith the capacity of attaining the supersensible. Faith is the actuation of freedom from all influence of the sensible world, this freedom having the scope of positing oneself through oneself. The self-certitude provided by faith does not require any further explanation, justification, or authorization. It is not based upon or determined by any other truth; rather every other truth is based upon it. This is the world of morality, the content and scope of freedom to which the transcendental viewpoint leads.

Instead of speaking of the divinity (*Gottheit*), Fichte speaks of the divine (*das Göttliche*), which, from the semantic viewpoint, is an even vaguer term. According to him, the divine becomes living and real in man. Like authentic incredulity and impiety, true atheism consists in rationalizing the consequences of one's own actions, in not obeying the voice of one's own conscience, in placing one's own judgment before God's judgment, and in making oneself God. Denying the fact of original sin, Fichte reduces all revealed religion to natural religion, wherein there is no dogma, all Biblical statements having value only in reference to moral action.

Critique. In general, Fichte starts with the illuministic positions of Spinoza, Rousseau, and Lessing and ends up in dissolving thought into action and destroying the very possibility of truth. Pursuing the logic of his predecessors, he adds only a Germanic preoccupation with deterministic morality. As his son later wrote, ''in the chain of [his] thoughts, everything is predetermined . . . so that . . . in the world of conscious natures, there is no room for free initiative'' (*Sämmtliche Werke* 5:vi).

Bibliography: Works. *Nachgelassene Werke,* ed. I. H. FICHTE, 3 v. (Bonn 1834–35); *Sämmtliche Werke,* ed. I. H. FICHTE, 8 v. (Berlin 1845–46; repr. 1964); *Werke,* ed. F. MEDICUS, 6 v. (Leipzig 1908–12); *Fichtes Briefwechsel,* ed. H. SCHULZ, 2 v. (Leipzig 1925–30). Literature. F. C. COPLESTON, *History of Philosophy* (Westminster, Md. 1946–) v.7. J. D. COLLINS, *A History of Modern European Philosophy* (Milwaukee 1954). X. LÉON, *Fichte et son temps,* 2 v. in 3 (Paris 1922–27). R. ADAMSON, *Fichte* (Edinburgh 1881). H. HEIMSOETH, *Fichte* (Munich 1923). M. WUNDT, *Fichte* (2d ed. Stuttgart 1937). R. W. STINE, *The Doctrine of God in the Philosophy of Fichte* (Philadelphia 1945). H. C. ENGELBRECHT, *Johann Gottlieb Fichte: A Study of His Political Writings, with Special Reference to His Nationalism* (New York 1933).

[C. FABRO]

Johann Gottlieb Fichte.

FICHTER, JOSEPH H.

Sociologist; b. Union City, NJ, June 10, 1908, d. New Orleans, LA, Feb. 23, 1994. In 1930 Fichter entered the New Orleans province of the Society of Jesus and was ordained a priest in 1942. He received his B.A. (1935) and M.A. (1939) from St. Louis University and a doctorate in sociology from Harvard University in 1947. Fichter spent most of his academic career teaching sociology at Loyola University in New Orleans, and also held the following academic appointments: Fulbright Professor, University of Muenster, Germany (1953–54); Visiting Professor, University of Notre Dame (1955–56); Fulbright Professor, Universidad Catolica de Chile (1960–61); Professor and Research Director, University of Chicago (1964–65); Chauncey Stillman Chair at Harvard University (1965–70); Professor, State University of New York at Albany (1971–72); and Favrot Chair of Human Relations, Tulane University (1973–74).

Joseph Fichter's research record includes 30 books and over 200 articles. The bulk of his work focused on aspects of Catholicism, including *Southern Parish* (1951), *Social Relations in the Urban Parish* (1954), *Parochial School* (1958), *Priest and People* (1965), *America's Forgotten Priests* (1968), *Rehabilitation of Clergy Alcoholics* (1982), *The Pastoral Provisions: Married Catholic Priests* (1989), *Wives of Catholic Clergy* (1992). Other books covered topics such as religion as an occupation, pain and healing, the Catholic Cult of the Paraclete, and the Unification Church. His sociological autobiography was published in two volumes: One Man Research (1973) and The Sociology of Good Works (1993).

Fichter was active in promoting social justice issues. In the 1930s he both defended organized labor and criticized corrupt union leadership, advocating the organization of white collar workers and pleading for more humane treatment of Mexican migrant laborers. In the 1940s he quietly achieved the first desegregation of Catholic colleges in the Deep South. In the early 1950s he developed a strategy to desegregate the entire New Orleans' Archdiocesan school system. In the 50s he wrote that reputed differences between the sexes was cultural in origin, and in 1966 he advocated the ordination of women in the Catholic Church.

Fichter served as president for the Society for the Scientific Study of Religion, the Southern Sociological Society, and as a member of the executive council of the American Sociological Association. In recognition of his stature in the field, the Association for the Sociology of Religion created the annual Fichter Research Award.

Bibliography: J.H. FICHTER, *One Man Research: Reminiscences of a Catholic Sociologist* (New York 1973); *The Sociology of Good Works: Research in Catholic America* (Chicago 1993). J. HADDEN and T. LONG, eds., *Religion and Religiosity in America: Studies in Honor of Joseph H. Fichter* (New York 1983).

[R.A. WALLACE]

FICINO, MARSILIO

Italian philosopher and leader of the Platonic Academy of Florence; b. Figline, Oct. 19, 1433; d. Florence, Oct. 1, 1499. Little is known of his youth and education, but he probably studied Latin, philosophy, medicine, and theology. His earliest writings date from about 1454 and show strong scholastic influences. He began studying Greek in 1456, and ultimately translated the complete writings of Plato (1463–73; printed Florence, 1484), Plotinus (1484–92; printed Florence, 1492), and Pseudo-Dionysius the Areopagite (1492; printed Florence, 1496). In 1462, Cosimo de'Medici granted Ficino the use of a number of Greek manuscripts and a villa at Careggi, where he devoted himself to the study of Platonic philosophy. There he was instrumental in founding the Platonic Academy, which became one of the foremost intellectual centers of Europe. At Careggi, Ficino wrote his major philosophical work, *Theologia platonica* (1469–74; printed Florence, 1482), and his *Commentary on Plato's Symposium* or *De amore* (1469; printed Florence, 1484). Ficino was ordained in 1473 and a year later wrote *De christiana religione* (printed Florence, 1476). With the expulsion the Medici from Florence in 1494, Ficino retired to the country.

As leader of the Platonic Academy, Ficino assumed the task of reviving PLATONISM, translating many works of the tradition into Latin. He was first led to an interest in Plato through the works of Augustine, who played a major role in the formation of Ficino's religious thought. He considered Aristotelian scholasticism to have degenerated into a series of antireligious philosophies, and envisioned the revived Platonism as a safeguard against this tendency.

Ficino saw religion as the identifying mark of man, distinguishing him from the lower animals. Philosophy and religion were considered parallel paths to truth: true religion (Christianity) and true philosophy (Platonism) ultimately must agree, for they stem from the same source, the contemplation of God. As the title of one of his letters indicates, ''Philosophy and Religion are Sisters.''

The hierarchical structure of Ficino's universe, derived in large measure from Neoplatonic sources, shows some originality. Ficino's universe is fivefold: God, angelic mind, rational soul, quality, and body. Rational soul, or man, has a place of preeminence as the connecting link between the immortal and the mortal. Man thus has a mobility wherein he can rise to God or fall to baseness, an idea further developed by Giovanni PICO DELLA MIRANDOLA.

According to Ficino's theory of natural appetite, the world demands that all things move toward their natural end. Man's end is the contemplation of, and union with, God; since this can rarely be achieved in life, personal immortality must be postulated. Much of the *Theologia platonica* is devoted to rational arguments for the immortality of the soul, drawn from Plato's *Phaedo,* Plotinus, and other sources.

In *De amore,* which animates Plato's Symposium with the Christian charity of Paul and Augustine, Ficino developed his notion of ''Platonic (or Socratic) love,'' as contrasted to ''vulgar love.'' The former concept, original with Ficino, is essentially a communion between friends based ultimately on the soul's love for God.

Ficino's influence, direct and indirect, was enormous. His translations and commentaries on the works of Plato and Plotinus were standard throughout Europe for several centuries. Traces of his thought are discernible in thinkers as diverse, geographically and intellectually, as J. COLET, the CAMBRIDGE PLATONISTS, HERBERT OF CHERBURY, and later deists in England; LEFÈVRE D'ETAPLES in France; and F. S. PATRIZI, G. BRUNO, and T. CAMPANELLA in Italy. His love theory is a basic ingredient in Renaissance literature, traces of it being found in Lorenzo de'Medici, Michelangelo, and Pietro Bembo in Italy; the Pléiade group and Scève in France; and E. Spenser in England.

Bibliography: *Opera* (Basel 1561; repr. 2 v. Paris 1641; rev. ed. Basel 1576; photo. repr. 2 v. in 4, Turin 1959); *Supplementum Ficinianum,* ed. P. O. KRISTELLER, 2 v. (Florence 1937), works not in 1576 ed.; *Marsile Ficin: Commentaire sur le ''Banquet'' de Pla-*

ton, ed. and tr. R. MARCEL (Paris 1956); ''Five Questions Concerning the Mind,'' *The Renaissance Philosophy of Man,* ed. E. CASSIRER et al. (Chicago 1948) 193–212; *Marsilio Ficino's Commentary on Plato's ''Symposium,''* tr. and ed. S. R. JAYNE (University of Missouri Studies 19.1; Columbia 1944). P. O. KRISTELLER, *The Philosophy of Marsilio Ficino,* tr. V. CONANT (New York 1943); *Studies in Renaissance Thought and Letters* (Rome 1956). R. MARCEL, *Marsile Ficin* (1433–1499) (Paris 1958), fullest bibliog.

[C. B. SCHMITT]

FIDEISM

A philosophical and theological doctrine or attitude that minimizes the capacity of the human intellect to attain certitude and assigns faith as a criterion of the fundamental truths. Thus, God's existence, the immortality of the soul, principles of morality, the fact of divine revelation, and the credibility of Christianity cannot be proved by reason alone, but must be accepted on authority. The term fideism (from the Latin *fides,* faith) was used for the first time by Eugene Ménégoz, *Réflexions sur l'évangile du salut* (Paris 1789), and was then applied to TRADITIONALISM and other theories of similar strain.

Forms. Fideism can be divided into two main forms: the broad sense and the strict sense. The former is any theory according to which the fundamental truths of the speculative and practical orders cannot be established by reason alone, but must be admitted on the authority of other men or because of a human, spontaneous propensity to do so. To this kind of fideism belong various theories. Some of them place a criterion of truth in common sense, be it conceived as a spontaneous impulse of instinct (Thomas Reid, d. 1796; Charles S. Peirce, d. 1914), or the common tenets of philosophical systems (Victor Cousin, d. 1867), or, again, universal reason (H. Felicité R. de Lamennais, d. 1854, in his later period); other theories connect the knowledge of truth with sentiment, as did Friedrich E. D. Schleiermacher (d. 1834), Friedrich H. Jacobi (d. 1819), Johann G. Herder (d. 1803), and William James (d. 1910); still others see an approach to the truth in ethical postulates, as I. Kant (d. 1804) and some of his followers did.

In the strict sense, fideism ascribes man's knowledge of basic truths to God's revelation. Such fideism is to be found mainly in the teaching of William of Ockham (d. 1349 or 1350), in Protestantism, in TRADITIONALISM, and in contemporary Christian EXISTENTIALISM.

From fideism in the strict sense one must distinguish semifideism, which holds that man reaches truth by reason, but with probability only and not with certitude. This form of fideism is accepted mainly by some scientists.

Origin and Development. Since fideism touches on the problem of the relationship between FAITH and reason, it can be traced back in some of its features to pagan philosophy, notably to the Sophists; and, in the Christian era, to the early patristic period, particularly to Tertullian's (d. 222 or 223) ''certum est quia impossibile'' (*De carne Christi* 5; *Patrologia Latina*, ed. J. P. Migne [Paris 1878–90] 2:760). However, the Sophists intended to show the incapacity of man's intellect to reach the truth; the negative position of the patristic period concerning man's intellect can be explained as a reaction against pagan philosophy rather than a denial of the natural capacity of the human intellect to reach the truth.

More precise expression of fideism occurred in the medieval Arabic thought, particularly in Algazel's (al-Ghazzālī, d. 1111) *Destruction of Philosophers,* in which he opposes his faith in the Koran to Avicenna's (d. 1036) philosophy. Subsequently his position was rejected by Averroës' (d. 1198) *Destruction of the Destruction.*

Strict fideism was advanced by WILLIAM OF OCKHAM. According to him, it is by faith alone that one attains certitude about God's existence, the immortality of the soul, and moral law. One finds a similar teaching in Nicolas of Autrecourt (d. *c.* 1350), and later in the teachings of Michel de Montaigne (d. 1592), Blaise Pascal (d. 1662), and Pierre D. Huet (d. 1721). Ockhamism, widely spread in Europe, influenced Protestantism. Luther rejected philosophy as an exaltation of reason and of nature. Consequently, he conceived faith as confidence able to justify. In his position, however, there are implied two aspects of faith, that Ménégoz, *op. cit.,* discerned in the position of the orthodox and liberal Protestants of his time, namely ''the gift to God of the heart'' and the adherence of the spirit to the revealed truth. By fideism Ménégoz meant *sola fides* that consists of the movement of oneself to God, independently of the adherence to certain beliefs or to revealed truths; such faith is justifying faith. Louis A. Sabatier (d. 1901), being in agreement with Ménégoz, finds in the Bible symbolic meanings only. The Bible expresses beliefs; faith expresses the movement toward salvation. Fideism means this movement realized by faith. Such a position, however, was criticized by some Protestants, especially by E. Doumerque in his *L'Autorité en matière de foi et la nouvelle école* (Paris 1892) and *Le Dernier mot du fidéisme* (Paris 1907).

Catholic usage of the term fideism, particularly in the teaching of the traditionalists, gives the opposite meaning to this term; fideism means the acceptance of the fundamental truth on the authority of God; hence faith becomes a criterion of truth.

Doctrine. Fideism presents in its negative aspect a critique of reason, which is made to appear unable to ascertain absolute truth through human effort. In its positive aspect it combats scepticism and agnosticism by inducing a specific source of certainty. This source is faith, an extrarational factor that allows man to grasp the fundamental truths immediately, particularly those in the field of religion, such as God's existence and the authority of the Bible. Faith provides an object for reason, and not only grace, as a subjective aid that helps man to attain the truth. This role faith plays with regard to basic natural truths, as well as to strict supernatural mysteries. These are tenets accepted also by the strict traditionalists.

One of the representatives of fideism, L. E. M. BAUTAIN (1796–1867), explains in greater detail the fideistic position, although with a flavor of ontologism, notably that man's reason is a passive faculty that can know the truths of the supernatural order and more subtle truths of the natural order only after having previously received the knowledge of them in germ. This germ is communicated by faith living in the Church, the Bible, the Prophets, the Apostles, and even poets. His most relevant work is *Philosophie du christianisme,* 2 v. (Paris 1835).

The ontological participation in the truth imparted to men by God was taught more clearly by A. Gratry (1805–72), a disciple of Bautain. Gratry maintains that there must be something of God in man in order for him to know God's existence (*La Logique,* 2 v. Paris 1855). It is a divine attraction present in every soul that enables men to experience God. Thus, by a sort of ''divine sense'' one recognizes Him (*De Le Connaissance de Dieu,* 2 v. Paris 1853).

Traces of fideism are noticeable also in contemporary thought, particularly in contemporary existentialism. Søren Kierkegaard (d. 1855) emphasized, mainly in his *Philosophical Fragments* (Copenhagen 1844), that one knows God's existence and the truth of the divine mission of Christ by faith alone; there are no rational proofs for those facts. A similar teaching has been advanced by Karl Barth (1886–1968), Rudolf Bultmann (1884–1976), and Martin Buber (1878–1965); and some traces of such a position are to be found in the writings of Gabriel Marcel (1889–1973) and in those of Karl Jaspers (1883–1969).

Ecclesiastical Documents. The Church's warnings against fideistic tenets are already found in the condemnation of the errors of Nicolas of Autrecourt, issued by Clement VI in 1347 (H. Denzinger, *Enchiridion symbolorum*, ed. A. Schönmetzer [Freiburg 1963] 1028–49). In 1835 and 1840, L. E. Bautain was compelled, with the approval of Gregory XVI, to sign theses contradicting his previous teaching and affirming that God's existence, the divinity of Mosaic and Christian revelation, the historical value of Christ's miracles can be proved with certitude; and that consequently, reason leads men to embrace faith, and it is not faith that must precede reason (Denzinger, 2751–56). In 1855 A. BONNETTY also signed theses reversing his previous doctrine by admitting that God's existence, the spirituality of the human soul, and man's liberty can be proved with certainty (Denzinger, 2812, cf. 2811, 2813–14). The same capacity of man's reason was sustained by Pius IX in his encyclical *Qui pluribus,* 1846 (Denzinger, 2775–80); by Vatican Council I (Denzinger, 3008–09, 3026, 3033); by Leo XIII in the encyclical *Aeterni Patris,* 1879 (Denzinger, 3135–38); and by Pius XII in his encyclical *Humani generis,* 1950 (Denzinger, 3875).

The Church's rejection of semifideism can be deduced from its insistence, in the above cited decrees, on the proofs with certitude of God's existence, of the spirituality of the soul, and of the credibility of divine revelation. The particularly important decree for this certitude is that of Vatican Council I (Denzinger, 3008–09, 3026). Besides, Innocent XI in 1679 condemned, among others, the error that the supernatural assent of faith stays with only probable knowledge of revelation, and even with fear that perhaps God did not speak to us (Denzinger, 2121). oreover, Pius X in the encyclical *Lamentabili* (1907) rejected the opinion that the assent of faith is based on a series of probable opinions (Denzinger, 3425); and in *Pascendi* (1910) he called attention to the decree of Vatican Council I, that man is capable of knowing with certainty, by natural reason, God's existence and the credibility of divine revelation through external signs, and not only through a subjective experience or inspiration (Denzinger, 3026, 3034).

Critique. Fideism rightly stresses the importance of faith against all varieties of scepticism, agnosticism, liberalism, and secularism. Fideism also plausibly defends the suprarational character of the mysteries of faith against the rationalistic tendency of accepting only what can be proved by reason. Finally, fideism shows clearly a moral need of divine revelation and faith.

However, fideism goes too far in its negative attitude toward the credibility of faith. If faith had no reasonable basis, it would be faith again that would lead us to faith. This would amount to complete relativism, since the credibility of faith would rely on a merely subjective basis, varying from one individual to another. Besides, since faith is essentially mediate cognition, it must be based on an immediately evident cognition in order to be acceptable to a reasonable being; otherwise, faith would be a blind assent; but ''nobody believes anything, if he previously does not think that it must be believed'' (''nullus credit aliquid nisi prius cogitaverit esse credendum''—St. Augustine, *Praed. sanct.* 2.5; *Patrologia Latina*, ed. J. P. Migne [Paris 1878–90] 44:962). Consequently, in daily life, one assents on the basis of the intrinsic evidence of the object; if this is lacking, one believes only when the credibility of the witness has been proved. Thus, in divine faith one believes when the veracity of the sources of belief is reasonably proved. Hence, even children, when they believe, rely on the authority of their parents; this authority is evident to them.

As to the certainty of the proofs, which is a concern of semifideism, one may notice that the proofs can become certain to those who understand them. Besides, the fact of revelation and its credibility can be proved historically and philosophically with certainty, just as other facts are proved. Finally, it would be imprudent for a reasonable being to accept something as true if it is not evidently true either in itself or on the authority of the relating witness.

See Also: FAITH; GOD, 7, 8.

Bibliography: General. S. HARENT, *Dictionnaire de théologie catholique*, ed. A. VACANT et al., (Paris 1903–50) 6.1:174–236. J. HASENFUSS, *Lexikon für Theologie und Kirche*, ed. J. HOFER and K. RAHNER (Freiberg 1957–65) 4:117–118. J. V. BAINVEL, *Dictionnaire apologétique de la foi catholique*, ed. A. D'ALÈS (Paris 1911–22) 2:17–94. G. ROTUREAU and Y. M. J. CONGAR, *Catholicisme* 4:1260–61. R. AUBERT, *Le Problème de l'acte de Foi* (3d ed. Louvain 1958). M. BRILLANT and M. NÉDONCELLE, *Apologétique* (Paris 1948). G. BRUNHES, *La Foi et sa justification rationnelle* (Paris 1928). É. DOMERGUE, *Les Étapes du fidéisme* (Paris 1906). R. GARRIGOU-LAGRANGE, *De revelatione,* 2 v. (5th ed. Rome 1950). E. MÉNÉGOZ, *Publications diverses sur le fidéisme,* 5 v. (Paris 1900–21). G. MONTI, *Apologetica scientifica della religione cattolica* (Turin 1922). L. A. SABATIER, *Esquisse d'une philosophie de la religion* (Paris 1897); *Les Religions d'autorité el la religion de l'esprit* (Paris 1903). G. DE BROGLIE, ''La Vrai notion thomiste des 'praeambula fidel,''' *Gregorianum* 34 (1953) 341–389. Particular. L. E. M. BAUTAIN, *Propositions générales sur la vie* (Strasbourg 1826); *La Morale de l'Évangile comparée à la morale des philosophies* (Strasbourg 1827); *De l'Enseignement de la philosophie en France au XIX*ᵉ *siècle* (Strasbourg 1833); *Philosophie morale,* 2 v. (Paris 1842); *La Chrétienne de nos jours,* 3 v. (Paris 1859–61). W. M. HORTON, *The Philosophy of the Abbé Bautain* (New York 1926; 2d ed. 1948). A. J. A. GRATRY, *De la connaissance de l'âme,* 2 v. (Paris 1857; 8th ed. 1920); *La Philosophie du crédo* (Paris 1861; 4th ed. 1902); *La Morale et la foi de l'histoire* (Paris 1868; 2d ed. 1871). J. MARIAS, *La filosofía del padre Gratry* (Madrid 1941). R. CRIPPA, ''Di un carattere distintivo tra lo spiritualismo cristiano italiano e quello francese,'' in *Motivi del pensiero contemporaneo* (Brescia 1950). A. W. CRAWFORD, *The Philosophy of F. H. Jacobi* (New York 1905). J. G. HERDER, *God: Some Conversations,* tr. F. H. BURKHARDT (New York 1949). K. BARTH, *Anselm; Fides quaerens intellectum,* tr. I. W. ROBERTSON (Richmond, Va. 1960); *Church Dogmatics,* tr. G. T. THOMSON et al. (New York 1955–). H. BOUILLARD, *Karl Barth,* 2 v. in 3 (Paris 1957). J. HAMFR, *Karl Barth,* tr. D. M. MARUCA (Westminster, Md. 1962). S. A. MATCZAK, *Karl Barth on God: The Knowledge of the Divine Existence* (New York 1962). A. C. COCHRANE, *The Existentialists and God* (Philadelphia 1956). D. E. ROBERTS, *Existentialism and Religious Belief* (New York 1957).

[S. A. MATCZAK]

FIDELIS OF SIGMARINGEN, ST.

Capuchin martyr; b. Mark Roy, Sigmaringen, Swabia, October 1578; d. Seewis, Präittigau, Switzerland, April 24, 1622. From December 1598 he studied at Freiburg-im-Breisgau, where he received doctorates in philosophy (1603) and canon and civil law (1611). Roy was tutor to noble children on a trip through France, Italy, and Spain (1604–10). He gave up the practice of law in Ensisheim, was ordained, and entered the Capuchins in Freiburg, Oct. 4, 1612, as Fidelis of Sigmaringen. In 1614 he went to Constance and Frauenfeld to study theology, and in 1617 began to preach. He was guardian at Rheinfeld (1618–19), Feldkirch (1619–20), Freiburg (1620–21), and again at Feldkirch from 1621 to his death. As a member of a Capuchin mission in Rhaetia dependent on Austria (Nov. 13, 1621) and on the Congregation for the PROPAGATION OF THE FAITH (Jan. 1622), Fidelis preached among the Grisons, who from 1608 had turned to Protestantism and were in revolt against Austria. He converted several important leaders; but when he went to Seewis against the advice of his friends, he was assaulted and slain in the church, April 24, 1622. In November 1622, after the Austrians had conquered the area, his relics were translated to Chur, and to Feldkirch. His beatification, initiated in 1623, was proclaimed March 12, 1729, and he was canonized June 26, 1746. On Feb. 16, 1771, he was called the proto-martyr of the Propagation of the Faith, and his cult was extended to the whole Church. Some of his extant writings have been published, and a number of vitae have been written. He is the patron of lawyers, the Sigmaringen, and the Hohenzollern.

Feast: April 24.

Bibliography: B. FISCHER, *Fidelis von Sigmaringen und seine Zeit* (Stein am Rhein 1991). R. SCHELL, *Fidelis von Sigmaringen* (Sigmaringen 1976). F. TOMANN, *Dreihundertfünfzig] Jahre St. Fidelis.* (Feldkirch 1972.) H. KORFF, *Biographica Catholica* (Freiburg 1927). P. WILLIBRORD DE PARIS, *Catholicisme* 4:1262–64. H. R. GUGGISBERG, *Die Religion in Geschichte und Gegenwart* 2:935.

[F. D. S. BORAN]

FIDELITY

A virtue allied to veracity (*see* TRUTHFULNESS), and indeed an integral part of that virtue, whose function it is to incline a person to the fulfillment of his promises. Whereas veracity inclines one to conform his speech to the judgment of his mind, fidelity disposes him to conform his deeds to his promissory commitments. The notion of fidelity is thus intimately associated with that of a promise, and the obligations of fidelity differ according to the different senses in which the term promise can be understood.

When a promise is contractual, i.e., when it has the force of a contract or a quasi-contract, it gives rise to an obligation in commutative justice. This obligation is a grave one and, where matters of importance are concerned, cannot be violated without serious sin. Thus, for example, conjugal fidelity and the promised payment of debts voluntarily contracted are grave obligations in conscience.

But when moral theologians refer to fidelity in its narrowest and most specific sense they do not have in mind the fidelity that obliges in virtue of commutative justice but are concerned rather with fidelity in the fulfillment of promises of a noncontractual kind, that is, with promises made spontaneously and out of pure liberality, and with no view to benefits received or expected. The obligations of fidelity understood in this sense bind less urgently than those arising from commutative justice, and their deliberate violation would not ordinarily involve grave sin.

However, it is not always easy to distinguish a simple promise binding only in fidelity from a gratuitous, unilateral contract that binds in commutative justice. The intention of the party making the promise is decisive in most cases, but in some circumstances the nature of what is promised, and the trouble and expense to which the promisee may be put by reason of his expectations, indicate that the promisor intends (or at least should intend) to bind himself seriously.

Bibliography: THOMAS AQUINAS, *Summa theologiae,* 2a2ae, 110.3 ad 5; 89.7; 98.3 ad 1 and 3. B. H. MERKELBACH, *Summa theologiae moralis,* 3 v. (Paris 1949) 2:497–500.

[P. K. MEAGHER]

FIDES ET RATIO

Pope JOHN PAUL II's thirteenth encyclical, *Faith and Reason,* issued on the feast of the Triumph of the Cross (Sept. 14, 1998). Addressed to the world's bishops, it is concerned with the relation between faith and reason, especially faith and philosophy in the contemporary world. It comprises an introduction, seven chapters, and a conclusion.

In the introduction (1–6), the pope notes that both Eastern and Western thought have asked the fundamental questions of human existence. In the West, the questions have been the special focus of philosophy, which uses reason to search for ultimate truth. Modern philosophy, however, has been so absorbed in the study of human subjectivity that it has neglected the search for transcendent truth or become skeptical of its attainability. This is a matter of concern to the Church, which as the bearer of the revelation of truth in Jesus Christ, has a special mission of service (*diakonia*) of the truth.

Chapter 1 (7–15) considers revelation, basing its treatment on *Dei Filius* of VATICAN I and *Dei verbum* of VATICAN II. God's revelation, known through faith, is distinct from and surpasses what reason can know. It is ''immersed in time and history'' through Jesus Christ, the incarnate Word of God. Only in Christ is the ultimate truth about human existence to be found. Revelation does not disable reason but drives it to extend its knowledge as far as possible. Christian revelation ''summons human beings to be open to the transcendent, while respecting both their autonomy as creatures and their freedom'' (15).

Chapter 2, ''*Credo ut intellegam* [I believe so that I might understand]'' (16–23), considers biblical teaching on faith and reason. Biblical texts reflect a ''conviction that there is a profound and indissoluble unity between the knowledge of reason and the knowledge of faith'' (16). The Old Testament writers understood the use of applying finite reason within the context of the human relation to the mystery of God. Saint Paul holds that reason can know God, but that this capacity has been damaged by human disobedience to God. The crucifixion of Christ challenges our habitual ways of thinking and overcomes any attempt to construct an account of the meaning of existence in purely human terms.

Chapter 3, ''*Intellego ut credam* [I understand so that I might believe]'' (24–35), speaks of the human search for truth, which is based ultimately in the human heart's desire for God. ''One may define the human being . . . as the one who seeks the truth'' (28), in particular, the truth about the meaning of life and death. The search for truth is not solitary but immerses us in communities and traditions. Most of what we know, we do not experience directly but believe on the testimony of others. The search for truth requires ''trusting dialogue and sincere friendship''; ''a climate of suspicion and distrust'' is destructive of it. Christian faith meets the human search, offering both ''the concrete possibility of reaching the goal'' and ''a person to whom they might entrust themselves'' (33).

Chapter 4 (36–48) surveys the history of the relationship of Christian faith with philosophy. The early apologists and church fathers used philosophy to express and defend Christian faith; at the same time they contributed to philosophy, purifying it of mythological elements. The medieval Scholastics continued this project, culminating in the work of THOMAS AQUINAS. Convinced of the harmony of faith and reason as coming from the same God, he gave reason its full scope, recognizing the autonomy of philosophy as well as its organic link to theology. But later medieval thought began an increasing separation between philosophy and faith, until in the 19th century much of Western philosophy explicitly opposed Christian revelation. Today, philosophy's search for truth and meaning has given way, even among many philosophers, to ''instrumental reason'' in the service of the market, technological power, and enjoyment. As a result, a nihilistic outlook, which claims that ultimate truth is unattainable and ''everything is fleeting and provisional'' (46), has gained strength. Philosophy needs faith, to recall it to its true goal, while faith needs philosophy, to temper its stress on feeling and experience and to save it from myth and superstition.

In chapter 5, ''The Magisterium's Interventions in Philosophical Matters'' (49–63), the pope states that the church has no official philosophy; philosophy must retain autonomy, ''faithful to its own principles and methods'' (49). But when philosophical opinions threaten the understanding of revealed truth, the church's magisterium must intervene. Such interventions serve right reason and are intended to stimulate philosophical inquiry. In the nineteenth century they defended reason against fideism and faith against rationalism. Today's chief problem is a ''deep-seated distrust of reason'' (55) and of ''universal and absolute statements.'' Philosophers must not set ''goals that are too modest''; they must not ''abandon the passion for ultimate truth'' (56).

Besides warning against errors, the church has also tried to promote a renewal of philosophy, as in the encyclical *AETERNI PATRIS* of Pope LEO XIII, which sparked a revival of THOMISTIC philosophy. Catholic philosophers who adopted more recent methods are also commended. Although the Second Vatican Council encouraged the study of philosophy, in the years since a lack of interest in philosophy has affected many Catholic faculties and even, as ''I cannot fail to note with surprise and displeasure,'' many theologians (61).

Chapter 6 (64–79) discusses ''The Interaction between Philosophy and Theology.'' Theology needs philosophy in order to understand the meaning of revealed truth and the way it is proclaimed. Neither the human sciences nor the traditional wisdom of non-Western cultures can take philosophy's place. The human sciences are helpful in studying human opinions but not in arriving at the objective truth in theology. The encounter with other cultures today is something like the encounter with Greek philosophy in early Christianity, but the church cannot neglect the universality of the human spirit across cultures nor ''abandon what she has gained from her inculturation in the world of Greco-Latin thought'' (72).

There is a circular, mutually enhancing relationship between philosophy and theology, as can be seen in the great philosopher-theologians ancient and modern, Eastern and Western Christian. Christian philosophy is ''a philosophical speculation conceived in dynamic union with faith'' (76), which gives philosophy material for reflection, while purifying it and keeping it humble. Faith, in turn, ''grows deeper and more authentic when it is wedded to thought and does not reject it'' (79).

Chapter 7 (80–99) lays out ''Current Requirements and Tasks'' for philosophy and theology. Scripture affirms that ''the world and human life do have a meaning'' (80), which is centered in Jesus Christ. But currently we are in a ''crisis of meaning'' (81). We are overwhelmed with data and conflicting theories, to the point where the question of meaning may itself seem to have no sense. ''To be consonant with the word of God,'' philosophy must recover its character as a search for the ultimate meaning of life and as ''the ultimate framework for the unity of human knowledge and action'' (81). It must acknowledge the human capacity to know objective truth. And it must be capable of transcending sense experience and speaking metaphysically. It must avoid ECLECTICISM, HISTORICISM, SCIENTISM, and a democratic pragmatism that bases moral values on majority vote.

Theology requires the belief that it is possible to know universally valid truth. It needs philosophy in order to clarify the relation between historical fact and enduring meaning in Scripture and to deal with the relationship between the permanent truth of dogmatic statements and their historical and cultural conditioning. MORAL THEOLOGY requires ''a philosophical ethics that looks to the truth of the good'' and is ''neither subjectivist nor utilitarian'' (98).

The ''Conclusion'' (100–108) reiterates that philosophy and theology need one another and stresses that training in philosophy is an important part of priestly formation. The pope addresses scientists, urging them not to lose sight of the need to join science with ''philosophical and ethical values'' (106). He concludes by invoking Mary, who gave herself in order that ''God's Word might take flesh'' (108), as an image for philosophy.

Bibliography: For the text of *Fides et ratio,* see: *Acta Apostolicae Sedis* 91 (1999): 5–88 (Latin); *Origins* 28, no. 19 (October 22, 1998): 317–347 (English).

[W. J. COLLINGE]

FIDES QUAERENS INTELLECTUM

Originally the subtitle of St. ANSELM's *Proslogion* (book to support the faith of the believer), this phrase became the motto of SCHOLASTICISM. For Anselm it signified the endeavor of one who has the faith to understand what he believes. One achieves this by putting his mind to the contemplation of God and by reflecting upon what he contemplates. It thus gives the basic method of Catholic theologians. Whereas, however, Anselm regards the proofs of God's existence as included in this process, St. Thomas Aquinas excludes them; furthermore, whereas Anselm regards this enquiry as being able not only to show the suitability of a doctrine but also to prove it, Aquinas allows only that it shows its suitability. Vatican I adopts this formula while giving it a more general sense: ''when reason, enlightened by faith, seeks its object with diligence, reverence, and moderation, it attains by God's gift some understanding (and that very fruitful) of the mysteries of the faith'' (*Enchiridion symbolorum,* 3016).

See Also: THEOLOGY; DOGMATIC THEOLOGY; METHODOLOGY (THEOLOGY); FAITH AND REASON; THEOLOGY, ARTICLES ON.

Bibliography: G. SÖHNGEN, *Lexikon für Theologie und Kirche,* ed. J. HOFER and K. RAHNER, 10 v. (2d new ed. Freiburg 1957–65) 4:119–120. F. CAYRÉ, *Patrologie et histoire de la théologie,* v.2 (4th ed. Paris 1947) 395.

[B. FORSHAW]

FIESOLE, GUIDO DA (FRA ANGELICO), BL.

Baptised Guido di Pietro (his father's name was Pietro); also known as Guido da Fiesole and Giovanni da Fiesole (John Faesulanus); Dominican priest and Florentine painter; b. near Vicchio di Mugello, Tuscany, Italy, *c.* 1386–87; d. La Minerva Friary, Rome, Italy, Feb. 18, 1455.

Guido was already a recognized artist at age 20, when he entered the Dominican monastery at Fiesole with his brother Benedetto. He took the religious name John of the Angels. Shortly thereafter, because of the Great Western Schism, Fra Giovanni and his brother (adherents to the Avignon claimant, Gregory XII) left Fiesole for the Dominican convent in Foligno, Umbria. The brothers moved to Cortonna to escape the pestilence that ravaged Foligno, and four years later made their way back to Fiesole where Giovanni remained for the next sixteen years.

As a young friar he worked at illuminating manuscripts such as the *Dominican Diurnal 3* (Laurentian Library, Florence), while his brother completed an exquisite set of choir books. From 1409, he continued his studies and was ordained priest at Fiesole in 1418. In the 1440s, he was appointed prior of San Marco (Florence), which he decorated with his paintings, and he held that office for three years. Pope Eugene IV wished to appoint him archbishop of Florence, but he declined in favor of Saint Antoninus.

Among his works are ''Coronation of the Virgin'' (Uffizi, Florence); ''Last Judgment''; and ''Deposition from the Cross'' (1433, S. Marco Museum, Florence). He also painted the frescoes in the cloister and cells of the remodeled monastery of S. Marco (1437), Florence.

During the last ten years of his life, Angelico was much in demand. In 1445, Eugene IV summoned him to the Vatican to work on the frescoes in the chapel of the Sacrament. These frescoes were later destroyed. In 1447, he began the ''Last Judgment'' frescoes in the S. Brixio Chapel, Orvieto cathedral (finished years later by Signorelli), but was summoned again to the Vatican by Nicholas V to paint scenes from the lives of SS. Stephen and Lawrence in the Nicholas Chapel. In 1449, he returned to Fiesole to become prior of San Domenico. He returned to Rome to finish work there, and it was there he died. The body of Bl. Fra Angelico now rests in S. Maria sopra Minerva, Rome.

John Paul II issued a *motu proprio,* Oct. 3, 1982, granting a liturgical cultus to the Dominicans for Fra Angelico, long known as *il beato Angelico* because of his ''angelic'' moral virtues. The Holy Father wrote: ''[E]ven today his art makes the way to God more accessible for us. And this is the purpose of sacred art. . . . the time has arrived to place him in his proper light in Church of God, to which he still continues to speak through his heavenly art.'' In 1984, he was declared patron of artists by Pope John Paul II.

Feast: Feb. 18 (Dominicans).

Bibliography: *Acta Apostolicae Sedis* 75 (1983) 796–99. V. ALCE, *Angelicus pictor: vita, opere e teologia del Beato Angelico* (Bologna 1993). U. BALDINI, *Beato Angelico* (Florence 1986). K. BERING, *Fra Angelico: Mittelalterlicher Mystiker oder Maler der Renaissance?* (Essen 1984). G. DIDI-HUBERMAN, *Fra Angelico: Dissemblance & Figuration,* tr. J. M. TODD (Chicago 1995). G. FALLANI, *Vita e opere di fra Giovanni Angelico* (Florence 1984). J. & M. GUILLAUD, *Fra Angelico: The Light of the Soul* (New York 1986). C. GILBERT, *A Renaissance Image of the End of the World: Fra Angelico and Signorelli at Orvieto* (University Park, Pa. 2001). A. HERTZ, *Fra Angelico* (Freiburg im Breisgau 1981). J. W. POPE-HENNESSY, *Fra Angelico* (Riverside, N.Y. 1990). M. SALMI, *Il beato Angelico* (Spoleto 1958). J. T. SPIKE, *Fra Angelico* (New York 1996). C. B. STREHLKE, *Angelico* (Milan 1998). G. VASARI, *Lives of the Artists; Biographies of the Most Eminent Painters, Sculptors and Architects of Italy,* abridged and edited by B. BURROUGHS (New York 1946). I. VENCHI, *Fra Angelico and the Chapel of Nicholas V* (Vatican City 1999).

[E. T. DE WALD/EDS.]

FIGLIUCCI, FELIX (FILLIUCIUS)

Humanist and theologian; b. Siena, Italy, *c.* 1525; d. Florence?, *c.* 1590. He studied philosophy at Padua and was in the service of Cardinal Del Monte, who later became Pope Julius III. Figliucci's reputation as a humanist was widespread. In 1551 he became a Dominican in Florence, taking the name Alexus. He wrote many works in Italian and translated Greek works into Italian. He attended the Council of Trent and translated its Latin Catechism into Italian.

Bibliography: *Biographical and Bibliographical Dictionary of the Italian Humanists and of the World of Classical Scholarship in Italy, 1300-1800* 2:1421. J. QUÉTIF and J. ÉCHARD, *Scriptores Ordinis Praedicatorum* (New York 1956) 2.1:263–264.

[E. A. CARRILLO]

FIGUEIREDO, JACKSON DE

Brazilian writer and Catholic lay leader; b. Aracajú, Sergipe, Oct. 9, 1891; d. Barra la Tijuca, Rio de Janeiro, Nov. 4, 1928. Though born a Catholic, he early absorbed the materialistic ideas prevalent among the intelligentsia. He matriculated at the law school of Bahia in 1909 and soon, through the Nova Cruzada movement, became a student leader in anticlerical and antisocial activities. Shortly thereafter, influenced by the works of Pascal and supported by Farias de Brito, he returned to the Church. In 1915 at Rio de Janeiro he met Leonel FRANCA, SJ, and Alceu Amoroso Lima, and under their tutelage came to understand that life has meaning only as a labor that can be offered to God. Since he perceived that only anarchy could follow a divorce between letters and the Church, he dedicated himself fully to the reestablishment of the Christian spirit. He founded the periodical *A Ordem* (1921), the principal vehicle for the diffusion of his ideas, and the Centro Dom Vital (1922), a religious-cultural institution. Unfortunately, he never succeeded in fully controlling his violent character, and this intemperance affected some of his work. His *Pascal e a Inquietação Moderna* is a carefully considered and revised work; *Cartas* (1932) are also noteworthy; they constitute, perhaps, his most positive, rich, and lasting contribution.

Bibliography: A. AMOROSO LIMA, *Estudos,* 1st series (2d ed. Rio de Janeiro 1929), 3d and 4th series (1930–31). H. NOGUEIRA, *J. de F.: O. doutrinário católico* (Rio de Janeiro 1927). J. S. FONTES, *J. de. F.: Sentido de sua obra* (Aracajú 1952). T. DE SILVEIRA, *J. de F.* (Rio de Janeiro 1945).

[A. STULZER]

FILARET (VASILIČI MIKHAILOVICH DROZDOV)

Russian theologian, metropolitan of Moscow; b. Kolomna (Moscow Region), Dec. 26, 1782; d. Moscow, Nov. 19, 1867. The son of the Orthodox archpriest of the cathedral in Kolomna, he studied at the seminary there (1791–99) and at Troïtskii (1800–03), and then taught Hebrew, Greek, poetry, and rhetoric in the Troïtskii seminary. In 1808 he became a monk and took the name Filaret (Philaret), but was called to St. Petersburg the same year as inspector and professor of philosophy in the seminary there. In 1809 he was ordained. He went to the St. Petersburg Ecclesiastical Academy as professor (1810) and rector (1812). He became bishop of Reval (1812), member of the HOLY SYNOD (1817), and archbishop (1821) and metropolitan of Moscow (1826). Filaret was brilliant and zealous and exercised enormous influence on the inner life and theology of the Russian Church and on Church-State affairs, although he encountered much opposition in some of his projects, such as the translation of the Bible into Russian and a new edition of the catechism. He sought legislation to force the conversion of the RASKOLNIKS and played an important role in efforts to reunite Catholics of the UKRAINIAN CATHOLIC CHURCH with the Orthodox. His hostility to the Catholic Church, especially to the pope, was constant, but he avoided the violent polemics common to Greek apologists. He favored the emancipation of the serfs. Filaret was a prolific writer, but much of his work was published only after his death. His principal theological work was his *Catechism* (1823), which was translated into several languages.

Bibliography: M. JUGIE, *Dictionnaire de théologie catholique* (Paris 1903–50) 12.1:1376–95. A. M. AMMANN, *Storia della Chiesa russa e dei paesi limitrofi* (Turin 1948), Ger. tr. (Vienna 1950). I. SMOLICH, *Russisches Mönchtum* (Würzburg 1953).

[J. PAPIN]

FILBY, WILLIAM, BL.

Priest, martyr; b. Oxfordshire, England, *c.* 1557–60 d. hanged, drawn, and quartered at Tyburn (London), May 30, 1582. Following his studies at Lincoln College, Oxford, Filby entered the seminary at Rheims, Oct. 12, 1579, and was ordained, March 25, 1581. He was active in the English mission for only a short time before his arrest in July and commitment to the Tower of London, Marshalsea, and back to the Tower. Following his sentencing on November 17 on the false charge of conspiring against the Government in Rome and Rheims, he was loaded with manacles for the rest of his life and deprived of his bedding for two of those months. With him suffered three others: BB. Thomas COTTAM, Luke KIRBY, and Laurence RICHARDSON. He was beatified by Pope Leo XIII.

Feast of the English Martyrs: May 4 (England).

See Also: ENGLAND, SCOTLAND, AND WALES, MARTYRS OF.

Bibliography: B. CAMM, ed., *Lives of the English Martyrs,* (New York 1905), II, 500–35. R. CHALLONER, *Memoirs of Missionary Priests,* ed. J. H. POLLEN (rev. ed. London 1924; repr. Farnborough 1969), I, nos. 12–14. J. H. POLLEN, *Acts of English Martyrs* (London 1891).

[K. I. RABENSTEIN]

FILCOCK, ROGER, BL.

Jesuit priest, martyr; *alias* Roger Nayler, Roger Arthur; b. ca. 1570 at Sandwich, Kent, England; d. Feb. 27, 1601, hanged, drawn, and quartered at Tyburn (London). He studied at Rheims (1588–90) and at St. Alban's Seminary, Valladolid, where he was ordained (ca. 1597). He applied to enter the Jesuits in Spain but was sent instead to the English Mission. En route he was captured at sea by the Dutch, but escaped to Kent in early 1598. Under the *alias* Roger Arthur he began his two–year ministry. Shortly after being admitted to the Society of Jesus by Fr. Henry GARNET, Filcock was betrayed by someone who had known him as a student at Valladolid, arrested (summer 1600), and imprisoned at Newgate before he could undertake his novitiate in Flanders. He was charged with being a priest on Feb. 23, 1601, and indicted three days later. The judge directed the jury to find him guilty of high treason although there was no evidence against him. When he and his former classmate at Valladolid, St. Mark BARKWORTH, were taken to the gallows for execution, they found that St. Anne LINE, for whom Filcock had acted as confessor, had just been executed. At the gallows Filcock denied treason, but admitted that he was ''a Catholic, a priest, and a member of the Society of Jesus.'' He was beatified by Pope John Paul II on Nov. 22, 1987 with George Haydock and Companions.

Feast of the English Martyrs: May 4 (England); Dec. 1 (Jesuits).

See Also: ENGLAND, SCOTLAND, AND WALES, MARTYRS OF.

Bibliography: R. CHALLONER, *Memoirs of Missionary Priests,* ed. J. H. POLLEN (rev. ed. London 1924). J. H. POLLEN, *Acts of English Martyrs* (London 1891). J. N. TYLENDA, *Jesuit Saints & Martyrs* (Chicago 1998) 65–66. D. DE YEPES, *Historia Particular de la persecución de Inglaterra* (Madrid 1599).

[K. I. RABENSTEIN]

FILIATION

The term filiation expresses the relation that exists by reason of the fact that the Second Person of the Holy TRINITY proceeds from the First by way of true GENERATION. For the procession of the LOGOS within the divine essence is generation in the strict sense, and this is clear both from revelation and from reasoning based on revelation.

In Scripture, especially in the OT, the phrase SON OF GOD is frequently employed in a figurative sense to denote a friend or a servant of God. In this sense Moses and the Prophets and, indeed, all just men are sons of God. But when Our Lord applied the term to Himself He was not using it in this qualified, figurative sense. He was not merely implying that He was a man closely united to God or officially representing God. He used the term literally; He meant that He was, in the fullest sense, the real, actual Son of the heavenly Father. In the NT, therefore, the term Son of God applied to Christ is meant to express His divinity, and it is in fact a statement of His real generation from the Father. Consequently, in the Prologue of the Fourth Gospel the Logos is called the ''only-begotten'' of the Father (Jn 1.14, 18). Earlier John had said, ''In the beginning was the Word, and the Word was with God; and the Word was God'' (Jn 1.1). The term the WORD, the LOGOS, gives one an insight into the way in which the Second Person of the Trinity proceeds from the First, namely, by generation.

Generation is described by St. Thomas as ''the origin from a conjoined living principle of a living being with a like nature'' (*Summa theologiae* 1a, 27.2). From this technical and rather succinct definition one sees that the notion of generation contains two essential marks: (1) the origin of one living being from another living being; (2) an offspring similar in nature to the parent.

Now there is a remarkable resemblance between the way in which a mental word or idea of some external object is conceived in the human mind and the ordinary biological process of generation. One often calls his ideas CONCEPTS. From the conjunction of an external object with the intellect there is produced a concept of the external object. And, hence, philosophers say that the external object plays the part of the father; the intellect, the part of the mother; and the concept resembles both its parents inasmuch as it is like the object but, at the same time, is modified somewhat by the particular understanding in which it is formed. But when one speaks of the generation of a concept in the human mind he is obviously using the term in an analogous sense. The formation of an idea of an extramental object is not, strictly speaking, generation at all. The process, however, may well be likened to the process of generation. But the procession of the Logos within the divine essence *is* generation in the strict sense of the word.

According to St. Thomas the Father contemplating the Divine essence generates therein the concept, or the Logos, of the divine essence, which is not merely like the divine essence but absolutely identical with it in nature. The concept that is begotten in the human mind—for instance, the concept of a pine tree—is something accidental to the mind that begets it; but whatever proceeds within the divine essence itself must be identical with the divine essence since there can be nothing accidental in God. The Logos, then, which is begotten of the Father, proceeds consubstantial with the Father, that is, having precisely the same divine nature as the Father, and yet really distinct from the Father in personality, as every son is distinct from the Father who begets him (*see* CONSUBSTANTIALITY).

In the divine act of cognition, therefore, every reality is present that is essential to the concept of generation. For there is the origin of one living being from another living being in such a way that this living being proceeds with the selfsame nature as its progenitor. The ordinary process of intellection requires that a concept shall be in some way similar to the object that, as has been noted, can be said to play the role of the father. The concept bears an ''intentional'' resemblance to the object with which it corresponds, that is to say, the object itself is not found in the human mind, but there is a representation of it or an intentional resemblance to it. But that which proceeds in the divine intelligence, namely, the Logos, is similar to the principle from which it proceeds, not merely in an intentional way, but in the most perfect possible way, namely, by substantial identity.

See Also: GENERATION OF THE WORD; PROCESSIONS, TRINITARIAN; RELATIONS, TRINITARIAN; TRINITY, HOLY, ARTICLES ON.

Bibliography: P. RICHARD, *Dictionnaire de théologie catholique*, ed. A. VACANT et al., 15 v. (Paris 1903–50; Tables générales 1951) 5.2:2353–2476. I. M. DALMAU, *Sacrae theologiae summa*, ed. Fathers of the Society of Jesus, Professors of the Theological Faculties in Spain, 4 v. *Biblioteca de autores cristianos* (Madrid 1945) 2.1:391–397.

[L. J. MCGOVERN]

FILIOQUE

A word, meaning ''and from the Son,'' added to the Nicene-Constantinopolitan Creed in the Latin Church after the phrase, ''the Holy Spirit . . . who proceeds from the Father.'' The *Filioque* has been the center of controversy almost from the time the Western church first inserted it into the Ecumenical Creed of Nicea-Constantinople in the sixth century. First a bone of contention between Rome (which did not add it to the Creed until the 11th century) and Charlemagne, and from the eighth century onwards the occasion for often bitter controversy and misunderstanding between the churches of the Eastern Orthodoxy and the Latin West.

History of the Doctrine. The doctrine of the double Procession of the Holy Spirit came into discussion early (*see* PROCESSIONS, TRINITARIAN). THEODORE OF MOPSUESTIA denied it and THEODORET OF CYR accused CYRIL OF ALEXANDRIA of error in holding it. The controversy reflected the tendency of the school of Antioch to interpret the Scriptures literally and to stress the distinction of Persons in the Trinity, in opposition to the school of Alexandria with its more analogical approach to Scriptures and its insistence on the unicity of deity. Later the Western Church, notably Saint AUGUSTINE, developed the Alexandrine thought; the Eastern Church that of Antioch and of Theodoret. Pope MARTIN I included the phrase ''and from the Son'' in his synodical letter to Constantinople (649), thereby causing irritation that was allayed by an explanation of MAXIMUS THE CONFESSOR: ''[The Latins wished] to show that He comes forth through Him and to expose the connection and immutability of the substance'' (*Patrologia Graeca* 91:136). In the 7th century the doctrine and the formula became common in Spain and were discussed in the Synod of Gentilly (767). Meanwhile the confession of faith of TARASIUS, PATRIARCH OF CONSTANTINOPLE, recited in the second Council of NICAEA, spoke of Procession ''from the Father through the Son.'' As doctrine this was attacked vehemently in the *LIBRI CAROLINI,* written reputedly by ALCUIN, Charlemagne's adviser, as imprecise and open to erroneous interpretation. The Synod of Frankfurt supported the condemnation, but ADRIAN I defended both the formula of Tarasius and its doctrine (*Patrologia Latina*, ed. J. P. Migne, 98:1249–52). CHARLEMAGNE, who had introduced the filioque into the Creed in his chapel, was unconvinced and bade Alcuin and others write against the phrase, ''through the Son.'' At the same time there was controversy in Palestine (807) which reached Rome and Aachen.

The filioque doctrine became a major cause of dissension between East and West when PHOTIUS, attacking the Western Church in general, made it the chief theological gravamen in his quarrel with NICHOLAS I. The controversy was revived at the Great Schism of 1054, when Constantinople employed the filioque as an argument against Rome, the Holy See having, in the meantime, inserted it into the Creed. It became the chief Greek accusation against the Latin Church and was based more and more on patristic grounds. Under the influence of Saint ANSELM, the Council of Bari (1098), where Greeks of Sicily were represented, formally affirmed both the addition and the doctrine. The Council of LYONS (1274), with the consent of the three Greek representatives of the Emperor MICHAEL VIII PALAEOLOGUS and (theoretically) of the Greek Church, defined the doctrine. The clergy and people of Constantinople, however, vehemently rejected it, in spite of the severe persecution employed by their emperor to impose acceptance. Beccus, first imprisoned for his opposition, then converted on reading the patristic evidence adduced by Nicephorus Blemmydes and made Patriarch by Michael, was later accused of heresy and exiled. Denial of the filioque in the East continued, and by the end of the 14th century its abjuration was required from converts. The Council of FLORENCE re-echoed the voice of Beccus. Its decree signed by Latins and Greeks defined that the Holy Spirit proceeds from Father and Son as from one principle and one spiration, "from" and "through" being equivalent and casual. But the union did not endure, and the old state of controversy returned.

The theological arguments for and against the filioque are well summarized in the speeches at Florence—in the sessions of March 17, 21, and 24, 1439. In John 15.26 it is stated: "The spirit of truth who proceeds from the Father," saying nothing of the Son; hence, asserted the Greeks, He proceeds from the Father only. The Latins adduced other texts: The Spirit receives from the Son (being); is sent by the Son (origin); is third in the formula of baptism (origin). The Creed teaches: "proceeds from the Father but is to be adored and glorified with Father and Son." The Greek Fathers were quoted on both sides; the Latin Fathers, however, all taught the filioque. Some of the Greeks maintained that the Father is the "sole fount of Divinity" (ATHANASIUS, PSEUDO-DIONYSIUS); JOHN DAMASCENE stated that "we do not say that the Spirit proceeds from the Son" (*Patrologia Graeca* 94:832). None used the phrase "proceeds from the Son." On the other hand, none ever wrote "from the Father only," but a great variety of expressions were employed: "springs from," "goes forth from," "Father and Son," "both," "Father through the Son." Analogies were used, such as that the Spirit is like the "steam" rising from the "water"; a "finger" of the "hand"; He is the Spirit of the Son, of truth, etc. The general Greek doctrine can be well summarized in Tarasius' words, "proceeds from the Father through the Son," and was the same as the Latin teaching, though less succinctly expressed. Beccus proved this assertion—the Greeks and Latins were really disputing over words rather than basic doctrine—after the Council of Lyons. In the Council of Florence, John of Montenero and BESSARION demonstrated it and the decree confirmed it.

The Filioque as an Addition to the Creed. After the doctrine had become current through the formulas approved by the synods of Toledo [16th (693), 11th (638), 4th (633), 3d (589)], and the longer formula of the first synod, written by Palentinus Pastor (*c.* 445), who had been inspired by LEO I's letters to Turibius, the filioque passed to nearby Gaul, where it was defended in the Synod of Gentilly (767) and in the *Libri Carolini.* From Gaul it came to Italy, as witnessed by the Council of Cividale (796–97). The Creed with the addition was introduced in Spain into the Mozarabic Rite before the *Pater Noster* (*c.* 589). Some two centuries later Charlemagne imposed its use, after the gospel, in his royal chapel of Aachen. Certain monks took the usage to Jerusalem where it aroused bitter theological controversy with the Greeks (807). Pope LEO III, appealed to by the Latin monks, sent in answer the form of the Creed recited in Rome and informed Charlemagne of his reply. The emperor held a council on the question in Aachen (809) and tried to obtain Leo's approval. "So do I think and hold," Leo replied in regard to the doctrine. On the matter of the addition, Leo stated: "We do not presume either in reciting or in teaching to add by inserting anything into that Creed." And he advised the emperor by slow stages to drop the recital of the Creed in the Mass. To stress his attitude he had two silver shields made, one with the Latin, the other with the Greek text of the Creed, neither with the addition; these he placed in front of the confession in Saint Peter's. The filioque, however, was finally inserted into the Creed also in Rome, probably *c.* 1013, at the insistance of the Emperor HENRY II. Even so, there were places where the filioque was omitted, e.g., Paris as late as 1240, without that implying any doubt about the doctrine. The addition was the subject of all 14 sessions in Ferrara of the Council of Ferrara-Florence. The Greeks asserted that any addition of a word or syllable to the Creed had been forbidden at EPHESUS (431); the Latins maintained that only change of the faith, and not of the words in the Creed, was intended. The decree of Florence defined that "the filioque was added to the Creed licitly and reasonably to expound the truth, and under the spur of necessity."

Later History. The unionistic effects of the Council of Florence soon faded and the filioque, both as addition and as doctrine, continued to be a chief subject of controversy. Old Catholics and Anglicans, Russian, Greek, Romanian, and Serbian Orthodox at Bonn in 1874 and 1875, agreed on its illegality as an addition, and tried to find a common basis of doctrine in six propositions taken from Saint John Damascene. The result was controversy among Russian theologians, and the assertion in a Council of Saint Petersburg in 1892 that "from the Father only" is part of Orthodox doctrine. In 1956 in conversations with Anglicans (who readily admit the illegitimacy of the addition but do not deny its truth or omit it from the Creed), the Russians held firm to their old positions. The Greek Churches also, though with less inflexibility, have the same views.

While the See of Rome insists that all the Eastern Churches that are in communion with it accept the doctrine of the filioque, it nevertheless does not impose its inclusion in the Creed. This is evidenced in the second Council of LYONS (though NICHOLAS III demanded it in 1278), Florence (though CALLISTUS III imposed it in 1457), CLEMENT VIII for the union of the Ruthenians (Ukrainians, Byelorussians) at Brest-Litovsk in 1596 (though the Ruthenians at the Council of Zamosc in 1720 imposed it on themselves). BENEDICT XIV in 1742 ruled that the Greeks were under no obligation to recite it, and such has since that time been the accepted position in the Eastern Catholic Churches.

Despite Latin efforts to minimize the doctrinal differences, the controversy over the *filioque* continued to divide East and West. In the 19th century Old Catholics and Anglicans, Russian, Greek, Romanian, and Serbian Orthodox meeting in Bonn (1874 and 1875), agreed that the unilateral addition of the phrase on the part of the West was illegitimate. The Old Catholics deleted the *filioque* from the Creed, and, at the request of the Greek and Russian delegates, the Bonn group endorsed six propositions taken from the works of Saint John Damascene as expressing ''the doctrine of the ancient undivided Church.'' Proposition three stated, ''The Holy Spirit proceeds from the Father through the Son.'' The attempt, however, to find in the works of Saint John Damascene a formula that expressed their common belief regarding the procession of the Holy Spirit, resulted in a controversy among the Russian Orthodox. As a result the Council of Saint Petersburg (1892) declared that ''from the Father only'' is a tenet of Orthodox doctrine. Nonetheless, in 1931 an Anglican-Orthodox Joint Doctrinal Commission reaffirmed that ''through the Son'' was useful as a unifying formula.

Altering the Creed. Although Russian theologians held firm to their position as recently as 1956 in conversations with Anglicans, the climate of the discussion changed noticeably as ecumenical efforts intensified in the years after Vatican II. At a meeting of the Joint Doctrinal Commission of Anglicans and Orthodox in Moscow in 1976, the Anglican delegates repudiated the *filioque* because the sentence in the Ecumenical Creed about the Spirit proceeding from the Father addresses the Spirit's eternal *procession*, not the historical *mission*; the interpolation of the *filioque* was made without universal agreement of the churches and the Creed constitutes the public confession of faith by the people of God in the Eucharist. The 1978 Lambeth Conference endorsed the Moscow statement and asked the churches of the Anglican communion to consider returning to the original wording of the Ecumenical Creed, that is, to drop the *filioque* from the text. In 1981 the Anglican Consultative Commission reported the responses of the individual provinces, but recommended that no unilateral alterations be made before the 1988 Lambeth Conference. Meanwhile in 1985 the Episcopal Church in America went on record in favor of dropping the *filioque* from the Creed.

Many Roman Catholic theologians, notably Yves Congar, favor deleting the *filioque* from the Creed ''as a gesture of humility and brotherhood on the part of the Roman Catholic Church which might have wide-reaching ecumenical implications'' (*I Believe,* III. 206). In May of 1973, the Greek Catholic hierarchy decided to follow the precedent of other Eastern churches in communion with the Roman See in suppressing the formula in the Greek text of the Creed. Pope John Paul II in several statements commemorating the 16th centenary of the Council of Constantinople quoted the third article of the Creed without the *filioque.*

The Faith and Order Commission of the World Council of Churches organized consultations in 1978 and 1979 to deal with the controversy. By way of a final report, the consultations drafted a memorandum stating, ''The restoration of unity is inconceivable if agreement is not reached on the formal and substantial justification for this formula.'' The memorandum, ''one of the most important and balanced statements ever produced on this thorny issue'' (Fahey, 667), asserts:

> the Son is indeed not alien to the procession of the Spirit, nor the Spirit to the begetting of the Son—something which has also been indicated in Eastern theology when it has spoken of the Spirit as 'resting upon' or 'shining out through' the Son, and insisted that the generation of the Son and the procession of the Spirit must be *distinguished* but not *separated.*

The report further noted that the Old Catholic Church had already suppressed the *filioque* in the liturgy and that the Anglican Communion was seriously considering a similar move. Among its recommendations was the suggestion ''that the original form of the third article of the Creed, without the *filioque*, should everywhere be recognized as the normative one and restored.'' In his preface to the report, however, Lukas Visher cautioned churches against taking separate decisions for ''the way to communion among the churches can be opened up only by an agreement for which they take joint responsibility.''

The International Consultation on Common Texts included a translation of *filioque* in the English version of the Ecumenical Creed, but put it in brackets with an indication that some churches do not use it.

Bibliography: J. N. D. KELLY, *Early Christian Creeds* (2d ed. London 1960). J. GILL, *The Council of Florence* (Cambridge, England 1959). K. WARE and C. DAVEY eds., *Anglican-Orthodox Dialogue: The Moscow Statement Agreed by the Anglican-Orthodox Joint Doctrinal Commission 1976* (London 1977). H. KÜNG and J.

MOLTMANN, "Conflicts About the Holy Spirit," *Concilium* 128 (New York 1979). *Spirit of God, Spirit of Christ. Ecumenical Reflections on the Filioque Controversy*, Faith and Order Paper 103 (Geneva 1981). Y. M. J. CONGAR, *I Believe in the Holy Spirit*, v. 3 (New York 1983). M. A. FAHEY, "Orthodox Ecumenism and Theology: 1978–83," *Theological Studies* 44 (1983) 625–92.

[J. GILL/B. L. MARTHALER]

FILIPPINI, LUCY, ST.

Foundress of the Pontifical Institute of the Religious Teachers Filippini; b. Tarquinia, Italy, Jan. 13, 1672; d. Montefiascone, March 25, 1732. As a child she helped her pastor to teach catechism. When she was 16, Cardinal Marc'Antonio BARBARIGO, Bishop of Montefiascone, sent her to a monastery of nuns, where under his guidance, she prepared for her future mission. She remained there until 1692, when she joined Bl. Rose Venerini (until Lucy took over completely in 1694) in the work of educating the poorer girls of the diocese (*see* VENERINI SISTERS). On Oct. 15, 1704, the community was formally established, receiving their rule and habit from the cardinal and pronouncing their Oblation. After the death of the cardinal in 1706, the community was called to Rome by CLEMENT XI, developing into the institute of today, which is under the sponsorship of the Apostolic Almoner. From 1828 to 1896 there was an organizational division in the institute, which has some 2,000 members in about 180 houses in Italy, England, Brazil, Canada, Switzerland, and the United States. Lucy, noted for great virtue, was beatified June 13, 1926, and canonized June 22, 1930.

Feast: March 25.

Bibliography: P. P. PARENTE, *Schoolteacher and Saint* (St. Meinrad, Ind. 1954). J. A. ABBO, *L'Istituto delle Maestre Pie Filippini e la Santa Sede* (Rome 1962). G. BASILE and G. CALABRESE, *Forever yes* (Philadelphia 1979). P. BERGAMASCHI, *From the Land of the Etruscans,* tr. M. MARCHIONE (Rome 1986).

[M. MARCHIONE]

FILIPPUCCI, ALESSANDRO FRANCESCO SAVERIO

Jesuit missionary in China and Japan for 32 years; b. Macerata, Italy, Jan. 5, 1632; d. Macau, Aug. 15, 1692. He became a Jesuit in 1651, and in 1658 was cured of a serious illness through the intercession of St. Francis Xavier. In 1660 he left for China, arriving there in 1663. At Macau he held the posts of novice-master and professor of literature until 1671, when he was assigned to parish work in Guangdong (Kwantung) Province. He saw his residence destroyed during an uprising against the Emperor in 1676. After serving as provincial for Japan from 1680 to 1683, and superior in Guangzhou (Canton) from 1683 to 1688, he was named visitor of the missions in China and Japan from 1688 to 1691. He collected the letters of St. Francis Xavier that were later included in Possuine's edition. He also wrote a work in defense of the Jesuits in the controversy of the CHINESE RITES (Lyons 1700).

Bibliography: L. PFISTER, *Notices biographiques et bibliographiques,* 2 v. (Shanghai 1932–34). *Dizionario ecclesiastico* 1:1118.

[B. LAHIFF]

FILLASTRE, GUILLAUME

The name of two French ecclesiastics.

Fillastre, Guillaume, French cardinal, canonist, humanist, geographer; b. Le Maine, *c.* 1348; d. Rome, Nov. 6, 1428. As *doctor juris utriusque* Fillastre taught law at Reims and was later dean there. He lived at the time of the WESTERN SCHISM, and first distinguished himself at the Synod of Paris, 1406, where Fillastre was the handpicked defender of BENEDICT XIII the antipope. But within the next three years—possibly at the Council of PISA (1409)—both Fillastre and his friend PETER OF AILLY changed their allegiance to the antipope JOHN XXIII, who named them cardinals in 1411. At the Council of CONSTANCE (1415–17) Fillastre called for the resignation of the three papal contenders, GREGORY XII, as well as his own former benefactors, Benedict XIII and John XXIII. Fillastre entered the controversy on CONCILIARISM when he insisted on the superiority of councils over the pope. The diary he kept at Constance became a principal source for the council. It was Fillastre's vote in the French "nation" during the last session of the council (1417) that ensured the election of Martin V as pope. Martin appointed Fillastre *legatus a latere* to France (1418) and later, archpriest of the Latern basilica. In 1422 he gave up his See of Aix, which he had held *in commendam* since 1414, for the See of Saint-Pons-de-Thomières. Besides his theological and canonical writings Fillastre annotated a number of Plato's works, and was much interested in Ptolemy's geography.

Fillastre, Guillaume, French abbot, bishop, statesman; b. Le Maine *c.* 1400; d. Ghent, Aug. 21, 1473. He may have been a nephew of the preceding. Fillastre was a Benedictine at Châlons-sur-Marne when he became abbot of Saint-Thierry of Reims (1431). In 1436 he received a doctorate in Canon Law from Louvain. He became bishop of Verdun in 1437, commendatory abbot of SAINT-BERTIN AT ST. OMER (1447), and bishop of Toul

(1449). He was already closely associated with Philip the Good of Burgundy when, in 1461, he became bishop of Tournai. Philip named him first councilor (1463) of his Council of State, and chancellor (1460) of the Order of Golden Fleece. He served on diplomatic missions to both the French king and the pope. His writings included a work entitled *La Toison d'Or, the Chronique de l'histoire de France,* and a French translation of *Troyennes istoires.* He left his wealth to the abbeys and dioceses he had governed.

Bibliography: L. SALEMBIER, *Dictionnaire de théologie catholique* 5.2:2343–52. G. MOLLAT, *Catholicisme* 4:1286–89. J. WODKA, *Lexikon für Theologie und Kirche* 2 4:128.

[J. F. JOLLEY]

FINAL CAUSALITY

The type of CAUSALITY exercised by the END (Lat. *finis*). In Aristotelian philosophy and in the medieval scholastic philosophy derived from it, the term ''cause'' had broader signification than in modern usage; it meant ''that on which something depends for its existence in any way,'' and not merely an extrinsic agent. According to Aristotle any corruptible substance depends for its existence on some other substance that has produced it (its efficient cause), on its intrinsic constituents (its formal and material causes), and on a goal, or *telos* (its final cause). This *telos* may be another substance for whose sake it has been produced (its *extrinsic* final cause); e.g., wheat is grown for the nourishment of man. Or it may simply be the full development of the substance itself (its *intrinsic* final cause), e.g., the maturity of the wheat plant. Thus the final cause need not preexist the process of which it is the cause, but may actually be the effect of this process. In this case it preexists only as a tendency in the efficient cause, as the tendency to mature growth preexists in the grain of wheat.

This article discusses the historical development of the concept of final causality in ancient and medieval philosophy and the value of the concept in various areas of philosophy and theology. (For the modern development of the concept and its use in the sciences, *see* TELEOLOGY.)

HISTORICAL DEVELOPMENT

Primitive man tended to interpret all phenomena in human terms, and hence was inclined to attribute purpose to all natural events. At the same time he was likely to think even of human behavior as determined by powers and traditional rules whose purpose is mysterious. Thus mythology often pictures the world as governed by an inscrutable and impersonal FATE, destiny, or necessity, to which even the gods are subject.

Greek Philosophy. Pre-Socratic GREEK PHILOSOPHY attempted to explain the world in terms of matter and forces, such as heat and cold, or in terms of quantitative proportions (Pythagoreans), and made little use of the concept of purpose. The atomistic systems, which were the most developed product of this first period of philosophic thought, positively rejected the concept. Thus EMPEDOCLES attributed the evolution of living things to chance combination of parts. Leucippus and DEMOCRITUS explained all things as chance combinations of atoms that had an innate tendency to fall; but their fall was in an infinite void, hence without any *telos.* This radical espousal of a cosmos without inherent purpose remains the classical position in opposition to the doctrine of final causality. It was later adopted by the Epicureans and revived during the Renaissance. (*See* ATOMISM; MATERIALISM.)

ANAXAGORAS, however, suggested that the flux of matter must originate with Mind, and Diogenes of Apollonia states explicitly:

> Such a distribution would not have been possible without Intelligence, namely, that all things should have their measure: winter and summer and night and day and rains and winds and periods of fine weather; other things also, if one will study them closely, will be found to have the best possible arrangement. [Simplicius, *Physics* 252.11.]

SOCRATES also seems to have held this conviction. It is forcefully put by PLATO, especially in the *Timaeus.* where he explains the visible universe as a result of a kind of compromise between reason, which produces order and purpose in all things, and necessity, which is a kind of material principle resisting the order that reason seeks to impose. Thus the world is intelligible as an imperfect imitation of Intelligence.

Aristotelian Analysis. ARISTOTLE (rightly, it seems) claimed to be the first to give an analytic account of final causality (*Meta.* 988b 10). For him the final cause is the ''cause of the causes,'' which must be known to give a complete explanation of any natural process. MATTER cannot exist without FORM, and form itself is produced in matter by some extrinsic AGENT, or efficient cause. The efficient cause does not produce an indeterminate action, however, since natural processes are observed to be regular. Hence, before the efficient cause begins to act it must be predetermined in a specific way to produce a definite effect. This predetermination, or specific tendency toward a goal, is final causality.

In intelligent beings this goal preexists in the knower as conscious purpose. In brute animals it preexists as an image of something desired. In plants and inanimate substances it preexists as NATURE, an unconscious inner tendency to specific activities or passivities.

Besides this innate purposiveness in the individual substances that make up the cosmos, there is also a general cosmic order; according to this, elements tend to form compounds; inanimate compounds are used as nourishment by plants; plants are similarly used by animals; and animals and all other things are used in the service of man. Man finds his happiness not in himself but in contemplation of the cosmic order and of the higher spiritual beings that it manifests. Not every phenomenon in the universe, however, has a purpose. The cosmos is not a single substance but many substances, each pursuing its own end—not all of them in perfect harmony. Furthermore, the material character of the visible world makes the activities of each substance liable to chance encounters and to frustration (*see* CHANCE). Hence it is not possible to use teleological explanation as a means of prediction. Rather it is a backward-looking analysis by which, from the observation of a goal already achieved, the steps that were necessary to its achievement are discovered.

Stoics and Neoplatonists. After Aristotle, the Stoics and Neoplatonists both defended finality without conceding it a really vital role. The Stoics held that the universe, including man, operates by an absolutely deterministic NATURAL LAW. In such a view, teleology is no longer found in individual substances but is the fixed pattern of the cosmos as a whole. The Neoplatonists tended to treat the order in the cosmos in a static, as opposed to a dynamic, sense and thus to reduce finality to exemplarity (a type of extrinsic formal causality). The universe became, for them, a hierarchy of more and more perfect imitations of the One rather than a system of diverse things, each seeking its own end and all coordinated by a First Mover.

Medieval Thought. The philosophers and theologians of the earlier Middle Ages (whether Jewish, Christian, or Islamic) remained within the Neoplatonist perspective, reinforced by the scriptural emphasis on divine providence and on the conception of God as the goal of the entire universe. The Christian apologists frequently stressed the argument for God's existence from order in the cosmos, but it is with St. JOHN DAMASCENE in the 8th century that the famous teleological proof for God's existence was first clearly formulated.

The renewal of ARISTOTELIANISM returned the concept of final causality to its central role. St. ALBERT THE GREAT and St. THOMAS AQUINAS organized both their philosophy and their theology on a teleological plan. They saw the whole universe as a plurality of beings, each endowed with a nature or principle of appropriate action; higher beings are endowed also with intelligence and free will. Under the governance of God, which is shared in a measure with created ministers, each of these beings tends toward its own goal, which is to reflect some specific aspect of God's perfection and to contribute to the universal order of the cosmos that is also His reflection. This reflection of God in nature, however, is not the best possible, since no created being or group of beings can be anything but an imperfect imitation of the infinite God. Nor is the order of nature infallible, since it is subject to chance, conflict, and sin. God's governance, however, ensures that the natural order cannot be wholly corrupted and that it will finally attain to the goal He has ordained for it.

According to St. Thomas, philosophy comes to a knowledge of the final causality of particular things by an observation of natural processes, since these for the most part (but not invariably) achieve their goal. The final causality of the universe as a whole, however, is mysterious and can only be conjectured, unless reason is aided by divine revelation.

The later scholastics turned away from this thoroughly teleological position. John DUNS SCOTUS, by his radical insistence on divine freedom, seemed to weaken the role of *telos* as the objective determinant of love. The dynamism of the world came to be seen more as an expression of inner indeterminacy and freedom than as goal-seeking activity. For the nominalists, led by WILLIAM OF OCKHAM, final causality is simply a name given to the efficient cause considered as producing an effect. It was this position, reinforced by the Platonic mathematicism of the Renaissance, that bore fruit in the denial of final causality by GALILEO and Francis BACON.

VALUE OF THE CONCEPT

Despite these various interpretations, the concept of final causality has great value when properly employed in philosophy and theology. This part of the article attempts to explain its value and use, treating successively of the philosophy of nature, metaphysics, and theology.

Philosophy of Nature. For Immanuel KANT the principle of finality is of heuristic value in science. Man, that he may give intelligible order to the data of experience, tends inevitably to see the world as if it were a construct designed for a purpose. The problem, however, is this: Is there in nature itself a teleological order that man must grasp in order to understand nature as it is?

Intimations of Finality. This problem is created first of all by the language used in talking about nature. It has been observed that no matter how antiteleological a scientist may be, he can only with the greatest difficulty avoid terms such as function, tendency, maturity, and growth. Sometimes he coins new words (e.g., teleonomy or directiveness) for teleology, which on examination could mean the same thing. The methods of modern analytical philosophy can be applied to scientific discourse to show that it is extremely difficult to eliminate every implication of means-goal relationships from the way one talks about the world, except by confining oneself to a purely mathematical language. The moment that a physical, dynamic interpretation is given to the mathematical formalism, this notion tends again to enter.

Psychological studies of children and of primitive peoples show that the concepts of causality and of final causality are not childish but are the product of psychological maturation. They represent the growing human being's achievement of self-conscious control over his own behavior and are his recognition of regularities in the environment that are independent of himself.

In applying the phenomenological method to experience, one again becomes aware not only that his own behavior in exploring experience is teleological, to the extent that it is a search for order and intelligibility, but also that he is confronted in his experience with objects that "go their own way," i.e., with patterns of behavior that are not his, but that he comes gradually to recognize and to understand. For example, the child playing with a dog comes to appreciate that the dog has a life of its own, analogous to that of the child, yet also very different. Certainly if experience did not manifest this teleological character of behavior to man, it would itself be of little value.

Existentialist philosophers similarly emphasize two facets of experience that give rise to teleological interpretations. One is the experience of LOVE, wherein one person feels himself drawn irresistibly to another, who becomes a goal. In this experience man discovers that, in a sense, his whole being is seeking for another person who is not possessed, and yet in being loved is somehow already his. Thus man is predetermined to union with another, and in the process of attaining the other discovers himself, since the other is almost more he than he is himself.

The other experience is that of FREEDOM. Love is not necessarily free; it may have the character of blind passion. Yet the most perfect love is one in which the self is given freely, so that in losing himself the lover finds himself, i.e., performs the most independent and deliberate of acts, a free act. Nevertheless some existentialists, such as J. P. Sartre, seem to deny the possibility of a real self-giving and self-finding, and also give to freedom an arbitrary and goalless character, as if man is free only when he acts without a motive (*see* EXISTENTIALISM).

Positivist and idealist philosophers are kept from any consideration of the teleological problems by their complete rejection of causal explanations. Marxists, on the other hand, return pretty much to the old Stoic position: there is no individual causality, but a universal dialectical trend inherent in the material universe as a whole. This position has much in common with that of P. TEILHARD DE CHARDIN, who detects in the universe a single evolutionary process moving toward a single goal.

Finality in Nature. Perhaps a more fruitful approach to the question is to consider the problem in its original terms. An examination of the world reveals certain obvious regular processes that repeat themselves again and again. These are noticed, however, in an ocean of other processes that appear random and unique. Science attempts to discover additional regularities in this sea of apparent randomness, proceeding on the conviction, based on experience, that a hidden order is often present. Science need not, however, make the dogmatic assumption of determination, viz, that all events in the world exhibit regularities, since in many well-explored situations events that are obviously casual can be found.

In discovering regular processes, which can be called natural, one also detects natural units, i.e., things that are the subjects of these processes and are relatively independent of the surrounding sea of events. If such units did not exist, it would be impossible to be sure even of regularities, since there is an unresolvable paradox in the notion of a process that has no subject and that comes to be from nothing. In the case of higher animals, such a unit is obvious in the ORGANISM. It is more difficult to identify in the case of the lower animals and plants, but this obscurity often yields to further observation. In the inanimate world, modern science has practically identified the free molecule and the free atom as such units.

Given a natural unit undergoing natural processes that can be observationally and even experimentally identified, the problem of analyzing and specifying each process remains. As Aristotle indicated, the notion of a process of natural change implies four aspects. The process goes on in a subject (material cause); it results in a modification of this subject (formal cause); it cannot in an exact sense be attributed to the subject itself, since a thing cannot produce itself or give what it does not yet have, but must be produced by another thing (efficient cause). The process, if regularly repeated, must end in a specific effect that gives it character and identity (final cause). This effect either must be destructive of the subject, or it must preserve and protect the subject, or it must contribute to the good of the system. If simply destructive, it cannot be said to be natural in a primary sense, because on the disappearance of the subject the process is no longer identifiable. Hence, in a natural process the effect is good or desirable and is sought as a preservation and development of the subject or of the system. But this specific effect must have been predetermined in the agent; otherwise it would not tend to reoccur regularly. How does it exist in the agent? It can be there only as the nature of the agent—i.e., its inner tendency to a certain sort of goal-directed behavior—or as the intelligence of an agent who is able to choose what sort of action he will perform to attain a desired goal. It is this directiveness of natural processes and of the things that produce them, which is not by chance or by strict necessity but to or for a goal, that is final causality in its primary sense. Goal-directed behavior is for the sake of the goal and depends upon the goal at least in direction or intention, without which it cannot be.

Such explanations are needed in studying the natural world because, with the element of chance in the universe, man cannot really predict the future. Any natural process may be frustrated. Hence scientific explanation is fundamentally backward-looking. It begins with some completed effect, a regularly reoccurring subject that has undergone a process by which it has come into existence and reached a stable existence in the world. Analysis, assisted by observation and experiment, can determine what factors were necessary for this process to reach its term. This is explanation in terms of final causality.

Metaphysics. Although the term metaphysical is often used to indicate any philosophical analysis and philosophy, in turn, is used to indicate any analysis of basic principles in a field of study, few philosophers have admitted the existence of METAPHYSICS, in the strict sense, as a valid discipline. Metaphysics, in the sense intended by the Aristotelian school, is a discipline based on the power of reason to prove the existence of spiritual substances—at least a spiritual part of man and a first principle that is independent of matter. It proposes that both spiritual and material substances can be studied in terms of the common notion of BEING, i.e., in terms of what is common to matter and spirit and dependent upon the same first principle. One of the problems of such a metaphysics is to determine whether the principles of causality discovered in a restricted sense, for the material realm, have universal and absolute validity, so that they apply to all being.

It is established in such a metaphysics that the First Efficient Cause, the Unmoved Mover, cannot itself have a cause, since it undergoes no process; on the other hand, it must be the ultimate final cause of all things that undergo any sort of process, whether a physical change or some sort of spiritual change analogous to physical change. Seeing that efficient and final causality are correlative, the First Efficient Cause must be also the Ultimate Final Cause; i.e., God creates and governs all things in view of His own perfection, which creatures share and imitate since there is no other ultimate perfection.

Nevertheless, it does not follow, as many philosophers have thought, that particular creatures lack a proper final causality of their own, any more than they lack a proper efficient causality. Since creatures truly participate in being by the gift of God, they also imitate Him in being true causes. Hence every created nature must either by nature or by choice seek an end that is its own perfection. Since creatures form a universe, there must also be a relation of lower to higher ends under the ultimate end. This fact of final causality does not, however, exclude the existence of chance events and of contingency. Every created good is finite and hence is the object of God's free choice. When God freely chooses to create something He does not make it to be necessary but contingent. Similarly, among material things the plurality of causes permits genuine chance, although this too falls under divine providence.

This method of establishing the universal necessity of final causality, beginning with induction from sense experience and then extending the physical principle to metaphysics by way of analogy based on a causal relation between God and the world, is not followed by all Thomists. Some Neothomists wish to establish this necessity by an analysis of the concept of being, showing that the notion of being must include the notion of ultimate determination. However, such a way seems open to accusations of verbalism. Other Neothomists wish to bypass the whole order of induction from external reality and to establish final causality in terms of necessary conditions of thought—a way open to objection as Cartesian or Kantian.

Theology. St. Thomas Aquinas uses the idea of finality to organize his entire theological scheme. Thus, in the *Summa contra gentiles,* bk. 3, he gives a broad panorama of the universe showing all things as going forth from God by creation and returning to God by finality. Angels and men attain to the contemplation of God and thus are intended by Him as true final causes in their own right, themselves forming a society. Thus the extrinsic final cause of the universe is God, whereas its intrinsic final cause is the contemplative society of rational creatures. The irrational universe, in turn, is ordered to the good of the rational universe. It serves man's physical needs and in this respect is not needed by the angels. But it serves both men and angels as a mirror in which they contemplate certain reflections of God that are not found in the spiritual universe. Also, through sharing in God's governance over the material universe, both men and angels participate in God's creative action. (*See* UNIVERSE, ORDER OF.)

In the *Summa theologiae* this conception is further developed, with emphasis being placed on the fact that man is a dynamic image of God, perfectly realized in Jesus Christ, in whom the whole visible cosmos is redeemed and consummated.

When discussing the finality attributed to Christ, Duns Scotus differs from Aquinas in hypothesizing (some of his disciples were less cautious) that the motive of the Incarnation was the perfecting of the universe, so that even if man had not sinned the Incarnation would have taken place. Aquinas, on the other hand, argues that the Incarnation was primarily for the sake of redeeming man from sin. Both Scotus and Aquinas agree that the universe has the Incarnation as its final cause, an elevation beyond its original goal; but for Aquinas this elevation is wholly a free act of mercy, occasioned by a tragic fall.

The argument from finality lies at the basis of the medieval scholastic ''arguments from convenience,'' since ''convenience,'' or ''fittingness,'' is seen by looking backward from an end already known to be accomplished. Post-Tridentine theology has become suspicious of this type of reasoning and tends to substitute in its place the methods of positive theology. However, the argument from convenience is legitimate if understood within its proper limits. Indeed, modern exegetical scholarship shows that the revelation contained in Scripture is fundamentally eschatological. The events of salvation history all take on their meaning in terms of the ultimate goal, the kingdom of God in which the whole cosmos is subject to Christ and He to God. Hence every theological problem must involve the question of the reference to the *eschaton,* from which all theological meaning is ultimately derived.

In current Catholic thought this great importance of finality is emphasized in the writings of Teilhard de Chardin, who has attempted to give a Christian synthesis of modern science by seeing the entire process of creation as directed to ''the Omega point.'' That this attempt has been illuminating and satisfying not only for Christians but for non-Christians seems to signalize the frustration modern man encounters when he looks for intelligibility in a purely mechanistic picture of the universe. The question is, however, whether this grandiose scheme does not suffer the same weaknesses that in the past have so often discredited teleology, namely, that it tries to explain the universe in a monistic manner, either ignoring sin and freedom or treating them as the product of a single law. The more modest concept of Aquinas—which sees the universe as a pluralistic structure of interrelated things and persons, each pursuing the tendency of its own nature or the choices of its free will, beset by chance and contingency but coordinated by God to a unified goal, yet to be attained only at the cost of tragedy—seems closer to reality and more compatible with the plurality of sciences and the data of revelation.

See Also: FINALITY, PRINCIPLE OF; NATURE.

Bibliography: P. A. R. JANET, *Final Causes,* 5th ed. tr. W. AFFLECK (New York 1905). R. GARRIGOU-LAGRANGE, *Le Réalisme du principe de finalité* (Paris 1932). A. MANSION, *Introduction à la physique aristotélicienne* (2d ed. Louvain 1946) 251–281. F. SOLMSEN, *Aristotle's System of the Physical World* (Ithaca, N.Y. 1960) 92–117. A. VAN MELSEN, *The Philosophy of Nature* (Duquesne Studies Philos. Ser. 2; Pittsburgh 1953) 159–161. M. A. BUNGE, *Causality* (Cambridge, Mass. 1959) ch. 2. A. PAP, *An Introduction to the Philosophy of Science* (Glencoe, Ill. 1962) 359–364. P. TEILHARD DE CHARDIN, *The Phenomenon of Man,* tr. B. WALL (New York 1959). B. M. ASHLEY, ''Research into the Intrinsic Final Causes of Physical Things,'' *American Catholic Philosophical Association. Proceedings of the Annual Meeting* 26 (1952) 185–194.

[B. M. ASHLEY]

FINALITY, PRINCIPLE OF

A principle commonly accepted by scholastic philosophers as one of the FIRST PRINCIPLES; it is succinctly stated by St. Thomas Aquinas: ''Every agent acts for an end'' (*C. gent.* 3.2), i.e., all beings when acting tend to some definite effect.

Explanation. The principle applies only analogously to intelligent and to nonintelligent beings. An intelligent being, qua intelligent, can know and freely elect the proximate end for which he is acting; a nonintelligent being, however, does not formally know the end to which its action tends, even though it is the agent tending to that end, i.e., even though the action is its own. Regardless of the agent acting, its tending toward an end (which scholastics regard as a CONDITION *sine qua non* of acting) connotes intelligence, inasmuch as such action is orderly. If intelligence is not manifested on the part of the agent that acts, then it is presupposed on the part of another being who directs the agent to so act. This other being may direct the agent in a wholly extrinsic manner, as a writer moves the pen to inscribe words, or it may direct the agent by placing certain tendencies or appetites within its very nature.

Tendency or APPETITE, in this context, must also be understood analogously. It may denote an intellectual, a sensory, or a natural appetite—the last being manifested by the empirically observable fact that all things tend to preserve their being (*Summa theologiae* 1a2ae, 94.2). End is then related to appetite as its object; it is something suitable, and hence GOOD, for the agent. It is suitable or good because the agent has a particular nature and because its tendencies are the basis for actions that realize or perfect that nature. Thus understood in this manner, the principle of finality implies a limited kind of determinism.

The principle of finality is closely related to the principle of INTELLIGIBILITY, which states that all being is intelligible. Those who deny the latter principle are led to reject the principle of finality, considering it anthropomorphist in inspiration. Francis BACON and Immanuel KANT thus attacked the validity of the principle of finality, and, more recently, so have Julian Huxley and Ernest Nagel. To obviate such criticism, one must bear in mind the following clarifications.

Clarifications. The principle does not claim, as some have misinterpreted it to, that every effect is for an end. It merely asserts that every agent acts for an end. Thus chance events do not invalidate the principle of finality (*see* CHANCE). Neither does the principle state that every agent actually attains the end for which it acts; even if impeded from attainment, the agent originates activity that is end-directed. In fact, at root, the denial of finality implies a denial of activity. Finality promotes activity; it moves the agent to such activity. If the agent did not act for an end, there would be no reason for it to act this way rather than that way. Being indifferent to all ends, it would be unable to act for any.

The ontological grounds for acting, and thus acting for an end, are rooted ultimately in the goodness of being. If being and the good were not convertible, there would be no activity (*see* TRANSCENDENTALS). Finality accounts as well for the regularity and UNIFORMITY manifested in the laws of nature. It makes nature predictable and scientific knowledge possible, thus providing the ontological basis for physical laws and for the moral NATURAL LAW.

It should further be noted that an end is sought because it is a principle of perfection; however, this does not necessarily imply that the end perfects principally the being acting for the end. In propagating its species, a plant acts for an end that is not so much its own perfection or good as it is the good of another. Then, too, not all elements within a system may act for the good of that system. Thus, in a sub-system encompassed within a larger whole, e.g., a parasite or mold within an organism, the parasite does not perfect the parent organism; rather it seeks its own good.

The fact that great caution must be exercised when identifying the particular end for which an agent acts does not nullify the general principle that agents do act for ends. Such ends are many and varied in the order of nature. While some are primary and others secondary, all are so interrelated as to manifest, to the discerning observer, the existence of God, the Author of nature (*see* GOD, PROOFS FOR THE EXISTENCE OF).

See Also: END; FINAL CAUSALITY; TELEOLOGY.

Bibliography: R. BUSA and C. NEGRO, *Enciclopedia filosofica* (Venice-Rome 1957) 2:438–439. A. WENZL, *Lexikon für Theologie und Kirche,* ed. J. HOFER and K. RAHNER (Freiburg 1957–65) 4:132–133. H. J. KOREN, *An Introduction to the Science of Metaphysics* (St. Louis 1955). V. E. SMITH, *Philosophical Physics* (New York 1950). R. GARRIGOU-LAGRANGE, *Le Réalisme du principe de finalité* (Paris 1932).

[G. F. KREYCHE]

FÍNÁN CAM, ST.

Irish abbot; b. County Kerry, Ireland, sixth century. It is thought that he was educated by St. Brendan of Clonfert (d. 578), and thus would have flourished in the sixth century (*see* BRENDAN, SS.). Fínán (Finnian or Fionain, fair-haired) Cam (the squinting) is probably the saint of Church Island, Lough Currane, County Kerry. His principal monastic foundation was made at Kinnity, County Offaly, under the Slieve Bloom mountains. In Kerry, Fínán is the object of local devotion, but in the vitae and in the public mind he has been hopelessly confused with Finan Lobur (the infirm), who, in fact, was never in Kerry.

Feast: April 7.

Bibliography: C. PLUMMER, comp., *Vitae sanctorum Hiberniae,* 2 v. (Oxford 1910) 2:87–95. J. F. KENNEY, *The Sources for the Early History of Ireland:* v.1, *Ecclesiastical* (New York 1929) 421–422. F. HENRY, ''Early Monasteries . . . (Co. Kerry),'' *Proceedings of the Royal Irish Academy* 58, sec. C (1957) 45–166. D. D. C. POCHIN MOULD, *The Irish Saints* (Dublin 1964) 158–159.

[D. D. C. POCHIN MOULD]

FINAN OF LINDISFARNE, ST.

Monk and bishop; d. Aug. 31, 661. He is called in Irish Fínán mac Rímedo and almost certainly was a native of Ireland. He was a monk at the Abbey of IONA before he succeeded AIDAN as bishop of LINDISFARNE, probably in 651. He set about extending the faith outside Northumbria and baptized Kings Peada (d. 656) of the Middle Angles and Sigebert (fl. 616–658) of the East Saxons. Later, he appointed bishops for their kingdoms: Diuma (d. 658) to the Middle Angles and CEDD, an Anglo-Saxon, to the East Saxons. At Lindisfarne he built a church, *more Scottorum,* a wooden structure with a thatched roof. He was an intransigent upholder of Celtic customs until his death. Pope LEO XIII extended his feast to the Scottish Church in 1898.

Feast: Jan. 19 (formerly Feb. 17).

Bibliography: BEDE, *Ecclesiastical History: The Annals of Ulster,* ed. and tr. W. M. HENNESSY and B. MACCARTHY, 4 v. (Dublin 1887–1901) v.1, under year 659. *The Martyrology of Tallaght,* ed. R. I. BEST and H. J. LAWLOR (H. Bradshaw Soc. 68; London 1931)

6. *A Dictionary of Christian Biography,* ed. W. SMITH and H. WACE, (London 1877–87) 2:516. L. GOUGAUD, *Christianity in Celtic Lands,* tr. M. JOYNT (London 1932) 138. *The Dictionary of National Biography From the Earliest Times to 1900* (London 1885–1900) 6:1305–06. G. BARDY, *Catholicisme* 4:1313. J. O'HANLON, *Lives of the Irish Saints,* 8 v. (New York) 2:610.

[C. MCGRATH]

FINCH, JOHN, BL.

Yeoman farmer, lay martyr; b. ca. 1548, Eccleston, Lancashire, England; hanged, drawn, and quartered at Lancaster, April 20, 1584. Although he was raised in a well–established Protestant family, Finch converted to Catholicism after seeing the contrast between Catholics and Protestants while spending time with cousins at the Inner Temple in London. Following his marriage his home in Lancaster became a center for Catholic activity. He was himself a catechist and sheltered refugee priests until his arrest on Christmas Day 1581. While he and Fr. George Ostliffe were being held, interrogated, and tortured in the house of the earl of Derby, it was rumored that Finch had betrayed the priest and other Catholics. When neither bribes nor torture compelled Finch to reveal information about the mission, he was taken to Fleet Prison, Manchester, then to the House of Correction. Upon his refusal to attend a Protestant service, he was dragged there across the rough stone pavement by his feet. He endured three months' maltreatment prior to trial at Lancaster, April 18, 1584. The night before his execution, he testified to the faith and converted some condemned felons. His cause was introduced in Rome, Dec. 4, 1886, leading to his beatification by Pius XI on Dec. 15, 1929.

Feast of the English Martyrs: May 4 (England).

See Also: ENGLAND, SCOTLAND, AND WALES, MARTYRS OF.

Bibliography: J. H. POLLEN, *Acts of English Martyrs* (London 1891).

[K. I. RABENSTEIN]

FINGLEY (FINGLOW), JOHN, BL.

Priest, martyr; b. at Barmby-in-the-Marsh (or Barneby near Howden), Yorkshire, England; d. Aug. 8, 1586, hanged, drawn, and quartered at York. He studied at Cambridge and at Rheims, where he was ordained to the priesthood March 25, 1581. The following month he entered the mission field in northern England. He was arrested, tried, and condemned for being a Catholic priest and reconciling English subjects to the ancient Church. Fingley was beatified by Pope John Paul II on Nov. 22, 1987 with George Haydock and Companions.

Feast of the English Martyrs: May 4 (England).

See Also: ENGLAND, SCOTLAND, AND WALES, MARTYRS OF.

Bibliography: R. CHALLONER, *Memoirs of Missionary Priests,* ed. J. H. POLLEN (rev. ed. London 1924). J. H. POLLEN, *Acts of English Martyrs* (London 1891).

[K. I. RABENSTEIN]

FINIS OPERANTIS

The traditional Latin expression signifying the purpose or intention of the agent in acting, prescinding from the consideration of the *finis operis* of the act in its substance (inner construction). In created acts, the *finis operantis* may or may not coincide with, though it can never alter, the *finis operis* of the act itself. There may be an indefinite number of interior motives on the part of the agent relative to the one act; an act of theft may be motivated by avarice, or revenge, or jealousy, etc.; the marital act may be motivated by charity, justice, or carnality. An evil motive cannot change the species of an act whose *finis operis* is good; nor can a good motive change the species of an act whose *finis operis* is evil.

The concept of *finis operantis* is used not only in regard to human acts but by analogy to understand more fully divine acts. In the consideration of the divine act of creation, theology distinguishes its *finis operantis* from its *finis operis*. God's end in creating (*finis operantis*) is His own absolute goodness, the love of which moves Him to communicate to creatures a participation in His own infinite perfection H. Denzinger, *Enchiridion symbolorum* 3002). God's necessary subsistence and His infinite beatitude, which it connotes (*Ibid.* 3001), preclude, in His extradivine acts, any end other than Himself. As He is the first efficient, exemplary cause, He must be the ultimate final cause of every created being.

See Also: FINIS OPERIS; END; FINAL CAUSALITY.

Bibliography: *Dictionnaire de théologie catholique,* ed. A. VACANT et al., (Paris 1903–50) 1:1522–26. W. KERN, *Lexikon für Theologie und Kirche,* ed. J. HOFER and K. RAHNER (Freiburg 1957–65) 4:139–140. P. J. DONNELLY, ''St. Thomas and the Ultimate Purpose of Creation,'' *Theological Studies* 2 53–83; ''The Vatican Council and the End of Creation,'' *ibid.* 4 (1943) 3–33.

[M. R. E. MASTERMAN]

FINIS OPERIS

Finis operis is a traditional Latin expression signifying the end, object, or good immanent in an act to which it tends by the interior dynamism of its very being (ontologically, essentially, and necessarily), prescinding from the subjective motives of the agent of the act, or of any particular circumstances under which it is performed. The end specifies the very being and substance (inner construction) of the act.

The *finis operis* of a human act serves as the invariable basis for the consideration of any other aspect of its morality. The act of justice is ordered to give to others that which is their due; the marital act is essentially constituted by the end to which the natural physiological act is directed [cf. Pius XII, Address to Midwives, Oct. 29, 1951, *Acta Apostolicae Sedis,* 43 (1951) 835–854; L. Lochet, ''Les Fins du mariage,'' *Nouvelle revue théologique* 73 (1951) 449–465].

The *finis operis* of the divine act of creation is the communication of divine goodness to creatures, whereby each creature by reason of its nature mirrors the divine perfections according to the degree of its participation in divine goodness. Intellectual creatures by their love and praise of the divine goodness attain their own beatitude, which is the secondary end (*finis operis*) of their creation. In reality, however, the primary and secondary ends are identical, for the intellectual creature's own beatitude is the attainment of the intrinsic essential divine goodness known and loved in the beatific vision.

See Also: FINIS OPERANTIS; END; FINAL CAUSALITY.

Bibliography: *Dictionnaire de théologie catholique,* ed. A. VACANT et al., 15 v. (Paris 1903–50; Tables générales 1951–), Tables générales 1:1522–26. W. KERN, *Lexikon für Theologie und Kirche,* ed. J. HOFER and K. RAHNER, 10 v. (2d, new ed. Freiburg 1957–65) 4:139–140. C. SCHAHL, *La Doctrine des fins du mariage dans le théologie scolastique* (Paris 1948).

[M. R. E. MASTERMAN]

FINITE BEING

Finite being, deriving from the Latin *finis* for end, boundary, or limit, means the same as limited being. It can be understood in either a quantitative or a qualitative sense. Examples of the former are things limited in dimensions, weight, or speed; these are known through experience and present no special difficulty. The qualitatively finite, as opposed to this, designates a limited possession of some perfection that admits of levels or degrees. As a concept it has long been present in the philosophical thought of both East and West, although it underwent a noteworthy evolution at the beginning of the Christian era.

Notion of Finite. For classical Greek thought the finite was the perfect, which meant the completed, the determinate or well-defined, or the intelligible (since definition itself is delimitation). The infinite, as opposed to this, was the imperfect, the unfinished, the indeterminate and formless (matter), or the unintelligible. ''Nature,'' said ARISTOTLE, ''flies from the infinite, for the infinite is unending or imperfect, and nature ever seeks an end'' (*Gen. animal.,* 715b 14). It was only in the early centuries of the Christian era, influenced first by PHILO JUDAEUS and the Neoplatonism of PLOTINUS, then by Christian thinkers, especially CLEMENT OF ALEXANDRIA and GREGORY OF NYSSA, that the present notion, of qualitative infinity as the supremely perfect, begin to appear and to be applied to God. From this point on, the finite was understood to be a lower level of being, one that possessed in a limited (and therefore imperfect) way some attribute or property that Infinite Being (God) posessed in an unlimited (and therefore supremely perfect) manner. Finite thus became a primary notion for describing the status of creatures, all of which are by nature finite, as compared with their Creator, the infinite plenitude of all perfection.

Explanatory Principles. What is required to explain the existence of something finite? It is a fundamental tenet of Christian philosophers, and of almost all metaphysicians of both East and West, that no finite being can be self-sufficient or self-existent, but must depend on Infinite Being as its ultimate source. Limitation in a being's nature always requires some higher cause outside of that being, since no thing can determine its own nature to possess this or that degree of perfection and no other. If it did, it would then be at once cause and effect of its own self. By the same token, if the cause is itself finite, it requires still another cause. Since a causal chain where *all* the members are only finite in nature can never contain an adequate cause for any of the members, ultimately there must be an infinite source that possesses the perfection in question, not from another, or by PARTICIPATION, but of its own nature and in unlimited fullness. From this infinite source all the finite possessors of an attribute receive it or participate in it, each according to its own finite capacity.

Thus the first requisite for something to be finite is an external cause, ultimately an infinite cause. The second requisite is a composition of elements within the being itself that results from and reflects the limiting action of its external cause. According to St. THOMAS AQUINAS (*De pot.* 1.2; ST 1a, 50.2 ad 3–4; 75.5 ad 1, 4) and the Thomistic school, possession of some perfection, a participated perfection, requires a duality or composition of two correlative, but nonidentical, elements within the finite being: one to explain the participated perfection, which of itself has no particular limit since it is found in different beings in different degrees; the other to explain the limited capacity of this particular participant. St.

Thomas utilized the terms POTENCY and ACT, found already in Aristotle with a somewhat different connotation, to describe this internal composition of a limiting principle with the perfection that it limits.

How the Finite Is Known. Since finite is essentially a relative or comparative term, a being cannot be known as finite except by comparison with something more perfect. Opinions differ as to whether the ultimate term of comparison can be merely another finite being or whether it must be some kind of infinity. Claiming that it is unnecessary to have explicit knowledge of God as infinite being before recognizing that creatures are finite, theistic philosophers have commonly argued from the finitude of creatures to the infinity of God. In recent times, however, some Christian philosophers, e.g., Maurice BLONDEL, Joseph MARÉCHAL, Karl Rahner, and Johannes Lotz, hold that to know a being explicitly as finite, one must refer simultaneously, if only vaguely and implicitly, to something without limits, such as being and goodness. Drawing their inspiration partly from the Augustinian tradition, partly from St. Thomas, and partly from the insights of modern philosophers like HEGEL, they point out that to know a limit as a limit is at least to think of or desire the unlimited.

Despite minor differences, Catholic philosophers and theologians agree that man's knowledge of the finite, for the mind able and willing to recognize it, points towards the infinite source and final end of all being, GOD.

See Also: INFINITY OF GOD; LIMITATION; POTENCY; GOD, PROOFS FOR THE EXISTENCE OF.

Bibliography: F. SUÁREZ, *Disputationes Metaphysicae*, Disp. 31, sect. 13 in *Opera Omnia,* Vivés ed. v.26. W. N. CLARKE, ''The Limitation of Act by Potency,'' *The New Scholasticism* 26 (1952) 167–194. G. GIANNINI, *Enciclopedia filosofica* (Venice-Rome 1957) 3:54–58.

[W. N. CLARKE]

FINK, LOUIS MARY (MICHAEL)

Bishop; b. Triftersberg, Bavaria, July 12, 1834; d. Kansas City, Kans., March 17, 1904. He was the son of Peter and Barbara (Hecht) Fink. About 1850 he came to St. Vincent Archabbey, Westmoreland County, Pa., as one of Archabbot Boniface Wimmer's recruits. He took his vows in the Order of St. Benedict on Jan. 6, 1854, and was ordained on May 28, 1857. After serving as pastor in several parishes, he was named prior of St. Benedict's Priory, Atchison, Kans., in 1868. At the request of John B. Miège, SJ, Vicar Apostolic of Kansas and of the Indian Territory, Fink was made coadjutor bishop and consecrated on June 11, 1871. Miège resigned at the end of 1874, and on May 22, 1877, Kansas was made a diocese with its see at Leavenworth. Fink, faced with the problems of a frontier state, established ''Christian Forts'' (mission centers) in areas where land was available. Catholic immigrants were then directed to these districts through colonization societies, railroad brochures, and the Catholic press. This campaign successfully established Catholic settlements for which Fink provided a resident pastor and a parochial school. When grasshoppers destroyed the crops in 1874, he collected alms in the Eastern states for his needy settlers. His pastoral letters, reflecting the rural character of his diocese, linked the Biblical world of the husbandman with the lives of his people. He was a vigorous promoter of the American Federation of Catholic Societies, and he also encouraged Catholics to join the Farmers' Alliance, forerunner of the Populist Movement. As Catholic immigrants were increasingly attracted to Kansas City, Fink turned his attention to problems of urban industrialism. He recognized the necessity of unions, but opposed the closed shop and, in the interests of family, encouraged the abolition of Sunday work. Fink moved his residence to Kansas City after his diocese was divided in 1887.

[P. BECKMAN]

FINLAND, THE CATHOLIC CHURCH IN

Located in northern Europe, the Republic of Finland is bordered by Sweden and the Gulf of Bothnia on the west, Norway on the north, Russia on the east, and the Gulf of Finland, which separates southern Finland from Estonia. With its heavily forested landscape of rolling plains dotted by hills and numerous lakes and streams, Finland possesses natural resources that include lumber, silver, copper, iron ore, and other minerals. Finland's economic strength depends on the export of timber products as well as electronics, chemicals, machinery, and other manufactured products.

Finland was part of Sweden from the early Middle Ages until 1809, when it became an autonomous grand duchy of the Russian Empire. On Dec. 6, 1917, Finland proclaimed its independence. During World War II, Finland ceded 17,778 square miles (Finnish Karelia and Viborg) to the USSR, and many people living in this area relocated westward to escape communist control and retain their Finnish culture. The Finns are of mixed East Baltic and Scandinavian origin. Ecclesiastically, Finland has formed the Catholic Diocese of Helsinki (Swedish Helsingfors) since 1955, which diocese is immediately subject to the Holy See. The bishop of Helsinki is a member of the Nordic Bishops' Conference.

Capital: Helsinki.
Size: 130,145 sq. miles.
Population: 5,167,485 in 2000.
Languages: Finnish, Swedish; Lapp and Russian are spoken in various regions.
Religions: 6,980 Catholics (1%), 5,975 Greek Orthodox (1%), 4,599,060 Evangelical Lutherans (89%), 555,470 without religious affiliation.

Catholic Origins and Growth to 1500. Finland was settled by the 8th century, and the inhabitants lived in relative peace for 400 years until the region gave way to Swedish explorers in the 12th century. Archeological finds in ancient settlements bear witness to Christian practices—both of the Eastern and Western churches—among these conquerers. As a result of a crusade in 1155 under the Swedish king St. ERIC IX JEDVARDSSON, and of other expeditions in 1239 and 1293, the counties of Finland proper, Häme and West Carelia were united with Sweden. St. Henrik, the patron saint of Finland, was an English-born bishop of Uppsala who accompanied St. Eric on his first crusade to Finland. While the king returned to Sweden, Henrik stayed in Finland to continue the work of the Church; he died a martyr's death in January 1156 at the hands of a peasant who had been excommunicated for manslaughter.

Finland's first bishop, Thomas (d.1248), was also English. His diocese at Turku (Swedish Åbo) was suffragan to the archbishop of Uppsala. The Dominicans founded a convent near the Diocese of Turku in 1249 and greatly influenced the region's spiritual life. Their liturgy was adopted by the Diocese of Turku.

The 14th century saw the arrival of Franciscans, while Bridgettines founded the monastery of Naantali in 1445. Close relations were maintained with both Scandinavia and the rest of Europe, and many Finnish students studied at the University of Paris. Among the most prominent bishops of the 14th and 15th centuries were HEMMING (d. 1366), friend of St. BRIDGET OF SWEDEN, who rebuilt the cathedral, destroyed by the Russians in 1318, and who was beatified in 1514; Magnus Tavast (d. 1450), powerful organizer of ecclesiastical life; Olaus Magnus (d. 1460), sometime professor in Paris, procurator of the English nation there, and twice rector of its faculty of arts; and Magnus Säerkilax (d. 1500), who energetically promoted the religious education of the people. Evidence of the flowering of Catholic ecclesiastical culture during this period still appears in the cathedral of Turku and in some 100 medieval churches yet standing. The development of ecclesiastical culture in Finland was interrupted during the late Middle Ages by Sweden's wars with Denmark and Russia. The last Catholic bishop, Arvid Kurck (1464–1521), was drowned in the Gulf of Bothnia while fleeing the Danish invasion in 1522.

Success of Protestantism. Unlike other parts of Scandinavia, Sweden and Finland exhibited no degeneration within the Church at the close of the Middle Ages, although its position, as elsewhere in Europe, was increasingly vulnerable. Its political power and economic resources made possible magnificent cultural achievements and active social work, but also gave rise to envy and ill-will from the monarchy, nobility, and burghers alike. Except among the mendicant orders, interest in theology declined, and the philosophical training of the clergy was often rooted in NOMINALISM. Moreover, a deep cleft developed between the theologians and humanists. To the laity, whose general education stressed the usual Christian truths, the hierarchy was more impressive as an organization than as a priestly body entrusted with the administration of the Sacraments; there was little understanding for the position of Rome within the Church.

When Lutheran reformers appeared in Scandinavia, they quickly gained the support of the monarchy and a following among the nobles and burghers. In Sweden King Gustav Vasa (1523–60) succeeded in breaking down the political and economic position of the Church by giving evangelical preachers a free hand, while outwardly keeping the customary forms and services of the Church, and denying any intention of establishing LUTHERANISM or any other Protestant form. Meanwhile the Catholic clergy were gradually replaced by Lutherans. In the Swedish grand duchy of Finland the process was similar but proceeded at a slower pace. Canon Peter Särkilax, who had studied at Wittenberg, was the first Lutheran preacher. In 1528 Gustav Vasa appointed the aged Dominican Martin Skytte a bishop; while Skytte's consecration had been without doubt valid it was not confirmed by the pope. In 1538 Masses in Swedish were celebrated in the cathedral together with ceremonial alterations. In 1538 Michael Olavi Agricola (*c.* 1508–57), Lutheran bishop of Turku and disciple of MELANCHTHON, published the first Finnish Church handbook, which was followed by a Finnish version of the New Testament (1548) and a vernacular Massbook (1549). Agricola was a moderate who accepted among other beliefs the traditional teaching on the Sacrament of Penance. Feasts such as Corpus Christi and the Assumption of the Blessed Virgin continued to be celebrated far into Lutheran times; the elevation at Mass was retained until the end of the 16th century; pictures were tolerated in churches in both Finland and Sweden, and those with Old Testament emphasis added. Due to this moderated change, disturbances such as those that occurred among the Swedish peasantry were avoided. The AUGSBURG CONFESSION was not introduced into Finland until 1593. Two years later Catholicism was forbidden within the country.

During the reigns of John III, King of Sweden (1568–92), and his son Sigismund III (1592–1604), there were attempts at a Catholic revival. Many Finnish students attended Jesuit colleges in western Europe. But after Sigismund's uncle, the Protestant Duke of Södermanland, seized power as Charles IX (1604–11), the REFORMATION was victorious, and a reorganization of church life on Lutheran principles was implemented. Credit is due to the Lutheran church for furthering general education. The first Finnish translation of the entire Bible was printed in 1640. The rigorous rules of the Church led to PIETISM, a 17th-century movement of German and English inspiration. While the influence of the ENLIGHTENMENT on the Swedish-speaking educated classes created a chasm between ecclesiastical and cultural life, burgeoning Finnish nationalism in the 19th century caused the formation of a new Finnish-speaking educated class, recruited partly among the Swedish-speaking people and partly among the Finnish-speaking clergy and their families.

Catholicism after 1781. In 1781 Catholics in Swedish-controlled Finland were granted religious liberty, although missionary work and conversions continued to be prohibited. In Vyborg in 1799 a parish, subject to the archdiocese of Mogilev, was founded by the Polish Dominicans to care for military personnel serving in the Russian Army, and a church dedicated to Saint Hyacinth was consecrated. A similar parish was founded in Helsinki in 1860, and Holy Mass was celebrated there in a small wooden church on the island fortress of Suomenlinna. Prohibition against leaving the Lutheran Church was abolished in 1869.

In 1809 Finland became a grand duchy under the Russian crown, bequeathed by Sweden following that country's defeat in the War of the Third Coalition. As part of Russia, the Finnish Church fell under the Archdiocese of Mohilev, which had its episcopal see in St. Petersburg. Under a policy of Russification enacted during the 1890s, Finnish culture, as well as Church autonomy, survived only with great difficulty. The first Finnish priest following the Reformation, W. v. Christierson (d. 1945), was finally ordained in Paris in 1903. A year after the proclamation of Finnish independence in 1919, the vicariate apostolic of Finland was created and entrusted to the Dutch Sacred Heart Fathers. With the help of German forces Finland waged a victorious civil war against residual Russian authority, and full religious liberty was granted in 1923. During World War II Finland eventually fought with Germany, not in support of Hitler's policies but rather because siding with Germany allowed them to

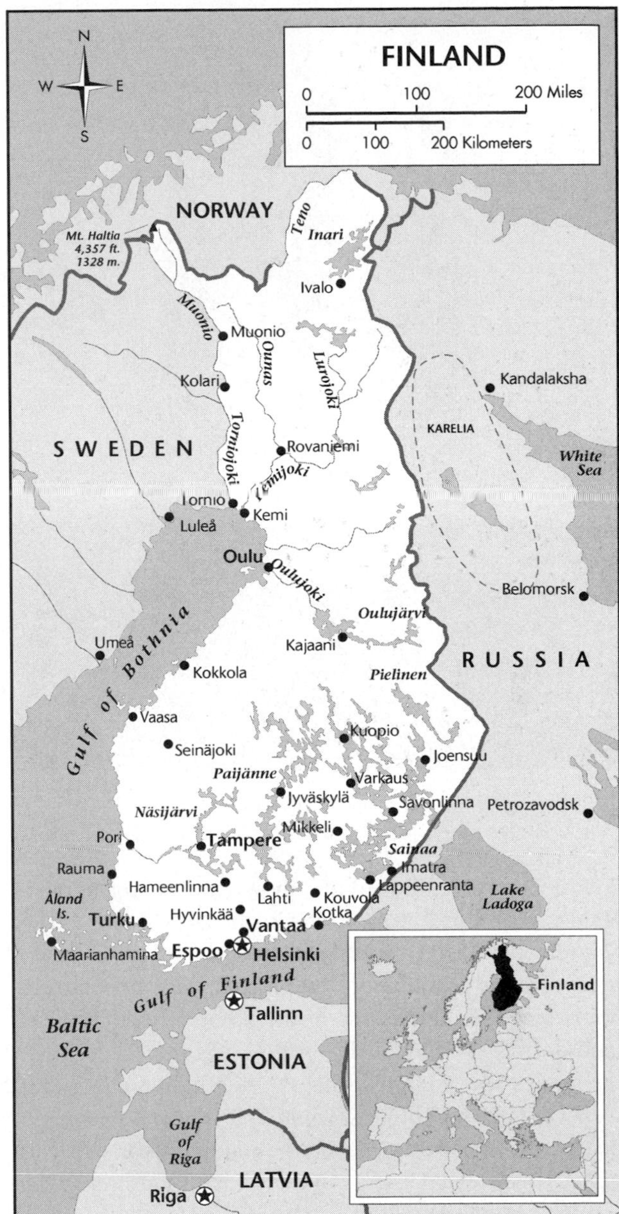

fight Russia. Axis defeats led to the progressive loss of Karelia to the USSR in 1940 and 1944, and two of Finland's four Catholic parishes were lost.

World War II was not the first time the Karelians had been the subject of dispute. As early as the 14th century East Karelia was united with Novgorod, thus providing Russian Orthodoxy inroads into Finland. Part of Russian Karelia was controlled by Sweden-Finland from 1580–1617; it included an Orthodox Karelian population that was subjected to harsh persecution. In 1721 East Karelia was given by Sweden to Russia. After the incorporation of all Finland into the Russian Empire in 1809 the position of Finnish Orthodox improved. An Orthodox

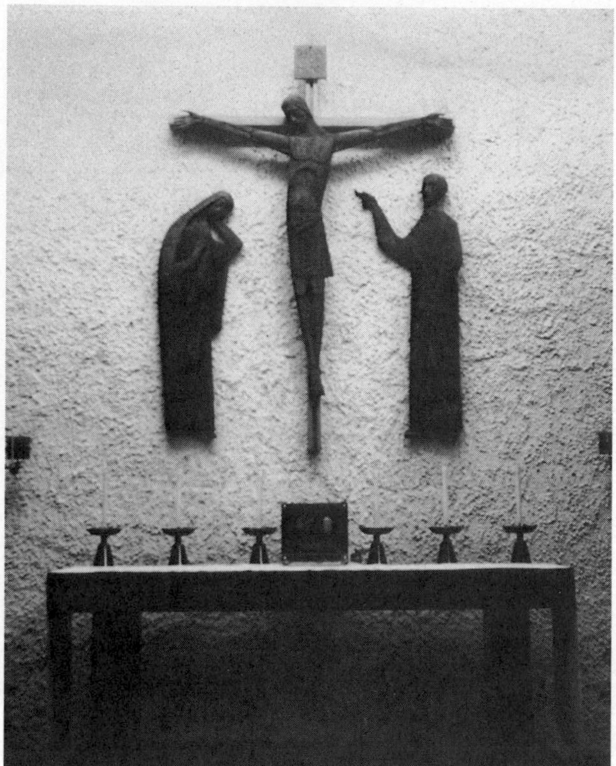

Sanctuary of a Catholic church, Jyuaskyla, Finland.

archdiocese was founded in Viborg (moved to Kuopio in 1944), with a bishop in Helsinki. In 1921 the Orthodox Church was freed from its dependence on Russia; it was recognized as autonomous by the patriarch of Constantinople in 1923. At the time of the Soviet invasion of Finland during World War II, Orthodox Karelians living in the lands ceded to the USSR left their homes and moved westward. The Orthodox Church in Finland eventually became independent of Moscow, and many parishes converted from Old Church Slavonic to Finnish-language sermons by the late 20th century.

The Church in Cold-War Europe. As the national church of Finland, the Evangelical Lutheran Church maintained a solid economic position throughout the second half of the 20th century, and retained active contacts with other Lutheran churches in Scandinavia. It had an archbishop in Turku and seven bishops. Theological faculties were established at the state-run University of Helsinki and at the Swedish Academy of Åbo. Teaching of religion remained compulsory in all Finland's schools, although by 2000 children of minority faiths were given non-Lutheran options. Despite the lack of equivalent state funding, the Catholic Church also dedicated itself to education in Finland during this period. Studium Catholicum, an institute for mutual cultural interchange founded in 1951, was directed by the Dominicans. Dutch Sisters of the Sacred Heart of Jesus in Moerdijk directed two orphanages, while Sisters of the Most PRECIOUS BLOOD came from the United States to run an English-language commercial school and a well-regarded secondary school in Helsinki. At Myllyjärvi, near Helsinki, two foreign secular priests of the Greek rite directed a center for ecumenical contacts. A Catholic union of students and graduates, Academicum Catholicum, a youth organization called Juventus Catholica, and two Catholic women's societies also flourished in the second half of the 20th century.

The Modern Church. Through the 20th century the Catholic Church of Finland continued to be respected as a religious community officially recognized by the state, although by rule of the law of religious liberty enacted in 1923 the foundation of monasteries remained prohibited. However, evangelical and other efforts to strengthen the Church continued. The Bridgettines arrived in 1986 from Sweden and four Carmelites came from the United States in 1989. The Missionaries of Charity established their first house in Finland in 1999. A priests' council was established in 1967 and the diocesan pastoral council followed in 1974. In 1983 the Diocesan Center North Helsinki, Stella Maris, was established. By 2000 Finland contained seven parishes administered by 5 secular and 15 religious priests, and 36 sisters. With a small and diminishing population, conversions remained few, usually coming from the country's intellectual circles. Catholic authors, such as Göran Stenius, and scholars contributed to Finland's cultural life.

While social issues would continue to spark controversy between Lutheran and Catholic interests, significant ecumenical advances included the Roman Catholic Church's membership in the Finnish Ecumenical Council after 1968. In 1985, as part of the ceremonies for the dedication of the St. Henrik altar at Santa Maria sopra Minerva in Rome, the Finnish Lutheran bishop, the Orthodox bishop, and the Roman Catholic bishop were received together by the pope. Four years later, in June of 1989, Pope John Paul II was received in Finland by both Catholics and non-Catholics, a reflection of the success of the Church's ecumenical efforts. In 1991 Lutheran Archbishop John Vikstrom participated in the celebration of the Feast of St. Bridget in St. Peter's Basilica, and in 1999 Vikstrom's successor traveled to the Vatican for a private audience with the pope. Additionally, in 1988, Uusi, Finland was the site of the fifth meeting of the international commission of Catholic and Orthodox theologians, a group working toward a greater understanding between these faiths.

Bibliography: G. SCHWAIGER, *Die Reformation in den nordischen Ländern* (Munich 1962). L. S. HUNTER, ed., *Scandinavian Churches* (London 1965). K. S. LATOURETTE, *Christianity in* *a Revolutionary Age: A History of Christianity in the Nineteenth and Twentieth Centuries* (New York 1958–62) v.2, 4. *The Church of Finland* (Pieksämäki 1963). G. SENTZKE, *Finland: Its Church and Its People* (Helsinki 1963). U. TOIVOLA, ed., *Introduction to Finland, 1960* (2d ed. Porvoo 1963). E. K. JUTIKKALA, ed., *Suomen historian kortasto: Atlas of Finnish History* (Porvoo 1959). E. K. JUTIKKALA and K. PIRINEN, *A History of Finland,* tr. P. SJÖBLOM (New York 1962). I. RACZ, *Suomen keskiajan taideaarteita* (Helsinki 1960), art treasures of medieval Finland. A. SINISALO et al., *Kauneimmat Kirkkomme* (Jyväskylä 1962), Finland's most beautiful churches. L. PINOMAA, ed., *Finnish Theology Past and Present* (Helsinki 1963). *Bilan du Monde* 2:368–373.

[J. GALLÉN/EDS.]

FINN, FRANCIS JAMES

Jesuit, teacher; b. St. Louis, Mo., Oct. 1859; d. Cincinnati, Ohio, Nov. 2, 1928. He was the son of John and Mary (Whyte) Finn, both Irish immigrants. After several years at St. Louis University, he entered the Jesuit novitiate at Florissant, Mo., on July 10, 1877. Further studies were interrupted by teaching at St. Mary's College, Kans. (1881–83, 1884–85); St. Xavier College, Cincinnati (1885–86); and Marquette University, Milwaukee, Wis. (1888–90). He studied philosophy and theology at Woodstock College, Woodstock, Md. (1883–84, 1886–88, 1890–93), and was ordained in 1893. In 1897 he began his 31-year stay at St. Xavier's College and Church in Cincinnati. He was active in parish work and established a nationwide circulating library, but his most notable work was his fiction for young people. At St. Mary's he had observed the effect of good books on the young, and after a day in class he would reward his students by reading his plays or stories to them. When confined to bed for long periods at Woodstock, he wrote reminiscences of his teaching days. His most popular work was *Tom Playfair* (1891), which his publisher (Benziger) then called ''the most successful book for Catholic boys and girls ever published in the English language.'' His 27 books were translated into many foreign languages.

[W. E. SHIELS]

FINNEY, CHARLES GRANDISON

American revival preacher; b. Warren, Conn., Aug. 29, 1792; d. Oberlin, Ohio, Aug. 16, 1875. His family migrated in 1794 to Oneida County, N.Y., where he was educated in rural schools. He taught school for several years, attended a private academy in Connecticut, studied law, and practiced as an attorney. Converted in 1821, he studied for the Presbyterian ministry under a local pastor and was ordained in 1824. Finney began preaching revivals in western New York and attracted national attention by his stress on emotional appeal and new measures, such as ''the anxious seat.'' In 1829 he accepted a pastoral charge in New York City and in 1835 published his controversial *Lectures on Revivals of Religion.* His insistence on freedom of the will and the ability of sinners to repent caused his separation from the Presbyterian Church in 1836 and led to divisions in the church the following year. Finney taught theology at Oberlin College and served as pastor of the Congregational Church in Oberlin until 1872. He was president of Oberlin from 1851 to 1866.

Bibliography: C. F. FINNEY, *Memoirs* (New York 1876). G. F. WRIGHT, *Charles Grandison Finney* (New York 1891). W. R. CROSS, *The Burned-Over District: The Social and Intellectual History of Enthusiastic Religion in Western New York 1800–1850* (Ithaca 1950). W. G. MCLOUGHLIN, *Modern Revivalism* (New York 1959).

[R. K. MACMASTER]

FINNIAN, SS.

The name of several Irish saints, of whom two are important.

Finnian of Clonard, abbot; b. Leinster, Ireland; d.549, Annals of Ulster. Finnian, or Finian, was one of the most important personalities in early Irish monastic history, he studied in Leinster before going to Wales, where he visited several important Welsh monasteries. Upon returning to Ireland, he made his principal foundation at Clonard (three miles east of Kinnegad on the Dublin-Galway road), one of the first great Irish monasteries. It combined Irish and Welsh monastic traditions and teachings. From Clonard, monastic enthusiasm spread throughout Ireland. Finnian's students included such Irish saints and monastic founders as COLUMBA OF IONA, BRENDAN, Kieran of Clonmacnois, and KENNETH OF DERRY. Finnian is the author of the oldest of the surviving Irish PENITENTIALS, compiled sometime after 525.

Feast: Dec. 12.

Finnian of Moville, abbot; b. north of Ireland; d. 579, Annals of Ulster, or 576, Annals of Inisfallen. After having studied at the famous Scottish priory of WHITHORN, founded by St. NINIAN, he made his own principal foundation at Moville, near Newtownards on Strangford Lough, Ireland. Surviving evidence presents Finnian—who is sometimes known also as Findbarr, both names meaning ''fair-haired''—as a notable scholar. There are chronological difficulties in the belief that he taught COLUMBA OF IONA, and there appears to be no real historical basis for the legend that the two saints quarreled over a stolen copy of the Psalter.

Feast: Sept. 10.

Bibliography: Finnian of Clonard. J. F. KENNEY, *The Sources for the Early History of Ireland:* v.1, *Ecclesiastical* (New York 1929) 374–376. P. GROSJEAN, ''Mention de S. Finnián de clúain Iraird . . . ,'' *Analecta Bollandiana* 72 (1954) 347–352. *The Irish Life of Saint Finnian of Clonard,* ed. E. HICKEY (Tara 1996). K. W. HUGHES, ''S. Finnian of Clonard,'' summary of thesis, *Bulletin of the Institute of Historical Research* 25 (1952) 76–78; ''The Cult of St. F. of Clonard . . . ,'' *Irish Historical Studies* 9 (1954–55) 13–27; ''The Historical Value of the Lives of St. F. of Clonard,'' *English Historical Review* 69 (1954) 353–372; ''The Offices of St. F. of Clonard . . . ,'' *Analecta Bollandiana* 73 (1955) 342–372; ''Additional Note on the Office of St. F. of Clonard,'' *ibid.* 75 (1957) 337–339. A tr. of Finnian's penitential in J. T. MC NEILL and H. M. GAMER, *Medieval Handbooks of Penance* (New York 1938) 86–97. **Finnian of Moville.** J. F. KENNEY, *The Sources for the Early History of Ireland:* v.1, *Ecclesiastical* (New York 1929) 390–391. O. DAVIES, ''Movilla Abbey,'' *Ulster Journal of Archaeology* 8 (1945) 33–38. A. BUTLER, *The Lives of the Saints,* ed. H. THURSTON and D. ATTWATER (New York 1956) 3:531–532. For the legend of the quarrel with Columba, D. D. C. POCHIN MOULD, *The Irish Saints* (Dublin 1964) 95–97, 169–171.

[D. D. C. POCHIN MOULD]

FINTAN, SS.

There are several Irish saints of this name.

Fintan of Clonenagh, Irish abbot; d. 603. He founded the monastery of Clonenagh, County Laois, under the Slieve Bloom Mountains. He was closely associated with St. Columba of Terryglass, and his regime at Clonenagh was noted for extreme asceticism.

Feast: Feb. 17.

Fintan of Rheinau, Irish hermit; b. Leinster?, Ireland; d. Rheinau, 876? On his way home from a pilgrimage to Rome, he joined the hermits on the island of Rheinau in the Rhine near Schaffhausen. As a patron of the abbey of RHEINAU, he is still the object of local devotion. His Latin vita (*Monumenta Germaniae Scriptores rerum Merovingicarum* 15:503–506) contains what may be the first mention of ''Ceili Dé'' or CULDEES, as well as the first Irish sentences recorded on the Continent. His Sacramentary is extant.

Feast: Nov. 15.

Fintan of Taghmon, Irish abbot; d. 635. He studied at Irish monasteries, then went to Scotland. But COLUMBA OF IONA, before he died, had said that Fintan must go back to Ireland to found a monastery. Fintan's principal foundation was at Taghmon, County Wexford. A number of churches in Scotland (where he was called Munnu) were dedicated to him and perhaps were personal foundations.

Feast: Oct. 21.

Bibliography: F. of Clonenagh. J. F. KENNEY, *The Sources for the Early History of Ireland:* v.1, *Ecclesiastical* (New York 1929) 384–386. A. BUTLER, *The Lives of the Saints,* ed. H. THURSTON and D. ATTWATER (New York 1956) 1:356–357. D. D. C. POCHIN MOULD, *Irish Saints* (Dublin 1964). **F. of Rheinau.** J. F. KENNEY, *The Sources for the Early History of Ireland:* v.1, *Ecclesiastical* (New York 1929) 602–603, 704–705. L. GOUGAUD, *Les Saints irlandais hors d'Irlande* (Louvain 1936). A. BUTLER, *The Lives of the Saints,* ed. H. THURSTON and D. ATTWATER (New York 1956) 4:350. J. HENNIG, ''Liturgical Veneration of Irish . . . Switzerland,'' *Iris Hibernia* 3 (1957) 23–32; *Lexikon für Theologie und Kirche,* ed. J. HOFER and K. RAHNER (Freiburg 1957–65) 4:137–138. **F. of Taghmon.** J. F. KENNEY, *The Sources for the Early History of Ireland:* v.1, *Ecclesiastical* (New York 1929) 449–450. A. BUTLER, *The Lives of the Saints,* ed. H. THURSTON and D. ATTWATER (New York 1956) 4:170. ADAMNAN, *Life of Columba,* ed. and tr. A. O. and M. O. ANDERSON (New York 1961). D. D. C. POCHIN MOULD, *Irish Saints* (Dublin 1964).

[D. D. C. POCHIN MOULD]

FIORETTI, THE

The full and original title of this 14th-century Franciscan literary classic is *I Fioretti di San Francesco* (The Little Flowers of St. Francis). It is an anonymous translation of the *Actus Beati Francisci et Sociorum Ejus,* written *c.* 1325 by Fra Ugolino Boniscambi of Montegiorgio in the Marches of Ancona and Fermo; for the last 100 years it has been the most popular book on St. FRANCIS OF ASSISI. Recent archival research by G. Pagnani has proved that the author did not belong to the Brunforte family of Sarnano. Though his years of birth and death are not known, he is mentioned in local documents of 1319 and 1342. In 1331 he testified in Naples against Andrea da Gagliano, a follower of the rebellious Minister General MICHAEL OF CESENA. Fra Ugolino sought to reform the Franciscan Order from within by writing and dictating about 20 previously unrecorded anecdotes about Francis and his first companions ''as revealed by their successors which were omitted in his biographies but which are also very useful and edifying.'' His principal source was a Brother James of Massa who had known several of the saint's companions. To a score of vivid, even humorous stories about the Poverello, Fra Ugolino added a series of chapters narrating the mystical experiences of several saintly friars of his own times and province, notably, Bl. John of La Verna and Bl. Conrad of Offida.

The basic purpose of the whole work, which has an organic inner unity, was to stimulate a return to the unique contemplative-and-active spirituality of the founder, as exemplified in the lives of his early companions and later disciples in the Marches. Some of the latter had sympathized with the reform movement of the Franciscan SPIRITUALS but, unlike them, refused to leave the order to practice their ideal. The remarkable popularity of the *Actus* during the 14th century thus sowed the seeds of the Observant reform. Hence it must be considered a proto-Observant rather than a Spiritual manifesto. Its historicity has been questioned because passages dealing with the controversial ELIAS OF CORTONA are inaccurate and partisan, and it describes a meeting between Brother Giles and St. Louis of France that is apocryphal. (*See* GILES OF ASSISI, BL.; LOUIS IX, KING OF FRANCE, ST.) However, the substance of half a dozen of its original anecdotes involving St. Francis has been confirmed by independent sources. The supreme value of Fra Ugolino's contribution lies in the fundamental authenticity of his spiritual profile of the Poverello.

Several anonymous Italian translations of the *Actus* were made c. 1375. Pagnani has identified a version in the dialect of the Marches. But it was one of the two extant Tuscan translations that became a classic of medieval Italian literature, owing to the limpid beauty and enchanting simplicity of its style. The impressive narrative talent of the unknown friar translator made him a worthy contemporary of Petrarch and Boccaccio. Selecting a bouquet of 53 of the most appealing chapters in the *Actus,* he aptly titled it *I Fioretti di San Francesco.* To them he added an original masterpiece of his own, *The Five Considerations on the Holy Stigmata,* which he compiled from the *Actus,* the *legendae* by THOMAS OF CELANO and St. BONAVENTURE, and the oral traditions of the friars at Mount La Verna.

Several other indirectly related addenda have been included in 15th-century manuscripts and various modern editions of *The Little Flowers of St. Francis,* such as short lives of Brothers Juniper and Giles, excerpts from the latter's *Golden Sayings,* and a miscellany of additional chapters from the *Actus* or other Franciscan compilations.

First printed at Vicenza in 1476, the *Fioretti* became a favorite target of some Protestant reformers, e.g., Pier Paolo Vergerio. F. Buonarroti's edition of 1718 rescued it from oblivion, and that of A. Cesari in 1822 launched it on a course of ever-spreading popularity that elevated it to the status of ''the breviary of the Italian people'' and a classic of world literature. Paul SABATIER's preliminary edition of the *Actus* in 1902 and the publication of the important Little-Phillipps manuscript in 1914 stimulated further research, which has culminated in recent studies and annotated editions that have significantly clarified the historical background of this deservedly famous yet relatively unstudied early Franciscan literary gem.

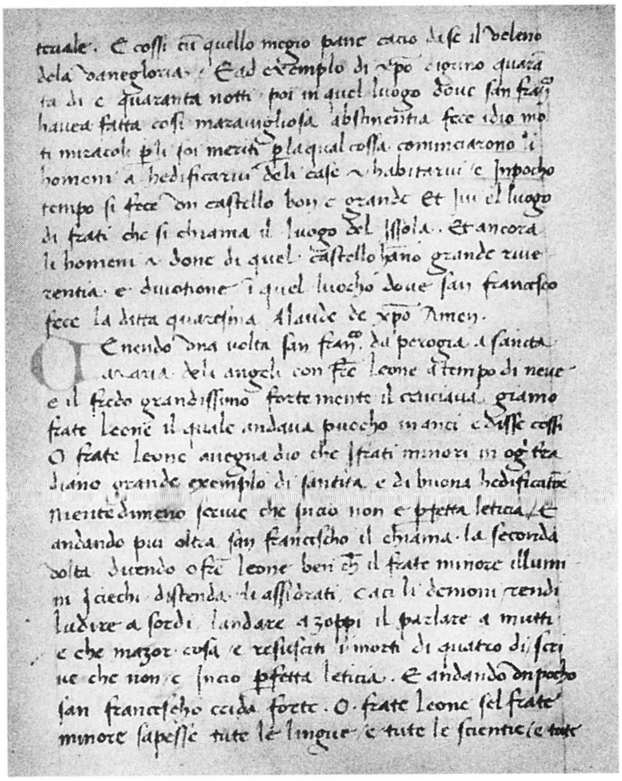
tuale. E cossi cu quello megio pane caccio da se il veleno
dela vanegloria. E ad exemplo di xpo ieiunò quaranta
di e quaranta notti poi in quel luogo dove san fran
haveva fatta cossi maravegliosa abstinentia fece idio mo
ti miracoli per li soi meriti per laqual cossa comminciarono li
homeni a hedificarvi dele case a habitarvi e inpocho
tempo si fece un castello bon e grande et lì è el luogo
di frati che si chiama il luogo del isola. Et ancora
li homeni e done di quel castello hano grande reve
rentia e devotione in quel luocho dove san francesco
fece la ditta quaresima. A laude de xpo Amen.
Venendo una volta san franc. da perogia a sancta
maria deli angeli con frate leone a tempo di neve
e il freddo grandissimo fortemente il cruciava. chiamò
frate leone il quale andava puocho inanci e disse cossi
O frate leone avegna dio che frati minori in ogni terra
diano grande exemplo di santita e di buona hedificatione
niente di meno scrive che in ciò non è perfetta letitia. E
andando piu oltra san francescho il chiama la seconda
volta dicendo o frate leone ben che il frate minore illumi
ni i ciechi distenda li assiderati caci li demoni rendi
ludire a sordi landare a zoppi il parlare a mutti
e che mazor cosa e resusciti i morti di quatro di scrivi
ne che non è in ciò perfetta letitia. E andando unpocho
san francescho crida forte. O frate leone sel frate
minore sapesse tute le lingue e tute le scientie e tute

Folio from a 15th-century Italian manuscript of ''The Little Flowers of St. Francis.'' (Cod. Vat. Lat. 10191, fol. 30r)

Bibliography: *Actus beati Francisci et sociorum ejus,* ed. P. SABATIER (Paris 1902). Important recent eds. with useful introd., nn., and bibliog. *Gli scritti di San Francesco e ''I Fioretti,''* ed. A. VICINELLI (Milan 1955); *I fioretti di San Francesco,* ed. B. BUGHETTI and R. PRATESI (Florence 1960), with most additional parts; *I fioretti di San Francesco,* ed. R. PRATESI and G. V. SABATELLI (Florence 1960), with only *The Considerations; I fioretti di San Francesco,* ed. G. PAGNANI (Rome 1959); *The Little Flowers of St. Francis,* ed. and tr. R. BROWN (Garden City, NY 1958), with added parts and extensive bibliog. S. CLASEN, ''Zur Problematik der Fioretti,'' *Wissenschaft und Weisheit* 25 (1962) 214–218. L. CELLUCCI, *Le leggende francescane del secolo XIII nel loro aspetto artistico* (2d ed. Modena 1957). G. PAGNANI, ''Il codice di Fabriano dei *Fioretti* di San Francesco,'' *Studia Picena* 25 (1957) 1–23; ''Contributi alla questione dei *Fioretti di San Francesco,*'' *Archivum Franciscanum historicum* (Quaracchi-Florence 1909–) 49 (1956) 3–16. O. ENGLEBERT, *St. Francis of Assisi: A Biography,* tr. E. M. COOPER, 2d ed. by I. BRADY and R. BROWN (Chicago 1966).

[R. BROWN]

FIRE, USE AND SYMBOLISM OF

From time immemorial, man has observed through experience the ambivalent character of fire. As a gift of the gods, the source of light and heat, it conditions the sphere of well-being, of life, and of the divine and celestial world. At the same time, as a destructive force, it enters organically into the chaotic and infernal aspects of this world and the next. Prometheus in stealing fire from heaven undoubtedly did not think of this destructive side of fire. However, the two forms of fire interpenetrate. The anger of the god of heaven is armed with lightning, his divine majesty is surrounded by an awe-inspiring fire. On the other hand, the violence of devouring fire is not merely negative, for fire can purify, renew, and rejuvenate.

General Use and Symbolism. The Greek and Roman—and general Indo-European—belief in the positive character of fire is revealed in the first place by the religious respect that surrounds the burning fire of the hearth. It is a begetting male power, it promotes the fecundity of women and cattle, and it guarantees the fertility of the fields. It is a magical means (pyromancy) for unveiling the future and of attaining immortality (the story of Demeter and Demophon in Greek mythology). The Spartan kings carry fire from the hearth on their campaigns. From the period of the Antonines, fire is borne before the emperor, probably to attest and honor his numinous character. The destructive force of fire is put into practice in various magical purification rites, such as the fire-walk. By submitting thus to the curative, cathartic, and apotropaic virtues of fire, man frees himself from impurities and contaminations and protects himself against the ascendency of evil powers. This destructive character of fire, moreover, does not exclude a positive result. The use of fire in certain initiations, the ''baptism of fire'' found among the Gnostics and the role of fire once in vogue in several Oriental Christian liturgies, all tend to bring about, in a real or symbolic fashion, the spiritual renewal of the believer. It is this aspect of fire that gives so marked a typological value to the legend of the phoenix, whose self-destruction on its pyre guarantees an eternal renewal of youth.

When a member of a family died in ancient Rome, the hearth-fire was extinguished as a sign of grief. However, the corpse was not deprived of the presence of fire, since a concentrated, symbolic, and convenient form of light was provided by candelabra, torches, and lamps. Light surrounded the bier; it was carried in the funeral procession; and it kept watch at the tomb. Originally fire performed an apotropaic role, driving away malevolent spirits, or even the practical role of lighting the way or kindling the pyre. In the Christian era, in the eyes of both pagans and Christians, it symbolized remembrance, prayer, and eternal life, or, at least, contact between the world of the living and that of the dead. Cremation, however utilitarian it became, took on, in the first centuries of the Empire, a cathartic and perhaps divinizing character. In the imaginary funeral obsequies connected with imperial apotheosis, the total cremation of the ''wax double'' furnished assurance that the emperor had rejoined the gods body and soul. The negative aspect of fire is maintained fully only in the mythological conception of the river of fire (Pyriphlegethon) surrounding the infernal abode.

In Religion. The positive aspect of fire is connected more strictly with the domain of the numinous in a twofold way. As the object of cult itself, fire, although not attaining among the Greeks and Romans the veneration that it inspired in India (Agni) and Iran (fire-temples), was personified to some degree in the goddess VESTA. Fire is employed as a means in honoring divinity. Divine manifestations, moreover, comprise fiery aspects that seem to be essential elements in all theophanies, as is clear from the Old Testament. Hence, Christianity has not abandoned the use of lighted lamps and candles, which, from the time of St. Jerome, was given a place in the cult of the martyrs. ''Eternal fires'' were found in Greek and Roman temples in honor of certain gods or, even symbolizing the numinous character of the state or the emperor—or both. ''Ever-burning lamps,'' as that of Athena Polias in the Erechtheum and that in the Temple of Jerusalem, represented the perpetuity of worship. The sanctuary lamp, which, however, was not introduced before the middle of the 13th century, symbolizes the Real Presence of Christ in the Eucharist. Lamps and lights were an indispensable element in pagan festivals, and the flames of candles and lamps flooded the celebrations of Christian worship with such joyous light that from the 5th century, at least, writers believed that the illuminated churches constituted a prefiguration of heaven. This joyous aspect of fire is connected also with a metaphorical meaning whereby the Bible often expresses its conception of the brightness and glory of God and His beneficent illumination of His servants. Likewise on the numinous plane, the destructive character of fire receives an incarnation, so to speak, in the figure of the god Vulcan. As an instrument of worship, the altar fire, both in Greece and Rome, as well as in Jerusalem, is the medium par excellence by which the material offerings of men may make a favorable impression on divinity. Destructive fire, especially in the form of lightning, or shooting stars, or comets, lends itself easily and universally to literal and metaphorical applications. In Israel, especially, fire of this kind is regarded as the instrument and image of God's anger. God punishes, tries, judges, and destroys by fire.

On the cosmological side, fire plays an essential role in the philosophy of HERACLITUS and in STOICISM. In Christian theology, it has a central place in the punishment of the damned and in the traditional teaching on purgatory (*see* FIRE OF JUDGMENT).

Bibliography: A. CLOSS et al., *Lexikon für Theologie und Kirche,* ed. J. HOFER and K. RAHNER, 10 v. (2d new ed. Freiburg1957–65) 4:106–110. C. M. EDSMAN, *Die Religion in Geschichte und Gegenwart* 2:927, with bibliog.; *Le Baptême de feu* (Leipzig 1940); *Ignis divinus* (Lund 1949). A. E. CRAWLEY, J. HAS-

TINGS, ed., *Encyclopedia of Religion and Ethics* 13 v. (Edinburgh 1908–27) 6:26–30. *Encyclopedic Dictionary of the Bible*, tr. and adap. by L. HARTMAN (New York 1963) 775. J. G. FRAZER, *Myths of the Origin of Fire* (London 1930). F. HEILER, *Erscheinungsformen und Wesen der Religion* (Stuttgart 1961). R. MAYER, *Die biblische Vorstellung vom Weltenbrand* (Bonn 1956). L. M. R. SIMONS, *Flamma aeterna* (Amsterdam 1949). J. MORGENSTERN, *The Fire upon the Altar* (Leiden 1963).

[G. SANDERS]

FIRE OF JUDGMENT

An expression used by the majority of exegetes and theologians in connection with the second coming of Christ. The conflagration pictured as taking place on that day searches out the works of all men (even those of the just, for whom it is a cleansing from all guilt) and hence is a judgment of fire.

Just as in the Old Testament (Is 66.15–17; Jl 2.1–3; Ps 96[97].3) the judgments of God were usually accompanied by fire, so also in the New Testament (1 Cor 3.13; 2 Thes 1.8; 2 Pt 3.12) it is stated that the final judgment of the Lord will be accompanied by fire. Will this fire of judgment be a metaphorical or real fire?

Considering the fire of judgment insofar as it will try every man's works in order to determine if they were according to, or contrary to the laws of God, the more common opinion is that the fire will be a metaphorical one. Except for Origen, almost all Scripture scholars and theologians agree with St. Thomas that the judgment will take place mentally (*Summa theologiae* 3a Suppl., 88.2). The reason for the metaphor of fire is that fire shows forth the following qualities: (1) *clarity*—God's judgment will be luminously clear and according to truth; (2) *ardor*—divine justice will meet out vengeance on works of impiety with zeal and power; (3) *subtlety*—divine judgment will search out even the most secret of human actions in an admirable way. The judgment, then, will be ''as of fire'' for the good as well as for the bad.

As for the conflagration that will accompany and manifest the Day of the Lord, this fire is depicted as real. The just who have not yet died before the coming of Christ pass through the fires of that dreadful time. The fire could have a twofold effect: (1) the effect of killing them and reducing their bodies to ashes; and (2) a spiritual effect, since it could be employed by divine justice to purge and purify them for venial sins and the temporal punishment that still remained. This would be an instantaneous purgatory. As for those who are in mortal sin, it would be the beginning of their eternal punishment.

The fire of that day would not harm those who have been completely free of sin (e.g., the Blessed Virgin Mary and the infants who died in their baptismal innocence), neither would it in any way harm those who have completely expiated their faults in this life or in purgatory.

Concerning the last day, many things will remain obscure until they are revealed. But this much should be firmly believed: all the actions of men, even the most sacred and hidden, must be judged, rewarded or punished.

See Also: JUDGMENT, DIVINE (IN THEOLOGY); PAROUSIA.

Bibliography: F. SUÁREZ, *In 3am Summa theologiae S. Thomae,* 59 (disp. 57, sec. 1; Vivès ed. v.19). R. BELLARMINE, ''De ecclesia quae est in purgatorio,'' Bk. 2, ch. 1 (*De controversiis*). A. MICHEL, *Dictionnaire de théologie catholique,* ed. A. VACANT et al., 15 v. (Paris 1903–50; Tables générales 1951–) 5.2:2239–46. E. LUSSIER, ''The Universal Conflagration at the Parousia,'' *Catholic Biblical Quarterly* 12 (1950) 243–247. *Encyclopedic Dictionary of the Bible,* tr. and adap. by L. HARTMAN (New York 1963), from A. VAN DEN BORN, *Bijbels Woordenboek* 498–504, 1728–39.

[M. GRIFFIN]

FIRMIAN

An old South Tyrolean family that gave several bishops to the Church.

Leopold Anton Eleutherius, b. Munich, May 27, 1679; d. Salzburg, Oct. 22, 1744. He was successively dean of Salzburg in 1713, bishop of Levant in 1718, bishop of Seckau in 1724, and bishop of Laibach in 1727; he became archbishop of Salzburg in 1727. He founded houses for retreats and missions under the Jesuits. His edict of emigration against Protestants in 1731 caused about 22,000 of them to leave, most of them for Prussia.

Leopold Ernst, his nephew, count and cardinal; b. Trent, Sept. 22, 1708; d. Passau, March 13, 1783. He was bishop of Seckau in 1739 and administrator of Trent in 1748. In 1763 he became bishop of Passau and was made a cardinal in 1772. In addition to his interest in the scientific training of the clergy, he supported missions for the laity.

Leopold Max, count; b. Trent, Oct. 11, 1766; d. Vienna, Nov. 29, 1831. He was suffragan bishop of Passau in 1787, bishop of Levant in 1800, administrator of Salzburg in 1818, and archbishop of Vienna in 1822.

Bibliography: M. SCHELLHORN, *Lexikon für Theologie und Kirche*, ed. J. HOFER and K. RAHNER (Freiburg 1957–65) 4:143–144.

[L. WEISENSEL]

FIRMICUS MATERNUS, JULIUS

Junior V(ir) C(larissimus), 4th-century apologist and polemicist; b. Syracuse, date unknown; d. after 350. An aristocrat of senatorial rank, he was reared in paganism and went through three successive careers: advocate, astrologer, and Christian polemicist. He wrote *Matheseos libri VIII* (*c.* 334–337), the longest systematic account of astrology in the Latin language. Converted to Christianity probably within the next decade, he decided to turn his pen to the defense of his adopted religion. The result, written *c.* 346, was the 80-page essay *De errore profanarum religionum.* The book yields valuable information on the Oriental religions, which had chiefly supplanted other pagan cults in the Roman Empire.

On Christianity and its spirit Firmicus was less well informed. He addressed his book to the Emperors Constans and Constantius and in fiery terms exhorted them to allow no religious liberty and to stamp out by drastic and violent means every vestige of pagan belief and cult, destroying the shrines and temples. This was the earliest-known instance of an appeal by a Christian to ''the secular arm'' to enforce Christianity and destroy other religions without mercy. The Emperors apparently elected not to adopt Firmicus's intemperate and intolerant advice.

Firmicus was a bookish man. He endeavored to write in a Ciceronian style and borrowed data freely from Cicero's *De natura deorum.* Like the apologists, he used euhemeristic methods to discredit the putative divinity of sundry pagan gods. Among his other unacknowledged sources were CLEMENT OF ALEXANDRIA (*Protrepticus*), ARNOBIUS THE ELDER, IRENAEUS, and CYPRIAN. While he quoted the Bible (70 quotations or allusions), he did so mostly from the pages of Cyprian's *Testimonia* rather than directly.

Firmicus's book lay in oblivion for 1,200 years until the Reformation. It survived in a solitary minuscule codex, written in Germany in the 9th or 10th century. Matthias FLACIUS ILLYRICUS, Lutheran Church historian, found the codex in a monastery at Minden and published the first (unsatisfactory) edition at Strassburg in 1562. The codex is now in the VATICAN (Vatican Palatinus Latinus 165). The attempt by G. Morin to identify Firmicus as the author of the *Consultationes Zacchaei et Apollonii* has been rejected by most scholars.

Bibliography: Editions. *Matheseos,* ed. W. KROLL et al., 2 v. (*Bibliotheca scriptorum Graecorum et Romanorum Teubneriana*; 1897–1913); *De errore,* ed. C. HALM (*Corpus scriptorum ecclesiasticorum latinorum* 2; 1867); ed. K. ZIEGLER, v.3 of *Das Wort der Antike*; ed. R. BEUTLER (Munich 1953); ed. and tr. G. HEUTEN (Brussels 1938); *Works,* ed. and tr. C. FORBES (*Ancient Christian Writers*; 1965). G. MORIN, ed., *Consultationes Zacchaei et Apollonii* (Florilegium Patristicum 39; 1935). **Literature.** G. MORIN, *Revue Bénédictine* 46 (1934) 456–459; *Jahrbuch für Liturgiewissenschaft* 13 (1936) 185–188. P. COURCELLE, *Revue de l'histoire des religions* 146 (1954) 174–193, on the *Consultationes.* J. LENZENWEGER, *Lexikon für Theologie und Kirche* 2 4:144. F. BOLL, *Paulys Realenzyklopädie der klassichen Altertumswisschenschaft* 6.2 (1909) 2365–79.

[C. A. FORBES]

FIRMILIAN OF CAESAREA

Chiefly remembered for his intemperate support of St. CYPRIAN against St. STEPHEN I; bishop from *c.* 230; d. Tarsus, 268 (feast in the Greek Church, Oct. 28). A friend of ORIGEN, he was highly esteemed throughout the East. He took part in various synods: at Iconium (*c.* 230) against Montanist baptism (*see* MONTANISM); at Antioch where (*c.* 252) the bishops rallied in condemning the Novatianist schism (*see* NOVATIAN AND NOVATIANISM); and again (*c.* 264) for the protracted trial of its heretical bishop, PAUL OF SAMOSATA. His known views contributed to Paul's deposition, though Firmilian himself had died at Tarsus on his way to the synod's final session. In his sole surviving letter (preserved in translation as *Ep.* 75 among Cyprian's letters) he commended Cyprian for repudiating any baptism administered outside the Church, and poured fresh scorn on Pope Stephen's more favorable attitude and on his claims. Stephen threatened to excommunicate Firmilian and many other Eastern bishops, but DIONYSIUS OF ALEXANDRIA pleaded on their behalf with both Stephen and his successor Sixtus II.

Bibliography: CYPRIAN, *Opera omnia,* ed. G. HARTEL, 3 v. (*Corpus scriptorum ecclesiasticorum latinorum* 3.1–3.3; 1868–71). EUSEBIUS, *Historia Ecclesiastica* 6:27, 46.3; 7:5.1, 14, 28.1, 30.4–5. J. CHAPMAN, *Catholic Encyclopedia* 6:80–81. G. BARDENHEWER, *Geschichte der altkirchlichen Literatur* 2:312–314.

[M. BÉVENOT]

FIRMIN OF AMIENS, ST.

First Bishop of the Diocese of Amiens, France, third-century martyr. He seems to have been a native of Pamplona in Navarre. He was converted to Christianity by (St.) Honestus, a disciple of (St.) Saturninus of Toulouse, and consecrated bishop by Honoratus of Toulouse. Firmin became a missionary in southern France. Later, after some years in northern France, he decided to settle at AMIENS, where, according to tradition, he was the first bishop. He was martyred there sometime during the reigns of Maximian and Diocletian (284–305). A church, at first dedicated to the Blessed Virgin and now known as Saint-Acheul's, was built over his tomb. His relics were translated to the cathedral in the seventh century. There is much that is obscure in the life of Firmin since no mention of him is found before the eighth century. In 1186 his relics were translated to Pamplona. Sources of the eighth and ninth centuries for Amiens name a second Bp. Firmin of Amiens, a confessor (feast: Sept. 1). The son of a senator converted by the first Firmin, he was renowned for his missionary work in the region of Amiens. It is often thought that Bishop Firmin the martyr and Bishop Firmin the confessor were one and the same man.

Feast: Sept. 25.

Bibliography: L. DUCHESNE, *Fastes épiscopaux de l'ancienne Gaule* (Paris 1907–15) 3:122–127. A. BUTLER, *The Lives of the Saints,* ed. H. THURSTON and D. ATTWATER (New York 1956) 3:632–633. G. BARDY, *Catholicisme* 4:1318–19. J. L. BAUDOT and L. CHAUSSIN, *Vies des saints et des bienheueux selon l'ordre du calendrier avec l'historique des fêtes* (Paris 1935–56) 9:514–516.

[J. A. CORBETT]

FIRST COMMUNION

By the fourth century infants and adults generally celebrated baptism, anointing, and Communion in the same ceremony, as is maintained today in many Eastern Rite churches. In the course of time, confirmation became an independent rite, reserved to the bishop. Infant baptism, *quam primum,* gradually became a universal practice. Infants continued to receive communion but the practice varied and eucharist began to be separated from baptism, severing the unity of the sacraments of initiation. The Fourth Lateran Council in 1215 (c. 21) stated that communion was not obligatory until one reached the ''age of reason,'' (about the age of seven), the age in which children are supposed to be capable of distinguishing right from wrong and therefore responsible for their conduct. Theologians and canonists of the time differed in their interpretation of this canon but the discussion resulted in the age of reason as important criteria for determining the obligation of receiving the sacraments. The Council of Trent confirmed the Decree of the Lateran Council but did not condemn the ancient practice (Council of Trent, Sess. 21, chap. 4).

By the High Middle Ages, denying Communion to infants was no longer a question. The focus on the transcendence of the Eucharist and the fear of receiving an unworthy communion led to such strict requirements for reception of communion that adults themselves only rarely received the sacrament. The Jansenist movement in the 17th and 18th centuries demanded a rigorous preparation comprised of a precise recital of the catechism, rigorous penitential practices to insure a worthy communion and the delay of first communion until adolescence. This regimen made the Holy Eucharist a reward for virtue and not the ''remedy by which we are freed from our daily faults and preserved from serious sin'' (Council of Trent, Sess. 13, chap. 2).

The decree of St. PIUS X *Quam Singulari* (Aug. 8, 1910), changed the age for First Communion from adolescence to about seven years of age in the Latin Rite. Pius X determined three criteria for reception of first communion: the child can distinguish between good and evil, knows the difference between ordinary bread and eucharistic bread and is able to receive communion with devotion ''becoming his years.'' The change in age met with negative reaction in many parts of the Catholic world. Concerns were raised about the capability of younger children to understand the doctrinal concepts and whether the children would continue catechism classes once they had received their first communion.

The French clergy as well as other episcopates dealt with these issues by distinguishing between a ''private communion'' celebrated within the family and a ''solemn Communion'' that took place during adolescence and was preceded by an extensive catechesis and thorough knowledge of the catechism as requirement for reception of communion. First Communion, since the 17th century, had already taken on a life of its own, becoming a public ritual, a solemn ceremony undertaken by all the members of a same age group at the same time, usually adolescents. In many countries, First Communion also symbolized the passage from childhood into youth. The ceremony of solemn communion included rituals such as the renewal of baptismal promises, the lighting of candles and a consecration to the Blessed Virgin Mary. The youth usually wore white clothing or armbands as a symbol of the innocence of childhood. White also symbolized that the child be as pure and sinless as possible for the reception of a worthy communion. Children were given prayer books, rosaries and holy cards as well as a certificate of First Holy Communion. Gradually, the Solemn Communion ceremony of adolescents, with almost no change, became the First Communion celebration for younger children.

The *Decree on the Church's Missionary Activity*, the *Decree on the Ministry and Life of Priests* of Vatican II, the *Order of Christian Initiation of Adults*, the *Code of Canon Law* (1983), and the *Catechism of the Catholic Church* (1994) restored the early church understanding of the unity of baptism, confirmation, and Eucharist as sacraments of initiation. The *Order of Christian Initiation of Adults* mandates their reception in one ceremony for unbaptized adults and children of catechetical age. There is no uniform sequence of reception of the sacraments of initiation for those baptized in infancy. The practice in the United States and many other countries admits of wide variations in age and sequence of reception. The First Communion rite, since it is not a universal ritual, has therefore never been revised and consequently never explicitly linked to baptism and confirmation. In many countries, the expectation that confession precede the first communion of children gives First Communion a closer relationship to penance than to baptism or confirmation. *The Instruction on the Worship of the Eucharist* (May 25, 1967) 14, encourages a liturgical catechesis based on the principal rites and prayers of the Mass (particularly the eucharistic prayer) and emphasizes the relationship of the Mass to daily life. The instruction states that these principles should be noted particularly with regard to First Communion so that it will be seen as the full incorporation into the Body of Christ. The primary focus of First Communion preparation is to enable the children, as full members of Christ's Body, to take part actively with the people of God in the eucharist, share in the Lord's table and in the community of their brothers and sisters (DMC, 12). The ecclesial significance of First Communion at the present time is that it gives the child a sense of belonging and a new relationship with the Church.

Bibliography: L. ANDRIEUX, *La Premiere Communion* (Paris 1911). C. CASPER, G. LUKKEN, and G. ROUWHORST, eds., *Bread of Heaven: Customs and Practices Surrounding Holy Communion. Essays in the History of Liturgy and Culture* (Kampen, Netherlands 1995). J. DELUMEAU, ed., *La Premiere Communion: Quatre siecles d'histoire* (Paris 1987). P. TURNER, *Ages of Initiation: The First Two Christian Millennia* (Collegeville, Minn. 2000).

[C. DOOLEY]

FIRST PRINCIPLES

In the traditional sense of the term, SCIENCE is KNOWLEDGE that is both discursive and complete in itself. It proceeds by way of DEMONSTRATION; hence, a demonstrated truth is one that impels the assent of the INTELLECT, presupposing a prior assent to the truths upon which it is based. If science has for its proper object demonstrated truth, that is, conclusions or mediately known propositions, it must base its demonstrations upon premises that are immediately known as indemonstrable truths, otherwise called first principles. This article explains the Aristotelian-Thomistic doctrine of first principles, with accent on their nature, origin, and habitual use.

Postulate, hypothesis, and principle. The expression ''first principles'' itself indicates that there are distinctions among principles. At the lowest level are propositions that are actually demonstrable, but are posited and utilized without being demonstrated. These are principles only insofar as they are accepted by one considering an argument; depending upon his position, they are regarded as postulates or hypotheses. A PROPOSITION is a POSTULATE (Lat. *postulare,* to ask) if the one considering it has no opinion of his own or holds a contrary one; we ''ask'' him, as it were, to admit it for the sake of demonstration. Should the auditor judge the proposition likely, giving some assent to it, it is called a hypothesis. In this case he does not merely agree to the use of the proposition for purposes of demonstration, but accepts it because it seems probable and he feels it can be proved.

Such is the meaning usually associated with the term ''hypothesis,'' although this is not its original meaning. Etymologically the word has an extension similar to that of PRINCIPLE. Deriving from ὑποτίθημι, meaning ''to put under,'' hypothesis was something posed as a foundation for reasoning. As such, it included indemonstrable truths, even the most proper and absolute. Since the term ''presuppose'' also has its origin in ὑποτίθημι, one can hold that a hypothesis, in its original sense, is a proposition ''presupposed'' to a demonstration, while in a later sense it comes to be one that is accepted as demonstrated, though it is neither indemonstrable nor actually demonstrated. Ambiguity can be avoided by using the term ''hypothesis'' in the more restrictive sense of proposition accepted as demonstrated, and leaving the term ''principle'' for the original meaning.

According to ARISTOTLE, ''a principle in a demonstration is an immediate proposition,'' while ''an immediate proposition is one which has no other proposition prior to it'' (*Anal. post.* 72a 7). In such a proposition, the predicate is so connected with the subject that the relationship affirmed between them admits of no middle term.

Common and proper principles. The terms involved offer a further basis for distinguishing principles. ''Among the principles used in the demonstrative sciences, some are proper to each science and some are common to all. . . .'' (*ibid.* 76a 37). This equivalently distinguishes between definitions and axioms.

Definitions. While a DEFINITION as such is not yet a proposition, any proposition that directly applies a definition to the thing defined is an immediate proposition. The same applies to a proposition that is founded immediately upon a definition, in which the predicate is so directly related that it seems to need no explanation and to flow from the definition. It is enough, for example, to know that a right angle is generated by a perpendicular erected on a straight line to know that all right angles are equal. Proper principles are always immediate, with the immediacy, so to speak, of definitions. Their designation as ''proper principles'' arises from the fact that their definitions derive from the proper subject matter of a particular science.

Axioms. From this it can be gathered that common principles or axioms go beyond the limits of a particular science, that the truth they convey has a common value for all science. They are also common in the sense that they express thoughts or opinions that all accept and share. Their terms are so simple and current, their evidence so compelling, that one can apply to all of them what Aristotle said of first principles, namely, that they are the best known, so well known, in fact, that no one can be mistaken about them. It is in this very firmness, founded upon their characteristic of being most known, that their priority resides, as well as their dignity in the scale of knowledge. This is why they are called first principles or axioms (Gr. ἄξιος, meaning fitting), which St. THOMAS AQUINAS renders as *dignitates* or *maximae propositiones.* In modern discussions of METHODOLOGY, however, the term ''axiom'' takes on a different meaning (*see* AXIOMATIC SYSTEM).

Certitude and Truth. Aristotle affirms that all principles must be believed and understood better than conclusions (*ibid.* 72a 25–39). Since the knowledge contained in conclusions derives from principles, the latter cannot be logically antecedent without at the same time being more certain. One hardly admits the truth of a conclusion with conviction unless the principles upon which it is based exclude the possibility of the contradictory conclusion being true. Thus the immediate evidence of principles is always greater than the participated evidence of conclusions.

All things being equal, common principles enjoy a certain superiority over proper principles; this does not mean, however, that proper principles must be demonstrated from common principles. The terms of the former also are joined without need of a third term, and their evidence comes from proper considerations. Yet, while independent from the viewpoint of knowledge, they are not independent from the viewpoint of CERTITUDE. Actually, common principles would not be the most common if they were not included in the proper, and the proper are not such because they are totally different from the common, but rather because they imply an addition to the common. Thus the truth of a common principle is found, although only implicitly, in the truth of a proper principle, so that if the first is not true, the second cannot be true either. Again, the certitude of common principles can be greater than that of proper principles only because of the greater simplicity of the former, although they share this certitude, so to speak, with proper principles.

Knowledge of principles. Except for one who studies a science, knowledge of principles proper to that science is not indispensable. Nor is there need to know such principles before taking up the science, for it is understood that the instructor begins by laying down these principles. Thus, for Aristotle, θέσις (thesis) is equivalent to proper principle. Whatever the discipline in which one engages, however, the possession of axioms or common principles is a prerequisite. Proper principles are already a part, initial though it be, of a science or particular treatise, while axioms are completely prior to any science. Thus BOETHIUS has formulated the classical distinction between immediate propositions that are such for specialists alone (*quoad sapientes tantum*) and immediate propositions that are such for all (*quoad omnes*). These are further subdivided into immediate propositions that are readily seen (*quod nos*), and those not recognized as such (*quoad se tantum*) that require a posteriori DEMONSTRATION, such as the existence of God (*see* GOD, PROOFS FOR THE EXISTENCE OF). Thus not all immediate propositions are principles, for the criterion of a principle is that it be better known to us, and even to all in the case of first principles.

Origin of first principles. Two extremes, INNATISM and EMPIRICISM, are to be avoided when accounting for first principles. According to innatism, man possesses first principles by nature. For LEIBNIZ, man has them as virtual knowledge, while for KANT he knows certain a priori propositions that have no other foundation than the condition of the knowing subject. In their different ways, each tries to explain why principles are so easily known, and yet safeguard their universality and necessity. Empiricism, on the other hand, refuses to recognize any universality or necessity in first principles; it classifies them as knowledge acquired from the senses and remaining wholly dependent upon sense, so that any assent given them is consequent on experience and knowledge of the particular. (*See* KNOWLEDGE, THEORIES OF.)

Some of Aristotle's expressions, such as ''prerequisite experience'' and ''necessary induction,'' might be interpreted empirically, while St. Thomas makes statements that might be taken in the sense of innatism, such as ''seeds that preexist in us'' (*De ver.* 11.1), ''knowledge put into us by God as author of nature'' (*C. gent.* 1.7). Both, however, concur in the doctrine that man possesses a potency or ability to acquire first principles, without this potency's being superior to the actual possession of such principles themselves (cf. *Anal. post.* 99b 33).

Role of Experience. According to Aristotle, the preliminary knowledge of principles involves the following stages: SENSATION, memory, EXPERIENCE, all of which are associated with SENSE KNOWLEDGE from the exterior SENSES all the way to the COGITATIVE POWER. Again, according to Aristotle, principles are not derived from experience without coming also from UNIVERSALS. Moreover, while aware of difficulties involved in interpreting some texts (e.g., *Anal. post.* 100a 6), we hold that the universal itself is not directly reducible either to experience or to principles. It is true that experience does include a certain grasp of the universal, the grasp of a universal that is confused, so to speak. But this is not actually possible unless the cogitative power compares and brings together singulars to achieve some notion of unity. If the cogitative faculty remains a *ratio particularis* and is always concerned with singulars, it certainly does not furnish the experience that Aristotle describes as ''the universal now stabilized in its entirety within the soul, the one beside the many which is a single identity within them all'' (100a 7–8). Under the latter formality, which is its proper formality, the universal is the object of no power save the intellect. But again, even the universal is not a principle, since the principle comes from the universal (cf. 100b 1–5). To distinguish the two, one need only have recourse to the definition of principle as a proposition. It thus appears that universals are nothing more than noncomplex, simple notions that constitute the terms of the proposition-principle.

Thus the universal stands between experience and first principles in such a way that sense knowledge is required only for the acquisition of terms, but does not enter into the formation of principles themselves. The proximate source of principles is not sense experience but intellectual comprehension, and this as formulated in the IDEA.

Role of Induction. This raises the further problem of how first principles are related to induction. ''It is clear,'' says Aristotle, ''that we must get to know the primary premises by induction, for the method by which even sense perception implants the universal is inductive'' (*Anal. post.* 100b 3–5). The term ''induction'' can be correctly applied to knowledge of complex expressions or propositions, for it commonly signifies the passage from a truth established in the singular case to the same truth known in all its universality. And while the fulcrum of induction is experience, the experience from which principles proceed is that of complexes and the induction contingent upon their formation. Such experience alone can assume the role of moving and determining the intellect to effect the composition found in the proposition. In its contact with singular reality, experience sketches out, one might say, both the basic notions and their relations to one another; thus, from the point of view of the acquisition of principles, of ''how'' they are born in us, one must say they come from experience but that they are obtained by way of induction.

Content and Assent. Having said this, one must specify that induction accounts for the origin of principles without explaining their content in any way. Since the knowledge attained in principles is that of propositions, the ultimate explanation for assent should be in terms of the absolute adherence we give propositions. Here the knowledge of terms furnishes the basic explanation, since immediate and absolute EVIDENCE is what compels assent. To invoke experience and induction alone would be to change the proposition into an object of discourse wherein our adherence would be conditioned by some antecedent adherence to the singulars of experience. This would make the principle something ''better known,'' without accounting for its superiority or its greater certitude with respect to previous knowledge. Aristotle located the universal between experience and principles, and St. Thomas explained knowledge of principles through knowledge of terms, because both regarded experience and induction as a necessary condition for the origin of principles; yet they also held that the knowledge of terms and their connection, as seen by the simple light of the intellect, is the unique formal reason for the assent we give them.

Grasped in its entirety, this doctrine steers a middle road between empiricism on the one hand, which finds all truth in the senses, and rationalistic innatism on the other, which assigns no role to the intellect except that of reenacting experience.

Habits and first principles. A HABIT is a stable disposition whose stability is ultimately determined by its OBJECT. The habits of the speculative intellect, namely, understanding, science, and wisdom, dispose it to attain necessary TRUTH. All three habits make use of first principles.

Understanding. The first of the intellectual habits, UNDERSTANDING, is directly concerned with principles. Scholastics call it *intellectus*, the name of the faculty from which it comes, a fact that is intelligible from what has already been said, since only by its own power does the intellect attain the truth of first principles. Experience supplies antecedent knowledge, but the terminal point of the induction itself specifies the habit of first principles.

Science. The second habit is that of SCIENCE. Each science has its proper subject and, if it demonstrates properties, necessarily proceeds from principles proper to that subject. Nothing prevents a science from also using common principles, provided that these be used in conjunction with proper principles and that they be applied in the context of the particular subject matter. Geometry, for instance, is not concerned with being and nonbeing in an absolute sense, but rather as applied to magnitudes. ''Sciences do not use first principles in all their generality, as applicable to all being, but only as much as needed according to content of their subject matter'' (Thomas Aquinas, *In 4 meta.* 5.591).

Wisdom. The third speculative habit is WISDOM, also known as METAPHYSICS. Its subject is BEING AS BEING in all its universality, as opposed to the beings studied in particular sciences. This immediately suggests the possibility that metaphysics has certain functions regarding principles whose terms are common. In fact, the coincidence in universality sets metaphysics apart as the only habit treating of first principles in themselves, making them the object of its consideration apart from simply using them.

Relation to metaphysics. Following Aristotle, St. Thomas assigns to metaphysics the role of establishing common notions and then defending first principles against those who deny them (*In 6 eth.* 5.1181–1183). In what can this role consist, if the comprehension of terms inducing assent already belongs to the habit of understanding? The answer is implicit in the question: Such a role must be granted to understanding in the exact measure required for assent itself. The point is that confused knowledge of terms suffices for making a JUDGMENT regarding their connection, that principles can be known quite certainly even though their terms be common. The habit of understanding is satisfied with grasping the universals found at the beginning of intellectual knowledge. The knowledge of *communia,* which is proper to wisdom, is, on the contrary, a distinct knowledge; one achieves it only by distinguishing the multiple acceptations of common terms. It is one thing to admit that it is impossible to be and not to be simultaneously; it is another to know whether the expression ''to be'' designates essential or accidental being, extramental or intentional being, or actual or potential being. In thus making common terms precise, the metaphysician might give the impression that he is a lexicographer or one compiling a vocabulary—Aristotle seems to do this in book five of his *Metaphysics*—but not everyone can control all the acceptations of these terms, and their distinction is a sign of the superiority of wisdom over understanding.

Defense of Principles. As for the defense of first principles, methods depend as much on the principles denied as on the reasons alleged in their negation. One such method could deal with the single case, in an argument *ad hominem,* if it happens that in confusing different senses of a term or playing on its ambiguity, someone should pretend to give examples of the falsity of the principle. Another method might utilize a demonstration to show, again *ad hominem,* that to deny some principle one must deny another that is even more common and more evident. This suggests that the defense of first principles is finally or radically rooted in the systematic defense of the most common principles, those so implied in all knowledge that to deny them is to deny knowledge itself. This is how Aristotle defends the principles of contradiction and of the excluded middle in book four of the *Metaphysics.* A number of his arguments are still useful against arguments more subtle than those of the ancient SOPHISTS.

Number of First Principles. Contemporary metaphysicians, including those in the Aristotelian and Thomistic traditions, regard it as one role of wisdom to discuss first principles, particularly to determine their names, their formulations, and their number. All agree in selecting from the following those principles they consider among the first: the principle of contradiction, of the excluded middle, of noncontradiction, of identity, of intelligibility, of sufficient reason, of causality, of finality, and even a principle of substance. St. Thomas employed the first two, usually formulating these in terms of affirmation and denial. Such apparently logical formulations displease some metaphysicians, possibly because they suspect an IDEALISM that might accept such principles as laws of thought, but of thought unrelated to extramental being. These thinkers prefer a principle stated in terms of being and nonbeing, that is, it is impossible to be and not to be, which was also formulated by St. Thomas (*In 1 anal. post.* 5.7). But this impossibility is hardly satisfying if the opposition of being to nonbeing be regarded as the object respectively of affirming and denying. Moved by a desire to find the foundation for this in being itself, some fasten upon the intelligibility of being, upon its transcendental truth, and therefore, upon its noncontradiction or its transcendental unity. Thus, it would seem, the principle of intelligibility as well as that of identity have become principles, one might even say ''principles of being,'' meaning by this that their value is not limited to knowledge alone. Furthermore, the TRANSCENDENTALS are the basic foundation for all knowledge, and might on this account be called principles; we leave open the question whether or not they conform to the general conditions already set down for axioms. At any rate, the tendency for discussions of first principles to move toward the problem of being in itself shows the metaphysical character of studies concerning these principles.

See Also: CONTRADICTION, PRINCIPLE OF; EXCLUDED MIDDLE, PRINCIPLE OF; IDENTITY, PRINCIPLE OF; CAUSALITY, PRINCIPLE OF; FINALITY, PRINCIPLE OF; SUFFICIENT REASON, PRINCIPLE OF; INTELLIGIBILTY, PRINCIPLE OF.

Bibliography: L. M. RÉGIS, *Epistemology,* tr. I. C. BYRNE (New York 1959). D. J. B. HAWKINS, *Being and Becoming* (New York 1954). J. MARÉCHAL, *Le Point de départ de la métaphysique,* 5 v. (3d ed. Paris 1944–49), v. 5 *Le Thomisme devant la philosophie critique* (2d ed.). P. COFFEY, *Epistemology,* 2 v. (New York 1917; repr. 1958). L. FUETSCHER, *Die ersten Seinsund Denkprinzipien* (Philosophie und Grenzwissenschaften 3, nn. 2–4; Innsbruck 1930). J. RICKABY, *The First Principles of Knowledge* (London 1888).

[E. TRÉPANIER]

FISCHER, JOHANN KASPAR FERDINAND

Baroque composer and keyboard virtuoso; b. Germany, 1650?; d. Rastatt, March 27, 1746?. Reliable biographical details are unavailable, but it is known that by 1695 he was music director to Margrave Ludwig of Baden. It is also evident, from his music, that he had captured the spirit of the late baroque French instrumental style of J. B. LULLY and helped introduce it into Germany. Like much baroque music, Fischer's compositions were first published in great sets. Among them are *Journal de Printemps* (1695), charming orchestral or dance suites following the French order; *Musikalisches Blumen-Büschlein* (1696), keyboard suites; *Vesperae* (1701), Vesper psalms for eight voices and instrumental accompaniment; *Ariadne Musica* (1715), preludes and fugues in 20 keys together with ricercars for the church seasons (this became the model for J. S. BACH'S *Well-Tempered Clavier*); *Litaniae Laurentiae* (1711), eight litanies and four Marian antiphons for voices and instruments; and *Blumenstrauss* (1732), organ preludes and fugues in as many church modes, together with a toccata and finale for each group.

Bibliography: *Sämtliche Werke für Klavier und Orgel*, ed. E. VON WERRA (Leipzig 1906); *Journal de Printemps*, in *Denkmäler Deutscher Tonkunst* 10.1 (Leipzig 1902); *Ariadne* in *Liber organi*, ed. E. KALLER (Mainz-New York 1931), v.7. K. NEF, *Geschichte der Sinfonie und Suite* (Leipzig 1921). G. FROTSCHER, *Geschichte des Orgelspiels und der Orgelkomposition*, 2 v. (2d ed. Berlin 1959). K. SEITZ, *Die Musik in Geschichte und Gegenwart*, ed. F. BLUME (Kassel-Basel 1949–) 4:264–269. J. R. MILNE, *Grove's Dictionary of Music and Musicians*, ed. E. BLOM, 9 v. (5th ed. London 1954) 3:143–144. W. APEL, *Masters of the Keyboard* (Cambridge, Mass. 1947). M. F. BUKOFZER, *Music in the Baroque Era* (New York 1947). A. PLOTINSKY, ''The Keyboard Works of Johann Kaspar Ferdinand Fischer'' (Ph.D. diss. City University of New York, 1978). D. M. RANDEL, ed., *The Harvard Biographical Dictionary of Music* (Cambridge, Massachusetts 1996) 270. N. SLONIMSKY, ed., *Baker's Biographical Dictionary of Musicians, Eighth Edition* (New York 1992) 544. S. WOLLENBERG, ''Johann Caspar Ferdinand Fischer'' in *The New Grove Dictionary of Music and Musicians, vol. 6*, ed. S. SADIE (New York 1980) 607–609.

[D. BEIKMAN]

FISH, SYMBOLISM OF

The fish as a food and as a symbol occupies an important position in the history of religions and in the cults of the gods and of the dead. In many cases the fish appeared as an article prohibited in the diet because of its sacral nature. Thus the liturgical laws of Egyptian priests demanded abstention from it. The venerators of Onuris, Hatmehit, Hathor, and Neith regarded the fish as sacred. The Syrian goddess Atargatis (identified with the *Magna Mater*) was honored with a fish-offering, and her priests sanctified themselves by eating it. The people, who were not permitted to eat it, offered fishes of gold and silver.

Pre-Christian Cults. In Syrian culture the fish became a symbol of happiness and life. The votaries of the Babylonian fish-god Oannes appear on monuments clad in a garment imitating a fish. Funeral repasts on Syrian monuments show the fish as an offering in the cult of the dead. Among the Carthaginians, the fish was used as a sacrifice to Tanit, Baal Hammon, and the Punic Saturnus. Punic-Roman altars have been discovered that show the fish as a votive offering. The Etruscans and Romans knew of a propitiatory offering of fish to ward off lightning. Fish was a sacrificial gift in the cult of *Dea Tacita* on the Roman Feast for the Dead, and fish offerings were well known in the cult of Hecate.

There was a strict prohibition against eating fish in the mystery cult of Eleusis, and the statutes of the Pythagoreans insisted on abstinence from it. Popular medicine forbade fish for the diet of those suffering from epilepsy, the ''sacred sickness.'' Among the Greeks it was customary to honor the goddess of the dead with a fish-offering, but not the gods of heaven. The burning of a fish sacrifice constituted the usual commemoration of the dead. There are a great number of inscriptions, monuments, and literary sources to prove this for the period between 2000 B.C. and Christian times, extending from Babylon, the Hetites Asia Minor, Macedonia, and the Greek Islands, to Punic Latin Africa, Gaul, Italy, Dalmatia, and the Danube provinces. The Jews regarded fish as the preferred food for the *cena pura,* the supper preceding the Sabbath with which the solemnity began.

Christian Symbolism. In Christian art and literature, the fish appears as an acrostic and as a symbol (*see* ICHTHUS). The abbreviation ΙΧΘΥΣ, for Ἰησοῦς Χριστὸς, Θεοῦ Υἱὸς Σωτήρ (Jesus Christ, Son of God, Savior), was current by the end of the 2d century. The Sibylline Oracles (8.217–280) refer to it, and Lactantius (*Div. inst.* 7.16–20), Eusebius (*Vita Constant.* 5.18), and Augustine (*Civ.* 18.23) also employ it. It can be seen on a great number of Christian sepulchral monuments, such as the inscription of Licinia Amias in Rome, the famous inscription of PECTORIUS in Autun, the inscription of Eutychianus at Perugia, and the silver plaque on the sarcophagus of St. PAULINUS at Trier. It was used as a phylactery at the doors of Christian houses and tombs and as an amulet on gems, medals, and rings; it is found also in the mosaics of Christian basilicas, such as the Constantinian church of the Nativity at Bethlehem and S. Apollinare in Classe at Ravenna.

Symbol of Christ. Side by side with this acrostic, the fish appears as a symbol of Christ in inscriptions, art, and

Symbolism of the Fish, early Christian stone epitaph.

literature. The East and West knew it at the end of the 2d century, as is proved by the much discussed inscription of ABERCIUS of Asia Minor and by TERTULLIAN (*De baptismo* 1). The fish is seen also as a food in banquet scenes on frescoes in the catacombs of Rome, including those of Peter and Marcellinus, Priscilla, and St. Callistus; it decorates Christian sarcophagi such as that of Livia Primitiva in the Louvre and that in the tomb of St. Matthias in Trier, and it appears in pictures showing Christ and the Apostles at the Last Supper, e.g., in the mosaic in S. Apollinare Nuovo at Ravenna, on the ivory of Count Stroganoff in the Walters Art Gallery at Baltimore, and in the Cathedral of Milan.

There are Christian lamps bearing the image of the fish, and some have its form. It has its place on Christian glasses and cups, on Eucharistic spoons, on epitaphs such as those in the catacombs of St. Agnes and St. Sebastian, and in the Coemeterium Soteris in Rome, in Christian baptisteries such as that of Cuicul in Numidia, and in basilicas such as that of Parenzo. The corpus of archeological material collected and published by F. J. DÖLGER shows the far-reaching influence and extent of the acrostic and the symbol.

Acrostic and Eucharistic Symbol. Several interesting questions in this regard have still to be answered. Is the acrostic older than the symbol? Is the symbol derived from the acrostic, or vice versa? What is the origin of the symbol? How is one to explain the Eucharistic meaning that clings to the symbol from its earliest appearance to the end of its use among Christian types. Of all the symbols in which the early Christians attempted to embody, and at the same time perhaps to conceal, the concepts of their faith, the fish is the most obscure in point of origin. V. Schultze, H. Achelis, and C. R. Morey derive the fish-symbol from the acrostic. Dölger derives the acrostic from the symbol. There seems to be a twofold root beneath the theology of the fish in Christian antiquity. The acrostic most probably goes back to Gnostic circles with their fondness for alphabetic mysticism and magic formulas. The origin of the symbol should perhaps be sought in the long history of the fish as a sacral food in the cults of the ancient world. Achelis's theory, according to which the fish-symbol grew out of the recognition of Christ as the Son of God on the occasion of His Baptism, rests entirely on the phrase of Tertullian (*De baptismo* 1): *Nos pisciculi secundum* ΙΧΘΥΝ *nostrum Jesum Christum in aqua nascimur*; this theory is not satisfactory.

Theory of Indian Origin. The theories of Pischel and C. Schmidt, who derived the Christian type from the savior-fish in Indian mythology, have not found the approval of scholars. A thorough review of the relations of primitive Christianity with India shows that a contact may have been established with Indian religion and symbolism in northwest India as early as the 1st century. But such a relation could not have been of sufficient intimacy or duration to justify the derivation of the Christian symbol from

Indian sources. Moreover, the parallel between the Indian savior-fish and the Christian symbol is not a striking one.

F. Münter's and A. Jeremias's derivation of the fish-symbol from a putative Jewish symbolical association of the zodiacal sign of the fishes with the Messiah does not deserve confidence. Schultze's reference of the symbol to Mt 7.9–10 (''Or if he ask for a fish, will he give him a serpent?'') is not convincing because the figure is so natural that a symbolical interpretation seems forced. Heuser's attempt to connect the symbol in its Eucharistic aspect with the ''Multiplication of Loaves and Fishes'' and the ''Supper on the Sea of Tiberias'' fails because the citations from the Fathers that he adduces are all after Augustine (d. 430).

A careful examination of ancient customs concerning the use of fish as a sacral food discounts the theories of S. Reinach, A. Dufourcq, and F. Cumont, according to whom the Christian symbol arose out of, or was strongly influenced by, the sacral repasts of the priests and worshipers of Atargatis and Derketo. In eating fish that was the incarnation of their divinity these cultists identified themselves with the object of their worship. The contrast between the pagan banquets and the Christian Eucharist is too strong. The eating of the sacral fish by *worshipers,* contrary to the assumption of the theories mentioned above, is nowhere found in pagan cults. In some cases it was practiced by priests, but for the most part the fish appeared in pagan religions as an article prohibited in the diet on account of its sacral nature.

One may contrast with this the fish offered by faith ''to the friends'' in the epitaph of Abercius. It is important to note that this epitaph, with the first instance of the Christian Eucharistic fish-symbol, was found in Phrygian Hieropolis in the middle of Asia Minor, where the Syrian goddess Atargatis, identified with the *Magna Mater,* was honored with a fish-offering. Dölger believes it natural to see the Christian fish-symbol here as an unusually apt opposition to pagan usages devised in the interest of propaganda and especially aimed at the cult of Atargatis and the cult of the Kabeiroi or Thracian Horsemen.

While there cannot be any doubt that the post-Constantinian Church employed such practices, everything known of the Church of the 2d century is sharply contradictory to the assumption that it permitted itself such devices on pivotal points of faith. Where such parallels existed, the apologists, e.g., JUSTIN MARTYR, explained them as pagan imitations of Christian usages. Though they were mistaken, one can see how they judged such matters.

Goodenough has recently expressed the opinion that the symbolism of the fish originated in pagan cults, was adopted by the Jewish religion, and passed from there to Christian usage. Though both the acrostic and the symbol appear almost at the same time in the sources, it seems that the symbol, fish=Christ, originated before the acrostic.

Bibliography: H. ACHELIS, *Das Symbol des Fisches und die Fischdenkmäler der römischen Katakomben* (Marburg 1888). R. PISCHEL, *Der Ursprung des christlichen Fischsymbols* (Berlin 1905). C. R. MOREY, ''The Origin of the Fish-Symbol,'' *Princeton Theological Review* 8 (1910) 93–106, 231–246, 401–432; 9 (1911) 268–289. F. J. DÖLGER, ΙΧΘΥΣ, 5 v. (Rome-Münster 1910–27; 2d ed. Münster 1928–43). I. SCHEFTELOWITZ, ''Das Fischsymbol im Judentum und Christentum,'' *Archiv für Religionswissenschaft* 14 (1911) 1–53. V. SCHULTZE, ΙΧΘΥΣ (Griefswald 1912). F. CUMONT, *Paulys Realenzyklopädie der klassischen Altertumswissenschaft,* ed. G. WISSOWA et al. 9.1 (1914) 844–850. E. R. GOODENOUGH, *Jewish Symbols,* v. 5 (Bollingen Ser. 37; New York 1956) 3–61. J. QUASTEN, *Patrology,* 4 v. (Westminster, Md. 1950–86) 1:171–175, literature.

[J. QUASTEN]

FISHER, JOHN, ST.

Cardinal bishop of Rochester, England, humanist and martyr; b. Beverley, Yorkshire, 1469; executed, London, July 22, 1535. He was the son of a merchant, was educated at the Minster school, and, about 1482, entered Michaelhouse, which was later absorbed into Trinity College, Cambridge. He earned his B.A. degree in 1488 and his M.A. in 1491, when he became a fellow of Michaelhouse and was ordained. Three years later he was elected proctor, then master of Michaelhouse, and president of Queens College in 1505.

Episcopal Career. In 1504 he became bishop of Rochester. His official affiliation with the university brought him to the notice of Lady Margaret Beaufort, mother of Henry VII. He became her confessor and consultant in the use of her wealth. Out of this association were created the readerships of divinity at Oxford and Cambridge (1503) and the foundations of Christ's College (1505) and St. John's College (1511), Cambridge. In 1501 he earned his D.D. degree and was elected vice chancellor of the University and chancellor three years later. It was his unique distinction to receive a lifetime appointment to this office in 1514. To raise the standard of preaching, he obtained a papal bull granting the university the right to appoint 12 priests to preach anywhere in the country. At the death of Lady Margaret in 1509 he was concerned about the foundation of St. John's, since she had not completed her testamentary provisions. Fisher assigned to the College lands she had given him. It is to Lady Margaret that we owe the sermons preached at her request on the penitential Psalms; these were published in 1509 and reprinted seven times before Fisher's death. Commemorative sermons on Henry VII and on Lady Margaret were published in that year also.

In 1511 Fisher encouraged ERASMUS to come to Cambridge to teach Greek. Upon the publication of the latter's Greek New Testament, Fisher was persuaded to learn the language and received his first lessons from Erasmus in 1516. Their friendship led Erasmus to write: "He is the one man at this time who is incomparable for uprightness of life, for learning, and for greatness of soul."

The coming of Lutheranism drew Fisher into controversy. He wrote eight books against various heresies. Since these were in Latin, they are seldom considered in estimates of his fame, but in his own time they gave him a leading position among European theologians. Two anti-Lutheran sermons have survived. The first was preached at a burning of heretical books at St. Paul's Cross on May 12, 1521; the second at the abjuration of Robert Barnes on Feb. 11, 1526.

Conflict with Henry VIII. In June 1527 WOLSEY first put to Fisher the problem posed by Henry VIII's adaptable conscience. Had the pope exceeded his powers in granting a dispensation for the marriage of Henry with Catherine, his brother's widow? Fisher promised to study the question. In September he declared his judgment in favor of the marriage; and in his defense of Catherine at the Legatine Court, May 1529, he incurred the king's resentment. He increased the royal displeasure by leading the opposition in the House of Lords to bills passed by the Commons as remedies for their grievance against the clergy. Two years later, in convocation, he spoke against accepting the king as supreme head of the Church of England.

This continued opposition fixed Henry's determination to silence the aged bishop. The first move was to implicate him in the affair of Elizabeth BARTON, the nun of Kent. His name was included in a bill of attainder (January 1534) on the grounds that he had not reported her "revelations" to the king. He was fined £300. By then his feeble health confined him to his diocese of Rochester. He left it for the last time when summoned to appear at Lambeth on April 13, 1534, to take the oath to the new Act of Succession. Both he and Sir Thomas MORE spurned the oath. They were prepared to accept the line of succession as coming within the province of Parliament, but the Act, as formulated, presumed the legality of the divorce and implied a repudiation of the pope's authority.

Imprisonment and Execution. After a grant of time for reconsideration, Fisher and More again refused the oath and were sent to the Tower on April 17, 1534. There

Saint John Fisher. (©Bettmann/CORBIS)

Fisher remained without trial until June of the next year. He was cared for by his brother, Robert, who had long been his steward as well as a member of parliament for Rochester, and whose death early in 1535 spared him the details of John's trial. While a prisoner, Fisher wrote for his half sister Elizabeth, a Dominican nun, his *Spiritual Consolation* and *Ways to Perfect Religion.*

At the end of 1534 a new Act of Treason was passed, condemning those who maliciously refused to the king any of his titles, including that of supreme head of the English Church. In the same Parliament, Fisher and More were both attaindered under the Act of Succession for refusing the oath and condemned to life imprisonment and loss of goods. At several interrogations in the Tower the questions regarding the acceptance of the king as supreme head were met with silence. Fisher, however, was tricked into making a denial by Richard Rich, the attorney general, who on May 7, 1535, pretended that the king wanted Fisher's opinion as a matter of conscience and that the answer would not be used in evidence against him. As a priest, Fisher could not refuse to answer and he stated that "the king was not, nor could not be, by the law of God, Supreme Head." Henry was further angered when he heard that the new pope, Paul III, created Fisher a cardinal priest of the title of St. Vitalis. Fisher was brought to trial on June 17, 1535, and charged with high treason. He admitted the words he had spoken to Rich, but claimed that it was a privileged occasion and that he had not spoken in malice. This plea was ignored and he was condemned to death, the execution to occur on June 22. His body, after lying naked on the scaffold all day, was given a rough burial in the churchyard of All Hallows near the Tower, and his head was displayed on London Bridge. As his place of burial attracted many who venerated him, his body was reburied in the Tower church of St. Peter-ad-Vincula near that of his fellow martyr, St. Thomas More. Cardinal John Fisher was beatified on Dec. 9, 1886, and canonized on May 19, 1935.

Feast: July 9.

Bibliography: *English Works of John Fisher*, ed. J. E. B. MAYOR (Early English Text Society, extra series 27; 1876); *Sacri sacerdotii defensio contra Lutherum* (1525), ed. H. K. SCHMEINK (*Corpus Catholicorum* 9; Münster 1925); *Defense of the Priesthood*, tr. P. E. HALLETT (London 1935). R. BAYNE, ed., *Life of Fisher* (Early English Text Society, extra series 117; 1921). P. HUGHES, *Earliest English Life of Saint John Fisher* (London 1935). E. P. BELLABRIGA, *De doctrina beati Joannis Fisher in operibus adversus Lutherum conscriptis* (Rome 1935). F. VAN ORTROY, ed., "Vie du bienheureux martryr Jean Fisher, cardinal, Évéque de Rochester (1535)," *Analect Bollandiana* 10 (1891) 121–365; 12 (1893) 97–287. T. E. BRIDGETT, *Life of Blessed John Fisher* (London 1902). E. E. REYNOLDS, *Saint John Fisher* (New York 1956). P. HUGHES, *The Reformation in England*, 3 v. (London 1950–54) v.1. A. HUMBERT, *Dictionnaire de théologie catholique*, ed. A. VACANT et al. (Paris 1903–50) 5:2555–61. A. BUTLER, *The Lives of the Saints*, rev. ed. H. THURSTON and D. ATTWATER (New York 1956) 3:45–49. J. GILLOW, *A Literary and Biographical History or Bibliographical Dictionary of the English Catholics from 1534 to the Present Time*, repr. (New York 1961) 2:262–270. *The Dictionary of the National Biography from the Earliest Times to 1900*, repr. (London 1938) 7:58–63.

[E. E. REYNOLDS]

FISHERMAN'S RING

The gold ring that holds the pope's private seal; it is so called because on it St. Peter is depicted fishing from a boat, the name of the reigning pope being around the edge. Although several of the Apostles were fishermen, Peter was the leader of those whom Christ called to be fishers of men (Lk 5.10). The earliest mention of the fisherman's ring is in a letter of Clement IV to his nephew in 1265; he says that popes sealed their private letters with the seal of the fisherman, whereas public papal documents were sealed with leaden bulls. From the 15th century the fisherman's ring has been used to seal the class of official documents called briefs. At the death of a pope the cardinal camerlengo destroys his fisherman's ring and on the election of a new pope places a new ring on his finger.

[B. FORSHAW]

FITCH, WILLIAM BENEDICT (BENEDICT OF CANFIELD)

Capuchin Friar Minor, a spiritual writer who exercised an outstanding influence, especially on 17th-century spirituality; b. Little Canfield, Essex, England, 1563; d. Paris, Nov. 21, 1610. Fitch was the third son of William Fitch, Lord of the manor of Little Canfield by his second wife Ann, *nee* Wiseman. He was brought up a Protestant. He went to London to read law, being admitted to the Middle Temple in 1580. While a student he was much moved by a chance reading of *The Book of Resolution* by Robert PERSONS, SJ, and was received into the Church, Aug. 1, 1585. He then crossed to France and entered the Capuchins in Paris, March 23, 1587. After finishing his novitiate, he went, apparently, to Italy to study theology, and was probably ordained there.

Back in France by 1592, from which date his spiritual teaching began to circulate in manuscript form, he was appointed novice master and, later, guardian at Orleans, remaining there until 1597, when, after being elected definitor, he moved to Paris. He was highly regarded as a director of souls, and was a prominent leader in spiritual and ecclesiastical reform.

On returning to England, in 1599, as a missionary, he was taken prisoner on arrival, and spent more than two years in captivity, chiefly at Wisbech. At the request of Henry IV, he was released and resumed his former active apostolate in France, again, holding high office in his society. In 1607, his name was included on a list of candidates considered suitable for the office of bishop in England that the nuncio in Paris, Maffeo Barberini (later URBAN VIII), submitted to Rome. During these years he published his chief work, *The Rule of Perfection* (Paris 1609), and *The Christian Knight* (Paris 1609), a work written during his imprisonment in England. He died with a reputation for great holiness of life.

His spiritual teaching, contained mostly in the *Rule of Perfection,* a work printed in numerous editions in various languages, consists, essentially, in seeking perfection through conformity to the will of God.

He was a master of spiritual writing and his work influenced (among others) Madame Acarie (*see* MARIE DE L'INCARNATION, BL.), Cardinal BÉRULLE, and St. VINCENT DE PAUL. His lack of clarity and precision led to criticism of his work, and during the quietist crisis *The Rule of Perfection* was put on the Index (1689). Most modern authorities, however, consider his teaching to be entirely orthodox.

Bibliography: OPTATUS VAN VEGHEL, *Benoît de Canfield, 1562–1610: Sa vie, sa doctrine et son influence* (Rome 1949). J. BROUSSE, *The Lives of Ange de Joyeuse and Benet Canfield,* ed. T.

A. BIRRELL, from R. ROOKWOOD'S tr. of 1623 (New York 1959). J. DAGENS, *Bérulle et les origines de la restauration catholique, 1575–1611* (Bruges 1952). *Lexicon Capuccinum* (Rome 1951) 192–193, gives a considerable bibliography. L. COGNET, *Post-Reformation Spirituality* (New York 1959).

[C. REEL]

FITERO, ABBEY OF

Former Cistercian monastery, probably the first in Spain, in the Diocese of Tarazona, Navarre province, near the Ebro River. Originally founded at Yerga in 1140 by Alfonso VII of Castile with monks from Scala Dei (affiliation of MORIMOND), it was moved to Niencebas in 1146 and to Fitero in 1152 under Abbot Raymond Serrat, who founded the military order of CALATRAVA in 1158. The church has a cenotaph of Rodrigo XIMÉNEZ DE RADA, Archbishop of Toledo (1210–47), who contributed to the building of the church, hoping to be buried there. Fitero, abbey *nullius* and one of the most important Cistercian cloisters in Spain, flourished until its suppression in 1834. It has recently been restored and has pastoral care of the town. The abbey church (now the parish church), the cloister, and the chapter hall have excellent examples of ogival architecture. The church, built *c.* 1200, is typically Cistercian in its main altar, five chapels, ambulatory, and three naves. The chapter hall is Romanesque-ogival, and the early 16th-century cloister is Gothic-plateresque.

Bibliography: M. ARIGITA Y LASA, *Cartulario de Fitero* (Pamplona 1900). T. BIURRUN SÓTIL, *El arte romanico en Navarra* (Pamplona 1936). M. COCHERIL, *Dictionnaire d'histoire et de géographie ecclésiastiques,* ed. A. BAUDRILLART et al. (Paris 1912–) 15:944–948, 952.

[J. PÉREZ DE URBEL]

FITTON, JAMES

Missionary; b. Boston. Mass., April 10, 1805; d. Malden, Mass., Sept. 15, 1881. He was the son of Abraham Fitton, an English wheelwright, and Sarah (Williams) Fitton of Wales. He attended public schools in Boston and Virgil Barber's Academy in Claremont, N.H. Bishop Benedict FENWICK personally supervised his theological studies and ordained him on Dec. 23, 1827. Fitton's labors were divided between urban pastoral assignments and missionary posts in Connecticut, western and central Massachusetts, and Rhode Island. After ministering to the Passamaquoddy people in Maine (1828) and the scattered Catholics of Vermont (1829), he was assigned to Hartford, Conn., in July 1830. There and at Worcester, Mass. (1836–43), he organized the Catholics, opened new schools, promoted temperance societies, lectured, and compiled devotional books. A pioneer in Catholic education, he founded Mt. St. James' Seminary, Worcester, which became the College of the Holy Cross. He was editor of the Hartford *Catholic Press* and author of *The Youth's Companion* (1833), *The Triumph of Religion* (1833), *Familiar Instructions* (n.d.), and *St. Joseph's Manual* (1877). He wrote his best-known work, *Sketches of the Establishment of the Church in New England* (1872), while he was pastor (1855–81) of the Church of the Most Holy Redeemer in East Boston, where he had been transferred after having served (1844–55) at Newport, R.I.

Seal made by the Fisherman's Ring of Pope Paul IV.

Bibliography: R. H. LORD et al., *History of the Archdiocese of Boston in the Various Stages of Its Development, 1604–1943,* 3 v. (New York 1944). L. P. MCCARTHY, *Sketch of the Life and Missionary Labors of Rev. James Fitton* (Boston 1908).

[W. L. LUCEY]

FITZALAN, HENRY

Twelfth Earl of Arundel; b. *c.* 1511; d. Feb. 24, 1580 (O.S. 1579). HENRY VIII was his godfather and Fitzalan spent his early career in his service. He served as governor of Calais (1540–43), expending his energy and his own money in improving the town's military strength. The title came to him at the death of his father in January 1544. At the siege of Boulogne he was ''marshall of the field'' and led the storming of the town. On his return to England he was appointed lord chamberlain, a post he filled for the rest of Henry VIII's reign. During the reign of Edward VI, first Protector Somerset and then the earl of Warwick succeeded in destroying Fitzalan's influence in the government. When Edward VI died, he feigned cooperation with Warwick while contriving to secure the accession of MARY TUDOR. Under Queen Mary, he filled a variety of governmental and diplomatic positions. ELIZABETH I retained him in all the posts he had held in the previous reign, but he was not trusted. He led the Roman Catholic party, opposed the 1559 intervention in Scotland, favored lenient treatment for MARY STUART at the time of her imprisonment, supported the plan to marry her to his widowed son-in-law, the Duke of Norfolk (father of Philip HOWARD, who inherited the earldom of Arundel in 1580), and was aware of the Ridolfi Plot. As a result of his implication in the plot, he was placed under guard and did not secure his liberty until December 1572. He passed the remainder of his life in seclusion.

Bibliography: *The Boke of Henrie, Earle of Arundel* (Harleian MS 4107), printed in Jeffery's *Antiquarian Repertory,* v.2 (London 1807). M. A. TIERNEY, *The History and Antiquities of the Castle and Town of Arundel,* 2 v. (London 1834). P. HUGHES *The Reformation in England* (New York 1963).

[V. H. PONKO]

FITZGERALD, EDWARD

Bishop; b. Limerick, Ireland, Oct. 28, 1833; d. Hot Springs, Ark., Feb. 21, 1907. Fitzgerlad came to the U.S. with his parents in 1849 and was educated for the priesthood at the Barrens, Perry County, Missouri; Mt. St. Mary Seminary of the West, Cincinnati, Ohio; and Mount St. Mary's College and Seminary, Emmitsburg, Md. He was ordained for the Diocese of Cincinnati, Aug. 22, 1857, and was assigned as pastor to St. Patrick's, Columbus, Ohio, a parish then under interdict and in a state of rebellion against Abp. John B. Purcell because of a dispute with the trustees. Fitzgerald restored peace and remained nine years as pastor.

On Feb. 3, 1867, he was consecrated bishop of Little Rock, Ark., a see that had been vacant since 1862 because of the Civil War. His diocese, comprising the state of Arkansas and the Indian Territory (now the state of Oklahoma), contained only 1,600 Catholics, five priests, four parishes, and three houses of Sisters of Mercy. Fitzgerald brought to the diocese Benedictine monks from St. Meinrad, Ind.; Holy Ghost Fathers from Pittsburgh, Pa.; two distinct communities of Benedictine nuns; the Sisters of Charity of Nazareth, Ky.; and the Sisters of Mercy from St. Louis, Mo. By introducing these orders, he prepared for the influx of German, Polish, and Italian immigrants who settled in the state in the late 19th century.

In 1870 Fitzgerald attended Vatican Council I, where he was one of seven North American bishops who opposed the definition of papal infallibility, and the only one of the seven present at the final vote (July 18, 1870), when he voted *non placet.* After the definition, however, he was among the first to indicate his acceptance of the dogma. In 1883, Fitzgerald represented the Province of New Orleans, La., at the conference of U.S. bishops at Rome. The following year he took part in the Third Plenary Council of Baltimore. In 1906 after Fitzgerald had suffered a paralytic stroke (Jan. 21, 1900), John B. Morris, Vicar-General of the Diocese of Nashville, Tenn., was appointed coadjutor. The diocese then had 41 churches, including St. Andrew's Cathedral dedicated in 1881; 33 missions with churches; 26 secular priests and 34 religious; 272 sisters; and a Catholic population of 20,000.

See Also: LITTLE ROCK, DIOCESE OF.

[J. E. O'CONNELL]

FITZGIBBON, MARY IRENE, SISTER

Social worker; b. Kensington, England, May 11, 1823; d. New York City, Aug. 14, 1896. When Catherine Fitzgibbon was nine years old, her family went to the U.S. and settled in St. James's parish, Brooklyn, N.Y. After receiving her early education in the parish school, she entered the Sisters of Charity, Jan. 10, 1850, and took the name of Sister Mary Irene. She taught in St. Peter's Academy, Barclay Street, New York City, until 1858, when she was appointed sister servant (superior) at St. Peter's Convent. Abandoned children were frequently left on the convent doorstep, and, at the request of Abp. John MCCLOSKEY, Sister Mary Irene was chosen to care for these infants. With Sister Teresa Vincent McCrystal and three other sisters, she initiated a work that gradually expanded to the care of 100,000 children. The Foundling Asylum, later known as the New York Foundling Hospital, was opened on Oct. 11, 1869. To provide for its maintenance, Sister Irene organized (November 1869), with the aid of Mrs. Paul Thébaud, the Foundling Asylum Society, a laywomen's auxiliary. In 1873 the hospital site was moved to East 68th Street, where it remained until its building on Third Avenue was opened in 1958.

Sister Irene initiated two important phases of foundling work: the boarding department and the shelter. The first provided for the care of children by foster parents in their homes. For such foster care and also for legal adoption, she established procedures that conformed to state and city regulations. The shelter aided needy unmarried mothers, keeping mother and child together and saving babies by a wet-nurse program. The rehabilitation of unwed mothers became Sister Irene's special work, for which she established three institutions associated with the New York Foundling Hospital: St. Ann's Maternity Hospital (1880), Hospital of St. John for Children (1881), and Nazareth Hospital, Spuyten Duyvil, New York City, for convalescent children (1881). In 1894 Seton Hospital for tubercular male patients was erected next to Nazareth Hospital; she also opened a temporary day nursery for preschool children of working mothers. During her 27 years as superior of Foundling Hospital, she developed techniques for reducing the spread of disease that were imitated by hospitals throughout the U.S.

Bibliography: M. DE L. WALSH, *The Sisters of Charity of New York, 1809–1959,* 3 v. (New York 1960).

[M. L. FELL]

FITZPATRICK, EDWARD AUGUSTUS

Educator, author, editor; b. New York City. Aug. 29, 1884; d. Milwaukee, Wis., Sept. 13, 1960. He was the son of Thomas and Ellen (Radley) Fitzpatrick. His undergraduate and graduate studies were completed in 1911 at Columbia University, New York City, with the Ph.D. Two years later he married Lillian V. Taylor. After teaching in the public high schools of New York, Fitzpatrick was appointed to the Wisconsin State Board for Public Affairs and devoted the rest of his life to educational work in Wisconsin. He served on the University of Wisconsin staff in Madison, Wis. (1919–23), and became dean (1924–39) of the Marquette University Graduate School, Milwaukee. From 1928 until his death he served also as chancellor, and as president of Mount Mary College, Milwaukee. Fitzpatrick edited *The Public Servant* (1916–17), *Hospital Progress* (1924–27), and the *Catholic School Journal* (1929–60). He published articles and books, including *Industrial Citizenship* (1927), *Foundations of Christian Education* (1929), *I Believe in Education* (1938), *How to Educate Human Beings* (1950), *Exploring a Theology of Education* (1950), and *La Salle, Patron of All Teachers* (1951).

[E. KEVANE]

FITZSIMON, HENRY

Missionary and writer; b. Dublin, Ireland, 1566; d. Dublin, 1643. He was the son of Nicholas, alderman of Dublin, and was related to several notable families of the Pale. He was educated as a Protestant at Oxford, but became reconciled to the Catholic Church through Thomas Darbishire, SJ, in Paris. After further studies at Pont-à-Mousson, he entered the Society of Jesus in 1592 at Tournai. He completed his theological course at Louvain and

Edward Fitzgerald.

returned to Ireland in 1597. For two years he labored, with brilliant success, to arrest the growth of Protestantism in Dublin and the Pale. When he was arrested and imprisoned in Dublin Castle, he continued his defense of Catholicism from his cell by engaging in controversy with such opponents as Meredith Hanmer and John Rider. Exiled in 1604, he spent the next 26 years chiefly in the Low Countries where he published many books on theology, spirituality, and history. He was unofficial agent of the Irish mission. For his own safety and that of the Jesuits in Ireland, his return to the mission was opposed by Father Christopher HOLYWOOD. However, he returned to Ireland in 1630. He was sent to France on business in 1632, but the letter of the Jesuit general forbidding him to return to Ireland arrived too late. Fitzsimon got back to Ireland, but henceforth his ministry had to be conducted secretly and his name disappears altogether from the Jesuit correspondence after 1635. The account of his last years and death dates from after the Cromwellian conquest.

Bibliography: Archives (unpublished) of the Society of Jesus, Rome. E. HOGAN, *Life, Letters and Diary of Henry Fitzsimon* (Dublin 1881). C. SOMMERVOGEL, *Bibliothèque de la Compagnie de Jésus* (Brussels-Paris 1890–1932) 3:766–768.

[F. FINEGAN]

FLACIUS ILLYRICUS, MATTHIAS

The Latinized name of Matthias Vlachich, Lutheran theologian; b. Albona, Istria, March 3, 1520; d. Frankfurt am Main, March 11, 1575. After his father's death he was placed under the tutelage of his uncle, Baldo Lupetino, provincial of the Francicans and a Lutheran sympathizer. Flacius studied for the priesthood at Venice, Basel, and Tübingen before he enrolled at the University of WITTENBERG. There he became a confirmed Lutheran and entered into a new period of his life, a period characterized by a violent hatred of the papacy and a passionate defense of what he considered to be the pure Lutheran doctrine. He held the chair of Hebrew at Wittenberg from 1544 to 1549 and in these years developed a violent aversion to the theological position of P. MELANCHTHON. Flacius opposed Melanchthon's Augsburg and Leipzig INTERIMS on the grounds that they were compromises and concessions to the papacy. He became the leader of the GNESIOLUTHERAN party along with such other prominent Lutherans as Nikolaus AMSDORF and Nikolaus Gallus. The Lutheran split originated over the question of nonessentials (*adiaphora*).

Melanchthon argued that only theological essentials were important and concessions could be made on minor, i.e., nonessential points. Flacius bitterly opposed such views and began a vitriolic campaign against his opponents whom he regarded as traitors to LUTHER. His assault began with the publication in 1549 of his *Wider das Interim* and continued in a series of personal attacks upon Melanchthon. In 1555 while at the University of Jena, Flacius produced his own version of Luther's works, and four years later he wrote the *Book of Confutation,* the most important statement of his position. He held that any ceremony, no matter how trivial, if commanded by God and germane to theology was important and could not be glossed over. His theological position and his violent nature were the reasons for his frequent moves, i.e., from Jena to Regensburg, Antwerp, Frankfurt, and Strassburg, and finally back to Frankfurt, where he was to remain.

Among his other works were the Biblical dictionary, *Key to Sacred Scripture* (1567), and the *Glossary of the New Testament* (1570). However, much of his fame rests upon the *Ecclesiastica historia . . .* begun in 1559 and completed in 1574. This work, known since the third edition (Nuremberg 1757) as the *Magdeburg Centuries,* is the product of a group known as the CENTURIATORS. Written by centuries, and covering the period to 1400, it is polemical and propagandist in scope, designed to prove the validity of the Lutheran position and to attack the Catholic Church. Although the *Centuries* contains much that is erroneous and false, it forced Catholics and Protestants alike to reexamine their position. The most famous Catholic reply was the *Annales ecclesiastici* of Caesar BARONIUS, the first volume of which appeared in 1588.

Flacius' position in Reformation history is important because he focused attention upon the interpretation of Lutheran theology. At the same time he created a serious rift between the strict and liberal interpreters of Martin Luther that has persisted until the present day.

Bibliography: W. PREGER, *Matthias Flacius Illyricus und seine Zeit,* 2 v. (Erlangen 1859–61). E. SCHAUMKELL, *Beitrag zur Entstehungsgeschichte der Magdeburger Centurien* (Ludwigslust 1898). P. POLMAN, ''Flacius Illyricus,'' *Revue d'histoire ecclésiastique* 27 (1931) 27–73. K. A. VON SCHWARTZ, *Die theologische Hermeneutik des Matthias Flacius Illyricus* (Munich 1933). L. HAIKOLA, *Gesetz und Evangelium bei Matthias Flacius Illyricus* (Lund 1952). P. MEINHOLD, *Lexikon für Theologie und Kirche* (Freiburg 1957–65) 4:161–162. G. MOLDAENKE, *Die Religion in Geschichte und Gegenwart* (Tübingen 1957–65) 2:971.

[C. L. HOHL, JR.]

FLAGELLATION

There are three stages in the history of flagellation in the Christian Church: (1) as a punishment it was in use from the 4th century; (2) as a form of voluntary penance it developed especially from the mid-11th century; and (3) as a feature of public penitential processions it began in the 13th century.

Penal Flagellation. Scourging was frequently a punishment for delinquent clerics. It was also administered to laymen, mostly to slaves, but occasionally also to free men. More generally, however, it was a feature of monastic discipline. In the East it is mentioned in the rule of PACHOMIUS (*Reg.* 163, in the Latin version of Jerome, *Patrologia Latina* 23:81d); in the West in the rules of CAESARIUS OF ARLES [*Opera* two (Maredsous 1942) 107], AURELIAN OF ARLES (*Patrologia Latina* 68:392), BENEDICT (only in cases of obstinate incorrigibility: ch. 28, ed. R. Hanslik; *Corpus scriptorum ecclesiasticorum latinorum* 60:84), and frequently in that of COLUMBAN [*Regula coenobialis;* ed. G. S. M. Walker, *Sancti Columbani opera* (Dublin 1957) 142–181]. AUGUSTINE states that it was used in episcopal courts (*Ep.* 133; *Patrologia Latina* 33:510). Councils from the 5th to the 7th centuries legislated for flagellation of monks (C. J. von Hefele, *Histoire des conciles d'après les documents originaux*, tr. and continued by H. Leclercq, 10 v. in 19 (Paris 1907–38) 2:905), as also did monastic customaries (*Usus ordinis Cisterciencis,* 70; *Patrologia Latina* 166: 1444; Lanfranc, *Decreta pro ordine OSB,* 18; *Patrologia Latina* 150:504). As a punishment for ecclesiastics it was recognized by Canon Law as late as the 17th century.

Voluntary Flagellation. This was a natural development from the penal form. Its motives are: expiation of personal sin and the sins of others, self-conquest, the impetration of divine graces and favors, and especially conformity with Christ in his Passion. In the early Church the martyrs were regarded as closest to Christ; but after the persecutions, the austerities of monastic life were esteemed the nearest equivalent to martyrdom. Monks were the first to adopt scourging as a systematic ascetic exercise, and the practice spread to the clergy and laity, becoming common throughout the Middle Ages. PETER DAMIAN, by his advocacy and example, was influential in stabilizing the practice, first at FONTE AVELLANA, and later in CAMALDOLESE monasteries, at MONTE CASSINO, and elsewhere [*De laude flagellorum; Patrologia Latina* 145:679–686; *Epistolae,* 5.8; *Patrologia Latina* 144:350–352; 6.27, *ibid.* 414–417; J. Leclercq, ''Inédits de saint Pierre Damien,'' *Revue Bénédictine* 67 (1957) 154].

As penal flagellation had long been part of the regular discipline of monasticism, the term ''discipline'' now came to be applied to voluntary penance, signifying the usage, the scourge used, or the individual strokes. The ''discipline of rule'' or custom became part of the observance of medieval religious orders. It was prescribed and regulated for certain days, especially during the penitential seasons. Similarly, provision for this kind of corporal penance was made in practically all religious rules composed or revised from the 16th to the 18th centuries. Undertaken with the sanction of a religious rule or the guidance of a spiritual director, such corporal penance has continued to be sanctioned by the Church. Without such safeguards it can lead to abuses and aberrations.

Penitential Processions of Flagellants. Originating in Perugia in May 1260 amid the misery of the wars of GUELFS AND GHIBELLINES and the disastrous plague of 1259, processions were stimulated by the eschatological prophecies of JOACHIM DA FIORE, who had predicted the coming of ''the third age'' for 1260. Instigated by the Umbrian hermit, Rainier Fasani, hundreds or even thousands, preceded by the cross and the clergy, made their way through the city, chanting and crying out for peace, scourging themselves to blood. Fasani's *Disciplinati* spread from Perugia throughout central and northern Italy, and beyond the Alps into Alsace, Bavaria, Hungary, Bohemia, and Poland. Good effects were noted in Perugia, but the spirit of the movement rapidly deteriorated. Severe measures were taken against the flagellant bands by the bishops of Poland, and in 1261 the processions were forbidden by the Holy See.

As a result, the movement abated and did not revive until the disastrous years of the Black Death (1348–50), when with astonishing rapidity numerous bands of antiecclesiastical flagellants reappeared throughout Europe. Although condemned and prohibited by CLEMENT VI (Oct. 20, 1349), many continued to exist, and in the early 15th century they were reinforced by the adherence of Beghards (*see* BEGUINES AND BEGHARDS) and the followers of John WYCLIF. They were still active in 1481.

Quite distinct from these fanatical and heretical groups were the associations of *Disciplinati,* common especially in Italy from *c.* 1350 until the end of the 16th century. These confraternities were under the control of the Church and were approved and supervised by such bishops as Charles BORROMEO. Similarly, occasional penitential processions of flagellants were held, such as those of VINCENT FERRER. They provoked the opposition in Paris of Jean GERSON, but they were common in the Netherlands and in Austria in the 17th and 18th centuries, and survived in Italy into the 19th. They were encouraged also by Jesuit and Franciscan missionaries in the newly evangelized regions of Asia and Latin America.

Bibliography: P. BAILLY, *Dictionnaire de spiritualité ascétique et mystique* 5:392–408. É. BERTAUD, *ibid.* 3:1302–11. L. GOUGAUD, *Devotional and Ascetic Practices in the Middle Ages,* tr. G. C. BATEMAN (London 1927). G. ALBERIGO, ''Contributi alla storia delle confraternite dei disciplinati e della spiritualità laicale nei secc. XV e XVI,'' *Il movimento dei disciplinati nel settimo centenario dal suo inizio* (Spoleto 1962) 156–252. G. MEERSSEMAN, ''Études sur les anciennes confréries dominicaines,'' *Archivum Fratrum Praedicatorum* 20 (1950) 5–113; 21 (1951) 51–196; 22 (1952) 5–176. P. TACCHI VENTURI, *Storia della Compagnia di Gesù in Italia* (2d ed. Rome 1950) v.1.2. W. FERNER, *Die Geisselmanie oder der Flagellantismus in den Mönchs- und Nonnenklöstern,* ed. G. FRUSTA (3d ed. Stuttgart 1922). G. M. MONTI, *Le confraternite medievali dell'alta e media Italia,* 2 v. (Venice 1927). O. J. BLUM, *St. Peter Damian* (Washington 1947) 114–120. J. LECLERCQ, *Saint Pierre Damien: Ermite et homme d'Église* (Rome 1960).

[F. J. COURTNEY]

FLAGELLATION (IN THE BIBLE)

The Mosaic Law regulated the conduct of society in a threefold way by enacting legislation concerning the conduct of its subjects as individuals, as citizens, and as members of a religious society. The basis of penal legislation was strict retribution (Ex 21.24; Lv 24.17; Dt 19.21). Flagellation was prescribed in two cases that involved sexual crimes (Lv 19.20; Dt 22.18). Judges were permitted to use their own discretion in imposing the sentence of flagellation (Dt 25.1). The number of blows was limited to 40 (Dt 25.3). The Mosaic Law did not specify the instrument to be used. It was presumably the *šēbeṭ* (rod) or the *šôṭ* (whip, scourge). The latter was either a single–lash whip or a multilashed flagellum. The varied references to scourging indicate that the practice was well known among the people. It was limited to crimes that did not embrace capital punishment. The sapiential books

"Flagellation of Christ," 17th-century painting. (©Elio Ciol/CORBIS)

contain numerous references to the use of the rod [Ps 2.9; 88(89).33; Prv 10.13; 13.24; 14.3; 22.15; 23.13; 26.3; 29.15]; the Hebrews did not "spare the rod" in the correction of children.

In Assyrian law flogging was a common penalty. The number of stripes varied according to crimes, but usually numbered between 20 and 100. Babylonian law as found in the Code of HAMMURABI (par. 202) prescribed it only for the striking of a superior and limited it to 60 stripes. Egyptian task masters are often pictured with a rod or a flagellum.

Roman law limited beating by rods to citizens. Slaves and noncitizens were subjected to scourging. The whips were constructed from leather or chain lashes. Frequently the ends were armed with small leaden balls or metal objects. A similar object seemed to be in the mind of Roboam, who stated: "My father beat you with whips (*šôṭîm*), but I will beat you with scorpions (*'aqrabbîm*)" (1 Kgs 12.11, 14). The latter were the metal–tipped ends of the flagellum. The Romans inflicted scourging on recalcitrant slaves, on political prisoners withholding information, and on criminals condemned to death by crucifixion. They also meted out death by scourging either intentionally or accidentally.

According to Lk 23.16, 22; Jn 19.1, Pontius Pilate imposed flagellation on Jesus as an attempted substitute for crucifixion, not as a prelude to it; but his plan was thwarted. According to Mt 27.26; Mk 15.15, the flagellation of Jesus occurred after the imposition of His death sentence. Actually, the scourging proved to be a prelude to the crucifixion, not a substitute for it. But Pilate's initial move led to confusion regarding the sequence of events in Matthew and Mark and to the erroneous conclusion of some exegetes that Jesus was scourged twice. That Christ suffered at the hands of the Roman soldiers leaves the number of blows struck a matter that cannot be settled. Had He suffered at the hands of the Temple police, His punishment likely would have been limited to the customary 40 blows less one, such as St. Paul suffered on at least five occasions (2 Cor 11.24). The other Apostles had received the Jewish flagellation at least once (Acts 5.40–41).

Bibliography: J. BLINZLER and G. MESTERS, ''Geisselung,'' *Lexikon für Theologie und Kirche,* ed. J. HOFER and K. RAHNER 10 v. (2d, new ed. Freiburg 1957–65) 4:608–610. *Encyclopedic Dictionary of the Bible,* tr. and adap. by L. HARTMAN (New York 1963) from A. VAN DEN BORN, *Bijbels Woordenboek* 786–788.

[G. T. KENNEDY]

FLAGET, BENEDICT JOSEPH

First bishop of Bardstown, Ky., diocese (now Louisville archdiocese); b. Contournat, France, Nov. 7, 1763; d. Louisville, Feb. 11, 1850. Orphaned at the age of two, Flaget with his brothers was left to the care first of an aunt, then of an uncle, Canon Benoît Flaget at Billom. At 17 he enrolled at the Sulpician university at Clermont, then a seminary, and in 1783 entered the Society of Priests of St. Sulpice. After his ordination at Issy *c.* 1788, he taught theology at Nantes until the French Revolution forced him back to Billom. In 1792 he joined the Sulpicians at St. Mary's Seminary, Baltimore, Md., with his colleague John Baptist David and seminarian Stephen T. Badin. Enrollment was so limited at the seminary that Bp. John Carroll was forced to use the Sulpicians in the missions, and Flaget was sent to the French settlement of Fort Vincennes, Ind., where, in the two years before he was recalled by his superiors, he transformed the spiritual and material life of the townsmen. His short assignment as professor at Georgetown College, Washington, D.C., was followed by an abortive attempt to found a college in Havana, Cuba. He returned to Baltimore where he taught at the seminary for eight years.

Flaget's nomination to the newly created see of Bardstown, Ky., in 1808 came as a distasteful shock to him, and he journeyed to France to enlist the aid of the Sulpicians in protest. When he realized that Rome would take no refusal, he gathered recruits for his new diocese, among them Simon BRUTÉ, who accompanied him to Baltimore. Flaget was consecrated by Bishop Carroll in St. Patrick's church, Baltimore, on Nov. 4, 1810; his installation in Bardstown took place in Badin's cabin on June 9, 1811.

Carroll's prophecy that in Flaget all factions would be united was soon realized. Before many months had passed, he had visited every Catholic settlement in Kentucky. On Dec. 21, 1811, he ordained Guy Chabrat, the first priest to be ordained in Kentucky. During that winter he established St. Thomas Seminary, and in the summer

Benedict Joseph Flaget.

confirmed almost 1,300 people in three states. By 1812 the Sisters of Loretto and the Sisters of Charity of Nazareth had been founded by the missionaries Charles Nerinckx and John David respectively. In his report to Rome in 1815 Flaget could claim that Kentucky counted 10,000 Catholics with 10 priests, 19 churches or chapels, one monastery, and two convents. On Aug. 8, 1819, the cathedral at Bardstown was consecrated, and two days later Flaget consecrated David as his first coadjutor.

The next 13 years were spent as a missionary covering territory that ultimately embraced more than 35 dioceses in Kentucky, Tennessee, Indiana, Ohio, Illinois, Wisconsin, and Michigan, the region between the Great Lakes on the north and the 35th degree of north latitude on the south, from the Alleghenies in the east to the Mississippi River in the west. Flaget also made visitations to St. Louis, Detroit, Vincennes, Cincinnati, and Knoxville. He called the first synod of Bardstown, 1812; consecrated Bp. George Whitfield and attended the first provincial council of Baltimore in 1829; and consecrated Bp. Francis Kenrick for Philadelphia in 1830. In 1832 he resigned the bishopric and David was appointed in his place. However, the uproar that ensued led Rome to reverse the action, and in 1834 Chabrat was consecrated as his second coadjutor. In 1835 when Flaget made his first *ad limina* visit to Rome, he petitioned for the removal of the see from Bardstown to Louisville. At the request of Pope Gregory XVI he spent two years visiting every diocese in France in the interest of the Propagation of the Faith, and by the time of his departure for his diocese in 1839, all France regarded him as a saint capable of working miracles.

When Martin J. Spalding, his third coadjutor, was consecrated in 1848, Flaget retired to spend his remaining two years in prayer. He witnessed the laying of the cornerstone of the new cathedral of the Assumption in Louisville. Six months later he was laid to rest in its crypts where his remains are still entombed. His 40 years as bishop spanned one of the most vital periods in American Catholic history; his was one of the most influential voices in the councils, and in the creation and staffing of new dioceses. In his own jurisdiction he proved to be an expert administrator, a man not of words but of deeds.

Bibliography: J. H. SCHAUINGER, *Cathedrals in the Wilderness* (Milwaukee 1952); *Stephen T. Badin: Priest in the Wilderness* (Milwaukee 1956). M. J. SPALDING, *Sketches of the Life, Times and Character of the Rt. Rev. Benedict Joseph Flaget* (Louisville 1852). R. J. PURCELL, *Dictionary of American Biography*, ed. A. JOHNSON and D. MALONE, 20 v. (New York 1928–36; index 1937; 1st suppl. 1944; 2d suppl. 1958) 6:445–447. C. LEMARIÉ, *A Biography of Msgr. Benedict Joseph Flaget,* 3 v. (Bardstown 1992).

[J. H. SCHAUINGER]

FLANAGAN, EDWARD JOSEPH

Founder of Boys Town; b. Roscommon, Ireland, July 13, 1886; d. Berlin, Germany, May 15, 1948. He came to the U.S. in 1904 and received his B.A. degree at Mount St. Mary's College, Emmitsburg, MD, in 1906. After a year at St. Joseph's Seminary, Dunwoodie, NY, he attended the Gregorian University in Rome, but lung trouble obliged him to return to the U.S. He later studied theology at Innsbruck, Austria, where he was ordained for the Archdiocese of Omaha, NE, July 26, 1912. Although he had no formal training in social work, his solicitude for derelict men prompted him to open his Workingmen's Hotel in Omaha in 1914. He became convinced that rehabilitation must begin during the impressionable years of youth and that environment was more vital than heredity, and he discarded the hotel in 1917 in favor of a protectory for unfortunate boys. In 1922, after establishing two temporary homes, he purchased Overlook Farm, ten miles west of Omaha, where he founded the present Boys Town.

Boys Town incorporated many of Flanagan's ideas for the rehabilitation of youth. His familiar adage, "there is no such thing as a bad boy," expressed his conviction that except for organic disorders, man is not born with maladjustments, but sometimes develops them because of extrinsic factors. The varied academic, vocational, and recreational facilities that he established were designed as a corrective for deficient environment. Although he made no attempt to proselytize among inmates accepted from all religious, national, and racial groups, religion played a significant part in his program of self-government under mature tutelage. Flanagan possessed a rare talent for capturing the public imagination, and was universally recognized as an authority on juvenile delinquency. In 1947, at the invitation of the supreme commander of the Pacific theater, Gen. Douglas MacArthur, he visited Japan and Korea to assist their governments in meeting complex youth problems. He was in the process of conducting a similar mission to central Europe when harassments by communists in Austria hastened his untimely death from a heart ailment.

[H. W. CASPER]

FLATHERS, MATTHEW, BL.

Priest, martyr; *alias* Matthew Major; b. ca. 1580 at Weston, Otley, Yorkshire, England; d. March 21, 1608, hanged, drawn, and quartered at York under James I. Three months after his ordination at Arras on March 25, 1606, Matthew was sent to English mission. He was discovered almost immediately by government emissaries, who, after the Gunpowder Plot, had redoubled their vigilance. He was brought to trial on the charge of receiving orders abroad, i.e., from the Vatican, and condemned to death. By an act of unusual clemency, the sentence was commuted to banishment for life. Undaunted, Flathers returned to England in order to fulfill his mission, and, after ministering for a brief time to oppressed Catholics in Yorkshire, was again apprehended. Flathers was offered his life on condition that he take the recently enacted Oath of Allegiance. On his refusal, he was condemned to death and taken to the common place of execution outside Micklegate Bar, York. He was beatified by Pope John Paul II on Nov. 22, 1987 with George Haydock and Companions.

Feast of the English Martyrs: May 4 (England).

See Also: ENGLAND, SCOTLAND, AND WALES, MARTYRS OF.

Bibliography: R. CHALLONER, *Memoirs of Missionary Priests,* ed. J. H. POLLEN (rev. ed. London 1924). J. H. POLLEN, *Acts of English Martyrs* (London 1891). D. DE YEPES, *Historia Particular de la persecución de Inglaterra* (Madrid 1599).

[H.G. WINTERSGILL/K. I. RABENSTEIN]

Father Flanagan with young orphan boy from publicity still. (©Bettmann/CORBIS)

FLAVIAN, PATRIARCH OF CONSTANTINOPLE, ST.

Reigned 446 to 449; d. Hypaepa, Lydia. A priest of Constantinople known for his moderation, Flavian succeeded PROCLUS as bishop of that see. Eusebius of Dorylеum in a session of the permanent Synod of Constantinople on Nov. 8, 448, forced Flavian to take cognizance of the heretical expressions used by the archimandrite EUTYCHES, godfather of the imperially powerful eunuch Chrysaphius, and Flavian had to accede to his condemnation and deposition (November 22). Upon the appeal of Eutyches to the emperor and the greater Churches of the East and Rome, Pope LEO I complained against Flavian's failure to refer the matter to him for judgment. When he did receive the acts of the synod, Leo supported the bishop of Constantinople's position in his famous *Tome* to Flavian. In preparation for the Council of Ephesus in 449, convoked by the emperor to vindicate Eutyches, Flavian's synod of 448 was investigated, and he was forced to present a profession of his faith. The council itself was conducted by DIOSCORUS OF ALEXANDRIA, who managed it in such fashion that Flavian was condemned, deposed, and exiled on Aug. 8, 449. He died soon after, but not before sending an appeal to the pope, who responded by branding Dioscorus's council *Illud latrocinium*—the Robber Synod. Upon the accession of Marcian and PULCHERIA in 451, the bones of Flavian were buried with honor in the Church of the Apostles in Constantinople, and he was exonerated at the Council of CHALCEDON. Three of his letters are preserved among the works of St. Leo (*Patrologia Latina,* ed. J. P. Migne 54:723, 743).

Feast: Feb. 18.

Bibliography: *Acta conciliorum oecumenicorum* (Berlin 1914–) 2.2.1:77–79. P. BATIFFOL, *Le Siège apostolique* (Paris 1924). T. G. JALLAND, *The Life and Times of St. Leo the Great* (London 1941). F. X. MURPHY, *Peter Speaks Through Leo* (Washington

1952). A. GRILLMEIER, A. GRILLMEIER and H. BACHT, *Das Konzil vom Chalkedon: Geschichte und Gegenwart* (Würzburg 1951–54) 1:195–198. P. GALTIER, *ibid.*, 350–353. H. CHADWICK, ''The Exile and Death of Flavian of Constantinople,'' *Journal of Theological Studies* 6 (1955) 16–34.

[P. T. CAMELOT]

FLAVIGNY-SUR-MOSELLE, ABBEY OF

Benedictine priory for men, later a Benedictine abbey for women, in the present Diocese of Nancy, France. The priory was founded on the banks of the upper Moselle *c.* 1020 in the former Diocese of Toul, on land originally given to the Abbey of Saint-Vanne of VERDUN-SUR-MEUSE (*c.* 950) by Bp. Berengar of Verdun, who transferred there the relics of one of his 5th-century predecessors, St. Firmin. A large tower from the 12th-century and the late 15th-century church show by their size the importance of Flavigny in the Middle Ages. After the abbey was joined to the Congregation of Saint-Vanne and Saint-Hydulphe in 1640, Flavigny experienced a revitalization. Its most famous superior was Dom CEILLIER, prior from 1733 to 1761, who was author of the important *Histoire des auteurs sacrés et ecclésiastiques.* The priory was suppressed in 1791. In 1824 the buildings received a new community, a Benedictine abbey for women made up of Benedictine nuns, formerly of Vergaville (Diocese of Metz). They remained at Flavigny until 1904, when they were forced to leave France. Since 1924 the old priory buildings have been used as a school for mentally retarded children, conducted by the Dominican Sisters of the Presentation of Mary from Tours.

Bibliography: A. DEDENON, *Histoire du prieuré bénédictin de Flavigny-sur-Moselle* (Nancy 1936). H. DAUPHIN, *Le Bienheureux Richard, abbé de Saint-Vanne* (Louvain 1946) 167–169. J. VILLEROT-REBOUL, ''Dom Remi Ceillier et le prieuré de Flavigny-sur-Moselle,'' *Annales de l'est,* 5th ser., 10 (1959) 161–172.

[J. CHOUX]

FLAVIGNY-SUR-OZERAIN, ABBEY OF

Former BENEDICTINE monastery in the town that has taken its name, in Côte d'Or, France, Diocese of Autun (present-day Diocese of Dijon). This much-fought-over abbey was founded in the 8th century by a Burgundian noble and was much favored by CHARLES MARTEL. Almost immediately, however, the monks and the bishops of Autun entered into a long-lasting struggle over control of the abbey. The presence at the abbey of the relics of St. Reine (or Regina) of Alise, an Autun marytr, had already given it great renown before it became part of the CLUNIAC REFORM movement in the late 10th century. But despite its Cluniac affiliation and its much later incorporation into the MAURIST congregation (1644), the abbey was the prey of the bishops of Autun and later of the Jesuits and had a notable controversy with the Franciscans concerning the relics of St. Reine. The abbey was suppressed in 1790 during the French Revolution; although destroyed, it again became popularly known when J. B. H. LACORDAIRE, the 19th-century Burgundian restorer of the DOMINICANS, founded a novitiate at Flavigny. Today the motherhouse of the Dominicaines missionaires des Campagnes is in the village. Only the crypt of the old monastery is still in existence.

Bibliography: *Monumenta Germaniae Historica: Scriptores* (Berlin 1826–) 3:150–152; 8:502–503, a catalogue of the abbots of Flavigny from 755 to 1096. *Gallia Christiana,* v. 1–13 (Paris 1715–85), v. 14–16 (Paris 1856–65) 4:454–465. D. A. MORTIER, *Flavigny: L'Abbaye et la ville, 720–1920* (Paris 1920). R. GAZEAU, *Catholicisme. Hier, aujourd'hui et demain,* ed. G. JACQUEMET (Paris 1947–) 4:1337–39.

[L. GAILLARD]

FLEMING, PATRICK

Historian of the Irish Saints; b. Christopher Fleming, Lagan, County Louth, Ireland, 1599; d. Beneschau, near Prague, Bohemia, Nov. 7, 1631. At 18 Fleming entered the Franciscan Order of Strict Observance, taking the religious name Patrick. He was sent to Rome, Louvain, and Douai for studies. During his years on the Continent he came under the influence of the Donegal-born scholar and rector of Louvain, Hugh WARD, who persuaded Fleming to devote research to the collection of materials on the Irish saints. While studying at St. Isidore's College in Rome, Fleming became the close friend of Hugh MacCaughwell (later archbishop of Armagh), enjoying an intimate intellectual relationship with him.

In 1631 at the age of 32, Fleming was made first president of the Irish College of the Immaculate Conception at Prague. This was a year of great political and social strife on the Continent during the Thirty Years' War (1618–48). The city of Prague was being besieged by the Elector of Saxony, and while fleeing from the capital with several of his companions, Fleming was set upon by a mob of enraged Calvinist peasants who murdered him. In addition to a *Life of St. Columba,* a *Biography of Bishop MacCaughwell,* and a *Chronicle of St. Peter's Monastery in Ratisbon,* Fleming left, unpublished, a valuable *Collectanea sacra* that was edited and published 30 years after his death.

Bibliography: J. S. CRONE, *Concise Dictionary of Irish Biography* (Dublin 1928). J. WARE, *The Antiquities and History of Ire-*

land (Dublin 1705). T. COOPER, *The Dictionary of National Biography from the Earliest Times to 1900* (London 1885–1900) 7:281–282.

[E. J. MURRAY]

FLEMING, THOMAS

Franciscan archbishop of Dublin (1623–55); b. 1593; d. 1655. The son of William Fleming, baron of Olane (Slane), Fleming was educated at Douai and in St. Anthony's Franciscan college at Louvain. He taught philosophy and theology there until, on Oct. 23, 1623, he was appointed to the See of Dublin; he was consecrated in St. Anthony's on Dec. 30, 1623. He went to Dublin, where the ministry of the Church, although exercised in private with a precarious toleration from the government, was threatened by the violent action of firebrands such as Paul Harris and Patrick Cahill, diocesan priests, and diehard opponents of the regulars. Fleming's tact, zeal, and vigilance were conspicuous in his bringing into being the Pastoral College in Louvain, in his interest in those of Douai and Antwerp, in his holding of a provincial Synod near Portarlington, County Kildare (1640) to implement the decrees of Trent and strengthen diocesan discipline, and in his patronage of the mission to Scotland. A friend of Luke WADDING, the Irish historian, he conspicuously encouraged at home and abroad Irish hagiographical and historical writing. In the crises of the Confederation of Kilkenny he adopted a middle-of-the-road policy.

Bibliography: B. H. BLACKER, *The Dictionary of National Biography from the Earliest Times to 1900* (London 1885–1900) 7:288. C. GIBLIN in *Father Luke Wadding: A Commemorative Volume* (Dublin 1957) 529–533 and *passim.* P. F. MORAN, *History of the Catholic Archbishops of Dublin* (Dublin 1864) 294–411. J. T. GILBERT, ed., *History of the Irish Confederation,* 7 v. (Dublin 1882–91). M. J. HYNES, *The Mission of Rinuccini* (Dublin 1932).

[J. J. MEAGHER]

FLETE, WILLIAM

Augustinian hermit and mystic; b. Fleet, Lincolnshire, England, *c.* 1325; d. probably at Lecceto, Italy, *c.* 1390. He entered the Augustinian Order *c.* 1339 and achieved the title *baccalarius formatus* at Cambridge by the year 1353. Renouncing the opportunity to continue his studies for the *magisterium,* he left England July 17, 1359, for Italy and the celebrated Augustinian monastery at Lecceto (San Salvadore di Selva di Lago), near Siena, where he became a member of the community in September. He lived an almost exclusively eremitical life from then on.

Flete was a friend, confidant, and quasi disciple of St. CATHERINE OF SIENA. They met on numerous occasions (first in 1367), and Catherine addressed several letters to him, four of which have survived. One may discern his influence on her Augustinian theological formation from 1368 to 1374. When Catherine returned from Avignon in 1377, having persuaded Pope Gregory XI to return to Rome, she visited Lecceto and revealed the basic tenets of her spirituality to Flete, who arranged them and wrote them down. The document is known as her *Spiritual Document.* Later St. Catherine tried in vain to persuade him to leave his hermitage in order to take a more active part in the apostolate. Despite her disappointment, she remained on friendly terms with the reluctant friar, and before she died appointed him spiritual head of her *famiglia* or group of disciples.

Flete is the author of a spiritual treatise *De remediis contra temptationes,* written probably in Cambridge during the years 1352–58. In 1380, perhaps on the occasion of St. Catherine's death, he broke his long silence and sent three letters to his brethren in England. All three letters are strong appeals for a return to pristine fervor through both interior and exterior reform. The first letter, addressed to all the members of the English province, is a kind of commentary on the Rule of St. Augustine.

Bibliography: B. HACKETT, *William Flete, O.S.A., and Catherine of Siena: Masters of Fourteenth-Century Spirituality,* ed. J. ROTELLE (Villanova 1992).

[R. J. WELSH/B. HACKETT]

FLEURY, ANDRÉ HERCULE DE

French cardinal and statesman; b. Lodève, Languedoc, June 22, 1653; d. Paris, Jan. 29, 1743. He studied in Paris at the colleges of Navarre, Louis-le-Grand, Harcourt, and the Sorbonne. He was tonsured in 1666, and made canon of Montpellier in 1668; he became chaplain in 1675 of Queen Marie Thérèse, and in 1678 of Louis XIV, who made him bishop of Fréjus in 1699. Fleury pursued social and religious reforms in his diocese, which was invaded by armies in 1702 and 1707. He carefully observed the reforms of the Council of Trent and took a sound theological position toward JANSENISM in 1711 when he censured P. Quesnel in letters to Cardinal Noailles, and also in an episcopal letter of 1714. He resigned the see in 1715 to become tutor to Louis XV, for whose spiritual life he showed solicitude. In 1717 Fleury entered the Académie Française. He used his position on the Jansenistic Council of Conscience (in charge of church benefices) to work for religious peace, order, and unity.

Having been a respected counselor of LOUIS XV during the regencies of the Dukes of Orleans and Bourbon, Fleury became prime minister in fact from June 1726 until his death. He was made a cardinal in September 1726. His policies were not fixed but were characterized by frugality and concern for peace. He stabilized the currency and the national credit, which had suffered from the extravagance and wars of Louis XIV. Commerce flourished, and France regained her position as arbiter of European affairs.

Fleury intervened reluctantly in the Wars of the Polish and Austrian Successions. His temporizing with the political and religious aspects of Jansenism was unpopular with both sides, and his quiet policy was not appreciated, but the years of his ministry were the happiest of the reign of Louis XV. He failed, however, to familiarize the king with matters of government.

Bibliography: G. HARDY, *Le Cardinal de Fleury et le mouvement janséniste* (Paris 1925). A. M. WILSON, *French Foreign Policy during the Administration of Cardinal Fleury, 1726–1743* (Cambridge, Mass. 1936). M. DE SARS, *Le Cardinal de Fleury, apôtre de la paix* (Paris 1942). R. CHALUMEAU, *Catholicisme. Hier, aujourd'hui et demain*, ed. G. JACQUEMET (Paris 1947–) 4:1344–45.

[W. E. LANGLEY]

FLEURY, CLAUDE

Church historian, educator, and jurist; b. Paris, Dec. 6, 1640; d. Paris, July 14, 1723. The son of a lawyer from Normandy, he was educated in the Jesuit College of Clermont, studied law, was called to the bar at 18 years of age, and practiced law in Paris for about ten years. During this period he read assiduously in civil and Canon Law, history, literature, and archeology. He became a friend and protegé of Bossuet, whom he met in the salon of Guillaume de Lamoignon, first president of the parliament of Paris. He was introduced to and accepted by the intellectual celebrities of France—Bossuet, Louis BOURDALOUE, Boileau-Despréaux, etc. At this time he wrote *l'Histoire du droit francais and l'Institution au droit ecclesiastique,* both published in Paris some years later, the first in 1674 and the second in 1677. Meantime, in 1669, he was ordained and through Bossuet was introduced into the French court, where he held positions most of his remaining years. In 1672 he became tutor to the Princes of Conti, whom Louis XIV wished educated with the Dauphin. When this task was completed in 1680, he became tutor to the legitimized son of Louis XIV and Louise de la Vallière. When the young Count died in 1684, the King named Fleury abbot of Loc-Dieu in the Diocese of Rodez. Until 1689 he assisted Bossuet in the administration of his diocese. Then through FÉNELON he was recalled to court to be tutor of the grandsons of Louis XIV, the young dukes of Burgundy, of Anjou, and of Berry. For 16 years he held this position. In recognition of his services he was made prior of Notre-Dame d'Argenteuil in 1706. A quiet and holy man, averse to disputes, he held aloof from the Jansenist difficulties of Port-Royal. In the controversy between Bossuet and Fénelon over quietism, he retained the friendship of both. He was a member of the French Academy, succeeding Jean de La Bruyère in 1691. He wrote a number of educational works that connect him with the ideas of Port-Royal and of the Oratory, such as *Traité du choix et de la méthode des études* (Paris 1686), which was translated into Spanish, German, and Italian and reprinted eight times in Paris. His *Les Moeurs des Israélites* (Paris 1681) anticipated the approach of Voltaire in dealing with the manners and customs of nations and was followed by his *Les moeurs des chrétiens* (Paris 1681) and the *Catéchisme historique* (Paris 1683). Fleury's most important work was the monumental *Histoire ecclésiastique* (20 v. Paris 1690–1720), from Christian origins to 1414. This clearly evidenced Fleury's Gallican tendencies, and was considered a standard reference throughout the 18th century. Even more obviously Gallican was his *Discours sur les libertés de l'Église gallicane* (Paris 1724), written in 1690 but published posthumously.

Bibliography: F. GAQUÉRE, *La Vie et les oeuvres de C. Fleury* (Paris 1925). C. CONSTANTIN, *Dictionnaire de théologie catholique* 6.1:21–24. A. DODIN, *Dictionnaire de spiritualité ascétique et mystique* 5:412–419. J. CALVET, *Catholicisme* 4:1343–44.

[M. M. BARRY]

FLICHE, AUGUSTIN

University professor, historian of the Gregorian Reform; b. Montpellier, France, Nov. 19, 1884; d. there, Nov. 20, 1951. He studied in Paris, becoming a doctor of letters in 1912. He was professor of medieval history at Montpellier from 1919 to 1946 and a member of the Académie des Inscriptions et Belles-lettres from 1941 until his death. He began his career with the publication of his dissertation *Le Règne de Philippe Ier, roi de France, 1060–1106* (Paris 1912). Shortly afterward he centered his interest on the history of GREGORY VII and the GREGORIAN REFORM and produced *La Polémique religieuse à l'époque de Grégoire VII* (Paris 1914), *Les Prégrégoriens* (1916), *Saint Grégoire VII* (1920), and the trilogy *La Réforme grégorienne* (1924–27). He contributed *La Chrétienté médiévale* to the series *Histoire du monde,* edited by Cavaignac, *L'Évolution de l'Europe 883 à 1125* to the Glotz series, and numerous journal articles. His greatest undertaking was the *Histoire de l'Église depuis les origines jusqu'à nos jours,* a series on the history of the Church that he planned and organized with the cooperation of Msgr. Victor MARTIN. The first volume appeared in 1934. Before his death Fliche had edited 15 volumes, written by a number of Catholic historians selected for this scholarship. Fliche lectured widely throughout Europe; his work was recognized by Pope Pius XII and several European universities.

Bibliography: C. E. PERRIN, *Revue Historique* 208 (1952) 382–383. J. R. PALANQUE, *La Vie intellectuelle* 25 (June 1953) 139–153. *Études médiévales offertes à M. le doyen A. F. de l'Institut par ses amis, ses anciens élèves* (Paris 1952).

[J. J. MUZAS]

FLODOARD (FRODOARD) OF REIMS

Historian; b. Epernay?, *c.* 894; d. Reims, March 28, 966. He was involved in the synod of Ingelheim (948) and in the episcopal disputes of his time. As canon at Reims, he had charge of the archives. He was elected bishop of Noyon-Tournai (951), but was not installed. In about 930 he wrote in epic hexameter the *De triumphis Christi sanctorumque Palestinae,* the *De triumphis Christi Antiochae gestis,* and the *De triumphis Christi apud Italiam.* The last of these is the most important, since it touches on contemporary events. His *Annales,* covering the years 919 to 966, is a basic source for the history of northern France and Germany for that period. In 946, he finished the important *Historia Remensis ecclesiae* (History of the Church of Reims), in four books. The *Annales* and *Historia* relate ecclesiastical reaction to contemporary events. The author often cited his sources and reproduced the documents.

Bibliography: Editions. *Patrologia Latina* 135; *Les Annales de Flodoard,* ed. P. LAUER (Paris 1905); *Monumenta Germanica: Scriptores* 3:363–408; poems in *Patrologia Latina* 135:491–886; *Historia Remensis ecclesiae,* ed. J. HELLER and G. WAITZ in *Monumenta Germanica: Scriptores* 13:405–599. **Literature.** H. PLATELLE, *Catholicisme* 4: 1348. T. SCHIEFFER, *Lexikon für Theologie und Kirche* (Freiburg 1957–65) 4:169.

[B. LACROIX]

FLOOD

A cataclysmic event narrated in Gen 6:5–9:19. The account is the theological center of the GENESIS account of prehistory in chaps. 1 –11 (*see* PRIMEVAL AGE IN THE BIBLE). God was heartbroken because human wickedness and violence had corrupted his good creation, and He determined to destroy all created things; but after finding NOAH to be righteous, God decided to preserve Noah and his family. God then had Noah preserve specimens of all living creatures so as to be able to populate a renewed creation in a new world order. The Genesis account is a composite of ancient Israelite traditions and reflects the influence of flood stories from other Near Eastern peoples (*see* GILGAMESH EPIC). Several New Testament authors refer to the Genesis story in exhortations to watchfulness and to faith.

Terminology. Various Old Testament writers vividly describe both the well-known frequent flash floods and ordinary seasonal flooding using common Hebrew words, but for the Genesis flood the authors reserved the word *mabbûl,* using the term 12 times. Outside Genesis, the word occurs only in Ps 29:10. There YHWH is described as enthroned above the *mabbûl,* a reference to the waters above the dome described in Gen 1:7 (see also Gen 7:11). The Deuterocanonical book of Sirach (44:17) and the Dead Sea Scrolls' Genesis Apocryphon (12:10) refer to the Genesis flood using *mabbûl.* The Septuagint translators used the Greek word κατακλυσμός where the Hebrew had *mabbûl,* and also in Sir 40:10; 44:17–18, and 4 Macc 15:31 in references to the Genesis flood. But in other places, the translators used κατακλυσμός for ordinary generic floods (Ps 32 [31]:6; Nah 1:8; Sir 21:13; 4 Macc 15:32). In the New Testament κατακλυσμός always refers to the Genesis flood (Matt 24:38–39; Luke 17:27; 2 Pet 2:5).

Literary Character of Gen 6:5–9:19. For more than two centuries scholars have recognized the presence of distinguishable sources in the Pentateuch. In the Genesis flood account at least two distinct sources were woven together, often referred to as the YAHWIST source (Y) and the PRIESTLY source (P). The older J segments use YHWH (''Lord'' or ''Yahweh'') as God's name and depict God in more anthropomorphic terms. For example, in 6:6, the Lord's heart grieved; in 7:16b, the Lord shut Noah and those with him in the ark, and in 8:21, the Lord smelled the pleasing aroma of Noah's sacrifice. The P source uses the common Hebrew word *'elōhîm* (''God'') for the deity and favors genealogies, precise numbers and dates. Examples in the Flood narrative include the repeated emphasis on Noah and his sons as the ancestors of all humanity, the precise dimensions of the ark in 6:15, and the exact dates on which the flood began and ended in 7:11 and 8:13. P also favors the themes of blessing and covenant reflected in 9:3, 7 and 6:18; 9:8–17. The presence of these sources in the flood narrative becomes evident in multiple doublets and inconsistencies. In 6:22 Noah does all that ''God'' (P) commanded, and in 7:5 Noah does all that the ''Lord'' (J) commanded. In the P source, God commands Noah to preserve one male-female pair of every living creature (6:19–20; 7:15–16). In J, the Lord calls for seven pairs of clean animals and birds, but single pairs of those that are unclean (7:2–3). In J the destruction is a consequence of rainfall (7:4,12), while in P it comes when the fountains of the great deep burst and the windows of the heavens are opened (7:11).

In P the flood continues for more than a year (7:11,24; 8:3,5,13–14), while in J it is 40 days and 40 nights (7:4,6,10,12). When J elements are extracted from the account, the P components form a complete and consistent narrative. While the earlier J tradition was substantially preserved in the blending of the traditions, gaps between some components suggest that parts may have been omitted, for example, the instructions to build the ark.

The doublets and differences in the sources were skillfully woven into a unified narrative with an extended palistrophe, a narrative device that divides a story in two, so that many events and details in the first half of the account mirror or parallel details and events in the second half. The Lord's decision to destroy creation in 6:5–8 (J), announced by God to Noah in 6:11 (P) finds a parallel in the Lord's decision to never again destroy creation in 8:21–22 (J), announced to Noah in 9:8–17 (P). The names of Noah's three sons at 6:10 are repeated at 9:18–19. God's promised covenant with Noah and his family in 6:18 is fulfilled at 9:9–17. The Lord's command for Noah and the animals to enter the ark in 7:1, followed by the account of Noah and the animals entering the ark in 7:7–8 is paralleled by God's command that Noah and the animals leave the ark in 8:16–17, followed by an account of their exiting the ark in 8:18–19. The waters swell and lift the ark, covering the mountains in 7:18–20. The waters recede, the mountains appear, and the ark comes to rest in 8:3–5. Only Noah and those with him in the ark were left in 7:23, and God remembered Noah and all the wild animals and all the domestic animals that were with him in the ark in 8:1. The elaborate structure contributes to the narrative flow, with everything centered on God's remembrance of Noah in 8:1.

Significance. The main character of the composite biblical account is God. Noah, described as perfectly obedient (6:22; 7:5), does not even speak. The reason for the flood is the grief in the Lord's heart because humans' hearts were inclined continually and only toward evil (6:5–6) and because human sin had spoiled what had been God's ''very good'' creation (6:11–13, see Gen 1:31). After the flood, when the Lord recognizes that the flood has not changed the inclination of human hearts toward evil, He decides to never repeat the destruction (8:21). Prior to the flood, increasingly pervasive human sin brings curses upon the ground (3:17; 4:11) and the ultimate curse, the flood itself. In the renewed created order after the flood, God's new response to human sin is blessing and covenant (9:1–17). To counter violence, bloodshed, and vengeance, Noah and his offspring, acting with God's authority, are made accountable for preserving all life, animal and human. In God's new order, humanity is charged with limiting vengeance and keeping lawlessness from spoiling the new creation. The story of Noah and his sons that follows the flood account (9:18–29) illustrates this new order. God is not even present as a character. Noah, speaking for the first and only time, curses Ham and Ham's descendant Canaan for their sin. Noah blesses Shem and Japheth for their righteous behavior.

The use of the Hebrew word *mabbûl* in the Genesis flood account and in Ps 29:10, along with the reference to the fountains of the great deep and the windows of the heavens in 7:11 and 8:2, suggests that the P tradition understood the flood as a near return to the formless chaotic void of the P account of creation in Gen 1:2. The ''wind'' (*rûaḥ.*) with which God stops the flood in 8:1 is the same ''wind'' (*rûaḥ.*) of God that hovered over the waters of the great deep in 1:2; but the renewed world after the flood populated by the people and animals God saved with Noah in the ark is far different from the ordered and sevenfold good creation of Genesis 1. The original harmony between humans and nature and among humans themselves has been altered. Now animals will fear and dread human dominion (9:2). Because the original abundance of nourishing trees and vegetation is no more, humans are permitted to kill and eat animals for food (9:3), and because the potential for murder remains, God ordains societal punishment of murderers so that desire for revenge will not again degenerate into limitless lawlessness (9:6).

This P tradition of understanding supplements and develops themes present in the earlier J tradition. In J's flood account, ''rain water,'' was the instrument of destruction of all living things (7:4); in J's creation account, it was acknowledged as essential for life (2:5–9). Sin, initiated by the first man and woman's disobedience (3:1–7), becomes increasingly pervasive in J's accounts of Cain's murder of his brother (4:1–16), Lamech's polygamy and ruthless vengeance (4:19–24), and the use of status and power to exploit and abuse the weak and defenseless (6:1–4). Each story illustrates a growing alienation between the Lord and humanity, between human and human, and between humanity and nature. In the J account, what would seem to be advances in civilization are progressive movements away from the Lord and the Lord's intended order (4:20–22) until the Lord regrets having made anything (5:7). For J, the Lord's new direction after the flood comes when the Lord smells the pleasing odor from Noah's sacrifice (8:20–22). Sacrificial worship is the remedy for human hearts' continued inclination toward evil. Noah's sacrifice of some of every clean animal and bird explains why in J it was necessary for Noah to bring more than one pair of each clean creature onto the ark. In the J tradition, covenant and blessing come into the picture in the Lord's call to Abram in Gen 12:1–3, while for P, sacrificial worship does not come until God gives Moses instructions for the conduct of the sacrificial cult beginning at Exodus chapter 35.

In the New Testament, in Matt 24:37–39 and Luke 17:26–27, Jesus likened the coming of the kingdom of God to the coming of the flood that caught Noah's contemporaries unaware. Jesus' followers are called to constant vigilance so as to be prepared when the Son of Man appears. The author of 2 Peter includes the flood among examples of instances where God punished human sinfulness (2:4). Then in 3:3–7, the author offers the destruction by the flood as proof that the judgement is coming and will actually occur. The author of 1 Pet 3:20–21 refers to the ark, whose inhabitants were saved through water, as prefiguring baptism that saves from sin. The author of the Epistle to the Hebrews presents Noah as an example of faith who, warned by God about the unforseen coming destruction, obeyed the warning, and became heir to the righteousness that comes in accord with faith (Heb 11:7).

Other Flood Traditions. While flood traditions were widespread among many ancient civilizations, three from Mesopotamia are of special interest in relation to the Genesis account: Atrahasis, Gilgamesh Tablet XI, and Ziusundra (J. B. Pritchard, ed. *Ancient Near Eastern Texts*, pp. 42–44, 93–97, 104–6). The accounts of the dimensions for the ark in Genesis and for the ship in the Akkadian Gilgamesh story illustrate the nature of the many parallels in the narratives. In Genesis, P describes the ark as 450 feet long, 75 feet wide, and 45 feet high (a biblical cubit = 1.5 feet). It had three decks, a pitched roof, and a door in its side (6:15–16). In Gilgamesh, the ship is a cube, 180 feet to each side. There are six decks, seven levels, and a sectioned floor plan (*Ancient Near Eastern Texts* p. 93).

The many such parallels in these accounts with the Genesis flood story do not suggest direct literary dependence. The manifold differences between details in these accounts and those of Genesis, especially in their depiction of the deities and their motives and their interpretation of events, make these accounts significant to understanding and interpreting the Genesis account. An example is the Genesis account of the Lord's smelling of the pleasing odor of Noah's sacrifice (8:21). In Gilgamesh, ''The gods smelled the savor, The gods smelled the sweet savor, The gods crowded like flies about the sacrificer'' (*Ancient Near Eastern Texts* p. 95).

Historical and Scientific Issues. The composite character of the Biblical account and the variations in details within the Mesopotamian accounts suggest that no one of these is an account of a particular historical flood. Floods were common in ancient Mesopotamia, and occasionally devastated whole cities; but no scientific, geological, or historical evidence even suggests that at one time a single flood totally wiped out all of civilization in ancient Mesopotamia, let alone the whole world. That marine fossils are commonly found in mountainous areas throughout the world is the result of geological uplifts. Periodically, news accounts appear about wood that is claimed to be from the ark, recovered on modern Mt. Ararat in Turkey. Carbon 14 tests consistently show that the wood is from the current era, about 1600 years old. The wood is thought to come from the ruins of an ancient monastery that served as a pilgrims' hostel.

The various flood accounts from Mesopotamia suggest that experiences with devastating local floods helped human imaginations to construct accounts of an even worse flood in the distant past that did almost destroy humanity. The accounts reflect the helplessness that humans experience in the face of raging flood waters capable of devastating entire cities. The accounts similarly reflect belief that such natural phenomena were expressions of divine power and will, brought on out of spite or irritation or capriciousness. Because some humans survived each local flood, in each account some humans survive, sometimes due to chance, and other times to the intervention of a sympathetic divine power.

The ancient authors of the Genesis flood story wove their Israelite traditions around one such devastating flood to create a compelling story about their God and His relationship with humanity. The scientific or historical accuracy of the biblical narrative, measured by modern human standards, is irrelevant to the accounts' abiding theological significance.

Bibliography: W. BRUEGGEMANN, *Genesis* (Atlanta, 1982). A.F. CAMPBELL and M.A. O'BRIEN, *Sources of the Pentateuch: Texts, Introductions, Annotations* (Minneapolis, 1993). N. COHN, *Noah's Flood: The Genesis Story in Western Thought* (New Haven, 1996). A. DUNDES, ed.,*The Flood Myth.* (Berkeley, 1988). W.G. LAMBERT and A.R. MILLARD, *Atra-Hasīs: The Babylonian Story of the Flood* (Winona Lake, IN, 1999). J. B. PRITCHARD, *Ancient Near Eastern Texts Relating to the Old Testament* (Princeton 1955). J.W. ROGERSON, *Genesis 1–11* (Sheffield, 1991). G. J. WENHAM, *Genesis 1–15* (Waco, TX, 1987). C. WESTERMANN, *Genesis 1–11* (Minneapolis, 1984).

[J. E. JENSEN]

FLOREFFE, MONASTERY OF

Second house of the PREMONSTRATENSIANS, Diocese of Namur, formerly Liège. It was founded and endowed by Count Gottfried of Namur in 1121–22, and has always held a place of prominence in the order; one of the provinces, the Circaria Floreffiae, was named after it. Floreffe founded seven daughterhouses, maintained 22 parishes, and had three convents under its guidance. It

Benozzo Gozzoli, self-portrait, detail of the "Journey of the Magi" fresco in the chapel of the Medici-Riccardi Palace in Florence. Gozzoli's signature for the large fresco series is painted on the band of his headgear.

had its own college at Louvain. In 1560 it managed to end its previous incorporation as a benefice of the Diocese of Namur. It had 61 religious when suppressed in 1797. When an attempt to reestablish Floreffe in 1842 proved unsuccessful, the monastery was converted into a college conducted by the diocesan clergy. The 103 carved 17th-century choirstalls are a reminder of former magnificence.

Bibliography: C. L. HUGO, *S. Ordinis Praemonstratensis annales,* 2 v. (Nancy 1734–36) 1:75. J. and V. BARBIER, *Histoire de l'abbaye de Floreffe,* 2 v. (Namur 1890–92). L. H. COTTINEAU, *Répertoire topobibliographique des abbayes et prieurés,* 2 v. (Mâcon 1935–39) 1:1155–56. N. BACKMUND, *Monasticon Praemonstratense,* 3 v. (Straubing 1949–56) 2:373–378. *Monumenta Germaniae Historica: Scriptores* (Berlin 1826–) 16:618–631.

[N. BACKMUND]

FLORENCE

City on both banks of the Arno River, in Tuscany, central Italy. It was an economic and artistic center in the late Middle Ages and Renaissance, and its dialect became the standard vernacular of Italy. Since 1420 Florence has been the capital of an archdiocese.

Medieval chroniclers report that *Florentia Tuscorum* was founded by Caesar (59 B.C.), and recent studies indicate that it is unlikely that modern Florence was derived from an Etruscan city. The Roman city, the focus of north-south roads at the foot of the Apennines, by A.D. 200 was a commercial center, having an aqueduct, baths, a theater, and other public monuments. It was the capital of the sixth region of DIOCLETIAN'S Diocese of Italy (Tuscany and Umbria) and *c.* 300 began to suffer from the economic crisis of the ROMAN EMPIRE. Heavy taxes, rural impoverishment, and a decline in trade caused politicoeconomic difficulties.

Early Christian History. Christianity came to Florence *c.* 200. In the small Christian community there were several martyrs under DECIUS, to one of whom, St. Miniatus, a basilica was dedicated. Felix, the first known bishop, attended the Council of Rome against the Donatists (313). St. Ambrose consecrated a basilica in Florence (394), where religious life flourished under St. Zenobius (*c.* 412). Bishop Podius organized pastoral care and instituted many parishes.

Stilicho and the Romans thwarted the sudden attack on Florence by the Ostrogoths under Radagaiso (405), but the city did not recover. In 541 the Byzantines defended it against Totila. Under the Lombards, who replaced the Byzantines, Florence had a duke and a royal court. The Franks placed it under a count in their reorganization. Charlemagne was in Florence for Christmas (786). LOTHAIR I in the *Constitutio Olonensis* (825) assigned Florence one of eight schools for students for the priesthood. The Franks fostered monasteries, which later influenced both the city and the diocese. Ottonian immunity contributed to the growth of church property, which became more and more important. Margrave Hugh of Tuscany founded many monasteries, which became centers of reform. Countess Matilda of Canossa (Tuscany), under whom the commune took form, sided with the papacy against the empire in the investiture struggle.

In the 10th and 11th centuries religious life flourished. St. ROMUALD and St. JOHN GUALBERT founded the first reform cenobite monasteries, especially CAMALDOLI and VALLOMBROSA. The cathedral chapter, reformed under Benedict IX (1032–45), led a life in common. The German emperor attended Pope Victor II's Council of Florence (1055), which promulgated stringent rules against simony and concubinage. Nicholas II (1058–61), the former Gerhard of Burgundy, had been bishop of Florence (1046–58). During the rise of the commune, the bishops were important in political life.

Several forms of autonomy, especially economic, developed in Florence and were defended against feudal lords who controlled the land around the city. Florence reduced them to obedience one by one and had them build houses within its walls and live there part of the year. Even the imperial envoys, associated with the feudal lords, came to terms with the commune. Against imperial rights, Florence was allied with the pope, then the strongest opponent of the emperor. When common goods had to be administered and collective rights defended, powers were delegated to a limited number of citizens (*boni homines*). The first consuls appeared in 1138. The first evidence of the commune in action was the war against Fiesole (1123), fought for territory, political hegemony, and diocesan boundaries. Fiesole was taken and destroyed. The commune built new walls (1172–75) and divided the city into quarters and sixths, each of which furnished representatives to the consular magistracy.

The commune developed as a federation of groups (*arti*). At first, there were two associations: the Society of the Torri or nobles (*optimates*), and the bourgeois Arte of Calimala, which headed the *arte* of the refining and dyeing of wool cloth, Florence's first and most important bourgeois industry. In time, divers industries and trades separated and formed independent *arti,* later to divide into major and minor *arti.* At its peak, the organization of *arti* clashed with and defeated the nobility, upsetting the consular constitution. A new supreme official, the podestà, was chosen first from the citizenry and then from foreigners.

Guelfs and Ghibellines. The internal antagonisms of the commune became a struggle between GUELFS and Ghibellines. After a long conflict, the Ghibellines, aided by FREDERICK II, drove the Guelfs into exile. On Frederick's death (1250), the Guelfs returned and promulgated a new constitution. A new magistracy was created beside the podestà, the *capitano* of the people, to look out for their interests. In 1252 Florence coined the first gold florins. Ghibellines returned with Manfred when SIENA defeated Florence at Montaperti (1260). In 1265 DANTE was born, and in 1266 the battle of Benevento marked the end of the Hohenstaufen-Church conflict and the triumph of Italian Guelfs. Florence, backed by the popes and the kings of Naples (House of Anjou), became a bulwark of Guelfism.

At Colle in 1267 Florence avenged the defeat at Montaperti, and at Campaldino in 1289 it fixed its hegemony over Ghibelline Arezzo. Cardinal Latino negotiated a peace (1279) that sought to end party rivalries and smooth the way to a new form of government, the primate of the *arti.* The major *arti* first had access to government, and then the minor *arti* (corporative trade groups of the *popolo minuto*), sanctioned by Giano della Bella's *Ordinamenti di giustizia* (1293). In 1300 Guelfs split into Blacks and Whites over how Guelfism should be expressed (Blacks intransigent, Whites somewhat moderate) and over independence of the Angevins and the popes. Whites first held a series of priorships, to one of which Dante belonged; but in 1301 the Blacks seized power with the support of Boniface VIII and banished White leaders. Dante died in exile in Ravenna (1321). The hopes of the Whites for a political revolution caused by the arrival of Emperor HENRY VII in Italy were ended with his death in 1313. Florence had recourse to Charles of Calabria, king of Sicily, for aid against Castruccio Castracani of Lucca, who defeated Florence in 1325. The deaths of Castruccio and Charles of Valois in 1328 freed Florence from an Italian threat and a foreign enemy.

"The Eucharist," one of the reliefs of the Sacraments by the Tuscan sculptor Andrea Pisano (1290?–1348) on the Campanile of the cathedral at Florence. (Alinari-Art Reference/Art Resource, NY)

After winning territory from nearby Pistoia, Arezzo, Cortona, and Siena, Florence was defeated by Pisa in a contest over the possession of Lucca; and the great banking houses of Peruzzi and Bardi failed. Walter of Brienne, Duke of Athens, accepted rule of the city but was ex-

Skyline of Florence, with the dome of the Cathedral of Santa Maria del Fiore (the Duomo) visible at right, and the tower of the Palazzo Vecchio at far left. (©Michael Lewis/CORBIS)

pelled in 1343 after a year of misrule. The war of the ''Eight Saints'' (1375) was fought against the papal legate William of Noellet (d. 1394), who attempted to take Florence. Afterward party conflict raged stronger in the city. In 1378 the proletariat of workers (Ciompi), excluded from corporative rights and rule, seized power, making Michele di Lando gonfalonier. Democratic rule lasted to 1382, when the oligarchy was restored under Maso degli Albizi. Capture of Pisa (1406) and Leghorn (1421) gave Florence access to the sea.

The Medici. The rule of the Albizi lasted until Cosimo de' Medici, a shrewd politician and rich merchant, replaced it (1434), founding a dynasty that reached its peak under his grandson, Lorenzo the Magnificent (1469–92). The aspirations of the oligarchs out of power exploded in the PAZZI plot, to which Lorenzo's brother Giuliano fell victim; but Lorenzo survived to consolidate his hold on the city. Not only did he rule well, assuring external peace with painstaking alliances, but he fostered internal growth; under him Florence attained its economic, artistic, and intellectual peak in the Renaissance. He was surrounded with humanist genius: Poliziano PICO DELLA MIRANDOLA, Marsilio FICINO, the Camaldolese theologian and humanist Ambrogio Traversari (1386–1439), and others. In his Biblioteca Laurenziana he collected codices of Greek and Latin classics. Great artists worked for him; Michelangelo was raised in his house. At the time of his death, Girolamo SAVONAROLA was denouncing the corruption of morals in the new age. Savonarola obtained the expulsion of Piero, Lorenzo's son, who ceded Florentine land to Charles VIII of France, and he established a Christian republic that was intended to be the center of a disciplinary reform of the Church. The oligarchy reacted, however, and the friar's dream vanished with him on his pyre (1498).

After being briefly out of power, the Medici returned in 1512, protected by two Medici popes, Leo X and Clement VII. In 1530 the republic came to an end following a siege by Emperor CHARLES V. Duke Alessandro (1510–37), who belonged to a collateral branch of the Medici, became lord of Florence. During the ensuing principate, Florence's history was regional rather than municipal. The ducal dynasty died out in 1737 and was replaced by Francis II of Lorraine. Except for the Napoleonic period (1801–14), the Lorraine dynasty ruled until 1859, when Leopold II (d. 1870) left after a plebescite voted annexation to the kingdom of Italy, of which Florence was the capital (1865–70).

Façade of the Pazzi Chapel, designed by Filippo Brunelleschi, located in the cloister of the church of Santa Croce. (Alinari-Art Reference/Art Resource, NY)

Religious life flourished from the 12th century onward. The faith inspired Florence's greatest creations. They included Dante's *Divine Comedy* and the Cathedral of S. Maria del Fiore, consecrated by Eugene IV (1430). The convents of S. Maria Novella, S. Spirito, S. Croce, and the Charterhouse were founded. A number of medieval saints claimed Florence as their native city: the recluse St. Verdiana (1182?–1242?), St. Julia of Certaldo, Bl. Joan of Signa, Bl. Umiliana de' Cerchi, and Bl. Villana De Botti (1332–60). The Servites (Servants of Mary) were founded in Florence by the seven saints (1233–49). The 17th ecumenical council, transferred from Basel to Ferrara, met in Florence (1439–43). St. ANTONINUS PIEROZZI, OP, founder of the Convent of San Marco, where Fra ANGELICO worked, was a virtuous and strong archbishop (1446–59). The reform of morals and of the Church that emanated from San Marco had its most fervent apostle in Savonarola, leader of Florence's late fifteenth-century spiritual Republic. In the 17th century Florence produced new saints: CATHERINE OF RICCI, Mary Magdalene de' PAZZI, and Hippolytus Galantini (founder of a congregation of lay catechists). Archbishop della Gherardesca founded the major seminary (1712). Under Cardinal Elia Dalla Costa (1932–61), who founded the minor seminary (1937), were held the Etruscan Council (1934) and two diocesan synods. The University of Florence (1348) moved to Pisa (1472); it was reconstituted in 1923, and is one of the largest in Italy.

CATHARI were prevalent in the 13th century and had a bishop in Florence; PATARINES were condemned by a diocesan synod (1327). Protestantism had almost no influence in the diocese, though PETER MARTYR Vermigli was born there. The Jansenist tendencies of Bp. Scipione de' Ricci of Pistoia did not affect the people of the city.

Bibliography: G. LAMI, *S. Ecclesiae Florentinae monumenta,* 4 v. (Florence 1758). R. GALLUZZI, *Storia del Granducato di Toscana sotto il governo di casa Medici,* 9 v. (Florence 1781). F.

SCHEVILL, *Medieval and Renaissance Florence,* 2 v. (New York 1963). A. PANELLLA, *Storia di Firenze* (Florence 1949). R. DAVIDSOHN, *Storia di Firenze,* 5 v. (Florence 1956–62), tr. of the German (Berlin 1896–1927). M. LOPES PEGNA, *Firenze dalle origini al Medioevo* (Florence 1962). *Annuario dell' Arcidiocesi di Firenze, 1965. Annuario Pontificio* (Rome 1912–) (1964) 152. G. BRUCKER, *Renaissance Florence* (New York 1969). E. COCHRANE, *Florence in the Forgotten Centuries 1527–1800* (Chicago 1973). R. GOLDTHWAITE *The Building of Renaissance Florence* (Baltimore 1980). R. TURNER, *The Renaissance in Florence* (London 1997).

[E. SCOZZAFAVA]

FLORENCE, COUNCIL OF

By the bulls *Doctoris gentium* of Sept. 18 and *Pridem ex iustis* of Dec. 30, 1437, Pope EUGENE IV transferred the Council of BASEL to Ferrara. There it opened on Jan. 8, 1438, under the presidency of Cardinal ALBERGATI. Eugene arrived on January 24. The first sessions were occupied in asserting the canonical validity of the council, in declaring null the sanctions voted in Basel against it, and in imposing penalties on opponents. For voting the council was divided into three estates: prelates, abbots and religious, and lower church dignitaries—the consent of two-thirds of each estate being needed for a conciliar decision.

At Ferrara. The Greeks arrived in Venice on February 8 and in Ferrara, March 4–7: the emperor John VIII Palaeologus and his brother Demetrius; the patriarch of Constantinople, Joseph II; with Gregory, the emperor's confessor, 20 metropolitans (five of whom acted also as procurators of the patriarchates of ALEXANDRIA, ANTIOCH, and JERUSALEM); deacons, monks, and courtiers. There were in all about 700. All their expenses in coming, returning, and maintaining themselves in Italy were to be paid by the pope. At the solemn inauguration on April 9, besides the Greeks, there were 118 Latin prelates. John VIII, however, had requested a delay of four months before any doctrinal discussion, to allow the Western secular powers time to send representatives, since from them he wanted military help for CONSTANTINOPLE, which was threatened by the Turks. To satisfy Latin impatience, in June discussions about PURGATORY were instituted between two committees of ten. The Latins proposed a purgation of punishment by fire; the Greeks, accepting the possibility of relief for the departed, denied fire and asserted that souls await the Last Judgment before entering on their final state. No agreement had been reached when the plague descended on Ferrara. Isidore, Metropolitan of Kiev and All Russia, arrived during this time (August 1438).

The council proper began on October 8. Cardinal BESSARION of Nicaea (one of the six spokesmen of the Greeks) gave an opening address and then Mark EUGENICUS, Metropolitan of Ephesus, introduced the subject chosen by the Greeks: the legitimacy of the addition by the Latins of the words *FILIOQUE* to the NICENE CREED. In 13 sessions, from October 8 to December 13, the Greeks contended that any addition to the creed, even of a word or syllable, even if true, had been forbidden by the Council of EPHESUS (431). Bessarion spoke in two sessions and Mark Eugenicus in all the rest. The Latins interpreted the prohibition of Ephesus as referring to the faith expressed by the creed, not to the formula of expression. Of the six appointed Latin orators, Andrew of Rhodes, OP; Aloysius of Forli, OFM; and especially Cardinal CESARINI were the principal speakers. No agreement was reached. Instead the Greeks, weary, nostalgic, and discouraged, wanted to go home. Eugene, in financial straits, was in arrears in his payments to them and was threatened by Milanese troops. He persuaded the Greek delegation to go to Florence (Jan. 10, 1439) and to discuss the doctrine of the *Filioque.*

At Florence. After a preliminary meeting of two committees of 40 on February 26, there were eight sessions between March 2 and 24. The Latins contended that within the Blessed Trinity the Holy Spirit proceeds from the Father and from the Son (*ex Patre Filioque*); the Greeks, that He proceeds from the Father only. John of Montenero was the sole speaker for the Latins; Mark Eugenicus, for the Greeks. Five sessions were spent largely in discussing which side had the more accurate texts of a few passages from the Fathers, especially from Basil's *Adversus Eunomium.* In the sixth, Mark quoted the Scriptures, the councils, and the Fathers as all supporting the Greek position. In the seventh and eighth, Montenero used the same sources in favor of the Latin doctrine. The result was a stalemate.

During the following two months in an atmosphere of frustration and pessimism, the Latins urged more sessions; the Greeks, weary of discussion, demanded another road to union, otherwise they would go home (April 11). Meetings of committees bore no fruit. The Latins presented an accurate statement of doctrine (*cedula*); the Greeks amended it into ambiguity. Urged to clarify their reply, they again refused and threatened to depart (May 21). As a last resort Eugene addressed the council on May 27, congratulating, encouraging, chiding, and exhorting. His words gave a new impulse to the efforts for union.

The Greek prelates believed that every saint, precisely as a saint, was inspired by the Holy Spirit and therefore could not err in faith. If they expressed themselves differently, their meanings must substantially agrcc. At this stage of the council this axiom was pressed by those Greeks who favored union. Latin saints stated that the

Holy Spirit "proceeds from Father and Son"; Greek saints (as abundantly quoted by Montenero, Bessarion, and others) variously wrote "comes forth from," "issues from," "springs from," "the Father," "the Father and the Son," "from Both," "from the Father through the Son." The patriarch TARASIUS had said: "proceeds from the Father through the Son." Once the Greeks accepted that the Latin Fathers had really written *Filioque* (they could not understand Latin), the issue was settled (May 29). The Greek Fathers necessarily meant the same; the faiths of the two Churches were identical; union was not only possible but obligatory (June 3); and on June 8 the Latin *cedula* on the Procession was accepted by the Greek synod. On June 10 Joseph II died and was buried in the church of S. Maria Novella.

During the next six weeks the Latins gave the Greeks *cedulae* on the primacy (*see* PRIMACY OF THE POPE) and the Eucharist (which were explained in two sessions, June 16, 18), and on purgatory. There were difficulties and tensions and concessions on both sides before agreement was reached. More friction arose over the wording of the decree, composed of the *cedulae* previously agreed on, to which an introduction and conclusion were added. The resulting *Laetentur caeli* was promulgated in solemn session, July 6, 1439, signed by Eugene and 116 Latins and by the emperor with 32 Greeks, four of whom acted as proxies of Alexandria, Antioch, and Jerusalem. Both groups agreed that the Holy Spirit proceeds from the Father and the Son as from one principle and spiration, the Latin "from" and the Greek "through" being equivalent and causal. In the Eucharist, rites in fermented and unfermented bread are both valid. After death some souls are purified by purgatorial punishments; others immediately receive their eternal destiny in hell or, with different degrees of beatitude, in heaven. The pope is the successor of St. Peter, head and teacher of the whole Church, and successor to the plenitude of power given by Christ to St. Peter; the usual precedence of the patriarchates is included.

As the Greeks departed, two representatives of the Armenians arrived from Caffa (August 13). In the bull *Moyses vir Dei* (September 4), Eugene challenged the ecumenicity of the Council of CONSTANCE when it decreed conciliar supremacy (*see* CONCILIARISM [HISTORY OF]) and condemned Basel for daring to "depose" him. Union with the Armenians was promulgated on Nov. 22, 1439, in *Exultate Deo* (the Decree for ARMENIANS). On Feb. 4, 1440, by *Cantate Domino,* union was established with the Coptic Church of Egypt and, after the council went to the Lateran in Rome (Sept. 24, 1443), unions were concluded with certain Syrians (April 30, 1444) and with Chaldeans and Maronites of Cyprus (Aug. 7, 1445). When the council ended is not certain, for no document of closure is extant. In the meantime, to fulfill the obligation undertaken in Florence, Eugene had raised a crusade to drive the Turks from Europe. Only Poland and Hungary by land and Burgundy and Venice with the papal ships by sea took part. At Varna (Nov. 10, 1444) the Christian army was defeated, and Cesarini and King Ladislas of Poland-Hungary were killed. A powerful argument for union, namely, aid for Constantinople, thereby lost all its force.

Conclusion. The union with the Greeks did not last long. Mark Eugenicus, its one consistent Greek opponent, found ready support in the ill-educated monks and populace of Constantinople, and the majority of the bishops, themselves with little theological formation, yielded to popular pressure. All the intellectuals remained constant—Mark, against union; and for union, Bessarion, Isidore, Dorotheus of Mitylene, Metrophanes (successor of Joseph II) with at least five others (of the 18 episcopal Greek signatories), and Patriarch GREGORY III, successor of Metrophanes.

The reason commonly given for the general defection is that the union was never genuine, and was signed under duress. That some of the Greeks suffered hardship from the pope's inability to pay them punctually, and that their prolonged stay in Italy and ill success in convincing the Latins in argument distressed and depressed them is clear. The Greeks also desired to obtain help for their homeland. But that these influences did not amount to duress is shown by the events themselves. After the unsuccessful sessions in Ferrara the Greeks were prepared to return home. Also, after the sessions in Florence they twice gave the pope an ultimatum. In neither case, however, was there the slightest sign of their being cowed by want or oppressed by the plight of their country; on the contrary, they resisted Latin pressure obstinately. Similarly, it is said that the emperor, determined on union for his own ends, allowed no freedom of speech. In the sessions Greeks spoke as frequently as Latins and in all the sessions but 2, i.e., in 19 out of 21 (or, including the deliberations on purgatory, in all but 3, i.e., in 23 out of 26) the Greek spokesman, Mark Eugenicus, was the sole constant opponent of union, and that with the emperor's consent. Besides, Mark (as he himself later testified) always spoke freely in the Greek private meetings, did not sign the decree, and was taken back to Constantinople in the imperial ship. It must be concluded, therefore, that the Greeks in Italy, though suffering certain disabilities, retained freedom of action and expression; that in Florence all who signed the decree did so freely, though in some cases influenced more by example than by conviction; and that in Constantinople they again followed the prevailing example and recanted. Consequently, in Constantinople itself there was sharp division. The emperor, though himself faithful to the union, did little to impose it. It was not officially promulgated till Dec. 12, 1452, by Isidore of Kiev as papal legate, under the shadow of Turkish attack. Mahomet captured Constantinople on May 29, 1453, and the union there ended. Elsewhere the unions continued until Turkish arms prevailed.

Effects. *Laetentur caeli* is an infallible document, the only one of the council. The union it expressed in Florence was real and, in a sense, model. It defined that the Latin faith and the traditional Greek faith were identical and allowed difference in their expression. It did not impose on the Greeks the addition of the *Filioque* to the creed; it approved difference in Eucharistic rite. Thus it established the sound principle of any union, identity of faith with liberty in rite, that has since been followed by the Ukrainians, the Rumanians, and many others. As regards the primacy, though the definition and the previous explanation of it were more general, the Greeks probably regarded it as a canonical, not a theological, question. A more important effect of the council was perhaps the check it gave to conciliarism. The Councils of Constance and Basel had tended to alter the traditional constitution of the Church by making councils, nearly always in session, into the supreme authority of the Church, with power in the hands of the lower clergy. The fact of union and the definition of the primacy in Florence, together with the intense antipapalism of Basel, though it did not kill conciliarism, certainly rendered it largely harmless. Further, the council stimulated interest in the Christians of Abyssinia and India, occasioning the voyages of discovery that ended by opening China in the East and America in the West.

Bibliography: Sources. *Concilium Florentinum: Documenta et scriptores* (Rome 1940–), esp. v. 5 *Acta graeca,* ed. J. GILL and v. 6 *Acta latina,* ed. G. HOFMANN. E. CECCONI, *Studi storici sul Concilio di Firenze* (Florence 1869). S. SYROPULOS,'Απομνημονε ύματα, ed. and tr. R. CREYGHTON as *Vera historia unionis non verae* (The Hague 1660). Literature. C. J. VON HEFELE, *Histoire des conciles d'après les documents originaux,* tr. and continued by H. LECLERCQ, 10 v. in 19 (Paris 1907–38) v. 7. J. GILL, *The Council of Florence* (Cambridge, Eng. 1959); *Eugenius IV: Pope of Christian Union* (Westminster, Md. 1961); *Personalities of the Council of Florence* (New York 1964). T. FERGUSON, ''The Council of Ferrara-Florence and Its Continued Historical Significance,'' *Saint Vladimir's Theological Quarterly* 43:1 (1999) 55–77. G. E. DEMACOPOULOS, ''The Popular Reception of the Council of Florence in Constantinople 1439–1453,'' *Saint Vladimir's Theological Quarterly* 43:1 (1999) 37–53. G. ALBERIGO, ed., *Christian Unity: The Council of Ferrara-Florence 1438/39–1989* (Louvain 1991).

[J. GILL]

FLORENCE OF WORCESTER

Benedictine chronicler and monk of Worcester Priory; d. July 7, 1118. The *Chronicon ex chronicis* attributed to him is one of the earliest Latin world chronicles to be compiled in England after BEDE. Up to 1073 it is principally an enlargement of the annals of MARIANUS SCOTUS, taking over his chronology and making use of other sources including the *Anglo-Saxon Chronicle,* Asser's *Life of Alfred,* and Coleman's *Life of Wulfstan.* From 1082 it is an important independent source, though it also includes extracts from the works of EADMER and other contemporary historians. The exact nature of the author's contacts with WILLIAM OF MALMESBURY and ORDERICUS VITALIS has still to be established. The chronicle became a standard source for later medieval historians. Though the work was undertaken at the instigation of WULFSTAN, Bishop of Worcester (d. 1095), there is evidence that it was still in its early stages in 1103. Florence appears to have collected materials and may have written the entries up to 1110 or 1113 at the latest. It is, however, just possible that the whole chronicle in its present form is the work of John of Worcester, who certainly compiled the continuation from slightly before the death of Florence until 1140.

Bibliography: *Chronicon ex chronicis,* ed. W. HOWARD (London 1592), complete; ed. B. THORPE, 2 v. (London 1848–49); tr. T. FORESTER (London 1854). *The Chronicle of John of Worcester, 1118–40,* ed. J. K. H. WEAVER (Oxford 1908). *The Vita Wulfstani of William of Malmesbury,* ed. R. R. DARLINGTON (Camden 3d ser. 40; London 1928) xv–xviii. R. R. DARLINGTON, *Anglo-Norman Historians* (London 1947). V. H. GALBRAITH, *Historical Research in Medieval England* (London 1951) 19–22. A. D. VON DEN BRINCKEN, *Studien zur lateinischen Weltchronistik bis in das Zeitalter Ottos von Freising* (Düsseldorf 1957) 173–181.

[M. M. CHIBNALL]

FLORENSKIĬ, PAVEL ALEKSANDROVICH

Russian philosopher, theologian, and scientist; b. Tiflis, 1882; place and date of death unknown. After studying mathematics and philosophy at the University of Moscow, he declined an offer to teach mathematics there. Instead he studied at the Moscow Theology Academy, taught philosophy and history there from 1908, and was ordained an Orthodox priest (1911). Florenskiĭ impressed contemporaries as a mathematician, physicist, philosopher, theologian, poet, historian, musician, archeologist, astronomer, engineer, polyglot, and mystic. Most of his writings could not be published because of the closing of the theological academies after 1917; but his dissertation, *The Pillar and Foundation of Truth: An Essay on Orthodox Theodicy in Twelve Chapters,* was printed in 1914 and attracted wide attention. After the revolution Florenskiĭ accepted a post in the main office of the electrical industry. In 1927 he invented a noncoagulating machine oil called dekanite. Also he wrote a standard textbook on dielectrics. His refusal to renounce Holy Orders caused his imprisonment several times. Because of his scientific reputation he dared in 1929 to address a meeting of engineers in Leningrad dressed in cassock and priest's cap. This act greatly displeased the Communists. In 1935 Florenskiĭ was sentenced to ten years in a concentration camp. Rumors of his death reached Sergeĭ BULGAKOV in 1943 and were heard by Russian refugees in 1946, but they were never verified.

In his metaphysics and in his theology of the Trinity Florenskiĭ applied the notion of consubstantiality. He divided all philosophical systems into rationalistic (*homoiousian*) and Christian (*homoousian*). The former, he believed, recognized generic likeness only, whereas the latter admitted consubstantiality, since it is the philosophy of ideas and of reason, the philosophy of personality and creative achievement. Florenskiĭ's repetition of the doctrine of KHOMIAĪAKOV on SOBORNOST (togetherness) as the principle of Church organization evoked sharp criticism from BERDĪAEV. Florenskiĭ's natural theology was based on living religious experience as the sole method of knowing dogmas "in a personal encounter with God." Following SOLOV'EV he defined "Sophia" (Wisdom) as a precosmic hypostatic concentration of divine prototypes. Thus in his outlook the cosmos, purified in Christ, becomes with Sophia a part of the Absolute merging in a total unity. Without the metaphysics of the Incarnation, however, the connection between the "two worlds" remains obscure and the concept of Sophia can result only in a philosophical incompleteness.

Bibliography: B. SCHULTZE, *Russische Denker* (Vienna 1950). N. O. LOSSKIĬ, *History of Russian Philosophy* (New York 1951). V. V. ZEN'KOVSKIĬ, *History of Russian Philosophy,* tr. G. L. KLINE, 2 v. (New York 1953).

[J. PAPIN]

FLORENTINA, ST.

Virgin; fl. in or near Seville, *c.* 600. She and (St.) Fulgentius (of Écija) were born between their Greek-named brothers (SS.) LEANDER and ISIDORE, both of whom became bishops of SEVILLE. Leander, who seems to have endowed Florentina (Florence) with a convent, wrote for her and her community the *De institutione virginum et contemptu mundi,* known in manuscripts from Betica (ninth century), San Millan (11th), SILOS (11th), and MONTE CASSINO (13th). The work exalts consecrated virginity and offers a "rule" of 31 chapters for virgins in monasteries. Isidore dedicated his *De fide catholica contra Judaeos* to Florentina. Her relics, discovered with those of Fulgentius near Guadalupe (*c.* 1330), were shared between the ESCORIAL and Murcia (1593). The cult of Florentina, patroness of Plasencia, dates from the 15th century.

Feast: June 20.

Bibliography: A. C. VEGA, *S. Leandri Hispalensis De institutione virginum et contemptu mundi* (Escorial 1948), originally pub. in *La Ciudad de Dios* 159 (1947) 357–394. J. MADOZ, *Analecta Bollandiana* 67:407–424. G. BARDY, *Catholicisme* 4:1349. A. M.. ZIMMERMANN, *Kalendarium Benedictinum: Die Heiligen und Seligen des Benediktinerorderns und seiner Zweige* (Metten 1933–38) 2:340–341.

[E. P. COLBERT]

FLORENTINI, THEODOSIUS

Swiss Catholic leader in educational, charitable, and social work, founder of two religious congregations; b. Münster, Graubünden canton, Switzerland, May 23, 1808; d. Heiden, Appenzell canton, Feb. 15, 1865. He joined the Capuchins (1825) and was ordained (1830). After teaching theology in the Capuchin house of studies in Baden, Switzerland, he became superior there (1838). Government suppression of religious houses caused him to flee to Alsace (1841). Upon his return he became active in the renewal of Swiss Catholic life, mainly in the fields of education and charitable works. To effectuate his plans Florentini founded the Teaching Sisters of the Holy Cross (1844) and the Sisters of Mercy of the HOLY CROSS (1856). By 1865 these two congregations had 441 members. For the former group Florentini drew up a plan of elementary education. In 1856 he reopened the former Jesuit college in Schwyz and developed for it a program of humanistic studies and industrial training.

Florentini believed that a solution of the labor problem was among the most urgent needs of his time, and he developed a social theology as well as an active reform program. He advocated model factories, to be established and even managed by religious orders as examples of shops run according to the principles of justice and charity. Some factories were opened at Florentini's instigation. In them he tried to bring about a "better distribution of revenue between dead money and working energy." In each new attempt he utilized lessons learned from previous failures. Florentini's most important enterprise was the cloth factory that he took over in 1860 in Oberleutensdorf, Bohemia, then part of Austria-Hungary. The higher clergy and nobles were well-disposed toward the project, which anticipated later developments in enlightened social management but which proved economically unprofitable.

When Florentini became vicar-general of the Diocese of Chur in 1860, he undertook new pastoral projects and helped inaugurate the Swiss bishops' conferences. He was also a noted preacher and author of many popular spiritual works. His unselfish labors won him the esteem of both Catholics and non-Catholics.

Bibliography: V. GADIENT, *Der Caritasapostel Theodosius Florentini* (2d ed. Lucerne 1946). A. BÜNTER, *Die industriellen Unternehmungen von P. Theodosius Florentini* (Freiburg 1962). B. VON MEHR, *Lexikon für Theologie und Kirche*, 10v. (2d, new ed. Freiburg 1957–65) 4:170.

[A. BÜNTER]

FLORENTIUS, RADEWIJNS

Cofounder with Gerard GROOTE of the BRETHREN OF THE COMMON LIFE; b. Leerdam, Holland, *c.* 1350; d. Deventer, March 24, 1400. Returning as a master of arts from the university in Prague, he heard a sermon by Groote, became his disciple, and at his insistence proceeded to ordination. In Deventer, center of the so-called DEVOTIO MODERNA, he joined Groote in his apostolate among poor clerical scholars. Gathering a number of these together as the Brethren of the Common Life, he thus fulfilled the desire of Groote to found such a community. In 1386 Windesheim became the center of the brotherhood, and other foundations soon followed. THOMAS À KEMPIS lived under Radewijns' care at Deventer for seven years and, when he came to write his master's biography, depicted Radewijns as one who drew others to Christ not by subtle argument, but by the humility of his way of life.

Bibliography: T. À KEMPIS, ''The Life of Florentius,'' *The Founders of the New Devotion,* tr. J. P. ARTHUR (St. Louis 1905) 81–162. T. P. VON ZIJL, *Gerard Groote, Ascetic and Reformer, 1340–1384* (Washington 1963). F. VANDENBROUCKE, *Lexikon für Theologie und Kirche* (Freiburg 1957–65) 8:964–965.

[M. S. CONLAN]

FLORES GARCÍA, MARGARITO, ST.

Martyr, priest; b. Feb. 22, 1899, Taxco, Guerrero, Diocese of Chilapa, Mexico; d. Nov. 12, 1927, Tulimán, between Chilapa and Chilpancingo. From the age of 12, Margarito dedicated himself to God's service, while working in the fields to help support his poverty-stricken family. He entered the seminary at Chilapa and was ordained priest (1924). Soon thereafter he was appointed professor in the seminary. He took refuge in Mexico City during the persecution and attended the academy of San Carlos. After he was arrested, then released there, he decided to return to Chilapa, where the vicar general had named him pastor of the parish at Atenango del Rio, Guerrero. He was captured upon his arrival, humiliated, and led to Tulimán where he was shot. Fr. Flores was both beatified (Nov. 22, 1992) and canonized (May 21, 2000) with Cristobal MAGALLANES [*see* GUADALAJARA, MARTYRS OF, SS.] by Pope John Paul II.

Feast: May 25 (Mexico).

Bibliography: J. CARDOSO, *Los mártires mexicanos* (Mexico City 1953).

[K. I. RABENSTEIN]

FLORES VARELA, JOSÉ (JOSEPH) ISABEL, ST.

Martyr, priest; b. Nov. 20, 1866, Santa María de La Paz, San Juan Bautista de Teúl, Zacatecas, Archdiocese of Guadalajara, Mexico; d. June 21, 1927, Zapotlanejo's cemetery, Jalisco, Archdiocese of Guadalajara. Flores was among the most distinguished graduates of the seminary of Guadalajara. After his ordination (1896) he worked in various parishes (Teocaltiche, Zapotlanejo, Tonalá, and Matatlán), where he promoted First Friday devotions and founded Marian associations. A long–time friend denounced him before the municipal authorities at the outbreak of the revolution. He was captured en route to a ranch to celebrate Mass, imprisoned for three days, and offered his freedom in exchange for allegiance to Plutarco Elías Calles. Upon his refusal, he was beheaded. Fr. Flores was both beatified (Nov. 22, 1992) and canonized (May 21, 2000) with Cristobal MAGALLANES [*see* GUADALAJARA, MARTYRS OF, SS.] by Pope John Paul II.

Feast: May 25 (Mexico).

Bibliography: J. CARDOSO, *Los mártires mexicanos* (Mexico City 1953). J. DÍAZ ESTRELLA, *El movimiento cristero: sociedad y conflicto en los Altos de Jalisco* (México, D.F. 1979). V. GARCÍA JUÁREZ, *Los cristeros* (Fresnillo, Zac. 1990).

[K. I. RABENSTEIN]

FLÓREZ, ENRIQUE

Scholar; b. Villadiego (Burgos), July 21, 1702; d. Madrid, May 5, 1773. An Augustinian since 1718, he had moderate success as a theologian in Alcalá (*Theologia,* 5 v., 1732–38), but the chief result of the regime of study and seclusion he followed for the last 40 years of his life was the first 29 volumes of the *España sagrada* (1747–75), still in publication. In this gigantic task of putting order into Spanish history, diocese by diocese, he received the generous help of many other Spanish scholars, a subsidy from Ferdinand VI, and ecclesiastical privileges from Benedict XIV. The work is still valuable for the many sources edited therein and today is itself the object of historical study. Flórez's *Clave historical* (1743; 18th ed. 1854) is a handbook of European history. His *Memorias de las reinas católicas* (1761, 1945) is a scholarly work. In 1765 he published the *Viage santo* of Ambrosio de Morales (d. 1591), whose work he had inherited at Alcalá. The *Medallas* (3 v., 1757–73) is a study of Hispano–Roman and Visigothic coins. His edition of the *Commentary on the Apocalypse* by BEATUS OF LIÉBANA (1770) was the only one in print until 1930. His fervent and purposeful scholarship was not entirely without fault. Flórez's voluminous correspondence is scattered.

Bibliography: F. MÉNDEZ, *Noticias sobre la vida, escritos y viajes del . . . Flórez* (2d ed. Madrid 1860); *Indice-catálogo de la biblioteca del padre E. Flórez,* ed. A. C. VEGA (Madrid 1952). *Enciclopedia universal illustrada Europeo-Americana,* 70 v. (Barcelona 1908–30; suppl. 1934–) 24:150–152. B. SÁNCHEZ ALONSO, *Historia de la historiografía española,* 3 v. (Madrid 1941–50) v.3. M. VALLEJO GIRVES, ''Enrique Florez y sus contemporaneos ante la Intervencion de Gregorio Magno en obispados de la Espana bizantina,'' *Hispanica Sacra* 49 (1997) 655–673.

[E. P. COLBERT]

FLORIANS (FLORIACENSES)

Italian monastic congregation. JOACHIM DA FIORE, the great Calabrian ''prophet'' and mystic was the abbot of the Cistercian Corazzo, but in pursuit of a stricter life he founded, in 1189, S. Giovanni in Fiore, a new abbey in a remote wilderness of Calabria. In his concept monks, detached from worldly cares and dedicated to contemplation in severe penances, were to herald the third and final phase of salvation, the kingdom of the Holy Spirit. The legal framework of the new organization was similar to that of the Cistercians, but the discipline and spirituality anticipated those of the Franciscans. In 1196 Celestine III approved the new congregation, which spread quickly throughout Italy, numbering in the middle of the 13th century about 40 houses. By the end of the 15th century, however, most houses had become depopulated and impoverished. In 1505 the Abbey of Fiore returned to the fold of the Cistercians and other communities were eventually absorbed by the Carthusians or Dominicans. In the 17th century the abbeys that had rejoined Cîteaux became members of the Cistercian Congregation of Calabria, ending the independent life of Florians.

Bibliography: F. RUSSO, *Gioacchino da Fiore e le fondazioni florensi in Calabria* (Naples 1959). G. PENCO, *Storia del monachesimo in Italia* (Rome 1961).

[L. J. LEKAI]

Archdiocese/Diocese	Year Created
Archdiocese of Miami	1968
Diocese of Orlando	1968
Diocese of Palm Beach	1984
Diocese of Pensacola-Tennessee	1975
Diocese of St. Augustine	1870
Diocese of Saint Petersburg	1968
Diocese of Venice	1984

FLORIDA, CATHOLIC CHURCH IN

Admitted (1845) to the Union as the 27th state, Florida is a peninsula between the Atlantic Ocean on the east and the Gulf of Mexico on the west. It is bounded on the north by Georgia and Alabama. The capital is Tallahassee. Miami is the largest city. In addition to the Metropolitan See of Miami there are six dioceses in the state (Orlando, Palm Beach, Pensacola-Tallahassee, St. Augustine, St. Petersburg, and Venice) which together form the ecclesiastical Province of Miami.

The tribes who inhabited Florida before the coming of Europeans hunted animals and gathered roots and shellfish. They lived along the extensive coastline and waterways, using the dugout canoe, and moved continually according to food supply. These natives were known as the Apalachees (in the Panhandle), Timucuas (north central), Tequestas, and Calusas (both in south Florida). As Europeans arrived, the Seminoles rebelled and were defeated. Most were forcibly removed to Oklahoma, but small bands fled to the Everglades and the Lake Okeechobee area to live on reservations.

The first recorded European in Florida was the Spaniard Juan Ponce de León. In 1513 he landed on Florida's northern Atlantic coast during the Easter season and named the newly discovered land *Pascua Florida*. Subsequently, Flordia's history falls into three distinct time periods. The Colonial period, beginning in 1565, was dominated by the Spanish, and lasted about 200 years. During this period, for a brief time between 1763 and 1821, Spain ceded the territory to Britain. Later, Florida came under American control.

The Colonial Period. In 1549 the Dominican Luis Cancer made the first real attempt to evangelize Florida. He encountered the native Tocabaga near Tampa Bay, a people who disliked the Spanish because of previous unsavory encounters with them. The Tocabaga bludgeoned Cancer to death, and he became the first in a series of martyr missionaries in colonial North America.

On Sept. 8, 1565, Pedro Menéndez de Avilés founded St. Augustine, the first permanent European set-

Sacred Heart Catholic Church, Tampa, Florida. (©Tony Aruza/CORBIS)

tlement in what would become the United States. Menéndez's 1,000 colonists included four diocesan priests, who founded America's first parish (*San Agustín*) and its first mission to the Native Americans (*Nombre de Dios*). In 1566 Menéndez enlisted Jesuits to evangelize Florida's natives—three came. Pedro Martínez, S.J., was martyred by aborigines near the mouth of the St. John's River. Francisco Villareal, S.J., established a mission on the shores of Biscayne Bay (Miami), while Juan Rogel, S.J., founded San Antonio de Padua Parish (near Ft. Myers Beach) among the Calusa in March 1567. However, various unfavorable conditions forced the Jesuits to leave Florida by mid-1569.

The Franciscans arrived in 1573 to take up the missionary enterprise. By 1595 they claimed 1,500 converts among the Timucuans of Northeast Florida and the Guale of coastal Georgia and South Carolina. Headquartered at their St. Augustine convent which was constructed in 1605, the Franciscans created a separate province, *Santa Elena*, for the Florida missions in 1612. That same year, Francisco de Pareda, O.F.M., published a catechism and confessional guide in Spanish and Timucuan. The friars' linguistic studies led them to produce catechetical and devotional works, as well as dictionaries and grammars in native languages. By 1675 the Franciscan missions reached their apex with about 75 friars serving in 38 missions (*doctrinas*), which extended as far north as the South Carolina coast, as far south as modern-day Ocala, and as far west as present-day Mariana, and included about 30,000 baptized natives from four major tribal groups.

In Florida, Native Americans lived a sedentary village-based lifestyle when the Spanish arrived. Following the previously established model of *reducción* first implemented in Mexico, the friars created separate autonomous native Christian enclaves, largely segregated from what was considered the corrupting contact with Spaniards. Besides evangelization and pastoral care, the friars were engaged in teaching European arts and crafts, as well as improving agricultural techniques. The Apalachee were so successful as agriculturalists that they not only fed Spanish Florida, but also exported foodstuffs to Cuba.

After 1675, the Florida missions declined. The native population decreased due to 17 major epidemics between 1513 and 1675. Moreover, fewer friars were sent to Florida and those who did come were less capable than the first. The Florida missions came to an end as a result of Queen Anne's War (1702–1708). Governor James Moore of Carolina, with a force of approximately 500 English colonists and 1,000 Creeks, systematically destroyed them all. Consequently, about 10,000 to 12,000 Christian natives were carried off to South Carolina as slaves. Others escaped to neighboring tribes, while nearly 3,000 were killed and about 300 found refuge in St. Augustine.

While the Franciscans ministered to the natives, diocesan priests maintained pastoral care of the colonists and soldiers at St. Augustine (1565) and at Pensacola (1698). Florida was under the ecclesiastical authority of Santiago de Cuba until 1763, when Havana took over jurisdiction. The first episcopal visitation to Florida was in 1606, when Juan de Altamirano confirmed 981 colonists and mission natives. Florida's second episcopal visitation was made by Gabriel Calderón during ten months in 1674–75, when he ordained seven *creoles* to the priesthood in St. Augustine. About one-third of the Franciscans of *Santa Elena* Province in the 17th century were *creoles*, that is Florida-born Spanish colonials. Visiting the *doctrinas* north and west of St. Augustine, Calderón confirmed 13,152 natives, commenting favorably on their piety, devotion, and practice. Florida's third episcopal visitor was Bishop Dionisio Resino, who arrived at St. Augustine in 1709, but remained only three months. When Francisco de San Buenaventura y Tejada came to St. Augustine to take up episcopal residence in 1735, he quickly set about to ameliorate the spiritual decadence he found. In 1736 he confirmed 630 colonists, along with 143 slaves and free African Americans. Buenaventura left in 1745 to become the bishop of Yucatán. Florida's next resident bishop did not arrive until 1754, Pedro Ponce y Carrasco, whose poor health limited his stay to ten months. The last colonial resident bishop was Pedro Agustín Morell, the bishop of Santiago de Cuba, who after having been made prisoner by the British who invaded Cuba, was eventually shipped to St. Augustine in December 1762. That spring he confirmed 639 persons before returning to Cuba.

In 1687, 11 fugitive slaves escaped from South Carolina to St. Augustine. Spanish authorities granted them their freedom, but required them to become Catholic and work on fortifications, especially St. Augustine's *Castillo*. By 1738, 38 households of former slaves were settled by authorities two miles north of St. Augustine at Santa Teresa de la Gracia Real de Mosé, the first legally free African-American community in what became the United States. Eligible males served in a free African-American militia stationed at nearby Fort Mosé, St. Augustine's first line of defense against an English land attack.

British Control. When Spain ceded Florida to Britain in 1763, Fort Mosé and its adjacent settlement was abandoned. Its 87 residents, along with about 300 remaining Catholic natives, as well as most Spanish colonists from St. Augustine and Pensacola, were transported to Havana, along with church records and furnishings. The British disposed of church property in St. Augustine as they saw fit. The Franciscan convent was converted into barracks (today the site of the Florida National Guard Headquarters); the provisional parish church of *La Soledad* was renamed St. Peter's Anglican Church.

As a British possession from 1763 to 1783, Florida lacked both priests and Catholics. In 1768 Andrew Turnbull founded New Smyrna as an indigo and cotton plantation. Collecting 1,403 Italians, Greeks, and mostly Minorcans as indentured servants, Turnbull, whose wife was Catholic, enlisted a Minorcan priest, Pedro Camps, to care for the spiritual needs of the colony. The enterprise soured; with inadequate food, clothing, and shelter, the colonists died at alarming rates. Frustrated with Turnbull's malfeasance, the plantation's residents set off on foot for St. Augustine to seek redress. The British governor released them from their indentures and allowed them to settle in St. Augustine. By November 1777, the British permitted the opening of San Pedro Catholic Church for the spiritual care of the refugees. Camps remained their pastor until his death in 1790. The descendants of this group, many of whom still reside in St. Augustine, provide a direct link between contemporary Florida Catholicism and its colonial past.

At the end of the American Revolution, both East and West Florida were ceded back to Spain, beginning the second Spanish colonial period from 1783 to 1821, during which time Pensacola usually had only one priest, whereas St. Augustine had as many as five Irish priests in the 1790s. As early as 1597, Richard Arthur served as pastor in St. Augustine, the first of a long line of Irish-born priests in Florida. The Irish had the advantage of being bilingual, a fact that was especially useful when Irish soldiers of the Hibernian Regiment were stationed at St. Augustine during the 1780s.

There had not been a permanent parish church in St. Augustine since 1702. In 1784 two priests from the Irish College at Salamanca, Thomas Hassett and Michael O'Reilly, arrived. Soon thereafter, Hassett lobbied royal authorities for a new parish church. The edifice was formally opened on Dec. 8, 1795, not by Hassett, who had been transferred to New Orleans, but by O'Reilly. In another major contribution, Hasset founded a free Catholic school for the Minorcans in 1787, probably the first such school in what is now the United States.

From 1783, Florida was under the supervision of Louis William Du Bourg, bishop of Louisiana and the Floridas. In 1787 East Florida had 900 whites and 490 African-American slaves; Pensacola, the capitol of West Florida, had only 265 inhabitants, while St. Augustine had 469. Catholics represented less than 50 percent of the total population of the two Floridas. Conversions to Catholicism were few, despite legal incentives. The practice of the faith was even less encouraging. In 1790, only seven people made their Easter duty in Pensacola, which had an overall population of 572. The following year, even after strenuous efforts by a visiting bishop, only 70 completed their Easter duty. The Spanish colonial enterprise in Florida was declining politically and spiritually.

Early American Period. Florida became a U.S. territory in 1821 and a state in 1845. With the creation of the Diocese of Charleston in 1820, Florida was included in the jurisdiction of the bishop of Charleston, John England, until 1825, when the apostolic vicariate of Alabama and the Floridas was created under Michael Portier. By 1827, Portier had "sublet" his Florida jurisdiction to Bishop England until 1829, when the Diocese of Mobile was created, with Portier as its head. As a result, neither Portier nor England had the means to oversee Florida effectively. During this period, Pensacola's St. Michael's

Parish erected its first permanent church building in 1833. When the Diocese of Savannah was created in 1850, its first bishop, Francis X. Gartland, oversaw Catholicism in Florida. In February 1852 Gartland traveled by ship from Savannah to dedicate St. Mary, Star of the Sea Church in Key West.

In 1857, territory east of the Apalachicola River became the apostolic vicariate of Florida (land west of the river remained with the Diocese of Mobile until 1968). The vicar apostolic, Augustin VEROT, a 53-year-old French Sulpician, who had taught at St. Mary's College, Baltimore, then later was pastor of St. Paul's Parish, Ellicott Mills, arrived in St. Augustine in June 1858. The vicariate contained four parishes, eight missions, several stations, but only three priests. Pastorates at Tallahassee and Key West were vacant. The biggest parish, St. Augustine, had 952 white and 376 African-American Catholics, while St. Mary's in Key West had about 350 parishioners. Florida's Panhandle, under the Diocese of Mobile, had three parishes, two missions, and two priests. The state had neither parochial schools nor any other Catholic institutions. Despite these privations, which only increased with wartime conditions, Verot energetically undertook the challenges of his widespread mission territory.

In May 1859 he traveled to Europe in search of personnel. With the seven priests he recruited from France, he was able to assign pastors in Tallahassee and Key West, and by 1860 founded new parishes in Tampa, Fernandina, and Mandarin. He journeyed to New England and French Canada in 1859. In Hartford, CT, he enlisted five Sisters of Mercy, and in Montreal, three Christian Brothers, who proceeded in the fall of 1860 to open schools for girls and boys in St. Augustine, which served Catholics, Protestants, and free African Americans. When the war between the states broke out, Verot supported the Southern cause and in July 1861 was appointed the bishop of Savannah, while retaining charge of Florida.

The war wrecked havoc on Verot's development plans. Both Catholic schools in St. Augustine closed. By the war's end, Verot characterized the pastoral situation in Georgia and Florida as ''a heap of smoking ruins.'' Four churches were ruined and the people were demoralized and impoverished. Not only did the war liquidate his assets, but debts remaining from his prewar expansion left him a pauper.

Undaunted, Verot initiated a physical and spiritual reconstruction program. He begged money from the Society of the Propagation of the Faith in France and from parishes in the Northeast, some proceeds from which he invested in a series of successful parish missions conducted by the Redemptorists during 1868 and 1869. He also commenced a limited experiment to educate newly freed slaves by recruiting from France the Sisters of St. Joseph, who opened in 1867 their first Catholic school for African Americans in St. Augustine. By 1876 they had over 360 students in seven such schools. In 1868 he engaged the Sisters of the Holy Names, of Montreal, to found in Key West a similar school. At first the Sisters opened an academy for whites, but by 1876 they had also opened St. Francis Xavier School for African Americans.

A Frontier Diocese. After relinquishing Savannah, Verot became the first bishop of St. Augustine in 1870, governing territory created from his former apostolic vicariate. Following his death in 1876, Irishman John Moore was named bishop in 1877. William Kenny, the first American bishop (1902–13), was, in turn, succeeded by Irish-born Michael Curley, who served from 1914 to 1921, when he was translated to Baltimore.

In 1880 Florida had almost 269,500 residents; 50 years later it had just under 968,500. During this period, Florida Catholics numbered about 3 percent of the state's population. New urban centers developed, the result of the introduction of the railroad along both of Florida's coasts by the 1890s, an improvement which brought commerce and tourism. Whereas, in 1880 only 10 percent of the population lived in cities, about 36 percent lived there by 1920. In 1900 Jacksonville was Florida's largest city with 28,249 persons, followed by Pensacola (17,747), Key West (17,144), and Tampa (15,839).

Moore enthusiastically responded to Florida's first growth spurt. When he took over in 1877, he was responsible for eight parishes, 12 missions, and eight diocesan and two religious priests; by his death in 1901, the diocese contained 15 parishes, 25 missions, 14 diocesan priests, and 17 religious priests. He introduced several important initiatives: the on-going recruitment of Irish-born priests; the ordination of the first native diocesan priest (Edward A. PACE in 1885); the requirement of an annual report from each parish; the introduction of the Benedictines of St. Vincent Abbey to pastorally oversee three West Coast counties (where some German-speaking people resided) and to start a college in 1887 (St. Leo's College, Florida's first Catholic college); and the recruitment of the New Orleans Jesuits in 1888, to whom he gave exclusive pastoral care of the southern half of his diocese in 1889. Headquartered in Tampa, the Jesuits also opened a high school for boys there in 1899. By 1920, 21 Jesuits served six parishes, 12 missions, and 46 stations in South Florida.

Moore also changed the focus of the diocesan Sisters of St. Joseph from teaching African Americans to running academies for whites, and from being a predominantly French community to being a predominantly Irish one. Also under his direction, in 1882, the Sisters of the Holy Names began work in Tampa, where they founded an academy.

Immigration was different in Florida compared to many other states. European immigrants were not numerous. Beginning in 1868, Cubans emigrated to Key West, as a result of a war of independence on their island. In response, the Holy Name Sisters, in 1873, opened a school for Cuban girls. By 1885, Key West had the largest concentration of Catholics in the state: 7,000 Cubans, 648 whites, and 70 African Americans. In 1886 Cubans, as well as Spaniards and Italians, began settling in Tampa, attracted to work in the cigar industry recently translated from Key West. By 1890 about 3,000 people from these three ethnic groups resided in Tampa; by 1920 there were 9,000. Tampa's Jesuits responded to this multilingual and multiethic challenge by founding new parishes. Meanwhile, both the Sisters of St. Joseph and the Sisters of the Holy Names inaugurated academies in the 1890s to serve these immigrants.

As was typical throughout the South, many Florida Catholics lacked access to a church or a priest on a regular basis, hence the domestic church was essential in keeping Catholicism alive. Wealthy benefactors, such as Edward Bradley, Kate Jackson, Mother Katherine Drexel, Mrs. Edward Morrell (Louise Drexel), and James McNichols played an indispensable role in the building of churches and schools, as did the benefactors of the Catholic Church Extension Society.

World War I to World War II. Bishop Michael Curley was so successful at recruiting priests from his native Ireland that by 1920 about 80 percent of Florida's 38 diocesan priests were Irish-born and over 50 percent of them were under 35 years of age. By 1921 Curley had enough secular clergy to begin to entrust the pastoral care of South Florida to diocesan priests, and not just to the Jesuits.

In 1920 Florida's largest parishes generally did not exceed 650 households, the average parish having about 500. By 1940, although the largest parishes contained around 2,000 households, the average parish still held only about 350. In 1920 the diocese had 30 parishes, with a Catholic population of approximately 51,000; in 1940, 62 parishes served an estimated 66,000 Catholics, a modest 29 percent increase. In the same period, the state population jumped from 968,470 to 1,897,414, a substantial 96 percent increase. Catholics represented about 5 percent of the state's population in 1920, but only about 3.5 percent in 1940. In 1920 only 36.5 percent of Floridians lived in urban areas, while 55.1 percent lived there in 1940.

Curley's successor was Irish-born Patrick Barry (1922–40). By 1937 he had 127 priests, 71 of whom were diocesan, and 60 percent of whom were Irish-born because Barry continued recruiting priests from Ireland. He introduced into the diocese the Adrian Dominican Sisters and the Allegany Franciscan Sisters, who soon made contributions in Catholic education, hospital administration, and ministry to African Americans. In 1940 the Adrian Dominicans founded Florida's second Catholic college, Barry College for women at Miami Shores.

Individuals, mostly from the Northeast, and the Extension Society, continued as important benefactors during this period. By far the biggest challenge for Barry, the pastors and parishioners was managing the effects of the Depression. A parish building boom of the 1920s created a diocesan debt of $1.6 million by 1928. In response to the problems exacerbated by the Depression, Barry collectivized and centralized parish finances so that the diocese might refinance parish debts. Yet despite his diocesan consolidation, pastors still (up to 1940) maintained a significant amount of independence and discretionary power.

Postwar Consolidation. During Joseph Hurley's episcopacy (1940–67), Florida Catholicism grew in population and developed in complexity. In 1940 Florida was the 27th most populated state with 1.9 million residents, by 1960 it was the tenth most populated with 4.9 million people. At that time Florida Catholics represented 11.9 percent of the state's population. Catholics increased in number from approximately 66,000 in 1940 to 753,000 in 1968, an increase of 1,041 percent. Already by the late 1940s the suburban parish had become the model for new parishes, and by 1968 the average parish increased to about 1,000 households, with the largest at 3,500 households.

Hurley consolidated power by means of heavy taxation of parishes in order to fund his extensive real estate purchases for parochial and institutional expansion and to centralize diocesan services. He assumed much of the former discretionary power of pastors. Although he continued to recruit priests from Ireland, he also stressed native vocations. Nevertheless, Irish priests reached their apex in numbers and influence under Hurley's leadership. The number of diocesan priests doubled, as did the number of parishes. By the late 1950s, Hurley had founded a diocesan hospital, organized a system of diocesan high schools, and established missions for Latino farm workers.

In 1958 the southern one-third of Hurley's diocese was erected as the Diocese of Miami, with Pittsburgh native Coleman Carroll as its first bishop (1958–77). Like Hurley, Carroll was a consolidator and builder. Within his first ten years, he presided over the establishment of 45 parishes, 17 parish schools, 58 new churches, 11 new high schools, and introduced 35 religious communities. He also invited the Vincentian Fathers to staff two seminaries he founded as a stimulus to native vocations. St. Vincent de Paul Seminary produced its first ordination class in 1968. Carroll was also a prominent community leader, responding to Cuban exiles with several creative programs and organizing a Human Relations Board for Miami to address racial injustice.

Changing Times. Both Hurley and Carroll attended the Second Vatican Council, and in the years after Vatican II, both favored gradualism and caution in the implementation of the letter and spirit of the Council. The postconciliar period coincided with major shifts in American culture, the papacy of John Paul II, and the continued growth of Catholicism in Florida.

In 1968 Miami became an archdiocese, with St. Petersburg and Orlando created as new dioceses. The Panhandle, long under the jurisdiction of Mobile, AL, became part of the Diocese of St. Augustine. A fifth Florida diocese was created in 1975, Pensacola-Tallahassee, and a sixth and seventh in 1984, Palm Beach and Venice. In 1969 the dioceses joined together to form the Florida Catholic Conference, an agency designed to represent the Church's position on policy and social issues and to coordinate its action statewide. It works with government agencies, as well as other religious groups, in addressing such matters as immigration, education and right-to-life issues.

This multiplication of dioceses in Florida reflected the rapid population and institutional growth. By 1990 Florida was the fourth largest state in population, with 13.2 million residents, of whom 1.7 million or 13 percent were Catholic. The 2000 census counted 15.9 million Floridians, of whom approximately 2.1 million or 14 percent are Catholic. Miami has the highest percentage of Catholics with 21 percent, while Pensacola-Tallahassee has the lowest with 5 percent.

At the dawn of the 21st century Florida Catholicism faces a number of challenges, some of which include: secularism, the size of parishes (the average parish is about 2,000 households); fewer priests per Catholic; multiculturalism (the 2000 census reports that Florida is 16.8 percent Latino, 14.6 percent African American, 1.7 percent Asian, and 3 percent other ethnic groups); increased bureaucratization on the diocesan and parish levels; the continued implementation of Vatican Council II, especially evangelization, ecumenism, interfaith dialogue, and lay spirituality and initiatives. Florida Catholicism's long tradition of adaptability, flexibility, and creativity, derived from its frontier missionary past, may be expected to serve it well in the future.

Bibliography: H. P. CLAVREUL, *Notes on the Catholic Church in Florida, 1565–1876* (Saint Leo, Abbey, FL, n.d.). M. J. GEIGER, *The Franciscan Conquest of Florida, 1573–1618* (Washington 1937). L. G. DE ORÉ, *The Martyrs of Florida, 1513–1616*, ed. and tr. M. J. GEIGER, *Franciscan Studies* 18 (St. Bonaventure, NY 1936). V. F. O'DANIEL, *Dominicans in Early Florida* (New York 1930). M. V. GANNON, *The Cross in the Sand: The Early Catholic Church in Florida, 1513–1870* (Gainesville 1965); *Rebel Bishop: The Life and Era of Augustin Verot* (Milwaukee 1964). M. J. MCNALLY, *Catholic Parish Life on Florida's West Coast, 1860–1968* (St. Petersburg 1996); *Catholicism in South Florida, 1868–1968* (Gainesville 1984). G. R. MORMINO, *The Immigrant World of Ybor City: Italians and Their Latin Neighbors in Tampa, 1885–1985* (Urbana, IL 1987).

[M. J. MCNALLY]

FLORILEGIA

The word florilegium comes from the Latin words *flores* (flowers) and *legere* (to gather, to collect). It corresponds exactly to the word anthology, which derives from the Greek. It denotes a collection of flowers, the word flowers being used metaphorically, not to mean literary artifices with which an author embellishes his work, but rather to designate excerpts from earlier writings. This article confines itself to a study of Christian florilegia.

Terminology. A separate study, or monograph, on florilegia has not yet been undertaken. As a first step toward this end, a complete inventory of all florilegia needs to be made. Following are many of the terms by which florilegia are designated in the catalogues of manuscripts and printed works. This list, in which Greek and Latin words are mixed together, includes terms common to a number of collections, as well as terms that are applied to only one collection: *Alphabetum, Analecta, Anthologia, Apomnêmoneumata, Apophthegmata, Aurifodina, Breviloquium, Candela, Collationes, Collectanea, Communiloquium, Deflorationes, Delucidarium, Dieta salutis, Eclogae, Epitome, Evergétinon, Excarpsus, Excerpta, Exerceptiones, Fasciculus, Floretum, Florilegium, Flosculi, Glaphyra, Gnomai, Gnomica, Gnomologion, Hiera, Liber pancrisis, Loci communes, Manipulus, Margarita, Melissa, Mensa spiritualis, Milleloquium, Miscellanea, Oculus moralis, Panarion, Pandectes, Parallela (sacra), Paterika, Pharetra, Philocalie, Polyanthea, Pré spirituel, Promptuarium, Rapiarium, Reductorium, Resina scriptuarum, Rosarium, Rosetum, Scarapsus, Scintillae, Sophologium, Speculum, Stillae verborum, Stromates, Sylloge, Sylva locorum communium, Themata, Thesaurus, Via salutis, Viridarium.*

Literary Genre. Florilegia belong to gnomic or sententious literature, but within this type of literature they differ from collections of original thoughts or anonymous proverbs in that they consist of borrowed literature. In other words, they are compilations of excerpts (Latin, *excerpta*) taken from earlier authors. The role of the compiler is expressed by the Latin verbs *carpere, decerpere, deflorare,* and *colligere.* The origin of this literary genre is intertwined with the beginnings of world literature. In Christian literature, the genre appears in the first Christian generations with the collections of the *logia* of the Lord or the Apostles and with the lists of *auctoritates* and *testimonia,* which were the earliest efforts toward a catechism, liturgical formularies, or Christian legislation. Later, there developed the anthologies of *sententiae* (*see* SENTENCES AND SUMMAE), of which ISIDORE OF SEVILLE was the first great compiler and which found their masters in SCHOLASTICISM. The history of Christian florilegia has been traced in ''Florileges,'' *Dictionnaire de spiritualitéascétique et mystique. Doctrine et histoire,* ed. M. Viller et al. (Paris 1932–) 5:435–512. The present study is confined to their classification and evaluation.

Classification. Florilegia can be classified according to the sources they use or according to their objectives. If classified according to their sources, florilegia are either profane, Christian, or a mixture of both. Although the profane florilegia are not the concern of this article, the mixed florilegia, because they borrow from both profane and sacred writers, are usually of Christian inspiration and are of interest in a study of Christian florilegia. In the classification of Christian florilegia according to sources, one can distinguish Biblical, patristic, Biblical-patristic, and mixed (sacred-profane) anthologies. At times a florilegium was compiled from the works of a single author, and in such case serves as an indication of his influence.

If classified according to the objectives that motivated the compiler, Christian florilegia cover the entire field of ecclesiastical disciplines. Thus, one finds florilegia that comment on Sacred Scripture, the valuable ''exegetical chains.'' Still others try to prove or defend a specific point of doctrine—these are the dogmatic or apologetic florilegia. Liturgical florilegia furnish formulas of prayers for those participating in religious ceremonies. Other florilegia provide preachers with citations and examples, and are called homiletic sententiaries. Among these one must distinguish between collections of plans or excerpts of sermons laid out according to the liturgical year and those that are the result of the study of the art of preaching; there are also alphabetical lists of quotations on vices and virtues, on the spiritual life, and on prayer. Canonical florilegia codify the jurisprudence of the Church, and spiritual anthologies gather together traditional teachings on various aspects of the Christian life, such as spiritual combat and the way of perfection. In the field of ethics, P. Delhaye distinguishes between educational anthologies (among which one should set apart *Mirrors of Princes*) and anthologies aimed at moral edification. M. Richard divides Greek florilegia into three groups: the Damascan, the sacred-profane, and the monastic florilegia.

Value. Florilegia may transmit excerpts of works that no longer exist; in some rare instances, it may even happen that these excerpts are of sufficient quantity and quality to allow a reconstruction of the general physiognomy of the original work. More often, however, the original works from which the compilers borrowed have survived; yet it is useful, even indispensable, to refer to the work as it was transmitted and interpreted through the florilegia when establishing the critical text of the work in question. Florilegia preserve interesting versions of Biblical and patristic texts, valuable either for the textual history of the Scriptures and the Fathers or for the history of their influence. As collections of citations of ancient authors, florilegia give a precise idea of the influence of these authors in the history of thought and literature. Further, by revealing what works have been commonly read in the past, they furnish information on the culture of a given period and on the condition of ancient and medieval libraries. However, it must be noted that the compilers did not always refer directly to the sources that they quoted; often they cited only already existing florilegia. Many anthologies are preceded by letters of advice or by prologues in which the compilers make explicit the reason for their collection. In the absence of such prefaces, however, their intentions can easily be determined by examining the plan and the contents of the collection, lists of *capitula* being significant in this regard. Knowledge of the compiler's objectives makes it possible to pass judgment on the methods he used to attain his end. By unveiling the didactic and pedagogic processes of reasoning and memorization implicit in the florilegia, one can penetrate the psychology of the compilers, of the scribes who copied and multiplied their work, and of their readers. A world of preoccupations, problems, proposed solutions, and realizations becomes intelligible, thanks to the florilegia, which are witnesses of a past no longer accessible except by the mirror of these writings.

Limitations. Florilegia, like all digests and excerpts, have their limitations. Selection, which is the basis of the work, implies discrimination. The compilers retain only what is considered useful for their ends, thus often ignoring nuances, explanations, and transitions. They preserve only the lapidary phrase, the punch line, the paradoxical sentences easy to memorize. Briefly, florilegia have a tendency to schematize, to devitalize the original idea, sometimes so much so that a sentence, taken out of its original context and used in the florilegia, no longer conveys its original meaning. Compilers were not always able or willing to transcribe faithfully, either because they did not understand certain passages of their model or because the model itself was defective for various reasons. It is quite possible that they copied from texts that had become illegible or that they tried to give passages a meaning alien to that of the author. Precaution is therefore necessary in using these collections. Before basing an argument on any one of the excerpts it is essential to refer first, whenever possible, to the text of the original work.

See Also: MEDIEVAL LATIN LITERATURE.

Bibliography: H. M. ROCHAIS, et al., *Dictionnaire de spiritualité ascétique et mystique. Doctrine et histoire,* ed. M. VILLER et al. (Paris 1932–) 5:435–512. H. M. ROCHAIS, ''Contribution à l'histoire des florilèges ascétiques de haut moyen âge latin: Le *Liber scintillarum,*'' *Revue Bénédictine* 63 (1953) 246–291.

[H. M. ROCHAIS]

FLORINUS, ST.

Fl. Rhaetia, Switzerland, seventh century. He was educated by Alexander, a priest of St. Peter's Church, who resigned his office in his favor after the young man's ordination. The early accounts of his life (*Bibliotheca hagiographica latina antiquae ct mediae aetatis,* 2 v. 3063–3065), written for the edification of the reader, are in large part unreliable. They recount a number of miracles supposed to have been worked by the saint. He was reported to have been buried in his parish church, but his relics were later transferred to the collegiate church of St. Florinus in Koblenz, Germany, and to the Abbey of Schönau in the Archdiocese of Trier. He is venerated as the patron of the Diocese of Chur.

Feast: Nov. 17.

Bibliography: *Analecta Bollandiana* 17 (1898) 199–204. O. SCHEIWILLER, ''Der hl. Florin von Remüs,'' *Zeitschrift für schweizerische Geschichte* 32 (1938) 241–256; 33 (1939) 71–90, 155–167.

[B. CAVANAUGH]

FLOROVSKY, GEORGE

Scholar and prominent Russian Orthodox theologian in the West; b. Odessa (Ukraine), Aug. 28, 1893, of a priest's family; d. 1974. Georges Vasilievich Florovsky (Georgij Vasilievich Florovskij) received a solid philosophical and scientific training at that city's university, under such renowned professors as N. N. Lange, B. Babkin, and I. P. Pavlov. His first published works were on laboratory experiments and classical philology. In 1920, fleeing Bolshevik occupation of his country, he settled in Sofia (Bulgaria), where he was drawn into the ''Eurasian'' group of Prince N. S. Trubeckoy, opposed to the older Russian currents of the Westernizers and the Slavophiles, through its insistence on the merits of Asian and Tartar values in Russian culture and world mission. Florovsky's personal position, however, evolved towards the acceptance of Byzantine-Orthodox culture as the true vocation of Russia.

Between 1922 and 1926 he resided in Prague as a lecturer in the philosophy of law at the Russian University Center, established by Russian emigrés. When the Russian Theological Institute of St. Sergius opened in Paris, Florovsky was among the first to join the faculty as professor of patristics (1926). In 1932 he was ordained a priest for the Russian Exarchate of Western Europe, under the jurisdiction of the Patriarch of Constantinople.

In Paris, Florovsky developed his thesis on the irreplaceable value of the intellectual experience of the Fathers of the Church for Christian dogma and theology. His two books on the Eastern and Byzantine Fathers produced during this period offer a powerful vision of Christian thought, forever grounded in that golden age of theology. The latter's impact—or the lack of it—on Russian theology was the object of his next major work, *The Ways of Russian Theology* (1937), which stirred a memorable conflict within the Russian emigré intelligenzia. His basic thesis was offered for discussion at the First International Congress of Orthodox Theologians in Athens (1936). At this time he became more and more engaged in the Ecumenical Movement in its different stages, often fighting almost singlehanded in order to keep it open to Orthodox insights. His later contribution to the World Assembly in Evanston, Ill. (1954), eased the way for the Russian Orthodox Church and other Eastern Churches into the World Council of Churches (New Delhi 1961).

In 1948 Florovsky moved to New York City in order to teach at St. Vladimir's Orthodox Theological Seminary, where as dean (1951–55) he insisted on high academic standards and was instrumental in starting the prestigious *St. Vladimir's Seminary Quarterly* (1950). During this same period, he lectured at Columbia University (1950–55), the Holy Cross Greek Orthodox Theological School in Brookline, Mass. (1955), Harvard Divinity School (1956), and Princeton (1961). On the occasion of his 80th birthday, shortly before his death, the Pontifical Institute for Oriental Studies in Rome published a Festschrift (1973) in his honor.

Influence. Florovsky left a mark in several fields of Christian doctrine and life, well beyond the strictly Russian boundaries of his Orthodox allegiance. His impact is particularly felt in his emphasis on the Hellenic quality of Orthodoxy, his anti-Nestorian Orthodox Christology, and his desire for true collegiality.

The age of the Fathers of the Church is for Florovsky, not just a stage in the development of theology, but a real turning point of Christian thought towards Orthodoxy, obtained through the happy marriage of the original Christian message and Greek thought, and duly adapted (baptized) to the needs of the former. To neglect the heritage of the Fathers would mean to go back to a stage of theological uncertainty and a breeding ground of christological heresies.

His view of orthodox Christology is that obtained and fully understood only through the suffered experience of the Eastern Church, as witnessed by the early ecumenical councils, and particularly Chalcedon. In order to safeguard true doctrine against the Nestorian temptation of Western Christianity, Florovsky propounds "asymmetric Christology" as a guarantee of hypostatic union in Christ.

The Russian word *SOBORNOST*, which translates as collegiality, is key to Florovsky's ecclesiology. *Sobornost* sets Christ at the core of the church, which is His extension as Christified humanity—the Augustinian *Christus totus, caput et membra*—made one in Christ, through the action of the Spirit and the ministry of the successors of the Apostles. Intensive catholicity, made present in the local church, would express adequately the fullness of ecclesiality, before recourse to any wider form of the church.

See Also: RUSSIAN THEOLOGY.

Bibliography: Y. N. LELOUVIER, *Perspectives russes sur l'Eglise. Un théologian contemporain: Georges Florovsky* (Paris 1968). B. MONDIN, *Georges Florovsky e la sintesi neopatristica*, I. *Grandi teologi del secolo ventesimo*, II. *Teologi protestanti e ortodissi* (Torino, Borla 1969) 291–314. D. NEIMAN and M. SHATKIN, eds., *The Heritage of the Early Church. Essays in Honor of Rev. G. V. Florovsky. Orientalia Christiana periodica* 195 (Rome 1973). A. BLANE, ed., *Russia and Orthodoxy. Essays in Honour of Georges Florovsky*, 2 v. (The Hague-Paris 1974–76). G. H. WILLIAMS, "Georges Vasilievich Florovsky: His American Career (1948–1965)" *The Greek-Orthodox Theological Review* 9 (1965). A complete list of G. Florovsky's writings in D. NIEMAN and M. SHATKIN, 437–451 (to 1969). An American edition of his works in: G. V. FLOROVSKIJ, *Collected Work*, 5 v. (Belmont, Mass. 1972–79).

[G. ELDAROV]

FLORUS OF LYONS

Carolingian author; b. probably Spain, late 8th century; d. Lyons, France, 860. In Lyons *c.* 800, he was the most important cultural figure in the school founded there by LEIDRADUS. Nearly all the official acts of the See of Lyons under Bishops Leidradus (798–814), AGOBARD (814–840), Amulo (840–852), and REMIGIUS (852–875) were performed under his influence or direction, even though they do not bear his signature. His role in the dispute between AMALARIUS of Metz and GOTTSCHALK OF ORBAIS was important, but his writings were more often concerned with the liturgy, exegesis, and Canon Law. The *Liber de imaginibus* of Pseudo–Agobard attributed to him is by CLAUDIUS OF TURIN, also from the school of Lyons. Most of Florus's works are of a collective nature, but their importance lies in what he selected. His works include: a compilation from 12 FATHERS OF THE CHURCH on the Epistles of St. Paul (in MS), an *Expositio missae* (ed. P. Duc, Belley 1937), an edition of the Martyrology, sentences of St. AUGUSTINE on predestination and grace, works against Amalarius, who had usurped the See of Lyons (*Patrologia Latina* 119:72–96), a treatise against JOHN SCOTUS ERIUGENA (*Patrologia Latina* 119:102–250), three treatises against Gottschalk, and a collection of canons of Troyes (in MS), from which have been published a *De electione episcoporum* and a *De lege et canone.*

Bibliography: Works. *Patrologia Latina,* ed. J. P. MIGNE (Paris 1878–90) 119:9–422; 121:1083–1134. *Monumenta Germaniae Historica: Poetae* (Berlin 1826–) 2:509–566. **Literature.** M. MANITIUS *Geschichte der lateinischen Literatur des Mittelalters* (Munich 1911–31) 1:560–567. F. STEGMÜLLER *Repertorium biblicum medii aevi* (Madrid 1949–61) 2:2274–91. A. WILMART, "Sommaire de l'exposition de Florus sur les épîtres," *Revue Bénedictine* 38 (1926) 205–216; "La Collection de Bède le Vénérable sur l'apôre," *ibid.* 16–52; "Une Lettre sans adresse écrite vers le milieu du IXe siècle," *ibid.* 42 (1930) 149–162. C. CHARLIER, "Les Manuscrits personnels de Florus de Lyon et son activité littéraire," *Mélanges E. Podechard* (Lyon 1945) 71–84; "La Compilation augustinienne de Florus sur l'apôtre: Sources et authenticité," *Revue Bénedictine* 57 (1947) 132–186. I. FRANSEN, "Les Commentaires de Bède et de Florus sur l'apôtre et saint Césaire d'Arles," *ibid.* 65 (1955) 262–266. J. M. HANSSENS, *Amalarii episcopi opera liturgica omnia,* 3 v. *Studi e Testi* 138–140; 1948–50), "Introductio," 1:39–224, *passim.* P. BELLET, "El Liber de imaginibus sanctorum bajo el nombre de Agobardo de Lyon obra de Claudio de Turín," *Analecta Sacra Tarraconensia* 26 (1953) 151–194. H. QUENTIN, *Les Martyrologes historiques du moyen âge* (Paris 1908). J. SZÖVÉRFFY, *Die Annalen der lateinischen Hymnendichtung. Ein Handbuch* (Berlin 1964–65) 1:232–235.

[P. BELLET]

FLOWER, RICHARD, BL.

Lay martyr; *vere* Floyd or Lloyd; alias Graye, Fludd; b. *c.* 1567 in Anglesey (Diocese of Bangor), North Wales; d. Aug. 30, 1588, hanged at Tyburn (London). Flower, the younger brother of Fr. Owen Lloyd, was arrested in London (1588) and condemned for assisting Fr. William Horner, a seminary priest. He suffered with Bl. Fr. Richard LEIGH and the blessed laymen Edward Shelley, Richard Martin, John Roche (all beatified in 1929), and St. Margaret WARD. He is frequently confused with Fr. William WAY, who used the alias Flower. Bl. Richard Flower was beatified by Pope John Paul II on Nov. 22, 1987 with George Haydock and Companions.

Feast of the English Martyrs: May 4 (England).

See Also: ENGLAND, SCOTLAND, AND WALES, MARTYRS OF.

Bibliography: R. CHALLONER, *Memoirs of Missionary Priests,* ed. J. H. POLLEN (rev. ed. London 1924). J. H. POLLEN, *Acts of English Martyrs* (London 1891).

[K. I. RABENSTEIN]

FLOWERS, SYMBOLISM OF

Flowers have frequently been understood as signs of a larger reality, and individual species have been used metaphorically as symbols. Though the Bible mentions nearly 100 species of flora, few of the flowers can be positively identified. Even the lilies of Christ's *logion* in Mt 6.28 are not the flower known today. In the Scriptures generally the life and death cycle of plants is primarily a sign of the transitory nature of life; the blossoming and withering of flowers illustrate particularly the swift passage of beauty. ''Man, born of woman, is short-lived and full of trouble, like a flower that springs up and fades'' (Jb 14.1). ''For the sun rises with a burning heat and parches the grass, and its flower falls and the beauty of its appearance perishes. So too will the rich man wither in his ways'' (Jas 1.10). Because flowers signal the spring (Sg 2.12), and because of their fragrance and beauty, and yet precisely because they pass so quickly, they acquired a further symbolic meaning. A great and lasting presence of flowers is to be a sign of the Messianic kingdom. ''The desert and the parched land will exult; the steppe will rejoice and bloom. They will bloom with abundant flowers . . .'' (Is 35.1).

Symbols played a prominent role in early Christian art; for example, in the catacombs of Domitilla, Praetextatus, and Callistus, and in the mosaics at Ravenna and the vault of the mausoleum of St. Constance in Rome, where garlands of flowers signify the paradisial state of the saints. Various flowers were used to designate persons and virtues. The lily as a sign of virginity is among the most ancient. The full development of this type of symbolism came in the late Middle Ages when flowers became part of an elaborate sign language, which was a major catechetical tool. The Renaissance added some of the flower symbolism of pagan times. The most important flowers were the lily (representing purity, Christ, Mary, and especially the Annunciation) and the rose, which had a wide variety of meanings depending on its color or the presence or absence of thorns, etc. The violet signified humility; the hyacinth, power or peace; the daisy, innocence; the tulip, prayer; the sunflower, soul longing for God; the lotus, eloquence; the marigold, jealousy. The passion flower illustrates the popular propensity to find symbolic representation, each of its many parts having been suggestive of an instrument of Christ's passion. Contemporary Christian symbolism is drawn mainly from the Bible and is less extravagant.

Bibliography: G. FERGUSON, *Signs and Symbols in Christian Art* (New York 1959). J. WILPERT, *Roma sotterranea: Le pitture delle catacombe romane* (Rome 1903). H. LECLERCQ, *Dictionnaire d'archéologie chrétienne et de liturgie* (Paris 1907–53) 5.2:1693–99. J. DANIÉLOU, *Sacramentum futuri* (Paris 1950). L. BEHLING, *Die Pflanze in der mittelalterlichen Tafelmalerei* (Weimar 1957). K. WESSEL, *Die Religion in Geschichte und Gegenwart* (Tübingen 1957–65) 6:545–548.

[G. D. HUCK]

FLOYD, JOHN

Jesuit theologian and controversialist; b. Cambridgeshire, England, 1572; d. Saint-Omer, France, Sept. 15, 1649. Admitted to English College, Reims (1588), he proceeded to Rome, where he entered the English College (1590). He joined the Society of Jesus in 1592. On the mission in England at the time of the Gunpowder Plot (1605) he visited Father Edward Oldcorne in Worcester Gaol and was himself captured and imprisoned. A year later he was exiled but afterward returned to England and underwent several further imprisonments. Floyd spent much of the later part of his life abroad, mostly at the English Jesuit College of Saint-Omer. He enjoyed a great reputation as a theologian and controversialist and wrote many books in defense of the Catholic cause against the English Protestants. He also defended in print, against certain of the English Catholic clergy and against the Sorbonne, the policy of the papacy in temporarily withholding a bishop from the Church in England. He used various pseudonyms: Daniel of Jesus, I. R. Student in Divinity, Fidelis Annosus, and Hermanus Loemelius.

Bibliography: T. COOPER, *Dictionary of National Biography from the Earliest Times to 1900* (London 1885–1900) 7:344–345. *Publications of the Catholic Record Society* v.37. J. GILLOW, *A Literary and Biographical History or Bibliographical Dictionary of the English Catholics from 1534 to the Present time* (New York 1961) 2:300–306. C. SOMMERVOGEL et al., *Bibliothèque de la Compagnie de Jésus* (Brussels-Paris 1890–1932) 3:812–818. A. F. ALLISON, ''John Gerard and the Gunpowder Plot,'' *Recusant History* 5 (1959) 43–63. A. F. ALLISON and D. M. ROGERS, *A Catalogue of Catholic Books in English . . . 1558–1640,* 2 v. (London 1956).

[A. F. ALLISON]

FOCHER, JUAN

Franciscan lawyer and author, date and place of birth unknown; d. Mexico City, 1572. Of French origin, Focher had already received the doctorate in law in Paris before entering the Franciscan Order in the Province of Aquitania. He went to New Spain in 1540 and spent the rest of his life there. In the complex problems of beginning Church organization, his personality and training made him something of an oracle, consulted by episcopal chapters and committees. His treatises cover the main problems of colonization and evangelization of the period, and are of special importance for religious history and for the development of Mexican civil law. They demonstrate a systematic theory of evangelization for the Americas and show its application, thereby constituting the manual for the Franciscan missionaries in New Spain and the source, in great part, of the inspiration of their methods and practices. His *Itinerarium catholicum* is universally considered as the first attempt at a manual of systematic missiology in which is stated, for the first time, the theory of the royal vicarship in the Indies to explain the relations between Spain and the Native American Church. His numerous works were circulated at the end of the 19th century among bibliophiles, but they are largely unknown and unpublished.

Bibliography: J. FOCHER, *Itinerario del misionero en América,* tr. A. EGUILIZ (Madrid 1960).

[A. EGUILUZ]

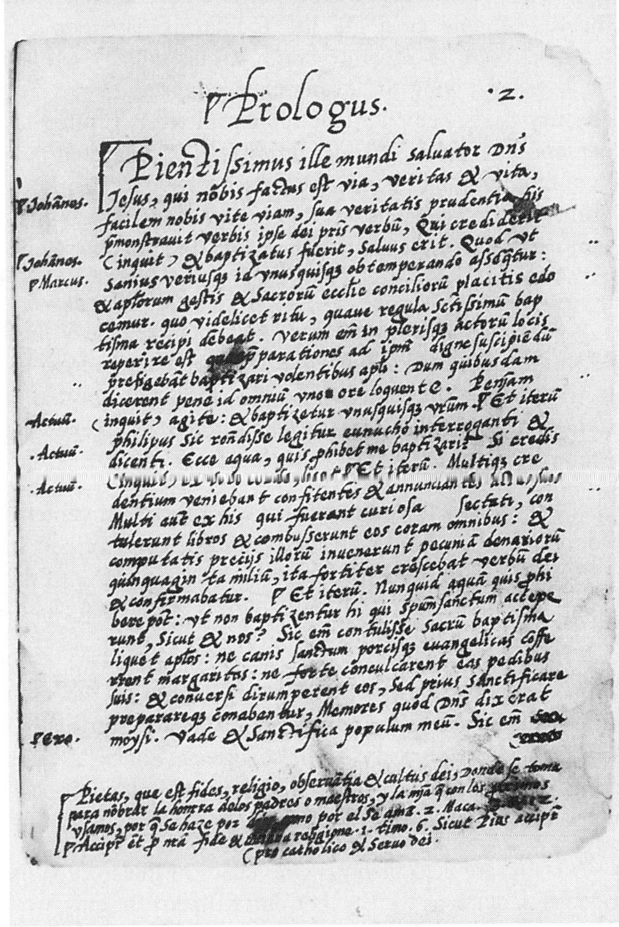

Manuscript prologue page from "Tractatus de Baptismo et Matrimonie Noviter Conversorum ad Fidem," 16th century, by Juan Focher.

FOCOLARE MOVEMENT

The worldwide Focolare Movement (Work of Mary) embodies a specific form of spirituality best described as the Gospel seen from the perspective of unity; the aim is to strive for the unity Jesus prayed for on the night before he died; "Father, may they all be one" (see Jn 17:21). Focolare had its origin in 1943 in Trent, Italy, when a young schoolteacher, Chiara Lubich, together with a few young women, amid the devastation of World War II, came to see that there is but one ideal that can never fail. This "ideal" is God, who is love. They focused their lives on the gospel and many others followed. Within a few months, over 500 people had joined them in living what was emerging as a new spirituality in the Church: the "spirituality of unity," which is based on the mutual love inherent in Jesus' new commandment. It is a way of going to God together, which brings about a change in individuals, in groups and society, uniting people beyond all their differences.

In 1962 Focolare was initially approved by Pope John XXIII, and received the continued blessing of Pope Paul VI, who on Feb. 8, 1978, said to a group of its members: "Be faithful to your inspiration which is so modern and so fruitful." The movement spread to every continent and came into special prominence in 1977 when its foundress, Chiara Lubich, was awarded the Templeton Prize for progress in religion.

The spirituality of the Focolare Movement bears striking kinship with the spirit of the Second Vatican Council. The council frequently recalls the promise of Jesus to be present wherever two or more are united in his name (Mt 18.20). The council's stress on unity is well known. "For the promotion of unity belongs to the innermost nature of the Church" (*Gaudium et spes* 42). These are only two of the fundamental points of the spirituality of the movement.

The Focolare Movement has many branches, including five that are movements in their own right, though animated by an identical spirituality and represented in the

General Coordinating Council of Focolare in Rome and locally. At the core are the focolarini, lay men and women living in separate communities called Focolare houses. Following the evangelical counsels of poverty, chastity, and obedience, the focolarini work as other lay persons in regular jobs and professions. Their goal is to maintain unity and hence the presence of the risen Lord. Some married persons, while continuing to live in their families, participate fully in the life of the Focolare houses.

Also part of the Focolare Movement are the Volunteers, who emerged in the wake of the Hungarian Revolution of 1956. They are lay people wholly committed to living the spirituality of unity and, through it, to renewing society.

The young generations make up three Movements known as the Gen (New Generation), first formed in 1966. They are divided according to their age into the Gen II for teenagers and young adults; Gen III for children; and the Gen IV for the little ones.

The priests' movement is made up of diocesan priests committed to living the Focolare spirituality. Often the life of unity of these priests brings about a transformation of parish life. Seminarians living this spirit make up the GenS (Gen Seminarians).

There are also bishops who share in the spirituality of the Focolare, as well as men and women religious, who are associated with Focolare while continuing to live in their own communities. Focolare spirituality helps them to see how the specific charism of their founders can be lived in the present time. They also cultivate a rapport of unity with other religious orders and congregations. Young religious living this spirit form the GenR (Gen Religious).

Between 1966 and 1984, a further development saw the emergence of large-scale but less formally organized bodies within the Focolare: New Humanity, New Families, Youth for a United World, Young for Unity, Parish Movement; all of these aim to bring a spirit of unity into their respective environments and fields of endeavor.

At the international headquarters of the Focolare, the president (who according to its statutes will always be a lay woman) is helped by a council in which all branches of the Focolare and all aspects of the life of its members are represented. The Focolare throughout the world is organized in 75 ''zones'' (i.e., geographical territories), each with its own council acting in unity with the international headquarters.

Wherever the Focolare Movement exists various ecumenical activities take place. Of particular interest is the Ecumenical Center of Ottmaring, Germany, where Lutherans and Catholics work together, though they live in separate communities. Over the years, the Focolare has built relationships with many ecclesial movements and associations within the Catholic Church. The movement is present throughout the Christian world and has also spread, particularly since 1977, among non-Christian religions.

The Focolare carries on social, cultural, and economic activities in many countries. Every year summer meetings called Mariapolis (City of Mary), are held for those who wish to come into contact with Focolare. The goal of the Mariapolis is to generate the presence of Christ in the community through the practice of mutual and constant charity. Permanent Mariapolises exist in Italy, Africa, Argentina, and Brazil. The movement operates ''New City'' publishing houses in many countries. The Focolare monthly magazine *New/Living City*, is devoted to the spirituality of the movement, and is published in 24 languages. In the United States the Mariapolis Luminosa, New City Press, and *Living City* magazine are located in Hyde Park, N.Y. In 1991 the movement launched the ''Economy of Sharing,'' a set of guidelines intended to reconcile the often conflicting worlds of economics and solidarity.

On the vigil of Pentecost 1998, during the meeting of ecclesial movements and new communities with Pope John Paul II, Chiara Lubich described the essence of that something new the Focolare offers. ''Holy Father, you identified love as the 'inspiring spark' of all that is done under the name of Focolare, and it is really true. It is the driving force of our movement. Being love and spreading love is our general aim. In fact, the Focolare Movement is called to bring an invasion of love into the world.''

Bibliography: J. GALLAGHER, *A Woman's Work: A Biography of the Focolare Movement and Its Founder* (New York 1990). C. LUBICH, *May They All Be One* (New York 1997); *Unity and Jesus Forsaken* (New York 1997).

[R. D. TETREAU/G. BRANDL/A. LINGLEY]

FOIK, PAUL JOSEPH

Librarian, educator, author; b. Stratford, Ontario, Canada, Aug. 14, 1879; d. Austin, Texas, March 1, 1941. He was the son of John and Joanna (Dameck) Foik. After arriving in the U.S. in 1900, he entered the Congregation of Holy Cross in 1901. Following ordination on June 30, 1911, at the University of Notre Dame, Ind., he went to The Catholic University of America, Washington, D.C., where he obtained his Ph.D. the next year. After serving as librarian and archivist at Notre Dame from 1912 to

1924, he moved to St. Edward's University, Austin, Tex., where he filled a number of positions, including those of librarian, archivist, professor of foreign languages, professor of American history, and dean of the College of Arts and Letters. Professionally active, he was an officer in several Texas historical associations, chairman of the Texas Knights of Columbus Historical Commission, and a member of the advisory board of the Texas Centennial Commission. He was founder of the Irish National Library Foundation and of the library section of the National Catholic Educational Association. He was also cofounder of the Catholic Library Association, which he served as vice president and member of the executive council. Foik was well known as an editor, his principal work being the first four volumes of *Our Catholic Heritage in Texas 1519–1950* (1936). He served also as associate editor of *Mid–America* and chairman of the editorial board of the *Catholic Periodical Index.* He wrote articles for the *Encyclopedia Americana* and the *Dictionary of American Biography,* and contributed to the major Catholic historical journals. He published a book on *Pioneer Catholic Journalism in the U.S.* (1930), as well as several brochures on Catholic history in the Southwest.

Bibliography: Archives, Holy Cross Provincialate, Priests' Society of the Indiana Province, South Bend, Ind. Archives (Catholic), Austin, Tex.

[J. P. GIBBONS]

FOLCWIN, ST.

Bishop of Thérouanne; b. late eighth century; d. Ekelsbecke, on the Ysar, France, Dec. 14, 855. A member of an illegitimate branch of the CAROLINGIAN DYNASTY, he became bishop of Thérouanne, Pas-de-Calais, France, *c.* 816–17. As bishop he attended the Synod of Paris (846) and those at QUIERCY (849) and Soissons (853). In 843 he was responsible for bringing the relics of St. OMER OF THÉROUANNE to the Abbey of SAINT-BERTIN. Folcwin was buried there, and his body was translated in 928 and again in 1181. The bishop's life was written in the 10th century by a monk of Saint-Bertin, also named FOLCWIN, who later became abbot of Lobbes.

Feast: Dec. 14.

Bibliography: *Vita* in *Monumenta Germaniae Scriptores* (Berlin 1825–) 15:423–430. L. DUCHESNE, *Fastes épiscopaux de l'ancienne Gaule,* 3 v. (2d. ed. Paris 1907–15) 3:135. *Bibliotheca hagiographica latina antiquae ct mediae aetatis,* 2 v. (Brussels 1898–1901; suppl. 1911) 3079. A. M.. ZIMMERMANN, *Kalendarium Benedictinum: Die Heiligen und Seligen des Benediktinerorderns und seiner Zweige,* 4 v. (Metten 1933–38) 3:434. A. DUMAS, *Catholicisme* 4:1407–08.

[C. R. BYERLY]

FOLCWIN OF LOBBES

Benedictine abbot, chronicler; b. *c.* 935; d. 990. In 948 he became a monk at SAINT–BERTIN, near Thérouanne, where Saint FOLCWIN, his great uncle, was bishop. In 965, designated abbot of LOBBES by Bp. Everaclus of Liège, he is supposed to have received the abbatial blessing at Cologne on Christmas Day in the presence of Emperor Otto I. Only in 1881 was it rediscovered that Folcwin of Saint-Bertin and Folcwin of Lobbes were the same man. His intelligent use of documentary evidence and his distrust of mere oral tradition give him special importance as a writer. His works include a history of the abbots of Saint-Bertin, written 961–962 (*Patrologia Latina* 136:1181–1278; *Monumenta Germaniae Historica: Scriptores* 13:606–634); a life of Saint Folcwin of Thérouanne, written between 970 and 972 (*Patrologia Latina* 137:535–542; *Monumenta Germaniae Historica: Scriptores* 15.1:424–430); a history of the abbots of Lobbes, written between 972 and 980 (*Monumenta Germaniae Historica: Scriptores* 4:54–74); and a history of the miracles of Abbots URSMAR and Erminus of Lobbes, written *c.* 980 (*Monumenta Germaniae Historica: Scriptores* 15.2:832–842).

Bibliography: J. WARICHEZ, *L'Abbaye de Lobbes depuis les origines jusqu'en 1200* (Tournai 1909), *passim.* M. MANITIUS, *Geschichte der lateinischen Literatur des Mittelalters* (Munich 1911–31) 2:210–214. A. DUMAS, *Catholicisme* 4:1407. G. BAADER, *Lexikon für Theologie und Kirche* (Freiburg 1957–65) 4: 193.

[W. E. WILKIE]

FOLIOT, GILBERT

English abbot and bishop; b. *c.* 1110 of a well-connected Anglo-Norman family; d. Feb. 18, 1187. Trained in Roman and Canon Law and theology, he taught in the schools before becoming a monk at Cluny *c.* 1132 and, subsequently, was prior of Abbeville. Chosen by King Stephen in 1139 to be abbot of Gloucester, he won the friendship of Archbishop Theobald, who in 1148 secured his election to the See of Hereford, where he speedily became the most respected bishop in England. Disappointed in his expectation of succeeding Theobald at Canterbury by the election of Thomas BECKET, whom he disliked, and unappeased by his translation to London in 1163, Foliot, after quarrelling with Becket at Clarendon and Northampton, became the leading spirit of the opposition to the exiled Archbishop, though by no means entirely the King's man. In a war of pamphlets his letter *Multiplicem* stands out as a rhetorical masterpiece and bitter summary of charges against Becket. Twice excommunicated, Foliot was unreconciled when Becket was murdered, but accepted the Archbishop's canonization with good grace. As bishop, Foliot was frequently a papal judge–delegate and helped to establish the personnel of his cathedral. He owes his celebrity to his share in the great controversy between HENRY II and St. Thomas, and while his action is comprehensible, he does not emerge as an attractive or saintly figure. He remains an enigma. Although upright, austere, energetic, and influential, his character contained elements of ambition, rigidity, harshness, and, possibly, even duplicity. His correspondence with many of the leading men of his time is an important source for the political history of England in the mid-12th century.

Bibliography: Works. G. FOLIOT, *Epistolae Patrologia Latina,* ed. J. P. MIGNE (Paris 1878–90) 190:739–1068. **Literature.** G. G. PERRY, *Dictionary of National Biography from the Earliest Times to 1900* (London 1885–1900) 7:358–360. M. D. KNOWLES, *The Episcopal Colleagues of Archbishop Thomas Becket* (Cambridge, Eng. 1951). F. L. CROSS, *The Oxford Dictionary of the English Church* (London 1957) 511–512. A. MOREY and C. N. L. BROOKE, *Gilbert Foliot and His Letters* (Cambridge 1965).

[M. D. KNOWLES]

FOLKSTONE, ABBEY OF

The first nunnery of Anglo-Saxon England, was built by King Eadwald of Kent *c.* 630 for his daughter Eanswith, its first abbess (*c.* 614–640). The destruction of the abbey was begun by the incursions of the sea and completed by Danish invaders, perhaps in 867. In 927 King Athelstan granted the land to Christ Church, Canterbury, to be refounded as a priory for monks, dedicated to St. Mary and St. Eanswith. After the Norman Conquest the house became an alien cell of Lonlay, Normandy, but later returned to English allegiance. When the sea again undermined the site, the monks, in 1137, moved for safety to a new church. Here, in what is now the parish church, St. Eanswith's reputed relics are still preserved, although nothing remains of the monastic buildings that were surrendered to King Henry VIII on Nov. 15, 1535.

Bibliography: W. DUGDALE, *Monasticon Anglicanum* (London 1655–73); best ed. by J. CALEY et al., 6 v. (1817–30) 1:97, 451, 4:672–675. L. H. COTTINEAU, *Répertoire topobibliographique des abbayes et prieurés,* 2 v. (Mâcon 1935–39) 1:1167.

[F. CORRIGAN]

FOLLOWING OF CHRIST (IN THE CHRISTIAN LIFE)

In the earliest Christian writings the concept of identification with Christ was the fundamental and all-pervading notion. TERTULLIAN's apothegm *Christianus alter Christus* found manifold expression throughout patristic literature and was admirably synthesized by ISIDORE OF SEVILLE (*Sententiae* 1.30.4): ''Christ is one in Himself and in us'' (*unus in se et in nobis est Christus*). CYPRIAN summed up the following of Christ: ''We ought to cling to His words, to study His teachings, and to imitate His life'' (*De unitate ecclesiae* 1.2). The perfect realization of this ideal was found in the martyr. IGNATIUS OF ANTIOCH pleaded in his letter to the Romans: ''Let me imitate the passion of my Lord.'' In this same spirit the ascetics embraced a life of total dedication. ''Let Christ be your life's breath'' was the admonition of ANTHONY OF EGYPT.

With the CHRISTOLOGICAL controversies of the 4th century the simple devotion of early Christianity assumed a more theological expression. Although the Doctors of the Church insisted upon the reality of Christ's human nature as the exemplary cause of all holiness, they referred to man's likeness to God as the special end of the Incarnation. In the Greek Fathers this idea was especially emphatic. In the East, however, stress was placed on the redeeming act of Christ, who raised us to a share in His divinity; in the West there was more emphasis on our imitation of Him: ''What does it mean to be a disciple of Christ if we do not copy His compassion and imitate His humility?'' (Ambrose, *Sermo* 29). These two aspects of Christological devotion, reverence for the divinity of the Word Incarnate and imitation of the sacred humanity of Jesus, were combined in the teaching of St. Augustine: ''In His divinity He dwells within our souls; in His humanity He sets before our eyes the example of His life and thereby draws our hearts to Himself'' (*Sermo* 264). In the 11th century PETER DAMIAN summed up this tradition: ''It is truly great to die for Christ, but not less noble to live for Him'' (*Sermo 32;* PL 144:6803).

With St. BERNARD the Christology of the West turned strongly toward the mysteries of Christ's human life. Bernard's affective trend in spirituality influenced subsequent writers. The Cistercian mystics developed profound love for the Sacred Humanity. Their prayer was a progression from the contemplation of Christ in the Scriptures and liturgy to the experience of union with Him and thence to imitation of His acts. The culmination of this devotion is to be found in the Franciscan tradition of deep emotional response to the mysteries of Jesus' human life and suffering. The stigmata of St. FRANCIS, the poetic tradition of the STABAT MATER, and the *Meditationes vitae Christi* find theological basis in the writings of St. BONAVENTURE and in the teaching of DUNS SCOTUS that love has precedence over knowledge.

Following more closely in the patristic tradition, the Dominicans developed a theological approach to the love of Christ. For St. THOMAS AQUINAS contemplation is wisdom in the intellect, charity in the will, and peace in the heart. Devotion is the gift of oneself to God, rather than complacency or enjoyment of Him. Thomas treated the mystery of the Incarnation as the principal work of Divine Providence and taught that every action of Christ was meant to lead men toward God. But the primary object of devotion is always the Person of the Word (*Summa Theologiae* 2a2ae, 82.1, 3).

The greatest mystic of the Dominican Order, CATHERINE OF SIENA, remained Thomistic in doctrine, but was more intuitive and practical in her zeal for the Church and her participation in Christ's suffering. Dominican mysticism in Germany under TAULER and HENRY SUSO took an affective turn in attempting to follow Christ to the cross, that is, by the willing acceptance of suffering, and thus win a share in His love.

The epitome of medieval piety is found in the *Vita Christi* of LUDOLPH OF SAXONY—a work that combines patristic and medieval spirituality with such clarity and unction that it merits to be called the book of the imitation of Jesus Christ. It is not so much a biography as a set of meditations on the life of Christ. The considerations are filled with tender reverence for "the exemplar of all holiness, the Lord Jesus Christ, who came from heaven that He might go before us on the road to eternal life." The prayers that conclude each meditation open the way, through love of Christ's humanity, to that penetration to the depths of His divinity whereby the medieval saints strove to form their souls in the image of Him who is the Image of the invisible God.

See Also: IMITATION OF CHRIST.

Bibliography: Sources, *Enchiridion asceticum,* ed. M. J. ROUËT DE JOURNEL (4th ed. Barcelona 1947). M. F. TOAL, ed. and tr., *The Sunday Sermons of the Great Fathers,* 4 v. (Chicago 1958–62). BONAVENTURE, *The Mind's Road to God,* tr. G. BOAS (New York 1953). CATHERINE OF SIENA, *The Dialogue,* tr. and ed. A. THOROLD (Westminster, MD 1950). H. SUSO, *Little Book of Eternal Wisdom,* in *The Exemplar,* ed. N. HELLER. tr. A. EDWARD, 2 v. (Dubuque 1962) v.2. Literature. P. POURRAT, *Christian Spirituality in the Middle Ages,* tr. S. JACQUES (New York 1924; repr. Westminster, MD 1953). J. LECLERCQ el al., *La Spiritualité du moyen âge* (Paris 1961). G. SITWELL, *Spiritual Writers of the Middle Ages* (New York 1961). F. CAYRÉ, *Spiritual Writers of the Early Church,* tr. W. W. WILSON (New York 1959). J. GAUTIER et al., eds., *Some Schools of Catholic Spirituality,* tr. K. SULLIVAN (New York 1959). J. QUASTEN, *Patrology,* 3 v. (Westminster, MD 1950–). F. VERNET, *Medieval Spirituality* (St. Louis 1930). M. GRABMANN, *The Interior Life of St. Thomas Aquinas,* tr. N. ASHENBRENER (Milwaukee 1951). C. MARMION, *Christ the Ideal of the Monk,* tr. a Nun of Tyburn Convent (London 1926). E. BERTAUD and A. RAYEZ, *Dictionnaire de spiritualité ascétique et mystique. Doctrine et histoire,* ed., M. VILLER et al. (Paris 1932) 3:765–766. J. C. DIDIER, Catholicisme 5:1263–71. P. J. MULLINS, *The Spiritual Life According to St. Isidore of Seville* (Washington 1940). T. A. CARROLL, *The Venerable Bede: His Spiritual Teachings* (Washington 1946). O. J. BLUM, *St. Peter Damian: His Teaching on the Spiritual Life* (Washington 1947).

[P. J. MULLINS]

FONCK, LEOPOLD

Exegete and founder, under Pius X, of the PONTIFICAL BIBLICAL INSTITUTE; b. Wissen, near Düsseldorf, Germany, Jan. 14, 1865; d. Vienna, Austria, Oct. 19, 1930. He made his humanistic studies at Kempen, Germany, and his philosophical and theological studies at the Gregorian University, Rome. Ordained in 1889, he entered the Society of Jesus in Germany in 1892. His biblical studies, begun at the Gregorian under R. Cornely, were continued from 1893 to 1899 in England, Egypt, and Palestine and at the Universities of Berlin and Munich. He taught NT exegesis at the University of Innsbruck from 1901 to 1908, when he was invited to the Gregorian. That was the age of the crisis of Modernism. In 1907, PIUS X published the decree *LAMENTABILI* and the encyclical PASCENDI; in 1909 he founded the Pontifical Biblical Institute in Rome and made Fonck its first rector. The directives of Pius X determined all of Fonck's work and thought.

For the next 20 years, Fonck devoted himself to this institute. As rector from 1909 to 1919 (though exiled to Switzerland during the war years, 1915–19), he formed its library, museum, publications, courses, and scientific method and prepared the founding of a filial institute in Jerusalem. Thereafter, he served as professor and as editor of *Biblica.* He was also a consultor of the PONTIFICAL BIBLICAL COMMISSION. His last years were spent in Prague and Vienna, where he devoted himself to the ministry.

Among the several books by Fonck on biblical topics, the best-known are his *Parabeln des Herrn im Evangelium* (Innsbruck 1902, 4th ed. 1927) and *Wunder des Herren* (Innsbruck 1903, 3d ed. 1907); the former appeared in English as *The Parables of the Gospels*, tr. G. O'Neill (New York 1915, 3d ed. 1918).

Bibliography: *Biblica* 11 (1930) 369–372. U. HOLZMEISTER, *Dictionnaire de la Bible* 3:310–312. P. NOBER, *Lexikon für Theologie und Kirche* 2 4:194–195.

[S. MC EVENUE]

FONSECA, PETER DA

Philosopher; b. Proença-a-Nova, Portugal, 1528; d. Lisbon, Nov. 4, 1599. He entered the Society of Jesus in 1548, studied at the University of Evora, and spent a number of years as teacher of philosophy and theology in the University of Coimbra. A man of great tact and finesse, he was appointed to important committees by his religious superiors and was sent on several delicate missions. He was one of six Jesuits appointed to work out the Jesuits code of education, the *Ratio Studiorum.* From 1567 to 1592 he held such offices in the society as rector, general's assistant, superior of a professed house, and visitor; contrary to what one sometimes reads, he was never provincial. After Portugal was incorporated under the crown of Spain (1582), Philip II used Fonseca's influence and ability to remedy the moral and social evils of Lisbon. Fonseca reminded his contemporaries of St. Ignatius Loyola by reason of his prudence, his choice of apostolic works, and his manner of accomplishing his goals.

Fonseca is best known, however, for his contribution to the renaissance of SCHOLASTICISM in the 16th century. He wrote a popular text in dialectics and an introduction to philosophy; but his most important work was his four-volume *Commentarii in libros Metaphysicorum Aristotelis* (Lisbon 1577–89). With a humanist's taste and philological background, Fonseca attended to textual criticism and always tried to get as accurate a Greek reading as possible. The Greek is accompanied by Fonseca's own translation. The commentary tries to interpret Aristotle strictly according to Aristotle himself; but after the commentary Fonseca adds a number of special questions in which he treats, in a personal fashion and sometimes at great length, almost all philosophical questions.

Though Thomistic in a broad sense, Fonseca nevertheless taught that the human intellect has a direct knowledge of singulars; that created existence is only an intrinsic mode of a finite essence; that primary matter is not altogether potency; and that the principle of individuation adds something positive to a thing's essence. Fonseca was one of the first to utilize *scientia media* (God's knowledge of hypothetical future free actions) as a means of reconciling human freedom with divine foreknowledge, predestination, and efficacious grace. Luis de MOLINA probably arrived at the doctrine of *scientia media* independently of and before Fonseca, but this point is still debated.

Bibliography: L. MORATI, *Enciclopedia filosofica* (Venice-Rome 1957) 2:474–475. M. SOLANA, *Historia de la filosofía Española: Época del Renacimiento,* 3 v. (Madrid 1941) 3:339–366, J. RABENECK, ''Antiqua Legenda de Molina Narrata Examinatur,'' *Archivum historicum Societatis Jesu* 24 (1955) 295–326. P. DA FONSECA, *Commentarii in libros metaphysicorum Aristotelis,* ed. G. OLMS (Hildesheim 1964).

[A. BENEDETTO]

FONTBONNE, SAINT JOHN, MOTHER

Mother superior, educator, and second foundress of the Sisters of St. Joseph, b. Bas-en-Basset, France, March 31, 1769; d. Lyon, Nov. 22, 1843. Jeanne Fontbonne was the daughter of Michel Fontbonne and Benoîte Theillière, the second oldest of five surviving children. She was educated by the Sisters of St. Joseph in Bas-en-Basset, where two of her aunts taught in the school. Later she completed her studies at Le Puy-en-Velay. On July 1, 1778, she and her sister Marie accompanied their aunts to a new foundation at Monistrol, where they were to become the first postulants. Bas-en-Basset and Monistrol are located about mid-way between Le Puy and Saint-Etienne, in the department of Haute-Loire.

On Dec. 17, 1778, Marie and Jeanne received the religious habit and the names of Sisters Saint Teresa and Saint John, respectively. Sister Saint John's leadership qualities were already evident, and she was elected superior of Monistrol in 1785. She immediately undertook the establishment of a training school where the poor could learn a trade, and obtained financial help from a wealthy citizen, Madame de Chantemule. Bishop de Galard encouraged her efforts; the hospital and schools progressed.

With the outbreak of the Revolution in 1789, the work of the sisters was in danger. Bishop de Galard, who had refused the constitutional oath, was forced to flee. Father Ollier, the local pastor, took the oath and became hostile toward the sisters, who also refused to swear allegiance to the new government. On Sept. 29, 1792, most of the sisters abandoned their convent and returned to their families. Mother Saint John remained along with her sister and Sister Martha. They continued their charitable work in the hospital in secular dress, but Father Ollier's insistence that they participate in the religious services that he conducted eventually drove them away, and on Oct. 14, 1792, they returned to the Fontbonne family home in Bas, where they observed the rule as much as possible.

Late in 1793, the three sisters were imprisoned at Monfranc (St-Didier-en-Velay), where others, including their aunts, were later condemned. Here they continued their life of prayer. They rejoiced as the day of their execution drew near, only to learn that they had been spared by the fall of Robespierre (July 27, 1794). When liberated, they returned to the Fontbonne home, where they resumed a life of service while in secular dress. Mother Saint John always regretted that she was not worthy to die as a martyr, but other great works awaited her.

In 1807, the need for religious education among the generation raised during the Revolution was imperative. Joseph Cardinal Fesch of Lyon, the uncle of Napoleon, through the intermediary of the Vicar General Father Claude Cholleton, called Mother Saint John to direct a group of women in St-Etienne, called the ''Black Daughters,'' or popularly, ''the Sisters of a Happy Death,'' because they attended the sick and the dying. She left her home on Aug. 14, 1807, to meet this unknown group, in whom she found kindred spirits. She gave them the Rule of the Sisters of St. Joseph that Father Médaille had drawn up and taught them to temper their austerities and combine the interior life with service to others. On July 14, 1808, she received twelve of them into the Congregation at the Maison Pascal. Father Piron addressed them in these words: ''You are but few, my daughters, but like a swarm of bees, you shall spread yourselves everywhere . . . . But, while increasing, preserve always the humility and simplicity which should characterize the Daughters of St. Joseph.''

Shortly afterward, another group at Rue Micarême joined the sisters. This establishment became the first motherhouse. Other foundations appeared; old ones were restored. Soon the necessity of a common novitiate became apparent. Formerly each house prepared its own postulants and novices; however, under the Napoleonic system, centralization was in order. In 1816, Mother Saint John obtained property, formerly a Carthusian Monastery, adjoining buildings, and the Château Yon, all located in the Croix-Rousse section of Lyon. This site, rue des Chartreux, became the motherhouse of the Sisters of St. Joseph of Lyon.

Other motherhouses were formed from Lyon, including Chambéry, Gap, Bourg, Annecy, and Bordeaux. Former foundations, now restored, became independent motherhouses, such as Le Puy, Clermont-Ferrand, and Saint-Vallier. In 1836, Mother Saint John accepted an appeal from Bishop Joseph Rosati of St. Louis, Missouri, in the United States, and sent six sisters, among them her two nieces, followed by two other sisters who were trained as instructors to the deaf. This group became the seed that gave birth to over thirty congregations of Sisters of St. Joseph in the United States and Canada. In 1831, sisters went to Italy where they formed independent foundations. Under Mother Saint John's leadership, the congregation expanded to include over 240 houses with 3,000 sisters.

In 1839, Mother Saint John resigned her office, and Mother Sacred Heart replaced her. She spent her remaining days in prayer and simple tasks, often giving conferences to the sisters, some of which have been preserved. She died on Nov. 22, 1843, at the motherhouse in Lyon. She is revered by the Sisters of St. Joseph as the second foundress, and as an example of the charity and humility encouraged by Father Médaille. Many buildings in American foundations bear her name, and her memory remains alive on both sides of the Atlantic.

Bibliography: SISTER M. K. LOGUE, *Sister of St. Joseph of Philadelphia* (Westminster MD 1950). SISTER OF ST. JOSEPH OF BRENTWOOD, *Mother Saint John Fontbonne* (New York 1936). Soeurs de Saint-Joseph, Fédération Française, *Par-del toutes frontières* (Strasbourg 1998).

[M. H. KASHUBA]

FONTE, PEDRO JOSÉ

Thirty-first archbishop of Mexico; b. Linares, Aragon, May 13, 1777; d. June 11, 1839. In 1802, the year of his ordination, Pedro José de Fonte y Hernández de Miravete was invited by the archbishop of Mexico, Francisco Javier de Lizana y Beaumont, to become his vicar-general and provisor.

After Archbishop Lizana died in 1811, the See of Mexico remained vacant until Fonte was consecrated June 29, 1816. When Mexico became independent, Archbishop Fonte returned to Spain. Following the recognition of Mexican independence by Spain in 1837, Pope Gregory XVI ordered him either to return to his see or to resign. Fonte chose resignation.

The first four years of his reign passed uneventfully since the movement for independence had all but collapsed with the execution of Morelos. In April of 1820 news of the Riego revolt in Spain and the readoption of the Constitution of 1812 reached Mexico. Fundamentally, the archbishop espoused political conservatism, but loyalty to the crown overrode his personal convictions. All Church leaders swore allegiance to the constitution, and in July the archbishop defended its freedom of the press, guarantees of political liberty and equality, and suppression of the Inquisition. In spite of the increasing anticlericalism demonstrated by the Spanish Cortes, Fonte remained loyal, even when all his suffragans during 1821 swore allegiance to Agustín de Iturbide, the conservative army commander who declared for independence.

When Iturbide's victory seemed assured, Fonte prepared to leave the country, but Capt.–Gen. Juan O'Donojú persuaded him to delay his departure. The archbishop agreed to remain if the King would accept the Treaty of Córdoba signed by Iturbide and O'Donojú in late August. When Iturbide entered Mexico City in triumph, the archbishop met him at the doors of the cathedral and intoned a solemn *Te Deum* of thanksgiving. He counseled his clergy to obey the new government, but he himself refused to participate.

His last important act as reigning archbishop was to report to the regency on Oct. 19, 1821, the results of his

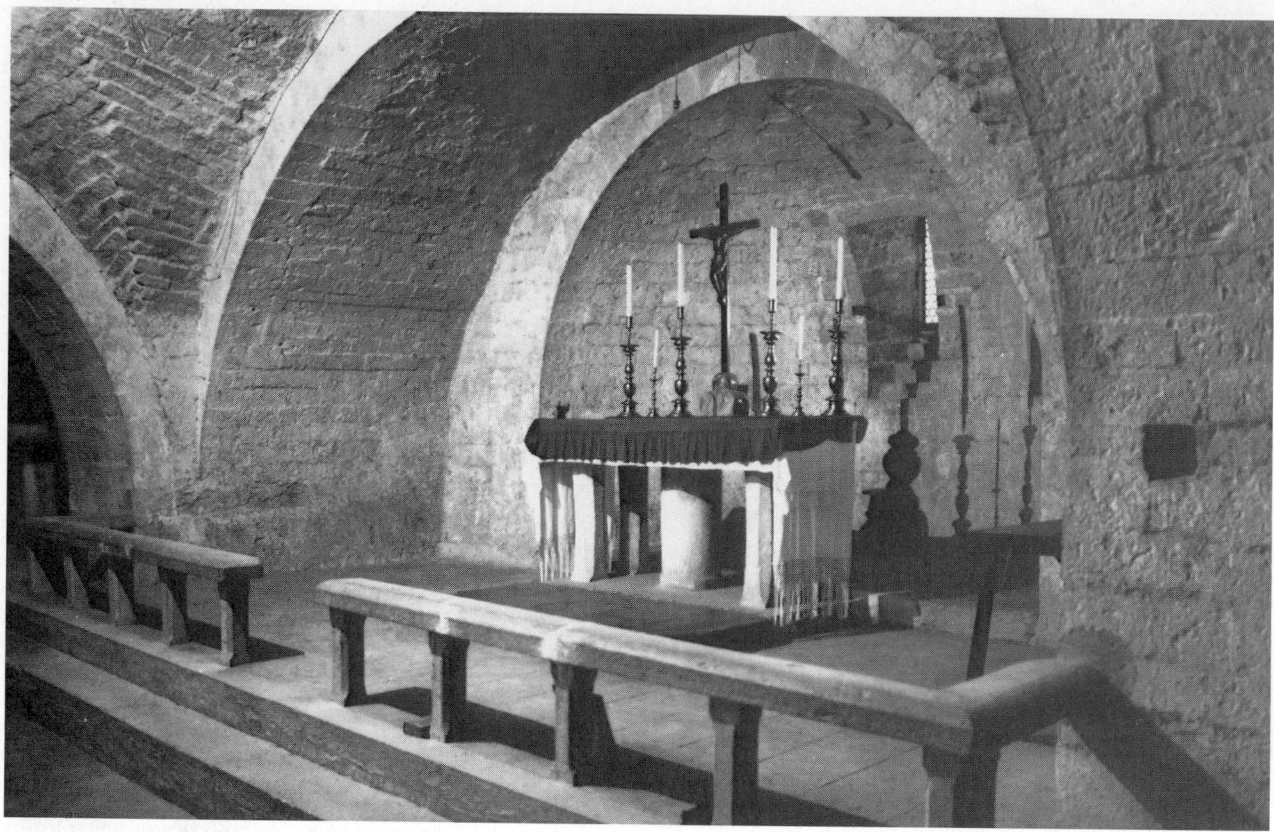

Altar inside the Monastery of Fonte Avellana, Italy.

deliberations with his cathedral chapter and a junta of bishops on the question of filling ecclesiastical vacancies. The consensus was that patronage had ended with independence, and that until Mexico received a new concession from the Holy See, the bishops had the power to appoint. In April of 1822 the Ministry of Justice and Ecclesiastical Affairs rejected this contention, but by this time the Spanish government had repudiated the Treaty of Córdoba and Fonte was ready to depart.

Bibliography: J. TRINIDAD BASURTO, *El arzobispado de México* (Mexico City 1901). K. M. SCHMITT, "The Clergy and the Independence of New Spain," *Hispanic American Historical Review* 34 (1954) 289–312.

[K. M. SCHMITT]

FONTE AVELLANA, MONASTERY OF

Camaldolese monastery in the Apennines, Diocese of Cagli-Pergola (former Diocese of Gubbio), central Italy. Tradition ascribes its founding (*c.* 1000) to Ludolf (d. 1047), a disciple of St. ROMUALD. It flourished under St. PETER DAMIAN (d. 1072) and became known for writings on asceticism, liturgy, and canon law (AVELLANA COLLECTIO), as well as for its role in the Gregorian reform. Papal protection was granted in 1076. It was head of an eremitical congregation of 18 monasteries, eight hermitages, and 15 priories (which came under papal protection in 1301) until 1325, when it was made an abbey. After being made commendatory in 1392, it fell into decline (*see* COMMENDATION). In 1569 the congregation was suppressed and attached to that of CAMALDOLI. The monastery was suppressed (1808–14 and 1866–1875) and restored as a hermitage in 1935. The Romanesque chapel and the scriptorium are noteworthy. Many saints lived at Fonte Avellana: DOMINIC LORICATUS, JOHN OF LODI, ALBERTINUS, and some 50 others.

Bibliography: A. PAGNANI, *Storia dei Benedettini Camaldolesi* (Sassoferrato 1949). L. H. COTTINEAU, *Répertoire topobibliographique des abbayes et prieurés,* 2 v. (Mâcon 1935–39) 1:1179–80. R. GAZEAU, *Catholicisme. Hier, aujourd'hui et demain,* ed. G. JACQUEMET (Paris 1947–) 4:1422. S. HILPISCH, *Lexikon für Theologie und Kirche,* ed. J. HOFER and K. RAHNER, 10 v. (2d, new ed. Freiburg 1957–65) 4:197–198. *L'eremitismo in Occidente nei secoli XI e XII* (Milan 1965).

[C. M. ROGGI]

FONTENELLE (SAINT-WANDRILLE), ABBEY OF

Benedictine abbey near Caudebec-en-Caux on the right bank of the Seine River, in the Archdiocese of ROUEN, north France. It was founded in 649 by St. WANDRILLE (d. 668) and his nephew in the forest of Jumièges near the Roman road from Harfleur to Paris. Under the protection of Abp. OUEN OF ROUEN and Queen BATHILDIS, it grew to 300 monks in 80 years. Its abbots include Ansebert (678–696); Hugh (723–732), the pluralist nephew of Charles Martel (bishop of Rouen, Paris, and Bayeux, and abbot of Fontenelle and JUMIÈGES); and ANSEGIS (823–833), the compiler of Carolingian capitularies. St. WULFRAM OF SENS (d. 697) evangelized Frisia from Fontenelle, the shrine of his relics was a pilgrimage center (1008 to the 16th century). Revived by Gerwold (787–811) after a brief decline, Fontenelle became known for its hagiographies and for the *Gesta abbatum Fontanellensium* (written 834–845, in *Monumenta Germaniae Historica: Scriptores*, 11:270–304). The monks fled the Northmen (852) but returned (960) under Mainardus, a monk of Saint-Bavon in Ghent, to flourish under good abbots; there were 77 monks in 1340. The abbey was placed in COMMENDATION (1546), was pillaged by Huguenots (1562), joined the MAURISTS (1636), and was rebuilt. In 1791 it was suppressed, sold, and partly destroyed, but it was restored in 1894 by the archbishop of Rouen with monks from LIGUGÉ. French law caused the monks to withdraw to Belgium (1901–23) and to Réray (1923–31) before they returned in 1931. Abbot Joseph Pothier (1898–1923) and Lucien David were important revivers of GREGORIAN CHANT (*see* SOLESMES). Fontenelle founded FÉCAMP (659), MONT-SAINT-MICHEL (965), Préaux (1034), Grestain (1036), Saint-Benoît-du-Lac in Quebec, Canada (1912), and several priories (7th–18th century).

Bibliography: *Gesta sanctorum patrum Fontanellensis coenobii (Gesta abbatum Fontanellensium)*, ed. F. LOHIER and J. LAPORTE (Rouen-Paris 1936). C. F. TOUSTAIN and R. P. TASSIN, *Histoire de l'Abbaye de Saint-Wandrille, 1604–1734,* ed. J. LAPORTE (St. Wandrille 1936). F. LOT, *Études critiques sur l'Abbaye de Saint-Wandrille* (Paris 1913). L. H. COTTINEAU, *Répertoire topo-bibliographique des abbayes et prieurés*, 2 v. (Mâcon 1935–39) 2:2921–24. O. L. KAPSNER, *A Benedictine Bibliography: An Author-Subject Union List,* 2 v. (2d ed. Collegeville, Minn. 1962) 2:270–271.

[J. LAPORTE]

FONTEVRAULT, CONVENT OF

Former French double monastery, about 11 miles southeast of Saumur, Maine-et-Loire, France. It was established, probably in 1101, in what was at the time a remote area, by ROBERT OF ARBRISSEL, a renowned preacher and hermit who had inspired many of both sexes to recognize their vocation to the monastic life. The new house attracted special attention when it revived a type of institution not uncommon in western Europe during the early Middle Ages but now little known; it was one of the famous medieval Double MONASTERIES, having communities of men and women living separate existences within a single precinct, both under the single rule of an abbess. The nuns were always the major element there and lived under the BENEDICTINE RULE with observances that demanded an austere and strictly enclosed life. The male community included both clergy and laity and, for a while at least, lived under the Rule of St. AUGUSTINE.

From its earliest days Fontevrault won the highest reputation, and the size of its community increased: in 1248 the abbey claimed to have a total population of 700 and in 1297 was said to have 360 nuns. It was greatly venerated by King HENRY II of England, who was a generous benefactor to the house, and by his son, King Richard I, who believed he owed his release from captivity to the prayers of its nuns. Both kings were buried at Fontevrault, where their tombs may still be seen along with those of Henry's wife, Eleanor of Aquitaine, his daughter Joan of Sicily, and his daughter-in-law, Isobel of Angoulême. In 1173 the abbey was exempted from episcopal visitation. Fontevrault gradually developed into a religious order that included houses in France and Spain, as well as five in England. In the mid-13th century, JACQUES DE VITRY warmly praised the life of this order.

The abbesses of Fontevrault were not infrequently of high birth, including in their number various members of the royal houses of France. In the 15th century the 26th abbess, Mary of Brittany, found the order in great decay and put forward vigorous new statutes, which under her immediate successors were widely adopted within the order, whose numbers were now much reduced. Later on the situation improved. When the order was suppressed in 1790, it had 59 monasteries. In 1824 there began an attempt to revive the order, and houses were established at Chemillé, Brioude, and Boulaur, but none of these now remain.

After being used as a prison since 1804, the considerable remains of the Abbey of Fontevrault have recently been taken over as an ancient monument. The imposing, Romanesque conventual church, dedicated in 1119, is largely intact, as are the adjoining cloister, chapter house, and refectory (for the most part of 16th century date). A remarkable feature is the huge, 12th-century octagonal kitchen.

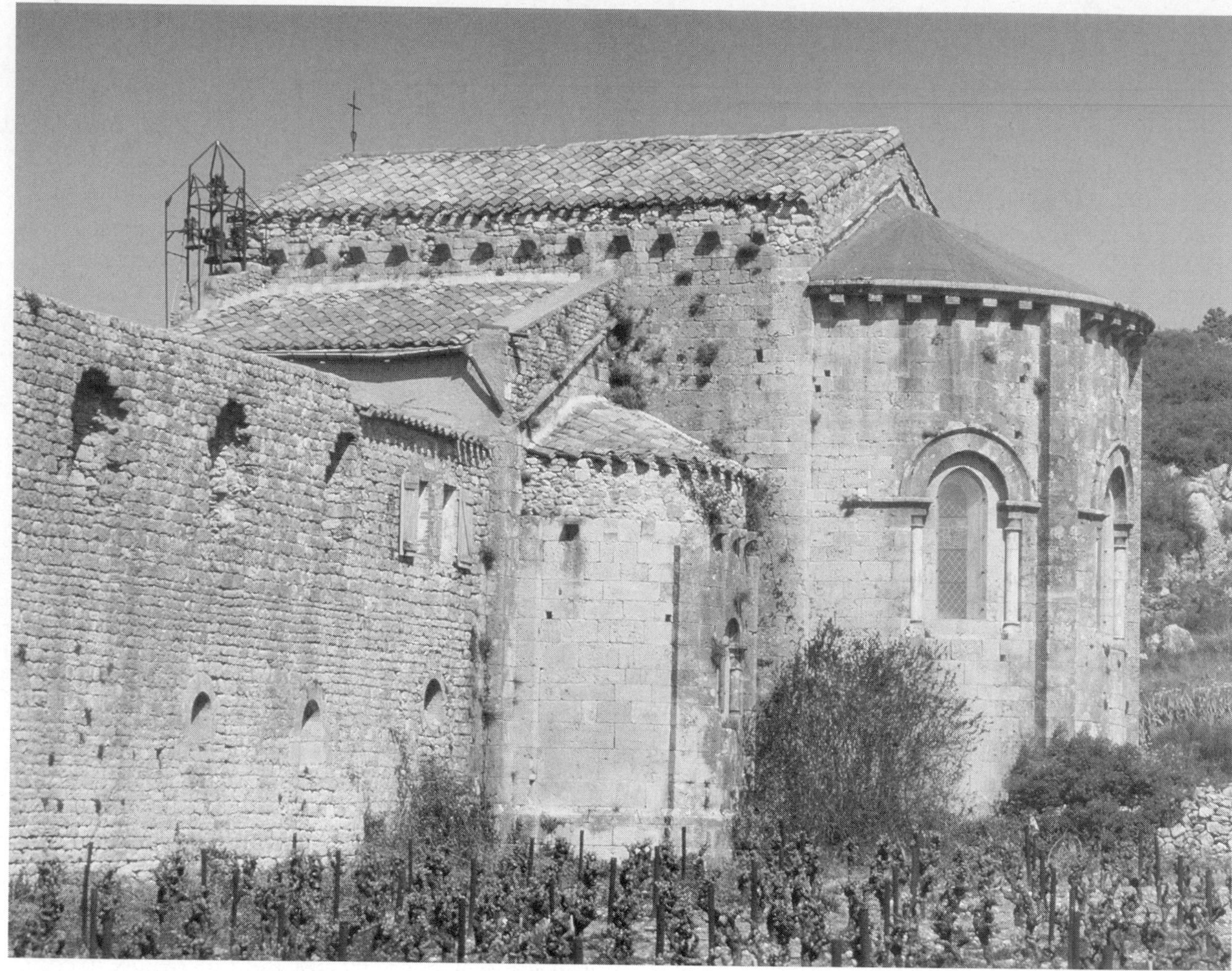

Abbey of Fontfroide, near Beziers, France. (©Michael Busselle/CORBIS)

Bibliography: H. NICQUET, *Histoire de l'ordre de Font-Evraud* (Paris 1642). *Congrès archéologique de France* 77 (1911) 48–64, for architecture. *Histoire de l'ordre de Fontevrault (1100–1908)*, by the religious of Sainte-Marie-de-Fontevrault, 3 v. (Auch 1911–15). L. H. COTTINEAU, *Répertoire topobibliographique des abbayes et prieurés*, 2 v. (Mâcon 1935–39) 1:1185–88, for bibliography. R. NIDERST, *Robert d'Arbrissel et les origines de l'ordre de Fontevrault* (Rodez 1952).

[J. C. DICKINSON]

FONTFROIDE, ABBEY OF

Former French abbey, first Benedictine, later Cistercian, in the Diocese of Narbonne, the present-day Diocese of Carcassonne. Fontfroide was founded by BENEDICTINES in 1093, but was acquired by the Abbey of Grandselve in 1142, both houses becoming affiliated with CLAIRVAUX in 1145. From this date the community grew rapidly. In 1149, it founded Poblet in Spain, and in 1242, Valbonne in the French Pyrenees. The CISTERCIANS of Fontfroide played an important role in the fight against the ALBIGENSES. The martyred PETER OF CASTELNAU (d. 1208) was a member of the community. The famous abbot of Fontfroide, Jacques Fournier, became BENEDICT XII (1334–42). After the mid-15th century Fontfroide was under commendatory abbots and subsequently lost much of its wealth and membership. In 1768 it had ten professed monks and an annual revenue of 14,000 *livres.* In 1783 the abbot's portion of the monastic income was granted to the Diocese of Perpignan. Fontfroide was suppressed during the French Revolution in 1791, but was reoccupied by the Cistercians of Sénanque in 1858. The community was ousted again by the French government in 1901. In 1919 the returning monks were resettled in the former Benedictine abbey of Saint-Michel de Cuxa, Fontfroide having been sold. The surviving church of Fontfroide was constructed in the late 12th century and is a fine example of early Cistercian Gothic.

Bibliography: É. CAPELLE, *L'Abbaye de Fontfroide* (Paris 1903). C. BOYER, *Abbaye de Fontfroide* (Carcassonne 1932). U. CHEVALIER, *Répertoire des sources historiques du moyen-âge. Topobibliographie,* 2 v. (Paris 1894–1903) 1:1142. L. H. COTTINEAU, *Répertoire topobibliographique des abbayes et prieurés,* 2 v. (Mâcon 1935–39) 1:1188–89. M. B. BRARD, *Catholicisme. Hier, aujourd'hui et demain,* ed. G. JACQUEMET (Paris 1947–) 4:1429–30.

[L. J. LEKAI]

FOOLHARDINESS

A vice opposed to the virtue of fortitude by way of excess. Fortitude, or courage, moderates the passions or emotions of fear and daring; it is concerned with threatening evils that are difficult either to endure or to overcome. Fortitude has two functions: it strengthens a man to the endurance of an evil or to an attack upon it, depending upon which of the alternatives is judged reasonable. Foolhardiness is opposed to fortitude by facing danger and attacking when true virtue would choose rather to flee or to endure the evil. Not only does foolhardiness attack unnecessarily and unreasonably, but it is also likely to attack with greater violence than is warranted by the circumstances. Foolhardiness may be caused by presumption, as when one overestimates his own powers to repel evil (cf. *Summa theologiae* 2a2ae, 127.2 ad 1); by anger, which can lead to an attempt to repel an aggressor with unnecessary violence or to punish him; or by vainglory, for an attack against evil may come from an unreasonable desire to assert one's own will and gain esteem. It can arise from a contempt for life or for other goods that are risked, or from other causes.

Foolhardiness—like the other offenses against fortitude—is sinful, but its gravity depends on its causes and its effects. If temerity or foolhardiness leads one to put some great good in serious jeopardy or inflict grave harm unnecessarily, the sin is a grave one.

Bibliography: THOMAS AQUINAS, *Summa theologiae* 2a2ae, q. 127.

[J. HENNESSEY]

FORBES, ALEXANDER PENROSE

Episcopalian bishop, leader of the OXFORD MOVEMENT in Scotland; b. Edinburgh, June 6, 1817; d. Dundee, Oct. 8, 1875. He was educated at Edinburgh and at Haileybury College, England, before going to Madras, India, in the East India Company's service. From 1840 to 1844 he attended Oxford University, where he came under the influence of Edward B. PUSEY and other Tractarians. After a brief ministry, he was consecrated bishop of Brechin in the Episcopal Church (1847). As a result of his primary charge (1857) dealing with the eucharistic presence and sacrifice, he was tried in 1860 by his fellow bishops, censured, and admonished. His main theological work, inspired by Pusey and written with his assistance, was *An Explanation of the Thirty-nine Articles of the Church of England* (1867–68), an Anglo-Catholic interpretation of the THIRTY-NINE ARTICLES. Forbes hoped for a better understanding between ANGLICANISM and other churches, especially the Roman Catholic, and in pursuit of this goal corresponded with Father V. de Buck, SJ, the Bollandist, and with DÖLLINGER. He was coeditor with his brother, Rev. George Hay Forbes, of the *Arbuthnott Missal,* (1864), and he wrote *Kalendars of Scottish Saints* (1872).

Bibliography: W. PERRY, *Alexander Penrose Forbes* (London 1939).

[J. QUINN]

FORBES, JOHN

A notable Capuchin Friar Minor of the Belgian Province; b. Aberdeenshire, *c.* 1570; d. Termonde, Flanders, Aug. 4, 1606. He was the second son of John, 8th Lord Forbes, by his first wife, Margaret Gordon, daughter of the 4th Earl of Huntly, leader of the Scottish Catholics at the time of the Reformation. His father, resolutely anti–Catholic, divorced his Catholic wife, and reared John as a Protestant. John was converted to Catholicism through the secret care of his mother, elder brother, and uncle, James Gordon, SJ. He evaded a marriage that his father had arranged for him by escaping in disguise to Flanders. There he joined the Capuchins at Tournai (1593), receiving the name Archangel, as had his brother, also a Capuchin, who had died in 1592. Paul V, at the request of prominent Scottish Catholics and of Archangel's father, sanctioned (1596) the friar's return to Scotland for the purpose of settling an age–long family feud and assisting the Catholic cause. Archangel, however, pursued his studies at Lille and was ordained. He held important offices among the Belgian Capuchins and won many converts. He died as a result of ministering to the plague–stricken. He is recognized as the *de jure* 9th Lord Forbes.

Bibliography: FATHER CUTHBERT, *The Capuchins,* 2 v. (London 1928). A. and H. TAYLER, eds., *The House of Forbes* (Aberdeen 1937). *Lexicon Capuccinum* (Rome 1951) 121.

[C. REEL]

Charles de Forbin-Janson.

FORBIN-JANSON, CHARLES DE

Bishop, founder of the Holy Childhood Association; b. Paris, Nov. 3, 1785; d. Aygalades, his family's castle near Marseilles, July 11, 1844. After being appointed auditor of the Council of State by Napoleon I (1805), he joined the CONGRÉGATION, and perhaps the KNIGHTS OF THE FAITH. He entered the Saint Sulpice seminary (1808), and was ordained (1811). He modified his intention to go to China after consulting Pius VII, who urged him to help re-Christianize France after the FRENCH REVOLUTION. Together with Abbé Jean Bauzan he founded the Missionnaires de France, later known as Fathers of MERCY, and served with them until 1823, except in 1817 when he was sent on a mission to Syria. Consecrated bishop of Nancy (1824), he was zealous in preaching but neglected diocesan administration and alienated his clergy. As an opponent of GALLICANISM he refused to sign the Gallican DECLARATION OF THE FRENCH CLERGY. When the revolution of 1830 unseated King Charles X, Forbin-Janson, an ardent monarchist, fled France, leaving to a coadjutor the administration of his diocese. At the request of bishops Benedict FLAGET and John PURCELL, Gregory XVI encouraged him to undertake a missionary tour in the U.S. Between 1839 and 1841 he preached widely and successfully in many cities, including Boston, New York, Philadelphia, Detroit, St. Louis, and New Orleans. At the invitation of the American bishops he attended the Fourth Provincial Council of BALTIMORE (May 1840). During the next two years he preached very frequently in Canada and the U.S. and evangelized the Native Americans. He helped Pauline JARICOT establish the Society for the PROPAGATION OF THE FAITH. In 1843 he founded the Pontifical Association of the Holy Childhood.

Bibliography: F. ROYER, ''Charles de Forbin-Janson, Missionary Bishop,'' *Americas* 10 (1953) 179–196. P. LESOURD, *Un Grand coeur missionnaire, Monseigneur de Forbin-Janson* (Paris 1944). P. GUILDAY, ''Four Early Ecclesiastical Observers in America,'' *Amercian Ecclesiastical Review* 85 (1931) 239–244. J. LEFLON, *Catholicisme. Hier, aujourd'hui et demain,* ed. G. JACQUEMET (Paris 1947–) 4:1442–43.

[E. G. DROUIN]

FORCE AND FEAR (CANON LAW)

Canon law adopted definitions of force and fear from Roman law. Force is pressure from a greater thing that cannot be resisted—*Vis autem est maioris rei impetus, qui repelli non potest* (*Corpus iuris civilis, Digesta* 4.2.2). Fear is trepidation of mind, caused by an immediate or future danger—*Metus est instantis vel futuri periculi causa mentis trepidatio* (*Corpus iuris civilis, Digesta* 4.2.1). Force results in the mere physical propulsion of the victim, who gives no voluntary response. Such force is called physical, absolute, or passive force. If a force is not overpowering, it may still cause fear in the victim. Fear, as St. Thomas Aquinas observed, may result in a voluntary act that would not have been performed if a harm or evil had not been inflicted or threatened (*Summa theologiae* 1a2ae, 6.6). This is moral, conditioned, conditional, causative, or active force and is more frequently simply called fear.

Types of fear. Fear is slight if it is caused by a harm or evil that is inconsequential. Fear is reverential if it is the trepidation normally found in the child-parent relationship and is, of its nature, slight. Fear is qualified-reverential if the trepidation inherent in the child-parent relationship is augmented by insistencies, harassments, or similar factors; in that case it becomes grave. Fear is grave in an absolute sense if it is serious enough to sway a resolute person; in a true though relative sense, it is grave if it is sufficient to sway a given person because of this person's age, temperament, or other qualities.

Fear is extrinsic if caused by a free agent distinct from the victim; intrinsic, if it arises from the subject's own being (e.g., conscience) or the force of nature. Fear is induced directly if the agent intends a certain act to be performed by the victim or indirectly if such an act is not intended by the agent. Fear is justly induced if (1) the victim deserves the harm or evil inflicted or threatened; (2) the agent has the right to inflict or threaten the harm or evil; and (3) the threats are made or the harm inflicted in a way provided by law. Fear is unjustly induced if (1) the victim does not deserve the harm or evil inflicted or threatened; (2) the agent does not have the right or authority to inflict or threaten the harm or evil; or (3) legal procedures are violated.

Principles and application. All acts that are the result of physical force are invalid (*Codex iuris canonici* c. 125 §1; *Codex canonum ecclesiarium orientalium* c. 932 §1). Acts that are the result of fear, though it be grave and unjust, are not invalid unless this is provided in the law, but such acts are subject to nullification by judicial sentence (*Codex iuris canonici* c. 125 §2; *Codex canonum ecclesiarium orientalium* c. 932 §2). The canons on fear are designed to protect human freedom, to curtail injury and injustice, and to preclude the unhappy effects that result from coerced actions.

Renunciation of an Office or Benefice. Resignation from an ecclesiastical office is null and void if it is caused by grave, unjustly inflicted fear (*Codex iuris canonici* c. 188; *Codex canonum ecclesiarium orientalium* c. 968). The gravity may be absolute or relative, the injustice substantial or in manner.

Holy Orders. No one ever has the right to force a man to receive orders (*Codex iuris canonici* c. 1026). Physical violence invalidates the Sacrament of Holy Orders (*Codex iuris canonici* c.125 §1; *Codex canonum ecclesiarium orientalium* c. 932 §1).

Religious. Entry into the novitiate is invalidated by physical force or grave fear brought to bear either upon a candidate or a superior receiving a candidate (*Codex iuris canonici* c. 643 §1, 4°; *Codex canonum ecclesiarium orientalium* cc. 450, 5° and 517 §1). The same canonical provisions obtain for religious profession as for entry into the novitiate (*Codex iuris canonici* cc. 656, 4° and 658; *Codex canonum ecclesiarium orientalium* cc. 464, 3°; 527, 3°; and 532).

Marriage. Marriage is invalid if entered into through force or grave fear from without so that the victim, in order to free himself, is forced to choose marriage (*Codex iuris canonici* c. 1103; *Codex canonum ecclesiarium orientalium* c. 825).

Vows and Oaths. The law nullifies any vow made as the result of grave, unjust fear (*Codex iuris canonici* c. 1191 §3; *Codex canonum ecclesiarium orientalium* c. 889 §3). In the Latin Church, the law also nullifies an oath extorted by force or grave fear (*Codex iuris canonici* c. 1200 §2).

Crimes. Under Latin discipline, physical force completely eliminates delictual imputability. In laws of purely ecclesiastical origin, grave fear generally eliminates delictual imputability; however, if an act is intrinsically evil or tends to the harm of souls, grave fear lessens but does not exclude imputability (*Codex iuris canonici* cc. 1323, 1324).

Bibliography: T. L. BOUSCAREN and J. I. O'CONNOR, comps., *Canon Law Digest* (Milwaukee 1934–). J. V. BROWN, *The Invalidating Effects of Force, Fear and Fraud upon the Canonical Novitiate* (Catholic University of America Canon Law Studies 311; 1951). J. G. CHATHAM, *Force and Fear as Invalidating Marriage: The Element of Injustice* (Catholic University of America Canon Law Studies 310; 1950); ''Force and Fear Invalidating Marriage: Rota Decisions, 1940–1946,'' *Jurist* 18 (1958) 39–78. D. LAZZARATO, *Iurisprudentia pontifica de metu, cc. 214 et 1087* (Vatican City 1956). L. MAFFEO, *I vizi della volontà nell'ordine sacro* (Turin 1960). A. MCCOY, *Force and Fear in Relation to Delictual Imputability and Penal Resonsibility* (Catholic University of America Canon Law Studies 200; 1944). L. BENDER, ''Metus indirecte incussus et validitas matrimonii,'' *Ephemerides iuris canonici* 13 (1957) 9–18.

[J. G. CHATHAM]

FORCE AND MORAL RESPONSIBILITY

Moral responsibility presupposes that a human act is voluntary. A voluntary act, whether of commission or omission, is one in which the cause or moving principle is within the agent, and one which the agent performs consciously and with awareness of the relevant moral circumstances. A person is therefore morally responsible when he knows what he is doing and is free in the sense that, at least interiorly, he is able to act or not to act.

When something is done through physical force or violence, the source or principle of the act is external to the agent. However, not every action that has its source in an external principle is necessarily to be attributed simply to force. In addition, the will, the intrinsic principle from which human and moral action proceeds, must not concur in what is done. Hence, for an action to be violent or forced, and therefore in no sense morally attributable to an agent, not only must its cause be external, but the agent's will must contribute nothing—indeed, must be opposed to—what is done. A clear instance of such an action would be the case of a man who is pushed and in falling accidentally strikes and injures another. Such an action is not voluntary and involves no moral responsibility.

Force, being physical in nature, cannot directly affect an act of the will itself, which is immaterial in nature. Acts issuing directly from the will itself are interior and are called *elicited* acts; other acts are under the control of the will, yet are performed by other powers, e.g., the members of the body. These are called *commanded* acts of the will. Acts elicited by the will are always voluntary. Even God, in moving the will, cannot force its act, for its forced act would be a contradiction, at once voluntary and involuntary.

Acts commanded by the will, however, are subject to physical force. It is with regard to these that the question of responsibility may arise when something is done under force. Clearly, if there is no reasonable way open to resist physical aggression, no responsibility is incurred in passive acquiescence in the action. If the action in question is morally evil, the will in its interior, elicited act should not concur. Whether or not external resistance is to be attempted depends upon particular circumstances and judgment of prudence as to whether resistance would serve any useful purpose.

Actions done because of physical force should be distinguished from actions done out of fear [*see* FEAR (MORAL ASPECT)] or because of compulsion in the psychological meaning of the term.

Bibliography: THOMAS AQUINAS, *Summa theologiae* 1a2ae, 6.4–5. B. H. MERKELBACH, *Summa theologiae moralis*, 3 v. (3d ed. Paris 1938) 1:72–75.

[J. A. OESTERLE]

FORCELLINI, EGIDIO

Priest and lexicographer; b. Campo sul Piave, Belluno, Italy, Aug. 26, 1688; d. there, April 5, 1768. He was educated at the Padua seminary, which he entered in 1704. He spent seven years (1724–31) as director of the seminary at Ceneda, near Treviso, and the last three years of his life in retirement in his native town. Otherwise, the Padua seminary was his home from boyhood and its library the focus of his work. He first collaborated with Jacopo Facciolati on a number of projects in Greek, Latin, and Italian grammar and lexicography, especially on a new edition (1718) of the then-standard Latin dictionary of Calepinus (first published 1502).

The deficiencies of the ''Calepinus'' led to the planning of a thoroughly new work, which was to be marked by breadth of coverage, with gleanings from rare authors, coins, and inscriptions, close attention to orthography and arrangement of meanings, and generous provision of illustrative examples. This work, the *Totius latinitatis lexicon,* Forcellini completed after about 40 years of prodigious toil, but he never saw it in print.

The first edition, dated 1771 (four folio volumes from the Padua seminary press), was followed by five other Italian editions and a number of transalpine and American reprints and adaptations. The best edition is that edited by F. Corradini and G. Perin (Padua 1864–1920; reprinted, with some additional material in the appendixes, Padua 1940). Until the *Thesaurus linguae latinae* (1900–) was completed, the Forcellini dictionary stood as the fundamental monument of Latin lexicography.

Bibliography: J. E. SANDYS, *History of Classical Scholarship* (New York 1958) 2:374–377; 3:243. A. ZARDO, *Enciclopedia Italiana di scienzi, littere, ed arti* (Rome 1929–39) 15:662. G. BELLINI, *Storia della tipografia del seminario di Padova, 1684–1938* (2d ed. Padua 1939) 219–221; 255–267; 352–354; *Le cinque edizioni padovane del Lexicon totius latinitatis* (Padua 1942). S. SERENA, *S. Gregorio Barbarigo e la vita spirituale e culturale nel suo seminario di Padova,* 2 v. (Padua 1963). M. E. COSENZA, *Biographical and Bibliographical Dictionary of the Italian Humanists and of the World of Classical Scholarship in Italy, 1300–1800* (Boston 1962) 2:1453–55; 5:729. Prefaces of earlier eds. of the Forcellini *Lexicon* repr. in 1864–1920 ed., l:xvii–xlviii.

[B. M. PEEBLES]

FORD, FRANCIS XAVIER

Bishop, missionary; b. Brooklyn, N.Y., Jan. 11, 1892; d. Canton, China, Feb. 21, 1952. He was the son of Austin B. Ford, publisher of the *Irish World,* the New York *Freeman's Journal,* and the *Monitor.* His mother, Elizabeth (Rellihan) Ford, was a teacher and newspaper woman. Ford attended St. Francis Preparatory School, Brooklyn, and Cathedral College, New York City, where he became interested in the newly founded Catholic Foreign Mission Society. In 1912 he became the first seminarian to enter the society's headquarters at Hawthorne, N.Y. He was ordained in 1917, and was one of the first four Maryknoll Missioners to leave for the Orient the next year. As superior of the Maryknoll mission in Yeoungkong, South China, he opened the first Maryknoll seminary for Chinese students in 1921 and the following year welcomed the first group of Maryknoll Sisters. In 1925 he became prefect apostolic of a new mission among the Hakkas in northern Kwangtung (Meihsien), with Kaying as its center. This prefecture became the vicariate apostolic of the same area in 1935 (a diocese in 1946), and Ford was named titular bishop of Etenne. He was consecrated by Maryknoll's cofounder, Bp. James A. Walsh, on Sept. 21, 1935. Ford remained in South China during World War II, directing limited mission work and caring for refugees from the coastal areas occupied by the Japanese. Five years later, with the arrival of the Communists from the North, he became the object of a systematic campaign of molestation and abuse. Arrested in December 1950 on charges of ''anti-Communist, counterrevolutionary, and espionage activities,'' he was transferred to prison in Canton in April 1951. During the 200-

mile trip he was subjected to public display and Communist ridicule at every stop. Subsequent interrogations and the rigors of Communist jail ended in his death, which was not revealed until Aug. 16, 1952.

Bibliography: F. X. FORD, *Come, Holy Spirit: Thoughts on Renewing the Earth as the Kingdom of God* (New York 1976). R. A. LANE, ed., *Stone in the King's Highway: Selections from the Writings of Bishop Francis X. Ford* (New York 1953). J. DONOVAN, *The Pagoda and the Cross: The Life of Bishop Ford of Maryknoll* (New York 1967). R. SHERIDAN, *Compassion: The Spirit of Francis X. Ford, M.M.* (New York 1982). M. (CHAI) TSAI, "Bishop Ford, Apostle of South China," *American Ecclesiastical Review* 127 (Oct. 1952) 241–47.

[W. J. COLEMAN]

FORD, THOMAS, BL.

Priest, martyr; b. Devonshire, England; d. hanged, drawn, and quartered at Tyburn (London), May 28, 1582. After receiving his master's degree from Trinity College, Oxford, Ford was a fellow for about three years. Having entered the English College, Douai in 1570, Ford became one of the first three of its students to be ordained (March 1573 at Brussels). He continued his studies until his return to England, May 2, 1576. There he was chaplain to Edward Yate and his Bridgettine guests at Lyford, Berkshire. Ford was arrested with St. Edmund CAMPION (July 17, 1581) and committed to the Tower (July 22), where he was submitted to torture three times. He and Bl. John SHERT stood trial together on an absurd charge of conspiracy at Rome and Rheims—where he had never been, and on dates when he was in England. Both were condemned November 21 and were executed with Bl. Robert JOHNSON. All three were beatified by Pope Leo XIII.

Feast of the English Martyrs: May 4 (England).

See Also: ENGLAND, SCOTLAND, AND WALES, MARTYRS OF.

Bibliography: R. CHALLONER, *Memoirs of Missionary Priests,* ed. J. H. POLLEN (rev. ed. London 1924; repr. Farnborough 1969). J. H. POLLEN, *Acts of English Martyrs* (London 1891).

[K. I. RABENSTEIN]

FOREIRO, FRANCISCO

Portuguese Dominican theologian and Scripture scholar who played a prominent role in the Council of Trent; b. *c.* 1510; d. Lisbon, Jan. 10, 1581. His academic achievements in Greek and Hebrew attracted King John III of Portugal, who sent him with Francisco de VITORIA to pursue his studies at Paris. Upon his return, Foreiro won fame as a theologian and preacher. He was eventually the King's personal theologian. King Sebastian retained Foreiro in this post and in 1561 sent him to the Council of Trent. Foreiro's preaching was so acclaimed there that he was appointed to preach every Wednesday of Lent. The first secretary of the INDEX OF FORBIDDEN BOOKS, he also served on the commission for the reform of the Breviary and Missal and helped to compose the Roman Catechism. In 1568 he was elected provincial of Portugal and, when freed from this office, devoted his waning years to study. He wrote commentaries on all the Prophets and on Job as well as meditations on the Gospels and a Hebrew lexicon.

Egidio Forcellini.

Bibliography: E. FILTHAUT, *Lexikon für Theologie und Kirche* (Freiburg 1957–65), 4:201.

[A. SMITH]

FOREST, JOHN, BL.

Franciscan priest, martyr; b. Oxford, England, 1471; d. hanged at Smithfield (London), May 22, 1538. At age 20, Forest was accepted into the Observant Franciscans at Greenwich. He studied theology at Oxford and may have earned a doctorate. He is known as the confessor to Queen Catherine of Aragon, and appears to have been provincial in 1525, when he threatened to excommunicate the brethren who opposed Cardinal Wolsey's legatine powers. The Observants as a whole and Fr. Forest in particular attracted Henry VIII's displeasure by opposing his divorce, although there was an attempted reconciliation in February 1533. Nevertheless, he was imprisoned at Newgate before Fr. William Peyto gave his famous sermon in front of the king at Greenwich (1534). In his confinement Fr. Forest corresponded with the queen and Bl. Thomas ABELL and wrote a book or treatise against King Henry. When Forest refused to make an act of abjuration before Cranmer at Lambeth (April 8, 1538), he was sentenced to death by hanging and his remains burned. The statue of "Darvell Gatheren," which had been brought from the church of Llanderfel in Wales, was thrown on the pile of firewood; thus fulfilling the popularly believed prophecy that this holy image would set a forest on fire. He was beatified by Pope Leo XIII on Dec. 9, 1886.

Feast: May 22 (Franciscans). Feast of the English Martyrs: May 4 (England).

See Also: ENGLAND, SCOTLAND, AND WALES, MARTYRS OF.

Bibliography: R. CHALLONER, *Memoirs of Missionary Priests,* ed. J. H. POLLEN (rev. ed. London 1924; repr. Farnborough 1969). J. H. POLLEN, *Acts of English Martyrs* (London 1891). J. THADDEUS, *Life of Bl. John Forest* (London 1888); *The Franciscans in England 1600–1859,* 15 v. (London 1898).

[K. I. RABENSTEIN]

FORGIVENESS OF SINS

In Catholic teaching SIN is an offense against God resulting in a state or condition of GUILT, in which the sinner is estranged from God, deprived of His grace and friendship, and under a juridical necessity of paying the debt of punishment incurred by his transgression. By the forgiveness of his sin the sinner is reconciled to God and restored to divine favor, and his liability to punishment is remitted. Since it is God who is offended in sin, the forgiveness of it must always come from Him, at least mediately. That God is willing and ready to exercise His divine prerogative of forgiveness with regard to all sinners who are disposed to pardon is clear in both Old and New Testaments (Is 43.25; 44.22; Ez 18.21–23; Mt 6.14; Lk 6.37; Jas 5.15, etc.). Forgiveness is offered and received in Christ (Jn 1.29; Rom 4.27; 1 Cor 15.3; Gal 1.4; 1 Pt 2.25; 3.18). Christ Himself claimed the authority to forgive sins (Mk 2.1–12; Mt 9.2–8; Lk 5.17–26), and He delegated it to his Apostles to be exercised by themselves and their legitimate successors in the Sacrament of PENANCE [H. Denzinger, *Enchiridion symbolorum,* ed. A. Schönmetzer (32d ed. Freiburg 1963) 1667–93]. Forgiveness of sin may be obtained also apart from the Sacrament through perfect CONTRITION, which includes at least an implicit desire to receive the Sacrament. Contrition or sorrow for sin is a universally necessary condition of pardon. The sorrow for sin required for forgiveness must involve an element of divine love, for it is impossible that a soul should be received to grace and put in right relationship to God if it is not prepared to love God. Moreover, this readiness to love God cannot conceivably exist without the repentant sinner being prepared also to love other children of the same heavenly Father (2 Jn 4.20–21). In the Christian way of life, therefore, an individual's willingness to forgive injuries done to himself is a ready test, easy to apply, of the sufficiency of his own dispositions to receive pardon (Mt 6.14–15; 18.21–35; Mk 11.25–26).

[T. A. PORTER]

FORGIVENESS OF SINS (IN THE BIBLE)

Sin, in the Bible, is a personal offense and a revolt against God. It makes man impure and excludes him from religious worship. By it the personal bond of the covenant is broken, so that man separates himself from God and provokes His wrath. *See* SIN (IN THE BIBLE). To reestablish this personal relationship and appease God's wrath, man offers God gifts and sacrifices and seeks forgiveness by the intercession of God's favored ones, by true repentance, and by interior submission to God.

In the Old Testament. Many Hebrew words are used to express forgiveness: *sālaḥ,* "to forgive" [always with God as subject (1 Kgs 8.30, 39; Is 55.7; Dt 29.19)]; *nāśā',* "to take away" [Ps 31(32).5]; *kipper* "to cover, make atonement for" (if man is subject, Ex 32.30), or, "to forgive" [if God is subject, Ps 64(65).4]; various forms of the root *ksy,* "to cover" [Ps 31(32).1; 84(85).3]; and *māḥâ,* "to wipe out" [Is 43.25; Ps 50(51).3]. So also, sins are said to be blotted out, purged away, covered, remembered no more, cleansed, and washed. And it is God Himself who cleanses, washes, and, in fact, "creates" anew.

One way to win someone's forgiveness is to present a gift (Gn 32.21). Sacrifices, too, appease Yahweh. After the census that was considered to be a crime, David offered holocausts and PEACE OFFERINGS (2 Sm 24.25). *See* CENSUS (IN THE BIBLE). The SIN OFFERING, prominent in postexilic times, atoned for a sin committed in ignorance (Lv 4.1–5.13). Yet in an early and primitive conception, no sacrifice could atone for deliberate sins (Nm 15.30–31). To expiate the sin of withholding dues from

God or man the guilt offering or sacrifice of reparation was offered (Lv 5.14–26; 7.1–7; Nm 5.5–8). Annually on the Day of ATONEMENT (Yom Kippur) the covenanted people confessed their sins and atoned for them by expiatory sacrifices. The high priest sprinkled the blood of the animals on the covering of the ARK OF THE COVENANT, because for the Israelites the blood was the seat of life, through which one made atonement [Lv 16.14–16; 17.11; *see* BLOOD, RELIGIOUS SIGNIFICANCE OF (IN THE BIBLE)].

Also through the intercession of His favored ones, e.g., Moses, God forgave His people (Ex 32.32–34). The intercession of the Servant of Yahweh (Is 52.13–53.12) went beyond that of Moses. The Servant's giving up His life as ''an offering for sin'' (Is 53.10; *see* SUFFERING SERVANT, SONGS OF) recalled the ritual of Leviticus ch. 16. Yahweh forgave directly, too. For example, David was absolved of the sentence of death after his humble acknowledgment of guilt (2 Sm 12.13), although he and his family were to be punished severely. The prophetic doctrine (Hos 14.2–7; Is 1.18–20; Jer 3.22–23) called for repentance, conversion, and return to the covenant of God in order to obtain forgiveness. Certain Psalmists extolled contrition as a means to forgiveness: ''Should I offer a holocaust, you would not accept it. My sacrifice, O God, is a contrite spirit; a heart contrite and humbled, O God, you will not spurn'' [Ps 50(51).18–19; 24(25).7–11, 18; 31(32).1–6; 37(38. 2–9, 18–19; 129(130); 143(144).1–2]. Psalm 102 (103) is a hymn praising God's compassion for contrite sinners.

Just as the Exile was the punishment for rebellion, so the restoration and the new covenant would entail a cleansing from sin, forgiveness, and, positively, a new spirit of fidelity to God [Jer 31.31–34; Ez 36.16–36; Psalm 50(51)]. Pardon for sin was also very much emphasized by the consoling prophet who wrote Deutero-Isaiah (Is 40.1–2; 44.22; 53.4–7, 8d, 10–12).

In the New Testament. With the coming of the Kingdom of God, the messianic redemption, which consisted in pardon for sins through Christ's expiation (Rom 3.21–26), created the new people of God, freed from sin and reconciled with God (Rom 5.1–11).

Forgiveness was proclaimed in the Gospels by Jesus Himself (Mt 9.1–7, 10–13; Lk 7.47–49; 15.1–32; *see also* Mt 6.12; Lk 11.4). The divine prerogative of pardoning sin was transferred to Jesus in His role as Servant of Yahweh (Mt 8.17; Lk 4.18–21; 18.31–34; Acts 2.23; 3.13, 18, 26; 4.27–38; 8.32–35). Like sin, forgiveness had taken on a personal nuance with Ezekiel (Ez 14.12–23; ch. 18; 33.10–20) and was so represented in the parables of Christ (Mt 13.3–9, 18–23; 25.14–46). In the LORD'S PRAYER, divine forgiveness parallels the forgiveness that a man gives to those offending him (Mt 6.12). The Servant of the Lord gave His life as a ransom for the multitude (Mt 20.28); His blood was poured out for the remission of sins (Mt 26.28). After His Resurrection, Jesus declared: ''repentance and remission of sins should be preached in His name to all the nations, beginning from Jerusalem'' (Lk 24.47).

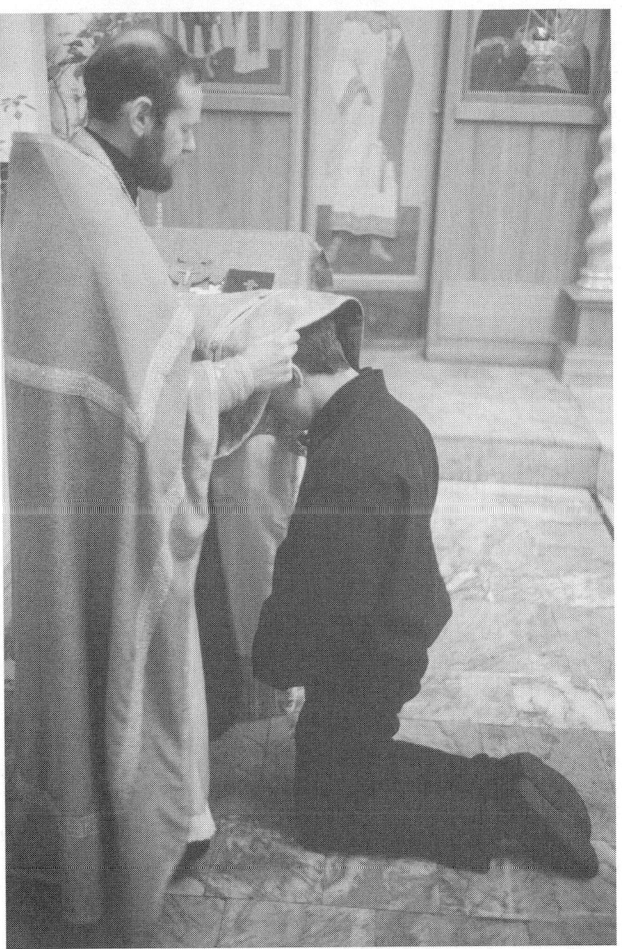

Father Aleksandr Stepanov absolving prisoner at Metalostroy Prison, Saint Petersburg, Russia. (©Steve Raymer/CORBIS)

St. Paul often personified sin and described the sinner as a slave to this archenemy of God. Consequently he considered the pardon of sin as an emancipation. God not only pardons the sinner but transfers him into the resurrected life of Christ through Christ's death (Rom 6.1–11; Gal 2.19–20). A man redeemed by Christ becomes a new creature (2 Cor 5.17; Gal 6.15), a new man (Eph 4.22–24; Col 3.9–10), in contrast with the old man subject to sin. ''He has rescued us from the power of darkness and transferred us into the kingdom of his beloved Son, in whom we have our redemption, the remission of our sins'' (Col 1.13–14). The motivation for this transformation is, simply, God's love (Rom 5.8–9).

Johannine theology speaks of sin in the singular as affecting all mankind. John the Baptist pointed out Jesus as ''the lamb of God, who takes away the sin of the world'' (Jn 1.29). Because He was the light of the world and life itself, Christ could rescue man from darkness and death (Jn 8.12; 9.5, 39; 11.25–26; 12.35–36, 46–50). As a result of His glorification He gave the Spirit to His Apostles that they might forgive sins (Jn 20.23). Toward the end of his life, John the Evangelist repeated that Christ appeared in order to ''take our sins away'' (1 Jn 3.5), that His blood was the source of pardon for sin (1 Jn 1.7), and that He continues to be the advocate and the propitiation for the sins of all men (1 Jn 2.1–2, 12).

So also in the Epistle to the Hebrews Jesus is described as the one who by offering His precious blood purifies Christians from every stain (Heb 9.14), saves man (5.1–10), and creates a way back to God (10.19–20).

See Also: GUILT (IN THE BIBLE); CONVERSION, I (IN THE BIBLE); EXPIATION (IN THE BIBLE); REDEMPTION (IN THE BIBLE); SIN (IN THE BIBLE).

Bibliography: V. TAYLOR, *Forgiveness and Reconciliation* (New York 1960). J. GIBLET, *The God of Israel: The God of the Christians,* tr. K. SULLIVAN (New York 1961) 149–163. C. R. SMITH, *The Bible Doctrine of Sin and the Ways of God with Sinners* (London 1953). *Encyclopedic Dictionary of the Bible,* tr. and adap. by L. HARTMAN (New York 1963), from A. VAN DEN BORN, *Bijbels Woordenboek* 803–808. W. A. QUANBECK, G. A. BUTTRICK, et al., eds., *The Interpreters' Dictionary of the Bible,* 4 v. (Nashville 1962) 2:314–319. T. C. VRIEZEN and K. STENDAHL, *Die Religion in Geschichte und Gegenwart*[3], 7 v. (3d ed. Tübingen 1957–65) 6:507–513.

[J. LACHOWSKI]

FORM

From the Latin *forma,* a term signifying figure or shape or ''that which is seen'' (Gr. εἶδος) and having many derived meanings, such as kind, nature, and species. In early philosophical usage it came to signify the intrinsic determinant of quantity from which figure or shape results, and then to mean the intrinsic determinant of anything that is determinable. Thus the term is employed in such expressions as ''form of contract,'' ''form of worship,'' and ''form of a Sacrament.'' In its stricter philosophical usage, however, it is limited to signifying the intrinsic PRINCIPLE OF EXISTENCE in any determinate essence, a definition that applies to both accidental and substantial form. In a further extended usage, every SPECIES OR NATURE, whether in itself material or existent as immaterial, is called a form, although it may not be strictly a formal principle. In this manner it is not unusual to speak of the angelic form, or even of the form of God, as signifying the nature or essence of the angel, or of God. Hence, form is sometimes used as a synonym for ESSENCE or nature. Similarly, the formal cause, in Aristotelian and scholastic philosophy, is frequently identified with the essence (τὸ τί ἦν εἶναι), as that in virtue of which the essence, even of material and composite entities, is precisely what it is.

This article is concerned primarily with the philosophical significance of the term form and treats this in two parts: the first presents a history of the development of the concept of form; the second, a systematic analysis of the concept from the viewpoint of scholastic philosophy.

History of the Concept of Form

This survey (taken mainly from F. Aveling's earlier one) first enumerates the kinds of form discussed by philosophers; the development of these kinds is then traced through the Greek, medieval, modern, and contemporary periods.

Kinds of Form. The various kinds of form recognized in philosophy include the following. Substantial form, in material entities, is what determines or actuates primary matter to become a specific substantial nature or essence, as the form of hydrogen, of horse, or of man (*see* MATTER AND FORM). It is defined by ARISTOTLE as the first ENTELECHY of a physical body, and it may be such that it is merely the determinant of matter, in which case it is called a corporeal substantial form, or it may exceed, as it were, the potentiality of matter, in which case it is called a spiritual or subsistent form. Accidental form is what determines a substance to one or other of the accidental modes, such as quantified, qualified, relationed, etc. (*see* CATEGORIES OF BEING). As the existence of an ACCIDENT is an inexistence, or one of inherence in an existent subject, it always connotes a subject of inherence. A separated form is one that exists apart from the matter it actuates. No accidental form can thus be separated, nor can corporeal substantial forms. The form of man, the human soul, becomes a separated form at death. An accidental form, because it modifies and determines substance, is sometimes referred to as an inhering form. The term is employed to emphasize the distinction of accidental from substantial forms. These latter do not inhere in matter, but are coprinciples with it in the constitution of material substances.

Forms of knowledge, according to I. KANT, are forms of (1) intuition, viz, space and time, and (2) thought, viz, the 12 categories by which all judgments are conditioned: unity, plurality, totality; reality, negation, limitation; substantiality, causality, relation; possibility, existence, and necessity. All of these are a priori forms and under them, as content, fall all of humanity's intuitions and judgments.

Greek Thought. The doctrine of form in Greek philosophy made its first appearance with PLATO. While not denying that the things of ordinary experience possess something like form, Plato turned his primary attention to the exemplars that corporeal shapes or forms might imitate. This led him to postulate the existence of a world of Forms or Ideas that subsist in themselves and are the immutable objects of man's highest knowledge. (For the historical development of this Platonic conception, *see* IDEA.) Plato's doctrine was criticized by his student, Aristotle, particularly on the point of the separate existence of Forms. For Aristotle, forms exist, but they exist in matter. The Aristotelian doctrine of forms stems from the notion of substance, and particularly from that of material substance as composed of matter and form. In some texts Aristotle identifies form with essence, and this because substance is what it is essentially by reason of the substantial form; it would be a mistake, nonetheless, to suppose that his doctrine leaves no room for a distinction between the two.

Medieval Thought. The Aristotelian distinction between matter and form, and its more basic formulation in the doctrine of potency and act, is central in the philosophy and theology of St. THOMAS AQUINAS, the principal spokesman for medieval scholasticism. For him, substantial form is an ACT, the principle of activity, and that by which things actually exist (*Summa theologiae* 1a, 66.1–2). Moreover, it is one. Thus man exists as man, in virtue of his substantial form, otherwise known as the human soul (*see* SOUL, HUMAN). That the rational soul is the unique form of the body is also of faith [H. Denzinger, *Enchiridion Symbolorum*, ed. A. Schönmetzer (Freiburg 1963) 900, 902, 1440, 2828]. Man is learned or healthy in virtue of the accidental forms of learning or health that inhere in him; these may be present or absent without detriment to his humanity. Both kinds of form, it may be noted, are individuated by something extrinsic to themselves: substantial forms by quantified matter, and accidental forms by their subject of inherence (*see* INDIVIDUATION). The incorporeal subsistent form of man, though continuing to exist when separated from the body, retains its relationship to the matter by which it was individuated.

This doctrine is common to most scholastics, but it should be noted that DUNS SCOTUS and others taught, in opposition to St. Thomas's doctrine of one substantial form, a plurality of forms in individuals. Thus, while according to Aquinas man is all that he is substantially (corporeal, animal, rational, Socrates) in virtue of his one soul, according to Scotus each determination (generic or specific) adds a new form to man. In this way, man would be corporeal in virtue of a corporeal form, animal in virtue of a superadded animal form, etc., until he becomes Socrates in virtue of his ultimate personal form (*Socrateitas*). WILLIAM OF OCKHAM also distinguished between a rational and a sensitive soul in man, and taught that the latter is corruptible. (*See* FORMS, UNICITY AND PLURALITY OF.)

Modern Thought. The principal alternative systems in the modern period that profess to give an account of corporeal substances are those of Descartes, Locke, Mill, and the materialists. R. DESCARTES placed the essence of bodies in extension in three dimensions, thus identifying quantified substance with quantity and in no way accounting for substantial differences. Each substance possesses a ''preeminent attribute, which constitutes its nature and essence and to which all others relate.'' To this J. LOCKE added the qualities of substance, making its essence consist of its primary qualities or properties (extension, figure and mobility, divisibility and activity). Locke regarded substantial form as ''wholly unintelligible,'' maintaining that the search for this and like entities is fruitless. J. S. MILL, considering substance from a psychological rather than from an ontological viewpoint, defined it by its relation to sense perception as an external and permanent possibility of human sensations. Akin to this is the doctrine of many materialists and positivists, who attempt to explain the nature of matter or substance as a series of sensations. All of these theories, as well as that of Kant mentioned above and those of the idealists, are strongly influenced by the epistemologies of their proponents (*see* KNOWLEDGE, THEORIES OF; QUALITY).

Contemporary Thought. In recent philosophy the term *form* rarely occurs, and the issues concerning the relationships between matter and form are no longer argued, the term matter being generally used without reference to form. Yet the problems that have traditionally been solved in terms of matter and form continue to be discussed. Examples are the problem of the one and the many, that of the universal and the particular, and that of the changeable and the changeless. These are discussed by thinkers such as W. JAMES and H. BERGSON, J. Dewey and G. SANTAYANA, and A. N. WHITEHEAD and B. RUSSELL. An occasional approximation to earlier thought is found in expressions such as the ''eternal objects'' of Whitehead or the ''realm of essence'' of Santayana. Although not explicitly stated, therefore, the problem of form and its meaning still lies dormant in contemporary thought.

Bibliography: F. AVELING, *The Catholic Encyclopedia*, ed. C. G. HERBERMANN et al., 6:137–39 (New York 1907–14; suppl. 1922). M. J. ADLER, ed., *The Great Ideas: A Syntopicon of Great Books of the Western World,* 1:526–542 (Chicago 1952); v.2, 3 of *Great Books of the Western World*. F. C. COPLESTON, *History of Philosophy* (Westminster, Md., 1946–). A. CARLINI, *Enciclopedia filosofica*, 2:477–492 (Venice-Rome 1957). A. MICHEL, *Dictionnaire* *de théologie catholique*, ed. A. VACANT et al., 6.1:541–588 (Paris 1903–50; Tables générales 1951–). J. B. LOTZ, *Lexikon für Theologie und Kirche*, ed. J. HOFER and K. RAHNER, 4:203–205 (2d new ed. Freiburg 1957–65). R. EISLER, *Wörterbuch der philosophischen Begriffe*, 1:436–443 (4th ed. Berlin 1927–30). R. P. PHILLIPS, *Modern Thomistic Philosophy,* 2 v. (Westminster, Md. 1934; repr. 1945). E. J. WATKIN, *A Philosophy of Form* (New York 1935).

[W. A. WALLACE]

Systematic Analysis

Form is the term commonly used to designate the determinate aspects humans apprehend in things. This part of the article investigates such a notion of form systematically, treating of quantitative form, qualitative form, and intelligible form, and concluding with an analysis of the concept of formal causality.

Quantitative Form. The shape of a triangular bar and the shape of a square desk top are quantitative forms. They are configurations of actual matter that are definite down to the minutest detail; that is, they are determinate. They must be the shapes of actual things, for otherwise they would not exist independently of thought; yet the kind of stuff of which they are quantitative forms is quite irrelevant to human understanding of them as such forms. Thus triangularity and squareness are abstract, and this in two ways: they leave out of consideration all possible materials that can be formed triangularly or squarely, and they also omit all deviations from actual straightness that occur in attempts to produce perfectly triangular or square surfaces in matter. This twofold abstractness results from the omission of all features that are irrelevant to understanding what it is to be triangular and what it is to be square. Thus does the human understanding apprehend some determinate aspect of the thing understood; this exists in the mind not with the properties of a physical existent but with the abstractness of an act of understanding. By contrast, the things that do exist in a physical way are determinate in every detail. Consequently, they are only approximations to their idealized quantitative aspects.

Some of the quantitative forms humans apprehend in nature can serve as models for forms engendered by him in matter when he produces artifacts. Thus a table top that is approximately square has been formed by man in accordance with a model made on paper or one existing only in his imagination. The model possesses the determinate form called squareness just as truly as does the actual table; however, its manner of existence is different, and so is its degree of approximation to the idealized squareness known through understanding. Thus one and the same formality (form considered abstractly as that by which something is determinate) can exist actually in matter, or representationally in the imagination, or meaningfully in the understanding.

Number and Measurement. A similar analysis holds for the quantitative form called number, which is used in a practical way to signify groupings of things; here, however, the imagined groupings and one's understanding of them can be exact replicas of actual physical multiplicities. This is so because numbers are more abstract than abstract shapes. Consequently, for numerical distinction any one means of identifying units suffices; the determinate aspects of their actual configurations can be left out of consideration.

In general the term quantitative form refers to any static or dynamic aspect of EXTENSION that can be considered in itself or as an actual aspect of things found in nature. The determinate aspects of such extension can be known with great precision by measurement.

Form and Matter. The determinate is contrasted with the determinable, that is, with what is capable of being formed in some manner. This latter is called matter or substrate; it designates what is formed and what remains when one form replaces another. The wood of a table about to be built is determinate as wood; nevertheless it is further determinable, since an arrangement of parts can be introduced into a pile of wood to form a table. When the wood has received these determinations, however, it is still receptive to further ones: it can be arranged, for example, as part of a room ensemble, or the table can be disassembled and the wood formed into some entirely different thing. Because the receiver of these new determinations is merely physical, and in no way cognitive, a new determination is acquired in each instance only at the expense of a previously existing one. This is so because a form that is actually present in a substrate forms the substrate determinately and thereby excludes other similar forms. Any one form must cease to be present actually when a contrary form replaces it.

The forms that result from the arrangement of parts presuppose the existence of parts, which are themselves determinate and further determinable. Consequently, the term quantitative form applies universally to the extended aspects of the most basic parts of material being as well as to the largest and most complex system of parts. But it is by the latter type of quantitative form that one customarily distinguishes kinds of living things. The same criterion is commonly used in the sciences of botany and zoology, and even paleontology, which primarily studies traces of the quantitative forms of living things preserved in the earth's crust. (*See* QUANTITY.)

Qualitative Form. Inseparable from the quantitatively determinate aspects of things are determinate aspects that correspond to a person's various abilities to be directly aware of his or her body and its environment. By sight and taste and touch, for example, one can detect determinate aspects that are called qualitative forms or sensory qualities—"forms" because they are actual determinations of things, "qualities" because they are of a particular kind (Lat. *quale*) for each external sense. Such aspects are directly indicative of differences other than differences of mere extension. They are forms *sui generis* and provide the initial diversity in one's apprehension of matter. Their number corresponds to the number of ways in which humanity can make direct sensory contact with things. Thus sensible qualitative form is any aspect of anything that can make an initial impression upon any human sense. The quantitative forms resulting from the limits of the extension of material beings, it should be noted, are not apprehended initially but only by means of the sense qualities. The triangular shape of a steel bar, for example, may be apprehended either in the contrast of the color of the steel with the visual appearances of its surroundings or in the contrast of its hardness and coolness with the tactile impressions of its surroundings, but not directly and initially.

Forms Related to Sense. Humanity's view of the material universe is predetermined in that the senses are able to detect some formal aspects but not others. Yet, through technology, people have devised instruments to extend the normal range of the senses and to detect formalities that are otherwise too minute, too gross, or too distant for accurate discrimination. Through such instruments, formal aspects of things not discernible by any sense (e.g., molecular structure) can be represented to the senses. These may be referred to as reductively sensible, even though they are not directly apprehended by the senses.

Mechanical Explanation. The discovery of such formal aspects and the entities corresponding to them—such as atoms and molecules—has led some in the history of thought to attempt to explain all sensory forms mechanically, i.e., as nothing more than subjective impressions produced by the motion of particles of matter. Thus DEMOCRITUS posited atoms and the void as the only true realities and asserted that sense qualities exist for man but not in things themselves; similarly, contemporary mechanists hold that sense perception is but a biochemical function of brain cells. One difficulty for such mechanical viewpoints is that the basic entities of one age tend to be replaced by new ones in succeeding ages, thus giving rise to repeated revolutions in mechanistic thought. Another is that mechanical phenomena alone are rendered more intelligible by mechanical explanations. For example, a mechanical explanation proposes that puttylike sodium, combining with gaseous chlorine, forms crystalline salt. The crystalline structure of salt can be explained in terms of the quantitative forms of its components, but this explanation sheds no light on the different qualitative properties found in salt and in its components when taken by themselves. Yet another difficulty for MECHANISM is that no direct contact with matter is possible for man except through his senses and through formal aspects that are inseparable from them. To cast doubt upon the senses is thus to characterize all sensory information, and all theory elaborated from it (mechanism included), as nothing more than an illusion.

The alternative to rejecting SENSE KNOWLEDGE or reducing it to some inexplicable, albeit real, element in human experience is to recognize the mechanical viewpoint as but one of many limited viewpoints arising in human understanding, according as a person singles out one or other formal aspect as preeminently intelligible.

Intelligible Form. Since the senses can apprehend only what is actually present to them, they are cognitively formed, or informed, by the determinate aspects of all things that can make an impression upon a sense organ. Through the repetition of sensory impressions, many things that are first discriminated as novelties come to be familiar. For example, bread and butter and coffee are easily recognizable by their visual appearances and their customary aromas and textures. If a mistake in identifying coffee by such sensory signs occurs, the sense of smell or of taste is usually invoked to decide the issue, since for most people to be coffee means to have a certain aroma or taste. But this may not be the decisive CRITERION for all. Some, for example, may want assurance that the ingredients are known to have been obtained from a coffee tree; others may wish a chemical analysis to determine that the beverage has the chemical components found in coffee beans. Each of these methods of identification—the regular recurrence of the same sensory signs in the same combination (with incidental variations), the regular derivation of the thing in question from the same kind of source, and the invariability of the chemical components and quantitative form of the individual molecule of the kind of thing in question—is sufficient for the practical purposes of identification. Moreover, all three viewpoints, when added together, constitute part of the answer to the question as to what coffee really is. Such grouping of characteristics is the work of the human INTELLECT; its result is what is known as intelligible form.

The name ABSTRACTION is commonly used of the process by which the intelligible form is derived from sensory experience. The CONCEPT it attains is abstract; there can be no concrete representation of it in itself, although its intelligible content can often be exemplified. Thus human understanding of animal as a sentient organism can be exemplified by any individual animal. While the concept is immaterial, however, it can be said to be formal, or to be a form, because it informs human intellect, even if in a general and abstract way. Its generality and abstractness do not militate against its being a form, since one formal aspect may encompass another, as the concept of color includes concepts of red, blue, and green. When many limited formal aspects are included within a more general formal aspect, however, this is always done at the expense of the determinateness of the more general. Thus to include green in the category of color and to include color in the category of quality is to proceed from determinate to general notions. It is this way, incidentally, that the notion of form itself is arrived at. The partiality of individual intelligible viewpoints obtained by abstraction from experience need not hinder human attempts at understanding the universe, for in thought itself one can compare them and derive more general but equally informative intelligible forms as a result. (*See* APPREHENSION, SIMPLE; KNOWLEDGE, PROCESS OF.)

Formal Causality. Although formal aspects that are exclusive of one another considered in themselves may be included in some more general category in thought, the same is not true for forms outside of thought, such as the quantitative forms of bodies. Forms of the same kind exclude one another from the same substrate. But many forms not of the same kind can exist in the same substrate. Thus a body that is living may also be sentient and soft and warm, although it cannot be warm and cold at the same time. Similarly, what are materially the same parts may be informed by different forms at both the substantial and the accidental level. Thus combinations of chemicals may be salt or living flesh, depending upon the form of the whole of which the chemicals are the components. The principle of formation in this case is called substantial form to indicate that it gives to that which it forms its very being in the order of SUBSTANCE. By contrast, accidental forms are aspects that may always be found with the kind of thing in question but are not thought to characterize it fully. Hardness is an essential quality of diamonds, although the substance of diamond is carbon; and humans have many reflex actions similar to those found in unicellular organisms, although they are defined as rational animals because reason is the dominating characteristic in their acting and being.

Form comes into being when the composite of which it is the form comes into being. Thus the properties of salt arise simultaneously with the chemical union of sodium and chlorine by their mutual action upon one another. While the sculptor is the sole efficient cause of the statue he produces in stone, the stone and the figure with which he informs it exert mutual causality upon each other.

Both substantial and accidental forms are said to be educed from the potency of their corresponding matter under the action of the efficient cause. The rational soul of man, however, so transcends matter in its intellectual activities that it cannot originate from matter by a process of eduction (*see* SOUL, HUMAN, ORIGIN OF).

Form passes out of existence when the whole of which it is the form is destroyed. When salt is broken down to its component chemical parts, the properties of salt cease to exist in them; similarly, the remains of a once living body act entirely according to their chemical natures and not as parts of living matter. Forms are physically inseparable from things; the act of apprehension, however, can separate them from matter and permit judgments about their nature, kinds, and characteristics.

From these considerations it may be seen that the causality of form is that of an intrinsic cause and, as such, one that requires the receptive action of some appropriate matter. Form and matter exercise their special causality by a mutual communication of their own being; their proper effect is the composite that results from their union. Both form and matter obtain their actual existence from the existence of this composite, even though the form may have preexisted potentially in the matter (and previous composite) from which it was educed. And neither form nor matter can exercise its causality unless there is a proper proportion between them, and unless an efficient cause acts to bring about the composite's formation. (*See* CAUSALITY; EFFICIENT CAUSALITY; FINAL CAUSALITY.)

Bibliography: F. J. COLLINGWOOD, *Philosophy of Nature* (Englewood Cliffs, N.J. 1961). V. E. SMITH, *The General Science of Nature* (Milwaukee 1958). L. L. WHYTE, ed., *Aspects of Form* (New York 1951). J. GOHEEN, *The Problem of Matter and Form in the 'De Ente et Essentia' of Thomas Aquinas* (Cambridge. Mass. 1940). P. H. J. HOENEN, *The Philosophy of Inorganic Compounds*, tr. P. COHEN (West Baden Springs, Ind. 1960).

[F. J. COLLINGWOOD]

FORM CRITICISM, BIBLICAL

Term used for the method of interpreting the books of the New Testament, particularly the Gospels, by investigating not only the literary *forms* employed in their composition, but also the preliterary *formation* of these writings. This method will be considered here according to its objective, its nature, its classification of various types in the Gospels, and its value for exegesis; a historical, bibliographical synthesis of the studies connected with this method will then be given, followed by a brief account of the literary genres employed in the New Testament apart from the Gospels.

Objective. The theory of the Biblical literary genres and its practical application as a hermeneutical method originated and developed in the field of Old Testament studies. Around 1920 this method was extended to the field of New Testament studies, more particularly to the study of the Gospels. Here, where it received the name of form criticism (*Formgeschichte,* history of forms), it underwent certain adaptations caused by the difference in subject matter, without however concealing its ancestry. H. GUNKEL, in the Old Testament field, went beyond the theory of the written documents (J, E, D, and P) older than the present Pentateuch and penetrated back to literary units, complete in themselves, classifiable according to types, units that were born and grew in the life of the people and that were ordinarily transmitted by oral tradition. Similarly, in the New Testament field, M. Dibelius and R. Bultmann went beyond the two-source theory (Mark and Q) in the solution of the Synoptic problem and penetrated back to small units, classified according to type, that were born and developed and transmitted orally in the early Christian community before these units were gathered and wrought into the Gospels by the Evangelists.

The objective of the form-criticism school is, in fact, to offer a genetic explanation for the accomplished fact of the Gospels as the outcome of earlier oral traditions. For this purpose literary forms are analyzed as an intermediary step in the process, on the supposition that from the ''forms,'' conclusions can be drawn regarding the ''formation.'' This method purports to go behind the four Gospels back to the original GOSPEL; it seeks to carry the modern Christian back into the life of the early Christian community in order that he may, with it and like it, hear the original preaching of the gospel (M. Dibelius).

Method. In order to attain this objective, the method requires that these three steps must be taken: (1) the literary units must be isolated; (2) they must be classified according to types; (3) their place of origin and transmission must be determined.

Isolation of Units. For the purpose of isolating the literary units, the Gospels offer data sufficiently firm for laying the foundations of a working hypothesis. The Gospels give clear evidence of being collections; they are compositions in the sense of being composite, made up of preexisting parts. This can be seen in the grouping of units around a common theme, in the repetition of certain catchwords, and in certain numerical arrangements (groups of three each, seven each, etc.); the transitions, the literary sutures, the framework around the units, etc., can easily be apprehended. This apprehension, of which one becomes reasonably sure in an attentive reading of any individual Gospel, becomes all the more certain when one Gospel is compared to another; in parallel pericopes there is only a change in the framework, in the introduction or the conclusion, in the position of a unit within the whole narrative, etc. In this way it is possible to arrive at a clear distinction between what is redactional and what is traditional; the redactional part is due to individual Evangelists, while the traditional part is the material derived from an earlier stage of oral transmission. The last step in the method is that of progressive analogy, i.e., from a series of units isolated with certainty, it is legitimate to conclude by analogy to others less certain or even doubtful.

Classification by Types. The units thus isolated are then classified according to types. Strictly speaking, the criteria of classification should be formal, i.e., drawn up on the basis of form; actually, various scholars combine three kinds of criteria: formal, thematic (according to the different themes), and purposive (according to different intentions or tendencies). This is quite legitimate because the theme often determines the selection of the form that is used, and the purpose has a strong effect on the style. Since many of the literary units are very short, formal criteria alone would not be sufficient for a satisfactory classification. Other criteria, such as those of literary or topical motifs or those of ''tone,'' can easily be brought under the criteria mentioned above. Theoretically, according to the leading scholars of the form-criticism school, form is a great superpersonal power; in reality, many doubtful, intermediate, or contaminated forms are encountered. In such cases the investigator can simply set forth the state of the material and not attempt a rigorous classification, or he can work over the material for the purpose of bringing it under exact forms. For the sake of classification, recourse may be had to a comparison with literatures that are historically or culturally close to the New Testament literature, especially to rabbinical or Hellenistic religious literature. The names given to types and subtypes are of but subordinate value; of much more importance is the exact description of the type. This is necessary for the sake of overcoming differences in terminology.

Origin and Transmission of the Units. To each type and to each unit belonging to this type there is assigned a *Sitz im Leben,* a certain situation in life, in which it receives and transmits its own proper form. One thus passes from the form back to its formation, from the literary fact back to its preliterary history. The *Sitz im Leben* is a concept, not in the historical, but in the literary sense. It is not a determination established by coordinates of space, time, or person. There is no intention or even possibility of drawing from the form conclusions regarding the date, place, or author of the analyzed form. Rather, it is in the activity of the community that the literary type has its situation in life—the community's worship, catechesis, and apologetics. As the literary type is a genus, so also its situation in life is generic. To find the situation in life of a genus, its form is helpful, since the form has been determined by the necessities and motives of the life of the community. This is the analytical way. Moreover, a unified picture of the life of this community may be obtained by bringing together and reconstructing into a unified whole the scattered, casual data of the other New Testament writings, the Acts of the Apostles, and the Epistles. This is the constructive process. This double process is completed by a comparative view, since the phenomenon of oral transmission is not limited to the early Christian community. The technique of such transmission in Judaism has been recognized and investigated, and the laws governing the oral transmission of popular traditions have been studied [see M. Jousse, *Le style oral et mnémotechnique chez les Verbo-moteurs* (Paris 1925)]. Moreover the apocrypha and the Synoptic Gospels themselves, when compared one with the other, can reveal certain tendencies that play a part in the transmission of this material. Such comparative material has a purely formal application, i.e., to discover the technique of transmission; it would be hazardous to use it for passing judgment on the contents.

When this third stage of study is finished, the literary method has not the right to advance without further ado to the facts, to pass positive or negative judgments on their historicity. This is the task of historical criticism, which, however, makes use of the literary method both as an instrument and as a preliminary step. Thus the form-criticism method seeks to classify the literary types and to describe the history of their transmission, but nothing else. It has not the right, in its own name, to decide that something is pure invention or actual fact.

Descriptive Classification. A primary, obvious classification divides the isolated pericopes into deeds and sayings, narratives and discourses; in such a division the criterion according to theme coincides with the criterion according to form. However, since narratives usually include dialogues, statements, and maxims and since sayings generally appear in the context of a narrative, one more criterion is needed for making a clearer division; this is the purpose of the passage. A deed may be told for its own sake, for the sake of the person who does it, or for the sake of a saying that serves as its climax. This diversity of purpose usually conditions the form and for this reason leaves certain traces in the style. Thus, for example, neither the purely thematic criterion of miracle nor the purely formal criterion of story would be sufficient, because the whole purpose of a miracle story might be to lead to the statement of some teaching. In the case of sayings, the difficulty in classifying them is much less, because the circumstances in which they are placed are often merely redactional; and they disappear when the pericope or literary unit is isolated in separating the part derived from tradition from the work of the redactor.

For the public life of Jesus, excluding the Passion narrative, the classification according to type that is commonly accepted is that of R. Bultmann—prescinding from his opinions on historicity, which are foreign to the method as such. L. Randellini has summed up the various types and illustrated them by examples. This classification is schematized below.

It is to be noted that, granted the cases that fall between the various types as well as the diversity of opinion among the scholars, no classification can be perfect. Thus for Bultmann disputations and didactic dialogues are reckoned as subtypes of apothegms. On the other hand, Dibelius calls paradigm what Bultmann calls apothegm, and he establishes a major type that he calls *Novelle* (short story), which frequently coincides with the miracle story. The sayings in the first person often coincide with the legal sayings, and it is not always easy to decide between the sapiential exhortations and the prophetic admonitions, etc.

Deeds. Certain literary units in the Gospels are concerned primarily with recounting the doings or deeds of Jesus. Besides special stories that cannot well be classified under a more general heading, there are miracle stories, cultic and biographical legends, and possibly, if understood in a special sense, myths.

The point of interest in miracle stories lies in the miracle that is recounted. In the most common type of miracle, the cure of a person who is ill, the narrative shows three steps in its development: (1) description of the sick man and his sickness and of others who are present; (2) the performance of the miracle, with certain gestures or words, which in the case of an exorcism may consist in a dialogue with the demon in the possessed man; (3) the effects of the miracle, especially the reaction of those present. The description is usually very sober; naturalness and power stand out. The motif of faith appears frequently. The tripartite scheme, mentioned above, grows quite clearly out of the theme. Miracle stories have their place in the preaching of the Apostles both as testimony to the person of Jesus and as signs of the salvation already at work.

Cultic and biographical legends are pious stories that explain a cultic act or exalt a saint. (According to Bultmann, the concept of legend excludes historicity; according to Dibelius, it prescinds from it.) The Last Supper would be a cultic legend, with ultimate cultic significance. The story of the sinful woman in Lk 7.36–50 would be a biographical legend, with ultimate hagiographical reference. Since Christ is over and above every saint and since the whole interest of the Evangelists is concentrated in Him, legends are less common in the Gospels than in Acts. The story of Zachaeus in Lk 19.1–10 could be a biographical legend. The story of Judas's suicide in Mt 27.3–10 (cf. Acts 1.18–20) could be an etiological legend connected with a certain place. In other cases there remain only some legendary motifs. The purpose of the community in recounting legends is the honor of a saint, edification, or imitation.

The concept of myth must be adapted if examples of it are to be found in the Gospels. Dibelius finds a mythical style throughout St. John's Gospel, without derogating from its historicity. For Bultmann's idea of myth in the Gospels and the need for giving modern significance to their mythical language, *see* DEMYTHOLOGIZING.

Under the heading of special stories would come the stories of Jesus' baptism, temptations in the desert, transfiguration, triumphal entry into Jerusalem, etc. Neither the theme nor the manner of development is constant. The style shows a certain amplitude and dramatic movement. No useful purpose is served in grouping these stories under a common heading, and exegetes study each one by itself.

Sayings of Jesus. The principal types of Jesus' sayings are: (1) discussions and dialogues; (2) sapiential sayings; (3) prophetic sayings; (4) legal sayings; (5) sayings in the first person; (6) parables. Note that the division into sapiential, prophetic, and legal sayings reechoes the classical division in Jer 18.18: instruction from the priests, counsel from the wise, messages from the prophets.

The occasion of a discussion may be a miracle that has just been recounted, something done by Jesus or His disciples, or a polemical question. Didactic dialogues usually begin with a sincere question. The answer may be another polemical question, a quotation from Scripture, or a maxim. The style strives for brevity, intensity, effectiveness. Bultmann claims that these disputes were born in the apologetic and polemic atmosphere of the community. M. Albertz [*Die Synoptischen Streitgespräche* (Berlin 1921)], while granting the apologetic and didactic purpose of the community, derives the original form from Jesus Himself.

Sapiential sayings are a clear-cut type, with numerous parallels in the Old Testament. It is sufficient here to cite a few examples: exhortation (Mt 10.16), question (Lk 6.39), maxim (Mt 5.14), macarism (Mt 5.3–12), argument *a minore ad maius* (Mt 10.29). Bultmann regards metaphors, hyperboles, antitheses, parallelisms, and paradoxes as ornamental motifs. Such sayings have their *Sitz im Leben* in the teaching of the community, and the principles of thematic grouping by means of key words plays a part in their transmission. Bultmann adds the principle of duplication, amplification, analogous creation, and false attribution.

Prophetic sayings include proclamations of salvation (Mt. 11.5–6), threats of woe (Lk 6.24–26), and warnings (Lk 21.34–36). Apocalyptic prediction is represented, e.g., by the foretelling of the destruction of the Temple (Mk 13.2). Noticeably absent are prophetic visions and the classical formulas of the Old Testament, "The word of the Lord to . . ." and "Thus says the Lord," etc.

Some of the legal sayings have their *Sitz im Leben* in the laws and customs of the Jews (Mk 7.15; 2.27); others give practical rules for the life of the Christian community (Mt 18.1–20). The *Sitz im Leben* of the latter is the counseling and instructing of the community.

As for sayings in the first person, Jesus proclaims His mission, His office, and His commission to the Apostles (Mt 15.24; Lk 10.18) in the first person.

In the generic term of parable certain related forms can be included. In the use of imagery the figurative element is combined with the doctrinal one without the use of a particle of comparison (Lk 6.43–45). In the metaphor the doctrinal element is not explicitly stated but is implied in the imagery (Mt 7.13). In the simile or comparison the two elements are joined by an explicit particle of comparison (Lk 7.31–35). Common to all three types is their combining of the two elements, the material one on the mundane level and the transcendent one on the religious level; likewise common to all three is the didactic religious purpose. The formal difference between them is slight. The parable in the strict sense uses a story as the material element. Its construction is usually quite simple: the introduction announcing the comparison, the narration of the story, at times with an emphatically marked climax ("I assure you"), and the conclusion or application joined to the preceding by different formulas. The narrative style follows the laws of the folk epic (A. Olrik), e.g., in brevity, economy of personages, construction of little scenes in which only two persons are involved, unencumbered dialogues, and linear development. The parables originated in a Palestinian environment, and the early Christian community transmitted them with didactic purposes in view, adapting the application to their concrete needs.

Apothegms. These are minute scenes in which an important saying is placed. The statement is the center of interest; it determines the brevity of the scene, and it usually comes at the end. Bultmann, who introduced the Greek term ἀπόφθεγμα, regards the scene as a pure invention created for the sake of finding a place for the saying. He thus turns most of the disputes and didactic dialogues into subtypes of apothegms. Dibelius employs the neutral term παράδιγμα, and he abstains from passing any judgment on its historicity.

Passion Narratives. The account of Christ's Passion is a unique case, and therefore it cannot be subject to classification. Here the principal task of the form-criticism school has no place; one can merely admit the uniqueness of this kind of narrative. However, the secondary task of form criticism is pertinent—to analyze the history of the tradition (which, showing remarkably fixed form and concord, precedes the redaction of the Gospels) and to discover the religious motives that sustain and impel the transmission of the tradition in the bosom of the early Church.

The Passion, joined to the Resurrection, is, first of all, the central theme of the Apostolic KERYGMA. The Gospels develop in narrative form what many passages elsewhere in the New Testament, both in Acts and in the Epistles, proclaim in brief form. In the narrative development, the kerygma becomes articulate in dogma and theology, especially in its frequent recourse to the Old Testament prophecies. Subordinate to the theological interest, an apologetic and even polemic interest is revealed, which has recourse to the arguments of Christ's own preaching. In the second place, the Passion narrative holds a privileged place in Christian worship. Traces of it are found in the hymns of Phil 2.6–11; 1 Tm 3.16; 1 Pt 1.18–21; 2.21–24; 3.18–22; and in the heavenly liturgy of Rv 5.6–14, while explicit references to the Passion are made in the Eucharist and Baptism rites. Mention should be made here of the radical theory of G. Bertram, a disciple of A. Deissmann, who finds in the Christian cult the origin of the apotheosis or deification of the hero Jesus. In the third place, the Passion narrative shows an exemplaric interest, presenting the self-sacrificing Jesus as a model for Christian living.

Resurrection Narratives. It is difficult to reduce to one common type the various accounts of the apparitions of the risen Christ. Certain common motifs; however, can be seen: the disciples' lack of faith, Christ's sudden appearances, the disciples' fear, their recognition of Him, and their joy. Some of these motifs coincide with apparition motifs in the Old Testament. Actually, however, the variety of motifs is predominant. It is evident that before the tradition was fixed in writing, a consecutive narrative of the apparitions had not been formed, as was the case with the Passion. On the contrary, the *Sitz im Leben* of these narratives is very clear: they are witnesses of a decisive fact, and they are adduced as such with theological and apologetic value. The Resurrection event is joined to the Passion in the most simple formulas of the Apostolic kerygma. (It is logical that the rationalist critics declare these narratives to be pure inventions of the Christian community.)

Infancy Narratives. Apart from the Davidic descent and the virginal birth of Jesus, an account of His childhood does not form part of the programmatic preaching of the Apostles. It is absent from the samples of the kerygma in Acts, as well as from the Gospels of Mark and John, and the episodes of the INFANCY NARRATIVES in Matthew are quite different from those in Luke. This is the specific problem of the Infancy narratives. It has led some Catholic scholars to compare them with Old Testament and even extra-Biblical narratives. P. Gaechter sees behind Luke's version a tradition originating in Jerusalem, and he makes an analysis of the history of the tradition. R. Laurentin finds in Luke's redaction a collection of imitations of the story of Samuel's childhood or a procedure typical of MIDRASH. For Matthew's Infancy Gospel certain extra-Biblical parallels are adduced from narratives of the life of Moses. These literary findings, which in some way imply judgments on the historicity of the narratives, have provoked a contrary reaction that has completely stopped further study in this field. Prescinding from questions of historicity, it is beyond dispute that Annunciation accounts in Luke repeat a consecrated schema used in such accounts in the Old Testament, and likewise certain are the cases of coincidence of motifs and literary formulas with passages in Samuel and extra-Biblical texts.

Evaluation. Form-criticism, or as it is called in German, *die formgeschichtliche Methode* (the method of the history of forms), can be considered from the viewpoint of its objective or from that of the method it employs. Its objective is to go back from the written Gospels to the preliterary oral stage in which tradition was in the course of formation; it is a sort of paleontology of the Gospels (Dibelius). This objective is, in itself, quite legitimate, and historically it supplanted a literary criticism that had already exhausted itself. But one must remember that a literary reality cannot be adequately identified with the process of its formation, that is, that the Gospels cannot be adequately explained without the Evangelists. Finally, the canonical and authoritative texts for the Church are the four Gospels, not some hypothetical or probable forms that may have existed before them. Form criticism, therefore, is a licit, interesting, and promising undertaking; but it cannot be called the only task of Gospel exegesis. Viewed as a method, *die formgeschichtliche Methode* is precisely that—a method of work. As such, it is neutral and disposable, to be evaluated according to its usefulness and its results. But it should not be forgotten that any method, especially one that is concerned with the sciences of the spirit, suffers under the influence of those who use it. For this reason it is very difficult to pass a neutral judgment on a method that, in theory, is neutral. Nevertheless, an evaluation will be attempted here, following the three stages of the method as described.

Value of Isolation of Units. To isolate the literary units of which the Gospels are composed is relatively easy and reliable. Likewise, the isolation of the editorial work that was done on the oral tradition can be achieved with sufficient certitude; the wide agreement of exegetes in this regard confirms the results. (In the Old Testament there is not the same favorable situation of the presence of three or even, at times, four parallel documents.) In otherwise doubtful places, what is lacking in objective evidence is supplied by the picture of the whole that the investigator has seen in formation or that he has brought with him. The method, however, becomes more uncertain or even dangerous when it pursues more and more minute divisions, separating a maxim from its scene, breaking a binary formula into its component parts, or isolating a piece from its natural series. The shortest is not always the oldest. Together with the aggregative force of thematic or formal combination, there are also at work the forces of selection, of partial citation, etc., as shown by the use of the Old Testament in the New Testament. Uncontrolled analysis can lead to an atomism that loses sight of the large or even the small connections. Bultmann is not free from this defect.

Value of Classification by Types. Every classification simplifies the understanding of an object and permits, by comparison, the appreciation of the individual. The convergence of the three criteria—theme, form, and purpose—can guarantee the results. Classification places the literary units in a new context, which means placing them in a new light. But it would be sterile to be content with a pure, quasi-botanical classification. The dangers in such a step are the following.

There is a danger of carelessly confusing the form and the thematic criteria and of drawing inferences as a result of such confusion. The same theme of miracle may appear in the form of miracle story or in the form of apothegm; the same form of miracle story may hold for a tempest theme or a deafmute theme. Therefore, before drawing conclusions it is necessary to determine clearly whether the differences are those of theme or of form.

Another danger is to apply foreign types to the Gospels and to draw unwarranted conclusions from them. Bultmann borrowed the term and type of apothegm from Greek literature. Actually, however, such a type is found in many different literatures, and therefore it could be useful for seeking the differential of the Gospels. The type of legend is taken from medieval Christian literature—written, not oral; but in Bultmann it is surcharged with a negative evaluation that has been imposed on it by the ENLIGHTENMENT. Dibelius's term of *Novelle* (short story) is not felicitous, and the deficiencies in the term myth are evident. Moreover, in using a type that is common to other literatures, there is the danger of jumping from analogy to dependence, e.g., to explain the stories of Jesus' miracles as imitations of Greek miracle stories created for the purpose of setting up Christian, in opposition to pagan, propaganda.

A third danger is to define a type so as to raise it to an absolute norm for judging all the individual units that may fall under this type. In assuming that the pure form is the original, primary one, a certain pure type is reconstructed that is never met with in any individual case, and then this pure type is applied as the ideal norm on the individual unit until they are equalized. The result is a mechanical stylization of life as if in a laboratory. Bultmann, for instance, finds that precise topographical data do not correspond to the style of the apothegm, and therefore, when they occur in Gospel apothegms, he considers them very suspicious. One runs the risk of going in a vicious circle in thus defining a certain literary genre with absolute rigor, applying this definition to the literary units, and then drawing conclusions. Bultmann is frequently guilty of such faulty methodology, thereby falsifying the form-criticism method in its very birth. It should be noted, however, that the fault lies not in using a well-established form as a criterion but in turning it into an absolute criterion.

A final danger lies in passing, without further ado, from conclusions regarding the form to judgments regarding historicity: e.g., it is cultic, hence not historical. As far as mere terminology regarding the form is concerned, one is justified in saying that it is a legend and that therefore it is not history. What this means is that the matter is narrated in the form of a legend, not in the form of history—nothing more. But it is wrong to draw the conclusion that since the thing is told in the form of a legend the thing itself is legendary, not historical. Such a conclusion is to leap from a judgment regarding the form to a judgment regarding the historicity. Naturally, the question concerning the historicity interests the investigator. Yet it is a question that cannot be answered by merely typological criteria: other ''real'' criteria (concerning the things themselves) must be added to these. Dibelius, in general, is cautious in his conclusions, modestly skirting this field. On the contrary, according to E. Schick, this is the capital sin of Bultmann: to jump from conclusions regarding the form (which are often merely hypothetical) to judgments of historicity, i.e., nonhistoricity. It is clear that frequently a judgment that something is not historical is simply a prejudgment (prejudice) placed at the end of the study. L. Köhler says of Bultmann's analyses of Jesus' disputes that they seek to find how they could have come into being, on the supposition that they are not historical. And Bultmann himself lays the burden of proof on anyone who wishes to go back from the Gospel text to the life of Jesus.

Part Played by the Community. With the classification according to the various literary forms the work is not yet finished. The next step is to investigate the history of the forms. This is where the *Geschichte* (history) of the *formgeschichtliche Methode* fits in: to go back through the "forms" to the "formation," back from the four Gospels to the original one gospel, from the Evangelists to the community. Thus there appears a new view of oral tradition, a new view of the early Church and its life. Before the Scripture there was oral tradition, as a living force united with Jesus, as a force that was, to a large extent, formative, so that Scripture is, to a large extent, a fixing of the oral tradition. The bearer of this tradition—tradition in the sense both of the act of transmitting and of the material transmitted—was the early Christian community, the early Church. Scripture was born in the Church and from the Church; the New Testament is the Church's book. This Church displayed a life of many different activities: it proclaimed the good news, it preached, it defended itself, it celebrated its liturgy. This rich and varied life vitalized the transmitted material and its fixed form in writing; it produced a living book—the New Testament.

In a certain sense, therefore, this new method has, no doubt, made an important contribution; and for this reason it has been welcomed, though with various degrees of reserve, by many Catholic scholars. Yet, if the investigator twists these concepts, the method can turn out to be catastrophic. Instead of a faithful transmission by controlled witnesses pledged to preserve, interpret, and actualize the material, we are offered a tradition that preserves but little and invents almost everything, indebted more to Judaism and Hellenism than to Jesus, a tradition that cannot bring us with certainty to the person and life of Jesus. "Of the life and personality of Jesus practically nothing can be known." This tradition can lead us merely to the early Christian community. Yet this community is not the Church as it is shown to be in the other writings of the New Testament and even in certain passages of the Gospels, but a community borrowed from a positivistic and romantic sociology that has already become outdated in the scholarly field of history and literature. It is an anonymous, amorphous community, an undifferentiated mass, without personalities; it is creative in a strict sense, collectively engaged in a work of invention. This community scarcely remembers Jesus, but it compensates for this by having a fantastically prodigious power of creation. It has created something marvelously new without anyone's being able to explain who created the community itself. It is precisely this that has discredited a *Formgeschichte* directed by certain determined religious conceptions or negations: the Gospels are first cut up into minute literary units, these are then dissolved in an amorphous community, and the result is set forth as a scientific explanation of the Gospels.

Historical and Bibliographical Conspectus. Although the opinions of the leading proponents of this method have already been mentioned, it will be useful to set forth here a brief historical synthesis of many of the scholars connected with this theory, together with the basic bibliographical data.

Early Background. It was from Johann Gottfried von HERDER that the first intuitions arose regarding this theory: the early preaching, oral tradition, the Apostles' preaching and the instruction of the first communities, the Palestinian and Hellenistic color; see his *Vom Erlöser der Menschen. Nach unseren drei ersten Evv.* (Leipzig 1796); *Nach Jo-Ev.* (Leipzig 1797). J. K. L. Gieseler developed the theory of the common oral tradition, with its conservative and formative principles, and he compared this with the tradition of the Rabbis; see his *Historisch-kritischer Versuch über die Entstehung und die frühesten Schicksale der schriftlichen Evangelien* (1818). This was followed by the period of literary criticism of the New Testament until, at the end of the century, there was a return to the ideas of Herder. C. F. G. Heinrici, in his book *Die Entstehung des New Testament* (Leipzig 1899) and in several articles, separated the Gospels from other surrounding literary works, in practice distinguished tradition from redaction, pointed to the formation of the traditions in the early preaching and teaching, and found their roots in the life of the community. H. Gunkel's influence was felt after World War I, and in about a year the new school was born. Decisive for the community and cult aspect of the theory was the work of Adolf Deissmann, *Licht vom Osten* (Tübingen 1908).

Basic Studies. Urged on by Gunkel, or on the strength of their own independent efforts, five men produced the following basic works: (1) M. Dibelius, *Die Formgeschichte des Evangelium* (Tübingen, January 1919); (2) K. L. Schmidt, *Der Rahmen der Geschichte Jesu* (Berlin, March 1919); (3) R. Bultmann, *Die Geschichte der synoptischen Tradition* (Göttingen, March 1921); *History of the Synoptic Tradition,* tr. J. Marsch (New York 1963); (4) M. Albertz, *Die synoptischen Streitgespräche* (Berlin, May 1921); (5) G. Bertram, *Die Leidengeschichte Jesu und der Christuskult* (Göttingen 1922).

These scholars remained active until the beginning of World War II, publishing books and articles and contributing to the second edition of the dictionary *Die Reli-*

gion in Geschichte und Gegenwart: Bertram, ''Entstehung des Christentums'' 1:1531–35; Bultmann, ''Evangelien: Gattungsgeschichtlich''2:418–422, ''Urgemeinde'' 5:1408–14; Schmidt, ''Formgeschichte'' 2:638–640, ''Geschichtschreibung im New Testament'' 2: 1115–17, ''Jesus Christus'' 3:110–115; Dibelius, ''Bibelkritik des New Testament'' 1:1033–35. The following are other works by these authors that should be cited: Bertram, ''Die Bedeutung der Kultgeschichtlichen Methode für die ntl. Forschung'' [*Theologische Blätter* 2 (1923) 25–36], in which he made his own method somewhat different by a different terminology; Bultmann, *Jesus* (Berlin 1926) and the first edition of his collected articles, *Glauben und Verstehen* (Tübingen 1933). Dibelius, ''Zur Formgeschichte der Evangelien'' *Theologische Rundschau* 1 (1929) 185–216 and other articles in which he widened the field of study, such as ''Zur Formgeschichte des New Testament ausserhalb der Evangelien'' *Theologische Rundschau* 3 (1931) 207–242; ''Stilkritisches zur Apostelgeschichte'' *Eucharisteion für H. Gunkel* 2 (1923) 27–49; ''Rabbinische und evangelische Erzählungen'' *Theologische Blätter* 11 (1932) 1–12. Schmidt, ''Die Stellung der Evangelien in der allgemeinen Literaturgeschichte'' *Eucharisteion für H. Gunkel* 2 (1923) 50–134; ''Die Persönlichkeitsfrage im Urchristentum'' *Theologische Blätter* 3 (1925) 153–161.

Reaction. Comments and criticisms on the new school or new method were not slow in making their appearance, and they came from different sides. On the Protestant side the following studies in criticism of this theory may be mentioned. O. Cullmann, ''Les recéntes études sur la formation de la tradition evangelique'' *Revue d'histoire et de philosophie religieuses* 5 (1925) 459–477, 564–579. E. Fascher, ''Die formgeschichtliche Methode: eine Darstellung und Kritik'' *Beihefte zur Zeitschrift für die Neutestamentliche Wissenschaft* 2 (1924). L. Köhler, ''Das formgeschichtliche Problem des New Testament'' in *Sammlung gemeinverständlicher Vorträge und Schriften aus dem Gebiet der Theologie und Religionsgeschichte* (Tübingen 1925). M. Goguel, ''Une nouvelle école de critique évangelique'' *Revue d'histoire des religions* 2 (1926) 114–160.

On the Catholic side the following critical studies, among others, have been published. H. Dieckmann, ''Die formgeschichtliche Methode und ihre Anwendung auf die Auferstehungsberichte'' *Scholastik* 1 (1926) 379–399. F. M. Braun, ''Une nouvelle école d'éxégèse'' *La Vie intellectuelle* (1931) 180–199; *Où en est le problème de Jésus* (Brussels 1932); ''Formgeschichte'' *Dictionnaire de la Bible*, supplemental ed. L. Pirot, et al. 3 (1938) 312–317. E. Florit, *Il metodo della ''Storia delle Forme'' e sua applicazione al racconto della passione* (Rome 1935).

Although the attitude of Catholic scholars has been rather negative, efforts are being made to distinguish the method used in this theory from the whole theory itself. During World War II, E. Schick brought out his *Formgeschichte und Synoptikerexegese: eine kritische Untersuchung über die Möglichkeit und die Grenzen der formgeschichtlichen Methode* (New Testament Abhandlungen 18, Münster 1940). This Catholic study, which explains the new method, evaluates it with balanced judgment and endeavors to apply it, is a work of basic importance and is still very useful. (Extensive use of it has been made in preparing this article.) After the war, various Catholic scholars began to accept the method as purged of the errors contained in the rest of the system. Special mention should be made of T. Soiron, who was able, in 1941, to publish (at Freiburg) his work, *Die Bergpredigt Jesu: formgeschichtliche, exegetische und theologische Erklärung.* However, although K. H. Schelkle defended his thesis, *Die Passion Jesu in der Verkündigung des New Testament,* in 1941, it was not until 1949 that he was allowed to publish it (at Heidelberg). Other Catholic scholars who have published valuable studies on this matter are L. Cerfaux, L. Léon-Dufour, H. Schürmann, A. Vögtle, J. Dupont, F. Mussner, the commentators in the Regensburg New Testament, etc. Abundant and clear information can be found in L. Randellini, ''La tradizione evangelica,'' *Introduzione al New Testament* (Brescia 1961) 35–138.

After 1950 there appeared a new method and school that extended and integrated the results of form criticism by paying more attention to the intelligent and important work that the Evangelists did on the material they received from tradition. W. Marxsen gave the name of *Redaktionsgeschichte* (redaction history) to this new method. Some of the main representatives of this school, with their important studies, are G. Bornkamm, ''Matthäus als Interpret der Herrenworte'' *Theologische Literzturzeitung* 79 (1954) 341–346; H. Conzelmann, *Die Mitte der Zeit: Studien zur Theologie des Lukas* (Tübingen 1954); W. Marxsen, *Der Evangelist Markus: Studien zur Redaktionsgeschichte des Evangeliums* (Göttingen 1956).

Other New Testament Literary Genres. The form-criticism school has concentrated its efforts on the Synoptic Gospels, with only an occasional excursus (e.g., by Dibelius) on the Acts of the Apostles.

The New Testament Epistles can be all grouped in one common literary genre, though with certain differences among them, from the short personal note to Philemon through the letters occasioned by certain situations, such as Galatians and 2 Corinthians, up to those Epistles, such as Romans and Hebrews, that approach the form of a theological treatise.

The Revelation to St. John belongs to the apocalyptic literary genre that was highly developed in the late extra-Biblical religious literature of the Jews. It evidently gives more space to eschatological visions, which are described in symbolic terms, than to visions concerning actual history related in allegorical style.

Although all these writings are strictly literary works, the incorporate a certain amount of preliterary, traditional material. To some extent, therefore, they too can be analyzed according to the principles of the history of tradition, yet without the advantage of a possible Synoptic comparison, as in the case of the Gospels. According to Bornkamm (*Die Religion in Geschichte und Gegenwart* 1:1002–05) the following types of literary genre may be mentioned as found in these writings: kerygmas, in which the faith is briefly set forth, and creeds, in which it is professed (1 Cor 15.3–5; 8.6); hymns (Phil 2.6–11); sermons made up of a kerygmatic argument from Scripture combined with an exhortation to repentance (Acts 2.22–39); and admonitions, which occur toward the end of many of the Epistles and which contain, among other things, lists of vices and virtues (Rom 1.29–31), comparisons taken from everyday life (1 Cor 9.24), and advice on the various states of life (Eph 5.21–6.9).

[L. ALONSO SCHÖKEL]

FORMOSUS, POPE

Pontificate: Oct. 6, 891 to April 4, 896. Of Roman origin, Formosus played an important role in papal affairs for more than a quarter of a century before becoming pope. He was consecrated bishop of Porto in 864 by Pope NICHOLAS I, who selected him to lead the missionary party that went to Bulgaria in 866 at the request of King Boris. Formosus was so successful in that venture that Boris sought to have him made an archbishop to serve as head of an autonomous Bulgarian church. It was a request that Nicholas denied, perhaps because he suspected that it had more to do with Formosus' ambition than with Boris' wishes. Formosus took an active part in the proceedings of the Roman synod of 869, which denied the right of PHOTIUS to be Patriarch of Constantinople. In 869 and again in 872 he served as papal legate on missions sent to the West Frankish and the East Frankish kingdoms. He played an important role in the complex maneuvering by Pope JOHN VIII that ended in 875 with the selection of Charles the Bald, king of the West Franks, to succeed Louis II as emperor. But Formosus' prominent role in the papal affairs was abruptly interrupted in 876, when he and a circle of prominent clerical and civil officials were forced by John VIII to flee Rome. When the fugitives refused the papal command to return to Rome, John VIII excommunicated them. After several years in exile in the West Frankish kingdom, Formosus was permitted to return to Rome and was restored to his see at Porto by POPE MARINUS I. In 885 he as bishop of Porto was called on to consecrate Pope STEPHEN V, and he himself was elected pope in 891.

As had been the case since the pontificate of Nicholas I (858–867), appeals continued to flow to the Roman curia requiring decisions by the pope. Although Photius had been deposed as patriarch in 886, opposing parties in Constantinople were still seeking to resolve problems associated with his patriarchate, especially the issue of the legality of his ordinations. Asked for a ruling on this matter, Formosus insisted that those ordained by Photius must surrender their positions, a decision that impeded the efforts of those in Constantinople anxious to put an end to the Photian schism and to make peace with Rome. Disputes arising from challenges to the jurisdiction of metropolitans and from contested episcopal elections continued to be appealed to Rome; Formosus made every effort to assure that papal authority in settling such matters was honored. At the urging of Archbishop Fulk of Reims, Formosus lent his support to the cause of Charles the Simple in his struggle against Eudo, count of Paris, for kingship of the West Frankish kingdom.

These activities reminiscent of the pontificates of such great Carolingian popes as ADRIAN I (772–795) and Nicholas I were in fact misleading in terms of the actual situation facing the papacy and the PAPAL STATE as the ninth century neared its end. The problem, long in the making, was fundamental. Since the pontificate of STEPHEN II (752–757) the survival of the Papal State and the capability of the pope to act independently on behalf of the Christian community had depended on a protector willing and able to guarantee the territorial integrity and the autonomy of the Papal State and allow the pope freedom of action in religious affairs. The Carolingian dynasty had filled that role since the time of King PEPIN III. However, by the end of the ninth century that family was fast approaching its end.

This emerging chaos was particularly evident in Italy, creating a situation which threatened the very existence of the Papal State. When Formosus became pope, Guido (Guy) of Spoleto—long an antagonist of popes John VIII and Marinus I—had emerged as the leading actor on the Italian scene. Guido was able by force of arms to establish himself as king of Italy and then in 891 to compel Pope STEPHEN V to crown him emperor and his son Lambert king of Italy. His past behavior left no doubt that he would have little respect for the ancient privileges of the Papal State. Guido's ascendancy raised the urge in Rome to seek a more benevolent protector for St. Peter. The leading candidate was Arnulf, king of the East Franks, to whom Pope Stephen V had already made overtures about intervention in Italy.

By the time of the election of Formosus, Guido seemed to be consolidating his position as master of Italy. He compelled Formosus to crown his son Lambert as emperor, assuring Spoletan control of that office. Complaints about his aggression against residents of the Papal State mounted. All of which combined to persuade Formosus in the summer of 893 to renew his predecessor's plea to Arnulf to help St. Peter and his people against ''the evil Christians'' of Spoleto. Arnulf invaded Italy in late 893, drove Guido out of Pavia, but then returned to his own realm without taking decisive action. Guido died soon after, leaving Lambert as emperor and king of Italy. In response to new papal appeals Arnulf led another expedition into Italy in 895 and marched victoriously to Rome, where he overpowered the Spoletan defenders and took over the city in early 896. Formosus immediately crowned him emperor, but what seemed a papal triumph was fleeting. While leading a campaign against Lambert Arnulf suffered an incapacitating stroke that ended any possibility of his utilizing his imperial office on behalf of the pope and the Papal State.

Shortly after Arnulf's coronation, Formosus died, but his presence on the Roman scene was not yet ended. With Arnulf disabled, Lambert of Spoleto quickly recovered control of Rome. He and his mother, Agiltrude forced Pope STEPHEN VI to convene a synod in 897 to consider the fitness of Formosus for the papal office. The dead pope's body, already buried nine months, was exhumed and placed in full regalia on a throne before the synod. With Pope Stephen VI presiding, a series of charges derived from Formosus' activities throughout most of his past career were addressed to the cadaver whose ''responses'' were relayed to the assemblage by a terrified deacon standing beside the corpse. At the end of what was later dubbed a *horrennda synoda,* Formosus' pontificate was declared illegal and all of his acts were declared void, including his ordinations. His body was then stripped of its insignia and vestments and consigned to a common grave from whence it was to be thrown into the Tiber, but it was spared that fate by a hermit who recovered and re-interred it.

This ''cadaveric synod'' divided Rome and the Papal State into pro- and anti-Formosan parties whose bitter animosity became increasingly violent. As reward for his role in the trial, Pope Stephen was deposed and strangled by the pro-Formosans. Although Pope JOHN IX (898–900) sought to clear the name of Formosus, Pope SERGIUS III (904–911) revived the decrees of the cadaverous synod, touching off not only a new round of violence but also the pamphlet writing of Auxilius and Eugenius Vulgarius in defense of Formosus. By the time the vicious rivalry over the Formosan issue ended, irreparable damage had been done to the established order in the Papal State. The constant turmoil caused by the rivalry of these factions created a setting that allowed a powerful Roman family, founded by Theophylactus, an official in the papal administration, to seize control of elections to the papal office, to exploit papal resources, and to dominate the governance of Rome and the Papal State during the first half of the tenth century.

Bibliography: *Liber Pontificalis,* ed. L. DUCHESNE, 3 v., 2n ed. (Paris 1955–1957) 2: 227. *Regesta Pontificum Romanorum ab condita ecclesia ad annum post Christum MCXCVIII,* ed. P. JAFFÉ, 2 v., 2d ed. (Leipzig 1885–88) 2: 435–439. *Formosi papae epistolae quotquot ad res Germanicas spectant,* ed. G. LAEHER, *Monumenta Germaniae Historica, Epistolae,* vol. 7: *Epistolae Karolini Aevi* (Berlin 1928) 366–370. J. D. MANSI, *Sacrorum conciliorum, nova et amplissima collectio,* 54 v. (Paris 1901–1920; reprinted Graz, 1960–1961), 18A: 101–174. *Flodoard von Reims, Die Geschichte der Reimser Kirche,* Liber IV, chs. 1–3, ed. M. STRATMANN, *Monumenta Germaniae Historica, Scriptores* 36 (Hannover, 1998) 363–378. E. DÜMMLER, *Auxilius und Vulgarius: Quellen und Forschungen zur Geschichte des Papsttums im Anfange des zehnten Jahrhunderts* (Leipzig 1866); *Gesta Berengarii Imperatoris. Beiträge zur Geschichte Italiens im Anfange des zehnten Jahrunderts* (Halle 1871) (In these two studies, DÜMMLER edits and comments on the main texts that emerged from the quarrel over Formosus' trial, including the tracts by Auxilius and Eugenius Vulgarius.) L. DUCHESNE, *The Beginnings of the Temporal Sovereignty of the Popes, A.D. 754–1073,* tr. A. H. MATTHEW (London 1908) 167–216. C. J. HEFELE, *Histoire des conciles d'après les documents originaux,* tr. H. LECLERCQ, vol. 4, part 2 (Paris 1911), 708–719. G. DOMENCI, ''Il papa Formoso,'' *La Civilità Cattólica* 75, no. 1 (1924) 106–120; 518–536; 75, no. 2 (1924) 121–135. J. DUHR, ''La concile de Ravenna, 895. La réhabilitation du pape Formose,'' *Recherches de science religieuse* 22: 541–579. F. X. SEPPELT, *Geschichte des Papsttums. Eine Geschichte der Päpste von den Anfängen bis zum Tod Pius X,* vol. 2: *Das Papsttums im Frühmittelalter. Geschichte des Päpste von Regierungsantritt Gregors des Grossen bis zum Mitte des ll. Jahrhundert,* (Leipzig 1934) 328–331. A. FLICHE, *L'Europe occidentale de 888 à 1125,* Histoire générale: Histoire du Moyen Age 2 (Paris 1941) 41–59, 110–131. É. AMANN and A. DUMAS, ''L'Église au pouvoir des laïques (888–1037),'' *Histoire de l'Église depuis les origines jusqu'a nos jours,* ed. A. FLICHE and V. MARTIN 7 (Paris 1948) 15–25. F. DVORNIK, *The Photian Schism. History and Legend* (Cambridge 1948) 202–232. J. HALLER, *Das Papsttum: Idee und Wirklichkeit,* vol. 2: *Der Aufbau* (Basel 1951) 190–194. G. ARNALDI, ''Papa Formoso e gli imperatori della casa di Spoleto,'' *Annali della Facultà di Lettera di Napoli,* 1 (1951) 85–104. H. ZIMMERMANN, *Papstabsetzungen des Mittelalters* (Graz, Vienna, and Cologne 1968) 49–76. A. LAPÔTRE, ''Le pape Formose. Étude sur les rapports du Saint-Siège avec Photius,'' in *Études sur la papauté au IXe siècle, 2 vols.* (Turin 1978) 1: 1–120. M. BACCHIEGA, ''Papa Formoso: processo di cadavere,'' *Gli Antagoniste* (Foggio 1983). W. HARTMANN, *Die Synoden der Karol-*

ingerzeit im Frankenreich und in Italian (Paderborn, Munich, Vienna, and Zurich 1989) 388–396. P. LLEWELLYN, *Rome in the Dark Ages* (London 1993) 286–315.

[R. E. SULLIVAN]

FORMS, UNICITY AND PLURALITY OF

A subject of controversy in the Middle Ages that can be understood only in terms of the Aristotelian doctrines it presupposes. This article therefore treats the presuppositions on which the controversy was based, its origins, its historical development, and a brief evaluation of its importance in the history of thought.

Presuppositions. The thesis of unicity or plurality of forms is philosophical in nature. It is an application to a concrete fact of the Aristotelian metaphysical doctrines of potency and act and of matter and form (*see* POTENCY AND ACT; MATTER AND FORM). It applies to all substances composed of matter and form. It may be formulated thus: whether in one individual, remaining essentially one, there are many substantial forms or only one. The essence of a natural thing is constituted from two principles: one potential, undetermined in itself yet determinable, namely, matter; the other actual, the determining factor that makes the thing what it is, namely, FORM. Incomplete in themselves, they tend naturally to unite so as to constitute one individual substance, the *hoc aliquid,* or composite, which, although possessing several perfections and activities, is essentially one. Three factors are essential in becoming: the starting point of the change, PRIVATION; its end, form; and an underlying subject, or substratum, persisting through the process. The substratum, though numerically one before the change, plays a double part: one positive, persisting in every transmutation, matter; the other negative, the absence of the preceding form, privation. Privation, however important in becoming, does not survive as a constituent element (*Phys.* 190a 14–192a 33; *Meta.* 1032a 15–1033b 19, 1055b 11, 1069b 32–4). The crux of the problem consists in determining (1) whether primary matter is absolutely passive potency or contains some actuality of its own (*potentia activa*); (2) whether privation is the disappearance of all previous forms or is an incomplete form (*incohatio formae*); and (3) whether substantial form, including virtually all preceding forms, confers on primary matter its complete and specific determination, and alone actualizes all its perfections and activities, or imparts one perfection only. In the first alternative, one must posit oneness of form; in the latter, plurality of forms.

Origins of the controversy. In the height of the controversy, JOHN PECKHAM asserted that the unicity thesis originated from the Averroist leaders (*Registrum epistolarum,* ed. C. T. Martin, *Rerum Britannicarum medii aevi scriptores,* 224 v. [London 1858–96; repr. New York 1964—] 3:842). The theory is Aristotelian in origin, not Averroist; the question was debated years before the Averroist movement arose (*see* AVERROISM, LATIN). It impinged on the schoolmen with Avicenna's *De anima* (Venice 1508, v. 7, fol. 26v–27v), and was formulated by DOMINIC GUNDISALVI (GUNDISSALINUS) in his own *De anima* [ed. J. T. Muckle, *Mediaeval Studies* 2 (1940) 44–7]. The discussion turned on the oneness of soul, admittedly a different question; but by systematically presenting Avicenna's statement and introducing the catchword ''substance,'' Gundissalinus supplied the main features of the problem and set the basis of the unity thesis: the vegetative, sensitive, and rational, though separately three distinct substances, united in man are one simple substance. Nevertheless, in his *De processione mundi* (ed. G. Bülow, *Beiträge zur Geschichte der Philosophie und Theologie des Mittelalters* 24.3:30) and *De unitate* (ed. P. Correns, *ibid.* 1.1:8) he popularized Avicebron's theories on matter and form, on the various degrees of forms, and other tenets, thus providing the pluralists with their fundamental principles.

Historical development. The full implications of the problem dawned on the masters slowly and gradually. In its first phase it was restricted to psychology; later, when its metaphysical issue was grasped, it was extended to all composites.

Prior to Aquinas. In its earliest stage the investigation, after the pattern of Avicenna and Gundissalinus, centered in the plurality or unity of the soul in man. JOHN BLUND (before 1210) and ROLAND OF CREMONA (1229–30) first broached the subject. Both supported the unity theory. Roland's proofs foreshadowed St. Thomas Aquinas's: Since one thing has one being (*unicum esse*), it can have but one first perfection. And if the first imparts complete perfection, the second or third serves no purpose. The pluralists argued from the embryo-genesis theory, which later, with the support of Aristotle's *De generatione animalium* (736a 35–736b 5), became their strongest evidence throughout the controversy. With PHILIP THE CHANCELLOR (d. 1236) the inquiry moved from the unity of soul to the unicity of substance: ''whether the sensitive and rational are rooted in the same substance.'' Some held that man possesses one soul comprising three distinct incorporeal substances, each exercising a special vital function. Others maintained that they were not three substances, but powers, or faculties, rooted in one soul, one substance. Philip's presentation of the question set the standard for the first half of the thirteenth century.

St. ALBERT THE GREAT, perceiving its general and wider principles, brought the inquiry one step further. He identified substance and form, distinguished by Philip and others. Albert's considered view appears in *De unitate intellectus:* "In my writings I repeatedly repudiated the pluralist theory as an absurdity. Its inventors were not Aristotelians, but some Latins who knew not the nature of the soul. It is a fatal error to assert that one subject possesses many [*plures* with the manuscripts, not *possibiles,* as in the printed text] substances, for substances cannot be but forms" (*Omnia opera,* ed. A. Borgnet, 9:455). See S. Vanni-Rovighi, "Alberto Magno e l'Unità della forma sostanziale nell'uomo," *Studi in onore di Bruno Nardi* (Firenze 1955) 2:753–778.

To sum up, Aristotle was claimed by all litigants, and the supporters of unicity appealed also to Augustine. ADAM OF BUCKFIELD, ROGER BACON, and Geoffrey of Aspall (see A. B. Emden, *A Biographical Register of the University of Oxford to* A.D. *1500,* 3 v. [Oxford 1957–59] 1:60–61) were all pluralists; and so were, according to their own principles, ROBERT GROSSETESTE, THOMAS OF YORK, and St. BONAVENTURE. RICHARD FISHACRE and RICHARD RUFUS OF CORNWALL remained undecided. But Philip the Chancellor, HUGH OF SAINT-CHER, JOHN OF LA ROCHELLE, the *Summa Fratris Alexandri,* WILLIAM OF AUVERGNE, Pseudo-Grosseteste's *De anima,* and St. Albert all defended the unity of substance in man, however imperfectly they understood it. Yet by admitting a medium uniting soul and body, or by distinguishing between substance and form, they showed their incomplete grasp of its implications. Even Albert, not being aware of the full implications of potency and act, failed to tackle certain difficulties, such as the elementary forms in inorganic bodies (*mixta*). By granting exceptions, they weakened its metaphysical and universal value [see D. A. Callus, "The Origins of the Problem of the Unity of Form," *The Dignity of Science,* ed. J. A. Weisheipl (Washington 1961) 121–149; O. Lottin, *Psychologie et Morale aux XIIe et XIIIe siècles* (2d ed. Gembloux 1957) 1:463–479].

Thomistic Teaching. St. THOMAS AQUINAS brought the unicity thesis to its full maturity. Recognizing the confusions on the fundamental issue, he restated the problem anew. His innovation consists in linking the traditional thesis with Aristotelian doctrine, regarding it not as psychological but as metaphysical, based on the principle of CONTRADICTION. An exact concept of *esse* and unity, of primary matter and substantial form, and of the distinction between substantial and accidental form enabled him to demonstrate the intrinsic incompatibility of plurality of forms, whether juxtaposed, or hierarchically coordinated, or however disposed. Nothing is absolutely one except by one form, by which a thing has being, for a thing has both being and unity from the same source. If, therefore, a human being were living by one form, animal by another, and man by a third, it would follow that he is not absolutely one. If the intellectual soul is the form of the body, it is impossible that there be another substantial form besides the intellectual soul, as it is impossible for any accidental disposition or other medium to come between the body and the soul or between any substantial form and its matter. Since the intellectual soul virtually comprises all inferior forms, it does by itself whatever the imperfect forms do in other things (*Summa Theologiae,* 1a, 76.1, 3–8; *De anim.* 6, 9–11; *De spir. creat.* 1–3).

Primarily a philosophical problem, it became theological by implication. But the question itself was not new, and it had been debated peacefully until theological inferences impinged on it. The crisis flared up during Thomas's second regency in Paris (1269–72). His dictum that "all previous forms disappear with the advent of the substantial form" (*Quodl.* 1.4.1, Easter 1269) aroused fierce opposition from some theologians. The crucial issue concerned Christ's identity living and dead. Was Christ, living and dead, the same man? Was His body numerically the same on the cross and in the grave? Does the soul perfect the body immediately or by means of corporeity? Thomas answered that, soul and body being hypostatically united with the Divine Person in life and death, Christ living and dead was identically, or *simpliciter,* the same man. But since the soul makes the body human, at their separation, the soul remaining the same, Christ's body was the same in a certain respect, or *secundum quid* (*Quodl.* 2.1, Christmas 1269; *ibid.* 3.2.2, Easter 1270; *ibid.* 4.5.1, Easter 1271; cf. *Summa Theologiae* 3a, 50.5, Naples 1273). The form of corporeity, not being distinct from the specific form but one and the same with it, does not remain (*Quodl.* 12.7.1, Christmas 1270).

The univocity thesis was impugned, but not condemned, in Paris. It was included in neither the 1270 nor the 1277 syllabus. There is no foundation for a story that it was proscribed and that Thomas was excommunicated. This arose from a misinterpretation of ROGER MARSTON [*Quaestiones disputatae* (Quaracchi 1932) 116–117; see D. A. Callus, "The Problem of the Unity of Form and Richard Knapwell, OP," *Mélanges offerts a Étienne Gilson* (Toronto-Paris 1959) 151–156].

The Oxford Crisis. Spared in Paris, the thesis was attacked at Oxford. The Dominican archbishop of Canterbury, ROBERT KILWARDBY, on March 18, 1277, forbade the teaching that "the vegetative, sensitive, intellective principles are one simple form [12]. The absolute potentiality of prime matter [3]; the absence of any incomplete form in privation [4]; the immediate union of substantial form with prime matter [7, 16]; and the equivocal predication of a living and dead body [13]'' were also not to be taught (*Chartularium universitatis Parisiensis,* 4 v. [Paris 1889–97] 1:558–560). Peter of Conflans, archbishop of Corinth, however, remonstrated with Kilwardby for condemning irreproachable theses, especially that of the unity of form, upheld as true doctrine by many masters. Kilwardby riposted that it is unintelligible that the specific form of the composite performs the activities of all imperfect forms, and at its presence they all pass away. This theory, he said, is false and against sense experience, faith, and morals. The true unity of forms consists in the aggregate of all incomplete forms, essentially different but coordinated, each performing its proper action, and thus constituting with the complete form one composite.

Kilwardby's *Apologia* prompted two vigorous replies—one from GILES OF ROME with the *Contra gradus et pluralitates formarum* (before April of 1278), the other from GILES OF LESSINES with his *De unitate formae* (July of 1278), which is a constructive, comprehensive, and dignified treatise, in which all Kilwardby's arguments are objectively confuted. The unity thesis was attacked by WILLIAM DE LA MARE in his *Correctorium Fratris Thomae,* but it was defended by THOMAS OF SUTTON in the *Contra pluralitates formarum* and in *De productione formae substantialis* (*see* CORRECTORIA). HENRY OF GHENT discussed the question in Paris without taking sides (*Quodl.* 1.4, 1276). Later, mainly because of theological prejudices, he stated that there are two forms in man but one in other compounds (*Quodl.* 2.2, Christmas 1277; *ibid.* 3.6, Easter 1286; etc.). And so it continued to be freely ventilated in the schools.

The controversy reached its final climax with Kilwardby's successor, John Peckham, who on Oct. 29, 1284, ratified the prohibition, singling out the unity tenet as a source of many absurdities. A long and painful struggle ensued between him and the English Dominicans. The crux of the dispute converged on whether the unicity thesis was compatible with Catholic doctrine. Peckham claimed that it was impossible, without the plurality theory, to safeguard the teaching on the Incarnation, the Eucharist, the resurrection of the body, and other Catholic articles. The Dominicans argued that the problem was not theological, but primarily philosophical, and therefore either answer was consistent with the faith. Since all Catholic doctrines could be explained effectively by either view, it could be discussed freely as an opinion. Moreover, since, on Peckham's own confession, this question was reserved to the Holy See, it was outside the archbishop's competency.

WILLIAM DE HOTHUM, Dominican provincial, pointed out to Peckham that the proper way of determining a philosophical issue, when either solution might be adopted without danger to faith, was not by condemnation but by a solemn disputation. RICHARD KNAPWELL undertook this task in his disputed question ''Whether faith about the essence of human nature united to the Word requires us to posit many forms.'' His purpose was not to attack the pluralist view nor to defend his own, but to show that both opinions could equally safeguard Catholic faith. He expounded them objectively, replied to both objections, and concluded: ''All this is said without dogmatizing, or injury to a better opinion.'' Peckham, however, on April 30, 1286, condemned the unity thesis in itself and in all its implications as heretical and fruitful of heresies, and excommunicated its defenders (*Rerum Britannicarum medii aevi scriptores* 3:921–923). Contrary to Peckham's expectation and pressure, Rome did not ratify his censure. The reaction to the condemnation was strongly felt, and it was criticized vigorously in Paris (cf. GODFREY OF FONTAINES, *Quodl.* 3.5.207–208, 211; Christmas 1286). Knapwell disappeared from Oxford, but ROBERT OF ORFORD, Thomas of Sutton, WILLIAM OF MACCLESFELD, and others vindicated the Thomist thesis.

The condemnation did not stop the controversy. It continued in scholastic disputations, treatises, and commentaries on the *Sentences* and on Aristotle. The condemnation had no juridical effect outside Peckham's province; yet it painfully hampered the freedom of discussion, causing perplexities and anguish of minds (cf. Henry of Ghent, Godfrey of Fontaines, *loc. cit.*). In Oxford the hindrance was more deeply felt. JOHN BACONTHORP, as late as the first half of the fourteenth century, is a striking example. Comparing Oxford with Paris, he deplored that, whereas the Parisians were free to accept whatever opinion they preferred, the Oxford masters were compelled to discuss it in Peckham's terms [*Quaest. in 3 sent.* 19.1 (Cremona 1618) 119–124; see D. A. Callus, ''The Problem . . . and Richard Knapwell,'' 123–160].

Evaluation. The controversy was not a conflict between Dominicans and Franciscans. They certainly had a prominent share in it; but other religious and secular masters in theology and arts joined issue. Nor was it a hair-splitting question. Indeed it was of the highest metaphysical importance. It is an explanation of the essential unity of man and of any composite. The answer betrays two concepts of unity: composite unity and simple unity. The pluralists, considering the components in the structure of the composite as substantial entities, posited unity of composition, although they varied considerably in their interpretations. Thomas Aquinas, establishing the transcendental relation of matter and form on potentiality and actuality and on the real composition of essence and the act of being, necessarily postulated one simple substance, or form, in all composites. He made it the cornerstone of his metaphysics and a fundamental tenet of his synthesis [cf. *Acta Apostolicae Sedis* 6 (1914) 385]. The conflict, therefore, was between two opposite tendencies; two different interpretations of potentiality and actuality, of matter and form; two different methods of approaching philosophical problems. For the metaphysicians, the controversy over unicity or plurality of forms is of universal significance and permanent value, and it is as relevant in the twenty-first century as it was in the thirteenth.

See Also: SCHOLASTICISM; ESSENCE AND EXISTENCE.

Bibliography: É. H. GILSON, *History of Christian Philosophy in the Middle Ages* (New York 1955) 416–420, 735–740, complete bibliog. D. A. CALLUS, "The Problem of Plurality of Forms in the Thirteenth Century. The Thomist Innovation," *L'Homme et son destin d'après les penseurs du moyen-âge* (Louvain 1960); *The Condemnation of St. Thomas at Oxford* (Aquinas Papers 5; Oxford 1946); "Two Early Oxford Masters on the Problem of Plurality of Forms: Adam of Buckfield—Richard Rufus of Cornwall," *Revue néo-scolastique de philosophie* 42 (1939) 411–445. A. C. PEGIS, *St. Thomas and the Problem of the Soul in the Thirteenth Century* (Toronto 1934). T. CROWLEY, *Roger Bacon: The Problem of the Soul in His Philosophical Commentaries* (Louvain 1950). R. ZAVALLONI, *Richard de Mediavilla et la controverse sur la pluralité des formes* (Philosophes médiévaux 2; Louvain 1951). A. FOREST, *La Structure metaphysique du concret selon S. Thomas d'Aquin* (Paris 1956). M. DE WULF, *Le Traité "De unitate formae" de Gilles de Lessines* (Les Philosophes belges 1; Louvain 1901).

[D. A. CALLUS]

FORNARI-STRATA, MARIA VICTORIA, BL.

Widow, foundress and abbess; b. Genoa, Italy, 1562; d. there, Dec. 15, 1617. In 1589 after nine years of marriage to Angelo Strata (Strada), she was widowed; she made a vow of chastity and lived quietly with her six children until they were settled in life. Five of them became religious; the sons, Franciscans; the daughters, Regular Canonesses. She was then free to carry out her desire to found an order of contemplative nuns devoted to the mystery of Mary's Annunciation and hidden life in Nazareth. Through the financial assistance of Vincenza Lomellini, she built a convent, and Bernardino Zannoni, SJ, drew up the constitutions, which were approved by CLEMENT VIII on March 15, 1604. Maria Victoria and ten companions were clothed in the habit; a year later they made solemn vows (Sept. 7, 1605). Each nun added "Maria Annunziata" to her baptismal name, and the order became known as the "Celestial Annunciades" from their sky-blue scapulars and mantles to distinguish them from the order founded by St. JOAN OF FRANCE (VALOIS). The Italians called them "Le Turchine" or "Blue Nuns." The order spread to Pontarlier (1612) and Vezou (1613) in Burgundy and then to Germany. The cloister is unusually rigid; the nuns devote their time to making vestments and altar linens for poor churches. Pope LEO XII beatified Maria Victoria in 1828.

Feast: Sept. 12.

Bibliography: F. A. SPINOLA, *Vita . . . di Maria Vittoria . . .* (Genoa 1649). F. DU MORTIER, *La Bienheureuse Marie-Victoire Fornari, fondatrice des Annonciades célestes* (Paris 1902). C. W. CURRIER, *History of Religious Orders* (New York 1896) 406–408. P. FOURNIER, *Dictionnaire d'histoire et de géographie ecclésiastiques,* ed. A. BAUDRILLART (Paris 1912) 3:409–412. A. BUTLER, *The Lives of the Saints,* ed. H. THURSTON and D. ATTWATER, 4 v. (New York 1956) 3:547–548.

[G. M. GRAY]

FORNICATION

Sexual intercourse between an unmarried man and an unmarried woman who are not closely related. It is thus distinguished from adultery, in which at least one of the parties is married, and from incest, in which there is a close relationship either of blood or affinity between the parties. Fornication, objectively considered, is always gravely sinful. It is one of the sins that excludes those guilty of it from the kingdom of Christ and of God (Eph 5.5; cf. 1 Cor 7.2; 10.8; Gal 5.19). This doctrine is confirmed by natural reason, which holds that the generative act is legitimate only when performed by a man and woman bound to each other by the tie of marriage. The unwed are not responsibly related to each other so as to provide a stable family situation in which possible issue of their union can be properly cared for and brought to maturity. Sexual relations between persons unmarried to each other are a type of activity that, per se, can result in injury to offspring and to the community, which is likely either to be burdened with their care, or to be deprived of the sort of increment it has the right to expect as the fruit of the union of its male and female members. Moreover, if irresponsible and promiscuous sexual behavior were legitimate, this would cause the institution of marriage, so necessary to the social good, to be less desirable, and it would provide occasion for much disorder and strife.

Bibliography: THOMAS AQUINAS, *Summa theologiae* 2a2ae, 154.2–3. B. DOLHAGARAY, *Dictionnaire de théologie catholique,* ed. A. VACANT et al., 15 v. (Paris 1903–50; Tables générales 1951–) 6.1:600–611. F. ROBERTI et al., *Dictionary of Moral Theology,* ed. P. PALAZZINI et al., tr. H. J. YANNONE et al. from 2d Ital. ed. (Westminster, Md. 1962) 515.

[L. G. MILLER]

FORNICATION (IN THE BIBLE)

Israel's legal tradition did not specifically prohibit sexual intercourse between an unmarried man and an unmarried woman. Unmarried women living in the paternal home were expected to be chaste since their chastity was a matter of respecting their fathers' authority and his economic interests. Thus, Deuteronomic legislation stipulates that a man who seduces an unmarried woman is to pay 50 shekels, as a form of bride price, to her father (Dt 22.28–29; see Ex 22.14–16). Subsequently he was not allowed to divorce her. If a man discovers that a woman was not a virgin at the time of their marriage and wished therefore to divorce her, substantiation of the charge meant that she was to be put to death because she had committed a serious sexual offense that affected the entire community (Dt 22.20–21). Legislation in Leviticus stipulated the death penalty for the daughters of priests who served as sacred prostitutes themselves because their sacrilegious behavior dishonored and tainted their fathers (Lv 21.9).

In English translations of the New Testament the Greek word *porneia* is often translated as "fornication." In fact, *porneia* is a general term meaning "sexual immorality" or "immoral sexual behavior." Specific connotations of the term can sometimes be construed from the contexts in which the term appears. Thus, Acts 15.20, 29 uses the term *porneia* as a summary of the kinds of sexual immorality cited in Leviticus 18. Influenced by the biblical image of the marital covenant to describe the covenantal relationship between Yahweh and Israel, the Book of Revelation uses "fornication" as a metaphor for idolatry and idolatrous practices (Rv 2.21; 14.8; 17.2, 4; 18.3; 19.2).

Most of the New Testament texts that employ the term *porneia* use it in a general sense. Thus, "fornication" is a common item on the lists of vices scattered here and there throughout the New Testament (Mk 7.21, etc.). Paul exhorts the Corinthians and the Thessalonians to "shun fornication" (1 Cor 6.18; 1 Thes 4.3). Like most of the moralists of his day, Paul gives sexual intercourse with a prostitute as an example of *porneia*, but he says nothing about the marital status of either the man or the woman involved in the activity. No New Testament text specifically mentions sexual intercourse between an unmarried man and an unmarried woman.

The meaning of the "exception clause" (Mt 5.32; 19.19) often translated as "except for the case of fornication (*porneia*)" in Matthew's version of Jesus' sayings on divorce is widely debated. The most plausible interpretation is that the clause refers to adultery. Roman law in force at the time that Matthew's gospel was written considered a husband's failure to divorce an adulterous wife to be a capital offense.

Bibliography: R. F. COLLINS, *Divorce in the New Testament*, GNS 38 (Collegeville, Minn. 1992); *Sexual Ethics and the New Testament: Behavior and Belief* (Companions to the New Testament; New York 2000).

[R. F. COLLINS]

FORT AUGUSTUS, ABBEY OF

Benedictine abbey at the south end of Loch Ness, Diocese of Aberdeen, Scotland; dedicated to St. Benedict. The fort, built by the English (1729) to keep the Highlanders in check after the Jacobite rising (1715) and named after the third son of George II, was abandoned and sold (1867). The new owner, Lord Lovat, offered it to the English Benedictines (1876), who transformed it into the present abbey and school. The foundation was the successor and continuation of the pre-Reformation Scottish abbey at Regensburg, which had become a seminary (1862), and whose last returning monk was a member of the new community, which had ties also with the English abbey at Lamspring, Hanover. The abbey, still part of the English Congregation, has produced several archbishops and bishops. The Priory of St. Andrew (Edinburgh), founded from Fort Augustus in 1930, has since moved to North Berwick. St. Anselm (Washington, D.C.) and St. Gregory (Portsmouth, R.I.) were founded as priories from Fort Augustus, though both are now independent. In 1964 Fort Augustus had 31 priests, three clerics, and 14 brothers; its school, opened in 1878, had 157 boys.

Bibliography: O. BLUNDELL, *Kilcumein and Fort Augustus* (Fort Augustus 1914). M. DILWORTH, "Two Necrologies of Scottish Benedictine Abbeys in Germany," *Innes Review,* 9 (1958) 173–203. *Fort Augustus Abbey, Past and Present* (Fort Augustus 1963). *The Catholic Directory for the Clergy and Laity in Scotland, 1964* (Glasgow 1964). O. L. KAPSNER, *A Benedictine Bibliography: An Author-Subject Union List,* 2 v. (2d ed. Collegeville, Minn. 1962): v. 1, author part; v. 2, subject part, 2:256.

[L. MACFARLANE]

FORTEM VIRILI PECTORE

Five-strophe office hymn that was traditionally prescribed for Vespers and Lauds in the common of feasts of holy women. It was composed by Cardinal Silvio Antoniano (1540–1603), who along with Robert BELLARMINE, under the chairmanship of BARONIUS, was a member of the commission that was responsible for the corrections and changes made in the Roman BREVIARY by Pope Clement VIII. The common of holy women was added to the Breviary at this time (1602). The hymn is inspired by Prv 31.10, where the valiant woman is described. The meter is iambic dimeter.

Bibliography: J. JULIAN, ed., *A Dictionary of Hymnology* (New York 1957) 1:382. M. BRITT, ed., *The Hymns of the Breviary and Missal* (new ed. New York 1948) 378–379. J. CONNELLY, *Hymns of the Roman Liturgy* (Westminster MD 1957) 156–157.

[J. P. MCCORMICK]

FORTESCUE, ADRIAN

Writer on oriental churches and Roman liturgy; b. Jan. 14, 1864; d. Letchworth, England, Feb. 11, 1923. He was of the family of St. Adrian Fortescue, martyred in 1539 under Henry VIII. His father Edward Bowles Knottesford Fortescue (1816–1877) built the church at Wilmcote in Warwickshire in the most advanced spirit of the Oxford Movement. In 1850 he became Provost of the St. Ninian Scottish Episcopal Cathedral at Perth. Through his first wife, Francis Spooner, he became connected with Cardinal Manning and the Archbishop of Canterbury, Archibald Tait. Among the seven children born from this marriage were George, who became the Keeper of Printed Books in the British Museum, and his heir, Edward Francis, who was an expert on the Armenian church. For fourteen years Edward was the President of the Association for Promoting the Unity of Christendom (A.P.U.C.). After the death of his first wife, he married Gertrude, the daughter of Reverend Sanderson Robins. Together they entered the Roman Catholic Church in 1872.

The second child of this marriage, Adrian Henry Timothy, was baptized in the Sacred Heart Church, Eden Grove, London, on Jan. 24, 1874, and educated at the Jesuit school at Boulogne–sur–Mer in France and at St. Charles, Bayswater, London. In 1891 he entered Scots College, Rome (Ph.D. 1894) and then to the theological college at Innsbruck. He was incardinated a priest in the Archdiocese of Westminster, where he served at St. Boniface (The German Church) in Whitechapel, as well as at Walthamstow, Ongar, Colchester, Enfield, Witham, and Maldon. After earning the degree of Doctor of Divinity in 1905, he spent a year traveling and studying in the Near East.

During this period he produced his first major work *The Orthodox Eastern Church* (Catholic Truth Society, 1908, third edition, 1911). Also at this time he contributed the first of 110 articles (about 250,000 words) to the original *Catholic Encyclopedia*. On his return to London, he was asked to found a parish in Letchworth in Hertfordshire. He and his cousin Charles Spooner designed the church, which was dedicated to St. Hugh of Lincoln. The opening ceremony was marked by a Mass in the Roman rite as well as by a Byzantine–rite (Melkite) liturgy. *The Tablet* reported the church as a place ''where the services (always strictly liturgical) are carried out in a manner which might well be imitated.'' In 1912, at the suggestion of Herbert Thurston, he wrote his second major work, *The Mass* (Longmans, second edition, 1913). He wrote the preface and edited *A Roman Missal* (tenth edition, New York 1951). In 1918 *The Ceremonies of the Roman Rite Described* first appeared. Until the reforms of the 1960s this volume made the name Fortescue almost synonymous with the Roman liturgy, and it was reproduced many times, as recently as 1996 by St. Austin Press. Fortescue lectured frequently on the Oriental liturgies, and in 1919 he was made consultor of the Congregation for the Oriental Church.

Bibliography: J. MCCARTHY, *Adrian* (Cleveland 1999). J. G. VANCE, *Adrian Fortescue: A Memoir* (New York 1924). *The Wisdom of Adrian Fortescue,* ed. M. DAVIES, (Fort Collins, Co. 1999).

[J. MCCARTHY]

FORTESCUE, ADRIAN, BL.

Knight of St. John, Martyr; b. Hertsfordshire *c.* 1476; d. London, July 8, 1539. The Fortescues were an ancient, noble family dating from the period of the Norman conquest. Adrian's mother was Alice Boleyn, aunt of the future queen. Adrian was the second son. He married Anne Stonor *c.* 1499 and was knighted in 1503. In 1503 he was named a commissioner of levying ''aids'' and in 1511 commissioner for the peace—both in Oxfordshire. In 1513 he was at the ''battle of the spurs,'' and in 1520 at the ''field of the cloth of gold'' in special attendance upon Queen Catherine. In 1530 he stood high in the King's favor, receiving lands from the estates of Wolsey. Perhaps he owed this favor to his close relationship to Anne Boleyn. About this time he married Anne Rede. In 1532 he was admitted as a ''knight of devotion'' of St. John of Jerusalem and in 1533 he joined the ''fraternity'' of the Blackfriars. In 1534 he was arrested and placed in the Marshalsea prison for the best part of a year. In 1539 he was again arrested and his name included in the Act of Attainder against Margaret Pole and others. The charges against him are most vague: that he traitorously refused his duty of allegiance and that he ''hath commyted diverse and sundrie detestable and abominable treasons.'' He was executed on July 8 or 9, 1539, and beatified by Leo XIII in 1895.

Feast: July 11 (Knights of Malta; Archdiocese of Birmingham).

Bibliography: T. FORTESCUE, *A History of the Family of Fortescue* (2d ed. London 1880). B. CAMM, *Lives of the English Martyrs,* 2 v. (London 1904). G. K. FORTESCUE, *Dictionary of National Biography from the Earliest Times to 1900* (London 1885–1900; repr. with corrections, 21 v., 1908–09, 1921–22, 1938; suppl. 1901–) 7:476–477.

[B. C. FISHER]

FORTITUDE, GIFT OF

The gift of the Holy Spirit that adds to acts of the infused virtues, the heroism that some circumstances of life demand. This gift moves the soul to intense acts in the areas of all the virtues, with no anxiety about results. Since it makes practical decisions, fortitude is directed by the gift of COUNSEL. Together, both gifts move the soul to confident activities that are beyond the reach of the virtues alone. Fortitude achieves the fourth Beatitude, an insatiable desire for works of justice that the soul constantly satisfies with acts of virtue. The fruits of the gift are patience, a quiet self-containment in the presence of vexatious details, and longanimity, the ability to endure with composure even very long periods of suffering.

Bibliography: A. ROYO, *The Theology of Christian Perfection*, ed. and tr. J. AUMANN (Dubuque 1962) 474–481. L. M. MARTÍNEZ, *The Sanctifier*, tr. M. AQUINAS (Paterson 1957) 135–141, 232–240, 284–289.

[P. F. MULHERN]

''Fortitude,'' marble sculpture by Nicola Pisano, from the pulpit of the Bapistry of Pisa Cathedral, Italy. (©Dennis Marsico/ CORBIS)

FORTITUDE, VIRTUE OF

Courage of soul that enables a person to adopt and adhere to a reasonable course of action when faced with the danger of death or other grave peril. In a wide sense fortitude can be understood as a general virtue, i.e., as a characteristic of all virtue, because of its very nature any true virtue must be firm and not readily subject to change. However, it is also considered as a specific virtue with the specific function of giving the soul firmness by controlling impulses, on the one hand of fear and on the other of foolhardiness, that might otherwise cause it to deviate from the path of virtue. Fortitude has as its subject the ''irascible'' APPETITE. The virtue strengthens this appetite against the passion of fear and curbs it in its immoderate stirrings of daring or audacity. Opposed to it by way of defect is the vice of cowardice; and by excess, the vice of foolhardiness.

Different conceptions of fortitude, or courage, and the virtues associated with it are to be found in the philosophers of classical antiquity, in the Bible, and in the writings of the Fathers. It is not possible to coordinate these different usages with precision (Gauthier, 487–532). However, it is clear that Christianity has assigned greater value to the passive aspect of courage, its willingness to endure suffering—or if need be, death—in the cause of God's justice, than to the active aspect that is manifest in acts of valor in war and in the performance of other great and noble deeds. In Christian theology the supreme act of the Christian virtue of fortitude is martyrdom (*see* MARTYRDOM, THEOLOGY OF). This, together with the Christian insistence upon gentleness, meekness, clemency, the forgiveness of injury, etc., has served as an excuse for some writers, such as Nietzsche, Marx, Renan, to denounce Christianity because it has made men unmanly and too ready to suffer evil rather than to fight against it. Without doubt there are circumstances in which virtue calls for vigorous and aggressive action, but it is a mistake to think that Christian morality does not take this into account. The virtue of fortitude has two acts: to attack (*aggredi*) is no less characteristic than to endure (*sustinere*).

Of these two acts, however, endurance is the more difficult and requires greater depth of manly courage, other things being equal. When an evil threatens, its objective existence generally helps moderate an excessive impulse to attack; but fear and the difficulties involved in endurance must be coped with by sheer virtue. In attacking evil, man has at least some hope that he will overcome it, some hope that he will prove stronger than the threat; but in endurance he submits to an evil that seems stronger than himself. Again, attack is made in the face of a danger that is still in some measure a future thing; but endurance already oppresses the victim. Furthermore, attack is usually of relatively brief duration; but endurance is long and continuous. However, endurance in this context is not to be regarded as mere passive submission to danger and suffering; it involves, more importantly, a strong action of the soul holding steadfastly to the good and refusing to yield to fear or pain.

The cardinal virtue of fortitude is conceived as strengthening the soul against the fear of death or comparable affliction. The virtues that are its potential parts—MAGNANIMITY, MAGNIFICENCE, PATIENCE, and PERSEVERANCE make the soul steadfast when confronted by lesser evil.

Bibliography: THOMAS AQUINAS, *Summa theologiae* 2a2ae, 123–125. F. L. B. CUNNINGHAM, ed., *The Christian Life* (Dubuque 1959) 655–668. R. A. GAUTHIER, ''Fortitude,'' *The Virtues and States of Life*, ed. A. M. HENRY, tr. R. J. OLSEN and G. T. LENNON (Theology Library 4; Chicago 1957) 487–531; *Magnanimité: L'Idéal de la grandeur dans la philosophie païenne et la théologie chrétienne* (Paris 1951). J. PEIPER, *Fortitude and Temperance*, tr. D. F. COOGAN (New York 1954).

[T. C. KANE]

FORTUNATUS, VENANTIUS HONORIUS CLEMENTIANUS

Poet and bishop of Poitiers; b. near Treviso, Venezia, *c.* 530; d. *c.* 609. Fortunatus was reared in Aquileia and educated in Ravenna (*c.* 552), where he studied rhetoric, grammar, and law. Cured of an eye disease through the intercession of St. MARTIN OF TOURS *c.* 565, he embarked on a pilgrimage of gratitude, the route of which can be traced by poems he composed at Mainz, Cologne, Trier, Metz, Verdun, Rheims, Soissons, Paris, and finally Tours, where he met Bishop Euphronius before he proceeded to Poitiers.

On a visit to Holy Cross convent in Poitiers, Fortunatus met the former Queen RADEGUNDA, who had taken the veil after fleeing from her husband, King Clotaire I of the Franks. He was persuaded to become the director of Radegunda and her spiritual daughter Agnes, abbess of the monastery, where there were about 200 nuns. His devotion to the nuns manifested itself in the constant exchange of gifts, letters, poems, and culinary delicacies. Fortunatus served for a time as steward for the convent and later, after receiving Holy Orders, as chaplain.

In 568 Radegunda received a relic of the true cross from the Byzantine Emperor JUSTIN II, and Fortunatus composed a series of hymns to commemorate the event. His *Vexilla Regis Prodeunt* and the *Pange Lingua Gloriosi Lauream Certaminis* were eventually incorporated into the liturgy of Holy Week. After the deaths of Radegunda and Agnes (*c.* 587), Venantius took up his travels once more and visited the Merovingian King Sigebert, as well as neighboring prelates, St. Felix of Nantes, St. Leontius of Bordeaux, and particularly St. GREGORY OF TOURS, who encouraged him to publish a collection of his poetry. During his lifetime, Fortunatus edited ten books of poetry; one book was published posthumously.

Elected bishop of Poitiers (*c.* 599), Fortunatus held that office for about ten years, but his fame rests on his literary achievements. A Christian gentleman of refinement, even of fastidiousness, Fortunatus has been accused of indulgence in flattery and a euphemistic characterization of contemporaries. His personal life was devout, and by the close of the 8th century his tomb was venerated as that of a saint. Although his name is not included in the Roman martyrology, several French and Italian dioceses venerate him as a saint.

He composed prose lives of St. HILARY OF POITIERS, St. Germain of Paris (*see* GERMAIN, SS.), St. Radegunda, and several local patron saints, as well as hagiographical poems, including a *Vita S. Martini* in 2,243 hexameters. His poetry embraces elegies, panegyrics, and eulogies on grief, death, virginity, patriotism, and womanhood, as well as toasts, inscriptions, epithalamia, and letters in poetical form to friends or hosts.

Fortunatus was a facile poet; but his true merit rests on allusions to contemporary events, persons, and places, depicting the refinement of Christian life and thought during the coarse and harsh Merovingian era. Although he avoided theological allegory, faults in prosody undermine his stature as a poet, and monotony intrudes in his versification. His literary cult declined appreciably after the 16th century.

Bibliography: B. ALTANER, *Patrology,* tr. H. GRAEF (New York 1960) 601–603. F. J. E. RABY, *A History of Christian-Latin Poetry from the Beginnings to the Close of the Middle Ages* (2d ed. Oxford 1953) 86–95. F. LEO and B. KRUSCH, *Monumenta Germaniae Auctores antiquissimi* (Berlin 1825–) v.4. B. KRUSCH and W. LEVISON, *Monumenta Germaniae Scriptores rerum Merovingicarum* (Berlin 1825–) 7.1:205–224, 337–428. H. LECLERCQ, *Dictionnaire d'archéologie chrétienneet de liturgie,* ed. F. CABROL, H. LECLERCQ and H. I. MARROU (Paris 1907–53) 5.2: 1892–97. S. A. BLOMGREN, *Studia Fortunatiana,* 2 v. (Upsala 1933–34); in *Eranos* 48 (Göteborg 1950) 150–156, classics. B. DE GAIFFIER, *Analecta Bollandiana* 70:262–284, cult.

[A. H. SKEABECK]

FORTUNE

A chance event whose *per accidents* cause is an agent operating by deliberate intention; more commonly referred to as luck. In his *Physics* (197a 35–197b 1), ARISTOTLE treats CHANCE as a genus, with fortune and the special type of chance that is not traceable to deliberate intention as its species. He also uses the notion of fortune, as something more known to man, to manifest the notion of chance. The latter is, like the operation of NATURE itself, difficult for the human intellect to grasp clearly. Yet one can see in human affairs that, at times, something happens to an intended effect that is beyond the intention or expectation of the agent, as when a person digging a grave finds a buried treasure.

Unlike chance, fortune or luck is called good or bad depending on the event that happens to the agent. Good luck is often identified with happiness, especially by those who think that the goods dispensed by fortune play a significant part in determining man's happiness. Misfortune, on the other hand, is usually associated with any unintended harm that comes to the agent.

Various notions of good and evil result in correspondingly different notions of fortune and misfortune. By reason of their identification of the good with the objects of desire, the Roman Stoics associated fortune with moral virtue. Since sorrow comes from a present evil, in their view the wise or virtuous man is careful to forestall any evil or misfortune; failing that, he reconciles his desires to what he cannot prevent. Good fortune is important to the extent that it is helpful in the ''art of living.'' (*See* STOICISM.)

Niccolò MACHIAVELLI, comparing fortune to a ''raging river,'' advises his prince to yield to its violence when necessary, but to provide for any reoccurrence ''when the weather becomes fair,'' so that the ''waters may pass away by canal.'' In particular undertakings he advises the prince to ''direct his actions according to the spirit of the times'' in such a way that he may anticipate fortune and be ready to receive it. He concludes that, since fortune changes while men remain the same, men will be successful when they are in agreement with fortune and unsuccessful when they are at odds with it. He further notes that ''fortune is a woman'' and thus yields more readily to the young and the bold man.

Finally there are those who identify fortune with fate, and the latter, in turn, with the PROVIDENCE OF GOD. Both identifications are associated with one type or other of absolute determinism in the universe.

See Also: CHANCE; FATE AND FATALISM.

Bibliography: M. J. ADLER, *The Great Ideas:A Syntopicon of Great Books of the Western World,* 2 v. (Chicago, 1952); v.2, 3 of *Great Books of the Western World.* 1:179–192, 515–525. A. CIOTTI, *Encyclopedia filosofica,* 4 v. (Venice-Rome 1957) 2: 503–504.

[R. A. KOCOUREK]

FORTY HOURS DEVOTION

A continuous period of public prayer ''before the face of the Lord'' recommended by Pope Clement VII in Graves et diuturnae (1592). ''Forty Hours'' seems to have originated in Milan (ca. 1527), where the devotion (involving Masses, eucharistic exposition, processions, litanies and special prayers) rotated through the city's numerous churches, creating a year-round cycle of prayer and supplication. In 1731, Clement XII republished, in Italian, the instructions for Forty Hours ceremonies to be followed as issued two decades earlier by Clement XI. While this ''Clementine Instruction'' was of obligation only in Rome, its use elsewhere was encouraged.

Forty Hours remained popular until the late 20th century. By decree of June 21, 1973 the Congregation for Divine Worship issued a revised ritual, ''Holy Communion and Worship of the Eucharist Outside Mass'' (HCWE). HCWE does not specifically mention the Forty Hours Devotion. Instead, it simply recommends with the local Ordinary's consent and when suitable numbers of people will be present, in churches where the Eucharist is regularly reserved solemn exposition of the Blessed Sacrament once a year for an extended, even if not strictly continuous period of time. ''This kind of exposition,'' says HCWE 82, ''must clearly express the cult of the blessed sacrament in its relationship to the Mass. The plan of the exposition should carefully avoid anything which might somehow obscure the principal desire of Christ in instituting the eucharist, namely, to be with us as food, medicine, and comfort.'' When continuous exposition is not possible because of too few worshipers, the Blessed Sacrament may be replaced in the tabernacle during the scheduled periods of adoration, but no more often than twice each day (HCWE 88). The Host should be consecrated in the Mass which immediately precedes the exposition and after Communion placed in the monstrance upon the altar. Mass ends with the prayer after Communion, and the concluding rites are omitted. The priest then may locate the Blessed Sacrament on an elevated, but not too lofty or distant throne, and incense it (HCWE 93–94). Prayers, scriptural readings, religious silence, homilies or exhortations, congregational singing, and part of the Liturgy of the Hours should be employed during the exposition (HCWE 95–96). This extended exposition is interrupted for Masses celebrated through that period.

[N. D. MITCHELL]

FORTY MARTYRS, SS.

Soldiers martyred near the end of the DIOCLETIAN PERSECUTION; d. March 323. These 40 martyrs probably belonged to the famous Roman Legion XII stationed in Lesser Armenia at Sebaste, the modern Sivas, Turkey. The Eastern Roman Emperor, Licinius, ordered all soldiers to sacrifice to idols. These 40 soldiers refused. While awaiting trial before Agricola, the governor, they composed ''The Testament of the Forty Holy Martyrs of Christ,'' which H. Delehaye considered to be an authentic and accurate historical account of the faith in the 4th century. The governor ordered them exposed naked on a frozen lake. The slow death provided time to persuade them to apostatize. One did. But another soldier declared his Christian faith and took the apostate's place.

Feast: March 10.

Bibliography: A. BUTLER, *The Lives of the Saints*, rev. ed. H. THURSTON and D. ATTWATER, 4 v. (New York 1956) 1:541–544. O. V. GEBHARDT, *Acta Martyrum selecta* (Berlin 1902) 166–181. H. DELEHAYE, *American Catholic Quarterly Review* 24 (Jan. 1899) 161–171; *Les Passions des martyrs et les genres littéraires* (Brussels 1921) 184–235. P. FRANCHI DE' CAVALIERI, *Note agiografiche* 7 (*Studi e Testi* 49; 1928) 155–184.

[E. G. RYAN]

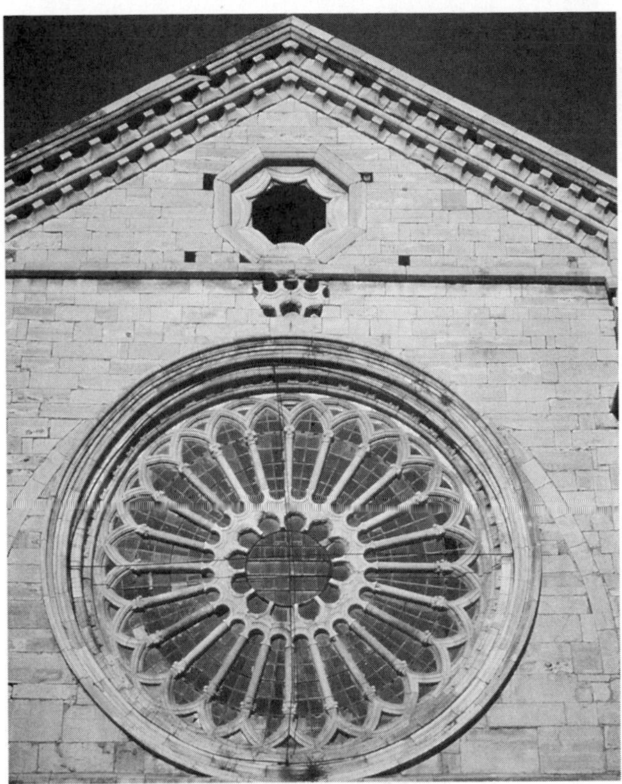

Stained glass window at Fossanova Abbey, Latium, Italy. (©John Heseltine/CORBIS)

FOSCARINI, PAOLO ANTONIO

Philosopher and theologian; b. Montalto Uffugo (Calabria, Italy), *c.* 1565; d. there, June 10, 1616. He entered the Carmelite Order and distinguished himself as a preacher, mathematician, and professor in philosophy and theology at Messina and Naples. In 1607 he was nominated vicar-provincial and in 1608 elected provincial of Carmelite Province of Calabria. His writings were: *Ordinationes et exercitia quotidiana* (Cosenza 1611), *Institutionum omnis generis doctrinarum tomis VII comprehensarum syntaxis* (Cosenza 1613), which can be considered a course in methodology; and *Trattato della divinatione naturale cosmologica* (Naples 1615), part of an unpublished *Institutiones.* Foscarini however became famous by his *Lettera sopra l'opinione de' Pittagorici, e del Copernico della mobilitá della terra, e stabilitá del sole, e del nuovo Pittagorico sistema del mondo, al reverendiss. P.M. Sebastiano Fantone, Generale dell'Ordine Carmelitano* (Naples 1615). In this letter he follows Copernicus's theory as proposed by Galileo, defending it as true and not in contradiction with Holy Scripture. His letter was put on the Index, March 3, 1616.

Bibliography: A. DE S. PAUL, *Dictionnaire de théologie catholique,* ed. A. VACANT (Paris 1903–50)12.1:53–55. A. FRANCO, ''Paulus Antonius Foscarini,'' *Analecta Ordinis Carmelitarum Discalceatorum* 2 (1911) 461–468; 493–504; 524–527. C. NARDI, *Notizie di Montalto in Calabria* (Rome 1954) 257–302, discusses the process against Foscarini. N. PICARD, *Lexikon für Theologie und Kirche,* ed. J. HOFER and K. RAHNER (Freiburg 1957–65) 4:225–226.

[H. SPIKKER]

FOSSANOVA, ABBEY OF

Former Cistercian abbey 60 miles south of Rome, Diocese of Terracina, Italy; now occupied by Conventual Franciscans. Pope Innocent II gave the 11th-century Benedictine monastery of St. Stephen to Cistercians from HAUTECOMBE (1135), and Frederick I Barbarossa and Innocent III favored it to make it one of the most important Cistercian foundations in Italy. It is known for drainage (*fossa nuova*) of the swamps and colonization of south Italy with seven daughterhouses. Its well-preserved Burgundian Gothic church, the first such structure in the south (1208), influenced later Italian architecture. In 1274 Thomas Aquinas died at Fossanova. The commendatory abbatial title was held by cardinals from the Renaissance to 1795, when Pius VI gave Fossanova to Cistercians of Casamari. It was suppressed during Napoleonic rule (1812) and revived by Carthusians (1826).

Bibliography: A. SERAFINI, *L'Abbazia di Fossanova e le origini dell'architettura gotica nel Lazio* (Rome 1924). H. HAHN,

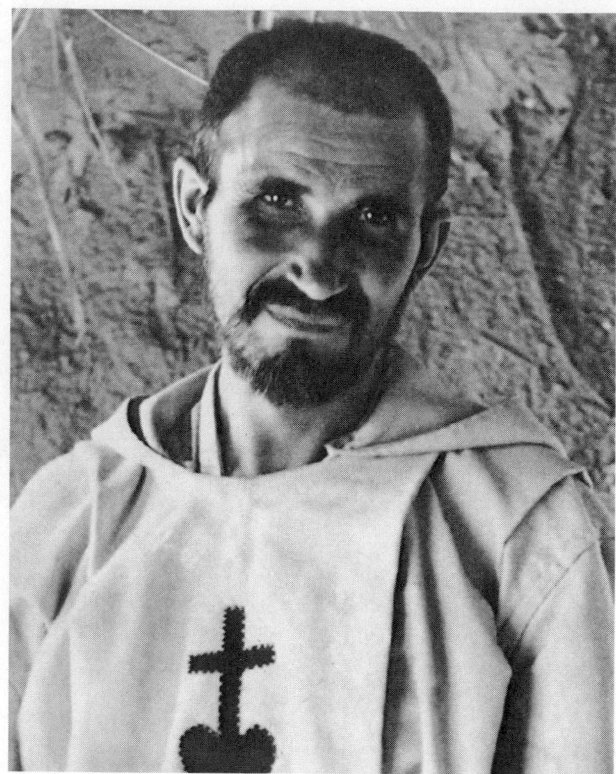

Charles Eugène De Foucauld.

Die frühe Kirchenbaukunst der Zisterzienser (Berlin 1957). U. CHEVALIER, *Répertoire des sources historiques du moyen-âge. Topobibliographie,* 2 v. (Paris 1894–1903) 1150. L. H. COTTINEAU, *Répertoire topobibliographique des abbayes et prieurés,* 2 v. (Mâcon 1935–39) 1:1200. K. SPAHR, *Lexikon für Theologie und Kirche,* ed. J. HOFER and K. RAHNER, 10 v. (2d, new ed. Freiburg 1957–65) suppl., *Das Zweite Vatikanische Konzil: Dokumente und Kommentare,* ed. H. S. BRECHTER et al., pt. 1 (1966) 4:226.

[L. J. LEKAI]

FOUCAULD, CHARLES EUGÈNE DE

Hermit; b. Strasbourg, France, Sept. 15, 1858; d. Tamanrasset, Algeria, Dec. 1, 1916. Foucauld, who came from a distinguished and devout family, was left an orphan in 1864 and was entrusted to the care of his maternal grandfather, De Morlet, a retired colonel. While pursuing his secondary studies at Strasbourg and Nancy, he lost his faith. So deeply did he plunge into dissipation that he had difficulty in completing his military education at Saint-Cyr (1876) and at the cavalry school in Saumur (1878). He received a commission as a second lieutenant, but he was discharged for disorderly conduct at the garrison of Pont-à-Mousson (1881). He was soon restored to his rank and regiment during a native revolt in the Sahara. In the ensuing eight-month campaign he turned from his dissolute ways and distinguished himself in the field for bravery and leadership qualities. When he returned to France, he could not adjust to garrison life and resigned his commission. Then he returned to the Sahara to engage in exploration. After a year spent in Algiers studying local language and customs he passed two years in the desert disguised as the Jewish servant of a rabbi (1883–84). His topographical, ethnological, social, and military findings were published as *Reconnaissance au Maroc, 1883–1884* (1888), which won for him recognition from the Geographical Society of Paris.

So deeply had the desert solitude and the religiousness of the Muslims impressed Foucauld that he became reconciled to the Church of Abbé Henri Huvelin (October 1886). With characteristic intensity he began to live a life of prayer and asceticism. On a pilgrimage to the Holy Land, he joined the TRAPPISTS in the Monastery of Notre Dame des Neiges in Nazareth (1890) but soon transferred to a poorer house at Akbès in Syria (1890–96). In search of greater poverty and self-sacrifice he transferred to the Abbey of Staoüeli in Algeria (1896). The superior there sent him to Rome to study theology, but he left the Trappists before ordination and returned to Nazareth to live as a hermit (1897–1900). In 1901 he was ordained at Viviers.

Thereupon he went back to the Sahara and established a hermitage at Beni-Abbès on the Morocco-Algeria frontier. He sought to bring Christianity to the Muslim desert tribes, not by preaching but by good example. By his life of contemplation and charity he aimed to show himself as a man of God and as "the universal brother," and thereby to prepare the way for later missionaries. In his hermitage, which he called "la Fraternité du Sacré-Coeur de Jésus," he kept the Blessed Sacrament always exposed and spent long hours in adoration. In 1905 he penetrated deeper into the Sahara and set up his hermitage in the Ahaggar Mountains near Tamanrasset. Respected by the Tuareg tribesmen, Foucauld was able to learn a great deal concerning their customs and language. He was murdered by a maurading band belonging to the fanatical Senusi sect. Foucauld had no disciples during life, but the publication of his personal papers inspired the founding of the LITTLE BROTHERS OF JESUS (1933) and the LITTLE SISTERS OF JESUS (1936). The first steps toward Foucauld's beatification were taken by the prefect apostolic of Ghardaia in 1927. In 1947 the relevant documents were forwarded to Rome.

Bibliography: *Oeuvres spirituelles* (Paris 1958), anthology. R. BAZIN, *Charles de Foucauld, Hermit and Explorer,* tr. P. KEELAN (London 1923). A. FREMANTLE, *Desert Calling* (New York 1949). M. CARROUGES, *Soldier of the Spirit: The Life of C. de F.,* tr. M. C. HELLIN (New York 1956). J. F. SIX, *Witness in the Desert,* tr. L. NOEL (New York 1965); ed., *Spiritual Autobiography of C. de F.* (New

York 1964); *Dictionnaire de spiritualité ascétique et mystique. Doctrine et histoire*, ed. M. VILLER et al. (Paris 1932–) 5:729–741.

[A. J. WOUTERS]

FOUNDATIONAL THEOLOGY

The terms ''foundational theology'' or ''fundamental theology'' as commonly understood within Roman Catholic theology refer to the introductory tract that treats the nature, possibility, and existence of revelation. In some versions, it also includes an analysis of the nature of Christian faith and a treatment of the nature, method, and sources of theology. Since the divine revelation in Jesus is the basis of the Church, Roman Catholic theology labels the discipline that deals with the existence and content of that revelation foundational or fundamental theology. The term ''fundamental theology'' is a very literal translation of the Latin *theologia fundamentalis* and was for a long time the title given to the discipline. The term ''foundational theology,'' however, has been used by many (especially Bernard LONERGAN) to signify a conception of the discipline that interprets the foundations of theology in a way different from that of traditional neo-scholasticism. Whereas the neo-scholastic treatment emphasized the nontheological and the apologetical task of the discipline, Lonergan develops foundational theology as a specific functional specialty within theology. Many have adopted Lonergan's term ''foundational'' in order to distance themselves from a view of the discipline that in their opinion is too naturalistic in that it uses philosophical and historical arguments without consideration of any Christian or religious preunderstanding. Nevertheless, the terms ''foundational'' and ''fundamental'' theology are often used today indiscriminately and often represent merely the choice of a different English term.

From Apologetics to Foundational Theology. The history of Christian apologetics up to the ENLIGHTENMENT is one of individual apologies being argued against specific heresies. The Enlightenment's critique of prophecies, miracles, and supernatural revelation struck at the foundations of Christian belief. Johann Sebastian von DREY, one of the initiators of the German TÜBINGEN SCHOOL, argued that a new type of apologetics was necessary. Such an apologetics should go beyond the medieval preambles of faith, namely, those philosophical truths that could be proven independently and prior to faith. It should provide a foundation for Christian faith and theology through a defense of revelation. Drey explicated the program for this discipline within his writing on the organization of theological disciplines in the modern university, with their increased specialization. Theology came to be divided into exegetical, historical, systematic, and practical studies. Catholic theology identified a division of foundational and systematic theology. The goal of foundational theology was to defend the presuppositions of theology, whereas the goal systematic theology was to give an exposition of Christian doctrine.

Modern Preamble of Faith. Henri Bouillard, one of the initiators of a theological movement known as ''la nouvelle théologie'' (the new theology), sought to retrieve a more integrated vision of the relation between the natural and the supernatural. The movement in reality recovered elements of patristic and scholastic theology that modern neo-scholasticism had neglected. It criticized the extrinsicism of neo-scholasticism and argued for a more intrinsic relation between human nature and divine grace and between the love of God and the knowledge of God.

Bouillard's conception of foundational theology retrieves Thomas Aquinas's notion of the preambles of faith, but give it a new role under the conditions of modernity. Bouillard notes that modern fundamental theology developed precisely when modernity stood under the impact of the Enlightenment and DEISM. Deism criticized the existence of supernatural divine revelation, but not the existence of God. The Enlightenment criticized concrete historical religions that invoked prophecies and miracles as a justification of their belief in a special supernatural revelation. Therefore, neo-scholastic fundamental theology sought to demonstrate the possibility and existence of supernatural revelation, the truth of Christian revelation, and the truth of the Catholic church.

Bouillard recognized that the modern situation deals only with the denial of revelation or the God of Abraham, Isaac, and Jacob, but also with the denial of the God of philosophers. Not deism, but atheism is the challenge today. The classical approach to the preambles of faith presupposed the rational and philosophical demonstration of the existence of God, the immortality of the soul, and the principles of morality. Its successor retrieved and also went beyond these demonstrations, taking up their task in the face of modern atheism and the loss of the divine in modern culture. Influenced by Maurice BLONDEL, this approach sought to integrate the natural and philosophical with the religious by appealing to an experience of transcendence that avoided the sharp separation between the philosophical and the religious. The task of foundational theology is then to explicate the interrelation between the philosophical and the religious experience of transcendence in elaborating an approach to the knowledge of God.

Formal and Existential Phenomenology. Karl RAHNER's *Foundations of the Christian Faith* transforms fundamental theology in a decisive way in terms of its addressee, method, and content. Rahner sees foundational theology not simply an apologetic. Rather, it should deal with the possibility of the "unbelief of the believer." It should itself explicate the philosophical mediation of faith. It should convincingly illumine the meaning of the Christian faith not just to the non-Christian or non-Catholic, but to the believers themselves.

Rahner's conception is labeled a "formal-fundamental" theology. This name calls attention to two aspects of his theology. On the one hand, it highlights the phenomenological and existential analysis of the human person as open for God. It explicates the possibility within human knowing and will for human persons to be hearers of God's word and receivers of God's revelation. On the other hand, it emphasizes that foundational theology is more than a formal analysis of human nature and human subjectivity. It uncovers the fact that human beings are immersed in history in their openness to God and oriented toward history in their search for an answer to their quest for the meaning of the mystery of God. This theology explicates that meaning is found in history in the encounter with a history of salvation that culminates in God's definitive revelation in Jesus Christ.

Rahner's treatment of the traditional demonstration of the existence of God illustrates his understanding of foundational theology. He acknowledges the validity of the proofs, but he maintains that they presuppose a pre-understanding or experiential anticipation of the meaning of what they should demonstrate. Rahner stands within the tradition of the "new theology" but nuances it by maintaining that the desire for God is not a desire based upon an abstract human nature. It is a desire embedded in a historical human nature that has received a historical call from God. His term "SUPERNATURAL EXISTENTIAL" expresses this historical characteristic of human nature. (Rahner appropriates the term "existential" from Martin HEIDEGGER, his teacher, who used it to refer to those categories specific to human nature, such as historicity and self-understanding.) Bernhard Welte has developed an analogous approach. Appropriating Heidegger's phenomenological analysis of the historicity of human nature and of the changing nature of language, thought, and metaphysics, Welte elaborates the pre-understanding of Christian salvation within the finite openness in human nature to the infinite.

Theological Aesthetics. Hans Urs von BALTHASAR has argued for the fundamental theological significance of a theological aesthetics that focuses on a dramatic action of God and Christ and the logic of that action for foundational theology. Balthasar contends that much of modern theology has insufficiently attended to the aesthetic dimension. This neglect had dominated certain strands of modern Protestant theology, but also influenced some modern Roman Catholic theological approaches that unfortunately neglect the classic Catholic emphasis on the aesthetic and sacramental. Against a fundamental theological method that focuses upon the human pre-understanding or the a priori condition of revelation within human rationality, Balthasar emphasizes the aesthetic contemplation of the Christian drama of revelation in his development of the fundamental theological implications of aesthetics. He points to an aesthetic model whereby the encounter with the aesthetic object influences, changes, and challenges the subject. Through contemplating the form of Christ manifest in the dramatic action of His suffering, death, and Resurrection, one opens oneself to this form and becomes conformed with Christ.

In developing theological aesthetics that display a Christian Trinitarian logic and drama, Balthasar cautions against the appeal to an anthropological, existential, or transcendental starting point within foundational theology. The danger is that the starting point does not remain simply a starting point or beginning, but can become a standard or measure that limits what is to be grasped. Just as an aesthetic experience transforms the subject, so too should God's action in Jesus transform our subjectivity. In his critique of an anthropocentric starting point as the foundation of theology, Balthasar has sought to pick up and develop Karl Barth's criticism of liberal Protestant theology, but in a way that remains sensitive to a Catholic sacramental understanding of the analogy of being and analogy of faith.

Practical Political Theology. Johann Baptist Metz, a student of Rahner, has developed a foundational theology that seeks to overcome what he perceives as the limitations of Rahner's approach. Metz argues that Rahner has overemphasized personal subjectivity, has failed to take sufficiently into account social and political praxis, and has not confronted the moral and religious implications of the Holocaust. The horrors of Auschwitz speak against a fundamental theological conception that underscores on human autonomy and human transcendence over nature. Such an ANTHROPOCENTRICISM interprets human history in terms of a continuous evolutionary progress. It views this history as culminating in the modern European West with its established freedoms. Such a view overlooks the suffering victims of this history. It expresses instead the viewpoint of the victors. It is Eurocentric rather than polycentric.

In contrast, Metz proposes a foundational theology that is a political theology or, more precisely, a practical hermeneutic of Christianity. Such a foundational theology is indeed defined by the challenge of modernity and the Enlightenment. Metz, however, does not interpret this challenge as a purely theoretical or as a merely philosophical critique of Christianity. It is also, and primarily, a practical challenge and a political critique. The fundamental theological response to this challenge entails a practical hermeneutic and an emphasis on practice as its central point. Christian theology has a practical logos. The belief in God entails the affirmation of specific practice implied within Christian belief. Such a belief entails a conversion and a discipleship. It requires a discipleship of solidarity of hope in the God of Jesus and in Jesus' practice of solidarity with society's outcasts and victims. The God of Jesus is a God of the living and the dead. This God promises resurrection and thereby affirms all to be subjects by affirming their identities and hopes even in the face of suffering, death, and injustice. The Christian community advocates a discipleship and a ''dangerous memory'' that is in solidarity with those who have unjustly suffered in the past and it proclaims a hope in resurrection that gives justice and meaning to life. The logos of Christian practice is a logos involving memory, solidarity, and hope. Such a logos differs from a more theoretical logos, for it criticizes the progressive understanding of history through its conviction that Christian apocalypticism entails an ''interruption'' of a human history of domination.

In Germany, Helmut Peukert, a student of Metz, has sought to develop foundational theology by bringing Metz's emphasis upon memory and a discipleship of solidarity with those who have suffered unjustly in confrontation with 20th-century philosophy, especially epistemology and the philosophy of science. Peukert criticizes the more empirical and positivist conceptions of rationality as insufficient because they are unable to deal adequately with suffering, especially the suffering and death of past victims of injustice. Foundational theology develops an understanding of meaning and rationality based upon a hope in the resurrection and in the ultimate vindications of those who have suffered and died.

Diverse Publics and Criteria. David Tracy has proposed that the various branches of theology should be distinguished with reference to their specific social location, public or reference group, characteristic mode of argumentation, and distinctive religious and ethical stance. Each branch of theology seeks to provide both an interpretation of a religious tradition and an explication of the religious dimension of the contemporary situation. Fundamental theology relates primarily but not exclusively to the public represented by the academy, whereas systematic theology relates primarily, though not exhaustively, to the Church. Fundamental theology consequently employs a mode of argument that suitable to the approach and methods of an established academic discipline in interpreting the truth claims of the religious tradition. Moreover, it offers arguments that all reasonable persons should acknowledge as reasonable even if these persons are neither religious believers nor members of a Christian church. In addition, fundamental theology has a distinctive ethical and religious stance. Though the fundamental theologian might be personally a believer, in arguments his personal faith or beliefs may not serve as warrants or backings of truth. His claims of the truth for the Christian faith must be argued on public grounds.

Such a conception of foundational theology relies on the link established within the sociology of knowledge between social location and types of argumentation and modes of commitment. Some critics question whether the awareness of the social conditioning of knowledge throws the notion of public rationality into question. Tracy's more recent work has taken up the significance of the ambiguity of interpretation, the importance of conversation, and the fragmentary character of knowledge for theology and foundational theology.

Critique of Foundationalism. Classical pragmatic philosophers such as Charles Pierce and Wilfrid Sellars as well as neo-pragmatists such as Richard Rorty, Richard Bernstein, and Robert Brandom have criticized various forms of foundationalism. They criticize a subjective foundationalism. based upon introspection of the human consciousness (e.g., R. DESCARTES's method, starting point, and search for clear and distinct ideas). In addition, they criticize the foundationalism of positivism and empiricism (e.g., John LOCKE's evidentialism, which equates true belief and evidential belief). Alongside this pragmatic critique, recent hermeneutical theory has underscored the role of one's pre-understanding as well as the horizon of one's embeddedness within a cultural historical tradition. Moreover, recent theories of deconstructive as well as postmodern analysis have underscored the ambiguity of meaning. All of these tendencies have influenced contemporary formulations of foundational theology.

For some contemporary Protestant theologians this critique of foundationalism has reinforced the traditional Lutheran critique of metaphysics and of natural theology. Hans Frei and George Lindbeck have strongly argued against an apologetic anthropological approach. Lindbeck appeals to Ludwig WITTGENSTEIN's understanding of language and its interrelation with life praxis to advance a cultural-linguistic understanding of theology that stresses a community's narratives and life practices. If Tracy argued that one can defend the notion of Christian claims via ''publicly acceptable criteria,'' Lindbeck underscores the linguistic and communitarian context of adjudication. Ronald Thiemann and William Placher explicitly take up the critique of foundationalism. Thiemann develops a narrative theology and bases Christian theology on revelation in a way that takes into account the pragmatic critique of foundationalism. Placher advocates an unapologetic theology.

Roman Catholic theologians, on the other hand, have incorporated the critique of foundationalism within foundational theology itself. Fiorenza argues that the critique of foundationalism does not entail the absence of any foundations. Instead, it requires a multiplicity of foundations and the awareness that every foundation is located within a web of interpretation and within a community of discourse. This procedure involves a broad reflective equilibrium (a term widely used within current political and moral philosophy influenced by John Rawls) whereby foundational theology brings together diverse grounds and reasons. Just as diverse cords are interwoven to form a strong rope, so too are diverse sources brought together to form the warrants for Christian belief. Thus foundational theology brings into reflective balance diverse tasks: the hermeneutical task of interpreting what is paradigmatic and normative within the tradition, the critical task of analyzing the warrants stemming from practice, and the philosophical task of explicating the appropriate background theories (philosophical, ethical, and anthropological). All of these tasks are interrelated and dependent on each other. The result shows the importance of diverse foundations, each influencing each other in the interpretation and warrant for Christian faith. Such a method takes up traditional topics within foundational theology, such as the foundation of the Church and the Resurrection of Jesus. These involve not only historical and existential arguments, but also a hermeneutical. interpretation that attends to the Church's reception of Jesus, evident in the diverse literary forms of its interpretation and in the living out of this reception in practice. The testimony and practice of the Christian community should be explicated in a way that acknowledges diverse foundations and varied warrants for the Christian faith.

Diverse Currents and Directions. These diverse currents within foundational theology show the vitality and the richness of the field. Not only are there basic agreements about the nature of fundamental theology, but there are also important disagreements. There is basic agreement on the importance and necessity of foundational theology within Roman Catholic theology, the need to deal with the challenges of the modernity and the Enlightenment, and the integration of foundational theology within theology in general. The disagreements include the degree to which a metaphysical defense and a transcendental philosophical approach is essential to the fundamental theological approach and whether foundational theology should be much more hermeneutical and praxis oriented. Whereas all take seriously the challenge of the modem Enlightenment, not everyone interprets this challenge in the same way and not everyone shares the same assessment of modernity. Some appeal to public reasons or public rationality as the avenue through which an apologetic should approach. Others view such a public rationality as a fiction of the modem Enlightenment. Consequently, the latter argue that foundational theology should take much more seriously the radical pluralism of philosophical worldviews and the increasing reality of religious diversity at a time when even local communities are becoming more multicultural and multireligious.

The emergence of the critique of modernity as Eurocentric and as dominated by a one-dimensional technological rationality has gained force with postmodern and postcolonial philosophical currents. This critique suggests that foundational theology needs to examine the extent to which its own methods and arguments have the limitations and presuppositions of the very positions it is contesting. In addition, the postmodern critique of traditional metaphysics as it emerges in Emmanuel Levinas's emphasis upon our vulnerability before the other highlights an ethic of responsibility for the other that is intrinsically linked with an ethic of belief. Christian foundational theology has always underscored the role of testimony for a knowledge of history and the importance of personal testimony and love for knowledge. The current task of foundational theology is to show further how the Christian community's testimony to Jesus and its solidarity with the other is central to the theoretical tasks of foundational theology.

Bibliography: H. U. VON BALTHASAR, *The Glory of the Lord: A Theological Aesthetics,* v. 1, *Seeing the Form,* tr. E. LEIVA-MERIKAKIS (New York 1982). A. DULLES, *The Craft of Theology: From Symbol to System* (New York 1992). F. S. FIORENZA, *Foundational Theology: Jesus and the Church* (New York 1984); ''Fundamental Theology and Its Principal Concerns Today: Towards a Non-Foundational Foundational Theology,'' *Irish Theological Quarterly* (1996) 118–39; ''The Relation between Fundamental and Systematic Theology,'' *Irish Theological Quarterly* (1996) 140–60; ''The Resurrection of Jesus and Roman Catholic Fundamental Theology,'' in *The Resurrection,* ed. G. O'COLLINS, D. KENDALL, and S. DAVIS (New York 1997) 213–248. H. FRIES, *Foundational Theology* (Washington, D.C. 1996). J. FARRELLY, *Belief in God in Our Time* (Collegeville, Minn. 1992). C. GEFFRÉ, *The Risk of Interpretation: On Being Faithful to the Christian Tradition in a Non-Christian Age* (New York 1987). A. J. GODZIEBA, *Bernhard Welte's Fundamental Theological Approach to Christology* (New York 1994). D. C. KAMITSUKA, *Theology and Contemporary Culture: Liberation, Postliberal and Revisionary Perspectives* (New York 1999). R. LATOURELLE and R. FISICHELLA, eds., *Dictionary of Fundamental Theology* (New York 1994). J. LIVINGSTON and F. S. FIORENZA, *Modern Christian Thought: The Twentieth Century,* v. 2 (Upper Saddle River, N.J. 2000). J. B. METZ, *A Passion for God: The Mystical Political Dimension of Christianity* (Mahwah, N.J. 1998). G. O'COLLINS, *Retrieving Fundamental Theology:*

The Three Styles of Contemporary Theology (New York 1993). H. PEUKERT, *Science, Action, and Fundamental Theology: Toward a Theology of Communicative Action* (Cambridge 1994). K. RAHNER, *Foundations of Christian Faith: An Introduction to the Idea of Christianity* (New York 1978). J. E. THIEL, *Nonfoundationalism* (Minneapolis 1994). D. TRACY, *The Analogical Imagination* (New York 1981); *Plurality and Ambiguity: Hermeneutics, Religion, Hope* (Chicago 1994).

[F. S. FIORENZA]

FOUNDATIONALISM

Foundationalism seeks to discover whether there exist ultimate bases and foundations of human knowledge, and if so, to discover what these are. Though the term is newly minted, it designates an ancient and honorable concern among nearly all of the major philosophers of the Western tradition. The earliest example is Aristotle's compelling logical argument in the *Posterior Analytics* that, insofar as knowledge is based on evidence, and that evidence in turn is articulated in premises, and those premises rest on still other premises—eventually we will need to reach premises that are not just ''prior and better known'' than the conclusions drawn from them, but that are themselves not dependent upon any prior knowledge, being instead those that are self-evident or evident simply in terms of themselves alone.

Problematic status. Despite the tradition of persistent and perennial search for foundations that has seemingly characterized all previous philosophy, the inventors of the new term ''foundationalism'' want the designation to be taken as a form of criticism and even opprobrium. What could be worse, they ask in effect, than that spectacle of futility and irrelevance that has been exhibited by Western philosophers in their obsessive preoccupation with the foundations of human knowledge. Instead, philosophers should open themselves to the dawning of that new day, ushered in by the likes of Richard Rorty and his associates among the so-called Post-Analysts, in which we shall no longer worry over the question of whether our knowledge be with or without adequate foundations.

It must not be thought, however, that this apparent bland dismissal of concern with the foundations of knowledge is philosophically frivolous. Richard Bernstein, for example, has made the very telling point that even on its face any such enterprise as that of trying to discover the absolute foundations of any and all human knowledge is bound to be a futile attempt to find some fancied Archimedean point, from which all knowledge might be levered and suspended. Still more to the point have been the sorts of arguments developed by Alvin Plantinga and Nicholas Wolterstorff. Oversimplifying their arguments somewhat, what they are apparently concerned to point out is that any ultimate or absolute foundational truths upon which all the rest of our human knowledge would need to be based presumably would have to be either of two kinds. Either they would have to be truths of a purely formal kind, such as we are familiar with from logic and mathematics, and which do indeed seem to require no other evidence of their truth than just those very truths themselves. Or, as an alternative, they might be truths of simple observation or perception. For what other evidence can one have of such simple truths as ''I am wearing shoes,'' or ''There is a tree outside my window,'' other than that I just do perceive these things to be the case?

Accordingly, having established this much, Plantinga and Wolterstorff immediately proceed to give the *coup de grace* to any remaining and still struggling Foundationalists. For so far from the purely formal truths of logic and language being able to provide us with a foundational knowledge upon which we might be able to base our remaining knowledge of the world, it turns out that any and all purely formal truths, being no more than mere logical or linguistic truths, are in principle totally incapable of providing us with the slightest knowledge of the world or the way things are. Hence they are quite irrelevant for purposes of any foundationalism. And no less embarrassing is the case regarding ordinary observational or perceptual truths. Not only are such truths unable to provide us with unshakable foundations for our human knowledge, but it would appear, particularly from recent researches in the logic of science, that any and all perceptions and supposed data of observation are entirely relative to the conceptual schemes or frameworks in terms of which our perceptions and observations take place. Hence we have only to change our operative frameworks, and what we perceive will no longer be the same at all. And with that, the hope that experience and observation might provide us with an ultimate foundation for our knowledge of the world and of reality simply goes out the window.

What, then, is the consequence of such a demise and destruction of any and all forms of foundationalism, so far as human knowledge is concerned? Presumably, the answer that the Post-Analysts would give is that henceforth it shall be pragmatism, and not realism, that must be the order of the day, so far as human knowledge is concerned. Catholic thinkers have surely been on the defensive with regards to this sort of epistemological nihilism. T. Russman's *Prospectus for the Triumph of Realism,* however, is a skillful rehabilitation of foundationalism along Aristotelian and Thomistic lines.

See Also: REALISM.

Bibliography: R. J. BERNSTEIN, *Beyond Objectivism and Relativism,* (Philadelphia, Pa. 1983). A. PLANTINGA and N. WOLTER-

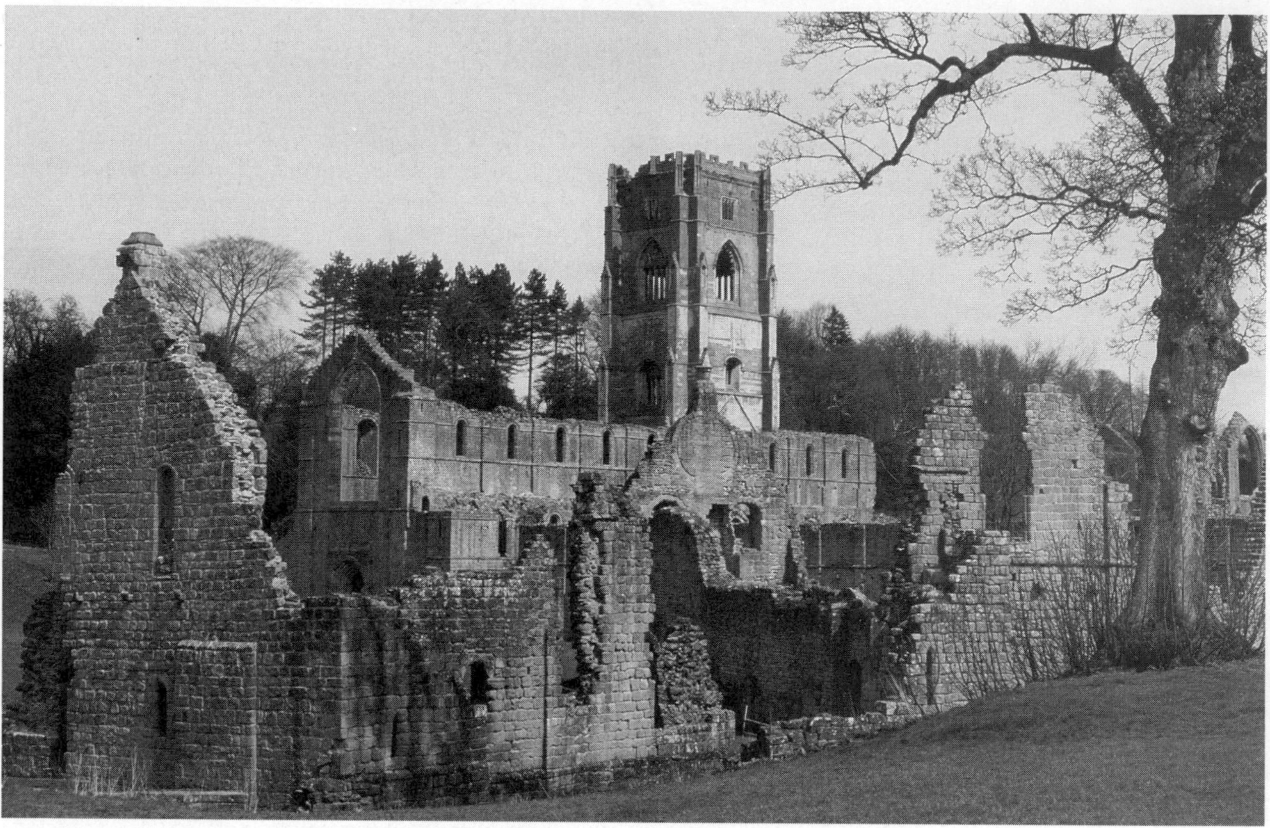

The ruins of Fountains Abbey stand within a heritage site on the Yorkshire Dales, England. (©Adam Woolfitt/CORBIS)

STORFF, eds., *Faith and Rationality* (Notre Dame, Ind./London 1983). T. A. RUSSMAN, *A Prospectus for the Triumph of Realism* (Macon, Ga. 1987).

[H. B. VEATCH]

FOUNTAINS ABBEY

Former Cistercian abbey, near Ripon, Yorkshire, England. Although the south and midland regions of England had been ''monasticized'' by the BENEDICTINES in the 10th century, the north of England was largely neglected until after the Norman Conquest, the great pioneer abbey in the area being the Cistercian Abbey of RIEVAULX. The most distinguished of the earlier monastic foundations of the area was probably the house of Black Monks at St. Mary's, York. Prior Richard and some of the monks there soon felt the pull of the Cistercian way of life as they saw it exemplified at Rievaulx and began to agitate for reform. Archbishop THURSTAN OF YORK heard of their plans and came to visit St. Mary's, but the abbot refused him admission. A scene of violence followed. Thurstan excommunicated the monks and withdrew, together with Prior Richard and the reform party of 12 monks. They spent Christmas Day with Thurstan, who on Dec. 26, 1132, led them to a site three miles from Ripon where the new community of Fountains Abbey was established. Richard was elected first abbot. The monks decided to follow the rule of the CISTERCIANS, and BERNARD OF CLAIRVAUX sent them one of his monks, Geoffrey, to teach them the Cistercian way of life. But after two years of extreme poverty and privation the monks felt they could carry on no longer and petitioned Bernard to receive them into CLAIRVAUX (1134). Bernard reluctantly agreed, but then the dean of York, Hugh, who had been a friend to the new abbey from its foundation, decided to give up his rich benefices and enter Fountains as a simple monk. He gave the abbey his great fortune and his fine library: from this time onward Fountains prospered. A foundation charter was drawn up. The abbey reached its greatest influence under the third abbot, HENRY MURDAC. In 1143 the See of York fell vacant, and King Stephen proposed to fill it with a royal clerk, his nephew WILLIAM FITZHERBERT. Murdac and the monks of Fountains led a successful resistance to this apparently scandalous appointment. Bernard and the Cistercian Pope EUGENE III were solicited, and Stephen had to accept Murdac as archbishop in his nephew's place. Unfortunately Murdac proved to be ineffective as archbishop, and after his death William was restored.

By the time of Bernard's death (1153), Fountains was the mother of seven daughter foundations, but the abbey quickly passed from austerity to laxity by way of the successful pursuit of power. The abbey church was completed in splendid style by 1245. Extravagance and mismanagement reduced the monks to poverty in the next generation. The Scots Wars hindered their recovery; in 1319 Edward II exempted them from royal taxation. Their later history was one of litigation over property. When the abbey was dissolved by Henry VIII in 1539, it was worth about £1,000 per annum and housed an abbot, a prior, and 30 monks.

Bibliography: W. DUGDALE, *Monasticon Anglicanum* (London 1655–73); best ed. by J. CALEY et al., 6 v. (1817–30) 5:286–314. *The Victoria History of the County of Yorkshire*, ed. P. M. TILLOTT (London 1961). F. L. CROSS, *The Oxford Dictionary of the Christian Church* (London 1957) 516. D. KNOWLES, *The Monastic Order in England, 943–1216* (2d ed. Cambridge, Eng. 1962). D. KNOWLES, *The Religious Order in England*, 3 v. (Cambridge, Eng. 1948–60). D. KNOWLES and R. N. HADCOCK, *Medieval Religious Houses: England and Wales* (New York 1953) 108.

[E. JOHN]

FOUR CROWNED MARTYRS

D. *c.* 304, at the beginning of the DIOCLETIAN PERSECUTION. Roman tradition lists them as four brothers, Severus, Severian, Carpophorus, and Victorinus, who held offices of trust in Rome; they were sentenced to death by public beating, and were buried as martyrs three miles from Rome on the Lavican Way. But they are confused with the five Pannonian stonemasons, Nicostratus, Claudius, Symphorian, Castorius, and Simplicius, who, having refused to sacrifice to the gods under Diocletian, were enclosed in leaden boxes and drowned. Modern hagiographers have not been able to distinguish the two groups.

By Pope GREGORY I THE GREAT's time the church built over the relics of these martyrs was considered ''an old church.'' Pope LEO IV repaired the church in 847. After a fire destroyed the church, Pope PASCHAL II had the church rebuilt and discovered two urns of relics under the altar.

Feast: Nov. 9 (formerly Nov. 8).

Bibliography: A. BUTLER, *The Lives of the Saints,* rev. ed. H. THURSTON and D. ATTWATER, 4 v. (New York 1956) 4:293–295. *Acta Sanctorum* Nov. 3:748–784. H. DELEHAYE, *Analecta Bollandiana* 32 (1913) 63–71; *Les Passions des martyrs . . .* (Brussels 1921) 328–344. L. DUCHESNE, *Mélanges d'archéologie et d'histoire* 31 (1911) 231–246. P. FRANCHI DE' CAVALIERI, *Note agiografiche,* 3 (*Studi e Testi* 24; 1912) 57–66. J. P. KIRSCH, *Historisches Jahrbuch der Görres-Gesellschaft* 38 (1917) 72–97.

[E. G. RYAN]

Exterior detail of the north facade of Florence's Or San Michelle church, showing the Four Crowned Martyrs. (©David Lees/CORBIS)

FOUR MASTERS, ANNALS OF THE

A title (*Annales quattuor magistrorum*) first used by John COLGAN in the preface to his *Acta Sanctorum Hiberniae* (Louvain 1645). The *Annals* are a historical compilation of the Kingdom of Ireland made at the Franciscan friary in Donegal (1632–36) and cover events from ''forty days before the Flood'' to the year 1616. The Four Masters were headed by Michael O'CLERY (Ó Clérigh), known as Tadhg an tSleibe before he became a friar in Louvain. He was sent by the Franciscans to Ireland to collect materials for their great enterprise of publishing the antiquities and hagiographical texts of early Ireland. His had been a learned family that had compiled the evidence of native Irish learning for more than three centuries. He gathered about him Peregrine O'Duignan (Cúcoigcríche Ó Duibhgennáin) of Leitrim, Farfassa O'Mulconny (Fearfassa Ó Maolconaire) of Roscommon, and a relative, Peregrine O'Clery (Cúcoigcríche Ó Clérigh). These were the principal workers on the project, but P. Walsh has shown that others, Muiris, son of Torna Ó Maolconaire, and Conaire Ó Clérigh, also had worked on the project for a short time.

The importance of the *Annals* lies in the fact that they present a synthesis of materials still in existence, enabling historians to establish the general reliability of the Four Masters. This allows greater assurance of truth for such periods for which the *Annals* are the only documents, and for which the originals have long since disappeared. The material was prepared directly for the printer, even to the title, preface, and necessary approbation, but none of the Four Masters ever saw the work in print. Michael O'Clery had planned the project and Fergal Ó Gara was the patron who paid the collaborators, while the community furnished them with food and lodging. Many of the manuscripts were obtained on loan and often a money deposit was required until a book should be returned. It remained for John O'Donovan to edit the *Annals* with an English translation, copious notes, and indexes.

Bibliography: *Annala Rioghachta Eireann: Annals of the Kingdom of Ireland by the Four Masters*, ed. J. O'DONOVAN, 7 v. (Dublin 1951). J. F. KENNEY, *The Sources for the Early History of Ireland: v.1, Ecclesiastical* (New York 1929) 43–44. P. WALSH, *Gleanings from Irish Manuscripts* (Dublin 1933); *The O'Cleirigh Family of Tír Conaill* (Dublin 1939); ''Dating of the Irish Annals,'' *Irish Historical Studies* 2 (1940–41) 355–375, esp. 373–375; *The Four Masters and Their Work* (Dublin 1944); *Irish Men of Learning*, ed. C. Ó LOCHLAINN (Dublin 1947).

[R. T. MEYER]

FOURIER, PETER, ST.

Cofounder of a religious order, pioneer in the establishment of elementary schools; b. Mirecourt, Lorraine, Nov. 30, 1565; d. Gray, Franche-Comté, Dec. 9, 1640.

Peter Fourier was educated at the Jesuit University at Pont-à-Mousson, entered the Order of Canons Regular of St. Augustine in 1585 at the Abbey of Chamounsey, was ordained in 1589, and received his doctorate in patristic theology in 1595, graduating with highest honors. When offered a choice of three parishes, he selected Mattaincourt, a morally lax parish and known as ''Little Geneva'' because of Calvinistic influences.

By personal mortification, austerity, and a deep prayer life, Fourier restored religious fervor to his parishioners, to many lax clergy, and to many Protestants who were converted to the Catholic faith. As pastor he organized the Guild of St. Sebastian for men, the Rosary Society for women, and the Immaculate Conception Society (now the Sodality of Mary) for young girls. He established a charitable fund to assist destitute parishioners, and inaugurated a court of justice to help unfortunate victims of malice.

Fourier was aware that the success of Calvinism and the lack of religious zeal among the uneducated villagers stemmed from ignorance of the truths of faith. His original intention of establishing a religious community of schoolmasters for the education of village boys met with disapproval from Rome. However, with the cooperation of Alix LE CLERC, a young girl of solid religious principles, he began in 1597 the foundation of a religious community of women who were to devote themselves to the teaching of religious and secular subjects to poor girls in free elementary schools. It was his belief that the uneducated girl was even more dangerous to society than the uneducated boy because of the important role of women in the upbringing of children. The new community received papal approval in 1616 under the title Canonesses Regular of St. Augustine of the Congregation of Our Lady, and enjoyed rapid growth in France.

Many educators have been inspired by Fourier's insight and his understanding of the educational and psychological needs of children. The use of the group method of instruction as opposed to the tutorial system, of visual instruction, and division of students according to abilities in reading rather than in age groups were ideas he utilized far in advance of his time.

In 1621, by order of the bishop of Toul, Fourier undertook the reform of the houses of the Canons Regular in Lorraine. His mission was not enthusiastically received, but by 1629 the original observance was reestablished and the Canons Regular of Lorraine had formed the Congregation of Our Savior. Fourier was elected their superior general in 1632.

Peter Fourier was beatified in 1730 and canonized in 1897 by LEO XIII.

Feast: Dec. 9.

Bibliography: P. FOURIER, *Pierre Fourier: a correspondance, 1598–1640*, ed. H. DERRÉAL and M. CORD'HOMME, 5 v. (Nancy 1986–1991). *Saint Pierre Fourier en son temps,* proceedings of a 1991 colloquy by the Diocese of Saint-Dié and University of Nancy, ed. R. TAVENAUX (Nancy 1992). B. BONTOUX, *Saint Pierre Fourier* (Paris 1949). L. PINGAUD, *Saint Peter Fourier,* tr. C. W. W. (New York 1905). M. CORD'HOMME, *Un Éducateur du XVIe siècle: Saint P. Fourier* (Moulins 1932). R. BAZIN, *Take This Child,* tr. M. A. GELSON (Boston 1948); *Blessed Alix Le Clerc,* tr. M. ST. L. WEST (London 1947). H. DERREAL, *Un missionnaire de la Contre'Réforme* (Paris 1965), extensive bibliography. D. MAST, *Man of Lorraine* (Baltimore 1966). W. LAWSON, *Pierre Fourier: Canon Regular, Parish Priest, Founder of the Congregation of Our Lady* (London 1969). M. C. TIHON, *Saint Pierre Fourier* (Paris 1997).

[M. V. GEIGER]

FOURNET, ANDRÉ HUBERT, ST.

Cofounder of the Daughters of the Holy Cross of ST. ANDREW; b. Maillé, near Poitiers, France, Dec. 6, 1752; d. La Puye, near Poitiers, May 13, 1834. Born of well-to-do and pious parents, Fournet reacted to the heavy religious atmosphere of his home with a certain irreverence and frivolity. While studying law and philosophy at Poitiers, he enlisted in military service and had to be brought out by his parents' influence. He was sobered by the counsel and example of his uncle, Jean Fournet, a dedicated and holy priest of the poor parish of Hains. He studied for the priesthood and was ordained (1776). After a brief curacy with his uncle he became vicar of the small church of St. Phèle (1779) and parish priest of St. Pierre (1781) in Maillé. Fournet was respected for his conviviality and his generosity to the poor, but his own parish house was run with austerity. He refused to take the oath required by the CIVIL CONSTITUTION OF THE CLERGY but ceded the church (September 1791). He continued to minister, saying Mass in homes, fields, and barns. His bishop, however, compelled him to flee to Spain in 1792. Fournet returned secretly to Maillé in 1797 and said Mass in a barn. He was continually hunted by the republican police and had some narrow escapes—once even posing as a dead man. After Napoleon became first consul, Fournet began to minister openly, but the unsettled religious conditions led to his assuming a much wider pastoral responsibility than before the French Revolution. Some churches around Maillé were suppressed; some priests apostatized, and others joined the PETITE ÈGLISE. In 1797 Fournet had become acquainted with St. Jeanne Élisabeth BICHIER DES AGES. He suggested that she establish a religious community to provide care for the sick and to educate the poor. He wrote the rule for the Daughters of the Holy Cross of St. Andrew. In 1820 he retired as parish priest of Maillé and moved to La Paye to direct the growth of the community. He was beatified on May 16, 1926, and canonized on June 4, 1933.

Feast: May 13.

Bibliography: L. RIGAUD, *Vie du bon Père André-Hubert Fournet* (2d ed. Poitiers 1885). J. SAUBAT, *André-Hubert Fournet,* 2 v. (Poitiers 1924–25). *Acta Apostolicae Sedis* 25 (1933) 417–428. J. L. BAUDOT and L. CHAUSSIN, *Vies des saints et des bienheueux selon l'ordre du calendrier avec l'historique des fêtes,* 12 v. (Paris 1935–56) 13:122–130. A. BUTLER, *The Lives of the Saints,* ed. H. THURSTON and D. ATTWATER, 4 v. (New York 1956) 2:303–305.

[T. P. JOYCE]

FOURNIER, ST. JOHN, MOTHER

Foundress of the Sisters of St. Joseph of Philadelphia; b. Arbois, France, Nov. 13, 1814; d. Philadelphia, Pa., Oct. 15, 1875. Her parents, Claude and Jeanne Marie (Ramboz) Fournier, christened her Julie. She entered (1828) the Order of the Immaculate Conception, making her vows in 1832. Attracted by the foreign missions, she transferred to the Sisters of St. Joseph of Lyons, who were planning an American foundation in St. Louis, Mo. She received the habit June 16, 1836, as Sister St. John, and after preparation for teaching the deaf, she went to teach in St. Louis. She remained there until 1847, when Bp. Francis P. Kenrick requested that she and three other sisters be assigned to St. John's Orphanage in Philadelphia. In 1848, Mother St. John opened St. Patrick's parochial school, Pottsville, Pa., and supported it by funds from an adjoining academy. The following year she agreed to Kenrick's request to staff St. Joseph's, Philadelphia's first Catholic hospital, which the sisters were forced to relinquish ten years later for lack of funds. In 1858, under Kenrick's successor, Bp. John Neumann, she established a permanent motherhouse, Mt. St. Joseph, at Chestnut Hill, Pa., later adding a wing (1860), a chapel (1866), and an academy building (1873). During the Civil War she sent 14 sisters to nurse in field and "floating" hospitals. Having established two orphanages and 38 parochial and private schools during her service in Philadelphia, Mother St. John, on the advice of Bp. J. F. Wood, remained independent of the St. Louis generalate set up in 1860. Papal approbation for the rule was obtained by the Philadelphia community in 1896.

Bibliography: M. K. LOGUE, *Sisters of St. Joseph of Philadelphia, 1847–1947* (Westminster, Md. 1950). M. L. SAVAGE, *The Congregation of St. Joseph of Carondelet* (2d ed. St. Louis 1927).

[C. M. AHERNE]

FOURSQUARE GOSPEL, INTERNATIONAL CHURCH OF THE

This church, an evangelistic, Pentecostal church, was founded (1921) by Aimee (Kennedy) Semple MCPHERSON at Los Angeles, Calif. In its essential theological orientation, the Foursquare Gospel Association is a pentecostal church, but it developed as the personal following of a single dynamic revival preacher, rather than growing out of any preexisting pentecostal fellowship. Mrs. McPherson was ordained (1921) as pastor of the First Baptist Church in San Jose, Calif., but her movement was only very loosely associated with the Baptist Church and became an independent denomination soon afterward, although she herself always claimed membership in the Baptist Church. With a natural flair for showmanship and public relations, she soon attracted a large following. In 1921 she formed the Echo Park Evangelistic Association, and two years later she dedicated the Angelus Temple in Los Angeles, the center of her Foursquare Gospel Church. The Lighthouse of International Foursquare Evangelism (L.I.F.E.) Bible School was established in 1923, and evangelists trained there became the missionaries and pastors of Foursquare Gospel churches throughout the U.S.

As an evangelist, Mrs. McPherson preached Protestant fundamentalism and placed particular stress on baptism by the Spirit that cleanses from inner sin and declares itself by the charismatic signs of faith healing and speaking with tongues. In this respect, she belonged to the pentecostal tradition. Faith healing became an important element in her revival services and in the church she organized. She also drew on the premillenarian tradition to emphasize the imminent Second Coming in her sermons. The new denomination survived a series of scandals involving her disappearance (1926) and charges of misappropriated funds and acrimonious quarrels between Mrs. McPherson and her mother over control of the Angelus Temple (1927–31). Aimee McPherson continued to dominate the Foursquare Gospel Church until her death in 1944.

The International Church of the Foursquare Gospel confesses the unity and Trinity of God and the Incarnation and Redemption of Christ. It holds the verbal inspiration and sufficiency of the Scriptures, the ability of all humans to repent and accept Christ as their personal Lord and Savior, and the second blessing of sanctification by the Holy Spirit; and it looks to the Second Coming of Christ. Indeed, the term ''foursquare'' in its name refers to the four foundational tenets of Pentecostalism: (1) salvation, (2) baptism by the Spirit, (3) divine physical healing, and (4) the Second Coming of Christ. Baptism and the Lord's Supper are accepted as divine ordinances. In its government, a central board oversees the entire denomination, appointing field supervisors to direct local churches, which are, in their turn, governed by a council elected from the congregation. A central ordination and missionary board passes on the qualifications of candidates for the ministry and the foreign missions. Services are primarily evangelistic and make provision for the healing of the sick. A number of foreign missions and various kinds of charitable work are supported.

Bibliography: A. S. MCPHERSON, *Faith Healing Sermons* (Los Angeles 1921); *The Four Square Gospel* (Los Angeles 1949); *This is That* (Los Angeles 1923); *In the Service of the King* (New York 1927). W. G. MCLOUGHLIN, *Modern Revivalism* (New York 1959). N. B. MAVITY, *Sister Aimee* (Garden City, NY 1931). F. S. MEAD, S. S. HILL and C. D. ATWOOD, *Handbook of Denominations in the United States*, 11th edition (Nashville 2001)

[R. K. MACMASTER/EDS.]

FOURTEEN HOLY HELPERS

A group of 14 saints traditionally venerated together, especially in Germany (feast, August 8). They are three bishops, DENIS OF PARIS (feast, October 9; invoked against headache and rabies), Erasmus, called ELMO (June 2; invoked against colic and cramp), and BLAISE (February 3; invoked against throat troubles); three virgins, BARBARA (December 4; invoked against lightning, fire, explosion, and sudden and unprepared death), MARGARET (July 20; invoked against possession and by pregnant women), and CATHERINE OF ALEXANDRIA (November 25; invoked by philosophers, students, wheelers, etc.); three knightly patrons, GEORGE (April 23; protector of soldiers), Achatius (June 22), and Eustace (September 20; invoked by hunters); the physician Pantaleon (July 27; invoked against tuberculosis); the monk GILES (September 1; invoked against epilepsy, insanity, and sterility); the deacon Cyriac (August 8; invoked against demoniac possession); the martyr Vitus (June 15; invoked against epilepsy and ''Vitus dance''); and the giant CHRISTOPHER (July 25; invoked by travelers in difficulties). Latin terms for these helper saints were manifold: *auxiliatores, auxiliantes, intercessores, adiutores, coadiutores, adiuvantes* or simply *quatuordecim sancti.* Calling a saint a *Nothelfer,* a ''Helper in Need,'' was current German usage from the late 12th century. Judging from earlier medieval art it would seem that Leonard of Noblat originally had the place of Cyriac. In fact, in southern Germany, including Nuremberg, it is Leonard, not Cyriac, who appears most often until *c.* 1520. Down to the 16th century certain localities made special substitutions; thus SS. Nicholas, Sixtus, Wolfgang, Sebastian, or Oswald might be counted a Helper. The Diocese of Augsburg, probably under the influence of the monastery of Sankt MAGNUS OF FÜSSEN, added a 15th name, St. Magnus.

The cult was advanced first by the Dominicans, later by the Cistercians and the Benedictines. The nobility, the urban aristocracy, and the *bourgeoisie* were equally favorable to the cult, and powerful religious movements and the plague years of the 14th century may have been responsible for its promotion. Its attraction lay in the power of the group as a whole, although individual saints were later assigned a special patronage; churches and altars dedicated to one of the 14 included the remainder of the group as subsidiaries.

The earliest pictorial witness of the cult is a fresco in the Dominican church of St. Blaise in Regensburg (*c.* 1320). In Nuremberg the cult developed and spread extensively in the 14th and 15th centuries; it was especially fostered there by the Dominican sisters of St. Catherine's. Having been diffused throughout southern Germany and the German-speaking Alps, the cult was carried into central Germany from Bamberg. Elsewhere only sporadic traces of it can be found. Veneration reached its high point in the mid-15th century with the Vierzehnheiligen pilgrimage on the Upper Main River in the Diocese of Bamberg. The feast of the Holy Helpers was given its own Office and Mass, probably the result of the pilgrimage. Soon confraternities began to develop. The origins of *Vierzehnheiligen* are outlined in a work printed in 1519; it reports that the son of a shepherd of the Cistercian monastery of Langheim, while watching sheep in a district originally called Frankenthal, had a vision *c.* 1445 of a group of 14 children with the Child Jesus in their midst; the Child told the shepherd that these were the 14 Holy Helpers, who from this spot wished henceforth to dispense their favors. (Thirty-three years prior to this book appearance, a Holy Helper altar in Langenberg, near Gera, Thuringia, had already pictorially portrayed the miracle.) Immediately a chapel was built on the site of the alleged apparition, and its altar was dedicated in 1448. Destroyed in 1525 during the PEASANTS' War, the shrine was rebuilt on a larger scale and dedicated in 1543. The cornerstone of the present basilica was laid in 1743 and the new baroque edifice, one of the most important of 18th-century German churches (by Balthasar Neumann), was dedicated in 1772. Pilgrimage processions, organized by parishes and confraternities, are still frequent and Vierzehnheiligen remains one of the most important pilgrim shrines of the Dioceses of Bamberg and Würzburg.

The earliest iconography of the Fourteen Holy Helpers displays them in a single row, headed by St. Christopher. Often they are grouped around the figures of the Madonna and Child or around the figure of St. Christopher carrying the Holy Child in his arms. Not infrequently they are grouped around the Man of Sorrows. Baroque art preferred to use a Root of Jesse motif, with the saints among the branches. At the Vierzehnheiligen shrine and in numerous wayside shrines that stand along Franconia's pilgrimage routes to Vierzehnheiligen, the Holy Helpers are depicted in a circle surrounding the Child; often it is a circle of 14 children as in the original apparition. Artistic monuments to the Helpers include late Gothic paintings, such as those by Hans Burgkmair, Lucas Cranach, and Matthias GRÜNEWALD.

Feast: Aug. 8.

Bibliography: Literature. H. WEBER, *Die Verehrung der heiligen vierzehn Nothelfer* (Kempten 1886). H. GÜNTER, *Legenden-Studien* (Cologne 1906). J. KLAPPER, "Die vierzehn Nothelfer im deutschen Osten," *Volk und Volkstum* 3 (1938) 158–192. J. DÜNNINGER, "Die Wallfahrtslegende von Vierzehnheiligen," in *Festschrift für Wolfgang Stammler* (Berlin 1953) 192–205. G. SCHREIBER, "Die vierzehn Nothelfer in Volksfrömmigkeit und Sakralkultur," (Schlern-Schriften 168; Innsbruck 1959) 261–310.

[J. DÜNNINGER]

Lauda ſantte Katarine uirginis ma-tiris
O Sacra ſantta Virgo benedeta
Chaterina beata.
dal padre eterno amata
de chriſto redemptor uera ſeruente.
O uirgo ſacra cum tuo benigne prece
humilia el creator:
che da pieta da nui lieui ſtanece.

"St. Catherine of Alexandria," standing in walled garden with her wheel and attributes of a martyr; page from "Laude devotissime et sanctissime," written by Leonardo Giustiani, 1517.

FOX, GEORGE

Founder of the society of FRIENDS (Quakers); b. Drayton-in-the-Clay (Fenny Drayton), Leicestershire, July 1624; d. London, Jan. 13, 1691. He was one of five or six children brought up in a household of piety. His father, a weaver, and his mother shared deep religious convictions. Fox was apprenticed to a shoemaker, and later was often referred to as a cobbler. In 1643, he began almost four years of restless wandering in search of enlightenment, until he was convinced that immediate revelation of truth comes from God to the individual in an experience of illumination. To Quakers, this is known as the Inner Light, Inward Light, or Light Within. Fox wrote in his *Journal,* "These things I did not see by the help of man, nor by the letter, though they are written in the letter, but I saw them in the light of the Lord Jesus Christ, and by His immediate Spirit and powers, as did the holy men of God, by whom the Holy Scriptures were written." He started a preaching ministry in 1647, but the beginning of his movement is usually dated 1652, the year of his vision on Pendle Hill. In this year Fox made his home at Swarthmore Hall, near Ulverstone, the house of Judge

George Fox. (Archive Photos)

Thomas Fell, vice-chancellor of the Duchy of Lancaster. In 1669, he married Margaret Fell, who had been a widow for eight years. Fox's compelling zeal attracted followers among the Friends of the Truth and the Seekers. After 1652, with Swarthmore Hall as the center, the Quaker movement grew in spite of persecution and the frequent imprisonment of Fox and his followers. The ''Valiant Sixty'' (actually 66), as they were called, traveled widely as missionaries of Quakerism. Fox himself made missionary journeys to Ireland (1669), the West Indies and North America (1671–72), and Holland (1677 and 1684). Among his disciples were James Nayler, Robert BARCLAY, and William PENN. Fox had great organizational ability, which enabled him to devise individualistic outlets in a larger complex for unity: the Particular Meeting, a local group, joins with other Particular Meetings in a Monthly Meeting, which in turn joins other similar Meetings in a Quarterly Meeting; these in turn form the Yearly Meeting. Fox left no theological treatises. His *Journal* was published posthumously in 1694, and edited by N. Penney in 1911.

Bibliography: G. FOX, *Book of Miracles,* ed. H. J. CADBURY (Cambridge, Mass. 1948). P. HELD, *Der Quäker George Fox* (Basel 1949). A. GORDON, *The Dictionary of National Biography from the Earliest Times to 1900,* 63 v. (London 1885–1900; repr. with corrections, 21 v., 1908–09, 1921–22, 1938; suppl. 1901–) 7:557–562. A. N. BRAYSHAW, *The Personality of George Fox* (London 1933). M. SCHMIDT, *Die Religion in Geschichte und Gegenwart,* 7 v. (3rd ed. Tübingen 1957–65)[3] 2:1010. E. RUSSELL, *The History of Quakerism* (New York 1942).

[C. S. MEYER]

FOXE, RICHARD

Bishop of Winchester, England, Lord Privy Seal to Henry VII and Henry VIII, founder of Corpus Christi College, Oxford; b. Ropesley, near Grantham, Lincolnshire, 1447 or 1448; d. probably at the castle of Wolvesey in Winchester, Oct. 5, 1528. Most probably, he studied for a time at Magdalen College, Oxford, but he took the degree Doctor of Canon Law from the University of Paris. There he was ordained and became secretary to Henry, Earl of Richmond later Henry VII. Foxe was present at Bosworth Field in 1485 and soon afterward was appointed principal secretary of state and keeper of the privy seal. For the next 30 years he occupied a high place in the councils of the realm and was constantly employed in diplomatic and other secular business. During this period he went from one bishopric to another, but for the most part, until he withdrew from public affairs, he administered his ecclesiastical responsibilities by deputy. He became bishop of Exeter (1487); of Bath and Wells (1492); of Durham (1494), where he was probably resident for a time; and of Winchester (1501). With the rise of Thomas WOLSEY he withdrew from public life to concentrate on the care of his diocese and the advancement of learning. He resigned the privy seal in 1516. His most lasting work was the foundation of Corpus Christi College, Oxford, the first statutes of which are dated 1517. He was blind for some years before his death.

Bibliography: *Letters of Richard Fox, 1486–1527,* ed. P. S. and H. M. ALLEN (Oxford 1929). *The Register of Richard Fox, Lord Bishop of Durham, 1494–1501,* ed. M. P. HOWDEN (Durham 1932). A. B. EMDEN, *A Biographical Register of the University of Oxford to A.D. 1500,* 3 v. (Oxford 1957–59) 715–719. T. FOWLER, *The Dictionary of National Biography from the Earliest Times to 1900* (London 1885–1900) 7:590–596. F. L. CROSS, *The Oxford Dictionary of the Christian Church* (London 1957) 517.

[V. PONKO, JR.]

FOXE'S BOOK OF MARTYRS

John Foxe (1516–87) entitled his work *Actes and Monuments of these latter and perillous dayes, touching matters of the Church, wherein ar comprehended and described the great persecutions & horrible troubles, that have bene wrought and practised by the Romishe Prelates, speciallye in this Realme of England and Scotlande, from the yeare of our Lorde a thousande, unto the tyme nowe present. Gathered and collected according to the true copies & wrytinges certificatorie as wel of the parties them selves that suffered, as also out of the Bishops Registers, which wer the doers thereof, by John Foxe.* The title gives the scope, the viewpoint, and the methodology of the work. The preface of the first English edition (1563) contained among other matters a dedication to Queen Elizabeth I and an address "To the Persecutors of Gods truth, commonly called Papists." Another address contrasts it with the *Golden Legend;* however, it is broadly within that tradition. It is a martyrology and a church history. The 1570 edition had the title . . . *the Ecclesiasticall history contaynyng the Actes and Monumentes of thynges passed in every kynges tyme in this Realme* . . . . Seven subsequent editions followed, bearing the title *Book of Martyrs* (1576, 1583, 1596, 1610, 1632, 1641, 1684). In 1837 the modern eight-volume edition was launched by S. R. Cattley and revised in 1870 by Josiah Pratt.

The work was severely attacked by S. R. Maitland as dishonest and inaccurate. Mozley has done much to rehabilitate its reputation. Haller has placed Foxe fully into the context of his time and demonstrated the meaning of the work as a polemic against Roman Catholicism and an apologetic for the Elizabethan church. Foxe was inaccurate at times, but the charge of dishonesty is unjust. He could be negligent of chronology, discursive, and prejudiced. In citing documents he is usually reliable and the large amount of original source material he quoted directly still gives usefulness to his work, although it must be used with care. Abridgments and revisions of his book were made for partisan purposes or for profit.

Foxe was influenced greatly by the CENTURIATORS of Magdeburg. Originally his work was called *Rerum in ecclesia gestarum narratio* (1559), but he expanded it greatly in the first English edition. The work ranges from the 1st century to the end of Mary I's reign (1558). The materials from the 14th and 16th centuries are particularly voluminous. Foxe supplied the English reading public with an account of the work of Luther, Zwingli, and other Continental figures; most notable, however, is the narrative of the church in England during the 14th, 15th, and 16th centuries. E. Gordon Rupp said, "Foxe's *Book* counted in English history as much as Drake's drum." It was accepted as authoritative by most Englishmen of 2½ centuries; therefore its historical importance as a work of ecclesiastical historiography is preeminent.

Bibliography: W. HALLER, *The Elect Nation: The Meaning and Relevance of Foxe's Book of Martyrs* (New York 1963). H. C. WHITE, *Tudor Books of Saints and Martyrs* (Madison 1963). J. F. MOZLEY, *John Foxe and His Book* (London 1940). S. R. MAITLAND, *Six Letters on Fox's Acts and Monuments* . . . (London 1837). S. LEE, *The Dictionary of National Biography From the Earliest Times to 1900,* 63v. (London 1885–1900) 7:581–590.

[C. S. MEYER]

FOY, ST.

Virgin martyr under Dacian; b. Agen, France, *c.* 290; d. there, 303. She is known in the various European languages as Faith, Fe, Fede, Fides, and Getreu. The *passio* of St. Foy is similar to that of St. AGATHA; also, before being beheaded she was roasted on a griddle, as was St. LAWRENCE. She should not be confused with the daughter of St. Sophia who was martyred at Rome with her sisters Hope and Charity. In the ninth century the body of St. Foy was removed from Agen to Conques, where it was venerated by pilgrims, some of whom were on their way to SANTIAGO DE COMPOSTELA, and by Crusaders. Until approximately 1050 her reliquary was displayed behind a screen of chains left by former prisoners, who attributed their release to her intercession. In art she appears with a griddle, the martyr's palm, the sword of her martyrdom, and sometimes the dove that reputedly brought her the martyr's crown.

The most famous representation of St. Foy is on a reliquary commissioned in 949 by Bp. Étienne of Clermont, abbot of Conques. The saint is shown as somewhat older than she was at the time of her martyrdom. She is seated on a throne in a hieratic pose. Her blue enameled eyes are the first reported in the history of art. Later the figure was decorated with jewels given by pilgrims. The two small tubes she holds have been identified as flower vases or as parts of her griddle. The reliquary was one of the "Majestés d'or" brought to the Synod of Rodez in 1161. She is represented also on the portal of the Last Judgment in the church of St. Foy, Conques, where she kneels before the abbot's chair and is blessed by the hand of God.

Feast: Oct. 6.

Bibliography: H. GREEN, *Little Saint* (New York 2000). K. M. ASHLEY and P. SHEINGORN, *Writing Faith: Text, Sign & History in the Miracles of Sainte Foy* (Chicago 1999). *The Book of Sainte Foy,* tr. P. SHEINGORN and *The Song of Sainte Foy,* tr. R. L. A. CLARK (Philadelphia 1995). BERNARDUS SCHOLASTICUS, *Liber miraculorum sancte Fidis,* ed. L. ROBERTINI, critical ed. (Spoleto 1994). G. GOYAU, "Rodez," *The Catholic Encyclopedia,* ed. C. G. HERBERMANN, 16 v. (New York 1907–14; suppl. 1922) 13:108. A. BUTLER, *The Lives of the Saints,* ed. H. THURSTON and D. ATTWATER, 4 v. (New York 1956). J. EVANS, *Art in Mediaeval France, 987–1498* (New York 1948). K. KÜNSTLE, *Ikonographie der christlichen Kunst,* 2 v. (Freiburg 1926–28). L. RÉAU, *Iconographie de l'art chrétien,* 6 v. (Paris 1955–59). R. REY, *L'Art roman et ses origines* (Paris 1945). C. BERNOUILLI, *Die Skulpturen der Abtei Conques-en-Rouergue* (Basel 1956), reviewed by M. AUBERT, *Gazette des beaux-arts* 50 (1957) 237.

[B. E. FOYE]

FRANCA, LEONEL

Founder and first rector of the Pontifical Catholic University of Rio de Janeiro, spiritual leader and writer; b. São Gabriel, Rio Grande do Sul, Brazil, Jan. 6, 1893; d. Rio de Janeiro, Sept. 3, 1948. After completing his early studies in Bahia, he attended the Jesuit Colégio Anchieta in Novo Friburgo, Rio de Janeiro, until he entered the Society of Jesus on Nov. 12, 1908. Upon completion of his liberal arts studies in São Paulo (1912), he studied philosophy at the Gregorian University, Rome. Returning to Brazil (1915), he taught for five years at the Colégio S. Inácio, Rio de Janeiro. He went back to Rome (1920) for theology at the Gregorian and was ordained on July 26, 1923. After his tertianship at Oya, Spain (1925), he pronounced his solemn vows on Feb. 2, 1926, at the Colégio Anchieta, which had become the scholasticate; there for two years he taught philosophy and was prefect of discipline. In 1928 Franca returned to the Colégio S. Inácio, where he remained until his death.

From his youth Franca was the victim of a heart ailment and received the Anointing of the Sick five times, but his frail health did not prevent him from exercising an extraordinary influence, particularly on the intellectual levels and among the nation's leaders. He was also a dedicated confessor and especially gifted as a spiritual director. He organized and for years was president of the Association of Catholic Professors in Rio de Janeiro and for a long time was ecclesiastical assistant in various centers of Catholic Action. Cardinals Sebastian Leme and Jaime de Barros Cámara held him in high esteem and entrusted him with important religio-political missions. He also enjoyed great prestige in government circles, and his influence as counselor of ministers and of members of Parliament brought about favorable decisions in various questions of national scope, e.g., legislation on divorce, laws in favor of religious instruction in government controlled schools, and the appointment of chaplains to the armed forces. The President of the Republic, Getúlio Vargas, invited him to run for senator.

Franca was a prolific writer and lecturer. At his death more than 200 lectures on apologetics, education, and sociology were found in his files. He published 14 books, the best known being *Nocoes da História da Filosofia* (currently in its 18th edition), *O Divórcio, A Psicologia da Fé, A Crise do Mundo Moderno* (translated into Spanish), *A Imitação de Cristo, A Igreja, A Reforma, e a Civilização* (translated into Dutch), *O Livro dos Salmos,* and a study of the RATIO STUDIORUM. He contributed to numerous journals until he devoted his time exclusively to the periodical *Verbum,* which he founded (1944) as the Catholic University magazine. When the foundation of the university was decided upon in the Brazilian Plenary Council of 1939, Cardinal Leme entrusted the work to the Society of Jesus in the person of Franca. He organized first the Catholic Faculties of Rio de Janeiro with chairs in law, philosophy, sciences, and letters. On Dec. 12, 1940, he was named the first rector. In March 1941 he inaugurated courses for both men and women. In 1942 the government officially recognized the Catholic Faculties. Franca founded (1943) the School of Social Service. In 1946 the federal government granted the institution the official title of university, and in the following year the Holy See raised it to the rank of pontifical university. Finally, in 1948, Franca obtained the government's authorization to install the faculty of engineering. This was the last note in his diary.

Bibliography: L. G. DA S. D'ELBOUX, *O Padre Leonel Franca, S.J.* (Rio de Janeiro 1953).

[L. G. S. D'ELBOUX]

FRANCA, SS.

Two saints of the Middle Ages.

Franca, virgin; fl. 11th century. She was a recluse in her home of Fermo, Italy, before seeking religious vows from the local bishop and entering a convent, possibly San Angelo in Pontano. In her later years she once again retired to her hermitage. The chief source of information on her is an almost contemporary *passio* composed by an anonymous monk [*Analecta Bollandiana* (1957) 75:288, 294–298].

Feast: Oct. 1.

Franca Visalta of Piacenza, abbess; b. Piacenza, Italy, 1173; d. Plectoli (Pittoli), near Piacenza, April 25, 1218. Her parents were the count of Visalta and his noble wife. Franca was accepted at the BENEDICTINE convent of San Siro in Piacenza at the age of seven and received the regular Benedictine habit at the age of 14. She manifested a great love for prayers, fasting, and other austerities. Her care of the sick and love of the poor, with whom she shared her bread, greatly edified her companions. In *c.* 1198 she was unanimously elected abbess, and she took great interest in religious discipline and strict observance of the rule. After spending 30 years at San Siro, Franca transferred to the CISTERCIAN convent at Plectoli and became superior of the new foundation. She died at the age of 43 and was buried at Plectoli. In 1559 her body was removed to the church of St. Franca in Piacenza. Her cult was confirmed by Pope GREGORY X in 1273.

Feast: April 26.

Bibliography: *Acta Sanctorum* April 3:383–407. A. MANRIQUE, *Annales cistercienses,* 4 v. (Lyon 1624–59) v.3, 4. A. G.

TONONI, *Compendio della vita di s. Franca* (Piacenza 1892). *Cistercienser-Chronik* 8 (1896) 95–102, 137–143, 175–182. I. BIANCHEDI, *Luci di una stella* (Padua 1936). *Analecta Bollandiana* 56 (1938) 455. A. M. ZIMMERMANN, *Kalendarium Benedictinum: Die Heiligen und Seligen des Benediktinerorderns und seiner Zweige,* 4 v. (Metten 1933–38) 2:105–108.

[M. B. MORRIS]

FRANCE, ANATOLE

French poet, novelist, critic; b. Paris, April 16, 1844; d. Saint-sur-Loire, Oct. 13, 1924. He was the son of a Parisian bookstore owner and bibliophile, and was educated at the Collège Stanislas. He began his literary career (under a pen name for Jacques Anatole François Thibault) rather inauspiciously in 1873 with the publication of *Poèmes dorés,* tepid imitations of Parnassian verse. Long an admirer of (Joseph) Ernest RENAN, France imitated him in tempering knowledge with skepticism to combat what he considered the prevailing dogmatism. Like VOLTAIRE, he argued for a kind of pragmatic humanism that barred any basic metaphysical and spiritual considerations and considered reason and justice the only redemptive factors in a universe corrupted by materialism.

His *Crainquebille* (1902; adapted for the theater, 1905) is a cleverly veiled treatment of the Dreyfus case. Crainquebille, like Dreyfus, appears as the innocent victim of shamefully partisan political justice. *Les Dieux ont soif* (1912) denounces religious and political fanaticism; France's narrow conception of humanism leads him to confuse dogma, law, and established order with constraint and repression of thought. This attitude was probably what led to all his works being put on the Index in 1922. Reacting to the scientific and positivistic currents prevalent in literature, he wrote and edited four volumes of literary criticism, *La Vie littéraire* (1888–92). This work, however, is more a compendium of France's own literary preferences and aversions than a balanced analysis of the literature of his time. His reputation rests mainly on the wit and wry humor that salts all his writings, however wrongheaded or superficial they may appear to the modern reader. He was elected to the French Academy and received the Nobel Prize for Literature in 1921. It is curious that he should be remembered best for some of his least objectionable stories, such as ''Le Jongleur de Notre Dame,'' and ''Pierre Nozière.''

Bibliography: A. FRANCE, *Anatole France par lui-même,* ed. J. SUFFEL (Paris 1954). E. P. DARGAN, *Anatole France, 1844–1896* (New York 1937). A. FRANCE, *Oeuvres complètes illustrées,* ed. L. CARIAS and G. LE PRAT, 25 v. (Paris 1925–35).

[R. T. DENOMMÉ]

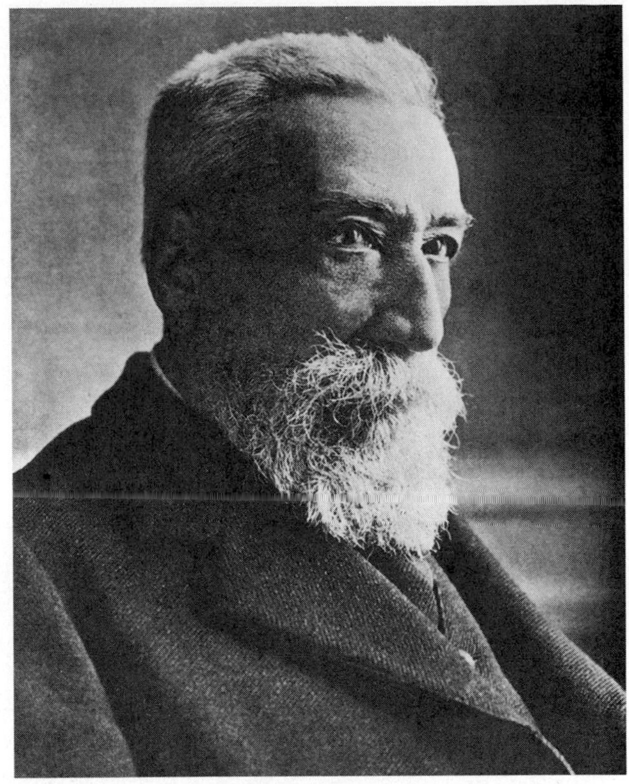

Anatole France.

FRANCE, THE CATHOLIC CHURCH IN

Once known as Gaul, the republic of France is located in Western Europe. It is bounded on the north by the English Channel, Belgium, and Luxemborg; on the east by Germany, Switzerland, and Italy; on the south by Spain and the Mediterranean Sea; and on the west by the Bay of Biscay. This entry presents discussion of the Church in France from 500 to the present; for information on the Church in France prior to the year 500, *see* GAUL, EARLY CHURCH IN.

The Middle Ages: 500 to 1515

The Merovingian Period. While Christianity is known to have been practiced in the city of Lyons by 120, it was not until the year 500 that the barbarian nations known as Gaul underwent a transition after its people united with the Gallo-Romans and brought new values to Christianity. The chief political institution of this new people—kingship—played a vital role in the religious history of France throughout the Middle Ages and beyond. First of all, there was the conversion of CLOVIS, king of the FRANKS, which precipitated the conversion of all his people. The Gallo-Roman bishops, who had dis-

Capital: Paris.
Size: 212,918 sq. miles.
Population: 59,329,691 in 2000.
Languages: French; regional dialects including Alsatian, Corsican, Provençal, Flemish, Breton, Basque, and Catalan are spoken in various regions.
Religions: 50 million Catholics (84%), 1.5 million Muslims (2%), 1.2 million Protestants (2%), 600,000 Jews (1%), 1 million Orthodox, 6 million without religious affiliations.

trusted the heretical ARIANISM of the other barbarian kings, gave full support to this new Frankish dynasty. Several years later, the Burgundians finally abjured Arianism under the influence of AVITUS OF VIENNE while CAESARIUS OF ARLES assured the victory of Catholicism in the regions of the lower Rhône. Thus in the early 6th century, unity of faith in Gaul had been achieved.

Meantime, the king became an anointed ruler. A period of ''political Augustinianism'' manifested itself in the ''ministerial concept of kingship.'' The king lived surrounded by clerics who formed the nucleus of a ''Hofkapelle'' from which the bishops were recruited. As the patron of churches the king summoned councils, eventually transforming the canons of these councils into CAPITULARIES, e.g., the council of Orléans (511) and the council of Paris (614). Above all, he exercised a sovereign right over church property, which had, in large part, been originally donated by him.

The end of urban life left the Church in Gaul comprised of rural parishes, and so it remained until the end of the *ancien régime.* From the 5th century, bishops had to send priests outside the mother church to serve the *vici, villae,* and *castra,* parishes that were often founded by nobles. Because such parishes were assured an endowment by their founders, they remained proprietary churches of a powerful laity, and intellectual, spiritual, and moral debasement of the clergy resulted for many years. Yet, this same clergy distinguished itself by the services it rendered in care of the poor (*matricula*) and the ransom of prisoners. In the Merovingian period the character of the clergy changed. A benefice was now linked to the parish, while the councils imposed discipline upon the peasant priest: CELIBACY, the interdict of banquets, etc. Meanwhile, culture reached its lowest ebb. There were no schools, much less universities. The few writers of the day were mediocre, GREGORY OF TOURS being the most characteristic. As a result, the religion of the people was very coarse. Although the councils made obligatory both Sunday Mass attendance and Easter Communion, these were but external practices of a religion entangled with superstition and ORDEALS. However, PILGRIMAGES, often to legendary saints, preserved a certain spirit of Christianity, the most famous pilgrimage of the era being the one to Tours.

As a result of the spiritual mediocrity under the MEROVINGIANS more perfect souls aspired to the monastic life. Consequently Irish monasticism flowered in France with St. COLUMBAN's Rule enjoying an extraordinary diffusion. For a long time, and in all regions, the influence of the *Scotti* was felt. In time, however, the Columban monasteries united themselves to the BENEDICTINE RULE, the most famous of the Benedictine monasteries being Fleury (SAINT-BENOÎT-SUR-LOIRE), which prided itself on housing the relics of St. Benedict himself.

The Carolingian Period. The CAROLINGIAN period was essentially one of Church reform pursued by a dynasty which was, admittedly, as Frankish as the Merovingians, but which was inspired by a coherent blending of the Christian spirit, the Bible, and the Fathers, in particular St. Augustine. This Carolingian reform began with the collaboration of three men: CHARLES MARTEL, whose policy it was to support Christianizing missions in Germany; St. BONIFACE, an Anglo-Saxon monk who interpreted the Benedictine Rule in a missionary sense; and Pope GREGORY II, who gave the enterprise the approval of Rome. This alliance of France and the papacy, which was to become one of the main themes of the country's religious history, was confirmed in 751 when PEPIN III was crowned king of the Franks, and again in 754 when Pope STEPHEN II went to Quiercy to request aid from the king against the LOMBARDS in Italy.

This Franco-papal alliance was first put to the service of reform. The councils of Soissons and Les Estinnes (742) interrupted the secularization of Church property, but obliged the churches to lodge royal hunting parties. CHARLEMAGNE followed up this early reform by bringing order to the Church, imposing the *Hadriana Collectio* and the Gregorian Sacramentary throughout his empire. But he wanted to be the sole master of the Church and even intervened in such dogmatic matters as ICONOCLASM and ADOPTIONISM, e.g., the LIBRI CAROLINI. The crowning of Charlemagne as Emperor of the West (800) gave him even more prestige: his empire had a certain mystique which contributed further to the myth of the ''Carolingian peace.'' Charles summoned to the Frankish court writers such as PAUL THE DEACON and THEODULF OF ORLÉANS from all over the Christian West to give luster to a Carolingian renaissance. During his own reign, however, this renaissance became primarily a reform of the education of the clergy.

The content and the spirit of Carolingian culture presented itself as a return to tradition. Ancient texts were accepted and became the norm of thought and life, e.g., the old canonical collections, the Grammar of Priscian; those texts that had been lost were forged, e.g., the FALSE DECRETALS, the DONATION OF CONSTANTINE. The Carolingians tried not only to live the *vita apostolica,* but to reconstitute the society of the Old Testament; no period was more Biblical, more ready to prefer the commandments of the Church over the demands of interior life. A century without philosophers and without mystics, the Carolingian era was one of moralists, especially Christian moralists who never forgot the requirements of salvation. Thus it was a century marked by great revivals, such as that of 829, and by an obsession with penance closely linked to the PENITENTIALS.

The Gregorian and Bernardian Reforms. The 10th and first half of the 11th centuries were the age of FEUDALISM par excellence, the age in which the Church fell under the power of laymen. Within this anarchy a popular religion took shape, a religion expressed in the earliest medieval drama, the Chansons De Geste; pilgrimages to SANTIAGO DE COMPOSTELA or to Jerusalem; and Roman pilgrimages. It was a religion of HERMITS, especially in western France.

During the second half of the 11th century, reform became the ambition of the Holy See. This GREGORIAN REFORM began in eastern France with Pope LEO IX, originally from Alsace, and with Cardinal HUMBERT OF SILVA CANDIDA, a former monk of MOYENMOUTIER. The reform was extended to all France by special legates, such as HUGH OF DIE. It at first focused on the morals of the clergy, as evidenced by the councils of Vienne and Tours (1059), but it presupposed Rome's initiative, and this entailed a shift in the ecclesiastical structure by which a centralized papacy gained at the expense of the local diocesan. Naturally this did not occur without resistance from the bishops.

During this era, the popes, who were often in serious conflict with the Roman emperor (*see* INVESTITURE STRUGGLE), found refuge in France. In gratitude they loaded the Capetian Dynasty with privileges such as the title ''very Christian king.'' It was this close relationship with the popes that led to that French devotion to St. Peter which is illustrated on the Miégeville portal at Saint-Sernin of Toulouse. This closeness between the papacy and France led to the election of French popes c. 1100, the first being URBAN II. Then in 1107, at the council of Troyes, Pope PASCHAL II upheld IVO OF CHARTRES's theory of investiture; the French Pope CALLISTUS II extended it to the whole Roman Empire through the Concordat of Worms.

The Gregorian reform was also a spiritual reawakening. Urban II fostered community life under the Rule of St. Augustine for various groups of canons (*see* CANONS REGULAR) as well as for the cathedral chapters. These canons then played a considerable role in developing hospitals, in parish life in the suburbs of towns, and in the sheltering of pilgrims. In 1095 the same Urban preached and organized the First CRUSADE at the council of Clermont. France responded with two armies, one from the north, one from the Midi. To defend the CRUSADERS' STATES established in the Holy Land, a new congregation, the TEMPLARS, was founded in France and was soon imitated by the KNIGHTS OF ST. JOHN. Both orders received numerous donations, making them important economic powers. Reform did not limit itself to the secular Church; the old religious orders also rejuvenated them-

Archdioceses	Suffragans
Aix	Ajaccio, Digne, Fréjus Toulon, Gap, Nice
Albi	Cahors, Mende, Perpignan-Elne, Rodez
Auch	Aire, Bayonne, Tarbes/Lourdes
Avignon	Montpellier, Nîmes, Valence, Viviers
Besançon	Belfort-Montbéliard, Nancy, Saint-Claude, Saint-Dié, Verdun
Bordeaux	Agen, Angoulême, Luçon, Périguex, Poitiers, La Rochelle
Bourges	Blois, Chartres, Clermont, Le Puy-en-Velay, Limoges, Orléans, Saint-Flour, Tulle
Cambrai	Arras, Lille
Chambéry	Annecy (and also the diocese Saint-Jean-de-Maurienne, Tarentaise)
Lyon	Autun, Belley-Ars, Dijon, Grenoble, Langres, Saint-Etienne
Paris	Créteil, Evry-Corbeil-Essonnes, Meaux, Nanterre, Pontoise, Saint-Denis, Versailles
Reims	Amiens, Beauvais, Châlons, Soissons
Rennes	Quimper, Saint-Brieuc, Vannes
Rouen	Bayeux, Coutances, Evreux, Le Havre, Sées
Sens	Moulins, Nevers, Troyes (as well as the Prelature nullius of Mission de France, or Pontigny)
Toulouse	Carcassonne, Montauban, Pamiers
Tours	Angers, Laval, Le Mans, and Nantes

The Archdioceses of Marseilles and Strasbourg and the Diocese of Metz are immediately subject to the Holy See.

selves. CLUNY had been restored since the 10th century; in 1098, CÎTEAUX was founded. BERNARD OF CLAIRVAUX, the most famous Cistercian monk, did not content himself with the life of a contemplative religious, but exercised a prodigious influence on his time: he was the preacher of the Second Crusade, and supervisor of the monarchy's choice of worthy bishops, the champion of the primacy of the pope. Bernard was even able to impose his own candidate, Innocent II, on France during the schism of 1130. While Bernard gave the popular religion of France elements that still predominate today—devotion to Mary, to the Passion, etc.—he was also a traditionalist, hostile to all innovation, especially in theology, where he clashed with ABELARD. With Bernard stood the canons of SAINT-VICTOR, who revived theology and mysticism (*see* VICTORINE SPIRITUALITY).

This same era was characterized further by new institutions: by ''communes,'' that owed much to the ideal of *communio* from which they drew their name; by the

Interior of Sainte–Chapelle, Sainte–Chapelle, Paris, built 1243–1248. (©Robert Holmes/CORBIS)

GUILDS that for a long time had remained of pagan inspiration but were gradually becoming confraternities. Rivalry between the nascent towns helped to spur the development of Gothic art and church architecture. The Gallery of Kings was created at Notre-Dame in Paris, and the Virgin became the protectress of the kingdom.

The 13th Century. The second half of the 12th century was an age of decline for the Church. King PHILIP II AUGUSTUS scandalized his contemporaries by his political cynicism. The Gregorian reform slowed down, and henceforth the reformers would be foreigners. In fact, toward 1200, France had become the home of the CATHARI and WALDENSES, the most widespread and virulent heretics of the period. In the face of this danger to the faith, St. DOMINIC devised new forms of the apostolate, such as public debates between heretic and preacher friar. Dominic's society of itinerant and mendicant preachers, organized in Toulouse, was a success, and in 1215 his order was extended to the whole Church. It was in France especially that the Dominicans found their first recruits; the friary of Saint-Jacques in Paris was their most famous house. For a long time proper evangelical action in response to the heretics in Languedoc was impossible, for the cruelties of the northern Crusaders against the ALBIGENSES (*see* LOUIS VIII, KING OF FRANCE) had provoked even the hesitant in southern France finally to rally to heresy. The peace treaty of 1229 did found a university in Toulouse to combat heretical error, but at the same time an institution of repression, the INQUISITION, was organized there.

Earlier, the University of Paris had been founded. At the time, there was a veritable popular movement in university circles, which would have been animated by an anticlerical spirit if the MENDICANT ORDERS had not been able to counteract it. Dominicans and Franciscans, in effect, early constituted a university-oriented clergy, their recruits often coming from that school. The University of Paris was the prototype of medieval universities both in its statutes and in its dynamism, for throughout the Middle Ages it had the best teachers and the largest number of students. It also assured the formation of a new type of man, the ''intellectual.'' Likewise, a new culture and a new collective mentality were being formed.

Because the mendicants presented themselves as the militia of the Holy See they clashed with the secular clergy: with the secular teachers of the University of Paris as well as with the secular parish priests to whom the mendicants meant competition because of their preaching.

Notre-Dame–en–vaux and fountain, 12th–13th Century, Chalons–sur–Mame, France. (©Elio Ciol/CORBIS)

These conflicts would continue until the end of the Middle Ages, with Rome most often upholding her ''militia.''

The new institutions in France were fruitful, thanks to LOUIS IX (d. 1270), a king whose religious spirit was exceptional. This remarkably cultivated prince reformed his kingdom and ruled with justice. Reflecting the austerity of his private life, he followed a policy of public economy that favored the little people. He achieved peace with England. His Crusades, which were the first to have a missionary character via contacts with the MONGOLS, earned Louis a reputation that would consolidate his dynasty. At the same time, Gregorian reforms continued; the king appointed excellent bishops; diocesan synods were held regularly and led to the composition of *Statuts* such as those of Nîmes that were effective throughout the whole area. Books such as the *Évangiles des domées* (Sunday Gospels) and the *Livre des métiers* (Guild Book) by Étienne Boileau revealed a vital and socially effective Christianity.

The Close of the Middle Ages. With the death of the son of Louis IX the century of knights ended. A new literature developed for the bourgeoisie: the FABLIAU and the second half of the *Roman de la Rose.* The king's chancery was no longer the monopoly of the clergy and passed into the hands of the legists. The best representative of the new spirit was Guillaume de Nogaret, for ten years the impetus behind the religious policy of King PHILIP IV and an enthusiastic promoter of reform ideas imbibed from his contemporary spiritual milieu. Nogaret was a master in the art of propaganda and thus able to give the king the support of all three Estates of his kingdom. The struggle he inspired against Pope BONIFACE VIII was as dramatic as it was useless: nothing, in fact, gravely divided the two powers except the theology of ''direct power'' (*see* UNAM SANCTAM) and the nationalism of Nogaret. The excommunication of the king forced Nogaret to push the battle as far as the criminal attempt at Anagni. The death of Boniface allowed Philip to influence the entire Church by having his satellite, Bertrand de Got, elected Pope CLEMENT V. Clement saw his office only as a means to exploit the Church. During this pontificate, the Holy See was domesticated by France, which imposed on the pope the suppression of the Templars (*see* VIENNE, COUNCIL OF), while the Sacred College was weighted with French cardinals.

The transfer of the Holy See from Rome to Avignon was a result of a new policy issued by a college of French cardinals that stated that only French popes could be elected. These popes now established themselves in Provence, and this new papal capital drained the resources of the French Church. Not unnaturally this Avignon papacy favored France. JOHN XXII excommunicated Flanders, while NEPOTISM became commonplace as cardinals pursued personal politics. Prodigiously wealthy due to the accumulation of benefices, cardinals were often protectors of the arts, thus preparing the way for the RENAISSANCE. In this manner, there developed an Avignonese civilization closely tied to that of the western basin of the Mediterranean.

What was the responsibility of France for the beginning of the WESTERN SCHISM? Cardinal de la Grange, who represented the French King Charles V in Rome, had followed an equivocal policy during the early months of URBAN VI's troubled reign. The king quickly rallied to antipope CLEMENT VII once he was elected, and exerted pressure on his bishops to do the same. Certain areas of France, however, especially the southwest, which was under English domination, continued to resist Clement (now in Avignon) and to support Urban in Rome. At the same time Charles chased any students and teachers who followed Urban out of Paris and transformed the university into a sort of royal council, making adherence to Clement VII an article of its diplomatic program. Although the alliance between Charles and Clement was very profitable to both parties, it ended at the death of Clement VII. In an attempt to end the schism, Charles VI called a veritable national council which decided to remove France from obedience to the pope at Avignon. An ordinance withdrew this pope's right to name any prelates, substituting the ''liberties of the Gallican church'' for papal reservations. The French Parlement established doctrine. Thus, the schism favored the development of a national religious conscience, and marked the birth of GALLICANISM. The affirmation of the autonomy of the Gallican Church within the universal Church was contemporary with the Gallicanism of theologians who asserted the superiority of the council over the pope (*see* CONCILIARISM). This doctrine, which was defended by such sincere theologians as GERSON, became a weapon in the hands of the king, and was given form with the PRAGMATIC SANCTION of Bourges in 1438. Thus the king of France became the absolute master of the Church in France. Henceforth he acted as sole judge of the recruiting of bishops. No council, not even a provincial one, could be held without his sanction. He assured the unity of this Church through the legateship conferred on Cardinal d'Amboise in 1501. About 1500 the king allowed the formation of so-called ''mitered'' families, administrators, from generation to generation, of the same dioceses, transforming such dioceses into veritable seigneurial estates. The French king eventually determined that his domination would be stronger if it were shared with the pope. Accordingly Francis I signed a new concordat with Pope LEO X in 1516 that remained in effect until 1790 and that later inspired the CONCORDAT OF 1801.

Serious decadence resulted from this royal meddling in ecclesiastical affairs, a decadence stimulated by the multiplied dispensations and privileges that resulted from the Western Schism. By 1500 simony was prevalent in the episcopate, for the bishop was now primarily a lord occupied with the administration of his province, not a resident diocesan. His first concern was with the material wealth of the Church, which, reconstituted in the second half of the 15th century, permitted the full development of flamboyant Gothic art.

Reforms and Pre-Reformation. In 1500 the French king summoned a council at Pisa, thinking to take upon himself the role of champion of Church reform. In reality the Pisa council served only to compromise true reform due to its partisan politics. And what was meant by ''reform''? Was it to be reform of the morals of the clergy, of the organization of the Church, or was it to be an awakening of religious sentiment? At the waning of the Middle Ages reform presented itself under each of these diverse facets. Although the secular clergy of the 15th century was generally too dependent on the monarchy to be receptive to reform, nevertheless, several of its number presented coherent programs of reform, notably Gerson, who until the beginning of the 16th century enjoyed an extraordinary audience. Gerson's ideas on education were taken up again at the end of the century by J. Standonck, who represented the Flemish milieu of the *DEVOTIO MODERNA* in Paris. All the religious orders partially reformed themselves during the 15th century. Each mendicant order gave birth to a reform group of Observants. At

''Tres Riches Heures by Jean,'' Duke of Berry, Paris, 15th century.

Cluny Jacques d'Amboise attacked COMMENDATION as responsible for much of the moral decadence. An analogous movement took place in convents for women, e.g., at FONTEVRAULT.

Another type of reform occupied certain humanists who, in the light of ancient texts, pursued the discovery of a new art of living, always at the risk of appearing too liberal to the Sorbonne, which remained attached to SCHOLASTICISM and where Noël Béda exerted a veritable despotism. GAGUIN, Fichet, and Budé and especially LEFÈVRE D'ÉTAPLES and ERASMUS represented the new spirit. Lefévre, molded by the culture of the Florence of Marsilio FICINO and heir to the mystical tradition of the Middle Ages, published and commented on a new edition of St. Paul three years before Luther. Erasmus, who often sojourned in Paris, where he was in touch with the humanistic and reform milieu, published his *Nouveau Testament* in 1516.

The religious life of laymen was likewise transformed toward the middle of the 14th century, aided per-

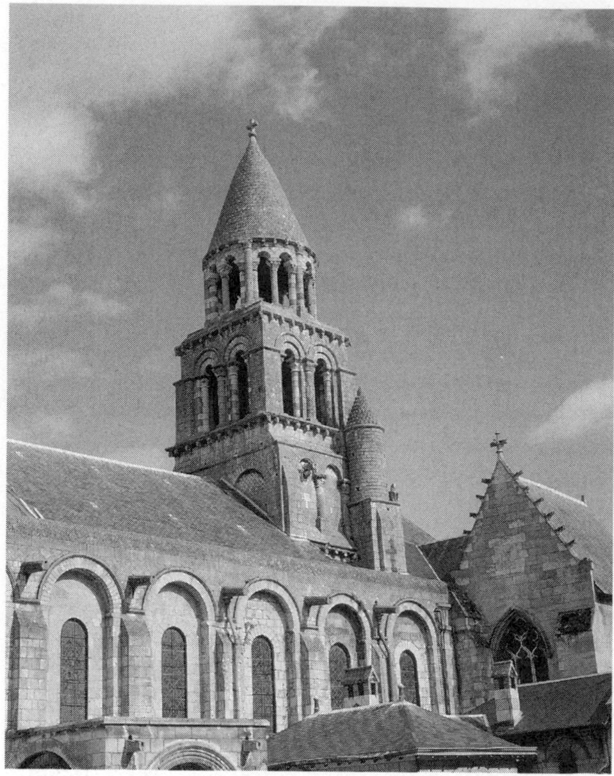

Bell tower on Church of Notre Dame la Grande, Poitiers, France. (©Ric Ergenbright/CORBIS)

haps by the Black Death. There followed a somber century: the Pietà, the DANCE OF DEATH, Holy Sepulchers, and the ARS MORIENDI all presupposed and supported an acute sense of sin, fear of the Last Judgment, remembrance of the Passion, and trust in Christ the Savior. This same religion excited popular movements such as the flagellants of St. VINCENT FERRER (*see* FLAGELLATION) and the penitents of the Franciscan Brother Richard (*c.* 1428–31). There was also a whole popular evangelical movement connected with the *Bible historiale,* the French translation of the ''histories'' and the ''moralities'' of the Bible. At the same time, the use of the Books of Hours became widespread, and works of piety such as the golden legends, manuals for confession, and ''lucidaires'' or laymen's guides, multiplied. Printing increased diffusion. The most important of these works was *Internelle Consolacion,* a French translation of the IMITATION OF CHRIST.

The trials France underwent at the close of the Middle Ages purified and internalized religious sentiment. The Christian of 1500 was characterized first of all by his *teatralità:* his taste for mystery plays, for dramatized sermons such as those of Olivier Maillard and for exaggeratedly expressionistic iconography. He was characterized by triumphalism, which manifested itself in processions of the Holy Sacrament and coronations of Mary, by his Christian sense of history as seen in the great PASSION PLAYS; he was characterized by his good conscience, his need for reassurance being reflected by his mathematical piety, his interest in indulgences, his passive confidence in the Church and priests and his recourse to the manuals of casuistry. Familiarity with the Bible increased; Christ came to be viewed more and more as the only Savior. Yet, religion remained very external, often limited to the letter of the commandments of the Church and far removed from the idea of salvation through faith. French Lutheranism in one way would benefit from these changes, but in another, would compromise this Catholic reform, which did not have the time to develop fully even its limited promise.

Bibliography: S. BERGER, *La Bible française au moyen-âge* (Paris 1884). É. MÂLE, *L'Art religieux du XIIe siècle en France* (5th ed. Paris 1947); *L'Art religieux du XIIIe siècle* (8th ed. Paris 1948), Eng. tr. from 3d Fr. ed. D. NUSSEY (New York 1913); *L'Art religieux de la fin du moyen-âge en France* (5th ed. Paris 1949). C. V. LANGLOIS, *La Vie en France au moyen-âge de la fin du XIIe au milieu du XIVe siècle,* 4 v. (Paris 1924–28). J. EVANS, *Life in Medieval France* (rev. ed. New York 1957). *Histoire spirituelle de la France* (Paris 1964). A. LATREILLE et al., eds., *Histoire du catholicisme en France,* 3 v. (rev. ed. Paris 1962–63). **Merovingian and Carolingian.** P. IMBART DE LA TOUR, *Les Paroisses rurales du IVe au IXe siècle* (Paris 1900). É. LESNE, *Histoire de la propriété ecclésiastique en France,* 6 v. in 8 (Lille 1910–43). E. SALIN, *La Civilisation mérovingienne,* 4 v. (Paris 1950–59). *Études mérovingiennes* (Paris 1953). **Gregorian.** P. IMBART DE LA TOUR, *Les Élections épiscopales dans l'Église de France du IXe au XIIe siècle* (Paris 1890). L. PAULOT, *Un Pape français, Urbain II* (Paris 1903). L. GAUTIER, *Là Chevalerie,* ed. J. LEVRON (rev. ed. Grenoble 1960). G. B. LADNER, *The Idea of Reform* (Cambridge, MA 1959). **13th century.** M. SEPET, *Saint Louis* (Paris 1898). J. GUIRAUD, *Histoire de l'Inquisition au Moyen-Âge,* 2 v. (Paris 1935–38). L. HALPHEN et al., *Aspects de l'Université de Paris* (Paris 1949). L. BUISSON, *König Ludwig IX, der Heilige, und das Recht* (Freiburg 1954). **Late Middle Ages.** N. VALOIS, *La France et le Grand Schisme d'Occident,* 4 v. (Paris 1896–1902). C. SAMARAN and G. MOLLAT, *La Fiscalité pontificale en France au XIVe siècle* (Paris 1905). G. MOLLAT, *The Popes at Avignon, 1305–1378,* tr. J. LOVE (New York 1963). G. LIZERAND, *Clément V et Philippe le Bel* (Paris 1911). J. RIVIÈRE, *Le Problème de l'Église et de l'état au temps de Philippe le Bel* (Paris 1926). V. MARTIN, *Les Origines du gallicanisme,* 2 v. (Paris 1939). Y. RENOUARD, *La Papauté à Avignon* (Paris 1954). **Reforms.** J. B. SCHWAB, *Johannes Gerson, Professor der Theologie und Kanzler der Universität Paris* (Würzburg 1858). P. IMBART DE LA TOUR, *Les Origines de la Réforme,* 4 v. (Paris 1905–35; v.1, 2d ed. 1948). A. RENAUDET, *Préréforme et humanisme à Paris pendant les premières guerres d'Italie, 1494–1517* (2d ed. Paris 1953). E. ROY, *Le Mystère de la Passion en France du XIVe au XVIe siècle,* 2 v. (Dijon 1903–04). M. VLOBERG, *La Vierge et l'Enfant dans l'art français,* 2 v. (Paris 1933).

[E. DELARUELLE]

The Rise of the Modern Church: 1515–1789

In 1515 the Church in France was in as disordered a state as it had been a century before at the end of the

Western Schism. For guidance in matters of unity and welfare it became accustomed to look for the person of the king, who in turn, through his control of the appointment to benefices, supplied bishops who had slight regard for their religious duties.

The Concordat of Francis I. Francis I (1515–47) agreed to a concordat with the papacy (1516) that, while removing the long-term threat of a French schism, also won him the formal recognition of his right to nominate candidates for the most important benefices. This concordat, which remained in force until the French Revolution, made it unnecessary for French kings to abandon Catholicism in order to gain control of the goods of the Church. This Gallican trend was furthered by the decree of the Council of Sens (1528) that made French bishops responsible for the reform of all religious orders in France, and by the decree of the king (1540) that gave Parlement sole competence in matters of heresy. Sentiment for reform did not come from royal or episcopal circles except in the case of Guillaume BRIÇONNET of Meaux, who gathered around him a circle of Christian humanists. Though this group eventually moved toward Lutheranism, Briçonnet's attempts to have Catholicism preached in his dioceses sets him apart from the other French bishops.

The Huguenots and Civil War. During the reign of Henry II (1547–59) royal action severely limited the inroads of Lutheranism. However, circumstances at the time of Henry's accidental death resulted in an influx of Calvinist ministers into France that reached its peak about 1562. This influx effected political changes and divided the allegiance of the nobility. The signing of the Treaty of Cateau-Cambrésis (1559) ended the long series of wars in Italy dating back to 1494 and limited the chance of the lesser nobles to make a career of the army. These men, who had begun to duplicate the extravagant manners of the Italian Renaissance, were finding their fixed income from the rent of peasants insufficient, especially in an era of inflation resulting from the influx of gold from the New World. In 1560 royal pensions were sharply reduced, thereby forcing them to become "clients" of the greater nobility. The seizure of Church lands seemed a way out of a dilemma. The three great noble families—the GUISEs, the Montmorencies, and the Bourbons, all of whom had gained a large number of clients—were involved in a struggle to dominate Henry's young successor, Francis II (1559–60). The Guises supported the royal family and Catholicism in order to further their own interests. The Montmorencies were split on religious issues: the Duke of Montmorency was loyal to the king and to Catholicism though he opposed the Guises, while the Admiral de Coligny, his nephew, supported the HUGUENOTS.

Aristide Briand.

The premature death of Francis II (December 1560) and the accession of his 11-year-old brother Charles IX (1560–74) shifted the balance of power. With the support of the Estates-General of 1560, the king's mother, CATHERINE DE MÉDICIS, assumed the position of regent. With the consequent decline of the power of the Guises, the Huguenots, led by the Bourbon Louis de Condé, took the initiative.

Despite attempts at conciliation, by April 11, 1562, France was involved in a religious and political civil war. After the ST. BARTHOLOMEW'S DAY Massacre on Aug. 25, 1572, when many Huguenots were murdered, the conflict became more bitter and culminated in strong anti-royal sentiment among the Huguenots and the formation of the fanatical Catholic League by followers of the king.

Henry IV and Reform. From the time of the murder of Henry III (1574–89) until 1594, France was in a state of anarchy that finally ended with the acceptance by all of France of Henry of Navarre, leader of the Bourbons. As Henry IV (1589–1610), he abjured Calvinism and brought a solution to the religious crisis by means of the Edict of Nantes (1598), which guaranteed the Huguenots the right to retain their religion and gave them 100 fortified towns for their protection until animosity subsided.

Archbishop Marcel Lefebvre. (Archive Photos)

As a result of the Wars of Religion the expansion of Calvinism in France was halted, and political stability, based on a growing desire for a strong monarch, was restored. But the religious life of the nation worsened despite the earnest activities of the Jesuits and Capuchins. In the rural areas a forceful Christianity was disappearing because of war and neglect. Among the intellectuals the skepticism of Montaigne and Charron became dominant. Yet during the reign of Henry IV steps toward reform were taken by Cardinal Jacques DUPERRON and Bp. Jean Camus. The assassination of Henry IV brought his wife, MARIE DE MÉDICIS, to power as regent for Louis XIII (1610–43). Though France faced a period of civil unrest that lasted into the 2d decade of the century, this religious reform continued. Despite the refusal (1614) of the Third Estate to accept the enforcement of the decrees of the Council of Trent in France and the continuing hostility of the government to these decrees on the grounds that they threatened the privileges of the Gallican Church, the Assembly of Clergy of 1615 accepted them. Under the inspiration of the Jesuits, the leaders of the First Estate resisted Gallicanism and worked for reform in the episcopacy and the regular clergy. The latter was begun by Cardinal de LA ROCHEFOUCAULD in 1622 and continued by Cardinal RICHELIEU. New congregations were established, and by 1630 there were 15,000 monasteries and convents in France, half of which had been founded since the end of the Wars of Religion.

The religious quickening that occurred during the first half of the 16th century was the work also of outstanding spiritual leaders. St. FRANCIS DE SALES, Bishop of Geneva and founder of the Visitation nuns, emphasized that perfection is a goal attainable by all men. Pierre de BÉRULLE, founder of the French Oratory, concentrated on the grandeur of God and the necessity of mortification. St. VINCENT DE PAUL, founder of the Lazarists and the Sisters of Charity, influenced by both St. Francis de Sales and Cardinal Bérulle, worked for the conversion of rural France and the establishment of charitable institutions. Jean Jacques OLIER founded the Sulpicians (1643) to improve the secular clergy through the foundation of diocesan seminaries. This period witnessed also a great French missionary effort led by the Jesuits, Capuchins, and Récollets.

The Role of Richelieu. The reign of Louis XIII was dominated by Cardinal Richelieu, who served as first minister of France from 1624 until his death in 1642. From the time of his consecration as bishop of Luçon (1607) until his entry into political life after the Estates-General of 1614, Richelieu planned sincerely for Church reform, though his interests were also political. He restrained the independence of the nobles and the Huguenots, accomplishing the latter through the Peace of Alcais of 1629, which ended Huguenot political power and their possession of the 100 fortified towns. Beyond the borders of France, Richelieu renewed the war against the Hapsburgs that had ended in 1559. French aid to the Lutheran states of Denmark and Sweden and to the Protestant princes of northern Germany, and, finally, direct French intervention in 1635 prolonged the Thirty Years' War and wakened the power of the Hapsburg dynasty.

Mazarin and the Fronde. The Italian-born Cardinal MAZARIN succeeded Richelieu in power and was master of France until 1661. He concluded the Thirty Years' War and furthered the great decline of Spanish political influence through the Treaty of the Pyrenees (1659). Within France, however, a growing hostility erupted against Mazarin and the Spanish regent, Anne of Austria. The anti-Italian spirit dated back into the 16th century and was especially strong among the clergy because of resentment that so many Italians held important French benefices. The anti-Spanish feeling gained momentum through the long wars with the Hapsburgs. This animosity resulted in the Fronde (1648–53), a rebellion begun by Parlement but carried on by the nobles, who found their political importance declining.

Louis XIV and Absolutism. During his long reign (1643–1715), Louis XIV achieved the goal of a strong

French state planned by Francis I, Henry IV, and Richelieu. He became his own first minister after Mazarin's death (1661), and by checking the threat of the Fronde and adopting a successful fiscal policy, he succeeded in reinforcing the monarchy and reducing the influence of the nobles to the functions of courtiers. His plans for full control of the state included religious affairs as well. He revoked the Edict of Nantes in 1685 since the presence of two religions limited the power of the crown. The Church was brought further under royal authority when the Assembly of Clergy of 1682 was pressured to accept the Four Articles. This formulation of Gallicanism emphasized the separateness of the French Church and the superiority of a general council over the pope. At issue was the *régale,* the rights of the king regarding appointments to benefices not included in his privileges. The Four Articles were revoked by the king in 1693 after strong opposition from INNOCENT XI, who had annulled them in a rescript on April 11, 1682. Louis gave up his pretensions to the control of some benefices not specified in the Concordat of 1516. Louis' power was felt in the territory of Rome itself over the matter of the *droit d'asile* (right of asylum), in which matter Innocent struggled to limit the abuses of ambassadorial immunity and to retain sovereignty in his own capital.

The Fate of Jansenism. The theology of Cornelius JANSEN, Bishop of Ypres (1510–76), which emphasized predestination, human unworthiness, and the irresistibility of grace, survived the condemnation of his book, the *Augustinus,* by the Holy Office on Aug. 1, 1641, and spread through Belgium, Holland, and France. Through the activity of Jean DUVERGIER DE HAURANNE, Abbé of St. Cyran (1581–1643), it spread to the Convent of PORT-ROYAL and was kept in prominence by the efforts of the ARNAULD family, the brilliant *Provinciales* of Blais PASCAL, and the leaders of Parlement who were sympathetic to Gallicanism and Calvinism. After the death of the influential supporter of the Jansenists, the Duchess of Longuevill, Louis XIV moved strongly against them, even when they supported Gallicanism and his own anti-Roman policies. He destroyed Port-Royal (1710) and enforced the papal bull *UNIGENTIUS* of April 8, 1713, which denounced the Jansenist propositions of Pasquier QUESNEL (1634–1719). However, Jansenism remained as a sentiment in France in the seminaries and in Parlement. The Jansenists had their revenge on the Jesuits, their determined opponents, when, through the influence of Parlement, the Society of Jesus was ordered expelled from France in 1763.

Madame Guyon and Quietism. The mystical theories of Miguel de Molinos, as adapted by Madame GUYON, attracted a group of followers in France in the 1680s and 1690s. QUIETISM was a reaction against the

Bronze Sculptures atop the roof of Notre–Dame Cathedral, Isle de la Cite, Paris. (©Robert Holmes/CORBIS)

overly organized spiritual life of the 17th century, and in its French version emphasized resignation and pure love of God. Madame Guyon had some support among the French clergy, especially Archbishop FÉNELON. The strongest opponent of this movement was Jacques BOSSUET, court bishop and theoretician of divine right absolutism. Through his effort, Madame Guyon was imprisoned in 1695 and Fénelon was silenced four years later. The condemnation of Quietism brought the contemplative life under suspicion. Jansenism had already deemphasized the efficacy of prayer and this reaction against Quietism completed the damage at a time when the Church in France was in need of all of its spiritual force. The government, meanwhile, faced the task of maintaining the absolutist structures of Louis XIV without a Louis XIV. The nobles and Parlement began to regain their lost power and the kings were progressively separated from the people by a growing bureaucracy. This problem was aggravated by the inept and inattentive behavior of Louis

Street café and Notre Dame Cathedral, Evreux, France. (©Franz-Marc Frei/CORBIS)

XV (1715–74) and the inability of Louis XVI (1774–91) ever to understand the crises he faced.

The Church and the Enlightenment. The attitude of the Church to the theories of the 17th-century scientists and the philosophies constructed upon them was multifold but disastrous. Some clerics were attracted to the ideas of Pierre GASSENDI and Daniel HUET, which ideas derived from the philosophy of MONTAIGNE and CHARRON and opposed that of DESCARTES. This resulted in a fideistic skepticism. The greater number of philosophers and theologians remained conservative, if we except the appearance of an occasional philosopher such as Leonart LESSIUS, and either ignored or condemned new trends of thought. As a consequence, men such as Descartes found themselves cut off from the established tradition and forced to forge their own answers to the pertinent question raised by investigations of thc new science: if man had been so long mistaken about the organization of the universe, could he know anything with certitude? By the end of the 17th century Newton and Leibniz had restored humanity's confidence in itself. However, this new creature placed his assurance not in faith and reason, but in reason alone. The thinkers of the 18th century were weary with the endless quarrels among Jesuits, Jansenists, Quietist, and scholastics. Aware that the world was not the world of Aristotle and Ptolemy, and searching for a means of making human beings happy, they accepted the new faith in reason. Voltaire, Diderot, and the other philosophes, inspired by Newton's laws, Leibniz's optimism, and the destructive criticism of the old order by Bayle and Montesquieu, worked to build a utopia in this world. Their religion was a DEISM that professed belief in creation by a Supreme Being and the progress of creation wholly by means of natural laws. For the middle class and for many clerics, already repelled by the growing worldliness of French churchmen, the ideas of the philosophes were irresistible. Their religion, however, did not become Deism, but simple indifference. (*See* ENLIGHTENMENT.)

The leaders of the Church in France did not protest the government's suppression of the Jesuits (1763), thus allowing the destruction of the one group that had entered into fruitful controversy with the philosophes. In 1766 Louis XV established a Commission of Regulars composed of five laymen and five archbishops. By 1781 these enemies of exempt religious had caused the disappearance of nine religious orders and the rapid decline of most others. Though the commission had been instituted to reform the orders, which was needed, they worked without papal approval either to destroy or to bring under episcopal and royal control the religious life of France. Rather than prescribing a gradual reform of such abuses as abbeys held *in commendam,* the commission demanded immediate acceptance of arbitrary legislation.

The Eve of Revolt. Because the bishops of France in the 1780s were all nobles, the Church was now identified with the aristocracy and the monarchy. The rural clergy, who received little support or attention from the episcopacy, formed a clerical proletariat. In the meantime the financial crisis of the government, growing since the wars of Louis XIV, reached its climax with the calling of an Assembly of Notables (1787) to remedy the failures in the system of taxation. The Notables, hoping to gain further power in their 70-year struggle against the crown, refused to assent to the taxation of the notables and clergy and called for an Estates-General. In this fateful meeting of 1789, approved by Parlement and dominated by the aristocracy, the middle class (given its first chance to speak in 175 years and united by its desire to gain a place in society) seized power for itself. In the following years the Church, because of its association with the aristocracy, suffered from the havoc and destruction brought by the revolution.

Bibliography: J. R. BOULENGER, tr., *The Seventeenth Century* (New York 1933). A. L. GUÉRARD, *The Life and Death of an Idea: France in the Classical Age* (New York 1928). P. HAZARD, *The European Mind: The Critical Years, 1680–1715,* tr. J. L. MAY (New Haven 1953); *European Thought in the 18th Century: From Montesquieu to Lessing,* tr. J. L. MAY (New Haven 1954). G. LEFEBVRE, *The Coming of the French Revolution, 1789,* tr. R. R. PALMER (Princeton 1947). J. LOUGH, *An Introduction to 17th-Century France* (New York 1954); *An Introduction to 18th-Century France* (New York 1960). V. MARTIN, *Le Gallicanisme et la réforme catholique* (Paris 1919); *Le Ballicanisme politique et le clergé de France* (Paris 1929). J. W. THOMPSON, *The Wars of Religion in France, 1559–1576* (Chicago 1909).

[J. M. HAYDEN]

Revolution, Restoration, and Reform: 1789–1965

The history of the Church of France after 1789 is dominated by three problems: the conflict with the more liberal society issuing from the French Revolution; the development of an industrial working class opposed to the aristocracy and all its manifestations; and the confrontation with contemporary civilization.

1789 to 1814. Under the *ancien régime,* the state was Catholic, and the king was considered a religious personage, a ''bishop of the exterior.'' At the start of the French Revolution, the Constituent Assembly of 1789 could not imagine a Church separated from the state. It legislated on religious matters as the king had done. Under the diverse influence of Gallicanism, Jansenism, Protestantism, and the Enlightenment, the Assembly enacted the CIVIL CONSTITUTION OF THE CLERGY. This legislation created a schismatical Constitutional Church, and split the country religiously into two opposing groups. The revolution became increasingly hostile to the Church and by 1792 sought to destroy it, along with the monarchy with which it had been intimately allied. Later the Constitutional Church suffered persecution also. An attempt was made to dechristianize the country, and to replace Christianity with the cult of the goddess of Reason (1793), the cult of the Supreme Being (1794), THEOPHILANTHROPY (1797), and the DECADI cult (1798). In this condition of semi-anarchy, leftist, republican, and irreligious France triumphed over rightist, monarchist, and Catholic France.

The decade of revolution revealed the dechristianization already extant in some regions of the country and promoted the phenomenon; but by 1799 the majority of the people desired the restoration of the Catholic religion. In Vendée the greater part of the populace had taken up arms to defend their altars. With order restored under the Consulate, Bonaparte (*see* NAPOLEON I) sought to unify two mutually hostile segments of France arrayed against each other in civil war. He negotiated with PIUS VII the CONCORDAT OF 1801. A few bishops among those who had refused to resign their sees, as the pope demanded, joined the schismatic PETITE ÉGLISE. The new concordat governed church-state relations until 1905. It did not recognize Catholicism as the state religion but as the religion of the majority of the French people. It permitted the government to name the bishops, who were then canonically instituted by the pope. Bishops in turn were given the right to select pastors and curates. The regular clergy, scorned by the public, was not mentioned in the pact. This concordat was a compromise in which the Church agreed to liberty of conscience and to a legal parity with the Protestants and Jews. Confiscated ecclesiastical goods were not restored, but the state obligated itself to a reimbursement of the clergy. However, Bonaparte, on his own authority, immediately appended to the concordat the Organic Articles, which withdrew the state's concessions. One result of this procedure was that the Church lost confidence in this French government, which was no longer Catholic and which was to manifest hostility to this faith. Gradually the Church became accustomed to turn for help to the Holy See and Gallicanism gave way to ULTRAMONTANISM.

Highlighting the period of the First Empire (1804–14) was the conflict between Napoleon I and Pius VII (who came to Paris in 1894 to consecrate the emperor). The Continental Blockade provided the occasion for this great church-state dispute, but the underlying cause was imperial despotism. From 1809 to 1814 the pope was Napoleon's prisoner, during which time he agreed to the so-called CONCORDAT OF FONTAINEBLEU (1813), which he soon disavowed. This dramatic conflict was terminated by the collapse of the empire. Its sole lasting effect was to increase the authority and prestige of the papacy. The empire had succeeded in its aim of restoring religious peace but it had failed to enslave the Church to the state.

1814 to 1830. The religious history of the Restoration period (1813–30) was that of the failure of an attempt at a partial return to the *ancien régime.* During the reigns of Louis XVIII and Charles X, counterrevolution, the dominant ideology, found its outstanding proponents in the theocratic Joseph de MAISTRE and the traditionalist Louis de BONALD. The reactionary political outlook, to which the newly appointed bishops such as Hyacinthe de QUELEN subscribed, was tinged with a Gallicanism that defeated the project of a new concordat in 1817. Administrative pressure, the laws in the press (1822) and on sacrilege (1825), and other legislative measures all favored the religious reconquest of society. Indicative of the means utilized to effect this reconquest was the activity of the KNIGHTS OF THE FAITH, a secret society that worked in the shadow of a pious society called the CONGREGATION, and that encountered violent opposition from a Voltairean bourgeoisie. The outcome was the expulsion of the Jesuits from teaching (1828) and the explosion of anticlericalism in the Revolution of 1830, which overthrew Charles X. The religious policy of the Restoration was mostly a failure; it had one good feature in that it permitted priests, sorely tried for a quarter of a century, to replenish their ranks and to build up a new vitality.

1830 to 1848. The July Monarchy was coterminous with the reign of Louis Philippe (1830–48), head of the cadet branch of the Bourbons. It began in an antireligious atmosphere. It was at this time that the first attempt was made at conciliation between the Church and society issuing from the revolution. The leaders in this movement of Catholic liberalism were Hugues Félicité de LAMENNAIS, LACORDAIRE, and MONTALEMBERT, whose organ was the short-lived newspaper *L'Avenir.* They championed liberty under every form. Above all, they upheld liberty of religion to be obtained by the complete separation of church and state. This program horrified the ecclesiastical authorities. Unfortunately, Lamennais was not a sound theologian, and *L'Avenir* was condemned by GREGORY XVI in the encyclical *Mirari vos* (1832). The principal Catholic demand under the July Monarchy was for liberty of education. During the Restoration the Church had tried, under the lead of Denis FRAYSSINOUS, to Catholicize the university, but after 1830 the university freed itself of this control. Under the July Monarchy the Church endeavored to obtain freedom for Catholic secondary education but the Chamber refused to grant it. As a result of the Catholic assaults on the university, the Jesuits were obliged to close their homes. On the other hand, the bourgeoisie were responsible for the passage of the Guizot Law (1833), which left to the Church supervision of primary education; they were motivated by fear lest popular unbelief menace the social structure. As a result of the influence of Lamennais and the anticlericalism of the government, ultramontanism made great progress. One effect was the gradual supplanting of the Gallican by the Roman liturgy. Another was the remarkable revival of the regular clergy, a phenomenon that was evident to a slight degree between 1830 and 1848 and that attained its full development later during the Second Empire.

1848 to 1852. Its liberal position in dealing with the anticlerical July Monarchy won for the Church widespread popular approval during the Revolution of 1848 and at the beginning of the Second Republic (1848–52). For the second time hope rose for a conciliation with the society issuing from the revolution. But the economic and social crisis that resulted from the revolutionary days of July 1848, in the course of which Archbishop AFFRE of Paris was slain, revived the division of the country into two blocs, with the Church taking its stand solidly on the right. Moreover, the hostility of the republicans was unleashed by the French military expedition to Rome, which overthrew the Roman Republic and restored Pius IX to control of the STATES OF THE CHURCH.

The Revolution of 1848 had brutally posed the social problem that arose from the destruction of the corporations by the French Revolution and from the birth of modern industry. Only a few Catholics grasped the situation as early as the time of the July Monarchy; these men formulated solutions, which later were given the name of social Catholicism. These forerunners manifested two diverse tendencies. Armand de MELUN was a pioneer leader in the conservative trend. The democratic direction was represented by *Ere nouvelle* (1848), whose political ideals were the liberal ones formerly proposed by *L'Avenir.* In the reaction to the stormy days of June 1848, social Catholicism suffered a blow from which it did not recover until the Third Republic.

Fear of socialism brought the middle class close to the Church on the political level. This was evident in the Falloux Law (1850), which granted the Church freedom for secondary education and representation in the council of the university. This law has been of capital importance in the religious history of contemporary France, because it assured the partial re-Christianization of the middle class, which had become completely imbued with the rationalist philosophy of the 18th-century Enlightenment. At the same time, the Falloux Law accentuated the rivalry, born during the July Monarchy, between intransigent or authoritarian Catholics, who found the law insufficient, and liberal Catholics, who were pleased with it. These two groups conflicted also over another great problem. The intransigents, led by Louis VEUILLOT and Bp. Louis PIE, condemned the type of society issuing from the revolution and sought to destroy it, whereas the liberal group, led by Montalembert, Albert de Broglie, and Bp. Félix DUPANLOUP, aimed rather to improve it. Thus the dispute between the Church and society was further complicated by a quarrel among Catholics themselves.

1852 to 1879. The Church, dominated as it was by intransigent Catholics, supported for the most part the dictatorship inaugurated by Louis Napoleon in the coup d'état of Dec. 2, 1851, followed by the establishment of the Second Empire (1852–70). Motivating in part this outlook was the Church's eagerness for the reestablishment of order and appreciation for the official homages that the new regime lavished on the Church. The only hostile Catholic groups were the legitimists, who were partisans of the elder branch of the Bourbons, and the liberals. The situation of the latter became still more painful in 1864 with the publication of the encyclical QUANTA CURA and the SYLLABUS OF ERRORS, despite the famous distinction made by Bishop Dupanloup between the thesis and the hypothesis. When VATICAN COUNCIL I solemnly defined the doctrines of papal primacy and infallibility in 1870, it dealt a death blow to Gallicanism.

The drive to unify Italy led in 1859 to a war that revealed disquieting perspectives in regard to the papal temporal power. Since NAPOLEON III and the Church viewed this problem differently, the alliance between them loosened until 1869 when republican opposition caused it to be tightened once more.

1870 to 1918. After the fall of the Second Empire, there followed a brief period introduced by the insurrection of the Paris commune. During this uprising, violently hostile to the Church, Abp. Georges DARBOY of Paris was shot to death. In the National Assembly, which governed the country until 1876, monarchists and Catholics comprised the majority. Great pilgrimages at this time to PARAY-LE-MONIAL revealed the persistence of vain hopes for a return to the Christian state. The Church did gain one advantage by obtaining (1875) freedom of higher education, which permitted it to found several Catholic faculties.

The republicans, positivist in spirit, came into power between 1876 and 1879. They disdained Catholicism as an obscurantist force destined soon to disappear. To precipitate this event they launched a threefold offensive that aimed to destroy religious congregations, Catholic education, and the Concordat of 1801. The onslaught was conducted in two stages. During the first one (1879–89) most congregations were dissolved (1880) and primary education was made compulsory, with public schools gratuitous and nonsectarian.

During the ensuing period of appeasement (1889–98), LEO XIII launched the third attempt at conciliation between the Church and the modern world. In pursuance of his policy of RALLIEMENT he issued *Au milieu des sollicitudes* (1892). This encyclical sought to deter French Catholics from jeopardizing their religion any longer by combating republican institutions; instead it advised Catholics to accept them. Most Catholics, however, refused either to abandon their monarchical ideal or to distinguish between the struggle against hostile legislation and the struggle against the Third Republic. The Ralliement had already collapsed when the Dreyfus Affair revived the battle between the right and the left and gave the signal for a second wave of anticlericalism and LAICISM (1898–1906), more violent than the first. It was started by Pierre Waldeck-Rousseau and resulted in further expulsions of religious congregations (1901). Justin Émile Combes was mainly responsible for the prohibition of congregations to teach (1904), the rupture of diplomatic relations with the Holy See (1904), and the abrogation of the concordat by the law separating Church and State (1905). Aristide Briand supervised as *rapporteur* the passage of this last law, which caused the Church to lose an annual budget of 35 million francs and the bulk of its possessions, because it conformed to Pius X's decision and refused to accept the juridical status bestowed on it.

At the beginning of the Third Republic, the conservative tradition of the social Catholicism was maintained in the workers' circles (*Oeuvre des cercles ouvriers*), in which the leading figures were Charles LA TOUR DU PIN and Albert de Mun. These circles enjoyed a measure of success for a while and then declined because of their undemocratic character. The encyclicals *RERUM NOVARUM* (1891) and *Au milieu des sollicitudes* (1892) gave rise to the movement of democratic priests, overly concerned with politics and journalism. Later came Sillon, led by Marc SANGNIER and the popular education movement, which had very brilliant moments c. 1900 before being dissolved by Pius X (1910), chiefly because it seemed to claim that Christianity implied democracy. Beginning in 1904 the Semaines sociales elaborated a doctrine for social Catholicism, but these ideas won support from no more than a minority of French Catholics.

The intellectual activity of the Church in France remained deficient after the Revolution because the clergy focused on the struggle against the adversaries of Catholicism, their activities absorbed by the work of ecclesiastical reconstruction. APOLOGETICS was continually behind the times. Young intellectuals who came under the influence of POSITIVISM, theological Liberalism, and Freemasonry (which in France had become irreligious) fell away from the faith. With the foundations of the Catholic faculties, the Church took note of this deficiency and underwent a veritable intellectual renaissance. This in turn gave rise to the crisis of MODERNISM, which occurred at the point where rationalist criticism encountered the rebirth of clerical studies. There was a question, for a time at least, of bringing the Catholic religion into harmony with the intellectual and moral needs of the time. French Modernism was above all Biblical (with LOISY as chief representative) and philosophical (with BLONDEL, LE ROY, and LABERTHONNIÈRE as leading exponents). Its errors drew a papal condemnation that affected the Church outside as well as within France. INTEGRALISM, which arose as part of the anti-Modernist reaction following the condemnation, retarded the intellectual activity of French Catholicism until after World War I.

1919 to 1945. After World War I international and financial problems relegated to the background of French politics the religious question, which was henceforth looked upon with greater serenity under the influence of the ''ex-service men'' spirit. The law regarding religious congregations was not put into effect. The Concordat of 1801 remained in force in Alsace-Lorraine even after the region's return to France. Relations with the Holy See were reestablished and permitted the negotiation of an accord that won for the Church the legal status that it had lacked since the separation. A last outbreak of militant anticlericalism appeared after the 1924 elections and attempted to question most of these changes. Its failure was due to the quick, resolute action of the Féderation nationale catholique and, above all, to its lack of popular support.

Taking advantage of the changed climate, Benedict XV and Pius XI overcame the opposition of the French hierarchy and resumed the Ralliement policy of Leo XIII, which Pius X had renounced. Catholics, who had been almost unanimously hostile to the separation of church and state, had since come to realize that although it had reduced the Church to poverty, it had also won for it liberty, independence, and an inestimable increase in dignity. They became accustomed to accepting separation as a permanent condition. On the other hand, Pius XI in 1926 condemned the ACTION FRANÇAISE of Charles MAURRAS who compromised the Church by assembling against the government a clientele of Catholic conservatives, integralists, nationalists, and monarchists. Action Française did not submit until 13 years later, but meanwhile its influence over youth had gradually declined. This second Ralliement, which constituted the fourth attempt to reconcile the Church, did not, to be sure, resolve all the problems that had plagued the Church for 135 years, but it did blunt their sharpness and relegated them permanently to the background. Henceforth both state and church tended to respect the nation's diverse spiritual families. If the traditional struggle between the two powers did not cease, it was carried on with much less intensity, except in regard to the school question.

After the great turning point of the French Revolution, the next great turning point in the history of the Church in France occurred between 1919 and 1926. The political problem had by 1919 ceased to be as important as the social problem. Gradually it became clear that the social problem was merely one aspect of a third problem, which was posed by contemporary civilization itself.

In the years following 1926 the changed political climate became stabilized. The state maintained correct or good relations with the clergy. Collusion between Catholics and monarchists ceased. No longer was the royalist party represented in the Chamber. Catholics no longer formed a single bloc; they divided in their positions and became pluralists. Some of them formed a republican party whose inspiration was Christian, the Parti démocrate populaire; its importance was quite modest, but it enjoyed a certain role in the Assembly between the two world wars.

During World War II the French regime (1940–44) under Marshal Pétain was conservative and favorable to the Church. It abolished the legislation affecting religious congregations and granted financial assistance to private schools. The hierarchy supported this government at first and then, like the rest of the country, detached itself from it and opposed the creation of a state youth movement and measures of racial discrimination.

The liberation government was dominated by the left-wing parties, but it was not anticlerical because Catholic participation in the resistance movement was widespread and because many militant Catholics were part of this government and of succeeding governments, although Catholic membership in government ministries had been a rarity before World War II. Only the office of Minister of National Education remained inaccessible to Catholics. The governments of both the Fourth and Fifth Republics granted financial aid to Catholic schools. The Mouvement républicaine populaire (MRP), successor to the Parti démocrate populaire and, like it, Christian in inspiration without being sectarian, won the largest number of votes after the liberation, because of a temporary weakness of the right-wing parties. On the political, social, and intellectual levels, the left wing of the MRP was composed of small groups of Catholics with very advanced, even progressivist ideas, bordering on those of the Communists.

A symmetrical development assured to social Catholicism a larger following within and without the Catholic fold. Social Catholicism saw its program put into effect by legislation, notably in regard to family allowances and social insurance. Christian syndicalism, whose modest beginnings dated back to 1887, was organized in 1919 with the creation of the Conféderation française de Travailleurs chrétiens. As a result of its earlier efforts this confederation grew rapidly after World War II.

Although the Church was for the most part freed from the political problem, it became aware that in place of the seemingly static world of the 19th century, a new world was evolving, whose future was as uncertain as the situation of Catholicism in the French sector of this world. The Church accepted also a newly developed type of spirituality.

Spiritual Renaissance. By the mid-20th century, France could no longer be regarded as almost entirely Catholic, as dechristianization had made deep inroads. The two anticlerical outbreaks during the Third Republic accentuated the trend toward dechristianization, especially in some regions. Another factor in the spread of dechristianization was industrial growth, one effect of which was the creation of proletarian areas that had little or no contact with traditional Christianity. *Le Christ dans le banlieu* (1943) by Y. Daniel and H. Goding (Eng. tr. *France Pagan,* 1949; by M. Ward) revealed the existence of this little-known dechristianized society existing alongside Christian society. A school of religious sociology founded by G. Le Bras was formed to study this phenomenon.

In the 19th century Catholics regarded their religion mostly in its moral aspects: they admired its organization, respected its prescriptions, which supplied them with a way of life, honored the virtues exemplified by the saints, and practiced sentimental devotion to the rosary, the month of Mary, the souls in Purgatory, etc. Beginning at the end of the 19th century a theological renaissance, a return to the faith of numerous intellectuals, the progress of Biblical studies, and the LITURGICAL MOVEMENT oriented fervor more directly toward God. Missals were substituted for prayerbooks to be read during Mass. The mystical life became more frequently looked upon as a prolongation of the life of grace. The Catholicism of conformism and individualism, of law and obligation, pious practices, and sentiment gave way to a Catholicism at once personal and more social, inspired by the theological virtues and growing stronger by practice, a Catholicism that aimed at making the life of a Christian a life of permanent prayer, a thoroughly human activity directed not only toward the salvation of the individual but also toward that of the world. To win victories the orientation of this Catholicism was no longer political but apostolic. While this new orientation banished egoism, it also impelled some zealous young Catholics into rash activism in critical situations.

During the 20th century LOURDES became a world-renowned center for pilgrimages. Other shrines in France, such as LA SALETTE, were also very popular. A large percentage of modern canonized or beatified martyrs and confessors were French, and many who had been put to death during the French Revolution were beatified in this period.

Another characteristic of the Church that became increasingly entrenched during the 20th century was the increasing number of religious congregations devoted mainly to the active apostolate. Many of these, while established in France, later spread throughout the world.

Intellectual Activities. On the intellectual plane, the modern renaissance had a character of objectivity as the human respect characteristic of the bourgeois Catholicism of the 19th century disappeared. Catholic literature enjoyed a brilliant revival, the first signs of which appeared before 1914. Georges BERNANOS, Paul CLAUDEL, and François Mauriac became among the best-known Catholic literary lights. The high level of this literary revival was sustained by the creation of the Semaine des Ecrivains catholiques, replaced after World War II by the much more substantial Semaine des Intellectuels catholiques. Catholic publishers produced great collections pertaining to all realms of religious thought and activity. From the Catholic press came numerous periodicals and newspapers.

Domestic Missionary Movements. To make the world Christian, the focus of missionary groups turned to natural social communities. Before World War II this apostolate was conducted through the specialized agencies of CATHOLIC ACTION. After the war, the job was spread among various missionary movements, certain geographical areas and certain classes in society treated much like mission territories. Following the example of the Belgian Young Christian Worker movement, in 1926 Catholic France organized Jeunesse ouvrière chrétienne française (JOC), the aim of which was to have catholic laymen of a certain group exercise an apostolate among other laymen of the same group and in the same milieu. The Catholic Association of French Youth, established in 1886, developed in this same spirit of social Catholicism. Between 1927 and 1931 the group was transformed into a federation of specialized movements, each focused around young persons of a different social milieu. Among the other specialized movements that arose after 1926 were the Agricultural Christian Youth (JEC), Young Christian Student (JEC), and the Independent (i.e., middle-class) Christian Youth (JIC). Corresponding movements for young women and for adults came into being later. In addition Catholic Action groups of a more general type also appeared.

Another notable feature of the Catholic revival was the birth of a domestic missionary movement among the clergy. In 1941 the Mission de France was created to remedy the inconveniences involved in the partitioning of the country into dioceses that left the most dechristianized regions deprived of priests. This apostolate was conducted among the workers and also in parishes, and involved a specialized group of priests who sought to reestablish the presence of the Church in a dechristianized class. These WORKER PRIESTS began their labors in 1941 and shared the same life of labor as other workers. Unfortunately some priests lacked sufficient preparation and engaged in temporal activities that sometimes compromised the integrity of the priesthood. Pius XII put an end to the experiment on 1954, but Paul VI permitted its revival in 1965 with certain modifications.

The missionary spirit was also applied to parish life, and it was here that it found the widest field of action, thanks to the revival of preaching and especially of the liturgy carried out in a community spirit centered on the celebration of Mass and the distribution of the Sacraments. In rural districts priests organized themselves into communities so that they could serve dechristianized nearby parishes.

To restore the stability of the Church after the French Revolution and its aftermath, the Church in France needed changes in its organization. The Concordat of 1801 prevented such reorganization as long as it remained in effect, and following the separation of church and state, Pius X did not sanction meetings of the hierarchy due to the fear they would further expand the law of separation. However, by the late 1800s new problems made clear the need for a new type of organization, and in 1919 a commission of French cardinals and archbishops was created. In 1951 the entire episcopate held its first plenary meeting; four others would meet by 1965. Several permanent episcopal commissions formed, as well as an episcopal secretariat, laying the groundwork for the French Church's transformation into an episcopate receptive and responsive to contemporary problems.

Vocations. Once the law of separation went into effect the social and financial considerations that once induced many peasant families to direct one of their sons toward the priesthood ceased to exist. This resulted in the gradual disappearance of a rather ineffectual type of priest. It also cut recruitments quickly to less than half of what they had been. Then, too, the regular clergy were affected by the law concerning religious congregations, as well as by the wretched material situation of most priests since 1905. This drop in recruitment was especially noticeable in rural areas, while among urban working-class areas vocations remained characteristically few. World War I heightened the crisis: by 1929 the number of secular priests dropped to 46,500, and by 1965 to 40,000. On the other hand, the regular clergy considerably increased its membership during the same period: among the 20,000 religious men there were 7,000 priests within France (apart from those living abroad in mission areas) by 1965. Teaching brothers totaled 5,000 in France, plus 1,500 more in the missions. There were about 117,000 religious women in France and several thousand other French nuns working in the missions.

French Foreign Missionary Activity. Despite the difficulties of French Catholicism, its missionary role in the first half of the 20th century was a leading one. This labor had begun with the increase in vocations in 1830 and developed very rapidly after 1860 because of French colonial expansion. Missionaries frequently arrived before the soldiers. The privileges France possessed in the Near East resulting from the ''capitulations'', and in China because of the Treaty of Tien Tsin (1858) facilitated the work of various French religious institutes, many of which were founded during this period. The HOLY GHOST FATHERS, the White Fathers, and the Society of the AFRICAN MISSIONS made great gains in evangelizing Africa. The Fathers of the Sacred Hearts, the MARIST FATHERS, and the SACRED HEART MISSIONARIES dedicated themselves to work in Oceania.

Bibliography: A. DANSETTE, *Destin du catholicism français, 1926–1956* (Paris 1957); ''Contemporary French Catholicism,'' in *The Catholic Church in World Affairs,* ed. W. GURIAN and M. A. FITZSIMONS (Notre Dame, IN 1954) 230–174. J. LEFLON, *La Crise révolutionnaire, 1789–1846* (Fliche-Martin 10; 1949); *L'Église de France et la révolution de 1848* (Paris 1948). R. AUBERT, *Le Pontificat de Pie IX* (Fliche-Martin 21; 2d ed. 1964). H. DANIEL-ROPS, *Histoire de l'Égilse de Christ,* 10 v. (Paris 1948–65) v 8, 9, 10; v. 8 *The Church in an Age of Revolution, 1789–1870,* tr. J. WARRINGTON (New York 1965), v.9, 10 in course of tr. K. S. LATOURETTE, *Christianity in a Revolutionary Age: A History of Christianity in the 19th and 20th Centuries,* 5v. (New York 1958–62) v.1, 2, 4. A. LATREILLE, *L'Église catholique et la Révolution française,* 2 v. (Paris 1946–50). S. DELACROIX, *La réorganisation de lé de France après la révolution, 1801–1809* (Paris 1962—). J. BRUGERETTE, *Le prêtre français et la société contemporaine,* 3 v. (Paris 1933–38). J. P. MARTIN, *La nonciature de Paris et les affaires ecclésiastiques de France sous le rè de Louis-Philippe (1830–48) Empire de 1852 à 1869* (Paris 1930). W. GURIAN, *Die politschen und sozialen Ideen des französischen Katholizismus, 1789–1914* (München-Gladbach 1929). J. B. DUROSELLE, *Les débuts du catholicisme social en France, 1822–1870* (Paris 1951). H. ROLLET, *L'action social des catholiques en France, 1871–1914,* 2 v. (Paris 1947–58). G. HOOG, *Histoire du catholicisme social en France, 1871–1931* (Paris 1942; new ed. 1946). J. N. MOODY, ed., *Church and Society: Catholic Social and Political Thought and Movements* (New York, 1953), *see* pt. 2 ''Catholicism and Society in France.'' L. CAPÉRAN, *L'invasion* *laïque: de l'avènement de Combes au vote de la séparation, 1905–1945* (Paris 1935); *Histoire contemporaine de la laïcité française,* 3 v. (Paris 1957–61). L. V. MÉJAN, *La séparation des églises et de l'état* (Paris 1959). L. CROUZIL, *Quarante ans de séparation, 1905–1945* (Paris 1946). W. BOSWORTH, *Catholicism and Crisis in Modern France: French Catholic Groups at the Threshold of the Fifth Republic* (Princeton, NJ 1962). G. LE BRAS, *Introduction à l'histoire de la pratique religieuse en France,* 2 v. (Paris 1942–45). F. BOULARD, *An Introduction to Religious Sociology: Pioneer Work in France,* tr. M. J. JACKSON (London 1960).

[A. DANSETTE]

The Mid-20th Century and Beyond

With the establishment of the Third Republic in 1870, and only interrupted by German occupation during World War II, France was able to maintain a republican form of government. For the French Church, Vatican II (1962–65) represented the realization of a great hope and the vindication of a distinctive national experience. It also marked the beginning of a period of self-doubt and internal tension that brought it to a very different situation by the close of the 20th century.

The French at Vatican II. The chief contribution to Vatican II by the French was made by theologians who in the decades preceding the council had been involved in a concerted effort to make the expression of Catholic teaching more informed by tradition and more relevant to modern times. This New Theology, which stressed the pastoral aspects of dogmas, had encountered many difficulties in the past and its exponents were suspected and put aside. The writings of Henri de LUBAC, Yves CONGAR, Jean DANIÉLOU, and their colleagues and disciples inspired influential bishops not only from their own country but also from many others. These theologians, held suspect in some quarters, were vindicated by the fact that they were among the experts chosen for the drafting and revision of the conciliar documents. Their mark appears distinctly on the texts on liturgy, revelation, ecclesiology, ecumenism, and missions. *Gaudium et spes* reflected an optimism typical of the influence of TEILHARD DE CHARDIN.

About 20 percent of the French bishops were also active participants at the council; their 210 interventions related mostly to the two constitutions on the Church, *Lumen gentium* and *Gaudium et spes.* They also addressed issues concerning the Christian apostolate, especially of the laity. On that last topic, despite the interventions of Cardinal LIÉNART and Bishop Ménager, the conciliar documents did not take into account the experience of French Catholic Action. On the documents on Ecumenism, Religious Liberty, and Non-Christian religions, French Archbishop Marcel LEFEBVRE, superior of the Holy Ghost Fathers, placed himself directly in opposition to the majority of his colleagues; he also took the lead in the resistance to the doctrine of episcopal collegiality.

The French Episcopal Conference. An immediate result of the Vatican II was the establishment of the French Episcopal Conference in 1964. The French hierarchy had a relative experience of episcopal collegiality since 1919 when an Assembly of Cardinals and Archbishops (ACA) began to meet occasionally. Between 1951 and 1960, the French episcopate held four plenary assemblies. In 1945 a general secretariat of the ACA was created in charge of preparing and coordinating the decisions of that body. In 1961 the position of adjunct secretary for pastoral matters was created, with the purpose of coordinating the initiatives and actions of many dioceses (pastorale d'ensemble). It was also in 1961 that a new regional structure was added that supplanted the traditional provincial division. The new structure established nine Apostolic Regions, reflecting cultural and even linguistic identities: Ile-de-France, North, West, Center, East, South-East, Midi, Provence-Mediterranée, and Center-East. The statutes of the French Episcopal Conference, first confirmed by the Holy See in 1966, were revised in 1975 in favor of a more democratic participation with all members of the episcopate electing the officers. The higher instance is the Permanent Council—president, vice president, nine elected members (one by apostolic region), the archbishop of Paris (and eventually a cardinal, if none is already present)—that meets monthly. An important secretariat was also instituted, with a general secretary and four adjunct secretaries: Information-communication (also the spokesman of the Conference); pastoral service; apostolate of the laity; and administrative, financial, and juridical matters. Fifteen episcopal commissions (Family, Rural World, Independent Milieus, Youth, Migrants, Clergy, Religious, Liturgy, Public Opinion, Social, Religious Education, Exterior Missions, Christian Unity) and six episcopal committees (Finance, Mission de France, Maritime, Relations with Judaism, France-Latin America, and Canon Law) were established. In addition a bureau doctrinal of six members was placed in charge of theological matters. Finally, three episcopal groups (groupes épiscopaux) assured a direct link between the bishops and Christian communities, charismatic renewal, and the Réalités of tourism and leisure, to which was added a National Council for Solidarity.

The Conference of Bishops also sponsored several national services. The Centre national de l'enseignement religieux was in charge of pastoral catechetics in the country. The Centre national de pastorale liturgique (1965) continued the works of the Centre de pastorale liturgique, founded in 1943. The Service national du catéchuménat coordinated the baptismal preparation of adult converts, and the Service biblique, évangile et vie organized and supported the many groups and associations interested in Biblical popularization. These groups published documents and magazines dealing with their objects of specialization.

In conformity with the reforms of Vatican II, each diocese established a council of priests (conseil presbytéral) and a pastoral council, in which the laity could participate. Religious men and women were organized in two Conferences of Major Superiors of France, with subdivisions at the regional level. The dearth of ordained ministries forced the ordinaries to commit many responsibilities to équipes animatrices of lay and religious men and women. They assumed charge of small parishes, often organizing Assemblées dominicales en l'absence de prêtres (ADAP) and serving as chaplains to schools, jails, and hospitals.

Liturgical Reform. Of the changes wrought by conciliar decisions, the most pervasive was in the area of liturgical reform. Many experts who contributed to the renewal of the liturgy were French or had been trained in France, among them A.-G. Martimort, L. Bouyer, J. Daniélou, and P. Jounel. These reformers based their recommendations on the many attempts at renewal and experimentation that had been tried during the 1940s and 1950s, both on the theoretical level (under the influence of the journal *La Maison-Dieu*) and the practical one (pilot communities, such as the one at Saint-Séverin, Paris). It later became plain that the reforms implemented were often poorly prepared and imprudently pushed through. Presenting, on occasion, the image of an iconoclastic and disorderly church, these reforms baffled many conventional faithful and scandalized the rest. Traditional devotions were disparaged, cherished customs such as *communion solennelle* were abandoned, and new rituals were invented that had little to do with the conciliar norms. In particular, the complete elimination of Latin exacerbated and brought into the public arena a rift that had long existed between conservative and progressive Christians within France.

A Time of Crisis. The crisis soon became apparent via the conflicts of the Action catholique. This form of apostolate of the laity had evolved along the lines of social or class distinctions, under the control of the hierarchy that commissioned the baptized Christians to represent the Church in their milieu. As their activity became more directed to social and political changes than to mission, this notion of mandatum was challenged and eventually abolished (1975). The successive tensions between the leaders of the different movements and the hierarchy (especially the crisis of the Jeunesse Etudiante Chrétienne [JEC] in 1965) brought a dilution of what had been for decades the store of Catholic elites and of religious and priestly vocations. At the same time, an identity crisis seriously affected the French clergy, as significant numbers abandoned the priesthood or religious life, and seminary recruitment reached its lowest point since the French Revolution. The turmoil of May 1968, a period of political unrest and systematic questioning of traditional values that started in the university community, revealed the uncertainty of a society in transition. It also demonstrated the weakness of the Catholic community in addressing these challenges and, above all, its divisions. At the dogmatic level, the tension was compounded by the reactions to the encyclical *Humanae vitae* (1968), of which the French bishops had given a pastorally sensitive interpretation.

By the late 1960s the divisions of the French Church were clear. Opposition, which had serious political connotations, existed between a left wing, often under Marxist influence, that advocated deep changes and wanted Christians to be fully involved in the transformation of society, and a right wing that promoted a return to order and tradition based on their interpretation of the Christian message. The leaders of the French episcopate who had been associated with Vatican II had either died (cardinals Roques, Richaud, Veuillot), resigned (Cardinal Liénart, Archbishop Lefebvre), or received Roman appointments (cardinals Garonne, Villot). They left to their successors the difficult task of controlling growing tensions and preserving some kind of order and homogeneity. Either individually or through documents issued by the Episcopal Conference, the majority of bishops endorsed a moderately progressive course that also reflected this rift.

Religion and Politics. Since the time of the French Revolution, the attitude of the Church vis-à-vis political issues had been consistent: a desire to influence society through political choices balanced by the need to maintain the independence of the Church. A situation now existed wherein a significant number of committed Catholics desired to improve and even change French society in the name of Christianity. One area of influence was social justice and the treatment of the poor both in internal and external policies (especially the matter of decolonization, which was very important at the time). Questions related to military disarmament were also raised. On these matters the *Politique, Église et Foi,* issued by the Conference of Bishops in 1972, represented a milestone in its acknowledgment of a diversity of political choices compatible with the Christian message and its delineation of ''normative evangelical and moral criteria'' for making decisions on social and political issues. The position of French Catholics was shown to be conservative in the election of May 10, 1981, when only

20 percent of practicing Catholics gave their vote to socialist President François Mitterand.

The Church and Social Issues. Once in power, Mitterand attempted to expand the reaches of the *Loi Debré* which, since its inception in 1959 under the leadership of President Charles de Gaulle, regulated the recognition of Catholic schools by the state and offered limited government support to students in exchange for moderate regulatory control. The final version of the proposed law appeared to many defenders of Catholic education a complete takeover by the state. In response a massive demonstration was organized in Paris that drew over 1,400,000 participants and successfully stopped the law's passage in the National Assembly.

Further attempts to reform education were resisted by the laity, as many bishops were reluctant to endorse a position they feared might be exploited at the political level. The same episcopal reluctance to intervene in matters involving politics was also evident in the moderate official positions expressed during Parliamentary discussion on the issue of contraception (*Loi Newirth,* 1967) and of the legalization of abortion (*Loi Weil,* 1974).

A Church Divided. The growing division within French Catholicism was publicly revealed in 1976 as the result of a rebellion led by Archbishop Lefebvre. The former archbishop of Dakar rejected several of Vatican II's decisions, especially as they were implemented in France. Desiring to preserve the traditional liturgical rites established after Trent, Lefebvre maintained a classical conception of the priesthood. In July 1976, he ordained the first priests trained according to these principles at the Fraternity St. Pius X at Écone, Switzerland. The Lefebvre affair had a deep political component, revealed the frustration of many Catholics with the changes they had been forced to accept, and indicated their desire for a clearer identity. While Lefebvre was excommunicated in 1988, after consecrating four bishops, negotiations conducted in Rome resulted in the reintegration of many of his followers in the Catholic communion.

Another disagreement among French Catholics was the question of catechetics. In the early 1960s most of the country's 220,000 catechists were lay women (84 percent). In response to the need for a better pedagogy of the faith, the classical presentation by questions and answers—in use in all dioceses since 1937—was replaced by a progressive method focusing more on the experience of children than on the content of the Christian message. A *Directory of Pastoral Catechetics* (*Directoire de Pastorale catéchétique*), issued in 1964 by the Conference of Bishops, was followed by a profusion of manuals adapted to all possible situations. The results of the new methodology were disappointing and in 1976 the bishops resolved to recenter the courses on prayer and faith. A comprehensive series of programs, or *parcours*, was established, with a reference book collecting fundamental documents titled *Pierres vivantes* (1981) that presented the salvation history beginning with the Exodus in the Old Testament and Pentecost in the New. In 1985, after many complaints and the intervention of the Congregation of the Doctrine of the Faith, a second edition beginning the history with the creation story in Genesis and the infancy narratives in the New Testament was published. A similar desire to improve the content of the resources available to educators resulted in a comprehensive catechism for adults (1991). By 1998, only 55,000 catechists were teaching the tenets of Catholicism in France, a reflection more of declining numbers of practicing Catholics than of the Church's commitment to catechetics.

Religious leaders long recognized the need to expose a faith many nominal Catholics seemed to know imperfectly. The success of the 1992 publication CATECHISM OF THE CATHOLIC CHURCH illustrated a need for this education. In response, Catholic universities and institutes expanded their continuing education offerings to include courses for the laity on par with the level of academic scholarship in existence in the period preceding Vatican II. Contributors to the journal *Communio* (founded 1975) represented an influential group of young philosophers and theologians who successfully worked to restore religious understanding to a high level.

Reform and Renewal. The desire for reforms within the Church reflected a widely held desire for a ''return of the sacred,'' a renewed interest in the transcendental elements of faith, particularly individual prayer. This tendency was encouraged by Rome through several key ecclesiastical appointments. The choice of a successor of the archbishop of Paris, Cardinal Marty, in 1981, was perceived by many as an important test. The selection of J. M. Lustiger (b. 1926), a former curé of Paris and successor at Orléans of the controversial Bishop G. Riobé, was indicative enough of a new type of leadership. Lustiger, a convert from the Jewish faith, had remained aloof from general ecclesiastical stances while serving as chaplain of the Sorbonne and a pastor. He soon put his mark on the diocese, stressing the need for a stronger presence, based on a renewed and deeply spiritual sense of Catholic identity. His attention to the problem of priestly recruitment and education of the laity was soon noted and imitated by his peers.

About the same time, a new archbishop was chosen at Lyon, A. Decourtray (1923–94), formerly of Dijon, was soon perceived as an open and traditional pastor. Both cardinals exhibited a willingness to address contemporary issues with rigor and clarity, displaying a rare ability to intervene in public debates and to use the media. Their influence was notable in the appointments of comparable bishops, distinguished by their intellectual and spiritual capacities and in the support given to fresh forms of Catholic ventures.

Another indication of a renewal in the French Catholic church was the growth of charismatic fraternities (*le Renouveau*), which echoed a movement begun in the Anglo-Saxon world that was based on a strong sense of community and association in prayer and action in society. Examples include Lion de Juda (1973), Chemin-neuf (1973), and Emmanuel (1976), to which can be added the older l'Arche (founded by Jean Vanier in 1964 and present in more than 17 countries) and the Foyers de charité, which started at Chateauneuf-de-Galaure in 1936 around the mystic Marthe Robin (1902–81). After their official recognition by the French bishops in 1982, these groups developed in many dioceses, often receiving a particular mission, such as the responsibility for a parish or a shrine. The international intellectual movement known as OPUS DEI took root in France in 1956, another example of a new association constituting a new source of influential lay and clerical elites.

A Secular Society. As the French Church entered the third millennium, its members continued to weather the unstable philosophical heritage of the French Revolution. In the postmodern world, many in the Church sought to transcend the combativeness characteristic of French Catholicism, most apparent between liberal and conservative interpretations of the Christian message. Such attempts at unification—which some have viewed as a reflection of changing attitudes within Western culture overall in the wake of the two World Wars—were encouraged by the papacy, particularly Pope John Paul II. The appointment of bishops who viewed the Church as an active moral presence in the world was supported by a new, younger elite who considered surrendering to worldly values a mistake made by their predecessors. Instead, this elite prefered an aggressive presentation and defense of Christian values.

In this era of multicultural awareness, many in the French Church supported the desire by other religious denominations—Orthodox and Protestant, but also Jewish and Muslim—to replace the traditional laïcité of the state with a more emphatic expression of religious freedom that would allow diverse faiths to be acknowledged within French society and valued in the name of culture and the defense of human values. The influence of Pope John Paul II marked the first evidence of a shift in this matter: It is quite significant that the reception the pope received during his second pastoral visit to Lyon (1986) was exceedingly warmer than was his 1981 reception in Paris.

The Catholic Presence. Reflecting a trend within Christian religions as a whole, surveys of Sunday mass attendance and reception of the sacraments taken between 1960 and the early 1990s revealed a slow but persistent decline in quantitative participation in religious life. In 1966 the proportion of regular participants at the Sunday mass or *messalisants* was calculated to be about 23 percent, but it had dropped to 12 percent by 1990. The number of occasional Catholics seemed most in decline, according to drops in the frequency of baptisms (421,295 in 1998), weddings, and funerals. While many of these *Catholiques festifs* were thought to have been dismayed by the changes associated with Vatican II, it might well have been that their attitude more reflected the influence of secularization and the retreat from Christian values common throughout the Western world. Many French citizens declaring themselves to be Catholic did not adhere to the major points of the Creed, such as the belief in the Trinity or the resurrection of Christ.

The importance, for the French Church, of public communication was reflected by the number and diversity of its publications. Two major publishers existed: the Centre National de Presse Catholique, which printed 26 titles, including the daily *La Croix*; and the Association Nationale de la Presse Catholique de Province, which produced 29 titles. The Chrétiens-Mídias was created in 1988, in direct association with the Episcopal Commission for Public Opinion, to coordinate diocesan activities with the goal of asserting a Catholic presence and fostering a dialogue in the fields of art and culture. The Church was also present over the airwaves, with such local radio stations as Radio-Notre-Dame in Paris (1981) and Radio-Fourvières in Lyon (1982). On national television, the Sunday program *Le jour du Seigneur* regularly included live broadcast of the Mass.

By 1998 there were 30,709 parishes in France. Private elementary and secondary schools (*écoles privées*) had about 20 percent of the total student population, and 90 percent of these private schools were Catholic. There were also five Catholic institutes of higher education, at Angers, Lille, Lyon, Paris, and Toulouse. In 1998 the Catholic clergy in France included five cardinals, 28 archbishops, 180 bishops, 27,781 priests, 3,858 brothers, and 55,087 sisters divided between 40,000 cathedrals, churches, and smaller chapels.

Accepting Religious Diversity. By 2000 13 percent of the population of France was immigrant. Due to an increased influx of Muslims during the late 20th century, Islam grew to become the second largest religion in France, with historian Alain Besançoin going so far as to posit that the nation now housed more Muslims than practicing Catholics. The assimilation of this growing

Muslim population into French society was a major challenge to both the state and the Church. In fact, French Catholics remained somewhat adverse to social accommodation of other religions, although at the official level cooperation was successfully attempted. For example, the 1994 funeral of Cardinal Decourtray concluded with an interreligious celebration in front of the Lyon cathedral, and involved representatives of France's significant Jewish community.

Despite the majority position still held by Catholics in France, in an age of increasing toleration of differences dialogues following the lines of Catholic ecumenism first presented by Y. Congar in 1937 were strengthened with other Christian communities. In addition to the exchanges existing around the community of Taizé or the informal Groupe des Dombes, official dialogues between Protestant and Catholics continued to produce declarations touching on such practical issues as the celebration of baptism and marriages.

Given the French Church's long and complex history, the growing tolerance of religious differences that developed in the closing years of the 20th century did not satisfy all the nation's Catholics. Some openly dissented from a vision that, in their eyes, succumbed to an illusive spirit of ''restoration,'' inconsistent with decades of French Catholic experience. Such tolerance was in some circles decried as utterly impossible in the postmodern age. Another concern of this faction involved fragmentation of the Church into rival ''chapels'' that would leave the institution more divided than ever. Held up as proof of the viability of this concern was the removal of Bishop Jacques Gaillot of Evreux in February of 1995. The bishop's removal was not justified by any dogmatic deviation, but by his lack of ''communion'' with the other bishops. The passionate reactions by the right wing to Gaillot's dismissal, as well as the organized left-wing protest encountered by Pope John Paul II on his 1996 visit to France, both illustrated that ideological polarization remained a serious problem in the country. However, the difficulties experienced by the Church in France, while a consequence of its long and unique history, may have also resulted from the stresses facing Catholicism, and indeed organized religion as a whole throughout an increasingly secularized Western world.

Bibliography: C. CALDWELL, ''The Crescent and the Tricolor,'' *Atlantic* 286:5 (2000), 20–34. G. CHOLVY AND Y.-M. HILAIRE, *Histoire religieuse de la France contemporaine,* III. *1930–88* (Paris 1988). R. DARRICAU and B. PEYROUS, ''Les communautés nouvelles en France 1967–1987,'' *Nouvelle revue théologique* (1987) 712–729. J.-M. DONEGANI and G. LESCANE, *Catholicisme en France* (Paris 1986). C. GRÉMION and P. LEVILLAIN, *Les lieutenants de Dieu. Les évêques de France et la République* (Paris 1986). M. HEBRARD, *Révolution tranquille chez les catholiques. Voyage au pays des synodes diocesains* (Paris 1989). D. HERVIEU-LÉGER, *Vers un nouveau christianisme? Introduction à la sociologie du christianisme occidental* (Paris 1987). P. LADRIÈRE and R. LUNEAU, *Le retour des certitudes. Événements et orthodoxie depuis Vatican II* (Paris 1987). M. LAUNAY, *L'Église et l'École en France XIXe- XXe siècles* (Paris 1988). D. MAUGEREST, ed., *Le Discours social de l'Eglise catholique de France. 1891–1992* (Paris 1995). P. PIERRARD, *Les laïcs dans l'Église de France* (Paris 1988). J. POTEL, *L'Église catholique en France. Approches sociologiques* (Paris 1994). E. POULAT, *Une Église ébranlée. Changement, conflit et continuité de Pie XII à Jean-Paul II* (Paris 1980). J. SUTTER, *La vie religieuse des Français à travers les sondages d'opinion (1944–76)* (Paris 1984). B. VASSOR-ROUSSET, *Les évêques de France en politique* (Paris 1986). G. CHOLVY AND Y.-M. HILAIRE, *Histoire religieuse de la France contemporaine,* III, *1930–1988* (Paris 1988).

[J. M. GRES-GAYER/EDS.]

FRANCES D'AMBOISE, BL.

Carmelite prioress; b. Thouars, France, May 9, 1427; d. Couëts, near Nantes, France, Nov. 4, 1485. A daughter of Louis d'Amboise, viscount of Thouars, she became the wife of Peter II, duke of Brittany (d. 1457). Noted for her charity to the poor and sick, the childless widow resisted even the request of King Louis XI that she marry again. In 1463 she founded at Vannes the first cloister of Carmelite nuns in France, and in 1467, entered this convent and received the habit from the prior general, John SORETH. She died as prioress of Our Lady of Couüts and was buried there. In the convent as at court she combined a practical sense of affairs with a life of prayer and love of neighbor and followed with interest the fortunes of her country. Some of her conferences to the nuns survive in manuscript. Her cult was approved in 1863 by Pope Pius IX.

Feast: Nov. 4.

Bibliography: F. RICHARD, *Vie de la bienheureuse Françoise d'Amboise, duchesse de Bretagne et religieuse carmélite,* 2 v. (Paris 1865). A. DAIX, *La Merveilleuse odyssée de Françoise d'Amboise* (Paris 1930). V. WILDERINK, ''Les *Exhortations* de la bienheureuse Françoise d'Amboise,'' *Carmelus* 11 (1964) 221–266. J. TEMPLÉ, *Catholicisme* 4:1558–59.

[E. R. CARROLL]

FRANCES OF ROME, ST.

Foundress of the Oblates of St. Frances; b. Rome, Italy, 1384; d. there, March 9, 1440. She was born into a noble Roman family of Busso and was married very young, in obedience to the wishes of her parents, to Lorenzo dei Ponziani, a wealthy landowner in the Trastevere district. Her saintly activity brought some ray of hope to the troubled years between 1400 and 1440, when furious internal struggles and natural calamities devastated the city of Rome. She aided the poor with great generosity and provided for the care of the sick in the city hospitals, especially Santa Maria in Cappella, which the Ponziani family was administering with papal consent. Here Frances was an example of modesty in dress and in her way of life for the 35 years in which she devoted herself to spiritual and temporal works of mercy. Her fame spread to Viterbo, Siena, Arezzo, Florence, Bologna, and the Marches, and naturally in Rome. On Aug. 15, 1425, she founded a group of Oblates of Olivetan Benedictines attached to the church of Santa Maria Nuova. Although at first not living in community, the group was later reorganized, adopting the common life to facilitate their dedication to works of mercy. Its constitution was approved by Pope EUGENE IV in 1433, and they were housed in a convent in the Tower of the Specchi, in the neighborhood of Campidoglio, where on March 21, 1436, the widowed Frances herself retired. Immediately after her death the process of canonization was begun, and after repeated attempts she was canonized by PAUL V on May 29, 1608. Her tomb is in Santa Maria Nuova.

Feast: March 9.

Bibliography: FRANCES, OF ROME, *Jubilation dans la lumière divine,* transcript of 20 visions (Paris 1989). *Acta Sanctorum* March 2:89–219. P. J. LUGANO and C. ALBERGOTTI, *La Nobile Casa delle Oblate di S. Francesca Romana in Tor de' Specchi, nel V centenario dalla fondazione, 1433–1933* (Vatican City 1933). P. J. LUGANO, ''L'istituzione delle Oblate di Tor de' Specchi, secondo i documenti,'' *Rivista storica benedettina* 14 (1923) 272–308, esp. 292–293; ed., *I processi inediti per Francesca Bussa dei Ponziani (Santa Francesca Romana) 1440–1453* (*Studi e Testi* 120; 1945). L. BERRA, A. MERCATI and A. PELZER, *Dizionario ecclesiastico,* 3 v. (Turin 1954–58) 1:1162. J. MATTIOTTI, *Il dialetto romanesco del Quattrocento,* ed. G. CARPANETO (n.s. 1995), 15th-century biography with glossary and bibliography. A. MONTONATI, *Le mani che guarirono la città: storia di santa Francesca Romana* (Cinisello Balsamo 1985). E. BONA, *Francesca Romana la santa di Roma* (Sestri Levante 1969). F. P. KEYES, *Three Ways of Love* (New York 1963). H. MONTESI FESTA, *Santa Francesca Romana* (Turin 1931). BERTHEM-BONTOUX, *Sainte Françoise Romaine et son temps, 1384–1440* (Paris 1931). A. M. ZIMMERMANN, *Kalendarium Benedictinum: Die Heiligen und Seligen des Benediktinerorderns und seiner Zweige,* 4 v. (Metten 1933–38) 1:304–307. G. C. FULLERTON, *The Life of St. Frances of Rome* (London 1855). A. BUTLER, *The Lives of the Saints,* ed. H. THURSTON and D. ATTWATER, 4 v. (New York 1956) 1:529–533.

[M. MONACO]

FRANCESCHI, GUSTAVO JUAN

Philosopher and sociologist; b. Corsica, 1871; d. Montevideo, June 11, 1957. He was an outstanding figure in the Argentine clergy during the first half of the 20th century because of his abilities and the excellent use he made of them. Before becoming a priest he had a reputation as an oceanographer and an author with a beautiful style. After his ordination in 1902, he became an outstanding preacher, stressing particularly the social doctrines of the Church and frequently speaking in the public squares and streets of Buenos Aires. He was chaplain of the chapel of El Carmen for 30 years, and during that time he served as secretary for the Argentine Social League and promoted social study clubs. He frequently served as chaplain for the national prison, and he was clerical adviser for the Catholic Students' Center and the Catholic Teachers' Union. He directed the review *Justicia Social* and contributed frequently to *El Trabajo,* the organ of the Catholic Workers' Groups. In 1916 he began teaching philosophy at the Catholic University of Buenos Aires, and from 1917 to 1941 he was professor of sociology and Catholic social thought in the major seminary of Buenos Aires. From 1933 until his death he directed the review *Criterio* (founded March 1928 by Atilio Del'Oro Maini) and wrote a weekly article for it. These articles, written in a clear logical style on a variety of important topics, were read by both intellectuals and nonintellectuals. Some of them, as well as articles published in other periodicals, were collected and published in book form: *La democracia y la iglesia* (1918); *Los cículos de estudios sociales* (1822); *Tres estudios sobre la familia* (1823); *La angustia contemporánea* (1929); *Keyserling* (1929); *Fundación social de la propiedad privada en la República Argentina; Las circunstancias sociales de Pío XI* (1933); *La Iglesia* (1935); *En el humo del incendio* (1938); *Visión espiritual de la guerra* (1940); *El deber actual de los Católicos* (1940); *Manantiales de nuestra fe* (1941); and *El pontificiado romano* (2 v. 1945). In this last work, as in all his writings, Franceschi showed himself to be a theologian, a moralist, a philosopher, and a well-balanced historian, always well informed on his subjects. He was much influenced by French thought and was very skillful in adapting it to Argentine circumstances. He was a canon of the cathedral and in 1933 was named a domestic prelate. He did outstanding work through his writings in spreading Catholic doctrine and defending the interests of the Church.

Bibliography: O. N. DERISI, ''Monseñor Franceschi apóstol providencial de la verdad,'' *Revista Eclesiástica Argentina* 1.4 (1958) 38–41.

[G. FURLONG]

FRANCESCO MARIA OF CAMPOROSSO, ST.

Italian Capuchin lay brother; b. Camporosso (Imperia), Italy, Dec. 27, 1804; d. Genoa, Sept. 17, 1866. After joining the Capuchins (1821), he exchanged his baptismal name, Giovanni, for Francesco Maria and pronounced his solemn vows in 1825. For the next 40 years he served in the friary in Genoa as almsgatherer (questor). During his daily begging rounds of the city his deportment, spiritual advice, and catechetical instruction deeply impressed the different classes of people whom he met. During the cholera epidemic (1866) he nursed the plague-stricken in their homes. He contracted the disease and died a martyr of charity. His remains are enshrined in the Capuchin church of the Most Holy Conception in Genoa. He was beatified June 30, 1929, and canonized Dec. 8, 1962.

Feast: Sept. 17.

Bibliography: L. DE ECHAVARRI-URTUPIÑA, *Un apóstol de la caridad* (Pamplona 1962). A. DA VARAZZE, *Il beato Francesco da Comporosso* (3d ed. Genoa 1929). C. DE PÉLISSANE, *Une Victime de la charité au XIXe siècle: Le Bienheureux François de Camporosso* (2d ed. Paris 1929). *Lexicon Capuccinum* (Rome 1951) 620–621. *Analecta Ordinis Fratrum Minorum Cappuchinorum* 79 (1963) 185–194. A. BUTLER, *The Lives of the Saints,* ed. H. THURSTON and D. ATTWATER, 4 v. (New York 1956) 3:586–587.

[T. MACVICAR]

FRANCHI DE' CAVALIERI, PIO

Italian scholar and hagiographer; b. Veroli, Aug. 31, 1869; d. Rome, Aug. 6, 1960. After studies in classical philology, he was given the post of a *scriptor* or researcher in the Vatican Library (1896) under Cardinal Franz Ehrle; he served as honorary conservator of the Sacred Museum of the library from 1921 to 1948. He worked on catalogues of manuscripts with Vatasso, editing the list of Latin manuscripts (1902), and with A. Mercati, the Greek manuscripts (1923). He also brought out editions of the *Rotulo di Giosuè* (1905) and the *Menologion of Basil* (1907), and with H. Lietzmann he published *Specimina Codd. graec. Vaticani* (Bonn 1910 and 1929). His principal concern, however, was hagiography, and he published nine volumes of *Note agiografiche* in the *Studi e Testi* series and wrote articles for the *Römische Quartalschrift, Rivista di archeologia cristiana, Nuovo bollettino di archeologia cristiana,* and *Studi romani.* In 1956 he presented the library with a precious collection of ancient coins; he was looked upon as the dean of Roman hagiographers.

Bibliography: J. RUYSSCHAERT, *Atti della Pontificia Accademia Romana di Archeologia* 30 (1960–61) 61–69. N. VIAN, *L'Osservatore Romano* 224 (25 Sept. 1960) 5; 230 (Oct. 2, 1960) 5.

[P. ROCHE]

FRANCIA, ANNIBALE MARIA DI, BL.

Founder of the Rogationist Fathers of the Heart of Jesus and the Daughters of Divine Zeal, known as ''the father of orphans and the poor''; b. July 5, 1851, Messina, Sicily, Italy; d. there, June 1, 1927.

Annibale was the son of a noble family headed by Francis di Francia, Marquis of Santa Catarina, and his wife Anna Toscano. When Annibale was two, his father, who was papal vice-counsel to Pius IX, died. Stories about Annibale's days in a Cistercian boarding school (1858–66) describe acts of the heroic compassion which characterized his entire life. When the school was closed during the Revolution of 1866, the Sicilian poet Felice Bisazza tutored him. Annibale used his writing skills to compose articles for his uncle's periodical, *La Parola Catolica*, poetry (*The Hymns of July First*), prayers, and pamphlets.

At 18 Annibale recognized his call to the priesthood. A month before his ordination (March 16, 1878), he encountered a blind youth, Francis Zancone, who introduced him to the need for charity. Thereafter he joyfully dedicated himself to the spiritual and temporal relief of the most neglected, beginning in the neighborhood of Avignone in Messina. He established evening and boarding schools for boys, a kindergarten for girls, and orphanages dedicated to Saint Anthony of Padua (to whom Annibale later built a shrine in Messina). Like others who heroically give of themselves he encountered opposition, but received the support of his archbishop, Giacomo Cusmano, and John Bosco. For the physically poor, especially children in the Anthonian orphanages, he begged from door to door. For the spiritually poor he prayed ''to the harvest master to send workers to the field'' (Mt. 9:38).

For the purpose of praying for vocations to the priesthood and religious life and for caring for needy children and the poor, Francia formed the Rogationists Fathers and Daughters of Divine Zeal. Melanie Calvat, one of the visionaries of La Salette, spent a year at the female institute (1897–98) helping Francia firmly establish it following some setbacks. Orphanages run by the sisters multiplied quickly after 1902 to meet each new crisis in Italy (e.g., earthquake, cholera, war). The Rogationists have expanded beyond the borders of Italy to other countries in Europe, Argentina, Brazil, India, the Philippines, Rwanda, and the United States. Additionally, to invite others to unite spiritually to pray for vocations, he established a Holy Alliance for bishops, prelates, and priests, as well as the Pious Union of Evangelical Prayer for laity.

For many years Annibale was the spiritual director for the writings of the Luisa Piccarreta (1865–1947; cause opened February 1994), who recorded private revelations on the Divine Will. Among the 19 volumes to which he gave the *nihil obstat* were *The Virgin Mary in the Kingdom of the Divine Will* and *The Hours of the Passion of Our Lord Jesus Christ.*

Throughout his life Blessed Annibale conscientiously fulfilled his priestly obligations, showed Christ–like love to the most vulnerable, and trusted completely in Divine Providence. In beatifying Annibale di Francia on Oct. 7, 1990, Pope John Paul II held him up to the Church as the ''authentic precursor and zealous teacher of the modern pastoral ministry of vocations.''

Feast: May 31 (Rogationists).

Bibliography: L. PICCARRETA, *The Clock of Passion*, ed. A. DI FRANCIA (Oria, Italy 1921). F. VITALE, *Il canonico Annibale Maria di Francia nella vita e nelle opere* (Messina 1939). L. ALESSANDRÀ, *La Madonna negli scritti e nell'opera del can. Di Francia* (Rome 1972). P. BORZOMATI, ed., *Annibale di Francia: la chiesa e la povertà* (Rome 1992), v. 18 of Religione e società, includes bibliographical references. N. CLEMENTE, *Io l'amo i miei bambini* (Padua 1973). A. SCELZO, *Padre Annibale M. di Francia: una vita copiata dal Vangelo* (Rome 1990). *Insegnamenti* 13, no. 2 (1990): 830. *L'Osservatore Romano,* Eng. ed., no. 28 (1997): 9; no. 31 (1997): 1.

[K. I. RABENSTEIN]

FRANCIS DE SALES, ST.

Bishop of Geneva, founder of the Order of the Visitation, and Doctor of the Church; b. Thorens, Savoy, Aug. 21, 1567; d. Lyons, Dec. 28, 1622.

Francis lived in what was the independent Catholic Duchy of Savoy, which, with its capital in Turin, straddled the Alps. His birthplace was on the French side of the Alps, some 30 miles south of Geneva. This city, once part of Savoy, had been controlled by John Calvin's followers since 1536, and its bishop had taken refuge in Annecy. By Francis's time the ''wars of religion'' had given way to a tentative truce but no true tolerance.

His parents, Francis de Boisy and Frances de Sionnaz, were staunch Catholics and loyal members of Savoyard nobility. His father destined his first-born Francis for a career in public life. After two years of primary school in LaRoche, and three years at the College Chappuisien in Annecy, Francis attended the Jesuit College de Clermont in the University of Paris from 1578 to 1588. He studied humanities then philosophy, adding courses on theology by his own choice and without his father's knowledge.

After a brief stay in Savoy Francis went to the University of Padua to study law. There he continued his theological studies and his spiritual formation, assisted in both by his spiritual director, Antonio Possevino, SJ (1534–161) a noted theologian and church diplomat. Together they worked out a set of ''spiritual exercises'' to help him cultivate devotion in a typical student milieu. His law studies, far from being neglected, led to a doctorate in both canon and civil law and high praise from his professor, Guido Pancirolo.

In Paris Francis experienced a crisis that arose in part from his reading of theology and confronting the controversial topic of predestination. As a young man of 19, he became convinced that he was predestined to hell. Much as he prayed, he still felt that, because of his sins, he would be among the damned; for him the worst part was the prospect of being unable to love God for eternity. Deliverance from the temptation came when he could pray: ''Whatever may happen, O Lord . . . I will love you always . . . at least in this life will I love you if it is not given me to love you in eternal life.'' Kneeling before a statue of Our Lady of ''Good Deliverance,'' he prayed the Memorare and then, standing, found himself ''perfectly and entirely healed.''

As he pursued his studies of law and theology at Padua, the question of predestination arose again as he questioned whether he could accept the position of Augustine and Aquinas as it was being taught, or if he had to reach an understanding more attuned to the scriptural truth of God's will to save all, and to the reality of human free will. The resolution of this crisis again found expression in prayer. Mindful of the fallibility of his own thinking, Francis cautiously yet confidently opted for the more positive view, convinced that God's name is not ''the one who condemns,'' but ''the one who saves [Jesus].'' His experience of this crisis, in its moral and intellectual phases, was formative of his spirituality with its emphasis on human capacity to love in the present moment, and on the prior unconditional goodness and love of God.

Ever since his early years he felt called to priesthood, but Francis's father knew nothing of this and had other plans for his eldest son—admission to the bar at Chambery, a proposed marriage and appointment to the Senate of Savoy. Francis agreed to the first of these plans, was coolly polite about the second, but refused the third. Meanwhile without his knowledge efforts were made in Rome to obtain for Francis the recently vacated position of provost, a post second to the bishop. The nominating letters arrived on May 7, 1593, and the next day, Francis asked his father's permission to take holy orders. The nomination as provost served as an enticement, and finally, M. de Boisy gave Francis his blessing. By the end of that year Francis had received all the minor and major orders, being ordained to the priesthood on December 18. He was installed as provost by Claude de Granier, bishop of Geneva in exile in Annecy.

In September 1594 Francis volunteered to undertake a mission to the Chablais, a part of the diocese where the Catholic faith had been banned by Calvinists for more than 50 years. The duke of Savoy had regained tentative control over the region, and wanted his Catholic religion to be restored in it. Bishop de Granier agreed to send two priests into the area. At first Francis and his cousin, Louis, had to stay at an armed castle some ten miles from Thonon, the regional capital, venturing forth to contact local officials and to preach wherever a few people would dare listen to them.

After a year and a half of seemingly futile efforts, multiple trials and frustrations, Francis's perseverance began to bear fruit: conversions, of civic leaders and of increasing numbers of citizens, tardy but necessary backing from the duke, four more priests to help, and the 1598 Treaty of Vervins, which promised a more stable and peaceful Savoy. By September the new situation of Catholics in the Chablais could be celebrated in Thonon. The duke arrived and proceeded to give the remaining Calvinists the choice of embracing the Catholic faith or of leaving his territory. As a trained jurist Francis saw a multiplicity of religions as a threat to the state's unity, and did not openly opposed the duke's measures. But as a priest and missionary, he much preferred persuasion, and never lost hope for a rapprochment among divided Christians, even though his three clandestine meetings with Theodore de Beze, Calvin's successor, showed how unlikely this was.

In 1597 Francis acceded to the request of Bishop de Granier to be named his coadjutor. The following year he took the ailing bishop's place in an ad limina visit to Rome, during which Pope Clement VII invited Francis to appear before a distinguished ''jury'' of cardinals and theologians, so that they might be as impressed as he was with the learning and piety of the bishop-elect.

In January 1602 Francis left for Paris. His official mission had to do with establishing the faith in a part of the diocese which the duke had given over to France. In that regard results were disappointing, but Francis's presence in Paris was a remarkable success. He interacted with a circle of spiritual leaders at the home of Barbe Acarie, where all the recent currents of spirituality were represented. Francis learned from all these trends, but he identified most with Teresa of Avila's approach, ''in which the solid, evangelical virtues were much preferable to visions, revelations, and ecstasies'' (A. Ravier). During these months Francis served as Madame Acarie's confessor; he influenced the circle to endorse her inspiration to bring the reformed Carmelites to France, and he encouraged Bérulle to do the same for Philip Neri's Oratory—in which Bérulle eventually found his own vocation.

''Saint Francis de Sales,'' by Giovanni Battista Tiepolo. (©Archivo Iconografico, S.A./CORBIS)

Francis also made a grand impression on the court and on Henry IV himself, who was struck by the priest's evangelical preaching and positive accessible piety and tried to entice de Sales to remain in France. Francis declined the offer made, as well others made in 1608 and 1619.

On his way back to Annecy, Francis received word of the death of Msgr. de Granier, and prepared for his episcopal ordination, which took place in the church of his baptism in Thorens. He later wrote that on that day ''God took me from myself to take me to himself and give me to his people.'' He gave himself to a full range of pastoral activities: he preached, taught catechism, worked for the reform of his clergy and of local monasteries, visited every parish, including those in remote Alpine villages, and more and more took on a ministry of spiritual direction both in person and by letter.

In 1604 he was invited to give the Lenten sermons in Dijon, the capital of Burgundy. There Francis met Baroness Jane Frances Fremyot de CHANTAL (1572–1641), a young widow with four small children. The spiritual rapport between Francis and Jane was immediate and mutual, and four months later Francis agreed to be her spiritual director. Thus began a relationship which would grow into one of the most celebrated spiritual friendships in the history of the church. For six years the friendship deepened through multiple letters they exchanged and through the visits Jane made to Savoy. The widow de Chantal had a desire to give herself totally to God but did not know what that might mean, especially in view of her children. Francis affirmed her in her existing responsibilities, but also encouraged her to nurture her inner desire until God's further inspiration would show the way. An idea they first discussed in 1607 bore fruit in 1610 in the creation of a new religious congregation, the Visitation of Holy Mary, a community of prayer open to women whose health or age prevented them from joining an existing order. To the end that the community could spread beyond Savoy into France, Francis and Jane saw this modest beginning evolve into a religious order with vows and enclosure (1618). In retrospect Francis saw this foundation as ''the fruit of the trip to Dijon,'' i.e., as flowing from his providential encounter with Jane de Chantal and marked by their respective contributions and by their common spirit.

In 1618 Francis was a member of a Savoyard delegation to the French court; they were to negotiate a marriage between Christine of France, sister of King Louis XIII, and Victor Amedee, crown prince of Savoy. In Paris Francis was much in demand as a preacher and spiritual director; he was again in contact with spiritual leaders such as Berulle and Vincent de Paul; with Mother de Chantal he established a Visitation community in Paris (with Vincent as its chaplain); he met several times with Angelique Arnauld, at that time an experienced convent reformer, who felt drawn to the Visitation; finally he again overcame the efforts of the cardinal of Paris to make him his coadjutor.

Francis returned to his dear Annecy after a year's absence, but his health was failing, and he dreamed of retirement. His brother was named coadjutor but there were two trips Francis had to make: one by order of the pope to oversee a monastic election in Piedmont, the other by order of the duke to be part of a Savoyard delegation to greet King Louis XIII at Avignon. On the return trip, at Lyons, he suffered a cerebral hemorrhage and died in the gardener's cottage of the Visitation monastery on Dec. 28, 1622. After some delays his will was found and his body duly returned to Annecy, arriving there on January 24.

Writings. Francis's life and ministry provided the matrix and motivation for all his writings—26 volumes in the *Oeuvres completes*. During the time in the Chablais when few would come to hear him, Francis explained Catholic doctrine in a series of short tracts which were copied (possibly printed) and clandestinely circulated. Francis hoped one day to rework and expand these ''meditations,'' to produce a book to help preachers win over Calvinists ''by a style that is not only instructive but affective.'' He never realized this larger project, but after his death a partial manuscript was found and published in 1672 under the title of *Controversies*. From the same period and ministry came the first book Francis himself published, *The Defense of the Standard of the Cross* (1600), a thorough explanation (in response to Protestant objections) of Catholic theology and practice in regard to venerating the cross or crucifix.

The ministry of spiritual direction led Francis to publish a very different kind of book in 1608. One of his directées, Madame de Charmoisy, had moved from Annecy for a time, and so he put in writing some of his advice on prayer and Christian living. These she shared with Fr. Fourier, a Jesuit, who strongly urged Francis to prepare them for publication. The resulting *Introduction to a Devout Life* was an immediate success, and Francis began to gather other memos he had written to directées, and worked them into an expanded second edition by September, 1609. Finally in 1619 he published the definitive edition, which continues to be recognized as a classic of Christian spirituality.

Prior to writing the *Introduction*, Francis had begun to write a ''booklet'' about the love of God and a sequel about love of neighbor. He eventually produced a substantial volume, divided into 12 ''Books''—all on love for God. While his subject was the practice of love for God, the first four Books contain theological and philosophical underpinnings for the rest. Books five through nine are the core of the *Treatise on the Love of God*, while the last three show how love of God reigns over all other loves, subsumes all the virtues and gifts and is exercised in everyday life. Though less accessible and less popular than the *Introduction*, the *Treatise*, which appeared in 1616, is seen as Francis's major work, comprehensive without being academic. Its teaching on the various forms and states of prayer owes much—as he says in the preface—to the experience of the early Visitation sisters and that of other directées.

Francis delivered many sermons, only one of which was published in his lifetime. Many others have come down to us: some in his own writing—either fully written out or, more frequently, as sketchy notes for his own use in preaching; others transcribed as he spoke and/or immediately afterward, by ''secretaries'' skilled in the art of memory (*ars memorativa*) and in reconstituting oral presentations. Recent studies have affirmed the basic reliability of these transcriptions and the advantage they have of giving an accurate idea of what and how Francis preached.

The Spiritual Conferences fall into this last category; in fact until very recently three transcribed sermons were included in collections of conferences. Most of the latter were informal, sometimes out-of-door discussions with the first Visitation community, and all were in implicit dialogue with it. A first unauthorized publication prompted Jane de Chantal to prepare the ''true spiritual conferences'' in 1629. Subsequent editions and translations have varied in their accuracy, contents, and order of presentation. The text published in the 1969 Pléiade edition of his *Oeuvres* surpasses them all, and is utilized in a recent English translation.

At Clermont College Francis had learned the art of letter writing and he practiced it both in formal correspondence with popes and princes and in personal letters of spiritual direction and friendship. His complete works contain over 2,000 letters, estimated to be one tenth of what he actually wrote. Many of these are letters of a gifted spiritual director. Though written to specific directées in unique circumstances, they have been published in a variety of collections beginning in 1626, and continue to speak to Christians in very different circumstances.

Other short writings, *opuscula*, which for the most part Francis wrote but did not see published, comprise the last five volumes of the *Oeuvres*. Included are a early work on the *Song of Songs*, the spiritual exercises he wrote in Padua, advice to confessors, and many texts related to the Visitation community.

This corpus of published and unpublished works contains a widely recognized spirituality, a ''devout'' or simply Christian humanism, possible in any calling or circumstance, a ''spirituality for all.'' Some parts of it were written for specific audiences, but according to Francis contemplative religious can benefit from reading the *Introduction*, and lay people do benefit from the *Spiritual Conferences*. Underlying all his life and writings can be seen an adaptable spirituality which (1) is rooted in the human heart-center and extends to all facets of life, (2) finds peace in the midst of busyness and in a dynamic conception of prayer and discernment, and (3) sees God acting in ordinary human relationships—in community, family and especially in friends. His experience convinced him that spiritual friendship is necessary for those living ''in the world,'' himself included. The relationship with St. Jane de Chantal so shaped both of them that it can be said that theirs is a common spirituality expressed in different voices.

These writings also contain a less-well-recognized theology. On some topics Francis can be called Scotist or Molinist, but what he developed over the years, while not a systematic or ''school'' theology, was a pastoral synthesis of those theological points ''which concern for the service of souls and 24 years spent in sacred preaching lead me to think are most conducive to the glory of the Gospel and of the Church.'' Some of the theological topics he dealt with are the primacy of love, the question of grace and free will, a theology of praise, an analysis of ''God's will,'' the nature of the Church, the sufficiency of scripture, and the role of Mary and the saints. Francis's theology, then, like his writing, was intimately linked to his ministry. It served as a solid foundation for his spiritual teaching and for his psychologically astute spiritual direction.

Francis was beatified in 1661, canonized in 1665, and declared a doctor of the Church in 1877. In 1854 he was named patron of the deaf and in 1923 that of writers and journalists. Shortly after the Second Vatican Council Pope Paul VI wrote: ''None of the recent doctors of the Church knew better than St. Francis de Sales how to anticipate, with the profound intuition of his wisdom, the deliberations of the Council'' [*Acta apostolicae sedis* LIX (1967), 115]. That wisdom is becoming better known through the attraction of his writings, through scholarly studies and through religious organizations claiming the saint as founder or patron, as they renew themselves in his spirit, notably Visitation Sisters, Missionaries of St. Francis de Sales, Oblates of St. Francis de Sales, Salesians of Don Bosco, and the St. Francis de Sales Association.

Feast: Jan. 24.

Bibliography: *Oeuvres*, 27 volumes (éd. complète, Annecy 1892–1964). *Oeuvres*, ed. A. RAVIER and R. DEVOS, (*Pléiade* edition Paris 1969). *Francis de Sales, Jane de Chantal, Letters of Spiritual Direction*, tr. P. M. THIBERT, intro. by W. WRIGHT and J. POWER (New York 1988). *Spiritual Conferences* tr. I. CARNIERO, 2 vols. (Bangalore, India 1995, 1998). *Sermon Texts on Saint Joseph by Francis de Sales*, tr. and ed. J. CHORPENNING (Toronto 2000). P. SEROUET, ''François de Sales'' in *Dictionnaire de spiritualité et mystique*, V, 1057–1097. A. RAVIER, *Francis de Sales: Sage and Saint* (San Francisco 1988). E.-M. LAJEUNIE, *Saint Francis de Sales: The Man, the Thinker, His Influence*, 2 vols. (Bangalore, India 1986 and 1987). W. WRIGHT, *Bond of Perfection: Jeanne de Chantal and François de Sales* (New York 1985). R. CHAMPAGNE, *François de Sales ou la passion de l'autre* (Montreal 1998). J. LANGELAAN, *The Philosophy and Theology of Love according to St. Francis de Sales* (Lewiston, N.Y. 1994). T. A. MCGOLDRICK, *The Sweet and Gentle Struggle: Francis de Sales on the Necessity of Spiritual Friendship* (Lanham, Md. 1996). H. BORDES and J. HENNEQUIN, eds., *L'Unidivers Salésien: Saint François de Sales hier et aujourd'hui* (Paris 1994). H. LEMAIRE, *Les Images chez François de Sales* (Paris 1962). E. STOPP, *A Man to Heal Differences: Essays and Talks on St. Francis de Sales* (Philadelphia 1997).

[J. POWER]

"Saint Francis of Assisi Presenting His Rule to Pope Innocent III," part of 14th-century fresco cycle by Giotto, Assisi, Italy.

FRANCIS OF ASSISI, ST.

Founder of the Order of Friars Minor, the Order of Saint Clare, and the Order of Brothers and Sisters of Penance. b. Assisi, c. 1182; d. there, Oct. 3, 1226.

His father, Pietro di Bernardone, was a textile merchant; his mother was named Pica. He was baptized John, but was called Francesco, that is, Francis. Having received the usual liberal arts education of the period, he knew Latin and possessed some knowledge of French. His wealth and love of life made him a flamboyant leader of Assisi's youth. In the feuding between Assisi and Perugia he was imprisoned (1202–03). Afterwards, a debilitating illness brought him to a realistic awareness of his strengths and weaknesses. In 1205 he dreamt about joining a campaign against Apulia, but after a dream promising him glory, he changed his plans and at Spoleto returned to Assisi. Soon after, he met a leper and began a life of continuous conversion. A short while later, he entered the abandoned church of San Damiano on the outskirts of Assisi where he heard a voice from the cross calling him to rebuild the house of God. Taking his inheritance he used the money to fulfill the mandate, severed relations with his father, and dramatically and publicly renounced dependence on his father, Pietro. After hearing the missionary discourse in the Gospel of Matthew 10: 5–14 on Feb. 24, 1209, he embraced poverty and gave his life to preaching penance and peace.

Early Days of the Order. He began attracting followers and when there were a dozen, Francis drew up a form of life consisting of Gospel passages and some practical norms of living. Francis and his brothers presented the document to Pope Innocent III who approved it orally in 1209 or 1210. They then returned to the chapel of Our Lady of the Portiuncula (Santa Maria degli Angeli) in the valley below Assisi. Clare was invested there March 18–19, 1212 into a new way of life and thus the Second Order was founded. The preaching of Francis and his brothers initiated in Italy a strong penitential movement, which spread elsewhere among the laity, and later developed into the Third Order.

To reactivate the Church's mission to spread the Gospel Francis attempted a journey to Syria in 1212, but was shipwrecked in Dalmatia. A second journey to Morocco was thwarted by his illness in Spain (1213–14). Meanwhile, the order had expanded considerably. In 1217 the order was organized into provinces. In 1219 during the Fifth Crusade Francis traveled to the Middle East where he tried in vain, at Damietta, to convert the Sultan of Egypt, Malik al-Kamil. Meanwhile during Francis's absence from Italy there arose internal difficulties among the brothers that clearly showed how much the legally unstable order depended upon the personality of its founder.

After his return to Italy in 1220, Francis requested the pope to name as cardinal-protector Cardinal Hugolino, a man who later, as Pope Gregory IX, played an important role in the formation of the order. In the same year Francis, who remained minister general until his death, accepted Peter Cathanii as his vicar. The rule, which had developed until that time without much direction, was revised and promulgated in 1221 at the Chapter of the Mats in Assisi, with 3,000 friars in attendance. Caesar of Speyer incorporated the related Scripture passages into this, the earliest extant rule (*regula non bullata*). After the death of Peter Cathanii in 1221, Francis independently appointed Brother Elias of Cortona as vicar-general. The demand for a stronger juridical structure in the order resulted in a definitive rule (*regula bulata*), approved by Honorius III, Nov. 29, 1223.

Death and Afterlife. Francis devoted himself to the spiritual growth of his brothers by means of circular letters and admonitions. He traveled and preached throughout the countryside, but he repeatedly interrupted his activity to retreat to a solitary hermitage. On Dec. 25, 1223, at Greccio he organized the now famous crib ceremony in the description of which it becomes evident that he was a deacon. The date of his ordination to the diaconate is unknown. On the mountain of Alvernia (La Verna) he received the stigmata on Sept. 14, 1224 (the first documented stigmatization). Plagued during the last years of his life with blindness and serious illness, he died at S. Maria degii Angeli (Portiuncula), Assisi during the evening of Oct. 3, 1226. The next day he was buried in Assisi at the church of Saint George. Two years later on July 16, 1228 in Assisi, Gregory IX enrolled Francis in the catalogue of the saints. A day later on the 17th, Gregory laid the cornerstone of a new church (built later by Brother Elias of Cortona) that was destined to shelter Francis' remains. At this same time, Gregory IX charged Thomas of Celano to write the saint's biography; he completed it by early January 1229 at the latest. In 1230 the lower church of S. Francesco was near enough to completion that Francis' remains were solemnly interred there on May 25. For fear that relics might be stolen, the location of the grave was kept secret. After many attempts in 1570, 1607, and 1806, the grave was located in 1818, and its surroundings were expanded into a crypt-church. The Church commemorates Francis' death on October 4 and the feast of the Stigmata on September 17. The order, moreover, celebrates the first approval of the rule (renewal of vows) on April 16, the *translatio* on May 25, the canonization on July 15, and the discovery of the grave on December 12. Franciscans further celebrate his death with a special *transitus* ceremony on the evening of October 4.

Francis is venerated as spiritual father by the three branches of the First Order (Franciscans, Franciscan Conventuals, and Capuchins), the branches of the Second Order of Poor Clares (Urbanists, Colettines, Capuchinesses, etc.), the Franciscan Third Order Regular, approximately 30 male congregations, more than 400 communities of Franciscan Sisters, and numerous lay communities of the Third Order Secular.

The miracles Francis performed during his lifetime and after his death have not followed a single pattern, but have answered all kinds of human requests. He is venerated not only by Catholics but, especially since the 19th century, by Protestants as well; there is also a Protestant Third Order of St. Francis. His apostolate of peace and his example of fraternal charity have captured today's imagination. His profoundly Christian love of creation (*Canticle of the Brother Sun*) exemplifies his appreciation of God's generous gifts of creation. All that is speaks and proclaims the glory of God. Francis' vision of creation in its profound origins as a generous outpouring of God's love has not always been properly understood. In recent times romantic enthusiasts have often encouraged a superficial praise for creation in and of itself rather in the wondrous beauty of its origin and destiny. However, the publication of a critical edition of Francis' writings by Cajetan Esser in 1974 have gone a long way to remedy that situation. In 1979 John Paul II proclaimed Francis to be the patron saint of ecology.

Feast: Oct. 4.

Bibliography: K. ESSER, *Die Opuscula des Hl. Franziskus von Assisi: Neue textkritische edition* (Grottaferrata 1976). R. ARMSTRONG, J. HELLMANN, and W. SHORT, eds., *Francis of Assisi: Early Documents*, 3 vols. (New York 1999–01). L. BOFF, *Saint Francis: A Model for Human Liberation*, tr. J. DIERCKSMEIER (New York 1982). A. FORTINI, *Francis of Assisi*, tr. H. MOAK (New York 1981). R. MANSELLI, *St. Francis of Assisi*, tr. P. DUGGAN (Chicago 1988).

[R. ARMSTRONG]

FRANCIS OF GERONIMO, ST.

Jesuit preacher and social worker; b. Grottaglie, near Taranto (Apulia), Italy, Dec. 17, 1642; d. Naples, May 11, 1716. He was the eldest of 11 children, and spent his boyhood in a residence of secular priests who lived in a community. In 1658 he entered the Jesuit college at Taranto and later attended the Gesù Vecchio, Naples, where he was ordained March 18, 1666. After a year as prefect at the Collegio dei Nobili, he entered the society in July 1670. Following his novitiate, he spent a year with an experienced missionary preaching in the Province of Otranto. He then returned to Naples, completed his studies at the Gesù Nuovo in 1675, and was solemnly professed.

After his profession he asked to be assigned to the mission in Japan, but was told that his mission was to be Naples. He was appointed regular preacher at the church of the Gesù Nuovo and began a lifetime of preaching to the Neapolitans and the people of the surrounding countryside. Three great interests consumed his life: his *Oratorio delle Missioni;* the organization of a citywide ''family Communion'' on the third Sunday of each month; and his numerous sermons, often preached outdoors and to those unaccustomed to frequenting churches.

To further his preaching work, he organized an auxiliary whose primary purpose was to support the missionaries. The organization, which he called *Oratorio delle Missioni,* was made up of ordinary workmen whom he himself enlisted. At first they aimed only at material aid for the missions; they raised money, prepared altars, vestments, etc., and arranged for the sermons. But before long the members entered into the spirit of the apostolate and rivaled one another in enrolling an audience for the sermons. Francesco formed the auxiliary into a sort of cooperative that gave financial assistance to its sick members and also provided funeral expenses.

The absorbing interest of his life was his preaching. His sermons were always well planned, short, and energetic. He scorned no means that would help his hearers; for example, he might hold a skull aloft for them to look at, or he might bare his shoulders and apply the discipline. Every Sunday he preached in the city several times. On Tuesdays, unfailingly he preached on Our Lady in the church of S. Maria. Other days he preached generally in towns outside the city, and some days it is recorded that he preached as many as 40 times. This seems less an exaggeration when it is realized that it was his custom to preach wherever he could find listeners. He went where he would find sinners to convert. If a section of the city developed a bad reputation, he went there and preached. He preached on street corners, in dark alleys, in the public squares, on the city docks, on the decks of prison ships in the harbor. The Jesuit archives contain the voluminous outlines of his sermons, each minutely developed, and in view of his tireless zeal their estimated number of 10,000 does not seem too large.

Francesco became interested in social agencies to aid in the permanent reclamation of his many converts. Two refuges for reformed women are credited to him in Naples, as well as an asylum for deserted children. Nothing was beyond his interest, and he formed charitable groups to prepare for his own work among the convicts and even among the slaves on the Turkish ships that put into the Bay of Naples.

Francesco published nothing, apart from a record of outstanding events in his preaching career, which he wrote at the behest of his superiors (cf. Boero, 67–181).

His obsequies were said to surpass the homage that Naples gave its kings, but the Neapolitan rulers never had the hold over the hearts of their subjects this apostle still has. He was canonized in 1839. His body lies in his native Taranto, but he is one of the patron saints of the city of Naples.

Feast: May 11.

Bibliography: F. VAN ORTROY, *The Catholic Encyclopedia,* ed. C. G. HERBERMANN, 16 v. (New York 1907–14; suppl. 1922) 6:218–219. C. SOMMERVOGEL, *Bibliotèque de la Compagnie de Jésus,* 11 v. (Brussels-Paris 1890–1932) 3:1358; 11:1462–69. G. BOERO, *S. Francesco di Girolamo e le sue missioni dentro e fuori di Napoli* (Florence 1882).

[P. F. MULHERN]

FRANCIS OF OSUNA

Franciscan priest whose writings greatly influenced St. Teresa; b. Osuna, Sevilla province, Spain, *c.* 1497; d. 1542 (place unknown). Although he was born of parents attached to a noble household, little is known of Osuna's early life. As a young friar he was sent to the University of Salamanca where, without neglecting his studies, he devoted considerable time to prayer and contemplation. He spent the years 1527 to 1531 mostly in Seville. Later he was chosen to represent his Order at chapters in Toulouse (1532) and Paris (1533). Afterwards he spent some time in Flanders, but the cold, damp climate affected his always delicate health. At some time between 1530 and 1535, his Order elected him Franciscan commissary general to the Indies, an office he never exercised, either because of ill health or because he felt his vocation lay in writing. From Flanders he returned to Spain. The circumstances of his death are unknown.

Osuna is known chiefly for his *Abecedario Espiritual* (Spiritual Alphabet), 1527, which so greatly influenced St. Teresa. The work is in six parts, treating respectively of the Passion, asceticism, prayer and the contemplative life, love, poverty and riches, and of Christ's wounds.

Bibliography: E. A. PEERS, *Studies of the Spanish Mystics,* 2 v. (2d ed. rev. London 1951), v.1 includes a full bibliography. R. P. FIDÈLE DE ROS, *Un Maître de sainte Thérèse* (Paris 1937). *Enciclopedia Universal Ilustrada Europea–Americana* 44 (Barcelona 1908–30) 991–992.

[K. E. POND]

FRANCIS OF PAOLA, ST.

Founder of the MINIMS; b. Paola, province of Cosenza, Calabria, Italy, March 27, 1416; d. Tours, France, April 2, 1507. He was the second son of Giacomo d'Alessio and his wife, Vienna da Fuscaldo. When 12 he spent a year at the Franciscan friary of San Marco and then accompanied his parents on a pilgrimage to Rome and Assisi. With their permission, he then sought a secluded region at Paola to live as a hermit. He later moved to a remote cave by the sea but was discovered by some hunters who spread the fame of his virtues. Although he would frequently return to his grotto, he believed that God now wished him to dedicate himself to an apostolic life. At 19 he received his first followers, thus laying the foundations of his order. Francis became the defender of the poor and oppressed and did not fear to plead their cause before Ferrante I of Aragon and Louis XI of France. His last 25 years were spent in France, where he was called by Louis XI, then near death. Though unwilling at first to leave Italy, at the insistence of SIXTUS IV he left for Paris and prepared the king for a happy death. At the court of the Valois he was instrumental in restoring peace between France and Brittany by advising the marriage of the Dauphin, Charles, to Anne of Brittany, and between France and Spain by counseling Louis XI to return the counties of Rousillon and Cerdagne to Spain. While at court he became the tutor of the future Charles

St. Francis of Paola, engraving. (©Bettmann/CORBIS)

VIII. His miracles were numerous, and because many were connected with the sea, he was declared patron of seafarers by PIUS XII on March 27, 1943. He was canonized on 1 May 1519, by LEO X, and has enjoyed particular veneration in Latin countries, where he is honored by the devotion of the ''Thirteen Fridays.'' His iconography is rich with illustrious names as Bartolomé Murillo, Diego Velázguez, Francisco Goya, Giovanni B. Tiepolo, Giovanni B. Piazzetta, Giulio Romano, and others. He appears in the *Torquemada* of Victor Hugo, and is the subject of a sonata by Franz Liszt, *St. Francis of Paola Walking on the Waters.* Francis' letters are preserved in a collection edited by F. Preste, *Centuria di lettere di S. Francesco di Paola* (Rome 1665).

Feast: April 2.

Bibliography: F. RUSSO, *Bibliografia di S. Francesco di Paola* (Bollettino Ufficiale dei Minimi Suppl. Rome 1957). G. M. ROBERTI, *S. Francesco di Paola: Storia della sua vita* (2d ed. Rome 1963). G. VEZIN, *Saint François de Paule, fondateur des minimes, et la France* (Paris 1971). G. VANZILLOTTA, *A Royal Adventure, St. Francis of Paola* (New York 1975). G. J. SIMI and M. M. SEGRETI, *Saint Francis of Paola: God's Miracle Worker Supreme* (Rockford, Ill. 1977). P. ADDANTE, *Il processo cosentino e turonense a Francesco di Paola* (Bari 1979). F. GRILLO, *San Francesco di Paola nella storia e nella leggenda* (Cosenza 1984). N. MISASI, *In provincia: l'ambiente calabrese al tempo dei Borboni* (Sala Bolognese 1984).

[A. BELLANTONIO]

FRANCISCAN FRIARS OF THE ATONEMENT

(SA, Official Catholic Directory #0530); officially known as the Society of the Atonement (Societas Adunationis, TOR), and popularly known as Graymoor or Atonement friars; a branch of the Third Order Regular of St. Francis of Assisi, founded in 1898 by Lewis Thomas WATTSON (Father Paul, SA). The Atonement friars are comprised of priests and brothers who are engaged in social, ecumenical, and pastoral ministries in the United States, Canada, England, Italy, and Japan.

Foundation. Wattson, who, as an Episcopalian clergyman, held pastorates in Kingston, New York, and Omaha, Nebraska, wished to begin ''a preaching order like the Paulists,'' based on the ideas of St. Francis, especially in the observance of religious poverty. On July 9, 1893, while reading from St. Paul, he found the word ''atonement'' and chose it as the name for his proposed community. Several years later he met Lurana Mary White (1870–1935), who, as Mother Lurana, SA, subsequently founded the FRANCISCAN SISTERS of the Atonement. On Oct. 7, 1898, they pledged themselves to God to establish the Society of the Atonement.

The foundation was made that December when Mother Lurana went to Graymoor. Father Paul arrived the following October and spent the first winter in an abandoned paint shack. In 1900 the first small building was erected on the friars' property, the Mount of the Atonement. For the next several years the two communities struggled to survive against the threats posed by paucity of numbers, poverty, and the ostracism by their fellow Anglicans.

On Oct. 30, 1909, in the sisters' chapel at Graymoor, Father Paul, Mother Lurana, and 15 followers were received into the Catholic Church. Permission for this singular event was granted by Pius X through the apostolic delegate to the United States, Diomede Falconi, OFM. Shortly after, the group was received into the Franciscan order. Father Paul was ordained on July 16, 1910, at St. Joseph's Seminary, Yonkers, New York, by Abp. John Farley of New York. During the next 30 years, Father Paul's efforts were expended for the Church, for Graymoor, and for Christian unity.

In 1951 the friars received their *decretum laudis* from the Holy See; the decree of final approbation was granted in 1960. The constitutions agree substantially with those of the Friars Minor, with whom the Graymoor friars have a decree of aggregation (1932). The priests and clerics recite the Divine Office in choir each day. All members wear the grayish-brown habit fastened at the waist by a cord to which is attached the Franciscan rosary of the Joys of Our Lady; and a crucifix is worn about the neck. The motto of the community is ''All for Christ and the Salvation of Men.''

Chair of Unity Octave. In 1908 Father Paul instituted the Chair of Unity Octave, a prayer crusade for religious unity from January 18 to 25. Pius X approved the practice in 1909; in 1916 Benedict XV extended it to the universal Church. Pius XII, in a letter (Nov. 1, 1957) urged the octave's observance to be spread as widely as possible. In 1959 John XXIII recommended it to all the faithful. The U.S. hierarchy in 1921 agreed to observe the octave in each diocese; this resolution was renewed in 1957 at the annual bishops' meeting in Washington, D.C.

Other Activities. Graymoor friars direct St. Christopher's Inn at Graymoor (opened in 1909), a hospice for homeless and jobless men. They are engaged in domestic and overseas missionary work, parish administration, chaplaincies, pastoral outreach, campus ministries, retreats, and spiritual direction. Many friars work with the homeless, HIV/AIDS patients, people seeking recovery from alcoholism and substance abuse. From 1903 to 1973, the society published the *Lamp,* a monthly periodical devoted to Christian unity and the missions. Between the years 1935 and 1969, the Atonement friars produced the Ave Maria Hour, a transcribed radio program on the lives of saints.

In 1949 the Atonement friars established their first overseas mission in the diocese of Yokohoma, Japan. This was followed by the establishment of a community in Rome and England. At the start of the 21st century, the friars operate parishes in the United States, Canada, and England; they have communities in the United States, Canada, England, Japan, and Italy. The motherhouse is in Graymoor, Garrison, New York.

Bibliography: D. GANNON, *Father Paul of Graymoor* (New York 1951). T. CRANNY, *Father Paul: Apostle of Unity* (Peekskill, N.Y. 1955). E. F. HANAHOE, ed., *One Fold* (Garrison, N.Y. 1959).

[T. CRANNY/EDS.]

FRANCISCAN MARTYRS OF GEORGIA

The title refers to five Friars Minor—Pedro de Corpa, Blas Rodríguez, Miguel de Añon, Antonio de Badajóz, and Francisco de Veráscola—who were slain in 1597 in the territory of the present-day Diocese of Savannah. Though the territory was then called La Florida, to distinguish these missionaries from others martyred in territory that is now part of the state of Florida, the term ''of Georgia'' is used to identify them.

These five Spanish missionaries—four priests and one lay brother—were laboring in the region then known as Guale. The event that occasioned their slaying was the polygamous infidelity of Juanillo, the son of a Guale cacique. A baptized Christian sacramentally married, Juanillo had openly taken a second wife. Called to task by the missionary in Tolomato, the headstrong young man took offense at the correction. Fearing that he would be impeded in succeeding to the position of cacique of the tribe, he organized a revolt against the authority of the missionaries. He rounded up a group of nonbaptized natives, who, under cover of night, came to Tolomato. On the morning of Sept. 14, 1597, Juanillo and his followers invaded the house where Fray Pedro was preparing for the celebration of Sunday mass for his flock. Without further ado, he slew the priest with blows of a stone-hatchet.

The following day the rampant natives moved on to the nearby settlement of Tupiquí, where they found Fray Blas preparing to offer mass with his people. The invaders allowed him to celebrate mass, after which he spoke words of farewell and exhortation to the faithful who had gathered. Though the friar sought to persuade the rebels to desist from their bloody intention, they refused to abandon their plan, beyond postponing action for two days. They then bashed his head with clubs and threw his body to the vultures.

Crossing the channel, the rebels came to St. Catherines Island (then called Guale). They had previously sent word to the cacique of the island to slay Fray Miguel and the lay brother Fray Antonio, the two friars missioned there. Hoping to save them, however, the cacique planned to send them to another island, where he knew that the faithful natives would give them safe haven. The warning did not arrive in time to save them from the rebels. The priest offered a last mass and gave viaticum to his assistant. The rebels slew both Fray Miguel and Fray Antonio with blows from a tomahawk.

The slaying of the fifth victim, Fray Francisco, took place on a date not explicitly indicated in the sources. For some days he had been absent from his mission on Asao (now St. Simons Island) when the revolt broke out and his brethren had been slain. Pressured by the rebels, the natives on the island, who had not embraced the Gospel in any great number, were persuaded to join the revolt. When within a few days the friar arrived back at his post, a group of young braves who had formerly been his friends overpowered him as he pulled into the land. On the shore of the island they clubbed him to death. Thus within the period of one week all five missionary friars working in Guale were put to death.

From the time of their martyrdom there was a constant recognition that their death was a witness to Gospel values. Their cause for canonization was formally opened in the Diocese of Savannah in 1983, and ten years later forwarded to the Congregation for the Causes of Saints in Rome for consideration.

Bibliography: M. GEIGER, *The Franciscan Conquest of Florida* (Washington 1937). M. HABIG, *Heroes of the Cross* (Paterson, N.J. 1947). J. T. LANNING, *The Spanish Missions of Georgia* (Chapel Hill, N.C. 1935).

[A. WYSE]

FRANCISCAN SISTERS

This entry reports on the congregations of religious women that look to St. Francis of Assisi for inspiration. Most follow the Third Order Regular Rule of St. Francis. For the historical development of the rule, *see* FRANCISCANS, THIRD ORDER REGULAR. Some have papal approbation; others are established with episcopal approval in a particular diocese. The members of these communities profess simple vows of poverty, chastity, and obedience. Each congregation is governed by constitutions designed according to its own specialized mission and particular ministries. In most cases the inventory that follows gives the official title of the congregation, the acronym each uses, and a number in brackets that refers to its listing in the *Official Catholic Directory*, where the location of its headquarters, and current statistics can be found.

St. Joseph's Convent, motherhouse of the Franciscan School Sisters of Milwaukee, Wisconsin.

Many of these congregations are members of the Franciscan Federation Third Order Regular of the Sisters and Brothers of the United States, an organization comprised of male and female religious in the United States, Canada, and the Caribbean who follow the Third Order Regular Rule of St. Francis. The mission of the Federation is to promote exploration and study of Franciscan evangelical life and its implications for contemporary society. The Federation provides national and regional opportunities to collaborate, gather, and celebrate so that the brothers and sisters can better live the Third Order Regular call to conversion, contemplation, poverty and humility.

In 1991 the members restructured the Federation into six geographic regions. The goal of regionalization and regional steering committee is to provide service to the members of the Federation and to increase grassroots participation and networking among the members.

See Also: POOR CLARES.

[R. RODDY]

Bernardine Sisters of the Third Order of St. Francis (OSF) [1810]. A congregation founded in Cracow, Poland, in 1457, when St. JOHN CAPISTRAN established the reformed branch of the Friars Minor in that city. A group of tertiaries, ladies of the Cracovian nobility, desiring to lead a life in common like that of the daughters of Bl. ANGELINA OF MARSCIANO in Italy, formed an active community of the Third Order of St. Francis. Because these Franciscan sisters attended liturgy in a church dedicated to the then recently canonized St. Bernardine of Siena, they became known as the Bernardines. St. Agnes, the first convent of the Bernardine Sisters, was erected in Cracow in 1457; from it a new foundation, that of St. Joseph, was established in the same city in 1646; St. Joseph Convent gave rise to the Sacred Heart Convent, which was founded at Zakliczyn-on-the-Danube in 1883. From there, the Bernardine sisters came to the United States in 1894.

During the first decades of its existence, the community was engaged in caring for the aged, nursing the sick, and instructing the poor. In time, however, the Bernardines became strictly contemplative; although they remain such in Poland, they engage in active work in the United States. The first American house of the congregation was opened at Mt. Carmel, Pennsylvania, in 1894. Thaddeus Jachimowicz, pastor of St. Joseph's parish, petitioned the Zakliczyn convent for sisters to educate the children of the parish. Mother Jadwiga Jurkiewicz obtained a dispensation from the cloister for the sisters who were appointed to this apostolate and sent three sisters, under the direction of Mother Veronica Grzedowska, to Mt. Carmel. In the course of a year circumstances forced the sisters to move to Reading, Pennsylvania, where they received a gift of ten acres of land from Msgr. George Bornemann that became the site for their permanent home. In 1901 the novitiate was established; in 1912 the first general chapter was held in which Mother Hedwig Leszczynska was elected the first general superior. Until 1918 the community remained under the jurisdiction of the Reformed Friars Minor in Poland. Because of disrupted communications with Europe caused by World War I, the congregation became diocesan in 1918. That year it received provisional approbation of its constitutions, and on May 6, 1941, the Holy See gave final approval to the constitutions, and the community returned to its former status of a pontifical congregation.

Originally engaged in elementary grade teaching and care of orphans, the community gradually extended its activities. Teaching, the major interest of the sisters, was expanded to include kindergarten through college, and to this was added social work, hospital care, nursery care, and retreats for women. The sisters progressively spread their apostolate to foreign lands. In 1937 Mother Angela Wojtkowiak established a convent at Dom Feliciano, Brazil, by amalgamating into the American community a group of ten European Bernardines who had migrated from Cracow to Brazil in 1926, but found conditions for expansion and growth too difficult without outside help. In 1957 the community extended its apostolate to Africa, when the superior general, Mother Mary Chrysostom Yadusky, opened a house in Cape Palmas, Liberia. Geographically the community is divided into four provinces: Sacred Heart, Reading, Pa.; Holy Name of Mary, Stamford, Conn.; Holy Rosary, Farmington, Mich.; and Immaculate Conception, Porto Alegre, Brazil. The general motherhouse and central novitiate are located at Villanova, Pa.

Bibliography: Archives, General Motherhouse, Villanova, Pa., Sacred Heart Provincial House, Reading, Pa., St. Joseph Convent, Cracow, and Sacred Heart Convent, Zakliczyn, Poland.

[R. JAMESON]

Congregation of the Servants of the Holy Child Jesus of the Third Order Regular of St. Francis (OSF) [1980]. An international Franciscan community founded in 1855 by Antonie Werr to minister to the needs of women who were neglected by society; in particular, prisoners, prostitutes and the destitute poor. The sisters first came to the United States in 1929 and established their first foundation at Staten Island, New York. Their principal ministries are in social work, health care and teaching.

[A. COOPER]

Congregation of the Sisters of the Third Order of St. Francis of Perpetual Adoration (FSPA) [1780]. This congregation, also known as the Franciscan Sisters of Perpetual Adoration, is a papally approved apostolic congregation founded in 1849. A group of six women and men, their pastor, Father Anton Keppeler, and his assistant, Father Mathias Steiger, all members of the Third Order of St. Francis, emigrated from their parish in Ettenbeuren, Bavaria, to Milwaukee, Wisconsin, to be of service to the Church among German immigrants. The women, Ottilie Dirr, Anna Ritter, Maria Saumweber, Theresia Moser, Maria Eisenschmid, and Creszentia Eberle, formed a religious community under the direction of Anton Keppeler, with Ottilie, (Mother Aemiliana), as Superior. Keppeler and Steiger died of cholera in 1851.

In 1860 the founders, overwhelmed with the domestic duties they had assumed at St. Francis Seminary (1856) adjacent to their property, left the small community. With the election of Sister Antonia Herb as superior and the support of Reverend Michael Heiss, rector of the seminary, the sisters again focused their efforts on the original purposes of the founders. They transferred the motherhouse to Jefferson, Wisconsin, (1864); then to La Crosse (1871), where Heiss had become bishop. At St. Rose Convent, the motherhouse, the sisters intensified their preparation to teach children in elementary and secondary parish schools. Their work at the seminary terminated when some 30 sisters stationed at or near the seminary severed connections with the La Crosse motherhouse and established an independent congregation.

The early ministries in educating immigrant children, caring for orphans, ministering to the sick, and spreading the Gospel among the Native Americans were later extended to African Americans in the South, the poor in Appalachia, and to the people of China, El Salvador, Guam, Zimbabwe, and Cameroon. The sisters today are focusing energy on the ever-evolving ministry of accompanying people on their spiritual journeys. They also sponsor a healthcare system, Viterbo University, four spirituality centers and a center for holistic living.

Through their social justice ministries, the Sisters try to serve as agents of change both in individual lives and in society. They also provide diverse educational programs, resources and direct ministry to the disadvantaged around the globe. The mission of the congregation is also expressed in partnerships with others seeking Franciscan values and goals without formal membership.

[R. HOPHAN/M. LANG/G. MCDONALD]

Congregation of the Third Order of St. Francis of Mary Immaculate (OSF) [1710]. Mother Alfred Moes and Father Pamfilo da Magliano established this first Franciscan Sisterhood in Illinois on Aug. 2, 1865. Papal Approbation was first received in 1909, with the most recent renewal in 1985. The strong Franciscan tradition imparted by Father Pamfilo and the charism experienced by Mother Alfred remain vital in the Joliet Sisters and their Associates. With a heritage of simplicity, versatility, and ingenuity in responding to the needs of God's people, the Congregation has ministered in most of the United States of America, with extensions in Central Brazil since 1963. Sisters have been engaged in a variety of ministries, including education (early childhood, special, primary, secondary, higher, and religious), pastoral ministry, administration, social work, child care, care of the sick and elderly, and ministry to the incarcerated.

[M. VOELKER]

Franciscan Handmaids of the Most Pure Heart of Mary (FHM) [1260]. A diocesan congregation originally called Franciscan Handmaids of Mary and founded in Savannah, Ga., in 1916, by Mother Theodore and Rev. Ignatius Lissner of the Society of the African Missions. Their purpose was to meet the challenge of proposed state legislation requiring that African-American children be educated only by members of their own race. The new community began its work in St. Anthony's school, Savannah. Scarcity of vocations and the timely invitation of Cardinal Patrick Hayes to staff a nursery prompted a small band of sisters to move to New York City in 1924 and establish their provincial house. The sisters minister in education, pastoral care, and social work.

[M. C. ALEXANDER]

Franciscan Hospitaller Sisters of the Immaculate Conception (FHIC) [1270]. A congregation of papal approbation founded in Lisbon in 1871 by Mother Maria Clara of the Child Jesus and Rev. Raimundo dos Anjos Beirao. The congregation sought to address the needs of the poor and abandoned. The sisters established foundation in Angola, Brazil, Spain, South Africa, the Philippines, Mexico and the United States (1960). The sisters minister in schools and hospitals, as well as other ministries devoted to meeting the needs of the poor and disenfranchised.

[R. RODDY]

Franciscan Missionaries of Mary (FMM) [1370]. A congregation with papal approbation (1896, 1984), founded in 1877 in Ootacamund, Madras, India, by Hélène de CHAPPOTIN DE NEUVILLE (Mother Mary of the Passion). The generalate of this congregation, established specifically for work in the foreign missions, has been in Rome since 1882, when the community was joined to the Franciscan Order. The sisters minister in 77 countries and 70 nationalities divided into 55 provinces. In the United States, where the sisters established themselves in 1903, the provincial house is in the Bronx, New York.

The sisters combine contemplative and active life and follow the rule of the Third Order Regular of St. Francis. Mother Marie Hermine de Jésus (Irma Grivot) and six companions were martyred during the Boxer Rebellion in China in 1900. They were beatified in 1946 and canonized on Oct. 1, 2000. Another China missionary, 26-year-old Maria Assunta PALLOTTA, was beatified in 1954. The foundress, Mother Marie of the Passion, was declared Venerable in June, 1999. The sisters serve in education, social service, medicine, nursing, and catechetics. In the United States they sponsor Franciscan Children's Hospital and Rehabilitation Center, Brighton, Massachusetts, and St. Francis Hospital, noted for open-heart surgery, in Roslyn, New York.

Bibliography: M. T. DE MALEISSYE, *A Short Life of Mary of the Passion (Helen de Chappotin), Foundress of the Franciscan Missionaries of Mary* (Bandra, Mumbrai, 2000). S. JUSTINA FANEGO, *In Order to Give Life: A Community That Delivered Itself up to Death* (2000).

[M. MOTTE]

Franciscan Missionaries of Our Lady (OSF) [1380]. A community that originated in 1854 in Calais, France, through the amalgamation of seven autonomous congregations. In November of 1866 the constitutions were submitted to the Holy See. In the spirit of the Franciscan rule, the sisters devote themselves to teaching and to the care of the sick and aged. After the union of 1854 the congregation spread rapidly throughout Europe and elsewhere. By 1964 there were houses in Europe, England, Ireland, Scotland, North and South America, and in the mission fields of Ethiopia, Madagascar, and Mozambique. There were six novitiates, located in France, Portugal, Scotland, Argentina, the United States, and

Ethiopia. The sisters arrived in the United States in 1911 and ministered in health care. The first foundation in the United States was established in Monroe, Louisiana. In 1966 the provincial house of the North American Province was established in Baton Rouge, Louisiana.

[R. BOYLE]

Franciscan Missionaries of St. Joseph (SMSJ) [1410]. A congregation with papal approbation (1939), founded by Cardinal Herbert VAUGHAN and Alice (Mother Mary Francis) Inghan, (d. 1890) at St. Joseph's College, Mill Hill, London, England, on Sept. 8, 1883. The sisters, popularly known as Mill Hill Sisters, have as their special purposes the domestic management of ecclesiastical colleges, teaching and medical work in the missions, and various branches of child care.

[M. T. SHARRATT]

Franciscan Missionary Sisters of Our Lady of Sorrows (OSF) [1390]. A congregation founded in China in 1939 by Bishop Raphael Angelo Palazzi, OFM. The congregation adopted its current name in 1948. In 1959, due to the threat of suppression by the Communists, Bishop Palazzi moved the sisters to Hong Kong. In 1952, under the leadership of Mother Mary Leola, the congregation moved from Hong Kong (Macao) to the United States, where it eventually established a provincial house in Beaverton, Oregon. In the United States the sisters ministered in education, retreats, and social work. In 1969 the sisters opened a mission in Taiwan. The sisters minister in retreat houses, pastoral ministry, and the missions, in Oregon, California, British Columbia, Taipei (Taiwan) and Shatin (Hong Kong).

[A. WARREN]

Franciscan Missionary Sisters of the Divine Child (FMDS) [1340]. A diocesan congregation founded on August 15, 1927, by William Turner, Bishop of Buffalo, N.Y. (1919–36). The chief purpose of the congregation is to proclaim the Gospel message through education, pastoral ministry, and spiritual guidance. The motherhouse is located in Williamsville, New York. On Dec. 4, 1957, Robert E. Lucey, archbishop of San Antonio, granted permission to organize a group of lay assistants known as the Daughters of St. Francis. Members dedicate a year or more of their lives to apostolic work.

[M. A. FASANELLO/M. KRANTZ]

Franciscan Missionary Sisters of the Immaculate Conception (OSF) [1350]. A pontifical congregation, founded in Mexico City in 1874 by Father Refugio Morales, OFM, and Dolores Vásquez (Sister Maria de la Cruz de Cristo Crucificado). Because of the religious persecution in Mexico, houses were set up in the United States in 1926 and in Central America in 1928. Worldwide the congregation is known as Hermanas Franciscanas de la Inmaculada Concepcion.

The Congregation is organized into five provinces: two in Mexico, two in Central America, and one in the United States. In 1980 the sisters opened two mission houses in Peru, South America, and in the following years it extended itself into Spain, Portugal, Rome, and Africa. In the United States province, the sisters serve in schools, hospitals, parish pastoral ministry, two homes for the aged, and a retreat house.

[M. ULLOA]

Franciscan Missionary Sisters of the Infant Jesus (FMIJ) [1360]. A congregation of pontifical right founded by Barbara (Sister Mary Joseph of the Infant Jesus) Micarelli on Dec. 25, 1879 in Aquila, Italy. The sisters ministered to the poor, the orphaned, and abandoned. After a wide expansion in Italy the sisters came to Latin America (Boliva and Peru) in the early part of the 20th century. They were established in the United States in 1961 at the invitation of Bishop Celestine Damiano, of Camden, New Jersey. Their ministry is primarily in pastoral care, evangelization, education, and health care. In the United States they serve in the dioceses of Camden and Trenton in New Jersey and Arlington in Virginia. The congregation also has foundations in the Philippines, Belgium, Germany, Albania, and Cameroon.

[R. RODDY]

Franciscan Sisters, Daughters of the Sacred Hearts of Jesus and Mary (OSF) [1240]. A congregation with papal approbation, founded in 1860 by Mother Maria Clara Pfaender in Salzkotten, Germany. The sisters are engaged in educational, nursing, pastoral and social services, and spiritual renewal in Germany, France, Holland, Indonesia, Brazil, Nigeria, Malawi, Rumania, and the United States. The ministry of the sisters has varied according to the needs of time and place. In Europe through the years they have undertaken nursing in hospitals, in homes, and even on the battlefields. They have also served in various phases of teaching and the sheltering of the aged and orphans.

The U.S. province—with headquarters in Wheaton, Illinois, since 1947—dates from 1872, when Rev. E. A. Schindel of St. Louis, Missouri, sought to establish a hospital in St. Louis. His request came when the stringent laws of the Kulturkampf made a U.S. foundation desirable for the welfare of the larger congregation. In 1875 five more sisters bound for the United States mission drowned when the German steamer *Deutschland* ran aground in a storm off the coast of England. The faith and heroism of these sisters during the crisis are immortalized in the poem ''The Wreck of the *Deutschland*,'' by Gerard Manley HOPKINS.

The work of the community in the United States extended to the states of Missouri, Iowa, Indiana, Illinois, Wisconsin, and Colorado. The generalate of the congregation is located in Rome.

[M. M. KEEVEN/D. ANDERSON]

Franciscan Sisters of Allegany (OSF) [1180]. At the request of John Timon, CM, first bishop of the Diocese of Buffalo, N.Y., four friars were commissioned to serve in the diocese by the Minister General of the Order of Friars Minor. In 1855 the four friars arrived in Ellicottville, N.Y., accompanied by Nicholas Devereaux, their benefactor.

The friars' missionary duties expanded to many towns and villages, prompting Bishop Timon to invite Father Pamfilo da Magliano, OSF, superior of the little band of missionaries, to seek the aid of the Sisters of the Third Order.

On April 25, 1859, Father Pamfilo founded the Franciscan Sisters of Allegany. On that date he received Mary Jane Todd, a Franciscan Tertiary, as the first novice and gave her the religious name Sister Mary Joseph. The ceremony took place in the Chapel of St. Bonaventure College and Seminary, Allegany, N.Y.

Mary Anne O'Neil (Sister Mary Theresa), the third novice received by Father Pamfilo, was elected the first general superior. She served in this capacity for 52 years though not consecutively. Mother Teresa established some 38 foundations in education and health care ministries. She is considered the co-foundress of the congregation. With the assistance of Diomede Cardinal Falconio, OFM, Mother Teresa received final approbation of the congregation by Pope St. Pius X in 1913.

The Allegany Sisters are the first congregation of women religious founded in the United States to go to the foreign missions. In 1879 two sisters went to the British West Indies (Jamaica); in 1946 and 1965 the sisters went to Brazil and Bolivia respectively. By the late 1990s, the sisters were co-foundresses of native Franciscan congregations in Brazil and Bolivia.

[G. E. DONOVAN]

Franciscan Sisters of Baltimore (OSF) [1200]. The Franciscan Sisters of Baltimore (also known as the Franciscan Sisters of Mill Hill), had their origin in 1868 when five sisters of the Church of England, under the leadership of Mary Basil, were received into the Catholic Church by Reverend (later Cardinal) Herbert Vaughan of Westminster. As members of the Society of St. Margaret, they had been working for the poor in the slums of East London, England. In the year of their reception as Franciscans in 1870, they resumed this same activity. Three years later they established a motherhouse at Mill Hill, London, with Mary Basil (Mother Mary Francis) as superior. Obtaining papal approval in 1880, they were known as the Franciscan Sisters of St. Mary, Mill Hill.

At the request of Vaughan and Archbishop James Gibbons (later James Cardinal Gibbons of Baltimore), four sisters arrived in the city in 1881. In 1882 they took charge of St. Elizabeth Home and St. Francis Xavier School for African-American children. In 1885, with the help of additional sisters, their educational work was extended to Richmond, Virginia, and in 1889 to Norfolk, Virginia. Until the end of segregation in 1954, the sisters were engaged solely in the African-American apostolate. From the beginning of their apostolate in the United States, the congregation was incorporated under the title of Franciscan Sisters of Baltimore. In 1902 Vaughan again requested the help of sisters to assist the Mill Hill Missionaries in the Vicariate of the Upper Nile in Africa. Leading this venture was Mother Mary Paul Murphy of New York. In 1952 this mission group became a separate community known as the Franciscan Missionary Sisters for Africa.

In 1954 the original congregation transferred the general motherhouse from Mill Hill to Baltimore, and in 1982 the Franciscan Sisters of Baltimore became an independent papal congregation. The sisters are presently engaged in a variety of ministries: education, social service, catechesis, pastoral ministry, and retreat work.

[S. J. KENNET-DAWSON]

Franciscan Sisters of Chicago (OSF) [1210]. A congregation with papal approbation (1939) founded Dec. 8, 1894, in Chicago, Illinois. The foundress, Josephine Dudzik (Mother Mary Theresa, 1860–1918) was a Franciscan tertiary and a prefect of the 3,000-member St. Stanislaus Kostka Rosary Sodality Society in Chicago. She dedicated herself to alleviating the misery of the poor and the aged whom she observed through the windows of her workshop while engaged in professional tailoring. Her plan to organize her tertiary companions who were willing to join her in a common life of prayer and work was confided to her friend, the superior of the parish tertiaries, Rose Wisinska (1850–1917), who later became co-foundress as Mother Mary Anna. At a meeting of the Third Order members on Oct. 1, 1893, the plan was presented and the group of women gathered in November of 1894. Guided by her pastor and spiritual director, Father Vincent Barzynski, CR (1838–99), Josephine promised never to abandon this congregation. Despite many hardships, she persevered in organizing the new religious family and was successful in inspiring her followers with her ideals of charity and self-sacrifice. Mother Mary Theresa Dudzik was named Venerable in 1994.

The Sisters continue to minister in education, healthcare, pastoral and social service and sponsor eldercare facilities and services in the Archdiocese of Chicago, Ill.; Cleveland, Ohio; Joliet, Ill.; Lafayette, Ind., and Louisville, Ky.

[M. C. LAWRENCE/F. C. RADKE]

Franciscan Sisters of Christian Charity (OSF) [1230]. A Congregation founded in 1869 by Theresa Gramlich, Rosa Wahl, and three companions in Manitowoc, Wisconsin, under the guidance of Rev. Joseph Fessler, to meet the catechetical and educational needs of the area. Within a few years the ministry of the sisters included health care. Primary concerns for the religious and professional formation of its members led the Congregation to establish Holy Family Academy and Normal School at the Motherhouse, Holy Family Convent. Manitowoc, in 1885. This school was the forerunner of Holy Family College, now Silver Lake College, a four-year, co-educational, liberal arts and professional college, founded in 1935, and sponsored by the congregation.

In the mid-1930s the Sisters began missionary work in the southwestern part of the United States, where they accepted eight schools on Native American reservations in Arizona. In 1964 they accepted a foreign mission in Lima, Peru. Since the 1960s, the Congregation, in addition to its educational and health care ministries, has responded to the growing needs of the Church by extending its services to include hospital pastoral ministry, various forms of parish ministry, service to African Americans, Latinos, immigrant peoples, and to the poor and needy. Members serve in numerous dioceses and archdioceses throughout the United States and in Lima, Peru.

[D. M. KESSLER]

Franciscan Sisters of Little Falls, Minn. (OSF) [1310]. A Franciscan congregation established in the Diocese of St. Cloud in 1891 by 16 women who were formerly associated with the Missionary Franciscan Sisters of the Immaculate Conception. The community is made up of associates and vowed members. Ministries include care of the sick and aged, education, parish and retreat ministries, spiritual direction, and social services. Sponsored ministries include Clare's Well, a spirituality farm; the Spiritual Center, a sabbatical program for men and women religious; St. Francis Music Center and St. Francis Health and Recreation Center.

[J. WELLE]

Franciscan Sisters of Mary (FSM) [1415]. The Franciscan Sisters of Mary came into being in 1987 with the reuniting of the Sisters of St. Mary (SSM), St. Louis, Mo., and the Sisters of St. Francis (OSF), Maryville, Mo. Both congregations had a common founding in 1872 by Mary Odilia Berger. This first congregation was known as the Sisters of St. Mary. In 1894, seven SSM, guided by Mary Augustine Giesen, formed a new religious congregation known as the Sisters of St. Francis of Maryville, Missouri. In 1987, after many years of prayerful study, the two congregations reunited. The ministry of the congregation embraces varied expressions of compassion and healing, including health care, pastoral services, homeless teens with children, birth center and hospitality to women. From the foundation center in St. Louis, Missouri, the sisters serve in the United States and Brazil.

[J. MOTZEL]

Franciscan Sisters of Mary Immaculate (FMI) [1500]. A congregation with papal approbation (1933). Although the sisters established their motherhouse in Colombia in 1893, the community had begun in Ecuador in 1888, when seven sisters from Switzerland, led by Mother Caritas Brader (1860–1943), went there to engage in teaching. Unfavorable political conditions forced them to move to Colombia. The congregation subsequently established schools and missions in Panama, Costa Rica, Ecuador, Peru, Mexico, Guatamala, El Salvador, Honduras, Cuba, Africa, Romania, and the United States. The sisters are engaged in teaching, nursing, catechetics, domestic work, and the staffing of charitable institutions. In 1932 they were invited to Amarillo, Texas, by Bishop Rudolph A. Gerken (1927–1943). The United States headquarters and novitiate are located in Amarillo, Texas. The sisters are represented in the Dioceses of Amarillo, Tex., and in the archdioceses of Santa Fe and Los Angeles. Mother Caritas Brader was declared venerable in 1999.

[M. N. ROONEY]

Franciscan Sisters of Oldenburg (OSF) [1720]. On Jan. 6, 1851, a Franciscan religious from Vienna, Austria, Sister Theresa Hackelmeier, joined Father Joseph Rudolph, pastor at Oldenburg, Ind., to help him begin a school for the children of his German immigrant parishioners. Three postulants awaited her arrival. A log cabin convent, a school for girls, and a home for orphans were built.

Despite a devastating fire in 1857, the congregation grew and staffed numerous elementary schools in southern Indiana. The first school outside Indiana opened in St. Louis, Mo., in 1859. Expansion followed in Kentucky, Ohio, Illinois, and Kansas. In 1892 the sisters took up the education of African-American children, first in Indianapolis, Ind., and later, in 1911, in Kansas City, Mo. The sisters began work with the Spanish-speaking people of

New Mexico in 1918. In answer to an appeal from the Jesuits in Montana, the Congregation accepted two missions on the Crow Indian Reservation in 1934. Five years later, six sisters began a mission in Wuchang, China. In 1960 the sisters accepted missions in Papua New Guinea.

Currently, the sisters are engaged in a variety of ministries, mainly in education and catechesis, as well as pastoral ministry to the poor and marginalized.

[F. KENNEDY]

Franciscan Sisters of Our Lady of Lourdes (OSF) [1710]. A congregation with papal approbation, founded in 1877 by Maria Catherine (Mother Alfred) Moes (1828–1899) and her sister, Catherine (Sister Barbara) Moes. They came to the United States from Remich, Luxembourg, intending to teach and first resided with the School Sisters of Notre Dame in Milwaukee, Wis. In 1856 they entered the Marianite Sisters of the Holy Cross at Notre Dame, Indiana.

When differences arose between the European and American branches of that community, Mother Alfred and three other sisters petitioned Father Pamfilo da Magliano, OFM, of Allegany, N.Y., to receive them as Franciscans. They adopted the Franciscan habit June 1, 1863, and became known as the Franciscan Sisters of Joliet, Illinois. Two years later they established a Congregation with Mother Alfred as general superior. Shortly after Mother Alfred left office, she responded to an invitation to establish an academy in Minnesota. She succeeded in opening two academies in 1877 in the towns of Owatonna and Rochester, Minn. Bishop Thomas Foley of Chicago (1870–79) expressed concern over the transfer of sisters to Minnesota in a letter to the superior at Joliet on Dec. 23, 1877. He wrote that Mother Alfred could not return to Joliet, and declared that the other sisters would have to choose between Joliet and Rochester. By the end of the month, 24 sisters had decided to join Mother Alfred.

With the approval of Bishop Thomas Grace of St. Paul, Minn., the Franciscan Sisters of the Congregation of Our Lady of Lourdes became a separate foundation in Rochester. The sisters continued classroom and music instruction in the academies and accepted invitations to work in parish schools. In 1894 they opened the Winona Seminary for Young Ladies, an academy for the elementary and secondary education of girls. In 1907, college courses were offered at the seminary; five years later it was chartered as the College of Saint Teresa, which remained in operation until 1989.

Although originally teachers, the sisters also began nursing after a tornado struck Rochester in 1883. In 1889 Saint Mary's Hospital, built by the sisters and staffed by Dr. W. W. Mayo and his sons, opened. Later additions made it one of the largest privately owned hospitals in the United States. In 1986 Saint Mary's, under the continued sponsorship of the sisters, became part of the Mayo Medical Center.

For many years the sisters also conducted hospitals in Ohio and Colorado and homes for the aged in Minnesota. Responding to the call of Pope John XXIII, in 1962 they began to minister in Latin America, including the founding of a colegio in Bogota, Colombia, where they continue to minister today. Since 1955 the Congregational Center has been at Assisi Heights in Rochester. The sisters serve throughout the United States and in Columbia, South America.

[M. L. REILLY]

Franciscan Sisters of Our Lady of Perpetual Help (OSF) [1430]. A congregation with papal approbation (1939) founded in St. Louis, Mo., on May 29, 1901. The cofounders, Mother M. Solana Leczna (1867–1919), Mother M. Ernestine Matz (1873–1957), and Mother M. Hilaria Matz (1881–1948), were members of the Franciscan Sisters of Joliet, Illinois. At the beginning of the 20th century, the purpose of the new congregation was to meet the needs of immigrants, particularly of Polish descent, settling in the Mississippi and Missouri Valleys. The sisters serve in about seventeen states in pastoral care, teaching, health care, youth ministry, and social services.

[M. I. JANOTA/A. P. WILKEN]

Franciscan Sisters of Peace (FSP) [1425]. A diocesan institute (Archdiocese of New York) established in 1986. The founding 112 sisters of this institute had been members of the Franciscan Missionary Sisters of the Sacred Heart of St. Francis (Peekskill, N.Y.). The sisters trace the roots of their charism to that of their European founders: Gertrude Paul, Constanza Huber and Pellegrina Santelamezza, who founded the Tertiary Franciscans for Apostolic Mission in Gemona, Italy, on Dec. 5, 1865. (The congregation later became known as the Franciscan Missionary Sisters of the Sacred Heart.) The sisters minister in education, health care, and pastoral ministry in the eastern United States. Their congregational center is located in Haverstraw, N.Y.

[R. RODDY]

Franciscan Sisters of Penance and Charity of Tiffin, Ohio (OSF) [1760]. This congregation was founded as a diocesan community in 1869 by Joseph Bihn, pastor of St. Joseph Church in Tiffin, and by Elizabeth Schaefer, a widow from the same parish. The original purpose of the community was to provide a home for orphans and the elderly following the U.S. Civil War. As the number of sisters gradually increased, the scope of their ministry extended to include teaching, hospital work, care of pilgrims and retreatants, pastoral ministry, and missionary work in the United States and Mexico. The orphanage was phased out in the 1930s but St. Francis Home for the elderly remains a vibrant institution, providing acute care, assisted living, and independent living for the elderly. Papal approbation was requested in 1955 and initial approval was granted by the Holy See in 1962. In their general assembly of 1994 the sisters agreed to focus their concerted efforts on living out the goals of contemplation/action, care of creation, peacemaking, and concern for the poor.

[H. LINDER]

Franciscan Sisters of St. Joseph of Hamburg, New York (FSSJ) [1470]. A congregation with papal approbation founded in 1897 by Mother M. Colette Hilbert (1865–1938) in Trenton, N.J. In 1898 Mother M. Colette established the community's motherhouse and a school near Corpus Christi Church, Buffalo, N.Y. In 1928 the motherhouse was transferred to its present site in Hamburg, N.Y. The congregation engages in education, health care, and social service ministries in several dioceses throughout the United States. The congregation sponsors Immaculata Academy, a high school for young women in Hamburg and Marycrest Manor, a skilled nursing facility in Livonia, Mich., and Hubert College, a four-year college in Hamburg.

[P. TIRONE]

Franciscan Sisters of the Atonement (SA) [1190]. A congregation with papal approbation, commonly known as the Graymoor or Atonement Sisters. The Society of the Atonement, composed of the Friars and Sisters of the Atonement, was founded at Graymoor, Garrison, N.Y., in 1898 by Rev. Paul James WATTSON and Mother Lurana Mary White, both of whom were then members of the Episcopal Church. In 1908, Father Paul inaugurated the Chair of Unity Octave, now called the Week of Prayer for Christian Unity. In October of 1909, the Friars and Sisters were corporately received into the Roman Catholic Church with the permission of Pope Pius X. The Society honors Mary under the title of Our Lady of the Atonement.

The word ATONEMENT indicates the twofold vocation of the Society: through a life of prayer, work, and sacrifice, they seek to atone for sin and to draw all persons to union, ''atonement'' with God, in the spirit of Christ's prayer, ''That all may be one'' (Jn 17:21). The congregation is involved in a variety of ministries: ecumenism; religious education and catechetical ministries; social welfare and community development; health care; hospital chaplaincies; pastoral ministry; home visitation; adult social day care; child day care and kindergartens; youth ministry; justice and peace work; and guest and retreat houses. The sisters minister in the United States, Canada, Ireland, Italy, Japan, Brazil, and South Africa.

[M. F. FLANIGAN/A. GRIFFITTS]

Franciscan Sisters of the Poor (SFP) [1440]. A papal congregation begun in Aachen, Germany, on Oct. 3, 1845, by Frances Schervier (1819–1876) for service to the sick and the poor. By 1851 Mother Frances Schervier and 23 companions professed a rule of life based on the Rule of the Third Order Regular of St. Francis. Mother Frances and her companions were noted for their compassionate response to the needs of the time. In 1858 six sisters arrived in Cincinnati, Ohio, at the invitation of Mrs. Sarah Peter, a wealthy widow, to begin the congregation's ministry in health care in the United States. Those pioneer sisters were responsible for building many hospitals, nursing during the U.S. Civil War, and maintaining an orphanage after the war. As time passed, numerous hospitals were established in the Midwest and Eastern parts of the United States. In April 1959, by decree of the Sacred Congregation for Religious, the Congregation of the Sisters of the Poor of St. Francis was officially divided into two autonomous religious congregations, each of Pontifical Right. The sisters in the United States and Italy became known as the Franciscan Sisters of the Poor. In 1960 and later in 1978 the Franciscan Sisters of the Poor established ministries in Brazil and Senegal. The sisters' vision of healing and hope continues today through their healing ministry to the sick and the poor.

International leadership is located in Brooklyn, N.Y., with regional leadership based in Cincinnati, Ohio, Rome, Italy, and Goiania, Go, Brazil. Frances Schervier was beatified on April 28, 1974 by Pope Paul VI.

[M. L. SAHM]

Franciscan Sisters of the Sacred Heart (OSF) [1450]. A congregation with papal approbation (1898) whose motherhouse is in Frankfort, Ill. This community stems from a congregation founded in Baden, Germany, by Rev. Wilhelm Berger in 1866. Berger, pastor of the village church of Seelbach, began the congregation to serve the poor and the sick in their homes. The first motherhouse, known as Maria Hilf, was established in 1867. Despite the services rendered by the sisters in 18 military hospitals during the Franco-Prussian War, the hostile measures of Bismarck's Kulturkampf forced the community to seek missions outside of Germany. The need for sisters in the United States was brought to the attention of Mother M. Anastasia Bischler, the first superior general (1874–1908), by Rev. Dominic Duehmig, pastor of St. Mary's Church, Avilla, Ind., who at that time was visiting his native Germany.

On May 17, 1876, Mother Anastasia and three companions sailed for the United States and were welcomed to the Diocese of Fort Wayne, Ind., by Bishop Joseph Dwenger (1872–93). Later that year 23 more sisters came to the United States where they eventually formed an independent congregation: the Franciscan Sisters of the Sacred Heart. Their first headquarters was established on a run-down farm in Duehmig's parish in Avilla. The farmhouse was remodeled to accommodate the sisters and to serve elderly persons who were given shelter in what came to be known as the Sacred Heart Home for the Aged. In 1883 the motherhouse and novitiate were transferred to Joliet, Ill.; the novitiate (1953); and the motherhouse (1964) were moved to St. Francis Woods in Frankfort, Ill. The sisters' first educational institution, a public elementary school, was opened in Avilla in 1877. Two more schools followed at Hessen Cassel, Ind. (1878), and Dyer, Ind. (1879). Further foundations, both schools and hospitals, were made in Indiana and Illinois before the end of the 19th century. By 1963 the community had extended its work into California.

Bibliography: M. HEIMBUCHER, *Die Orden und Kongregationen der katholischen Kirche*, 2 v. (3d. ed Paderborn 1932–34) 2:36.

[M. A. BRITTON]

Franciscan Sisters of the Sorrowful Mother (SSM) [4100]. A congregation with papal approbation that was founded in Rome, Italy, by Mother Frances of the Cross (Amalia Streitel, 1844–1911), a native of Mellrichstadt, Germany. Having been educated by the Franciscan Sisters of Maria Stern in Augsburg and having experienced religious life in both Franciscan and Carmelite convents, she went to Rome in 1883 at the request of Father Franziskus Maria Jordan to organize a new community of sisters. Both soon discovered that their views concerning the foundation were divergent. The conflict was resolved in 1885 when the cardinal vicar of Rome, Lucido Maria Parocchi (1883–1903), appointed as spiritual director of the small community Rev. Dr. George Jacquemin (d. 1920) and named the new congregation Sisters of the Sorrowful Mother. A rented dwelling close to St. Peter's Basilica became the first motherhouse in Rome. In accord with the instruction and example of their foundress, the sisters practice special devotion to Our Lady under the title of Sorrowful Mother.

From Italy the community spread to Germany, Austria, the West Indies, and the United States, where the first foundation (St. Francis Hospital) was made in 1889 in Wichita, Kansas. The sisters also have missions in Wisconsin, Minnesota, New Jersey, and Oklahoma. The Sisters of the Sorrowful Mother sponsor the Marian Health System and minister as educators, chaplains, social workers, counselors, pastoral associates, and retreat directors. The congregation is divided into two provinces, a European province and a United States-Caribbean province, with its generalate in Rome, Italy. The foundress's cause for beatification is in process.

[D. DIRKX]

Hospital Sisters of the Third Order of St. Francis (OSF) [1820]. A congregation with papal approbation, founded in Münster, Germany, in 1844 by Father Christopher Behrensmeyer. The founder had belonged to the Order of Friars Minor until 1811, when his order was dispersed during the Napoleonic conquest. The congregation was founded on July 2, 1844, at the Shrine of Our Lady of Telgte, near Münster. The sisters began their work in the homes of the sick and in hospitals that they established for the physically and mentally ill. At the time of Father Christopher's death on June 2, 1858, there were ten hospitals in Germany and Silesia. Later the sisters extended their apostolate to Poland, Holland, Czechoslovakia, the United States, China, and Japan.

Twenty sisters arrived in New York in 1875. Under the direction of the Bishop of Alton, Ill., they proceeded into various parts of Illinois to carry on their nursing activities. St. John's Hospital, in Springfield, Ill., became the center for the religious and professional training of the sisters. In 1930 the sisters transferred their provincial motherhouse to a site about six miles northeast of Springfield, Ill. Msgr. Joseph Straub, as director of the community, supervised the construction of the new headquarters, which includes St. Francis of Assisi Church and St. Clare of Assisi Adoration Chapel.

At the present time the American province sponsors thirteen hospitals that comprise Hospital Sisters Health System. The sisters of the American province are also represented in Germany, Poland, the Czech Republic, Japan, Korea, and India.

[M. C. KELLEY/M. O'CONNOR]

Missionary Franciscan Sisters of the Immaculate Conception (MFIC) [1360]. An apostolic Institute of pontifical right founded in 1873 by Elizabeth (Mother Mary Ignatius) Hayes (1821–94), a convert from Anglicanism. She founded the first mission of the congregation in Belle Prairie, Minn., in 1873 and the second mission five years later in Augusta, Ga. The sisters serve among the poor and marginalized in some eleven countries in social services, education, and catechetical instruction. Provincial houses are located in Newton, Mass.; Montreal, Canada; Brisbane, Australia; and Aitape, Papua New

Guinea. Missions currently are in Ireland, England, Egypt, Bolivia, Peru, and Chad.

[G. FOYSTER]

Missionary Sisters of the Immaculate Conception of the Mother of God (SMIC) [2760]. The Missionary Sisters of the Immaculate Conception of the Mother of God were founded in 1910 in Santaém, Párá, Brazil, by Bishop Amando Bablmann, OFM, and Mother Immaculata of Jesus (Elizabeth Tombrock) together with four Brazilian Conceptionist nuns of the Ajuda Monastery in Rio de Janeiro. The new foundation, designated a branch of the Conceptionist Order, was named the Missionary Poor Clares of the Immaculate Conception. The Conceptionist Rule was followed until 1922 when a decree of reorganization was issued by the Holy See. The Rule of the Third Order of St. Francis was adopted in 1925, and in 1929 the order was granted the status of an apostolic congregation of pontifical right and given the name Missionary Sisters of the Immaculate Conception of the Mother of God. The generalate was transferred from Brazil to the United States in 1924.

Initially, the congregation served the people of the Amazon Region of Northern Brazil, mainly through the education of youth. The congregation spread to other areas of Brazil; to Germany (1915); the United States (1922); China (1931); and later to Taiwan (1949); Namibia (1962); and the Philippines (1996). As an international community with a missionary charism, the congregation encourages and promotes collaboration and exchange among the provinces, but mission experiences are sought primarily in the country of origin. The focus of ministry includes rural and urban health care, education at various levels, pastoral care, and social work.

Bibliography: D. FLOOD, OFM, *Room for One More* (Saco Printing Co. 1993). F. L. LAUGHLIN, *As a Seal on My Heart* (West Paterson, N.J. 1992).

[R. C. GONZALEZ]

Missionary Sisters of the Third Order of St. Francis (FMSC) [1400]. A congregation with papal approbation, this community, whose motherhouse is located in Rome and whose work is in education and the missions, was founded in 1860 at Gemona, Italy. Under the guidance of Father Gregorio Fiorvante dalle Grotte di Castro, OFM, the new community was endowed for a time by a French duchess, Laura Leroux, who wished to place her patrimony in the service of some good work.

On Dec. 9, 1865, the sisters began their work in the United States at the request of the Franciscan Friars in New York City. In 1869 they purchased the site of their provincial house and novitiate at Mt. St. Francis in Peekskill, N.Y. There they began an academy for girls, which was transferred in 1900 to Highland Falls, N.Y., and called Ladycliff Academy. Growth of the academy and of Ladycliff College (chartered in 1933) necessitated the erection of a new Ladycliff Academy at Mohegan, N.Y., in 1961.

The sisters spread their teaching apostolate into New Jersey (1871) and Pennsylvania (1874), as well as in New York State. An important phase of their work began in 1879 with the care of neglected children at St. Joseph's Home in Peekskill. In 1949 Cardinal Francis Spellman requested the sisters to assume the care and supervision of the children at Lt. Joseph P. Kennedy, Jr., Home in the Bronx, N.Y. Four sisters from the U.S. province were sent to do mission work among the native Americans of Bolivia in 1960.

The sisters are engaged in ministry in Chile, Peru, Italy, India, Cyprus, Turkey, Congo, Bolivia, France, Lebanon, Bulgaria, the Philippines, the United States, Switzerland, Lithuania, the Czech Republic, Luxembourg, Ecuador, Albania, and the Republic of Central Africa. In 1986, 115 sisters in the American province opted to start a new diocesan community. The remaining sisters carry on works in education, health care, administration, and pastoral ministry.

[M. R. CONLON]

School Sisters of St. Francis (OSF) [1680]. The School Sisters of St. Francis Congregation was founded April 28, 1874, in New Cassel, Wis., by Mother Alexia Hoell, Mother Alfons Schmid, and Sister Clara Seiter. These sisters left their community in Schwarzach, Germany, to minister to the German immigrants in America. Within the next decade, School Sisters staffed schools across the United States. By 1887 a new motherhouse was built and dedicated in Milwaukee.

The congregation is an international community working in eleven countries worldwide, mainly in the United States. Provinces are also located in Europe, India, and Central America. Sisters are involved in education, pastoral ministry, social services, health care, and the fine arts. In addition to vowed members, the community has an associates program, comprised of men and women who share in the congregation's mission.

[I. DEGER]

School Sisters of St. Francis of Christ the King (OSF) [1520]. An international congregation with papal approbation that traces its roots to the School Sisters of St. Francis of Assisi founded in Graz, Austria, in 1843. After being sent to run an academy for girls in Maribor, Austria, (now Slovenia), circumstances dictated that they form a new congregation, which became independent on

Sept. 13, 1869. This congregation later came to be known as the School Sisters of St. Francis of Christ the King. In October of 1909, four sisters arrived in the United States to work among the Slavic immigrants of the Kansas City area. The sisters expanded their ministries to serve as educators, housemothers of an orphanage, housekeepers, musicians, sacristans, cooks, and mentors. These ministries took them to the Chicago archdiocese and the Joliet diocese. In 1926 an 88-acre tract of land was purchased in Lemont, Ill. Mt. Assisi Convent, the provincial center and novitiate, Mt. Assisi Academy, Alvernia Manor, and Our Lady of the Angels House of Prayer are located on this site. Through these and a number of parishes within the archdiocese of Chicago and the Joliet diocese the sisters engage in their principal ministry, education, particularly religious education.

[T. A. QUINCY]

School Sisters of the Third Order Regular of St. Francis (OSF) [1690 Pittsburgh and 1700 Bethlehem]. The School Sisters of the Third Order Regular of St. Francis trace their roots to the community of Mother Frances (Antonia) Lampel in Graz, Austria, in 1843 and continued by Mother Hyacinth (Magdalene) Zahalka in a new foundation in Bohemia in 1888. Originally founded for the education and Christian formation of young women in Austria and Bohemia the sisters soon embraced other ministries as the needs of the Church grew. On Oct. 30, 1911, Mother Hyacinth, accompanied by Sister Georgia Cerney, sailed for America but died in Pittsburgh on March 10, 1912. The new general superior, Mother Xavier Furgott, came to Pittsburgh in May of 1913 to initiate plans for a future foundation. On Aug. 15, 1913, six sisters arrived in America and began staffing schools in parishes of the diocese of Pittsburgh. In 1946 the community in Pittsburgh received the status of a province.

In 1957, because of increased membership and numerous vocations from the eastern part of Pennsylvania, the province was divided into two provinces: the Pittsburgh Province, serving western Pennsylvania, and the Bethlehem Province, serving eastern Pennsylvania, New Jersey, and Massachusetts. Presently, the Pittsburgh Province ministers in western Pennsylvania, Texas, and Arizona. The Bethlehem province serves the eastern United States. Changes and adaptations following Vatican II resulted in the broadening of areas of ministry. The sisters respond to the needs of today's Church through ministries in education, parish social ministry, pastoral ministry, retreat work and spiritual direction, and pastoral care. Today the congregation has provinces in Rome, Czech Republic, Slovak Republic, and the United States (Pittsburgh and Bethlehem, Pennsylvania). Sisters also minister in Chile, South Africa, Aima-Ata, Kazakstan, and Warsaw, Poland. They have a Formation House in Kerala, India.

[F. PARANA]

Sisters of St. Felix of Cantalice. See separate entry under that heading.

Sisters of St. Francis, Clinton, Iowa (OSF) [1540]. Near the end of the Civil War, a young widow named Caroline Cambron Warren visited the Trappist Abbey in Gethsemani, Ky. While there, she was asked by the abbot to conduct a school for poor girls. She agreed and was employed immediately. By the time the school session began in May of 1863, Mrs. Warren had been joined by her niece, Sally Walker. In 1864, Lizzie Lillis joined the other two. The three began to live a communal life of work and prayer. Shortly thereafter, Mrs. Warren was received as a Franciscan tertiary, and on Jan. 21, 1866, all three women became Franciscan tertiaries. After the ceremony, Bishop Lavialle of Louisville, Ky., declared that the Sisters of the Third Order of St. Francis was established with his approbation. Abbot Benedict Berger was appointed their spiritual director.

Abbot Benedict's first endeavor was to see that the sisters were trained properly. He persuaded Mother Antonia of the Oldenburg Franciscans to set up a separate novitiate for these women, and nine women entered the separate novitiate in Oldenburg, Ind. After completing their studies, the sisters made vows for a year and returned to Gethsemani in 1868. The abbot had built a new motherhouse and school named Mount Olivet, not far from Gethsemani Abbey, but Bishop McCloskey prevailed upon the sisters to move to Shelbyville, Ky. Our Lady of Angels Academy opened there in 1874. The school in Shelbyville was recognized as a superior institution, but there were many academies in the area and the school was located in an area that was very anti-Catholic. The sisters' welfare did not improve, and many times they had to resort to begging just to provide a little food.

In spite of the hardships, women continued to ask admittance, and schools were opened in Fancy Farm, Hardinsburg, Knottsville, Lebanon, Louisville, St. Mary's, and Whitesville, Ky. In 1888 two Jesuit priests gave a mission at Shelbyville and, seeing the destitute situation of the sisters, urged them to apply for acceptance into the diocese of Dubuque, Iowa. On Sept. 21, 1890, the first twelve sisters left for Iowa.

Upon reaching Iowa, some of the sisters went directly to the schools where they were to teach. Those sisters not yet employed were graciously given food and lodging by the Dubuque Franciscan Sisters. On Jan. 6, 1891, the last of the sisters left Dubuque for Anamosa, where the motherhouse was to be established. In 1891, Rev. James Murray, pastor of St. Patrick Parish in Clinton, asked for teachers. In 1893, Father Murray was instrumental in helping the sisters obtain the Chase property in Clinton. The large building on the property became the motherhouse. It was named Mount St. Clare, and Mount St. Clare Academy was opened on the premises. New property was purchased, and a seven-storey building was built in 1910. In 1918, the school was extended to include a junior college, Mount St. Clare College. Hospitals were opened in Grinnell and Burlington, Iowa, and in Macomb, Ill. Schools of nursing were opened in Macomb and Burlington. In 1914 a health-care facility for the elderly was opened in Clinton in the first Mount St. Clare building, then called Mount Alverno Home for the Aged. The sisters staffed parish schools in many Iowa towns as well as in Illinois, Nebraska, Minnesota, Ohio, Missouri, and California. In 1960, the congregation staffed a school and clinic in Freeport, Bahamas. In 1964, four sisters went to staff a school in Chulucanas, Peru. Following the Second Vatican Council, many sisters who had been involved in education and health care turned their attention to social services, peace and justice works, pastoral ministry, campus ministry, early childhood education, AIDS ministry, legal aid to the poor, hospital chaplaincy, prison ministry, and home care for the elderly. In 1988, an associate program was inaugurated, and in 2000 a temporary commitment program was authorized.

[S. MCCARTHY]

Sisters of St. Francis Congregation of Our Lady of Lourdes (OSF) [1530]. Mother Adelaide Sandusky of the Rochester, Minnesota Franciscan Sisters, responded to the invitation of Bishop Joseph Schrembs of Toledo, Ohio, and came with 23 Sisters to minister to the educational needs of immigrants in the parishes in 1916. By 1930 the growth and development of the Ohio community brought about its separation and establishment as an autonomous diocesan congregation with Mother M. Adelaide as the first elected general superior. The generalate and corporate headquarters of the sisters is situated on an 89-acre campus in Sylvania, Ohio. Sisters' residences, Rosary Care Center, Lourdes College, St. Francis Education Center, Sophia Counseling Center, the Franciscan Center, Franciscan Services Corporation, which administers health and human services in Ohio and Texas, and Convent Park Apartments for independent senior living are located on or adjacent to the Sylvania campus. The sisters' mission extends to 15 other states.

[M. B. MROZ/K. ZIELINSKI]

Sisters of St. Francis of Assisi (OSF) [1705]. In 1849, a small band of lay Franciscans left Ettenbeuren, Bavaria, and came to America to become missionaries to the German immigrants in Wisconsin. Amidst hardship and struggles, these women organized the Sisters of St. Francis of Assisi. In their personal and corporate lives the sisters are dedicated to the Franciscan values of living simply and serving the poor, seeking personal transformation, working toward right relationships with all people through justice, respect, hospitality and peace making, and reverencing God within themselves and others and in all creation. Ministries are as diverse as the women who serve them: administrators; teachers; health-care providers; social workers and counselors; campus, prison and parish ministers; childcare workers; artists and musicians. Community members are located across the United States and in Taiwan.

The congregation sponsors Canticle Court Inc. and Juniper Court, Inc., St Francis, Wis., corporations offering affordable housing and independent living for the older adult in a community environment. Cardinal Stritch University, located in Milwaukee, Wis., is the largest Franciscan institution in the United States. Marian Center for Nonprofits leases space to nonprofit agencies that respond to human needs through education, the arts, and social justice. St. Ann Center for Inter-generational Care, also in St. Francis, Wis., is a nationally recognized non-institutional daycare alternative for persons of all ages. Shepherd Hall meets the special daycare needs of persons with dementia. St. Coletta's of Illinois, located in Palos Park, provides group home living for profoundly disabled persons, a day school, and a workshop where those with developmental challenges can learn skills needed to earn a living. St. Coletta and Cardinal Cushing Schools of Massachusetts, located in Braintree and Hanover, provide residential and educational services to school-age youngsters with developmental challenges, adult living units with vocational training, and a day school for those with severe, multiple disabilities. Cushing Residence, a funded housing complex for senior citizens located on the Hanover campus, engages services provided by students in vocational training. St. Coletta of Wisconsin, Jefferson, serves the needs of adults with disabilities. In addition, the congregation maintains Liteh Kindergarten in Taipei, Taiwan.

[M. LUNZ]

Sisters of St. Francis of Penance and Christian Charity (OSF) [1630]. A congregation with papal approbation (1869) founded in 1835 by Marie Catharina Daemen (1787–1858) in Heijthuijsen, province of Limburg, Holland. Daemen was a Franciscan tertiary engaged in works of charity at Maaseik, Belgium. In 1827 she went to Heijthuijsen, where she formed a group of tertiaries devoted to similar works. Under the direction of the local pastor, Petrus van der Zandt, and with the approval of Bp.

Cornelius van Bommel of Liège, the tertiaries assumed the Franciscan habit and formed a religious community in 1835. Daemen, now known as Mother Magdalen, became the first superior. Expansion outside Holland began in 1854 when a house was established in Germany. Subsequent foundations were made in Poland (1867), Indonesia (1870), Brazil (1872), the United States, and Tanganyika (now Tanzania; 1959). In 1874 the sisters began their work in the United States at Stella Niagara (Holy Name Province) in the diocese of Buffalo, N.Y. Two other provinces are located in Denver, Colo., (Sacred Heart Province; 1939) and Redwood City, Calif. (St. Francis Province; 1939). In 1991, the sisters of the Sacred Heart Province established a mission in Chiapas, Mexico.

Bibliography: L. MASON, *Life of Mother Magdalen* (Niagara, N.Y. 1935). M. P. JONES, *He Chose Catherine* (New York 1959). M. HEIMBUCHER, *Die Orden und Kongregationen der katholischen Kirche*, 2 v. (3d. ed Paderborn 1932–34) 2:41–42.

[M. G. MILLER]

Sisters of St. Francis of Perpetual Adoration (OSF) [1640]. A congregation with papal approbation (formerly known as the Poor Sisters of St. Francis Seraph of Perpetual Adoration) founded in 1863 by Aline (Mother Maria Theresia) Bonzel in Olpe, Westphalia, Germany, for the purpose of serving the sick, the aged, and orphans and of educating youth. The sisters maintain perpetual adoration of the Blessed Sacrament in the congregation. By the time of Mother Maria Theresia's death in 1905, the congregation had spread to several parts of Germany and to the United States. In 1930 her remains were transferred to a special crypt at the general motherhouse in Olpe, and her cause for beatification has since been introduced in Rome. The sisters came to the United States because of the oppressive laws of the Kulturkampf. On Dec. 14, 1875, six sisters arrived in Lafayette, Ind., at the invitation of Joseph Dwenger, Bishop of Fort Wayne. In 1886 the foundations made in Indiana, Nebraska, and Ohio were constituted as an American province. In 1932 the whole congregation was divided into four provinces: two in Germany and two in the United States. Since 1993 there are four provinces: St. Elizabeth Province, Cologne, Germany, the Immaculate Heart of Mary Province, for the area east of the Mississippi River, with its headquarters in Mishawaka, Ind., the St. Joseph province, for the western states, with its headquarters in Colorado Springs, Colo., and the Immaculate Conception province, Baybay, Leyte, Philippines.

[M. F. PETERS/C. GENTRUP]

Sisters of St. Francis of Philadelphia (OSF) [1650]. The Sisters of St. Francis of Philadelphia, formerly known as the Glen Riddle Franciscans, were founded in 1855 by Mother Mary Francis (Anna Maria) Bachmann, Sister Margaret (Barbara) Boll and Sister Bernardine (Anna) Dorn with the support of St. John Neumann, Bishop of Philadelphia, Pa. They became the first American community of Franciscan women following the Third Order Regular Rule of St. Francis. Throughout their history, they have been dedicated to serve the poor, the marginalized, and oppressed, directly and indirectly, by ministering in the United States, the Carribean, Central America, Europe, and Africa. Ministries include education, spiritual direction and pastoral care, health care, and counseling. Five other congregations: the Sisters of the Third Franciscan Order (Syracuse, N.Y.; 1860); Sisters of St. Francis of the Third Order Regular (Williamsville, N.Y.; 1863); the Sisters of St. Francis of the Immaculate Virgin Mary Mother of God (Millvale, Pa.; 1871); the Sisters of St. Francis of the Immaculate Virgin (Hastings-on-Hudson, N.Y.; 1893); and the Sisters of St. Francis of the Providence of God (Pittsburgh, Pa.; 1922), trace their roots to the Sisters of St. Francis of Philadelphia.

[E. KULAEZ]

Sisters of St. Francis of Savannah, Missouri (OSF) [1670]. The origin of this congregation of sisters began in Vöcklabruck, Austria, where the sisters provided day nurseries for children whose parents worked in factories. In 1850 Fr. Sebastian Schwarz organized a group of women who formed a community of sisters under the leadership of Mother Franziska Wimmer. As the community grew it branched out to other charitable services. In August of 1922, upon invitation from the Benedictines in Conception, Mo., twelve of these sisters came to Conception. The first superior and foundress was Mother Pia Feitenschlager. In 1935 the community moved to Chillicothe, Mo., and remained there until the purchase of the Dr. Nichols' Sanatorium in Savannah, Mo., in 1957. With the move to Savannah they established La Verna Heights Retirement Center, a nursing home for women. Besides the care of the elderly and infirm, the sisters established Subasio Center in the Provincial House for the care of persons with HIV/AIDS. The sisters remain involved in the education of adults and children and in various other social works.

Bibliography: M. A. SPAK, *Die Armen Schulschwestern vom Dritten Orden des hl. Franziskus zu Voecklabruck* (Vienna 1950).

[K. REICHART]

Sisters of St. Francis of the Holy Cross (OSF) [1550]. A diocesan congregation founded in 1874 by Edward Francis Daems, OSC, a missionary who worked in northeastern Wisconsin from 1851 to 1879. Fr. Daems established a religious society of women to assist in ministering to the Catholics who were immigrating from Canada and Europe. The community had its beginning in the work of Christine Rousseau, Pauline LaPlant, and Mary Pius Doyle, who in 1868 staffed a new parish school at Bay Settlement, Wis. They and a fourth woman were received into the Third Order of St. Francis in 1874 and were granted episcopal approbation by Bishop Francis Xavier Krautbauer of Green Bay in 1881. The sisters continue their work with new immigrants while continuing their ministries in education, health care, and pastoral work in Wisconsin and Nicaragua.

[D. SHALLOW/U. SCHUMACHER]

Sisters of St. Francis of the Holy Eucharist of Independence, Missouri (OSF) [1560]. A diocesan congregation established in 1893 in the diocese of Kansas City-St. Joseph and dedicated to the works of the active apostolate. The sisters trace their origin from the Franciscan convent of Grimmenstein, Switzerland, begun in 1378. In the latter part of the 19th century, five sisters, led by Mother M. John Hau, came to the United States to settle in Nevada, Mo. In 1900 they became an independent community with their own motherhouse and novitiate. In 1977 a mission was opened in Rodrigues Alves, Acre, Brazil, and in 1982 the motherhouse was moved to Independence, Missouri.

[M. J. PETERS]

Sisters of St. Francis of the Holy Family (OSF) [1570]. A congregation with papal approbation whose motherhouse is located at Mount St. Francis, Dubuque, Iowa (established in 1878). The community was founded in Herford, Germany, by Mother Xavier (Josephine Termehr, d. 1892) and approved by Bp. Konrad Martin of Paderborn in 1864. During the 11 years that the congregation existed in Germany the sister cared for children at Haus Bethlehem, a Herford orphanage, and nursed wounded soldiers during the Austro-Prussian and Franco-Prussian Wars. In recognition of their services, the King of Prussia, William I, awarded the sisters the Iron Cross in 1872, but only three years later Bismarck's Kulturkampf forced them to leave Germany and go to the United States. The exiled community sailed from Rotterdam on the *Caland* and landed in New York on Sept. 5, 1875. The little band, comprised of Mother Xavier, 17 sisters, seven novices, and four postulants, went directly to Iowa City, Iowa, where they staffed the German department of St. Joseph's Institute in 1875 and opened Mount St. Mary's Orphanage in 1876. Their stay in Iowa City terminated in 1878, when the community transferred to Dubuque to open the diocesan orphanage. In 1880 they built their first motherhouse; in 1925 a new and larger motherhouse was erected on the present site. The sisters serve numerous dioceses throughout the United States, as well as Africa and Central America.

[M. R. ROSEMEYER/D. HEIDERSCHEIT]

Sisters of St. Francis of the Immaculate Conception (OSF) [1580]. A diocesan congregation established in 1890 when Mother Mary Pacifica Forrestal (1859–1948) and four companions assumed directorship of the diocesan orphanage in Metamora, Ill., at the request of John Lancaster Spalding, Bishop of Peoria. As the community grew the sisters' ministry extended to elementary education and care of the aging. The congregation is involved in teaching, parish work, care of the elderly, religious education, social work, hospital chaplaincy, retreats, spiritual direction, adult literacy, and prison ministry. These ministries are based in the dioceses of Peoria, Springfield, and Joliet, Ill., with a mission on Standing Rock Indian Reservation in the diocese of Rapid City, South Dakota.

[V. BUTKOVICH]

Sisters of St. Francis of the Immaculate Heart of Mary (OSF) [1590]. A congregation with papal approbation (1943) whose generalate is in Dillingen an der Donau, Bavaria, Germany. In the United States, the provincialate is located in Hankinson, N. Dak. The community traces its origin to a group of women (perhaps originally BEGUINES) whom Count Hartmann of Dillingen endowed with a convent in 1241. These religious adopted the rule of the Franciscan Third Order and led a strictly cloistered life for the greater part of their early history. Then, in 1774, the community changed to a semicloistered form of life and began educating girls. In 1913 the community sent sisters to the United States, where they opened a convent at Collegeville, Minn., in 1913. The provincial motherhouse in the United States was established in Hankinson, N. Dak., in 1928. After 1936 the congregation expanded from Dillingen to Brazil, Switzerland, Spain, Italy, India, and Albania. The sisters of the Hankinson province are largely engaged in healthcare, care for the elderly, and childcare, as well as education and catechesis.

Bibliography: M. P. KOCH, *Die Franziskanerinnen in Dillingen, 1241–1829* (Landshut, Germany 1956). M. HEIMBUCHER, *Die Orden und Kongregationen der katholischen Kirche*, 2 v. (3d. ed Paderborn 1932–34) 2:29.

[M. P. FORREST]

Sisters of St. Francis of the Immaculate Virgin Mary Mother of God (OSF) [1620]. A congregation with papal approbation whose motherhouse is located in Millvale (Pittsburgh), Pa. The congregation is also known as the Millvale Franciscans. The congregation takes its heritage from the Franciscan Sisters of Philadelphia (formerly the Glen Riddle Franciscans) founded in 1855. In 1864 sisters went to Pittsburgh to solicit financial aid for their proposed hospital in Buffalo. While in Pittsburgh, a prominent Catholic physician, Dr. Philip

Weisenberger, urged them to begin a hospital to serve the German immigrants. These sisters opened a 30-bed hospital. Soon afterwards the sisters began to teach in the elementary and high schools in the diocese. Today the work of the congregation focuses on education, health care, social services, and pastoral care. The sisters own and sponsor Mt. Alvernia, an all-female high school, as well as Mt. Alvernia Day Care and Learning Center located on their motherhouse campus. The congregation was the first in Pittsburgh to establish a volunteer program open to single men and women who commit themselves for a year of service with the poor while living a simple Franciscan lifestyle. The congregation largely serves in the Pittsburgh area; however, sisters minister throughout the United States, as well as Africa, Canada, and Puerto Rico.

[L. WESOLOWSKI]

Sisters of St. Francis of the Martyr St. George (OSF) [1600]. A congregation with papal approbation founded in Thuine, Germany, in 1869 by Pauline (Mother Anselma) Bopp (1835–87) under the direction of Rev. Gerhard Bernhard Dall (d. 1874) for the purpose of nursing the sick in their homes and caring for orphans. Community members are engaged in teaching, nursing, and social work in Brazil, Germany, Holland, the United States, Japan, Sumatra, and Africa. The sisters came to the United States in 1923, where they established their motherhouse and novitiate in Alton, Ill.

[M. I. ROHNER]

Sisters of St. Francis of the Mission of the Immaculate Virgin (OSF) [1510]. A community that traces its origin to the congregation founded in 1855 by John Nepomucene NEUMANN, Bishop of Philadelphia, and later known as the Glen Riddle Franciscans (now known as the Sisters of St. Francis of Philadelphia). On July 2, 1882, the Franciscan Sisters of Buffalo, N.Y., a community that in 1861 became independent of Bishop Neumann's original foundation in Philadelphia, went to New York City at the request of Father John C. DRUMGOOLE to assist him in the care of orphaned and destitute children at the Mission of the Immaculate Virgin. As the work at the mission expanded, it was deemed advisable to form another independent community, the Sisters of St. Francis, Conventuals of the Third Order. The separation took place in July of 1893, and Mother Mary Catherine was elected the first superior general of the new congregation. The original motherhouse at Mount Loretto, the extensive new site of the children's home on Staten Island, N.Y., was later transferred to Hastings-on-Hudson, N.Y. While continuing the child care at Mt. Loretto, the sisters expanded their apostolate to include health care in hospitals, day clinics, and nursing homes, as well as in education. They also serve as pastoral associates.

[J. A. RANIERI/R. S. SMITH]

Sisters of St. Francis of the Providence of God (OSF) [1660]. The congregation was founded in 1922 to preserve the faith of Lithuanian immigrants and their children and eventually extended its ministry to the broader Church. Based in Pittsburgh, Pa., the congregation is the fifth foundation of the Sisters of St. Francis of Philadelphia (formerly the Glen Riddle Franciscans) established by St. John Neumann of Philadelphia in 1855. Over the years the congregation staffed hospitals, elementary and secondary schools, and provided catechesis for public school children. Since Vatican II its ministries aim to meet contemporary needs with the new immigrants, the homeless, the poor, the disadvantaged, and the imprisoned. Sisters also provide spiritual direction, retreats, and the use of hermitages on their grounds. Since 1938 they have been meeting the educational, spiritual, and social needs of the people in various parts of Brazil, where they are based in São Paulo. They maintain schools and a social center, engage in parish ministry in areas where priests are few, work with base communities, provide health care, and assist the poor in literacy and housing programs, as well as food and clothing distribution.

Bibliography: M. C. POPP, *History of the Sisters of St. Francis of the Diocese of Pittsburgh, Pa., 1868–1938* (Millvale, Pa. 1939).

[M. JASKEL]

Sisters of St. Francis of the Third Order Regular Williamsville, New York (OSF) [1800]. This community of the Sisters of St. Francis of the Third Order Regular stems from the Sisters of St. Francis of Philadelphia (formerly the Glen Riddle Franciscans), who were founded in 1855 in Philadelphia by Mother Mary Francis Bachmann with the help of St. John Neumann, bishop of Philadelphia. In 1861, responding to the needs in Buffalo, N.Y., a new foundation was established by Sister Mary Margaret Boll. As women at the service of life, the sisters are involved in education at various levels, health care, care of the elderly, pastoral work, counseling and spiritual direction, mission work, communications, social services, and prayer ministry. The sisters minister primarily in western New York, but also serve in four other states, as well as in Kenya, East Africa.

[B. LEISING]

Sisters of St. Joseph of the Third Order of St. Francis (SSJ-TOSF) [3930]. A congregation with papal approbation (1917) founded on July 1, 1901, by Mothers Mary Clara Bialkowski and Mary Felicia Jaskulski.

Guided by Rev. Luke Pescinski, pastor of St. Peter's Church in Stevens Point, a group of Polish sisters separated from the School Sisters of St. Francis, Milwaukee, to respond to the dire religious and social need for teachers of immigrant children in the growing Polish parishes of the Midwest and across the country. The sisters first responded to health-care needs in 1939, procuring the tuberculosis sanatarium just outside Stevens Point. Shortly afterwards they responded to calls for service in small hospitals in several states, including an integrated hospital in Mississippi. In 1949, the Congregation built Marymount Hospital on convent grounds in Garfield Heights, Ohio, the only hospital it currently sponsors. Inspired by the Second Vatican Council, with laity serving in Catholic schools and hospitals, some sisters responded to unmet needs such as ministry to the mentally and physically handicapped and their care-givers; organizational work in poor areas; pastoral roles in parishes, dioceses, hospitals, nursing homes, and senior apartments; sponsorship of ecumenical spirituality centers; and missionary work in Puerto Rico, Peru, Brazil, and South Africa. In 1943, St. Joseph Motherhouse and Novitiate were transferred to South Bend, Ind., centrally located to the three provinces in Stevens Point, Garfield Heights, and Bartlett (Ill.). In 1990, the congregation centralized offices in Stevens Point.

[J. M. PEPLINSKI]

Sisters of the Sorrowful Mother of the Third Order of St. Francis (SSM) [4100]. A congregation with papal approbation, dedicated to works of Christian charity, and following the rule of the Third Order Regular of St. Francis. It was founded in Rome, Italy, by Mother Frances of the Cross (Amalia Streitel, 1844–1911), a native of Mellrichstadt, Germany. Having been educated by the Franciscan Sisters of Maria Stern in Augsburg and having experienced religious life in both Franciscan and Carmelite convents, she went to Rome in 1883 at the request of Father Franziskus Maria Jordan to organize a new community of sisters. Both soon discovered that their views concerning the foundation were divergent. The conflict was resolved in 1885 when the cardinal vicar of Rome, Lucido Maria Parocchi (1883–1903), appointed as spiritual director of the small community Rev. Dr. George Jacquemin (d. 1920) and named the new congregation Sisters of the Sorrowful Mother. A rented dwelling close to St. Peter's Basilica became the first motherhouse in Rome. In accord with the instruction and example of their foundress, the sisters practice special devotion to Our Lady under the title of Sorrowful Mother. From Italy the community spread to Germany, Austria, the West Indies, and the United States, where the first foundation (St. Francis Hospital) was made in 1889 in Wichita, Kansas. The sisters established themselves in Wisconsin, Minnesota, New Jersey, Pennsylvania, Oklahoma, New Mexico, and Iowa. Mother Frances' cause for beatification was introduced at Rome in 1947.

Bibliography: A. REICHERT, *Mother Frances Streitel, Her Life and Work,* tr. C. DOMINIONI (Milwaukee 1948).

[M. C. KOLLER]

Sisters of the Third Franciscan Order (OSF) [1490]. The Sisters of the Third Franciscan Order, Syracuse, N.Y., were founded in 1860 by Mother Mary Bernadine Dorn, one of the original group of the first native community of Sisters of St. Francis established in the United States (known as the Glen Riddle Franciscans). When the Conventual Franciscans accepted parishes in Syracuse and Utica, N.Y., they invited the Glen Riddle Sisters to join them and to staff the schools. The sisters accepted in March of 1860. The following November, with the approbation of Bp. John McCloskey of Albany, N.Y., the foundation in Syracuse was established. Four years later, the Sisters' first motherhouse and chapel in Syracuse were dedicated. In 1883 Mother Marianne Cope led a group of sisters to Hawaii to care for individuals with leprosy. She relinquished her position as superior general to become superior of the missions in Hawaii, where she remained for 35 years. In 1932 the order received the decree of papal approbation.

Dedicated primarily to education, the community developed a program of teacher training, including maintenance of Duns Scotus House of Studies at Catholic University of America, for the sisters in graduate work. St. Francis Normal School opened at the motherhouse in 1934 and later became Maria Regina College. The community's hospital medical centers include the only Catholic hospitals in Hawaii. The community has around 300 professed sisters who minister in education, healthcare, social services, and retreats throughout the United States and Peru.

[M. C. DORAN/C. WALTER]

Sisters of the Third Order of St. Francis (OSF) [1770]. A congregation with papal approbation (1899) established in 1877. (The Franciscan Sisters of Rock Island, Ill., merged with the East Peoria sisters in 1989.) The East Peoria sisters stem from the Franciscan Sisters of the Holy Family of Dubuque, Iowa, who were canonically established in Herford, Germany, in 1864, and who came to the United States in 1875 during the Kulturkampf. The German community of 29 members settled first in Iowa City, Iowa, in 1875 and in 1878 established a motherhouse in Dubuque. Later, a few of the sisters went to Peoria to found a hospital. Bp. John Lancaster Spalding, first bishop of the Diocese of Peoria (1877–1908), seeing that the sisters were struggling in poverty and were without proper hospital facilities, offered to help, provided that the sisters would agree to establish their own independent community in his diocese. After consulting with their superior in Dubuque, the sisters consented to his request in 1877. Bp. Spalding then set about choosing the site for the future St. Francis Hospital and Motherhouse and helped the sisters draw up the constitutions of the community. Sister Mary Frances Krasse was elected the first superior of the new congregation, called the Sisters of the Third Order of St. Francis. The apostolate of the sisters consists in caring for the sick, poor, injured, aged, and dying. The congregation conducts hospitals in Illinois and Michigan, and nursing homes in Iowa and Illinois. The community maintains a formal in-service program for the education of the junior sisters.

[M. C. JAMES/M. E. FLANNERY]

St. Francis Mission Community (OSF) [1505]. Established in 1981 as an autonomous province of the Franciscan Sisters of Mary Immaculate [1500]. The 20 professed sisters minister in education, parish ministry, and pastoral care in the dioceses of Amarillo and Lubbock, Tex., as well as the archdiocese of Los Angeles.

[R. RODDY]

FRANCISCAN SPIRITUALITY

Franciscan spirituality motivates a way of following Christ that is based on the gospels. It embraces a diversity of vocations: lay and clerical, contemplative and active, academic and pastoral, married and celibate. Emerging out of the high middles ages, it emphasizes the humanity of Jesus Christ as the mystery of God's presence in human flesh. After the Second Vatican Council critical editions and new translations of primary sources inaugurated new approaches to study of texts that are foundational for Franciscan spirituality. First among these are the writings of Francis of Assisi, which, although not exclusively, are important for the Franciscans of the First Order. The writings of Clare have also developed in importance for the Second Order of Poor Clares. In regard to the lay movement of the Third Order, which today comprises both the Secular Franciscan Order and many canonically established religious communities, there are a number of important texts. The experience of these early lay Franciscans, who embraced a life of conversion, served the poor and experienced mystical contemplation, have become more important for understanding the foundational Franciscan experience. Angela of Foligno and Jacopone da Todi are here selected as examples of the lay Franciscan penitental movement. The first part of this article will examine the writings of these four figures as examples of the foundational inspiration for the ongoing development of Franciscan spirituality.

The second part of the article will treat initial theological insights and developments offered by three early Franciscan theologians: ANTHONY OF PADUA, BONAVENTURE, and JOHN DUNS SCOTUS. The development of the full 800-year tradition of Franciscan spirituality is beyond the scope of this article, but it will conclude by identifying several common characteristics that continue to identify the Franciscan spiritual tradition.

Foundations. Francis of Assisi (d. 1226) acknowledges that his conversion began when the Lord led him to live among the lepers. It was among lepers that the Spirit transformed for him what ''seemed bitter . . . into sweetness of body and soul'' (I 124) [cf. *Francis of Assisi: Early Documents* listed below]. Francis's loving acceptance of those who had been hatefully rejected was his way of ''leaving the world'' of power, conceit, and its death-dealing divisions. From this point forward, Francis considered himself a ''lesser brother,'' and accepted every human being he encountered as a generous gift of God and, therefore, his brother or sister.

Having found a new home among the lepers and the beggars, Francis found a new home in the Church and a new understanding of Church. He came upon the three abandoned churches in Assisi of St. Mary of the Portiuncula, San Damiano, and St. Peter that were falling into ruin. By rebuilding these churches, he began to care for the wounds of the Church. He was equally at home in the Church and in the houses of lepers. Both places opened his heart to hear the Word of God and to embrace those different from himself. Just as he experienced the cross of Christ in the poverty of lepers, so in the human vulnerability and weaknesses of the larger community— that is Church—he entered into the same mystery of the cross. The first prayer he taught his brothers was an ecclesial prayer: ''We adore You, Lord Jesus Christ, in all your churches throughout the whole world and we bless you because by your holy cross you have redeemed the world'' (I 124–25). This is an older liturgical formula that Francis adapted by adding to it his own words: ''Lord Jesus, . . . in all your churches throughout the world,'' and ''holy.'' For Francis every church and every house of lepers was a place of sacred encounter with the cross of the Lord Jesus.

The church of St. Mary of the Portiuncula was especially important to him because there Francis honored Mary, who first conceived the Word of God by the same Spirit that penetrated his own heart. It was there, in obedience to the command of Christ, he received the Body of Christ she first brought into the world. Only in the

Church, where Francis could find the Body of Christ, could he find the source, the beginning, and the power for his gospel life of peace and reconciliation: ''I implore all of you brothers to show all possible reverence and honor to the most holy Body and Blood of our Lord Jesus Christ in Whom that which is in heaven and on earth has been brought to peace and reconciled to almighty God'' (I 117).

From the houses of lepers and the churches Francis moved into the world with new ears for the Gospel. The more he embraced the Gospel, the more the ''poverty and humility of Our Lord Jesus Christ'' (I 70) became the concrete and practical plan for his own life. Courageously he announced peace: ''Let us pay attention to what the Lord says: 'Love your enemies and do good to those who hate you, for Our Lord Jesus Christ, Whose footprints we must follow, called His betrayer a friend and willingly offered Himself to His executioners. Our friends therefore, are all those who unjustly inflict upon us distress and anguish, shame, injury, sorrow and punishment, martyrdom and death''' (I 79). Francis's acceptance of distress and anguish, martyrdom and death were at the heart of his mission to serve the Lord as a ''pilgrim and stranger'' on the highways and byways of the world. In his Testament Francis acknowledged that he and his brothers in their gospel life and preaching had one greeting for all: ''The Lord revealed a greeting to me that we should say: 'May the Lord give you peace''' (I 125–26).

In his mystical experience of the stigmata on Mount La Verna two years before he died, Francis embraced Christ, his Brother, on the cross. It was an embrace so intimate it marked his flesh. The stigmatized Francis received Christ's wounded flesh in his own flesh. This has often been interpreted as affirmation of his unconditional embrace of what the Spirit revealed to him: ''a form of life according to the Gospel.'' Francis embraced Christ in lepers, in the Church and, ultimately through the stigmata, in himself. On Mt. La Verna he received the gift of ecstatic peace.

After that mystical experience he composed his famous work The Canticle of Brother Sun. In this *Canticle*, Francis makes it clear that only when brothers and sisters humble themselves with their Brother, who humbled himself on the cross, can they make God's name known. To give praise to God, they must be humble not only before the lepers of the world, the non-Christians across the sea, and before the needs of each other, but they must also be humble before the very earth under their feet and even the sun above their heads. All elements of the created universe are brothers and sisters and share with Francis a common origin from the same God. All creation is called to share in the communion of praise offered by the whole church together with the Virgin Mary and all the angels and saints. The legacy he left for his brothers was that they were to promote throughout the world *The Canticle of Brother Sun* as a song of communion and praise. He requested that it be sung before they preach. *The Canticle* was his message of peace.

''The Marriage of St. Francis and Poverty,'' detail of fresco by Giotto in the Lower Church, Basilica of S. Francesco, Assisi, Italy.

Clare of Assisi (d. 1253) was the first woman to follow Francis, and in her own right she became a foundress of the Second Order, a new way of contemplative life for women. She was the first woman to write a rule of life for women. Living with her sisters in the monastery of San Damiano, she emphasized the necessity of peace in their relationships with each other in order that their spirits might soar toward contemplation of the mystery of the Incarnate Word. This is captured in Clare's Fourth Letter to Agnes: ''Gaze upon that mirror each day, O Queen and Spouse of Jesus Christ, and continually study your face within it. . . . Indeed blessed poverty, holy humility and inexpressible charity are reflected in that mirror, as with the grace of God you can contemplate them throughout the entire mirror . . . that is, the poverty of Him who was placed in a manger . . . the holy humility, the blessed poverty, the untold labors and burdens that He endured . . . the ineffable charity that led Him to suffer on the wood of the Cross and to die there the most shameful death'' (Cf. *Clare of Assisi: Early Documents*, 48).

Poverty, humility, and charity are conditions and rewards of a life focused on penetrating the great mystery of how God creates and loves in God's own free and eternal choice for the incarnation of the Son. Contemplation is the shared journey of the sisters into direct experience of the heart of the great Christian mystery of God's love, the Word made flesh. In the ''mirror'' of that mystery, the sisters see the intimate reality of themselves. Christ, the fullest expression of God's life and love, is the mirror of all that God creates and loves. Contemplation is to ponder, experience, and embrace all that is found in the heart of Christ, who is the perfect example of self-giving love.

Clare's single-minded focus on the great mystery of God's love empowered her and her sisters to ''be a mirror and an example for those living in the world'' (CA:ED, 55). Their life of contemplation in a bond of peace and free from accumulation of possessions was not only a life for themselves—it was also a life to serve as example for others, calling others into the heart of the mystery of God's greatest revelation of love. In the bull of canonization issued by Alexander IV, he recognized this aspect of Clare's vocation: ''Her life is an instruction and a lesson to others who learned the rule of living in this book of life'' (CA:ED, 180). Moved by the example of Francis and inspired by the Spirit, Clare and her sisters focused all their energies toward a life of fullest freedom from what is not necessary in order to gaze in the mirror, that is, to know a peace that sees clearly and experiences profoundly God's love revealed in the ''ineffable charity'' of Christ on the cross.

Angela of Foligno (d. 1309) exemplifies the development of ecstatic experience among Franciscan lay penitent women. After the death of her husband and reception into the Third Order, she directed her attention to the service of lepers, the poor, and the sick. In this she began to perceive and experience how Christ had died for her. Overwhelmed at the gift of God's generous love, she was moved one day to strip herself of all her clothing before the cross: ''I was inspired with the thought that if I wanted to go to the cross, I would need to strip myself in order to be lighter and go naked to it.'' (LaChance, 126). Stripped of her sins and possessions, her spiritual experience becomes intense, affective, and imaginative. Description of these experiences is preserved in her *Memorial*, the text written by her confessor Brother Arnaldo. To him she poured out her soul between 1290 and 1296, and step by step she describes her sharing in the self-emptying of Christ crucified that lead her through suffering, pain, joy, and darkness to ''a state of joy so great that it is unspeakable. In it I knew everything I wanted to know, possessed all I wanted to possess. I saw the All Good. In this state the soul delights in the All Good'' (LaChance, 203).

The cross was the inspiration of her prayer and visions, and through these she received the grace to return the love to Christ crucified which he had given to her. In this manner, she experienced the cross deep within herself and she entered intensely into the experience of Christ, who made himself ''poor of goods, . . . poor of friends, . . . poor of himself to the point of helplessness'' (LaChance, 288). Through this self-emptying focus on the cross she entered into a radical new experience of God. She writes: ''The more perfectly and purely we see, the more perfectly and purely we love. As we see, so we love. Therefore, the more we see of Jesus Christ, God and man, the more we are transformed into him by love'' (LaChance, 242).

Jacopone da Todi (d. 1306) lived as a lay Franciscan penitent for 10 years after the death of his wife. Although he eventually joined the First Order, his vernacular writing, *The Lauds*, a poetic diary of his own experience, was shaped by his lay penitential life. Jacapone emphasized that poverty and obedience of the cross are key insights for following Christ: ''poverty is having nothing, wanting nothing, and possessing all things in freedom'' (Huges, 186). On the cross Christ obediently embraces all that is mortally human and therein the obedience of the cross is recapitulation of all of creation into the peace and harmony of God's eternal plan. So Jacopone exults: ''Since I gave my will to God, all things are mine and I am one with them in love, in ardent charity.'' Jacopone was amazed at the wonder of all the gifts of creation. The more he let them go, the more beautiful they became, and the more he connected to them. His poverty became his peace.

Initial Theological Developments. Anthony of Padua (d. 1231) was among the first of the trained theologians to join the First Order. Francis acknowledged and approved his theological vocation: ''I am pleased that you teach sacred theology to the brothers providing that, as contained in the Rule, you 'do not extinguish the spirit of prayer and devotion' during study of this kind'' (I 107). Anthony captured Francis's vocation of preaching and composed two sermon collections: the Sunday Sermons (1223–30) and the *Festal Sermons* (1230–31). He gave much of his energy to teaching theology in order to support the mission of gospel preaching. He was a master of the spiritual interpretation of scripture, and he crafted his gospel message to be practical encouragement for people of all vocations. Like Francis, Anthony of Padua taught that the humility, poverty, and suffering of Jesus is at the heart of the Gospel and is the only way to understand and effect among peoples the gospel message of peace. Anthony writes: 'only the poor, that is the humble, have the gospel preached to them, because their emptiness makes them receptive, while the proud are unwilling to receive anything'' (Lynch, 28–29).

Bonaventure (d. 1274), especially after his election as minister general of the order, devotes his theological and literary skills to deepen the spiritual insights that flowed from Francis. He applied his interpretations and synthesis of Augustinian theories of exemplarism and illumination to the Franciscan mystical journey. This earned him the title Seraphic Doctor. His spiritual masterpiece, *The Journey of the Soul into God*, models the pilgrim's contemplative assent after the pattern of Francis's seraphic embrace of the poor crucified Christ. Bonaventure identifies the spiritual journey in a very succinct way: ''There is no other path but through the burning love of the crucified'' (Cousins, 54).

From the outset of the spiritual journey, Bonaventure insists that the true goal of contemplation is the ecstatic peace of union with God. Since the soul's desire for peace can only be fulfilled through and in a humble desire for God, the text outlines a path to peace through ''six levels of illumination by which, as if by steps or stages, the soul can pass over to peace through ecstatic elevations of Christian wisdom'' (Cousins, 54). Bonaventure understands peace (*pax*) to mean ''right order,'' specifically, the order of divine love as shared within the Trinity and as poured out into creation. Receptivity is the root of the ''right order'' of peace. Such a vision understands that everything is a pure gift from God and everything is invitation to an intimate sharing of God's love generously poured out upon all creatures. True order is not a static ''thing'' imposed, but a dynamic relationship of love that is freely shared.

Bonaventure's insistence on the necessity of receptivity for acquiring peace can be seen in how he opens the first chapter: ''Here begins the speculation of the poor person in the desert'' (Cousins, 59). Like Francis, Bonaventure's journey to God begins in poverty. The inherent poverty of the human person is embedded in the very fact that, as a creature, one is in no way equal to God; rather, the creature, essentially and totally, depends upon God the Creator. This is a poverty of absolute and radical dependency on God, which in turn opens the creature to God, the overflowing giver and source of every good gift. Poverty is fundamentally openness and receptivity. Everything exists not only in relationship to God's loving presence, but since only God can truly fulfill the inherent poverty and need of the created human person, the poverty of created existence reveals also the richness of the divine presence. Ultimately, poverty indicates that all of creation and every creature is a gift freely and generously given.

The journey of the soul ends with the poverty of the cross. The disorder of sin must be reordered by the love of the cross whereby the highest becomes the lowest and the richest becomes the poorest. On the cross God becomes poor. Cruciform love leads the wayfarer into the very core of the mystery of God's self-giving love. Here, the root of the soul's union with God is the poverty of the reciprocal self-emptying of the divine into the human and the human into the divine. The fruit of this union is the soul's *transitus* into the ecstatic peace of God's love. The two meet and become one through and in the seraphic love of Christ crucified. In the gift of Christ's cross, like Francis, one receives peace.

John Duns Scotus (d. 1308), in his unique approach to the absolute predestination of Christ, offers an important theological cornerstone for the development of Franciscan spirituality. He taught that the mystery of the incarnation resides first and foremost deep in the mystery of the free gift of God's goodness and love. Jesus is the ''first born of every creature'' (Col 1, 15), and the incarnation of the Word is therefore conditioned neither to creation nor to human sin. Rather, creation itself is ordered within God's eternal design that the Word become flesh. All creation therefore exists because of and for the sake of the gift of the incarnate Christ, who is the full manifestation of God's love. All creation mirrors the gift of God's Word because all exist in view of the incarnate Word, and no human sin can destroy the eternal design that manifests God's goodness. Creation, that is, each and every creature, even in the singular uniqueness or ''thisness'' (*haecceitas*) of each individual reality, is a gift and is infinitely loved by God. Considering, however, the historical reality of sin, this divine love does in fact become redemptive but in the great eternal scheme of God's plan for creation this redemptive aspect is an accidental rather than an essential aspect of God's love for creation. For example, in the third *Ordinatio* John Scotus writes: ''I say that the incarnation of Christ was not foreseen as occasioned by sin, but as immediately foreseen from all eternity by God as a good more proximate to the end. Thus Christ in his human nature is seen as closer to the end [God had in mind in creating]'' (McElrath, 153). Scotus' teaching on the Immaculate Conception is to be understood in this context. In the primary mystery and eternal plan that the Word of God is to take flesh, Mary is and remains a model of God's divine original intention.

Characteristics. *Poverty.* The fundamental disposition of Franciscan spirituality is openness to God, the giver of every gift. It refers everything back to God. Francis of Assisi saw poverty exemplified in Christ and it becomes the gospel value he embraced as he followed the ''poverty and humility of Our Lord Jesus Christ.'' Clare embraced radical poverty to foster a life of contemplation of the poor Christ. Bonaventure taught poverty is the first step of the spiritual journey toward God. Jacopone da Todi believed that poverty was having nothing in order to possess all things in freedom. Subsequently, Spiritual Franciscans John Peter Olivi (d. 1298) and Ubertino da Casale (d. 1341) insisted that strict poverty was key to authentic living of the Rule. With Angelo of Clareno (d. 1337), poverty took on an eschatological significance necessary for the renewal of the whole Church. Later in the 15th century, the First Order Observant movement attempted to recapture and promote a simpler life of strict poverty as it was found in the tradition of the rural or more eremitical friaries. John Capistran (d. 1456) and James of the Marshes (d. 1476) were strong promoters for this renewal of poverty in the life of the First Order.

Humility. Francis identified humility as a sister to poverty. Humility is grateful acceptance of God's gifts, especially the gift of God's Son in Word and Eucharist. Both of these aspects of the mystery of the incarnation are sacraments of the humility of God. In the conclusion of his *Later Rule* Francis writes that the brothers are ''to observe the poverty, humility and Holy Gospel of our Lord Jesus Christ'' (I 106). Poverty and humility not only have gospel implications but also ecclesial ones. The brothers are to live the gospel ''submissive and subject'' to Holy Church. This humble submission to the Church is consistent with his vision of the gospel life that the brothers no matter where they find themselves are ''not to engage in arguments or disputes but [are] to be subject to every human creature for God's sake'' (I 89). According to Thomas of Celano (d.1260) the ''humility of the Incarnation'' describes the process of Francis's conversion and is the identifying characteristic of the spiritual disposition of all the brothers.

Compassion. Clare is the first to mention explicitly two basic characteristics of Franciscan compassion. In her contemplation Clare gazes in the mirror and sees Him ''who was placed in a manger'' and Him who suffered ''on the wood of the cross'' (CA:ED, 48). Crib and cross characterize the compassion of Christ who fully embraced the human condition in the helplessness of an infant and in the suffering of a shameful death. This is the compassion of God. In *The Major Life of Francis*, Bonaventure explains that it is ''through compassion [God] transformed him [Francis] into Christ'' (II 586). Compassion is the basis for service to the poor. This characteristic was pronounced among Third-Order lay Franciscans. In addition to Angela of Foligno and Jacapone da Todi, St. Elisabeth of Hungary (d. 1231), St. Rose of Viterbo (d. 1252), St. Margaret of Cortona (d. 1297) and even St. Louis IX (d. 1270) were notable examples of an active compassion that embraced others in their helplessness and suffering.

Jesus Christ—The Incarnate Word. The characteristics of poverty, humility and compassion flow from the vision and the experience of Christ as he is found in the texts of the gospel. The incarnate Christ in the crib and on the cross is the central spiritual focus that captures the dynamic of Franciscan spirituality. This fosters the affections and, in some cases, encourages ecstatic mystical experiences. As already indicated above, Clare saw Christ as the ''mirror'' into which one must gaze. Angela threw herself naked on the cross to embrace her Divine Lover. Bernadine of Siena (d. 1444), following the Christ-centered spirit of Scotus, preached the holy name of Jesus. In his sermon *The Glorious Name of Our Lord Jesus Christ* he taught that everything that pertains to salvation and to the glory of the final age is revealed in the name of Jesus: ''O glorious name, O gracious name, O lovely and worthy name.'' St. Leonard of Port Maurice promoted the devotion of the Stations of the Cross as a way to foster affective prayer based on the human suffering of Christ. Francesco de Osuna (d. 1540) developed a method of recollection that placed emphasis on alertness of heart and intensity of desire. Human affections, desire and imagination are all aspects of Franciscan prayer that center on the mystery of the incarnation.

Within this central characteristic of emphasis on the humanity of Christ, the role of Mary is always prominent. The incarnation of the Word of God can never be honored apart from her who conceived the Word and gave the Word human flesh. Francis often praised the ''Mother of our most holy Lord Jesus Christ, Spouse of the Holy Spirit'' (I 141), and he even held that to follow Christ in poverty is to follow Mary: ''He [Christ] wished, together with the most Blessed Virgin, His mother to choose poverty in the world beyond all else'' (I 46). Bonaventure continues the Marian tradition by identifying Mary as the Advocate of the Franciscan Order. Lawrence of Brindisi (d. 1619) in his famous *Mariale* demonstrates that Marian spirituality flows out of the devotion to the universal primacy of Christ and is directed toward her consent to and participation in the mystery of the Word made flesh. In modern times, Maximilian Kolbe (d. 1941) renewed and further developed this same Marian aspect of Franciscan devotion to the mystery of the Incarnation.

Finally, all these characteristics can be brought together under the umbrella of piety (*pietas*). In the modern use of English the word is weak; but in Bonaventure's use of the term, it is a rich use of the ancient Roman word that characterizes familial relationships. In Franciscan spirituality, the virtue of piety reconciles the family of creation. It flows from participation in the mystery of the incarnation: ''Truly this is the virtue that binds all creatures together, and gives power to all things having the promise of the life, that now is and is yet to come'' (II 595).

Bibliography: Sources. E. MENESTÒ and S. BRUFANI et al., eds., *Fontes Franciscani* (Assisi 1995). R. ARMSTRONG, J. HELLMANN, and W. SHORT, eds., *Francis of Assisi: Early Documents*, 3 vols. (New York 1999–01). R. ARMSTRONG, ed., *Clare of Assisi: Early Documents* (New York 1989 & St. Bonaventure NY 1990). B. PREZEWOZNY, tr. *Life of St. Anthony: Assidua (1232)* (Padua 1984). ANGELA OF FOLIGNO, *Angela of Foligno*, ed. P. LACHANCE (New York, 1993). ANTHONY OF PADUA, *S. Antonii Patavini Sermones Dominicales et Festivi*, eds. B. COSTA et al. (Padua 1979). BONAVENTURE, *The Soul's Journey into God*, in *Bonaventure*, tr. E. COUSINS (New York 1979). BONAVENTURE, *Disputed Questions on the Knowledge of Christ*, tr. Z. HAYES (St. Bonaventure NY 1992). FRANCISCO DE OSUNA, *The Third Spiritual Alphabet*, tr. M. GILES (New York 1981). JACOPONE DA TODI, *Jacapone da Todi: The Lauds*, tr. S. and E. HUGES (New York 1982). **Studies.** M. BLASTIC, ''Franciscan Spirituality,'' in *The New Dictionary of Spirituality* (Collegeville Minn. 1993). A. BLASUCCI, ''Frères Mineurs: Spiritualité franciscaine,'' *Dictionnaire de Spiritualité, Ascetique et Mystique*, vol. 5 (Paris 1962). L. BOFF, *Saint Francis: A Model for Human Liberation*, tr. J. DIERCKSMEIER (New York 1982). L. BOFF, *The Prayer of Saint Francis: A Message of Peace for the World Today*, tr. P. BERRYMAN (Maryknoll, NY 2001). D. BURR, *Olivi and Franciscan Poverty* (Philadelphia 1989). M. CARNEY, *The First Franciscan Women: Clare of Assisi and Her Form of Life* (Quincy Ill. 1993). S. CLASEN, *St. Anthony: Doctor of the Church* (Chicago 1973). J. HAMMOND, *''Seeking Peace through Prayer'': Bonaventure's Journey of the Mind into God.* (Quincy 2002). J. A. HELLMANN, ''The Spirituality of the Franciscans'' in *Christian Spirituality: High Middle Ages and Reformation*, ed. J. RAITT (New York 1987). E. LECLERCQ, *The Canticle of Creatures: Symbols of Union* (Chicago 1978). E. MENESTÒ, *Angela da Foligno Terziaia Francescana* (Spoleto 1992). D. NIMMO, *Reform and Division in the Medieval Franciscan Order* (Rome 1987). I. PETERSON, *Clare of Assisi: A Biographical Study* (Quincy Ill. 1993) W. SHORT, *The Franciscans* (Collegeville Minn. 1989). R. SORRELL, *St. Francis of Assisi and Nature* (New York 1988).

[J. M. HAMMOND/J. A. HELLMANN]

FRANCISCAN SPIRITUALS

Strict observers of the rule and testament of St. FRANCIS OF ASSISI. Their centers were hermitages in central Italy, where LEO OF ASSISI and many of the first companions of Francis survived, and in Provence. They accepted the doctrines of JOACHIM OF FIORE on the approaching ''age of the Holy Spirit,'' which was to be preceded by the coming of ANTICHRIST, and inaugurated by a barefooted order of contemplatives, which they identified with themselves. The breach between them and the Franciscan Conventuals was widened by the condemnation of Gerard of Borgo San Donnino's *Introduction to the Eternal Gospel* (1254), an edition of Joachim's works, which Gerard regarded as the Bible of the new age, and by the resignation of the Joachimite minister general, (Bl.) John of Parma (1257). It was completed by relaxations of the rule of poverty after St. BONAVENTURE's death (1274).

The views on poverty and some of the theological and philosophical theories of the Provençal Spiritual PETER JOHN OLIVI were condemned in 1283, but his subsequent appointments as lector at Florence and Montpellier were vindications of his orthodoxy. Although a Joachimite, Olivi was a moderate, condemning the excesses of the Spirituals and accepting the legitimacy of the resignation of CELESTINE V, whom many Spirituals identified with the ''angel pope'' of pseudo-Joachimite prophecy. The ardent Spiritual JACOPONE DA TODI witnessed the COLONNA manifesto against BONIFACE VIII. Olivi's disciples were persecuted before and after his death (1298). He was venerated as a saint, and his lay followers, the Provençal BEGUINES, gave considerable trouble to the INQUISITION.

In the March of Ancona a number of Spirituals, among them ANGELUS CLARENUS, author of the *Historia septem tribulationum,* an account of the Spirituals from the end of the life of St. Francis, were imprisoned in 1275 for 15 years. After a stay in Armenia, they returned to Italy and were formed by Celestine V into a hermit order called the CELESTINES. They retired to Greece at the election of Boniface VIII but returned because of the persecutions of the Conventuals. During the pontificate of CLEMENT V, Angelus, now their general, was at the Curia seeking papal recognition for his order.

From 1309 to 1312 there was a papal inquiry into the state of the order and the doctrines of Olivi, representatives of both parties being summoned to the Curia. The case of the Spirituals and the defense of Olivi were undertaken by Olivi's disciple, UBERTINO OF CASALE. Four of Olivi's doctrines were condemned, and Ubertino's plea for the separation of the Spirituals was rejected. After Clement's death the Tuscan Spirituals seized three hermitages; those of Provence took the convents of Narbonne and Beziers, electing their own superiors and adopting a special short and skimpy habit. Upon the election of JOHN XXII (1316), a delegation sent by them to Avignon was refused a hearing and its members imprisoned. Three bulls were issued against the Tuscan Spirituals, who had taken refuge in Sicily, and against those of Provence, four of whom were burned at Marseilles (1318) for refusing to abandon their peculiar habits. Olivi's *Lectura super Apocalipsim* was condemned in 1320.

The ideals of the Spirituals were revived by the Observants, whose founder, John de Valle, was almost certainly a disciple of Angelus Clarenus. Their aspirations are reflected in such works as the *Speculum perfectionis* and the FIORETTI (*see* FRATICELLI).

Bibliography: E. GLEASON, "Sixteenth Century Italian Spirituali and the Papacy," in *Anticlericalism in Late Medieval and Early Modern Europe* (Leiden 1993) 299–307. S. BRUFANI, "Angela da Foligno e gli Spirituali," in *Angela da Foligno, Terziaria Francescana* (Spoleto, Italy 1992) 83–104. T. MACVICAR, *The Franciscan Spirituals and the Capuchin Reform* (St. Bonaventure, N.Y. 1986). R. MANSELLI, *Spirituels et Beguins du Midi,* trans. J. DUVERNOY (Toulouse 1989). B. MCGINN, trans., *Apocalyptic Spirituality: Treatises and Letters of Lactanius, Adso of Montier-en-Der, Joachim of Fiore, the Franciscan Spirituals, and Savonarola* (New York 1976), bibliography. J. PAUL, "Les Spirituels, l'Eglise et la Papaute," in *Chi erano gli Spirituali* (Assisi 1976) 221–262. R. G. MUSTO, "Queen Sancia of Naples and the Spiritual Franciscans," in *Women of the Medieval World* (Oxford 1985). R. LERNER, *Heresy and Literacy, 1000–1530* (Cambridge 1994) 186–204.

[D. L. DOUIE]

FRANCISCAN THEOLOGICAL TRADITION

Contemporary study of the Franciscan theological tradition breaks with the custom, established by earlier generations of scholars, of speaking of a uniform Franciscan school, with a perennial core of fixed and unalterable positions. The comparison of vernacular and academic theologians, some of them previously ignored, prompts an appreciation of the diversity among Franciscan theologians throughout the medieval period. Nevertheless, men and women, drawn to the Franciscan worldview from varying social and political strata, often appear to have shared a common sensibility vis-à-vis the theological concerns that marked their experience of the evangelical life. Questions regarding the possibility of knowing and loving God, the relationship between the current society and the world to come, respect for creation as expression of the goodness of God, free will and revelation, the uniqueness of Christ in personal and cosmic history, together with other concerns, often elicited creative, if not always harmonic responses from those who identified with the gospel proposal of FRANCIS OF ASSISI.

Sometime after Nov. 29, 1223, Francis of Assisi sent a brief letter to his confrere, Anthony of Padua, approving his intention to teach theology to the brothers near Bologna as long as study, like any other work, did not extinguish prayer and devotion. Bologna is the same city where Franciscan hagiographical sources note the Poverello earlier demanded the abandonment of the first friary linked to academics. Site of the earliest European university, Bologna is emblematic of the controversy that surrounded theological studies in the Minorite community from the beginning. Unlike their fellow mendicants, the Dominicans, the early Franciscans did not always recognize an intrinsic link between their evangelical vocation and academic theology.

Francis of Assisi, though not trained in the academic discipline of theology, is considered a vernacular theologian who displayed a profound knowledge of Scriptural and Patristic sources cultivated in liturgical prayer, preaching, and reflective literary composition. He reminds the brothers in the *Testament* (1224) that respect is due to theologians because they minister God's word of spirit and life to the world. Although he described himself as a simple, uneducated man, his writings reveal an educated layman, transformed by God's word and committed to spreading his interpretation of the Christian calling through various venues, including the medium of the written text. The themes he developed in native Umbrian and acquired Latin, such as the goodness of the Triune God, following the poor Christ, the symbolic nature of the world, the dynamics of Gospel fraternity, virtues and vices, and the importance of the Eucharist and the Mother of God, are among the salient insights later Franciscan theologians explored in the cloister, the pulpit, and the classroom.

The cloister of San Damiano was the locus of Clare of Assisi's theological reflection. As a companion of Francis from the earliest days, she focused on the community of sisters, poverty, and Christ. Clare, like Francis, received no formal theological education but was likewise convinced of her experience of the divine and the corresponding responsibility of conveying her faith in word and example. Her *Form of Life* (1253), the first religious rule written by a woman, and the *Testament* (1247–1253) evoke a vision of community as the matrix of evangelical ministry and contemplation of Christ. Her *Letters to Agnes of Prague* (1234–1253) written perhaps with the assistance of another early companion of Francis, Brother Leo, demonstrate Clare's ability to synthesize sources from monastic theology within a Franciscan framework of radical poverty and ecstatic prayer. Others after Clare, like Angela of Foligno, who in the *Memorial* (1296–1297) describes her spiritual itinerary, would continue to find poverty, inside and outside the cloister, conducive to contemplation of the crucified Christ.

Paris School. Many of Francis's other companions came from the educated ranks of society, as his biographer, Thomas of Celano, relates in *The Life of Saint Francis* (1228–1229). Their previous intellectual formation favored the academic theological reflection apparent in their formal preaching and teaching. The missionary thrust beyond the borders of Europe and expansion into areas within Europe where literate and educated, yet unorthodox formulations of the faith flourished, necessitated preaching different from the popular approach the Poverello had employed so successfully. The concomitant entrance into urban areas, where academic faculties were located, facilitated the friars' growing interest in the cultivation of theological study. Beginning with Bologna as early as 1220, houses dedicated to study or *studia*, and other friaries with lectors for the instruction of the brothers, appeared throughout Europe. The English Minorite Roger Bacon boasted that already by the 1230s the brothers had brought learning into every city; however, two cities, Paris and Oxford, became the intellectual centers identified, in particular, with the nascent Franciscan theology.

The Franciscans arrived in Paris as early 1217 and established a house of studies in 1224 with the assistance of a confrere theologian, Haymo of Faversham. The decision in 1236 of the secular regent master, ALEXANDER OF HALES, to enter the fraternity and transfer his chair of theology to the Franciscan *studium* provided the friars with the opportunity to receive a university degree at their own school. Alexander, together with JOHN OF LA ROCHELLE, guided the Minorite school until their deaths in 1245 when they were replaced by ODO RIGALDUS and WILLIAM OF MELITONA. Each master made a substantial contribution, much of which is remains unedited, to the formation of the friars; however, Alexander of Hales remains the dominant figure of the early Parisian *studium.* He introduced the *Sentences* of Peter Lombard into the curriculum and, without neglecting biblical sources, utilized Aristotelian philosophy. Alexander's emphasis on theology as a science included the notion of theological knowledge as *sapientia* or wisdom, which became a hallmark of the Franciscan approach to education. The *Summa* (1245–1256) of Alexander, edited by John of La Rochelle and completed by William of Melitona, together with the *Disputed Questions* and the *Gloss on the Sentences* (1223–1227), treated themes such as the contingency of the world, divine knowledge, the person as the *imago Dei*, the Incarnation of Christ, and the vision of God as Good.

Alexander's student BONAVENTURE received the habit of the friars in 1243 and became the most influential of the regent masters at the Parisian *studium.* Although Bonaventure's course of study concluded in 1254, he was not recognized as a master of theology until 1257 due to the conflict between the mendicant and secular masters at the university. Elected general minister of the Franciscan order in the same year, he served in this capacity until his death in 1274 at the Second Council of Lyon. The academic works of the Seraphic Doctor included disputed questions, sermons, biblical commentaries and the *Commentary on the Sentences* (1250–1252). Bonaventure's university writings present a cosmic vision of emanation, creation, incarnation, redemption, and return. The trinity of persons, not the unity of God, is the starting point of theology. Pastoral and administrative responsibilities as minister general promoted an integration of previously held Augustinian and Neoplatonic positions into a synthesis dominated by the Gospel paradigm of Francis of Assisi and his eschatological role in salvation history. The *Journey of the Mind into God* (1259), the *Major Life of Saint Francis* (1260–1262) and the *Collations on the Six Days* (1273) illustrate Bonaventure's appropriation of the Poverello as source and stimulus for theology. Later confreres, including Gilbert of Tournai, Walter of Bruges, John Pecham, Matthew of Aquasparta, and Richard of Middleton, would frequently follow the trajectory of his teaching.

Introduced to Bonaventure's apocalyptic views as a student in Paris, PETER JOHN OLIVI also pondered the heritage of the Poverello, the institution and purpose of the Minorite order, and the ages of history marking the approaching eschaton. Upon leaving Paris, Olivi was appointed lector in southern France, then Florence, and again in Provence, where he died in 1298. His utilization of the Joachimite tradition in the *Lecture on the Apocalypse* (1296–1297), his stance on poverty in the *Questions on Evangelical Perfection* (1274–1279), and his teachings concerning the Virgin Mary and marriage provoked censure and condemnation from some, and admiration and imitation from others. Olivi's biblical and sentence commentaries, selected questions, and sermons illustrate a broad range of interests from the proper study of Scripture and the person of Jesus Christ to the economic aspects of religious poverty and the nature of free will.

Oxford School. Like Paris, Oxford was an influential center of medieval Franciscan theology. Thomas of Eccleston's chronicle, *On the Coming of the Friars Minor to England* (1258–1259), claims that the friars arrived in the university town in 1224. ROBERT GROSSETESTE served as the first prominent, secular lector for the newly arrived Minorite community until 1235. After being named bishop of Lincoln, Grosseteste provided other secular masters for the Oxford *studium,* who also received episcopal appointments throughout the British Isles. Adam Marsh, friar and student of Grosseteste, took a chair of theology in 1247, becoming the first of many Franciscan regents at Oxford. The combination of theology and science cultivated by Grosseteste and Marsh found a proponent in Roger Bacon, who, critical of the theological methodology of the Parisian friars, insisted on the epistemological priority of experience and a requisite, reciprocal relationship between science and wisdom. Bacon entered the Franciscan order in 1257, already having taught in the faculty of arts in Paris and Oxford. His *Opus Maius, Opus Minus, Opus Tertium, Letter to Clem-*

ent IV (1266–1268), and compendiums to the study of philosophy and theology explored the correlation between Church and culture and the possibility, albeit unrealized, of interdisciplinary unity among the scientific, philosophical, and theological branches of knowledge.

John DUNS SCOTUS, most probably a native of the small Scottish town of Dun near the English border, studied and taught in Oxford and Paris until his death in 1308 at the Minorite *studium* in Cologne. The ''Subtle Doctor'' produced a wealth of theological and philosophical works delineating the direction of academic Franciscan theological reflection for centuries. Among his edited works are *On the First Principle, Quodlibetal Questions*, and sections of the *Ordinatio*. Scotus directed his acute ability for philosophical analysis toward the integration of Aristotle into theological method, thereby providing a systematic, metaphysical foundation for positions on Christ, the Immaculate Conception, the sacraments, morality, the univocity of infinite and finite being, the contingency of creation, and individuation. His teaching on the principle of individuation, *haecceitas*, allowed for the appreciation of every contingent being and the freedom of God's revelatory actions in salvation history. Consequently, he held that the incarnation of Christ was not dictated by sin, but, rather, the desire that humanity, together with all of creation, be united to God in the most intimate bond. Throughout his theological texts, Scotus defended reason yet underlined the primacy of love over knowledge, concluding that the essence of beatitude is the love of God.

WILLIAM OF OCKHAM, another prolific friar educated at Oxford, was the last major figure representing the Franciscan theological tradition before the Reformation. Controversial and innovative in both theology and politics until his death in 1347, Ockham elaborated reasoned, nuanced positions on Christology, Mariology, the sacraments, divine freedom, and creation and divine power in his commentaries on the *Sentences* (1317–1321). Drawn into the events surrounding the turbulent papacy of John XXII, he defended the received Franciscan interpretation of evangelical poverty in the *Opus nonaginta dierum* (1332). Other texts, like the *Quodlibetal Questions* (1323–1327) and the *Treatise on Imperial and Pontifical Power* (1347), indicate, respectively, Ockham's willingness to revise previous theological views on the absolute power of God and consider contested political and ecclesial issues.

With few exceptions, the reception and interpretation of Duns Scotus's opus dominated the Franciscan theological tradition after the Reformation to the end of the 19th century. Certainly the writing of Bonaventure, whose synthesis of the spiritual life was widely diffused through vernacular translations, and the writings of others like Peter John Olivi, whose views on evangelical life found favor among the reform minded, were not forgotten. The Franciscan *studia*, both among the Conventual and Observants after the division of the Minorite Order in 1517, continued to introduce students to a wide diversity of theological texts, often abbreviated, from the Franciscan tradition. Friars on university faculties and elsewhere, however, preferred to comment upon and develop selected Scotist themes in textbook form throughout the Counter-Reformation and Enlightenment. The turn toward historical-critical studies in the 19th century, especially in Germany, resulted in renewed academic interest in diverse representatives of Franciscan theology. Romano Guardini, Wolfhart Pannenberg, Paul Tillich, Hans Urs von Balthasar, Karl Rahner, and Joseph Raztinger are among the theologians of the 20th century who looked to the broad Franciscan tradition in the formulation of their theological worldviews.

The last decades of the 20th century proffered historical studies in Europe and the Americas on myriad aspects of the Franciscan theological tradition, including new perspectives on previously marginalized or forgotten male and female figures. A critical appreciation of the past with an openness to the present possibilities of dialogue may offer the best prospective for the reception of the Franciscan theological tradition in the future. The contemporary quest for truth and the experience of the divine, concern for the environment and social justice, the desire to unite authentic spirituality and science, and respect for a pluralism of belief and culture in the midst of globalization, are but few of the areas where the resources of the Franciscan tradition continue to provide potential inspiration and insight.

Bibliography: K. OSBORNE, ed., *The History of Franciscan Theology* (St. Bonaventure, N.Y. 1994). B. MCGINN, *The Flowering of Mysticism: Men and Women in the New Mysticism 1200–1350* (New York 1998). J. MERINO, *Storia della filosofia francescana,* tr. L. FIOCCHI (Milan 1993). F. X. PUTALLAZ, *Figure francescane alla fine del XIII secolo,* tr. C. MARABELLI, (Milan 1996). B. ROEST, *A History of Franciscan Education (c. 1210–1517)* (Leiden 2000).

[T. J. JOHNSON]

FRANCISCANS, FIRST ORDER

The popular name for the Order of Friars Minor (O.F.M.), founded by St. Francis of Assisi in 1209. The formal English term, ''Friars Minor,'' is a literal translation of the Latin *fratres minores* (''Lesser Brothers''). Over the centuries the Order of Friars Minor has split into several independent congregations. Their common history is treated in this article.

The Lesser Brothers emerged from the ''form of Gospel life'' chosen by Francis (1181/82–1226) and his first companions in Assisi. Research into their origins over the past quarter of a century has emphasized the essentially lay origins of the movement. Their call ''to follow in the footsteps of Jesus Christ'' led Francis and his brothers ''to leave the world'' by rejecting the structures of Assisi's communal life to live at the margins of society among the poor and the outcasts. Although the life of these early ''Lesser Brothers'' had a strong eremetical element, they also were convinced they had an evangelical mission to their society. Supporting themselves by whatever trade they knew or by begging, they engaged in informal street preaching to call their hearers to a committed Christian life. The little band received initial papal approval in 1209. What quickly set the Lesser Brothers apart from many other lay penitential groups was their phenomenal expansion, both numerical and geographical. By 1217, they had decided to spread north of the Alps and to the Crusader States, even to Muslim ''unbelievers.'' By 1221, there were between three and five thousand brothers.

Both the Lesser Brothers' rapid growth and their desire to gain official canonical recognition of their novel way of life led them to develop greater internal organization. They soon began conforming to many of the patterns of traditional religious life. A formal version of Francis's Rule of Life was definitively approved in 1223. At the same time, the complexion of the community was quickly changing, as more and more clerics were drawn to the apostolic ideals of the brotherhood. The popes, especially Gregory IX, who canonized Francis in 1228, recognized in the Franciscan movement a potent instrument to implement the pastoral reform vision of the Fourth Lateran Council and increasingly intervened to oversee and channel its growth to this end.

Early Developments. The attitude of Francis himself toward these developments continues to be debated by historians. In any event, whether viewed as a betrayal or a providential evolution, by mid-century the life of the Lesser Brothers was largely focused on the official pastoral ministry of the Church, especially doctrinal and moral preaching and the hearing of confessions. A predominantly lay brotherhood had become an order of educated clerics; the friars largely abandoned their rural hermitages, settling down in urban residences similar to those of canons regular, following a traditional conventual routine with churches to accommodate their growing clientele. To support these apostolic tasks, the earlier strict poverty was relaxed by several Papal interventions. The study houses of the Order in such academic centers as Paris and Oxford produced some of the greatest masters of Scholastic theology, such as Bonaventure (+1274), John Duns Scotus (+1308), and William of Ockham (+1347).

Illustration of Franciscan Monk, 18th-century watercolor by Baltasar Jaime Martinez Compañon, from ''Book of the Bishopric of Trujillo, Peru.'' (©Archivo Iconografico, S.A./ CORBIS)

This rapid transformation provoked serious external and internal crises. Many clergy resented what they viewed as the intrusion of the new mendicant orders—armed with papal privileges—into the pastoral ministry entrusted to them. Largely exempt from the local hierarchy, the friars' churches were drawing away their audience and their incomes. Their complaints found a voice in a strong theological attack on both the life and ministry of the mendicant orders mounted by several prominent theologians of the University of Paris between 1254 and 1271. The brothers, led by Bonaventure (General Minister from 1257 to 1274), responded by constructed an ideology justifying their pastoral ministry in the Church. They saw their mission as grounded in their perfect observance of the life of Christ and his apostles, particularly evident in their distinctive renunciation of the ownership

Franciscan Monks standing at base of cross, New York. (©CORBIS)

of property and the use of money. Supported by the papacy, the Franciscans beat back the attempt of some bishops to suppress or restrict them at the Second Council of Lyons in 1274. In 1279 Nicholas III issued an apostolic constitution, *Exiit Qui Seminat*, which upheld the Franciscan ideology on poverty as official church teaching and also ruled on disputed points of religious observance among the friars. The latter points to the severe crisis of identity that was tearing apart the Order from within.

Poverty Controversy. A vocal minority had resisted the new orientations from the outset; by the end of the century, reacting against what they saw as increasing laxism among the main body of brothers, a protest movement, known as the Spirituals, formed. Influenced by the apocalyptic views of JOACHIM OF FIORE, the Spirituals considered Francis as a prophetic sign of a coming age of renewal in the Church. Any betrayal of his practice of poverty ''to the letter' could therefore only be viewed as surrender to the forces of the carnal institutional Church of a passing age. The increasingly acrimonious debate within the Order eventually led to outright schism on the part of the Spirituals and their eventual suppression in a series of decisions by John XXII between 1317 and 1329. However, in the process John also re-interpreted *Exiit*, condemning the characteristic Franciscan doctrine of the absolute poverty of Christ. The elected leadership of the Order, aided by the writings of William of Ockham, refused to submit to these decisions; they rejected John as a false Pope, seeking refuge in Bavaria with the Emperor Louis IV. The vast majority of the Order remained faithful to John, but with the theoretical underpinnings of their distinctive observance now undercut, the Lesser Brothers soon conformed to the pattern of common ownership of property customary among other religious.

During the latter part of the 14th century, however, a certain reaction to this accommodation set in, with small groups of friars seeking permission to retire to remote houses to live a more primitive form of Franciscan life. Besides attempting to conform to the earlier practice of poverty, this movement, known as the Observant reform, also stressed the eremetical dimension of Franciscan life and the fundamental equality of all friars. These aims originally limited the reformers' engagement in organized pastoral ministries. As the movement gained momentum in the 15th century, tensions within the Order increased between these ''Observant'' friars and those who wished to maintain the now-traditional practices, known as ''Conventuals.'' This was partially due to the fact that more and more Observants, such as Bernardino of Siena (+1444), were increasingly engaged in the ministry of itinerant popular preaching, thus bringing them into pastoral competition with their Conventual brethren. Wishing to preserve and promote their vision of Franciscan life, the Observants sought protection from superiors they viewed as lax. The papacy acquiesced, granting them virtual autonomy within the structures of the Order in 1446. However, the acrimony between the two parties only continued to increase, finally forcing an ultimate solution: in 1517, Pope Leo X divided the Order into two independent congregations, the Friars Minor of the Regular Observance and the Friars Minor Conventual.

More Divisions. The Regular Observance thus created in 1517 had merged together various local reforms with differing standards. Very quickly, friars dissatisfied with the settlement initiated movements of ''stricter observance,'' leading to the further splintering of the Franciscan Order. The largest of these, originally known as the Friars Minor of the Eremetical Life, but popularly called Capuchin Friars (''the brothers with little hoods'') because of their distinctive habit, quickly achieved autonomy in 1528. Characterized by their zeal for the ideals of the primitive Franciscan fraternity and for an intense blending of its contemplative and missionary energies, the Capuchins grew rapidly, playing a prominent role as popular preachers during the Counter-Reformation. They gained total independence as a third congregation of Friars Minor, under their own general minister, in 1619.

Robed Capuchin Franciscan friars, Capuchin Seminary of St. Mary, Crown Point, Indiana.

Other groups seeking a more austere life also appeared, although they remained under the jurisdiction of the Observant General: the Discalced, led by Peter of Alcantara (+1562), in Spain and Portugal; the Reformed, concentrated in Italy and Eastern Europe; and the Recollects, in France, Germany, the Low Countries, and the British Isles. These three families of ''stricter observance'' gained considerable autonomy within the Observant branch, organized into their own provinces with their own distinctive statutes. Despite—or because of—this process of continual fragmentation, the Franciscans flourished during the Counter-Reformation and Baroque periods. They were notably active as missionaries: the Observants and Capuchins within the Spanish, Portuguese, and French colonial dominions, the Conventuals in Eastern Europe. By 1760, the Order reached its peak membership, totaling 130,000 friars in the three congregations.

The next century brought a series of wrenching crises for the Franciscans. First, the Enlightenment reform policies of Spain, Portugal, France, and the Austrian Empire drastically limited recruitment to the Order. Then, in the wake of the French Revolution, governments inspired by liberal anti-clerical ideologies suppressed religious houses in a number of European countries. Finally, Bismarck's *Kulturkampf* banished the friars from much of Germany in 1875. The breakdown of communal life and the challenge of modern values caused a lack of identity for many Franciscans. By 1880, the three branches of Friars Minor had been reduced to a total of only 25,000 friars. However, new ground for expansion providentially appeared at this point in the rapidly growing church in the United States.

Move to the Americas. Franciscans had been in the Americas from the very beginnings of European exploration. Between 1493 and 1820 almost 8,500 Spanish Franciscans—most members of the Regular Observance—set out for the New World. In what is now the United States, the first permanent Franciscan missions among Native Americans date to the late 16th century. Friars arrived in Florida in 1573, gradually establishing a chain of 36 missions, but the native population was soon depleted due to disease, desertion, and incursions by English raiders. By the early 18th century, only a few Christian Indians remained in the vicinity of St. Augustine. Franciscans also accompanied the Spanish colonizing expedition to New Mexico in 1598, quickly establishing missions among the Pueblo nation. Later efforts extended the evangelizing ef-

Holy Cross Friary, Mt. Calvary, Wisconsin.

forts of Spanish friars to Texas in 1716, Arizona in 1767, and California in 1769. The Franciscan presence in the Southwest began to unravel in the late 18th century, as Spanish and then Mexican policies of secularization gradually forced the withdrawal of the friars from these areas. Franciscans were also active in the French colonies. Recollect friars labored along the St. Lawrence and the Great Lakes beginning in 1615; the Capuchins in Acadia from 1632, and in Louisiana from 1722. This presence was dramatically curtailed when New France was ceded to England in 1763.

Although a few missionaries and refugee friars continued to minister in the United States in the early 19th century, Franciscans were able to establish a stable and enduring presence only with the great waves of European immigrants that arrived between 1840 and 1920. The oldest Franciscan jurisdictions presently in the United States trace their origins to friars who came to labor among German-speaking immigrants. Observant friars arrived in Cincinnati in 1844, Conventuals in Texas in 1852, and Capuchins in Wisconsin in 1857. As Italian and Eastern European immigrants began arriving later in the century, friars from those nations arrived to serve them, forming new jurisdictions. The needs of this immigrant population greatly shaped Franciscan life and ministry in the United States, establishing it in patterns quite different from the experience of most friars in Europe. In America, the predominant ministries were parishes and schools; the demands of these institutions forced the modification of the more monastic style of Franciscan life characteristic in Europe, especially in the many smaller houses. But America proved to be fertile soil for Franciscans; by 1960, the Observant friars, generally called simply Franciscans in the United States, were organized into six provinces and several smaller units, with 3,600 friars; the Capuchins into five jurisdictions with 1,100 friars, and the Conventuals into four provinces with 1,000 friars.

New Developments. Meanwhile, in the late 19th century the Order in Europe began experiencing both a numerical and a spiritual rebirth. All three branches of the Order attempted to reestablish Franciscan life by fostering a return to traditional observances and the Order's intellectual tradition. In terms of Franciscan institutional history, the great event of this period was the Leonine Union of 1897, whereby the Recollect, Discalced, and Reformed families were merged back into the Regular Observance to create one Order of Friars Minor (O.F.M.). Participating in the neo-Scholastic revival of the period, the three Franciscan congregations established general study houses in Rome and attempted to recover the distinctive insights of Bonaventure and John Duns Scotus. The period of historical retrieval culminated in the late 1960s with new critical attention on the writings of Francis himself.

This coincided with the massive efforts to renew the Order's life and mission in the wake of the Second Vatican Council. The consequent attempts over the next 30 years to redefine the Franciscan charism and refound the Order on that basis resulted in both liberating and creative ventures and wrenching internal dislocations. Franciscans of all three of the major branches have been part of the general phenomenon of the decline of vocations to religious life, especially in the industrialized nations where the Order had been most strongly established in recent centuries. At the dawn of third Christian millennium, the Friars Minor (O.F.M.) worldwide numbered 17,000, with 1,800 in the United States; the Capuchins numbered 11,300, with 730 in the U.S.; and the Conventuals numbered 4,500, with 620 in the U.S. At the same time, the perennial tendency of Franciscans to form new splinter movements again emerged. Two of these have experienced rapid growth: the Franciscan Friars of the Immaculate, which was recognized as an institute of papal right in 1998, and the Franciscan Friars of the Renewal, an American congregation established in New York in 1987.

Bibliography: M. ALBERZONI, et. al., *Francesco d'Assisi e il primo secolo di storia francescana* (Turin 1997). R. ARMSTRONG, J. HELLMANN, and W. SHORT, eds., *Francis of Assisi: Early Documents*, 3 vols. (New York 1999–2001). L. IRIARTE, *Franciscan History* (Chicago 1982). D. NIMMO, *Reform and Division in the Medieval Franciscan Order: From Saint Francis to the Foundation of the Capuchins* (Rome 1987).

[D. V. MONTI]

FRANCISCANS, SECOND ORDER

The Order of St. Clare, better known as the Poor Clares, dates back to Palm Sunday, 1212, when St. Clare received the habit from St. Francis of Assisi, opening the way for women to join the Franciscan movement. After a very brief stay with the Benedictines of San Paulo and a few months at Sant Angelo with a group now believed to be Beguines, Clare and her first followers, including her blood sister, Agnes, were taken by Francis to San Damiano, the small chapel where he had first heard a voice from the crucifix calling him to ''Rebuild my church.'' Within the enclosure of that monastery the sisters would live the same gospel life as the friars, a life centered around poverty, minority, and community. Francis gave these first Poor Ladies, as he liked to call them, a very brief ''form of life'' which committed them to ''having nothing'' either as individuals or as community. Church authorities regarded this non-ownership as being too risky for enclosed women who, unlike the friars, were not free to go out and to work or beg.

In 1215, the Fourth Lateran Council, concerned about the religious groups springing up all over Europe, decreed that new religious communities had to accept one of four existing rules. Francis had already received verbal approval of his rule, but Clare and her sisters had not. The Benedictine rule was closest to the way the sisters were living, but it did not include the Franciscan charism of absolute poverty. Therefore, in 1215–16 Clare applied for and received an indult from Innocent III giving her and her new community the Privilege of Poverty by which ''no one can compel you to accept possessions.'' As part of this same effort to place the new San Damiano community on more solid canonical footing, Francis ''almost forced'' Clare to assume the role of abbess, a service she would give to her sisters the remaining 40-some years of her life.

Appointed by Honorius III as papal legate, Cardinal Hugolino of Ostia in 1219 gave the Poor Sisters a new constitution, the Rule of Hugolino. Benedictine in character, it lacked the communal poverty so important to Clare's understanding of her form of life. When Hugolino was elected to the papacy in 1227 Clare asked for a renewal of the Privilege of Poverty that had been given her some ten years earlier and this was granted in 1228. Foundations made by the community at San Damiano accepted this Privilege of Poverty but other monasteries continued to follow Hugolino's Form of Life, retaining communal ownership. All were Benedictine by rule rather than being officially incorporated into the Franciscan family.

During the next decades the rapid multiplication of monasteries claiming the same basic inspiration as the Damianites, as the sisters were sometimes called, prompted Innocent IV in 1247 to write still another Form of Life, which, although incorporating Clare and her followers into the Franciscan Order, still permitted communal ownership of property. This rule was never widely accepted by the sisters.

Around this time Clare began work on her own Form of Life which took its inspiration from Francis, including his emphasis on absolute poverty, but also incorporated elements from the legislation of Hugolino and Innocent IV. However, all of these diverse sources were modified by the lived experience of the sisters at San Damiano, making this the first rule written by a woman for women. When Innocent IV came to visit Clare on her deathbed, she requested papal approval of her Form of Life. This she received on Aug. 9, 1253, two days before she died.

Known today as the Primitive Rule, Clare's Form of Life was accepted by the community of San Damiano and by a few other monasteries; others, however, continued to observe either the Rule of Hugolino or that of Innocent IV. In 1263 St. Bonaventure, as minister general of the Franciscan Order, petitioned Pope Urban IV to bring some unity into the observance of Clare's followers. The pope responded by issuing still another rule, which came to be know as the Urbanist Rule; once again communal ownership of property was permitted. This document was the first to use the title ''Order of St. Clare.''

By 1316, a hundred years after the order's inception, there were 372 Poor Clare monasteries located in places as diverse as Syria, France, Belgium, Spain, Germany, Bohemia, Sweden, Denmark, Cyprus, Greece, and England. New foundations were made in mission lands as the sisters followed and sometimes preceded the evangelizing efforts of the friars. In the early 1400s a return to the original inspiration of Clare, especially in regard to poverty, was initiated by Colette of Corbie; her reform movement came to be known as the Colettine observance. The Order also suffered from the persecutions of this period. In 1539, when all monasteries were suppressed in England, women who wished to become Clares had to go to the Continent to do so. It would be two and half centuries before the order would be reintroduced. In France the Poor Clares of Lyon were condemned to death but were saved from execution by the prior death of Robespierre. But Josephine Leroux, a Poor Clare from Valenciennes, was martyred along with five Ursuline Sisters. Similar hardship, persecution, imprisonment threatened communities in Germany, Spain, Portugal and other countries, yet the order continued to grow and spread.

For more than 700 years the Poor Clares have kept the same form of life: living a purely contemplative religious life in an enclosed community, relating to each other as sister to sister, practicing the total poverty of ''possessing nothing'' either individually or communally, and offering a life of personal and liturgical prayer as intercession for all God's people. They form a worldwide order of about a thousand monasteries.

The Poor Clares came to the United States in 1875 in the persons of Mother Maddalena Bentivoglio and her sister, Constance, who were commissioned by Pius IX to start a monastery of the Primitive observance in what was then mission country. They opened the first permanent monastery in Cleveland in August 1877, but when other Clares from Germany, led by Mother Veronica von Elmendorff, arrived later that year, Mother Maddalena moved on, first to New Orleans and finally to Omaha, Nebraska where she succeeded in establishing the protomonastery of all those using the initials OSC. The Cleveland monastery became the first U.S. foundation of Colettines, i.e., those using the initials PCC.

All Poor Clare monasteries are autonomous, each with its own abbess, council, chapter, and novitiate and its own nuancing of Clare's original charism. In 1950 the Holy See urged all contemplative monasteries to federate for the purpose of sisterly support and communication. At present there are five such federations in the United States: the Bentivoglio Federation and the Holy Name Federation, which include all the houses that trace their beginning to Mother Maddelena; the Federation of Mary Immaculate which unites the Colettine Poor Clares; the-Federation of the Capuchin Poor Clares who came to the U.S. from Mexico in 1981; and the Poor Clares of Perpetual Adoration who began in the U.S. in 1921 and who have their own PCPA association with their own Constitution based on the Rule of St. Clare. The first Canadian foundation of Colettine Poor Clares was made in Valleyfield, Quebec in 1902. In the western part of Canada several monasteries owe their origin to and are members of the Bentivoglio federation in the United States.

Bibliography: R. ARMSTRONG, *Clare of Assisi: Early Documents* (New York 1988). M. D. FRANE, ed., *Clarion Call: Eight Centuries of Franciscan Poor Clare Life* (Jamica Plain, Mass. 1993). C. O'BRIEN, *The Story of the Poor Clares* (Limerick 1992). I. OMAECHEVARRIA, *Las Clarissas a traves de los siglos* (Madrid 1972).

[M. E. BEHA]

FRANCISCANS, THIRD ORDER REGULAR

The Third Order Regular of Saint Francis traces its historical and spiritual origins to the ancient Order of Penance, the medieval penitential movements, and to Saint Francis of Assisi. Men and women anxious to live a deeper spiritual life looked to Francis of Assisi to give them a ''form of life.'' *The Letter to the Faithful*, in both the earlier and later editions, embodies this elemental rule of life for lay people living in the world. In time, many of these brothers and sisters of penance left their homes to live either in hermitages or in common life bound by the religious vows of poverty, chastity, and obedience and engaging in the works of mercy. The first official approbation of this movement in Italy was given by Nicholas V, July 20, 1447, in the apostolic letter *Pastoralis officii*, in which he recommended that these tertiaries constitute themselves as a true mendicant order by holding a general chapter for the election of a visitator or general superior, compiling their own statutes, and selecting their own proper religious habit.

History. From the beginning the rule of life of the Third Order Regular was substantially that of the secular third order, which had been approved by Nicholas IV in the bull *Supra montem*, Aug. 18, 1289. As the order developed revisions were made, particularly at the chapter of Florence in 1472. Further revisions in the rule and constitutions, done in the 16th century by Bonaventura da Vicenza, were approved in 1549. During the course of the centuries other congregations of the Third Order had arisen in Dalmatia, Germany, France, Holland, Spain, Belgium, and Portugal. With the intention of unifying the internal life of all tertiary Franciscans, Leo X promulgated by means of the bull *Inter cetera*, Jan. 20, 1521 another rule composed of 10 chapters. This rule, which remained in effect until 1927, did not, however, bind the tertiaries of Italy, Spain, Belgium, and Dalmatia. Sixtus IV granted in 1473 the privilege of exemption and, in 1479, the special privileges enjoyed by all Franciscans.

In the 16th century the Italian congregation, also called the congregation of Lombardy—of which the present male branch of the Third Order Regular of Saint Francis is the continuation—united within itself tertiary groups in Italy, Sicily, and Dalmatia. The congregation of Belgium joined in 1650, and some congregations of southern Germany as well. The rule and constitutions of that period, revised in 1639, 1734, and 1888 were replaced by new legislation in the 20th century. The rule given by Pius XI, Oct. 4, 1927 was extended to all the modern congregations of regular tertiaries of both sexes. New constitutions for the male branch, approved by the same pope on March 7, 1929, were amended and revised in 1940, 1953, 1959, 1969, 1973, and 1992. The Third Order Regular is a member and active participant, along with the Friars Minor, the Conventuals, and the Capuchins, in the conference of Franciscan Ministers General.

Growth in the 20th Century. Events that took place in Italy from 1860 to 1873 brought about in great part the suppression of the order by the civil government. The number of provinces in Italy was reduced to two, namely, the province of Sicily and that of Umbro-Picena (today, Assisi). The dawn of the 20th century saw the order almost extinct, but it found new life as a result of the union of the Spanish congregation, May 13, 1906 and the establishment in the United States, at Loretto, Pa., of the Province of the Sacred Heart. The Spanish congregation had originated in the 13th or 14th century and was approved as a regular order in 1442 by Eugene IV. Suffering many suppressions in the early 19th century, it was revived through the leadership of Fray Antonio Ripoll. The province of the Sacred Heart was made up from two communities of Franciscan Tertiary brothers, one at Spalding, Nebraska and the other at Loretto, Pa., which sought and obtained permission to join the Third Order Regular. Two Italian friars, Jerome Zazzara and Anthony Balestieri, were sent to assist the process of union. The province was established in 1910.

On Oct. 11, 1912, Pius Dujmovic of the Dalmatian province was elected minister general and remained in office for nearly eight years. He promoted the work of restoration by personally visiting the provinces in Italy and the U.S. He began publication of the *Analecta T.O.R.*, the official publication of the Order. His efforts were seriously handicapped during World War I when again the order suffered heavily in Italy and Dalmatia. On Aug.12, 1920, Arnaldo Rigo of the Spanish province was elected minister general and guided the order for 12 years. In that same year a group of friars from Sacred Heart Province formed the Commissariate of the Immaculate Conception to care for Italian immigrants in the diocese of Altoona, Pa. In 1925 this commissariate was established as a province. In 1924 the Spanish province established a commissariate in North America with houses in New York, New Jersey, Texas and Mexico. Later, friars living and working in Texas and Mexico were gathered into the Vice Province of Santa Maria de Guadalupe. The following year, 1925, the Dalmatian province established a commissariate in Pittsburgh, Pa., to care for Croatian immigrants. In 2001, few friars continued to minister in the United States but many served Croatian immigrants in Germany.

The pattern of growth continued through the general administrations of six successive minister generals. Giovanni Parisi, nominated May 26, 1936, expressed a desire that the order extend itself to the foreign missions. In 1938, the Congregation for the Propagation of the Faith assigned a territory in the diocese of Patna, India. Under the leadership of Father Eugene George, then minister provincial, friars from the Province of the Sacred Heart began this work. In 1971, this mission was established as the province of Saint Thomas the Apostle. In 1996, two commissariates were additionally formed: that of Saint Francis in Ranchi and the other of Saint Louis in Bangalore. Most recently, in 1999, the commissariate in Ranchi was raised to the status of a vice province.

During the generalate of John Bocella, (1947–1965), mission territory in Paraguay was entrusted to the care of friars from the Assisi Province in 1951 and additional territory in the same country entrusted to friars from the Immaculate Conception province in the U.S. in 1960. Both of these groups of friars with indigenous vocations were formed into the Vice Province of Saint Anthony in 1992. In 1955, the Tertiaries of Albi, France, along with their missions in Brazil, were united to the Third Order Regular. This group of friars was founded in 1866 by Francis M. Causade and approved in 1873. They may be considered to be a revival of the ancient French Franciscan congregation known as the ''Picpus'' founded in 1287 by Barthélemy Béchin. In 1962, the U.S. Province of the Sacred Heart accepted another Brazilian mission in the diocese of Borba. All of the friars working in Brazil along with native vocations now form the Vice Province of Nossa Senhora de Aparecida established in 1992.

The generalate of Louis Secondo (1964–1977) was marked by an extraordinary general chapter given over to the mandate of the Second Vatican Council to return to the spirit of the founder and to adapt to the signs of the times. Consultation among the members of the provinces resulted in experimental constitutions (1969) that, after the period of experimentation, were later examined and codified. During his term the collaborative work on a new Rule was begun with the Madrid Conference of 1974. It would be completed by his successor.

In 1982, the minister general, Roland Faley (1977–1983), formally united two additional diocesan congregations with the Third Order Regular. The Franciscan Familiars of Saint Joseph, a community organized by the vicar apostolic of Marianhill (Republic of South Africa) in 1923 to live and work among the Zulu people was established as the Vice Province of Saint Joseph. And in the same year, the Congregation of Native Brothers of Saint Vincent de Paul organized in 1877 by Fr. Luigi Piccinelli in Ceylon (Sri Lanka) to care for orphans and to teach was established as the Vice Province of Our Lady of Sri Lanka.

In 1991, a small group of friars in Gothenburg, Sweden, was united to the TOR under the leadership of general minister, José Angulo Quilis (1983–1995). This group, originally Lutheran, shared an attraction to St. Francis and welcomed men and women in need of personal care or spiritual guidance. Today they comprise the Delegation of Saint John the Baptist. In 1999, under the guidance of minister general Bonaventure Midili (1995–), the Delegation of Saint Bonaventure was established in Bangladesh.

Notable Figures. Several members of the order have made notable contributions to studies. John P.M. Doyle (1874–1952) of the Sacred Heart Province (U.S.) taught philosophy and theology at St. Francis College and Seminary and edited four books on these sciences. Raniero Luconi (1878–1951) was a historian and for many years editor of the *Analecta, T.O.R.*. Bartolomé Salvá (1867–1956) was a student and editor of the works of Bl. Raymond Lull. Historians Raffaele Pazzelli, Lino Temperini and Gabriele Andreozzi have written extensively about the penitential charism and history of the Third Order of Penance.

Inclusive Third Order Regular. Beginning in the late 1950s there had been some attempt to dialogue with male tertiary congregations who followed the common rule of the TOR (1927). This dialogue was expanded in the 1970s to include the many women's congregations who also followed that rule. Encouraged by the mandate of Vatican II to return to the historical and spiritual sources, this expanded and inclusive dialogue moved slowly toward the creation of a new rule. With approximately 200 superiors general, representing 35 countries and almost 200,000 Third Order Regular religious, and after much study and deliberation, the text for the new rule was approved in March 1982. It received papal approbation on Dec. 8, 1982. These varied male and female congregations known collectively as the Brothers and Sisters of the Third Order of Saint Francis are represented internationally by the International Franciscan Conference (CFI) with executive offices in Rome, Italy. The president of the CFI joins with the general minister of the Secular Franciscan Order (SFO) and the four ministers general (OFM, OFM Conv, OFM Cap, and TOR) to form the Conference of the Franciscan Family through which they have a common voice. In the United States, the Franciscan Federation with executive offices in Washington, D.C., serves as the umbrella organization and voice for the 12,000 plus male and female members of the TOR in the U.S.

Bibliography: M. CARNEY and T. HORGAN, eds., *Rule and Life of the Brothers and Sisters of the Third Order Regular of Saint Francis: Rule and Commentary* (Washington, D.C. 1999). L. TEMPERINI, *Penitential Spirituality in the Franciscan Sources* (Franciscan Federation Publications 1983). R. PAZZELLI, *St. Francis and the Third Order: The Franciscan and Pre-Franciscan Movement* (Chicago 1989). M. SLOWICK, *The Franciscan Third Order Regular in the U.S.: Origins, Early Years, and Recent Developments* (Tiffin, Ohio 1999). E. SAGGAU, *A Short History of the Franciscan Federation, Third Order Regular of the Sisters and Brothers of the U.S. 1965–1995* (Franciscan Federation Publications 1995).

[L. SECONDO/G. SCHINELLI]

FRANCISCANS, THIRD ORDER SECULAR

An autonomous lay order, properly called the Secular Franciscan Order (formerly ''Third Order of St. Francis''). It is open to men and women, married and single, as well as to diocesan bishops, priests, and deacons who are not members of religious orders. It is the only lay Franciscan order. Its members are bound by a life commitment to live the gospel according to their state of life. They are organized into local self-governing ''fraternities'' assisted by regional, national, and international fraternities. A minister general, elected by the S.F.O. general chapters, leads the S.F.O. with a general council at the international level. Each level of fraternity also has a spiritual assistant from one of the religious orders of Franciscan men and women.

Origins. When Francis of Assisi decided to enter into conversion (penance), in his own words, he ''left the world,'' that is, he began reducing his personal material needs in order to be free to love and serve the Lord. St. Francis was the first of a long line of ''Penitents from Assisi''—all within a larger penitential movement which dates from the beginning of the Church. Some Franciscan Penitents became celibate brothers (friars) in a religious order of men (the ''First Order''), and women like St. Clare became cloistered sisters (the ''Second Order''). Most Franciscan Penitents were not called by God to leave their marriages and children, nor their ordinary lives. Francis's *Letter to All the Faithful*, describing what it means to be part of the penitential (conversion) process, is used to introduce the new S.F.O. *Rule*.

Various editions of a Rule and other instructions for lay Franciscans were approved by the Holy See to help them in their conversion process. In 1893 Pope Leo XIII issued a new Rule for the ''Third Order Secular of St. Francis.'' This new Rule changed the direction of growth in the Order from an autonomous lay order to a quasi religious order subject to the authority of Friars of the three branches of the First Order and the Third Order Regular. This artificially divided the one S.F.O. into four orders. ''Third Order Secular'' Franciscans took up many customs of religious orders, none of which were appropriate for a lay order.

The New Rule. In 1976 Pope Paul VI approved a new Rule of the S.F.O. that reasserts the basic autonomy and unity of the order and its interdependence with other Franciscan men and women in the world. At the same time it affirms the independence of the S.F.O. from the Friars' Orders. The Holy See approved the *General Constitutions* of the S.F.O. in 1995. These were revised by the S.F.O. General Chapter of 1999, and the revisions were approved in 2000.

Franciscan brothers and sisters of the various Franciscan religious orders now help S.F.O. Fraternities as ''spiritual assistants.'' A tangible sign of their decision to convert their hearts, usually a Tau cross, is worn by the Seculars to show who they are. However, the testimony of their love for one another, their dedication to living the gospel of Jesus within the Catholic Church, and their care for the poor are the clearest signs of conversion.

Model for Lay Spirituality. The Second Vatican Council called all the orders in the Church, religious and lay, to study their roots in order to renew their life within the Church. The new Rule of Paul VI for the S.F.O. enables lay Franciscans to return to their original calling within the Church. The focus of the new Rule is on conversion, on opening hearts to the work of the Holy Spirit, to enable Franciscan laity to live their baptismal vocation. The new S.F.O. Rule sets the gospel of Jesus as the anchor of spiritual life. Secular Franciscans are to read and live the gospel, ''going from Gospel to life and life to Gospel.'' In the Rule there are five specific areas of ministry for Secular Franciscans: (1) formation of each other in gospel living, (2) promotion of family life, (3) working for peace and justice for all peoples, (4) protection of all of Creation, (5) reverence for work as a gift from God. Secular Franciscans are to be active members of their parish churches and dioceses, leading by their good example. Eucharist and the Liturgy of the Hours, active care for the poor, and a desire to be leaven in society are marks of Secular Franciscan life.

Bibliography: R. PAZZELLI, *St. Francis and the Third Order* (Quincy, Ill. 1982). R. ARMSTRONG, J. HELLMANN, W. SHORT, eds., *Francis of Assisi: Early Documents*, v.1 and 2 (Hyde Park, N.Y. 1999–2000). R. STEWART, *De Illis Qui Faciunt Penitentiam: The Rule of the Secular Franciscan Order* (Rome 1991). L. BACH, *Catch Me a Rainbow* (Lindsborg, Kan. 1990).

[N. F. THOMPSON]

FRANCK, CÉSAR AUGUSTE

Important composer of the romanticist period; b. St. Croix (Liège), Belgium, Dec. 22, 1822; d. Paris, Nov. 8, 1890. Although by birth a Walloon, he became absorbed into French culture, was naturalized in 1873, and is regarded as a French composer. He studied at the Liège and Paris conservatories, becoming organ professor at the latter in 1872. He had aspired to a career as virtuoso pianist, and concentrated practice gave him an abnormal handstretch that influenced his creative pianism. Although three early piano trios (1841) suggested what was to follow, it was only between 1860 and 1862 that his first really important music appeared, *Six Pièces* for organ—a direct consequence of his appointment in 1858 as organ-

César Auguste Franck. (Corbis/Bettman)

ist at Sainte-Clothilde, where he could give full vent in his extemporizations to his simple and ardent faith. His religiosity has been distorted; the picture painted by his adoring pupil Vincent d' INDY is one of a bigoted and consummate prig. This he was not; he was simply a good man and a staunch believer, who spoke to God through his music. The gallery of Sainte-Clothilde, his house in Boul' Mich, and later the organ room at the conservatory thronged with young musicians (not all his pupils) who were introduced there to the beauties of Bach and Beethoven and his own improvisations. His ''liturgical'' compositions are undistinguished; his concert works, however, reflect his spiritual preoccupation as well as his improvisatory technique. There are few composers whose sincerity is so overt as was his in everything he wrote.

Musically he may be regarded as the father of modern harmony. He formulated a distinctive school of composers whose style was basically contrapuntal in structure yet lyrical in intent; and he moved French music from operatic domination to an ''absolute'' and symphonic position. His own output was not large, but it includes several masterpieces among the genres he essayed. Such are his monumental oratorio, *Les Béatitudes;* his violin sonata, string quartet, and piano quintet; and his extended orchestral works, notably the *Symphonic Variations* and *D-Minor Symphony*, both popular perennials of the concert repertory. His organ works and the two great solos for piano are acknowledged classics of their instruments.

Bibliography: C. VAN DEN BORREN, *César Franck* (Brussels 1950). N. DEMUTH, *César Franck* (New York 1949); *French Piano Music* (London 1959). N. DUFOURCQ, *César Franck* (Paris 1949). M. EMMANUEL, *César Franck* (Paris 1930). V. D'INDY, *César Franck,* tr. R. H. NEWMARCH (New York 1910). L. VALLAS, *César Franck,* tr. H. FOSS (London 1951). M. COOPER, *French Music* (London 1951). A. SALAZAR, *Music in Our Time,* tr. I. POPE (London 1948). P. DEWONCK, ''César Franck, 'maître de la musique moderne,''' *Revue Belge de Musicologie* 52 (1998) 73–84. J. FERRARD, ''L'œuvre por orgue de César Franck: Sources et Éditions,'' *Revue Belge de Musicologie* 45 (1991) 163–180. M.-L. JAQUET-LANGLAIS, ''The Organ Works of Franck: A Survey of Editorial and Performance Problems,'' in *French Organ Music from the Revolution to Franck and Widor,* ed. L. ARCHBOLD and W. J. PETERSON, tr. M. DIRST and K. MARSHALL (Rochester 1995) 143–188. M. G. KAUFMANN, '''Caesar Franck; Ein Deutscher!': Der Versuch einer Vereinnahmung der Französischen Musik-kultur im 'Dritten Reich,''' *Musik und Kirche* 69 (1999) 326–333. J. QUITIN, ''Le Retour de Franck à Liège,'' *Revue Belge de Musicologie* 45 (1991) 85–96. R. SMITH, *Toward an Authentic Interpretation of the Organ Works of César Franck* (Hillsboro, N.Y. 1983); *Playing the Organ Works of César Franck* (Hillsboro, N.Y. 1997).

[N. DEMUTH]

FRANCKE, AUGUST HERMANN

German Pietist, Protestant educational theorist, sense realist, and practical reformer; b. Lübeck, March 22, 1663; d. Halle, June 8, 1727. After studying for the Lutheran ministry at the Universities of Erfurt and Kiel, he received his degree from Leipzig in 1685. Francke founded a Bible study club, the Collegium Philobiblicum, that attracted Philipp Jakob SPENER, the court preacher at Dresden who converted Francke to PIETISM. In 1689 Francke won the post of lecturer on the Bible at the University of Leipzig, but his Pietist views angered the Lutheran clergy who forced his resignation. The newly founded University of Halle then offered him a professorate in Greek and Oriental languages and later in theology and a pastorate in the adjoining town of Glaucha. For the remaining 36 years of his life Francke taught at the university and preached to his parishioners at Glaucha.

Francke's work in education exerted great influence throughout the Protestant sections of the Germanies. In 1692 at Glaucha he opened an elementary school supported by alms to educate the poor. As an innovation he used needy university students as tutors, who in return received guidance and free attendance at the university lectures in Halle. Soon after the rich demanded and received a Latin school for their sons. In 1695 Francke started an orphans' school that ran a printing press, paper mill, book store, and dispensary. Within three years this practical school, taught by university students, numbered 100 resident pupils and 500 day scholars.

Student teachers trained in Francke's teacher's seminaries carried throughout Europe and incorporated into elementary and secondary schools his main educational ideas: special care and training for orphans; training of teachers; emphasis on practical subjects—vernacular, arithmetic, geography, useful arts, foreign language—and practical piety in everyday life. As a professor, Francke, together with his collaborators, succeeded in making Halle the first modern university by substituting German for Latin as the lecture language; placing scientific studies alongside law, medicine, and theology; and introducing the principle of ACADEMIC FREEDOM made operative through research. Other European universities followed the example of Halle, and in the United States, the Johns Hopkins University in Baltimore, Md., in 1867 took it as its model and became the first graduate school in the Americas.

Bibliography: J. E. WISE, *The History of Education: An Analytic Survey from the Age of Homer to the Present* (New York 1964). H. RECHTMANN, *Lexicon der Pädagogik* 2 (Freiburg 1962) 68–70.

[E. G. RYAN]

FRANCO LIPPI, BL.

Carmelite lay brother; b. Grotti, near Siena, Italy, Dec. 3, 1211; d. Siena, Dec. 11, 1291. After a scandalous life as a *condottiere*, he was blinded in battle at the age of 50 and vowed to change his life and go on at pilgrimage to SANTIAGO DE COMPOSTELA if cured. St. James answered his prayers, and his sight was restored. After visiting Rome, he returned to Siena to take up the penitential life of a hermit, which he continued when he later became a CARMELITE lay brother. Living in a little cell close to the chapel of Our Lady, he overcame various temptations of the devil and was comforted by appearances of Our Lord and Our Lady. He was said to have enjoyed also the gift of prophecy. His body was exhumed 50 years after death, and part of his relics were taken to Cremona, while the remainder are still venerated in the Carmelite church in Siena. His cult was approved by Pope CLEMENT V in 1308, and he has been in Carmelite liturgy since 1672. Many 17th-century confraternities, especially in Spain, were dedicated in his honor. He should not be confused with another Sienese Francis, the Blessed Servite Francesco of Siena (d. 1328), as is done in G. Lombardelli's *La Vita del b. Franco Sensese da Grotti* (Siena 1590).

Feast: Dec. 11.

Bibliography: "Catalogus sanctorum ordinis carmelitarum," in B. M. XIBERTA Y ROQUETA, *De visione Sancti Simonis Stock* (Rome 1950) 284, 294, 305, 312.

[E. R. CARROLL]

FRANCO OF COLOGNE

Medieval music theorist; fl. 1250–80. Nothing is known of his life except that he was a papal chamberlain and preceptor of the Hospital of St. John of Jerusalem at Cologne. The only reference to his compositions is a statement by Jacob of Liège about a three-part motet heard in Paris. The same writer describes Franco as *Teutonicus* (German), perhaps to distinguish him from an earlier Franco of French birth. His reputation rests on one genuine treatise, *Ars cantus mensurabilis* (c. 1260), which presents a system of setting down music whereby rhythmical and metrical matters are dealt with clearly, logically, and scientifically. Previous methods had tended to be ambiguous and vague, hindering the development of polyphony. Franco's system found many imitators in Italy, France, and England, and some aspects remained in force until the 16th century. His definitions of discant, hocket, copula, and organum are classics of their kind, combining brevity, accuracy, and pertinent musical illustration.

Bibliography: Texts of treatise in *Scriptorum de musica medii aevi nova series*, H. COUSSEMAKER, 4 v. (Paris 1864–76) 1:117–136, Eng. tr. in *Source Readings in Music History*, O. STRUNK (New York 1950) 139–159. M. GERBERT, *Scriptores ecclesiastici de musica sacra potissimum* 3 v. (Milan 1931) 3:1–16, slightly less reliable. G. REESE, *Music in the Renaissance* (rev. ed. New York 1959). H. BESSELER, *Die Musik in Geschichte und Gegenwart*, ed. F. BLUME (Kassel-Basel 1949–) 4:688–698. S. T. WARNER, *Grove's Dictionary of Music and Musicians*, ed. E. BLOM 9 v. (5th ed. London 1954) 3:478–480. F. DE COLONIA, "Ars cantus mensurabilis." in *Corpus scriptorum de musica, vol. 18*, ed. G. REANEY and A. GILLES (Rome 1974) 23–82. A. HUGHES, "Franco of Cologne" in *The New Grove Dictionary of Music and Musicians, vol. 6*, ed. S. SADIE (New York 1980) 794–797. D. M. RANDEL, ed., *The Harvard Biographical Dictionary of Music* (Cambridge 1996) 280. N. SLONIMSKY, ed. *Baker's Biographical Dictionary of Musicians, Eighth Edition* (New York 1992) 569.

[D. STEVENS]

FRANGIPANI

A noble Roman family influential in affairs of the papacy and the Empire from the early 11th to the end of the 13th century. The name first appears in 1014, when a Leo *de Imperio or de Imperatore qui vocatur Frangapane* signed a *placitum* relative to the abbey of Farfa. *De imperatore* shows adherence to the imperial cause, and it has been suggested that the *qui vocatur* indicates the then recent origin of the family name. Another witness to the 1014 agreement was a Petrus de Imperato, head of the city militia; the name appears in Roman records from 960 on. *De imperatore* without "Frangipane" is found frequently until 1042, then disappears. The family name has various forms: Fragapane and Frajapane (1014), Fricapanem (1094), Fraiapanem (1116); and in the 12th century Friapane and Fraiapanis vary with Fragenspanem or Frangenspanem.

The legend connecting the origin of the family with the old Roman Anicii and the name with an 8th-century member, Flavius, who provided bread (*frangebat panem*) for the people during a famine, is without foundation.

In Rome the Frangipani possessed the large holdings extending along the Palatine, the Forum, Via sacra, Coliseum, and the Circus Maximus, and centered in the fortified tower near the Arch of Titus. This tower, the *Turris cartularia* temporarily housed a portion of the papal archives. In the beginning of the 12th century the family was divided into three branches: de Cartularia, de Septizonio, and de Gradellis, and acquired many lands in Campagna, Marittima, and Terracina. They held Ninfa in fief from the pope until 1213, and dominated Marino, Torri, Astura, and Cisterna until these yielded to GAETANI influence in the 13th century; Nemi was acquired by the Frangipani in the 16th century.

Increasingly prominent during the GREGORIAN REFORM, the Frangipani vacillated as circumstances demanded between supporting the papacy and the Empire, always opposing the other baronial families, first the PIERLEONI, then the Annibaldi and the Gaetani. In 1061 *Cencio* Frangipani supported Hildebrand in obtaining the election of ALEXANDER II, and in 1084 he aided Robert Guiscard's entry into Rome to liberate GREGORY VII. Under Cencio's son *Giovanni,* URBAN II received hospitality and refuge in 1093 at the *Turris cartularia,* and in 1108 PASCHAL II entrusted the government of Benevento to *Leone* Frangipani.

When Emperor HENRY V went into Italy, the Frangipani shifted to the imperial side. *Cencio II*, a follower of Henry V, took GELASIUS II prisoner in 1118. This opposition to the papacy continued under CALLISTUS II, who destroyed the Frangipani towers to obtain their submission. The Frangipani reached the height of their power when their candidate, HONORIUS II, was elected in 1124. They continued more or less loyal to the papacy during the 12th century, but in the following century they took part in the uprisings against the papacy and aided FREDERICK II against GREGORY IX and INNOCENT IV. They sold their strongholds in Rome to the Emperor and received them back from him in fief; with his help they rebuilt the destroyed *Turris cartularia.* Toward the end of Frederick II's reign the Frangipani shifted again to the papal side, and because of this defection Frederick took back their fiefs to Taranto and Otranto.

Frangipani influence in Rome declined at the close of the 13th century. The Neapolitan branch continued into the 17th century. Families elsewhere claimed descent from the Frangipani of Rome and assumed the name. The Frangipani of Croatia, who held Modrus, Tersato, and the island of Veglia, claimed descent from the Roman house, but on the basis of false documents. The Frangipani of Friuli, who also claimed a Roman origin, held Tarcento and Castel Porpeto; this family is still extant. It is uncertain whether ANTIPOPE Innocent III (Lando of Sezze) 1179, and Leo de Monumento, supporter of Henry VI, belonged to the Frangipani family.

The following are prominent members of the Roman branch of the Frangipani family: *Aldruda,* Countess of Bertinoro, who in 1174, with Guglielmo Marchesella of Ferrara, led the troops who freed Ancona from the siege of the Germans. *Jacoba,* wife of Graziano Frangipani of Settisoli, friend and follower of St. Francis of Assisi (buried near his tomb in the Assisi basilica). *Guglielmo,* d. 1337, archbishop of Patras (1317), who excommunicated the Catalonian Company in 1331. *Muzio,* husband of Julia Strozzi and leader of the papal auxiliaries to France in 1569. *Silvester* (*Ignatius Ciantes*), Dominican; b. 1594; d. 1667; provincial of the order in Sicily, then in Apulia, Calabria, and later England; author of several ecclesiastical works. *Pietro Francesco Orsini* (BENEDICT XIII), Dominican; b. 1649; d. 1730; son of *Giovanna* Frangipani of Tolpha.

A number of the members of the Neapolitan branch are noteworthy: *Giovanni,* Count of Astura, famous for the capture of Conradin of Swabia in 1268. *Fabio Mirto,* d. March 17, 1587; governor of the Marches and of Perugia, 1559; bishop of Cajazzo, 1537, of Barletta-Nazareth, 1572; participant in the Council of Trent, 1562 to 1572, 1577 to 1587; nuncio to Paris, 1568 to 1572. *Ottavio Mirto,* nephew of Fabio, son of *Sylvio Frangipani Mirto;* b. 1542 or 1543; d. 1612; bishop of Cajazzo, 1572; governor of Bologna under Gregory XIII; bishop of Tricario, 1592; nuncio to Cologne and the Low Countries, 1587 to 1596, to Brussels, 1596 to 1606; archbishop of Taranto, 1605. *Ottavio Fraja,* Benedictine; b. 1783; d. 1843; librarian at Monte Cassino, collaborator of Cardinal Angelo MAI, noted paleographer.

Bibliography: General. L. FRANGIPANE, *Geneologia dei Frangipane signori di Castello e Tarcento* (Udine 1891). F. SABATINI, *La famiglia e le torri dei Frangipane in Roma* (Rome 1907). F. EHRLE in *Mélanges offerts à M. Émile Chatelain* (Paris 1910) 448–85. P. FEDELE, ''Sull'origine dei F.,'' *Archivio della Societá romana di storia patria* 33 (1910) 493–506. E. D. THESEIDER, *Enciclopedia Italiana di scienzi littere ed arti*, 36 v. (Rome 1929–39) 16:23–24. G. OPITZ, *Lexikon für Theologie und Kirche*, ed. J. HOFER and K. RAHNER, 10 v. (2d, new ed. Freiburg 1957–65) 4:252–54. Special. P. FEDELE, ''Il leopardo e l'agnello di casa Frangipane,'' *Archivio della Società romana di storia patria* 28 (1905) 207–17. E. D'ALENÇON, *Frère Jacqueline* (new ed. Paris 1927). J. QUÉTIF and J. ÉCHARD, *Scriptores Ordinis Praedicatorum,* 5 v. (Paris

1719–23); continued by R. COULON (Paris 1909–); repr. 2 v. in 4 (New York 1959) 2.2:620–21. E. JALLONGHI, ''D. Ottavio Frajo Frangipane, archivista cassinese, 1763–1843,'' *Bulletino dell'Istituto storico ital. . . . e Archivio Muratoriano* 47 (1932) 227–45.

[M. G. MCNEIL]

FRANK, JACOB

Jewish pseudo-Messiah; b. Korolowska (Podolia), Poland, *c.* 1726; d. Offenbach (Hesse), Germany, 1791. Frank flourished in a time of economic and political insecurity for the Jewish community and of spiritual confusion resulting from the exposure of the messianic pretensions of Shabbetai Zevi (*see* SHABBATIÏSM), which, while disillusioning many of the latter's followers, persuaded many others that his conversion to Islam was a necessary condition to the fulfillment of his messianic claims.

Having grown up in an atmosphere filled with mystical aberration and superstition, and having received a poor Jewish education, Frank was attracted early to the teachings of the Shabbatians whom he met in Turkey, where he had settled as a merchant. Adapting the beliefs and practices of this semi-Islamic cult to his purposes, he returned to Podolia in 1755, where, through clandestine meetings characterized by mystical formulas and erotic behavior, he assumed leadership as the reincarnation of Shabbetai Zevi, the second person of a trinitarian doctrine.

The Jewish community, scandalized by the activities of the Frankists, reported them, to the authorities in 1756, resulting in Frank's expulsion from Poland as a Turk and his followers' excommunication by the rabbis for gross violations of Jewish observance and morality. As anti-Talmudists and Trinitarians, the sectarians sought relief from the archbishop of Podolia, who granted them his protection and convened a public disputation between them and the rabbis. This concluded with the Jewish community being compelled to pay their opponents a heavy indemnity and publicly burning copies of the Talmud. Reappearing in Podolia, Frank convinced his adherents to adopt Christianity as a cover for their messianic expectations, and in 1759 the Frankists negotiated with the Catholic Church for their conversion, requesting another public disputation, wherein they attempted unsuccessfully to demonstrate a Talmudical basis for the blood accusation.

After a pomp-filled conversion ceremony, which included the participation of the royal house, reports of non-Christian preachings and practices by the converts confirmed the Church authorities' growing suspicion of Frank's hypocrisy. After a trial for heresy in 1760, he was imprisoned for 13 years, during which time he vigorously propagandized his cause. He was released by the Russians in 1772 at the first partition of Poland.

Leaving Poland, Frank had some success in Moravia, and finally established himself in a palace in Offenbach, giving himself the title of baron. Supported by the gifts of his devotees, he and his daughter, Eve, ''the Holy Lady,'' lived a life of luxury. After Frank's death, Eve assumed the leadership of the sect, but her father's supporters did not transfer their loyalty to her, either in spirit or in coin, and at her death in 1816 she was destitute. As for the Frankists, they merged into their surroundings, eventually disappearing as a sect.

Bibliography: S. M. DUBNOW, *History of the Jews in Russia and Poland,* tr. I. FRIEDLANDER, 3 v. (Philadelphia 1946) 1:211–220. H. H. GRAETZ, *History of the Jews,* ed. and tr. B. LÖWY. 6 v. (Philadelphia 1945) 5:271–290. J. R. MARCUS, *The Jew in the Medieval World* (Cincinnati 1938) 279–283. *Encyclopaedia Judaica: Das Judentum in Geschichte und Gegenwart* (Berlin 1928–34) 6:1071–80.

[R. KRINSKY]

FRANKENBERG, JOHANN HEINRICH

Archbishop of Malines and primate of Belgium (1759–1801); b. Grosglogau, Silesia, Sept. 18, 1726; d. Breda, Holland, June 11, 1804. As the scion of an old Silesian noble family, he studied philosophy in Breslau and theology at the Collegium Germanicum in Rome, where, when still a young student, he drew the attention of Pope Benedict XIV. In 1750, he was ordained and made assistant to the apostolic vicar and later archbishop of Gorizia, Karl Michael Count Attems. He was dean of the Chapterhouse in Prague (1754) and dean of Bunzlau, Bohemia (1755). On Jan. 20, 1778, Frankenberg was appointed archbishop of Malines by MARIA THERESA, and he was created a cardinal by Pope Pius VI.

JOSEPHINISM, the system that Maria Theresa had introduced into her patrimonial dominions, was felt only mildly in the Belgian Church, so that Cardinal Frankenberg could discharge his office of metropolitan without great difficulty. As early as 1782, however, Emperor Joseph, disregarding the totally different Belgian conditions, thwarted the attempt of the Belgian episcopate to proceed collectively in the problem of mixed marriages, which had become acute because of the Emperor's proclamation of his Tolerance Decree on Dec. 13, 1781. In 1786, in the matter of the erection of a general seminary at Louvain, the ruler provoked the public opposition of Cardinal Frankenberg, who refused to send his pupils to the seminary founded and conducted by the government.

Frankenberg was called to Vienna, where the Emperor tried in vain to win the archbishop over to his views. Back in Malines, supported by the other Belgian bishops, he continued his opposition until in August 1789, a popular uprising forced the Emperor formally to decree the reestablishment of the episcopal seminaries. But when open civil war broke out in October, the cardinal fled in order to escape imprisonment. When Austrian rule and, in its wake, religious peace, were reestablished, Frankenberg returned to his diocese. A few years later, he opposed French measures hostile to the Church, and was forced to leave the country (1797). The cardinal went first to Borken, in Münsterland, and, when the Prussians expelled him, to Breda.

Bibliography: H. BENEDIKT, *Neue deutsche Biographie* (Berlin 1953–) 5:349–350. H. HOFFMANN, *Schlesische Lebensbilder* v.4 (Breslau 1931).

[F. MAASS]

FRANKFURT SCHOOL

The Frankfurt School, most famous for its Critical Theory, was conceived in 1922 by Felix Weil. His family fortune provided for both the inauguration of the Frankfurt Institute of Social Research in Frankfurt, Germany and the financial independence necessary for its members to perform the envisaged social research and theoretical speculation both there and elsewhere, especially in the United States, during the period of exile caused by Nazism. Officially erected in 1923, the Institute only began to develop the approach which later characterized it in 1930 under the leadership of Max Horkheimer (1895–1973). He remained director of the Institute until his retirement. He and Theodor Adorno (1903–1969) are most closely identified with both the Institute and the development of its Critical Theory. Among others associated with the institute, the more well known are W. Benjamin, F. Pollock, and especially in the United States, P. Tillich, E. Fromm, H. Marcuse, and J. Habermas.

General Theory. In order to produce a new critical theory, the Frankfurt School attempted a fusion of Marx's socio-economic with Freud's psychoanalytic critique. Originally directed precisely against the capitalist economic system and its concomitant implicit ontology, the new Critical Theory soon widened its scope to include the "whole (of reality)," which it deemed to be a "totally administered world," and, hence, destructive of individual human persons, their freedom, their pleasure, their being. Thus, "the (empirical) whole is the untrue." Consequently, Critical Theory rejected both the more recent positivism, empiricism, and scientism as well as the older classical metaphysical systems, because both inherently tend to accept and equate any given particular state of reality with reality pure and simple. According to Critical Theory, the malaise of modern man is rooted specifically in the Enlightenment, but can be traced all the way back to the dawn of human consciousness and reflective thinking. The exploitation of nature and the alienation of humanity involved in this beginning have intensified steadfastly and culminated in the capitalist economic system, whose own proper fruit has been the mass culture and consumer civilization, so typical of the West, but inexorably infecting all mankind. The result is the total and seemingly incurable alienation of man—not only economic, social, cultural, but also ontological.

A Theological Dimension. Although some thinkers associated with the Frankfurt School have remained steadfastly atheistic, there is discernible in the writings of especially Benjamin and the later Horkheimer and Adorno what has been termed a theological dimension. Thus Adorno and Horkheimer have been led to the conclusion that, since "the whole is the untrue," the appeal to or "longing for the entirely other" is not absolutely reprobate, although it "is, to be sure, a nonscientific wish." However, on the basis of their fear of and opposition to the cheap reconciliation advocated in customary metaphysical systems (German Idealism) and the reduction of everything to the status of means in contemporary empiricist scientism, they remain decidedly dedicated to their Negative Dialectic. By it alone can the temptation to absolutize the present moment be overcome. Thus their admittedly impressive achievement remains but a negative critique. Hence their noble aim of overcoming the split in human consciousness, of reconciling subject and object, person and nature, of restoring paradise (the influence, however implicit and unreflective, of the Jewish background of many members of the Frankfurt School ought never be overlooked) was essentially beyond attainment. The thin line between Judeo-Christian negative theology and rationalist agnosticism is strikingly manifest in their thought.

Writings. Horkheimer and Adorno not only thought together, they also wrote together *Dialectic of Enlightenment* (New York 1944, 1972). The foundation of Critical Theory, as well as of all their later writings, was provided by that book along with Horkheimer's *Eclipse of Reason* (New York 1947, 1974) and Adorno's *Minima Moralia* (Frankfurt, 1951, 1976). Their entire work can be viewed, as they themselves viewed it, as "a critique of philosophy, and therefore (it) refuses to abandon philosophy." Their journey, starting in the culture of assimilated German Jewry, took them through classical Greek and modern European philosophy as well as the Marxist and Freudian critiques to a head-on confrontation with contemporary mass-consumer culture, created by technological rationalism. They were philosophers characterized by a refusal to accept human suffering, by a demand for justice in a world where injustice at least seems to triumph. Hence they were led to define the human being as the "Longing for the Entirely Other," the title of what may be termed Horkheimer's last will and testament (*Die Sehnsucht nach dem ganz Anderen*, Hamburg 1970). For theistic thinkers their writings are clearly an inspiration and a challenge, for the philosophy of religion an especially fertile source of new insights about the transcendent, both human and divine.

Bibliography: Suhrkamp Verlag of Frankfurt, Germany, has published the collected works of T. Adorno and is publishing those of M. Horkheimer. T. ADORNO, *Negative Dialectics* (New York 1972); *Jargon of Authenticity* (Evanston 1973). T. ADORNO et al., *The Positivist Dispute in German Sociology* (New York 1976). M. HORKHEIMER, *Die Sehnsucht nach dem ganz Anderen* (Hamburg, 1979); *Critical Theory* (New York 1972); *Critique of Instrumental Reason* (New York 1974). M. JAY, *The Dialectical Imagination* (Boston 1973). K. OPPENS et al., *Über Theodor W. Adorno* (Frankfurt 1970). H. SCHWEPPENHÄUSER, ed., *Theodor W. Adorno zum Gedachtnis* (Frankfurt 1971).

[R. KRESS]

FRANKS

A people of Germanic origin who played a decisive role in shaping western European history during four centuries extending from the late 5th to the late 10th century. During that period the term "Frank" assumed different meanings depending on the historical situation.

The Franks were mentioned for the first time in Roman written texts in the 3rd century in connection with Germanic raids across the Rhine frontier. The term, meaning "hardy" or "brave", referred not to a unified political and ethnic entity, that is, not to a *gens* or nation, but to loose, constantly shifting confederations involving various related tribes, each with its own name, living east of the lower Rhine. From time to time these tribes joined hands temporarily to raid Roman territory, to defend against other Germanic groups, or to fight other confederations. From the late 3rd century onward the Roman imperial government began to utilize members of what one modern authority called "this swarm of tribes" for a variety of purposes: settlement as war prisoners on abandoned farm land west of the Rhine; recruitment as auxiliaries in army units assigned throughout the Roman empire; acceptance as imperial allies (*foederati*) granted lands in return for military service. Some tribes continued to raid Roman territory in search of booty to take back to their original lands east of the Rhine. This ambiguous relationship, continuing throughout the 4th and 5th centuries, resulted in the settlement of many Franks on Roman soil, especially along the northeast frontier. Archaeological evidence, chiefly from grave sites, demonstrates that these newcomers adapted many aspects of Gallo-Roman life without entirely abandoning their Germanic culture or their connections with the Germanic world east of the Rhine. Some individual Franks even rose to high status in the Roman world as generals and even consuls. But in the larger picture marking the decline and dissolution of the Roman Empire, the Franks remained an obscure, relatively insignificant force.

Tribal Migrations. As the 5th century progressed that picture began to change. On the larger scene entire Germanic "nations" led by well-established kings migrated en masse into the western part of the Roman Empire and eventually established independent kingdoms: VISIGOTHS, VANDALS, Burgundians, Ostrogoths, ANGLO-SAXONS. So complete was the dismemberment of the Empire that after 476 there ceased to be an emperor in the West. Roman Gaul was decisively affected by this process. The Burgundians occupied the Rhône valley, and the Visigoths took control of the lands south of the Loire River. The territory between the Loire and the Rhine, increasingly under control of military figures who claimed to represent the Roman government, provided the setting in which the Franks began to make their mark on history. Unlike the Germanic nations noted above, the Franks did not take possession of this area as a politically unified people. Rather, different groups from the "swarm of tribes" that together comprised the Franks slowly penetrated south and west from their original homeland on the right bank of the lower Rhine, a process that was often facilitated by the Roman imperial government. As the infiltration continued and the newcomers took up permanent residence, the tribal groups became more effectively organized under chiefs whose role was fundamentally military. Two such groupings became especially important. One involved Franks who moved south on both sides of the Rhine to establish an area of dominance centered around Cologne; this group would later be known as the Ripuarian Franks. The second group, called the Salian Franks, originally settled just south of the mouth of the Rhine in Batavia. From there the Salians expanded southward, eventually establishing control over old Roman cities such as Cambrai, Tournai, and Arras, and over the Gallo-Roman population that had long occupied that area. During that expansion the Salian Franks usually supported the authorities claiming to represent the Roman imperial government, especially in military operations such as those mounted to halt the intrusion of the Hunnic ruler Attila into Gaul or to block the Visigoth kingdom from expansion north of the Loire. For that effort the Salian leaders were well rewarded, as is illustrated by the rich contents of tomb of King Childeric (reigned 458–481) found at Cambrai in 1653. Childeric's career also made it clear that the newcomers were slowly replacing the Romans as the effective rulers of northern Gaul.

The Merovingians. It was a Salian king, CLOVIS (reigned 481 or 482–511) and the dynasty he founded, the MEROVINGIANS, who elevated the Franks to a central position in western part of the Roman Empire. One of Clovis' chief accomplishments was his unification of the ''swarm of tribes'' into a single political entity, an end Clovis achieved by the brutal murder of the leaders of rival tribes of Franks. He and his sons mounted a series of military campaigns that established Frankish rule over all of Gaul except small territories occupied by the Gascons, the Bretons, and the Visigoths in Septimania. While conquering Gaul the Merovingians also asserted their authority in varying degrees over Germanic peoples living east of the Rhine, including the Thuringians, the Alemanni, the Bavarians, and the Saxons. The might of the Franks was felt even in northern Italy as a result of their involvement in the sequence of events that witnessed the end of the Ostrogothic kingdom and the establishment of the Lombard kingdom. By the end of the Merovingian dynasty in 751 a succession of kings of Frankish descent had created *Francia*, a term used to describe a unified political entity that represented the most powerful and the most enduring of all the Germanic kingdoms established in the western part of the Roman Empire.

But the Frankish leaders of the Merovingian dynasty had achieved more. Despite the violence and brutality that characterized their rule, the Merovingian kings played a key role in creating a milieu in which the Frankish newcomers and the established Gallo-Roman elite gradually intermixed to create an aristocracy whose members considered themselves Franks, increasingly defined as freemen of any ethnic origin who accepted the overlordship of a Frankish king. The melding of Germans and Gallo-Romans was encouraged by the Merovingian system of government, which vested authority in a king as a war leader and his personal followers who were rewarded for serving the king loyally. By dispersing their wealth gained from seizure of the Roman public lands, from booty acquired through military victories, and from property confiscated from their political enemies, the kings were able to draw to their court both Frankish and Gallo-Roman aristocrats eager for wealth and status. Through family ties and friendship bonds those who had the king's trust drew an ever widening circle toward identification with the cause of the king. Religion provided another matrix linking the two populations. One of the highlights of Clovis' reign was his conversion to orthodox Christianity; in contrast with other Germanic kings who were Arians, Clovis thereby became the champion of the religion accepted by the bulk of the population in the West. Clovis' Frankish companions soon followed the example of their leader, thereby becoming Christians who shared a common ground with the Gallo-Roman aristocrats. The Frankish warriors who often received grants of land in return for their loyalty to their king found it sensible to adopt the prevailing agricultural system based on large estates tilled by a dependent population; this accommodation provided another common ground to share with their Gallo-Roman counterparts. All of these factors combined to erode slowly the distinctions between Franks and Gallo-Romans, forming in the process a homogeneous elite, which increasingly conceived themselves as Franks, that is, free men living under the overlordship of a Frankish ruler. The end product was the formation of the last of the Germanic *gentes* who shared in the dismemberment of the Roman Empire, the ''Frankish nation'', a nation formed *after* the great migrations through a process of assimilation and accommodation that provided elements of strength which permitted the Franks to play a decisive role in the development of the post-Roman western Europe world.

The Carolingian Dynasty. During the course of the 7th and early 8th centuries the Merovingian kings were increasingly stripped of their power and wealth by the very same aristocratic families that had long supported them in their rise to power. Finally, in 751 one of those factions brought the Merovingian dynasty's rule over the kingdom of the Franks to an end. That faction was led by a member of a powerful aristocratic family of Frankish origins, later known as the CAROLINGIANS. In many ways the new rulers sought to continue the Frankish ways of their Merovingian predecessors. They titled themselves ''kings of the Franks''. They continued to be successful warrior kings, greatly expanding their political sway by subduing the Frisians, the Saxons, the LOMBARDS in Italy, the Avars in the Danube valley, Muslims in northeastern Spain, and the Aquitainians. These conquests allowed the kings to continue rewarding their followers, thus sustaining the aristocracy whose members counted themselves Franks. The Carolingian rulers retained the basic structures of government that had emerged under Merovingian rule in a fashion that prolonged the Frankish flavor of their rule; one of their chief concerns as rulers was to make more effective the political mechanisms which allowed the central government to restrain the ambitions of aristocratic families. They lent their efforts to strengthening the Christian establishment by putting the weight of royal authority behind a religious reform movement and a vigorous missionary undertaking. The kings played a key role in nurturing a cultural renaissance which gave new vigor to a concern that had long been significant in Gallo-Roman society, that is, the preservation of the

Roman cultural heritage and the religious tradition of the patristic age. To the extent that Carolingian rule could be equated with the Franks, it could fairly be said that during the first half of the 9th century the Franks had achieved a position that allowed them to share center stage among the major powers in the Mediterranean world. Their political sway over the western European portion of the old Roman empire was unchallenged. They stood as equals to Roman emperors in Constantinople and the Muslim caliphs in Baghdad and Cordoba. They were widely recognized as the guardians of the Christian establishment in the West, a role symbolized by their protectorate over the papacy and the Papal States. Intellectual leaders from all over the West—Italy, Spain, Ireland, Anglo-Saxon England—were drawn to the Frankish court and to Frankish monasteries to share in shaping the CAROLINGIAN RENAISSANCE.

However, the Carolingian regime fostered developments that began to efface its Frankish characteristics. From the moment that he took power, PEPIN III, the first Carolingian king, modified the role of blood ties rooted in a Germanic past as the basis of royal authority in favor of religious sanction bestowed by the ecclesiastical establishment, including the Roman Pope. The concept of king as ruling by the grace of God, nourished by the revival of learning and given shape by the experience gained from governing an increasingly diverse population and from royal leadership in reforming religious life, eventually convinced Charlemagne, his religious and intellectual counselors, and the Pope that the title ''emperor of the Romans'' better suited reality than did ''king of the Franks''. The priestly function implied in the Carolingian concept of the imperial office radically redefined the responsibilities of the ruler and of his subjects in ways that effaced the old Frankish idea of the warrior king and his warrior followers to the point where that ethos survived only in a mythology that provided the substance of great epic poems compiled later in the Middle Ages. The bonds that linked the warrior king to his followers for the purpose of gathering the fruits of war were slowly transformed during the Carolingian period into bonds involving a lord–vassal relationship based on personal allegiance of a vassal to a lord in return for a benefice, usually a grant of land, made by a lord to his vassal in order to permit the vassal to perform specified personal services. This transformation laid the basis for the feudal order in which the royal office, civic responsibility, and the public welfare had an entirely different meaning than did the original Frankish monarchy. The Carolingian reform created a religious establishment carrying a Roman stamp that set it a considerable distance apart from that which had taken shape under the rule of the Merovingian Franks. And the Carolingian cultural renaissance produced an intellectual, literary, and artistic milieu that had little association with anything Frankish. In short, although the Carolingian regime did not consciously disassociate itself from its Frankish roots, it blurred to some degree the Germanic elements that had played an important role in giving original shape to post-Roman world in western Europe.

That the age of the Franks had passed was made especially clear by political developments of the last half of the 9th century. What had once represented a united Francia, the realm of the Franks, now became a collection of independent kingdoms whose Frankish rulers of the Carolingian dynasty were eventually replaced by other ruling families with little or no connection to the Franks. For a brief span two of these kingdoms were known as the kingdom of the East Franks and the kingdom of the West Franks. However, in time each of these kingdoms fragmented into local lordships whose populations were linked by ties that had little to do with ethnic origins. Occasionally a late Carolingian king called attention to his Frankish heritage or was criticized for forgetting it. Eventually, the term ''Franks'' virtually disappeared from the vocabulary of the West, except for a territory known as Franconia. The Muslims often referred to the crusaders as Franks, and of course one of the major national states that emerged from the Middle Ages was called France. But these names had little to do with the remarkable people who from an obscure existence along the lower Rhine frontier came to dominate the history of western Europe for four centuries and to create the foundations upon which western Europe's remarkable history eventually was built.

See Also: ARIANISM; CAROLINGIAN REFORM; FEUDALISM.

Bibliography: O. BERTOLINI and C. VIOLANTE, *I Germani. Migrazioni e regni nell'Occidente già romano: I Franci* (Milan 1965). E. ZÖLLNER, *Geschichte der Franken bis zur Mitte des sechsten Jahrhunderts* (Munich 1970). R. FOLZ, A. GUILLOU, L. MUSSET, and D. SOURDEL, *De l'antiquité au monde médiéval* (Paris 1972). E. JAMES, *The Origins of France: From Clovis to the Capetians* (London and Basingstoke 1982). K. F. WERNER, *Les origines (avant l'an mil)* (Paris 1984) 207–496. H. H. ANTON, J. FLECKENSTEIN, R. SCHIEFFER, R. VERHULST, and A. PATSCHOVSKY, ''Franken; Frankenreich'', in *Lexikon des Mittelalters* 4/1 (Munich and Zurich 1987) cols. 689–728. P. PERRIN and L.-C. FEFFER, *Les Francs*, 2 v. (Paris 1987). E. JAMES, *The Franks* (London and New York 1988). R. SCHNEIDER, *Das Frankenreich*, (2nd ed. Munich 1990). R. COLLINS, *Early Medieval Europe, 300–1000* (New York 1991). R. KAISER *Die Franken: Roms Erben und Wegbereiter Europas?* (Idstein 1997); extensive bibliography.

[R. E. SULLIVAN]

FRANSEN, PIETER FRANS

Theologian, author; b. Doornik (Tournai), Belgium, Dec. 10, 1913; d. Heverlee (Louvain) Belgium, Dec. 2, 1983. Fransen entered the Society of Jesus in 1930 and completed his philosophy and theology studies at the theological faculty of the Society in Louvain. Ordained to the priesthood in 1943, he earned a doctorate in theology at the Gregorian University in Rome in 1947. From 1947 to 1967, he taught dogmatic theology at the Jesuit Theological Faculty at Louvain and then Heverlee. He also taught alternate semesters at the University of Innsbruck. In 1966, Fransen was named Dean of the theology faculty at Heverlee. He was instrumental in the formation of the Center for Ecclesiastical Studies, a consortium of several religious orders and congregations which collaborated in the educational formation of their candidates for priesthood.

When the bilingual division of the Catholic University of Louvain became inevitable in 1968, the Faculty of Theology, which already included Irish Franciscans and students of the American College, instituted an English-speaking section of the Faculty in 1969. Fransen was named chairman of the newly created English program and ordinary professor at the University, responsible for the areas of sacramentology, ecclesiology, grace, mystical theology and the hermeneutics of conciliar texts. Fransen continued at the University until his death in 1983 but also lectured and taught courses on every continent. He served on the editorial boards of *Louvain Studies, Bijdragen, Collationes, Tijdschrift voor Theologie* and contributed about 200 articles to various periodicals. The major themes of his writings are found in *Divine Grace and Man* (Desclee 1962); *Intelligent Theology,* 3 v. (1969); *New Life of Grace* (1971). He edited and contributed to *Authority in the Church* (Louvain 1983).

Theology. Although Fransen wrote in the areas of ecclesiology, sacramentology, mystical theology and ecumenism, his best known works were studies of the Council of Trent and the renewal of the concept of grace. His doctoral work on *The Indissolubility of Christian Marriage in the Case of Adultery: Canon Seven of the Twenty-Fourth Session of the Council of Trent* (1947) was the beginning of his life-long interest in the critical exegesis of conciliar texts. His general principles of interpretation asserted that in matters of faith, not even the pope or bishops possess the truth. All human thoughts and formulae always fall short of God's fullness. The truth is entrusted to the whole Church and the sum total of the Church's teaching will never exhaust the mystery that is God. God is the only source of authority and thus, all reflection on faith is a ministry, a service of the Word. A council is the Church in action at a given time and a given place in history. A dogma is not an endpoint as much as a new beginning and must be reinterpreted in dialogue with the *sensus fidei.*

In contrast to the handbooks of theology, Fransen formulated three hermeneutical principles: in dogmatic texts, only the central assertion in a decree or canon is defined, any subsequent interpretations do not have the same authority; with regard to pontifical documents, there is a need to distinguish carefully between declarations of faith addressed to the universal Church and replies given to one bishop or conference of bishops; and, finally, every text should be read in the spirit in which it was written. This attention to the linguistic and historical contexts of a given historical period can free the Church from a fundamentalism which presumes that dogmas are free from historical evolution. Conciliar texts must be subject to the same kind of literary criticism given to Biblical texts.

Koinonia. Fransen's familiarity with the mystical theology of Jan van Ruysbroeck enabled him to develop a positive theology of grace, emphasizing neither redemption from sin nor intermittent actual auxilliary proddings to good and from evil, but communion with the triune God. In this communion, God and man are in an interpersonal encounter and dialogue, through which God divinizes man and man is divinized by God. The *leit motif* of Fransen's theology of grace is best expressed thus: the more grace divinizes us humans, the more it humanizes us. God and man are not hostile rivals, but friendly partners. It is for this purpose and within this horizon that God created the world in the first place. Salvation by grace is not primarily of the fallen world, from sin, but primarily of the created world, its consummation into celestial communion and glory.

This emphasis on divine-human communion also pervades his understanding of the Church, the Sacraments, and all salvation history. Against a sort of ''metaphysical clericalism,'' whose inherent thrust divides the Church into ''above'' and ''below,'' Fransen emphasized the Church as *koinonia* or communion. To understand the Sacraments properly, one must begin with and concentrate on their content, namely, grace. And grace is the communion of the divine with the human. In history, this communion is humanly actualized in what has come to be termed Faith and Sacrament. Hence, one properly always speaks of Faith and the Sacraments of the Faith. Faith and Sacrament are equally incarnations or embodiments of God's saving will/grace in human nature and history. Sacraments are the symbolic, ritual celebrations of this saving grace by the faith-full. These faith-full are to be thought of primarily as the whole communion of the Church, consequently as the individual members of this communion.

Christ is the perfect communion of the human and divine. As this perfect communion was not centripetal, selfish, and for itself, but centrifugal, sharing and for others, so must all Christian, ecclesial, and sacramental reality and realities also be. Fransen's theology is intent upon showing that insistence upon the specialness of Christ and the Church is not inconsistent with insistence on the universality of salvation for all men and women, for ''God wills that all should be saved and come to the knowledge of the truth'' (1 Tim 2:4–6). Clearly, then, one of his favorite theological texts was from Augustine:

> I referred only to the true religion that *now* is called *Christian*. . . . For the reality itself, which we now call the Christian religion, was present among the early people, and, . . . was never absent from the beginning of the human race: so the true religion which already existed, now began to be called Christian . . . not that in former time it was not present, but because it received this name at a later date'' (*Retract.* 1.12.3; *Patrologia Latina,* ed. J. P. MIGNE, 217 v. 34, 128).

One best understands both the life and theology of Piet Fransen if one understands them as the illustration and illumination of another beloved statement of Augustine: *Quia amasti me, fecisti me amabilem.*

Bibliography: H. E. MERTENS and F. DE GRAVE, eds., *Hermeneutics of the Councils and Other Studies* (Leuven 1985) 55–66 (a full listing of Fransen's publications and a selection of 18 articles in Flemish, French, German, and English on various topics). *The New Life of Grace* (New York 1969). *Intelligent Theology,* v. 1–3 (Chicago 1967, 1968, 1969).

[R. KRESS]

FRANZELIN, JOHANNES BAPTIST

Cardinal, theologian; b. Aldein, Tyrol, April 15, 1816; d. Rome, Dec. 11, 1886. After completing his preliminary training at the Franciscan college in Bolzano, he entered the Jesuit novitiate at Graz in 1834. He later spent six years teaching in Austrian Poland. In 1845, he was sent to Rome to pursue a course in theology, but in 1848, he was driven from the Eternal City by the anti-Jesuit sentiment of the Italian revolution. His theological studies were completed at the University of Louvain. After his ordination in 1849, Franzelin was assigned to teach Scripture at the Jesuit scholasticate at Vals near Le Puy. In 1850, he was recalled to Rome to teach Oriental languages and lecture on dogmatic theology at the Gregorian University. He was named prefect of studies and confessor at the German College in Rome in 1853. Four years later he was called to occupy the chair of dogmatic theology at the Gregorian University. As professor he published an almost complete theology course that was widely used.

Chief among his works (all issued in Rome) are the *De Sacramentis in genere* (1868), *De Eucharistiae sacramento et sacrificio* (1868), *De Deo Uno* (1870), *De Deo Trino* (1869), *De Verbo Incarnato* (1870), and *De divina Traditione et Scriptura* (1870). In addition to teaching, Franzelin acted as consultor to various Congregations of the Roman Curia, including the Holy Office. In his theological lectures at the university he tried to open new vistas. He left no branch of learning untouched in his attempts to draw up a synthesis. By applying this knowledge he tried to give theology a more positive orientation. In this attempt he parted company with many of his predecessors and contemporaries who regarded theology as an abstract and speculative discipline, far removed from the empirical sciences.

During Vatican Council I, Franzelin acted as papal theologian. In this capacity he was asked to prepare a draft of the constitution *Dei Filius* on the nature of the Church. Franzelin's draft was rejected by the Council fathers in the form in which it was submitted. It was drastically revised, and eventually accepted and promulgated. In the consistory of April 3, 1876, Franzelin was named a cardinal by Pius IX. He was appointed to membership on several Congregations and made prefect of the Sacred Congregation of Rites. Honors did little to change the man; he remained an exemplar of the rule of his religious order.

Bibliography: N. WALSH, *John Baptist Franzelin* (Dublin 1895). C. SOMMERVOGEL, *Bibliotèque de la Compagnie de Jésus,* 11 v. (Brussels-Paris 1890–1932) 3:950–951. H. HURTER, *Nomenclator literarius theologiae catholicae,* 5 v. in 6 (3d ed. Innsbruck 1903–1913) 5.2:1507–09. J. COURTADE, *Catholicisme* 4: 1564–66. P. BERNARD, *Dictionnaire de théologie catholique,* ed. A. VACANT (Paris 1903–50) 6.1:765–767.

[C. R. MEYER]

FRASSATI, PIER GIORGIO, BL.

Lay youth, member of the Dominican Laity, patron of youth. b. April 6, 1901, Turin, Italy; d. there, July 4, 1925. Pier Giorgio Frassati, marked by youthful vitality, optimism, and charity, combined a love of politics, sports, outdoor life, study, and piety. His agnostic father, Alfredo Frassati, founder and owner of the liberal Turin daily *La Stampa*, was appointed senator of the Kingdom (1913). His mother, Adelaide Amelia, saw that her children received religious training. Pier Giorgio began his studies (1910) in the state school in Turin with his younger sister Luciana, but was later sent to the Jesuit school (1913). The following year, he enrolled in the Apostleship of Prayer and the Company of the Most Blessed Sacrament. After graduating from high school (1918), he studied mineralogy in the Faculty of Industrial Mechanical Engineering at the Royal Polytechnic of Turin in order to ''serve Christ among the miners.'' At the university, he became active in many Christian groups. He joined the Italian Catholic Students Federation (1919), the St. Vincent de Paul Society (1919), the university Nocturnal Adoration Group (1920), the newly founded Popular Party (1921) that promoted Catholic teaching based on *Rerum Novarum*, and the *Milites Mariae* of the Young Catholic Workers (1922). He became a member of the Dominican Laity (1922), taking the name Girolama in honor of the Dominican Savanarola to the surprise of many who thought of him as a sportsman or political activist. During his father's tenure as Italian ambassador to Berlin (1920), Pier Giorgio worked with Father Karl Sonnenschein to seek out and assist the poor, just as he did in Turin. There he also became friendly with Karl Rahner and his family.

At the age of 24, Frassati was stricken with acute poliomyelitis of which he died after five days of terrible suffering. On his deathbed he gave money and instructions to his sister to continue to see to the needs of the families dependent upon his charity. Thousands of the poor he had helped without public knowledge attended his funeral. He was buried in Pollone, where on July 16, 1989, Pope John Paul II prayed at his tomb. His body has since been transferred to Turin's cathedral.

Frassati's cause for beatification was opened in 1932 but suffered delays. Pope John Paul II beatified ''the man of the eight beatitudes'' (May 20, 1990) saying: ''The secret of his apostolic zeal and holiness is . . . in prayer, in persevering adoration, even at night, of the Blessed Sacrament, in his thirst for the Word of God, which he sought in Biblical texts; in the peaceful acceptance of life's difficulties, in family life as well; in chastity lived as a cheerful, uncompromising discipline; in his daily love of silence and life's 'ordinariness.'''

Feast: July 4 (Turin).

Bibliography: F. ANTONIOLI, *Pier Giorgio Frassati* (Rome 1985). C. CASALEGNO, *Una vita di carità* (Casale Monferrato 1990). R. CLAUDE, *Le rayonnement de Pier–Giorgio Frassati, d'après les ''Testimonianze'' de don Cojazzi* (Tournai 1946). A. COJAZZI, *Pier Giorgio Frassati*, tr. H. L. HUGHES (London 1933); *Pier Giorgio Frassati: testimonianze* (Turin 1977). R. FECHTER, *Frassati; leben eines jungen katholiken in dieser zeit* (Munich 1935). L. FRASSATI, *La carità di Pier Giorgio* (Rome 1951); *Mon frère Pier Giorgio; les dernières heures* (Paris 1952); *L'impegno social, e giudizi sul carattere* (Rome 1953); *Mio fratello Pier Giorgio; vita e immagini* (Genoa 1959); *Mio fratello Pier Giorgio; la morte* (Turin 1960); *Pier Giorgio Frassati, i giorni della sua vita* (Rome 1975); *Il cammino di Pier Giorgio* (Milan 1990). G. A. SCALTRITI, *Pier Giorgio Frassati e il suo Savonarola* (Rome 1979).

[K. I. RABENSTEIN]

FRASSINELLO, BENEDETTA CAMBIAGIO, BL.

Married woman, founder of the Benedictine Sisters of Providence *(Benedettine della Provvidenza);* b. Oct. 2, 1791, Langasco (near Genoa), Italy; d. March 21, 1858, Ronco Scrivia, Italy. She was the daughter of Giuseppe and Francesca Cambiagio, who moved to Pavia while Benedetta was still young. Following a mystical experience in 1811, Benedetta wanted to devote herself to prayer in a convent, but instead she complied with her family's wishes and married Giovanni Battista Frassinello (Feb. 7, 1816). In 1818, the couple agreed to live together in perpetual continence while caring for Benedetta's younger sister Maria, who suffered from intestinal cancer. Following her death (1825), they both chose to enter religious life: Giovanni joined the Somachi, while Benedetta took the habit of the Ursulines. Illness forced Benedetta to leave the convent and return to Pavia, where she decided to help abandoned girls. Giovanni left his monastery also to assist her in this task. Although Benedetta was appointed ''Promoter of Public Instruction'' and they publicly vowed perfect chastity, the couple suffered criticism for their unusual relationship. That impelled them to turn over their work to the bishop (1838) and retire to the village of Ronco Scrivia. In 1833, with her husband and five companions, Benedetta founded the educational Institute of Benedictine Sisters of Providence, which continues its work in Italy and Peru. Benedetta was beatified at Rome by Pope John Paul II, May 10, 1987.

Feast: May 10.

Bibliography: G. GUDERZO, I problemi socioeconomici di Pavia 'restaurata' e la risposta religiosa di Benedetta Cambiagio Frassinello, *Studi e fonti di Storia lombarda. Quaderni milanesi* 17–18 (1989) 56–73. *Acta Apostolicae Sedis* 1987, 690. *L'Osservatore Romano*, Eng. ed., 21 (1987) 18–19.

[K. I. RABENSTEIN]

FRASSINETTI, GIUSEPPE

Pastor, writer, and founder of the Sons of Mary Immaculate (FSMI); b. Genoa, 1804; d. there, Jan. 2, 1868. The brother of Bl. Paola Frassinetti, he was ordained in 1827. After laboring in the ministry at S. Pietro di Quinto al Mare, he became pastor of S. Sabina in Genoa in 1839, where he remained thereafter. His intensely active pastoral apostolate won for him the reputation of being ''the Italian curé d'Ars.'' Besides busying himself with many other works, Frassinetti was a voluminous writer whose works went through many editions. These include: *Compendio della teologia dogmatica* (Genoa 1839; 26th ed.

Turin 1903); *Gesù Cristo regola del sacerdote* (Florence 1852; 11th ed. Genoa 1899); *Il conforto dell'anima divota* (Naples 1852; 14th ed. Rome 1906); *Manuale pratico del parocho novello* (Novara 1863; 10th ed. Turin 1902); *Compendio della teologia morale di S. Alfonso* (2 v. Genoa 1865–66; 11th ed. Turin 1948); and many others. Frassinetti's cause for beatification was introduced at Rome in 1939.

Bibliography: C. OLIVARI, *Della vita e delle opere del servo di Dio, sac. Guiseppe Frassinetti* (Rome 1928). *Acta Apostolicae Sedis* 31 (Rome 1939) 617–619. P. PALAZZINI, *Enciclopedia cattolica* 5 (Rome 1949–54) 1703. E. MANGENOT, *Dictionnaire de théologie catholique* 6 (Paris 1903–50) 769–770.

[J. C. WILLKE]

FRASSINETTI, PAOLA ANGELA MARIA, ST.

Also Paula; founder of the Congregation of Sisters of St. Dorotea (Dorotheans); b. March 3, 1809, Genoa, Italy; d. June 11, 1882, Rome. The only daughter of the five children of John and Angela Frassinetti, Paola's four brothers became priests. When her mother died in 1818, her aunt took charge of the family until her own death in 1821. After that, Paola cared for the household. She was educated at home by her father and brothers. Bronchial problems caused her to go to Quinto al Mare (Genoa) in 1830, where she lived with her brother (Ven.) Giuseppe FRASSINETTI, a priest. She served as the parish housekeeper and taught the local girls. When Paola's ill health frustrated her attempts to join a religious congregation, she founded her own institute, the Dorotheans, at St. Clara's (Aug. 12, 1834), which was dedicated to the education of girls from all walks of life. After difficult early years, the institute received papal approval in 1863. Paola remained superior general until her death; after 1841 she resided in Rome. She saw the Dorotheans spread through Italy and abroad to Portugal and Brazil. In 1876, Frassinetti suffered the first of several paralyzing strokes. She died peacefully of pneumonia at the mother house, St. Onofrio in Rome, where she is buried. Frassinetti, patron of the sick, was beatified in 1930, and canonized March 11, 1984 by Pope John Paul II.

Feast: June 11.

Bibliography: *Acta Apostolicae Sedis* 77 (1985): 923–928. *L'Osservatore Romano,* Eng. ed., no. 13 (1984): 3. H. CASHIN, *A Great Servant of God, Mother Paola Frassinetti . . .* (Staten Island, N.Y. 1951). H. TRINKLER, *Die andere Möglichkeit* (Freiburg, Switzerland 1977). J. UNFREVILLE, *A Foundress in 19th Century Italy: Blessed Paula Frassinetti and the Congregation of the Sisters of St. Dorothy* (New York 1944).

[F. G. SOTTOCORNOLA]

FRATICELLI

Term of contempt for heretical Franciscans; these can be divided into two branches.

Fraticelli de Paupere Vita. These were the successors of the Franciscan SPIRITUALS and were directed by ANGELUS CLARENUS, who returned to Italy in 1318 and died in 1337. The CLARENI had hermitages in Rome, in central Italy, and in Naples, where Angelus's friend Philip of Majorca, brother of Queen Sancia of Naples, arrived in 1329, and was joined by the surviving Spirituals from Provence and Sicily. Philip preached against Pope JOHN XXII, and a bull of 1340 describes him as "the promotor and ruler of a heretical sect." In 1362 a process was directed against Louis of Durazzo, the cousin of Joanna I, because he had protected the Fraticelli. On that occasion they were said to be divided into three groups, one of which was called the "followers of brother Philip of Majorca." The courts of Aragon and Sicily also protected them. Writing in Latin and Italian, the pamphleteers, defending the Fraticelli's separation from the Franciscan Order, show considerable familiarity with the works of the Fathers, with the early Franciscan writings, including those of the Spirituals, and with the manifestos against John XXII, whom, with his successors and adherents, they regarded as heretical because of John's condemnation of the Franciscan doctrine of the poverty of Christ (*see* POVERTY CONTROVERSY). Their Joachimism (*see* JOACHIM OF FIORE) makes it likely that some of the later Joachimite treatises emanated from their circle, and there may be some connection between them and the hermits with whom COLA DI RIENZO lived after his first exile from Rome. Part of the sect subsequently became orthodox. In 1473 various groups of Clareni hermits, distinguished by their short, skimpy habits, were united to the Franciscan Observants but enjoyed considerable autonomy until 1563, when the two bodies were finally amalgamated. At that time the Clareni had 21 hermitages.

The Fraticelli de Opinione. The followers of MICHAEL OF CESENA were given this designation. Their resistance to John XXII received considerable support among the Franciscans and, outside the order, even as far away as Persia. In 1331 the two Franciscan chaplains of Sancia of Naples were accused of corresponding with the former minister general and of maintaining that John XXII was no longer pope. One of them, Andrea de Gagliano, was later tried by the Inquisition but was absolved. In the late 14th and 15th centuries the sect was confined mainly to Italy and gained adherents during the WESTERN SCHISM. Their propaganda provoked answers from orthodox circles; from the Tuscan hermit John de Cellis, a correspondent of St. CATHERINE OF SIENA; and from St. JAMES OF THE MARCHES, the companion of St. BERNARD-

INE OF SIENA, who with St. JOHN CAPISTRAN acted as an inquisitor against them. The Fraticelli were organized as a church with their own minister general, bishops, priests, and women preachers. Many members of the sect became victims of the INQUISITION; a certain Fra Michael da Calci was burned at Florence (1389), and others at Rome (1467). Certain groups escaped to Greece in the mid-15th century, but little trace of the sect has been found elsewhere; nor has it been possible to establish connections between them and the HUSSITES and other heretics.

Bibliography: F. EHRLE, ''Die Spiritualen: Ihr Verältnis zum Franziskanerorden und zu den Franticellen,'' *Archiv für Literatur- und Kirchengeschichte des Mittelalters,* 1 (Freiburg 1885–1900) 509–569. F. TOCCO, *Studii francescani* (Naples 1909). D. DOUIE, *The Nature and the Effect of the Heresy of the Fraticelli* (New York 1978).

[D. L. DOUIE]

FRAVASHI

In Zoroastrianism, the name of the protective spirits, one of which is assigned to each man or woman belonging to the camp of Ahura Mazda and fighting for him against the forces of evil. Originally they seem to have been rather like the *Marutah* in India or the Teutonic *Walküren.* In the *Yasht* (*see* AVESTA) dedicated to them, they are invoked not only for victory in battle but more often for fecundity. They survive man's earthly existence, but they are believed to have existed even before he was born. As surviving spirits of the dead they, like the Roman *manes,* are supposed to come back to earth at a given time of the year, when festivals are held to welcome them.

Bibliography: J. DUCHESNE-GUILLEMIN, *La Religion de l'Iran ancien* (Paris 1962).

[J. DUCHESNE-GUILLEMIN]

FRAYSSINOUS, DENIS

French bishop, apologist; b. Curières (Aveyron), May 9, 1765; d. St. Géniez (Aveyron), Dec. 12, 1841. He was a Sulpician (1788–1806) and was ordained in 1789. After engaging in pastoral work secretly during the French Revolution, he taught dogmatic theology at the seminary of St. Sulpice in Paris (1800–06). In 1801, he began to attract wide attention for his outstanding sermons and conferences, which were suspended from 1809 to 1814 by order of Napoleon I. Louis XVIII named him court preacher and royal almoner. In 1819, he became vicar-general of the Archdiocese of Paris, and in 1822 titular bishop, grand master of the university (minister of public instruction), member of the French Academy, and of the Chamber of Peers, with the title of count. From 1824 to 1828 he acted as minister of ecclesiastical affairs. During the July Revolution (1830) he retired from public affairs and lived in Rome for two years. From 1833 to 1838, Frayssinous, a royalist in politics, dwelt in Prague and Görz as tutor for Count Henri de Chambord, who was later a claimant to the French throne, supported by the Legitimists. From 1838 to 1841 he resided at St. Géniez.

In 1818, Frayssinous published Les Vrais principes de l'Église gallicane, reflecting his moderate GALLICANISM similar to that of BOSSUET. His conferences, published as Defense du christianisme (3 v. 1825), went through many editions and were translated into English, Italian, Spanish, and German. Frayssinous was the outstanding Catholic apologist during the early Restoration period.

Bibliography: A. GARNIER, *Frayssinous: Son rôle dans l'Université sous la Restauration, 1822–1828* (Paris 1925); *Frayssinous et la jeunesse* (Paris 1931). L. GRIMAUD, *Histoire de la liberté d'enseignement en France,* v.5 (Paris 1950). J. DUTILLEUL, *Dictionnaire de théologie catholique,* ed. A. VACANT (Paris 1903–50) 6:794–797. C. LEDRÉ, *Catholicisme* 4:1574–75.

[L. P. MAHONEY]

FREDEGARIUS

The 16th-century name for the author of a universal chronicle, whose final part, a continuation of the *Historia Francorum* of GREGORY OF TOURS from 585 to 642, is almost the unique source of Frankish history for the period it covers. The chronicle contains many curiosities, such as the earliest legend of the Trojan origin of the Franks, the sole report of the first Slavic kingdom (ruled by the Frank Samo), and glimpses of what Gaul knew of the Byzantine world. For all the barbarism of its language, it is a major witness to the culture of its time.

The work grew out of an existing compilation of world chronology and history, which Fredegarius interpolated and augmented with an epitome of Gregory of Tours's *Histories,* bks. 1–4. He then added an original chronicle, which ends in 642 but alludes to events as late as 658. Why Fredegarius stopped is unknown; he meant to continue to his own time. Though the chronicle has been attributed to as many as three authors, writing at different times, recent opinion favors a single author, probably a Burgundian, writing *c.* 658 to 660, whose testimony is rarely that of an eyewitness.

Equally important, interesting, and barbaric in language are the eighth-century continuations of Fredegarius, which were commissioned by Childebrand, a brother of CHARLES MARTEL, and his son Nibelung. They constitute a Carolingian family chronicle between 642 and 737 to the death of King Pepin I (768).

Bibliography: Editions. *Chronicon,* ed. B. KRUSCH, *Monumenta Germaniae Historica: Scriptores rerum Merovingicarum* 2:1–168. J. M. WALLACE-HADRILL, ed. and tr., *The Fourth Book of the Chronicle of Fredegar with Its Continuations* (New York 1960). Literature. J. M. WALLACE-HADRILL, ''Fredegar and the History of France,'' *Bulletin of the John Rylands Library* 40 (1958) 527–550. W. GOFFART, ''The Fredegar Problem Reconsidered,'' *Speculum* 38 (1963) 206–241.

[W. GOFFART]

FREDERICK II (THE GREAT), KING OF PRUSSIA

Reigned 1740 to 1786; b. Berlin, Jan. 24, 1712; d. Potsdam, Aug. 17, 1786.

Early Life. He was the oldest of four surviving sons born to King Frederick William I of Prussia and Princess Sophia Dorothea of Hanover. His tutor, Duhan de Jandun, instilled in him a deep love of French culture. The curriculum set up for the crown prince by his father, the ''Soldier King,'' strongly emphasized military training. Frederick rebelled against the Spartan drill and the king's stern Calvinism. After the failure of an attempt to flee to England (Aug. 4, 1730), he was arrested and imprisioned in the fortress of Kuestrin. Completely submitting to his father's will, he was freed after a year. Still under restrictions, he was gradually reinstated. In 1733 he married Elizabeth Christine of Brunswick-Bevern. The marriage was not harmonious and remained childless. In Rheinsberg, an estate he had received from his father, the crown prince spent the happiest years of his life. Here he found time to study and to write. Enjoying the company of the congenial intelligentsia, he corresponded with many prominent men of letters, such as Voltaire. The best-known of his early writings is *Antimachiavel* (1740), a lofty refutation of immorality in politics.

Kingship. He succeeded to his father's throne May 31, 1740. At the beginning of his 46-year reign Frederick II abolished the use of torture for criminals and lifted press censorship. The death of the Hapsburg Emperor Charles VI and the accession of Maria Theresa provided Frederick with the opportunity of renewing ancient but questionable claims to some Silesian territories. He invaded Silesia (December 1740) and initiated the War of the Austrian Succession, which involved the electors of Bavaria and Saxony as well as the kings of England and France. By the Treaty of Dresden (1745) Frederick remained in possession of Silesia but acknowledged Maria Theresa's husband (Francis of Lorraine) as Holy Roman emperor. The acquisition of Silesia made Prussia a European power. During the next 11 years Frederick made remarkable efforts to improve agriculture and manufacturing. He balanced the budget, produced a substantial surplus, and, in an age of intense dynastic conflict and shifting alliances, increased his army and concluded the convention of Westminster with England. In the meantime, France, Russia, and some smaller states became Austria's allies. Frederick's sudden invasion of Saxony precipitated the Seven Years' War (1756–63). Strategy and courage enabled him to oppose a powerful coalition and the death of Tsarina Elizabeth removed Russia from the war and saved Frederick. The Peace of Hubertusburg restored the status quo. Peace, save for the brief war over the Bavarian Succession (1778–79) and the first partition of Poland (1772), by which he gained Western Prussia (without Danzig and Thorn), characterized his remaining years. Dismissing the divine theory of kingship, Frederick II considered himself the ''first servant of the State.'' He worked incessantly for the welfare of his subjects. Many of his reforms were directed to the administration of justice. The independence of law courts was established as a principle. But Frederick was an avowed cynic who believed in power and in power alone. He was an autocrat whose tight personal rule was sustained by the strict, though grudging, obedience of the

Frederick II (The Great), King of Prussia. (©Bettmann/CORBIS)

noble bureaucrats. Contemptuous of all beliefs, he practiced religious toleration, but there was no freedom of thought in Prussia. For the achievements of German culture Frederick had nothing but scorn—a feeling that was reciprocated by the leading German intellectuals. The myth of Frederick's "German mission" has long been shattered.

Religious Policy. His relations with the Catholic Church remained strained despite some friendly gestures. When he annexed Silesia, he solemnly promised to respect the Catholic religion, to which about half of his new subjects adhered. But soon discriminatory laws and fiscal policies caused deep concern. The introduction of Prussia's anticlerical marriage practice was bitterly resented. Conforming to the pattern of absolutism, he used (and misused) his prerogatives to interfere in the internal affairs of the Diocese of Breslau, and to establish a tight control over the hierarchy and benefices. He disregarded the fact that such prerogatives were derived from privileges granted only to Catholic sovereigns on the basis of a treaty with the Holy See. Toward the Jesuits he assumed a benevolent attitude after the suppression of their order. The members of the extinct society were encouraged to carry on their work as educators.

Bibliography: G. RITTER, *Friedrich der Grosse* (3d ed. Heidelberg 1954). G. P. GOOCH, *Frederick the Great* (New York 1947). E. SIMON, *The Making of Frederick the Great* (Boston 1963). For Frederick II's relations with the Catholic Church see L. PASTOR, *The History of the Popes from the Close of the Middle Ages,* (London–St. Louis 1938–61) 36, 38, 39. *Oeuvres,* 30 v., ed. J. D. E. PREUSS et al. (Berlin 1846–57); *Politische Correspondenz,* 46 v., ed. G. DROYSEN et al. (Berlin 1879–1939). R. B. ASPREY, *Frederick the Great: The Magnificent Enigma* (New York 1986). R. PEYREFITTE, *Voltaire et Frédéric II* (Paris 1992). D. E. SHOWALTER, *The Wars of Frederick the Great* (London and New York 1996). G. MACDONOGH, *Frederick the Great: A Life in Deed and Letters* (New York 2000). D. FRASER, *Frederick the Great: King of Prussia* (New York 2000). T. SCHIEDER, *Frederick the Great,* ed. and trans. by S. BERKELEY and H. M. SCOTT (New York 2000).

[H. W. L. FREUDENTHAL]

FREDERICK I BARBAROSSA, ROMAN EMPEROR

Reign: March 4, 1152, to June 10, 1190; b.1122 or 1123, the son of Frederick II, Duke of Swabia, and Judith, the daughter of Henry the Black. His reddish-blond hair earned him the sobriquet "Barbarossa," which means "Red Beard" in Italian. In 1147 he became Duke of Swabia upon the death of his father and accompanied his uncle, Conrad III, on the unsuccessful Second Crusade. Frederick was elected king of Germany on March 4, 1152 after Conrad's death. His lineage made him an ideal choice to bring reconciliation to Germany, since his Hohenstaufen father was a brother of the preceding king, and his mother was sister to Henry the Proud, who had been leader of the Guelphs, Conrad's main opposition.

Frederick hoped to reestablish the power of empire, which had been weakened during the struggle between popes and emperors during the eleventh and early twelfth centuries. After his coronation he predicted the restoration of the greatness of imperial Rome. He considered himself the heir of the caesars and had no difficulty including his own legislation with that of Justinian and the emperors of antiquity. He saw Roman law as a vehicle for extending his power, especially in regard to the papacy. Frederick called his state the *sacrum imperium,* or "Holy Empire," and he believed himself to have been chosen by God to foster an institution that was the cornerstone of world order, the source of peace and justice. Although his vision had something in common with that of post-Constantinian emperors, his was an empire governed by medieval mechanisms, especially customary law, and its medieval roots were fundamental to it. The veneration of CHARLEMAGNE as a saint during the Christmas season of 1165 was meant to enhance Frederick's own imperial prestige as the ostensible heir of the FRANKS and the Saxons as well the ancients.

In Germany Frederick tried to fulfill the hope of reconciliation that his election portended. He offered important offices and dignities to his Guelph uncle Welf VI, and he was eventually able to satisfy the demand of Henry the Proud's son and heir, Henry the Lion, to return the Duchy of Bavaria, which had been given by Conrad to the Babenburg family. The Babenburg Henry Jasomirgott was compensated with the newly created Duchy of Austria, which was granted on generous terms. But years later, when Henry the Lion refused to support him during a crucial Italian campaign, Frederick blamed his defeat in Italy on him and was eventually able drive him from power.

As the perfidy of Henry the Lion demonstrated, a German policy based solely upon the accommodation of German princes could only have modest success. It was necessary for Frederick to build power that was independent of the high aristocracy, and he had certain advantages, since he could use his legal position as sovereign against the nobility. He also increased the size of royal estates and attempted to give them a geographic cohesion that would make them governable. Within these lands he built towns and castles and placed ecclesiastical institutions under his protection. He employed to a greater extent than his predecessors *ministrales,* a servile class of men who were hardly serfs, to govern those lands directly under royal control. There were no exact equivalents to *ministrales,* who were often quite talented soldiers, and who occasionally became quite wealthy in other countries

In spite of the Frederick's energy and intelligence, his success in Germany was limited and led to no unified kingdom. The princes may have been too firmly entrenched because of the weakness of the monarchy during the INVESTITURE CONTROVERSY, and monarchy itself too archaic in its structure. There was no fixed capital and no class of administrators. Income was always uncertain. German nationalist historians have looked wistfully at his reign, but he had no nationalist aspirations, not as later centuries would understand them.

Certainly Frederick's long involvement in Italy was detrimental to his success in Germany. Frederick made six expeditions to Italy, where he spent 16 of his 38 years in power. Numerous and complex were his reasons for devoting so much of his time there. He was enamored with the classical tradition, and Italy was the home of the Roman Empire, but there were factors more compelling than historical romanticism. It has been conjectured that he hoped to create a basis for a territorial state from a central grouping of lands that included northern Italy as well as Burgundy and Switzerland. Clearly the cities of northern Italy had been the beneficiaries of the increase in trade and population that had taken place over the previous several hundred years, and they could provide Frederick with a revenue that was greater than that of either the French or English king. In addition Italy was the seat of the papacy, and in an age when society was perceived as the "Church," it was in Frederick's interest to remain on good terms with the popes or to dominate them. A strong Norman state in southern Italy, which could threaten his influence in Rome, further complicated the situation.

Nevertheless, the future of his rule in Italy looked bright at the beginning of his reign. In 1153 at Constance his delegation reached an accommodation with the papacy that promised to benefit both pope and emperor. In addition there were a group of Italian cities that were uncomfortable with the dominance of Milan, the most powerful city in northern Italy, and they looked to the emperor for support. Although Pope HADRIAN IV crowned Frederick emperor in 1155, and although he was able to dominate Lombardy after he destroyed Milan in 1162, Italian politics became bramble from which he could never completely extricate himself. All Italian cities shared a sense of independence and a reluctance to support Frederick financially. They chafed under imperial administrators and their demands for *regalia,* certain political and economic prerogatives that Frederick claimed as his own. Milan was rebuilt with the help of

Frederick I Barbarossa, Roman Emperor.

its neighbors. In regard to the papacy, Frederick's understanding of imperial authority made him sensitive to papal aspirations, both real and imagined, and his inability to intervene effectively in the southern Italy for a sustained period of time made him a poor ally to the popes. In 1160 he sided with Antipope VICTOR IV in the disputed election of Alexander III and began an 18-year schism that had disastrous consequences for his Italian policy. The cities of Lombardy supported Alexander, who worked closely with them. In a moment of imperial weakness, they formed an alliance known as the LOMBARD LEAGUE and built a strategically placed fortress named after the pope, Alessandria, as an act of defiance. Abandoned by his cousin, Henry the Lion, before whom he may have knelt to beg for help, he was decisively defeated by the League at Legnano in 1176. He was able to salvage a respectable peace, but he could not dictate terms.

Yet Frederick was far from broken. In 1180 he was able not only to drive Henry the Lion into exile but also to fragment the base of power that Henry had created by subdividing his estates. In spite of his defeat at Legnano he was able to collect a healthy subsidy from Lombardy and to establish his own power base in Tuscany. He arranged a marriage between his son Henry and Constance, the woman who would become the heiress to the Norman kingdom of the *mezzogiorno,* which might have given his son mastery in Italy and hegemony in Europe if Henry VI had not died prematurely.

Therefore Frederick still had great power and position when news reached Europe in 1187 that Jerusalem had fallen to Muslim forces. He, along with the kings of England and France, vowed to free the Holy City. The emperor, who led the largest contingent, took an overland route to Palestine, and in 1190, in what is now Turkey, he fell from his horse in a rapidly moving stream and drowned. In latter times a legend, which had originally grown up around his grandson, Frederick II, was transferred to him. Frederick, it claimed, did not die on a crusade, but rather he sleeps in a cave, to be awakened when Germany will again need him.

Bibliography: H. SIMONSFELD, *Jahrbücher des deutschen Reiches unter Friedrich I* (Leipzig 1908). OTTO OF FREISING, *The Deeds of Frederick Barbarossa,* tr. C. C. MIEROW (New York 1953). U. BALZANI, *Italia, papato e impero nella prima metà del secolo XII* (Messina 1930). G. BARRACLOUGH, tr., *Medieval Germany, 911–1250,* 2 v. (Oxford 1938). P. MUNZ, *Frederick Barbarossa, A Study in Medieval Politics* (Ithaca, NY 1969). R. MANSELLI and J. RIEDMANN, ed., *Federico Barbarossa nel dibattito storiografico in Italia e in Germania,* Annali dell'Istituto storico italo-germanico 10 (Bologna 1982). F. CARDINI, *Il Barbarossa: Vita, Trionfi, e Illusioni di Federico I, Imperatore* (Milan 1985). H. FUHRMANN, *Germany in the High Middle Ages c. 1050–1200,* tr. T. REUTER (Cambridge 1986). F. OPLL, *Friederich Barbarossa* (Darmstadt 1990). A. HAVERKAMP, *Medieval Germany 1056–1273,* tr. H. BRAUN and R. MORTIMER (Oxford 1988); *Friederich Barbarossa Handlungsspielräume und Wirkungsweisen des staufischen Kaisers* (Sigmaringen 1992). T. E. CARSON, *Barbarossa in Italy* (New York 1994). A. PLASSMANN, *Die Struktur des Hofes unter Friedrich I. Barbarossa nach den deutschen Zeugen seiner Urkunden* (Hannover 1998). K. GÖRICH, *Die Ehre Friedrich Barbarossa: Kommunication, Konflikt und politisches Handeln im 12. Jahrhundert* (Darmstadt 2001).

[T. E. CARSON]

FREDERICK II, ROMAN EMPEROR

Reigned Nov. 22, 1220 to Dec. 13, 1250. Frederick was born in Jesi, a small city on the eastern side of the Italian peninsula on Dec. 26, 1194. His father was the Emperor Henry VI of the Hohenstaufen family (d. 1197) and his mother was Constance, daughter of Norman King Roger II of Sicily. Frederick inherited the crown of the Kingdom of Sicily through his mother. He was crowned Roman emperor in St. Peter's on Nov. 22, 1220 and ruled until he died on Dec. 13, 1250. His reign was marked by a long and difficult conflict with the papacy. In its aftermath, the empire was permanently weakened. Although the papacy emerged victorious, it did not enhance papal authority and prestige.

Since Frederick was only four years old when Henry VI died, and since the imperial title was not hereditary, he was not immediately elected emperor. Frederick was crowned king of Sicily in 1198, but turbulence and civil war marked his minority there. An old supporter of his father, Markward of Anweiler, claimed the throne for himself. Since the papacy had long claimed the overlordship over the Kingdom of Sicily, Pope Innocent III intervened to support the rights of young Frederick. With the pope's support, Markward and his allies were defeated. Innocent did not want Frederick to reassert Hohenstaufen claims in Germany or in central Italy, but after an electoral dispute and a civil war in which Otto of Brunswick emerged victorious, Innocent had no choice but to support young Frederick as the king of Germany. The German princes opposed to Otto elected Frederick king of Germany and emperor-elect in 1211. Frederick spent the next eight years in his German lands reasserting Hohenstaufen rule.

Innocent was not only concerned about the political implications of Frederick's new position. The pope had worked vigorously to reestablish papal secular authority over the Papal States in Central Italy and to eliminate the practice that was common in many parts of Christendom by which kings and princes participated in the election of bishops. The issue had already arisen in Sicily over the election of the archbishop of Palermo in 1209. Frederick's relationship with the Church was further complicated by the large number of fiefs that Innocent had given to the bishops of the realm. The conflict between papal authority and rights in the Kingdom of Sicily and Frederick's royal power would complicate relations with the papacy during his entire reign.

In November 1220 Innocent III's successor, Pope Honorius III, placed the crown of Roman emperor on Frederick in St. Peter's. During the coronation Frederick took the cross again and vowed to lead a crusade to the Holy Land. At Honorius's request he promulgated a series of constitutions that protected the rights of the Church and the clergy in imperial and royal lands. After his coronation Frederick returned to Sicily and began to regain control of the kingdom.

The pope wanted Frederick to lead an army to the Holy Land immediately but Frederick delayed. He spent three years organizing his government and reclaiming royal rights in Sicily. He founded the University of Naples in 1224. It was the first university established by a secular ruler in Europe. There are many stories about Frederick's love of learning. If we can believe all of them he was interested in mathematics, poetry, science, philosophy, and languages. He did write a book on the art of falconry that remained a standard work for centuries.

Pope Honorius became increasingly unhappy with Frederick. The pope died in 1227, and Pope Gregory IX, the new pope, excommunicated the emperor after Frederick's first expedition to the Holy Land was aborted by illness. In spite of his excommunication, Frederick returned to the Holy Land, concluded a peace treaty with the Moslem ruler, Sultan al-Kamil of Egypt. Its terms granted Frederick control of Jerusalem for ten years.

Pope Gregory was not placated by Frederick's success. Instead of lifting the ban of excommunication, the pope called for an invasion of Kingdom of Sicily. Frederick's father-in-law, John of Brienne, led the papal army. Frederick sailed back to Italy and quickly restored order to his kingdom. After extensive negotiations, he concluded a peace treaty with the papacy in 1230. Gregory lifted Frederick's excommunication, and the emperor reaffirmed the Church's rights in the Kingdom of Sicily.

In 1231 Frederick promulgated the *Constitutions of Melfi,* the first legal codification issued by a European secular ruler. These laws replaced all earlier legislation in the Kingdom of Sicily. As soon as the papacy learned of the plan for a new codification, Gregory warned Frederick not to issue any laws that would infringe upon ecclesiastical rights. As in 1220, the papacy wanted to influence the content of Frederick's legislation. The *Constitutions of Melfi,* which became the law of the land in the Kingdom of Sicily, were augmented with new legislation for centuries afterwards. They were commented upon by the most important Southern Italian jurists, and remained in force until 1809 in Southern Italy and until 1819 in Sicily.

The relationship between Frederick and Gregory deteriorated from 1231 to 1239. Frederick claimed authority over parts of Central Italy that infringed on papal lands, and Gregory accused the emperor of ignoring or destroying ecclesiastical liberties. Frederick also tried to reestablish imperial control over the Italian city-states in Northern Italy. In 1239, after Frederick had suffered defeats in Northern Italy, Gregory excommunicated him again. The pope accused Frederick of heresy, of injuring the rights of the church in Sicily, and of hindering the recovery of the Holy Land. Gregory died a short time later. When Innocent IV became pope in 1243 after a long interregnum, he pursued a vigorous campaign against Frederick. In 1245 he convened a council in Lyon and summoned the emperor to answer for his crimes. Frederick moved slowly toward Lyon, but Innocent condemned him before his arrival. The pope deposed him from his imperial and royal offices and called for a crusade against him. It was the first time that a pope had used the crusade against a Christian ruler.

Although Frederick continued his war with the papacy after Lyon, he had little success. The Lombard city-states were too rich and powerful to be subdued with the

Frederick II, Roman Emperor. (Archive Photos, Inc.)

limited resources Frederick had. On Dec. 13, 1250 Frederick died in Castel Fiorentino near Foggia. After his death, the German empire and the Kingdom of Sicily were separated forever. The Hohenstaufen vision of an empire stretching from the North Sea to Sicily ended with a long imperial interregnum that lasted until 1270 and with the pope's appointment of a French monarch to rule the Kingdom of Sicily.

Bibliography: J. HUILLARD-BRÉHOLLES, *Historia diplomatica Friderici Secundi, sive constitutiones, privilegia, mandata, instrumenta quae supersunt istius Imperatoris et filiorum ejus: Accedunt epistolae Paparum et documenta varia,* 7 v. in 12 (Paris 1852–61; reprint Bologna 1963). L. WEILAND, ed., *Constitutiones et acta publica imperatorum et regum* (Monumenta Germaniae historica, Legum sectio, 4.2; Hannover 1896, reprint Hannover 1963). E. WINKELMANN. ed., *Acta imperii inedita seculi XIII et XIV,* 2 v. (Innsbruck 1880–85; reprint Aalen 1964). *Das Falkenbuch Friedrichs II.: Cod. Pal. Lat. 1071 der Biblioteca Apostolica Vaticana,* D. WALZ and C.A. WILLEMSEN, ed., (Graz 2000, tr. C. A. WOOD and F. M. FYFE, Stanford 1943, reprint Stanford 1961). *Die Konstitutionen Friedrichs II. für das Königreich Sizilien,* W. STÜRNER (Monumenta Germaniae historica, Constitutiones et acta publica imperatorum et regum, 2, suppl.; Hannover 1996; tr. J. M. POWELL, Syracuse 1971).

Bibliographie zur Geschichte Kaiser Friedrichs II. und der letzten Staufer, C. A. WILLEMSEN, ed. (Monumenta Germaniae historica, Hilfsmittel 8; Munich 1986). E. KANTOROWICZ, *Frederick the Second, 1194–1250,* tr. E. O. LORIMER (New York 1957). T. C. VAN CLEVE, *The Emperor Frederick II of Hohenstaufen, immutator mundi* (Oxford 1972). W. STÜRNER, *Friedrich II.* (2 v. Darmstadt 1992). D. ABULAFIA, *Frederick II: A Medieval Emperor* (London 1992).

[K. PENNINGTON]

FRÉDOL, BÉRENGER (BERENGARIUS FREDOLI)

Cardinal and canonist; b. Lavérune (southern France), *c.* 1250; d. 1323. At first a professor of Canon Law at Bologna, he became bishop of Béziers in 1294, a cardinal in 1305, cardinal bishop of Tusculum (after June 10, 1309), and major penitentiary (before Sept. 2, 1311). In the pontificate of Boniface VIII, Bérenger's flair for diplomacy made him an important figure in relations between the Holy See and the Kings of France and Aragon; in that of Clement V (1305–14) he was at times the Pope's sole confidant and counselor. And if he adroitly terminated the posthumous trial of Boniface VIII, he played a more questionable role in the suppression of the TEMPLARS, particularly in the famous case of the confession of the Grand Master, Jacques de Molay. As a canonist he was one of those commissioned in 1296 by Boniface VIII to compile the *LIBER SEXTUS*; in addition, he wrote a fine treatise on excommunication and interdict [ed. E. Vernay, *Le ''Liber de excommunicatione'' du Cardinal Bérenger Frédol* (Paris 1921)] and has been credited with a manual on confessional practice. His inclination for cataloguing, attested by inventories of the *Corpus Iuris* from Gratian to the Sext, of the *Summa* of HOSTIENSIS (''Oculus copiosae''), and of the *Speculum* of DURANTI THE ELDER (1306), is a sign of a clear and orderly, if somewhat systematic, turn of mind.

Bibliography: J. F. VON SCHULTE, *Die Geschichte der Quellen und der Literatur des kanonischen Rechts,* 3 v. in 4 pts. (Stuttgart 1875–80; repr. Graz 1956) 2:180–182. P. VIOLLET, *Histoire Littéraire de la France* 34 (1914) 62–178. G. LIZERAND, ''Les dépositions du grand maître Jacques Molay,'' *Moyen-âge* 26 (1913) 81–106. G. A. L. DIGARD, *Philippe le Bel et le Saint-siège de 1285 à 1304,* 2 v. (Paris 1936) 1:261–263. A. VAN HOVE, *Commentarium Lovaniense in Codicem iuris canonici*, v.1–5 (Mechlin 1928–); v.1, Prolegomena (2d ed. 1945) 1:368, 464. G. MOLLAT, *Dictionnaire de droit canonique,* ed. R. NAZ, 7 v. (Paris 1935–65) 5:905–907; *Catholicisme* 4:1577–78. A. TEETAERT, ''La *Summa de poenitentia: Quoniam circa confessiones* du cardinal B. F. Senior,'' *Miscellanea moralia in honorem eximii domini Arthur Janssen,* 2 v. (Louvain 1948–49) 567–600.

[P. LEGENDRE]

FREE CHURCHES

The title given in England and Wales to religious bodies, previously known as Dissenters or NONCONFORMISTS, that are not in communion with the Church of England or the Catholic Church. The term came into common use late in the 19th century and generally refers to the Methodists, English Presbyterians, Congregationalists, Baptists, Quakers, Unitarians, Churches of Christ, Plymouth Brethren, various Pentecostal sects, and, recently, Mormons. During the 19th century, Nonconformists agitated for disestablishment and promoted the principle of voluntaryism which held that the church ought to be spiritually independent of the state, that establishment of any one denomination was unjust to all others, and that state endowment of any religion must be rejected as a corrupting influence. In 1892, under the leadership of the Methodist Hugh Price Hughes and the Baptist John Clifford, a National Free Church Council was established in Manchester. It was intended to be a loose association of local councils and at its annual meeting a wide range of theological and religious questions were to be discussed. The efforts of J. H. Shakespeare of the Baptist Union led to the founding of the Federal Council of Evangelical Free Churches (1919), which excluded Unitarians and allotted representation on the basis of each denomination's membership. These two bodies united as the Free Church Federal Council (1940). Most Free Church bodies also joined with the established Churches of England and Scotland in the British Council of Churches (1942). The influence of the Free Churches in public and religious affairs of England has tended to decline with their numbers.

Bibliography: H. DAVIES, *The English Free Churches* (New York 1952). E. K. H. JORDAN, *Free Church Unity* (London 1956). F. L. CROSS, *The Oxford Dictionary of the Christian Church* (London 1957) 526–527, 963.

[W. HANNAH]

FREE WILL

Sometimes called free choice or free decision (Latin *liberum arbitrium*), free will is an ability characterizing man in the voluntary activity of choosing or not choosing a limited good when this is presented to him. It is the basis for asserting man's unique dignity among creatures, as well as for maintaining that he is a person. On it is founded much of the tradition of Western law and morality. Again, it has important consequences in the social order; a person's outlook on man as a strictly determined being or as an autonomous moral person is bound to condition, to some extent, his attitude toward the rehabilitation of criminals and of the mentally ill.

In view of the long history of the concept of free will, and the divergence of views regarding it, this article first sketches the evolution of the concept and its status in modern thought, and then gives a detailed analysis based on the teaching of scholastic philosophers. Arguments against free will are mentioned here only in passing, since these are given fuller treatment elsewhere.

History of the Concept of Free Will

The main stages in the development of the notion of free will may be characterized as follows: the philosophical bases were first proposed by Greek thinkers; these were then developed systematically by patristic and medieval writers, under the influence of the Christian religion; then controversies arose in later scholasticism, traceable largely to the Protestant Reformation and its underlying causes; and these were followed, finally, by the diversity of views that typifies modern thought on the subject.

Greek Origins. The early Greeks generally believed that inanimate things, as well as human beings and the gods themselves, were subject to the fates. Consequently these thinkers did not attempt to change the order of things, but sought to be in harmony with the rest of the universe. Again, in the ancient world freedom was viewed more in a political than in a metaphysical setting. The free man was the one who could participate in the political order, who, unlike the slave, was not ruled by someone above him. Nevertheless, even then certain philosophies contained implicit suggestions of human free choice.

Pre-Socratics. The followers of Pythagoras seem to have simultaneously advocated both freedom and determinism. In their theory of METEMPSYCHOSIS, they argued that the state of a man in his new life depended on actions he performed in his previous life. At the same time they held that all things in the universe were interconnected with an unknown, but probably discoverable, series of number relationships, and that whoever found the key to these would be able to control human affairs. The SOPHISTS taught that man, by clever argument, could change the course of human events; they also argued over whether or not a man deliberated about acts he performed. From this it may be inferred that they acknowledged some degree of free choice in man, even if the outcome was subject to the will of the fates. The Eleatics necessarily denied human freedom, in consequence of their pantheistic monism. Similarly DEMOCRITUS, and the Greek atomists generally, adhering as they did to a strict mechanism, denied contingency of any kind in the universe.

Classical Thinkers. It was with SOCRATES that the Greek notion of human freedom shifted emphatically from a political concept to the psychological notion of individual subjective freedom. Socrates was one of the first Greek philosophers to stress the need for internal self-control. External authority had broken down under the attacks of the Sophists. Consequently the new law Socrates taught was based not so much on external authority as on the mastery (Gr. ἐγκράτεια) each man has of himself. Since, for Socrates, no man does evil knowingly, and since his future depends upon what he knows, man must possess some degree of freedom.

Plato's myth of reincarnation implied moral responsibility. In fact, the whole of the *Republic* may be described as an extension of Socrates's notion of ἐγκράτεια. Aristotle himself did not explicitly discuss either liberty or free will, although both concepts can be found in his works. He disagreed with the teaching of PLATO and Socrates that a wicked man is necessarily ignorant of what is good. Experience, he said, shows otherwise; a man who is truly good can still choose what is evil.

Later Evolution. Like the Eleatics, the Stoics denied freedom of choice as a result of their materialistic pantheism, holding, as they did, that all changes in the universe were due to inexorable laws. For them, a man could be called free only if he willingly accepted these laws. PHILO JUDAEUS held that man's freedom is rooted in his intelligence. PLOTINUS taught that the human soul is free so long as it does not become involved in the world of matter. Moses MAIMONIDES, on the other hand, maintained the freedom of the will in an unqualified way.

Patristic and Medieval Development. With the introduction of Christianity into the mainstream of Western thought, free will came to be studied in more detail. Two teachings of the Christian religion influenced this development. One was that man was created by God and commanded to obey a divine moral law; at the same time, he was promised an eternal reward or punishment. But reward or punishment imply that a man has free choice, for otherwise such sanctions are meaningless. The second was that the first man had incurred original sin and that man, as a result, needed redemption by grace.

Patristic and medieval writers were not so much concerned to prove the existence of free will as they were to establish the roots of freedom, its relation to reason, and its theological implications. St. EPHREM THE SYRIAN, for example, taught that man has freedom; that this freedom is rooted in his intellect and will; and, because of this, that man is the image of God. Other patristic writers defended free will against the pagan teaching that fate ruled the universe.

Augustine and Anselm. In the early Church St. AUGUSTINE was beyond question the greatest exponent of the Christian teaching on human freedom. His major concern was to reconcile man's freedom in relation to contingent acts with the foreknowledge God necessarily possesses. Augustine insisted on the freedom of the human will; yet he insisted on the necessity of grace as a basis of merit. He also asserted that an omnipotent and omniscient God would necessarily know, from all eternity, the infinite number of motives to which the will of each man might consent.

By the time Augustine composed his treatises, the Latin term *libertas* had several meanings in the Christian world. It could mean freedom of the will, or freedom as opposed to slavery—whether this is slavery to sin or slavery to death. Consequently when St. ANSELM OF CANTERBURY took up a discussion of liberty he distinguished between the power to choose what is good or evil (*arbitrium*) and the power to choose what is actually good for one's nature (*libertas*). For St. Anselm, free choice is not so much an ability to choose between good and evil as it is an ability to maintain rectitude of the will.

Thomistic Doctrine. St. THOMAS AQUINAS argued that man is free with respect to finite goods but that he is determined to the infinite good. That is to say, the human person, encountering a finite object, can accept or refuse it; he can do so because the object can appear either as good, since it has actuality, or as lacking in good, since it lacks the actuality possessed by a different object. Aquinas held that a human person would not be free if he directly encountered an infinite good his intellect clearly recognized as such. But since man, in this life, is not confronted directly with an infinite good, he is not necessitated by the objects of this world. To reconcile the contingency of human choice with God's foreknowledge, Aquinas emphasized that man is in time whereas God is outside time, and that past, present, and future are simultaneously present to the Divine Mind. Thus *fore*knowledge, while meaningful to man, has no counterpart in God.

Yet God is not only omniscient, He is omnipotent; and in His omnipotent providence He brings into actuality all events that have happened, that are happening, and that will happen in the universe. This raises a problem: If an omniscient and all-provident God also effects whatever happens in the universe, how can God's activity be reconciled with man's freedom?

Later Scholasticism and Protestantism. Among Catholic philosophers and theologians two main positions have been formulated to solve this problem. Both positions claim their origin as further refinements of the teaching of St. Thomas, and both were developed in answer to the positions of Luther and Calvin.

Dominican and Molinist Theories. Dominican theologians for the most part teach that God premoves each man toward his freely chosen goal, because every act of a creature requires that God first move the creature. This premotion is in conformity with the nature of the creature premoved. Thus an infinitely powerful God infallibly premoves man, a free agent, to choose a particular goal freely, while premoving other creatures toward their goals with necessity. God's premotion is inevitable in view of his omniscience. Since it is inevitable, it may be called a decree, and in this sense is logically prior to divine knowledge of creatural activity. (*See* PREMOTION, PHYSICAL.)

The Molinist position differs from the Dominican chiefly in two respects: instead of referring to a divine premotion, Molinists think it more precise to speak of a divine concurrence with man's will; and, secondly, they hold that God's knowledge of what a free being would choose, if the necessary conditions were supplied, is logically prior to His decree of concurrence or premotion. (*See* CONCURRENCE, DIVINE.)

St. Thomas himself notes that part of the difficulty in resolving the question of God's premotion and of man's free choice lies in the need to use a more apt terminology when speaking about God, since terms can be predicated of God only analogically. In the problem at hand terms such as premotion or foreknowledge are applied to God as if He existed in time, whereas He is an infinite being existing outside of time.

Protestant Reformers. Among the controversies of the Reformation, the doctrine of free will was a crucial point of difference between Protestant and Catholic theologians. Martin LUTHER and John CALVIN strongly denied freedom of the will, basing their arguments on scriptural texts, especially those of St. Paul. Luther concluded that man is predestined to such an extent that he can never truly be said to have power over his own fate. Luther did not deny all human freedom; but he believed that the freedom man possessed after original sin was not enough freedom to allow him to work out his redemption.

Calvin's denial of free will went further than Luther's. He asserted that man cannot perform a good act unless necessitated to it by God's grace, and that man can in no way resist such grace. It is absurd, said Calvin, to speak of man cooperating with grace, because this implies the possibility of rejection on man's part. *See* PREDESTINATION (IN NON-CATHOLIC THEOLOGY).

Modern Thought. Consequent on the 16th-century discovery of large numbers of regular movements in the universe, some philosophers attempted to extend physical determinism to the sphere of human action. This inclination still persists, although it is counterbalanced by other tendencies in modern thought that defend the reality of freedom.

Determinists. Thomas HOBBES held that the notion of free subject was as self-contradictory as that of round quadrangle. Deliberation, for Hobbes, was nothing more than a succession of desires and aversions, each counterbalancing the other, until a final state was reached. This final state Hobbes called ''the will act.'' Since each desire and aversion had been caused, Hobbes concluded that the will act itself was caused; hence the will act is not free. Yet he maintained that man does have freedom to act, since he can act once he has willed it.

B. SPINOZA concluded that only God is a free cause and that all human actions are subject to strict determinism. J. O. de La Mettrie, on the basis of his materialism, also denied freedom of the will. Arthur SCHOPENHAUER taught that a man knows the successive acts of his will *after* they have occurred, but that he does not foresee his future acts. Man only thinks he is free; if he were actually so, he would be able to foresee his future acts. J. F. Herbart's denial of free will resulted from his initial assumption that the methods and presuppositions of psychology are identical with those of physics.

Descartes, Hume, and Schelling. The writers mentioned above may safely be characterized as determinists; others cannot be located in a neat category, because their works contain elements of both determinism and freedom. René DESCARTES, for example, wavered between Jansenism and Molinism. David HUME held that from one standpoint man's acts are free, whereas from another standpoint they are not. He asserted that man's choice is necessitated as much as that of any material agent. Acts of choice are strictly determined by preceding feelings or motives, as well as by character. Nevertheless, since man himself makes the choice, in this respect he may be called free. Friedrich SCHELLING held that man's actions are simultaneously predictable and free. Man himself makes a choice, but his choices are determined by his character, which, in turn, is the result of previous choices. Freedom, for Schelling, is fundamentally the power of choosing between good and evil.

Proponents of Free Will. A variety of positions may be found also among advocates of free will. Some preserve deterministic elements in their teachings. N. MALEBRANCHE, for example, saw that if his position on causality were carried far enough, it would deny human responsibility for any acts. Not wishing to go to this extreme, he asserted that religion and morality would be meaningless unless man is free. G. W. LEIBNIZ held for freedom of choice, although his theory should likewise have ended in a mitigated form of determinism. He held that, while free acts must be motivated by reason, reason must judge to be best what seems to be best.

Some writers accept freedom of the will as a given fact but deny any attempts at a strict demonstration. Blaise PASCAL, for example, said that freedom could be known only by means of a religious experience. Immanuel Kant held that it could not be demonstrated scientifically, but that it is implicit in the CATEGORICAL IMPERATIVE. Similarly, contemporary existentialists are prone to accept free choice as a foundation for their philosophical positions. Karl JASPERS, for example, maintains that each man is a unique being who goes beyond what he already is, and locates his new state of being in the process of exercising his freedom. Martin HEIDEGGER states that, within certain limits, man can be responsible for his destiny by freely choosing his possibilities, especially his destiny to death. Jean Paul SARTRE affirms that freedom is a distinctive characteristic of man. Gabriel Marcel and Emmanuel Mounier teach that man realizes himself as a person only in his acts of commitment. (*See* EXISTENTIALISM; PERSONALISM.)

Philosophical Analysis of Free Will

The foregoing history of the concept of free will shows not only the diversity of thought on this subject, but also the necessity of distinction and definition when attempting to analyze man's free activity. Scholastic philosophers, pursuing such a program, have arrived at refined notions of free will, its distinction from voluntarity and related concepts, and various influences to which it is subjected. The following is a survey of common scholastic teaching in this area.

Preliminary Distinctions. The term free will is customarily regarded as an accurate translation of the Latin expression *liberum arbitrium;* yet the more exact translation is free choice or free decision. One reason for objecting to ''free will'' is that this expression is interpreted too often to mean that every voluntary act is by definition a free act preceded immediately by an act of deliberation. Such is not the case.

Voluntarity. The designation ''voluntary'' means that an act was, at one time or another, willed freely; but it does not always mean that an act here and now being performed is a free act. Acts that have become ingrained as habits were perhaps at one time willed; and insofar as they were once willed and arose from the will principle, they may be called voluntary; but once established as habits, they should no longer be called free. Other acts resulting from a previous act of choice may also be called voluntary, but not, strictly speaking, free. These are virtually voluntary acts, that is to say, acts that, once chosen, are executed without requiring a new act of choice. A man who has chosen to go for a walk does not have to continue making a choice for each step he takes while walking. Insofar as he chose to be doing what he is doing, his act is virtually voluntary, although not completely free. (*See* VOLUNTARITY.)

Deliberation. Again, not every act a man performs is voluntary. The actions a man performs are commonly divided into human acts (*actus humanus*) and acts of man (*actus hominis*); a HUMAN ACT is one following some kind of deliberation, whereas an act of man is not preceded by deliberation. A reflex movement of the body, for example, would be an act of man and not a human act.

Definition of Free Will. To avoid confusing freedom with voluntarity and nondeliberate acts, free will is usually defined as the freedom possessed by a human being who, encountering an object he evaluates as finite, may choose whether or not to yield to the attraction of that object.

Such a definition obviously requires further exposition and clarification. Any object, insofar as it is actual and attractive, may be called a GOOD. Yet the WILL can be attracted to such an object only so far as it recognizes this as some kind of good. A good that can satisfy only to a limited extent is called a particular or finite good, whereas one that can satisfy in every conceivable respect is called the universal or supreme good (*see* GOOD, THE SUPREME).

According to St. Thomas Aquinas, the human will is strictly determined in its nature toward an object recognized intellectually as the universal good. (According to DUNS SCOTUS, the human will, absolutely speaking, would not be necessitated even in this case.) For St. Thomas, then, freedom of choice is exercised only with regard to objects recognized as particular goods. A man is not determined to these because particular goods may be viewed in two opposing ways: (1) they may be seen as good, i.e., according to the proportionate good they possess when compared to the universal good; or (2) they may be seen as lacking in good, i.e., to the extent that they lack goodness when measured against the universal good. Thus, any finite good can be considered under an aspect of desirability or undesirability when compared to the universal good. As desirable, it can attract the will; as undesirable, it cannot.

Further Distinctions. Assuming that the object in question is a particular good, further notions are helpful for clarifying what is meant by freedom of the will. These include the concepts of freedom of exercise, freedom of specification, elicited and commanded acts of the will, license, indifference, and spontaneity.

Exercise and Specification. Freedom of exercise is freedom to adopt or reject a particular good. This is the basic freedom of the will. Freedom of specification, on the other hand, is freedom to choose between one particular good and another, when several such goods are available. This is not found in every case involving freedom of the will. A person who elects to achieve a goal may find that only one particular good is available to achieve it. In such an eventuality he has no freedom of specification.

Commanded and Elicited Acts. Freedom of exercise and freedom of specification both apply to elicited acts of the will, as distinguished from commanded acts. Elicited acts are those taking place within the will itself; e.g., acts of desire or of choice. Commanded acts are those desired or chosen by the will, yet executed by another power. Suppose, for example, that an athlete desires to run faster than any man has ever run before. His desire is an elicited act; but his act of desire alone will not accomplish the result he seeks. He can accomplish this only by his ability to run. In such a case he is free to seek the goal; whereas he is not necessarily free to attain it.

License. Freedom of the will should not be confused with license. License is the ability to choose an object that, although satisfying, does not perfect the nature of the chooser. The ability to consume poisoned food or to read a salacious book is license, not freedom, because poisoned food or such reading do not make a person more human—they work against his humanity. Freedom, as opposed to license, is the capacity of a person to pursue, without extrinsic or intrinsic necessity, goods that can fulfill his nature.

Indifference. Freedom of will may be defined also as a condition of indifference with regard to finite goods. Such indifference can be understood either as indifference within the will itself or as indifference within the object. Indifference within the will is further subdivided into active and subjective. Active indifference is the neutrality of the will to act or not to act for a finite object. Subjective indifference (sometimes called formal indifference) is the neutrality of the will precisely as the subject in which active indifference is rooted. Indifference within the object (sometimes called objective indifference) is the dual aspect presented by a finite object whereby it can be considered from one standpoint as possessing desirable attributes, and from another standpoint as lacking the attributes possessed by another desirable object.

With these distinctions understood, freedom of the will may be more accurately described as the active indifference in virtue of which the will has dominion over its own act, through its power over the last practical judgment of the intellect, which presents the finite object to the will as a good to be adopted.

Spontaneity. Such freedom is not to be confused with spontaneity. Spontaneity signifies something arising within a thing from its internal principles and independently of external agents. The life activities of a plant are spontaneous; yet they are not free, since they arise from internal necessity.

Faculties Acting on the Will. The most important of the powers of the soul that influence choices of will is obviously the INTELLECT (*see* FACULTIES OF THE SOUL). The will is necessitated toward anything that is understood to be in some way satisfying; such understanding is a function of the intellect. Therefore a person's choice of an object is partly guided by his intellect. On the other hand, since even understanding of an object is a finite good for the person considering it, he may refuse to acquire a complete understanding, and his truncated intellectual act may thus result in a distorted concept of the object. Because of this, he may be attracted toward an object that here and now he considers good, whereas a more complete understanding of the same object would have presented it as undesirable.

The will can also be affected indirectly by objects of the sense powers, insofar as such objects are presented with a vividness rarely found in intellectual activity. Sense impressions and physical states, as a consequence, can influence a person's intellectual deliberation and choice. Examples of physical states are: (1) an inherited physical makeup whereby one person tends to react more readily and with greater emotion than another; (2) organic dispositions at certain ages of life—e.g., the youth, with his whole future open to him, is more optimistic, less cautious, and more subject to physical drives than the middle-aged man; and (3) organic modifications acquired by an individual himself. Some of the latter may be purely transitory, such as the effect of stimulants or depressing agents. Others may be more or less fixed, such as the pathological condition set up in the nervous system as the result of an addiction to dope.

Free Will and Unconscious Influences. The powers and contents of mind referred to above are considered as existing in the field of CONSCIOUSNESS at the time they exert their influence. Other contents of mind, outside the field of consciousness, can be shown also to influence a person's act of choice. Because of such unconscious influences, some writers have argued that a man cannot be called free in his choice, because he is not aware of everything affecting him at the time. This objection, however, does not hold, because the act of free choice is itself made on the basis of conscious judgments. Free will should be considered more as an ability to select between influences, than as an absence of influences. One's own awareness is witness to the fact that he chooses consciously. If his belief is illusory in this case, then no datum of consciousness would seem to have any truth value.

Free Will and Mental Illness. It has also been objected that freedom of the will has been outmoded by what is called "the irresistible impulse." The term is defined in various ways, but the common note is that of a deprivation (sometimes called a destruction) of the free agency of the individual so that he has an uncontrollable impulse to act. Yet it is inaccurate to speak of an irresistible impulse; it would be more correct to say that the impulse was unresisted. It is generally held by psychiatrists that even in severe cases of an obsessive-compulsive reaction a patient *could* continue resisting the "compulsive" urge, even though this would require an enormous expenditure of anxiety. Uncommon effort may be required for a neurotic to reject the object of a compulsive urge; but this is far different from saying that his will has been destroyed. Again, weakened resistance to an unresisted impulse may be more or less severe at different times for the same neurotic; these are mitigating circumstances in determining the morality of his actions, but it is] incorrect to say, on this account, that his will has been destroyed. If his will were destroyed, it would be impossible both practically and theoretically for a physician to cure him. After the unconscious content influencing a patient has been uncovered, the major effect of therapy is to have the patient choose a more constructive mode of action.

Freedom of will has also been denied in the case of psychotic patients. Psychosis may be generally described as a condition where the sufferer is markedly out of contact with some area of reality and is not aware that he is out of contact. (The psychotic who is hallucinating, for example, sincerely believes that the voice commanding him to kill his children is real.) Therefore, the objector argues, since the psychotic does not possess the true knowledge required for making a free choice, he is not free. To answer this objection, the notion of responsibility must be clarified and a distinction made between subjective responsibility and objective responsibility. By responsibility is meant the capacity to determine one's own acts, or the capacity to be deterred by sanctions or consequences. A person has subjective responsibility if he has freedom to act or not in accordance with his evaluation of the object and, while acting, is aware that he might have done otherwise. A person has objective responsibility if his choice is made on the basis of a true understanding of the situation in which he makes his decision. In the case of the man hallucinating, he would be subjectively responsible if he were free to act or refuse to act on the commands he heard from the voice; but he would not be objectively responsible if he were not in possession of objectively true knowledge, and thus was not free to make an objectively true choice. He would not be guilty of his act, even though subjectively responsible. It must be kept in mind, of course, that here it is a question of a psychotic's action as directly rooted in his psychosis. It is not necessarily true that every action this same individual would perform is totally lacking in responsibility, because he may have some degree of mental clarity in other areas of his life.

See Also: FREEDOM; CHOICE.

Bibliography: A. M. FARRER, *The Freedom of the Will* (London 1958). J. DE FINANCE, *Existence et liberté* (Lyon 1955). A. M. MUNN, *Free-will and Determinism* (London 1960). K. W. RANKIN, *Choice and Chance* (Oxford 1961). P. NOLAN, *Saint Thomas and the Unconscious Mind* (Washington 1953). R. ZAVALLONI, *Self-determination*, tr. V. BIASIOL and C. TAGESON (Chicago 1963). J. R. CAVANAGH and J. B. MCGOLDRICK, *Fundamental Psychiatry* (3d ed. Milwaukee 1964). R. P. MCKEON, *Freedom and History* (New York 1952). A. ANTWEILER, *Das Problem der Willensfreiheit* (Freiburg 1955). O. LOTTIN, *Psychologie et morale aux XIIe et XIIIe siácles*, 6 v. (Louvain-Gembloux 1942–60). Y. SIMON, *Traité du libre arbitre* (Liége 1951). P. RICOEUR, *Philosophie de la volonté*, 2 v. in 3 (Paris 1950–60). M. J. ADLER, ed. *The Great Ideas: A Syntopicon of Great Books of the Western World*, 2 v. (Chicago 1952) 1:991–1012; 2:251–69, 1071–1101. D. MACKENZIE, J. HASTINGS, ed., *Encyclopedia of Religion and Ethics*, 13 v. (Edinburgh 1908–27) 6:124–27. F. BATTAGLIA, *Enciclopedia filosofica*, 4 v. (Venice-Rome 1957) 3:18–41. J. BAUCHER, *Dictionnaire de théologie catholique*, ed. A. VACANT et al., 15 v. (Paris 1903–50) 9.1:660–703. A. MICHEL, *ibid.* 15.2:3322–87. E. SCHOTT, *Die Religion in Geschichte und Gegenwart*, 7 v. (3d ed. Tübingen 1957–65) 6:1719–25.

[P. NOLAN]

FREE WILL AND GRACE

The way in which the fact of man's free choice is reconciled with the fundamental Christian truth of his total dependence on the grace of God is, ultimately, a mystery. The Catholic Church has always believed and taught both truths while allowing its theologians full liberty to attempt to explain their compatibility. This article concentrates on the history of the problem.

Sovereignty of Grace. Catholic belief in the sovereignty of grace holds that no free act leading to salvation can be performed unless it is initiated, sustained, and brought to completion by the merciful gift or grace of God. To deny this is to destroy the whole meaning of the gospel of Jesus Christ (see, e.g., Jn 6.44; 15.5; Phil 2.13; 2 Cor 3.5; Rom 11.6), as the Church affirmed in its vigorous reaction to Pelagianism (H. Denzinger *Enchiridion symbolorum*, 222–230, 371–397; *see* PELAGIUS AND PELAGIANISM). It even accepted with approval the judgment of the author of the *Indiculus* that the Pelagians are "very impious defenders of free will" (*Enchiridion symbolorum* 238).

With the rise of NOMINALISM in philosophical and theological teaching, a latent Pelagianism came to infect many facets of popular piety and preaching. Against this tendency the voice of the Reformation thundered the absolute sovereignty of grace. Yet, as Augustine had observed, the question of the interrelation of grace and man's free act is so difficult that "there are some persons who so defend God's grace as to deny man's free will" (*Grat. et lib. arb.* 1.1; *Patrologia Latina* 44:881). The Reformation theologians were heirs of nominalism's EXTRINSICISM as well as foes of its naturalism, and they could only conceive of FREE WILL and grace as standing in opposition to one another, not as set in a relationship of harmony and subordination.

Affirmation of Free Will. In the context of the strong statements of the Reformers [which at least some contemporary Protestant theology interprets in a way entirely acceptable to Catholics—see J. Dillenberger and C. Welch, *Protestant Christianity* (New York 1958) 33] the Church defined as a dogma that even sinful man has a truly free will (*Enchiridion symbolorum* 1555). This conviction it has from the revelation that the process of salvation is man's dialogue of love with Him who first loved man (1 Jn 4.10–11; Mt 22.37–40). This same fidelity to the Gospel would constrain it to reject the pseudo-Augustinianism of Baius (*Enchiridion symbolorum* 1939, 1966; *see* BAIUS AND BAIANISM) and C. JANSEN (Jansenius) (H. Denzinger, *Enchiridion symbolorum* 2003), which would consider the gift of grace as an irresistible attraction that necessitates man's action, destroying freedom.

Catholic Theology. Every Catholic theology maintains that man's supernatural act is produced both by his free will and by God's grace, but the relationship between them is not that of two independent causes mutually cooperating. On the contrary, the free consent is itself a gift of grace. While one legitimately speaks of "cooperating with grace" (*Enchiridion symbolorum* 379, 397, 1525), this cooperation is given to men by the gracious God. He so gives it to men that it is truly theirs, but it is theirs without ceasing to depend on the saving good pleasure of God. God and man act on totally different planes. Only the divine freedom is absolutely independent. Man's freedom is a creaturely freedom, and even in its free activity it is dependent on Subsistent Freedom. Yet this dependence does not do away with human freedom, for God's causality transcends every category of cause man can imagine. It gives lesser causes their own action in a way that is totally in harmony with their natures. Beings that are not free He moves to an activity that is determined; beings that are free He moves to an activity that is free and responsible while not ceasing to be the product of grace. Herein there is mystery, but not absurdity.

Theological Controversy. The years that followed Trent's solemn definition of the dogma of human liberty in the presence of efficacious GRACE found theologians trying to explain in rational terms how the sovereign efficacy of God's grace is compatible with the psychological dominion of man's own act that is essential to his liberty. Luis de MOLINA, SJ, wrote his famous *Concordia liberi arbitrii cum gratiae donis . . .* (Lisbon 1588), in which he postulated a *SCIENTIA MEDIA* as the special way God foresees the future free act of man prior to determining to give him the efficacious grace that will unfailingly bring about the free action. At the same time Domingo Báñez, OP, was expounding an approach to the problem in terms, he believed, of the principles of St. Thomas Aquinas (e.g., *Summa theologiae* 1a, 19.8; 105.5; 1a2ae, 10.4 ad 3; 112.3). He totally rejected the *scientia media* as an unnecessary innovation and as implying that God is somehow dependent on His creature (*see* BÁÑEZ AND BAÑEZIANISM). Thence developed the debate between Bañezianism and Molinism, which the Church has refused to decide (*Enchiridion symbolorum* 2564). The unresolved debate remains as an occasion of suspicion to orthodox Protestant theology; e.g., Karl Barth distrusts any Catholic affirmation of the sovereignty of divine grace that leaves room for a *scientia media* (*Kirchliche Dogmatik* 2.1:640–657).

The theologies of the Jesuit and the Dominican schools remain irreconcilably opposed in their manner of explaining how grace is efficacious to move the human will to its free act of encounter with God, but both affirm the fact that it is. Since faith is more concerned with revealed realities than theological explanations, the Church can tolerate the conflict.

The issue is not dead. It is a legitimate task of theology to seek a formula by which to express the complex data of the problem. In recent years there have been new efforts to express this reality within the general terms of the opposing camps (Bañezian: H. Guillermin, Marín-Sola, R. Garrigou-Lagrange, J. Maritain; Molinist: M. de la Taille, A. Michel, B. Lonergan, A. d'Alés, C. Boyer). Others (A. Sertillanges, C. Baumgartner), shunning both the *scientia media* and the physical premotion, are content to appeal to the transcendent character of the mysterious divine action.

See Also: GRACE, ARTICLES ON; CONGREGATIO DE AUXILIIS; GRACE, CONTROVERSIES ON; GRACE AND NATURE; MOLINISM; SYNERGISM.

Bibliography: C. BOYER, *Dictionnaire de théologie catholique*, Tables générales 1:1862–68. K. RAHNER, *Lexikon für Theologie und Kirche*, ed. J. HOFER and K. RAHNER, 10 v. (2d new ed. Freiburg 1957–65) 4:996–997. F. STEGMÜLLER, *ibid.* 4:1002–10. M. J. FARRELLY, *Predestination, Grace, and Free Will* (Westminster, Md. 1964). R. GUARDINI, *Freedom, Grace, and Destiny,* tr. J. MURRAY (New York 1961). B. LONERGAN, "St. Thomas' Thought on *Gratia Operans,*" *Theological Studies* 3 (1942) 533–578; *Insight* (New York 1957) 662–664. T. U. MULLANEY, "The Basis of the Suarezian Teaching on Human Freedom," *Thomist* 11 (1948) 1–17, 330–369, 448–502; 12 (1949) 48–94, 155–206. M. PONTIFEX, *Freedom and Providence* (New York 1960). N. DEL PRADO, *De gratia et libero arbitrio,* 3 v. (Fribourg 1907). H. RONDET, *Gratia Christi* (Paris 1948).

[C. REGAN]

FREE WILL AND PROVIDENCE

That God has a providence implies that He has omniscience and OMNIPOTENCE and that His providence extends to all things. A question concerning man's FREE WILL arises. How can this exist if his every action is eternally foreseen and determined?

Pre-Christian Thought. Among the Greeks the denial of freedom was common. In the universe there is an inescapable law, devoid of intelligence and love, determining every event, binding men and gods. This is destiny, necessity, or inflexible fate. Even those who admitted a supreme being's existence, providence, and man's freedom did not always clearly perceive these realities. Thus Plato held to a hierarchy of gods; Aristotle was a monotheist. Both discussed human liberty not as a special power of the will but more in a political or social context.

Jewish thought asserted the existence of divine providence and human freedom. Deuteronomy clearly stated the ability to choose between good and evil. If Josephus' statement (*Antiquities* 18.1.3–5) is accepted, at the time of the second Temple the Sadducees, to safeguard man's liberty, denied God's influence in his actions. The Essenes are pictured as having been absolute determinists. The Pharisees seemed to have held a middle position, admitting the creature's liberty in certain matters.

Christian Thought. With a deeper notion of man's supernatural DESTINY, the question of human liberty under the mysterious influence of predestination to grace and final glory became more complex in the Christian Era. Gnosticism, which in some cases rejected responsibility, and Manichaeism, with its denial of freedom, gave no answer. Augustine set forth the difficulty when he wrote that some so defend the grace of God that they deny man's free will; and others so defend man's free will that they deny the grace of God (*Grat. et lib. arb.* 1.1; *Patrologia Latina* 44:881). He himself maintained that the divine precepts of the Old and New Testaments would be worthless without freedom (*ibid.* 2.2, *Patrologia Latina* 44:882; 2.4, *Patrologia Latina* 44:883).

St. Thomas Aquinas affirmed both divine providence and man's freedom. God's knowledge and existence are not the same as those of His creatures. He does not know things successively but with one eternal act; otherwise He would be subject to change and imperfection (*Summa theologiae* 1a, 14.4; 14.7). Nor does He exist in time (*Summa theologiae* 1a, 14.13 ad 3). Thus the manner and limitations of created intelligence and power must not be ascribed to Him. On the other hand man is free. If he were not, counsels, exhortations, precepts, prohibitions, rewards, and punishments would be purposeless (*Summa theologiae* 1a, 83.1). To harmonize these two truths Thomas distinguished between primary and secondary causality. To be free the creature need not be the first but only the secondary cause of his actions. An analogy is proposed. When man makes something, he works on an already existing thing, yet he is the real cause of what is produced. God is the first cause of all things; man, acting under His influence, is the true secondary cause of his own actions (*Summa theologiae* 1a, 83.1 ad 3).

This reasoning applies both to natural and supernatural providence, but with a difference. Strictly speaking the former is not beyond human understanding; yet such understanding is incomplete. Man's knowledge of the divine essence is not proper but analogical; this is imperfect because it is only proportional. The teaching of faith, while only morally necessary here, increases certitude. In the supernatural order, however, man's liberty under grace and predestination to eternal life is a mystery; the created intelligence alone cannot prove it; an appeal to faith is, therefore, absolutely necessary.

The core of the argument on faith is had in the Church's response to various errors. Martin Luther maintained that divine providence and omnipotence were incompatible with human freedom. Original sin also left permanent damage. Free will exists only in God. If applied to man, it should be restricted to things below him, such as the right to use or not use his goods or possessions. In matters of salvation or damnation he is a captive either to the divine will or to that of Satan. M. Baius taught that without grace man is not free; he can only sin.

The Council of Trent affirmed that in Adam's sin man lost his original innocence; his will, though weakened, remains free; under the influence of actual grace it can consent or dissent (H. Denzinger, *Enchiridion symbolorum*, ed. A. Schönmetzer (32d ed. Freiburg 1963)1521, 1554). St. Pius V asserted that even without grace man naturally has the choice between good and evil (*Enchiridion symbolorum* 1927). Vatican Council I mentioned both divine providence and man's freedom:

> All things which He founded God by His providence protects and governs, ''reaching from end to end mightily and governing all things well'' (cf. Wis 8.1). ''For all things are naked and open to His eyes'' (Heb 4.13), even those things which are future by the free actions of creatures.'' [H. DENZINGER, *Enchiridion symbolorum* 3003.]

In the post-Tridentine period a controversy arose among Catholic theologians concerning the divine influence and human freedom. Luis de MOLINA, SJ, proposed his system of *SCIENTIA MEDIA*. From all eternity God knows what use each individual will make of his free will. With His aid the creature makes its own self-determination; His decree, either absolute or permissive, follows such choice (*see* MOLINISM). Domingo Báñez, OP, maintained an eternal but free PREDETERMINATION of man's actions (*see* BÁÑEZ AND BAÑEZIANISM).

Depending on its concept of God and human freedom, modern philosophy often gives a different picture. When it denies the supernatural order, as does Deism, it rules out consideration of the mystery of grace and free will. When it is materialistic it denies true liberty. Many psychologists hold that man's conviction of freedom as the result of personal experience is an illusion.

Bibliography: AUGUSTINE, *The Problem of Free Choice*, tr. and annot. M. PONTIFEX (*Ancient Christian Writers* 22; 1955). A. D'ALÈS, *Providence et libre arbitre* (2d ed. Paris 1927). V. J. BOURKE, *Will in Western Thought* (New York 1964). J. DE FINANCE, *Existence et liberté* (Lyons 1955). A. C. GIGON, *Divinae scientiae causalitas quoad res temporales humanamque libertatem* (Fribourg 1948). R. HOURCADE, ''Prescience et causalité divines,'' *Bulletin de Littérature Ecclésiastique* 39 (1938) 181–203. L. JERPHAGNON, *Servitude de la liberté? Liberté-providence-prédestination* (Paris 1958). M. PONTIFEX, *Freedom and Providence* (New York 1960). C. SPICQ, ''Liberty according to the N.T.,'' *Spiritual Life* 6 (1960) 323–336. W. G. THOMPSON, ''The Doctrine of Free Choice in Saint Bonaventure,'' *Franciscan Studies* 18 (1958) 1–8.

[E. J. CARNEY]

FREEDOM

The various meanings of the term ''freedom'' center around three main themes. The first is the possibility of the subject to act as he will to satisfy his tendencies, aspirations, and the like (freedom of action as opposed to constraint, servitude, etc.; civil and political liberties, etc.). The second is the power of self-determination without any necessitation in willing, if only from pressures of a nature slightly distinct from the ego (freedom of willing, free will, as opposed to NECESSITY). The third is the fulfillment of the reasoning subject by the internal domination of reason, of superior motivations over feelings and over inferior motivations (rational freedom). This article sketches the historical development of the various notions of freedom and then presents a systematic analysis of topics relating to freedom that are of particular interest to Catholics.

HISTORICAL DEVELOPMENT

The history of the concept of freedom may be conveniently divided into periods corresponding to those of ancient, patristic, medieval, modern, and contemporary thought.

Ancient period. Man's first awareness of things outside himself naturally led him to an early appreciation of the first type of freedom mentioned above. SOCRATES and PLATO, impressed with the idea of servitude, presented its correlative as a liberation internal to man. The evildoer who thinks he is free because he can satisfy his desires is himself a slave. Only the wise and virtuous man in whom reason rules is truly free. Can man freely choose between true and false freedom? The Socratic theory, which identifies virtue and wisdom, is interwoven in the answer. Sin comes only from ignorance of the true GOOD. This logically seems to exclude freedom of choice properly speaking. In any event, Plato conceived of freedom in the third sense already mentioned.

ARISTOTLE rejected the Socratic principle; for him, evil can knowingly be willed, although not as evil. However, there is no agreement among scholars as to whether or not Aristotle affirmed the existence of free will. He admits of choice (Gr. προαίρεσις) preceded by deliberation. Both concern means alone. Deliberation ends upon a person's accepting one means as the most appropriate. There is neither deliberation nor choice about the end. Again, Aristotle gives the practical syllogism as the application of a general rule to a particular case. Passion can impede the correct use of the principles of reason and substitute for them another rule (e.g., pleasure to be sought). Aristotle's notion of freedom is thus not clearly defined and is difficult to distinguish from spontaneity, just as the will is poorly distinguished from desire. Similarly, the idea of free will is not made precise; the word itself (αὐτεξούσιον) appears only later in Greek philosophy with the problem of morality, and thenceforth occupies a prominent place in philosophical thought.

Paradoxically, the Stoics, holding for a strict causal determinism (a revival of the old notion of FATE), assert most strongly that man has the power to be master of himself and to arrive at virtue; and they maintain an opposition between what depends on man and what does not. The wise man who has himself conquered virtue is superior to the gods. They strive to reconcile the two seemingly contradictory positions by showing that human acts, although conditioned by their antecedents, are man's very own and truly proceed from him, much like a cylinder that, once thrown on a plane, rolls by itself. In fact, the Stoics consider true freedom as an acceptance of necessity. It has its perfection in the wise man who is free from passions and emotions and is master of himself through submission to universal reason. No less paradoxically, EPICURUS and his followers, although materialists, admit of freedom of choice, freeing themselves from the fear of destiny. To ensure such freedom they posit an indeterminism in the physical world by acknowledging, in atoms undergoing falling motion, the power to deviate from the vertical.

In the Hellenistic period many treatises on destiny appeared, and the first meaning of freedom found energetic defenders (e.g., Alexander of Aphrodisias, second and third centuries A.D.). The problem of reconciling freedom with divine foreknowledge and providence had already arisen by this time.

Patristic era. Christianity, or more precisely Judeo-Christianity, emphasized the idea of freedom: freedom of God in creation, in calling men to salvation, and so on; freedom of man, without which precepts and sanctions would have no meaning. The fact that a free act involves an eternal destiny gave to the problem of freedom a tragic aspect completely overlooked by the Greeks, Aristotle in particular. The specifically Christian problem of the harmony between freedom and grace further complicated the problem of the harmony between divine knowledge and freedom. Moreover the Christian message, with St. Paul in particular, was presented as a liberation: the Christian is torn from servitude to sin, to the flesh, and to the letter of the law in order to enjoy freedom of spirit.

The Fathers of the Church, in fact, at first appeared concerned with defending free will against the fatalism of the Gnostics and the Manichaeans (St. IRENAEUS, ORIGEN, METHODIUS OF OLYMPUS, GREGORY OF NYSSA, etc.). Knowledge does not change the nature of its object; what is foreseen as free is free (St. AUGUSTINE). BOETHIUS was more precise. He clarified the idea of ETERNITY, that in God there is not foreknowledge but knowledge, so that what is future for man is present for God. The problem of freedom and grace came to the fore with the Pelagian controversy (*see* PELAGIUS AND PELAGIANISM). In what sense and to what point is man, a fallen creature and enslaved to sin, free? How can God move man toward good without infringing upon his freedom, and so on? The Latin Middle Ages would remain under the influence of the Augustinian problematics.

Middle ages. In the early scholastic period, Saints ANSELM OF CANTERBURY and BERNARD OF CLAIRVAUX are the two outstanding figures. Anselm considered freedom essentially as the power to retain rectitude of the will for love of this very rectitude. It is inseparable from the will and perdures even in the sinner who cannot recover his lost rectitude. St. Bernard distinguished three freedoms: a natural freedom that is contrary to necessity; another, the effect of grace, that frees from sin; and a third, an effect of glory, that frees from suffering. The will is essentially free, and in man this freedom effects a special resemblance to God.

The thinkers of the high scholastic period dealt more rigidly with the nature of the will's freedom, some relating it to reason, others to the will, still others to both. St. THOMAS AQUINAS saw it as an attribute of the will insofar as the latter is rational. He based his theory of the free act on the distinction between the order of specification, in which intelligence is primary, and that of exercise, in which the will has primacy. Only the good in general, the Absolute Good, can necessarily determine the will in the order of specification. But in the latter case, although this necessity does away with freedom of choice, it does permit a freedom of spontaneity. Man participates in such freedom here on earth to the degree that he is led by the Holy Spirit. It must be noted that, since divine motion respects natures, God can move the will with no detriment to its freedom. (*See* FREE WILL; CAUSALITY, DIVINE.)

John Duns Scotus gives freedom a particular emphasis as that which characterizes the will and differentiates it from ''natural'' powers. The will is the sole cause of its decision, the role of the intellect being merely that of proposing its object. Even when faced with the Absolute Good, the will strictly retains the possibility of refusing its assent. The theology of Scotus tries to avoid anything that would place in God a dependence of will on intellect.

The nominalist school further accented the voluntarist and indeterminist tendency. Physical and moral laws are completely subject to the divine mind, and a type of theological determinism begins to appear. This does not always deny free will but views it as necessarily determined by God and in reality as nonexistent. THOMAS BRADWARDINE and John WYCLIF are representative of this tendency.

Modern period. Such theories found an echo among the reformers. For M. LUTHER and J. CALVIN, among others, free will no longer exists in man, who is fallen and totally enslaved to his desires. It is basically incompatible with the foreknowledge and sovereign dominion of God.

The controversy raised by such opinions afforded Catholic theologians the opportunity to study the nature of freedom and of its compatibility with divine knowledge, providence, and action. As regards the first topic, Thomists maintained the nondetermining character of motives, whereas F. SUÁREZ and the Molinists held for the possibility of acting or not acting, all conditions required for action being present, and ''all'' being understood to include divine motion. On the other hand, Thomists and St. Robert BELLARMINE held that the will always follows the last practical judgment, a point on which Suárez disagreed. The second topic gave rise to the systems of D. Báñez and L. de MOLINA and their variations. Báñez emphasized the primacy of divine action, which infallibly predetermines the will to determine itself freely. Suárez, on the other hand, was careful to safeguard the psychological reality of free will, but he faced serious problems also, particularly in his theory of the *SCIENTIA MEDIA*. These two systems have confronted each other throughout the history of Catholic theology (*see* CONCURRENCE, DIVINE; PREDETERMINATION; PREMOTION, PHYSICAL).

The problems of philosophers during this period differed from those of the theologians. While T. HOBBES professed determinism, R. DESCARTES vigorously affirmed freedom in God and in man. In God freedom is absolute and operates with essences and truths as well as with existences. This indifference is one aspect of God's infinite perfection, of His supreme independence. Freedom is in some way infinite in man too; in this way it is in him the mark of the Creator. Man can oppose the clearly known good simply to assert his freedom. However, this indifference is not purely and simply a perfection in man, who does not create the true and the good. On the contrary, the infinity of freedom in man, insofar as it goes beyond the extent of understanding, is the cause of error and sin, for man can affirm and will something whose truth and worth he does not perceive clearly. Perfect freedom, for him, would be an irresistible and fully spontaneous adherence to the clearly perceived good. Descartes cites an example of this in consenting to the evidence of the *Cogito*. The Cartesian notion of freedom oscillates between the second and the third meanings cited at the beginning of this article.

For B. SPINOZA, something is free if it exists because of the sole necessity of its nature and if it alone determines itself to act. Only one being fits this definition, God or SUBSTANCE, whose freedom and necessity are identical. There is no freedom of choice in God, for this would place contingency in Him; things derive from Him as conclusions from a principle. Again, there is no freedom of choice in man, whose activity is determined not only by his own essence but by the action of other beings (modes). Human freedom in the third meaning, however, does exist; it consists in freedom from passions or affections and in determination by reason, and comes about because of ''knowledge of the third kind,'' which grasps things through their highest reason, *sub specie aeternitatis.*

G. W. LEIBNIZ rejected this necessitarianism and attempted to restore the freedom of choice. In his view, the free act is characterized by (1) spontaneity, a characteristic common to every activity since the substance, or

MONAD, is alone the cause of all its determinations; (2) intellectuality; and (3) contingency, in the sense that the opposite act does not imply any logical or metaphysical contradiction. Decision is always the result of judgments, affections, tendencies, ''little perceptions,'' and the like, which converge in the soul at a moment coinciding with the autonomous development (with no external command) of the monad. A ''freedom of indifference'' would violate the principle of SUFFICIENT REASON, whose discovery Leibniz attributed to himself. Thus he never went beyond psychological determinism and considered the free subject an immaterial automaton. In his opinion, God Himself is determined by His perfection to the choice of the better.

Eighteenth-century EMPIRICISM and MATERIALISM completely rejected free will. Freedom is an attribute of man, not of the will, and it consists in the power man has to determine his actions (including his internal acts) by his will when faced with possible alternatives. But the will is necessarily moved by the attraction of pleasure and especially, according to J. LOCKE, by the desire to escape ''uneasiness,'' although Locke acknowledged in man the power to suspend his decision to make the choice clearer. According to D. HUME, internal facts appear to be as completely dependent upon their antecedents as are external facts. Yet these writers were deeply interested in freedom in the first meaning. In this period, the development of liberal ideas in politics and economics put an end to the old regime and created a new type of society.

I. KANT stated the problem of freedom in original fashion. The pure reason, requiring that phenomena be linked among themselves according to causal determinism, excludes the freedom of the phenomenal world but allows the possibility of freedom in the noumenal world, of which it knows nothing (*see* PHENOMENA; NOUMENA). But the practical reason sees in the fact of obligation a determination by pure reason that implies freedom. In reality Kant has two ideas of freedom: one negative, the power to begin a series of phenomena, and the other positive, the autodetermination of practical reason (or will) in positing moral law. How is negative freedom reconciled with the determinism in this view? In his *Die Religion innerhalb der Grenzen der blossen Vernunft* (Königsberg 1793), Kant acknowledges a timeless choice that determines the intelligible character governing the complete unfolding of empirical existence for every man. This idea was to appear many times in the future, for example, with F. W. J. SCHELLING and A. SCHOPENHAUER.

Contemporary period. The notion of freedom is much used in contemporary philosophy but with very different meanings, a diversity already seen in post-Kantian IDEALISM. J. G. FICHTE exalted the creative freedom by which the ego set up for itself a world where morality was to be practiced (The Vocation of Man), while G. W. F. HEGEL located true freedom in man's having within himself the reason for his own activity. Such a notion of freedom excludes contingency; it is an inclusive and internalized necessity. Concretely it is realized within a well-organized state. This notion of freedom as the perfect penetration of man by reason, as the realization of the true ego (i.e., the rational ego), is common to the rationalist-idealist tradition of the nineteenth and twentieth centuries, as exemplified by F. H. BRADLEY and B. Bosanquet.

Whereas the positivistic empiricism of J. S. MILL recognized only freedom in the first meaning—and scientific determinism spread this conception—Marxism adopted and transposed certain Hegelian ideas into materialism. True freedom is what all of humanity will possess when men control the physical and social mechanisms that dominate them at present. Freedom is necessity that is understood and utilized. There is no free will. Because they make no distinction between theory and practice, the Marxists speak of liberation (i.e., from the mastery of a determinism imposed by science and technology) rather than of freedom. Man learns what freedom is by liberating himself. They insist on the dialectical connection between determinism and freedom; without determinism freedom is impossible, because man cannot act upon nature.

Among the defenders of free will, apart from traditional SPIRITUALISM, may be cited C. Renouvier. In the last quarter of the nineteenth century, an antirationalist and antideterminist reaction appeared in the form of pragmatism, the philosophy of contingency developed by W. JAMES. Unfortunately, the assertion of freedom has often been separated from a finalist metaphysics that alone renders it intelligible.

H. BERGSON stressed the freedom of spirit as opposed to the determinism of matter. The free act is the continuous expression of the underlying ego, which continually reconstitutes itself so that one state can never be reduced to a previous state. Determinism proceeds from an illusion that expresses pure spiritual duration in terms of space.

More recently some claim to have found a defense for freedom in the indeterminism of quantum mechanics.

Existential or existentialist thinkers since S. A. KIERKEGAARD insist on the irrational side of freedom as the generator of ANXIETY. Choice plays an important role in the ontology of J. P. Sartre, for whom freedom is conscious awareness and existence. It precedes the entire order of reason and in this sense, but in this sense alone, it is ''absurd.'' The radical choice is that by which being-for-itself puts itself, in an absolutely contingent fashion, into being-in-itself as its negation. Such a freedom has no limit but the impossibility of self-renunciation. No nature or order of values is before or above it; it itself creates values.

For N. HARTMANN and others, freedom encounters a world of values to be realized, but it can move toward realization only by choosing among them. This necessity is the radical evil. On the other hand, human freedom is interpreted by the theory of ''levels of being,'' each of which is free with respect to the inferior levels.

Among contemporary Thomists, Jacques Maritain has studied the problem of freedom more profoundly than any other (*see* THOMISM). Freedom of choice presupposes freedom of spontaneity, common to everything that lives and acts, but it must lead to the freedom of ''autonomy and exultation.'' This is the opening out of a personality whose aspirations nothing harms or contradicts, either as a human personality or as a personality in general. Moreover, Maritain draws attention to the ontological basis of freedom by relating it to the Thomistic doctrine of EXISTENCE.

SYSTEMATIC ANALYSIS

Among the topics associated with freedom that merit more detailed consideration are its ontological basis, its relationships to God, and its particular relation to the person.

Ontological basis. In its metaphysical essence, freedom implies autodetermination of the subject more than it does nonnecessity. Its various types stem from the various ways of considering the subject, which can be (1) man as determined from without; (2) more particularly, man as determining his internal or external acts by his will; (3) deeper still, in the willing subject, the ego as not completely determined by nature, circumstances, motives, and the like; or (4) the superego, as opposed to the ego and to the id. To understand the bond between freedom broadly associated with BEING in this way, one must consider being not only as an ESSENCE, as a determination to be this or that, but also as an existent actuality.

A purely essentialist notion of being tends to conceive the bond between various beings after the fashion of a logical connection; in its extreme form, this is found in the rationalist determinism of Spinoza and somewhat less in that of Leibniz. In reality, the ACT by which the subject exists and subsists in his incommunicable individuality, and this in accordance with the demands of his essence, is the root of his activity and spontaneity. His activity is his own inasmuch as it is the expression and realization of this radical actuality.

Spontaneity increases with the ontological level of being. Being is more unified and more itself, its activity more its own and more autonomous, the more it is being and the more it approaches the sufficiency and independence of Subsistent Being. But below the level of SPIRIT, this spontaneity remains entirely determined by the nature of the agent and the concrete conditions of its exercise. With spirit there appears a new kind of spontaneity. Spirit, of course, acts according to its nature, or essence, but its nature is not to be simply a nature, not to be simply what it is, but to be somehow everything. Its essence is ''open'' and its aspirations can be satisfied by the Absolute alone. In this way it escapes from determinism. Other existents, being only what they are, can act only according to what they are at a given moment. But spirit is not imprisoned by any particular determination, by any end or value; it can transcend them all. This condition of the spirit can be referred to as ontological freedom. In spirit, in fact, there ''freely'' appears the positive indetermination of being as such, its eminence over its various determinations. Freedom of action is rooted in this ontological freedom.

Obviously, for a spirit incarnate in matter, the exercise of this power of surpassing is conditioned by what it has of the nonspiritual within itself. Human freedom is essentially impure and its field of immediate action is quite diminished.

Freedom in no way constitutes an irrational exception in being, as was believed under the influence of determinist thought. On the contrary, it is nonfreedom that marks a decadence in being. For St. Thomas, free action as action ''by itself'' has primacy over any action that is determined by a given nature, which is action ''by another'' (*De pot.* 3.15). The mystery of freedom is basically the mystery of being itself, of the existent. This is why, if every act clearly makes existence manifest, the free act does so to an eminent degree. The essence of the will does not explain such behavior in these circumstances; only the existent can remove such indetermination. Insofar as freedom implies the contingency of the act in the choice of a finite good, the mystery that it envelops is also that of FINITE BEING, of NONBEING in being itself. Finally, insofar as created freedom expresses the (at least radical) possibility of failure, it implies nonbeing not only on the part of the object but also on the part of the subject.

Freedom and God. Two points here merit consideration: freedom in God and man's freedom before God.

God's freedom. As PURE ACT of being, dependent on nothing, not even on a nature that might differ so little as to be His act and for Him a given, God is freedom. Some thinkers, such as C. Secrétan (1815–95), even consider this freedom as the principle of divine being (''I am what I will''). This implies two impossibilities: self-causation, in the strict sense, and the contingency of the Absolute Being. Divine existence can be called a free act only if one understands by this the independence and unconditional character of Absolute Being. Such a freedom is also a necessity because Absolute Being cannot not exist (contingency is a defect of being). Only He exists by Himself alone; His existence is neither a pure fact nor the effect of necessity that is a priori with respect to Him. God simply *is.*

Neither is there freedom of choice in the love that God has for Himself, which is the internal aspect of His necessity, although He does have freedom of choice with regard to other beings. God is determined neither to create, nor to create a particular type of world, nor to impress a determined course on its history. To think otherwise would be to include this world among the conditions without which God would not be God. The Divine Being is sufficient unto Himself; His worth does not depend upon the beings He establishes, nor is He better for having created (better for man, indeed, but this is true only insofar as man exists). This poses a difficulty, which was accentuated by Spinoza, for indetermination and contingency seem thus to be attributed to God. Had God created another world, His act would have been different; and since His act and His being are inseparable, His being would have been other than it is. Here it is pointless to make, as some do, a distinction between God and His choice, to presume that such a distinction can be reconciled with the SIMPLICITY OF GOD and that it does not introduce nonbeing or POTENCY in Him. Even though it is claimed that the determination God gives Himself proceeds from His plenitude and presupposes no lack within Him, there is still the presence of this determination itself that must be explained, and this can proceed ad infinitum. In reality, here one encounters the mystery of free causality. It is proper to the THING that it cannot produce a different effect unless it is modified in its being. It is proper to spirit to be able to give rise to different effects without so changing. For the finite spirit, acts are specified by their objects, and the contingency of objects reflects back on the acts. On the other hand, God is not involved in a network of relationships, for He gives and receives nothing. Contingency, multiplicity, and the diversity of beings that He establishes cannot affect His unique, identical, and necessary act. Man's reason cannot very well grasp the ''how'' of this. The affirmation of divine freedom guarantees the contingency of the universe but transfigures it at the same time; such contingency is no longer absurd and distressing, as the existentialists hold, but rather it becomes the expression of a loving freedom. The world's entire value stems from its appearing to be the result of a free gift.

Man's freedom before God. There is no need to examine here the particular problems encountered in reconciling human freedom of choice with divine knowledge and providence (*see* PREDESTINATION; PROVIDENCE OF GOD). The more general difficulty is the following. If man can begin a chain of events, he seems to be a creator and to possess within himself something that does not depend upon God. Human freedom thus seems to limit the universality of divine action. In fact, some thinkers, for example, H. Höffding (1843–1931), have asserted that to admit free will is to admit a kind of polytheism. Without entering into an examination of theories that have tried to clarify the problem of divine CONCURRENCE, one may note that a correct understanding of the relation between freedom and being can shed much light on the problem. The relation of created freedom to God is then seen as an aspect of the relation of participated being to Absolute Being (*see* PARTICIPATION). God is this very relationship at its maximum intensity. Human freedom participates in divine freedom, but it no more limits divine freedom than finite being limits Infinite Being. On the contrary, divine freedom and OMNIPOTENCE are manifested by the ability of beings to determine themselves, to be in some way ''causes of themselves''—a capacity that itself comes from their ''openness'' to the Absolute. The free act reveals the infinite depth of the Spirit who makes its originator be an ''image of God.'' Thus in every way human freedom bespeaks dependence upon God; it does not limit God. The participated character of human freedom is here the fundamental truth. To specify the ''how'' of this must be left to various systems of explanation, though none offers complete satisfaction.

The real problem lies in the matter of choosing EVIL, for one would not wish to place responsibility for this on God. But the possibility of sinning, far from perfecting freedom, limits it. Man sins to the extent that he participates only imperfectly in divine freedom. Sin is the expression of the nothingness in the creature. It is the negation or ''rupture'' of the divine movement toward good; and as such, it is the work exclusively of the creature. Although contrary to the divine will, sin is permitted by this will, which wishes beings to be what they are and to act according to their nature. Divine action (grace) and human freedom must not be considered as contradictories, as though man is freer when less ''moved'' by God; it is the opposite, rather, that is true.

Human freedom, participating in God's freedom, perfects itself as freedom only to the extent that it allows itself to be completely enveloped by God.

Freedom and person. Freedom appears as the act proper to the PERSON. Metaphysically speaking, the person is radically composed of two elements: (1) SUBSIS-

TENCE, that is, individual existence proper to a unit that is relatively autonomous and incommunicable, fully ''in itself''; (2) spirituality or an intellectual nature, together with all this implies for openness to being, values, and so on, and for the ability to enter into communication with other persons. This latter aspect is particularly stressed in contemporary thought. But freedom exhibits the person in this twofold characterization: (1) Not only does the free act show the existent as existent, but eminently as *this* existent. My free act is mine; I alone am responsible (whereas a truth is true for all). Moreover, freedom completes individuality, adding to natural differences or those owed to circumstances that stem from various choices. (2) The free act is expressive of a spiritual nature insofar as this act involves going beyond particular values. The awareness of freedom is nothing more than the awareness of this power of surpassing and of the opening out toward the Absolute. In this way the person is rendered present to himself, in possession of himself, as opposed to the dispersion and the alienation of the thing. This enables the person truly to give himself in a selfless LOVE.

Authentic or spiritual love and freedom are thus closely related; both express the superabundance of the spiritual existent. True love implies freedom, and it is itself a liberator. It is obvious from this that freedom is a condition for the establishment of a true SOCIETY of persons. PERSONALITY and freedom progress on an equal footing. This implies that the person must be placed in conditions conducive to the full operation of his power of self-determination, and this normally implies a certain amount of freedom in the first meaning mentioned at the beginning of this article. Only a really strong personality can find in servitude the opportunity to affirm his proper freedom. The education of the person will thus leave some play for freedom, even though this involves some risk; one need not attempt to prevent every deviation by external restraints. The virtuous act must proceed from within, and this presumes the subject's recognition and acceptance of moral values as his own. When the Good, with whom the subject identifies himself through love, completely determines him and conditions and envelops the very good of his subjectivity and freedom, it is then that he is fully self-determined, fully free, and fully a person.

See Also: CONTINGENCY; FREEDOM, INTELLECTUAL; FREEDOM, SPIRITUAL; FREEDOM OF RELIGION; FREE WILL.

Bibliography: M. J. ADLER, ed. *The Great Ideas: A Syntopicon of Great Books of the Western World,* 2 v. (Chicago 1952) 1:991–1013. R. EISLER, *Wörterbuch der philosophischen Begriffe,* 3 v. (4th ed. Berlin 1927–30) 3:571–597. J. BAUCHER, *Dictionnaire de théologie catholique,* 15 v. (Paris 1903–50) 9.1:660–703. A. GUZZO and V. MATHIEU, *Enciclopedia filosofica,* 4 v. (Venice-Rome 1957) 3:18–37. K. RAHNER et al., *Lexikon für Theologie und Kirche,* 10 v. (Freiburg 1957–65) 4:325–337. M. J. ADLER, *The Idea of Freedom,* 2 v. (Garden City, N.Y. 1958–61). J. MARITAIN, *Freedom in the Modern World,* tr. R. O'SULLIVAN (New York 1935); *Existence and the Existent,* tr. L. GALANTIÈRE and G. B. PHELAN (New York 1948). R. P. MCKEON, *Freedom and History* (New York 1952). R. N. ANSHEN, ed., *Freedom: Its Meaning* (New York 1940).

[J. DE FINANCE]

FREEDOM, INTELLECTUAL

Human freedom is the possibility of self-determination as opposed to dependence on the power and compulsion of others: negatively, ''being free *from*'' (a certain unfetteredness in relation to other things and to oneself: detachment, separation); positively, ''being free *to*'' (ability to dispose of other things and of oneself: power, dominion). Being human, FREEDOM is never absolute and unlimited but relative and in many respects limited; but it is precisely thus that it displays its various levels and forms. Intellectual freedom (in contrast to more practical specifications of it, such as freedom of will, choice, decision, action) means in general terms freedom of the INTELLECT, of thought, of the mind in general, and thus insofar as every man is a spiritual being, it is a capability and a right of every man; it has further the special meaning of the freedom of intellectuals, those whose work is principally of the mind, and is thus, insofar as such men are in the special service of truth and beauty, a capability and right precisely of scholars (working in the natural sciences and other intellectual fields), artists, and writers. Insofar as intellectual freedom is especially called for within a university, in teachers and students, in research, teaching, and study, it is called ACADEMIC FREEDOM (from Plato's school of philosophy in the grove of the hero Academus).

History. The whole history of the human mind is a history of the freedom of the mind, constantly realized anew in new historical situations and forms. But when freedom of the mind, intellectual freedom, appears as a program, a social and indeed political demand, a right of the individual person over against State, Church, and society, its history has to be seen against the background of something with a wider content, human rights, those inalienable rights, because inseparably bound up with the dignity of the human person, to recognition and respect for the essential conditions of its existence. The prehistory of these rights reaches back not only to the secularized ideas of the English and French ENLIGHTENMENT about natural rights, the right to freedom of conscience, of Calvinist inspiration, and scholastic natural law (Thomas Aquinas, Francisco de Vitoria), but right back to Greek antiquity (Stoa) and to the preaching of the New Testament (man as the IMAGE OF GOD and as set free into the freedom of the children of God). Constitutional demands in this field, which had to some extent been asserted in England from the 17th century and largely implemented, were consolidated and given an explicit basis in natural law in the Bill of Rights of Virginia in 1776, the first specialized catalogue of universal human and civil rights (note especially article 1 on personal freedom and equality, article 12 on freedom of the press, and article 16 on freedom of conscience and FREEDOM OF RELIGION). While the Declaration of Independence of the United States of America, 1776, contains a sentence in general terms on the rights of man, the *Déclaration des droits de l'homme* of the French National Assembly, 1789, treats the matter at length; article 11 is of great importance in relation to this particular subject: ''La libre communication des pensées et des opinions est un des droits les plus précieux de l'homme; tout citoyen peut donc parler, écrire, imprimer librement, sauf à répondre de l'abus de cette liberté dans les cas déterminés par la loi.'' Thence derive similar statements in all modern constitutions, including finally the United Nations Declaration on Human Rights: article 18—''Everyone has the right to freedom of thought, conscience and religion; this right includes freedom to change his religion or belief, and freedom, either alone or in community with others and in public or private, to manifest his religion or belief in teaching, practice, worship and observance''; article 19—''Everyone has the right to freedom of opinion and expression; this right includes freedom to hold opinions without interference and to seek, receive and impart information and ideas through any media and regardless of frontiers.'' Finally, there is the requirement laid down by Pope John XXIII in his encyclical *PACEM IN TERRIS*: ''By the natural law, every human being has the right to freedom in searching for truth and in expressing and communicating his opinions, and in pursuit of art, within the limits laid down by the moral order and the common good. And he has the right to be informed truthfully about public events.''

Theological Basis. The Church, aiming to orientate itself by the gospel, has not less but more reason than the thinkers proceeding from the idea of natural law not only to set a theoretically high value on human freedom in every context but also to realize it in practice to the greatest possible extent. The gospel of Jesus Christ is meant, indeed, to bring man true freedom. But man cannot achieve it himself. Man in the concrete just does not live as the Stoics' sovereign being of pure reason, capable of following the law of reason, but finds himself constantly in bondage and fettered to the things and powers of this world and, above all, to himself: ''For I do not do the good that I wish, but the evil that I do not wish, that I perform . . . . Unhappy man that I am! Who will deliver me from the body of this death?'' (Rom 7.19, 24). God through Jesus Christ (Rom 7.25) helps man, the unfree, to cancel out his own slavish, sinful self and win a new, free self: ''For freedom Christ has made us free'' (Gal 4.31; cf. Jn 8.36).

Thus the basis and origin of man's freedom does not lie in man himself, he being by nature the slave of sin, but in the freedom of God, the freedom of His grace setting man free in Christ. This freedom is made present by the Spirit: ''where the Spirit of the Lord is, there is freedom'' (2 Cor 3.17). Freedom from what and for what? Freedom from the slavery of sin for God's saving grace; from the oppressive compulsion of the Law for the gospel, the liberating message of God's reign and the salvation of man in faith and service of his neighbor; from the annihilating power of death for eternal life in God's glory, in the ''glorious freedom of the children of God'' (Rom 8.21). For the Christian who desires to be given this freedom, everything depends on his not wanting to dispose, by his own power, of himself but letting God, the liberator, dispose of him: in trusting faith and self-giving love for God and his fellow men.

The Church, as the community of these who are truly free in Christ, is by no means a colony on earth of citizens of heaven without interest in conditions in this world. Rather, it takes part, though with prudent detachment, in the trade and traffic of the world (1 Cor 7.29–31), rejoices with those who rejoice and weeps with those who weep (Rom 12.15). It is required to practice OBEDIENCE toward secular authority (Rom 13.1–7) and be socially constructive itself by settling the various conflicts within it (1 Cor ch. 5–7) and building everything up in a love that is not limited to its own community, but is, in principle, without limits (1 Cor ch. 8–14). In this active love of neighbor in the world and for the world, which comes from the love of God, there is revealed the real and not merely notional freedom of Christians and of their Church (cf. Rom 8.31–39). How far it goes is shown by Augustine's *ama, et fac quod vis* (love, and do what you will).

Precisely as being a gift from God, ever newly given, freedom is at the same time a task for man, to be ever newly conquered—not only in the world but also in the Church. It was necessary even in Paul's time for him to intervene energetically in the Church on behalf of freedom as lived by the individual person and individual group: against, for instance, the traditionalist legalism of the Jewish Christians, who wished to impose the prescriptions of their Law on the Gentile Christians (Gal), and against the arrogance of those who passed judgment on others' personal decisions of faith and conscience (Romans ch. 14; 1 Cor ch. 8 and 10). In all this, Paul never means unbridled willfulness, in which the individual, in simulated freedom, proposes himself as his own god, but true freedom, which is freedom in order (1 Cor 14.33, 40; cf. Rom 8.2). True freedom, coming from love, does not destroy but constructs, in the service of one's neighbor and of the community.

Historical Realization. The freedom of Christians and of the Church in the New Testament cannot simply be copied. Rather, it must be realized anew, historically, in new forms within each historical situation. Over and over again this will assuredly call for a struggle against lovelessness, servility, cowardice, power politics, force, hypocrisy, and, above all, against fear, and a struggle for a loving readiness for self-sacrifice, candor, courage, magnanimity, and tolerance. But this struggle takes different forms in the age of the Roman persecutions and in that of the Christian Byzantine Empire, in the theocratic High Middle Ages and in the time of the absolutist princes of the Enlightenment. In the present age, which is one not only of DEMOCRACY but also of overt or covert totalitarianism in East and West, the manifold realization of freedom, and of intellectual freedom in particular, in the Church (and especially in THEOLOGY) is of special importance. What is involved in intellectual freedom in the Church of today?

(1) Freedom of thought and research: the right to dedicate oneself without hindrance to the discovery of TRUTH and to form a personal opinion or conviction in accordance with the results of research (freedom of opinion, freedom of conscience). (2) FREEDOM OF SPEECH and teaching: the right, without hindrance, to put forward one's own scholarly opinions and convictions, in private and public (and especially in academic form). (3) Freedom to write and to publish: the right, without hindrance, to disseminate one's own scholarly convictions and opinions in written form (freedom of the press).

Practical norms: (1) The only norm in any intellectual activity must be, not an externally imposed law, but solely the truth; fear of the truth is unworthy of a Christian. (2) Every intellectual, in self-critical service of the truth, will be on his guard against premature conclusions and intellectual pride. (3) All fields of learning, and equally the authority of the State and the teaching authority of the Church, have to refrain strictly from overstepping their own frontiers. (4) For the good of one's neighbor and for the sake of the community (whether of State or Church) limitations of freedom are possible, but never according to the principle of totalitarianism: freedom as far as necessary, restraint as far as possible; but always according to the principle of SUBSIDIARITY, which applies in the Catholic Church: freedom as far as possible, restraint as far as necessary.

See Also: FREEDOM, INTELLECTUAL (IN THE CHURCH); INTELLECTUAL LIFE.

Bibliography: *Liberté et vérité,* ed. professors of the University of Louvain (Louvain 1964). "Reading on Book Selection and Intellectual Freedom 1954–1961," comp. R. W. GREGORY, *American Library Association Bulletin* 56 (February 1962) 145–49. M. FELTIN et al., *Christianity and Freedom* (London 1955). A. HARTMAN, *Bindung und Freiheit des katholischen Denkens* (Frankfurt 1952). H. KÜNG, *The Council, Reform and Reunion,* tr. C. HASTINGS (New York 1962); "The Church and Freedom," *Commonweal* 78 (1963) 343–53; *Freedom To-day* (New York 1966). J. C. MURRAY, *We Hold These Truths* (New York 1960). D. A. O'CONNELL, *Christian Liberty* (Westminster, Md. 1952). K. RAHNER, *Free Speech in the Church* (New York 1959); *Theological Investigations,* v.2, tr. K. H. KRUGER (Baltimore 1964). *Freedom and Man,* ed. J. C. MURRAY (New York 1965).

[H. KÜNG]

FREEDOM, SPIRITUAL

The freedom of the children of God under grace. This is infinitely more than the independence and the power of the will to do as it pleases. It includes the real capacity of the will to do good and avoid evil, but in the higher perspective of the freedom wherewith Christ has made us free (Gal 4.31). Sin, on the other hand, by which a human being created to the image and likeness of God refuses to share in God's freedom, must be seen as the loss of that freedom for which God has created man and Christ has redeemed him.

Freedom and Law. The Epistle to the Romans ch. 7 deplores the miserable situation of the man whose concept of freedom is self-centered and who is externally submitted to the written law. Such a man cannot understand that God's law is a law of freedom: "The Law indeed is holy and the commandment holy and just and good" (v. 12). With this unspiritual attitude a man is a slave of sin and as such cannot really be subject to God's law. True subjection to God's law, the gift of God's loving will, can be understood and embraced only when a man opens his heart, humbly and gratefully, to God's love and the needs of his neighbor. Man, who by his self-centeredness is a prisoner under the law (v. 23), still remains to some extent the image of God and therefore feels that the law is something good. He gives a limited approval to it. But he does not really and sincerely identify himself with God's law, or see that it is written in his inmost being, or find in it a call to his deepest and best possibilities. But he still desires full freedom and cries out: "Unhappy man that I am! Who will deliver me from the body of this death?" (v. 24). The response is St. Paul's hymn on the spiritual freedom conferred by the law of the Spirit: "For the law of the Spirit of the life in Christ Jesus has delivered me from the law of sin and of death" (Rom 8.2).

The external law alone could not generate true freedom. It found man a slave, selfish and closed in his attitude toward God, toward his neighbor, and therefore also toward the law. This attitude robbed the law of its strength (Rom 8.3). True freedom—a sharing in God's own blessed freedom—for which God had created man, was lost on earth through Adam's sin. It was lost through the attitude that sees freedom not as coming from God and returning to God, but as man's independence of God.

Through Christ and in Christ full freedom, a total sharing in God's love and liberty, returned again to earth. Christ in His human nature was anointed by the fullness of the Holy Spirit, who is the "gift of Himself." Before Christ could baptize the believers in the Holy Spirit, thus giving them a spiritual understanding of His own law that is "spirit and life" (Jn 6.3), the Spirit had to descend visibly upon Him and rest upon Him. In the life-giving power of the Holy Spirit Christ fulfilled the loving will of the Father and made Himself a sacrifice for man's redemption. The power of the same Spirit raised Him again to life. Thus the glorified Lord "is the spirit" (2 Cor 3.17)—He who gave Himself in holocaust and was visibly accepted. It is He who through his Spirit writes the new law in man's heart (Heb 8.10)—He who fulfilled it in the Easter mystery. Through a living faith He gives man a spiritual understanding of the law. "Where the Spirit of the Lord is, there is freedom" (2 Cor 3.17).

Freedom in Grace. The freedom of the children of God presupposes, therefore, a living faith in the paschal mystery (cf. Jn 7.39). It presupposes Baptism in the fire of the Holy Spirit, trust in Him, the state of grace, and the supernatural virtue of charity. The loss of the life of grace means also the loss of spiritual freedom; and growth in grace, faith, hope, and charity brings growth in spiritual freedom.

Negatively, the liberty of the children of God presupposes a liberating death: death to the deadly "freedom" of selfishness, to the glorification of self and of one's own will. Consequently, there is no possibility of spiritual freedom without a constant struggle against the works of the flesh listed in some detail by St. Paul: "immorality, uncleanliness, licentiousness, idolatry, etc." (Gal 5.19–20).

This must be kept in mind when it is said that spiritual freedom means being "not under the law but under grace" (Rom 6.14). Renewed in mind by the gift of the Holy Spirit, the free Christian not only does not slavishly submit himself to those laws that impose a minimum of external duty; he accepts wholeheartedly and gratefully the law of faith. He tries constantly to live ever more in accordance with the liberating truth of the gospel. He follows the law of grace. He is really free because he allows himself "to be led by the Spirit of God" (Rom 8.14).

Positively, spiritual freedom coincides with this total and grateful dependence on the grace of God. "If you are led by the Spirit, you are not under the law . . . . If we live by the Spirit let us also walk" (Gal 5.18, 25).

Spiritual freedom is a life in accordance with the "talents," the gifts of God. Those who are led by the Spirit follow in all things the supreme rule: "How shall I make a return to the Lord for all the good he has done for me?" [Ps 115 (116B).12(3)]. Through the grace of the Holy Spirit and in perfect obedience to this grace, the Christian accepts everything as a gift of God and glorifies God by making everything a means of unselfish love for God and for neighbor.

Spiritual freedom, then, has as its condition and result the crucifixion of one's lower nature with its passions and desires (Gal 5.24). But in uniting the Christian with the paschal mystery it means essentially joy and peace (Gal 5.22). This joy and the other fruits of the Spirit give one the strength to be victorious in the struggle against the behavior natural to his lower selfishness, in order to fulfill the law of Christ. Spiritual freedom manifests itself in a thinking and a behavior that correspond to the evangelical law expressed in the Sermon on the Mount and the Farewell Discourse. Only those who let themselves be led by the Spirit of Christ can love one another as Christ has loved them. The demands of fraternal love do not diminish one's spiritual freedom; rather, they fulfill it. It is precisely this spiritual freedom that makes the disciple of Christ renounce some actions not forbidden by a general law, when such self-denial strengthens the bonds of unity and contributes to the salvation of one's neighbor. "For none of us lives to himself, and none dies to himself" (Rom 14.7). This constant openness to others and care for them purifies man, making him more spiritual, more like Christ, and hence more free.

Both a useless multiplication of external precepts and a slavish and mechanical obedience are opposed to spiritual freedom, since both suffocate spiritual energy and hinder constant watchfulness for the real needs of one's neighbor and the community. But spiritual freedom by no means involves lawlessness. It unites one with Christ and so causes one to bear the burdens of another in the spirit of Christ. It helps one to submit himself in the right way to the laws of Church and society, integrating everything in the spirit of solidarity.

Bibliography: B. HÄRING, *The Life of Christ,* v.1, tr. E. G. KAISER (Westminster, Md. 1961) 99–122.

[B. HÄRING]

FREEDOM OF RELIGION

The most authoritative statement of Catholic teaching on religious freedom is the *Declaratio de Libertate Religiosa* of VATICAN COUNCIL II. It solemnly proclaims that all men, and all religious communities, have a strict right to religious freedom: a right that is based on the dignity of the human person. It praises contemporary legal systems that recognize and uphold this right, and deplores the fact that in many countries it is infringed. The present article is concerned with the main arguments and considerations that have formed Catholic thinking about religious freedom, and the main positions represented at the Council. For the broader historical background of the Council's Declaration, *see* CHURCH AND STATE.

Religious Freedom at the Time of Vatican Council II. A glance at the state of religious freedom in the world during the 1960s may help to explain why the question received conciliar treatment. No previous ecumenical council had dealt with the topic. Two considerations in particular seem to have urged attention to it.

Violations under Communist Regimes. First, consideration was prompted by the persecution of religion under Communist regimes, which, as Pope Pius XII said, ''in the end reject and deny the rights, the dignity, and the freedom of the human person.'' Forty years after the Russian revolution of 1917, at least 186 bishops of the Roman Catholic Church alone had been executed or imprisoned, and at least 67 million Catholics were undergoing religious persecution to a greater or less degree. In terms of the number of souls affected, this was estimated to be the greatest religious persecution in history. Temporary alleviations of it were dictated by political considerations rather than by recognition of the right to religious freedom, and overtures for the easing of pressures were hindered by the danger that religious leaders would appear to condone antireligious regimes and thus confuse or demoralize the faithful.

A Soviet directive of 1934 made explicit the permanent object of the campaign:

> Instruction in any type of religious ceremony as well as the performance of any type of religious ceremony or rite and any other type of religious influencing of the younger generation is forbidden and is punishable by law.
>
> Elementary and secondary schools are to insure the antireligious indoctrination of the pupils. Education and training are to be evaluated as foundations for the active battle against religion and its influence on students and adults. [RSFSR Statute on Secondary Schools (1934) text 263.]

Modern educational techniques enable practical hostility to religion to be exercised most effectively by antireligious education, systematically conducted. The primary criterion for testing the sincerity of alleged concessions to, and in general the real acknowledgment of, the right to religious freedom is not to be sought in the release or nonimprisonment of bishops and priests, or in the diplomatic honors or other privileges accorded to them, but in the freedom of religious education—real, sustained, and peaceful freedom, without penalties of any kind, for parents to provide their children with formation in their own religious traditions.

A general account of Communist policies can be summarized under three headings. (1) In the Soviet Union the main target of attack was the Orthodox Church. At first persecution was direct; then, after a generation of antireligious education, every effort was made to convert the reduced Orthodox Church into an instrument of the state. It was in the Ukraine and in Lithuania, Latvia, and Estonia that the Catholic Church suffered direct and violent persecution—in 1946 more than 500 priests of the Diocese of Lvov alone were in prison—and pressure was applied to absorb Eastern Rite Catholics into the Orthodox Church. (2) In China, Christianity was attacked chiefly on the pretext that it was an instrument of European and Catholic imperialism; Taoism was attacked as ''counter-revolutionary.'' Within the first decade after 1949, all but five of 2,500 Chinese Catholic priests had been executed or imprisoned, and systematic antireligious education had attained a perfection and effectiveness not previously known. (3) In Eastern Europe the position remained more complex. Christianity is part of several national traditions; and the forces of antireligion were connected with the Soviet Union. Indirect persecution, e.g., by the imposition of crippling taxes on churches and religious schools, had therefore become more common. In 1965, East German customs officials seized copies of the New Testament as imperialist propaganda. Parish meetings, religious processions, children's recitals at the Christmas crib, the traditional blessings of the fields—these and many other activities often were stopped. Frequently, antireligious measures were even more direct. Catholic bishops such as Cardinals MINDSZENTY, STEPINAC, Beran, and SLIPYJ, and Protestant leaders such as Bishops Dibelius, Ordass, and Radvansky underwent ''trials'' and suffered maltreatment, imprisonment, deportation, or isolation from clergy and people; they must rank with the heroes of any period of Christianity. Many Catholic bishops of Communist-dominated countries were prevented from attending Vatican Council II, and Pope Paul VI, in opening the second session, pointed to their vacant benches as a symbol of ''a wound inflicted upon the Council itself.'' Religious freedom, he said, is a fundamental human right violated in many modern countries by principles and methods of intolerance.

Modern Recognition of the Right. A second consideration that urged the topic upon the Council was the demand for religious freedom that had been mounting in modern times. John MILTON and John LOCKE pleaded for it (except for Catholics and atheists) in the 17th century, VOLTAIRE and Jean Jacques ROUSSEAU in the 18th. The right to religious freedom for all was recognized by the two great 18th-century revolutions, by the French in theory, and by the American in theory and practice. It has been acknowledged by an increasing number of states through the 19th and 20th centuries and is recognized in various forms in the constitutions of many modern states. This recognition expresses one of the deepest convictions of what may loosely be called "the modern mind." Since many Council fathers believed that the Church's most urgent task was to begin "a dialogue with the modern world," it was natural that they should be anxious for a statement of the Catholic attitude toward religious freedom.

Such a statement could not be formulated by simply observing existing situations. No single description could cover the position in traditionally Catholic countries. In Spain a section of the *Fueros de los Espagnoles,* requiring that the spiritual unity of the nation be maintained, forbade "ceremonies and external manifestations other than those of the Catholic religion." Spain's 30,000 Protestants felt that this rendered ineffective another section of the *fueros* that recognized the right of non-Catholics to "nonmolestation in their religious beliefs," and in the early 1960s the Spanish foreign minister (Señor F. M. Castiella) was working for the more practical acknowledgment of this right by the recognition of religious minorities in Spain. In Italy the Catholic faith is the official state religion and, although the right to religious freedom is constitutionally recognized, it was sometimes claimed that, in the first decade or so of the Republic, non-Catholics suffered certain disabilities. In Ireland there is no established church; the constitution (art. 44.2) guarantees freedom of conscience and the free profession and practice of religion to every citizen, and state aid is given to schools without discrimination among the churches that manage the schools.

In the newly independent countries of Asia and Africa the situation confronting the Council fathers was more varied, more complex, and more unpredictable. Freedom in these countries was often conceived as simply freedom from the former colonial powers. Frequently there was no long tradition of pluralism, political or religious, and the existence of any organized "opposition" was often seen as inimical to the state. In some countries no clear distinction was made between state and society; in others the basis of social organization is the tribe. For these and other reasons some of the usual preconditions of religious freedom were lacking, and there were in some places suggestions that an unpleasant modern version of the principle *cuius regio, eius religio* was in the making; e.g., in (Buddhist) Sri Lanka measures were taken against Catholic schools, and in the (Muslim) Sudan Christian missionaries suffered persecution on the score of their being agents of the former colonial powers. But in many countries religion was free, and Christians were prominent in works of primary, secondary, and technological education and in social and political leadership. The Catholic Church worked rapidly to develop local (i.e., native) hierarchies and bodies of clergy and religious, which seem to be a necessary, though obviously not a sufficient, condition of its freedom.

The Doctrine of St. Thomas Aquinas. Turning to Catholic theology on religious freedom, perhaps the most influential, as well as the most representative account of one strong element in the theology is in the treatise *De fide* in the *Summa Theologiae* of St. THOMAS AQUINAS, specifically in the treatment of unbelief (*Summa tehologiae* 2a2ae, 10–12). It is important to remember that by *infideles* (unbelievers) St. Thomas meant non-Catholics of every kind, Christian or otherwise. His views may be summarized in his answers to three questions.

Should Unbelievers Be Forced to Accept the Faith? St. Thomas distinguished between those who had never been Catholics and those who once were Catholics but had lapsed into unbelief. According to his teaching, unbelievers who have never been Catholics must not be forced to embrace the faith. The act of faith is by its nature a free act; without an interior free choice of the will there is no valid act of faith at all. It is therefore wrong in any way to force Jews or pagans to become Christians (*Summa theologiae* 2a2ae, 10.8); it is an offense against natural justice (3a, 68.10).

In the case of Catholics who have lapsed into unbelief by joining another denomination (*haeretici vel schismatici*) or by abandoning Christianity altogether (*apostatae*), the teaching of St. Thomas is quite different: they should be compelled, even by physical force, to resume membership in the Church and practice of the faith. The basis for this position is that it is proper that a person be compelled, if necessary by physical force, to honor a promise (here, presumably, the baptismal promises). The Church should seek the return of one who lapses, and always welcome him back to spiritual communion. But if he is obstinate, and there seems to be no hope of his return, she must set the eternal salvation of the many above the mortal life of one man, banish him from the Church by excommunication, and see that the secular power banishes him from the world by death. Only prudential considerations would urge a different policy: if the unbeliever had support of such strength as to threaten schism, he might be left alone; but otherwise there must be no leniency in his punishment (*Summa theologiae* 2a2ae, 10.8, 11.3–4).

Should the Children of Jews and Other Unbelievers Be Baptized against Their Parents' Wishes? St. Thomas held without qualification that it is never permissible to baptize a child against the wishes of the parents. For the natural order of things demands that, before a child comes to the age of discretion, he should be cared for by his parents, in matters both of body and soul. It would therefore be a violation of natural justice if he were taken away from his parents or baptized against their wishes (*Summa theologiae* 2a2ae, 10.12; 3a, 68.10).

Should the Religious Rites of Unbelievers Be Tolerated? Given that unbelievers must not be forced to accept the Catholic religion, may they be permitted to practice their own? St. Thomas answered that tolerance is permissible if it leads to some great good or prevents some great evil. Jews may therefore be permitted to practice their rites, since these prefigured the Christian faith and in a way bear witness to it. The rites of other unbelievers, however, having neither truth nor utility to commend them, should not be tolerated except to prevent some greater evil, e.g., civil unrest, scandal, or the placing of obstacles to the salvation of those who, if left in peace, might gradually be converted to the faith. For these reasons, St. Thomas concluded, the Church has sometimes extended toleration to pagan and heretical worship when unbelievers were in large numbers (*Summa theologiae* 2a2ae, 10.11).

Modern Developments in Thomism. St. Thomas clearly did not credit the unbeliever with a *right* to practice and profess his religion. In this and several other points many modern Catholics have followed St. Thomas, though with important modifications and developments. Their main positions may be summarized under two headings.

Opposition to the Use of Force. It has been held consistently, and without St. Thomas' restriction to those who were never Catholics, that no one must ever be forced to accept the Catholic faith. Modern writers have never condoned the use of secular power to enforce an initial acceptance of, or a return to, the Church. Pius XII's statement in *MYSTICI CORPORIS* is unconditional: ''If it were ever to happen that, contrary to the unvarying doctrine of this Apostolic See, a person was compelled against his will to embrace the Catholic Faith, we could not, for the sake of our office and our conscience, withhold our censure'' [*Acta Apostolicae Sedis* 35 (1943) 243]. This has been accepted unreservedly by Catholic writers.

The ''Thesis-Hypothesis'' Theory. The question remained, should (or may) an unbeliever be permitted to adhere to his own religion, or even to none? The answer was most often given in terms of the curiously titled ''thesis-hypothesis'' theory. The *thesis* asserted that the state has the obligation to acknowledge the Catholic Church as the only religious society with a God-given right to public existence and action, and to recognize this by law. In principle, other religions should have no legal right to public existence and action, and ought to be repressed by the state, for error and evil run counter to the rational and moral nature of man, to the common good of society, and to the right of people to be protected from occasions of defecting from the truth. On the *hypothesis,* however, that such a constitutional arrangement is unfeasible, the Church may forego her right to establishment as the one true religion of the state, and not oppose the legal tolerance of other religions.

When is the thesis applicable, and when the hypothesis? A common interpretation was that in nations where the majority of the citizens were Catholic, the thesis applied; in others, it was permissible to accept the hypothesis. This naturally led to the charge that the attitude of Catholics in regard to religious freedom was highly ambiguous—where they were in a minority, they demanded it; where in a majority, they refused it. The charge was echoed by some Catholic writers. But many others had the courage of their logic and avowed it quite frankly, as did the authors of a widely used American Catholic textbook who wrote: ''The fact that the individual may in good faith think that his false religion is true gives no more right to propagate it than the sincerity of the alien anarchist entitles him to advocate his abominable theories in the United States, or than the perverted ethical notions of the dealer in obscene literature confer upon him a right to corrupt the morals of the community'' [J. A. Ryan and F. J. Boland *Catholic Principles of Politics*]. Nor did these writers fear that such an attitude could be turned against Catholics in countries in which they were in a minority. First, they insisted, Catholic worship and preaching, being true, do not harm the community; second, no non-Catholic state can logically take this attitude, since no non-Catholic sect claims to be infallible. Hence the famous remark of Louis VEUILLOT to non-Catholic liberals, ''I demand from you, in the name of your principles, that freedom which I refuse you in the name of my own.'' Such remarks were widely quoted as a warning to enlightened people against Catholic obscurantism. Ryan and Boland sought to reassure their non-Catholic fellow Americans on the score that a Catholic state in America was too remote in time and probability to disturb a practical man. But clearly the fact remained that such considerations did not demand, or even allow for, universal religious freedom as a matter of principle.

Another group of writers sought to show that interpretations of the thesis-hypothesis theory that failed to demand religious freedom for all were self-defeating. Four levels in the argument can be distinguished. First, at the merely prudential level, there is the danger that if Protestants or Muslims are denied religious freedom in Catholic states, Catholic minorities may (in retaliation) be denied it in Protestant or Muslim states. Second, at a higher level, the Church as a whole forfeits respect, for if she claims for herself a freedom that she denies others, she will be thought insincere and unjust; indeed, some Catholic theologians believed that she would be opportunist and Machiavellian. Third, at a quite different level, a social order that discriminates against groups within it on account of the beliefs that they hold, or which stifles open and rational discussion of important questions, is inimical to the growth of truth in men's hearts. Fourth, at perhaps the highest level, since the act of faith is by its nature a free act, the Church should favor the policy of religious freedom for all as most conducive to a climate in which men can make the act of faith in the most salutary manner that is possible.

The Demand for Religious Freedom in Principle. Policy is not principle. Even the foregoing arguments in favor of freedom would not establish universal religious freedom as required in principle. The positive arguments in favor of religious freedom as a matter of principle have been developed along other lines.

First, it is necessary to recall Catholic principles about the duty to follow conscience. The history of the medieval debates on the issue has been traced by Dom Odon Lottin. Most writers before St. Thomas held that conscience could be binding only insofar as it was in conformity with the law of God. But St. Thomas, from his earliest treatment of the subject, insisted that conscience, whether correct or mistaken, is always binding, in the sense that to act against conscience is always wrong. To evaluate a person's moral performance is to evaluate the performance of his will; the ''proper object'' of the will is the good, not as it is in itself, but as it is presented by the reason, which is just what is meant by the judgment of conscience. The conclusion is clear: it is always wrong to act against conscience, provided that it has been formed in good faith. So confident was St. Thomas of his conclusion that he applied it absolutely: if a man's conscience judges faith in Christ or abstinence from fornication to be sinful, then such faith or such abstinence would be sinful (*Summa theologiae* 1a2ae, 19.5, cf. *In 2 sent.* 39.3.3; *De ver.* 17.3–4; *De malo* 2.2).

St. Thomas did not draw the further conclusion that the act that follows conscience is good. But in the 18th century St. ALPHONSUS LIGUORI (*Theologia Moralis* 1.6) saw that this was entailed by St. Thomas's principles, and practically every Catholic moralist has followed him since then. Three quotations show the position of Catholic thought on the question:

> Whether in theory conscience be correct or mistaken, an action will have in fact whatever evil or goodness conscience attributes to it. [A. Vermeersch, *Theologiae Moralis Principia* (Rome 1923) 1:293.]

> Provided it be certain, an erroneous conscience shows a man what is God's will for him, in exactly the same way as does a correct one. [E. Genicot, *Institutiones Theologiae Moralis,* ed. A. Gortebecke (Brussels 1951) 1:42.]

> If our conscience tells us that we ought to perform a particular act, it is our moral duty to perform it. [F. C. Copleston, *Aquinas* (London 1955) 220.]

These conclusions are in the minds of the writers who argue for religious freedom as a matter of principle. Their main lines of argument can be sketched under three headings.

The Individual's Right to Follow Conscience. The first argument claims to establish the individual's strict *right* to follow his conscience in matters of religious choice, profession, and worship. Versions have been proposed by Bernard Olivier, OP, and E. D'Arcy. The form of the argument is: ''X has a strict duty to follow his conscience'' entails ''X has a strict right to follow his conscience.'' For the more intimately a given ''object'' is connected with the integrity of the human person, the more stringently is it protected for him by natural justice. When the ''object'' is life itself, St. Thomas argued—and all Catholics agree—not even the jeopardy of many innocent people can so abrogate the right to life of an innocent man as to sanction the directly intentional killing of him as a means to their safety. The conclusion holds a fortiori if the ''object'' is a person's moral integrity, for human rights are derived from human ends. The more closely an ''object'' is tied to the sovereign end of the sovereign person's existence, the more sacrosanct is his right to it; and substantial fidelity to moral duty is a necessary (this is not to say a sufficient) condition of attaining that end. Therefore, given the premise that it is always one's duty to follow conscience once it is formed in good faith, one has the *right* to freedom to follow it; and this must hold most especially in the area in which moral duty bears most intimately upon the attainment of one's end, namely with regard to one's relationship with God—religious choice, profession, and worship.

Who is the other party affected by this right? Every ascription of a right to a given person contains an implicit reference to some other identifiable person or persons against whom he can validly claim the right. In the debate concerning religious freedom the other party is the state. The argument concludes that the state, whether on its own behalf or at the behest of the Church, may not use its powers to force or induce a person to adopt a particular religion or to prevent or dissuade him from following that religious belief which his conscience requires him to follow. Two lines of argument lead to this conclusion. The first reasons that to answer otherwise is to imply that the state is empowered to prevent or hinder a person from achieving his sovereign end and require him to breach his personal moral obligations, and to credit it with the right to violate natural justice. The second leads to the next argument advanced by modern writers who hold that religious freedom is required in principle.

Limits of the Competence of the State. The previous argument began with the individual person and ended with the state; the second begins with the state and ends with the person. Two points are basic to it.

The first is a principle that was given its most authoritative statement by Pius XII: ''In the pre-Christian era the public authority, the state, was as competent in the religious domain as in profane matters. The Catholic Church was aware that her divine Founder had transmitted to her the sphere of religion, the religious and moral direction of men, to the fullest extent, and independent of the power of the state'' [*Vous avez voulu, ActApS* 47 (1955) 677]. This suggests that the state is not empowered to enjoin or forbid attitudes and conduct in religious matters as it is competent to do in other fields; and this immediately prepares one for the conclusion that the state has no warrant for applying pressure for or against a given religious faith.

The other basic point is made by drawing a clear distinction between SOCIETY and the STATE, a distinction implicit, it is claimed, in many earlier Catholic documents. In terms of this distinction it is argued that the state is simply one of the means—admittedly a very important means—used by society to attain its purposes. Since substantial fidelity to conscience in religious matters is a necessary condition for attaining the supreme purpose of the human person, it cannot be within the state's power to interfere with the citizen's freedom to be faithful to his conscience in religious matters.

It would be simplistic to conclude baldly that ''the state therefore has no competence in the field of religion.'' A satisfactory theory of the human person, the state, the Church, and their mutual relationships cannot be fashioned by seeing the strict implications of these two principles alone. Many other factors are relevant—a people's history and experience; its stage of cultural, economic, technical, and political development; its shared moral code; its tribal or national temperament; its characteristic *Weltanschauung;* and its religious beliefs. All these and many other factors determine the kind of state it fashions. The state is not a sort of Platonic form that all actual states must identically instantiate; different societies may demand different functions of the states they create to serve their purposes. The Swedish and American peoples, for example, expect very different social services from their respective states, and neither can claim to have *the* correct program. In this and other fields there is a whole range of possibilities that, provided the demands of justice owed to individuals and groups are respected, may all satisfy the strict requirements of Christian social and political principles. With regard to religion, at least one thing is necessary: that the state recognize and protect religious freedom. It is perfectly proper for a people, if it chooses, to have the state do more, as in the Federal Republic of Germany, where the state contributes a proportion of public revenue to the various churches. But it may not do less.

The most complete statement in English of this second line of argument is that of John Courtney Murray, SJ. He has proposed reasons for preferring this approach to the first sketched above, suggesting that it does greater justice to the multiplicity of elements in the problem, beginning as it does, not with a ''single insight—the exigence of the free human person for religious freedom,'' but with ''a complex insight—the free human person under a government of limited powers'' [*Theological Studies*].

Faith a Free Act. French writers were prominent in the development of a third line of argument. The argument is based on the nature of the act of faith, two aspects of which lead toward the same conclusion.

First, faith is the gift of God alone. There are, in turn, two aspects to this. (1) Although natural truths about God are, at least in principle, discoverable by natural reason, supernatural truths, the proper object of faith, can be known only because God chose to reveal them—through revelation in the strict sense. (2) Nor is this enough. Faith requires the work of God *within* a person; God's immediate action upon the soul is absolutely necessary if one is to be able to embrace divine revelation *sicut oportet.* This was true even of those who saw Jesus and his works with eyes of the flesh: ''No one can come to me unless the Father who sent me draw him'' (Jn 6.44). Hence faith is the gift of God alone; the conclusion is that religious faith not only may not, but quite literally cannot, be given or imposed or required by the state.

Second, faith involves, of its very nature, the completely free assent of the soul to the divine revelation and action. In *Mystici Corporis* Pius XII, citing a constitution of Vatican Council I, declared, ''That faith without which it is 'impossible to please God' must be the completely free 'homage of intellect and will''' (*loc. cit.* 243). Freedom is absolutely necessary for a valid act of faith; the state therefore acts unjustly if it requires such faith of any person, or even if it destroys or lessens that condition of freedom in which such an act can validly be made.

Answers to Objections. An important part of the case of those who argued for religious freedom as a demand of principle was their handling of objections. They were often accused of being at odds with ''traditional Catholic doctrine,'' and in large measure they met this general charge by answering specific objections. It is sufficient to cite the four most important objections with an indication of the typical lines of reply.

First, it was objected that the claim of a universal right to religious freedom involves assumptions of religious indifferentism or doctrinal relativism. A statement of Ryan and Boland is typical of many: ''The men who defend the principle of toleration for all varieties of religious opinion assume either that all religions are equally true or that the true cannot be distinguished from the false'' (*op. cit.*). The Catholic writers whose arguments have just been sketched draw on no such assumptions; indeed, they completely reject them. They all believe in the Catholic Church as the one true Church founded by Christ. They draw, as has been seen, on three groups of data that have nothing to do with the indifferentist or relativist premises imputed in the objection. It is true that the premises lead to the claim for universal religious freedom; but the converse is not true (*p implies q* does not entail *q implies p*).

Second, it was objected that ''error has no rights.'' This maxim was taken to be axiomatic, and the full consequences were put forward, not simply as the theory of one school, but as Catholic teaching. For instance, Reginald Garrigou-Lagrange, OP, wrote, ''The Church claims that *the truth* alone has the right to be protected. Since therefore it is certain that she alone possesses the whole truth, she alone has the right to protection. . . . In a Catholic state, she will often tolerate non-Catholics in order to avoid greater evils'' [*De Revelatione* (Rome 1929–31) 2:453]. The maxim embodies a confusion of categories, viz, the logical fallacy committed by allocating concepts to logical types to which they do not belong, in this case, by assigning a predicate that falls under one category to a subject that falls under another. For a given predicate, there is a finite range of subjects of which it may be meaningfully affirmed or denied; if it is ascribed to a subject lying outside that range, the result is not false, but meaningless. For instance, the predicate ''having wheels'' may be affirmed or denied of motor-cars, armchairs, or clocks, but not —that is, not meaningfully—of jokes, sonnets, or sonatas. So with the predicate ''having rights''; it can be meaningfully ascribed *only to persons,* either individual persons, or groups of them. Rights can be meaningfully claimed or disclaimed for a person, a family, a voluntary association, a state; but not for a proposition, a theory, an argument, or a doctrine. In its literal acceptance then, the maxim ''Error has no rights'' is meaningless; it is in the same logical case as the sentence ''Error has no wheels.''

Third, another objection began with the principle that one is obliged to prevent evil when it lies in one's power to do so. If another person is bent on doing wrong, but cannot do so without one's assistance or acquiescence or at least noninterference, then one is bound to prevent him; to allow him to act is to share his guilt. But—the objection proceeds—pagan and heretical religions are wrong. If, therefore, a person or group is bent on practicing or preaching them, a Catholic government that could prevent it is obliged to do so. But, in the first place, it is never permissible to use unjust means, even in order to secure a good end or to prevent a great evil. Since the right to religious freedom is a right in strict justice, no purpose, however exalted, can justify its violation. Second, Pius XII, dealing with the objection without reference to the question of the strict *right* to religious freedom, rejected in very explicit terms the major premise of the objection, viz, the claim that one is always obliged to prevent evil when it lies in one's power to do so. In an address to Italian Catholic jurists, he observed, ''God has not given to human authority any such absolute and universal mandate in the field of either faith or morals. Such a mandate is unknown to the common convictions of mankind, to the Christian conscience, to the sources of revelation, and to the practice of the Church'' [''Ci riesce,'' Acta Apostolicae Sedis].

Fourth, it was charged that the claim that religious freedom is a universal human right runs counter to traditional Catholic doctrine, in particular, that it was condemned by 19th-century popes. For example, GREGORY XVI wrote in *Mirari vos,* Aug. 15, 1832: ''Indifferentism is the fetid source that gives rise to the mistaken view, or rather madness, that everyone is entitled to freedom of conscience'' (H. Denzinger, *Enchiridion symbolorum* 2730). PIUS IX explicitly repeated the condemnation, and in his SYLLABUS OF ERRORS condemned the proposition ''Every man is free to embrace and to profess the religion which, by the light of reason, he believes to be true'' (H. Denzinger, *Enchiridion symbolorum* 2915). It must be noted, however, that the Church's teaching authority is not exercised *in vacuo,* but according to the demands created by the needs of man and society, and by the spread of false teachings. Furthermore, it is necessary to distinguish between an ideology and the institutions to which it gives rise; the latter may be sound, although the former is false.(*see* JOHN XXIII) [''Pacem in terris,'' Acta Apostolicae Sedis]. The popes condemned the ideology that based freedom of conscience on three false doctrines, viz, that the human conscience is *exlex,* subject to no law, not even God's; that all religions are equally true or valuable, or that religious truth cannot be known with certainty; and that the state is omnicompetent, so that the Church herself is to be incorporated in and subordinate to the state. These are false doctrines, and were condemned as such by the popes, but the condemnation does not extend to the institution of religious freedom that did in fact, in some places, come from them, but can be based on other, true, doctrinal and rational foundations. This statement may be compared with one from an Anglican source noting that toleration ''is generally held to merit commendation when it issues from respect for the natural rights of the human person to freedom of belief, but condemnation when it is due to mere indifference'' [*Oxford Dictionary of the Christian Church*].

Vatican Council II. Between the end of the first session of Vatican Council II and the opening of the debate on religious freedom in the second session, two important papal statements on the question were made. One occurred in the encyclical letter *PACEM IN TERRIS.* In setting out the rights that arise from the dignity of the human person, John XXIII wrote: ''Every human being has the right to honor God according to the dictates of an upright conscience, and therefore the right to profess his religion in private and in public'' (*loc. cit.* 260). The other statement was made by Paul VI in his address at the opening of the second session, in the course of which he protested against the persecution that kept some bishops from attending the Council, and said: ''It grieves and distresses us to see that in many countries religious freedom, together with the other principal human rights, are violated by the doctrines and practices of men who will not tolerate opinions different from their own: opinions about politics, about racial questions, about religion of every kind. We deplore the fact that such injustice is done anywhere to people who sincerely and openly profess their religion'' (*loc. cit.*). Three points in these statements need to be emphasized. First, religious freedom is not presented simply as the lesser of two evils, to be tolerated for the sake of avoiding a greater evil. The popes speak of it as a strict *right,* whose violation is an *injustice.* Second, the right is not claimed simply for Catholics, nor based upon the objective truth of a person's belief; it is seen as a human right, tied to conscience and the (subjective) sincerity of faith. Third, the individual's religious freedom is not restricted to interior belief; it extends to public profession.

Drafts of the Declaration on Religious Freedom. These two papal statements were greatly encouraging to those fathers of the Council who hoped for a declaration of the right to religious freedom. A draft for such a declaration was prepared by the Secretariate for Promoting Christian Unity. It was introduced in a *relatio* presented by Bp. Emile De Smedt of Bruges, Belgium. The claim for the right was based on the principle that a man can attain his ultimate end only by faithfully following the dictates of conscience: ''The man who obeys his conscience obeys God himself.'' The draft was debated in the second session of the Council, but no vote was taken; in the months that followed a great number of *animadversiones* were received from the fathers and incorporated into a second draft. It was found that the majority of the fathers agreed with the substance of its principal thesis; but there were many amendments sought in expression, argument, and structure.

The minority opposed to the central thesis, which in the event turned out to be small numerically, argued along four main lines: (1) The draft seemed to favor religious and doctrinal indifferentism. (2) It ran counter to traditional Catholic doctrine, especially as taught by the 19th-century popes. (3) It ignored the axiom that error has no rights; only cynicism could extend the same rights indifferently to truth and error. (4) The proposed argument made a logically illegitimate move from the subjective order of conscience to the objective order of right. The Secretariate proposed answers to the first three questions along the lines already indicated. The fourth objection it answered by showing that, in the draft, the starting point was the human person in the objective factual state of contemporary society.

The amended draft was debated at the third session, rewritten once more, and finally adopted by the fourth. It was solemnly proclaimed at the close of the Council under the title *Declaratio de Libertate Religiosa.* The subtitle is noteworthy: *On the right of the person and of communities to social and civil freedom in religious matters.* The central thesis is stated as follows: ''It is an injustice done to the human person, and to the order laid down for men by God, if a man is denied the free exercise of religion in society: saving a just public order.''

After an introduction, which summarizes the reasons for interest in the problem and its principal elements, the Declaration falls into two parts.

A General Account of Religious Freedom. Three levels are distinguished: the human person, religious communities, and the family.

The human person, in matters concerning religion, has a strict right to freedom, i.e., to immunity from force, be it from individuals, from social groups, or from any human power. The right should be recognized in the legal structure of society, and established as a strict right at law.

Two sorts of reason are given. First, every man, being endowed with reason, free-will, and social responsibility, has an obligation to seek the truth, and embrace it when found: especially in religious matters. But he must do this in ways that fit his rational and social nature: by free inquiry, by learning from and engaging in discussions in which one man helps another find the truth that he believes himself to have found. God's commands are mediated to man by conscience; if he is to make his way to God, he must faithfully follow conscience in all his activity. The right to religious freedom is therefore based, not in a person's subjective attitudes, but in human nature itself.

This right demands that a person be not forced to act against his conscience, nor prevented from following it. For the exercise of religion consists above all in free interior acts, which no human power can command or prevent. But further, the social nature of man requires that these interior acts be given external and corporate expression. To deny a person the freedom of such expression would therefore be an injustice.

Second, religious acts transcend the earthly and temporal order. Since, therefore, the civil authority is charged with serving the common temporal good, it would be exceeding its competence if it presumed to direct or restrain such acts.

Religious communities, the Declaration continues, must be credited with the same right to immunity from force as is the person, for such communities are required both by the social nature of man and the nature of religion itself.

The freedom to which they are entitled, given that they respect the just demands of public order, involves a number of constitutive rights: the right to perform public worship, and to prepare their members for religious life and belief by suitable instruction and encouragement; the right to freedom from interference by the civil body in choosing, educating, appointing, and transferring their ministers, in communicating with their authorities and other religious communities in other parts of the world, and in erecting buildings and administering their affairs; the right to bear public witness to their beliefs by the spoken and written word, given respect for the rights of others; the right to show the special contribution their doctrines can make to social order and the enrichment of human life; and the right to hold assemblies and form associations of an educational, cultural, and charitable nature.

The family has the right to order its own religious life, under the direction of the parents; and parents have the right to decide the way that their children are to be educated in their own religious tradition. The civil authorities must therefore recognize the right of parents to decide what sort of schools their children shall attend, without any penalties being imposed, whether directly or indirectly. The rights of parents are violated if their children are forced to attend schools that are not in harmony with their own beliefs, or where the only education given excludes any religious formation.

The Declaration then specifically considers the implications of these rights for civil law. Since it is the special business of the law to preserve and foster human rights and duties, it must ensure the religious freedom of all citizens, and thus the conditions that foster religious life. In some circumstances, the state may give special recognition to a particular religious community; but in such cases, it must recognize and protect the religious freedom of all other citizens and communities. In all circumstances, the civil authorities must make sure that the equality of all citizens before the laws is never, whether overtly or covertly, violated for religious reasons. It is very wrong, then, if the civil authorities, through force or fear, ever impose or prevent the free profession or change of religion; and this is worst of all when force is used to eradicate or stifle religion altogether.

Finally, the Declaration insists on one's duty to exercise religious freedom with personal and social moral responsibility. One must consider the rights of other people, and treat them with justice and humanity. It is for the civil authorities to protect its citizens from abuses of religious freedom, though invoking restrictions, of course, only when necessary.

Religious Freedom in the Light of Revelation. It is possible only to summarize the heads of doctrine in this very rich statement.

Since the act of faith is by its nature a free act, it is only voluntarily that a man can accept God's revelation. A condition of religious freedom, therefore, conduces to a situation in which one can best accept God's invitation to the Christian faith.

Although possessed of all the power of the Godhead, Our Lord forced no one to believe; gentle and humble of heart, He worked miracles to win men to belief, but rebuked the Apostles for suggesting prodigies that smacked of violence, and said that punishment for unbelief should be left to the Day of Judgment; it was not by force but by being lifted up on the cross that He drew men most powerfully to Himself. After Pentecost, the Apostles followed Our Lord's example. In proclaiming the right of the human person to religious freedom, the Church has therefore followed the spirit and mind of the gospel; and though there have been actions in the history of the people of God that lapsed from the spirit, the Church has always taught that no man may be forced to embrace the faith.

The Catholic Church claims freedom for herself under two descriptions: as a spiritual authority founded by Christ and charged to preach the gospel to every creature; and as a society of human beings entitled to live in civil society according to the commandments of the Christian faith.

The faithful are reminded that an element in the formation of their consciences must always be the teaching of the Church. They are urged to pray constantly for all men and to do everything they can to bring them to the truth of Christ by word, witness, and example, but always in the spirit of Christ's gentleness and love, full of respect for the dignity of the free human person.

Finally, the Council welcomes the religious freedom upheld in many contemporary legal systems, but deplores its infringement in many other countries. It is God's will that the human family should respect the right to religious freedom in human society and so, through the grace of Christ and the power of His Spirit, enter into the far more exalted freedom ''wherewith Christ has made us free.''

See Also: CHURCH AND STATE.

Bibliography: F. L CROSS, *The Oxford Dictionary of the Christian Church* (London, 1957). J. C. MURRAY, *The Problem of Religious Freedom* (pa. Westminster, Md. 1965), a basic survey of the recent theological development. Surveys with bibliographical aids. A. F. CARRILLO DE ALBORNOZ, *Roman Catholicism and Religious Liberty* (Geneva 1959); *The Basis of Religious Liberty* (New York 1963). J. N. MOODY, ''Church and State,'' *Catholic Encyclopedia*, suppl.2. Studies representative of the development. E. D'ARCY, *Conscience and Its Right to Freedom* (New York 1962). A. HARTMANN, *Toleranz und christlicher Glaube* (Frankfurt 1955). J. LECLER, *L'Église et la souveraineté de l'état* (Paris 1946); ''Toleration and the Reformation,'' tr. FRATRES SALVETE *Acta Apostolicae Sedis* 55 (1963) 855–56. T. L. WESTOW, 2 v. (New York 1960); ''La Papauté moderne et la liberté de conscience,'' *Études* 249 (1946) 289–309. J. LECLERCQ, *Jean de Paris et l'ecclésiologie du XIII e siécle* (Paris 1942). G. LAMB, *Tolerance and the Catholic: A Symposium*, tr. (New York 1955). DOM O. LOTTIN, *Psychologie et Morale aux XII e et XIII e siècles* (Louvain 1942–49) 2:354–406. J. C. MURRAY, ''St. Robert Bellarmine on the Indirect Power,'' *Theological Studies* 9 (1948) 491–535; ''Governmental Repression of Heresy,'' *Catholic Theological Society of America, Proceedings* 3 (1948) 26–101. A. OTTAVIANI, F. J. CONNELL, J. C. FENTON, and G. W. SHEA in *American Ecclesiastial Review* 123–128 (1950–53), *passim.*, articles, including defenses of the ''thesis-hypothesis'' position. J. A. RYAN and F. J. BOLAND, *Catholic Principles of Politics* (New York 1947) 318. A. VERMEERSCH, *Tolerance,* tr. W. H. PAGE (New York 1913). A. DULLES, ''John Paul II on Religious Freedom,'' *The Thomist* 65 (2001) 161–178.

[E. D'ARCY]

FREEDOM OF RELIGION (IN U.S. CONSTITUTION)

The meaning of the religious clauses of the First Amendment to the Federal Constitution has been one of the most challenging aspects of constitutional law, and has significant social implications. These clauses read, ''Congress shall make no law respecting an establishment of religion, or prohibiting the free exercise thereof.''

1. GENESIS OF THE RELIGION CLAUSES

The principles contained in this declaration of religious liberty had a long and tortuous path to follow before they finally became a part of the U.S. Constitution. At the time of the Revolutionary War the majority of the colonies had established churches, but when the framers of the Constitution convened in Philadelphia, the religious status of the several states varied from full and perfect freedom to absolute establishment of Protestantism [*See* CHURCH AND STATE IN THE U.S. (LEGAL HISTORY)]

The diversity of religious systems was matched by the diversity of religious backgrounds of the delegates to the Constitutional Convention. Almost all religious denominations were represented, including several Baptists and Catholics. The Catholic representatives were Daniel Carroll and Thomas Fitzsimmons.

Agitation for Religious Guarantees. When the delegates to the Constitutional Convention met in 1787 to draft a federal constitution there was already a strong sentiment in favor of religious liberty. No attempt was made in the convention fully to codify this attitude. The principal preoccupation with religious liberty in the convention dealt with test oaths. Charles Pinckney of South Carolina submitted the following provision, ''But no religious test shall ever be required as a qualification to any office or public trust under the United States.'' After brief opposition the proposal was adopted. With slight modifications it was finally approved in the form as it now appears in Article 6 of the Constitution.

In the state conventions called to ratify the proposed Constitution of the United States, opposition to this limited guarantee of religious liberty was expressed. The majority of the delegates approved of the action but expressed the opinion that further guarantees were necessary. Several states recommended specific amendments. New Hampshire proposed the following amendment:

> Congress shall make no laws touching religion, or to infringe the rights of conscience.

Virginia requested an amendment providing:

> That religion, or the duty which we owe to our Creator, and the manner of discharging it can be

> directed only by reason and conviction, not by force or violence, and therefore all men have an equal natural and unalienable right to the free exercise of religion according to the dictates of their conscience, and that no particular sect or society ought to be favored or established, by law, in preference to others.

The states of North Carolina, New York, and Rhode Island, while not proposing a specific amendment, issued declarations of principles in conjunction with ratification. The principles of religious liberty, expressed in these declarations, followed the language of the Virginia proposal. Strong statements of the need for an amendment prohibiting religious liberty were expressed in other states, notably Pennsylvania and Maryland, but they were not adopted as formal recommendations.

In some of the states it was not deemed necessary to request an amendment, for it was asserted that the federal government was not given any power over religion. Oliver Ellsworth of Connecticut, writing under the name of ''Landholder,'' expressed this idea in the Dec. 10, 1787 issue of the *Connecticut Courant* in answer to a charge that the Constitution did not contain a bill of rights. He said, ''Nor is liberty of conscience, or of matrimony or burial of the dead [referred to]; it is enough that Congress have no power to prohibit either, and can have no temptation.''

Others felt that a bill of rights was absolutely necessary; the leading exponent of this position was Thomas Jefferson. In a letter to James Madison on Dec. 20, 1787, he indicated that he was quite concerned because the Constitution did not carry a bill of rights.

> I will now tell you what I do not like. First, the omission of a bill of rights, providing clearly, and without the aid of sophism, for freedom of religion, freedom of the press, protection against standing armies, restriction of monopolies, the eternal and unremitting force of the habeas corpus laws, and trials by jury in all matters of fact triable by the laws of the land, and not by the laws of nations.

But Madison did not feel quite as strongly as Jefferson. He was well aware of a rising demand for another convention to revise the Constitution, but preferred to have amendments adopted by the Congress.

The debate in the state conventions called to ratify the Constitution clearly indicated that the primary concern was to eliminate legal preference for one or more religions. Many letters, written frequently by men who were outstanding in their communities, demonstrated a fear that possibly the federal government might establish a national religion. They evidenced no attitude of hostility toward religion but rather the desire to prevent by law the extension of legal preference for one sect over another.

Joseph Story, one of the leading contemporary authorities on the Constitution and later associate justice of the Supreme Court, made the following observation:

> Probably at the time of the adoption of the Constitution, and of the amendment to it now under consideration, the general, if not the universal sentiment in America was, that Christianity ought to receive encouragement from the State so far as it was not incompatible with the private rights of conscience and the freedom of religious worship. An attempt to level all religions, and to make it a matter of State policy to hold all in utter indifference, would have created universal disapprobation if not universal indignation . . . . The real object of the amendment was . . . to exclude all rivalry among Christian sects, and to prevent any national ecclesiastical establishment which should give to a hierarchy the exclusive patronage of the national government.

The following article appeared in the *Federal Gazette,* titled, ''Remarks on the First Part of Amendments to the Federal Constitution Moved on the Eighth Instant in the House of Representatives''

> The next article [First Amendment] established religious liberty, and all of those political rights, which by various tricks of state have been wounded through its means, on the firmest ground. The tender, the almost sacred rights of conscience, says this inestimable article, shall by no means, on no account be abridged or interfered with. No self righteous or powerful church shall set up its impious domination over all of the rest. Every pious man may pay the Divine Author of his existence the tribute of thanksgiving and, adoration in the manner of his forefathers.

This article was extraordinarily significant. It was reprinted in the *Massachusetts Centinal* on July 4, 1789, and appeared in many other leading newspapers throughout the states. It is frequently credited with being instrumental in helping to create a public understanding of the issues involved in the move for an amendment on religious liberty.

Debate on the Proposed Amendment. While these official and unofficial utterances are significant, the important statements were those made at the time that the amendment was under active consideration. This phase of the legislative process commenced on June 8, 1789, when James Madison rose in the House and said:

> The amendments which have occurred to me, proper to be recommended by Congress to the

> State Legislatures, are these: . . . Fourthly, That in Article 1st, Section 9, between clauses 3 and 4 to be inserted these clauses, ''The civil rights of none shall be abridged on account of religious belief or worship, nor shall any national religion be established, nor shall the full equal right of conscience in any manner or on any pretext be infringed.''

This was an amendment to a section of the original Constitution that was a limitation upon Congress alone. It set forth that portion of the Bill of Rights which Madison deemed to be proper to restrict the power of the Federal government in matters of religion. On June 8, 1789, this draft was referred to the committee of the whole.

On July 21 the committee of the whole was discharged and a select committee was appointed to receive and consider Madison's propositions. This committee was composed of the following state representatives: John Vining, of Delaware; James Madison, of Virginia; Abraham Baldwin, of Georgia; Roger Sherman, of Connecticut; Aedamus Burke, of South Carolina; Nicholas Gilman, of New Hampshire; George Clymer, of Pennsylvania; Egbert Benson, of New York; Benjamin Goodhue, of Massachusetts; Elias Boudinot, of New Jersey; and George Gale, of Maryland. Vining was named chairman of the Committee.

In the House. On July 28 the select committee reported out the fourth proposal of Madison in the following manner:

> Article I, Section 9 between paragraphs 2 and 3 insert: ''no religion shall be established by law, nor shall the equal rights of conscience be infringed.''

It is to be observed that the term ''national'' was dropped after having been incorporated specifically in Madison's initial recommendation. The report of the committee was tabled.

On August 7 the Congress reenacted the Northwest Ordinance, which in part provided, ''Religion, morality and knowledge being necessary to good government and the happiness of mankind, schools and the means of education shall be forever encouraged.''

On August 13 the House of Representatives resolved itself into a committee of the whole to consider the report of the select committee. Again, on August 15, the House resolved itself into a committee of the whole with Representative Boudinot of New Jersey in the chair. Fortunately, the Annals of Congress are unusually complete in the significant debate that ensued. The Annals preserve the comments of the more influential members of the House. So important is the legislative history of the amendment that it is necessary to set forth in detail the entire debate:

> Mr. Sylvester (New York) had some doubts of the propriety of the mode of expression used in this paragraph. He apprehended that it was liable to a construction different from what had been made by the committee. He feared it might be thought to have a tendency to abolish religion altogether.
>
> Mr. Vining (Delaware) suggested the propriety of transposing the two members of the sentence.
>
> Mr. Gerry (Massachusetts) said it would read better if it was, that no religious doctrine shall be established by law.
>
> Mr. Sherman (Connecticut) thought the amendment altogether unnecessary, inasmuch as Congress had no authority whatever delegated to them by the Constitution to make religious establishments; he would, therefore, move to have it struck out.
>
> Mr. Carroll (Maryland)—As the rights of conscience are, in their nature, of peculiar delicacy, and will little bear the gentlest touch of governmental hand; and as many sects have concurred in opinion that they are not well secured under the present Constitution, he said he was much in favor of adopting the words. He thought it would tend more towards conciliating the minds of the people to the Government than almost any other amendment he had heard proposed. He would not contend with gentlemen about the phraseology, his object was to secure the substance in such a manner as to satisfy the wishes of the honest part of the community.
>
> Mr. Madison (Virginia) said, he apprehended the meaning of the words to be, that Congress should not establish a religion, and enforce the legal observation of it by law, nor compel men to worship God in any manner contrary to their conscience. Whether the words are necessary or not, he did not mean to say, but they had been required by some of the State Conventions, who seemed to entertain an opinion that under the clause of the Constitution, which gave power to Congress to make all laws necessary and proper to carry into execution the Constitution and the laws made under it, enabled them to make laws of such a nature as might infringe the rights of conscience, and establish a national religion; to prevent these effects he presumed the amendment was intended, and he thought it as well expressed as the nature of the language would admit.
>
> Mr. Huntington (Connecticut) said that he feared, with the gentleman first up on this subject; that the words might be taken in such latitude as to be extremely hurtful to the cause of religion. He understood the amendment to mean what had been expressed by the gentleman from Virginia; but others might find it convenient to put another construction upon it. The ministers of their congregations to the Eastward were maintained by the

contributions of those who belonged to their society; the expense of building meeting-houses was contributed in the same manner. These things were regulated by by-laws. If an action was brought before a Federal Court on any of these cases, the person who had neglected to perform his engagements could not be compelled to do it; for a support of ministers of building of places of worship might be construed into a religious establishment.

By charter of Rhode Island, no religion could be established by law; he could give a history of the effects of such a regulation; indeed the people were now enjoying the blessed fruits of it. He hoped, therefore, the amendment would be made in such a way to secure the rights of conscience, and a free exercise of the rights of religion, but not to patronize those who professed no religion at all.

Mr. Madison thought, if the word, ''National,'' was inserted before religion, it would satisfy the minds of honorable gentlemen. He believed that the people feared one sect might obtain a preeminence, or two combine together, and establish a religion to which they would compel others to conform. He thought if the word ''national'' was introduced, it would point the amendment directly to the object it was intended to prevent.

Mr. Livermore (New Hampshire) was not satisfied with that amendment; but he did not wish them to dwell long on the subject. He thought it would be better if it were altered, and made to read in this manner, that ''Congress shall make no laws touching religion, or infringing the rights of conscience.''

Mr. Gerry did not like the term ''national,'' proposed by the gentleman from Virginia, and he hoped it would not be adopted by the House. It brought to his mind some observations that had taken place in the conventions at the time they were considering the present Constitution. It had been insisted upon by those who were called antifederalists, that this form of Government consolidated the Union; the honorable gentleman's motion shows that he considers it in the same light. Those who were called anti-federalists at that time, complained that they had injustice done them by the title, because they were in favor of a Federal Government, and the others were in favor of a national one; the federalists were for ratifying the Constitution as it stood, and the others not until amendments were made. Their names then ought not to have been distinguished by federalists and anti-federalists, but rats and anti-rats.

Mr. Madison withdrew his motion, but observed that the words ''no national religion shall be established by law,'' did not imply that the Government was a national one; the question was then taken on Mr. Livermore's motion, and passed in the affirmative, thirty-one for, and twenty against it.

The House began consideration of the report of the Committee of the Whole on Aug. 19, 1789. The next day, Fisher Ames moved that the proposed religious amendment be altered so as to read: ''Congress shall make no law establishing religion, or to prevent the free exercise thereof, or to infringe the rights of conscience.'' This motion was accepted by the House.

It is reported in the *Journal of the House* for Friday, August 21 that the third article was again debated and finally agreed to in this slightly different form: ''Third. Congress shall make no law establishing religion, or prohibiting the free exercise thereof, nor shall the rights of conscience be infringed.'' This action of August 21 is not noted in the Annals of Congress. The next day congressmen Benson, Sherman, and Sedgwick were appointed to arrange the articles for delivery to the Senate, and on the 24th, the clerk of the House was ordered to present the Senate with a ''fair engrossed copy of the said proposed articles of amendment with a request for concurrence.''

In the Senate. On Tuesday, Aug. 25, 1789, there was read in the Senate the House draft of the articles on religion. >From one of the senators present that day, we learn that the Senate discussed the amendments to the Constitution sent from the House of Representatives. They were not well received by Ralph Izard (South Carolina), John Langdon (New Hampshire) and Robert Morris (Pennsylvania). Izard moved that they should be postponed until the next session. Langdon seconded, and Morris got up and spoke against the amendment. The motion was defeated and Monday was assigned for consideration of the amendments.

It was moved in the Senate on September 3 to amend the House draft of article three by striking out the words ''Religion or prohibiting the free exercise thereof,'' and inserting ''One Religious Sect or Society in preference to others.'' This motion was defeated. A motion for reconsideration was then passed, and a motion to strike the House-proposed third article was defeated. In lieu of the suggested third article, it was moved to adopt the following: ''Congress shall not make any law, infringing the rights of conscience, or establishing any Religious Sect or Society.'' This too failed. The debate continued. Another motion was defeated that would have amended the House's third article to read: ''Congress shall make no law establishing any particular denomination of religion in preference to another, or prohibiting the free exercise thereof, nor shall the rights of conscience be infringed.'' Oddly, the Senate then moved to accept the third article just as it had been received from the House, namely, "Congress shall make no law establishing religion or prohibiting the free exercise thereof, nor shall the rights of conscience be infringed." But this also failed to pass. Finally, it was passed in the affirmative that they adopt the wording of the House, but with the deletion of the words "nor shall the rights of conscience be infringed."

On Sept. 9, 1789, the necessary two-thirds of the Senate concurred in adopting a draft proposed by the Senator from Connecticut, Oliver Ellsworth. It reads as follows:

> To erase from the third article the word "*Religion*" and insert "*articles of faith or a mode of worship*"—And to erase from the same article the words "*Thereof, nor shall the rights of conscience be infringed,*" and insert—"*of Religion; or abridging the freedom of speech, or of the press.*"

The proposed amendment that would have prohibited the states from infringing the rights of conscience was also erased in the Ellsworth draft.

On September 10 the House received word of the Senate action and on the 19th the House reconsidered their proposed amendments, as these had been changed by the Senate.

On Sept. 21, 1789, the House informed the Senate it could not agree to the wording approved by the Senate and that it desired a conference. Accordingly, a committee of conference was named, composed of Senators Oliver Ellsworth, of Connecticut; Charles Carroll, of Maryland; and William Paterson, of New Jersey; together with Representatives James Madison, of Virginia; Roger Sherman, of Connecticut; and John Vining, of Delaware. By the 24th of the month the House had agreed to the committee's present wording of the First Amendment:

> Congress shall make no law respecting an establishment of religion, or prohibiting the free exercise thereof.

In the process of arriving at this agreement the conferees deleted the proposal that would have applied directly to state action. There is no satisfactory evidence as to who is the author of this wording. The following day, September 25, the Senate concurred in the resolution of the House requesting the President to submit the amendments to states.

Ratification. A determination of the meaning of the First Amendment must of necessity consider the attitude of the conventions called for the purpose of the ratification of the new amendments to the Constitution, and also the expressed attitude of the people during the time that ratification was being debated. The three most important steps in ascertaining the meaning of the amendments are: (1) the recommendations made by the states; (2) the proposals in the first Congress and the debate thereon; (3) the developments in the process of ratification. Unfortunately, historical records are incomplete with respect to the attitude of the ratifying conventions. It is known that some conventions did not give any specific attention to the amendment on religion but adopted the Bill of Rights as submitted by Congress.

The one ray of light that we have from historical records shone from the Virginia Assembly. On Sept. 28, 1789, three days after the concurrence by the Senate and the House on the 12 amendments, Senators R. H. Lee and William Grayson, of Virginia, wrote to the governor of the state submitting the amendments and saying:

> It is with grief that we now send forward proposals inadequate to the purpose of real substantial amendments, and so far short of the wishes of our country [state].

On Dec. 12, 1789, the majority of the Virginia Senate postponed ratification of the amendments until the next session. Among the amendments that did not meet with their approval was the First Amendment. The *Journal of the Virginia Senate* for Dec. 12, 1789, reads as follows:

> The third [first] amendment recommended by Congress does not prohibit the rights of conscience from being violated or infringed; and although it goes to restrain Congress from passing laws establishing any national religion, they might, notwithstanding, levy taxes to any amount for the support of religion or its preachers; and any particular denomination of Christians might be so favored and supported by the general government, as to give it a decided advantage over the others, and in the process of time render it powerful and dangerous as if it was established as the national religion of the country.
>
> This amendment then, when considered as it relates to any of the rights it is pretended to secure, will be found totally inadequate, and betrays an unreasonable, unjustifiable, but a studied departure from the amendment proposed by Virginia, and other states for the protection of these rights. We conceive that this amendment is dangerous and fallacious, as it tends to lull the apprehensions of the people on these important points; without affording them security, and mischievous because by setting bounds to Congress it will be considered as the only restriction on their power over these rights, and thus certain powers in the Government which it has been denied to possess, will be recognized without being properly guarded against abuse.

This document is particularly significant because it demonstrates that the Virginians who were

> probably the leaders in the whole movement for disestablishment felt that the proposed amendment did not live up to th spirit or the letter of the recommendation made by the state of Virginia when ratifying the Constitution. This is additionally significant when consideration is given to the fact that other states had adhered to the recommendation of Virginia, i.e., North Carolina, Rhode Island, and New York.

Several of the senators who filed this report had a continuous relationship with the development of religious liberty in Virginia. For example, Anderson and Pride were on the committee which originally reported the Virginia bill for establishing religious freedom. Though Virginia finally ratified the First Amendment, the document in 1789 containing the Virginia Senate's interpretation of the First Amendment was circulated widely throughout the colonies. For example, it appeared in the *Daily Advertiser,* New York, N.Y., for Jan. 26, 1790. It also was reprinted in the *Virginia Independent Chronicle,* Richmond, for Dec. 12, 1789. We can only speculate as to whether the other states when ratifying the amendment placed the same interpretation upon it as the Virginia Senate. However, it is a matter of historical record that several of the states were affected by the attitude of Virginia with respect to religious freedom. Presumably, they gave mature consideration to the interpretation placed upon the religious amendment by the Senate of the State of Virginia.

With respect to the other states the record is meager. The records of the debate in the Delaware General Assembly do not divulge what was discussed on the floor of either the House of Delegates or the Council. Final ratification occurred on Jan. 27, 1790.

The state of Pennsylvania formally ratified the present ten amendments on March 10, 1790. Again there is no historical record of the debate on the amendments. Of more than a little interest are the conclusions reached in the state constitutional convention, which was held in 1790, during the same time that the Pennsylvania Assembly was debating the proposed amendments. The Pennsylvania constitution of 1776 stated that:

> All men have an unalienable right to worship Almighty God according to the dictates of their own consciences.

The new Constitution repeated this declaration but significantly added the following:

> That no preference shall ever be given by law, to any religious establishment or mode of worship.

Undoubtedly, there is a relationship between the religious amendment recommended by Congress and the language adopted by the delegates to the state constitutional convention. This is particularly true when one considers the emphasis on the term "preference" by the First Congress during the formulation of the religious amendment.

In the state of New York the Senate ratified the amendments on Feb. 24, 1790, without significant debate.

New Hampshire ratified the Federal Bill of Rights on Jan. 25, 1790. The absence of debate or newspaper comment indicates that the New Hampshire legislators did not think that there was any substantial conflict between the proposed amendments on religion and the recommendation that the state had made when it ratified the Constitution.

Similarly, the records fail to disclose any debate preceding ratification by Maryland.

The state of Connecticut did not ratify the Federal Bill of Rights but extensively considered the proposed amendments. The convention was still debating over the form of the amendments when Virginia ratified the Bill of Rights on Dec. 17, 1791, and since three-fourths of the states had already ratified the Bill of Rights, it automatically became law. Similarly, Massachusetts failed to ratify the Bill of Rights. It does not appear from historical records that there was any discussion of religion in the legislative tribunal called for the purpose of ratifying the recommended amendment nor is there any significant discussion in the newspapers of the time.

Georgia also failed to ratify the amendments. No evidence is available concerning the reasons for the failure of Georgia to ratify, and there is no historical documentation of the attitude of Georgia with respect to the religious amendment. However, it is known that in the constitution of 1789 Georgia had declared that all persons should have "free exercise" of their religion.

The amendments were submitted to the South Carolina convention on Jan. 4, 1790, and approved on Jan. 19, 1790. It will be recalled that South Carolina was one of the states that had specifically recommended an amendment with respect to religion. The lack of debate indicated that it felt that the essence of its proposal was incorporated in the religious amendment proposed by the Federal government.

Rhode Island ratified the Bill of Rights of the Constitution at the same time. There is some evidence in the official journal of Rhode Island indicating that there was a debate on the religious issue. The record, however, is so sketchy and contains so many deletions and interruptions that it is difficult to determine the attitude of the Rhode Island convention.

Public Opinion. An examination of the newspapers published during the ratification period discloses few comments on the First Amendment. Undoubtedly, this is due to several factors. In the first place, the amendment did not arouse extended debate in the conventions called to ratify the amendments to the Constitution. Secondly, there had been rather extensive comment on the amendment during the time that it was being debated in the First Congress. Consequently, there was a fairly good understanding of the religious amendment and a conviction that it was substantially in harmony with the attitude of the majority of the states with respect to the relationship between Church and State. It reflected the mainstream of thinking respecting religious liberty. Though there was no significant newspaper comment, the Founding Fathers, who as legislators formulated the First Amendment, expressed their views of the proper relationship between Church and State on frequent occasions. Their statements give us an invaluable insight into the thinking of the men who were primarily responsible for framing the First Amendment.

The Carrolls. It is interesting to examine the opinions of the Carrolls. This outstanding Catholic family was in close contact with the constitutional development of religious liberty in the U.S. Charles Carroll, of Carrolltown, was a senator from Maryland in the First Congress. More important, he was chairman of the Senate Conferees in the committee of conference that was responsible for the final structure of the First Amendment. Fortunately, his views on the Church-State relationship have been preserved in several documents. He frequently expressed his opinion that any preference and discrimination because of religion was constitutionally objectionable. He had approved the ban upon religious tests in Article 6 of the U.S. Constitution, and he led the forces in Maryland in favor of ratifying this amendment. He felt that the use of government funds to aid religion so long as there was no preference given to one sect was constitutional. In the Maryland State Legislature he sponsored various laws which favored impartial state support of religion. None of his writings contain evidence that he believed that the Federal government should have been denied the opportunity to engage in similar expenditures.

Daniel Carroll, cousin of Charles Carroll, also served in the First Congress of the United States and took an active part in the debate on the religious amendments. At various times as a state legislator he had demonstrated his willingness to use governmental funds to aid religion. He had been a staunch advocate of the passage of an action to provide relief for widows and children of Protestant clergy. Moreover, as president of the Maryland Senate he introduced a bill "to incorporate certain persons in every Christian church or congregation throughout this state."

Though not a legislator, a third member of the Carroll family, namely, Bp. John Carroll, was particularly active in the field of religious liberty. Historical records contain many letters and debates of Bishop Carroll in which he consistently expressed the broad principle of religious liberty embraced in the First Amendment as it was originally understood. On Jan. 30, 1789, Bishop Carroll answered a series of letters appearing in the *Columbia Magazine* that attacked Catholic citizens. He said:

> After having contributed in proportion to their numbers, equally at least with every other denomination to the establishment of independence, and run every risk in common with them, it is not only contradictory to the avowed principles of equality in religious rights but a flagrant act of injustice to deprive them of those advantages to the acquirement of which they so much contributed.

Edward Humphrey, in *Nationalism and Religion in America* (Boston 1924), said that the Carrolls were largely instrumental in reading into the Federal Constitution a principle of religious freedom drawn from the framers of the Declaration of Independence that all men are created equal and are endowed by the Creator with certain unalienable rights.

This equality of religion was a dominant note in the thinking of the Carrolls and certainly it was constantly expressed by them, together with others in the First Congress and in the ratifying conventions. It is the key to an understanding of the meaning of the First Amendment, as it was understood by the Founding Fathers and prominent men of that day.

Bibliography: F. AMES, *Works* (Boston 1809). M. P. ANDREWS, *History of Maryland* (Garden City, N.Y. 1929). S. H. COBB, *The Rise of Religious Liberty in America* (New York 1902). J. ELLIOT, ed., *The Debates in the Several State Conventions on the Adoption of the Federal Constitution . . . Together with the Journal of the Federal Convention,* 5 v. (Washington 1836–59). *Records of the Federal Convention of 1787,* ed. M. FARRAND, 4 v. (rev. ed. New Haven 1911–37). P. L. FORD, ed., *Essays on the Constitution of the United States, Published during Its Discussion by the People 1787–1788* (Brooklyn 1892). M. V. GEIGER, *Daniel Carroll: A Framer of the Constitution* (Washington 1943). P. K. GUILDAY, *The Life and Times of John Carroll, Archbishop of Baltimore, 1735–1815,* 2 v. (New York 1927). W. MACLAY, *Journal,* ed. E. S. MACLAY (New York 1890). J. C. MEYER, *Church and State in Massachusetts from 1740 to 1833* (Cleveland 1930). A. P. STOKES, *Church and State in the United States,* 3 v. (New York 1950). F. N. THORPE, *Constitutional History of the United States,* 3 v. (Chicago 1901); ed., *Federal and State Constitutions, Colonial Charters, and Other Organic Laws of the State, Territories, and Colonies Now or Heretofore Forming the United States of America,* 7 v. (Washington 1909). A. W. WERLINE, *Problems of Church and State in Maryland During the Seventeenth and Eighteenth Centuries* (South Lancaster, Mass. 1948). Records of Federal Conventions and Legislative Sessions. U.S. Constitution, *Constitution of the United States of America . . . Annotations of Cases Decided by the Supreme Court of the United States to June 30, 1952,* ed. E. S. CORWIN (82nd Cong., 2d sess. Senate Document 170; Washington 1953). U.S. Congress, *The Debates and Proceedings in the Con-*

gress of the United States . . . >From March 3, 1789 to May 27, 1824, inclusive, half-title: *Annals of the Congress of the United States,* 42 v. (Washington 1834–56) v.1–2. J. B. SCOTT, *James Madison's Notes of Debates in the Federal Convention of 1787* (New York 1918). U.S. Congress, Senate, *Journal of the First Session of the Senate of the United States of America* (New York 1789). State Journals and Records. *Journal of the House of Representatives* (New York 1777–95); *Journal of the Senate, 1790,* South Carolina Archives, Columbia; *Journal of the Virginia Senate, December 12, 1789* (Richmond 1928); *Meetings of the Council of Delaware, 1777–1792* (Dover 1928); *Rhode Island Journal.*

[G. E. REED]

IMPACT ON THE NEW NATION.

Mr. Justice Felix Frankfurter, speaking of the religion clauses of the First Amendment when giving his concurring opinion in *McCollum v. Board of Education,* 333 U.S. 203 (1948), said, ''The mere formulation of a relevant constitutional principle is the beginning of the solution of a problem, not its answer'' (333 U.S. at 212). This observation aptly summarizes developments between the date of the congressional adoption of the First Amendment (1789) and 1840. It was a period of erratic but steady growth of the principle of religious liberty.

Federal Action. An important factor in assessing the impact of the religion clauses of the First Amendment is the limitation of the amendment to action of the Federal government. The House and Senate conferees stressed this limitation in 1789 when they refused to adopt the proposal of the House that would have made it unconstitutional for a *state* to violate the equal rights of conscience. The limitation of the Bill of Rights to Federal action was confirmed by the Supreme Court of the U.S. in the case of *Barron v. Baltimore,* 7 Peters 243, decided in 1833.

Treaties. Despite this limitation the federal government was able to promote religious liberty through treaties and various types of federal legislation. Article V of the treaty with Spain (1819) ceding Florida to the U.S. provided:

> The inhabitants of the ceded territories shall be secure in the free exercise of their religion without restriction. [8 U.S. Stat. at Large 252.] The growth of this principle is reflected in the legislation providing for a territorial government of Florida, 1822. Section 5 of the enabling congressional legislation provided that:

> No law shall be valid which . . . shall lay any person under restraint, burthen, or disability, on account of his religious opinions, professions or worship; in all of which he shall be free to maintain his own, and not burdened with those of another [3 U.S. Stat. at Large 654.]

This attitude had been anticipated in the treaty ceding Louisiana to the U.S. (1803). Article II of this treaty had stated that:

> The inhabitants shall be maintained and protected in the free enjoyment of their liberty, prosperity and the religion which they profess. [8 U.S. Stat. at Large 200.]

The next year Congress had passed a law erecting Louisiana into territories. This act had spelled out the precepts of religious liberty in detail, stating in summary that no law would be valid that imposed a disability on account of religious opinions or worship. In 1805 Congress had passed an act for the government of Louisiana, section 30 of which said:

> That the Constitution shall contain the fundamental principles of religious liberty. [2 U.S. Stat. at Large 331.]

These treaty and enabling law provisions are particularly significant since a large number of the people in these areas were of Catholic persuasion. Moreover, the constitutions of the several states carved out of the Louisiana Territory exemplified this mandate of religious liberty.

The same Congress that adopted the First Amendment enacted the Northwest Ordinance of 1787, Article I of which provided that:

> No person, demeaning himself in a peaceable and orderly manner, shall ever be molested on account of his mode of worship, or religious sentiments, in the North West Territory. [1 U.S. Stat. at Large 50.]

This principle of freedom of religion radiated to a large section of the country through organic laws that left no doubt about the commitment of the federal government to the basic principles of religious liberty. Other legislation was later to delineate the principles enunciated, but it is clear that these treaties and early enabling laws were the primary contributions to the development of the concept of religious liberty in the area between the Atlantic coast and the Mississippi River. They emphasized the concept of individual religious freedom and the ''free exercise'' concept of the First Amendment. They were silent on the principle of ''no establishment.'' In this respect they were similar to the House provision rejected by the conferees considering the Bill of Rights.

Thanksgiving and Chaplains. The concept of religious freedom did not, during this period, preclude the official recognition of God. Thus, on the day that the report of the conference committee was accepted (Sept. 24, 1789), the House adopted a resolution:

> That a joint committee of both Houses be directed to wait upon the President of the United States, to

> request that he would recommend to the people of the United States a day of public thanksgiving and prayer, to be observed by acknowledging with grateful hearts, the many signal favors of the Almighty God. [I Annals of Congress 913.] During the rest of this period all of the presidents, with the exception of Jefferson, proclaimed national days of prayer and religious observance.

In 1790 the House adopted a resolution, "that chaplains of different denominations be appointed to the Congress" (Annals, I, p. 932). The next year congressional legislation provided for chaplains in the Military Establishment Law (1 US Stat. at Large 223). This legislation was extended in 1792. Chaplains were provided for the Navy in 1794 (1 U.S. Stat. at Large 350). In 1800 the Congress directed that:

> The Commanders of all ships and vessels in the Navy having chaplains on board, shall take care that divine services be performed in a solemn orderly and reverent manner twice a day, and a sermon preached on Sunday, unless bad weather or some extraordinary accident prevent it; and that they cause all, or as many of the ship's company as can be spared from duty, to attend every performance of the worship of Almighty God. [2 U.S. Stat. at Large 45.] At the turn of the century the pattern of legislation, both federal and state, continued to disclose a willingness and desire to recognize officially God and the beneficial effect of religion. There was no significant protest outside of Jefferson's refusal to proclaim days of prayer.

Incorporation of Churches. Madison did not object to the appointment of chaplains in 1789 though later, after he had retired from active political life, he wrote a treatise arguing that the practice was not consistent with religious freedom—a thesis that has not been accepted. Madison took a strict view also on the incorporation of religious bodies. In 1811 he vetoed a bill to incorporate the Protestant Episcopal Church of Alexandria,

> Because the bill exceeds the rightful authority to which governments are limited by the essential distinction between civil and religious functions and violates in particular the Article of the Constitution of the United States which declares that, "Congress shall make no law respecting a religious establishment."

The Annals of Congress do not record the debate on the veto message, but the issue of the *National Intelligencer* for Feb. 23, 1811, records a portion of the debate; Mr. Timothy Pitkin from Connecticut stated that

> He had no idea that the Constitution precluded Congress from passing laws to incorporate religious bodies for the purpose of enabling them to hold property. He had always held the Constitution to intend to prevent the establishment of a National Church, such as the Church of England, a refusal to subscribe to the tenents of which was to exclude a citizen from office. The veto was sustained by a vote of 90 to 27, but this vote should be interpreted in the light of the fact that Mr. Benjamin Pickman, Jr., of Massachusetts, said:
>
> It appeared to him that the bill was not an important one, a refusal to pass which would be productive of any serious injury; and yet that a full discussion of the principles that it involved would occupy the whole of the remainder of the session.

In line with Rep. Pitkin's views was an editorial entitled "Democratic Qualms," appearing in the *Baltimore Federal Republican and Commercial Gazette* for Feb. 26, 1811. The editorial stated:

> What was the meaning of the Constitution in providing against a religious establishment? Does any man but Mr. Madison imagine it was to prevent the District of Columbia from engaging legal church regulations, and from exercising corporate rights in their congregations? Does The Legislature of Maryland believe it is creating a religious establishment when it is occupied in granting charters to the churches of the different sects of Christians as often as they apply? Where all are equally protected and accommodated, where each sect and congregation has its own establishment, modified according to its wishes and sanctioned in that modification by law, the best security exists against "a religious establishment," that is to say, one pre-eminent establishment which is preferred and set up over the rest against which alone the constitutional safeguard was created.

This was the first legislation to fall as a result of the application of the First Amendment. The fact is that it reflected a very special condition that existed in Virginia, namely, the associating of establishment with incorporation.

Madison also vetoed a bill that provided for a grant of land to a Baptist church in Salem, Miss. This position did not display the general attitude of the Congress or that of the executive office during this period.

In 1803 Jefferson as President concluded a treaty with the Kaskaskia people providing for the payment of $100 annually to a Catholic priest to perform religious ceremonies for the Native Amricans and to educate them (7 U.S. Stat. at Large 74). Starting in 1819 Congress commenced annual appropriations of money for mission boards to Christianize and educate native peoples. This became a standard and well-accepted policy during this period.

Many church-related schools also received congressional grants of land and money. In 1833, for example,

Congress granted land to Georgetown College (6 U.S. Stat. at Large 538). These facts are recited not in an endeavor to interpret the First Amendment but rather to indicate the nature and direction of its development.

Scant Judicial Review. There is no body of judicial precedent interpreting the amendment during this period. The only case reaching the Supreme Court of the U.S. was *Terret v. Taylor,* 9 Cranch 43 (1815), which involved the validity of laws turning over confiscated glebe land in Virginia to public officials. In declaring the law unconstitutional, Justice Joseph Story, speaking for the Supreme Court, said:

> Consistent with the constitution of Virginia, the legislature could not create or continue a religious establishment which would have exclusive rights and prerogatives, or compel the citizens to worship under a stipulated form or discipline, or to pay taxes to those whose creed they could not conscientiously believe. But the free exercise of religion cannot be justly deemed to be restrained, by aiding with equal attention the votaries of every sect to perform their own religious duties, or by establishing funds for the support of ministers, for public charities, for the endowment of churches, or for the sepulture of the dead. [9 Cranch at 49.]

This language came close to representing the contemporary attitude with respect to Church and State.

State Constitutions. It is important to examine the constitutional reaction of the states during this period to determine whether their organic law reflected the impact of the First Amendment. This would only demonstrate the indirect action of the amendment for, as heretofore observed, it was a limitation on the federal government and not the states. Yet the amendment was, to a certain extent, a codification of the religious sentiments of the day, and as such, it could be expected to have significant influence.

Uniform Enactments. Twenty-one states adopted constitutions during this time. Seven contained the following provision:

> That all men have a natural and indefeasible right to worship Almighty God according to the dictates of their own consciences; that no man can of right be compelled to attend, erect or support any place of worship or maintain any ministry, against his consent; that no human authority can, in any case whatever, control or interfere with the rights of conscience, and no preference shall ever be given by law, to any religious establishments or modes of worship. This language was first incorporated in the Pennsylvania Constitution of 1790, which was adopted in convention at Philadelphia at the same time and place where delegates from Pennsylvania ratified the First Amendment. The relationship or impact of the First Amendment on the formulation of this language is still open to speculation, but it will be observed that it contains the guarantee of free exercise and a bar against legal preference for a religious establishment. Certainly, the proximity of time, place, and common interest gave the respective delegates an opportunity for an exchange of opinion. States adopting this same language during the period under consideration were Kentucky, 1792; Tennessee, 1796; Ohio, 1802; Indiana, 1816; Illinois, 1818; and Arkansas, 1836. Language substantially similar may be found in the constitutions of Vermont, 1791; Delaware, 1792; New Hampshire, 1792; Georgia, 1798; Missouri, 1820; Michigan, 1835; and Florida 1838.

Private Schools. No state constitution adopted during this period provided that money could not be used in aid of a sectarian school. The constitution of Michigan, however, provided that:

> No money shall be drawn from the treasury for the benefit of religious societies, or theological or religious seminaries.

No other state constitutional provisions reveal this concept. On the other hand, the Ohio constitution of 1802 provided:

> The laws shall be passed by the legislature which shall secure to each and every denomination of religious society in each surveyed township, which now is or which may hereafter be formed in the State, an equal participation according to their number of adherents, of the profits arising from the land granted by Congress for the support of religion, agreeable to the ordinance or act of Congress making the appropriation.

The Missouri Enabling Act of 1812 had similar language. Despite this diversity, the constitutions were remarkably similar. All contained a free exercise provision spelled out in detail, and most of them had a "no establishment" clause detailed in terms of *no preference.* This obviously was the accepted concept of religious liberty during this period. Modified establishments did persist as late as 1833 in Massachusetts and several of the other New England states, but by 1840 very little remained except vestigial aspects of establishment that were retained more by tradition than by usage. Several states retained test oaths, notably, Maryland, North Carolina, Tennessee, Mississippi, Arkansas, and Pennsylvania.

Of course, this does not mean that all the constitutional aspects of religious liberty had been translated into action. It was during the latter part of this period that Nativism took root. In 1834 the Ursuline Convent in Charlestown, Mass., was burned to the ground. More trouble was to come and more open flouting of the constitutional guarantees of religious liberty. The gap between the law and actual practice was a wide one, but this was due to a variety of factors, none of which specifically involved the First Amendment.

Many social and philosophical factors such as the growth of the public schools, the influx of immigrants, the anticlerical philosophy of the French Revolution, and the fear of Rome would eventually result in movements that would reshape state constitutions and place a new and different gloss of interpretation on the First Amendment. However, the basic concept of religious liberty is most accurately shown in the treaties, congressional enactments, and state constitutions that were adopted before 1840. This was the period when the momentum, developed during the constitutional period, generated laws accurately reflecting the fundamental meaning and purpose of the First Amendment.

Bibliography: C. A. BEARD, *The Republic* (New York 1943). E. CHANNING, *A History of the United States,* 6 v. (New York 1905–25). S. H. COBB, *The Rise of Religious Liberty in America* (New York 1902). R. J. GABEL, *Public Funds for Church and Private Schools* (Washington 1937). E. B. GREENE, *Religion and the State* (New York 1941). P. SCHAFF, *Church and State in the United States* (New York 1888). F. N. THORPE, *Federal and State Constitutions, Colonial Charters and Other Organic Laws of the State, Territories, and Colonies Now or Heretofore Forming the United States of America,* 7 v. (Washington 1909). W. W. WINTHROP, *Military Law and Precedents* (reprint Washington 1920). J. ELLIOT, ed. *The Debates in the Several State Conventions on the Adoption of the Federal Constitution . . . Together with the Journal of the Federal Convention,* 5 v. (Washington 1836–59). U.S. Congress, *The Debates and Proceedings in the Congress of the United States . . . From March 3, 1789 to May 27, 1824, inclusive (Annals of the Congress of the United States)* 42 v. (Washington 1834–1856) 1:914, 932, 1043. U.S. President, *A Compilation of the Messages and Papers of the Presidents,* comp. J. D. RICHARDSON, 20 v. (New York 1917).

[G. E. REED]

FREEDOM OF SPEECH (IN CHURCH TEACHING)

The right of the individual to express or communicate in a more or less public way his views without interference from other individuals or groups or from social authority. It is distinguished from freedom of the press insofar as it is the freedom to disseminate one's views by word of mouth (including right of access to radio and television) rather than by the printed word. Insofar as speech implies an overt external activity, the freedom here considered is one over and above intellectual FREEDOM, which strictly taken is a freedom within the unindictable confines of the person himself. Because the communication of views, ideas, and theories may have and generally does have social repercussions, this right and its limitations present problems that perennially vex the minds of philosophers, theologians, and political scientists.

Men differ in assigning limits or denying limits to this freedom accordingly as they differ on the nature of the society or community within which the right is claimed; on the effectiveness or power of words to influence or determine action; on the likelihood of truth triumphing over error by its own sheer weight; on the existence and importance of basic principles for well-ordered community life and the right and duty of protecting such principles from irresponsible and inflammatory attack; and on the practical possibility of limiting or containing something as volatile as expression of opinion. Thus, one who questions whether men have as yet acquired any clear and unchanging truths, whether there are truths whose denial would jeopardize social life, and whether verbal attacks can do any real or demonstrable harm will naturally be at odds with one who is convinced that there are at least some basic truths permanently valid, that among these are some whose denial will undermine the structure of social life, that normal people can reach the reasonable judgment that certain forms of attack upon these principles will ordinarily corrode or destroy them in the minds of the immature and the unbalanced, that while truth will eventually prevail it may do so too late to avert serious and irreparable harm.

General Catholic Attitude. In the past the Church in her general teaching and Catholic theologians in their writings, while acknowledging a right (and even an inalienable one) of the individual to express his mind, have tended to emphasize strongly the limits of this right. The Church's attitude would appear to flow from its conviction that both reason and revelation do declare at least some immutable principles, that among these principles are those on which peace and public order hinge, that society is vested with power to oppose and restrain attacks upon public order, even though the attack at a given moment be mounted only by words and speech.

More recently this attitude, or this emphasis, has been questioned by some Catholic theologians, who share a regard for the individual person and his rightful autonomy, an understandable fear based on experience of excesses perpetrated in the name of public order by entrenched groups in control of public power, and a belief that in modern life—given the proliferation of means of communication that level all barriers to movement of thought and exchange of views—it is impractical and unrealistic to attempt to dam the flow of opinion. These thinkers would prefer to discard the negative and repressive forms of reaction; to accentuate the positive by confronting the false, the unwholesome, and the dangerous with an ever more effective presentation and defense of truth and objective values; and trust to the maturity and responsibility of intelligent and educated public opinion to select and hold fast that which is good.

Specific Areas of Freedom and Limitations. It is inevitable that the Catholic Church, which considers itself divinely founded and preserved, which claims to be entrusted with a doctrine divinely revealed and to be equipped with effective divine assistance in maintaining this revealed message, will admit freedom in more restricted areas than societies that make no such claim. To the extent, however, that the divine message is coupled with human modes of presentation or with arrangements, directions, and discipline consistent with but not in all ages or in all situations demanded by the revealed message, the Church appears ready to recognize more explicitly and sympathetically freedom of speech within the household.

The areas in which freedom may be claimed may be divided into four, the first of which is that of doctrine definitively fixed by the supreme doctrinal authority of the Church. The second is likewise one of doctrine and teaching, but in which the teaching has never been clearly fixed. The third is one in which the divine message is not immediately involved, where consequently the role of the Church has been rather the pastoral one of practical guidance (setting up norms for worship; approving forms of monastic and religious life; conceding indulgences; establishing rules for fast, abstinence, etc.). The fourth is the area of current administrative decisions, contemporary planning, and policy either by the supreme authority or by lower authority, e.g., by local bishops or by the heads of religious orders and congregations (especially in the administration of schools, hospitals, and social institutions directed by religious congregations).

In regard to the first area, if the Church takes seriously its claim to be able to define the sense of divine revelation it cannot tolerate within the Church a freedom that would in effect contain a denial of its infallible teaching authority.

In the second area, one in which there is still room for modification of the Church's position, voiced dissent would not involve a denial of the Church's right; nevertheless, the one invoking freedom should realize that the Church will generally regard the traditional viewpoint as enjoying a strong presumption of truth, and that a pastoral concern for the faithful will urge the Church to exact from the one claiming freedom patience, sobriety in expression of a newer viewpoint, and circumspection in propounding his views. Certainly in more recent times (e.g., Pius XII's encyclical *DIVINO AFFLANTE SPIRITU* and the "Instruction on the Historical Truth of the Gospels" emanating from the PONTIFICAL BIBLICAL COMMISSION (April 1964) ecclesiastical authorities have tried to safeguard a legitimate freedom for scholars, even when they voice views at variance with positions long held within the Church, and at the same time to protect the children of the Church from hasty acceptance of theories that may ultimately prove unsatisfactory or of theories that when not fully understood may lead the uninformed or the poorly informed to question related truths that belong to the unchangeable doctrine of the Church. Pastors in the Church may, then, at times act to restrain public expression or discussion, while allowing private discussion in circles competent to understand and sift the issues involved.

The same restrictions of freedom will prevail in the area of long-standing discipline and Catholic life. One who invokes freedom to challenge and adversely criticize arrangements incorporated in the constitutions and rules of religious congregations, centuries-old practices of Catholic life, and historic usages in public worship may be expected to present his views in a manner that displays the courtesy of charity toward Catholics and the Catholicism of the past and avoids so far as possible disruption of Catholic life and unlovely factions within the people of God. Those in authority, out of concern for the continuity of Christian life and worship, may be expected to manifest reserve at times in dealing with those who advocate sudden and violent changes, or to modulate the stridency that at times marks and mars free speech.

In the fourth area, freedom of speech presents the special difficulty that it usually involves an attack upon (or at least a pointed criticism of) living men and women here and now vested with authority ultimately derived from Christ. Within the Church some account must be taken of this circumstance, and the one choosing to exercise freedom may be held to manifest his acknowledgment of the authority, even as he decries its unfortunate exercise. It does not seem that freedom here will be unduly hampered if it be exercised by respectful and private remonstrance to the ones whose official action is considered imprudent or unfair or pointlessly rigorous and then (if no redress is secured) by quiet recourse to higher authority before the aggrieved parties carry their case to the public.

The tensions generated by the exercise of free speech in this sector may be substantially reduced if the directive of Vatican Council II is wholeheartedly accepted and the grounds for later criticism removed or diminished by affording those who are subject to authority a chance to be heard before decisions are made or actions taken. Toward the end of the chapter on the laity (37) in the Constitution on the Church, the council states that

> they [the laity] should openly reveal to them [their pastors] their needs and desires with that freedom and confidence that is fitting in children of God and brothers in Christ. By reason of their knowledge, competence, achievements, they may express and sometimes have even the duty of expressing their opinions in regard to things that concern the good of the Church. Let this be done, when the occasion arises, through channels established for this purpose by the Church. Let it always be done in truth, with courage and prudence, with reverence and love for those who by reason of their sacred office represent the person of Christ. . . . Let them [pastors] willingly avail themselves of the prudent counsel of the laity. . . . Let them thoughtfully in Christ weigh with paternal love the projects, suggestions and desires of the laity.

Although freedom of speech within the Church and the limits of that freedom will never be established to the satisfaction of all, the problems it raises will be notably reduced if those who must ''guard the deposit'' concede freedom to those who labor to relate that deposit to the needs of the time and to contemporary development, and if these in turn honestly and sympathetically assess the responsibility that weighs upon those in authority in the Church to turn over to future generations whole and unimpaired the message and patrimony received from Christ and his Apostles.

See Also: AUTHORITY, ECCLESIASTICAL

Bibliography: LEO XIII, ''Immortale Dei'' (Encyclical Nov. 1, 1885) *Acta Sanctorum* (Antwerp 1643–; Venice 1734–; Paris 1893–) 18 (1885) 161–80; Eng., *Catholic Mind* 34 (Nov. 8, 1936) 425–29; ''Libertas'' (Encyclical letter, June 20, 1888) *Acta Sanctorum* 20 (1888) 593–613; Eng. *Tablet* 72 (July 14, 1888) 41–46. JOHN XXIII, *Acta Apostolicae Sedis* 55 (1963) 257–304, encyclical. J. LECLERCQ, *La Liberté d'opinion et les Catholiques* (Paris 1963). Y. M. J. CONGAR, *Vraie et fausse réforme dans l'Église* (2d ed. Paris 1953). A. HARTMANN, *Toleranz und christlicher Glaube* (Frankfurt 1955). J. LECLERQ, *Toleration and the Reformation*, tr. T. L. WESTOW, 2 v. (New York 1960). J. MARITAIN, *The Person and the Common Good,* tr. J. J. FITZGERALD (New York 1947). J. C. MURRAY, *We Hold These Truths* (New York 1960). D. A. O'CONNELL, *Christian Liberty* (Westminster, Md. 1953). K. RAHNER, *Free Speech in the Church* (New York 1959). *Liberté et verité* (Louvain 1954), collection of essays by professors of the Catholic University of Louvain on occasion of the bicentennial of Columbia University.

[S. E. DONLON]

FREEMAN, WILLIAM, BL.

Priest, martyr; *alias* Mason; b. Menthorpe or Manthorp (?), East Riding, Yorkshire, England, *c.* 1558; d. hanged, drawn, and quartered at Warwick, Aug. 13, 1595. Freeman was born into a recusant Catholic family, but he outwardly conformed to the Anglican Church. After receiving his baccalaureate degree from Magdalen College, Oxford (1581), he lived in London, where he witnessed the martyrdom of Bl. Edward STRANSHAM (1586). Freeman was so impressed by Stansham's example that he converted, studied at Rheims, and was himself ordained priest in 1587. For six years following his return to England, Freeman ministered in Warwickshire, where his life was interconnected with that of William Shakespeare. He was arrested in January 1595 in the home of Mrs. Heaths, whose son Freeman was tutoring, and executed as a traitor seven months later despite his protest of loyalty. He was beatified by Pius XI on Dec. 15, 1929.

Feast of the English Martyrs: May 4 (England).

See Also: ENGLAND, SCOTLAND, AND WALES, MARTYRS OF.

Bibliography: R. CHALLONER, *Memoirs of Missionary Priests,* ed. J. H. POLLEN (rev. ed. London 1924; repr. Farnborough 1969). J. H. POLLEN, *Acts of English Martyrs* (London 1891).

[K. I. RABENSTEIN]

FREETHINKERS

Those who contend that reason can attain to a truth that has been contradicted, obscured, or distorted by the official doctrines of a religious body which lays claim to divine revelation and the consequent right to compel assent to its teachings. In a more restricted sense, freethinkers are those 17th-, 18th- and 19th- century philosophers and scientists, e.g., Anthony Collins, (1676–1729), Lord Shaftesbury (1671–1713), Denis Diderot, Thomas PAINE, Charles DARWIN, and Herbert SPENCER, who maintained that the teachings of Christianity—as contained in Scripture, in the writings of approved theologians, and in the pronouncements of the various churches—were an impediment to the progress of science and enlightened morality. To achieve desired scientific progress and ameliorate various social evils, they insisted it was necessary for the scientist and the philosopher to be free in their thinking and liberated from the limitations imposed by religious authorities. In France, those who assumed this attitude were called *libres penseurs, libertins, esprits forts, or franc-pensants;* in Germany, the term was *Freigeister or Freidenker.*

The term ''freethinker'' was first used by William Molyneux in a letter to John LOCKE (1697), in which the former called John Toland (1670–1722) ''a candid freethinker.'' Fifteen years later, the term appeared in print again, in Jonathan Swift's *Sentiments of a Church of En-*

gland Man. Swift referred to ''the atheists, libertines, despisers of religion, that is to say, all those who usually pass under the name of Free-thinkers.'' After the publication of Anthony Collins's *Discourse of Free-Thinking, Occasion'd by the Rise and Growth of a Sect called Free-Thinkers* (1713), the term was in common use. However, a certain ambiguity still attached to it, so that when Ambrose Philips began publishing his weekly journal, *The Freethinker,* in 1718, he was able to use the term freethinker to denote simply one who is ''free from prejudice.''

John M. Robertson, in his *A Short History of Freethought* (London 1899, 3d ed. 1915), defines freethinking as ''a conscious reaction against some phase or phases of conventional or traditional doctrine in religion on the one hand, a claim to think freely, in the sense not of disregard for logic but of special loyalty to it, on problems to which the past course of things has given a great intellectual and practical importance; on the other hand, the actual practise of such thinking.''

Early History. Throughout the history of Western thought, the problem that gave rise to the modern freethinkers occurred repeatedly within the context of various religious traditions. Each time it fostered a conflict between religious authorities and intellectuals whose scientific and philosophical inquiries led them to question the validity of the doctrines and sacred writings of the religion generally accepted in their society.

Greeks. The first Greek philosophers, Thales, Anaximander, and Anaximenes (sixth century B.C.), when pursuing their scientific inquiries into the nature, genesis, and function of the physical universe, found it necessary to reject the Homeric and Hesiodic accounts of how the gods had produced and continued to govern the world. Xenophanes (*c.* 500 B.C.) openly scoffed at the common anthropomorphic conception of the Greek gods. HERACLITUS, living in the same era, wrote, ''Hesiod is the teacher of most men; they suppose that his knowledge was very extensive, when in fact he did not know night and day, for they are one.'' Heraclitus is reported as having said also that Homer deserved to be cast out of the lists and flogged. The fifth–century atomists denied the possibility that the gods could affect the earth in any fashion; rather, they said, all occurrences in the universe were the result of the chance movements of indivisible bits of matter. They also denied the immortality of the soul. SOCRATES was condemned to death (399 B.C.) on the charge that he did not believe in the gods of the Athenian state. PLATO, in his *Republic* and various other dialogues, argued that the accounts of the Greek gods given by Homer and Hesiod could not be accepted in any literal sense, and that children ought not be exposed to the immorality contained in such tales. (*See* GREEK PHILOSOPHY.)

Romans. In the first century B.C., Lucretius carried on, among the Romans, the same sort of freethinking that had been championed by the Greek atomists. Lucretius's explicitly stated aims in composing his lengthy philosophical poem, *De rerum natura,* have been the aims of most freethinkers since that time: to give a natural, materialistic explanation of all physical and social phenomena, and thereby eliminate from the minds and hearts of men the paralyzing fears that stem from believing that the gods have brought this world and man into being, that the gods intervene in the affairs of men, that the gods can be moved by sacrifices, and that there is an afterlife in which men will be judged and punished by the gods. (*See* MATERIALISM.)

Muslims. The Muslim world, with its official religious teaching based on the Qur'ān, has had its own freethinkers, who found their reason in conflict with orthodox religious doctrine. Ibn-Ishāq al-KINDI (9th century), a devotee of Greek learning at Baghdad, gave considerable impetus to the development of a new school of Islamic theology, a kind of modernism that aimed at a reinterpretation of the Qur'ān along lines that would permit a reconciliation of Greek learning and Islamic doctrine. The resulting Mu'tazilite school, however, was soon challenged by a resurgence of fundamentalism. Then, in the 11th century, Omar Khayyām, the mathematician, astronomer, and poet whom J. M. Robertson calls ''the most famous of all Eastern Freethinkers,'' openly rejected the limitations of Islamic orthodoxy. In the same century, AVICENNA made a new attempt to provide a philosophical interpretation of the Qur'ān and thus to reconcile orthodoxy and science; but his efforts served to provoke Algazel's fundamentalist *Destruction of the Philosophers.* Finally, AVERROËS, a 12th-century Arab living in Spain, reasserted the claims of reason over religious faith in his *Destruction of the Destruction,* aimed at ALGAZEL, and in his three sets of commentaries on the works of Aristotle. (*See* ARABIAN PHILOSOPHY.)

Christians. In the early Christian period the Manichaeans, who claimed that they were Christians, propounded a fanciful, but would-be scientific account of the genesis of the universe and its functioning, along with an interpretation of Scripture in accordance with the demands of their ''science.'' However, orthodox Christianity asserted itself so powerfully that in the nineth century the Greek scholar and patriarch PHOTIUS was considered by many to be a dangerous freethinker because he had maintained in a sermon that earthquakes were the result not of divine anger, but of natural causes. In the same centur JOHN SCOTUS ERIUGENA gave a metaphysical explanation of reality in his Neoplatonic *De divisione naturae* that incurred severe ecclesiastical censures for its supposed heterodoxy.

In the 13th century, the influence of Averroës provided the occasion for the rise of a group of freethinking Christians, the Latin Averroists, who discounted the value of revelation and theology and accorded first place to reason and Aristotelian philosophy, which they regarded as the greatest accomplishment of human thought. (*See* AVERROISM, LATIN.)

Modern Development. With the rise of modern science the tension between orthodoxy and reason became acute for many. The celebrated affair of Galileo GALILEI is a case in point. In addition, the Renaissance humanists provided the beginnings of a ''higher criticism'' of Scripture that questioned the generally accepted notions concerning the dates, authorship, and historical backgrounds of the various books of the Bible. With respect to the difficulties of both scientists and Scripture critics, the conflicts were exacerbated by a failure on the part of orthodox theologians to distinguish clearly between the message of revelation and its cultural matrix, a failure that was repeated at other times of intellectual crisis, e.g., on the occasion of Darwin's publication of his *Origin of Species* (1859). In the 17th-century B. SPINOZA had incurred the wrath of the orthodox, both Christian and Jew, with the publication of his *Tractatus theologico-politicus,* in which he anticipated much of the German 19th–century higher criticism of Scripture and presented a plea for freedom of thought and speech in religious matters. At approximately the same period, the British Deists were beginning to publish their objections to revealed religion (*see* DEISM). Shortly thereafter, the French ENCYCLOPEDISTS made their contribution to freethought on the Continent. The 1789 Declaration of the Rights of Man showed the influence of freethinking in its statement that ''no one is to be interfered with on account of his opinions, even on the subject of religion, so long as their manifestation does not disturb public order as established by law.''

Early in the 19th century, Robert Owen (1771–1858), English social reformer, gave evidence of the continuing conflict between science and revealed religion. On a visit to the U.S. in 1830, he challenged the American clergy in general to debate with him a set of freethinking propositions: that all religions are founded in ignorance; that all religions are opposed to the laws of nature; that religion is the principal cause of strife among men; that religion is the principal cause of human vice and misery; and that all religions are maintained only through the ignorance of the many and the tyranny of the few. For Americans, however, freethinking came to be typified by Robert Ingersoll (1833–99), lawyer, politician, author, and lecturer. As a result of his popular lectures on such subjects as ''Some Mistakes of Moses'' (1879) and ''Why I Am an Agnostic'' (1896), Ingersoll earned for himself the sobriquet of ''The Great Agnostic.''

Numerous organizations of freethinkers were established in Europe and America in the 18th and 19th centuries. Freemasonry's Grand Lodge, founded in London in 1717, was originally an association of freethinkers. Other organizations of freethinkers were the Theophilanthropists of France, the Abrahamites in Bohemia, Ernst Haeckel's Monistic Society in Rome, the National Secular Society in England, the International Freethinkers' League in Brussels, the American Rationalist Association, the American Secular Union, and the Freethinkers of America. Numerous freethinking publications sprang up. Robertson, in his *A History of Freethought in the Nineteenth Century* (2 v. London 1929), lists, for example, 13 such periodicals that began publication in England between 1819 and 1850.

Influence on Catholics. Within the Catholic Church, the pressures exerted by those who desired an adjustment in traditional teaching to bring Catholicism in line with advances in the sciences and in higher criticism were met by Pope Pius IX's encyclical *QUANTA CURA* (1864) and its list of 80 propositions that came to be known as the Syllabus of Errors. The last of these anathematized propositions summarized the position Pius IX wished to condemn: ''The Roman pontiff can and should reconcile and align himself with progress, liberalism, and modern civilization.'' Pius X continued Pius IX's policy in his encyclical *PASCENDI* (1907), which condemned the Modernist tendencies that manifested themselves at the turn of the century.

The term freethinker has become somewhat archaic in the second half of the 20th century, largely because the kinds of pressures formerly exerted by church and state to exact intellectual conformity in religious matters have generally given way to a respect for religious freedom and for freedom of thought in general. Within the Catholic Church, moreover, a conciliating factor has been the approval of new directions in scriptural interpretation, particularly in Pope Pius XII's *DIVINO AFFLANTE SPIRITU* (1943), and the consequent removal of much of the troublesome tensions that formerly existed. Finally, the deliberations of Vatican Council II have resulted in *an aggiornamento* that encourages a fuller rapprochement between the Church and contemporary intellectual movements.

See Also: THEOPHILANTHROPY; SCIENTISM; RATIONALISM; ATHEISM.

Bibliography: E. TROELTSCH and E. H. BLAKENEY, *Encyclopedia of Religion and Ethics*, ed. J. HASTINGS (Edinburgh 1908–27) 6:120–124. K. ALGERMISSEN, *Lexikon für Theologie und Kirche*, ed. J. HOFER and K. RAHNER (Freiberg 1957–65) 4:318–322. K. HUTTEN,

Die Religion in Geschichte und Gegenwart (Tübingen 1957–65) 2:1093–96. J. M. WHEELER, *Biographical Dictionary of Freethinkers* (London 1889). J. E. COURTNEY, *Free-thinkers of the Nineteenth Century* (London 1920). C. WATTS, *A Defence of Secular Principles* (London 1871); *The Philosophy of Secularism* (London 1871).

[R. Z. LAUER]

FRELICHOWSKI, STEFAN WINCENTY, BL.

Diocesan priest, martyr; b. Jan. 22, 1913, Chelmza, Poland; d. Feb. 23, 1945 in the concentration camp at Dachau (near Munich), Germany. As a Polish Scout prior to his entry into the seminary, Stefan ''acquired a particular sensitivity to the needs of others'' (John Paul II, beatification homily). He was ordained a priest in 1937. He was working at his first assignment as a parish priest at Torun when he was arrested with several other priests by the Gestapo and released after a few days. On Oct. 18, 1939, he was again stopped and sent to Oranienburg–Sachsenhausen. Over the course of the next 14 months, he was transferred successively to ''Fort Seven,'' Stutthof, Grenzdorf, Oranienburg-Sachsenhausen, and finally Dachau (Dec. 13, 1940). At each stop along the way, Frelichowski witnessed to the love of Christ through his humble service to others. During the typhus epidemics at Dachau (1944–45), he risked his life to bring forbidden material and spiritual comfort to the afflicted and dying until he himself contracted the disease, then developed pneumonia. He died in the camp hospital at age 32—just two months before the end of the war. The decree of Frelichowski's martyrdom was signed on March 26, 1999. Pope John Paul II beatified Frelichowski on June 7, 1999 at Torun, Poland, the city where two peace treaties were signed and a colloquium was held between Catholics and Calvinists, because he was a peacemaker.

Bibliography: *Acta Apostolicae Sedis* (1999): 639–40.

[K. I. RABENSTEIN]

FRELINGHUYSEN, THEODORE JACOBUS

Dutch Reformed pastor, influential in the growth of PIETISM and the development of the GREAT AWAKENING in America; b. Hagen, Westphalia, Germany, Nov. 6, 1692; d. after May 1747. He was the son of a Reformed pastor, and he studied for the ministry in Germany and Holland. In 1717 he was ordained by the Coetus of Embden, Holland, and given a pastoral charge in East Friesland. In 1719 he accepted a call to the Dutch congregations in the Raritan Valley of New Jersey.

From his arrival in 1720, Frelinghuysen sought to combat the formalism of worship and the laxity of his congregations. His sermons stressed personal conviction of sin, true repentance, faith, and the work of the Holy Spirit in regeneration. He encouraged private prayer meetings and lay preaching. His new approach and free use of excommunication led some parishioners to appeal to Henricus Boel, a conservative New York pastor, and involved Frelinghuysen in controversy from 1723 to 1732. He was active in the movement for greater autonomy for the Dutch Reformed churches in America beginning in 1737 and favored the wider use of English in services (*see* REFORMED CHURCHES, II: NORTH AMERICA). He cooperated closely with the Presbyterians, particularly Gilbert Tennent, and in 1739–40, George WHITEFIELD. His sermons were published in English translation by William Demarest (New York 1856).

Bibliography: P. H. B. FRELINGHUYSEN, *Theodorus Jacobus Frelinghuysen* (Princeton 1938). F. J. SCHRAG, *Pietism in Colonial America* (Chicago 1948). C. H. MAXSON, *The Great Awakening in the Middle Colonies* (Chicago 1920).

[R. K. MACMASTER]

FRENCH REVOLUTION

The French Revolution (1789–99), whose religious history alone is here recounted, was not merely a violent and decisive overthrow of the political and social structures of the French kingdom; it was also a spiritual and religious drama. After demolishing the traditional ecclesiastical structure of one of the oldest Catholic countries of Europe, the revolutionaries aimed to formulate valid principles of organization for all modern societies, while prescinding from the Church's traditional doctrines or opposing them.

This aspect of the crisis in France during the last decade of the 18th century greatly impressed contemporary observers and later historians. Joseph de Maistre, in his *Considérations sur la France* (1796), described the Revolution as a death struggle between Christianity and a diabolical philosophy and as a trial permitted by Providence to revivify Catholicism. Abbé Augustin de Barruel's *Mémoires pour l'histoire du Jacobinisme* (1797) saw in it the fruit of a plot hatched by philosophers, freemasons, and fanatics to destroy the Church. Edgar Quinet in *La Révolution* (1865) interpreted it as an essentially religious conflict whose goal was the triumph of the spirit of enquiry and of liberty over the ''ancient belief'' that formed the basis of political despotism. Still later, ''scientific'' historians rejected these earlier interpretations as too systematic and too philosophical. François Alphonse Aulard (1849–1928) and Albert Mathiez (1874–1932) studied

Bonfire and celebration after the taking of the Bastille, engraving by Berthault, after drawing by Prieur, July 14, 1792, Paris. (Archive Photos)

the religious aspects of the disturbance, but denied that the Revolution was a premeditated war against the Church. They brought out the role of circumstances and of necessity (financial, national security) in the decisions taken against the Church. According to them, national renovation could not be effected unless the revolutionary leaders could attract powerful religious support. Lacking the support of the old Church, which had become hostile, they turned to the new "revolutionary religions." Finally, contemporary historiographers invite us to place the revolutionary phenomenon as it appeared in France behind every ideological and reform movement that disturbed Europe and even the entire Western world about the beginning of the 19th century. Although it was in France that the conflict between traditional religion and the new spirit erupted and proceeded to extreme lengths, one cannot separate the history of the vicissitudes of French Catholicism from that of the upheavals that have affected the Catholic Church and other denominations elsewhere and that have changed among peoples everywhere traditional concepts of relations between the state and religion.

Religious Situation in France in 1789. From the beginning of the 18th century throughout all Christian Europe "enlightened" minds and innovators, such as writers, political figures, administrators, and economists, examined "God's case," as Paul Hazard termed it, on a metaphysical plane, and also the Roman Catholic Church's case, on a political and social plane. The "philosophers" rejected divine revelation and the authority of the ecclesiastical magisterium and replaced them, in the name of reason, with "natural religion" or more rarely with outright atheism. They complained that the clergy, especially the papacy, was domineering, intolerant, and scandalously wealthy; and they condemned Catholicism for its social shortcomings, its complete disregard for civic-mindedness, and its alliance with despotism. Incredulity was restricted mostly to the aristocracy and intelligentsia. The middle classes were often hostile to the clergy, especially to the regular clergy, and disliked the Holy See and its ultramontane defenders. Among the masses religious practice remained regular, but it was mixed with much ignorance and was based more on conformity than on solid devotion (*see* ENLIGHTENMENT).

In France the *Cahiers de doléances,* drawn up in 1789 with a view to a meeting of the Estates-General, manifested a widespread attachment to the national religion, but they contained numerous criticisms of the ecclesiastical institution and revealed an eagerness to see the Church reform and bring the fullness of its influence to bear on the reform of the state. The *Cahiers* demanded that the clerical class surrender its privileges, especially its exemption from direct taxation, and a part of its immense real estate holdings, which occupied about one-tenth of the country. They showed great hostility toward religious congregations, especially of men, which were considered too numerous, useless, and contrary to human nature because of their vows of chastity and obedience. Convinced supporters of GALLICANISM wished to limit papal authority over the national clergy. In this respect they were in accord with the disciples of JANSENISM, who were very hostile to the Roman Curia and to PIUS VI (1775–99), who pursued them with his condemnations in France, in Italy, and in German-speaking countries. Supported by philosophers who advocated tolerance, Protestants demanded complete liberty of conscience and of worship.

On the whole there was no evidence in any part of France at the beginning of the Revolution of an intention to destroy Catholicism. Patriots no more intended to knock down the altar than to overthrow the throne. They had not even a common program for Church-State relations. No one imagined the possibility of establishing a regime of separation similar to that recently set up in the U.S. Furthermore, all differences were hidden by the unanimity of hopes. Everyone believed that the eliminating of abuses, the revivifying of institutions, and the establishment of a new constitution ''on the sacred foundation of religion'' would require the cooperation of bishops and priests; all expected such cooperation. The Catholic Church seemed to be held in much higher respect in France than in Austria or in the Rhineland. It seemed that in case of difficulty the Church could rely for defense on the devout King Louis XVI and on the deep attachment of a population that had never envisioned throwing aside its Catholic tradition.

Attempt to reorganize the National Church (May 1789 to April 1792). During its first year, the Constituent Assembly made decisions whose direct or indirect effects were to upset the Church's status and to alarm Catholics.

Louis XVI (with Marie Antoinette) taking oath of loyalty to the French Constitution, 1790, engraving. (Archive Photos)

On the night of Aug. 4, 1789, the deputies abolished all privileges of individuals and of social groups. Thenceforth the clergy could no longer exist in the state as a distinct order or class, enjoying precedence, the right to levy certain taxes (tithes), and the power to administer its own holdings and to consent to imposts sought by the king. In the future ecclesiastics were to be citizens on the same level as others and, like them, subject to the law.

Nationalization of ecclesiastical property followed in November of 1789. To circumvent the danger of public insolvency, the Assembly heeded the suggestion of TALLEYRAND-PÉRIGORD, Bishop of Autun, and legislated the seizure of the extensive properties belonging to the Church and the sale of it to benefit the state treasury. The Assembly promised that in exchange the state would guarantee an appropriate salary to ecclesiastical functionaries and would assume responsibility for maintaining hospitals, schools, and foundations that had been up to then the Church's care. This confiscation raised some protests, including the indignation of the Holy See; but it was carried out without great difficulty. Purchasers of ''national property'' continued to fear a return to the past and became determined adversaries of the Church, which persisted in condemning the operation.

At this time the Constituent Assembly, by way of prologue to the political constitution, proclaimed the Declaration of the Rights of Man, inspired by the American Declaration of Independence but more general and universal in character. It declared all men free and equal in rights, with freedom to think and write as they wish; it promised further that no one should be harassed for his opinions, even on religion. The ecclesiastical delegates accepted this moderate formula of tolerance, as well as the complete civil equality of Protestants. Pius VI, however, severely censured the principles contained in the declaration as contrary to revelation and impregnated with an indifferentism capable of leading to the ruin of the true religion (March 10, 1791).

Dissolution of religious congregations was the next step. In the spring of 1790 the Assembly decided to reform religious congregations as a measure indispensable to the public welfare; and it did so without consulting Rome. Religious vows were forbidden in the name of the inalienable liberty of the individual. Congregations not devoted to nursing or teaching were suppressed. Religious houses with few members were united. Religious men and women were authorized to leave their convents. These measures resulted very soon in the desertion of the houses of male religious, which were thereupon confiscated. The congregations of women resisted the pressure of local authorities much longer. Their convents, havens of retreat for priests and laymen who were dissatisfied with the religious reforms, were treated with increasing severity by the government until all were closed and the nuns dispersed (August 1792).

Although it had stripped the clergy of its privileges, the Assembly denied any hostile intentions against the Church. Indeed the majority of the clerical deputies still believed in 1790 that the Gallican Church, once purified, would find a worthy place in the ''regenerated'' state. Relations between the Revolution and the Church were changed decisively by the CIVIL CONSTITUTION OF THE CLERGY (July 12, 1790). Without consulting the Holy See, the Constituent Assembly enacted on its own authority a new statute concerning the Catholic clergy as part of its program of administrative and social reforms. It then demanded that priests, as salaried civil servants, take a civil oath to uphold the Civil Constitution. This threatened the enfeoffment of the clergy to the civil power and a break between the Gallican Church and Rome. Another effect of the law was to divide clergy and laity into two hostile groups. The constitutionals, or jurors, supported the Civil Constitution; the nonjurors, or refractory element, opposed it. Pius VI's solemn condemnation of the Civil Constitution (March-April 1791) caused the majority of the faithful to lean toward the refractory. As a result many Catholics detached themselves from the patriots and sided with the ''aristocrats,'' who were resolved to restore the *ancien régime* with the help of foreign arms if necessary.

The dream of harmonious collaboration between the Revolution and the Church disappeared. Toward the end of 1790 violent anticlerical manifestations broke out in Paris and throughout France. Most of the bishops feared for their lives and fled the country. They joined the royalists, who in Germany and Italy were trying to organize a league of Christian princes that would save the Church and King Louis XVI, by now a prisoner of the Revolution. European rulers hesitated to engage in a very hazardous ideological war, which Pius VI regarded as inevitable. In May of 1791 the French government severed diplomatic relations with the Holy See; and in September it seized AVIGNON, a part of the States of the Church. The pope was convinced that the Jacobins in Paris were spreading their propaganda in order to rouse peoples everywhere to insurrections against the throne and the altar. Within France and throughout all western Europe the revolutionary ideal and Roman Catholicism seemed to be in tragic opposition. Cardinal Zelada, the papal secretary of state, affirmed: ''A most cruel and uncompromising war against religion has been openly declared by the dominant party.''

The Legislative Assembly declared war on Emperor Leopold II of Austria (April 20, 1792). Soon afterward it decreed the deportation beyond French borders of all nonjuring priests suspected of conspiring against the state. Louis XVI, who had endeavored to prevent the enforcement of this last measure and who was suspected of connivance with foreign powers, was dethroned in a violent Parisian insurrection (Aug. 10, 1792). The collapse of the throne led to a ferocious attack against Catholicism.

Dechristianization (May 1792 to October 1794). Historians have coined the term ''dechristianization'' to describe the assault by the Legislative Assembly and its successor, the National Convention, against Roman Catholicism and then against all forms of Christianity. This persecution involved the deportation of ecclesiastics and the condemnation of some of them to death; the closing of churches, the wholesale destruction of religious monuments and symbols; the prohibition of worship, religious teaching, and propaganda; the secularization of the state and its institutions; and the condemnation of all ancient religious traditions. Attempts were made to replace ''superstition'' with revolutionary and civic religions. Dechristianization coincided almost exactly with the Reign of Terror, i.e., with the establishment of a centralized, dictatorial, and bloody regime that arose because of the Revolution's implacable war on a Europe allied against it. Dechristianization was also the consequence of a growing aversion, even hatred toward the Church and the religious ideal, and of a determination to "extirpate fanaticism," a resolve that characterized some political leaders and the populace under their influence.

Stages of Dechristianization. There were two outbreaks of dechristianization corresponding to what is called the "little terror," during the summer and autumn of 1792, and the "great terror," from September 1793 to August 1794.

Since the Legislative Assembly had to wage war against Austria, Prussia, Sardinia, and the French *émigrés*, it feared the internal disorders caused by the rivalry between juring and nonjuring priests and by the collusion of the latter, who maintained a strong ascendancy over the populace, with the enemies of the Revolution. The government therefore decreed the arrest and exile of nonjuring priests, who were regarded as models of disobedience to the laws. While the Austrians and Prussians were invading France from the northeast, local authorities imprisoned suspects somewhat at random. In Paris a mob became panic-stricken at the news of the approaching enemy, invaded the prisons, and indiscriminately massacred the prisoners as "accomplices of foreign powers" (Sept. 2–4, 1792). Many of the victims have been beatified (*see* PARIS, MARTYRS OF).

The confusion that followed the collapse of the throne permitted the installation at Paris of an insurrectionary city council, the Commune, which exercised discretionary authority, apart from that of the Assembly. It forbade public manifestations of worship, such as processions, midnight Mass at Christmas, and the wearing of clerical garb. It likewise despoiled churches to amass silver and bronze for national defense. These measures affected the clergy and worship of the Constitutional Church as well as the nonjurors. Actions of this kind were applauded by Cordelier and Jacobin clubs, by popular societies, and by the majority of the Legislative Assembly, whose Girondist deputies were very antireligious. The Assembly even decided to remove the clergy from its function as keepers of the census (the last social function they still performed) and to confine this work to lay officials.

However, these oversystematic procedures ran the risk of deeply wounding popular sentiment, especially in the provinces, and prudent political figures sought to slow down the application of them and to avoid their spread.

Under the National Convention the dechristianizing movement began anew in the summer of 1793, spread across France, and lasted until at least the autumn of 1794 and the Thermidorean reaction. The external and internal situation had become very grave. With England and Spain allied with the enemies of the Revolution, France was besieged by land and sea on all its frontiers by the First European Coalition. At the same time it was torn asunder domestically by terrible civil revolts, notably by the uprising in the Vendée, where the Catholics, who were also royalists, fought with extraordinary intensity to retain the nonjuring "good priests." A federalist insurrection set the large cities of the provinces against Paris and went so far as to make a compact with foreign countries. The Convention, dominated by the Mountain faction, sought by every means to reduce the French to submission. Thus it sent throughout the country commissioners armed with discretionary powers to crush the enemies of the Republic. Some of these envoys, with the complicity of local clubs, stirred up popular wrath against "fanaticism and its henchmen." They forbade all public and private worship. After tracking down priests, the revolutionists compelled them to marry and to abjure the priesthood (*deprêtriser*). Priests who resisted, along with their religious or lay accomplices, were arraigned before revolutionary tribunals. A law of Oct. 21, 1793, made all suspected priests and all persons who harbored nonjurors liable to death on sight. Condemnations multiplied. Sometimes they were carried out in batches. Thus 135 priests were shot to death at Lyons in the *mitraillades* (November of 1793). In Compiègne 16 Carmelites were executed; in Orange, 32 Ursulines. The Church has honored a number of these victims as martyrs (*see* COMPIÈGNE, MARTYRS OF; ORANGE, MARTYRS OF; ARRAS, MARTYRS OF; LAVAL, MARTYRS OF; VALENCIENNES, MARTYRS OF).

Once the "conspirators" were crushed, the attempt was made to replace "superstitious and hypocritical cults" by the cult of the Republic and of natural morality. Civic celebrations were organized in honor of Liberty and of the "Goddess Reason," whose feast was commemorated in Notre Dame Cathedral in Paris (November of 1793) and later in several provincial cathedrals. If these celebrations were not the Saturnalia depicted by the enemies of the Revolution, they inevitably repelled believers as sacrilegious parodies. Henceforth churches were devoted to popular meetings or transformed into shops. It was forbidden to attempt to reopen them for religious services. Protestants also had their churches closed and their services stopped. Some zealots of the Mountain went so far as to close Masonic lodges. All propaganda, all teachings other than those imparting Republican doctrines, were forbidden in popular societies.

To erase the memory of ancient traditions, it was considered insufficient to "demolish the temples that proclaimed the imbecility of our fathers" and to demolish belfries and crosses. Localities bearing names of saints were renamed, and children were given civic first names. Finally, in October of 1793, the Convention abolished the Gregorian calendar, in use among Christian peoples, and replaced it with a revolutionary calendar without Sundays or saints' feast days; the foundation of the Republic was taken as the year I. This was supposed to signify humanity's entrance upon a new era.

Scope and Limits of the Dechristianization Movement. This desperate effort to ''uproot fanaticism'' from the earth and from souls was the act of a small minority to whom circumstances had momentarily permitted the exercise of almost unlimited authority: Girondists during the Legislative Assembly, the Mountain during the National Convention, members of the Paris Commune and of the Jacobin clubs. Among them were jurists; intellectuals; lawyers, such as Pierre Chaumette; journalists, such as Jacques Hébert or Jean Marat; former religious, such as Joseph Fouché; members of the middle class who led the *sans-culottes* of the towns; and artisans and workmen, but not the lowest classes. This attests to the existence of a strong current of resentment against the Church, mixed with a rationalist ideology that was in good measure a tributary of the philosophical ideas of the preceding period, although not entirely so. This current continued for a long time after the Revolution.

It would be inaccurate to attribute the entire responsibility for the dechristianizing movement to the Jacobins or to regard all of them indiscriminately as atheists who denied all transcendent morality. The political leader who enjoyed the largest audience in the club of the Jacobins and who dominated the government committees and the Convention during the Reign of Terror was Maximilien ROBESPIERRE. He professed a form of DEISM inspired by Jean Jacques ROUSSEAU. Once in power, he sought to impose by law on all citizens belief in a Supreme Being and in the immortality of the soul (*see* SUPREME BEING, CULT OF THE). He did not favor the Church, nor did he advocate clemency toward it, but he disapproved the excesses of dechristianization as a discredit to the Revolution. His opposition to some members of the National Convention was not without bearing on his fall (July 28, 1794).

These distinctions were scarcely understood outside France. Most Christian peoples, Catholics and Protestants alike, viewed the religious persecution as the crowning point of the collective fury called the Reign of Terror, which could be explained only as a satanic blow against all that was most respectable in civilization. Beginning with the summer of 1794, the French Republic went from victory to victory and occupied Belgium, the Rhineland, and Savoy. In these Catholic countries it put into effect some of the Revolution's ecclesiastical legislation and measures. All western Europe was seized with dread lest the spread of the antireligious movement prove irresistible. Aversion to the Revolution increased still more because of the sympathy some of its victims inspired. The thousands of refugee or banished priests, religious, and bishops who had settled in Rome, Italy, Spain, Switzerland, Germany, England, and the U.S. (where a handful of Sulpicians founded in Baltimore the first Catholic seminary) demonstrated, on the whole, a dignity under trial and piety amid their hardships that won them great respect, even in the opinion of the antipapist British. The *émigrés* contributed not a little to confirming abroad the conclusion that France was the scene of an explosion of antireligious hate that was truly satanic.

Although the tempest that had been sweeping over France left ruins in its wake, it did not destroy all religious life, even momentarily. The Catholic masses opposed dechristianization with heroic resistance. Not all the Catholic clergy who were attached to Roman orthodoxy left France. Out of 135 bishops 25 refused to emigrate, and some spent the entire period of the Reign of Terror hidden in the vicinity of Paris. Other bishops sought to maintain the direction of their dioceses through authorized representatives. In Paris the Sulpician Jacques ÉMERY prudently directed the archiepiscopal council; in Lyons the Vicar-General Linsolas courageously organized itinerant missions. Priests and also many religious women who transformed themselves into unassuming schoolmistresses lived and worked clandestinely with the cooperation of the local inhabitants, especially in mountain and forest regions far from administrative centers, such as Jura, Haute Loire, and Lot. Nonjuring priests in western France found shelter among the insurgents of the Vendée.

In the Constitutional Church there was a relatively large number of priests and even of bishops who abdicated their faith, but there were also men of character, such as Henri GRÉGOIRE, Bishop of Loir-et-Cher, who was a deputy in the National Convention and always defended courageously the rights of religious conscience.

The prohibition of worship could be enforced in very unequal measure in different regions and in different periods. Even in Paris, where the promoters of dechristianization were most determined, religious services in secret could not be completely prevented. In the various departments of France the situation varied according to the zeal of local authorities and, above all, according to the resistance of the populace. There were whole regions, as in Brittany, where the prerevolutionary situation hardly changed. Areas with strong religious tradition succeeded in inaugurating missions entrusted to itinerant priests endowed with regular faculties, who were assisted by catechists and utilized the interval between visits from one parish to another to strengthen their spiritual lives. Even in more tepid regions the populace indicated by its attitude that, at the least sign of change in the political scene, it would demand the reopening of churches and schools where children could receive education based on traditional religion and morals.

It was this passive resistance, this evident determination of the people that brought about the progressive abandonment of dechristianization measures, beginning with the day when the Thermidorean Convention let the revolutionary government fall into disgrace, after the elimination of Robespierre.

Separation of Church and State (September 1794 to November 1799). During the year III the Thermidorean Convention turned gradually toward a regime of separation of Church and State. Force of circumstances rather than doctrinal convictions guided it. To lighten the public financial burden, the government decided first to cease paying salaries to the clergy. Implied in this was the abandonment of the Constitutional Church. To free itself from inextricable difficulties, the Convention next promised the free exercise of all religions, subject to precautions necessary to keep public order. This principle was even inserted in the new political constitution of the year III (promulgated in October of 1795), which initiated the Directory regime. This meant that the state would consider itself alien to religious questions and would guarantee to all citizens freedom of conscience and of religious practice.

Unlimited government tolerance was, however, impossible in a nation that was prey to the most profound political and moral divisions and that contained partisans of diverse cults engaged in continual rivalry and bickering. For five years the Directory shifted from complete abstention in regard to religion to half-hearted attempts at accommodation with the Catholic Church, to enforcement, and even to renewal of measures of surveillance and repression of Catholicism. This inconsistent attitude offered no security to any creed and succeeded in discrediting a regime that was very unpopular anyway because of the prolongation of the war, financial bankruptcy, and increasing anarchy.

Attempt at Tolerance and the Revival of Catholicism. From October of 1795 to September of 1797 the government sought to be tolerant. Catholic priests reappeared, and public worship resumed. The rival Constitutional and Roman Churches tried to reorganize. They disputed bitterly with one another over the faithful as clientele. But the Constitutional clergy were weakened by defections and by the low esteem in which the laity held them. On the other hand, the orthodox clergy suffered from divisions in their own ranks. Some priests preached prudence and submission to the authorities, but the majority, especially those who had returned from exile, refused reconciliation with the Republic and censured its laws and its representatives. The Directory thought it prudent to impose on ministers of religion a promise to obey the Republic's laws. In the summer of 1796 it made a somewhat ambiguous attempt to negotiate with the pope to get him to impose submission of the refractory clergy. When this failed and when resistance continued, the Directory stiffened its policy and accused Catholics of seeking to be "aloof, dominant, and persecuting." Furthermore, anti-Catholic prejudice remained very strong in government circles. The Directory imposed the revolutionary calendar and the decadi feasts on which the magistrates had to preach a civic religion (*see* DECADI, CULT OF). One of the directors, Louis Larevellière-Lépeaux, even pretended to be the prophet of a new religion of his own invention, called THEOPHILANTHROPY. The minister Joseph Lakanal was active in organizing a secular type of education that removed pupils from any semblance of religious cult.

The elections in the year V (March–April of 1797) manifested a strong popular movement against those in power and in favor of complete religious liberty and the recall of deported priests. In the elections Catholics, hoping to restore the Church to its old position, allied with the royalists, who were enemies of a republican form of government. The Directory used this as a pretext to disregard the elections by the *coup d'état* of 18th Fructidor (September 4) and to call in question the whole policy of religious appeasement.

New Anti-Catholic Offensive. As a result severe persecution started again and lasted two years (September of 1797 through November of 1799). Under the pretext of seeking guarantees of loyalty, the Directory imposed on priests an oath of "hate for the royalty" to which they could not subscribe. Against nonjuring priests the Directory revived the deportation legislation of the previous period and caused 2,000 priests to be arrested (of whom 500 belonged to departments in annexed Belgium). While waiting to transport them to Guiana, officials herded them into prisons and onto convict ships at Rochefort and neighboring ports under conditions so inhuman that many died. Although executions were relatively rare, annoyances were incessant. Catholic worship was no longer tolerated even for the Constitutional Church. The Directory hoped that it would wear down its opponents and put an end to the Church and its priests; it expected that eventually the populace would forget about them.

The victories won outside France by the armies of the Republic seemed to foretell the ruin of Catholicism in every country under French rule. As early as 1796 some directors wished to take advantage of the brilliant success of Gen. Napoleon Bonaparte in Italy by having him advance to Rome and attack the Holy See. Bonaparte refused, unwilling to jeopardize his conquests by stirring up the wrath of the Italian masses, whom he knew to be attached firmly to their religious traditions. He was satisfied to conclude with Pius VI the Treaty of Tolentino (February of 1797), which imposed on the pope rigorous neutrality but left him independent and in possession of Rome. This act permitted Napoleon to pose as the savior of the Holy See in the eyes of Italian and French Catholics (*see* NAPOLEON I).

Bonaparte's departure for Egypt and numerous incidents between French occupation troops and Italian princes in central and southern Italy allowed the Directory finally to dispatch to Rome Gen. Louis Berthier's army, which dispersed the papal court and proclaimed the Roman Republic (February of 1798). Pius VI, although 81 years old and ill, was seized and taken as a prisoner to France, where he died (Aug. 29, 1799). On this day the total destruction of the Holy See seemed to many to be accomplished. It might have appeared practically impossible to proceed to the election of a new pope in Europe, where the Second Coalition had stirred up war everywhere or to restore Catholicism in France after seven years of merciless persecution.

Religious Pacification (November of 1799 to July of 1802). Actually, the Jacobin government, as it was called in Catholic circles, was condemned by its inconsistency and injustices and by the intense desire of all Frenchmen for peace. When Gen. Bonaparte returned from Egypt, he took advantage of his popularity and of the discredit of the Directory to effect his *coup d'état* of 18–19 Brumaire (Nov. 9–10, 1799) and to seize power amid general approval. Within two years Napoleon as First Consul restored religious peace in France and in Europe. Once he became First Consul, he declared the Revolution ended but promised to guarantee its ''conquests,'' such as liberty of opinion and of belief, equality among religions, and the sale of religious property. Napoleon used exhortation and force to unite the French. He permitted the return of the refugee priests, from whom he demanded only a simple promise of fidelity to the constitution. Public worship resumed. Churches that had not been confiscated were allowed to reopen, but control over them was disputed between the Constitutional and the orthodox clergy. Each group claimed full authority to the exclusion of the other. The First Consul was surrounded by counselors who had been members of the Jacobin assemblies and who were very hostile to the restoration of Gallican and monarchist bishops to their former sees. Napoleon did not, however, lean toward the Constitutional Church or seriously consider making Protestantism the official religion of the new state, because he had already decided in favor of the Roman Church.

Experience had taught Napoleon to rule men according to the wish of the majority. In France and also in Belgium, the Rhineland, Italy, and in other territories annexed to France, the majority of the population was Catholic and much attached to the Holy See. These Catholics would not overlook the violence of the religious quarrels or submit to the laws of the established government except on the advice of their ''good priests'' or on the pope's orders. It was, therefore, necessary to negotiate with Rome, but at the same time to advance so cautiously that there would be neither victor nor vanquished among the partisans of the different religions, and to act so firmly that the papacy would be unable to take revenge for the Revolution and oblige Napoleon to compromise his principles and his conquests. It was with these considerations in mind that the government of the Consulate entered into negotiations (November of 1800) with PIUS VII, who had recently arrived in Rome to reestablish the papal government. The new pope was more inclined than his predecessor to enter into an accord with the French government, since he judged this indispensable to save religion in Europe.

The accord was incorporated in the CONCORDAT OF 1801, which was signed July 15, 1801, and promulgated April 18, 1802. It guaranteed full liberty of worship to the Roman Catholic apostolic religion (implicitly rejecting the Civil Constitution of the Clergy), the reestablishment of the hierarchy in communion with the Holy See, and the payment of an adequate salary to the clergy in compensation for the loss of their landed property confiscated and sold during the Revolution. But it did not make Catholicism the national or dominant religion, because Napoleon wanted to safeguard the freedom of dissident religions and the equality of religions recognized by the Republic. The silence of the concordat concerning religious congregations resulted in the disappearance of one group among the clergy and the transfer to others of the social services that they performed. The Concordat was, therefore, a promise of restoration of Catholicism in France and in the countries belonging to it; but this restoration did not involve any compensation for past losses, nor did it bestow any future concessions or special privileges.

Emperor Napoleon I was responsible for the observation of tolerance and for what must be called the laicizing of the state. He gave legal recognition to Protestant and Jewish worship and obliged all creeds to live on good terms under the watchful eye of the government. This situation was so novel in comparison with the *ancien régime* that Catholics found difficulty in accepting it. Its emancipation of religious dissidents, however, was in conformity with the Revolution's decrees.

So well was the formula of the Concordat adapted to existing conditions and to the mentality of the time in France and throughout most of western Europe that many neighboring states tried to obtain from the Holy See a similar accord during the following quarter-century. In France the Concordat survived its author. The Restoration period did not succeed in replacing it, even though it regarded a return to the prerevolutionary regime as essential. Despite numerous changes of government, France retained the concordat for 104 years, until the Third Republic legislated the separation of Church and State (December of 1905).

Prolongation of the Conflict. The mass of French Catholics interpreted the Concordat of 1801 as proof of the Revolution's failure in its attempt at dechristianization. But some conservative philosophers and, still more, some ultramontane theologians continued to deplore the Church's impaired status in comparison with the *ancien régime;* even more did they bewail the partial victory of Revolutionary principles over Catholic doctrine. The Church could indeed forgive and forget the plundering, the bloody persecution, even the sacrilegious overthrow of the Holy See during the Revolution. It could also consent to deal with the new, secularized states to obtain the blessings of peace and to safeguard religious liberty. It could not and would not, however, tolerate the propagation of those doctrines championed by the Revolution that were injurious to God and to society. Among them was the substitution of popular sovereignty for authority emanating from God. Unacceptable to the Church also was the concession of equal rights to religious truth and error implied in the phrases ''liberty of opinion'' and ''liberty of conscience.'' The proclaimed equality among individuals seemed contrary to traditional teachings about the providential inequality of conditions.

This explains the effort by the Church, particularly by the papacy, for more than a century to condemn and refute the ''principles of 89'' and to repel the Revolution, which was conceived thenceforth less as an historic event than as a doctrine of revolt and of negation that had taken hold of the human mind as a result of a false philosophy and had caused the diabolic insurrection of man against God. If several popes, notably Gregory XVI, Pius IX, and Pius X, waged a relentless struggle against the Revolution, it was because they attributed to it the essential responsibility for the spread of such modern errors as doctrinal indifferentism, rationalism, naturalism, and liberalism and because they saw in it a series of innovations dangerous to the individual, the family, and society, including civil marriage, secularized education, and separation of Church and State.

Liberal Catholics proposed, at times with tenuous arguments, that the Church reexamine the message and significance of the Revolution and the conditions of its promulgation; but for a long time this proposal went unheeded. The Church considered war on Catholicism as the basic aim of the Revolution, against which it must take an irreversible counterrevolutionary stand. The appeasement of this antagonism between Church and Revolution demanded, especially in the 20th century, new and terrible trials by mankind. It required also a pacifying of the antireligious fury that characterized the spiritual heirs of the Revolution, a more serene and detailed examination of the philosophical contents of the Declaration of the Rights of Man, a more minute and exact knowledge of the origin of some decisions and of the historic chain of events between 1789 and 1799. In fine, it necessitated a long labor of reconciliation between the Catholic Church and the modern world.

Bibliography: P. DE LA GORCE, *Histoire religieuse de la Révolution française,* 5 v. (Paris 1909–23). A. LATREILLE, *L'Église catholique et la révolution française,* 2 v. (Paris 1946–50). J. LEFLON, *La Crise révolutionnaire 1789–1846* (Fliche-Martin 20; 1949). C. LEDRÉ, *L'Église de France sous la Révolution* (Paris 1949). F. MOURRET, *A History of the Catholic Church,* tr. N. THOMPSON, 8 v. (St. Louis 1930–57) v. 7. H. DANIEL-ROPS, *L'Église des révolutions: En face des nouveaux destins (Histoire de l'Eglise du Christ* 6.1; Paris 1960). Dansette v. 1. A. AULARD, *La Révolution française et les congrégations* (Paris 1903); *Christianity and the French Revolution,* tr. LADY FRAZEN (London 1927). A. MATHIEZ, *Les Origines des cultes révolutionnaires, 1789–92* (Paris 1904); *Contributions à l'histoire religieuse de la Révolution française* (Paris 1907); *La Révolution et l'Église* (Paris 1910); *Rome et le clergé français sous la Constituante* (Paris 1911); *La Question religieuse sous la Révolution* (Paris 1929). A. SICARD, *L'Ancien clergé de France,* 3 v. (Paris 1893–1903; v. 1, 5th ed. 1912); *Le Clergé de France pendant la Révolution,* 3 v. (new ed. Paris 1912–27). P. PISANI, *L'Église de Paris et la Révolution,* 4 v. (Paris 1908–11). C. H. TILLY, *The Vendée* (Cambridge, Mass. 1964).

[A. LATREILLE]

FREPPEL, CHARLES ÉMILE

French theologian, apologist, writer; b. Obernai (Bas-Rhin), France, June 1, 1827; d. Angers, Dec. 22, 1891. After studying at the seminary in Strasbourg, he was ordained (1849) and then became director of St. Arbogaste College in Strasbourg (1851), professor of homiletics, and later of patristics, at the Sorbonne (1855), consultor in the preparations for Vatican Council I (1869), and bishop of Angers (1869). During Vatican Council I he was an energetic supporter of papal infallibility. In 1880 he was elected deputy to the French Chamber, where he was a stalwart upholder of the Church and the monarchy. As a teacher and writer he was noted more for brilliance than for profundity. His voluminous writings included more than 40 titles in 80 volumes. Apart from his numerous pastoral letters and speeches as bish-

Charles Émile Freppel.

op, his best-known works are *Études sur les Pères des trois premiers siècles* (11 v. 1859–93), a history of the sacred eloquence of the Fathers of the Church full of allusions to contemporary history; *Bossuet et l'éloquence sacrée au 17e siècle* (2 v. 1893); his study on the life of Christ written by RENAN, *Examen critique de la Vie de Jésus par E. Renan* (1863, 15th ed. 1866), which was widely read; and, still more popular, *La Révolution française* (1889), which went through many editions. Freppel was a brilliant orator and very combative. He was one of the most-discussed figures in the French hierarchy, especially because of his sharp, but not always objective, opposition to growing laicism. The impulse that Freppel gave to the social movement in French Catholicism did not advance much beyond the moralizing stage because of his opposition to state action in social problems. At the first Catholic congress on the social question, held at Angers, Freppel presided and claimed that moral renovation and private initiative sufficed to provide the essential remedies for social wrongs. Freppel's hostility to the Third Republic was shortsighted, and it reduced his political influence. His most lasting service was the foundation of the University of Angers (1875).

Bibliography: E. TERRIEN, *Mgr. Freppel, apologiste et défenseur des droits de l'Église* (Paris 1927); *Mgr. Freppel, sa vie, ses ouvrages, ses oeuvres, son influence et son temps,* 2 v. (Angers 1931–32). E. MANGENOT, *Dictionnaire de théologie catholique* 6 (Paris 1903–50) 1:798–800. C. LEDRÉ, *Catholicisme* 4:1583–85.

[V. CONZEMIUS]

FRERE, RUDOLPH WALTER HOWARD

Anglican bishop, liturgist, musicologist; b. Cambridge, England, Nov. 23, 1863; d. Mirfield, Yorkshire, April 2, 1938. From Trinity College, Cambridge, he went to Wells Theological College and was ordained in 1889. As curate (1887–92) of St. Dunstan's, Stepney, within reach of the British Museum manuscript collections, he laid the foundation for his intensive lifelong research into medieval chant and liturgy. In 1892 he was professed in the new Anglican Community of the Resurrection and he was superior from 1902 to 1912 and from 1917 to 1922. In 1923 in Westminster Abbey he was consecrated bishop of Truro. He took an active part in the MALINES CONVERSATIONS. His principal works are editions of the *Winchester Troper* (*see* LITURGICAL MUSIC, HISTORY OF), the *Sarum Gradual, Consuetudinary, Ordinal, and Tonal;* the *Hereford Breviary* and *Hymns Ancient and Modern* (historical ed., 1909); articles in *Grove's Dictionary of Music and Musicians* (3d ed.), *The Oxford History of Music* (2d ed.), *Journal of Theological Studies,* and *Church Quarterly Review.*

See Also: SARUM USE.

Bibliography: C. S. PHILLIPS et al., eds., *Walter Howard Frere: A Memoir* (London 1947). W. SHAW, *Die Musik in Geschichte und Gegenwart,* ed. F. BLUME (Kassel-Basel 1949–) 4:911.

[L. ELLINWOOD]

FRESCOBALDI, GIROLAMO

Distinguished baroque composer and Vatican organist; b. Ferrara, *c.* August 1583; d. Rome, March 1, 1643. As a youth he had a voice of great beauty, and studied organ with Francesco Milleville, a Ferrarese who became organist of Voltera. In 1694 he became organist and cantor of the Congregation of St. Cecilia. He was appointed organist of Santa Maria, Trastevere, Rome, in January 1607, but left in June for a year in the Netherlands.

At Antwerp Frescobaldi published his first volume of five-part madrigals (Phalese 1608) and returned to Italy, where he published his second book of four-voice fantasies in Milan (1608). In November 1608 he was appointed organist at St. Peter's, Rome, where, according to G. Baini, 30,000 persons came to hear his first performance. Dissatisfied with the pay, he took a leave of ab-

Girolamo Frescobaldi.

sence in 1628, to be organist to Ferdinando II de' Medici, Grand Duke of Tuscany, in Florence. Because of political upheaval, he left Florence in April 1634 and was directly reinstated at St. Peter's, where he played until his death. Some records mention him as organist of S. Lorenzo in Montibus during his last year. J. J. FROBERGER was his pupil from September 1637 to April 1641 and handed down his method, spreading it to Germany.

His music is remarkable for its high intelligence and artistic taste. All his extraordinary talents are combined in one work, the *Ricercare con obligo di cantare la quinta parte senza toccarla,* from the *Messa della Madonna,* of the *Fiori Musicali.* Here it is provided that a fifth part, a theme of six notes, may be superimposed over the four manual parts, presumably to be sung by the player. The realization by Guilmant has been reprinted by Bonnet and others. Although best known for his organ works, he composed a comparable number of choral and instrumental pieces. Transcriptions of his better-known instrumental works have been made by B. Bartók, O. RESPIGHI, and several other composers.

Bibliography: *Orgel- und Klavierwerke,* ed. P. PIDOUX, 5 v. (Kassel 1950–54); *Fiori musicali,* in *Les Grands maîtres anciens de l'orgue,* ed. J. BONNET and A. GUILMANT (Paris 1922) v. 1, with biog. by A. GUILMANT; *Fiori musicali,* ed. F. GERMANI (Rome 1936); *Ausgewählte Orgelwerke,* ed. H. KELLER, 2 v. (Leipzig-New York 1943). A. MACHABEY, *Gerolamo Frescobaldi Ferrarensis* (Paris 1952). H. F. REDLICH, ''G. F.,'' *Music Review* 14 (1953) 262–274. M. REIMANN, *Die Musik in Geschichte und Gegenwart,* ed. F. BLUME (Kassel-Basel 1949–) 4:912–926. F. GEHRING, *Grove's Dictionary of Music and Musicians,* ed. E. BLOM, 9 v. (5th ed. London 1954) 3:494. M. F. BUKOFZER, *Music in the Baroque Era* (New York 1947). P. H. LÁNG, *Music in Western Civilization* (New York 1941). C. ANNIBALDI, ''Palestrina and Frescobaldi: Discovering a Missing Link,'' *Music and Letters* 79 (1998) 329–345. N. J. BARKER, ''Analytical Issues in the Toccatas of Girolamo Frescobaldi'' (Ph.D. diss. Cornell University 1995). I. GODT, ''Frescobaldi's Viol? An Unsolved Mystery,'' *Consort* 46 (1990) 10–15. F. HAMMOND, ''The Influence of Girolamo Frescobaldi on French Keyboard Music,'' *Recercare* (1991) 147–167. F. KRUMMACHER, ''Phantastik und Kontrapunkt: Zur Kompositionsart Frescobaldis,'' *Die Musikforschung* 48 (1995) 1–14. A. NEWCOMB, ''Girolamo Frescobaldi'' in *The New Grove Dictionary of Music and Musicians,* ed. S. SADIE, v. 6 (New York 1980) 824–835.

[L. SEARS]

ISBN 0-7876-4009-3